The Consumer Credit and Sales
Legal Practice Series

CONSUMER BANKRUPTCY LAW AND PRACTICE

Seventh Edition   With CD-Rom

Henry J. Sommer

John Rao, Editor and Contributing Author
Susan A. Schneider, Contributing Author for Chapter 16

National Consumer Law Center
77 Summer Street, 10th Floor   Boston, MA 02110

www.consumerlaw.org

About NCLC

The National Consumer Law Center, a nonprofit corporation founded in 1969, assists consumers, advocates, and public policy makers nationwide who use the powerful and complex tools of consumer law to ensure justice and fair treatment for all, particularly those whose poverty renders them powerless to demand accountability from the economic marketplace. For more information, go to www.consumerlaw.org.

Ordering NCLC Publications

Order securely online at www.consumerlaw.org, or contact Publications Department, National Consumer Law Center, 77 Summer Street, Boston, MA 02110, (617) 542-9595, FAX: (617) 542-8028, e-mail: publications@nclc.org.

Training and Conferences

NCLC participates in numerous national, regional, and local consumer law trainings. Its annual fall conference is a forum for consumer rights attorneys from legal services programs, private practice, government, and nonprofit organizations to share insights into common problems and explore novel and tested approaches that promote consumer justice in the marketplace. Contact NCLC for more information or see our web site.

Case Consulting

Case analysis, consulting and co-counseling for lawyers representing vulnerable consumers are among NCLC's important activities. Administration on Aging funds allow us to provide free consulting to legal services advocates representing elderly consumers on many types of cases. Massachusetts Legal Assistance Corporation funds permit case assistance to advocates representing low-income Massachusetts consumers. Other funding may allow NCLC to provide very brief consultations to other advocates without charge. More comprehensive case analysis and research is available for a reasonable fee. See our web site for more information at www.consumerlaw.org.

Charitable Donations and Cy Pres Awards

NCLC's work depends in part on the support of private donors. Tax-deductible donations should be made payable to National Consumer Law Center, Inc. For more information, contact Suzanne Cutler of NCLC's Development Office at (617) 542-8010 or scutler@nclc.org. NCLC has also received generous court-approved *cy pres* awards arising from consumer class actions to advance the interests of class members. For more information, contact Robert Hobbs (rhobbs@nclc.org) or Rich Dubois (rdubois@nclc.org) at (617) 542-8010.

Comments and Corrections

Write to the above address to the attention of the Editorial Department or e-mail consumerlaw@nclc.org.

About This Volume

This is the Seventh Edition of *Consumer Bankruptcy Law and Practice* with a 2004 companion CD-Rom. The Seventh Edition and 2004 CD-Rom supersede all prior editions, supplements, and CDs, which should all be discarded. Continuing developments can be found in periodic updates to this volume and in NCLC REPORTS, *Bankruptcy & Foreclosures Edition*.

Cite This Volume As

National Consumer Law Center, Consumer Bankruptcy Law and Practice (7th ed. 2004).

Attention

ISBN 1-931697-62-0 (this volume)
ISBN 0-943116-10-4 (Series)

Library of Congress Control Number 2004114739

About the Authors

Henry J. Sommer, the author, is Supervising Attorney at the pro bono Consumer Bankruptcy Assistance Project in Philadelphia. Previously, he was the head of the Consumer Law Project at Community Legal Services in Philadelphia, where he worked for over 21 years. He has also served as a Lecturer-in-Law at the University of Pennsylvania Law School. He is Editor in Chief of *Collier on Bankruptcy* and the entire Collier line of bankruptcy publications published by Matthew Bender and Co. He is the author of *Consumer Bankruptcy: The Complete Guide to Chapter 7 and Chapter 13 Personal Bankruptcy* (John Wiley & Sons, 1994) as well as numerous articles on bankruptcy law. He is the co-author of *Collier Family Law and the Bankruptcy Code* (Matthew Bender). He is a former member of the Federal Judicial Conference Advisory Committee on Bankruptcy Rules and the Federal Reserve Board Consumer Advisory Council. He is a member of the National Bankruptcy Conference, a Fellow of the American College of Bankruptcy, and a member of the American Law Institute. He is also President of the National Association of Consumer Bankruptcy Attorneys, Vice President of the Coalition for Consumer Bankruptcy Debtor Education, and former Chairman of the Eastern District of Pennsylvania Bankruptcy Conference. He was the first recipient of the Vern Countryman Consumer Law Award.

John Rao, the editor and a contributing author, is an NCLC attorney with a focus on consumer bankruptcy, foreclosures, and credit law. He is the co-editor of the Sixth Edition of this manual, co-author of *Repossessions and Foreclosures* (5th ed. 2002), contributing author to *Student Loan Law* (2d ed. 2002), and head of NCLC's Advice and Assistance Project. He is also a contributing author to *Collier on Bankruptcy* and the *Collier Bankruptcy Practice Guide*. For 18 years, he had a bankruptcy and consumer law focus at Rhode Island Legal Services, and was a managing attorney there. He is a member of the board of directors for the National Association of Consumer Bankruptcy Attorneys and the American Bankruptcy Institute.

Susan A. Schneider, the contributing author for the family farmer bankruptcy chapter, is an Associate Professor of Law and Director of the Graduate Agricultural Law Program at the University of Arkansas School of Law. She has also taught at William Mitchell College of Law and at the Drake University Summer Agricultural Law Institute. Her private practice and consultation experience include agricultural law work with firms in Arkansas, Minnesota, North Dakota and Washington, D.C. She served as a staff attorney at Farmer's Legal Action Group, Inc. and at the National Center for Agricultural Law Research and Information. She has published numerous articles on agricultural law subjects, served as the President of the American Agricultural Law Association (AALA) in 2004, and continues to serve on the AALA Board of Directors.

Acknowledgments: We are particularly grateful to Eric Secoy for editorial supervision; Nathan Day for editorial assistance; Shirlron Williams for assistance with cite checking; Shannon Halbrook for production assistance; Xylutions for typesetting services; Mary McLean for indexing, and Neil Fogarty of Law Disks, for developing the CD-Rom accompanying this volume, including Law Disks' Bankruptcy Forms. This Seventh Edition is based on the contributions of the many individuals who have worked on the prior six editions and also on the sixteen supplements to those editions. We want to thank all of these individuals, even though they are too numerous to list individually here. But special mention must be made of Gary Klein, for his numerous contributions over the years to prior editions and supplements.

What Your Library Should Contain

The Consumer Credit and Sales Legal Practice Series contains 16 titles, updated annually, arranged into four libraries, and designed to be an attorney's primary practice guide and legal resource in all 50 states. Each manual includes a CD-Rom allowing pinpoint searches and the pasting of text into a word processor.

Debtor Rights Library

2004 Seventh Edition with CD-Rom, Including Law Disks' Bankruptcy Forms

Consumer Bankruptcy Law and Practice: the definitive personal bankruptcy manual, with step-by-step instructions from initial interview to final discharge, and including consumers' rights as creditors when a merchant or landlord files for bankruptcy. Appendices and CD-Rom contain over 130 annotated pleadings, bankruptcy statutes, rules and fee schedules, an interview questionnaire, a client handout, and software to complete the latest versions of petitions and schedules.

2004 Fifth Edition with CD-Rom

Fair Debt Collection: the basic reference in the field, covering the Fair Debt Collection Practices Act and common law, state statutory and other federal debt collection protections. Appendices and companion CD-Rom contain sample pleadings and discovery, the FTC's Official Staff Commentary, *all* FTC staff opinion letters, and summaries of reported and unreported cases.

2002 Fifth Edition, 2004 Supplement, and 2004 CD-Rom

Repossessions and Foreclosures: unique guide to VA, FHA and other types of home foreclosures, servicer obligations, motor vehicle and mobile home repossessions, threatened seizures of household goods, tax and other statutory liens, and automobile lease and rent-to-own default remedies. The CD-Rom reprints relevant UCC provisions and numerous key federal statutes, regulations, and agency letters, summarizes hundreds of state laws, and includes over 150 pleadings covering a wide variety of cases.

2002 Second Edition, 2004 Supplement, and 2004 CD-Rom

Student Loan Law: student loan debt collection and collection fees; discharges based on closed school, false certification, failure to refund, disability, and bankruptcy; tax intercepts, wage garnishment, and offset of social security benefits; repayment plans, consolidation loans, deferments, and non-payment of loan based on school fraud. CD-Rom and appendices contain numerous forms, pleadings, interpretation letters and regulations.

2004 Third Edition with CD-Rom

Access to Utility Service: the only examination of consumer rights when dealing with regulated, de-regulated, and unregulated utilities, including telecommunications, terminations, billing errors, low-income payment plans, utility allowances in subsidized housing, LIHEAP, and weatherization. Includes summaries of state utility regulations.

Credit and Banking Library

2003 Fifth Edition, 2004 Supplement, and 2004 CD-Rom

Truth in Lending: detailed analysis of *all* aspects of TILA, the Consumer Leasing Act, and the Home Ownership and Equity Protection Act (HOEPA). Appendices and the CD-Rom contain the Acts, Reg. Z, Reg. M, and their Official Staff Commentaries, numerous sample pleadings, rescission notices, and two programs to compute APRs.

National Consumer Law Center ■ **77 Summer Street** ■ **10th Floor** ■ **Boston MA** ■ **02110**
(617) 542-9595 ■ **FAX (617) 542-8028** ■ **publications@nclc.org**
Order securely online at www.consumerlaw.org

2002 Fifth Edition, 2004 Supplement, and 2004 CD-Rom	**Fair Credit Reporting:** the key resource for handling any type of credit reporting issue, from cleaning up blemished credit records to suing reporting agencies and creditors for inaccurate reports. Covers credit scoring, privacy issues, identity theft, the FCRA, the new FACT Act, the Credit Repair Organizations Act, state credit reporting and repair statutes, and common law claims.
2002 Second Edition, 2004 Supplement, and 2004 CD-Rom	**Consumer Banking and Payments Law:** unique analysis of consumer law (and NACHA rules) as to checks, money orders, credit, debit, and stored value cards, and banker's right of setoff. Also extensive treatment of electronic records and signatures, electronic transfer of food stamps, and direct deposits of federal payments. The CD-Rom and appendices reprint relevant agency interpretations and pleadings.
2000 Second Edition, 2004 Supplement, and 2004 CD-Rom	**The Cost of Credit: Regulation and Legal Challenges:** a one-of-a-kind resource detailing state and federal regulation of consumer credit in all fifty states, federal usury preemption, explaining credit math, and how to challenge excessive credit charges and credit insurance. The CD-Rom includes a credit math program and hard-to-find agency interpretations.
2002 Third Edition, 2004 Supplement, and 2004 CD-Rom	**Credit Discrimination:** analysis of the Equal Credit Opportunity Act, Fair Housing Act, Civil Rights Acts, and state credit discrimination statutes, including reprints of all relevant federal interpretations, government enforcement actions, and numerous sample pleadings.

Consumer Litigation Library

2004 Fourth Edition with CD-Rom	**Consumer Arbitration Agreements:** numerous successful approaches to challenge the enforceability of a binding arbitration agreement, the interrelation of the Federal Arbitration Act and state law, class actions in arbitration, collections via arbitration, the right to discovery, and other topics. Appendices and CD-Rom include sample discovery, numerous briefs, arbitration service provider rules and affidavits as to arbitrator costs.
2002 Fifth Edition, 2004 Supplement, and 2004 CD-Rom	**Consumer Class Actions: A Practical Litigation Guide:** makes class action litigation manageable even for small offices, including numerous sample pleadings, class certification memoranda, discovery, class notices, settlement materials, and much more. Includes contributions from seven of the most experienced consumer class action litigators around the country.
2004 CD-Rom with Index Guide: ALL pleadings from ALL NCLC Manuals, including Consumer Law Pleadings Numbers One through Ten	**Consumer Law Pleadings on CD-Rom:** Over 1000 notable recent pleadings from all types of consumer cases, including predatory lending, foreclosures, automobile fraud, lemon laws, debt collection, fair credit reporting, home improvement fraud, rent to own, student loans, and lender liability. Finding aids pinpoint the desired pleading in seconds, ready to paste into a word processing program.

Deception and Warranties Library

2004 Sixth Edition with CD-Rom	**Unfair and Deceptive Acts and Practices:** the only practice manual covering all aspects of a deceptive practices case in every state. Special sections on automobile sales, the federal racketeering (RICO) statute, unfair insurance practices, and the FTC Holder Rule.
2003 Second Edition, 2004 Supplement, and 2004 CD-Rom	**Automobile Fraud:** examination of title law, odometer tampering, lemon laundering, sale of salvage and wrecked cars, undisclosed prior use, prior damage to new cars, numerous sample pleadings, and title search techniques.
2001 Second Edition, 2004 Supplement, and 2004 CD-Rom	**Consumer Warranty Law:** comprehensive treatment of new and used car lemon laws, the Magnuson-Moss Warranty Act, UCC Articles 2 and 2A, mobile home, new home, and assistive device warranty laws, FTC Used Car Rule, tort theories, car repair and home improvement statutes, service contract and lease laws, with numerous sample pleadings.

National Consumer Law Center ■ **77 Summer Street** ■ **10th Floor** ■ **Boston MA** ■ **02110**
(617) 542-9595 ■ **FAX (617) 542-8028** ■ **publications@nclc.org**
Order securely online at www.consumerlaw.org

NCLC's CD-Roms

Every NCLC manual comes with a companion CD-Rom featuring pop-up menus, PDF format, Internet-style navigation of appendices, indices, and bonus pleadings, hard-to-find agency interpretations and other practice aids. Documents can be copied into a word processing program. Of special note is *Consumer Law in a Box*:

December 2004 CD-Rom

Consumer Law in a Box: a CD-Rom combining *all* documents and software from 16 other NCLC CD-Roms. Quickly pinpoint a document from thousands found on the CD through keyword searches and Internet-style navigation, links, bookmarks, and other finding aids.

Other NCLC Publications for Lawyers

issued 24 times a year

NCLC REPORTS covers the latest developments and ideas in the practice of consumer law.

2003 First Edition with CD-Rom

The Practice of Consumer Law: Seeking Economic Justice: contains an essential overview to consumer law and explains how to get started in a private or legal services consumer practice. Packed with invaluable sample pleadings and practice pointers for even experienced consumer attorneys.

2002 First Edition with CD-Rom

STOP Predatory Lending: A Guide for Legal Advocates: provides a roadmap and practical legal strategy for litigating predatory lending abuses, from small loans to mortgage loans. The CD-Rom contains a credit math program, pleadings, legislative and administrative materials, and underwriting guidelines.

National Consumer Law Center Guide Series are books designed for consumers, counselors, and attorneys new to consumer law:

2002 Edition

NCLC Guide to Surviving Debt: a great overview of consumer law. Everything a paralegal, new attorney, or client needs to know about debt collectors, managing credit card debt, whether to refinance, credit card problems, home foreclosures, evictions, repossessions, credit reporting, utility terminations, student loans, budgeting, and bankruptcy.

2002 Edition

NCLC Guide to Mobile Homes: what consumers and their advocates need to know about mobile home dealer sales practices and an in-depth look at mobile home quality and defects, with 35 photographs and construction details.

2002 Edition

NCLC Guide to Consumer Rights for Immigrants: an introduction to many of the most critical consumer issues faced by immigrants, including international wires, check cashing and banking, *notario* and immigration consultant fraud, affidavits of support, telephones, utilities, credit history discrimination, high-cost credit, used car fraud, student loans and more.

2000 Edition

Return to Sender: Getting a Refund or Replacement for Your Lemon Car: Find how lemon laws work, what consumers and their lawyers should know to evaluate each other, investigative techniques and discovery tips, how to handle both informal dispute resolution and trials, and more.

Visit **www.consumerlaw.org** to order securely online or for more information on all NCLC manuals and CD-Roms, including the full tables of contents, indices, listings of CD-Rom contents, and **web-based searches of the manuals' full text.**

National Consumer Law Center ■ 77 Summer Street ■ 10th Floor ■ Boston MA ■ 02110
(617) 542-9595 ■ FAX (617) 542-8028 ■ publications@nclc.org
Order securely online at www.consumerlaw.org

Finding Aids and Search Tips

The Consumer Credit and Sales Legal Practice Series presently contains sixteen volumes, ten supplements, and sixteen companion CD-Roms—all constantly being updated. The Series includes over 10,000 pages, 100 chapters, 100 appendices, and over 1000 pleadings, as well as hundreds of documents found on the CD-Roms, but not found in the books. Here are a number of ways to pinpoint in seconds what you need from this array of materials.

Internet-Based Searches

www.consumerlaw.org

Electronically search every chapter and appendix of all sixteen manuals and their supplements: go to www.consumerlaw.org/keyword and enter a case name, regulation cite, or other search term. You are instantly given the book names and page numbers of any of the NCLC manuals containing that term.

www.consumerlaw.org

Current indexes, tables of contents, and CD-Rom contents for all sixteen volumes are found at www.consumerlaw.org. Just click on *The Consumer Credit and Sales Legal Practice Series* and scroll down to the book you want. Then click on that volume's index, contents, or CD-Rom contents.

Finding Material on NCLC's CD-Roms

Consumer Law in a Box CD-Rom

Electronically search all sixteen NCLC CD-Roms, including thousands of agency interpretations, all NCLC appendices and almost 1000 pleadings: use Acrobat's search button* in NCLC's *Consumer Law in a Box CD-Rom* (this CD-Rom is free to set subscribers) to find every instance that a keyword appears on any of our sixteen CD-Roms. Then, with one click, go to that location to see the full text of the document.

CD-Rom accompanying this volume

Electronically search the CD-Rom accompanying this volume, including pleadings, agency interpretations, and regulations. Use Acrobat's search button* to find every instance that a keyword appears on the CD-Rom, and then, with one click, go to that location on the CD-Rom. Or just click on subject buttons until you navigate to the document you need.

Finding Pleadings

Consumer Law Pleadings on CD-Rom and Index Guide

Search five different ways for the right pleading from over 1000 choices: use the *Index Guide* accompanying *Consumer Law Pleadings on CD-Rom* to search for pleadings by type, subject, publication title, name of contributor, or contributor's jurisdiction. The guide also provides a summary of the pleading once the right pleading is located. *Consumer Law Pleadings on CD-Rom* and the *Consumer Law in a Box CD-Rom* also let you search for all pleadings electronically by subject, type of pleading, and by publication title, giving you instant access to the full pleading in Word and/or PDF format once you find the pleading you need.

Using This Volume to Find Material in All Sixteen Volumes

This volume

The Quick Reference at the back of this volume lets you pinpoint manual sections or appendices where over 1000 different subject areas are covered.

---

* Users of NCLC CD-Roms should become familiar with "search," a powerful Acrobat tool, distinguished from "find," another Acrobat feature that is far slower and less powerful than "search." The Acrobat 5 "search" icon is a pair of binoculars with paper in the background, while the "find" icon is a pair of binoculars without the paper. Acrobat 6 uses one icon, a pair of binoculars, that brings you to a menu with several search options.

Summary Contents

Contents

Chapter 6   **Counseling the Consumer Debtor: Does Bankruptcy Provide the Best Solution and, If So, How and When?**

Chapter 9   Automatic Stays and Turnover of Property

Chapter 10

Exemptions

Chapter 11   Dealing with Secured Creditors

Chapter 14

The Discharge: Protecting It and Using It

Contents

Chapter 15 **Attorney Fees for Debtor's Counsel in Consumer Bankruptcy Cases**

Chapter 16 **Chapter 12 Bankruptcy: Family Farmer Reorganizations**

Chapter 17   Consumers As Creditors in Bankruptcy: Selected Topics

Contents

Appendix E   Selected Forms Promulgated by the Administrative Office of the U.S. Courts

Appendix F   Sample Completed Bankruptcy Schedules to Institute Case

Appendix G   Sample Bankruptcy Pleadings and Other Forms

CD-Rom Contents

How to Use/Help

Acrobat 6.0 Problem

Map of CD-Rom Contents

Bankruptcy Statutes

Bankruptcy Rules, Fees

Bankruptcy Forms Software

Bankruptcy Forms, Pleadings

Search This Manual

Contents of NCLC Publications

Consumer Education Brochures, Books

Order NCLC Publications, CD-Roms

Chapter 1   About This Manual

1.1 Bankruptcy As a Remedy for Consumer Debtors

1.1.1 Overview

The past twenty years have seen an explosive increase in the already easy availability of consumer credit in the United States.[1] The significantly higher debt loads carried by more and more American consumers, particularly those of low and moderate income, render them and their families vulnerable to enormous financial difficulties when they suffer income interruptions.[2] Exorbitant interest rates and fees that quickly accumulate upon a default have left more families than ever vulnerable to a financial death spiral when they experience even a short term drop in income or an emergency expense that disrupts their debt payments. Aggressive creditors regularly threaten to throw debtors' lives into chaos, through foreclosures, repossessions, levies, executions, garnishments, collection harassment, and utility shut-offs.

In many cases bankruptcy is the only option that will bring order, rational planning and permanent or at least temporary relief to people who are under immense financial pressure. Bankruptcy provides an effective means of leveling the playing field between debtors and creditors, and it can profoundly improve the well-being of individuals and families.

It should come as no surprise, then, that over one and one-half million families file consumer bankruptcy cases each year. As credit expands and bankruptcy becomes increasingly central to our economic and legal systems, ever larger numbers of consumers and businesses seek bankruptcy relief. Bankruptcy gives them an opportunity to reorder their finances and obtain a fresh start.

It has become impossible to ignore bankruptcy. Not only is bankruptcy an important option to offer a client with financial difficulties, but it also frequently affects individuals and corporations with whom a client may be involved through employment, marriage, a tenancy, a consumer relationship, or as party to a lawsuit. Bankruptcy can eliminate both long and short term debts, with a minimum of effort in many cases, and can upset the firmest of expectations about consumer, landlord-tenant, and even marital relationships. Large municipal governments, like Orange County, California, have filed bankruptcy cases with potentially significant implications for all residents.

As the importance of bankruptcy increases, so does the need for low and moderate income clients to have access to the bankruptcy system. Unfortunately, though, because of high filing and attorney fees, it is those with low and moderate incomes who have had the least access to bankruptcy. This book is intended to serve as a guide for those interested in providing high quality bankruptcy representation to consumers, particularly for those advocates serving consumers with low and moderate incomes.

1.1.2 The Bankruptcy Reform Act and Subsequent Amendments

1.1.2.1 Passage of the Bankruptcy Reform Act

On October 1, 1979, a new and far-reaching consumer protection law went into effect.[3] That law, the federal Bankruptcy Code,[4] may well be the most important federal legislation ever passed, in terms of its benefits for consumers. In its first years, the Code demonstrated its enormous potential as an area for creative advocacy on behalf of low and moderate income people, as well as its utility as a source

---

1   *See* Lawrence M. Ausubel, *Credit Card Defaults, Credit Card Profits and Bankruptcy*, 71 Am. Bankr. L.J. 249 (1997).

2   *See* Elizabeth Warren & Amelia Warren Tyagi, The Two-Income Trap: Why Middle Class Mothers & Fathers are Going Broke (2003); Teresa A. Sullivan, Elizabeth Warren & Jay Lawrence Westbrook, The Fragile Middle Class: Americans in Debt (2000).

3   The effective dates of different portions of the Bankruptcy Reform Act, Pub. L. No. 95-598, 92 Stat. 2549 (1978) are established by § 402 of that Act, as amended by the 1984 amendments. The Bankruptcy Reform Act of 1978 as a whole consisted of four titles. Title 1 enacted a new title 11 of the United States Code, the Bankruptcy Code, which went into effect on October 1, 1979. Title II contained amendments to title 28 of the United States Code. Title III contained amendments to other acts and title IV contained transitional provisions.

4   The new title 11 is commonly referred to as the Bankruptcy Code, in contrast to the prior law, which was known as the Bankruptcy Act. In this manual that distinction will be maintained: "the Code" will refer to the law now in effect, and "the Act" will refer to prior law.

of quick, concrete, and far-reaching relief in the day-to-day circumstances of financially troubled individuals. The burgeoning number of bankruptcies in recent years has been matched by a tidal wave of interpretive case law.

1.1.2.2 Consumer Bankruptcy Amendments of 1984

The significant benefits of the new Bankruptcy Code for consumer debtors were noted early on by creditors as well. Within a year after the Code's effective date, the consumer credit industry mounted a drive to drastically cut back on the relief obtainable in bankruptcy and, in some ways, to tilt the law in creditors' favor even more than it had been under the prior Bankruptcy Act.

Despite an intense lobbying and public relations campaign, the credit industry's efforts were largely rebuffed. Congress did pass, in the Bankruptcy Amendments and Federal Judgeship Act of 1984,[5] a package of consumer bankruptcy amendments. But those amendments were mere shadows of the creditors' original proposals, narrowly tailored to meet the few abuses of the Code that might actually be occurring.[6]

While they did have important effects, usually detrimental, in the cases of a minority of debtors, the 1984 amendments did not alter the basic rights of consumers to bankruptcy relief. Indeed, in several ways the 1984 amendments clarified and strengthened consumer rights.[7] Their net effect in most cases was probably a slight increase in the paperwork required and nothing more. Hence, the importance of bankruptcy law to low and moderate income consumers, and the opportunities for its development on their behalf, continued unabated.

1.1.2.3 Bankruptcy Judges, United States Trustees, and Family Farmer Bankruptcy Act of 1986

In 1986, Congress again made substantial changes in the Bankruptcy Code, passing the Bankruptcy Judges, United States Trustees, and Family Farmer Bankruptcy Act of 1986.[8] Besides adding a substantial number of new bankruptcy judgeships in many judicial districts, the 1986 Act made the many changes necessary to institute a phased-in United States trustee system to handle many administrative functions formerly handled by the court. It also created a new chapter 12 of the Bankruptcy Code especially tailored

to meet the needs of family farmers in financial distress in ways that neither chapter 11 nor chapter 13 could offer.[9] Chapter 12 is discussed at length in Chapter 16, *infra*. The 1986 amendments also made a number of other changes, mostly minor, affecting consumer bankruptcies. The most significant of these changes was the elimination of a mandatory discharge hearing in most cases.[10]

1.1.2.4 The Bankruptcy Reform Act of 1994

In the waning hours of the 103d Congress, lawmakers addressed bankruptcy once more, passing the Bankruptcy Reform Act of 1994.[11] That Act, the culmination of four years of legislative efforts, made changes to numerous parts of the Bankruptcy Code, making more changes than any legislation since the original enactment of the Bankruptcy Reform Act of 1978. In addition, after substantially amending the Code, Congress created a National Bankruptcy Review Commission to study whether further changes should be made.[12] The Commission issued its report on October 20, 1997.[13] The report recommends a variety of controversial changes to the provisions of the Code governing consumer bankruptcy cases, but these recommendations have been ignored by Congress.[14]

Among the many changes made by the 1994 Act in the area of consumer bankruptcy were some which benefited consumers and some which were detrimental to them. On the positive side, the amounts of the federal exemptions under Code section 522(d), as well as most other dollar amounts in the Code, were doubled, and a mechanism was built into the Code for automatic cost-of-living adjustments in the future.[15] The dollar limits for chapter 13 eligibility

---

5 Pub. L. No. 98-353, 98 Stat. 333 (1984).

6 For a short review by this author of the 1984 amendments specifically directed at consumer bankruptcies, see Henry J. Sommer, *Consumer Bankruptcy Amendments of 1984*, 31 Prac. Law 45 (Jan. 1985).

7 See, for example, 11 U.S.C. § 525(b), prohibiting discrimination by private employers, discussed in Chapter 14, *infra*.

8 Pub. L. No. 99-554, 100 Stat. 3088 (1986).

9 Chapter 12 of the Bankruptcy Code expired on January 1, 2004. However, Pub. L. No. 108-369, 118 Stat. 1749 (2004), enacted on October 25, 2004, extended chapter 12 through June 30, 2005, with a retroactive effective date of January 1, 2004. *See* § A.2.10, *infra*.

10 11 U.S.C. § 524, as amended in 1986, made the discharge hearing discretionary with the court unless the debtor intended to reaffirm a debt. *See* § 8.8, *infra*.

11 Pub. L. No. 103-394, 108 Stat. 4106 (generally effective with respect to cases filed on or after October 22, 1994). The bill's provisions dealing with the effective date of the amendments are reprinted in Appendix A.2.8, *infra*. The amendments themselves have been integrated into the revised Bankruptcy Code reprinted in Appendix A.1, *infra*.

12 Bankruptcy Reform Act of 1994, Pub. L. No. 103-394, tit. VI, 108 Stat. 4106.

13 Nat'l Bankruptcy Review Comm'n, Bankruptcy: The Next Twenty Years, Final Report (Oct. 20, 1997). The report is available on the Review Commission website: www.nbrc.gov.

14 For a discussion of the Review Commission's recommendations, see Gary Klein, Consumer Bankruptcy in the Balance: the National Bankruptcy Review Commission's Recommendations Tilt Toward Creditors, 5 Am. Bankr. Inst. L. Rev. 293 (1997).

15 11 U.S.C. §§ 104, 522(d), as amended by the Bankruptcy Reform Act of 1994, Pub. L. No. 103-394, 108 Stat. 4106. *See* § 10.2.2, *infra*.

were also substantially increased, with similar adjustments to be made in the future.[16] The third of these adjustments became effective on April 1, 2004, and the adjusted numbers are used throughout this manual. Future adjustments will be reflected in the annual supplements to this manual.

In addition, the 1994 amendments overruled (but only for future mortgages) the Supreme Court's misguided decision in *Rake v. Wade*,[17] which had required debtors curing mortgage arrears to pay thousands of dollars of additional interest, and reinstated the law most circuits had followed before that decision.[18] Congress also partially overruled the Court's decision in *Nobelman v. American Savings Bank*,[19] which had prohibited the stripping down of many mortgage liens in chapter 13, by creating additional categories of mortgages which could be modified.[20]

In addition, the 1994 amendments clarified the law in areas in which there had been conflicting court decisions, such as those concerning when a debtor loses the right to cure a default on a mortgage,[21] how to determine whether a lien impairs an exemption,[22] how to determine property of the estate when a case is converted from chapter 13 to chapter 7,[23] whether a late-filed claim should be allowed,[24] whether a student loan grantor can discriminate against a debtor based on a discharged debt,[25] and whether condominium and cooperative fees are dischargeable.[26]

Unfortunately, the amendments also contained a number of provisions detrimental to consumers, including a weakening of the protections with respect to reaffirmation,[27]

several new exceptions to discharge, including an additional exception to the chapter 13 discharge,[28] and procedural changes that will increase the time and costs necessary to process consumer bankruptcy cases.[29]

Finally, the many other changes made by the amendments included a broad abrogation of sovereign immunity, intended to reverse the result in two harmful Supreme Court cases which had limited the Code's original waiver of sovereign immunity,[30] a package of amendments intended to strengthen the rights of a debtor's dependent spouse, former spouse, or children to receive alimony, maintenance, support and, in some cases, property settlements,[31] tough new provisions to regulate non-attorney bankruptcy petition preparers,[32] and procedural provisions concerning jury trials[33] and appeals.[34]

1.1.2.5 Other Amendments to the Code

Over the years, Congress has occasionally made other amendments to the Bankruptcy Code, usually tucked away in appropriations bills that received little scrutiny. Some of these amendments, for example, have greatly limited the dischargeability of student loans,[35] family support obligations owed to governmental units,[36] and criminal restitution.[37] Despite much talk about a bankruptcy overhaul in 1998, largely instigated by a consumer credit industry media and lobbying campaign,[38] only one set of changes to the Bankruptcy Code actually became law in the first few years

---

16 11 U.S.C. §§ 104, 109(e), as amended by the Bankruptcy Reform Act of 1994, Pub. L. No. 103-394, 108 Stat 4106. *See* § 12.2.3, *infra*.

17 508 U.S. 464, 113 S. Ct. 2187, 124 L. Ed. 2d 424 (1993).

18 11 U.S.C. § 1322(e), as enacted by the Bankruptcy Reform Act of 1994, Pub. L. No. 103-394, 108 Stat. 4106. *See* § 11.6.2.7, *infra*.

19 508 U.S. 324, 113 S. Ct. 2106, 124 L. Ed. 2d 228 (1993).

20 11 U.S.C. § 1322(c)(2), enacted by the Bankruptcy Reform Act of 1994, Pub. L. No. 103-394, 108 Stat. 4106. *See* § 11.6.1.2, *infra*.

21 11 U.S.C. § 1322(c)(1), enacted by the Bankruptcy Reform Act of 1994, Pub. L. No. 103-394, 108 Stat. 4106. *See* § 11.6.2.2, *infra*.

22 11 U.S.C. § 522(f)(2), as enacted by the Bankruptcy Reform Act of 1994, Pub. L. No. 103-394, 108 Stat. 4106. *See* §§ 10.4.2.2, 10.4.2.3, *infra*.

23 11 U.S.C. § 348(f), as enacted by the Bankruptcy Reform Act of 1994, Pub. L. No. 103-394, 108 Stat. 4106. *See* § 4.7.4, *infra*.

24 11 U.S.C. § 502(b)(9), as enacted by the Bankruptcy Reform Act of 1994, Pub. L. No. 103-394, 108 Stat. 4106. *See* § 13.4.3, *infra*.

25 11 U.S.C. § 525(c), as enacted by the Bankruptcy Reform Act of 1994, Pub. L. No. 103-394, 108 Stat. 4106. *See* § 14.5.5.2, *infra*.

26 11 U.S.C. § 523(a)(16), as enacted by the Bankruptcy Reform Act of 1994, Pub. L. No. 103-394, 108 Stat. 4106. *See* § 14.4.3.14, *infra*.

27 11 U.S.C. § 524(c), (d), as amended by the Bankruptcy Reform Act of 1994, Pub. L. No. 103-394, 108 Stat. 4106. *See* § 14.5.2, *infra*.

28 11 U.S.C. §§ 523(a)(14)–(16), 1328(a), as enacted and amended by the Bankruptcy Reform Act of 1994, Pub. L. No. 103-394, 108 Stat. 4106. *See* §§ 14.4.1, 14.4.3.12–14.4.3.14, *infra*.

29 11 U.S.C. §§ 341(d), 342(c), and Fed. R. Bankr. P. 7004, as enacted or amended by the Bankruptcy Reform Act of 1994, Pub. L. No. 103-394, 108 Stat. 4106. *See* §§ 1.4.2, 8.4.2, *infra*.

30 11 U.S.C. § 106, as amended by the Bankruptcy Reform Act of 1994, Pub. L. No. 103-394, 108 Stat 4106 (effective with respect to cases pending on or after October 22, 1994), overruled Hoffman v. Connecticut Dep't of Income Maintenance, 492 U.S. 96, 109 S. Ct. 2818, 106 L. Ed. 2d 76 (1989) and United States v. Nordic Vill., 503 U.S. 30, 112 S. Ct. 1011, 117 L. Ed. 2d 181 (1992). *See* § 13.3.2.2, *infra*. However, some of the 1994 amendments have been found to be unconstitutional. *See* § 13.3.2.2, *infra*.

31 11 U.S.C. §§ 362(b)(2), 507(a)(7), 522(f)(1), 523(a)(15), and 547(c)(7), as amended or enacted by the Bankruptcy Reform Act of 1994, Pub. L. No. 103-394, 108 Stat. 4106. *See* §§ 3.5, 9.4.5, 10.4.2.3, 10.4.2.6.4, 14.4.3.13, *infra*.

32 11 U.S.C. § 110, as enacted by the Bankruptcy Reform Act of 1994, Pub. L. No. 103-394, 108 Stat. 4106. *See* § 15.6, *infra*.

33 28 U.S.C. § 157(e), as enacted by the Bankruptcy Reform Act of 1994, Pub. L. No. 103-394, 108 Stat. 4106. *See* § 13.2.7, *infra*.

34 28 U.S.C. §§ 158, 1334(c)(2), as amended by the Bankruptcy Reform Act of 1994, Pub. L. No. 103-394, 108 Stat. 4106. *See* §§ 2.4.3, 13.10.1, *infra*.

35 *See* § 14.4.3.8, *infra*.

36 *See* § 14.4.3.17, *infra*.

37 *See* § 14.4.3.7, *infra*.

38 *See* § 1.4.4.1, *infra*.

after the report of the National Bankruptcy Review Commission. This is the Religious Liberty and Charitable Donation Protection Act of 1998.[39] The amendments made by this Act protect bona fide and reasonable religious and charitable contributions[40] from being attacked and recovered from the donee as fraudulent transfers.[41] In addition, the amendments permit debtors to continue to make such contributions after bankruptcy in cases filed under chapter 7 and chapter 13.[42]

The 108th Congress, which began in January 2003, has again seen a massive effort by the consumer credit industry to make sweeping changes to the Bankruptcy Code, but has not to date enacted significant bankruptcy legislation.[43] The sunset date for chapter 12 was again extended in 2002 to January 1, 2004,[44] and again in 2004 to June 30, 2005.[45]

1.1.3 Bankruptcy's Past As Neglected Remedy

Despite its potential importance to consumer clients, the use of bankruptcy law is avoided by some attorneys. These practitioners see bankruptcy as an intimidating maze of paperwork in an unfamiliar and sometimes (for rural offices) inconvenient forum. And, perhaps, a touch of the old-time stigma still remains from the early days of consumer debtor representation, which saw bankruptcy as a lazy cop-out, either for client or lawyer, if not just a bit immoral.

In legal services offices, the disfavored status of bankruptcy has sometimes been officially announced as a principle of office priorities, bankruptcy being a matter which could be left to the private attorneys who traditionally handled bankruptcies in their community. More troubling, though, is the narrow view of bankruptcy which such policies evince—bankruptcy only as an easy way out for judgment-proof debtors.

Offices which have excluded bankruptcy from their practice have excluded a remedy which can be used to better or more easily deal with those problems which they traditionally handle in other ways. To say "we don't do bankruptcies" is basically not much different than saying "we don't file complaints." In many cases bankruptcy is the best way to prevent loss of housing, utility service, income, a car or driver's license necessary to maintain or gain employment, or even freedom, as imprisonment may result from failure to comply with orders to pay support or other indebtedness.[46] Bankruptcy has certainly provided millions of people with relief from the incessant collection calls, letters, and other harassment tactics that accompany unpaid debts. Yet, presumably, the clients of some attorneys do not have that remedy available to them.

1.1.4 Making Bankruptcy Available to Consumer Clients

It is incumbent upon those who represent financially troubled clients to have a basic knowledge of what can be accomplished through the use of bankruptcy. Not only may such knowledge save a client thousands of dollars, a home, a car, or a job, but it may accomplish these desired results better, faster, and with less expenditure of attorney and client resources than any other means. The bankruptcy court may be a more favorable forum for the raising of affirmative claims and may dispose of them more quickly. Moreover, it may be malpractice not to make available to clients the powerful tools available in bankruptcy for solving their problems.

Probably even more important is the impact of bankruptcy practice on creditor behavior in a particular community. The use of bankruptcy when appropriate often makes a lasting impression, and the ever-present threat of bankruptcy in subsequent cases causes many creditors to become a lot more reasonable than they were before in settling cases and in dealing with their customers. Practitioners have sometimes found regular and skillful use of bankruptcy remedies to have greater deterrent effect than a dozen class actions. The creditor facing an attorney known for filing class actions usually is of the firm belief that it has little to worry about because it firmly believes all of its practices are legal (at least in the particular case involved). But the creditor facing an attorney known to be well-versed in bankruptcy will know, or soon learn, that it stands to lose money in almost every case the bankruptcy attorney handles and that every case is one in which it can be forced to be reasonable, if indeed bankruptcy leaves any claim to be reasonable about.

Of course, bankruptcy is not always the preferable remedy and consumer attorneys should not hesitate to bring

---

39 Pub. L. No. 105-183, 112 Stat. 517. The amendments made by this Act affect cases pending on or after the date of the Act (June 19, 1998).

40 The contributions must be made to a qualified donee under the Internal Revenue Code. The amount may not exceed fifteen percent of the debtor's gross income unless a larger contribution is consistent with the debtor's past pattern of contributions.

41 Protections from avoidance have been added to both 11 U.S.C. §§ 544 and 548. The law overrules cases such as *In re* Newman, 203 B.R. 468 (D. Kan. 1996) and *In re* Gomes, 219 B.R. 286 (Bankr. D. Or. 1998) which had found charitable contributions to be constructive fraudulent transfers within the meaning of the Bankruptcy Code. *See* §§ 10.4.2.6.2, 10.4.2.6.5, *infra*.

42 *See* §§ 12.3.3, 13.9.2.2, *infra*.

43 Pub. L. No. 107-8, 115 Stat. 10 (2001) (extending chapter 12 until May 31, 2001); Pub. L. No. 107-17, 115 Stat. 151 (2001) (extending chapter 12 until September 30, 2001).

44 Pub. L. No. 108-73, 117 Stat. 891 (2003).

45 Pub. L. No. 108-369, 118 Stat. 1749 (2004).

---

46 Such debt-related imprisonment still exists in some places. *See, e.g.*, Judice v. Vail, 430 U.S. 327, 97 S. Ct. 1211, 51 L. Ed. 2d 376 (1977). Moreover, virtually every state imposes imprisonment for failure to pay child or spousal support.

class actions whenever appropriate. The well-rounded advocate should know how to use all kinds of remedies, often in conjunction with each other, as tools to effect her clients' objectives.

1.2 The Focus of This Manual— Bankruptcy Practice for Consumer Debtors and Family Farmers

This manual provides the basic information needed to best utilize the tools that bankruptcy provides to consumer debtors. Of necessity, most of what follows is also applicable to debtors who have had small businesses; many consumer clients are, after all, simply businesspeople who have fallen upon hard times and no longer operate their businesses. However, while this manual may be of some use in cases in which debtors seek to continue operating their businesses, advocates will have to look elsewhere for assistance in handling the more complex problems which can arise in such an undertaking.

Chapter 16, *infra,* deals extensively with the issues and problems arising in the representation of family farmers under chapter 12 of the Bankruptcy Code. Although most of the concepts and strategies involved in such representation are similar to those applicable to chapter 13, there are a number of provisions and subjects which are either more akin to chapter 11 principles or unique to chapter 12.

Although this manual is primarily oriented toward representing debtors, Chapter 17, *infra,* provides a basic outline for representing consumers as creditors: that is, when a merchant, landlord, lender, or other entity with whom an individual consumer is involved files bankruptcy. The treatment of this topic provided in Chapter 17, *infra,* is far from exhaustive, and anyone seeking to aggressively represent a creditor in the bankruptcy process is encouraged to utilize other resources.

This manual is also not intended to be a treatise. Although it contains a thorough discussion of those substantive issues which are most common and important, it is neither exhaustive nor comprehensive on all of bankruptcy law. In general, for the issues discussed, only a few leading cases, along with the applicable statutes and rules, are cited. Because it is now possible to find at least one bankruptcy court opinion taking almost any position on a given issue, lower court decisions contrary to the text of this manual are not always noted. Appellate decisions normally are cited, however, whether or not they agree with the author. Again, for further research, the authorities at the end of this Chapter and in the Bibliography should be consulted.

1.3 How to Use This Manual

1.3.1 Purpose of the Manual

This manual is intended to serve as a basic resource to advocates, both attorneys and paralegals working with attorneys, handling bankruptcy cases. It is meant to provide an introduction for the novice considering her first bankruptcy case and also a useful tool for the expert who has handled many such cases. It should be serviceable both as a quick reference in offices with substantial libraries as well as a fairly complete basic resource in those offices which maintain only a minimal library immediately accessible.

Naturally, offices doing many bankruptcies will wish to purchase other comprehensive texts on the subject, as well as a subscription to at least one bankruptcy reporting service. Suggestions for these are listed at the end of this Chapter. Those offices may also wish to develop forms, checklists, and other materials tailored to their own particular needs, for use in addition to or instead of those in this manual.

1.3.2 Organization of the Manual

To facilitate its use by the various constituencies to which it is addressed, the manual is divided into several parts. Although there are frequent cross-references, each part has a different purpose.

The first part, consisting of the first four chapters, is intended to provide an introductory "nuts and bolts" understanding of how bankruptcy works. To keep these chapters relatively non-technical, they contain many references to later chapters for in-depth discussion of particular topics.

The next four chapters contain a step-by-step practice guide on how to handle a case from the moment that bankruptcy is first considered until events that occur after the case is over. Together, the first eight chapters should provide the reader with a basic knowledge of what happens in a typical consumer bankruptcy. The remaining chapters may then be consulted as necessary.

Chapters 9 through 15, *infra,* contain a more detailed discussion of the legal issues frequently arising in consumer bankruptcy cases. As these issues are so often present, those who practice regularly in bankruptcy courts should eventually become knowledgeable in the areas covered by these chapters as well as those preceding them.

Finally, Chapter 16, *infra,* contains a discussion of issues involved in representing family farmers in cases under chapter 12 of the Bankruptcy Code and Chapter 17, *infra,* addresses issues related to representing consumers as creditors when a merchant, landlord or other entity is in bankruptcy.

The manual includes a set of appendices that contain basic bankruptcy reference materials. These materials have been substantially updated and revised for this Seventh Edition. They should be used in preference to older editions and supplements which no longer present accurate versions of current law. As new supplements are published, they should be consulted for the most current available materials. And because the supplements are published yearly, interim materials such as *NCLC REPORTS* should also be consulted.

Appendix A, *infra,* reprints the text of the U.S. Bankruptcy Code[47] as well as selected provisions of other relevant statutes. Appendix B, *infra,* reprints the Federal Rules of Bankruptcy Procedure as amended through December 2004. Appendix C, *infra,* reprints the Judicial Conference Schedule of Fees.

Appendix D, *infra,* includes, as blank reproducible forms, those Official Forms promulgated by the federal Judicial Conference which are generally relevant to consumer bankruptcy practice. These forms were substantially altered in the past few years, so it is important not to rely on old forms, including those reproduced in prior editions of this manual. The forms found in Appendix D, *infra,* can be copied and used in actual cases although, as discussed below, it will usually be more efficient to use either a specialized bankruptcy document preparation program or the word-processing files containing the same forms that are included on the CD-Rom accompanying this volume.

Appendix E, *infra,* contains some other reproducible forms which, though not "official," are in common use. Although they may be filed as is in most jurisdictions, local practice may impose different requirements.

Following the blank official forms, there are two appendices containing other sample forms, pleadings, letters and other documents. Appendix F, *infra,* contains sample completed bankruptcy schedules illustrating how to prepare an initial filing. Many commonly occurring issues encountered in filling out the official forms are addressed. Appendix G, *infra,* contains more than one-hundred-fifty model pleadings and form letters for representing consumer debtors. The Appendix also includes sections on forms commonly used in chapter 12 and by consumers as creditors.

The forms in Appendices F and G, *infra,* are intended to serve as a guide for addressing issues which commonly arise in consumer bankruptcy practice. A listing of these forms can be found both in the table of contents and at the beginning of each Appendix in the back of the volume.

Appendix H, *infra,* is a sample bankruptcy interview form which can be filled out either by an advocate or by clients directly. It may need to be edited to accommodate local practice. Appendix I, *infra,* is a sample handout for clients, which answers many common bankruptcy questions.

One other helpful resource is the bibliography of articles and books on consumer bankruptcy which precedes the appendices. A separate farm bankruptcy bibliography is found in § 16.9, *infra.*

Finally, these practice aids are included on the CD-Rom which accompanies this volume, allowing rapid computer searches, editing of pleadings with word-processing software, and copying source materials directly into briefs. The CD-Rom contains all the material found in *Consumer Bankruptcy Law and Practice*'s Appendices, Index, and Quick Reference. In addition, this CD-Rom contains petitions, schedules, and other official bankruptcy forms that may be completed using various word-processing programs. These forms are part of an *unsupported* version of Law Disks' *Bankruptcy Forms.*

1.3.3 Using This Manual As a Research Tool

1.3.3.1 This Manual Does Not Contain Citations to Every Relevant Case

The number of reported cases on consumer bankruptcy issues has far outstripped the space in this book to catalogue them. The text of the manual discusses a wide variety of issues that may arise in consumer cases. The footnotes contain case law which will serve as a starting point for research. We have attempted, whenever possible, to include the relevant court of appeals decisions on the topics discussed as well as other cases which support the arguments a consumer may wish to make. However, do not expect to find all relevant cases on any topic or cases in each jurisdiction. Further research into case law is likely to be necessary.

This book identifies arguments which support the consumer position on most issues. For this reason, the footnotes contain many more cases which provide support for the consumer debtor than cases which support creditors. However, when there are court of appeals cases on both sides of an issue, we have attempted to be inclusive.

Because many bankruptcy issues overlap more than one bankruptcy topic, this book contains many cross references. Careful attention to the cross references will often yield additional relevant case law. Other valuable research tools are discussed at the end of this Chapter.

1.3.3.2 NCLC Case Consulting and Other NCLC Manuals

Consumer law questions on issues other than bankruptcy often arise in the context of a bankruptcy case. For example, bankruptcy clients are often the victims of debt collection abuses and may have causes of action to remedy those

---

47 The full Code is reprinted with the exception of chapter 9 and subchapters III and IV of chapter 7, which are not relevant to consumers.

abuses. Similarly, creditor overcharges can often result in overstated claims. Many of these issues are covered at length in other books in this NCLC series. The Consumer Credit and Sales Legal Practice Series contains books, for example, on fair debt collection, fair credit reporting, the cost of credit, truth in lending, repossessions and foreclosures, and sales of goods and services, which are as exhaustive as this treatment of bankruptcy.

In addition, NCLC has established a low-cost case consulting service. NCLC can provide additional research, pleadings, briefs, or other litigation support on a wide variety of consumer issues. More information about this service is available on a card in the front of this manual or by calling 617-542-8010.

1.4 The Governing Law

1.4.1 Statutory Materials

1.4.1.1 The Bankruptcy Code

The most important source of law in bankruptcy cases is, of course, the statute itself. The Bankruptcy Code, which is title 11 of the United States Code, was meant to be a comprehensive body of law, gathering from other parts of the United States Code all those provisions dealing with the substantive law of bankruptcy.

As with any comprehensive code, frequent reference to the definitions is critically important. The definitions applicable throughout the Bankruptcy Code are contained in section 101 of the statute. Among the many terms defined are "claim," "consumer debt," "creditor," "debtor," "entity," "governmental unit," "judicial lien," "lien," "statutory lien," "security interest," "person," and "transfer." In addition to these general definitions, various other chapters of the Code contain definitions of other terms applicable only to those chapters.

The first chapter of the Code also contains rules of construction.[48] Most important among these is the use of the phrase "after notice and a hearing." Depending on the circumstances, this phrase may not mean that a hearing will actually take place. Other rules explain use of the words "or," "includes," and "order for relief."

Chapter 1 also provides an explanation of the Code's structure. One should always remember that chapters 1, 3, and 5 of the Code are applicable to all proceedings under any chapter of the Code unless a provision of that specific chapter provides otherwise.[49] In contrast, chapters 7, 9, 11, 12, and 13 are only applicable to cases brought under those chapters respectively.

The Bankruptcy Judges, United States Trustees, and Family Farmer Bankruptcy Act of 1986[50] enacted amendments to the Bankruptcy Code to accommodate the phase-in of the United States trustee program nationwide and to take the place of the former chapter 15 of the Code which dealt with the pilot U.S. trustee program that previously existed. These amendments have become operative in almost every district.[51]

1.4.1.2 Other Relevant Statutes

Other statutory materials relevant to bankruptcy cases are found outside the Bankruptcy Code itself. Most importantly, the jurisdictional provisions relevant to bankruptcy are found in title 28 of the United States Code.[52] Additionally, a small number of government benefit programs now have their own bankruptcy dischargeability provisions which have been codified with the program authorization rather than in the Bankruptcy Code itself.[53] Similarly, some taxation issues relevant to bankruptcy cases and debts discharged in bankruptcy are found in title 26, generally known as the Internal Revenue Code.[54]

Finally, some bankruptcy law, particularly portions of statutes which provide implementation dates, is not codified at all. These provisions can only be found by reviewing the enacted public law itself.[55]

Throughout this book, full citation to this material is provided to the best source available. With few exceptions, relevant statutory material is also reprinted in Appendix A, *infra.*

1.4.2 The Federal Rules of Bankruptcy Procedure

Complementing the statute's mostly substantive provisions are the Federal Rules of Bankruptcy Procedure, also known as the Bankruptcy Rules, which were promulgated by the Supreme Court in 1983 and amended at various times since then.[56] These rules provide detailed guidelines in numerous areas not specifically covered by the Code. They cover the procedures not only for administering the bank-

---

48 11 U.S.C. § 102.
49 11 U.S.C. § 103.

50 Pub. L. No. 99-554, 100 Stat. 3088.
51 Pub. L. No. 99-554, § 302, 100 Stat. 3088. The U.S. trustee program now operates in every district except those in North Carolina and Alabama. *See* § 2.7, *infra.*
52 *See* Appx. A.2.1, *infra.*
53 *See, e.g.,* Appx. A.2.2, *infra.*
54 *See* Appx. A.2.2, *infra.*
55 *See, e.g.,* Appxs. A.2.3–A.2.10, *infra.*
56 The Rules of Bankruptcy Procedure as amended through the publication date of this manual are reprinted in Appendix B, *infra.* The Rules are now to be cited as the Federal Rules of Bankruptcy Procedure (Fed. R. Bankr. P.) as opposed to the "Bankruptcy Rules" under prior law. Fed. R. Bankr. P. 1001.

ruptcy petitions themselves, but also for proceedings within or related to the principal bankruptcy case.[57]

The rules' distinction between a "case" and a "proceeding" is important to keep in mind. Although nowhere specifically defined, the word "case" encompasses the bankruptcy petition itself, seeking the relief provided by the Code, and includes within its scope all controversies which arise as to that petition.[58] A "proceeding," on the other hand, concerns a dispute which arises within a case, or which is related to a case.[59]

"Proceedings" are themselves divided into two categories. Those which are considered more significant or complex are classified as "adversary proceedings" and governed by Part VII of the rules. Rule 7001 contains a list of the matters that fall in this category, including proceedings to recover money or property (with certain exceptions), to determine the validity or priority of a lien or interest in property (*except* proceedings to avoid judicial liens or non-possessory non-purchase money security interests under section 522(f)), to obtain approval pursuant to section 363(h) for a sale of joint property by the trustee, to object to or revoke a discharge, to obtain an injunction or other equitable relief, to determine the dischargeability of a debt, to obtain most declaratory judgments, and to determine a claim or cause of action removed to a bankruptcy court.

Generally, the adversary proceeding rules, Rules 7001–7087, provide for a lawsuit within the bankruptcy case. With some exceptions (such as service of process which can be done by mail more easily),[60] these rules conform closely to the Federal Rules of Civil Procedure and are numbered to correspond to those rules.[61] For example, Rule 7004 corresponds to Fed. R. Civ. P. 4. As of December 1, 2000, all of the federal discovery rules, including the disclosure requirements contained in Fed. R. Civ. P. 26, will be applicable in every district and bankruptcy court. Bankruptcy courts are no longer authorized to alter or opt out of these requirements by local rule.[62]

Disputes which are not considered adversary proceedings, such as requests for relief from the automatic stay,[63] are called "contested matters" and are governed by Rule 9014.[64] Generally, this rule provides for a more summary procedure akin to motion practice, to which only certain of the adversary proceeding rules apply, and in which an answer is not always required, depending on local rules and practice. However, it is important to note that the applicable rules do incorporate various adversary proceeding rules including those governing discovery,[65] default, and summary judgment.[66] Further, the applicability of the various adversary proceeding rules in contested matters may be expanded or restricted by the court.[67]

Even with the detailed statute and rules, however, there are many procedural questions to which there are no clear answers. Moreover, any rule which is in conflict with the statute is not valid.[68]

Under the Federal Rules of Bankruptcy Procedure, it continues to be important to determine whether there are also supplemental local rules or unusual local procedural practices. When in doubt as to procedure, it is best to check with the clerk of the local bankruptcy court, who will usually be quite cooperative. A failure to be aware of such rules could have dire consequences, because their force and effect equal those of the Bankruptcy Rules.[69] Because the rules specifically provide authority for supplemental local rules,[70] it may also be useful to suggest to the local bankruptcy court that it promulgate particular rules which would codify or improve current practices.

1.4.3 The Official Bankruptcy Forms

Lastly, official bankruptcy forms have been promulgated for use in bankruptcy cases. These are detailed examples of what various documents in a case are to contain. The Bankruptcy Rules provide that papers filed must conform substantially to the Official Forms.[71]

The official bankruptcy forms were substantially amended in recent years to make many of the forms clearer and more

---

57 The Bankruptcy Rules cover proceedings in bankruptcy cases even when those proceedings are before district court judges. Fed. R. Civ. P. 81(a)(1); Fed. R. Bankr. P. 1001; *see* Hedges v. Resolution Trust Corp., 32 F.3d 1360 (9th Cir. 1994) (Fed. R. Civ. P. 11 does not apply when district court is reviewing bankruptcy decision; proper authority is Fed. R. Bankr. P. 9011).

58 Fed. R. Bankr. P. 1002; 11 U.S.C. §§ 301, 303.

59 1 Collier on Bankruptcy ¶ 3.01[4][b] (15th ed. rev.).

60 The procedures for service under Fed. R. Bankr. P. 7004 were amended by the Bankruptcy Reform Act of 1994, Pub. L. No. 103-394, 108 Stat. 4106, to require service on insured depository institutions by certified mail in most cases. *See* Fed. R. Bankr. P. 7004(h); § 13.3.2.1, *infra*.

61 Certain other Federal Rules of Civil Procedure, applicable to all bankruptcy matters, and not just adversary proceedings, are incorporated in Part IX of the Bankruptcy Rules. *See, e.g.*, Fed. R. Bankr. P. 9024 (incorporating Fed. R. Civ. P. 60).

62 However, Fed. R. Bankr. P. 9014(c) provides that the mandatory disclosure requirements of Fed. R. Civ. P. 26, as incorporated by Fed. R. Bankr. P. 7026, do not apply in contested matters.

63 The automatic stay obtained by filing a bankruptcy petition is discussed in detail in Chapter 9, *infra*.

64 Advisory Committee Note to Fed. R. Bankr. P. 9014. The only exceptions to this principle are those few matters specifically designated as "applications" in particular rules, which normally do not give rise to actual disputes. *See, e.g.*, Fed. R. Bankr. P. 1006(b) (application to pay filing fee in installments).

65 Fed. R. Bankr. P. 7028–7037.

66 Fed. R. Bankr. P. 7055, 7056.

67 Fed. R. Bankr. P. 9014.

68 28 U.S.C. § 2075.

69 *See, e.g.*, *In re* Adams, 734 F.2d 1094 (5th Cir. 1984) (failure to properly list creditor's address on mailing matrix required by local rule resulted in debt being excepted from discharge as not "duly scheduled").

70 Fed. R. Bankr. P. 9029.

71 Fed. R. Bankr. P. 9009; *see also, e.g.*, Fed. R. Bankr. P. 1007(b).

understandable, to conform them to statutory changes, and to protect somewhat the privacy of debtors and their dependents. The forms, as amended, are reprinted in Appendix D, *infra,* and are available on the CD-Rom which accompanies this volume, along with software templates of the forms which advocates may use to complete the forms in particular bankruptcy cases.

1.4.4 Other Issues Concerning Sources of Law

1.4.4.1 Pending Legislation and Amendments to the Rules

Nearly every year there are a variety of efforts to amend the Bankruptcy Code, rules, and official forms. Some of these efforts come to fruition and others do not. Careful attention to the progress of those amendments and their effective dates is required.

Over the past few years, legislative proposals that would make dramatic changes in consumer bankruptcy law have garnered substantial support in Congress. Because they would make bankruptcy harder and more expensive for individual debtors, the possibility of future Code amendments making bankruptcy more difficult and expensive should be factored into any advice given to clients about delaying bankruptcy. Other potential changes to the rules and forms also are currently percolating through the system.[72]

Changes are made to this manual through annual supplements reflecting changes in the law as of their publication deadlines. Significant amendments are also reported in our bimonthly publication, *NCLC REPORTS Bankruptcy and Foreclosures Edition.*

1.4.4.2 Local Bankruptcy Rules

In addition to the Bankruptcy Rules, practitioners should refer to any local rules[73] and local practice to fill in gaps in interpretation. Pursuant to the policy of the federal Judicial Conference, local bankruptcy rules are generally numbered to correspond to the Federal Rules of Bankruptcy Procedure to which they relate. Some courts may also promulgate local "procedural orders" applying to all cases before that court. Many courts have local forms which are to be used in particular situations, including forms for chapter 13 plans (although any such form that abridged statutory rights would be invalid). Consequently, in each jurisdiction, attorneys should consult the court clerk concerning all local rules, forms, orders, and customs.[74]

In some instances, there may be important ways in which the local rules conflict with the national rules or even with the Bankruptcy Code. When necessary, these conflicts should be pointed out to the local committee which drafted the rules or to the judges who adopted them. When clients' rights are affected, it is appropriate to challenge the rules and they should certainly be invalidated when they are inconsistent with the national rules, the official forms, or the Code.[75]

1.4.4.3 Case Law Under the Code

Over the years, many bankruptcy cases under the Code have reached the Supreme Court. Although the Supreme Court's definitive holdings reach only limited specific issues in bankruptcy law, two important guiding principles have been enunciated on several occasions. First, as expected, the plain language of the statute controls.[76] Second, the Court has repeatedly held that it will not find congressional intent to overrule law under the prior Bankruptcy Act absent a clear statement by Congress to that effect.[77] Because of the latter principle, it is important to review precedent under the

---

rules commensurate with the cost of printing. *See* Judicial Conference Schedule of Fees at ¶ 18 (reprinted following 28 U.S.C.A. § 1930 and as Appx. C, *infra*). Obviously, the fee, if any, varies from jurisdiction to jurisdiction. Local rules and forms are also usually available on local courts' websites, accessible through www.uscourts.gov.

75 *See* Fed. R. Bankr. P. 9029 (local rules may not be "inconsistent with" the national rules or "prohibit or limit the use of the Official Forms"). Local rules also must be promulgated by the district court judges (rather than the bankruptcy court) with appropriate opportunity for notice and comment. *Id.*; *see, e.g., In re* Petro, 276 F.3d 375 (7th Cir. 2002) (striking down local rule requiring chapter 13 debtors to file affidavit every six months listing income along with copies of paycheck stubs); *In re* Wilkinson, 923 F.2d 154 (10th Cir. 1991) (striking down local rule requiring district court permission to move for rehearing as inconsistent with Fed. R. Bankr. P. 8015); *In re* Steinacher, 283 B.R. 768 (B.A.P. 9th Cir. 2002) (invalidating local rule requiring short cure period for any debtor who had previous chapter 13 case pending within six months before current case).

76 *E.g.,* Toibb v. Radloff, 501 U.S. 157, 111 S. Ct. 2197, 115 L. Ed. 2d 145 (1991); Johnson v. Home State Bank, 501 U.S 78, 111 S. Ct. 2150, 115 L. Ed. 2d 66 (1991); Pennsylvania Dep't of Public Welfare v. Davenport, 495 U.S. 552, 110 S. Ct. 2126, 109 L. Ed. 2d 588 (1990); United States v. Ron Pair Enterprises, Inc., 489 U.S. 235, 109 S. Ct. 1026, 1030, 103 L. Ed. 2d 290 (1989). However, whether some of the Supreme Court's recent decisions purporting to rely on the Code's plain language have actually comported with that language is quite debatable. *See, e.g.,* Rake v. Wade, 508 U.S. 464, 113 S. Ct. 2187, 124 L. Ed. 2d 424 (1993) (holding that a mortgage arrearage is an allowed secured claim that must be paid interest under 11 U.S.C. § 1325(a)(5)(B)).

77 *E.g.,* Dewsnup v. Timm, 502 U.S. 410, 112 S. Ct. 773, 116 L. Ed. 2d 903 (1992); Kelly v. Robinson, 479 U.S. 36, 107 S. Ct. 353, 93 L. Ed. 2d 216 (1986); Midlantic Nat'l Bank v. New Jersey, 474 U.S. 494, 106 S. Ct. 755, 88 L. Ed. 2d 859 (1986).

---

72 Proposed changes may be reviewed at www.uscourts.gov.
73 Fed. R. Bankr. P. 9029.
74 Courts are empowered to charge fees for copies of their local

Bankruptcy Act as well as cases under the Bankruptcy Code in researching unresolved bankruptcy questions.

Since 1978, a substantial body of case law from the bankruptcy courts has been reported. In addition, appellate decisions in each jurisdiction have created a pool of binding precedent which must be examined before advocating on bankruptcy issues. In a bankruptcy court, it is generally only circuit court precedent which is considered binding. District court decisions and bankruptcy appellate panel decisions[78] have *stare decisis* effect in bankruptcy, but because of the potential for inconsistent decisions from different judges of the same district court, they are generally not considered binding even on bankruptcy judges in the district in which they arose.[79]

Additionally, state courts have ruled on issues directly or indirectly related to bankruptcy, most notably in the areas of state exemptions, dischargeability of certain debts, and lien rights of secured creditors. As is discussed more fully below, many bankruptcy issues turn on questions of state law. As the body of bankruptcy case law continues to grow, careful research will generally uncover helpful decisions if not binding precedent on virtually any issue.

1.5 Other Resources for Practicing Under the Bankruptcy Code

1.5.1 Legislative History

1.5.1.1 The Bankruptcy Reform Act of 1978

In dealing with legal questions about bankruptcy, the first places to look, of course, are the statute itself and the Federal Rules of Bankruptcy Procedure, the relevant parts of which are included in Appendices A and B, *infra,* as well as relevant case law. Often, these will not provide sufficient answers, and other sources must be consulted.

Generally, the most important indicator of what Congress meant in a particular section of the Code is the legislative history. Because of the long gestation periods which produced both the final law and the later amendments, there are a number of parts to the legislative history.[80]

The first major document in the evolution of the 1978 Bankruptcy Code was the report of the Commission on the Bankruptcy Laws.[81] The Commission, a special body set up by Congress, proposed a precursor to the final legislation and in its report explained its reasons for the provisions contained in its proposed bill. In the many areas in which the Bankruptcy Reform Act is identical or similar to the Commission's proposal, the report of the Commission is an excellent explanatory authority.

Even more important are the House[82] and Senate[83] reports which accompanied the bills first passed by those two bodies (H.R. 8200 and S. 2266 of the 95th Congress). As these bills were in most respects identical to the final Act, the reports accompanying them are the most comprehensive and definitive explanation of congressional intent for many provisions.

Unlike most legislation, the Bankruptcy Reform Act never went to a conference committee of the two houses, so there is no conference report regarding how the differences between the House and Senate bills were reconciled. Instead, there are long and detailed floor statements by the sponsors in each house, who had met and worked out the differences among themselves. The floor statement of Representative Edwards[84] explains each change in the House bill which resulted from the compromises reached, and similarly the statement of Senator DeConcini[85] explains each change in the Senate bill.

Thus, in using the legislative history, the floor statements, which are the latest explanations, must be consulted first to see if there was any change from the previous bills, and if so whether any explanation for the change was given. Next, the report of each house and finally the Commission report should be checked. For very detailed research the many volumes of hearings,[86] reflecting the views of numerous

---

78 See § 2.4.3, *infra,* for discussion of bankruptcy appellate panels.

79 *See In re* Rheuban, 128 B.R. 551 (Bankr. C.D. Cal. 1991) (bankruptcy judge in multi-judge district need not follow decisions of the district court); *In re* Johnson-Allen, 67 B.R. 968 (Bankr. E.D. Pa. 1986) (bankruptcy court should make every effort to follow decisions of district court where it is sitting). Similarly, bankruptcy appellate panel decisions are not binding on district or bankruptcy judges in districts of the circuit other than where the panel sits. *In re* Selden, 121 B.R. 551 (D. Or. 1990); *see* Bank of Maui v. Estate Analysis, Inc., 904 F.2d 470 (9th Cir. 1990) (bankruptcy appellate panel decisions do not bind the district courts).

80 A good discussion of the Code's legislative history is found in

Kenneth N. Klee, *Legislative History of the New Bankruptcy Code,* 54 Am. Bankr. L.J. 275 (1980).

81 Report of the Commission on the Bankruptcy Laws of the United States, H.R. Doc. No. 93-137 (1973) (hereafter "Commission Report"). The Commission Report is available, among other places, in Collier on Bankruptcy app. vol. B (15th ed. rev.).

82 H.R. Rep. No. 95-595 (1977).

83 S. Rep. No. 95-989 (1978).

84 124 Cong. Rec. H11,089–H11,116 (daily ed. Sept. 28, 1978).

85 124 Cong. Rec. S17,406–S17,434, (daily ed. Sept. 7, 1978).

86 *Hearings on H.R. 31 and H.R. 32 Before the Subcomm. on Civil and Constitutional Rights of the House Comm. on the Judiciary,* 94th Cong. (1975–1976); *Hearings on S.235 and S.236 Before the Subcomm. on Improvements in Judicial Machinery of the Senate Comm. on the Judiciary,* 94th Cong. (1975); *Hearings on S.2266 and H.R. 8200 Before the Subcomm. on Improvements in Judicial Machinery of the Senate Comm. on the Judiciary,* 95th Cong. (1977); *Hearings on H.R. 8200 Before the Subcomm. on Civil and Constitutional Rights of the House Comm. on the Judiciary,* 95th Cong. (1977).

parties on various provisions, are also available, as well as some congressional debate on earlier versions of the bill.[87]

1.5.1.2 The 1984 Amendments

Like the Bankruptcy Reform Act, the 1984 amendments, particularly those concerning consumer bankruptcy, evolved through a lengthy process of hearings and reports followed by a last minute frenzy of compromises. As with the 1978 Act, there is no formal conference report and no explanation of many of the final provisions other than in statements on the floor of Congress by their sponsors.

The jurisdictional sections of the 1984 amendments, in particular, were determined almost entirely on the floor and in unreported conferences. Therefore, to the extent that there is legislative history, it is to be found in the floor statements of June 29, 1984[88] and in the earlier statements and debates concerning the amendment offered by Representative Kastenmeier to the original House Bill,[89] as that amendment in large part formed the basis of the final enactment.

The other provisions of the 1984 amendments emerged from a variety of sources. The consumer bankruptcy amendments were the result of successive revisions of a bill originally proposed by the consumer finance industry. A weakened version of that bill passed the Senate in 1983, and the Senate report[90] on that version is helpful in interpreting provisions that were not substantially changed in the final bill. However, many provisions of the Senate bill were further altered in a later compromise in the House, which produced the final language of the consumer amendments. There are only floor statements, particularly those of Representative Rodino,[91] who sponsored the compromise, to explain those changes, though for a few sections other portions of the legislative history are also relevant.[92] Again, for further research, there are several volumes of hearings as well as earlier versions of many provisions of the amendments which may be consulted.[93]

1.5.1.3 The 1986 Amendments

The legislative history of the 1986 amendments is somewhat less ample. The United States Trustee program, first conceived and discussed in the legislative history of the 1978 Bankruptcy Reform Act, was the subject of several competing bills in the House and Senate. Similarly, the plight of family farmers led to the hurried introduction of a number of bills to remedy their situation. There were hearings[94] and reports[95] in both houses of Congress and a final conference report resolving differences between the two houses.[96]

1.5.1.4 The Bankruptcy Reform Act of 1994

Like much other bankruptcy legislation, the Bankruptcy Reform Act of 1994 was passed in a flurry of last minute activity, so there is no conference report detailing the final compromises between the House and Senate versions of the bill. Instead, these compromises were worked out as the bill was being considered in the House Judiciary Committee and during the time between its passage out of that committee and its consideration on the House floor. The final explanation of the bill is contained in floor statements made when it was considered on the House floor.[97] This explanation is mostly identical to the House report on the bill,[98] except as to those provisions that were changed after the bill was voted out of the House Judiciary Committee. A comparison of the final bill to the bill which had previously passed the Senate[99] and its accompanying committee report[100] sheds further light on the decisions and compromises that were made in the legislative process.

---

87 Large portions of the legislative history are reprinted in Collier on Bankruptcy app. (15th ed. rev.) along with a detailed description of the legislative process, and at 1978 U.S.C.C.A.N. 5786–6573.

88 130 Cong. Rec. H7471–H7497 (daily ed. June 29, 1984); 130 Cong. Rec. S8887–S8900 (daily ed. June 29, 1984).

89 130 Cong. Rec. E1107–E1110 (daily ed. Mar. 20, 1984); 130 Cong. Rec. H1832–H1854 (daily ed. Mar. 21, 1984).

90 S. Rep. No. 98-65 (1983).

91 130 Cong. Rec. H1721, H1722 (daily ed. Mar. 19, 1984); 130 Cong. Rec. H1807–H1832 (daily ed. Mar. 21, 1984); 130 Cong. Rec. H1941, H1942 (daily ed. Mar. 26, 1984).

92 For example, the amendments to 11 U.S.C. § 1325(b) and 11 U.S.C. § 1329 were adopted virtually verbatim from a proposal made and explained by the National Bankruptcy Conference in hearings on the amendments. *See Oversight Hearings on Personal Bankruptcy Before the Subcomm. on Monopolies and Commercial Law of the House Comm. on the Judiciary*, 97th Cong. 181–222 (1981-1982).

93 *See Oversight Hearings on Personal Bankruptcy Before the*

Subcomm. on Monopolies and Commercial Law of the House Comm. on the Judiciary, 97th Cong. (1981-1982).

94 *Hearings on H.R. 4128 and H.R. 4140 Before the Subcomm. on Monopolies and Commercial Law of the House Comm. on the Judiciary*, 99th Cong. (1986); *Hearings on H.R. 1397 and H.R. 1399 Before the Subcomm. on Monopolies and Commercial Law of the House Comm. on the Judiciary*, 99th Cong. (1985); *Hearings on S. 705, S. 1342, S. 1516, and H.R. 2211 Before the Subcomm. on Admin. Practice and Procedure and the Subcomm. on Courts of the Senate Comm. on the Judiciary*, 99th Cong. (1985); *Hearings on S. 1923 Before the Senate Comm. on the Judiciary*, 99th Cong. (1985).

95 H.R. Rep. No. 99-764 (1986); H.R. Rep. No. 99-178 (1985); S. Rep. No. 99-269 (1986).

96 H.R. Rep. No. 99-958 (1986).

97 140 Cong. Rec. H10,752–H10,773 (daily ed. Oct. 4, 1994).

98 H.R. Rep. No. 103-835 (1994), *reprinted in* 1994 U.S.C.C.A.N. 3340.

99 S. 540, 103d Cong. (1994).

100 S. Rep. No. 103-168 (1993).

1.5.2 Rules Advisory Committee Notes

The Federal Rules of Bankruptcy Procedure were accompanied by advisory committee explanatory notes, as was each amendment to those rules. These notes are available in a number of published versions of the rules[101] and, like the legislative history, are the most authoritative explanation of the drafters' intent. On questions of rule interpretation, therefore, they should be the first source consulted.

1.5.3 Treatises and Texts[102]

Collier on Bankruptcy. Of the many treatises and texts on bankruptcy law which have been available, one has become by far the most frequently used and is a bible to many judges and practitioners.[103] Any office doing a substantial amount of bankruptcy work should have access to *Collier on Bankruptcy*,[104] which includes among its authors two of the principal congressional staff persons who worked on drafting the legislation.[105] A substantially revised edition of this treatise was published in 1996. References in this manual have been updated to reflect this revised edition.

Numerous other treatises, texts, and handbooks are also available. Some of the most popular and useful ones include, in alphabetical order by author:

Richard I. Aaron, *Bankruptcy Law Fundamentals.* This text, another one volume general treatment of bankruptcy, contains an often interesting, but sometimes uneven discussion of some of the issues arising in consumer and business bankrupcies.[106] It is supplemented by an annual maintenance service.

Arnold Cohen & Mitchell W. Miller, *Consumer Bankruptcy Manual* (2d ed.). A one-volume practice manual for attorneys handling chapter 7 and chapter 13 cases, it competently but somewhat less comprehensively covers many of the same topics as this manual. As the Cohen and Miller volume provides guidance for those who represent creditors, it would be an excellent addition to any library wishing to expand its materials on consumer bankruptcy.[107]

Collier Bankruptcy Manual (3d ed.). A shorter version of the treatise, this three-volume set is less comprehensive than the treatise and it is not in the library of many judges who have the full *Collier* treatise instead. An accompanying three-volume *Collier Forms Manual* may also be purchased, which contains the forms in the standard *Collier* treatise.[108]

Daniel R. Cowans, *Bankruptcy Law and Practice* (7th ed.). One of the most useful texts for consumer bankruptcy practice under the old Act was Cowans, *Bankruptcy Law and Practice,* which has since been updated.[109]

W. Homer Drake, Jr., *Bankruptcy Practice for the General Practitioner* (3d ed.). This text offers little discussion of consumer bankruptcy issues and would not add a great deal to what is contained in this manual.[110]

W. Homer Drake, Jr. & M. Regina Morris, *Chapter 13 Practice and Procedure* (2d ed.). A one-volume text on most aspects of chapter 13, this work offers a fairly complete discussion of many chapter 13 issues, as well as a number of forms.[111]

David G. Epstein, *Bankruptcy and Related Law in a Nutshell* (6th ed.). This short text is a very good, easy-to-read, and concise explanation of much substantive bankruptcy law with especially helpful discussions of trustees' avoiding powers.[112]

---

101 The Federal Rules of Bankruptcy Procedure are published as a part of the United States Code Annotated, and in paperbound form. Collier Pamphlets 2004 (3 volumes, including code, rules, portable pamphlet, $149.00). In addition to sections of the legislative history and the Rules Advisory Committee Notes, this edition now includes a brief editorial commentary on each Code section and rule as well as some case annotations and a smaller, portable version of the Code and rules. A one-volume compilation of the Code and rules, along with the Federal Rules of Civil Procedure and Federal Rules of Evidence, is published by West Group Publishing Co. ($48.00). A two-volume paperback version containing the Code, rules, forms and commentary is available from West Group for $139.00. A smaller sized "Mini-Code" and "Mini-Rules" are available from AWHFY, L.P., 3950 Doniphan, Suite E, El Paso, TX 79922 ($22.00 for each volume or $35.00 for a combined volume).

102 The prices listed for various publications are for informational purposes only. They are based on information available to NCLC at the time of the publication of this manual. Updated information can be obtained directly from the relevant publisher.

103 Author's disclaimer: This sentence is taken verbatim from the first edition of this manual, written several years before the author became a contributing author to *Collier*, and then Editor-in-Chief of *Collier.*

104 This treatise is published by Matthew Bender ($2570.00 per set of sixteen volumes; annual maintenance is $1747.50). This publication is also available on CD-Rom ($1920.00, approximate annual maintenance is $1930.00) with a variety of other Matthew Bender bankruptcy publications, including Collier Bankruptcy Cases 2d (price varies depending upon publications purchased).

105 Richard B. Levin and Kenneth N. Klee, both of whom served on the staff of the House subcommittee, which put a large portion of the new law into its final form, are consulting editors of the 15th edition.

106 Publisher is West Group ($199.00; annual maintenance is approximately $87.00).

107 Publisher is West Group ($176.00; annual maintenance is approximately $98.00).

108 Publisher is Matthew Bender ($572.00; annual maintenance is approximately $340.00). Collier Forms Manual costs $437.00; annual maintenance is approximately $261.00.

109 This text is published by Lexis Publishing Co. (multi-volume, $535.00).

110 Publisher is West Group ($225.00; annual maintenance is approximately $31.00).

111 Publisher is West Group ($176.00; annual maintenance is approximately $82.00).

112 Publisher is West Group ($25.00).

Herzog's Bankruptcy Forms and Practice (9th ed.). A two-volume form book covering all aspects of bankruptcy practice, this work is the latest edition of a longstanding bankruptcy reference.[113]

Bankruptcy Service, Lawyers Edition. A newer treatise of fifteen volumes, this set might be consulted in addition to *Collier* for detailed explanations and extensive case annotations as to different sections of the Code.[114] Subscribers also receive a monthly "Current Awareness Alert" discussing developments in bankruptcy law.

Morgan D. King, *Discharging Taxes in Bankruptcy.* A one-volume text on the intersection of tax law and bankruptcy, this book contains useful information about Internal Revenue Service procedures and forms, as well as sample forms and pleadings.[115]

Keith M. Lundin, *Chapter 13 Bankruptcy.* The three-volume second edition of this text by a respected bankruptcy judge contains much practical information, presented in a coherent, accessible form. It is primarily a practical guide, so that the case citations are not extensive, and some general bankruptcy topics are discussed only to a limited degree.[116]

Patrick A. Murphy, *Creditors' Rights in Bankruptcy* (2d ed). A good one-volume text which, while oriented to creditors, contains useful information.[117]

Norton Bankruptcy Law and Practice (2d ed.). This service consists of a seven-volume treatise, soft-cover versions of the Code and rules, a monograph binder, and a monthly newsletter.[118] It contains sections written by a large number of respected bankruptcy practitioners and other authorities who provide a discussion of many areas of the law. It also seems to be gaining some degree of acceptance as a recognized authority.

Alan N. Resnick, *Bankruptcy Law Manual* (5th ed.). This text is still another one-volume work, not focused particularly on consumer bankruptcy, attempting to emphasize practical aspects of bankruptcy.[119]

Alan N. Resnick, Henry J. Sommer, & Contributing Authors, *Collier Bankruptcy Practice Guide.* This six-volume work is intended to be the practice manual counterpart to the *Collier* treatise.[120] It is primarily oriented toward business bankruptcies although it contains some material on consumer cases.

Henry J. Sommer, *Collier Consumer Bankruptcy Practice Guide.*[121] This one-volume practice guide is devoted to the nuts and bolts of representing consumers and creditors in consumer bankruptcy cases. It contains some material that is similar to that in this manual, as well as other material, including material pertaining to representing creditors, that is not found in this manual. It may also be purchased on a CD-Rom that contains other Matthew Bender publications including *Collier Family Law and the Bankruptcy Code*, *Collier Consumer Bankruptcy Forms*, the *Collier Bankruptcy Manual*, and the *Collier Exemption Guide.*

Henry J. Sommer & Margaret Doe McGarity, *Collier Family Law and the Bankruptcy Code.* This one-volume text is the only comprehensive treatment of the growing areas of intersection between bankruptcy and family law, going far beyond the limited discussion possible in this manual. It is essential for practitioners doing significant amounts of work in family law areas in which bankruptcy may arise, as well as for bankruptcy practitioners who must confront family law issues in their practices.[122]

George M. Triester, *Fundamentals of Bankruptcy Law* (5th ed.). A one-volume overview of bankruptcy law.[123]

Rosemary E. Williams, *Bankruptcy Practice Handbook* (2d ed.). Another one-volume how-to-do-it guide for relatively inexperienced attorneys, this text contains a number of useful tips, but virtually no discussion of substantive bankruptcy law.[124]

John Williamson, *Attorney's Handbook on Consumer Bankruptcy and Chapter 13* (27th ed., 2004). An inexpensive paperbound volume, this handbook is oriented to private attorneys representing consumers. Although it contains some useful information and forms, on the whole it is considerably less comprehensive than this manual.[125]

Another useful resource, particularly for debtors seeking to handle their own cases, is *How to File for Bankruptcy.*[126] It is published by Nolo Press, which is a nonprofit organization dedicated to assisting non-lawyers with self-help legal remedies. While there are numerous self-help guides to bankruptcy presently flooding the market, *How to File for Bankruptcy* is probably the best, most detailed and easiest to understand. Note that it is important, if the book is recommended to a client, to point out the need for the most recent

---

113 Publisher is West Group ($340.00; annual maintenance is approximately $296.00).

114 This treatise is published by West Group (15 volumes, $2825.00; annual maintenance is approximately $1225.00).

115 Publisher is Kings Press, Suite 222, 7080 Donlon Way, Dublin, CA 94568, or www.bankruptcybooks.com ($197.60).

116 Publisher is Wiley Law Publishing ($315.00; annual maintenance is approximately $135.00).

117 Publisher is West Group ($170.00; annual maintenance is approximately $141.00).

118 Publisher is West Group ($1494.50; annual maintenance is approximately $725.00). A two-volume paperback set of the Code and rules is also available separately for $139.00. The monthly newsletter, the Norton Bankruptcy Law Advisor, may be purchased separately for $598.00 per year.

119 Publisher is West Group ($298.00; annual maintenance is approximately $62.00).

120 Publisher is Matthew Bender ($1393.00); annual maintenance is approximately $880.00.

121 Publisher is Matthew Bender ($207.00).

122 Publisher is Matthew Bender ($207.00).

123 Publisher is American Law Institute ($129.00).

124 Publisher is West Group ($290.00; annual maintenance is approximately $105.00).

125 Publisher is Argyle Publishing, Lakewood, CO ($37.95).

126 The publisher is Nolo Press, Berkeley, CA, and the suggested retail price is $20.97. It is available at a discount in many bookstores.

edition, incorporating recent amendments, updated forms, and commentary. Many bookstores stock older versions of self-help manuals and forms which do not include current versions of necessary documents. Clients should also be advised of the many pitfalls of proceeding *pro se*, which should be recommended only in the simplest cases and only when there is no possibility of legal representation.

Potential *pro se* debtors, as well as other debtors and non-attorneys interested in learning more about bankruptcy, may also be referred to *Consumer Bankruptcy: The Complete Guide to Chapter 7 and Chapter 13 Personal Bankruptcy*,[127] which is an abridged version of this manual. However, they should also be advised that the print version of this book has not been updated to incorporate the 1994 amendments or later amendments and case law.

1.5.4 Reporting Services

Because much of the initial case law developed under the new Code is found in decisions of the bankruptcy courts, which are not reported in the Federal Supplement or other standard reporters, and because federal district court bankruptcy decisions are no longer reported in the Federal Supplement, access to a bankruptcy reporting service is essential.[128] Several competing services are available.

West Bankruptcy Reporter (B.R.). A product of the mammoth West system, this reporter publishes full text opinions of the bankruptcy courts. It offers the advantage of being tied into the West Digest and the West keynote system. The weekly advance sheets also offer a newsletter of very recent developments and a bibliography of recent articles on bankruptcy.[129] According to *The Bluebook: A Uniform System of Citation* (17th ed.), Table 1, the *West Bankruptcy Reporter* should be cited if a case is reported therein, with other reporting services cited only if a West reporter citation is not available.

Bankruptcy Court Decisions (Bankr. Ct. Dec. (LRP)). Also a full-text service, this publication is often more current than West. Containing some bankruptcy news beyond its decision reprints and a calendar of bankruptcy seminars, it comes out every two weeks. One useful feature is a table of cases based upon different sections of the statute.[130]

Collier's Bankruptcy Cases 2d (Collier Bankr. Cas. 2d (MB)). Another full-text service, similar to *Bankruptcy Court Decisions*, this reporter also appears biweekly but contains fewer decisions. Besides a table of cases keyed to statute sections and to *Collier* treatise sections, it also contains a useful Shepard's-like citator for cases it reports.[131]

BNA Bankruptcy Law Reporter. This weekly newsletter does not contain full text opinions. It is often the most current journal and contains news articles about bankruptcy developments and pending legislation. A daily version is available through legal research services such as Westlaw and Lexis.[132]

Collier Bankruptcy Case Update. This newsletter is delivered weekly by e-mail or monthly in hard copy to its subscribers. It contains summaries of all recent bankruptcy decisions, helpfully organized by the Code sections to which they pertain.[133]

1.5.5 Periodicals

From time to time articles on bankruptcy appear in the various law reviews and other periodicals. Many appear in the *American Bankruptcy Law Journal*,[134] in the *American Bankruptcy Institute Law Review*,[135] or in the *Annual Survey of Bankruptcy Law*.[136] In addition, a *Bankruptcy Developments Journal* is published by Emory Law School[137] and there is a commercial publication, *The Journal of Bankruptcy Law and Practice*,[138] which contains some articles pertaining to consumer bankruptcy. A selected bibliography of recent bankruptcy articles is contained at the end of the text of this manual.

Another useful publication for updated news on consumer bankruptcy issues is the biweekly publication *Consumer Bankruptcy News* which contains articles and reports of recently decided cases.[139]

And last, but hardly least, the National Consumer Law Center distributes six times a year a *Bankruptcy and Foreclosures Edition* of *NCLC REPORTS* to each neighborhood

---

127 Publisher is John Wiley & Sons, Inc., New York, NY ($24.95).

128 Federal court of appeals decisions concerning bankruptcy continue to be reported in the Federal Reporter, as well as in the Bankruptcy Reporter.

129 Publisher is West Group ($5364.00; annual maintenance is approximately $2000.00). The cost for advance sheets is $495.00 per year. The West Bankruptcy Digest which was formerly provided free of charge with West's Bankruptcy Reporter now must be purchased separately ($1620.00).

130 Publisher is LRP Publications, c/o Axon Group, West Palm Beach, FL ($895.00 per year). A set of volumes 1–41 is $4100.00.

131 Publisher is Matthew Bender ($1642.00 per year; CD-Rom is $1352.00).

132 Publisher is Bureau of National Affairs, Washington, D.C. ($1256.00 per year for print edition, $1446.00 per year for electronic edition, or $1760.00 per year for both; those prices include cost of renewal).

133 Publisher is Matthew Bender ($404.00 per year for either the print or e-mail edition, or $450.00 for both).

134 Publisher is National Conference of Bankruptcy Judges, 235 Secret Cove Dr., Lexington, SC 29072 ($65.00 per year).

135 Publisher is West Group ($127.00 per year).

136 Publisher is West Group ($367.00 per year).

137 The cost is $32.00 for two issues per year. This publication is also available on the Internet at www.law.emory.edu/BDJ/bdjhome.htm.

138 Publisher is West Group ($364.00 per year).

139 Publisher is LRP Publications, c/o Axon Group, West Palm Beach, FL ($295.00 per year).

legal services office and to other subscribers.[140] The report contains new developments, new ideas, model forms, and reprints of important source materials, keeping this manual and its bound supplements current with the latest developments.

1.5.6 Citator

Fortunately, with all the different reporting services providing multiple citations for most opinions, there is a citator that allows easy cross-referencing, *Shepard's Bankruptcy Citations*.[141]

1.5.7 Computer Assisted Legal Research

One of the fastest and most thorough methods of bankruptcy research is use of any of the several computer assisted legal research services that are now available, for example, Lexis and Westlaw. These systems contain a full-text database of bankruptcy cases, and usually also contain many

unreported decisions, as well as a citator. The Lexis and Westlaw databases also contain public record information that may be necessary, including UCC filings, bankruptcy records, and various bulletins, law reviews, and newsletters. These services are now available over the Internet. A useful entry point for Lexis is the bankruptcy practice page at www.lexis.com which offers easy access to cases, statutes, rules, forms, the Collier publications, Shepard's, public records, news articles, and other secondary materials.

In addition, a number of publishers, including Matthew Bender/Lexis and West Publishing Co. now publish CD-Rom versions of case reports and treatises. Each version contains the full text of virtually all bankruptcy decisions that are available, with an updating service for recent cases, as well as the texts and treatises sold by the particular publisher. The cases and texts can be searched using words or phrases when doing research. The Matthew Bender/Lexis CD-Rom of bankruptcy cases can be purchased in a form that includes *Shepard's Bankruptcy Citations.*

Finally, the text of the Bankruptcy Code, like the rest of the United States Code, the Federal Rules of Bankruptcy Procedure, and local bankruptcy court rules are available on the Internet. Many other useful materials, such as court decisions and law review articles, are also available through various websites offering free legal resources.

---

140 The cost of the *Bankruptcy & Foreclosure Edition* is $60.00. The full set of four editions (also including *Consumer Credit & Usury Edition, Debt Collection & Repossession Edition,* and *Deceptive Practices & Warranties Edition*) includes twenty-four issues and costs $175.00 annually.

141 Seven-volume set for $1486.00; annual maintenance is $932.00.

Chapter 2

What Is Bankruptcy? Some General Concepts

2.1 A Definition

In essence, a voluntary[1] bankruptcy case is a legal proceeding, brought by a debtor, that seeks relief specifically provided for by a federal statute, the Bankruptcy Code.[2] The bankruptcy case must be brought in the United States District Court, which has jurisdiction over all bankruptcy cases, but bankruptcy cases are normally automatically referred to the bankruptcy court for the district, a unit of the district court.[3] Therefore, the actual bankruptcy petition is filed with the bankruptcy court.

2.2 Relief Available in Bankruptcy

For individuals, there are two types of relief that are usually used. The first is liquidation under chapter 7 of the Code. In a liquidation case, often referred to as a straight bankruptcy, all of the debtor's nonexempt[4] assets are converted to cash and distributed to creditors according to certain statutory rules. At the end of the proceeding, the individual debtor receives a discharge, which absolves him or her from any responsibility to pay most debts and also provides various other protections.[5]

The second type of relief is a reorganization,[6] or adjustment, of the debtor's financial affairs. Although such a reorganization may be available to individuals under both chapters 11[7] and 13 of the Code, chapter 13 is more beneficial for virtually every consumer debtor.[8] It is less expensive and it also offers a number of protections not found in chapter 11.[9] In a chapter 13 case, the debtor proposes a plan for payment of some or all of his or her debts, within certain statutory guidelines.[10] The plan is then carried out under court supervision with the court protecting the debtor, and usually all of the debtor's property, from creditors. At the end of the case, as in a chapter 7 case, the debtor receives a discharge from personal liability on most debts, as well as other protections.

Neither discharge by itself protects the debtor's property from creditors with valid liens on the property. However, the Code offers a number of ways, particularly in chapter 13, for debtors to obtain full or partial relief from secured claims in most cases.[11]

2.3 Purposes of Bankruptcy

The purposes of bankruptcy are usually described as twofold: (1) a fresh start for the debtor and (2) equity among creditors. In most cases involving consumer debtors, the first is by far the more significant, because there are typically few assets to be distributed, equitably or otherwise, to the creditors involved.

The "fresh start" concept encompasses the statutory goal of allowing individuals who have become mired in debt to free themselves from that morass and to engage in newly productive lives unimpaired by their past financial prob-

---

1 Most bankruptcies are voluntary petitions filed by debtors. The Bankruptcy Code also provides for involuntary bankruptcy proceedings filed by creditors. 11 U.S.C. § 303. These are quite rare in consumer cases and are discussed in Chapter 13, *infra*.

2 11 U.S.C. §§ 101–1330.

3 28 U.S.C. §§ 157(a), 1334(a).

4 Certain assets, called exempt assets, may be retained by individual debtors in bankruptcy. A detailed discussion of exemptions is contained in Chapter 10, *infra*.

5 See Chapter 14, *infra*, for a detailed discussion of discharge protections.

6 Although chapter 13 functionally offers much the same type of reorganization relief as chapter 11, the term "reorganization" is often used as a term of art to refer to chapter 11. This term will therefore be avoided herein in referring to chapter 13, which will be referred to simply as "chapter 13."

7 The Supreme Court has held that individual debtors may file under chapter 11, whether or not they have an ongoing business. Toibb v. Radloff, 501 U.S. 157, 111 S. Ct. 2197, 115 L. Ed. 2d

145 (1991). A discussion of the relief available to debtors under chapter 11 is, for the most part, beyond the scope of this manual. *See* § 6.3.4, *infra*.

8 Individual family farmers may also file under chapter 12, discussed in Chapter 16, *infra*.

9 For example, Chapter 13 provides for a broader discharge and a stay of most actions against codebtors. It also does not allow creditors to propose, vote on, or approve the debtor's plan. Chapter 11 is normally used only in business reorganization cases. However, if an individual cannot utilize chapter 13 or does not wish to proceed under that chapter, the lack of an ongoing business does not bar chapter 11 relief. *See* Toibb v. Radloff, 501 U.S. 157, 111 S. Ct. 2197, 115 L. Ed. 2d 145 (1991); § 6.3.4, *infra*.

10 The requirements for a chapter 13 plan are discussed in Chapters 7 and 12, *infra*.

11 See Chapters 10 and 11, *infra*, for discussion of the debtor's rights with respect to secured creditors.

lems. It avoids the kind of permanent discouragement that would prevent a person from ever becoming reestablished as a hard-working member of society, striving to find the good life and fulfill the American Dream. The Supreme Court has described the fresh start as "a new opportunity in life, unhampered by the pressure and discouragement of pre-existing debt."[12] Functionally, then, bankruptcy serves to grease the wheels of a capitalist economy, offering a safety valve which somewhat tempers its harshness for those who do not fare well in free-market competition. At the same time, it adds to the dynamism of the society, encouraging risk-taking and expansion of new enterprises by limiting the risk involved and by offering a new start to those who fail.

The goal of equity among creditors is achieved by the fair distribution of the debtor's assets according to established rules, set forth in the statute, which guarantee identical treatment to similarly situated creditors. This guarantee, and various provisions that require creditors to disgorge certain assets obtained by them shortly before bankruptcy,[13] are meant to discourage creditors from rushing to be the first to execute on or to repossess property from a struggling individual or business. Thus, the specter of bankruptcy sometimes causes creditors to negotiate with debtors, because the aggressive dismemberment of debtors' assets could force those debtors to seek relief from the bankruptcy court.

2.4 The Bankruptcy Court

2.4.1 Status Under the Bankruptcy Reform Act As Amended in 1984

Under the 1984 amendments to the Bankruptcy Reform Act, the bankruptcy court is a "unit" of the federal district court in each judicial district.[14] Its powers, however, are greatly diminished compared to those that were originally contemplated by the drafters of the 1978 Act. Bankruptcy judges are appointed for terms of fourteen years by the courts of appeals which have jurisdiction over the various districts;[15] the judges have a status and power roughly equivalent to United States magistrate judges. Because the bankruptcy court is a part of the district court, statutes

applicable to the federal district courts, as well as the Federal Rules of Evidence, generally are applicable in bankruptcy proceedings.

The records of the bankruptcy court are kept by the clerk of the court. Typically, there is a case docket listing all filings and orders in each bankruptcy case. The case docket notes the filing of each adversary proceeding, which then has its own separate docket. In addition, there is a separate claims docket, listing the claims filed in the case. All of these dockets—and, in many courts, the complete contents of all documents filed in a case—are accessible electronically over the Internet through a system called PACER.[16] The fees for such access are set forth in the Judicial Conference Schedule of Fees.[17] They may be waived by the court in order to avoid unreasonable burdens and to promote public access to the information. Courts have used the power to waive fees to give free PACER access to legal services programs.

2.4.2 Jurisdiction

A principal goal of the 1978 Bankruptcy Reform Act had been to simplify a jurisdictional scheme which had caused endless litigation for the previous eighty years under the Bankruptcy Act of 1898. This simplification was to be accomplished by giving the bankruptcy court broad and pervasive jurisdiction over all matters related in any way to the bankruptcy case.[18] But granting such broad jurisdiction to a non-Article III court was found unconstitutional by the United States Supreme Court.[19]

The 1984 amendments attempted to meet the Supreme Court's objections in a variety of ways, most of which involved removing matters from the jurisdiction of the bankruptcy court. Under the amendments, all matters arising under the Bankruptcy Code (title 11 of the United States Code), or arising in or related to cases under title 11, are initially referred by the district court to the bankruptcy court,[20] or may arrive in the bankruptcy court by removal from another court.[21] However, some matters will not stay in the bankruptcy court. The statute provides for a complex system of mechanisms to transfer cases or proceedings to the district court or to state courts, often depending upon the type of proceeding involved. These include devices such as

---

12 Local Loan Co. v. Hunt, 292 U.S. 234, 244, 54 S. Ct. 695, 78 L. Ed. 1230 (1934); *see also* H.R. Rep. No. 95-595, at 117, 118 (1977) (fresh start is the "essence of modern bankruptcy law"; chapter 13 designed to ensure "the debtor is given adequate exemptions and other protections to ensure that bankruptcy will provide a fresh start"; whether debtor uses chapter 7 or 13, premise of the Code is that "bankruptcy relief should be effective, and should provide the debtor with a fresh start").

13 These provisions, termed the "avoiding powers," are discussed in Chapter 10, *infra*.

14 Pub. L. No. 98-353, 98 Stat. 343 (1984); *see* Appx. A.2.4, *infra*.

15 28 U.S.C. § 152.

16 Information about accessing PACER may be obtained at http://pacer.psc.uscourts.gov/ or by calling (800) 676-6856.

17 Reprinted in Appendix C, *infra*.

18 See the sources cited in § 1.5.1.1, *supra,* for a discussion of the evolution of the 1978 Act.

19 N. Pipeline Constr. Co. v. Marathon Pipe Line Co., 458 U.S. 50, 102 S. Ct. 2858, 73 L. Ed. 2d 598 (1982).

20 28 U.S.C. § 157(a).

21 28 U.S.C. § 1452. It is assumed that cases removed under this section to the district court will initially be referred to the bankruptcy court handling the related bankruptcy case. *See* Fed. R. Bankr. P. 9027(f).

discretionary abstention and mandatory abstention, discretionary withdrawal to the district court and mandatory withdrawal to the district court, and referral to bankruptcy judges as masters.[22] In some proceedings bankruptcy judges are permitted to enter final orders, and in others they are allowed only to submit proposed findings of fact and conclusions of law to the district court.[23] The procedures effectuating this jurisdictional scheme are discussed elsewhere in this manual.[24]

These jurisdictional complexities added in 1984 did not affect most routine bankruptcy cases, which are resolved entirely in the bankruptcy court. However, for more unusual matters, the statute's many twists and turns have caused considerable confusion and litigation, not unlike that which existed before 1978, thus ending the hopes of many that such wasteful expenditures of time and money could finally be eliminated.

Corresponding to the court's broad initial jurisdiction are provisions for nationwide service of process. Many proceedings arising in or related to a bankruptcy case may be commenced in the court where that case is pending even if that court is in Maine and the defendant is in Hawaii.[25] However, a case or proceeding may be transferred to another district in the interest of justice or for the convenience of the parties.[26]

Furthermore, proceedings already commenced elsewhere may be removed by a party to a district court that has bankruptcy jurisdiction.[27] This provision may be of tremendous assistance in obtaining a better forum or other procedural advantages in a particular case. It should be noted, though, that the receiving court may choose to remand the proceeding, and that such a decision is not reviewable by appeal or otherwise except by the district court.[28]

Finally, assuming a matter is properly referred to it, the bankruptcy court, in some circumstances, may conduct jury trials in cases in which the right to a jury trial exists.[29] The

district court in a bankruptcy case may issue writs of *habeas corpus*[30] and the bankruptcy court may issue any other order, process, or judgment necessary to carry out its functions.[31] The bankruptcy court generally has all the powers of a court of equity, law, and admiralty.[32]

2.4.3 Appeals

There are two possible avenues for appeals from the bankruptcy court. The path to be taken depends upon the wishes of the parties and the practice adopted by the federal district court and judicial circuit where the bankruptcy court is located.

In the case of a final judgment, order or decree, when a bankruptcy court is authorized to enter one, an appeal is normally taken to the district court.[33] Further appeals from the district court decision may then be taken to the court of appeals, provided the district court's order is also a final order.[34] However, there is no statutory provision explaining what is or is not a final judgment, order, or decree, and some uncertainty remains.[35]

The only exception to this general rule is when a bankruptcy appellate service ("BAPS") has been established by the judicial council of the circuit to hear appeals arising in the district where the case is pending.[36] An appeal from a bankruptcy court order may be taken to a panel of three bankruptcy judges appointed to the BAPS instead of to the district court only if (1) all parties consent and (2) the district

---

22 *See* 28 U.S.C. § 157.

23 28 U.S.C. § 157(b), (c).

24 See Chapter 13, *infra,* for further discussion of jurisdictional issues.

25 28 U.S.C. § 1409. There are, however, certain venue limitations on actions for small amounts of money or property, on post-petition claims brought by or against a trustee, and on actions brought by a trustee as successor to the debtor or creditors. 28 U.S.C. § 1409(b)–(e).

26 28 U.S.C. § 1412.

27 28 U.S.C. § 1452. Exceptions to this principle are proceedings in the United States Tax Court and civil actions by governmental units to enforce their police or regulatory powers. Removed proceedings will normally be referred to bankruptcy judges like all other proceedings. Fed. R. Bankr. P. 9027(f). See Chapter 13, *infra,* for discussion of removal.

28 28 U.S.C. § 1452(b). *But see* Pacor Inc. v. Higgins, 743 F.2d 984 (3d Cir. 1984) (decision may be reviewed if jurisdictional issues involved).

29 28 U.S.C. §§ 157(e), 1411. See § 13.2.7, *infra,* for further discussion of jury trials in the bankruptcy court.

30 While 28 U.S.C. § 2256, specifically permitting bankruptcy courts to issue writs of *habeas corpus*, was repealed in 1984, the issuance of such writs could possibly be delegated to bankruptcy courts pursuant to 28 U.S.C. § 157. *See* § 13.4.5, *infra*.

31 11 U.S.C. § 105(a).

32 While 28 U.S.C. § 1481, specifically conferring these powers upon the bankruptcy court, was repealed in 1984, 28 U.S.C. § 151 grants bankruptcy judges "the authority conferred under this chapter with respect to any action suit or proceeding . . . except as otherwise provided by law or by rule or order of the district court." United States v. Energy Resources, Inc., 495 U.S. 545, 549, 110 S. Ct. 2139, 109 L. Ed. 2d 580 (1990) (bankruptcy courts, as courts of equity, have broad power to modify creditor-debtor relationships). See generally Chapter 13, *infra,* for further discussion of bankruptcy jurisdiction.

33 28 U.S.C. § 158(a).

34 28 U.S.C. § 158(d).

35 See Chapter 13, *infra,* for discussion of what orders are final orders.

36 *See* 28 U.S.C. § 158(b). The courts of appeals for the First, Sixth, Eighth and Tenth Circuits have established appellate panels for all or some of the districts within their circuits. The First Circuit panel hears appeals from all districts in the circuit. The Sixth Circuit appellate panel hears appeals arising only in the Northern and Southern Districts of Ohio. The Eighth Circuit panel hears appeals arising anywhere in the circuit except those arising in the districts of North Dakota and South Dakota. The Tenth Circuit's panel hears appeals arising throughout the circuit except for those arising in the District of Colorado.

judges for the district, by majority vote, authorize referral of appeals to the appellate panel.[37]

Appellate procedure for interlocutory orders and decrees is somewhat different. An appeal to either a three-judge bankruptcy appellate panel or the district court (whichever is applicable) is permitted only with the leave of that panel or district court.[38] At least one bankruptcy appellate panel has held that only a showing of exceptional circumstances will justify the granting of such leave to appeal.[39] However, when the district court or appellate panel takes an appeal of an interlocutory order, there is then a further right of appeal to the court of appeals for that circuit.[40]

The procedure for appeals to a district court or bankruptcy appellate panel is governed by the Federal Rules of Bankruptcy Procedure.[41] These rules are similar to the Federal Rules of Appellate Procedure, but they differ in several significant respects, most notably in the ten-day time limit for such appeals.[42] The Federal Rules of Appellate Procedure govern cases appealed to the court of appeals.[43]

2.5 The Bankruptcy Estate

2.5.1 Contents of the Estate

The term *bankruptcy estate* describes the aggregation of property rights that can be administered by the court in a bankruptcy case. The estate is created upon the commencement of the case and it generally consists of all interests of the debtor in any kind of property as of that time.[44] It includes interests in community property, entireties property, and other property which cannot be attached under state law, such as the right to receive various kinds of income in the future.[45] Moreover, property comes into the bankruptcy estate free from restrictions conditioned on insolvency or the filing of a bankruptcy case.[46]

The estate also includes property recovered by the trustee,[47] proceeds or rents of property already in the estate,[48] pre-petition causes of action or claims possessed by

---

37   28 U.S.C. § 158(b). Parties required to consent probably include all those with any adversarial interest in the proceeding. *See In re* Odom, 702 F.2d 962 (11th Cir. 1983). Under the statute as amended, if a bankruptcy appellate panel is authorized to hear appeals, consent is presumed unless the appellant elects, at the time of filing the appeal, to have the appeal heard in district court, or any other party so elects, by a separate writing, within thirty days after service of the notice of appeal. 28 U.S.C. § 158(c)(1).

38   28 U.S.C. § 158(a), (b); Fed. R. Bankr. P. 8001(e); *see* § 13.10.1, *infra.*

39   *In re* Nat'l Shoes, 20 B.R. 672 (B.A.P. 1st Cir. 1982).

40   28 U.S.C. § 1292; Conn. Nat'l Bank v. Germain, 503 U.S. 249, 112 S. Ct. 1146, 117 L. Ed. 2d 391 (1992).

41   Fed. R. Bankr. P. 8001–8019. See Chapter 13, *infra,* for further discussion of appellate procedure in bankruptcy cases.

42   Fed. R. Bankr. P. 8002(a). As the ten-day period now includes intervening holidays and weekends, a decision on whether to appeal has to be made relatively quickly. *See* Fed. R. Bankr. P. 9006(a).

43   Advisory Committee Note to Fed. R. Bankr. P. 8001.

44   11 U.S.C. § 541. *See, e.g., In re* Nejberger, 934 F.2d 1300 (3d Cir. 1991) (even though debtor's liquor license had expired pre-petition, right to make late renewal application comes into the estate); Miller v. Shallowford Cmty. Hosp., Inc., 767 F.2d 1556 (11th Cir. 1985) (debtor's right to receive insurance benefits existing on date bankruptcy was filed held property of the estate even though right to benefits became apparent under state

law only after that date); NLT Computer Services v. Capital Computer Sys., 755 F.2d 1253 (6th Cir. 1985) (fact that monies had been paid into registry of district court in interpleader action did not prevent them from becoming property of the estate in a subsequent bankruptcy). However, property belonging to a debtor's children is not property of the estate. *In re* Biancavilla, 173 B.R. 930 (Bankr. D. Idaho 1994).

45   *See, e.g., In re* Parsons, 280 F.3d 1185 (8th Cir. 2002) (real estate commissions attributable to pre-petition contracts were property of estate); *In re* Yonikus, 996 F.2d 866 (7th Cir. 1993) (contingent right to receive workers' compensation in the future was property of the estate); *In re* Lonstein, 950 F.2d 77 (1st Cir. 1991) (debtor's vested interest in bequest under will was property of the estate); Sierra Switchboard Co. v. Westinghouse Elec. Corp., 789 F.2d 705 (9th Cir. 1986) (emotional distress claim was property of the estate); Smoker v. Hill & Associates, Inc., 204 B.R. 966 (N.D. Ind. 1997) (contingent interest in employer's profit-sharing plan was property of estate to extent attributable to pre-petition earnings); Morris v. Philadelphia Elec. Co., 45 B.R. 350 (E.D. Pa. 1984) (fuel assistance grants to which debtor was entitled on date of bankruptcy held property of estate despite the fact that they were to be paid directly to utility); *In re* Wicheff, 215 B.R. 839 (B.A.P. 6th Cir. 1998) (debtor's right to receive insurance commissions after bankruptcy based upon pre-petition sales of insurance was property of estate); *In re* Dibiase, 270 B.R. 673 (Bankr. W.D. Tex. 2001) (stock options were property of estate even though they were subject to forfeiture if debtor's employment terminated prior to one year of employment); *In re* Edmonds, 273 B.R. 527 (Bankr. E.D. Mich. 2000) (contingent interest in employer's profit-sharing plan was property of estate to extent attributable to pre-petition earnings); *In re* Scanlon, 10 B.R. 245 (Bankr. S.D. Cal. 1981) (right to receive sales commission is property of estate). *But see In re* Chappo, 257 B.R. 852 (E.D. Mich. 2001) (employment bonus received post-petition not property of estate when employer retained right to modify or terminate bonus plan at any time before distribution).

46   11 U.S.C. § 541(c)(1)(B); *see In re* Knapp, 137 B.R. 582 (Bankr. D.N.J. 1992) (when only reason that creditor revoked debtor's credit card was the filing of a bankruptcy case, that revocation was invalid under the Code, and chapter 13 debtor had right to continue using card).

47   The bankruptcy trustee is discussed in § 2.6, *infra.* The trustee may recover property from other parties in various ways, discussed in Chapter 10, *infra,* along with the debtor's power to recover exempt property.

48   *See, e.g.,* Bradt v. Woodlawn Auto Workers Fed. Credit Union, 757 F.2d 512 (2d Cir. 1985) (insurance payment for collision repairs to automobile that was property of the estate was also property of the estate because payment constituted proceeds of property of the estate); *see also In re* Bumper Sales, Inc., 907 F.2d 1430 (4th Cir. 1990) (section 552(b) protects security interests in after-acquired property when such property constitutes proceeds of property already in the estate); *cf. In re* Jones,

debtor,[49] interests in insurance policies,[50] and various other interests set forth in 11 U.S.C. § 541. In each case, however, the estate's interest in such property is no greater than the debtor's interest at the time of the filing of the bankruptcy petition.[51] And, in addition to the debtor's interest in property, if only one spouse in a community property jurisdiction files a petition, the estate may sometimes include the other spouse's share of all community property.[52]

Although most property acquired by the debtor after commencement of the case does not come into the estate,[53] there are exceptions for certain types of property acquired within 180 days of filing. These exceptions include property acquired by bequest or inheritance,[54] through a spousal property settlement or divorce decree,[55] or as a beneficiary of life insurance. The 180 days runs from the date the original bankruptcy petition is filed, even if a case is converted from one chapter to another.[56] Also, in a chapter 13 case, all property and earnings acquired during the pendency of the case (unless the case is converted to another chapter) are property of the estate.[57]

---

908 F.2d 859 (11th Cir. 1990) (post-petition increases in value of property created by post-petition payments do not constitute proceeds within the meaning of § 552(b)).

49 *See* Wieburg v. GTE Southwest, Inc., 272 F.3d 302 (5th Cir. 2001) (employment discrimination claim was property of estate); *In re* Crysen/Montenay Energy Co., 902 F.2d 1098 (2d Cir. 1990) (debtor's right to collect accounts receivable is property of the estate); *In re* Cottrell, 876 F.2d 540 (6th Cir. 1989) (personal injury action is property of the estate even though action is not assignable under state law and may be prosecuted by chapter 7 trustee); Jones v. Harell, 858 F.2d 667 (11th Cir. 1988); Krank v. Utica Mut. Ins. Co., 109 B.R. 668 (E.D. Pa.) (once cause of action becomes property of the estate, debtor may not bring suit unless that property is abandoned by the trustee), *aff'd*, 908 F.2d 962 (3d Cir. 1990) (table); *see also* § 2.6, *infra*.

50 *See In re* Titan Energy, Inc., 837 F.2d 325 (8th Cir. 1988) (bankruptcy court has jurisdiction over suit to determine scope of insurer's liability to the debtor, but may abstain from hearing dispute. The estate does not normally include the proceeds of an insurance policy, unless the debtor is the beneficiary of the policy. *In re* Edgeworth, 993 F.2d 51 (5th Cir. 1993) (malpractice policy proceeds were not property of estate); First Fid. Bank v. McAteer, 985 F.2d 114 (3d Cir. 1993) (credit life insurance proceeds not property of the estate; proceeds belong to creditor/beneficiary rather than estate); Counties Contracting & Constr. Co. v. Constitution Life Ins. Co., 855 F.2d 1054 (3d Cir. 1988) (debtor's interest in reinstating lapsed policy during policy's "grace period" is property of the estate and is extended by operation of 11 U.S.C. § 108, but unless policy is reinstated, debtor cannot collect benefits).

51 *See* Universal Bonding v. Gittens & Sprinkle Enterprises, Inc., 960 F.2d 366 (3d Cir. 1992) (when monies paid to contractor had to be held in trust for laborers and materialmen, estate could gain only legal title to those funds, which would be held in trust for benefit of laborers and materialmen); *In re* Crossman, 259 B.R. 301 (Bankr. N.D. Ill. 2001) (trustee could not sell right to future payments under structured personal injury settlement when such sale was prohibited by state law and settlement agreement); *In re* Thompson, 253 B.R. 823 (Bankr. N.D. Ohio 2000) (trustee could not compel turnover of prorata refund for future months' rental fees, which debtor would have been able to obtain if she had moved from residence, when debtor had not elected to move).

52 11 U.S.C. § 541(a)(2); *see In re* Fingado, 995 F.2d 175 (10th Cir. 1993) (property acquired by married couple through an instrument indicating joint ownership was community property under New Mexico law and therefore was property of the bankruptcy estate); *cf. In re* LaNess, 159 B.R. 916 (Bankr. S.D. Cal. 1993) (estate did not include community property not yet divided after couple's divorce, because § 541(a)(2) refers to property of the debtor and the debtor's spouse, and the couple was no longer married when the bankruptcy case was filed).

53 11 U.S.C. § 541(a)(6); Patrick A. Casey, P.A. v. Hochman, 963 F.2d 1347 (10th Cir. 1992) (patent on device invented by debtor after bankruptcy petition filed was not property of the estate); *In re* Clark, 891 F.2d 111 (5th Cir. 1989) (salary paid post-petition pursuant to a pre-petition contract not property of the estate in chapter 7); *In re* Swanson, 36 B.R. 99 (B.A.P. 9th Cir. 1984). *But see In re* Froid, 109 B.R. 481 (Bankr. M.D. Fla. 1989) (post-petition renewal commissions for insurance policies sold pre-petition are property of the estate because no post-petition services were performed by the debtor).

54 11 U.S.C. § 541(a)(5); *see In re* Newman, 903 F.2d 1150 (7th Cir. 1990) (distribution from spendthrift trust within 180 days of petition is not property of the estate under § 541(a)(5) because it is not acquired by bequest, devise or inheritance); *In re* Roth, 289 B.R. 161 (Bankr. D. Kan. 2003) (post-petition distribution from an *inter vivos* trust that occurred after settlor's death and within 180 days of petition was not "bequest, devise, or inheritance"); *In re* Hendricks, 22 B.R. 572 (Bankr. W.D. Mo. 1982) (rights accruing to the debtor within 180 days under wrongful death statute held property of the estate). A debtor's effort to disclaim an interest in an inheritance may not be effective. *See In re* Kolb, 326 F.3d 1030 (9th Cir. 2003) (pre-petition disclaimer was invalid because debtor had already "accepted" interest in trust by listing it as an asset in a loan application); *In re* Chenoweth, 3 F.3d 1111 (7th Cir. 1993) (debtor who inherited property within 180 days after bankruptcy case filed could not disclaim inheritance and thereby keep property out of estate; debtor became entitled to acquire property, for purposes of 11 U.S.C. § 541(a)(5), when testator died, not when will was probated); *In re* Cornell, 95 B.R. 219 (Bankr. W.D. Okla. 1989); *see also In re* Stevens, 112 B.R. 175 (Bankr. S.D. Tex. 1989) (pre-petition disclaimer of interest in estate is avoidable by the trustee as a fraudulent transfer); *cf. In re* Simpson, 36 F.3d 450 (5th Cir. 1994) (pre-bankruptcy disclaimer of any interest in deceased father's estate was not a fraudulent transfer because the debtor never had a state law interest in the disclaimed property); *In re* Atchison, 925 F.2d 209 (7th Cir. 1991) (pre-petition disclaimer of inheritance prevents property from vesting in the debtor or her estate).

55 However, several courts have held that alimony or support rights, as opposed to property settlements, are not included within this provision. *In re* Wise, 346 F.3d 1239 (10th Cir. 2003); *In re* Jeter, 257 B.R. 907 (B.A.P. 8th Cir. 2001). Several courts have also held that rights to child support belong to the child and not to the divorcing spouse. *E.g., In re* Poffenbarger, 281 B.R. 379 (Bankr. S.D. Ala. 2002). For conflicting decisions on whether entireties property of which a debtor becomes sole owner pursuant to a divorce within the 180 days may still be exempted under 11 U.S.C. § 522(b)(2)(B), see § 10.2.3.2, *infra*.

56 *In re* Carter, 260 B.R. 130 (Bankr. W.D. Tenn. 2001).

57 11 U.S.C. § 1306(a); *see* § 12.8, *infra*; *cf. In re* Meade, 84 B.R.

Even very limited and remote property interests are included in the debtor's bankruptcy estate. For example, bare legal title to property, as a trustee or as a convenience co-tenant, brings an interest in that property into the estate.[58] Property of the debtor in the hands of a creditor after repossession also comes into the estate, subject to the creditor's lien.[59] Similarly, a mere possessory interest without legal title is sufficient to bring property into the estate.[60] Such property may not be available for actual administration by the trustee however, as the estate's interest is usually limited to the debtor's interest.[61] The nature of that interest is generally determined under state law.[62] If the debtor has no right under state law to transfer the property, the trustee usually does not have that right either.

Significant issues may arise when two or more people jointly own property and only one of the co-owners files a bankruptcy case.[63] Although the debtor's partial interest in the property clearly comes into the estate, the Code mandates some protection of the interests of the nondebtor co-owner.[64]

---

106 (Bankr. S.D. Ohio 1988) (wages earned by chapter 7 debtor pre-petition are property of the estate even if unpaid, but wages earned post-petition are not).

58 *See* Ga. Pac. Corp. v. Sigma Serv. Corp., 712 F.2d 962 (5th Cir. 1983) (debtor had interest in property subject to constructive trust); *see also In re* Crabtree, 871 F.2d 36 (6th Cir. 1989) (under Florida law, debtor owns property in fee although deed named debtor as trustee, when no beneficiary is named and no declaration of trust recorded); *cf.* T & B Scottdale Contractors, Inc. v. United States, 866 F.2d 1372 (11th Cir. 1989) (debtor had no interest in funds being held in joint account when funds were clearly deposited to satisfy secured claim of third party); *In re* Newcomb, 744 F.2d 621 (8th Cir. 1984) (debtor had no interest in escrowed funds when, at time of petition, condition of escrow agreement had been fulfilled). *But see In re* Thena, 190 B.R. 407 (D. Or. 1995) (property seized under criminal forfeiture statute was not property of estate even though no criminal charges had yet been brought).

59 United States v. Whiting Pools, Inc., 462 U.S. 198, 103 S. Ct. 2309, 76 L. Ed. 2d 515 (1983); *In re* Knaus, 889 F.2d 773 (8th Cir. 1989). *But see In re* Lewis, 137 F.3d 1280 (11th Cir. 1998) (under Alabama law, debtor no longer has possessory right or title to an automobile after repossession so that only a right of redemption comes into the estate). The *Lewis* decision fails to explain its inconsistency with *Whiting Pools*. And at least one court in the Eleventh Circuit has limited *Lewis* to its questionable roots in Alabama law. *In re* Littleton, 220 B.R. 710 (Bankr. M.D. Ga. 1998).

60 *In re* Atl. Bus. & Cmty. Corp., 901 F.2d 325 (3d Cir. 1990); *In re* 48th St. Steakhouse, Inc., 835 F.2d 427 (2d Cir. 1987); *In re* Mumpfield, 140 B.R. 578 (Bankr. M.D. Ala. 1991) (vendee in contract for sale of real property who became chapter 13 debtor had a property interest that became property of the estate even though vendor had terminated contract and sought eviction, because debtor was still in possession of the property).

61 *See, e.g.,* Davis v. Cox, 356 F.3d 76 (1st Cir. 2004) (debtor had only contingent interest in funds held in escrow account pursuant to divorce court order and, based on equities and preliminary injunction issued upon filing of divorce, IRA funds were held by debtor in constructive trust); *In re* Baum, 22 F.3d 1014 (10th Cir. 1994) (although debtor was settlor and trustee of trusts for his children, he did not have power to revest property in himself, so trust assets were not property of bankruptcy estate); Chiu v. Wong, 16 F.3d 306 (8th Cir. 1994) (constructive trust imposed upon debtor's homestead so that equitable interest of trust beneficiary was not property of bankruptcy estate); *In re* Columbia Gas Sys., Inc., 997 F.2d 1039 (3d Cir. 1993) (estate's interest did not include property subject to constructive trust created by federal common law, to extent that trust property can be traced when commingled with other property); Mid-Atlantic Supply v. Three Rivers Aluminum Co., 790 F.2d 1121 (4th Cir.

1986) (property held in trust belongs to beneficiary); *In re* N.S. Garrott & Sons, 772 F.2d 462 (8th Cir. 1985) (estate's interest in property subject to constructive trust); *In re* Schmitt, 215 B.R. 417 (B.A.P. 9th Cir. 1997) (property granted to debtor in a revocable trust did not become property of estate because state law deemed such property to belong to grantors of trust); *In re* Dally, 202 B.R. 724 (Bankr. N.D. Ill. 1996) (money in custodial accounts for debtor's children established under Uniform Gifts to Minors Act not property of estate); *In re* Amos, 201 B.R. 184 (Bankr. N.D. Ohio 1996) (van titled in debtor's name was property of her boyfriend, who paid for it and was beneficial owner pursuant to express trust); *see also In re* Corrigan, 93 B.R. 81 (Bankr. E.D. Va. 1988) (estate has no interest in portion of military retirement pay awarded to ex-wife under final decree of divorce). *But see In re* Kemp, 52 F.3d 546 (5th Cir. 1995) (pre-petition commissions purportedly escrowed by debtor's employer were property of estate); *In re* First Capital Mortgage Loan Corp., 917 F.2d 424 (10th Cir. 1990) (en banc) (escrow funds recovered by the trustee pursuant to avoiding powers become property of the estate and escrow depositor holds only a general unsecured claim); *In re* Beatrice, 296 B.R. 576 (B.A.P. 1st Cir. 2003) (property that debtor claimed to have put in trust for children was property of the estate because debtor retained incidents of ownership including power to terminate trust); *In re* Ross, 162 B.R. 863 (Bankr. D. Idaho 1993) (debtor's power to revoke "living trust" was property of bankruptcy estate and trustee could exercise revocation power). In some cases, the trustee's avoiding powers may defeat the unrecorded interest of the beneficiary of a constructive trust. *Compare In re* Omegas Group, 16 F.3d 1443 (6th Cir. 1994) (constructive trust is a legal fiction which, absent pre-bankruptcy judicial action impressing a trust on property, does not create a property interest in the party who claims a constructive trust interest); Belisle v. Plunkett, 877 F.2d 512 (7th Cir. 1989) (equitable ownership could be defeated by bona fide purchaser under state law) *with In re* Howard's Appliance Corp., 874 F.2d 88 (2d Cir. 1989) (contra). The holding of *Omegas Group* has been substantially narrowed in subsequent cases. *See In re* Morris, 260 F.3d 654 (6th Cir. 2001). *See generally* 11 U.S.C. § 544; § 10.4.2.6.2, *infra*.

62 *See, e.g., In re* Yeary, 55 F.3d 504 (10th Cir. 1995) (chapter 13 debtors' pre-petition settlement agreement had not effectuated a transfer of stock but merely created a security interest under state law, so stock was property of the estate); *In re* Crysen/Montenay Energy Co., 902 F.2d 1098 (2d Cir. 1990); *see also* W. United Life Assurance Co. v. Hayden, 64 F.3d 833 (3d Cir. 1995) (debtor had no interest in periodic payments made to her under structured settlement of lawsuit, because she had executed pre-petition assignment of her rights that was valid under state law); Goldberg v. N.J. Lawyer's Fund, 932 F.2d 273 (3d Cir. 1991) (issue of whether trust exists is determined under state law).

63 *See In re* Mantle, 153 F.3d 1082 (9th Cir. 1998) (proceeds of sale of house which was community property are also community property and therefore proceeds were property of estate).

64 11 U.S.C. § 363(h); *see In re* Persky, 893 F.2d 15 (2d Cir. 1989)

Counsel must exercise care in identifying and listing a debtor's various interests in property. Failure to properly list property of the estate in the debtor's schedules may be grounds to deny or revoke the debtor's discharge[65] and may give rise to claims by creditors or the trustee against the unlisted property.[66]

Most consumer debtors will find that they can exempt all or almost all property of their estate.[67] Even property which cannot be exempted is often of little interest to the trustee, because of the cost of liquidation, including payment of liens and taxes, and is therefore abandoned or sold back to the debtor.[68]

2.5.2 Pensions and Spendthrift Trusts

Particularly thorny issues arise in evaluating whether the beneficiary's interest in pensions, retirement funds, certain employee benefit accounts, and spendthrift trusts come into the estate. Section 541(c)(2) of the Bankruptcy Code provides that "[a] restriction on the transfer of a beneficial interest of the debtor in a trust that is enforceable under applicable nonbankruptcy law is enforceable in a case under this title." This provision means that when the beneficiaries of a trust cannot lose their interests in that trust to a creditor outside of bankruptcy, they are equally protected in the bankruptcy case.[69]

For many years, courts reached various conclusions about whether this provision of section 541(c)(2) protects ERISA-qualified pension plans by excluding them from a debtor's bankruptcy estate. The issue was whether the "anti-alienation" provision protecting ERISA-qualified pensions[70] constituted "applicable nonbankruptcy law" such that those pensions could not be transferred to a debtor's bankruptcy estate.[71]

Fortunately, in 1992 the Supreme Court cleared up the morass of case law in the area and concluded that ERISA does protect debtors' pensions.[72] The Court held that a debtor's interest in an ERISA-qualified pension is outside the estate based on section 541(c)(2).[73] The entire plan, including after-tax contributions, is excluded from the estate, because the entire plan is subject to the anti-alienation language.[74] If a plan is an ERISA plan and has the anti-alienation language, it does not matter whether the plan is also tax-qualified.[75]

(although state law allows execution on one spouse's interest in a tenancy by the entireties, bankruptcy court must evaluate detriment of sale to nondebtor spouse under § 363(h)(3)); *In re* Nelson, 129 B.R. 427 (Bankr. W.D. Pa. 1991) (jointly-owned property could not be sold under § 363(h) when co-owning nondebtor spouse had occupancy rights for the duration of her life). On remand, the bankruptcy court in *In re* Persky, 134 B.R. 81 (Bankr. E.D.N.Y. 1991) held that retroactive application of § 363(h) to sell the interest of a nondebtor spouse who was not involved in any debtor-creditor relationship would violate the takings clause of the Fifth Amendment to the United States Constitution because it was not a public use that would justify a taking. *See also In re* Lyons, 995 F.2d 923 (9th Cir. 1993) (proceeding by trustee seeking authority to sell property pursuant to § 363(h) must be adversary proceeding and not a motion).

65 11 U.S.C. § 727(a)(2), (4), (5), 727(d); *see* §§ 14.2, 14.3, *infra.*

66 *See* Krank v. Utica Mut. Ins. Co., 109 B.R. 668 (E.D. Pa. 1990), *aff'd*, 908 F.2d 962 (3d Cir. 1990) (debtor may not enforce pre-petition cause of action not listed in his schedules without reopening bankruptcy case and allowing trustee an opportunity to enforce or abandon the claim); *see also* Vreugdenhill v. Navistar Int'l Transp. Corp., 950 F.2d 524 (8th Cir. 1991) (claim belonging to debtor was not abandoned back to debtor at close of case, even though trustee knew of claim, because debtor had not formally scheduled it as property). A debtor's failure to schedule a pre-petition cause of action may also bar the debtor from pursuing that cause of action under the doctrine of judicial estoppel. *See* § 7.3.4.2.2, *infra.*

67 11 U.S.C. § 522; *see* Chapter 10, *infra.*

68 11 U.S.C. § 554; *see* §§ 3.5, 8.3.8, *infra.*

69 *See In re* Frank-Hill, 300 B.R. 25 (Bankr. D. Ariz. 2003) (funds held in trust in Individual Indian Money Account by U.S. Dept.

of Interior subject to restrictions on transfer and not property of estate).

70 29 U.S.C. § 1056(d)(1). "ERISA" is the Employee Retirement Income Security Act of 1974.

71 *Compare, e.g., In re* Harline, 950 F.2d 669 (10th Cir. 1991) (ERISA anti-alienation provision constitutes "applicable nonbankruptcy law") *with In re* Dyke, 943 F.2d 1435 (5th Cir. 1991) (ERISA does not protect pensions because "applicable nonbankruptcy law" encompasses only state law protections).

72 Patterson v. Shumate, 504 U.S. 753, 112 S. Ct. 2242, 119 L. Ed. 2d 519, *motion granted*, 505 U.S. 1239 (1992). Based on this holding, it would seem that a claim that can be secured by a debtor's ERISA plan, such as a tax claim, cannot be an allowed secured claim, because an allowed secured claim is secured by property of the estate. *See* Internal Rev. Serv. v. Snyder, 343 F.3d 1171 (9th Cir. 2003) (tax lien on ERISA plan cannot create an allowed secured claim); *In re* Wingfield, 284 B.R. 787 (E.D. Va. 2002).

73 *But see In re* Harshbarger, 66 F.3d 775 (6th Cir. 1995) (funds that chapter 13 debtors wished to use to repay pre-petition loan from ERISA plan were not excluded from the estate).

74 *In re* Conner, 73 F.3d 258 (9th Cir. 1996).

75 *In re* Sewell, 180 F.3d 707 (5th Cir. 1999) (ERISA plan excluded from estate even if acts of employer rendered plan not tax-qualified); *In re* Craig, 204 B.R. 756 (D.N.D. 1997); *In re* Bennett, 185 B.R. 4 (Bankr. E.D.N.Y. 1995) (ERISA plan need not be tax-qualified; Supreme Court's decision had looked only to nonalienation provisions; *In re* Hanes, 162 B.R. 733 (Bankr. E.D. Va. 1994) (pension plan need not be tax-qualified to be "ERISA-qualified"); *see also* Raymond B. Yates, M.D., P.C. Profit Sharing Plan v. Hendon, 124 S. Ct. 1330, 158 L. Ed. 2d 40 (2004) (working owner of business that has at least one non-owner employee who is not owner's spouse can be employee protected by ERISA); *In re* Stern, 345 F.3d 1036 (9th Cir. 2003), *cert. denied*, 124 S. Ct. 1671 (2004) (when plan covered only owner and his spouse, owner was not protected by ERISA); *In re* Baker, 114 F.3d 636 (7th Cir. 1997) (ERISA violations did not render ERISA inapplicable, even if debtor violated his duties as trustee and exposed employer to extra taxes). *But see* Morlan v. Universal Guar. Life. Ins. Co., 298 F.3d 609 (7th Cir. 2002) (unlike ERISA pension benefits, ERISA welfare plan benefits are assignable); *In re* Adams, 302 B.R. 535 (B.A.P. 6th Cir. 2003) (ERISA exempts § 403(b) plans from trust require-

Some issues nevertheless remain. Debtors who have filed bankruptcy cases while in the process of rolling over their pension funds into another plan have been faced with claims that the funds were not in an ERISA plan on the date of bankruptcy and were therefore not excluded from the estate.[76] The policy of protecting pension plan benefits should prevail in this situation, but it is better to avoid such situations if at all possible by deferring either the bankruptcy case or the rollover so that the bankruptcy case is filed while the funds are in a qualified plan.[77] It does seem clear, though, that a plan does not lose its ERISA protections simply because it is funded in whole or in part by an employee debtor[78] or because the debtor has the right to receive a lump-sum distribution.[79]

There are also issues with respect to non-ERISA plans. For example, the *Patterson* Court pointed out that at least two types of retirement accounts do not qualify under ERISA and therefore are not entitled to its protection. These accounts are certain pensions established by governmental entities or religious organizations and individual retirement accounts (IRAs).[80] The treatment of these types of retirement accounts, along with other employee benefit plans not subject to ERISA's anti-alienation language, must still be analyzed on a case-by-case basis.[81]

It should be noted that some government and church pensions may have been established with provisions similar to the anti-alienation provisions in ERISA plans or may qualify for protection under state law.[82] And if the debtor has no right to reach the funds in a plan, the estate can have no greater rights. Thus, for example, when a county employee could not reach the funds in his retirement plan while he was still employed by the county, the trustee had no right to compel turnover of those funds.[83] Similarly, IRAs may also be protected from alienation under state law.[84]

Non-retirement employee benefit plans may also be protected, depending on whether they come within the ambit of ERISA's anti-alienation language or alternative protections of the plan or state law. The benefits under some plans may not be vested so that they cannot be reached by debtors or their estates. One critical issue may be whether receipt of the funds is contingent upon additional services from the debtor or some other future event.[85] Alternatively, other plans may qualify as state law spendthrift trusts, so that they cannot be

---

ment so they are included in property of estate).

76   *See In re* Toone, 140 B.R. 605 (Bankr. D. Mass. 1992) (funds were not in ERISA plan during rollover process and were property of estate even though tax law treated them as if they were in a plan during that period); *see also In re* Barshak, 106 F.3d 501 (3d Cir. 1997) (decided under Pennsylvania state exemption laws). The *Barshak* result was subsequently overruled by an amendment to Pennsylvania's exemption laws. *Cf. In re* Goldman, 182 B.R. 622 (Bankr. D. Mass. 1995) (funds being rolled over could be exempted under state law, even though amount rolled over to IRA exceeded amount that could be deposited to qualify for exemption), *aff'd*, 192 B.R. 1 (D. Mass. 1996); *In re* Nudo, 147 B.R. 68 (Bankr. N.D.N.Y. 1992) (state exemption statute protecting plan funds also protected funds to which debtor had access upon terminating employment, but which could be rolled over into another exemptible qualified account).

77   *See In re* Latta, 189 B.R. 222 (N.D. Ga. 1995) (pension plan proceeds withdrawn for purpose of rollover after chapter 7 case filed were not property of the estate).

78   *In re* Rueter, 11 F.3d 850 (9th Cir. 1993) (employee-funded plan excluded from bankruptcy estate); *In re* Conner, 165 B.R. 901 (B.A.P. 9th Cir. 1994) (plan excluded despite fact that it included employee after-tax contributions), *aff'd*, 73 F.3d 258 (9th Cir. 1996).

79   Whetzal v. Anderson, 32 F.3d 1302 (8th Cir. 1994) (retired debtor's right to immediate distribution did not become estate property).

80   Patterson v. Shumate, 504 U.S. 753, 112 S. Ct. 2242, 2249, 119 L. Ed. 2d 519, *motion granted*, 505 U.S. 1239 (1992).

81   *See, e.g., In re* Walker, 959 F.2d 894 (10th Cir. 1992) (plans not containing anti-alienation language were not excluded from estate, but could be exempted under Oklahoma law).

82   *In re* Moses, 167 F.3d 470 (9th Cir. 1999) (medical group retirement plan was spendthrift trust under California law and therefore excluded from estate under § 541(c)(2)); Morter v. Farm Credit Services, 937 F.2d 354 (7th Cir. 1991) (teacher's retirement account qualifies as spendthrift trust under state law and is excluded from estate); *In re* Fink, 153 B.R. 883 (Bankr. D. Neb. 1993) (teacher's retirement annuity plan was a trust and also subject to restrictions on transfer enforceable under non-bankruptcy law, so it was not property of the estate). *But see In re* Swanson, 873 F.2d 1121 (8th Cir. 1989) (teacher's retirement fund is property of the estate).

83   *In re* Sanders, 969 F.2d 591 (7th Cir. 1992).

84   *In re* Yuhas, 104 F.3d 612 (3d Cir. 1997) (state law deemed IRA to be a trust and exempted it from claims of creditors); *In re* Meehan, 102 F.3d 1209 (11th Cir. 1997) (IRA excluded from estate because state law prohibited garnishment of debtor's interest); *see* Velis v. Kardanis, 949 F.2d 78 (3d Cir. 1991) (IRA included in estate because debtor had reached age allowing free withdrawal); *In re* Nelson, 180 B.R. 584 (B.A.P. 9th Cir. 1995) (ERISA did not preempt state law exempting IRAs); *In re* Kramer, 128 B.R. 707 (Bankr. E.D.N.Y. 1991) (IRA does not qualify as spendthrift trust under New York law); *In re* Howerton, 21 B.R. 621 (Bankr. N.D. Tex. 1982) (individual retirement annuity contracts property of the estate).

85   *In re* Parsons, 280 F.3d 1185 (8th Cir. 2002) (real estate commissions earned prior to petition were property of estate); *In re* Ryerson, 739 F.2d 1423 (9th Cir. 1984) (severance pay sufficiently rooted in pre-bankruptcy past considered property of estate); *In re* Haynes, 679 F.2d 718 (7th Cir. 1982) (future military retirement pay conditioned upon performance of future obligations is not property of estate); Denedai v. Preferred Capital Markets, Inc., 272 B.R. 21 (D. Mass. 2001) (interest in stock options was property of estate to extent options resulted from pre-petition efforts); *In re* Edmonds, 263 B.R. 828 (E.D. Mich. 2001) (contingent interest in employer's profit sharing plan was property of estate); *In re* Chappo, 257 B.R. 852 (E.D. Mich. 2001) (bonus awarded after bankruptcy petition was filed not property of estate because employer could have decided not to grant bonus); *In re* Siverling, 72 B.R. 78 (Bankr. N.D. Ga. 1987) (debtor subject to future military recall); *In re* Kervin, 19 B.R. 190 (Bankr. S.D. Ala. 1982) (renewal premiums earned by debtor's post-bankruptcy servicing of old insurance policies not property of estate).

alienated for purposes of bankruptcy.[86] Generally, though, a spendthrift trust cannot be created by its beneficiary and such "self-settled" trusts are not protected under state laws.[87] However, two states, Alaska and Delaware, have recently changed their laws to permit protection of self-settled spendthrift trusts if the assets in those trusts were not generated through fraudulent transfers.

The laws regarding spendthrift trusts vary widely from jurisdiction to jurisdiction. However, most states allow trusts to be established that protect the beneficiary's interest from creditors, as long as the beneficiary has no right to obtain trust funds whenever she desires. Those trusts are excluded from the debtor's bankruptcy estate under section 541(c)(2).[88] However, once funds are distributed or withdrawn from any qualified trust account, they presumably lose their protection.[89]

Another situation that can arise is that of the debtor whose pension has been divided in a divorce proceeding, usually pursuant to a Qualified Domestic Relations Order (QDRO). Most courts have held that such an order divests the debtor of any property rights in the pension rights that were transferred by the QDRO to the debtor's former spouse.[90] If the former spouse who received such a transfer later becomes a bankruptcy debtor, that spouse's interest should be deemed a pension interest with the same protections as the debtor would have had with respect to that interest.[91]

The debtor must list pensions and other trust interests in Schedule B of the bankruptcy schedules whether or not they come into the estate.[92] Any argument that the interest is outside the estate should be carefully noted on Schedule B with a reference to section 541(c)(2).

Issues also continue to arise in determining whether retirement funds or other trust interests that do come into the estate qualify for exemption. It should not be assumed that no exemption applies.[93] And nothing prevents a debtor from

---

86 *Compare In re* Lowenschuss, 171 F.3d 673 (9th Cir. 1999) (pension plan not a spendthrift trust under Pennsylvania law because debtor was settlor, administrator, and sole beneficiary of the pension plan, exercised control over the pension plan, and had the power to terminate the pension plan and distribute the proceeds to himself); *In re* Kaplan, 97 B.R. 572 (B.A.P. 9th Cir. 1989) (pension plan in which debtor is sole beneficiary as well as trustee is property of the estate); *In re* Davis, 125 B.R. 242 (Bankr. W.D. Mo. 1991) (profit-sharing plan not valid spendthrift trust under state law); *In re* Council, 122 B.R. 64 (Bankr. S.D. Ohio 1990) (trustee can reach debtor's deferred compensation plan when plan allows distribution in the event of unforeseeable emergency); *In re* Klayer, 20 B.R. 270 (Bankr. W.D. Ky. 1981) (retirement plan is property of estate when trust held invalid) *with In re* Wilcox, 233 F.3d 899 (6th Cir. 2000) (anti-assignment provision in city charter was enforceable restriction on alienation); *In re* Johnson, 191 B.R. 75 (Bankr. M.D. Pa. 1996) (tax-deferred annuity, though not ERISA plan, contained spendthrift trust clause enforceable under state law); *In re* Kleist, 114 B.R. 366 (Bankr. N.D.N.Y. 1990) (employee savings plan meeting certain IRS Code requirements is spendthrift trust under New York law even though debtor could withdraw funds at any time); SSA Baltimore Fed. Credit Union v. Bizon, 42 B.R. 338 (D. Md. 1984) (when government employee had no choice in connection with government's contribution to Civil Serv. Retirement and Disability Fund and would not currently receive annuity, fund was spendthrift trust under state law and excluded from bankruptcy estate). To the extent that some of these cases involved ERISA plans, the issue of whether the plan is a spendthrift trust is no longer significant after the Supreme Court's decision in *Patterson v. Shumate,* discussed above. However they continue to be instructive on the principles for determining whether a retirement plan is a spendthrift trust.

87 *See In re* Lowenschuss, 171 F.3d 673 (9th Cir. 1999) (pension plan not a spendthrift trust under Pennsylvania law because debtor was settlor, administrator, and sole beneficiary of the pension plan, exercised control over the pension plan, and had the power to terminate the pension plan and distribute the proceeds to himself); *In re* Shurley, 115 F.3d 333 (5th Cir. 1997) (assets placed in spendthrift trust by debtor were not protected from creditors by Texas law applicable to spendthrift trusts, but other trust assets were protected).

88 *See* Drewes v. Schonteich, 31 F.3d 674 (8th Cir. 1994) (trusts created for benefit of debtor's caretaker and charitable institution were spendthrift trusts excluded from bankruptcy estate); *In*

re Neuton, 922 F.2d 1379 (9th Cir. 1990) (percentage of trust which qualifies as valid spendthrift trust under California law is not property of the estate); *In re* Newman, 903 F.2d 1150 (7th Cir. 1990) (trustee cannot reach valid spendthrift trust under Missouri law); *In re* Fitzsimmons, 896 F.2d 373 (9th Cir. 1990) (forfeiture on alienation provision in land trust prevents beneficiary's interest in trust from passing to bankruptcy trustee and may be given effect under § 541(c)(2)); *In re* Robbins, 826 F.2d 293 (4th Cir. 1987); *cf. In re* Brown, 303 F.3d 1261 (11th Cir. 2002) (Florida law did not protect funds in self-settled spendthrift trust from creditors); *In re* Jordan, 914 F.2d 197 (9th Cir. 1990) (trust established by debtor's employer as compensation for personal injury not spendthrift trust under Washington law); *In re* Meyers, 139 B.R. 858 (Bankr. N.D. Ohio 1992) (fact that state held debtor's lottery winnings to be paid annually in the future did not create spendthrift trust); *see also In re* Moody, 837 F.2d 719 (5th Cir. 1988) (post-petition distribution from spendthrift trust may be attached by post-petition creditors).

89 *See* Velis v. Kardanis, 949 F.2d 78 (3d Cir. 1991) (pension and Keough plans are included in the bankruptcy estate to the extent of any distribution). *But see In re* Coumbe, 304 B.R. 378 (B.A.P 9th Cir. 2003) (income distributions were property of estate but *corpus* distributions were not); *In re* Bresnahan, 183 B.R. 506 (Bankr. S.D. Ohio 1995) (funds distributed from pension plan and placed in debtor's bank account were property of estate, but could be exempted under Ohio law protecting pension funds).

90 *See* § 14.4.3.5, *infra.*

91 *In re* Nelson, 322 F.3d 541 (8th Cir. 2003); *In re* Lalchandani, 279 B.R. 880 (B.A.P. 1st Cir. 2002) (interest in ERISA plan obtained by debtor through QDRO was not property of estate); *In re* Farmer, 295 B.R. 322 (Bankr. W.D. Wis. 2003); *In re* Satterwhite, 271 B.R. 378 (Bankr. W.D. Mo. 2002) (anti-alienation provisions of Uniform Services Spouse's Protection Act caused interest in pension of debtor's former spouse to be excluded from estate).

92 *See* § 7.3.4.2.2, *infra.*

93 A pension or other trust interest may be exempt under either state or federal law. Such exemptions are not preempted by ERISA. *In re* Schlein, 8 F.3d 745 (11th Cir. 1993). See § 10.2.2.10, *infra,* for a discussion of pension exemptions.

claiming that property is outside the estate (on Schedule B), but nevertheless listing an applicable exemption (on Schedule C) in the alternative.

2.5.3 Tax Refunds and the Earned Income Tax Credit

The right to receive a tax refund is clearly property of the estate.[94] The debtor may also have a property interest in excessive withholding by an employer for the then-current tax year which becomes a part of a refund due after the filing of the bankruptcy.[95] When such withholdings do result in a refund, the refund is often prorated over the entire year, with the pre-bankruptcy portion considered property of the estate.[96] However, in many jurisdictions, trustees do not check whether there has been excessive withholding from the debtor's pay during the tax year the bankruptcy case is filed, probably because it is usually eligible for exemption. Debtors' counsel should be sure to check local practices on this issue.

Debtors' rights to various tax credits which arise pre-petition have also been held to come into the estate,[97] but there is some precedent for distinguishing the right to an earned income tax credit.[98] The courts that have concluded that the earned income tax credit is always excluded from the estate base their decision on a belief that a debtor can have no legal or equitable interest in the credit prior to receiving it, or at least claiming it by filing a return.

Because the right to a credit cannot be determined at least until the end of the tax year, the argument that it should not be included in the estate is strongest when bankruptcy is filed prior to the end of the relevant tax year.[99] A slightly weaker argument can be made when the debtor files bankruptcy before claiming the credit by filing a return. In that event, the debtor can argue that there is not yet a cognizable entitlement to the credit.[100]

It is also plausible to argue that the mere filing of the return does not create an interest in the credit, because the credit does not come into existence until it is determined by the government. It follows, then, that the credit does not come into the estate unless it is actually mailed or received pre-petition.[101]

Prior to commencing a bankruptcy case, counsel should consider how a tax refund will be treated in the bankruptcy process. Careful efforts should be made to set up the case in a way that maximizes the debtor's ability to obtain the benefit of the credit.

---

94 *In re* Barowsky, 946 F.2d 1516 (10th Cir. 1991); *see In re* Canon, 130 B.R. 748 (Bankr. N.D. Tex. 1991) (when trustee made proper demand for tax refund constituting property of the estate, IRS is required to pay trustee, even though it had paid the refund to the debtors); *see also* United States v. Michaels, 840 F.2d 901 (11th Cir. 1988) (IRS can recoup tax refund paid to debtor which should have been paid to trustee as property of the debtor's estate).

95 Turshen v. Chapman, 823 F.2d 836 (4th Cir. 1987); *In re* Doan, 672 F.2d 831 (11th Cir. 1982); *cf. In re* Christie, 233 B.R. 110 (B.A.P. 10th Cir. 1999) (tax refund attributable to overpayment made after bankruptcy petition was filed, from post-petition earnings and borrowings, was not property of estate).

96 *In re* Barowsky, 946 F.2d 1516 (10th Cir. 1991); *In re* Rash, 22 B.R. 323 (Bankr. D. Kan. 1982); *In re* Koch, 14 B.R. 64 (Bankr. D. Kan. 1982); *see In re* Aldrich, 250 B.R. 907 (Bankr. W.D. Tenn. 2000); *see also In re* Lambert, 283 B.R. 16 (B.A.P. 9th Cir. 2002) (prepayment of current year refund pursuant to special provision in tax legislation treated as refund for current year, not prior year, even though amount of prepayment was calculated based on income for prior year). *Compare In re* Bading, 154 B.R. 687 (Bankr. W.D. Tex. 1993) (estate entitled to prorated portion of return calculated based on one-half of joint refund even through debtor was unmarried on petition date) *with In re* Kleinfeldt, 287 B.R. 291 (B.A.P. 10th Cir. 2002) (joint income tax refund not divided between husband and wife because husband earned all of the income on which return was based).

97 Segal v. Rochelle, 382 U.S. 375, 86 S. Ct. 511, 15 L. Ed. 2d 428 (1966). Although *Segal* was decided under the Bankruptcy Act rather than the Code, the language of Code section 541(a)(1) is at least as broad as the language on which the *Segal* holding is based. *See In re* Prudential Lines, Inc., 928 F.2d 565 (2d Cir. 1991) (debtor's pre-petition net operating loss carry forward is property of the estate).

98 *In re* Searles, 445 F. Supp. 749 (D. Conn. 1978); *In re* Hurles, 31 B.R. 179 (Bankr. S.D. Ohio 1983); *see also In re* Hankerson, 133 B.R. 711, 717 (Bankr. E.D. Pa. 1991), *rev'd on other grounds*, 138 B.R. 473 (E.D. Pa. 1992) (earned income tax credit does not arise until a tax return is filed). Even if the earned income tax credit is deemed to be property of the estate, it usually may be exempted, either by using a wild card exemption or an exception for public assistance benefits under the federal bankruptcy exemptions or state exemption law. *See* § 10.2.2.11, *infra*.

99 *See In re* Pratavadi, 281 B.R. 816 (Bankr. W.D.N.Y. 2002) (ruling on related issue that taxes due from debtor are not prorated unless debtor elects to file a split-year return in year bankruptcy case was filed). *But see In re* Johnston, 222 B.R. 552 (B.A.P. 6th Cir. 1998), *aff'd*, 209 F.3d 611 (6th Cir. 2000); *In re* Montgomery, 219 B.R. 913 (B.A.P. 10th Cir. 1998), *aff'd*, 224 F.3d 1193 (10th Cir. 2000) (earned income tax credit is available to the debtor and becomes property of the estate during the tax year not at year end). These cases require proration of the earned income tax credit on the same basis as the balance of the return.

100 *In re* Hankerson, 133 B.R. 711, 717 (Bankr. E.D. Pa. 1991) (earned income tax credit does not arise until a tax return is filed), *rev'd on other grounds*, 138 B.R. 473 (E.D. Pa. 1992); *see also In re* Meza, 243 B.R. 538 (Bankr. M.D. Fla. 1999) (earned income credit not property of estate because on date bankruptcy petition was filed, dependent child had not lived with debtors for requisite six months). *But see In re* Luongo, 259 F.3d 323 (5th Cir. 2001) (date of filing return irrelevant).

101 Some support for this argument can be derived from *In re* Searles, 445 F. Supp. 749 (D. Conn. 1978) and *In re* Hurles, 31 B.R. 179 (Bankr. S.D. Ohio 1983). *But see* Segal v. Rochelle, 382 U.S. 375, 86 S. Ct. 511, 15 L. Ed. 2d 428 (1966) (pre-petition business-generated loss carry-back tax refund comes into the estate).

When possible, the simplest way of ensuring that a debtor will retain control over a tax refund, whether or not it includes an earned income tax credit, is to wait for the refund to be received before filing bankruptcy. Most debtors are easily able to use such funds pre-petition for consumable necessities or for tangible property that can be exempted once bankruptcy is filed.[102]

Obviously, this strategy of delaying the filing pending receipt of a tax refund may not be appropriate if the tax refund is subject to pre-petition interception by the Internal Revenue Service on a government claim. In certain circumstances, the government can seize both an overpayment of withholding taxes and the earned income tax credit.[103] The potential interception of a tax refund can be a consideration in favor of filing sooner rather than later. An earlier filing may also make sense if the petition can be filed before January 1 and the practice in the debtor's jurisdiction is to consider tax refunds as property of the debtor only after January 1.

If the refund is seized either before or after filing, the preference,[104] post-petition transfer,[105] and set-off[106] provisions of the Code may apply in some cases, enabling the debtor to reverse the transfer.[107]

Another way of protecting the right to a tax refund may be to elect to apply it to the following year's taxes. It has been held that when debtors have made an irrevocable election to apply a tax overpayment to their next year's taxes they no longer have an overpayment or a right to a refund, and therefore no longer have a property interest in the funds.[108]

Whether or not there is an argument that the refund or tax credit is not part of the estate, it is always a good idea to evaluate whether there is an applicable exemption. In many cases a debtor can assert an exemption to protect a tax refund or the earned income tax credit based on the federal wild card exemption or a state wild card exemption.[109] Similarly, the earned income tax credit may qualify for exemption based on state or federal exemptions for public assistance benefits.[110]

2.6 The Bankruptcy Trustee

In every case under chapter 7 or chapter 13 of the Code, a trustee is appointed by the United States trustee, or if no United States trustee exists in the district, by the court.[111] The trustee's basic role is to represent the interests of the unsecured creditors.[112]

The trustee's duties in carrying out this role are set forth in the statute. They can include collecting property of the estate, invalidating certain transfers made by the debtor, objecting (if appropriate) to a claim of exemption, objecting to discharge, liquidating any nonexempt property and distributing it to creditors with valid claims, and making a final accounting to the court and to the United States trustee.[113] The trustee may sue or be sued as the representative of the estate in order to determine claims by or against the estate.[114]

---

102 For a discussion of exemption planning, see § 10.4, *infra*.

103 *See* Sorenson v. Sec'y of the Treasury, 475 U.S. 851, 106 S. Ct. 1600, 89 L. Ed. 2d 855 (1986) (earned income tax credit can be intercepted to recoup welfare payments made in default of the taxpayer's child support obligations).

104 11 U.S.C. § 547; *see* § 10.4.2.6.4, *infra*.

105 11 U.S.C. § 549; *see* § 10.4.2.6.6, *infra*.

106 11 U.S.C. § 553; *see* §§ 10.4.2.6.7, 13.3.2.2, *infra*. *Compare In re* Hankerson, 133 B.R. 711 (Bankr. E.D. Pa. 1991) (pre-petition tax intercept set aside pursuant to § 553(b)) *with In re* Stall, 125 B.R. 754 (Bankr. S.D. Ohio 1991) (tax intercept not set-aside). *In re* Hankerson was reversed. Hankerson v. Dep't of Educ., 138 B.R. 473 (E.D. Pa. 1992). The district court held that the recovery of a pre-petition set-off from the federal government was barred by sovereign immunity, which would no longer be true under the amended version of 11 U.S.C. § 106.

107 New limits on use of these powers against governmental units based on the Eleventh Amendment and sovereign immunity have emerged from recent Supreme Court decisions. *See* § 13.3.2.2, *infra*.

108 *In re* Block, 141 B.R. 609 (N.D. Tex. 1992) (debtors no longer had interest in $11,000 tax refund when then had elected to apply it to estimated taxes); *In re* Simmons, 124 B.R. 606 (Bankr. M.D. Fla. 1991) (once debtor made election it was irrevocable, and overpayment of taxes no longer existed).

109 11 U.S.C. § 522(d)(5); *see* § 10.2.2.6, *infra*. However, an exemption may not protect a right to a tax refund from a pre-petition right to set-off, at least absent the ability to avoid the right to set-off. *In re* Luongo, 259 F.3d 323 (5th Cir. 2001).

110 *See* § 10.2.2.11, *infra*; *see also In re* Goldsberry, 142 B.R. 158 (Bankr. E.D. Ky. 1992) (earned income credit exempt as "public assistance" under Kentucky law); *In re* Jones, 107 B.R. 751 (Bankr. D. Idaho 1989) (state exemption for federal public assistance benefits); *In re* Taylor, 99 B.R. 371 (Bankr. S.D. Ohio 1989) (state exemption for "poor relief" payments). However, the federal exemption of certain wages from garnishment does not extend to wages withheld for taxes even if they are still in the hands of the employer. Kokoszka v. Belford, 417 U.S. 642, 94 S. Ct. 2431, 41 L. Ed. 2d 374 (1974) (construing 15 U.S.C. § 1671). A different result might be reached based on state law restrictions on garnishment. *In re* Davis, 136 B.R. 203 (Bankr. D. Iowa 1991) (earned income tax credit exempt in Iowa as public assistance). *But see In re* Collins, 170 F.3d 512 (5th Cir. 1999) (earned income tax credit not exempt as public assistance under Louisiana law); *In re* Wallerstedt, 930 F.2d 630 (8th Cir. 1991) (Missouri protection for "earnings" does not apply to tax refund); *In re* Rutter 204 B.R. 57 (Bankr. D. Or. 1997) (earned income tax credit not exemptible public assistance); *In re* Goertz, 202 B.R. 614 (Bankr. W.D. Mo. 1996) (same).

111 11 U.S.C. §§ 701, 1302. Sections 701 and 1302 were amended, effective upon the United States trustee program becoming operational in a district, to provide that the United States trustee appoints the chapter 7 interim trustee and the chapter 13 trustee. There is a now a United States trustee in every judicial district except for those in Alabama and North Carolina.

112 *But see In re* Andrews, 49 F.3d 1404 (9th Cir. 1995) (chapter 13 trustee represents all creditors).

113 11 U.S.C. § 704. The trustee lacks standing, however, to object to the dischargeability of particular debts. *See, e.g., In re* Dunn, 83 B.R. 694 (Bankr. D. Neb. 1988).

114 Wieburg v. GTE Southwest, Inc., 272 F.3d 302 (5th Cir. 2001)

In a typical chapter 7 consumer case, there is no nonexempt property, so the trustee's duties are limited. In such cases, she evaluates the debtor's schedules, statements, and exemption claims, and ensures that the debtor carries out the stated intentions with respect to property securing consumer debts.[115] The trustee participates in and, in many districts, presides at the meeting of creditors.[116] The trustee also may make inquiries of the debtor to determine whether to file objections to discharge or whether the filing of the case is otherwise improper. Trustees, probably at the urging of the United States trustee, have increased their efforts in this regard, sometimes making unreasonable and burdensome requests for information from the debtor. While the debtor, under 11 U.S.C. § 521(3), has a duty to cooperate with the trustee, the debtor does not have a duty to do the trustee's work nor to expend significant funds or do substantial work (such as obtaining documents not already in the debtor's possession) to comply with such requests. In many cases, the appropriate response to a request for documents or information the debtor does not possess is to give the trustee information about where they may be obtained and a release authorizing the trustee to obtain them. Finally, in some places, the trustee also files a report with the court stating any objections to the discharge or to exemption claims.

The chapter 13 trustee has considerably more to do. Unlike in chapter 7 cases, where the trustee is one of a number who can be chosen from a panel in each district, there is usually only one trustee, a "standing trustee," to handle all chapter 13 cases in a particular district or part of a district.[117] In addition to most of the duties of a chapter 7 trustee, a chapter 13 trustee must attend all hearings on the value of property subject to liens or on confirmation or modification of the debtor's plan, receive and disburse payments according to the debtor's plan, make sure the debtor is making payments,[118] advise the debtor on non-

legal matters, and assist the debtor in performance of the plan.[119] In the past the diligence of chapter 13 trustees in performing the last two duties of advice and assistance has varied widely among districts.

Both chapter 13 and chapter 7 trustees are accountable for the performance of their statutory duties and may generally be held liable for failure to perform them.[120] Courts have differed on the extent of a bankruptcy trustee's immunity from suit.[121]

However, it is clear that the bankruptcy trustee is not a judicial officer with the power to resolve disputed issues arising in a bankruptcy proceeding. The trustee is a party with equal status to other persons interested in the outcome of the case. If there is a disputed issue, the trustee may file or respond to a contested matter or an adversary proceeding and seek resolution by the court. The trustee, like other parties, is also required to take and respond to discovery. *Ex parte* communications between the trustee and the bankruptcy judge are prohibited.[122]

Depending on the type of matter involved, then, the trustee may be either a friend or a foe of the debtor. Naturally, it is important to distinguish these situations carefully and to be familiar with how the trustee sees her role. An active trustee may closely scrutinize the debtor's affairs, sometimes to help the debtor and sometimes to help the creditors. Some trustees may be interested in asserting the debtor's counterclaims or defenses,[123] while others may

---

(trustee should have been allowed to join or ratify debtor's employment discrimination case); Tanenbaum v. Smith, Friedman & Associates, 289 B.R. 800 (D.N.J. 2002) (settlement of debtor's pre-petition personal injury claims reached without consent of chapter 7 trustee voided); *see, e.g.*, Bellini Imports v. Mason & Dixon Lines, Inc., 944 F.2d 199 (4th Cir. 1991) (failure to name trustee as defendant when pursuing administrative claims precludes enforcement of those claims against the estate).

115 This duty, set forth in 11 U.S.C. § 704(3), is discussed in Chapter 11, *infra*.

116 Fed. R. Bankr. P. 2003(b)(1) provides that the United States trustee shall preside at the meeting of creditors unless the court has designated a different person. In many places, that designee is the interim trustee. In chapter 13 cases, the designee will generally be the standing chapter 13 trustee. See Chapter 3, *infra*, for discussion of the meeting of creditors.

117 11 U.S.C. § 1302(d) was replaced by 28 U.S.C. § 586(b) in the 1986 amendments, providing for appointment of standing chapter 13 trustees by the United States trustee when a United States trustee has been appointed.

118 Many chapter 13 trustees post their records of payments by debtors and of payments to creditors on the Internet, where they

can be accessed by debtors, creditors, and their counsel.

119 11 U.S.C. § 1302(b).

120 *See, e.g., In re* Gorski, 766 F.2d 723 (2d Cir. 1985) (Chapter XIII trustee in case under Bankruptcy Act ordered to pay $500 or other compensation to creditors damaged by his failure to act when debtors made no plan payments for thirty-three months); *In re* Nash, 765 F.2d 1410 (9th Cir. 1985) (chapter 13 trustee held liable to debtors for distributing funds to creditors after receiving notice of voluntary dismissal of case).

121 *Compare* Conn. Gen. Life Ins. v. Universal Ins. Co., 838 F.2d 612 (1st Cir. 1988) (trustee liable for willful and deliberate violation of fiduciary duties); Yadkin Valley Bank & Trust Co. v. McGee, 819 F.2d 74 (4th Cir. 1987) (no absolute immunity from civil damages for negligence in performing duties) *with* Gregory v. United States, 942 F.2d 1498 (10th Cir. 1991) (trustee has absolute immunity for executing bankruptcy judge's orders); Bennett v. Williams, 892 F.2d 822 (9th Cir. 1989) (trustee acting within scope of authority has quasi-judicial immunity from suit for discretionary acts); Mullis v. United States Bankruptcy Court, 828 F.2d 1385 (9th Cir. 1987) (trustee has absolute quasi-judicial immunity from civil damages for acts within the scope of official duties).

122 Fed. R. Bank. P. 9003(a).

123 As successor-in-interest to property of the estate, the trustee has full power to raise claims of the debtor. *See, e.g., In re* Scaife, 825 F.2d 357 (11th Cir. 1987); *see also* Bauer v. Commerce Union Bank, 859 F.2d 438 (6th Cir. 1988) (trustee is properly substituted as party plaintiff for debtor when cause of action becomes property of estate); Tanenbaum v. Smith, Friedman & Associates, 289 B.R. 800 (D.N.J. 2002) (court could deem debtor's post-petition settlement of pre-petition cause of action void because trustee did not participate in settlement). However,

not. As will be seen in the following chapters, knowing the predilections of a particular trustee may be of considerable help in choosing the correct bankruptcy strategy.

2.7 The United States Trustee

The 1986 amendments to the Bankruptcy Code and related legislation made the United States trustee program, which had begun in 1979, permanent and expanded it nationwide. Every judicial district, with the exception of those in Alabama and North Carolina, is part of a larger United States Trustee District, served by a United States trustee and one or more assistant United States trustees. For political reasons, neither Alabama nor North Carolina has a United States trustee.[124]

In 1991 the Bankruptcy Rules were amended to require notice to the United States trustee, either by the clerk or by the parties, in numerous areas of bankruptcy practice. The amended rules should be checked carefully to avoid overlooking these service requirements.

The function of the United States trustee is to remove the bankruptcy court from administrative matters, leaving the court to perform its primary function of resolving disputes that arise among parties in the bankruptcy case and related proceedings. Thus, the United States trustee takes over such functions as appointing and supervising trustees, convening the meeting of creditors, and monitoring fees charged by bankruptcy attorneys. All of these tasks were formerly performed by the court.[125]

The United States trustee is also given the right to move for dismissal of a case under chapter 7 for substantial abuse of the provisions of the Code, and for dismissal of cases under all chapters for undue delay in filing required documents.[126] The United States trustee's role in a bankruptcy case beyond the duties enumerated in the statute remains unclear.[127] However, the United States trustee is prohibited from *ex parte* contacts with the court concerning particular cases[128] and, like the bankruptcy trustee, must submit disputes, in the appropriate manner, to the court for resolution.

---

if a case is in chapter 13, or is converted to chapter 13, the debtor has the right, pursuant to 11 U.S.C. § 1306(b), to control litigation on behalf of the estate. *In re* Wirmel, 134 B.R. 258 (Bankr. S.D. Ohio 1991) (chapter 7 trustee lost control of debtor's civil rights case upon conversion of debtor's bankruptcy case to chapter 13).

124 Under Pub. L. No. 99-554, § 302(d)(3), 100 Stat. 3088 (1986), as amended by Pub. L. No. 106-518, 114 Stat. 2410 (2000), the judicial districts in North Carolina and Alabama will not have a United States trustee unless they opt to have one. The exclusion of districts in only two states from the program was held to be an unconstitutional violation of the bankruptcy uniformity clause of the United States Constitution by the Ninth Circuit Court of Appeals. St. Angelo v. Victoria Farms, Inc., 38 F.3d 1525 (9th Cir. 1994). However, as the districts without a United States trustee are not in the Ninth Circuit, the court ordered no remedy for the violation.

125 *See In re* Plaza de Diego Shopping Ctr., Inc., 911 F.2d 820 (1st Cir. 1990) (district court abused its discretion by selecting a trustee because such duty is exclusive responsibility of the United States trustee). In Alabama and North Carolina judicial districts, many of these duties are performed by a court official called the bankruptcy administrator.

126 11 U.S.C. §§ 707(a)(3), 707(b), 1307(c)(9), 1307(c)(10); *see* Fed. R. Bankr. P. 1017.

127 *See* United States Trustee v. Price Waterhouse, 19 F.3d 138 (3d Cir. 1994) (United States trustee has standing to appeal); *In re* Revco, 898 F.2d 498 (6th Cir. 1990) (United States trustee has standing to appeal the bankruptcy court's refusal to appoint an examiner in a chapter 11 case; under certain circumstances the appointment of an examiner is required upon request of the trustee).

128 Fed. R. Bankr. P. 9003(b).

Chapter 3

Chapter 7 Bankruptcy (Straight Bankruptcy): The Basic Steps

3.1 General Explanation of Chapter 7 Bankruptcy

When most people think of bankruptcy, they think of the type of bankruptcy provided for in chapter 7 of the Code, a liquidation proceeding often called straight bankruptcy. This type of bankruptcy has by far been the most popular type of proceeding for individuals. Although the percentage of debtors choosing chapter 7 has diminished somewhat since enactment of the Code because of the advantages that chapter 13 offers, chapter 7 continues to be the chapter most frequently utilized, and it remains an important option for consumer debtors.

This Chapter describes the routine steps in a typical liquidation case, from beginning to end, with emphasis on the procedures in "no-asset" cases. (A "no-asset" case is one in which none of the debtor's assets are available to be sold for the benefit of unsecured creditors because all of the assets are exempt[1] or encumbered by liens[2] to the full extent of their value.) Chapters 5 through 8, *infra,* then provide a detailed practical guide on how to prepare and handle a bankruptcy case.

In a liquidation case, all of the debtor's non-exempt assets are distributed to creditors and the debtor receives a bankruptcy discharge. From the beginning of the case until its conclusion, each step in the process is directed toward one or both of these ends.

3.2 Commencement of the Case

3.2.1 Who May File?

3.2.1.1 General Rules

Any individual residing, domiciled, or having property or a place of business in the United States may file a chapter 7 bankruptcy.[3] The individual need not be insolvent and no other test must be met (although in very limited circumstances a chapter 7 case may be dismissed by the court for bad faith or "substantial abuse").[4] A person, whether a citizen or not, may file a bankruptcy case even if the person does not reside in the United States, as long as the person has assets in the United States.[5]

Although a debtor may file on her own behalf, an individual generally may not file as trustee on behalf of some other person.[6] This rule may cause occasional problems in cases in which parents have title to encumbered property in trust for their children. However, the child may be able to file, claiming as exempt her interest as beneficiary of the trust.[7] It may also be possible for the trustee of a trust, by filing a chapter 13 case, to secure the benefits of the automatic stay and to prevent loss of the property, if adequate protection is provided to the secured creditors involved.[8] An incompetent person has also been held eligible

---

1 Exempt property is property that the debtor may retain in a liquidation case. *See generally* Ch. 10, *infra.*

2 Property fully encumbered by a valid lien not voided by the trustee or the debtor during the bankruptcy through use of their various powers (*see* Ch. 10, *infra*), is not considered an asset available to unsecured creditors as the secured party has superior rights to the property.

3 11 U.S.C. § 109. Subject to certain limitations, corporations and partnerships may also file under chapter 7, because they are within the definition of "person" under the Code. 11 U.S.C. § 101(41).

4 11 U.S.C. § 707. See Chapter 13, *infra,* for discussion of dismissal and the substantial abuse provision added by the 1984 amendments.

5 *See, e.g.,* Bank of Am., N.T. & S.A. v. World of English, N.V., 23 B.R. 1015 (N.D. Ga. 1982) (bank account in United States); *In re* McTague, 198 B.R. 428 (Bankr. W.D.N.Y. 1996) (resident of Canada with $194.00 bank account).

6 *In re* Kirby, 9 B.R. 901 (Bankr. E.D. Pa. 1981).

7 *See In re* Nesset, 33 B.R. 326 (Bankr. D.N.M. 1983).

8 *See In re* Foster, 19 B.R. 28 (Bankr. E.D. Pa. 1982) (trustee's bare legal title sufficient to invoke automatic stay); *see also* Fed. Home Loan Mortgage Corp. v. Wynn, 29 B.R. 679 (Bankr. D.N.J. 1983). See generally § 2.5, *supra,* for a discussion of trust property as property of the trustee's bankruptcy estate.

to file a case under the Code. It may be possible for an attorney or relative to file the petition as "next friend" to the debtor, or for a court-appointed guardian to file the petition.[9] Bankruptcy may also be filed for an incompetent person pursuant to a sufficiently broad valid power of attorney, when evidence of the power of attorney is filed with the petition.[10] However, if there is a court appointed guardian, only that person has the authority to file for the debtor[11] and one court has held that an appointed conservator cannot file bankruptcy on behalf of an absent debtor whose whereabouts were unknown.[12]

Although an executor or administrator of an estate cannot file a bankruptcy petition because a probate estate is not an entity eligible to file a bankruptcy case, if the debtor dies during the case, especially if the case is a chapter 7 case, the case will usually continue. Federal Rule of Bankruptcy Procedure 1016 provides that death or incompetency of the debtor shall not abate a chapter 7 case. In such circumstances, the rule requires that the estate is to be administered and the case concluded, to the extent possible, as if the death or incompetency had not occurred. The debtor's interests

may have to be represented by a personal representative with the legal authority to represent the estate.[13]

3.2.1.2 Effect of Prior Bankruptcy Cases on Eligibility to File

One limitation exists on the broad right to file under chapter 7. An individual is not eligible to file a petition if, within the preceding 180 days, (1) she was the debtor in a bankruptcy case dismissed for willful failure to abide by orders of the court or to appear before the court in proper prosecution of the case or (2) she requested and obtained voluntary dismissal of a bankruptcy case following the filing of a request for relief from the automatic stay provided by section 362.[14]

In interpreting this provision with respect to involuntary dismissals, it is important to note that filing a petition within 180 days of an involuntary dismissal is not improper unless the failure to abide by court orders or to appear was willful.[15] Because this determination is not one that the clerk can normally make upon filing of the later case, such a dismissal should occur only if, after a motion to dismiss by some party in interest, the court finds the requisite willfulness as a matter of fact.[16] Absent a specific court order issued for cause, involuntary dismissals do not preclude the debtor from filing a new case under the Code, unless they fall within the parameters of section 109(g).[17]

Simply failing to make payments of filing fees, or plan payments in a prior chapter 13 case, should not, without more, be considered willful so as to preclude a successive filing for 180 days.[18] Nor should failure to appear at the

---

9 Fed. R. Bankr. P. 1004.1, promulgated in 2002, provides that a legally appointed representative may file a petition on behalf of an infant or incompetent person. If no such representative exists, such a person may file a petition by next friend. Prior case law had generally been consistent with these rules. *In re* Murray, 199 B.R. 165 (Bankr. M.D. Tenn. 1996) (parent could file petition on behalf of seven-year-old debtor as "next friend" of debtor); *In re* Smith, 115 B.R. 84 (Bankr. E.D. Va. 1990) (power of attorney does not allow wife to file on behalf of her incapacitated husband; however incapacitated person may file through court-appointed guardian); *In re* Jones, 97 B.R. 901 (Bankr. S.D. Ohio 1989) (guardian for incompetent debtor may file chapter 13); *In re* Zawisza, 73 B.R. 929 (Bankr. E.D. Pa. 1987) (attorney filed as "next friend"); *cf. In re* Brown, 163 B.R. 596 (Bankr. N.D. Fla. 1993) (petition filed on behalf of debtor by his wife, who signed it without indicating that signature was in representative capacity, was a nullity).

10 *In re* Hurt, 234 B.R. 1 (Bankr. D.N.H. 1999). *But see In re* Curtis, 262 B.R. 619 (Bankr. D. Vt. 2001) (general power of attorney is insufficient to authorize filing case for another person); *In re* Harrison, 158 B.R. 246 (Bankr. M.D. Fla. 1993) (petition on which debtor's name was signed by another, purportedly based upon later-submitted power of attorney, was a nullity, because there was no indication on petition that it was signed based on power of attorney and there were no exigent circumstances making it impossible for debtor to sign his own petition).

11 It is unclear whether a state conservatorship may deprive a debtor-ward of the right to file a bankruptcy case. *See In re* Kjellsen, 53 F.3d 944 (8th Cir. 1995) (if a guardian has been appointed for an incompetent person, only the guardian has authority to file a bankruptcy petition); *In re* Woods, 248 B.R. 322 (Bankr. W.D. Tenn. 2000) (petition dismissed for cause when not authorized by conservator); *see also In re* Blumeyer, 297 B.R. 577 (Bankr. E.D. Mo. 2003) (incarcerated person could file chapter 11 case despite existence of statutory trustee appointed by state court).

12 *In re* King, 234 B.R. 515 (Bankr. D.N.M. 1999) (distinguishing the situation of an absent debtor from one who is otherwise incapacitated).

13 *See In re* Lucio, 251 B.R. 705 (Bankr. W.D. Tex. 2000) (debtor's daughter could not appear for deceased debtor at meeting of creditors; personal representative of estate could appear).

14 11 U.S.C. § 109(g). See Chapter 9, *infra,* for further discussion of this provision and the automatic stay.

15 Given the language of the statute and its purpose of preventing abuse, it seems clear that a failure to appear before the court must be "willful" to justify dismissal of a subsequent petition filed within 180 days. *See In re* Arena, 81 B.R. 851 (Bankr. E.D. Pa. 1988). *But see In re* Smith, 851 F.2d 747 (5th Cir. 1988) (subsequent petition precluded when first petition dismissed for lack of proper prosecution, apparently without consideration of willfulness).

16 *In re* Montgomery, 37 F.3d 413 (8th Cir. 1994) (issue of willfulness is to be decided when later bankruptcy is filed, but debtor has burden of showing that earlier dismissal was not due to willful failure to prosecute case); *see also In re* Arena, 81 B.R. 851 (Bankr. E.D. Pa. 1988) (party moving for dismissal has burden of proof); *In re* Quinones, 73 B.R. 333 (Bankr. D. P.R. 1987) (same). *But see In re* Bigalk, 813 F.2d 189 (8th Cir. 1987). Regardless of when the determination of willfulness is made, it is clear that the debtor must receive notice and an opportunity to introduce evidence that the conduct in question was not willful before the court may dismiss a new petition under section 109(g). *In re* Bradley, 152 B.R. 74 (E.D. La. 1993).

17 11 U.S.C. § 349(a).

18 *See In re* Howard, 134 B.R. 225 (Bankr. E.D. Ky. 1991) (debtors

meeting of creditors in a prior case, by itself, be grounds for dismissal of a subsequent filing.[19] A new petition may even be proper while a prior petition is still pending.[20]

There is also some question concerning the scope of the subsection covering voluntary dismissals[21] "following" requests for relief from the automatic stay.[22] The obvious purpose of this provision is to prevent debtors from repeatedly filing new bankruptcy cases and obtaining new automatic stays after relief was requested or granted in previous cases.[23] With this purpose in mind, it is not unreasonable to read the word "following" to imply some causal connection between the request for relief and the new filing.[24] Surely the provision was not meant to apply when there is a voluntary dismissal and a new case after a request for relief from the stay is denied,[25] withdrawn, or settled favorably to the debtor.[26] These situations were not among Congress's concerns when it passed section 109(g). Similarly, the provision should not apply when the voluntary dismissal and new case are remote in time from the request for relief from the stay, for example, when a request for relief was filed several years before the dismissal and has nothing to do with

the new case. Nor should debtors who requested dismissal before the filing of a motion for relief from stay, but who did not obtain a dismissal order until after such a motion, be considered within the scope of the bar to refiling.[27] Moreover, the existence in the Code of specific limitations on refiling strongly suggests that courts are precluded from issuing more general injunctions precluding future filings.[28]

Nonetheless some courts do enter dismissal orders, not based directly on section 109(g), that prohibit a debtor from filing another case for a period of time, usually 180 days.[29] In extremely rare cases, courts may dismiss a bankruptcy case with prejudice, which precludes a debtor from ever discharging the debts involved in that case.[30] It is important to distinguish between these two types of dismissal, because courts sometimes use "with prejudice" language when they intend only to preclude refiling for a period of time.[31]

3.2.1.3 Eligibility to File a Case Does Not Assure Discharge of Debts

Apart from eligibility to file a chapter 7 case, however, there are also certain requirements for obtaining a chapter 7 discharge. Because the discharge is usually the main goal of filing, few people who do not meet these requirements should voluntarily[32] start a chapter 7 case. The various bars to discharge are listed in section 727(a) of the Code. Most are discussed at greater length elsewhere in this manual.[33] The provisions which most commonly present problems are those that deny a discharge when the debtor has received a bankruptcy discharge in a case filed less than six years earlier, with some exceptions for chapter 13 cases,[34] and when the debtor has committed certain acts with an intent to hinder, delay, or defraud a creditor.[35]

---

who fell behind in payments and did not attend dismissal hearing not precluded from refiling when failure to pay was due to job loss); *In re* Dodge, 86 B.R. 535 (Bankr. S.D. Ohio 1988); *In re* Samuel, 77 B.R. 520 (Bankr. D. Pa. 1987); *see also In re* Hollis, 150 B.R. 145 (D. Md. 1993) (*pro se* debtor's failure to follow rules, due to ignorance of them, does not warrant dismissal of case with prejudice or a finding of willfulness under § 109(g)); § 9.7.3.1.5, *infra. But see In re* McIver, 78 B.R. 439 (D.S.C. 1987).

19 *In re* Dodge, 86 B.R. 535 (Bankr. S.D. Ohio 1988); *In re* Arena, 81 B.R. 851 (Bankr. E.D. Pa. 1988).

20 *See In re* Saylors, 869 F.2d 1434 (11th Cir. 1989) (second bankruptcy may be filed while first case still pending in some situations); *In re* Cormier, 147 B.R. 285 (Bankr. D. Me. 1992) (court could consider whether change in circumstances justified filing of second case); *In re* Strause, 97 B.R. 22 (Bankr. S.D. Cal. 1989) (filing of chapter 13 case was not barred by pending chapter 7 case when debtor's discharge would have been granted but for court's administrative delays).

21 Failing to respond to a motion to dismiss in the prior case does not make the dismissal voluntary. *In re* Gamble, 72 B.R. 75 (Bankr. D. Idaho 1987).

22 11 U.S.C. § 109(g)(2).

23 It does seem clear that the 180 days cannot be measured from date creditor obtained relief from stay. *In re* Berts, 99 B.R. 363 (Bankr. N.D. Ohio 1989).

24 *See In re* Luna, 122 B.R. 575 (B.A.P. 9th Cir. 1991) (application of § 109(g) is discretionary with the court); *In re* Patton, 49 B.R. 587 (Bankr. M.D. Ga. 1985) (when new case begun two weeks after voluntary dismissal caused no prejudice to creditor, it was not abusive filing prohibited by § 109(g)); *see also* § 9.7.3.1.5, *infra. But see* Kuo v. Walton, 167 B.R. 677 (M.D. Fla. 1994) (when 11 U.S.C. § 109(g) applies, dismissal is mandatory and not discretionary); *In re* Keziah, 46 B.R. 551 (Bankr. W.D.N.C. 1985) (application of § 109(g) not limited to abusive filings after voluntary dismissal).

25 *In re* Jones, 99 B.R. 412 (Bankr. E.D. Ark. 1989).

26 *See, e.g., In re* Milton, 82 B.R. 637 (Bankr. S.D. Ga. 1988) (motion for relief which was settled between the parties does not preclude subsequent filings within 180 days).

27 *In re* Hicks, 138 B.R. 505 (Bankr. D. Md. 1992).

28 *In re* Frieouf, 938 F.2d 1099 (10th Cir. 1991) (bankruptcy court could not enjoin all access to bankruptcy court beyond 180 day period provided in § 109(g), but it could bar discharge of particular debts listed in prior bankruptcy case for a longer period); *see also* § 9.7.3.1.5, *infra*. The question of willfulness related to the dismissal of the prior bankruptcy should not be confused with issues of good faith in the existing bankruptcy. *See generally In re* Chisum, 847 F.2d 597 (9th Cir. 1988).

29 *See* 11 U.S.C. § 349(a). Note that an order barring a future case can only be entered "for cause." Presumably, as a due process matter, a finding of cause can only be entered after notice and a hearing. Thus, the practice of barring future cases for 180 days whenever a case is dismissed is improper.

30 *See* 3 Collier on Bankruptcy ¶ 349.02[2] (15th ed. rev.).

31 *See In re* Tomlin, 105 F.3d 933 (4th Cir. 1997) (although court used words "with prejudice," it intended only to prohibit refiling for 180 days).

32 Involuntary bankruptcies, rare in consumer cases, are provided for in 11 U.S.C. § 303. *See* Ch. 13, *infra*.

33 *See* Ch. 14, *infra*.

34 11 U.S.C. § 727(a)(8), (9); *see* §§ 14.2.2.8, 14.2.2.9, *infra*.

35 11 U.S.C. § 727(a)(2); *see* § 14.2.2.2, *infra*.

3.2.2 The Initial Forms

Although the bankruptcy filing process may seem intimidating at first, a voluntary case is actually started by the debtor[36] filing a simple two-page petition,[37] along with a statement of the debtor's social security number or lack thereof.[38] If no schedule of liabilities is filed with the petition, a list of creditors must also be submitted.[39] All of the documents in a bankruptcy case may be filed electronically, as discussed in a later chapter.[40]

The fee for filing the petition, comprising a statutory filing fee of $155.00 and other fees imposed by the courts, is currently $209.00,[41] which is normally paid at the time of filing. The fee for a husband and wife filing together as a joint case is the same as for an individual filing alone.[42] The court will accept the petition without the fee if it is accompanied by an application to pay the fee in installments over the next 120 days.[43] Unfortunately, the statute specifically provides that the base filing fee of $155.00 may not be waived for debtors who cannot afford it.[44] If the fee is not ultimately paid, or if the required forms are not filed, the case will normally be dismissed.[45]

A number of other forms must also be filed either concurrently with the petition or shortly thereafter.[46] These include the debtor's statement of affairs and schedules,[47] a disclosure of attorney fees,[48] and a statement of intentions with respect to property securing consumer debts.[49] In many districts local rules or administrative orders may prescribe another form or two, such as a matrix of creditors' names and addresses for use in preparing mailing labels and, in some districts, a verification of this matrix.[50]

3.2.3 Proper Venue for Bankruptcy Case

Under section 1408 of title 28 of the United States Code, a debtor may commence a bankruptcy case in any federal judicial district in which the domicile, residence, principal place of business, or principal assets of the debtor have been located for 180 days prior to the petition, or for a longer portion of that 180 days than any other district. The language of the statute referring to the district meeting the test for "the longer portion of such one-hundred-and-eighty-day period" suggests that only one district can satisfy the requirement for residence.[51] However, there may be more than one venue that fits the statute's description, for example, if the debtor's residence and principal place of business have been in two different districts for 180 days. Occasionally, debtors file in an incorrect venue, either inadvertently or intentionally, especially if that venue is more convenient or offers some other advantage.

Incorrect venue does not deprive the bankruptcy court of jurisdiction over the case. However, the court may dismiss or transfer the case to a proper venue if a party files a motion for it to do so.[52] Sanctions may also be assessed against an attorney who knowingly files a case in an improper venue.[53]

---

36 *See In re* Carter, 285 B.R. 61 (Bankr. N.D. Ga. 2002) (case could be converted after discharge without vacating discharge order). Under the Bankruptcy Code, the person filing the petition is called the "debtor" rather than the "bankrupt" as the latter term was thought to have a pejorative meaning.

37 Fed. R. Bankr. P. 1002(a); *see* Official Form 1, Appx. D, *infra.* Relief under chapter 7 may also be obtained by a debtor who converts from another chapter, such as chapter 13. *See* § 4.7.2, *infra.*

38 Fed. R. Bankr. P. 1007(f); *see* Official Form 21, Appx. D, *infra.* Technically, this statement is not filed, but rather "submitted" to the clerk, because it is not included in the documents that are docketed and kept in the court file for the case.

39 Fed. R. Bankr. P. 1007(a)(1).

40 *See* § 7.1.4, *infra.*

41 28 U.S.C. § 1930(a). In addition to the $155.00 filing fee provided by 28 U.S.C. § 1930(a), the federal Judicial Conference decided to assess an additional noticing fee of $39.00 in connection with all chapter 7 and chapter 13 filings pursuant to 28 U.S.C. § 1930(b). The federal Judicial Conference also decided to add yet another $15.00 fee to be paid at the outset of a chapter 7 case to provide the funds necessary for additional compensation to chapter 7 trustees mandated by 11 U.S.C. § 330(b)(2), as amended by the Bankruptcy Reform Act of 1994, Pub. L. No. 103-394, 108 Stat. 4106 (1994). *See* Appx. C, *infra.* The noticing fee and trustee fee, like the filing fees, can be paid in installments, and the form application to pay the filing fee in installments has been modified to accommodate this possibility. *See* Official Form 3, Appx. D, *infra*; Fed. R. Bankr. P. 1006.

42 11 U.S.C. § 302. *But see In re* Allen, 186 B.R. 769 (Bankr. N.D. Ga. 1995) (gay couple could not file joint petition unless legally married). No court has yet ruled on whether the federal Defense of Marriage Act precludes legally married gay couples from filing a joint bankruptcy petition.

43 28 U.S.C. § 1930(a); Fed. R. Bankr. P. 1006(b); *see* Official Form 3, Appx. D, *infra.* Under the rule, the time for payment of any installment may be extended for cause until up to 180 days from the petition filing date.

44 28 U.S.C. § 1930(a) (codifying United States v. Kras, 409 U.S. 434, 93 S. Ct. 631, 34 L. Ed. 2d 626 (1973)). The additional fees should be waivable by the courts for indigent debtors, because they are imposed under 28 U.S.C. § 1930(b). *See* § 13.6, *infra.* A form for an application to waive the noticing fee and trustee fee can be found at Form 7, Appendix G.3, *infra.*

45 11 U.S.C. § 707; Fed. R. Bankr. P. 1017(b), (c).

46 Fed. R. Bankr. P. 1007 deals with the filing date for these forms.

47 Fed. R. Bankr. P. 1007(a)(1), (b). See blank Official Forms 6 and 7 in Appendix D, *infra*, and the completed versions in Appendix F, *infra.* This rule also requires a statement of executory contracts and unexpired leases. That statement is now Schedule G of Official Form 6.

48 Fed. R. Bankr. P. 2016(b); *see* Forms 21, 22, Appx. G.3, *infra.*

49 11 U.S.C. § 521(2)(A). See blank Official Form 8 in Appendix D, *infra*, and the completed version in Appendix F, *infra.*

50 The clerk of the local bankruptcy court may be consulted as to these requirements. *See also* Ch. 7, *infra.*

51 *In re* Handel, 253 B.R. 308 (B.A.P. 1st Cir. 2000).

52 *Id.*

53 *In re* Pannell, 253 B.R. 216 (S.D. Ohio 2000).

The court may also transfer a case to a different venue in the interest of justice or for the convenience of the parties.[54]

3.3 First Steps After Filing

The filing of a voluntary chapter 7 petition "constitutes an order for relief" under that chapter.[55] This means that the process of granting the relief requested is automatically set in motion.

An interim trustee, chosen from the panel of trustees established in the district,[56] is immediately appointed.[57] However, in most cases, this trustee will have little to do until later in the case except, perhaps, to peruse the papers filed. If the debtor has filed an application to pay the filing fee in installments, the court issues an order setting the dates for those payments.

The filing of the petition operates to effectuate the automatic stay provided for in section 362 of the Code.[58] With a few limited exceptions, the stay prevents further proceedings or acts against the debtor or the debtor's property by anyone, except in the bankruptcy court, with respect to any claims arising before commencement of the case. The stay has the general purpose of freezing the debtor's property so that it may be examined and administered in the bankruptcy case. The statute also requires any entity holding property that the trustee[59] may use, sell, or lease, or that the debtor may exempt, to deliver that property to the trustee forthwith.[60]

Normally, within a few weeks after filing, the court mails to all creditors, the debtor, and the debtor's attorney, a notice of the stay and of the date and place set for the section 341(a) meeting, also known as the first meeting of creditors.[61] This meeting is normally scheduled for a date twenty to forty days after filing of the petition[62] and must be at least twenty days after the notice.[63] It may be held at the court or at any other place that the United States trustee or bankruptcy administrator deems to be convenient to the parties.[64]

The notice also contains deadlines for creditors who wish to file claims or complaints raising objections to discharge[65] or to the dischargeability of a particular debt.[66] Under the rules, the deadline for complaints objecting to discharge or requesting determination of certain dischargeability issues is sixty days after the first date set for the meeting of creditors.[67] If the case appears to be a no-asset case, the court will notify creditors that claims should not be filed unless they later receive notice that there are assets.[68]

3.4 The Section 341(a) Meeting (Meeting of Creditors)

The debtor's first, and often only, appearance at any kind of a hearing usually occurs at the section 341(a) meeting (meeting of creditors).[69] This proceeding is intended to give the various parties a chance to examine the debtor and her affairs. In practice, the meeting allows the trustee to learn whatever she feels is necessary to perform the trustee's duties.

Despite the name, creditors rarely appear at the meeting of creditors in a consumer bankruptcy case. Some of those who do attend are there only because they are unsophisticated and believe that the notice they received compels their attendance. Others may occasionally come to ask questions for discovery purposes.[70] And a few creditors (particularly retail stores whose credit card agreements give them questionable purchase money security interest claims) have sometimes attended in order to coerce debtors to enter into inadvisable reaffirmation agreements.[71]

The meeting itself is usually conducted by the interim trustee or the United States trustee.[72] It may last from three to thirty minutes and consists of a series of routine questions,[73] generally covering most of the information in the statement of affairs and schedules.[74] These are typically propounded to the debtor by the interim trustee,[75] who

---

54 28 U.S.C. § 1412.

55 11 U.S.C. § 301.

56 This panel is established by the United States trustee if one exists, otherwise by the bankruptcy administrator for the court. 28 U.S.C. §§ 586(a), 604(f).

57 The appointment is made by the United States trustee if one exists, otherwise by the court. 11 U.S.C. § 701.

58 *See* Ch. 9, *infra.*

59 Under chapter 13, the debtor may exercise the trustee's power to use, sell, or lease property. 11 U.S.C. §§ 1303, 1304. *See generally* Ch. 12, *infra.*

60 11 U.S.C. §§ 542, 543; *see* § 9.9, *infra.*

61 See Official Form 9, reprinted in Appendix D, *infra,* for the commonly used versions of these forms.

62 Fed. R. Bankr. P. 2003(a). If the meeting is not at a location staffed by the United States trustee, it may be held up to sixty days after the filing. *Id.*

63 Fed. R. Bankr. P. 2002(a)(1).

64 Fed. R. Bankr. P. 2003(a).

65 There are various grounds upon which a party may object to the debtor's discharge. 11 U.S.C. § 727(a); *see* Ch. 14, *infra.*

66 A creditor may contest the discharge of a particular debt in certain circumstances. 11 U.S.C. § 523; *see* Ch. 14, *infra.*

67 Fed. R. Bankr. P. 4004(a), 4007(c).

68 Fed. R. Bankr. P. 2002(e).

69 This meeting is provided for in 11 U.S.C. § 341.

70 See Chapter 8, *infra,* for further discussion of this procedure.

71 It is usually a bad idea to agree to these reaffirmation agreements at the meeting of creditors. *See* § 14.5.3, *infra;* Helping Your Client Do the Wash: The Effect in Bankruptcy of PMSI Claims Created by Revolving Credit Accounts, 12 NCLC REPORTS *Bankruptcy and Foreclosures Ed.* 37 (Jan./Feb. 1994).

72 *See* Fed. R. Bankr. P. 2003(b).

73 The questions usually asked in one district are set out in Forms 45, 48, Appx. G.7, *infra.*

74 See blank forms in Appendix D, *infra,* and the completed versions in Appendix F, *infra.*

75 The interim trustee has been previously appointed under 11 U.S.C. § 701.

normally becomes the permanent trustee.[76] The debtor is usually asked to produce photo identification and documentary proof that the social security number listed on the statement of social security number is correct. The bankruptcy judge is not permitted to attend the meeting, so that she is not influenced by any information brought out there.[77] It is somewhat unclear whether evidentiary rules apply, and the trustee (who, in essence, is another party to the case) does not have the authority to resolve any disputes that arise other than disputes about how to conduct the meeting.[78] Any dispute or challenge to the trustee's procedures must be resolved by the judge, much like a dispute arising in a deposition, if any party feels strongly enough about the issue to pursue it. Although creditors new to bankruptcy may not realize it, it is clear that the trustee has no power to rule on any question concerning the stay, discharge, or any other dispute between a creditor and the debtor.

Under the 1994 amendments to the Code the trustee was given additional duties to perform at the meeting of creditors. The trustee is required to "orally examine" the debtor to assure that the debtor is aware of several things, including the potential consequences of seeking a discharge in bankruptcy, its effects on the debtor's credit history, the debtor's ability to file under a different chapter of the Code, the effect of receiving a discharge, and the effect of reaffirming a debt.[79] In practice, most trustees give much of this information in writing and ask if the debtor has read it.[80] Although it is a good idea, naturally, to prepare the debtor to respond appropriately to these questions, there are no apparent consequences if the debtor expresses a lack of awareness in response to the trustee's inquiries, except perhaps that the debtor will be asked to read or reread the written information provided by the trustee.

3.5 After the Meeting of Creditors

3.5.1 Exempt and Encumbered Property

What happens after the meeting of creditors depends to some extent on whether there are substantial assets in the bankruptcy estate that are neither exempt[81] nor encumbered, and that are thus available for the unsecured creditors.

In all cases, unless some party successfully objects, the debtor retains property claimed as exempt.[82] Although abandonment may be sought before the case ends, on motion by the trustee, debtor, or some other party, it usually occurs automatically at the end of the case. The trustee generally abandons all property in which there is little or no nonexempt equity by declining to administer the property and closing the case.[83] When the property is abandoned, the trustee in effect disclaims interest in it, and ownership status reverts to whatever it was prior to the bankruptcy. Ordinarily, once property is abandoned by the trustee, that decision is irrevocable.[84] However, property which has not been scheduled is not deemed abandoned and the trustee may reopen the case to administer such property if it is later discovered. Rights to such property therefore may not revest in the debtor at the closing of the case.[85] Moreover, when abandonment is sought by motion, the parties must comply with the procedural requirements of the rules.[86]

81　Exempt property is property that the debtor may retain in a liquidation case. *See generally* Ch. 10, *infra.*

82　11 U.S.C. § 522(*l*); Taylor v. Freeland & Kronz, 503 U.S. 638, 112 S. Ct. 1644, 118 L. Ed. 2d 280 (1992); *see* § 10.3, *infra.*

83　11 U.S.C. § 554. Once the trustee has filed a final report certifying that the estate has been fully administered, if no objection is filed within thirty days, there is a presumption that full administration has taken place regardless of whether the case is closed. Fed. R. Bankr. P. 5009. Once the presumption is in place, all property scheduled which has not been administered is deemed abandoned unless the court orders otherwise. 11 U.S.C. § 554(c); *see In re* Potter, 228 B.R. 422 (B.A.P. 8th Cir. 1999) (court could order that contingent remainder interest remain part of estate as unadministered asset when case was closed).

84　*In re* Wornell, 70 B.R. 153 (W.D. Mo. 1986); *In re* Enriquez, 22 B.R. 934 (Bankr. D, Neb. 1982). *But see In re* Woods, 173 F.3d 770 (10th Cir. 1999) (court may revoke deemed abandonment of property under section 554(c) pursuant to Fed. R. Bankr. P. 9024); *In re* Alt, 39 B.R. 902 (Bankr. W.D. Wis. 1984) (revocation of mistaken abandonment permitted). The revocability of an abandonment often turns on whether the debtor fully disclosed the interest in property involved. *Compare In re* Bryson, 53 B.R. 3 (Bankr. M.D. Tenn. 1985) (abandonment irrevocable when trustee knew of debtor's interest in lawsuit that, after abandonment, resulted in large recovery, and no objection was filed at time of abandonment) *with In re* Schmid, 54 B.R. 78 (Bankr. D. Or. 1985) (abandonment revoked when debtor's interest in lawsuit was insufficiently listed in the schedules).

85　*See In re* Baudoin, 981 F.2d 736 (5th Cir. 1993) (lender liability claim scheduled as "any possible claim against creditor for actions taken against debtor," with value listed as "undetermined" was not properly scheduled and therefore was not deemed abandoned at end of case); Vreugdenhill v. Navistar Int'l Transp. Corp., 950 F.2d 524 (8th Cir. 1991).

86　Fed. R. Bankr. P. 6007; *see* Seward v. Devine, 888 F.2d 957 (2d Cir. 1989) (abandonment without notice to creditors is ineffective); *see also In re* Killebrew, 888 F.2d 1516 (5th Cir. 1989) (assets had never been abandoned by trustee).

76　Creditors may vote to elect a trustee if a sufficient number of creditors are present. 11 U.S.C. § 702. A sufficient number is almost never present in consumer cases, so the interim trustee then becomes the permanent trustee. 11 U.S.C. § 702(d).

77　11 U.S.C. § 341.

78　The questions typically propounded, as well as other guidelines set for § 341(a) meetings and administration of chapter 7 cases by the Executive Office of the United States Trustees, can be found in the Chapter 7 Trustee Handbook published by that office, available at www.usdoj.gov/ust/library/trusteelib.htm. *See also* Form 46, Appx. G.7, *infra.*

79　11 U.S.C. § 341(d).

80　A sample form used by many trustees is reprinted in Form 47, Appendix G.7, *infra.*

Various other proceedings may sometimes take place, such as motions to avoid liens on exempt property.[87] In cases in which there is property securing a consumer debt,[88] and the debtor has filed a statement of intention[89] to redeem the property,[90] surrender it, or reaffirm the debt,[91] that intention must be performed.[92] The normal deadline for the debtor's performance is forty-five days after the statement is filed, but the court may extend that deadline for cause if the debtor so requests before it expires.[93] And, in any case, the debtor's substantive rights with regard to the property should not be affected by the debtor's failure to meet the deadline,[94] which serves only as a guideline as to when the required events should occur.

In cases in which property remains in the estate, it is normally administered by the trustee, except when the property has little value. In such cases, called "nominal asset cases," if it appears that the trustee intends to administer the property, the debtor may request that the property be abandoned[95] on the grounds that it would not provide any meaningful distribution to creditors after the costs of administration were paid.[96]

---

87 See § 10.4.2, *infra,* for discussion of lien avoidance motions.

88 "Consumer debt" is defined at 11 U.S.C. § 101(8).

89 The statement of intention is required by 11 U.S.C. § 521(2), a 1984 amendment. See § 11.4, *infra,* for further discussion of this provision.

90 Redemption is provided for in 11 U.S.C. § 722. See § 11.5, *infra,* for discussion of redemption.

91 Reaffirmation of debts is permitted in some circumstances by 11 U.S.C. § 524(c). See § 14.5.2, *infra,* for discussion of reaffirmation.

92 11 U.S.C. § 521(2)(B).

93 11 U.S.C. § 521(2)(B). The intention clearly need not be performed before the forty-fifth day. *See, e.g., In re* Grace, 85 B.R. 464 (Bankr. S.D. Ohio 1988) (sanctions imposed against creditor that prematurely repossessed car that debtor intended to surrender).

94 11 U.S.C. § 521(2)(C); *see* Lowry Fed. Credit Union v. West, 882 F.2d 1543 (10th Cir. 1989) (Bankruptcy Code provides no penalty for debtor's failure to comply with statement of intention and no remedy for creditor). See also § 11.4, *infra,* for other cases taking varying positions on this issue.

95 Any party in interest may request that the court order the trustee to abandon property if the trustee does not do so voluntarily. 11 U.S.C. § 554(b). See § 8.3.8, *infra,* for further discussion of abandonment of property. See also Form 88, Appendix G.10, *infra,* for an example of a motion for abandonment.

96 Any sale of estate assets involves some administrative expense to the trustee, and these costs must be paid before creditors receive anything. If only a small amount of property can be sold, all of the proceeds would likely go to the trustee and none to creditors, thus defeating the purpose of the sale, which is to benefit creditors. Congress specifically disapproved of the sale of assets in nominal-asset cases. H.R. Rep. No. 95-595, at 93 (1977). The amount of assets considered to be nominal varies from district to district, and ranges from under $500.00 to about $3000.00. *See, e.g., In re* Kusler, 224 B.R. 180 (Bankr. N.D. Okla. 1998) (criticizing trustee for selling encumbered property which would not realize significant dividends for creditors); *In re* Maropa Marine Sales Serv. & Storage, Inc., 92 B.R. 547

3.5.2 *Liquidation of Non-Exempt Property*

If the estate has more than nominal assets, they must be turned over to the trustee at or after the creditors meeting.[97] Usually, the debtor is offered the option of paying their value to the trustee instead.[98] The trustee then collects any other property of the estate that is neither exempt nor abandoned, and liquidates the estate, that is, converts it to cash. The trustee must normally give twenty days notice of intent to sell the property. Any party, including the debtor, may object within specified time limits to the proposed sale, which may be a private sale or a sale by public auction.[99] If an asset is partially exempt, the debtor's exemption should be paid in cash from the proceeds prior to distribution of any proceeds to creditors or for administrative expenses.

3.5.3 *Filing and Allowance of Claims*

While the non-exempt assets of the estate are being liquidated, the trustee receives and evaluates all claims filed by creditors, objecting to them if they are improper.[100] Unless an objection is filed, a proof of claim in proper form is deemed allowed.[101] Any objections filed commence contested matters under Rule 9014[102] and are ruled upon by the

---

(Bankr. S.D. Fla. 1988) (trustee's sale of asset subject to lien of undersecured creditor would be abusive); *see also In re* Nelson, 251 B.R. 857 (B.A.P. 8th Cir. 2000) (granting motion compelling trustee to abandon real estate in which there was no equity).

97 Although 11 U.S.C. § 521(4) literally requires debtors to turn all property of the estate over to the trustee, such a transfer does not occur in practice. The trustee normally takes constructive possession of estate property in a consumer bankruptcy case, not actual possession. *In re* Figueira, 163 B.R. 192 (Bankr. D. Kan. 1993). Generally, all of the property is exempt or encumbered and therefore not available for distribution to creditors, so there would be no purpose served by physical transfer of assets to the trustee. *See also* 4 Collier on Bankruptcy ¶ 521.12 (15th ed. rev.).

98 *In re* Bailey, 234 B.R. 7 (Bankr. D.R.I. 1999) (approving compromise in which debtor paid trustee slightly less than amount that sale of debtor's home would have generated under "best case scenario"). The debtor may use exempt assets or property which does not belong to the estate for this purpose. Most practically, because post-petition income is not part of the chapter 7 estate, a debtor can use post-petition savings to buy back non-exempt property interests from the trustee.

99 Fed. R. Bankr. P. 6004.

100 The debtor usually has no interest in whether particular creditors are paid, but in rare cases may wish to object to a claim if the disallowance of a particular creditor's claim would mean that more funds will be available to pay a nondischargeable debt or that the debtor would receive estate property in excess of the amount necessary to pay all allowed claims with interest. *See* 11 U.S.C. § 726(a)(6).

101 11 U.S.C. § 502(a).

102 However, if the objection is joined with a claim for relief of a kind specified in Fed. R. Bankr. P. 7001 (for example, bringing into question the extent of a lien), the adversary proceeding rules apply. Fed. R. Bankr. P. 3007.

court. Once the status of the claims has been determined and the deadline for filing claims has expired, the distribution to creditors is made.

3.5.4 Distribution of Property to Creditors

After the estate has been liquidated and the amounts of the claims have been determined, the trustee is in a position to make distributions of the estate's property to creditors. The distribution to creditors is carried out according to priority rules in the Bankruptcy Code, which serve to effectuate various policy decisions of the drafters regarding which creditors should be paid first. Distributions to creditors are generally known as "dividends."

Under the statutory distribution scheme, to the extent that any asset is partially encumbered, the claims of creditors with liens on that asset are paid from the proceeds of sale prior to distribution to unsecured creditors. Briefly, the order of distribution is as follows (although many of these categories are rarely applicable in consumer cases):

(1) Senior liens granted to secure credit obtained by the trustee or the debtor during the case under 11 U.S.C. § 364(d) (normally for operation of the debtor's business), in the amount of the allowed secured claim.

(2) Secured claims of creditors in the amount of their allowed secured claims[103] and in order of lien priority,[104] in property not abandoned (when there is a non-exempt interest in the property which can be liquidated by the trustee).

(3) Junior liens granted to secure credit under 11 U.S.C. § 364(d), in the amount of the allowed secured claim.

(4) "Super priority" unsecured claims granted to creditors who have been harmed by failure of the debtor or trustee to provide adequate protection[105] of their interests in property during the case. 11 U.S.C. § 507(b).

(5) Administrative expenses, including costs of preserving the estate, taxes incurred by the estate,[106] payments to the trustee, attorneys, accountants, and so forth, and certain specified expenses of creditors helping the estate. 11 U.S.C. §§ 507(a)(1), 503(b).[107]

(6) Certain unsecured claims, in involuntary cases only. 11 U.S.C. § 507(a)(2).

(7) Allowed unsecured claims for wages, salaries, vacation, severance, or sick pay earned from the debtor within ninety days before the filing of the petition or cessation of a debtor's business, whichever occurred first, up to $4925.00 per claimant. 11 U.S.C. § 507(a)(3).

(8) Allowed unsecured claims for contributions to employee pension or benefit plans arising from services within 180 days before the filing of the petition or the cessation of business, whichever occurred first, up to $4925.00 times the number of employees, minus the amount paid under (7) above. 11 U.S.C. § 507(a)(4).

(9) Allowed unsecured claims of persons engaged in the production or raising of grain, for grain or its proceeds, against debtors who own or operate grain storage facilities, or of United States fishermen, up to $4925.00, against debtors operating fish produce storage or processing facilities. 11 U.S.C. § 507(a)(5).

(10) Certain allowed unsecured claims from the deposit of money by consumers who had deposited money for the purchase, lease, or rental of property or services not provided, up to $2225.00 per individual. 11 U.S.C. § 507(a)(6).[108]

(11) Certain allowed claims for debts to a spouse, former spouse, or child of the debtor that are in the nature of alimony, maintenance, or support. 11 U.S.C. § 507(a)(7).[109]

---

103   The allowed secured claim may be less than the debt owed to the creditor. It cannot exceed the creditor's interest in the collateral. 11 U.S.C. § 506; *see* Ch. 11, *infra*.

104   *See In re* Darnell, 834 F.2d 1263 (6th Cir. 1987); Pearlstein v. United States Small Bus. Admin., 719 F.2d 1169 (D.C. Cir. 1983). Secured creditors' claims may be equitably subordinated in some cases to those of other secured or unsecured creditors under either bankruptcy or state law. *See* 11 U.S.C. § 510; Small v. Beverly Bank, 936 F.2d 945 (7th Cir. 1991) (equitable subordination considered under Illinois law).

105   See Chapter 9, *infra*, for explanation of adequate protection of creditors' interests in property during the case.
      See also In re Campbell, 205 B.R. 288 (Bankr. D. Colo. 1997) (payments that were to be made pursuant to chapter 13 plan and that were denominated as "adequate protection payments" were not in fact true adequate protection payments, but rather simply plan payments, and therefore failure to make payments did not create super priority claim).

106   Post-petition interest on post-petition tax claims also appears to be a priority claim. *In re* Mark Anthony Constr. Co., 886 F.2d 1101 (9th Cir. 1989); *In re* Allied Mech. Services, Inc., 885 F.2d 837 (11th Cir. 1989).

107   Administrative expenses include only debts for services to the extent they are actually utilized by the trustee or the estate. *In re* Subscription Television of Greater Atlanta, 789 F.2d 1530 (11th Cir. 1986); *In re* Thompson, 788 F.2d 560 (9th Cir. 1986).

108   *See* § 17.5.5, *supra*. It has been held that tenants' security deposits fall within this priority. *In re* River Vill. Associates, 161 B.R. 127 (Bankr. E.D. Pa. 1993), *aff'd*, 181 B.R. 795 (E.D. Pa. 1995). One court has held that debts owed by a money order issuer to stores that sold money orders to consumers do not fall within this priority, even though the store had obtained assignments of the consumers' rights. *In re* Northwest Fin. Express, Inc., 950 F.2d 561 (8th Cir. 1991).

109   This subsection excludes debts that have been assigned, but that exclusion does not affect a debt that is merely being collected by a state agency for the benefit of the debtor's former spouse. *In re* Gray, 269 B.R. 881 (Bankr. N.D. Ala. 2001) (portion of claim filed by state that would go to children's grandmother for their support was a priority claim, but portion that would be retained by state pursuant to assignment was not); *In re* Maiten, 225 B.R. 246 (Bankr. M.D. Fla. 1998).

(12) Certain allowed unsecured claims of governmental units, for example, taxes, specified in 11 U.S.C. § 507(a)(8).[110] However, tax penalty claims are given this priority only if they are in compensation for actual pecuniary loss.[111] As in cases concerning dischargeability of taxes, there is sometimes an issue regarding whether a particular claim is a tax at all.[112]

(13) Certain allowed unsecured claims based on responsibilities to the government related to its oversight of the banking industry. 11 U.S.C. § 507(a)(9).[113]

(14) Timely-filed general unsecured claims and certain tardily-filed claims. 11 U.S.C. § 726(a)(2).

(15) Other general unsecured claims filed after the deadline for filing claims. 11 U.S.C. § 726(a)(3).[114]

(16) Allowed claims for fines, penalties, forfeitures, or multiple, exemplary, or punitive damages. 11 U.S.C. § 726(a)(4).

(17) Interest at the legal rate on all claims paid, from the date of filing. 11 U.S.C. § 726(a)(5).

(18) The debtor. 11 U.S.C. § 726(a)(6).

If there are certain types of community property involved,[115] distribution follows a somewhat different order. That community property is segregated from other property of the estate and the estate is distributed in several stages. Within each stage, except the first two stages, the order set forth above is applied. The stages are:

(1) The claims set out in (1) through (4) above, in that order from property to which they are applicable.

(2) Claims for administrative expenses, which can also be paid from other property of the estate, as justice requires. 11 U.S.C. § 726(c)(1).

(3) Community claims[116] against the debtor or the debtor's spouse, from community property in the estate, except to the extent that the community property is solely liable for debts of the debtor. 11 U.S.C. § 726(c)(2)(A).

(4) Community claims against the debtor not paid under (3) above, from community property in the estate that is solely liable for debts of the debtor. 11 U.S.C. § 726(c)(2)(B).

(5) Claims against the debtor, including community claims not paid under (3) and (4) above, from property of the estate other than the community property involved. 11 U.S.C. § 726(c)(2)(C).

(6) Community claims against the debtor or the debtor's spouse not already paid, from all remaining property of the estate. 11 U.S.C. § 726(c)(2)(D).

After distribution, the trustee makes a final report and accounting to the court, which then concludes the case.

In most cases involving consumer debtors, of course, no distribution is made to any of the parties listed above, because there are no assets to distribute. In such cases, depending upon local practice, the trustee may or may not make a report to the court,[117] setting forth any objections to discharge or the claim of exemption.[118]

---

110 Section 507(a)(8) was formerly numbered § 507(a)(7). Pre- and post-petition interest on priority tax claims have also been held to constitute priority claims. *In re* Garcia, 955 F.2d 16 (5th Cir. 1992) (pre-petition interest on priority tax claim entitled to same priority); *In re* Bates, 974 F.2d 1234 (10th Cir. 1992) (same); *see In re* Hanna, 872 F.2d 829 (8th Cir. 1989) (post-petition interest on pre-petition taxes). The Supreme Court has ruled that the three-year time period in section 507(a)(8) is tolled during the time that the automatic stay in an earlier case prevents the taxing authority from collecting. Young v. United States, 535 U.S. 43, 122 S. Ct. 1036, 152 L. Ed. 2d 79 (2002). Although the decision at one point states that the look back period is "tolled during the pendency of a prior bankruptcy petition," the holding and rationale of the decision would seem to make it inapplicable to any time period that a prior petition was pending, during which the taxing authority was not stayed from collecting. Finally, in an involuntary bankruptcy case, the three-year period dictated by § 507(a)(8) commences when the involuntary petition is originally filed. *In re* Rassi, 140 B.R. 490 (Bankr. C.D. Ill. 1992).

111 *In re* Hovan, 172 B.R. 974 (Bankr. W.D. Wash. 1994), *aff'd*, 96 F.3d 1254 (9th Cir. 1996); *In re* Mako, Inc., 135 B.R. 902 (E.D. Okla. 1991).

112 *See In re* DeJesus, 243 B.R. 241 (Bankr. D.N.J. 1999) (motor vehicle surcharge debt was not an excise tax); *see also* § 14.4.3.1.1, *infra*.

113 This provision was added to the Code to assist the government's attempts to recover assets from individuals involved with failed banks and savings and loans.

114 Prior to the 1994 amendments, some courts had held that the failure to mention tardily-filed priority claims in this section meant that tardily-filed priority claims could be paid ahead of timely-filed non-priority claims. *In re* Century Boat Co., 986 F.2d 154 (6th Cir. 1993) (late-filed priority claim should receive priority in distribution, at least if the priority creditor did not receive notice of the case and files its claim before the trustee makes any distribution of estate, provided that there is no bad faith on the part of the priority claimant and no undue prejudice to other creditors). Other courts rejected this reasoning, holding that late-filed priority claims had to be paid after timely-filed claims. *In re* Mantz, 151 B.R. 928 (B.A.P. 9th Cir. 1993), *rev'd*, 33 F.3d 59 (9th Cir. 1993). The 1994 amendments resolved this issue, amending 11 U.S.C. § 726(a)(1) to provide that tardily-filed priority claims are to be paid before general unsecured claims in chapter 7 cases, as long as the priority claims are filed before the trustee commences distributions to creditors.

115 The bankruptcy estate includes all community property of the debtor and the debtor's spouse that is (1) under sole, equal, or joint management or control of the debtor, or (2) liable for an allowable claim against either the debtor or the debtor and the debtor's spouse. 11 U.S.C. § 541(a)(2).

116 A "community claim" is defined at 11 U.S.C. § 101(7).

117 In some districts, it is presumed that if the trustee does not object to exemptions a report is unnecessary because the exemptions will be granted under 11 U.S.C. § 522(*l*) without the filing of a report.

118 The procedures for litigating the objections are discussed in Chapters 8 and 14, *infra*. The current Federal Rules of Bank-

3.6 The Discharge and Discharge Hearing

The final step in a straight bankruptcy is usually the granting of the debtor's discharge. This discharge is effective as to all debts except certain taxes, some debts not listed by the debtor in the schedules, debts for alimony or spousal and child support, most fines and penalties owed to governmental units, most student loans, debts which were or could have been listed in a prior bankruptcy in which discharge was denied or waived, certain debts incurred by driving while intoxicated, certain debts of individuals involved in the banking or savings and loan industry, and debts which have been ruled nondischargeable during the case.[119] Other exceptions to the discharge include federal criminal restitution debts, debts incurred to pay nondischargeable federal taxes, certain condominium and cooperative fees,[120] and certain court fees and costs owed by prisoners.[121] Also, to the extent a secured creditor's lien has not been disallowed, avoided, or satisfied, that creditor normally will retain the right to bring an *in rem* action to enforce its lien.[122]

In any case in which the debtor wishes to reaffirm a debt, if the debtor was not represented by an attorney in negotiating the reaffirmation agreement, the court is required to hold a discharge hearing.[123] The court may, in its discretion, hold discharge hearings in other cases but such hearings are rare.

Because of the strong policy against reaffirmation agreements, which are unfairly coerced by some creditors, the Code requires a careful explanation of reaffirmation to the debtor by the court at the discharge hearing, or by an attorney if the debtor is represented in connection with the proposed reaffirmation.[124] Unless the debt is secured by real property of the debtor, or an attorney representing the debtor in the reaffirmation agreement files a written declaration that the agreement is a fully informed and voluntary act of the debtor that does not impose undue hardship on the debtor or the debtor's dependents, the reaffirmation agreement must then be approved by the court.[125] The court may only approve the agreement if it (1) does not impose undue hardship on the debtor or the debtor's dependents and (2) is in the best interest of the debtor.[126]

Once the discharge has been entered, a no-asset chapter 7 case is complete, except for a notice of discharge sent out by the court to the debtor and all creditors.[127] Unless new property comes into the estate within 180 days of the filing of the original petition,[128] there is nothing further to be done by the court and the case is closed.[129] Once a case is closed, further action may still be possible in the bankruptcy court, including actions to provide relief for the debtor, but reopening the case will be a prerequisite.[130]

---

ruptcy Procedure do not provide for the trustee's report required by prior rules, stating only that any objections to exemptions must be filed within thirty days after the conclusion of the meeting of creditors or the filing of any amendment to the exemptions and any objection to discharge must be raised by an adversary proceeding. Fed. R. Bankr. P. 4003(b), 7001.

119 11 U.S.C. §§ 523, 727(b). See Chapter 14, *infra,* for discussion of debts which are not discharged. Certain types of debts, listed in 11 U.S.C. § 523(a)(2), (4), (6) and (15) are discharged unless a creditor files an adversary proceeding during the bankruptcy case to have them found nondischargeable.

120 *See* §§ 14.4.3.12, 14.4.3.13, 14.4.3.15, *infra.*

121 *See* § 14.4.3.16, *infra.*

122 *See* § 14.5.3, *infra; see also, e.g.,* Estate of Lellock v. Prudential Ins. Co. of Am., 811 F.2d 186 (3d Cir. 1987); Chandler Bank of Lyons v. Ray, 804 F.2d 577 (10th Cir. 1986).

123 The discharge hearing was made discretionary in all cases except those in which a reaffirmation agreement was negotiated by the debtor without representation by an attorney by the Bankruptcy Reform Act of 1994, Pub. L. No. 103-394, 108 Stat. 4106 (1994). *See* § 14.5.2, *infra.*

124 See § 14.5.2, *infra,* for detailed discussion of reaffirmation agreements.

125 11 U.S.C. § 524(d). Under the 1994 amendments, the affidavit must also state that the attorney fully advised the debtor of the legal effect and consequences of the reaffirmation and of a default on the reaffirmation agreement.

126 11 U.S.C. § 524(d).

127 If there are assets being administered, the discharge is usually entered before distribution occurs and the case remains open until administration of the assets is completed by the court's approval of the trustee's final report.

128 11 U.S.C. § 541(a) provides that certain property acquired after filing becomes part of the estate. *See* § 2.5, *supra.*

129 Closing of the case is an administrative act which occurs separately from the entry of discharge. Courts vary widely in how quickly this occurs. Occasionally, the debtor will want the case closed more quickly than the normal course (for example, to commence a new case in a jurisdiction which does not allow a debtor to maintain two open cases simultaneously). An informal request to the clerk may be sufficient or, if necessary, a motion can be filed. In asset cases, the discharge does not await the completion of administration of the estate. Filing of claims and distribution to creditors may continue after discharge, and the case is closed only after the trustee has filed a final report on this process.

130 11 U.S.C. § 350(b); Fed. R. Bankr. P. 5010.

Chapter 4

Chapter 13 Bankruptcy: The Basic Steps

4.1 General Explanation of Chapter 13

Chapter 13 bankruptcy gives the debtor the opportunity to adjust his or her financial affairs without having to liquidate current assets. Rather than being designed to pay debts out of those assets, a chapter 13 case usually involves payment of debts out of future income (although the debtor may also choose to make some payment out of current assets). The debtor is allowed to keep and use all property, whether exempt or not, and to pay some or all debts according to a plan approved by the court. At the completion of this plan (or, in some cases, earlier) the debtor receives a discharge which, with several significant exceptions, is similar to the discharge received in a chapter 7 case.

This Chapter describes the sequence of events in a typical chapter 13 case. Many of these events are quite similar to those in a chapter 7 bankruptcy. Chapters 5 through 8, *infra,* will then provide a detailed guide to the steps the debtor's counsel must take in preparing and handling the case.

4.2 Commencement of the Case

4.2.1 Who May File?

Chapter 13 is available to "individual[s] with regular income"[1] who reside, are domiciled, or have a place of business or property in the United States. An infant or incompetent person may be a debtor in a chapter 13 case.[2]

To qualify as an "individual with regular income," one must be "any individual whose income is sufficiently stable and regular to enable such individual to make payments under a plan under chapter 13."[3] This definition was clearly intended to encompass not only wage earners, but also recipients of government benefits, alimony or support payments, or any other regular type of income.[4] The question of how regular the income must be is left to case law but, as types of income such as commissions are meant to be included, it is clear that the debtor need not receive payments at particular or rigid intervals.

It is clear that the spouse of an individual with regular income may file a joint case with that individual.[5] Probably a spouse or other living partner of a person with regular income, who has no independent source of income, may also file a petition without the other spouse or partner. As the definition is directed toward whether the debtor will have funds available for a plan, if such a debtor can show a regular allowance from the living partner for expenses, she should be eligible to file chapter 13.[6] Regular payments from friends or other family members, who do not live with the debtor, should also qualify as regular income, although problems related to documentation may arise. A letter or affidavit from the friend or family member would satisfy most trustees, but when disputes arise, testimony and documentary evidence in the form of canceled checks may be required.

Besides the requirement of regular income, a second limitation on eligibility to file chapter 13 not present in chapter 7 is the amount of debt. Although the limits do not pose problems for most consumer debtors, chapter 13 is not available to debtors (or debtor couples) with over $307,675.00 of non-contingent, liquidated, unsecured debts

---

1 11 U.S.C. § 109(a), (e).

2 Fed. R. Bankr. P. 1004.1 provides that a legally appointed representative may file a petition on behalf of an infant or incompetent person. If no such representative exists, such a person may file a petition by "next friend." Prior case law had generally been consistent with these rules. *See In re* Kjellsen, 53 F.3d 944 (8th Cir. 1995) (guardian has authority to file); *In re* Murray, 199 B.R. 165 (Bankr. M.D. Tenn. 1996) (parent could file chapter 13 petition on behalf of seven-year-old debtor as "next friend" of debtor); *In re* Smith, 115 B.R. 84 (Bankr. E.D. Va. 1990) (guardian may file on behalf of incapacitated debtor, although wife by virtue of power of attorney may not); *In re* Jones, 97 B.R. 901 (Bankr. S.D. Ohio 1989) (guardian for incompetent debtor may file chapter 13). In *In re* Zawisza, 73 B.R. 929 (Bankr. E.D. Pa. 1987), an attorney, as "next friend," filed on behalf of an incompetent, who had no validly appointed guardian or representative.

However, a trust is not "an individual with regular income." *In re* W.F.C. Real Estate Trust #1, 236 B.R. 90 (Bankr. S.D. Fla. 1999). See § 3.2.1.1, *supra,* for discussion of whether a trustee may file a case.

3 11 U.S.C. § 101(30).

4 H.R. Rep. No. 95-595, at 119 (1977).

5 11 U.S.C. § 109(e); *see also* 11 U.S.C. § 302.

6 *In re* Rowe, 110 B.R. 712 (Bankr. E.D. Pa. 1990) ($200.00 monthly contribution from son is sufficient as regular income for purpose of eligibility for chapter 13). See § 12.2.2, *infra,* for further discussion of the regular income requirement.

or over $922,975.00 of non-contingent, liquidated, secured debts.[7] As in chapter 7, though, the debtor need not be insolvent.

Also, as in chapter 7 bankruptcies, an individual whose prior bankruptcy was dismissed within the previous 180 days may not be eligible for chapter 13 relief. Code section 109(g) bars a debtor from filing a new case if the prior case was (1) dismissed for willful failure of the debtor to abide by orders of the court or to appear before the court in proper prosecution of the case or (2) voluntarily dismissed following a request for relief from the automatic stay of section 362 of the Code.[8]

A major advantage of chapter 13 is the absence of the bars to discharge found in chapter 7.[9] A chapter 13 discharge may be obtained by a debtor who has received a chapter 7 discharge within the six years before filing, or who would not be granted a discharge due to some other provision in chapter 7.[10] The only impediments to discharge in a chapter 13 case are the requirements for a plan, discussed below, and the possibility that the discharge could, in some cases, be revoked on the grounds that it was fraudulently obtained.[11]

4.2.2 The Initial Forms

A chapter 13 bankruptcy case is commenced by the filing of a two-page petition which in form is identical to a chapter 7 petition but which is completed somewhat differently.[12] The petition must be accompanied by $194.00 in fees whether the petition is individual or joint (including a $155.00 filing fee and a $39.00 noticing fee imposed by the federal Judicial Conference),[13] or an application to pay the fees in installments.[14] If an application to pay in installments is filed, the debtor need not pay the fees at the time of filing; the fees may be paid over a period up to 120 days, which the court can extend to 180 days for cause.[15] However, no waiver of the $155.00 filing fee is permitted.[16] If the debtor is not prepared to file schedules with the petition, a list of creditors and their addresses must be supplied.[17]

In addition to the petition, the debtor must file a statement of social security number,[18] schedules,[19] and a statement of financial affairs.[20] A disclosure of attorney fees[21] and chapter 13 plan are also required.[22] Except for the statement of social security number, if these documents are not filed with the petition, they may be filed within fifteen days afterward.[23] The schedules and statement of financial affairs for a chapter 13 filing are identical to those required in chapter 7. There are only two significant differences in the filings required under the two chapters. First, chapter 13 debtors may omit a statement of intentions with regard to property securing consumer debts.[24] Second, a chapter 13 plan is required.[25]

The debtor is given great leeway in formulating the plan, subject to only a few requirements. The most important of the provisions usually required, which are discussed in greater detail elsewhere[26] in this manual, are listed below:

---

7   11 U.S.C. § 109(e). The debt limits are subject to the inflation adjustments provided under 11 U.S.C. § 104(b) and are discussed further in § 12.2.3, *infra.* The amount of secured debt may be measured by the value of the security rather than the amount of the claim. *Compare In re* Day, 747 F.2d 405 (7th Cir. 1984) *with In re* Morton, 43 B.R. 215 (Bankr. E.D.N.Y. 1984). *In re* Belknap, 174 B.R. 182 (Bankr. W.D.N.Y. 1994), holds that a debt is a secured debt for the purpose of calculating the debt limits even if it is secured by property that is not property of the debtor, though there are strong arguments to the contrary. The debt limitations of § 109 are not jurisdictional. They do not, for example, preclude conversion of a case to a chapter under which the debtor qualifies. Rudd v. Laughlin, 866 F.2d 1040 (8th Cir. 1989); *In re* Wenberg, 94 B.R. 631 (B.A.P. 9th Cir. 1988), *aff'd,* 902 F.2d 768 (9th Cir. 1990).

8   11 U.S.C. § 109(g). See § 3.2.1, *supra,* and § 9.7.3.1.5, *infra,* for further discussion of this provision, which was added by the 1984 amendments, and of the automatic stay.

9   11 U.S.C. § 727(a). See § 14.2.2, *infra,* for discussion of objections to discharge.

10 See § 12.10, *infra,* for discussion of chapter 13 cases after prior bankruptcies.

11 11 U.S.C. § 1330; *see In re* Hicks, 79 B.R. 45 (Bankr. N.D. Ala. 1987) (discussing requirements for revoking confirmation); *In re* Scott, 77 B.R. 636 (Bankr. N.D. Ohio 1987) (debtor fraudulently concealed identity). See § 14.3, *infra* for further discussion of revocation of discharge.

12 Official Form 1, Appx. D, *infra.* The venue rules for chapter 13 are the same as for chapter 7. *See* § 3.2.3, *supra.*

13 The initial fee for chapter 13 is now somewhat lower than for chapter 7, because there is no $15.00 trustee surcharge at the outset of the case. In the long term, though, the total fees for chapter 13 are likely to be higher, because trustee's fees will be collected on payments made under the plan.

14 Fed. R. Bankr. P. 1006; Official Form 3, Appx. D, *infra.* The noticing fee may also be paid in installments. Fed. R. Bankr. P. 1006. A form for an application to waive the noticing fee can be found at Form 7 in Appendix G.3, *infra.* See modified application to pay fees in installments. Official Form 3, Appx. D, *infra.* See also § 3.2.2, *supra,* and § 13.6.2, *infra,* for further discussion of filing fee issues, including waiver of filing fees and recent fee increases.

15 Fed. R. Bankr. P. 1006(b)(2) states that the fee is ordinarily payable within 120 days of filing, but that this period may be extended to 180 days from filing for cause shown.

16 28 U.S.C. § 1930(a).

17 Fed. R. Bankr. P. 1007(a)(1).

18 Fed. R. Bankr. P. 1007(f). Technically, this statement is not filed, but rather "submitted" to the clerk, because it is not included in the documents that are docketed and kept in the court file for the case.

19 Fed. R. Bankr. P. 1007(b)(1); Official Form 6, Appx. D, *infra.*

20 Fed. R. Bankr. P. 1007(b)(1); Official Form 7, Appx. D, *infra.*

21 Fed. R. Bankr. P. 2016(b).

22 Fed. R. Bankr. P. 3015.

23 Fed. R. Bankr. P. 1007(c), 2016(b), 3015(b).

24 *See* §§ 7.3.6, 11.4, *infra;* Official Form 8, Appx. D, *infra.*

25 See generally Chapters 7 and 12, *infra,* for a detailed discussion of the chapter 13 plan.

26 *See generally* §§ 11.6–11.8, 12.3–12.9, *infra.*

- All claims given priority by 11 U.S.C. § 507[27] must be paid in full;[28]
- The present value[29] of payments on unsecured claims must be at least equal to what would be paid in a chapter 7 liquidation;[30]
- With respect to each allowed secured claim provided for by the plan, either (1) the holder of the claim must accept the plan, (2) the plan must provide for payments with a present value[31] in the amount of the claim and continuance of the lien, or (3) the debtor must surrender the property securing the claim to the creditor;[32] and
- If a party in interest objects to the plan, the plan must either commit all of the debtor's disposable income for three years or pay unsecured claims in full.[33]

Lastly, local rules or practice may require certain other papers to be filed, either with the petition or shortly thereafter. All documents in a case may be filed or submitted electronically, as discussed in a later chapter.[34]

4.2.3 Conversion from Chapter 7 Proceedings

Another way of obtaining chapter 13 relief is through conversion from a chapter 7 case. Any debtor who has begun a chapter 7 case may convert it to a chapter 13 case at any time during the case provided the debtor is eligible for relief under chapter 13.[35] A court determination that debts are nondischargeable in chapter 7 does not preclude conversion and, in fact, conversion may be the best strategy in such a situation given the broader discharge available in chapter 13.[36] Similarly, any person who has commenced a chapter 13 case may elect to convert it to a chapter 7 case.[37] A debtor may convert a case from chapter 7 to chapter 13 as of right only if the case was commenced as a chapter 7 case; if the case had previously been converted to chapter 7, a second (or third) conversion may occur only with the court's permission.[38]

A few courts have held that a debtor who has already once converted a case from another chapter to chapter 7 may not be permitted to convert it to chapter 13 thereafter, even at the discretion of the court.[39] This reading of Code section 706 is at odds with normal rules of statutory construction. Section 706(a) of the Code provides that *the debtor* may convert a case to another chapter as a matter of right if the case has not been previously converted. Section 706(c) states that *the court* may not convert a case to chapter 13 unless the debtor so requests. Because the debtor has an absolute right to convert the case when the case has not been previously converted, section 706(c) would make no sense unless there were other situations when the court could convert the case to chapter 13 in addition to those in which the debtor could convert the case. Those situations, obviously, would be those in which the debtor requested conversion after there had been a prior conversion, as the court is not permitted to convert the case to chapter 13 except at the request of the debtor.[40]

---

27 These types of debts are listed in § 3.5, *supra.*

28 11 U.S.C. § 1322(a)(2); *see* § 12.3.5, *infra.*

29 The concept of present value arises from the language "value as of the effective date of the plan" in 11 U.S.C. § 1325(a)(4). Basically, it envisions a total of payments which equals the amount creditors would receive in a liquidation case plus interest over the term of the plan. See discussion in § 12.3.1, *infra.*

30 11 U.S.C. § 1325(a)(4). See § 12.3.1, *infra,* for discussion of this standard.

31 *See* 11 U.S.C. § 1325(a)(4); § 12.3.1, *infra.* For these purposes, the total of payments to the creditor would be the allowed secured claim plus interest.

32 11 U.S.C. § 1325(a)(5). See § 11.6, *infra,* for discussion of this standard.

33 11 U.S.C. § 1325(b). See § 12.3.3, *infra,* for discussion of this requirement.

34 *See* § 7.1.4, *infra.*

35 11 U.S.C. § 706(a); *see In re* Finney, 992 F.2d 43 (4th Cir. 1993) (even debtor who had failed to cooperate with trustee and to disclose pre-petition transfers had right to convert from chapter 7 to chapter 11, but court could then *sua sponte* consider whether reconversion to chapter 7 was warranted); *In re* Miller, 303 B.R. 471 (B.A.P. 10th Cir. 2003) (debtor had one-time right to convert to chapter 13 that could not be denied on any basis not set forth in conversion provisions); *In re* Martin, 87 B.R. 20 (E.D. La. 1988) (absolute right to convert even after chapter 7 discharge granted), *aff'd,* 880 F.2d 857 (5th Cir. 1989); *In re* Stern, 266 B.R. 322 (Bankr. D. Md. 2001) (eligibility determined on date of petition, so debtor could not convert case based upon discharge in chapter 7 of unsecured debts above

eligibility level); *In re* Sobin, 99 B.R. 483 (Bankr. M.D. Fla. 1989); *In re* Walker, 77 B.R. 803 (Bankr. D. Nev. 1987). *But see In re* Kuntz, 233 B.R. 580 (B.A.P. 1st Cir. 1999) (right to convert may be denied in "extreme circumstances," but delay in notifying trustee of inheritance did not warrant denial); *In re* Markovich, 207 B.R. 909 (B.A.P. 9th Cir. 1997) (bankruptcy court did not have power to revoke chapter 7 discharge to permit conversion to chapter 13); *In re* Jones, 111 B.R. 674 (Bankr. E.D. Tenn. 1990) (debtor may not convert after chapter 7 discharge is granted unless revocation of that discharge would not harm creditors).

36 *Compare* 11 U.S.C. § 727 *with* 11 U.S.C. § 1328. *See* Ch. 14, *infra.* One court has held that a case may be converted for this reason even after the debtor's chapter 7 discharge is granted. *In re* Caldwell, 67 B.R. 296 (Bankr. E.D. Tenn. 1986). After discharge, however, it may be less problematic to simply refile under chapter 13, because such filing is not barred by any provision of the Code. *See* § 12.10, *infra.*

37 11 U.S.C. § 1307(a).

38 11 U.S.C. § 706(a), (b); *see In re* Masterson, 141 B.R. 84 (Bankr. E.D. Pa. 1992); *In re* Walker, 77 B.R. 803 (Bankr. D. Nev. 1987) (section 706(a) constitutes an absolute ban on reconversion); *In re* Hollar, 70 B.R. 337 (Bankr. E.D. Tenn. 1987).

39 *E.g., In re* Hanna, 100 B.R. 591 (Bankr. M.D. Fla. 1989); *In re* Carter, 84 B.R. 744 (D. Kan. 1988).

40 In jurisdictions where reconversion is problematic, filing a new case under chapter 13 after completion of the chapter 7 case is nevertheless possible, because such refiling is permitted under the Code. *See* § 12.10, *infra.* This strategy would not work, of

4.3 First Steps After Filing

As in a chapter 7 case, the filing of a petition operates as an order for relief and sets the bankruptcy process in motion.[41] A trustee, usually the standing trustee for the district,[42] is appointed and, if the debtor has applied for it, an order is entered for payment of the filing fee in installments.

The filing of a petition immediately puts into effect the automatic stay,[43] which prevents creditors from taking any further actions against the debtor or the debtor's property with respect to claims arising prior to commencement of the case. The filing of a chapter 13 case also effectuates a stay of actions against most non-filing codebtors who are obligated to pay claims against the debtor.[44] Creditors must obtain the permission of the bankruptcy court before proceeding with any of the acts prohibited by either stay.[45] In the case of the stay of actions against codebtors, this permission may be granted to the extent that:

- The codebtor was the principal debtor who received the consideration on the claim; or
- The debtor's plan proposes not to pay the claim; or
- The creditor would be irreparably harmed by the stay.[46]

The statute requires that, as of the commencement of the case, any entity holding property that the trustee[47] may use, sell, or lease, or that the debtor may exempt, must deliver that property to the trustee.[48] Because the debtor in a chapter 13 case generally has a right to possess[49] all property of the estate, the trustee must then deliver the property to the debtor.

The debtor must begin making plan payments within thirty days after filing of the plan, unless the court orders otherwise.[50] This requirement makes possible quicker pay-

ment to creditors and also gives the court some evidence of the debtor's ability to pay, a consideration in confirmation of the plan.[51] At the debtor's request, the court will issue a wage deduction order to cover the plan payments.[52] These payments are retained by the trustee pending confirmation of the plan and, if a plan is not confirmed, they are returned to the debtor after deduction of administrative costs.[53] The failure to commence payments as required may be grounds for dismissal of the case.[54]

Within a relatively short time after the petition is filed, the clerk issues the notice of the section 341(a) meeting of creditors.[55] This form also provides notice to creditors of the automatic stay and of the deadlines for filing their claims with the court.[56] Usually, it also gives notice of the date set for the confirmation hearing and the deadline for objections to confirmation.[57]

4.4 The Meeting of Creditors and Other Pre-Confirmation Activities

The meeting of creditors, required in each case by section 341(a) of the Code, is normally scheduled between twenty and fifty days after the date the bankruptcy petition is filed.[58] If the meeting is to be held at a place not regularly staffed by the United States trustee's office, it may be held as much as sixty days after the order for relief.[59]

The primary purpose of the section 341(a) meeting (the meeting of creditors), as in a chapter 7 case, is to provide the trustee and the creditors the opportunity to examine the debtor and determine whether there are any grounds for objecting to the plan. The trustee inquires generally into the information presented in the statement and plan, including the debtor's ability to make the proposed payments. The debtor is usually asked to produce photo identification and documentary proof that the social security number listed on the statement of social security number is correct. Despite the popular name for the proceedings, creditors rarely appear in most judicial districts, and the bankruptcy judge is not permitted to be present.[60]

---

course, if the need to reconvert is based on a creditor action, such as foreclosure, which will be completed before the new case can be filed.

41 11 U.S.C. § 301.

42 *See* § 2.6, *supra.*

43 11 U.S.C. § 362. *See generally* Ch. 9, *infra.*

44 11 U.S.C. § 1301. The stay applies only to individuals liable on "consumer debts" and does not apply if the cosigner became liable in the ordinary course of her business. *See* Ch. 9, *infra.*

45 11 U.S.C. §§ 362(d), 1301(c). However, if neither the debtor nor codebtor makes a written objection to a request for relief from the codebtor stay sought because the plan does not propose full payment of the claim, the stay is automatically modified as requested. 11 U.S.C. § 1301(d). See Ch. 9, *infra,* for further discussion of this procedure.

46 11 U.S.C. § 1301(c).

47 In a chapter 13 case, the debtor exercises most of the trustee's powers to use, sell, or lease property. 11 U.S.C. §§ 1303, 1304.

48 11 U.S.C. §§ 542, 543; *see* § 9.9, *infra.*

49 11 U.S.C. § 1306(b).

50 11 U.S.C. § 1326(a)(1). Payments may not be made to the debtor's attorney rather than the trustee unless the court so orders. *See In re* Barbee, 82 B.R. 470 (Bankr. N.D. Ill. 1988).

51 11 U.S.C. § 1325(a)(6).

52 See Forms 10 and 11, Appendix G.4, *infra,* for a sample request for a wage order. Some courts have local rules and forms governing requests for wage orders. See § 12.6.1, *infra,* for further discussion of payment orders.

53 11 U.S.C. § 1326(a)(2); *see In re* Brown, 118 B.R. 1008 (Bankr. E.D. Mo. 1990). *But see In re* Beam, 229 B.R. 454 (D. Or. 1998) (Internal Revenue Service could levy on debtor's funds in hands of trustee and receive funds that would otherwise be returned to debtor upon dismissal), *aff'd,* 192 F.3d 941 (9th Cir. 1999).

54 11 U.S.C. § 1307(c)(4).

55 Fed. R. Bankr. P. 2002(a), 2003.

56 Official Form 9, Appx. D, *infra.*

57 Fed. R. Bankr. P. 2002(b).

58 Fed. R. Bankr. P. 2003(a).

59 *Id.*

60 11 U.S.C. § 341(c).

The meeting is likely to last between five and thirty minutes, generally following the pattern of routine questions asked in a chapter 7 case.[61] In some districts, the proceeding serves as an opportunity for the debtor to negotiate with creditors or the trustee in order to obviate any objections to the plan.

The debtor may wish to file claims on behalf of certain creditors who have not filed themselves, in order to protect the purposes of the plan.[62] For example, a debtor who wants a secured or nondischargeable claim to be paid through the plan should file a claim on behalf of that creditor if the creditor does not file its own claim. This filing may be done after the first date set for the meeting of creditors or within 120 days thereafter (210 days if the creditor is a governmental unit).[63]

In many jurisdictions, absent such a filing, the debtor's plan payments will be distributed to other creditors who do file claims. Such a result can frustrate the purpose of the bankruptcy entirely. It thus is crucial to check the claims docket at regular intervals to make sure that the necessary claims are submitted and, when required, to submit them within the deadline on the creditor's behalf.

During or after the meeting, the trustee must decide whether to object to any of the claims filed. The debtor may also object to the amount, validity, secured status, or any other aspect of a claim.[64] Ultimately, all disputes on these matters must be resolved by the bankruptcy judge, who sometimes considers them in conjunction with the confirmation hearing.

Various other proceedings may take place as well, such as motions to avoid liens on exempt property of the debtor,[65] or creditors' motions for relief from the automatic stay.[66]

4.5 The Confirmation Hearing

The confirmation hearing may occur on the same day as the meeting of creditors or some time within the next several months, depending upon local practice.[67] In either case, the court must give at least twenty-five days notice of the date of the hearing.[68] The purpose of the hearing is to provide a basis for ruling on whether the plan will be confirmed, to inquire into whether the requirements of chapter 13 are met,[69] and to hear any objections to confirmation and any evidence or argument that is necessary. Objections to confirmation must be timely filed and served on the debtor, trustee, and any other entity ordered by the court, as well as transmitted to the United States trustee.[70] Local rules often set specific deadlines for such objections.[71] The hearing may also encompass other matters related to confirmation, such as objections to claims or disputes about valuation of property.

Under local practice in some jurisdictions, the debtor and/or her counsel may not be required to attend the confirmation hearing if the standing trustee is recommending confirmation. Although the court often rules on confirmation at the hearing, there is no requirement that it do so. If confirmation is denied, the debtor is normally allowed an opportunity to amend the plan to meet the court's objections.[72]

The effect of confirmation is to bind the debtor and all creditors of the debtor to the terms of the plan.[73] Normally, the trustee then begins payments to creditors under the plan. Confirmation also revests title to all property of the estate in the debtor, free and clear of any creditor's claim, except as otherwise provided in the plan or order confirming the plan.[74] If the plan is completed successfully, there are normally no possible impediments to the debtor's discharge.[75] However, in very limited circumstances, the court

---

61 *See* § 3.4, *supra.* A sample list of questions asked in first meetings is found in Form 48, Appendix G.7, *infra.*

62 11 U.S.C. § 501(c). See §§ 8.4.1, 8.4.2, 13.4.3, *infra,* for discussion of claims filed by the debtor.

63 Fed. R. Bankr. P. 3004, 3002(c).

64 Under 11 U.S.C. § 502(a), a "party in interest" may object to a claim. The advisory committee note to Fed. R. Bankr. P. 3007 recognizes both that parties other than the trustee may object and that a counterclaim may be joined with such an objection. The procedure for filing and objecting to claims is discussed in Chapters 8 and 13, *infra.*

65 See § 10.4.2, *infra,* for discussion of lien avoidance motions.

66 See § 9.7, *infra,* for discussion of motions for relief from the stay.

67 At least one district court has held that scheduling the first meeting and the confirmation hearing for the same day is improper. *In re* Robinson, 22 B.R. 497 (W.D. Va. 1982). Usually, if a creditor who is objecting to confirmation so

requests, the hearing is postponed.

68 Fed. R. Bankr. P. 2002(b). The procedure for the confirmation hearing and objections to confirmation is governed by Fed. R. Bankr. P. 3015.

69 Issues concerning these requirements are discussed in Chapter 12, *infra. See generally In re* Dues, 98 B.R. 434 (Bankr. N.D. Ind. 1989).

70 Fed. R. Bankr. P. 3015(f).

71 *See In re* Carbone, 254 B.R. 1 (Bankr. D. Mass. 2000) (objection not timely because it was not received by clerk within time period allowed by local rule); *In re* Duncan, 245 B.R. 538 (Bankr. E.D. Tenn. 2000) (objection not timely filed under local rule even though filed before confirmation).

72 11 U.S.C. § 1323.

73 11 U.S.C. § 1327(a); *see In re* Bonnano, 78 B.R. 52 (Bankr. E.D. Pa. 1987) (discussing the effects of confirmation); *see also* § 12.11, *infra.*

74 11 U.S.C. § 1327(c); *see also* § 12.8, *infra.*

75 11 U.S.C. § 1328(a). The objections to discharge available in chapter 7 cases under 11 U.S.C. § 727(a) are not available in chapter 13 proceedings. 11 U.S.C. § 103(b); *see also In re* Daniels, 163 B.R. 893 (Bankr. S.D. Ga. 1994) (creditor could not have chapter 13 case reopened and discharge revoked based upon creditor's mistake in filing proof of claim). *But see In re* Escobedo, 28 F.3d 34 (7th Cir. 1994) (confirmation of plan that did not pay priority claims in full was "nugatory" and case could be dismissed even though there was no appeal of confirmation order and debtor had completed plan payments).

may revoke an order of confirmation, if a party in interest can show that the confirmation order was procured by fraud.[76]

4.6 Modification of the Plan and Post-Petition Transactions

For various reasons, the debtor may wish to modify the plan that was originally submitted. Such modifications can usually be accomplished with little difficulty. Before confirmation, the plan may be modified as a matter of course, as long as the modified plan meets the requirements of chapter 13. If a claim holder has filed an acceptance of the plan (a consideration only relevant in the case of some secured or priority claims),[77] the acceptance is deemed to apply to the modified plan unless the holder's rights are modified and the holder withdraws its acceptance.[78]

After confirmation, the procedure is slightly different. The plan may be modified by the debtor unless, after notice and a hearing, the modification is disapproved.[79] A creditor may not object to a modification if its rights would not be altered by the modified plan.[80] Given the Code's definition of "notice and a hearing,"[81] it is unlikely that disapproval could occur without a hearing, provided the debtor or some other party requests one. In most cases, an uncontested modification is approved without a hearing and any objection to a post-confirmation modification is resolved by the court after a hearing. Although there is no requirement that a debtor establish good cause for modification,[82] the plan as modified must, of course, meet the requirements of the Code.[83]

One of the most common reasons for modification is to cure post-petition mortgage defaults.[84] The debtor may also wish to provide for post-petition transactions that arise from an unforeseen emergency or change in the debtor's circumstances. Post-petition claims may generally be provided for in the initial plan, but will be disallowed if the claimant knew or should have known that the trustee's prior approval of the debtor's incurring the obligation was practicable and was not obtained.[85] Post-petition obligations may also be incurred with the trustee's permission and paid outside the plan.[86]

Because a post-petition claim may only be filed by the holder of the claim and not by the debtor,[87] and because a post-petition claim may be paid through the plan only if the plan provides for it, which is the debtor's choice,[88] the inclusion of post-petition claims in a chapter 13 plan occurs only when both the debtor and the creditor agree to that procedure. If a post-petition claim is filed and provided for by the plan, it is discharged along with other debts when the debtor completes the plan or receives a hardship discharge, whether or not it has been paid in full.[89] Otherwise, a post-petition claim survives the chapter 13 discharge at the end of the case.

The holder of an unsecured claim or the trustee may also move for modification of the plan.[90] The principal reason for such a motion would be a change in the debtor's income or expenses that would enable the debtor to make larger payments for the remainder of the plan.[91] Normally, a modification of the plan at a creditor's request should not be granted without a hearing unless the debtor consents. As the Bankruptcy Rules are not fully clear on the procedure for post-confirmation modification, local practice may vary. Debtors should be sure to oppose any plan modification to which they do not fully consent.

---

76 11 U.S.C. § 1330(a). Even if the order of confirmation is revoked, the debtor should generally have an opportunity to propose a modified plan. 11 U.S.C. § 1330(b). *But see In re* Scott, 77 B.R. 636 (Bankr. N.D. Ohio 1987). Simply failing to list a creditor is not, without more, grounds for revoking an order of confirmation. *See In re* Hicks, 79 B.R. 45 (Bankr. N.D. Ala. 1987) (failure to inform court of new obligations incurred during case is not fraud sufficient to revoke confirmation).

77 Unsecured claimants have no right to accept or reject the plan, but acceptance by a secured claimant may be necessary under 11 U.S.C. § 1322(a)(2) or § 1325(a)(5) if the provisions of those sections are not otherwise met.

78 11 U.S.C. § 1323(c).

79 11 U.S.C. § 1329. The procedure for modification of a plan after confirmation is governed by Fed. R. Bankr. P. 3015(g). See § 8.7.3, *infra,* for further discussion of plan modification.

80 *In re* Eason, 178 B.R. 908 (Bankr. M.D. Ga. 1994) (doctrine of *res judicata* bars the litigation of issues already decided by confirmation of plan).

81 11 U.S.C. § 102(1).

82 *In re* Davis, 34 B.R. 319 (Bankr. E.D. Va. 1983); *see* 8 Collier on Bankruptcy ¶ 1329.02 (15th ed. rev.).

83 *See In re* Farquhar, 112 B.R. 34 (Bankr. D. Colo. 1989) (modified plan which discriminates among unsecured creditors may not be approved).

84 *In re* Mendoza, 111 F.3d 1264 (5th Cir. 1997); *In re* Hoggle, 12 F.3d 1008 (11th Cir. 1994) (debtor could modify plan to cure post-confirmation default; *In re* McCollum, 76 B.R. 797 (Bankr. D. Or. 1987); *see* § 11.6.2, *infra.*

85 11 U.S.C. § 1305.

86 Payments outside the plan are not made through the trustee. See discussion in Chapter 12, *infra. See also In re* Edwards, 190 B.R. 91 (Bankr. M.D. Tenn. 1995) (overruling creditor's objection to debtor incurring post-petition debt because debtor would still be able to complete payments under confirmed plan, to which creditor had not objected).

87 11 U.S.C. § 1305(a).

88 11 U.S.C. § 1322(b)(6).

89 *See* 8 Collier on Bankruptcy ¶ 1305.03 (15th ed. rev.).

90 11 U.S.C. § 1329(a).

91 See § 12.3.3, *infra,* for discussion of motions to increase plan payments.

4.7 Options in the Event of Failure to Complete the Plan

4.7.1 Overview

In some cases, usually due to loss of income, the debtor is unable to complete the plan as proposed. In such situations four options are available—a hardship discharge, a plan modification, conversion to chapter 7, or dismissal—each of which has somewhat different consequences.

4.7.2 Hardship Discharge

The Code provides for a hardship discharge if the debtor's problems are caused by circumstances for which the debtor is not justly accountable.[92] Such circumstances need not be catastrophic; they need only be circumstances that make it impossible for the debtor to complete the plan.[93] Such circumstances may include the debtor's death or a serious deterioration in the debtor's financial circumstances.[94] A hardship discharge may be granted at any time after confirmation, provided that unsecured creditors have received as much as they would have received in a chapter 7 liquidation.[95] Thus there need not have been the full payment of priority claims normally required in a chapter 13 case.

It is unclear what happens to holders of allowed secured claims after a hardship discharge. Presumably, if they have retained their liens under the plan, they still have liens in the amounts of their allowed secured claims left unpaid.[96] If a creditor did not retain a lien or if its allowed secured claim was fully paid before the hardship discharge, its claim would be discharged, and no lien would remain.[97] As to other claims, the debtor receives a discharge equivalent to that granted in a chapter 7 case, and not the broader chapter 13 discharge that the debtor would have received upon completion of the plan.[98]

A hardship discharge may be granted only if modification of the plan is not practicable.[99] Thus, the Code seems to prefer modification whenever possible. In many cases the debtor, too, has good reason to prefer that remedy.

4.7.3 Modification

It is often possible to modify the plan, under the provisions discussed above, to accommodate new problems as they arise. The payments under the plan may be reduced, or even terminated, if the plan, as modified, still complies with the requirements of chapter 13.

The advantages of modification are that the broader "full compliance" discharge of chapter 13 is preserved, and the hardship discharge tests need not be met. Normally, however, the priority claims and allowed secured claims provided for in the plan must still be paid, and if they cannot be paid modification may be impracticable. Modification is discussed in more detail elsewhere in this manual.[100]

4.7.4 Conversion to Chapter 7

The debtor has an absolute right to convert a case to chapter 7,[101] without any showing of hardship, and in most cases such a conversion provides the same relief as the hardship discharge. A new set of schedules generally need not be filed; however, a statement of intention must be

92 11 U.S.C. § 1328(b).

93 *In re* Bandilli, 231 B.R. 836 (B.A.P. 1st Cir. 1999) (circumstances need not be catastrophic, but temporary relapse of medical condition which did not affect income was insufficient); *In re* Edwards, 207 B.R. 728 (Bankr. N.D. Fla. 1997).

94 *In re* Graham, 63 B.R. 95 (Bankr. E.D. Pa. 1986); *In re* Bond, 36 B.R. 49 (Bankr. E.D.N.C. 1984); *see also* Fed. R. Bankr. P. 1016. *But see In re* Roberts, 279 F.3d 91 (1st Cir. 2002) (no abuse of discretion in denying hardship discharge to debtor who made no attempt to modify the plan or to sever her case from her husband's, actions that in all likelihood would have been allowed by the bankruptcy court and might have permitted her to obtain a discharge).

95 11 U.S.C. § 1328(b). Again, the present value as of the effective date of the plan is the relevant figure. *See* 11 U.S.C. § 1325(a)(4); § 12.3.1, *infra.*

96 In most cases, the plan will provide for the creditor's retaining the lien until the allowed secured claim is paid in order to meet the confirmation standard of 11 U.S.C. § 1325(a)(5). In a case in which there is doubt about this issue, conversion to chapter 7 may be a better option than a hardship discharge, because the 1994 amendments make clear that a pre-conversion valuation remains in effect in chapter 7 and that pre-conversion payments are to be credited against the allowed secured claim. 11 U.S.C. § 348(f)(1)(B); *see also In re* Bunn, 128 B.R. 281 (Bankr. D. Idaho 1991) (following conversion from chapter 13 to chapter 7, debtor could redeem vehicle by paying only the balance due on amount of allowed secured claim; unsecured claim is dis-

charged); *In re* Tlusick, 122 B.R. 728 (Bankr. W.D. Mo. 1991) (after conversion to chapter 7, debtor could redeem vehicle by paying unpaid balance of secured claim).

97 *See In re* Penrod, 50 F.3d 459 (7th Cir. 1995) (confirmed chapter 11 plan which did not specifically preserve creditor's lien extinguished lien of creditor that had participated in reorganization, even if creditor could have successfully objected to plan); *In re* Lee, 162 B.R. 217 (D. Minn. 1993) (court can confirm plan which calls for release of retained lien upon full payment of the allowed secured claim even if that occurs before end of plan term); *In re* Nicewonger, 192 B.R. 886 (Bankr. N.D. Ohio 1996) (same); *see also* § 12.11, *infra.*

98 The exceptions to discharge found at 11 U.S.C. § 523(a) are applicable to a hardship discharge. 11 U.S.C. § 1328(c)(2). See Chapters 6 and 14, *infra,* for a discussion of the difference between chapter 7 and chapter 13 discharges.

99 11 U.S.C. § 1328(b)(3).

100 *See* §§ 8.7.3, 8.7.4.2, 12.3.3.5, *infra.*

101 11 U.S.C. § 1307(a). *But see In re* Spiser, 232 B.R. 669 (Bankr. N.D. Tex. 1999) (case could not be converted after both debtors had died). The Bankruptcy Rules provide that the debtor need only file a notice of conversion, and that no court order is necessary to effect the conversion. Fed. R. Bankr. P. 1017(d).

submitted within thirty days after the order of conversion is entered or before the first date set for the meeting of creditors, whichever is earlier.[102]

The debtor must also file a supplemental schedule of debts arising since the chapter 13 case was initially filed.[103] These will be treated as if they arose prior to the commencement of the case.[104] Thus, when applicable, the automatic stay prevents creditor action on these debts, and they may be discharged.[105] After the conversion, the debtor's non-exempt property, if any, is liquidated, and the debtor receives a chapter 7 discharge.

Prior to the 1994 amendments to the Code, some courts had held that the property of the estate in a converted case included all property acquired after the petition was filed and before the conversion.[106] However, it is now clear that property acquired post-petition may be included in the chapter 7 estate only if the case is converted in bad faith.[107] In addition, any post-petition increase in the value of property acquired pre-petition should not be included in the estate after conversion.[108] And even in cases in which post-petition property is found to be property of the estate, the debtor should be entitled to exempt post-petition earn-ings held by the trustee and other property acquired after the chapter 13 case was filed, at least to the extent of applicable exemptions.[109]

If there is non-exempt property in the estate, it is liquidated regardless of what the unsecured creditors have already received under the plan (at least to the extent necessary to pay all creditors in full). Therefore, in cases in which the debtor has non-exempt assets and can meet the requirements, a hardship discharge is often preferable to conversion.

On the other hand, an advantage of conversion is that it allows post-petition debts arising before conversion to be treated as if they arose pre-petition.[110] These debts may thus be discharged if they are dischargeable under chapter 7.[111] This rule may make conversion an attractive option if the debtor has significant unsecured post-petition debts.

Conversion of the case does not create a new automatic stay when relief from the stay has been previously granted.[112] It may sometimes be possible, however, to move to have a stay reimposed if the debtor can ensure that the creditor's rights will be protected.[113]

The debtor may wish to convert if the reasons for the initial choice of chapter 13 no longer apply. For example, the debtor may have chosen chapter 13 to protect property, such as an automobile, from repossession.[114] If that property is later destroyed or is no longer of value to the debtor, chapter 13 may no longer be necessary.

Conversion may also be advantageous when the debtor is unable to complete her plan and is ineligible for a hardship discharge, yet wishes to obtain a discharge of unsecured debts or to preserve the effect of lien avoidance or other orders obtained under chapter 13.[115] If a case is voluntarily

---

102 Fed. R. Bankr. P. 1019(1); *see* Official Form 8, Appx. D, *infra.* Additional (post-petition) debts to existing creditors, such as utilities, should be listed to ensure that they are discharged.

103 Fed. R. Bankr. P. 1019(5).

104 11 U.S.C. § 348(d); *In re* Deiter, 33 B.R. 547 (Bankr. W.D. Wis. 1983).

105 It is not uncommon, for example, for post-petition utility arrearages to be discharged following conversion from chapter 13 to chapter 7.

106 11 U.S.C. § 1306(a); *In re* Calder, 973 F.2d 862 (10th Cir. 1992); *In re* Lybrook, 951 F.2d 136 (7th Cir. 1991); Resendez v. Lindquist, 691 F.2d 397 (8th Cir. 1982); *In re* Winchester, 46 B.R. 492 (B.A.P. 9th Cir. 1984); *cf. In re* Young, 66 F.3d 376 (1st Cir. 1995) (1994 amendments show congressional intent that property be determined as of date chapter 13 case was commenced); *In re* Williamson, 804 F.2d 1355 (5th Cir. 1986) (homestead exemption eligibility determined as of date of first bankruptcy filing); Koch v. Myrvold, 784 F.2d 862 (8th Cir. 1986) (property inherited after 180 days from filing of chapter 11 case not property of estate when case converted to chapter 7); *In re* Bobroff, 766 F.2d 797 (3d Cir. 1985) (property acquired during chapter 13 case would not become property of estate after conversion to chapter 7).

107 11 U.S.C. § 348(f); *see In re* Bejarano, 302 B.R. 559 (Bankr. N.D. Ohio 2003) (no bad faith in converting case after acquisition of tax refunds and personal injury claims); *In re* Wiczek-Spalding, 223 B.R. 538 (Bankr. D. Minn. 1998) (taking advantage of Code protections is not bad faith on part of debtor who converted to chapter 7 to exclude employee severance pay from property of estate).

108 *In re* Slack, 290 B.R. 282 (Bankr. D.N.J. 2003); *In re* Page, 250 B.R. 465 (Bankr. D.N.H. 2000); *In re* Horton, 130 B.R. 326 (Bankr. D. Colo. 1991); *see also* Warren v. Peterson, 298 B.R. 322 (N.D. Ill. 2003) (property was implicitly valued by confirmation order at value listed on schedules and that valuation applies if case converted to chapter 7).

109 Arkison v. Plata, 958 F.2d 918 (9th Cir. 1992); *In re* Brown, 118 B.R. 1008 (Bankr. E.D. Mo. 1990). *But see* Resendez v. Lindquist, 691 F.2d 397 (8th Cir. 1982).

110 11 U.S.C. § 348(d); *In re* Deiter, 33 B.R. 547 (Bankr. W.D. Wis. 1983).

111 *See* Ch. 14, *infra.*

112 *See generally In re* State Airlines, 873 F.2d 264 (11th Cir. 1989) (conversion from chapter 11 to chapter 7 does not trigger new stay).

113 A stay may be available under 11 U.S.C. § 105 particularly as to property which might be liquidated for the benefit of unsecured creditors. This stay may allow a debtor facing foreclosure to obtain the benefit of an applicable homestead exemption in the liquidation process.

114 See generally Ch. 11, *infra,* for a discussion of the use of chapter 13 in dealing with secured creditors.

115 11 U.S.C. § 348(f)(1)(B); *accord In re* Bunn, 128 B.R. 281 (Bankr. D. Idaho 1991); *see* § 8.7.4, *infra; see also In re* Archie, 240 B.R. 425 (Bankr. S.D. Ala. 1999) (debtor permitted to redeem property without further payment when allowed secured claim had been paid in full prior to conversion); *In re* Tluscik, 122 B.R. 728 (Bankr. W.D. Mo. 1991) (debtor may redeem property after conversion to chapter 7 at the amount of unpaid balance of secured claim determined in chapter 13 case); *In re* Hargis, 103 B.R. 912 (Bankr. E.D. Tenn. 1989) (effect of lien

or involuntarily dismissed, rather than converted, liens avoided in the bankruptcy are reinstated.[116]

Conversion to chapter 7 can also be ordered against the debtor's will upon request of a party in interest, such as a creditor. The court may order conversion only "for cause," such as unreasonable delay to the prejudice of creditors, failure to file a timely plan, failure to commence plan payments, denial of confirmation along with denial of time to file a modified plan, a material default by the debtor in performance of a plan, revocation of confirmation, or termination of a plan according to its own terms.[117] However, if the debtor is a farmer, the Code provides that the court may not convert the case to chapter 7 unless the debtor so requests.[118] There are also some situations in which, because of the scope of relief available in chapter 11 or 12, conversion to those chapters may be an alternative to remaining in chapter 13.[119]

4.7.5 Dismissal

Occasionally, dismissal may be preferable to any of the other options. The debtor may at any time obtain dismissal as of right unless the case was previously converted from another chapter.[120] This route may be particularly attractive if it appears that the case may be converted to chapter 7 against the debtor's will and if the debtor has non-exempt property that she does not wish to see liquidated. It is doubtful whether the right to a dismissal continues after the case has been converted.[121]

A dismissal places the debtor and the creditors where they were before the case began. Unless the court orders otherwise, a dismissal vacates most bankruptcy orders and returns the parties as much as possible to the status quo prior to the petition.[122] The trustee should return to the debtor any funds that she is still holding.[123] In some cases, this option

may be preferable to all of the other alternatives discussed above, leaving the debtor to deal with creditors as if no bankruptcy had occurred. Obviously, to the extent that creditors have been paid before the case is dismissed, the debtor is entitled to the benefit of these payments. Some debts may have been completely paid, or partially paid to an extent sufficient for the debtor to work out an agreement directly with the creditors on the remaining balances due.

Dismissal, like conversion, can also be ordered against the debtor's will, for cause, at the request of any party. In addition to the reasons that might justify conversion, the court may also dismiss the case for failure to pay required fees and charges or for failure to file required documents.[124]

4.8 Discharge

The final step in a successfully completed chapter 13 case, or in one ended under the hardship provisions,[125] is the discharge. A discharge must be granted by the court "as soon as practicable" after completion of all payments under a confirmed plan.[126] There is no possibility of any further objection to discharge at this point. Thereafter, the discharge is revocable only if it was obtained by fraud, and then only if the fraud first came to an objector's attention after the discharge and is raised within a year of the discharge.[127]

The discharge hearing provisions of section 524 apply to chapter 13 cases as well as to chapter 7.[128] Thus, the debtor must seek court approval for any reaffirmation agreement on a consumer debt which is neither secured by real property nor negotiated by an attorney who certifies that it is fully informed, voluntary, and does not pose any hardship for the debtor or the debtor's dependents.[129] The debtor must also receive the "Miranda warnings" about the consequences of reaffirmation at a discharge hearing in every case in which there is a reaffirmation agreement, if the reaffirmation was not negotiated by the debtor's attorney who advised the debtor of those consequences.[130]

The discharge received in a chapter 13 case is often broader than that received in a chapter 7 case. It includes all debts "provided for"[131] by the plan, except:

---

avoidance won in chapter 13 preserved after conversion to chapter 7).

116 11 U.S.C. § 349; *see In re* Sadler, 935 F.2d 918 (7th Cir. 1991).

117 11 U.S.C. § 1307(c).

118 11 U.S.C. § 1307(e). This provision is in accord with the general bar against involuntary bankruptcies involving farmers. *See* 11 U.S.C. § 303(a).

119 11 U.S.C. § 1307(d). For example, when the chapter 13 debt limits make dismissal unexpectedly likely under 11 U.S.C. § 109(e), conversion to chapter 11 remains possible. Rudd v. Laughlin, 866 F.2d 1040 (8th Cir. 1989); *In re* Wenberg, 94 B.R. 631 (B.A.P. 9th Cir. 1988), *aff'd*, 902 F.2d 768 (9th Cir. 1990). See § 6.3.4, *infra*, for a brief discussion of chapter 11 and Chapter 16 for a discussion of chapter 12.

120 11 U.S.C. § 1307(b). See § 13.9.1, *infra*, for further discussion of the right to dismiss a chapter 13 case.

121 The relevant section, 11 U.S.C. § 1307(b), permits dismissal of "a case under this chapter." It is likely that after conversion the case would no longer be under chapter 13 and the right to dismiss would be lost.

122 11 U.S.C. § 349(b).

123 *In re* Nash, 765 F.2d 1410 (9th Cir. 1985). *But see In re* Witte,

279 B.R. 585 (Bankr. E.D. Cal. 2002) (when debtor's house had been sold pursuant to court order prior to dismissal, proceeds held by trustee were not plan proceeds that had to be returned to debtor and had to be turned over to holders of liens on house).

124 11 U.S.C. § 1307(c)(2), (9), (10).

125 11 U.S.C. § 1328(b).

126 11 U.S.C. § 1328(a).

127 11 U.S.C. § 1328(e). See § 14.3, *infra*, for further discussion of revocation of discharge.

128 11 U.S.C. § 103(a); *see* § 3.6, *supra*.

129 11 U.S.C. § 524(c). See Chapter 14, *infra*, for further discussion of reaffirmation agreements.

130 11 U.S.C. § 524(d).

131 11 U.S.C. § 1328(a). See Chapter 14, *infra*, for further discussion of the chapter 13 discharge.

- Long-term debts with final payments due after the completion of the plan that are cured in the plan;
- Most support and alimony payments;
- Many unpaid student loan debts;
- Certain drunk driving debts; and
- Certain criminal fines and restitution debts ordered in connection with a criminal sentence.[132]

Thus, the chapter 13 discharge may eliminate liability on many debts not dischargeable in a chapter 7 case, including those incurred through fraud or false pretenses, willful and malicious injuries, marital property settlements, and certain fines or penalties. However, as in chapter 7, to the extent that a secured creditor's lien has not been disallowed, avoided, or satisfied, that creditor most likely will retain the right to bring an *in rem* action to enforce its lien.[133]

Promptly after the discharge, a notice of discharge is mailed to all creditors and the trustee.[134] The debtor and the debtor's attorney also receive a copy of this notice. Notice of the discharge order normally marks the last activity in the case, although the case may be formally closed later. However, even after the case is closed, the debtor has a broad right to have a case reopened if additional relief is necessary.[135]

---

132   11 U.S.C. § 1328(a).

133   *See* § 14.5.3, *infra*; *see also, e.g.*, Estate of Lellock v. Prudential Ins. Co. of Am., 811 F.2d 186 (3d Cir. 1987); Chandler Bank of Lyons v. Ray, 804 F.2d 577 (10th Cir. 1986).

134   Fed. R. Bankr. P. 4004(g).

135   11 U.S.C. § 350(b); Fed. R. Bankr. P. 5010.

Chapter 5   Getting All the Necessary Facts

5.1 Introduction to Part II of the Manual

5.1.1 How These Chapters Fit In

Chapters 5 through 8, *infra,* unlike the first four chapters, are intended primarily to be a practice guide for practitioners handling consumer bankruptcy cases. To put the practices outlined into a meaningful context, the reader should have a general grasp of the basic concepts of bankruptcy set out in Chapters 1 through 4, *supra.*

These next four chapters describe all of the necessary steps involved in representing consumer debtors in bankruptcy cases. They can serve as a "cookbook" for bankruptcy novices and also a useful self-checkup for those who have already handled many bankruptcy cases. As most of the steps involved in chapter 7 and chapter 13 cases are identical or at least similar, both types of proceedings are considered together.

5.1.2 Roles for Non-Attorneys

As will quickly become apparent, most of the tasks involved in handling a bankruptcy case can be ably accomplished by non-attorney legal workers with a relatively small amount of training. This situation presents a significant advantage to busy offices. Of course, an attorney involved in a case prepared by non-attorneys must supervise and take ultimate responsibility for handling the case. The attorney should review the case prior to filing and at various points thereafter, with particular attention to ascertaining that non-routine circumstances are handled properly.

5.1.3 Use of the Materials in the Manual

To facilitate thorough and competent preparation of bankruptcy cases, this manual also contains a number of other materials. Appendix D, *infra,* contains the Official Bankruptcy Forms in a format suitable for copying. However, for offices with a significant volume of practice, there are now many commercially available computer programs which generate completed high quality forms with input in a standard format. This volume comes with an unsupported version of one such program, *Bankruptcy Forms,* by Law Disks. Appendices E through I, *infra,* contain annotated forms and checklists which should prove useful in most cases. All of these forms and checklists are also on the CD-Rom accompanying this volume. Appendix I, *infra,* contains four form brochures for clients answering common bankruptcy questions. These materials can and should be altered as necessary to meet the needs of particular clients and offices.

Each office or program must decide for itself the exact division of labor between attorney, legal worker, and client which best serves its purposes. While one office may choose to have a paralegal bankruptcy specialist handling most aspects of the case, another may decide that it is appropriate to have many of the details attended to by a secretary or a group with whom the office works. Still others may wish to require clients to do much of the leg work of obtaining necessary information, relying on a detailed questionnaire to guide them. Finally, some will prefer the more traditional method of having most steps taken by an attorney.

5.2 The Importance of Getting All the Facts

Before a bankruptcy case can be filed, it is necessary that a decision be made that bankruptcy is, in fact, the best vehicle for dealing with the problems facing a particular client. Indeed, most of the legal analysis that occurs in a typical consumer bankruptcy case involves comparing bankruptcy with other possible avenues of relief.

An absolutely necessary prerequisite to such consideration, just as in most other legal analysis of real world problems, is knowledge of all the relevant facts. Although it may sometimes be possible to rule out bankruptcy based upon knowledge of only a few facts (for example, that the client does not wish to lose certain property that cannot be saved in bankruptcy), it is never possible to recommend bankruptcy safely without a thorough knowledge of the facts. Without such knowledge, unknown property (such as the right to a tax refund) may be lost in bankruptcy, major debts may turn out to be nondischargeable or unaffected because of security interests, or undervalued property might be determined to be non-exempt and lost.

Of equal importance is the fact that, without complete information, an attorney may not be able to utilize fully the bankruptcy for the debtor's maximum benefit. Substantial hardship may be caused, for example, if a creditor is not notified of the automatic stay before the debtor's car is repossessed because no one checked to see if the debtor was behind in payments to that secured creditor. The debtor's right to avoid or modify a lien may be lost because the existence of the lien is not discovered in the fact-gathering stage of the case. Moreover, debts not listed in the bankruptcy papers might survive a discharge;[1] even if they are discovered during the pendency of the case and can be included, they may lead to additional fees for the debtor and more work for the debtor's attorney.[2]

Finally, much of the information which should be sought early is necessary in any case for proper completion of the bankruptcy forms. It makes sense, then, to obtain this information before, rather than after, there is a commitment to pursue a bankruptcy instead of other possible strategies.

5.3 Methods of Gathering Information

5.3.1 The Initial Interview

The steps necessary to assure complete information will vary somewhat from case to case. For example, if no real estate is involved, a title search might not be necessary; if a client has clearly kept organized and complete records counsel may often rely upon them with little risk.

Normally, the first step is an interview with the client. In addition to the establishment of a relationship, this interview will usually serve to quickly identify most cases in which bankruptcy is not appropriate. Regardless of whether the possibility of a bankruptcy is first broached by a client who believes it is necessary or an attorney whose initial reaction to the case leads in that direction, a few questions will usually reveal the most likely impediments to a successful bankruptcy.

These initial questions should be asked early to get an overview of the client's problems:

- What types of debt are causing the most trouble?
- How were the debts incurred and are they secured?
- What significant assets does the client have?
- How much income does the debtor have available

which is not committed to unavoidable expenses?
- How imminent is creditor action which may limit the client's options?

The answers to these general questions (which, of course, must be put in terms the client understands) will reveal not only the likelihood of relief in a bankruptcy but also many other dimensions of the client's problems: their causes, their scope, whether they are likely to continue or recur, and whether other solutions seem obviously preferable. They can lead naturally into a broad discussion of the problems most troubling to the client.

5.3.2 Filling in the Complete Picture

Once bankruptcy is being seriously considered, and has perhaps been tentatively decided upon, much more information is necessary. Only after all of this information is gathered can bankruptcy be finally recommended. Again, the principal source of information is usually the client, but methods of tapping this source may vary.

Many bankruptcy specialists have clients do much of the information-assembling on their own, through use of a detailed questionnaire phrased in easily understandable terms. One such questionnaire is suggested in Appendix H, *infra.* Practitioners using questionnaires cite two principal advantages. First, they save time, and encourage the client to gather much information prior to a detailed interview. Second, use of a form questionnaire, even if it is completed by the attorney or by the attorney's staff, minimizes the possibility of any later misunderstanding (or malpractice claim) concerning whether the client was asked a particular question.

Whether or not a questionnaire is used, it is important to conduct a careful interview to assure the completeness and accuracy of the data obtained. Even the simplest written questions may not be understood by some clients, and clients may be confused about the purpose of others. They may fail to list debts they wish to pay, or property they do not consider "really" theirs.

The oral and written questions to clients should always be supplemented and checked by obtaining every shred of documentation the client possesses regarding his or her financial situation. Consumer debtors may not realize that security interests have been taken in their property; they may also be unaware of defenses and counterclaims available to them. In addition, the documents will usually provide precise information on the amounts due and the addresses of creditors.

---

1 11 U.S.C. § 523(a)(3). See § 14.4.3.3, *infra,* for discussion of dischargeability of unscheduled debts.

2 The fee currently set by the Administrative Office of the U.S. Courts for an amendment adding a creditor is $26.00. It may be waived upon application to the court in cases of indigent debtors. See § 13.6, *infra,* for discussion of filing documents *in forma pauperis.*

5.3.3 Frequently Missed Information

5.3.3.1 Introduction

Certain types of information, in particular, are frequently overlooked in the handling of bankruptcy cases, especially by practitioners who rely exclusively on questions on the official forms as their interview guide. Given the broad definitions of property and claims in the Code, the forms by themselves are not adequate as a means of inquiring into nontraditional types of assets and debts.

Some of the most commonly missed items in the cases of consumer debtors are listed below. Regardless of the method used to elicit information from a client, inquiry should always be made into the following matters.

5.3.3.2 Property

Among the types of property clients often forget in reporting their assets are long-dormant accounts with savings institutions, such as banks and credit unions. Especially in the case of the latter, the client may not have access to a share balance (deposit) that was required to secure a loan. Nonetheless, such a balance belongs to the client and may become important to the case. Similarly, pledged goods, such as those in the hands of pawnbrokers, are often not considered by clients to be "their own." In each of these cases, as much property as possible should be withdrawn from the hands of others prior to bankruptcy. Not only can this property be converted to exempt assets, if necessary,[3] but the return of the property will avoid later difficulties caused by reluctance of the holding party to relinquish it after the bankruptcy.[4]

Other types of property that clients may not recognize include entitlement to tax refunds or credits, rights to alimony or support arrearages or marital property settlements,[5] rights to inheritance or life insurance proceeds from someone who has recently died or may soon pass away,[6] security deposits given to landlords or utilities, accrued vacation pay, future commissions from sales positions, salary or pension rights, legal claims against third parties,[7] leasehold interests which are of value, shares in housing, shopping, agricultural or other cooperatives, the right to collect money owed to the debtor, and entitlements to government grants such as energy assistance grants.[8] It is crucial to know about all of these interests, both to ensure that they will not be lost and to take full advantage of them. Depending on the circumstances, a bankruptcy petition might be postponed until a tax refund is received or vacation pay or other entitlements are exhausted.[9]

Lastly, insurance interests are often overlooked. Clients may have life insurance with a cash value or credit insurance that can be terminated and "cashed in" at the time of bankruptcy.[10] On the other hand, whether clients have fire or automobile insurance may be an important factor in providing "adequate protection"[11] to creditors who might otherwise be entitled to possession of their security. Local practice usually determines the extent to which the trustee or court will inquire into such nontraditional assets, but there is no excuse for the debtor's counsel being less than fully informed and prepared for all possible problems that might arise.

5.3.3.3 Liabilities

Naturally, the opportunity for discharge of debts in bankruptcy should be used to its fullest, and every conceivable liability should be searched out and considered in weighing the advantages of a petition. Clients do not always realize that they have certain types of debts, especially if payment has not been demanded. Just as a legal claim may be a form of property, so too may a legal claim give rise to a liability if the client is the potential defendant. The terms of a lease or land installment sales contract may be important, espe-

---

3　See Chapter 6, *infra,* for discussion of such "exemption planning." Goods constituting security for a debt should not be transferred, because doing so may risk objections under 11 U.S.C. § 727(a)(2) or 11 U.S.C. § 523(a)(6). *See generally* §§ 14.2.2.2, 14.4.3.6, *infra.*

4　See § 9.4.3, *infra,* for discussion of banks freezing debtors' accounts after a bankruptcy case is filed and § 9.9, *infra,* for discussion of the duty to turn over property of the debtor after filing.

5　Property acquired as a result of a marital settlement or divorce decree within 180 days *after* a bankruptcy case is filed is considered property of the bankruptcy estate. 11 U.S.C. § 541(a)(5); *see* § 2.5, *supra.*

6　If the debtor acquires such rights within 180 days after a bankruptcy is filed, the rights become property of the bankruptcy estate. 11 U.S.C. § 541(a)(5); *see* § 2.5, *supra.*

7　Such legal claims, if not disclosed in the bankruptcy schedules, may later be barred by the doctrine of judicial estoppel. *See* § 7.3.4.2.1, *infra.*

8　*See In re* Thompson, 253 B.R. 823 (Bankr. N.D. Ohio 2000) (debtor's right to partial refund of monies paid to move into retirement community if she moved out within one-hundred months was property of the estate, but trustee had no right to require debtor to move in order to liquidate property). *But see In re* Ball, 201 B.R. 210 (Bankr. N.D. Ill. 1996) (trustee not entitled to cash payment received post-petition in lieu of debtor's accrued sick and vacation days, because payment was discretionary with employer and debtor had no right to receive the money). See § 2.5, *supra,* for further discussion of unusual property interests that may come into the bankruptcy estate.

9　More information concerning the appropriate timing of a bankruptcy filing is contained in § 6.5, *infra.* A more complete discussion of tax returns and their impact on timing a bankruptcy may be found in § 2.5.3, *supra.*

10　See § 12.9.3.3, *infra,* for the possibilities of rejecting executory contracts for credit insurance.

11　Creditors are entitled to "adequate protection" of their interests in collateral as a condition of maintaining the automatic stay. *See* Ch. 9, *infra.*

cially if it is possible to modify them in a chapter 13 case,[12] or if an unfair lease or rent-to-own contract is found.[13] Debts of others for whom clients have cosigned are not usually considered by clients as their own liabilities. Similarly, clients are rarely aware of possible deficiencies remaining after property is repossessed in satisfaction of secured debts, or after vacating a rental property, voluntarily or involuntarily, before the expiration of a lease.

In many states a person is automatically liable for necessaries provided by a third party to an individual's dependents, or for welfare payments provided; few clients are aware of such liabilities. Divorce-related debts, such as money owed on a property settlement, division of marital liabilities, or alimony and child support may also be overlooked. Utility bills paid regularly may be omitted by a client because they are not perceived as comparable to a loan or other long-term debt, or because the client is current on a payment agreement to cure a long-term arrearage. A client may not think it necessary to mention that a driver's license was revoked because of an old tort judgment or fines which may be dischargeable.[14] Likewise, if public benefit overpayments are being deducted from current benefits, a client may feel that fact has little to do with bankruptcy and fail to list such overpayments as debts.[15] A debtor who has been involved in running a business may not realize that sales or payroll taxes which the business failed to pay may become the debtor's liability.

Special care must also be taken to inquire into debts likely to be treated differently in bankruptcy. Unpaid taxes must be carefully analyzed to determine their dischargeability and priority status.[16] Are there large liabilities for student loans, support, or alimony?[17] Has there been recent, improvident use of credit cards, in excess of the credit limits imposed?[18] Clients should be advised, at the same time, of the likely loss of their credit cards due to a bankruptcy.[19]

Bankruptcy clients also may not always recognize when a debt is or may be a secured debt. Some clients, for example, co-sign on debts for others and offer their own property as collateral. This practice is particularly common among elderly clients who are looking for a way to help their adult children. Similarly, as home equity lending becomes more prevalent, clients may forget about second or third mortgages which have not been aggressively collected. And most clients rarely understand (and in some cases may never even know) when a judgment lien has been entered. Often, judgment liens secure a debt after a consumer has been sued on a debt or after a divorce property settlement.

As the presence of a security interest greatly affects the impact of bankruptcy,[20] looking for these types of debts on real property, if necessary by ordering a title search, is very important. Similarly, cars may be used as collateral for lenders other than those making the loan which allowed the client to purchase the car.

Unfortunately, related issues arise with credit card debts and finance company loans. Several retailers claim to have security interests in property purchased with their credit cards. Similarly, some finance company loans which appear to be unsecured have provisions which purport to take personal property as collateral.[21] As discussed elsewhere in this manual, many of those interests are worthless or cannot be documented by the lender.[22] Nevertheless, it is important to be aware of whether these interests exist in formulating an appropriate bankruptcy strategy.[23]

Finally, many debtors ask that certain debts be omitted from their bankruptcy papers because of embarrassment about notifying particular creditors, or because of a continuing intent to repay. The answer to this request must always be that every existing liability has to be listed (including personal debts to family members and friends). The debtor's signature on the schedules is a certification under penalty of perjury that the information provided is complete and accurate. Upon learning this fact, some debtors may instead choose to pay off a particular debt prior to filing so that there is no liability to be listed, although they should be advised of the ramifications if a creditor receives an avoidable preference.[24]

5.3.3.4 Other Aspects of Financial Affairs

Finally, careful inquiry must be made into other areas of the client's affairs that are likely to generate issues if a bankruptcy case is filed. For example:

---

12 See Chapter 12, *infra,* for a discussion of tenants' rights in chapter 13 cases and executory contracts.

13 See § 11.8, *infra,* for discussion of rent-to-own contracts and § 12.9, *infra,* for a general discussion of leases in bankruptcy.

14 See § 14.5.5.1, *infra,* for discussion of restoring drivers' licenses through bankruptcy.

15 See § 14.5.5.4, *infra,* for discussion of discharging public benefit overpayments.

16 See § 14.4.3.1, *infra,* for discussion of taxes that are not dischargeable and methods of obtaining a debtor's tax records.

17 These debts are all, to some extent, nondischargeable in chapter 7 and are usually priority claims. 11 U.S.C. §§ 507(a)(7), 523(a); *see* §§ 12.3.5, 14.4, *infra.*

18 This behavior may cause problems if the creditor claims the debts were incurred under false pretenses and that they are nondischargeable. 11 U.S.C. § 523(a)(2); *see* § 14.4.3.2, *infra.*

19 See § 8.4.2, *infra,* for discussion of the practice of requiring debtors to give up their credit cards.

20 *See* Ch. 11, *infra.*

21 Other creditors, most notably credit unions, may assert that a credit card account is secured by the debtor's automobile or home based on a cross-collateral clause in the card agreement or in other loan agreements the debtor has with the creditor. *See* § 14.5.3, *infra.*

22 *See* § 14.5.3, *infra.* It is likely to cost the creditor more to repossess and resell the property than the property is worth. These claimed "interests" are thus used more for their threat value, than for their real economic worth.

23 *See* §§ 10.4.2.4, 11.4, 11.5, 14.5.2, *infra.*

24 *See* § 10.4.2.6.4, *infra.*

- Are payroll deductions being made, such as to a credit union, that the client can terminate? If so, that step usually prevents later complications of trying to recover money deducted after a bankruptcy is filed. It also increases the client's available income.
- Has the client made any pre-bankruptcy transfer or disposition of property which could cause problems?[25]
- Does the client remember giving a financial statement to any creditor which was not completely true?[26]
- Has there been recent excessive or unusual use of a credit card?[27]
- Are there any criminal prosecutions pending related to bad checks, theft of utility service, conversion of collateral, or other liabilities on debts?[28]
- Is any property that the debtor owns or possesses hazardous or alleged to be hazardous, giving rise to potential liabilities or a diminution in the property's value?[29]

5.3.4 Other Sources of Information

Depending upon the complexity of a client's debt situation, and the completeness of the information obtained from the client, it may be necessary to seek further information elsewhere. One source which should not be overlooked is the creditor to whom a debt is or may be owed. Especially if they think it may be to their benefit, as in a chapter 13 case, creditors are usually quick to respond to inquiries regarding the balance due and the security interests they have. And the same letter which requests this information can also serve notice upon the creditor that it must henceforth communicate only with the attorney and not with the client.[30]

In addition, a credit report, which can be used to check or supplement previous information, may be obtained by the client at no cost or for a small fee.[31] Tax returns, recent pay stubs, and bank statements also will provide information useful in handling the case. Similarly, past appraisals, lien or title searches, or previous years' tax returns may be necessary or helpful. If there are likely to be tax issues, records should be obtained from taxing authorities to ensure that the potential for discharging taxes is maximized by delaying the petition until expiration of an applicable reach back period if necessary.[32] In a few districts, aggressive trustees have been known to use their section 544 "strong arm" powers to avoid unperfected security interests in property such as automobiles,[33] creating equity in the property which the debtor cannot exempt and thereby causing the debtor to lose the property. A lien search may also indicate other liens which the debtor does not remember or know about, and which may be avoided or otherwise dealt with in the bankruptcy.[34] If the value of property is of significant importance, a current formal or informal appraisal may be required to get a full picture of the case.

If there are questions about previous bankruptcy cases filed by the debtor, such as the case number, date filed, or number of earlier cases, information on prior bankruptcy filings may be obtained from the bankruptcy court. Normally, this information is available electronically, through the PACER system[35] or another automated system. In addition, a national database of bankruptcy filings is available through Lexis.

If valuation of an automobile is an issue, the average wholesale and retail values for most models can be obtained from industry guides, such as the Kelley Blue Book and the NADA Used Car Guide. In addition, wholesale values are available on the Internet through the Kelley Blue Book at www.kbb.com, and also at www.autopricing.com or www.carprices.com. Uniform Commercial Code filing information often may be obtained through Lexis.

If valuation of real estate is in doubt, information about recent sales is available from websites such as

---

25 These transfers may be preferences or fraudulent transfers avoidable by the trustee or may give rise to an objection to discharge. *See* Ch. 6, *infra*.

26 If so, that statement may be grounds for a claim that the debt is nondischargeable under 11 U.S.C. § 523(a)(2). *See* § 14.4.3.2, *infra*.

27 This behavior can give rise to claims under 11 U.S.C. § 523(a)(2)(A) for fraud. Particular attention should be paid to the presumption of fraud based on pre-petition purchases of luxury items or use of a credit card for cash advances within sixty days of bankruptcy. 11 U.S.C. § 523(a)(2)(C); *see* § 14.4.3.2, *infra*.

28 *See* §§ 9.4.5, 14.5.5.5, *infra*.

29 If property owned or possessed by the debtor poses or is alleged to pose a threat of imminent and identifiable harm to public health or safety, that fact must also be disclosed in Exhibit C to the bankruptcy petition.

30 *See* Form 2, Appx. G.2, *infra*.

31 Beginning in late 2004, a consumer can obtain one free copy of a credit report per year. To obtain such a report from a nationwide consumer reporting agency, the consumer must make the request through a centralized source that the Federal Trade Commission is to set up through regulations. Usually, reports can also be obtained over the Internet directly from consumer reporting agencies and it may be wise to obtain one while the debtor client is in the attorney's office if a recent report is not already available. For more information on obtaining reports from reporting agencies, which charge about $8.00 per person when a free report is not available, see National Consumer Law Center, Fair Credit Reporting § 4.4.2.1 (5th ed. 2002 and Supp.).

32 See § 14.4.3.1.2, *infra*, for discussion of the dischargeability of taxes and the availability of federal tax records.

33 See § 10.4.2.6.2, *infra*, for discussion of the "strong arm" powers.

34 See Chapters 10 and 11, *infra*, for discussion of ways to deal with secured creditors.

35 Access to the PACER system, administered by the courts, is available at www.pacer.psc.uscourts.gov. A national search of bankruptcy filings can be made on PACER using the "U.S. Party/Case Index."

www.domania.com and www.homegain.com. In addition, multiple listings of homes currently on the market can be accessed through www.realtor.com.

5.4 Impressing upon Clients the Need for Full and Accurate Information

No matter what method is used to inquire into the client's situation, it is crucial that the client understand the importance of providing every detail requested. A lack of trust or other feeling on the part of a client that something should be concealed must be dispelled.

Usually the best way to do this is to paint a vivid picture of the worst consequences which can result from less than full disclosure, while at the same time emphasizing the confidentiality of the attorney-client relationship. It should be made clear that property not listed as exempt may be lost and that debts not reported may not be discharged. It should also be pointed out that there is often a filing fee for amending the papers, and (in a non-threatening manner, of course) that by giving incomplete or false information under oath on the bankruptcy forms the debtor risks not only losing the bankruptcy discharge but also criminal prosecution.

More than anything else, though, it should be emphasized that representation in the client's case may suffer if counsel has less than the whole story and that the real loser in this case will be the client. Once they understand this reality (which indeed is the central point of this Chapter) most clients realize the importance of a real effort on their part to help develop the facts of the case.

Chapter 6	Counseling the Consumer Debtor: Does Bankruptcy Provide the Best Solution and, If So, How and When?

6.1 Introduction

6.1.1 Explaining the Options to Clients

Whether, how, and when to file a bankruptcy petition is probably the most important single decision made in a bankruptcy case. Like most questions of legal strategy, it is rarely simple. It involves the interplay of a number of factors. Many of these are unique to each client; others turn on state law, custom, or practice in a community, or the provisions of the Bankruptcy Code. This chapter describes the considerations and alternatives which should be explored in the representation of consumer debtors, as well as steps that could improve the debtor's position before a bankruptcy case is filed.

Naturally, it is important early on to explain to clients the options being considered, and what they would entail. In cases in which bankruptcy is a serious possibility, the general principles and procedures involved should be discussed.[1] Often, it is necessary to dispel some of the common myths that exist about bankruptcy, for example, that debtors will lose all of their property, or that the law prohibits the acquisition of property or credit after bankruptcy.

In many cases, it is also crucial to deal with the perceived stigma of bankruptcy. The moral overtones of not paying one's debts (which, of course, are constantly reinforced by those to whom debts are owed) are frequently forgotten by those who deal with such problems on a daily basis. The idea of bankruptcy, which represents a declaration of sorts that a debtor does not intend to pay, may be difficult for clients to accept at first, especially if they have been continually and sincerely insisting to creditors that they do intend to make good on their obligations.

For these clients, some counseling is especially helpful. They should be reminded that bankruptcy is their right under the law, provided for in the Constitution, intended to provide a fresh start for those in precisely their situation, and that big corporations, like Texaco, Macy's, T.W.A., and Penn Central, and famous people, such as Jerry Lewis, Mickey Rooney, Tammy Wynette and even former Treasury Secretary John Connally, have not hesitated to utilize this right. It might help to point out that the "stigma" of bankruptcy is largely a creation of creditors who have every reason to make bankruptcy appear unattractive, and that bankruptcies are not generally publicized in newspapers or elsewhere, although they are a matter of public record. Some clients might find comfort in the fact that the Bible itself provides for periodic release from debts:

> At the end of every seven years thou shalt make a release. And this is the manner of the release: every creditor shall release that which he hath lent unto his neighbor and his brother; because the Lord's release hath been proclaimed.[2]

Lastly, the alternatives to bankruptcy must be explained. What are the likely results of doing nothing? Are there other ways available to defend against the largest and most troublesome debts? What would be the consequences of waiting until later before filing a bankruptcy petition?

6.1.2 Methods of Explaining Bankruptcy

Certainly the most common method of explaining these subjects is through a face-to-face discussion during the client interview. Not surprisingly, many bankruptcy specialists have found that doing this job can be both time-consuming and repetitive. For that reason, some have chosen to give most of this general information in written form and to supplement that information in the interview. A model client information brochure is provided in Appendix I, *infra*.[3] Some bankruptcy practice manuals contain similar

---

1 The 1984 Bankruptcy Amendments specifically require a debtor's attorney to certify that the debtor has received an explanation of the relief available under the different chapters of the Code. The required certification is now incorporated into the bankruptcy petition form. *See* Official Form 1, Appx. D, *infra*.

2 *Deut.* 15:1–2.

3 In addition, the American Bar Association publishes a short pamphlet entitled "Bankruptcy and Alternatives" (fifty copies for $2.50) and a longer booklet, "Your Guide to Consumer

materials. Clients seeking further information may also be referred to books about bankruptcy for lay audiences, which are available in most public libraries.[4] They may also be able to access a wealth of information on the Internet at websites like www.uscourts.gov/library/bankbasic.pdf, but they should be cautioned that the Internet can also be a source of misinformation.[5]

The National Consumer Law Center's *NCLC Guide to Surviving Debt*[6] is a good introduction for individual consumers to a variety of strategies for dealing with consumer debt. The *NCLC Guide to Surviving Debt* includes chapters on dealing with debt collectors, setting priorities for debt payments, raising defenses to debt collection lawsuits, preventing evictions, and negotiating mortgage workout agreements among other things. Basic bankruptcy information is also included.

The *NCLC Guide to Surviving Debt* was written by NCLC staff for use by individual consumers and their advocates. The book thus provides a useful supplement to what you can offer in a basic bankruptcy or debt counseling consultation.[7]

6.2 Advantages and Disadvantages of Bankruptcy

6.2.1 Advantages: The Uses of Bankruptcy

6.2.1.1 Discharge of Most Debts

In a sense, most of this manual is devoted to describing the advantages of bankruptcy for consumer debtors and showing how to make the most of those advantages. Before a client can make an intelligent decision on a course of action, the advantages applicable to that client's case, and the disadvantages, if any, must be explained.

The principal goal of most bankruptcies is to achieve the total discharge of most unsecured debts. Bankruptcy is a relatively quick and easy way to end the creditor harassment (though, of course, there are other ways to curtail this),[8] hardship, anxiety, and marital stress normally associated with debt overload.

6.2.1.2 Protection of Property and Income from Unsecured Creditors

Bankruptcy is often the only sure way to protect a debtor's property from execution by unsecured creditors. Bankruptcy may provide total protection for a home, car, or other vital property. The amount of property debtors are allowed to protect from creditors through use of exemptions in bankruptcy is, in many states, far greater than the amount they can protect in state law execution processes.[9]

Even when state exemptions from execution are similar to or better than the federal bankruptcy exemptions or when the federal exemptions are not available, bankruptcy allows the debtor to avoid having to assert the exemptions repeatedly in response to the execution attempts of different creditors. Once a bankruptcy case is filed, an unsecured creditor holding a dischargeable claim, including a dischargeable tax claim, is ordinarily stayed from ever obtaining a lien on the debtor's property, even a lien that, had it been obtained prior to bankruptcy, could not have been eliminated by the bankruptcy.[10] Normally bankruptcy also

---

Credit and Bankruptcy" ($1.00). The American Bar Association now publishes a booklet entitled "Your Legal Guide to Consumer Credit" which contains a seven-page section on bankruptcy and other alternatives for dealing with debts ($2.00).

4 *See, e.g.,* Henry J. Sommer, Consumer Bankruptcy: The Complete Guide to Chapter 7 and Chapter 13 Personal Bankruptcy (1994) (an abridged version of this manual with additional materials on alternatives to bankruptcy and other topics); Stephen Elias et al., How to File for Chapter 7 Bankruptcy (11th ed. 2004); Kenneth J. Doran, Personal Bankruptcy and Debt Adjustment: A Step-By-Step Guide (2d ed. 1995); Janice Kosel, Bankruptcy: Do It Yourself (1986). Because some of these sources may not reflect the most recent changes to the Code, rules and forms, clients should be advised that they may not be entirely accurate. Another useful book for clients who decide to file a bankruptcy case is John Ventura, Fresh Start!: Surviving Money Troubles, Rebuilding Your Credit, Recovering Before or After Bankruptcy (1992). Another resource, available for use by bankruptcy attorneys at no charge from King's Press at www.bankruptcybooks.com is Morgan D. King & Nancy Finley-King, How to Rebuild Your Credit (4th Ed. 1998).

5 For example, the website www.bankruptcy.com contains creditor propaganda urging people not to file bankruptcy cases.

6 (2002 ed.).

7 The *NCLC Guide to Surviving Debt* can be ordered for $19.00 per copy (with discounts for bulk orders) by calling NCLC at (617) 542-9595.

---

8 Harassment by collection agencies and by certain attorneys acting as debt collectors is regulated by the Fair Debt Collection Practices Act, 15 U.S.C. §§ 1692–1692*o*. Actions of creditors may violate state tort law on the grounds of intentional infliction of emotional distress or invasion of privacy, as well as state statutes dealing with unfair and deceptive practices. *See* National Consumer Law Center, Fair Debt Collection § 4.2.7 (5th ed. 2004).

9 The federal and state exemption laws are discussed in Chapter 10, *infra*.

10 This issue is complicated in some cases when tax lien creditors have a pre-petition interest in the debtor's property pursuant to state law that may be perfected post-petition. 11 U.S.C.

serves to prevent any garnishment of wages or other income after the petition is filed. This result, in turn, may protect a client's job if the client's employer does not favor multiple wage garnishments.[11] Even recoupment of social security or other public benefit overpayments should be preventable by a timely bankruptcy petition.[12]

6.2.1.3 Tools for Eliminating or Modifying Secured Debts

Under the Code, bankruptcy gives debtors mechanisms to deal with most secured creditors. Many types of liens may be eliminated, either because they impair exemptions,[13] or because they are in reality undersecured.[14] In a chapter 13 case, payments on most other secured debts can be lowered,[15] and a reasonable time can be gained to cure any defaulted secured debt.[16] Often, one or more of these aspects of bankruptcy will make it possible for a client to retain a home, car, or furniture that would otherwise be lost.

6.2.1.4 Automatic Stay

Sometimes, the most valuable feature of a bankruptcy is the automatic stay, gained instantaneously upon the filing of a petition. The stay forces an abrupt halt of most creditor actions against the debtor, including repossessions, garnishments or attachments, utility shut-offs, foreclosures, and evictions.[17] Many of these collection actions can thereafter be permanently prevented.[18] The stay is also an effective way (though, again, hardly the only way) to end creditor collection efforts, with contempt, or money damages, and attorney fees as available remedies for violations of the stay.[19] Furthermore, the stay affords the debtor a breathing spell—a chance to sort things out—through the additional time gained to solve problems.

In addition to the automatic stay available in every bankruptcy case, chapter 13 provides a special automatic stay of creditor actions against most people who are codebtors with the debtor.[20] This codebtor stay, which can relieve creditor pressure on friends or relatives of the debtor, may be an important reason to file a chapter 13 case.

6.2.1.5 Other Protections Available Through Bankruptcy

Bankruptcy may offer the only possible way for a client to keep or regain a driver's license subject to revocation because of an unpaid accident judgment.[21] Keeping the license, in turn, may mean employment and income for the client's family. Bankruptcy may, in some cases, literally mean freedom for a debtor who might otherwise be incarcerated for failure to pay support obligations,[22] or as a result of a contempt proceeding involving some other debt.[23] Even for taxes that cannot be discharged, a chapter 13 case may save the debtor thousands of dollars in interest and penalties.[24] The Code also protects the debtor from many types of discriminatory action by governmental units and private employers on the basis of unpaid debts discharged in bankruptcy.[25] Nor can a private party take any action intended to coerce payment of such debts.[26]

6.2.1.6 Litigation Advantages of the Bankruptcy Forum

An important factor to consider in opting for bankruptcy is the opportunity to litigate disputes with creditors in a federal court, which has at least initial jurisdiction over such disputes after a case has been filed.[27] In some places the bankruptcy court may provide a far more sympathetic forum than the local state court, and it may be far more familiar with the applicable law. It may also offer procedural advan-

---

§ 362(b)(3); *see In re* Parr Meadows Racing Ass'n, Inc., 880 F.2d 1540 (2d Cir. 1989).

11 Garnishments are limited by the Consumer Credit Protection Act, 15 U.S.C. § 1674, as is the employer's right to discharge employees due to garnishment. The laws of many states further restrict the extent to which wages may be garnished.

12 See § 14.5.5.4, *infra,* for discussion of the discharge of debts arising out of public benefits programs.

13 See § 10.4.2, *infra,* for discussion of liens which impair exemptions.

14 See Chapter 11, *infra,* for discussion of liens which can be modified because they are undersecured.

15 See Chapter 11, *infra,* for discussion of the right to modify secured claims in chapter 13 cases.

16 See § 11.6.2, *infra,* for discussion of the right to cure defaults within a reasonable time in chapter 13 cases.

17 See Chapter 9, *infra,* for discussion of the automatic stay.

18 The creditor normally may not have the stay lifted prior to the end of the case, except in certain specified circumstances. 11 U.S.C. § 362(d); *see* Ch. 9, *infra.* If the debt is discharged during the case, 11 U.S.C. § 524(a) prevents any act to collect it after the case is over, though some liens may survive bankruptcy.

19 11 U.S.C. § 362(h). For discussion of remedies for violation of the stay order, see § 9.6, *infra.*

20 See § 9.4.4, *infra,* for discussion of the codebtor stay, which is also available in chapter 12 cases.

21 Normally, such revocation cannot be continued after discharge of the judgment. Perez v. Campbell, 402 U.S. 637, 91 S. Ct. 1704, 29 L. Ed. 2d 233 (1971); *see* § 14.5.5.1, *infra.*

22 Dischargeability of these obligations is discussed in Chapter 14, *infra.* See also Chapter 12, *infra,* for discussion of use of chapter 13 in support cases.

23 *See, e.g.,* Judice v. Vail, 430 U.S. 327, 97 S. Ct. 1211, 51 L. Ed. 2d 376 (1977). The bankruptcy court or district court may exercise its *habeas corpus* powers to end a debt-related incarceration. *See also* Ch. 3, *infra.*

24 Generally, no post-petition interest need be paid on unsecured tax claims that are paid through a chapter 13 plan, even if they are priority claim. *See* § 12.3.5, *infra.*

25 11 U.S.C. § 525; *see* § 14.5.4, *infra.*

26 11 U.S.C. § 524(a); *see* Ch. 14, *infra.*

27 28 U.S.C. § 1334(a), (b), (d); *see* § 13.2, *infra.*

tages, such as greater discovery rights[28] or the ability to serve distant defendants.[29] Other rights, such as statutes of limitations[30] or sovereign immunity,[31] may also be affected to the client's advantage.

In sum, then, bankruptcy may be the best way, if not the only way, to save a home, a job, a car, or thousands of dollars for a client. It may even mean a debtor's freedom, literally as well as figuratively.

6.2.2 Reasons for Not Filing a Bankruptcy Case

6.2.2.1 Overview

Despite all of the possible advantages that bankruptcy may provide, there are many valid reasons for choosing not to file a petition. Some of these concern problems in the cases of particular clients, and others relate simply to the fact that bankruptcy is not the only means to address a client's legal problems and may not be necessary.

6.2.2.2 Loss of Property in Bankruptcy

One consequence of a chapter 7 bankruptcy is the loss of non-exempt property (or its value in cash). For most consumer clients this potential loss is not a problem because consumer debtors rarely have any non-exempt property. Except in those few states which not only have low exemptions but also have opted out of the federal exemptions,[32] the amount of property a debtor is allowed to keep is relatively generous; only debtors with equity substantially over $18,000.00 per debtor in a home, $2950.00 in a car, or $9850.00 in household goods and certain other property are likely to have any problems under the federal exemptions.[33] Some states have more generous exemptions. Even when a debtor has non-exempt property, a chapter 13 bankruptcy often presents a viable alternative through which debtors may retain all of their possessions.

6.2.2.3 Effect on Credit and Reputation

Invariably, a bankruptcy will be part of a debtor's credit history for as long as the law allows, which is ten years

under the Fair Credit Reporting Act.[34] The effect this notation will have on future credit is less predictable, but it is an understandable concern to many clients.

There is no definite response to this concern. However, clients should be reminded that if they have substantial debts, and especially if they are in default, their credit histories are already poor. In the eyes of some creditors, a bankruptcy that wipes the slate clean will be an improvement. Not only will the potential customer be free of other financial obligations, but she will also be unable to obtain a chapter 7 discharge, in most cases,[35] for another six years. For these reasons, some creditors have been known to actively solicit recent bankruptcy debtors.

In any case, the available research on the subject is inconclusive.[36] It is fair to say is that each credit decision turns on the bias of the individual creditor and that most creditors look more to a potential customer's current income situation, and its stability, than anything else.[37] Most creditors have chosen not to exclude automatically all of the millions of people who have filed a bankruptcy case, especially if a few years have passed since the filing. Indeed, as credit standards have loosened in recent years, bankruptcy debtors have regularly been offered new credit, even while they are still in bankruptcy, though often on fairly unfavorable terms. And clients should also be reminded that they always have the option of voluntarily paying a favored creditor with whom they wish to maintain a line of credit, either before the bankruptcy (though preferences of over $600.00 within ninety days should be avoided if possible)[38] or afterward.[39] It is often possible for a client to pay off a low balance on at least one credit card prior to bankruptcy, so that the creditor need not be listed on the schedules. In

---

28 Basically, the Rules of Bankruptcy Procedure incorporate the liberal federal discovery rules. Fed. R. Bankr. P. 7026–7037, 9014.

29 The venue provisions of 28 U.S.C. § 1408 essentially provide for nationwide service of process. *See* § 13.3.2.1, *infra.*

30 *See* 11 U.S.C. § 108.

31 *See* 11 U.S.C. § 106; *see also* § 13.3.2.2, *infra.*

32 See § 10.2.1, *infra,* for discussion of states' rights to opt out of the federal exemptions.

33 See § 10.2, *infra,* for discussion of the interplay of the dollar limits among the federal exemption provisions.

---

34 15 U.S.C. § 1681c(a)(1); *see also* § 8.9, *infra.*

35 *See* 11 U.S.C. § 727(a)(8), (9); *see also* § 14.2.2, *infra.* However, the continued availability of a chapter 13 discharge within six years may soon come to be understood by creditors.

36 One study, albeit somewhat dated, is contained in D. Stanley & M. Girth, Bankruptcy: Problem, Process, Reform 62–65 (1971). This study found wide regional variations in ability to obtain credit. However seventy percent of those interviewed had made major purchases on credit since bankruptcy, and only about one-third found credit harder to get after bankruptcy. A similar number found no change and eight percent found getting credit easier; twelve percent had not tried to obtain credit.

37 Each creditor uses its own mix of closely guarded criteria including income, assets, job stability, and so forth.

38 See § 10.4.2.6.4, *infra,* for a discussion of preferences. While there is nothing illegal or immoral about a debtor making a preferential transfer before bankruptcy, the trustee may avoid many such transfers if she chooses. Therefore, if the property to be transferred can be claimed as exempt in the bankruptcy, the debtor may be advised to transfer it after the bankruptcy to eliminate the risk of avoidance of the transfer by the trustee.

39 These debts may or may not be reaffirmed. A debtor may choose to continue payments after bankruptcy without reaffirming the obligation. *See* § 14.5.2, *infra.*

most such cases, the creditor will then permit continued use of the credit card after bankruptcy.[40]

As discussed earlier, the effect of a bankruptcy on a client's reputation in the community is almost always imperceptible. However, in a small town, especially if debts are owed to local people, the stigma of bankruptcy cannot be entirely discounted. The potential harm can only be evaluated locally, on a case-by-case basis, and weighed against the advantages that bankruptcy has to offer. Again, the possibility of voluntarily paying selected debts should not be overlooked if that would ameliorate the problem.

6.2.2.4 Possible Discrimination After Bankruptcy

6.2.2.4.1 *The available protections*

Closely related to the problem of reputation is that of discrimination against debtors who have filed bankruptcy cases. To a large extent, the Bankruptcy Code alleviates this problem.

Under the Code, governmental units[41] generally may not discriminate on the basis of a bankruptcy filing.[42] Thus, a housing authority or student loan agency cannot deny benefits to a client based upon a previously discharged debt.[43] Similarly, utilities may not deny service based upon a bankruptcy or discharged debts.[44] Nor may any private employer discriminate with respect to employment or terminate employment based upon bankruptcy or debts discharged in bankruptcy.[45] Clients can be assured that the law protects them in this regard and that they will be able to enforce their rights in court, if necessary.

However, the distinction between discrimination based upon bankruptcy or debts discharged in bankruptcy and discrimination based upon future financial responsibility or ability should be carefully explained.[46] That is, a client

should be told that even creditors who are precluded from discrimination based on bankruptcy may refuse new credit or other services if the refusal is properly based on other considerations.[47]

The law regarding discrimination by other private entities, such as creditors who provide essential services, is not as clear. It should be pointed out that this type of discrimination is extremely rare, especially in more urban areas where many providers of goods and services are available to a client. It would be most likely to occur in a small town, where only one merchant offers a particular product or service. In that case, at least if it can be shown that later discrimination was an attempt to coerce payment of a debt, the client would also have a remedy.[48]

Again, the situation can best be assessed locally, on a case-by-case basis. Normally discrimination against debtors who have filed bankruptcy cases is not a problem, but if a practitioner is in doubt, the chapter 13 standing trustee or a more experienced bankruptcy attorney may be consulted.

6.2.2.4.2 *Medical debts*

Medical debts to doctors or hospitals with whom a patient would like to have a continuing relationship are often a source of concern. Particularly in small communities where there may be few health care providers, clients may worry that a discharge will leave them with few options for future care.

One response is that, if the client cannot pay the debts anyway, the doctor or hospital involved may have little concern about a bankruptcy discharge. Often a frank discussion with a sympathetic doctor about inability to pay will allay any concern about future refusal to provide service.

A second option is for the debtor to agree to make voluntary payments after the bankruptcy.[49] In extreme cases, even reaffirmation of a particular debt may be appropriate.[50] Before taking such drastic action, however, the debtor should be reminded that the ethical obligations of doctors and hospitals should preclude their refusal to provide service to patients who are in extreme need. Moreover, even the most recalcitrant doctor will generally provide care if cash payments or medical coverage is offered, and many hospitals have a legal obligation under state or federal law to provide free medical care.[51]

---

40 Indeed, it has been held that, at least in the case of a chapter 13 debtor, a creditor has no right to revoke a non-delinquent credit card based solely on a bankruptcy filing, because under 11 U.S.C. § 541(c)(1)(B) the pre-petition property rights of the debtor become property of the bankruptcy estate notwithstanding any contractual provision that gives an option to terminate the contract upon a bankruptcy filing. *In re* Knapp, 137 B.R. 582 (Bankr. D.N.J. 1992).

41 The term "governmental unit" is defined in 11 U.S.C. § 101(27).

42 11 U.S.C. § 525(a); *see* § 14.5.4, *infra*.

43 *In re* Gibbs, 9 B.R. 758 (Bankr. D. Conn. 1981), *later proceeding at* 12 B.R. 737 (Bankr. D. Conn. 1981), *aff'd* 76 B.R. 257 (D. Conn. 1983); *see also* 11 U.S.C. § 525(c) (clarifying that discrimination in the granting of student loans is prohibited).

44 11 U.S.C. § 366. However, utilities may be able to demand adequate assurance of future payments. *See* § 9.8, *infra*.

45 11 U.S.C. § 525(b); *see* § 14.5.4, *infra*.

46 The legislative history makes clear that it is not prohibited discrimination to take into account such factors as financial responsibility and ability to repay, if this is done with all people and not just those who have filed bankruptcy cases. H.R. Rep.

No. 95-595, at 81 (1977); *see* Ch. 14, *infra*.

47 As with any discrimination issue, questions may arise about whether a creditor's articulated reason for refusing credit or services is a pretext for bankruptcy discrimination.

48 11 U.S.C. § 524(a) prohibits any act to collect a discharged debt. *See* § 14.5, *infra*.

49 11 U.S.C. § 524(f). As discussed above, a refusal to provide service which is directed at coercing payments on a discharged debt is an actionable violation of the discharge injunction.

50 11 U.S.C. § 524(c); *see* § 8.8.2, *infra*.

51 For example, the Hill-Burton uncompensated care assurance

In summary, there is no completely satisfactory answer to questions about future health care because a doctor has no legally enforceable obligation to provide care to a debtor who has discharged prior medical debts. However, the problem should rarely affect access to needed care.

6.2.2.5 Clients' Feelings of Moral Obligation

Another factor mitigating against bankruptcy may be the client's personal feelings on the subject. This difficult subject, which is generally outside a lawyer's training, must be discussed carefully and with understanding. Remember, it is not easy for clients suddenly to decide to seemingly discard those values which may have guided them since childhood.

Usually, it is best to remind the client of other values which must also be considered. Besides the fact that bankruptcy is a right guaranteed by law and provided for in the Constitution[52] and even the Bible,[53] a client should consider the hardship bankruptcy may avoid for her family. It may be the only way to provide the family with food, clothing, and shelter in hard times. Very often, clients decide that the moral obligation to provide for loved ones outweighs the obligation to pay their creditors.

It may also be possible to explore chapter 13 with clients who wish to pay some or all of their debts. In some cases, a chapter 13 bankruptcy may provide a viable mechanism for repaying creditors as well as solving other problems, if the debtor has sufficient income. Lastly, clients should be reminded that filing a bankruptcy case does not prevent them from voluntarily paying their debts at a later time if they wish.[54] This realization, too, provides comfort to those who cannot come to terms with the idea of turning their backs on their creditors forever.

6.2.2.6 Cost of Filing a Bankruptcy Petition

Besides any attorney fee, bankruptcy carries an out-of-pocket cost, normally $209.00 in a chapter 7 case and $194.00 in a chapter 13 case.[55] Occasionally, other fees may raise this figure somewhat. And, in a chapter 13 case, the trustee is usually entitled to a commission of up to ten percent of the payments made through the plan.[56] Also, in some cases, various utilities may require security deposits to ensure future service.[57]

These costs, like those other tangible costs, must be weighed in deciding whether to file a bankruptcy case. Usually, however, the other factors discussed in this Chapter are considerably more important.

6.2.2.7 Is Bankruptcy Necessary?

The question of fees leads back to a more basic issue. In some states, there are debtors who are totally judgment-proof at the time they seek advice. Legally, creditors can do virtually nothing to harm these clients.

In such cases, several other factors must be considered. Is the client likely to fall further into debt? For some clients the answer is no; their debts arose before they lost a job because of layoff, disability, or retirement. For many, though, there is a prospect of medical bills, or other continuing financial problems which will result in greater debt. For most, there is also a slight possibility of a motor vehicle accident or other incident creating a large liability.

Some debtors have only a few debts and have strong defenses to each. For those debtors, the best avenue might be either litigation or settlement outside of bankruptcy court. This decision may also depend on whether resources are available to make the alternative of vigorous litigation a possibility.

Still others, if they have more than modest incomes, may be able to avoid bankruptcy by reevaluating their lifestyle or the budget choices they make. In extreme cases, if such debtors choose to file, they will be vulnerable to a claim of bad faith or "substantial abuse" of chapter 7.[58] When appropriate, such debtors might be referred to a debt counseling process.

In all of these cases, a client should be advised to bear in mind that the same relief in bankruptcy will almost always be available later,[59] but that filing a bankruptcy case now

---

requirements apply to hospitals which have received federal funds. *See* 42 C.F.R. §§ 124.501–124.518. Hospitals are also limited in turning away patients with medical emergencies by the Emergency Medical Treatment and Women in Active Labor Act, 42 U.S.C. § 1395dd, and may have other obligations to serve the community due to their charitable status.

52   U.S. Const. art. I, § 8 provides that Congress has the power to establish uniform bankruptcy laws.

53   *See Deut.* 15:1–2.

54   11 U.S.C. § 524(f).

55   The filing fee for each chapter under 28 U.S.C. § 1930(a) is $155.00. Under 28 U.S.C. § 1930(b), the federal Judicial Conference decided to assess an additional noticing fee of $39.00 in connection with all chapter 7 and chapter 13 filings, so that the initial fee for a chapter 13 case now totals $194.00. In addition, the federal Judicial Conference has mandated a $15.00 fee for chapter 7 debtors to pay compensation to chapter 7 trustees. The

---

noticing fee and trustee fee, like the filing fees, can be paid in installments, and the form application to pay the filing fee in installments has been modified to accommodate this possibility. Fed. R. Bankr. P. 1006; *see* Appx. D, *infra*. Moreover, these two fees should be waivable by the courts for indigent debtors, because they are imposed under 28 U.S.C. § 1930(b). *See* § 13.6, *infra*. See Form 7, Appendix G.3, *infra*, for an Application to Waive Administrative Fees. See also § 3.2.2, *supra*, for discussion of recent fee changes.

56   However, debts paid outside the plan in a chapter 13 case may not be subject to the commission. *See* Ch. 12, *infra*.

57   11 U.S.C. § 366(b); *see* § 9.8, *infra*.

58   *See* § 13.9.2, *infra*.

59   A warning, however, should be added, that if the client's situation changes greatly, or if the law changes, for example, the state opts out of the federal exemptions, bankruptcy may not be

may impair the right to file another case in years to come.[60] Thus, unless a judgment-proof debtor expects to soon acquire non-exempt property, she may wish to wait.

Ultimately, the client must make a choice. Do the advantages of bankruptcy outweigh the disadvantages? Will bankruptcy in some way have a positive effect on that client's life? Obviously, for many consumer clients who face real threats that bankruptcy can eliminate, the answer is yes. But even those clients who are not in danger of sustaining a tangible loss may value the peace of mind that comes from having their burden of debt lifted. Whether they arise from the hope of someday making it out of a life of poverty, or simply from the anxiety of constantly feeling pressure to pay what is owed, these feelings should not be discounted. Thus, the decision of an informed client as to whether to file a bankruptcy petition should almost always be respected.[61]

6.2.2.8 The Case in Which Bankruptcy Offers No Help or Is Unavailable

6.2.2.8.1 When bankruptcy will not help

Finally, there are some cases in which bankruptcy is the wrong tool to use and in which none of the advantages listed above will be realized.

One such situation is that of the debtor whose debts are fully secured by security interests or other liens that cannot be eliminated or modified through bankruptcy, and who does not have sufficient income to remedy a default even with all of the help bankruptcy provides. Unless there is some special advantage to litigating in bankruptcy court, bankruptcy will not solve the basic problems this debtor faces. At most, it may discharge the debtor's personal liability for the debts and gain the advantage of the automatic stay for a month or more.[62] Although in some cases these results could be worthwhile, in many it will not ultimately benefit the client.

The problem of clients in these predicaments is often that their current expenses exceed their income. Because bankruptcy (except for chapter 13's ability to stretch out or reduce certain types of short-term expenses) basically deals with assets and liabilities, it does not directly address this problem in most cases.

The opposite situation can also sometimes cause problems. If a debtor has substantial and valuable unencumbered property which cannot be exempted, a premature bankruptcy will generally hasten loss of the property rather than prevent it. Because unsecured creditors would have to obtain judgment liens or levies on the debtor's property under state law, execution outside bankruptcy may be quite slow. On the other hand, liquidation of non-exempt property generally occurs quickly in the bankruptcy process. And, as unsecured creditors are entitled to the present value of non-exempt property in chapter 13, a case under that chapter could be quite costly. In this situation, the best option is probably to advise the client to wait at least until execution on the property appears imminent, unless the client can afford the necessary chapter 13 case.

Another potentially difficult situation arises when a client holds property in trust for children or other relatives. Because a trust may not file a bankruptcy petition, it may be difficult to gain the protection of bankruptcy for such property. However, in some cases relief may be possible if the beneficiaries of the trust file cases on their own behalf, which could protect their beneficial interests in the property. Alternatively, a trustee's bare legal title may be sufficient to invoke the automatic stay while a creditor secured by the property in question is paid through the trustee's chapter 13 plan.[63]

6.2.2.8.2 Clients who have filed prior bankruptcy cases

Some clients may be barred from filing a bankruptcy altogether for some period of time. If a client was the debtor in a bankruptcy dismissed in the previous 180 days, and that dismissal was (1) for willful failure to abide by court orders or to appear in court in proper prosecution of the case or (2) a voluntary dismissal following a request for relief from the automatic stay of section 362, then that client is not eligible to be a debtor until 180 days after the dismissal.[64] Occasionally, a court has entered, or a client has agreed to, an order that bars the client from filing a new case for some specified period of time or that purports to limit the client's protection under the automatic stay. Such an order or agreement may sometimes be reconsidered, or challenged in a later case, but otherwise it may be a significant hurdle.[65] In any event, if a client has filed prior bankruptcy cases in the recent past, the situation must be examined carefully to determine whether a new case is likely to succeed or whether it will fail for the same reasons that the prior cases failed. Debtors' attorneys should not become participants in

---

as attractive in the future. This advice may be somewhat more risky at present, because Congress is considering legislation which would overhaul the bankruptcy law and undermine consumer relief. *See* § 1.4.4.1, *supra.* Careful attorneys may wish to keep a list of clients who were advised to delay bankruptcy in order to bring them back to the office for a further consultation if changes to the Code become imminent.

60 11 U.S.C. § 727(a)(8), (9). See § 14.2.2.8, *infra,* for a discussion of the bar to future chapter 7 cases.

61 However, an attorney is not necessarily obligated to represent the client in the course of action chosen.

62 *See* Ch. 9, *infra.*

63 *See In re* Foster, 19 B.R. 28 (Bankr. E.D. Pa. 1982). See also § 2.5, *supra,* for discussion of trust property.

64 11 U.S.C. § 109(g). See § 3.2.1, *supra,* for discussion of this provision. *See also* § 9.7.3.1.5, *infra.*

65 *See* § 9.7.3.1.5, *infra.*

their clients' efforts to abuse the bankruptcy process by filing repeated cases that have no chance of success.

Lastly, some clients may stand to gain little from a chapter 7 bankruptcy because they cannot receive a discharge due to a prior bankruptcy. For these clients the prospect is somewhat brighter. In most cases, a chapter 13 case is still available to provide significant relief.[66] When a client is advised not to pursue bankruptcy or makes that choice after consultation, additional counseling may be necessary. For example, such clients are likely to need advice about non-bankruptcy approaches to debt problems and their consumer rights. Much of that information is collected in NCLC's publication the *NCLC Guide to Surviving Debt*.[67]

6.3 Choosing the Type of Bankruptcy Case

6.3.1 Introduction

Bound up with the decision of whether to file a bankruptcy case is the question of which type of bankruptcy offers the greatest benefit to a client. Although this decision may be changed at least once as of right by converting the case after it is filed, it is nonetheless of obvious importance to ultimately settle upon the chapter offering the greatest advantages for a client.

6.3.2 Considerations Favoring Chapter 7

For many consumer debtors, straight bankruptcy, now provided for in chapter 7 of the Code, has traditionally been the remedy chosen. There are a number of reasons why chapter 7 usually meets the needs of the low-income debtor in particular.

First, one of the main factors leading to a chapter 13 case—the desire to protect non-exempt property—is rarely present. A low-income debtor in most states will rarely have any non-exempt property. Nor will she be likely to have any excess income, over and above that necessary for living expenses, with which to pay unsecured creditors through a chapter 13 plan.[68]

Thus, unless a chapter 13 petition is necessary for some specific reason, such as those discussed below, many consumer debtors will not desire it. They can obtain a quick and easy fresh start in life through a chapter 7 case which will discharge most of their debts. Even if the debtor has one or

two secured creditors who must be dealt with, a chapter 13 plan may not be necessary. Debtors can handle some secured creditors as well, or better, in a chapter 7 case, by utilizing the devices for reducing or eliminating their liens that are available in that type of case,[69] or by dealing with their claims outside the bankruptcy court.[70]

A small number of consumer debtors have a different problem. The amounts of their debts exceed the limitations for eligibility to file a chapter 13 case. If a debtor's secured non-contingent liquidated debts exceed $922,975.00, or unsecured non-contingent liquidated debts exceed $307,675.00, the Code denies that debtor access to chapter 13.[71] As these limits are not doubled for a husband and wife filing together, the debt limits may sometimes dictate that only one spouse, or each spouse separately, file a chapter 13 case if the individual spouse's debts alone are within the statutory limits.[72]

Moreover, an important factor to remember is that a subsequent chapter 13 case may be filed at any time after a chapter 7 case.[73] Thus, if a chapter 13 case is not necessary at the time the debtor wants to file, it may still be filed later if circumstances change. There is no chapter 13 counterpart to the six-year bar to a new chapter 7 discharge after a prior bankruptcy case.

6.3.3 Considerations Favoring Chapter 13

Probably the most common reason for filing a chapter 13 case on behalf of a consumer client is the presence of one or more secured creditors who cannot be satisfactorily handled in any other way. One frequent example is a bank or finance company that is about to repossess a client's car. Few legal steps prevent repossession as quickly and effectively[74] as a

---

66 *See* § 12.10, *infra.*

67 The *NCLC Guide to Surviving Debt* can be ordered for $19.00 per copy (with discounts for bulk orders) by calling NCLC at (617) 542-9595.

68 One requirement of chapter 13 is that all priority claims, including the trustee's fees and priority taxes, must be paid in full, 11 U.S.C. § 1322(a)(2).

69 11 U.S.C. §§ 506, 522, 722; *see* Chs. 10, 11, *infra.*

70 However, even if the debtor does not do so, the creditor may shift litigation to the bankruptcy court by filing a proceeding to lift the automatic stay or for reclamation of property, or by removal. See Chapters 9, 11 and 13, *infra,* for discussion of these topics.

71 11 U.S.C. § 109(e). See Chapter 12, *infra,* for more detailed discussion.

72 Alternatively, they may choose to file a chapter 11 case. *See* § 6.3.4, *infra.*

73 *See* Johnson v. Home State Bank, 501 U.S. 78, 111 S. Ct. 2150, 115 L. Ed. 2d 66 (1991). However, it is not clear whether a chapter 13 case may be filed while a chapter 7 case is still pending. Normally, conversion would be appropriate in those circumstances. *See* Ch. 4, *supra. But see In re* Saylors, 869 F.2d 1434 (11th Cir. 1989) (chapter 13 case may be filed while chapter 7 case still pending if debtor has received discharge and only lack of trustee's administrative acts delays closing of case); *In re* Strause, 97 B.R. 22 (Bankr. S.D. Cal. 1989) (filing of chapter 13 case not barred by pending chapter 7 case when discharge would have been granted but for court's administrative delays); § 12.10, *infra.*

74 The repossession is prohibited upon filing by the automatic stay provided for in 11 U.S.C. § 362. *See* Ch. 9, *infra.*

chapter 13 petition and plan, which can also usually lower the monthly payments and perhaps the balance due.[75] Similarly, a chapter 13 case can be used to halt a mortgage foreclosure, giving the client time to cure a default and, in some cases,[76] a chance to lower the payments or principal due.

As mentioned above, other reasons to file a chapter 13 case spring from deficiencies in the relief available under chapter 7. If the debtor does have non-exempt property, it is protected in chapter 13, though its present value must usually be paid to unsecured creditors over the course of the plan.[77] And, if the debtor has obtained a chapter 7 discharge in a case filed within the previous six years, it is likely that the only real option in bankruptcy is chapter 13.[78]

Another feature of chapter 13 which may sometimes be important is the broader discharge it provides. Many debts that are not dischargeable in chapter 7 may be discharged in chapter 13. These include some taxes;[79] debts incurred by use of false financial statements, false pretenses, or fraud; willful and malicious torts; fraud in a fiduciary capacity; certain restitution obligations; and debts with respect to which a previous bankruptcy discharge was denied or waived.[80]

Even for the nondischargeable debts, such as alimony, maintenance, or support arrearages, or for debts like taxes which must be paid in a chapter 13 case because they are priority debts,[81] a chapter 13 plan may still benefit the debtor by allowing her to stretch out the payments over a longer period than would otherwise be possible and perhaps avoid interest and penalties. In addition, most of the possible objections to a chapter 7 discharge, such as fraudulent transfer, concealment of property, or inability to explain loss of assets, may not be raised in a chapter 13 case.[82]

A decision to file under chapter 13 sometimes depends on how likely it is that these questions will arise. Some debts are dischargeable in chapter 7 unless the creditor affirmatively files a complaint seeking a declaration of their non-dischargeability.[83] When an objection to discharge or dischargeability is not predictable, it may be preferable to commence a chapter 7 case and later convert to chapter 13, if necessary.

Another reason to file a chapter 13 case is to help a client who does want to pay her debts but needs the protection of the bankruptcy court and, perhaps, the "discipline" of a chapter 13 plan. Chapter 13 usually offers this client, in addition, an end to finance charges and late charges on unsecured claims, and possibly less detriment (when there is any) to the debtor's credit history[84] and reputation. However, such a client should be reminded that most of these advantages are available without a chapter 13 case; she may pay all or part of any debt voluntarily after a chapter 7 case, without the deadlines and extra costs of a chapter 13 plan.

Occasionally, the filing of a chapter 13 case is required because a client cannot afford to pay her bankruptcy attorney fees except by installments as part of a chapter 13 plan.[85] Attorneys should be careful not to abuse this device; the bankruptcy courts and United States trustees are giving greater scrutiny to chapter 13 cases which seem to have been filed primarily so that the debtor's attorney could "use the chapter 13 trustee as his collection agent."[86]

Finally, if there is significant doubt as to whether any bankruptcy is the right solution, but for some reason the debtor must file a petition before that doubt is finally resolved, chapter 13 usually offers a safer course than chapter 7. The debtor may voluntarily dismiss a case commenced under chapter 13 at any time as a matter of right.[87] The same is not true of a case commenced under chapter 7 (or later converted to a chapter 7). In a chapter 7 case, dismissal may occur only with leave of the court, and may be refused if it appears to prejudice the rights of creditors.[88]

---

75 However, if the value of the collateral is quite low, the debtor could choose to redeem the property in a chapter 7 case. 11 U.S.C. § 722; *see* § 11.5, *infra*.

76 A claim for which there is a security interest in the debtor's principal residence may only be modified by a chapter 13 plan in certain circumstances. 11 U.S.C. § 1322(b)(2), (c)(2); *see* § 11.6.1, *infra*.

77 11 U.S.C. § 1325(a)(4); *see* § 12.3.1, *infra*.

78 11 U.S.C. § 727(a)(8), (9). The six-year bar cannot be evaded by filing a chapter 13 case within the six years after an earlier petition and then converting the case to chapter 7 after the six years has run. *In re* Burrell, 148 B.R. 820 (Bankr. E.D. Va. 1992). When a chapter 13 case is impossible for some reason, exempt property may nevertheless be protected in a chapter 7 case even if a discharge is not available. 11 U.S.C. § 522(c). 11 U.S.C. §§ 727(a)(8) and (9) prohibit another chapter 7 discharge within this period. Those subsections do not bar the filing of another chapter 7 case, in which exemptions would still be available. For at least a few debtors, that may be the best alternative as they would receive the benefit of the automatic stay and their exempt property would thereby be preserved despite the lack of a discharge.

79 Certain taxes may be nondischargeable in a chapter 7 case, and yet not be priority claims (which must be paid in full under chapter 13). An example of such a tax might be an income tax over three years old for which a return was never filed.

80 Discharge of these debts is barred by 11 U.S.C. § 523(a) in a chapter 7 case. *See* Ch. 14, *infra*. The exceptions to discharge for student loans and certain drunk-driving debts formerly found only in chapter 7 have been carried over to chapter 13 as of 1991. *See* §§ 14.4.3.8, 14.4.4.3.9, *infra*.

81 11 U.S.C. § 1322(a)(2).

82 However, a court may well consider outrageous behavior to be violative of the "good faith" requirement of 11 U.S.C. § 1325(a)(3). *See* § 12.3.2, *infra*.

83 11 U.S.C. § 523(c) specifies these types of debts.

84 The evidence as to this point is mixed. *See* § 6.2.2.3, *supra*.

85 See § 15.4, *infra*, for further discussion of payment of attorney fees through the chapter 13 plan.

86 *See, e.g., In re* San Miguel, 40 B.R. 481 (Bankr. D. Colo. 1984).

87 11 U.S.C. § 1307(b); *see In re* Eddis, 37 B.R. 217 (E.D. Pa. 1984); *see also In re* Nash, 765 F.2d 1410 (9th Cir. 1985); § 13.9.1, *infra*.

88 Voluntary dismissal is sometimes denied. *See* § 13.9, *infra*.

6.3.4 *Use of Chapter 11 by Consumer Debtors*

In *Toibb v. Radloff*,[89] the Supreme Court held that individual debtors may file under the reorganization provisions of chapter 11 of the Bankruptcy Code. While even a cursory review of the chapter 11 process is beyond the scope of this manual, some basic information about chapter 11 from the perspective of consumer creditors is available in Chapter 17, *infra*.

For the great majority of consumer debtors, chapter 11 is not the right choice. Most of the relief available in chapter 11 is available for individuals in chapter 13 at a much lower cost in time and money.

However, a limited number of debtors might choose chapter 11 over chapter 13 in the following situations:

- The debtor is ineligible to file under chapter 13 because of non-contingent, liquidated, secured debt in excess of $922,975.00 or non-contingent, liquidated, unsecured debt in excess of $307,675.00.[90]
- The debtor cannot pay priority tax claims within the five-year period permitted under chapter 13, but could do so within the time permitted under chapter 11.[91]
- The debtor seeks to avoid commitment of all disposable income over three years to a plan as would be required by the "ability to pay" test of Code section 1325(b),[92] which is not applicable in chapter 11.

Chapter 11 cases tend to be expensive[93] and complicated. Unlike a chapter 13 case, a chapter 11 case may not be dismissed as of right;[94] a plan may ultimately be proposed by creditors over the debtor's objection;[95] creditors generally must vote on the plan;[96] there is no codebtor stay;[97] and the same exceptions to discharge found in chapter 7 apply.[98] For this reason, it is advisable to perform a thorough review to make certain that chapter 11 is necessary. It also may be helpful to obtain expert assistance or a practice manual which covers chapter 11 in some detail.

6.4 Should Both Spouses File?

In cases in which both a husband and wife are represented, an additional question presents itself—whether both spouses should file, or only one of them. The answer to this question is that it is usually preferable for both to file. The filing fee is the same for joint cases as for an individual case and can provide both spouses the advantages of a bankruptcy discharge.[99] Most often, many debts are jointly owed; a spouse who does not file thus remains liable as a codebtor, and may continue to be pursued by creditors.[100]

When a joint bankruptcy case is filed, the debtors file joint schedules, statements and other papers, reducing the amount of work necessary as compared to the filing of two separate cases. However, the filing of a joint bankruptcy does not automatically consolidate the cases of the two debtors; such consolidation, which would consolidate the estates of the debtors, must be ordered by the court.[101] This issue is significant primarily in cases in which one spouse has non-exempt property that will be distributed (or much more non-exempt property than the other spouse) and some or all of the debts are not joint debts. In such cases, the creditors of the spouse with more non-exempt property have an interest in opposing consolidation so they do not have to share that spouse's non-exempt property with creditors of the other spouse.[102]

The decision to file jointly, if appropriate, must be made at the outset of the case. Numerous courts have held that a spouse cannot be added to an existing bankruptcy petition after it is filed.[103] If an existing debtor's spouse seeks to file subsequently to the initial spouse's petition, the best option might be a separate filing under the same chapter and a request for joint administration of the two cases.[104]

There are several exceptions to the general rule that both spouses should file. The most obvious is the situation in

---

89   501 U.S. 157, 111 S. Ct. 2197, 115 L. Ed. 2d 145 (1991).

90   11 U.S.C. § 109(e); *see* § 12.2.3, *infra.*

91   *Compare* 11 U.S.C. § 1322(a)(2), (c) *with* 11 U.S.C. § 1129(a)(9)(C), which permits six years after the date of assessment. This situation would be very rare. In chapter 11 present value payments on the priority tax debts would be required.

92   *See* § 12.3.3, *infra.*

93   The filing fee for chapter 11 is currently $830.00. 28 U.S.C. § 1930(a)(3). In addition, fees to the United States trustee of at least $250.00 per quarter are required until the case is closed, converted, or dismissed. 28 U.S.C. § 1930(a)(6). There are also other costs, including those of preparing and mailing disclosure statements and ballots for creditor voting.

94   *Compare* 11 U.S.C. § 1112 *with* 11 U.S.C. § 1307.

95   11 U.S.C. § 1121.

96   11 U.S.C. §§ 1125, 1129.

97   *See* § 9.4.4, *infra*; *cf.* 11 U.S.C. § 1301.

98   11 U.S.C. § 523(a).

99   *See* Form 7, Appendix G.3, *infra,* for an application to waive the noticing fee. See also § 3.2.2, *supra,* for discussion of other issues relating to filing fees.

100 However, in many chapter 13 cases, such pursuit is at least temporarily prohibited by 11 U.S.C. § 1301, which stays actions against codebtors. See Chapter 9, *infra,* for discussion and exceptions.

101 11 U.S.C. § 302(b).

102 *See In re* Reider, 31 F.3d 1102 (11th Cir. 1994) (substantive consolidation is abuse of discretion in case in which creditor can show it will thereby inequitably receive lesser share of assets because it relied on credit of one spouse); Robert B. Chapman, *Coverture and Cooperation: The Firm, the Market, and the Substantive Consolidation of Married Debtors,* 17 Bankr. Dev. J. 105 (2000).

103 *See, e.g., In re* Morgan, 96 B.R. 615 (Bankr. N.D. W. Va. 1989); *In re* Kirkus, 97 B.R. 675 (Bankr. N.D. Ga. 1987).

104 Fed. R. Bankr. P. 1015(b).

which one spouse does not wish to participate. After an explanation of the disadvantages of such a course of action to that spouse, most of the advantages of bankruptcy can still be obtained by filing a petition on behalf of the willing spouse.

A second exception is the case in which one spouse is barred from filing by a prior bankruptcy or, if the case proposed is a chapter 7 case, by some likely objection to discharge. Similarly, if a chapter 13 case is advisable, some debt of the non-filing spouse,[105] for example, a very large priority debt which must be paid, or a debt above the chapter 13 debt limitations, might make a viable case impossible.

Probably the most important case in which it is necessary to deviate from the general rule is the situation in which filing for only one spouse would protect property. Occasionally, this may mean not filing for a spouse with non-exempt property. However, creditors can then usually continue to proceed against that property.[106] The more likely reason is the presence of substantial amounts of entireties property or other jointly-owned property in excess of the federal exemption levels, which under state law are not reachable by a creditor of only one spouse. In such cases, if only one spouse files, and the state, rather than federal, exemptions are chosen, all of that spouse's interest in such property may be claimed as exempt, at least as to creditors of only the filing spouse.[107] Then, after the bankruptcy, those creditors[108] will be unable to reach the joint property because their claims have been discharged.[109] The advantages of one spouse filing in such situations, then, are obvious.

Finally, it is necessary to remember the effects of the bankruptcy on community debts and community property in community property states. Although the considerations involved will vary with the different community property laws, most community property generally becomes a part of the estate, and most community claims usually are discharged even if only one spouse files.[110] Thus, most or all of a spouse's property and debts may be affected by the

bankruptcy regardless of whether he or she joins in the petition. This factor may bring either advantages (discharge) or disadvantages (loss of property) to a non-filing spouse, and should be considered carefully.

6.5 Considerations of Timing and Events Prior to Filing

6.5.1 Reasons to File Quickly

A final factor to be considered in deciding on a course of action is the timing of the petition. Even after the debtor decides that a bankruptcy should be filed, in many cases it is advisable to wait before filing.

Of course, in some cases, a debtor has no choice but to file immediately. Prompt action may be necessary to forestall a repossession, eviction, execution sale, or utility shut-off. In some cases, a debtor may wish to file immediately before, or even after, foreclosure, if there is a possibility that the debtor will be able to effectuate a cure of a mortgage default through a chapter 13 plan.[111] It may also be the only way to stay a state court proceeding and thereby avoid much unnecessary work therein. Filing before the expiration of a statute of limitations or a period for redemption can provide the debtor with an extension of the time period to commence a lawsuit or take other action.[112] Another occasional reason for a quick bankruptcy is an expectation[113] of soon acquiring non-exempt property. Such property does not usually become part of the estate after filing.[114] In all of these cases, a bankruptcy can be filed almost instantaneously, if necessary, under the current rules.[115]

6.5.2 The Effects of Pre-Bankruptcy Transfers or Other Actions

6.5.2.1 Fraudulent Acts, Conveyances and Preferences

One of the prime reasons for a delay before filing stems from the possible effects, both negative and positive, of

---

105 11 U.S.C. § 1322(a)(2).

106 *But see* 11 U.S.C. § 1301 (staying actions against codebtors in chapter 13 cases); Ch. 9, *infra*.

107 11 U.S.C. § 522(b)(2)(B). *But see* Sumy v. Schlossberg, 777 F.2d 921 (4th Cir. 1985); *In re* Grosslight, 757 F.2d 773 (6th Cir. 1985); Napotnik v. Equibank, 679 F.2d 316 (3d Cir. 1982) (limiting the exemption possible under 11 U.S.C. § 522(b)(2)(B)). For discussion of the joint property exemption, see § 10.2.3.2, *infra*.

108 An exception is the secured creditor whose rights were not impaired by the bankruptcy.

109 In a few jurisdictions, courts have also ruled that even when there are joint creditors, a bankruptcy filed by one spouse who chooses the exemption for entireties property can protect the entireties property from their claims. *See* § 10.2.3.2, *infra*.

110 11 U.S.C. §§ 524(a)(3), 541(a)(2); *see In re* Morgan, 286 B.R. 678 (Bankr. E.D. Wis. 2002) (trustee permitted to liquidate home where debtor's estranged wife and children lived because, as community property, it had become property of the estate and it had not been exempted by debtor).

111 *See* § 11.6.2.2, *infra*.

112 11 U.S.C. § 108(b); *see* Thomas v. GMAC Residential Funding Corp., 309 B.R. 453 (D. Md. 2004) (right of rescission under Truth in Lending Act extended by sixty days after filing of bankruptcy petition).

113 This expectation would have to be something less than an entitlement, as the latter would probably be property of the estate under 11 U.S.C. § 541.

114 Certain property acquired within 180 days of filing does become a part of the estate, for example, property acquired by inheritance or marital property settlement. 11 U.S.C. § 541(a)(5). In addition after-acquired property becomes part of the estate in a chapter 13 case. 11 U.S.C. § 1306; *see* § 2.5, *supra*.

115 *See* § 7.2, *infra*.

pre-bankruptcy transfers. Some transfers already made may dictate a delay in filing, and it may be advisable to take time to make others before filing in order to gain maximum advantage from the case.

Several types of acts fall into the class of transfers that dictate delays; some of these may affect a discharge in chapter 7 proceedings. If the debtor, with intent to hinder, delay or defraud creditors, has transferred, removed, destroyed, mutilated or concealed her property within one year prior to the filing of a petition, a successful objection to a chapter 7 discharge may be brought.[116] This definition may include the transfer of specific property subject to a security interest in favor of a creditor, but only if the requisite intent existed.[117] If it seems likely that such an objection will be raised, it may be prudent to delay filing a chapter 7 case, if possible, until a year has passed since that act. Even after that year, a trustee may still seek to recover a fraudulent transfer,[118] and a secured creditor may still raise a claim of willful and malicious conversion of the collateral, but only to seek an exception to the discharge of that particular creditor's claim in a chapter 7 case.[119]

Usually less serious are two other types of transfers. These are preferences and those types of fraudulent conveyances made without actual intent to defraud creditors. The worst possible result of these transfers is a reversal of the transfer by the bankruptcy trustee.[120] Briefly, an avoidable preference in an individual bankruptcy is a transfer of property worth more than $600.00 from an insolvent debtor to a creditor on account of an antecedent debt, that allows that creditor to receive more than it would otherwise receive in a chapter 7 liquidation case, made within ninety days before filing (or one year before filing if the creditor is an insider).[121] Thus, large payments to some creditors prior to bankruptcy may be set aside by the trustee if they were made within the stated time periods. If the client cares, as she may if the payment was made to a friend or relative, it may be better to delay filing until after the applicable preference period has passed. However, it should be stressed that there is nothing improper or illegal about making a preferential payment. The only possible negative consequence is avoidance of the transfer by the trustee.

A fraudulent transfer may also be set aside by the trustee. Basically, the trustee's power extends to a transfer or obligation made within one year before filing, either (1) for the purpose of hindering, defrauding, or delaying creditors, or (2) for which the debtor did not receive reasonably equivalent value at a time that the debtor was insolvent or was about to incur debts beyond her ability to pay.[122] In addition, a transfer which could be set aside under a state fraudulent transfer statute can usually be set aside by the trustee at any time within the period allowed by that statute (usually longer than one year).[123] Again, this possibility may be of no concern to the debtor but if it is, it may be advisable to wait, if possible, before filing.

On the other hand, some preferences and fraudulent transfers may be set aside by the debtor within the same time periods allowed the trustee. Generally, if the transfer was involuntary, the debtor did not conceal the property, and the debtor could have exempted the property involved, then the debtor may set aside the transfer.[124] Thus, if the debtor plans to make use of this power, it may be crucial to file the petition before the time period has run.

Finally, section 523(a)(2)(C) of the Code creates a rebuttable presumption that consumer debts aggregating more than $1225.00 owed to a single creditor, for cash advances or "luxury goods and services" obtained within sixty days before a bankruptcy case was filed, were fraudulently incurred.[125] If the debtor plans to file a chapter 7 case and has recently incurred that type of debt, it is usually better, if possible, to wait until the sixty-day period has passed. Waiting out this period does not guarantee dischargeability. However, absence of the presumption may make creditor challenges to dischargeability much less likely.

6.5.2.2 Exemption Planning

There are also steps a debtor can sometimes take prior to filing to improve her ability to retain property. Most of these come under the general rubric of exemption planning. Basically, exemption planning means arranging the debtor's affairs so that a maximum amount of property can be claimed under the exemption provisions, and a minimum amount is lost to creditors in the bankruptcy. It is much akin to tax planning, which is the way people arrange their affairs to take maximum advantage of the tax laws. In the opinion of most commentators, it is perfectly legal under present law, at least if not done to excess.[126]

---

116 11 U.S.C. § 727(a)(2).

117 *See* § 14.2, *infra.*

118 The trustee may be able to avoid a fraudulent transfer under 11 U.S.C. § 544. *See* § 10.4.2.6.2, *infra.*

119 11 U.S.C. § 523(a)(6); *see* Ch. 14, *infra.*

120 11 U.S.C. §§ 544, 547, 548. However, in some states, some types of fraudulent conveyances constitute crimes as well.

121 11 U.S.C. § 547. The terms "transfer," "insider," and "insolvent," are all defined in 11 U.S.C. § 101. See § 10.4.2.6.4, *infra,* for further explanation of preferences.

---

122 11 U.S.C. § 548; *see* § 10.4.2.6.5, *infra.*

123 11 U.S.C. § 544; *see* § 10.4.2.6.2, *infra.*

124 11 U.S.C. § 522(h). See § 10.4.2.6.5, *infra,* for examples and further discussion.

125 *See* § 14.4.3.2.3.2, *infra.*

126 *In re* Stern, 317 F.3d 1111 (9th Cir. 2003) (purposeful conversion of non-exempt assets to exempt assets on eve of bankruptcy not fraudulent per se); *In re* Carey, 938 F.2d 1073 (10th Cir. 1991) (no intent to defraud found when debtor mortgaged non-exempt equity in residence and fully disclosed transaction); *In re* Bowyer, 932 F.2d 1100 (5th Cir. 1991) (use of assets to create exempt equity in home not improper when debtors had not yet formed plan to file bankruptcy); *In re* Armstrong, 931 F.2d 1233 (8th Cir. 1991); *In re* Holt, 894 F.2d 1005 (8th Cir. 1990) (conversion of non-exempt assets into exempt assets on

A number of steps can be taken to take advantage of the exemption provisions. For example, some states require the debtor to file a homestead deed in order to claim the state homestead exemption. Assets that are not exempt, such as cash above the amounts allowed, can be spent on household goods and clothing (each item must be worth less than $475.00 if the federal exemptions are used), life insurance, or other items in categories in which the debtor has unused exemptions (assuming the federal exemptions or similar state exemptions are available). If there is non-exempt equity in a debtor's home, the possibility of obtaining a second mortgage (again using the money to purchase exempt assets) should be weighed against loss of that equity (or against paying that amount in a chapter 13 case).[127] All of these steps are nothing more than a rearrangement of a debtor's assets. Unless there is established case law in a jurisdiction finding them not permissible, these steps should be relatively free from risk.[128]

It is also important to remember property owed to the debtor. Tax refunds due[129] are always considered part of the estate and are claimed by the trustee if they are not exempt.[130] Thus, if the refund due is greater than the debtor's unused exemptions, it may be better to wait until it arrives and spend it on exempt assets before filing the bankruptcy petition. In some areas, exemption planning may even come down to waiting until the debtor's pay day to file, as careful trustees may seek out any non-exempt wages or vacation pay owed the debtor for the previous few days.[131] If no unused exemptions remain, prepaid rent could also pose a problem; in a few areas trustees and judges may consider the remaining portion of a month's prepaid rent, as well as any security deposits to landlords or utilities, to be assets.[132] Arrangements for a temporary refund may be worked out if no money is presently owed to the utility companies. Similarly, trustees have occasionally even been known to claim bank deposits as assets because checks which have been written have not yet cleared by the date of filing. Local practice regarding these types of property varies greatly and should be investigated. In most areas, trustees do not inquire into these small amounts due the debtor. And, of course, if the debtor has significant unused exemptions to cover these amounts, there is no cause for concern.

A debtor may also take steps to ensure that no new non-exempt property comes into the bankruptcy estate after filing. Such property could come into the estate, for example, if the debtor receives or becomes entitled to acquire it by bequest, devise, or inheritance, as a result of a marital

---

eve of bankruptcy is not necessarily fraudulent); *In re* Johnson, 880 F.2d 78 (8th Cir. 1989) (mere fact of conversion of property into exempt assets does not establish fraud); *In re* Bradley, 294 B.R. 64 (B.A.P. 8th Cir. 2003) (conversion of non-exempt assets to exempt assets permissible under Arkansas law); *In re* Wadley, 263 B.R. 857 (Bankr. S.D. Ohio 2001) (debtor's sale of motorcycle and use of proceeds to acquire exempt assets was permissible). H.R. Rep. No. 95-595, at 361 (1977) states that this practice is not fraudulent with respect to creditors, and permits the debtor to make full use of the exemptions to which she is entitled under law. For a discussion of prior law, see Resnick, *Prudent Planning or Fraudulent Transfers: The Use of Non-Exempt Assets to Purchase or Improve Exempt Property on the Eve of Bankruptcy*, 31 Rutgers L. Rev. 615 (1978). However, some courts have held that transfers designed to maximize exemptions are fraudulent even under the Code. Clients must be advised that there is a risk that the transfers will be avoided, and that there is even a risk to their discharge. Most of these cases have involved state exemption law, large amounts of money, and conduct intended to conceal the transfers. *See, e.g., In re* Sholdan, 217 F.3d 1006 (8th Cir. 2000) (ninety-year-old's conversion of virtually all assets into exempt homestead found fraudulent and exemption denied); *In re* Tveten, 848 F.2d 871 (8th Cir. 1988) ($700,000.00 transfer to exempt assets found fraudulent and discharge denied); Ford v. Poston, 773 F.2d 52 (4th Cir. 1985) (conversion of non-exempt property to exempt property is normally permissible, but a court may find extrinsic evidence of an attempt to defraud creditors); *In re* Reed, 11 B.R. 683 (Bankr. N.D. Tex. 1981), *aff'd*, 700 F.2d 986 (5th Cir. 1983) (debtor denied discharge due to pre-bankruptcy rearrangement of property); *see also In re* Levine, 134 F.3d 1046 (11th Cir. 1998) (transfer of assets into exempt annuities was fraudulent transfer under Florida law); *In re* Coplan, 156 B.R. 88 (Bankr. M.D. Fla. 1993) (debtors who moved to Florida and filed bankruptcy case shortly thereafter, claiming unlimited Florida homestead exemption, held to be limited to amount of the homestead exemption in their prior state of residence, because they acknowledged that move was motivated by desire to obtain greater exemption).

127 *See* 11 U.S.C. § 1325(a)(4); § 12.3.1, *infra*.

128 In the unlikely event a court finds the property non-exempt because of such actions, the debtor will still be able to save it through payment of its value in a chapter 13 plan, or perhaps by

voluntary dismissal of the case. Therefore, if there is doubt about whether a transfer might be considered fraudulent, a chapter 13 case should be seriously considered from the outset.

129 See § 2.5.3, *supra*, for further discussion of tax refunds and withholdings.

130 United States v. Michaels, 840 F.2d 901 (11th Cir. 1988) (Internal Revenue Service permitted to recoup tax refunds paid to debtors because they should have been paid to chapter 7 trustee).

131 *See, e.g., In re* Sexton, 140 B.R. 742 (Bankr. S.D. Iowa 1992); *In re* Meade, 84 B.R. 106 (Bankr. S.D. Ohio 1988) (wages earned by debtor but not yet paid on date of petition were property of the estate). In many states, most or all of a debtor's accrued wages are exempt from garnishment, and wages are also protected from garnishment by the Consumer Credit Protection Act. 15 U.S.C. §§ 1671–1677. Such exemptions may also be applicable if the state and federal non-bankruptcy exemption scheme is utilized by the debtor in a bankruptcy case. *See In* re Irish, 303 B.R. 380 (Bankr. N.D. Iowa 2003); *In re* Maidman, 141 B.R. 571 (Bankr. S.D.N.Y. 1992). *See generally* § 10.2.3, *infra*. Some states also have specific exemptions for accrued wages applicable to bankruptcy cases.

132 It should be possible to exempt prepaid rent under 11 U.S.C. § 522(d)(1), the federal homestead exemption, which is broadly worded to permit exemption of an interest in property used as a residence or a similar state exemption. Indeed, if such an exemption is available the debtor may use non-exempt cash to prepay rent and claim that asset as exempt. *See In re* Casserino, 290 B.R. 735 (B.A.P. 9th Cir. 2003) (prepaid rent could be exempted under Oregon homestead exemption).

property settlement or divorce decree, or as a beneficiary of a life insurance policy or death benefit plan. If the situation warrants, it may be advisable to temporarily change the will or insurance policy giving rise to the possible entitlement, and to arrange marital settlements accordingly. As most of these steps involve the acts of persons other than the debtor (for example, the testator or owner of an insurance policy), there is little likelihood that they could adversely affect the debtor's case.[133]

Finally, exemption planning should be distinguished from a process by which debtors transfer property completely out of their estate. It is not permissible, for example, for a debtor to give valuable property to a spouse or other relative shortly before bankruptcy, without return of fair consideration, in order to keep it from coming into the bankruptcy estate.[134] Such conduct may be considered an effort to defraud the estate and may give rise to a challenge to discharge, avoidance of the transfer as fraudulent or even, in serious cases, to criminal prosecution.[135]

6.5.3 Other Reasons for Delaying a Petition

6.5.3.1 Anticipation of Further Debt

It is sometimes said that a bankruptcy should not be filed until a client's debt load has peaked. If the client anticipates further unavoidable liabilities, such as medical bills, the bankruptcy should, if possible, be delayed until after these are incurred. The object of this delay, of course, is to gain maximum benefit from the discharge.

This advice may be somewhat more risky at present than under normal circumstances, because Congress is considering legislation which would overhaul the bankruptcy law and undermine consumer relief.[136] If such legislation is passed it may apply to cases filed on or after the date the amendments become law. Careful attorneys may wish to keep a list of clients who were advised to delay bankruptcy in order to bring them back to the office for a further consultation if changes to the Code become imminent.

However, this delay must be carefully distinguished from another type of behavior—that of obtaining goods or ser-

vices under false pretenses with no intent of paying for them. Debts incurred in this manner may be declared non-dischargeable in a chapter 7 case.[137] Fortunately, the line between these two courses of action is not as difficult to draw as it might at first seem. In general, the courts have found nondischargeable only the most obvious examples of debts incurred with no intent to pay, for example, pre-bankruptcy vacation trip and credit card shopping spree debts.[138] Expenses for medical bills and other necessities are rarely challenged.

6.5.3.2 Paying Favored Creditors

Clients may wish to delay a bankruptcy until after they have paid creditors whose claims they do not want to see discharged, for example friends or the grantors of credit cards they hope to keep. As noted above, such payments, if over $600.00 and within the applicable preference period, could be set aside by the bankruptcy trustee. Thus, if a client wants to pursue this course of action, and ensure that the creditor retains the payment, the petition must be delayed until after the preference period has run.[139]

In most cases, it is preferable not to delay a bankruptcy for this purpose, but rather to pay the creditor after the petition is filed, using either exempt assets or post-petition income. There is no impediment to this course of action in a chapter 7 case and usually it will not be questioned in a chapter 13 case.[140]

6.5.3.3 Delay of a Petition As a Strategy to Forestall Harm to Clients

Finally, there will be occasions when, for purposes of litigation strategy, a bankruptcy petition should be delayed. For example, a client defending against an eviction or mortgage foreclosure may also desire a bankruptcy. By waiting to file the petition until delay of eviction or foreclosure is no longer possible in state court litigation, a good advocate can take advantage of the automatic stay arising from the bankruptcy to gain additional time during which the client may remain in her residence. This additional time can be invaluable to a client who may later be able to settle the housing problem, either outside the bankruptcy or in a chapter 13 case. At the least, the client will have more time to find another place to live. There is certainly nothing unethical about timing a legitimate and necessary bank-

---

133 *But see In re* Green, 986 F.2d 145 (6th Cir. 1993) (in unusual situation of debtor who, having a contractual right to receive property under a will, agreed to give up that right, the exercise of a power of appointment to terminate the debtor's rights under a will was found to be a fraudulent transfer).

134 *E.g., In re* White, 28 B.R. 240 (Bankr. E.D. Va. 1983) (absent consideration, pre-bankruptcy transfer from one spouse to another not permitted). However, a fair trade of property for consideration should be allowed. *See In re* Armstrong, 931 F.2d 1233 (8th Cir. 1991) (transfer of home to father found proper when father paid fair consideration).

135 11 U.S.C. § 727(a)(2); 18 U.S.C. § 152; *see* § 14.2, *infra*.

136 *See* § 1.4.4.1, *supra*.

137 *See* § 14.4.3.2, *infra*.

138 *Id.*

139 Further discussion of preferences is found in § 10.4.2.6.4, *infra*.

140 However, paying more to one creditor than to another while a chapter 13 case is pending, even outside the plan, could be considered an unfair classification of debts or evidence that the debtor can afford to pay more under the disposable income test. *See* §§ 12.3, 12.4, *infra*.

ruptcy to obtain the maximum advantage for the client. Of course, filing a bankruptcy petition solely for the purpose of delay is quite a different matter and would likely be found unethical,[141] or cause for sanctions against the debtor, the debtor's counsel, or both.[142]

6.5.3.4 Tax Reach Back Periods

The dischargeability of certain taxes and their possible treatment as priority debts (which must be paid in full in chapter 13 cases) will depend on various time periods

having passed.[143] Investigation concerning the exact date of expiration of these time periods is essential if discharging taxes is an objective of the case.[144] Many debtors have been disappointed by an attorney's miscalculation of the relevant dates, which can be complicated by tolling periods and special tax rules. Possible malpractice claims can result.

Delay until the date of expiration of the periods is appropriate if there will not be other harmful consequences in the interim. If delay creates other risks, those risks must be weighed against the benefit of discharging the taxes involved.

---

141 *See* Model Rules of Prof'l Conduct R. 3.1; Fed. R. Bankr. P. 9011(a).

142 Cinema Serv. Corp. v. Edbee Corp., 774 F.2d 584 (3d Cir. 1985).

143 See § 14.4.3.1, *infra,* for detailed discussion of ways to obtain and analyze tax information.

144 In some cases, returns must be filed to first start the clock running. *Id.*

Chapter 7

Preparing and Filing the Papers

7.1 Introduction

7.1.1 Some General Principles

Once it has been decided that bankruptcy is appropriate in a particular case, most of the remaining work is relatively routine. A good deal of it involves preparation of the necessary papers for the initial filing. This Chapter provides a detailed step-by-step description of how to prepare and file the forms used in a typical bankruptcy case.

Preparing a bankruptcy case is mostly a matter of filling in the blanks on a standard set of forms. As with any legal document, an important goal of this exercise is to convey information as clearly and completely as possible. If necessary, the preparer should not hesitate to supplement the answers given with notes indicated by asterisks or otherwise. The annotated forms in Appendix F provide an example of the completed papers, but need not (and should not) be followed verbatim in any particular case. It is reassuring to remember that mistakes made in completing the forms may ordinarily be corrected later without great difficulty by amendment.[1]

In answering the various questions posed in the Official Forms, it is important to have a general understanding of the purpose of those questions. The overall purpose is to give the court, the trustee, and the creditors a full and accurate picture of the debtor's case. Knowing the reason for a question enables the debtor's attorney to ensure that the question is answered in a way that provides the necessary information.

Knowing the purpose of a question is also important in presenting the client's case in the best possible truthful light. For example, in questions of property valuation, estimates on the low side of a possible range of values (often forced-sale value) are usually used to maximize the amount of property that can be claimed within the dollar limits of the exemptions allowed.[2] Similarly, it is often important to give a low estimate of the amount of a claim against the debtor, taking into account all possible defenses and setoffs, if it may not be fully eliminated by the discharge. However,

these general rules cannot be applied in every case. In some instances it may be advantageous to give a higher estimate of the value of an encumbrance on a piece of property if the strategy is ultimately to have the trustee decide to abandon the property because it has no equity available for creditors.[3] In other cases, property should be given a higher estimated value to preclude a creditor that is seeking relief from the stay from arguing that the debtor has admitted to having no equity in the property.[4]

In every case it should be borne in mind that the trustee and creditors will have an opportunity (of which they may or may not make good use) to examine the client concerning the information given. However, these parties do not usually have a great interest in going over the affairs of the typical consumer debtor with a fine-tooth comb, as they might in the case of a higher-income debtor or business person who is far more likely to have something of significance to hide.

7.1.2 Obtaining the Forms

Some bankruptcy practitioners who do not handle large numbers of cases make use of bankruptcy forms printed by various commercial suppliers and usually available from sellers of legal stationery for about eight to fifteen dollars a set. These preprinted forms are used for a number of reasons. They are easily obtained and they follow the required format.

However, there are also some inconveniences in using the commercial forms. The spaces provided for answers to some questions may be much larger or smaller than necessary in most consumer cases. Moreover, the problem of obtaining the money to pay for the forms from either the client or the office's funds may create more inconvenience in bookkeeping and other ways than it is worth.

For these reasons, offices doing substantial numbers of bankruptcy cases generally use computer programs as described in the next section of this manual. For offices which do not currently have ready access to such a program, reproduction of blank Official Forms is the simplest alternative. Those found in Appendix D, *infra*, for example, can be copied and filled in as required for a particular case. The

---

1 Fed. R. Bankr. P. 1009. See Chapter 8, *infra*, for discussion of amendment procedures.

2 See Chapter 10, *infra*, for a detailed discussion of exemptions.

3 See § 3.5, *supra*, for discussion of abandonment.

4 See § 9.7.3.2, *infra*, for discussion of grounds for relief from the automatic stay.

content and overall format of these forms is identical to the Official Forms prescribed by the Judicial Conference of the United States.

Preprinting of bankruptcy forms by an office will often save money in the long run. The total number of pages used may be less than that in the commercial forms, and answers that are virtually always the same in consumer bankruptcies[5] may be preprinted on the forms themselves and then changed manually if necessary. The rules make clear that the papers filed need not conform precisely to the Official Forms, so that some consolidation or routine cross-referencing may be possible (for example, between Schedules B and C which are usually lists of the same property). It may also be possible to include a statement that certain questions are not applicable unless otherwise indicated.

However, the rules do require substantial conformance to the Official Forms,[6] both to assure the completeness of the information sought and to supply a uniformity that facilitates quick reviews and locating of desired information by participants in the case. For this reason, it is not advisable to deviate too much from the Official Forms. It may be a good idea to submit proposed forms to the local bankruptcy court before putting them into use.

7.1.3 Computer Programs

It is common for offices which handle large numbers of bankruptcy cases to use word processing programs, or to purchase special computer programs which generate bankruptcy forms based on input data. There are a wide range of such programs now on the market and, of course, they vary in cost and quality. One such program, *Bankruptcy Forms* by Law Disks, is provided free of charge on the CD-Rom accompanying this volume. This version of *Bankruptcy Forms* is *unsupported*.

Every office desiring to computerize bankruptcy practice should make its own decision about which program works best for the needs of its clients. Most of the programs are marketed through demonstration disks and it is useful to obtain as many as possible before making a final decision.

There are a number of considerations to keep in mind in selecting the appropriate program. Most importantly, the program must work well with the configuration of computer equipment available in a particular office. Certain programs are designed to work best with particular systems, software or printers, so each office should try to obtain a good match.

In addition, all judicial districts permit, or will soon permit, electronic filing of bankruptcy forms, which can be a great convenience, especially for offices located at some distance from the courthouse. If electronic filing is to be used it is important to find a program that is compatible with the standards for electronic filing set by the relevant bankruptcy court clerk's office.

Also importantly, some programs print forms which comply more closely to the Official Forms than others. It is probably a good idea to obtain a set of completed forms from the contemplated program or to print sample forms from the demonstration disk. If they vary significantly from the Official Forms, prior approval for their use should probably be obtained from the clerk of the local bankruptcy court. Similarly, it is important to determine whether the forms generated will meet the requirements of local rules, administrative orders, or community custom. For example, some districts have model chapter 13 plans that practitioners are strongly encouraged to use.

Another consideration, and one which is sometimes more difficult to evaluate, is the degree to which the forms allow entry of complete information. On some programs it is difficult to input anything but the most routine information, to edit the actual forms, or to modify the standard bankruptcy plan, making it difficult to handle complicated cases. A large degree of flexibility is optimal.

A final consideration is whether adequate support will be available from the publisher of the program. The ability to get assistance is often crucial in getting the program to run well. It is sensible to check on the availability of help, including the hours help is available and the number of servicers, before buying any sort of expensive software. The vendor should be asked for references who can be called for their views about the program.

For offices which prefer not to use special bankruptcy forms preparation software an additional option is to input blank forms into a word processing program. Information for individual cases can then be input into the form directly on the computer. This, in effect, is what is offered by the CD-Rom accompanying this volume, *Bankruptcy Forms* by Law Disks. NCLC does not offer technical support for this program; technical support must be purchased separately from Law Disks.

7.1.4 Electronic Filing of Documents

All of the bankruptcy courts have adopted or are in the process of adapting their procedures and systems to permit the electronic filing of documents.[7] In some districts electronic filing is, or soon will be, required of all bankruptcy attorneys. In most bankruptcy courts, it is also possible to access any electronically-filed document (and sometimes other documents) over the Internet and thereby obtain a copy of the document without a trip to the bankruptcy court

---

5 For example, the answers to items 26–32 on Schedule B will almost always be "none" for consumer filings.

6 *See, e.g.,* Fed. R. Bankr. P. 9009.

7 Information on courts that have adopted electronic filing can be obtained from the local courts' websites, accessible through www.uscourts.gov or from the PACER website at http://pacer.psc.uscourts.gov.

or paying for copies. (There is, however, usually a charge of seven cents a page for accessing documents over the court's PACER system, which may be waived for indigent clients.) Unfortunately, there are some variations in the procedures that the various courts are adopting, which are generally set forth in local rules. However, all of the courts appear to require that the documents be filed in Adobe Acrobat's PDF format,[8] and attorneys who file documents (or at least documents requiring a filing fee) must provide a credit card to which filing fees may be charged.

There are obvious advantages to electronic filing of documents for virtually all attorneys who file any significant number of bankruptcy cases, particularly those whose offices are not near the courthouse. Much travel time and expense can be saved by avoiding trips to the courthouse to file documents or by avoiding fees of couriers who perform that task. Emergency cases or other documents can be filed from any location with Internet access when the clerk's office is not open.

---

8 An Acrobat (PDF) file is a kind of electronic photograph of the original file. First, the attorney prepares the bankruptcy petition and schedules using their software program: for example, Microsoft Word, Corel WordPerfect, or a specialized bankruptcy program. When finished, the file must be converted into Acrobat. The Acrobat PDF file is then sent to the bankruptcy court via the Internet.

The principal method of creating PDF files is to use the "full" Adobe Acrobat program (not the free Acrobat Reader). When the full Adobe Acrobat program is installed on a computer, any file can be duplicated as an Acrobat (PDF) file. Besides using Adobe Acrobat to create the PDF version, there are other methods. WordPerfect versions 9, 10, and 11 have an internal PDF generator. Some of the specialized bankruptcy programs include a PDF converter to save the petition as a PDF document for you. However, such users will likely find that they still need to use Adobe Acrobat or other software for pleadings not covered by the bankruptcy forms software, such as custom motions, complaints, and adversary proceedings. Free and low-cost third party (non-Adobe) PDF converters may be found on the Internet. For example, see www.primopdf.com for a free PDF print driver which creates Acrobat PDF files. For best quality on screen however, the full Adobe Acrobat program is better than the free converters.

Scanning is another method of creating a PDF file, by using Adobe Acrobat or some other software program. However, the attorney generally needs a scanner only to make PDF versions of exhibits which exist only on paper, such as a mortgage or a contract. In general, bankruptcy petitions are not scanned; the PDF copies are created using Adobe Acrobat software (or some third-party PDF generator). In the most progressive bankruptcy courts, nothing in the initial bankruptcy filings needs to be scanned, and the court accepts signatures in the format of "S/Attorney Signature" and "S/Debtor Signature" as a certification that the original document was signed. However, other courts require the page with the debtor's signature to be scanned. This is a matter to be checked in the local bankruptcy rules, available at www.uscourts.gov. *See In re* Wenk, 296 B.R. 719 (Bankr. E.D. Va. 2002) (attorney sanctioned for electronically filing petition with debtor's electronic signature when debtor had not signed petition).

All of the major commercial bankruptcy software programs now may be used to file documents electronically.[9] For most offices, electronic filing requires some investment in computer hardware or software compatible with the courts' systems. New office procedures are also usually necessary to deal with receipt of electronic notices, accounting for credit card payments to the court, and storage of electronic files.

7.2 The Papers Necessary to Start a Case

7.2.1 Forms Usually Filed

Normally, a bankruptcy case is started by filing several documents at once. In a chapter 7 case the documents are the petition, which is the pleading that actually starts the case, a statement of the debtor's social security number, the debtor's statement of financial affairs and schedules, a statement of intentions with respect to property securing consumer debts, and a disclosure of attorney fees paid or promised.[10]

In a chapter 13 case, the documents are quite similar; they are the petition, the statement of the debtor's social security number, the statement of financial affairs and schedules, the chapter 13 plan, and the attorney fee disclosure.[11] The statement of affairs and schedules filed in a chapter 13 case are the same as those which are filed in a chapter 7 case.

In addition, local rules may require one or two other papers. Many bankruptcy courts require the debtor to provide, either at the time of filing or shortly thereafter, a form (commonly known as the "matrix") to create mailing labels to be used by the court.[12] Also commonly mandated is a form summarizing the plan in a chapter 13 case.

The Bankruptcy Rules do not state the number of copies of the petition, statements, and schedules to be filed, leaving that matter to local rules.[13] The rules require only one copy

---

9 The documents produced by the Lawdisks program accompanying this manual must be converted to PDF format for electronic filing, which may require purchase of Adobe Acrobat.

10 Fed. R. Bankr P. 1007(b), (f). Fed. R. Bankr. P. 2016(b) requires this last form to be filed within fifteen days after the petition unless the court orders otherwise. The easiest practice is probably to file it with the schedules and statement of affairs at the outset of the case.

11 Fed. R. Bankr. P. 1007(b), (f). The statement of intentions with regard to property securing consumer debts is probably not required in a chapter 13 case. See discussion of this form at § 7.3.6, *infra*.

12 The failure to properly list a creditor's address on such a form could lead to a debt being excepted from discharge as not "duly scheduled." *In re* Adams, 734 F.2d 1094 (5th Cir. 1984). See § 14.4.3.3, *infra*, for further discussion of this exception to discharge.

13 The former rules specifying the number of copies required were abrogated by the 1987 amendments to the rules.

of the chapter 13 plan and fee disclosure statement,[14] though local rules may impose additional requirements. Usually, again possibly excepting documents required by local rule, all of the forms may be filed in a single package. Many courts require two holes to be punched at the top of the forms. However, local practices regarding these procedures vary and should be checked. In any event, the clerk is not permitted to reject the filing of any paper because it is not presented in proper form.[15] However, the court may thereafter require that a defective filing be corrected.

Lastly, the initial filing must be accompanied by a filing fee of $155.00, plus a $39.00 noticing fee. In addition, in chapter 7 cases, the debtor must also pay an extra $15.00 to be used for trustee compensation, raising the total fees in chapter 7 to $209.00. If the debtor cannot pay all of these fees at the time of filing, and has not paid any money to an attorney, she may instead file an application requesting permission to pay the filing fee in installments. This application is normally granted as a matter of course.[16] Usually, only one copy of the application and a proposed order need be filed.[17] Moreover, some courts have waived the noticing fee (and should similarly waive the chapter 7 trustee surcharge) upon the filing of an affidavit of indigency and a request for a waiver because the fees are imposed under 28 U.S.C. § 1930(b).[18]

7.2.2 The Emergency Bankruptcy, or How to Prepare a Bankruptcy Case in Under Ten Minutes

It is sometimes necessary to file bankruptcy immediately in order to utilize the automatic stay[19] to stop some possibly imminent harm from befalling a client. In such cases, it is often impossible to gather the necessary information and prepare all of the required papers quickly enough.

Fortunately, the Bankruptcy Rules provide a solution for this problem. They allow a debtor to commence a case by filing only the two-page bankruptcy petition, along with the statement of social security number and a list of the debtor's creditors and their addresses.[20] The number of copies of these forms required is the same as in a bankruptcy in which all the forms are filed together. The filing must also include the filing fee or an application to pay the fee in installments and, if possible, an application for waiver of a portion of the fees.

After these few documents are filed, the rules require that the remainder of the usual forms be filed within fifteen days.[21] The court may further extend the deadline for all of the forms to be filed upon application, for cause shown.[22]

If the remaining required forms are not filed, the case is usually dismissed. Dismissal may be acceptable to the debtor, if bankruptcy later proves to be the wrong course of action,[23] as the dismissal is normally without prejudice.[24] However, it cannot be assumed that the case will always be dismissed. A chapter 13 case may be converted to chapter 7.[25] And, if creditors or the trustee object to dismissal of a chapter 7 case, the court may allow the case to proceed, possibly affording creditors the equivalent of an involuntary bankruptcy case without requiring them to satisfy the normal prerequisites for such a proceeding.[26]

7.2.3 Timing the Filing of Multiple Cases

Offices filing several bankruptcies during a short time period may wish to check with the clerk of the bankruptcy court as to how the date of filing affects the dates of later proceedings, such as the section 341 meeting of creditors.

---

14 Fed. R. Bankr. P. 3015, 2016.

15 Fed. R. Bankr. P. 5005(a).

16 Fed. R. Bankr. P. 1006(b). Note that the filing fee must be paid in full before debtor's counsel receives any fee. Fed. R. Bankr. P. 1006(b)(3). In a few districts, contrary to the express language of the rule, courts require part of the filing fee to be paid when a petition is filed with an application to pay the fee in installments. Appellate challenges to such practices should be considered.

17 Official Form 3; *see* Appx. D, *infra.*

18 See § 13.6, *infra,* and Form 7, Appendix G.3, *infra,* for an application to waive administrative fees. See also Appendix C and § 3.2.2, *supra,* for discussion of the chapter 7 trustee surcharge.

19 See Chapter 9, *infra,* for discussion of the automatic stay.

20 Fed. R. Bankr. P. 1007(a), (c), (f), 3015. Most commercial form sets provide a form for the list of creditors. *See also* Appx. E, *infra.* This right to file only a bare petition is not meant to be used routinely for debtors when there is no emergency. A number of bankruptcy courts have indicated their displeasure with attorneys who regularly fail to file the complete package of documents at the outset of the case, especially when the later documents are not promptly filed. *See, e.g., In re* Waddell, 21 B.R. 450 (Bankr. N.D. Ga. 1982).

21 Fed. R. Bankr. P. 1007(c), 3015. The statement of intentions with regard to property securing consumer debts has a somewhat different deadline. *See* § 7.3.6, *infra.* The deadlines may not be strictly enforced in all jurisdictions. *But see In re* Casteel, 85 B.R. 741 (Bankr. W.D. Mich. 1988) (court to strictly enforce deadline prospectively).

22 Fed. R. Bankr. P. 1007(c), 3015. The rules provide that the application for extension must be made on notice to the United States trustee and the trustee in the case. Fed. R. Bankr. P. 1007(c), 3015.

23 Of course, a case should not be filed if there is no intention of proceeding, because that type of a filing solely for delay would not be in good faith as required by Fed. R. Bankr. P. 9011.

24 11 U.S.C. § 349(a). But see 11 U.S.C. § 109(g), discussed at § 3.2.1, *supra,* and § 9.7.3.1.5, *infra,* which bars a new case within 180 days after involuntary dismissal for willful failure to appear before the court to prosecute the case. It is doubtful that failure to file papers is a failure to appear before the court. In most cases failure to file papers is also not "willful" within the meaning of the Code.

25 11 U.S.C. § 1307(c).

26 See § 13.8, *infra,* for discussion of involuntary bankruptcy.

Especially when the court is located at some distance from the office, it is obviously a more efficient use of resources to have more than one meeting scheduled for a single date. Such scheduling can often be accomplished by filing several bankruptcy cases simultaneously. Even if the cases cannot be filed together, however, it is worthwhile to check with the court, the trustee, or the United States trustee on the possibility of having several scheduled for hearings on the same day. (Such inquiry must be made promptly, however, because the notice of the meeting of creditors is usually sent out shortly after the case is filed.)

7.3 Forms at the Outset of the Case

7.3.1 Official and Unofficial Forms

Most of the forms filed at the outset of the case are Official Forms promulgated by the Judicial Conference of the United States and are reprinted in Appendix D, *infra*. The CD-Rom accompanying this volume also contains *Bankruptcy Forms,* software templates of the Official Forms. A few forms, such as the attorney fee disclosure[27] are not officially promulgated, but nevertheless are standardized forms in common use. Those forms are reprinted in Appendix E, *infra*.

The Advisory Committee Note to Federal Rule of Bankruptcy Procedure 9009 states that the forms used should substantially comply with the Official Forms. The Introduction and General Instructions for the Official Forms states that a form will be in substantial compliance if it contains the complete substance of the information required by the Official Forms. Thus, for example, typefaces can be changed and the instructions in the forms can be deleted. Of course, when necessary, continuation sheets may be attached to provide complete information.

The instructions state that courts may not reject forms because they are presented in novel or unfamiliar formats. The only requirements other than complete substantive information are that the forms be printed on one side only, with two prepunched holes at the top of the document and an adequate top margin so that the caption and text are not obscured. In many localities, the requirement of prepunched holes is waived. Local practice should be checked.

In filling out the forms, it is important to check boxes which state "none," if "none" is the appropriate answer. Additionally, if the answer to a question is "none" or "not applicable" it is necessary to so indicate. However, when multiple choices are contained in the Official Form, it is acceptable to file a form which contains only the choice selected.

It is also acceptable, especially in emergency situations, to file legible handwritten forms or to indicate that required information is the most complete available and that it will be supplemented by amendment or otherwise.[28]

All of the official bankruptcy forms were modified in 1995 to include the information which must be provided by non-attorney bankruptcy petition preparers under Bankruptcy Code section 110, added by the 1994 amendments. The failure to provide this information will lead to serious sanctions against a petition preparer.[29]

7.3.2 The Bankruptcy Petition (Official Form 1) and the Statement of Social Security Number (Official Form 21)

The actual bankruptcy petition, which is the document that officially begins a case, is a two-page form with boxes for information to be filled in as appropriate. Its content is prescribed by the Official Forms.[30]

The petition must include all names, including fictitious or trade names, that the debtor has used over the previous six years and the last four digits of the debtor's social security number.[31] In a similar vein, the petition requests basic information about the chapter chosen by the debtor, the type of case being filed (individual, joint, partnership, corporate, or otherwise), the number of creditors and the debtor's assets and liabilities, bankruptcy cases filed by the same debtor within the prior six years,[32] and pending related[33] cases. It also sets forth that the debtor(s) meets the basic venue[34] and jurisdictional prerequisites for the chapter selected. The averments of the petition must be verified by the debtor's signature, under penalty of perjury.[35]

---

27 *See* § 7.3.8, *infra*.

28 Fed. R. Bankr. P. 1009 allows amendments to be made as a matter of course, at any time before the case is closed. *See* § 8.3.2, *infra*.

29 11 U.S.C. § 110; *see* § 15.6, *infra*.

30 Official Form 1. A copy of this form is included in Appendix D, *infra*, as well as in word-processing format on the CD-Rom accompanying this volume.

31 Fed. R. Bankr. P. 1005.

32 This information is requested because a discharge in a prior case could bar a discharge in the present case. 11 U.S.C. § 727(a)(8), (9); *see* §§ 14.2.2.8, 14.2.2.9, *infra*. Additionally, dismissal of the prior case within 180 days of the present case may render the debtor ineligible for relief. 11 U.S.C. § 109(g); *see* § 3.2.1, *supra*; § 9.7.3.1.5, *infra*.

33 A case is defined as related if filed by a spouse, partner, or affiliate of the debtor.

34 See Chapter 13, *infra,* for discussion of venue. Venue problems occur most often with debtors who have recently moved or who are employed in a judicial district other than that in which they reside.

35 *See In re* Harrison, 158 B.R. 246 (Bankr. M.D. Fla. 1993) (petition on which debtor's name was signed by another, purportedly based upon later-submitted power of attorney, was a nullity, because there was no indication on petition that it was signed based on power of attorney and there were no exigent circumstances making it impossible for debtor to sign his own petition).

The petition in every consumer chapter 7 case must also contain an averment by the debtor that she is aware of and understands the choice available between relief under chapter 7, chapter 11, chapter 12, and chapter 13 of the Code. This averment is contained in the box in which the debtor signs the petition.

In addition, to reinforce the importance of an informed choice of chapter, every consumer chapter 7 bankruptcy petition must contain a separately signed declaration by the debtor's attorney that she has explained the relief available under chapters 7, 11, 12, and 13.[36] Lastly, the debtor must state on the petition whether or not she owns or possesses property that poses or has been alleged to pose an imminent threat of identifiable harm to public health or safety. If the debtor does own or possess such property, the possible harms must be identified on Exhibit C to the petition in order to notify the trustee, who might be responsible for the property, and other parties who might be affected.[37]

The petition must be filed with the clerk of the bankruptcy court, who transmits a copy to the United States trustee.[38] Except for occasional problems concerning venue, or whether a particular debtor is eligible for chapter 13, the petition itself rarely gives rise to any issue in a case. Even with respect to the latter problem, the court normally refers to the schedules rather than to the petition in deciding the issue.

The debtor must submit to the clerk, with the petition, a verified statement that sets forth the debtor's full social security number or states that the debtor does not have a social security number.[39] This statement is not made a part of the official court file, so the debtor's social security number is not available to the general public or over the Internet. However, the social security number is included in the notice of the § 341(a) meeting mailed to creditors.[40]

7.3.3 Notice from the Clerk of Chapters Under Which Relief Is Available

Section 342(b) of the Code requires the clerk of the bankruptcy court to give each consumer debtor a notice indicating each chapter under which such individual may proceed, prior to the filing of the petition. When this requirement was first added, some clerks had required the debtor to file a form acknowledgment of notice from the

clerk regarding the types of relief available to satisfy the dictates of section 342(b).[41] This form is no longer in use, except in a few districts where it is required as a matter of local practice or where it is required of *pro se* debtors. It is a good idea to check with the local clerk's office about whether any form acknowledgment is required when a petition is filed.

Apparently, it is contemplated that the requirements of section 342(b) are now met by that portion of the bankruptcy petition in which a chapter 7 debtor certifies awareness of the various chapters under which she may proceed and the debtor's attorney certifies that she explained the relief available under each chapter.[42] In any event, the failure to file or receive the acknowledgment of notice, even in those places where it is still required, does not invalidate a bankruptcy petition.[43]

7.3.4 The Bankruptcy Schedules (Official Form 6)

7.3.4.1 Overview

Each debtor who files a bankruptcy case, under any chapter, must submit schedules A through J (Official Form 6). The main purpose of these schedules is to give an exact picture of the debtor's assets, liabilities, and budget, as of the date of filing, in a uniform manner that facilitates administration of the case. This section describes generally how the schedules are to be completed, but local rules may impose additional requirements, such as a requirement to alphabetize creditors.

7.3.4.2 Schedules A, B, and C: The Debtor's Property

7.3.4.2.1 Schedule A—real property

Schedule A is the list of the debtor's real property. In this schedule the debtor must list all legal, equitable, and future interests in real property. As with all the schedules, if the debtor has no such interests, the schedule should state "none." Leasehold interests must be listed separately in Schedule G.[44] If the debtor's interest in a particular property is other than a full possessory interest in fee simple (as in the case, for example, of a life estate or the beneficial interest in property held in trust), a careful description of the debtor's actual interest should be provided.[45] Similarly, if there are

---

36 This declaration is incorporated into Official Form 1. *See* Appx. D, *infra*.

37 This declaration is incorporated into Official Form 1, and a form for Exhibit C, if necessary, is part of that Official Form. *See* Appx. D, *infra*.

38 Fed. R. Bankr. P. 1002.

39 Fed. R. Bankr. P. 1007(f). The statement should be made on Official Form 21, reprinted in Appendix D, *infra*, and available as well in word-processing format on the CD-Rom accompanying this volume.

40 Fed. R. Bankr. P. 2002(a)(1).

---

41 A copy of this notice is reprinted in Appendix E, *infra*.

42 Official Form 1; *see* Appx. D, *infra*.

43 *See In re* Bryant, 51 B.R. 729 (Bankr. N.D. Miss. 1985).

44 *See* § 7.3.4.4, *infra*.

45 A review of some of the unusual types of property interests

limits on the debtor's access to the property (as, for example, in some divorce agreements), the nature of the limitation should be described.

It is more important to list accurately the nature of the interest, than to fit it into the available space. Footnotes or supplemental pages should be supplied when necessary.

If the debtor is married, the schedule must indicate whether the property is owned by the husband, the wife, jointly, or as community property, regardless of whether the petition is filed jointly. If the property is owned jointly, whether or not by spouses, the box describing the nature of the debtor's interest should so indicate and an appropriate adjustment reflecting the extent of the debtor's ownership interest should be made to the value.

The value of the property interest should also be given without deduction for any secured debts, such as mortgages, which are listed in the last column and described more fully in Schedule D. As noted earlier,[46] value should be listed at the amount most helpful to the debtor's case that can truthfully be given. Usually, if the property is to be claimed as exempt or if it may be worth less than the amount of any liens affecting it, the best valuation will be on the low side of the possible range. If the property is likely to be the subject of a motion for relief from stay, a higher choice may be preferable. If the value seems to be above the exemption amount, it may be appropriate to give a value that takes into account liquidation costs, such as a broker commission, trustee fees, trustee's professionals' fees, transfer taxes, and the interest and escrow portions of the mortgage payments that would not be made while the house is awaiting sale. If such items are deducted, that fact should be noted on the schedules to avoid any confusion.

Sometimes, there may be uncertainty as to how to estimate the value of one spouse's undivided and unalienable interest in certain types of joint property which cannot be sold without the consent of both spouses. In such cases, as the trustee may have a right to partition the property,[47] it is probably best to indicate the value of a one-half ownership as one-half the total value of the property, but with a note explaining that the debtor could not sell his or her share for

that amount.[48] The same approach is appropriate for other interests in jointly-held property when the joint owner is not a debtor.[49] Similarly, if the debtor has a life estate or other non-fee-simple interest in the property, the value assigned should account for the limited nature of the interest.

Lastly, courts vary regarding the specificity they demand in the description of real property. Usually, the address and a brief description is sufficient. Courts in some districts, however, may require a full legal description including the metes and bounds from the deed.

7.3.4.2.2 Schedule B—personal property

Schedule B is a list of the debtor's personal property. Schedule B should contain a list of all of the debtor's interests in personal property together with a description and the location of the property. In addition to tangible possessions, all other types of interests should be set out in this schedule, including causes of action, eligibility for government grants such as energy assistance, security deposits with landlords or utilities, support or alimony owed to the debtor, earned income tax credits, retroactive social security awards, and so forth.[50] Property the debtor is purchasing under a rent-to-own agreement should also be listed if the debtor wants to treat the rent-to-own agreement as a credit sale rather than an executory contract.[51] Because of the potential consequences of failing to list property in the schedules,[52] it is always better to be over-inclusive, rather than under-inclusive. It is especially important to list all claims or causes of action the debtor may have so that the

---

which may come into the debtor's estate is provided in § 2.5, *supra*.

46 *See* § 7.1.1, *supra*.

47 11 U.S.C. § 363(h). Under section 363(h), the appropriate inquiry is whether the benefit to the estate accruing from sale of the property would outweigh the detriment to the co-owner occurring due to partition. Courts may apply a variety of factors in making such a determination. *Compare, e.g., In re* McCoy, 92 B.R. 750 (Bankr. N.D. Ohio 1988) (partition refused because of psychological and emotional stress on mentally handicapped co-owner); *In re* Coombs, 86 B.R. 314 (Bankr. D. Mass. 1988) (partition denied on ground of psychological stress to handicapped co-owner); *In re* Ray, 73 B.R. 544 (Bankr. M.D. Ga. 1987) (partition refused) *with In re* Vassilowitch, 72 B.R. 803 (Bankr. D. Mass. 1987) (partition authorized). *See* § 2.5, *supra*.

48 See Appendix F, *infra*, for an example of completed Schedules.

49 The co-owners, however, may lack standing to object to the disposition of the debtor's interest in the jointly-held property even if it is liquidated and sold without their knowledge to a third party. *See In re* Globe Inv. & Loan Co., 867 F.2d 556 (9th Cir. 1989).

50 A review of some of the less common types of property interests which may come into the debtor's estate is provided in § 2.5, *supra*.

51 *See* § 11.8, *infra*.

52 In egregious cases of omitted assets, criminal prosecution is possible. 18 U.S.C. § 152. Similarly, an exemption may be denied if the debtor conceals assets. *In re* Yonikus, 996 F.2d 866 (7th Cir. 1993) (contingent right to receive workers' compensation in the future not disclosed in schedules could not be exempted when court found intentional and bad faith concealment of asset). Also, failure to schedule property that is not exempted will preclude that property from being deemed abandoned at the close of the case pursuant to 11 U.S.C. § 554(c). *See* Vreugdenhill v. Navistar Int'l Transp. Corp., 950 F.2d 524 (8th Cir. 1991); *In re* Shondel, 950 F.2d 1301 (7th Cir. 1991) (debtor's failure to list liability policy as an asset justified reopening bankruptcy case for benefit of tort liability claimant); Krank v. Utica Mut. Ins. Co., 109 B.R. 668 (E.D. Pa. 1990), *aff'd*, 908 F.2d 962 (3d Cir. 1990) (once cause of action becomes property of the estate, debtor may not bring suit unless that property is abandoned by the trustee).

debtor is not prevented from pursuing them after bankruptcy under the doctrine of judicial estoppel.[53]

Although the categories of property set out in schedule B are quite detailed, it is not critical to list each piece of property in the right category as long as it is listed somewhere. Note that the instructions also require that an "x" be placed in any category for which the debtor has no property and that, for married debtors, the property be listed as that of the husband, or wife, or as joint or community property.

Once more, there is considerable variation among courts as to the degree of specificity they require in descriptions of property. In view of the small values involved, some might allow low-income debtors to group property broadly in categories such as "used clothing" or "assorted household goods, each item worth under $400." Others require much more specific lists. One frequently used compromise is to list major appliances and furniture, with the latter designated more or less by room, for example, "2 bedroom sets," "kitchen set," and so forth.[54] It is normally a good idea also to include a catchall of "miscellaneous household goods," to cover all of the other items with values too small to warrant individual listings.

As for valuation, there is quite a bit of leeway. Usually, the value given takes into account the proposed method of liquidation by distress sale, without deduction for liens or exemptions.[55] A good way to convey this concept to clients is to ask them for the "tag sale" or "garage sale" value of specific items. In completing this schedule it is important to bear in mind the very low sale value of most used furniture and appliances. Because of this low value, the trustee will have little interest in the personal property of consumer clients, except perhaps for a few large items.

Some categories of property present more tricky problems of valuation. The value of a cause of action, for example, should be discounted for the contingency of success and ultimate collectability.[56] These considerations should be explained by a short note. Sometimes a similar note can explicate a seemingly low valuation on other property. For example, a relatively new car given a low value might be described as "inoperable, 120,000 miles" if those were the facts. In every case, of course, the trustee and creditors will have an opportunity to demand more detail later. Amendments to the schedule are also possible.[57] Therefore, the consequences of an innocently imperfect description of assets are not grave.

Alternatively, if the value of property is truly unknown, it is often best to simply state the value as "unknown," leaving it to the trustee and creditors to assess the value on their own. This treatment of a cause of action has the advantage of ensuring the debtor will not be accused of undervaluing it, and has been deemed sufficient by the Supreme Court.[58]

---

53 *See* Burnes v. Pemco, 291 F.3d 1282 (11th Cir. 2002) (debtor who intentionally failed to disclose employment discrimination case in schedules barred from pursuing claim for monetary damages but not claim for injunctive relief); Hamilton v. State Farm Fire & Cas. Co., 270 F.3d 778 (9th Cir. 2001) (debtor judicially estopped from bringing insurance claims not listed in schedules); *In re* Coastal Plains, Inc., 179 F.3d 197 (5th Cir. 1999); Wolfork v. Tackett, 273 Ga. 328, 540 S.E.2d 611 (2001) (failure to list tort claim that arose during pendency of chapter 13 judicially estopped debtor from pursing claim in state court). *But see In re* Barger, 348 F.3d 1289 (11th Cir. 2003) (employment discrimination claim not barred when debtor's counsel inadvertently failed to schedule claim; trustee could substitute for debtor in seeking damages and debtor could seek injunctive relief); *In re* Baldwin, 307 B.R. 251 (M.D. Ala. 2004) (judicial estoppel did not apply because debtor was not aware of lender liability claim when bankruptcy filed and later promptly amended schedules); *In re* Smith, 293 B.R. 786 (Bankr. D. Kan, 2003) (when symptoms of injury from weight reduction drug did not appear until after bankruptcy was filed, debtor's claim accrued post-petition and was not estate property); IBF Participating Income Fund v. Dillard-Winecoff, Ltd. Liab. Co., 275 Ga. 765, 573 S.E.2d 58 (2002) (fact that claim was not scheduled produced no advantage for debtor because bankruptcy case was ultimately dismissed); Chicon v. Carter, 258 Ga. App. 164, 573 S.E.2d 413 (2002) (tort claim that arose after confirmation of plan not part of bankruptcy estate and debtors obtained no unfair advantage by not disclosing it); *In re* Carter, 258 B.R. 526 (Bankr. S.D. Ga. 2001) (chapter 13 debtors' failure to list tort claim that arose post-confirmation and not necessary for maintenance of plan did not judicially estop them from pursing claim); Hoffman v. Truck Driving Academy, Inc., 777 So. 2d 151 (Ala. Civ. App. 2000) (no judicial estoppel when creditor failed to show it was prejudiced by debtor's failure to disclose claims in bankruptcy); Period Homes, Ltd. v. Wallick, 275 Ga. 486, 569 S.E.2d 502 (Ga. 2002); Johnson v. Si-Cor, 107 Wash. App. 902, 28 P.3d 832 (2001) (no evidence that failure to disclose claim benefited debtor). The failure to schedule an asset may sometimes be cured by reopening the bankruptcy case and amending the debtor's schedules. *In re* Lopez, 283 B.R. 22 (B.A.P. 9th Cir. 2002) (debtor should have been permitted to reopen and amend to schedule cause of action because, even if claim had been intentionally concealed, asset could be administered to benefit creditors); *In re* Rochester, 308 B.R. 596 (Bankr. N.D. Ga. 2004) (debtor allowed to reopen bankruptcy case to add products liability claim as debtor's failure to list claim in original schedules was not intentional or in bad faith). The debtor's failure to schedule a cause of action should not preclude the trustee from pursuing the action. Parker v. Wendy's Int'l, Inc., 365 F.3d 1268 (11th Cir. 2004).

54 Failure to give a description which at least puts the trustee on notice of the likely value of the property (and of the wisdom of further inquiry) may be cause for denying an exemption of property not properly disclosed. Payne v. Wood, 775 F.2d 202 (7th Cir. 1985) (holding that debtors could not exempt insurance proceeds received after destruction of certain property not fairly disclosed in schedules).

55 Security interests and exemptions should be listed separately in Schedule D and C respectively.

56 *See In re* Polis, 217 F.3d 899 (7th Cir. 2000) (Truth in Lending cause of action was fully exempt because, when discounted for contingency of success, it was within exemption limits).

57 Fed. R. Bankr. P. 1009; *see* § 8.3.2, *infra.*

58 Taylor v. Freeland & Kronz, 503 U.S. 638, 112 S. Ct. 1644, 118 L. Ed. 2d 280 (1992) (cause of action described but valued as "unknown" was sufficient to put trustee on notice of the exemption); *see also In re* Adair, 253 B.R. 85 (B.A.P. 9th Cir.

As with real estate, it is important to describe accurately the nature of the debtor's interest if it is other than a full ownership interest in fee simple. A legal or beneficial interest in a trust, for example, should be explained with as much detail as possible. Similarly, in a divorce scenario, a non-filing spouse's interest in property under a state law equitable distribution provision should be described. Footnotes to the schedule or supplemental pages should be filed if necessary to provide full and complete information. Some care is also required in valuing property in which the debtor holds an unusual interest. Legal restrictions on use or access to property can lower its value.

One other question which sometimes arises in connection with Schedule B is how to treat property in which the debtor has an interest, but which do not become property of the bankruptcy estate.[59] An example of this kind of property is the debtor's interest in certain ERISA-qualified pensions.[60] Because Schedule B is a list of all the debtor's property interests and not just those which come into the estate, the best practice is to list the debtor's interest with a notation that it is excluded from the estate, together with a statutory reference. In the case of a pension and most other non-estate property, the appropriate reference will be 11 U.S.C. § 541(c)(2). Often the claim that property is not part of the estate should be coupled with an exemption claim, raised in the alternative in Schedule C.

7.3.4.2.3 Schedule C—property claimed as exempt

Schedule C is the debtor's list of property claimed as exempt. Normally, it is permissible to incorporate by reference much of the listing in Schedules A and B in order to avoid repetition.[61] As always, though, local practice should be checked.

Schedule C must, first of all, state whether the debtor is utilizing the state exemptions or the federal bankruptcy exemptions. (Often, there may be no choice because the state has opted out of the latter.) Because a detailed explanation of this and other exemption issues follows in a later chapter,[62] only a few other points need be made here regarding completion of this schedule.

Obviously, the goal in completing this schedule is to exempt as much as possible, preferably all of the client's property. In the case of most low-income clients, that is not

difficult. If all property cannot be exempted, the debtor should consider exemption planning prior to filing the petition.[63]

Another strategy that is effective, if the debtor has a relatively small amount of property that cannot be exempted, is to claim exemptions in a manner that will discourage the trustee from liquidating any particular item. For example, if the debtor has five valuable household items and a car, with a total value of $2400.00 over the amount that can be exempted, the debtor may exempt all but $400.00 in value of each item, assuming the exemptions afford that flexibility, either through a wild card exemption or a total exemption amount for a variety of personal property items. The trustee would then be less likely to liquidate these items than if one item worth $2400.00 was not exempted.

Similarly, if not all property can be exempted, it is better to leave as non-exempt the property which the trustee is least likely to liquidate, such as a cause of action which would involve litigation expenses, or all or part of a joint interest in real estate. For example, if a debtor using the federal exemptions has an interest in real estate worth $18,450.00, and $3000.00 in cash or other liquid assets, the debtor might exempt only $16,435.00 worth of the real property interest, using the remainder of the exemption for the liquid assets under the wild card provisions of section 522(d)(5).[64] Although a trustee probably would demand the non-exempt cash from the debtor, it is unlikely that he or she would invest the time and expense necessary to liquidate a $2025.00 interest in real estate.

The items listed in Schedule C should be checked against Schedules A and B to be sure nothing has been inadvertently omitted. For each item, the specific applicable exemption statute should be listed. Most often, the value given in Schedule C for the exemption equals the value given in Schedules A and B, except that lien amounts can and should be deducted. If the federal exemptions are available (and under some state statutes as well), property which would not normally appear to be exempt may be exempted under the "wild card" exemption.[65] When exemptions contain monetary limits, two or more different exemptions that are applicable to the same property can be combined. Therefore, it should be fairly rare to completely omit any property interest from Schedule C unless it is an interest which the trustee is unlikely to liquidate or an interest which the debtor is willing to surrender.

It is also important to exempt property as to which the right of redemption is to be exercised. Otherwise, unless the property is sure to be abandoned, the right to redeem may be jeopardized.[66] Similarly, if property is subject to liens or transfers avoidable under section 522,[67] the property should

---

2000) (debtors had no duty to volunteer information about settlement offer on cause of action listed in schedules and ultimately abandoned by trustee when settlement offer was received after schedules were filed and trustee never sought further information during case).

59 *See* § 2.5, *supra.*

60 *See* § 2.5.2, *supra.*

61 However, any cross reference should be to specific items listed as a general claim of exemption for "assets of the petitioner" probably does not satisfy the requirements of the statute. *In re* Andermahr, 30 B.R. 532 (B.A.P. 9th Cir. 1983).

62 *See* Ch. 10, *infra.*

63 *See* Ch. 6, *supra.*

64 *See* § 10.2.2.6, *infra.*

65 11 U.S.C. § 522(d)(5); *see* § 10.2.2.6, *infra.*

66 See § 11.5, *infra,* for discussion of right to redeem.

67 See § 10.4, *infra,* for discussion of lien avoidance.

be claimed as exempt before the avoiding powers are exercised.[68]

There is no need to use exemptions on property the trustee cannot reach, that is, to the extent property is subject to a non-avoidable lien. Only equity in the property over and above the lien need by exempted. For example, if a debtor owns a $50,000.00 home subject to a $46,000.00 mortgage, only the debtor's interest—the $4000.00 equity above the mortgage—need be claimed as exempt.

Finally, the importance of careful attention to Schedule C is underscored by 11 U.S.C. § 522(*l*) which provides that property listed as exempt is exempt unless a party-in-interest objects. As there is a strictly enforced deadline for objecting to exemptions, it is to the debtor's advantage to be certain that all good faith exemptions are listed.[69] Such listing shifts the burden to the trustee and creditors to raise timely objections if any are available.[70]

It may also be important, in light of several recent cases, to specify that the debtor is exempting the debtor's entire interest in the property listed.[71] Some courts have held, erroneously, that listing an item and an amount means only that the debtor has reserved that amount out of the item's total value as exempt.[72] While in most cases a fair reading of the other schedules listing the same amount as the total value of the debtor's interest in the property makes clear that the debtor indeed does intend to claim as exempt the total value of her interest, it may be safest to specify this fact on Schedule C itself. It should be remembered, however, that Schedule C (and all the debtor's schedules) may be amended as of right at any time before the close of the case so that

mistakes and oversights are easily corrected.[73] Amended exemption schedules are then subject to objection for the time period provided in the rules.[74]

7.3.4.3 Schedules D, E, and F: Information About Creditors

7.3.4.3.1 In general

Schedules D, E, and F divide all of the client's liabilities into three categories: those to secured creditors, those to unsecured creditors entitled to priority, and those to unsecured creditors without priority.

In filling out these schedules, it is of critical importance to list the correct name and address of the creditor. If the correct name or address is not listed and, consequently, the creditor fails to receive notice, the dischargeability of a debt may be affected.[75] With respect to state and federal government creditors, the clerk of the bankruptcy court is required to maintain a register of addresses at which agencies wish to receive notice.[76] If an agency has listed its address in that registry, that address should be used, because it provides a safe harbor from any later claims that the wrong address was used.[77] Also, if the debtor knows that a person to be included on a list of creditors or in the schedules is an infant or incompetent person, the debtor should include, in addition, the name, address, and legal relationship of any person who would be served with process in an adversary proceeding brought against the infant or incompetent person in accordance with Federal Rule of Bankruptcy Procedure 7004(b)(2).[78] Normally, this person would be the parent or guardian of the infant or incompetent person.

The other information, regarding the account number, the amount of debt, the date incurred, whether there are codebtors, and the consideration for the claim is usually less crucial but, of course, should be answered as accurately as possible. When accurate information is unavailable, the debtor's best estimate is usually sufficient as long as it is made in good faith. In most consumer cases the amount listed in the schedules has little relevance, because if assets are available,

---

68 Because § 522(h) allows avoidance of liens on property "which the debtor could have exempted," it may not be necessary to list the property as exempt before the lien is avoided under that section. However, because § 522(f) contains different wording, it is safer as a general practice to claim the debtor's interest in the property as exempt, with an explanatory note about planned lien avoidance if appropriate.

69 Fed. R. Bankr. P. 4003(b) provides that objections to exemptions must be made within thirty days of the meeting of creditors unless more time is granted within that period.

70 Taylor v. Freeland & Kronz, 503 U.S. 638, 112 S. Ct. 1644, 118 L. Ed. 2d 280 (1992).

71 This should be done by stating explicitly "the debtor exempts the full amount of the estate's interest in this property," because even an exemption of "all" or "100 percent" may lead to questions about whether the debtor means "all of the exemption" or "all of the property." *See In re* Mercer, 158 B.R. 886 (Bankr. D.R.I. 1993), *aff'd*, 170 B.R. 759 (D.R.I. 1994), *aff'd*, 53 F.3d 1 (1st Cir. 1995) (claim of "100 percent" found to mean "100 percent of the available exemption").

72 *E.g., In re* Hyman, 967 F.2d 1316 (9th Cir. 1992); *see also In re* Wick, 276 F.3d 412 (8th Cir. 2002) (erroneously holding that, even though debtor listed value of stock options as unknown and trustee did not object to exemption, property was only partially exempt because trustee expressed interest in asset and debtor supposedly made statements suggesting she "understood" options to be only partially exempt).

---

73 Fed. R. Bankr. P. 1009.

74 Fed R. Bankr. P. 4003(b) allows objections within thirty days after amendment. *See* § 10.3.3, *infra*.

75 11 U.S.C. § 523(a)(3). Dischargeability may be similarly affected by failure to list a correct address in a mailing matrix, if one is required by local rule. *In re* Adams, 734 F.2d 1094 (5th Cir. 1984); *see* § 14.4.3.3, *infra*. Although section 523(a)(3) is not applicable to chapter 13 cases in which the debtor completes a plan, the claim of an unlisted creditor without actual notice of the case is probably also not discharged because the claim is not provided for under the plan. *See* 11 U.S.C. § 1328(a).

76 *See* Fed. R. Bankr. P. 5003(e).

77 *See* Fed. R. Bankr. P. 5003(e).

78 Fed. R. Bankr. P. 1007(m).

they are paid according to the creditor's proof of claim rather than according to the debtor's schedules.[79]

For joint petitions only the debtor must list whether the debt is owed by the husband, the wife, or as a joint or community debt. The schedule should note the existence of a co-obligor (other than a spouse with whom the debtor has filed jointly) by a check in the appropriate box labeled "codebtor" and by providing the necessary information about the codebtor in Schedule H.[80]

If there is any chance that the amount of a debt will continue to be relevant after bankruptcy (as with secured or nondischargeable debts), the schedules should not contain an admission of a debt larger than the debtor will later maintain to be due. If the amount of the debt is contingent, unliquidated, or in dispute, that should be noted in the appropriate place. Whether a debt is contingent or unliquidated may be important if the debtor has large debts that make her ineligible for chapter 13.[81] A debt is usually considered contingent if payment is not yet due and will not become due unless a particular event occurs in the future. An example of a contingent debt is a guarantor's obligation to pay a debt only if the principal obligor does not pay. A debt is unliquidated when the debtor has a legal obligation to pay some amount of money, but the amount has not yet been fixed. An example of an unliquidated debt is an auto accident claim for which the debtor acknowledges liability, but the amount of the liability has not yet been fixed. By listing such debts and having them discharged, the debtor can often avoid having to fight over the details concerning the validity or amount of the debt.

It is always wise to check the column which lists a debt as disputed if there is any doubt about the validity of the debt or the amount the creditor claims due. Noting the debt as disputed should prevent a later claim by the creditor that the schedules constitute an admission by the debtor of the validity or extent of the creditor's claim.

Because debts that are not listed are sometimes not discharged, it is of obvious importance to list every conceivable claim against the client so that the discharge may be used to maximum advantage. As discussed above in a previous chapter, this may necessitate prompting the client to remember various types and categories of frequently overlooked debts.[82] It may also mean listing debts that appear on a client's credit report, even if the client does not recognize them and they appear to be erroneously reported. There is ordinarily no disadvantage to listing these debts and noting that they are disputed.

7.3.4.3.2 Schedule D—secured debts

Schedule D lists all secured creditors. This schedule should include all creditors that hold liens, even if they are undersecured, and even if their liens can later be avoided by the debtor or trustee.[83] Creditors holding security deposits also should be listed here, as well as creditors holding less noticeable types of security interests, such as those in the refunds of credit insurance. Similarly, banks and other savings institutions with a right of setoff against the debtor's accounts should be considered secured for the amounts in such accounts. (But normally, with good planning, all money will be withdrawn prior to bankruptcy and therefore these creditors will be unsecured.)[84] Again, if the debtor intends to treat a rent-to-own contract as a credit sale of property subject to a security interest, the rent-to-own debt should be included in this schedule.[85] There is a box in the Official Form for the debtor to check if there are no secured creditors at all.

If the debtor disputes whether a claim is secured, it should be listed in Schedule D, along with the fact that the security interest is disputed. Again, as with all of the forms, the goal should be clarity in depicting the client's affairs. As long as clarity is achieved, even errors as to placement in the proper schedule will not be of great importance.

Although there is no place on the form to list the amount of arrears owed on a long-term secured debt such as a mortgage, it may be a good idea to include that information if the debtor has filed chapter 13 and intends to cure those arrears. This inclusion may help eliminate confusion about the nature of the debtor's plan.

Finally, some care should be taken in Schedule D to identify undersecured creditors, particularly in chapter 13, and to list the amount of the unsecured portion in the appropriate box. These figures may help in a later attempt to determine the creditor's allowed secured claim.[86]

---

79 There may occasionally be an issue under 11 U.S.C. § 109(e) concerning debt limits for eligibility for chapter 13 to which such estimates are relevant. *See* § 12.2, *infra*. There also may be issues which arise under § 707(b) or § 1325(a)(3), (4), or (b) concerning the debtor's purposes in filing, good faith, or the amount which must be paid to unsecured creditors under a chapter 13 plan. See §§ 13.9.2.2 and 12.3, *infra*, respectively. At most, the amounts listed in Schedule D are evidence of the debtor's belief about what such creditors are owed at the outset of the case. They should not be conclusive proof of the amount of the debt even against the debtor.

80 *See* § 7.3.4.5, *infra*.

81 See § 12.2.3.2, *infra*, for further discussion of contingent and unliquidated debts.

82 *See* § 5.3.3.3, *supra*.

83 *See* Ch. 10, *infra*.

84 *See* § 6.5, *supra*.

85 *See* § 11.8, *infra*.

86 *See In re* Gabor, 155 B.R. 391 (Bankr. N.D. W. Va. 1993) (claim of creditor holding security interest in debtor's car was treated as totally unsecured under § 506(a) because debtor's wife had absconded with car, debtor had no knowledge of her whereabouts, and therefore estate's interest in the car was worthless); § 11.2, *infra*. The same issues also may be relevant to a determination of whether a chapter 13 debtor meets the debt limitations under § 109(g). *See* § 12.2.3, *infra*.

7.3.4.3.3 Schedule E—priority debts

Schedule E lists the different categories of debt that may have priority under the Code. The Official Form has boxes that should be checked to designate the types of priority debt or to note that the debtor has no priority obligations.

In order to complete this schedule, the practitioner must first determine which claims, if any, fall into the priority categories set out in 11 U.S.C. § 507.[87] If the creditor has a lien, the debt should be placed in Schedule D whether or not the creditor would otherwise be entitled to a priority.[88] (If there is neither a lien nor an applicable priority, the debt belongs in Schedule F as unsecured, non-priority.) In some cases, only part of a debt will be entitled to priority status. With respect to each priority debt, the amount entitled to the priority and the amount not entitled to priority should be listed separately in the appropriate column on the schedule. In other words, the non-priority portion of the debt is listed on Schedule E, not Schedule F.

By far the most common type of priority debt owed by consumer clients is taxes. It should be noted, however, that not all tax claims are entitled to priority, and only those which are at least partially priority claims and also are unsecured should be listed in Schedule E. This determination is especially important because priority tax claims must be paid in full in chapter 13 and they are nondischargeable in chapter 7. In a chapter 7 case, if there are assets in the estate, it is important to make sure that such nondischargeable tax debts are listed as priority claims, so that they will be paid first.[89] However, if there are no assets, and if there is any doubt as to priority status, the taxes should be listed in Schedule F (unless secured by a lien) so as not to make any admission as to nondischargeability.

Other types of priority debts occasionally found in consumer cases are those for alimony, maintenance, or support arrears,[90] or wages or consumer deposits, which sometimes exist if the client had a small business. As in the case of taxes, if there is any doubt whether a debt to a spouse or former spouse is in the nature of nondischargeable alimony, maintenance, or support,[91] the debtor should claim the debt to be a dischargeable property settlement and list it on Schedule F (unless it is likely to be paid from assets of the estate).

Because wages and consumer deposit claims are normally dischargeable, there need be no hesitation about listing any such possible priority claims on Schedule E in chapter 7 cases. In chapter 13, however, more care should be exercised because an admission of priority status will carry a requirement that the particular debt be paid in full under the debtor's plan.[92]

7.3.4.3.4 Schedule F—general unsecured debts

All of the client's remaining debts are included on Schedule F. The general principles stated above apply here with equal force, and all possible claims should be listed. Often forgotten are the contingent subrogation claims which may be available to codebtors who later pay off a claim, including those on mortgages guaranteed by the Veterans Administration or Federal Housing Administration and those on guaranteed student loans.[93] Though such persons are often unlikely to pursue the client, or even know they have a right to do so, it is good practice to list them as creditors as well, with an indication that the debt is not a separate one to be added to the total amount owed.[94] If such listing is done, codebtors will be given notice of the case, and any possible claims they have will be extinguished.

Another frequently overlooked category of debt is a continuing obligation to pay prorated amounts on a prepetition contract for services. When the contract calls for deferment of a lump sum balance due at the outset of the agreement, such as with many condominium assessments, those debts may be dischargeable.[95]

Courts vary on the specificity required in completing the section of the form detailing the consideration for the debt

---

87　See § 3.5, *supra*.

88　11 U.S.C. § 507(a) which defines types of priority debts is applicable only to unsecured claims.

89　It is also important to make sure that a timely proof of claim is filed on behalf of the creditor, by the debtor if not by the creditor, because a trustee can pay an unsecured claim in chapter 7 only if a proof of claim has been filed. *See* § 8.5, *infra*.

90　There may be issues regarding whether a debt owed is in the nature of alimony, maintenance, or support and thus a priority debt, or in the nature of a property settlement and therefore not entitled to priority. For discussion of this dichotomy, see § 14.4.3.5, *infra*. A debtor in a particular case, depending upon the circumstances, may wish to argue that a debt is not a priority debt, but is rather a property settlement (which is a dischargeable general unsecured claim), or that a debt is in the nature of alimony, maintenance, or support, so that it will be accorded priority treatment if assets of the estate are liquidated. *See generally* Henry J. Sommer & Margaret Doe McGarity, Collier Family Law and the Bankruptcy Code. The treatment of the debt in the debtor's schedules should be consistent with the strategy desired.

91　*See* § 14.4.3.5, *infra*.

92　11 U.S.C. § 1322(a)(2).

93　See Appendix F, *infra*, for example of completed form. *See also In re* Barnett, 42 B.R. 254 (Bankr. S.D.N.Y. 1984) (debt to guarantor of student loan must be scheduled); *In re* McCrady, 23 B.R. 193 (Bankr. W.D. Ky. 1982) (codebtor who paid note could not sue debtor who had given him notice of bankruptcy).

94　Though government guarantors of mortgages rarely pursue a debtor after foreclosure, the failure to discharge the personal liability to the Veteran's Administration (VA), for example, may leave a debtor ineligible for a new veteran's mortgage. If the debt is discharged, the VA may not discriminate based on previous nonpayment. 11 U.S.C. § 525(a); *see* § 14.5.4, *infra*.

95　*See In re* Rosteck, 899 F.2d 694 (7th Cir. 1990) (condominium assessments falling due post-petition on a pre-petition contract are dischargeable). Dischargeability of condominium assessments is now addressed by 11 U.S.C. § 523(a)(14) and is discussed in § 14.4.3.14, *infra*.

and the date the debt was incurred. In the case of credit card debts, courts will usually accept a general description such as "credit card" or "miscellaneous purchases" made on "various dates."

Finally, even though the Official Form is not formatted to easily input an obligation that is owed to two separate creditors, it is a good idea to include both creditors in the schedule. Probably, the easiest way to do so is to enter the creditors' names separately in two boxes with a notation that it is the same debt so that it does not affect the total.[96] This approach is also useful with respect to an obligation assigned to another entity or to a collection agency for purposes of collection. Including both the original creditor and the collection agency or assignee in both the schedule and the mailing matrix ensures that both get notice of the bankruptcy and that any claim of either of them is discharged.

7.3.4.4 Schedule G: Unexpired Leases and Executory Contracts

Schedule G, the schedule of unexpired leases and executory contracts, is required in all cases. It is designed primarily to put the trustee on notice of leases or other executory contracts which might be assumed or rejected because of their potential benefit or cost to the estate.[97] Although the issues which might be raised by the schedule are rarely of great importance in consumer cases, the schedule is not difficult to complete.

An executory contract is broadly defined as one for which significant aspects of performance remain due on both sides. An unexpired lease is one that has not yet terminated by its terms.[98] If, as is common, the debtor has no unexpired leases or executory contracts, the debtor should check the box marked "none."

For most consumer debtors, a residential lease will be the only entry on this form. These should probably be listed even if the lease is only a month-to-month oral agreement. Occasionally, the debtor may have an automobile lease, an ongoing employment contract, or a pending sale agreement for goods or real estate. These should be listed as well.

In those cases which include unexpired leases or other executory contracts, the listing must include a statement of the debtor's interest. The other party to the contract may also be listed as a creditor in the applicable schedule, particularly if there has been a default on the contract. This listing will ensure notice of the bankruptcy to that party. On the other hand, some debtors would rather not give their landlords notice that they are filing a bankruptcy case. If the debtor does not owe money to the lessor, perhaps because there is

a month-to-month lease, there is no requirement that the lessor be listed as a creditor or included in the mailing matrix for notices in the case.

One other issue that may occasionally arise is how to treat a rent-to-own contract for consumer goods. For the reasons discussed in a later chapter, there is a significant advantage and considerable precedent for treating these contracts as security agreements rather than executory contracts.[99] Consequently, the rent-to-own obligation should generally be listed in Schedule D as a secured debt.

7.3.4.5 Schedule H: Codebtors

The debtor's codebtors, other than a spouse in a joint case, should be listed in Schedule H. The instructions for the Official Form provide that, in community property states, a married debtor not filing a joint case should always report the name and address of the non-debtor spouse, together with any other names used by the non-debtor spouse within the previous six years. As discussed above, codebtors may also be listed as creditors in Schedule F due to any potential subrogation claims that could arise if the codebtors later pay off the obligation. However, even if they are not listed in that schedule, their claims are ordinarily discharged as long as they receive notice of the case.[100]

7.3.4.6 Schedules I and J: Income and Expenses

The last two parts of Official Form 6 are schedules I and J which require a complete disclosure of the debtor's income and expenses. In chapter 7 cases, these schedules are intended to provide information that could help a bankruptcy court to determine whether a chapter 7 case might be a "substantial abuse" and therefore subject to dismissal under 11 U.S.C. § 707(b).[101] In chapter 13 cases, schedules I and J allow the trustee and interested creditors to determine whether the debtor's plan is feasible and whether it is in compliance with plan requirements.[102] Creditors and the trustee may look to these schedules to decide whether to object to confirmation under 11 U.S.C. § 1325(b), the "ability-to-pay" test.[103] The court may also look to these schedules to decide whether the plan is the debtor's best effort,[104] and whether there is cause for extending the plan beyond the

---

96 See completed Official Forms found in Appendix F, *infra.*

97 *See* § 12.9, *infra.*

98 See § 12.9, *infra,* for a fuller discussion of the Code's treatment of unexpired leases and executory contracts.

99 *See* § 11.8, *infra.*

100 Unscheduled creditors' claims are discharged if they receive notice of the case. *See* § 14.4.3.3, *infra.* The debtor's counsel can make sure that they receive notice by including codebtors on the mailing matrix or any other notice list.

101 See § 13.9.2.2, *infra,* for discussion of the "substantial abuse" test.

102 See § 7.3.7, and Chapter 12, *infra,* for a fuller discussion of chapter 13 plans.

103 See § 12.3.3, *infra,* for discussion of the "ability to pay" test.

104 See § 14.2.2.9, *infra,* for discussion of the "best effort" requirement, relevant under 11 U.S.C. § 727(a)(9).

usual three years.[105]

Schedule I must include income for both spouses in a joint case and also when one spouse files a chapter 12 or chapter 13 case individually, unless the spouses are separated and a joint petition is not filed. Income contributions to the debtor by persons not married to the debtor should generally be listed separately in the schedule as "other monthly income." This listing is of particular importance in chapter 13 cases in which the income contributions are necessary to meet the regular income eligibility requirement or to make the plan feasible.[106]

When income from a business or farm is included, a detailed statement of the business revenues must be attached. When expected income is not likely to be received, such as alimony or support payments that have not historically been paid, this circumstance should be noted in order to present a realistic picture. Although food stamps and certain other public benefits are not treated as income for many purposes, they should nevertheless be considered income for the purpose of the bankruptcy filing. The existence of food stamps in Schedule I, for example, will be offset by the debtor's food expense in Schedule J, and may explain what otherwise appears to be an unrealistic budget.

Because the form requires information about anticipated increases or decreases in income of more than ten percent in the year following the filing of the plan, any significant non-speculative expected changes should be listed. For example, if unemployment benefits are due to terminate within a year of the petition, the date of termination should be given.

Schedule J requires information about the expenses of the debtor and the debtor's family. A box is provided on the Official Form to be checked by spouses who have filed a joint case but keep separate households. Such debtors are instructed to file separate schedules of expenditures, with the second schedule labeled "spouse." When household expenses are paid by persons whose income or contributions are not included in Schedule I, it is best to list the expense as zero with an appropriate note about how it is paid.

When there are regular expenses from operation of a farm or business, a detailed statement of those expenses must be attached. For chapter 13 cases, it is necessary to work out the debtor's plan before finishing the expense schedule, because the debtor must list on that schedule the amount to be paid into the plan.

In listing the debtor's income and expenses, particularly the latter, the purposes of the forms should be kept in mind. A good faith effort to be accurate is always required, but budgets are flexible and budgeting for the future is an inexact science. Many debtors have only a vague idea of what they spend for various items, and have often spent less

than necessary for things like home maintenance and clothing because they were trying to make debt payments they no longer will have to make. The debtor's expenses usually can be estimated, within the limits of realistic planning, in a way that presents the case in a favorable light. In chapter 7, for example, it is not wise to show a great deal of income not needed for reasonable living expenses of the debtor and the debtor's dependents if that can truthfully be avoided, because some courts might find the availability of such income to dictate a dismissal for "substantial abuse" of chapter 7. A catchall category, such as "miscellaneous expenses" can be added to reflect the various items not specifically listed, and other categories, such as the substantial expenses for school expenses and haircuts in a large family may also need to be added. However, such income is rarely likely to be a problem; the overwhelming majority of debtors filing chapter 7 bankruptcies have barely enough income to meet the most basic family expenses.[107]

In chapter 13, the debtor's income and expenses must support the debtor's position that sufficient disposable income is available to fund the proposed plan. If, for example, the debtor's income is only barely sufficient to fund the necessary payments required under chapter 13, some care may be necessary to use the lowest possible reasonable estimates of the debtor's expenses so that the plan will not appear infeasible. In other cases, it will be to the debtor's advantage to minimize disposable income which would otherwise be paid to unsecured creditors.[108] In that event, the maximum good faith estimate of anticipated necessary expenses should be used.

It is not uncommon for debtors to estimate poorly their expenditures on items such as food, clothes, and transportation. Counsel should make every effort to get an appropriate good faith estimate that supports the debtor's goals for the case. Ideally, the budget will show the sum of the debtor's expenses and payments under the plan to be just a bit less than her income. Items frequently overlooked on the expense side are child care costs (including diapers), home maintenance costs, and irregular expenses such as schoolbooks and auto maintenance. Because the income and expense information requested are estimates of future income and expenses, there is some latitude to go back to the debtor to obtain good faith estimates consistent with the debtor's objectives. There is probably little need for concern that a low-income client's expenses will appear too high, as bankruptcy judges are more accustomed to middle-class debtors who typically have much higher expenses.

---

105 See § 12.6.3, *infra,* for discussion of the requirements for extending a plan over more than three years.

106 *See* §§ 12.2.2, 12.5, *infra.*

107 Of course, there is no requirement that a chapter 7 debtor show a positive cash flow. It is therefore quite common for chapter 7 debtors to schedule substantially greater expenses than income. Having greater expenses than income is, after all, how they got into substantial debt before the bankruptcy case.

108 *See* § 12.3.3, *infra.*

7.3.4.7 Declaration Concerning Debtor's Schedules

The Official Form schedules include a separate "declaration" page. This page contains the debtor's oath under penalty of perjury that the debtor has read the schedules and that they are true and correct to the best of her knowledge, information, and belief. Joint debtors must each sign the declaration page.

The meeting with the debtor to review the schedules is another opportunity to explain the bankruptcy process as well as the purposes of the information contained in the schedules. It is a good idea to allow the debtor as much time as the debtor needs to read over all the schedules and statements. A practitioner can then spend some time with the debtor to explain the meeting of creditors and anything else anticipated concerning future progress of the case.[109]

7.3.4.8 The Summary of Schedules

Accompanying the schedules is a form summarizing debts, property, income, and expenses. The form is self-explanatory. After the summary is filled out, it is usually inserted at the front of the schedules for filing, or elsewhere if required by local practice.

7.3.5 The Statement of Financial Affairs (Official Form 7)

The statement of financial affairs (Official Form 7) is also required in both chapter 7 and chapter 13 cases. Every question must be answered, but the form is simple to fill out. Each question has a box labeled "none" which should be checked if that is the appropriate response to a given question.

Spouses filing a joint petition may file a single statement. In cases under chapter 12 or 13, married debtors must provide information for both spouses whether or not a joint petition is filed, unless the spouses are separated and a joint petition is not filed. Debtors engaged in business must provide the requested information for all unincorporated businesses as well as for their personal affairs.

Questions 1 to 18 must be answered by every debtor, but questions 19 to 25 are required only for debtors who have been engaged in business[110] within the six years preceding bankruptcy.

The first two questions on the statement of financial affairs address the debtor's income history. The information to be included in response to these questions goes back two years and therefore may be different from the expected future income included in Schedule I.[111] The income figures provided should be in terms of gross income, not take-home pay. Although income is usually not relevant to a chapter 7 case, which deals primarily with assets and liabilities, a statement of high income or one which does not fit in with other information provided may prompt further investigation. It may also trigger an inquiry by the United States trustee or the court as to whether the filing of a chapter 7 case is a substantial abuse of that chapter.[112]

The next eight questions concern recent transfers or losses of property by the debtor. Using the responses to these questions, the trustee can sometimes avoid transfers or seek proceeds due the debtor.[113] Because debtors themselves may exercise avoiding powers,[114] especially with respect to executions on their property, accurate information here is important to protect these rights. Lastly, the answers to these questions could point out possible impediments to discharge, such as transfers to hinder or defraud creditors.[115]

The first part of question 3 requests information about loans and other debts on which more than $600.00 was repaid within the ninety days prior to the bankruptcy. The second part deals with payments of any amount made to or for the benefit of creditors who were "insiders"[116] within the year prior to the bankruptcy regardless of the amount. The trustee may be able to recover these payments as preferences.[117] Again, in most cases, the trustee will not be interested in pursuing small amounts of money, even if they are somewhat above the $600.00 threshold, especially if they are not easily collectible. Local practice varies as to the specificity required in answering this question. In some places it may be sufficient to state that "monthly payments" or "several payments" of a particular amount were made to some or all creditors if the aggregate to any single creditor is under $1000.00 or so. If the trustee is interested, she may then inquire further. Even though they would not ordinarily be avoidable as preferences, the question appears to seek information about payments to secured creditors, such as mortgagees and car lenders, as well as to unsecured creditors.

---

109 *See* Ch. 8, *infra.*

110 Being "in business" is defined for the purposes of Official Form 7 in the Official Form. It includes debtors who are officers, directors, managing executives or persons in control of a corporation; partners other than limited partners; sole proprietors or self-employed. Family farmers are included.

111 Note that the two year period is not identical in questions 1 and 2. Question 1 refers to the present calendar year and the "two years immediately preceding this calendar year." Question 2 refers to the "two years immediately preceding the commencement of this case."

112 See § 13.9.2.2, *infra,* for discussion of the "substantial abuse" test.

113 See § 10.4, *infra,* for discussion of avoiding powers.

114 *See* § 10.4, *infra.*

115 11 U.S.C. § 727(a)(2); *see* § 14.2.2, *infra.*

116 Insider is defined as it is in the Bankruptcy Code, 11 U.S.C. § 101(31). It includes relatives and certain business relations of the debtor. Relative is in turn defined at 11 U.S.C. § 101(45) and includes an "individual related by affinity or consanguinity within the third degree by the common law, or individual in a step or adoptive relationship within such third degree."

117 See § 10.4, *infra,* for discussion of avoiding powers.

Question 4 seeks information about all lawsuits and administrative proceedings involving the debtor which are pending or were terminated within the previous year. It also seeks the details of any execution, seizure, or garnishment in the previous year.[118] The information required is minimal; the debtor need only provide the caption, case number, nature of proceeding, court, and status of the case. Such information may help uncover creditor actions which can be set aside by the trustee or debtor. It also may lead to a further source of information about the debtor's affairs. In addition, property seized or levied upon may still belong to the debtor and may come into the estate if it has not been sold. The question also recognizes that lawsuits brought by the debtor may, in fact, be assets of the debtor that can benefit the estate. When such claims of the debtor are listed, they should also be included in Schedule B as property of the debtor and in Schedule C as exempt, if possible.

Question 5 requests information about repossessions, foreclosures, deeds in lieu of foreclosure, and returns of property. They may also give the trustee an opportunity to recover property for the estate.

Question 6, concerning assignments and receiverships, is rarely applicable to consumer cases, as those mechanisms normally concern business insolvencies in the few situations when they are still used. Like the preceding questions, this question is intended to identify property that might be recovered by the trustee.

Question 7 seeks information about large gifts or charitable contributions in the year before bankruptcy. Because gifts, by definition, are without consideration, the trustee reviews the answer to this question to determine whether recoverable property may have been lost to the estate.[119] The debtor need not list ordinary and usual gifts to family members (such as birthday or holiday gifts) if they total less than $200.00 per recipient. Similarly, charitable contributions aggregating $100.00 or less to a single recipient need not be listed.

Question 8, seeking information as to gambling, theft, or fire losses, is designed to explain lost assets. It is also sometimes used to smoke out dishonest debtors who use this section to account for the sudden disappearance of large amounts of property. In some cases, this question will help the trustee discover the availability of a claim to insurance proceeds which might substitute for the lost property.

Question 9 seeks disclosure of payments made for debt counseling or bankruptcy within one year before the case by or on behalf of the debtor. In addition to payments made to third party debt counselors and prior attorneys, payments made in connection with the debtor's existing case should be included. Payments made by persons other than the debtor must also be disclosed. The question's purpose is to assist in

court supervision of attorney fees paid to debtors' counsel and occasionally to turn up exploitative debt counseling or other bankruptcy related scams.[120]

The next question, number 10, again looks for transfers which can be set aside, including fraudulent transfers.[121] Any transfers that were not in the ordinary course of the business or financial affairs of the debtor (such as payments for normal household expenses) and that are not listed elsewhere in the statement should be listed in response to question ten. It is important to remember that the granting of a security interest is a transfer within the meaning of this question,[122] as is any payment to any entity not listed in answering the previous questions. Also included are involuntary transfers other than repossessions and returns.

Questions 11 and 12 concerning closed financial accounts and safe deposit boxes are designed to determine if the debtor has hidden or transferred any assets that could potentially benefit the estate. The answers to these questions, in some cases, are also used to trace the debtor's assets. Closed financial accounts must be listed, whether they were in the debtor's name or for the benefit of the debtor. They may include bank accounts, certificates of deposit, credit union accounts, pension funds, brokerage accounts, and other types of financial accounts. Safe deposit boxes must be listed only if they contained cash, securities, or other valuables within the year prior to the bankruptcy. In some jurisdictions, trustees will routinely request additional information about the contents of safe deposit boxes or statements from the closed accounts.

Question 13 requests information about setoffs by a bank or any other entity within the ninety days preceding the case, again because the trustee or debtor may have the option to recover the setoff.[123] Debtors who have had setoffs against their accounts during that period must list the name and address of the creditor, the date of the setoff, and the amount of the setoff.

Question 14 deals with property held by the client but belonging to another person. Especially if large amounts of such property exist, or if the property seems to encompass things that most people would own themselves, such as household goods or clothing, the trustee might inquire further. Property held in trust for another or in a Uniform Transfer to Minors account should also be listed here.

Question 15 requires prior addresses of the debtor within the previous two years. The answer to this question some-

---

118 Such transfers may be preferences or fraudulent transfers. 11 U.S.C. §§ 547, 548.

119 See § 10.4.2.6.5, *infra,* concerning fraudulent transfers.

120 *See generally* Ch. 15, *infra*; National Consumer Law Center, Unfair and Deceptive Acts and Practices § 5.1.12 (5th ed. 2001 and Supp.). This question should help the court and the trustee identify issues involving petition preparers under 11 U.S.C. § 110, but there is evidence that some less scrupulous petition preparers are failing to list their fees in filling out the answer to this question. Failure to disclose the fee is a violation of section 110(h). *See* § 15.6, *infra.*

121 11 U.S.C. §§ 544, 548; *see* Ch. 10, *infra.*

122 11 U.S.C. § 101(54).

123 11 U.S.C. § 553; *see* § 10.4.2.6.7, *infra.*

times provides a clue to the trustee or a suspicious creditor of additional interests of the debtor in real estate or a way to begin an investigation of potential hidden assets. It may also help creditors verify the identity of the debtor.

Question 16 requests information concerning spouses and former spouses, but only for debtors who have lived in community property states in the previous six years. Such debtors must list the name of the debtor's spouse or any former spouse who resided with the debtor in a community property state. This information is necessary because the community property provisions of the Bankruptcy Code[124] often will cause a debtor's bankruptcy case to affect the property and debts of a spouse or former spouse in a community property state, even if the spouse or former spouse has not joined in the bankruptcy case.

Question 17 seeks information concerning potential environmental liabilities of the debtor. Although few debtors have such liabilities, any debtor who has received a notice that she may have an environmental violation, or who is subject to a judicial or administrative proceeding under an environmental law, must provide information in response to this question.

Question 18 is intended to identify debtors who have been in business in the previous six years. Every debtor must either answer the question or check the box marked "None." If the debtor has been in business, information identifying the business must be provided and questions 19–25 must be answered.

Questions 19–25 are applicable to debtors who have owned or operated businesses, including family farms, partnerships, and sole proprietorships, within the six years prior to the case. Information must be provided about the business, the business books and records, inventories, present and former business partners, officers, directors, and shareholders, as well as withdrawals or distributions made to insiders.

The debtor's statement of financial affairs, like the schedules, must be signed by the debtor or debtors under penalty of perjury. For almost all consumer debtors, the responses to the questions in the statement of financial affairs are routine. It is likely that the trustee will engage in little more than a cursory review of the statement and it will have little impact on the case. Obviously, though, thorough answers are appropriate, because any attempt to obfuscate is only likely to lead to problems and perhaps a claim that the debtor is seeking to hide assets. To the extent that the debtor intends to seek to recover exempt property from creditors, the answers in the statement should be consistent with the debtor's theory for that recovery.[125]

7.3.6 The Statement of Intention with Regard to Property Securing Consumer Debts

Another required document in chapter 7 cases is the statement of intention regarding property securing consumer debts.[126] This document must state certain intentions of the debtor, as of the date of its filing, with regard to any property, real or personal, that serves as collateral for a "consumer debt."[127] The statement must be filed within thirty days after the debtor files a petition under chapter 7, or on or before the date of the section 341 meeting of creditors, whichever is earlier, unless the court, for cause, extends the deadline for filing.[128] As a practical matter, it is normally filed with the statement of affairs and schedules in a chapter 7 case.

The Bankruptcy Rules provide that the statement of intention must be prepared as prescribed by Official Form 8.[129] That form requires a listing of all property subject to security interests securing consumer debts, and the names of the creditors holding liens on the property. The rules also require that the statement be served on the trustee and each creditor named in the statement on or before the date the statement is filed.[130]

It is important to note what this section does and does not require. It requires only that the debtor state (1) whether the property will be surrendered or retained, (2) whether it will be claimed as exempt, (3) whether the debtor intends to redeem the property, and (4) whether the debtor intends to reaffirm the debt secured by the property.[131] If property is to be retained, the Official Form[132] offers the debtor the option of indicating an intention, if applicable, to: (1) claim the property as exempt,[133] (2) redeem pursuant to 11 U.S.C. § 722,[134] or (3) reaffirm pursuant to 11 U.S.C. § 524(c).[135]

But there is no requirement that the debtor choose one of the options provided under the Code or in the Official Form even if the debtor cannot exempt the property and check the box stating that option.[136] A debtor may choose to retain the

---

124 11 U.S.C. §§ 524(a)(3), 541(a)(2); *see* § 2.5, *supra*; § 14.5.1.4, *infra*.

125 *See* Ch. 10, *infra*.

126 11 U.S.C. § 521(2); *see* Official Form 8, Appx. D, *infra*.

127 Consumer debt is defined at 11 U.S.C. § 101(8).

128 11 U.S.C. § 521(2)(A).

129 Fed. R. Bankr. P. 1007(b)(2). A completed form is included in Appendix F, *infra*.

130 Fed. R. Bankr. P. 1007(b)(2).

131 11 U.S.C. § 521(2).

132 Official Form 8; *see* Appx. D, *infra*.

133 *See* Ch. 10, *infra*.

134 *See* § 11.5, *infra*.

135 *See* § 14.5.2, *infra*.

136 *See* Lowry Fed. Credit Union v. West, 882 F.2d 1543 (10th Cir. 1989) (Code does not limit debtor to choice between redemption or reaffirmation); Homeowners Funding Corp. of America v. Belanger, 128 B.R. 142 (E.D.N.C. 1990), *aff'd*, 962 F.2d 345 (4th Cir. 1992); *In re* Windham, 136 B.R. 878 (Bankr. M.D. Fla. 1992); *In re* Stefano, 134 B.R. 824 (Bankr. W.D. Pa. 1991). *But see In re* Edwards, 901 F.2d 1383 (7th Cir. 1990); *In re* Bell, 700

property subject to the creditor's security interest and state law rights whatever they may be.[137] When this option is chosen, assuming the debtor has an exemptible interest in the property,[138] the debtor should ordinarily check only the box indicating an intent to exempt the property. In such cases, based on local practice, it may also be advisable to include a note that makes clear the debtor's intention to continue payments.

There is also nothing in section 521 stating that a debtor may not change her intentions. Like other statements and schedules, this statement may be amended at any time before the time period for performance of the intention expires.[139] Although it is doubtful that any negative consequences result from failing to act in accordance with the statement of intention,[140] it is normally advisable to file amendments to the statement when the debtor's plans change and to serve them, as required, on the trustee and any affected creditors.[141]

The debtor is normally required to follow through on the stated intention within forty-five days, but that deadline should be seen more as a guideline for when redemption or reaffirmation should occur, if they are going to happen. The Code makes clear that the statement of intention does not alter any of the debtor's substantive rights as they previously existed.[142]

In most chapter 7 cases, completion of the statement of intention is quite simple. Generally, chapter 7 debtors retain all of their property, as they claim their interests in all of it as exempt. (If there is significant non-exempt property the debtor usually chooses chapter 13 rather than chapter 7.)[143] The fact that the property is encumbered by a secured creditor's lien does not prevent the debtor from claiming her interest, subject to the lien, as exempt. In many cases the lien may be partially or totally avoidable in bankruptcy.[144] Few debtors reaffirm their debts[145] or redeem more than one or two items under section 722.[146]

Probably the greatest uncertainty about section 521(2) when it was enacted was whether a statement of intentions had to be filed in a chapter 13 case as well as in a chapter 7 case. The text of the section, requiring filing "within thirty days after the date of the filing of a petition under chapter 7

of this title or on or before the date of the meeting of creditors, whichever is earlier," strongly indicates that it is meant only to apply to chapter 7. However, the 1984 amendments also amended 11 U.S.C. § 1302(b)(1) to incorporate among the chapter 13 trustee's duties the chapter 7 trustee's duty under section 704(3), to "ensure" the debtor's performance of the intentions in the statement.

The most likely explanation for these contradictory signals is that the amendment to section 1302 was a drafting error in the last-minute congressional rush to put together a compromise bill. Drafting errors with respect to renumbering Code provisions to accommodate the 1984 amendments were, unfortunately, quite frequent.[147]

Moreover, the options that may be designated in the statement of intentions do not really fit chapter 13. They omit the most common methods for dealing with secured debts under that chapter, which are payment of an allowed secured claim under a plan and curing a default within a reasonable time.[148] In fact, earlier versions of section 521(2) would have required the debtor to choose among only the options of surrender, redemption, or reaffirmation, which is further evidence that the drafters only had chapter 7 cases in mind.[149] This intent is also indicated by the use of the term "schedule of assets and liabilities" in the text of section 521(2), as no such schedules existed in chapter 13 when the amendment was passed. Finally, a statement of intentions is largely superfluous for chapter 13, as most or all of the information it conveys should already be available in the chapter 13 schedules and plan.

Fortunately, this question was almost entirely resolved by the Bankruptcy Rules in 1991. Bankruptcy Rule 1007(b)(2) requires the filing of such a statement only in chapter 7 cases. Even if some conflict in the statutory language remains, it is extremely unlikely that any debtor would be penalized or even faulted for following the express language of the Bankruptcy Rules.

In any case, the function of the statement of intention is simply one of notice. It is intended to meet creditors' complaints at congressional hearings that they could not get necessary information from debtors' attorneys and were not permitted to contact *pro se* debtors at all. Except in those courts that have held that the form requires a debtor to either reaffirm, redeem, or surrender the collateral, it should impose little burden on debtors, because it changes none of their substantive rights.[150]

F.2d 1053 (6th Cir. 1983). The instructions for Official Form 8 under the category of property to be retained now states: "Check any applicable statement."

137 *See* § 14.5.2, *infra.*

138 Because a possessory interest is eligible for exemption, the debtor will virtually always have an exemptible interest.

139 Fed. R. Bankr. P. 1009(b); *see* § 8.3.2, *infra.*

140 *See* § 11.4, *infra.*

141 Fed. R. Bankr. P. 1009(c).

142 11 U.S.C. § 521(2)(C); *see In re* Eagle, 51 B.R. 959 (Bankr. N.D. Ohio 1985) (debtors who stated intention to reaffirm debt not barred from redeeming property instead).

143 See § 6.3, *supra,* for discussion of this choice.

144 See § 10.4, *infra,* for discussion of avoiding liens.

145 See §§ 8.1 and 14.5.2, *infra,* for discussion of reaffirmation.

146 See § 11.5, *infra,* for discussion of redemption.

147 See, for example, 11 U.S.C. § 362, which had been given two subsections numbered as (b)(9), and 11 U.S.C. § 523, which had two subsections designated as (a)(9). Section 1302(b)(1) was renumbered to accommodate the renumbering of section 704. The numbering errors in the 1984 amendments were corrected in the 1986 amendments. However, no clarifying change was made with respect to § 1302(b)(1).

148 See § 11.4, *infra,* for discussion of these alternatives.

149 H.R. 4876, 97th Cong. § 7 (1981).

150 See § 11.4, *infra,* for a discussion of the requirement in § 521(2)(B) that the debtor perform the stated intentions within

7.3.7 *The Chapter 13 Plan*

7.3.7.1 Introduction

The most important document filed in a chapter 13 case is usually the debtor's proposed plan. This plan, which only the debtor can propose, sets out how the debtor wishes to reorganize her financial situation. Its purpose, then, is to make clear how the debtor desires payments and distributions to be made in the case. The plan may be modified as of right before confirmation and also, with the court's permission, after confirmation in certain circumstances.[151]

7.3.7.2 Form of Plan

The form of the plan is not prescribed by the rules or the statute. As long as the plan meets all of the requirements of the statute, and clearly describes how creditors will be paid, its form should be acceptable.[152] Most practitioners draft a standard plan that may then be modified to suit the needs of each case. Several examples are contained in Appendix G, *infra*.

In some jurisdictions, chapter 13 trustees promulgate form plans, which are sometimes even "required" by local rules. This procedure is probably not objectionable, as long as it does not in any way impair the debtor's flexibility in utilizing all of the options provided by chapter 13.[153] Practitioners in a jurisdiction with a form plan should take care to add, delete or modify form provisions, as necessary, to create a chapter 13 plan which meets the debtor's objectives. The need to comply with a form should never be a basis for limiting a chapter 13 debtor's substantive rights.

7.3.7.3 Required Provisions and Confirmation Standards

There are only a few plan provisions that are required by the statute. First, the plan must provide for full payment of all claims entitled to priority under section 507 of the Code, unless the holder of such a claim agrees otherwise.[154]

Notably, these claims must be paid even if they would have been discharged in a chapter 7 case filed by the debtor. Most important among them are usually those for administrative expenses, which include the trustee's commission and, in cases handled by private attorneys, any unpaid portion of the debtor's attorney fee as approved by the court. The trustee's commission, to cover both compensation and expenses, can vary from two to ten percent of the payments although it may occasionally be reduced in unusual cases.[155] Some courts have held that the trustee's percentage fee must be calculated as a percentage of amounts the trustee receives from the debtor and disburses to creditors, and not on the total amount the trustee receives from the debtor including the percentage fee,[156] but the fee is not always calculated that way. The Code sets a minimum trustee's commission of five dollars per month unless the court orders otherwise.[157] Therefore, if the debtor wishes to pay less than that amount, perhaps because five dollars per month would constitute a disproportionate part of the payments in a low-payment plan, the plan should include a provision permitting a lower trustee's fee. The confirmation order could then serve as the order required for an exception to the general rule.[158]

A second requirement is that the plan provide for submission of "all or such portion" of the debtor's future income as is necessary for the execution of the plan.[159] Conceivably, in an exceptional case, a debtor might propose to make no payments through the trustee and therefore submit no income. Whether such a plan would be deemed to meet this requirement is unclear;[160] there is little to be lost in making the attempt if it seems appropriate, as a disapproved plan can normally be modified as necessary to gain confirmation.

Third, if the plan classifies claims, it must provide the same treatment for each claim in a particular class. This provision is intended to prevent unfair discrimination against disfavored creditors. As discussed later in this

---

a specified time and the conflicting case law on this provision.

151 See § 8.7.3, *infra*, for discussion of modification procedure.

152 *See In re* Maloney, 25 B.R. 334 (B.A.P. 1st Cir. 1982) (plan not meeting requirement that it provide for submission of earnings or income to trustee as necessary for the plan was not adequate).

153 *See In re* Walat, 89 B.R. 11 (E.D. Va. 1988) (upholding local rule requiring form chapter 13 plan when form did not impinge on debtor's substantive rights to devise plan provisions).

154 11 U.S.C. § 1322(a)(2). See Chapter 3, *supra*, for a list of these claims. However interest on those claims is not required by § 1322(a)(2). *See In re* Hageman, 108 B.R. 1016 (Bankr. N.D. Iowa 1989). If a plan pays more than the debtor would otherwise be required to pay in order to pay all expected priority claims, the plan can later be modified to provide for lower payments if some priority claim holders never file claims. When the debtor

---

does not choose to file a claim for a non-filing priority creditor, there seems to be no reason why the debtor could not argue that unfiled priority claims should not be looked to under this section, as they would not be paid even if the higher plan payments continued. *See In re* Int'l Horizons, Inc., 751 F.2d 1213 (11th Cir. 1985) (late-filed claims may not be paid).

155 *See, e.g., In re* Eaton, 1 B.R. 433 (Bankr. M.D.N.C. 1979) (fees can be adjusted for equitable reasons; *see also* 8 Collier on Bankruptcy ¶ 1302.05[1][a] (15th ed. rev.).

156 *E.g.*, Pelofsky v. Wallace, 102 F.3d 350 (8th Cir. 1996). *But see In re* BDT Farms, Inc., 21 F.3d 1019 (10th Cir. 1994).

157 11 U.S.C. § 330(c) actually sets the minimum trustee compensation at $5.00 per month. Although the trustee's commissions in the aggregate are designed to cover both compensation and expenses of the trustee, 28 U.S.C. § 586(e), there is no requirement that the fee in any particular case include expenses. Therefore, the minimum compensation is also the minimum commission.

158 *See* 8 Collier on Bankruptcy ¶ 1302.02[5][a] (15th ed. rev.).

159 11 U.S.C. § 1322(a)(1).

160 See § 12.4, *infra*, for further discussion of plan requirements.

manual,[161] the courts have not yet agreed as to which classifications are fair. While it is clear that secured claims, priority claims, claims with codebtors, and possibly claims that are nondischargeable may be treated separately, there is considerable difference of opinion as to discrimination between other groups of unsecured claims. Some potential classifications, which on their face appear discriminatory, may in fact be allowable based on principles of equitable subordination.[162]

With the exception of the above mentioned requirements, chapter 13 generally provides total flexibility as to the order of distribution. No particular scheme is required, although most plans call for payment of priority and secured debts before other debts. Some debtors may wish to have priority administrative expenses paid first so that the debtor's attorney can be paid.[163] Sometimes, it might be advisable to pay some priority claims later in the event that the case is converted to a chapter 7 proceeding, in which those claims would be discharged. In such a case, it would be to the debtor's advantage to pay first the secured creditors holding non-avoidable liens that would remain in existence after a chapter 7 case, rather than unsecured dischargeable priority claims. However, such a plan would likely meet with loud objections from the trustee, at least if her claim for administrative expenses were deferred, especially because section 330(c) requires trustee compensation of five dollars per month from any plan distribution. Generally, however, priority status does not entitle a claim to payment before all others, but merely to full payment as provided in section 1322(a)(2), sometime during the plan.[164]

The payments and distributions need not be equal. The plan may provide for graduated payments over time, or annual payments,[165] or even a lump sum payment from the debtor's property. However, the court may disapprove such a plan if it finds it to be not in good faith or not feasible.[166] The plan may provide for payments over any period of time up to five years,[167] although specific court approval, upon good cause shown, is needed for plans that last longer than three years.[168]

The court may[169] also disapprove a plan if it does not meet certain standards as to secured claims provided for in the plan. Unless the holder of such a claim has accepted the plan, the court may require that the debtor either surrender the property securing the debt or propose in the plan to make payments having a present value at least as great as the amount of the allowed secured claim, with the creditor retaining its lien.[170] In order to achieve the latter result, unless the full amount of the allowed secured claim is paid immediately, the plan should provide for interest on the amounts outstanding. Although the Supreme Court has set guidelines for deciding the issue, there may still be some dispute regarding the appropriate rate of interest, so at least in courts which have not already decided the issue the plan may provide for the lowest arguably proper rate.[171]

Similarly, the court may refuse to confirm a plan[172] if it does not meet both of two tests requiring payments in some circumstances to unsecured creditors.[173] The first is the "best interests of creditors" test and is set out in 11 U.S.C. § 1325(a)(4). This test requires the property to be distributed under the plan to unsecured creditors to have a present value not less than the amount those creditors would receive in a chapter 7 liquidation. Put another way, the present value of payments under the plan must be at least equal to the value of the debtor's non-exempt property (minus hypothetical costs of administration in a chapter 7 case) in order to satisfy the test.[174] The second test is based on the debtor's ability to pay and is set out in 11 U.S.C. § 1325(b). It requires that unsecured creditors either be paid in full or that the debtor commit to the plan all of her "disposable income" for at least three years. Disposable income is essentially defined as all income not needed by the debtor for maintenance and support of the debtor and the debtor's dependents.[175]

---

161 See Ch. 12, *infra.*

162 See 11 U.S.C. § 510(c). *But see* U.S. v. Noland, 517 U.S. 535, 116 S. Ct. 1524, 134 L. Ed. 2d 748 (1996) (non-pecuniary loss tax penalties may not be subordinated to other unsecured claims in derogation of legislatively established priority scheme).

163 *In re* Tenney, 63 B.R. 110 (Bankr. W.D. Okla. 1986).

164 11 U.S.C. § 1322(b)(4) gives the debtor flexibility to pay priority claims concurrently with other unsecured claims.

165 *In re* Fiegi, 61 B.R. 994 (Bankr. D. Or. 1986).

166 See 11 U.S.C. § 1325(a)(3), (a)(6); *see also* § 12.5, *infra.*

167 It should be noted that although the plan must call for payments to be made within a period not to exceed five years, the five-year limitation may run from the date the first payment under the plan becomes due following confirmation, rather than from the date of bankruptcy filing. *See* West v. Costen, 826 F.2d 1376 (4th Cir. 1987); *In re* Endicott, 157 B.R. 255 (W.D. Va. 1993); *see also In re* Martin, 156 B.R. 47 (B.A.P. 9th Cir. 1993); *In re* Black, 78 B.R. 840 (Bankr. S.D. Ohio 1987) (Bankruptcy Code contains

no provision for dismissing a chapter 13 case because payments extend over sixty-six months, if the plan complied with the duration limitations of the Code at the time of confirmation); *In re* Eves, 67 B.R. 964 (Bankr. N.D. Ohio 1986) (modification which could have been effective before five years following first payment after plan confirmation was timely, even though proposed modification was filed more than five years after first plan payment was made).

168 11 U.S.C. § 1322(c).

169 The court has discretion to approve such a plan. *See* § 12.7, *infra.*

170 See discussion of present value in § 11.6.1.3, *infra.*

171 See § 11.6.1.3, *infra,* for discussion of present value interest rate.

172 *See* § 12.7, *infra.*

173 *See* § 12.3, *infra.*

174 Because in both a chapter 7 and a chapter 13 case administrative expenses would be paid, the deduction for those expenses in either type of case must be taken into account. For further discussion of the best interests of the creditors test, see § 12.3.1, *infra.*

175 11 U.S.C. § 1325(b)(2). For further discussion of the ability to pay test, see § 12.3.3, *infra.*

7.3.7.4 Other Plan Provisions Permitted

In addition to the criteria set forth above, the Code offers some guidance as to what the plan may do but establishes few limitations. Under section 1322(b), the plan may classify claims (as long as it does not unfairly discriminate), modify the rights of holders of secured claims except those secured only by a security interest in real property that is the debtor's principal residence,[176] provide for curing or waiving any default, provide for payments on unsecured claims to be concurrent with those on secured claims, provide for curing defaults on long-term debts, provide for post-petition claims, provide for payment of claims through the sale of property, and provide for assumption or rejection of any executory contract or unexpired lease.

Moreover, the plan may include any other appropriate provision not inconsistent with title 11. Thus, except when there is an express provision of the Code, practically the only limitation on a chapter 13 plan is the advocate's imagination. Such provisions might[177] include liquidation of property by the debtor to pay certain claims;[178] higher payments on debts which are nondischargeable in chapter 13;[179] payment of some debts outside the plan;[180] priority status for post-petition utility defaults (to be deemed adequate assurance of future payment under section 366);[181] rejection of leases or executory contracts for credit insurance, health spas and other dubious bargains;[182] exemption of all property recovered by the trustee unless the applicable exemption is exhausted; avoidance of liens under section 522;[183] liquidation of property by the debtor to pay certain claims;[184] vesting of all property of the estate and the right to use it in the debtor;[185] and so forth. Many provisions that may be appropriate in a particular case are included in the annotated forms in Appendix G, *infra*.

7.3.7.5 Formulating the Plan

As a practical matter, when formulating a chapter 13 plan, practitioners should keep several broad principles in mind. A strategy must be designed for priority, secured, and unsecured debts which meets the debtor's objectives, consistent with the Code and the debtor's available income. Legitimate priority debts generally must be paid in full, unless the creditor agrees otherwise. A secured debt may be treated in one of five ways, depending on the circumstances: 1) pay it in full in the plan, 2) cure the default, 3) treat it outside the plan and let the lien ride through unaffected by bankruptcy, 4) avoid the lien and treat the debt as unsecured, or 5) surrender the property securing the debt. Unsecured creditors are entitled to at least what they would receive if the debtor's estate were liquidated in chapter 7 (the "best interest of the creditors' test"). All of these options and requirements of the Code are discussed above and elsewhere in this manual.

The debtor must have sufficient income to pay at least the amounts necessary to meet these standards for secured, priority, and unsecured debts as the plan is designed, plus the trustee's commission. In so providing, there is no need to accept any creditor's proof of claim as a given. It is possible to object to a creditor's characterization of a claim as priority or secured, to the amount that the creditor is claiming, or to the creditor's right to a claim at all.[186]

Once the amounts listed above are committed to the plan, it is necessary to return to the debtor's budget to check whether the debtor has additional disposable income. If so, the trustee or a creditor will probably object if most of that income is not paid to the unsecured creditors under the ability to pay test.[187]

Unless there are only one or two debts, it is usually impossible to specify the precise amounts that will actually be paid to different creditors under the plan. In most cases, the ultimate distribution is dependent on a number of events which occur only after formulation of the plan. For example, the amount of a secured claim may be disputed. If the plan provides for a certain level of payments to the trustee, the amount to be distributed to claims paid after the disputed claim is calculable only after the amount of the disputed secured claim has been determined. Moreover, not all creditors file claims; nationally, forty percent do not. Thus the amount each unsecured creditor receives from the total

---

176 However, under 11 U.S.C. § 1322(c), the rights of certain residential mortgage holders may be modified. *See* § 11.6.1.2, *infra*.

177 It should be noted that some of the provisions discussed have never been contested in court. It is likely that some would not be allowed in some bankruptcy courts, given those courts' decisions under chapter 13.

178 *See* § 12.6.5, *infra*.

179 *See* § 12.4, *infra*.

180 *See* § 12.4.4, *infra*.

181 See § 9.8.2.2, *infra,* for discussion of adequate assurance to utilities.

182 See § 12.9, *infra,* for discussion of executory contracts and leases.

183 *But see In re* McKay, 732 F.2d 49 (3d Cir. 1984) (under Rules of Bankruptcy Procedure, lien avoidance under 11 U.S.C. § 522(f) must be by motion). See Chapter 10, *infra,* for discussion of lien avoidance procedures.

184 *See* § 12.6.5, *infra*.

185 *See* § 12.8, *infra*.

186 *See* § 13.4.3, *infra*.

187 As discussed above, in some cases it may be appropriate to reevaluate the budget at this stage and to increase certain expenses, if possible in good faith, in order to minimize the necessary payments to unsecured creditors. *See* § 7.3.4.6, *supra*. It is also appropriate to withhold payments under the "ability to pay test" pending an objection by a party-in-interest. The test only applies to preclude confirmation if there is an objection by the trustee of the holder of an allowed secured claim. *See* § 12.3.3, *infra*.

allocated to unsecured claims depends upon how many other unsecured creditors file their claims.

For these reasons, the plan need not specify how much each creditor will receive;[188] it may simply describe the order of distribution in sufficient detail so the trustee will know how to proceed once the amounts of all allowed claims are known. So long as the amounts paid into the plan by the debtor appear to be sufficient to meet the requirements outlined above, the plan should be confirmed. In any case, as mentioned earlier, modifications are freely allowed if a problem does arise.

A plan formulated as prescribed above, which does not specify how much each general unsecured creditor will receive, is known as a "pot plan" or a "base plan" because it simply provides a residual pot of money for unsecured creditors after all other claims have been paid.[189] Its advantages, which stem from its flexibility in dealing with the unpredictability of claims, are described above.

Some practitioners, however, prefer to file a "percentage plan." This type of plan specifies that each general unsecured creditors will receive a certain percentage of its claim. The advantage of this type of plan, which is typically calculated on the assumption that all creditors will file claims, is that the debtor may not have to pay all of her disposable income if not all creditors file claims. Precisely because of this possibility, some courts refuse to approve percentage plans if the trustee or a creditor objects to the plan.[190] Percentage plans also leave the debtor uncertain regarding how much the ultimate plan payments will be until all secured claims and priority claims have been determined, and until the claims deadline has passed. In addition, a percentage plan may require the debtor to object to unsecured claims filed in excessive amounts, because such claims would increase the debtor's payments.[191] (If a pot plan has been filed, the debtor is not concerned if one unsecured creditor files an excessive claim, because that will simply reduce the other creditors' share of the pot.) And, for the same reason, if an unscheduled creditor files a claim or

is later discovered, many percentage plans cannot provide for that creditor's claim except through amendment of the plan, thereby allowing its discharge at the end of the case under section 1328 unless an amendment is made.

7.3.8 Other Forms

7.3.8.1 Overview

Aside from the papers already described, there are one or two other forms which usually must be filed. These rarely require much work to prepare.

7.3.8.2 Disclosure of Fees

In every case, under Federal Rule of Bankruptcy Procedure 2016(b), a disclosure of fees paid to the debtor's attorneys must be filed. The purpose of this form is to allow the court and the United States trustee, who also must receive a copy, to monitor fees to make sure they are reasonable. A form for this disclosure comes with most commercially printed sets.[192] Because no fee is paid to legal services or pro bono attorneys by their clients, completion of this form should pose little difficulty for them. Attorneys charging fees must provide some specificity about the services to be provided. The degree of specificity required varies to some extent based on local rule, the preferences of the United States trustee or local judges, and community custom.[193] If the debtor was assisted by a non-attorney bankruptcy petition preparer, as defined in section 110 of the Bankruptcy Code, the preparer must file a similar statement, required by Code section 110(h)(1).[194]

7.3.8.3 Application to Pay Filing Fee in Installments

If the filing fee is not paid in full at filing, the debtor must file an application to pay it in installments. The form for this application is provided in Official Form 3, a fill-in-the-blanks format which can be photocopied to save time.[195] The form also contains a proposed order for payments in installments. This application may not be filed, however, if the debtor has paid anything to her attorney in connection with the bankruptcy.[196] As discussed above, it may sometimes be possible to file an application to waive some of the filing fees.[197]

---

188   *See In re* Parker, 15 B.R. 980 (Bankr. E.D. Tenn. 1981), *aff'd*, 21 B.R. 692 (E.D. Tenn. 1982) (plan need not describe exactly how trustee would make payments).

189   These terms are used to describe different things in different places. In some places, the "pot" refers only to money that will be paid to unsecured creditors.

190   *In re* Bass, 267 B.R. 812 (Bankr. S.D. Ohio 2001).

191   *See In re* Roberts, 279 F.3d 91 (1st Cir. 2002) (plan which provided that debtor would pay fixed amount to trustee but also provided specified percentage return to unsecured creditors required debtor to pay larger of the two amounts); *In re* Rivera, 177 B.R. 332 (Bankr. C.D. Cal. 1995) (chapter 13 case dismissed, even though debtors had made all payments required under plan, because payments did not provide unsecured creditors sixty-five percent return provided for in plan). This problem might be avoided in a carefully drafted plan by including a provision which automatically decreases the percentage paid to each unsecured creditor to the extent that claims exceed the total anticipated by the debtor.

192   See discussion of this form in Chapter 15, *infra*, and a copy of the form itself in Appendix E, *infra*.

193   A more complete discussion of this issue is contained in § 15.3, *infra*. See also Appendices E and G, *infra*, for sample forms.

194   A form for this statement has been promulgated by the Administrative Office of the United States Courts. *See* Appx. E, *infra*.

195   See Appendix D, *infra*, for a reproducible form.

196   Fed. R. Bankr. P. 1006(b)(3).

197   *See* § 7.2.1, *supra*.

7.3.8.4 Motion for Extension of Time to File Required Documents

If the schedules, statements, or plan cannot be filed within fifteen days of the petition, a motion for additional time must be filed or the case may be dismissed.[198] A simple form for this purpose can easily be prepared for repeated use.[199] Such an application should show cause for the extension and be served on the trustee, if any, and the United States trustee.[200] Most courts routinely grant a two to three week extension of time if requested before the papers are due.[201] Some courts require proposed orders to be attached to these papers and local practice should be checked.

7.3.8.5 Forms Required by Local Rules or Practice

Finally, local practice may require other papers, and may dictate the size of the paper to be used, whether backers are needed, and so forth. Most districts now require a form to be used in preparing notices, to be filed either with the petition or shortly thereafter. Practitioners should consult local rules or the clerk's office for these and any other requirements.

7.4 Signing, Verification, and Filing

Once all of the forms are prepared and reviewed, they must be signed by the attorney of record and the debtor(s), as well as verified by the debtor(s). In appropriate circumstances, a petition may be signed and filed by another on behalf of a debtor pursuant to a power of attorney.[202]

The attorney normally signs two documents—the petition (including Exhibit B to the petition in chapter 7 cases involving primarily consumer debts) and the disclosure of attorney fees. Those signatures, like any other signatures on pleadings, constitute certifications that the documents meet the requirements of Fed. R. Bankr. P. 9011.[203] The debtor signs the petition (in two places if a chapter 7 case is filed) and statement of intentions, and verifies the schedules and statement of financial affairs. Either the attorney or the debtor may sign the chapter 13 plan. Under federal law, a notarized signature to a verification is not necessary if the signer certifies its truth under penalty of perjury.[204]

Every document prepared by a non-attorney bankruptcy petition preparer, as defined by section 110 of the Code, must contain the signature and printed name and address of the preparer.[205] It must also contain the social security number of the preparer and the printed names and social security numbers of all other individuals who prepared or assisted in preparation of the document, and attach separate certifications by each person who prepared the document.[206] The failure to comply with these requirements will render the violators subject to serious sanctions.[207]

It is always important to have a client carefully review the documents before signing and to point out any inaccuracies. This review serves as a final check on their correctness, and also prevents any later misunderstanding in which the client might claim that the forms were not properly prepared.

Once the papers have been signed and verified, they are ready for filing.[208] With the filing of the complete set of documents, or just the petition, statement of social security number, and list of creditors with the required fee (or application to pay the filing fee in installments if necessary), the bankruptcy case is officially commenced.

---

198 *See* Fed. R. Bankr. P. 1007(c). Failure to file timely schedules without an extension of time could lead to loss of substantive rights such as exemptions, even if the case is not dismissed. *See* Petit v. Fessenden, 80 F.3d 29 (1st Cir. 1996) (debtor's exemptions disallowed when schedules not timely filed).

199 *See, e.g.,* Forms 3–5, Appx. G.3, *infra.*

200 Fed. R. Bankr. P. 1007(c).

201 *Id.; see* § 7.2.2, *supra.*

202 *In re* Ballard, 10 Bankr. Ct. Dec. (LRP) 1328 (Bankr. N.D. Cal. 1987); *see* § 3.2.1, *supra.*

203 *See In re* Jerrels, 133 B.R. 161 (Bankr. M.D. Fla. 1991) (attorney sanctioned pursuant to Rule 9011 for falsely certifying that he had explained debtor's choices of various bankruptcy chapters).

204 28 U.S.C. § 1746 provides that an unsworn declaration "under penalty of perjury" shall have the same force and effect as a sworn statement.

205 11 U.S.C. § 110(b), (c). Spaces for this information have been added to each official bankruptcy form in which it is likely to be required.

206 11 U.S.C. § 110(c)(2). See the various official bankruptcy forms.

207 11 U.S.C. § 110(b), (c), (i), (j); 18 U.S.C. § 156; *see* § 15.6, *infra.*

208 In districts that permit electronic filing, local rules typically require documents containing original signatures that are electronically filed to be stored in paper form by the debtor's attorney for a period of two to five years following expiration of all time periods for appeals after entry of a final order terminating the case or proceeding.

Chapter 8

After the Papers Are Filed

8.1 Introduction

Once the decision to file a bankruptcy has been made and acted upon by commencement of the case, the remainder of many a routine bankruptcy case seems anticlimactic. Although numerous complications can occur, and significant steps must sometimes be taken on behalf of the debtor, quite often only a few formalities are left after the filing of the initial papers. This Chapter describes those events which occur in every case, and also how to handle some of the other proceedings that may arise during the pendency of the case.

8.2 Advice to Clients

It is important to advise the client immediately about what will occur. The client should understand what has happened and what will happen next. She should be told about the notices that will be issued by the court. These include the Notice of Appointment of a Trustee and the Notice of the Section 341(a) Meeting of Creditors, which is normally combined with other notices of deadlines, and so forth.[1]

Any obligations to make payments, including installment payments of the filing fee,[2] payments under a chapter 13 plan and outside the plan,[3] and security deposits for utility service,[4] should be carefully explained and set forth in writing.[5] In most cases any or all of these payments will be due within a month or two after the case is filed. Chapter 13 plan payments must begin within thirty days after the plan is filed, unless the court orders otherwise.[6]

Clients also should know their rights under the automatic stay provisions—that creditors are not permitted to seek payment of any debts,[7] and that any creditor that does take any action should be advised of the bankruptcy, with the creditor's contact reported to the person handling the case. In general debtors should be advised not to pay any prebankruptcy debt (except in cases in which debts will remain after bankruptcy or in which they are being paid outside a chapter 13 plan). Debtors should not enter into new credit transactions without consultation, especially in chapter 13, as the trustee's permission is usually needed.[8]

As in any case, clients must advise their attorneys of any change in address. The court should then also be advised, because all notices will otherwise go to the debtor's old address.[9] Similarly, any property acquired that would become a part of the estate, for example, inheritances, marital property settlements or life insurance proceeds,[10] should be reported so the schedules filed with the court can be amended[11] if necessary. And, of course, a chapter 7 debtor should not dispose of any property that is not exempt, because the trustee can, and probably will, demand that it be turned over to her.[12] In some places local practice may require the trustee's permission even to use property of the estate, although this practice is questionable and may be successfully challenged if a chapter 13 case has been filed[13] or if the property is exempt.[14]

---

1 Fed. R. Bankr. P. 2002, 4004(a), 4007(c); Official Form 9, Appx. D, *infra*.

2 *See* § 3.2.2, *supra*.

3 See Chapter 12, *infra*, for discussion of payments outside the plan.

4 See § 9.8, *infra*, for discussion of utility deposits.

5 See sample letters which may be used in chapter 7 and 13 cases. Forms 16, 17, Appx. G.3, *infra*.

6 11 U.S.C. § 1326.

7 For further discussion of the automatic stay, see Chapter 9, *infra*.

8 *See* 11 U.S.C. §§ 1305(c), 1328(d). As a practical matter, most large creditors will be aware of these provisions and will not usually grant credit without the trustee's approval.

9 Fed. R. Bankr. P. 4002(5) requires the debtor to file a statement of any change of address.

10 See 11 U.S.C. § 541(a)(5) for a list of properties acquired after filing which may come into the estate. In a chapter 13 case generally property acquired after bankruptcy filing is property of the estate, but it is not necessary to amend the schedules of assets to reflect that property unless it is property that is also within the scope of § 541(a)(5) and therefore deemed to be property held as of the commencement of the case.

11 The Federal Rules of Bankruptcy Procedure require amendment within ten days after the information comes to the debtor's knowledge or such further time as the court allows. For procedure to amend, see § 8.3.2, *infra*.

12 Technically, the trustee can demand such turnover immediately. 11 U.S.C. § 521(4).

13 See § 12.8, *infra*, for a discussion of property use in chapter 13 cases.

14 See Chapter 10, *infra*, for a discussion of exempt property after filing.

8.3 Events Which May Occur Prior to the Section 341 Meeting of Creditors

8.3.1 Notice of the Automatic Stay and Turnover Requirement

Although all creditors should receive a notice of the automatic stay as part of the notice of the meeting of creditors, that notice may not be sufficient to protect the debtor's rights. It may not be mailed until weeks, or even months, after the petition is filed; in the meantime, creditors without notice might take action harmful to the debtor. A creditor without notice of the case will normally not be found to have willfully violated a stay it knew nothing about.

Thus, if there is any chance that a creditor might act to the debtor's detriment soon after the case is commenced, notice should be given by the debtor's advocate that the stay is in effect. Certainly such notice should be given, by certified mail if possible and if necessary preceded by a telephone call or facsimile transmission, to forestall any threatened foreclosure, repossession, execution, or utility shut-off. When time is especially short, such as when a bankruptcy is filed immediately before a scheduled foreclosure sale, a special effort to provide notice should be made. This effort might include advance notice of the filing to the creditor or the creditor's attorney as long as threatened action cannot be taken early to thwart the debtor's purpose in filing bankruptcy.[15] If a utility shut-off or repossession is imminent, the debtor may choose to provide personal notice to the repossessing agent or utility employee by waiting at or near the property involved. Similarly, posting notice of the bankruptcy on a car which is about to be repossessed should be sufficient. If any of these latter actions are taken, a witness is helpful in the event of a later case based on a creditor's violation of the stay.

Special notice may also be appropriate in cases involving creditors prone to harassing collection efforts and those filing legal proceedings in state courts. And it may be necessary to notify courts where actions against the debtor are pending as well. In chapter 13 cases, the letter should also mention the stay of actions against codebtors, if it is applicable.[16]

If, after notice, a creditor or judicial officer acts in violation of the stay, debtor's counsel may file a motion to have that party held in contempt of court, including claims for damages and attorney fees.[17] It is well established that the stay is automatic, that no further court order is necessary to restrain a creditor, and that actual notice of the bankruptcy, even without official notice from the court, is sufficient.[18] Appropriate sanctions that can be sought from the bankruptcy court include actual damages, punitive damages, and orders to pay the attorney fees and costs of the party enforcing the stay.[19] The debtor is also entitled to an order undoing the action that violated the stay.

Additionally, the filing of a case puts into effect the automatic turnover provisions of sections 542 and 543 of the Code. Under these sections, any entity holding property the trustee may use, sell, or lease (powers exercised by the debtor in chapter 13 cases),[20] or that the debtor may exempt, must turn over such property to the trustee. Because the debtor may exempt equity in property subject to a lien, or even an interest in property when there is no measurable equity,[21] this turnover should include any property held by creditors which has been repossessed or is subject to a possessory lien.[22] Here, too, notice by certified mail of the property-holder's obligation is appropriate, followed up by court action if necessary.[23]

8.3.2 Amendments to Statements or Schedules

When an amendment is necessary, whether due to inadvertence, mistake, on an unexpected change in circumstances, the procedure is quite simple. Under current Bankruptcy Rules, the debtor may amend the initial papers as a matter of course at any time before the case is closed.[24] The

---

15   Advance notice might also provide a later basis to challenge unnecessary costs, such as an auctioneer's fee for a canceled sale. Early notice of a bankruptcy case should cause the creditor to eliminate any avoidable costs related to a stayed proceeding or sale in order to minimize the claim which will later be filed in the case.

16   See Chapter 9, *infra,* for discussion of the automatic stay and the stay against codebtors.

17   *See* § 9.6, *infra;* Forms 24, 25, Appx. G.4, *infra.*

18   *See, e.g.,* Fid. Mortgage Investors v. Camelia Builders, 550 F.2d 47 (2d Cir. 1976).

19   11 U.S.C. § 362(h). Cases and issues relating to stay violations are discussed in § 9.6, *infra.*

20   See § 12.8, *infra,* for further discussion of the debtor's power to use, sell, or lease property in chapter 13.

21   See Chapter 10, *infra,* for further discussion of what property may be exempted.

22   See § 9.9, *infra,* for further discussion of the turnover provisions and examples.

23   *See* Forms 36, 37, Appx. G.5, *infra.*

24   Fed. R. Bankr. P. 1009; *In re* Olson, 253 B.R. 73 (B.A.P. 9th Cir. 2000); *see also In re* Kaelin, 308 F.3d 885 (8th Cir. 2002) (while a debtor may be barred from amending to exempt property that has been concealed, or in other circumstances of bad faith, debtor who promptly amended to exempt cause of action after he first learned about it was permitted to claim exemption even though he intended to abandon cause of action that would have benefited creditors). But see § 10.3.2, *infra,* citing a few cases holding that the claimed exemptions may not be amended after a certain time. The rules are not so liberal that they allow a single spouse's petition to join the other spouse, creating a joint

procedure requires the filing of an amended document verified by the debtor.[25] The amended document should be filed with the same number of copies as the original document, and signed or verified in the same manner as the document being amended.[26]

The rules also provide that "[t]he debtor shall give notice of the amendment to the trustee and to any entity affected thereby."[27] Generally, notice of an amendment to the debtor's exemptions should be sent to all creditors. Notice should also be sent to creditors added by amendment so that they may protect their rights (although other creditors may be affected as well). In certain cases, the late filing of an amendment adding a creditor could prejudice the right to discharge a debt.[28] Therefore, the debtor's counsel should make sure that the creditor receives notice of the amendment and a copy of the notice of the meeting of creditors as soon as possible. Because the court will send out notices when a creditor is added, there is a $26.00 fee for filing such an amendment. However, this fee can be waived upon application to the court for good cause.[29] For all other amendments, there is no fee.

Adding a creditor to the schedules may not be sufficient to bring about the discharge of the creditor's claim in a chapter 13 case if the deadline for filing proofs of claims has already passed, because a chapter 13 case discharges only those claims provided for in the plan.[30] If the debtor's plan is worded in such a way that a tardily filed claim is provided for, the debtor may be able to file a claim on behalf of the creditor under Federal Rule of Bankruptcy Procedure 3004 or seek an extension of time to file such a claim.[31] If the debtor or the creditor files a late proof of claim and no party objects that the claim is tardy, the claim is allowed.[32]

8.3.3 Avoiding Transfers of Exempt Property

As discussed in detail below, the Code gives debtors a wide range of powers to avoid transfers, including various liens on property.[33] Many of these powers are intended to protect the full use of the exemptions provided by the Code or by state and federal non-bankruptcy law.

In some cases in which a transfer, such as a lien, may be avoided by the debtor, it may save time to attempt to obtain a stipulation from the lienholder or transferee that the transfer is null and void. Occasionally a letter to the creditor, accompanied by a proposed stipulation,[34] will accomplish this stipulation. The letter might also let the creditor know that if court action is necessary, the losing party is sometimes liable for costs.[35]

If a stipulation is not obtained, the safest course of action is to seek avoidance of the transfer by the court prior to discharge. The language of sections 522(f) and (h) indicates that lien avoidance is not self-executing, and must be initiated by the debtor. The best practice is to do so before the case is closed.[36] In that way, there will be no loose ends or possibility of later problems once the discharge is granted at the end of the case.

The Federal Rules of Bankruptcy Procedure set out the procedure for lien avoidance. When a debtor seeks to avoid a lien under section 522(f) (applicable to judicial liens and certain non-purchase money security interests), a motion should be filed in accordance with Rule 9014 (governing contested matters).[37] For all other types of lien avoidance, or other exercises of avoiding powers, an adversary proceeding is required.[38] It is unclear whether the rules permit lien avoidance to be done through a provision in the debtor's chapter 13 plan, as some courts had permitted under the prior rules.[39]

Regardless of the method chosen, it is good practice to follow through once an order has been obtained. The order proposed to the court may include a provision requiring the lienholder or transferee to take all steps necessary to terminate the lien.[40] Once it has been signed, it can be forwarded to the lienholder accompanied by a request that termination of the lien be recorded in all necessary records offices, and that evidence of such action be sent to the debtor's counsel. However, in most cases it may be more expeditious for the debtor's attorney simply to file the bankruptcy court order in

---

case, by amendment. A spouse who has not joined in the petition originally must file a new petition, which would commence that spouse's case as of the date of its filing. *In re* Austin, 46 B.R. 358 (Bankr. E.D. Wis. 1985); *In re* Perkins, 51 B.R. 272 (Bankr. D.D.C. 1984).

25 *See* Forms 17, 18, Appx. G.2, *infra*.

26 Fed. R. Bankr. P. 1008.

27 Fed. R. Bankr. P. 1009; *see In re* Govoni, 289 B.R. 500 (Bankr. D. Mass. 2002) (order granting amendment to exemption schedule vacated because notice not provided to judicial lienholder).

28 *See* 11 U.S.C. § 523(a)(3). For further discussion of this issue, see § 14.4.3.3, *infra*.

29 Judicial Conference Schedule of Fees § 4, *reprinted in* Appx. C, *infra. See* Form 81, Appx. G.10, *infra*.

30 11 U.S.C. § 1328(a).

31 *In re* Moore, 247 B.R. 677 (Bankr. W.D. Mich. 2000).

32 11 U.S.C. § 502(a).

33 See Chapters 10 and 11, *infra,* for discussion of these powers.

34 *See* Form 77, Appx. G.9, *infra*.

35 Although their authority to do so is somewhat unclear, some courts have provided by local rule that creditors who unsuccessfully oppose lien avoidance proceedings are also liable for attorney fees. Additionally, Fed. R. Bankr. P. 9011 may provide a basis to claim fees and costs if opposition to a lien avoidance is unfounded. Such a motion may be enhanced if the creditor had an opportunity to assent to the relief requested and refused.

36 11 U.S.C. § 546(a)(2) may preclude certain lien avoidance proceedings once a case has been closed. See § 10.4.2.2, *infra,* for discussion of lien avoidance after discharge.

37 Fed. R. Bankr. P. 4003(d).

38 Fed. R. Bankr. P. 7001.

39 For further discussion of lien avoidance in a chapter 13 plan, see § 10.4.2.2, *infra*.

40 *See* Form 75, Appx. G.9, *infra*.

the appropriate records offices. The latter procedure ensures that a client's rights are fully protected and does not require waiting for the lienholder to act.

8.3.4 Redemption

Another important right that the debtor may exercise against secured creditors in a chapter 7 case is the right to redeem certain personal property by paying the lienholder the value of the property.[41] As with lien avoidance, it is probably easiest to attempt a stipulated settlement regarding redemption prior to filing for judicial enforcement. Of course, such a settlement must involve the lienholder's agreement on the value of the property. It could also involve an agreement by the lienholder not to seek to enforce the lien as long as the stipulated amount is paid in agreed-upon installments, either with or without reaffirmation of the debtor's personal liability.[42] A few courts have held that redemption agreements are subject to court review and therefore should be filed with the bankruptcy court.[43]

If an agreement cannot be reached, debtor's counsel should seek judicial enforcement of the right to redeem. It is unclear whether the rules require that this enforcement be done by complaint, as a "proceeding . . . to determine the validity . . . or extent of a lien,"[44] or whether it may be done by motion.[45] If there is a dispute about valuation, preparations for proof of value at trial must be made.[46] For the reasons stated above, and also because the protection of the automatic stay is lost thereafter[47] as to lien enforcement, the redemption proceeding should be filed before the discharge is granted. To meet the requirements of section 521(2)(B), redemption should normally be initiated within forty-five days after the filing of the Statement of Intentions, unless the court extends that deadline.

8.3.5 Complaints on Dischargeability

On occasion, it may be advisable for strategic reasons for the debtor to seek a determination regarding the dischargeability of a particular debt.[48] Such action can resolve the issue of whether a debt is being discharged once and for all, in the forum of the debtor's choice, and the debtor may obtain specific injunctive relief as well.[49] For example, if a particular tax is to be discharged, having the bankruptcy court specifically order the taxing authority to cease collection attempts may be preferable to raising the discharge as a defense later in some other forum. Similarly, it is almost always a good idea to obtain a determination in bankruptcy court on the dischargeability of a student loan when undue hardship is an issue.[50]

The procedure for seeking a determination of dischargeability is governed by the adversary proceeding rules.[51] Thus, a complaint stating the relief sought must be filed and served. Unlike complaints of creditors raising the nondischargeability of certain debts,[52] such a complaint may be filed at any time.[53]

8.3.6 Objections to Claims of Creditors

In those cases in which creditors do file claims, and particularly when they file secured or priority claims, an objection to a claim may be crucial to the debtor's case. Such an objection may mean the difference between success and failure of a chapter 13 plan or the reduction of a secured debt by thousands of dollars.[54] An objection may allege that the claim has not been timely filed or that it is improper or excessive for some other reason.[55]

An objection to a claim may raise any defense the debtor has against the creditor who filed the claim. It may also seek a determination that the claim is only partially secured, or not secured at all because the value of the property encumbered is less than the amount of the claim.[56]

Under current rules, there is no fixed deadline for filing an objection, but as the claim is allowed unless an objection is filed, the objection should be filed by the debtor[57] before

---

41　See § 11.5, *infra,* for further discussion of redemption.

42　See §§ 8.8.2, 14.5.2, *infra,* for further discussion of reaffirmation.

43　*See* § 11.5.5, *infra.*

44　Fed. R. Bankr. P. 7001.

45　Fed. R. Bankr. P. 6008.

46　For a discussion of valuation problems, see Chapter 11, *infra.*

47　The automatic stay is terminated by the discharge, except as to property of the estate, in which case the stay continues until the case is closed (usually on or soon after the date of discharge in a no-asset case). 11 U.S.C. § 362(c). When the case is closed, unadministered property is deemed abandoned and is no longer part of the estate. 11 U.S.C. § 554(c).

48　See § 14.4, *infra,* for a more complete discussion of dischargeability issues.

49　The provisions of 11 U.S.C. § 523(c), however, strongly suggest that it would not be in the debtor's interest to raise dischargeability issues under 11 U.S.C. § 523(a)(2), (4), (6) or (15), because if the creditor fails to assert nondischargeability under these sections, the debt is automatically rendered dischargeable.

50　See § 14.4.3.8, *infra,* for a discussion of the dischargeability of student loans.

51　Fed. R. Bankr. P. 7001.

52　See § 14.4, *infra,* for a discussion of such complaints.

53　Fed. R. Bankr. P. 4007(b).

54　See Chapters 11 and 12, *infra,* for a discussion of objections to secured claims and the treatment of such claims in a chapter 13 plan. See also Forms 59–68, Appendix G.8, *infra,* for examples of objections.

55　See § 13.4.3, *infra,* for further discussion of timeliness and other requirements for claims.

56　11 U.S.C. § 506; *see* Ch. 11, *infra.*

57　In some places a trustee will file an objection if the debtor alerts her to existing defenses, but the debtor should not rely on the trustee unless the trustee's filing is certain to achieve the debtor's goals.

distribution of dividends begins in a chapter 13 case,[58] or before the case is closed in a chapter 7 case. The rules stipulate that the objection must be in writing[59] and must be mailed or delivered to the claimant, the trustee, and the debtor at least thirty days prior to a hearing on the objection.[60] If the objection is joined with a demand for relief of the kind specified in Rule 7001, it becomes an adversary proceeding.[61] Otherwise, the matter is governed by Rule 9014. In either case, discovery should be available and the matter can be treated as a fully contested lawsuit between the debtor and creditor.

8.3.7 Other Disputes That May Arise

Various other types of disputes may occur between the debtor and creditors before (or after) the meeting of creditors. Perhaps the most common dispute putting the debtor on the defensive is a creditor's motion for relief from the automatic stay. Strategies for defense of these actions are discussed in a later chapter.[62] Less frequently, a creditor may file a complaint seeking reclamation of property from the estate.[63] Both of these types of cases usually bring disputes regarding secured claims to a head early in the case. Occasionally, a creditor files a complaint objecting to discharge or seeking a determination that a particular debt is nondischargeable.[64] It is also possible 1) that a motion to dismiss will be filed if there has been some procedural defect or if the debtor has not made required chapter 13 plan payments, or 2) that a proceeding may be filed alleging that a chapter 7 case constitutes a "substantial abuse" of the Code.[65]

There may also be other issues that the debtor should bring to the court's attention. One method of doing so is by filing a complaint seeking declaratory relief regarding the issue in dispute. If the issue is one which frequently recurs, a class action should be considered. Further discussion of such litigation is contained in Chapter 13, *infra*.

8.3.8 Retaining Non-Exempt Property in Chapter 7 Cases

In consumer chapter 7 bankruptcies, although the trustee pretty clearly has a right to take possession of non-exempt property prior to the section 341 meeting of creditors,[66] this turnover rarely occurs. All parties involved usually recognize that when such property is of limited value the simplest method of disposition is to sell it back to the debtor, who may purchase it with exempt assets or post-petition income. For example, the debtor's automobile may be worth two thousand dollars more than the amount which can be exempted. Usually, terms can be arranged for a payment to the trustee in lieu of turning over the car for a sale in which the debtor would receive the exempted amount in cash. That payment should normally be something less than two thousand dollars in order to reflect the trustee's avoided liquidation costs.[67] As long as the case will not be delayed, the trustee should be also willing to accept the payment in installments. If difficulties do arise, the case can be converted to a chapter 13, in which the debtor has the absolute right, in essence, to do the same thing—to pay the value of the non-exempt property over time.[68]

If the total value of the non-exempt property in a chapter 7 case is small, for example, less than one or two thousand dollars, it should also be possible to argue, in a chapter 7 case, that the property should not be sold because the proceeds of a sale would be largely or totally consumed by administrative expenses and thus would be of little or no benefit to creditors, especially if the assets are not liquid assets such as a bank account. In many cases, even if the debtor does not pursue such an argument, the trustee either declines to administer (that is, sell) such property or formally abandons it.[69] Under the prior Bankruptcy Act many courts dealt with nominal-asset cases by ordering abandonment of the property back to the debtor and Congress made clear its desire that this procedure should continue under the Code.[70] The Executive Office of the United States Trustees also has policies discouraging the administration of assets worth only small amounts.

---

58 Theoretically an objection could be resolved even after the distribution begins, with a return of any dividends wrongfully paid. *See* Advisory Committee Note to Fed. R. Bankr. P. 3007. However, recovery of such funds may be difficult. In some courts, the trustee files a motion to allow claims that have been filed, and any objection must be raised in response to that motion.

59 Fed. R. Bankr. P. 3007.

60 *Id.*

61 *Id.*

62 *See* § 9.7, *infra.*

63 *See* § 11.3.2, *infra,* for a discussion of reclamation complaints.

64 *See* Chapter 14, *infra,* for a discussion of these types of complaints.

65 *See* § 13.9, *infra,* for discussion of dismissal proceedings.

66 11 U.S.C. § 521.

67 The source of the payment may be exempt property of the debtor or property which does not come into the estate such as post-petition wages in a chapter 7 case. A post-petition gift to the debtor also may provide cash which the debtor can use to pay the trustee.

68 See Chapters 11 and 12, *infra,* for further discussion of chapter 13 cases.

69 11 U.S.C. § 554.

70 *See* H.R. Rep. No. 95-595, at 93–95 (1977). For further discussion of abandonment of property under 11 U.S.C. § 554, see § 3.5, *supra.*

8.3.9 Commencement of Payments in Chapter 13 Cases

Pursuant to 11 U.S.C. § 1326(a), the debtor must commence making payments pursuant to her plan within thirty days after a chapter 13 plan is filed. Payments to the trustee must be retained by the trustee until the plan is confirmed or confirmation is denied. If the plan is confirmed, the payments are distributed in accordance with the plan.[71] If confirmation is denied, the trustee returns the payments to the debtor after deducting allowed administrative expenses.[72]

Often, payments to the trustee are made through wage deductions forwarded by the debtor's employer. A court order, normally obtained by motion of the debtor or the trustee depending on local practice, is necessary to effectuate such payments pursuant to section 1325(c).[73] If such an order is to be effectuated, the debtor must be advised that it sometimes takes several weeks for the employer to begin making the deductions and that the debtor must pay directly to the trustee any plan payments that become due before the deductions begin.

If the plan proposes to cure a default on a secured claim and to maintain current payments to be paid directly to the creditor, the debtor also must make regular payments to the secured creditor as they come due.[74] In most jurisdictions this obligation can be discharged by payments made directly to the secured creditor, thereby avoiding a trustee's commission, but in some places such payments are usually made through the chapter 13 trustee. Local practice should be reviewed.

In some cases, the first months of a chapter 13 plan create a significant hardship for a debtor because of the confluence of required utility deposits, installment payments on the filing fee, and the need to commence plan payments. One potential solution is to propose a plan featuring graduated payments to the trustee, with lower payments in the first several months and higher payments thereafter. As long as the total to be paid over the life of the plan meets the requirements of the Code,[75] the plan is feasible,[76] and the payments in each given month commit the debtor's full disposable income,[77] graduated payment plans should be confirmed without a problem.

8.3.10 Rule 2004 Examinations

In rare instances in consumer cases, either before or after the meeting of creditors, the debtor may be ordered by the court to attend an additional examination. A creditor, the trustee, or any party in interest can seek an examination of the debtor (or any other entity) pursuant to Federal Rule of Bankruptcy Procedure 2004. The permissible scope of such an examination is broad, but not unlimited.[78] Motions[79] for such examinations are rare in consumer cases, but increasing due to the desire of credit card companies to pursue nondischargeability claims based on fraud. A motion for an examination can be opposed (and a subpoena can be quashed) on the ground that it would not serve a legitimate purpose consistent with the scope of examination defined in the rule.[80] The examination cannot be used for the purpose of abuse or harassment.[81]

In situations in which a creditor comes to court unprepared with evidence to establish a dischargeability case or when a complaint is filed without sufficient grounds pursuant to Federal Rule of Bankruptcy Procedure 9011, the creditor's failure to conduct a Rule 2004 examination can be used by the debtor as a sword. By failing to avail itself of the opportunity to examine the debtor, a creditor is open to the argument that the reasonable inquiry requirements of Rule 9011 have not been met, or that attorney fees should be awarded to the debtor under section 523(d) in a nondischargeability action.[82]

8.4 The Meeting of Creditors

8.4.1 Preparation

In many a routine chapter 7 bankruptcy, the only real event of any importance between filing and discharge is the meeting of creditors, sometimes colloquially called the "first meeting of creditors" or the "section 341(a) meeting" in honor of the relevant statutory provision. While it may pose occasional problems, this proceeding is usually routine and uneventful.

---

71 11 U.S.C. § 1326(a)(2).

72 11 U.S.C. § 1326(a)(2). *But see In re* Beam, 229 B.R. 454 (D. Or. 1998), *aff'd*, 192 F.3d 941 (9th Cir. 1999) (Internal Revenue Service could levy on debtor's funds in hands of trustee and receive funds that would otherwise be returned to debtor upon dismissal).

73 *See* § 12.6.1, *infra*.

74 *See* § 11.6.2, *infra*.

75 *See* § 7.3.7, *supra*; Ch. 12, *infra*.

76 *See* § 12.5, *infra*.

77 *See* § 12.3.3, *infra*.

78 The examination "may relate only to the acts, conduct, or property or to the liabilities and financial condition of the debtor, or to any matter which may affect the administration of the debtor's estate, or to the debtor's right to a discharge." The scope of examination if the debtor operates a business may include inquiries about the operation of the business. Fed. R. Bankr. P. 2004(b).

79 Some courts have local rules which allow examinations to be held on notice subject to objection by the party being examined. *See* 9 Collier on Bankruptcy ¶ 2004.01[2] (15th ed. rev.).

80 *In re* Eagle-Picher Indus., Inc., 169 B.R. 130 (Bankr. S.D. Ohio 1994).

81 *In re* Fearn, 96 B.R. 135 (Bankr. S.D. Ohio 1989).

82 *In re* Chinchilla, 202 B.R. 1010 (Bankr. S.D. Fla. 1996).

Despite the attorney's knowledge that the meeting of creditors is rarely anything to worry about, most debtors cannot believe that it will all be so simple; many expect their creditors to turn out in force to grill them about why they are not paying their just obligations. Therefore, it is important to give the client a detailed explanation of the procedure, and the questions that are likely to be asked, in much the same manner one would use in preparing for a trial or deposition.

Usually this preparation will not be difficult, as most trustees tend to ask the same questions in every case. Because the questions center on the schedules and statements already filed, it is essential to review these carefully with the client, paying particular attention to the items claimed as exempt and the values given them. It is sometimes a good idea to give the debtor a copy of all or part of these documents to take home and review, although doing so may only heighten the anxiety of some clients.

It is also necessary to assemble whatever documents are required to be brought to the meeting under local practice. In all jurisdictions, the trustee will wish to see a social security card or other documentary proof of the debtor's social security number. In some, the trustee may request deeds, titles to motor vehicles, tax returns, pay stubs, rent receipts, bank statements, real estate tax assessment documents, etcetera. These requests are often made in a notice sent to the debtor before the meeting. In a few places, local rules list documents that must be brought to the meeting. If an advocate is in doubt about these requirements, local practice can usually be easily checked. In any event, it is a good idea to bring the entire file in case something is needed.

The meeting of creditors is a good time to check which creditors have filed proofs of claim. Because generally the only creditors that will be paid in a chapter 13 case (or in those few chapter 7 cases in which there are dividends) are those for whom proofs of claim are filed, a debtor's counsel should make sure to file claims on behalf of any creditors who have not filed and whom the debtor wants to pay. The debtor may file such claims at any time during the 120 days after the first date set for the meeting of creditors.[83] In addition, it is useful to check the claims filed at this time, as

well as shortly after the deadline for filing claims,[84] to determine whether there are any claims to which the debtor wishes to object.

8.4.2 Procedure at the Meeting of Creditors

The debtor must attend the meeting of creditors.[85] If the debtor does not attend, it is often possible to obtain at least one postponement of the meeting. However, failure to attend or to obtain a postponement will ordinarily lead to dismissal, unless a reasonable excuse is provided.[86] In exceptional cases of hardship, including illness or incarceration, the personal appearance of the debtor may be excused, upon a motion filed by the debtor, and the debtor may be examined by telephone or by written interrogatories.[87]

The proceeding is likely to be short and informal in the case of a typical consumer debtor. Despite its name, it is rarely graced by the presence of any creditors. Indeed, neither trustees nor creditors show much interest in the cases of most consumer debtors.

---

83 Fed. R. Bankr. P. 3004. Specifically, the deadline is thirty days after the expiration of the deadline set in Fed. R. Bankr. P. 3002(c). The time for a governmental unit to file a claim was extended by the 1994 amendments to 180 days after the order for relief, 11 U.S.C. § 502(b)(9), so the debtor also has a longer deadline to file a claim for a governmental unit. Notice of such a claim is given to the creditor, and it may then file its own claim, which supersedes that filed by the debtor, unless the deadline for the creditor to file a claim has passed. 11 U.S.C. § 502(b)(9). Even after the deadline has passed, some courts have allowed a creditor to amend a proof of claim filed by the debtor on the creditor's behalf. *See, e.g., In re* Kolstad, 101 B.R. 492 (Bankr. S.D. Tex. 1989), *aff'd*, 928 F.2d 171 (5th Cir. 1991).

84 This deadline is ninety days after the first date set for the meeting of creditors. Fed. R. Bankr. P. 3002(c). However, governmental units are given 180 days from the date of the order for relief (normally, the date the petition was filed) to file their claims. 11 U.S.C. § 502(b)(9). It does not appear that a creditor is given additional time to file a superseding claim under Fed. R. Bankr. P. 3004 when the debtor files a claim shortly before the claims deadline. Advisory Committee Note to Fed. R. Bankr. P. 3004. *But see In re* Kolstad, 101 B.R. 492 (Bankr. S.D. Tex. 1989) (creditor allowed to amend debtor's timely-filed claim), *aff'd*, 928 F.2d 171 (5th Cir. 1991).

85 11 U.S.C. § 343.

86 *But see In re* Dinova, 212 B.R. 437 (B.A.P. 2d Cir. 1997) (case could not be dismissed without notice and a hearing after debtor failed to attend § 341 meeting, notwithstanding legend in notice of meeting that "failure by the debtor(s) to appear . . . shall result in dismissal of the case upon ex parte order").

87 *See In re* Bergeron, 235 B.R. 641 (Bankr. N.D. Cal. 1999) (debtor with severe dementia and other medical problems excused from testifying when wife had already testified); *In re* Vilt, 56 B.R. 723 (Bankr. N.D. Ill. 1986); *In re* Sullivan, 30 B.R. 781 (Bankr. E.D. Pa. 1983) (debtor's brother, who had the debtor's power of attorney, could appear in debtor's place); *In re* Edwards, 2 B.R. 103 (Bankr. S.D. Fla. 1979) (debtor in military service in Philippines and wife available to testify); *see also In re* Oliver, 279 B.R. 69 (Bankr. W.D.N.Y. 2002) (debtor's failure to appear because he had died prior to meeting was not cause for dismissal because Fed. R. Bankr. P. 1016 provides that a chapter 7 case in which the debtor dies should ordinarily proceed to its conclusion). *But see In re* Davis, 275 B.R. 864 (B.A.P. 8th Cir. 2002) (bankruptcy court did not abuse its discretion in dismissing case of incarcerated debtor who made no attempt to make arrangements to conduct creditors meeting by means other than personal appearance). See also the cases on attendance at discharge hearings cited in § 8.8.2, *infra*. In many cases, it may be a good idea to request that the trustee agree to such a procedure in advance. Form pleadings may be found in Forms 50 and 51, Appendix G.7, *infra*.

There are several reasons for this lack of interest. Probably paramount is the feeling that there are rarely any assets worth pursuing in such cases and that the cost in time and effort required of the trustee and creditors is not justified by the benefits achieved. Unless the trustee can obtain property for the estate worth thousands of dollars, her fee will not be significantly increased in a chapter 7 case.[88] Most creditors realize that there is little they can accomplish at the meeting other than perhaps some discovery. Some creditors will appear to find out the location of their collateral and to attempt to negotiate its future disposition. Often, though, the only ones to show up are unsophisticated creditors who are under the misimpression that they are required to attend.

Local practice does, however, vary from jurisdiction to jurisdiction. In a few localities, for example, it is relatively common for creditors to appear in chapter 13 cases in order to negotiate with the debtor's counsel and the trustee concerning various provisions of the plan. If this occurs, it is important to remember that the trustee has no power to make a final decision on whether a particular plan will be confirmed. When issues are contested, the trustee or a creditor may file an objection, and the debtor may present opposition if necessary and obtain judicial resolution.[89] Frequently, even when issues are raised at the meeting of creditors, neither the trustee nor any creditor will go to the effort necessary to formally raise the appropriate objection.

The purpose of the meeting is to obtain further information about the debtor's case, particularly regarding the debtor's assets and liabilities. This information is obtained through a set of routine questions usually propounded by the presiding officer, who may be the trustee or the United States trustee depending on local rules. In a few jurisdictions, the debtor's attorney may pose questions as in a direct examination.

The questions typically seek to check the accuracy of the schedules and statements filed and, in a chapter 13 case, the debtor's ability to perform under her plan.[90] It is not uncommon for information somewhat inconsistent with the previously filed documents to come out, but it is rare that any serious problems arise. Usually any discrepancies can be cured by amendment.[91]

The questions may also go to the right to a discharge. These questions are rarely very detailed unless a particular creditor has appeared to seek information on a debt that it claims is nondischargeable. Then the proceeding may become, for all practical purposes, a deposition by that creditor.

By and large though, the questions asked parallel those in the official forms that the debtor has already answered, and

have similar purposes.[92] They seek information concerning fraudulent transfers, preferences, former bankruptcies and, usually, how the debtor fell into financial difficulty. Unless an answer arouses suspicion, the questions are rarely followed up. In many districts, though, trustees are careful to ask about types of property frequently not listed by debtors, such as tax refunds, security deposits, and the like. If the procedures suggested in this manual have been followed, no surprises should surface. However, even if new property is uncovered, it usually can still be claimed as exempt by amendment of the schedules or statement.

As the bankruptcy judge is not present at the meeting, disputes may occasionally arise either between the debtor and creditors, or between the debtor and the trustee. For example, the debtor's counsel may object to certain questions for any one of several reasons, such as privilege, the Fifth Amendment,[93] relevance, or repetitiousness. Although neither the statute nor the rules address how such disputes are to be resolved, it is clear that neither the trustee nor the United States trustee can issue enforceable orders. The procedure usually followed is similar to that of a deposition—an instruction to the client not to answer, if necessary, with the dispute reserved for the court's decision if a party seeks to compel an answer.

Similarly, there is sometimes confusion about how much a debtor may consult counsel during the examination. In most jurisdictions, the practice is quite liberal; the client is allowed to confer with counsel before answering a question and counsel is allowed to interject clarifying remarks when necessary.

Occasionally a debtor cannot produce photo identification, a social security card, or some other document demanded by a trustee. Again, it must be remembered that the trustee has no authority to require such documents, and even the United States trustee, who supervises the trustee, does not have such authority. Usually the demand for a particular document results from a direction to the trustee from the United States trustee, or perhaps a particular trustee's interpretation of such a direction. If the document is not produced the only thing the trustee can do is move to dismiss the case, and in that event it is for the court to decide whether the document is really necessary. Nothing in the Bankruptcy Code or the Federal Rules of Bankruptcy Procedure requires a debtor to produce either photo identification or any other particular documents. Indeed, the Code does not even require that the debtor have a social security

---

88 The amount of the trustee's compensation is set by 11 U.S.C. §§ 326(a) and 330(b).

89 *See* § 8.6, *infra*.

90 See sample lists of questions in Forms 44 and 45, Appendix G.7, *infra*.

91 See § 8.3.2, *supra,* on procedure for amending.

92 The purposes of the questions are discussed in Chapter 7, *supra*.

93 Discharge cannot be denied for refusal to answer a question on this ground unless the debtor has first been granted immunity with respect to the matter involved. 11 U.S.C. § 727(a)(6). Trustees are also constrained by other Constitutional protections. *See, e.g., In re* Truck-A-Way, 300 B.R. 31 (E.D. Cal. 2003) (*ex parte* order allowing trustee's entry, search, and seizure of debtor's property without probable cause or a warrant violated Fourth Amendment).

number.[94] Therefore, unless there is a legitimate question about the debtor's identity or social security number, especially if the documents demanded by the trustee do not exist or are not in the debtor's possession, there is little likelihood that a court would require them. Often, a trustee may back down without even filing a motion. Of course, in some cases, the course of least resistance and expense may be to have the debtor obtain the documents demanded by the trustee.

One practice that has arisen in some bankruptcy courts is a request that debtors surrender all credit cards still in their possession at the time of the meeting of creditors. Although most debtors are quite willing to relinquish the cards, if they have not already done so, some may have legitimate objections to this procedure, especially regarding necessary accounts which may not even be in default. If the debtor wishes to retain possession of the cards the request for their surrender should be opposed. Most judges and trustees admit that they lack specific authority for the turnover of the cards absent a request by the creditors involved, and they will not pursue the issue, especially if the debtor has shown good reason for retaining the cards. Indeed, it has been held that, at least in the case of a chapter 13 debtor, a creditor has no right to revoke a non-delinquent credit card based solely on a bankruptcy filing and the debtor may continue to use the card.[95]

Another issue that crops up frequently in some jurisdictions involves creditors who attend meetings seeking to pressure debtors into signing reaffirmation agreements. These creditors often threaten the debtor with repossession of items of personal property pursuant to questionable or non-existent security interests.[96] For the reasons discussed more fully later in this manual, reaffirmation of debts is rarely a good idea.[97] Clients may need to be reassured, however, that repossession is unlikely, and that if the clients simply refuse to allow a creditor to enter their home to repossess, the creditor will need to obtain a court order permitting repossession.[98] It may also be necessary to assure clients that representation will be provided in any post-bankruptcy action filed by the creditor seeking to obtain possession of the claimed collateral. However, few creditors take the trouble to pursue the matter that far. In the unusual instance in which that occurs, a vigorous defense raising issues concerning the validity of the security interest, and perhaps its use to circumvent the bankruptcy discharge, normally results in the creditor finding a graceful way to end the proceeding and deciding it will seek to concentrate its future efforts on debtors represented by less diligent attorneys.

Recent class action cases filed against certain major retailers concerning their reaffirmation practices turned up some horror stories about creditor behavior at meetings of creditors. In some cases, creditor representatives (who earned commissions for each reaffirmation) convinced debtors to sign reaffirmation agreements without the knowledge of the debtor's attorney, often because the attorney was in the meeting room with other clients and the trustee. As the agreements were never filed with the court, neither the attorney nor the court system was aware of the existence of these agreements. Debtors nevertheless paid under the agreements when billed after bankruptcy.

Practices such as these require educating clients prior to the meeting of creditors concerning the disadvantages of reaffirmation agreements. Perhaps even more importantly clients should be told to report any direct contact by a creditor, not only for advice before making a decision, but also so that sanctions against the creditor may be considered.

In chapter 7 cases only, the 1994 amendments to the Bankruptcy Code added one additional procedure to the meeting of creditors. The trustee must orally examine the debtor to "ensure" that the debtor is aware of several things.[99] The legislative history makes clear that the sole purpose of this examination is informational.[100] Thus, there should be no consequences if the debtor expresses lack of awareness or confusion in the face of the trustee's examination.

The first subject of the required examination is the debtor's awareness of the potential consequences of bankruptcy on a person's credit history. However, other than the fact that bankruptcy appears on a credit report for ten years, it is hard to see what a trustee can say on this topic. If the idea was to convince a debtor not to file a bankruptcy case, the information would come too late; the bankruptcy has already been filed by the time of the meeting and cannot be removed from a credit history. Moreover, as the legislative history

---

94 *In re* Merlo, 265 B.R. 502 (Bankr. S.D. Fla. 2001). The Statement of Social Security Number submitted with the petition and schedules provides that the debtor may check a box indicating that she does not have a social security number. *See* Official Form 21, Appx. D, *infra.*

95 *In re* Knapp, 137 B.R. 582 (Bankr. D.N.J. 1992) (under 11 U.S.C. § 541(c)(1)(B) the pre-petition property rights of the debtor become property of the bankruptcy estate notwithstanding any contractual provision that gives an option to terminate the contract upon a bankruptcy filing).

96 Very often the creditors involved have claimed that they have a security interest pursuant to a credit card agreement. These security interests, if they exist, are difficult, if not impossible, to enforce. They are generally based on an adhesion contract which is mailed to the debtor with the card and in the case of a revolving charge, it is often impossible to determine whether the secured claims have been paid off.

97 *See* §§ 8.8.2, 14.5.2, *infra.*

98 For a more complete discussion of the issues, see National

Consumer Law Center, Repossessions and Foreclosures (5th ed. 2002 and Supp.). *See also Helping Your Client Do the Wash: The Effect in Bankruptcy of PMSI Claims Created by Revolving Credit Accounts*, 12 NCLC REPORTS *Bankruptcy and Foreclosures Ed.* 37 (Jan./Feb. 1994).

99 11 U.S.C. § 341(d).

100 H.R. Rep. No. 103-835, at 43 (1994), *reprinted in* 1994 U.S.C.C.A.N. 3340.

states,[101] the trustee cannot and should not prognosticate about how bankruptcy will affect future credit, or that dismissal would improve the debtor's chances of obtaining credit. Some creditors give credit to recent bankruptcy debtors. Indeed, if the debtor's income is freed from payment on numerous obligations, the debtor may have a better chance of obtaining credit. And, because many creditors do not distinguish between chapter 7 and chapter 13 cases on credit reports, the trustee cannot and should not predict that the debtor's credit will be better if the case is converted to chapter 13.

The second topic is the debtor's ability to file a petition under a different chapter. This information is presumably to ensure the debtor knows that chapter 13 is also available. However, the debtor will already have been informed of that fact both by counsel (who must swear in the petition that this information was given) and by the clerk, who must give notice of the chapters available to every debtor.[102]

The third topic is the effect of receiving a discharge of debts under the Code. This information includes not only the fact that the discharge eliminates liability on most debts, but also the risks of and procedures for reaffirming debts.[103] In this context, the debtor should be informed that a debt may be paid voluntarily after discharge without a reaffirmation which waives the protections of the discharge.[104] As the legislative history points out,[105] most debtors who reaffirm debts will no longer receive the warnings about the dangers of reaffirmation given by the court, so it is important that this information be given by the trustee.

In most cases trustees will attempt to minimize the time necessary for this examination by giving out the information in written form and then inquiring whether the debtor has read it.[106] If the debtor is given such a handout and has questions about it, the time following the creditors' meeting is a good time for the debtor's attorney to answer these questions.

Finally, in a chapter 13 case, the meeting of creditors may provide a good opportunity for the debtor to file any priority or secured claims that creditors have not already filed and that the debtor wants to pay under the plan.[107] The reason for these filings, as discussed above, is to ensure that the money the debtor is paying into the plan in order to deal with these creditors does not go instead to pay dischargeable unsecured claims. For the same reason, it is probably good practice to

file at this time any other claims the debtor wishes to pay, both in chapter 13 cases and in chapter 7 cases which will involve a distribution to unsecured creditors. These claims may include nondischargeable debts and claims upon which friends or relatives have cosigned (so they are paid, at least in part, by any distribution).[108] The time limits provided for in the rules for creditors to file claims are outlined in the notice of the creditors' meeting.[109]

8.5 Chapter 7 Cases—After the Meeting of Creditors

In the typical no-asset bankruptcy, there is little to be done between the creditors' meeting and the discharge. Proceedings commenced by the debtor, such as for lien avoidance or redemption, may be litigated, as well as proceedings concerning dischargeability of debts and other matters. Amendments to the schedules or statement of affairs may be necessary. However, amendments that add creditors may not always be of value after the deadline for filing a nondischargeability complaint has passed.[110]

If the debtor has more than nominal non-exempt assets, of course, they are turned over or their value is paid to the trustee who, as described in an earlier chapter, liquidates them.[111] Such events rarely occur because consumer debtors with non-exempt assets usually opt for chapter 13. However, when this does occur, it is important for the debtor to check to make sure that claims are filed for debts that may be nondischargeable, in order to maximize the amount that is paid toward those debts from the assets of the estate.[112]

In some districts, the trustee files a report to the court concerning whether she objects to the exemptions claimed or to the discharge of the debtor. The necessity of this report,

---

101 *Id.*

102 *See* Official Form 1, Appx. D, *infra*; 11 U.S.C. § 342(b).

103 H.R. Rep. No. 103-835, at 43 (1994), *reprinted in* 1994 U.S.C.C.A.N. 3340.

104 11 U.S.C. § 524(f).

105 11 U.S.C. § 524(f).

106 11 U.S.C. § 524(f). A sample of this form is reprinted as Form 47, Appendix G.7, *infra*.

107 Occasionally, there may be cases in which an exception to this general rule is appropriate, if the main purpose of the plan is other than to pay particular secured creditors. See Chapter 11, *infra*, for a more detailed discussion.

108 Because these debts have to be paid by the debtor or others even after the discharge, it is to the debtor's advantage to make sure the maximum amount possible is paid on these debts during the bankruptcy case. See Chapter 14, *infra*, for a discussion of nondischargeable debts in chapters 7 and 13.

109 Fed. R. Bankr. P. 3002(c); Official Form 9, Appx. D, *infra*. The time limit for a debtor's claim on behalf of a creditor is found in Fed. R. Bankr. P. 3004.

110 See Chapter 14, *infra*, for a discussion of creditors not listed in the schedules prior to the first meeting. Some courts have allowed the addition of creditors even after the closing of the case in no-asset chapter 7 cases. *In re* Rosinski, 759 F.2d 539 (6th Cir. 1985); *In re* Stark, 717 F.2d 322 (7th Cir. 1983); *In re* Adams, 41 B.R. 933 (D. Me. 1984); *In re* Soures, 19 B.R. 798 (Bankr. E.D. Va. 1982) (permission to add creditor after discharge granted when no prejudice to creditor in no-asset case). *But see In re* Swain, 21 B.R. 594 (Bankr. D. Conn. 1982) (debtors denied permission to amend schedules to add creditor after discharge).

111 *See* Ch. 3, *supra*.

112 *See In re* Danielson, 981 F.2d 296 (7th Cir. 1992) (debtor not permitted to file untimely claim for Internal Revenue Service, which would have allowed distributions from the estate that would have reduced nondischargeable tax liability).

which was required under a provision of the prior rules not included in the current rules,[113] is questionable because under the Code the exemptions are self-executing if no objection is filed.[114]

The trustee or any creditor who wishes to object to the exemptions claimed must file such objections in writing and serve them within thirty days after the conclusion of the meeting of creditors (or, if later, the date of any amendment to the exemptions claimed).[115] Thereafter, there must be a hearing on the objections, at which the objecting party has the burden of proving the exemptions are not properly claimed.[116]

8.6 Chapter 13 Confirmation Hearing

In a chapter 13 case, the next step after the section 341 meeting is normally the confirmation hearing, which may be held on the same day or anytime up to several months later.[117] In some cases it is not possible to conclude the confirmation hearing until many months after the creditors' meeting, pending the court's decision on objections to priority or secured claims; without such a decision there is no way to determine whether the plan pays such claims in full,[118] as is usually required for confirmation.[119]

The procedures followed at the confirmation hearing vary greatly. If neither the trustee nor any creditor objects to confirmation, the hearing usually takes only a few minutes, and the court simply enters an order of confirmation finding that the plan complies with all of the provisions of chapter 13.[120] The debtor's attendance may not be necessary. In fact, some bankruptcy judges actively discourage counsel from bringing their clients to the confirmation hearing, so that the debtors will not lose another day's pay. Other judges do not even require that counsel be present when there is no objection; they simply sign the confirmation order in chambers. Local practice in this regard should be checked.

If there are objections or if the court has questions of its own, testimony and argument may be taken regarding the debtor's income, ability to pay, and other matters.[121] Normally, objections are filed prior to the hearing,[122] but they may be filed as late as the hearing itself if the court sets that deadline for their filing.[123] A creditor that has not filed a proof of claim generally does not have standing to object to the plan.[124] The substantive issues likely to be raised by objections are discussed in later chapters.[125]

Lastly, in some districts the court may require counsel to present a proposed order of confirmation[126] or an application for confirmation. As is required in other proceedings, inquiry should be made into local practice on these matters prior to the date of the hearing. The day of the confirmation hearing is a good time to determine what claims have been filed, especially in jurisdictions in which the deadline for filing claims has already expired. If only a few claims have been filed, the plan may provide more than enough payments to pay all filed claims in full. If that is the case, it is obviously in the debtor's interest to modify the plan to lower either the amount or the number of payments. Otherwise, because of the way some trustees' computers are programmed, the debtor may continue to make payments to the trustee even after all claims have been paid.

Because the debtor has the absolute right to modify the plan prior to confirmation,[127] it may be wise to file a modified plan to deal with anticipated objections to confirmation that are not likely to be rejected by the court. Usually, if the court denies confirmation, the debtor is also given an opportunity to file a modified plan. Once the debtor

113 *Compare* Fed. R. Bankr. P. 4003 *with* R. Bankr. P. 403(b).

114 11 U.S.C. § 522(*l*). For further discussion of exemption practices, see Chapter 10, *infra.*

115 Fed. R. Bankr. P. 4003(b).

116 Fed. R. Bankr. P. 4003(c).

117 At least one district court has held that when a creditor objects, it is improper to hold the confirmation hearing on the same day as the first meeting. *In re* Robinson, 22 B.R. 497 (W.D. Va. 1982). Some courts wait until three months after the meeting of creditors have passed before holding the confirmation hearing so that all claims (except perhaps governmental claims) will have been filed by the date of the hearing.

118 See § 13.4.3, *infra,* for further discussion of objections to claims.

119 See Chapters 11 and 12, *infra,* for discussion of confirmation requirements.

120 *See In re* Hines, 723 F.2d 333 (3d Cir. 1983) (trustee's recommendation is sufficient basis for confirming plan); *In re* Dues, 98 B.R. 434 (Bankr. N.D. Ind. 1989) (absent objection, full evidentiary hearing is not required).

121 At this hearing the burden of proof and the burden of going forward concerning an objection should be placed on the objecting party. *In re* Mendenhall, 54 B.R. 44 (Bankr. W.D. Ark. 1985); *In re* Flick, 14 B.R. 912 (Bankr. E.D. Pa. 1981).

122 The objections must consist of more then simply checking a box on the proof of claim form rejecting the plan. They must state specific grounds for objections. *In re* DeSimone, 17 B.R. 862 (Bankr. E.D. Pa. 1982).

123 Fed. R. Bankr. P. 3015(f) provides that objections to confirmation must be filed and served upon the debtor and the trustee, as well as transmitted to the United States trustee, prior to confirmation. It is not clear whether a local rule may permissibly set an earlier deadline for such objections. *See In re* Gaona, 290 B.R. 381 (Bankr. S.D. Cal. 2003) (objections untimely under local rule); *In re* Harris, 275 B.R. 850 (Bankr. S.D. Ohio 2002) (objections filed after deadline established in clerk's notice were untimely); *In re* Carbone, 254 B.R. 1 (Bankr. D. Mass. 2000) (objection not timely because it was not received by clerk within time period allowed by local rule); *In re* Duncan, 245 B.R. 538 (Bankr. E.D. Tenn. 2000) (objection not timely filed under local rule even though filed before confirmation).

124 *In re* Stewart, 46 B.R. 73 (Bankr. D. Or. 1985); *see In re* Hansel, 160 B.R. 66 (S.D. Tex. 1993) (holder of untimely filed proof of claim lacks standing to object to confirmation).

125 *See* Chs. 11, 12, *infra.*

126 *See* Form 9, Appx. G.3, *infra.*

127 11 U.S.C. § 1323.

files a modified plan, the court must base its confirmation decision on that modified plan.[128]

8.7 Administration of the Chapter 13 Plan

8.7.1 Trustee Payments to Creditors

Once the chapter 13 plan has been confirmed, the trustee usually takes over the administrative details. Although the debtor may have been making payments for some time, no distribution is made until after confirmation. If the time for filing claims has not yet elapsed,[129] there may be further delays before all claims are determined and allowed. In the interim, objections to other claims, as well as other disputes that arise, may be litigated.

It is a good idea to monitor the trustee's payments periodically once distribution has begun. Most trustees allow convenient access to their records, often on the Internet or otherwise by computer modem, and some mail computer printouts to debtors or their counsel. It is not uncommon for computer-ordered payments from a trustee's office to deviate from either the plan or the claims actually filed. In that event, it is important to bring the problem to the trustee's attention before incorrect amounts have been paid.[130] An occasional check on the progress of the plan can also reveal any other budding problems, such as a delinquency in the debtor's payments.

Finally, it is common for creditors to credit payments received from the trustee in a manner which is inconsistent with the debtor's plan. For example, current payments of principal and interest may be lumped together with payments made on the arrears and credited in ways that will not lead to reinstatement of a mortgage debt upon completion of the plan. All amounts paid may be credited exclusively to the interest arrears so that there is no principal reduction commensurate with the debtor's payments and new late charges continue to accrue. It is therefore a good idea to monitor the debtor's account statements in order to catch these problems before the plan is completed.[131] Alterna-

tively, pre- or post-discharge litigation may be necessary based on the creditor's failure to comply with the confirmed plan.[132]

8.7.2 Post-Petition Claims

Once distribution has begun, events normally flow smoothly for the duration of the plan, with the debtor or the debtor's employer[133] sending payments regularly to the trustee for distribution. The Code provides for incorporation of certain post-petition claims (debts incurred after the petition) into the plan;[134] however, such debts may also be paid outside the plan. Allowable post-petition claims may include debts for post-petition taxes[135] and consumer debts for property or services necessary for the debtor's performance under the plan.[136] Regardless of whether the post-petition claims are to be paid through the plan or outside it, creditors often require the trustee's approval before any significant obligation is incurred.[137] Such approval is rarely difficult to obtain,[138] though local practices may vary.

When the debtor, trustee, and creditor do not agree that a post-petition claim should be paid through the plan, there may be different results. Only a creditor may file a post-petition claim, so that a debtor may not force a post-petition creditor into the plan involuntarily.[139] If a creditor does not choose to file a claim, the post-petition claim will survive the bankruptcy and can be enforced in non-bankruptcy courts to the extent that it is not paid.[140] Similarly, the debtor

---

128 *In re* Nielsen, 211 B.R. 19 (B.A.P. 8th Cir. 1997).

129 Fed. R. Bankr. P. 3002(c) allows the filing of claims up to three months after the first date set for the meeting of creditors.

130 Although a trustee is probably liable for such improper payments and can often recoup them from improperly paid creditors, it is far better to avoid having to litigate that issue.

131 When a debtor suspects that payments have not been credited properly, a "qualified written request" under the Real Estate Settlement Procedures Act (RESPA) may be sent to the creditor which will trigger an obligation on the part of the creditor (or servicer) to provide information relating to the account. *See* 12 U.S.C. § 2605(e); *see also Little Known RESPA Provision Offers Relief from Servicer Problems*, 15 NCLC REPORTS *Consumer Credit and Usury Ed.* 21 (May/June 1997). For a sample request form, see Form 69, Appendix G.4, *infra*.

132 *See* § 12.11, *infra*.

133 See § 12.6.1, *infra*, for discussion of wage orders requiring employers to remit a portion of the debtor's paycheck to the trustee.

134 11 U.S.C. § 1305.

135 *See In re* Ripley, 926 F.2d 440 (5th Cir. 1991) (income tax is payable post-petition, when return is due, rather than pre-petition when quarterly payments were due, for the purpose of determining whether post-petition claim for taxes is timely). Post-petition taxes are not entitled to administrative expense status, regardless of whether the governmental entity files an allowable post-petition claim. *In re* Gyulafia, 65 B.R. 913 (Bankr. D. Kan. 1986).

136 *See* 11 U.S.C. § 1305(a); *In re* Roseboro, 77 B.R. 38 (Bankr. W.D.N.C. 1987). *But see In re* Farquhar, 112 B.R. 34 (Bankr. D. Colo. 1989) (claims based on fire damage to debtor's property are not allowable as post-petition claims).

137 *See* 11 U.S.C. § 1305(b).

138 *See* Form 73, Appx. G.8, *infra*; 11 U.S.C. §§ 1305, 1328(d).

139 *In re* Seyden, 294 B.R. 418 (Bankr. S.D. Ga. 2002) (debtor did not have standing to file post-petition tax claim); *In re* Benson, 116 B.R. 606 (Bankr. S.D. Ohio 1990) (debtor could not file claim for post-petition rent-to-own creditor); *In re* Hester, 63 B.R. 607 (Bankr. E.D. Tenn. 1986); *In re* Pritchett, 55 B.R. 557 (Bankr. W.D. Va. 1985); *In re* Nowak, 17 B.R. 860 (Bankr. N.D. Ohio 1982).

140 *In re* Dunn, 83 B.R. 694 (Bankr. D. Neb. 1988) (post-petition claims not discharged because they were not provided for in the plan); *In re* Lewis, 33 B.R. 98 (Bankr. W.D.N.Y. 1983) (leave of court obtained to sue debtor in state court while chapter 13 case

may choose not to provide for post-petition claims in the plan for a variety of reasons, including the inability to control which post-petition claims are filed and the possibility that they may exceed what the debtor can pay.

If a creditor and the debtor both want the claim to be treated under the plan, and the claim is filed and allowable under 11 U.S.C. § 1305(a)(2) and 1305(c),[141] a modification of the plan may be necessary to accommodate the claim. Modification may be accomplished either by increasing the payments or the length of the plan and perhaps separately classifying the claim so it is paid in full. At least one court has held that, if the debtor refuses to apply for the necessary modification, the claim cannot be allowed and it will be retained by the creditor for enforcement outside the bankruptcy.[142] This result seems clearly correct, as Code section 1322(b)(6) is a permissive provision. The debtor may provide for post-petition claims in the plan, but is not required to do so.

Post-petition claims that are filed and allowed are normally discharged by a chapter 13 discharge if they are provided for in the plan. However, if the trustee's approval of a post-petition debt could have been obtained by the debtor but was not obtained, that debt survives the discharge to the extent it has not been paid.[143]

8.7.3 Modification of the Plan

Debtors often need to modify their plans after confirmation, either to raise payments to accommodate post-petition claims or to lower the payments because the debtor has had a change of circumstances. One such change of circumstances may occur if the debtor loses use of a car that serves as collateral for a secured claim being paid under the plan, through its destruction, repossession, inoperability, or other cause, or if the debtor no longer needs the vehicle. Although some courts have erroneously refused to permit a debtor to modify a plan in order to surrender a vehicle and treat the secured creditor's claim as unsecured,[144] others have permitted such modifications.[145] The Code permits modifica-

tion of the "amount of the distribution to a creditor" to "take into account any payment of such claim other than under the plan,"[146] which should include surrender or repossession of the vehicle. In addition, a court may reconsider a claim under Code section 502(j) and, under Federal Rule of Bankruptcy Procedure 3008, the court's reconsideration may allow or disallow a claim, increase or decrease the amount of a prior allowance, accord the claim a different priority, or give rise to any other appropriate order.[147] A court reconsidering a claim can reclassify a secured claim as unsecured and grant a motion modifying the amount of payments to the creditor accordingly.[148] Alternatively, the debtor may wish to modify a plan to use insurance proceeds available due to a car's destruction (which typically serve as additional collateral because the creditor is named as loss payee) to purchase a new vehicle that can serve as substitute collateral for the creditor's claim.

The trustee or a holder of an unsecured claim may also seek plan modification, if the debtor's financial circumstances have improved since confirmation.[149] However, the debtor probably need not prove changed circumstances to establish grounds for a modification.[150] The requirements for modification are set out in 11 U.S.C. § 1329, and basically provide that the modified plan must meet all the tests for confirmation of the original plan.[151] The procedure,

---

pending). If the case is converted to chapter 7 and the claim is dischargeable, a post-petition claim is discharged. 11 U.S.C. § 348(d); *see* § 8.7.4, *infra.*

141 The trustee or debtor may object to allowance of the claim under this section if the creditor knew or should have known that obtaining the trustee's approval of the debt was practicable and that approval was not obtained.

142 *In re* Nelson, 27 B.R. 341 (Bankr. M.D. Ga. 1983); *see also In re* Smith, 192 B.R. 712 (Bankr. E.D. Tenn. 1996) (local rule providing that post-petition claim must be paid one-hundred percent unless creditor affirmatively consents otherwise and payments on other claims may not be reduced due to post-petition claim unless debtors comply with local rule procedures).

143 11 U.S.C. § 1328(d).

144 *E.g., In re* Nolan, 232 F.3d 528 (6th Cir. 2000).

145 *E.g., In re* Zieder, 263 B.R. 114 (Bankr. D. Ariz. 2001); *In re*

Townley, 256 B.R. 697 (Bankr. D.N.J. 2000); *see also In re* Hernandez, 282 B.R. 200 (Bankr. S.D. Tex. 2002) (debtor could modify plan to surrender collateral to secured creditor in payment of secured claim); *In re* Morris, 289 B.R. 783 (Bankr. S.D. Ga. 2002) (establishing procedure requiring that creditors who obtain relief from stay to repossess chapter 13 debtors' vehicles file amended claims, to which parties could object, or else their allowed secured claims would be deemed paid in full).

146 11 U.S.C. § 1329(a)(3).

147 Rules Advisory Committee Note to Fed. R. Bankr. P. 3008.

148 *In re* Zieder, 263 B.R. 114 (Bankr. D. Ariz. 2001). However, a trustee cannot unilaterally reduce the creditor's secured claim. *In re* Davis, 314 F.3d 567 (11th Cir. 2002).

149 See discussion of the "ability-to-pay test" in Chapter 12, *infra.* *See In re* Gronski, 86 B.R. 428 (Bankr. E.D. Pa. 1988) (substantial change in circumstances necessary to permit creditor to impose modification on debtor requiring increase in payments); *see also* 8 Collier on Bankruptcy ¶ 1329.03 (15th ed. rev.). *But see In re* Witkowski, 16 F.3d 739 (7th Cir. 1994) (plan could be modified on motion of trustee even though there was no change in circumstances since confirmation); *In re* Perkins, 111 B.R. 671 (Bankr. M.D. Tenn. 1990) (changed circumstances not statutory prerequisite to trustee's motion to modify). The court may not order a particular modification of the plan. *In re* Muessel, 292 B.R. 712 (B.A.P. 1st Cir. 2003).

150 *See In re* Larson, 122 B.R. 417 (Bankr. D. Idaho 1991) (no requirement of proof of changed circumstances by debtor required for modification); *see also* 8 Collier on Bankruptcy ¶ 1329.02 (15th ed. rev.).

151 *See In re* Black, 292 B.R. 693 (B.A.P. 10th Cir. 2003) (debtor could not circumvent sixty-month maximum plan period by modification that labeled payments made over first twenty-eight months as "lump sum contribution"); *In re* Jourdan, 108 B.R. 1020 (Bankr. N.D. Iowa 1989) (debtor may modify plan to change treatment of creditor when plan as amended meets all

prescribed by Federal Rule of Bankruptcy Procedure 3015(g), requires the filing of a motion,[152] along with the proposed modification, and at least twenty days notice to the debtor, the trustee, and all creditors of the time for filing objections and of a hearing to consider any objections.[153] A copy of the notice is also transmitted to the United States trustee, and all notices must be accompanied by a copy of the modification or a summary thereof.[154] Any objection to the proposed modification gives rise to a contested matter under Federal Rule of Bankruptcy Procedure 9014, and must be served on the debtor, the trustee and any other entity designated by the court, and transmitted to the United States trustee.[155] If a modification sought by the debtor is unopposed, no hearing is normally held[156] and the modification is approved. Once approved, it binds all parties.[157]

Usually a hearing is held on any request for modification by a party other than the debtor, unless the debtor expressly agrees to it.[158] However, as with many issues that affect a debtor's rights, it is best to affirmatively file an objection to the relief requested, because a response guarantees that the debtor will obtain a hearing.

8.7.4 Debtor's Inability to Complete the Plan

8.7.4.1 Failure to Make Plan Payments

Unfortunately, many debtors encounter difficulties of various sorts in completing their chapter 13 plans as originally confirmed. These difficulties may arise due to loss of income, unexpected expenses, marital problems, or other causes.

Sometimes financial problems prevent debtors from making required plan payments as they come due. When the debtor misses payments, the debtor should be encouraged to catch up if possible. Most trustees are quite willing to accept delinquent plan payments as long as the debtor does not fall too far behind. However, in serious cases the trustee may request dismissal based upon the debtor's failure to comply with the plan.[159]

In other cases the debtors are unable to keep up with current mortgage payments that must be made outside the plan. Generally this problem will give rise to a motion by the secured creditor for relief from the stay to commence or continue foreclosure proceedings.[160] In the event of such a motion the best response, if possible, is for the debtor to catch up before the motion is heard. Most secured creditors will agree to allow a debtor to catch up because they know that, if the debtor brings the delinquent payments to a hearing on a motion for relief from stay, the bankruptcy judge will probably deny relief. Other creditors will agree not to foreclose immediately and to allow the debtor an opportunity to catch up on payments, if the debtor in return agrees to future relief from the stay if the post-petition payments are not brought current. In general, it is a good idea to avoid such agreements, except as a last resort when no modification of the plan or defense to relief from stay is possible.[161]

When these issues come to a head, either by motion to dismiss or motion for relief from stay, several options must be considered if the debtor cannot cure payment defaults within a reasonable time. Often, if not always, the debtor can still obtain full or partial bankruptcy relief by utilizing one of the strategies discussed below.

8.7.4.2 Plan Modifications That Enable the Debtor to Complete the Plan

The most preferable option when addressing a problem in completing the plan is often modification, following the procedure described above.[162] Modification may allow the chapter 13 plan to proceed to conclusion by lowering the payments to a level the debtor can afford or by extending the payments. It may also be possible to modify the plan to terminate earlier than originally proposed. As long as all of the requirements of chapter 13 are met, such as full payment of priority debts, this type of modification should be allowed. However, if the claims of secured creditors have not yet been satisfied, the termination of the plan may pose difficulties unless arrangements can be made with those creditors. If the plan is modified, the debtor preserves the right to the broader chapter 13 discharge, which is important

---

requirements of Code); *In re* Perkins, 111 B.R. 671 (Bankr. M.D. Tenn. 1990) (trustee's proposed modified plan may not be confirmed when it does not pass the feasibility test for confirmation).

152   *See* Forms 128, 129, Appx. G.12, *infra*.

153   The notice must be specific in describing the modification. *See In re* Friday, 304 B.R. 537 (Bankr. N.D. Ga. 2003). The court may limit the notice required to include only creditors affected by the proposed modification. Fed. R. Bankr. P. 3015(g).

154   Fed. R. Bankr. P. 3015(g).

155   *Id.*

156   The phrase "after notice and a hearing" is construed in accordance with 11 U.S.C. § 102(1).

157   *In re* Rincon, 133 B.R. 594 (Bankr. N.D. Tex. 1991) (creditor which had not objected to modified plan lost right to amend proof of claim in a manner inconsistent with the modified plan). In some courts, no order approving the modification is necessary and it becomes effective immediately, subject only to disapproval upon a timely objection. *See In re* Taylor, 215 B.R. 882 (Bankr. S.D. Cal. 1997).

158   *See* 8 Collier on Bankruptcy ¶ 1329.06 (15th ed. rev.).

159   If the debtors can catch up, at any time before the hearing on a dismissal motion based on missed payments, it is unlikely that the court would actually dismiss the case.

160   The creditor may also seek to have the case dismissed pursuant to 11 U.S.C. § 1307(c).

161   See § 9.7, *infra*, for a discussion of defenses to motions for relief from stay.

162   *See* § 8.7.3, *supra*.

in cases in which there are unsecured debts that are not dischargeable in chapter 7.[163]

8.7.4.3 Obtaining a Hardship Discharge

A second possibility is to apply for a hardship discharge. This discharge is granted when the failure to complete payments is "due to circumstances for which the debtor should not justly be held accountable,"[164] but only if modification is impractical and the value of payments to unsecured creditors, as of the effective date of the plan, is not less than the amount they would have received had the case originally proceeded as a chapter 7 liquidation.[165] In most consumer cases these tests should not be difficult to meet.[166] The debtor need not pay all priority claims to obtain a hardship discharge; however, secured creditors that have not yet been fully paid normally retain their liens for the unpaid amounts of their allowed secured claims, thus possibly posing problems that must be resolved. Lastly, the hardship discharge is not as broad as the normal chapter 13 discharge, but rather is coextensive with the chapter 7 discharge, which may mean that fewer debts will be discharged. However, if seventy percent of the unsecured claims have been paid, a hardship discharge will not bar a subsequent chapter 7 discharge within six years, as would a chapter 7 discharge.[167]

The procedure for obtaining a hardship discharge is set forth in Federal Rule of Bankruptcy Procedure 4007(d). If the debtor files a motion for a hardship discharge, the court gives notice to all creditors of the motion and of the deadline for filing a complaint to determine the dischargeability of a debt under Code section 523(c). If a hardship discharge is granted, the court then determines the issues raised by any complaint that is timely filed.

8.7.4.4 Conversion to Chapter 7

A third choice when addressing failure to complete a chapter 13 plan is conversion of the case to a chapter 7 case. Conversion may be done by the debtor as of right,[168] and may also be requested by creditors for various reasons.[169] The procedure for a debtor to convert a case to chapter 7 is set forth in Federal Rule of Bankruptcy Procedure 1017(d), which provides that the conversion is effectuated when the debtor files a notice of conversion with the clerk.[170] The conversion is deemed to take place when the notice is filed.

In cases filed prior to the effective date of the 1994 amendments to the Bankruptcy Code, conversion posed problems because some courts had held that property that the debtor acquired after filing the chapter 13 case became property of the chapter 7 estate in the converted case.[171] Other courts had held to the contrary.[172] The 1994 amendments added section 348(f) of the Code which largely resolved this issue by clarifying that property of the estate in a case converted to chapter 7 from chapter 13 does not include property acquired after the original petition was filed.[173] The only exception to this rule is when the case is converted in "bad faith," in which case the court can order that property acquired during the chapter 13 case becomes property of the chapter 7 estate.[174] There is little guidance regarding what a bad faith conversion might be.[175] Presum-

---

163 See § 14.4.1, *infra,* for discussion of the difference between the chapter 7 and chapter 13 discharges.

164 11 U.S.C. § 1328(b). At least one court has found that death is such a circumstance. *In re* Bond, 36 B.R. 49 (Bankr. E.D.N.C. 1984).

165 11 U.S.C. § 1328(b).

166 *In re* Bandilli, 231 B.R. 836 (B.A.P. 1st Cir. 1999) (circumstances need not be catastrophic, but temporary relapse of medical condition which did not affect income was insufficient); *In re* Edwards, 207 B.R. 728 (Bankr. N.D. Fla. 1997) (hardship need not involve catastrophic circumstances). *But see In re* Roberts, 279 B.R. 396 (B.A.P. 1st Cir. 2000) (no abuse of discretion in denying hardship discharge to debtor who made no attempt to modify the plan or to sever her case from her husband's, actions that in all likelihood would have been allowed by the bankruptcy court and might have permitted her to obtain a discharge).

167 11 U.S.C. § 727(a)(9).

168 11 U.S.C. § 1307(a). *But see In re* Spiser, Bankr. N.D. Tex. 1999) (case could not be converted after both debtors had died).

169 11 U.S.C. § 1307(c). For example, unsecured creditors may request conversion if there are non-exempt assets that could be liquidated for their benefit when required plan payments are not being made.

170 A sample form for this notice is provided in Appendix G, *infra.*

171 *E.g., In re* Calder, 973 F.2d 862 (10th Cir. 1992); *In re* Lybrook, 951 F.2d 136 (7th Cir. 1991). Moreover, some courts held that the debtor could not obtain return of payments to the chapter 13 trustee even if they were otherwise exemptible. *Compare* Resendez v. Lindquist, 691 F.2d 397 (8th Cir. 1982) (payments under confirmed plan still in hands of chapter 13 trustee could not be exempted in case converted to chapter 7) *with In re* Plata, 958 F.2d 918 (9th Cir. 1992). *See also* § 4.7.4, *supra.*

172 *See, e.g., In re* Young, 66 F.3d 376 (1st Cir. 1995); *In re* Bobroff, 766 F.2d 797 (3d Cir. 1985); *see also In re* Williamson, 804 F.2d 1355 (5th Cir. 1986) (conversion from chapter 11 to chapter 7); Koch v. Myrvold, 784 F.2d 862 (8th Cir. 1986) (seemingly limiting the holding in Resendez v. Lindquist, 691 F.2d 397 (8th Cir. 1982)).

173 11 U.S.C. § 348(f)(1)(A); *In re* Stamm, 222 F.3d 216 (5th Cir. 2000) (wages of debtor in hands of chapter 13 trustee at time of conversion not property of chapter 7 estate and must be returned to debtor).

174 11 U.S.C. § 348(f)(2).

175 *See In re* Bejarano, 302 B.R. 559 (Bankr. N.D. Ohio 2003) (using conversion provisions to protect assets acquired after petition but before conversion not bad faith); *In re* Wiczek-Spalding, 223 B.R. 538 (Bankr. D. Minn. 1998) (taking advantage of Code provisions is not bad faith on part of debtor who converted to chapter 7 to exclude employee severance pay from property of estate).

ably, a conversion could be found in bad faith if the debtor never really had intended to proceed under chapter 13. Courts should not find bad faith in cases in which the debtor is unable to complete a plan due to financial hardship, even if the debtor has acquired significant property interests since the original filing.

However, if the debtor had significant non-exempt property at the outset of the chapter 13 case, that property is considered property of the estate to the extent the debtor retains it at the time of conversion. Such property can be liquidated by a chapter 7 trustee if the case is converted, even if the debtor has made some payments to unsecured creditors. In this situation the hardship discharge, if available, is usually a better alternative, and even dismissal may be preferable to conversion.

The 1994 amendment to section 348(f) also clarifies the law regarding treatment of secured claims in converted cases. Any valuations of property previously made in the chapter 13 case are binding in the converted case.[176] This provision could help or hurt the debtor, depending upon whether the property is appreciating or depreciating and depending upon the purpose of the valuation. For example, if the valuation is in determination of an allowed secured claim, the creditor benefits if the property has since depreciated and the debtor benefits if it has appreciated. In the determination of exemptions, creditors cannot benefit from an increase in the debtor's equity,[177] but the debtor may be precluded from lowering the value for exemption purposes if the property has depreciated. To the extent that these rules would work a significant hardship on the debtor, it may be wise to consider dismissal of the chapter 13 case and the filing of a new chapter 7 petition instead of conversion, subject to the limits on refiling in Code section 109(g).[178]

In addition, the amendment provides that allowed secured claims are reduced in the converted case to the extent that they have been paid in the chapter 13 case. Again resolving a split in the case law,[179] this change makes clear that a creditor cannot be paid twice on an allowed secured claim in the same bankruptcy case. Thus, for items of property that the debtor may redeem under section 722,[180] the debtor need pay only the unpaid balance of the allowed secured claim to complete the redemption in the converted case.[181]

In any case, post-petition debts are included in the ultimate chapter 7 discharge,[182] which could be a major advantage if the debtor has incurred significant new debts after filing. These debts would be included in a chapter 13 hardship discharge only if the trustee's approval had been obtained and they had been incorporated into the plan.[183]

On the other hand, although priority claims would be discharged to the extent allowed in chapter 7, secured claims and claims that are nondischargeable in chapter 7 would remain to be dealt with after discharge. And if objections to a discharge are possible under 11 U.S.C. § 727 conversion to chapter 7 may not be advantageous to the debtor.

If the debtor cannot obtain approval of a modified plan, is ineligible for a hardship discharge, and yet still wishes to obtain some bankruptcy relief, conversion may be the only option. Because voluntary or involuntary dismissal reinstates not only all pre-petition debts but also all avoided liens,[184] conversion may be necessary in such cases to retain the benefit of successful litigation under chapter 13.[185]

8.7.4.5 Dismissal

A final option is dismissal, also available to a chapter 13 debtor as of right in any case not previously converted from another chapter.[186] Pursuant to Federal Rule of Bankruptcy Procedure 1017(d), the debtor may obtain a voluntary dismissal by filing a motion stating the debtor's entitlement to dismissal. An involuntary dismissal may also occur on motion of the chapter 13 trustee, the United States trustee, or a creditor.

Dismissal may be preferable if the debtor cannot meet the hardship test or "best interests" test[187] for a hardship discharge and if the debtor stands to lose significant non-exempt property in a conversion to chapter 7. Dismissal, to the extent possible, returns the parties to the status quo prior

---

176   11 U.S.C. § 348(f)(1)(B). This treatment is accorded uncontested valuations contained in the debtor's plan, once they are made binding on all parties by confirmation. 11 U.S.C. § 1327(a); Warren v. Peterson, 298 B.R. 322 (N.D. Ill. 2003).

177   *In re* Slack, 290 B.R. 282 (Bankr. D.N.J. 2003); *In re* Page, 250 B.R. 465 (Bankr. D.N.H. 2000); *see also* § 4.7.4, *supra*.

178   *See* § 9.7.3.1.5, *infra*.

179   *See* § 11.6.1.3.3, *infra*.

180   *See* § 11.5, *infra*.

181   11 U.S.C. § 348(f)(1)(B); *In re* Archie, 240 B.R. 425 (Bankr. S.D. Ala. 1999) (debtor permitted to redeem property without further payment when allowed secured claim had been paid in full prior to conversion); *see also In re* James, 285 B.R. 114 (Bankr. W.D.N.Y. 2002) (creditor's post-discharge repossession

of automobile, for which debtor had paid entire allowed secured claim before conversion to chapter 7, was action to collect unsecured debt and violated discharge injunction). Although this case suggests it may not be necessary, the safer course is to file a motion to redeem the property without further payment in such a situation.

182   11 U.S.C. § 348(d). Moreover, 11 U.S.C. § 348(a) provides that the conversion date would be the date of the order for relief. Because 11 U.S.C. § 348(b) applies 11 U.S.C. § 727(b) to that date, all debts arising before the conversion date are discharged. *See In re* Deiter, 33 B.R. 547 (Bankr. W.D. Wis. 1983); *see also In re* Winchester, 46 B.R. 492 (B.A.P. 9th Cir. 1984).

183   11 U.S.C. § 1328(c), (d); *see* § 8.7.2, *supra*.

184   11 U.S.C. § 349.

185   *See In re* Hargis, 103 B.R. 912 (Bankr. E.D. Tenn. 1989) (effect of lien avoidance won in chapter 13 preserved after conversion to chapter 7).

186   11 U.S.C. § 1307(b). If the case was originally filed under another chapter dismissal by leave of court may be obtainable by motion. 11 U.S.C. § 1307(c); *see* § 13.9.1, *infra*.

187   See Chapter 12, *infra,* for discussion of the "best interest of creditors" test in chapter 13.

to the bankruptcy, negating many benefits that the debtor might already have obtained, such as the avoidance of liens.[188] Nonetheless, the debtor might find it preferable to deal with creditors outside of bankruptcy rather than subject non-exempt assets to immediate liquidation. If the case is dismissed, all trustee payments to creditors immediately cease, and property in the hands of the chapter 13 trustee should be promptly returned to the debtor.[189]

Once the case is dismissed, the debtor has the option to file again under either chapter 13 or chapter 7. However, if this option is in the debtor's interest, some care should be taken that the anticipated subsequent case will not be barred by section 109(g).[190]

It should be noted that both the right to dismiss and the right to convert may be lost by the debtor who does not exercise them in a timely manner. Once the case is converted to a chapter 7 case, perhaps on request of creditors, the chapter 13 right to dismiss the case ceases to exist. Similarly, once a case is dismissed over the debtor's objection, no further right to convert exists. Thus it is important to exercise these rights before an involuntary conversion or dismissal. Although a new chapter 7 petition could usually be filed after a chapter 13 case is dismissed,[191] it would entail needless effort and a new filing fee. The consequences of an involuntary conversion can be worse; conversion may mean the loss of non-exempt property that is critical to the debtor's affairs.

8.8 The Discharge and the Discharge Hearing

8.8.1 Overview

Once the time for objecting to a discharge has passed in a chapter 7 case, with a few limited exceptions, the debtor is entitled to a discharge.[192] Similarly, once the debtor has completed the payments required by a confirmed chapter 13 plan, even if the payments are completed early by a lump sum payment, the debtor is entitled to a discharge.[193] Once the payments are completed, it is too late for any party to move for modification of the plan.[194]

Although the Code as originally enacted required that the court hold a discharge hearing in every case, a discharge hearing is now required only when the debtor desires to reaffirm a debt and was not represented by an attorney in negotiating the reaffirmation agreement.[195] Otherwise, it is discretionary with the court and few courts now hold discharge hearings when there is no reaffirmation involved.

When a discharge hearing is held, the Code clearly provides that the debtor must attend.[196] If the discharge hearing is not one which is required by the Code because of a reaffirmation agreement, it should be possible to convince a court to waive the required appearance of the debtor when attendance at the hearing would cause real hardship.[197] Indeed, several courts have announced that Congress did not really mean what it said, and that the debtor need not attend in all cases.[198]

Whether or not a discharge hearing is held, the debtor ultimately receives a discharge order from the court, which in chapter 7 cases conforms in general to Official Form 18. The chapter 7 discharge order contains a general explanation of the discharge and is mailed by the clerk as a matter of course to the debtor, the debtor's attorney, and all creditors shortly after the deadline for objections to discharge has expired unless the debtor has not completed payments on the

---

188 11 U.S.C. § 349; *see In re* Sadler, 935 F.2d 918 (7th Cir. 1991) (once case is dismissed, avoided preferences are reinstated irrespective of whether a new case is contemplated or filed). However, if limitations periods on avoidance have not expired, collateral estoppel may apply in the subsequent case.

189 *In re* Nash, 765 F.2d 1410 (9th Cir. 1985); *In re* Slaughter, 141 B.R. 661 (Bankr. N.D. Ill. 1992). *But see In re* Brown, 280 B.R. 231 (Bankr. E.D. Wis. 2002) (funds in hands of trustee subject to levy by Internal Revenue Service); *In re* Witte, 279 B.R. 585 (Bankr. E.D. Cal. 2002) (when debtor's house had been sold pursuant to court order prior to dismissal, proceeds held by trustee were not plan proceeds that had to be returned to debtor, and had to be turned over to holders of liens on house).

190 See § 3.2.1, *supra,* and § 9.7.3.1.5, *infra,* for a discussion of 11 U.S.C. § 109(g) and other issues connected with serial bankruptcy filings. Additionally it should be noted that, unless there is some change in circumstances, a subsequent chapter 13 case may be alleged to be filed in bad faith. *See generally* § 12.3.2, *infra.*

191 A new petition is expressly barred after an involuntary dismissal only if the debtor willfully disobeyed court orders or willfully failed to appear to prosecute the case, and then only for 180 days. 11 U.S.C. § 109(g); *see* § 3.2.1, *supra.*

192 Fed. R. of Bankr. P. 4004(c) (stating exceptions such as non-payment of filing fee, pendency of an objection to discharge, motion to dismiss for substantial abuse, or motion to extend time for filing of such objection or motion).

193 11 U.S.C. § 1328(a); *In re* Smith, 237 B.R. 621 (Bankr. E.D. Tex. 1999); *In re* Bergolla, 232 B.R. 515 (Bankr. S.D. Fla. 1999).

194 11 U.S.C. § 1329(a); 8 Collier on Bankruptcy ¶ 1329.08 (15th ed. rev.).

195 11 U.S.C. § 524(d).

196 See Chapter 14, *infra,* for further discussion of this requirement.

197 *In re* Mensch, 7 B.R. 804 (Bankr. S.D.N.Y. 1980) (debtor suffered disabling stroke); *In re* Keefe, 7 B.R. 270 (Bankr. E.D. Va. 1980) (debtor suffered mental breakdown); *In re* Garber, 4 B.R. 684 (Bankr. C.D. Cal. 1980) (use of "shall" in § 524 is directory, not mandatory); *In re* Killett, 2 B.R. 273 (Bankr. E.D. Va. 1980) (debtor in England serving in U.S. Air Force).

198 See § 14.5.2, *infra,* for further discussion of reaffirmation agreements.

filing fees or there is a pending objection to discharge, motion to extend time for filing such an objection, or motion to dismiss the case. The debtor can move to delay the granting of the discharge for thirty days to negotiate a possible reaffirmation agreement with a creditor.[199] The debtor should be encouraged to keep a copy of the discharge order, a list of creditors scheduled in the bankruptcy, a list of property claimed as exempt,[200] and copies of any orders entered during the course of the proceedings in a safe place in case issues arise later about the disposition of the case.

8.8.2 Reaffirmation of Debts

The principal stated purpose of the discharge hearing is to advise debtors of their rights, especially with regard to reaffirmation of debts. In a well-handled case, this counsel should already have been provided by the debtor's attorney. Without doubt, the best advice in this regard is simply that reaffirmation is rarely a good idea. Reaffirmation, which in essence is a promise to pay a debt despite its discharge, effectively waives the benefits of discharge as to that particular debt[201] and should be advised only in exceptional circumstances.[202] Perhaps, if a debtor is in economic default, that is, behind in payments on a secured debt, and does not wish to pursue chapter 13 to deal with the problem, reaffirmation might be appropriate in exchange for a creditor's forbearance. Similarly, if it is unlikely that any recovery of a deficiency would be sought after foreclosure on a mortgage, either because the value of the collateral far exceeds the debt or because deficiency judgments are barred in the jurisdiction, then little harm can be done by reaffirming that debt. In either case, the debt should not be reaffirmed in an amount exceeding the value of the collateral;[203] there may also be ways to save the debtor's property without reaffirmation.[204]

Many debtors (and attorneys) are under the misimpression that no payment may be made to a creditor after bankruptcy unless the debt is reaffirmed. This is not correct.[205] Usually, the results sought by reaffirmation of a debt can be obtained just as well by simply continuing to make regular voluntary payments on a debt. For example, a creditor will rarely foreclose on its security or pursue a cosigner if payments on a debt are current. Although it is reassuring for the debtor to have a promise from the creditor that it will not exercise the right to foreclose given it by the common "bankruptcy clause"[206] in consumer contracts, this agreement can often be negotiated without a reaffirmation which again obligates the debtor personally. The debtor usually has some leverage in negotiating such an agreement, because there may be issues as to defenses the debtor may raise, or a dispute as to the value of the security.[207]

In any case, creditors should be put on notice that they risk substantial litigation if they threaten to exercise their rights under bankruptcy clauses to foreclose or pursue cosigners either to force a reaffirmation or to obtain valuable collateral. There is a good argument that the effect of such clauses is nullified by section 541(c)(1) of the Code, which provides that the debtor's interest in property comes into the estate free from any provision that gives an option to modify or terminate that interest upon filing of a bankruptcy.[208] Because under section 522(b) the debtor exempts an interest in property that is in the estate, this protection should be passed on to the debtor along with that interest in property. Moreover, bankruptcy clauses are obviously adhesion clauses, never really bargained over between debtor and creditors. As such their use can probably be challenged as unconscionable and unfair and deceptive acts.[209] They might also be found to violate the good-faith requirements of section 1-203 of the Uniform Commercial Code. And finally, the exercise of such rights can be swiftly prevented or reversed by converting the case to a chapter 13 bankruptcy, or by filing a new chapter 13 case if the previous case has already ended. Because chapter 13 provides both that a plan may waive a default[210] and that a prior bankruptcy is no bar to filing,[211] debtors are fully within their rights to utilize a new chapter 13 case to prevent such creditor abuses.

Despite its clear disadvantages, many debtors agree to reaffirmation, especially if they do not have counsel in negotiating with the creditor. It is in these situations that the discharge hearings can serve an important purpose. The

---

199 Fed. R. Bankr. P. 4004(c)(1).

200 Such property is not liable for any debt that arose before commencement of the case. 11 U.S.C. § 522(c). It is somewhat unclear whether exempt property can be reached by a creditor whose debt is reaffirmed. Because the better view is that a reaffirmed debt does not first arise after the petition, such property should still be protected from liability on that debt.

201 Fed. R. Bankr. P. 4004(c)(2). See § 14.5, *infra,* for a discussion of reaffirmation agreements.

202 Preprinted materials, such as the handout reprinted in Appendix I, may assist the attorney in conveying this information to the client. *See* Appx. I.2, *infra.*

203 See Chapter 11, *infra,* for methods to reduce the debt to equal the value of the collateral.

204 See § 14.5.2, *infra,* for a more detailed discussion of reaffirmation.

205 11 U.S.C. § 524(f).

206 This clause usually provides that the filing of a bankruptcy case constitutes a default under the contract.

207 See Chapter 11, *infra,* for further discussion of how such disputes arise.

208 *See* § 14.5.3, *infra.*

209 The use of other similar boilerplate clauses, neither bargained over nor understood by most debtors, has been found to be unfair by the Federal Trade Commission. *See* Am. Fin. Services Ass'n v. Fed. Trade Comm'n, 767 F.2d 957 (D.C. Cir. 1985). See also National Consumer Law Center, Unfair and Deceptive Acts and Practices § 4.3.4 (5th ed. 2001 and Supp.) for a fuller discussion of the FTC's unfairness analysis as it applies to adhesion contracts.

210 11 U.S.C. § 1322(b)(3).

211 11 U.S.C. § 727(a)(8) and (9) bar only chapter 7 discharges within certain periods after an earlier case. *See* Ch. 12, *infra.*

judge's main duty is to advise debtors of the dangers of reaffirmation, of the fact that reaffirmation is not required, and of the debtor's right to rescind the reaffirmation within sixty days after it is filed with the court or, if later, up to the date of the discharge.[212]

An attorney who represents a debtor in negotiating a reaffirmation agreement on a consumer debt[213] must also counsel the debtor about the advisability of reaffirmation. The attorney must then file a declaration with the court stating that the reaffirmation is a fully informed and voluntary agreement that does not impose an undue hardship on the debtor or a dependent of the debtor.[214] The attorney's declaration must also state that the attorney fully advised the debtor as to the legal effect and consequences of the agreement and of any default under the agreement. Attorneys should think carefully about possible malpractice liability before signing such a declaration, in view of the uncertainties of most debtors' future income and expenses.

In all reaffirmations of consumer debts not negotiated by an attorney for the debtor, except those secured by real property, the court has the duty to decide whether to approve the reaffirmation agreement. Such agreements may be approved only if they do not impose an undue hardship on the debtor or a dependent of the debtor and they are in the best interests of the debtor.[215]

8.8.3 Procedure When There Is a Discharge Hearing

If the court decides to have a discharge hearing even though there will be no reaffirmation of debts, the discharge hearing is usually a very brief affair, with nothing to be said by the debtor or the debtor's counsel. In fact, in many jurisdictions, debtors' counsel are not required to attend the hearing in such cases. The court usually warns the debtor about creditors trying to collect their debts or obtain reaffirmations in the future, and lets the debtor know that bankruptcy is a serious business. Generally, the court then advises prudence in future credit transactions and wishes the debtor good luck. Given the potential for mind-numbing repetition, some judges give this message to all the debtors scheduled on a particular day en masse. Others give it once,

to the first debtor to appear, and then simply ask the debtors appearing later whether they heard what was said to the first debtor, saying that the same applies to them. A few judges do, however, repeat the message, with slight variations, for each debtor who appears.

If a reaffirmation agreement is proposed for approval, most courts require prehearing filing, or the filing at the hearing, of a motion and a proposed order.[216] The court may (and should) then examine the debtor closely to determine if she understands what reaffirmation means and whether reaffirmation is really in the debtor's best interest. If it is not, the reaffirmation should not be approved.[217]

8.9 After Discharge

Once the discharge has been granted and all related litigation has ended, one or two steps normally remain to be taken in representing the debtor. These final details may be quite important in particular cases and should not be neglected.

Public records must often be modified to reflect what has occurred in the bankruptcy. For example, liens may no longer exist or may have been modified. Debtor's counsel should be sure that any record of such liens has been corrected or that bankruptcy court orders modifying or avoiding liens are properly recorded in the appropriate registry. Normally, this has been done as part of the lien avoidance process,[218] but it is important to check the records when closing a case.

In some jurisdictions it is a matter of practice to notify courts where proceedings have been pending that the discharge has been granted or that certain judgments are void or satisfied by payment.[219] Technically, this notice is not necessary, because the effect of the discharge is automatic, but local practice or the dictates of court etiquette may make it advisable.

Credit reports should also be checked thirty to sixty days after discharge to verify whether creditors are properly reporting information about discharged debts as required by the Fair Credit Reporting Act.[220] All debts discharged in the bankruptcy case should show a zero balance and be noted as having been included in the bankruptcy.[221] If the client's

---

212 11 U.S.C. § 524(c)(2). If court approval is required, the agreement normally becomes effective only when the approval is granted. In all other cases, unless the agreement provides otherwise, the effective date is the date of filing with the court. 11 U.S.C. § 524(c)(3). After discharge and passage of sixty days from the date of the reaffirmation agreement it may be difficult to rescind a reaffirmation agreement. *See In re* Jones, 111 B.R. 674 (Bankr. E.D. Tenn. 1990) (discharge may not be revoked in order to create additional opportunity to rescind reaffirmation agreement).

213 Consumer debt is defined in 11 U.S.C. § 101(8).

214 11 U.S.C. § 524(c)(3).

215 11 U.S.C. § 524(c)(6); *see* § 14.5.2, *infra*.

216 *See* Forms 116, 117, Appx. G.11, *infra*. Fed. R. Bankr. P. 4008 requires a motion for approval of reaffirmation to be filed before or at the hearing.

217 See § 14.5.2, *infra*, for further discussion of standards for approval of reaffirmation.

218 See Chapters 10 and 11, *infra*, for further discussion of lien avoidance.

219 See Chapter 14, *infra*, for further discussion of the discharge.

220 For detailed discussion of the Fair Credit Reporting Act (FCRA), 15 U.S.C. §§ 1681–1681x, see National Consumer Law Center, Fair Credit Reporting (5th ed. 2002 and Supp.).

221 Fed. Trade Comm'n, Official Staff Commentary § 607, item 6; *see also* National Consumer Law Center, Fair Credit Reporting

credit reports still show balances owed on discharged debts, steps should be taken to have the client send letters demanding correction of the report, with letters sent to both the creditor furnishers of information and the credit reporting agencies. If the report is not corrected, it may be necessary to initiate litigation to enforce the debtor's rights under the Fair Credit Reporting Act.[222]

Finally, there is some very important advice to be given to clients. They should be made fully aware of the meaning of their discharge so they are not misled into paying discharged debts. They should be told to report any contacts by creditors so that advice can be given and steps taken against those creditors if necessary. Debtors should also be advised of the other protections arising from their discharge, particularly against any governmental and employer discrimination.[223]

Most importantly, clients must be told not to ignore legal actions brought against them after bankruptcy. Many clients are under the impression that the bankruptcy makes any further action to protect their interests unnecessary. While perhaps technically true with respect to some debts,[224] as a general rule it is advisable to seek the advice of counsel if sued by a creditor after discharge. Some creditors may wrongfully institute legal actions to collect a discharged debt and, while this type of action can usually be rectified, early intervention and assertion of the bankruptcy discharge can prevent later complications, such as harm caused by a wrongful execution. Other creditors may seek to foreclose on a valid lien or to collect a debt that a creditor claims was not discharged, such as a student loan. In these cases, the debtor needs counsel as much as ever. The solution may be a new chapter 13 bankruptcy or any one of numerous other defensive strategies. These strategies may include the possible reopening of the bankruptcy case for a proceeding to determine dischargeability of the debt or, in some jurisdictions, to schedule a creditor not previously listed.[225]

Preprinted materials or a form letter may save time and assure that these warnings are clearly conveyed.[226] Regardless of the method used (interview, letter, or both), it is appropriate to ensure that there are no new or undiscovered legal problems and to give the client a clear understanding of the new post-bankruptcy situation.[227] Normally, that situation should be a good deal better than that which existed when the client first came into your office.

---

§ 7.8.4.10.2 (5th ed. 2002 and Supp.).

222 The credit reporting agency must first be notified that the information is disputed before an action may be brought under the FCRA against the creditor furnisher. *See* National Consumer Law Center, Fair Credit Reporting § 10.2.3 (5th ed. 2002 and Supp.). The inaccurate reporting of a pre-petition debt with the intent to coerce a debtor into paying the debt may also pursued as an automatic stay or discharge injunction violation. *E.g.*, *In re* Goodfellow, 298 B.R. 358 (Bankr. N.D. Iowa 2003) (reporting of discharged debt as ninety days past due violated discharge injunction); *In re* Singley, 233 B.R. 170 (Bankr. S.D. Ga. 1999); *In re* Sommersdorf, 139 B.R. 700 (Bankr. S.D. Ohio 1992) (bank's actions in placing notation of debt charge-off on codebtor's credit report violated stay); *see also* §§ 9.4.3, 9.4.4, *infra*.

223 See § 14.5, *infra*, for further discussion of these protections.

224 *See* Ch. 14, *infra*.

225 See § 8.5, *supra*, and § 14.4.3.3, *infra*, for discussion of this possibility.

226 *See* Form 118, Appx. G.11, *infra*.

227 Debtors may also appreciate receiving information on how to avoid credit problems after bankruptcy. *See* Appx. I.3, *infra*.

Chapter 9

Automatic Stays and Turnover of Property

9.1 Introduction

Simply by filing a bankruptcy petition, a debtor brings to his or her aid an instrument of awesome breadth and power—the Bankruptcy Code's automatic stay. Few other legal steps that may be taken on behalf of a consumer can bring about relief so simply, so effectively, and so dramatically. The stay provisions of the Code,[1] along with the other related provisions that are discussed in this Chapter, take effect the instant a case is filed, from that moment placing the debtor and the debtor's property under the protection of the bankruptcy court.

The power of these provisions extends to many sorts of actions which may be taken against consumers, including some that at first glance do not appear to be debt-related. These actions are stopped, totally and immediately, by the filing of a two-page bankruptcy petition.[2] Indeed, the certainty of obtaining such relief is often a prime factor in the decision to file a case. In some situations, there may be no other remedy as effective, and usually none is as simple. For clients who have come to an attorney's office at the last possible minute before some serious adverse action, the automatic stay may provide the only practical solution. And for other clients, for whom all other legal steps have failed, it may provide one last way to at least postpone a crisis while the debtor seeks relief in the bankruptcy court.

9.2 Purpose of the Automatic Stay

The basic purpose of the stay is to protect the debtor and his or her property. As stated in the House Report on the Bankruptcy Code:

> The automatic stay is one of the fundamental debtor protections provided by the bankruptcy laws. It gives the debtor a breathing spell from his creditors. It stops all collection efforts, all harass-

ment, and all foreclosure actions. It permits the debtor to attempt a repayment or reorganization, or simply to be relieved of the financial pressures that drove him into bankruptcy.[3]

Functionally, the stay also freezes the debtor's assets as of the date of filing, preventing individual creditors from picking away at them for their own benefit and to the detriment of the ultimate goals of the bankruptcy. In chapter 7 liquidation cases, the stay guarantees the protection of the debtor's property or equity therein, both so it can be exempted to provide a fresh start and so non-exempt property can be fairly distributed to creditors. In chapter 13, the stay ensures protection of property that may be necessary not only for the debtor's fresh start but also for the success of the debtor's plan.

Along with other provisions governing property of the estate, the stay permits the bankruptcy court to deal with all aspects of the debtor's situation in an orderly manner. It prevents, at least until such time as the bankruptcy court allows, other courts and parties from interfering with or complicating the bankruptcy process. Virtually all activity concerning the debtor and the debtor's property thus comes into a single forum to be handled in accordance with the (usually) overriding purposes of the bankruptcy.

9.3 Duration of the Stay

The duration of the automatic stay can vary significantly depending upon the circumstances. Theoretically it can be ended almost immediately, if the circumstances require, by the court granting relief to affected parties. Such circumstances, usually dealing with very perishable property, are almost never present in cases involving consumer debtors.[4] As a practical matter, the stay usually is not lifted by the court in much less than thirty days; and it may last for the

---

1 11 U.S.C. § 362.

2 The bankruptcy petition which commences a case may be filed before most of the schedules and statements that usually accompany it, if necessary. *See* § 7.2, *supra.* The automatic stay goes into effect even if there is a defect in the petition. Wekell v. United States, 14 F.3d 32 (9th Cir. 1994) (stay went into effect with respect to individual listed as a debtor, even if her spouse lacked authority to file bankruptcy case on her behalf).

3 H.R. Rep. No. 95-595, at 340 (1977); *see In re* Ionosphere Clubs, Inc., 922 F.2d 984 (2d Cir. 1990) (breathing spell from creditors is a principal purpose of automatic stay).

4 *See In re* Delaney-Morin, 304 B.R. 365 (B.A.P. 9th Cir. 2003) (reversing stay relief order entered based on grounds not alleged in motion at hearing debtor did not attend because *ex parte* relief not appropriate in case in which mortgage creditor alleged defaults).

duration of the case, a matter of three to six months in a chapter 7 case and up to five years in a chapter 13 case.[5]

Technically, the statute[6] provides that the stay continues until the following dates:

To the extent the stay is based upon provisions barring an act against property of the estate, the earlier of:

- The date such property is no longer property of the estate (usually the date property is abandoned, or the date it is deemed abandoned at the close of the case under 11 U.S.C. § 554(c));
- The date on which the stay is terminated by order of the court, or by inaction of the court upon a request for relief from the stay.[7]

To the extent the stay is against any other act, the earliest of the following:

- The date the case is closed;[8]

- The date the case is dismissed;[9]
- The date a discharge is granted or denied;
- The date on which the stay is terminated by order of the court.[10]

Practically, however, the benefits of the stay may last a good deal longer. A lazy or inefficient opponent may not pay attention to when the bankruptcy ends, and thus may not reinstitute actions promptly (assuming there remains an action to reinstitute after the stay is terminated). While the court notifies all parties that the stay is in effect, usually as part of the notice of the meeting of creditors,[11] and debtor's counsel may also give a notice of the stay, there is normally no specific notice that the stay is terminated at the end of the case. In the interim a creditor may give up on or simply forget the course of action originally planned. In either case, much additional time may pass, sometimes years, to the benefit of the debtor. Indeed, a statute of limitations, which is extended, if necessary, until thirty days after termination of the stay,[12] may run before any action is taken.

If a case is dismissed, and a new filing is appropriate, a new automatic stay comes into effect.[13] However, counsel should take care that the subsequent filing is in good faith and not barred by the 180 day limit of 11 U.S.C. § 109(g).[14] If relief from the stay is granted or the stay is terminated during a case, conversion of the case to another chapter does not create a new stay.[15]

9.4 Scope of the Automatic Stay

9.4.1 Legal Proceedings

The acts prohibited by the automatic stay are set out in a series of overlapping statutory provisions.[16] This section discusses those provisions.

5 Some courts have held that the stay is supplemented or supplanted by the chapter 13 plan after confirmation, because 11 U.S.C. § 1327(a) makes the plan binding upon all creditors. These courts have held that after confirmation even a lack of adequate protection or other grounds which would be available to lift the § 362 stay would not be sufficient to obtain court permission to proceed against the debtor. *See In re* Schewe, 94 B.R. 938 (Bankr. W.D. Mich. 1989) (stay continues in force after confirmation of debtors' chapter 13 plan); *In re* Lewis, 8 B.R. 132 (Bankr. D. Idaho 1981); *see also* Sec. Bank of Marshalltown, Iowa v. Neiman, 1 F.3d 687 (8th Cir. 1993) (property acquired by chapter 13 debtor during case continues to be property of the estate protected by the stay after it vests in the debtor upon confirmation); *In re* Harlan, 783 F.2d 839 (9th Cir. 1986); *In re* Ellis, 60 B.R. 432 (B.A.P. 9th Cir. 1985); *In re* Evans, 30 B.R. 530 (B.A.P. 9th Cir. 1983) (section 362 inapplicable after confirmation, absent post-confirmation default in carrying out plan); *In re* Brock, 6 B.R. 105 (Bankr. N.D. Ill. 1980); §§ 9.4.2, 12.8, 12.11, *infra*; *cf. In re* Mann Farms, Inc., 917 F.2d 1210 (9th Cir. 1990) (confirmed plan may bind parties on some issues, but not on others). *But see In re* Thomas, 91 B.R. 117 (N.D. Ala. 1988) (creditor which did not file proof of claim entitled to relief from stay because confirmed plan does not provide for its claim); *In re* Hines, 20 B.R. 44 (Bankr. S.D. Ohio 1982) (secured creditor who failed to file timely claim under former R. Bankr. P. 13-302(e)(1) could proceed against collateral if adequate protection not provided). See also discussion of Fed. R. Bankr. P. 3003, 3004 in § 11.6.1.3, *infra*.

6 11 U.S.C. § 362(c)–(e). If the court does not act within thirty days after the filing of a motion seeking relief from stay to take an action against property of the estate, the stay may terminate as to that action automatically. 11 U.S.C. § 362(e); *see* § 9.7.2, *infra*.

7 Unlike many orders, an order granting relief from the stay does not take effect until ten days after it is entered, so that a debtor or other party may seek a stay pending appeal. However, the order granting relief from the stay can specifically provide otherwise. Fed. R. Bankr. P. 4001(a)(3). For a discussion of stay pending appeal, see §§ 9.7.3.3.3, 13.10.4, *infra*.

8 *See In re* Bryant, 95 B.R. 857 (Bankr. M.D. Ga. 1989) (court will not reopen closed case to consider motion for relief from stay).

9 *In re* DeJesus Saez, 721 F.2d 848 (1st Cir. 1983) (ten day stay of enforcement of judgments, applicable to adversary proceedings, does not serve to preserve stay for ten days after petition dismissed); *In re* Barnes, 119 B.R. 552 (S.D. Ohio 1989) (same).

10 An order granting relief from the stay does not take effect until ten days after it is entered. Fed. R. Bankr. P. 4001(a)(3). For a discussion of stay pending appeal, see §§ 9.7.3.3.3, 13.10.4, *infra*.

11 *See* Official Form 9, Appx. D, *infra*.

12 11 U.S.C. § 108(c); *see, e.g.,* Valley Transit Mix of Ruidoso, Inc. v. Miller, 928 F.2d 354 (10th Cir. 1991).

13 *See In re* Cont'l Airlines, 928 F.2d 127 (5th Cir. 1991) (automatic stay implemented in second case precludes appeal of claim denied in prior case). The new stay will even bar actions allowed by the court pursuant to relief from stay proceedings in the prior case. Carr v. Sec. Sav. & Loan Ass'n, 130 B.R. 434 (D.N.J. 1991).

14 *See* §§ 3.2.1, 4.2.1, *supra*; § 9.7.3.1.5, *infra*.

15 *In re* State Airlines, Inc., 873 F.2d 264 (11th Cir. 1989).

16 11 U.S.C. § 362(a).

The stay bars "the commencement or continuation, including the issuance or employment of process, of a judicial, administrative, or other action or proceeding against the debtor that was or could have been commenced before the commencement of the case . . . or to recover a claim against the debtor that arose before the commencement of the case."[17] Thus, almost all forms of civil legal actions are brought to an abrupt halt.[18] The only possible exceptions to this provision, are actions that do not arise out of circumstances existing prior to the case and do not pertain to a claim[19] that existed prior to the case.[20] However, many of those actions may still be barred by a different provision of section 362(a).

One illustrative issue, which arises with more frequency in business bankruptcy cases, is how to treat tort claims in cases in which the acts giving rise to liability occur pre-petition, but in which no injury is discovered until after the commencement of the tortfeasor's bankruptcy case. Many courts have held that the victim has a pre-petition claim which is subject to the automatic stay.[21]

Among the many types of legal proceedings affected by the automatic stay are attachments,[22] garnishments[23] and executions, evictions,[24] and almost all family-related court proceedings, including custody, divorce,[25] and some support cases.[26] A proceeding against the debtor commenced in the federal district court or court of appeals is stayed, notwithstanding the fact that they are "higher" courts than the bankruptcy court.[27] Even proceedings in which the debtor is sued solely in a fiduciary capacity,[28] and proceedings based on admittedly nondischargeable debts,[29] are prohibited un-

---

17 11 U.S.C. § 362(a)(1).

18 11 U.S.C. § 362(a)(1); Sunshine Dev. Inc. v. Fed. Deposit Ins. Corp., 33 F.3d 106 (1st Cir. 1994) (FDIC is not exempt from stay when acting as receiver or conservator because it is not exercising regulatory powers excepted by 11 U.S.C. § 362(b)(4)); *In re* Colonial Realty Co., 980 F.2d 125 (2d Cir. 1992) (provisions of Federal Deposit Insurance Act giving Federal Deposit Insurance Corp. (FDIC) rights superior to a bankruptcy trustee did not make automatic stay provisions inapplicable to FDIC). *But see* Rexnord Holdings Inc. v. Bidermann, 21 F.3d 522 (2d Cir. 1994) (ministerial act of a court clerk in entering judgment which had been ordered prior to bankruptcy filing did not violate stay because it was not a continuation of a legal proceeding); *In re* Roxford Foods, Inc., 12 F.3d 875 (9th Cir. 1994) (automatic stay does not prohibit lawsuits filed in bankruptcy court where debtor's bankruptcy case is pending); *In re* Geris, 973 F.2d 318 (4th Cir. 1992) (stay does not prevent foreclosure on real estate not owned by debtor even if debtor has personal liability on debt secured by mortgage).

19 "Claim" is defined extremely broadly in 11 U.S.C. § 101(5), to include contingent, unmatured, non-monetary and many other types of rights. *See* Ohio v. Kovacs, 469 U.S. 274, 105 S. Ct. 705, 83 L. Ed. 2d 649 (1985).

20 One court of appeals has held that claims arising directly from the act of filing a petition in bankruptcy, such as a cause of action for abuse of process under state law, are not covered by the stay. However, according to that court such claims are within the exclusive federal bankruptcy jurisdiction and may not be litigated in state court. Gonzalez v. Parks, 830 F.2d 1033 (9th Cir. 1987).

21 *See* Grady v. A.H. Robins Co., 839 F.2d 198 (4th Cir. 1988); *cf. In re* Cent. R.R. Co. of N.J., 950 F.2d 887 (3d Cir. 1991) (claim does not exist until claimant discovers injury and knows, or has reason to know, its cause).

22 *In re* Matthews, 184 B.R. 594 (Bankr. S.D. Ala. 1995) (IRS levy notices and tax refund seizures violated stay and discharge injunction).

23 *See In re* Roberts, 175 B.R. 339 (B.A.P. 9th Cir. 1994) (state franchise tax board violated stay by continuing to accept payments from debtor's employer pursuant to pre-petition garnishment).

24 *In re* Smith Corset Shops Inc., 696 F.2d 971, 976 (1st Cir. 1982); *In re* Butler, 14 B.R. 532 (S.D.N.Y. 1981); *In re* Lowry, 25 B.R. 52 (Bankr. E.D. Mo. 1982); *see also In re* Goodman, 991 F.2d 613 (9th Cir. 1993) (unlawful detainer action against sublessee debtor's sublessor by owner of property violated stay).

25 While it is clear that such actions are stayed, the stay will often be lifted by the court, upon a proper request, for cause. *See* § 9.7, *infra*. One case discussing the stay of a divorce action, and refusing to lift the stay, is *In re* Pagitt, 3 B.R. 588 (Bankr. W.D. La. 1980). *See also* H.R. Rep. No. 95-595, at 343, 344 (1977). *See generally* Henry J. Sommer & Margaret Doe McGarity, Collier Family Law and the Bankruptcy Code ¶ 5.03.

26 Carver v. Carver, 954 F.2d 1573 (11th Cir. 1992) (action seeking to collect divorce obligations from chapter 13 debtor's wages violated automatic stay); *In re* Kearns, 161 B.R. 701 (D. Kan. 1993) (contempt proceedings in a support case may violate the automatic stay); *In re* Farmer, 150 B.R. 68 (Bankr. N.D. Ala. 1991) (state court order to incarcerate chapter 13 debtor unless support payments are made from wages violates automatic stay); *In re* Tweed, 76 B.R. 636 (Bankr. E.D. Tenn. 1987) (petition for contempt of child support order violated stay); *In re* Marriage of Lueck, 140 Ill. App. 3d 836, 489 N.E.2d 443 (1986) (child support contempt proceedings violated automatic stay). Some prior holdings in this area, particularly concerning actions establishing or modifying the amount of a support award were legislatively overruled by the 1994 amendments to 11 U.S.C. § 362(b)(2) applicable to cases filed after October 22, 1994. *E.g., In re* Stringer, 847 F.2d 549 (9th Cir. 1988) (motion for modification of support award violates stay); Amonte v. Amonte, 17 Mass. App. Ct. 621, 461 N.E.2d 826 (1984) (continuation of support proceedings was stayed by bankruptcy when no final judgment existed prior to bankruptcy filing date). 11 U.S.C. § 362(b)(2); *see* § 9.4.5, *infra*. *See generally* Henry J. Sommer & Margaret Doe McGarity, Collier Family Law and the Bankruptcy Code ¶ 5.03[3]–[6].

27 *See* Constitution Bank v. Tubbs, 68 F.3d 685 (3d Cir. 1995) (district court judgment was void, and therefore court of appeals had no jurisdiction, when it was entered in violation of stay, even though district court purported to enter judgment *nunc pro tunc* to date prior to bankruptcy filing).

28 *In re* Panayotoff, 140 B.R. 509 (Bankr. D. Minn. 1992) (proceeding to remove debtor as personal representative of decedent's estate violated stay); *In re* Colin, 35 B.R. 904 (Bankr. S.D.N.Y. 1983) (suit against debtor in his capacity as a trustee was stayed).

29 *See In re* Merchant, 958 F.2d 738 (6th Cir. 1992) (actions to collect nondischargeable student loan violate stay); *In re* Arneson, 282 B.R. 883 (B.A.P. 9th Cir. 2002) (stay applies to bar enforcement of debt found non-dischargeable in earlier bankruptcy case). *But see In re* Cady, 315 F.3d 1121 (9th Cir. 2002) (after creditor obtains judgment of non-dischargeability, it may proceed against property of the debtor but not property of the

less the court grants relief from the stay. Also enjoined are administrative proceedings such as those to revoke drivers' licenses,[30] to intercept tax refunds,[31] or to determine and collect overpayments of public benefits,[32] as well as arbitrations and other less formal proceedings.[33] Appeals of all proceedings against the debtor are also stayed.[34]

No further steps may be taken in any stayed proceedings without the permission of the bankruptcy court.[35] Thus, the act of continuing the date of a foreclosure sale violates the stay, although several appellate courts have held otherwise on the theory that such a postponement merely preserves the status quo.[36] Ongoing discovery must also be discontinued. Similarly, civil contempt proceedings for alleged discovery order violations are stayed. Counsel bringing an action against the debtor has a duty to take action to halt a

non-bankruptcy court's actions.[37] However, the provision pertaining to legal proceedings is subject to several limited exceptions, discussed below.[38]

It is important to note that 11 U.S.C. § 362 bars only actions against the debtor, and not those brought by the debtor.[39] The debtor's actions may be continued after commencement of the case, although the trustee may acquire an interest in the action and a party may be able to remove the action to the bankruptcy court.[40] Occasionally it is not clear whether an action is against the debtor or brought by the debtor, for example, when a debtor's counterclaim predominates or when a defendant/debtor has filed an appeal. The answer to this question turns on whether the action was brought initially by or against the debtor.[41] When the origi-

---

estate); *In re* Embry, 10 F.3d 401 (6th Cir. 1993) (once creditor obtained determination that debt was nondischargeable in chapter 7 case due to false pretenses, creditor could proceed against property that was not property of the estate without violating the automatic stay). Note, however, that exempted property is protected during and after the case. 11 U.S.C. § 522(c); *see* § 10.5, *infra*.

30 *In re* Duke, 167 B.R. 324 (Bankr. D.R.I. 1994) (stay prohibited state from suspending debtor's driver's license for failure to pay judgment).

31 *In re* Herron, 177 B.R. 866 (Bankr. N.D. Ohio 1995) (student loan creditor's failure to act to reverse post-petition tax refund intercept after notice of bankruptcy was willful stay violation); *In re* Stucka, 77 B.R. 777 (Bankr. C.D. Cal. 1987).

32 Lee v. Schweiker, 739 F.2d 870 (3d Cir. 1984); *see* § 9.4.3, *infra*.

33 *See, e.g., In re* King Mem'l Hosp., 5 B.R. 192 (Bankr. S.D. Fla. 1980) (state certificate of need process for hospital stayed).

34 *See, e.g.,* Raymark Indus. v. Lai, 973 F.2d 1125 (3d Cir. 1992) (appeal stayed even though debtor had posted deposit to stay execution pre-petition); Sheldon v. Munford, Inc., 902 F.2d 7 (7th Cir. 1990) (appeal stayed even when appellant-debtor had filed *supersedeas* bond).

35 Dean v. Trans World Airlines, 72 F.3d 754 (9th Cir. 1996) (involuntary dismissal of action against debtor violated the stay); Ellis v. Consol. Diesel Elec. Corp., 894 F.2d 371 (10th Cir. 1990) (dismissal of case against debtor violates stay); Pope v. Manville Forest Products Corp., 778 F.2d 238 (5th Cir. 1985) (dismissal of case against debtor is precluded by the stay); *In re* Westwood Lumber, Inc., 113 B.R. 684 (Bankr. W.D. Wash. 1990) (voluntary dismissal of case against debtor to allow state court case to go forward against others violates stay); *In re* Weed, 6 B.C.D. 606, 2 C.B.C. 2d 994 (Bankr. S.D. Iowa 1980) (discovery in district court case not allowed without lifting of stay); *see In re* Knightsbridge Dev. Co., 884 F.2d 145 (4th Cir. 1989) (post-petition entry of arbitration award violates stay when arbitrators had not completed their deliberations before the petition was filed); *In re* Tampa Chain Co., 835 F.2d 54 (2d Cir. 1987) (appeal of defendant in adversary proceeding cannot be dismissed after that defendant became debtor in his own bankruptcy case). *But see* Picco v. Global Marine Drilling Co., 900 F.2d 846 (5th Cir. 1990) (subsequent blanket order granting relief from stay validates prior dismissal of action against debtor in violation of stay).

36 Taylor v. Slick, 178 F.3d 698 (3d Cir. 1999) (postponement of foreclosure sale to new date does not violate stay); *In re* Peters, 101 F.3d 618 (9th Cir. 1996) (creditor did not violate stay by continuing foreclosure sale date after plan confirmation).

37 Eskanos & Adler, Prof'l Corp. v. Leetien, 309 F.3d 1210 (9th Cir. 2002) (failure to dismiss or stay pending collection action against debtor was willful violation of stay); *In re* Braught, 307 B.R. 399 (Bankr. S.D.N.Y. 2004) (creditor willfully violated stay by failing to take affirmative action to vacate state court judgment entered in violation of stay); *In re* Atkins, 176 B.R. 998 (Bankr. D. Minn. 1994) (creditors' attorney was in contempt of automatic stay injunction when he failed to abort a pre-petition process that led to the debtor's post-petition arrest on a bench warrant for contempt of discovery order after attorney had notice of the debtor's bankruptcy).

38 *See* § 9.4.5, *infra*.

39 *In re* U.S. Abatement Corp., 39 F.3d 563 (5th Cir. 1994) (creditor's motion with respect to debtor's counterclaim did not violate stay because counterclaim was not claim against the debtor); Koolik v. Markowitz, 40 F.3d 567 (2d Cir. 1994) (debtor's appeal of judgment on counterclaim against debtor was stayed because counterclaim was an action or proceeding against debtor); Brown v. Armstrong, 949 F.2d 1007 (8th Cir. 1991) (automatic stay does not apply to the debtor's action against the Farmers Home Administration); Mar. Elec. Co. v. United Jersey Bank, 959 F.2d 1194 (3d Cir. 1991) (automatic stay can preclude claims against the debtor without staying debtor's counterclaims; claims and counterclaims could be disaggregated so that a defendant-debtor's counterclaims could proceed); Martin-Trigona v. Champion Fed. Sav. & Loan Ass'n, 892 F.2d 575 (7th Cir. 1989) (automatic stay inapplicable to debtor's lawsuit); Carley Capital Group v. Fireman's Fund Ins. Co., 889 F.2d 1126 (D.C. Cir. 1989) (debtor's appeal of judgment in action filed by debtor not stayed); *see also In re* Mann Farms, Inc., 917 F.2d 1210 (9th Cir. 1990) (debtor's lawsuit not affected by pendency of bankruptcy case except to the extent debtor bound itself under confirmed plan). Even counterclaims against the debtor in the bankruptcy court may be barred. *In re* Lessig Constr., Inc., 67 B.R. 436 (Bankr. E.D. Pa. 1986).

40 See Chapter 13, *infra*, for discussion of removal of litigation to bankruptcy court.

41 *In re* Delta Airlines, 310 F.3d 953 (9th Cir. 2002) (but appeal could proceed in cases of non-debtor co-defendants); Delpit v. Comm'r Internal Revenue Serv., 18 F.3d 768 (9th Cir. 1994) (appeal from Tax Court proceeding was stayed because it was continuation of what was originally an administrative proceeding to collect taxes from the debtor); Nielsen v. Price, 17 F.3d 1276 (10th Cir. 1994) (stay did not apply to appeal in adversary proceeding initiated by debtors in prior bankruptcy); Alpern v. Lieb, 11 F.3d 689 (7th Cir. 1993) (appeal from dismissal of suit originally filed by debtor was not stayed); Farley v. Henson, 2 F.3d 273 (8th Cir. 1993) (debtor's appeal in action brought

nal action was brought against the debtor, the action may be stayed, even if the debtor would prefer that it go forward.[42]

It is also quite clear that, except as provided in 11 U.S.C. § 1201 or § 1301,[43] the stay does not affect acts against codebtors.[44] However, a creditor cannot pursue community property or entireties property owned jointly by the debtor and a codebtor, even if acquired after the bankruptcy, because section 362(a)(1) prohibits any legal action to recover a pre-petition claim against the debtor and a "claim against the debtor" includes a claim against the debtor's property.[45]

9.4.2 Acts Directed at the Debtor's Property

Several provisions protect, in various ways, the property owned by the debtor at the time of filing. They prohibit:

- The enforcement, against the debtor or against property of the estate, of a judgment obtained before the commencement of the case under title 11;[46]
- Any act to obtain possession of property of the estate or property from the estate or to exercise control over property of the estate;[47]
- Any act to create, perfect, or enforce any lien against property of the estate;[48] and
- Any act to create, perfect, or enforce any lien to the extent that such lien secures a claim that arose before the commencement of the case under title 11.[49]

These provisions have slightly different effects depending upon whether a judgment or a lien is involved. A judgment obtained prior to filing cannot be enforced against either the debtor or property of the estate. This bar covers most injunctive as well as monetary judgments.[50] And because legal proceedings are also stayed as to pre-petition claims, only a judgment which arose solely out of post-petition claims can be enforced against the debtor without violation of the stay.[51]

The provisions prohibiting acts to obtain possession or to utilize liens against property of the estate apply regardless of when the claim arose, as property of the estate is essentially frozen, to be administered only by the bankruptcy court.[52] In

---

against debtor was stayed); Carley Capital Group v. Fireman's Fund Ins. Co., 889 F.2d 1126 (D.C. Cir. 1989) (debtor's appeal of judgment in action filed by debtor not stayed); Ingersoll-Rand Fin. Corp. v. Miller Mining Co., 817 F.2d 1424 (9th Cir. 1987); Commerzanstalt v. Telewide Sys., Inc., 790 F.2d 206 (2d Cir. 1986); Teachers Ins. & Annuity Ass'n of Am. v. Butler, 803 F.2d 61 (2d Cir. 1986); Freeman v. Internal Revenue Serv., 799 F.2d 1091 (5th Cir. 1986); Cathey v. Johns-Manville Sales Corp., 711 F.2d 60 (6th Cir. 1983); Ass'n of St. Croix Condo. Owners v. St. Croix Hotel Corp., 682 F.2d 446 (3d Cir. 1982); *see also* Ellison v. Northwest Eng'g Co., 709 F.2d 681 (11th Cir. 1983). *But see* Mason v. Oklahoma Turnpike Auth., 115 F.3d 1442 (10th Cir. 1997) (Code did not prevent debtor's appeal in action originally brought against debtor but did stay plaintiff's cross appeal); Koolik v. Markowitz, 40 F.3d 567 (2d Cir. 1994) (appeal by debtor plaintiff from adverse judgment on defendant's counter-claim was stayed); *In re* Lyngholm, 24 F.3d 89 (6th Cir. 1994) (minority view that trustee or debtor may continue any action, regardless of how it began, without relief from stay); Accredited Associates, Inc. v. Shottenfeld, 292 S.E.2d 417 (Ga. Ct. App. 1982) (result turns on which party filed appeal); Kessel v. Peterson, 350 N.W.2d 603 (N.D. 1984) (appeal by debtor plaintiff from adverse judgment on defendant's counterclaim was stayed).

42 *See In re* Hoffinger Indus., Inc., 329 F.3d 948 (8th Cir. 2003) (appeal by debtor in action in which debtor was defendant was stayed); Borman v. Raymark Indus., Inc., 946 F.2d 1031 (3d Cir. 1991) (debtor's appeal of judgment against it is stayed). Nothing prevents the debtor from seeking relief from the stay for cause, in order to allow the appeal to go forward. *See* § 9.7.3.2.1, *infra*.

43 *See* § 9.4.4, *infra*.

44 Queenie, Ltd. v. Nygard Int'l, 321 F.3d 282 (2d Cir. 2003) (appeal stayed as to defendant who had filed a bankruptcy case and his wholly-owned corporation, but not as to other defendants); Credit Alliance Corp. v. Williams, 851 F.2d 119 (4th Cir. 1988); Fortier v. Dona Anna Plaza Partners, 747 F.2d 1324 (10th Cir. 1984); Williford v. Armstrong World Indus., 715 F.2d 124 (4th Cir. 1983); Wedgeworth v. Fibreboard Corp., 706 F.2d 541 (5th Cir. 1983); Austin v. Unarco Indus., 705 F.2d 1 (1st Cir. 1983); Pitts v. Unarco Indus., 698 F.2d 313 (7th Cir. 1983); HBA East, Ltd. v. JEA Boxing Co., 796 S.W.2d 534 (Tex. App. 1990); *see also In re* Am. Hardwoods, Inc., 885 F.2d 621 (9th Cir. 1989) (court lacks power to institute non-automatic stay pursuant to 11 U.S.C. § 105 to protect non-debtor guarantors); *cf. In re* Replogle, 929 F.2d 836 (1st Cir. 1991) (determinations made in non-stayed case which affect the estate's interests because of debtor's guarantee are not binding in the bankruptcy case).

45 11 U.S.C. § 102(2); *see In re* Passmore, 156 B.R. 595 (Bankr. E.D. Wis. 1993) (creditor could not attach post-petition wages of debtor's spouse, as they were community property in which debtor had an undivided interest).

46 11 U.S.C. § 362(a)(2).

47 11 U.S.C. § 362(a)(3).

48 11 U.S.C. § 362(a)(4).

49 11 U.S.C. § 362(a)(5).

50 Certain judgments obtained by governmental units to enforce police or regulatory powers may be enforced. 11 U.S.C. § 362(b)(4); *see* § 9.4.5, *infra. But see In re* Watson, 78 B.R. 232 (B.A.P. 9th Cir. 1987) (judgment held nondischargeable may be executed without relief from stay).

51 *See* Taylor v. First Fed. Sav. & Loan Ass'n of Monessen, 843 F.2d 153 (3d Cir. 1988); *In re* Petruccelli, 113 B.R. 5 (Bankr. S.D. Cal. 1990). Note that such judgments cannot be enforced against property of the estate. However, some post-petition claims can be collected only as administrative claims in the context of the debtor's bankruptcy proceeding. *See* 11 U.S.C. § 503; *see also In re* Creative Cuisine, Inc., 96 B.R. 144 (Bankr. N.D. Ill. 1989) (lessor cannot collect claim for post-petition rent in state court). And creditors may not use the subterfuge of claiming that payments extracted from the debtor are for post-petition services when they are really applied to pre-petition debts. *In re* Lansdale Family Restaurants, Inc., 977 F.2d 826 (3d Cir. 1992).

52 Similarly, the provision against exercising control over property of the estate prevents third parties from attempting to enforce claims which have come into the bankruptcy estate. *In re* McConville, 84 F.3d 340 (9th Cir. 1996) (deed of trust granted by debtor to secure post-petition loan was lien on property of the

a chapter 13 case, this freeze can be very important because, generally, all property the debtor acquires during the entire time the case is pending becomes property of the estate.[53] The prohibition of acts to obtain possession also applies to property not owned by, but in possession of, the estate, such as leased property, even if the lease was terminated prior to the case.[54] And it applies to any other property in which the

debtor has any interest,[55] to intangible property rights as well as to tangible property.[56]

The stay also prevents any action to create, perfect or enforce a lien against property of the estate.[57] Although this provision prevents renewal or extension of most expiring

---

estate which was void under § 362(a)(4)); *see In re* Sherk, 918 F.2d 1170 (5th Cir. 1990) (non-debtor wife may not bring fraudulent transfer action outside bankruptcy based on claim which had passed, in part, into husband's bankruptcy estate); *In re* Crysen/Montenay Energy Co., 902 F.2d 1098 (2d Cir. 1990); § 12.8, *infra.* See § 2.5, *supra,* for a discussion of what property comes into the estate. However, post-petition transfers of estate property may be authorized by the court pursuant to 11 U.S.C. § 363. The relevant portions of this provision are made applicable to debtors in chapter 13 by 11 U.S.C. § 1303.

53 11 U.S.C. § 1306(a); Sec. Bank of Marshalltown, Iowa v. Neiman, 1 F.3d 687 (8th Cir. 1993) (property acquired by chapter 13 debtor during case continues to be property of the estate protected by the stay after it vests in the debtor upon confirmation); *In re* Kolenda, 212 B.R. 851 (W.D. Mich. 1997) (automobile acquired post-confirmation was property of the estate protected by stay). *But see In re* Fisher, 203 B.R. 958 (N.D. Ill. 1997) (vesting of property of estate in debtor at confirmation deprives that property of stay protection afforded to property of the estate), *rev'g* 198 B.R. 721 (Bankr. N.D. Ill. 1996); *In re* Sak, 21 B.R. 305 (Bankr. E.D.N.Y. 1982); *In re* Adams, 12 B.R. 540 (Bankr. D. Utah 1981) (all of debtor's property except that used to fund plan is no longer property of the estate after confirmation, under 11 U.S.C. § 1327(b)). One possible way to avoid the potential problem of property losing its character as property of the estate in jurisdictions where that is at issue is to provide in the plan for such property to vest in the debtor at the end of the case, because § 1327(b) provides that confirmation vests estate property in the debtor only if the plan does not provide otherwise. This provision will extend the protection of the stay. For an example of such plan language, see Form 8, Appendix G.3, *infra. See In re* Clark, 207 B.R. 559 (Bankr. S.D. Ohio 1997) (post-confirmation wages were property of estate protected from IRS levy for post-petition taxes when plan clearly provided that property of estate did not revest in debtors upon confirmation); *In re* Lambright, 125 B.R. 733 (Bankr. N.D. Tex. 1991); *In re* Petrucelli, 113 B.R. 5 (Bankr. S.D. Cal. 1990); *In re* Denn, 37 B.R. 33 (Bankr. D. Minn. 1983); *see also* § 9.3, *supra,* §§ 12.8, 12.11, *infra.*

54 *In re* Convenient Food Mart No. 144, Inc., 968 F.2d 592 (6th Cir. 1992); *In re* Atl. Bus. & Cmty. Corp., 901 F.2d 325 (3d Cir. 1990) (mere possessory interest in property triggers stay); *In re* 48th St. Steakhouse, 835 F.2d 427 (2d Cir. 1987) (same); *In re* Sudler, 71 B.R. 780 (Bankr. E.D. Pa. 1986); *In re* Gibbs, 9 B.R. 758 (Bankr. D. Conn. 1981); *In re* A.L.S. Inc., 3 B.R. 107 (Bankr. E.D. Pa. 1980); *see also In re* Di Giorgio, 200 B.R. 664 (C.D. Cal. 1996) (declaring unconstitutional state statute which permitted execution on writ of possession despite tenant's bankruptcy filing), *appeal dismissed as moot,* 134 F.3d 971 (9th Cir. 1998). *But see In re* Pinetree, Ltd., 876 F.2d 34 (5th Cir. 1989) (debtor's interest in property by unrecorded deed from related entity not protected by automatic stay when debtor did not assert its interest pre-petition). The protection of possessory interests after lease termination does not apply to some leases of non-residential real property. 11 U.S.C. § 362(b)(10).

55 Missouri v. U.S. Bankruptcy Court, 647 F.2d 768 (8th Cir. 1981); *see also* Borman v. Raymark Indus., 946 F.2d 1031 (3d Cir. 1991) (§ 362(a)(3) protects property of the estate even if it is not in the debtor's possession); *In re* McCall-Pruitt, 281 B.R. 910 (Bankr. E.D. Mich. 2002) (state violated stay by accepting funds arising from pre-petition tax garnishment after bankruptcy case was filed). *But see* United States v. Inslaw, 932 F.2d 1467 (D.C. Cir. 1991) (party's use of property in its possession under claim of right does not violate stay); *In re* Lockard, 884 F.2d 1171 (9th Cir. 1989) (surety bond to protect debtor's creditors not property of the estate so that state court action to collect on bond not stayed).

56 *See In re* Gaskin, 120 B.R. 13 (D.N.J. 1990) (post-petition termination of "interest credit agreement" by FmHA violates automatic stay); Scrima v. John Devries Agency Inc., 103 B.R. 128 (W.D. Mich. 1989) (purported post-petition cancellation of insurance policy void); *In re* R.S. Pinellas Motel P'ship, 2 B.R. 113 (Bankr. M.D. Fla. 1979). Even a debtor's interest in a liability insurance policy is property subject to the automatic stay. *In re* Minoco Group of Companies, Ltd., 799 F.2d 517 (9th Cir. 1986) (prepaid policy may not be cancelled by the issuing company without relief from the stay); Tringali v. Hathaway Mach. Co., 796 F.2d 553 (1st Cir. 1986). Similarly, it is a violation of the stay to unilaterally terminate a license or a contract with the debtor. *In re* Computer Communications, Inc., 824 F.2d 725 (9th Cir. 1987); *see also In re* Carroll, 903 F.2d 1266 (9th Cir. 1990) (termination of management agreement post-petition violates stay); *In re* Nejberger, 120 B.R. 21 (E.D. Pa. 1990) (post-petition termination of liquor license due to failure to pay pre-petition taxes violates stay), *aff'd,* 934 F.2d 1300 (3d Cir. 1991); *In re* North, 128 B.R. 592 (Bankr. D. Vt. 1991) (suspension of chiropractor's license for failure to pay pre-petition taxes violates stay); *In re* Pester Ref. Co., 58 B.R. 189 (Bankr. S.D. Iowa 1985); *cf.* Hazen First State Bank v. Speight, 888 F.2d 574 (8th Cir. 1989) (stay does not prevent contract from expiring by its own terms); Holland Am. Ins. Co. v. Succession of Roy, 777 F.2d 992 (5th Cir. 1985).

57 *In re* Avis, 178 F.3d 718 (4th Cir. 1999) (§ 362(a)(5) prevented attachment of federal tax lien to property acquired by estate due to inheritance of property by the debtor); *In re* Glasply Marine Indus., 971 F.2d 391 (9th Cir. 1992) (stay prohibits creation of new property tax liens after petition filed); Makoroff v. City of Lockport, 916 F.2d 890 (3d Cir. 1990) (perfection of tax lien post-petition violates stay); *In re* Parr Meadows Racing Ass'n, Inc., 880 F.2d 1540 (2d Cir. 1989). A 1994 amendment to the Code added 11 U.S.C. § 362(b)(18), which overrules these cases. That section creates an exception to the stay for the creation or perfection of a statutory lien for an *ad valorem* property tax that comes due after the filing of the bankruptcy petition. *But see* Mann v. Chase Manhattan Mortgage Corp., 316 F.3d 1 (1st Cir. 2003) (mortgage company adding charges to debtor's account in its internal bookkeeping, absent any overt attempt to collect the fees, did not violate automatic stay); *In re* Stanton, 303 F.3d 939 (9th Cir. 2002) (increase in lien on debtors' home due to new advances on loan to corporation that they had guaranteed did not violate stay); *In re* Knightsbridge Dev. Co., 884 F.2d 145 (4th Cir. 1989) (creditor did not violate stay by amending its *lis pendens* post-petition).

liens while the stay is in effect,[58] another provision of the Code effectively extends an existing lien until at least thirty days after the stay expires if renewal or extension of the lien is stayed.[59]

Finally, these provisions generally prevent the creation, perfection, or enforcement of any lien against the debtor's property, even if it is not property of the estate, for example, most property acquired after the filing of the bankruptcy case or property abandoned in a chapter 7 case, if the lien secures a pre-petition claim.[60]

Thus, repossessions and sales of repossessed property are clearly enjoined.[61] If relief from the stay is subsequently granted to allow the sale of estate property to go forward, the creditor may be required to re-advertise and provide new notice of the sale to all interested parties including the debtor.[62]

The applicability of the stay to acts against property of the estate often turns on difficult questions about whether the debtor had a property interest at the time the case was filed.[63] Generally, however, even a very limited interest brings the stay into effect. For example, probate proceedings concerning an estate from which the debtor may inherit property are stayed.[64] The stay may halt even evictions, foreclosures, or other transactions that are nearly complete, depending upon

the state law as to the debtor's interest.[65]

In particular, the relationship of the stay to rights of redemption under state law has been the subject of frequent litigation. Here, too, the applicable state law may be critical, especially if the creditor must take some further action, such as obtaining a deed, after the redemption period runs.[66] When a creditor need take no affirmative act to assert its rights after the redemption period, the debtor's only protection may come from section 108 of the Code, which extends a redemption period to sixty days after the petition is filed if it would otherwise have expired earlier.[67] It is unclear

---

58 *In re* Lobherr, 282 B.R. 912 (Bankr. C.D. Cal. 2002) (renewal of judgment violated stay and was void). A 1994 amendment to 11 U.S.C. § 362(b)(3) permits acts to maintain or continue perfection of a lien in certain limited circumstances.

59 *See* 11 U.S.C. § 108(c); *In re* Hunter's Run Ltd. P'ship, 875 F.2d 1425 (9th Cir. 1989); *In re* Morton, 866 F.2d 561 (2d Cir. 1989). Additionally, note that perfection of certain types of liens which relate back to an event occurring pre-petition is permitted under 11 U.S.C. § 362(b)(3). *See* Equibank v. Wheeling Pittsburgh Steel, 884 F.2d 80 (3d Cir. 1989). *But see In re* Larson, 979 F.2d 625 (8th Cir. 1992) (stay did not prohibit a filing of mortgage addendum to extend duration of existing lien).

60 *In re* Brooks, 871 F.2d 89 (9th Cir. 1989) (creditor cannot re-record deed after bankruptcy to perfect interest in debtor's property by changing incorrect property description); *In re* Sedgwick, 266 B.R. 185 (Bankr. N.D. Cal. 2001) (creditors could not obtain lien on debtor's property after confirmation of plan, regardless of whether property was still property of estate); *In re* Passmore, 156 B.R. 595 (Bankr. E.D. Wis. 1993) (creditor could not attach post-petition wages of debtor's spouse, even though they were not property of the estate, because they were community property in which debtor had an undivided interest).

61 *In re* Reed, 102 B.R. 243 (Bankr. E.D. Okla. 1989) (post-petition sale of repossessed collateral violates automatic stay); *In re* Koresko, 91 B.R. 689 (Bankr. E.D. Pa. 1988) (debtor retains right to redeem vehicle after repossession; post-petition sale violates stay).

62 *See also* § 9.4.1, *supra.*

63 *See* United States v. Pelullo, 178 F.3d 196 (3d Cir. 1999) (debtor had no interest in assets which had been divested by a criminal forfeiture order prior to bankruptcy petition).

64 *In re* Molitor, 183 B.R. 547 (Bankr. E.D. Ark. 1995) (probate proceedings that occurred without relief from the stay were void; stay protected trustee's right to be involved in distribution of probate estate).

65 *See, e.g., In re* 48th St. Steakhouse, 835 F.2d 427 (2d Cir. 1987) (notice of lease termination to debtor's sublessor violated stay); *In re* Aponte, 82 B.R. 738 (Bankr. E.D. Pa. 1988) (tenant's bare possessory interest triggers stay); *In re* Evans, 22 B.R. 608 (Bankr. D. Neb. 1982) (debtor retained interest in pawned goods during redemption period); *In re* Jones, 20 B.R. 988 (Bankr. E.D. Pa. 1982) (debtor retained interest in home after sheriff's sale); *In re* Gambogi, 20 B.R. 587 (Bankr. D.R.I. 1982) (post-eviction possessory interest in leased property sufficient to activate stay); *In re* Jenkins, 19 B.R. 105 (D. Colo. 1982) (debtors retained interest in property subject to deed of trust foreclosure until redemption period had run). See also cases cited above in this subsection and § 9.7.3.2.4, *infra.*

66 *In re* Brown, 126 B.R. 767 (N.D. Ill. 1991) (non-bankruptcy law determines whether IRS levy terminates debtor's interests in bankruptcy); *In re* Lambert, 273 B.R. 663 (Bankr. N.D. Fla. 2002) (post-petition issuance of tax deed based on pre-petition sale of tax certificate violated stay because it was not mere ministerial act); *In re* Cooper, 273 B.R. 297 (Bankr. D.D.C. 2002) (resale of debtor's property after first foreclosure sale purchaser failed to comply with terms of sale was stayed by bankruptcy petition filed before resale occurred because debtor had right of redemption); *In re* Davenport, 268 B.R. 159 (Bankr. N.D. Ill 2001) (action of tax sale purchaser in seeking tax deed violated stay because debtor still had equitable and beneficial interest in property after tax sale); *see* Fish Mkt. Nominee Corp. v. Pelofsky, 72 F.3d 4 (1st Cir. 1995) (stay prevented state court order terminating debtor's right of redemption during bankruptcy case); *In re* Garber, 129 B.R. 323 (Bankr. D.R.I. 1991) (state law right of redemption comes into the estate precluding sale of seized property by creditor). *But see In re* Rodgers, 333 F.3d 64 (2d Cir. 2003) (when right to redemption from tax sale expired before bankruptcy petition was filed, automatic stay did not prevent delivery of deed to tax sale purchaser).

67 11 U.S.C. § 108; *In re* Canney, 284 F.3d 363 (2d Cir. 2002) (Vermont strict foreclosure); *In re* Tynan, 773 F.2d 177 (7th Cir. 1985); Johnson v. First Nat'l Bank of Montevideo, 719 F.2d 270 (8th Cir. 1983) (automatic transfer of property under Minnesota law would not violate stay); *see also* Counties Contracting & Constr. Co. v. Constitution Life Ins. Co., 855 F.2d 1054 (3d Cir. 1988) (statutory grace period for payment on insurance policy is extended sixty days by bankruptcy filing; at end of sixty days policy expires); *In re* McCallen, 49 B.R. 948 (D. Or. 1985) (stay applied when further creditor action required to complete foreclosure); *In re* Jenkins, 19 B.R. 105 (D. Colo. 1982) (stay applies when further action required of creditor or third party after running of redemption period). Neither the requirement of a ministerial act by a court clerk after the running of the redemption period nor the retention of greater rights by the debtor during the redemption period is sufficient to bring the automatic stay into effect. *In re* Carver, 828 F.2d 463 (8th Cir.

whether this period can be further extended under the broad powers granted to the bankruptcy court under 11 U.S.C. § 105.[68] However, even when the right of redemption expires, the creditor must seek relief from the stay to file an action against the debtor for possession of the property.[69]

9.4.3 Other Acts Prohibited by the Stay

The automatic stay also prohibits:

- Any [other] act to collect, assess or recover a claim against the debtor that arose before the commencement of the case;[70]
- The setoff of any debt owing to the debtor that arose before the commencement of the case against any claim against the debtor;[71] and
- The commencement or continuation of a proceeding before the United States Tax Court concerning the debtor.[72]

These provisions round out the stay's protections. Creditors may not engage in any collection activity, nor in any other acts to try to force the debtor to pay a pre-petition claim.[73] This prohibition encompasses all types of collection

attempts: by mail, by phone, in person or through third parties.[74] As noted earlier, the word "claim" is broadly defined to include not only rights to payment, regardless of whether they are liquidated, contingent, matured, disputed, or secured, but also many rights to equitable remedies.[75] Administrative recoupments of public benefits, such as social security or welfare, based upon a claim of overpayment or fraud, are not allowed.[76] If a collection motivation is

1987); *In re* Manum, 828 F.2d 459 (8th Cir. 1987). However, other courts have found the stay applicable regardless of the necessity of further creditor action. *See, e.g., In re* Dohm, 14 B.R. 701 (Bankr. N.D. Ill. 1981). Also, if a creditor fails to object to a chapter 13 plan extending the right to redemption, he may be bound by that confirmed plan. *See In re* Bennett, 29 B.R. 380 (W.D. Mich. 1981).

68 *Compare* Johnson v. First Nat'l Bank of Montevideo, 719 F.2d 270 (8th Cir. 1983) *with* Bank of Ravenswood v. Patzold, 27 B.R. 542 (N.D. Ill. 1982).

69 11 U.S.C. § 362(a)(3).

70 11 U.S.C. § 362(a)(6).

71 11 U.S.C. § 362(a)(7). *But see In re* Holford, 896 F.2d 176 (5th Cir. 1990) (certain recoupments allowed if they arise from the same transaction).

72 11 U.S.C. § 362(a)(8). *But see* Cheng v. Comm'r Internal Revenue Serv., 938 F.2d 141 (9th Cir. 1991) (automatic stay does not apply to appeal of tax court proceeding).

73 *See In re* Diamond, 346 F.3d 224 (1st Cir. 2003) (threat to take action at real estate commission to have broker's license revoked could violate stay); *In re* Flynn, 143 B.R. 798 (Bankr. D.R.I. 1992) (credit union violated stay by communicating with debtor to seek reaffirmation when it knew she was represented by counsel); *In re* Guinn, 102 B.R. 838 (Bankr. N.D. Ala. 1989) (termination of credit union membership and refusal to accept mortgage payments violate stay); *In re* Sechuan City, Inc., 96 B.R. 37 (Bankr. E.D. Pa. 1989) (creditor's posting of signs in lobby of hotel that debtor restaurant does not pay its bills violates automatic stay; creditor's first amendment arguments rejected). Even revocation of a debtor's probation motivated by desire to coerce payment of a pre-petition restitution debt has been held to violate the stay. *See* § 9.4.5, *infra. But see In re* Duke, 79 F.3d 43 (7th Cir. 1996) (erroneously holding that a non-threatening, non-coercive letter to the debtor seeking reaffirmation of a debt did not violate the stay); Brown v. Pa. State

Employees Credit Union, 851 F.2d 81 (3d Cir. 1988) (credit union's letter informing debtor that it would not do further business with her unless she reaffirmed debt does not violate stay); Morgan Guaranty Trust Co. v. Am. Sav. & Loan, 804 F.2d 1487 (9th Cir. 1986) (a holder in due course's presentment of pre-petition notes executed by the debtor does not violate the stay). The *Duke* decision was narrowly construed by at least one bankruptcy court, which found a creditor in contempt for simply mailing a proposed reaffirmation agreement directly to a debtor who was represented by counsel. *In re* Seelye, 243 B.R. 701 (Bankr. N.D. Ill. 2000). Communications seeking reaffirmation of debt may also violate other consumer protection laws, regardless of whether they violate the stay. *See* Sears, Roebuck & Co. v. O'Brien, 178 F.3d 962 (8th Cir. 1999) (state law prohibiting creditor from communicating with debtor represented by counsel was not preempted by federal bankruptcy law); Greenwood Trust Co. v. Smith, 212 B.R. 599 (B.A.P. 8th Cir. 1997) (creditor's direct communication with debtor represented by attorney violated state consumer credit laws); Sturm v. Providian Nat. Bank, 242 B.R. 599 (S.D. W. Va. 1999) (state law claims for unfair debt collection not preempted by automatic stay provisions).

74 *See In re* Crudup, 287 B.R. 358 (Bankr. E.D.N.C. 2002) (letter sent to debtor's in-laws was attempt to collect debt); *In re* Draper, 237 B.R. 502 (Bankr. M.D. Fla. 1999) (repeated invoices requesting payment and sent to debtor with payment coupon and return envelope violated the stay even though they acknowledged bankruptcy filing and stated that they were for "informational purposes only").

75 11 U.S.C. § 101(5).

76 Lee v. Schweiker, 739 F.2d 870 (3d Cir. 1984); Crabtree v. Veterans Admin., 31 B.R. 95 (Bankr. S.D. Ohio 1983). However, some types of "recoupment" may be allowed if previous payments to a debtor reduce or eliminate any entitlement to future benefits and are not otherwise considered as collectible debts. *In re* Kosadnar, 157 F.3d 1011 (5th Cir. 1998) (employer could reduce debtor's paychecks to recoup prior advances that were overpayments to debtor); *In re* Mullen, 696 F.2d 470 (6th Cir. 1983) (military readjustment allowance not considered a debt); *see also In re* Malinowski, 156 F.3d 131 (2d Cir. 1998) (state agency could not reduce debtor's unemployment benefits to repay overpayment on prior claim; reduction was setoff and not recoupment because two unemployment claims covered separate periods and were not same transaction); *In re* Univ. Med. Ctr., 973 F.2d 1065 (3d Cir. 1992) (Department of Health and Human Services (HHS) not permitted to withhold Medicare payments to hospital based upon pre-petition debts of hospital to HHS); *In re* Gullett, 230 B.R. 321 (Bankr. S.D. Tex. 1999) (recoupment of erroneously paid workers' compensation benefits violated stay when recoupment was not permitted by state law); *In re* Gaither, 200 B.R. 847 (Bankr. S.D. Ohio 1996) (recoupment of unemployment compensation overpayment from post-petition benefits does not violate stay as claims arise out of same transaction); *In re* Howell, 4 B.R. 102 (Bankr. M.D. Tenn. 1980) (administrative determination of overpayments not

shown, the withholding of a student's transcript or other benefits normally provided to non-debtors is also prohibited.[77] Similarly, creditors may not exercise a right of setoff against the debtor's property, such as bank accounts, without violating the stay,[78] nor may they garnish the debtor's wages,[79] or collect their debts from property of the debtor, such as energy assistance payments, that comes into their hands.[80] The reporting of a debt to a credit bureau is a violation of the stay if done with the intent to coerce a debtor into paying a pre-petition debt.[81] Even the acceptance of payroll deductions authorized by the debtor before the bankruptcy on payments for a pre-petition debt constitutes an act to collect that debt and thus is a violation of the stay.[82]

The interception of tax refunds to pay student loans or other debts being collected by the government is another example of an act that is stayed.[83] Although it is sometimes not easy to determine the date the intercept actually occurred, if it occurred after the bankruptcy case was filed it is normally possible to have the intercepted funds returned to the debtor.[84]

However, the Supreme Court has held that a "freeze" on a debtor's bank account, by a bank to which the debtor owes money, does not constitute a setoff prohibited by the stay.[85] The court held that a temporary freeze, while a creditor seeks relief from the stay in order to exercise a right of setoff is permissible. However, a more permanent freeze should be considered differently. If a creditor does not promptly seek relief from the stay in order to setoff its debt, the Supreme Court's decision should not be considered applicable.[86] Moreover, cases prohibiting a setoff or freeze in contravention of a confirmed plan providing for different treatment of the creditor's claim remain good law.[87] In addition, there is no right to setoff pre-petition debts against post-petition deposits in an account.[88] And any freeze or setoff for credit card debts or overdrafts on consumer lines of credit is usually prohibited by non-bankruptcy law.[89]

---

stayed but overpayments themselves were simply unsecured claims to be treated as others).

77 *In re* Merchant, 958 F.2d 738 (6th Cir. 1992) (although student loan debt found nondischargeable, school's refusal to release transcript violates stay); *In re* Gustafson, 934 F.2d 216 (9th Cir. 1991) (refusal to release transcript violates stay, but state university held immune from money damages); Loyola Univ. v. McClarty, 234 B.R. 386 (E.D. La. 1999) (damages imposed for refusal to release transcript); *In re* Scroggins, 209 B.R. 727 (Bankr. D. Ariz. 1997) (parochial school's withholding of transcript to collect debt violated stay); *In re* Carson, 150 B.R. 228 (Bankr. E.D. Mo. 1993) (threats to prevent student from attending graduation and to withhold transcript violated stay); *In re* Parham, 56 B.R. 531 (Bankr. E.D. Va. 1986) (student transcript); *In re* Olson, 38 B.R. 515 (Bankr. N.D. Iowa 1984) (refusal of medical services until pre-petition debt paid was contempt); *In re* Ware, 9 B.R. 24 (Bankr. W.D. Mo. 1981).

78 *See In re* Scharff, 143 B.R. 541 (Bankr. S.D. Iowa 1992) (creditor violated stay by withholding pension checks to repay debt to pension plan); *In re* Figgers, 121 B.R. 772 (Bankr. S.D. Ohio 1990) (creditor's set-off rights are fixed as of date of filing despite conversion from one chapter to another). See also § 10.4.2.6.7, *infra*, for discussion of rights to setoff a creditor may later exercise. *But see In re* McMahon, 129 F.3d 93 (2d Cir. 1997) (utility's application of pre-petition deposit to pre-petition debt was not prohibited setoff because it was recoupment under New York law).

79 *In re* Warren, 7 B.R. 201 (Bankr. N.D. Ala. 1980); *see also In re* Carlsen, 63 B.R. 706 (Bankr. C.D. Cal. 1986).

80 *In re* Morris, 45 B.R. 350 (E.D. Pa. 1984); *see also In re* Farmers Markets, Inc., 792 F.2d 1400 (9th Cir. 1986) (state could not condition transfer of liquor license it held on payment of pre-petition taxes).

81 *In re* Singley, 233 B.R. 170 (Bankr. S.D. Ga. 1999).

82 *In re* Hellums, 772 F.2d 379 (7th Cir. 1985); *In re* Briggs, 143 B.R. 438 (Bankr. E.D. Mich. 1992) (credit union's notice to debtor that it would continue to apply post-petition earnings to pre-petition debt unless requested not to do so constituted violation of stay); *In re* Brooks, 132 B.R. 29 (Bankr. W.D. Mo. 1991) (refusal to disgorge payroll deductions on demand constitutes willful violation of stay); *see also In re* O'Neal, 165 B.R. 859 (Bankr. M.D. Tenn. 1994) (retention of loan payment automatically withdrawn from checking account violated stay).

83 *In re* Blake, 235 B.R. 568 (Bankr. D. Md. 1998) (Department of

Education violated stay by causing setoff of tax refund to pay student loan).

84 *See In re* McCall-Pruitt, 281 B.R. 910 (Bankr. E.D. Mich. 2002) (state violated stay by accepting funds arising from pre-petition tax garnishment after bankruptcy case was filed). If the intercept was for a loan held by the United States Department of Education, a refund may be obtained by contacting the U.S. Department of Education, Debt Collection Service. If the loan is held by a guarantor contact the guarantor, or the guarantor and the Department of Education. If these contacts fail, the Department of Education's General Counsel should be contacted and, of course, an action can be brought in the bankruptcy court for turnover of the property, damages, and attorney fees.

85 Citizens Bank of Md. v. Strumpf, 516 U.S. 16, 116 S. Ct. 286, 133 L. Ed. 2d 258 (1995). See § 10.4.2.6.7, *infra*, for a discussion of the implications of such a freeze on the creditor's right of setoff.

86 *In re* Holden, 217 B.R. 161 (D. Vt. 1997) (IRS could not permanently hold debtors' refund to coerce payment of much smaller debt already addressed in debtors' chapter 13 plan); *In re* Orr, 234 B.R. 249 (Bankr. N.D.N.Y. 1999) (credit union violated stay by freezing funds and not seeking relief from stay for over two months); Town of Hempstead Employees Fed. Credit Union v. Wicks, 215 B.R. 316 (Bankr. E.D.N.Y. 1997) (four month administrative freeze without filing of motion for relief from automatic stay violated stay).

87 *In re* Cont'l Airlines, 134 F.3d 536 (3d Cir. 1998) (reaffirming principles in earlier chapter 13 decision prohibiting IRS setoff after confirmation of plan providing for payment of tax debt through plan).

88 *In re* Dunning, 269 B.R. 357 (Bankr. N.D. Ohio 2001) (punitive damages awarded when bank admitted setoffs of pre-petition debts against post-petition deposits as a matter of course); *In re* Harris, 260 B.R. 753 (Bankr. D. Md. 2001); *In re* Orr, 234 B.R. 249 (Bankr. N.D.N.Y. 1999) (credit union had no right to setoff except as to funds on deposit on petition date which were not withdrawn after the petition was filed); *In re* Schwartz, 213 B.R. 695 (Bankr. S.D. Ohio 1997).

89 The Fair Credit Billing Act prohibits such setoffs. 15 U.S.C. § 1666h(a); *see Bank Setoffs: Federal Prohibition on Credit Card Debt Often Ignored*, 20 NCLC REPORTS, *Bankruptcy and Foreclosures Ed.* 5 (Sept./Oct. 2001).

Usually, the best way to prevent such a freeze from occurring is to ensure that the debtor has no money deposited, at the time the bankruptcy petition is filed, with any institution that is a creditor. When possible, the debtor should also try to make sure that all checks written on such accounts have cleared prior to the petition date. If that cannot be done, the debtor may want to consider withdrawing all funds from the account, advising the payees on the undeposited checks not to deposit those checks, and paying the payees with cash, money orders, or replacement checks drawn on a different account.

The Internal Revenue Service (IRS) has been one of the most frequent adversaries in litigation regarding these issues. The IRS now appears to give some recognition to the necessity that it seek relief from the stay before it can set off a tax refund against a pre-bankruptcy tax debt, perhaps because, in several instances, the IRS has been held in contempt for setting off tax refunds without getting relief from the stay.[90] However, despite these cases, it is often difficult to have tax refunds released to a debtor, because the IRS claims a right to "retain" them;[91] in some districts, questionable standing orders of the court have given the IRS blanket relief from the automatic stay for the setoff of mutual debts.[92] The Supreme Court's decision with respect

to bank account freezes will undoubtedly provide the IRS with additional arguments for retaining at least those refunds owed to the debtor at the time the petition is filed. In any case, it is clear that there is no right to setoff if the tax debt is a pre-bankruptcy debt and the right to a refund is a post-bankruptcy debt, so the IRS would have no justification for freezing the debtor's funds in that situation.[93]

9.4.4 The Automatic Stay Protecting Codebtors in Chapter 13

In chapter 13 cases, another type of automatic stay also goes into effect. This stay prohibits any act or civil legal action to collect all or part of a consumer debt of the debtor from any codebtor.[94] The codebtor need not be personally liable on the debt; it is sufficient that the codebtor put up security for the obligation.[95] Congress found this provision to be necessary because in many instances under the old Chapter XIII codebtors were pursued by creditors as soon as a debtor filed a case, leading ultimately to the failure of the Chapter XIII plan.[96]

One problem which arises not infrequently is the reporting of a bankruptcy on the credit report of a codebtor, even though the codebtor has not filed a bankruptcy case. Although creditors have argued that such a report accurately reflects that the particular debt is being paid in a bankruptcy plan, the report may be actionable if it inaccurately appears from the report that the codebtor has filed a bankruptcy case.[97] Even if the report is accurate, it may be a violation of the codebtor stay if it is made with the intent to coerce payment by the codebtor.[98]

---

90   *In re* Price, 103 B.R. 989 (Bankr. N.D. Ill. 1989) (that notice was sent out inadvertently by IRS computer is no defense), *aff'd*, 42 F.3d 1068 (7th Cir. 1994); *In re* Hebert, 61 B.R. 44 (Bankr. W.D. La. 1986) (IRS in contempt for attempting to collect interest on its claim outside chapter 13 plan); *In re* Cudaback, 22 B.R. 914 (Bankr. D. Neb. 1982) (IRS action to enforce pre-bankruptcy tax lien is contemptuous); *In re* Hackney, 20 B.R. 158 (Bankr. D. Idaho 1982) (IRS in contempt for refusing to release refund when confirmed plan gave debtors right to pay debt in installments); *In re* Holcomb, 18 B.R. 839 (Bankr. S.D. Ohio 1982) (IRS required to turn over tax refunds to chapter 13 trustee); *see also* United States *ex rel.* Internal Revenue Serv. v. Norton, 717 F.2d 767 (3d Cir. 1983) (IRS may not offset money due to debtors against pre-petition claim which was provided for in confirmed chapter 13 plan; § 362 also bars such setoff before confirmation); United States v. Holden, 258 B.R. 323 (D. Vt. 2000) (debtors awarded damages for IRS's administrative freeze of tax refund that was contrary to terms of confirmed chapter 13 plan). In seeking damages or an injunction for violation of the stay against the IRS, issues related to federal sovereign immunity or the Anti-Injunction Act may arise. For a further discussion of those issues, see §§ 9.6 and 13.3.2.2, *infra*.

91   Both the Third and Fourth Circuit Courts of Appeals have held that, perhaps depending in some cases on state law, an IRS "freeze" on a debtor's tax refund is a setoff that is prohibited by the automatic stay. United States v. Reynolds, 764 F.2d 1004 (4th Cir. 1985); United States *ex rel.* Internal Revenue Service v. Norton, 717 F.2d 767 (3d Cir. 1983); *cf. In re* Murry, 15 B.R. 325 (Bankr. E.D. Ark. 1981) (retention by IRS was not a prohibited setoff).

92   Such orders have not always withstood scrutiny. *See In re* Internal Revenue Service Liabilities & Refunds in Chapter 13 Proceedings, 30 B.R. 811 (M.D. Tenn. 1983) (vacating standing order allowing *ex parte* relief from stay); *In re* Willardo, 67 B.R. 1014 (Bankr. W.D. Mich. 1987) (local rule violated due process clause as well as Bankruptcy Code). *But see In re* Wilkerson, 22

B.R. 728 (Bankr. E.D. Wis. 1982) (offset against tax refund for past due child support payable through IRS permitted); *In re* Murry, 15 B.R. 325 (Bankr. E.D. Ark. 1981) (relief from stay granted for setoff against tax refund).

93   See § 2.5.3, *supra*, for further discussion of when tax refunds become due and § 10.4.2.6.7, *infra*, for further discussion of limitation of right to setoff to mutual debts only.

94   11 U.S.C. § 1301; *see In re* Holder, 260 B.R. 571 (Bankr. M.D. Ga. 2001) (perfection of lien was an act to collect barred by codebtor stay and therefore was void); *In re* Sommersdorf, 139 B.R. 700 (Bankr. S.D. Ohio 1992) (bank's actions in placing notation of debt charge-off on codebtor's credit report violated stay).

95   *In re* Harris, 203 B.R. 46 (Bankr. E.D. Va. 1994) (conveyance of jointly-held property to foreclosure sale purchaser violated codebtor stay even though non-debtor spouse's personal liability on joint mortgage had been discharged in prior bankruptcy case).

96   H.R. Rep. No. 95-595, at 122 (1977).

97   For a discussion of claims brought under the Fair Credit Reporting Act, see National Consumer Law Center, Fair Credit Reporting (5th ed. 2002 and Supp.).

98   *In re* Singley, 233 B.R. 170 (Bankr. S.D. Ga. 1999); *In re* Sommersdorf, 139 B.R. 700 (Bankr. S.D. Ohio 1992) (bank's actions in placing notation of debt charge-off on codebtor's credit report violated stay).

There are several limitations upon this stay. It applies only to "consumer debts,"[99] and it does not apply to codebtors who became obligated in the ordinary course of their business.[100] It ends automatically if a chapter 13 case is closed, dismissed, or converted to a chapter other than chapter 12.

In several situations, the stay is effective as of the filing of the case, but may be lifted by the court upon request of a creditor or other party in interest. Such a request could be grounded upon the fact that the chapter 13 debtor was really the cosigner, and the non-filing individual received the consideration for the claim.[101] However, the issue in such cases is not whether the cosigner is the primary obligor or secondary obligor; cosigners are protected if they are also liable, along with the debtor, on a debt which provided a benefit to the debtor.[102] Relief from the codebtor stay is also available upon a showing of irreparable harm to the creditor caused by the stay.[103]

In addition, the codebtor stay will be lifted upon a creditor's motion to the extent that the proposed plan does not provide for full payment of the claim.[104] Thus, if a plan proposes to pay ten percent of a claim, relief from the stay may be granted as to the remaining ninety percent.[105] As discussed in a following chapter, the need to retain the codebtor stay justifies separate classification of debts involving codebtors in a chapter 13 plan so that those debts will receive full payment even when the debtor cannot afford to pay other creditors in full.[106]

The fact that a creditor will be paid late does not by itself justify relief from the stay if payment will be made in full.[107] Less clear is what happens when unearned interest is involved. Normally, unearned interest is not considered part of an unsecured claim in chapter 13,[108] and not paid in a plan. Therefore, it should not be taken into account in deciding whether the "claim" is paid in full.[109] However, some courts have held otherwise, stating that a codebtor may be pursued to the extent that post-bankruptcy interest is not paid in the plan.[110]

The procedure by which creditors may obtain relief from the codebtor stay is similar to that followed for relief from the section 362 automatic stay, discussed below, except in a few respects. A creditor that files a motion for relief from the codebtor stay based upon allegations that the plan will not pay its claim in full need not obtain a court order terminating the stay, if that motion is not opposed. If the debtor or codebtor does not file a response to the motion and serve it upon the creditor within twenty days, the codebtor stay is terminated to the extent requested by the creditor.[111] It is

---

99 Consumer debt is defined at 11 U.S.C. § 101(8). The term includes legal fees incurred for a non-business purpose. Patti v. Fred Ehrlich, Prof'l Corp., 304 B.R. 182 (E.D. Pa. 2003) (state court action to collect divorce legal fees violated codebtor stay). The term probably does not include a tax debt. *See In re Westberry*, 215 F.3d 589 (6th Cir. 2000) (tax debt not a consumer debt); *In re Pressimone*, 39 B.R. 240 (N.D.N.Y. 1984); *In re Stovall*, 209 B.R. 849 (Bankr. E.D. Va. 1997) (personal property tax not a consumer debt); *In re Goldsby*, 135 B.R. 611 (Bankr. E.D. Ark. 1992); *In re Reiter*, 126 B.R. 961 (Bankr. W.D. Tex. 1991). It also may not include tort liability. *In re Alvarez*, 57 B.R. 65 (Bankr. S.D. Fla. 1985). See also § 13.9.2.2, *infra*, for cases concerning definition of "consumer debt."

100 11 U.S.C. § 1301(a)(1).

101 11 U.S.C. § 1301(c)(1); *see, e.g., In re Jones*, 106 B.R. 33 (Bankr. W.D.N.Y. 1989). However, this principle is a narrow one. Even if a debtor's non-filing spouse also benefited from the debt and that debt was a community claim against community property of both spouses, the non-filing spouse did not receive the consideration for a debt rather than the spouse in bankruptcy. *In re Lopez Melendez*, 145 B.R. 740 (D. P.R. 1992). Only if all the consideration at the time of the original transaction went to the codebtor does this exception apply. *In re Motes*, 166 B.R. 147 (Bankr. D. Mo. 1994) (codebtor stay applied because loan to purchase mobile home benefited both debtor and spouse when it was made, even though non-debtor spouse had obtained full title to mobile home by time of bankruptcy).

102 *In re Zersen*, 189 B.R. 732 (Bankr. W.D. Wis. 1995).

103 11 U.S.C. § 1301(c)(3); *e.g., In re Case*, 148 B.R. 901 (Bankr. W.D. Mo. 1992) (creditor would suffer irreparable harm if not permitted to file a timely claim against deceased codebtor's estate).

104 11 U.S.C. § 1301(c); *see In re Fink*, 115 B.R. 113 (Bankr. S.D. Ohio 1990) (student loan creditor entitled to relief from stay to pursue codebtors because plan did not provide for full payment of claim). *But see In re Bonanno*, 78 B.R. 52 (Bankr. E.D. Pa. 1987) (chapter 13 plan providing that stay would continue throughout plan was binding upon creditors who did not object to it despite plan's failure to provide for full payment); *In re Weaver*, 8 B.R. 803 (Bankr. S.D. Ohio 1981) (same). 8 Collier on Bankruptcy ¶ 1327.02[1] (15th ed. rev.). Other courts have

refused to give effect to such plan provisions. *In re Britts*, 18 B.R. 203 (Bankr. N.D. Ohio 1982) (creditor not bound by such a clause unless it specifically adopts plan after notice of clause); *In re Rolland*, 20 B.R. 931 (Bankr. W.D.N.Y. 1982) (such a clause is inconsistent with provisions of chapter 13).

105 However, the codebtor is required to pay the amounts not paid under the plan only as they fall due, and not immediately, if there has been no prior acceleration of the debt. *In re Matula*, 7 B.R. 941 (Bankr. E.D. Va. 1981); Int'l Harvester Employee Credit Union, Inc. v. Daniel, 13 B.R. 555 (Bankr. S.D. Ohio 1981). *But see In re Jacobsen*, 20 B.R. 648 (B.A.P. 9th Cir. 1982) (creditor could sue comaker immediately for amount not included in plan). The stay should not be lifted if the only reason a claim is not being paid under the plan is the creditor's own failure to file a timely claim. *In re Francis*, 15 B.R. 998 (Bankr. E.D.N.Y. 1981).

106 11 U.S.C. § 1322(b)(1); *see* § 12.4.2, *infra*.

107 Harris v. Fort Oglethorpe State Bank, 721 F.2d 1052 (6th Cir. 1982).

108 11 U.S.C. § 502(b)(2).

109 *In re Alls*, 238 B.R. 914 (Bankr. M.D. Ga. 1999). For discussion of whether a plan may separately classify cosigned debts and pay post-petition interest on such debts, see § 12.4.2, *infra*.

110 Southeastern Bank v. Brown, 266 B.R. 900 (S.D. Ga. 2001) (creditor may pursue codebtor for post-petition interest, but debtor may prevent this claim by separately classifying creditor and paying interest through plan); *In re Leger*, 4 B.R. 718 (Bankr. W.D. La. 1980); *see also In re Bradley*, 705 F.2d 1409 (5th Cir. 1983) (holding codebtors could be pursued for interest as it came due; debtor apparently did not argue that unearned interest was not part of the unsecured claim).

111 11 U.S.C. § 1301(d).

important to note that this exception applies to only one of the grounds for relief from the codebtor stay (failure to propose payment in full), and it has no effect if a response to the creditor's motion is timely filed and served. Also, the time limits set forth in section 362(e) for court determination of a motion for relief are not made applicable to the section 1301 codebtor stay.[112] Finally, the burden of proof should be on the party seeking relief from the codebtor stay to prove that the grounds for relief exist.[113]

9.4.5 Exceptions to the Automatic Stay

The breadth of the automatic stay is narrowed slightly by eighteen exceptions listed in section 362(b). Many of these exceptions have little bearing in consumer cases (such as those concerning commodity futures or Department of Housing and Urban Development foreclosures on multiple-family dwellings). Some, though, are occasionally significant.

The stay does not automatically prohibit commencement or continuation of criminal proceedings.[114] Thus, a criminal case based upon a bad check can continue without violation of the stay.[115] This exception, however, does not necessarily protect a private creditor who instigates such proceedings in an attempt to collect a debt.[116] The exception also does not include the collection of a monetary liability imposed as part of a probation program or as restitution in a criminal case.[117]

However, it is less clear whether a court could, under the guise of continuing a criminal case, substitute jail time for unpaid restitution as an element of the punishment for the crime. The Supreme Court did not fully resolve this issue in the *Davenport* case, but implied that restitution orders may not be enforced during bankruptcy at all and at least two courts have so held.[118] However, if the debtor does not pay according to the restitution order and then fails to either pay the order during the case or obtain a discharge of the debt,[119] the consequences may be severe.

It is unclear whether contempt proceedings are stayed. The answer may turn on the distinction between civil and criminal contempt.[120] When the contempt proceeding is intended to coerce payment of a debt, as opposed to upholding the dignity of the court, the stay almost certainly applies.[121]

Also excepted from the automatic stay is the collection of alimony, maintenance, or support from property that is not property of the estate.[122] Thus, in a chapter 7 case, post-petition income can be collected and retained by an obligee

---

112   11 U.S.C. § 362(e).

113   *In re* Root, 203 B.R. 55 (Bankr. W.D. Va. 1996) (creditor failed to meet burden of showing irreparable harm); *In re* Burton, 4 B.R. 608 (Bankr. W.D. Va. 1980) (citing 5 Collier on Bankruptcy ¶ 1301.01[5][6] (15th ed. rev.)); *cf.* 11 U.S.C. § 362(g).

114   11 U.S.C. § 362(b)(1); *In re* Gruntz, 202 F.3d 1074 (9th Cir. 2000) (*en banc*) (criminal child support proceeding was not stayed); *see In re* Sims, 101 B.R. 52 (Bankr. W.D. Wis. 1989) (incarceration of debtor for failure to pay fine imposed in lieu of jail sentence does not violate stay). For further discussion, see § 9.4.6, *infra.*

115   However such a case may be enjoined by the court under 11 U.S.C. § 105. *See* § 9.4.6, *infra; see also In re* Bicro Corp., 105 B.R. 255 (Bankr. M.D. Pa. 1989) (creditor enjoined from participating in criminal proceeding against debtor when central purpose of creditor's participation had been to procure payment on a debt).

116   *In re* Brown, 213 B.R. 317 (W.D. Ky. 1997) (creditor violated stay and discharge injunction by filing criminal complaint to collect debt); *In re* Muncie, 240 B.R. 725 (Bankr. S.D. Ohio 1999) (creditor violated stay when it initiated criminal charges, its attorney prosecuted charges, and its motive was to collect the debt); *In re* Barboza, 211 B.R. 450 (Bankr. D.R.I. 1997) (state and creditor sanctioned for using probation hearing to collect debt).

117   Pennsylvania Dep't of Public Welfare v. Davenport, 495 U.S. 552, 110 S. Ct. 2126, 109 L. Ed. 2d 588 (1990); *In re* Carlin, 274 B.R. 821 (Bankr. W.D. Ark. 2002) (arrest intended solely to collect debt not within exception); *In re* Washington, 146 B.R. 807 (Bankr. E.D. Ark. 1992); *see also In re* Gandara, 257 B.R. 549 (Bankr. D. Mont. 2000) (§ 549 could be used to invalidate payment made in exchange for dismissal of criminal bad check

case, even if payment was not prohibited by automatic stay). But see 11 U.S.C. § 1328(a)(2) making restitution obligations imposed as part of a criminal sentence nondischargeable in chapter 13. For further discussion of these issues, see §§ 14.4.3.7 and 14.5.5.5, *infra.*

118   *In re* Rainwater, 233 B.R. 126 (Bankr. N.D. Ala. 1999) (granting writ of *habeas corpus* to debtor imprisoned for failure to pay criminal restitution that was provided for in chapter 13 plan), *vacated,* 254 B.R. 273 (N.D. Ala. 2000); *In re* Walters, 219 B.R. 520 (Bankr. W.D. Ark. 1998) (municipality violated stay by arresting debtor to coerce payment of restitution debt); *see also In re* Coulter, 305 B.R. 748 (Bankr. D.S.C. 2003) (state probation department was bound by debtor's chapter 13 plan and was enjoined from holding probation hearing based on nonpayment of restitution provided for in plan).

119   Many criminal restitution orders are nondischargeable, in chapter 7 or in chapter 13. *See* §§ 14.4.3.7, 14.4.3.11, *infra; see also In re* Gruntz, 202 F.3d 1074 (9th Cir. 2000) (*en banc*) (criminal child support proceeding not stayed).

120   One court has held, however, that a federal district court civil contempt proceeding is not stayed. *See* U.S. Sprint Communications Co. v. Buscher, 89 B.R. 154 (D. Kan. 1988).

121   *In re* Goodman, 277 B.R. 839 (Bankr. M.D. Ga. 2001) (arrest warrant arising out of contempt proceeding to coerce compliance with discovery was not part of a criminal proceeding and was stayed; creditor had duty to ensure that warrant was not enforced after bankruptcy filed); *In re* Foster, 100 B.R. 174 (Bankr. D. Del. 1989) (contempt proceeding against debtor for failing to pay a judgment is stayed). *But see* Miller v. Miller, 813 P.2d 353 (Idaho 1991) (state court contempt proceeding against chapter 13 debtor to coerce payment of post-petition support arrearage does not violate stay). *See generally* Henry J. Sommer & Margaret Doe McGarity, Collier Family Law and the Bankruptcy Code ¶ 5.03[3][iii].

122   11 U.S.C. § 362(b)(2)(B). *But see In re* Stringer, 847 F.2d 549 (9th Cir. 1988) (prior to 1994 amendments, exception applied only to collection of support that has been awarded by a pre-petition order and action to modify order is not within exception). *See generally* Henry J. Sommer & Margaret Doe McGarity, Collier Family Law and the Bankruptcy Code ¶ 5.03[3]–[6].

for this purpose, but property of the estate cannot be collected (at least until it has gone out of the estate because it is exempt or abandoned).[123] In a chapter 13 case, on the other hand, because all property acquired by the debtor is property of the estate unless the plan or confirmation order provides otherwise,[124] all actions to collect alimony, support, or maintenance are usually stayed.[125] Notably, unlike other exceptions, section 362(b)(2)(B) does not permit "the commencement or continuation of a proceeding" to obtain alimony, maintenance or support, even with respect to property that is not property of the estate. It permits only the collection of payments.

Some judicial proceedings with respect to alimony, maintenance, or support are permitted under a more narrow exception. Section 362(b)(2)(A) of the Code provides an exception to the stay for the commencement or continuation of proceedings to establish paternity or to establish or modify an order of alimony, maintenance, or support.[126] This exception is carefully worded so that it does not permit proceedings to enforce such orders.[127] However, once an order for current support is entered by a state family court, the bankruptcy court is likely to permit relief from the stay in most cases in which the debtor does not comply with it.[128]

Certain acts to perfect or continue perfection of security interests in property, mainly Uniform Commercial Code (U.C.C.) filings which relate back to their creation, are also permitted,[129] as are proceedings and enforcement of some non-money judgments pursuant to governmental regulatory powers.[130] Courts have disagreed regarding whether some or all criminal or non-criminal forfeiture proceedings come within the latter exception.[131] Even when there is a regulatory action, courts look carefully to determine whether the real goal of the proceeding is to collect money from the debtor.[132]

---

123 11 U.S.C. § 522(c)(1) allows exempt property to be pursued for these debts.

124 11 U.S.C. § 1306(a).

125 Carver v. Carver, 954 F.2d 1573 (11th Cir. 1992) (action seeking to collect divorce obligations from chapter 13 debtor's wages violated automatic stay); *In re* Steenstra, 280 B.R. 560 (Bankr. D. Mass. 2002) (revenue department's attempt to attach chapter 13 debtor's wages and causing debtor's arrest to compel payment violated stay); *In re* Price, 179 B.R. 209 (Bankr. E.D. Cal. 1995) (refusal to terminate wage assignment and continued collection of payments after notification of chapter 13 case violated stay); *In re* Farmer, 150 B.R. 68 (Bankr. N.D. Ala. 1991) (state court order to incarcerate chapter 13 debtor for failing to pay support would violate automatic stay); *see also* Sec. Bank of Marshalltown, Iowa v. Neiman, 1 F.3d 687 (8th Cir. 1993) (property acquired by chapter 13 debtor during case continues to be property of the estate protected by the stay even after it vests in the debtor upon confirmation of a plan). *But see In re* Bernstein, 20 B.R. 595 (Bankr. M.D. Fla. 1982); *In re* Adams, 12 B.R. 540 (Bankr. D. Utah 1981). Both cases hold that only property necessary to fund the plan is property of the estate after confirmation, and that other property can be pursued for alimony, maintenance or support, unless the plan provides otherwise. *See also* § 9.4.2, *supra*; § 12.8, *infra*. *See generally* Henry J. Sommer & Margaret Doe McGarity, Collier Family Law and the Bankruptcy Code ¶ 5.02.

126 11 U.S.C. § 362(b)(2)(A); *see* Allen v. Allen, 275 F.3d 1160 (9th Cir. 2002) (appeal of dissolution proceeding not stayed to extent it sought to modify support).

127 The new exception thus does not affect the holdings in the cases cited above.

128 *See generally* Henry J. Sommer & Margaret Doe McGarity, Collier Family Law and the Bankruptcy Code ¶ 5.03[3].

129 11 U.S.C. § 362(b)(3); *see* Equibank v. Wheeling Pittsburgh Steel, 884 F.2d 80 (3d Cir. 1989); *In re* Yobe Elec., Inc., 728 F.2d 207 (3d Cir. 1984) (filing of mechanics lien permitted when, under state law, it related back to date materials installed); *In re* Boggan, 251 B.R. 95 (B.A.P. 9th Cir. 2000) (mechanic did not have to turn over debtor's car, held pursuant to mechanic's lien because maintaining possession of car was necessary to preserve existence of lien); *see also In re* Parr Meadows Racing Ass'n, Inc., 880 F.2d 1540 (2d Cir. 1989) (pre-petition but not post-petition tax lien interests may be perfected); *cf.* United States v. ZP Chandon, 889 F.2d 233 (9th Cir. 1989) (maritime lien for seaman's wages may be enforced notwithstanding the automatic stay). The result in the *Parr Meadows* case was overruled, for property tax liens only, by the enactment of 11 U.S.C. § 362(b)(18) in 1994.

130 11 U.S.C. § 362(b)(4). 11 U.S.C. § 362(b)(4) was enacted by Pub. L. No. 105-277 (1998) to replace former 11 U.S.C. § 362(b)(4) and (5). Although the language is slightly different, adding entities enforcing the Chemical Weapons convention and references to section 362(a)(3) and (6), it appears that the new language has substantially the same meaning as the former language. Fed. Reserve Board v. MCorp, 502 U.S. 32, 112 S. Ct. 459, 116 L. Ed. 2d 358 (1991) (Federal Reserve Board administrative action to enforce banking regulation is within exception to the stay); Alpern v. Lieb, 11 F.3d 689 (7th Cir. 1993) (a proceeding to impose Rule 11 sanctions on debtor was exempt from stay as an exercise of police or regulatory powers); *In re* Wade, 948 F.2d 1122 (9th Cir. 1991) (state bar's disciplinary action against attorney may proceed under the police power exception to the automatic stay). *But see In re* PMI-DVW Real Estate Holdings, L.L.P., 240 B.R. 24 (Bankr. D. Ariz. 1999) (condemnation proceeding was not within exception for police and regulatory actions).

131 *Compare In re* James, 940 F.2d 46 (3d Cir. 1991) (state forfeiture action involving alleged proceeds of criminal activity comes within police power exception); *In re* Chapman, 264 B.R. 565 (B.A.P. 9th Cir. 2001) (civil forfeiture action was within exception to stay to extent government sought money judgment or possession of property, but government could not enforce money judgment without relief from stay) *and In re* Smith, 176 B.R. 221 (Bankr. N.D. Ala. 1995) (same) *with In re* Finley, 237 B.R. 890 (Bankr. N.D. Miss. 1999) (forfeiture proceeding against debtor charged with drunk driving was civil proceeding and not within police and regulatory powers exception); *In re* Bell, 215 B.R. 266 (Bankr. N.D. Ga. 1997) (*in rem* civil forfeiture proceeding directed at debtor's property was not permitted by exception for police and regulatory actions); *In re* Thomas, 179 B.R. 523 (Bankr. E.D. Tenn. 1995) (post-petition non-criminal forfeiture proceeding that could not have been brought pre-petition was stayed) *and In re* Goff, 159 B.R. 33 (Bankr. N.D. Okla. 1993) (civil forfeiture action that had no remedial purpose and was intended to make money was not within exception).

132 *See* Ohio v. Kovacs, 469 U.S. 274, 105 S. Ct. 705, 83 L. Ed. 2d 649 (1985); *In re* Berg, 230 F.3d 1165 (9th Cir. 2000) (court's imposition of sanctions on attorney was exercise of regulatory

Another exception to the automatic stay allows negotiation of checks which were delivered pre-petition.[133] And yet another permits taxing authorities to conduct an audit to determine tax liability, issue a notice of deficiency, make a demand for tax returns, and make an assessment for any tax along with a notice and demand for payment.[134] Similarly, there is an exception to the stay which permits the creation

of post-petition statutory liens for property taxes.[135] Still other exceptions to the stay exist, but they are rarely applicable in consumer bankruptcy cases.[136]

Finally, it is clear that proceedings and actions pursued by the debtor against others are not stayed.[137] Although this situation may occasionally become complicated when there are claims and counterclaims in one action or multiple parties, the distinction can and should be made; the debtor's action should be permitted to proceed.[138]

9.4.6 Non-Automatic Stays

None of the inclusions or exceptions to the automatic stay in any way limits the general injunctive power of the court, under section 105(a) of the Code, to stay other actions.[139] Thus, if the automatic stay is found to be not applicable to a criminal proceeding based upon a bad check, the court may nonetheless be persuaded that the purpose of the action is really to collect the liability and thus to circumvent the bankruptcy. Some bankruptcy courts have held that when restitution is a likely result, the prosecution of criminal actions can be enjoined.[140] However, several appellate decisions have not looked favorably on such injunctions, holding them violative of the principles of federal-state court comity.[141] One possible alternative method is an in-

---

power); Nat'l Labor Relations Bd. v. Cont'l Hagen Corp., 932 F.2d 828 (8th Cir. 1991) (NLRB order may be enforced by court of appeals except that back pay award must be enforced in bankruptcy proceedings); *In re* Commonwealth Companies, Inc., 913 F.2d 518 (8th Cir. 1990) (government may pursue debtor to obtain judgment, but not enforcement of judgment, under False Claims Act notwithstanding automatic stay); United States v. Nicolet, 857 F.2d 202 (3d Cir. 1988) (government can seek judgment for clean-up costs for hazardous waste site but cannot enforce judgment); *In re* Commerce Oil Co., 847 F.2d 291 (6th Cir. 1988) (state can establish liability for violation of pollution control law as long as it does not seek to collect); Equal Employment Opportunity Comm'n v. McLean Trucking Co., 834 F.2d 398 (4th Cir. 1987) (EEOC can proceed against debtor for injunction including claim for back pay, but would be subject to automatic stay if its monetary claims were reduced to judgment); Brock v. Morysville Body Works, 829 F.2d 383 (3d Cir. 1987) (OSHA citation enforceable against debtor to extent it ordered abatement of safety violations, but not to extent it imposed monetary penalty); *In re* Corporation de Servicios Medicos Hospitalarios, 805 F.2d 440 (1st Cir. 1986) (action to enforce government's contractual rights does not qualify as an exercise of "police power"); Nat'l Labor Relations Bd. v. Edward Cooper Painting, Inc., 804 F.2d 934 (6th Cir. 1986); United States v. Jones & Laughlin Steel Corp., 804 F.2d 348 (6th Cir. 1986); Cournoyer v. Town of Lincoln, 790 F.2d 971 (1st Cir. 1986); Equal Employment Opportunity Comm'n v. Rath Packing Co., 787 F.2d 318 (8th Cir. 1986) (automatic stay does not apply to Title VII actions brought by the EEOC); *In re* Dunbar, 235 B.R. 465 (B.A.P. 9th Cir. 1999) (state agency proceedings to revoke contracting license of debtor if he did not pay restitution to homeowners and pay for state's costs violated stay), *aff'd*, 245 F.3d 1058 (9th Cir. 2001); *In re* Berkelhammer, 279 B.R. 660 (Bankr. S.D.N.Y. 2002) (removal of physician debtor from list of Medicaid-eligible physicians based on non-payment of pre-petition debts was based on pecuniary motivations and therefore violated stay); *In re* Massenzio, 121 B.R. 688 (Bankr. N.D.N.Y. 1990) (license revocation against insurance agent violates stay when government unit uses the sanction in attempt to enforce pre-petition monetary claim). *But see* Eddleman v. United States, 923 F.2d 782 (10th Cir. 1991) (exception in § 362(b)(4) allows the government to take actions which affect property of the estate).

133 11 U.S.C. § 362(b)(11); *see In re* Roete, 936 F.2d 963 (7th Cir. 1991). Even though the post-petition presentment of a check and the creditor's receipt of funds from the debtor's account may fall within this exception to the automatic stay, the debtor should be able to recover the funds as the post-petition transfer is avoidable under section 549. *See In re* Thomas, 311 B.R. 75 (Bankr. W.D. Mo. 2004); *In re* Franklin, 254 B.R. 718 (Bankr. W.D. Tenn. 2000); *see also* § 10.4.2.6.6, *infra*.

134 11 U.S.C. § 362(b)(9). However, no lien may attach as a result of an assessment unless the tax is a debt of the debtor that will not be discharged in the case and the property or its proceeds are transferred out of the estate to, or otherwise revested in, the debtor. 11 U.S.C. § 362(b)(9).

135 11 U.S.C. § 362(b)(18).

136 *See* 11 U.S.C. § 362(b).

137 *In re* Berry Estates, Inc., 812 F.2d 67 (2d Cir. 1987).

138 *See* § 9.4.1, *supra*.

139 *In re* Gruntz, 202 F.3d 1074 (9th Cir. 1999) (*en banc*) (bankruptcy courts have injunctive power under § 105 to impose stay on actions excepted from the automatic stay). However, the Anti-Injunction Act of the Internal Revenue Code may limit the court's power. *See* Laughlin v. Internal Revenue Serv., 912 F.2d 197 (8th Cir. 1990) (Anti-Injunction Act precludes entry of order requiring additional specificity in levy served on chapter 13 trustee to collect amounts due under confirmed chapter 13 plan); *In re* Am. Bicycle Ass'n, 895 F.2d 1277 (9th Cir. 1990) (Anti-Injunction Act precludes a bankruptcy court from enjoining IRS levy of non-debtor attorney's receipts under a chapter 13 plan); *In re* Becker's Motor Transp., Inc., 632 F.2d 242 (3d Cir. 1980).

140 *In re* James, 10 B.R. 2 (Bankr. W.D.N.C. 1980) (criminal case based upon alleged worthless checks enjoined because it would frustrate bankruptcy process); *see* Howard v. Allard, 122 B.R. 696 (W.D. Ky. 1991) (preliminary injunction may issue against county attorney preventing prosecution of bad faith bad check charges); *In re* Cancel, 85 B.R. 677 (N.D.N.Y. 1988) (debtor entitled to injunction preventing state from taking action to enforce restitution during pendency of chapter 13 case). For similar holdings, see *In re* Reid, 9 B.R. 830 (Bankr. M.D. Ala. 1981); *In re* Caldwell, 5 B.R. 740 (Bankr. W.D. Va. 1980).

141 *In re* Fussell, 928 F.2d 712 (5th Cir. 1991) (refusal to enjoin criminal prosecution for "hindering enforcement of security interest" as bad faith attempt to collect dischargeable debt); *In re* Heincy, 858 F.2d 548 (9th Cir. 1988) (court should not enjoin collection of restitution without examining other remedies available to allow restitution payments in the context of chapter 13 plan); *In re* Davis, 691 F.2d 176 (3d Cir. 1982) (injunction not

junction that prevents a creditor from receiving or profiting from any restitution order.[142] If such orders against creditors became a predictable response to the initiation of bad check prosecutions for collection purposes, such prosecutions would soon be few in number.

Similarly, the action of a private employer in discharging an employee,[143] or of some other entity which would affect the debtor's income or expenses, might well be enjoined under section 105 if such an injunction is necessary for success of a chapter 13 plan. An injunction in such cases is not automatic upon filing; it must be specifically sought.[144] A court may also occasionally be persuaded that an injunction against a creditor collecting from a non-debtor third party is necessary for the success of the plan.[145]

Furthermore, the court may use its powers under section 105 to reinstitute the automatic stay if it has previously been terminated.[146] Thus, if the stay was allowed to terminate

through inadvertence, or if a substantial change in circumstances has occurred since a court order lifting the stay, the court may renew all or some of its protections. An order granting relief from the stay may also be superseded by the provisions of a confirmed chapter 13 plan, at least if the creditor has had fair notice that the plan proposes to alter the order.[147]

9.5 Notice of the Automatic Stay

Creditors are notified officially of the automatic stay in the notice of the meeting of creditors.[148] Unfortunately, from the debtor's perspective, this notice is not always adequate for several reasons. First, the notice is not mailed until weeks, and occasionally months, after the petition is filed. Second, when it is mailed, it goes only to creditors listed in the schedules or statement. Landlords or other entities to whom no debts are owed are not included in these lists. Although the notice mailed to creditors by the court explains the automatic stay to some extent, few unsophisticated creditors who receive it have a clear understanding of all of the acts that are prohibited.

The only solution to this problem is for the debtor's advocate to give additional notice of the stay, at least as to creditors and others who might violate the stay without prompt, clear notice. This notice should be sent by certified mail, return receipt requested, immediately after the petition is filed.[149] If time is a critical factor, a telephone call or fax preceding the mailed notification may be appropriate. The debtor's notice can be much more specific than the official notice, tailored to the action the recipient is likely to take. Copies of the notice should be sent to both the party stayed and the party's attorney, so no excuse of communication problems is possible. In the case of the Internal Revenue Service, to suspend or forestall collection actions such as a wage levy, notice should be given to the Revenue Officer on the case as well as to the IRS Special Procedures Staff in the District Office collection branch for the relevant jurisdiction. Lastly, if appropriate, the notice can advise that the debtor will seek to have violators of the stay held in contempt and held liable for unfair practices, with damages and attorney fees assessed against them.

---

proper, but possibility of later relief from restitution order, if not overturned on state court appeal, left open); Barnette v. Evans, 673 F.2d 1250 (11th Cir. 1982); United States v. Carson, 669 F.2d 216 (5th Cir. 1982); Pennsylvania v. Barone, 23 B.R. 761 (E.D. Pa. 1982) (injunction not proper when prosecution stated it would not seek restitution).

142 *See In re* Redenbaugh, 37 B.R. 383 (Bankr. C.D. Ill. 1984); *In re* Holder, 26 B.R. 789 (Bankr. M.D. Tenn. 1982); *In re* Lawson, 22 B.R. 100 (Bankr. S.D. Ohio 1982); *see also In re* Bicro Corp., 105 B.R. 255 (Bankr. M.D. Pa. 1989) (creditor enjoined from participating in criminal proceeding against debtor when central purpose of creditor's participation was to procure payment on a debt); *cf. In re* Roussin, 97 B.R. 130 (D.N.H. 1989) (refusal to enjoin state court contempt proceeding for failure to comply with state court order in aid of execution on pre-petition debt because creditor would not profit from remedy).

143 A discharge or other employment discrimination based upon the bankruptcy or a pre-petition debt is specifically prohibited. 11 U.S.C. § 525(b); *see* Ch. 14, *infra.*

144 However, the 1986 amendments to the Bankruptcy Code now permit the court to act *sua sponte* pursuant to 11 U.S.C. § 105 notwithstanding any provision of the Code providing that a party in interest must raise an issue. This amendment abrogates the rule propounded in *In re* Gusam Restaurant Corp., 737 F.2d 274 (2d Cir. 1984).

145 *See In re* Drexel Burnham Lambert Group, Inc., 960 F.2d 285 (2d Cir. 1992).

146 *In re* Martin Exploration Co., 731 F.2d 1210 (5th Cir. 1984); *In re* Twenver, Inc., 149 B.R. 950 (D. Colo. 1993) (four-part test to establish grounds for injunctive relief must be met); *In re* Bailey, 111 B.R. 151 (W.D. Tenn. 1988); *In re* Casner, 302 B.R. 695 (Bankr. E.D. Cal. 2003) (court issued preliminary injunction under § 105 enjoining mortgage foreclosure to allow debtors time to complete refinancing and modify chapter 13 plan); 9 Collier on Bankruptcy ¶ 4001.03 (15th ed. rev.); *see In re* Gledhill, 76 F.3d 1070 (10th Cir. 1996) (reimposition of stay may be sought by motion under Fed. R. Bankr. P. 9024; adversary proceeding seeking injunction not necessary). The best practice is to continue to proceed on both tracks because the standard for relief from judgment under Rule 9024 and the showing required to obtain a stay under 11 U.S.C. § 105 are not necessarily the same. *See also In re* Krueger, 88 B.R. 238 (B.A.P. 9th Cir. 1988) (court can reinstate case so as to void subsequently held foreclosure sale when case was dismissed in

violation of debtor's right to notice and hearing).

147 *In re* Garrett, 185 B.R. 620 (Bankr. N.D. Ala. 1995); *see also In re* Simpson, 240 B.R. 559 (B.A.P. 8th Cir. 1999) (failure of creditor to appeal confirmation of plan that provided for cure of mortgage default rendered mortgage creditor's appeal of order denying relief from stay moot); § 12.11, *infra.*

148 Official Form No. 9, Appx. D, *infra.*

149 *See In re* Calder, 907 F.2d 953 (10th Cir. 1990) (failure to provide notice together with debtor's continued litigation activity in the stayed action equitably precludes the debtor from later claiming the protection of the automatic stay with regard to that action).

9.6 Enforcing the Stay

It has long been held that actions taken in violation of the stay are void.[150] This principle means that any actions taken after the bankruptcy filing, including foreclosure sales, repossessions and judgments, are without effect.[151] This rule applies whether or not the violator acted with knowledge of the stay, though there are limited exceptions to this general rule.[152]

Courts have the power to undo violations of the stay by injunction, by avoiding post-petition transfers under 11 U.S.C. § 549,[153] and, if appropriate, by ordering other statu-tory and equitable remedies as discussed below. Numerous courts have held, for example, that post-petition credit union deductions or repossessed automobiles must be returned.[154]

The Bankruptcy Code contains a specific cause of action against a creditor who causes injury[155] to an individual[156] by a willful violation of the section 362 stay.[157] A willful

---

150   Kalb v. Feuerstein, 308 U.S. 433, 60 S. Ct. 343, 84 L. Ed. 370 (1940); *see, e.g., In re* Knightsbridge Dev. Co., 884 F.2d 145 (4th Cir. 1989) (arbitration award entered in violation of stay is void); *In re* La. Ship Mgmt. Inc., 761 F.2d 1025 (5th Cir. 1985); *In re* Posner, 700 F.2d 1243 (9th Cir. 1983); Borg-Warner Acceptance Corp. v. Hall, 685 F.2d 1306 (11th Cir. 1982); Butzloff v. Quandt, 397 N.W.2d 159 (Iowa 1986); *see also In re* Smith, 876 F.2d 524 (6th Cir. 1989). *But see In re* Coho Res., Inc., 345 F.3d 338 (5th Cir. 2003) (violations are merely "void-able" and are subject to discretionary "cure" through annul-ment of stay); Riley v. United States, 118 F.3d 1220 (8th Cir. 1997) (responsible party tax assessment was not invalid due to notice of proposed assessment that was issued in violation of stay); Matthews v. Rosene, 739 F.2d 249 (7th Cir. 1984) (when debtor inexcusably and unreasonably delayed contempt petition for almost three years, ordinary rule that orders issued in violation of stay are void would not be applied due to laches).

151   *E.g.*, 40235 Wash. St. Corp. v. Lusardi, 329 F.3d 1076 (9th Cir. 2003) (tax foreclosure auction in violation of stay was void even though bankruptcy case later dismissed); *In re* Schwartz, 954 F.2d 569 (9th Cir. 1992) (IRS violation of stay was void, not voidable); *In re* 48th Street Steakhouse, Inc., 835 F.2d 427 (2d Cir. 1987); *In re* Shamblin, 878 F.2d 324 (9th Cir. 1989) (tax sale held in violation of the stay is void); *In re* Ward, 837 F.2d 124 (3d Cir. 1988) (foreclosure sale occurring in violation of the stay is void); *see also* Lampe v. Xouth, Inc., 952 F.2d 697 (3d Cir. 1991) (legal action commenced in violation of the stay is void and cannot be referred to the bankruptcy court). *But see In re* Siciliano, 13 F.3d 748 (3d Cir. 1994) (court had authority to annul stay in proper circumstances, validating acts taken in violation of stay); Easley v. Pettibone Mich. Corp., 990 F.2d 905 (6th Cir. 1993) (actions in violation of stay are voidable and shall be voided absent limited equitable circumstances); Fed. Deposit Ins. Corp. v. Shearson-American Express, Inc., 996 F.2d 493 (1st Cir. 1993) (even if an attachment violated the stay, an unappealed bankruptcy court order finding that the stay had not been violated was not subject to collateral attack, so that the attachment was deemed valid).

152   *E.g., In re* Smith, 876 F.2d 524 (6th Cir. 1989) (post-petition sale of repossessed car is void even though bank had no notice of stay; debtor found not to have remained "stealthily silent"); Zestee Foods, Inc. v. Phillips Foods Corp., 536 F.2d 334 (10th Cir. 1976). *See generally* Kennedy, *The Automatic Stay in Bankruptcy*, 11 U. Mich. J.L. Reform 177 (1978). See also cases cited in § 9.4.6, *supra*.

153   See § 10.4.2.6.6, *infra*, for discussion of that section. Although a debtor or trustee may not, under § 549(c), be able to avoid a transfer of real property to a good faith purchaser without knowledge of the bankruptcy and for fair equivalent value (unless a copy or notice of the bankruptcy petition has been filed in the county recording office before the transfer has become so far perfected that it could not be overturned by bona fide purchaser) most courts have held that § 549(c) does not protect a transfer that violated the automatic stay. *See In re* Cueva, 371 F.3d 232 (5th Cir. 2004) (section 549(c) does not create excep-tion to protect transfers that are void under section 362(a)); 40235 Wash. St. Corp. v. Lusardi, 329 F.3d 1076 (9th Cir. 2003) (same); *In re* Ford, 296 B.R. 537 (Bankr. N.D. Ga. 2003); *see also In re* Ward, 837 F.2d 124 (3d Cir. 1988) (sale not perfected and therefore not within exception). When a trustee or debtor does not seek to avoid a transfer of property under § 549(c), a non-debtor party having an interest in the property may have standing to seek avoidance of an action in violation of the stay. *In re* Donovan, 266 B.R. 862 (Bankr. S.D. Iowa 2001) (holder of first mortgage on debtor's home had standing to seek de-claratory judgment that issuance of tax deed violated automatic stay because tax deed, if not voided, would extinguish its mortgage).

154   *In re* Knaus, 889 F.2d 773 (8th Cir. 1989) (property seized in violation of the stay must be returned; failure to return it constitutes an actionable violation of the stay); *In re* Smith, 876 F.2d 524 (6th Cir. 1989) (post-petition sale of repossessed car is void); *In re* Hellums, 772 F.2d 379 (7th Cir. 1985) (post-petition payroll deductions must be returned); *In re* Sharon, 234 B.R. 676 (B.A.P. 6th Cir. 1999) (damages awarded for willful vio-lation of stay when creditor refused to return car after tender of adequate protection); *In re* Berscheit, 223 B.R. 579 (Bankr. D. Wyo. 1998) (adequate protection not required as a prerequisite to turnover). Some courts have required adequate protection of the creditor's interest as a prerequisite to return of automobiles repossessed prior to the petition. These issues are discussed in § 9.9.3, *infra*. *In re* Taylor, 7 B.R. 506 (E.D. Pa. 1980); *In re* Brooks, 132 B.R. 29 (Bankr. W.D. Mo. 1991) (post-petition payroll deductions); *In re* Fry, 122 B.R. 427 (Bankr. N.D. Okla. 1990) ($25,000.00 in punitive damages awarded for failure to return repossessed mobile home); *In re* Miller, 10 B.R. 778 (Bankr. D. Md. 1981), *aff'd*, 22 B.R. 479 (D. Md. 1982); *In re* Newman, 1 B.R. 428 (Bankr. E.D. Pa. 1979).

155   *See In re* Roman, 283 B.R. 1 (B.A.P. 9th Cir. 2002) (injury can be as minimal as costs expended in going to an attorney's office).

156   Several courts have held that use of the term "individual" in the statute does not preclude an award of damages under § 362(h) to a corporate debtor. *E.g., In re* Chateaugay Corp., 112 B.R. 526 (S.D.N.Y. 1990); *In re* Bair Island Marina & Office Ctr., 116 B.R. 180 (Bankr. N.D. Cal. 1990).

157   *See* Pettitt v. Baker, 876 F.2d 456 (5th Cir. 1989). In 1998, Congress enacted 26 U.S.C. § 7433(e) which provides a damage remedy against the United States for willful stay violations by the IRS in situations not covered by § 362(h). This new provi-sion will primarily benefit non-individual debtors, because dam-ages for willful violations with respect to individuals are avail-able under § 362(h). The new provision, specifically 26 U.S.C. § 7433(e)(2)(B), also contains some confusing language which provides that administrative and litigation "costs," even in an action under § 362(h), may only be awarded under 26 U.S.C. § 7430, which may mean that exhaustion of administrative

violation is one committed knowingly; no malice need be shown.[158] Even when a violation begins innocently, refusal to rectify it after notice of the case renders it willful.[159] Similarly, a willful violation occurs when a creditor fails to act affirmatively to prevent an action prohibited by the stay, for example, by failing to prevent the sheriff from selling the debtor's property at a post-petition sheriff's sale.[160] In such cases, section 362(h) provides for actual damages,[161] costs and attorney fees[162] as well as, if appropriate, punitive damages.[163]

An issue in some cases is whether the creditor has received actual notice. For damages to be available, the debtor must prove notice of the stay to the party enjoined.[164]

remedies is required to recover such costs. Although IRS regulations define these costs to include "legal fees," Treas. Reg. 301.7433-1(b), this provision mentioning only "costs" should not be read to limit the right to "attorney fees" under section 362(h). Alternatively, the language could be read to simply limit the hourly rate for attorney fees to that found in § 7430.

158 *See* Fleet Mortgage Group, Inc. v. Kaneb, 196 F.3d 265 (1st Cir. 1999) (willfulness does not require intent to violate stay); *In re* Lansdale Family Restaurants, Inc., 977 F.2d 826 (3d Cir. 1992) (willfulness does not require an intent to violate the stay, it requires only that acts which violate the stay be intentional acts); *In re* Ketelsen, 880 F.2d 990 (8th Cir. 1989); *In re* Bloom, 875 F.2d 224 (9th Cir. 1989); Haile v. New York State Higher Educ. Services Corp., 90 B.R. 51 (W.D.N.Y. 1988); *In re* Coons, 123 B.R. 649 (Bankr. N.D. Okla. 1991) (knowledge of bankruptcy case makes action taken by creditor willful); *cf.* 11 U.S.C. § 523(a)(6) (referring to willful *and* malicious acts); *In re* Lafanette, 208 B.R. 394 (Bankr. W.D. La. 1996) (IRS did not willfully violate stay when it diverted debtor's tax refund to child support agency, because IRS had no notice of bankruptcy case). *But see In re* Skinner, 90 B.R. 470 (D. Utah 1988) (actions not willful when creditor received notice of stay, but did not read it; nonetheless creditor could be held in civil contempt), *aff'd*, 917 F.2d 444 (10th Cir. 1990).

159 *In re* Carrigg, 216 B.R. 303 (B.A.P. 1st Cir. 1998) (creditor's failure to return repossessed vehicle after notice of case sanctioned as willful violation of stay even though creditor had not had notice of case when vehicle was repossessed); *In re* Abrams, 127 B.R. 239 (B.A.P. 9th Cir. 1991) (retention of repossessed automobile after receiving notice of the stay is willful); Nissan Acceptance Corp. v. Baker, 239 B.R. 484 (N.D. Tex. 1999) ($23,000.00 damages for refusal to turn over vehicle and applying proceeds of canceled extended service contract to debt); Carr v. Sec. Sav. & Loan Ass'n, 130 B.R. 434 (D.N.J. 1991) (refusal to return repossessed automobile); *In re* Coats, 168 B.R. 159 (Bankr. S.D. Tex. 1993) (county and constable liable for $36,000.00 damages and attorney fees for refusal to release property which had been seized pursuant to pre-petition execution for forty-one days after they received notice of bankruptcy); *In re* Brooks, 132 B.R. 29 (Bankr. W.D. Mo. 1991) (refusal to return post-petition payroll deductions); *In re* Holman, 92 B.R. 764 (Bankr. S.D. Ohio 1988); *In re* Stephen W. Grosse, Prof'l Corp., 84 B.R. 377 (Bankr. E.D. Pa. 1988), *aff'd*, 96 B.R. 29 (E.D. Pa. 1989), *aff'd*, 879 F.2d 857 (3d Cir. 1989) (table); *In re* Maas, 69 B.R. 245 (Bankr. M.D. Fla. 1986). See § 9.9, *infra,* for a further discussion about recovering property after bankruptcy which was repossessed prior to the date of the petition.

160 *In re* Mims, 209 B.R. 746 (Bankr. M.D. Fla. 1997) (creditor had duty to dismiss garnishment proceeding after bankruptcy filed); *In re* Sams, 106 B.R. 485 (Bankr. S.D. Ohio 1989).

161 In addition to recovery of any payments made to the creditor that violated the stay, loss of use damages are available if property is repossessed or retained in violation of the stay.

Similarly, lost wages should be recoverable for time that the debtor must spend in court. *In re* See, 301 B.R. 549 (Bankr. N.D. Iowa 2003) (debtor awarded actual damages consisting of lost wages and travel expenses). Emotional distress damages are also available. Fleet Mortgage Group, Inc. v. Kaneb, 196 F.3d 265 (1st Cir. 1999); *In re* Rijos, 263 B.R. 382 (B.A.P. 1st Cir. 2001) (debtors must be given opportunity to put on evidence of damages); *In re* Flynn, 185 B.R. 89 (S.D. Ga. 1995); *In re* Covington, 256 B.R. 463 (Bankr. D.S.C. 2000) (emotional distress damages awarded without need for medical testimony); *In re* Lohbauer, 254 B.R. 406 (Bankr. N.D. Ohio 2000) ($3000.00 emotional distress damages based on debtors' testimony); *In re* Johnson, 253 B.R. 857 (Bankr. S.D. Ohio 2000) (same); *In re* Lord, 270 B.R. 787 (Bankr. M.D. Ga. 1998) (lost wages due to lack of wrongfully held car, plus wages improperly garnished after petition filed due to failure to end garnishment, plus attorney fees); *In re* Holden, 226 B.R. 809 (Bankr. D. Vt. 1998). *But see In re* Aiello, 239 F.3d 876 (7th Cir. 2001) (debtor could not recover for "purely emotional injury" when there were no other damages); *In re* Stinson, 295 B.R. 109 (B.A.P. 9th Cir. 2003) (to be entitled to emotional distress damages, debtor must have suffered significant economic loss caused by the willful violation of the automatic stay).

162 If the court finds a willful violation of the stay, the debtor is entitled to all reasonable attorney fees and costs; the court does not have discretion to award less. *In re* Stainton, 139 B.R. 232 (B.A.P. 9th Cir. 1992). Attorney fees should include any fees necessary to obtain or protect an award under § 362(h) on appeal. *In re* Roman, 283 B.R. 1 (B.A.P. 9th Cir. 2002). Attorney fees and costs may be awarded against the Internal Revenue Service under § 362(h), at least if it has filed a proof of claim. Taborski v. Internal Revenue Serv., 141 B.R. 959 (N.D. Ill. 1992); *see also In re* Walsh, 219 B.R. 873 (B.A.P. 9th Cir. 1998) (debtor also entitled to attorney fees for work done on appeal); *In re* Seal, 192 B.R. 442 (Bankr. W.D. Mich. 1996) (debtor can recover damages from payments due to the creditor in other chapter 13 cases, if necessary). The Tax Reform Act of 1998 now establishes that the filing of a proof of claim by the Internal Revenue Service is not required for an award of costs and attorney fees in an action under § 362(h). *See* 26 U.S.C. § 7433(e). However, the Act limits the hourly rate that can be recovered for attorney fees. 26 U.S.C. § 7430.

163 *In re* Ocasio, 272 B.R. 815 (B.A.P. 1st Cir. 2002) (ratio of 9:1 between punitive damages and compensatory damages was not excessive); *In re* Henry, 266 B.R. 457 (Bankr. C.D. Cal. 2001) ($65,700.00 in punitive damages awarded against mortgage holder who contacted debtors ninety-three times post-petition); *In re* Shade, 261 B.R. 213 (Bankr. C.D. Ill. 2001) (punitive damages may be awarded even if there are no compensatory damages); *In re* Meeks, 260 B.R. 46 (Bankr. M.D. Fla. 2000) ($35,000.00 punitive damages for repossession with notice of automatic stay); *In re* Timbs, 178 B.R. 989 (Bankr. E.D. Tenn. 1994) (punitive damages awarded against attorney who failed to take affirmative steps to end wage garnishment; actions were willful even if attorney had not understood the law); *see, e.g., In re* Kortz, 283 B.R. 706 (Bankr. N.D. Ohio 2002) ($51,000.00 punitive damages and equitable subordination of mortgage to remedy mortgage company's "belligerent" violations of stay).

164 *See* Price v. Rochford, 947 F.2d 829 (7th Cir. 1991) (commencing lawsuits without notice of the stay is not actionable under § 362(h)); *In re* Abt, 4 B.R. 527 (Bankr. E.D. Pa. 1980) (repos-

A telephone call or fax to a creditor or its counsel provides such notice,[165] though later problems of proof could arise when the notice is not in writing. Similarly, if the filing occurs at the last minute to prevent a foreclosure sale, repossession, or utility termination, it may be a good idea to tell the client to inform the creditor or the creditor's agent directly, at the location of the threatened action. Even posting a copy of the petition on property that is likely to be repossessed should be sufficient notice to the creditor and the repossessing agent.

In addition to remedies under section 362(h), the debtor also has remedies for violation of the automatic stay as contempt of a court order.[166] The legislative history of section 362(h) makes clear that Congress was granting an additional remedy to debtors beyond those already in existence.[167] Neither remedy may be available, however, if it was unclear whether an act was barred by the stay.[168]

Contempt sanctions can be imposed regardless of whether the violation is in willful disregard of the stay.[169] So long as the enjoined party knows of the stay, it is responsible for the consequences.[170] The duty is on creditors, especially those

regularly involved with bankruptcy cases, to establish procedures that ensure compliance with the stay, in order that bankruptcy cases proceed smoothly.[171] Indeed, if either a creditor or its collection agent has knowledge of the case, the creditor may be held in contempt for any post-petition collection attempts by its agent.[172] Additionally, reliance in good faith on the advice of an attorney that actions are not barred by the stay is no defense.[173] Nor is "computer error" a valid defense.[174]

The sanctions that may be imposed for contempt are similar to those available under section 362(h), except that punitive damages are not available.[175] They may include fines and attorney fees, in appropriate cases, against both the violator and any attorneys who advised such violations.[176]

---

session of automobile by several creditors without notice of stay was not contempt). For further discussion of notice of the stay, see § 9.5, *supra*.

165 *In re* Carter, 16 B.R. 481 (W.D. Mo. 1981) (stating that if creditor's counsel had doubts about representations of debtor's counsel, it was incumbent upon creditor's counsel to verify filing with bankruptcy court), *aff'd*, 691 F.2d 390 (8th Cir. 1982); *In re* Coons, 123 B.R. 649 (Bankr. N.D. Okla. 1991) (phone call from debtor's attorney to creditor is sufficient notice of stay to make subsequent violations willful).

166 It is quite clear that a violation of the stay's prohibitions constitutes contempt of court. Jove Eng'g Inc. v. Internal Revenue Serv., 92 F.3d 1539 (11th Cir. 1996) (contempt remedy available when § 362(h) not applicable); *In re* Pace, 67 F.3d 187 (9th Cir. 1995); *In re* Carter, 691 F.2d 390 (8th Cir. 1982); Fid. Mortgage Investors v. Camelia Builders, 550 F.2d 47 (2d Cir. 1976). Contempt proceedings in bankruptcy cases are governed by Fed. R. Bankr. P. 9020. *See* § 13.2.8, *infra*; *see also In re* Del Mission Ltd., 98 F.3d 1147 (9th Cir. 1996) (state found in contempt for failing to promptly return taxes it had been ordered to repay debtor after violation of stay).

167 130 Cong. Rec. H1942 (daily ed. Mar. 26, 1984) (remarks of Rep. Rodino); *see also In re* Skinner, 917 F.2d 444 (10th Cir. 1990); *In re* Wagner, 74 B.R. 898 (Bankr. E.D. Pa. 1987).

168 United States *ex rel.* Internal Revenue Serv. v. Norton, 717 F.2d 767 (3d Cir. 1983).

169 McComb v. Jacksonville Paper Co., 336 U.S. 187, 191, 63 S. Ct. 497, 93 L. Ed. 599 (1949); Perry v. O'Donnell, 759 F.2d 702 (9th Cir. 1985); Vuitton et Fils S.A. v. Carousel Handbags, 592 F.2d 126 (2d Cir. 1979); *In re* Demp, 22 B.R. 331 (Bankr. E.D. Pa. 1982), *aff'd*, 17 Clearinghouse Rev. 1129 (E.D. Pa. 1983); *see also In re* Skinner, 90 B.R. 470 (D. Utah 1988) (actions not willful when creditor received notice of stay, but did not read it; nonetheless creditor could be held in civil contempt), *aff'd*, 917 F.2d 444 (10th Cir. 1990); *In re* Womack, 4 B.R. 632 (Bankr. E.D. Tenn. 1980) (filing fee and attorney fees awarded even though no contempt found).

170 *See, e.g., In re* Kilby, 100 B.R. 579 (Bankr. M.D. Fla. 1989) (landlord responsible for property lost during eviction in viola-

tion of the stay), *aff'd*, 130 B.R. 259 (N.D. Ill. 1991).

171 *In re* Perviz, 302 B.R. 357 (Bankr. N.D. Ohio 2003) (creditor must assure that bankruptcy notices sent to an internally improper, but otherwise valid, corporate address are forwarded in a prompt and timely manner to the correct person/department); *In re* Price, 103 B.R. 989 (Bankr. N.D. Ill. 1989) (IRS threat to levy against debtor violates stay even though notice was generated by computer; IRS had no procedures in place to prevent notices from being sent out in violation of the stay); *In re* Stucka, 77 B.R. 777 (Bankr. C.D. Cal. 1987) (failure to adopt procedures to prevent stay violations rendered violations "willful" and "wanton"); *In re* Stalnaker, 5 Bankr. Ct. Dec. (LRP) 203 (Bankr. S.D. Ohio 1978).

172 *In re* Mauck, 287 B.R. 219 (Bankr. E.D. Mo. 2002) (notice to mortgage servicing agent at payment address sufficient to render later notice of foreclosure a willful violation by both servicing agent and mortgage holder); *In re* Fultz, 18 B.R. 521 (Bankr. E.D. Pa. 1982) (creditor had notice); *In re* Fowler, 16 B.R. 596 (Bankr. S.D. Ohio 1981) (agent's knowledge imputed to creditor).

173 *In re* Taylor, 884 F.2d 478 (9th Cir. 1989). However, under such circumstances punitive damages may not be available. *In re* Ketelsen, 880 F.2d 990 (8th Cir. 1989).

174 *In re* Campion, 294 B.R. 313 (B.A.P. 9th Cir. 2003) (failure of debt collector's computer to match debtor's name with name in its database did not render violation non-willful); *In re* Rijos, 263 B.R. 382 (B.A.P. 1st Cir. 2001) (creditor's "computer did it" defense allegedly caused by installation of new software system rejected); *In re* Chateaugay Corp., 112 B.R. 526 (S.D.N.Y. 1990); *In re* McCormack, 203 B.R. 521 (Bankr. D.N.H. 1996) (computer error defense called a "non-starter").

175 *In re* Dyer, 322 F.3d 1178 (9th Cir. 2003) (although attorney fees may be awarded and mild non-compensatory fines may be necessary under some circumstances, serious punitive penalties not available for civil contempt).

176 *See* Hubbard v. Fleet Mortgage Co., 810 F.2d 778 (8th Cir. 1987) (upholding imposition of $7,649.00 fine, plus attorney fees, plus cancellation of mortgage); Borg-Warner Acceptance Corp. v. Hall, 685 F.2d 1306 (11th Cir. 1982); *In re* Gustafson, 111 B.R. 282 (B.A.P. 9th Cir. 1990) (attorney fees awarded to recompense debtor for action necessary to obtain school transcript withheld in violation of stay); *In re* Timbs, 178 B.R. 989 (Bankr. E.D. Tenn. 1994) (punitive damages awarded against collection agency's attorney under § 362(h)); *In re* Stephen W. Grosse, Prof'l Corp., 84 B.R. 377 (Bankr. E.D. Pa. 1988) (sanctions against attorney upheld), *aff'd*, 96 B.R. 29 (E.D. Pa. 1989), *aff'd*, 879 F.2d 857 (3d Cir. 1989) (table).

Many courts have held that damages for contempt may also be awarded.[177]

Note also that the same actions which can be penalized as violations of the automatic stay might also be unfair trade practices under state law.[178] In some cases it may be a good idea to seek this remedy in the alternative because of the availability of enhanced damages. But, in any event, the bankruptcy court has exclusive jurisdiction over sanctions for violation of the automatic stay itself.[179]

Another issue which unfortunately often arises concerns the remedies available against government entities for violations of the stay. If the stay is violated through state action as defined for purposes of the civil rights laws, remedies under 42 U.S.C. § 1983 may be available against the officials who violate the stay under color of law.[180] Such remedies may be available because a violation of 11 U.S.C. § 362 may be considered a denial of rights secured by federal law for purposes of section 1983.[181] If such an action were successful, then attorney fees would also be proper under the Civil Rights Attorney's Fees Award Act, 42 U.S.C. § 1988.[182]

In light of Supreme Court cases taking a narrow view of the Bankruptcy Code's original provisions regarding waiver of sovereign immunity,[183] there had been some doubt about whether damages are available against state and federal governmental entities for violating the automatic stay. Such issues should no longer arise with respect to the federal government, because the 1994 amendments to the Code specifically abrogated sovereign immunity with respect to section 362.[184] Although the same amendment attempted to abrogate states' Eleventh Amendment immunity, it is doubtful that Congress could do so under its Article I powers.[185]

Several courts have held that when the government violates the stay in attempting to collect a tax claim, the debtor's claim for damages and attorney fees under section 362(h) arises out of the same transaction or occurrence as the government's claim, so that sovereign immunity is waived.[186] At least if the state government has filed a claim in the bankruptcy case, the state should be deemed to have submitted itself to the bankruptcy court's jurisdiction.[187]

Even when remedies are precluded under section 362(h) based on the Supreme Court sovereign immunity decisions,[188] contempt remedies may remain available.[189] However, punitive damages may not be authorized.[190]

One further issue is the best way to go forward procedurally in seeking a remedy for a violation of the stay.

---

177 *In re* Zartun, 30 B.R. 543 (B.A.P. 9th Cir. 1983); *In re* Batla, 16 B.R. 392 (Bankr. N.D. Ga. 1981); *In re* Reed, 11 B.R. 258 (Bankr. D. Utah 1981); Springfield Bank v. Caserta, 10 B.R. 57 (Bankr. S.D. Ohio 1981); *In re* Walker, 7 B.R. 216 (Bankr. D.R.I. 1980). However, damages may be denied when no notice of the stay is given. *In re* Smith Corset Shops, 696 F.2d 971 (1st Cir. 1982); *see In re* Ketelsen, 880 F.2d 990 (8th Cir. 1989) (no damages proved in case in which FmHA seized the debtor's tax refund in violation of the stay; however attorney fees awarded). *But see In re* Walters, 868 F.2d 665 (4th Cir. 1989) (award for damages for emotional distress resulting from contempt is impermissible). Disallowance of a secured claim may also be an appropriate sanction. *In re* Carrigan, 109 B.R. 167 (Bankr. W.D.N.C. 1989) (secured creditor's pre-petition arrearage claim of nearly $5000.00 disallowed and punitive damages awarded). The debtor may wish to argue against such a sanction when the only benefit would be to other unsecured creditors.

178 *See In re* Aponte, 82 B.R. 738 (Bankr. E.D. Pa. 1988). Relief under other theories should also be considered. *See* Vahlsing v. Commercial Union Ins. Co., 928 F.2d 486 (1st Cir. 1991) (damages for abuse of process, negligence and other theories unsuccessfully sought).

179 Halas v. Platak, 239 B.R. 784 (N.D. Ill. 1999) (because state court had no jurisdiction to sanction stay violations, prior state proceeding could not be *res judicata* on issue of whether sanctions for such violations were proper); *see also* E. Equip. & Serv. v. Factory Point Nat'l Bank, 236 F.3d 117 (2d Cir. 2001) (actions based upon stay violations must be brought in bankruptcy court and state law tort claims for same acts were preempted by federal law).

180 Judges and similar officials, however, have immunity for their violations of the stay. *See In re* 1736 18th Street, N.W., 97 B.R. 121 (Bankr. D.D.C. 1989) (city rent administrator has judicial immunity for conducting rent proceeding in violation of the stay).

181 Maine v. Thiboutot, 448 U.S. 1, 100 S. Ct. 2502, 65 L. Ed. 2d 555 (1980).

182 *Id.*; *see also* § 15.5.2, *infra*.

183 United States v. Nordic Village, 503 U.S. 30, 112 S. Ct. 1011, 117 L. Ed. 2d 191 (1992); Hoffman v. Connecticut Dep't of Income Maintenance, 492 U.S. 96, 109 S. Ct. 2818, 106 L. Ed. 2d 76 (1989).

184 11 U.S.C. § 106(a). However, punitive damages may not be awarded under this provision, and there are limitations on attorney fees, at least against the federal government. *See* § 13.3.2.2, *infra*. In addition, the Tax Reform Act of 1998 provides for claims against the Internal Revenue Service for damages based on willful violations of § 362. 26 U.S.C. § 7433(e).

185 See Seminole Tribe of Fla. v. Florida, 517 U.S. 44, 116 S. Ct. 1114, 134 L. Ed. 2d 252 (1996) and § 13.3.2.2, *infra*, for discussion of sovereign immunity and Eleventh Amendment issues.

186 *In re* Lile, 161 B.R. 788 (S.D. Tex. 1993); *In re* Boldman, 157 B.R. 412 (C.D. Ill. 1993); Taborski v. Internal Revenue Serv., 141 B.R. 959 (N.D. Ill. 1992).

187 11 U.S.C. § 106(b); *In re* Burke, 200 B.R. 282 (Bankr. S.D. Ga. 1996).

188 *See* § 13.3.2.2, *infra*.

189 *See* Small Bus. Admin. v. Rinehart, 887 F.2d 165 (8th Cir. 1989) (affirming award of actual damages, costs and attorneys fees); *In re* Colon, 114 B.R. 890 (Bankr. E.D. Pa. 1990) (*Hoffman* case bars damages under § 362 but not under court's contempt power); *In re* Price, 103 B.R. 989 (Bankr. N.D. Ill. 1989) (IRS not immune from suit for violations of the stay), *aff'd*, 130 B.R. 259 (N.D. Ill. 1991); *see also* United States v. McPeck, 910 F.2d 509 (8th Cir. 1990) (§ 106(b) waives sovereign immunity to the extent of the government's claim); *In re* Fernandez, 132 B.R. 775 (M.D. Fla. 1991) (waiver of sovereign immunity under § 106(a) found). *But see In re* Gustafson, 934 F.2d 216 (9th Cir. 1991) (governmental units are immune from money damages for violating stay); *In re* Pearson, 917 F.2d 1215 (9th Cir. 1990) (same).

190 *See* Small Bus. Admin. v. Rinehart, 887 F.2d 165 (8th Cir. 1989).

Although several courts have held that relief under section 362(h) is available by motion,[191] it may be preferable to proceed by complaint pursuant to the adversary rules, especially if injunctive relief or a contempt remedy is sought.[192] This procedure will eliminate any potential issues about the due process rights of the defending party. In many, if not all cases, careful practice requires seeking statutory remedies together with relief for contempt in the alternative.[193]

Expeditious action to protect the debtor's rights is generally advisable, especially if damages may be mitigated, but a remedy is available even after the bankruptcy case is terminated.[194] Prompt action is particularly important if the stay violation involves proceedings in a state court. It is almost always better to seek to enforce the stay in the bankruptcy court, which is usually more familiar with and sympathetic to the stay than a state court, than to allow the state court to rule on whether the stay applies. Although the Ninth Circuit has held that the bankruptcy court can still find such a state court ruling to be erroneous and therefore void as a violation of the stay,[195] other courts have ruled otherwise and refused to overturn a state court's decision.[196]

9.7 Proceedings Seeking Relief from the Stay

9.7.1 Proceedings Must Be Commenced by Motion

While the scope of the stay is broad and the sanctions to enforce it are powerful, the duration of its protections may be short-lived. A common creditor response to the bankruptcy petition is to file a proceeding seeking relief from the automatic stay. The court may grant relief, upon motion of a party, terminating, annulling,[197] modifying, or conditioning the stay. Only the bankruptcy court has the power to grant relief from the automatic stay.[198]

Federal Rule of Bankruptcy Procedure 4001(a) specifically provides that the proper method of proceeding "shall" be by motion under Bankruptcy Rule 9014.[199] Indeed, the stay may not be eliminated without court approval even if the parties agree to relief.[200] The trustee and, if the court orders, other creditors are entitled to notice of any agree-

191 Fed. R. Bankr. P. 9014; *see In re* Zumbrun, 88 B.R. 250 (B.A.P. 9th Cir. 1988); *In re* Karsh Travel, Inc., 102 B.R. 778, 780, 781 (N.D. Cal. 1989); *In re* Hooker Investments, 116 B.R. 375, 378 (Bankr. S.D.N.Y. 1990); *In re* Forty-Five Fifty-Five, Inc., 111 B.R. 920, 922, 923 (Bankr. D. Mont. 1990); *see also In re* Rijos, 263 B.R. 382 (B.A.P. 1st Cir. 2001) (debtors denied due process when bankruptcy court denied motion for stay sanctions without conducting evidentiary hearing); *In re* Elegant Concepts Ltd., 67 B.R. 914, 917 (Bankr. E.D.N.Y. 1986) (court, approving procedure of filing motion for sanctions, suggested that adversary proceeding might be more appropriate, but noted that adverse party raised no procedural objections and thereby waived any procedural irregularity); *In re* Herbert, 61 B.R. 44, 45 (Bankr. W.D. La. 1986) (because creditor was properly served under Rule 9014 and creditor failed to raise any procedural objections, motion for sanctions was appropriate, even if, as court suggested, adversary proceeding was more appropriate).
192 Fed. R. Bankr. P. 7001–7087.
193 *See, e.g.,* Forms 24, 25, 27, Appx. G.4, *infra.* See also § 13.2.8, *infra,* concerning the contempt power of the bankruptcy court.
194 Price v. Rochford, 947 F.2d 829 (7th Cir. 1991); *In re* Davis, 177 B.R. 907 (B.A.P. 9th Cir. 1995). In some instances the case may need to be reopened pursuant to 11 U.S.C. § 350(b).
195 *In re* Gruntz, 202 F.3d 1074 (9th Cir. 2000) (*en banc*); *accord In re* Rainwater, 233 B.R. 126 (Bankr. N.D. Ala. 1999), *vacated,* 254 B.R. 273 (N.D. Ala. 2000); *see also In re* Dunbar, 245 F.3d 1058 (9th Cir. 2001) (administrative agency ruling).
196 *E.g., In re* Singleton, 230 B.R. 533 (B.A.P. 6th Cir. 1999); *see also In re* Coho Res., Inc., 345 F.3d 338 (5th Cir. 2003) (state courts have jurisdiction to determine whether a pending action is stayed by a ruling of the bankruptcy court, but should consider deferring close questions involving the applicability of the automatic stay to the bankruptcy court).

197 Annulment of the stay is usually sought by parties seeking to validate an innocent violation of the stay in circumstances in which relief from the stay would have been granted, if it had been sought. *See In re* Soares, 107 F.3d 969 (1st Cir. 1997) (annulment should not be granted to validate foreclosure when mortgagee knew of bankruptcy and failed to inform state court); Franklin v. Office of Thrift Supervision, 31 F.3d 1020 (10th Cir. 1994) (power to annul stay should rarely be used, probably only in cases of claimants who were honestly ignorant of stay); *In re* Siciliano, 13 F.3d 748 (3d Cir. 1994) (court had authority to annul stay in proper circumstances); *In re* Melendez Colon, 265 B.R. 639 (B.A.P. 1st Cir. 2001) (decision to annul stay made without request from creditor or opportunity for debtor to argue issue was abuse of discretion); *In re* Brown, 251 B.R. 916 (Bankr. M.D. Ga. 2000) (party seeking annulment of stay has burden of proving that annulment would not negatively impact any other creditors); *In re* Adams, 215 B.R. 194 (Bankr. W.D. Mo. 1997) (although creditor innocently violated stay, annulment not granted when relief from the stay would not have been granted had it been sought).
198 *In re* Gruntz, 202 F.3d 1074 (9th Cir. 2000) (*en banc*).
199 Fed. R. Bankr. P. 4001(a)(1). Normally this motion should be heard in the bankruptcy court where the bankruptcy case is pending, although other courts may have concurrent jurisdiction over some of the issues that arise. *In re* Baldwin-United Corp. Litig., 765 F.2d 343 (2d Cir. 1985); *see In re* LPM Corp., 300 F.3d 1134 (9th Cir. 2002) (prior order directing debtor to pay rent was not order granting relief from stay, so execution on debtor's bank account when debtor did not pay violated stay); *see also* NLT Computer Services Corp. v. Capital Computer Sys., Inc., 755 F.2d 1253 (6th Cir. 1985) (fact that monies had been paid into district court registry did not remove them from jurisdiction of bankruptcy court once a bankruptcy was filed). One court of appeals has held that, at least in some cases when a motion for relief has been filed, an oral order granting relief from the stay is sufficient, even if it is not memorialized by a subsequent written order. Noli v. Comm'r of Internal Revenue Serv., 860 F.2d 1521 (9th Cir. 1988).
200 *In re* Fugazy Express, 982 F.2d 769 (2d Cir. 1992).

ment to terminate the stay before it is approved, if a motion for relief from stay was not previously served.[201] For the same reason, a pre-petition agreement by the debtor that the stay will not apply to a particular creditor cannot be enforced.[202]

The rule dictating that a motion be filed to seek relief reflects the view that, due to the expedited treatment that the Code affords to stay litigation, a request for relief from the stay should be a discrete proceeding that can be disposed of without the trappings of a full adversary proceeding. A request for relief from the stay may not be honored if it is filed as an adversary proceeding commenced by a complaint, or joined with any claim for relief that would require an adversary proceeding.[203] At a minimum, the party seeking relief from the stay in that fashion should be deemed to have waived the right to a prompt hearing, because the normal timetable for an adversary proceeding does not accommodate the deadlines of Code section 362(e).[204] If such ancillary claims are permitted at all, they should normally be deferred until after the creditor's right to relief from the stay has been determined, so that the debtor does not lose discovery rights and other rights available in adversary proceedings.

Rule 9014 provides that no answer is required to a motion, unless the court directs otherwise.[205] Nonetheless, it is often useful to file an answer in order to frame the issues to be presented as defenses to the motion. Moreover, some courts grant relief by default when answers are not filed, despite the clear contrary language of the rules.[206] Because

Rule 9014 provides only that there be "notice and opportunity for hearing," it is usually wise to file at least a request for a hearing on the motion. Local rules and practice should be checked carefully in this regard.

9.7.2 Time Limits for Court Actions

The Code sets out strict time limits for stay litigation involving stays of acts against property. Section 362(e) provides that at least a preliminary hearing on a request for relief from the stay must be held within thirty days; if that hearing is not held, the stay is automatically terminated.[207] If the court at the preliminary hearing finds that there is a "reasonable likelihood that the party opposing relief" from the stay will prevail in the stay litigation, the stay can be continued until the conclusion of a final hearing. This finding may sometimes be made without the taking of evidence,[208] but there must be at least an opportunity for the movant to be heard.[209]

Under a 1994 amendment to the Code, the final hearing must be concluded within thirty days after the conclusion of the preliminary hearing. If it is not, the stay of acts against property is terminated unless the thirty day period is extended with the consent of the parties or for a specific time that the court finds is required by compelling circumstances.[210]

These time limits were meant to prevent a bankruptcy judge from simply ignoring a motion to lift the stay and thus denying the moving party an appealable order through which to seek review. However, there still may be ways in which the time limits can be avoided by a court that is determined to take longer to decide a stay motion. First, parties may be pressured into "consenting" to a continuance of the hearing; few litigants can refuse a judge's strong suggestion that they agree to a postponement. Second, the time period runs from the conclusion of the preliminary hearing. A court may fail to conclude that hearing, while finding that the stay should be continued pending a final hearing, thereby preventing the commencement of the thirty-day period. Finally, it is not clear that conclusion of a hearing is the same thing as rendering a decision on the stay motion. A court may be able to conclude the hearing but reserve decision on the motion for relief from the stay for a longer period of time.

---

201 Fed. R. Bankr. P. 4001(d).

202 Farm Credit of Cent. Fla., ACA v. Polk, 160 B.R. 870 (M.D. Fla. 1993); *see also In re* Riley, 188 B.R. 191 (Bankr. D.S.C. 1995) (pre-petition agreement to waive protections of automatic stay could not be enforced after cure of default that gave rise to agreement); *In re* Madison, 184 B.R. 686 (Bankr. E.D. Pa. 1995) (pre-petition agreement not to file a bankruptcy case for 180 days was void because it violated public policy).

203 These types of claims for relief are listed in Fed. R. Bankr. P. 7001. *See, e.g., In re* Harvey, 13 B.R. 608 (Bankr. M.D. Fla. 1980) (stay proceeding dismissed when commenced in improper form). *But see* Pursifull v. Eakin, 814 F.2d 1501 (10th Cir. 1987) (relief from stay proper on motion to abstain in adversary proceeding when trustee had notice such relief would be sought).

204 *In re* Med. Plaza Associates, 67 B.R. 879 (W.D. Mo. 1986); *see* 9 Collier on Bankruptcy ¶ 4001.02[1] (15th ed. rev.).

205 The rule previously required a specific court order that an answer be filed, but was amended so courts could require answers to motion by local rule. *See In re* Allstar Bldg. Products, 809 F.2d 1534 (11th Cir. 1987) (decided under prior wording of rule), *rev'd on other grounds,* 834 F.2d 898 (11th Cir. 1987) (*en banc*). In most other respects, proceedings under Rule 9014 are covered by the same rules as adversary proceedings, which in general conform to the Federal Rules of Civil Procedure. *See* Fed. R. Bankr. P. 9014, 7001–7087; § 1.4.2, *supra.*

206 It is, of course, also inappropriate for a court to enter relief from the stay on the basis of an *ex parte* affidavit, except in the limited circumstances described in Fed. R. Bankr. P. 4001(a)(2) [for-

merly Rule 4001(a)(3)]. *See* First Republicbank Dallas v. Gargyle Corp., 91 B.R. 398 (N.D. Tex. 1988).

207 *In re* Wedgewood Realty Group, Ltd., 878 F.2d 693 (3d Cir. 1989); *In re* River Hills Apartments Fund, 813 F.2d 702 (5th Cir. 1987); *see also In re* Looney, 823 F.2d 788 (4th Cir. 1987) (overcrowded docket does not excuse failure to meet time limits).

208 Satter v. KDT Indus., 28 B.R. 374 (S.D.N.Y. 1982).

209 *In re* Looney, 823 F.2d 788 (4th Cir. 1987).

210 11 U.S.C. § 362(e).

Several important points must be remembered with respect to these time limits. First, they apply only to the automatic stay. A judge may always reinstitute that stay by order, or issue a separate injunction staying certain acts.[211] Second, they apply only to the stay of acts against property. Third, while the section 1301 stay of actions against codebtors in chapter 13 cases may also be challenged under the rules by a motion,[212] the time limits in section 362 do not apply to such a proceeding,[213] nor would they apply to any other request for relief joined with a request for relief from the stay. For such other relief, which might require a more extensive final determination of rights, a slower pace is permitted for the remainder of the proceedings. Finally, the time limits may be waived by the party seeking relief, either explicitly or implicitly.[214]

9.7.3 Defending Against Motions for Relief from the Stay

9.7.3.1 Procedural Questions

9.7.3.1.1 Parties

Normally, any proceeding must include as parties all persons who will be ordered by the court to do something or whose interests will be seriously affected if the action is successful. Thus, both Federal Rule of Civil Procedure 19 and Federal Rule of Bankruptcy Procedure 7019 generally provide that such indispensable parties must be joined. While these rules are not specifically incorporated in Federal Rule of Bankruptcy Procedure 9014, that rule does provide that notice shall be given to the party against whom relief is sought.[215]

In a proceeding for relief from the stay it seems clear that joinder of the debtor and the trustee is almost always necessary. The former typically has possession of property, or will be the defendant in legal proceedings if the stay is lifted, and usually has a strong interest in continuation of the stay. The latter also has at least a possible interest in almost every case involving property. Indeed, because of the chapter 13 trustee's important role, the Code expressly provides that she appear and be heard at any hearing that concerns the value of property subject to a lien, a frequent issue in stay litigation.[216]

Thus, one of the first issues which can be raised is whether the court should dismiss the proceeding for lack of an indispensable party. A motion to dismiss on these grounds may be necessary when a motion for relief from the stay has been filed only against the trustee or only against the debtor.[217] In such a case, a good argument can be made that the proceeding must be dismissed so that the thirty-day time limit will begin to run only when all of the proper parties have been notified and joined in the proceeding. Any other result would allow a party seeking relief from the stay to sue only some of the necessary parties, and then to add others when the thirty days is about to run, giving those others inadequate time to prepare a defense.

In some cases there may also be questions about the standing of the moving party to seek relief from the automatic stay. Some courts have held that a mortgage servicing company with no beneficial interest in the underlying mortgage did not have standing to file a motion for relief from the stay and that only the holder of the mortgage could file such a motion.[218]

9.7.3.1.2 Discovery

Either party may take discovery in connection with a motion for relief from stay.[219] Although the full range of federal discovery opportunities are available, the short time limits require that discovery be completed with great speed to be meaningful. The normal time period allowed by the rules to provide discovery is in every case too long a period to wait unless the parties agree that the stay can continue pending discovery. Thus an order for expedited discovery must be sought if any discovery is needed, and it should be granted by the court. Such discovery can then be pursued just as it would be in any other contested proceeding.

---

211 *In re* Wedgewood Realty Group, Ltd., 878 F.2d 693 (3d Cir. 1989) (stay can be reimposed on grounds similar to those which would warrant a preliminary injunction); *In re* Kozak Farms, 47 B.R. 399 (W.D. Mo. 1985); *see, e.g., In re* Fulghum Constr. Corp., 5 B.R. 53 (Bankr. M.D. Tenn. 1980) (preliminary injunction issued by court prior to automatic expiration of stay prevented order of possession to creditors); *In re* Walker, 3 B.R. 213 (Bankr. W.D. Va. 1980) (stay renewed on assumption it had expired due to time limits); *In re* Feimster, 3 B.R. 11 (Bankr. N.D. Ga. 1979); *see also* § 9.4.6, *supra.*

212 Fed. R. Bankr. P. 4001(a).

213 By its terms, § 362(e) applies only to requests for relief from the § 362(a) stay of acts against property. *See In re* Small, 38 B.R. 143 (Bankr. D. Md. 1984).

214 *In re* Alderson, 144 B.R. 332 (Bankr. W.D. La. 1992) (creditor waived benefit of time limits when it set the hearing date beyond thirty days itself and because its motion sought additional relief—abandonment—in addition to relief from stay); *In re* Small, 38 B.R. 143 (Bankr. D. Md. 1984) (party who files discovery requests due beyond the thirty-day period and seeks other relief implicitly waives thirty-day hearing requirement); *In re* Wilmette Partners, 34 B.R. 958 (Bankr. N.D. Ill. 1983).

215 *See In re* Ctr. Wholesale, 759 F.2d 1440 (9th Cir. 1985) (cash collateral order allowing debtor's use of sale proceeds subject to

lien of junior secured party was void when inadequate notice was given to that party and adequate protection was not provided).

216 11 U.S.C. § 1302(b)(2).

217 *See In re* DiBona, 7 B.R. 798 (Bankr. E.D. Pa. 1980) (joinder of trustee ordered on grounds that he was indispensable party).

218 *In re* Morgan, 225 B.R. 290 (Bankr. E.D.N.Y. 1998), *vacated on other grounds sub nom. In re* Nunez, 2000 WL 655983 (E.D.N.Y. Mar. 17, 2000).

219 Fed. R. Bankr. P. 9014.

9.7.3.1.3 Defenses and counterclaims

To the extent there are defenses or counterclaims which reduce or eliminate the right of the party seeking relief from the stay to proceed after the stay is lifted, they should be relevant to stay litigation and raised therein.[220] For example, if a debtor claims that a lien does not exist because it was rescinded under the Truth in Lending Act, the stay should not be lifted to permit enforcement of that lien.[221] Or, if a debtor's defenses and counterclaims reduce the balance owing on an automobile loan to an amount that does not justify lifting of the stay,[222] then evidence of those defenses should be allowed.

Notwithstanding these points, a number of questions existed under the prior law as to whether counterclaims could be raised and determined in stay litigation, due to the narrow jurisdiction of the bankruptcy courts.[223] These questions have not been totally laid to rest under the Code despite the fact that the bankruptcy court's expanded jurisdiction includes such counterclaims.[224]

Thus, an unsettled problem can arise when one of the parties to the case does not feel ready to engage in an extensive trial of the counterclaim. The party seeking relief from the stay may protest that the counterclaims have nothing to do with the stay litigation.

The legislative history of the stay provision points to a compromise solution. The House Report states that the hearing "will not be the appropriate time at which to bring in other issues, such as counterclaims against the creditor *on largely unrelated matters*. Those counterclaims are not to be handled in the summary fashion that the preliminary hearing under this provision will be."[225]

Thus Congress apparently contemplated that counterclaims and defenses on related matters should be considered in stay litigation. The new rules can be read consistently with this approach. While they do foreclose the actual pleading of counterclaims in response to a motion, they certainly do not preclude the debtor from raising the existence of defenses and counterclaims in defending against the motion. If the counterclaims and defenses are related to the creditor's claim, they can then be considered to the extent it is necessary to determine whether they are reasonably likely to be successful, as might be done in a preliminary injunction proceeding.[226] However, the final litigation of the issues raised would ordinarily be deferred until later in the case.[227]

9.7.3.1.4 Burden of proof

The Code provides that the burden of proof in stay litigation is on the party seeking relief from the stay as to the issue of the debtor's equity in property and on the party opposing relief on all other issues.[228] While this provision is not as clear as it might be, it apparently means that whenever

---

220 *See In re* Allstar Bldg. Products, Inc., 809 F.2d 1534 (11th Cir.), *rev'd on other grounds*, 834 F.2d 898 (11th Cir. 1987) (*en banc*); United Companies Fin. Corp. v. Brantley, 6 B.R. 178 (Bankr. N.D. Fla. 1980) (defenses and counterclaims striking at the heart of plaintiff's lien should be considered); 9 Collier on Bankruptcy ¶ 4001.02[2] (15th ed. rev.); *see also In re* Errington, 52 B.R. 217 (Bankr. D. Minn. 1985) (Farmers Home Administration not entitled to adequate protection when it was enjoined from foreclosing by court orders totally unrelated to automatic stay).

221 *In re* Gurst, 75 B.R. 575 (Bankr. E.D. Pa. 1987).

222 The question of how value can play a role in stay litigation is discussed below, in § 9.7.3.3.1, *infra*.

223 *See* Kennedy, *The Automatic Stay in Bankruptcy*, 11 U. Mich. J.L. Reform 230–232 (1978).

224 See generally § 13.2, *infra*, for discussion of bankruptcy court jurisdiction.

225 H.R. Rep. No. 95-595, at 344 (1977) (emphasis supplied). The Senate Report, S. Rep. No. 95-989, at 55 (1978), is somewhat more restrictive, but should not be considered meaningful because the Senate Bill did not include the expanded jurisdiction of the final statute. *See also In re* Montgomery, 262 B.R. 772 (B.A.P. 8th Cir. 2001) (transfer avoidance claims must be litigated in separate proceeding, and failure to have filed such proceeding may have influenced court to grant relief from stay).

226 Payment Plans, Inc. v. Strell, 717 F.2d 25 (2d Cir. 1983) (fact that creditor's lien was unperfected considered in denying relief from stay); *In re* Bialac, 694 F.2d 625, 627 (9th Cir. 1982) (when debtor's defenses and counterclaims directly involve question of debtor's equity, they should be heard in stay proceeding); Societa Internazionale Turismo v. Lockwood, 14 B.R. 374 (Bankr. E.D.N.Y. 1981) (creditor denied relief on ground that it had "no real claim" even though it had state court default judgment); *see also In re* Rice, 82 B.R. 623 (Bankr. S.D. Ga. 1987) (relief from stay must be denied if evidence supports conclusion that lien will be held invalid in a collateral proceeding); *In re* Gellert, 55 B.R. 970 (Bankr. D.N.H. 1985) (continuing the stay on the ground of an available defense to the claim requires a showing analogous to the showing necessary for a preliminary injunction including "likelihood of success on the merits"). *But see* Farm Credit Bank of Omaha v. Franzen, 926 F.2d 762 (8th Cir. 1991) (counterclaims previously concluded in state court proceeding cannot be considered). *See generally Using Consumer Defenses In Response to a Motion for Relief From Stay in Chapter 13*, 12 NCLC REPORTS *Bankruptcy and Foreclosures Ed.* 29 (Sept./Oct. 1993).

227 3 Collier on Bankruptcy ¶ 362.08[6] (15th ed. rev.) seems to interpret the legislative history similarly, stating that a *res judicata* determination on counterclaims should not be made when the court decides on relief from the stay, but that they may be raised and considered by the court at that time. *See* Grella v. Salem Five Cent Sav. Bank, 42 F.3d 26 (1st Cir. 1994) (relief from stay determination did not have preclusive effect with respect to trustee's preference claim); Estate Constr. Co. v. Miller & Smith Holding Co., 14 F.3d 213 (4th Cir. 1994) (failure to raise fraud claim at hearing on relief from stay did not preclude raising it in a later proceeding); D-1 Enterprises, Inc. v. Commercial State Bank, 864 F.2d 36 (5th Cir. 1989) (order granting relief from stay did not resolve debtor's lender liability claim against creditor); *In re* Vigil, 250 B.R. 394 (Bankr. D.N.M. 2000) (determination that debt was in nature of alimony, maintenance or support in stay proceedings was not binding in later dischargeability proceeding).

228 11 U.S.C. § 362(g); *see In re* Allstar Bldg. Products, Inc., 834 F.2d 898 (11th Cir. 1987) (*en banc*) (party opposing creditor's motion for relief has burden on claim that security interest is not properly perfected).

equity is at issue, the party seeking relief must prove it. Thus, if the question of equity is central to whether a creditor's interest is adequately protected from harm because of the stay, the creditor probably must prove that the debtor lacks sufficient equity to provide adequate protection.[229] If a debtor asserts that equity in a property by itself provides adequate protection, as discussed below, and the creditor fails to offer sufficient evidence on the question of equity, the debtor should prevail.[230]

Regardless of which party has the ultimate burden of proof on a motion for relief from stay, the creditor always must carry an initial burden of production on the grounds alleged for the motion. A creditor's failure to carry this burden of going forward to show grounds for relief should result in a decision for the debtor.[231]

9.7.3.1.5 Effect of prior bankruptcy cases involving the same debtor

One problem that has received substantial judicial attention is the repetitious filing in bad faith of new bankruptcy petitions by debtors seeking to reinvoke the automatic stay after it has been lifted in their earlier cases. In their zeal to prevent this abuse, a few bankruptcy courts ruled that a determination between two parties in a prior proceeding for relief from the automatic stay was *res judicata* as to all future stay litigation between those parties.[232] These courts went so far as to hold that the prior determination prevented

a new stay from even coming into effect in a new case.[233] According to those decisions, the only possible remedy for a debtor seeking to invoke the stay in a new or converted case would be to obtain relief from the prior judgment under Federal Rule of Bankruptcy Procedure 9024, which incorporates the standards of Federal Rule of Civil Procedure 60.[234]

Such holdings were incorrect and have largely been rejected or overruled.[235] The principles of *res judicata* apply only if a later proceeding involves the same transactional facts.[236] Yet, under the cases discussed above, a debtor would be forever barred from invoking the stay by a new petition, even in a new case several years later when the debtor's circumstances had changed dramatically and the prior default with the creditor had been totally cured. When there is any change of circumstances, *res judicata* is not applicable.[237]

The appropriate principles to look to in this situation are those of collateral estoppel (also known as issue preclusion). To the extent that the facts and the law have been actually litigated and determined, were essential to the judgment in the previous case, and have not changed since then, the parties are bound by those determinations.[238] However, if factual or legal issues were not previously litigated, either because of changed circumstances or because a default judgment was entered in the previous proceeding,[239] those issues must be decided in the second proceeding for relief from the stay.

A few courts, mostly located in the Central District of California, have concluded that they have power to make and enforce *in rem* orders as to the property against which

---

229 3 Collier on Bankruptcy ¶ 362.10 (15th ed. rev.). *But see In re* Gauvin, 24 B.R. 578 (B.A.P. 9th Cir. 1982) (debtor always has burden on adequate protection).

230 *In re* Raymond, 99 B.R. 819 (Bankr. S.D. Ohio 1989); *In re* Boisvert, 4 B.R. 664 (Bankr. D. Mass. 1980).

231 *In re* Anthem Communities/RBG, Ltd. Liab. Co., 267 B.R. 867 (Bankr. D. Colo. 2001) (court denied relief *sua sponte* to creditor who failed to meet initial burden of production); *see, e.g., In re* Sonnax Indus., Inc., 907 F.2d 1280 (2d Cir. 1990).

232 In a related development, some creditor attorneys have attempted to obtain stipulations from debtors in one bankruptcy which preclude the same debtors from invoking the automatic stay in future bankruptcies. Although it should go without saying that such stipulations should be assiduously avoided in the first instance, when they have been entered it should be argued that they are void. Among the arguments against the validity of such stipulations are that the provisions of 11 U.S.C. § 362 are mandatory upon filing and that the benefits of the stay cannot be waived. Allowing waiver would encourage creditors to attempt to impose a pre-bankruptcy waiver in many form contracts, in which there is a significant imbalance in bargaining power. Farm Credit of Cent. Fla., ACA v. Polk, 160 B.R. 870 (M.D. Fla. 1994) (pre-petition agreement by debtor not to contest motion for relief from stay in any later bankruptcy was not self-executing or binding on the debtor); *see also In re* Pease, 195 B.R. 431 (Bankr. D. Neb. 1996) (pre-petition contractual provision that waived automatic stay was unenforceable). *But see In re* Franklin, 802 F.2d 324 (9th Cir. 1986) (bankruptcy court has jurisdiction to construe stipulation entered in prior bankruptcy).

233 *In re* Bystrek, 17 B.R. 894 (Bankr. E.D. Pa. 1982).

234 *In re* Durkalek, 21 B.R. 618 (Bankr. E.D. Pa. 1982).

235 *In re* Taylor, 77 B.R. 237 (B.A.P. 9th Cir. 1987); *In re* Norris, 39 B.R. 85 (E.D. Pa. 1984); *In re* Artishon, 39 B.R. 890 (Bankr. D. Minn. 1984).

236 Restatement (Second) of Judgments § 24 cmt. f; *accord In re* Darling, 141 B.R. 239 (Bankr. M.D. Fla. 1992) (stay motion in chapter 11 case involved different issues than previously granted stay motion of same creditor in same debtor's prior chapter 7 case).

237 *In re* Bumpass, 28 B.R. 597 (Bankr. S.D.N.Y. 1983); *see also In re* Metz, 820 F.2d 1495 (9th Cir. 1987) (filing of successive bankruptcies does not necessarily show bad faith and may be perfectly proper); *In re* Johnson, 708 F.2d 865 (2d Cir. 1983) (court must inquire into facts to determine if change of circumstances occurred before concluding that second chapter 13 case is improper after dismissal of earlier case); *In re* Chisum, 68 B.R. 471 (B.A.P. 9th Cir. 1986) (filing four successive bankruptcies was not in bad faith when changed circumstances explained each filing), *aff'd*, 847 F.2d 597 (9th Cir. 1988); *cf. In re* Strause, 97 B.R. 22 (Bankr. S.D. Cal. 1989) (existence of pending chapter 7 case when chapter 13 case is filed is not automatic ground for relief from stay; court must determine whether chapter 13 case is in bad faith).

238 Restatement (Second) of Judgments § 27.

239 A default judgment does not meet the requirement that issues be actually litigated, so collateral estoppel does not apply. Restatement (Second) of Judgments § 27 cmt. e.

relief from stay is requested if there has been a consistent pattern of abusive refiling.[240] Such orders purport to grant stay relief to the creditor with respect to the property involved such that no new automatic stay can arise which affects that property. The grounds for this practice are questionable for many of the same reasons because, when entering such an order, the court may determine the rights of unknown parties who are not present in the bankruptcy process. In addition, the grounds and scope for stay relief are set out in detail in the Code and rules in a way which seems to preclude judges from fashioning additional equitable remedies. As for the unwarranted filing of new petitions in bad faith, there are other ways of dealing with the problem. The court has ample sanctions, strengthened by the Federal Rules of Bankruptcy Procedure,[241] to discourage this practice.

In addition, Code section 109(g) provides statutory guidelines which explicitly articulate the standard for determining when repeat filings are not permissible. That section renders ineligible for relief under the Code any individual who within the previous 180 days has 1) suffered dismissal of a case for *willful* failure to abide by orders of court or to appear before the court or 2) requested and obtained *voluntary* dismissal "following" the filing of a request for relief from the section 362 stay. A companion provision in section 349(a) makes clear that, except as provided in section 109(g), the dismissal of a case, whether voluntary or involuntary, does not prejudice the debtor with regard to the filing of a subsequent petition.[242] These provisions make clear that a court does not have authority to enjoin debtors from filing future cases or to dismiss repeat filings except under the terms specified in the statute.[243]

These provisions were intended to be carefully targeted only at the type of repetitive filing in which there is rarely a justification for the new bankruptcy. Their precise language should be strictly construed, with careful attention paid to the statute's distinction between voluntary and involuntary dismissal. Thus, an involuntary dismissal following a request for relief from the stay does not bar a new case (unless it was for willful failure to abide by court orders or to appear). And a voluntary dismissal may be willful, but it does not bar a second filing unless it follows a request for relief from the stay.

The limitations on new bankruptcy cases after an involuntary dismissal do not apply if that dismissal was for reasons other than the debtor's willful malfeasance as specified in section 109(g). As the issue of willfulness is usually not litigated when the first case is dismissed, it normally must be raised by a motion to dismiss the second case;[244] the initial filing of the second petition cannot be barred because the court clerk has no way of knowing whether the previous case met the willful malfeasance test. For the same reason, there can be no argument that the automatic stay does not come into being in the second bankruptcy case based simply on an alleged violation of § 109(g).[245] It also would be improper for the court in the earlier case to enjoin a new filing within 180 days, especially if there had been no showing of willfulness in the earlier case, nor any notice that the right to refile would be considered at the dismissal hearing.[246]

Courts have generally recognized that willful malfeasance means more than inadvertence or even reckless disregard for the duties involved.[247] Thus, a dismissal for failure to make payments, or to appear in court, should not by itself bar a new case within 180 days.[248] However, the

---

240   *See In re* Fernandez, 212 B.R. 361 (Bankr. C.D. Cal. 1997), *aff'd on other grounds*, 227 B.R. 174 (B.A.P. 9th Cir. 1998).

241   Fed. R. Bankr. P. 9011(a); *In re* Eisen, 14 F.3d 469 (9th Cir. 1994) (history of prior bankruptcy filings and dismissals justified dismissal of debtor's petition as one filed in bad faith; sanctions imposed on debtor for frivolous filing); *see also In re* Ulmer, 19 F.3d 234 (5th Cir. 1994) (Rule 9011 sanctions imposed on counsel for filing improper petition in violation of § 109(g)); *In re* Taylor, 884 F.2d 478 (9th Cir. 1989) (Rule 9011 sanctions may not be imposed on debtor or attorney for multiple filings absent finding that successive petitions were filed in bad faith); *In re* Jones, 41 B.R. 263 (Bankr. C.D. Cal. 1984) (sanctions of $500.00 against debtor and attorney filing debtor's fifth and sixth bankruptcy petitions); *In re* Eck, 34 B.R. 11 (Bankr. M.D. Fla. 1983) ($500.00 attorney fees awarded when debtor dismissed and filed new case on date of stay hearing). For a general discussion of the propriety of chapter 13 after previous bankruptcy cases see § 12.10, *infra*.

242   11 U.S.C. § 349(a) currently refers to section 109(f) rather than 109(g). This reference is to a prior codification and is thus purely a technical error.

243   *See* § 3.2.1, *supra*; *see also In re* Frieouf, 938 F.2d 1099 (10th Cir. 1991) (court may not enjoin filings by a debtor beyond the statutory 180 day limit but may enjoin discharge of debts listed in prior dismissed case for a three-year period); *In re* Jones, 192 B.R. 289 (Bankr. M.D. Ga. 1996); *In re* Friend, 191 B.R. 391

(Bankr. W.D. Tenn. 1996). *But see In re* Casse, 198 F.3d 327 (2d Cir. 1999) (court has power to enjoin future filings for period longer than 180 days).

244   *In re* Montgomery, 37 F.3d 413 (8th Cir. 1994) (also holding that debtor has burden of showing that prior dismissal was not for willful failure to attend or prosecute case); *see also* § 3.2.1, *supra*.

245   *In re* Flores, 291 B.R. 44 (Bankr. S.D.N.Y. 2003).

246   *In re* Surace, 52 B.R. 868 (Bankr. C.D. Cal. 1985). *But see In re* Tomlin, 105 F.3d 933 (4th Cir. 1997) (interpreting bankruptcy court order dismissing case "with prejudice" as one imposing a bar to refiling within 180 days).

247   *In re* Lewis, 67 B.R. 274 (Bankr. E.D. Tenn. 1986); *In re* Fulton, 52 B.R. 627 (Bankr. D. Utah 1985); *In re* Morris, 49 B.R. 123 (Bankr. W.D. Ky. 1985).

248   *In re* Howard, 134 B.R. 225 (Bankr. E.D. Ky. 1991) (failure to make plan payments debtors were unable to make and failure to appear at creditors' meeting not willful); *In re* Chmura, 63 B.R. 12 (Bankr. D.N.J. 1986); *In re* Glover, 53 B.R. 14 (Bankr. D. Or. 1985); *In re* Fulton, 52 B.R. 627 (Bankr. D. Utah 1985); *In re* Nelkovski, 46 B.R. 542 (Bankr. N.D. Ill. 1985); *see also In re* Hollis, 150 B.R. 145 (D. Md. 1993) (*pro se* debtor's failure to follow rules, due to ignorance of them, does not warrant dismissal of case with prejudice or a finding of willfulness under § 109(g)).

addition of other facts in a particular case may prove willfulness.[249] The debtor must be permitted an opportunity to introduce evidence that the conduct in question was not willful before the court may dismiss a new petition under section 109(g).[250]

Debtors' attorneys have had to litigate how broadly to construe the prohibition of filings after voluntary dismissals when there has been a request for relief from the stay. If read literally, it could prevent a new case even if the debtor had successfully defended against a request for relief from the stay in the first bankruptcy, or if the creditor who had requested relief had subsequently been paid in full.[251] Moreover, there is no time limit as to how long before the dismissal the request for relief may have been filed. Thus, the section could be applicable even when the request for relief was filed five years before the voluntary dismissal and was based upon circumstances totally different than those existing when the second case is filed. In view of the potential unfairness of such results, courts have read a causal relationship into the word "following" in section 109(g), which was used instead of the more common "after" or "subsequent to," and have refused to dismiss a second bankruptcy when the rights of the party who sought relief from the stay in the first case have not been prejudiced.[252]

Finally, some courts have held that if a repeat bankruptcy case is dismissed under section 109(g), the 180 day period from the prior case may either be renewed for an additional 180 days[253] or tolled during the period that the automatic stay in the later case was in effect.[254]

9.7.3.2 Grounds for Relief

9.7.3.2.1 *For cause*

The first of the grounds listed in the statute for relief from the stay is a catchall. It provides that the stay may be lifted "for cause." While it is clear that a lack of adequate protection, as discussed below, is one such cause, the provision is meant to allow courts considerable discretion to grant relief for other reasons. Thus, legal proceedings against the debtor that have nothing to do with bankruptcy, such as child custody cases, would ordinarily be allowed to go forward. Similarly, the court may lift the stay with respect to other activities that will have no effect on the bankruptcy. As a catchall provision, this ground for relief is also used to remedy a variety of other situations in which the stay is not deemed necessary by the court.[255]

---

249 *In re* Correa, 58 B.R. 88 (Bankr. N.D. Ill. 1986) (dismissal warranted when, during previous bankruptcy, debtor had "voluntarily and intentionally" abused cocaine resulting in failure to comply with directives of the court); *In re* Patel, 48 B.R. 418 (Bankr. M.D. Ala. 1985) (the debtor's two prior chapter 13 petitions had been dismissed for failure to make payments).

250 *In re* Bradley, 152 B.R. 74 (E.D. La. 1993).

251 Most courts have taken a sensible approach to this aspect of § 109(g). *See In re* Jones, 99 B.R. 412 (Bankr. E.D. Ark. 1989) (voluntary dismissal after unsuccessful motion for relief from stay in first case does not trigger 180 day limitation on subsequent filing); *In re* Milton, 82 B.R. 637 (Bankr. S.D. Ga. 1988) (motion for relief from stay which was settled between the parties does not preclude new filing for 180 days).

252 *In re* Sole, 233 B.R. 347 (Bankr. E.D. Va. 1998) (§ 109(g) not applicable when no connection between stay motion and dismissal); *In re* Duncan, 182 B.R. 156 (Bankr. W.D. Va. 1995) (same); *In re* Santana, 110 B.R. 819 (Bankr. W.D. Mich. 1990) (dismissal denied when second case filed within five days of prior voluntary dismissal because motion for relief filed in previous case had been withdrawn); *In re* Patton, 49 B.R. 587 (Bankr. M.D. Ga. 1985) (dismissal denied when creditor was not prejudiced and refiling was not "abusive"); *see* 2 Collier on Bankruptcy ¶ 109.08 (15th ed. rev.); *see also In re* Eason, 166 B.R. 793 (E.D.N.Y. 1994) (section 109(g) inapplicable when debtors requested dismissal prior to motion for relief from stay even though dismissal order was entered after motion was filed); *In re* Hutchins, 303 B.R. 503 (Bankr. N.D. Ala. 2003) (refusing to apply strict language of statute when it would lead to absurd results); *In re* Bates, 243 B.R. 466 (Bankr. N.D. Ala. 1999) (§ 109(g) not applicable when dismissal order was entered by mistake); *In re* Hicks, 138 B.R. 505 (Bankr. D. Md. 1992) (section 109(g) inapplicable when debtors requested dismissal prior to motion for relief from stay even though dismissal order was entered after motion was filed). *But see* Kuo v. Walton, 167

B.R. 677 (M.D. Fla. 1994) (court has no discretion to create exceptions to § 109(g)).

253 *In re* McIver, 78 B.R. 439 (D.S.C. 1987).

254 *In re* Carty, 149 B.R. 601 (B.A.P. 9th Cir. 1993) (period may be tolled as a matter of court's discretion, but would not be in this case because creditor sat on his rights by doing nothing until ten months after the second bankruptcy was filed).

255 *See, e.g.*, Claughton v. Mixson, 33 F.3d 4 (4th Cir. 1994) (relief from stay granted to permit effectuation of state court equitable distribution order which had distributed marital assets prior to bankruptcy in light of fact that debtor's estate had sufficient assets to pay all creditors even after distribution); *In re* Robbins, 964 F.2d 342 (4th Cir. 1992) (stay lifted to permit state court to enter equitable distribution judgment, with bankruptcy court retaining jurisdiction to determine allowance of claim created by state court judgment); *In re* White, 851 F.2d 170 (9th Cir. 1988) (stay lifted to allow divorce proceeding to continue in state court; state court may determine spouses' respective property rights but not enforce them); Casperone v. Landmark Oil & Gas Corp., 819 F.2d 112 (5th Cir. 1987) (relief granted to liquidate claim but not to decide dischargeability); Pursifull v. Eakin, 814 F.2d 1501 (10th Cir. 1987) (stay lifted to allow determination of lease validity under state law by state court); *In re* MacDonald, 755 F.2d 715 (9th Cir. 1985) (stay lifted to allow state courts to decide spousal support modification issues); *In re* Busch, 294 B.R. 137 (B.A.P. 10th Cir. 2003) (relief granted to allow state divorce court to determine debtor's equity in former marital home); *In re* Pieri, 86 B.R. 208 (B.A.P. 9th Cir. 1988) (stay lifted to allow landlord to pursue cross-complaint against debtors in state court, because landlord could appropriately set-off her claim against those of the debtors); *In re* Roberge, 188 B.R. 366 (E.D. Va. 1995) (court granted relief to allow determination of vested equitable distribution rights of debtor's spouse in state court), *aff'd*, 95 F.3d 42 (4th Cir. 1996); *In re* Hohenberg, 143 B.R. 480 (Bankr. W.D. Tenn. 1992) (relief from stay granted to pursue divorce, custody, alimony and support in

This section is also sometimes used by parties seeking to proceed with litigation that does affect the debtor's financial condition. In some cases, creditors argue that litigation on a nondischargeable debt should be allowed to proceed. Courts may consider various factors in deciding such matters, including whether the debt would clearly be nondischargeable if the plaintiff prevailed and how far the proceedings elsewhere had progressed.[256] When state court litigation is already in progress, the bankruptcy court may grant relief from the stay on facts similar to those which would justify abstention under the statute.[257] On the other hand, the bankruptcy court may well be persuaded to determine a dischargeability issue itself in a trial before allowing the debtor to be subjected to proceedings in other courts.

Other grounds that might constitute cause may exist when the debtor is only a nominal party in litigation involving others.[258] However, if the debtor's interests are significantly involved, or if there is a possibility of duplicative or burdensome litigation for the debtor, the stay should not be lifted because that action would undermine the purpose of the bankruptcy.[259] Such an action could, though, proceed as to all other parties.[260]

One other type of cause averred in a number of cases is the failure of a debtor to make current payments on a mortgage or other secured obligation. Generally, if the creditor's interest is adequately protected (as discussed in the next subsection), the stay should not be lifted solely for this reason.[261] Obviously, a creditor's refusal to accept payments or inaccuracies in crediting payments also should preclude it from obtaining relief under this theory.[262] Another common response, as discussed in a prior chapter, is to modify the plan to include a cure of the post-petition default.[263] However, if the failure to pay is prolonged or the collateral is depreciating, and there is no prospect for cure, a court may decide that there is no purpose in maintaining the stay.[264] Often, in chapter 12 or chapter 13 cases, the court articulates the reason for relief from stay as "failure to comply with the plan."[265]

The failure to make post-petition payments might also in some circumstances result in the creditor being allowed a claim for a priority administrative expense.[266] However, this claim is important only if assets of the estate are ultimately liquidated under chapter 7 or if the debtor ultimately fails to cure the delinquency, but still wishes to complete a chapter 13 plan.

On the other hand, if the debtor is in compliance with a confirmed plan, the grounds for a creditor to obtain relief from the stay are extremely limited. Courts have generally held that confirmation of the plan is *res judicata* on issues such as adequate protection and that a creditor is bound by

---

256 *See, e.g., In re* Bogdanovich, 292 F.3d 104 (2d Cir. 2002) (stay should not have been lifted to permit entry of judgment on jury verdict and appeals because it was not clear whether debt was nondischargeable); *In re* Wilson, 116 F.3d 87 (3d Cir. 1997) (relief from stay granted to allow creditor to appeal adverse judgment in state proceeding alleging what would have been willful and malicious injury, because appeal was sole means for creditor to pursue case without bankruptcy court effectively sitting as appellate court for state court judgment); *In re* Loudon, 284 B.R. 106 (B.A.P. 8th Cir. 2002) (relief granted allowing state court to determine liability and damages but limiting enforcement of any judgment); *In re* Dixie Broad., 871 F.2d 1023 (B.A.P. 11th Cir. 1989) (debtor's apparent bad faith in filing bankruptcy considered a factor in allowing state court specific performance lawsuit to go forward); *In re* Harris, 4 B.R. 506 (S.D. Fla. 1980) (action allowed to proceed after declaratory judgment that judgment for plaintiff would be *res judicata* on all facts necessary to show nondischargeability).

257 *E.g., In re* Kissinger, 72 F.3d 107 (9th Cir. 1995) (relief granted for completion of trial on large claim which needed to be determined before chapter 11 reorganization could be completed). See § 13.5, *infra*, for a further discussion of mandatory and discretionary abstention. *See also In re* Tucson Estates, Inc., 912 F.2d 1162 (9th Cir. 1990).

258 *See In re* Fernstrom Storage & Van Co., 938 F.2d 731 (7th Cir. 1991) (relief from stay allowed for creditor to proceed against debtor's insurers); *In re* Holtkamp, 669 F.2d 505 (7th Cir. 1982) (personal injury action allowed to go forward when insurer assumed full financial responsibility); *In re* Traylor, 94 B.R. 292 (Bankr. E.D.N.Y. 1989) (relief from stay granted to allow accident victims to proceed against debtor's insurer even though their claim against the debtor had been discharged); *In re* Honosky, 6 B.R. 667 (Bankr. S.D. W. Va. 1980) (stay lifted to extent necessary to proceed with suit against debtor which would be defended by insurance company that would be liable for a judgment).

state court, but other unsecured creditors given leave to participate in state court proceedings concerning property of the estate and bankruptcy court retained jurisdiction to control disposition of property of the estate); *In re* Palmer, 78 B.R. 402 (Bankr. E.D.N.Y. 1987) (relief granted to adjudicate state law matrimonial rights, but not to enforce them).

259 *Compare In re* Hawaiian Mini Storage Sys., Inc., 4 B.R. 489 (Bankr. D. Haw. 1980) *with In re* Cloud Nine, Ltd., 3 B.R. 202 (Bankr. D.N.M. 1980).

260 *See, e.g.*, Stone's Pharmacy, Inc. v. Pharmacy Accounting Mgmt., Inc., 875 F.2d 665 (8th Cir. 1989) (debtor not a necessary party to lawsuit; lawsuit allowed to go forward as to other parties).

261 *See* Household Fin. Corp. v. Adams, 27 B.R. 582 (D. Del. 1983); *In re* Mathews, 208 B.R. 506 (Bankr. N.D. Ill. 1997) (stay relief inappropriate after debtor missed two post-petition mortgage payments, especially given an $8000.00 equity cushion); *In re* Mannings, 47 B.R. 318 (Bankr. N.D. Ill. 1985); *In re* Davis, 11 B.R. 680 (Bankr. E.D. Pa. 1981); *see also In re* Can-Alta Properties, Ltd., 87 B.R. 89 (B.A.P. 9th Cir. 1988) (when creditor is protected by equity, debtor must be given a reasonable opportunity to propose and implement a confirmable plan); *In re* Raymond, 99 B.R. 819 (Bankr. S.D. Ohio 1989) (sporadic post-confirmation payments alone is not ground for relief from stay when no evidence established amount of post-confirmation arrears or value of collateral); *In re* Heath, 79 B.R. 616 (Bankr. E.D. Pa. 1987) (relief denied when creditor protected by equity cushion).

262 *In re* Alvarez, 101 B.R. 176 (B.A.P. 9th Cir. 1989).

263 *See* §§ 8.7.3, 8.7.4, *supra*.

264 *E.g., In re* Wieseler, 934 F.2d 965 (8th Cir. 1991).

265 *E.g.*, Reinbold v. Dewey County Bank, 942 F.2d 1304 (8th Cir. 1991).

266 Grundy Nat'l Bank v. Rife, 876 F.2d 361 (4th Cir. 1989).

the terms of the plan.[267] Even if the creditor's motion would have been granted prior to plan confirmation, the creditor is usually deemed to have waived its rights by not raising them in opposition to confirmation of a plan that did not protect them.[268]

9.7.3.2.2 Lack of adequate protection

Many motions seeking relief from the stay are based on the grounds that the movant does not have "adequate protection" for an interest in property. The provision of adequate protection is a basic concern of the Code, and thus what is meant by that term is of critical importance.

Yet adequate protection is not defined, except by example in section 361. We are told what does not provide adequate protection—the granting of a priority status as an administrative expense claim.[269] Thus, even if the assets of the estate clearly would cover such priority claims, an offer to allow such status is not sufficient. Examples of what can be sufficient include cash payments to compensate for a decrease in value of collateral due to use or depreciation, or providing an additional or replacement lien that is clearly sufficient to compensate any loss due to the stay or other situations in which adequate protection is required.[270]

Adequate protection is probably best described by the Code's language stating that it must insure the protected party's realization of the "indubitable equivalent" of that party's interest in the property in question.[271] While there is no definition of "indubitable equivalent" either, the concept is apparent. In a situation involving the automatic stay, adequate protection has been provided if there is no reasonably foreseeable way that the protected party's interest in the property can be economically harmed by continuation of the stay. Ultimately, whether adequate protection has been provided is a question of fact to be decided by the bankruptcy court.[272]

The Code contemplates that the debtor will propose methods of providing adequate protection that are intended to satisfy a party who might seek relief from the stay. Besides those mentioned above, these might include a cash security deposit, procurement of a guarantor, obtaining insurance,[273] or anything else that protects the interests of the other party. There are no limits on what might satisfy this requirement except those of the imagination.

One of the most common and important examples of adequate protection for a secured creditor is the existence of an equity "cushion." For example, in the case of a $60,000.00 mortgage on a $100,000.00 house, the existence of $40,000.00 in equity provides protection to the creditor. Even if the stay is continued for quite a while, the creditor should still easily be able to fully satisfy its claim, by foreclosure if necessary, when the stay is lifted.[274] In other words, unless the collateral is worth less than the claim or will depreciate so much that it might not fully satisfy the claim, adequate protection is normally provided by an equity cushion. If the possibility of destruction is eliminated, usually by insurance, real estate collateral values will, in most cases, remain high enough to provide adequate protection. With depreciating collateral, such as motor vehicles, it may also be necessary to provide, through a chapter 13 plan or by agreement with the creditor, for periodic cash payments which will reduce the claim at least as fast as the value of the collateral decreases.[275] The court may monitor or reconsider the situation at later dates to ensure that the creditor is protected.[276]

---

267 *E.g.*, Chevy Chase Bank v. Locke, 227 B.R. 68 (E.D. Va. 1998); *see also In re* Carvalho, 335 F.3d 45 (1st Cir. 2003) (bifurcation of a creditor's claim into secured and unsecured portions is not annulled by the mere act of granting relief from the automatic stay); § 9.4.6, *supra*; § 12.11, *infra*.

268 *See* § 12.11, *infra*.

269 11 U.S.C. § 361(3).

270 *See In re* Besler, 19 B.R. 879 (Bankr. D.S.D. 1982); *see also* 11 U.S.C. § 361(1), (2). Adequate protection does not include protection against lost "opportunity costs" incurred by not being able to immediately foreclose on collateral and reinvest the proceeds. United Sav. Ass'n of Tex. v. Timbers of Inwood Forest Associates Inc., 484 U.S. 365, 108 S. Ct. 626, 98 L. Ed. 2d 740 (1988). That decision must be applied retroactively. *In re* Cimarron Investors, 848 F.2d 974 (9th Cir. 1988). A guaranty by a non-debtor party may serve as adequate protection when that guaranty is secured by sufficient collateral. *E.g.*, *In re* T.H.B. Corp., 85 B.R. 192 (Bankr. D. Mass. 1988). Adequate protection is also required in other situations besides stay litigation. *See* 11 U.S.C. § 364(d)(1)(B). However, the discussion here will concentrate on automatic stay cases.

271 11 U.S.C. § 361(3).

272 *In re* O'Connor, 808 F.2d 1393 (10th Cir. 1987) (whether adequate protection provided was a question of fact subject to review under "clearly erroneous" standard).

273 The courts are divided as to whether Federal Housing Administration insurance or Veterans Administration guarantees on home mortgages can constitute adequate protection. *Compare In re* Roane, 8 B.R. 997 (Bankr. E.D. Pa.), *aff'd*, 14 B.R. 542 (E.D. Pa. 1981) *with In re* Britton, 9 B.R. 245 (Bankr. E.D. Pa. 1981).

274 Cases applying this principle include: *In re* Heath, 79 B.R. 616 (Bankr. E.D. Pa. 1987) (thirty-nine percent equity cushion in property appraised at $32,000.00); *In re* Shockley Forest Indus., 5 B.R. 160 (Bankr. N.D. Ga. 1980) (additional security provided collateral which far exceeded claim); *In re* Breuer, 4 B.R. 499 (Bankr. S.D.N.Y. 1980) (debtor's agreement to cure default promptly plus cushion of $21,000.00 were adequate protection); *In re* Rogers Dev. Corp., 2 B.R. 679 (Bankr. E.D. Va. 1980) (fifteen percent to twenty percent equity cushion gave adequate protection); *In re* McAloon, 1 B.R. 766 (Bankr. E.D. Pa. 1980) ($20,000.00 mortgage on $28,000.00 property has adequate protection); *see also In re* McKillips, 81 B.R. 454 (Bankr. N.D. Ill. 1987) (adequate protection payments necessary when equity cushion eroding, but only to the extent of the erosion).

275 *See* 11 U.S.C. § 361(1); *In re* Stembridge, 287 B.R. 658 (Bankr. N.D. Tex. 2002) (adequate protection payments must be credited towards amounts to be paid under § 1325(a)(5)(B) to satisfy allowed secured claim).

276 *See In re* Pitts, 2 B.R. 476 (Bankr. C.D. Cal. 1979) (small equity

There is sometimes a question as to how much of an equity cushion the creditor is entitled to have. It seems clear from the statute that it is not necessarily the amount originally bargained for in the transaction, but rather can be considerably less. The purpose of the provision is to allow the court to decide what is adequate to protect the creditor's interest, even if the creditor once had better than adequate protection.[277]

This consideration in turn raises the question of whether equity encumbered by soon-to-be-avoided liens should be counted in calculating amounts of equity available as a cushion.[278] The better view is that the equity should be considered unencumbered, once the court is satisfied that the liens will be avoided, because the main determinant is the amount of equity that will actually be available to satisfy the creditor seeking relief from the stay.[279] For the same reason, liens junior to that of the party seeking relief should not be considered in determining adequate protection.[280]

Perhaps the most useful concept of adequate protection in the foreclosure or repossession context, because the debtor will often have little or no equity in the property at issue, is the concept of cash payments to compensate the creditor for the collateral's depreciation.[281] This provision of the Code allows the debtor to propose a plan in a chapter 13 case which, in effect, cures or pays off the debt on a car or home. As long as the debtor makes the plan payments, the creditor is adequately protected within the meaning of the Code.

Alternatively, when the debtor cannot afford the necessary plan, it may occasionally be an option to provide an additional or replacement lien which can constitute adequate protection.[282] For example, if the debtor owns two cars and only one is encumbered, a lien on the second may be offered to the secured creditor as adequate protection. Of course, the risk in doing so is that the creditor will then have a security interest in both automobiles rather than just one. If payments cannot be made the debtor might lose both. For this reason, the strategy is advisable only in the most extreme cases.

Thus, in opposing a creditor's claim that adequate protection has not been provided, it is necessary to show that the creditor will not be economically harmed by continuation of the stay. Even if no equity can be shown, the stay may be continued if the creditor's then-current interest is protected.[283] For example, a tenant may offer to make payments on a lease equivalent to what the lessor would receive by renting the property at that time to another tenant,[284] or a debtor may propose payments on an automobile loan that protect the creditor against depreciation.

Finally, it should be pointed out to the court that section 362(d) does not require termination of the stay when there is no adequate protection. The stay may be modified to provide a time limit for some action, or conditioned, for example, upon monthly payments being made or other risks to the property being eliminated.[285] Partial relief may be granted to allow the litigation of certain rights to proceed in state court, with the final issue of the property's disposition to remain with the bankruptcy court. In short, even if there is no possibility of providing adequate protection, every effort should be made to salvage some of the benefits of the stay for the debtor.

9.7.3.2.3 Lack of equity or necessity for effective reorganization

Section 362(d)(2) sets forth one other basis for relief from the automatic stay that is applicable to consumer cases.[286] This ground is limited to acts against property and requires proof of two coexisting facts. These are:

- That the debtor does not have an equity interest in the property; and
- That such property is not necessary for an effective reorganization.

cushion with court monitoring every few months sufficient to provide adequate protection).

277 *In re* San Clemente Estates, 5 B.R. 605 (Bankr. S.D. Cal. 1980); *see also In re* Ahlers, 794 F.2d 388 (8th Cir. 1986) (considering the extent to which a creditor is entitled to adequate protection for potential delays associated with foreclosure), *rev'd on other grounds*, 485 U.S. 197 (1988). *But see In re* Tucker, 5 B.R. 180 (Bankr. S.D.N.Y. 1980) ($6,500.00 cushion on $88,000.00 property inadequate when liens increasing at $25.00 per day, no payments were offered, no insurance was in existence, and no successful plan was likely); *In re* Lake Tahoe Land Co., 5 B.R. 34 (Bankr. D. Nev. 1980) (dicta stating that for land a forty percent to fifty percent cushion is necessary); *In re* Pitts, 2 B.R. 476 (Bankr. C.D. Cal. 1979).

278 For discussion of lien avoidance, see § 10.4, *infra*.

279 Although the decision is vague, *In re* McAloon, 1 B.R. 766, 768 n.12 (Bankr. E.D. Pa. 1980), indicates that the court considered the fact that liens were avoided under 11 U.S.C. § 522(f).

280 *In re* Indian Palms Associates, Ltd., 61 F.3d 197 (3d Cir. 1995) (junior liens are disregarded in determining senior lienholder's equity cushion for adequate protection purposes); *In re* Mellor, 734 F.2d 1396 (9th Cir. 1984).

281 11 U.S.C. § 361(1). When the creditor's interest in the property is declining because of the accrual of more senior liens, such as property taxes, adequate protection may consist of payments in the amount of the debtor's monthly property tax liability. *In re* Busconi, 135 B.R. 192 (Bankr. D. Mass. 1991).

282 11 U.S.C. § 361(2).

283 *In re* Alyucan Interstate Corp., 12 B.R. 803 (Bankr. D. Utah 1981).

284 *In re* Dabney, 45 B.R. 312 (Bankr. E.D. Pa. 1985) (lease payments constituted adequate protection).

285 *See, e.g., In re* Polvino, 4 B.R. 677 (Bankr. W.D.N.Y. 1980) (stay modified to continue, provided debtors obtained confirmation of plan, paid back real estate taxes, mortgage payments, and arrearages, and avoided other liens within six weeks).

286 11 U.S.C. § 362(d)(3) is applicable only to single asset real estate cases, which are defined under section 101 to exclude cases involving residential real estate with fewer than four units.

The purpose of this provision is to allow creditors to proceed against property that is of no value to either the debtor or the estate insofar as the bankruptcy case is concerned. If there is no equity in property that can be exempted by the debtor or sold by the estate and if the property is not needed in a reorganization of the debtor's affairs, there is no reason that the property is needed for bankruptcy purposes.[287]

Conversely, the stay should not be lifted if it protects some interest in property that the debtor may exempt under section 522, because allowing a creditor to proceed outside the bankruptcy court could jeopardize the exemption and thus the debtor's fresh start. Similarly, if there is equity in property that is not exempt, the court usually prefers that it be disposed of in the normal bankruptcy liquidation process.[288] And if the property is necessary for an effective reorganization, the purposes of the bankruptcy reorganization provisions are protected by the continuation of the stay even when the debtor has no equity.

Because of poor drafting, a threshold question has arisen over whether these provisions are even applicable to consumer cases. Generally, the term "reorganization" is applied only to cases under chapter 11 of the Code, usually used for business reorganization. A few courts have interpreted the use of this term to mean that section 362(d)(2) is only partially applicable or not applicable at all to chapter 13 cases, in which the process is usually described as "rehabilitation" or "adjustment of debts" rather than "reorganization."[289] One such court thus found that the stay may be lifted only upon the grounds stated in section 362(d)(1).[290]

An alternative result based upon a finding that section 362(d)(2)(B) is inapplicable would be that the party seeking relief from the stay in a chapter 13 or chapter 7 case need only meet the lack-of-equity ground of section 362(d)(2)(A), because there is no "reorganization" at all. While for most purposes the determination of a lack of equity would also be a determination of a lack of adequate protection, such is not always the case. There may be significant equity over and above the lien of the creditor seeking relief from the stay that would protect that creditor's claim, even if that equity is encumbered by junior liens.[291]

Moreover, because adequate protection can be provided by other means, for example, by periodic payments, permitting the stay to be lifted upon a simple showing of no equity would seriously undermine the concept of adequate protection, by not allowing use of these other means specifically mentioned in the statute.

The more accepted and better view is that chapter 13 cases, at least, were meant to be included within the term "reorganization."[292] This view also received some Congressional recognition by clarifying amendments proposed in both the House and Senate versions of technical amendments to the Code.[293] In terms of the purpose of the stay, it is just as necessary to protect completion of a chapter 13 plan as it is to protect completion of a corporate reorganization, and the term "reorganization" should be deemed to include such cases.[294]

In cases in which relief is sought under these provisions, questions of how property is to be valued necessarily become crucial. Should the property be given a liquidation value, a wholesale value, or a replacement-cost value?[295] As of what date should the property be valued? The answers to these questions, in many cases, will determine whether relief from the stay is granted.

Generally, at this stage of the case it is in the debtor's interest that a high value, such as the replacement value, be placed on the property, to show that equity exists and that the creditor is adequately protected.[296] It can be argued that section 362(d)(2) is at least partially concerned with the possibility of the debtor having to replace property necessary for a reorganization if the stay were lifted and that, therefore, the replacement value is the proper criterion for determining the debtor's equity in stay proceedings.

On the other hand, the debtor's counsel should be careful to assess what effect a high valuation could have later in the

---

287 For purposes of this subsection, equity is the difference between the value of the property and the total value of the liens on the property. Stewart v. Gurley, 745 F.2d 1194 (9th Cir. 1984). However, it probably can be successfully argued that invalid or avoidable liens should not be counted.

288 However, this process could include a release to a secured creditor later in the case if that was deemed in the interest of the estate. 11 U.S.C. § 725; *see* § 11.3.4, *infra*.

289 *In re* Feimster, 3 B.R. 11 (Bankr. N.D. Ga. 1979).

290 *Id.*

291 *See In re* Indian Palms Associates, Ltd., 61 F.3d 197 (3d Cir. 1995) (although junior liens are disregarded in determining senior lienholder's equity cushion for adequate protection purposes, they are counted in determining equity under § 362(d)(2)).

292 *In re* Pittman, 8 B.R. 299 (D. Colo. 1981); *In re* McAloon, 1 B.R. 766 (Bankr. E.D. Pa. 1980); *In re* Zellmer, 6 B.R. 497 (Bankr. N.D. Ill. 1980); *see also In re* Purnell, 92 B.R. 625 (Bankr. E.D. Pa. 1988).

293 A technical amendments bill, S.658, was passed by both the House and Senate in the 96th Congress, but died at the end of that Congress without being passed into law. Later technical amendments in 1984 did not ultimately include the clarifying language.

294 This view is also adopted by 3 Collier on Bankruptcy ¶ 362.07[4] (15th ed. rev.).

295 *See* Associates Commercial Corp. v. Rash, 520 U.S. 953, 117 S. Ct. 1879, 138 L. Ed. 2d 148 (1997) (replacement value must be used in valuing creditor's allowed secured claim for purposes of 11 U.S.C. § 1325(a)(5) if automobile is to be retained by debtor during term of plan). Although the valuation issues are not identical under sections 1325 and 362, a debtor may be able to use this case to advantage in the context of arguing for a higher valuation of property for the purposes of automatic stay litigation. *See generally* § 11.2, *infra*.

296 *But see In re* George Ruggiere Chrysler-Plymouth, 727 F.2d 1017 (11th Cir. 1984) (corporate debtor successfully argued for lower value when it wished to remit that amount to creditor to provide adequate protection).

case. For example, that same high value might well be the amount found necessary to redeem the property from a lien under section 722 or to satisfy an allowed secured claim under section 1325(a)(5).[297] Although it can be argued that different values should be used in those situations because the purpose of the valuation is different,[298] it is likely that the court's earlier determination of value in the stay proceedings will be of great importance.

In chapter 13 cases, the debtor's testimony is usually sufficient to prove the necessity of assets for a reorganization. If the property is a house in which the debtor lives, the burdens and expense of a forced move, along with higher housing costs, can easily be shown to have enough disruptive potential to cause failure of a chapter 13 plan. Similarly, if the property in question is an automobile necessary for transportation to work or other important family business, it is not difficult to prove the deleterious effects on a plan that would be caused by its loss. As for "luxury" items, such as entertainment equipment or a second car not needed for work, the test is somewhat more difficult. When it can be shown that saving the property is a prime motivation for the plan, and that its loss will cause the debtor to give up on the plan, it should be possible to argue that this property, too, is necessary for an effective reorganization.[299] Of course, all of these possibilities are based upon the assumption that an effective reorganization or plan can otherwise be accomplished. If it cannot, then logically the property cannot possibly be necessary for an effective reorganization.[300]

9.7.3.2.4 Leases

Special problems are posed under the stay provisions in cases that involve leases.[301] While it may be quite possible for a debtor to give a lessor adequate protection, perhaps in the form of a security deposit, it is usually difficult to argue that the debtor has equity in the leased premises unless the debtor has a long-term lease at a rate below current market values, or receives other benefits from remaining in possession, such as the special rights available in public housing or in a rent-control jurisdiction. Also, as to the property's necessity for an effective reorganization, it is usually somewhat harder to argue that moving to other leased premises is as great a hardship as losing a home owned by the debtor, because the lease usually guarantees only a short term of residency in any case. (Again, if rent control laws include eviction controls, stronger arguments can be made.)[302]

The greatest problems of persuasion arise because the debtor, by means of the stay, could, in effect extend a lease beyond the term to which she was otherwise entitled, and in some cases retain possession of property in which she otherwise had no rights whatsoever still in existence.

The most difficult cases are those in which the debtor's tenancy and right of possession, but not actual possession, are validly terminated before the bankruptcy is filed. In such cases, many bankruptcy courts have been loath to continue the stay, holding that the debtor has no legal interest in the property and there is no lease that the debtor or trustee may assume under section 365.[303] According to these courts, if the debtor and the estate have no legal interest in the property, then cause exists for lifting the stay, just as it would if the debtor were simply a squatter who had moved in after the commencement of the bankruptcy. They have held that if the debtor cannot assume the lease, perhaps because it is impossible to cure a default promptly as required by section 365, then there is no reason to allow the stay to continue.[304]

Despite these holdings, there are several reasons why the stay should be continued as to a leased property, even if the tenancy has ended or will soon end. These arguments are most convincing in cases in which the lessor has adequate protection and the continuation of the stay is necessary to an effective reorganization. One argument is that the effect of the stay is to nullify a prior judgment for possession and termination of tenancy. Because sections 362(a)(2) and 362(a)(3) in effect prevent any actions to enforce prepetition judgments or recover property in the possession of the debtor, at least one court has held that their intent is to "erase" such judgments and terminations.[305] The stay's provisions are meant to allow use by the debtor of property,

---

297 See Chapter 11, *infra,* for a discussion of these provisions and the valuation approaches they have engendered.

298 In determining the amount of an allowed secured claim under section 506(a), value is determined "in light of the purpose of the valuation and of the proposed disposition or use of the property." *See also In re* George Ruggiere Chrysler-Plymouth, 727 F.2d 1017 (11th Cir. 1984) (value for stay litigation purposes was amount particular secured creditor could realize upon sale after deduction of expenses in its usual course of disposing of property); 3 Collier on Bankruptcy ¶ 361.04 (15th ed. rev.).

299 Grundy Nat'l Bank v. Stiltner, 58 B.R. 593 (W.D. Va. 1986) (when debtor's primary purpose in filing bankruptcy is to save home, an "irrebuttable presumption" is created that the home is necessary to effective reorganization); *see also In re* McAloon, 1 B.R. 766 (Bankr. E.D. Pa. 1980) (court found property necessary upon debtor's testimony that he would not remain in chapter 13 if it were lost).

300 *In re* Canal Place Ltd. P'ship, 921 F.2d 569 (5th Cir. 1991) (creditor entitled to relief from stay when chapter 11 debtor has no prospect of reorganizing within a reasonable period of time); *In re* Sutton, 904 F.2d 327 (5th Cir. 1990); *In re* Sun Valley Ranches, 823 F.2d 1373 (9th Cir. 1987); *In re* Aries Enterprises, 3 B.R. 472 (Bankr. D.D.C. 1980).

301 *See generally In re* Reice, 88 B.R. 676 (Bankr. E.D. Pa. 1988).

302 *See In re* Gibbs, 9 B.R. 758 (Bankr. D. Conn. 1981), *later proceeding at* 12 B.R. 737 (Bankr. D. Conn. 1981). See also discussion of leases in Chapter 12, *infra.*

303 See § 12.9.2, *infra,* for discussion of lease assumption under § 365.

304 *In re* GSVC Restaurant Corp., 10 B.R. 300 (S.D.N.Y. 1980); *In re* Mimi's of Atlanta, Inc., 5 B.R. 623 (Bankr. N.D. Ga. 1980); *In re* Greco, 5 B.R. 155 (Bankr. D. Haw. 1980); *In re* Racing Wheels, 5 B.R. 309 (Bankr. M.D. Fla. 1980); *In re* Aries Enterprises, 3 B.R. 472 (Bankr. D.D.C. 1980).

305 *In re* Mulkey of Mo., 5 B.R. 15 (Bankr. W.D. Mo. 1980).

such as collateral which would otherwise be repossessed, including property which the debtor does not technically "own."

Even if this argument is not accepted, as long as adequate protection is provided, there is no economic harm to the lessor, compared to what could otherwise be realized by renting the property. The substitution of money for the right of possession is in accord with a long line of recent cases holding that residential rental real estate is a fungible consumer good and not a unique interest for which money is no substitute.[306] This argument is especially compelling in the bankruptcy court, which as a court of equity must consider the "balance of hurt." When a lessor cannot show any real harm resulting from the stay, and protests only the continued occupancy by people to whom she does not choose to rent, the bankruptcy court should not feel compelled to lift the stay preventing eviction of the debtors.

For the same reasons, the fact that there is no lease for the debtors to assume is also not in itself cause for the stay to be lifted. Section 362 need not be read as limited by section 365, because the latter has other purposes. In a business case, for example, a long-term lease may be a valuable asset and the right to assume the lease may mean continued occupancy at below-market rents or the ability to assign the lease in exchange for a large cash payment. Such is not likely to be the case in a consumer case. If there is not an assumable lease, continued occupancy may still be allowed, but only with adequate protection, for example, rent payments at the market rate the lessor could otherwise receive.

Lessors sometimes argue that the automatic rejection of a lease by a chapter 7 trustee under Code section 365(d)(1), which occurs in virtually every case involving a tenant, terminates the lease. This argument is incorrect, because the rejection simply abandons the lease back to the debtor.[307] Therefore, rejection of a residential lease under section 365 does not necessarily mean that the lessee may not continue in possession. It only means that the court must consider the lease in light of bankruptcy law provisions such as the right to adequate protection.[308]

These arguments are significantly strengthened by the 1984 amendments to the Code, which for the first time recognized the differences between residential and nonresi-

dential leases. Section 365(c)(3) now prohibits the assumption of a lease terminated prior to a bankruptcy only in the case of a nonresidential lease. Section 365(d)(4) provides that property be immediately surrendered to a lessor after rejection only if the lease is a nonresidential lease. And section 362(b)(9) makes clear that the stay applies even when a residential lease has expired, by excepting from the stay only nonresidential leases which have expired. The obvious implication of these provisions pertaining to nonresidential leases is that residential tenants are not bound by them, and may be allowed to remain in a property even when a lease has been rejected or terminated.[309] They make more clear that, when a lessor is adequately protected, nothing in the Code requires granting the lessor relief from the automatic stay and imposing the hardships of eviction on a bankruptcy debtor.

Thus, although some early case law was not encouraging, there are strong arguments for the continuation of the stay with respect to leased property even after the lease terminates. However, the doubt about the case law in this area militates in favor of filing before the debtor's rights under the lease are terminated under state law whenever that is possible.[310]

9.7.3.3 Tactics in Stay Litigation

9.7.3.3.1 Valuation problems

Necessarily, the tactics to be followed in litigating to preserve the automatic stay vary from case to case. Certain issues, however, are likely to recur frequently, and certain strategies are likely to be repeatedly useful.

One problem that will very often arise is that of proving the value of property.[311] Although the party seeking to lift the stay has the initial burden on the question of equity, it will normally be necessary to have evidence ready to rebut that party's proof. Obtaining such evidence is not always easy.

In some cases the debtor's testimony may be sufficient. If property was recently purchased at arms-length, the price may be a good indication of value. The debtor may also have

---

306 *See* Javins v. First Nat'l Realty Corp., 428 F.2d 1071 (D.C. Cir. 1970) (warranty of habitability implied through comparison of leased housing with other consumer goods); Centex Homes Corp. v. Boag, 128 N.J. Super. 385, 320 A.2d 194 (Super. Ct. Ch. Div. 1974) (specific performance of sales agreement denied because realty not unique); Case Note, 48 Temple L.Q. 847 (1974).

307 See cases cited in § 12.9.1, *infra*.

308 *In re* Braniff Airways, 783 F.2d 1283 (5th Cir. 1986) (when there is a lease, adequate protection consists of reasonable value of debtor's use and occupancy). *But see In re* Miller, 103 B.R. 353 (Bankr. D.D.C. 1989) (once lease is rejected, landlord is entitled to relief from stay when debtor proposes to pay only current monthly rent).

309 *But see In re* Williams, 144 F.3d 544 (7th Cir. 1998) (bankruptcy court did not abuse discretion in granting relief from stay for lessor to continue eviction proceedings in which state court could better assess debtor's defenses); Robinson v. Chicago Hous. Auth., 54 F.3d 316 (7th Cir. 1995) (relief from stay appropriate if lease terminated and the debtor has no way to revive lease under state law).

310 *See* Bennett v. St. Steven Terrace Apartments, 211 B.R. 265 (N.D. Ill. 1997) (lease does not terminate until judgment is entered in forcible detainer case; no stay relief appropriate because debtor retains rights in the leased property).

311 Valuation issues arise in many different bankruptcy contexts. It is important to think through how valuation in one context may impact other valuation issues which are likely to arise in the case. *See* § 9.7.3.2.3, *supra*; §§ 10.3.3, 11.2, 11.5.5, *infra*.

knowledge (supplemented by certified copies of deeds or other sale documents presented in evidence) of recent sale prices of similar properties. Neighbors or friends may be able to offer testimony about the value of their properties. Generally, a landowner's testimony as to the value of his or her land is admissible without further qualification.[312]

More common is the use of experts in property appraisal. Their expertise, of course, allows them to render opinions regarding the value of property. In most places real estate appraisers are available to testify; in larger cities they may be employed full time in that profession, while in other areas they are usually real estate brokers. In either case, paying their fees may be a real hardship for some clients. In cases in which appraisers are necessary, however, this relatively small investment may save thousands of dollars for a client.

For appraisals of property other than real estate, obtaining an expert may be difficult. In cases involving motor vehicles or mobile homes, standard industry guides may be acceptable as evidence, and in many areas, auctioneers are willing and able to testify to the value of consumer goods. When property such as an automobile is worth less than the standard value for that model based on, for example, mechanical problems, testimony of a mechanic or used car dealer may be necessary.

One way to ease the problem of proof, and in some cases shift the costs, is to engage in pretrial discovery on issues of value. If a request for an admission of value is denied by an opposing party and that value is later proved, the party denying the request can be required to pay for the costs of proof on that issue, including attorney fees.[313] Thus, it may be possible to obtain a written appraisal inexpensively and request that its authenticity and correctness be admitted, or even to simply request that a specific valuation be admitted. If the valuation is not admitted, then the cost of successful testimony can usually be shifted.

Similarly, if there may be a problem of admissibility, a request for admissions can demand that an opponent admit or deny the accuracy of sources such as the NADA used car guides, and the fact that they are regularly used as indicators of value in the trade. Especially given the costs and expenses of proving disputed issues at trial, a request for admissions can result in a stipulated value which meets the debtor's needs and, on occasion, to withdrawal of a poorly grounded motion.

9.7.3.3.2 Other tactics

Discovery may be helpful, as always, in narrowing the issues or pointing up flaws in an opponent's case. In any case, because of the time deadlines involved in stay litigation, a motion for expedited discovery is usually necessary to complete discovery within the thirty days before the preliminary hearing. One positive result of such a motion is often a quick stipulation from the party seeking relief from the stay agreeing that the hearing (and the stay) can be continued beyond the thirty day deadline.

Discovery may also demonstrate that the motion for relief from the stay is frivolous. It has become increasingly common for mortgage servicing companies to make errors in crediting bankruptcy debtors' payments and to file motions for relief from the stay when a debtor is current in post-petition payments. In such cases, sanctions against the moving party may be warranted.[314]

Other aggressive litigation strategies in fighting to preserve the stay may pay similar dividends. As discussed earlier, counterclaims and defenses probably can be considered and they definitely should be asserted. Many parties seeking relief from the stay expect little in the way of defense, and when faced with strong opposition, may decide they are getting more than they bargained for. If their motions meet answers raising questions of equity, laches, Truth in Lending or other consumer statutes,[315] they may well choose not only to delay the initial hearing but also to agree to a settlement favorable to the debtor. Alternatively, it is common for parties to agree to continue or dismiss a motion for relief from stay until an underlying question about the validity of a counterclaim or defense can be resolved in a separate proceeding.

In any case, it is unlikely that the court will want to decide a complicated case within the short time provided for the preliminary hearing. The debtor can then take advantage of the section 362(e) provisions allowing the preliminary hearing to be continued for up to thirty days, arguing that the pleadings and discovery to date show a reasonable likelihood that she will prevail at the final hearing. Of course, if the party seeking relief from the stay has not cooperated in discovery, additional grounds exist for continuing the hearing. It should always be pointed out that that party will have another day in court, that the continuation of the stay is only like a preliminary injunction, and that the harm to that party is relatively slight in comparison to the potential for harm to the debtor.

Finally, it should be remembered, and argued forcefully, that while the statute provides that relief from the stay may be granted in certain circumstances, that relief need not be complete lifting of the stay. Lesser relief, such as conditioning the stay on certain actions of the debtor or modifying it to give the debtor a reasonable period of time to relinquish property or get other affairs in order, is expressly contem-

---

312 Joe T. Dehmer Distributors Inc. v. Temple, 826 F.2d 1463 (5th Cir. 1987); United States v. 3698.63 Acres of Land, 416 F.2d 65, 67 (8th Cir. 1969); United States v. Sowards, 370 F.2d 87 (10th Cir. 1966).

313 Fed. R. Bankr. P. 7037 (incorporating Fed. R. Civ. P. 37(c)); *In re* Sweeten, 56 B.R. 675 (Bankr. E.D. Pa. 1986).

314 *See In re* Gorshtein, 285 B.R. 118 (Bankr. S.D.N.Y. 2002); *In re* Kilgore, 253 B.R. 179 (Bankr. D.S.C. 2000).

315 *See* Form 31, Appx. G.4, *infra*.

plated by section 362(d) and should be granted, when appropriate, under the court's equitable powers.[316]

9.7.3.3.3 Stays pending appeal

If an appeal is contemplated after the automatic stay is terminated by order of the court or otherwise, it may be essential to obtain a stay pending appeal. The rules provide a ten day delay in the effectiveness of an order granting relief from stay in order to provide time to seek a stay pending appeal, but a court may order otherwise.[317] Therefore, if a possible appeal is contemplated, a debtor should argue against any language in the court's order changing the normal ten day delay of relief from the stay. Absent a stay, property may be sold, litigation terminated unfavorably, or both.[318] In that event, an appeal may be rendered moot.[319]

9.8 Utility Services in Bankruptcy Cases

9.8.1 No Utility May Deny Service Within Twenty Days After Bankruptcy

Closely akin to the automatic stay provisions of Code section 362 are the provisions regarding refusal to provide utility service in section 366. While the general purpose of this section closely parallels that of the automatic stay, its operation and effect are somewhat different.

The first part of section 366 sets forth a general rule for at least the first twenty days after the petition is filed. No utility[320] may "alter, refuse, or discontinue service or dis-

criminate against" the debtor solely on the basis of an unpaid pre-petition debt or the filing of a bankruptcy case during that time period.

This subsection clearly prohibits a utility with notice of the case from shutting off the debtor's utility service in the first twenty days after the bankruptcy petition is filed. Thus, what was said earlier in this Chapter about giving notice to creditors and sanctions for violations of the automatic stay[321] applies equally in the utility context. Swift court relief, as well as possible fines and attorney fees, should be available for illegal shut-offs.[322]

One problem that may occasionally arise is a shut-off which is ostensibly based not merely on the unpaid debt, but rather on defective equipment, an illegal hookup by the customer, or some other reason. Naturally, such cases boil down to a problem of proof, with special attention being given to why the utility happened to terminate service immediately after bankruptcy. If the utility has at any time stated that a payment of money will cure the problem, it should not be hard to show that the shut-off was an attempt to collect money, rather than to protect the public from unsafe equipment.

More complicated is the question of obtaining service if it was discontinued prior to the bankruptcy. Section 366(a) requires that the utility service be reinstated, because it cannot be "refused" solely on the basis of the unpaid debt. If service is refused due to an unpaid debt, section 366 is violated.[323] However, a clever utility may argue that it requires an initial deposit from all customers and therefore is not refusing service based upon the unpaid debt.[324] The

---

316 *See In re* Cox, 251 B.R. 446 (Bankr. W.D.N.Y. 2000) (bankruptcy court adopted policy which discouraged stay motions by over-secured lenders unless lenders gave debtors notice of opportunity to cure default in post-petition payments).

317 Fed. R. Bankr. P. 4001(a)(3); *In re* Banks, 253 B.R. 25 (Bankr. E.D. Mich. 2000) (damages awarded against creditor who proceeded to evict debtor before expiration of ten days from order granting relief from stay).

318 *See* Fish Mkt. Nominee Corp. v. Pelofsky, 72 F.3d 4 (1st Cir. 1995) (automatic stay ended immediately upon dismissal of case).

319 *In re* Nat'l Mass Media Telecomm. Sys., Inc., 152 F.3d 1178 (9th Cir. 1998) (when foreclosed property was sold to nonparty, appeal from order granting relief from stay to permit foreclosure became moot; *see also In re* Highway Truck Drivers & Helpers Local 107, 888 F.2d 293 (3d Cir. 1989); *In re* Weston, 110 B.R. 452 (E.D. Cal. 1989) (foreclosure sale occurring after dismissal held valid because debtor had not obtained stay pending appeal); § 13.10.4, *infra*.

320 The term "utility" covers any supplier of utility services with a monopoly position. The legislative history of § 366 states: "This section is intended to cover utilities that have some special position with respect to the debtor, such as an electric company, gas supplier, or telephone company that is a monopoly in the area so that the debtor cannot easily obtain

comparable services from another utility." S. Rep. No. 95-987, at 60 (1978), *reprinted in* 1978 U.S.C.C.A.N. 5846. The cases have given the term a similarly broad reading. *In re* Gehrke, 57 B.R. 97 (Bankr. D. Or. 1985) (electric co-op. association is a utility); *In re* Hobbs, 20 B.R. 488 (Bankr. E.D. Pa. 1982) (condominium owners association that sells electricity to condominium owner treated as a utility for purposes of § 366); *In re* Good Time Charlie's Ltd., 25 B.R. 226 (Bankr. E.D. Pa. 1982) (shopping mall providing electricity is a utility). Another purpose of the section is to assure that a debtor can obtain vital services, so that the elimination of monopolies by deregulation should not free providers of services such as water, gas, electricity, and telephone from the requirements of section 366. *See* 3 Collier on Bankruptcy ¶ 366.05 (15th ed. rev.); *accord* One Stop Realtour Place, Inc. v. Allegiance Telecomm., Inc., 268 B.R. 430 (Bankr. E.D. Pa. 2001) (deregulated local telephone service provider was "utility" under § 366).

321 *See* §§ 9.5, 9.6, *supra*; Forms 39–41, Appx. G.6, *infra*.

322 *See, e.g., In re* Smith, 170 B.R. 111 (Bankr. N.D. Ohio 1994) (actual damages and attorney fees awarded for willful disconnection of telephone service after notice of bankruptcy).

323 *In re* Whittaker, 882 F.2d 791 (3d Cir. 1989); *In re* Tarrant, 190 B.R. 704 (Bankr. S.D. Ga. 1995) (city utility ordered to pay damages and attorney fees for violating sections 362 and 366 by demanding pre-petition debt repayment as condition of reconnection).

324 *See In re* Roberts, 29 B.R. 808 (E.D. Pa. 1983) (deposit required before service provided when non-bankruptcy customer would be required to post deposit).

answer to this contention lies in whether the utility is "discriminating" on the basis of that debt. Under the utility's normal practices, would a deposit have been required of a new customer, or to effectuate a reinstatement of service if a customer had paid the back bill in full? In most cases the answer to this question is no, and in fact many state or local utility regulations provide that service can be reinstated if even a part of the prior bill is paid, with an agreement to pay the rest in installments. If such is the case, then a refusal to reinstate when the bill has not been paid should be considered discrimination solely on the basis of the unpaid debt.[325] However, a reasonable reconnection fee, if charged to all customers whose service is reinstated, could probably be required in these cases.

9.8.2 A Utility May Be Able to Discontinue Service If the Debtor Does Not Furnish Adequate Assurance of Future Payment

9.8.2.1 Procedure

Section 366(a) is significantly limited by section 366(b) which provides that a utility may "alter, refuse or discontinue service" if the debtor does not, within twenty days after filing of a voluntary petition, furnish adequate assurance of future payment.

The statutory section cited above reads, at first glance, as if it is self-executing, and it is generally understood to mean that the utility may terminate service after twenty days without special permission from the court if it does not believe adequate assurance has been provided.[326] If that is the local understanding, then it behooves the debtor to come to some agreement with the utility as to what is adequate assurance before the twenty days has run. Counsel should become familiar with local practice regarding adequate assurance because, for example, some utilities do not require deposits or other forms of adequate assurance except in extraordinary cases. If there is any doubt about local practice, counsel may wish to send a letter to all utilities, immediately upon filing the bankruptcy petition, stating that the debtor is prepared to provide adequate assurance, but that none will be provided unless a request is made by the utility.[327] In cases in which there is a dispute, the debtor must seek the court's intervention along with preliminary relief if the utility will not agree to continue service.

However, a utility may take substantial risks in terminating service when the debtor has tendered what she believes to be adequate assurance. The second sentence of section 366(b) states that "[o]n request of a party in interest and after notice and a hearing, the court may order reasonable modification of the amount . . . necessary to provide adequate assurance." Thus, the "parties in interest" required to seek court modification of a deposit or security with which they do not agree include the utility providers.

At least one court has suggested that there is a presumption that the deposit terms permitted by state utility regulations set the maximum a utility can demand without court modification.[328] If a utility does not seek a determination regarding adequate assurance before altering service, it can be strongly argued that it is in contempt of the requirements of section 366(b) if a court later determines the amount that had been tendered by a debtor to be sufficient for adequate assurance.[329] This reading, which places utilities terminating service without court permission at risk of contempt, more closely parallels the operation of the automatic stay provisions, as well as the executory contract provisions,[330] as section 366 was intended to do.[331]

9.8.2.2 Adequate Assurance of Future Payment

9.8.2.2.1 Methods of adequate assurance

The term "adequate assurance" is not defined in the Code, except to the extent that examples are given. Those examples are a "deposit or other security."[332] Certainly, the former of these is the most common in consumer cases. However, it is clear from the statute that there are other possibilities, including the voluntary granting of a lien on property of the debtor to be available in the event of a post-petition delinquency. In some states it may be possible to have a pre-petition security deposit applied to provide post-petition adequate assurance.[333] Still another way of giving adequate assurance, at least in a chapter 13 plan in which significant payments are being made, would be the granting of priority status to any delinquent debt for post-petition utility service. This result is clear both from the

---

325 *See In re* Whittaker, 882 F.2d 791 (3d Cir. 1989); *In re* Kiriluk, 76 B.R. 979 (Bankr. E.D. Pa. 1987).

326 *See, e.g.*, 3 Collier on Bankruptcy ¶ 366.03 (15th ed. rev.); *see also In re* Stagecoach Enterprises, Inc., 1 B.R. 732 (Bankr. M.D. Fla. 1979).

327 *See In re* Am. Investcorp & Dev. Co., 155 B.R. 300 (Bankr. D.R.I. 1993) (section 366 places burden on debtor to furnish adequate assurance within twenty days).

328 *In re* Kiriluk, 76 B.R. 979 (Bankr. E.D. Pa. 1987).

329 *See, e.g., In re* Tabor, 46 B.R. 677 (Bankr. S.D. Ohio 1985) (utility fined $250.00 as sanctions for contempt of court and $526.00 in damages for applying amount tendered to pre-petition debt and requesting excessive amount as adequate assurance).

330 See § 12.9, *infra,* for a discussion of § 365.

331 3 Collier on Bankruptcy ¶ 366.02 (15th ed. rev.).

332 11 U.S.C. § 366(b).

333 *In re* Cole, 104 B.R. 736 (Bankr. D. Md. 1989) (pre-petition security deposit which constituted exempt property of the estate could be used as post-petition adequate assurance). This strategy may not be available when the deposit secures a pre-petition delinquency.

legislative history,[334] and because there is no specific exclusion of the granting of an "administrative expense" (and thus priority status) in section 366 similar to that in section 361.[335] In short, adequate assurance may be given in any way that protects the utility from an unreasonable risk of nonpayment, even if it falls short of an absolute guarantee.[336]

9.8.2.2.2 Adequate assurance not always required

Other questions also arise as to the necessity for adequate assurance. Several of these concern the interplay of section 366 with state customer service regulations which govern the utilities. One question is whether normal shut-off procedures required by such regulations can be omitted by the utility. While the utility may argue that section 366(b), which allows termination after twenty days, overrides state regulations, there are several reasons that this argument should not prevail. The first is that the overriding effect of the Supremacy Clause comes into effect only if there is a conflict between the state and federal law. Section 366(b) says only that the utility "may" discontinue service, not that it "shall" do so. If there are other reasons why, under state laws, the utility cannot discontinue service, then there is nothing which requires that those reasons be ignored.

For example, it is clear in most places that service cannot be terminated if the bill is fully current. The mere filing of a bankruptcy petition should not suddenly give the utility the right to terminate in such a case. Another indication that it was not the intent of Congress to give the utilities greater rights than they already have under state law is that "discrimination," prohibited in section 366(a), is conspicuously omitted from the actions allowed in section 366(b) if adequate assurance is not provided. This conclusion is also supported by statements in the original Report of the Bankruptcy Commission that the term "adequate assurance," in a slightly different context, is not intended to give the non-debtor party greater rights in a case than it would otherwise have.[337]

Thus, if the state regulations do not require any deposit for continuance of service to someone who pays a prior utility bill before termination, it can also be argued that it would be discrimination to require a deposit from a debtor in bankruptcy whose utility bills are current.[338] Alternatively, the debtor's past record of prompt payments should be considered, in itself, adequate assurance.[339] Similarly, if a utility never requires a deposit from a new customer, then it should not be able to require one from a bankruptcy debtor, because that would be discrimination based upon the unpaid debt.[340]

A 1984 amendment to the Bankruptcy Code clarified these principles, by adding to section 366(a) an explicit prohibition of discrimination with respect to service based merely upon the filing of a bankruptcy. There is no exception in section 366(b) to this prohibition.[341]

9.8.2.2.3 Amount necessary for adequate assurance

Utilities often demand a deposit equal to the amount required of new customers under state utility regulations. Such regulations should set an upper limit on the amount of a deposit required.[342] While it is clear that the bankruptcy court has the power to set a lower deposit than required by such regulations for reinstatement,[343] the utility should have a heavy burden to show its entitlement to a deposit higher than the legal limit under state law deemed reasonable by the

---

334 H.R. Rep. No. 95-595, at 350 (1977).

335 Va. Elec. & Power Co. v. Caldor, Inc., 117 F.3d 646 (2d Cir. 1997) (availability of administrative expense claim can be a component of adequate assurance; court need not order a security deposit or other assurance); *see In re* Hennen, 17 B.R. 720 (Bankr. S.D. Ohio 1982) (every chapter 13 plan to include provision setting aside deposit out of initial payments to the trustee, to be held in reserve as adequate assurance for future service); *In re* George C. Frye Co., 7 B.R. 856 (Bankr. D. Me. 1980); *see also In re* Steinebach, 303 B.R. 634 (Bankr. D. Ariz. 2004) (debtors delinquent in utility payments could provide for deposit in plan, for which utility could file proof of claim); *In re* Epling, 255 B.R. 549 (Bankr. S.D. Ohio 2000) (approving plan provision requiring any utility seeking a deposit to file an administrative claim to be paid by the trustee).

336 *In re* Keydata Corp., 12 B.R. 156 (B.A.P. 1st Cir. 1981); *see* Form 43, Appx. G.6, *infra*.

337 Bankruptcy Commission Report, vol. 2, at 156, 157. The term "adequate assurance" in the Commission's original bill was

derived from § 2-609 of the Uniform Commercial Code, and thus the comments and interpretations of that section may be useful in determining its meaning.

338 *See In re* Heard, 84 B.R. 454 (Bankr. W.D. Tex. 1987); *In re* Coury, 22 B.R. 766 (Bankr. W.D. Pa. 1982); Form 42, Appx. G.6, *infra*. However, in a case in which a previous security deposit was applied to pay the pre-bankruptcy debt, a utility may argue that it has the right to maintain the security deposit it would have been holding had the debt been paid in full.

339 *In re* Steinebach, 303 B.R. 634 (Bankr. D. Ariz. 2004) (utility has no unreasonable risk of nonpayment from debtor current in payments); *In re* Demp, 22 B.R. 331 (Bankr. E.D. Pa. 1982).

340 *But see* Hanratty v. Philadelphia Elec. Co., 907 F.2d 1418 (3d Cir. 1990) (utility may require adequate assurance in bankruptcy even if it does not normally require security deposits from its new non-corporate customers).

341 *In re* Coury, 22 B.R. 766 (Bankr. W.D. Pa. 1982); *In re* Shirey, 25 B.R. 247 (Bankr. E.D. Pa. 1982); *see also In re* Begley, 41 B.R. 402 (E.D. Pa. 1984), *aff'd*, 760 F.2d 46 (3d Cir. 1985).

342 *See In re* Steinebach, 303 B.R. 634 (Bankr. D. Ariz. 2004) (when utility not entitled to deposit under state regulations, those regulations provide guidance supporting decision that no deposit necessary under § 366(b)); *In re* Kiriluk, 76 B.R. 979 (Bankr. E.D. Pa. 1987). For a discussion of utility deposit regulations, see National Consumer Law Center, Access to Utility Service §§ 3.7, 3.8 (2d ed. 2001 and Supp.).

343 3 Collier on Bankruptcy ¶ 366.03 (15th ed. rev.); *see also* Sharon Steel Corp. v. Nat'l Fuel Gas Distrib. Corp., 871 F.2d 1217 (3d Cir. 1989) (court, not local regulating authority, has power to set terms under which service must be provided); *In re* Cunha, 1 B.R. 330 (Bankr. E.D. Va. 1979).

state regulatory body for even the worst cases.[344] Adequate assurance need not be the equivalent of a guaranty of payment.[345] When the pre-petition debt is small, the debtor and utility may also agree that the debtor will pay the pre-petition debt as adequate assurance and waive the automatic stay with respect to that debt.[346] However, it should be added that there seems to be nothing which would prevent the bankruptcy court from ordering continued service conditioned on prompt payments and specifically allowing a waiver of normal state termination procedures, with or without an additional court order, if those payments are not made.[347] The debtor may, in fact, propose such a solution as a last resort if it is impossible to otherwise provide adequate assurance. Obviously, such a waiver of state protections involves significant risk to the client and should be considered only with the greatest caution.

The guidelines to be used in determining the amount necessary for adequate assurance have slowly emerged from case law. Although the precise amount varies from case to case, the courts have tended to look to "all of the circumstances" including the pre-bankruptcy history of the debtor, the nature of the debtor, how much was owed, the previous course of dealing and conduct on the part of the utility, the stability of the debtor's present circumstances, the speed with which the utility may terminate service, the frequency of payments, and the likely usage of the utility in months to come.[348] Other factors that might be considered include the time of year (a deposit of one average monthly payment could pay for six months' heating service in non-winter months), the possibility of sureties, and the likely availability of energy assistance for some consumers. One reported case that considered the matter used most of these factors and finally set a deposit approximately equal to one upcoming winter month's bill, payable in three monthly installments by the debtor, with the utility to refund half of the deposit, with interest, a year later, and the other half according to its normal practice. The court also provided for speedy termination in the event of nonpayment.[349]

9.8.2.2.4 Post-petition termination procedures

Once the debtor has provided adequate assurance to a utility, the involvement of the bankruptcy court normally ends. Absent a contrary procedure specifically ordered by the court or agreed to by the debtor as part of the adequate assurance, state law will govern the treatment of post-petition debts.[350] Thus, any termination procedures required by state law or consumer rights provided by state law are applicable to debts arising after adequate assurance has been provided.[351]

9.8.2.2.5 Possible special protections for customers of governmental utilities

Finally, there is a significant question as to the interplay of section 366 with section 525 of the Code, which prohibits discrimination by a governmental unit with respect to the granting of a "license, permit, charter, franchise, or other similar grant," solely because of bankruptcy or because of nonpayment of a debt discharged in bankruptcy. Assuming that the right to use normally monopolized utility service is some sort of license or grant, there is a good argument that the two sections must be read together in those frequent cases in which utilities are also "governmental units."[352] Reading these two sections together would mean that there could be no discrimination by such utilities based upon dischargeable debts and that bankruptcy debtors should be treated the same as persons who never had a debt to the utility.[353] Because consumers in the latter category need not supply a deposit for continued service, bankruptcy debtors should not be required to do so either. Following the same rationale, for a reinstatement of service, debtors should have the same rights as someone who had no previous debt to the utility or to any of the other creditors listed in the petition. If such persons need not pay a deposit to obtain service under the utility's normal practices, then debtors should be given the same treatment.

In support of this argument, it should be noted that nothing in section 366 requires the utility to demand a deposit. Therefore, there is no contradiction between section 366 and section 525, and normal rules of statutory construction require that every effort be made to read the two sections harmoniously.

9.9 Turnover of Property Under Section 542

9.9.1 The General Rule

The commencement of the case also activates two other automatic provisions relating to the debtor's property—sections 542 and 543. These sections require turnover to the

---

344 *See In re* Hennen, 17 B.R. 720 (Bankr. S.D. Ohio 1982) (utility could not demand deposit in excess of that set by state regulation without violating § 366(a)).

345 *In re* Adelphia Bus. Solutions, Inc., 280 B.R. 63 (Bankr. S.D.N.Y. 2002).

346 *In re* Wells, 280 B.R. 701 (Bankr. S.D. Ala. 2001).

347 Va. Elec. & Power Co. v. Caldor, Inc., 117 F.3d 646 (2d Cir. 1997) (availability of administrative expense claim can be a component of adequate assurance; court need not order a security deposit or other assurance beyond remedies already available to utility under bankruptcy law).

348 *In re* Cunha, 1 B.R. 330 (Bankr. E.D. Va. 1979).

349 *Id.*

350 Begley v. Philadelphia Elec. Co., 760 F.2d 46 (3d Cir. 1985).
351 *Id.*
352 "Governmental unit" is defined at 11 U.S.C. § 101(27).
353 See discussion of § 525 in Chapter 14, *infra.*

trustee of property in which the debtor has an interest. Both of these sections have similar provisions; section 543 applies to "custodians,"[354] such as sheriffs or receivers legally appointed to take charge of the debtor's property,[355] and section 542 applies to all other "entities."[356]

Very simply, section 542 requires that any entity, other than a custodian, in possession, custody, or control of property that the trustee[357] may use, sell, or lease, or that the debtor may exempt, must immediately deliver to the trustee such property or the value of such property, unless the property is of inconsequential value or benefit to the estate. Its purpose is to assist in the gathering up of all property of the estate for the liquidation or reorganization that will take place in bankruptcy, as well as to effectuate the debtor's right to claim exemptions.

This general rule has few exceptions, stated in later subsections and not often applicable in consumer cases. Except for these, the rule normally applies to all property of the estate, because an individual debtor may usually choose to exempt any property of the estate,[358] that is, any property in which the debtor has any legal or equitable interest.[359] It applies no matter where the property is located and no matter how it was acquired by the entity in possession.[360] The rule also applies to recorded information, such as records subject to an attorney's lien.[361]

9.9.2 Questions of Scope: Secured Parties in Possession

Unfortunately, due to poor drafting of the statute, a question arose as to whether an entity must surrender property in which the debtor's present interest does not include a possessory interest but only something less, such as a right of redemption, for example, an automobile validly repossessed just prior to the bankruptcy. Noting that only property of the estate can be used, sold, or leased under section 363, some courts concluded that the estate's property was only

the right of redemption in such cases, and not the right of possession, so that turnover was not required.[362]

This interpretation was unduly narrow, in that little would remain of section 542 if it were adopted. The principal purpose of section 363 is to allow the debtor to continue to use, sell, or lease property that the creditor could otherwise repossess due to its security interest in the property. Indeed, even "cash collateral," such as bank deposits subject to a right of setoff by the bank, may be used if adequate protection is provided.[363] Thus, it is evident that the debtor need not have a right to retain possession as of the commencement of the case in order to use, sell or lease property. For the same reason, if a debtor claims as exempt an equity interest in a repossessed vehicle, it is hard to see how that interest could be delivered except by return of the entire vehicle.

Most courts and commentators accepted this interpretation and found that turnover of property is required whenever the estate has any interest in that property.[364] For chapter 11 cases, the Supreme Court has explicitly held that, at least when the debtor has more than bare legal title, turnover is required.[365] Although the Court expressly declined to rule on the issue with respect to non-chapter 11 cases,[366] the logic employed in its decision also dictates turnover in chapter 13 cases in which property is necessary for the debtor's rehabilitation[367] and perhaps in chapter 7

---

354 "Custodian" is defined at 11 U.S.C. § 101(11).

355 *In re* Skinner, 213 B.R. 335 (Bankr. W.D. Tenn. 1997) (sheriff who seized debtor's truck based upon writ of execution was custodian required to turn over truck to trustee).

356 "Entity" is defined at 11 U.S.C. § 101(15).

357 In a chapter 13 case the debtor exercises most of these trustee powers. *See* § 12.8, *infra.*

358 See Chapter 10, *infra,* for a discussion of what property may be exempted.

359 11 U.S.C. § 541. *But see In re* Charter Co., 913 F.2d 1575 (11th Cir. 1990) (debtor may not obtain turnover of funds claimed due on a disputed contract claim).

360 *But see In re* James, 940 F.2d 46 (3d Cir. 1991) (court may not order turnover of currency confiscated as proceeds of drug transaction).

361 11 U.S.C. § 542(e). It should be noted that § 543 requires custodians to turn over "any property of the debtor transferred to" them, probably a broader collection of property interests than that covered by § 542.

362 *See, e.g., In re* Avery Health Ctr., 8 B.R. 1016 (W.D.N.Y. 1981), *overruled by* United States v. Whiting Pools, Inc., 462 U.S. 198 (1983); *cf. In re* Smith, 921 F.2d 136 (8th Cir. 1990) (IRS not required to turn over tax overpayment when no timely claim for a refund was made by taxpayer before the bankruptcy).

363 11 U.S.C. § 363(c). *But see In re* Lyons, 957 F.2d 444 (7th Cir. 1992) (trustee could not compel turnover of retirement funds, even though they were estate property, when debtor had no right to withdraw them or use them).

364 *In re* Pester Ref. Co., 845 F.2d 1476 (8th Cir. 1988); Carr v. Sec. Sav. & Loan Ass'n, 130 B.R. 434 (D.N.J. 1991) (repossessed collateral must be returned); *see* 5 Collier on Bankruptcy ¶ 542.02 (15th ed. rev.) (secured creditor in possession must turn over property).

365 United States v. Whiting Pools, Inc., 462 U.S. 198, 103 S. Ct. 2309, 176 L. Ed. 2d 515 (1983); *see also In re* Challenge Air Int'l, Inc., 952 F.2d 384 (11th Cir. 1992) (third party required to turn over to chapter 11 debtor funds subject to IRS levy).

366 United States v. Whiting Pools, Inc., 462 U.S. 198, 208 n.17, 103 S. Ct. 2309, 76 L. Ed. 2d 515 (1983).

367 *In re* Sharon, 234 B.R. 676 (B.A.P. 6th Cir. 1999); *In re* Gaimo, 194 B.R. 210 (E.D. Mo. 1996) (funds in bank account subject to pre-petition IRS levy subject to turnover power in chapter 13 case); *In re* Attinello, 38 B.R. 609 (Bankr. E.D. Pa. 1984); *In re* Robinson, 36 B.R. 35 (Bankr. E.D. Ark. 1983). *But see In re* Kalter, 292 F.3d 1350 (11th Cir. 2002) (following prior *Lewis* decision, repossessed vehicle not property of the bankruptcy estate based on operation of Florida certificate of title statute); *In re* Lewis, 137 F.3d 1280 (11th Cir. 1998) (under Alabama law, debtor no longer has possessory right or title to an automobile after repossession so that only a right of redemption comes into the estate). The *Lewis* and *Kalter* decisions fail to explain their inconsistency with United States v. Whiting Pools,

cases in which the right of redemption could be exercised.[368] Thus, the turnover provisions should be very useful in regaining possession of repossessed automobiles, pledged goods,[369] goods subject to garagemen's, warehousemen's or artisans' liens, and any other property seized legally or illegally by an entity prior to the bankruptcy.[370] A willful failure to turn over assets seized pre-petition may constitute an actionable violation of the automatic stay.[371] Additionally, failure to turn over property in a timely fashion may result in disallowance of a creditor's claim.[372]

9.9.3 Procedure

Theoretically, a party obligated to turn over property should do so immediately upon notice of the case. Sometimes this turnover happens, especially when courts have made clear that it is required. Thus, the first step which should be taken on behalf of the debtor is to give the creditor or other party in possession notice of the case, both informal and formal, in a manner similar to that used to give notice of the automatic stay.

In practice, however, many holders refuse to turn over property. Many simply do not believe that they are required to do so, because these provisions are not nearly as clear as those setting out the automatic stay. In such cases, there is no alternative but to obtain a court order for turnover, seeking immediate interlocutory relief if necessary.[373] Continuing to exercise control over property of the estate is a violation of the automatic stay as well as section 542.[374] Sanctions under section 362(h) or a contempt order, including damages and attorney fees, are also available.[375]

Some creditors (primarily automobile lenders) have claimed that adequate protection payments are a prerequisite to turnover. Courts are divided on this issue.[376] In jurisdictions which do require adequate protection payments prior to turnover, negotiation of the value of the property and the amount of appropriate adequate protection may be necessary.[377] In chapter 13 cases, adequate protection will often consist of payments under the plan.[378] If that is the case, the only required showing should be that plan payments are being made.

Finally, it is important to give notice of the case promptly to any holder of property not only to obtain a turnover, but also to prevent the complications that could arise from a transfer to a third party by a holder without notice. It is clear that the holder incurs no special liability for such a transfer,[379] and thereafter the property may not be recoverable, although there are good arguments that it does remain property of the estate because rights were frozen as of the filing of the case.[380]

Inc., 462 U.S. 198, 103 S. Ct. 2309, 76 L. Ed. 2d 515 (1983) and have not been followed by other courts. *See In re* Moffett, 356 F.3d 518 (4th Cir. 2004) (repossession did not terminate debtor's interest under Virginia law and turnover required); *In re* Robinson, 285 B.R. 732 (Bankr. W.D. Okla. 2002). Indeed, even the Eleventh Circuit appears to be backing away from the decision, distinguishing a case under Georgia law based upon an opinion of the Georgia Supreme Court. *In re* Rozier, 376 F.3d 1323 (11th Cir. 2004), *relying upon answer to certified question,* Motors Acceptance Corp. v. Rozier, 278 Ga. 52, 597 S.E.2d 367 (2004).

368 *See In re* Gerwer, 898 F.2d 730 (9th Cir. 1990) (trustee may obtain turnover from secured party in possession in chapter 7 case).

369 *In re* Dunlap, 143 B.R. 859 (Bankr. M.D. Tenn. 1992) (property in possession of pawnbroker must be turned over to chapter 13 debtors if debtors provide adequate protection).

370 *See, e.g., In re* Stage, 85 B.R. 880 (Bankr. M.D. Fla. 1988) (engagement ring held by debtor was conditional gift under state law in which the debtor had a cognizable interest). *But see In re* Boggan, 251 B.R. 95 (B.A.P. 9th Cir. 2000) (mechanic did not have to turn over debtor's car, held pursuant to mechanic's lien because maintaining possession of car was necessary to preserve existence of lien, and maintaining possession was therefore within exception to stay provided by § 362(a)(3)).

371 *In re* Knaus, 889 F.2d 773 (8th Cir. 1989) (refusal to turn over property lawfully seized pre-petition after being given notice of the stay constitutes violation of the automatic stay remediable pursuant to § 362(h)); *In re* Abrams, 127 B.R. 239 (B.A.P. 9th Cir. 1991) (retention of repossessed automobile after receiving notice of the bankruptcy is a willful violation of the stay); *see In re* Diviney, 211 B.R. 951 (Bankr. N.D. Okla. 1997) (compensatory damages and $40,000.00 in punitive damages awarded when lender failed to return repossessed automobile after the dismissal of debtors' chapter 13 case was vacated), *aff'd,* 225 B.R. 762 (B.A.P. 10th Cir. 1998); *see also* § 9.6, *supra.*

372 11 U.S.C. § 502(d); *see In re* Davis, 889 F.2d 658 (5th Cir. 1989) (IRS entitled to a reasonable time to turn over property before its claim is disallowed).

---

373 *See* Form 37, Appx. G.5, *infra.* A complaint rather than a motion is required by Rule of Bankruptcy Procedure 7001. *In re* Estes, 185 B.R. 745 (Bankr. W.D. Ky. 1995); *In re* Riding, 44 B.R. 846 (Bankr. D. Utah 1984). Under 28 U.S.C. § 157(b)(2)(E) the matter is a core proceeding.

374 *In re* Hill, 174 B.R. 949 (Bankr. S.D. Ohio 1994).

375 *See* §§ 9.6, 9.9.2, *supra;* Gen. Motors Acceptance Corp. v. Ryan, 183 B.R. 288 (M.D. Fla. 1995) (retention of property was stay violation; creditor cannot wait until debtor files turnover complaint after receiving request for turnover); *In re* Cordle, 187 B.R. 1 (Bankr. N.D. Cal. 1995) (failure to turn over insurance proceeds violated stay and justified sanctions); *In re* LaTempa, 58 B.R. 538 (Bankr. W.D. Va. 1986).

376 *Compare, e.g., In re* Nash, 228 B.R. 669 (Bankr. N.D. Ill. 1999) (creditor could retain automobile; adequate protection required as a prerequisite to turnover); *In re* Fitch, 217 B.R. 286 (Bankr. C.D. Cal. 1998); *In re* Young, 193 B.R. 620 (Bankr. D.D.C. 1996); *In re* Richardson, 135 B.R. 256 (Bankr. E.D. Tex. 1992) (in failing to adequately insure repossessed automobile, chapter 13 debtor failed to satisfy the adequate protection precondition for turnover) *with In re* Sharon, 234 B.R. 676 (B.A.P. 6th Cir. 1999); *In re* Berscheit, 223 B.R. 579 (Bankr. D. Wyo. 1998) (adequate protection not required as a prerequisite to turnover).

377 *See* §§ 8.2.7.3, 8.7.2.1, *supra.* Proof of insurance may also be required.

378 *See* § 9.7.3.2.2, *supra.* For chapter 7 cases, other forms of adequate protection may be necessary.

379 11 U.S.C. § 542(c).

380 See discussion of 11 U.S.C. §§ 549 and 550 in § 10.4.2.6.6, *infra,* as to voidability of post-petition transfers.

9.9.4 Issues of Possession After Turnover

It must be noted that section 542 requires turnover of property to the trustee, and not to the debtor.[381] Nowhere does the Code clearly spell out the procedure that should be used to transfer such property to the debtor in cases in which it seems clear the debtor should have possession of it. Thus, for example, if property that the debtor may exempt in a chapter 7 case is turned over to the trustee, the trustee may not feel free to relinquish it immediately to the debtor before the exemptions are approved.

It seems fairly obvious that the intent of the Code is that debtors should have possession of exempt property during the case; they are not expected to relinquish their household goods pending approval of the exemptions claimed. In fact, the exemptions are approved automatically if there is no objection to them.[382] Moreover, such goods are rarely of any use to the trustee who would incur needless expense in storing and preserving them. In view of all these considerations, and the general purpose of the exemptions to allow the debtor to maintain a modest standard of living, there can be little doubt that property claimed as exempt should be immediately relinquished to the debtor by a trustee to whom it is turned over under section 542, at least absent a serious dispute about the exemption claim.

---

381 At least one court has held that creditors may not request turnover when the trustee fails to do so. *In re* Perkins, 902 F.2d 1254 (7th Cir. 1990).

382 11 U.S.C. § 522(*l*); *see* § 10.3.4, *infra*.

Until this issue is definitively resolved, however, it is best to avoid having to litigate it. As much exempt property as possible should be in the debtor's possession on the date the case is commenced. All monies should be withdrawn from bank accounts, so that access to them is not prevented because they were turned over to the trustee or frozen. If possible, the filing should be delayed until after receipt of a tax refund, because the Internal Revenue Service also frequently pays such refunds to the trustee rather than to the debtor.

In chapter 13 cases, the situation is somewhat more clear. Because section 1306 provides that the debtor is to remain in possession of all property of the estate, there is no reason for the trustee to retain any property turned over to him or her. Such property should be promptly delivered to the debtor. Indeed, it is unfortunate that there is no provision requiring turnover directly to the debtor to obviate the necessity for any trustee involvement, because in most cases, the right to use, sell, or lease property is that of the debtor, exclusive of the trustee.[383]

Finally, it should be noted that much of what has been said above applies equally to property obtained by the trustee through use of other powers. The trustee has a wide range of ways to gather property into the estate and to avoid pre-bankruptcy transfers of property. Many of these are discussed in the context of the debtor's exemptions, in the next chapter of this manual.

---

383 11 U.S.C. § 1303. See § 12.8, *infra*, for a more detailed discussion.

Chapter 10   Exemptions

10.1 Introduction

10.1.1 Importance of the Exemption Provisions

For most consumer debtors, no section of the Bankruptcy Code is more important than section 522, which governs the debtor's rights in relation to exempt property. It is a section which makes enormous advances in debtors' rights. On the whole, the exemption provisions in the Code make bankruptcy much more attractive to consumers than the previous law, and give better protection to their property than can be had under the law governing execution in most states.

Indeed, the availability of exemptions is usually key to the determination of whether to file a bankruptcy in the first place, and also the determination as to which type of bankruptcy case to file.[1] If the debtor has significant amounts of property that are not exempt, and thus would be lost in a chapter 7 liquidation, a chapter 13 case is usually preferable. And in a chapter 13 case, the value of non-exempt property may determine the minimum that must be paid to unsecured creditors;[2] if that amount cannot be paid through the plan, then a chapter 13 case may not be feasible.

The exemption provisions are closely related to other parts of the Code. For example, they give the debtor many of the trustee's powers to avoid pre-petition transfers of property, as well as some additional powers over and above those of the trustee, all of which are discussed in this Chapter. The turnover provisions of section 542 specifically require that property that is in the possession of a third party and that the debtor can exempt must be turned over to the trustee.[3] Similarly, the right to redeem certain types of property from liens under section 722 applies only to exempt or abandoned property.[4] And many of the protections after discharge bear a direct relationship to what property has been exempted.[5]

10.1.2 Definition of Exempt Property

The Code contains no formal definition of the terms "exemption" or "exempt property." Fundamentally, these are the designations given to the property that the debtor is permitted to retain in a chapter 7 liquidation. Other than the exempt property, virtually all of the debtor's interests in property that have significant value are transferred to the trustee for the benefit of creditors.

With some exceptions, discussed later in this Chapter, exemptions do not affect valid security interests or other liens on property of the debtor.[6] A debtor must usually pay the secured creditor the amount of its secured claim to eliminate a lien. As the lien can be thought of as diminishing the debtor's interest in the encumbered property, only the value of the interest remaining after subtraction of the lien amount need be claimed as exempt.

The procedure for claiming exemptions is not fully spelled out in the Code. Although section 522(1) states that the debtor shall "file a list" of property claimed as exempt, the questions of when, where and how this list is to be filed are left to the Rules of Bankruptcy Procedure. The rules require the debtor to file the claim of exemption with the schedules at the outset of a case.[7]

Exemptions are claimed and determined with respect to the debtor's property at the outset of the case, except to the extent additional property becomes property of the estate thereafter, in which case the value of property is determined on the date the property becomes property of the estate.[8] Ordinarily, if a case is converted to chapter 7 from chapter 13, property acquired since the filing of the petition need not be claimed as exempt as it is not property of the estate in the converted case unless it would have been property of the estate on the date the chapter 13 petition was filed.[9]

---

1. For a general discussion of these decisions, see Chapter 6, *supra.*
2. 11 U.S.C. § 1325(a)(4). See discussion of the "best interests of creditors" chapter 13 test in § 12.3.1, *infra.* This test is also applicable in chapter 12 cases. *See* § 16.5.4.1, *infra.*
3. See § 9.9, *supra,* for discussion of the turnover provisions.
4. See § 11.5, *infra,* for discussion of the right to redeem property.
5. 11 U.S.C. § 522(c); *see* § 10.5, *infra.*

---

6. *In re* Sloma, 43 F.3d 637 (11th Cir. 1995) (debtor's claim that annuity payments were exempt did not affect bank's security interest in annuity, which debtor had assigned as collateral for loan).
7. Fed. R. Bankr. P. 4003(a); Official Form 6, Sch. C, Appx. D, *infra.*
8. 11 U.S.C. § 522(a)(2). See § 2.5, *supra,* for a discussion of the limited types of property which may come into the estate after filing.
9. 11 U.S.C. § 348(f)(1) (with exception for bad faith conversions in § 348(f)(2)).

The Code also does not specify when exempt property loses its previous character as property of the estate. Is it when the list is filed (at the commencement of the case in most instances)?[10] At the latest, it should be when the time for objections[11] has passed.[12]

Similarly, the Code does not address the question of who shall possess exempt property during the period before the time for objections has run. Courts have generally assumed that the debtor has the right to remain in possession of exempt property throughout the case;[13] it is hard to imagine debtors delivering all of their household goods to the trustee. However, if the property comes into the hands of the trustee, because of a turnover or avoidance of a transfer, there are no guidelines as to when the trustee must deliver it to the debtor in a chapter 7 case. Presumably, in view of the purposes of exemptions discussed below, this turnover should be done promptly.[14] It is clear in a chapter 13 case that prompt delivery to the debtor is required, because the debtor is entitled to possession of all property of the estate.[15]

10.1.3 Purposes of Exemptions

Historically, the purpose of exemption laws has always been to allow debtors to keep those items of property deemed essential to daily life. Without this bare grubstake, it was feared that debtors could not retain the minimum of dignity and self-respect to which all members of a society are entitled. Perhaps more importantly to some, it was feared that stripping debtors of all of their property would increase the chances of their becoming public charges, unable to maintain themselves without assistance.

In the bankruptcy context, exemptions serve the overriding purpose of helping the debtor to obtain a fresh start. They allow the debtor to come out of the process with not only a minimum amount of dignity, but also the essentials upon which to build a new life. They leave at least a basic vestige of the possessions that the debtor has acquired over a lifetime, so that the debtor may proceed to move forward, rather than spend time struggling simply to exist.

These policies have been judged, by state legislatures and by Congress, to be more important than satisfying the claims of unsecured creditors (and, in bankruptcy, some secured creditors) out of certain items of the debtor's property. The Bankruptcy Code gave new strength and protection to these principles, and eliminated many of the creditor practices which, over the years, had come to undermine them.

10.2 What Property Is Exempt?

10.2.1 The Choice of State or Federal Exemptions

In many states, a debtor may choose from two sets of exemptions. As under the prior law, a debtor in any state may choose to utilize the exemptions provided by state law and by federal non-bankruptcy law (for example, laws protecting social security benefits and veterans benefits, and so forth). If the debtor chooses the state exemptions, then certain other property of the estate not normally subject to process under state law may also be claimed as exempt.

The Code also provides a comprehensive list of special federal exemptions that are applicable only in bankruptcy cases. Debtors may choose these exemptions as an alternative to the traditionally available exemptions, as long as their state of domicile has not "opted out" of the federal exemption scheme.[16] The "opt out" provision, adopted as a last-minute compromise to secure passage of the Code, allows any state to pass a law prohibiting the use of the special federal bankruptcy exemptions. While this concept is unusual, it has not been successfully challenged.[17] Currently,

---

10 *In re* Peterson, 897 F.2d 935 (8th Cir. 1990) (exemptions are fixed and vested at the time of petition, so debtor's death eight months after filing the petition does not constitute an abandonment of the debtor's homestead exemption or cause the exemption to lapse back into the estate).

11 Objections to exemptions are discussed in § 10.3.3, *infra*.

12 *In re* Gamble, 168 F.3d 442 (11th Cir. 1999); *In re* Hahn, 60 B.R. 69 (Bankr. D. Minn. 1985); *see* Kennedy, *Automatic Stays Under the New Bankruptcy Law*, 12 U. Mich. J.L. Ref. 3, 38 n.158 (1978); § 10.3.4, *infra*; *see also* Wissman v. Pittsburgh Nat'l Bank, 942 F.2d 867 (4th Cir. 1991); Christy v. Heights Fin. Corp., 101 B.R. 542 (C.D. Ill. 1987).

13 However, a debtor must be careful in using property, especially cash, the exemption of which might ultimately be in dispute. *See In re* Walker, 83 B.R. 14 (B.A.P. 9th Cir. 1988) (order may be entered denying debtor use of funds in pension plan when the exempt character of those funds is in dispute); *see also* 11 U.S.C. § 363 (insofar as it relates to use of property by a debtor).

14 *But see In re* Salzer, 52 F.3d 708 (7th Cir. 1995) (erroneously holding that Indiana execution procedures permit a bankruptcy trustee to hold property after the deadline for objecting to exemptions has run until the trustee obtains an appraisal of the property; pro se debtor waived argument that commercial property in question was totally exempt); Greene v. Balaber-Strauss, 76 B.R. 940 (S.D.N.Y. 1987) (trustee could wait until she completed her administrative duties; decision is poorly reasoned, confusing the issue of discharge with that of exemptions, which are provided regardless of discharge).

15 11 U.S.C. § 1306(b); *see* § 12.8, *infra*.

---

16 11 U.S.C. § 522(b). In cases where a state opts out after the petition is filed, federal exemptions are available. *See* Hollytex Carpet Mills v. Tedford, 691 F.2d 392 (8th Cir. 1982) (law in effect on date of petition governs exemptions throughout the case); *In re* Boozer, 4 B.R. 524 (Bankr. N.D. Ga. 1980).

17 A fairly strong argument can be made that the provision allowing states to opt-out is unconstitutional. Article 1, section 8 of the Constitution gives Congress the power to establish "uniform laws on the subject of bankruptcy" and it could be argued that the opt-out provision is a non-uniform law. While the previous Act's complete deference to state exemption laws was upheld against such a challenge, there may be a difference now that there is a federal standard for exemptions which states may reject. Put another way, may Congress delegate to the states the

thirty-five states have such a law,[18] and in those states, debtors may utilize only the state and federal non-bankruptcy exemptions.[19] (A state may also opt out of the federal bankruptcy exemptions and pass its own bankruptcy exemptions, which may be different from its normal exemptions from execution.)[20] By repealing these laws, of course, those states can opt back into the federal exemptions.[21]

Occasionally a debtor who is domiciled or who resides in an opt-out state may still utilize the federal exemptions,

depending upon the precise wording of the opt-out statute. Because "domicile" is usually defined as a permanent home, from which a person may be away for a period of time but to which the person intends to return, a person may be domiciled in a different state than that in which the person resides temporarily. Thus, a debtor who is domiciled in a state that has opted out for its *residents* may reside in a second state temporarily, even if it is an opt-out state, file in the first state (the debtor's domicile) within ninety days after the move, and claim the federal bankruptcy exemptions because the debtor is not a resident of the first state and the state opted out only for residents.[22] Conversely, if a state has opted out only for persons domiciled in the state, debtors who are residents but intend to return to another permanent domicile would be able to claim the federal exemptions.[23]

In any case, even when a state has opted out of the federal bankruptcy exemptions, the remaining provisions of section 522 remain applicable to enhance the exemptions that are available to the debtor; a state may not opt out of those provisions.[24]

Assuming that the debtor's state has not opted out, the debtor must choose the applicable exemptions. In some states, the state exemptions may be more liberal than the federal exemptions, particularly with respect to homesteads, pensions and insurance interests.

The choice between state and federal exemptions is normally made by designation in Schedule C, the schedule of exemptions that is filed with the debtor's other bankruptcy schedules.[25] The designation is sufficient if one set of statutory references is used rather than the other. Under the rules, that schedule can later be amended, including presumably to change from federal to state exemptions or vice versa.[26] In a joint filing of a husband and wife, both spouses must choose the same exemption scheme.[27] If the spouses cannot

---

right to deprive citizens of federal rights applicable only in bankruptcy cases? *See* Michael Terry Hertz, *Bankruptcy Code Exemptions: Notes on the Effect of State Law*, 54 Am. Bankr. L. J. 339, 341–344 (1980). The argument that the opt out provision violates the Constitution's requirement for a uniform bankruptcy law has been rejected in several cases. *In re* Storer, 58 F.3d 1125 (6th Cir. 1995) (also holding that opt out did not violate privileges and immunities, due process, supremacy, or equal protection clauses of Constitution); *In re* Sullivan, 680 F.2d 1131 (7th Cir. 1982). However, several opt-out statutes have been found unconstitutional for other reasons. State exemptions provided by Maryland have been found to so greatly discriminate against non-home owners that they thwart the Congressional policy of nondiscrimination and thus violate the Supremacy Clause. *See In re* Locarno, 23 B.R. 622 (Bankr. D. Md. 1982). But this reasoning has been rejected by at least one court of appeals. Rhodes v. Stewart, 705 F.2d 159 (6th Cir. 1983). In addition, the Maryland statute required, as a condition precedent to claiming a homestead exemption, that the debtor attempt to negotiate payment agreements with creditors. This provision has also been found to violate federal bankruptcy policy and thus the Supremacy Clause. *In re* Smith, 23 B.R. 708 (Bankr. D. Md. 1982); *In re* Davis, 16 B.R. 62 (Bankr. D. Md. 1981). Indiana's exemption scheme making certain property available to tort creditors in bankruptcy, but not to contract creditors was upheld, however, without express consideration of the Supremacy Clause. *In re* Ondras, 846 F.2d 33 (7th Cir. 1988).

18 The following states have opted out: Alabama, Alaska, Arizona, California, Colorado, Delaware, Florida, Georgia, Idaho, Illinois, Indiana, Iowa, Kansas, Kentucky, Louisiana, Maine, Maryland, Mississippi, Missouri, Montana, Nebraska, Nevada, New York, North Carolina, North Dakota, Ohio, Oklahoma, Oregon, South Carolina, South Dakota, Tennessee, Utah, Virginia, West Virginia and Wyoming. Arkansas and New Hampshire, which previously had opted out, subsequently repealed their opt-out laws. *See In re* Gardner, 139 B.R. 460 (Bankr. E.D. & W.D. Ark. 1991).

19 When a state has opted out, the argument that the federal bankruptcy exemptions may in some way limit a more expansive state law exemption has been rejected. *In re* Thompson, 867 F.2d 416 (7th Cir. 1989); *In re* Taylor, 861 F.2d 550 (9th Cir. 1988). The exemptions available are those in effect on the date of the bankruptcy petition. Amendments to the state exemptions cannot be retroactively applied to bankruptcies pending before the effective date of the state statute, even where the petition was involuntary. *In re* Peacock, 119 B.R. 605 (Bankr. N.D. Ill. 1990), *aff'd*, 125 B.R. 526 (N.D. Ill. 1991). Similarly, if a state repeals its opt-out law, exemptions are governed by the law in effect on the date of the petition. *In re* Gardner, 139 B.R. 460 (Bankr. E.D. & W.D. Ark. 1991).

20 *See In re* Bloom, 5 B.R. 451 (Bankr. N.D. Ohio 1980).

21 *See In re* Gardner, 139 B.R. 460 (Bankr. E.D. & W.D. Ark. 1991).

---

22 *See In re* Schultz, 101 B.R. 301 (Bankr. N.D. Fla. 1989); *In re* Hawkins, 15 B.R. 618 (Bankr. E.D. Va. 1981) (as Virginia exemptions were available for residents only, opt-out could not apply to non-resident).

23 *In re* Arispe, 289 B.R. 245 (Bankr. S.D. Fla. 2002) (resident alien who was not domiciled in Florida or any other state was not subject to Florida exemption laws, including opt-out, and could claim federal exemptions).

24 Owen v. Owen, 500 U.S. 305, 111 S. Ct. 1833, 114 L. Ed. 2d 350 (1991) (§ 522(f) treats federal and state exemptions equally and a state cannot opt out of the Code's lien avoidance provisions by passing exemption statutes which purport to exclude property subject to liens).

25 *See In re* Pierce, 214 B.R. 550 (Bankr. E.D.N.C. 1997) (in court statement by the debtor does not reflect a choice of exemptions particularly as mentioning a "wild card" exemption could reflect either state or federal law), *rev'd on other grounds*, 231 B.R. 890 (E.D.N.C. 1998).

26 *See* § 10.3.2, *infra*.

27 11 U.S.C. § 522(b); *see* Seung v. Silverman, 288 B.R. 174 (E.D.N.Y. 2003) (requiring New Jersey debtor to use New York exemptions rather than federal exemptions in joint case because her New York domiciliary husband could only choose New York exemptions, a questionable result).

agree upon which exemptions to choose, they are deemed to have chosen the federal exemptions.[28] They also, however, have the option of filing two separate petitions, with each spouse electing the exemptions of his or her choice.[29] Even when a state has opted out of the federal exemptions, it may be possible to assert the state exemptions separately for each debtor,[30] as section 522(m) of the Code provides that each debtor's exemptions must be treated separately.

10.2.2 The Federal Bankruptcy Exemptions

10.2.2.1 In General

The property that can be claimed as exempt under the federal bankruptcy exemptions (in states that have not opted out) is listed in section 522(d) of the Code. The list itself, adopted originally by the Bankruptcy Commission, was later generally followed in the Uniform Exemptions Act.[31] Although Congress made some changes in drafting the Code and in later amendments, the commentary to the Uniform Act, therefore, is a good place to look for interpretive assistance.

Because the exemptions may be claimed by each debtor individually,[32] a husband and wife filing a joint case are each entitled to the full exemption amounts listed for each category of property in section 522(d), effectively doubling those amounts for jointly held property. (In many states there is a presumption that property acquired during the

marriage is jointly owned.) However, the same provisions would probably prevent the application of one spouse's unused exemption amount to the separate property of the other spouse.[33]

As a result, problems occasionally arise from the wording of some of the exemptions. For example, if there are two jointly- held motor vehicles, each worth $2575.00, each joint debtor could only exempt one-half of the value of one car because the motor vehicle exemption applies to the debtor's interest in one motor vehicle.[34] This result would leave the equivalent of one vehicle not exempted under that subsection. One simple solution to this problem would be a pre-bankruptcy trading of interests so that each spouse owned one car in full. Then each could exempt the full $2575.00 value of his or her car. Thus, pre-bankruptcy exemption planning may be especially important in joint filings.

The list of federal exemptions was amended in 1994 to double the previous dollar amounts of exemptions permitted, most of which had gone unchanged since 1978. Under Code section 104(b), the dollar amounts of the federal bankruptcy exemptions are now adjusted every three years to take into account changes in the cost of living. The most recent of these adjustments was effective on April 1, 2004.

10.2.2.2 Homestead—§ 522(d)(1)

The largest specific dollar amount applicable to particular property is the $18,450.00 that each debtor may claim as a homestead exemption.[35] This exemption, like all of the other exemptions, applies only to the debtor's interest in property, that is, the equity over and above liens. Hence, a debtor with a one-half interest in a $60,000.00 jointly-owned home encumbered by a $30,000.00 mortgage, has a $15,000.00 interest in that home (1/2 x [$60,000.00–$30,000.00]). Being not more than a $18,450.00 interest, the debtor's interest would be fully exempt. However, it is important to remember that in subtracting liens to determine equity, precomputed but as yet unearned interest should not be included. Only the current "payoff figure" due on the lien can properly be considered owing.[36]

As discussed earlier, two joint owners may exempt an interest of $36,900.00 under this exemption. In fact, they may add an additional $1950.00 to that figure (or to any

28   11 U.S.C. § 522(b).

29   *But see* Fed. R. Bankr. P. 1015(b) (court may order joint administration of husband's and wife's individual petitions and fix time in which they must choose same set of exemptions). If the husband and wife filed under different chapters, such joint administration would be far less likely.

30   *In re* Cheeseman, 656 F.2d 60 (4th Cir. 1981); *In re* Bartlett, 24 B.R. 605 (B.A.P. 9th Cir. 1982); *In re* Smith, 27 B.R. 30 (Bankr. D. Ariz. 1982); Manufacturers & Traders Trust Co. v. Borst, 128 Misc. 2d 691 (N.Y. Sup. Ct. 1984); *see also* John T. Mather Mem'l Hosp. v. Pearl, 723 F.2d 193 (2d Cir. 1983) (based upon interpretation of state law); § 10.2.3.1, *infra*. *But see In re* Talmadge, 832 F.2d 1120 (9th Cir. 1987) (California's exemption scheme allowing spouses single set of exemptions does not violate Equal Protection and can be enforced despite § 522(m)); Stevens v. Pike County Bank, 829 F.2d 693 (8th Cir. 1987) (state could limit couple to one homestead exemption in bankruptcy); *In re* Granger, 754 F.2d 1490 (9th Cir. 1985) (state exemption scheme which did not provide separate exemptions for husband and wife enforced in bankruptcy); First Nat'l Bank v. Norris, 701 F.2d 902 (11th Cir. 1983) (section 522(m) does not create separate state exemptions for joint debtors); *see also In re* Pruitt, 829 F.2d 1002 (10th Cir. 1987) (where only one homestead is allowed to a couple, value of single debtor's interest is computed by taking one half of the difference between value of property and homestead exemption).

31   13 U.L.A. 371-406.

32   11 U.S.C. § 522(m).

33   *In re* Cunningham, 8 Bankr. Ct. Dec. (LRP) 863, Bankr. L. Rep. (CCH) ¶ 68,578 (Bankr. D. Mass. 1980) (husband's exemption may not be used for wife's property); *In re* Crum, 6 B.R. 138 (Bankr. M.D. Fla. 1980) (tax refund allocated between spouses according to monies withheld); *In re* Colbert, 5 B.R. 646 (Bankr. S.D. Ohio 1980) (wife could not claim exemption on joint tax refund if she had no earnings that year).

34   11 U.S.C. § 522(d)(2).

35   11 U.S.C. § 522(d)(1).

36   *In re* Parenteau, 23 B.R. 289 (B.A.P. 1st Cir. 1982).

other exemption) because a different subsection permits each to exempt an interest of $975.00 in "any property."[37]

The homestead exemption is applicable to interests in either real or personal property, and therefore it clearly includes mobile homes, houseboats, shares in a cooperative, and so on.[38] It also clearly includes non-ownership interests such as leases.[39] The property must be a residence of the debtor or a dependent of the debtor, though it does not appear necessary that it be the principal residence.[40] The debtor need not necessarily be occupying the property on the date of the petition.[41] A burial plot may also be exempted under this subsection.

Unlike some state exemption schemes, the federal bankruptcy homestead exemption does not explicitly apply to proceeds of the sale of a homestead.[42] However, when a home is sold after bankruptcy is filed, the exemption is preserved because section 522(a)(2) explicitly states that exemptions are to be determined as of the date the bankruptcy petition was filed.[43] It is less clear whether a debtor may use the federal homestead exemption to exempt proceeds of a sale of a home which occurred prior to filing. This uncertainty can frequently be avoided with careful pre-bankruptcy exemption planning.[44]

10.2.2.3 Motor Vehicle—§ 522(d)(2)

A debtor may exempt an interest of up to $2950.00 in one motor vehicle under section 522(d)(2). It is important to note the limitation in this provision to one vehicle per debtor. Again, the exemption need be applied only to the debtor's interest over and above any security interest or other lien. And an interest in excess of the $2950.00 amount may sometimes be picked up using another exemption, such as the exemption for any property,[45] or in some cases, the exemption for tools of a trade.[46]

10.2.2.4 Household Goods, Etcetera—§ 522(d)(3)

Section 522(d)(3) allows a debtor to exempt an interest of up to $475.00 in value in any item of household furnishings, household goods, wearing apparel, appliances, books, animals, crops, or musical instruments held primarily for the personal, family or household use of the debtor or the debtor's dependents. Like the other exemptions, this exemption may be doubled in a joint case to include items of up to $950.00 in value if jointly owned by the debtors.[47] There is an aggregate dollar limit of $9850.00 per debtor on the property that can be exempted under this subsection. This limit was raised from $4000.00 by the 1994 amendments and is adjusted for inflation every three years.[48] Thus, especially in joint cases in which the limit is doubled, all of the household belongings of most debtors may be saved under this provision.

One question which may occasionally arise concerns the definition of the term "item." When several related pieces of property may be considered a "set" worth over $475.00, disputes could occur as to whether that set is an item. For example, it is not clear whether each chair in a dining room set, or each spoon in a set of silver, or each speaker in a stereo system, should be considered to be an item apart from the set as a whole.[49] Common sense should prevail in dealing with these issues, and except in cases in which the debtors have a great deal of valuable property, trustees have little interest in litigating about the exemption of a few household goods.

The scope of the subsection may also raise questions. It will not generally include motor vehicles, though a lawn tractor might be an exception.[50] Similarly, most items spe-

---

37 11 U.S.C. § 522(d)(5).

38 *See In re* Meola, 158 B.R. 881 (Bankr. S.D. Fla. 1993) (travel trailer qualified as exempt under Florida homestead exemption for a "dwelling house").

39 *In re* Princiotta, 49 B.R. 447 (Bankr. D. Mass. 1985) (debtor's interest in land installment sale contract could be exempted under this section); *see* Uniform Exemption Act, § 4, cmt. (4), 13 U.L.A. 379; *see also In re* Casserino, 290 B.R. 735 (B.A.P. 9th Cir. 2003) (Oregon homestead exemption applied to prepaid rent on leasehold interests); *In re* Johnson, 288 B.R. 130 (B.A.P. 8th Cir. 2003) (lien interest awarded by divorce court was interest in residence that could be exempted); *cf. In re* Moody, 862 F.2d 1194 (5th Cir. 1989) (debtor's attempt to fraudulently transfer residence pre-petition does not deprive the debtor of homestead exemption under Texas law when the property is brought back into the estate).

40 *But see In re* Tomko, 87 B.R. 372 (Bankr. E.D. Pa. 1988) (exemption not allowed in vacation home because debtors lived elsewhere most of the year).

41 *In re* DeMasi, 227 B.R. 586 (D.R.I. 1998) (debtor who owned a remainder interest in home, had resided there previously and intended to reside there again was permitted to claim property as exempt).

42 *See In re* Healy, 100 B.R. 443 (Bankr. W.D. Wis. 1989) (debtors not entitled to exemption in proceeds of pre-petition sale of homestead absent evidence that proceeds would be reinvested in residence which debtors planned to occupy); *see also, e.g., In re* Williamson, 844 F.2d 1166 (5th Cir. 1988) (proceeds of sale of exempt property exempt under Mississippi homestead provision).

43 *See* § 10.3.3, *infra*; *see also In re* Reed, 940 F.2d 1317 (9th Cir. 1991) (where property is sold prior to abandonment by trustee, debtors are entitled to exemption from the proceeds, but trustee may claim balance).

44 *See* § 6.5.2.2, *supra*.

---

45 11 U.S.C. § 522(d)(5).

46 11 U.S.C. § 522(d)(6); *see* § 10.2.2.7, *infra*.

47 *In re* Lambert, 10 B.R. 11 (Bankr. N.D. Ind. 1980).

48 11 U.S.C. § 104(b).

49 *See In re* Wahl, 14 B.R. 153 (Bankr. E.D. Wis. 1981) (each knife, fork or spoon in a set of silver considered an item; court looked to *Webster's Dictionary* for guidance).

50 *See In re* Jones, 5 B.R. 655 (Bankr. M.D.N.C. 1980) (garden tractor exempt as household good). There has also been some litigation about whether a mobile home can be considered a household good for the purposes of the lien avoidance provision

cifically listed elsewhere in the exemption provisions, such as jewelry,[51] are not usually included. Other items, such as guns, may be subject to a dispute because it is unclear whether they are household goods.[52] Although the provision is not specifically limited to personalty, it may be hard to use section 522(d)(3) to have real property exempted (except possibly for some fixtures and the like).

Finally, items used *primarily* for business purposes are not meant to be included.[53] The language limiting the exemption to items used *primarily* for "personal, family, or household use," derived from the Truth in Lending Act,[54] does make this limitation clear. However, under that Act, the case law and Federal Reserve Board interpretations and staff opinions have given that phrase a fairly broad meaning, and should be consulted if questions arise.[55] The same phrase is used in the Code's definition of "consumer debt," discussed elsewhere in this manual.[56]

It seems safe to say that, except for debtors who conduct a business in their home, this exemption should be applicable to just about all of the personal property normally kept at the debtor's residence that is not specifically mentioned in other exemptions.[57] It is clear that the scope of the exemption extends beyond necessities, as it does not include, as do some others,[58] only amounts "reasonably necessary for the support of the debtor." The section is concerned only with how the property is used, and not whether it might be considered a luxury.

10.2.2.5 Jewelry—§ 522(d)(4)

Each debtor is allowed to exempt up to $1225.00 worth of jewelry, as long as it is held primarily for personal, family,

or household use of the debtor or a dependent. As with the household goods exemption, unused exemptions applicable to "any property" may be used to increase this amount. For example, a jewelry item worth $1300.00 may be exempted using the $1225.00 jewelry exemption plus $75.00 worth of the exemption applicable to any property (sometimes referred to as the "wild card" exemption).

Some questions may arise under this provision concerning whether a particular item is classified as jewelry or wearing apparel.[59] If the item is worth under $475.00, it is usually to the debtor's benefit for it to be considered the latter, because a larger total exemption is available for wearing apparel worth less than $475.00 per item. On the other hand, if the debtor has items worth more than $475.00, the debtor's use of other exemptions will determine which interpretation is more favorable in a particular case. If none of the exemption for "any property" has been used and all of the jewelry exemption has been used, then it is preferable to argue that the items are wearing apparel so that on each item any value in excess of the $475.00 available for wearing apparel may be exempted (until the wild-card exemption is exhausted). However, if the jewelry exemption has not yet been used, it is preferable to argue that the item is jewelry so that the amount available only for jewelry can be used so the wild-card exemption can be saved for some other property. In any event, case law developed under the various state exemption laws pertaining to jewelry and wearing apparel will be relevant to the argument.

A common issue under this subsection arises with respect to wedding rings, engagement rings and other jewelry with great sentimental value. The monetary value of those items can sometimes exceed the amount of the available exemptions. Most trustees do not make a practice of taking a debtor's personal jewelry unless it is very valuable, but there is no way to make this guarantee about a particular item to a nervous debtor contemplating bankruptcy. In such situations, it may make sense to obtain an appraisal, because it is not uncommon for debtors to have an inflated opinion about the value of jewelry which is based in sentiment rather than reality. After appraisal, if the jewelry still cannot be exempted under any combination of available provisions, local practice should be checked. In some jurisdictions, given the practice of trustees, there may be little cause for worry. Further, as discussed in an earlier chapter, a trustee who is interested in selling valuable jewelry may be willing to sell it to the debtor or a relative of the debtor in order to avoid liquidation costs and the hardship caused by sale of a highly personal item.[60] Finally, if a sale cannot be avoided, the debtor will receive the amount of the exemption in cash, and that cash can be used to purchase a substitute item.

---

applicable to nonpossessory, nonpurchase-money security interests in exempt household goods. See § 10.4.2.4 infra.

51 11 U.S.C. § 522(d)(4).

52 Most of the litigation on this issue had taken place in the context of lien avoidance motions. See § 10.4.2.4 infra.

53 See In re Reid, 757 F.2d 230 (10th Cir. 1985) (debtor's "classic religious paintings," worth $187,000.00 and pledged as collateral for business loans, were primarily used for business and are not household furniture exemptible under Oklahoma law).

54 15 U.S.C. § 1602(h).

55 See National Consumer Law Center, Truth in Lending § 2.2.3 (5th ed. 2003).

56 11 U.S.C. § 101(8); see § 13.9.2.2, infra.

57 See In re Ratliff, 209 B.R. 534 (Bankr. E.D. Okla. 1997) (computer and printer were household goods for purposes of Oklahoma exemptions); In re Beard, 5 B.R. 429 (Bankr. S.D. Iowa 1980) (stereo components and Betamax are household goods); In re Coleman, 5 B.R. 76 (Bankr. M.D. Tenn. 1980) (stereo system constitutes household furnishings). The Fourth Circuit has adopted a slightly more limited definition, finding "household goods" to mean those items of personal property typically found in or around the home and used by a debtor or the debtor's dependents to support and facilitate day-to-day living within the home. In re McGreevy, 955 F.2d 957 (4th Cir. 1992).

58 See, e.g., § 522(d)(11)(B), (C), (E).

59 See, e.g., In re Fernandez, 855 F.2d 218 (5th Cir. 1988) (under Texas law jewelry may be exemptible as clothing); In re Hazelhurst, 228 B.R. 199 (Bankr. E.D. Tenn. 1998) (jewelry could be considered wearing apparel under Tennessee exemptions).

60 See § 8.3.8, supra.

10.2.2.6 Any Property—§ 522(d)(5)

One of the most important of the federal exemptions is the exemption which can be applied to "any property," sometimes called the "wild card." The amount of this exemption is $975.00 per debtor, plus any unused amount of the homestead amount from subsection (d)(1) up to $9250.00 per debtor. The applicability of the unused homestead exemption to any property, sometimes called the "homestead pourover," was originally intended to equalize home owners and renters but was significantly reduced when a $3750.00 limit was added in 1984. That limit was raised in 1994 and is adjusted every three years to take into account changes in the cost of living.[61] It gives tremendous flexibility to both home owners and renters, as many home owners may not choose to or need to use the entire homestead exemption for their residences. And as there is no requirement that any portion of the homestead exemption be used on a home as a prerequisite to qualifying for the homestead pourover, renters can get the benefit of a total wild card exemption worth $10,225.00.[62]

As noted above, this exemption can be used in conjunction with any other specific exemption to pick up value in excess of the amount provided by the particular exemption, for example, the remaining $50.00 on a $3000.00 car.[63] It can also be applied to any possible property interest, including intangibles, non-liquid property, causes of action, tax refunds, cash, public benefits already received, and so forth.[64] If the wild card exemption is not used in the debtors' initial exemption claim, it remains available to be raised by way of amendment to protect property which the trustee unexpectedly contends is to be non-exempt.[65]

10.2.2.7 Tools of the Trade—§ 522(d)(6)

Each debtor may exempt up to $1850.00 worth of implements, professional books, or tools of the trade that belong to the debtor or a dependent of the debtor. This exemption, too, may overlap with some of the others. For example, a motor vehicle sometimes can be claimed as exempt under this subsection as well as subsection (d)(2) if it is used by the debtor in his or her trade (beyond normal commuting.)[66] Thus, a vehicle worth $4800.00 per debtor could be claimed by combining these sections. Three way combinations, including the wild card exemption, are also possible.[67] Additionally, the spouse of a debtor may claim equipment as exempt even if that spouse only handles the business end of the enterprise.[68] As with jewelry, it may be preferable to argue that a particular item falls within the household goods exemption, that is, is held primarily for personal, non-business use, if its value is under $475.00, or if the tools of trade exemption has been exhausted on other property.

There are often significant questions as to whether farm equipment or livestock are included within this exemption or similar exemptions under state law. Although the importance of the issue is diminished in the federal scheme by the relatively low amount of the exemption, it has been raised in a number of reported cases.[69] Similar issues may arise in connection with home office equipment.[70]

---

61 11 U.S.C. § 104(b). The most recent adjustment became effective on April 1, 2004.

62 *See In re* Martin, 140 F.3d 806 (8th Cir. 1998) (no requirement that the debtor use any portion of the homestead exemption on a home in order to qualify for the homestead pourover).

63 Augustine v. United States, 675 F.2d 582 (3d Cir. 1982) (section 522(d)(5) exemption may be used to exempt tools of trade in excess of $750.00 limit applicable at that time).

64 4 Collier on Bankruptcy ¶ 522.09[5] (15th ed. rev.); *In re* Smith, 640 F.2d 888 (7th Cir. 1981) (Truth in Lending claim could be exempted under 11 U.S.C. § 522(d)(5)); *In re* Laird, 6 B.R. 273 (Bankr. E.D. Pa. 1980) (arbitration award); *In re* Collins, 5 B.R. 675 (Bankr. N.D. Cal. 1980) (credit union account); *In re* Nichols, 4 B.R. 711 (Bankr. E.D. Mich. 1980) (wage withholdings and tax refunds); *In re* Cramer, 3 B.R. 428 (Bankr. D. Ariz. 1980) (business inventory).

65 *See* § 10.3.2, *infra.*

66 *Compare In re* Breen, 123 B.R. 357 (B.A.P. 9th Cir. 1991) (carpenter may avoid nonpossessory, nonpurchase-money security interest on pick-up truck considered to be tool of the trade); *In re* McNutt, 87 B.R. 84 (B.A.P. 9th Cir. 1988) (truck used in dry-wall business exempt as tool of debtor's trade); *In re* Lyall, 191 B.R. 78 (E.D. Va. 1996) (if car was necessary for debtor's work as an architect, it was tool of trade under Virginia law even if it was a luxury car); *In re* Graettinger, 95 B.R. 632 (Bankr. N.D. Iowa 1988) (pick-up truck is tool of trade in debtor's business as grain bin salesperson); *and In re* Dubrock, 5 B.R. 353 (Bankr. W.D. Ky. 1980) (real estate broker and salesman may claim automobile as tool of the trade) *with In re* Johnston, 842 F.2d 1221 (10th Cir. 1988) (pick-up truck used only for commuting not tool of trade under Wyoming law) *and In re* Damron, 5 B.R. 357 (Bankr. W.D. Ky. 1980) (mechanic and factory worker may not claim automobile as tool of the trade if they could carry on occupation without car).

67 *See* § 10.2.2.6, *supra.*

68 *In re* Meckfessel, 67 B.R. 277 (Bankr. D. Kan. 1986); *see also In re* Lampe, 331 F.3d 750 (10th Cir. 2003) (wife-debtor had joint ownership interest in farm equipment so her exemption could be added to husband's exemption).

69 *Compare In re* Walkington, 42 B.R. 67 (Bankr. W.D. Mich. 1984) (cattle found tools of trade under federal law) *with In re* Patterson, 825 F.2d 1140 (7th Cir. 1987) (cattle and farm machinery not tools of trade). *See In re* Heape, 886 F.2d 280 (10th Cir. 1989) (breeding livestock are tools of a livestock farmer's trade under Kansas law); *In re* Stewart, 110 B.R. 11 (Bankr. D. Idaho 1989) (horses necessary for debtor's work as a yardman were tools of trade under Idaho law); *In re* Siegmann, 757 P.2d 820 (Okla. 1988) (tractor, front-end loader and flat-bed trailer are tools of farmer's trade under Oklahoma law).

70 *See In re* Clifford, 222 B.R. 8 (Bankr. D. Conn. 1998) (facsimile machine used to submit bids and keep in touch with clients is a tool of the trade).

10.2.2.8 Unmatured Life Insurance—§ 522(d)(7)

The subsection providing an exemption for unmatured life insurance, as distinguished from the subsection following it, is for those interests in life insurance owned by the debtor which do not have a cash or loan value. Thus, any interest in term insurance can be exempted in full under this subsection.

Credit life insurance is specifically excluded from the coverage of this subsection. And, if the debtor is merely the beneficiary of a policy insuring the life of a living person and owned by someone other than the debtor, no exemption need be used, because generally the debtor has no property interest in that policy. (However, if the insured dies within 180 days after the bankruptcy petition is filed, the debtor's interest in the proceeds does become property of the estate,[71] and can be exempted under section 522(d)(11), discussed below.)[72] It is important to note that the debtor need not be the person insured by the life insurance contract for this exemption to apply.

10.2.2.9 Accrued Dividend, Interest, or Loan Value of Life Insurance—§ 522(d)(8)

Interests in life insurance policies which do have a cash value may be exempted to the extent of $9300.00 per debtor under subsection (d)(8). From this amount must be subtracted any amounts that are used by the insurance company to continue premium payments under a contract which provides for automatic payments out of the accrued value.[73]

Unlike the exemption provided by the previous subsection, this exemption may only be applied to policies insuring the life of the debtor or someone of whom the debtor is a dependent. Nonetheless, because life insurance can be a relatively liquid type of property, if a debtor has excess liquid assets prior to filing a case that cannot be otherwise exempted, this exemption provides a way to exempt a substantial additional amount through a pre-bankruptcy purchase of life insurance.[74]

10.2.2.10 Health Aids—§ 522(d)(9)

A debtor may exempt an unlimited amount of professionally prescribed health aids for the debtor or a dependent of the debtor. This exemption clearly covers such items as wheelchairs and artificial limbs. Arguably, it is much broader, and could include specially equipped automobiles, or even normal automobiles essential to receiving medical treatments.[75] It is also possible that property prescribed for therapy, such as swimming pools, could be included.[76]

Some guidance on these issues may be obtained from the income tax cases dealing with the medical expenses deduction. These cases have allowed deductions for a home elevator[77] and automobile modifications to accommodate a disabled person.[78] However, the deductions are allowed only to the extent they do not increase the value of the property on which they are installed.[79] A good argument can be made that the bankruptcy exemption should be more broadly construed due to its different purpose. First, the tax cases are also concerned with distinguishing expenses from capital expenditures, and that concern is what led to the limitation on deductions which increase the value of property. In addition, the exemption's principal purpose is to preserve for the debtor that property necessary because of health problems. It would do little good to preserve the special automobile equipment without the automobile, so arguably the entire specially equipped vehicle can be claimed as exempt. Moreover, there is no reason in bankruptcy to only allow part of the value of a home improvement to be exempted because the rest can later be recouped upon sale of the house. If the home and improvement are lost because of such an interpretation, the purpose of the exemption would be defeated.

10.2.2.11 Disability, Retirement and Other Benefits Replacing Wages—§ 522(d)(10)

Because of the Code's broad definition of property of the bankruptcy estate,[80] a debtor's entitlement to receive various benefits in the future has for the first time become subject to the claims of creditors. Rights to such entitlements must therefore be exempted if they are to be saved for the debtor's future use. Thus, section 522(d)(10) exempts the right to

---

71 11 U.S.C. § 541(a)(5)(C).

72 *See also* BancOhio Nat'l Bank v. Walters, 724 F.2d 1081 (4th Cir. 1984) (where debtors claimed unmatured life insurance policies as exempt under § 522(d)(7), proceeds of policy acquired within 180 days of petition were included in that exemption).

73 Such payments are also specifically excepted from the turnover requirements of § 542. 11 U.S.C. § 542(d).

74 *See In re* O'Brien, 67 B.R. 317 (Bankr. N.D. Iowa 1986). *But see In re* Mueller, 867 F.2d 568 (10th Cir. 1989) (purchase of insurance policy three days before bankruptcy where debtor already had insurance contained badges of fraud on creditors so as to make it non-exempt under Kansas law).

75 *But see* Uniform Exemption Act § 5, 13 U.L.A. 380 (which has different wording limiting exemption to aids necessary to enable individual to work or sustain health).

76 *See In re* Johnson, 101 B.R. 280 (Bankr. W.D. Okla. 1989) (water treatment system recommended by physician qualifies as professionally prescribed health aid under Oklahoma law), *aff'd*, 113 B.R. 44 (W.D. Okla. 1989).

77 Hollander v. Comm'r of Internal Revenue, 219 F.2d 934 (3d Cir. 1955).

78 Rev. Rul. 70-606, 1970-2 C.B. 66.

79 Rev. Rul. 59-411, 1959-2 C.B. 100.

80 11 U.S.C. § 541; *see* Ch. 2, *supra*.

receive, in the future, social security, unemployment, welfare, disability, and illness benefits.[81] Alimony and support payments are also exempt but only to the extent reasonably necessary for the support of the debtor and any dependents of the debtor.[82] (In some states that have opted out of the federal exemptions, there may be a question with respect to whether alimony payment arrearages are exempted.)[83]

Similarly, payments under most pension plans and many employee benefit plans are exempt to the extent reasonably necessary for the support of the debtor and the debtor's dependents.[84] A determination of whether a pension is reasonably necessary for the support of a debtor and any dependents requires an examination of the debtor's age, health, earning capacity, present and future financial needs and ability to reestablish a retirement fund.[85] The courts have generally rejected exemptions under this section in cases of middle- and upper-income debtors with no present need for support or right to receive the payments.[86] In such cases, the state exemptions may provide superior protection.[87] An issue has also arisen about whether this provision protects only distributions under such plans or the funds in the plan as a whole.[88] This issue should be resolved in favor of the debtor's position because there would be no value to protecting payments under a plan, when the funds in the plan itself can be liquidated, and because the exemption is for the debtor's prospective "right to receive" the payment.[89]

---

81 11 U.S.C. § 522(d)(10)(A), (B), (C). Worker's compensation benefits probably fall within this category or within § 522(d)(11)(D) or (E) (payments on account of personal injuries or in compensation for loss of future earnings). *See In re* Cain, 91 B.R. 182 (Bankr. N.D. Ga. 1988); *In re* Evans, 29 B.R. 336 (Bankr. D.N.J. 1983); *In re* LaBelle, 18 B.R. 169 (Bankr. D. Me. 1982). Benefits under privately purchased disability policies may be able to be exempted only under § 522(d)(10)(E), which limits the exemption to amounts reasonably necessary for support. *In re* Wegrzyn, 291 B.R. 2 (Bankr. D. Mass. 2003). *But see In re* Lambert, 9 B.R. 799 (Bankr. W.D. Mich. 1981). Similarly a Federal Employers' Liability Act settlement for an injury that led to disability was determined by one court to be exempt under § 522(d)(10)(C). *In re* Albrecht, 89 B.R. 859 (Bankr. D. Mont. 1988). However, the mere fact that a debtor is in bad health does not transform unrestricted lottery winnings paid as an annuity into an annuity paid on account of illness. *In re* Skog, 144 B.R. 221 (Bankr. D.R.I. 1992). And benefits that bear no relation to lost income normally do not fall within this provision. *In re* Chavis, 207 B.R. 845 (Bankr. W.D. 1997) (proceeds of accidental death or dismemberment policy not exemptible under § 522(d)(10), but were exemptible under § 522(d)(11). When in doubt, a debtor should claim all possible exemptions.

82 11 U.S.C. § 522(d)(10)(D). It is unclear whether the court can examine an award to determine whether its true purpose is support as it can do in determining dischargeability under § 523(a)(5). *See In re* Milligan, 342 F.3d 358 (5th Cir. 2003) (because § 522(d)(1)(D) did not have language contained in § 523(a)(5) regarding true purpose of award, court could not look behind labels in decree); *In re* Ellertson, 252 B.R. 831 (Bankr. S.D. Fla. 2000) (divorce decree payments not exemptible because they were not in nature of support despite labels in divorce decree); *In re* Bentley, 245 B.R. 684 (Bankr. D. Kan. 2000) (court cannot look behind state court label); *In re* Sheffield, 212 B.R. 1019 (Bankr. M.D. Fla. 1997) (life insurance proceeds that debtor received from policy that former husband was required by divorce decree to maintain did not constitute alimony because insurance requirement in decree was reciprocal and therefore not in the nature of support); § 14.4.3.5.3, *infra*. It seems fairly clear that child support and awards for the benefit of someone other than the debtor need not be exempted because they can be considered to be held in trust for the real intended beneficiary. See Hughes, *Code Exemptions: Far-Reaching Achievement*, 28 DePaul L. Rev. 1025, 1033 n.57 (1979) and cases cited therein.

83 *See In re* Poffenbarger, 281 B.R. 379 (Bankr. S.D. Ala. 2002) (while right to child support arrearages was in reality property of debtor's children, there was no exemption for alimony arrearages under Alabama law).

84 11 U.S.C. § 522(d)(10)(E); *In re* Brucher, 243 F.3d 242 (6th Cir.

2001) (exemption of IRAs allowed under § 522(d)(10)(E)); *In re* Carmichael, 100 F.3d 375 (5th Cir. 1996) (debtor's rights in IRA could be exempted under § 522(d)(10)(E)); Jurgenson v. Chalmers, 248 B.R. 94 (W.D. Mich. 2000) (IRA exemptible under federal exemption provision); *In re* Lightbody, 240 B.R. 545 (Bankr. E.D. Mich. 1999) (county deferred compensation plan was a "similar plan" even though debtor could withdraw money for unforeseen emergency); *In re* Yee, 147 B.R. 624 (Bankr. D. Mass. 1992) (IRA intended to be included); *In re* Hickenbottom, 143 B.R. 931 (Bankr. W.D. Wash. 1992) (same); *In re* Cilek, 115 B.R. 974 (Bankr. W.D. Wis. 1990) (IRA intended to be included); *In re* Bell, 119 B.R. 783 (Bankr. D. Mont. 1988) (IRA intended to be included); *In re* Johnson, 36 B.R. 54 (Bankr. D.N.M. 1984); *In re* Miller, 33 B.R. 549 (Bankr. D. Minn. 1983) (court looked to future retirement needs in exempting interest in profit-sharing plan); *see also In re* Andersen, 259 B.R. 687 (B.A.P. 8th Cir. 2001) (annuity purchased with lump sum from inheritance for purpose of retirement income could be exempted under § 522(d)(10)(E)). *But see In re* Rousey, 347 F.3d 689 (8th Cir. 2003) (some IRAs are not exempt under § 522(d)(10)(E)), *cert. granted sub nom.* Rousey v. Jacoway, 124 S. Ct. 2817 (2004); Weidman v. Shapiro, 299 B.R. 429 (E.D. Mich. 2003) (annuity bequeathed to debtor by her mother not replacement for lost income or future earnings); *In re* Collett, 253 B.R. 452 (Bankr. W.D. Mo. 2000) (payments under annuity established by testamentary trust not within scope of exemption because not under plan on account of illness, disability, death, age, or length of service).

85 *In re* Hamo, 233 B.R. 718 (B.A.P. 6th Cir. 1999); *In re* Fisher, 63 B.R. 649 (Bankr. W.D. Ky. 1986).

86 *See In re* Moffatt, 959 F.2d 740 (9th Cir. 1992) (annuity established in contemplation of bankruptcy with quarterly payments of $4370.00 beginning immediately after bankruptcy was not reasonably necessary to debtor when he and his wife had income in excess of $90,000.00 per year); *In re* Kochell, 732 F.2d 564 (7th Cir. 1984) (pension plans not necessary to support of forty-four-year old physician); *In re* Clark, 711 F.2d 21 (3d Cir. 1983) (funds not needed by forty-three-year-old therapist).

87 See cases cited later in this subsection.

88 Patterson v. Shumate, 504 U.S. 753, 112 S. Ct. 2242, 2249 n.5, 119 L. Ed. 2d 519, 530 n.5 (1992).

89 *In re* Carmichael, 100 F.3d 375 (5th Cir. 1996) (debtors could exempt both right to receive current payments from IRA and right to receive payments in the future); *In re* Marsella, 188 B.R. 731 (Bankr. D.R.I. 1995); *In re* Yee, 147 B.R.624 (Bankr. D. Mass. 1992).

It is important to note that the Supreme Court has ruled that ERISA-qualified pension and employee benefit plans do not come into a debtor's bankruptcy estate at all.[90] When benefit plans are not in the estate, the debtor need not claim them as exempt. However, if there is any doubt about whether the plan is excluded from the estate, there is no reason not to claim the exemption in the alternative. When a plan does not qualify under ERISA, whether or not it is exemptible under section 522(d)(10)(E), applicable non-bankruptcy law restrictions on transfer[91] may result in the plan being excluded from the estate. Alternatively, state law exemptions,[92] which are often more generous than section 522(d)(10), may be available.[93]

Except in the case of Social Security and SSI benefits,[94] property traceable to benefits already received may have to be exempted under other provisions of the federal exemptions. If so, this requirement is a departure from some of the federal non-bankruptcy laws protecting income benefits such as veterans benefits, under which accrued benefits were also exempt from execution.[95] Thus, a debtor who has saved from such benefits a substantial amount of money that cannot all be claimed as exempt, perhaps because of a large retroactive payment, may be better off choosing the alternative of the state and federal non-bankruptcy exemptions.[96]

As noted above, some types of property covered by this provision, for example, alimony, child support, and private retirement plans, are exempt only to the extent reasonably necessary for the support of the debtor and the debtor's dependents. This limitation was included primarily to prevent wealthy people with enormous amounts of income from such sources from protecting all of that income in bankruptcy. With this purpose in mind, the courts are likely to be relatively liberal in deciding what amounts are reasonably necessary for support. Although the statute gives no guidance, judges who see mostly middle-class debtors usually approve a living standard that supports a middle-class lifestyle.[97]

---

90 Patterson v. Shumate, 504 U.S. 753, 112 S. Ct. 2242, 119 L. Ed. 2d 519 (1992). The Supreme Court pointed out, however, that at least two types of retirement accounts do not qualify under ERISA and, therefore, are not entitled to its protection. These are certain pensions established by governmental entities or religious organizations and individual retirement accounts (IRAs). Protection for those plans will have to be sought under § 522(d)(10)(E), state law exemptions, or claims that they are not property of the estate because under applicable non-bankruptcy law they have the same inalienability as the Supreme Court found in ERISA plans. For further discussion of the latter issues, see § 2.5.2, *supra.*

91 Applicable non-bankruptcy law restrictions on transfer of pensions and employee benefit plans are enforceable by all debtors through 11 U.S.C. § 541(c)(2) whether or not state exemptions are chosen. *See* § 2.5.2, *supra. See generally* Patterson v. Shumate, 504 U.S. 753, 112 S. Ct. 2242, 119 L. Ed. 2d 519 (1992). The Supreme Court will determine whether these restrictions protect IRA accounts in reviewing *In re* Rousey, 347 F.3d 689 (8th Cir. 2003), *cert. granted sub nom. Rousey v. Jacoway,* 124 S. Ct. 2817 (2004).

92 State law exemptions (as opposed to restrictions on transfer) are available only to those who claim state exemptions under 11 U.S.C. § 522(b)(2). *In re* MacIntyre, 74 F.3d 186 (9th Cir. 1996) (section 403(b) plan fully exempt under California law); *In re* Schlein, 8 F.3d 745 (11th Cir. 1993) (Florida exemption for employee benefit plans protected debtor's SEP-IRA accounts and was not preempted by ERISA); *In re* Walker, 959 F.2d 894 (10th Cir. 1992) (Oklahoma exemption provisions protected debtor's non-ERISA retirement plans and were not preempted by ERISA); *In re* Buzza, 287 B.R. 417 (Bankr. S.D. Ohio 2002) (Ohio exemption covering self-settled IRA not preempted by ERISA); *see* § 10.2.1, *supra.*

93 In jurisdictions where both federal and state law exemptions are available, state exemptions may offer superior protection. Such would be the case where state exemptions are not limited to amounts reasonably necessary for the support of the debtor or the debtor's dependents. *See, e.g.,* Hovis v. Wright, 751 F.2d 714 (4th Cir. 1985) (employee contributions to teacher retirement fund held exempt under South Carolina law).

94 Since the Bankruptcy Code was passed, Congress has amended the Social Security Act to make clear that benefits thereunder are not subject to the bankruptcy laws and thus should not become property of the estate. 42 U.S.C. §§ 407, 1383(d); *see In re* Buren, 725 F.2d 1080 (6th Cir. 1984). Therefore, they need not be exempted to be preserved for the debtor. This protection should apply not only to the right to receive benefits, but also to the benefits already received. *See* Philpott v. Essex County Welfare Bd., 409 U.S. 413, 93 S. Ct. 590, 34 L. Ed. 2d 608 (1973); *In re* Frazier, 116 B.R. 675 (Bankr. W.D. Wis. 1990) (exemption covers not only future benefits but also lump sums received prior to bankruptcy filing). Similar protections are likely to be found for Veterans benefits and perhaps other federal benefits with statutory language similar to the anti-alienation provisions of the Social Security Act.

95 *Compare In re* Treadwell, 699 F.2d 1050 (11th Cir. 1983) (decided prior to the amendment discussed above) *and In re* Moore, 214 B.R. 628 (Bankr. D. Kan. 1997) (retirement funds already received were not exempt but social security funds received were exempt) *with In re* Donaghy, 11 B.R. 677 (Bankr. S.D.N.Y. 1981) (recently received lump sum payments could be exempted under § 522(d)(10)(E) even though "right to receive" no longer technically existed).

96 *See* Philpott v. Essex County Welfare Board, 409 U.S. 413, 93 S. Ct. 590, 34 L. Ed. 2d 608 (1973) (social security benefits in bank account could not be attached); *In re* Smith, 242 B.R. 427 (Bankr. E.D. Tenn. 1999) (veteran's benefits received by widow of veteran exempt even though they were used to purchase a certificate of deposit); *In re* Crandall, 200 B.R. 243 (Bankr. M.D. Fla. 1995) (debtor's bank account, which consisted solely of social security benefits, exempt under Social Security Act); *In re* Bresnahan, 183 B.R. 506 (Bankr. S.D. Ohio 1995) (retirement fund distribution deposited in debtor's bank account was still exempt under Ohio exemption law).

97 *See, e.g., In re* Hendricks, 11 B.R. 48 (Bankr. W.D. Mo. 1981); *In re* Lambert, 9 B.R. 799 (Bankr. W.D. Mich. 1981). *But see In re* Thurston, 255 B.R. 725 (Bankr. S.D. Ohio 2000) (under similar state exemption court found $14,000.00 support arrearages not necessary for support of debtor with no dependents earning $38,000.00); Hughes, *Code Exemptions: Far-Reaching Achievement,* 28 DePaul L. Rev. 1025, 1033 nn.60, 61 (citing cases which have set varying standards); *see also* Vukowich, *The Bankruptcy Commission's Proposal Regarding Bankrupts' Exemption Rights,* 63 Cal. L. Rev. 1439, 1461, 1462 (1975) (citing cases and recommending amount "reasonably essential

Another question likely to arise concerns the definition of the term "public assistance." Obviously, welfare cash payments are included. It also seems clear that supplements such as food stamps and energy assistance should come within this category.[98] The question becomes slightly closer with housing subsidies. Payments under Section 8, which reduce a family's rent to a certain percentage of income, can be analogized to food stamps, which reduce food costs to a certain percentage of income. And from there it should not be difficult to extend the principle to mortgage interest subsidies and the subsidy inherent in living in public housing, where rent is limited to a certain percentage of income. Similar issues arise with regard to the federal earned income tax credit, other tax credits, and other subsidy programs.[99]

It is usually not necessary to claim all of these benefits as exempt, although it may often be safer to do so. Trustees are unlikely to show much interest in such benefits, because they are probably not transferable, and may therefore be abandoned as of no value to the estate.[100] If a trustee does show interest, the schedules and claim of exemption can be amended at that time. Also, there are questions about the appropriate value to assign to these benefits. Should the right to receive welfare be valued as if it will continue through the close of the case? Or is it value only nominal, as it is not really transferable and may end the next day if other income appears or if durational limits apply? Must all workers who have paid social security taxes list a vested or non-vested contingent right to receive social security benefits when they retire or become disabled? Local practice, which usually does not require the listing of such assets, generally provides a guide as to such questions. In general, because of the contingencies involved, when benefits are listed as an asset, listing the value as "unknown" makes the most sense.

10.2.2.12 Rights to Compensation for Injury or Losses—§ 522(d)(11)

The last category listed among the federal bankruptcy exemptions covers the right to receive, and property traceable to, payments for various types of injury or loss.[101] These include crime-victim reparations awards, as well as payments, not to exceed $18,450.00, on account of bodily injury of the debtor or a person upon whom the debtor is dependent (but not including pain and suffering or pecuniary loss).[102] They also cover wrongful death awards based upon the death of someone of whom the debtor was a dependent, payments on life insurance that insured the life of someone of whom the debtor was a dependent, and payments in compensation for loss of future earnings of the debtor or one upon whom the debtor was a dependent.

---

or needed by an average and reasonable person"); Plumb, *The Recommendations of the Commission on the Bankruptcy Laws—Exempt and Immune Property*, 61 Va. L. Rev. 1, 94, 95 (1975). The language "reasonably necessary for support," also contained in § 1325(b), is discussed further in § 12.3.3, *infra*.

98 *See* Morris v. Philadelphia Elec. Co., 45 B.R. 350 (E.D. Pa. 1984) (energy assistance).

99 *See* Flanery v. Mathison, 289 B.R. 624 (W.D. Ky. 2003) (earned income credit exempt as public assistance under Kentucky law); *In re* Brasher, 253 B.R. 484 (M.D. Ala. 2000) (earned income credit exempt as public assistance under Alabama law); *In re* Wilson, 305 B.R. 4 (Bankr. N.D. Iowa 2004) (federal commodity program payments based on determination of need were public assistance under Iowa law); *In re* Koch, 299 B.R. 523 (Bankr. C.D. Ill. 2003) (child tax credit available to affluent taxpayers not in nature of public assistance, but refundable child tax credit available only to lower income taxpayers was); *In re* Tomczyk, 295 B.R. 894 (Bankr. D. Minn. 2003) (federal earned income credit and state equivalent were "relief based on need" and therefore exempt under Minnesota law); *In re* Longstreet, 246 B.R. 611 (Bankr. S.D. Iowa 2000) (earned income credit exempt as public assistance under Iowa law); *In re* Fish, 224 B.R. 82 (Bankr. S.D. Ill. 1998) (earned income credit exempt as public assistance under Illinois law); *In re* Barnett, 214 B.R. 632 (Bankr. W.D. Okla. 1997) (earned income credit exempt under Oklahoma law protecting earnings from personal services); *In re* Goldsberry, 142 B.R. 158 (Bankr. E.D. Ky. 1992) (earned income credit was public assistance under Kentucky law); *In re* Jones, 107 B.R. 751 (Bankr. D. Idaho 1989) (earned income tax credit is exempt as public assistance payment under Idaho law); *In re* Murphy, 99 B.R. 370 (Bankr. S.D. Ohio 1988) (earned income tax credit is exempt as a "poor relief" payment under Ohio law). *But see In re* Collins, 170 F.3d 512 (5th Cir. 1999) (earned income credit not exemptible under Louisiana law protecting public assistance payments); *In re* Trudeau, 237 B.R. 803 (B.A.P. 10th Cir. 1999) (earned income credit not personal services earnings exempt under Wyoming law); *In re* Annis, 229 B.R. 802 (B.A.P. 10th Cir. 1999) (earned income credit not public assistance or earnings exempt under Oklahoma law); *In re* Rutter 204 B.R. 57 (Bankr. D. Or. 1997) (earned income credit not exemptible public assistance); *In re* Goertz, 202 B.R. 614 (Bankr. W.D. Mo. 1996) (earned income credit not exempt under Missouri law). *See generally* § 2.5.3, *supra*. State exemption law may also explicitly provide an exemption for the earned income credit. *See In re* Sanderson, 283 B.R. 595 (Bankr. M.D. Fla. 2002) (citing newly enacted Florida exemption for earned income credit).

100 See § 3.5, *supra,* for a discussion of abandonment of property under 11 U.S.C. § 554.

101 Because § 541(a)(5) of the Code brings life insurance proceeds acquired within 180 days of the bankruptcy filing into the estate, one court has held that such insurance proceeds must be exempted under this subsection, notwithstanding the fact that the unmatured policy was properly claimed as wholly exempt at the time the bankruptcy was initiated. Cyrak v. Poynor, 80 B.R. 75 (N.D. Tex. 1987). Other courts have found that properly the insurance policy protects any subsequent proceeds. *See* BancOhio Nat'l Bank v. Walters, 724 F.2d 1081 (4th Cir. 1984).

102 Because this exemption provision, unlike § 522(d)(1), (3), (4), (5), (6) and (8) does not refer to the debtor's aggregate interest, the debtor may exempt an amount up to the statutory dollar limit for each accident giving rise to exemptible damages. *In re* Comeaux, 305 B.R. 802 (Bankr. E.D. Tex. 2003); *In re* Chavis, 207 B.R. 845 (Bankr. W.D. Pa. 1997) (proceeds of accidental death or dismemberment); *In re* Marcus, 172 B.R. 502 (Bankr. D. Conn. 1994). *But see In re* Christo, 192 F.3d 36 (1st Cir. 1999) (dollar limit applies to personal injury claims in the aggregate rather than to each claim).

It is important to note, first, that this exemption category does include property that can be traced to the listed benefits, as well as the benefits themselves.[103] This inclusion may pose difficult problems of tracing past payments, but to the extent exemption planning can maximize traceability, it should be carefully considered. Second, some but not all of the payments listed are limited to amounts reasonably necessary to the support of the debtor and the debtor's dependents.[104] The comments made with respect to this limitation in section 522(d)(10) are equally applicable here.[105]

One category has a specific dollar limit: $18,450.00 on account of personal bodily injury.[106] This category not only explicitly excludes pain and suffering and compensation for pecuniary loss (the latter being covered by a separate provision), but also implicitly seems to exclude punitive damages. It is unclear how the bankruptcy court will be able to divide lump sum awards or settlements into these component parts.[107] Because the burden of proof in objections to exemptions is on the party objecting to the exemptions,[108] the exemption should be allowed unless the objector can demonstrate that a specific portion of the award is not exempt.[109] It is also unclear to what extent damage recoveries, or the right thereto, for non-bodily injuries such as

discrimination or invasion of privacy, may be protected.[110] While these may not be covered by subsection (D) of § 522(d)(11), which is limited to personal bodily injuries, some portions of them may be deemed compensation for loss of future earnings, and thus exempt under subsection (E).[111]

In light of these considerations, it may be worthwhile to attempt to obtain a favorable designation of a damage award or settlement, if possible, prior to bankruptcy for the purposes of exempting as much property as possible under these provisions when permissible.

It may also be a good idea, prior to bankruptcy, to structure settlements or to place the proceeds of awards in spendthrift trusts which are valid under state law, in order to exclude them from the debtor's estate.[112]

10.2.3 Using the State and Federal Non-Bankruptcy Exemptions

10.2.3.1 Federal Bankruptcy Modifications of These Exemptions

In cases in which the federal bankruptcy exemptions are either not chosen or not available, debtors may use the exemptions in effect on the date the bankruptcy case is filed[113] provided for by state[114] or local law and by federal

103 *See In re* Miller, 36 B.R. 420 (Bankr. D.N.M. 1984) (real estate lot traced to payment for loss of future earnings; party objecting to exemption had burden of proof on tracing).

104 *In re* Collins, 281 B.R. 580 (Bankr. M.D. Pa. 2002) (life insurance proceeds reasonably necessary for young widowed mother); *In re* Cramer, 130 B.R. 193 (Bankr. E.D. Pa. 1991) (personal injury award of $20,000.00 reasonably necessary for support of disabled debtor whose only other income is social security disability); *In re* Gallo, 49 B.R. 28 (Bankr. N.D. Tex. 1985) (life insurance proceeds of $275,000.00 reasonably necessary for support of unemployed, possibly disabled debtor with two young children); *see also In re* Collopy, 99 B.R. 384 (Bankr. S.D. Ohio 1989) ("dependent" under Ohio exemption scheme may include someone physically, but not financially dependent on the insured).

105 *See* § 10.2.2.11, *supra*.

106 This amount is adjusted every three years pursuant to 11 U.S.C. § 104(b).

107 *See In re* Scotti, 245 B.R. 17 (Bankr. D.N.J. 2000) (award is exemptible unless it was for pain and suffering with no bodily injury).

108 Fed. R. Bankr. P. 4003(c).

109 *See In re* Barner, 239 B.R. 139 (Bankr. W.D. Ky. 1999) (trustee had burden of proving purpose of award); *In re* Blizard, 81 B.R. 431 (Bankr. W.D. Ky. 1988) (objecting trustee failed to meet his burden of proving portion of award attributable to personal bodily injury exceeded available exemption amount); *In re* Harris, 50 B.R. 157 (Bankr. E.D. Wis. 1985) (under Fed. R. Bankr. P. 4003(c), objectors had burden of showing how much of insurance settlement was attributable to pain and suffering); *see also In re* Sidebotham, 77 B.R. 504 (Bankr. E.D. Pa. 1987) (pain and suffering damages excluded only if clearly separable and far out of proportion to injuries). *But see In re* Patterson, 128 B.R. 737 (Bankr. W.D. Tex. 1991) (debtor failed to meet court ordered burden to establish basis for undivided settlement payment); *In re* Hill, 5 B.R. 518 (Bankr. S.D. Ohio 1980) (under similar Ohio exemption debtor has burden of proof that award

claimed exempt was for trauma or injury rather than pain and suffering or pecuniary loss).

110 Several courts have concluded, probably erroneously, that a "personal bodily injury requirement" in a state law exemption precludes use of that exemption to protect proceeds of a sexual harassment lawsuit. *In re* Hanson, 226 B.R. 106 (Bankr. D. Idaho 1999); *In re* Ciotta, 222 B.R. 626 (Bankr. C.D. Cal. 1999). These courts assume that personal bodily injury can only be manifested by actual physical injury and that the basis on which damages are calculated (lost wages) establishes the nature of the injury. *See In re* Lynn, 13 B.R. 361 (Bankr. W.D. Wis. 1981) (award for loss of consortium with spouse arising out of personal injury to spouse is an award on account of injury exempt under 11 U.S.C. § 522(d)(11)(D)).

111 *See* Plumb, *The Recommendations of the Commission on the Bankruptcy Laws—Exempt and Immune Property*, 61 Va. L. Rev. 1, 94, 95 (1975).

112 11 U.S.C. § 541(c)(2); *see* § 2.5.1, *supra*; *see also* Walro v. Striegel, 131 B.R. 697 (S.D. Ind. 1991) (annuity contract containing proceeds of personal injury action does not constitute valid spendthrift trust under Indiana law).

113 *In re* Wolf, 248 B.R. 365 (B.A.P. 9th Cir. 2000) (debtor could not take advantage of exemption enacted after petition, even if property interest not acquired until after enactment).

114 It is not totally clear what effect state law exceptions to general exemption statutes have in bankruptcy (for example, where exemptions are not applicable to executions by certain creditors). It is likely that these exceptions will not be preserved in bankruptcy, at least in part based on the preemptive effect of section 522(c). *In re* Weinstein, 164 F.3d 677 (1st Cir. 1999) (exceptions to homestead exemption under Massachusetts law do not apply in bankruptcy); *In re* Kim, 257 B.R. 680 (B.A.P.

non-bankruptcy law.[115] The term "local law" presumably includes Indian Tribal law, and any other provisions applicable to a particular locality. (For convenience, this collection of exemptions will sometimes be referred to simply as the "state exemptions.") Some states have special state exemptions applicable only in bankruptcy cases.[116] The property that the debtor may exempt in bankruptcy under a state exemption scheme probably also includes any property that is not subject to execution under state law, such as contingent tort claims.[117] And state exemption rights are significantly enhanced by the Bankruptcy Code in several ways.

First, debtors have available to them all of the other protections of section 522. Any waiver of exemptions is unenforceable, regardless of whether exemptions could be waived under state law.[118] The extensive powers to avoid pre-bankruptcy transfers of exempt property all are applicable to the state as well as the federal exemptions, because the sections providing them refer to exemptions claimed under section 522(b), which includes both sets of exemptions.[119] And exempt property is permanently protected after the bankruptcy under section 522(c), as discussed later in this Chapter.[120]

Certain states, however, have narrow limitations in their exemption schemes which apply under some conditions to prevent property from being exempt. Some courts had given effect to these limitations by concluding that liens may not be avoided on such property because the property is not exempt in the first instance.[121] Those decisions were overruled by the United States Supreme Court.[122]

In addition, debtors in bankruptcy may be able to take advantage of section 522(m) which provides that the exemption section applies separately with respect to each debtor in a joint case. In states where a single exemption is granted to a household, this provision could mean that each debtor is entitled to claim that exemption, especially if a two separate bankruptcy cases are filed.[123]

9th Cir. 2001) (state procedural law permitting court to consider debtor's post-petition use of property cannot override bankruptcy principle that property of estate and exemptions are determined on petition date), *aff'd*, 35 Fed. Appx. 592 (9th Cir. 2002); *In re* Scott, 199 B.R. 586 (Bankr. E.D. Va. 1996) (state law exception to exemption making it inapplicable to debts arising from intentional torts is not applicable in bankruptcy); *see In re* Cooley, 72 B.R. 54 (N.D. Ala. 1987), *aff'g* 67 B.R. 229 (Bankr. N.D. Ala. 1986); Michael Terry Hertz, *Bankruptcy Code Exemptions: Notes on the Effect of State Law*, 54 Am. Bankr. L. J. 339, 353, 354 (1980); Stern, *State Exemption Law in Bankruptcy: The Excepted Creditor as a Medium for Appraising Aspects of Bankruptcy Reform*, 33 Rutgers L. Rev. 70 (1980); *see also* § 10.3.3, *infra*. *But see In re* Ondras, 846 F.2d 33 (7th Cir. 1988) (Indiana permitted to opt for exemption scheme treating tort and contract claims differently).

115 Such federal non-bankruptcy exemptions include social security benefits, 42 U.S.C. § 407; veterans benefits, 38 U.S.C. § 5301; Railroad Retirement Act annuities and pensions, 45 U.S.C. § 231m; civil service retirement benefits, 5 U.S.C. § 8346; Foreign Service Retirement and Disability payments, 22 U.S.C. § 4060; compensation payments for injury or death from war risk hazards, 42 U.S.C. § 1717; wages of master and seamen, 46 U.S.C. § 11109; Longshoremen's and Harbor Worker's Compensation Act death and disability benefits, 33 U.S.C. § 916; government employees' benefits for work-related injuries leading to disability or death; 5 U.S.C. § 8130; military survivors' benefits, 10 U.S.C. § 1450(i); military annuities, 10 U.S.C. § 1440. The Supreme Court has held that pension plans covered by ERISA do not come into the estate at all. Patterson v. Shumate, 504 U.S. 753, 112 S. Ct. 2242, 119 L. Ed. 2d 519 (1992). Note that this holding is applicable regardless of whether the debtor utilizes state or federal bankruptcy exemptions. *See* § 2.5.2, *supra*.

116 *See, e.g., In re* Reaves, 285 F.3d 1152 (9th Cir. 2002) (prior determination that debtor could not exempt car under regular state law exemptions did not preclude exemption under special state exemptions for bankruptcy cases); *cf. In re* Williams, 280 B.R. 857 (B.A.P. 9th Cir. 2002) (debtor could not claim normal state exemption in property when state court had denied claim of same exemption). *But see In re* Cross, 255 B.R. 25 (Bankr. N.D. Ind. 2000) (special bankruptcy exemptions unconstitutional).

117 *In re* Williams, 293 B.R. 769 (Bankr. W.D. Mo. 2003) (unliquidated personal injury claims exempt). *But see* Howe v. Richardson, 193 F.3d 60 (1st Cir. 1999) (fact that property could not be attached was not equivalent to being exempt under Rhode Island law; issue depended on state law); *In re* Wishcan, 77 F.3d 875 (5th Cir. 1996) (debtor's personal injury claim could not be exempted under Louisiana state exemptions; debtor does not

appear to have argued that property was exempt because it was not subject to process under state law); Tignor v. Parkinson, 729 F.2d 977 (4th Cir. 1984) (property not exempt though not subject to process because of specific provisions of state law); *see also In re* Ford, 638 F.2d 14 (4th Cir. 1981).

118 11 U.S.C. § 522(e); *In re* Thompson, 884 F.2d 1100 (8th Cir. 1989) (waiver of state law exemptions by voluntary encumbrance of property does not preclude lien avoidance); *In re* Howell, 51 B.R. 1015 (M.D.N.C. 1985); *see also* § 10.4.1, *infra*.

119 *See* Owen v. Owen, 500 U.S. 305, 111 S. Ct. 1833, 114 L. Ed. 2d 250 (1991).

120 *See* § 10.5, *infra*.

121 *See In re* Owen, 877 F.2d 44 (11th Cir. 1989) (where homestead exemption does not attach under state law to residence, because liens arose before homestead attached, liens on residence may not be avoided); *In re* McManus, 681 F.2d 353 (5th Cir. 1982) (state scheme which renders all personal property subject to chattel mortgages non-exempt precludes lien avoidance).

122 Owen v. Owen, 500 U.S. 305, 111 S. Ct. 1833, 114 L. Ed. 2d 250 (1991); *see also In re* Betz, 273 B.R.313 (Bankr. D. Mass. 2002) (state law could not limit lien avoidance on increased exemption amounts). *But see* Owen v. Owen, 961 F.2d 170 (11th Cir. 1992) (on remand, court concluded lien could not be avoided because it had not attached to a preexisting interest of the debtor in property); *In re* Pederson, 230 B.R. 158 (B.A.P. 9th Cir. 1999) (same).

123 *In re* Cheeseman, 656 F.2d 60 (4th Cir. 1981) (each spouse could claim householder exemption where both were employed). *But see In re* Talmadge, 832 F.2d 1120 (9th Cir. 1987) (California's exemption scheme upheld allowing spouses only a single set of exemptions); Stevens v. Pike County Bank, 829 F.2d 693 (8th Cir. 1987) (state could limit couple to one homestead exemption in bankruptcy); *In re* Granger, 754 F.2d 1490 (9th Cir. 1985) (Oregon exemption scheme did not permit doubling exemptions for husband and wife); First Nat'l Bank of

Lastly, debtors have the right to redeem property claimed as exempt, through use of section 722. As discussed in a later chapter,[124] this right can be extremely important in dealing with purchase money or possessory security interests in chapter 7 cases.

However, debtors may still have to comply with state procedural requirements for claims of exemptions. For example, in states that require debtors to file a declaration of homestead prior to the use of that exemption, courts are split on the question of whether that requirement is also a prerequisite to claiming a state homestead exemption in bankruptcy.[125] The precise wording of the state statute involved and previous state case law interpreting it may be determinative.[126]

Debtors may also occasionally have problems in proving that they have been domiciled in a state where they have recently moved for the requisite period of time to claim that state's exemptions—the 180 days preceding the petition or a longer period within those 180 days than in any other place.[127] When it appears that debtors have recently moved to take advantage of more generous exemptions in a particular state, courts may closely scrutinize whether they have actually changed their domicile.[128]

10.2.3.2 Exemption of Property Not Subject to Process

Debtors who claim the state exemptions in bankruptcy may also be able to take advantage of another special provision that protects certain jointly owned property. This provision[129] allows the debtor to claim as exempt "any interest in property in which the debtor had, immediately before the commencement of the case, an interest as a tenant by the entirety or joint tenant to the extent such interest as a tenant by the entirety or joint tenant is exempt from process under applicable non-bankruptcy law."[130]

The intent of this provision is to protect that property which a creditor of only the debtor (and not of both joint tenants) could not have levied upon as of the date that the bankruptcy was filed. In this way it duplicates what the debtor could have kept out of the estate under the prior Act; there the trustee only had rights in that property of the debtor which a creditor of that debtor alone could attach. One example of such property is property owned as tenants by the entireties, in states where such property can be levied upon only by a joint creditor of the cotenants.[131] If one

---

Mobile v. Norris, 701 F.2d 902 (8th Cir. 1983); *In re* Thompson, 4 B.R. 823 (E.D. Va. 1980) (husband and wife could not both claim householder exemption where they were living together and only husband was employed), *rev'g* 2 B.R. 380 (Bankr. E.D. Va. 1980); *see also* § 10.2.1, *supra*.

124 Redemption is discussed in § 11.5, *infra*.

125 *Cf. In re* Michael, 49 F.3d 499 (9th Cir. 1995) (debtors could claim Montana homestead exemption after petition filed); *In re* Renner, 822 F.2d 878 (9th Cir. 1987) (homestead declaration defective and therefore exemption disallowed); Zimmerman v. Morgan, 689 F.2d 471 (4th Cir. 1982) (homestead not exempt); *In re* Martin, 20 B.R. 235 (B.A.P. 9th Cir. 1982) (debtor could file post-petition claim for homestead); *see also In re* Nguyen, 211 F.3d 105 (4th Cir. 2000) (debtors had complied with procedural requirements for claiming homestead exemption under Virginia law, which was construed liberally in favor of debtor); *In re* Niland, 825 F.2d 801 (5th Cir. 1987) (homestead declaration upheld); Smoot v. Wolfe, 271 B.R. 115 (W.D. Va. 2001) (debtors required to file Virginia homestead declaration within five days after first date set for meeting of creditors); *In re* Govoni, 289 B.R. 500 (Bankr. D. Mass. 2002) (right to amend state law declaration of homestead terminated as of petition filing date); *In re* Collins, 24 B.R. 485 (Bankr. E.D. Va. 1982) (Virginia debtors required to file claim of property to be exempted on or before date of petition).

126 *See In re* Zibman, 268 F.3d 298 (5th Cir. 2001) (debtors who had sold Texas homestead before bankruptcy and had not reinvested proceeds in another homestead within six months as required by Texas exemption law could not claim proceeds as exempt even though six months had not run as of date of petition).

127 11 U.S.C. § 522(b)(2)(A).

128 *See, e.g., In re* Ring, 144 B.R. 446 (Bankr. E.D. Mo. 1992) (rejecting claim that debtors had changed their domicile to Florida in view of evidence that they intended to remain in Missouri); *see also In re* Drenttel, 309 B.R. 320 (B.A.P. 8th Cir. 2004) (debtors who lived in Arizona for less than ninety days before filing petition in Minnesota allowed to use Minnesota

---

homestead exemption on property purchased in Arizona); *In re* Tanzi, 297 B.R. 607 (B.A.P. 9th Cir. 2003) (debtors not permitted to use Florida homestead exemption because § 522(b)(2)(A) must be applied no differently in involuntary case; 180-day period runs from petition date rather than date on which order for relief was entered).

129 11 U.S.C. § 522(b)(2)(B).

130 If the property is not located in the state where the debtor resides, the applicable law is the law in the state where the property is located. *In re* Gillette, 248 B.R. 845 (Bankr. M.D. Fla. 1999).

131 These states are Delaware, District of Columbia, Florida, Indiana, Michigan, Maryland, Missouri, Montana, Mississippi, North Carolina, Pennsylvania, Rhode Island, Vermont, Virginia, and Wyoming. In other states, such as Massachusetts, tenancies by the entirety may be partially exempt from claims of one spouse's creditors. Courts have come to sometimes strange results in attempting to effectuate those exemptions, as nearly as possible, under the Bankruptcy Code. *See In re* McConchie, 94 B.R. 245 (Bankr. D. Mass. 1988) (trustee given rights of a hypothetical creditor, under 11 U.S.C. § 544(a)(1) to attach but not sell debtor's interest). *But see* United States v. Craft, 535 U.S. 274, 122 S. Ct. 1414, 152 L. Ed. 2d 437 (2002) (federal tax lien may attach to entireties interest). The *Craft* decision should not alter the debtor's rights as to creditors other than those making claims under federal law. *See In re* Hutchins, 306 B.R. 82 (Bankr. D. Vt. 2004) (applying *Craft* to two liens securing federal criminal fines); *In re* Dahlman, 304 B.R. 892 (Bankr. M.D. Fla. 2003) (federal criminal obligation); *In re* Greathouse, 295 B.R. 562 (Bankr. D. Md. 2003) (*Craft* did not give trustee greater powers); *In re* Knapp, 285 B.R. 176 (Bankr. M.D.N.C. 2002) (*Craft* did not enhance trustee's rights).

Additionally, in those states where a tenancy by the entireties may be subjected to execution by a creditor of either spouse, the bankruptcy court must nevertheless apply the provisions of 11 U.S.C. § 363(h) before property is liquidated for the benefit of creditors of one joint tenant only. *See In re* Persky, 893 F.2d 15 (2d Cir. 1989); § 12.6.5, *infra*.

cotenant files a bankruptcy and claims the state exemptions, then such an interest in entireties property may be claimed as exempt, at a minimum from creditors holding claims against only that cotenant.[132]

Presumably, joint property could be claimed under this exemption even if the co-owner also files a bankruptcy.[133] Indeed, the two co-owners should both be able to claim their interests in entireties property as exempt, even in a joint case, because section 522(m) states that this provision should apply separately to each debtor.[134] However, because courts have not agreed on these issues, it is safer to file a petition for only one of two co-tenants if that will suffice to effectuate the relief sought.

It is important to note several other aspects of this subsection:

- It applies to both real and personal property;
- It is unlimited in value;
- It is applicable to any interest.

Thus, debtors with significant amounts of property that fall within these provisions may be far better off choosing the state rather than the federal exemptions. However, as discussed below, the case law in the jurisdiction in which the case is filed should be carefully researched before that step is irrevocably taken.

The original purpose of this subsection was to preserve the protection given under the previous Bankruptcy Act to certain property which could not be levied upon under state law.[135] Under the Act such property was usually not considered a part of the bankruptcy estate. Without the new subsection, debtors utilizing the state exemptions, either by choice or because their state had opted out, would have been worse off than before the Code was enacted. Their interests in property such as entireties property or other property not subject to state law process would have, for the first time, been brought into the estate under section 541's broadened definition of property of the estate.[136] Such property, then, would have been available to their creditors, even though it had not been under state law, unless it could be exempted. And as it never had been available to creditors under state law, state exemption laws did not take such property into account, so that state exemption provisions were insufficient to protect it. Section 522(b)(2)(B) was meant to fill this breach.

But section 522(b)(2)(B) does more than simply duplicate the results under the prior Act. Under the Act the debtor's interests in property which could not be levied upon did not come into the estate or were abandoned by the trustee.[137] However, to a large degree the effect of the bankruptcy on joint debts had been vitiated by judicially created law which allowed joint creditors to obtain a stay of the discharge to pursue entireties property.[138] The Code, which gives these property interests the same status and protections as all other exempt property, intended to preclude this result. Thus, as discussed below, pursuit of such property during or after the case by a pre-bankruptcy creditor should be prohibited by section 522(c), and any judicial lien obtained by such creditor should be avoidable by the debtor under section 522(f).[139]

---

132 *In re* Ford, Jr., 638 F.2d 14 (4th Cir. 1981), *aff'g* 3 B.R. 559 (D. Md. 1980); *In re* Thacker, 5 B.R. 592 (Bankr. W.D. Va. 1980) (all applying the exemption language); *In re* Shaw, 5 B.R. 107 (Bankr. M.D. Tenn. 1980); *see also In re* Martin, 269 B.R. 119 (Bankr. M.D. Pa. 2001) (exemption allowed even though debtor became sole owner of property within 180 days pursuant to divorce decree, because entireties tenant always was seized of the whole of the property as of petition date); *cf. In re* Steury, 94 B.R. 553 (Bankr. N.D. Ind. 1988) (separate chapter 7 cases of husband and wife consolidated to the extent necessary to allow trustee to liquidate property held by the entireties for the benefit of joint creditors). *But see In re* Weiss, 4 B.R. 327 (Bankr. S.D.N.Y. 1980) (because creditor could reach one spouse's interest in New York entireties property, exemption was not applicable).

133 *But see* Ragsdale v. Genesco, 674 F.2d 277 (4th Cir. 1982) (joint debtors could not exempt or avoid lien on entireties property subject to judgment lien of creditor).

134 *In re* Bunker, 312 F.3d 145 (4th Cir. 2002), *aff'g* Thomas v. Peyton, 274 B.R. 450 (W.D. Va. 2001) (entireties property claimed as exempt in joint case could be administered only for benefit of joint creditors).

135 It is less clear what happens to property not subject to process, which is not within the scope of § 522(b)(2)(B) but which is brought into the bankruptcy estate, where the state exemptions are applicable. The answer may depend on the particulars of state law. *Compare* Howe v. Richardson, 193 F.3d 60 (1st Cir. 1999) (fact that property could not be attached was not equivalent to being exempt under Rhode Island law; issue depended on

state law) *and* Tignor v. Parkinson, 729 F.2d 977 (4th Cir. 1984) (property not exempt though not subject to process due to specific provisions of state law) *with In re* Mitchell, 73 B.R. 93 (Bankr. E.D. Mo. 1987) (holding property exempt where, *inter alia*, claim not subject to garnishment), *aff'd*, 855 F.2d 859 (8th Cir. 1988) *and* Scarlett v. Barnes, 121 B.R. 578 (W.D. Mo. 1990) (cause of action for legal malpractice is exempt because it could not be attached under state law).

136 See § 2.5, *supra*, for a discussion of property of the estate.

137 See § 3.5, *supra*, for a discussion of abandonment of property.

138 Phillips v. Krakower, 46 F.2d 764 (4th Cir. 1931), was the first of these cases, most of which were in the Fourth Circuit. The correctness of their result had been questionable even under the Act and Rules, which required the discharge to be granted "forthwith." Former R. Bankr. P. 404(d); *see In re* Cantwell, 7 Bankr. Ct. Dec. (LRP) 807 (E.D. Pa. 1980), *appeal dismissed as moot* 639 F.2d 1050 (3d Cir. 1981).

139 *See* S. Rep. No. 95-989, at 76 (1978), H.R. Rep. No. 95-595, at 362 (1977) ("The debtor may avoid [any] judicial lien on any property to the extent that the property could have been exempted in the absence of the lien."). However, notwithstanding the fact that the theoretical underpinnings of *Krakower* have disappeared with the inclusion of entireties property interests in the estate, some courts (mostly in the Fourth Circuit) have continued to follow *Krakower* even under the Code. *See, e.g.*, Chippenham Hosp. Inc. v. Bondurant, 716 F.2d 1057 (4th Cir. 1983); *In re* Menefee, 22 B.R. 425 (Bankr. E.D. Va. 1982); *see also* Paeplow v. Foley, 128 B.R. 429 (N.D. Ind. 1991) (although creditor could pursue lien on property held by entireties during

Despite the history and intent of section 522(b)(2)(B), most courts of appeals have interpreted that section far more restrictively. Ignoring early decisions and other authorities which had discussed the issue,[140] the Third Circuit Court of Appeals refused to avoid a lien on entireties property claimed as exempt under section 522(b)(2)(B).[141] The court held that as the property as a whole could be reached by the lien creditor, it did not fall within the exemption provision, even though the *debtor spouse's interest*, which the language of the statute actually looks to, could not be reached by any creditor. Citing no legislative history to support its views, or to refute the analysis of legislative history in an earlier Fourth Circuit decision,[142] the court strongly implied that it would refuse to find property exempt under section 522(b)(2)(B) whenever (but perhaps only to the extent that) a husband and wife had joint creditors.[143]

The Third Circuit's decision was subsequently followed by the First, Fourth, Sixth, and Eighth Circuit Courts of Appeals.[144] The Sixth Circuit cases have held that entireties property not protected from joint creditors by other exemp-

tion provisions can be liquidated in the bankruptcy for the benefit of joint creditors.[145] They also held, however, that when a joint creditor does not timely object to the use of the section 522(b)(2)(B) exemption, it is barred from pursuing the entireties property after the bankruptcy.[146] Only the Seventh Circuit Court of Appeals, interpreting an Indiana statutory exemption of entireties property, has come to the result that was intended by Congress.[147]

The net result of the decisions limiting the use of section 522(b)(2)(B) is that, where they are applicable, the principal use of this exemption may be in those cases in which all or almost all of the debts involved are debts of only one spouse.[148] In such cases, at least, the entireties property is protected from liquidation or (if there are small joint debts) only a small portion of it may be found non-exempt under section 522(b)(2)(B).[149] It seems clear from language of

---

bankruptcy case, failure to do so prior to discharge precludes that option), *aff'd*, 972 F.2d 730 (7th Cir. 1992). As discussed in the text, this result is contrary to express provisions of 11 U.S.C. § 522.

140 *See* Ray v. Dawson, 14 B.R. 822 (E.D. Tenn. 1981), *aff'g* 10 B.R. 680 (Bankr. E.D. Tenn. 1981); *In re* Gibbons, 17 B.R. 373 (Bankr. D.R.I. 1982); *In re* Buck, 17 B.R. 168 (Bankr. D. Haw. 1982); *In re* Phillos, 14 B.R. 781 (Bankr. W.D. Va. 1981); *In re* Lunger, 14 B.R. 6 (Bankr. M.D. Fla. 1981); *In re* Woolard, 13 B.R. 105 (Bankr. E.D.N.C. 1981); Norton, Bankruptcy Law and Practice § 26.09 (property that did not come into estate under prior Act is exempt under § 522(b)(2)(B)); Marc S. Cohen & Kenneth N. Klee, *Caveat Creditor: The Consumer Debtor Under the Bankruptcy Code*, 58 N.C. L. Rev. 681, 690, 691 (1980); William T. Vukowich, *Debtor's Exemption Rights Under the Bankruptcy Reform Act*, 58 N.C. L. Rev. 769, 792 (1980); Douglas R. Rendleman, *Liquidation Bankruptcy Under the '78 Code*, 21 Wm. & Mary L. Rev. 575, 596 (1980); R.L. Hughes, *Code Exemptions: Far Reaching Achievement*, 28 DePaul L. Rev. 1025, 1028 (1979).

141 Napotnik v. Equibank, 679 F.2d 316 (3d Cir. 1982).

142 *In re* Ford, 638 F.2d 14 (4th Cir. 1981).

143 The *Napotnik* court did not explain how this entireties property would be distributed once it did come into the estate. Would it be distributed only to joint creditors who might have reached it outside of bankruptcy? The Code provides no basis for believing that such a bifurcated system of distribution was contemplated. Yet, if all creditors shared in the property, then those who could not have reached it otherwise would receive a windfall.

144 *In re* Edmonston, 107 F.3d 74 (1st Cir. 1997); *In re* Garner, 952 F.2d 232 (8th Cir. 1991), *rev'g* Garner v. Strauss, 121 B.R. 356 (W.D. Mo. 1990); Sumy v. Schlossberg, 777 F.2d 921 (4th Cir. 1985); *In re* Grosslight, 757 F.2d 773 (6th Cir. 1985). These cases should perhaps be reevaluated, based on federal preemption, in light of the Supreme Court's decision in Owen v. Owen, 500 U.S. 305, 111 S. Ct. 1833, 114 L. Ed. 2d 350 (1991). *See In re* Weinstein, 164 F.3d 677 (1st Cir. 1999) (exceptions to state law exemption do not apply in bankruptcy). *But see In re* Tyree, 116 B.R. 682 (Bankr. S.D. Iowa 1990) (trustee could not liquidate homestead held jointly by debtor and non-debtor spouse).

145 *In re* Grosslight, 757 F.2d 773 (6th Cir. 1985); *see also In re* Oberlies, 94 B.R. 916 (Bankr. E.D. Mich. 1988) (Michigan law requires that property be liquidated for the benefit of joint creditors only). *But see In re* Ballard, 65 F.3d 367 (4th Cir. 1995) (when non-debtor spouse dies during the bankruptcy case, the bankruptcy estate becomes sole owner of the property and joint creditors no longer have the right to be paid ahead of non-joint priority creditors from the proceeds of the property).

146 *In re* Dembs, 757 F.2d 777 (6th Cir. 1985); *see* Taylor v. Freeland & Kronz, 503 U.S. 638, 112 S. Ct. 1644, 118 L. Ed. 2d 280 (1992) (extending the holding in *Dembs*). *But see In re* Williams, 104 F.3d 688 (4th Cir. 1997) (even though no objection to exemption was filed within time permitted, debtor's of interest in entireties property not protected from joint creditors).

147 *In re* Hunter, 970 F.2d 299 (7th Cir. 1992). The same result, prohibiting an *in rem* proceeding by a joint creditor against the entireties property claimed as exempt after an Indiana debtor had discharged his indebtedness in a non-joint case was reached in *In re* Paeplow, 972 F.2d 730 (7th Cir. 1992). *See also* Great S. Co. v. Allard, 202 B.R. 938 (N.D. Ill. 1996) (applying Illinois law and permitting debtor to avoid judicial lien on interest in entireties property claimed as exempt under § 522(b)(2)(B)).

148 Despite the restrictive holdings cited above, it may nonetheless be worthwhile to claim the entireties exemption as to all creditors, because that exemption will be allowed if no party timely objects. Taylor v. Freeland & Kronz, 503 U.S. 638, 112 S. Ct. 1644, 118 L. Ed. 2d 280 (1992); *In re* Dembs, 757 F.2d 777 (6th Cir. 1985). Certainly, as there are strong arguments that restrictive holdings are wrong, there is nothing unethical about doing so and there may be little risk of adverse consequences where a chapter 13 case is filed that may be dismissed as a matter of right or where there is no alternative to bankruptcy in any case. *But see In re* Williams, 104 F.3d 688 (4th Cir. 1997) (even though no objection to exemption was filed within time permitted, debtor's exemption of interest in entireties property construed to mean only exemption from non-joint creditors).

149 Somerset Sav. Bank v. Goldberg, 166 B.R. 776 (D. Mass. 1994) (debtor could claim property held as tenant by entireties as exempt because creditor was not permitted to execute on property under Massachusetts law); *In re* Pernus, 143 B.R. 856 (Bankr. N.D. Ohio 1992) (all of debtor's interests in entireties property were exempt where debtor had no unsecured joint creditors). However, even if the debtor's interest is not exempt under section 522(b)(2)(B), there remains the issue of valuing that interest. A number of courts, particularly in New York, have

section 522(b)(2)(B), as well as the case law that, when there are joint creditors, only that amount of the property that is equal to the amount of the joint unsecured debts is not exempt.[150] This result should occur even if both spouses file a joint bankruptcy case, because their exemptions are claimed individually and no consolidation of the estates occurs in a joint case unless it is specifically ordered.[151] Ordinarily, such consolidation would be improper, as it would seriously diminish the rights of joint creditors to the benefit of other creditors. After the bankruptcy, the exempt property is protected because the debt of the cotenant who filed the bankruptcy has been discharged. Even if the other entireties cotenant dies during or after the bankruptcy, leaving the bankruptcy debtor as the sole owner, the exemption protects the property.[152] And it is also important to remember that even if the debtor's interest in joint property is not exempt, the trustee may still be prohibited from liquidating it for the benefit of creditors by 11 U.S.C. § 363(h) which requires the court to consider the hardship to the non-debtor spouse that would be caused by liquidation.[153]

Thus, the state exemptions, as enhanced by the Code, may have a great deal to offer to some debtors, even in states where they have relatively low dollar limits. Of course, debtors in states which have opted out of the federal bankruptcy exemptions have no choice but to make the most of the state provisions. But all other debtors' advocates should carefully consider that option as well, as in some cases it may provide greater benefits than the federal exemption provisions.

10.3 Procedure for Claiming Exemptions

10.3.1 The Initial Claim

The Bankruptcy Code itself says little regarding the procedure for claiming exemptions, other than that the debtor or a dependent shall "file a list" of property claimed exempt.[154] If the debtor does not file such a list, a dependent of the debtor may do so.[155] The procedure for a dependent claiming exemptions is set out in Federal Rule of Bankruptcy Procedure 4003(a), which sets the deadline for filing as thirty days after the debtor's deadline for filing. It is not clear whether the debtor may thereafter amend or object to the exemptions to alter the dependent's claim.[156]

The Bankruptcy Rules require this list to be filed by a debtor as part of the schedules of property. As discussed in Chapter 7, *supra*, the list is to be set forth on Schedule C of Official Form 6.[157] Failure to file a timely schedule of exemptions may be a basis for an objection to the exemptions.[158] The property must be at least fairly specifically described.[159] If it is not, the debtor may later encounter problems in protecting property that was not specifically listed, or the proceeds of such property.[160]

---

used a method of subtracting the value of the non-debtor spouse's life and survivorship interests from the total value of the property, leaving a very small value for the estate in most cases. *Cf. In re* Van der Heide, 164 F.3d 1183 (8th Cir. 1999) (one half of value of property became property of estate and debtor was entitled to one half of state homestead exemption). *But see In re* Cordova, 73 F.3d 38 (4th Cir. 1996) (when debtor acquired, through divorce decree within 180 days of petition, full ownership of property previously held by entireties, debtor's full ownership interest became property of estate subject to claims of all creditors pursuant to § 541(a)(5)(B) and not exemptible under § 522(b)(2)(B)). *See generally In re* Persky, 893 F.2d 15 (2d Cir. 1989).

150 *See, e.g., In re* Edmonston, 107 F.3d 74 (1st Cir. 1997); Sumy v. Schlossberg, 777 F.2d 921, 922 (4th Cir. 1985) (debtor loses benefit of exemption *to the extent of joint claims*); *In re* Grosslight, 757 F.2d 773, 776 (6th Cir. 1985) (debtor's interest *in portion of entireties property reachable by joint creditors* not exempt); *see also In re* Eads, 271 B.R. 371 (Bankr. W.D. Mo. 2002) (if entireties property not fully exempt due to existence of joint creditor, proceeds of sale of property must first be divided—with non-debtor spouse's share distributed to her—and then joint creditors could be paid from debtor's share, with any remaining funds from that share distributed to debtor).

151 11 U.S.C. § 302(b); *see In re* Bunker, 312 F.3d 145 (4th Cir. 2002).

152 *In re* Birney, 200 F.3d 225 (4th Cir. 2000).

153 *See In re* Persky, 893 F.2d 15 (2d Cir. 1989); Henry J. Sommer & Margaret Doe McGarity, Collier Family Law and the Bankruptcy Code ¶ 2.06[3]; § 12.6.5, *infra. But see In re* Morgan, 286 B.R. 678 (Bankr. E.D. Wis. 2002) (equitable factors of § 363(h) do not apply to former community property because, as entire asset in debtor's bankruptcy estate, no interest of the non-debtor spouse was being sold).

154 11 U.S.C. § 522(*l*).

155 11 U.S.C. § 522(*l*). *But see In re* Alexander, 288 B.R. 127 (B.A.P. 8th Cir. 2003) (debtor's spouse could not assert exemption in property that had already been found non-exempt after debtor's claim of exemption). It has been held that even where the debtor files a list, a dependent of the debtor may supplement that list if other exemptions are available and unclaimed. *In re* Crouch, 33 B.R. 271 (Bankr. E.D.N.C. 1983). However, a non-debtor dependent may not supplement an incomplete list of federal exemptions with state exemptions. *In re* Homan, 112 B.R. 356 (B.A.P. 9th Cir. 1989).

156 A debtor may also be able to assert a non-debtor spouse's exemptions in community property, depending on state law. *See In re* Perez, 302 B.R. 661 (Bankr. D. Ariz. 2003) (debtor could assert community's exemptions in community property).

157 *See* § 7.3.4.2.3, *supra*.

158 *See* Petit v. Fessenden, 80 F.3d 29 (1st Cir. 1996) (debtor's exemptions disallowed when schedules not timely filed). If the schedule of exemptions is not timely filed, a motion for enlargement of time may be filed on the basis of excusable neglect under Fed. R. Bankr. P. 9006(b)(1). *See In re* Fetner, 218 B.R. 262 (Bankr. D. Colo. 1997) (requiring procedure to file late exemptions which meets the requisites of the Rule).

159 *In re* Andermahr, 30 B.R. 532 (B.A.P. 9th Cir. 1983); *In re* Wenande, 107 B.R. 770 (Bankr. D. Wyo. 1989) (exemption denied where property not listed with sufficient particularity); *In re* Hill, 95 B.R. 293 (Bankr. N.D.N.Y. 1988) (same); *In re* Elliott, 31 B.R. 33 (Bankr. S.D. Ohio 1983).

160 *See* Preblich v. Battley, 181 F.3d 1048 (9th Cir. 1999) (trustee's

In some jurisdictions, debtors must be careful to make clear that they are claiming their entire interest in particular items of property as exempt. Some courts have held that if a debtor claims a homestead exemption of a specified amount in a particular property and does not also clearly assert that this amount is the total value of the debtor's interest in the property, the trustee may later sell the property and reserve for the debtor from the proceeds the dollar amount claimed as exempt.[161] Often, it should be obvious that the debtor is claiming her entire interest, because the amount claimed as exempt is the same amount as is listed as the value of the debtor's equity elsewhere on the debtor's schedules. Nonetheless, in order to prevent problems of this type, it is probably wise to state on the schedule of exemptions that, unless otherwise noted, the debtor claims as exempt the entire amount of the estate's interest in all property listed.[162]

10.3.2 Amending the Claim of Exemption

Under the rules, any part of the schedules, including the exemption claim, may be amended as a matter of right before the case is closed.[163] Presumably, an amendment may include a change from the state to the federal exemption scheme or vice versa.[164] Under similar language in the prior rules, some courts had imposed time limitations on the right to amend the exemption claim, holding that the claim became "finalized" after the time for objections to exemptions had passed.[165] However, the current rules' provision for extending the time for objections to thirty days after any amendment[166] lays those decisions to rest. A debtor may sometimes even be allowed to reopen the case after discharge to amend the exemptions.[167] It has been held, however, that a debtor cannot exempt property which has been knowingly concealed from the trustee.[168] Additionally, some courts have held that a trustee's or creditor's detrimental

---

time for objecting to exemptions only began to run when debtor clarified that exemption claim covered escrow accounts as well as wages); *In re* Yonikus, 996 F.2d 866 (7th Cir. 1993) (debtor's exemption for workers' compensation claim denied after debtor had initially fraudulently concealed existence of the claim); Payne v. Wood, 775 F.2d 202 (7th Cir. 1985) (debtors not permitted to exempt insurance proceeds of property not listed; intent to conceal property inferred); *In* re Bauer, 298 B.R. 353 (B.A.P. 8th Cir. 2003) (clearly untruthful and bad faith disclosure of home's value as $80,000.00, when it was worth over $200,000.00, justified sustaining objection to exemption amendment filed only after trustee determined true value of property); *In re* Bogert, 104 B.R. 547 (Bankr. M.D. Ga. 1989) (trustee permitted to withdraw no asset report after learning debtor did not adequately describe his pension plan). *But see In re* Rutherford, 73 B.R. 665 (Bankr. W.D. Mo. 1986) (debtor entitled to insurance proceeds when exempt property destroyed by fire despite undervaluation on schedules). The debtor may encounter similar problems in not specifically describing property in an amended exemption. However, the description need only be sufficient to put the trustee on notice of the nature of the property and the amount of the exemption. Taylor v. Freeland & Kronz, 503 U.S. 638, 112 S. Ct. 1644, 118 L. Ed. 2d 280 (1992) (cause of action described but valued as "unknown" was sufficient to put trustee on notice of the exemption).

161 *E.g., In re* Alsberg, 68 F.3d 312 (9th Cir. 1995) (erroneously holding that, even though debtor's interest was totally exempt at time of filing, appreciation of interest above exemption amount was not exempted); *In re* Hyman, 967 F.2d 1316 (9th Cir. 1992). The *Alsberg* holding is wrong based on 11 U.S.C. § 522(a)(2) which fixes the exemptions as of the date of filing. *See In re* Polis, 217 F.3d 899 (7th Cir. 2000) (TILA claim should be valued for exemption purposes based on fair market value, discounted for contingency, on date of bankruptcy petition). The decision also creates a perverse incentive for trustees to hold estates open as long as possible in order to wait for property to appreciate and disincentives for debtors to make repairs and improvements to property while a case is pending.

162 However, the debtor must still give a dollar value for the interest in property if that is possible. The debtor cannot simply state that each item is totally exempt. *In re* Bell, 179 B.R. 129 (Bankr. E.D. Wis. 1995); *see also* Mercer v. Monzack, 53 F.3d 1 (1st Cir. 1995) (listing property as "100 percent" exempt under particular subsections of § 522(d) without giving value

---

found to mean one-hundred percent of the available exemption under those subsections, so trustee could claim amount realized that was not within the scope of the exemption provisions cited); *In re* Jackson, 194 B.R. 867 (Bankr. D. Ariz. 1995) (debtors should have listed property as "100 percent exempt" in addition to claiming exemption in amount that they stated was the value of the property); *cf. In re* Soost, 262 B.R. 68 (B.A.P. 8th Cir. 2001) (debtor who claimed interest in property as exempt in amount of $1.00 could only avoid lien to that extent). This decision is incorrect because it did not follow the lien avoidance formula in 11 U.S.C. § 522(f)(2) and section 522(f) refers to exemptions to which the debtor "would have been entitled" but for the lien, suggesting that technically the property is not able to be exempted until the lien is avoided. Nonetheless, the decision points up the need to clearly state that the debtor's entire interest is being exempted.

163 Fed. R. Bankr. P. 1009; *In re* Michael, 163 F.3d 526 (9th Cir. 1998) (debtors had right to amend even after discharge if case not yet closed); *In re* Williamson, 804 F.2d 1355 (5th Cir. 1986); *see also* Lucius v. McLemore, 741 F.2d 125 (6th Cir. 1984); *In re* Shirkey, 715 F.2d 859 (4th Cir. 1983); Redmond v. Tuttle, 698 F.2d 414 (10th Cir. 1983) (exemptions may be amended at any time before case is closed); *In re* Doan, 672 F.2d 831 (5th Cir. 1982) (reversing a denial of debtor's motion to amend schedules to add exemption claim).

164 *In re* McQueen, 21 B.R. 736 (Bankr. D. Vt. 1982).

165 *In re* Mertsching, 4 B.R. 519 (Bankr. D. Idaho 1980) (debtor forced to pay trustee $50.00 costs in order to modify exemptions to meet previous objection of trustee which was sustained); *In re* Lyon, 6 Bankr. Ct. Dec. (LRP) 343, 2 Collier Bankr. Cas. 2d (MB) 561 (Bankr. D. Kan. 1980) (local rule provided that exemption finalized if no objection within fifteen days after § 341 meeting); *In re* Duggan, 4 B.R. 709 (Bankr. N.D. Tex. 1980) (debtor could not change to federal exemptions fifteen days after trustee's statement of exempt property filed). Objection time limits are discussed in § 10.3.3, *infra*.

166 Fed. R. Bankr. P. 4003(b); 9 Collier on Bankruptcy ¶ 4003.02[2] (15th ed. rev.).

167 *In re* King, 27 B.R. 754 (Bankr. M.D. Tenn. 1983).

168 *In re* Wood, 291 B.R. 219 (B.A.P. 1st Cir. 2003); *In re* Dorricott, 5 B.R. 192 (Bankr. N.D. Ohio 1980); *see also* Payne v. Wood, 775 F.2d 202 (7th Cir. 1985). *But see In re* Moody, 862 F.2d 1194 (5th Cir. 1989) (attempted fraudulent transfer of property

reliance on the debtor's original claim of exemption may limit later amendment.[169] These courts do not fully address why prejudice to the creditor in the absence of bad faith on the part of the debtor should be sufficient to affect the right to amend nor why there should be an exception that does not exist in the Federal Rules of Bankruptcy Procedure. Other courts have required the debtor who amends to include property brought into the estate by the trustee to pay the fees and costs of expended by the trustee in obtaining the property.[170] At least with respect to property obtained by the trustee under the turnover and avoiding powers, the Code specifically provides that the exempted property is liable for its aliquot share of the costs and expenses of recovering the property.[171] And a debtor may not, after the case is filed, convert non-exempt property into exempt property to claim it as exempt.[172]

One type of situation in which an amendment may be necessary is the case in which property acquired after the petition is filed becomes property of the estate.[173] The debtor is permitted to amend the exemption schedules to exempt such property if it fits within applicable exemption limits, regardless of whether a discharge has already been entered.[174]

Any amendment, of course, should comply with Bankruptcy Rule 1009 which requires service on all parties affected by an amendment; in the case of amended exemptions, service should presumably be made on the trustee and all creditors, except creditors already being paid in full.[175]

Perhaps also, if the time for filing claims has run, the amendment need not be served on creditors who did not file claims. Failure to make proper service may extend the deadline for objections.[176]

10.3.3 Objections to Exemptions

The Code allows objections to claims of exemption by "a party in interest," again specifying no procedure.[177] The procedure is provided by Bankruptcy Rule 4003(b), though the rule does not prescribe any particular form for the objection.[178] In most cases the party who would be likely to object is the trustee. However, the rules make clear that any creditor has standing to file objections to exemptions.[179]

In some districts, trustees still file reports of any objections to exemptions as well as a recommendation concerning discharge. In any case, all objections to exemptions must be filed within thirty days after the conclusion of the meeting of creditors or the filing of any amendment to the exemption list, unless a motion for an extension of the deadline is filed within that period and the court grants the motion.[180] Bankruptcy Rule 1009 requires that notice of any amendment of the exemptions be given to any entity affected by it, which

---

did not preclude debtor from later claiming homestead exemption under Texas law).

169 *See In re* Kaelin, 308 F.3d 885 (8th Cir. 2002) (debtor could exempt recently discovered cause of action because debtor had acted promptly to amend exemptions after learning of its existence); *In re* Osborn, 24 F.3d 1199 (10th Cir. 1994) (stating that a limited exception to the general permissibility of amendments could exist if the debtors were equitably estopped, but declining to find exception applicable where misrepresentations relied upon by creditors were not made by both husband and wife debtors); Hardage v. Herring Nat'l Bank, 837 F.2d 1319 (5th Cir. 1988) (creditor may change litigation posture in reliance on debtor's initial exemption claim resulting in prejudice precluding amendment); *In re* Goswami, 304 B.R. 386 (B.A.P. 9th Cir. 2003) (debtors had right to amend exemptions for purpose of lien avoidance absent bad faith or prejudice).

170 *In re* Arnold, 252 B.R. 778 (B.A.P. 9th Cir. 2000); *In re* Myatt, 101 B.R. 197 (Bankr. E.D. Cal. 1989) (where trustee conducts litigation based on belief that litigation costs and fees would be paid from recovery of non-exempt property, debtor's later amendment of exemptions to include recovered property may be conditioned on payment of trustee's expenses).

171 11 U.S.C. § 522(k)(1).

172 *In re* Blue, 5 B.R. 723 (Bankr. S.D. Ohio 1980).

173 Certain types of property acquired within 180 days after the petition is filed, such as inheritances, life insurance proceeds and property settlements, become property of the bankruptcy estate. 11 U.S.C. § 541(a)(5).

174 *In re* Notargiacomo, 253 B.R. 112 (Bankr. S.D. Fla. 2000); *In re* Magness, 160 B.R. 294 (Bankr. N.D. Tex. 1993).

175 *See In re* Casani, 214 B.R. 459 (D. Vt. 1997) (all creditors

should be served); *In re* Govoni, 289 B.R. 500 (Bankr. D. Mass. 2002) (order granting amendment to exemption schedule vacated because notice not provided to judicial lienholder).

176 *Compare In re* Woodson, 839 F.2d 610 (9th Cir. 1988) (creditor's objection to amendment was timely on thirty-first day after amendment because creditor had not been served with debtor's amendment, even though the creditor had actual knowledge of the asset about which the amendment was made) *and In re* Robertson, 105 B.R. 440 (Bankr. N.D. Ill. 1989) (deadline for objecting to amended exemption did not apply where trustee had no notice of amendment) *with In re* Peterson, 929 F.2d 385 (8th Cir. 1991) (objection to amended exemption untimely where creditor had actual notice of the amendment by virtue of service of the trustee's objection ten months earlier).

177 11 U.S.C. § 522(*l*).

178 *See In re* Spenler, 212 B.R. 625 (B.A.P. 9th Cir. 1997) (objection to exemption was timely even though it did not conform to local rule).

179 Fed. R. Bankr. P. 4003(b).

180 *Id.*; Fed. R. Bankr. P. 9006(b)(3); *In re* Bernard, 40 F.3d 1028 (9th Cir. 1994) (creditors meeting is not concluded until after two adjournments caused by debtors' failure to cooperate, so objection was timely); *In re* Kahan, 28 F.3d 79 (9th Cir. 1994) (trustee's objection to amendment was timely objection, because amendment was not merely a clarification of prior schedule). Rule 4003(b) was amended in 2000 to overrule cases that had held that the court had to grant the extension prior to the expiration of the thirty days. *E.g., In re* Laurain, 113 F.3d 595 (6th Cir. 1997); *In re* Stoulig, 45 F.3d 957 (5th Cir. 1995). An objection to an amended exemption claim may only raise issues concerning the amendment if the time for objecting to the initial claim has run. *In re* Kazi, 985 F.2d 318 (7th Cir. 1993); *In re* Payton, 73 B.R. 31 (Bankr. W.D. Tex. 1987); *see also In re* Alderton, 179 B.R. 63 (Bankr. E.D. Mich. 1995) (grant of extension of time to file dischargeability complaint did not extend deadline for objecting to exemptions).

usually would include the trustee and all creditors, so that they have an opportunity to object.[181] Objections that are not timely filed cannot be considered.[182] Once the deadline has passed, converting a case from another chapter to chapter 7 does not start a new thirty-day period to object, as the property of the estate does not change.[183]

Copies of the objections must be served on the trustee, the person filing the exemption claim (usually the debtor), and that person's attorney.[184] At the hearing on the objections, the objecting party has the burden of proof.[185] Exemption statutes should be construed liberally in favor of the debtor.[186]

As in other areas of bankruptcy procedure, questions of value may be critical in objections to exemption claims. In general, the discussion in Chapter 9, *supra*, of methods to prove value for stay litigation purposes is equally relevant here.[187] However, while the goal in that type of litigation may be to prove a high value for property, in exemption claims the debtor usually attempts to prove the property to have a low value, within the exemption limits. While it can be argued that the different purposes of the valuations should lead to different values in each case, it is certainly preferable to try to be consistent, which means carefully planning strategy from the outset. In fact, at least if value is determined in one proceeding and the purpose of valuation is the same in a subsequent proceeding, collateral estoppel may bar the debtor from relitigating the question of value.[188]

In any case, the debtor usually should argue that for exemption purposes the "fair market value" of section 522(a)(2) is liquidation value, because the purpose of the valuation is to see if liquidation of the property will produce cash in excess of the exemption amount.[189] There is no point in selling the debtor's property if all of the proceeds after the costs of sale will go back to the debtor.

The value should be determined as of the date the petition was filed, and any appreciation since then should be considered property acquired post-petition that is not a part of the estate.[190] Conversion of a case from one chapter to another does not change the relevant date for calculating value for the purpose of determining exemptions.[191] Similarly, a change in the applicable exemption law following the filing of the case does not apply; the law in effect at the time of filing determines the property which may be exempted.[192] Even if the property would no longer be consid-

---

181 *See In re* Banke, 267 B.R. 852 (Bankr. N.D. Iowa 2001) (creditor had until thirty days after actual notice of amended exemption to object); *see also* § 10.3.2, *supra*.

182 Taylor v. Freeland & Kronz, 503 U.S. 638, 112 S. Ct. 1644, 118 L. Ed. 2d 280 (1992). *But see In re* Young, 806 F.2d 1303 (5th Cir. 1986) (objection allowed where debtor had notice of trustee's objection prior to deadline even though actual objection filed after deadline). Some courts had held, incorrectly, that an untimely objection to an exemption could be sustained where the exemption claim has "no statutory basis" or no "good faith statutory basis." *E.g., In re* Peterson, 920 F.2d 1389 (8th Cir. 1990); *In re* Sherk, 918 F.2d 1170 (5th Cir. 1990). Those decisions have been overruled by the United States Supreme Court. Taylor v. Freeland & Kronz, 503 U.S. 638, 112 S. Ct. 1644, 118 L. Ed. 2d 280 (1992); *see* § 10.3.4, *infra*.

183 *In re* Smith, 235 F.3d 472 (9th Cir. 2000); *In re* Bell, 225 F.3d 203 (2d Cir. 2000); *In re* Slack, 290 B.R. 282 (Bankr. D.N.J. 2003); *In re* Rogers, 278 B.R. 201 (Bankr. D. Nev. 2002); *In re* Beshirs, 236 B.R. 42 (Bankr. D. Kan. 1999) (conversion does not start new objection period); *In re* Brown, 178 B.R. 722 (Bankr. E.D. Tenn. 1995) (conversion does not trigger a new period to object to exemptions); *In re* Halbert, 146 B.R. 185 (Bankr. W.D. Tex. 1992) (conversion to chapter 7 did not create new time period for objections to exemptions); *In re* Robertson, 105 B.R. 440 (Bankr. N.D. Ill. 1989). *But see In re* Alexander, 236 F.3d 431 (8th Cir. 2001) (chapter 7 trustee permitted to raise objection to new Schedule C in chapter 7 case converted from chapter 13 when debtor claimed same exemption that had been disallowed in chapter 13 case); Weissman v. Carr, 173 B.R. 235 (M.D. Fla. 1994) (time period began to run again after chapter 7 meeting of creditors in converted case).

184 Fed. R. Bankr. P. 4003(b).

185 Fed. R. Bankr. P. 4003(c).

186 *E.g., In re* Wallerstedt, 930 F.2d 630 (8th Cir. 1991).

187 *See* § 9.7.3.3.1, *supra*.

188 *In re* Bohrer, 19 B.R. 958 (Bankr. E.D. Pa. 1982).

189 *In re* Walsh, 5 B.R. 239 (Bankr. D.D.C. 1980). *But see In re* Windfelder, 82 B.R. 367 (Bankr. E.D. Pa. 1988) and cases cited therein.

190 11 U.S.C. § 522(a)(2); *In re* Rappaport, 19 B.R. 971 (Bankr. E.D. Pa. 1982); *see also In re* Harris, 886 F.2d 1011 (8th Cir. 1989) (debtors could not claim exemption in proceeds of property of estate, where apparently property of the estate had not previously been claimed as exempt, when proceeds came into existence under state law only because of event occurring post-petition); *In re* Finn, 151 B.R. 25 (Bankr. N.D.N.Y. 1992) (property valued as of filing date for lien avoidance purposes). *But see In re* Alsberg, 68 F.3d 312 (9th Cir. 1995) (erroneously holding that, even though debtor's interest was totally exempt at time of filing, when debtor first claimed exemption long after the petition was filed, trustee could object that appreciation of interest above exemption amount was not exempted); *In re* Hyman, 967 F.2d 1316 (9th Cir. 1992) (when debtor's interest was not totally exempt at time of petition, appreciation could not be exempted). Both of these cases should be distinguishable from the more typical situation where the debtor promptly claims the entire equity as exempt at the time of the petition and no timely objection is filed. At that point the estate has no interest that can appreciate. *See In re* Polis, 217 F.3d 899 (7th Cir. 2000) (TILA claim should be valued for exemption purposes based on fair market value, discounted for contingency, on date of bankruptcy petition). Both cases also rely on the peculiar wording of the California homestead exemption statute.

191 11 U.S.C. § 348(a); *see In re* Hall, 1 F.3d 853 (9th Cir. 1993) (value of property in converted case is determined as of date of original bankruptcy petition filing); *In re* Kaplan, 97 B.R. 572 (B.A.P. 9th Cir. 1989). It is unclear whether the *Hall* decision is still valid precedent. The decision was withdrawn and then subsequently reaffirmed by the Ninth Circuit without reissuing the decision. See *In re* Hall, 41 F.3d 502 (9th Cir. 1994) and 42 F.3d 1399 (9th Cir. 1994); *see also In re* Alsberg, 68 F.3d 312 (9th Cir. 1995). It would appear that the reasoning of the court, albeit limited, nevertheless continues to have persuasive value.

192 *In re* Marcus, 1 F.3d 1050 (10th Cir. 1993).

ered exempt, the same principle applies.[193] Exemptions are determined as of the filing of the petition.

Of course, if the property is sold during the bankruptcy case, the sale price is normally the best evidence of its value, unless a change in value since the petition date can be proved.[194] When property is sold by the bankruptcy trustee during the bankruptcy case and unexpected proceeds are realized, the debtors should be allowed at a minimum to amend the exemption claim and thereby obtain the maximum exempt share of the funds raised.[195]

10.3.4 Absent Successful Objections, the Exemptions Are Allowed

If no timely and successful objection to the debtor's exemptions is made, the exemptions listed by the debtor are automatically allowed.[196] Untimely objections cannot be entertained by the court, whether or not the original exemption was proper.[197]

This rule means that the trustee or a creditor can dispute an exemption only by affirmatively filing a timely objection.

For this reason, debtor's attorneys should not acquiesce to a request to turn over to the trustee property which the debtor claims as exempt. In practice, as often as not, the trustee never files the necessary objection. In those instances in which an objection is actually filed on time, the debtor can then litigate the question of whether the property is actually exempt.

Debtors should also beware of trustees' attempts to indefinitely extend the time for objections. Some trustees have indefinitely "adjourned" the meeting of creditors to prevent the conclusion of the meting, from which the time period begins to run. Such adjournments should not be permitted, because they render the deadline for objections meaningless.[198] Other trustees have attempted in other ways to keep their options open without litigating an objection.[199]

Given the burden on the trustee and the creditors to raise timely objections, the debtor should be careful to make all appropriate exemption claims at the outset of the case, when possible.[200] It is to the debtor's advantage to fully describe the property, including its value and any features which would decrease its value if it were sold, and then to list the basis for the exemption. Obviously, the limit on this principle is one of good faith. Bad faith exemption claims that are not grounded in fact or law not only create the risk of a successful objection, but also expose debtors and their counsel to the risk of sanctions.[201]

Once property is exempt by virtue of the expiration of the deadline for objections, nothing prevents the debtors from using or otherwise disposing of their exempt interest.[202]

---

193 *In re* Alexander, 239 B.R. 911 (B.A.P. 8th Cir. 1999) (homestead determined as of petition date); *In re* Beshirs, 236 B.R. 42 (Bankr. D. Kan. 1999) (property that was exempted as tool of trade was still exempt after conversion even though no longer used as tool of trade).

194 Fitzgerald v. Davis, 729 F.2d 306 (4th Cir. 1984).

195 Armstrong v. Hursman, 106 B.R. 625 (D.N.D. 1988); *see* § 10.3.2, *supra*.

196 11 U.S.C. § 522(*l*); *see* Taylor v. Freeland & Kronz, 503 U.S. 638, 112 S. Ct. 1644, 118 L. Ed. 2d 280 (1992); *In re* Sadkin, 36 F.3d 473 (5th Cir. 1994) (even if exemption is without merit, failure of any party to file a timely objection results in allowance of exemption); *In re* Green, 31 F.3d 1098 (11th Cir. 1994) (if no party challenges debtor's valuation of asset claimed as fully exempt, debtor is entitled to exempt the entire asset regardless of what the value ultimately proves to be); *In re* Morgan-Busby, 272 B.R. 257 (B.A.P. 9th Cir. 2002) (deadline for objections includes objections based on valuation of property clearly claimed as exempt); *In re* Chaparro Martinez, 293 B.R. 387 (Bankr. N.D. Tex. 2003) (court has no jurisdiction over debtors' personal injury settlement proceeds, even though in excess of claimed exemption, because debtors claimed one-hundred percent of claim as exempt and trustee failed to file timely objection). *But see In re* Wick, 276 F.3d 412 (8th Cir. 2002) (erroneously holding that, even though debtor listed value of stock options as unknown and trustee did not object to exemption, property was only partially exempt because trustee expressed interest in asset and debtor supposedly made statements suggesting she "understood" options to be only partially exempt); Petit v. Fessenden, 80 F.3d 29 (1st Cir. 1996) (if exemption claim is not filed timely, automatic allowance after objection period does not occur); *In re* Clark, 266 B.R. 163 (B.A.P. 9th Cir. 2001) (ambiguous exemption claim construed against debtor when debtor claimed as exempt "five lots listed in qualified retirement plan" and plan did not exist).

197 Fed. R. Bankr. P. 4003(b); Taylor v. Freeland & Kronz, 503 U.S. 638, 112 S. Ct. 1644, 118 L. Ed. 2d 280 (1992); *see* § 10.3.3, *supra*.

198 *In re* Smith, 235 B.R. 472 (9th Cir. 2000) (trustee could not adjourn § 341 meeting indefinitely; rules required specific place and time); *In re* Clark, 262 B.R. 508 (B.A.P. 9th Cir. 2001) (trustee must announce date of continued creditors meeting within reasonable time, not to exceed thirty days); *In re* Hurdle, 240 B.R. 617 (Bankr. C.D. Cal. 1999) (trustee could not adjourn meeting with no new date scheduled to avoid deadline); *In re* Levitt, 137 B.R. 881 (Bankr. D. Mass. 1992) (trustee's failure to announce an adjourned date and time within thirty days of the initial meeting of creditors means that meeting must be deemed closed as of the initial date); *see also* 3 Collier on Bankruptcy ¶ 341.02[5][g] (15th ed. rev.). *But see In re* DeCarolis, 259 B.R. 467 (B.A.P. 1st Cir. 2001) (adjournment without setting new date could extend time for objections if amount of extension reasonable under circumstances).

199 *In re* Thomas, 236 B.R. 573 (Bankr. E.D.N.Y. 1999) (trustee could not file "no asset report," close case, and still retain right to reopen if cause of action proved to have unexpected value).

200 Note, however, the right to amend. See § 10.3.2, *supra*.

201 *See* Fed. R. Bankr. P. 9011. It is unclear whether sanctions for bad faith exemptions are possible after the time for objecting to the actual exemption has passed.

202 Wissman v. Pittsburgh Nat'l Bank, 942 F.2d 867 (4th Cir. 1991) (debtors may pursue an exempt cause of action in order to recover their exemption); Ball v. Nationscredit Fin. Serv. Corp., 207 B.R. 869 (N.D. Ill. 1997) (exempt property revests in debtor when time to object to exemptions expires); Seifert v. Selby, 125 B.R. 174 (E.D. Mich. 1989) (absent timely objection, exempt property revests in the debtor and is no longer property of the estate); *cf. In re* Reed, 940 F.2d 1317 (9th Cir. 1991) (although

When a single piece of property is only partially exempt, the debtor may retain the entire property until the trustee pays the value of the exemption to the debtor in cash.[203] Importantly, this rule means that the debtor can continue to reside in property which the trustee may liquidate without responsibility to the trustee for rent or other payments.[204] Moreover, under section 522(k), the trustee must pay the entire exemption amount to the debtor before the trustee can use the proceeds of the sale to pay any costs or fees in connection with the sale.[205]

10.4 Making the Most of Exemptions

10.4.1 Exemption Planning

Section 522 of the Code provides many protections and powers in connection with debtors' exemption rights. The exemptions, whether state or federal, are non-waivable for bankruptcy purposes, even if state law would normally allow a waiver of exemptions.[206] And the debtor's powers to enhance the exemptions, to be discussed below, are also non-waivable.[207] In essence, the exemption provisions federalize all of the law applying to bankruptcy exemptions, except for the actual items which can be claimed as exempt by a debtor utilizing the state exemptions.[208] Under this uniform bankruptcy system, dependents of the debtor may claim exemptions if the debtor does not,[209] and the exemptions are automatically allowed if no objection is filed.[210]

As discussed in an earlier chapter,[211] the amount of property that may be claimed as exempt can be greatly increased, if necessary, by careful exemption planning. For example, cash in a non-exemptible bank account can be used to pay down a mortgage to create exemptible home equity.[212] Although there was some question as to the propriety of exemption planning under the prior Act, the federalization of most bankruptcy exemption law should somewhat ease those doubts that existed before. However, some courts have found the movement of very large amounts of money into exempt property to be fraudulent, at least with respect to state exemptions.[213]

10.4.2 Avoiding Powers of the Debtor

10.4.2.1 General Principles

One of the most far-reaching and exciting changes made by the Bankruptcy Reform Act was its grant to the debtor of the power to avoid (nullify) many types of pre-bankruptcy

---

debtor is entitled to exemption when no one timely objects to the exemption, the trustee is entitled to proceeds of sale to the extent they exceed the actual dollar value of the exemption); *In re* Salzer, 52 F.3d 708 (7th Cir.) (reading Indiana law to delay revesting of exempt property in debtor), *aff'd*, 68 F.3d 312 (9th Cir. 1995).

203 *In re* Szekely, 936 F.2d 897 (7th Cir. 1991). *But see In re* Salzer, 52 F.3d 708 (7th Cir. 1995) (erroneously holding that Indiana execution procedures permit a bankruptcy trustee to hold property after the deadline for objecting to exemptions has run until the trustee obtains an appraisal of the property; pro se debtor waived argument that commercial property in question was totally exempt); Greene v. Balaber-Strauss, 76 B.R. 940 (S.D.N.Y. 1987) (trustee could wait until she completed her administrative duties). The latter decision is poorly reasoned, confusing the issue of discharge with that of exemptions, which are provided regardless of discharge.

204 *In re* Szekely, 936 F.2d 897 (7th Cir. 1991).

205 *In re* Allen, 203 B.R. 925 (W.D. Va.), *aff'd sub nom.* Scott v. U.S. Trustee, 133 F.3d 917 (4th Cir. 1997) (table).

206 11 U.S.C. § 522(e); *In re* Howell, 51 B.R. 1015 (M.D.N.C. 1985); *see* Dominion Bank of Cumberlands v. Nuckolls, 780 F.2d 408 (4th Cir. 1985).

207 11 U.S.C. § 522(e); *see In re* Hebert, 301 B.R. 19 (Bankr. N.D. Iowa 2003) (waiver of homestead exemption unenforceable due to § 522(e)).

208 *See* Owen v. Owen, 500 U.S. 305, 111 S. Ct. 1833, 114 L. Ed. 2d 250 (1991). *But see In re* Golden, 789 F.2d 698 (9th Cir. 1986) (giving effect to substantive limitation on California homestead exemption which requires that proceeds of sale of homestead be reinvested in new home within six months to maintain exemption). It should be noted that California's ex-

emption is thus broader than the federal exemption. *See also* § 10.2.1, *supra.*

209 11 U.S.C. § 522(*l*).

210 11 U.S.C. § 522(*l*); Taylor v. Freeland & Kronz, 503 U.S. 638, 112 S. Ct. 1644, 118 L. Ed. 2d 280 (1992). In fact, a creditor's failure to file a timely objection can preclude that creditor from later challenging the debtor's exemptions when the debtor attempts to use the bankruptcy code's avoiding powers. *In re* Hahn, 60 B.R. 69 (Bankr. D. Minn. 1985); *see also* 9 Collier on Bankruptcy ¶ 4003.03[3] (15th ed. rev.); § 10.3.4, *supra.*

211 See § 6.5.2.2, *supra,* for a discussion of exemption planning and its legitimacy.

212 *In re* Bowyer, 932 F.2d 1100 (5th Cir. 1991); *In re* Bradley, 294 B.R. 64 (B.A.P. 8th Cir. 2003) (use of non-exempt assets to purchase exempt homestead did not constitute fraud necessary to deny Arkansas homestead exemption); *see also In re* Carey, 938 F.2d 1073 (10th Cir. 1991) (debtor's negotiation of a mortgage which prepaid a prior mortgage and created exemptible home equity does not constitute fraud).

213 *Compare* Hanson v. First Nat'l Bank in Brookings, 848 F.2d 866 (8th Cir. 1988) *with In re* Sholdan, 217 F.3d 1006 (8th Cir. 2000) (ninety-year-old's conversion of virtually all assets into exempt homestead found fraudulent and exemption denied) *and* Norwest Bank Neb. v. Tveten, 848 F.2d 871 (8th Cir. 1988). Two of these decisions of the Eighth Circuit dealing with exemption planning were issued on the same day. They reach different conclusions based on facts which on close reading are not meaningfully distinguishable. If anything, the two decisions illustrate the care necessary in exemption planning and the potential for fact-intensive decision-making by courts finding a debtor's manipulation of Code provisions unpalatable. *See also In re* Stern, 345 F.3d 1036 (9th Cir. 2003) (conversion of assets from non-exempt forms into exempt forms is not, in and of itself, sufficient to establish fraud absent other facts showing fraud); *In re* Armstrong, 931 F.2d 1233 (8th Cir. 1991) (exemption planning which is legitimate under state law is legitimate for bankruptcy purposes).

transfers of exempt property. This set of powers, contained in section 522, opened up an entirely new area in which debtors can greatly expand upon the exemption rights given to them by state or federal law. Because this area was new, it was largely uncharted when the Code was enacted. Since then, numerous courts, including the Supreme Court on several occasions, have interpreted the lien avoidance provisions of section 522(f).

The power to avoid transfers is expansive due, in part, to the broad definition of the word "transfer." Section 101(54) includes within this term any lien, execution sale, setoff, or any other mode of disposing of or parting with an interest in property, whether voluntarily or involuntarily, including foreclosure of the debtor's equity of redemption.

The debtor, with certain limitations, may thus invalidate numerous types of transfers, and recover valuable interests in property, as long as those interests can be claimed as exempt. Put another way, if the interest in property involved fits within the exemption scheme utilized by the debtor and if the interest is impaired by a transfer of a type covered by section 522, then that transfer may be avoided.[214] But if only a portion of the transferred property may be claimed as exempt, the transfer may be avoided only to that extent.[215]

Courts have disagreed about whether a debtor seeking to avoid a lien on a particular property can rely upon the fact that an exemption claimed with respect to that property was finalized because no party objected to it.[216] Because the creditor had an opportunity to object to the value claimed as exempt, and the exemption is deemed allowed if no objection is filed, the creditor should not be given a second opportunity to question valuation or other issues in the lien avoidance proceeding.[217] However, some courts have drawn a distinction, holding that Code section 522(f) requires an independent finding that the property is, in fact, exemptible

and the creditor is not bound by the automatic exemption of property claimed as exempt when no objection is filed.[218]

The avoiding powers may be invoked even if the debtor has no equity in a particular property, as long as the debtor can claim some interest in that property as exempt, even a mere right to possession or to redemption.[219] Nor is it necessary to show that the debt upon which a transfer is based is a dischargeable debt before the transfer can be avoided. The statute seems clear that nondischargeability of an underlying debt is no defense to an otherwise proper action to avoid a transfer that impairs an exemption.[220] And, despite a few early lower court decisions to the contrary, it is clear that the avoiding powers are equally available in chapter 7 and chapter 13.[221]

10.4.2.2 Procedure for Use of Avoiding Powers

The Federal Rules of Bankruptcy Procedure prescribe the procedure to be followed for lien avoidance by the debtor. Rule 4003(d) provides that lien avoidance under 11 U.S.C. § 522(f) shall be by motion in accordance with Bankruptcy Rule 9014.[222] However, transfer or lien avoidance under 11

---

214 *See In re* Snyder, 279 B.R. 1 (B.A.P. 1st Cir. 2002) (debtor could avoid lien that impaired state homestead exemption even though debtor had amended exemptions after having originally claimed federal exemptions and having lost lien avoidance motion based on those exemptions); *In re* Dardar, 3 B.R. 641 (Bankr. E.D. Va. 1980) (section 522(f) only applicable to property claimed exempt).

215 *In re* Jordan, 5 B.R. 59 (Bankr. D.N.J. 1980). As the issue is whether property may be claimed as exempt, and exemptions are determined as of the petition date, property is valued as of the petition date for purposes of the debtor's avoiding powers. 11 U.S.C. § 522(a)(2); *In re* Finn, 151 B.R. 25 (Bankr. N.D.N.Y. 1992).

216 *Compare* Great S. Co. v. Allard, 202 B.R. 938 (N.D. Ill. 1996) (creditor bound in lien avoidance action by determination under section 522(1) that property is exempt) *and In re* Carruthers, 87 B.R. 723 (Bankr. N.D. Ga. 1988) *with In re* Morgan, 149 B.R. 147 (B.A.P. 9th Cir. 1993). *See also* § 10.3.4, *supra*.

217 Great S. Co. v. Allard, 202 B.R. 938 (N.D. Ill. 1996); *In re* Indvik, 118 B.R. 993 (Bankr. N.D. Iowa 1990); *In re* Hahn, 60 B.R. 69 (Bankr. D. Minn. 1985); 9 Collier on Bankruptcy ¶ 4003.03[3] (15th ed. rev.).

218 *In re* Schoonover, 331 F.3d 575 (7th Cir. 2003); *In re* Morgan, 149 B.R. 147 (B.A.P. 9th Cir. 1993.

219 *In re* Bland, 793 F.2d 1172 (11th Cir. 1986) (*en banc*); *In re* Brown, 81 B.R. 432 (N.D. Ohio 1985); *In re* Lovett, 11 B.R. 123 (W.D. Mo. 1981), *opinion vacated on other grounds*, 23 B.R. 760 (W.D. Mo. 1982); *In re* Kursh, 9 B.R. 801 (Bankr. W.D. Mo. 1981); *In re* Van Gorkom, 4 B.R. 689 (Bankr. D.S.D. 1980); *see also In re* Sherwood, 94 B.R. 679 (Bankr. E.D. Cal. 1988) (debtor could avoid lien on household goods destroyed by post-petition fire and thereby obtain insurance proceeds held by the creditor). *Contra In re* Boteler, 5 B.R. 408 (Bankr. S.D. Ala. 1980). Section 522(f) was clarified in 1994 to eliminate any doubt on this issue, so that cases like *Boteler* can no longer be considered as valid precedent. *See* § 10.4.2.3, *infra*.

220 Walters v. U.S. Nat'l Bank of Johnstown, 879 F.2d 95 (3d Cir. 1989) (debtor may avoid lien of creditor whose claim is nondischargeable on ground of fraud); *In re* Liming, 797 F.2d 895 (10th Cir. 1986); *In re* Krajci, 7 B.R. 242 (Bankr. E.D. Pa. 1980), *aff'd*, 16 B.R. 462 (E.D. Pa. 1981); *In re* Gantt, 7 B.R. 13 (Bankr. N.D. Ga. 1980); *see also In re* Clark, 217 B.R. 943 (Bankr. M.D. Fla. 1998) (debtor had lien avoidance powers even though he was denied a discharge); *In re* Sullivan, 83 B.R. 623 (Bankr. S.D. Iowa 1988) (although general rule is that lien avoidance is not dependent on dischargeability of underlying debt, under Iowa law homestead property could not be exempted to the extent impaired by child support judgment).

221 *In re* Hall, 752 F.2d 582 (11th Cir. 1985); *see also* James B. McLaughlin, Jr., *Lien Avoidance by Debtors in Chapter 13 of the Bankruptcy Reform Act of 1978*, 58 Am. Bankr. L. J. 45 (1984); 8 Collier on Bankruptcy ¶ 1300.81 (15th ed. rev.).

222 For a sample motion to avoid judicial lien, see Form 74, Appendix G.9, *infra*. As in all contested matters under Rule 9014, however, the adversary proceeding service rules that apply have special requirements for serving insured depository institutions. *In re* Hamlett, 322 F.3d 342 (4th Cir. 2003) (judgment properly vacated when officer of institution not served).

U.S.C. § 522(h), which is often a more complicated matter, requires an adversary proceeding initiated by complaint.[223]

At least some avoidance actions carry with them a right to trial by jury. The Supreme Court has made clear that a defendant to a fraudulent conveyance action who has not filed a proof of claim in the bankruptcy case has a right to jury trial that is protected by the Seventh Amendment.[224]

It is the debtor's burden to file a lien avoidance proceeding; if none is filed, all liens on the debtor's property, including otherwise exempt property, will normally survive the bankruptcy.[225]

The statute does not specify whether lien avoidance under section 522(f) has to take place prior to discharge, and as exemptions are afforded continued protection after the bankruptcy, they could continue to be impaired after the bankruptcy by an otherwise avoidable lien. Presumably, then, an action to avoid a lien may be filed after the discharge.[226]

Unlike many of the other Bankruptcy Rules, the Rules providing for debtor lien avoidance set no time limits. And because lien avoidance is a personal right which does not affect the administration of the bankruptcy case, there is no need for the bankruptcy case to be reopened in order for the debtor to avoid a lien.[227]

Contrastingly, most actions to avoid transfers under section 522(h) are subject to a statute of limitations.[228] They must be brought within two years of the order for relief (the date a voluntary petition is filed) or by the date the case is closed or dismissed, whichever is earlier. In cases brought on or after October 22, 1994, if a trustee is first appointed or elected within two years of the order for relief, the limitations period may be extended (beyond two years after the order for relief) until the expiration of one year after the appointment of that trustee or until the case is closed or dismissed, whichever is earlier. To be safe, it is better to avoid liens and other transfers within the limitations period and prior to discharge whenever possible.

It may also be possible to include in a chapter 13 plan provisions which effectuate the avoidance of transfer upon confirmation.[229] Although the Rules provide that a motion or complaint are necessary in a "proceeding" to avoid a lien, it can be argued that where the lien is avoided in the plan, no separate "proceeding" is necessary. Otherwise, the Rules might conflict with section 1322(b)(10) which allows plans to incorporate any appropriate provision not inconsistent with the Code.[230] Although one provision of chapter 13 appears to indicate that the plan cannot modify the rights of

---

223   Fed. R. Bankr. P. 7001; *see, e.g.*, Connelly v. Marine Midland Bank, 61 B.R. 748 (W.D.N.Y. 1986) (proceeding by motion deprives the bankruptcy court of jurisdiction).

224   Granfinanciera, S.A. v. Nordberg, 492 U.S. 33, 109 S. Ct. 2782, 106 L. Ed. 2d 26 (1989); *see* § 13.2.7, *infra*.

225   Fed. Deposit Ins. Corp. v. Davis, 733 F.2d 1083 (4th Cir. 1984). *But see In re* Penrod, 50 F.3d 459 (7th Cir. 1995) (default rule in chapter 11, based on language of section 1141(c), is that if confirmed plan provides for creditor but is silent about whether creditor retains its lien, that lien is automatically extinguished). The *Penrod* rationale should apply equally in chapter 13 under section 1327(c). Of course, if liens are paid off in a chapter 13 plan, they are also eliminated, and there are other options for treatment of liens under the Code as well. *See* Ch. 11, *infra*.

226   *In re* Goswami, 304 B.R. 386 (B.A.P. 9th Cir. 2003) (debtors have right to amend exemptions after case closing for purpose of lien avoidance absent bad faith or prejudice); *In re* Ricks, 89 B.R. 73 (B.A.P. 9th Cir. 1988) (creditor's action to execute on lien after bankruptcy does not constitute sufficient prejudice to bar reopening of case to avoid lien); *In re* Yazzie, 24 B.R. 576 (B.A.P. 9th Cir. 1982) (post discharge avoidance allowed where no prejudice to creditor from delay); *In re* McDonald, 161 B.R. 697 (D. Kan. 1993) (local bankruptcy rule that required lien avoidance motions to be filed at least five days before date set for discharge was invalid and court could allow reopening of case for motion to avoid lien unless equitable considerations dictated otherwise); First Nat'l Bank of Park Falls v. Maley, 126 B.R. 563 (W.D. Wis. 1991); Hassler v. Assimos, 53 B.R. 453 (D. Del. 1985) (creditors not prejudiced by delay in failing to move to avoid lien until after discharge and thus lien avoidance not barred by laches); Beneficial Fin. Co. of Va. v. Lazrovitch, 47 B.R. 358 (E.D. Va. 1983) (debtors entitled to reopen cases after discharge to avoid liens); *In re* Orr, 304 B.R. 875 (Bankr. S.D. Ill. 2004) (case could be reopened for lien avoidance four years after case was closed even though debtor no longer had interest in property); *In re* Mailhot, 301 B.R. 774 (Bankr. D.R.I. 2003) (debtor allowed to avoid judicial liens seven years after discharge); *In re* Baskins, 14 B.R. 110 (Bankr. E.D.N.C. 1981); *In re* Smart, 13 B.R. 838 (Bankr. D. Ariz. 1981); *see also In re* Goydoscik, 94 B.R. 72 (Bankr. W.D. Pa. 1988) (section 550(e) does not prevent reopening case to avoid a lien); *In re* Babineau, 22 B.R. 936 (Bankr. M.D. Fla. 1982) (liens can be avoided after confirmation of chapter 13 plan). *But see* Hawkins v. Landmark Fin., 727 F.2d 324 (4th Cir. 1984) (court has discretion to refuse to reopen a case for amend-

ment of exemptions and lien avoidance). A post-bankruptcy transfer of property may cut off the right to avoid a lien as to that property. *In re* Vitullo, 60 B.R. 822 (D.N.J. 1986); *In re* Carilli, 65 B.R. 280 (Bankr. E.D.N.Y. 1986). However, a debtor could argue that all exemption rights are fixed as of the date of the petition so a post-petition transfer is irrelevant.

227   *In re* Keller, 24 B.R. 720 (Bankr. N.D. Ohio 1982); *In re* Schneider, 18 B.R. 274 (Bankr. D.N.D. 1982). *But see In re* Bianucci, 4 F.3d 526 (7th Cir. 1993) (debtors could not reopen bankruptcy case to avoid lien two years after closing of case, and five months after they became aware of the lien, when creditor had been prejudiced by payment of expenses to enforce lien); Hawkins v. Landmark Fin., 727 F.2d 324 (4th Cir. 1984).

228   11 U.S.C. § 546(a); *see* § 10.4.2.6.8, *infra*; *see also* Zilkha Energy Co. v. Leighton, 920 F.2d 1520 (10th Cir. 1990) (two-year limitation period runs from date of filing and applies to successor to chapter 11 debtor). Note that the limitations period does not apply to transfers avoidable under sections 522(f), 549 or 724(a).

229   McLaughlin, *Lien Avoidance by Debtors in Chapter 13 of the Bankruptcy Reform Act of 1978*, 58 Am. Bankr. L. J. 56 (1984); 8 Collier on Bankruptcy ¶ 1300.81 (15th ed. rev.). *But see In re* Commercial W. Fin. Corp., 761 F.2d 1329 (9th Cir. 1985) (Bankruptcy Rules require individual proceedings against investors whose security interests trustee wished to avoid in chapter 11 case); *In re* McKay, 732 F.2d 44 (3d Cir. 1984) (chapter 13 lien avoidance must be by motion).

230   *But see In re* Commercial W. Fin. Corp., 761 F.2d 1329 (9th Cir. 1985); *In re* McKay, 732 F.2d 44 (3d Cir. 1984) (lien avoidance must be by motion rather than in plan).

a creditor secured only by a security interest in the debtor's residence, it was held under the prior rules that at least those transfers that do not come within the narrow definition of "security interest," defined as "a lien created by agreement,"[231] can be avoided through the plan.[232] However, to avoid doubt on these issues, the best practice is to seek to avoid the lien in a separate proceeding rather than to rely on a plan provision.

Whatever the method used, the debtor's counsel should be sure to obtain an order giving complete relief, including a requirement that the transferee (usually a creditor) take all steps necessary to reflect the avoidance of the transfer in state and local recording offices,[233] or else an order suitable for filing in those offices by the debtor's counsel. Keep in mind as well that if a separate action is necessary to recover property subsequent to avoidance of a transfer of that property, it must be brought within one year.[234]

10.4.2.3 Power to Avoid Judicial Liens— § 522(f)(1)(A)

10.4.2.3.1 Extent of the power to avoid judicial liens

Section 522(f)(1)(A) gives the debtor an unqualified right to avoid any judicial lien that impairs an exemption, subject only to an exception for certain family-related debts. As the term "judicial lien" is defined broadly[235] to include levies, judgment liens (including confessed judgments)[236] and liens obtained by sequestration or any other legal or equitable proceeding,[237] this section provides a powerful tool for the debtor. To the extent a creditor's lien is avoided, the creditor becomes an unsecured creditor and the lien cannot attach to property that the debtor acquires after the petition is filed.[238]

Occasionally there is a dispute as to whether a particular lien is a judicial lien,[239] sometimes involving liens granted in divorce proceedings.[240] In such cases, careful analysis of the Code's definition is required. However, some of the

---

231 11 U.S.C. § 101(51).

232 *In re* Jordan, 5 B.R. 59 (Bankr. D.N.J. 1980).

233 *See* Form 75, Appx. G.9, *infra*.

234 11 U.S.C. § 550(f); *see* § 10.4.2.7, *infra*.

235 11 U.S.C. § 101(36).

236 *In re* Gardner, 685 F.2d 106 (3d Cir. 1982); *In re* Bensen, 262 B.R. 371 (Bankr. N.D. Tex. 2001) (garnishment lien on bank account avoided); *see also In re* Bistansin, 95 B.R. 29 (Bankr. W.D. Pa. 1989) (lien created by sheriff's levy is avoidable judicial lien); *cf. In re* Duden, 102 B.R. 797 (D. Colo. 1989) (lien which would impair the debtor's ability to alienate property post-petition is avoidable even though it may not presently attach to debtor's property as a judicial lien because of state homestead exemption).

237 *In re* Thomas, 215 B.R. 873 (Bankr. E.D. Mo. 1997) (debtor could avoid garnishment lien on wages in employer's possession); *In re* Waltjen, 150 B.R. 419 (Bankr. N.D. Ill. 1993) (debtor could avoid garnishment lien on wages still in employer's possession). *But see In re* Lucas, 21 B.R. 794 (Bankr. W.D. Mich. 1982) (lien given to secure appeal bond held security interest and not judicial lien).

238 *In re* Marshall, 204 B.R. 838 (Bankr. S.D. Ga. 1997). However, the holder of a nondischargeable claim might be able to pursue non-exempt property acquired after the bankruptcy.

239 *See, e.g., In re* Nichols, 265 B.R. 831 (B.A.P. 10th Cir. 2001) (foreclosure decree did not transform mortgage into judicial lien); *In re* James, 304 B.R. 131 (D.N.J. 2004) (lien arising from unpaid motor vehicle insurance surcharges was non-avoidable statutory lien); *In re* Concrete Structures, Inc., 261 B.R. 627 (E.D. Va. 2001) (Virginia mechanics' lien, though enforced judicially, is a statutory lien); *In re* Liberman, 244 B.R. 557 (E.D.N.Y.) (mortgage foreclosure judgment not avoidable), *aff'd*, 225 F.3d 646 (2d Cir. 2000) (table); Mozingo v. Pa. Dept. of Labor and Industry, 234 B.R. 867 (E.D. Pa. 1999) (lien for overpayments of unemployment compensation was statutory lien that simply became choate upon recordation); *In re* Washington, 238 B.R. 852 (M.D. Fla. 1999) (Florida attorney's charging lien not a judicial lien), *aff'd in relevant part*, 242 F.3d 1320 (11th Cir. 2001); *In re* Felizardo, 255 B.R. 85 (Bankr. S.D. Fla. 2000) (Florida attorney's charging lien, though reduced to judgment, was not judicial lien); *In re* Rouse, 145 B.R. 546 (Bankr. W.D. Mich. 1992) (tax refunds intercepted for payment of support delinquency and held by "Friend of the Court" considered subject to judicial lien); *In re* Frost, 111 B.R. 306 (Bankr. C.D. Cal. 1990) (California tax lien avoided as judicial lien); *In re* MacLure, 50 B.R. 134 (Bankr. D.R.I. 1985) (landlord's lien, though statutorily authorized, required resort to judicial process and was thus judicial lien); *In re* Barbe, 24 B.R. 739 (Bankr. M.D. Pa. 1982) (lien for overpayments of unemployment compensation held judicial lien due to requirement of recordation).

240 *In re* Pederson, 875 F.2d 781 (9th Cir. 1989) (lien granted in divorce proceedings was judicial lien), *aff'g* 78 B.R. 264 (B.A.P. 9th Cir. 1987); Maus v. Maus, 837 F.2d 935 (10th Cir. 1988) (property settlement agreement incorporated into divorce decree gives rise to an avoidable judicial lien); Boyd v. Robinson, 741 F.2d 1112 (8th Cir. 1984) (lien awarded by court in marital dissolution action held not a judicial lien); *In re* Rittenhouse, 103 B.R. 250 (D. Kan. 1989) (lien awarded in divorce decree is not avoidable); *In re* Duncan, 85 B.R. 80 (W.D. Wis. 1988) (lien granted in divorce proceedings constitutes avoidable judicial lien); *In re* Chestnut, 50 B.R. 309 (Bankr. W.D. Okla. 1985) (attorney's lien granted by divorce decree was avoidable); *In re* Wicks, 26 B.R. 769 (Bankr. D. Minn. 1982) (lien granted in marital dissolution agreement held a security interest and not judicial lien), *aff'd*, 741 F.2d 1112 (8th Cir. 1984); *see also* Mead v. Mead, 974 F.2d 990 (8th Cir. 1992) (holding lien created by fraud judgment to be a reinstatement of divorce lien not avoidable under holding of *Farrey*); *In re* Borman, 886 F.2d 273 (10th Cir. 1989) (debtor's wife entitled to nondischargeable, non-avoidable equitable lien based on divorce decree); *In re* Donahue, 862 F.2d 259 (10th Cir. 1988) (divorce decree which awarded former spouse money judgment and awarded debtor real property subject to the money judgment creates a lien in favor of the former spouse; bankruptcy court must determine whether lien is avoidable). This issue was not resolved by the Supreme Court decision in Farrey v. Sanderfoot, 500 U.S. 291, 111 S. Ct. 1825, 114 L. Ed. 2d 337 (1991). However the *Farrey* decision does limit the avoidance of liens arising in domestic relations proceedings when they are created in connection with transfer of the property to which the lien simultaneously attaches. *See* § 10.4.2.3.2, *infra*. *See generally* Henry J. Sommer & Margaret Doe McGarity, Collier Family Law and the Bankruptcy Code ¶ 7.04[3].

difficult questions about whether certain divorce-related liens are judicial liens have been rendered moot by a Code provision, added in 1994, that makes many divorce-related liens non-avoidable if they are liens for debts owed to a spouse, former spouse or child of the debtor that is in the nature of alimony, maintenance or support.[241]

The power to avoid judicial liens extends to every type of exempt property, without limitation, including property exempted under a wild card provision.[242] Unlike some of the other avoiding powers, the lien need not have been obtained within a certain time period before the bankruptcy petition.[243] Even if the lien has caused the property to have been removed from the debtor's possession or the debtor has transferred the property after the petition, it can be avoided, forcing the return of the property.[244]

In some cases, courts had refused to avoid liens because of provisions in state exemption laws which they read to prevent the debtor from claiming any exemption in bank-

ruptcy which could be impaired.[245] For the reasons discussed earlier, these cases ignored clear congressional intent and the Supremacy Clause.[246] For the most part these decisions have been overruled by the Supreme Court.[247] In *Owen v. Owen* the Court held that a state law limiting exemptions from execution to property that is not subject to certain liens does not preclude avoidance of those liens under section 522(f).[248]

In 1994, responding to several cases which had misconstrued the lien avoidance provisions, Congress amended section 522(f) to specifically set forth a general arithmetic formula for determining whether a lien could be avoided

---

241 11 U.S.C. § 522(f)(1)(A); *see In re* Lowe, 250 B.R. 422 (Bankr. M.D. Fla. 2000) (lien could be avoided because it secured property settlement debt rather than debt for alimony, maintenance or support). Although the wording of this provision is confusing, its intent is clear. *See* § 10.4.2.3.2, *infra*.

242 *In re* Groff, 223 B.R. 697 (Bankr. S.D. Ill. 1998) (debtors could avoid lien that impaired their equitable interest in property being purchased under land installment sales contract); *In re* Garcia, 149 B.R. 530 (Bankr. N.D. Ill. 1993) (wages in the hands of an employer can be exempted under Illinois wild card provision so that lien giving rise to the wage garnishment can be avoided), *aff'd*, 155 B.R. 173 (N.D. Ill. 1993).

243 *In re* Naples v. London, Bankr. L. Rep. (CCH) ¶ 67,422 (Bankr. D. Conn. 1980). However, the avoiding power may not extend to liens that were already on a property when the debtor acquired it. *See* § 10.4.2.3.2, *infra*.

244 *In re* Bagley, 1 B.R. 116 (Bankr. E.D. Pa. 1979) (sheriff ordered to return automobile seized under a levy); *see also In re* Chiu, 304 F.3d 905 (9th Cir. 2002) (debtor could avoid lien on escrowed proceeds of sale of homestead that had been claimed as exempt in schedules and sold after petition date); *In re* Brown, 734 F.2d 119 (2d Cir. 1984) (debtor could exempt and avoid judicial lien on cash proceeds of execution sale of property where proceeds were still in hands of state court commissioner); *In re* Fairchild, 285 B.R. 98 (Bankr. D. Conn. 2002) (debtor need only have interest in property at time of fixing of lien and not when motion to avoid is filed); *In re* Carroll, 258 B.R. 316 (Bankr. S.D. Ga. 2001) (lien avoidance based on interests held on date of petition. In a development necessitated in part by the limitation on avoiding preferences worth less than $600.00, discussed in § 10.4.2.6.4, *infra*, debtors in some states have successfully recovered garnished wages still in the hands of their employers by avoiding the lien which gave rise to the garnishment. Bryant v. Gen. Elec. Credit Corp., 58 B.R. 144 (N.D. Ill. 1986); *In re* Lafoon, 278 B.R. 767 (Bankr. E.D. Tenn. 2002) (debtor could avoid lien on garnished wages despite procedural waiver caused by failure to claim state law exemption at time of garnishment); *In re* Buzzell, 56 B.R. 197 (Bankr. D. Md. 1986); *see also In re* Rowell, 281 B.R. 726 (Bankr. N.D. Ala. 2001) (debtor could avoid lien on garnished funds, even those paid erroneously by court clerk to creditor, because state court had not entered condemnation order terminating debtor's interest in wages).

245 *See In re* Dixon, 885 F.2d 327 (6th Cir. 1989) (Ohio exemption scheme does not contemplate any homestead exemption absent execution on judgment; therefore liens may not be avoided in bankruptcy as impairing a debtor's exemption); *In re* Owen, 877 F.2d 44 (11th Cir. 1989) (where homestead exemption does not attach under state law to residence as against judicial liens which attached first, liens on residence may not be avoided). The *Dixon* decision has been overruled by the 1994 amendments to the Bankruptcy Code which now define what it means to impair an exemption. 11 U.S.C. § 522(f)(2); *In re* Holland, 151 F.3d 547 (6th Cir. 1998); *see* H.R. Rep. No. 103-835, at 53 (1994), *reprinted in* 1994 U.S.C.C.A.N. 3340, 3362.

246 *See* § 10.2.1, *supra*.

247 Owen v. Owen, 500 U.S. 305, 111 S. Ct. 1833, 114 L. Ed. 2d 250 (1991); *In re* Maddox, 15 F.3d 1347 (5th Cir. 1994) (prior case law of circuit on this issue had been overruled by *Owen*); *see also In re* Snow, 899 F.2d 337 (4th Cir. 1990) (debtors entitled to avoid judicial lien on personal property based on back rent even though state law provided that exemption does not apply to claims for rent); *In re* Kinnemore, 181 B.R. 516 (Bankr. D. Idaho 1995) (landlord's lien could be avoided despite state statute excluding exempt property from protection with respect to claims for unpaid rent).

248 *In re* Henderson, 18 F.3d 1305 (5th Cir. 1994) (judicial lien could be avoided even though no execution on the lien was possible because lien was unenforceable as to homestead); *In re* Coats, 232 B.R. 209 (B.A.P. 10th Cir. 1999) (same); *In re* Shafner, 165 B.R. 660 (Bankr. D. Colo. 1994) (lien impaired exemption even though it did not technically attach to exempt property, because of its practical effects on debtor's ability to encumber or dispose of property); *see also In re* Watts, 298 F.3d 1077 (9th Cir. 2002) (California law limiting judicial liens to surplus equity did not prevent lien from attaching and thereby becoming avoidable). This principle may not apply, however, to debtors who fail to meet the condition for declaring the state law exemption in the first instance. *See In re* Amiri, 184 B.R. 60 (B.A.P. 9th Cir. 1995) (failure to timely file for homestead exemption under state law precludes avoidance of lien); *In re* Wall, 127 B.R. 353 (Bankr. E.D. Va. 1991) (same); *cf. In re* Johnson, 184 B.R. 141 (Bankr. D. Wyo. 1995) (lien could be avoided as long as homestead exemption existed on date of bankruptcy petition); *In re* Pinner, 146 B.R. 659 (Bankr. E.D.N.C. 1992) (failure to claim property as exempt at time creditor obtained judgment did not preclude avoidance of creditor's lien); *see also* § 10.2.3.1, *supra*. The *Owen* decision should invalidate state laws that purport to exclude from exempt status wages that are subject to a garnishment lien. *But see In re* Youngblood, 212 B.R. 593 (Bankr. N.D. Ill. 1997) (discussing such a statute in case in which debtor apparently did not argue that statute was invalid under *Owen*).

under that section.[249] Section 522(f)(2) specifies that a judicial lien is avoidable to the extent that the lien, plus all other liens on the property, plus the amount of the exemption that the debtor could claim if there were no liens on the property exceeds the value that the debtor's interest in the property would have in the absence of any liens.[250] The liens used in the calculation should be those that existed on the date of the bankruptcy petition.[251] Once a lien has been avoided, it is not counted for the calculation of whether other liens impair exemptions.[252] And the formula does not apply to judgments arising out of mortgage foreclosures.[253]

As the legislative history makes clear, this language adopts the conclusion of those cases holding that a debtor who has no equity in a property may still avoid liens on the property.[254] It also overrules cases which had held that a partially secured creditor could protect against lien avoidance that portion of its lien which exceeds the value of the collateral, and similar cases which had held that a debtor could not avoid a lien to the extent that the amount of the lien exceeded the debtor's exemption.[255] Finally, by focusing on the dollar amount of the exemption in defining when an exemption is impaired, the amendment overrules cases that had held that a debtor's exemption was not impaired unless the creditor was executing on that lien.[256]

10.4.2.3.2 Limitations on power to avoid judicial liens

As with the other avoiding powers, if the lien only partially impairs the exemption, only that part may be avoided. Thus, if a $3000.00 judgment lien encumbers a house worth $17,000.00, in which an interest of $15,000.00 can be claimed as exempt and in which an interest of $2000.00 is not exempt, only $1000.00 worth of the lien can be avoided.[257] The other $2000.00 is deemed an encumbrance on that interest in the house which is not exemptible.

---

249 The 1994 amendments generally apply in cases filed on or after October 22, 1994. However, as the new section was intended to clarify rather than change existing law, liens should be avoidable based on the formula contained in the amendment regardless of when the case was filed. As a clarification of what Congress believed existing law to be, this result should apply even if application of the amendment is required to overrule case law of a jurisdiction which had previously limited judicial lien avoidance. *See* 140 Cong. Rec. H10764 (daily ed. Oct. 4, 1994).

250 *See In re* Kolich, 328 F.3d 406 (8th Cir. 2003) (formula required avoidance of lien even though it was senior to non-avoidable lien of subsequent mortgagee); *In re* Miller, 299 F.3d 183 (3d Cir. 2002) (total value of property used even though only one co-owner filed); *In re* Silveira, 141 F.3d 34 (1st Cir. 1998) (applying formula to partially avoid lien); *In re* Hanger, 217 B.R. 592 (B.A.P. 9th Cir. 1998), *aff'd* 196 F.3d 1292 (9th Cir. 1999) (same); *In re* Cozad, 208 B.R. 495 (B.A.P. 10th Cir. 1997) (in applying formula to jointly-held property when only one debtor is in bankruptcy, formula must be followed literally and total of liens and exemption must be subtracted from only debtor's interest in property). *But see In re* Lehman, 205 F.3d 1255 (11th Cir. 2000) (total value of property used even though only one co-owner filed); *In re* Nelson, 192 F.3d 32 (1st Cir. 1999) (despite language of statute, lien avoidance formula applied only to debtor's fifty percent interest in property); *In re* Snyder, 249 B.R. 40 (B.A.P. 1st Cir. 2000) (value of one entireties cotenant's interest deemed to be one-hundred percent of value of property), *aff'd*, 2 Fed. Appx. 46 (1st Cir. 2001); *In re* Lehman, 223 B.R. 32 (Bankr. N.D. Ga. 1998) (despite language of statute, court deducted liens from entire value of property, not just debtor's interest), *aff'd*, 205 F.3d 1255 (11th Cir. 2000).

251 *In re* Salanoa, 263 B.R. 120 (Bankr. S.D. Cal. 2001) (first trust deed taken into account even though it was paid in full after the petition).

252 It is not clear whether liens must be avoided in reverse order of priority, that is, the most junior judicial lien first, as some courts have held. *E.g., In re* Hanger, 217 B.R. 592 (B.A.P. 9th Cir. 1998), *aff'd* 196 F.3d 1292 (9th Cir. 1999); *In re* Jochum, 309 B.R. 327 (Bankr. E.D. Mo. 2004). An earlier version of the statute would have required this ordering, but the priority language was deleted from the final version. *See* S.540, § 303, 103d Cong. (1994).

253 11 U.S.C. § 522(f)(2)(C). Because judgments arising out of mortgage foreclosures are not normally considered to be avoidable judicial liens, this provision will have little impact. Courts have held that deficiency judgments are not protected by this provision. *See In re* Hart, 328 F.3d 45 (1st Cir. 2003) (deficiency judgment not a lien arising out of mortgage foreclosure); *In re* Been, 153 F.3d 1034 (9th Cir. 1998) (§ 522(f)(2)(C) did not

protect judgment lien obtained by creditor's suit on note after its junior lien on another property was extinguished by senior lienholder's foreclosure sale); *In re* Carson, 274 B.R. 577 (Bankr. D. Conn. 2002) (deficiency judgment not a lien arising out of a mortgage foreclosure); *In re* Smith, 270 B.R. 557 (Bankr. W.D.N.Y. 2001) (same); *In re* Pascucci, 225 B.R. 25 (Bankr. D. Mass. 1998) (deficiency judgment lien was not a judgment arising out of a mortgage foreclosure).

254 *In re* Higgins, 201 B.R. 965 (B.A.P. 9th Cir. 1996); *In re* McQueen, 196 B.R. 31 (E.D.N.C. 1995) (prior Fourth Circuit case law overruled by 1994 amendments); *In re* Thomsen, 181 B.R. 1013 (Bankr. M.D. Ga. 1995); H.R. Rep. No. 103-835, at 52–54 (1994), *reprinted in* 1994 U.S.C.C.A.N. 3340, 3361–3363. The legislative history also states that the legislation overruled *In re* Simonson, 758 F.2d 103 (3d Cir. 1985), in which the court had held that a judicial lien could not be avoided if it was senior to a non-avoidable mortgage and the non-avoidable mortgages on the property exceeded the value of the property. *See also In re* Holloway, 81 F.3d 1062, 1069 n.10 (11th Cir. 1996) (recognizing that prior case law not applicable to post-amendment cases). *But see In re* Soost, 262 B.R. 68 (B.A.P. 8th Cir. 2001) (court, seemingly confused by irrelevant fact that debtor claimed $1.00 exemption in property, found it "difficult to fathom" how debtor could avoid lien on property in which he had no equity).

255 H.R. Rep. No. 103-835, at 52–54 (1994), *reprinted in* 1994 U.S.C.C.A.N. 3340, 3361–3363; *see In re* Toplitzky, 227 B.R. 300 (B.A.P. 9th Cir. 1998) (formula in 1994 amendments precluded creditor from retaining its lien by paying debtor amount of equity in property above senior lien).

256 H.R. Rep. No. 103-835, at 52–54 (1994), *reprinted in* 1994 U.S.C.C.A.N. 3340, 3361–3363; *In re* Holland, 151 F.3d 547 (6th Cir. 1998).

257 *See In re* Silveira, 141 F.3d 34 (1st Cir. 1998) (explaining partial lien avoidance).

On the other hand, when the total value of the liened property can be claimed as exempt, then any amount of liens can be avoided, because even if only a few dollars worth of liens remained, they would impair the exemption. Hence, if a house with $15,000.00 of equity in excess of a mortgage is claimed as totally exempt, all judgment liens on that house may be avoided under this section no matter what their amount.[258] When only some liens may be avoided, the most junior avoidable liens are presumably the ones which impair the debtor's exemption.[259]

In *Farrey v. Sanderfoot*,[260] the Supreme Court held that section 522(f)(1) can only be used to avoid the fixing of a lien on a debtor's pre-existing interest in property. Unless the debtor had an interest in the property *before* the lien attached to the property, the lien cannot be avoided. In applying this principle to a lien granted in a divorce decree that conveyed jointly held property to the debtor, the Court found that the divorce decree extinguished the debtor's pre-existing undivided half-interest in the marital home and granted him a new fee simple interest. The Court therefore concluded that the simultaneously created lien for the benefit of the debtor's former spouse did not attach to a pre-existing interest of the debtor in property and that section 522(f)(1) was not available to avoid the lien. The Court assumed without deciding that the divorce decree did create a judicial lien. It also left open the possibility that a divorce decree lien could be avoided if it attached to property that had previously been titled only in the name of the debtor spouse.[261]

The Eleventh Circuit extended the *Farrey* rationale to a debtor who obtained a homestead in a jurisdiction where an unsatisfied judgment had previously been recorded against him.[262] The judgment automatically fixed as a lien on property in that jurisdiction when it was acquired by the debtor. The court concluded that the lien could not be avoided because it did not fix on a pre-existing interest of the debtor in property. While this ruling seems on the surface like a reasonable extension of *Farrey*, it is inconsistent with the congressional purpose in allowing the avoidance of judicial liens[263] and illogically gives more protection to a judgment lien creditor that had no lien when it obtained a judgment than to one with a judgment lien interest in the debtor's property that arose at the time it obtained its judgment.[264]

Similarly, a few courts had refused to avoid judicial liens that were senior to non-avoidable liens to the extent that the junior non-avoidable liens exceed the debtor's exemptions.[265]

---

258 *See In re* Galvan, 110 B.R. 446 (B.A.P. 9th Cir. 1990) (unsecured portion of under-secured judicial lien is avoidable as it impairs debtor's right to fully realize homestead exemption); *In re* Sajkowski, 49 B.R. 37 (Bankr. D.R.I. 1985); *see also In re* Magosin, 75 B.R. 545 (Bankr. E.D. Pa. 1987) (discussing lien avoidance methodology). The Supreme Court in *Owen* specifically cited two bankruptcy court decisions which clearly set forth this method of determining which liens could be avoided. 111 S. Ct. at 1838, n.5 (citing *In re* Brantz, 106 B.R. 62, 68 (Bankr. E.D. Pa. 1989) and *In re* Carney, 47 B.R. 296 (Bankr. D. Mass. 1985)). Decisions to the contrary have also been specifically overruled by legislation. *See, e.g., In re* Wrenn, 40 F.3d 1162 (11th Cir. 1994); *In re* Sanders, 39 F.3d 258 (10th Cir. 1994); *In re* Menell, 37 F.3d 113 (3d Cir. 1994); *see also* § 10.4.2.3.1, *infra*.

259 *In re* Hoffman, 28 B.R. 503 (Bankr. D. Md. 1983); *see* Owen v. Owen, 500 U.S. 305, 111 S. Ct. 1833, 114 L. Ed. 2d 250 (1991) (if property would be exempt "but for" the lien, then lien can be avoided).

260 500 U.S. 291, 111 S. Ct. 1825, 114 L. Ed. 2d 337 (1991).

261 *See In re* Parrish, 7 F.3d 76 (5th Cir. 1993) (divorce lien attaching to debtor's preexisting separate property could be avoided); *In re* Stoneking, 225 B.R. 690 (B.A.P. 9th Cir. 1998) (debtor could avoid lien which first attached to property when it was held with spouse as community property despite fact that it later became debtor's separate property, because lien fixed on property at time debtor had interest in property). *See generally* Henry J. Sommer & Margaret Doe McGarity, Collier Family Law and the Bankruptcy Code ¶ 7.04.

262 Owen v. Owen, 961 F.2d 170 (11th Cir. 1992). Interestingly, this decision is the Court of Appeals' decision following the Supreme Court's remand in Owen v. Owen, 500 U.S. 305, 111 S. Ct. 1833, 114 L. Ed. 2d 250 (1991). *See also In re* Scarpino, 113 F.3d 338 (2d Cir. 1997) (same result under New York law); *In re* Pederson, 230 B.R. 158 (B.A.P. 9th Cir. 1999) (same result under California law); *cf. In re* Kuehnert, 271 B.R. 434 (Bankr. D. Conn. 2001) (debtor who owned real property as joint tenant with non-debtor husband and who became owner of entire property through post-petition divorce transfer could avoid lien on entire property because she had always held undivided interest in entire property); *In re* Ulmer, 211 B.R. 523 (Bankr. E.D.N.C. 1997) (debtor who had owned property as entireties cotenant before lien attached had interest in property when lien attached due to transmutation of debtor's interest at divorce); *In re* Cooper, 197 B.R. 698 (Bankr. M.D. Fla. 1996) (debtor could avoid lien that attached after she had title to property even though she had not established homestead exemption before lien attached); *In re* Conyers, 129 B.R. 470 (Bankr. E.D. Ky. 1991) (relying on the Supreme Court decision in *Owen* to avoid a lien based on a judgment which arose before the debtor acquired the otherwise exempt homestead).

263 Congress enacted section 552(f)(1)(A) to protect the debtor's right to exempt property and to eliminate an otherwise unsecured creditor's "race to the courthouse" to obtain a lien before the debtor declared bankruptcy. *See* Farrey v. Sanderfoot, 500 U.S. 291, 111 S. Ct. 1825, 1830, 114 L. Ed. 2d 337 (1991).

264 The decision also goes beyond the Supreme Court's expressed concern in *Farrey* with protecting against fraudulent transfers of property which is already subject to a lien to a third person who could avoid that lien in bankruptcy. Farrey v. Sanderfoot, 500 U.S. 291, 111 S. Ct. 1825, 1830, 114 L. Ed. 2d 337 (1991); *cf. In re* Garcia, 155 B.R. 173 (N.D. Ill. 1993) (debtor could avoid lien obtained by creditor on wages prior to bankruptcy if wages were claimed as exempt and state court had not yet entered final wage deduction order).

265 *See, e.g., In re* Duncan, 43 B.R. 833 (Bankr. D. Alaska 1984); *see also In re* Simonson, 758 F.2d 103 (3d Cir. 1985) (where non-avoidable junior mortgages, when added to senior mortgage, exceeded the value of the property, intervening judicial liens not avoidable because even if judicial liens did not exist property would still be fully encumbered; court did not discuss the possible operation of § 506(d) to render the junior mortgages void, and ignored dissent's application of § 522(i)(2) to preserve avoided judicial liens for the benefit of the debtor); *In re*

As discussed above,[266] these decisions were overruled by Congress in the Bankruptcy Reform Act of 1994.

The 1994 amendments also added an exception to the power to avoid judicial liens. In order to better protect a spouse, former spouse, or child who is owed alimony, maintenance, or support, section 522(f)(1)(A) now provides that liens securing such debts cannot be avoided, as long as the debt is actually in the nature of alimony, maintenance, or support.[267] However, this exception does not apply if the debt has been assigned to any other entity, such as a state welfare department.[268]

10.4.2.3.3 Avoidance of liens on property exemptible under section 522(b)(2)(B)

A final issue which may arise under this section is whether a lien may be avoided if that lien is on joint property, such as property owned as tenants by the entireties, where but for the lien the property could be claimed as exempt under section 522(b)(2)(B). Creditors have argued that because the lien made such property subject to process immediately before the commencement of the case, the property could not be claimed as exempt in the first place under section 522(b)(2)(B), and that therefore the avoiding powers do not even come into play. This argument is refuted by the legislative history, which states that the "debtor may avoid a judicial lien on any property to the extent that the property could have been exempted in the absence of the lien."[269] Hence, if the interest in joint property is subject to

process and is thus non-exempt only because of a judicial lien, then that judicial lien should be avoidable to the extent the property could otherwise be exempted.[270] In any case, there should be no doubt that, to the extent a creditor has a judicial lien on the interest of only one of two entireties cotenants, and that interest is exemptible under section 522(b)(2)(B), the creditor's lien is avoidable.[271]

10.4.2.4 Power to Avoid Nonpossessory, Nonpurchase-Money Security Interests in Certain Items—§ 522(f)(1)(B)

Certainly one of the most potent of the avoiding powers is that provided by section 522(f)(1)(B)[272]—the power to avoid nonpossessory, nonpurchase-money security interests in the following items:

- Household furnishings, household goods, wearing apparel, appliances, books, animals, crops, musical instruments, or jewelry that are held primarily for the personal, family, or household use of the debtor or a dependent of the debtor;[273]

Patterson, 139 B.R. 229 (B.A.P. 9th Cir. 1992) (permitting judicial lienholder to prevail over debtor's claim of exemption because judicial lien was senior to a consensual lien; court ignored § 522(i)(2)).

266 *See* § 10.4.2.9, *infra*; § 10.4.2.3.1, *supra*.

267 A drafting error in the statute may defeat the legislative intent to protect debts in the nature of support. Read literally, section 522(f)(1)(A) permits avoidance of "a judicial lien . . . (ii) to the extent that such debt—(II) includes a liability designated as alimony, maintenance, or support, unless such liability is actually in the nature of alimony, maintenance or support." The statute should have read "unless such liability is *not* actually in the nature of alimony, maintenance, or support." *See In re* Kestella, 269 B.R. 188 (Bankr. S.D. Ohio 2001) (divorce lien on debtor's retirement plan secured alimony or support obligations and could not be avoided); *In re* Allen, 217 B.R. 247 (Bankr. S.D. Ill. 1998) (debtor could not avoid liens for support and attorney fees deemed in nature of support); *In re* Willoughby, 212 B.R. 1011 (Bankr. M.D. Fla. 1997) (husband who owed support to former wife not permitted to avoid lien on residence owned jointly with new wife, but new wife entitled to avoid lien to extent it impaired her interest because she did not owe support).

268 11 U.S.C. § 522(f)(1)(A)(ii)(I); *In re* Christie, 218 B.R. 27 (Bankr. D.N.J.), *vacated on other grounds*, 222 B.R. 64 (D.N.J. 1998).

269 H.R. Rep. No. 95-595, at 362 (1977). This reading of the statute is also supported by the concern in the legislative history that the debtor not be harmed by losing the "race to the courthouse,"

H.R. Rep. No. 95-595, at 126 (1977). *But see* Napotnik v. Equibank, 679 F.2d 316 (3d Cir. 1982). See § 10.2.3.2, *supra,* for discussion of *Napotnik. See also* Ragsdale v. Genesco, Inc., 674 F.2d 277 (4th Cir. 1982) (joint debtors could not exempt or avoid lien on entireties property subject to judgment lien of joint creditor).

270 This argument is greatly enhanced by the similar rationale for the Supreme Court decision in Owen v. Owen, 500 U.S. 305, 111 S. Ct. 1833, 114 L. Ed. 2d 250 (1991). The issues might be relitigated even in those jurisdictions with binding appellate case law, based on an argument that those cases were overruled by *Owen. See* Massie v. Yamrose, 169 B.R. 585 (W.D. Va. 1994) (judicial lien held by creditor of only one of two entireties tenants was avoidable, even though it was not presently enforceable, because it could at some future attach to the debtor's interest, and thereby impair it, if the entireties tenancy ended). *But see In re* Arango, 992 F.2d 611 (6th Cir. 1993) (lien on the debtor's rights in entireties property did not impair his ability to exempt those rights because the creditor could not execute on the lien). This case was overruled by the 1994 amendments, creating § 522(f)(2), discussed in § 10.4.2.2, *supra. See In re* Holland, 151 F.3d 547 (6th Cir. 1998).

271 *See In re* Patenude, 259 B.R. 481 (Bankr. D. Mass. 2001) (judicial lien on only debtor's interest in property held as tenants by entireties impaired exemption even though creditor had no present right to execute on lien).

272 This provision, formerly designated as § 522(f)(2), has been upheld against a constitutional challenge based on the takings clause of the Fifth Amendment. *In re* Thompson, 867 F.2d 416 (7th Cir. 1989).

273 A mobile home has been held not to be a household good within the meaning of this provision. *In re* Coonse, 108 B.R. 661 (Bankr. S.D. Ill. 1989); *cf. In re* Rhines, 227 B.R. 308 (Bankr. D. Mont. 1998) (rifle, shotgun, computer and VCR were household goods); *In re* Crawford, 226 B.R. 484 (Bankr. N.D. Ga. 1998) (rifle and computer were household goods); *In re* Di-Palma, 24 B.R. 385 (Bankr. D. Mass. 1982) (mobile home is a household good). A gun has also been held not to be a household

- Implements, professional books, or tools of the trade of the debtor or the trade of a dependent of the debtor; and
- Professionally prescribed health aids for the debtor or a dependent of the debtor.[274]

As the above list illustrates, this avoiding power extends to most, but not quite all, exempt tangible personal property of the debtor that is not in the creditor's possession.[275] The definition of household goods has been construed broadly under this section to include all items kept in or around the home and used to facilitate the day to day living of the debtor and the debtor's dependents,[276] all items normally used by the debtor or the debtor's dependents in or about a residence,[277] or personal property normally found in or around a home which allows the debtor or the debtor's dependents to live in a convenient or comfortable manner or has entertainment or recreational value.[278] It is not limited to necessities,[279] nor is it limited to those items encompassed within the restrictive definition of household goods used by the Federal Trade Commission in its Credit Practices Rule.[280]

These items need not be within the value limitation set forth in section 522(d)(3), as long as they have been validly claimed as exempt under some subsection or combination of subsections in section 522(d) or other applicable exemption law (including a wild card provision).[281] Thus, if a motor vehicle is claimed as exempt using the motor vehicle exemption, but is also used as a tool of the debtor's trade,[282] a nonpossessory, nonpurchase-money lien on that vehicle may be avoided.[283] The dispute in such cases often centers on the definition of "tools of trade" under state or federal law, because many states have an exemption for tools of trade that is large or unlimited in amount.[284]

Disputes concerning tools of the trade will only be increased by an incomprehensible 1994 amendment which purports to create an exception to the power to avoid nonpossessory nonpurchase-money security interests on tools of the debtor's trade, farm animals, or crops in certain cases. Section 522(f)(3) states that if certain conditions are met and the items in question exceed $5000.00 in value, such a lien cannot be avoided. However, among the conditions which must be met are that the state either permits the debtor to claim exemptions that are unlimited in amount, except to the extent that property is encumbered by a consensual lien, or the state prohibits avoidance of consen-

---

good. *In re* McGreevy, 955 F.2d 957 (4th Cir. 1992) (defining household goods as those items of personal property typically found in or around home and used by debtor or his dependents to support and facilitate day-to-day living within the home); *In re* Barrick, 95 B.R. 310 (Bankr. M.D. Pa. 1989); *see also* § 10.2.2.4, *supra*.

274 A water treatment system recommended by a doctor has been held to be a professionally prescribed health aid within the meaning of this provision. *In re* Johnson, 101 B.R. 280 (Bankr. W.D. Okla.), *aff'd*, 113 B.R. 44 (W.D. Okla. 1989).

275 It may also be possible to recover property that was repossessed by a creditor who had held a nonpossessory nonpurchase-money security interest. *In re* White, 203 B.R. 613 (Bankr. N.D. Tex. 1996) (debtor could avoid security interest even though creditor had obtained possession through judicial proceedings); *In re* Vann, 177 B.R. 704 (D. Kan. 1995) (debtors allowed to avoid lien on tool of trade and recover it from creditor even though tool had been repossessed prior to bankruptcy filing).

276 *In re* McGreevy, 955 F.2d 957, 960 (4th Cir. 1992).

277 *In re* Barrick, 95 B.R. 310 (Bankr. M.D. Pa. 1989); *In re* Bailey, 74 B.R. 450 (Bankr. N.D. Ind. 1987).

278 *In re* Courtney, 89 B.R. 15 (Bankr. W.D. Tex. 1988); *In re* Bandy, 62 B.R. 437 (Bankr. E.D. Cal. 1986).

279 Fraley v. Commercial Credit, 189 B.R. 398 (W.D. Ky. 1995) (stereo and camcorder were household goods); *In re* Doss, 298 B.R. 866 (Bankr. W.D. Tenn. 2003) (fifty-inch television was household good); *In re* Gebhart, 260 B.R. 596 (Bankr. S.D. Ga. 2000) (forty-inch television was household good; no exception for luxury items).

280 *In re* Reid, 121 B.R. 875 (Bankr. D.N.M. 1990) (Federal Trade Commission definition at 16 C.F.R. § 444.1(i) rejected as too restrictive).

281 *In re* Liming, 797 F.2d 895 (10th Cir. 1986); First Nat'l Bank of Park Falls v. Maley, 126 B.R. 563 (W.D. Wis. 1991) (lien may be avoided on optometrist's equipment exempt under combina-

tion of tool of trade and wild card exemptions); *see also In re* Reid, 757 F.2d 230 (10th Cir. 1985) (valuable paintings pledged as collateral for business loans not household furniture that is exempt under Oklahoma law so that non-possessory non-purchase money liens on those paintings could not be avoided). It is possible, however, for some goods to be exempted under state law, yet not held for the personal, family or household use of the debtor. *See In re* Thompson, 750 F.2d 628 (8th Cir. 1984).

282 *See* § 10.2.2.7, *supra*.

283 *See* Dominion Bank of Cumberlands v. Nuckolls, 780 F.2d 408 (4th Cir. 1985) (restaurant equipment exempted with homestead exemption is subject to lien avoidance as tool of trade); *In re* Graettinger, 95 B.R. 632 (Bankr. N.D. Iowa 1988) (liens could be avoided in pick-up truck exempted as motor vehicle, because truck was a tool of debtor's trade); *In re* Meyers, 2 B.R. 603 (Bankr. E.D. Mich. 1980) (motor vehicle used only for commuting not a tool of trade, but if it were, lien could be avoided). *But see In re* Moore, 5 B.R. 669 (Bankr. S.D. Ohio 1980) (vehicle must be claimed exempt under tool-of-trade exemption to avoid lien using tool-of-trade avoidance power). Even a mobile home, exempted under § 522(d)(5), may be considered as household goods or furnishings, according to one court. *In re* Dipalma, 24 B.R. 385 (Bankr. D. Mass. 1982).

284 *See* § 10.2.2.7, *supra*; *see also In re* Heape, 886 F.2d 280 (10th Cir. 1989) (lien avoided in debtors' breeding livestock on ground that livestock is tool of breeder's trade); *In re* Thompson, 867 F.2d 416 (7th Cir. 1989) (debtor's state law exemption of tools of trade is not in any way limited by federal limitation of that exemption to $750.00); *In re* Taylor, 861 F.2d 550 (9th Cir. 1988) (logging equipment worth $50,000.00 could be freed from non-possessory non-purchase money security interest); *In re* Erickson, 815 F.2d 1090 (7th Cir. 1987) (baler and haybine were tools of trade so security interest therein could be avoided); *In re* La Fond, 791 F.2d 623 (8th Cir. 1986) (Bankruptcy Code's definition of "farmer" given at 11 U.S.C. § 101(20) is not determinative for the purpose of avoiding non-possessory non-purchase money lien on farm equipment as tool of trade); Dominion Bank of Cumberlands v. Nuckolls, 780 F.2d 408 (4th Cir. 1985) (lien may be avoided on restaurant equipment used to operate business out of home); *In re* Taylor, 73 B.R. 149 (B.A.P. 9th Cir. 1987) (liens on log truck and trailer avoidable), *aff'd*, 861 F.2d 550 (9th Cir. 1988).

sual liens. Because no state has unlimited exemptions, and no state could have had, consistent with the Supremacy Clause, a law prohibiting avoidance of liens in bankruptcy, it is not clear that the exception can be invoked in any state.[285] The legislative history does make clear that the exception applies only to exemptions claimed under state exemption schemes, and has no applicability to a debtor choosing the federal bankruptcy exemptions.[286] It also states that the $5000.00 limit, if it is ever applicable, is calculated separately for each debtor in a joint case.[287] When the exception is applicable, the $5000.00 limit is designed to free $5000.00 of equity in tools of the trade from liens, not to limit the amount of the lien that could be avoided to $5000.00.[288]

Issues may also arise as to whether or not a purchase-money security interest exists.[289] For example, the debtor may have entered into a series of credit purchases with cross-collateral clauses. These clauses secure each purchase with property previously purchased, even if that property had been fully paid for, through language stating that the property purchased in each transaction is security for subsequent purchase transactions. In such cases, it has been held that no purchase-money security interest exists, even as to the last item purchased. Under the former provisions of the Uniform Commercial Code, the term purchase-money security interest had been narrowly defined to exclude any transactions in which the agreement purports to make collateral secure a debt other than its own price.[290] The revised Uniform Commercial Code takes no position on the issue, leaving it for courts to decide, presumably in light of prior case law.[291] Thus, whenever such clauses exist, stating that the collateral will secure future indebtedness, it should be

held that no purchase-money security interest exists, even if there has been no later indebtedness.[292] Certainly, when a refinancing has occurred, and the collateral in fact secures indebtedness other than its price, any possible purchase money character should be extinguished.[293] And similarly, if a loan involves other funds besides the purchase price (perhaps even those used to buy insurance), then property purchased using only some of the proceeds should not be considered subject to a purchase money security interest.[294]

In addition, it should be noted that the Federal Trade Commission has promulgated a rule which makes the taking of certain nonpossessory, nonpurchase-money liens in personal property an unfair trade practice.[295] The rule can be used in litigation asserting the unfair practice, and in at least one instance has been used in bankruptcy to avoid otherwise non-avoidable liens.[296]

10.4.2.5 Power to Exempt Property Recovered by Trustee—§ 522(g)

A power of the debtor somewhat less likely to be used is provided in section 522(g). This provision allows the debtor to exempt any property that the trustee recovers using the various trustee powers to recover property.[297] Thus, if such property comes into the trustee's hands, the debtor may claim it as exempt, as long as the pre-bankruptcy transfer of

---

285 *Compare In re* Ehlen, 202 B.R. 742 (Bankr. W.D. Wis. 1996) (section 522(f)(3) inapplicable in Wisconsin), *aff'd* 207 B.R. 179 (W.D. Wis. 1997) *and In re* Zimmel, 185 B.R. 786 (Bankr. D. Minn. 1995) (Minnesota did not allow unlimited exemptions or permit debtors to waive exemptions, so section 522(f)(3) was inapplicable) *with In re* Parrish, 186 B.R. 246 (Bankr. W.D. Wis. 1995) (Wisconsin law prohibited the avoidance of consensual liens, so debtor could only avoid security interest to extent of $5000.00 interest in tractor).

286 H.R. Rep. No. 103-835, at 56, 57 (1994), *reprinted in* 1994 U.S.C.C.A.N. 3340, 3365, 3366.

287 *Id.*

288 *In re* Duvall, 218 B.R. 1008 (Bankr. W.D. Tex. 1998) (also holding that $5000.00 limit does not apply to each tool individually).

289 See National Consumer Law Center, Repossessions and Foreclosures Chapter 3 (5th ed. 2002) for a detailed discussion of the existence and duration of purchase money security interests.

290 *In re* Freeman, 956 F.2d 252 (11th Cir. 1992) (security interest lost its purchase money character when debt consolidated with other debts under Alabama law); *In re* Manuel, 507 F.2d 990 (5th Cir. 1975); *In re* McCombs, 126 B.R. 611 (N.D. Ala. 1989); *In re* Johnson, 1 Bankr. Ct. Dec (LRP) 1023 (Bankr. S.D. Ala. 1973); *see* National Consumer Law Center, Repossessions and Foreclosures § 3.8.4.5 (5th ed. 2002 and Supp.).

291 Official Comment 8 to Uniform Commercial Code § 9-103.

292 Southtrust Bank v. Borg-Warner Acceptance Corp., 760 F.2d 1240 (11th Cir. 1985); *In re* Jones, 5 B.R. 655 (Bankr. M.D.N.C. 1980). *But see* Pristas v. Landaus of Plymouth, 742 F.2d 797 (3d Cir. 1984) (Pennsylvania Goods and Services Statute provided a method of apportioning payments so purchase-money character retained even if later sales made); *In re* Mattson, 20 B.R. 382 (Bankr. W.D. Wis. 1982) (purchase-money character not lost if consolidation agreement provides clear and fair way to apportion payments among items of collateral).

293 *In re* Matthews, 724 F.2d 798 (9th Cir. 1984); *In re* Freeman, 124 B.R. 840 (N.D. Ala. 1991), *aff'd*, 956 F.2d 252 (11th Cir. 1992); *In re* Cameron, 25 B.R. 410 (Bankr. N.D. Ga. 1982); Rosen v. Associates Fin. Services Co., 17 B.R. 436 (Bankr. D.S.C. 1982). *But see In re* Billings, 838 F.2d 405 (10th Cir. 1988) (where purpose of refinancing substantially appears to be to allow the debtor more favorable repayment terms, almost no new money advanced, and agreement stated specific intent to continue purchase-money status, refinancing may not extinguish purchase money character of original lien).

294 *In re* Mulcahy, 3 B.R. 454 (Bankr. S.D. Ind. 1980). *But see In re* Griffin, 9 B.R. 880 (Bankr. N.D. Ga. 1981) (fact that collateral secured finance and insurance charges did not render security interest non-purchase money).

295 16 C.F.R. § 444; *see* National Consumer Law Center, Unfair and Deceptive Acts and Practices § 5.1.2.1 (5th ed. 2001 and Supp.).

296 *In re* Raymond, 103 B.R. 846 (Bankr. W.D. Ky. 1989).

297 Most of these powers are discussed below in the context of the debtor's right to use them under § 522(h). Sections 542 and 543 are discussed in § 9.9, *supra*. Although the avoiding powers of sections 544 through 549 are not specifically enumerated in section 522(g), they are encompassed by the inclusion of section 550 under which the trustee actually recovers the property transferred in an avoided transfer.

the property from the debtor was not voluntary and the debtor did not conceal the property. The debtor may also exempt the property, under section 522(g)(2), if the debtor could have avoided the transfer because the transfer was pursuant to a nonpossessory, nonpurchase-money security interest.[298]

In some cases, under both section 522(g)(1) and section 522(h), an issue may arise as to whether the transfer avoided by the trustee was a voluntary transfer.[299] For example, there is no question that a debtor who pays money with a gun to his or her head has made an involuntary transfer. Would it be much different if the debtor paid a large utility arrearage upon the threat of a shut-off of heating or water service to a home in which the debtor's children live (or perhaps an elderly or sick relative)? What about a debtor threatened with lesser evils, for example, repossession of property necessary for daily existence, such as a refrigerator?[300] Thus, a seemingly voluntary transfer made under threat of foreclosure or based on misrepresentations about the circumstances of the transfer may be found to be involuntary for purposes of section 522(g) or (h).[301]

It is also a little unclear whether section 522(g) is really an expansion of the debtor's powers to exempt property or rather, in fact, a limitation. Because under section 522(b) the debtor already may claim exempt property from any property of the estate, and because property of the estate under section 541(a)(3) and (4) includes property recovered by the trustee under sections 543, 550, 551, 553 and 723, section 522(g) seems to add only a right to exempt property recovered by the trustee under sections 510(c) and 542.[302] But section 522(g) does not allow the property to be exempted if it was transferred voluntarily or concealed by the debtor. This provision could mean that property which could be otherwise claimed as exempt under section 522(b) may not be claimed as exempt because of the limitations in section 522(g).[303] On the other hand, the legislative history states that the several provisions of section 522 are cumulative,[304] and therefore if property can be exempted under section 522(b), section 522(g) should not impair that right.[305] In any event, if the trustee acquires property other than through use

---

298 *In re* Flitter, 181 B.R. 938 (Bankr. D. Minn. 1995) (debtor may exempt property recovered by trustee if debtors could have avoided transfer under § 522(f), even if transfer was voluntary). The reference in § 522(g)(2) to § 522(f)(2) is a technical error; it should be a reference to § 522(f)(1)(B). Section 522(f)(2) was redesignated as § 522(f)(1)(B) by the 1994 amendments, but Congress neglected to change the reference in § 522(g)(2). It appears that this subsection would allow the debtor to recover goods repossessed pursuant to a nonpossessory, nonpurchase-money security interest if that repossession was first avoided by the trustee, because there are really two transfers being avoided—the repossession and the granting of the original security interest. The repossession, being involuntary, fits within § 522(g)(1); the original grant of the security interest does not, because it was voluntary, but it does come within § 522(g)(2). Thus, the debtor, who could have avoided the security interest, would not lose the right to exempt such property simply because the trustee avoided the transfer first. *But cf. In re* Vann, 177 B.R. 704 (D. Kan. 1995) (security interest could be avoided through simply using § 522(f) even after goods had been repossessed); *In re* Meadows, 75 B.R. 357 (W.D. Va. 1987) (same).

299 *See, e.g.,* Berman v. Forti, 232 B.R. 653 (D. Md. 1999) (although consent to judgment against debtors was voluntary, transfer effected by judgment itself was involuntary); *In re* Rollins, 63 B.R. 780 (Bankr. E.D. Tenn. 1986) (property transferred pursuant to insurance policy required by mortgage is voluntary transfer).

300 *See In re* Via, 107 B.R. 91 (Bankr. W.D. Va. 1989) (payment made to creditor to avoid garnishment was involuntary), *aff'd, In re* Via, Clearinghouse No. 45,232 (W.D. Va. 1990); *In re* Taylor, 8 B.R. 578 (Bankr. E.D. Pa. 1981) (threat of sheriff sale of home forced involuntary transfer); *In re* Reaves, 8 B.R. 177 (Bankr. D.S.D. 1981) (creditor applied unfair pressure).

301 *In re* Davis, 169 B.R. 285 (E.D.N.Y. 1994) (sale/leaseback agreement in which debtor executed a deed to avoid a threatened foreclosure was set aside as a fraudulent transfer under 11 U.S.C. § 548).

302 One possible exception to this statement is property claimed under section 522(b)(2)(B), which can only be claimed exempt to the extent of "any interest the debtor had immediately before commencement of the case."

303 *In re* Arzt, 252 B.R. 138 (B.A.P. 8th Cir. 2000) (debtors could not exempt property recovered by trustee because transfer of property had been voluntary); *In re* Milcher, 86 B.R. 103 (Bankr. W.D. Mich. 1988); *In re* Lamping, 8 B.R. 709 (Bankr. E.D. Wis. 1981); *In re* Lanctot, 6 B.R. 576 (Bankr. D. Utah 1980) (debtors could not claim property recovered by trustee avoidance of non-perfected conventional security interests); *see In re* Wilson, 694 F.2d 236 (11th Cir. 1982) (section 522(g) is a limitation on general power to exempt any property of estate, and does not apply to property not brought into estate by trustee avoiding powers enumerated therein); *see also In re* Duncan, 329 F.3d 1195 (10th Cir. 2003) (debtor not entitled to homestead exemption in property recovered by trustee as fraudulent transfer to tenancy by entireties based on § 522(g) even though trustee failed to object to debtor's claim of exemption in property within thirty-day period under Fed. R. Bankr. P. 4003(b); trustee recovered, and debtor could not exempt, all interests in property that had been transferred under Wyoming law); *In re* Glass, 60 F.3d 565 (9th Cir. 1995) (trustee need not have first recovered property transferred by debtor in order to object to exemption under § 522(g)); *In re* Kelsey, 270 B.R. 776 (B.A.P. 10th Cir. 2001) (when debtor withdrew money from joint account with wife he became owner of funds, so all of the funds later transferred to her were his property). One solution to the problem of obtaining possession of property recovered by the trustee when it cannot be claimed as exempt is to convert to chapter 13 wherein the debtor has a right to possession of all property of the estate. *See* § 12.8, *infra.*

304 S. Rep. No. 95-989, at 77 (1978); H.R. Rep. No. 95-595, at 363 (1977).

305 In some cases, there may be an issue regarding whether the trustee recovered property or whether it was in the estate all along. *See In re* Moody, 862 F.2d 1194 (5th Cir. 1989) (attempted fraudulent transfer of property did not preclude debtor from later claiming homestead exemption under Texas law; *In re* Pancratz, 175 B.R. 85 (D. Wyo. 1994) (transfer of property to self-settled spendthrift trust was invalid, so property was property of the estate at outset of case and § 522(g) was inapplicable).

of the provisions listed in section 522(g), section 522(g) does not prevent the debtor from exempting the property.[306]

In any case, it is not very likely that such disputes will arise often under section 522(g), as it will be a rare case in which the trustee bothers to avoid a transfer of property that the debtor may claim as exempt.[307] Indeed, it is unusual for trustees to avoid the small transfers involved in consumer cases at all; when the only result will be more exempt property for the debtor rather than proceeds for the creditors, trustees have no incentive to do so.[308] Except in cases in which the trustee would recover a substantial amount of non-exempt property along with the exempt property, the trustee's avoiding powers, and thus section 522(g), are not likely to be used often in consumer cases. When they are used though, prejudgment interest may be available to enhance the award.[309]

Occasionally, when the trustee does move to avoid an unperfected lien on a car or other property, however, it may cause problems for the debtor by creating non-exemptible equity in the property. (For example, the trustee may avoid a security interest of $6000.00 on an $8000.00 vehicle. The debtor usually would not be able to exempt the equity created because a security interest is usually a voluntary transfer of property and because applicable law may not permit an exemption in that high an amount.) In such cases, the trustee may attempt to liquidate the property if the debtor does not pay the trustee its value.[310] And when the trustee does avoid a transfer, the debtor's exempt share of the property recovered can be reduced by a pro rata share of the costs and expenses of avoiding the transfer.[311]

10.4.2.6 Debtor's Right to Utilize Trustee's Avoiding Powers—§ 522(h)

10.4.2.6.1 Overview

More likely to be used are the provisions of section 522(h), which give the debtor the wide panoply of avoiding powers available to the trustee under sections 544, 545, 547, 548, 549, 553 and 724(a) in cases in which the trustee does not choose to avoid a transfer.[312]

The use of these powers is subject to the same limitations as section 522(g); the transfer to be avoided cannot have been a voluntary transfer, and the debtor may not use these powers to exempt property that was concealed by the debtor. The discussion above on voluntariness under section 522(g) is equally applicable to this section.[313]

In some cases, especially under chapter 13, a debtor may be able to convince a trustee to exercise an avoiding power the debtor cannot use because the transfer was voluntary, especially if it will mean greater dividends for unsecured creditors. It may even be possible to provide that the trustee will do so as part of the chapter 13 plan.[314] The debtor has a right to possession of any property recovered in this manner (though it cannot be exempted).[315] When a plan does provide for the trustee to avoid a transfer, the trustee's prior concurrence in such a provision should be sought if possible. Because the recovery of such property for use in funding the plan can also be enormously helpful to the debtor in paying priority or secured claims, debtor's counsel might even offer to draw up all of the necessary papers for use by the trustee. Perhaps because such methods of invoking the chapter 13 trustee's powers are available, some courts have held that all chapter 13 debtors, as debtors in possession, have full use of

---

306 McFatter v. Cage, 204 B.R. 503 (S.D. Tex. 1996). *But see In re* Glass, 164 B.R. 759 (B.A.P. 9th Cir. 1994) (debtor could not exempt property that had been voluntarily transferred to son, even though trustee had recovered property without using avoiding powers enumerated in § 522(g)), *aff'd*, 60 F.3d 565 (9th Cir. 1995); *In re* Dorricott, 5 B.R. 192 (Bankr. N.D. Ohio 1980) (holding under 11 U.S.C. § 522(g)(1) that debtor could not exempt concealed property even in case where trustee never recovered property for estate).

307 However, in those cases where the trustee does move to avoid a transfer, the debtor may be obligated to intervene in that action to protect his or her rights. *See* H.R. Rep. No. 95-595, at 362 (1977); *cf.* Wellman v. Wellman, 933 F.2d 215 (4th Cir. 1991) (debtor-in-possession in chapter 11 case precluded from avoiding transfer when avoided transfer would not benefit bankruptcy estate). This result should be different where the debtor can exempt an interest in the property once it is brought into the estate, even if there is no additional benefit to creditors.

308 In fact, where the amount recovered by the trustee can be substantially exempted so that the balance will pay only trustee fees, the trustee may be required to abandon the property in favor of the debtor. *In re* Melvin, 64 B.R. 104 (Bankr. W.D. Mo. 1986). *But see In re* Myatt, 101 B.R. 197 (Bankr. E.D. Cal. 1989) (where trustee conducts litigation based on belief that litigation costs and fees would be paid from recovery of non-exempt property, debtor's later amendment of exemptions to include recovered property could be conditioned on payment of trustee's expenses).

309 *In re* Chattanooga Wholesale Antiques, Inc., 930 F.2d 458 (6th Cir. 1991).

310 *See In re* Bagnato, 80 B.R. 655 (Bankr. E.D.N.Y. 1987) (although debtor did not properly preserve her rights in exempt property, trustee's failure to avoid lien prior to discharge prevented trustee from preserving lien to benefit the estate).

311 11 U.S.C. § 522(k)(1). *But see In re* Breen, 123 B.R. 357 (B.A.P. 9th Cir. 1991) (section 522(k)(1) not applicable where trustee recovers property through methods other than avoiding powers).

312 *See* Deel Rent-A-Car v. Levine, 721 F.2d 750 (11th Cir. 1983) (debtor may avoid transfer that trustee could have avoided even though transfer was pursuant to pre-bankruptcy execution on property that would not otherwise have been exempt due to liens eliminated by the execution); *cf. In re* Merrifield, 214 B.R. 362 (B.A.P. 8th Cir. 1997) (debtor could not use trustee's powers to avoid voluntary transfer that trustee had already sought to avoid).

313 *See* § 10.4.2.5, *supra*.

314 *In re* Johnson, 36 B.R. 381 (Bankr. D. Colo. 1982) (plan could provide for chapter 13 trustee to avoid fraudulent transfer).

315 11 U.S.C. § 1306; *see* § 12.8, *infra*; *see also In re* Walls, 17 B.R. 701 (Bankr. S.D. W. Va. 1982) (opinion is confusing as to why the debtor could not himself avoid the transfer).

the trustee's powers without the limitations in § 522(h).[316] However, other courts disagree.[317]

The debtor's powers under section 522(h) are otherwise the same as those of the trustee.[318] To use them, it is therefore first necessary to understand what powers the trustee has. The discussion below briefly describes each of the trustee's powers as well as the debtor's possible use of them.

10.4.2.6.2 The "strong-arm clause"—§ 544

Through the use of section 544, the trustee (and thus the debtor in many instances) is able to avoid a wide variety of transfers. Section 544(a) allows the trustee to avoid any transfer or obligation[319] incurred by the debtor that is voidable by:

- A creditor that extends credit to the debtor at the time of commencement of the case, and that obtains at that time and with respect to such credit a judicial lien on all property on which a creditor on a simple contract could have obtained such a judicial lien, whether or not such a creditor exists;
- A creditor that extends credit to the debtor at the time of the commencement of the case, and obtains, at such time and with respect to such credit, an execution against the debtor that is returned unsatisfied at such time, whether or not such a creditor exists;
- A bona fide purchaser of real property other than fixtures from the debtor against whom applicable law permits such transfer to be perfected, that obtains the status of a bona fide purchaser and has perfected such transfer at the time of the commencement of the case, whether or not such a purchaser exists.

In addition, section 544(b) bestows the power to avoid any transfer or obligation that is avoidable under applicable law by an actually existing creditor holding an unsecured claim.[320]

All of these rights depend on the powers given to creditors or purchasers under state or local law. They carry forward, mostly unchanged,[321] the powers the trustee had under the former Bankruptcy Act, so reference to case law under the Act continues to be useful. They make clear that the first three powers, relating to a "hypothetical" creditor, rather than actual existing creditors, assume that the hypothetical creditor had no knowledge of the transfer, to the extent that knowledge might otherwise bar the avoidance of a transfer.[322]

The most frequent use of the section 544(a) powers is the avoidance of unrecorded security interests and other liens. Section 9-301(1)(b) of the Uniform Commercial Code (UCC) gives a lien creditor priority over the holder of an unperfected UCC security interest.[323] A close examination of the nature and manner of perfection of a creditor's security interest may turn up avoidable transfers.[324] In many

---

316 *In re* Cohen, 305 B.R. 886 (B.A.P. 9th Cir. 2004); *In re* Freeman, 72 B.R. 850 (Bankr. E.D. Va. 1987); *In re* Ottaviano, 68 B.R. 238 (Bankr. D. Conn. 1986); *In re* Boyette, 33 B.R. 10, 11 (Bankr. N.D. Tex. 1983).

317 *See, e.g., In re* Stangel, 219 F.3d 498 (5th Cir. 2000); Hollar v. United States, 174 B.R. 198 (M.D.N.C. 1994) (chapter 13 debtor may not directly avoid transfer under § 548, case remanded to determine if requirements of 522(h) are met); *In re* Mast, 79 B.R. 981 (Bankr. W.D. Mich. 1987); *In re* Driscoll, 57 B.R. 322 (Bankr. W.D. Wis. 1986).

318 *See In re* Saults, 293 B.R. 739 (Bankr. E.D. Tenn. 2002) (debtor's procedural waiver of state exemption rights in bank account during state execution process did not prevent use of § 522(h) to recover funds).

319 Section 522(h) only speaks of incorporating the trustee's power to avoid transfers, not obligations. It is not clear whether it would be carried over to section 522(h) despite the failure to mention it specifically. Generally, unsecured obligations of the debtor are eliminated by the discharge, so that there would be no need to avoid them, and secured obligations involve a transfer of an interest in property that can be avoided. (The trustee may wish to avoid an obligation to prevent other creditors from being prejudiced.).

320 *See In re* Bushey, 210 B.R. 95 (B.A.P. 6th Cir. 1997) (open credit card account maintained by debtor qualified as existing creditor, even though balance was zero at some time between date of transfer and bankruptcy petition).

321 One change is the addition of bona fide purchaser status of § 544(a)(3).

322 *But see In re* Hamilton, 125 F.3d 292 (5th Cir. 1997) (remanding case to determine whether reasonably diligent inquiry could have given hypothetical bona fide purchaser inquiry notice that would defeat right to avoid trustee's deed); *In re* Weisman, 5 F.3d 417 (9th Cir. 1993) (under California law, bona fide purchaser is deemed to be on notice of and obligated to determine ownership status of persons who occupy real estate); *In re* Prof'l Inv. Properties, 955 F.2d 623 (9th Cir. 1992) (involuntary bankruptcy petition put trustee on constructive notice of creditor's interest under unrecorded instrument, so trustee could not invoke strong-arm powers); Watkins v. Watkins, 922 F.2d 1513 (10th Cir. 1991) (where hypothetical purchaser would have constructive notice of debtor's former wife's security interest granted by divorce decree of record, lien could not be avoided); *In re* Hagendorfer, 803 F.2d 647 (11th Cir. 1986) (constructive knowledge of mutual mistake will permit reformation of a security interest); McCannon v. Marston, 679 F.2d 13 (3d Cir. 1982) (trustee is charged with constructive knowledge that would be charged to any purchaser under state law).

323 *In re* Freeman, 72 B.R. 850 (Bankr. E.D. Va. 1987). An exception in the Uniform Commercial Code exists for purchase money security interests perfected within ten days. Similar exceptions exist in various other state lien statutes.

324 *See, e.g., In re* Crawford, 274 B.R. 798 (B.A.P. 8th Cir. 2002) (improperly perfected security interest in annuity); *In re* Ware, 59 B.R. 549 (Bankr. N.D. Ohio 1986). *Compare In re* Wuerzberger, 284 B.R. 814 (Bankr. W.D. Va. 2002) (no amendment to mobile home certificate of title required if assignor remains as servicing agent for assignee securitization trust; court adopts "conduit" theory that assignor/servicer can provide information to those inquiring about status of lien) *with In re* Wuerzberger, 271 B.R. 778 (Bankr. W.D. Va. 2002) (assignment by mobile home lender of all its interest to securitization

cases trustees have successfully asserted these rights when financing statements were incorrectly filed, thus rendering the security interest unperfected, or when a transaction denominated as a lease was found to be a disguised security interest with no financing statement filed.[325] (In these cases the debtor cannot exempt the equity created by the trustee's lien avoidance because the lien avoided was a voluntary transfer.) Similarly, the law in most states gives judicial lien creditors and bona fide purchasers priority over unrecorded or improperly recorded mortgages and many other unrecorded liens on real estate.[326] Depending upon state law, the power to avoid transfers that are not enforceable against a bona fide purchaser of real estate may permit the debtor to avoid foreclosure sale transfers that have not been completed by the filing of a deed.[327]

The "bona fide purchaser" power also allows the cutoff of other rights (in real property only), such as equities created by fraud, unperfected or constructive trusts,[328] and

in most states, unrecorded deeds.[329] In such proceedings, most often, one issue is whether the trustee can be considered a bona fide purchaser or whether she must be deemed to have constructive notice.[330]

Under section 544(b) certain other transfers may also be totally avoided, if they could have been avoided, even in part, by an actually existing unsecured creditor.[331] This provision allows the trustee to make use of applicable state laws to avoid fraudulent conveyances, bulk transfers in which the notices required by Article 6 of the Uniform Commercial Code were not given, and other types of transfers avoidable under state law by existing creditors.[332]

However, in 1998 Congress enacted a restriction on the trustee's right to use state fraudulent conveyance laws, and indeed upon creditor's rights to use such laws outside of bankruptcy, to recover religious or charitable contributions of the debtor. The Religious Liberty and Charitable Donation Protection Act of 1998[333] amended section 544(b) to provide that charitable contributions[334] to qualified religious or charitable entities or organizations,[335] that are protected

---

trust extinguished its lien). Problems with perfection of auto and mobile home security interests may occur when the loans are securitized.

325 *See, e.g., In re* Merritt Dredging Co., 839 F.2d 203 (4th Cir. 1998) ("rental" agreement creates avoidable unperfected security interest).

326 *See, e.g., In re* Burns, 322 F.3d 421 (6th Cir. 2003) (improperly witnessed mortgage subject to avoidance); *In re* Kroskie, 315 F.3d 644 (6th Cir. 2003) (mortgage on permanently affixed mobile home that was recorded at registry of deeds but not properly perfected under state mobile home statute may be avoided by trustee); *In re* Bridge, 18 F.3d 195 (3d Cir. 1994) (trustee's rights as hypothetical bona fide purchaser of real estate prevailed under New Jersey law over equitable lien created when mortgage was satisfied by refinancing but new mortgage was not recorded); *In re* Ryan, 851 F.2d 502 (1st Cir. 1988); *In re* Sandy Ridge Oil Co., 807 F.2d 1332 (7th Cir. 1987); *In re* Pac. Express, Inc., 780 F.2d 1482 (9th Cir. 1986); Thacker v. United Companies Lending Corp., 256 B.R. 724 (W.D. Ky. 2000) (defective mortgage avoidable even though it was recorded); *In re* Check, 129 B.R. 492 (Bankr. N.D. Ohio 1991) (trustee may avoid mortgage to debtor's attorney which was improperly certified by the attorney so as to be invalid under state law); *In re* Consol. Southeastern Group Inc., 75 B.R. 102 (Bankr. N.D. Ga. 1987) (unrecorded lien for utility services); *see also In re* Robertson, 203 F.3d 855 (5th Cir. 2000) (trustee could not avoid pre-petition divorce decree transfer of interest in house because judgment of divorce had been recorded in appropriate conveyance records); *In re* Seaway Express, 912 F.2d 1125 (9th Cir. 1990) (unrecorded security interest may be avoided by trustee even though failure to record could be blamed on the debtor). *But see In re* Donahue, 862 F.2d 259 (10th Cir. 1989) (unrecorded equitable lien held by debtor's wife pursuant to divorce decree could not be avoided due to unjust enrichment which would result). The trustee probably cannot avoid liens which were properly recorded as of the date of bankruptcy, but which subsequently lose that status under state law because no continuation statements were properly filed. *See* Gen. Elec. Credit Corp. v. Nardulli & Sons, Inc., 836 F.2d 184 (3d Cir. 1988).

327 *In re* Elam, 194 B.R. 412 (Bankr. E.D. Tex. 1996).

328 *In re* Seaway Express, 912 F.2d 1125 (9th Cir. 1990) (claim of constructive trust beneficiary can be avoided); Belisle v. Plun-

kett, 877 F.2d 512 (7th Cir. 1989) (leasehold interest held by debtor in constructive trust for others can be brought into estate by trustee); *In re* Tleel, 876 F.2d 769 (9th Cir. 1989) (constructive interest in property held by debtor's partners can be avoided); *In re* Crabtree, 871 F.2d 36 (6th Cir. 1989) (deed which failed to meet state law requirements for actual trust creates avoidable constructive trust); *In re* Quality Holstein Leasing, 752 F.2d 1009 (5th Cir. 1985) (trustee's rights superior to those claimed through beneficiary of constructive trust). *But see In re* Gen. Coffee Corp., 828 F.2d 699 (11th Cir. 1987) (constructive trust not avoidable).

329 *But see In re* Hartman Paving, Inc., 745 F.2d 307 (4th Cir. 1984) (deed of trust that would be invalid against bona fide purchaser not avoidable).

330 *E.g., In re* Probasco, 839 F.2d 1352 (9th Cir. 1988); McCannon v. Marston, 679 F.2d 13 (3d Cir. 1982).

331 The principle, adopted in the Code, that if a transfer could be avoided by any creditor it could be avoided by the trustee *in toto*, regardless of how small the actual creditor's claim, is known as the rule of Moore v. Bay, 284 U.S. 4, 52 S. Ct. 3, 76 L. Ed. 133 (1931), the Supreme Court case which first announced it. *See In re* Marlar, 267 F.3d 749 (8th Cir. 2001) (trustee could bring action based on existence of unsecured creditor with right to bring action even if another creditor had unsuccessfully brought fraudulent transfer action in state court).

332 *E.g., In re* Craig, 144 F.3d 587 (8th Cir. 1998) (debtor made indirect fraudulent transfer under North Dakota law when he directed that loan funds owed to him be used to pay for residence in wife's name); *In re* Levine, 134 F.3d 1046 (11th Cir. 1998) (transfer of assets into exempt annuities was fraudulent transfer under Florida law). *But see In re* Popkin & Stern, 223 F.3d 764 (8th Cir. 2000) (disclaimer of interest in estate was not avoidable under state law so transfer could not be avoided under § 544(b)).

333 Pub. L. No. 105-183, 112 Stat. 517 (1998), applicable to cases pending on or after June 19, 1998. The amendment applies to cases pending on or after the date of the Act.

334 The "charitable contribution" must meet the definition in section 548(d)(3), as amended by the same Act, and thus must consist of either a financial instrument or cash.

335 Section 544(b) incorporates § 548(a)(2), which incorporates the definition of "qualified religious or charitable entity or organi-

from avoidance under section 544 and under state law.[336] As discussed below,[337] section 548(a)(2) protects from avoidance religious or charitable contributions within the year prior to bankruptcy of up to fifteen percent of the debtor's gross income in the year they were made, or even more if consistent with past giving. Under the language of the provision, the fifteen percent limit applies to each transfer individually, even if the aggregate in a single year exceeds fifteen percent. However, at least one court has read the language to mean that if the fifteen percent limit is exceeded and there was no past giving no part of the contribution is protected.[338]

The debtor's rights to use the section 544 powers are somewhat limited by the incorporation of language from section 522(g) into section 522(h) excluding voluntary transfers. Many security interests and other transfers of property are voluntary, and those transfers will not be avoidable by the debtor even if they are avoidable by the trustee.[339]

The powers of section 544(a) can be used by the debtor to avoid various types of unperfected or improperly perfected[340] involuntary liens,[341] such as mechanics' or repairmen's liens, and tax liens, if they are subordinate to judicial liens or the rights of bona fide purchasers under state law. These powers can also be used to cut off various equitable rights in real property, such as constructive trusts, if those rights were not created voluntarily by the debtor.[342]

The section 544(b) power will likely be used most by debtors to attempt avoidance through incorporation of state fraudulent transfer laws.[343] In some twelve states this law is based on the Uniform Fraudulent Conveyance Act (UFCA). At least twenty-four others have adopted the Uniform Fraudulent Transfer Act (UFTA). Still other states have varying case law derived from the old English Statute of 13 Elizabeth.

A possible difficulty in using the UFCA is the question of whether it is applicable at all to involuntary transfers. This issue was resolved in the Uniform Fraudulent Transfer Act, which is clearly applicable to involuntary transfers. However, a specific provision was included in the UFTA to except "a regularly conducted, noncollusive foreclosure sale or execution of a power of sale . . . upon default under a mortgage, deed of trust or security agreement."[344] If avoidance of involuntary transfers is possible, then a wide variety of execution sales and defectively conducted foreclosures could be invalidated by debtors' use of this section. In each case, state law is the determining factor. This issue is further addressed below in the discussion of the section 548 avoiding powers for conveyances deemed fraudulent under federal law.

10.4.2.6.3 Statutory liens—§ 545

Under section 545, certain statutory liens may be avoided. These include any lien that first becomes effective upon insolvency or insolvency proceedings of various types, liens which could be defeated by a bona fide purchaser on the date of commencement of the case, liens for rent and liens of distress for rent. Such liens may be avoided even if they have already been enforced by a sale before the filing of the bankruptcy case.[345]

Among the liens possibly avoidable under this section are unfiled federal tax liens and, in certain cases, even recorded tax liens.[346] Under section 6323(a) of the Internal Revenue

---

zation" in § 548(d)(4), requiring the recipient of the contribution to be an entity described in § 170(c)(1) or 170(c)(2) of the Internal Revenue Code.

336 11 U.S.C. § 544(b)(2). The law overrules cases such as *In re* Newman, 203 B.R. 468 (D. Kan. 1996) and *In re* Gomes, 219 B.R. 286 (Bankr. D. Or. 1998).

337 *See* § 10.4.2.6.5, *infra.*

338 *In re* Zohdi, 234 B.R. 371 (Bankr. M.D. La. 1999).

339 *But see* § 10.4.2.6, *supra.*

340 *See* McLean v. City of Philadelphia, 891 F.2d 474 (3d Cir. 1989) (city's liens for utility service found avoidable based on failure to properly comply with state lien indexing law); *In re* Janmar, 6 B.C.D. 385, 1 C.B.C.2d 1051 (Bankr. N.D. Ga. 1980).

341 *In re* Fed'n of Puerto Rican Organizations, 155 B.R. 44 (E.D.N.Y. 1993).

342 Here again the meaning of "voluntary" in section 522(g) is unclear. Would a constructive trust created by the debtor's voluntary acts be a voluntary transfer if the debtor did not realize those acts would create a constructive trust?

343 *See, e.g.,* Havee v. Belk, 775 F.2d 1209 (4th Cir. 1985).

344 Section 3 of the Uniform Act creates a presumption that the value given for a transfer of this type is reasonably equivalent value. It may nevertheless be possible under the UFTA to challenge a foreclosure sale as not regularly conducted or non-collusive.

345 H.R. Rep. No. 95-595, at 371 (1977).

346 *In re* Sierer, 121 B.R. 884 (Bankr. N.D. Fla. 1990) (permitting avoidance of perfected federal tax liens on automobiles, money market account, household goods, stocks, IRA, tools, promissory note and cash, but not as to insurance), *aff'd,* United States v. Sierer, 139 B.R. 752 (N.D. Fla. 1991); *see* I.R.C. § 6323(b)–(e); S. Rep. No. 95-989, at 86 (1978); *see also In re* Hudgins, 967 F.2d 973 (4th Cir. 1992) (tax lien filed against Michael Hudgins, Inc. avoidable with respect to debtor's non-business assets, even though the corporation had ceased to exist prior to filing of the lien, because notice of lien did not put bona fide purchasers on notice that debtor's personal assets were liened); *cf. In re* Stanford, 826 F.2d 353 (5th Cir. 1987) (state tax lien not avoidable where it was good against bona fide purchaser under state law). Several other courts have held that a debtor may not avoid a properly filed tax lien due to the operation of § 522(c)(2)(B), which according to those courts prohibits exemptions from impairing the effect of a tax lien. *In re* Straight, 207 B.R. 217 (B.A.P. 10th Cir. 1997); *In re* Mattis, 93 B.R. 68 (Bankr. E.D. Pa. 1988); *In re* Perry, 90 B.R. 565 (Bankr. S.D. Fla. 1988); *cf. In re* Suarez, 182 B.R. 916 (Bankr. S.D. Fla. 1995) (section 522(c)(2) not applicable because notice of tax lien was not properly filed). However, these courts misread the statute. Section 522(c)(2)(B) refers to the effect of a tax lien on exempt property. It does not apply if that lien has been avoided pursuant to another section of the Code, and it contains no language limiting the avoiding powers of section 522(h). In any

Code, unfiled or improperly filed tax liens are not valid against a purchaser or judgment lien creditor. Under section 6323(h), even a filed tax lien is not valid against a bona fide purchaser of a motor vehicle or certain household goods.[347] In addition, debtors are likely to use section 545 in states where landlords' liens and distress for rent are common.[348] It can also be used in cases involving mechanics' liens,[349] innkeepers' liens, and other statutory liens, to the extent those liens are subject to the rights of bona fide purchasers under state law.[350] However, it should be noted that statutory liens may lose their character as statutory liens in some states once they are enforced, and thus become immunized to attack.[351] On the other hand, if the lien becomes effective only upon recordation, it may not be a statutory lien at all, but rather a judicial lien,[352] because it does not arise solely by force of a statute.[353]

10.4.2.6.4 Preferences—§ 547

10.4.2.6.4.1 In general

By far the most frequently used trustee avoiding power is the power to avoid preferences, codified in 11 U.S.C. § 547. With certain exceptions, set forth in section 547(c), the trustee may avoid any transfer of property of the debtor:

- To or for the benefit of a creditor;[354]
- For or on account of an antecedent debt owed by the debtor before such transfer was made;[355]
- Made while the debtor was insolvent;[356]
- Made

  (A) on or within ninety days before the date of filing of the petition[357] or

---

case, this issue does not arise if the trustee joins in the debtor's avoidance action. While this would be of little help to the debtor in chapter 7 cases in courts not permitting the exemption of property that was subject to a tax lien, it may be useful in chapter 13, as the debtor is entitled to possession of such property under § 1306(b) and the tax lien may secure a non-priority debt which is dischargeable. *See* United States v. Branch, 170 B.R. 577 (E.D.N.C. 1994) (objection that debtor could not utilize § 545 was rendered moot by chapter 13 trustee's joinder in action).

347 *But see In re* Berg, 121 F.3d 535 (9th Cir. 1997) (trustee not entitled to bona fide purchaser status and could not avoid tax lien); *In re* Janssen, 213 B.R. 558 (B.A.P. 8th Cir. 1997) (same); *In re* Walter, 45 F.3d 1023 (6th Cir. 1995) (trustee not entitled to protections that Internal Revenue Code § 6323(b)(2) gives to purchaser for full consideration).

348 *See, e.g., In re* Wedemeier, 237 F.3d 938 (8th Cir. 2001) (landlord's lien avoided).

349 *See In re* English, 112 B.R. 20 (Bankr. W.D. Ky. 1989) (mechanic's lien avoided where debtor had personal knowledge of intent to file lien but, in capacity of bona fide purchaser for value, could avoid lien which had not yet been perfected at time of filing); *In re* Saberman, 3 B.R. 316 (Bankr. N.D. Ill. 1980) (mechanic's lien avoided by debtor because under state law it would have been invalid against bona fide purchaser).

350 *In re* U.S. Leather, Inc., 271 B.R. 306 (Bankr. E.D. Wis. 2001) (water and sewer lien not perfected as of petition date); *see In re* America W. Airlines, 217 F.3d 1161 (9th Cir. 2000) (unperfected city tax lien was avoidable because it was not enforceable against bona fide purchaser on petition date); *In re* Loretto Winery, Ltd., 898 F.2d 715 (9th Cir. 1990) (trustee could not, as hypothetical bona fide purchaser, avoid statutory California producer's lien on partially processed grapes, because lien was good against bona fide purchasers).

351 *See In re* Mascenik, 6 Bankr. Ct. Dec. (LRP) 763 (D. Colo. 1980) (landlord's lien already enforced by sale could not be avoided).

352 *In re* Barbe, 24 B.R. 739 (Bankr. M.D. Pa. 1982).

353 See 11 U.S.C. § 101(53) defining "statutory lien."

354 The benefit may be indirect, as when a guarantor benefits from the payment of a debt of the debtor which she guaranteed. Because the guarantor would normally have a contingent claim against the debtor for contribution or indemnification in the event the guarantor ultimately paid the debt, the guarantor is a creditor who benefits from the transfer and has therefore received a preference. *See In re* Robinson Bros. Drilling, 877 F.2d 32 (10th Cir. 1989) (payments to non-insider creditors made at arms length are preferences subject to one-year limitations period because the payments ultimately benefit insider guarantors); Levit v. Ingersoll Rand Fin. Corp., 874 F.2d 1186 (7th Cir. 1989) (same); *In re* C-L Cartage Co., 899 F.2d 1490 (6th Cir. 1990) (same); *see also In re* Wesley Indus., 30 F.3d 1438 (11th Cir. 1994) (transfer of cash collateral that benefited insider within one year before petition could be a preference); cases cited in § 10.4.2.6.4.1, *infra.*

355 The transfer of a security interest in connection with a car loan, for example, is not on account of an antecedent debt. *In re* McFarland, 131 B.R. 627 (E.D. Tenn. 1990), *aff'd*, 943 F.2d 52 (6th Cir. 1991).

356 "Insolvent" is defined in 11 U.S.C. § 101(32) in a way that would include virtually all low-income debtors. Under that definition a debtor is solvent only if his or her assets exclusive of exempt property exceed his or her obligations. *In re* Babiker, 180 B.R. 458 (Bankr. E.D. Va. 1995); *see also In re* Taxman Clothing Co., 905 F.2d 166 (7th Cir. 1990) (costs of sale must be deducted in computing debtor's assets); *In re* Koubourlis, 869 F.2d 1319 (9th Cir. 1989) (creditor must present evidence to rebut presumption of insolvency and cannot simply question debtor's accounting methods); Porter v. Yukon Nat'l Bank, 866 F.2d 355 (10th Cir. 1989) (trustee need not present expert evidence concerning insolvency); *In re* Xonics Photochemical, Inc., 841 F.2d 198 (7th Cir. 1988) (contingent asset or liability must be reduced to its present or expected value for purposes of determining debtor's insolvency). Under 11 U.S.C. § 547(f) there is a rebuttable presumption that the debtor was insolvent during the ninety days prior to filing a case. Once the presumption is rebutted, the burden of persuasion may shift back to the debtor or trustee. Clay v. Traders Bank of Kan. City, 708 F.2d 1347 (8th Cir. 1983).

357 The ninety-day period is calculated by counting backward from the petition filing date. *In re* Nelson Co., 959 F.2d 1260 (3d Cir. 1992). Conversion from one chapter to another does not start the running of a new preference period. Vogel v. Russell Transfer, Inc., 852 F.2d 797 (4th Cir. 1988). The Code provides that a

(B) between ninety days and one year before the date of filing of the petition, if such creditor, at the time of such transfer was an insider;[358] and

- That enables such creditor to receive more than such creditor would receive if

(A) the case were a case under chapter 7 of the Code;

(B) the transfer had not been made; and

(C) such creditor received payment of such debt to the extent provided by the provisions of the Code.[359]

The basic purpose of this section is to promote equality among creditors by invalidating pre-bankruptcy seizures or transfers of the debtor's property that would give particular creditors more than they would receive in a chapter 7 liquidation. It also serves to deter creditors from engaging in a race to get at the debtor's property before bankruptcy, because they know that if they do obtain the property and perhaps hasten a bankruptcy, they will only have to surrender it to a trustee exercising the power to avoid preferences.[360]

The first issue in preference analysis is, of course, whether property of the debtor has been transferred at all. In some cases the debtor may merely be transferring property held in trust for others.[361] But if a party owing a debt to the debtor, as part of a transaction involving the debtor, pays that debt to a creditor of the debtor at the debtor's request, there has been a transfer of the debtor's property.[362]

---

transfer is perfected only when a bona fide purchaser from the debtor of real property or a judicial lien creditor on a simple contract for personal property or fixtures cannot acquire an interest superior to the trustee. 11 U.S.C. § 547(e). Thus, a transfer of a security interest normally occurs only when it has been perfected. *In re* Nelson Co., 959 F.2d 1260 (3d Cir. 1992) (transfer of judicial lien occurs when judgment is filed and docketed in county where debtor owns property). The period is not extended just because the final day for filing falls on a weekend or holiday. *In re* Greene, 223 F.3d 1064 (9th Cir. 2000); *In re* Butler, 3 B.R. 182 (Bankr. E.D. Tenn. 1980); *see also* Decatur Contracting v. Belin, Belin & Naddeo, 898 F.2d 339 (3d Cir. 1990). But a belated perfection of a security interest may be deemed under state law to relate back to the date it was granted. *In re* Hesser, 984 F.2d 345 (10th Cir. 1993); *see also* § 10.4.2.6.4.2, *infra*. For purposes of this section, a transfer made by check is deemed made when the check is honored. Barnhill v. Johnson, 503 U.S. 393, 112 S. Ct. 1386, 119 L. Ed. 2d 519 (1992).

358 "Insider" is defined at § 101(31) to include relatives of the debtor. "Relative" is defined at § 101(45). *See In re* Strickland, 230 B.R. 276 (Bankr. E.D. Va. 1999) (boyfriend of debtor's mother not an insider). Many of the cases involving insiders arise from payments on debts guaranteed by insiders. *See In re* Suffola, Inc., 2 F.3d 977 (9th Cir. 1993) (payment to outside creditor on debt guaranteed by insider was a payment for the benefit of the insider); *In re* Robinson Bros. Drilling, 877 F.2d 32 (10th Cir. 1989) (payments to non-insider creditors may be avoided as preferential going back one year from date of bankruptcy because debtor's insiders obtained release by virtue of the payments); Levit v. Ingersoll Rand Fin. Corp., 874 F.2d 1186 (7th Cir. 1989) (payments to non-insider creditors may be avoided if made during one year insider preference period if they benefited insiders who guaranteed the debts being paid); *see also In re* Westex Foods, Inc., 950 F.2d 1187 (5th Cir. 1992) (transfers by debtor garnishee to non-insider creditor in satisfaction of judgment against garnishee's president avoided because they benefited president, who was insider); *In re* C-L Cartage Co., 899 F.2d 1490 (6th Cir. 1990) (payments made within year before filing to bank in satisfaction of obligation to debtor's president and president's mother were avoidable).

The results, but not the reasoning, of many of these cases were overruled by a 1994 amendment creating a new § 550(c), which prohibits recovery of money or property transferred through insider preferences made more than ninety days before the petition from anyone other than the insider creditor who was preferred. However, this amendment does not prevent recovery from a non-insider when an insider was preferred during the ninety days pre-petition, nor does it prevent avoidance of the transfer without an affirmative recovery, which may be all that is necessary if, for example, the transfer was the granting of a lien on property.

359 The date on which the bankruptcy petition is filed rather than the date on which the turnover proceeding is filed is probably the

correct date for constructing a hypothetical chapter 7 case to determine how much the creditor would receive. *In re* Tenna Corp., 801 F.2d 819 (6th Cir. 1986). For the purpose of creating a hypothetical distribution, payments which the debtor has voluntarily agreed to make pursuant to a reaffirmation agreement are not included. *In re* Finn, 86 B.R. 902 (Bankr. E.D. Mich. 1988), *rev'd and remanded on other grounds*, 909 F.2d 903 (6th Cir. 1990). The fact that the debtor might have been able to exempt the property which was transferred is not a defense to a trustee's preference action. *In re* Noblit, 72 F.3d 757 (9th Cir. 1995); *see also* § 10.4.2.5, *supra*.

360 H.R. Rep. No. 95-595, at 177, 178 (1977).

361 Begier v. Internal Revenue Serv., 496 U.S. 53, 110 S. Ct. 2258, 110 L. Ed. 2d 246 (1990) (excise taxes which are supposed to be held by businesses in trust for the IRS are trust property of the IRS regardless of whether they are held in the debtor's general account; therefore payments of those funds to the IRS cannot be preferential even if made within ninety days of the debtor's bankruptcy); *see In re* Unicom Computer Corp., 13 F.3d 321 (9th Cir. 1994) (transfer of funds that were held in constructive trust was not a preference); *In re* Cal. Trade Technical Schools, Inc., 923 F.2d 641 (9th Cir. 1991) (debtor trade school's repayments of federal student assistance program monies effectively became trust funds upon their deposit and thus were not property of the debtor); *In re* Royal Golf Products Corp., 908 F.2d 911 (6th Cir. 1990) (payment to creditor by debtor's shareholder on behalf of debtor was a preferential transfer where debtor granted security interest to shareholder in exchange for payment, to the extent of the value of the security interest which depleted the estate); First Fed. of Mich. v. Barrow, 878 F.2d 912 (6th Cir. 1989) (unless creditor can trace funds held by debtor in commingled account, creditor cannot assert that payment was return of funds held in trust); *In re* Wey, 854 F.2d 196 (7th Cir. 1988) (no transfer made when debtor forfeits a down payment made in connection with a real estate contract); *In re* Bullion Reserve of N. Am., 836 F.2d 1214 (9th Cir. 1988) (payments by debtor to investor in "Ponzi" scheme were not a return of money held by debtor in trust; therefore a potentially avoidable transfer did occur).

362 *In re* Interior Wood Products, 986 F.2d 228 (8th Cir. 1993) (payment to unsecured creditor by purchaser of debtor's assets was a preference); *In re* Food Catering & Hous., Inc., 971 F.2d 396 (9th Cir. 1992) (same); *see also In re* Kemp Pac. Fisheries, 16 F.3d 313 (9th Cir. 1994) (payment by check from debtor's

In addition, all of the elements listed above must be present for a transfer to be considered a preference. Thus, if a validly secured creditor, with a security interest not otherwise avoidable, repossesses property worth less than the amount of the secured debt, no preference exists as that creditor would have had a right to that property or its full value in a liquidation.[363] But if an unsecured or partially secured creditor receives a payment on the debt within ninety days, that payment probably is a preference, as it will presumably be applied to that portion of the debt which is unsecured, and will allow the secured creditor to receive more than the total it would otherwise receive in a liquidation.[364] If property is transferred in exchange for a new debt, rather than an antecedent debt, no preference exists, nor does one exist if the property the creditor receives belongs to someone other than the debtor, such as a co-maker, including money that passes through the debtor's hands but is "earmarked" solely for payment to the creditor.[365] Of course, a transfer outside the specified time periods cannot

be a preference; section 547(e) sets forth rules for determining the date a transfer is deemed to have occurred.

10.4.2.6.4.2 Exceptions to preference avoiding power

The major exceptions to the preference section are listed in section 547(c).[366] The first is for exchanges that are intended to be and are in fact "substantially contemporaneous" exchanges for new value, for example, cash purchases, purchases paid for immediately by check, or security interests securing new value.[367] The Code does not define "substantially contemporaneous."[368] Also excepted are transfers

---

account, which bank honored despite the fact that account was temporarily overdrawn, was a transfer of debtor's property).

363 *See In re* Edl, 207 B.R. 611 (Bankr. W.D. Wis. 1997) (payment of fees to attorney was not a preference because attorney had equitable lien on divorce proceeds under state law). However, a security interest does not insulate a payment from being a preference if the security interest is in property owned by an entity other than the debtor, as that security interest would not provide better treatment for the creditor in the distribution of the *debtor's* assets. *In re* Virginia-Carolina Fin. Corp., 954 F.2d 193 (4th Cir. 1992).

364 *In re* Clark Pipe & Supply Co., 893 F.2d 693 (5th Cir. 1990); Porter v. Yukon Nat'l Bank, 866 F.2d 355 (10th Cir. 1989) (payment to under-secured creditor constitutes preference where unsecured claims would not be paid in full in liquidation); Drabkin v. A.I. Credit Corp., 800 F.2d 1153 (D.C. Cir. 1986); *In re* Lewis W. Shurtleff, Inc., 778 F.2d 1416 (9th Cir. 1985); *In re* McCormick, 5 B.R. 726 (Bankr. N.D. Ohio 1980).

365 *In re* Super. Stamp & Coin Co., 223 F.3d 1004 (9th Cir. 2000) (earmarking doctrine applied to prevent avoidance of transfer because transfer was funded by loans specifically designated for payment to transferee); *In re* Heitkamp, 137 F.3d 1087, 1088, 1089 (8th Cir. 1998); *In re* Ward, 230 B.R. 115 (B.A.P. 8th Cir. 1999) (earmarking doctrine protects lien obtained by creditor that refinanced debtor's auto loan because creditor's advance could be used only to pay auto loan). *But see In re* Bohlen Enterprises, Ltd., 859 F.2d 561 (8th Cir. 1988) (for earmarking doctrine to apply to funds lent to debtor to pay off an antecedent debt and thereby save payment from preference avoidance, debtor must have no control over the use of the non-debtor transferor's funds); *In re* Hartley, 825 F.2d 1067 (6th Cir. 1987) (debtor's transfer of security interest to third party who paid debtor's antecedent debt was a preference); *cf. In re* Hurt, 202 B.R. 611 (Bankr. C.D. Ill. 1996) (transfers to credit card grantors made by payments with balance transfer checks issued by new credit card grantor not protected by earmarking doctrine where funds made available by new creditor were not designated for particular specified creditors). One court has also held that no preference exists to the extent a creditor is paid more than the amount of its claim. *In re* Barge, 875 F.2d 508 (5th Cir. 1989). Presumably, however, a fraudulent transfer has occurred. *Id.*; *see* § 10.4.2.6.5, *infra*.

366 The creditor has the burden of establishing that it falls within one of the defenses. *In re* Chase & Sanborn Corp., 904 F.2d 588 (11th Cir. 1990).

367 11 U.S.C. § 547(c)(1); *see In re* Electronic Metal Products, Inc., 916 F.2d 1502 (10th Cir. 1990) (attorney's promise to continue working on litigation did not constitute new value); *In re* Kumar Bavishi & Associates, 906 F.2d 942 (3d Cir. 1990) (pre-petition payments of preexisting debts owed by debtor partnership to limited partners in exchange for partners personally guaranteeing loan to debtor partnership, which partnership was unable to obtain without guarantees, constituted transfers for new value); *In re* Chase & Sanborn Corp., 904 F.2d 588 (11th Cir. 1990) (corporate debtor's pre-petition payments to individual controlling another corporation for which the debtor corporation had guaranteed a debt constituted payments "for or on account of antecedent debt" despite contingent nature of guarantee); *In re* Spada, 903 F.2d 971 (3d Cir. 1990) (where three loans were consolidated into a new loan, a partial preference was granted to the extent that amount received by creditor was in excess of new value surrendered to debtor by creditor); *In re* Nucorp Energy, Inc., 902 F.2d 729 (9th Cir. 1990) (transfer of money from debtor to creditor in exchange for release of lien was not for new value where property subject to lien was valueless at time of transfer); *In re* Meredith Manor, Inc., 902 F.2d 257 (4th Cir. 1990) (advances and repayments pursuant to open credit line resulted in preferences to extent of difference between total preferences and total advances, provided that each advance could only offset transfers from the debtor prior to that particular advance); Lewis v. Diethorn, 893 F.2d 648 (3d Cir. 1990) (payment to settle case and thereby remove *lis pendens* constitutes exchange for new value); *In re* Allen, 888 F.2d 1299 (10th Cir. 1989) (transfer of interest under escrow agreement for money paid by creditor is exchange for new value); E.R. Fegert, Inc. v. Seaboard Sur. Co., 887 F.2d 955 (9th Cir. 1989) (payment to third parties which reduces surety's equitable lien is exchange for new value); *In re* Jet Fla. Sys., Inc., 861 F.2d 1555 (11th Cir. 1988) (restoration of debtor's prior status through forbearance of creditor does not constitute new value for payment); *In re* Bellanca Aircraft Corp., 850 F.2d 1275 (8th Cir. 1988) (payment made by creditor to other creditors of the debtor can constitute new value for debtor's payments); *In re* Pitman, 843 F.2d 235 (6th Cir. 1988) (transfer of mortgage is exchange for new value where it is made pursuant to an executory contract for sale of property and the debtor receives a deed at the time of transfer); *In re* Energy Co-op, Inc., 832 F.2d 997 (7th Cir. 1987) (release of existing liability not "new value"); *In re* Calvert, 227 B.R. 153 (B.A.P. 8th Cir. 1998) (release of security interest obtained when debt was first incurred did not provide new value).

368 *See In re* Dorholt, Inc., 224 F.3d 871 (8th Cir. 2000) (transfer of security interest can be substantially contemporaneous even if

made prior to the debtor's receipt of new value from the creditor, as long as the creditor obtained no other non-avoidable security for the new value.[369]

Similarly, payments on debts incurred in the ordinary course of business or financial affairs of the debtor and transferee are excepted.[370] This exception includes most payments for current utility services, goods bought with payment due in thirty days, and most charge accounts. Section 547(c)(2) applies equally to long-term and short-term debt.[371] To be within the ordinary course of business, the payments must be ordinary in relation to other business dealings between creditor and debtor, made according to ordinary business terms, and ordinary in relation to standards in the relevant industry.[372] Unusually late payments are ordinarily not excepted, however.[373] Payments made pursuant to settlement agreements have been found to be outside the ordinary course of a debtor's business.[374] Nor may a payment following a special or unusual request by a creditor for payment be considered to be within the ordinary course of business.[375] It is not clear whether a major loan of a type incurred only once or a few times in a debtor's lifetime would be considered to be in the ordinary course of the debtor's financial affairs.[376] The "ordinary course" language may also open the door to challenges of fraudulent or

---

security interest not perfected within time period allowed for relation back under § 547(e)(2)); *In re* Lewellyn & Co. Inc., 929 F.2d 424 (8th Cir. 1991) (new value can be given before or after the transfer; test is whether exchange is "substantially" contemporaneous); *In re* Arnett, 731 F.2d 358 (6th Cir. 1984) (thirty-three days later not substantially contemporaneous); *In re* Standard Food Services, Inc., 723 F.2d 820 (11th Cir. 1984) (check replacing earlier contemporaneous bounced check not substantially contemporaneous). The court may look to the intent of the parties in order to determine whether an "exchange" has really taken place. *See In re* Prescott, 805 F.2d 719 (7th Cir. 1986) (bank's taking possession of the debtor's certificate of deposit held not to be an exchange of value where bank simultaneously allowed overdrafts on debtor's other accounts). Also at issue may be the actual value of the property exchanged, as it bears on the issue of whether a *quid pro quo* was really intended. But at least one court of appeals has held that a valuation is not required. *In re* George Rodman, Inc., 792 F.2d 125 (10th Cir. 1986).

369 11 U.S.C. § 547(c)(4). *See generally* S. Technical College, Inc. v. Hood, 89 F.3d 1381 (8th Cir. 1996) (debtor's use of leased properties after payment to lessor constituted new value to extent lender did not have security therefor); *In re* Kroh Bros. Dev. Co., 930 F.2d 648 (8th Cir. 1991) (creditor may be able to assert "new value" defense even though it had received consideration for the new value from a third party); *In re* N.Y. City Shoes, Inc., 880 F.2d 679 (3d Cir. 1989). To assert this defense, the new value for each transfer must be given after the transfer that the debtor seeks to avoid. *In re* Toyota of Jefferson, Inc., 14 F.3d 1088 (5th Cir. 1994); *see also In re* Tenn. Chem. Co., 112 F.3d 234 (6th Cir. 1997) (date of receipt of check, rather than date check was honored, used to determine timing of new value).

370 11 U.S.C. § 547(c)(2); *see, e.g.,* Kleven v. Household Bank, 334 F.3d 638 (7th Cir. 2003) (payments on tax refund anticipation loans were in ordinary course of business, even if debtors had never had such a loan before); *In re* Jan Weilert, RV, Inc., 315 F.3d 1192 (9th Cir. 2003) ("ordinary business terms" encompasses wide range of practices of similarly situated debtors); Fid. Sav. & Inv. Co. v. New Hope Baptist, 880 F.2d 1172 (10th Cir. 1989) (payments made by lender to redeem investor's savings certificates are within ordinary course of business); *In re* Fulghum Constr. Corp., 872 F.2d 739 (6th Cir. 1989) (repayment of advances to debtor's sole shareholder, though irregular, were consistent with ordinary course of dealing between parties); *In re* Smith-Douglass, Inc., 842 F.2d 729 (4th Cir. 1988) (payment of interest as it comes due is in the ordinary course of business); *In re* Colonial Discount Corp., 807 F.2d 594 (7th Cir. 1987) (debtor's transaction typical of affairs over past twenty years); *In re* Powerine Oil Co., 126 B.R. 790 (B.A.P. 9th Cir. 1991) (payments made outside time for payment specified in the contract are not within the ordinary course of business); *In re* Loretto Winery, Ltd., 107 B.R. 707 (B.A.P. 9th Cir. 1989) (determination of ordinary course requires objective evaluation of similarly situated businesses). *See generally In re* Molded Acoustical Products, 18 F.3d 217 (3d Cir. 1994) (discussion of "ordinary business terms").

371 Union Bank v. Wolas, 502 U.S. 151, 112 S. Ct. 527, 116 L. Ed. 2d 514 (1991).

372 *In re* A.W. & Associates, 136 F.3d 1439 (11th Cir. 1998) (court must consider industry standards to determine whether payment was in ordinary course of business); *In re* Fred Hawes Org., 957 F.2d 239 (6th Cir. 1992). As with other exceptions in § 547(c), it is the transferee's burden to present evidence supporting the exception, such as evidence of normal industry practices. *See In re* Roblin Indus., 78 F.3d 30 (2d Cir. 1996).

373 *In re* Gateway Pac. Corp., 153 F.3d 915 (8th Cir. 1998); *In re* Xonics Imaging Inc., 837 F.2d 763 (7th Cir. 1988) (late payment of rent after grace period not in ordinary course of business); *In re* Ewald Bros., Inc., 45 B.R. 52 (Bankr. D. Minn. 1984). Late payments may sometimes be considered within the ordinary course of business if they are consistent with the pattern of prior payments and within the range of ordinary practices of similar firms. *In re* Tolona Pizza Products Corp., 3 F.3d 1029 (9th Cir. 1993); *In re* Yurika Foods Corp., 888 F.2d 42 (6th Cir. 1989) (evidence that payments are commonly made late both by particular debtor and by others in the industry supports conclusion that such payments are in ordinary course of business).

374 *In re* Richardson, 94 B.R. 56 (Bankr. E.D. Pa. 1988) (public housing tenants' payment made pursuant to settlement of eviction action found to be an avoidable preference).

375 *See, e.g., In re* Meredith Hoffman Partners, 12 F.3d 1549 (10th Cir. 1993) (escrow arrangement under which creditor received payments was not a normal financing relationship); *In re* J.P. Fyfe, Inc., 891 F.2d 66 (3d Cir. 1989) (payment made pursuant to special arrangement reached after creditor learned of debtor's financial problems not within ordinary course of business); *In re* Seawinds, Ltd., 888 F.2d 640 (9th Cir. 1989) (payments made under creditor pressure not within ordinary course); *In re* Craig Oil Co., 785 F.2d 1563 (11th Cir. 1986) (request "for a show of good faith" when debtor is in difficult financial straits takes a payment out of the ordinary course of business exception).

376 *See In re* Finn, 86 B.R. 902 (Bankr. E.D. Mich. 1988) (long-term loan is not within the debtor's ordinary course of business), *rev'd* 909 F.2d 903 (6th Cir. 1990) (incurring long-term consumer debt may be in ordinary course of debtor's affairs, depending upon the facts of the case); *see also* Union Bank v. Wolas, 502 U.S. 151, 112 S. Ct. 527, 116 L. Ed. 2d 514 (1991) (§ 547(c)(2) applies to long-term debt); *In re* Bishop, Baldwin, Rewald, Dillingham & Wong, 819 F.2d 214 (9th Cir. 1987)

unfair transactions in which security interests are taken in the debtor's property, or loans and refinancings prompted by extraordinary factors in the debtor's situation.

Certain security interests created within ninety days are also excluded from the preference category. These are:

- Security interests that secure new value given by the secured party to enable the debtor to acquire property and used by the debtor for that purpose, if perfected within twenty days after the debtor receives possession of the property;[377]
- Security interests in inventory or receivables, to some extent;[378] and
- Statutory liens that are not avoidable under section 545.[379]

Under section 547(c)(7) added by the 1994 amendments, a preference also may not be avoided if the transfer was a bona fide payment of a debt in the nature of alimony, maintenance, or support to spouse, former spouse or child of the debtor. The definition of what constitutes alimony, maintenance, or support is a flexible one, which has given rise to much litigation under the exception to discharge provisions of Code section 523(a)(5).[380] It is clear, however, that this exception to the preference avoiding power does not apply to debts that have been assigned to governmental units or to any other entity.[381]

Finally, one additional limitation was placed upon the avoidance of preferences by the 1984 Code amendments. Neither the trustee nor the debtor in a case filed by a consumer debtor may avoid a preference or preferences totaling less than $600.00 to a single creditor.[382] This provision, undoubtedly directed at consumer debtor preference actions against loan companies and utilities, reduces the number of preferences avoidable by debtors under 11 U.S.C. § 522(h).[383] It is important to note, however, that it applies only to section 547, and not to any of the other avoiding powers. Thus, for example, debtors may be able to use the lien avoidance provisions under section 522(f) to recover garnished wages still in the hands of their employers.[384] If the debtor retains a property interest in the garnished wages under state law, and the debtor can claim that interest as exempt using a wild card or some other exemption, the judicial lien on the wages resulting from the garnishment procedure may be voided and the funds returned to the debtor.[385]

10.4.2.6.4.3 Debtor's use of preference avoiding power

The debtor's use of the section 547 avoiding powers through section 522(h) can be quite varied. Levies and execution sales by otherwise unsecured creditors,[386] includ-

---

(payment as part of a Ponzi scheme not made in ordinary course of business).

377 11 U.S.C. § 547(c)(3); Fid. Fin. Services Inc. v. Fink, 522 U.S. 211, 118 S. Ct. 651, 139 L. Ed. 2d 571 (1998) (time period in Code takes precedence over longer perfection period in state law). The time period for perfection was changed from ten days to twenty days by the 1994 amendments to the Code. *See In re* Davis, 734 F.2d 604 (11th Cir. 1984); *In re* Arnett, 731 F.2d 358 (6th Cir. 1984). Nor can transfers outside the § 547(c)(3) time period be protected under the "contemporaneous exchange exception." *In re* Holder, 892 F.2d 29 (4th Cir. 1989); *In re* Tressler, 771 F.2d 791 (3d Cir. 1985) (agreeing that transfer perfected after time period is not protected by this provision or the "contemporaneous exchange" exception); *In re* Vance, 721 F.2d 259 (9th Cir. 1983). *But see In re* Dorholt, Inc., 224 F.3d 871 (8th Cir. 2000) (transfer of security interest can be substantially contemporaneous even if security interest not perfected within time period allowed for relation back under different Code provision).

378 11 U.S.C. § 547(c)(5).

379 11 U.S.C. § 547(c)(6); *In re* Lionel Corp., 29 F.3d 88 (2d Cir. 1994) (mechanic's lien could not be avoided under § 547). However, the statutory lien must be perfected as of the petition date for this exemption to apply. *In re* Nucorp Energy, Inc., 902 F.2d 729 (9th Cir. 1990).

380 *See* 14.4.3.5, *infra; see also* Henry J. Sommer & Margaret Doe McGarity, Collier Family Law and the Bankruptcy Code ¶¶ 6.04, 6.05.

381 11 U.S.C. § 547(c)(7)(A); *see In re* Neuman, 265 B.R. 904 (Bankr. N.D. Ohio 2001) (payments made to child support enforcement agency but then passed on to debtor's former

spouse were not made on debt that had been assigned and could not be avoided).

382 11 U.S.C. § 547(c)(8) (formerly § 547(c)(7)); *see In re* Holyfield, 50 B.R. 695 (Bankr. D. Md. 1985). This provision does not, however, allow a creditor receiving an avoided preference to retain the initial $599.99. *In re* Via, 107 B.R. 91 (Bankr. W.D. Va. 1989); *In re* Vickery, 63 B.R. 222 (Bankr. E.D. Tenn. 1986). It also does not shield particular transfers under $600.00 if the aggregate of all transfers to a creditor is at least $600.00. *In re* Hailes, 77 F.3d 873 (5th Cir. 1996); *In re* Clark, 217 B.R. 89 (E.D. Ky. 1995); *In re* Djerf, 188 B.R. 586 (Bankr. D. Minn. 1995); *In re* Alarcon, 186 B.R. 135 (Bankr. D.N.M. 1995).

383 *But see* § 10.4.2.3.1, *supra.*

384 *See* § 10.4.2.3, *infra.*

385 *In re* Thomas, 215 B.R. 873 (Bankr. E.D. Mo. 1997); *In re* Youngblood, 212 B.R. 593 (Bankr. E.D. Ill. 1997); *In re* Garcia, 155 B.R. 173 (N.D. Ill. 1993); *In re* Nunally, 103 B.R. 376 (Bankr. D.R.I. 1989); *In re* Buzzell, 56 B.R. 197 (Bankr. D. Md. 1986).

386 Deel Rent-A-Car v. Levine, 721 F.2d 750 (11th Cir. 1983); *In re* Bova, 272 B.R. 49 (Bankr. D.N.H. 2002) (avoiding attachment of real estate obtained to secure criminal restitution order); *In re* Rhoads, 130 B.R. 565 (Bankr. C.D. Cal. 1991) (recordation of abstract of judgment avoided as preferential); *In re* Hines, 3 B.R. 370 (Bankr. D.S.D. 1980) (execution sale avoided by debtors). However, a levy may be held to relate back to the date of the writ of execution under state law, at least in the Third and Fifth Circuits. *In re* Latham, 823 F.2d 108 (5th Cir. 1987); *In re* RAMCO Am. Int'l, 754 F.2d 130 (3d Cir. 1985); *see also In re* Lane, 980 F.2d 601 (9th Cir. 1992) (judgment lien related back to date creditor obtained *lis pendens* due to operation of § 547(e)(1), which deems transfer of real estate to have been perfected when a bona fide purchaser could not acquire a superior interest in the property); *In re* Wind Power Sys., Inc.,

ing wage garnishments[387] within ninety days prior to filing of the bankruptcy, are clearly avoidable. A payment made pursuant to a criminal restitution order can be recovered, even if it was made through a third party, such as a court clerk.[388] Tax refund intercepts made by the Internal Revenue Service on behalf of another entity, such as a state student loan guarantee agency, child support enforcement office or another governmental agency can be set aside as preferences if made within the ninety day look-back period. These types of transfers normally meet all of the required tests for preferences and are definitely considered involuntary. Additionally, payments made to and retained by collection agencies can be recovered directly from the agency.[389] The fact that a debt is nondischargeable should not affect the use of this power.[390] Thus, a debtor may be able to set aside a tax levy,[391] or perhaps other tax payments.[392]

Repossessions pursuant to valid security interests which could not otherwise be avoided generally do not constitute preferences.[393] However, if the security interest was extracted within the preference period in exchange for forbearance on a pre-existing debt,[394] or if new security during that period for a refinancing exceeds the new value given, then the security interest and any enforcement of it would constitute preferences. Also, if property of greater value than the debt has been acquired by the creditor because a sale has not yet been scheduled, because the creditor has chosen to exercise a right of strict foreclosure and keep the property, or because the creditor has acquired the property at a foreclosure sale, then the creditor may be deemed to have received a preference by recovering property of greater value than it would receive in a liquidation.[395]

---

841 F.2d 288 (9th Cir. 1988) (attachment lien by levy in California relates back to date on which creditor obtained a temporary protective order covering the debtor's assets); *In re* Ware, 99 B.R. 103 (Bankr. M.D. Fla. 1989) (judgment lien).

387 *In re* Wade, 219 B.R. 815 (B.A.P. 8th Cir. 1998) (debtor could avoid garnishment of wages earned within ninety days of petition); *In re* Pierce, 6 B.R. 18 (Bankr. N.D. Ill. 1980); *see also* Bank of Am. (USA) v. Stine, 252 B.R. 902 (D. Md. 2000) (state statute making exemptions inapplicable to wage garnishment did not preclude avoidance of garnishment as preference and exemption of proceeds), *aff'd sub nom. In re* Stine, 360 F.3d 455 (4th Cir. 2004). Some courts had held that under particular state laws the garnishment must have been first initiated within the ninety days. *In re* Conner, 733 F.2d 1560 (11th Cir. 1984); *In re* Riddervold, 647 F.2d 342 (2d Cir. 1981); *see also In re* Battery One-Stop Ltd., 36 F.3d 493 (6th Cir. 1994) (transfer occurred under Ohio law when notice of garnishment was served); *In re* Hagen, 922 F.2d 742 (11th Cir. 1991) (where attorney's charging lien was created prior to ninety-day period, transfer of amount of lien during preference period does not constitute avoidable preference). These cases do not properly recognize the provision in § 547(e)(3) that the transfer is not made until the debtor has acquired rights in the property. *See In re* Morehead, 249 F.3d 445 (6th Cir. 2001) (*Ridderwold* and *Coppie* ignore plain meaning of § 547(e)(3)); *In re* James, 257 B.R. 673 (B.A.P. 8th Cir. 2001) (transfers pursuant to garnishment order did not occur until debtor earned wages); *In re* Johnson, 239 B.R. 416 (Bankr. M.D. Ala. 1999) (transfer occurred when debtor acquired interest in wages); *In re* Kaufman, 187 B.R. 167 (Bankr. E.D. La. 1995) (same); *In re* Polce, 168 B.R. 580 (Bankr. N.D. W. Va. 1994) (same); *In re* Larson, 21 B.R. 264 (Bankr. D. Utah 1982); *In re* Cox, 10 B.R. 268 (Bankr. D. Md. 1981). They were also undermined by the Supreme Court's decision in Barnhill v. Johnson, 503 U.S. 393, 112 S. Ct. 1386, 118 L. Ed. 2d 39 (1992), which held that a transfer by check did not occur until the bank honored the check. *See In re* Freedom Group, 50 F.3d 408 (7th Cir. 1995) (*Barnhill* overruled cases that had held that notice of garnishment of bank account constituted transfer); *In re* Arway, 227 B.R. 216 (Bankr. W.D.N.Y. 1998) (*Riddervold* case overruled by *Barnhill*).

388 *In re* Kirk, 38 B.R. 257 (Bankr. D. Kan. 1984).

389 *In re* Mill St., Inc., 96 B.R. 268 (B.A.P. 9th Cir. 1989).

390 *See In re* Chase & Sanborn Corp., 904 F.2d 588 (11th Cir. 1990) (pre-bankruptcy fraud does not preclude avoiding preferential payments on the resulting debt); *In re* Car Renovators, 946 F.2d 780 (11th Cir. 1991) (nondischargeable restitution payment may be avoided as a preference).

391 *In re* Williams, 153 B.R. 74 (Bankr. S.D. Ala. 1992) (IRS levy on debtor's wages within 90 days before petition avoided as preference), *aff'd*, 156 B.R. 77 (S.D. Ala. 1993); *In re* Ballard, 131 B.R. 97 (Bankr. W.D. Wis.); *In re* RBT Roofing Structures, 42 B.R. 908 (Bankr. D. Nev. 1984), *aff'd*, 887 F.2d 981 (9th Cir. 1989). However, the actual fixing of a tax lien is not avoidable to the extent that it is a statutory lien not avoidable under 11 U.S.C. § 545. *In re* Biddle, 31 B.R. 449 (Bankr. N.D. Iowa 1983). Note, however, there are important issues related to sovereign immunity. *See* § 13.3.2.2, *infra*. Establishing a waiver of sovereign immunity is a necessary prerequisite to avoiding a tax levy as a preference.

392 Drabkin v. District of Columbia, 824 F.2d 1102 (D.C. Cir. 1987). Again the question of voluntariness arises. In view of the criminal penalties for nonpayment, are tax payments voluntary?

393 *See In re* Cannon, 237 F.3d 716 (6th Cir. 2000) (bank's charge backs against debtor's account for deposited checks returned for insufficient funds were based on security interest under Tennessee law).

394 In general it has been held that forbearance from taking an action which could be taken by the creditor, such as eviction or foreclosure, does not constitute new value. *See In re* Air Conditioning of Stuart, 845 F.2d 293 (11th Cir. 1988); *In re* Jet Fla. Sys., Inc., 841 F.2d 1082 (11th Cir. 1988) (landlord's forbearance in terminating lease does not constitute new value); *In re* Duffy, 3 B.R. 263 (Bankr. S.D.N.Y. 1980).

395 *In re* Andrews, 262 B.R. 299 (Bankr. M.D. Pa. 2001) (foreclosure sale can be avoided if secured claim was substantially less than property value obtained by creditor); *In re* Park N. Partners, Ltd., 85 B.R. 916 (Bankr. N.D. Ga. 1988) (creditor received preference when it purchased property of debtor at foreclosure sale, the value of which exceeded the amount of the debtor's secured obligation to the creditor); *In re* Fountain, 32 B.R. 965 (Bankr. W.D. Mo. 1983) (property purchased at foreclosure sale worth more than secured debt); *In re* Seidel, 27 B.R. 347 (Bankr. E.D. Pa. 1983) (truck returned to creditor worth more than secured debt); *see also In re* Missionary Baptist Found., 796 F.2d 752 (5th Cir. 1986) (question of the value of the transferred property arises which should be determined in the bankruptcy court); *In re* Winters, 119 B.R. 283 (Bankr. M.D. Fla. 1990) (foreclosure sale held to be preference). *But see In re* Ehring, 900 F.2d 184 (9th Cir. 1990) (creditor who purchased debtor's house at pre-petition foreclosure sale did not receive more from foreclosure than it would have in a liquidation, even though

Security interests in general, though, raise the thorny problems of voluntariness. Security interests are almost voluntary by definition. Section 101(51) defines security interest as a "lien created by agreement." But what of the security interest granted only under threat of dire consequences for example, foreclosure or eviction? Like the payment of utility arrearages under a threat of midwinter cutoff, rent arrearages under threat of eviction, or debt arrearages under threat of imprisonment, such a transfer can quite arguably be considered involuntary and made under duress.[396] Other transfers that might well be considered involuntary include those pursuant to contractual terms that a debtor does not understand.[397] As it is widely accepted that many of the terms used in consumer credit contracts are neither bargained for nor understood by consumers, this provision could result in setting aside wage assignments[398] and other security arrangements.

10.4.2.6.5 Fraudulent transfers—§ 548

Besides the power to avoid transfers fraudulent under state law that is bestowed upon the trustee through section 544, the Code also contains its own fraudulent transfer avoidance power, in section 548.

Under the Code's definition, the trustee may avoid a transfer or obligation if the transfer[399] or obligation was made or incurred within one year before the case was filed and:

(1) The transfer or obligation was made or incurred with actual intent to hinder, delay or defraud[400] any entity

to which the debtor was or became indebted, on or after the date that the transfer occurred or obligation was incurred or

(2)(A) The debtor received less than a reasonably equivalent value for the transfer or obligation and

(B)(i) the debtor was insolvent[401] on the date of the transfer or obligation or became insolvent as a result of the transfer or obligation, or

(ii) the debtor was engaged in business or was about to engage in a business or transaction with unreasonably small capital, or

(iii) the debtor intended to incur, or believed that he or she would incur, debts beyond his or her ability to pay.

Occasionally, consumer debtors may face the trustee's use of this avoiding power to undo gifts they have made during the year preceding bankruptcy.[402] Courts have considered, with varying results, whether charitable contributions are fraudulent transfers under this section.[403] And trustees have

---

creditor resold property pre-petition for more than amount of outstanding debt).

396 *See In re* Mason, 69 B.R. 876 (Bankr. E.D. Pa. 1987) (payments of rents into escrow pursuant to court order pending appeal held involuntary); *see also* § 10.4.2.5, *supra*.

397 *See In re* Davis, 169 B.R. 285 (E.D.N.Y. 1994) (sale/leaseback agreement in which the debtor executed a deed to avoid a threatened foreclosure found to be involuntary based on misrepresentations made by the transferee).

398 *In re* Peterson, 14 Clearinghouse Rev. 459, Clearinghouse No. 29,153 (Bankr. W.D. Mich. 1980) (wage assignment deemed involuntary due to lack of debtor understanding).

399 A threshold question is whether a transfer of the debtor's property has occurred at all. *See In re* Atchison, 925 F.2d 209 (7th Cir. 1991) (no transfer occurs under state law when debtor disclaims inheritance); *In re* Bright, 241 B.R. 664 (B.A.P. 9th Cir. 1999) (disclaimer of inheritance was not a transfer); *In re* Kellman, 248 B.R. 430 (Bankr. M.D. Fla. 1999) (adding wife's name as joint owner of bank account was done only as convenience to deal with possible disability of husband, so removal of her name was not transfer of any interest in account to husband). *But see In re* Green, 986 F.2d 145 (6th Cir. 1993) (in unusual situation of debtor who, having a contractual right to receive property under a will, agreed to give up that right, the exercise of a power of appointment to terminate the debtor's rights under a will was found to be a fraudulent transfer); *In re* Stevens, 112 B.R. 175 (Bankr. S.D. Tex. 1989).

400 Although a single "badge of fraud" may spur suspicion of

fraudulent intent, confluence of several badges can be conclusive evidence of actual intent to defraud. Max Sugarman Funeral Home Inc. v. A.D.B. Investors, 926 F.2d 1248 (1st Cir. 1991); *see also* Kelly v. Armstrong, 141 F.3d 799 (8th Cir. 1998) (presence of multiple badges of fraud shifts burden of production and persuasion to debtor).

401 It should be remembered that insolvency is defined at 11 U.S.C. § 101(32) as something other than normal balance sheet insolvency. In determining whether a debtor is insolvent, the liability on a contingent debt, such as a guarantee, is computed by multiplying the amount of the debt by the probability that the debtor would have to pay it. Covey v. Commercial Nat'l Bank of Peoria, 960 F.2d 657 (7th Cir. 1992).

402 *See, e.g., In re* Roosevelt, 220 F.3d 1032 (9th Cir. 2000) (trustee permitted to avoid transfer of property pursuant to marital settlement agreement because wife's relinquishment of community property income in debtor's professional education not considered value under § 548); Butler v. Nationsbank, 58 F.3d 1022 (4th Cir. 1995) (trustee permitted to recover payment made by debtor to satisfy her husband's debt); *In re* Trujillo, 215 B.R. 200 (B.A.P. 9th Cir. 1997) (trustee permitted to avoid transfer of vehicle titles to debtors' children, even though vehicles could have been exempted had they not been transferred). *Compare In re* Fornabio, 187 B.R. 780 (Bankr. S.D. Fla. 1995) (because homestead was completely exempt under Florida law, transfer of homestead to wife was not an attempt to hinder, delay, or defraud creditors) *with* Tavenner v. Smoot, 257 F.3d 401 (4th Cir. 2001) (fact that property was exemptible was not a defense to fraudulent transfer proceeding). *See also* Havoco of Am., Ltd. v. Hill, 197 F.3d 1135 (11th Cir. 1999) (creditor could not challenge as fraudulent, by way of objection to exemptions, transfer of property to entireties; adversary proceeding including wife as defendant was necessary); *In re* Loomer, 198 B.R. 755 (Bankr. D. Neb. 1996) (trustee could not recover alleged fraudulent transfer to pension plan because plan assets were protected from alienation, but trustee could obtain judgment against debtors, as parties benefited by transfer, which would be enforceable against non-ERISA, non-exempt assets).

403 *Compare In re* Young, 82 F.3d 1407 (8th Cir. 1996) (application of § 548 to church contributions violates Religious Freedom Restoration Act, 42 U.S.C. § 2000bb) *with In re* Tessier, 190

also attempted to avoid transfers for gambling losses as transfers made without reasonably equivalent value in exchange.[404]

Because some courts had allowed trustees to set aside religious contributions,[405] Congress amended section 548 to specifically protect most religious or charitable contributions from avoidance by the trustee. The Religious Liberty and Charitable Donation Protection Act of 1998[406] amended the Code to provide that charitable to qualified religious or charitable entities or organizations, that are protected from avoidance under section 548(a)(1)(B).[407] Such contributions are protected if they did not exceed fifteen percent of the debtor's gross income in the year they were made or, if they were greater than that amount, were consistent with past giving practices of the debtor.[408] Under the language of the provision, the fifteen percent limit applies to each transfer individually, even if the aggregate in a single year exceeds fifteen percent. However, courts have read the language to mean that if the fifteen percent limit is exceeded and there was no past giving no part of the contribution is protected.[409] The Act also defined, for purposes of section 548, as well as amendments to sections 544, 707(b) and 1325(b), the terms "charitable contribution" and "qualified religious or charitable entity or organization." Section 548(d)(3) defines "charitable contribution" as a contribution made by a natural person consisting or cash or a financial instrument, and section 548(d)(4) defines "qualified religious or charitable entity or organization" as an entity described in section 170(c)(1) or 170(c)(2) of the Internal Revenue Code.

The most important of section 548's provisions for consumer debtors is the provision which classifies as fraudulent any transfer that occurred within a year preceding the petition for less than reasonably equivalent value while the debtor was insolvent. As most consumer debtors are insolvent under the Code's definition in 11 U.S.C. § 101(32), this section allows the debtor to avoid any transfer (as transfer is broadly defined in section 101(54)) within the previous year[410] which was for less than reasonably equivalent value, as long as the transfer was not voluntary and the debtor did not conceal the property.[411]

A common use of this power by consumer debtors in the past was to avoid transfers such as mortgage foreclosures, tax sales,[412] repossessions or execution sales where the property in question was worth significantly more than the value received for it.[413] Despite seemingly clear language in the statute supporting such use, the Supreme Court held in *BFP v. Resolution Trust Corp.*,[414] that a regularly conducted, non-collusive foreclosure sale could not be avoided under section 548.

The court's holding appears to also preclude use of section 548 in cases where secured creditors sell property at public auctions pursuant to Article 9 the Uniform Commercial Code, but should leave open the possibility of challenging a private sale or a strict foreclosure pursuant to the provisions of that Article or in a mortgage context.[415] In the *BFP* opinion, the Supreme Court expressly limited its hold-

---

B.R. 396 (Bankr. D. Mont. 1995) (Religious Freedom Restoration Act found unconstitutional in § 548 case) *and In re* Young, 152 B.R. 939 (D. Minn. 1993) (trustee allowed to recover $13,450.00 in church contributions made by debtors). *In re* Young was remanded by the Supreme Court for reconsideration in light of the Supreme Court's decision that the Religious Freedom Restoration Act (RFRA) was unconstitutional (117 S. Ct. 2502 (1997)), and was reaffirmed by the appellate court to the extent that RFRA modified federal and not state law. 141 F.3d 854 (8th Cir. 1998). Other courts have found contributions to churches to be fraudulent transfers that do not violate RFRA. *In re* Bloch, 207 B.R. 944 (D. Colo. 1997); *In re* Rivera, 214 B.R. 101 (Bankr. S.D.N.Y. 1997). The issue was essentially mooted by The Religious Liberty and Charitable Donation Protection Act of 1998 amending sections 544 and 548 as discussed below.

404 *See In re* Chomakos, 69 F.3d 769 (6th Cir. 1995) (denying avoidance because debtors received reasonably equivalent value for their bets).

405 *E.g., In re* Newman, 203 B.R. 468 (D. Kan. 1996); *In re* Gomes, 219 B.R. 286 (Bankr. D. Or. 1998).

406 Pub. L. No. 105-183, 112 Stat. 517 (1998). The amendment applies to cases pending on or after the date of the Act.

407 The 1998 Act also redesignated the subsections of § 548, so that § 548(a)(1)(B) is the former § 548(a)(2).

408 11 U.S.C. § 548(a)(2).

409 *See also In re* Jackson, 249 B.R. 373 (Bankr. D.N.J. 2000) ($20,000.00 contribution fully avoided because it was not consistent with past practices).

410 Section 548(d)(1) governs how the one year is calculated. In the context of a judicial sale, one court of appeals has held that the significant transfer occurs on the date of the sale rather than the date on which the transfer is recorded. That court thus found a transfer to be outside of the year preceding the debtors' bankruptcy. Butler v. Lomas & Nettleton Co., 862 F.2d 1015 (3d Cir. 1988). An Illinois bankruptcy court, construing a peculiar Illinois tax sale statute, concluded that a transfer of property pursuant to a tax foreclosure sale occurs at the end of the statutory redemption period rather than on the date of sale. *In re* McKeever, 132 B.R. 996 (Bankr. N.D. Ill. 1991).

411 11 U.S.C. § 522(h).

412 At least one appellate court has held that in a proceeding to set aside a tax sale conducted by selling a tax sale certificate, the proceeding must be brought against the taxing authority as well as the tax sale purchaser. *In re* Slack-Horner Foundries, Inc., 971 F.2d 577 (10th Cir. 1992).

413 *See, e.g., In re* Hulm, 738 F.2d 323 (8th Cir. 1984).

414 511 U.S. 531, 114 S. Ct. 1757, 128 L. Ed. 2d 556 (1994).

415 *In re* Sherman, 223 B.R. 555 (B.A.P. 10th Cir. 1998) (*BFP* decision not applicable to tax sale with no competitive bidding); *In re* Fitzgerald, 255 B.R. 807 (Bankr. D. Conn. 2000) (BFP decision not applicable to strict foreclosure); *In re* Fitzgerald, 237 B.R. 252 (Bankr. D. Conn. 1999) (*BFP* not applicable to foreclosure without public sale); *In re* Wentworth, 221 B.R. 316 (Bankr. D. Conn. 1998) (tax forfeiture proceeding without judicial oversight or competitive bidding not governed by *BFP* decision); *In re* Grady, 202 B.R. 120 (Bankr. N.D. Iowa 1996) (*BFP* not applicable to land contract forfeiture). The *BFP* decision does not appear to apply at all to tax lien execution or other process which does not involve an auction. *See, e.g., In re* McKeever, 132 B.R. 996 (Bankr. N.D. Ill. 1991).

ing to mortgage foreclosures of real estate, stating that "the considerations bearing on other foreclosures and forced sales (to satisfy tax liens, for example) may be different."[416] For tax foreclosures which do not involve a formal sale of the property (for example, where the purchaser obtains a lien or a certificate rather than an actual deed), the *BFP* analysis should not be relevant.[417] Typically, the purchaser of a tax lien pays only the amount of delinquent taxes, an amount which bears no relationship to the value of the property. For this reason, there is no logical basis on which to conclude that the tax lien purchase price is a "reasonably equivalent value."

Obviously, the court's ruling also leaves open the possibility of using section 548 to avoid transfers pursuant to foreclosure sales that were not regularly conducted or that were collusive.[418] Additionally, sales may be challenged in most states where the price received is considered "grossly" inadequate.[419] The bankruptcy court, if that is the preferred forum, should have jurisdiction over an action to set aside a sale on state law grounds, because it would be an action to recover property for the estate.[420] Such an action, or an action raising other state law defects in the sale, may be brought directly in the bankruptcy court or by removal of a state court foreclosure proceeding.[421]

Alternatively, in certain states the transfer associated with a foreclosure is not completed until the occurrence of an event which occurs after the sale. If bankruptcy is filed in the period before the sale is complete under state law, there is no transfer to avoid, because the debtor still owns the property.[422] However, it may be a good idea to obtain and record an order to the effect that the sale process is stayed by bankruptcy if the fact of the auction has already been recorded. This recommendation would be especially prudent if the purchaser at sale is a third party.

Other creative uses of section 548 such as to avoid forfeitures under real estate sale agreements,[423] real estate installment sales contracts,[424] pawnbroker agreements[425] including automobile title pawns,[426] or extortionate charges under consumer contracts[427] should also be considered. Use of this avoiding power may be an effective way of remedying home equity scams, in which mortgagors in trouble are tricked into conveying title to their properties to those who say they will help them.[428] Similarly, the grant of a mortgage or other security interest by a cosigner or accommodation party who received no consideration in a transaction may be challenged, because only the value that the debtor received should be considered relevant under section 548. Such transactions may not always be considered involuntary in which case action by the trustee would be required.[429] When the one-year limitation period under section 548 has passed, it may be possible to seek to avoid such transfers pursuant to section 544 under a longer state law limitations period for fraudulent transfers.

---

416 *BFP*, 114 S. Ct. at 1757 n.3. *But see In re* McGrath, 170 B.R. 78 (Bankr. D.N.J. 1994) (applying *BFP* analysis to tax sales); *see also* § 10.4.2.6.6, *infra*.

417 *E.g., In re* Sherman, 223 B.R. 555 (B.A.P. 10th Cir. 1998) (*BFP* does not apply to Wyoming tax sale when statutory procedure does not provide for competitive bidding); *In re* Butler, 171 B.R. 321 (Bankr. N.D. Ill. 1994); *In re* McKeever, 132 B.R. 996 (Bankr. N.D. Ill. 1991). In Illinois, the property transfer is an administrative act based on prior sale of the *tax lien* and a failure to redeem; there is no property sale to which the *BFP* analysis could apply. *See also In re* Grandoe Country Club Co., Ltd., 252 F.3d 1146 (10th Cir. 2001) (*BFP* analysis applied because tax sale under state law subject to competitive bidding procedure).

418 *See In re* Ryker, 301 B.R. 156 (D.N.J. 2003) (avoiding foreclosure sale, which took place after having been postponed without new advertising advising potential bidders that debtor had in the interim paid seventy-five percent of the debt).

419 *See, e.g., In re* Schleier, 290 B.R. 45 (Bankr. S.D.N.Y. 2003) (sale invalid under New York law due to shocking inadequacy of sales price); Gumz v. Chickering, 19 Wis. 2d 625, 121 N.W.2d 279 (Wis. 1963). *See generally* Robert M. Washburn, *The Judicial Legislative Response to Price Inadequacy in Mortgage Foreclosure Sales*, 53 S. Cal. L. Rev. 843 (1980).

420 For a discussion of bankruptcy court jurisdiction, see § 13.2, *infra*.

421 *See, e.g., In re* Graves, 33 F.3d 242 (3d Cir. 1994) (sheriff's sale was voidable because purchaser had notice of unrecorded ownership interest of the debtor); *In re* Pontes, 280 B.R. 20 (Bankr. D.R.I. 2002) (tax sale invalidated based on due process grounds when state statute failed to require meaningful notice of the right to redeem property after tax sale); *In re* Edry, 201 B.R. 604 (Bankr. D. Mass. 1996) (foreclosure sale could be avoided under state law when mortgagee did not give amount of notice usually given in such sales and when price fell below state law standards of adequacy). For a discussion of removal of state court actions, see § 13.4.1, *infra*.

422 *See* § 11.6.2.2, *infra*.

423 *See In re* McConnell, 934 F.2d 662 (5th Cir. 1991) (forfeiture of $600,000.00 down payment under real estate sale agreement avoided as fraudulent transfer).

424 *In re* Grady, 202 B.R. 120 (Bankr. N.D. Iowa 1996) (*BFP* does not apply to forfeiture of real estate installment sale contract; property interest of $40,000.00 forfeited to satisfy $16,000.00 debt under the contract constituted fraudulent transfer).

425 *In re* Carter, 209 B.R. 732 (Bankr. D. Or. 1997) (forfeiture of right to redeem jewelry from pawnbroker was involuntary transfer avoidable by debtor under section 522(h)).

426 *In re* Jones, 304 B.R. 462 (Bankr. N.D. Ala. 2003) (debtor in title pawn transaction did not receive reasonably equivalent value); *In re* Bell, 279 B.R. 890 (Bankr. N.D. Ga. 2002) (pawnbroker preliminarily enjoined from selling car worth over $10,000.00 that was taken for failure to pay $5300.00 redemption price on $4000.00 loan).

427 For example, large check cashing fees or loan broker charges might be challenged as fraudulent transfers. In such cases, a major question will be whether the transfer was voluntary. *See In re* Wernly, 91 B.R. 702 (Bankr. E.D. Pa. 1988) ($1150.00 fee paid to check cashing company to cash check was not paid due to fraud or duress so as to make the payment involuntary and therefore avoidable).

428 *See, e.g., In re* Davis, 169 B.R. 285 (E.D.N.Y. 1992) (conveyance in sale/leaseback transaction based on misrepresentations of transferee and without understanding of consequences found to be involuntary).

429 *See* § 10.4.2.6, *supra*.

A major limitation on the use of section 548 should be noted, however. Under subsection 548(c), if a transfer is avoidable only under section 548, any transferee who takes for value and in good faith is given a lien on the interest transferred or may enforce the obligation incurred to the extent of the value given to the debtor.[430] If the creditor had executed on a previously unsecured debt, this lien might not be avoidable under any of the debtor's other avoiding powers. However, it could presumably be paid in installments in a chapter 13 plan.[431]

Several issues may arise where section 548(c) is invoked. The most important is probably that of good faith, because the subsection can only be invoked by a good-faith transferee. In many cases the transferee is the creditor or a party closely connected with the creditor. If the transferee knew of the debtor's insolvency, or even had reason to inquire into the financial straits of the debtor, good faith may be found lacking, especially if the value given was grossly inadequate.[432] Other problems may include a determination of how much value was given to the debtor if the amount of the debt was in dispute. Because the lien is measured by value given to the debtor, it seems fairly clear that costs incurred in the process of transfer should not be included in this figure.[433]

10.4.2.6.6 Post-petition transfers—§ 549

In line with the general principle that filing a bankruptcy freezes the debtor's property for administration by the bankruptcy court, section 549 allows the trustee to avoid most post-petition transfers of the debtor's property. Like the other avoiding powers, this power may be exercised by the debtor under Code section 522(h), if the property was not concealed and the transfer was not voluntary. As elsewhere in the Code, "transfer" is broadly defined to mean almost any parting with an interest in property.[434]

There are a number of exceptions to this general rule.[435] One of the most important protects third party transferors of the debtor's property that have no notice of the bankruptcy case.[436] The most typical example is a bank that transfers funds in a debtor's bank account to honor a check drawn by the debtor. However, section 549(a)(2)(A) protects only the party that makes the transfer, and not the transferee.[437] In addition, any transfer authorized by a specific Code provision[438] or by the bankruptcy court is not avoidable.[439]

Besides these exceptions, several others exist. Transfers made by a debtor against whom an involuntary case has been filed are protected, if they arise out of the debtor's normal affairs.[440] However, such transfers may be invalidated to the extent they are intended to satisfy pre-petition debts.[441] And there are two exceptions applicable only to real property.[442] A post-petition transfer of such property may not be avoided if it was sold to:

- A good faith purchaser;[443]
- Without knowledge of the bankruptcy;[444]
- For present fair equivalent value;[445]

---

430   *See In re* Sherman, 67 F.3d 1348 (8th Cir. 1995) (parents of debtors, who knew about suspicious nature of debtors' transfer of properties to them not entitled to lien as good faith transferees; bank to whom parents gave security interests and that had knowledge of some of the facts was not an immediate transferee from initial transferee that took in good faith and was therefore protected from recovery under § 550(b)); *In re* Jones, 304 B.R. 462 (Bankr. N.D. Ala. 2003) (title pawn lender given lien to extent it gave value).

431   See Chapter 11, *infra,* for a discussion of dealing with secured claims in chapter 13.

432   *In re* Armstrong, 285 F.3d 1092 (8th Cir. 2002) (casino transferee was not in good faith when it was on notice that debtor was having financial difficulties and might be insolvent); *In re* Carr, 40 B.R. 1007 (Bankr. D. Conn. 1984); *see* 5 Collier on Bankruptcy ¶ 548.07 (15th ed. rev.).

433   *In re* Richardson, 23 B.R. 434 (Bankr. D. Utah 1982). *But see In re* Jones, 20 B.R. 988 (Bankr. E.D. Pa. 1982) (including sheriff's costs in lien given to buyer).

434   *But see In re* McConville, 110 F.3d 47 (9th Cir. 1997) (creation

of a post-petition consensual lien is not a transfer of property for purposes of § 549).

435   If no exception applies, the transfer is avoidable, no matter how harsh the result. *See In re* Rice, 83 B.R. 8 (B.A.P. 9th Cir. 1987) (transferee has no rights in transferred property where it does not come within an exception to § 549).

436   11 U.S.C. § 549(a)(2)(A), incorporating 11 U.S.C. § 542(c).

437   *In re* Mills, 176 B.R. 924 (D. Kan. 1994) (transferee who received money when bank honored check post-petition received an avoidable transfer); *In re* W & T Enterprises, Inc., 84 B.R. 838 (Bankr. M.D. Fla. 1988) (bank honoring check payable to itself is liable for post-petition transfer).

438   For example a transfer made within the ordinary course of the debtor's business pursuant to 11 U.S.C. § 363 is not avoidable. *See In re* Dant & Russell, 853 F.2d 700 (9th Cir. 1988).

439   11 U.S.C. § 549(a)(2)(B); *see* Farm Credit Bank of Omaha v. Franzen, 926 F.2d 762 (8th Cir. 1991) (foreclosure sale held following relief from stay is not avoidable under section 549); Vogel v. Russell Transfer, Inc., 852 F.2d 797 (4th Cir. 1988). A debtor's transfer of exempt property or its proceeds is not avoidable because, once exempted, the property is not property of the estate. *In re* Reed, 184 B.R. 733 (Bankr. W.D. Tex. 1995). *But see* Manion v. Providian Nat'l Bank, 269 B.R. 232 (D. Colo. 2001).

440   11 U.S.C. § 549(a)(2)(A) (incorporating 11 U.S.C. § 303(f)).

441   11 U.S.C. § 549(b). *See generally In re* Texas Research, Inc., 862 F.2d 1161 (5th Cir. 1989).

442   *See In re* Shamblin, 890 F.2d 123 (9th Cir. 1989) (tax sale transfers claim rather than property under Illinois law so exceptions do not apply).

443   *See In re* Taft, 262 B.R. 55 (Bankr. M.D. Pa. 2001) (tax sale purchaser was not in good faith when it had reason to believe debtor had interest in property and was in bankruptcy).

444   *See In re* Allen, 816 F.2d 325 (7th Cir. 1987) (mortgagee/purchaser at foreclosure sale was not good faith purchaser without knowledge of the bankruptcy where mortgagee had been told bankruptcy petition would be filed that day).

445   *See In re* Shaw, 157 B.R. 151 (B.A.P. 9th Cir. 1993) (price of $36,049.00 at regularly conducted tax sale was not fair equiva-

• Unless a copy or notice of the bankruptcy petition was filed in the county recording office before the transfer was so far perfected that it could not be invalidated by a bona fide purchaser or judicial sale purchaser.[446]

To the extent that a good faith purchaser meets all of the requirements except present fair equivalent value, that purchaser has a lien to the extent of any present value given.[447] It should be noted, however, that this section speaks only of *present value* given in return for the property. This limitation means that to the extent a purchaser has taken the property in satisfaction of a prior debt, that purchaser is not protected.[448]

It is also important to note that the definition of "purchaser" in section 101 of the Code is "transferee of a voluntary transfer and includes immediate or mediate transferee of such transferee." Thus section 549(c) does not apply at all to involuntary transfers, a fact that seems to have escaped some courts considering such transfers (perhaps because it was never argued by the debtor or trustee). In general, therefore, section 549(c) does not protect involuntary sales carried out in violation of the automatic stay which, like most actions in violation of the stay, are void.[449]

The debtor may use section 549 in conjunction with the automatic stay provisions to invalidate involuntary post-petition transfers.[450] One example of a case in which the stay

might need such supplementation is a repossession ordered by a creditor without notice of the bankruptcy. Although the creditor would probably not be held in contempt as it had no notice of the case, the repossession could clearly be reversed. A setoff after the bankruptcy could be similarly undone. And in chapter 13 cases in which the debtor's post-petition income is property of the estate,[451] any deduction by a credit union from wages would be avoidable.[452] To prevent any problems in effecting this last type of avoidance, it is advisable to withdraw, before the bankruptcy, any prior authorization for such deductions that might muddy the issue of voluntariness.

For purposes of section 549, it has been held that a transfer by check occurs when the check is delivered.[453] However, due to recent Supreme Court precedent to the contrary under section 547,[454] more recent rulings under this section have held that the date of transfer by check occurs on the date it is honored.[455] For this reason, debtors must be careful to assure that any large check written shortly before the bankruptcy petition, such as a check for a mortgage payment, has been honored. Otherwise, there is a danger that the trustee could recover the funds from the payee of the check.[456]

10.4.2.6.7 Setoff—§ 553

The Code gives the trustee the power to avoid some, but not all, setoffs of mutual debts in the ninety days prior to filing of the petition.[457] If a setoff is otherwise permissible

---

lent value of property with a value of $76,000.00); *In re* Powers, 88 B.R. 294 (Bankr. D. Nev. 1988) (seventy-three percent of value not fair equivalent value).

446 11 U.S.C. § 549(c). The bona fide purchaser test in this section assumes a hypothetical purchaser with no notice of the transfer. *In re* Ward, 837 F.2d 124 (3d Cir. 1988); *see also* United States, *ex rel.* Agric. Stabilization Serv. v. Gerth, 991 F.2d 1428 (8th Cir. 1993) (obligation on pre-petition contract was not transformed by debtors assumption of contract into post-petition obligation against which creditor could offset post-petition debt); *In re* Konowitz, 905 F.2d 55 (4th Cir. 1990) (where interest taken by purchaser at pre-petition foreclosure sale was not perfected before bankruptcy was filed, sale was subject to avoidance); *In re* Walker, 861 F.2d 597 (9th Cir. 1988) (confirmation of foreclosure sale did not constitute requisite perfection of transfer under California's recording statute).

447 11 U.S.C. § 549(c).

448 *In re* Major, 218 B.R. 501 (Bankr. W.D. Mo. 1998) (credit bid by foreclosing creditor was not present fair equivalent value). *But see In re* T.F. Stone Co., 72 F.3d 466 (5th Cir. 1996) (price obtained at regularly conducted, non-collusive tax sale deemed present fair equivalent value under § 549(c)).

449 *See* 40235 Wash. St. Corp. v. Lusardi, 329 F.3d 1076 (9th Cir. 2003) (section 549(c) not available for transactions that are void because they occurred in violation of automatic stay); *In re* Schwartz, 954 F.2d 569 (9th Cir. 1991) (section 549(c) applies to unauthorized transfers of estate property which are not otherwise prohibited by the Code); *In re* Ford, 296 B.R. 537 (Bankr. N.D. Ga. 2003); *In re* Smith, 224 B.R. 44 (Bankr. E.D. Mich. 1998). *But see In re* Taylor, 884 F.2d 478 (9th Cir. 1989).

450 For discussion of the effect of the automatic stay on the validity of transfers see § 9.6, *supra*. *See also In re* Gandara, 257 B.R. 549 (Bankr. D. Mont. 2000) (section 549 could be used to

invalidate payment made in exchange for dismissal of criminal bad check case even if payment was not prohibited by automatic stay).

451 11 U.S.C. § 1306(a).

452 *In re* Shepherd, 12 B.R. 151 (E.D. Pa. 1981).

453 Quinn Wholesale, Inc. v. Northen, 873 F.2d 77 (4th Cir. 1989).

454 Barnhill v. Johnson, 503 U.S. 393, 112 S. Ct. 1386, 119 L. Ed. 2d 519 (1992) (transfer by check occurs when check is honored for purposes of preference analysis).

455 *In re* Oakwood Markets, 203 F.3d 406 (6th Cir. 2000); *see also In re* Mora, 199 F.3d 1024 (9th Cir. 1999) (transfer of cashiers check is on date of delivery, but suggesting that transfer of ordinary check is on date it is honored).

456 *See In re* Mora, 199 F.3d 1024 (9th Cir. 1999) (trustee recovered large payment deemed made to mortgage company by check transferring pre-petition funds that were deemed transferred after petition was filed).

457 The automatic stay prevents setoffs after the petition is filed, though the stay may be lifted if certain prerequisites are met and a creditor may "freeze" a debtor's account in anticipation of set off. Citizens Bank of Md. v. Strumpf, 516 U.S. 16, 116 S. Ct. 286, 133 L. Ed. 2d 258 (1995); *see* Ch. 9, *supra*. Generally, the right to setoff will involve a bank account or other "cash collateral" as defined in 11 U.S.C. § 363(a), which under 11 U.S.C. § 363(c)(2) cannot be used, that is, withdrawn from the bank, without notice and a hearing or consent of the creditor. No setoff probably occurs where the bank has foreclosed a valid security interest in an account. *See* Smith v. Mark Twain Nat'l Bank, 805 F.2d 278 (8th Cir. 1986); *cf. In re* Knudson, 929 F.2d

under non-bankruptcy law,[458] section 553 provides certain tests which must be met before it can be avoided. At the same time, section 553 preserves the right of setoff after a bankruptcy petition, except as prohibited elsewhere in the Code, such as by the automatic stay.

First, a setoff may be avoided or otherwise invalidated if it is not for a mutual debt. If the debtor owes the debt in a capacity other than that in which a debt is owed to the debtor, no mutuality exists and no setoff is permitted. For example, if the debtor has deposited money in his or her individual account, a setoff of that deposit against the debtor's obligation as a trustee for another person by the bank may be avoided, as it is against the debtor in a different capacity. This principle is frequently applied to set-offs involving debtors' IRA accounts.[459] Similarly, a creditor may not set off a pre-petition claim against a post-petition claim, both because of the express wording of section 553(a) and because the debts are not considered to be mutual.[460]

However, it is not always easy to determine whether mutual debts exist.[461] In particular, courts have disagreed about whether debts owed to different agencies of the same government are mutual debts.[462]

Second, a setoff may be avoided if it is exercised to satisfy a claim against the debtor other than an allowable claim. Thus, if defenses to the claim's allowance, including defenses to the claim itself, are successfully asserted, a setoff may be avoided.[463] However, one court of appeals had held that a creditor need not file a proof of claim as a prerequisite to asserting a right of set-off.[464] And a claim may be eligible for setoff even if it has not been reduced to judgment.[465]

Third, if a creditor exercising a setoff acquires its claim from another entity either after the filing of the petition or within ninety days before filing while the debtor was insolvent, the setoff may be avoided.[466]

Fourth, if a creditor exercising a setoff has caused the debtor to increase the amount owed by the creditor to the debtor (for example, by pressuring the debtor to "build up" its bank deposits) while the debtor was insolvent in order to obtain a setoff, the setoff so obtained may be avoided.[467]

Finally, a setoff may be avoided to the extent that it results in the creditor's improving its position over what it was either (1) ninety days prior to the filing of the petition or (2) if no "insufficiency" existed on that date, the first date an insufficiency existed.[468] The Code defines "insufficiency" as the "amount, if any, by which a claim against the debtor exceeds a mutual debt owing to the debtor by the holder of such claim."[469] For example, if the debtor owed $5000.00 to a bank and ninety days prior to the filing of the case had a deposit balance of $200.00, there would be an insufficiency on that date of $4800.00 ($5000.00 minus $200.00). If forty days prior to the filing the bank was then owed

---

458 *See In re* Capps, 251 B.R. 73 (Bankr. D. Neb. 2000) (debtor entitled to recover funds setoff by bank because they were social security benefits which bank was prohibited from seizing by 42 U.S.C. § 407(a)).

459 *In re* Mastroeni, 57 B.R. 191 (Bankr. S.D.N.Y. 1986); *In re* Gillett, 55 B.R. 675 (Bankr. S.D. Fla. 1985); *In re* Todd, 37 B.R. 836 (Bankr. W.D. La. 1984) (avoiding setoff of debt against debtor's IRA account); *see also In re* Bevill, Bresler & Schulman Asset Mgmt., 896 F.2d 54 (2d Cir. 1990) (creditor withholding income from government bonds which rightfully belonged to debtor was mere trustee holding debtor's funds and thus owed debtor no debt which could be set off).

460 Cooper Jarrett Inc. v. Cent. Trans., Inc., 726 F.2d 93 (3d Cir. 1984); *In re* Harris, 260 B.R. 753 (Bankr. D. Md. 2001) (credit union could not set off post-petition deposits against pre-petition debt or claim that security interest in account extended to those deposits); *In re* Kleather, 208 B.R. 406 (Bankr. S.D. Ohio 1997) (bank could not setoff pre-petition debt against post-petition deposits despite fact that debtor had withdrawn pre-petition deposits after petition was filed); *In re* Figgers, 121 B.R. 772 (Bankr. S.D. Ohio 1990) (to qualify for setoff, debts must be individual and pre-petition); *In re* Princess Baking Corp., 5 B.R. 587 (Bankr. S.D. Cal. 1980); *see also In re* Davidovich, 901 F.2d 1533 (10th Cir. 1990) (chapter 7 debtor's former partner not entitled to offset amounts debtor allegedly owed pursuant to post-petition real estate partnership defaults); *cf. In re* United Sciences of Am., Inc., 893 F.2d 720 (5th Cir. 1990) (mutuality created by agreement between bank and debtor depositor pursuant to which bank deposited proceeds of credit card transactions in debtor's account and debtor authorized bank to charge its account for charge backs and other fees); Braniff Airways, Inc. v. Exxon Co. U.S.A., 814 F.2d 1030 (5th Cir. 1987) (mutuality found where debtor had made unused prepayments to creditor holding claim). *But see In re* Bacigalupi, Inc., 60 B.R. 442 (B.A.P. 9th Cir. 1986). The case is distinguishable insofar as it involves a setoff against a state court judgment obtained by the debtor after filing bankruptcy. The setoff essentially allowed the creditor to recoup its counterclaim. The Internal Revenue Service has sometimes attempted to ignore a lack of mutuality. *See, e.g., In re* Glenn, 198 B.R. 106 (Bankr. E.D. Pa. 1996) (IRS

could not offset post-petition refund against pre-petition debt). *Glenn* was reversed at 207 B.R. 418 (E.D. Pa. 1997) on the issue of when the debtor acquires the right to a tax refund. *In re* Hammett, 21 B.R. 923 (Bankr. E.D. Pa. 1982) (post-petition setoff not permitted where debtor had post-petition claim for refund and IRS had pre-petition claim for taxes); *see also* § 2.5.3, *supra*. See also discussion of Internal Revenue Service actions in § 9.6, *supra*.

461 *See In re* Elcona Homes Corp., 863 F.2d 483 (7th Cir. 1988).

462 *See* United States v. Maxwell, 157 F.3d 1099 (7th Cir. 1998) (federal government a single entity for setoff purposes); *In re* Turner, 84 F.3d 1294 (10th Cir. 1996) (*en banc*), (United States is a unitary creditor for setoff purposes); Doe v. United States, 58 F.3d 494 (9th Cir. 1995). *But see* Westamerica Bank v. United States, 178 B.R. 493 (N.D. Cal. 1995) (mutuality did not exist for debts involving different agencies).

463 11 U.S.C. § 553(a)(1).

464 *In re* G.S. Omni Corp., 835 F.2d 1317 (10th Cir. 1987).

465 *In re* Bevill, Bresler & Schulman Asset Mgmt., 896 F.2d 54 (2d Cir. 1990).

466 11 U.S.C. § 553(a)(2).

467 11 U.S.C. § 553(a)(3); *see In re* Dutton, 15 B.R. 318 (Bankr. D.N.J. 1981).

468 11 U.S.C. § 553(b)(1).

469 11 U.S.C. § 553(b)(2).

$3000.00 and the debtor had a deposit of $2000.00 there would be an insufficiency on that date of only $1000.00 ($3000.00 minus $2000.00). If the bank then set off against the entire deposit, that setoff could be avoided in its entirety, because on the date of the setoff the bank's insufficiency position had improved to the extent of $3800.00 ($4800.00 minus $1000.00) an amount greater than the amount of the setoff. If, instead of $200.00, there had been $2500.00 on deposit ninety days before filing then the improvement in position would have been $1500.00 and that amount of the $2000.00 setoff would be avoidable.[470] And if the amount on deposit ninety days before the filing had been $6000.00 and then, three days before filing the debtor for the first time withdrew $3500.00, then the first insufficiency would be $1500.00. A setoff after that date would be avoidable to the extent that the insufficiency on the date of setoff exceeded $1500.00.[471]

Arguably, any deposit to a creditor bank is a transfer to the bank which could be avoided as a setoff if it improved the bank's position.[472] However, there was also a significant line of pre-Code cases holding that deposits in the ordinary course of business were not preferences.[473] In any case, such is rarely an issue with respect to the debtor's avoiding powers, as the deposit is normally a voluntary transfer and thus not avoidable under 11 U.S.C. § 522(h).

Also, it is important to note that section 553(b) addresses only setoffs prior to the filing of the petition. It does not appear that the improvement-in-position test applies at all to setoffs after filing, once the automatic stay is no longer in effect. Generally, such setoffs by creditors having the right to setoff for mutual debts are permissible, though they may be prohibited by a court in exercise of its discretion.[474] However, several courts have held that no setoff may be had against exempt property.[475] Setoff may also be prohibited when a creditor has expressly waived its setoff rights.[476] Creditors occasionally attempt to use the doctrine of "recoupment" to justify refusal to pay to the debtor or trustee money that they owe the debtor, claiming that it is reduced by money the debtor owed them with respect to the same transaction. This doctrine is quite limited.[477]

The right to setoff can be eliminated by a confirmed plan that does not preserve that right or modifies it.[478] In addition, a creditor waives its right to setoff to the extent that it releases funds held pre-petition that were subject to setoff, and cannot setoff against funds acquired from the debtor post-petition to collect a pre-petition debt.[479]

10.4.2.6.8 Liens securing fines, penalties and forfeitures—§ 724(a)

The final type of transfer that is avoidable by the trustee, and sometimes by the debtor, is described in section 724(a), which in turn incorporates section 726(a)(4). Because this

---

470 The bank's position would have improved from a deficiency of $2500.00 ($5000.00 minus $2500.00) to a deficiency of $1000.00 ($3000.00 minus $2000.00).

471 For an application of these principles in a case where a debtor avoided a setoff, see *In re* Duncan, 10 B.R. 13 (Bankr. D. Tenn. 1980). *See also* Durham v. SMI Indus., Corp., 882 F.2d 881 (4th Cir. 1989) (setoff may be recovered to the extent amount creditor received exceeded amount it paid); *In re* Moreira, 173 B.R. 965 (Bankr. D. Mass. 1994) (debtor could challenge setoff against credit union account to extent she could claim funds in account were exempt); *In re* Stall, 125 B.R. 754 (Bankr. S.D. Ohio 1991) (setoff of tax refund against pre-petition student loan obligation did not result in improvement of position); *In re* Fox, 62 B.R. 432 (Bankr. D.R.I. 1986) (avoiding Veterans Administration withholding of benefits to recover money paid out on a mortgage guarantee).

472 See S. Rep. No. 95-989, at 27 (1978) and H.R. Rep. No. 95-595, at (1977), stating the term "transfer" includes a deposit in a bank account. *See also In re* Bohlen Enterprises, Ltd., 859 F.2d 561 (8th Cir. 1988) (deposit not in ordinary course of business made for purpose of creating right of setoff is avoidable under § 553(a)(3)). *But see* Coral Petroleum, Inc. v. Banque Paribas-London, 797 F.2d 1351 (5th Cir. 1986).

473 *See* 5 Collier on Bankruptcy ¶ 553.03[5][b] (15th ed. rev.); *see also* Laws v. United Mo. Bank of Kan. City, 98 F.3d 1047 (8th Cir. 1996) (routine advances against uncollected deposits do not create a debt).

474 *See* Ch. 13, *infra.*

475 *In re* Alexander, 245 B.R. 280 (W.D. Ky. 1999) (IRS setoff to collect dischargeable pre-petition debt prohibited by § 522(c)); *In re* Jones, 230 B.R. 875 (M.D. Ala. 1999) (same); *In re* Sharp, 286 B.R. 627 (Bankr. E.D. Ky. 2002) (same); *In re* Killen, 249 B.R. 585 (Bankr. D. Conn. 2000) (same); *In re* Miel, 134 B.R. 229 (Bankr. W.D. Mich. 1991) (Internal Revenue Service could not carry out post-petition offset of dischargeable pre-petition taxes owed against tax refund claimed as exempt by debtor); *In re* Wilde, 85 B.R. 147 (Bankr. D.N.M. 1988); *In re* Haffner, 12 B.R. 371 (Bankr. M.D. Tenn. 1981); *see also In re* Monteith, 23 B.R. 601 (Bankr. N.D. Ohio 1982) (IRS not allowed to setoff against exempt property to collect dischargeable taxes). *But see* U.S. v. Luongo, 259 F.3d 323 (5th Cir. 2001) (IRS permitted to setoff pre-petition refund against discharged tax debt); *In re* Lares, 188 F.3d 1166 (9th Cir. 1999) (Idaho law permitted pre-bankruptcy exercise of contractual right of setoff against proceeds of homestead sale); *In re* Madigan, 270 B.R. 749 (B.A.P. 9th Cir. 2001) (long term disability insurer could not recoup from post-discharge claim for disability benefits based on pre-petition overpayment because benefits did not arise from same transaction); *In re* Pieri & Boucher, 86 B.R. 208 (B.A.P. 9th Cir. 1988) (landlord allowed to setoff claims against debtors' counterclaims, although debtors' counterclaims were listed as exempt).

476 *In re* Calore Express, 288 F.3d 22 (1st. Cir. 2002) (IRS waived its right of setoff by stating in proof of claim that its claim for pre-petition taxes was not subject to setoff; factual question as to whether waiver may have been later rescinded).

477 *See In re* Malinowski, 156 F.3d 131 (2d Cir. 1998) (state unemployment agency could not recoup overpayment arising from one period of unemployment from benefits due for a different period of unemployment); U.S. *ex rel* Postal Serv. v. Dewey Freight, 31 F.3d 620 (8th Cir. 1994).

478 *In re* Cont'l Airlines, 134 F.3d 536 (3d Cir. 1998).

479 *In re* Orr, 234 B.R. 249 (Bankr. N.D.N.Y. 1999); *In re* Kleather, 208 B.R. 406 (Bankr. S.D. Ohio 1997).

avoiding power is contained in chapter 7, it applies only in cases under that chapter, and not in chapter 13 cases.

Basically, this section allows avoidance of liens for penalties, fines, punitive damages, multiple damages, and the like, to the extent the amount secured by that lien does not represent compensation for actual pecuniary loss. Under this section, to the extent a tax lien secures penalties for late payment, for example, it can be avoided.[480] In cases involving judgment liens, this power will add little to the debtor's arsenal beyond the broader power which is available under 11 U.S.C. § 522(f)(1)(A).[481]

However, under some consumer contracts the power may be available to challenge that portion of a lien which represents a penalty, including, for example, late charges and prepayment penalties. In such cases one issue likely to arise for a debtor seeking to use the power is the voluntariness of the transfer. The debtor should argue that the imposition of the penalty represents a separate involuntary transfer from the underlying transaction granting the security interest.[482]

10.4.2.7 Other Limitations on Debtor's Use of Trustee Avoiding Powers

In addition to the overriding limitations on sections 522(g) and (h) that the debtor may not avoid any voluntary transfer or transfer where the debtor concealed property,[483] there are a number of other limitations on the debtor's avoiding powers.

Naturally, the avoiding powers are limited by the extent of the debtor's available exemptions. Subsection 522(j) permits exemption of particular property only to the extent that the exemption for that type of property is still available.

More importantly, the avoiding powers are subject to the limitations placed upon the trustee by sections 546 and 550. Section 546 sets a statute of limitations for avoidance actions at the earlier of 1) two years after the entry of the order for relief (normally the date of the petition) or 2) the time the case is closed or dismissed.[484] However, if a trustee is appointed or elected before the two years has run, there has been no prior trustee, and the case is not closed or dismissed, the time is extended to one year after the trustee is appointed or elected if that is later.[485] The limitations

period may be tolled if the debtor or others conceal material facts necessary to discover the avoidable transfer.[486] The limitations period may also be waived.[487]

Section 546 also subordinates the trustee's powers to any applicable law that allows perfection of an interest to relate back to an earlier date,[488] and to certain sellers' rights of reclamation of goods sold.[489]

10.4.2.8 Recovery of Property After Transfer Is Avoided

When a transfer is avoided, section 550 generally allows recovery of the transferred property (or its value in some cases) from both the initial transferee and a subsequent transferee.[490] In some cases, after an avoidance proceeding, a separate action must be brought under section 550 to recover the property that was transferred.[491]

---

480 *See, e.g., In re* Davis, 22 B.R. 523 (Bankr. W.D. Pa. 1982) (IRS lien avoided to extent it was penalty). *But see In re* DeMarah, 62 F.3d 1248 (9th Cir. 1995) (debtor could not use § 724(a) to avoid a tax lien due to operation of § 522(c)(2)).

481 *See* § 10.4.2.3, *supra*.

482 *See* §§ 10.4.2.5, 10.4.2.6, *supra*.

483 *But see* § 10.4.2.5, *supra*.

484 11 U.S.C. § 546(a). This amendment resolved confusion in the cases concerning how the statute of limitations was to be computed in cases where there initially was no trustee appointed.

485 11 U.S.C. § 546(a). This last time period is only relevant in cases commenced under chapter 11 and in involuntary cases, in which a trustee is not normally appointed at the outset of the

case. *In re* Bodenstein, 253 B.R. 46 (B.A.P. 8th Cir. 2000) (appointment of chapter 7 trustee in case converted from chapter 13 did not start one-year period because chapter 13 had been appointed previously; no tolling of period permitted when debtors did not conceal transfers and chapter 7 trustee had time to bring proceeding after conversion).

486 *See In re* Olsen, 36 F.3d 71 (9th Cir. 1994) (statute could be equitably tolled due to debtors' conduct failing to comply with duty to cooperate with trustee); *In re* Petty, 93 B.R. 208 (B.A.P. 9th Cir. 1988) (trustee allowed to reopen case and proceed with avoidance action where the debtor's interest in property was not properly disclosed).

487 *In re* Pugh, 158 F.3d 530 (11th Cir. 1998).

488 11 U.S.C. § 546(b); *In re* WWG Indus., Inc., 772 F.2d 810 (11th Cir. 1985); *see In re* Griggs, 965 F.2d 54 (6th Cir. 1992) (lender could correct absence of notation of its lien on mobile home pursuant to Kentucky law which permitted retroactive perfection of security interests); *In re* Yobe Elec., Inc., 728 F.2d 207 (3d Cir. 1984); *see also* 11 U.S.C. § 362(b)(3).

489 11 U.S.C. § 546(c), (d); *see, e.g., In re* Pester Ref. Co., 964 F.2d 842 (8th Cir. 1992); *In re* Griffin Retreading Co., 795 F.2d 676 (8th Cir. 1986).

490 11 U.S.C. § 550(a); *see In re* Bean, 252 F.3d 113 (2d Cir. 2001) (recovery under § 550 limited to value of debtor's equity interest that was transferred); *In re* Willaert, 944 F.2d 463 (8th Cir. 1991) (proceeds of sale of transferred property can be recovered); *cf. In re* Cohen, 300 F.3d 1097 (9th Cir. 2002) (when debtor transferred to her husband a cashier's check made payable to husband's creditor, creditor was only party that could exercise dominion and control and was therefore initial transferee). A party must have actual dominion or control over funds to qualify as a transferee. *See In re* Hurtado, 342 F.3d 528 (6th Cir. 2003) (when debtors transferred money to individual's bank account, that individual had dominion and control over the funds even though she used them as directed by debtors). Thus a bank receiving funds to be deposited in a bank account is normally not a transferee, because the person owning the account ordinarily controls that money. *In re* First Sec. Mortgage, 33 F.3d 42 (10th Cir. 1994).

491 *See In re* Cowan, 273 B.R. 98 (B.A.P. 6th Cir. 2002) (if avoidance of lien provides trustee with complete relief, no action under § 550 is necessary).

There are several major exceptions to the general right to recover property after a transfer is avoided, however. The debtor may not recover from any transferee subsequent to the initial transferee if that transferee has either (1) taken for value in good faith without knowledge of the voidability of the transfer or (2) taken from a prior transferee who has taken for value in good faith and without knowledge.[492] (In such cases, the only recovery can be the value of the property from the initial transferee.) It is the burden of the transferee to show good faith and lack of knowledge.[493] And, if an initial transferee acted in good faith,[494] the transferee, while returning the property, retains a lien for the cost or increase in value due to any improvements on the property, whichever is less.[495]

Finally, an action to recover property subsequent to the avoidance of a transfer must be commenced within one year after the avoidance, or before the case is closed, whichever comes first.[496]

10.4.2.9 Preservation of Avoided Transfers or Recovered Property

An important but often overlooked addition to the avoiding powers is the right to preserve avoided transfers for the benefit of the debtor. Subsection 522(i)(2) provides that a transfer avoided or property recovered by the debtor or the trustee may be preserved for the benefit of the debtor to the extent that the debtor may exempt that property under section 522(g) or could have avoided the transfer under section 522(f)(1)(B).[497]

The result, in effect, is that the debtor steps into the shoes of the holder of the avoided transfer *vis-a-vis* any other entity with rights junior to that holder, and thereby obtains rights superior to junior lienholders.[498] For example, if two joint debtors have a home worth $10,000.00 which has an $8000.00 judicial lien and a $10,000.00 mortgage junior to the judicial lien, the debtors, if they are able to exempt their $10,000.00 interest (as they could under the federal exemptions) may avoid the judicial lien under section 522(f)(1).[499] Without preservation of that lien (a transfer) for their benefit, however, this avoidance would not benefit the debtors, because it would merely move the mortgage up in priority from a position of being secured in the amount of $2000.00 and unsecured in the amount of $8000.00 to being fully secured in the amount of $10,000.00. By allowing the debtors to preserve the avoided judicial lien for their own benefit, the Code keeps the mortgage in its previous position, that is, secured only to the extent of $2000.00 and unsecured as to the remaining $8000.00. Needless to say, this power can be of great importance in cases in which there are multiple liens on a particular property.

It is unclear what, if any, affirmative action must be taken to preserve a transfer under section 522(i)(2). Unlike the trustee's power to have transfers preserved under section 551,[500] it appears that the preservation for the debtor may not be automatic, because the language of section 522(i)(2) states that a transfer "may be preserved," and not that it "is preserved." In view of this language, it is advisable to seek preservation affirmatively as part of the relief when a transfer is avoided, in order to eliminate any possible doubts as to this question. Proper recording of any order so obtained will have the practical benefit of preserving the value of the exemption for the debtor if, for example, the property is sold many years after bankruptcy and a title company is distributing the proceeds of sale.

---

492 11 U.S.C. § 550(b); *see In re* Bressman, 327 F.3d 229 (3d Cir. 2003) (law firms did not know that they were being paid with estate assets for representation in criminal case); *In re* Cohen, 226 B.R. 1 (B.A.P. 9th Cir. 1999) (when debtor gave funds to her husband, who then purchased cashiers check and sent it to creditor, husband was initial transferee). One court of appeals has held that actual rather than constructive notice must be shown to recover transferred property under section 550. *In re* Columbia Data Products, Inc., 892 F.2d 26 (4th Cir. 1989); Smith v. Mixon, 788 F.2d 229 (4th Cir. 1986).

493 *In re* Whaley, 229 B.R. 767 (Bankr. D. Minn. 1999) (transferee that did not produce evidence of good faith or lack of knowledge liable for recovery of preference).

494 Willful ignorance cannot constitute good faith under § 550. *In re* Harbour, 845 F.2d 1254 (4th Cir. 1988) (transfer recovered from initial transferee who kept herself willfully ignorant of the circumstances of the transaction even though she retained no funds from the transfer for herself).

495 11 U.S.C. § 550(e); *see, e.g., In re* Black & White Cattle Co., 783 F.2d 1454 (9th Cir. 1986). Improvements are defined in this section to include physical changes, repairs, payment of taxes, payments of any debt secured by a lien, and discharge of any lien superior to the rights of the trustee.

496 11 U.S.C. § 550(f).

497 *See In re* Bell, 194 B.R. 192 (Bankr. S.D. Ill. 1996) (because debtors' granting of security interest in vehicles was voluntary, when trustee avoided unrecorded security interests the liens were preserved for benefit of the estate and increased the

amount of non-exempt property, so that debtors had to pay increased amount to unsecured creditors under § 1325(a)(4) "best interests of creditors" test). Section 522(i) refers to § 522(f)(2) due to a technical error in which the 1994 amendments failed to conform § 522(i) to the redesignation of section 522(f)(2) as § 522(f)(1)(B).

498 However, the preservation of the lien gives no greater rights than those which the original lienholder possessed. *In re* Carvell, 222 B.R. 178 (B.A.P. 1st Cir. 1998).

499 *See* Kors, Inc. v. Howard Bank, 819 F.2d 19 (2d Cir. 1987); *In re* Losieniecki, 17 B.R. 136 (Bankr. W.D. Pa. 1981). *But see In re* Simonson, 758 F.2d 103 (3d Cir. 1985) (refusing to apply § 522(i)(2) or avoid liens where total of mortgages exceeded value of property even though intervening judicial liens rendered one mortgage largely unsecured). The *Simonson* case was overruled by the 11 U.S.C. § 522(f)(2), enacted in 1994. *See* § 10.4.2.3.1, *supra*.

500 *See In re* Van De Kamp's Dutch Bakeries, 908 F.2d 517 (9th Cir. 1990) (transfer avoided by trustee as fraudulent was automatically preserved for benefit of estate, regardless whether interest could have been avoided by competing creditor in pre-petition state court proceeding).

10.4.2.10 Limits on Availability of Debtor's Avoiding Powers As Applied to Liens Predating the Bankruptcy Reform Act

A flood tide of cases challenging the retroactive application of the debtor's powers to avoid pre-Code liens under 11 U.S.C. § 522(f) reached the United States Supreme Court in 1982. In *United States v. Security Industrial Bank*,[501] the Court held, in order to avoid reaching a difficult constitutional question, that Congress' failure to explicitly deal with retroactivity evidenced an intent that the avoiding powers were to apply only prospectively. Thus, it is now settled that nonpossessory, nonpurchase-money security interests which existed prior to enactment of the Bankruptcy Reform Act on November 6, 1978 cannot be avoided under section 522(f)(1)(B).[502] Given the rationale for the court's decision, it is likely that pre-enactment judicial liens are similarly immune from avoidance under section 522(f)(1)(A).[503] However, at least one court of appeals has held that because judicial liens, especially confessed judgments, were avoidable in some instances under the former Bankruptcy Act, pre-Code judicial liens may be avoided notwithstanding *Security Industrial Bank*.[504]

The Supreme Court expressly declined to decide whether its holding would apply to liens created in the gap period between enactment of the Code and its effective date, about one year later. The constitutional objections to avoidance in such cases have not been found substantial by most lower courts considering the issue, because once the statute was passed all creditors were placed on notice of the status of the liens created by contracts after November 6, 1978.[505] Based on this distinction, the major underpinning for the Supreme Court's ruling is not present for these "gap" liens. It may be significant that shortly after the *Security Industrial Bank* decision, the Court denied certiorari in the only court of appeals case that had expressly considered the gap issue, a decision holding that "gap period" liens could be avoided.[506] Since then, three other courts of appeals have also held that such liens are avoidable.[507]

The Supreme Court's decision also left unanswered a number of other questions. Is the lien created by a refinancing of a consumer debt after the effective date of the Code considered to be a post-Code lien? Creditors may argue that they are protected by a clause in their contracts stating that the lien in the original contract secures future indebtedness. This argument should fail because the parties agreed to a new contract after the Code, a contract in which the terms of the prior contract could be modified, and in which the provisions of the Code became implied terms.[508] Given the propensity of some finance companies to keep debtors as continuous customers by repeated refinancings over the years, any contrary holding would allow security interests in household goods to continue for many years.

Even less clear is the question of whether a new judicial lien is created by state law revival procedures, which in many places must be complied with periodically in order to maintain the lien or its priority. The answer to this question is likely to be found in a careful reading of state law.[509]

Finally, there will be issues as to the retroactivity of the debtor's other avoiding powers, under 11 U.S.C. § 522(h), which incorporate the trustee's powers. At least to the large extent that the trustee's powers are unchanged from prior law, debtors have good arguments that those powers are not barred by *Security Industrial Bank*. In every such case where the debtor exercises an avoiding power, the creditor's rights are impaired to no greater extent than they could have been before the Code, by the trustee's own exercise of his or her powers.[510]

In any case, the issue of retroactive application has become largely academic due to the passage of time. It has virtually disappeared, and it will reappear only to the extent the law is again changed.[511]

10.5 Protection of Exempt Property After Discharge

Still another important feature of the bankruptcy exemption scheme is the continuing protection given to exempt property after the discharge. Section 522(c) provides that, with a few exceptions, no creditor holding a pre-bankruptcy claim may ever execute against the property that has been claimed as exempt.

The principal significance of this subsection is that even creditors holding claims that were not discharged may not reach exempt property to execute on their still-valid claims.

---

501   459 U.S. 70, 103 S. Ct. 407, 74 L. Ed. 2d 235 (1982).

502   11 U.S.C. § 522(f)(2) was redesignated as 11 U.S.C. § 522(f)(1)(A) by the 1994 amendments to the Code.

503   *In re* White, 25 B.R. 339 (B.A.P. 1st Cir. 1982) (retroactive avoidance of judicial liens not permitted). Also, shortly after the Supreme Court decided *Security Industrial Bank*, the Court vacated and remanded *In re* Ashe, 669 F.2d 105 (3d Cir. 1982), a case which had previously upheld the retroactive avoidance of judicial liens under § 522(f). Commonwealth Nat'l Bank v. Ashe, 459 U.S. 1082 (1982).

504   *In re* Ashe, 712 F.2d 864 (3d Cir. 1983).

505   See, for example, *In re* Webber, 674 F.2d 796 (9th Cir. 1982), and cases cited therein.

506   *In re* Webber, 674 F.2d 796 (9th Cir. 1982).

507   *In re* Washburn & Roberts, Inc., 795 F.2d 870 (9th Cir. 1986); *In re* Ashe, 712 F.2d 864 (3d Cir. 1983); *In re* Groves, 707 F.2d 451 (10th Cir. 1983).

508   Marcus Brown Holding Co. v. Feldman, 256 U.S. 170 (1921).

509   *See* First Nat'l Bank & Trust Co. v. Daniel, 701 F.2d 141 (11th Cir. 1983) (consolidation note did not create new lien); *In re* Hickey, 32 B.R. 588 (Bankr. S.D. Ohio 1983) (continuation statement not a new lien).

510   *See In re* Ashe, 712 F.2d 864 (3d Cir. 1983).

511   *See In re* Wilson, 90 F.3d 347 (9th Cir. 1996) (1994 change to section 522(f) does not apply retroactively).

Thus, if a debt is not discharged because of a false financial statement, because the debt was not listed, because of fraud, or willful and malicious injury, or on a student loan, the debtor may nevertheless be fully protected from execution on that debt if she has no property except the property exempted in the bankruptcy case. The only exceptions to this general rule are debts for non-dischargeable taxes, support, or alimony, liens that are not avoided during the bankruptcy, and any student loans, scholarships, or grants obtained by fraud.[512]

This provision serves the obvious purpose of ensuring that the debtor's fresh start is not frustrated by pre-existing debts. It gives the exemptions a permanent character, protecting that minimum grubstake afforded by the exemption provisions (either state or federal) from almost every attack arising out of the debtor's pre-bankruptcy circumstances.

The protections of section 522(c) do give rise to some issues as to how the exemptions will be applied in later executions on nondischarged pre-bankruptcy debts. Clearly, property acquired after the bankruptcy is not protected, unless the debtor is able to exempt it under one of the provisions allowing exemption of the right to receive certain benefits in the future.[513] But does the exemption apply forever to the items exempted, or only to the extent of the value exempted?[514] In other words, is a debtor's increased equity in a home totally protected because the home was exempted in the bankruptcy? Certainly, such protection would further the purpose of protecting the debtor's basic necessities if the increase was caused simply by inflation. But the result might be different if the increased equity was purchased with after-acquired assets used to make mortgage payments. Similarly, with more liquid assets, such as bank accounts, difficult problems of tracing may arise in determining whether certain property was exempted in the bankruptcy.[515] A number of courts have held that, for example, even the right of setoff on exempt property is trumped by section 522(c).[516]

In such cases, there are also questions as to the interplay of the bankruptcy exemptions with the state's normal exemptions from execution. If certain property of the debtor is protected from execution by section 522(c), presumably the debtor may then claim other property as exempt under the state's exemption scheme in the execution. Does it make a difference if, in the bankruptcy, the debtor had been claiming property under the state exemption scheme already, rather than the federal bankruptcy exemptions? In order to promote equality of treatment, it should not.

---

512   11 U.S.C. § 522(c). However, these exceptions do not eliminate state law protections for property that would never have been subject to such claims outside of bankruptcy. *In re* Davis, 170 F.3d 475 (5th Cir. 1999) (*en banc*); *see also In re* Dishong, 188 B.R. 51 (Bankr. S.D. Fla. 1995) (tax lien preserved by § 522(c)(2) cannot be used to attach property acquired post-petition for payment of discharged taxes); *In re* Monteith, 23 B.R. 601 (Bankr. N.D. Ohio 1982) (IRS not permitted to setoff post-petition tax refund against *dischargeable* pre-petition tax debt). The existence of the exception does not of itself give creditors with excepted claims the right to levy on exempt assets during the bankruptcy case. *In re* Hebermehl, 132 B.R. 651 (Bankr. D. Colo. 1991). There may also be an exception for liens for nondischarged federal criminal fines. Although 18 U.S.C. § 3613(e) provides that such fines are not discharged and that liens for such fines shall not be voided in bankruptcy, it does not specifically permit the imposition of a lien after bankruptcy on property protected by § 522(c). However, 18 U.S.C. § 3613(a) provides that such fines are enforceable, notwithstanding any other federal law, against all property of the person fined except property listed in that subsection.

513   *E.g.*, 11 U.S.C. § 522(d)(10), (11).

514   *See In re* Farr, 278 B.R. 171 (B.A.P. 9th Cir. 2002) (section 522(c) applies only to extent of value exempted).

515   *See In re* Farr, 278 B.R. 171 (B.A.P. 9th Cir. 2002) (creditor holding non-dischargeable debt could enforce lien acquired post-petition on portion of debtor's equity that exceeded sum of senior liens and debtor's $100,000.00 California exemption claimed in chapter 7 case).

516   *See* § 10.4.2.6.7, *supra*.

Chapter 11   Dealing with Secured Creditors

11.1 Introduction

One of the greatest advances for consumers under the Bankruptcy Code came in the powers they were given with respect to secured debts. Under the prior Bankruptcy Act, relatively little could be done to protect consumer debtors from the holders of secured claims. A straight bankruptcy generally did not affect the status of otherwise valid liens or security interests and, as a practical matter, few Chapter XIII plans could get very far with respect to secured claims unless the holders of those claims agreed to the plan or were not affected by it. Now, in contrast, almost every conceivable type of secured claim can be altered in some way through bankruptcy, often to a tremendous degree and with very significant benefits for the debtor.

Some of the ways that the rights of secured creditors can be affected are covered in previous chapters of this manual, and those discussions are not repeated here. Chapter 9, *supra*, dealt at length with two of these areas: the automatic stay which, among other things, generally prevents lien creation, perfection, and enforcement once the petition is filed;[1] and the turnover provisions, through which the debtor may recover property from a secured party who has obtained possession of it prior to the case.[2] Chapter 10, *supra*, discusses the various powers of the debtor to avoid transfers, including some liens and security interests which impair the debtor's exemptions.[3] Through use of these powers the debtor can often entirely eliminate security interests in household goods, judicial liens, execution sales, garnishments, repossessions, setoffs, and other transfers of property which occurred before the debtor filed the bankruptcy case.

All of these powers discussed in previous chapters can, of course, enormously improve a debtor's position with respect to many secured claims. This Chapter is devoted to several additional ways in which the problems of secured claims may be lessened or removed. These methods may be used either in conjunction with those options already discussed or when those other remedies are not available.

11.2 Determination of the Allowed Secured Claim

11.2.1 The Concept of the Allowed Secured Claim

11.2.1.1 General Principles

Critical to an understanding of most of the provisions dealing with secured claims is a familiarity with a key concept in the Bankruptcy Code—the "allowed secured claim." Although not defined in the definition section of the Code,[4] the term is explained by section 506, which is applicable to cases under all chapters of the Code.[5]

Code section 506(a) provides that every claim filed which is secured by a lien on property, or subject to a setoff, is an allowed secured claim to the extent of the creditor's interest in the estate's interest in such property or in the amount subject to setoff.[6] To the extent that the creditor's interest, or the amount subject to setoff, is less than the total amount of the claim, the claim is an allowed unsecured claim. Put another way, a secured claim cannot be an allowed secured claim in an amount greater than the value of the estate's interest in the collateral. An under-secured claim which is

---

1   11 U.S.C. § 362; *see* § 9.4, *supra*.

2   11 U.S.C. §§ 542, 543; *see* § 9.9, *supra*.

3   11 U.S.C. § 522(f)–(h); *see* § 10.4.2, *supra*.

4   The term "claim," however, is defined at 11 U.S.C. § 101(5).

5   11 U.S.C. § 103(a).

6   Disputes sometimes arise about whether a particular transaction gave rise to a secured claim, a lease, or some other type of claim. For discussion of this issue see § 11.8 (rent-to-own contracts), § 12.9.1 (land installment sale contracts and motor vehicle leases), *infra*. In order for an allowed secured claim to exist, the estate must have an interest in the property. Unfortunately, several decisions of the Eleventh Circuit Court of Appeals have erroneously held that Florida and Alabama debtors do not have an interest in motor vehicles after repossession. *See* § 9.9.2, *supra*. There are also issues when a claim of the Internal Revenue Service is secured by an ERISA plan that is not property of the estate. Most courts have held the IRS's interest is not an allowed secured claim. Internal Revenue Serv. v. Snyder, 343 F.3d 1171 (9th Cir. 2003) (claim secured by ERISA plan not an allowed secured claim); *In re* Wingfield, 284 B.R. 787 (E.D. Va. 2002) (ERISA plan cannot create an allowed secured claim).

filed and allowed[7] is therefore divided, or "bifurcated," into two parts: (1) an allowed secured claim in an amount equal to the value of the collateral and (2) an allowed unsecured claim for any excess of the total claim over the value of the collateral.

One simple example is a debt, not otherwise subject to defenses or setoffs, in the amount of $2000.00 secured by an automobile worth $500.00. With respect to that creditor's claim, the debtor could request a determination that the claim be divided into an allowed secured claim of $500.00 and an allowed unsecured claim of $1500.00. Similarly, if, during the entire 90 days prior to the filing of the petition, a debtor had a bank account of $500.00 subject to setoff by a bank to which the debtor owed $2000.00, the court would determine that the bank had an allowed secured claim of $500.00 and an allowed unsecured claim of $1500.00.

The purpose of this concept is quite apparent. In accord with the general bankruptcy scheme, it looks to the actual interests of the parties existing at the time of the bankruptcy to determine their rights. A secured creditor's interest is measured by what it would receive at that time through enforcement of its lien, and that amount, of course, would be the value of the collateral. The Code, therefore, gives that secured creditor a better position than the unsecured creditors in bankruptcy only to that extent, even if the secured creditor's total claim is much greater than the value of the collateral, because in a practical sense the secured creditor can realize only that value due to its secured status. Its rights to property other than the collateral are no greater than those of other creditors. By treating the amount of the claim which is in excess of the value of the collateral as an unsecured claim, the Code prevents the secured creditor from exercising undue power or getting an unfair advantage in the bankruptcy case over the unsecured creditors out of proportion to the true value of its security interest. There is no special exception to these principles for liens held by the government.[8]

11.2.1.2 Limitations on Claim Bifurcation in Chapter 7

Unfortunately, the Supreme Court somewhat limited the application of the allowed secured claim concept in *Dewsnup v. Timm*.[9] There, despite clear statutory language in Code section 506(d) stating that a lien securing a claim that is not an allowed secured claim is void,[10] the Court held that a chapter 7 debtor could not have a lien declared void on the basis of that language, even though the lien did not secure a claim that was an allowed secured claim under section 506(a). Construing the language extremely narrowly, the Court held that it rendered a lien void only if it secured a claim that was disallowed under section 502 of the Code, such as a claim to which a valid defense existed.[11]

Thus, bifurcation of secured claims is generally relevant in chapter 7 only in the context of redemption under Code section 722, which is discussed later in this chapter,[12] and in cases in which the debtor originally filed under chapter 13 and then converted to chapter 7.[13] However, a few courts have limited *Dewsnup* to its facts and found that a totally unsecured lien does not come within the prohibition on bifurcation for chapter 7.[14] Additionally, an under-secured judicial lien can be avoided in chapter 7 under the formula created by 11 U.S.C. § 522(f)(2) because it impairs the debtor's exemption.[15]

11.2.1.3 Claim Bifurcation Alive and Well in Other Chapters

After *Dewsnup*, some creditors argued that the case prevents the use of bankruptcy to void under-secured liens in other contexts than the one presented by that case, including chapter 13. Such arguments were not successful for a number of reasons. First, the Supreme Court made clear in *Dewsnup* that it was limiting its holding to the case where a chapter 7 debtor relied solely on section 506(d) to render a

---

7 Filing and allowance of claims are provided for in 11 U.S.C. §§ 501 and 502.

8 *See In re* Voelker, 42 F.3d 1050 (7th Cir. 1994) (value of property subject to tax lien determines what debtor must pay to satisfy lien in chapter 13 plan; however, value of property exempt from levy under Internal Revenue Code must be included in determining allowed secured claim); *In re* Crook, 966 F.2d 539 (10th Cir. 1992) (sovereign immunity was not violated by chapter 12 plan stripping down mortgages held by government).

9 502 U.S. 410, 112 S. Ct. 773, 116 L. Ed. 2d 903 (1992).

10 11 U.S.C. § 506(d) so provides, with certain exceptions which were not pertinent in *Dewsnup*.

11 112 S. Ct. at 777, 116 L. Ed. 2d at 911. Based on a close reading of *Dewsnup*, an argument remains that a debtor may strip down a non-recourse loan in chapter 7. (A non-recourse loan is one in which the creditor's only option to collect is to foreclose on or repossess the collateral. Note that in some cases, state law may limit the creditor's remedies to recovery of the collateral.) Because, in the typical non-recourse situation, the creditor has no right to maintain an *in personam* action against the debtor, it follows that the creditor could not have an allowable unsecured claim against the estate for the amount by which it is under-secured. *See* 11 U.S.C. § 502(b)(1). Consequently, that creditor's lien is arguably void to the extent of the under-security under § 506(d) and *Dewsnup* because that portion of its claim would neither be secured nor allowable pursuant to § 502.

12 *See* § 11.5, *infra*.

13 *See* 11 U.S.C. § 348(f)(1)(B); § 11.6.1.3.3, *infra*.

14 *E.g., In re* Howard, 184 B.R. 644 (Bankr. E.D.N.Y. 1995) (unsecured judgment lien can be stripped off). *But see In re* Talbert, 344 F.3d 555 (6th Cir. 2003) (mortgage cannot be stripped off in chapter 7 case); Ryan v. Homecomings Fin. Network, 253 F.3d 778 (4th Cir. 2001) (wholly unsecured mortgage may not be stripped off in chapter 7); *In re* Laskin, 222 B.R. 872 (B.A.P. 9th Cir. 1998).

15 *See* § 10.4.2.3, *supra*.

lien void.[16] It therefore did not purport to affect the law in other chapters, such as chapter 12 and chapter 13. Second, the Court found a lack of legislative history indicating that Congress had intended section 506(d) to be used independently in this manner, a use which would have significantly changed the law in liquidation cases.[17] In contrast, there is clear legislative history indicating congressional intent that a chapter 13 debtor, for example, may free property from a lien by paying the lienholding creditor the present value of its allowed secured claim through a chapter 13 plan.[18] And third, *Dewsnup* does not deal with situations where section 506 operates in tandem with another Code section. In fact, it recognizes the debtor's right to redeem certain property in section 722,[19] which allows redemption by payment to the lienholder of the amount of its allowed secured claim.[20] Similarly, provisions in chapter 12 and 13 provide that a plan shall be confirmed if it provides for a secured creditor to be paid the amount of its allowed secured claim,[21] that (except as provided in the plan) the confirmation of the plan vests all property of the estate in the debtor free and clear of any lien of any creditor provided for in the plan,[22] and that the terms of the confirmed plan are binding upon all creditors.[23]

The Supreme Court explicitly recognized that most liens could be reduced to the value of their collateral ("stripped down") through a chapter 13 plan in *Associates Commercial Corp. v. Rash*.[24] In that case the Court discussed the amount by which a claim secured by a debtor's property could be stripped down in chapter 13.[25] And, as discussed below, since *Dewsnup* was decided, numerous courts of appeals have held that liens on other property, as well as some home mortgage liens, may still be stripped down through a chapter 13 plan.[26]

11.2.2 Procedure for Determining the Allowed Secured Claim

11.2.2.1 Overview of the Process

Any dispute concerning the amount of the allowed secured claim usually arises[27] as an objection filed by the debtor after the creditor has filed its claim.[28] The objection, filed under Bankruptcy Rule 3007, commences an adversary proceeding if it raises the validity and/or extent of the creditor's lien.[29] Therefore, it should often be filed in the form of a complaint.[30] However, if the only issue is the question of valuation, a motion under Bankruptcy Rule 3012 will suffice as a way to bring the matter before the court.[31]

If the secured creditor fails to file a proof of claim, the debtor may file a claim on behalf of the creditor in the amounts the debtor believes to be secured or unsecured.[32] Provided that the claims bar date has not passed, the creditor then has an opportunity to file its own claim, which would supersede the one filed by the debtor.[33] In either case, the debtor may then initiate a proceeding against the creditor, by complaint or (if valuation is the only issue) by motion, seeking a court order determining the amount of the claim.[34]

A complaint objecting to a secured claim can and should raise any and all defenses to the creditor's claim, because the claim may only be allowed to the extent it is enforceable

---

16 112 S. Ct. at 778, n.3, 116 L. Ed. 2d at 911, n.3.

17 112 S. Ct. at 779, 116 L. Ed. 2d at 912.

18 *See* 124 Cong. Rec. H11,107 (daily ed. Sept. 28, 1978) (remarks of Rep. Edwards); 124 Cong. Rec. S17,424 (daily ed. Oct. 6, 1978) (remarks of Sen. DeConcini) (secured creditor's lien retained under § 1325(a)(5) only secures the value of the collateral and is satisfied in full by plan payments equal to present value of allowed secured claim); H.R. Rep. No. 95-595, at 124 (1977).

19 112 S. Ct. at 776, 116 L. Ed. 2d at 909.

20 *See* § 11.5, *infra*.

21 11 U.S.C. §§ 1225(a)(5), 1325(a)(5); *see* §§ 11.6.1, 16.5.5.3, *infra*.

22 11 U.S.C. §§ 1227(b), (c); 1327(b), (c).

23 11 U.S.C. §§ 1227(a), 1327(a); *see* § 12.11, *infra*.

24 520 U.S. 953, 117 S. Ct. 1879, 138 L. Ed. 2d 148 (1997); *see also In re* McClurkin, 31 F.3d 401, 406 (6th Cir. 1994); *In re* Hammond, 27 F.3d 52, 56 (3d Cir. 1994).

25 *See* § 11.2.2.3, *infra*.

26 *See* §§ 11.2.2, 11.6.1.2, *infra*.

27 As discussed below in this subsection, some courts determine the allowed secured claim in chapter 13 cases, without an objection, in the context of confirming the debtor's chapter 13 plan.

28 However, the prior filing of a claim is probably not an absolute prerequisite for seeking a determination of the extent to which a claim is secured. Indeed, it is not at all clear that a secured claim even need be filed to be allowed. *See* § 11.6.1.3.3.2, *infra*. Nonetheless, the safer practice is probably for the debtor to file a claim on behalf of the creditor, as discussed in § 11.2.2, *infra*.

29 Fed. R. Bankr. P. 7001. The objection is a core proceeding under 28 U.S.C. § 157(b)(2)(K). *See generally* § 13.2.4, *infra*.

30 Fed. R. Bankr. P. 7003; *see* Form 65, Appx. G.8, *infra*.

31 *See* Advisory Committee Note to Fed. R. Bankr. P. 3012; *see also* Ontra, Inc. v. Wolfe, 192 B.R. 679 (W.D. Va. 1996) (separate adversary proceeding to determine value not necessary if value determined as part of proceeding seeking leave to sell property).

32 Fed. R. Bankr. P. 3004.

33 *Id.*

34 If the debtor is requesting a determination based on a claim filed by the debtor, the best practice may be to file a complaint seeking declaratory judgment that the claim is allowable only in the amounts reflected in the debtor's proof of claim. Even if the debtor does not seek a declaratory judgment setting the amount of the claim, the creditor may be bound by the debtor's claim, especially if the creditor received notice of the claim, failed to object to it or file a substitute claim, and accepted payments under a confirmed plan. Lawrence v. Educ. Credit Mgmt. Corp., 251 B.R. 467 (E.D. Va. 2000), *rev'd on other grounds sub nom. In re* Kielisch, 258 F.3d 315 (4th Cir. 2001).

against the debtor.[35] If the debtor (and thus the bankruptcy estate) no longer has the property which the creditor claims as collateral, because it was transferred, stolen or otherwise lost, the creditor does not have an allowed secured claim under the language of section 506.[36] Or, for example, the debtor may object that the claim is not secured at all, because the purported security interest is invalid.[37]

A creditor must attach evidence of granting and perfection of a claimed security interest to the proof of claim.[38] If it fails to do so an objection may be filed. An objection may also bring out the fact that such evidence does not exist, or does not comply with Uniform Commercial Code requirements that the collateral be adequately described.[39] The agreement may violate the requirement that the debtor's signature be reasonably legible and below the language concerning the claimed security interest.[40] If the security interest language is in small print, or buried in a credit card agreement, or appears only on a sales slip, unnoticed by the consumer, courts may deem it to be an unenforceable adhesion clause not knowingly signed by the debtor.[41] And consumers may sometimes be able to limit the security agreement to fewer items, or totally invalidate it, by challenging creditors' methods of applying payments to particular items purchased and arguing that the proper method is "first-in, first-out."[42] Similarly, a close reading of the agreement may reveal that it does not secure all of the amounts claimed by the creditor.[43]

Although some courts determine allowed secured claims as part of the plan confirmation process, the safest practice is to file a complaint or motion objecting to a secured claim, and to have the claim specifically determined in a separate proceeding. Absent such a proceeding, the claim may be presumed valid.[44] If the court does not affirmatively decide that the claim is not allowable for some particular reason, the claim may be allowed as filed, notwithstanding contrary provisions in the debtor's chapter 13 plan.[45] In any case, the

---

35   11 U.S.C. § 502(b)(1). It is not totally clear whether, if the creditor's claim is divided into a secured claim and an unsecured claim, the defenses of the debtor can be applied first to the secured claim rather than the unsecured claim. Certainly, a good argument can be made for this when the defense is in some way logically related to the lien in particular, rather than to the debt in general. *See In re* Jablonski, 70 B.R. 381 (Bankr. E.D. Pa. 1987) (Truth in Lending recoupment subtracted from secured portion of claim).

36   *In re* Gilsinn, 224 B.R. 710 (Bankr. E.D. Mo. 1997); *In re* Gabor, 155 B.R. 391 (Bankr. N.D. W. Va. 1993).

37   *See In re* Brigance, 234 B.R. 401 (W.D. Tenn. 1999) ("deferred presentment service" holding check which debtor had obligation to redeem within 14 days was not holder of a secured claim); *In re* Reese, 194 B.R. 782 (Bankr. D. Md. 1996) (creditor could not claim Uniform Commercial Code security interest in fixtures which had become part of debtor's realty).

38   Fed. R. Bankr. P. 3001(c), (d).

39   *In re* Esteves Ortiz, 295 B.R. 158 (B.A.P. 1st Cir. 2003) (installment sales agreement did not create security interest); *In re* Shirel, 251 B.R. 157 (Bankr. W.D. Okla. 2000) (phrase "all merchandise" in credit card application did not sufficiently describe collateral and therefore did not create security interest in refrigerator by debtor); U.C.C. § 9-203(1)(a); *see* National Consumer Law Center, Repossessions and Foreclosures § 3.2.3 (5th ed. 2002 and Supp.).

40   *In re* Nedeau, 24 B.R. 1 (Bankr. S.D. Fla. 1982).

41   *See In re* Jackson, 9 U.C.C. Rep. Serv. 1142 (W.D. Mo. 1971); *In re* Gibson, 234 B.R. 776 (Bankr. N.D. Cal. 1999) (cross-collateralization buried in small print was not enforceable); National Consumer Law Center, Unfair and Deceptive Acts and Practices §§ 4.4, 5.2.3 (5th ed. 2001 and Supp.). *But see In re*

Conte, 206 F.3d 536 (5th Cir. 2000).

42   *E.g., In re* Vandeusen, 147 B.R. 9 (Bankr. E.D.N.C. 1992), *aff'd*, 155 B.R. 358 (E.D.N.C. 1993); *In re* Coomer, 8 B.R. 351 (Bankr. E.D. Tenn. 1980); *see also In re* Freeman, 956 F.2d 252 (11th Cir. 1992) (where agreement provided no method of apportioning payments, purchase money character not preserved); Southeast Bank of Ala. v. Borg-Warner Acceptance Corp., 760 F.2d 1240 (11th Cir. 1985). See also cases cited in § 10.4.2.5, *supra*.

43   *E.g., In re* Stendardo, 991 F.2d 1089 (3d Cir. 1993) (mortgage holder was not entitled to recover amounts it paid for taxes and insurance after it had obtained a judgment absent specific authority in mortgage agreement).

44   11 U.S.C. § 502(a); *see* H.R. Rep. No. 95-595, at 352 (1977).

45   Cen-Pen Corp. v. Hanson, 58 F.3d 89 (4th Cir. 1995) (secured claim was not affected by chapter 13 case, notwithstanding provision of confirmed plan stating that lien of creditor was void, because no separate adversary proceeding had been filed to determine rights of creditor); *In re* Simmons, 765 F.2d 547 (5th Cir. 1985) (secured claim allowed as filed where debtor did not object, notwithstanding contrary provisions in confirmed chapter 13 plan); *In re* Hobdy, 130 B.R. 318 (B.A.P. 9th Cir. 1991); *see also In re* Bateman, 331 F.3d 821 (11th Cir. 2003) (although mortgage creditor's claim for arrearages had to be disallowed to extent it exceeded amount provided for in confirmed plan, the arrearages disallowed would remain owing after the case because plan could not modify mortgage creditor's secured claim); *In re* Tarnow, 749 F.2d 464 (7th Cir. 1984) (where secured claim was not filed timely and determined, a lien remained valid and was not affected by chapter 11 plan). However, some courts permit the plan confirmation proceeding to be the proceeding in which the valuation determination is made and do not require a separate proceeding for that purpose. If adequate notice is given to the creditor that this will occur, nothing in the Code appears to preclude this procedure. *In re* Fili, 257 B.R. 370 (B.A.P. 1st Cir. 2001) (secured claim filed before bar date but after confirmation hearing disallowed where creditor given fair notice that its claim would be disallowed under chapter 13 plan and creditor ignored the confirmation process); *In re* Wolf, 162 B.R. 98 (Bankr. D.N.J. 1993); *In re* Tucker, 35 B.R. 35 (Bankr. M.D. Tenn. 1983); *In re* Russell, 29 B.R. 332 (Bankr. E.D.N.Y. 1983) (both cases holding that a confirmed plan may determine the status of a claim filed by a secured creditor); *see also In re* Calvert, 907 F.2d 1069 (11th Cir. 1990). In any event, the fact that a plan has been confirmed does not necessarily preclude the debtor from challenging a proof of claim after confirmation. *In re* Enewally, 368 F.3d 1165 (9th Cir. 2004); *In re* Lewis, 875 F.2d 53 (3d Cir. 1989); *In re* Tomasevic, 275 B.R. 103 (Bankr. M.D. Fla. 2001) (debtor could seek reconsideration under § 502(j) of secured claim that was deemed allowed in confirmed plan); *In re* Adams, 264 B.R. 901 (Bankr. N.D. Ill. 2001) (debtor could seek valuation of allowed secured claim after confirmation if confirmed plan did not fix value of secured claim); § 12.11, *infra. But see In re* Bateman,

creditor involved must receive specific notice that a proceeding concerning its lien is taking place.[46] Even in jurisdictions where it is well known that the court will address the validity and extent of secured claims in the plan confirmation process, notice should include service of a copy of the plan detailing the proposed treatment of the claim, on any affected creditor.[47] The notice should also include a clear statement that the creditor's allowed secured claim will be determined at confirmation.[48] Moreover, to be safe, if the creditor is an insured depository institution, such notice should probably be made by certified mail addressed to an officer of the institution.[49]

Assuming the matter is not settled, the issue of value will ultimately be tried and determined by the court. As the proof of claim itself is normally prima facie evidence of the claim,[50] creditors will argue that the debtor has the burden of proof on this issue. However, this argument should fail. While the proof of claim is prima facie evidence under section 502(a), once the party objecting to the claim introduces contrary evidence, the claimant must then bear the ultimate burden of proof.[51]

The methods of contesting and proving value in this context will generally be the same as in the context of proceedings for relief from the automatic stay where value is an issue. Therefore, the discussion of that question in Chapter 9 of this manual may be helpful. Discovery is often useful, to find out whether the creditor has appraised the collateral and to determine how much the creditor has actually realized by foreclosure on other similar security. Requests for admission may be a way of shifting the cost of a successful proof of value to the creditor if it denies that value.[52] Ultimately, the debtor may have to be prepared to prove a value different from that testified to by the creditor's witnesses, which may require retention of an appraiser or other expert. However, creative discovery, requests for admission as to similar sales and use of industry guides, and so forth, or stipulations of undisputed facts, may provide ways to avoid this expense.

An important difference is that, unlike in proceedings for relief from the stay in which the debtor often tries to prove that the value of property is high so that there is equity in it, under section 506 the debtor's goal is to prove that the value of the property is as low as possible. A number of issues arise in this context, generally going to the language in section 506(a) that "value shall be determined in light of the purpose of the valuation and of the proposed disposition or use of such property."[53]

11.2.2.2 Date of Valuation

The first issue that arises under section 506 is the date as of which value should be determined. Depending upon whether the property is increasing or decreasing in value, it may be in the debtor's interest to argue for an earlier date or a later one, whichever will produce a lower value. Although there is little difference in most cases, the issue can be significant in cases of rapidly depreciating new automobiles, rapidly appreciating real estate, or property which has been damaged since the filing of the case.

Some courts, perhaps in the interest of simplicity, have chosen the filing date of the petition or plan as the valuation date in all cases, on the theory that the parties' rights are frozen as of that date in most other respects.[54] There are several arguments against this approach. First, in chapter 13 cases, there is language[55] that the creditor is entitled to the "value as of the effective date of the plan." While that phrase could be interpreted merely as stating a present value standard,[56] it has been held that the amount of the claim should be evaluated as of the date of the confirmation hearing.[57] Another, perhaps better, argument is that under

---

331 F.3d 821 (11th Cir. 2003) (objection to claim must be filed prior to confirmation; court did not address how debtor could object when claim filed after confirmation). If as a result of a decision on an objection a creditor has been overpaid, the trustee or debtor can recover the overpayment from the creditor. *See In re* Sims, 278 B.R. 457 (Bankr. E.D. Tenn. 2002); *In re* Stevens, 187 B.R. 48 (Bankr. S.D. Ga. 1995).

46   *See In re* White, 908 F.2d 691 (11th Cir. 1990) (bankruptcy court could not *sua sponte* disallow creditor's secured claim without specific notice to creditor that claim was to be challenged); *In re* Calvert, 907 F.2d 1069 (11th Cir. 1990) (specific notice must be given to holder of secured claim that court will determine extent to which its claim is secured at confirmation hearing; mere notice that confirmation hearing will be held is not sufficient); *In re* Shook, 278 B.R. 815 (B.A.P. 9th Cir. 2002) (when debtor listed claim as unsecured in schedules and plan did not specifically address creditor's claim, debtor could not seek to have claim deemed secured four-and-a-half years after confirmation). *But see In re* Karbel, 220 B.R. 108 (B.A.P. 10th Cir. 1998) (notice of motion mailed to creditor at address it had given for motions concerning mobile home transactions satisfied due process even though it concerned different type of collateral).

47   *See In re* King, 290 B.R. 641 (Bankr. C.D. Ill. 2003) (discussing requisites of notice required).

48   *See In re* Calvert, 907 F.2d 1069 (11th Cir. 1990). Absent such notice due process concerns may be implicated.

49   Fed. R. Civ. P. 7004(h).

50   Fed. R. Bankr. P. 3001(f); H.R. Rep. No. 95-595, at 352 (1977); S. Rep. No. 95-989, at 62 (1978).

51   *In re* Fid. Holding Co., 837 F.2d 696 (5th Cir. 1988); 9 Collier on Bankruptcy ¶ 3001.10 (15th ed. rev.).

52   Fed. R. Bankr. P. 7036 (incorporating Fed. R. Civ. P. 36); *see In re* Sweeten, 56 B.R. 675 (Bankr. E.D. Pa. 1986).

53   *See In re* Midway Partners, 995 F.2d 490 (4th Cir. 1993) (valuation determined in automatic stay proceeding not binding in claim allowance proceeding). *See generally* §§ 9.7.3.3.1, 10.3.3, *supra*.

54   *In re* Willis, 6 B.R. 555 (Bankr. N.D. Ill. 1980); *In re* Siegler, 5 B.R. 12 (Bankr. D. Minn. 1980); *In re* Adams, 2 B.R. 313 (Bankr. M.D. Fla. 1980); *see also In re* Hanson, 132 B.R. 406 (Bankr. E.D. Mo. 1991).

55   11 U.S.C. § 1325(a)(5)(B)(ii).

56   See discussion at § 11.6.1.3, *infra*.

57   *In re* Bernardes, 267 B.R. 690 (Bankr. D.N.J. 2001) (when purpose of valuation under § 506(a) is plan confirmation, holder

section 506(a) the purpose of the valuation is to protect the interest the creditor has at the time of valuation, because that would be all that could be realized were the creditor to obtain the property at that time. The creditor, after all, has an opportunity to force an earlier valuation by filing a complaint for relief from the stay. Some language in the legislative history suggests that the valuation under section 506 may well be different than an earlier valuation under section 362, but it is a bit unclear whether that language refers more to the different purposes of the valuations than to the different dates.[58] Using some of these rationales, a number of courts have used the date of the valuation proceeding (which is often the date of the confirmation hearing) as the critical date for valuation, looking to the value of the property as of that date.[59]

Finally, where there is a post-petition claim in a chapter 13 case, the court may choose the date the claim was filed as the valuation date. Some support for this approach is found both in the Code[60] and in the scant case law on the subject.[61] However, the statutory language in section 1305(b) calling for a determination "as of the date such claim arises" could also be read to call for valuation as of the date the post-petition debt was incurred.[62] Alternatively, the legislative history, which refers to the date of allowance,[63] could be interpreted as calling for valuation as of the date of the valuation proceeding.

11.2.2.3 Method of Valuation

11.2.2.3.1 Valuation standard

More controversial has been the issue of which method to use to determine value once a date has been chosen, an issue that has monetary significance in virtually every case. It is not surprising that many courts have addressed this issue.

Perhaps the easiest case is that of property which has been purchased quite recently in relation to the date of valuation. In such cases, courts have often looked simply to the price actually paid by a willing buyer to a willing seller, and adjusted it for any clear changes in the condition of the property.[64]

The more typical situation involves property of changing value that was purchased substantially in advance of the valuation date. The Supreme Court addressed this issue in the context of valuing a motor vehicle for purposes of a chapter 13 cramdown[65] in *Associates Commercial Corp. v. Rash*.[66] The court rejected the lower court's holding that the appropriate valuation would be the creditor's liquidation value and also rejected the creditor's argument that retail value was the correct figure to use. Instead, the court held that the language of section 506(a) dictated that the debtor's cost of replacing the property be used, but made clear that this cost would not include portions of the retail price that reflect costs a debtor would not incur to obtain a similar car in a similar condition, such as warranties, inventory storage, and reconditioning.[67] The court left to the bankruptcy courts, as triers of fact, the best way of determining replacement value based on the evidence presented.

11.2.2.3.2 Valuation of motor vehicles

Valuation issues arise most frequently, as they did in the *Rash* case, with respect to motor vehicles. Based upon *Rash*, debtors should have little trouble in convincing bankruptcy courts that creditors should not receive the retail value listed in various industry price guides, because that value includes items such as warranties, inventory storage, and reconditioning, precisely the items the Supreme Court held must be excluded from the value. Even when a vehicle is sold by a dealer "as is," some of these items are included.

Since *Rash*, courts have used a variety of different approaches to valuation of vehicles. Some courts have continued to use presumptive formulas, such as beginning at the midpoint between wholesale and retail value.[68] Others have begun with a presumption of retail value even though that

---

of crammed down mortgage not entitled to reconsideration of its claim based on post-confirmation increase in home value); *In re Kennedy*, 177 B.R. 967 (Bankr. S.D. Ala. 1995) (selecting the confirmation date approach, but collecting cases with a variety of holdings); *In re McLeod*, 5 B.R. 520 (Bankr. N.D. Ga. 1980); *see also In re Moreau*, 140 B.R. 943 (N.D.N.Y. 1992) (where property apparently greatly increases in value after valuation but before confirmation of chapter 13 plan, creditor was entitled to revaluation closer to confirmation date); *In re Crain*, 243 B.R. 75 (Bankr. C.D. Cal. 1999) (effective date of plan was ten days after confirmation order if no appeal taken).

58 S. Rep. No. 95-989, at 68 (1978).

59 *In re Weaver*, 5 B.R. 522 (Bankr. N.D. Ga. 1980); *In re Miller*, 4 B.R. 392 (Bankr. S.D. Cal. 1980); *In re Crockett*, 3 B.R. 365 (Bankr. N.D. Ill. 1980); *see also In re Pierce*, 5 B.R. 346 (Bankr. D. Neb. 1980) (value to be determined at date of § 722 redemption proceedings rather than date of petition).

60 11 U.S.C. § 1305(b).

61 *In re Klein*, 20 B.R. 493 (Bankr. N.D. Ill. 1982).

62 11 U.S.C. § 1305(b).

63 H.R. Rep. No. 95-595, at 427 (1977); S. Rep. No. 95-989, at 140 (1978).

64 *In re Two S Corp.*, 875 F.2d 240 (9th Cir. 1989) (price obtained through commercially reasonable sale by trustee was conclusive proof of value); *In re Willis, Jr.*, 6 B.R. 555 (Bankr. N.D. Ill. 1980); *In re Savloff*, 4 B.R. 285 (Bankr. E.D. Pa. 1980). However, because a new car depreciates significantly as soon as it leaves the dealer's lot, the price of a new car will rarely be its market value even a day after it was purchased.

65 *See* § 11.6, *infra*.

66 520 U.S. 953, 117 S. Ct. 1879, 138 L. Ed. 2d 148 (1997).

67 *Id.*, 520 U.S. at 964 n.6.

68 *E.g., In re Getz*, 242 B.R. 916 (B.A.P. 6th Cir. 2000); *In re Lyles*, 226 B.R. 854 (Bankr. W.D. Tenn. 1998); *In re Williams*, 224 B.R. 873 (Bankr. S.D. Ohio 1998); *In re Franklin*, 213 B.R. 781 (Bankr. N.D. Fla. 1997); *see also In re Renzelman*, 227 B.R. 740 (Bankr. W.D. Mo. 1998) (starting point of five percent less than retail value).

choice does not reflect the necessary deductions from retail value discussed in the *Rash* decision.[69] Others have taken evidence in an attempt to follow the Supreme Court's directives, sometimes coming out even below the wholesale value of the vehicle.[70]

Even if a particular method of valuation is used as a starting point by the court or by agreement between the parties, the debtor may offer evidence that the valuation of a particular vehicle should differ from the presumed value.[71] Initial presentation of relevant evidence by the debtor is especially important, as the debtor has the burden of coming forward with evidence to rebut the creditor's proof of claim, even though the ultimate burden remains on the creditor to prove its claim.[72]

The most promising line of argument for debtors is to focus on the Supreme Court's language that "replacement value" means the price a willing buyer in the debtor's trade, business, or situation would pay a willing seller to obtain property of like age and condition.[73] This language suggests that the market to look to should be the market of private sales of vehicles, such as those advertised by individuals in newspapers. The prices obtained in such sales, which are "as is" and do not include dealers' overhead such as showroom costs, are typically far below the retail values in industry guides.[74] Alternatively, debtors can base their valuations on values obtained in auction sales of similar vehicles following repossession. The prices realized at auction sales are also well below the retail value listed in industry guides. Such sales, which also do not have the dealer overhead involved, in fact are often touted by repossessing sellers as a perfect market of willing buyers and sellers in which to conduct a commercially reasonable sale in order to justify their repossession and deficiency collection practices.[75]

In order to prove the private market value of a debtor's vehicle, the debtor may of course present expert testimony of an auctioneer or similar witness. The debtor is also competent to give a value of the debtor's property,[76] but that value will be credible only to the extent the debtor provides persuasive reasons to justify it. If the debtor has attempted to sell the vehicle, or purchase a similar one, that experience may be a good basis for expressing an opinion on value. It may also be possible to obtain proof in the discovery process, through interrogatories requesting information about the price obtained at auction for similar vehicles which the creditor has recently repossessed, and requests for admission that newspaper ads accurately reflect the asking price for similar vehicles.[77] If a creditor denies such requests for admission, the cost of proving the truth of the statements can be shifted to the creditor. Moreover, a party responding to a request for admissions may not simply deny its truth without some investigation; thus, a creditor might even be sanctioned if it denied the truth without making reasonable inquiries, such as calling the telephone number listed in a newspaper advertisement.[78]

11.2.2.3.3 *Property other than automobiles*

With respect to household goods and other personal property without established industry guides to value, the problem of valuation is more difficult. The *Rash* decision's rejection of retail value for automobiles should clearly prevent purchase price, even from a used furniture store, from becoming the standard.[79] Again, the best guideline is probably the price that would be obtained at an auction, or in the garage sale market populated by individual buyers and sellers. In some areas there may also be people who, as an occupation, conduct yard sales for others and such people would also be good witnesses, as might a dealer or hobbyist who regularly frequents yard sales.[80] The debtor is also competent to give a value of the debtor's property,[81] but that value will be credible only to the extent the debtor provides persuasive reasons to justify it. Thus, a debtor might be instructed to go to a large number of sales and observe the prices of items similar to that in question. In many rural areas, auctioneers may be called to testify concerning the value of different items in that market. To avoid such expense, at least one court adopted its own depreciation

---

69 *In re* Russell, 211 B.R. 12 (Bankr. E.D.N.C. 1997).

70 *In re* McElroy, 210 B.R. 833 (Bankr. D. Or. 1997) (basing decision primarily on testimony of used car dealer).

71 *See In re* Jenkins, 215 B.R. 689 (Bankr. N.D. Tex. 1997) (encouraging the debtor and creditors bar to reach an accommodation for valuations subject to presentation of evidence in order to limit the court's involvement to special cases).

72 *See In re* Gates, 214 B.R. 467 (Bankr. D. Md. 1997) (proof of claim provides prima facie evidence relevant to valuation, subject to a burden on the debtor of coming forward with evidence sufficient to contradict it).

73 *Id.*, at n.2.

74 Some industry guides, such as the Kelly Blue Book (available at www.kbb.com), have a private party valuation for used cars that can be used for this purpose.

75 *See* National Consumer Law Center, Repossessions and Foreclosures § 10.9.3 (5th ed. 2002 and Supp.).

76 *See* § 11.3.2, *infra*.

77 *See Resolving Valuation Issues After Rash*, 16 NCLC RE-PORTS, *Bankruptcy and Foreclosures Ed.* 1 (July/Aug. 1997).

78 Fed. R. Civ. P. 36(a) (incorporated in Fed. R. Bankr. P. 7036).

79 There is substantial legislative history on valuation of personal property which justifies a lower valuation standard and which may even serve as a basis for distinguishing *Rash*. H.R. Rep. No. 95-595, at 124 (1977) ("Most often in a consumer case, a secured creditor has a security interest in property that is virtually worthless to anyone but the debtor. These items . . . have a high replacement cost. The mere threat of repossession operates as pressure on the debtor to pay the secured creditor [more than it would receive upon repossession].").

80 Under Federal Rules of Evidence 701 and 702, an individual may qualify as an expert or be permitted to express an opinion based upon knowledge and experience not possessed by the average person. *See* Advisory Committee Note to Fed. R. Evid. 702.

81 *See* § 11.3.2, *infra*.

standards for such property which depended on the purchase price and the time elapsed since the purchase.[82]

In the case of real estate, an appraisal is often necessary. As in other types of proceedings, there may be ways to avoid or minimize the costs involved. For example, if a court accepts an appraiser's testimony that a property is worth an amount denied by an opposing party in a request for admissions, that party can be required to pay the cost of the appraiser.[83] In other cases, the parties may agree to be bound by the appraisal of an appraiser that both trust, thereby avoiding the expense of the appraiser's court appearance. Often, an appraiser will give an estimate of value that the parties can accept (or which can be a basis for negotiation) based on less than a full-blown appraisal report. Other courts may allow, or require, testimony by affidavits. Finally, a request for production of documents or a request for admissions may turn up a useful appraisal in the creditor's files. It is not uncommon for foreclosing lenders to obtain a low appraisal of real estate in anticipation of foreclosure. In doing so, they hope to protect against a later claim that the property was sold at foreclosure for less than reasonable value.

In any case, it is a good idea for attorneys doing a significant number of bankruptcy cases to develop a relationship with at least one appraiser in whom they have confidence. The prospect of continued business from an attorney will make the appraiser much more willing to cooperate in minimizing costs in a particular case.

Again, a method of proof available in all such cases is to have the debtor testify as to the value of the property, especially when the opposing party has no first-hand knowledge of the property or its condition. Generally, under the Federal Rules of Evidence, a witness may testify as to the value of his or her own property.[84] Even if the debtor has no personal knowledge of the value of the property, the debtor may nevertheless testify as to any problems with the condition of the property which decrease its value below that of other property of the same model or type.

A common issue in valuations of real estate is whether liquidation costs should be deducted when the debtor proposes to retain and use the property. This issue is discussed in more detail in the section directly below. It is clear that no additional amount should be added for an assignment of rents taken as part of the creditor's collateral, because the rental value is already taken into account in determining the property's market value.[85]

11.2.2.3.4 Computation of value

When there are prior liens on property ahead of the lien which is to be valued, the amount of those liens must first be subtracted to determine if there is value over and above the prior liens. If the prior liens equal or exceed the value of the property, then the allowed secured claim of a creditor with a lower priority lien is equal to zero.[86] When making these calculations, debtor's counsel should make certain to account for tax and municipal liens which take first priority position in most jurisdictions by statute. These are frequently forgotten in the process of determining the allowed secured claims of junior creditors. If the debtor is not the sole owner of the property, the value of the debtor's fractional interest after deduction of liens must then be determined.

Under *Rash* the value should not include the costs involved in listing a property for sale with a real estate broker, because the debtor will not receive any services from a broker. Other costs of sale will also have to be examined under the rationale of *Rash*, which will necessitate reevaluation of decisions which had considered whether costs of sale should be deducted in determining value.[87]

Valuation issues can also arise when the property that secures a claim, or a portion of that property, is not property of the estate. For example if the debtor is a one-half owner of a property, the allowed secured claim should be determined by comparing the claim only to the debtor's one-half ownership interest, with the full amount of prior liens deducted from the value of that one-half interest.[88] If the property is owned by the entireties or by joint tenants with a right of survivorship, some courts also require calculation of the value of the survivorship interest.[89] If the debt is secured in whole or in part by an ERISA pension plan, or some other property that is not property of the estate, the value of the non-estate property should not be included in the computation of the allowed secured claim.[90]

An additional issue which may arise with respect to certain types of statutory liens, such as federal tax liens, is whether in assigning a value to property subject to a lien, the value of property exempt from levy should be included. (For example, the Internal Revenue Code exempts certain property from levy on tax liens.)[91] Two courts of appeals,

---

82 *In re* Willis, 6 B.R. 555 (Bankr. N.D. Ill. 1980) (for example, for furniture, the value is determined to be seventy-five percent of price in first year since purchase, fifty percent in second year, twenty-five percent in third year and zero percent thereafter).

83 *See* § 11.2.2.2, *supra*; Form 93, Appx. G.10, *infra*.

84 Joe T. Dehmer Distributors, Inc. v. Temple, 826 F.2d 1463 (5th Cir. 1987); Bingham v. Bridges, 613 F.2d 794 (10th Cir. 1980); Kinter v. United States, 156 F.2d 5 (3d Cir. 1946).

85 *In re* Thompson, 352 F.3d 519 (2d Cir. 2003).

86 *In re* Smith, 92 B.R. 287 (Bankr. S.D. Ohio 1988).

87 *In re* Taffi, 96 F.3d 1190 (9th Cir. 1996) (*en banc*).

88 *In re* Abruzzo, 249 B.R. 78 (Bankr. E.D. Pa. 2000) (tenancy in common).

89 *See In re* Pletz, 221 F.3d 1114 (9th Cir. 2000); *In re* Basher, 291 B.R. 357 (Bankr. E.D. Pa. 2003) (interest in entireties property should be determined by joint actuarial analysis).

90 Internal Revenue Serv. v. Snyder, 343 F.3d 1171 (9th Cir. 2003) (claim secured by ERISA plan not an allowed secured claim); *In re* Wingfield, 284 B.R. 787 (E.D. Va. 2002) (ERISA plan cannot create an allowed secured claim). *But see In re* Jones, 206 B.R. 614 (Bankr. D.D.C. 1997).

91 26 U.S.C. § 6334.

reversing lower courts, have held that all property subject to the lien must be included, even though some of it could not be seized by the Internal Revenue Service.[92] There is certainly a good argument that the lower courts were correct, because the purpose of the exemption from levy is defeated if the debtors have to pay the lienholder the value of the property that is exempt from levy. Other courts have read the Internal Revenue Code exemption to exempt property not just from a levy, as the Ninth Circuit held, but also from the tax lien itself.[93]

Finally, in some cases the estate's interest in the property securing a debt may be valueless because the property is gone. The property may have been destroyed, stolen, or lost to the debtor prior to the bankruptcy, or sold by the debtor subject to the lien. If the property is no longer owned by the debtor, the estate's interest in the property has no value. In such a case, the allowed secured claim is zero and the entire claim is deemed an allowed unsecured claim.[94]

11.3 Creditors' Efforts to Obtain Security After Bankruptcy Commenced

11.3.1 Overview

The first problem often faced by debtors with secured creditors is that of a creditor's attempt in the bankruptcy court to exercise the rights it would otherwise have available to seize or foreclose on the collateral. These attempts may come in a number of forms.

The most common method is the creditor's motion for relief from the automatic stay which is essentially a request for permission from the bankruptcy court to take action against the debtor outside the bankruptcy forum. These proceedings are discussed in detail in Chapter 9, *supra*.[95]

In an attempt to avoid the difficulties it might face in such a proceeding, or to add to the relief it could obtain, the creditor might file several other types of actions.

11.3.2 Reclamation of Property

Such creditor actions may occasionally include a Complaint to Reclaim Property, sometimes known as a Complaint in Reclamation. Although the Code does not specifi-

cally provide for such a proceeding, it seems fairly clear that the expanded jurisdiction of the bankruptcy court would include jurisdiction over the assertion of any valid rights that the creditor might have, including a right to gain possession of the collateral. However, these rights are clearly limited by specific provisions contained in the Code. Most important among these limitations is the automatic stay against lien enforcement in section 362(a). Unless the creditor meets the requirements for relief from the stay, there would be no point in proceeding to the question of the creditor's right to possession of the property, as the stay prohibits "any act" to enforce a lien.

Other limitations on the creditor's right to possession that could also be raised to defeat many reclamation complaints would include the debtor's powers under the exemption provisions in section 522,[96] the debtor's right to redeem under section 722,[97] the fact that a creditor is bound by a confirmed chapter 13 plan, giving the debtor the right to possession of the property in question,[98] or the fact that the creditor's lien may be found void under section 506(d) because the creditor is wholly or partially under-secured. Finally, a number of bankruptcy courts have held that they simply do not wish to become involved in creditors' attempts to circumvent normal state court proceedings and have abstained from ruling on creditor claims for repossession.[99] For this reason, creditors seeking possession of property usually file motions for relief from the automatic stay.

11.3.3 Abandonment of Property by the Trustee

Another tactic that is occasionally tried is to have the trustee abandon her interest in the property sought by the secured creditor. Under the previous Act, such abandonment left parties with interests in the property free to proceed outside of the bankruptcy court. A trustee may thus be asked by the creditor to voluntarily abandon the collateral, as the trustee may do under section 554(a), or the court may be requested by a creditor to order such abandonment under section 554(b).

It should first be noted that abandonment is proper only in situations where the property is either burdensome to the estate or of inconsequential value to the estate.[100] As the first of these conditions will rarely exist, creditors will usually attempt to prove the second, arguing that there is no non-exempt equity, or perhaps no equity at all in the property above the value of the liens.

---

92 *In re* Voelker, 42 F.3d 1050 (7th Cir. 1994); United States v. Barbier, 896 F.2d 377 (9th Cir. 1990), *rev'g* 84 B.R. 190 (D. Nev. 1989) *and* 77 B.R. 799 (Bankr. D. Nev. 1987).
93 *In re* Ray, 48 B.R. 534 (Bankr. S.D. Ohio 1985).
94 *In re* Gabor, 155 B.R. 391 (Bankr. N.D. W. Va. 1993) (where debtor's wife took automobile that secured loan and debtor did not know her whereabouts or whereabouts of vehicle, estate's interest in automobile had no value).
95 *See* § 9.7, *supra*.

96 See Chapter 10, *supra*, for further discussion of the debtor's powers under this section.
97 *See* § 11.5, *infra*.
98 11 U.S.C. § 1327(a); *see* § 12.11, *infra*.
99 *See In re* Calabria, 5 B.R. 73 (Bankr. D. Conn. 1980) (state court "far more able" to hear mortgage foreclosure claims).
100 11 U.S.C. § 554.

Especially where there is some equity, these arguments should fail. Any equity is property of the estate, even if claimed as exempt, because Congress has made clear that exempt property is part of the bankruptcy estate under the Code.[101] And property may have value to the estate in a non-monetary sense. In a chapter 13 case, it may be necessary to the production of income, or the necessity for the replacement of property may cause difficulties in completing a successful plan. Furthermore, in both chapters 7 and 13, the debtor may claim an interest of nominal value as exempt, making it clear that the interest is a part of the estate.[102]

More importantly, the limitations described above as to reclamation would also apply in cases where abandonment is sought. Technically, even the seeking of an abandonment might be considered a violation of the automatic stay against "any act" to enforce a lien, and a debtor can argue that relief from the stay is a prerequisite for seeking abandonment. Moreover, even if property is abandoned by the trustee, the automatic stay would still prevent any act to obtain possession from the debtor through enforcement of a lien or to collect a pre-petition claim, unless such relief from the stay has been granted by the court.[103] Although such acts would not violate the provisions of the stay pertaining to property of the estate, they would violate those provisions prohibiting any act to collect a pre-petition claim.[104]

Similarly, the abandonment provisions must be read together with other sections of the Code, for example, sections 506, 522, 722, and 1327. To the extent that abandonment runs counter to the purposes of those sections, it should not be allowed, and the property should be considered of value to the estate.[105] In addition, if property has vested in the debtor through confirmation of a chapter 13 plan,[106] the trustee no longer has an interest in the property that can be abandoned.[107]

Procedurally, abandonment cannot happen before the end of the case, except "after notice and a hearing." Because of the specific meaning given to those words by the Code,[108] the debtor must be certain to request a hearing if notice is given of possible abandonment of property about which the debtor is concerned, otherwise no hearing is likely to be held. In cases in which the trustee does decide to abandon property the court may prohibit that action. While the trustee does have considerable discretion on this subject, it was generally assumed under the prior Act that it was subject to control by the court.[109]

11.3.4 Disposition by the Trustee Under Section 725

Creditors also have sought to make use of section 725 of the Code which allows the trustee to "dispose of" property. Although the legislative history is not very illuminating, it appears that the purpose of this section is merely to supplement the other powers of the trustee where none of them seem applicable, and perhaps to provide a statutory basis for some types of voluntary reclamations when there is no objection by the trustee. (For example, if the estate has some significant interest in the property securing a claim, section 554 could not be used by the trustee.) By its very language, section 725 indicates that it is to be read together with the various other sections which control disposition of property, including sections 362, 506, 522, and 722. As in section 554, there is no indication that the trustee has the power to dispose of any interest of the debtor in property.

Nonetheless, trustees in a few places have attempted to sell homes and other property in chapter 7 cases, even though there is no equity available for unsecured creditors, in order to realize commissions and fees on such sales. These attempts are clearly improper.[110] Often, they may be prevented simply by bringing them to the attention of the United States trustee. If that is not sufficient, an objection to the sale should be filed with the court.

There is one situation, though, in which it is to the debtor's advantage to have the trustee sell property, regardless of whether there are significant proceeds for creditors. If the debtor will not be able to save a property from foreclosure, a sale by a bankruptcy trustee can sometimes avoid significant capital gains tax liability. Normally, when a property is sold at foreclosure, the owner of the property is liable for taxes on any capital gain over the property's basis. If a property is abandoned by the trustee, and later sold at foreclosure, this could mean a substantial tax liability for the debtor. But if the trustee sells the property, the estate incurs the tax liability and the debtor does not. However, the danger of debtors being saddled with such capital gains liabilities after foreclosure has been greatly reduced by new

---

101 H.R. Rep. No. 95-595, at 368 (1977). It is unclear how long exempt property remains property of the estate, however. See discussion of this issue in Chapter 10, *supra*.

102 See cases cited in § 10.4.2.1, *supra*.

103 *In re* Motley, 10 B.R. 141 (Bankr. M.D. Ga. 1981); *In re* Cruseturner, 8 B.R. 581 (Bankr. D. Utah 1981); *see also In re* Boback, 273 B.R. 158 (Bankr. E.D. Tenn. 2002) (distinguishing stay relief from abandonment); *In re* Shelton, 273 B.R. 116 (Bankr. W.D. Ky. 2002) (same).

104 11 U.S.C. § 362(a) (1), (5), (6).

105 *See In re* Hawkins, 8 B.R. 637 (Bankr. N.D. Ga. 1981).

106 11 U.S.C. § 1327(b). But see cases cited in § 9.4.2, *supra*, holding that when property of estate vests in the debtor it is no longer protected by provisions pertaining to property of the estate.

107 *In re* Stark, 8 B.R. 233 (Bankr. N.D. Ohio 1981).

108 11 U.S.C. § 102(1).

109 *See* 5 Collier on Bankruptcy ¶ 554.LH[1] (15th ed. rev.). Fed. R. Bankr. P. 6007(c) makes clear that, where any party objects, the court shall decide upon the propriety of abandonment.

110 *In re* Kusler, 224 B.R. 180 (Bankr. N.D. Okla. 1998) (criticizing trustee for selling encumbered property which would not realize significant dividends for creditors); *see In re* Williamson, 94 B.R. 958 (Bankr. S.D. Ohio 1988); *In re* Landenreau, 74 B.R. 12 (Bankr. W.D. La. 1987); *In re* Lambert Implement Co., 44 B.R. 860 (Bankr. W.D. Ky. 1984).

provisions of the Internal Revenue Code which allow a large capital gains tax exemption for sale of a residence as often as every two years.[111]

In the event that this section is used, its effect and operation is similar to that of section 554. The trustee may act only "after notice and a hearing." One authority, at least, states that any dispute concerning the trustee's proposed action must be resolved by the court.[112] Certainly, if state law procedural or substantive rights may be lost, the debtor should strongly oppose any attempt by the trustee to sell property that does not have significant non-exempt equity that would be available to unsecured creditors.[113] As a practical matter, this section should be little used in consumer cases, because it appears to be intended mainly to give flexibility in the disposition of property in a bankruptcy where there are non-exempt assets for the trustee to administer. Few bankruptcies involving consumer debtors involve any significant administration or distribution of assets by the trustee.

11.3.5 Holding of Cash Collateral by Creditors

A final and conceptually different way in which debtors may be deprived of certain property after bankruptcy, should also be mentioned. After filing a bankruptcy case, a debtor may suddenly find that a bank or credit union to which the debtor owes money refuses to allow withdrawals from the debtor's bank or share account. This refusal occurs because the bank or credit union, if it has a right of setoff under section 553,[114] is considered to be a holder of cash collateral.

If, under section 553, the bank retains a right of setoff, it may not exercise that setoff without first obtaining relief from the automatic stay.[115] However, it is not automatically required to turn over the property to the trustee or the debtor under section 542, because section 542(b) creates an exception excusing payment of a debt to the extent that it may be offset against a claim against the debtor. Moreover, section 542 requires turnover only of property the trustee may use, sell or lease or that the debtor may exempt. The trustee may not use, sell, or lease cash collateral without the creditor's consent unless the court, after notice and a hearing, finds that there is adequate protection[116] and approves such use.[117] In

addition, the debtor's exemption rights may also be defeated by a right of setoff allowed under section 553, just as they may be by a valid non-avoidable lien.[118]

The Supreme Court has held that the freezing of a debtor's account by a bank with a right of setoff does not violate the automatic stay. In *Citizens Bank of Maryland v. Strumpf*[119] the court held that an "administrative hold" on the debtor's account was not a setoff prohibited by Code section 362(a)(7) because it did not purport to permanently reduce the account.[120] The court also held that the freeze was not an exercise of control over the debtor's property because the bank account was only a promise by the bank to pay the depositor and the bank was merely refusing to perform on its promise.[121]

In any case, it is clear that a bank has no right of setoff against property acquired post-petition based upon a pre-petition debt.[122] To the extent the bank did not have a deposit to setoff against its debt at the time of the petition, it is the holder of an unsecured claim.

The problem of a bank account "freeze" and setoff can generally be prevented simply by making sure the debtor has no money in the account as of the date of the bankruptcy petition. If a debtor has not depleted bank accounts prior to bankruptcy, those accounts, or parts of them, may in effect be seized by the bank or credit union creditor. Once this has occurred, assuming that a valid right of setoff exists and unless there are defenses to the underlying claim or adequate protection can be provided, there may be little that can be done to recover the debtor's funds.

11.4 Statement of Intentions with Respect to Property Securing Consumer Debts

Section 521(2) requires the debtor to file a statement of certain intentions with respect to property securing consumer debts. The debtor need not state all of his or her plans on this statement. All that is required is a statement of whether the debtor intends to retain or surrender the collateral, whether it is claimed as exempt, and whether the debtor intends to reaffirm the debt. The Official Bankruptcy Form for the Statement of Intentions has been amended to clarify that it was not intended to require the debtor to choose redemption, surrender, or reaffirmation in every case.[123] The debtor may choose other options besides those listed on the

---

111 26 U.S.C. § 121; *see* National Consumer Law Center, Repossessions and Foreclosures (5th ed. 2002 and Supp.).

112 6 Collier on Bankruptcy ¶ 725.02 (15th ed. rev.).

113 *See In re* Landenreau, 74 B.R. 12 (Bankr. W.D. La. 1987); *In re* Lambert Implement Co., 12 B.C.D. 651 (Bankr. W.D. Ky. 1984).

114 See Chapter 10, *supra,* for a discussion of section 553.

115 11 U.S.C. § 362(a)(7).

116 For a discussion of the concept of adequate protection, see Chapter 9, *supra.*

117 11 U.S.C. § 363(c)(2). It would be difficult to provide adequate protection in such cases, except perhaps through granting of a lien which clearly exceeded the amount of the cash collateral in value.

---

118 However, several courts have held that no setoff may be had against exempt property. See § 10.4.2.6.7, *supra.*

119 516 U.S. 16, 116 S. Ct. 286, 133 L. Ed. 2d 258 (1995).

120 *Id.,* 116 S. Ct. at 289. See § 9.4.3, *supra,* for further discussion of when a bank account freeze is permissible.

121 *Id.,* 116 S. Ct. at 290.

122 *See* § 10.4.2.6.7, *supra.*

123 Official Bankruptcy Form 8, *reprinted in* Appendix D, *infra.* Advisory Committee Note to 1997 Amendment to Official Form 8.

form.[124] In many jurisdictions, for example, a debtor may choose to simply continue paying an automobile loan without either redeeming or reaffirming the debt.[125]

The statement of intention must be filed within thirty days of the filing of a chapter 7 petition or on or before the date of the meeting of the creditors, whichever is earlier.[126] The court, within that period, can also extend the deadline.[127] The statement must be served on the trustee and all creditors named in the statement on or before the date it is filed.[128] Thereafter, the debtor may amend it as of right at any time up to the time when performance is to take place under Code section 521(2)(B).[129] The statement is not required in chapter 13 cases, despite some slight ambiguity on the subject.[130]

Section 521(2) also requires that the debtor "shall perform his intention," within forty-five days after the statement is filed, or such additional time as the court for cause within that period allows. In most cases this is quite simple; if the debtor stated an intent to retain or exempt property, that has long since been accomplished. If the debtor's intention is to surrender the property, there is no requirement to deliver it or to execute a deed to effectuate the surrender, because the Code provision was not designed to provide a substitute for normal state law proceedings to enforce a creditor's rights to collateral.[131] The new provisions can be seen as setting a guideline for when redemption or reaffirmation should be accomplished if that is the debtor's intent. But, as the section expressly provides that it does not affect substantive rights,[132] it should not be a bar to redemptions, even if they are not accomplished by the deadline.[133] The forty-five day guideline may even prove helpful to a debtor who has no other way of stopping a foreclosure or repossession, because it may extend the time a debtor may retain possession of property.[134]

Although the chapter 7 trustee is supposed to "ensure that the debtor shall perform" the stated intention, the Code provides no mechanism for the trustee to use. As a practical matter, trustees will probably become involved if asked by a secured creditor, and that is likely only if the stated intention is redemption or reaffirmation. Presumably, the trustee could then bring the matter to the attention of the court for resolution, something the secured creditor could do just as easily on its own.

The statement of intention thus seems designed primarily as a way for secured creditors to obtain notice of what the debtor plans to do, and as a guideline to when redemption and reaffirmation should occur. However, because substantive rights are expressly left unaffected, the debtor may change his or her mind about what is planned and apparently would not have to file a new statement if that happened.[135] Also, there appears to be no sanction provided for failing to carry through on stated intentions.[136] At most, that conduct would give a secured creditor an additional argument in seeking relief from the automatic stay.[137]

124   *In re* Price, 370 F.3d 362 (3d Cir. 2004); *In re* Parker, 139 F.3d 668 (9th Cir. 1998); Capital Communications Fed. Credit Union v. Boodrow, 126 F.3d 43 (2d Cir. 1997); Lowry Fed. Credit Union v. West, 882 F.2d 1543 (10th Cir. 1989); Home Owners Funding Corp. of Am. v. Belanger, 128 B.R. 142 (E.D.N.C. 1990), *aff'd*, 962 F.2d 345 (4th Cir. 1992); 4 Collier on Bankruptcy ¶ 521.10 (15th ed. rev.). *But see In re* Burr, 160 F.3d 843 (1st Cir. 1998); *In re* Johnson, 89 F.3d 249 (5th Cir. 1996) (debtor who was in default on secured debt did not have right to retain collateral without either redeeming or reaffirming debt; decision limited to debtors in default at the time of filing); *In re* Taylor, 3 F.3d 1512 (11th Cir. 1993); *In re* Edwards, 901 F.2d 1383 (7th Cir. 1990); *see also* § 7.3.6, *supra*; Completed Official Form 8, Appx. F, *infra*.

125   *See In re* Parlato, 185 B.R. 413 (Bankr. D. Conn. 1995); § 11.5.4, *infra*.

126   11 U.S.C. § 521(2).

127   11 U.S.C. § 521(2).

128   Fed. R. Bankr. P. 1007(b)(2).

129   Fed. R. Bankr. P. 1009(b).

130   *See* § 7.3.6, *supra*; 4 Collier on Bankruptcy ¶ 521.10 (15th ed. rev.).

131   *In re* Theobald, 218 B.R. 133 (B.A.P. 10th Cir. 1998).

132   *See also In re* Price, 370 F.3d 362 (3d Cir. 2004); *In re* Peacock, 87 B.R. 657 (Bankr. D. Colo. 1988). *See generally In re* Winters, 69 B.R. 145 (Bankr. D. Or. 1986).

133   Lowry Fed. Credit Union v. West, 882 F.2d 1543 (10th Cir. 1989); *In re* Rodgers, 273 B.R. 186 (Bankr. C.D. Ill. 2002) (redemption not barred by expiration of forty-five days from

statement of intention); 4 Collier on Bankruptcy ¶ 521.10 (15th ed. rev.).

134   *See In re* Simpson, 147 B.R. 14 (Bankr. E.D.N.C. 1992) (debtor's counsel was justified in refusing to consent to relief from stay for creditor to complete foreclosure before expiration of forty-five-day period).

135   *See In re* Stefano, 134 B.R. 824 (Bankr. W.D. Pa. 1991); *In re* Eagle, 51 B.R. 959 (Bankr. N.D. Ohio 1985). However, the rules do provide for amending the statement. Fed. R. Bankr. P. 1009(b).

136   *In re* Crooks, 148 B.R. 867 (Bankr. N.D. Ill. 1993) (debtor's statement which erroneously stated intention to retain car did not preclude debtor from later surrendering it); *see also In re* French, 185 B.R. 910 (Bankr. M.D. Fla. 1995) (debtor was justified in refusing to sign reaffirmation agreement that added attorney fees to debt); *In re* Williams, 64 B.R. 737 (Bankr. S.D. Ohio 1986); *In re* Eagle, 51 B.R. 959 (Bankr. N.D. Ohio 1985).

137   *In re* Rathbun, 275 B.R. 434 (Bankr. D.R.I. 2001) (adopting opinion in *Donnell*); *In re* Donnell, 234 B.R. 567 (Bankr. D.N.H. 1999) (denying injunctive relief to enforce security interest and refusing to deny discharge of debt or dismiss case); *In re* Weir, 173 B.R. 682 (Bankr. E.D. Cal. 1994) (no implied cause of action or other remedy, except possibly relief from stay if debtors are in monetary default on obligation, if creditor believes debtors have not filed adequate statement of intentions); *In re* Bracamortes, 166 B.R. 160 (Bankr. S.D. Cal. 1994) (court would not compel debtor to amend statement of intentions to add allegedly omitted creditor; creditor could seek relief from stay if it felt its rights were violated).

11.5 Right of Redemption in Chapter 7 Cases

11.5.1 Purpose

One of the new provisions in the Bankruptcy Code when it was enacted in 1978 was section 722, which provides for a limited right of redemption in chapter 7 cases. In essence, it provides that for certain secured consumer debts the security interest may be eliminated upon payment to the creditor of the value of its collateral, that is, the amount of its allowed secured claim.

The purpose of this section, like that of section 506, is to prevent secured creditors from getting an unfair advantage out of proportion to the value of their security. Section 722, however, is aimed solely at preventing an unfair advantage over the debtor, rather than over the other creditors. Under prior law, a secured creditor had the right to demand full payment or to obtain a reaffirmation of a secured debt after bankruptcy, and to repossess or otherwise recover the collateral if such payment or reaffirmation did not occur. This often allowed the creditor to collect far more than the market value of the collateral due to the fact that the debtor could not easily replace the property securing the debt. Congress felt it was unfair for a creditor holding a security interest in some necessity like a refrigerator to demand payment of a debt of several hundred dollars when the collateral was worth only $50.00 on the market, simply because the item was irreplaceable for an indigent debtor who could not afford to purchase a new one.[138]

11.5.2 Limitations on the Right to Redeem

The redemption provision provides a simple procedure, within the chapter 7 case, for the debtor to remove a creditor's lien by paying the creditor the real value of the property. There are several limitations on that right, however. It is available only to individual debtors, and only with respect to certain property and certain debts. Specifically, it can only be used in cases of dischargeable consumer debts[139] secured by tangible personal property[140] which has been either exempted by the debtor or abandoned by the trustee. It is not available with respect to real estate or intangible liquid assets. And it is doubtful that redemption can occur without creditor agreement after a case is closed

(unless, perhaps, the case is reopened), though it can occur after the discharge has been entered.[141]

Although the operation of section 722 is normally quite straightforward, questions occasionally arise as to whether a debt incurred by the owner of a small business is a consumer debt, especially if combined with other debts later incurred for business purposes.[142] As the definition of "consumer debt" was derived from the definitions in the Truth in Lending Act,[143] case law and interpretations under that statute should prove helpful.

There may also be questions concerning whether property has been or can be claimed as exempt, because unless the property is exempted or abandoned, section 722 cannot be utilized. Generally, these questions are dealt with in those sections of this manual concerning exemptions[144] and abandonment.[145] In redemption cases, the questions usually arise when the debtor has no equity in the property and the creditor asserts that, therefore, it cannot be claimed as exempt. As discussed in Chapter 10, *supra*, so long as the debtor has any legal interest in property, that property may be claimed as exempt.[146] In any case, if the debtor does not have any equity, it should not be difficult to have the estate's interest abandoned by the trustee under section 554 of the Code.

It is clear that once any interest in the property is exempted, the entire property may be redeemed.[147] This is necessarily true because the debtor never has a right to exempt that property interest which is subject to the lien; the debtor may only exempt his or her own residual interest in the property. If the right to redeem were limited to the interest exempted, it could never reach any interest subject to a lien. Nor is the right of redemption limited to the dollar values of the exemption. If the debtor exempts some interest, then the remaining interest subject to the lien may be dealt with under section 722.[148] (However, if the debtor has non-exempt equity in the property, section 722 will not affect the estate's rights to the equity.)[149]

---

138 H.R. Rep. No. 95-595, at 127, 128 (1977).

139 "Consumer debt" is defined at 11 U.S.C. § 101(8).

140 The term "tangible personal property" has been interpreted broadly for this purpose. *In re* Walker, 173 B.R. 512 (Bankr. M.D.N.C. 1994) (a fixture such as vinyl siding could still be tangible personal property that was redeemable under § 722 in some cases).

141 *In re* Hawkins, 136 B.R. 649 (Bankr. W.D. Va. 1991).

142 *See In re* Runski, 102 F.3d 744 (4th Cir. 1996) (office equipment used for business purposes could not be redeemed because it was not intended primarily for personal, family, or household use); *In re* Boitnott, 4 B.R. 122 (Bankr. W.D. Va. 1980) (auto loan for vehicle used by family later consolidated with business loan held to be consumer debt).

143 15 U.S.C. § 1602(h); *see* National Consumer Law Center, Truth in Lending § 2.2 (5th ed. 2003).

144 *See* Ch. 10, *supra*.

145 *See* § 3.5, *supra*.

146 Once the property has been listed as exempt and the deadline for objecting to exemptions has run, the creditor will be barred from raising any issue about the validity of the exemption. 11 U.S.C. § 522(*l*); Fed. R. Bankr. P. 4003(b); *see* Taylor v. Freeland & Kronz, 503 U.S. 638, 112 S. Ct. 1644, 118 L. Ed. 2d 280 (1992).

147 6 Collier on Bankruptcy ¶ 722.04 (15th ed. rev.).

148 *Id.*

149 Indeed, there is some question whether the right of redemption exists where there is some non-exempt equity. *See* Bare, *The*

11.5.3 Redemption by Payment in Installments

A final issue is whether section 722 gives the debtor the right to pay the amount of the allowed secured claim in installments. Most courts have found that, because section 524 provides for reaffirmation *agreements*, both parties must concur in any arrangement for installment payments under section 722.[150] These courts generally have held that unless the creditor agrees otherwise, the debtor must redeem through cash payment of the redemption amount, and that neither the debtor nor the court can impose an installment arrangement upon the creditor.[151]

These decisions may present a problem to the debtor who cannot afford to pay the entire allowed secured claim in cash and is unwilling or unable to negotiate a reaffirmation agreement. Two possible solutions are treatment of the debt under chapter 13 or simply continuing the payments on the entire debt without reaffirming. (The latter solution would not permit the reduction of the debt to the value of the collateral.) Both of these options are discussed later in this chapter.

There may also be another way of overcoming the early decisions prohibiting redemption in installments without the creditor's consent. Section 521(2)(B), gives the court the authority to grant additional time for the debtor to perform an intended redemption. Thus, a debtor should have a clear right under that section to request additional time to redeem, by installments or otherwise.[152] None of the decisions which barred redemption in installments held that a court could not grant such a request under section 521(2)(B).

Still another option for a debtor who cannot afford to redeem in a lump sum is to obtain financing of the lump sum. If the vehicle is worth significantly less than the amount due on the existing car loan, or if the debtor is delinquent on the loan, financing a redemption may be the most advantageous alternative. Financing a redemption may cost less to the debtor than the alternatives of continuing to pay the original loan, obtaining another vehicle with a high-interest loan (if credit is available), or filing a chapter 13 case, which could require payments to other creditors as well as additional fees and costs.[153]

11.5.4 Secured Creditors Who Refuse to Agree to Continued Installment Payments

The secured creditor who refuses installment payments may also present a problem to the chapter 7 debtor who is current on payments for a secured debt such as an automobile loan or a mortgage. Secured creditors whom the debtor does not propose to affect in the bankruptcy will often simply continue to accept payments and not attempt to enforce their security interests as long as payments are current. Occasionally, however, a creditor will try to foreclose on the basis of a contract clause that makes the bankruptcy itself a default on the obligation.

Many courts have stated that, although a debtor has not reaffirmed a secured claim, a creditor holding that claim has no right to exercise its rights under such a clause as long as payments are current.[154] As discussed earlier, one theory supporting this result is that the protection of section 541(c), which invalidates bankruptcy clauses as to property of the estate, passes through to the debtor.[155] In addition it may be argued that in this context enforcement of such a contract clause is unconscionable or not in good faith under the Uniform Commercial Code or other law.[156] If such arguments are not effective, the debtor can usually obtain relief by converting the case to a chapter 13, if the case is still

---

Bankruptcy Reform Act of 1978, 47 Tenn. L. Rev. 567, 568 (1980) (suggesting that there is not a right of redemption in such cases).

150 *In re* Bell, 700 F.2d 1053 (6th Cir. 1983); *In re* Polk, 76 B.R. 148 (B.A.P. 9th Cir. 1987); *In re* Harp, 76 B.R. 185 (Bankr. N.D. Fla. 1987); *In re* Cruseturner, 8 B.R. 581 (Bankr. D. Utah 1981); *In re* Zimmerman, 4 B.R. 739 (Bankr. S.D. Cal. 1980); *In re* Miller, 4 B.R. 305 (Bankr. E.D. Mich. 1980); *In re* Stewart, 3 B.R. 24 (Bankr. N.D. Ohio 1980); *see also In re* Vinson, 5 B.R. 32 (Bankr. N.D. Ga. 1980) (debtor may not unilaterally reaffirm home mortgage).

151 In many cases, of course, the debtor may wish to avoid a reaffirmation agreement. For the considerations involved, see Chapter 8, *supra*, and Chapter 14, *infra*.

152 *See* 6 Collier on Bankruptcy ¶ 722.05[2] (15th ed. rev.).

153 Potential sources of redemption financing, albeit at high interest rates, are 722 Redemption Funding at (888) 278-6121 and Redemption Financial Services at (877) 265-8844.

154 *See, e.g.,* Lowry Fed. Credit Union v. West, 882 F.2d 1543 (10th Cir. 1989); Riggs Nat'l Bank v. Perry, 729 F.2d 982 (4th Cir. 1984); Home Owners Funding Corp. of Am. v. Belanger, 128 B.R. 142 (E.D.N.C. 1990), *aff'd*, 962 F.2d 345 (4th Cir. 1992); *In re* Brock, 23 B.R. 998 (Bankr. D.D.C. 1982); *In re* Corona, 1 Collier Bankr. Cas. 2d (MB) 899 (Bankr. C.D. Cal. 1980) (holding that repossession after bankruptcy would be an attempt to force reaffirmation of discharged debt and that creditor had no right to repossess if payments were current); 6 Collier on Bankruptcy ¶ 722.05[3] (15th ed. rev.); *see also* § 11.3.4, *supra*; *In re* Winters, 69 B.R. 145 (Bankr. D. Or. 1986) (secured creditor's attempt to enforce bankruptcy default clause after discharge constitutes impermissible attempt to collect on personal liability). *But see In re* Taylor, 3 F.3d 1512 (11th Cir. 1993); *In re* Edwards, 901 F.2d 1383 (7th Cir. 1990); *In re* Bell, 700 F.2d 1053 (6th Cir. 1983); *In re* Whitaker, 85 B.R. 788 (Bankr. E.D. Tenn. 1988). If the creditor is a governmental unit, then foreclosure is probably also prohibited by section 525. It could also be argued that by utilizing the bankruptcy clause the creditor is attempting to deny the right of the debtor to obtain a discharge in bankruptcy. See discussion of discrimination by private parties in Chapter 14, *infra*.

155 *See* § 8.8.2, *supra*.

156 *See* U.C.C. §§ 1-203, 2-302; *see also In re* Rose, 21 B.R. 272 (Bankr. D.N.J. 1982) (creditor's acceptance of payments after bankruptcy waived any contractual right to accelerate debt upon debtor's bankruptcy).

pending, or by commencing a new chapter 13 case after the chapter 7 case is closed. Once the debtor is in chapter 13, there are effective restraints on the secured creditor, as discussed later in this chapter.

Indeed, the threat of conversion to chapter 13, in which the creditor can be forced to accept installments and possibly reduced payments as well, or of other litigation, is usually sufficient to force a creditor to accept a redemption in which the allowed secured claim is reaffirmed and paid in installments. The threat may be so effective that the creditor may even agree to an arrangement more advantageous to the debtor—that the creditor will not enforce its security interest as long as certain payments on an amount reduced to the value of the collateral are made—without the debtor reaffirming the debt.[157] Nothing in the Code precludes such an arrangement, which has the significant advantage of eliminating any possible liability of the debtor for a later deficiency judgment based upon a reaffirmed debt in states where deficiency judgments are permitted.

However, if the debtor cannot convert to chapter 13, or file a chapter 13 case, and the debtor is in a judicial circuit in which the court of appeals has held that a creditor may repossess after bankruptcy if personal liability is not reaffirmed, the debtor may have few practical alternatives to reaffirming the debt. In such cases, the debtor's counsel should at a minimum resist a reaffirmation for more than the current value of the collateral and should not agree to any additional charges, such as attorney fees, being added to the debt.

An alternate approach, especially for appliances and items of personal property with relatively little value, is to ignore the security interest entirely and wait to see if the creditor takes post-bankruptcy action to repossess. Many creditors take no such action because repossession and resale is not economical. Moreover, debtors can be advised not to allow repossessing agents into their homes. The creditor cannot breach the peace in order to repossess. Usually, creditors who cannot achieve repossession of collateral simply give up, rather than incur the expense necessary to pursue *in rem* actions, like replevin, that are required in most states to force the debtor to surrender personal property.[158]

11.5.5 Uses in Practice

The right to redeem is used most often to reduce the amount payable on purchase money or possessory security interests in household goods such as appliances, and on both purchase-money and nonpurchase-money (or possessory)

security interests in motor vehicles. The former, unlike nonpossessory nonpurchase-money security interests in household goods and certain other items, are not avoidable under section 522.[159] Similarly, security interests in motor vehicles are not normally avoidable unless they are nonpurchase-money and nonpossessory and the vehicle is a tool of the trade of the debtor or a dependent.[160]

Except when the creditor agrees to installment payments, or the court permits them, consumer debtors use section 722 mainly to redeem items of low value, because the total value of the item must be paid in cash. (As discussed above, in cases in which there is collateral of higher value and where the creditor cannot be forced to accept installments, the debtor must use one of the other remedies discussed in this chapter.) When redemption for a cash payment is possible, it provides a simple procedure by which the debtor may eliminate the security interest as well as the debt (which is discharged) once and for all. In some cases, when the property has no resale value or is subject to more than one lien, a secured creditor's interest may be totally eliminated under section 722 if the liens ahead of that creditor are greater than the value of the property.[161]

The only factual issue that is likely to arise is the value of the property. The discussions of valuation elsewhere in this book have some relevance to redemption.[162] However, the Supreme Court decision adopting a replacement value standard can be distinguished for valuations related to redemption.[163] As a creditor has no risk of depreciation or destruction of collateral when redemption is made in a lump sum,[164] there is no reason to compensate the creditor at replacement value rather than at the amount available in a liquidation of the property.[165] As in cases involving the automatic stay or

---

157 See Form 62, Appendix G.8, *infra,* for a sample of such an agreement.

158 A variety of approaches to dealing with repossession of property are discussed in detail in National Consumer Law Center, Repossessions and Foreclosures (5th ed. 2002 and Supp.).

159 For a discussion of these rights, see Chapter 10, *supra.*

160 *See* § 10.4, *supra.*

161 *In re* Groth, 269 B.R. 766 (Bankr. S.D. Ohio 2001) (creditor who refused to accept surrender of boat required to allow debtor to redeem for one dollar); *In re* Williams, 228 B.R. 910 (Bankr. N.D. Ill. 1999) (redemption allowed for the amount required to obtain release of the lien); *In re* Altenberg, 6 B.C.D. 331, 1 C.B.C. 2d 807, (Bankr. S.D. Fla. 1980) (redemption allowed by payment of filing fee for notice of lien discharge to creditor whose lien was subordinate to lien which exceeded value of debtor's automobile).

162 *See* §§ 9.7.3.3.1, 11.2.2.3.3, *supra.*

163 Associates Commercial Corp. v. Rash, 520 U.S. 953, 117 S. Ct. 1879, 138 L. Ed. 2d 148 (1997).

164 This risk was a primary rationale for the Court's decision in *Rash. See In re* Dunbar, 234 B.R. 895 (Bankr. E.D. Tenn. 1999).

165 *In re* Weathington, 254 B.R. 895 (B.A.P. 6th Cir. 2000) (liquidation value for automobile redemption); *In re* Barse, 309 B.R. 109 (W.D.N.Y. 2004), *aff'g* 301 B.R. 404 (Bankr. W.D.N.Y. 2003) (wholesale value); *In re* Podnar, 307 B.R. 667 (Bankr. W.D. Mo. 2003) (trade-in value); *In re* Zell, 284 B.R. 569 (Bankr. D. Md. 2002); *In re* Ard, 280 B.R. 910 (Bankr. S.D. Ala. 2002); *In re* Henderson, 235 B.R. 425 (Bankr. C.D. Ill. 1999) (vehicle valued at foreclosure sale value, presumed to be Blue Book trade in value); *In re* White, 231 B.R. 551 (Bankr. D. Vt. 1999); *In re* Donley, 217 B.R. 1004 (Bankr. S.D. Ohio 1998)

exemptions, the date of valuation may be critical. Because the type of property subject to redemption usually depreciates in value over time, it is normally to the debtor's advantage to have the valuation date be the date of redemption rather than the date the bankruptcy petition was filed. At least one court has adopted that date as determinative,[166] and others have taken a similar approach, using the date of the valuation hearing.[167]

However, if a case has been converted from chapter 13 to chapter 7, any valuation of the property that occurred in the chapter 13 case will continue to apply for purposes of section 722.[168] By the same token, any payments made toward the allowed secured claim in the chapter 13 case will be credited toward the amount necessary to redeem after conversion to chapter 7.[169]

Section 722 is apparently meant to be used without resort to the court in the first instance. When the parties agree to value and terms, redemption is accomplished simply by paying the creditor.[170] Of course, when there is no agreement, the court's intervention is necessary, sought either by a motion to redeem,[171] or perhaps a complaint for declaratory judgment to determine that an amount tendered is, in fact, the amount of the allowed secured claim. The debtor need not wait until the time for dischargeability complaints has expired to file such a proceeding,[172] and normally should

act earlier, because once that time has expired the bankruptcy case is likely to be closed before the proceeding can be filed.[173]

Some retailers have responded to court hostility to their overly aggressive reaffirmation tactics[174] by instead insisting that consumers redeem personal property that is subject to a security interest through installment payments. As the personal property involved would have little or no value if it were repossessed, the redemption may be an unwise and expensive means for a debtor to retain the property. Creditors that encourage debtors to make this unwise choice may seek to use the redemption process to avoid the procedural requirements and court oversight necessary to obtain a valid reaffirmation.[175] Several courts have asserted authority to review and reject redemption agreements that are unfair to a debtor.[176]

11.6 Using Chapter 13 to Deal with Secured Creditors: The Chapter 13 Cramdown

11.6.1 Modification of Secured Creditors' Rights in Claims Not Secured Only by Real Estate That Is the Debtor's Principal Residence

11.6.1.1 In General

Perhaps the greatest powers to affect the rights of secured creditors are found in the provisions of chapter 13. Bankruptcy Code section 1322 provides that the debtor's plan may modify the rights of holders of most secured claims, other than some claims secured only by a security interest in real property that is the debtor's principal residence. In addition, section 1322(b)(3) and (b)(5) provide that as to any claim, including a claim secured only by the debtor's principal residence, the plan may provide for the curing of a default over a reasonable period of time.

Most of the flexibility given to the debtor in chapter 13 comes from the broad right to modify the rights of secured

---

(redemption of mobile home allowed for total payments of $1250.00 because that is what the creditor could recover if it repossessed and resold the home). Another reason to distinguish *Rash* for redemptions is specific legislative history related to valuations of personal property. The legislative history makes clear that replacement value is not the appropriate standard. H.R. Rep. No. 95-595, at 124 (1977); *see In re* Williams, 224 B.R. 873 (Bankr. S.D. Ohio 1998) (citing legislative history); § 11.2.2.3.3, *supra.*

166 *In re* Pierce, 5 B.R. 346 (Bankr. D. Neb. 1980); *see also* 6 Collier on Bankruptcy ¶ 722.05[1] (15th ed. rev.).

167 *In re* Podnar, 302 B.R. 49 (Bankr. W.D. Mo. 2003); *In re* King, 75 B.R. 287 (Bankr. S.D. Ohio 1987) (relevant date for determining value of collateral sought to be redeemed is the later of date on which debtor filed request to determine the value of the collateral or the date on which the request, if contested, is heard).

168 11 U.S.C. § 348(f)(1)(B), added by the Bankruptcy Reform Act of 1994, Pub. L. No. 103-394 (effective with respect to cases filed on or after October 22, 1994). *See also In re* Davis, 300 B.R. 898 (Bankr. N.D. Ill. 2003).

169 11 U.S.C. § 348(f)(1)(B); *In re* Archie, 240 B.R. 425 (Bankr. S.D. Ala. 1999).

170 Arruda v. Sears Roebuck & Co., 273 B.R. 332 (D.R.I. 2002), *aff'd*, 310 F.3d 13 (1st Cir. 2002). *But see In re* White, 231 B.R. 551 (Bankr. D. Vt. 1999) (court approval of redemption agreements required by local rule); *In re* Spivey, 230 B.R. 484 (Bankr. E.D.N.Y. 1999) (redemption agreement must be presented to court by motion for approval under Fed. R. Bankr. P. 6008), *rev'd*, 265 B.R. 357 (E.D.N.Y. 2001); *In re* Lopez, 224 B.R. 439 (Bankr. C.D. Cal. 1998) (same).

171 Fed. R. Bankr. P. 6008. See Form 59, Appendix G.8, *infra,* for a sample of such a motion.

172 *In re* Jewell, 232 B.R. 904 (Bankr. E.D. Tex. 1999).

173 If the debtor wishes to redeem property under § 722 after the bankruptcy case has been closed, and the debtor is unable to reach an agreement with the creditor on value or the terms of redemption, the debtor may request that the bankruptcy court reopen the case and resolve a motion to redeem. *See* Arruda v. Sears Roebuck & Co., 310 F.3d 13 (1st Cir. 2002).

174 *See* § 14.5.2.1, *infra.*

175 11 U.S.C. § 524(c), (d).

176 Fed. R. Bankr. P. 6008; *In re* White, 231 B.R. 551 (Bankr. D. Vt. 1999) (upholding general order that required filing of redemption agreements); *In re* Lopez, 224 B.R. 439 (Bankr. C.D. Cal. 1998). *But see In re* Spivey, 265 B.R. 357 (E.D.N.Y. 2001).

creditors.[177] In bankruptcy parlance, this right to limit the enforceability or change the terms of a creditor's contract over the creditor's objection is called a "cramdown."

The Code does not define the term "modify" which appears in section 1322(b)(2), so that presumably it may be given its broadest possible meaning, in other words, that any term of the contract is subject to change. Thus, except as limited by other Code provisions,[178] the debtor might propose to pay a lower total amount than originally agreed, to lower the amount of payments, to pay the claim over a longer period of time, to defer payments until after other debts are paid, to eliminate various oppressive terms, or even to eliminate totally the creditor's lien.

11.6.1.2 Limitations on Modifying Certain Debts Secured Only by Real Estate That Is Debtor's Principal Residence

11.6.1.2.1 In general

The debtor's rights to modify are subject to several major limitations. First, except to the extent of curing a default over a reasonable period of time, the right to modify does not extend to certain debts secured only by a security interest in real property that is the debtor's principal residence.[179] If a debt falls within this exception, set forth in Code section 1322(b)(2), and the debt is not subject to one of several exceptions to the exception discussed below, the plan may not alter the interest rate, payment amount or other terms of the mortgage.

In *Nobelman v. American Savings Bank*,[180] the Supreme Court interpreted section 1322(b)(2) and held that creditors whose claims are not subject to modification are also protected from having their liens stripped down to the value of the collateral pursuant to Code section 506. The Court held that even if a plan modified only the unsecured portion of a protected claim, the plan would still contravene section 1322(b)(2), because it would modify the rights of a creditor holding an allowed secured claim secured solely by real estate that is the debtor's principal residence.[181]

11.6.1.2.2 Security interests in the debtor's residence that are not protected by section 1322(b)(2)

The limitation in section 1322(b)(2), while important, is not as broad as it first appears. Many courts have held that the *Nobelman* holding does not apply in cases in which a junior mortgage is totally under-secured due to the fact that senior liens equal or exceed the value of the property. In *Nobelman* the Supreme Court rested its holding on the fact that the creditor, after bifurcation of its claim under section 506(a), had a secured claim as well as an unsecured claim, and therefore was a "holder of a secured claim."[182] When the creditor, after bifurcation, holds only an unsecured claim, it is not a "holder of secured claim" and does not come within the ambit of section 1322(b)(2).[183]

Furthermore, Congress has cut back significantly on the limitations on modification, and hence the *Nobelman* holding. Section 1322(c)(2) provides that *notwithstanding section 1322(b)(2)*, in a case in which the last payment on the original payment schedule for a claim secured only by a mortgage on the debtor's principal residence is due before the due date of the final plan payment, the plan may modify the creditor's rights pursuant to Code section 1325(a)(5). That section, as discussed below,[184] generally permits a debtor to pay only the allowed secured claim of a creditor, to modify payment terms and interest rates, and to treat the unsecured portion of an under-secured claim as an unsecured claim in the chapter 13 plan. Thus, debtors are permitted to modify many short term mortgages, mortgages on which the debtor's payments are nearly complete, and

---

unsecured claim, that is, if it has no rights other than to foreclose on the collateral, then those rights are not modified by strip-down. An example arises when a debtor files a chapter 7 followed by a chapter 13: the personal liability is extinguished by the chapter 7 discharge so that no modification occurs when only the secured portion of the debt is paid in chapter 13. This argument was rejected in *In re* Kirchner, 216 B.R. 417 (Bankr. W.D. Wis. 1997). A similar issue may arise in connection with a non-recourse loan.

182 508 U.S. at 328, 329.

183 *In re* Zimmer, 313 F.3d 1220 (9th Cir. 2003); *In re* Lane, 280 F.3d 663 (6th Cir. 2002); *In re* Pond, 252 F.3d 122 (2d Cir. 2001); *In re* Dickerson, 222 F.3d 924 (11th Cir. 2000); *In re* Tanner, 217 F.3d 1357 (11th Cir. 2000); *In re* Bartee, 212 F.3d 277 (5th Cir. 2000); *In re* McDonald, 205 F.3d 606 (3d Cir. 2000); *In re* Mann, 249 B.R. 831 (B.A.P. 1st Cir. 2000); Johnson v. Asset Mgmt. Group, Ltd. Liab. Co., 226 B.R. 364 (D. Md. 1998); Wright v. Commercial Credit Corp., 178 B.R. 703 (E.D. Va. 1995); *In re* Woodhouse, 172 B.R. 1 (Bankr. D.R.I. 1994); *In re* Kidd, 161 B.R. 769 (Bankr. E.D.N.C. 1993); *In re* Lee, 161 B.R. 271 (Bankr. W.D. Okla. 1993); *see also In re* Mooney, 301 B.R. 627 (Bankr. W.D.N.Y. 2003) (subsidy recapture amount on U.S. Dep't of Agriculture subsidized first mortgage counted for purposes of determining whether second mortgage was wholly unsecured); 8 Collier on Bankruptcy ¶ 1322.06[1][a] (15th ed. rev.). *But see In re* Barnes, 207 B.R. 588 (Bankr. N.D. Ill. 1997); *In re* Neverla, 194 B.R. 547 (Bankr. W.D.N.Y. 1996).

184 *See* § 11.6.1.3, *infra*.

---

177 For purposes of the provisions of chapter 13, and depending upon state law, many courts have held land installment sale contracts to be secured debts, because they serve the same function as mortgages. *See* § 12.9.1, *infra*.

178 *See* §§ 11.6.1.2–11.6.1.4, *infra*.

179 The determination of whether a property is the debtor's principal residence is made as of the date of the bankruptcy filing. *In re* Wetherbee, 164 B.R. 212 (Bankr. D.N.H. 1994) (debtor who no longer resided at property could modify mortgage on that property); *see also In re* Johnson, 269 B.R. 246 (Bankr. M.D. Ala. 2001) (creditor with mortgage on real estate where mobile home was situated but not on mobile home did not have lien on debtor's principal residence).

180 508 U.S. 324, 113 S. Ct. 2106, 124 L. Ed. 2d 228 (1993).

181 508 U.S. at 331, 332. This portion of the court's reasoning leads to an argument that if the mortgage holder has no basis for an

mortgages with balloon payments falling due before the end of the chapter 13 plan.[185] It is not surprising that Congress carved out these types of mortgages from those which could not be modified. Short-term mortgages and those with balloon payments are not usually purchase money mortgages, which section 1322(b)(2) was primarily drafted to protect. They are also more likely to carry high interest rates and other unfair terms, a fact Congress recognized in passing the Home Ownership and Equity Protection Act of 1994[186] at roughly the same time as the 1994 bankruptcy amendments. It is also not surprising that Congress would permit more flexibility for debtors who have nearly reached the end of their payments on long-term mortgages, as those debtors are typically long-time home owners, often elderly and often with a large amount of equity in their homes that could be lost in foreclosure.[187]

The limitation on modification in section 1322(b)(2) also does not apply if the creditor has other security besides the mortgage.[188] Many claims secured by real estate are also secured by household goods,[189] or at least the possible refund of proceeds from credit insurance.[190] Even in first mortgages, there are often clauses giving creditors security interests in appliances, rents or escrow accounts established for payment of taxes and insurance.[191] In other cases, the lender has also taken a security interest in other real estate, such as rental units owned by the debtor or farmland.[192] And

---

185 *In re* Paschen, 296 F.3d 1203 (11th Cir. 2002) (statutory exception to Code's anti-modification provision permits debtors to bifurcate and cram down under-secured, short-term home mortgages); *In re* Eubanks, 219 B.R. 468 (B.A.P. 6th Cir. 1998) (short term mortgage modifiable); *In re* Mattson, 210 B.R. 157 (Bankr. D. Minn. 1997) (§ 1322(b)(2) protections did not apply to loans maturing before end of plan); *In re* Young, 199 B.R. 643 (Bankr. E.D. Tenn. 1996) (debtors could strip down mortgage if last payment was due before final scheduled plan payment); *In re* Sarkese, 189 B.R. 531 (Bankr. M.D. Fla. 1995) (debtors could pay off mortgage which had ballooned prior to bankruptcy using the cramdown provisions of § 1325(a)(5)); *In re* Lobue, 189 B.R. 216 (Bankr. S.D. Fla. 1995) (debtor could pay matured mortgage through plan); *see also In re* Nepil, 206 B.R. 72 (Bankr. D.N.J. 1997) (loan on which creditor had obtained foreclosure judgment could be treated as loan on which final payment due before end of plan). *But see In re* Witt, 113 F.3d 508 (4th Cir. 1997) (stripdown not permitted under § 1322(c)(2), because it provides for modification of payments and not claims). The *Witt* court misreads § 1322(c)(2) because the statute plainly refers to "claims as modified."

186 Pub. L. No. 103-325, Title I, Subtitle B, 108 Stat. 2160 (1994) (codified largely at 15 U.S.C. § 1639). For a discussion of HOEPA, see National Consumer Law Center, Truth in Lending § 9.1 (5th ed. 2003).

187 *See* 8 Collier on Bankruptcy ¶ 1322.16 (15th ed. rev.).

188 *See* Lomas Mortgage v. Louis, 82 F.3d 1 (1st Cir. 1996); *In re* Hammond, 27 F.3d 52 (3d Cir. 1994); *In re* Graham, 144 B.R. 80 (Bankr. N.D. Ind. 1992) (when bank extended mortgages on real estate other than debtors' residence which contained clause stating the mortgages also secured existing indebtedness to the bank, original mortgage debt on residence became a debt secured by liens on the nonresidential properties).

189 As the Supreme Court's decision in *Nobelman* relied on the "plain meaning" of the statute, most courts have concluded that it has no bearing on situations where the creditor is secured by property other than the debtor's principal residence. *In re* Hammond, 27 F.3d 52 (3d Cir. 1994); *In re* Bouvier, 150 B.R. 24 (Bankr. D.R.I. 1993). The *Hammond* case was cited favorably as representing current law by the legislative history to the

1994 amendments to the Code. 140 Cong. Rec. H10,764 (daily ed. Oct. 4, 1994).

190 Transouth Fin. Corp. v. Hill, 106 B.R. 145 (W.D. Tenn. 1989); *In re* Pedigo, 283 B.R. 493 (Bankr. E.D. Tenn. 2002); *In re* Selman, 120 B.R. 576 (Bankr. D.N.M. 1990); *In re* Stiles, 74 B.R. 208 (Bankr. N.D. Ala. 1987). *But see In re* Washington, 967 F.2d 173 (5th Cir. 1992) (mere fact that debtor obtained credit life and disability insurance was not additional security, at least in case where insurance was voluntary and could be canceled by the debtors, and there was no language pledging the policy as security for the loan or assigning its proceeds to the creditor).

191 Sapos v. Provident Inst. of Sav., 967 F.2d 918 (3d Cir. 1992) (wall to wall carpeting, rents and profits); Wilson v. Commonwealth Mortgage Corp., 895 F.2d 123, 128, 129 (3d Cir. 1990) (appliances and furniture); Lutz v. Miami Valley Bank, 192 B.R. 107 (W.D. Pa. 1995) (security interest in rents); Secor Bank v. Dunlap, 129 B.R. 463 (E.D. La. 1991) (security interest also covered easements, rights, appurtenances, rents, royalties, mineral oil and gas rights and water rights and stock and all fixtures); *In re* Donadio, 269 B.R. 336 (Bankr. M.D. Pa. 2001) (security interest also covered escrow account for taxes and insurance); *In re* Stewart, 263 B.R. 728 (Bankr. W.D. Pa. 2001) (same, even though collateral not in hands of mortgage holder on petition date); *In re* Heckman, 165 B.R. 16 (Bankr. E.D. Pa. 1994) (security interest in rents placed mortgage outside scope of § 1322(b)(2)); *In re* Jackson, 136 B.R. 797 (Bankr. N.D. Ill. 1992) (modification permitted because rents are additional security); *In re* Jablonski, 70 B.R. 381 (Bankr. E.D. Pa. 1987) (security interest covered appliances and also rents, issues, and profits), *aff'd on other grounds*, 88 B.R. 652 (E.D. Pa. 1988); *In re* Reeves, 65 B.R. 898 (Bankr. N.D. Ill. 1986) (security interest also covered fixtures). *But see In re* Davis, 989 F.2d 208 (6th Cir. 1993) (neither requirement that debtor obtain fire insurance, absent the existence of proceeds from such insurance due to a fire, nor the mortgage language conveying interest in appurtenances, rents, royalties, profits, and fixtures appertaining to the real estate constituted additional security for purposes of § 1322(b)(2)). For a further discussion of rents as additional security, see *Stripping Down Residential Mortgages After Nobelman: Security Interest in Rents as Additional Security,* 12 NCLC REPORTS, *Bankruptcy and Foreclosures Ed.* 41 (Mar./ Apr. 1994).

192 Lomas Mortgage v. Louis, 82 F.3d 1 (1st Cir. 1996) (holder of mortgage on three unit building that included the debtor's residence not protected by 11 U.S.C. § 1322(b)(2)); *In re* Maddaloni, 225 B.R. 277 (D. Conn. 1998) (debtor occupied one unit of multifamily building); *In re* Del Valle, 186 B.R. 347 (Bankr. D. Conn. 1995); *In re* McVay, 150 B.R. 254 (Bankr. D. Or. 1993) (creditor holding security interest in property that was used by debtors as a "bed and breakfast" was not secured solely by debtor's principal residence); *In re* Foster, 61 B.R. 492 (Bankr. N.D. Ind. 1986) (security interest also covered farm on which residence was located); *In re* Leazier, 55 B.R. 870 (Bankr. N.D. Ind. 1985) (creditor held security interest in debtor's farm as well as residence); *see In re* Ramirez, 62 B.R. 668 (Bankr. S.D. Cal. 1986) (units at property were also used to generate

many banks have, either by law or by way of a deposit agreement, the right of setoff against a debtor's bank account.[193] A creditor is not permitted to release security interests in such other property in order to gain protection from the limitation in section 1322(b)(2).[194] Moreover, it is irrelevant whether a debtor retains the other property securing the debt after the petition is filed; the key issue is whether such other collateral existed on the date the petition was filed.[195] Indeed, there is no requirement that the additional security for the debt be property that belongs to the debtor.[196]

In deciding whether the agreement provides for security in other collateral, courts often consider whether the additional collateral provides something more to the creditor than might already exist as a component of its security interest in the real property.[197] However, the plain language of section 1322(b)(2) suggests that the protection against modification should not apply if any additional collateral is provided for in the security agreement, regardless of the value it provides independent of the debtor's principal residence, and it should not matter that the security interest is contained in "boilerplate" language commonly found in mortgage documents.[198] In some cases, the issue may turn on questions of state property law as to whether the collateral is an inherent component of the real property, or treated separately.

11.6.1.2.3 Right to cure defaults is not impaired by section 1322(b)(2)

In addition, the limitation of section 1322(b)(2) does not apply to the debtor's right to waive or cure a default on any secured claim, either under section 1322(b)(3) (for claims maturing before the end of the plan) or section 1322(b)(5)

(for claims maturing after the end of the plan.) Courts have held that when the plan otherwise conforms to section 1325(a) or section 1322(b)(5),[199] a plan may cure or waive a default even on a claim secured only by real property that is the debtor's principal residence because a cure is not a "modification."[200] Using this reasoning, courts have held that chapter 13 plans proposing to pay such claims in full may effectuate a cure under section 1322(b)(3) that is not a modification prohibited by section 1322(b)(2).[201] This interpretation was confirmed by the 1994 amendments to the Code. Section 1322(c)(1) refers to cures of defaults with respect to liens on a debtor's principal residence pursuant to 1322(b)(3) or (5), and states that the plan may propose such cures notwithstanding section 1322(b)(2).

In addition, section 1322(b)(3) may provide other tools for the debtor. As section 1322(b)(3) also refers to waiving a default, a debtor may be able to eliminate the effects of a due on sale clause that is asserted by a creditor as grounds for foreclosure.[202]

11.6.1.2.4 Section 1322(b)(2) not applicable to liens that are not security interests in real estate

Finally, the limitation by its terms applies only when the claim is secured solely by a "security interest" in the residence. A security interest, as defined by the Code, must be a lien created by agreement,[203] and the limitation is thus not applicable when the claim is secured by a judicial lien or a statutory lien.[204] Nor does the limitation apply to property

---

rental income). The *Ramirez* case was cited favorably as representing current law by the legislative history to the 1994 amendments to the Code. H.R. Rep. No. 103-835, at 46 n.13 (1994), *reprinted in* 1994 U.S.C.C.A.N. 3340. *But see In re* Marenaro, 217 B.R. 358 (B.A.P. 1st Cir. 1998) (fact that debtor's property was designated as three separate lots did not mean debt was secured by property other than residence when property had never been divided for other use).

193 *In re* Libby, 200 B.R. 562 (Bankr. D.N.J. 1996) (security interest in all money, securities and property in bank's possession, even if no such property was held by bank, constituted additional security); *In re* Crystian, 197 B.R. 803 (Bankr. W.D. Pa. 1996) (escrow funds and right to setoff against checking account constituted additional security).

194 *In re* Johns, 37 F.3d 1021, 1025 (3d Cir. 1994) (also holding that merger of mortgage into foreclosure judgment does not eliminate security); *In re* Baksa, 5 B.R. 184 (Bankr. N.D. Ohio 1980).

195 *In re* Groff, 131 B.R. 703 (Bankr. E.D. Wis. 1991) (debtor could surrender some of the property securing the debt other than the real estate after the petition was filed and still be permitted to modify claim secured by principal residence).

196 *In re* Bouvier, 160 B.R. 24 (Bankr. D.R.I. 1993).

197 *In re* French, 174 B.R. 1 (Bankr. D. Mass. 1994).

198 *In re* Hammond, 27 F.3d 52 (3d Cir. 1994).

199 See discussion in §§ 11.6.1.3, 11.6.2, and Chapter 12, *infra*.

200 *In re* Litton, 330 F.3d 636 (4th Cir. 2003); *In re* Clark, 738 F.2d 869 (7th Cir. 1984); Grubbs v. Houston First Am. Sav. Ass'n, 730 F.2d 236 (5th Cir. 1984) (*en banc*); *In re* Taddeo, 685 F.2d 24 (2d Cir. 1982); *see also* 8 Collier on Bankruptcy ¶ 1322.07[2] (15th ed. rev.).

201 *In re* Spader, 66 B.R. 618 (W.D. Mo. 1986); *In re* Larkins, 50 B.R. 984 (W.D. Ky. 1985); *In re* Williams, 109 B.R. 36 (Bankr. E.D.N.Y. 1989); *In re* Klein, 106 B.R. 396 (Bankr. E.D. Pa. 1989); *In re* Bolden, 101 B.R. 582 (Bankr. E.D. Mo. 1989). *But see* First Nat'l Fid. Corp. v. Perry, 945 F.2d 61 (3d Cir. 1991); *In re* Seidel, 752 F.2d 1382 (9th Cir. 1985).

202 *See In re* Garcia, 276 B.R. 627 (Bankr. D. Ariz. 2002) (due-on-sale clause violation could be cured under § 1322(b)(3)); 8 Collier on Bankruptcy ¶ 1322.07[2] (15th ed. rev.). *See generally Enforceability of Due On Sale Clauses*, 12 NCLC REPORTS *Bankruptcy and Foreclosures Ed.* 20 (Mar./Apr. 1995) (discussion of federal limitations on due on sale clauses as grounds for foreclosure).

203 11 U.S.C. § 101(51); *see also* 11 U.S.C. § 101(53).

204 *In re* Bates, 270 B.R. 455 (Bankr. N.D. Ill. 2001) (claim of tax sale purchaser for redemption amount can be paid under plan and treated like any other secured claim); *In re* McDonough, 166 B.R. 9 (Bankr. D. Mass. 1994); *In re* Cullen, 150 B.R. 1 (Bankr. D. Me. 1993); *In re* Seel, 22 B.R. 692 (Bankr. D. Kan. 1982) (limitation of 11 U.S.C. § 1322(b)(2) not applicable to mechanic's lien). These terms are mutually exclusive. H.R. Rep. No. 95-595, at 312 (1977); S. Rep. No. 95-989, at 25 (1978). *But see In re* Perry, 235 B.R. 603 (S.D. Tex. 1999) (assessment lien

that is the debtor's principal residence if it is not real property, as in the case of a mobile home which is not considered to be realty under state law.[205]

11.6.1.3 Provisions Dealing with Allowed Secured Claims Provided for by the Plan

11.6.1.3.1 Overview

In addition to section 1322(b)(2) and adequate protection, a third important factor in determining whether the court will approve the modification of a secured creditor's rights is compliance with section 1325(a)(5). Section 1325(a) provides that the court shall approve a plan if certain standards[206] are met. One of these is that of section 1325(a)(5), which states that as to each allowed secured claim provided for by the plan one of the following conditions should be met:

(A) The holder of the claim has accepted the plan; or

(B) (i) The plan provides that the holder of the claim retain the lien securing such claim;[207] *and* (ii) The value, as of the effective date of the plan, of property to be distributed under the plan on account of such claim is not less than the allowed amount of such claim; or

(C) The debtor surrenders the property securing such claim to such holder.

11.6.1.3.2 Creditor acceptance of plan or debtor's surrender of collateral

The first and third of these options are fairly simple. If the creditor consents to modification of its rights, by negotiated settlement or otherwise, there is no reason for the court to be concerned. A number of courts have held that a secured creditor who does not object to a plan may be deemed to have accepted it.[208] And if the debtor surrenders the collat-

eral to the creditor, that creditor, in effect, is no longer a secured creditor, but only an unsecured creditor with respect to whatever debt remains.[209] The debtor need not secure the creditor's consent to exercise the option to surrender the property securing the debt.[210]

11.6.1.3.3 Payment of allowed secured claim through plan when creditor does not accept plan

11.6.1.3.3.1 Lien retention and present value of payments

The most complicated provision is the second, which deals with retention of the property when the creditor does not consent to the plan. To meet this standard, the plan must specifically provide that the creditor retains a lien, that is, that the creditor will continue to have priority rights to the property subject to the lien.[211] However, some of the rights usually associated with the lien are necessarily limited by chapter 13, such as the right to repossess. The main purpose of the lien retention is to preserve the creditor's rights in the property if the plan ends in failure before the creditor receives the amount to which it is entitled on its allowed secured claim.[212] Once the allowed secured claim has been paid the lien may be eliminated, and the plan may so provide.[213] In such circumstances, it should be possible to

---

205 *In re* Thompson, 217 B.R. 375 (B.A.P. 2d Cir. 1998) (mobile home is personalty under New York law); *In re* Plaster, 101 B.R. 696 (Bankr. E.D. Okla. 1989); *see also In re* Johnson, 269 B.R. 246 (Bankr. M.D. Ala. 2001) (creditor with mortgage on real estate where mobile home was situated, but not on mobile home, did not have lien on debtor's principal residence); *In re* Thurston, 73 B.R. 138 (Bankr. N.D. Tex. 1987) (security interest in mobile home, without more, may not involve "real property" within meaning of § 1322(b)(2)); *cf. In re* Carter, 116 B.R. 156 (Bankr. W.D. Mo. 1990).

206 *See* Ch. 12, *infra.*

207 Absent such a provision the lien is eliminated upon confirmation. 11 U.S.C. § 1327(c).

208 *In re* Andrews, 49 F.3d 1404, 1409 (9th Cir. 1995); *In re* Szostek, 886 F.2d 1405 (3d Cir. 1989); *In re* Ruti-Sweetwater, Inc., 836 F.2d 1263 (10th Cir. 1988) (chapter 11 case); *In re* Brown, 108 B.R. 738 (Bankr. C.D. Cal. 1989).

---

of homeowners' association was a lien created by agreement and therefore a "security interest" and not modifiable).

209 The debtor may also choose to surrender only part of the collateral securing the debt, thereby reducing the allowed secured claim that must be paid. *In re* McCommons, 288 B.R. 594 (Bankr. M.D. Ga. 2002) (debtor could surrender some items of collateral and keep others); *In re* Groff, 131 B.R. 703 (Bankr. E.D. Wis. 1991) (debtor could surrender collateral other than residence plus thirty acres and pay only the value of remaining collateral). *But see In re* Williams, 168 F.3d 845 (5th Cir. 1999) (debtor had to either transfer entire property or pay claim).

210 *In re* White, 282 B.R. 418 (Bankr. N.D. Ohio 2002); *In re* Harris, 244 B.R. 557 (Bankr. D. Conn. 2000).

211 *See In re* Hanna, 912 F.2d 945 (8th Cir. 1990) (similar provision in chapter 12 case meant that creditor had to retain lien in herd of livestock, including offspring, rather than particular animals, and that herd had to be maintained at level to ensure lender was adequately protected). *But see In re* Pence, 905 F.2d 1107 (7th Cir. 1990) (where secured creditor failed to object to chapter 13 plan provision substituting collateral, creditor was bound by confirmed plan).

212 Section 1325(a)(5)(B)(i) does not require that a chapter 13 plan protect the lien holder from a diminution in value of the lien while the claim is being paid under the plan. *In re* Harris, 304 B.R. 751 (Bankr. E.D. Mich. 2004) (plan need not provide that automobile lender receive payments after confirmation in amount necessary to cover collateral's monthly depreciation).

213 *See* 124 Cong. Rec. H11,107 (daily ed. Sept. 28, 1978) (remarks of Rep. Edwards); 124 Cong. Rec. S17,424 (daily ed. Oct. 6, 1978) (remarks of Sen. DeConcini) (secured creditor's lien retained under § 1325(a)(5) only secures the value of the collateral and is satisfied in full by plan payments equal to present value of allowed secured claim). *But see In re* Day, 292 B.R. 133 (Bankr. N.D. Tex. 2003) (plan which provided for release of lien prior to completion of plan could not be confirmed over credi-

have the lien satisfied even before the plan is completed.[214] Occasionally, the debtor will be able to immediately pay the amount of the secured claim, either in cash or by transferring property, thereby giving the creditor present value. In some cases, a portion of the collateral may be divided from the remainder and transferred to the creditor.[215]

To meet the requirements of section 1325(a)(5), the plan must also provide that the present value of the payments to be made to the creditor under the plan equals the amount of the allowed secured claim.[216] This means that, if payments are to be made over time, the creditor must receive interest on the amount of the allowed secured claim so that the amount it ultimately receives is equivalent economically to what it would have received if the allowed secured claim had been immediately paid in cash.[217]

---

tor's objection because of potential effect of § 349(b)(3) if case dismissed).

214 *In re* Campbell, 180 B.R. 686 (M.D. Fla. 1995); *In re* Lee, 162 B.R. 217 (D. Minn. 1993); *In re* Rheaume, 296 B.R. 313 (Bankr. D. Vt. 2003); *In re* Castro, 285 B.R. 703 (Bankr. D. Ariz. 2002); *In re* Gray, 285 B.R. 379 (Bankr. N.D. Tex. 2002); *In re* Townsend, 256 B.R. 881 (Bankr. N.D. Ill. 2001); *In re* Shorter, 237 B.R. 443 (Bankr. N.D. Ill. 1999); *In re* Murry-Hudson, 147 B.R. 960 (Bankr. N.D. Cal. 1992); *see also In re* James, 285 B.R. 114 (Bankr. W.D.N.Y. 2002) (when debtor had paid full allowed secured claim before converting to chapter 7, creditor's post-discharge seizure of collateral violated discharge injunction because only the claim creditor had remaining was unsecured claim, which was discharged); *In re* Stoddard, 167 B.R. 98 (Bankr. S.D. Ohio 1994) (debtors could redeem property from lien for no additional payment after conversion to chapter 7 when they had already paid allowed secured claim in full during chapter 13 case); *In re* Pickett, 151 B.R. 471 (Bankr. M.D. Tenn. 1992) (lien satisfied during plan did not spring back into existence when case was converted to chapter 7); *In re* Hargis, 103 B.R. 912 (Bankr. E.D. Tenn. 1989) (lien satisfied during plan did not spring back into existence when case was converted to chapter 7). The result in these conversion cases was codified by § 348(f)(1)(B), added to the Code in 1994. If an allowed secured claim is partially paid in a plan, at least if the case is not dismissed, the creditor's interest in the property is only the remaining portion of the allowed secured claim. *See In re* Stevens, 130 F.3d 1027 (11th Cir. 1997) (creditor's interest in insurance proceeds resulting from destruction of vehicle collateral was limited to interest in vehicle as that interest was defined by plan); *In re* McCauley, 173 B.R. 453 (Bankr. M.D. Ga. 1994) (when debtor's vehicle was destroyed in accident, creditor could only keep amount of insurance proceeds equal to remainder of allowed secured claim); *In re* McDade, 148 B.R. 42 (Bankr. S.D. Ill. 1992) (same).

215 *In re* Kerwin, 996 F.2d 552 (2d Cir. 1993) (chapter 12 debtor could pay secured claim by transferring to holder portion of collateral equal to amount of claim). *But see In re* Williams, 168 F.3d 845 (5th Cir. 1999) (debtor had to either transfer entire property or pay claim).

216 For purposes of this requirement, the Supreme Court has held that the arrearages on a mortgage being cured under a chapter 13 plan are an allowed secured claim. Rake v. Wade, 508 U.S. 464, 473, 113 S. Ct. 2187, 2192, 2193, 124 L. Ed. 2d 424, 434 (1993). Congress subsequently overruled this decision for most mortgages by enacting § 1322(e). *See* § 11.6.2.7, *infra*.

217 See § 11.6.1.3.3.5, *infra*, for discussion of present value interest.

11.6.1.3.3.2 Filing of the secured claim

Preliminarily, if the debtor seeks to deal with a secured claim through the plan, there must first be an allowed secured claim. If the creditor does not file a claim, the debtor may have to do so on the creditor's behalf.[218] The Bankruptcy Rules provide that this may be done by the debtor at any time between the first date set for the meeting of creditors and 120 days thereafter.[219] It was held by some courts, under the prior bankruptcy rules, that if a secured claim was not filed and determined, it passed through the bankruptcy unaffected,[220] and could not receive greater distributions than unsecured claims.[221] Although the current rules seem to permit distribution to an allowed secured claim pursuant to a plan without regard to whether the claim was filed, it is still safest to make sure a secured claim is filed if it is to be provided for in the plan.

For this reason, it is generally a good idea to check the claims docket for the case shortly after the meeting of creditors. If a secured creditor whom the debtor proposes to pay in the plan has not filed a proof of claim, one should be filed on behalf of that creditor within the deadline in an amount consistent with the debtor's schedules and plan.[222]

---

218 Most courts and chapter 13 trustees expect a debtor to file a claim for the creditor if that claim is to be paid by the plan. However, the rules do not appear to require the filing of a secured claim in order for it to be allowed. *See* Fed. R. Bankr. P. 3002 ("an *unsecured* creditor or equity security holder *must* file a proof of claim" for the claim or interest to be allowed (emphasis added)); *see also In re* Babbin, 156 B.R. 838 (Bankr. D. Colo. 1993) (filing proof of claim not required for allowance of secured claim); 8 Collier on Bankruptcy 1300.71[1] (15th ed. rev.). Apparently, the intent of the rules is that only the chapter 13 plan will determine whether an allowed secured claim is to be paid, regardless of whether a proof of claim is filed. *But see In re* Baldridge, 232 B.R. 394 (Bankr. N.D. Ind. 1999) (notwithstanding language of rule, secured creditor must file a claim to receive plan distributions).

It does seem clear, however, that if no claim is filed and the chapter 13 plan does not provide for the secured creditor, the creditor's lien is not impaired by the bankruptcy. *In re* Thomas, 883 F.2d 991 (11th Cir. 1989); *see also* § 11.6.1.3.3.3, *infra*; § 12.11, *infra*.

219 Fed. R. Bankr. P. 3002(c), 3004. Rule 3004 does not appear to allow a creditor to file a superseding claim to a claim filed by the debtor or trustee if the bar date for claims has passed, because it only allows a claim filed pursuant to Rule 3002 or 3003(c), that is, within the time limits of those rules, to supersede the claim filed by the debtor or trustee. *See also In re* Hill, 286 B.R. 612 (Bankr. E.D. Pa. 2002) (discussing case law); Advisory Committee Note to Fed. R. Bankr. P. 3004.

220 *In re* Honaker, 4 B.R. 415 (Bankr. E.D. Mich. 1980); *In re* Robertson, 4 B.R. 213 (Bankr. D. Colo. 1980).

221 11 U.S.C. § 1322(a)(3) does not allow unfair classification of similar claims. *See* Ch. 12, *infra*; *see also In re* Price, 1 Collier Bankr. Cas. 2d (MB) 221, Bankr. L. Rep. (CCH) ¶ 67,287 (Bankr. N.D. Cal. 1979) (confirming plan but not allowing favored treatment to secured claim).

222 *See* Form 56, Appx. G.8, *infra*.

11.6.1.3.3.3 Plan need not provide for all secured claims

On the other hand in some cases the debtor may not wish to provide for a secured claim in the plan. Section 1325(a)(5) does not require the plan to provide for all secured claims; it merely sets forth standards to be met if the plan does provide for an allowed secured claim.[223] In such cases, the debtor may argue that the secured creditor will be bound by the plan in any case under section 1327(a) and unable to foreclose until after the plan is completed.[224] This course of action involves some risk, however, at least until the courts conclusively hold that section 1327(a) overrides the provisions under which the creditor could seek relief from the automatic stay.[225]

The debtor may decide not to provide for a secured creditor in the plan because the debtor is unable or unwilling to pay that creditor through the plan. For example, the debtor may owe a large mortgage to a relative who is not likely to foreclose. Or the debtor may be current on an automobile loan and may wish to continue payments outside the plan to avoid the trustee's charges.[226] Or the debtor may believe that the creditor will never seek to enforce its lien.[227]

Nothing in the Code requires that all secured claims be provided for in a chapter 13 plan.

11.6.1.3.3.4 Determination of allowed secured claim

Assuming that a secured claim is filed, it will be allowed in the amount requested unless an objection is raised.[228] If an objection is raised, the claim must then be determined and allowed. As discussed earlier in this chapter, if such a determination is sought, the allowed secured claim cannot be greater than the value of the collateral.[229] It may also be reduced to the extent that it is subject to defenses that the debtor may raise as objections to the claim. However, if the value of the collateral is greater than the amount claimed, the allowed secured claim can include interest earned to the date of confirmation, plus any reasonable fees, costs, and charges under the original agreement.[230]

---

223 There is no requirement that a chapter 13 plan provide for all secured claims. *See also In re* Bisch, 159 B.R. 546 (B.A.P. 9th Cir. 1993) (tax lien which was not provided for in plan remained enforceable after bankruptcy). *See generally In re* Evans, 66 B.R. 506 (Bankr. E.D. Pa. 1986), *aff'd*, 77 B.R. 457 (E.D. Pa. 1987).

224 *See In re* Rebuelta, 27 B.R. 137 (Bankr. N.D. Ga. 1983); *In re* Willey, 24 B.R. 369 (Bankr. E.D. Mich. 1982).

225 *In re* Penrod, 50 F.3d 459 (7th Cir. 1995) (default rule in chapter 11, based on language of section 1141(c), is that if confirmed plan provides for creditor but is silent about whether creditor retains its lien, that lien is automatically extinguished). The *Penrod* rationale should apply equally in chapter 13 under section 1327(c). *See In re* Pettit, 18 B.R. 832 (Bankr. S.D. Ohio 1982) (if secured claim not timely filed, operation of 11 U.S.C. § 1327(c) results in holder of secured claim losing the security). *But see In re* Hines, 20 B.R. 44 (Bankr. S.D. Ohio 1982) (secured claim holder may be entitled to full payment or surrender of collateral when plan does not provide full payment); *see also In re* Tarnow, 749 F.2d 464 (7th Cir. 1984) (claim that was disallowed only because it was filed late remains enforceable against debtor); *In re* Junes, 99 B.R. 978 (B.A.P. 9th Cir. 1989) (where federal tax lien was not provided for in chapter 13 plan it survived bankruptcy case unimpaired); § 11.6.1.4, *infra*.

226 *See In re* Delauder, 189 B.R. 639 (Bankr. E.D. Va. 1995) (permitting direct payment of auto loan pursuant to provisions for curing long term debt under § 1322(b)(5); court did not discuss, probably because debtor did not argue, the fact that § 1325(a)(5) does not require plan to provide for all secured debts).

227 Most holders of security interests in low-value personal property never seek to enforce them. In many cases, the debtor's attorney will know from experience that there is no danger of repossession. In other cases, holders of municipal or tax liens may be known to rarely foreclose on them or may be willing to arrange payments over much longer than five years. Similarly,

in some cases, there may be little fear that a family member intends to enforce a mortgage or other lien.

228 *See* § 11.2, *supra*.

229 *See* § 11.2.1, *supra*. The Supreme Court's *Nobelman* decision, affecting some home mortgages, does not affect the ability of the debtor to strip down other liens in chapter 13.

230 11 U.S.C. § 506(b); *In re* Auto Specialties, 18 F.3d 358 (6th Cir. 1994) (over-secured creditor entitled to add to its claim reasonable attorney fees provided for in loan agreement); Mack Fin. Corp. v. Ireson, 789 F.2d 1083 (4th Cir. 1986) (reasonable late charges permitted as part of over-secured creditor's allowed secured claim). This section is somewhat ambiguous as to whether interest must be allowed as part of the claim at the contract rate in every case. Some courts have held it need not be. *In re* Marx, 11 B.R. 819 (Bankr. S.D. Ohio 1981); *In re* Minguey, 10 B.R. 806 (Bankr. W.D. Wis. 1981); *see also In re* Kalian, 178 B.R. 308 (Bankr. D.R.I. 1995) (creditor not permitted to add interest at "default rate" that was higher than contractual pre-default rate). In United States v. Ron Pair Enterprise, Inc., 489 U.S. 235, 109 S. Ct. 1026, 103 L. Ed. 2d 290 (1989) the Supreme Court held that the plain language of 11 U.S.C. § 506(b) authorized the inclusion of post-petition interest in over-secured claims on nonconsensual liens (in that case a tax lien) as well as on liens created by agreement. In any case, however, if the interest is pursuant to an agreement, the creditor may not claim a rate higher than the agreement provides, even if it loses "opportunity costs." *In re* Anderson, 833 F.2d 834 (9th Cir. 1987). Interest payable to an over-secured creditor may also, in proper circumstances, be reduced on equitable grounds. *In re* Lapiana, 909 F.2d 221 (7th Cir. 1990). Several courts of appeals have held that this section allows attorney fees provided by an agreement even where prohibited by state law. *In re* Schriock Const. Co., 104 F.3d 200 (8th Cir. 1997); *In re* 286 Ltd., 789 F.2d 674 (9th Cir. 1986); Unsecured Creditors' Committee v. Walter E. Heller, 768 F.2d 580 (4th Cir. 1985). Such decisions have been criticized for, *inter alia*, ignoring section 502(b)(1) which separately disallows claims that are unenforceable against the debtor under applicable law. *See* Commentary, 8 Attorney's Fees Awards Reporter, No. 5, p. 19 (1985). In general, courts have strictly construed contractual provisions providing for fees and costs, and have disallowed unreasonable fees. *See, e.g., In re* Sublett, 895 F.2d 1381 (11th Cir. 1990) (denying interest on attorney fees not authorized by agreement); First Brandon Nat'l Bank v. Kerwin-White, 109 B.R. 626 (D.

In determining what fees are reasonable and thus may be allowed as part of the allowed secured claim, the issue is a question of federal law and the bankruptcy court need not award as much as the contract or state law might allow,[231] though section 506(b) appears to preclude an award greater than that provided in the contract.[232] Several courts have held that if the debt has been reduced to judgment, the applicable interest rate is no longer the contract rate, but rather the judgment interest rate.[233]

Some creditors also add to their claims, or otherwise attempt to charge, a variety of other amounts, such as bankruptcy monitoring fees,[234] duplicative escrow charges,[235] and duplicative interest charges.[236] It is critical to carefully examine and recompute claims filed by secured

creditors to insure that the claims are correct, and to object if they are excessive.[237] Once an objection is filed, a secured claim holder has the burden of producing evidence of the reasonableness of its fees and charges.[238]

11.6.1.3.3.5 Trustee's fee and present value interest

Once the allowed secured claim has been determined, it is then necessary to compute what payments will equal the present value of that claim. In order to do this it is also necessary to know the amount of the trustee's fees and expenses, if the claim is to be paid through the plan,[239] and also the interest rate to be applied.

The former can easily be learned from the trustee, but the latter had, until recently, been a matter of considerable dispute.[240] Creditors, naturally, argued for high interest rates, usually the contract rates, while debtors attempted to secure lower rates, such as the legal rate of interest provided by state law. The Supreme Court largely resolved this dispute in *Till v. SCS Credit Corp.*[241] The Court held that a formula method is to be used, with the prime rate of interest[242] as the starting point, adjusted by a factor for risk.[243] Although not setting any amount for the risk factor, the Court cited cases adding one to three percent to the interest rate. The amount added for risk should not be large and may be close to zero. If the creditor is significantly over-secured, the equity cushion will provide protection against risk. In other cases, assuming that risks of loss by fire or other damage are covered by insurance, as they typically are, the only real risk the creditor usually faces under a bankruptcy plan is the risk of a little delay in payments. If

---

Vt. 1990) (provision in agreement providing attorney fees for taking possession of collateral after default did not apply to taking possession through bankruptcy proceedings); *In re* Hatala, 295 B.R. 62 (Bankr. D.N.J. 2003) (language of mortgage permitted fees only for foreclosure proceeding, not subsequent fees). If the secured claim does not arise from an agreement, no post-petition fees, charges or penalties may be added, because § 506(b) allows only those provided for under the agreement under which the claim arose. *In re* Gledhill, 164 F.3d 1338 (10th Cir. 1999) (*Ron Pair* allows post-petition interest to nonconsensual secured creditors but not attorney fees); *In re* Brentwood Outpatient, Ltd., 43 F.3d 256 (6th Cir. 1994); *In re* Pointer, 952 F.2d 82 (5th Cir. 1992) (only creditors who have voluntary secured claims created by agreement may recover post-petition penalties, fees, and costs); *see also* § 11.6.2.7.1, *infra.*

231 *In re* Welzel, 275 F.3d 1308 (11th Cir. 2001) (*en banc*) (bankruptcy court must independently determine reasonableness of fees as a matter of federal law because § 506(b) preempts state law); *In re* Hudson Shipbuilders, Inc., 794 F.2d 1051 (5th Cir. 1986); *In re* 268 Ltd., 789 F.2d 674 (9th Cir. 1986); *In re* Clark, 299 B.R. 694 (Bankr. S.D. Ga. 2003) (fees not permitted by state law due to failure to give required notice were not allowable); *In re* Shaffer, 287 B.R. 898 (Bankr. S.D. Ohio 2002) (creditor not entitled to attorney fees for stay motion because such fees not authorized by statute nor enforceable under the contract).

232 *In re* Laymon, 958 F.2d 72 (5th Cir. 1992) (section 506(b) interest calculated at contract rate in case where no judgment existed; whether to use higher contract "default rate" depended upon the equities involved); *In re* Johnson-Allen, 67 B.R. 968 (Bankr. E.D. Pa. 1986); *see also* § 11.6.2.7.1, *infra.*

233 *E.g., In re* Presque Isle Apartments, Ltd. P'ship, 118 B.R. 331 (Bankr. W.D. Pa. 1990); *In re* Lehal Realty Associates, 112 B.R. 588 (Bankr. S.D.N.Y. 1990); *In re* Herbert, 86 B.R. 433 (Bankr. E.D. Pa. 1988); *see also In re* Guarnieri, 308 B.R. 122 (D. Conn. 2004) (after acceleration and judgment no late charges could accrue as no separate payments were due).

234 *See, e.g., In re* Stark, 242 B.R. 866 (Bankr. W.D.N.C. 1999) (mortgage company violated automatic stay by adding monitoring fees to debtors' monthly statements).

235 Such escrow charges are included in arrears that a creditor claims are due and then added again to the claim as an "escrow deficit."

236 *In re* Wines, 239 B.R. 703 (Bankr. D.N.J. 1999); *see also* § 13.4.3.4, *infra.* Many creditors add "interest on arrears" to their claims, even though the trustee computes and adds interest to the claim filed by the creditor.

237 For detailed discussion of objecting to such overcharges, see § 13.4.3.4, *infra.*

238 *In re* Atwood, 293 B.R. 227 (B.A.P. 9th Cir. 2003) (unsworn memorandum of counsel that did not include fee agreement or disclose its terms, and did not state what tasks were performed in the case, deprived claim of Rule 3001(f) presumption of validity); *In re* Coates, 292 B.R. 894 (Bankr. C.D. Ill. 2003) (once objection to claim is filed, party asserting claim must place into evidence terms of the fee contract with the attorney, time records, a copy of any judgment including fees, and receipts or invoices for expenses).

239 For a discussion of paying "inside" or "outside" the plan, see Chapter 12, *infra.*

240 A creditor waives the right to dispute the interest rate if creditor fails to assert its arguments prior to or at the confirmation hearing. *In re* Szostek, 886 F.2d 1405 (3d Cir. 1989); *In re* Blair, 21 B.R. 316 (Bankr. S.D. Cal. 1982).

241 124 S. Ct. 1951 (2004).

242 The prime rate of interest may be found on the Internet at: http://federalreserve.gov/releases/h15/data.htm#top.

243 To the extent that application of *Till* does not produce a lower rate, debtors who are on active duty in the armed forces may obtain plan confirmation of a present value interest rate of six percent pursuant to the Servicemembers Civil Relief Act. 50 U.S.C. app. § 527(c); *see In re* Watson, 292 B.R. 441 (Bankr. S.D. Ga. 2003) (plan modified to reduce interest rate from twelve percent to six percent while debtor on active duty).

the debtor falls more than a little behind in payments, the chapter 13 plan will normally fail. In that event, the plan will be inoperative and the contract terms will be restored, including the interest rates and late charge provisions set forth therein, which would typically compensate the creditor for any delay.

The Supreme Court held that an objecting creditor has the burden of going forward with evidence that the interest rate proposed by the debtor is inadequate.[244] It has been held that the chapter 13 trustee, as representative of the unsecured creditors, does not have standing to object to the alleged inadequacy of provisions dealing with secured creditors in the plan.[245]

Once the necessary figures are known, it is possible to compute what payments, over what period of time, will be sufficient to pay the allowed secured claim, plus the necessary interest, plus the trustee's fees. This can be done most easily by first applying the annual percentage rate to the allowed secured claim for the number of payments and the time period desired.[246] After these payments are calculated, the trustee's percentage fee may simply be added to each payment.[247]

11.6.1.3.3.6 Plans not complying with section 1325(a)(5) may be confirmed

A final question which arises as to section 1325(a)(5) is whether the court may, over a creditor's objection, approve a plan providing for a secured claim which does not pay the amount set forth in 1325(a)(5)(B). Although most courts seem to have assumed that payment of at least that amount is mandatory, the language of the section indicates otherwise. Unlike section 1322(a) which states that the plan must meet certain requirements, section 1325(a) states that the court shall confirm the plan if it meets certain standards and is silent as to plans which do not meet those standards. It does not state that such plans shall not be confirmed. Nor does it state, as does section 1129(a), that the court shall confirm the plan *only if* certain "requirements" are met. Given Congress' placement of the mandatory provisions for chapter 13 plans in section 1322(a), the better reading of the two sections together is that courts have discretion to confirm any plan that complies with section 1322(a) and must confirm a plan that complies with both sections 1322(a) and 1325(a).[248] In any case, it seems clear that if a creditor or trustee does not raise an objection under section 1325, the plan may be confirmed notwithstanding the fact that it does not meet all of the standards in that section. Most courts have interpreted a failure to object as the secured creditor's acceptance of the plan, which is an alternative to the requirement that present value interest be provided.[249]

It should also be remembered that the standards of section 1325(a)(5) apply only to those secured claims *provided for* by the plan.[250] In some cases a debtor may be unwilling or unable to make the payments a court might require under that section to one or more particular secured claims. In such cases it is perfectly permissible to state that the plan does not provide for those claims.[251] Although this may mean that the

---

244 124 S. Ct. at 1961.

245 *In re* Brown, 108 B.R. 740 (Bankr. C.D. Cal. 1989); *see also In re* Andrews, 49 F.3d 1404 (9th Cir. 1995) (trustee may not raise issues under § 1325(a)(5), but may raise issue of adequate protection of secured creditor under § 1325(a)(1)).

246 It is important to note that the rate must be applied to a declining balance. Thus, a ten percent rate on $100.00 to be paid over three years does *not* yield $30.00 interest. Tables setting out the necessary payments in amortizations providing equal payments throughout the plan are readily available in many places, such as the Appendix to Regulation Z under the Truth-in-Lending Act, which can be obtained from the Federal Reserve Board. There are also spreadsheet programs and inexpensive pocket calculators available which are programmed to do such calculations. However, there is no requirement that all plan payments be equal. The plan may provide for graduated payments, increasing over time as the debtor's situation is anticipated to improve, provided that the plan is feasible. Negative amortization is not per se impermissible. *See* Great W. Bank v. Sierra Woods Group, 953 F.2d 1174 (9th Cir. 1992) (chapter 11 case).

247 To compute the trustee's fee precisely, the debtor must determine what total payment will provide for both the fee and the desired payment to creditors. In jurisdictions where trustees are permitted to compute the fee as a percentage of the total payment, and not of the payment to creditors, one cannot simply add ten percent to the payments to creditors to determine the necessary fee. *In re* BDT Farms, 21 F.3d 1019 (10th Cir. 1994) (court deferred to United States trustee's interpretation that trustee entitled to collect percentage fee on all monies received, including monies used to pay trustee's fees). For example, if the payment to creditors is $9.00/month, the trustee's fee, at ten percent, would be $1.00 or ten percent of the total payment of $10.00 ($9.00 to creditors and $1.00 to trustee), rather than $.90. In districts where such trustees administer cases, for a ten percent fee the payment to creditors must be multiplied by 1.1111 to obtain the correct total payment. (This multiple is determined using the formula $10 + X = 10X$.) However, other trustees do compute the fee based on a percentage of the

amounts paid to creditors rather than a percentage of the total amount paid to the trustee. *See In re* Wallace, 167 B.R. 531 (Bankr. E.D. Mo. 1994), *aff'd sub nom.* Pelofsky v. Wallace, 102 F.3d 350 (8th Cir. 1996) (chapter 12 trustee could calculate percentage fee only based upon payments disbursed to creditors); *In re* Edge, 122 B.R. 219 (Bankr. D. Vt. 1990).

248 *In re* Chappell, 984 F.2d 775 (7th Cir. 1993) (secured creditor required to satisfy mortgage after being paid full amount of claim filed but no post-petition interest, pursuant to confirmed chapter 13 plan to which creditor did not object, that provided for payment of amount in proof of claim to satisfy claim); *In re* Szostek, 886 F.2d 1405 (3d Cir. 1989); *In re* Brady, 86 B.R. 166 (Bankr. D. Minn. 1988); *cf. In re* Escobedo, 28 F.3d 34 (7th Cir. 1994) (provisions of § 1322(a), unlike those of § 1325(a), are mandatory). *But see In re* Barnes, 32 F.3d 405 (9th Cir. 1994) (provisions of § 1325(a)(5) are mandatory, and plan not paying present value of allowed secured claim could not be confirmed over creditor's objection).

249 *See* § 11.6.1.3, *supra*.

250 *See* § 11.6.1.3.3.3, *supra*.

251 *In re* Evans, 66 B.R. 506 (Bankr. E.D. Pa. 1986), *aff'd*, 77 B.R. 457 (E.D. Pa. 1987); 8 Collier on Bankruptcy ¶ 1325.06[2][b] (15th ed. rev.).

holders of these claims are entitled to relief from the stay and will have to be dealt with outside of bankruptcy, that outcome may be preferable to trying to pay the allowed secured claims in the bankruptcy, particularly if the filing of the chapter 13 case stemmed from other problems.

11.6.1.4 Requirement of Adequate Protection

A second limitation on the rights of chapter 13 debtors to deal with secured creditors is the requirement of adequate protection to creditors that have liens on property used, sold, or leased by the debtor. At least until a plan is confirmed, it is clear that a creditor may request relief from the automatic stay if adequate protection has not been provided.[252] It is less clear whether this right continues after a plan is confirmed, because section 1327 states that the provisions of a confirmed plan bind each creditor. A number of courts have held that this section, in effect, overrides the creditor's preexisting right to adequate protection and eliminates the creditor's right to relief so long as the debtor is in compliance with a confirmed plan.[253]

11.6.2 Right to Cure Defaults on Long-Term Debts Including Mortgages on Debtor's Residence

11.6.2.1 Overview

There are certain claims that the debtor cannot pay within the time period of the proposed plan, which can never exceed five years,[254] simply because they are large long-term obligations that have many years of payments remaining before they are due to be fully satisfied. Section 1322(b)(5) allows the debtor to cure a default on such an obligation within a reasonable period of time without having to pay the entire debt balance within the time period of the plan. This provision can be utilized to cure both pre-petition and post-petition defaults.[255]

While section 1322(b)(3) may be used to cure defaults on short-term debts secured only by a security interest in the debtor's principal residence,[256] and such debts may be modified pursuant to sections 1322(c)(2) and 1325(a)(5), section 1322(b)(5) may in some cases be the only feasible remedy available with respect to defaults on long-term home mortgages. In addition, courts have generally ruled that land installment sales contracts are secured debts,[257] so that they too should be subject to the cure provisions of section 1322(b)(5), as well as the other provisions for dealing with secured claims.

11.6.2.2 Cure of Mortgages After Acceleration or Foreclosure Judgment

Although a few early cases held otherwise, it is now well established that defaults on long-term debts such as mortgages may be cured under this section even if there has already been an acceleration and/or judgment which caused the entire balance to become due.[258] Indeed, at least one state court has held that, because a confirmed plan deaccelerating a mortgage debt is binding on a creditor, if that creditor later gets relief from the automatic stay the creditor must begin its foreclosure anew by reaccelerating the debt.[259]

---

252 See Chapter 9, *supra,* for a further discussion of adequate protection.

253 *In re* Evans, 30 B.R. 530 (B.A.P. 9th Cir. 1983); *In re* Guilbeau, 74 B.R. 13, 14 (Bankr. W.D. La. 1987); *In re* Lewis, 8 B.R. 132 (Bankr. D. Idaho 1981); *In re* Brock, 6 B.R. 105 (Bankr. N.D. Ill. 1980). *But see In re* Andrews, 49 F.3d 1404 (9th Cir. 1995) (suggesting that plan's failure to provide adequate protection would justify objection to confirmation under 11 U.S.C. § 1325(a)(1)); *In re* Simmons, 765 F.2d 547 (5th Cir. 1985) (confirmed plan does not eliminate creditor's lien where no objection to the claim was filed or determined but plan called for claim to be treated as unsecured).

254 11 U.S.C. § 1322(c).

255 *In re* Mendoza, 111 F.3d 1264 (5th Cir. 1997) (debtor could modify plan to cure post-confirmation default); *In re* Hoggle, 12 F.3d 1008 (11th Cir. 1994) (debtor could modify plan to cure post-confirmation default); *In re* McCollum, 76 B.R. 797

(Bankr. D. Or. 1987); *In re* Simpkins, 16 B.R. 956 (Bankr. E.D. Tenn. 1982); *see also In re* Carvalho, 335 F.3d 45 (1st Cir. 2003) (lifting of stay did not preclude debtors from seeking to cure post-petition default and obtain bifurcation of creditor's claim when creditor did not initiate foreclosure proceedings after stay lifted and debtors continued to make plan payments); 8 Collier on Bankruptcy ¶ 1322.09[1] (15th ed. rev.).

256 *See* § 11.6.1.2, *supra.*

257 *In re* Johnson, 75 B.R. 927 (Bankr. N.D. Ohio 1987); *In re* Leazier, 55 B.R. 870 (Bankr. N.D. Ind. 1985); *In re* Britton, 43 B.R. 605 (Bankr. E.D. Mich. 1984); *In re* Love, 38 B.R. 771 (Bankr. D. Mass. 1983); *In re* Booth, 19 B.R. 53 (Bankr. D. Utah 1982); *see also* § 12.9.1, *infra. But see* Brown v. First Nat'l Bank in Lenox, 844 F.2d 580 (8th Cir. 1988); Shaw v. Dawson, 48 B.R. 857 (D.N.M. 1985). The treatment of such contracts as similar to mortgages under state law will often be determinative in deciding that they are to be treated like secured debts. If land installment sale contracts are held to be executory contracts, defaults on such contracts may still be cured. There would then be an issue whether such debts could be cured as long-term debts under § 1325(b)(5) or whether they must be cured "promptly" under § 365(b)(1)(A).

258 *In re* Thompson, 894 F.2d 1227 (10th Cir. 1990); *In re* Metz, 820 F.2d 1495 (9th Cir. 1987); *In re* Terry, 780 F.2d 894 (11th Cir. 1986); *In re* Clark, 738 F.2d 869 (7th Cir. 1984); Grubbs v. Houston First Am. Sav. Ass'n, 730 F.2d 236 (5th Cir. 1984) (*en banc*); *In re* Taddeo, 685 F.2d 24 (2d Cir. 1982) (to deprive debtors of the right to cure after an acceleration would undermine the purpose of the cure provisions); *see also In re* Glenn, 760 F.2d 1428 (6th Cir. 1985); *In re* Nelson, 59 B.R. 417 (B.A.P. 9th Cir. 1985). *But see In re* Roach, 824 F.2d 1370 (3d Cir. 1987) (under New Jersey law, debtor's right to cure home mortgage default expired when mortgagee obtained foreclosure judgment).

259 Fed. Nat'l Mortgage Ass'n v. Miller, 123 Misc. 2d 431, 473 N.Y.S.2d 743 (Sup. Ct. 1984).

In 1994, Congress codified those cases permitting cure after acceleration and judgment, by enacting section 1322(c)(1). That subsection provides that a default with respect to a lien on the debtor's principal residence may be cured under paragraph 1322(b)(3) or (b)(5) until such residence is sold at a foreclosure sale conducted in accordance with applicable non-bankruptcy law.

This statutory language suggests that a cure may be effectuated under chapter 13 as long as the sale has not been completed under state law as of the time of the bankruptcy petition. Thus, if any step in the sale remains to be taken, such as an order confirming the sale or delivery of a deed, the debt giving rise to the foreclosure may be cured pursuant to section 1322(b)(3) or (b)(5).[260]

---

260 *See In re* Randall, 263 B.R. 200 (D.N.J. 2001) (New Jersey foreclosure sale not complete until sheriff delivers deed to purchaser); McEwen v. Fed. Nat'l Mortgage Ass'n, 194 B.R. 594 (N.D. Ill. 1996) (sale not complete until court order of confirmation); *In re* Wescott, 309 B.R. 308 (Bankr. E.D. Wis. 2004) (same result under Wisconsin law); *In re* Pellegrino, 284 B.R. 326 (Bankr. D. Conn. 2002) (same result under Connecticut law); *In re* Faulkner, 240 B.R. 67 (Bankr. W.D. Okla. 1999) (Oklahoma foreclosure not completed until auction confirmed by court); *In re* Beeman, 235 B.R. 519 (Bankr. D.N.H. 1999) (New Hampshire foreclosure not completed until deed recorded); *In re* Tomlin, 228 B.R. 916 (Bankr. E.D. Ark. 1999) (Arkansas foreclosure not final until deed recorded); *In re* Donahue, 231 B.R. 865 (Bankr. D. Vt. 1998) (Vermont judicial foreclosure not complete until court order of confirmation filed in land records); *In re* Rambo, 199 B.R. 747 (Bankr. W.D. Okla. 1996) (sale not complete until court enters order confirming sale); *In re* Barham, 193 B.R. 229 (Bankr. E.D.N.C. 1996) (debtor may cure if foreclosure sale has not been completed by expiration of period for upset bid); *In re* Ross, 191 B.R. 615 (Bankr. D.N.J. 1996) (right to cure existed until delivery of sheriff's deed to purchaser); *In re* Jaar, 186 B.R. 148 (Bankr. M.D. Fla. 1995) (foreclosure sale not completed until certificate of sale filed with clerk of court); *see also In re* Brown, 249 B.R. 193 (Bankr. N.D. Ill. 2000) (buyer under real estate installment sales agreement still had right to cure after seller declared forfeiture because buyer had right to cure and reinstate contract under state law). The legislative history also suggests that the new provision was not intended to override decisions setting a later cutoff of the right to cure, stating that "if the state provides the debtor more extensive 'cure' rights (through, for example, some later redemption period), the debtor would continue to enjoy such rights in bankruptcy." H.R. Rep. No. 103-835, at 52 (1994), *reprinted in* 1994 U.S.C.C.A.N. 3340. Thus, the provision should be viewed as permissive, rather than restrictive; it does not state that no cure may occur after the property is sold if that is otherwise permitted by state law. Indeed, an earlier version of the bill, S.540, § 301, 103d Cong. (1994), would have permitted cure in any case in which the debtor retained "any legal or equitable interest, including a right of redemption." *But see* Colon v. Option One Mortgage Corp., 319 F.3d 912 (7th Cir. 2003) (right to cure under Illinois law is cut off upon completion of sale if time for redemption has run and does not continue until order confirming sale); *In re* Frazer, 284 F.3d 363 (2d Cir. 2002) (under Vermont strict foreclosure law, automatic stay does not permit debtor to redeem property after end of redemption period, except as extended for sixty days by 11 U.S.C. § 108(b); court did not consider application of § 1322(c)(1)); *In re* Smith,

---

11.6.2.3 Cure of Mortgages That Mature Before the Bankruptcy Case or Before the End of the Plan

Section 1322(c) also makes clear that the time period for cure under section 1322(b)(3) may extend beyond the last scheduled payment date on the mortgage, as many courts had held,[261] and overrules the result of those courts that had held otherwise.[262] Notwithstanding the limitations of section 1322(b)(5), section 1322(c)(1) clearly permits cure of home mortgages under section 1322(b)(3) as well as under section 1322(b)(5), and section 1322(c)(2) permits modification of mortgages that mature before the end of the plan. Therefore, a debtor may cure a mortgage with a balloon payment that has already fallen due, or that will fall due during the plan, by paying the balance over the course of a chapter 13 plan.[263]

Prior to the 1994 amendments, several courts of appeals held, for different reasons, that there was no right to cure a default once a foreclosure sale had taken place,[264] though by the operation of Code section 108 there was a sixty day tolling of any right to redeem.[265] Other courts have held that the right to cure may exist until the expiration of state law

---

85 F.3d 1555 (11th Cir. 1996) (dicta that right to cure does not exist during statutory redemption period); *In re* Froehle, 286 B.R. 94 (B.A.P. 8th Cir. 2002) (redemption period following tax sale under Iowa law not tolled beyond sixty-day period provided for in § 108(b), and debtor may not use cure provisions under chapter 13 to redeem property); *In re* Bebensee-Wong, 248 B.R. 820 (B.A.P. 9th Cir. 2000) (relief from stay granted to foreclosure sale purchaser was not abuse of discretion because under California law recording of trustee's deed related back to date of sale, which occurred before bankruptcy); *In re* McCarn, 218 B.R. 154 (B.A.P 10th Cir. 1998) (property was "sold" on date of foreclosure sale under Wyoming law); *In re* Ferrell, 179 B.R. 530 (W.D. Tenn. 1994).

261 Grubbs v. Houston First Am. Sav. Ass'n, 730 F.2d 236 (5th Cir. 1984); *In re* Spader, 66 B.R. 618 (W.D. Mo. 1986) (residential mortgage maturing pre-petition could be cured in chapter 13); *In re* Larkins, 50 B.R. 984 (W.D. Ky. 1985); *In re* Dochniak, 95 B.R. 100 (Bankr. W.D. Ky. 1988); *In re* McSorley, 24 B.R. 795 (Bankr. D.N.J. 1982); *In re* Simpkins, 16 B.R. 956 (Bankr. E.D. Tenn. 1982); *see* § 11.6.1.2.3, *supra*.

262 *In re* Harlan, 783 F.2d 839 (9th Cir. 1986); *In re* Seidel, 752 F.2d 1382 (9th Cir. 1985); *In re* Fontaine, 27 B.R. 614 (B.A.P. 9th Cir. 1982) (chapter 13 debtor may not cure pre-petition balloon payment default); *cf. In re* Clark, 738 F.2d 869, 874 (7th Cir. 1984) (suggesting that § 1322(b)(5) cure cannot extend beyond last payment date).

263 *In re* Chang, 185 B.R. 50 (Bankr. N.D. Ill. 1995); *see also In re* Jefferson, 263 B.R. 231 (Bankr. N.D. Ill. 2001) (section 1322(c)(1) permitted cure of lien obtained by condominium association on debtor's home if lien had not yet been foreclosed upon).

264 Justice v. Valley Nat'l Bank, 849 F.2d 1078 (8th Cir. 1988); *In re* Roach, 824 F.2d 1370 (3d Cir. 1987) (conclusion rests on New Jersey law); *In re* Glenn, 760 F.2d 1428 (6th Cir. 1985) (conclusion appears to be based on federal law); *see also In re* Tynan, 773 F.2d 177 (7th Cir. 1985).

265 *See* § 9.4.2, *supra*; *In re* Tynan, 773 F.2d 177 (7th Cir. 1985).

rights of redemption.[266] As discussed above, the language of section 1322(c)(1), enacted after these decisions, suggests that a cure can occur at least until every step of a foreclosure sale is completed and perhaps until all state law cure rights no longer exist.[267] Additionally, in the limited situations in which a foreclosure can be set aside pursuant to state law, the right to cure may be reinstated.[268]

11.6.2.4 Cure Permitted Even If Debtor Has No Personal Liability

A cure may also be effected under section 1322(b)(5) despite the fact that the debtor has no personal liability on the underlying obligation due to its discharge in a prior bankruptcy, as the creditor continues to have a claim, and a "claim against the debtor" is defined to include a claim against property of the debtor.[269] Similarly, a debtor who has taken over payments on a mortgage when a property has been transferred to him or her may cure despite the absence of personal liability on the original obligation.[270]

11.6.2.5 Length of Time Permitted for Cure

The Code does not define what period of time is "reasonable" for the purpose of section 1322(b)(5). Necessarily, this depends to some extent on the facts and circumstances of each case.[271] It is not safe to assume that cure over the entire length of the plan will be found reasonable,[272] although in many cases that long a time period is allowed.[273] Many bankruptcy courts routinely permit three to five years to cure a mortgage default, if necessary.

It may also be possible to obtain a longer period of time to cure by arguing that the time for a plan to run does not begin until confirmation of the plan. At least one court of appeals has held that the plan can run for sixty months from that date.[274] In any case, the amount of time a prior bankruptcy case was pending is not counted toward the sixty-month maximum for plan duration.[275]

---

266 *See In re* Chambers, 27 B.R. 687 (Bankr. S.D. Fla. 1983); *see also In re* Thompson, 894 F.2d 1227, 1230 n.6 (10th Cir. 1990) (suggesting that cure may be possible after foreclosure sale if no third-party purchaser present); 8 Collier on Bankruptcy ¶ 1322.09[6] (15th ed. rev.). *But see In re* Smith, 85 F.3d 1555 (11th Cir. 1996) (state law right to redeem cannot be exercised by curing the arrears in installments in bankruptcy; unclear whether entire balance due could be paid in installments).

267 *In re* Grassie, 293 B.R. 829 (Bankr. D. Mass. 2003) (debtor retains equity of redemption when bankruptcy petition was filed minutes after foreclosure sale and after memorandum of sale signed by purchaser but before memorandum signed by auctioneer); *In re* Benson, 293 B.R. 234 (Bankr. D. Ariz. 2003) (trustee's sale is not complete under Arizona law until the bid price is paid; sale invalidated as debtor filed bankruptcy after fall of auctioneer's hammer but before high bidder paid bid price); *In re* Brown, 282 B.R. 880 (Bankr. E.D. Ark. 2002) (judicial foreclosure not complete under Arkansas law until sale is confirmed by court; bankruptcy filed after sale but one day before sale confirmed); *see* § 11.6.2.2, *supra*; *see also In re* Schleier, 290 B.R. 45 (Bankr. S.D.N.Y. 2003) (clerk's time-stamp on bankruptcy petition created mere rebuttable presumption which debtor rebutted with evidence that petition was in possession of clerk and actually filed minutes before the completion of the sale). *But see* Colon v. Option One Mortgage Corp., 319 F.3d 912 (7th Cir. 2003) (right to cure under Illinois law is cut off upon completion of sale if time for redemption has run and does not continue until order confirming sale); *In re* Canney, 284 F.3d 363 (2d Cir. 2002) (under Vermont strict foreclosure law, automatic stay does not permit debtor to redeem property after end of redemption period, except as extended for sixty days by 11 U.S.C. § 108(b); court did not consider application of § 1322(c)(1)); *In re* Tucker, 290 B.R. 134 (Bankr. E.D. Mo. 2003) (deed of trust foreclosure sale complete under Missouri law even though bankruptcy filed before trustee's deed recorded).

268 *See* § 10.4.2.6.5, *supra*.

269 11 U.S.C. § 102(2); Johnson v. Home State Bank, 501 U.S 78, 111 S. Ct. 2150, 115 L. Ed. 2d 66 (1991).

270 *In re* Curinton, 300 B.R. 78 (Bankr. M.D. Fla. 2003) (debtor

could cure mortgage on home that was transferred to him from his business even though mortgage remained in corporation's name); *In re* Rosa, 261 B.R. 136 (Bankr. D.N.J. 2001) (debtor could cure default on mortgage on her property even though mortgage was in name of her spouse); *In re* Trapp, 260 B.R. 267 (Bankr. D.S.C. 2001) (debtor could cure mortgage with due on sale clause on property she had purchased from mortgagors); *In re* Rutledge, 208 B.R. 624 (Bankr. E.D.N.Y. 1997); *In re* Wilcox, 209 B.R. 181 (Bankr. E.D.N.Y. 1996) (debtor could pay off mortgage on inherited home even though under "reverse mortgage" provisions mortgage came due when debtor's father died); *In re* Everhart, 87 B.R. 35 (Bankr. N.D. Ohio 1988); *see also In re* Garcia, 276 B.R. 627 (Bankr. D. Ariz. 2002) (due-on-sale clause violation did not prevent debtor who had become owner of property from curing).

271 *In re* Steinacher, 283 B.R. 768 (B.A.P. 9th Cir. 2002) (invalidating local rule that required short cure period for any debtor who had previous chapter 13 case pending within six months before current case).

272 *In re* Coleman, 5 B.R. 812 (Bankr. W.D. Ky. 1980) (reasonable time not synonymous with three-year duration of typical plan).

273 *In re* Capps, 836 F.2d 773 (3d Cir. 1987) (sixty months); *In re* King, 23 B.R. 779 (B.A.P. 9th Cir. 1982) (cure over duration of plan not unreasonable); Philadelphia Sav. Fund Soc'y v. Stewart, 16 B.R. 460 (E.D. Pa. 1981) (three years, four months); *In re* Chavez, 117 B.R. 730 (Bankr. S.D. Fla. 1990) (three years); *In re* Harmon, 72 B.R. 458 (Bankr. E.D. Pa. 1987) (cure during period of five years not unreasonable); *In re* Johnson, 6 B.R. 34 (Bankr. N.D. Ill. 1980) (three years).

274 West v. Costen, 826 F.2d 1376 (4th Cir. 1987); *In re* Serna, 193 B.R. 537 (Bankr. D. Ariz. 1996) (sixty months run from due date of first payment after confirmation of plan); *see also* PNC Mortgage Co. v. Dicks, 199 B.R. 674 (N.D. Ind. 1996) (arrearages could be cured over remaining twenty-five year term of mortgage); *In re* Black, 78 B.R. 840 (Bankr. S.D. Ohio 1987) (no dismissal where payments extend over sixty-six months, if plan complied with duration requirements of the Code at the time of confirmation).

275 *In re* Martin, 156 B.R. 47 (B.A.P. 9th Cir. 1993).

11.6.2.6 Method of Maintaining Current Payments on Debts Being Cured

Most courts permit current payments on long-term obligations that are being cured to be paid outside the plan.[276] And, as the payments on long-term obligations are often higher than on any others, it is a common practice to make them outside the plan to avoid adding the substantial cost of the trustee's percentage fees and expenses (up to ten percent).[277]

However, some trustees and practitioners prefer payment of current mortgage payments through the chapter 13 trustee. This method has the advantage of making payment more likely if the debtor's payments to the trustee are made by wage deductions. It also provides a better method of keeping track of payments made, through the trustee's records, which avoids the necessity of trying to reconstruct a debtor's fragmentary records or canceled checks or money order receipts if a dispute later arises. Often, trustees who funnel current mortgage payments through their offices are able to greatly reduce their percentage fees because much more money is flowing through their systems.

11.6.2.7 Amount Necessary to Effectuate Cure

11.6.2.7.1 Attorney fees and costs

Another question arising under section 1322(b)(5) is the extent to which creditors may collect attorney fees and costs as part of the amount needed to cure. The answer usually turns upon the precise language of the contract and state law. Section 506(b) of the Code, applicable to determining the amount payable to the holder of an over-secured claim, provides for collection of such charges only if provided for in the parties' agreement.[278] Agreements departing from the standard "American rule" that each party must bear its own fees are to be strictly construed, especially when drafted by the creditor trying to collect fees.[279] In addition, many state statutes place significant limitations on fee arrangements[280] or prohibit them entirely.[281] Such state laws are usually read into any contract to which they are applicable as implied terms.

In any case, fees should be allowed in a cure situation only to the extent that they are reasonable and necessary.[282] Where a creditor's litigation is unsuccessful or unnecessary, it should not be rewarded by the assessment of attorney fees against the debtor.[283] Similarly, if the creditor does not provide adequate records to establish that its attorney fees are fair and reasonable, the fees should be denied.[284] The filing of a claim does not require an attorney, and thus no

---

276 Payments outside the plan are not made through the trustee. *See* Ch. 12, *infra.*

277 *In re* Land, 96 B.R. 310 (D. Colo. 1988); *In re* Burkhart, 94 B.R. 724 (Bankr. N.D. Fla. 1988); *In re* Erickson Partnership, 77 B.R. 738 (Bankr. D.S.D. 1987), *aff'd*, 83 B.R. 725 (D.S.D. 1988). *But see In re* Foster, 670 F.2d 478 (5th Cir. 1982) (trustee's commission must be paid on payments outside the plan). The *Erickson Partnership* decision noted a change in statutory language which may overrule the *Foster* result. *See* 8 Collier on Bankruptcy ¶ 1302.05[1][c] (15th ed. rev.).

278 *See* § 11.6.1.3.4, *supra.* For agreements entered into after October 22, 1994, section 1322(e) similarly requires that the creditor's right to collect attorney fees and costs must be provided for in the underlying agreement. *See In re* Plant, 288 B.R. 635 (Bankr. D. Mass. 2003) (§ 1322(e) rather than § 506(b) determines creditor's entitlement to pre-petition fees in chapter 13 cure situation).

279 *In re* Hatcher, 208 B.R. 959 (B.A.P. 10th Cir. 1997) (creditor had no right, under § 506(b) or otherwise, to post-petition attorney

fees in addition to fees provided for in mortgage contract); *In re* Romano, 174 B.R. 342 (Bankr. M.D. Fla. 1994) (interpreting ambiguous attorney fee provision in note against drafter); *In re* Kennedy Mortgage Co., 23 B.R. 466 (Bankr. D.N.J. 1982) (instrument did not allow fees when collection was by way of setoff); *In re* Roberts, 20 B.R. 914 (Bankr. E.D.N.Y. 1981) (participation in chapter 13 proceedings was not included in the attorney fees provision of the mortgage); *see also In re* United Nesco Container Corp., 68 B.R. 970 (Bankr. E.D. Pa. 1987) (equipment lease providing for attorney fees in the event of repossession would not be interpreted broadly so as to include attorney fees incurred by lessor in pursuing claim in bankruptcy court).

280 *In re* Wilder, 22 B.R. 294 (Bankr. M.D. Ga. 1982) (statutory attorney fees could not be collected for work that could have been performed by non-lawyers); *see also* § 11.6.1.3.3.4, *supra.*

281 *In re* Lake, 245 B.R. 282 (Bankr. N.D. Ohio 2000) (boilerplate fee provisions in a mortgage were not product of free and understanding negotiation and therefore were unenforceable under Ohio law); *In re* Bertsch, 17 B.R. 284 (Bankr. N.D. Ohio 1982) (assessment of bank's attorney fees against debtor disallowed as contrary to Ohio public policy).

282 *In re* McMullen, 273 B.R. 558 (Bankr. C.D. Ill. 2001) (flat fee covering attorney fees for entire foreclosure proceeding found excessive where not pro-rated to cover only services actually performed prior to bankruptcy filing); *In re* A.J. Lane & Co., 113 B.R. 821 (Bankr. D. Mass. 1990) (prepayment charge disallowed because it was unreasonable); *In re* Bailey, 23 B.R. 222 (Bankr. E.D. Pa. 1982) (attorney fees and costs denied for unsuccessful proceeding for relief from automatic stay). One bankruptcy court has held that it must make its own independent determination of whether fees are reasonable for the purposes of the Code, even if they have already been reduced to judgment by a creditor. *In re* Harper, 146 B.R. 438 (Bankr. N.D. Ind. 1992); *see also In re* Welzel, 275 F.3d 1308 (11th Cir. 2001) (*en banc*) (bankruptcy court must independently determine reasonableness of fees as a matter of federal law because § 506(b) preempts state law).

283 *In re* Crowley, 293 B.R. 628 (Bankr. D. Vt. 2003) (excessive time spent by creditor attorney in drafting default letters, a modification agreement, and for pursuing new legal theory in stay relief proceeding found to be unnecessary and not recoverable under note).

284 *In re* Harmon, 72 B.R. 458 (Bankr. E.D. Pa. 1987). The creditor and its counsel have the burden of proving that the fees requested are reasonable. *In re* Coates, 292 B.R. 894 (Bankr. C.D. Ill. 2003) (claim of mortgage servicer for attorney fees, foreclosure expenses, and other charges denied as servicer failed to produce evidence that would satisfy its burden of proving reasonableness); *In re* Staggie, 255 B.R. 48 (Bankr. N.D. Idaho 2000) (burden of proof not satisfied because counsel's billing summary failed to provide detailed break down of time entries).

attorney fees may be charged for that task.[285] Some courts have held that the inclusion in a proof of claim of any attorney fee incurred in connection with the bankruptcy case is improper unless the fee has been sought and approved under Federal Rule of Bankruptcy Procedure 2016, because the fee would be paid from property of the bankruptcy estate.[286] Other courts have held that a creditor may include an attorney-fee demand in a proof of claim without filing an application under Rule 2016 if the claim is sufficiently detailed and provides adequate notice to the debtor.[287] Indeed, at least one court has held that attorney fees may never be added to the amount due in a chapter 13 case.[288]

11.6.2.7.2 Interest on arrears

Another important question is how interest is to be computed when a long-term obligation is cured under section 1322(b)(5). Unfortunately, the Supreme Court, in *Rake v. Wade*,[289] rejected the holdings of most lower courts and held that a creditor may demand that interest be paid on arrears being cured through a chapter 13 plan. The Court reached this result by holding that the arrearages constitute a separate "allowed secured claim,"[290] notwithstanding that the definition of allowed secured claim in the Code encompasses the creditor's entire claim and does not carve out a special category of claims that would include only arrears.[291]

The Court held that interest on the arrears for the period preceding plan confirmation could be required with respect to an over-secured mortgage because section 506(b) of the Code permits creditors to demand pre-confirmation interest on any over-secured claim.[292] For the period after confirmation the Court found section 1325(a)(5) applicable to the "arrearage claim," and thus held that a creditor could demand present value interest[293] on the arrears as a condition of plan confirmation. However, because there is only a right to post-confirmation interest to the extent that the arrears constitute an allowed secured claim, a creditor who is under-secured may not demand post-confirmation interest to the extent it is not fully secured.[294]

In 1994, Congress overruled the result of *Rake v. Wade* by enacting a new section 1322(e) of the Code, which provides that in a cure of a default through a chapter 13 plan the interest or other charges that need be paid must be determined in accordance with the underlying contract and applicable state law.[295] The subsection makes clear that it is an exception to both section 506(b) and section 1325(a)(5), thus covering both bases for the *Rake* holding, and the legislative history leaves no doubt of Congress' intent to overrule that case.[296] Unfortunately, unlike any other provision of the 1994 amendments, section 1322(e) is only effective with respect to agreements entered into after the enactment date of the amendments, October 22, 1994.[297]

---

285 *See In re* E. Side Investors, 702 F.2d 214 (11th Cir. 1983); *In re* Noletto, 280 B.R. 868 (Bankr. S.D. Ala. 2001); *In re* Allen, 215 B.R. 503 (Bankr. N.D. Tex. 1997) (preparation of claim is ministerial act for which no attorney fees should be charged to debtor); *In re* Trombley, 31 B.R. 386 (Bankr. D. Vt. 1983); *In re* Banks, 31 B.R. 173 (Bankr. N.D. Ala. 1982). See also § 13.4.3.4, *infra*, for discussion of other "costs" which mortgage creditors attempt to collect.

286 *In re* Tate, 253 B.R. 653 (Bankr. W.D.N.C. 2000); *see also In re* Plant, 288 B.R. 635 (Bankr. D. Mass. 2003) (Rule 2016 application required if creditor's claim for fees contested by debtor); Powe v. Chrysler Fin. Corp., 281 B.R. 336 (Bankr. S.D. Ala. 2001) (private right of action under § 105 exists to enforce secured creditor's duty to adequately disclose attorney fees sought from debtors; nationwide class of debtors certified challenging creditor's disclosure); *In re* Noletto, 281 B.R. 36 (Bankr. S.D. Ala. 2000) (fees that are not properly claimed or disclosed with specificity, or omitted from an arrearage claim to be paid under debtor's plan, are per se unreasonable); *In re* Gifford, 256 B.R. 661 (Bankr. D. Conn. 2000) (court noted that in future cases it would follow *Tate* and require over-secured creditors to seek approval of fees under Rule 2016). *But see* Telfair v. First Union Mortgage Corp., 216 F.3d 1333 (11th Cir. 2000) (when mortgage company assessed fees on payments made directly to mortgage company outside the plan, and property of the estate had revested in the debtor at confirmation, Rule 2016 was not applicable).

287 *In re* Powe, 281 B.R. 336 (Bankr. S.D. Ala. 2001); *see also In re* Atwood, 293 B.R. 227 (B.A.P. 9th Cir. 2003) (proof of claim lacking specific detail fails to meet creditor's evidentiary burden on reasonableness of fees).

288 *In re* Burns, 16 B.R. 757 (Bankr. M.D. Ga. 1982) (section 506(b) applies only in liquidation cases).

289 508 U.S. 464, 113 S. Ct. 2187, 124 L. Ed. 2d 424 (1993).

290 113 S. Ct. at 2192, 2193.

291 *See* 11 U.S.C. § 506(a).

292 113 S. Ct. at 2191, 2192. Hence, creditors who are not over-secured cannot demand pre-confirmation interest.

293 113 S. Ct. at 2192, 2193; *see also In re* Cabrera, 99 F.3d 684 (5th Cir. 1996) (present value interest in cure had to be paid at rate provided in note).

294 *In re* Johnson, 203 B.R. 775 (Bankr. M.D. Fla. 1996); *In re* Arvelo, 176 B.R. 349 (Bankr. N.J. 1995).

295 *In re* Young, 310 B.R. 127 (Bankr. E.D. Wis. 2003) (note provision that interest due until paid in full not sufficient to require interest on arrearage under § 1322(e)); *In re* Bumgarner, 225 B.R. 327 (Bankr. D.S.C. 1998) (interest on arrears must be authorized both by contract and state law, and was not authorized by contract language permitting ongoing interest on principal); *see also In re* Trabal, 254 B.R. 99 (D.N.J. 2000) (interest on arrears required because mortgage "significantly more specific" than in *Bumgarner* by providing for payment of "all other sums, with interest"; no specific reference to bankruptcy arrears required); *In re* Koster, 294 B.R. 737 (Bankr. E.D. Mo. 2003) (note language required payment of interest on portion of arrearage attributable to principal and attorney fee advances but not late charges and "additional charges").

296 H.R. Rep. No. 103-835, at 55 (1994), *reprinted in* 1994 U.S.C.C.A.N. 3340.

297 Pub. L. No. 103-394, § 702(b)(2)(D), 108 Stat. 4106 (1994). The legislative history provides that for this purpose a refinancing is considered a new agreement. H.R. Rep. No. 103-835, at 55 (1994), *reprinted in* 1994 U.S.C.C.A.N. 3340; *see In re* Harding, 274 B.R. 173 (Bankr. D. Md. 2002) (modification agreement entered into after October 22, 1994 that modified

Thus, mortgages made before that date are still governed by the *Rake* holding.

11.6.2.8 Effect of Cure

The effect of a cure under section 1322(b)(5) is to nullify all consequences of the default.[298] Thus, in the case of a long-term mortgage, the debtor would normally be returned to the original amortization schedule once the default has been cured. Unfortunately, holders of long-term mortgages do not always comply with this principle, and debtors' attorneys may have to bring proceedings at the end of a chapter 13 plan to ensure that the cure is fully effectuated and not subverted by a mortgage holder's contrary bookkeeping practices.[299] The chances for success in such pro-

ceedings is enhanced if the chapter 13 plan specifically provided that once the mortgage is cured under the plan the debtor will be treated as if the default never existed and returned to the original amortization schedule.[300]

The cure provisions, then, are particularly useful in a case where the debtor is behind on a mortgage and the creditor refuses to allow the debtor to bring the payments up to date gradually. In essence, they provide a method of forcing the creditor to be reasonable, by giving the debtor a right to cure over a reasonable time, at least when the creditor has adequate protection and cannot obtain relief from the automatic stay.[301]

11.7 Use of Section 506 to Reduce Liens That Are Not Paid Under Section 1325(a)(5)

The allowed secured claim concept is effectuated by section 506(a) and 506(d) of the Code. Section 506(a) bifurcates the claim into its secured and unsecured portion and section 506(d) provides that "[t]o the extent that a lien secures a claim that is not an allowed secured claim [as determined under § 506(a)] *such lien is void* unless" such a claim was disallowed only because it was for unmatured alimony or support or such claim was not an allowed claim only because no entity filed a proof of claim.[302]

In *Dewsnup v. Timm*,[303] the Supreme Court held that section 506(d) could not be used independently of section 722 to void a lien in a chapter 7 case. Despite the clear statutory language of section 506(d), noted by the dissent, providing that a lien is void to the extent it does not secure an allowed secured claim, the Court based its decision on the fact that Congress had given no indication in the legislative history that it intended the section to act as an independent avoiding power in chapter 7 cases. However, the courts have not extended this ruling to chapter 13 cases.[304]

---

terms of 1986 mortgage was refinancing and governed by 1322(e)).

298 *See In re* Southeast Co., 868 F.2d 335 (9th Cir. 1989) (chapter 11 cure); *see also In re* Epps, 110 B.R. 691 (E.D. Pa. 1990) (debtor did not lose the benefit of Dep't of Housing and Urban Development forbearance agreement where pre-bankruptcy default on agreement was cured under chapter 13 plan). The House Report to the Bankruptcy Reform Act of 1994 reaffirms that this is the intent of Congress. "It is the Committee's intention that a cure pursuant to a plan should operate to put the debtor in the same position as if the default had never occurred." H.R. Rep. No. 103-835, at 55 (1994), *reprinted in* 1994 U.S.C.C.A.N. 3340.

299 *See, e.g.*, Chase Manhattan Mortgage Corp. v. Padgett, 268 B.R. 309 (S.D. Fla. 2001) (mortgagee waived its rights to charge debtor for post-petition escrow advances because it never notified debtors that they should increase monthly payments); *In re* Riser, 289 B.R. 201 (Bankr. M.D. Fla. 2003) (mortgage company not entitled to payments for any charges incurred before or during bankruptcy that were not provided for in confirmed plan); *In re* Chess, 268 B.R. 150 (Bankr. W.D. Tenn. 2001) (mortgage company that did not notify debtor of escrow increases or respond to trustee's customary motion to deem mortgage current at end of plan could not assert debtor was in arrears at end of plan); *In re* Wines, 239 B.R. 703 (Bankr. D.N.J. 1999) (debtor overcharged interest based on creditor misapplying payments received outside the plan to pre-petition arrears); *In re* McCormack, 203 B.R. 521 (Bankr. D.N.H. 1996) (mortgagee bank held liable for $10,000.00 punitive damages when it did not adjust its computer records to reflect effect of plan confirmation and sent debtor demand letter expressing intent to collect fees that were not due under plan); *In re* Ronemus, 201 B.R. 458 (Bankr. N.D. Tex. 1996) (creditor assessed $10,000.00, plus $3000.00 attorney and accountants' fees after discharge due to mortgagee charging late charges on current payments made during bankruptcy and for charging filing fee, attorney fees and expenses to debtor's escrow account without permission of court); *In re* Rathe, 114 B.R. 253 (Bankr. D. Idaho 1990); *In re* Ward, 73 B.R. 119 (Bankr. N.D. Ga. 1987) (late charges may not be added to current payments made pursuant to plan unless those payments are not made on time); *see also In re* Harris, 297 B.R. 61 (Bankr. N.D. Miss. 2003) (prohibiting mortgage lender from charging late fees based on delay by trustee in disbursing ongoing mortgage payments does not violate anti-modification restrictions in § 1322(b)(2)). *But see* Mann v. Chase Manhattan Mortgage Corp., 316 F.3d 1 (1st Cir.

2003) (mortgage company adding charges to debtor's account in its internal bookkeeping, absent any overt attempt to collect the fees, did not violate automatic stay). Servicers often violate RESPA's escrow requirements in the course of chapter 13 cases. *See generally* 12 U.S.C. § 2609; Reg. X, 24 C.F.R. § 3500.17; National Consumer Law Center, Repossessions and Foreclosures § 19.3.2 (5th ed. 2002 and Supp.).

300 *See, e.g.*, Form 8, Appx. G.3, *infra*.

301 See Chapter 9, *supra*, for a discussion of relief from the automatic stay.

302 (Emphasis added.) *But see* Dewsnup v. Timm, 502 U.S. 410, 112 S. Ct. 773, 116 L. Ed. 2d 903 (1992) (section 506(d) does not operate to void lien on unsecured portion of claim in chapter 7 case); *In re* Tarnow, 749 F.2d 464 (7th Cir. 1984) (lien not void where claim disallowed only because it was not timely filed); *see also* § 11.6.1.3.3.2, *supra*.

303 502 U.S. 410, 112 S. Ct. 773, 116 L. Ed. 2d 903 (1992).

304 *See* § 11.2.1, *supra*.

As discussed above,[305] when an allowed secured claim is provided for in a chapter 13 plan and the holder of the claim is paid the full present value of the allowed secured claim under section 1325(a)(5), the lien is satisfied and any remaining claim is only an unsecured claim, as fully dischargeable by the chapter 13 discharge as any other unsecured claim. The only exception to this general rule would be a claim at least partially secured solely by the debtor's principal residence, if under section 1322(b)(2) that claim could not be bifurcated.[306] In fact, if no claim is filed by an under-secured creditor for the portion of the claim found to be unsecured, the creditor is not entitled to any distributions on that part of the claim.[307]

Section 506 also should be available to provide a vehicle for reducing or eliminating a lien in a chapter 13 case in which the allowed secured claim is not fully paid through the chapter 13 plan, unless the holder of the claim is protected from modification by Code section 1322(b)(2). Whenever the debtor or some other party requests a determination of the value of an under-secured claim under section 506(a), or successfully objects to a secured claim on any basis, section 506(a) renders the creditor's claim an allowed unsecured claim to the extent that it exceeds the amount of the allowed secured claim as determined by the court. A chapter 13 plan may provide for treatment of the unsecured portion of the claim in the same manner as it provides for other unsecured claim holders, including a discharge of the unsecured portion of the claim, because the Code permits any plan provision not inconsistent with other provisions of the statute.[308] The plan can similarly provide that the lien is void to the extent it exceeds the allowed secured claim of the creditor because section 1325(a)(5)(B), providing for allowed secured claims, only requires that the holder of the claim retain the lien securing the allowed secured claim, and not the allowed unsecured portion of the claim.[309] Thus, at the end of the case, the personal liability

on the claim will be fully discharged and the lien will be reduced to the amount of the allowed secured claim, minus any principal payments made during the case.

The ultimate ramifications of such lien avoidance have not been addressed by many courts. For example, if $5,000.00 of a $15,000 lien is avoided, how are the monthly payments restructured? Are the next $5,000.00 in payments due deemed paid, or is the final $5,000.00 in payments excused? Generally, the reported decisions have resolved these issues by holding that a debtor who cures a mortgage default in chapter 13, but has a remaining balance on a stripped down lien, may not alter the monthly payment or interest rate, with the result being that the term of the loan is shortened.[310] And at least two courts have held that when a secured claim is bifurcated under section 506, any recoupment under the Truth in Lending Act or any payment on the arrears is applied to the allowed secured claim rather than to the allowed unsecured claim.[311]

11.8 Rent-to-Own Transactions in Bankruptcy

A comprehensive discussion of the myriad consumer issues arising in rent-to-own transactions is provided elsewhere in this series,[312] and is beyond the scope of this manual. For several reasons, bankruptcy court may be an excellent forum for consumer advocates who seek a remedy for the abuses of the rent-to-own industry.

Most importantly, the automatic stay provides probably the fastest and surest way to prevent continued harassment

---

305 *See* § 11.6.1.3, *supra.*

306 *See* § 11.6.1.2, *supra.* If a mortgage on a debtor's principal residence is not even partially secured, because the entire equity is encumbered by prior liens, *Nobelman* leaves open the argument that the mortgage may still be modified. In deciding that the creditor in that case was the holder of a secured claim, the Court held that "[p]etitioners were correct in looking to § 506(a) . . . to determine the status of the bank's secured claim. . . . But even if we accept petitioners' valuation, the bank is still the 'holder' of a 'secured claim,' because petitioners' home retains $23,500.00 of value as collateral." Nobelman v. Am. Sav. Bank, 508 U.S. 324, 113 S. Ct. 2106, 2110, 124 L. Ed. 2d 228 (1993). Thus, had the home been of no value to the creditors as collateral, the court would presumably have found that the bank was not the holder of a secured claim entitled to have its rights protected by § 1322(b)(2). A variety of courts have adopted this reasoning. *See* § 11.6.1.2.2, *supra.*

307 *In re* Burrell, 85 B.R. 799 (Bankr. N.D. Ill. 1988).

308 11 U.S.C. § 1325(b)(10).

309 *In re* Hart, 923 F.2d 1410 (10th Cir. 1991); Wilson v. Commonwealth Mortgage Corp., 895 F.2d 123 (3d Cir. 1990); *In re*

Hougland, 886 F.2d 1182 (9th Cir. 1989).

310 *In re* Bellamy, 962 F.2d 176 (2d Cir. 1992); *In re* Enewally, 276 B.R. 643 (Bankr. C.D. Cal. 2002); *In re* Murphy, 175 B.R. 134 (Bankr. D. Mass. 1994) (after bifurcation, debtor cannot amortize allowed secured claim over balance of the term of the mortgage); *In re* Brown, 175 B.R. 129 (Bankr. D. Mass. 1994) (arrearage portion of allowed claim cannot be assigned to the unsecured claim and discharged after bifurcation); *In re* Session, 128 B.R. 147 (Bankr. E.D. Tex. 1991); *In re* Franklin, 126 B.R. 702 (Bankr. N.D. Miss. 1991); *In re* Hayes, 111 B.R. 924 (Bankr. D. Or. 1990); *see also* Sapos v. Provident Inst. of Sav., 967 F.2d 918 (3d Cir. 1992); Fed. Nat. Mortgage Assn. v. Ferreira, 223 B.R. 258 (D.R.I. 1998) (debtor may cure with respect to secured portion of bifurcated claim).

311 *In re* Jablonski, 70 B.R. 381 (Bankr. E.D. Pa. 1987); *In re* Frost, 19 B.R. 804 (Bankr. D. Kan. 1982) (debtors allowed to allocate their most recent taxes (those which were priority and nondischargeable claims) to the secured portion of the bifurcated claim).

312 The following volumes of the National Consumer Law Center's Consumer Credit and Sales Legal Practice Series cover rent-to-own issues: Unfair and Deceptive Acts and Practices § 5.7.4 (5th ed. 2001 and Supp.); The Cost of Credit: Regulation and Legal Challenges § 7.5.3.2 (2d ed. 2000 and Supp.); Repossessions and Foreclosures § 17.3 (5th ed. 2002 and Supp.); Truth in Lending § 2.4.2 (5th ed. 2003).

of delinquent debtors by rent-to-own companies.[313] Because rent-to-own property in the debtor's possession becomes property of the estate upon filing of a bankruptcy case, the automatic stay immediately enjoins continued efforts by a rent-to-own creditor to collect delinquent payments or to recover property. If a rent-to-own creditor continues to seek payment or repossession, it will be liable pursuant to 11 U.S.C. § 362(h) for its violations of the stay.[314] Especially in view of some of the industry's traditional collection practices, the full range of section 362(h) remedies, including punitive damages, may be appropriate.[315]

Numerous potential issues arise in addressing how rent-to-own contracts should be treated in bankruptcy. The dealer will argue that the contract is a lease agreement representing an executory contract, and that the debtor's options are limited to assuming or rejecting the contract pursuant to 11 U.S.C. § 365.[316] The debtor should argue instead that the contract creates a secured debt, giving rise to the full panoply of remedies discussed in this chapter. In fact there is ample precedent for treating installment sale contracts for real property[317] and leases with purchase options[318] as security agreements. Many cases that have addressed the property interests created by rent-to-own contracts support the view that they should be treated as credit sales in bankruptcy cases.[319] However, although state law treatment of the transaction is not determinative, practitioners should check the current status of state law as many states have adopted industry sponsored legislation that exempts such contracts from Uniform Commercial Code Article 9, state retail installment sales acts, or other state credit legislation.[320] Treatment of the contract as a security agreement gives rise to rights such as the debtor's right to redeem,[321] the right to modify the creditor's rights or to cure any default,[322] and the right to limit the creditor's secured claim to the value of the collateral.[323]

Whether the contract is treated as executory, as a security agreement, or otherwise, the debtor should not forego the opportunity to litigate the amount of the rent-to-own company's proof of claim, if any, and to lodge such claims or counterclaims as the debtor may possess.[324] Such claims may include usury, unfair trade practices, Uniform Commercial Code claims, debt collection claims, and truth-in-lending or consumer leasing claims. Often the bankruptcy court will be the most sympathetic forum for debtors who seek to address these creditor abuses.

11.9 Automobile Title Pawn Transactions in Bankruptcy

Another fast-growing business preying on low income families is "title pawn" lending. The typical title pawn contract is a loan of a small amount of money, accompanied by a "pawn" of the automobile title to the lender and sometimes a lease-back of the car to the borrower. The effective interest rates in such transactions are often several hundred percent or more.[325]

---

313   11 U.S.C. § 362. See Chapter 9, *supra,* for a discussion of the automatic stay.

314   *See* § 9.6, *supra.* One bankruptcy case has addressed these issues in the context of a rent-to-own transaction. Mercer v. D.E.F., Inc., 48 B.R. 562 (Bankr. D. Minn. 1985).

315   Mercer v. D.E.F., Inc., 48 B.R. 562 (Bankr. D. Minn. 1985) ($6,500.00 actual and punitive damages plus attorney fees and costs).

316   *See* § 12.9, *infra.*

317   *In re* Johnson, 75 B.R. 927 (Bankr. N.D. Ohio 1987); *In re* Leazier, 55 B.R. 870 (Bankr. N.D. Ind. 1985); *In re* Britton, 43 B.R. 605 (Bankr. E.D. Mich. 1984); *In re* Booth, 19 B.R. 53 (Bankr. D. Utah 1982).

318   *See In re* Crummie, 194 B.R. 230 (Bankr. N.D. Cal. 1996) (GM "SmartBuy" contract deemed credit sale, not lease); *In re* Lewis, 185 B.R. 66 (Bankr. N.D. Cal. 1995) (General Motors "SmartBuy" contract deemed credit sale and not lease); *In re* Coors of Cumberland, Inc., 19 B.R. 313 (Bankr. M.D. Tenn. 1982); *see also In re* Celeryvale Transport, Inc., 822 F.2d 16 (6th Cir. 1987); Fogie v. Rent-A-Center, Inc., 867 F. Supp. 1398 (D. Minn. 1993) (rent-to-own contract was consumer credit sale under Minnesota law), *aff'd sub nom.,* Fogie v. Thorn Americas, 95 F.3d 645 (8th Cir. 1996). *But see In re* Powers, 983 F.2d 88 (7th Cir. 1993); *In re* Mahoney, 153 B.R. 174 (E.D. Mich. 1992); *In re* Charles, 278 B.R. 216 (Bankr. D. Kansas 2002) (while court might have reached different result under former U.C.C., agreement was clearly a lease under revised U.C.C. § 1-207(37)).

319   *See* S.C. Rentals v. Arthur, 187 B.R. 502 (D.S.C. 1995); *In re* Smith, 262 B.R. 365 (Bankr. E.D. Va. 2000); *In re* Burton, 128 B.R. 807 (Bankr. N.D. Ala.), *aff'd,* 128 B.R. 820 (N.D. Ala. 1989); *In re* Aguilar, 101 B.R. 481 (Bankr. W.D. Tex. 1989); *In re* Rose, 94 B.R. 103 (Bankr. S.D. Ohio 1988); *In re* Fogelsong, 88 B.R. 194 (Bankr. C.D. Ill. 1988); *In re* Brown, 82 B.R. 68 (Bankr. W.D. Ark. 1987); *In re* Puckett, 60 B.R. 223 (Bankr. M.D.

Tenn. 1986); Sight & Sound of Ohio, Inc. v. Wright, 36 B.R. 885 (Bankr. S.D. Ohio 1983); Murphy v. McNamara, 36 Conn. Supp. 183, 416 A.2d 170, 28 U.C.C. Rep. Serv. 911 (Super. Ct. 1979); Broad v. Curtis Mathes Sales, Co., Clearinghouse No. 36,376 (Me. Super. Ct. Feb. 7, 1984); *see also* 6 Collier on Bankruptcy ¶ 722.03 (15th ed. rev.). *But see In re* Glenn, 102 B.R. 153 (Bankr. E.D. Ark. 1989); *In re* Harris, 102 B.R. 128 (Bankr. S.D. Ohio 1989) (relying on special state lease-purchase statute); *In re* Huffman, 63 B.R. 737 (Bankr. N.D. Ga. 1986) (RTO contract lease not security agreement because of terminability); *In re* Martin, 64 B.R. 1 (Bankr. S.D. Ga. 1984) (seventy-seven payment freezer contract lease not security agreement because of terminability). *See generally* National Consumer Law Center, Unfair and Deceptive Acts and Practices § 5.7.4 (5th ed. 2001 and Supp.); National Consumer Law Center, Repossessions and Foreclosures § 14.3 (5th ed. 2002 and Supp.).

320   National Consumer Law Center, Repossessions and Foreclosures § 14.3 (5th ed. 2002 and Supp.).

321   11 U.S.C. § 722; *see* § 11.5, *supra.*

322   *See* § 11.6, *supra.* Given the unfairness of most rent-to-own contracts to the consumer, cure of a default may not be in the debtor's best interests.

323   11 U.S.C. § 506; *see* § 11.7, *supra.*

324   *See* Ch. 13, *infra*

325   *See* National Consumer Law Center, The Cost of Credit: Regulation and Legal Challenges § 7.5.2.3 (2d ed. 2000 and Supp.).

Courts have treated such transactions as disguised non-possessory security interests. Thus, the normal rights of cramdown in chapter 13 apply.[326] Chapter 13 thus provides a method of reducing the exorbitant finance charges, and often the amount of the secured claim owed to such lenders. Similarly, the right of redemption under section 722[327] may allow a debtor to eliminate the lien of such a lender by paying the value of the lender's allowed secured claim in cash.

Even if possession of the property has been lost prior to bankruptcy, it may be possible to regain the vehicle. In most cases, a section 542 turnover would be required if the creditor still has possession.[328] In some cases, the taking of possession or other acts to improve the creditor's position may also constitute an avoidable preference.[329]

---

326 *In re* Burnsed, 224 B.R. 496 (Bankr. M.D. Fla. 1998).

327 *See* § 11.5, *supra.*

---

328 *See* § 9.9, *supra*; *see also In re* Johnson, 289 B.R. 251 (Bankr. M.D. Ga. 2002) (automobile repossessed and not redeemed by debtor during grace period was subject to turnover because contract violated statutory requirements for auto title pawn loan). Even if the court determines that the debtor no longer has a property interest in the automobile based on the pre-petition expiration of the period for redeeming pawned property, the debtor may still be able to obtain turnover by setting aside the repossession of the automobile as a fraudulent transfer under § 548. *See In re* Bell, 279 B.R. 890 (Bankr. N.D. Ga. 2002); § 10.4.2.6.5, *supra.*

329 *In re* Mattheiss, 214 B.R. 20 (Bankr. N.D. Ala. 1997); *see* § 10.4.2.6.4, *supra.*

Chapter 12

Issues Arising in Chapter 13 Cases

12.1 Introduction

No part of the Bankruptcy Code caused more controversy or confusion in its early days than the greatly revised chapter 13. In drafting that chapter, Congress made an explicit effort to encourage greater use of its provisions, which had been rarely employed in most parts of the country under the prior Bankruptcy Act. Even where it had been used, practices under the old Chapter XIII varied widely among judicial districts, with substantial deviations from the strict terms of the Act.

The current chapter 13 contains many different provisions designed to make it more attractive to debtors, for the first time providing consumers with the flexibility to rearrange their affairs in plans that parallel the types of plans that corporations have long been able to devise. There are only a few basic requirements that chapter 13 plans must meet in order to provide some protections to creditors. Beyond these requirements, the debtor has enormous freedom to create a plan that best suits her circumstances.

Unfortunately, because chapter 13 was so new and so different, creditors and some judges initially resisted its liberality. Because little relevant case law existed under the old Act and because the legislative history was relatively scant, widely divergent opinions arose concerning the use of chapter 13. Some judges tried to apply concepts developed under prior law and failed to take into account adequately the congressional intent to liberalize the law. This judicial hostility to the new powers given to debtors, combined with some unfortunate "hard cases" of the type which made bad law, led to a rash of decisions which imposed new judge-made limitations found nowhere in the statute. Of course, there were also many decisions applying the statute more faithfully, but the result was a tremendous disparity in the extent to which chapter 13 was a viable vehicle for debtors in different judicial districts.

As experience under chapter 13 grew and cases reached the appellate courts, most of these problems disappeared. Further clarification came from Congress in 1984 and 1994, when new amendments addressed some of the most litigated issues. Hence, there is now a large body of law to turn to in interpreting chapter 13, and both knowledge and use of its liberal provisions have increased considerably. However, even today there are significant variations in local custom with respect to the types of plans that courts and trustees feel are appropriate.

12.2 Eligibility for Chapter 13

12.2.1 Introduction

A threshold issue, which has occasionally been troublesome, concerns eligibility to file a chapter 13 case. The basic provision governing this issue is section 109(e) of the Code. That section provides that to be a chapter 13 debtor, the debtor must:

- Be an individual with regular income or an individual with regular income and that individual's spouse;
- Owe non-contingent, liquidated unsecured debts of less than $307,675.00 on the date of filing; and
- Owe non-contingent, liquidated, secured debts of less than $922,975.00 on that date.

The dollar amounts in section 109(e) were increased by the Bankruptcy Reform Act of 1994 from the amounts originally enacted in 1978 to account for inflation. In accordance with that Act, these amounts were last adjusted on April 1, 2004 and will be adjusted every three years thereafter to account for changes in the cost of living.[1]

12.2.2 Individuals with Regular Income

In consumer cases, issues may arise as to any of these requirements, which could preclude the filing of a chapter 13 case. Probably the most common issue for low-income debtors is whether the debtor is an "individual with regular income." This phrase is defined in section 101(30) as an "individual whose income is sufficiently stable and regular to enable such individual to make payments under a plan under chapter 13." The legislative history makes clear that the intent of the statute is to include others besides wage earners, and to expand eligibility to recipients of public

---

1   11 U.S.C. § 104(b).

benefits such as welfare and social security, small business proprietors, and those supported by other income such as alimony or pensions.[2]

It is somewhat unclear, however, whether a spouse who is not separated or divorced is eligible to file without the other spouse filing jointly, if only the non-filing spouse brings income into the family. Quite arguably, a non-working spouse who receives a regular amount of income for expenses from the income-earning spouse could file alone. Indeed, a schedule of regular payments from the non-filing spouse to the trustee could even be ordered by the court as part of the plan under section 1325(c). Similarly, payments from other friends or relatives may sometimes satisfy the regular income requirement, as long as there is a reasonable assurance that the payments will continue.[3] If a hearing on this issue is held, proof in the form of testimony from the friend or relative and, if possible, documentary evidence concerning the regularity of prior financial support should be produced.

Regardless of its source, the amount of the debtor's income must be sufficient to fund payments under a plan. Presumably, this means that the income must be sufficient for a plan proposed by the debtor which complies with the Code.

The case law concerning who is an individual with regular income has so far been relatively scarce. Some creditors have argued that a husband and wife who operate a business should be considered partners, and thus not eligible for chapter 13.[4] The resolution of that challenge turned simply upon a finding that the requisites for establishing a partnership under state law had not been met.[5] However, even if an individual is a member of a partnership or a husband and wife are considered partners, the individuals who are partners should not be precluded from filing under chapter 13. Although a partnership cannot file a chapter 13 case, an individual who happens to be a partner is clearly eligible,

provided that the other eligibility requirements are met.[6] In such a case, the partnership's assets would not become property of the bankruptcy estate, but the individual's interest in the partnership itself would become property of the estate.[7] Similarly, the individual's liability for partnership debts would be considered a debt in the case, which could affect eligibility for chapter 13 under the debt limitations[8] unless such liability were considered to be contingent.

More often, courts are concerned about whether asserted regular income really exists. One debtor who provided the court with no factual evidence that he was earning regular income as a cabinetmaker sufficient to make the payments proposed was found ineligible to file a chapter 13 case.[9] Similarly, when a debtor with no past income merely anticipates future income, the case may be dismissed or converted to chapter 7, unless there is clear evidence that the income will be forthcoming.[10] Even when it appears on paper that the debtor's income is sufficient, the court may deem evidence of inability to make similar payments proposed under a previous plan to cast doubt on the debtor's stated budget.[11] And when the debtor's statement does not show income sufficient to make the necessary level of payments, it is likely that the court will find the debtor ineligible for chapter 13.[12] On the other hand, the income need not be absolutely assured; a farmer whose income is dependent on good weather and fair prices for crops should not be denied access to chapter 13 merely because his future income is somewhat speculative.[13] In many cases, these issues are resolved in the context of a determination about the feasibility of the plan rather than about whether the debtor has regular income.[14]

In view of these issues, a prudent approach would be to begin regularly setting aside an amount equal to the plan payments as soon as the case is filed, if not earlier. Under the Code, plan payments to the trustee must begin within thirty days after filing of the plan, which is usually before the meeting of creditors and confirmation of the plan, unless the court orders otherwise.[15] If such payments are regularly made or set aside, there can then be little doubt as to the

---

2 H.R. Rep. No. 95-595, at 13, 312 (1977); *see In re* Hammonds, 729 F.2d 1391 (11th Cir. 1984) (AFDC payments may be used to fund chapter 13 plan); *see also In re* Lapin, 302 B.R. 184 (Bankr. S.D. Tex. 2003) (withdrawals from individual retirement account could constitute portion of regular income needed for plan); *In re* Cole, 3 B.R. 346 (Bankr. S.D. W. Va. 1980).

3 *In re* Antoine, 208 B.R. 17 (Bankr. E.D.N.Y. 1997) (unemployed carpenter was individual with regular income because wife made oral commitment to devote her salary to plan); *In re* Varian, 91 B.R. 653 (Bankr. D. Conn. 1988) (commitment of non-filing spouse to make payments to trustee was sufficient to provide regular income); *In re* Campbell, 38 B.R. 193 (Bankr. E.D.N.Y. 1984) (contributions of relatives who had substantial interest in plan's success could constitute income needed for plan). *But see In re* Fischel, 103 B.R. 44 (Bankr. N.D.N.Y. 1989) (non-debtor's commitment to make payments was too tenuous where debtor and non-debtor were not related and there was no record regarding stability of shared living arrangement).

4 *In re* Ward, 6 B.R. 93 (Bankr. M.D. Fla. 1980).

5 *Id.*

6 *See* 8 Collier on Bankruptcy ¶ 1304.01[1] (15th ed. rev.); *see also* Biery, *Debt Adjustment under Chapter 13 of the Bankruptcy Reform Act of 1978*, 11 St. Mary's L. J. 473, 477 (1979); H.R. Rep. No. 95-595, at 320 (1977).

7 *See* 8 Collier on Bankruptcy ¶ 1304.01[1] (15th ed. rev.).

8 *See* § 12.2.3, *infra*.

9 *In re* Wilhelm, 6 B.R. 905 (Bankr. E.D.N.Y. 1980).

10 *In re* Mozer, 1 B.R. 350 (Bankr. D. Colo. 1979).

11 *In re* Burns, 6 B.R. 286 (Bankr. D. Colo. 1980) (holding alternatively that plan of such individuals not offered in good faith).

12 *In re* Terry, 630 F.2d 634 (8th Cir. 1980).

13 *In re* Fiegi, 61 B.R. 994 (Bankr. D. Or. 1986) (proceeds projected from annual harvests sufficiently regular income to make annual payments proposed in farmer's plan); *In re* Hines, 7 B.R. 415 (Bankr. D.S.D. 1980).

14 *See* § 12.5, *infra*.

15 11 U.S.C. § 1326(a)(1).

debtor's ability to perform under the plan. Conversely, the failure to make pre-confirmation payments often leads to dismissal of the case, unless the debtor provides a valid explanation or can modify the plan to abate or lower the payments.

12.2.3 Debt Limitations

12.2.3.1 Determining Whether Debts are Secured or Unsecured

Issues may also arise concerning the dollar-amount limitations on claims against debtors who file chapter 13 cases, limitations designed to exclude large businesses from evading the requirements of chapter 11.[16]

For these limits to be met, in some cases, it may be critical whether an under-secured debt is considered a secured or an unsecured debt. Depending upon the facts of a particular case, the debtor may wish to argue that the entire amount of a secured debt should be considered against the $922,975.00 limit on secured debts, or that only the amount of the allowed secured claim (equal to the value of the collateral)[17] should be measured against that limit, with the unsecured portion of the claim secured against the $307,675.00 limit on unsecured debts.

One early case considering this question illustrates the problem. *In re Ballard*[18] involved debtors who owed secured creditors over $350,000.00 (the limit on secured debts at the time), but whose property securing that debt was worth less than $350,000.00. The creditor asserted that the debtors were ineligible for chapter 13 because their secured debts were too high. It argued that claims are not filed or determined in a case until after the initial stages when the debtor's eligibility is decided, and that therefore the value of the collateral could not be looked to because the court would have to rely on the debtor's valuation in the schedules. (The creditor cited no reason why that valuation could not be challenged.)

The court rejected these arguments. It looked first to statements in the legislative history which referred to the $350,000.00 limit as a limit on "secured claims,"[19] and also to the statutory definition of "debt"[20] which incorporates the definition of "claim."[21] The court also found that because a debtor could almost always create a security interest,

practically at will, it would undermine the intent of the congressional limitations to allow the debtor to convert unsecured claims to secured claims in order to qualify for chapter 13. *Ballard* was later followed by all of the courts of appeals that have decided the issue to date.[22] Indeed, one court of appeals has gone so far as to hold that a debt secured by a lien that can be avoided by the debtor under Code § 522(f) should be considered an unsecured debt for eligibility purposes.[23]

Although the holding in *Ballard* and the cases which have followed it may often be helpful to consumer debtors with similar fact situations, at least as many debtors will have the opposite problem, in view of the lower limit on unsecured debts for chapter 13 eligibility.[24] These debtors will want to argue that Congress meant a distinction by using that word "debt" rather than "claim" in section 109(e), and that the *Ballard* court's reading of the definitions was superficial. The definition of "debt" as a "liability on a claim" could just as easily mean the total liability on a claim, whether secured or unsecured, before that claim is divided into its secured and unsecured parts under section 506(a). This result, too, has some support in the case law.[25]

Courts have similarly disagreed regarding whether a debt that is secured by property of someone other than the debtor should be considered a secured debt for purposes of section 109(e). It has been held that such debts should be considered secured debts as contemplated by that section,[26] and it has also been held that, because they are not secured by the debtor's property, they should be considered unsecured debts.[27]

---

16 H.R. Rep. No. 95-595, at 119 (1977).

17 11 U.S.C. § 506(a); *see* Ch. 11, *supra*.

18 4 B.R. 271 (Bankr. E.D. Va. 1980).

19 124 Cong. Rec. H11,089 (daily ed. Sept. 24, 1978) (remarks of Rep. Edwards) *and* 124 Cong. Rec. S17,406 (daily ed. Oct. 6, 1978) (remarks of Sen. DeConcini), *reprinted in* 1978 U.S.C.C.A.N. 6441, 6509.

20 11 U.S.C. § 101(12) defines "debt" as "liability on a claim."

21 11 U.S.C. § 101(5) defines "claim" as including a "right to payment, whether or not such right is . . . secured, or unsecured."

22 *In re Ficken*, 2 F.3d 299 (8th Cir. 1993); *In re Balbus*, 933 F.2d 246 (4th Cir. 1991); Miller v. United States *ex rel.* Farmers Home Admin., 907 F.2d 80 (8th Cir. 1990); *In re Day*, 747 F.2d 405 (7th Cir. 1984); *see also* Cavaliere v. Sapir, 208 B.R. 784 (D. Conn. 1997) (only secured portion of mortgage claims counted in determining chapter 13 eligibility when debtor had previously discharged personal liability in chapter 7); *In re Jerome*, 112 B.R. 563 (Bankr. S.D.N.Y. 1990). The court in *Balbus* rejected a creditor's argument that the hypothetical costs of liquidating the debtor's property should be deducted in determining the amounts of the secured and unsecured claims for this purpose.

23 *In re Scovis*, 249 F.3d 975 (9th Cir. 2001).

24 *See, e.g., In re Day*, 747 F.2d 405 (7th Cir. 1984); *In re Bobroff*, 32 B.R. 933 (Bankr. E.D. Pa. 1983).

25 *In re Holland*, 293 B.R. 425 (Bankr. N.D. Ohio 2002); *In re Morton*, 43 B.R. 215 (Bankr. E.D.N.Y. 1984).

26 Branch Banking & Trust Co. v. Russell, 188 B.R. 542 (E.D.N.C. 1995); *In re White*, 148 B.R. 283 (Bankr. N.D. Ohio 1992); *In re Gorman*, 58 B.R. 372 (Bankr. E.D.N.Y. 1986); *see also In re Lindsey*, Stephenson & Lindsey, 995 F.2d 626 (5th Cir. 1993).

27 *In re Tomlinson*, 116 B.R. 80 (Bankr. E.D. Mich. 1990).

12.2.3.2 Determining Whether Debts Are Liquidated and Non-Contingent

Further problems may arise in determining whether debts are liquidated or non-contingent and therefore countable toward the debt limitations. Neither term is defined in the Code, and thus state law concepts may come into play. As to these questions, all debtors filing chapter 13 cases will have a common interest—to classify the maximum number of debts as non-liquidated or contingent.

Regarding whether a debt is liquidated, the clearest cases are at the extremes. A note as to which a judgment has been entered and to which there are no defenses is perhaps the paradigm of a liquidated debt.[28] A tort claim for personal injuries and pain and suffering, which has not been adjudicated, is clearly unliquidated. Between the extremes, however, there is more doubt. If a debtor can assert any defense to a debt that is not foreclosed by *res judicata* or otherwise, it should be argued that the debt is not liquidated. Many of the definitions of "liquidated" suggest that when the amount owing is neither agreed upon nor fixed by operation of law the debt is not liquidated.[29] And even if the defenses go to only a part of the amount due, these definitions indicate that the debt as a whole should be considered unliquidated because its precise amount is not settled.[30] However, this test does not require that to be liquidated the debt must be *both* agreed upon and fixed by operation of law, so some

courts have held that if the amount claimed is readily ascertainable, it is liquidated even if the debtor disputes liability.[31]

The question of contingency is somewhat more complicated. Generally, a contingent debt is one which is dependent upon some future event that may never occur.[32] An example is an agreement to pay a debt if (and only if) another person does not do so.[33] Cosigners on debts may be in this position depending on the terms of the contract and state law. The exact status of a debt must always be determined by both the applicable law and the facts. There may be a dispute regarding whether the condition upon which the debt is contingent has occurred, which may in turn depend upon whether there were valid defenses that justified nonpayment by a principal debtor. Alternatively, the court may find that, due to known facts, the outcome of another proceeding need not be awaited for it to decide that the condition has occurred.[34] It may also find that, as a matter of state law, the creditors need not pursue other assets or co-obligors before looking to the debtor for payment.[35]

---

28   *See In re* Vaughan, 36 B.R. 935 (N.D. Ala. 1984) (readily calculable contract debt was liquidated); *see also In re* Papatones, 143 F.3d 623 (1st Cir. 1998) (debt which had been adjudicated by court but not yet reduced to a docketed judgment was liquidated); *In re* Hammers, 988 F.2d 32 (5th Cir. 1993) (bankruptcy court could not look behind judgment to determine that part of claim was not allowable when claim had already been adjudicated by another tribunal).

29   *In re* Horne, 277 B.R. 320 (Bankr. E.D. Tex. 2002) (debt was unliquidated when court had discretion in determining amount of damages); *see* Black's Law Dictionary 1079, 1080 (6th ed. 1990); *see also In re* Hull, 251 B.R. 726 (B.A.P. 9th Cir. 2000) (claim not liquidated because trial on the merits would have been necessary to liquidate claim); *In re* Verdunn, 160 B.R. 682 (Bankr. M.D. Fla. 1993), *aff'd*, 187 B.R. 996 (M.D. Fla. 1995) (alleged tax fraud claim was unliquidated because tax liabilities could not be readily determined from documents presented), *rev'd*, 89 F.3d 799 (11th Cir. 1996); *In re* Harbaugh, 153 B.R. 54 (Bankr. D. Idaho 1993) (tax claim was liquidated only to extent it was undisputed or capable of being easily determined without evidentiary hearing); *In re* Robertson, 143 B.R. 76 (Bankr. N.D. Tex. 1992) (IRS claim for almost $900,000.00 was contingent and unliquidated because IRS had not yet proved tax law violations, which debtor disputed); *In re* Lambert, 43 B.R. 913 (Bankr. D. Utah 1984) (debt subject to bona fide dispute not counted); *In re* King, 9 B.R. 376 (Bankr. D. Or. 1981).

30   *But see In re* Quintana, 915 F.2d 513 (9th Cir. 1990) (existence of a counterclaim does not reduce amount of claim for purposes of measuring amount of debt for eligibility under chapter 12).

31   United States v. Verdunn, 89 F.3d 799 (11th Cir. 1996) (federal income tax liabilities and penalties were liquidated because they were easily ascertainable through application of fixed legal standards); *In re* Knight, 55 F.3d 231 (7th Cir. 1995) (fact that debt is disputed does not make it unliquidated if amount claimed is easily ascertainable); *In re* Wenberg, 902 F.2d 768 (9th Cir. 1990) (where creditor's damages were unliquidated, but award of attorney fees to creditor was "readily ascertainable" and therefore liquidated, attorney fees award was included in computation of debts), *aff'g* 94 B.R. 631 (B.A.P. 9th Cir. 1988); *In re* Crescenzi, 69 B.R. 64 (S.D.N.Y. 1986). *But see In re* Ho, 274 B.R. 867 (B.A.P. 9th Cir. 2002) (substantial dispute about liability, requiring contested evidentiary hearing, can make debt unliquidated); United States v. May, 211 B.R. 991 (M.D. Fla. 1997) (debt found to be unliquidated because it could not be readily determined until Tax Court litigation was resolved).

32   Black's Law Dictionary 392 (6th ed. 1990); *see In re* Knight, 55 F.3d 231 (7th Cir. 1995) (debt is non-contingent if events giving rise to liability occurred before bankruptcy case was filed); *In re* Fostvedt, 823 F.2d 305 (9th Cir. 1987).

33   *But see In re* Marchetto, 24 B.R. 967 (B.A.P. 1st Cir. 1982) (Massachusetts co-maker who signs as accommodation party is liable as a maker and bound without prior recourse to the principal).

34   *See In re* Prince, 5 B.R. 432 (Bankr. W.D.N.Y. 1980) (court need not await outcome of chapter 7 proceeding concerning debtors' business to determine amount they would owe on loans they guaranteed where it was clear that over $100,000.00 in unsecured claims would not be paid in chapter 7 case).

35   *In re* Fostvedt, 823 F.2d 305 (9th Cir. 1987) (debtor was jointly and severally liable); *In re* Kaufman, 93 B.R. 319 (Bankr. S.D.N.Y. 1988) (liability of an agent for an undisclosed principal was unconditional under state law); *see In re* Kelsey, 6 B.R. 114 (Bankr. S.D. Tex. 1980) (creditors of partnership need not first pursue partnership assets before looking to assets of a partner).

12.2.3.3 Procedure for Determining Eligibility

The courts have also differed concerning whether a hearing is necessary to determine the amount of non-contingent liquidated claims. While some courts have held that such a hearing may be appropriate,[36] the Sixth Circuit has held that the court should normally rely solely upon the representations in the debtor's chapter 13 statement, provided that the representations are made in good faith.[37] The Sixth Circuit found that the dollar limits of section 109(e) are analogous to the amount in controversy jurisdictional requirement in federal diversity cases. Noting that section 109(e) states nothing about computing eligibility after a hearing on disputed claims, and that the Code contemplates that a chapter 13 case will move expeditiously to confirmation, the Sixth Circuit concluded that a hearing on threshold eligibility issues would defeat the Code's objectives.[38]

As in the diversity situation, the Sixth Circuit held that having a hearing on the merits of the claim at the outset of the case is unnecessary and that the case should not be dismissed unless it appears to a legal certainty that the debtor is not eligible.[39] If, based upon good faith statements in the debtor's schedules, it appears that the debtor meets the requirements of section 109(e) when the case is commenced, the case may proceed as a chapter 13, even if subsequent determinations prove that this initial determination was incorrect, because eligibility is determined as of the date the petition is filed.[40] In a similar vein, other courts have held that eligibility provisions contained in section 109 are not jurisdictional.[41] Obviously, this protects judgments and orders entered in a bankruptcy case from collateral attack on the basis of the provisions of section 109.[42]

12.2.3.4 Strategies for Avoiding Eligibility Problems

For the debtor, it is essential to avoid eligibility issues when possible. This may sometimes be accomplished simply by filing separate cases for a husband and wife rather than filing a joint petition. Because the debt limitation amounts would then apply separately to the debts of each, rather than to their combined debts as in a joint case,[43] the total amount of combined debt permitted can be increased to the extent that the debts owed are not joint obligations.

In other cases, if one spouse owes a large debt which exceeds the eligibility limits and the other does not, the goals of the bankruptcy may be accomplished by filing a chapter 13 petition for only the spouse not owing the large debt. In such a case, the codebtor stay would protect the non-filing spouse with respect to most joint debts[44] and the incomes of both spouses could be used to cure or satisfy the claims of secured creditors or other creditors.

If a large tort judgment is imminent, a chapter 13 petition may be filed before it is entered, even if a bankruptcy is not then contemplated, to preserve the option if it later becomes necessary. And debtors should be wary of agreeing to settlements or judgments that could push their liquidated debt totals near the limit. Because the key date is the date the petition is filed, other actions, such as settlements of disputed amounts, may still be taken after the bankruptcy case is filed which alter the debtor's debt amounts or the character of the debts as secured or unsecured without affecting the debtor's eligibility for chapter 13.[45]

Occasionally, a debtor with unsecured debts above the limit may have to file a chapter 7 case to deal with some of his or her debts, in the hope that the chapter 7 case will be sufficient. If it is not, the debtor may then be eligible to file a chapter 13 case because the unsecured debts have been discharged in the prior chapter 7 case.[46] However, because eligibility is determined as of the date of the petition, a debtor may not convert a chapter 7 case to chapter 13 based upon the discharge in the chapter 7 case of unsecured debts

---

36   *See, e.g., In re* Sylvester, 19 B.R. 671 (B.A.P. 9th Cir. 1982).

37   *In re* Lybrook, 951 F.2d 136 (7th Cir. 1991); *In re* Pearson, 773 F.2d 751 (6th Cir. 1985).

38   *In re* Pearson, 773 F.2d 751, 756, 757 (6th Cir. 1985). *But see* Lucoski v. Internal Revenue Serv., 126 B.R. 332 (S.D. Ind. 1991) (court may look beyond the schedules if it determines, within reasonable period of time, that debts exceed statutory limits).

39   *Pearson,* 773 F.2d at 757.

40   *Id.,* at 758; *see also In re* Ridgon, 94 B.R. 602 (Bankr. W.D. Mo. 1988) (court looked beyond debtors' schedules to find debtors ineligible only because schedules were filed in bad faith). Similarly, if a debt is contingent or unliquidated at the time of a chapter 7 petition, but becomes liquidated before a debtor converts a case to chapter 13, the debt must nonetheless be considered contingent or unliquidated, because the relevant date for determining its status is the date of the original bankruptcy petition. *In re* Bush, 120 B.R. 403 (Bankr. E.D. Tex. 1990). Even when debtors may have misrepresented their eligibility, if a creditor fails to raise the issue in a timely fashion and instead waits until after confirmation of a plan, a motion to dismiss will be denied because eligibility is not jurisdictional. *In re* Jones, 134 B.R. 274 (N.D. Ill. 1991).

41   Rudd v. Laughlin, 866 F.2d 1040 (8th Cir. 1989) (fact that debtors were ineligible for chapter 13 did not deprive bankruptcy court of jurisdiction necessary to enter valid order converting case to chapter 7); *In re* Jarvis, 78 B.R. 288 (Bankr. D. Or. 1987); *see also In re* Republic Trust & Sav. Co., 59 B.R. 606 (Bankr. N.D. Okla. 1986) (eligibility challenged in chapter 11).

42   *In re* Jarvis, 78 B.R. 288 (Bankr. D. Or. 1987).

43   11 U.S.C. § 109(e).

44   See § 9.4.4, *supra,* for discussion of the chapter 13 codebtor stay.

45   *See In re* Dally, 110 B.R. 630 (Bankr. D. Conn. 1990) (mortgage debts could not be excluded from total of secured debts based upon debtor's attempted Truth in Lending rescission of those debts after the bankruptcy petition was filed).

46   *See* Cavaliere v. Sapir, 208 B.R. 784 (D. Conn. 1997) (only secured portion of mortgage claims counted in determining chapter 13 eligibility when debtor had previously discharged personal liability in chapter 7); § 12.10, *infra* (a discussion of chapter 13 cases after prior bankruptcies).

above the eligibility level.[47] If a chapter 13 case follows closely after a chapter 7 case in such circumstances, a court may perceive the two filings as a bad faith subterfuge to avoid the chapter 13 dollar limitations.

Finally, the limitation on secured debts may be good reason to give a low or high estimate of the value of collateral, in case the court looks to that measure.[48] Like all of the decisions to be made, however, these strategies must be determined in the context of the entire case, which might for other reasons dictate settling a claim or giving a different estimate of the value of collateral in order to maintain the automatic stay.[49]

12.3 What Amount Must Be Paid to Unsecured Creditors?

12.3.1 The Best Interests of Creditors Test

No single question under the Code stirred more debate in the statute's early years than the issue of how much the debtor must pay to unsecured creditors in a chapter 13 plan. Hundreds of courts debated the question, coming to a fairly consistent, if vague, result. That result has now been codified by the 1984 amendments to the Code, and the legal issue has receded, except in occasional cases.

One standard delineating how much unsecured creditors are to receive in a chapter 13 case is known as the "best interests of creditors" test. The Code provides that, if all other requirements are met, the court "*shall* confirm a plan if . . . the value, as of the effective date of the plan, of property to be paid under the plan on account of each allowed unsecured claim is not less than the amount that would be paid on the claim [in a chapter 7 case]."[50] This test was inserted into the Code to ensure that general unsecured creditors would not be harmed by a debtor's choice of chapter 13 over chapter 7. By giving such creditors payments with a present value equivalent to the value of the debtor's non-exempt property, that is, including interest to compensate for delay in their receipt,[51] the Code gives them as much as they would have received in a chapter 7 liquidation.

Because the court must compare the chapter 13 distributions to the outcome of a chapter 7 case, the appropriate date

for valuing the non-exempt property that would be distributed to creditors is the filing date of the chapter 13 petition, because the filing date is the date of valuation in a chapter 7 case.[52] Property acquired after the petition is filed generally should not be included in the determination of what creditors would receive for purposes of the best interests of creditors test.[53]

Moreover, the court must take into account the costs of sale that would be incurred by a chapter 7 trustee,[54] which could include a capital gains tax on any increase in value of property since the debtor acquired it.[55] These costs would also include mortgage payments and other carrying costs from the date of the petition to the date of sale.

---

47 *In re* Stern, 266 B.R. 322 (Bankr. D. Md. 2001).

48 If the value of collateral test is used, however, it is not clear that the collateral would have to be only that belonging to the debtor. *See* § 12.2.3.1, *supra.*

49 See Chapter 9, *supra,* for a discussion of valuing collateral in the stay context.

50 11 U.S.C. § 1325(a)(4) (emphasis added).

51 For a discussion of present value and possible interest rates, see Chapter 11, *supra.* As to the latter, however, the court should also take into account the delay which occurs before creditors receive dividends in a chapter 7 case.

52 *In re* Nielsen, 86 B.R. 177 (Bankr. E.D. Mo. 1988).

53 *In re* Sanchez, 270 B.R. 322 (Bankr. D.N.H. 2001) (cause of action that arose after filing of bankruptcy petition not considered in best interests test); *see In re* Richardson, 283 B.R. 783 (Bankr. D. Kan. 2002) (insurance proceeds received post-confirmation are property of the debtor under § 1327(b) and may be used to pay off plan early); 8 Collier on Bankruptcy ¶ 1325.05[2][a] (15th ed. rev.); *see also In re* Britton, 288 B.R. 170 (Bankr. N.D.N.Y. 2002) (plan failed to satisfy "best interest of creditors" test as it did not provide for debtors' right to receive post-petition payments under annuity, which was property of the debtor's estate because annuity had been established pre-petition in settlement of personal injury claim). In rare cases, the debtor may acquire property after the petition that would be property of a chapter 7 estate due to § 541(a)(5) which brings into the estate marital settlements, life insurance proceeds, and inheritances acquired within 180 days of the petition. This property probably would be considered in the best interests test, at least if it were acquired prior to confirmation of the plan.

54 *In re* Dixon, 140 B.R. 945 (Bankr. W.D.N.Y. 1992) (ten percent cost of sale of real estate could be deducted from market value); *In re* Rivera, 116 B.R. 17, 18 (Bankr. D. P.R. 1990); *In re* Hieb, 88 B.R. 1019 (Bankr. D.S.D. 1988); *In re* Barth, 83 B.R. 204 (Bankr. D. Conn. 1983); 8 Collier on Bankruptcy ¶ 1325.05[2][d] (15th ed. rev.); *see also In re* Hardy, 755 F.2d 75, 77, 78 (6th Cir. 1985) (implicitly accepting administrative costs of liquidation as part of hypothetical liquidation analysis). In chapter 7 estates with small amounts of assets, the trustee fees and costs under § 326 often consume most of the assets.

55 *In re* Young, 153 B.R. 886 (Bankr. D. Neb. 1993); *In re* Dixon, 140 B.R. 945 (Bankr. W.D.N.Y. 1992); *In re* Card, 114 B.R. 226 (Bankr. N.D. Cal. 1990) (because the estate is assessed with a capital gains tax if it sells the property, the result is that where property has appreciated, but most of its value can be exempted, the debtor gains a "super homestead" exemption); *see* 26 U.S.C. § 1398 (taxation of a chapter 7 estate); *see also In re* Barden, 105 F.3d 821 (2d Cir. 1997) (trustee not permitted to use debtor's one time capital gains tax exclusion or stepped-up basis that was available to debtor for sale of debtor's principal residence); *In re* Winch, 226 B.R. 591 (Bankr. S.D. Ohio 1998) (trustee could not use debtor's capital gains exclusion even though it is no longer a one-time exclusion, because it was meant to make funds available for taxpayers' future living expenses). *But see In re* Popa, 238 B.R. 395 (N.D. Ill. 1999) (trustee can take debtor's capital gains exclusion for personal residence, which is no longer a one-time exclusion but may be claimed every two years); *In re* Kerr, 237 B.R. 488 (W.D. Wash. 1999) (same).

In some cases, the best interests test may require different unsecured creditors to receive different percentage recoveries. For example, if there is community property or entireties property involved, the Code's distribution rules give different rights to creditors depending upon whether they have joint or community claims.[56] The amount of non-exempt assets may be such that only priority creditors would receive distributions in a chapter 7 case. While questions might arise as to which claims to consider in determining whether this test is met,[57] there is no doubt that, unless the proposed plan meets the standard, a creditor may challenge it and the court need not confirm it.[58]

12.3.2 Use of the Good Faith Test Prior to the 1984 Amendments

When the Code first went into effect, many courts were dissatisfied that the best interests of creditors test looked only to the debtor's assets and not to income. Faced with plans proposing little or no payment to unsecured creditors from debtors who clearly had sufficient income to make substantial payments, they devised a wide variety of standards for confirming plans, under the general standard of section 1325(a)(3) that the plan be proposed in good faith. These standards often required "substantial" or "meaningful" payments to creditors holding unsecured claims; in one court, no plan proposing less than seventy-percent payment of such claims was approved.[59]

At the other end of the spectrum, many courts refused to view the good faith test as having any relevance to the amount paid to unsecured creditors. These courts, and most commentators,[60] looked to the more specific language of section 1325(a)(4) as being dispositive of what unsecured creditors must be paid. They pointed out that, although references in the legislative history of the Code mentioned Congressional intent to encourage or enable debtors to make substantial payments to unsecured creditors, there was no indication whatsoever that this was to be required.

The cases refusing to apply the good faith test to the amount paid under the plan also relied on a somewhat more substantial body of case law interpreting the term "good faith" under the prior Bankruptcy Act. These cases[61] pointed to a line of opinions under several chapters of that Act, holding "good faith" to have a narrower meaning.[62] Those opinions did not permit the "good faith" test to preclude taking advantage of the plain provisions of a statute. Rather, they held that good faith means honesty in fact, and the absence of extraordinary circumstances such as fraud, malfeasance or concealment of assets.[63] It appears to be conceded by all parties that this is the meaning of "good faith" in chapter 11 proceedings, and that mere "selfishness" or acting in one's own enlightened self-interest does not constitute bad faith.[64]

In addition, some of the courts that totally rejected use of the good faith test as a quantitative measure of payments of unsecured claims looked to the practical consequences. Perhaps most importantly for low-income debtors, requiring meaningful or substantial payments threatened to become a barrier to the other benefits of chapter 13, such as the right to cure defaults or the right to "cram down"[65] as to secured

---

56   11 U.S.C. § 726(c); *see In re* Chandler, 148 B.R. 13 (Bankr. E.D.N.C. 1992) (because § 522(b)(2)(B) permits exemption of entireties property from creditors not holding claims against both spouses, plan paying one-hundred percent to joint claims and 9.6% to non-joint claims satisfied best interests test).

57   *See In re* Weiss, 4 B.R. 327 (Bankr. S.D.N.Y. 1980) (court should look only to claims filed as of § 341 meeting in applying test).

58   *In re* Hardy, 755 F.2d 75 (6th Cir. 1985) (confirmation denied where unsecured creditors who would have received one-hundred percent payment in chapter 7 case were not provided interest in addition to one-hundred percent payment in chapter 13 plan); *In re* Beguelin, 220 B.R. 94 (B.A.P. 9th Cir. 1998) (unsecured creditor entitled to interest on claim when it would have received interest in chapter 7 liquidation); *see also In re* Williams, 3 B.R. 728 (Bankr. N.D. Ill. 1980). However, unless the present value of payments which an unsecured creditor, whether priority or non-priority, will receive is less than the amount it would receive in a liquidation case under chapter 7, there is no requirement that "present value payments," that is, interest, be paid over and above the creditor's claim. *In re* Young, 61 B.R. 150 (Bankr. S.D. Ind. 1986).

59   *See generally* Conrad K. Cyr, *The Chapter 13 "Good Faith" Tempest: An Analysis And Proposal For Change*, 55 Am. Bankr. L. J. 271 (1981).

60   *See, e.g.*, Biery, *Debt Adjustment under Chapter 13 of the Bankruptcy Reform Act of 1978*, 11 St. Mary's L. J. 473, 489 (1979); Kaplan, *Chapter 13 of the Bankruptcy Reform Act of 1978: An Attractive Alternative*, 28 De Paul L. Rev. 1045, 1051 (1979); Joe Lee, *Chapter 13 nee Chapter XIII*, 53 Am. Bankr. L. J. 303, 319 (1979); Merrick, *Chapter 13 of the Bankruptcy Reform Act of 1978*, 56 Denv. L. J. 585, 615 (1979).

61   *See, e.g.*, *In re* Harland, 3 B.R. 597 (Bankr. D. Neb. 1980); *In re* Cloutier, 3 B.R. 584 (Bankr. D. Colo. 1980).

62   *See, e.g.*, Sumida v. Yumen, 409 F.2d 654 (9th Cir. 1969); Gonzalez Hernandez v. Borgas, 343 F.2d 802 (1st Cir. 1965); *In re* Pine Hill Collieries Co., 46 F. Supp. 669 (Bankr. E.D. Pa. 1942); *see also* Neustadler, *Consumer Insolvency Counseling for California in the 1980s*, 19 Santa Clara L. Rev. 817, 910 n.345 (1979).

63   *In re* Wiggles, 7 B.R. 373 (Bankr. N.D. Ga. 1980); *In re* Thacker, 6 B.R. 861 (Bankr. W.D. Va. 1980); *In re* Cloutier, 3 B.R. 584 (Bankr. D. Colo. 1980); *In re* Keckler, 3 B.R. 155 (Bankr. N.D. Ohio 1980). Several courts have applied this meaning of good faith to refuse confirmation of plans which smacked of fraud. *See, e.g.*, *In re* Lockwood, 5 B.R. 294 (Bankr. S.D. Fla. 1980); *In re* Tanke, 4 B.R. 339 (Bankr. D. Colo. 1980); *In re* Ballard, 4 B.R. 271 (Bankr. E.D. Va. 1980).

64   Kane v. John-Manville Corp., 843 F.2d 636, 649 (2d Cir. 1988); *In re* Sun Country Dev., Inc., 764 F.2d 406 (5th Cir. 1985); *see* 7 Collier on Bankruptcy ¶ 1129.02[a] (15th ed. rev.) (discussing the meaning of "good faith" in 11 U.S.C. § 1129(a)(3), the provision which parallels the chapter 13 good-faith test).

65   See Chapter 11, *supra*, for a discussion of these rights.

creditors.[66] Low-income debtors could have been found, generally, to be too poor to be filing in good faith.

In view of these conditions, some courts found that, at least if the chapter 13 plan served any special rehabilitative purpose, meaningful payments to unsecured creditors should not be required of debtors who are unable to make them.[67] In a similar vein, other courts found that when no payments were to be made to any creditors, the case was merely a disguised liquidation, and there was no reason to allow it to proceed under chapter 13.[68] Some of these courts dismissed or converted such cases on jurisdictional grounds.[69] Presumably, most of these courts would have agreed that when the debtor makes some legitimate use of chapter 13, such as saving a home from foreclosure or providing for other payments to secured creditors, a chapter 13 case is permissible even if the debtor proposes no payments to unsecured creditors.

The courts, however, differed on what was a legitimate use and what was an abuse of chapter 13. A good number held that it was an abuse of chapter 13 to obtain a discharge of debts not dischargeable under chapter 7 without substantial payment of such debts.[70] A roughly equal number, though, held that such use of the broader discharge was contemplated by Congress and was not, in itself, an abuse constituting bad faith.[71] These latter cases were, and continue to be, the better reasoned insofar as they effectuate the differences in the discharge available under chapter 7 and chapter 13 as enacted by Congress.[72] Generally, the appel-

late courts held that the fact that the plan will discharge debts not dischargeable in a chapter 7 case can only be considered as a bar to confirmation if it is combined with other factors showing abuse in the court's consideration of all of the circumstances.[73] The same rationale applies to the dischargeability of debts in chapter 13 which have been specifically held nondischargeable in a prior chapter 7 case.[74]

One thing nearly all courts have agreed on is that a creditor that holds an unsecured claim that is not dischargeable in chapter 7 may not argue that, because its claim will be discharged in chapter 13, it will receive less than it would receive in a chapter 7 liquidation. The cases pointed to the plain language of section 1325(a)(4), which considers the amount the creditor "would be paid" in the chapter 7 case, and not whether the creditor would still have the right to pursue a nondischargeable claim after the case.[75]

Finally, a substantial number of courts held that whether unsecured creditors receive meaningful payments is a component of the good faith test, but that the court must consider all of the facts and circumstances of each case to determine if chapter 13 has been abused.[76] The circumstances that various courts listed as relevant included the following:

- Whether the percentage paid to unsecured creditors is "meaningful";[77]
- The ability of the debtor to pay;
- Whether the debtor is making his or her best effort;[78]
- Whether the debtor is making an "honest and sincere effort";
- The present and potential earnings of the debtor;

66 *See In re* Roy, 5 B.R. 611 (Bankr. M.D. Ala. 1980); *In re* Moss, 5 B.R. 123 (Bankr. M.D. Tenn. 1980); *In re* Cloutier, 3 B.R. 584 (Bankr. D. Colo. 1980).

67 *In re* Stollenwerck, 8 B.R. 297 (M.D. Ala. 1981); *In re* Zellmer, 6 B.R. 497 (Bankr. N.D. Ill. 1980); *In re* Johnson, 6 B.R. 34 (Bankr. N.D. Ill. 1980); *In re* Roy, 5 B.R. 611 (Bankr. M.D. Ala. 1980); *In re* Bellgraph, 4 B.R. 421 (Bankr. W.D.N.Y. 1980).

68 *See, e.g., In re* Terry, 630 F.2d 634 (8th Cir. 1980) (plan with no payments to any creditor cannot be confirmed, and debtor unable to make any payments is ineligible under 11 U.S.C. § 109(e), but there are no minimum percentages necessary); *In re* Wiggles, 7 B.R. 373 (Bankr. N.D. Ga. 1980); *see also In re* Seman, 4 B.R. 568 (Bankr. S.D.N.Y. 1980). *But see In re* Hardy, 56 B.R. 95 (Bankr. N.D. Ala. 1985) (plan could be confirmed despite fact that no creditor would receive any payment due to the fact that no creditor had filed a claim).

69 *In re* Wiggles, 7 B.R. 373 (Bankr. N.D. Ga. 1980).

70 *See, e.g., In re* Brown, 7 B.R. 529 (Bankr. S.D.N.Y. 1980); *In re* DeSimone, 6 B.R. 89 (Bankr. S.D.N.Y. 1980); *In re* Bloom, 3 B.R. 467 (Bankr. C.D. Cal. 1980); *In re* Cole, 3 B.R. 346 (Bankr. S.D. W. Va. 1980).

71 *In re* Street, 55 B.R. 763 (B.A.P. 9th Cir. 1985); *see, e.g., In re* Easley, 72 B.R. 948 (Bankr. M.D. Tenn. 1987); *In re* Thorson, 6 B.R. 678 (Bankr. D.S.D. 1980); *In re* McBride, 4 B.R. 389 (Bankr. M.D. Ala. 1980); *In re* Bonder, 3 B.R. 623 (Bankr. E.D.N.Y. 1980); *In re* Peoro, Bankr. L. Rep. (CCH) ¶ 67,413 (Bankr. N.D. Cal. 1980); *In re* Keckler, 3 B.R. 155 (Bankr. N.D. Ohio 1980); *see also* Neufeld v. Freeman, 794 F.2d 149 (4th Cir. 1986).

72 *See* § 14.4.1, *infra*; *In re* Chaffin, 816 F.2d 1070 (5th Cir. 1987), *modified*, 836 F.2d 215 (5th Cir. 1988). *Compare* 11 U.S.C. § 1328(a) *with* 11 U.S.C. § 523(a).

73 *In re* Chaffin, 816 F.2d 1070 (5th Cir. 1987), *modified*, 836 F.2d 215 (5th Cir. 1988); Educ. Assistance Corp. v. Zellner, 827 F.2d 1222 (8th Cir. 1987); *In re* Rimgale, 669 F.2d 426 (7th Cir. 1982); *see also In re* Rasmussen, 888 F.2d 703 (10th Cir. 1989) (where debtor who originally had debts in excess of chapter 13 debt limits had discharged all debts, except one debt held nondischargeable in chapter 7 case, and two weeks later filed chapter 13 case proposing to pay 1.5% of debt not discharged in chapter 7, which was only debt listed in chapter 13 statement, plan was not filed in good faith and was manipulation of the bankruptcy process).

74 *In re* Chaffin, 816 F.2d 1070 (5th Cir. 1987), *modified*, 836 F.2d 215 (5th Cir. 1988).

75 *See, e.g., In re* Klein, 57 B.R. 818 (B.A.P. 9th Cir. 1985).

76 *See In re* Polak, 9 B.R. 502 (W.D. Mich. 1981); *In re* Melroy, 7 B.R. 513 (E.D. Cal. 1980); *In re* Burrell, 6 B.R. 360 (N.D. Cal. 1980); *In re* Iacovoni, 2 B.R. 256 (Bankr. D. Utah 1980).

77 A few of the courts would have gone no further in their analysis of "all the circumstances" if this percentage were not also "substantial," regardless of the other circumstances. *See, e.g., In re* Iacovoni, 2 B.R. 256 (Bankr. D. Utah 1980). These holdings are squarely contrary to the 1984 amendments instituting an "ability-to-pay" test, discussed in § 12.3.3, *infra*.

78 This test seems at variance with the language of the statute which clearly distinguishes "good faith" and "best effort" as two different standards. *See* 11 U.S.C. § 727(a)(9).

- Whether the payments meet a "rule of thumb" requirement of ten percent of take home pay;[79]
- The length of the proposed plan;[80]
- Whether the debtor has been in bankruptcy before, especially if the six-year bar to a chapter 7 case is applicable;
- Whether the debtor is attempting to obtain a discharge of debts not dischargeable under chapter 7;
- The amount and type of debt involved;
- The extent to which secured claims are involved;
- The relation of attorney fees and administrative costs to the amount paid to unsecured creditors;
- Whether the debtor has created preferences or preferred classes of creditors;
- The availability of property that could be liquidated; and
- Whether the case is a disguised chapter 7 case.

Thus, consideration of all the circumstances, which apparently appealed to many bankruptcy courts as a compromise between the extreme positions on this question, meant different things to different judges. A decision to weigh all of the circumstances did not yield a clear and discernible standard by which the debtor could predict whether a plan would be approved or whether a chapter 13 case would be worthwhile. Moreover, it burdened the courts with innumerable subjective questions which, to be dealt with fairly, would take a great deal of time and expense to decide.

Ultimately, most of the courts of appeals addressed the good faith issue. The District of Columbia Circuit Court of Appeals held that the good faith standard is not aimed at the level of repayment to unsecured creditors at all and is directed only at honesty of intention.[81] The other circuit courts settled on a fairly liberal version of the "all of the circumstances" compromise, holding that the percentage of payment on unsecured claims is one factor to examine, but it is never the only factor.[82] All of these decisions left open the possibility of plans providing zero or nominal payment plans to unsecured creditors in cases in which they are

necessary and appropriate to achieve debtors' goals. Although the issue of repayment to unsecured creditors has since ceased to be a major factor in courts' determinations of good faith, other discussed factors in these decisions continue to be considered in courts' good faith analyses.[83]

12.3.3 The Ability to Pay Test

12.3.3.1 Introduction

Some of the issues that so troubled the courts that interpreted the good faith test were resolved by the 1984 amendments to the Bankruptcy Code. In a new section 1325(b), courts were given express instructions regarding whether and how to take into account the debtor's income. At the same time, by adding a new subsection separate and apart from the good faith standard, Congress made clear its intent that the good faith test revert to its more traditional meaning, which did not concern the size of the debtor's payments.[84]

Section 1325(b) provides that if (and only if) an unsecured creditor or the chapter 13 trustee objects to confirmation of the plan, the court must determine whether the plan either 1) pays the objecting creditor in full or 2) commits to the plan all of the debtor's "disposable income" for the next three years. "Disposable income" in turn is defined as income not reasonably necessary for the maintenance or support of the debtor or dependents of the debtor.[85] If a debtor is engaged in business, "disposable income" also excludes funds necessary for the continuation, preservation and operation of the business.[86] However, although the test requires payment into the plan of the amount of disposable income the debtor would have in the first three years of the plan, that amount may be paid over a longer period of time if the debtor chooses to do so, for example, in order to continue otherwise impermissible expenses or live with a budget that is less tight.[87]

---

79 *See In re* Curtis, 2 B.R. 43 (Bankr. W.D. Mo. 1979). This test also is contrary to the new ability-to-pay test if debtors cannot afford ten percent dividends. *See* § 12.3.3, *infra*.

80 *Compare In re* Henry, 4 B.R. 220 (Bankr. M.D. Tenn. 1980) (four month plan denied confirmation) *with In re* Poff, 7 B.R. 15 (Bankr. S.D. Ohio 1980) (denying confirmation to five year plan as too long unless at least seventy percent of unsecured claims paid).

81 Barnes v. Whelan, 689 F.2d 193 (D.C. Cir. 1982).

82 *In re* Smith, 286 F.3d 461 (7th Cir. 2002) (the fact that debts not dischargeable in chapter 7 and debtor could pay only ten percent of debt through plan not sufficient to find lack of good faith); *In re* Hines, 723 F.2d 333 (3d Cir. 1983); Flygare v. Boulder, 709 F.2d 1344 (10th Cir. 1983); *In re* Kitchens, 702 F.2d 885 (11th Cir. 1983); *In re* Estus, 695 F.2d 311 (8th Cir. 1982); Deans v. O'Donnell, 692 F.2d 968 (4th Cir. 1982); *In re* Goeb, 675 F.2d 1386 (9th Cir. 1982) (one percent plan confirmable unless evidence of bad faith); *In re* Rimgale, 669 F.2d 426 (7th Cir. 1982).

83 *See* § 12.3.4, *infra*.

84 *In re* Keach, 243 B.R. 851 (B.A.P. 1st Cir. 2000) (1984 disposable income amendment makes clear that meaning of good faith is simple honesty of purpose); *In re* Red, 60 B.R. 113 (Bankr. E.D. Tenn. 1986); 8 Collier On Bankruptcy ¶ 1325.04[1] (15th ed. rev.). *But see* Neufeld v. Freeman, 794 F.2d 149 (4th Cir. 1986) (looking to some of the factors it had listed prior to 1984 amendments, though not to percentage of payments to unsecured creditors). It is not clear whether the court in *Neufeld* considered the effect of the 1984 amendments.

85 11 U.S.C. § 1325(b)(2). "Dependent" may include a debtor's aging parent, even if the debtor provides less than half the parent's support. *In re* Tracey, 66 B.R. 63 (Bankr. D. Md. 1986). At least one court has held that a personal injury recovery may be taken into account in determining disposable income, notwithstanding the fact that it was exempt property. Watters v. McRoberts, 167 B.R. 146 (S.D. Ill. 1994).

86 11 U.S.C. § 1325(b)(2).

87 *In re* Mendoza, 274 B.R. 522 (Bankr. D. Ariz. 2002) (debtors could continue retirement contributions because plan extending

Section 1325(b) makes clear that a debtor need not have enough income to make substantial payments or, indeed, any payments to unsecured creditors. If a debtor has no disposable income over and above the amount to pay secured claims, then a plan may be confirmed without payments to unsecured creditors if the other requirements of chapter 13 are met. The legislative history[88] expressly states that the so-called zero payment plan is permissible in certain circumstances.[89]

Overall, the ability-to-pay test should lay to rest problems which had made chapter 13 virtually unavailable to low-income debtors in some districts. It should now be clear that, if the other specific requirements of chapter 13 are met, no debtor is too poor to file a chapter 13 case.

12.3.3.2 Procedure for Objections Based upon Section 1325(b)

The procedure for objections to confirmation of a plan under section 1325(b) is the same as that for other objections to confirmation and is thus governed by Federal Rule of Bankruptcy Procedure 3015(g). That rule requires that objections be filed with the court and served on the debtor and the trustee. They must be timely filed, within a time fixed by the court.[90] Normally, the objections will be based upon the debtor's schedules of current income and expenditures. It therefore behooves the debtor to complete those portions of the forms carefully, with both the ability-to-pay and feasibility tests[91] in mind. Because only the trustee or the holder of an allowed unsecured claim may file an objection, a creditor who has not filed a claim does not have standing to object to confirmation.[92]

Once an objection is filed, the creditor will have at least an initial burden of production.[93] Assuming that burden is met, the debtor may defeat the objection by proving one of two things. First, the debtor may show that an objecting creditor will be paid in full. Alternatively, the plan can be confirmed if the debtor is committing to the plan all of his or her "disposable income" for at least three years.

12.3.3.3 Full Payment Test

Obviously, the full payment test is met if all unsecured claims are to be paid in full. It may also be met if the objecting claimant can be separately classified and paid in full, even if other creditors will not receive full payment.[94] Occasionally, it may be worthwhile to amend the plan to add such classification to satisfy the troublesome creditor, especially if the debtor anticipates difficulty in meeting the alternative disposable income standard. However, if the trustee objects to confirmation, the "full payment" test will likely require that all filed unsecured claims be paid in full. Even then, though, it is likely that only full payment of the original claim is necessary, and not the payment of additional interest to give the creditor the present value of its money.[95]

12.3.3.4 Disposable Income Test

If an objection under section 1325(b) is filed and the full payment standard cannot be met, a plan of at least three years duration is probably mandatory.[96] The court must then determine whether the debtor has committed to the plan all of his or her "projected disposable income."

Because changes in income or expenses can rarely be foreseen, the court normally looks to the debtor's current financial situation to decide this issue. Although the legislative history contains little indication as to what expenses may be considered reasonably necessary and therefore properly deductible from the debtor's income, a different amendment passed in 1984 does offer some guidance. Section 523(a)(2)(C) defines "luxury goods or services" as those which are *not* reasonably required for the support of the debtor or the debtor's dependents. A necessary corollary to that definition is the principle that all other expenses are reasonably required for such support.[97]

This definition therefore strongly supports the argument that the court's inquiry under the "ability-to-pay" test should be limited to determining whether debtors have included expenses for luxuries in their budgets, rather than whether they conform to some predetermined level of expenses.[98] Courts cannot reasonably or fairly make decisions

---

more than thirty-six months paid unsecured creditors amount equal to debtors' disposable income for thirty-six months); *In re* Elrod, 270 B.R. 258 (Bankr. E.D. Tenn. 2001).

88 The ability-to-pay test was adopted from a proposal made by the National Bankruptcy Conference. *See Oversight Hearings on Personal Bankruptcy Before the Subcomm. on Monopolies and Commercial Law of the House Comm. on the Judiciary*, 97th Cong. 181–223 (1981–1982).

89 *Id.*, at 223.

90 *In re* Gaona, 290 B.R. 381 (Bankr. S.D. Cal. 2003) (objections untimely under local rule); *In re* Harris, 275 B.R. 850 (Bankr. S.D. Ohio 2002) (objections filed after deadline established in clerk's notice were untimely); *In re* Carbone, 254 B.R. 1 (Bankr. D. Mass. 2000) (objection untimely when filed after deadline set by local rule).

91 *See* § 12.5, *infra*.

92 *In re* Stewart, 46 B.R. 73 (Bankr. D. Or. 1985).

93 Educ. Assistance Corp. v. Zellner, 827 F.2d 1222 (8th Cir. 1987); *In re* Fries, 68 B.R. 676 (Bankr. E.D. Pa. 1986).

94 See § 12.4, *infra*, for a discussion of permissible classifications of claims.

95 *In re* Eaton, 130 B.R. 74 (Bankr. S.D. Iowa 1991); *see* 8 Collier on Bankruptcy ¶ 1325.08[3] (15th ed. rev.).

96 *In re* Peterson, 53 B.R. 339 (Bankr. D. Or. 1985).

97 *See In re* Jones, 55 B.R. 462 (Bankr. D. Minn. 1985).

98 *See, e.g., In re* Gonzales, 297 B.R. 143 (Bankr. D.N.M. 2003) (food budget of $700.00/month for father, mother, and two teenage children not unreasonable under circumstances, nor was support of adult child in household).

beyond that regarding what expenses are more necessary or truly necessary. Different debtors will have widely varying expenses for housing and transportation, depending on their age, mobility, and place of residence, yet all but luxury-style residences should be considered necessary. Similarly, some debtors will feel that parochial school or other items are absolutely required.[99] The court can realistically go no further than deciding whether clearly unnecessary luxuries are included in the budget, and they should not attempt to do so. And, if a debtor's total expenses are average or less than average, it is doubtful that the court should even look at the expenses individually, because such debtors could only afford luxuries by making sacrifices in other parts of their budgets.

The cases under section 1325(b) have generally followed these principles. It has been held that the debtor need not commit to the plan every last dollar that is not necessary for expenses and may preserve a small cushion to guard against life's unexpected events.[100] The debtor should not be required to borrow or withdraw money from a retirement plan to fund a chapter 13 plan.[101] Nor should the debtor be expected to commit income that may never be received because its receipt is uncertain or speculative.[102] On the other hand, courts have denied confirmation to debtors paying substantial private school tuitions[103] and making payments on an expensive sports car.[104] Moreover, the mere fact that income, such as social security benefits, may be exempt or not subject to alienation does not mean that the income is not considered in applying the disposable income test.[105]

Generally, if only one spouse files a chapter 13 case, the other spouse's income is not considered available for chapter 13 payments.[106] However, the availability of the non-filing spouse's income is considered in determining the debtor's necessary expenses, because that spouse is expected to share in paying the expenses and thereby reduce the amount the debtor needs to pay.[107] Therefore, there is usually no advantage with respect to disposable income in filing for only one spouse.

Courts have split on whether a debtor is permitted to use part of his or her income to make repayments on a loan from the debtor's pension plan.[108] The better view is that such a loan is a claim under the Code's broad definition of "claim" and, like any other claim may be paid under the plan.[109] Similarly, courts have not agreed about whether a debtor can continue contributions to a pension plan, even if those contributions are mandated by state law. The court should evaluate such contributions under § 1325(b) to determine whether they are reasonable and necessary, taking into account such factors as the debtor's age, the amount of the contribution, and the effects that terminating contributions could have on the debtor's fresh start.[110] And the disposable income test does not require the debtor to commit exempt assets, as opposed to income, to the plan.[111]

---

99 *See In re* Burgos, 248 B.R. 446 (Bankr. M.D. Fla. 2000) (private school tuition allowed as reasonable expense based on debtors' sincere religious beliefs).

100 *In re* Greer, 60 B.R. 547 (Bankr. C.D. Cal. 1986); *In re* Otero, 48 B.R. 704 (Bankr. E.D. Va. 1985); *see also In re* Smith, 207 B.R. 888 (B.A.P. 9th Cir. 1996) (necessity of life insurance premiums must be considered on case-by-case basis); *In re* Woodman, 287 B.R. 589 (Bankr. D. Me. 2003) (tobacco expenses allowed).

101 *In re* Solomon, 67 F.3d 1128 (4th Cir. 1995); *In re* Short, 176 B.R. 886 (Bankr. S.D. Ind. 1995); *In re* Stones, 157 B.R. 669 (Bankr. S.D. Cal. 1993); *see also In re* Smith, 222 B.R. 846 (Bankr. N.D. Ind. 1998) (debtor not required to take cash distribution from profit sharing plan when that would have caused her to incur significant taxes and penalties).

102 *In re* Killough, 900 F.2d 61 (5th Cir. 1990) (affirming confirmation of plan without requiring debtor to include projected overtime in calculating budget).

103 *In re* Lynch, 299 B.R. 776 (W.D.N.C. 2003) ($567.00 per month for Catholic school tuition not reasonable when debtors argued need for school that was "more advanced" and did not teach evolution); Univest-Coppell Vill., Ltd. v. Nelson, 204 B.R. 497 (E.D. Tex. 1996); *In re* Jones, 55 B.R. 462 (Bankr. D. Minn. 1985). *But see In re* Webb, 262 B.R. 685 (Bankr. E.D. Tex. 2001) (private school tuition was necessary for child with learning and emotional problems).

104 *In re* Rogers, 65 B.R. 1018 (Bankr. E.D. Mich. 1986); *see also In re* Hedges, 68 B.R. 18 (Bankr. E.D. Va. 1986) (plan including continued payment for recreational boat denied confirmation).

105 *In re* Freeman, 86 F.3d 478 (6th Cir. 1996) (exempt status of tax

refund under state law irrelevant to disposable income test); *In re* Hagel, 184 B.R. 793 (B.A.P. 9th Cir. 1995); *In re* Sohn, 300 B.R. 332 (Bankr. D. Minn. 2003) (projected exempt tax refunds under Earned Income Tax Credit program must be included in calculating disposable income).

106 *See In re* Bottelberghe, 253 B.R. 256 (Bankr. D. Minn. 2000). *But see In re* Hull, 251 B.R. 726 (B.A.P. 9th Cir. 2000) (under Washington state's community property laws, each spouse had vested interest in income of other spouse).

107 *In re* Nahat, 278 B.R. 108 (Bankr. N.D. Tex. 2002) (income of non-debtor spouse considered in debtor's case after deduction of payments on non-debtor's own credit cards; non-debtor spouse was not required to devote her income to paying husband's debts to detriment of her own creditors).

108 *Compare In re* Anes, 195 F.3d 177 (3d Cir. 1999); *In re* Harshbarger, 66 F.3d 775 (6th Cir. 1995) (payments not permitted) *with In re* Buchferer, 216 B.R. 332 (Bankr. E.D.N.Y. 1997). *See generally Pension Plan Loans in Bankruptcy*, 17 NCLC REPORTS *Bankruptcy and Foreclosures Ed.* 17 (Mar./Apr. 1999).

109 *In re* Buchferer, 216 B.R. 332 (Bankr. E.D.N.Y. 1997) (pension loan is non-recourse secured claim).

110 *In re* Taylor, 243 F.3d 124 (2d Cir. 2001); *In re* Guild, 269 B.R. 470 (Bankr. D. Mass. 2001); *cf. In re* Festner, 54 B.R. 532 (Bankr. E.D.N.C. 1985) (voluntary contributions to retirement plan and stock option plan not reasonably necessary).

111 *In re* Graham, 258 B.R. 286 (Bankr. M.D. Fla. 2001) (proceeds of personal injury settlement based on cause of action that was an exempted asset were not income); *In re* Kerr, 199 B.R. 370 (Bankr. N.D. Ill. 1996) (proceeds from sale of exempt homestead need not be committed to plan); *see also In re* Baker, 194 B.R. 881 (Bankr. S.D. Cal. 1996) (exempt life insurance proceeds not disposable income, but interest on proceeds would be disposable income). *But see* Barbosa v. Solomon, 235 F.3d 31 (1st Cir. 2000) (proceeds from sale of home, on which mortgage had been stripped off due to lack of equity prior to confirmation,

Because some courts had restricted debtors' tithing or other church contributions in applying the disposable income standard,[112] Congress amended the Code in 1998 to make clear that such contributions are permissible and need not be curtailed in order to pay more to creditors. The Religious Liberty and Charitable Donation Protection Act of 1998[113] amended section 1325(b) to provide that charitable contributions[114] to qualified religious or charitable entities or organizations,[115] in an amount not exceeding fifteen percent of the debtor's gross income in any year, are permissible expenses for a chapter 13 debtor under the ability to pay test. No similar change was made for chapter 12 debtors, however. The amendment does not require that the permissible contributions be made to a religious organization, perhaps because Congress feared constitutional church-state problems. Nor does it apply only if the debtor had made such contributions in the past.[116] Thus, a chapter 13 debtor may choose to pay up to fifteen percent of his or her income to charity rather than to creditors over the course of a chapter 13 plan.

Some judicial hostility to the provision is apparent in some of the first cases decided on charitable contributions in chapter 13 since the amendment was passed. A few courts have concluded that a contribution must be "reasonably necessary to be expended for the maintenance or support of the debtor" or the debtor's dependents.[117] Though this reading might be possible based on the ambiguous structure of the new provision, it clearly eviscerates the statutory language and ignores congressional intent.[118] The problem in holding that only "reasonably necessary" contributions can be made is illustrated by the difficulty in articulating standards to evaluate the size and type of contributions which are to be considered reasonably necessary for the maintenance and support of the debtor or the debtor's dependents.[119]

_____

required to be paid to creditors in modified plan when home sold for twice the value used for stripping of liens).

112 *See, e.g., In re* Sturgeon, 51 B.R. 82 (Bankr. S.D. Ind. 1985).

113 Pub. L. No. 105-183, 112 Stat. 517 (1998).

114 The "charitable contribution" must meet the definition in § 548(d)(3), as amended by the same Act, and thus must consist of either a financial instrument or cash.

115 Section 1325(b) incorporates the definition of "qualified religious or charitable entity or organization" in § 548(d)(4), which in turn requires the recipient of the contribution to be an entity described in § 170(c)(1) or 170(c)(2) of the Internal Revenue Code.

116 Compare 11 U.S.C. § 548(a)(2)(B) with 11 U.S.C. § 707(b), both of which appear to, in some cases, take past contributions into consideration.

117 *E.g., In re* Buxton, 228 B.R. 606 (Bankr. W.D. La. 1999).

118 *In re* Cavanagh, 250 B.R. 107 (B.A.P. 9th Cir. 2000) (Congress intended that contributions within limit be deemed reasonable and necessary); *In re* Kirschner, 259 B.R. 416 (Bankr. M.D. Fla. 2001) (court follows *Cavanagh* though requires debtors to provide ongoing documentation that contributions actually made during life of plan).

119 In *In re* Buxton, 228 B.R. 606 (Bankr. W.D. La. 1999) the court

12.3.3.5 Post-Confirmation Modification of Plan Based Upon Change in Circumstances

Finally, the ability-to-pay provisions also provide for unanticipated changes in the debtor's income or expenses. Section 1329(a) permits a debtor, unsecured creditor, or trustee to seek modification of the plan, raising or lowering payments, if the debtor's circumstances change substantially. Thus, when there has been a substantial and unanticipated change for the better in the debtor's financial condition after confirmation, the trustee or an unsecured creditor can move for a modification that increases the debtor's payments.[120] As a practical matter, however, this section is utilized primarily by debtors seeking to lower payments because of lower income or higher expenses, because the trustee and creditors will usually have no knowledge of changes in the debtor's situation.[121]

Although section 1329(a) does not by its terms limit creditors' motions to cases where there has been a change in income or expenses, any motions filed on other grounds, which could have been raised earlier, should be barred by the *res judicata* effect of the confirmation order.[122] Also, if

_____

seems to require that reasonableness be demonstrated by limited contributions made from otherwise discretionary income. This limitation swallows the rule.

120 See *In re* Arnold, 869 F.2d 240 (4th Cir. 1989) (debtor's income rose from $80,000.00 per year to $200,000.00 per year); *In re* Powers, 202 B.R. 618 (B.A.P. 9th Cir. 1996) (five hundred dollars increase in debtor's income justified plan modification, even after taking into account debtor's increased expenses); *In re* Fitak, 121 B.R. 224 (S.D. Ohio 1990) (sale of debtors' property 57 months after confirmation for $20,000.00 more than value estimated at time of confirmation was not an unanticipated change of circumstances justifying modification motion of creditor because property would have been expected to appreciate over time); *In re* Flennory, 280 B.R. 896 (Bankr. S.D. Ala. 2001) (receipt of tax refund was not change of circumstances that could not have been anticipated and did not justify modification). However, some courts have held that under a literal reading of section 1329, the ability to pay test of section 1325(b) is not applicable to post-confirmation modifications. *In re* Forbes, 215 B.R. 183 (B.A.P. 8th Cir. 1997); *In re* Anderson, 153 B.R. 527 (Bankr. M.D. Tenn. 1993). Moreover, if no objection to plan confirmation was made by a creditor on the basis of ability to pay, the issue may not later be raised for the first time by a motion to modify the plan, at least with respect to any income which might have been anticipated at the time of confirmation. *In re* Grissom, 137 B.R. 689 (Bankr. W.D. Tenn. 1992).

121 A few trustees do require annual reports of debtors' income and expenses. Their authority to do so is, at best, unclear. See Petro v. Mishler, 276 F.3d 375 (7th Cir. 2002).

122 *See, e.g., In re* Klus, 173 B.R. 51 (Bankr. D. Conn. 1994); *In re* Bonanno, 78 B.R. 52 (Bankr. E.D. Pa. 1987); 8 Collier on Bankruptcy ¶ 1329.03 (15th ed. rev.). For a discussion of the binding effect of a confirmed plan, see § 12.11, *infra. But see* Barbosa v. Solomon, 235 F.3d 31 (1st Cir. 2000) (plan may be modified without showing change of circumstances); *In re* Witkowski, 16 F.3d 739 (7th Cir. 1994) (changed circumstances not a prerequisite for trustee's motion to modify plan after

the debtor is able to complete payments under the original plan before a motion to modify is filed, the court is precluded from modifying the plan, because Code section 1329(a) permits modification only "before completion of payments under [the confirmed] plan."[123]

A few courts have tried to take into account possible increases in debtors' incomes in advance by requiring that plan payments increase by the same percentage as the debtor's income, or by some percentage of any additional income that the debtor receives.[124] These cases are misguided for several reasons. First, the legislative history gives no indication that such automatic increases were contemplated; the mechanism discussed in the proposal that led to the 1984 amendments was the motion to amend the plan.[125] Second, such automatic increases would create monitoring and verification problems, making it difficult for the court or the trustee to know when, or if, the debtor had completed payments under the plan. Finally, any automatic increase provision could not take into account inflation or other expenses which could decrease the debtor's *real* disposable income. A three percent salary increase in a period when the cost of living increases by six percent is a decrease in real income that leaves the debtor less able to afford plan payments. It is for precisely such reasons that the only proper method for increasing plan payments is a case by case approach through motions to amend chapter 13 plans.[126]

As the Ninth Circuit Court of Appeals held in *In re Anderson*,[127] a debtor should not be required to pledge increased plan payments upon later increases in income in order to obtain confirmation. The procedure of the bankruptcy court in that case, permitting the trustee to determine that plan payments should be increased without a motion to modify the plan, was disapproved as contrary to the statutory scheme which contemplates a modification motion as the appropriate vehicle to change plan payments.[128] Simi-

larly, it is not proper to condition plan confirmation on the debtor submitting future periodic reports of income with current pay stubs.[129]

12.3.4 Use of the Good Faith Test After the 1984 Amendments

Although use of the good faith test of 11 U.S.C. § 1325(a)(3) to challenge a plan based solely upon the amount of a debtor's payment to unsecured creditors[130] has been put to rest by the "ability to pay test,"[131] creditors have continued to invoke section 1325(a)(3) to challenge other perceived debtor abuses. Some courts have read the new "ability to pay" test as simply eliminating certain issues—those going to whether minimal payments to unsecured creditors evidence bad faith—from the "all of the circumstances" examination of good faith.[132] However, even when courts continue to evaluate the totality of the circumstances,[133] it should be argued that the inquiry into good faith should be limited to such issues as the debtor's honesty in completing the schedules and intention to effectuate a chapter 13 plan as proposed.[134] Nonetheless, some courts continue to impose limitations that are based on subjective judgments about the appropriate purposes for which a debtor

---

obligation to pay all disposable income at the end of three years to unsecured creditors, rather than specific amounts, debtors could be required to pay amounts that court determined were not necessary for support of debtor or dependents or operation of farm in order to obtain discharge, even though debtor would have to borrow to finance future operations).

129 Petro v. Mishler, 276 F.3d 375 (7th Cir. 2002).

130 *See* § 12.3.2, *supra.*

131 *See* § 12.3.3, *supra.*

132 *In re* Smith, 848 F.2d 813 (7th Cir. 1988); Educ. Assistance Corp. v. Zellner, 827 F.2d 1222 (8th Cir. 1987); *In re* Smith, 100 B.R. 436 (S.D. Ind. 1989). See § 12.3.2, *supra,* for discussion of earlier cases on good faith.

133 *See In re* Young, 237 F.3d 1168 (10th Cir. 2001) (plan could be in good faith despite debtor's conversion from chapter 7 in order to deal with non-dischargeable punitive damages award); *In re* Gier, 986 F.2d 1326 (10th Cir. 1993) (bankruptcy court did not err in denying confirmation after finding that there were discrepancies in debtor's testimony about available income, debtor was motivated by desire not to pay creditors rather than inability to pay them, chapter 13 case was filed before chapter 7 case was concluded and plan proposed to discharge debt that was non-dischargeable in chapter 7 case); *In re* LeMaire, 898 F.2d 1346 (8th Cir. 1990) (*en banc*); *In re* Okoreeh-Baah, 836 F.2d 1030 (6th Cir. 1988); *In re* Chaffin, 816 F.2d 1070 (5th Cir. 1987), *modified,* 836 F.2d 215 (5th Cir. 1988); Neufeld v. Freeman, 794 F.2d 149 (4th Cir. 1986).

134 Educ. Assistance Corp. v. Zellner, 827 F.2d 1222 (8th Cir. 1987); *In re* Keach, 243 B.R. 851 (B.A.P. 1st Cir. 2000); *In re* Gathright, 67 B.R. 384 (Bankr. E.D. Pa. 1986); *In re* Red, 60 B.R. 113 (Bankr. E.D. Tenn. 1986); *see also In re* Doersam, 849 F.2d 237 (6th Cir. 1988) (questionable listing of expenses combined with bulk of debts being student loans yielded finding that plan not proposed in good faith); 8 Collier on Bankruptcy ¶ 1325.04[1] (15th ed. rev.).

---

confirmation); *In re* Brown, 219 B.R. 191 (B.A.P. 6th Cir. 1998) (no substantial change of circumstances need be shown); *In re* Than, 215 B.R. 430 (B.A.P. 9th Cir. 1997) (no substantial and unanticipated changed circumstances required for trustee's motion to modify plan).

123 *In re* Profit, 283 B.R. 567 (B.A.P. 9th Cir. 2002); Bayshore Nat'l Bank v. Smith, 252 B.R. 107 (E.D. Tex. 2000), *aff'd,* 252 F.3d 1357 (5th Cir. Tex. 2001) (table); *In re* Casper, 154 B.R. 243 (N.D. Ill. 1993); *In re* Richardson, 283 B.R. 783 (Bankr. D. Kan. 2002); *In re* Jordan, 161 B.R. 670 (Bankr. D. Minn. 1993); *In re* Moss, 91 B.R. 563 (Bankr. C.D. Cal. 1988); 8 Collier on Bankruptcy ¶ 1329.08 (15th ed. rev.).

124 *See, e.g., In re* Akin, 54 B.R. 700 (Bankr. D. Neb. 1985); *In re* Krull, 54 B.R. 375 (Bankr. D. Colo. 1985).

125 *Oversight Hearings on Personal Bankruptcy Before the Subcomm. on Monopolies and Commerce of the House Comm. on the Judiciary,* 97th Cong. 215, 221 (1981–1982).

126 8 Collier on Bankruptcy ¶ 1325.08[4][b] (15th ed. rev.).

127 21 F.3d 355 (9th Cir. 1994).

128 *But see In re* Broken Bow Ranch, 33 F.3d 1005 (8th Cir. 1994) (where confirmed chapter 12 plan did provide for general

may use chapter 13, and which take into account the amount of the payments proposed.[135]

12.3.5 Payments to Unsecured Priority Creditors

One group of unsecured claims must normally be paid in full through the chapter 13 plan. Section 1322(a)(2) of the Code requires that the plan provide for payment in full of all claims entitled to priority under Code section 507(a), unless the holder of the claim agrees otherwise. A creditor who fails to object to a plan proposing less than full payment may be deemed to have agreed to it.[136] In any case, if such a plan is confirmed, the creditor is bound by it.[137]

The most common types of priority claims in chapter 13 cases are claims for administrative expenses, such as the debtor's attorney fees[138] or the trustee's fees,[139] and tax claims.[140] In some cases, debtors may owe debts in the nature of alimony, maintenance, or support that are priority claims.[141] Debtors who have been in business may also owe priority debts for wages or consumer deposits.[142] While attorney fees and trustee's fees are to be expected in most chapter 13 cases, the requirement that other priority claims be paid in full may be difficult for some debtors to meet.

It should be noted, however, that section 1322(a)(2) does not require that priority creditors receive the present value of their claims, that is, the claims plus interest, over the course of the plan, as does the best interests of creditors test.[143] Nor does it require that priority claims be paid before other claims. In some cases, a debtor may want to provide for payment of large priority claims only after the secured claims are paid in full. If that is done and the debtor is then for some reason unable to complete the plan, there is a better chance that the secured claims will have been satisfactorily dealt with by the time the plan fails, in which case the debtor may seek a hardship discharge[144] or choose to convert the case to chapter 7.[145] If the debtor chooses either of these alternatives, priority claims need not be paid in the bankruptcy case, although the unpaid priority taxes or support debts may not be discharged.[146]

Generally, a debtor should provide for payment of priority claims before general unsecured claims are paid, however. Then, if the plan fails before it can be completed, there will be a greater chance that priority claims have been paid in full or almost paid in full, which could keep open the option of modifying the plan, because any modified plan must also provide for full payment of priority claims.[147] Alternatively, if the debtor seeks a hardship discharge or converts to chapter 7, taxes or alimony or support obligations that would not have been discharged will no longer be owed if they have already been paid in the chapter 13 plan.

It is quite clear that a priority creditor need not be paid if it fails to file a claim.[148] Occasionally, taxing authorities will

---

135 *See, e.g.*, Noreen v. Slattengren, 974 F.2d 75 (8th Cir. 1992) (finding lack of good faith in plan of debtor who sought to eliminate liability for child sexual abuse with minimal payments); *In re* LeMaire, 898 F.2d 1346 (8th Cir. 1990) (*en banc*) (good faith found lacking in large part due to heinous nature of debtor's pre-petition acts); *In re* Gilmore, 217 B.R. 228 (Bankr. S.D. Ohio 1998) (debtor's pre-petition conduct in stopping payment on payday loan checks not evidence of bad faith); *In re* Hawes, 73 B.R. 584 (Bankr. W.D. Wis. 1987) (use of chapter 13 in part to block employer's efforts to enforce a covenant not to compete constitutes bad faith); *see also In re* Tucker, 989 F.2d 328 (9th Cir. 1993) (bankruptcy court failed to make sufficient factual findings about whether debtor had acted equitably); *cf. In re* Robinson, 987 F.2d 665 (10th Cir. 1993) (creditor who failed to argue in bankruptcy court that debt for improper sexual activities by pastoral counselor would have been nondischargeable as willful and malicious injury could not obtain reversal of confirmation order based on that argument).

136 *See In re* Lindgren, 85 B.R. 447 (Bankr. N.D. Ohio 1988); *In re* Hebert, 61 B.R. 44 (Bankr. W.D. La. 1986); *see also In re* Teligent, Inc., 282 B.R. 765 (Bankr. S.D.N.Y. 2002) (chapter 11 case interpreting similar language). *But see In re* Northrup, 141 B.R. 171 (N.D. Iowa 1991).

137 *In re* Riley, 204 B.R. 28 (Bankr. E.D. Ark. 1996) (tax debt was provided for by debtor's chapter 13 plan and thus discharged, even though modified plan omitted debt, when taxing authority had knowledge of case, participated in process and filed other proofs of claim); *see* § 12.11, *infra. But see In re* Hairopoulos, 118 F.3d 1240 (8th Cir. 1997) (tax claim was not provided for when Internal Revenue Service did not receive proper notice of conversion to chapter 13 and other significant dates); *In re* Escobedo, 28 F.3d 34 (7th Cir. 1994) (confirmation of plan that did not pay priority claims in full was "nugatory" and case could be dismissed even though there was no appeal of confirmation order and debtor had completed plan payments).

138 See § 15.4.1, *infra,* for a discussion of payment of attorney fees through a chapter 13 plan.

139 See § 7.3.7, *supra,* for discussion of the chapter 13 trustee's fees. Chapter 7 trustees sometimes seek priority treatment for their fees in cases converted from chapter 7, but some courts have held that they are limited to a percentage of chapter 7 disbursements, if any, by 11 U.S.C. § 326. See *In re* Murphy, 272 B.R. 483 (Bankr. D. Colo. 2002) and cases cited therein.

140 Not all tax claims are entitled to priority. *See* § 3.5, *supra.*

141 11 U.S.C. § 507(a)(7). It should be noted that such claims are not entitled to priority if they are not actually in the nature of alimony, maintenance, or support, or if they have been assigned. 11 U.S.C. § 507(a)(7). Also, claims for unmatured alimony or support are not allowable. 11 U.S.C. § 502(b)(5).

142 See § 3.5, *supra,* for discussion of the various types of priority debts.

143 *In re* Hageman, 108 B.R. 1016 (Bankr. N.D. Ind. 1989); *In re* Hieb, 88 B.R. 1019 (Bankr. D.S.D. 1988); *see* § 12.3.1, *supra; cf.* 11 U.S.C. § 1325(b)(4). Of course, if the priority claim would have been paid in full in a chapter 7 case, such present value interest would be required under the best interests of creditors test itself.

144 11 U.S.C. § 1325(b); *see* § 8.7.4, *supra.*

145 11 U.S.C. § 1307(a); *see* § 8.7.4, *supra.*

146 11 U.S.C. § 523(a)(1), (5), (15); *see* §§ 14.4.3.1, 14.4.3.5, 14.4.3.13, *infra.*

147 *See* § 8.7.4, *supra.*

148 Priority administrative expenses are exceptions to this rule. An entity seeking allowance of an administrative expense files a

fail to file claims for priority taxes; in such cases, provided the taxes were properly scheduled and the taxing authority had notice of the case, the taxes are discharged when the plan is completed, just as any other unsecured claim.[149] A similar analysis applies when a taxing authority fails to file a claim for the full amount that it later claims is owed. Generally, if the omitted amounts derive from a different year or a different transaction, courts will not allow them to be added to the taxing authority's proof of claim by amendment after the claims bar date has passed.[150]

However, if a priority alimony, maintenance, or support claim is not filed, the debt will not be discharged at the end of the case, because such claims (unlike tax claims) are nondischargeable under Code section 1328(a). Therefore, it is usually in the debtor's interest to file a claim for a priority support creditor, if the debtor can afford to pay the claim in the plan, to assure that the creditor is paid ahead of non-priority unsecured creditors.[151] Alternatively, if the claim is to be paid by the debtor directly to the creditor outside the plan, the debtor should ensure that his or her budget is adjusted to take into account such payments.

Some creditors, in an effort to receive payments which exceed the amount to which they are legitimately entitled, will file priority claims even when they have no right to priority treatment under the Code. For example, some utility companies commonly assert an inappropriate priority for pre-petition utility debts. Similarly, some secured creditors assert priority status even though priority claims, by definition, must be unsecured.[152] When bogus priorities are asserted, an objection to the claim is required, perhaps with a request for sanctions under Federal Rule of Bankruptcy Procedure 9011 if the claimed priority is frivolous.[153]

12.4 Classification of Claims

12.4.1 In General

One of the powers that chapter 13 gives to debtors is the right to designate classes of claims.[154] In essence, this is the right to treat some claims better than others in the chapter 13 plan. However, this right is subject to an important limitation. The plan may not "discriminate unfairly" against any class of claims.[155] Generally, this means that if certain claims are placed in a separate class for preferred treatment, some distinguishing characteristic of those claims must justify that preferred treatment, making it "fair."[156] Otherwise, one of the cardinal principles of bankruptcy, equality among creditors, would be undermined.

Unfortunately, chapter 13 gives little indication of what should be considered to be fair. It does make clear, because it allows classes of unsecured claims, that all unsecured claims need not be in the same class. Section 1322(b)(1) also refers to section 1122, which provides for classification of claims in chapter 11 cases. That section, in turn, provides a little more guidance. A claim may be placed in a class only if it is "substantially similar" to other claims in the class,[157] and a separate class of small unsecured claims may be created for administrative convenience.[158] The legislative history of this section further states that it is meant to codify preexisting case law.[159]

Although helpful, none of these guidelines fully prepared bankruptcy courts for all of the types of classifications that consumers would propose in chapter 13 cases. Some classifications have posed few problems; it is clear that secured claimants and priority claimants have greater rights in bankruptcy than unsecured claimants. Separate classifications of such claims merely carry forward the policies evident in the Code.[160] And, if the debtor wishes, there is no doubt that such claims may even be divided into separate classes for different treatment in order of their priority or lien status.[161]

As fairness depends on the order of payment as well as the amount, it would probably be considered unfair to pay creditors with a lower priority before those with a higher status, although in specific cases, some showing of fairness might be allowed.[162] However, section 1322(b)(4) does expressly permit payments on any unsecured claim to be

---

"request," which is not governed by the claims deadline but must normally be timely. 11 U.S.C. § 503(a).

149 *In re* Tomlan, 907 F.2d 114 (9th Cir. 1990); *In re* Richard, 50 B.R. 339 (E.D. Tenn. 1985); *In re* Rothman, 76 B.R. 38 (Bankr. E.D.N.Y. 1987); *see also* § 14.4.1, *infra*. It is also now clear, under § 502(b)(9), that late filed claims must be disallowed. However, the debtor probably has to object to such claims to ensure that they will be disallowed.

150 *See* § 13.4.3, *infra*.

151 See §§ 8.4.1, 8.4.2, *supra*, for a discussion of claims filed by the debtor.

152 11 U.S.C. § 507.

153 See § 13.4.3, *infra*, for a discussion of objections to claims. Fed. R. Bankr. P. 9011 requires twenty-one days prior notice of any request by a party for sanctions under that rule.

154 11 U.S.C. § 1322(b)(1).

155 11 U.S.C. § 1322(b)(1).

156 *See In re* Furlow, 70 B.R. 973 (Bankr. E.D. Pa. 1987).

157 11 U.S.C. § 1122(a).

158 11 U.S.C. § 1122(b). The debtor might wish to pay off a large number of small claims first in order to satisfy most of his or her creditors quickly, especially if future business with those claimants is contemplated. *See also In re* Ratledge, 31 B.R. 897 (Bankr. E.D. Tenn. 1983) (plan confirmed that proposed payment of first $500.00 and ten percent of remaining balance to all unsecured creditors); *accord In re* Terry, 78 B.R. 171 (Bankr. E.D. Tenn. 1987) (first $1000.00 and ten percent of remaining balance to be paid on unsecured claims).

159 S. Rep. No. 95-989, at 118 (1978); H.R. Rep. No. 95-595, at 406 (1977).

160 *In re* Stewart, 290 B.R. 302 (Bankr. E.D. Mich. 2003) (each secured claim may be separately classified, and secured claims need not be paid concurrently); *see* 7 Collier on Bankruptcy ¶ 1122.03[4][b], [c] (15th ed. 2003).

161 *See* 7 Collier on Bankruptcy ¶ 1122.03[4][b], [c] (15th ed. rev.).

162 *In re* Bagley, 7 B.R. 108 (Bankr. S.D. Ohio 1980).

made concurrently with payments on any secured claim or any other unsecured claim.[163] A few courts have required payment of the debtor's attorney fees concurrently with unsecured debts, despite their priority status, to assure that the debtor's attorney maintains an interest in the case.[164] Other courts have permitted payment of attorney fees prior to other claims.[165] Section 1322(b)(5) also permits unsecured claims with a final payment due after the conclusion of the plan to be dealt with in a different manner, through maintenance of payments and curing of defaults.[166]

12.4.2 Claims with Cosigners

The most commonly proposed classification confronted by the courts has been that providing for favored treatment (usually one-hundred percent payment) to creditors who have obtained cosigners on their claims. Because in consumer cases these cosigners are almost always the debtor's close friends or relatives, it is not surprising that debtors have wanted to place a higher priority on payment of these debts to avoid the bad feelings or embarrassment that could be engendered if the creditor sought payment from their cosigners. Debtors in such cases have argued that, for them, there was a substantial difference between these and other unsecured claims.

Although the courts had not been particularly sympathetic to these arguments,[167] Congress apparently did agree with them. The 1984 amendments to the Code specifically permit separate classification of claims with cosigners.[168] The legislative history recognized that practical differences exist between cosigned claims and other claims, and that those differences cause debtors to pay creditors voluntarily outside the plan if classification is not permitted, thereby jeopardizing their ability to make plan payments.[169] These practical

differences were found to justify separate classification.[170] Under the language of the amended section 1322(b)(1), debtors are permitted to separately classify and treat differently cosigned debt without showing that such treatment is fair.[171] Presumably, as some courts have held that creditors may proceed against cosigners in chapter 13 unless the plan proposes to pay the claim in full including interest,[172] separate classification of such claims can also be utilized to pay interest on them when no other creditors receive interest under the plan.[173] With no basis in the plain language of the Code, a few courts have held that separate classification of cosigned debts may not be used to pay a lower percentage of those claims than other unsecured claims—even when the cosigner is up to date on payments.[174] Others have permitted some discrimination in favor of cosigned claims but not discrimination they believe is disproportionate.[175] These cases are wrongly decided and may frustrate a debtor's plan. Additionally, unnecessary double payments may be made.[176]

12.4.3 Other Classifications

Debtors in chapter 13 cases have also proposed a number of other types of classifications. Several have classified separately debts that would likely be nondischargeable in a chapter 7 case or in both chapters 7 and 13. Although these claims are not given priority in liquidation, such classifications have been allowed by some courts.

For example, plans proposing favored treatment of child support arrearages were approved based on the nondischargeability of such debts and the different enforcement mechanisms available, for example, contempt of court.[177] In

---

163 The Supreme Court has held that, as to tax payments, a chapter 11 debtor may allocate payments to a particular tax liability if the allocation furthers the debtor's reorganization, despite the claims of the Internal Revenue Service that it had the right to allocate the payments due to their involuntary nature. United States v. Energy Res., Inc., 495 U.S. 545, 110 S. Ct. 2139, 109 L. Ed. 2d 580 (1990); *see* § 12.4.3, *infra.* The language of section 1322(b)(4) and the fact that a chapter 13 plan is, in all cases, completely voluntary in nature should militate for a similar result in chapter 13.

164 *See* § 15.4.1, *infra.*

165 *E.g., In re* Tenney, 63 B.R. 110 (Bankr. W.D. Okla. 1986).

166 *See* Joe Lee, *Chapter 13 nee Chapter XIII*, 53 Am. Bankr. L. J. 303, 313 (1979).

167 *See, e.g.,* Barnes v. Whelan, 689 F.2d 193 (D.C. Cir. 1982) (plan proposing one-hundred percent payment to cosigned debts and one percent to other debts discriminated unfairly; court left open possibility that complete equality of treatment might not be necessary, depending on the individual debtor's circumstances); *In re* Wade, 4 B.R. 98 (Bankr. M.D. Tenn. 1980); *In re* Iacovoni, 2 B.R. 256 (Bankr. D. Utah 1980).

168 11 U.S.C. § 1322(b)(1).

169 S. Rep. No. 98-65, at 17 (1983); *see also In re* Ross, 161 B.R.

36 (Bankr. C.D. Ill. 1993) (permitting separate classification of debt guaranteed by debtor's employer, who allegedly would have discharged debtor if debt was not paid).

170 S. Rep. No. 98-65, at 17 (1983). Despite the 1994 amendments, several courts have held that separate classification of codebtor claims is subject to the unfair discrimination test. *See, e.g., In re* Applegarth, 221 B.R. 914 (Bankr. M.D. Fla. 1998); *In re* Thompson, 191 B.R. 967, 971 (Bankr. S.D. Ga. 1996) (discrimination in favor of creditors with cosigners was intended to be "per se" fair discrimination). *But see In re* Hill, 268 B.R. 548 (B.A.P. 9th Cir. 2001) (debts incurred through debtor's use of mother's credit cards did not give rise to debtor's joint liability to card grantor, so debt was not eligible for separate classification).

171 *In re* Dornon, 103 B.R. 61 (Bankr. N.D.N.Y. 1989).

172 *See* § 9.4.4, *supra.*

173 Southeastern Bank v. Brown, 266 B.R. 900 (S.D. Ga. 2001); *In re* Monroe, 281 B.R. 398 (Bankr. N.D. Ga. 2002); *In re* Austin, 110 B.R. 430 (Bankr. E.D. Mo. 1990).

174 *E.g., In re* Markham, 224 B.R. 599 (Bankr. W.D. Ky. 1998).

175 *In re* Chacon, 202 F.3d 725 (5th Cir. 1999).

176 As a practical matter, creditors are unlikely to object to a plan as long as payments are being made by the codebtor.

177 *In re* Haag, 3 B.R. 649 (Bankr. D. Or. 1980); *In re* Curtis, 2 B.R. 43 (Bankr. W.D. Mo. 1979).

In re Leser[178] the Eighth Circuit Court of Appeals held that the strong public policy in favor of obtaining funds for child support claims, including those assigned to governmental units, dictated that they could be separately classified and paid more than other unsecured claims. Of course, now that Congress has made some child support debts priority claims,[179] there can be no doubt about the propriety of giving those debts more favored treatment.

Similarly, separate classification of student loan debts has been allowed by some courts.[180] Many of the same arguments applicable to child support debts also apply in the student loan context. As in the case of child support, the exception to the chapter 13 discharge for student loans is not one based on the fault of the debtor, or intended to punish the debtor. It was passed as part of a budget act as a way of providing revenues to the government.[181] Congressional action making the debt nondischargeable is, in itself, evidence that payment of student loan debts has special social importance. Therefore, it is entirely in keeping with these purposes to allow separate classification and greater payments which will increase the amount the government collects on such debts. At least one court has also pointed out that separate classification has another reasonable basis because, absent payment of a student loan, a debtor is often ineligible to obtain other financial assistance or to return to school.[182] For some courts, it has been a sufficient basis for classification that the debt is nondischargeable in chapter 13 and the debtor, therefore, has a significant interest in paying as much of it as possible.[183]

When such classifications have been rejected, it has often been, at least in part, due to a lack of proof that the claims would indeed be nondischargeable.[184] In any case, debtor should be able to cure and maintain payments on a long-term student loan pursuant to § 1322(b)(5), even if that means that the student loan creditor receives more than other unsecured creditors.[185] This may achieve the same practical result as separate classification, even in jurisdictions where separate classification is not otherwise allowed.

Likewise, when the Code provides special treatment for particular contracts, such as executory contracts and unexpired leases, that treatment can be carried out through classification. As discussed below,[186] to assume an executory contract or unexpired lease the debtor must promptly cure a default. The debtor may effectuate that cure by paying the arrears on the contract, even if those arrears might otherwise be an unsecured claim, prior to other claims.[187]

Other proposals have involved preferred treatment to creditors with a special relationship to the debtor or with claims of a special nature. Courts have sometimes approved more favored treatment for doctors, landlords, trade creditors necessary for continued operation of a business, attorneys, and even banks from whom future credit is needed.[188]

---

178 939 F.2d 669 (8th Cir. 1991); *see also* Henry J. Sommer & Margaret Doe McGarity, Collier Family Law and the Bankruptcy Code ¶ 8.07 (1992). *But see In re* Crawford, 324 F.3d 539 (7th Cir. 2003) (bankruptcy court did not abuse discretion in refusing to allow debtor to separately classify non-priority child support owed to county, implying that permitting classification would also have been within court's discretion).

179 11 U.S.C. § 507(a)(7) was added by the 1994 amendments to the Bankruptcy Code.

180 *In re* Tucker, 159 B.R. 325 (Bankr. D. Mont. 1993); *In re* Foreman, 136 B.R. 532 (Bankr. S.D. Iowa 1992); *In re* Boggan, 125 B.R. 533 (Bankr. N.D. Ill. 1991); *In re* Freshley, 69 B.R. 96 (Bankr. N.D. Ga. 1987). *But see In re* Groves, 39 F.3d 212 (8th Cir. 1994) (plan could not discriminate in favor of student loans solely due to their nondischargeability); *In re* Bentley, 266 B.R. 229 (B.A.P. 1st Cir. 2001) (plan paying student loan in full and only three percent on other claims was unfairly discriminatory); *In re* Sperna, 173 B.R. 654 (B.A.P. 9th Cir. 1994); *In re* Willis, 197 B.R. 912 (N.D. Okla. 1996); McCullough v. Brown, 162 B.R. 506 (N.D. Ill. 1994); *In re* Scheiber, 129 B.R. 604 (Bankr. D. Minn. 1991); *In re* Furlow, 70 B.R. 973 (Bankr. E.D. Pa. 1987) (separate classification of student loan debt not allowed without further explanation of reasons).

181 Omnibus Budget Reconciliation Act of 1990, Pub. L. No. 101-508, 104 Stat. 1388 (1990). A similar argument could be made with respect to criminal restitution debts and drunk driving debts that are nondischargeable in chapter 13, in that they were made nondischargeable by amendments designed to give greater amounts of money to victims. Criminal Victims Protection Act of 1990, Pub. L. No. 101-581, 104 Stat. 2865 (1990); *see In re* Etheridge, 297 B.R. 810 (Bankr. M.D. Ala. 2003) (debtor permitted to separately classify bad check debt that was subject of criminal proceedings).

182 *In re* Freshley, 69 B.R. 96 (Bankr. N.D. Ga. 1987) (separate classification of student loan debt allowed so debtor could return to school).

183 *In re* Boggan, 125 B.R. 533 (Bankr. N.D. Ill. 1991); *see also* 8 Collier on Bankruptcy ¶ 1322.05[2] (15th ed. rev.). *But see In re* Groves, 39 F.3d 212 (8th Cir. 1994) (plan could not discriminate in favor of student loans solely due to their nondischargeability); *In re* Sperna, 173 B.R. 654 (B.A.P. 9th Cir. 1994) (same); *In re* Willis, 197 B.R. 912 (N.D. Okla. 1996); McCullough v. Brown, 162 B.R. 506 (N.D. Ill. 1994); *In re* Scheiber, 129 B.R. 604 (Bankr. D. Minn. 1991); *In re* Furlow, 70 B.R. 973 (Bankr. E.D. Pa. 1987) (separate classification of student loan debt not allowed without further explanation of reasons).

184 *See In re* Gay, 3 B.R. 336 (D. Colo. 1980); *In re* Fonnest, 5 Bankr. Ct. Dec. (LRP) 1236, 1 Collier Bankr. Cas. 2d (MB) 383 (N.D. Cal. 1980).

185 *In re* Sullivan, 195 B.R. 649 (Bankr. W.D. Tex. 1996); *In re* Cox, 186 B.R. 744 (Bankr. N.D. Fla. 1995); *In re* Benner, 156 B.R. 631 (Bankr. D. Minn. 1993). *But see In re* Labib-Kiyarash, 271 B.R. 189 (B.A.P. 9th Cir. 2001) (different treatment of long-term debt under § 1322 (b)(5) still subject to scrutiny for unfair discrimination); *In re* Coonce, 213 B.R. 344 (Bankr. S.D. Ill. 1997).

186 *See* § 12.9.2, *infra*.

187 *In re* Davis, 209 B.R. 893 (Bankr. N.D. Ill. 1997). Assumption of the executory contract or lease renders the amount necessary to cure a priority administrative expense, which clearly can be separately classified. *In re* Klein Sleep Products, Inc., 78 F.3d 18 (2d Cir. 1996); *see* 4 Collier on Bankruptcy ¶ 503.06[6][b] (15th ed. rev.).

188 *In re* Hill, 4 B.R. 694 (Bankr. D. Kan. 1980) (physicians, dentists, lawyers); *In re* Kovich, 4 B.R. 403 (Bankr. W.D. Mich.

If the debtor must discriminate among creditors to maintain the income necessary for the plan, such discrimination is likely to be allowed.[189] Such decisions have been justified by the fact that these debts were more likely to be paid in the non-bankruptcy world and that the plan or even the debtor's well-being might be endangered, without payment to such creditors, for example, if the only doctor in town refused treatment because of a discharged debt.[190] The sparse legislative history on the subject also seems to support a broad view of the debtor's right to classify claims,[191] as does the justification given by Congress for separate classification of cosigned debts.[192] However, some courts decide these issues differently.[193]

Classification may also be used to designate which portion of a claim for federal taxes a debtor wishes to pay. Generally, the debtor will wish to classify tax claims to make sure that priority and secured tax claims are paid prior to general unsecured tax claims. The Supreme Court has specifically held that a chapter 11 debtor may so designate the payments under its plan,[194] so a chapter 13 debtor whose payments are, if anything, more voluntary than those of a chapter 11 debtor, should certainly be able to designate which tax years are being provided for in the plan. Occasionally, a debtor may also wish to separately classify pre-petition tax penalty claims and seek to have them equitably subordinated to other unsecured claims if, for example, the debtor would prefer to see the general unsecured creditors get paid rather than the taxing authorities. Most courts have held that, at least in some cases, tax penalty claims can be equitably subordinated.[195]

Finally, some courts have gone behind the classifications of debts explicitly stated in plans to find different treatment which has been implicitly granted to certain unsecured claims. This has usually occurred where debts are partially secured. In such cases, the partially secured debt should be divided into a secured claim and an unsecured claim.[196] Thus, full payment of the partially secured claim would mean full payment of the unsecured portion as well as the secured portion. Where this has been proposed and where other unsecured creditors were not to be paid in full, confirmation of the plan has been denied.[197]

12.4.4 Payments Outside the Plan

Another type of provision that may be a classification is the designation of certain claims to be paid "outside the plan." What this means is that the debtor will make payments on these claims directly to the creditor, instead of through the trustee. Such provisions may offer a number of advantages. They usually save the debtor from paying the trustee's fees and costs, of up to ten percent, on such debts, a factor that may be important in cases where the payments on one debt, such as a home mortgage, are particularly large.[198] Payments outside the plan may also avoid the

---

1980) (landlord); *In re* Sutherland, 3 B.R. 420 (Bankr. W.D. Ark. 1980) (trade creditors, medical debts, banks); *see also* Connors, *Bankruptcy Reform: Relief for Individuals with Regular Income*, 13 U. Rich. L. Rev. 219, 237 (1978). Similar issues arise in chapter 11 cases, where courts often allow full payment of creditors essential to the debtor's business through "first day orders" under the "critical vendor doctrine."

189 *See In re* Gallipo, 282 B.R. 917 (Bankr. E.D. Wash. 2002) (debtor allowed to separately classify and pay traffic fines because non-payment would have jeopardized her ability to get to work).

190 For a discussion of the principles applied in such cases, see Charles F. Vihon, *Classification of Unsecured Claims; Squaring a Circle?*, 55 Am. Bankr. L. J. 143 (1980).

191 *See Bankruptcy Act Revision: Hearings on H.R. 31 and H.R. 32 Before the Subcomm. on Civil and Constitutional Rights of the House Comm. on the Judiciary*, 94th Cong. 1425, 1426 (1976) (statement of Claude L. Rice).

192 *See* § 12.4.2, *supra.*

193 *See, e.g., In re* Jones, 138 B.R. 536 (Bankr. S.D. Ohio 1991) (debtor could not give favored treatment to loan from his retirement fund); *In re* Harris, 62 B.R. 391 (Bankr. E.D. Mich. 1986) (denying confirmation to plan providing greater payment to consumer creditors than to business creditors).

194 United States v. Energy Res., Inc., 495 U.S. 545, 110 S. Ct. 2139, 109 L. Ed. 2d 580 (1990).

195 Burden v. United States, 917 F.2d 115 (3d Cir. 1990); *In re* Virtual Network Services Corp., 902 F.2d 1246 (7th Cir. 1990); Schultz Broadway Inn v. United States, 912 F.2d 230 (8th Cir.

1990). *But see* U.S. v. Noland, 517 U.S. 535, 116 S. Ct. 1524, 134 L. Ed. 2d 748 (1996) (tax penalties that are post-petition administrative expenses cannot be subordinated).

196 11 U.S.C. § 506(a). See Chapter 11, *supra,* for a discussion of this section.

197 *In re* Cooper, 3 B.R. 246 (Bankr. S.D. Cal. 1980); *In re* Tatum, 1 B.R. 445 (Bankr. S.D. Ohio 1979); *In re* Bevins, 1 B.R. 442 (Bankr. S.D. Ohio 1979). *But see In re* Delauder, 189 B.R. 639 (Bankr. E.D. Va. 1995) (permitting direct payment of auto loan pursuant to provisions for curing long term debt under § 1322(b)(5) even though creditor was under-secured; *cf. In re* Dingley, 189 B.R. 264 (Bankr. N.D.N.Y. 1995) (plan which proposes to pay a present value interest rate to a secured creditor under § 1325(a)(5) which exceeds the minimum required to confirm the plan found to inequitably reduce the dividend to unsecured creditors thus warranting denial of confirmation).

198 For this reason, trustees have sometimes objected to payments outside the plan. Normally, courts have dismissed these objections. *In re* Aberegg, 961 F.2d 1307 (7th Cir. 1992); *In re* Grear, 163 B.R. 524 (Bankr. S.D. Ill. 1994) (proceeds of collateral could be paid directly to secured creditor without payment of trustee's fee); *see In re* Bettger, 105 B.R. 607 (Bankr. D. Or. 1989) (proceeds of sale of real estate could be paid directly to creditors); *see also In re* Beard, 45 F.3d 113 (6th Cir. 1995) (no fee payable on direct payments to creditors under chapter 12 plan); *In re* Wagner, 36 F.3d 723 (8th Cir. 1994) (same); 8 Collier on Bankruptcy ¶ 1302.05[1][c] (15th ed. rev.). *But see In re* Fulkrod, 973 F.2d 801 (9th Cir. 1992) (chapter 12 debtor may not avoid trustee commission by making payments directly to impaired creditors); *In re* Foster, 670 F.2d 478 (5th Cir. 1982) (payments may be made outside the plan in some cases, but they are still subject to trustee's percentage fee; courts should consider lowering percentage to reflect trustee's lesser responsibilities in such circumstances. The argument that no trustee fee is required on payments made directly to creditors was strength-

delays sometimes encountered when payments are made through the trustee. In any case, to the extent that the plan provides a creditor with a greater benefit from having payments made outside the plan, that designation does constitute a classification subject to the unfair discrimination test.[199]

On the other hand, some trustees and practitioners prefer payment of the current mortgage payments through the trustee. Payments through the trustee may be more likely to be made, especially if they are made through a wage-deduction order. Moreover, the trustee is able to easily provide an accounting of the payments, eliminating most disputes about whether payments have been made and obviating the need to reconcile the debtor's often fragmentary records of canceled checks and money order receipts. Although such payments are subject to the trustee's fee, in districts where current mortgage payments are routinely made through the trustee, the percentage fee is often at a much lower rate because the trustee's receipts are far higher.

12.4.5 Practical Considerations

It is generally in the debtor's interest to classify some claims. Large secured claims may be paid outside the plan to avoid considerable trustee expenses. Also it is usually advantageous to pay other secured claims, where liens cannot be avoided, and claims not dischargeable in chapter 13 or chapter 7, before general unsecured claims. If this is done, then after the chapter 13 case, or if later circumstances force a conversion to chapter 7 or dismissal, the debtor may have paid off, or at least reduced, those claims which would be most troublesome in chapter 7 or outside of bankruptcy. In addition, the debtor usually wants to provide for early payment of priority claims at least before other unsecured claims. Once these are paid, if circumstances change, the debtor may choose to modify the plan to terminate earlier, assuming that the other mandatory requirements of chapter 13 have also been met by then. If priority claims have not yet been paid in full, such modification is not available; the options may be limited to a hardship discharge, conversion to chapter 7, or dismissal.[200]

In view of the courts' general hostility to special treatment for certain unsecured debts, the debtor may not be able to provide for such treatment in the plan. However, other alternatives that accomplish a similar result may be available. The debtor may be able to propose a plan that gives a low percentage payment to all unsecured creditors, and then make *voluntary* payments outside the plan to the preferred creditors. Because the plan would not provide for these payments, however, the debtor would not be bound to make them under section 1327(a). Nor could the debtor formally promise the creditor that the payments would be made without running afoul of the reaffirmation provisions in section 524.[201] A creditor who receives continued voluntary payments is not likely to deny services on the basis of a bankruptcy. Thus, as long as the payments are not provided for in the plan or binding upon the debtor, and the plan otherwise complies with chapter 13 (large voluntary payments might run afoul of the ability-to-pay test[202] if an objection is raised on that basis), there should be no impediment to giving preferred treatment voluntarily to particular creditors outside the plan.[203]

12.5 Feasibility of the Plan

In drafting a plan, a consumer debtor's counsel must also be aware of section 1325(a)(6). This subsection requires that "the debtor will be able to make all payments under the plan and to comply with the plan." If the plan does not meet this standard, sometimes called the "feasibility" test, confirmation may be denied.

Thus, the schedules' property and budget figures must show sufficient income or other financial resources to enable the debtor to make the payments proposed. If the debtor does not present such evidence as is necessary to convince the court that payments can be made, the plan may be found not feasible.[204] Similarly, if the plan calls for a very large lump sum payment at the end of the plan, with no reasonable explanation of how the debtor will fund it, the plan will be found not to meet the feasibility test.[205] The court may

---

ened by the 1986 amendments, replacing language in § 1302(e)(2) that the fee be collected from "all payments under plans" with language in 28 U.S.C. § 586(e)(2) that the fee shall be collected from all payments received by the trustee, so that the cases prohibiting direct payment may no longer be good law. A number of courts, including at least one court in the Fifth Circuit, have found that the 1986 amendments overrule *Foster* and provide authority for permitting payments directly to a creditor without deduction of the trustee's commission on those payments. *In re* Donald, 170 B.R. 579 (Bankr. S.D. Miss. 1994); *In re* Burkhart, 94 B.R. 724 (Bankr. N.D. Fla. 1988); *In re* Wright, 82 B.R. 422 (Bankr. W.D. Va. 1988).

199 *In re* Haag, 3 B.R. 649 (Bankr. D. Or. 1980); *In re* Iacovoni, 2 B.R. 256 (Bankr. D. Utah 1980).

200 See § 8.7.4, *supra*, for a discussion of these options.

201 See § 14.5.2, *infra*, for a discussion of reaffirmation.

202 *See* § 12.3.3, *supra*.

203 *See In re* Iacovoni, 2 B.R. 256 (Bankr. D. Utah 1980).

204 *In re* Epps, 6 Bankr. Ct. Dec. (LRP) 379, 2 Collier Bankr. Cas. 2d (MB) 97 (Bankr. S.D.N.Y. 1980); *In re* Nance, 4 B.R. 50 (Bankr. W.D. Mo. 1980).

205 *In re* Fantasia, 211 B.R. 420 (B.A.P. 1st Cir. 1997) (plan not feasible when debtors offered no evidence to show they could carry out intent of making large balloon payment by refinancing a parcel of property); *In re* Gavia, 24 B.R. 573 (B.A.P. 9th Cir. 1982) (plan based upon sale of residence, which was not likely, denied confirmation); *In re* Seem, 92 B.R. 134 (Bankr. E.D. Pa. 1988) (plan to sell real estate at end of plan period was too speculative to meet test); *In re* Schenck, 67 B.R. 137 (Bankr. D. Mont. 1986). However, a balloon payment at the end of a plan is not always found infeasible. *See In re* Gregory, 143 B.R. 424 (Bankr. E.D. Tex. 1992) (plan with large balloon payment at end

consider whether necessaries such as potential medical expenses and clothing have been provided for,[206] and whether there is sufficient "cushion" or "play" in the budget to cover unexpected expenses and inflation.[207] Finally, it may simply find the expense estimates to be unreasonably low.[208]

In view of the possibility of such scrutiny, it is important to note on the schedules of income and expenditures such facts as coverage of all medical expenses by medical assistance, receipt of food stamps and emergency fuel grants, and any other non-cash variations from a normal budget. Even with these, a "cushion" for unexpected expenses is virtually unheard of for low-income people. The best way of showing ability to make payments is to begin making the monthly payments before the confirmation hearing, as section 1326(a) requires. If a debtor has demonstrated an ability to pay the monthly amounts provided in the plan, then few courts will deny a debtor the opportunity to at least try to comply with the plan.[209]

All of these considerations dictate careful construction of a reasonable budget which, if possible, allows a small cushion over and above the required plan payments. As the court may also look to ability to pay if an objection is filed under section 1325(b), however, this cushion should not be overly large, lest the court decide the debtor could pay more into the plan. Ultimately, the debtor must steer a course between the Scylla and Charybdis of feasibility and ability to pay to create the optimum chance of confirmation. The feasibility ceiling on payments may not be far above the ability-to-pay floor.

12.6 Other Plan Provisions

12.6.1 Payment of Debtor's Income Directly to Trustee

Section 1325(c) provides that, after confirmation,[210] the court may order any entity from whom the debtor receives income to pay all or part of that income directly to the trustee. Such an order, known as a "wage order," is often sought by private attorneys representing debtors (with their clients' concurrence) to ensure that they receive their own fees, which are priority administrative expenses, and to maximize the chance that payments will be made. The court may sometimes view an application for a wage order as a sign of the debtor's seriousness, and thus it may help obtain confirmation. Indeed, in some courts they are almost a requirement.

Most courts require a separate application or motion to be filed in order to obtain a wage order.[211] Because it is a court order, the court can enforce compliance with the wage order by a recalcitrant employer, if necessary.[212]

Such orders may offer less attraction in legal services cases, because they reduce the debtor's flexibility in budgeting and possibly deviating slightly from the established payment schedule if necessary. Still, they should be explained and offered as an option to clients who have doubts as to their self-discipline in making payments.

Clients should also know that there is a possibility that the court will enter a wage order regardless of their wishes.[213] In some courts this possibility is more remote than others. Some trustees now routinely request wage orders by motion for all employed debtors. When a debtor does not want a wage order entered, (for example, if the debtor does not wish an employer to know about the bankruptcy) opposition to a wage order should be made known to the trustee or the court. This may require a response opposing the trustee's motion.

One issue which has arisen with respect to subsection 1325(c) is whether it overrides the non-assignability provisions of the Social Security Act and of other federal laws which prohibit assignment or attachment of benefits. Looking to legislative history, which clearly contemplates the filing of chapter 13 cases by recipients of such benefits,[214]

---

based on proposed sale of debtors' home was not too speculative); *In re* Groff, 131 B.R. 703 (Bankr. E.D. Wis. 1991) (balloon payment on mortgage at end of plan permitted).

206 *In re* Washington, 6 B.R. 226 (Bankr. E.D. Va. 1980); *In re* Hockaday, 3 B.R. 254 (Bankr. S.D. Cal. 1980).

207 *In re* Lilley, 29 B.R. 442 (B.A.P. 1st Cir. 1983); *In re* Washington, 6 B.R. 226 (Bankr. E.D. Va. 1980) ($44.93/mo. cushion insufficient); *In re* Coleman, 5 B.R. 812 (Bankr. W.D. Ky. 1980) ($4.00/mo. cushion insufficient); *In re* Hockaday, 3 B.R. 254 (Bankr. S.D. Cal. 1980) ($10.00/mo. cushion insufficient); *In re* Howard, 3 B.R. 75 (Bankr. S.D. Cal. 1980).

208 *In re* Lucas, 3 B.R. 252 (Bankr. S.D. Cal. 1980).

209 *See In re* Ryals, 5 B.R. 522 (Bankr. E.D. Tenn. 1980) (court reluctant to judge what sacrifices a debtor can make).

210 Despite the language of § 1325(c), most courts enter such orders before confirmation. *See In re* Torres, 191 B.R. 735 (Bankr. N.D. Ill. 1996) (court has authority under § 105(a) to enter pre-confirmation wage order).

211 *See* Forms 10, 11, Appx. G.3, *infra*.

212 *In re* Worrell, 113 B.R. 236 (Bankr. E.D. Va. 1990).

213 *See In re* Berry, 5 B.R. 515 (Bankr. S.D. Ohio 1980).

214 S. Rep. No. 95-989, at 24 (1978); H.R. Rep. No. 95-595, at 312 (1977); *see In re* Hammonds, 729 F.2d 1391 (11th Cir. 1984) (Aid to Families with Dependent Children benefits); Regan v. Ross, 691 F.2d 81 (2d Cir. 1982) (state employee pension benefits subjected to income deduction order despite state law's anti-assignment provisions and despite provisions of Internal Revenue Code and Treasury regulations); *In re* Simmons, 94 B.R. 74 (W.D. Pa. 1988) (state teachers retirement fund subjected to deduction order despite state statute prohibiting assignment of rights to benefits); *In re* Cochran, 141 B.R. 270 (Bankr. M.D. Ga. 1992) (Code modified Anti-Assignment Act to allow assignment of debtor's tax refunds to United States trustee through income deduction order); *In re* Sampson, 95 B.R. 66 (Bankr. W.D. Mich. 1988) (payroll order could be entered in case of enlisted serviceman despite federal statute prohibiting assignment of pay); *In re* Wood, 23 B.R. 552 (Bankr. E.D. Tenn. 1982) (pension benefits subject to order to pay directly to trustee despite Employee Retirement Income Security Act); *In re* Williams, 20 B.R. 154 (Bankr. E.D. Ark. 1982) (seaman's wages). Those cases which dealt with funds held in

courts generally found the Bankruptcy Code to repeal the earlier statutes implicitly to the extent of allowing such orders (despite the objection of the Social Security Administration).[215] However, Congress then amended the Social Security Act to state that such repeal by implication was not intended.[216] Since that amendment, courts have become more reluctant to find that Congress intended to repeal by implication the anti-assignment provisions of federal benefits statutes.[217] Courts have also refused to enter payment orders against retirement plans that are not property of the estate.[218] However, other benefits, including assignable public assistance payments, can be subject to such an order.[219]

Another issue that has occasionally arisen is the practice of a few employers to charge the debtor a fee for complying with the wage order.[220] Such a fee may be challenged as discrimination based upon bankruptcy that violates section 525,[221] especially if it is not charged in other similar situations, such as attachments for child support, or as a violation of the automatic stay to the extent it is a taking of property of the estate. Perhaps, the best way to prevent assessment of a fee is to include language in the form of wage order submitted to the court that prohibits the employer from charging the debtor a fee for complying with the order.

Of course, with respect to any wage order, it is important to remember that the debtor may dismiss a chapter 13 case at any time as a matter of right if the case has not been converted from another chapter.[222] Therefore, the debtor always retains the right to end the assignment of benefits or of any other income almost instantly.

12.6.2 Payment of Interest and Penalties

Normally, post-petition interest, late fees, and other charges are not considered to be part of a creditor's claim.[223] Carried over from case law under the prior Act[224] is the principle that such charges are in the nature of penalties that will not be enforced by the bankruptcy court, a court of equity. Not even priority claims, such as unsecured debts for taxes, are entitled to interest,[225] which can be a significant advantage of chapter 13 for a debtor who has large tax debts.

Under the Bankruptcy Code a few exceptions to this general rule exist. As discussed earlier in this chapter,[226] a debtor may have to pay interest to meet the "best interests of creditors" test if the debtor has a substantial amount of non-exempt property. In addition, section 1325(a)(5) may require payment of interest, possibly at the contract rate, to give secured creditors the present value of their allowed secured claims,[227] and section 1322(b)(5) may require some payment of interest to cure a default on a long-term debt.[228] Moreover, if a debt is nondischargeable in chapter 13 and post-petition interest on that debt must be paid, then the debtor may choose to propose that such interest be paid either in the plan or by direct payments to the creditor.[229]

Thus, in drafting a plan one must be aware of the several possibilities as to interest rates. Particular claims may be entitled to no interest (such as most unsecured claims), to interest at a rate necessary to meet a present value test,[230] or possibly to interest at the contract rate.

ERISA plans are probably no longer good law in light of the Supreme Court's decision in Patterson v. Shumate, 504 U.S. 753, 112 S. Ct. 2242, 119 L. Ed. 2d 519 (1992), which held that the anti-alienation provisions in such plans prevent them from becoming property of the bankruptcy estate.

215 United States v. Devall, 704 F.2d 1513 (11th Cir. 1983); Michigan Employment Sec. Comm'n v. Jenkins, 64 B.R. 195 (W.D. Mich. 1986).

216 Pub. L. No. 98-21, § 336, 97 Stat. 65 (1983); *see In re* Buren, 725 F.2d 1080 (6th Cir. 1984); H.R. Rep. No. 98-25, at 82 (1983).

217 *In re* Roach, 94 B.R. 440 (W.D. Mich. 1988) (veterans' benefits not subject to order that payments be made directly to trustee).

218 *See* McLean v. Cent. States Pension Funds, 762 F.2d 1204 (4th Cir. 1985); *In re* Watkins, 95 B.R. 483 (W.D. Mich. 1988) (debtor's interest in pension plan could not be subject to payment order); *In re* Snipe, 276 B.R. 723 (Bankr. D.D.C. 2002).

219 *But see In re* Knapp, 294 B.R. 334 (W.D. Wash. 2003) (order to Internal Revenue Service to pay tax refunds to trustee violated sovereign immunity).

220 *See, e.g.,* United States v. Santoro, 208 B.R. 645 (E.D. Va. 1997) (administrative fee charged by U.S. Postal Service was improper because § 1325(c) payroll deduction was not a garnishment on which fee could be charged pursuant to 5 U.S.C. § 5520(a)); *In re* Hudson, 216 B.R. 244 (Bankr. W.D. Tenn. 1997) (payments to chapter 13 trustee not a garnishment), *aff'd,* 230 B.R. 542 (W.D. Tenn. 1999). *But see In re* Heath, 115 F.3d 521 (7th Cir. 1997) (bankruptcy court did not have jurisdiction to consider challenge to $50.00 fee charged by U.S. Postal Service for complying with wage order).

221 *See* § 14.5.4, *infra.*

222 11 U.S.C. § 1307(b); *see* § 13.9.1, *infra.*

223 11 U.S.C. § 502(b)(2).

224 *See, e.g., In re* Jones, 2 B.R. 150 (Bankr. M.D. Tenn. 1980) (and cases cited therein); *see also In re* Clayborn, 11 B.R. 117 (Bankr. E.D. Tenn. 1981) (attorneys fees for filing a claim could not be included in unsecured claim).

225 *In re* Hieb, 88 B.R. 1019 (Bankr. D.S.D. 1988); *In re* Young, 61 B.R. 150 (Bankr. S.D. Ind. 1986); *In re* Christian, 25 B.R. 438 (Bankr. D.N.M. 1982); *see also In re* Kingsley, 86 B.R. 17 (Bankr. D. Conn. 1988) (post-petition tax claim which was a priority administrative expense could be paid without addition of interest).

226 *See* § 12.3.1, *supra.*

227 *See* § 11.6.1.3, *supra.* Over-secured creditors may also claim post-petition interest to the date of confirmation under § 506(b).

228 *See* § 11.6.2, *supra.*

229 The permissibility of such a provision may hinge on whether that debt may be separately classified and treated differently in the relevant jurisdiction. *See* § 12.4.3, *supra.*

230 See § 11.2.2.2, *supra,* for a discussion of present value under 11 U.S.C. §§ 1325(a)(4) and 1325(a)(5). An over-secured creditor may also be entitled to interest pursuant to 11 U.S.C. § 506(b). *See* § 11.6.1.3.3.4, *supra.* However, it should never be the case that present value interest and interest under § 506(b) are awarded for the same time period.

12.6.3 Length of Plan

Although it contains provisions that set maximum limits on the length of plans, chapter 13 contains no minimum time period. A plan may not exceed three years in length, unless the court specifically finds that there is good cause for a longer plan, in which case a plan of up to five years may be approved.[231] The procedure for obtaining such approval is not set forth specifically in the Federal Rules of Bankruptcy Procedure. Many courts require that a separate application and order be filed, although it may be possible to incorporate the approval into the plan confirmation process.[232]

Good cause for a longer plan may be that the debtor needs the additional time to meet the tests of sections 1325(a)(4) or 1325(a)(5), by paying the present value of non-exempt property or the collateral securing a debt.[233] It may also be that four or five years is the minimum reasonable time in which a debtor can cure a default under section 1322(b)(5) on a long-term debt.[234] However, the debtor's desire to pay more to unsecured creditors may not be sufficient cause,[235] especially because a debtor can continue to pay creditors voluntarily after the end of the plan, if the debtor chooses, without being bound to do so.

It is clear that plans that last less than three years may be confirmed as of right, as long as they comply with the other tests of chapter 13, including the "ability-to-pay" test.[236] A plan may last only eighteen months,[237] or it may consist of only one payment, liquidating property designated by the debtor, if unsecured creditors are paid in full or if no party objects.

12.6.4 Adjustments in Trustee's Charges

A possible alternative to making large payments outside the plan is to request an adjustment in the percentage charged by the trustee for expenses and compensation. The justification for this would be that with respect to such large payments, the commission would be unduly large in proportion to the expense and work involved.

At least one court has adopted this principle and limited the percentage commission to only part of the debtor's monthly payments. However, in that case,[238] the payments were $6000.00 per month, far higher than those likely in the typical consumer bankruptcy. The court's limitation provided that the nine percent commission could be charged against only the first $600.00 paid per month, again a figure higher than that paid in chapter 13 cases filed by most debtors. Similarly, another bankruptcy court has held that it had discretion to adjust fees despite the fact that the trustee was serving in a district subject to the United States Trustee program.[239] However, in most cases, payments outside the plan have proved to be an easier way to deal with the problem of large trustee fees.

Another possible adjustment which may be requested is a reduction in the normal minimum fee of five dollars per month set forth in section 330(c). This fee must be paid unless the court orders otherwise, and such an order is appropriate in cases where low-income debtors can only afford very modest plan payments.[240] It should be considered proper to include a provision adjusting the minimum payment in a chapter 13 plan; if so, the order of confirmation would constitute the order required by section 330(c) for an exception to the usual minimum fee.[241]

---

231 11 U.S.C. § 1322(d). It should be noted that although the plan must call for payments to be made within a period not to exceed five years, the five year limitation may run from the date the first payment under the plan becomes due following confirmation, rather than from the date of bankruptcy filing. *See* West v. Costen, 826 F.2d 1376 (4th Cir. 1987); *In re* Endicott, 157 B.R. 255 (W.D. Va. 1993); *In re* Serna, 193 B.R. 537 (Bankr. D. Ariz. 1996) (sixty months runs from due date of first payment after confirmation of plan); *see also In re* Aubain, 296 B.R. 624 (Bankr. E.D.N.Y. 2003) (reinstating dismissed case so debtor could complete plan after expiration of sixty months); *In re* Brown, 296 B.R. 20 (Bankr. N.D. Cal. 2003) (refusing to dismiss case when debtor needed some extra time beyond sixty months to complete plan); *In re* Harter, 279 B.R. 284 (Bankr. S.D. Cal. 2002) (debtor could complete plan within reasonable time after five-year plan's scheduled completion date); *In re* Black, 78 B.R. 840 (Bankr. S.D. Ohio 1987) (Bankruptcy Code contains no provision for dismissing a chapter 13 case because payments extend over 66 months, if the plan complied with the duration limitations of the Code at the time of confirmation); *In re* Eves, 67 B.R. 964 (Bankr. N.D. Ohio 1986) (modification which could have been effective before five years following first payment after plan confirmation was timely, even though proposed modification was filed more than five years after first plan payment was made). Thus, a court may allow a debtor who has become a few months delinquent in a five-year plan to complete the plan.

232 See Form 7, Appendix G.3, *infra*, a plan which contains a paragraph that confirmation shall be deemed a finding that good cause exists for a five-year plan.

233 See § 11.2.2.2, *supra*, for discussion of these tests.

234 *In re* Masterson, 147 B.R. 295 (Bankr. D.N.H. 1992); *In re* Fries, 68 B.R. 676 (Bankr. E.D. Pa. 1986). See § 11.6.2, *supra*, for a discussion of curing such defaults.

235 *In re* Festa, 65 B.R. 85 (Bankr. S.D. Ohio 1986).

---

236 *See* § 12.3.2, *supra*.

237 *In re* Markman, 5 B.R. 196 (Bankr. E.D.N.Y. 1980).

238 *In re* Eaton, 1 B.R. 433 (Bankr. M.D.N.C. 1979).

239 *In re* Melita, 91 B.R. 358 (Bankr. E.D. Pa. 1988). *But see In re* Schollett, 980 F.2d 639 (10th Cir. 1992) (court had no authority to adjust standing trustee's fees in U.S. trustee district); *In re* Savage, 67 B.R. 700 (D.R.I. 1986).

240 8 Collier on Bankruptcy ¶ 1302.05 (15th ed. rev.).

241 *Id.*

12.6.5 *Liquidation of Property in Chapter 13*

Occasionally, non-bankruptcy law may prevent a debtor from selling property to realize exempt equity or to pay creditors. This may occur, for example, if only one of two cotenants by the entirety wishes to sell property that can be conveyed only by both spouses under state law. Or it may be that a sale of real estate is impossible to complete in time to prevent an imminent foreclosure.

In such cases, a chapter 13 plan that provides for the liquidation of property is often a solution. Filing the petition will stay all proceedings against the property, allowing time for a sale.[242] The plan[243] may then provide for the method of sale and the distribution of the proceeds, as well as the trustee's use of the power to partition entireties property under 11 U.S.C. § 363(h), if necessary.[244]

When liens on the property can be avoided to create exempt equity, it is advisable to do so before the sale is completed.[245] In some cases use of the bankruptcy process will thereby help a debtor preserve an exemption which is unavailable under state law because an execution sale is a prerequisite to claiming the exemption.

If sale of real property is contemplated, it is advisable to obtain a specific order authorizing the sale free and clear of liens, in order to satisfy any title insurance company doubts. The order requested should specify the distribution of the proceeds, and set the compensation of any real estate broker. This can generally be accomplished by a motion seeking such an order, naming all lienholders and other affected parties as respondents.[246]

Under 11 U.S.C. § 1322(b)(8) it is clear that property may be liquidated in a chapter 13 plan.[247] It is less clear whether such a provision obviates the necessity to submit some income to the trustee as required by 11 U.S.C. § 1322(a)(1).[248] To be safe, the plan should provide for at least minimal payments in addition to the liquidation of property.[249] Even when a mortgage will be cured and satisfied by the sale of property, the court may still require maintenance of current payments until the sale takes place unless there is adequate protection in the form of equity in the property.[250] In any case, the sale of property through a chapter 13 plan is often a useful device, especially if an impending foreclosure threatens the loss of a large amount of equity built up over years of ownership.

12.6.6 *Refinancing a Property During a Chapter 13 Case*

In times of low mortgage interest rates, even a bankruptcy debtor may be able to refinance her mortgage at a lower rate than the existing mortgage. Generally, if a debtor can show a good payment history in a chapter 13 plan of at least a year's duration, the debtor will qualify for a mortgage refinancing at relatively reasonable rates. Such a refinancing may be preferable to continuing to make payments under the chapter 13 plan, especially if the refinancing would lower the debtor's monthly payments. For debtors who anticipate having trouble keeping up with payments, it may be the only way to salvage the benefits of chapter 13.

It is generally preferable to refinance a mortgage as part of a plan or a modified plan, rather than to dismiss the chapter 13 case before refinancing and lose the discharge of

---

242 See Chapter 9, *supra,* for discussion of the automatic stay.

243 For an example of such a plan, see Form 12 in Appendix G.2, *infra.*

244 The trustee is permitted, with limited exceptions, to partition entirety or joint property that a single cotenant may not partition under state law. 11 U.S.C. § 363(h); *see In re* Belyea, 253 B.R. 312 (Bankr. D.N.H. 1999) (debtor could partition jointly held property under § 363(h) as part of chapter 13 plan confirmation process); § 2.5, *supra.* Under section 363(h), the appropriate inquiry is whether the benefit to the estate accruing from sale of the property would outweigh the detriment to the co-owner occurring due to partition. Courts may apply a variety of factors in making such a determination. *Compare, e.g., In re* Ray, 73 B.R. 544 (Bankr. M.D. Ga. 1987) (partition refused) *with In re* Vassilowitch, 72 B.R. 803 (Bankr. D. Mass. 1987) (partition authorized). *See generally* Henry J. Sommer & Margaret Doe McGarity, Collier Family Law and the Bankruptcy Code ¶ 2.06[3].

245 *See* § 10.4, *supra.*

246 *See* Form 56, Appx. G.7, *infra.* If the court has not approved the broker's fee in advance, it may not permit the payment of the fee from estate assets pursuant to § 330(a). In some districts, it may be necessary to obtain an order appointing the broker as a professional person in the case pursuant to § 327(a). *See In re* Haley, 950 F.2d 588 (9th Cir. 1991) (refusing commission to broker who had not been given approval to act as broker for debtor's property in chapter 11 case). Probably, a chapter 13 debtor who retains a broker is not subject to the provisions

governing employment of professionals by the trustee. However, some courts may feel otherwise if estate assets are to be used to pay the broker.

247 *But see In re* Anderson, 18 B.R. 763 (Bankr. S.D. Ohio 1982) (plan not feasible where its success contingent on sale of realty in adverse market), *aff'd,* 28 B.R. 268 (S.D. Ohio 1982).

248 *Compare In re* Smith, 51 B.R. 273 (Bankr. D.D.C. 1984) (motion to dismiss denied where already confirmed plan funded solely from sale of property) *with In re* Anderson, 21 B.R. 443 (Bankr. N.D. Ga. 1981) (liquidation of residence of unemployed debtor did not provide regular income necessary for chapter 13 eligibility).

249 Such payments could also be required to meet the ability to pay test under 11 U.S.C. § 1325(b), the best interests of creditors test under 11 U.S.C. § 1325(a)(4), or to pay priority claims in full as required by 11 U.S.C. § 1322(a)(2). *See* §§ 12.3.3, 12.3.1, 12.3.5, *supra.*

250 *In re* Gavia, 24 B.R. 573 (B.A.P. 9th Cir. 1982); *cf. In re* Vanasen, 81 B.R. 59 (D. Or. 1987) (allowing debtors reasonable time to sell property did not violate prohibition against modification of mortgage claims in § 1322(b)(2)); *In re* McCann, 27 B.R. 678 (Bankr. S.D. Ohio 1982) (such payments unnecessary where mortgage had been accelerated). Equity in the property protects the creditor from loss on its claim due to delay in the event that the expected sale falls through. *See* § 9.7.3.2.2, *supra.*

debts, lien avoidance rights, and other rights under chapter 13. If a plan has already been in effect for over thirty-six months, there should be little opposition to a modification that allows the debtor to pay off the remaining plan payments through a refinancing.[251] If the plan has been in effect for less than thirty-six months, a trustee or unsecured creditor may oppose such a modification on the grounds that the debtor should continue monthly payments for the remainder of the thirty-six months. A debtor should be able to make a good argument against such opposition, because by refinancing the remaining payments, which had been based on the debtor's ability to pay, the debtor is still making those payments. In essence, the debtor is simply taking on a mortgage to borrow the money for those payments, and will be paying that money back to the new lender. Requiring additional plan payments would make the debtor pay the money twice.

Plan provisions for refinancing a mortgage should give some thought to the mechanics of the process. To avoid problems arising at the last minute from an excessive pay off demand on an existing mortgage, the plan may provide for the debtor to pay such a demand at the closing of the new loan, with continued jurisdiction in bankruptcy court to resolve the dispute thereafter. If possible, the plan should also provide that remaining mortgage arrears be paid at the closing of the new loan, rather than through the trustee, so that the prior mortgage can be completely paid off at closing; absent a complete pay off the existing mortgage holder may balk at providing a mortgage satisfaction, without which the new lender may not be willing to close the new loan. Such a provision would also avoid the trustee's percentage fee on the remaining arrearage claim, which is one reason why a trustee might oppose it.

12.7 Do the Section 1325(a) Standards Set Mandatory Requirements?

One question which the courts have begun to confront is whether the bankruptcy court has discretion to confirm a plan that does not meet all of the tests of section 1325(a). It is clear that if these tests are met, as well as the other requirements of chapter 13, the plan must be confirmed.[252] But what of the case where they are not?

Most courts and commentators in the first years of practice under the Code, especially those cited earlier in this chapter who found good faith to be mandatory, appear to have assumed that all of the section 1325(a) tests must be met before a plan can be confirmed. More recently, however, courts have recognized that they have discretion to confirm a plan without all of these standards being met.

The language of chapter 13 indicates that Congress did intend these tests to be discretionary rather than mandatory. Unlike section 1322(a), section 1325(a) does not state that "the plan shall" have certain provisions. It states only that if those tests are met then confirmation is mandatory. Unlike section 1325(b), section 1325(a) does not state that a court "may not approve the plan" if certain tests are not met. And unlike section 1129 of the Code governing chapter 11 plans, section 1325 does not state that a plan shall be confirmed "only if" the listed standards are met. In view of the obvious difference in the language of these closely related sections, it seems clear that Congress did intend a distinction between the tests of section 1322(a) and those of section 1325(a).

Such a distinction makes sense in view of the policies of chapter 13. Giving discretion to the court to approve plans of debtors who cannot meet the "best interests of creditors" test, for example, or who cannot pay the full amount of an allowed secured claim over the course of the plan, enhances the flexibility of chapter 13. The court still has the discretion to prevent abuses; if creditors do not object to the plan, it is difficult to see why the court should deny confirmation. And, in line with the broad rehabilitative policy of chapter 13, there seems little reason to exclude automatically from relief debtors doing their best under such circumstances.

The positions discussed above have been adopted by several courts, including the Third Circuit Court of Appeals. In *In re Szostek*,[253] that court agreed that the standards set forth in section 1325(a) are not mandatory and that a plan can be confirmed that does not meet those standards.[254] In the *Szostek* case, the plan did not provide present value interest to a secured creditor, but the plan was confirmed after the creditor failed to object to confirmation. Alternatively, the court held that the failure to object to confirmation could be deemed to be acceptance of the plan under section 1325(a)(5)(A).[255]

Given this interpretation of section 1325(a), there are a number of other possible plan provisions that may become advantageous to the debtor. As to allowed secured claims, it might be possible to pay only a portion of the claim over the course of the plan and the rest after the bankruptcy, with the holder of the claim retaining its lien. Or the plan may

---

251 An example of a plan including such provisions is included in Appendix G, *infra*.

252 Petro v. Mishler, 276 F.3d 375 (7th Cir. 2002) (plan must be confirmed if standards of § 1325(a) met and court may not set additional requirements).

253 886 F.2d 1405 (3d Cir. 1989).

254 *See also In re* Escobedo, 28 F.3d 34 (7th Cir. 1994) (distinguishing § 1322(a), which does set mandatory requirements); *In re* Brady, 86 B.R. 166 (Bankr. D. Minn. 1988). *But see In re* Barnes, 32 F.3d 405 (9th Cir. 1994) (provisions of § 1325(a)(5) are mandatory, and plan not paying present value of allowed secured claim could not be confirmed over creditor's objection).

255 *In re* Szostek, 886 F.2d 1405, 1413 (3d Cir. 1989); *In re* Ruti-Sweetwater, Inc., 836 F.2d 1263 (10th Cir. 1988) (chapter 11 case); *In re* Brown, 108 B.R. 738 (Bankr. C.D. Cal. 1989). See also *In re* Escobedo, 28 F.3d 34 (7th Cir. 1994) (distinguishing § 1322(a), which does set mandatory requirements).

provide that the property becomes vested in the debtor without lien retention by the claim holder, giving some other protection in lieu of the lien.[256] Finally, the plan could provide for payment of less than the amount required by the "best interests of creditors" test, perhaps by paying, over time, only the total amount that would be paid in a liquidation, without the additional interest necessary for the "present value" calculation which the test would require.

In most cases, probably little would be lost by proposing some of these provisions, if appropriate. It seems clear that if no objection is raised to such a provision and the plan is confirmed, the provision will be binding on all creditors, even if it is later found contrary to chapter 13, by virtue of the *res judicata* effect of plan confirmation.[257] If an objection is filed and confirmation is denied, a debtor is normally given the opportunity to modify the plan to meet the objection which has barred confirmation.

12.8 Use and Possession of Property of the Estate

One of the principal advantages of chapter 13 is that the debtor has the right to possession of all property of the estate, whether exempt[258] or non-exempt. Section 1306 specifically provides that "the debtor shall remain in possession of all property of the estate." Although this language speaks only of "remaining" in possession, it seems clear that the section also applies to property the estate acquires after commencement of the case, pursuant to sections 542 and 543[259] or the various avoiding powers. The entire thrust of this section and section 1303 is to transfer to the debtor virtually all of the powers and rights that the trustee would otherwise have with respect to property of the estate.[260]

For the same reason, debtors are free to use, sell, or lease property of the estate in the same manner as they ordinarily did prior to the case. Although a slight problem of drafting makes this less than crystal clear in the Code,[261] it has been universally assumed that this was the intent of the Congress.[262] There would, after all, be little point in the debtor retaining possession of property if it could not be used. And section 363(e), which is incorporated into chapter 13 by section 1303, only provides for prohibiting or conditioning such use, sale, or lease of property when an entity having an interest in the property does not have adequate protection. Moreover, notice and a hearing are only required under section 363(b), also incorporated into chapter 13, when use, sale, or leasing not in the ordinary course of business is proposed. Finally, to require a hearing before each debtor could use his or her property would impose a monumental and needless burden on the court, and that was obviously not intended by Congress.

As mentioned above, however, parties with interests in such property have a right to adequate protection if the property is used, as provided under section 363(e). "On request," the court may prohibit or condition the use of a home or a car, for example, by requiring fire or collision insurance to protect a secured party against damage resulting from use. Such issues are normally decided at a hearing, which might well occur in conjunction with a hearing on a party's request for relief from the automatic stay, relief to which it might also be entitled if adequate protection is not furnished.[263] In any case, the issues are similar to those in a hearing on relief from the stay, and the debtor must assume the trustee's burden of proof on the issue of adequate protection under section 363(e).

Once a chapter 13 plan is confirmed, property of the estate vests in the debtor unless the plan or order confirming the plan provides otherwise.[264] Some courts have held that this

---

256 *In re* Pence, 905 F.2d 1107 (7th Cir. 1990).

257 11 U.S.C. § 1327(a); *In re* Szostek, 886 F.2d 1405 (3d Cir. 1989); *see* § 12.11, *infra;* 8 Collier on Bankruptcy ¶ 1327.02[1] (15th ed. rev.). *But see In re* Escobedo, 28 F.3d 34 (7th Cir. 1994) (holding that confirmation of plan that did not satisfy mandatory requirements of § 1322(a) was a nullity). Since *Escobedo*, a court in the Seventh Circuit has held that confirmation of a plan that did not satisfy § 1322(a) could not be attacked after the debtor received a discharge. *In re* Puckett, 193 B.R. 842 (Bankr. N.D. Ill. 1996).

258 For a discussion of rights to possess exempt property in chapter 7 cases, see § 10.1.2, *supra.*

259 For discussion of sections 542 and 543 see § 9.9, *supra.*

260 Cable v. Ivy Tech State College, 200 F.3d 467 (7th Cir. 1999) (after conversion to chapter 13, chapter 7 trustee automatically dropped from discrimination case and debtor became real party in interest with standing to prosecute case on behalf of bankruptcy estate); Murray v. Bd. of Educ., 248 B.R. 484 (S.D.N.Y. 2000) (chapter 13 debtor had standing to bring Title VII action even though she inadvertently omitted it from schedules); *In re* James, 210 B.R. 276 (Bankr. S.D. Miss. 1997) (chapter 13 debtor has right to control whether a pre-petition lawsuit should be settled); *see* 8 Collier on Bankruptcy ¶ 1303.01 (15th ed. rev.).

261 None of the sections incorporated into chapter 13 by section 1303 specifically grants the non-business debtor the right to use property of the estate in the ordinary course of business as does § 363(c)(1) for business debtors incorporated by § 1304. Presumably this is only because non-business debtors could not use, sell or lease property in the course of a business.

262 *See* 8 Collier on Bankruptcy ¶ 1303.01 (15th ed. rev.). "The chapter 13 debtor is vested with the identical rights and powers conferred upon a liquidation trustee under section 363, relating to the use, sale, and lease of property of the estate." *Id.* (citing identical language in S. Rep. No. 95-989, at 140 (1978)).

263 See Chapter 9, *supra,* for discussion of adequate protection and relief from the automatic stay. However, adequate protection rights may be lost by a party if they are not protected in a confirmed plan to which that party does not object. *In re* Minzler, 158 B.R. 720 (Bankr. S.D. Ohio 1993) (creditor could not prevail on motion for relief from stay due to lack of adequate protection on leases allegedly misclassified as secured claims because creditor was bound by confirmed plan to which it had not objected).

264 11 U.S.C. § 1327(b); *In re* Chaparro Martinez, 293 B.R. 387 (Bankr. N.D. Tex. 2003) (after confirmation exempt personal injury cause of action vested in debtor and debtor did not need

causes the property to lose the protection of the provisions of the automatic stay which protect property of the estate.[265] However, other courts have adopted the better view that the property continues to retain the character of property of the estate, albeit vested in the debtor, after confirmation.[266] To avoid problems in this regard, it is often advisable to provide in a chapter 13 plan that property of the estate does not vest in the debtor until the closing of the case.[267]

12.9 Unexpired Leases and Executory Contracts

12.9.1 Definition of Executory Contract

Another important feature of chapter 13 is found in section 1322(b)(7). This section provides that the debtor has the power to assume or reject any executory contract or unexpired lease. This is a power which may be exercised only by the trustee in a chapter 7 case, where an executory contract or unexpired lease is automatically deemed rejected unless the trustee assumes it within sixty days after the case is commenced.[268] Indeed, a default or anticipated difficulties with respect to an executory contract or lease may be a prime reason for choosing chapter 13.[269]

The Code does not define exactly what it means by the term "executory contract," and whether a particular contract is executory is sometimes an important question. Generally speaking, an executory contract is one "on which performance remains due to some extent on both sides."[270] Perhaps the prototype of such a contract is the unexpired lease, which is of course specifically included.

A more specific definition adopted by some courts classifies a contract as executory if "the obligations of both parties are so far unperformed that the failure of either party to complete performance would constitute a material breach and thus excuse the performance of the other."[271] However, other definitions have looked mainly to whether the debtor has an obligation other than one to pay money for property and services already received before the bankruptcy. If so, the contract is executory.[272]

Under any of these definitions, there are several types of executory contracts into which consumer debtors routinely enter. They include purchase and sale agreements for real

---

court approval to settle case or pay their attorney from proceeds); *see* 8 Collier on Bankruptcy ¶¶ 1327.03, 1327.04 (15th ed. rev.).

265 *In re* Fisher, 203 B.R. 958 (N.D. Ill. 1997), *rev'g* 198 B.R. 721 (Bankr. N.D. Ill. 1996); *see* §§ 9.3, 9.4.2, 9.4.5, *supra*.

266 Sec. Nat'l Bank of Marshalltown, Iowa v. Neiman, 1 F.3d 687 (8th Cir. 1993); *In re* Kolenda, 212 B.R. 851 (W.D. Mich. 1997).

267 *In re* Clark, 207 B.R. 559 (Bankr. S.D. Ohio 1997) (Internal Revenue Service violated automatic stay by levying on post-petition wages, which under plan provision were property of the estate). See sample chapter 13 plans, Forms 8 and 14, Appendix G.3, *infra*.

268 11 U.S.C. § 365(d). Once assumption or rejection occurs in a chapter 7 case, the consequences are basically the same as in a chapter 13 proceeding.

269 Although all leases of a debtor are usually deemed rejected by operation of law in chapter 7 cases, this usually has little practical effect. Most lessors are unaware that the bankruptcy has any effect on a lease where payments are current and, because they usually have no special desire to evict a rent-paying tenant, they continue to treat the lease as still in effect. However, a landlord may attempt to evict a tenant based upon the trustee's deemed rejection. In such cases, the debtor should be able to successfully argue that the trustee's rejection did not involve the debtor's interest except insofar as the trustee, by rejection, abandoned the leasehold interest back to the debtor. Rejection is not equivalent to the termination of a lease. *In re* Ranch House of Orange-Brevard, Inc., 773 F.2d 1166 (11th Cir. 1985); *In re* T.F.P. Res., Inc., 56 B.R. 112 (Bankr. S.D.N.Y. 1985); *In re* Storage Tech. Corp., 53 B.R. 471 (Bankr. D. Colo. 1985) (rejection is a breach of lease that may be waived, not a termination of lease). Several courts have adopted this interpretation to avoid a harsh result after an automatic chapter 7 rejection. *In re* Reed, 94 B.R. 48 (E.D. Pa. 1988) (rejection

results in abandonment of lease to debtor); *In re* Rodall, 165 B.R. 506 (Bankr. M.D. Fla. 1994) (same); *see also In re* Austin Dev. Co., 19 F.3d 1077 (5th Cir. 1994) (rejection of lease does not terminate lease with respect to parties that have not rejected it nor affect their rights); *In re* Szymecki, 87 B.R. 14 (W.D. Pa. 1988) (automatically rejected public housing lease is abandoned to debtor); *In re* Knight, 8 B.R. 925 (Bankr. D. Md. 1981); Dime Sav. Bank of N.Y. v. Pesce, 217 A.D. 299, 636 N.Y.S.2d 747 (1995). And the 1984 amendments to the Code support this interpretation. While they require a non-residential tenant to vacate a property if a lease is not assumed, 11 U.S.C. § 365(d)(4), they contain no such requirement for a residential tenant. In addition, if a landlord accepts rental payments after the expiration of the sixty-day period, the debtor may argue that any rejection of the lease has been waived. Another alternative might be for the debtor to convert to chapter 13 or begin a new chapter 13 case to assume the lease. *See In re* Sims, 213 B.R. 641 (Bankr. W.D. Pa. 1997) (chapter 13 debtor could assume lease that had been automatically rejected in prior chapter 7 case, because lease continued to exist after rejection). In a rare case, a chapter 7 trustee may seek to assume a residential lease with significant value. *See In re* Toledano, 299 B.R. 284 (Bankr. S.D.N.Y. 2003) (trustee permitted to assume and assign, for $150,000.00, debtor's rights in rent stabilized lease for Manhattan luxury apartment).

270 H.R. Rep. No. 95-595, at 347 (1977).

271 *In re* Texscan Corp., 976 F.2d 1269 (9th Cir. 1992) (insurance contract was not executory where failure of debtor to pay premiums would not relieve insurer of obligation to perform); *In re* Wegner, 839 F.2d 533, 536 (9th Cir. 1988); Jensen v. Cont'l Corp., 591 F.2d 477 (8th Cir. 1979); *In re* Columbia Gas Sys., Inc., 146 B.R. 106 (D. Del. 1992) (class action consent decree was not executory contract because failure of either to complete performance of obligations would not excuse performance of the other), *aff'd*, 50 F.3d 233 (3d Cir. 1995); Vern Countryman, *Executory Contracts in Bankruptcy*, 57 Minn. L. Rev. 439, 460 (1973). For one criticism of this definition see Mitchell R. Julis, *Classifying Rights and Interests Under the Bankruptcy Code*, 55 Am. Bankr. L. J. 233, 252–259 (1981).

272 *See* Shanker, *The Treatment of Executory Contracts and Leases in the 1978 Bankruptcy Code*, 25 Prac. Law. (No. 7) 11, 26. (1979).

estate,[273] options for the sale of real estate or other property,[274] most automobile leases,[275] layaway contracts,[276] contingent fee contracts with attorneys,[277] insurance contracts,[278] personal services contracts,[279] installment payment contracts for cemetery plots, book clubs, magazine subscriptions, health clubs, appliance or motor vehicle service contracts that are paid for in installments, and (if they are not considered credit sales) rent-to-own contracts.[280]

The Seventh Circuit Court of Appeals has held that an employee's agreement to participate in an Employee Stock Ownership Plan (ESOP) is not an executory contract which could be rejected to avoid the wage reduction involved while at the same time maintaining the employment that was a part of the contract.[281] And, there is considerable dispute regarding whether a covenant not to compete may be rejected as an executory contract.[282] The Third Circuit Court

of Appeals has held that a personal services contract, which could contain such a covenant, may be rejected.[283] And one court has held that a postnuptial agreement is an executory contract, at least if the parties are not yet divorced.[284]

Another type of contract that might present problems under this section is the land installment sales agreement, in which a debtor pays for property in installments, receiving a deed only when most or all of the payments have been made to the seller. A number of courts have held such arrangements to be executory contracts, and have required debtors wishing to maintain them to cure defaults promptly.[285] However, whether this must always be so may depend on the nature of the agreement and the applicable state law. In some places, retention of the deed may be functionally equivalent to taking a security interest,[286] placing the transaction within the ambit of secured claims covered by sections 1322(b)(2), (b)(5) and 1325(a)(5) rather than section 365. Such a situation would be more analogous to a creditor holding the title to an automobile as security, an arrangement which seems clearly outside the scope of the executory contract provisions.[287]

12.9.2 Assumption of a Lease or Executory Contract

In many cases, a debtor will have much to gain from assumption of an executory contract or unexpired lease. For example, if moving would cause a hardship, or if a residential lease has favorable terms, it is usually advantageous to keep it in effect. This may be particularly true in a rent control jurisdiction[288] or in public housing, as the debtor's

---

273 Such contracts remain executory and may be rejected even after one party has tendered performance. *In re* Alexander, 670 F.2d 885 (9th Cir. 1982). But courts may refuse to allow rejection of a purchase and sale agreement if they find that this was the sole purpose of the bankruptcy filing. *In re* Waldron, 785 F.2d 936 (11th Cir. 1986); *In re* Chinichian, 784 F.2d 1440 (9th Cir. 1986). *But see In re* W & L Associates, Inc., 71 B.R. 962 (Bankr. E.D. Pa. 1987).

274 *In re* Robert L. Helms Constr. & Dev. Co., 139 F.3d 702 (9th Cir. 1998) (*en banc*); *In re* Hardie, 100 B.R. 284 (Bankr. E.D.N.C. 1989).

275 *In re* Wallace, 122 B.R. 222 (Bankr. D.N.J. 1990). It is often difficult to tell whether an automobile transaction is a sale or a lease. It is usually to the debtor's advantage if the transaction is deemed a credit sale. *See In re* Mandrell, 246 B.R. 528 (Bankr. D.S.C. 1999) (applying "economic test" of whether debtor acquired substantial equity in vehicle, determining that transaction was not a lease); *In re* Crummie, 194 B.R. 230 (Bankr. N.D. Cal. 1996) (GM "SmartBuy" contract deemed credit sale, not lease); *In re* Lewis, 185 B.R. 66 (Bankr. N.D. Cal. 1995) (General Motors "SmartBuy" contract was a credit sale, not a lease). For a discussion of the distinctions between auto leases and credit sales for purposes of coverage of the Truth in Lending Act and the Consumer Leasing Act, see National Consumer Law Center, Truth in Lending § 10.2.3 (5th ed. 2003).

276 *In re* Davies, 27 B.R. 898 (Bankr. E.D.N.Y. 1983).

277 *In re* Aesthetic Specialities, Inc., 37 B.R. 679 (B.A.P. 9th Cir. 1984); *In re* Ashley, 41 B.R. 67 (Bankr. E.D. Mich. 1984).

278 *In re* Garnas, 38 B.R. 221 (Bankr. D.N.D. 1984).

279 *In re* Allain, 59 B.R. 107 (Bankr. W.D. La. 1986) (non-competition clause as well as remainder of dentist's contract for joint practice was rejected); *see also* Turner v. Avery, 947 F.2d 772 (5th Cir. 1991) (chapter 7 trustee could not assume debtor attorney contingent fee contracts with clients because under § 365(c)(1)(A) the trustee may not assume contract if other party has right to decline performance from substitute for original contracting party under state law; however, trustee was entitled to fees earned prior to filing of bankruptcy petition as property of the estate). *But see In re* Carrere, 64 B.R. 156 (Bankr. C.D. Cal. 1986) (television actress did not have right to reject personal services contract in chapter 11 case).

280 *See* § 11.8, *supra*.

281 *In re* Crippin, 877 F.2d 594 (7th Cir. 1989).

282 *Compare In re* Register, 95 B.R. 73 (Bankr. M.D. Tenn. 1989), *aff'd*, 100 F.3d 360 (M.D. Tenn. 1989) *and In re* Allain, 59 B.R.

107 (Bankr. W.D. La. 1986) (non-competition clause as well as remainder of dentist's contract for joint practice was rejected) *with In re* Don & Lin Trucking Co., 110 B.R. 562 (Bankr. N.D. Ala. 1990).

283 *In re* Taylor, 913 F.2d 102 (3d Cir. 1990). *But see In re* Udell, 18 F.3d 403 (7th Cir. 1994) (granting relief from the automatic stay to enforce injunction obtained under covenant not to compete because equitable claim for injunction, which could be obtained under state law in addition to damages, was not a "claim" as defined in 11 U.S.C. § 101(5)(B)).

284 *In re* Lawson, 146 B.R. 663 (Bankr. E.D. Va. 1992).

285 *In re* Terrell, 892 F.2d 469 (6th Cir. 1989); *In re* Streets & Beard Farm P'ship, 882 F.2d 233 (7th Cir. 1989); *In re* Speck, 798 F.2d 279 (8th Cir. 1986); *In re* Rose, 7 B.R. 911 (Bankr. S.D. Tex. 1981); *In re* Vertich, 5 B.R. 684 (Bankr. D.S.D. 1980).

286 *In re* Kane, 248 B.R. 216 (B.A.P. 1st Cir. 2000) (installment land sales contract not an executory contract), *aff'd*, 254 F.3d 325 (1st Cir. 2001); *In re* Rehbein, 60 B.R. 436 (B.A.P. 9th Cir. 1986); *see In re* Climer, 10 B.R. 872 (W.D. Tenn. 1977); *In re* Johnson, 75 B.R. 927 (Bankr. N.D. Ohio 1987); *In re* Adolphson, 38 B.R. 776 (Bankr. D. Minn.), *aff'd*, 38 B.R. 780 (D. Minn. 1983); *In re* Cox, 28 B.R. 588 (Bankr. D. Idaho 1983); *In re* Booth, 19 B.R. 53 (Bankr. D. Utah 1982).

287 Heartline Farms, Inc. v. Daly, 934 F.2d 985 (8th Cir. 1991); *In re* Rojas, 10 B.R. 353 (B.A.P. 9th Cir. 1981).

288 *See In re* Yasin, 179 B.R. 43 (Bankr. S.D.N.Y. 1995) (rent

occupancy may not otherwise be terminable even at the end of the lease term. (Staying beyond the term otherwise allowable may also be possible due to the operation of the automatic stay during the course of the plan.)[289]

The approval of the court is required for the debtor to assume an executory contract or lease.[290] The debtor must be willing to assume the burdens as well as the benefits of the contract; a debtor may not assume only its favorable aspects.[291] Once a lease is assumed, the rent due becomes a priority administrative expense, even if the debtor later decides to reject the lease.[292] Therefore, there should be no problem in separately classifying any pre-petition rent due and paying it before other debts.[293]

To assume a lease or executory contract, the debtor must be willing and able to cure any default promptly or must provide adequate assurance that the default will be promptly

cured.[294] If there has been a default, the debtor must also compensate the other party for any actual pecuniary loss resulting from the default, as well as provide adequate assurance of future performance under the contract or lease.[295] Such assurance is not required if no default exists.[296] It also may not be necessary if the default is a non-monetary default, especially if it is not curable after the bankruptcy case is filed.[297]

These requirements raise other issues. How promptly must the default be cured?[298] What is meant by adequate assurance?[299] "Promptness" will no doubt depend upon all of the circumstances of the individual case, including the amount in default, term of the contract or lease, and relative needs of the contracting parties. The phrase "adequate assurance" was adopted by the Commission on Bankruptcy Laws from the Uniform Commercial Code, section 2-609. According to the comment to that section and case law thereunder this might consist of a cosigner, or a deposit, or even a simple showing of cash flow or credit sufficient to perform under the contract.[300]

There may also be a dispute regarding whether, in fact, a default exists on the part of the debtor.[301] If it does not, no cure or adequate assurance is required by section 365(b). Naturally, such issues, whether relating to claims on consumer contracts or rights under implied warranties of habitability in residential leases, may be litigated in the bankruptcy court. However, disputes about the contract's validity or breach of the contract need not be resolved in determining whether the contract may be assumed, and may instead be

---

stabilized lease could be assumed by chapter 13 debtor, preserving right of renewal; even if lease is rejected it may be possible for tenant to renew lease).

289 See discussion of leases in Chapter 9, *supra*. For an example of a plan assuming a lease, see Form 14, Appendix G.3, *infra*.

290 *In re* Harris Mgmt. Co., 791 F.2d 1412 (9th Cir. 1986); *In re* Whitcomb & Keller Mortgage Co., 715 F.2d 375 (7th Cir. 1983). Although a formal motion under Fed. R. Bankr. P. 6006 to assume an executory contract may be better practice, it has been held that confirmation of a chapter 13 plan containing a provision for assumption of a lease constitutes court approval as required by 11 U.S.C. § 365(a). Dep't of Air Force v. Carolina Parachute Corp., 907 F.2d 1469 (4th Cir. 1990) (chapter 11 case); *In re* Hall, 202 B.R. 929 (Bankr. W.D. Tenn. 1996); *In re* Flugel, 197 B.R. 92 (Bankr. S.D. Cal. 1996); *In re* Aneiro, 72 B.R. 424 (Bankr. S.D. Cal. 1987). *But see* Sea Harvest Corp. v. Riviera Land Co., 868 F.2d 1077 (9th Cir. 1989) (nonresidential real property lease deemed rejected in chapter 11 case when not assumed by motion within applicable time limits). The *Sea Harvest* case may not be relevant to residential leases and executory contracts not involving real property, because there are normally no time limits for assumption, except when the court has set one pursuant to 11 U.S.C. § 365(d)(2). Federal Rule of Bankruptcy Procedure 6006 specifically applies to proceedings to assume *other than as part of a plan*.

291 Dep't of Air Force v. Carolina Parachute Corp., 907 F.2d 1469 (4th Cir. 1990); *see also In re* Pittman, 289 B.R. 448 (Bankr. M.D. Fla. 2003) (chapter 13 plan may not modify term in auto lease requiring lump sum payment of purchase option).

292 *In re* Klein Sleep Products, Inc., 78 F.3d 18 (2d Cir. 1996); *In re* Masek, 301 B.R. 336 (Bankr. D. Neb. 2003) (because debtors had assumed automobile lease, balance of amount due on lease was administrative expense even though car had been repossessed; *In re* Wright, 256 B.R. 858 (Bankr. W.D.N.C. 2001) (rejection damages were priority claim when debtor first assumed lease under confirmed chapter 13 plan and later modified plan to reject lease); *cf. In re* Badgley, 308 B.R. 293 (Bankr. E.D. Mich. 2004) (automobile lessor not entitled to administrative claim for post-petition lease payments once debtors amended plan prior to confirmation to provide for lease rejection, even though debtors' initial plan provided for lease assumption); *In re* Scott, 209 B.R. 777 (Bankr. S.D. Ga. 1997) (when no plan had been confirmed and court had not otherwise approved lease assumption, post-petition rent was not administrative expense).

293 *In re* Davis, 209 B.R. 893 (Bankr. N.D. Ill. 1997).

294 11 U.S.C. § 365(b)(1). However, a debtor need not pay a lease penalty for failure to perform non-monetary obligations under the lease in order to cure. 11 U.S.C. § 365(b)(2)(D); *see In re* Parker, 269 B.R. 522 (D. Vt. 2001) (cure requires payment only of amounts for which debtor, liable under non-bankruptcy law and in particular case, did not include attorney fees or repair and utility charges).

295 11 U.S.C. § 365(b)(1).

296 *In re* Perretta, 7 B.R. 103 (Bankr. N.D. Ill. 1980).

297 11 U.S.C. § 365(b)(2)(D); *see In re* Claremont Acquisition Corp., 186 B.R. 977 (Bankr. C.D. Cal. 1995) (automobile dealership permitted to assume franchise agreement despite having violated agreement by being closed for seven consecutive days), *aff'd*, 113 F.3d 1029 (9th Cir. 1997).

298 *See In re* Reed, 226 B.R. 1 (Bankr. W.D. Ky. 1998) (under circumstances of case, cure within six months was required on car lease); *In re* Yokley, 99 B.R. 394 (Bankr. M.D. Tenn. 1989) (two years too long under circumstances of case); *In re* Coors of N. Miss., 27 B.R. 918 (Bankr. N.D. Miss. 1983) (three years may be prompt depending upon circumstances).

299 These issues may be particularly troubling in cases of nonmonetary defaults. *See, e.g., In re* Yardley, 77 B.R. 643 (Bankr. M.D. Tenn. 1987) (default arising from tenant debtor's altercation with a security guard at his apartment complex).

300 *See* Don Fogel, *Executory Contracts and Unexpired Leases in the Bankruptcy Code*, 64 Minn. L. Rev. 341, 356–358 (1980).

301 *See, e.g., In re* Perretta, 7 B.R. 103 (Bankr. N.D. Ill. 1980) (lessor has waived right to prompt payment by accepting late payments, so late payment not a default).

resolved after the assumption.[302] Once the contract has been assumed, the rights of the parties may be determined under the law that would ordinarily be applicable, absent contrary provisions in the Bankruptcy Code.[303]

Finally, the non-debtor party to the lease or contract may argue that it cannot be assumed because it was validly terminated prior to the bankruptcy.[304] This issue is particularly likely to arise in a case when the bankruptcy petition has been filed on the eve of an eviction. A number of courts and authorities have held that this argument is correct, finding that there is no contract or lease to assume.[305]

The debtor seeking to assume has a number of strong counterarguments available, however. There may be questions as to whether the contract was validly terminated under state law,[306] or whether the debtor has a right to cure the default still available.[307] Section 108(b) of the Code may have extended such a cure period automatically to 60 days after the case was filed,[308] or the court may hold that the debtor has the right to cure under section 1322(b)(3).[309] At least one court has held that the effect on the automatic stay

is to "erase" a judgment for possession which would otherwise terminate a lease, returning the lease to viability.[310]

The debtor may also be able to argue that the contract was ended due to a nonpayment resulting from the debtor's insolvency. If the contract was ended pursuant to provisions of applicable law which allowed termination because of nonpayment, and that nonpayment was caused by the insolvency or financial condition of the debtor, it may be argued that the contract was, in fact, conditioned upon the insolvency or financial condition of the debtor. If it is, the termination is invalid under 11 U.S.C. § 365(e).[311]

In addition, section 365(c)(3) specifically prohibits assumption of a terminated lease only if the lease is for nonresidential real property. By implication, a residential lease may be assumed despite its prior termination. Similarly, although section 362(b)(10) provides an exception to the automatic stay as to nonresidential property under a lease which has expired before the case, there is no such exception for residential real property.[312] These distinctions were obviously not accidental. Congress intended to provide protection to consumer debtors against evictions when those evictions are based simply on tenants' pre-petition lease defaults or on tenants' bankruptcy filings.

12.9.3 Rejection of Leases or Executory Contracts

12.9.3.1 Overview

Problems are less likely to arise when the debtor chooses to reject an executory contract. This choice may be advantageous in a variety of situations, as many of the types of executory contracts listed above are unfair and burdensome to consumers. As discussed above,[313] it may also be possible to reject contracts imposing restrictions on the debtor, such as a covenant not to compete with a former employer or business in which the debtor was involved. Like assumption, rejection can be accomplished by a provision in a confirmed chapter 13 plan or by a separate motion.[314]

---

302 *In re* Orion Pictures Corp., 4 F.3d 1095 (2d Cir. 1993).

303 Wainer v. A.J. Equities, 984 F.2d 679 (5th Cir. 1993).

304 The automatic stay prevents the non-debtor party to a contract from acting to terminate the contract post-petition. *See In re* Computer Communications, Inc., 824 F.2d 725 (9th Cir. 1987).

305 *See, e.g.*, Robinson v. Chicago Hous. Auth., 54 F.3d 316 (7th Cir. 1995); *In re* Hospitality Associates, 6 B.R. 778 (Bankr. D. Or. 1980).

306 *See, e.g., In re* Dash, 267 B.R. 915 (Bankr. D.N.J. 2001) (lease had not been terminated when lessor had repossessed vehicle but had not notified debtor that lease was terminated); *In re* Gant, 202 B.R. 952 (Bankr. N.D. Ill. 1996) (lease not terminated because landlord's acceptance of rent check waived right to forfeiture of lease); *In re* Bronx-Westchester Mack Corp., 4 B.R. 730 (Bankr. S.D.N.Y. 1980).

307 *In re* Stolz, 197 F.3d 625 (2d Cir. 1999) (lease may be assumed even after judgment in state court eviction action based on tenant's possessory interest and unexpired right to cure under state law); Robinson v. Chicago Hous. Auth., 54 F.3d 316 (7th Cir. 1995) (tenant has right to assume terminated lease as long as tenant has any way to revive lease under state law); *In re* Windmill Farms, Inc., 841 F.2d 1467 (9th Cir. 1988) (lease may be assumed, even if it has been terminated, if state law gives lessee a right to prevent forfeiture); Moody v. Amoco Oil Co., 734 F.2d 1200 (7th Cir. 1984); Ross v. Metro. Dade County, 142 B.R. 1013 (S.D. Fla. 1992) (debtor could assume public housing lease because state anti-forfeiture doctrine gave right to prevent eviction through cure of default), *aff'd*, 987 F.2d 774 (11th Cir. 1993); *In re* Mims, 195 B.R. 472 (Bankr. W.D. Okla. 1996) (execution of writ of assistance is step in eviction process that terminates Oklahoma debtor's right to assume lease); *In re* Shannon, 54 B.R. 219 (Bankr. M.D. Tenn. 1985); *In re* Easthampton Sand & Gravel Co., 25 B.R. 193 (Bankr. E.D.N.Y. 1982); *see also In re* Di Giorgio, 200 B.R. 664 (C.D. Cal. 1996) (California statute permitting eviction after filing of bankruptcy found invalid), *vacated as moot*, 134 F.3d 971 (9th Cir. 1998).

308 *But see* Moody v. Amoco Oil Co., 734 F.2d 1200 (7th Cir. 1984).

309 Most of the cases considering section 365 have been under chapter 11, which has no comparable provision.

310 *In re* Mulkey of Mo., Inc., 5 B.R. 15 (Bankr. W.D. Mo. 1980) (denying relief from the stay because adequate protection provided and property necessary for reorganization).

311 *See In re* Computer Communications, Inc., 824 F.2d 725 (9th Cir. 1987); *see also* Shanker, *The Treatment of Executory Contracts and Leases in the 1978 Bankruptcy Code*, 25 Prac. Law. (No. 7) 11, 17, 18. (1979).

312 *In re* Reinhardt, 209 B.R. 183 (Bankr. S.D.N.Y. 1997) (debtor's possessory interest in residential lease protected by automatic stay as section 362(b)(10) exception does not apply).

313 *See* § 12.9.1, *supra*.

314 *In re* Milstead, 197 B.R. 33 (Bankr. E.D. Va. 1996) (rejection occurred upon confirmation of chapter 13 plan providing for rejection).

The effect of rejection is to give the other contracting party a damage claim.[315] The rejection is deemed a breach of the contract as of the time immediately prior to the filing of the bankruptcy petition.[316] As with any claim, the debtor may object to the amount claimed.[317] If the contract is secured, however, and is to be provided for in the plan, the plan may have to provide for the claim to be paid consistent with the chapter 13 standards for secured claims in order to obtain confirmation.[318]

12.9.3.2 Residential Leases

The rejection of a residential lease is advantageous to a debtor mainly when the debtor plans to move or has vacated the premises prior to the end of the lease term. The unpaid rent from the period prior to the bankruptcy usually becomes a general unsecured claim,[319] which is often paid little or nothing during the case. And the lessor's potential claim for lost rents is limited to one year's rent or fifteen percent of the rent due for the remaining term of the lease, whichever is more.[320]

However, payment for the period after the case is filed is treated somewhat differently. During the time between filing of the case and the debtor's rejection (and also after rejection, if the debtor stays on), the lessor may be entitled to receive from the estate the reasonable rental value of the property, often known as "use and occupancy payments."[321]

The rent agreed upon previously is usually deemed to be the fair value,[322] but the court may be persuaded to set the value at a higher or lower level.[323] If the rent provided for in the lease is greater than the fair value of the premises, it may thus be to the debtor's advantage to reject the lease (or simply not assume it) but remain in occupancy paying rent, if the lessor agrees[324] or the court allows the automatic stay to remain in effect.[325] In any case, once requested and allowed by the court, the use and occupancy expense will probably be considered an administrative expense, as a cost and expense of preserving the estate under 11 U.S.C. § 503(b)(1)(A).[326] Thus, in a chapter 13 case, it must be paid in full if filed as a priority claim, unless the case is dismissed, converted, or ended by a hardship discharge.[327]

In a both chapter 13 and chapter 7, because the claim for damages arising from rejection of the lease, including damages relating to post-petition use, is considered a pre-petition claim under section 502(g), that claim is normally dischargeable.[328] Therefore, if the debtor does not wish to continue payments to maintain possession of the property, the lessor cannot sue the debtor after a bankruptcy case for damages arising from post-petition use of the property.[329]

---

315 11 U.S.C. § 502(g). This result applies even if the non-debtor party to the contract might have had a right to specific performance in a non-bankruptcy forum. *See In re* Aslan, 65 B.R. 826 (Bankr. C.D. Cal. 1986). Also, the parties to the lease or contract are not relieved of other duties which are imposed upon them by law, such as statutes or regulations governing landlord-tenant relations. Saravia v. 1736 18th Street, N.W. Ltd. P'ship, 844 F.2d 823 (D.C. Cir. 1988). As rejection constitutes a breach by the estate, the consequences of the breach depend on state law. *See* Bargain Mart v. Lipkis, 212 Conn. 120, 561 A.2d 1365 (1989).

316 *In re* Miller, 282 F.3d 874 (6th Cir. 2002) (claim for damages based upon rejected lot lease was discharged even though vacant mobile home remained on lot after petition was filed); *In re* Aslan, 909 F.2d 367 (9th Cir. 1990); *In re* Beck, 272 B.R. 112 (Bankr. E.D. Pa. 2002) (claim for excess mileage under rejected automobile lease was pre-petition claim even if it arose post-petition and debtor had continued to make lease payments post-petition); *cf. In re* Werbinski, 271 B.R. 514 (Bankr. E.D. Mich. 2001) (landlord could collect post-rejection rent when debtors remained on premises after rejection).

317 See § 13.4.3, *infra,* for a discussion of objections to claims.

318 *See* Ch. 11, *supra. See generally* Leasing Serv. Corp. v. First Tenn. Bank Nat'l Ass'n, 826 F.2d 434 (6th Cir. 1987) (rejection of contract does not affect creditor's secured status).

319 *See In re* Whitcomb & Keller Mortgage Co., 715 F.2d 375 (7th Cir. 1983). The claim would become a secured claim, however, to the extent there was a security deposit or other security interest.

320 11 U.S.C. § 502(b)(6); *see In re* Highland Superstores, Inc., 154 F.3d 573 (6th Cir. 1998) (cap is to be applied only after any applicable damages are computed under lease and state law).

321 Farber v. Wards Co., 825 F.2d 684 (2d Cir. 1987); *cf. In re*

Freeman, 297 B.R. 41 (Bankr. E.D. Va. 2003) (administrative expense denied when lessor had sought relief from stay to evict debtor and debtor had not opposed motion or argued property was necessary to case); 3 Collier on Bankruptcy ¶ 365.04[7] (15th ed. rev.).

322 Farber v. Wards Co., 825 F.2d 684 (2d Cir. 1987).

323 Zagata Fabricators v. Super. Air Products, 893 F.2d 624 (3d Cir. 1990); *In re* Dant & Russell, Inc., 853 F.2d 700 (9th Cir. 1988).

324 Farber v. Wards Co., 825 F.2d 684 (2d Cir. 1987).

325 Zagata Fabricators v. Super. Air Products, 893 F.2d 624 (3d Cir. 1990); *In re* Thompson, 788 F.2d 560 (9th Cir. 1986) (where debtors only use part of leased premises, they must pay administrative expense only for use and occupancy of that portion); *see In re* Schnabel, 612 F.2d 315, 317 (7th Cir. 1980). However, some courts hold that where a lease is never assumed or rejected during a chapter 11 bankruptcy case, and presumably also a chapter 13 case, the lease "rides through" and is not affected by the case. *In re* Whitcomb & Keller Mortgage Co., 715 F.2d 375 (7th Cir. 1983); *In re* Cochise College Park, Inc., 703 F.2d 1339 (9th Cir. 1983); *In re* Werbinski, 271 B.R. 514 (Bankr. E.D. Mich. 2001) (landlord could collect post-rejection rent when debtors remained in premises after rejection); *see* 3 Collier on Bankruptcy ¶ 365.04[2][d] (15th ed. rev.).

326 4 Collier on Bankruptcy ¶ 503.04 (15th ed. rev.); *see also* Zagata Fabricators v. Super. Air Products, 893 F.2d 624 (3d Cir. 1990); *In re* Standard Furniture Co., 3 B.R. 527 (Bankr. S.D. Cal. 1980).

327 11 U.S.C. § 1322(a)(2).

328 Chateau Communities v. Miller, 252 B.R. 121 (E.D. Mich. 2000) (creditor violated automatic stay and discharge injunction by seeking money judgment for post-petition rent), *aff'd on other grounds*, 282 F.3d 874 (6th Cir. 2002). The fact that a lease may have by its terms automatically renewed for a new term does not convert it into a post-petition obligation. *See In re* Country Club Estates, 227 B.R. 565 (Bankr. S.D. Fla. 1998) (contract which was automatically renewed was still subject to assumption or rejection).

329 *In re* Maupin, 165 B.R. 864 (Bankr. M.D. Tenn. 1994).

12.9.3.3 Credit Insurance

Another common type of contract that could be considered executory is the purchase of credit insurance which accompanies many consumer loans.[330] More often than not, credit insurance is a very bad bargain for the consumer.[331] Rejection of the contract and termination of its benefits results in very little loss of real protection.

If a debtor attempts to reject such a contract in order to obtain a refund for the remaining term, the creditor or insurance company can be expected to argue that the insurance was paid in full by the debtor at the outset of the loan with part of the amount financed. However, the debtor can show in most contracts that nonpayment of the loan will excuse the insurer from its obligation to perform; thus, each party still has obligations which, if breached, excuse performance by the other making the contract executory under even the stricter definition discussed above. Moreover, the debtor can also point to the fact that such contracts typically provide for a refund for the remaining term if the loan is prepaid or, often, in the case of a default, making them more like installment contracts for which insurance is paid over a period of time. In fact, it is not uncommon for the creditor to make the actual payments on the debtor's behalf to the insurance company on an installment basis.

Creditors often take a security interest in the refund on credit insurance. If such a security interest is taken and is valid, there is little to be gained by rejecting the credit insurance on an otherwise unsecured debt which will not be paid in full under the plan. However, rejection of the insurance contract on a secured debt which must be paid in full under the plan could produce a refund of many hundreds, or even thousands, of dollars. This refund, even if held by the creditor as security, will ultimately go towards reducing the total amount payable.[332] When a creditor receives a credit insurance refund, counsel should ensure that an amended claim is filed to reflect the amount of the refund.

12.9.4 Procedure and Tactics

In a chapter 13 case, the debtor is not normally required to choose assumption or rejection until the time of confirmation of the plan.[333] However, the other party may force an earlier election by requesting the court to set a specified earlier date by which the choice must be made.[334] Additionally, although courts are split on this point, a lessor might seek relief from the stay prior to a decision on assumption or rejection, arguing that its interest in the property is not adequately protected.[335] Few lessors in consumer cases take advantage of either method of forcing an election.

Normally, it is to the debtor's advantage to wait until the last possible moment before choosing assumption or rejection, at least with leases. By waiting, the debtor can keep all options open and also postpone the time by which defaults must be promptly cured as part of an assumption. The non-debtor party to the executory contract or lease is bound to honor the contract until it is rejected.[336] During the period before assumption, the debtor can save money, making an immediate or prompt cure of the default easier. Alternatively, the savings can finance a move to another home.

As discussed earlier, during this interim period the debtor-lessee also builds up a debt for use and occupancy, usually at the agreed rate of rental payments. Current payments of rent after the bankruptcy is filed satisfy the debtor's only obligation to the lessor at this time, and usually keep the lessor satisfied to let the proceedings run their course (especially if the lessor is told that back rent payments will eventually be paid under the chapter 13 plan). A lessor who is satisfied with such an arrangement is unlikely to seek counsel to exercise the right to seek adequate protection[337] or to force an early election of assumption or rejection.

After weighing the factors involved, the debtor usually should assume or reject the lease by the time of confirmation.[338] If this is done, the consequences described above will transpire. If not, it is somewhat less clear what will happen. Presumably, the automatic stay is still in effect, but the debtor's failure to assume the lease when given the opportunity might be considered cause for relief from the stay under section 362(d).[339] On the other hand, especially if a lease contains burdensome clauses the debtor does not wish to assume, the debtor can argue that the stay should be continued, regardless of the failure to assume (or, for that matter, the conclusion of the lease term), as long as the

---

330 *See In re* Garnas, 38 B.R. 221 (Bankr. D.N.D. 1984) (insurance contract considered executory).

331 The credit insurance industry is not very well regulated. Consumers typically have a poor understanding of the nature of these policies and of their very limited benefits. *See generally* National Consumer Law Center, The Cost of Credit: Regulation and Legal Challenges Ch. 8 (2d ed. 2000 and Supp.).

332 *See In re* Waiwada, 248 B.R. 258 (Bankr. M.D. Pa. 2000) (contract provided that debtor could cancel life and disability insurance, but creditor permitted to retain refund and apply to balance of debt).

333 11 U.S.C. § 365(d)(2).

334 11 U.S.C. § 365(d)(2).

335 *Compare, e.g., In re* Sweetwater, 40 B.R. 733 (Bankr. D. Utah 1984) (relief from stay not available to lessor prior to assumption or rejection) *with In re* DeSantis, 66 B.R. 998 (Bankr. E.D. Pa. 1986) (contra).

336 *In re* Pub. Serv. Co. of N.H., 884 F.2d 11 (1st Cir. 1989).

337 See discussion of adequate protection in Chapter 9, *supra.*

338 It is unclear whether a chapter 13 plan can be modified after confirmation to assume or reject a lease. While section 365(d)(2) states that the election must be made before confirmation, section 1322(b)(7) allows a plan (and thus perhaps a modified plan) to provide for assumption or rejection of any lease or executory contract not previously rejected.

339 See discussion of relief from the stay in Chapter 9, *supra.*

lessor has adequate protection and continued occupancy is necessary for rehabilitation.[340]

It should be remembered, though, that because use and occupancy claims do have priority, the post-petition rental payments often will have to be paid in a chapter 13 case at some point.[341] However, if the case is converted to chapter 7 or found appropriate for a hardship discharge, such post-petition claims would normally be discharged just as most other unsecured priority claims are discharged in such cases.[342]

Consequently, even if a lease is not assumed, it is not clear that the debtor must therefore vacate the premises.[343] She simply may no longer have that leasehold interest. Also, if there is otherwise an entitlement to remain, as in public housing situations, an eviction may still be prohibited, especially where it would violate the section 525 prohibition on discrimination based solely on the discharged debt for back rent.[344]

The method for actually assuming or rejecting a lease or executory contract is not spelled out in the Code. As Code section 1322(b)(7) permits a plan to provide for assumption or rejection, it is presumably sufficient to simply include a provision in the chapter 13 plan to carry out the debtor's intent.[345] However, in a case under chapter 11, which has similar provisions, one court of appeals has held that a separate motion under Federal Rule of Bankruptcy Procedure 6006 is necessary.[346] But that rule, by its own terms,

provides that a motion is necessary to assume a lease or executory contract *other than as part of a plan.*

12.10 Chapter 13 Cases After Prior Bankruptcies

One important distinction between chapter 13 and chapter 7 is the debtor's right to file a chapter 13 case within six years of a prior bankruptcy case. This right exists because sections 727(a)(8) and (9), barring a chapter 7 discharge within six years after any chapter 7 case and many chapter 13 cases in which a discharge was granted, are clearly inapplicable in chapter 13, which has no comparable provision.[347] Every court that has considered whether a chapter 13 case may be filed within six years after a prior bankruptcy has agreed that this is the only possible meaning of the statutory provisions.[348]

Nevertheless, the hostility of some courts to what they perceive as abuse of chapter 13 has carried over to cases filed shortly after prior bankruptcies. Despite the statute's clear authorization, at least one court has denied confirmation of a plan that proposed full payment of those debts which had not been discharged in an earlier chapter 7 case. The court found that the chapter 7 case and the subsequent chapter 13 case combined to effectuate a plan which resulted in no payment to unsecured creditors. By that court's definition, such a plan failed the "good faith" test discussed earlier in this chapter.[349]

However, most courts have found nothing improper in the filing of a chapter 13 case after an earlier chapter 7 filing, at least when the combination is not a disguised liquidation.[350] At most, the earlier case should be considered in the determination of whether the later chapter 13 case is filed in good faith.[351] In *Johnson v. Home State Bank*,[352] the Supreme

---

340 See discussion of relief from the stay with respect to leases in Chapter 9, *supra*. However, some courts have held that where a lease is neither assumed nor rejected, it rides through the bankruptcy case unaffected. *See* § 12.9.3.2, *supra*. Therefore, failing to assume the lease may not relieve the debtor of burdensome lease terms, though if the debtor later leaves the property any liability for rent under the lease would probably be deemed discharged.

341 Post-petition rental expenses for property used by the debtor are usually considered administrative expenses under 11 U.S.C. § 507(a)(1) and are therefore priority claims required to be paid under 11 U.S.C. § 1322(a)(2), at least if the creditor files a claim. *See* § 12.3.5, *supra*.

342 A post-petition claim for rent due may usually be filed by a lessor under 11 U.S.C. § 365(g)(1), or perhaps 11 U.S.C. § 1305. While the discharge of post-petition rent may seem a harsh result for the lessor, it should be remembered that the lessor can protect itself against such a loss by demanding adequate protection in the form of a new security deposit, a cosigner, or other device. *See* § 12.9.3.2, *supra*.

343 *See In re* Adams, 65 B.R. 646 (Bankr. E.D. Pa. 1986) (rejection of lease does not automatically grant landlord relief from automatic stay or relieve landlord of necessity of resorting to state court eviction proceedings).

344 11 U.S.C. § 525(a); *see* § 14.5.5.3, *infra*.

345 *In re* Hall, 202 B.R. 929 (Bankr. W.D. Tenn. 1996); *In re* Flugel, 197 B.R. 92 (Bankr. S.D. Cal. 1996); *see* § 12.9.2, *supra*.

346 Sea Harvest Corp. v. Riviera Land Co., 868 F.2d 1077 (9th Cir. 1989). It should be noted, however, that this case involved pre-confirmation assumption of a lease, which is often necessary in chapter 11, due to the deadline for assuming leases of nonresidential real property in 11 U.S.C. § 365(d)(4). In most

chapter 13 cases, the leases involved will be of residential real property and therefore not subject to this deadline. In cases where assumption cannot occur pursuant to a plan because it must occur earlier, it is clear that merely filing an election to assume, rather than a motion the lessor may oppose, is not sufficient. *In re* Burger Boys, 94 F.3d 755, 763 (2d Cir. 1996); *see* § 12.9.2, *supra*.

347 11 U.S.C. § 103(b) provides that the provisions of subchapter II of chapter 7 apply only in chapter 7 cases.

348 *In re* Baker, 736 F.2d 481 (8th Cir. 1984); *In re* DeSimone, 6 B.R. 89 (Bankr. S.D.N.Y. 1980); *In re* Pearson, 4 B.R. 376 (Bankr. N.D. Ohio 1980); *In re* Ciotta, 4 B.R. 253 (Bankr. E.D.N.Y. 1980); *In re* Bonder, 3 B.R. 623 (Bankr. E.D.N.Y. 1980).

349 *In re* Diego, 6 B.R. 468 (Bankr. N.D. Cal. 1980).

350 *In re* Baker, 736 F.2d 481 (8th Cir. 1984); *In re* Gayton, 61 B.R. 612 (B.A.P. 9th Cir. 1986); *In re* Tauscher, 26 B.R. 99 (Bankr. E.D. Wis. 1982).

351 *In re* Taylor, 884 F.2d 478 (9th Cir. 1989); *In re* Metz, 820 F.2d 1495 (9th Cir. 1987); *In re* Ponteri, 31 B.R. 859 (Bankr. D.N.J. 1983); *see In re* Rasmussen, 888 F.2d 703 (10th Cir. 1989) (where debtor who originally had debts in excess of chapter 13 debt limits had discharged all debts, except one debt held

Court made clear that it is possible to file a chapter 13 case after a prior chapter 7 case. The court held that there was no per se bar to such a filing and that any allegations of abuse must be proved in connection with an objection to confirmation under the good faith standard.

The filing of a chapter 13 case during a still-pending chapter 7 case, on the other hand, sometimes is not permitted.[353] But when the debtor has already received a discharge in a prior chapter 7 case, the fact that the case has not been administratively closed should not affect the debtor's right to file a subsequent chapter 13 case.[354] And it has also been held that filing a new chapter 13 petition while a previously filed inactive chapter 13 is still pending is not absolutely barred, though it may be indicative of bad faith.[355]

A number of advantages to the debtor spring from the right to file a chapter 13 case after a chapter 7 case. The most obvious is the possibility of refuge from creditors and a fresh start in bankruptcy when a chapter 7 discharge is not available. Because a case initially filed as a chapter 13 case may be dismissed as a matter of right at any time by the debtor,[356] it could serve as a kind of holding action for a year or two until the six-year bar following a prior bankruptcy expired. If the plan were then dismissed before completion, a chapter 7 case would not be barred because section 727(a)(9) bars chapter 7 cases only after chapter 13 cases which have resulted in a discharge.[357]

Another possibility is that of successive chapter 13 cases, with one commenced, if necessary, immediately after discharge or dismissal of a previous case.[358] This could be particularly useful if new and unanticipated debts, such as a tort judgment or medical bills, arise after the first chapter 13 case is underway,[359] if debts not discharged in the first chapter 13 case continue to cause insurmountable problems for the debtor, or if problems develop in the first case. The first case may then be dismissed as a matter of right and a new chapter 13 (or chapter 7) case could be commenced. This strategy could also provide a way to reduce the payments necessary to meet the "best interests of creditors" test,[360] if the amount of non-exempt property owned by the debtor was substantially reduced between the filing of the first case and the second case. However, if a request for relief from the stay was filed in the first case, no new case may be commenced for 180 days after the voluntary dismissal of the first case.[361]

In considering these possible courses of action, practitioners should be aware that an unsympathetic court may find them to be not in good faith and may deny confirmation of the plan in the later chapter 13 case.[362] (The chapter 13 "good faith" test could not be used, however, to bar a chapter 7 discharge after a dismissed chapter 13 case, though there are a few cases that have held that a chapter 7 case can be dismissed for bad faith.[363]) Especially if it appears that the debtor has willfully incurred many new debts with the specific intent of filing a new chapter 13 case to discharge them, a court may be quite receptive to creditor arguments that the successive petitions are part of a fraudulent scheme and that confirmation should be denied. In such cases, debtors may run a significant risk not only of dismissal, but also of an involuntary conversion to chapter 7. Obviously, it is not good practice to subject debtors to such risks when they can be avoided, and debtors should be discouraged from such behavior which places not only their own cases, but also the credibility of liberal bankruptcy laws, in jeopardy.

---

nondischargeable in chapter 7 case, and two weeks later filed chapter 13 case proposing to pay 1.5% of debt not discharged in chapter 7, which was only debt listed in chapter 13 statement, plan was not filed in good faith and was manipulation of the bankruptcy process); *see also In re* Chisum, 68 B.R. 471 (B.A.P. 9th Cir. 1986) (filing of four successive bankruptcies not an abuse in circumstances of particular case), *aff'd*, 847 F.2d 597 (9th Cir. 1988).

352 501 U.S. 78, 111 S. Ct. 2150, 115 L. Ed. 2d 66 (1991).

353 *In re* Cowen, 29 B.R. 888 (Bankr. S.D. Ohio 1983).

354 *In re* Saylors, 869 F.2d 1434 (11th Cir. 1989); *In re* Keach, 243 B.R. 851 (B.A.P. 1st Cir. 2000); *see also In re* Strause, 97 B.R. 22 (Bankr. S.D. Cal. 1989) (filing of chapter 13 case not barred by pending chapter 7 case where debtor's discharge would have been granted but for court's administrative delays).

355 *In re* Whitmore, 225 B.R. 199 (Bankr. D. Idaho 1998) (fact that debtor's prior chapter 13 case was still pending for a few days after new chapter 13 case was filed was not in itself cause for dismissal of new case); *In re* Cormier, 147 B.R. 285 (Bankr. D. Me. 1992).

356 11 U.S.C. § 1307(b).

357 It is doubtful whether a chapter 13 case filed within six years of a prior bankruptcy could be converted to a chapter 7 after the six years expired because the filing date of the chapter 13 case would likely be deemed the filing date of the converted chapter 7, thus barring a chapter 7 discharge. In view of this likelihood, dismissal of the chapter 13 and the filing of a new chapter 7 case seems a safer course than conversion after the six years have run.

358 *See In re* Smith, 43 B.R. 319 (Bankr. E.D.N.C. 1984) (plan confirmed, with conditions, even though there had been three prior unsuccessful chapter 13 cases). But see 11 U.S.C. § 109(g), placing certain limitations on successive filings, discussed in Chapters 3 and 9, *supra*.

359 See also § 8.7.2, *supra,* concerning post-petition claims in chapter 13.

360 *See* § 12.3.1, *supra*.

361 11 U.S.C. § 109(g). See discussion of this 1984 amendment in Chapters 3 and 9, *supra*.

362 *See In re* Eisen, 14 F.3d 469 (9th Cir. 1994) (debtor's chapter 13 case dismissed as in bad faith where debtor had had several prior bankruptcy cases, one of which had been dismissed as in bad faith, and had made misrepresentations to court about prior cases and other facts).

363 *See* § 13.9.2.1, *infra*.

12.11 Confirmation of Plan Binds Debtor and All Creditors

The confirmation order is binding upon the debtor and all creditors.[364] Once the appeal period has passed, it is *res judicata* as to all issues which could have been raised in opposition to confirmation.[365] After confirmation, no creditor may take actions that are inconsistent with the plan.[366] Therefore, no creditor may later challenge the plan by arguing that it did not comply with some provision of chapter 13, such as the good faith requirement.[367] Similarly,

the trustee is bound by the confirmed plan and is responsible for rectifying any erroneous distributions.[368]

Even if a creditor has not been provided all that it is entitled to receive under the statute, such as present value interest for a secured creditor,[369] the creditor that does not timely assert those rights will lose them,[370] just as parties in

---

364 11 U.S.C. § 1327(a); *In re* Diviney, 225 B.R. 762 (B.A.P. 10th Cir. 1998) (unless expressly preserved by confirmed plan or order confirming plan, terms of pre-confirmation agreement regarding automatic stay did not survive confirmation); *In re* Garrett, 185 B.R. 620 (Bankr. N.D. Ala. 1995) (pre-confirmation order granting relief from automatic stay was superseded by provisions of confirmed plan; after confirmation binding effect of plan precludes relief from stay based upon events which occurred before confirmation). The binding effect of a confirmed plan extends to all those in privity with the debtor or a creditor. Sanders Confectionery Products v. Heller Fin., 973 F.2d 474 (6th Cir. 1992) (chapter 11 plan was binding on parent corporation of creditor and creditor's law firm, but not shareholder of a creditor). It applies to related proceedings, both core and non-core, which could have been brought. *Id.* However, a confirmed plan that is ambiguous may be construed against its drafter, the debtor. *See In re* Roberts, 279 F.3d 91 (1st Cir. 2002) (plan which provided that debtor would pay fixed amount to trustee but also provided specified percentage return to unsecured creditors required debtor to pay larger of the two amounts).

365 Corbett v. MacDonald Moving Services, Inc., 124 F.3d 82 (2d Cir. 1997) (lack of subject matter jurisdiction over particular issue dealt with by chapter 11 plan could not be raised after passage of time to appeal confirmation order); *In re* Ivory, 70 F.3d 73 (9th Cir. 1995) (even if order confirming plan erroneously gave debtor right to redeem property after expiration of redemption period, creditor could not collaterally attack unappealed confirmation order); *In re* Pence, 905 F.2d 1107 (7th Cir. 1990); *In re* Szostek, 886 F.2d 1405 (3d Cir. 1989); United States v. Edmonston, 99 B.R. 995 (E.D. Cal. 1989) (creditor could not contest debtor's eligibility for chapter 13 after confirmation); *In re* Bilal, 296 B.R. 828 (Bankr. D. Kan. 2003) (creditor bound by confirmed plan provision that rescinded mortgage under Truth in Lending act and declared creditor's lien void); *In re* Durham, 260 B.R. 383 (Bankr. D.S.C. 2001) (creditor who claimed to be lessor was bound by plan's provision treating it as secured creditor); *In re* Minzler, 158 B.R. 720 (Bankr. S.D. Ohio 1993) (creditor could not prevail on motion for relief from stay due to lack of adequate protection on leases allegedly misclassified as secured claims because creditor was bound by confirmed plan to which it had not objected); 8 Collier on Bankruptcy ¶ 1327.02[1] (15th ed. rev.); *cf. In re* Miller, 16 F.3d 240 (8th Cir. 1994) (motion to set aside confirmation of chapter 12 plan filed within ten days of confirmation order treated as timely motion for new trial under Fed. R. Bankr. P. 9023).

366 *In re* Talbot, 124 F.3d 1201 (10th Cir. 1997) (IRS not permitted to demand full payment of its lien when debtors sold home because lien was to have been paid through chapter 13 plan).

367 *In re* Gregory, 705 F.2d 1118 (9th Cir. 1983). The debtor may

modify the plan, however, if the modification meets the requirements of § 1329, even without a showing of cause. *In re* Jourdan, 108 B.R. 1020 (Bankr. N.D. Iowa 1989); *In re* Mosely, 74 B.R. 791 (Bankr. C.D. Cal. 1987); *see also In re* Penrod, 50 F.3d 459 (7th Cir. 1995) (confirmed chapter 11 plan which did not specifically preserve creditor's lien extinguished lien of creditor that had participated in reorganization, even if creditor could have successfully objected to plan). *But see In re* Escobedo, 28 F.3d 34 (7th Cir. 1994) (distinguishing mandatory requirements of § 1322(a), and holding that a trustee could obtain dismissal of a plan not complying with § 1322(a) even after an unappealed confirmation order).

368 *In re* Wilson, 274 B.R. 4 (Bankr. D.D.C. 2001) (when trustee—who began distributions after confirmation but before governmental claims bar date—made distributions to unsecured creditors of funds that should have gone to larger-than-expected governmental claims, trustee was required to recover erroneous distributions or reimburse estate).

369 First Nat'l Bank v. Allen, 118 F.3d 1289 (8th Cir. 1997) (failure to object to chapter 12 plan which provided for banks' secured claims, but not their unsecured claims constitutes waiver of the unsecured claims); *In re* Chappell, 984 F.2d 775 (7th Cir. 1993) (lien was eliminated and debt discharged upon full payment of creditor's claim for principal, without interest, pursuant to confirmed chapter 13 plan not providing for interest, to which creditor had not objected); *In re* Szostek, 886 F.2d 1405 (3d Cir. 1989); *In re* Echevarria, 212 B.R. 185 (B.A.P. 1st Cir. 1997) (creditor who failed to object to failure of plan to provide interest on secured claim was bound by plan and could not collect that interest after plan was completed); *see* § 11.6.1.3, *supra*; *see also In re* Harrison, 987 F.2d 677 (10th Cir. 1993) (creditor was estopped from arguing that its claim was partially unsecured when plan surrendered property to satisfy proof of claim filed by creditor that stated claim was fully secured; burden was on creditor to amend proof of claim or seek valuation of collateral prior to confirmation); *In re* Pence, 905 F.2d 1107 (7th Cir. 1990) (creditor could not object to substitution of collateral violating lien retention standard of § 1325(a)(5) in confirmed plan). *But see In re* Boyd, 11 F.3d 59 (5th Cir. 1994) (debtor's plan did not revest in debtor property that was never in estate to begin with because it had been conveyed through a foreclosure sale completed thirty-three months before bankruptcy; therefore creditor was not precluded by confirmation of plan from obtaining relief from the automatic stay).

370 *In re* Harvey, 213 F.3d 318 (7th Cir. 2000) (creditor waived any argument about plan provision voiding its lien upon payment of allowed secured claim by not objecting to confirmation); *In re* Herbert, 61 B.R. 44 (Bankr. W.D. La. 1986); *see also In re* Allen, 300 F.3d 1055 (9th Cir. 2002) (confirmed chapter 11 plan that did not incorporate terms of prior stay relief order and stipulation was nonetheless binding on creditor); *In re* Webb, 932 F.2d 155 (2d Cir. 1991) (creditor could not raise issue of property valuation in objecting to chapter 12 plan modification because creditor had not objected to valuation accepted by court at time of confirmation and creditor was bound by that valuation); *In re* Woods, 130 B.R. 204 (W.D. Va. 1990) (creditor

other proceedings may lose rights by default. For example, a plan provision finding that a student loan was dischargeable under the undue hardship provision of section 523(a)(8) was binding on the loan guarantee agency once the plan had been confirmed.[371] As noncompliance with any provision of chapter 13 or other applicable provisions of the Bankruptcy Code may be raised as an objection to confirmation under Code section 1325(a)(1), a creditor has few if any ways to challenge a confirmed plan other than under the very narrow grounds provided for seeking revocation of confirmation.[372]

However, even a provision of a confirmed plan may not be sufficient to invalidate a claim properly filed by a creditor. Some courts have held that the only method contemplated for challenging a filed proof of claim is the process of objecting to the claim.[373] Other courts have allowed the

provisions of a confirmed plan to govern over an inconsistent claim.[374] Still others have treated the issue as one of whether the creditor has received constitutionally sufficient notice that its property rights are in jeopardy, suggesting that if sufficient notice is given, a creditor may have its lien reduced by confirmation of a plan.[375]

The binding effect of confirmation can be important in requiring creditors to abide by the terms of the plan even after it has been concluded. If a plan provides that certain payments under the plan will cure a mortgage default, thereby bringing the debtor current on the mortgage, a mortgage lender may not add extra charges or pre-petition claims to the ongoing mortgage payments either during the plan or after it has been completed,[376] as some attempt to do.

---

could not argue that bankruptcy court had lacked jurisdiction to enter confirmation order when it did not raise the issue at time of confirmation); *cf. In re* Booth, 289 B.R. 665 (N.D. Ill. 2003) (plan provision providing for release of creditor's lien prior to completion of plan upon payment of secured portion of claim, although binding on creditor, was trumped by § 349(b)(1) upon dismissal of chapter 13, so lien revested in creditor for unpaid portion of full claim).

371 *In re* Andersen, 215 B.R. 792 (B.A.P. 10th Cir. 1998), *aff'd*, 179 F.3d 1253 (10th Cir. 1999). Note however that, upon objection, confirmation of a plan containing such a provision has been denied. *In re* Mammel, 221 B.R. 238 (Bankr. D. Iowa 1998); *see also In re* Pardee, 193 F.3d 1083 (9th Cir. 1999) (interest on student loan discharged pursuant to a provision of a confirmed plan). *But see In re* Banks, 299 F.3d 296 (4th Cir. 2002) (adversary proceeding required to discharge student loan or post-petition interest on student loan).

372 11 U.S.C. § 1330 allows revocation of confirmation to be sought only within 180 days of the confirmation order and only if the confirmation order was procured by fraud. It may be sought only by a creditor provided for in the plan. *In re* Fesq, 153 F.3d 113 (3d Cir. 1998) (confirmation may not be vacated under Fed. R. Bankr. P. 9024; revocation based upon fraud is only remedy); *In re* Robinson, 293 B.R. 59 (Bankr. D. Or. 2002) (Fed. R. Bankr. P. 9024 cannot be used to revoke confirmation); *In re* Slack, 280 B.R. 604 (Bankr. D.N.J. 2002) (bad faith not sufficient grounds for revocation of confirmation); *In re* Randolph, 273 B.R. 914 (Bankr. M.D. Fla. 2002) (revocation denied even though debtor made materially false statement because creditor did not prove intent to obtain confirmation by fraud). Revocation may not be sought if the alleged fraud was known in time to object to confirmation. *In re* Ritacco, 210 B.R. 595 (Bankr. D. Or. 1997); *In re* Hicks, 79 B.R. 45 (Bankr. N.D. Ala. 1987); *see also In re* Nikoloutsos, 199 F.3d 233 (5th Cir. 1999) (revoking confirmation based on debtor's failure to schedule judgment for $863,440.00 that had been entered against him); Young v. Internal Revenue Serv., 132 B.R. 395 (S.D. Ind. 1990) (reversing bankruptcy court's decision which had reconsidered plan confirmation on motion of IRS, which alleged it had been improperly treated).

373 *In re* Simmons, 765 F.2d 547 (5th Cir. 1985). The Fifth Circuit elaborated on the *Simmons* case in *In re* Howard, 972 F.2d 639 (5th Cir. 1992). There the court held that it is simply necessary to file an objection to a secured claim before the confirmation hearing to put the creditor on notice that its lien is at risk if it does not participate in confirmation proceedings. Thereafter, a confirmed plan may modify the lien of a creditor who has filed

a secured claim. *See also In re* Bateman, 331 F.3d 821 (11th Cir. 2003) (although mortgage creditor's claim for arrearages had to be disallowed to extent it exceeded amount provided for in confirmed plan, the arrearages disallowed would remain owing after the case because plan could not modify mortgage creditor's secured claim); Cen-Pen Corp. v. Hanson, 58 F.3d 89 (4th Cir. 1995) (adversary proceeding is required to challenge validity of lien); § 11.2.2, *supra*. The fact that a plan has been confirmed, however, does not necessarily preclude the debtor from challenging a proof of claim after confirmation. *In re* Lewis, 875 F.2d 53 (3d Cir. 1989).

374 *In re* Fili, 257 B.R. 370 (B.A.P. 1st Cir. 2001) (plan which provided for discharge and no distribution to secured creditor prevailed over timely-filed claim); *In re* Ramey, 301 B.R. 534 (Bankr. E.D. Ark. 2003) (plan provision with sufficient notice given is binding); *In re* Dickey, 293 B.R. 360 (Bankr. M.D. Pa. 2003) (same); *In re* Hudson, 260 B.R. 421 (Bankr. W.D. Mich. 2001) (confirmation can establish binding decision on amount of allowed secured claim and interest rate, but unsecured claim is normally established through claims allowance process); *In re* Jones, 271 B.R. 397 (Bankr. S.D. Ala. 2000) (confirmation order prevailed over timely claim filed after confirmation); *In re* Harnish, 224 B.R. 91 (Bankr. N.D. Iowa 1998) (when creditor was listed as unsecured in debtor's schedules and treated as unsecured in confirmed plan, plan did not preserve any lien creditor might have had; creditor had duty to monitor confirmation of plan); *In re* Wolf, 162 B.R. 98 (Bankr. D.N.J. 1993); *In re* Tucker, 35 B.R. 35 (Bankr. M.D. Tenn. 1983); *In re* Russell, 29 B.R. 332 (Bankr. E.D.N.Y. 1983).

375 *In re* Linkous, 990 F.2d 160 (4th Cir. 1993) (notice of confirmation hearing was not adequate to permit reduction of liens when it failed to state that court would consider valuation of security interests at confirmation hearing); *In re* King, 290 B.R. 641 (Bankr. C.D. Ill. 2003) (wholly unsecured lien may be stripped off as part of confirmation process because plan provision provided adequate notice to creditor); *see also In re* Shook, 278 B.R. 815 (B.A.P. 9th Cir. 2002) (when debtor listed claim as unsecured in schedules and plan did not specifically address creditor's claim, debtor could not seek to have claim deemed unsecured four-and-a-half years after confirmation). *See generally* 8 Collier on Bankruptcy ¶ 1327.02[2] (15th ed. rev.).

376 *In re* Riser, 289 B.R. 201 (Bankr. M.D. Fla. 2003) (mortgage company not entitled to payments for any charges incurred before or during bankruptcy that were not provided for in confirmed plan); *In re* Rathe, 114 B.R. 253 (Bankr. D. Idaho 1990); *In re* Brown, 121 B.R. 768 (Bankr. S.D. Ohio 1990) (mortgagee must treat debtor as current even where it claimed to have incorrectly computed its proof of claim).

The debtor must be treated as if the default had not occurred and she is current on payments.[377] Practitioners representing debtors who have cured mortgages should advise their clients to be alert to any charges added to their payments that may be related to the earlier default. If such charges are imposed, it may be necessary to enforce the terms of the confirmation order, reopening the chapter 13 case if it has already been completed. Such charges also violate the discharge injunction[378] and in many states additional damages and attorney fees may be available because imposition of illegal charges violates state usury or unfair trade practice laws.[379]

Although the binding effect of a confirmed plan often works in a debtor's favor, some courts have allowed creditors to use it as an argument against a debtor. For example, debtors have been prevented from claiming an exemption in the proceeds of the sale of their home when such an exemption precluded them from paying creditors the amount provided in their plan.[380] It has also been held, erroneously, that confirmation fixes the amount of a claim filed prior to confirmation to which no objection has been made, and the debtor may not later argue that the claim was overstated.[381]

---

377 *In re* Rathe, 114 B.R. 253 (Bankr. D. Idaho 1990); *see In re* Wines, 239 B.R. 703 (Bankr. D.N.J. 1999) (reconciling payments made with proof of claim and cure of default).

378 11 U.S.C. § 524(a)(2); *see* § 14.5.5.7, *infra*; *see also In re* Turner, 221 B.R. 920 (Bankr. M.D. Fla. 1998) (attorney fees and costs awarded for contempt based on accounting on secured debt inconsistent with completion of confirmed chapter 11 plan); *In re* Ronemus, 201 B.R. 458 (Bankr. N.D. Tex. 1996) (creditor assessed $10,000.00, plus $3000.00 attorney and accountants' fees after discharge due to mortgagee charging late charges on current payments made during bankruptcy and for charging filing fee, attorney fees and expenses to debtor's escrow account without permission of court).

379 *See generally* National Consumer Law Center, The Cost of Credit: Regulation and Legal Challenges (2d ed. 2000 and Supp.); National Consumer Law Center, Unfair and Deceptive Acts and Practices (5th ed. 2001 and Supp.).

380 *In re* Wolfberg, 255 B.R. 879 (B.A.P. 9th Cir. 2000).

381 Adair v. Sherman, 230 F.3d 890 (7th Cir. 2000) (debtor precluded from bringing action under Fair Debt Collection Practices Act alleging that proof of claim filed by creditor was excessive); *cf. In re* Lewis, 875 F.2d 53 (3d Cir. 1989) (confirmation does not necessarily preclude challenge to proof of claim); *In re* Fryer, 172 B.R. 1020 (Bankr. S.D. Ga. 1994) (confirmation did not bar Truth in Lending objection to claim, because objection did not implicate validity of any plan provision).

Chapter 13   Litigating in the Bankruptcy Court

13.1 Introduction

Under the Bankruptcy Act of 1898, consumer bankruptcy cases were almost uniformly handled in a routine manner by all parties involved, more as matters of administrative processing than as proceedings involving legal issues to be litigated. Few contested disputes arose in such cases, and most of those that did arise were resolved not in the bankruptcy courts, but rather in state courts, because of the limited jurisdiction of the bankruptcy referees under the Act. Virtually the only litigated matters that involved consumer debtors were complaints objecting to the discharge of particular debts, and even those cases had been forced into bankruptcy courts only by relatively recent amendments to the Act of 1898.

All of this has changed radically under the Bankruptcy Code. Not only does the Code make the basic bankruptcy case a much more attractive alternative for consumer debtors, but also other provisions in the Bankruptcy Reform Act have brought about a major expansion of many different kinds of consumer litigation in the bankruptcy courts.

Central to this change was the greatly expanded jurisdiction of the bankruptcy courts under the 1978 Act.[1] In the years since the Code was enacted, these courts have heard numerous and varied claims of types never before brought before them, including damage claims for injury to property[2] or for unfair trade practices,[3] Truth in Lending actions,[4] actions to rescind contracts,[5] and class actions under the Civil Rights Acts for enforcement of rights provided by federal welfare programs.[6]

Generally, the bankruptcy courts were quick to recognize and exercise their increased jurisdiction in these cases, although a few resisted.[7] Only when no significant relation existed between the cause of action and the bankruptcy's purpose or success was jurisdiction found to be lacking.[8]

Then, in 1982, new and major uncertainties arose, with the Supreme Court's decision in *Northern Pipeline Construction Co. v. Marathon Pipe Line Co.*,[9] which declared the entire bankruptcy jurisdictional scheme to be unconstitutional. For almost two years after that decision, the bankruptcy system operated under makeshift emergency jurisdictional rules which were themselves of questionable constitutionality.[10] Finally, on July 10, 1984, a new jurisdictional structure was enacted as part of the Bankruptcy Amendments and Federal Judgeship Act of 1984.[11] As discussed below, that scheme creates a host of different issues, not the least of which is the constitutionality of some of its own provisions under the *Northern Pipeline* case. This chapter considers how best to utilize the jurisdiction of the bankruptcy forum and some of the issues most likely to arise in bankruptcy litigation, including particularly the litigation of issues under non-bankruptcy law.

13.2 Bankruptcy Court Jurisdiction Under the 1984 Amendments

13.2.1 A Brief History[12]

In 1978, when Congress passed the Bankruptcy Reform Act, bankruptcy jurisdiction was identified as a primary area in need of reform. For the previous eighty years, under the Bankruptcy Act of 1898, few topics had been the subject of

---

1 *See* § 13.2, *infra.*

2 *E.g., In re* Thompson, 3 B.R. 312 (Bankr. D.S.D. 1980).

3 *E.g., In re* Fleet, 95 B.R. 319 (E.D. Pa. 1989) (mortgage counselors who referred clients to bankruptcy attorney committed unfair trade practices); *In re* Gibbs, 9 B.R. 758 (Bankr. D. Conn. 1981), *aff'd*, 76 B.R. 257 (D. Conn. 1983).

4 *E.g., In re* Claypool, 2 Collier Bankr. Cas. 2d (MB) 64 (Bankr. M.D. Fla. 1980).

5 *E.g., In re* Griffith, 6 B.R. 753 (Bankr. D.N.M. 1980).

6 *E.g.*, Morris v. Philadelphia Elec. Co., 45 B.R. 350 (E.D. Pa. 1984); *In re* Maya, 8 B.R. 202 (Bankr. E.D. Pa. 1981).

7 *See, e.g., In re* Universal Profile, 6 B.R. 194 (Bankr. N.D. Ga.

1980) (creating a "domestic relations exception" to the general grant of jurisdiction to avoid becoming involved in a marital dispute affecting property of the estate over which the court appeared to have exclusive jurisdiction).

8 *See In re* Turner, 724 F.2d 338 (2d Cir. 1983) (conversion action brought by debtor would have no impact on bankruptcy and was therefore not related to bankruptcy case).

9 458 U.S. 50, 102 S. Ct. 2858, 73 L. Ed 2d 598 (1982).

10 *See* Vern Countryman, *Emergency Rule Compounds Emergency*, 57 Am. Bankr. L. J. 1 (1983); *see also* § 13.2.1, *infra.*

11 Pub. L. No. 98-353, 98 Stat. 333 (1984).

12 For a more detailed recounting of how bankruptcy jurisdiction arrived at its present state, see Vern Countryman, *Scrambling to Define Bankruptcy Jurisdiction: The Chief Justice, the Judicial Conference, and the Legislative Process*, 22 Harv. J. on Legis. 1 (1985).

more litigation. The system that existed was one of piece-meal jurisdiction, and in larger corporate cases simultaneous litigation concerning the same bankruptcy debtor was often conducted in numerous courts. The bankruptcy courts had only limited powers, most of them tied to jurisdiction over the debtor's property. Beyond those powers, matters could be tried in the bankruptcy court only with the consent, express or implied, of the parties. Uncertainty as to jurisdiction continued to cause litigation and expense in many cases.

The 1978 Act sought to remedy all of these ills by creating a single court, the new bankruptcy court, with jurisdiction over all matters related in any way to the bankruptcy.[13] But when Congress refused to make that court a full-fledged federal court as defined by Article III of the Constitution, it sowed the seeds of new uncertainties. These reached fruition in the *Northern Pipeline* case,[14] when the new structure was rejected in its entirety by the Supreme Court.

For the next two years, the bankruptcy courts operated without any clear statutory authority, under an emergency rule giving them jurisdiction delegated from the district court. This rule created a new distinction between proceedings that were integral to the bankruptcy process and those that were only "related" to it, the latter being the type of case which the Supreme Court had found clearly beyond the power of a non-Article III judge. All cases and proceedings were referred initially to bankruptcy judges under the rule, but district courts retained the authority to review all bankruptcy court actions de novo. And in "related proceedings," unless the parties agreed otherwise, a bankruptcy judge was empowered only to enter a proposed order or judgment to be reviewed in every case by the district court. The rule contained a non-exhaustive list of proceedings that would not be considered "related." Finally, it expressly prohibited bankruptcy judges from conducting certain types of proceedings, including appeals from other bankruptcy courts and jury trials.

The emergency rule was immediately challenged in numerous courts on the grounds that it did not comply with the Supreme Court's decision in *Northern Pipeline*. Every court of appeals to consider the issue upheld the rule, however, and the Supreme Court declined to resolve the issue conclusively by denying certiorari whenever it was sought.[15] Ultimately, because no court of appeals had found it invalid

and because it appeared to work reasonably well, the emergency rule formed the basis of the jurisdictional scheme enacted in 1984.[16]

Thus, on July 10, 1984 yet another bankruptcy court jurisdictional scheme came into being.[17] This system was further embellished with several amendments affecting jurisdictional issues in the Bankruptcy Reform Act of 1994.[18] Because Congress again declined to give bankruptcy judges Article III status, but still attempted to keep most "related issues" in the bankruptcy system, mechanisms were once more necessary to prevent bankruptcy courts from deciding issues that the Supreme Court had reserved for Article III courts. And as no precise definition of how those issues could be identified has been given by the Supreme Court, there continues to be some doubt over whether the current structure is constitutional.[19]

To date, there have been no definitive Supreme Court decisions. However, the Supreme Court decision in *Granfinanciera, S.A. v. Nordberg*[20] contains a number of hints that at least part of this new jurisdictional scheme could be found unconstitutional when the issue is finally addressed, because it vests in the bankruptcy court powers that may only be exercised by district courts. As the composition of the Court changes and the Code becomes more entrenched, though, it becomes less likely that the present jurisdictional system will be fully scrapped.

---

13 *See* H.R. Rep. No. 95-595, at 220–230 (1977).

14 N. Pipeline Constr. Co. v. Marathon Pipe Line Co., 458 U.S. 50, 102 S. Ct. 2858, 73 L. Ed. 2d 598 (1982).

15 *See, e.g., In re* Stewart, 741 F.2d 127 (7th Cir. 1984); *In re* Kaiser, 722 F.2d 1574 (2d Cir. 1983); White Motor Corp. v. Citibank, 704 F.2d 254 (6th Cir. 1983); *In re* Hansen, 702 F.2d 728 (8th Cir. 1983); *In re* Braniff Airways, Inc., 700 F.2d 214 (5th Cir. 1983); *see also In re* Committee of Unsecured Creditors of F.S. Communications Corp., 760 F.2d 1194 (11th Cir. 1985).

16 *See* 130 Cong. Rec. E1107–E1110 (daily ed. Mar. 20, 1984) (remarks of Rep. Kastenmaier); 130 Cong. Rec. H1847–H1849 (daily ed. Mar. 21, 1984) (remarks of Rep. Kindness). The legislative history of the 1984 amendments on jurisdiction consists primarily of the floor debates that occurred on March 21, 1984 in the House of Representatives, and June 19, 1984 in the Senate (130 Cong. Rec. S7617–S7625), as well as the Conference Report of June 29, 1984 (130 Cong. Rec. S8887–S8900).

17 A drafting error in the 1984 amendments accidentally re-enacted, in section 121(a) of Pub. L. No. 98-353, 98 Stat. 333 (1984), the 1978 court system provisions that had been repealed eight sections earlier in section 113 of the same law. Courts have thus far agreed that section 121(a) was a mistake and ignored it. *See, e.g.*, Precon, Inc. v. JRS Realty Trust, 47 B.R. 432 (D. Me. 1985); *In re* Long, 43 B.R. 692 (Bankr. N.D. Ohio 1984).

18 Pub. L. No. 103-394, 108 Stat. 4106 (Oct. 22, 1994), *amending* 28 U.S.C. §§ 157, 1334, 158, 2075.

19 *See, e.g., In re* Mankin, 823 F.2d 1296 (9th Cir. 1987) (bankruptcy court jurisdiction over trustee's use of state fraudulent conveyance statute held constitutional). There was also litigation concerning whether the "retroactive" reinstatement of sitting bankruptcy judges by Congress, after their statutory authority expired on June, 1984, was constitutional. Those constitutional challenges failed. *In re* Benny, 812 F.2d 1133 (9th Cir. 1987); *In re* Koerner, 800 F.2d 1358 (5th Cir. 1986) (retroactive extension of term of office for bankruptcy judges does not violate appointments clause of the Constitution); *In re* Lombard-Wall Inc., 48 B.R. 986 (S.D.N.Y. 1985); *see also In re* Moens, 800 F.2d 173 (7th Cir. 1986) (challenge to constitutionality of BAFJA rendered moot where bankruptcy judge sitting pursuant to the Act resigns).

20 492 U.S. 33, 109 S. Ct. 2782, 106 L. Ed. 2d 26 (1989); § 13.2.7, *infra*.

As discussed below, jurisdictional provisions continue to give rise to frequent litigation over how they are to be interpreted. Although in many ways the new statute is similar to the prior emergency rule, and in some ways it reverts to pre-1978 law, it is identical to neither. Hence, a new body of case law defining the boundaries of the bankruptcy court's jurisdiction has emerged and will continue to develop over the years to come.

13.2.2 Initial Referral of Bankruptcy Matters to the Bankruptcy Courts

The 1984 amendments are structured on the premise that the power to decide all cases and proceedings involving bankruptcy ultimately resides in the federal district court. The statute confers this power in 28 U.S.C. § 1334, which gives the district court original and exclusive jurisdiction over all cases under title 11 (the Bankruptcy Code);[21] original but not exclusive jurisdiction over proceedings arising under title 11 or arising in or related to cases under title 11;[22] and exclusive jurisdiction over all property of the bankruptcy estate.[23] This section thus gives the district court essentially the same broad initial jurisdiction which was conferred upon the bankruptcy courts by the Bankruptcy Reform Act of 1978.

The breadth of the statutory grant of jurisdiction is vast but not unlimited. A number of courts have adopted the test set forth by the Third Circuit Court of Appeals for determining whether a proceeding is at least "related to" a bankruptcy case—whether the outcome of the proceeding could conceivably have any effect on the administration of the bankruptcy case.[24] However, the Supreme Court has declined to precisely define "related to" in the context of bankruptcy jurisdiction.[25]

Under the current scheme, virtually all bankruptcy matters are immediately referred by the district court to the bankruptcy court, which is now a "unit" of the district court.[26] A bankruptcy judge is thus analogous in some ways to a magistrate judge. This referral to the bankruptcy court occurs pursuant to section 157 of title 28, which sets forth

the fairly complicated division of responsibilities between the bankruptcy court and district court. The amendments give the district court discretion to refer any or all bankruptcy cases or proceedings, including those only related to the bankruptcy, to the bankruptcy judges for the district.[27] The district court also has discretion to refer actions which are related to the bankruptcy and which are pending in the district court at the time the bankruptcy is filed.[28] As a practical matter, district courts immediately refer all such cases and proceedings to their bankruptcy courts (generally by blanket order of referral), and in virtually every district there remains a separate bankruptcy court clerk's office to process all bankruptcy filings.[29] Indeed, when a blanket order of referral has been promulgated, actions relating to a bankruptcy case may not be filed with the district court and must be filed with the bankruptcy court.[30] Thus, in almost all cases, bankruptcy papers continued to be filed initially with the clerk of the bankruptcy court.

Once a matter is begun in the bankruptcy court, though, there is no assurance that it will stay there. Nor is there a single uniform way that it will be treated if it does remain. The new jurisdictional scheme deploys a variety of procedural mechanisms for the transfer or ultimate resolution of different types of proceedings. These mechanisms are discussed below.

13.2.3 The Bankruptcy Case

The bankruptcy case, that is the case under title 11 initiated by the filing of a petition under chapters 7, 9, 11, 12 or 13 of that title, continues to be within the province of the bankruptcy court for entry of the orders that are essential for bankruptcy relief.[31] The bankruptcy court may enter as final orders: the order for relief under each chapter;[32] orders distributing property of the estate and setting aside exemptions; discharge orders; and other similar orders in the main bankruptcy case. As with every type of matter referred to the

---

21 28 U.S.C. § 1334(a).

22 28 U.S.C. § 1334(b).

23 28 U.S.C. § 1334(e).

24 Pacor v. Higgins, 743 F.2d 984 (3d Cir. 1984); *see also In re* Time Constr., Inc., 43 F.3d 1041 (6th Cir. 1995) (bankruptcy court has jurisdiction over proceeding if outcome could alter debtor's rights, options or freedom of action). This jurisdiction continues for many purposes even after a case is dismissed or closed. *In re* Aheong, 276 B.R. 233 (B.A.P. 9th Cir. 2002); *see In re* McAlpin, 278 F.3d 866 (8th Cir. 2002) (objection to claim filed after chapter 13 case had been completed and closed was not within bankruptcy court's jurisdiction because it could have no effect on bankruptcy case).

25 *See* Celotex Corp. v. Edwards, 514 U.S. 300, 308 n.6, 115 S. Ct. 1493, 131 L. Ed. 2d 403 (1995).

26 28 U.S.C. § 151.

27 28 U.S.C. § 157(a). One court of appeals has held that it is also permissible for a district court to refer a core bankruptcy proceeding to a magistrate upon the parties' consent, but that the practice should be limited to situations in which there is a compelling need to do so. *In re* Nix, 864 F.2d 1209 (5th Cir. 1989); *see also In re* San Vicente Med. Partners Ltd., 865 F.2d 1128 (9th Cir. 1989) (consent to trial of bankruptcy matter before magistrate must be knowing and explicit).

28 *See* Philippe v. Shape, Inc., 103 B.R. 355 (D. Me. 1989). One court has held that a motion for directed referral is the appropriate means to request that such a case be referred. Thomas Steel Corp. v. Bethlehem Rebar Indus., 101 B.R. 16 (Bankr. N.D. Ill. 1989).

29 28 U.S.C. § 156(b). The remaining districts have a deputy clerk for bankruptcy, often in a separate office.

30 Vreugdenhil v. Hoekstra, 773 F.2d 213 (8th Cir. 1985); Cent. Nat'l Bank v. Kwak, 49 B.R. 337 (N.D. Ohio 1985).

31 28 U.S.C. § 157(b)(1).

32 *See* 11 U.S.C. §§ 301, 303(h).

bankruptcy court, however, the district court may withdraw the entire bankruptcy case or part of it from the bankruptcy court.[33]

13.2.4 Types of Proceedings

13.2.4.1 Adversary Proceedings, Contested Matters, and Applications

Generally, a "proceeding" is a litigated controversy in connection with the bankruptcy case, either a contested matter governed by Bankruptcy Rule 9014 or an adversary proceeding under Bankruptcy Rules 7001–7087. An "adversary proceeding" is essentially a lawsuit within the bankruptcy case and the rules governing such proceedings closely parallel the Federal Rules of Civil Procedure, requiring the proceeding to be commenced by a complaint, providing federal civil discovery procedure and the like.[34] Bankruptcy Rule 7001 specifies those types of proceedings that must be brought as adversary proceedings.[35]

Most other proceedings are "contested matters," essentially treated as motions within the main bankruptcy case. Bankruptcy Rule 9014, which governs contested matters, specifies that some but not all of the adversary proceeding rules ordinarily apply to such proceedings.[36] A few types of matters, usually very routine and uncontested, are designated as "applications," for example, an application to pay the filing fee in installments.[37]

13.2.4.2 Core and Non-Core Proceedings

Many of the bankruptcy procedural mechanisms revolve around the distinction between "core" and "non-core" proceedings. A bankruptcy judge may hear and enter final judgments and orders in any core proceeding, as defined by section 157(b)(2) of title 28.[38] In delineating core proceed-

ings, Congress attempted to identify proceedings within a bankruptcy case or arising under the Bankruptcy Code which did not fall into the category of "related" cases which the Supreme Court, in *Northern Pipeline*, prohibited a bankruptcy judge from deciding. Core proceedings include, "but are not limited to":[39]

(A) Matters concerning the administration of the estate;

(B) Allowance or disallowance of claims against the estate or exemptions from property of the estate, and estimation of claims of interest for the purposes of confirming a plan under chapter 11 or 13 of title 11 but not the liquidation or estimation of contingent or unliquidated personal injury tort or wrongful death claims against the estate for purposes of distribution in a case under title 11;[40]

(C) Counterclaims by the estate against persons filing claims against the estate;

(D) Orders in respect to obtaining credit;

(E) Orders to turn over property of the estate;

(F) Proceedings to determine, avoid, or recover preferences;

(G) Motions to terminate, annul or modify the automatic stay;

(H) Proceedings to determine, avoid, or recover fraudulent conveyances;

(I) Determinations as to the dischargeability of particular debts;

(J) Objections to discharges;

(K) Determinations of the validity, extent, or priority of liens;

(L) Confirmations of plans;

(M) Orders approving the use or lease of property, including the use of cash collateral;

(N) Orders approving the sale of property other than property resulting from claims brought by the estate against persons who have not filed claims against the estate; and

(O) Other proceedings affecting the liquidation of the assets of the estate or the adjustment of the debtor-creditor or the equity security holder relationship, except personal injury tort or wrongful death claims.[41]

---

33   *See* § 13.2.5, *infra*.

34   Fed. R. Bankr. P. 7001–7087; *see In re* Adair, 965 F.2d 777 (9th Cir. 1992) (procedure of taking direct testimony by written declaration complied with Federal Rules of Evidence and Federal Rules of Civil Procedure incorporated in Bankruptcy Rules).

35   At least one court of appeals has held that the requisites of an adversary proceeding can be waived by the parties. *In re* Vill. Mobile Homes, Inc., 947 F.2d 1282 (5th Cir. 1991).

36   Fed. R. Bankr. P. 9014 also provides that the court may order that additional adversary proceeding rules shall be applicable in a particular proceeding, or that some of the rules specified in Rule 9014 shall not be applicable.

37   Some types of applications, such as an application for attorney fees under Fed. R. Bankr. P. 2016(a), may be contested. The designation of such proceedings as applications is probably just a custom carried over from prior rules.

38   However, the bankruptcy court need not enter a final judgment. Teton Exploration Drilling, Inc. v. Bokum Res. Corp., 818 F.2d 1521 (10th Cir. 1987) (where bankruptcy court erroneously

treated matter as non-core, district court's adoption of bankruptcy court's opinion constituted valid judgment).

39   28 U.S.C. § 157(b)(2). Proceedings not specifically listed may be core proceedings if they concern fundamental functions of the bankruptcy court, such as determining the nature and extent of the estate. *In re* Goodman, 991 F.2d 613 (9th Cir. 1993) (proceeding brought by debtor-subtenant to enjoin unlawful detainer against tenant was core proceeding).

40   *See, e.g., In re* Manville Forest Products Corp., 896 F.2d 1384 (2d Cir. 1990); *In re* Meyertech Corp., 831 F.2d 410 (3d Cir. 1987) (creditor's breach of warranty action was a core proceeding seeking allowance of claim).

41   Because the question of a discharge is a core matter, the question whether someone violated the discharge injunction

This list is similar to the list of proceedings defined as not "related" under the emergency rule in effect from 1982 to 1984. Nevertheless, there are differences between the two lists, so that even courts that approved the emergency rule may not necessarily agree that every item on the list created by the 1984 Amendments may be delegated to a non-Article III court. And, of course, the Supreme Court never approved even the list set out in the emergency rule. Therefore, constitutional challenges may continue, particularly to proceedings found to be included in the last category, (O), listed above.[42]

If the bankruptcy court does not have core jurisdiction to decide a proceeding, then the proceeding falls into one of two other jurisdictional pigeonholes. In some cases, there is no jurisdiction for the court to decide the issue at all. In others, the issue is related to the bankruptcy case so that the court may exercise "non-core" jurisdiction, but may only recommend findings of fact and conclusions of law to the district court unless the parties consent to entry of a final judgment by the bankruptcy court. These issues are discussed in the two following subsections as is the procedure by which the court determines the extent of its jurisdiction.

13.2.4.3 Court's Determination of Jurisdictional Questions

The first question that must be answered in determining jurisdiction over a proceeding is whether there is any federal bankruptcy jurisdiction over the matter at all.[43] Some proceedings may be so remote from the bankruptcy that they will have no impact on the bankruptcy case and cannot be considered even to be related to it.[44] In such instances, the

bankruptcy court may never hear the proceeding, and a district court may hear it only if there is some non-bankruptcy basis for federal jurisdiction.

However, even in such cases, there may be bankruptcy jurisdiction over the property involved.[45] And when there is some effect on the bankruptcy estate or the administration of the case, the matter at least is a non-core, related proceeding.[46] Generally, each claim included in a proceeding must

---

must also be a core matter. *In re* Schatz, 122 B.R. 327 (N.D. Ill. 1990).

42 *See, e.g.*, Briden v. Foley, 776 F.2d 379 (1st Cir. 1985) (core bankruptcy proceeding with respect to a public right may constitutionally be decided by an Article I court).

43 Of course, constitutional limitations on the power of federal courts to resolve cases, such as the requirement of a "case or controversy" also may apply to preclude bankruptcy court decision-making. *In re* Kilen, 129 B.R. 538 (Bankr. N.D. Ill. 1991).

44 *See, e.g., In re* Boone, 52 F.3d 958 (11th Cir. 1995) (chapter 7 debtor's suit based upon post-petition cause of action would have no impact on bankruptcy case); Specialty Mills v. Citizens State Bank, 51 F.3d 770 (8th Cir. 1995) (damage action by debtor's lessee against a creditor based upon motion filed in bankruptcy case would not affect bankruptcy case); *In re* Gallucci, 931 F.2d 738 (11th Cir. 1991) (trustee's action to recover property which would not belong to bankruptcy estate is not related to bankruptcy case); *In re* Lemco Gypsum, Inc., 910 F.2d 784 (11th Cir. 1990) (dispute between debtor's landlord and purchaser of debtor's assets was non-related because it did not affect other creditors and could not have effect on debtor's estate); *In re* Bobroff, 766 F.2d 797 (3d Cir. 1985) (post-petition tort claim of debtor not within bankruptcy jurisdiction); Pacor, Inc. v. Higgins, 743 F.2d 984 (3d Cir. 1984) (determination of products liability action between original plaintiff and defen-

dant, where debtor was third party defendant, would not affect bankruptcy estate because it would not determine any rights of the debtor); *see also In re* Resorts Int'l, 372 F.3d 154 (3d Cir. 2004) (jurisdiction cannot be created by a confirmed plan when it does not otherwise exist); *In re* Gardner, 913 F.2d 515 (10th Cir. 1990) (where debtor had no interest in property following divorce order awarding property to debtor's ex-spouse, bankruptcy court lacked jurisdiction to determine whether ex-spouse's interests in property were superior to those of government); Home Ins. Co. v. Cooper & Cooper Ltd., 889 F.2d 746 (7th Cir. 1989) (district court must determine whether action is related to bankruptcy before circuit court can address merits of appeal); *In re* Hall's Motor Trans., 889 F.2d 520 (3d Cir. 1989) (bankruptcy court lacks jurisdiction to entertain action by purchaser of property from bankruptcy estate to enjoin enforcement of local zoning ordinance); *In re* Am. Hardwoods, Inc., 885 F.2d 621 (9th Cir. 1989) (bankruptcy court lacks jurisdiction to permanently enjoin creditor from enforcing state court judgment against non-debtor guarantors); Nat'l City Bank v. Coopers & Lybrand, 802 F.2d 990 (8th Cir. 1986) (action alleging accountant malpractice did not arise under or relate to bankruptcy proceeding). Similarly, in some cases where the debtor seeks to protect a non-debtor third party from liability at the hands of a creditor, the court may not have power to enter an injunction. *Cf.* United States v. Huckabee Auto Co., 783 F.2d 1546 (11th Cir. 1986) (bankruptcy court lacks jurisdiction to enjoin IRS from imposing tax liability on non-debtor third party even to the extent that such liability would affect debtor's ability to reorganize).

45 *See In re* Moody, 837 F.2d 724 (6th Cir. 1987) (district court had jurisdiction to make order affecting debtor's post-petition property in favor of bankruptcy trustee); *In re* Teel, 34 B.R. 762 (B.A.P. 9th Cir. 1983) (bankruptcy court retained exclusive jurisdiction over community property despite marital dissolution action in state court). *But see In re* McClellan, 99 F.3d 1420 (7th Cir. 1996) (bankruptcy court had no jurisdiction to make orders concerning ERISA plan that was excluded from bankruptcy estate); *In re* Edwards, 962 F.2d 641 (7th Cir. 1992) (bankruptcy court had no jurisdiction over lien priority dispute and purchaser of property after property had been sold free and clear of liens); *In re* Fietz, 852 F.2d 455 (9th Cir. 1988) (after confirmation of chapter 13 plan, if recovery of property of the estate can no longer affect the bankruptcy case and property of estate has vested in debtor, there is no bankruptcy jurisdiction).

46 *See, e.g., In re* Time Constr., Inc., 43 F.3d 1041 (6th Cir. 1995) (bankruptcy court has jurisdiction over proceeding if outcome could alter debtor's rights, options or freedom of action); Abramowitz v. Palmer, 999 F.2d 1274 (8th Cir. 1993) (action to impose constructive trust on non-debtor spouse's interest in home was related to bankruptcy case because home was purchased with fraudulently obtained funds and court needed to determine rights of spouse to fully and fairly resolve rights of debtor); *In re* Marcus Hook Dev. Park, Inc., 943 F.2d 261 (3d Cir. 1991) (test is whether proceeding could "conceivably" have any effect on the estate being administered in bankruptcy);

be analyzed separately because some claims may be related while others are not.[47]

Occasionally, a court may rule that it lacks jurisdiction over an issue in a bankruptcy proceeding, because of a prior binding ruling on that issue in state court. The application of the "Rooker-Feldman"[48] doctrine deprives a federal court of jurisdiction when its ruling on an issue effectively would require overturning a prior decision of the state court.[49] The doctrine exists independently of claim and issue preclusion.

Thus, whenever possible, the debtor should avoid a state court decision on an issue which might later be resolved in a bankruptcy proceeding, possibly by removal[50] or the filing of an independent bankruptcy court proceeding. If a state court decision is unavoidable, a debtor may seek to establish, based on the record, that the issues are different in the bankruptcy proceeding than they were in the state court. Alternatively, state court appeals or motions for reconsideration or for relief from judgment are not precluded unless the automatic stay applies to the action.[51]

If there is some basis for bankruptcy jurisdiction, the proceeding must be either a core proceeding or a non-core proceeding. In an adversary proceeding, the complaint, and also any counterclaim, cross-claim or third party complaint, must contain a statement of whether the action is core or non-core.[52] The determination of whether a proceeding is a core proceeding is to be made initially by the bankruptcy court, on its own motion or on motion of a party.[53] But if no motion has been made by a party, and the parties have not explicitly disagreed on the issue, there is probably no necessity for a formal determination at the outset of every proceeding. The mere fact that a proceeding involves an issue of state law does not make it a non-core proceeding.[54] Many of the proceedings listed as core proceedings involve issues of state law, and bankruptcy courts have always considered state law issues in some contexts.

The issue of whether a proceeding is core or non-core may not always be clear. It is probably correct to assume that any proceeding asserting a right created by the Bankruptcy Code, or which could only arise in bankruptcy, is a core proceeding.[55] If the proceeding is based upon state or federal

---

Robinson v. Michigan Consol. Gas Co., 918 F.2d 579 (6th Cir. 1990) (action brought by debtor's tenants against trustee and utility for wrongful discontinuation of utility service was related proceeding because recovery was sought from estate); Diamond Mortgage Corp. of Ill. v. Sugar, 913 F.2d 1233 (7th Cir. 1990) (corporate debtor's malpractice action against former attorneys was related to corporation's bankruptcy case because resolution might impact on assets available for distribution); Kaohani Ohana, Ltd. v. Sutherland, 873 F.2d 1302 (9th Cir. 1989) (bankruptcy jurisdiction exists whenever litigation may alter potential obligations arising out of claims pending against the estate); *In re* Contractors Equip. Supply Co., 861 F.2d 241 (9th Cir. 1988) (bankruptcy court had jurisdiction over suit between non-debtor third party and secured creditor because non-debtor was seeking to recover property in which debtor retained an interest); *In re* Majestic Energy Corp., 835 F.2d 87 (5th Cir. 1988) (bankruptcy court could determine effect of agreement related to debtor's stock after plan confirmation because issues presented were related to the debtor's bankruptcy case and parties had consented to bankruptcy court determination); *In re* Wood, 825 F.2d 90 (5th Cir. 1987) (case involved possible liability of estate for wrongful appropriation of assets); *In re* Xonics, Inc., 813 F.2d 127 (7th Cir. 1987) (payment to debtor's other creditors would depend on competing claims to pool of money); *In re* Dogpatch, U.S.A., Inc., 810 F.2d 782 (8th Cir. 1987) (outcome of proceeding would have effect on estate and possibly impose liability on the debtor); *In re* S. Indus. Banking Corp., 809 F.2d 329 (6th Cir. 1987) (cause of action arose because of bankruptcy proceeding and was based on bankruptcy law and debt alleged as setoff was owed by debtor). The bankruptcy court has the concurrent jurisdiction to determine a debtor's tax liability under 11 U.S.C. § 505(a), even if the parties have been granted relief from the stay to pursue litigation over the same issue in the United States Tax Court. United States v. Wilson, 974 F.2d 514 (4th Cir. 1992). However, the bankruptcy court may not determine tax liability if that liability has already been adjudicated by the Tax Court. *In re* Bunyan, 354 F.3d 1149 (9th Cir. 2004) (bankruptcy court lacked jurisdiction to consider issues previously decided by final orders of tax court); *In re* Teal, 16 F.3d 619 (5th Cir. 1994); *see also In re* Cody, Inc., 338 F.3d 89 (bankruptcy court lacked jurisdiction over issues of debtor's tax-exempt status that had already been decided in non-bankruptcy proceedings).

47 *See, e.g., In re* Reed, 94 B.R. 48 (E.D. Pa. 1988) (bankruptcy court could decide chapter 7 debtor's claims related to a post-petition fire insofar as fire damaged personal property of her estate, but could not determine whether landlord had properly fulfilled obligations as to leasehold interest acquired post-petition which was not property of the debtor's estate).

48 *See* D.C. Ct. of Appeals v. Feldman, 460 U.S. 462, 103 S. Ct. 1303, 75 L. Ed. 2d 206 (1983) (federal courts lack jurisdiction to consider issues which are "inextricably intertwined" with a state court's decision); Rooker v. Fid. Trust Co., 263 U.S. 413, 44 S. Ct. 149, 68 L. Ed. 362 (1923).

49 *E.g., In re* Abboud, 237 B.R. 777 (B.A.P. 10th Cir. 1999) (bankruptcy court would not decide objection to proof of claim when sole basis of objection had been raised in state court proceeding and rejected by state court); *In re* Ferren, 227 B.R. 279 (B.A.P. 8th Cir. 1998) (court lacked jurisdiction to resolve adversary proceeding seeking turnover of funds that had been disbursed pursuant to decision of state court to creditors whose claims had arguably been discharged), *aff'd*, 203 F.3d 559 (8th Cir. 2000). *Compare In re* Gruntz, 202 F.3d 1074 (9th Cir. 2000) (*en banc*) (state court ruling on applicability of automatic stay was subject to bankruptcy court's ultimate authority to determine scope of stay, so Rooker-Feldman doctrine does not apply) *with In re* Pope, 209 B.R. 1004 (Bankr. D. Kan. 1997) (review of state court determination that litigant's actions did not violate stay is barred by Rooker-Feldman).

50 *See* § 13.4.1, *infra.*

51 *See* § 9.4.1, *supra.*

52 Fed. R. Bankr. P. 7008(a).

53 28 U.S.C. § 157(b)(3).

54 28 U.S.C. § 157(b)(3); *see In re* Manville Forest Products Corp., 896 F.2d 1384 (2d Cir. 1990); *see also* § 13.2.4.2, *supra.*

55 *In re* Harbour, 840 F.2d 1165 (4th Cir. 1988); *In re* Wood, 825 F.2d 90 (5th Cir. 1987); *see In re* McLaren, 990 F.2d 850 (bankruptcy court could determine dischargeability of a debt as a core proceeding, and the validity of the debt was also a core

non-bankruptcy law, however, it must be examined further. Generally, if it is brought as a counterclaim or otherwise against a creditor of the debtor, the proceeding is considered a core proceeding.[56] If the proceeding is brought against a non-creditor third party, it usually is not a core proceeding.[57] If the proceeding is brought against the debtor by a person who is not a pre-petition creditor, the proceeding may or may not fit into any of the categories of core proceedings. In some cases, the determination may involve a claim-by-claim analysis, with some claims being core and some non-core.[58]

Even in cases in which jurisdiction is found, an additional issue which occasionally arises is the bankruptcy court's power to enter certain types of equitable relief requested by a party. Code section 105 generally gives the bankruptcy court power to issue orders, process and judgments "necessary or appropriate" to carry out the provisions of the Bankruptcy Code.[59] Section 105 is not, however, a substan-

tive grant of jurisdiction.[60] It also does not give the bankruptcy court unlimited power to create substantive rights or to issue equitable relief contrary to the Bankruptcy Code or applicable law.[61]

A few courts have used this principle to improperly limit the authority of bankruptcy courts to address creditor violations of the bankruptcy law. In some cases, courts have denied remedies under section 105 to parties seeking relief from creditor fraud or egregious violations of the discharge injunction on the basis that no private right of action exists under section 105.[62] These courts ignore the importance of the statutory power to issue orders, process and judgments necessary and appropriate to carry out the provisions of the Bankruptcy Code.[63] Clearly, in order to seek the court's use of that authority, a party in interest must bring the problem to the attention of the court, by complaint or otherwise, seeking to have the provisions of the Code effectuated— whether by restitution or some other equitable remedy.

---

issue), *superseding* 983 F.2d 56 (6th Cir. 1993); *see also* Moody v. Amoco Oil, 734 F.2d 1200 (7th Cir. 1984) (proceeding to assume contract under § 365 not a "related" case under emergency rule); *In re* Goldrich, 45 B.R. 514 (Bankr. E.D.N.Y. 1984) (action to enforce nondiscrimination provisions of 11 U.S.C. § 525 a core proceeding), *rev'd on other grounds*, 771 F.2d 28 (2d Cir. 1985). But see Granfinanciera, S.A. v. Nordberg, 492 U.S. 33, 109 S. Ct. 2782, 106 L. Ed. 2d 26 (1989), which may cast doubt on this proposition.

56 28 U.S.C. § 157(b)(2)(C), (O); *In re* Baudoin, 981 F.2d 736 (5th Cir. 1993) (debtor's lender liability suit against creditor was core proceeding). *But see In re* Brickell Inv. Corp., 922 F.2d 696 (11th Cir. 1991) (application for attorney fees against IRS is non-core proceeding even though request stems from core proceeding, but could be a related proceeding because bankruptcy court is not a "court of the United States" as specified in 26 U.S.C. § 7430); *In re* Castlerock Properties, 781 F.2d 159 (9th Cir. 1986). In addition, personal injury tort or wrongful death claims are expressly made non-core proceedings. *See* § 13.2.6, *infra*.

57 *See, e.g., In re* Cinematronics, Inc., 916 F.2d 1444 (9th Cir. 1990) (state law claims against corporate debtor's principal shareholder/president for his post-petition conduct were non-core where claims would not directly affect estate or confirmation of plan); Howell Hydrocarbons, Inc. v. Adams, 897 F.2d 183 (5th Cir. 1990) (RICO claims brought by seller of jet fuel against shareholders, officers, directors and managing agent of debtor buyer's parent corporation were non-core, non-related proceedings); Rosen-Novak Auto Co. v. Honz, 783 F.2d 739 (8th Cir. 1986) (action against debtor's insurer); *In re* Vinci, 108 B.R. 439 (Bankr. S.D.N.Y. 1989) (debtor's civil rights claim against non-creditor is a non-core related proceeding). *But see In re* Cassidy Land & Cattle Co., 836 F.2d 1130 (8th Cir. 1988) (debtor's action to foreclose on mortgage which constituted sole asset of bankruptcy estate is core proceeding in the nature of a turnover action); *In re* Arnold Print Works, 815 F.2d 165 (1st Cir. 1987) (debtor in possession's action to collect on contract made after bankruptcy as part of estate administration was core proceeding); *see also In re* Orion Pictures, 4 F.3d 1095 (2d Cir. 1993) (contract suit against party to executory contract that debtor wished to assume was non-core proceeding).

58 Halper v. Halper, 164 F.3d 830 (3d Cir. 1999).

59 *See In re* Hardy, 97 F.3d 1384 (11th Cir. 1996); Browning v. Navarro, 887 F.2d 553 (5th Cir. 1989) (section 105 is an

authorization under the anti-injunction act, 28 U.S.C. § 2283, giving the bankruptcy court power to vacate a fraudulent state court judgment held against the estate); *see also* 2 Collier on Bankruptcy § 105.01[2] (15th ed. rev.).

60 *See* Official Committee of Equity Sec. Holders v. Mabey, 832 F.2d 299 (4th Cir. 1987); *In re* Sequoia Auto Brokers Ltd., 827 F.2d 1281 (9th Cir. 1987) (section 105 is not a substantive grant of authority empowering bankruptcy judges to enter contempt orders).

61 Norwest Bank Worthington v. Ahlers, 485 U.S. 197, 108 S. Ct. 963, 99 L. Ed. 2d 169 (1988) ("Whatever equitable powers remain in the bankruptcy courts must and can only be exercised within the confines of the Bankruptcy Code."); *see also In re* Ionosphere Clubs, Inc., 922 F.2d 984 (2d Cir. 1990) (powers under § 105 cannot be exercised in derogation of other sections of the Code); *In re* Weissman, 126 B.R. 889 (Bankr. N.D. Ill. 1991) (bankruptcy judge has no power to alter priorities contained in the Code); *In re* Gerst, 106 B.R. 429 (Bankr. E.D. Pa. 1989) (bankruptcy court has power to issue injunction requiring that debtor's landlord repair conditions which constitute serious risk to health and safety of residents). *Compare In re* Am. Hardwoods, Inc., 885 F.2d 621 (9th Cir. 1989) (section 105 does not give the bankruptcy court power to permanently enjoin creditors from enforcing a judgment against non-debtor guarantors of a corporate debtor) *with In re* A.H. Robins Co., 880 F.2d 694 (4th Cir. 1989) (section 105 permits court to enjoin suit against non-debtor corporate officers and directors in order to effectuate debtor's confirmed plan).

62 *E.g.*, Cox v. Zale Del., Inc., 239 F.3d 910 (7th Cir. 2001); Pertuso v. Ford Motor Cr. Co., 233 F.3d 417 (6th Cir. 2000); Holloway v. Household Auto. Fin. Corp., 227 B.R. 501 (N.D. Ill. 1998) (no private right of action under § 105 to address creditors fraudulently filed or inflated proofs of claim); *In re* Wiley, 224 B.R. 58 (Bankr. N.D. Ill. 1998) (no private right of action to enforce discharge injunction), *vacated and modified on other grounds*, 237 B.R. 677 (Bankr. N.D. Ill. 1999). *But see* Malone v. Norwest Fin. Cal., Inc., 245 B.R. 389 (E.D. Cal. 2000) (section 105 creates right of action to enforce discharge injunction in action involving unfiled reaffirmation agreements).

63 Bessette v. Avco Fin. Services, Inc., 230 F.3d 439 (1st Cir. 2000) (section 524 may be enforced through section 105); *see also* § 14.5.5.7, *infra*.

Consumer Bankruptcy Law and Practice

One further issue which may arise involves the scope of the bankruptcy court's jurisdiction over a case after it has been closed or dismissed. Many matters "arising under" or "related to" a bankruptcy proceeding may be brought before the court after a case has ended, even if the case is not formally reopened.[64] Nothing in the Bankruptcy Code or title 28 of the United States Code precludes a bankruptcy court from exercising jurisdiction over such matters.

As a practical matter, all of the proceedings in a routine consumer bankruptcy case are normally considered core proceedings, so these new jurisdictional provisions have no significant effect on them. Such proceedings will generally continue to be heard in the bankruptcy court, subject to appeal to higher courts. Other proceedings, though, including many of the types of actions discussed later in this chapter, do raise issues as to where they should be heard. And the distinction between core proceedings and non-core proceedings is only the first step in resolving those issues under the bankruptcy jurisdictional scheme. Even if a proceeding is found to be a core proceeding, which the bankruptcy court may decide, there is no assurance that it will remain in that court.

13.2.4.4 Procedure in Non-Core Proceedings

If a proceeding is determined to be a non-core proceeding, it is still normally initiated in the bankruptcy court pursuant to the district court's referral. The proceeding may be heard by the bankruptcy court and that court may make interlocutory orders.[65] However, the bankruptcy judge may not enter a final judgment or order, unless all parties consent.[66] A party's consent is to be set forth in the pleadings.[67] However, consent may also be implied by a party's actions.[68] If such consent is not obtained, the bankruptcy court may only submit proposed findings of fact and conclusions of law to the district court.[69]

If (and only if) a party timely objects[70] to any of the proposed findings and conclusions, the district court must conduct a de novo review of the pertinent portions of proceedings.[71] Arguably, if no party objects, the district court must accept the proposed findings and conclusions of the bankruptcy court.[72] The failure to file objections to recommended findings of fact and conclusions of law has been held to constitute a waiver of any right to appeal a district court's order adopting such recommendations.[73]

64 *See, e.g., In re* Statistical Tabulating Corp., 60 F.3d 1286 (7th Cir. 1995) (bankruptcy court could reopen dismissed bankruptcy case to decide remand of appeal which was not mooted by dismissal); *In re* Universal Farming Indus., 873 F.2d 1334 (9th Cir. 1989) (appeal of case determining priority of interests in debtor's property not mooted by dismissal of underlying bankruptcy); *In re* Franklin, 802 F.2d 324 (9th Cir. 1986) (bankruptcy court could construe its order in a prior bankruptcy case which had not been reopened); *see also In re* Porges, 44 F.3d 159 (2d Cir. 1995) (bankruptcy court could retain jurisdiction over adversary proceeding after underlying bankruptcy case was dismissed); *In re* Carreher, 971 F.2d 327 (9th Cir. 1992) (bankruptcy court could retain jurisdiction over related fraud claims of the debtor after dismissing debtor's bankruptcy case); *In re* Morris, 950 F.2d 1531 (11th Cir. 1992) (bankruptcy court could retain jurisdiction over adversary proceeding after main chapter 11 case was dismissed); *In re* Smith, 866 F.2d 576 (3d Cir. 1989) (bankruptcy court could retain jurisdiction over adversary proceeding after bankruptcy case closed to complete litigation of related claims). Of course, certain matters may be mooted by the dismissal or close of the case. *See In re* Petty, 848 F.2d 654 (5th Cir. 1988) (court's jurisdiction over motion to have lease deemed rejected ends upon dismissal of case). *But see* Chapman v. Currie Motors, 65 F.3d 78 (7th Cir. 1995) (district court could relinquish jurisdiction over proceeding based upon state law after bankruptcy case dismissed); *In re* Querner, 7 F.3d 1199 (5th Cir. 1993) (bankruptcy court should not have retained jurisdiction over probate matter after bankruptcy case closed where bankruptcy judge had not become deeply involved in matter, had no special knowledge about probate and had no reason to believe outcome could affect bankruptcy estate).

65 *In re* Kennedy, 48 B.R. 621 (Bankr. D. Ariz. 1985).

66 28 U.S.C. § 157(c)(1), (2); *In re* Pioneer Inv. Services Co., 946 F.2d 445 (6th Cir. 1991).

67 Fed. R. Bankr. P. 7008(a).

68 *In re* Texas Gen.Petroleum Corp., 52 F.3d 1330 (5th Cir. 1995) (party that does not object to bankruptcy court's assumption of core jurisdiction consents to entry of final judgment by bankruptcy court); *In re* Johnson, 960 F.2d 396 (4th Cir. 1992) (by allowing bankruptcy judge to enter dispositive order parties impliedly consented to core jurisdiction); *In re* G.S.F. Corp., 938 F.2d 1467 (1st Cir. 1991) (consent implied by parties' filing settlement agreement for final approval by bankruptcy court); *In re* Men's Sportswear, Inc., 834 F.2d 1134 (2d Cir. 1987) (failure to object to bankruptcy court's assumption of core jurisdiction may constitute implied consent); *In re* Daniels-Head & Associates, 819 F.2d 914 (9th Cir. 1987). *But see* Advisory Committee Note to 1987 Amendment to Fed. R. Bankr. P. 7008; *see also In re* BNI Telecommunications, 246 B.R. 845 (B.A.P. 6th Cir. 2000) (admission in pleading that proceeding was core proceeding was not enough, in circumstances of particular case, to constitute consent).

69 28 U.S.C. § 157(c)(1); Fed. R. Bankr. P. 9033.

70 Pursuant to Fed. R. Bankr. P. 9033(b) objections must be filed within ten days after service of the proposed findings of fact and conclusions of law. Service of objections then triggers a ten-day period for a response by any other party. Further, pursuant to Rule 9033(c), upon request made prior to expiration of the ten-day period for objections, the bankruptcy judge is empowered to extend the time allowed for filing objections for up to twenty days.

71 28 U.S.C. § 157(c)(1); Fed. R. Bankr. P. 9033. Where it was shown that the district court conducted no hearing and did not consider the actual testimony in bankruptcy court, no de novo review occurred. *In re* Castro, 919 F.2d 107 (9th Cir. 1990). A party claiming that the district court had not conducted a de novo review has the burden of proof. The fact that the record remained with the clerk of the bankruptcy court is not sufficient to show that a de novo review has not been conducted by the district court. *In re* Dillon Constr. Co., 922 F.2d 495 (8th Cir. 1991).

72 There is no provision in Fed. R. Bankr. P. 9033 for review absent a timely objection.

73 *In re* Nantahala Vill., Inc., 976 F.2d 876 (4th Cir. 1992).

13.2.5 *Withdrawal to the District Court*

13.2.5.1 In General

Regardless of whether a matter is or is not a core proceeding, it may still come to be heard initially in the district court. The bankruptcy jurisdictional provisions provide that after the initial referral to the bankruptcy court a bankruptcy proceeding, or even the bankruptcy case itself in whole or in part, may be withdrawn back to the district court.[74] Withdrawal is discretionary in some cases and mandatory in others. Such withdrawal may be upon "timely" motion of a party or on the court's own motion.[75]

Because the withdrawal decision appears to be one that can be made only by the district court, any motion for withdrawal must be addressed to that court.[76] However, the 1987 Advisory Committee Note to Federal Rule of Bankruptcy Procedure 5011 indicates that the motion should be filed with the bankruptcy clerk.

Rule 5011 does not appear to clarify time limits for filing a motion for withdrawal.[77] It should be remembered, however, that a motion for withdrawal, whenever filed, does not operate as a stay of the proceeding in the bankruptcy court. If a stay pending determination of a motion for withdrawal is desired, a motion for a stay should be presented in the first instance to the bankruptcy judge.[78]

13.2.5.2 Mandatory Withdrawal

In certain classes of cases or proceedings, including core proceedings, if a party timely[79] moves for withdrawal to the district court, that motion must be granted. Such mandatory withdrawal upon motion must occur whenever the resolution of a proceeding "requires consideration of both title 11 and other laws of the United States regulating organizations or activities affecting interstate commerce."[80] Although the general purpose of this section is clear—to prevent bankruptcy courts from deciding, over the objections of a party, substantial questions under statutes such as the antitrust and securities laws—the precise scope of the section is not.

What is meant by "consideration of both title 11 and other laws?" Does the section apply to matters considering federal laws regulating interstate commerce but not title 11? It may not. Some courts have held that both bankruptcy law and other federal law issues must coexist for mandatory withdrawal to be proper.[81]

How much "consideration" is necessary for the section to apply? Presumably, there would have to be more than mere consideration of a federal commerce statute by way of analogy. The legislative history suggests that the interstate commerce statute must be material to the resolution of the proceeding.[82] Some courts have suggested that there must be a need for "substantial and material" consideration of such a statute for withdrawal to be required.[83] The Seventh

---

74 28 U.S.C. § 157(d).

75 28 U.S.C. § 157(d); *see* Anderson v. Fed. Deposit Ins. Corp., 918 F.2d 1139 (4th Cir. 1990) (district court's retention of jurisdiction after plaintiff filed bankruptcy and trustee was substituted as plaintiff effectively withdrew matter from bankruptcy court). Where a district court withdraws the reference after the bankruptcy court has rendered a decision, the district court may exercise its original jurisdiction to reshape relief. *In re* Moody, 899 F.2d 383 (5th Cir. 1990).

76 Fed. R. Bankr. P. 5011(a); *In re* Porter, 295 B.R. 529 (Bankr. E.D. Pa. 2003) (bankruptcy court has no authority to send case back to district court, because only district court may withdraw reference).

77 *See In re* IQ Telecommunications, Inc., 70 B.R. 742 (N.D. Ill. 1987) (motion before answer was due was timely, but motion made over one year after proceeding began was not timely).

78 Fed. R. Bankr. P. 5011(c); *In re* Morse Elec. Co, Inc., 47 B.R. 234 (Bankr. N.D. Ind. 1985); *see also In re* Roppolo, 111 B.R. 113 (Bankr. W.D. La. 1990) (request for stay of fraudulent conveyance proceedings pending resolution of motion for withdrawal denied).

79 There are currently no rules to determine timeliness under this section. However, a motion for withdrawal of reference presumably must be filed prior to dismissal or discharge. *In re* Mandalay Shores Coop. Hous. Ass'n, Inc., 58 B.R. 586 (N.D. Ill. 1986). One court has held that a motion for withdrawal more

than six months after the grounds for the motion were discovered is untimely. Laine v. Gross, 128 B.R. 588 (D. Me. 1991). That court was concerned that withdrawal was not sought until after a motion to dismiss had been resolved by the bankruptcy court.

80 28 U.S.C. § 157(d).

81 *In re* Anthony Tammaro, Inc., 56 B.R. 999 (D.N.J. 1986); *In re* Maislin Indus., 50 B.R. 943 (Bankr. E.D. Mich. 1985); *see also In re* Auto Specialties Mfg. Co., 134 B.R. 227 (W.D. Mich. 1990) (filing of RICO claim did not require withdrawal unless there was showing that claim was facially valid, that it presented questions of first impression, or that case required construction of both the Bankruptcy Code and the RICO statute); *In re* Chateaugey Corp., 109 B.R. 613 (S.D.N.Y. 1990) (although underlying case involved both bankruptcy and other federal law, where party sought injunction of that case, withdrawal was properly denied because court did not need to consider other federal law).

82 130 Cong. Rec. S6081 (daily ed. June 19, 1984) (remarks of Sen. DeConcini); *see, e.g.,* Dow Jones/Group W Television Co. v. NBC, Inc., 127 B.R. 3 (S.D.N.Y. 1991) (withdrawal denied where bankruptcy court had merely to apply settled principles of federal antitrust law to the proceeding).

83 *In re* Ionosphere Clubs, Inc., 922 F.2d 984 (2d Cir. 1990); *In re* Adelpi Inst., Inc., 112 B.R. 534 (S.D.N.Y. 1990) (requirement that matter require substantial and material consideration of other federal law excludes from mandatory withdrawal cases which involve only application of other federal law to particular set of facts); *In re* Carolina Produce Distributors, Inc., 110 B.R. 207 (W.D.N.C. 1990) (adversary proceeding under Perishable Agricultural Commodities Act did not involve substantial material question of both bankruptcy law and other federal law required only application of the other federal law to the facts and consideration of state law); *In re* Amfesco Indus., Inc., 81 B.R. 777 (E.D.N.Y. 1988) (question presented did not require substantial and material consideration of the copyright laws); *In re* White Motor Corp., 42 B.R. 693 (N.D. Ohio 1984); *see also In*

Circuit has stated that consideration means the interpretation, as opposed to the mere application of the non-bankruptcy statute, or the resolution of significant open issues of law.[84] Another court has stated that withdrawal is mandatory where the bankruptcy issues are secondary to the non-bankruptcy federal issues.[85]

Mandatory withdrawal may be a very real possibility in some consumer bankruptcy proceedings. For example, debtors may raise a variety of federal consumer protection laws by way of objections to claims or otherwise. In such cases, either party may move for, and possibly obtain, withdrawal of the proceeding to the district court. Naturally, whether the debtor will wish to make a motion for withdrawal will depend on a variety of factors, including the judges involved, the likelihood of delay, and other aspects of the case. The debtor may wish to argue that individual consumer protection cases are not what Congress had in mind when it described laws regulating interstate commerce. However, a motion for withdrawal is certainly an option which must be considered whenever it is available.

13.2.5.3 Discretionary Withdrawal

The district court may also withdraw any case or proceeding at its discretion, either upon motion of a party or upon its own motion. The standards for discretionary withdrawal are far from clear although the statute requires "cause."[86] Certainly, withdrawal makes sense when there is already related litigation in the district court.[87] Withdrawal may also be appropriate when the parties or the court believe that a case will have wide-ranging consequences and is likely to be reviewed de novo by the district court in any event. However, absent exceptional circumstances, it does not seem appropriate for a district court to withdraw the reference of a case or proceeding after receiving an appeal of a final order of the bankruptcy court, because such a withdrawal would frustrate the normal process of the appeal.[88]

13.2.6 Personal Injury and Wrongful Death Claims

A special exception to the broad categories of core proceedings was created by Congress for all personal injury tort and wrongful death claims against the debtor or the estate.[89] The 1984 amendments, in a provision probably designed to curb manufacturers seeking refuge in bankruptcy from asbestos and other product liability claims, require all such claims to be tried either in the district court in which the bankruptcy case is pending or the district court where the claim arose, as determined by the district court in which the bankruptcy is pending.[90]

Although the language of section 157(b)(5) is vague, it was probably not intended to include personal injury and wrongful death claims held by the debtor against a third party. Such claims are usually considered non-core proceedings, which can be heard in the bankruptcy court but not finally determined by that court without the consent of the parties.[91] There may also be disputes as to what types of claims qualify as personal injury claims.[92]

---

re Baker, 86 B.R. 234 (D. Colo. 1988) (withdrawal required where question as to dischargeability of debt required "substantial consideration" of 42 U.S.C. § 1983 and Bankruptcy Code dischargeability provisions).

84 *In re* Vicars Ins. Agency, Inc., 96 F.3d 949 (7th Cir. 1996).

85 Wooten v. Dep't of Interior, 52 B.R. 74 (W.D. La. 1985).

86 28 U.S.C. § 157(d); *In re* Parklane/Atlanta Joint Venture, 927 F.2d 532 (11th Cir. 1991) ("cause" is not an "empty requirement," but may be satisfied in a situation where bankruptcy court disposition of case might be unappealable); Halvajian v. Bank of N.Y., 191 B.R. 56 (D.N.J. 1995) (fact that bankruptcy court lacked supplemental jurisdiction under 28 U.S.C. § 1367 to hear third party state law indemnification claim that defendant wished to raise not cause for withdrawal, because claim could be raised in separate action); *see also In re* Canter, 299 F.3d 1150 (9th Cir. 2002) (granting mandamus to review withdrawal of reference that was inappropriate because bankruptcy court was already familiar with case and had already entered order and because withdrawal created inefficiency and disrupted bankruptcy administration). However, the district court will almost certainly refuse to exercise its discretion to withdraw a core matter, especially where the basis for core jurisdiction is the creditor's presumably voluntary filing of a proof of claim. *See* Bedford Computer Corp. v. Ginn Publ'g, Inc., 63 B.R. 79 (D.N.H. 1986). It would also likely be inappropriate for a district court to withdraw the reference *nunc pro tunc* in order to validate its own order entered in violation of the stay. *Cf.* Mission Indians v. Am. Mgmt. & Amusement, 840 F.2d 1394 (9th Cir. 1987) (reference withdrawn *nunc pro tunc* in conjunction with an order entered after order partially lifting stay).

87 *See* Carlton v. BAWW, Inc., 751 F.2d 781 (5th Cir. 1985); *cf.* Mar. Elec. Co. v. United Jersey Bank, 959 F.2d 1194 (3d Cir. 1991) (district court other than one in jurisdiction where bankruptcy case is filed may retain and exercise "related to" jurisdiction over case involving debtor which is already pending).

88 *In re* Hall, Bayoutree Associates Ltd., 939 F.2d 802 (9th Cir. 1991) (district court's decision to reach issue not raised on appeal cannot constitute a de facto withdrawal of the reference); *In re* Pruitt, 910 F.2d 1160 (3d Cir. 1990) (writ of *mandamus* issued directing district court to consider appeal from bankruptcy court order dismissing case, rather than withdraw reference after the dismissal); *see In re* Powelson, 878 F.2d 976 (7th Cir. 1989) (writ of mandamus issued directing district court to determine appeal of confirmation order rather than withdraw reference and substitute alternative non-appealable "interim" plan).

89 28 U.S.C. § 157(b)(2)(B), (O).

90 28 U.S.C. § 157(b)(5).

91 28 U.S.C. § 157(c); *see In re* Vinci, 108 B.R. 439 (Bankr. S.D.N.Y. 1989) (civil rights claim by debtor against non-creditor governmental entities is a non-core, related proceeding).

92 *See, e.g., In re* Littles, 75 B.R. 240 (Bankr. E.D. Pa. 1987) (claim under Fair Debt Collection Practices Act was not personal injury claim under § 157(b)(5)), *conclusions adopted,* Littles v. Lieberman, 90 B.R. 669 (E.D. Pa. 1988); *see also In*

This provision also was not meant to preclude bankruptcy courts from determining issues related to the dischargeability of claims against the debtor involving personal injury or wrongful death.[93] However, bankruptcy courts may be unwilling to exercise their discretion to liquidate those claims if they have not been liquidated elsewhere.[94]

Section 157(b)(5) requires personal injury tort and wrongful death claims to be tried in the district court. The section does not explicitly require that pretrial proceedings be in the district court, and this omission presumably was deliberate, to leave open the possibility of pretrial proceedings before a bankruptcy judge.[95]

Section 157(b)(2)(B) excludes from the core proceedings list "liquidation or estimation" of personal injury tort or wrongful death claims for purposes of distribution. The section thus does not appear to preclude estimation of these claims for purposes of deciding whether a plan may be confirmed.[96] It also does not preclude discretionary abstention which would allow such claims to be tried in state courts.

13.2.7 Jury Trials in the Bankruptcy Court

Unlike the temporary emergency rule governing bankruptcy jurisdiction from 1982 to 1984, the current jurisdictional statutes contain no prohibition of jury trials conducted by the bankruptcy court. The 1984 amendments specifically preserve the right to a jury trial with regard to personal injury and wrongful death claims.[97] However, that trial may not take place before a bankruptcy judge.[98] It is doubtful that this provision was intended to affect other rights to jury trials that previously existed.[99]

Other questions about jury trial rights in bankruptcy survived the 1984 amendments. Most importantly, these included the degree to which traditional jury trial rights are affected by the Code and the post-*Marathon* jurisdictional scheme and whether jury trials may be conducted by bankruptcy judges.

The first question was addressed by the Supreme Court in *Granfinanciera, S.A. v. Nordberg*.[100] The Court held that under the Seventh Amendment, a defendant in a preference or fraudulent conveyance action who has not filed a claim against the estate retains the right to trial by jury. The Court applied a traditional Seventh Amendment analysis and determined that a preference or fraudulent conveyance action is, by tradition, an action at law as to which jury trial rights are constitutionally preserved.[101] Presumably, in the future, a similar analysis will have to take place when jury trials are demanded, on an issue by issue basis.[102] Courts have held, for example, that there is no constitutional right to a jury trial in a dischargeability action.[103]

When the defendant files a claim against the estate, that party's right to a jury trial is waived.[104] In addition, other limitations on the availability of a jury trial, such as the necessity for a timely jury demand, continue to apply and jury trials may be denied for failure to comply with procedural requirements.[105]

100 492 U.S. 33, 109 S. Ct. 2782, 106 L. Ed. 2d 26 (1989).

101 *But see In re* Texas Gen.Petroleum Corp., 52 F.3d 1330 (5th Cir. 1995) (no jury trial existed in fraudulent transfer proceeding when only issue in proceeding was legal issue of standing).

102 *See generally In re* M & L Bus. Mach. Co., 59 F.3d 1078 (10th Cir. 1995) (no jury trial right in trustee's action under § 549, which was equitable in nature); *In re* O.P.M. Leasing Services, Inc., 48 B.R. 824 (S.D.N.Y. 1985); Macon Prestressed Concrete Co. v. Duke, 46 B.R. 727 (M.D. Ga. 1985).

103 *In re* McLaren, 3 F.3d 958 (6th Cir. 1993) (debtor has no right to jury trial in dischargeability proceeding); *In re* Hallahan, 936 F.2d 1496 (7th Cir. 1991) (debtor has no right to jury trial in dischargeability proceeding); *In re* Hooper, 112 B.R. 1009 (B.A.P. 9th Cir. 1990) (creditor has no right to jury trial in dischargeability proceeding).

104 Langenkamp v. Culp, 498 U.S. 42, 111 S. Ct. 330, 112 L. Ed. 2d 343 (1990); *see also* Billing v. Ravin, Greenberg & Zackin, 22 F.3d 1242 (3d Cir. 1994) (no right of jury trial for malpractice claim asserted as a defense to a proof of claim); *In re* EXDS, 301 B.R. 436 (Bankr. D. Del. 2003) (creditor could not vitiate waiver of jury trial right by withdrawing claim after it was filed). *But see* Smith v. Dowden, 47 F.3d 940 (8th Cir. 1995) (withdrawal of claim before fraudulent transfer proceeding was commenced rendered claim a nullity, so jury trial was not waived).

105 *See In re* Latimer, 918 F.2d 136 (10th Cir. 1990) (oral request for jury trial not sufficient; even if it had been, failure to combine jury request with request for transfer to district court resulted in waiver of right to jury trial); *In re* Wynn, 889 F.2d 644 (5th Cir. 1989) (party who participated in determination of proceeding without reminding court of his jury trial request waived his jury trial rights); *In re* Sand Hills Beef Corp., 199 B.R. 740 (D. Colo. 1996) (failure to request transfer to district court when jury trial was requested resulted in waiver of right to jury trial); *In re* Blackwell *ex rel*. Estate of I.G. Services, 279 B.R. 818 (Bankr. W.D. Tex 2002) (party that demanded jury trial waived right to jury by failing to move to withdraw reference, because bank-

re Gary Brew Enterprises, Ltd., 198 B.R. 616 (Bankr. S.D. Cal 1996) (employment discrimination claim was in nature of personal injury tort); *In re* Vinci, 108 B.R. 439 (Bankr. S.D.N.Y. 1989) (civil rights claim which did not involve bodily injury is not a claim for personal injury).

93 *See* 11 U.S.C. § 523(a)(6); 28 U.S.C. § 157(b)(2)(I); *see also* § 14.4.3.6, *infra*.

94 *Cf. In re* Saunders, 103 B.R. 299 (Bankr. N.D. Fla. 1988) (bankruptcy court can exercise discretion to have potentially nondischargeable debt liquidated in forum where parties had been litigating for two years prior to bankruptcy).

95 *In re* Chateaugay Corp., 111 B.R. 67 (Bankr. S.D.N.Y. 1990) (bankruptcy court could make initial determination regarding proper parties and statutory defenses). *But see* Pettibone Corp. v. Easley, 935 F.2d 120 (7th Cir. 1991) (bankruptcy judge cannot hear any part of a personal injury case).

96 1 Collier on Bankruptcy ¶ 3.06[2] (15th ed. rev.).

97 28 U.S.C. § 1411.

98 28 U.S.C. § 157(b)(5).

99 *See* 1 Collier on Bankruptcy ¶ 3.09[3] (15th ed. rev.); *see also In re* Graham, 747 F.2d 1383 (11th Cir. 1984) (interpreting prior statutory language that jury rights "provided by any statute" not affected by Bankruptcy Reform Act).

The fact that a proceeding is "core" under the jurisdictional scheme established by the 1984 amendments will not be dispositive in determining whether a jury trial right attaches.[106] Additionally, one court has held that a debtor may retain and assert certain jury trial rights following a bankruptcy petition.[107]

The *Granfinanciera* decision explicitly leaves open the other significant issue regarding jury trials in bankruptcy, that is, whether bankruptcy judges may conduct them. It has always been fairly clear that in non-core matters it would be uneconomic and inefficient to hold jury trials in bankruptcy courts unless the parties consented to entry of final judgment by the bankruptcy judge, because the parties would have a right to a trial de novo in district court.[108] However, after *Granfinanciera*, some core matters clearly carry jury trial rights and significant questions may arise as to whether they may be tried in bankruptcy court. That issue turns in part on whether the Seventh Amendment mandates a jury trial in front of an Article III judge.[109]

To the extent that there was also an issue concerning the bankruptcy court's statutory authority to conduct a jury trial, the situation was clarified by the Bankruptcy Reform Act of 1994.[110] That Act added 28 U.S.C. § 157(e), which provides that if there is a right to a jury trial in a proceeding a bankruptcy judge may hear, the bankruptcy judge may conduct the jury trial if specially designated by the district court to do so and with the express consent of all parties. The statute does not make clear whether the special designation is to be made once for all cases before a particular bankruptcy judge or on a case-by-case basis. At least some district courts have made blanket special designations for their bankruptcy judges.

The procedure for requesting a jury trial is set forth in Federal Rule of Bankruptcy Procedure 9015. The rule incorporates Federal Rules of Civil Procedure 38, 39, 47–51 and 81(c), making them applicable in bankruptcy cases, except that the demand for a jury trial must be filed in accordance with Bankruptcy Rule 5005. Separate consents or a joint consent to a jury trial must be filed no later than the deadline for such consents under local rules.[111]

13.2.8 Contempt Powers of the Bankruptcy Courts

The 1984 amendments also cast doubt upon the power of bankruptcy courts to enter contempt orders. A few courts have held that bankruptcy judges do not have the contempt power because they are not Article III judges.[112] But most have found that civil contempt proceedings, at least when the proceedings involve bankruptcy stays such as the section 362 automatic stay, are core proceedings in which the bankruptcy court may enter final orders.[113] Even those

---

ruptcy court could not unilaterally transfer proceeding to district court); *cf. In re* Corey, 892 F.2d 829 (9th Cir. 1989) (entity controlled by parties who had filed claims against the estate deemed to have filed a claim and therefore ineligible for jury trial).

106 The fairly substantial body of case law which concluded that there are no jury trial rights in core proceedings or in proceedings arising under a specific statutory provision of the Bankruptcy Code has been overruled. *See, e.g.*, Beard v. Braunstein, 914 F.2d 434 (3d Cir. 1990) (party's right to jury trial of claims raised in bankruptcy proceeding does not depend on whether proceeding is designated core or non-core); *In re* Harbour, 840 F.2d 1165 (4th Cir. 1988).

107 *In re* Jensen, 946 F.2d 369 (5th Cir. 1991) (where state court case is removed to bankruptcy court by a creditor, debtor retains jury trial rights notwithstanding voluntary decision to file bankruptcy); *see also* Germain v. Conn. Nat'l Bank, 988 F.2d 1323 (2d Cir. 1993) (filing of bankruptcy case did not waive any right chapter 7 trustee might have to a jury trial).

108 *See, e.g., In re* Orion Pictures, 4 F.3d 1095 (2d Cir. 1993) (bankruptcy court could not constitutionally conduct jury trial in non-core proceeding); *In re* Cinematronics, Inc., 916 F.2d 1444 (9th Cir. 1990) (withdrawal of reference repaired where non-core defendant demands jury trial to which it is entitled and parties do not consent to final judgment by bankruptcy court); Beard v. Braunstein, 914 F.2d 434 (3d Cir. 1990); *In re* Am. Cmty. Services, Inc., 86 B.R. 681 (D. Utah 1988); Macon Prestressed Concrete Co. v. Duke, 46 B.R. 727 (M.D. Ga. 1985); *In re* Morse Elec. Co., 47 B.R. 234 (Bankr. N.D. Ind. 1985). *But see In re* Hardesty, 190 B.R. 653 (D. Kan. 1995) (when jury trial demanded in non-core proceeding, withdrawal of reference not necessary until case is ready for trial).

109 *Compare In re* Clay, 35 F.3d 190 (5th Cir. 1994) (bankruptcy judge had no constitutional or statutory authority to conduct jury trial absent consent of the parties, even in core proceedings); *In re* Stansbury Poplar Place, Inc., 13 F.3d 122 (4th Cir. 1993) (bankruptcy judge has no statutory authority to conduct jury trial); *In re* Grabill Corp., 967 F.2d 1152 (7th Cir.1992) (bankruptcy judge not authorized to conduct jury trial); *In re* Baker & Getty Fin. Services, Inc., 954 F.2d 1169 (6th Cir. 1992) (bankruptcy judge not authorized to conduct jury trial); *In re* United Mo. Bank of Kansas City, 901 F.2d 1449 (8th Cir. 1990)

(bankruptcy judge lacks authority to conduct jury trial in preference action) *with In re* Ben Cooper, Inc., 896 F.2d 1394 (2d Cir. 1990), *reinstated after remand*, 924 F.2d 36 (2d Cir. 1991); *In re* Jackson, 118 B.R. 243 (E.D. Pa. 1990) (bankruptcy judge has authority to conduct jury trials in core proceedings); *In re* Kroh Bros. Dev. Co., 108 B.R. 228 (W.D. Mo. 1989) (bankruptcy judge has authority to conduct jury trials in core matters). All cases in this note were decided under the law as it existed prior to the 1994 amendment adding 28 U.S.C. § 157(e) discussed below.

110 Pub. L. No. 103-394, 108 Stat. 4106 (1994).

111 Fed. R. Bankr. P. 9015(b).

112 *E.g., In re* Sequoia Auto Brokers Ltd., 827 F.2d 1281 (9th Cir. 1987); *In re* Indus. Tool Distrib., Inc., 55 B.R. 746 (N.D. Ga. 1985); *In re* Omega Equip. Corp., 51 B.R. 569 (D.D.C. 1985).

113 *E.g., In re* Terrebonne Fuel & Lube, Inc., 108 F.3d 609 (5th Cir. 1997); *In re* Power Recovery Sys., Inc., 950 F.2d 798 (1st Cir. 1991) (bankruptcy courts have contempt powers provided that proper notice of procedures is given); *In re* Castro, 919 F.2d 107 (9th Cir. 1990) (bankruptcy court has civil contempt power to enforce discharge order in core proceeding); *In re* Schafer, 146 B.R. 477 (D. Kan. 1992) (bankruptcy court had power to find party in contempt for violating discharge injunction); *In re* DePew, 55 B.R. 106 (Bankr. E.D. Tenn. 1985); *see also* United

courts, however, have expressed doubt about the power to enter a criminal contempt order.[114] As most contempt proceedings in consumer cases have arisen out of automatic stay violations, for which there is now a statutory damage remedy under section 362(h),[115] this question is of less importance to consumer debtors than might otherwise have been the case.[116]

Because most courts have held that bankruptcy courts do have contempt powers,[117] Federal Rule of Bankruptcy Procedure 9020 was amended to eliminate the special procedures that had been adopted when the contempt power was in doubt, and to provide that a motion for an order of civil contempt is to be litigated as a contested matter under Rule 9014.[118]

13.3 Advantages of the Bankruptcy Court As a Forum

13.3.1 *Possibilities of a Fairer Result for the Consumer Client*

Depending on the circumstances, the bankruptcy court may be a preferable forum for the litigation of many types of cases that involve consumer debtors. When the debtor is in bankruptcy and has a choice of forums, a number of factors should be considered. But even if a client is not in bankruptcy, the litigation advantages offered by the federal bankruptcy forum may be so great that they justify filing a bankruptcy petition even if it otherwise might not be needed.

In many districts, the bankruptcy judges and federal judges may be a good deal more sympathetic to the consumer's case than judges in other local courts. Not only do bankruptcy judges regularly see the problems of debtors in trouble, but also they are generally more aware of the unfair creditor practices that often take place. Many bankruptcy judges are pleased to be presented with novel and creative cases that provide both a change of pace from routine bankruptcy matters and a means for ruling on unfair practices.

In addition, most bankruptcy judges are far more knowledgeable in commercial law, and often in consumer law, than the average state judge, because the cases they see usually involve such issues. To the extent that some bankruptcy judges are not yet familiar with consumer law, the concentration of a significant number of consumer cases in their courts will soon enhance their expertise. In addition, both bankruptcy and federal appellate judges may be more disposed, because of lower case loads and the greater availability of law clerk assistance, to consider carefully bona fide legal arguments on behalf of debtors.

Litigation in the bankruptcy case may provide a method of avoiding a forum in which the debtor has little chance of prevailing. In a rural area, it may be the only way to avoid a hostile state judge who hears every case filed in that particular locality. It may also provide a means to avoid courts that have become high-volume mills (usually for the benefit of debtors' adversaries) for eviction, foreclosure, and collection cases.

The bankruptcy system also offers better discovery than many state courts, because it is governed by the Federal Rules of Bankruptcy Procedure, which basically incorporate the liberal federal discovery rules. In busy metropolitan areas, litigation in bankruptcy court and federal court usually proceeds more quickly and expeditiously than in state courts serving the same jurisdiction.

States v. Revie, 834 F.2d 1198 (5th Cir. 1987) (district court can hold party in criminal contempt for failing to appear at hearing in bankruptcy court to show cause why he had not obeyed bankruptcy court order; bankruptcy court had jurisdiction at least to determine if its order was being obeyed).

114 *See* United States v. Guariglia, 962 F.2d 160 (2d Cir. 1992) (district court had authority to punish criminal contempt of bankruptcy court's order in first instance); *In re* Hipp, Inc., 895 F.2d 1503 (5th Cir. 1990) (bankruptcy court without power to preside over criminal contempt proceedings except perhaps those involving contempt committed in or near its presence); *see also In re* Dyer, 322 F.3d 1178(9th Cir. 2003) (no authority under § 105(a) to award criminal contempt sanctions); *In re* Magwood, 785 F.2d 1077 (D.C. Cir. 1986); *In re* Armstrong, 304 B.R. 432 (B.A.P. 10th Cir. 2004) (contempt order imposing fines for violations of litigation injunction was in nature of criminal contempt, which bankruptcy court did not have jurisdiction to impose); *In re* Lickman, 288 B.R. 291 (Bankr. M.D. Fla. 2003) (referring contempt matter to district court because bankruptcy court may not enter punitive or criminal contempt orders); *In re* Crabtree, 47 B.R. 150 (Bankr. E.D. Tenn. 1985). *But see In re* Ragar, 3 F.3d 1174 (8th Cir. 1993) (bankruptcy court order finding attorney in criminal contempt and giving ten days for attorney to request de novo hearing in district court was valid).

115 11 U.S.C. § 362(h); *see* § 9.6, *supra*. Sanctions imposed by the bankruptcy court pursuant to § 362(h) under this section have been held constitutional. Budget Services Co. v. Better Homes of Va., 804 F.2d 289 (4th Cir. 1986); *see also In re* Ark. Communities Inc., 827 F.2d 1219 (8th Cir. 1987) (bankruptcy court may impose sanctions under Fed. R. Bankr. P. 9011).

116 *But see* § 13.3.2.2, *infra*.

117 *E.g., In re* Terrebone Fuel & Lube, Inc., 108 F.3d 609 (5th Cir. 1997); *In re* Rainbow Magazine, Inc., 77 F.3d 278 (9th Cir. 1996).

118 *See* 2001 Advisory Committee Note to Federal Rule of Bankruptcy Procedure 9020.

13.3.2 *Avoidance of Substantive or Procedural Difficulties*

13.3.2.1 *In Personam* Jurisdiction, Venue and Service Requirements

In specific cases, a bankruptcy proceeding may offer a way around a difficult procedural problem which could prove fatal in any other forum. Certain provisions governing bankruptcy litigation make it a useful way to avoid such problems.

One extremely helpful provision allows nationwide service of process in most bankruptcy proceedings. Generally, any case within the district court's bankruptcy jurisdiction that involves the debtor, that is, relating in any way to the bankruptcy or the debtor's property,[119] may be filed in the bankruptcy court in which the bankruptcy case has been filed, regardless of whether the state or federal courts in that state would otherwise have had "long-arm jurisdiction" over the defendant.[120] There is no "minimum contacts" test which must be met before an out-of-state defendant can be sued in the forum district's bankruptcy court,[121] and so, in some cases, the bankruptcy court may be the only place other than a defendant's home state where litigation can be commenced against a particular party.

The major exception to this general venue provision applies to trustees who commence cases either to recover less than $1000.00 or, for consumer debts, less than $5000.00 (that is, against a consumer) in a district other than that where the defendant resides.[122] As this exception applies only to the trustee, it seems unlikely to affect litigation initiated by debtors. However, even if it were extended to debtors using the trustee's powers, it would affect very few cases—only those against other consumers or for under $1000.00.

Another exception to the general venue rules can occur under 28 U.S.C. § 1412. That section provides that even if venue is proper in the district where suit has been brought, the litigation may be transferred to any other district in the interest of justice and for the convenience of the parties.[123]

Because consumer debtors rarely have the resources to litigate in distant forums, it will be a rare case where an out-of-state defendant successfully invokes this provision to transfer a case commenced by a consumer client.

Moreover, service of process generally can be made by first class mail.[124] An exception to the general right to serve by first class mail was created by the Bankruptcy Reform Act of 1994,[125] which amended Federal Rule of Bankruptcy Procedure 7004 to provide that service of process on an insured depository institution in a contested matter or adversary proceeding must be made by certified mail unless certain requirements have been met.[126]

The 1994 amendments also added section 342(c) of the Code, which states that all notices required to be given by the debtor to a creditor must contain the debtor's name, address, and taxpayer identification (social security) number.[127] It may not always be clear what constitutes a notice under this provision. For example, is a motion a notice? It is probably simplest to routinely include the required information on any correspondence giving official notice to creditors.[128] However, section 342(c) also provides that failure to include this information does not affect the validity of the notice.

13.3.2.2 Sovereign Immunity

In some cases, sovereign immunity poses a complete bar to recovery of a particular claim in state or federal court. For certain purposes, the Bankruptcy Code provides a means to overcome this bar.

Especially as amended by the Bankruptcy Reform Act of 1994,[129] section 106 of the Code contains a broad abrogation

---

119 28 U.S.C. § 1334(b), (e).

120 28 U.S.C. § 1409(a).

121 *In re* Fed. Fountain, Inc., 165 F.3d 600 (8th Cir. 1999) (*en banc*) (nationwide service is constitutional); *In re* Hogue, 736 F.2d 989 (4th Cir. 1984) (finding nationwide service of process constitutional); *In re* G. Weeks Securities, Inc., 3 B.R. 215 (Bankr. W.D. Tenn. 1980).

122 28 U.S.C. § 1409(b). There are several other exceptions relating to debtors in business. *See* 28 U.S.C. § 1409(c), (d), (e); *In re* Little Lake Indus., Inc., 158 B.R. 478 (B.A.P. 9th Cir. 1993) (debtor in possession could bring preference action for less than $1000.00 only in defendant's home district).

123 *See In re* Good Hope Refineries, Inc., 4 B.R. 290 (Bankr. D. Mass. 1980); *cf.* Mar. Elec. Co. v. United Jersey Bank, 959 F.2d 1194 (3d Cir. 1991) (district court other than one in jurisdiction

where bankruptcy case is filed may retain and exercise "related to" jurisdiction over case involving debtor which is already pending). Presumably the debtor can remove a case like *Maritime Electric* to the district where the bankruptcy is pending or move to have the case referred there. *See* § 13.4.1, *infra*.

124 Fed. R. Bankr. P. 7004(b); *see In re* Park Nursing Ctr., Inc., 766 F.2d 261 (6th Cir. 1985) (service by mail is constitutional).

125 Pub. L. No. 103-394, 108 Stat. 4106 (1994).

126 Fed. R. Bankr. P. 7004(h). Process may be served by first class mail if 1) the institution has appeared by its attorney, 2) the court so orders after service of an application for such an order by certified mail on the institution, or 3) the institution agrees to waive service by certified mail and designates an officer to receive service. *See In re* Hamlett, 322 F.3d 342 (4th Cir. 2003) (default judgment vacated because service made on registered agent rather than officer of institution). Information about whether a particular entity is an insured depository institution may be obtained on the Federal Deposit Insurance Corporation's website at: http://www2.fdic.gov/structur/search/findoneinst.asp.

127 11 U.S.C. § 342(c); *see* H.R. Rep. No. 103-835, at 51 (1994), *reprinted in* 1994 U.S.C.C.A.N. 3340.

128 *See* Official Form 16A, Appendix D, *infra*.

129 Pub. L. No. 103-394, 108 Stat. 4106 (1994). Unlike most parts of the 1994 amendments, the amendments to § 106 were effective with respect to cases pending on the enactment date of

of sovereign immunity. Sovereign immunity is expressly abrogated with respect to a broad range of statutory provisions listed in section 106(a). Included among these are virtually all of the provisions which normally would give rise to claims against the government in bankruptcy.

A notable exception to the list is section 541 of the Code. The legislative history states that the amendment was not intended to permit a debtor to sue the government on a pre-bankruptcy cause of action when suit would otherwise have been barred by sovereign immunity.[130] But section 542 is included in the list, and section 542(b) permits a debtor to recover "a debt that is property of the estate and that is matured, payable on demand, or payable on order" except to the extent it may be offset under section 553.

The legislative history[131] states clearly that the amendment was intended to abrogate both federal sovereign immunity and state 11th Amendment immunity, overruling *Hoffman v. Connecticut Department of Income Maintenance*[132] and *United States v. Nordic Village Inc.*[133] In consumer cases, this history should remove any doubts about federal governmental monetary liability and the immunity of other entitites that are not states,[134] not only for transfer avoidance, but also for stay and discharge violations, as well as sanctions under Federal Rule of Bankruptcy Procedure 9011.[135]

However, the ability of Congress to abrogate the states' Eleventh Amendment immunity was severely limited by the Supreme Court's decision in *Seminole Tribe of Florida v. Florida*,[136] so it is questionable whether the provisions of § 106 abrogating states' immunity from suit are valid.[137] A few courts have found that section 106 was enacted pursuant to the privileges and immunities clause of the Fourteenth Amendment and is therefore valid,[138] but appellate courts

have found that *Seminole Tribe* invalidates section 106 insofar as it authorizes damage suits against a state.[139] This problem may be avoided occasionally if it is possible to argue that the entity being sued is not a state or an arm of a state.[140] In cases involving state action in which the state has not filed a proof of claim or otherwise waived its immunity,[141] debtors may be barred from suing for damages in the

---

October 22, 1994, even if they were on appeal. Pub. L. No. 103-394 § 702, 108 Stat. 4106 (1994); *In re* Price, 42 F.3d 1068 (7th Cir. 1994).

130 140 Cong. Rec. H10,766 (Oct. 4, 1994) (remarks of Rep. Brooks).

131 *Id.*

132 492 U.S. 96, 109 S. Ct. 2818, 106 L. Ed. 2d 76 (1989).

133 503 U.S. 30, 112 S. Ct. 1011, 117 L. Ed. 2d 181 (1992).

134 *See* Krystal Energy Co. v. Navajo Nation, 357 F.3d 1055 (9th Cir. 2004) (Indian tribe's immunity abrogated by § 106(a)). *But see In re* Mayes, 294 B.R. 145 (B.A.P. 10th Cir. 2003) (where debtor did not raise § 106 argument, tribe's common law immunity precluded lien avoidance motion).

135 Hanna Oil Co. v. Internal Revenue Serv., 198 B.R. 672 (W.D. Va. 1996).

136 517 U.S. 44, 116 S. Ct. 1114, 134 L. Ed. 2d 252 (1996).

137 Prior to the *Seminole Tribe* case at least one court of appeals had found § 106(a)'s abrogation of a state's Eleventh Amendment immunity to be constitutional. *In re* Merchants Grain, Inc., 59 F.3d 630 (7th Cir. 1995), *vacated and remanded*, 517 U.S. 1130 (1996).

138 *E.g., In re* Wilson, 258 B.R. 303 (Bankr. S.D. Ga. 2001); *In re* Arnold, 255 B.R. 845 (Bankr. W.D. Tenn. 2000); Lees v. Tenn. Student Assistance Corp., 252 B.R. 441 (W.D. Tenn. 2000), *aff'd on other grounds*, 264 B.R. 884 (W.D. Tenn. 2001); *In re*

Headrick, 200 B.R. 963 (Bankr. S.D. Ga. 1996); *In re* S. Star Foods, Inc., 190 B.R. 419 (Bankr. E.D. Okla. 1995).

139 *E.g.*, Nelson v. La Crosse County Dist. Atty., 301 F.3d 820 (7th Cir. 2002); *In re* Sacred Heart Hosp. of Norristown, 133 F.3d 237 (3d Cir. 1997); *In re* Estate of Fernandez, 123 F.3d 241 (5th Cir. 1997); *In re* Creative Goldsmiths of Wash., 119 F.3d 1140 (4th Cir. 1997); *In re* Martinez, 196 B.R. 225 (D. P.R. 1996). *But see In re* Hood, 319 F.3d 755 (6th Cir. 2003) (11th Amendment did not override Bankruptcy Clause), *aff'd on other grounds*, 124 S. Ct. 1905 (2004); *In re* Mitchell, 209 F.3d 1111 (9th Cir. 2000).

140 *In re* Lees, 264 B.R. 884 (W.D. Tenn. 2001) (student loan agency was not arm of state entitled to immunity).

141 Generally, a party that files a proof of claim is deemed to submit to the bankruptcy court's jurisdiction, at least as to a claim arising out of the same transaction that created the government's claim. Arecibo Cmty. Health Care, Inc. v. Puerto Rico, 270 F.3d 17 (1st Cir. 2001), *cert. denied*, 537 U.S. 813 (2002); *In re* Rose, 187 F.3d 926 (8th Cir. 1999) (state waived Eleventh Amendment with respect to claims for which it filed proofs of claim); *In re* Jackson, 184 B.R. 1046 (9th Cir. 1999) (state waived Eleventh Amendment with respect to tax claims by filing proof of claim); *In re* Burke, 146 F.3d 1313 (11th Cir. 1998) (state waived Eleventh Amendment by filing proofs of claim in debtors' cases); *In re* Straight, 143 F.3d 1387 (10th Cir. 1998); *In re* Rose, 227 B.R. 518 (W.D. Mo. 1997) (state waived Eleventh Amendment protection from being sued to determine dischargeability of student loan by filing claim for student loan debt); *In re* Bliemeister, 251 B.R. 383 (Bankr. D. Ariz. 2000) (state waived sovereign immunity by seeking summary judgment in adversary proceeding involving dischargeability of state's claim), *aff'd*, 296 F.3d 858 (9th Cir. 2002); *In re* Huffine, 246 B.R. 405 (Bankr. E.D. Wash. 2000) (state waived sovereign immunity by signing student loan participation agreement); *In re* Lazar, 200 B.R. 358 (Bankr. C.D. Cal. 1996); *In re* Burke, 200 B.R. 282 (Bankr. S.D. Ga. 1996); *see also In re* Innes, 184 F.3d 1275 (10th Cir. 1999) (state consented to litigation in federal court by signing participation agreement with U.S. Department of Education agreeing to oppose dischargeability complaints); *In re* Platter, 140 F.3d 676 (7th Cir. 1998) (state waived Eleventh Amendment immunity by filing dischargeability complaint); *In re* White, 139 F.3d 1268 (9th Cir. 1998) (sovereign immunity waived by participation in case through objection to plan confirmation and voting against plans); *In re* Barrett Refining Corp., 221 B.R. 795 (Bankr. W.D. Okla. 1998) (state could not undo waiver by withdrawing proof of claim). Cases concerning whether all agencies of a state or federal government are deemed a single entity for setoff purposes will be relevant. See cases cited below in this subsection. *But see* Magnolia Venture Capital Corp. v. Prudential Securities, Inc., 151 F.3d 439 (5th Cir. 1998) (venue provision in pledge agreement not sufficient to waive Eleventh Amendment immunity because official signing it was not shown to have authority to waive immunity); *In re* Creative Goldsmiths of Wash., 119 F.3d 1140 (4th Cir. 1997) (Eleventh Amendment immunity not waived by filing unrelated claim); *see also* 11 U.S.C. § 106(b).

bankruptcy court, and may still have to resort to devices used in other areas of the law, such as suits against state officers for injunctive relief. The *Ex parte Young* doctrine holds that an action brought against state officials in their individual capacities seeking prospective declaratory and injunctive relief for continuing violations of federal law is not barred by the Eleventh Amendment.[142] For example, a suit seeking a declaration that a particular action violates the automatic stay that may not be brought against the state normally could be brought for injunctive and declaratory relief against the state officer heading the relevant state agency.[143] The discharge itself is an injunction, which can be[144] enforced against a state officer,[145] as may the automatic stay, the discrimination protections,[146] the turnover requirements (except if seeking a money judgment)[147] and a confirmed plan.[148]

A suit for damages against the state caused by violations of federal bankruptcy law may not be brought even in the state courts, unless the state has waived its sovereign immunity. In another recent decision the Supreme Court has held that such a suit would offend the structure of the Constitution, which preserved state sovereignty.[149]

However, the Supreme Court has also held that because bankruptcy is an *in rem* proceeding, affecting the debtor's property, the bankruptcy case itself is not a suit against the state and the discharge of a debt to the state is not barred by the Eleventh Amendment.[150] The court's jurisdiction over the dischargeability of debt, just like its jurisdiction to confirm a plan of reorganization, derives not from jurisdiction over the state or other creditors, but rather from jurisdiction over debtors and their estates.[151] Similarly, court proceedings about the debtor's property, such as proceedings to avoid liens on the property, are not suits against the state.

As a limitation on the broad abrogation of sovereign immunity in section 106(a), the state and federal government extracted provisions limiting punitive damages and attorney fees awards. Section 106(a)(3) prohibits an award of punitive damages and limits attorney fee awards. However, this section should not be read to prohibit all monetary sanctions that are not compensatory damages. "Punitive damages" should be given its normal meaning, limited to cases in which that term has traditionally been used to describe a monetary award (as opposed to "sanctions" under Federal Rules of Bankruptcy Procedure 7037 or 9011). Attorney fees and costs are limited to those consistent with 28 U.S.C. § 2412(d)(2)(A) (the Equal Access to Justice Act).[152]

It is also unclear whether section 106(a)(3) is simply an exception to the abrogation of sovereign immunity, or whether it goes beyond that. Some governmental units, such as municipalities, never had sovereign immunity.[153] In other situations, such as actions for contempt, sovereign immunity is generally not implicated.[154] The structure of the new section 106 suggests that the punitive damages language in section 106(a)(3) is designed to modify and limit the general abrogation language in section 106(a), and not to create new restrictions on litigation against entities or on claims that never were barred by immunity. Similar issues exist with respect to application of the attorney fee limitations in section 106(a)(3).[155]

The sovereign immunity provisions were also clarified with respect to counterclaims against the government. Under new section 106(b) (formerly section 106(a)), such a counterclaim may be asserted only if the governmental unit has actually filed a proof of claim in the bankruptcy case.[156]

---

142 *See* Coeur d'Alene Tribe of Idaho, 531 U.S. 261, 269, 117 S. Ct. 2028, 138 L. Ed. 2d 438 (1997); Green v. Mansour, 474 U.S. 64, 106 S. Ct. 423, 88 L. Ed. 2d 371 (1985); *Ex parte* Young, 209 U.S. 123, 28 S. Ct. 441, 52 L. Ed. 2d 714 (1908); *In re* LTV Steel Co., 264 B.R. 455 (Bankr. N.D. Ohio 2001) (action to enforce automatic stay could be brought against state officials under *Ex parte Young* doctrine).

143 *In re* Ellett, 243 B.R. 741 (B.A.P. 9th Cir. 1999) (suit against state tax official to enjoin collection of taxes discharged in chapter 13 may proceed under *Ex parte Young* doctrine), *aff'd sub nom.* Ellett v. Goldberg, 254 F.3d 1135 (9th Cir. 2001), *cert. denied*, 534 U.S. 1127 (2002); *In re* DeAngelis, 239 B.R. 426 (Bankr. D. Mass. 1999).

144 *In re* Rainwater, 233 B.R. 126 (Bankr. N.D. Ala. 1999).

145 *In re* Lapin, 226 B.R. 637 (B.A.P. 9th Cir. 1998).

146 *In re* Kidd, 227 B.R. 161 (Bankr. E.D. Ark. 1998).

147 *In re* Zywiczynski, 210 B.R. 924 (Bankr. W.D.N.Y. 1997).

148 Maryland v. Antonelli Creditors' Liquidating Trust, 123 F.3d 777 (4th Cir. 1997).

149 Alden v. Maine, 527 U.S. 706, 119 S. Ct. 2240, 144 L. Ed. 2d 636 (1999).

150 Tenn. Student Assistance Corp. v. Hood, 124 S. Ct. 1905, 158 L. Ed. 2d 764 (2004).

151 *Id.*

152 This incorporates limits on the amount of fees, but not other substantive limitations of the EAJA. *See generally* §§ 15.5, 15.5.4, *infra*.

153 *See, e.g.,* Owen v. City of Independence, 445 U.S. 622, 100 S. Ct. 1398, 63 L. Ed. 2d 673 (1980); Mancuso v. New York State Thruway Authority, 86 F.3d 289 (2d Cir. 1996); Christy v. Pennsylvania Turnpike Comm'n, 54 F.3d 1140 (3d Cir. 1995); Metcalf & Eddy v. Puerto Rico Aqueduct & Sewer Auth., 991 F.2d 935 (1st Cir. 1993); *In re* Durant, 239 B.R. 859 (Bankr. N.D.N.Y. 1999) (county social services department was not an arm of the state entitled to immunity).

154 Because of the potential attorney fee limitation under section 106, it may make sense where sovereign immunity is implicated to continue to include a contempt claim when that claim is available.

155 *See* § 15.5, *infra*.

156 *See* Aer-Aerotron v. Texas Dep't of Transp., 104 F.3d 677 (4th Cir. 1997) (post-petition letters to debtor demanding payment did not constitute proof of claim for purposes of this section); Carrington Gardens Associates v. United States, 258 B.R. 622 (E.D. Va. 2001) (government waived sovereign immunity by filing proof of claim even though debtor's claim was not strictly a counterclaim where proof of claim was filed after adversary complaint was brought against agency), *aff'd*, 49 Fed. Appx. 427 (4th Cir. 2002) (table); *In re* Gibson, 176 B.R. 910 (Bankr. D. Or. 1994) (federal government considered one governmental

This reverses the result reached by some courts, which had held that a counterclaim could be asserted if the government had taken an action that could be deemed an "informal proof of claim."[157] As under prior law, the counterclaim must be a compulsory counterclaim, arising out of the same transaction or occurrence to come within this section.[158]

A debtor or trustee may also offset against a claim or interest of a governmental unit any claim against the governmental unit that is property of the estate.[159] However, in some cases courts will have to define whether different agencies of the same government are the same governmental unit for purposes of this section.[160]

Because actions may not be brought directly against a state that has not waived its immunity,[161] many proceedings seeking injunctive or declaratory relief may only be brought under the *Ex parte Young* doctrine.[162] Because civil contempt damages and attorney fees are considered prospective relief, they may be awarded against a state officer notwithstanding the state's Eleventh Amendment immunity.[163] Ad-

ditionally, non-bankruptcy limitations on and waivers of sovereign immunity remain applicable in bankruptcy.[164]

One other way of dealing with federal sovereign immunity problems may be available under the Tucker Act[165] and the "Little Tucker Act."[166] The latter statute permits non-tort suits for money damages arising under federal law to be brought against the federal government in district court if the amount sought is less than $10,000.00.[167] Thus, a debtor or trustee should be able to file such a proceeding arising under the Bankruptcy Code, or the Constitution or any other federal statute, in the district court. Probably, if the proceeding arises under the Code, it would automatically be referred to the bankruptcy court under the general order of reference applicable in that district court.[168]

13.3.2.3 Overcoming Barriers to Federal Court Access

The district court's broad bankruptcy jurisdiction may also be helpful in cases where a federal court is otherwise likely to abstain or refuse to hear a case under the doctrines announced in the *Pullman*[169] or *Younger*[170] cases and their progeny. The explicit provision by Congress of bankruptcy

unit, so proof of claim waived sovereign immunity for all agencies under predecessor to this provision); *see also* Lapides v. Bd. of Regents, 535 U.S. 613, 122 S. Ct. 1640, 152 L. Ed. 2d 806 (2002) (by removing action to federal court, a state waives Eleventh Amendment immunity, relying on Gardner v. N.J., 329 U.S. 565, 574, 67 S. Ct. 467, 91 L. Ed. 504 (1947), which held that filing a proof of claim waives a state's immunity); *In re* Stanley, 273 B.R. 907 (Bankr. N.D. Fla. 2002) (having waived immunity by filing proofs of claim, state could not reinstate immunity by withdrawing them).

157 *E.g.*, Sullivan v. Town & Country Nursing Home Services, Inc., 963 F.2d 1146 (9th Cir. 1992).

158 *See* Lazar v. California, 237 F.3d 967 (9th Cir. 2001) (state's proof of claim arose out of same transaction or occurrence as mandamus action against state seeking payment of claims from Underground Storage Tank Cleanup Trust); *In re* Price, 42 F.3d 1068 (7th Cir. 1994) (violation of automatic stay arose out of same transaction as government's tax claim); *In re* Graham, 981 F.2d 1135 (10th Cir. 1992) (section 106(a) requires claims against government to be compulsory counterclaims for sovereign immunity waiver under that subsection); *In re* Rebel Coal Co., 944 F.2d 320 (6th Cir. 1991) (preference claim arising from garnishment for fines did not arise from same transaction or occurrence as government's claim for remaining fines, so sovereign immunity not waived under section 106(a)); *cf.* United States v. Pullman Constr. Indus., Inc., 153 B.R. 539 (N.D. Ill. 1993) (preference action against Internal Revenue Service was compulsory counterclaim to government's claim for taxes).

159 11 U.S.C. § 106(c).

160 *See In re* Hal, Inc., 122 F.3d 851 (9th Cir. 1997) (federal government is unitary creditor for purposes of setoff rights); *In re* Turner, 84 F.3d 1294 (10th Cir. 1996) (*en banc*) (federal government is unitary creditor for bankruptcy purposes so debt owed to one agency may be set off against claim of another); Doe v. United States, 58 F.3d 494 (9th Cir. 1995) (all agencies of United States are a single governmental unit); § 10.4.2.6.7, *supra.*

161 Murphy v. Michigan Guar. Agency, 271 F.3d 629 (5th Cir. 2001); *In re* Mitchell, 209 F.3d 1111 (9th Cir. 2000).

162 *See Ex parte Young*, 209 U.S. 123, 28 S. Ct. 441, 52 L. Ed. 714 (1908).

163 *In re* Colon, 114 B.R. 890 (Bankr. E.D. Pa. 1990); *see also In*

re Bryant, 116 B.R. 272 (Bankr. D. Kan. 1990) (IRS had no defense of sovereign immunity where it violated discharge injunction), *aff'd*, 1991 WL 204911 (D. Kan. Sept. 9, 1991); *In re* Adams, 115 B.R. 59 (Bankr. D.N.J. 1990) (wage order entered against debtor employed by Navy did not violate sovereign immunity because order provided injunctive, not monetary, relief). *But see In re* Gustafson, 934 F.2d 216 (9th Cir. 1991) (state immune from money damages for violations of the stay without express consideration of potential contempt remedies).

164 *See In re* Epps, 110 B.R. 691 (E.D. Pa. 1990) (debtor's action against Dep't of Housing and Urban Development for equitable relief was not barred by sovereign immunity because it was permitted under Administrative Procedure Act).

165 28 U.S.C. § 1491. *See generally* Dennis M. Garvis & Frank W. Koger, *If at First You Don't Succeed . . .; An Alternative Remedy After Nordic Village*, 66 Am. Bankr. L.J. 423 (1992).

166 28 U.S.C. § 1346(a) (2).

167 28 U.S.C. § 1346(a) (2). Claims over $10,000.00 must be brought in the United States Claims Court. 28 U.S.C. § 1491. *But see* Bowen v. Massachusetts, 487 U.S. 879, 906 n.42, 108 S. Ct. 2722, 2738 n.42, 101 L. Ed. 2d 749, 771 (1988) (legislation upon which claim is based must be such that it can fairly be interpreted as mandating compensation by the federal government for damage sustained).

168 *See* Dennis M. Garvis & Frank W. Koger, *If at First You Don't Succeed . . .; An Alternative Remedy After Nordic Village*, 66 Am. Bankr. L.J. 423, 434 (1992). However, if the debtor is seeking damages against the IRS for violations of the automatic stay or discharge injunction, the debtor may file the action directly in the bankruptcy court. *See* 26 U.S.C. § 7433(e).

169 R.R. Comm'n of Texas v. Pullman Co., 312 U.S. 496, 61 S. Ct. 643, 85 L. Ed. 971 (1941). *See generally* James W. Moore et al., Moore's Federal Practice and Procedure ¶ 0203 (2d ed.).

170 Younger v. Harris, 401 U.S. 37, 91 S. Ct. 746, 27 L. Ed. 2d 669 (1971). *See generally* Charles A. Wright et al., Federal Practice and Procedure: Jurisdiction § 4251 *et seq.* (2d ed. 1988).

jurisdiction for proceedings related to the bankruptcy case may be sufficient to overcome these obstacles to federal court access which have been created by the Supreme Court. Thus, if a decision of an unclear state law question is clearly important to the debtor's successful bankruptcy, the nexus with the ongoing bankruptcy case may justify a federal court deciding a question from which it would have otherwise abstained under the *Pullman* doctrine.

Of course, to the extent either of these doctrines are seen as reflecting constitutional limitations on federal court jurisdiction, Congress has no power to infringe upon them. And there is also a strong likelihood that the federal courts will interpret their power to abstain "in the interest of justice," or "comity," or "respect for state law,"[171] and the mandatory abstention provisions in the bankruptcy jurisdictional scheme[172] to incorporate the *Pullman* and *Younger* doctrines.[173] It should be noted, however, that abstention is usually not appropriate in cases involving property of the debtor, over which the district court has exclusive jurisdiction.[174]

The bankruptcy jurisdictional scheme may also provide consumers with a way to avoid contractual arbitration clauses. Courts have held that such clauses can be inconsistent with Congressional intent to concentrate all bankruptcy litigation in a single forum—the bankruptcy court.[175]

Finally, the bankruptcy court may be a better place to litigate disputes with the Internal Revenue Service or other taxing agencies. Section 505(a) of the Code permits the bankruptcy court to determine the amount or legality of any tax, any fine or penalty relating to a tax, or any addition to a tax, whether or not it has been assessed, paid, or contested before the bankruptcy case.[176] For example, a bankruptcy court may determine whether a debtor is entitled to relief from tax liability under the "innocent spouse" provisions of the Internal Revenue Code.[177] The only exceptions to this rule are that the court may not determine the amount or legality of such claims if it has been previously contested and adjudicated by a judicial or administrative tribunal of competent jurisdiction,[178] and the court cannot determine a trustee's request for a refund before 120 days from the date the trustee requests the refund or, if earlier, the date the refund request is ruled upon by the governmental unit from which it requested.[179]

13.3.2.4 Recoupment Claims in Bankruptcy After Expiration of Limitations Periods

Bankruptcy court can also be an important forum for raising consumer claims against creditors after the statute of limitations on those claims has run.[180] In *In re Coxson*,[181] for example, the Fifth Circuit concluded that a Truth in Lending Act claim could be raised defensively by way of an adversary proceeding objecting to a proof of claim in a chapter 13 case—even though the limitations period had passed.[182]

When a creditor seeks to collect on a debt, many states and federal common law allow offset of claims that the debtor may have emerging from the same set of operative facts that gave rise to the debt—even if the limitations period has run.[183] In most states and under federal law, this process is known as recoupment. In some states there is a statutory basis for recoupment, while in others recoupment has developed as a common law remedy.

---

171 28 U.S.C. § 1334(c); *see* § 13.5, *infra*.

172 28 U.S.C. § 1334(c).

173 *See In re* Davis, 691 F.2d 176 (3d Cir. 1982) (injunction prohibiting bad check prosecution improper under *Younger* doctrine).

174 28 U.S.C. § 1334(e); *see also* H.R. Rep. No. 95-595, at 466 (1977) (stating that abstention in such cases would not be "in the interest of justice").

175 *In re* U.S. Lines, 197 F.3d 631 (2d Cir. 1999) (refusal to refer core proceeding to arbitration not an abuse of discretion); *In re* Knepp, 229 B.R. 821 (Bankr. N.D. Ala. 1999); *see also* § 13.3.2.5, *infra*; Mette H. Kurth, *An Unstoppable Mandate and an Immovable Policy: The Arbitration Act and the Bankruptcy Code Collide*, 43 UCLA L. Rev. 999 (1996).

176 Courts have generally found that the Tax Injunction Act, 28 U.S.C. § 1341, does not deprive bankruptcy courts of jurisdiction where the more specific grant of authority under section 505 applies. *See, e.g.*, Ellett v. Goldberg, 254 F.3d 1135 (9th Cir. 2001), *cert. denied*, 534 U.S. 1127 (2002); *In re* Stoecker, 179 F.3d 546 (7th Cir. 1999); City Vending of Muskogee, Inc. v. Oklahoma Tax Comm'n, 898 F.2d 122 (10th Cir. 1990); Carrollton-Farmers Branch v. Johnson & Cravens, 858 F.2d 1010 (5th Cir. 1988), *modified*, 867 F.2d 1517 (5th Cir.), *vacated on other grounds*, 889 F.2d 571 (5th Cir. 1989); Adams v. Indiana, 795 F.2d 27, 30 (7th Cir. 1986); *In re* Pontes, 310 F. Supp. 2d 447 (D.R.I. 2004).

177 26 U.S.C. § 6015(b), (c); *see In re* Hinckley, 256 B.R. 814 (Bankr. M.D. Fla. 2000) (debtor granted relief from liability). *But see In re* French, 255 B.R. 1 (Bankr. N.D. Ohio 2000) (only the agency could determine whether individual was "innocent spouse").

178 11 U.S.C. § 505(a)(2)(A); *see In re* Baker, 74 F.3d 906 (9th Cir. 1996); *see also* § 13.2.4.3, *supra*.

179 11 U.S.C. § 505(a)(2)(B).

180 Recoupment is more likely to be important in addressing secured and priority claims. Recoupment is also available against unsecured claims, but as many such claims are paid at less than their full amount the importance of recoupment for unsecured claims is diminished.

181 43 F.3d 189 (5th Cir. 1995).

182 *See Supreme Court Bars Most Rescission By Recoupment*, 16 NCLC REPORTS *Bankruptcy and Foreclosures Ed.* 17 (Mar./Apr. 1998); *cf.* Beach v. Ocwen Fed. Sav. Bank, 523 U.S. 410, 118 S. Ct. 1408, 140 L. Ed. 2d 566 (1998) (rescission by recoupment not allowed except where consistent with state law in the context of a foreclosure case).

183 A Supreme Court citation for this principle is Bull v. United States, 295 U.S. 247, 262, 55 S. Ct. 695, 79 L. Ed. 1421 (1935) in which the Court said: "[R]ecoupment is in the nature of a defense arising out of some feature of the transaction upon which the plaintiff's action is grounded. Such a defense is never barred by the statute of limitations so long as the main action itself is timely." *See also, e.g., In re* Monongahela Rye Liquors, 141 F.2d 864 (3d Cir. 1944).

Recoupment can similarly be used to raise otherwise untimely usury,[184] fraud, unfair trade practice,[185] warranty,[186] and other damage claims emerging from the facts giving rise to the formation of the loan contract.

Recoupment has been permitted in the bankruptcy process by objection to a creditor's proof of claim.[187] The creditor's claim is an action to collect the debt and the objection to the claim is effectively defensive. The underlying rationale is the same as with any recoupment; parties should not be required to pay sums to which they have an underlying defense. If anything, the principle should be stronger in bankruptcy, because a defense to one creditor's claim is likely to lead to greater recovery for other creditors.

When recoupment is expected to be raised in bankruptcy, it is a good idea to mark the claim in the schedules as "disputed." Additionally, careful practice may require listing the availability of a recoupment claim as an asset and exempting it at a nominal valuation if an exemption is available.

An occasional problem arises when a secured creditor does not file a proof of claim against which recoupment may be asserted. Because the liens associated with secured claims survive a discharge, these creditors retain their right to enforce a lien following bankruptcy. The best strategy in such cases is to file a proof of claim on behalf of that creditor pursuant to Federal Rule of Bankruptcy Procedure 3004.[188] That claim can expressly deduct the recoupment claim. Filing and serving such a claim will put the creditor in the difficult position of having to choose between filing a superseding claim and thereby setting up the opportunity for an adversary proceeding seeking recoupment, or ignoring the claim and accepting the potential *res judicata* consequences of having their claim resolved in the bankruptcy process.

13.3.2.5 Avoiding Mandatory Arbitration Agreements

With increasing frequency, mandatory arbitration clauses are appearing in consumer contracts of all kinds. These clauses force consumers to submit their claims to an arbitrator who issues a final, binding ruling on the merits, with virtually no opportunity for judicial review. Bankruptcy court can be a favorable forum for avoiding arbitration clauses so that consumer claims may be litigated in court.

The Federal Arbitration Act requires that where a valid and enforceable arbitration agreement exists, courts must halt their proceedings while an arbitrator determines the rights of the parties to the arbitration agreement and adjudicates the dispute in controversy.[189] This strong federal presumption that valid arbitration agreements should be enforced is often in direct conflict with the goal of bankruptcy jurisdiction to have one centralized forum for the prompt resolution of disputes affecting the bankruptcy estate.[190] This conflict between the Bankruptcy Code and the Federal Arbitration Act has led most courts to hold that, at least as to core proceedings, a bankruptcy judge may refuse to enforce an arbitration agreement and may stay any pending arbitration proceedings.[191]

In exercising discretion whether to enforce an arbitration agreement, bankruptcy courts generally consider the degree to which (1) the nature and extent of the litigation and evidence would make the judicial forum preferable to arbitration, (2) the extent to which special expertise is necessary to resolve the dispute, and (3) the extent to which the bankruptcy court may more efficiently and economically resolve the dispute without depleting estate assets.[192] Another factor given considerable weight is that bankruptcy courts can more appropriately consider the interests of

---

184 National Consumer Law Center, The Cost of Credit: Regulation and Legal Challenges § 10.6.6 (2d ed. 2000 and Supp.).

185 National Consumer Law Center, Unfair and Deceptive Acts and Practices § 7.3.5 (5th ed. 2001 and Supp.).

186 National Consumer Law Center, Consumer Warranty Law § 10.3.7 (2d ed. 2001 and Supp.).

187 *E.g., In re* Harvey, 2003 WL 21460063 (Bankr. E.D. Pa. June 9, 2003) (time-barred recoupment claim under Real Estate Settlement Procedures Act may be brought in response to mortgage lender's proof of claim); *In re* Maxwell, 281 B.R. 101 (Bankr. D. Mass. 2002) (debtor allowed to assert by way of recoupment time-barred claim under the Fair Debt Collection Practices Act against mortgage servicer); *In re* McNinch, 250 B.R. 848 (Bankr. W.D. Pa. 2000) (one-year statute of limitations for Truth In Lending Act damages claim did not apply to claim asserted by recoupment in response to creditor's proof of claim), *aff'd sub nom.* McNinch v. Harris Trust Sav. Bank, 281 F.3d 222 (3d Cir. 2001) (table); *In re* Jones, 122 B.R. 246 (W.D. Pa. 1990); *In re* Werts, 48 B.R. 980 (E.D. Pa. 1985); *In re* Bishop, 79 B.R. 94 (Bankr. D.D.C. 1987).

188 That rule sets a deadline for filing of thirty days after expiration of the bar date applicable to the case. *See* § 13.4.3.3, *infra*.

189 9 U.S.C. § 3. For a more detailed discussion of arbitration, see National Consumer Law Center, Consumer Arbitration Agreements (4th ed. 2004).

190 Zimmerman v. Cont'l Airlines, Inc., 712 F.2d 55 (3d Cir. 1983); *In re* Hemphill Bus Sales, Inc., 259 B.R. 865 (Bankr. E.D. Tex. 2001); *In re* Knepp, 229 B.R. 821 (Bankr. N.D. Ala. 1999).

191 *In re* Gandy, 299 F.3d 489 (5th Cir. 2002); *In re* United States Lines, Inc., 197 F.3d 631 (2d Cir. 1999); Selcke v. New England Ins. Co., 995 F.2d 688 (7th Cir. 1993); *In re* Spectrum Info. Techs., Inc., 183 B.R. 360 (Bankr. E.D.N.Y. 1995); *In re* Sacred Heart Hosp., 181 B.R. 195 (Bankr. E.D. Pa. 1995). If the dispute does not involve a core proceeding and arbitration will not undermine the administration of the estate, courts are more likely to enforce the arbitration clause. *In re* Crysen/Montenay Energy Co., 226 F.3d 160 (2d Cir. 2000); *In re* Nat'l Gypsum Co., 118 F.3d 1056 (5th Cir. 1997); Hays & Co. v. Merrill Lynch, Pierce, Fenner & Smith, Inc., 885 F.2d 1149 (3d Cir. 1989).

192 *In re* Hemphill Bus Sales, Inc., 259 B.R. 865 (Bankr. E.D. Tex. 2001); *In re* Slipped Disc Inc., 245 B.R. 342 (Bankr. N.D. Iowa 2000); *In re* Trident Shipworks, Inc., 243 B.R. 130 (Bankr. M.D. Fla. 1999); *In re* Edgerton, 98 B.R. 392 (Bankr. N.D. Ill. 1989).

creditors who are not a party to the arbitration agreement and who would likely be precluded from participating in the arbitration forum.[193]

These considerations generally favor resolution in the bankruptcy forum of claims and defenses raised as objections to a creditor's proof of claim, particularly where prompt adjudication of the claim is necessary to the plan confirmation process.[194] Similarly, the terms of a confirmed plan which provides for resolution of disputes other than through arbitration are normally binding on the parties.[195] In addition, an arbitration clause should not prevent a bankruptcy court from resolving creditor abuses involving the bankruptcy process itself, such as violations of the automatic stay and discharge injunction, as these proceedings are core proceedings involving the bankruptcy court's inherent power to enforce its own orders.[196]

13.4 Bringing a Matter Before the Bankruptcy Forum

13.4.1 Removal

13.4.1.1 In General

A dispute may be brought into the bankruptcy system in a number of ways. Depending upon the nature of the dispute and the tactics of the parties, most litigation takes place through either adversary proceedings or contested matters within the bankruptcy case.[197]

The most dramatic method of bringing a matter into bankruptcy court is through the removal of an action already pending in another court. Under 28 U.S.C. § 1452 nearly all actions over which the district court would have bankruptcy jurisdiction may be removed to the district court in the jurisdiction where the removed action is pending.[198] However, if the debtor's bankruptcy case is pending in a different court, removed cases may presumably then be consolidated or otherwise transferred to that court.[199] Removed cases are then referred, like other bankruptcy matters, to the bankruptcy court.[200] The power to remove an action may be exercised by either plaintiff or defendant at any stage of the proceedings in the case that is removed, provided the deadlines of the Federal Rules of Bankruptcy Procedure are met.[201]

One question which may arise is how to handle cases involving the debtor or estate property which were pending in the district court at the time bankruptcy was filed. Because removal is made to district court, it does not make sense to remove such an action unless it is pending in a

---

193 *In re* First Alliance Mortgage Co., 280 B.R. 246 (C.D. Cal. 2002) (arbitration of class TILA and UDAP claims against debtor mortgage lender would deplete estate assets and negatively impact creditors); *In re* United Companies Fin. Corp., Inc., 277 B.R. 596 (Bankr. D. Del. 2002) (arbitration agreement exclusion for bankruptcy proceedings interpreted as applying not just when borrower files bankruptcy but also when lender as debtor files bankruptcy); *e.g.*, *In re* Hemphill Bus Sales, Inc., 259 B.R. 865 (Bankr. E.D. Tex. 2001).

194 *See In re* Mintze, 288 B.R. 95 (Bankr. E.D. Pa. 2003) (noting impact on other creditors and questions about arbitrator's neutrality), *aff'd*, 51 Collier Bankr. Cas. 2d (MB) 300 (E.D. Pa. 2003); *In re* Hicks, 285 B.R. 317 (Bankr. W.D. Okla. 2002) (potential costs of arbitration would adversely affect debtor and creditors); *In re* Laroque, 283 B.R. 640 (Bankr. D.R.I. 2002) (denying enforcement of arbitration clause to decide Truth in Lending rescission issues); *In re* Serv. Marine Indus., Inc., 2000 WL 1673061 (E.D. La. Nov. 3, 2000) (staying the bankruptcy proceeding to allow a creditor to arbitrate an objection to its claim would prejudice the rights of all other creditors and delay the administration of the debtor's bankruptcy).

195 Ernst & Young L.L.P v. Baker O'Neal Holdings, 304 F.3d 753 (7th Cir. 2002) (chapter 11 case); *see also* § 12.11, *supra*.

196 *In re* Cavanaugh, 271 B.R. 414 (Bankr. D. Mass. 2001) (arbitration clause did not apply to dispute concerning violation of automatic stay because it did not involve contractual rights); *see In re* Grant, 281 B.R. 721 (Bankr. S.D. Ala. 2000); *see also In re* Startec Global Communications Corp., 300 B.R. 244 (D. Md. 2003) (arbitration clause referring to claims arising out of or connected with agreement did not encompass alleged violations of court orders but, even if it did, bankruptcy court did not abuse discretion in refusing to enforce clause).

197 *See* §§ 1.4.2, 13.2.4, *supra*.

198 *E.g.*, *In re* Mem'l Estates, 950 F.2d 1364 (7th Cir. 1991) (mortgage foreclosure case properly removed to bankruptcy court when property was debtor's principal asset and foreclosure would have affected debtor's estate); Gandy v. Peoples Bank and Trust Co., 224 B.R. 340 (S.D. Miss. 1998) (state law action would have effect on bankruptcy estate and therefore was related to bankruptcy case). Exceptions are tax court cases and civil actions by governmental units to enforce police or regulatory powers. A proceeding also may not be removed from an agency such as the National Labor Relations Board. *In re* Adams Delivery Serv., 24 B.R. 589 (B.A.P. 9th Cir. 1982). Presumably, the court's jurisdiction must be over the claim of the plaintiff in the case; as under other federal removal statutes, an anticipated federal defense to the claim, even if pleaded in the complaint, would not be sufficient. *See* Rivet v. Regions Bank of La., 522 U.S. 470, 118 S. Ct. 921, 139 L. Ed. 2d 912 (1998).

199 *See, e.g.*, *In re* Nat'l Developers, Inc., 803 F.2d 616 (11th Cir. 1986).

200 *See* § 13.2.2, *supra*.

201 *See, e.g.*, *In re* Massey, 3 B.R. 110 (Bankr. D. Colo. 1980) (removal after jury verdict had been set aside by judge).

district court different from that of the bankruptcy.[202] However, it may be appropriate to ask the district court to refer such matters to the bankruptcy court if they are related to the bankruptcy.[203]

The removal of an action is often both a surprise and a problem for an opposing party that is unfamiliar with the bankruptcy system. It may also be an excellent way to permanently alter the course of state court litigation that has been going unfavorably. Once the action is removed, federal procedural law (which may be more favorable to the debtor's case) will govern.[204] Substantive rights, such as the right of a party to a jury trial, should be unaffected.[205]

13.4.1.2 Procedure for Removal

The procedure for removal is governed by Federal Rule of Bankruptcy Procedure 9027, which requires that a notice of removal be filed with the clerk of the bankruptcy court for the district in which the action to be removed is pending. The notice must contain a short and plain statement of the facts which entitle the party filing the notice to removal, and a statement of whether the removed action is core or non-core. If it is non-core, there must also be a declaration of whether or not the party filing the notice consents to entry of final orders by the bankruptcy judge.[206] The notice must also be accompanied by a copy of all process and pleadings in the removed case.[207] A copy of the notice of removal must be served on all other parties to the removed action, and a copy of the notice must be filed with the court where the action was previously pending.[208]

It is critical, however, to be aware of the time limits within which removal is allowed. For cases pending when the bankruptcy case was commenced, Federal Rule of Bankruptcy Procedure 9027(a)(2) requires a notice of removal to be filed within ninety days after the order for relief (or thirty days after entry of an order terminating an automatic stay of the action to be removed, if later).[209] For cases initiated after the bankruptcy case is commenced, the deadline for removal is thirty days after the initial service of process.[210] Most courts have held that these time limits are mandatory and may not be waived.[211] However, the time may be extended pursuant to Federal Rule of Bankruptcy Procedure 9006(b), upon motion to the court to which the action is to be removed.[212]

13.4.1.3 Procedure After Removal

Upon removal, other parties to the case who have filed pleadings in the removed case are required to file a statement admitting or denying the allegation in the removal notice concerning the court's core or non-core jurisdiction.[213] That statement must also state, if the party alleges the action is non-core, whether the party consents to entry of final judgment by the bankruptcy court.[214] It must be filed within ten days of the notice of removal and be mailed to every other party.[215]

After a case has been removed, the parties may not proceed further in the court from which it was removed unless the case is later remanded to that court.[216] The bankruptcy court may issue any necessary orders and pro-

---

202 One court has held that any district court can exercise jurisdiction over a case related to a bankruptcy pending in another jurisdiction. Mar. Elec. Co. v. United Jersey Bank, 959 F.2d 1194 (3d Cir. 1991). That court suggests that a motion for change of venue under 28 U.S.C. § 1412 is necessary to have the case heard where the bankruptcy is pending. It is not clear whether the court would consider the removal option improper in these circumstances.

203 *See generally* Philippe v. Shape, Inc., 103 B.R. 355 (D. Me. 1989) (case pending in district court which is related to bankruptcy case would be referred to bankruptcy court); *In re* Shelbyville Mixing Ctr., Inc., 288 B.R. 765 (Bankr. E.D. Ky. 2002) (case cannot be removed from district court to bankruptcy court); Thomas Steel Corp. v. Bethlehem Rebar Indus., 101 B.R. 16 (Bankr. N.D. Ill. 1989) (case cannot be removed from district court to bankruptcy court; however, district court can entertain a motion for directed referral).

204 *In re* Miller, 90 B.R. 762 (Bankr. E.D. Pa. 1988); *In re* Vic Snyder, Inc., 22 B.R. 332 (Bankr. E.D. Pa. 1982) (Federal Rule of Civil Procedure 60, made applicable through then-applicable R. Bankr. P. 914, governed relief from judgment in removed action); *see* Fed. R. Bankr. P. 9027(g) (procedure after removal is governed by rules for adversary proceedings).

205 *See, e.g., In re* Jensen, 946 F.2d 369 (5th Cir. 1991) (after removal of a state court action by a creditor, debtor retained the right to a jury trial). *See generally* § 13.2.7, *supra*.

206 Fed. R. Bankr. P. 9027(a)(1).

207 Fed. R. Bankr. P. 9027(a)(1). See annotated forms in Appxendix G.11, *infra*. Although Rule 9027 requires filing of removal notices with the clerk "for the district," it appears that where a bankruptcy clerk has been appointed, filing with the bankruptcy court as a unit of the district court is contemplated. *See In re*

Hendersonville Condo. Homes, 84 B.R. 510 (M.D. Tenn. 1988). Where the record in the removed case is unavailable for reasons beyond the control of the removing party, the court is empowered to allow the record to be supplied by affidavit or otherwise. Fed. R. Bankr. P. 9027(h).

208 Fed. R. Bankr. P. 9027(b), (c). These notices must be given or filed "promptly" pursuant to Rule 9027, but the consequences of delay or failure to comply are unclear.

209 If process has not yet been served in such a case, it may be served in accordance with Fed. R. Bankr. P. 7004(f). *See* § 13.3.2.1, *supra*.

210 Fed. R. Bankr. P. 9027(a)(3); Creasy v. Coleman Furniture Corp., 763 F.2d 656 (4th Cir. 1985); *see In re* Eagle Bend Dev., 61 B.R. 451 (Bankr. W.D. La. 1986) (failure to serve process may extend the deadline).

211 *In re* McCallum, 7 B.R. 76 (Bankr. C.D. Cal. 1980).

212 Caperton v. A.T. Massey Coal Co., 251 B.R. 322 (S.D. W. Va. 2000).

213 Fed. R. Bankr. P. 9027(e)(3).

214 Fed. R. Bankr. P. 9027(e)(3). *But see* Allied Signal Recovery Trust v. Allied Signal, Inc., 298 F.3d 263 (3d Cir. 2002) (order permitting remand of case to state court in state other than that from which it had been removed is reviewable by mandamus).

215 Fed. R. Bankr. P. 9027(e)(3).

216 Fed. R. Bankr. P. 9027(c).

cess to bring all proper parties before the court. The judge may also order the removing party to file some or all of the record in the removed case.[217] A removed action is treated as an adversary proceeding in the bankruptcy court.[218] Pleading again is not necessary unless the court so orders.[219]

13.4.1.4 Remand of Removed Actions

Once a case has been removed, any of the other parties to the case can seek to have the case remanded. Under 28 U.S.C. § 1452(b), the court to which a claim or cause of action is removed may remand the claim or cause of action "on any equitable grounds." Federal Rule of Bankruptcy Procedure 9027(d) provides that a motion for remand must be brought and heard as a contested matter pursuant to the Rule 9014.[220] When the matter is core, presumably the bankruptcy judge is empowered to enter a final order remanding the case.[221] If non-core, a recommendation governed by Rule 9033 is probably appropriate unless all parties consent to final disposition by the bankruptcy court.[222]

Once entered, an order remanding a claim is not reviewable by the court of appeals by appeal or otherwise.[223] An order refusing to remand a claim removed pursuant to 28 U.S.C. § 1452 is also not reviewable by a court of appeals.[224] However, these limitations should not prevent

appeals to the district court, under 28 U.S.C. § 158(a), of final bankruptcy court orders requiring or denying remand.[225]

Generally, the decision with respect to remand is based upon the same type of considerations applicable to decisions on whether to abstain.[226] These considerations include the convenience of the parties, comity with state courts, judicial economy, and the likelihood of delay.[227]

Another issue which frequently arises in the context of a motion for remand is whether an entire action may be removed to the bankruptcy forum when many of the claims or parties have no relation to the bankruptcy case. It is generally agreed that the presence of such claims and parties does not destroy bankruptcy jurisdiction over the entire case.[228] However, many of the same courts holding that jurisdiction exists in such cases have proceeded to remand all or parts of these cases.[229]

13.4.2 Litigation of Other Claims Commenced by the Debtor

Even if the time limit for removal has expired or the debtor has decided not to remove an action in state court (continuation of any action against the debtor usually being stayed under 11 U.S.C. § 362(a)),[230] a dispute already pending elsewhere may still be brought into bankruptcy court. It

---

217 Fed. R. Bankr. P. 9027(e)(2).
218 Fed. R. Bankr. P. 9027(g).
219 *Id.*
220 *See generally* § 1.4.2, *supra.* It is not clear whether 28 U.S.C. § 1447 applies to cases removed under § 1452. *See* Advisory Committee Note to Fed. R. Bankr. P. 9027 (rule conforms substantially to 28 U.S.C. §§ 1446–1450). If it does, it requires a remand motion made on any basis other than lack of jurisdiction to be filed within thirty days of the notice of removal. *In re* Gold Messenger, Inc., 221 B.R. 259 (D. Colo. 1998). *But see In re* Ciclon Negro, Inc., 260 B.R. 832 (Bankr. S.D. Tex. 2001) (thirty-day limit does not apply).
221 *In re* Borelli, 132 B.R. 648 (N.D. Cal. 1991).
222 *See* 28 U.S.C. § 157(c)(1).
223 28 U.S.C. § 1452(b); Things Remembered v. Petrarca, 516 U.S. 124, 116 S. Ct. 494, 133 L. Ed. 2d 461 (1995) (court of appeals may not review order remanding case based upon defect in procedure or lack of jurisdiction regardless of whether removal was pursuant to 28 U.S.C. § 1452(a) or 28 U.S.C. § 1441(a)); *see also In re* Robertson, 258 B.R. 470 (M.D. Ala. 2001) (although court of appeals could not hear appeal of decision remanding case, district court had jurisdiction over such an appeal).
224 28 U.S.C. § 1452(b); *In re* Cathedral of Incarnation, 90 F.3d 28 (2d Cir. 1996); *see also In re* Bissonet Investments Ltd. Liab. Co., 320 F.3d 520 (5th Cir. 2003) (court of appeals could review decision not to remand that was based on jurisdiction rather than equitable grounds); *In re* Celotex Corp., 124 F.3d 619 (4th Cir. 1997) (court of appeals could review denial of remand to extent motion for remand was based on district court's alleged lack of jurisdiction); *In re* U.S. Brass Corp. 110 F.3d 1261 (7th Cir. 1997) (discussing possible exceptions to rule).

225 *See In re* Robertson, 258 B.R. 470 (M.D. Ala. 2001); *In re* Borelli, 132 B.R. 648 (N.D. Cal. 1991); Advisory Committee Note to 1991 Amendments to Fed. R. Bankr. P. 9027; *see also In re* Goerg, 930 F.2d 1563 (11th Cir. 1991) (right of review by Article III court is constitutionally required).
226 *See* § 13.5, *infra; see also* Reed v. Miss. Farm Bureau Mut. Ins. Co., 299 B.R. 804 (S.D. Miss. 2003) (remand required when mandatory abstention appropriate); *In re* Revco D.S., Inc., 99 B.R. 768 (N.D. Ohio 1989) (grounds for mandatory abstention require remand of removed action).
227 *See* Browning v. Navarro, 743 F.2d 1069 (5th Cir. 1984); *In re* Roper, 203 B.R. 326 (Bankr. N.D. Ala. 1996) (remanding to state court actions brought by debtors against creditors for unfair practices).
228 *See In re* Wood, 825 F.2d 90 (5th Cir. 1987) (non-debtor third party properly joined in core proceeding); *In re* Salem Mortgage Co., 783 F.2d 626, 634 (6th Cir. 1986); *In re* Red Ash Coal & Coke Corp., 83 B.R. 399 (W.D. Va. 1988) (bankruptcy court has non-core jurisdiction over removed actions including claims against non-debtor guarantors of debtor's notes); *In re* Auburn Med. Realty, 19 B.R. 113 (B.A.P. 1st Cir. 1982); *In re* Griffith, 6 B.R. 753 (Bankr. D.N.M. 1980); *In re* Greco, 3 B.R. 18 (Bankr. D. Haw. 1979); Kennedy, *The Bankruptcy Court Under the New Bankruptcy Law: Its Structure, Jurisdiction, Venue and Procedure*, 11 St. Mary's L.J. 251, 286–289 (1979). Indeed, a case may be related to the bankruptcy case even if the debtor is not a party. *In re* Maine Marine Corp., 20 B.R. 426 (Bankr. D. Me. 1982).
229 *In re* Bellucci, 9 B.R. 887 (Bankr. D. Mass. 1981); *In re* Griffith, 6 B.R. 753 (Bankr. D.N.M. 1980); *In re* Greco, 3 B.R. 18 (Bankr. D. Haw. 1979); *see also In re* Haw. Mini Storage Sys., Inc., 4 B.R. 489 (Bankr. D. Haw. 1980).
230 See Chapter 9, *supra,* for discussion of the automatic stay.

is well-established that the pendency of an action in one court does not bar a subsequent action in another for the same or similar relief.[231] The failure to remove the first lawsuit to the bankruptcy forum does not change this rule.[232]

The debtor may commence an adversary proceeding for damages, equitable, or declaratory relief to bring such a case before the bankruptcy forum. Often, such an adversary action may be framed as an objection to proof of claim. In such cases, a debtor may be able to address issues and present claims against a creditor holding a valid judgment, especially if it is a judgment by default.[233] By becoming the plaintiff, the debtor is often able to frame the litigation in the most advantageous way. The debtor may bring virtually any type of action based upon pre-petition claims,[234] and some post-petition claims, into the federal bankruptcy system (subject, of course, to abstention when the court deems appropriate).[235]

The debtor should list on the bankruptcy schedules and claim as exempt, if possible, any claims that the debtor plans to assert, also noting that the debts to the creditors involved are disputed. However, if claims are not discovered until later, the failure to schedule them initially is not fatal, because schedules may be amended,[236] and because there is rarely any prejudice to the creditor if schedules are amended during the case.[237] If a claim cannot be claimed as fully exempt, a chapter 7 debtor may suggest that the trustee become co-plaintiff. If the trustee is unwilling to bear this expense, the debtor may then be able to request that the trustee abandon the claim.[238] In chapter 13, the debtor normally has the right to fully control any litigation, because the debtor remains in possession of all property of the estate.[239]

13.4.3 Objections to Claims

13.4.3.1 Overview

Another way of raising issues in the bankruptcy court is by objecting to claims filed by creditors. There are many grounds for objections that might be filed. In a chapter 13 case, for example, debtors may object to claims that they do not want to pay if those claims have not been timely filed,[240] or if they do not otherwise conform to the rules.[241] Section

---

231 *In re* N. Pipeline Constr. Co., 6 B.R. 928 (Bankr. D. Minn. 1980), *rev'd on other grounds sub nom.* N. Pipeline Constr. Co. v. Marathon Pipe Line Co., 458 U.S. 50, 102 S. Ct. 2858, 73 L. Ed. 2d 598 (1982).

232 *Id.*

233 Unless a state has a compulsory counterclaim rule, counterclaims, including recoupment under the Truth in Lending Act, are not barred by a judgment on the creditor's claim and may be raised in a later proceeding. *See* Restatement (Second) of Judgments § 22; *see also In re* Hamlett, 63 B.R. 492 (Bankr. M.D. Fla. 1986). *But see In re* Trans State Outdoor Advertising Co., 140 F.3d 618 (5th Cir. 1998) (bankruptcy court could not redetermine tax liability that had been adjudicated in an administrative hearing); Kelleran v. Andrijevic, 825 F.2d 692 (9th Cir. 1987) (bankruptcy court could not disregard state court judgment of liability); § 13.4.3.3, *infra*.

234 *See, e.g., In re* Dobrowsky, 735 F.2d 90 (3d Cir. 1984) (insurance claim of the debtor); *In re* Russell, 181 B.R. 616 (M.D. Ala. 1995) (action brought for unfair sales practices); *In re* Carter, 177 B.R. 951 (N.D. Okla.) (rescinding mortgage based upon economic duress), *aff'd*, 45 F.3d 439 (10th Cir. 1994); *In re Daniel*, 137 B.R. 884 (D.S.C. 1992) (debtor and trustee awarded damages for wrongful repossession of mobile home); *In re* Fleet, 95 B.R. 319 (E.D. Pa. 1989) (class action seeking unfair trade practice damages for consumers injured by business whose services consisted solely of providing referrals to bankruptcy attorney); *In re* Arsenault, 184 B.R. 864 (Bankr. D.N.H. 1995) (denying interest to mortgagee that imposed excessive charges); *In re* Madison, 42 B.R. 302 (Bankr. E.D. Pa. 1984) (suit seeking judicial review of decision by HUD to deny assignment program benefits to debtor), *aff'd*, 60 B.R. 837 (E.D. Pa. 1986).

235 *See* § 13.3.2.3, *supra*; § 13.5, *infra*.

236 *See* § 8.3.2, *supra*.

237 *See* Ryan Operations, Gen. P'ship v. Santiam-Midwest Lumber

Co., 81 F.3d 355 (3d Cir. 1996) (suit on claim not listed in bankruptcy schedules not barred by judicial estoppel, as debtor had not attempted to play fast and loose with rules and failure to list claim had no impact on bankruptcy case); Donato v. Metro. Life Ins. Co., 230 B.R. 418 (N.D. Cal. 1999) (failure to disclose lawsuit as an asset on schedules did not judicially estop debtor from pursuing it); Elliott v. ITT Corp., 150 B.R. 36 (N.D. Ill. 1992) (failure to initially schedule debt as disputed or note cause of action and failure to deal with it in prior chapter 13 cases which had been dismissed did not estop debtors from raising consumer protection claims against creditor after those claims were discovered); *cf.* Payless Wholesale Distributors v. Alberto Culver Inc., 989 F.2d 570 (1st Cir. 1993) (intentional failure to list claims in bankruptcy warrants dismissal of later filed action based on those claims).

238 *See* § 8.3.8, *supra*.

239 11 U.S.C. § 1306(b); Cable v. Ivy Tech State College, 200 F.3d 467 (7th Cir. 1999) (chapter 13 debtor can bring claim in own name); Olick v. Parker & Parsley Petroleum Co., 145 F.3d 513 (2d Cir. 1998) (chapter 13 debtor has standing to litigate causes of action); Donato v. Metro. Life Ins. Co., 230 B.R. 418 (N.D. Cal. 1999) (chapter 13 debtor had standing to litigate prepetition causes of action); *In re* Wirmel, 134 B.R. 258 (Bankr. S.D. Ohio 1991) (conversion from chapter 7 to chapter 13 removed civil rights cause of action from trustee's control).

240 *See* § 13.4.3.2, *infra*.

241 *In re* Milton, 1990 WL 122048 (Bankr. S.D. Cal. Apr. 17, 1990) (IRS' claim disallowed because it did not state type of tax, tax period or amount and was therefore insufficient under Fed. R. Bankr. P. 3001); *see also* Greer v. O'Dell, 305 F.3d 1297 (11th Cir. 2002) (servicing agent could be real party in interest with standing to file a proof of claim); *In re* Sims, 278 B.R. 457 (Bankr. E.D. Tenn. 2002) (chapter 13 debtor has standing to object to claims and recover overpayments on inflated claims even if the base plan that confirmed in which amount debtor pays into plan will not change); *In re* Chain, 255 B.R. 278 (Bankr. D. Conn. 2000) (failure to attach any documentation to claim resulted in creditor being denied normal presumption that claim was valid). However, in most cases, defects in form will not cause disallowance of the claim without an opportunity for the creditor to cure the defect. *In re* Stoecker, 5 F.3d 1022 (7th Cir. 1993) (court could not disallow claim lacking required

502 of the Code also permits objections to claims on various other grounds, such as the inclusion of unmatured interest, which may be part of the "balance" on a loan in which interest is pre-computed.[242]

Even in a chapter 7 case, there may be a need to object to a claim. Under an erroneous Ninth Circuit decision,[243] a failure to object to a claim can give the claim *res judicata* effect, regardless of the fact that the claim is never served on the debtor and the fact that the case is a no-asset chapter 7 case in which objecting to the claim serves no purpose in the bankruptcy.

The rules do not set a time limit for objections to claims. However, in chapter 13 cases some courts have set deadlines by local rule, or issue an "order on claims" soon after the deadline for filing claims has passed, and will not consider objections filed after that order. It is not clear that such deadlines are valid, especially if the resolution of the objection is not necessary to the chapter 13 plan confirmation process, as the Federal Rules of Bankruptcy Procedure do not set a deadline.[244]

13.4.3.2 Claims Filed After Bar Date for Claims

A creditor's failure to file a timely proof of claim is often a convenient basis to strike a claim which the debtor does not want to pay at all. The time limit for filing claims in cases under chapters 7, 12 and 13 in most instances is ninety days from the first date set for the meeting of creditors.[245]

Claims by governmental units may be filed until 180 days after the order for relief.[246] (The order for relief is normally the date the petition is filed.)

If a claim is not filed on time and an objection to the claim is filed, the claim should be disallowed.[247] However, the court may sometimes find that some other filing by the creditor with the court served as a timely informal proof of claim.[248] The situations in which a court may extend the

---

Most courts rejected this approach, however, and had found the rule to be valid. *E.g., In re* Johnson, 156 B.R. 557 (Bankr. N.D. Ill. 1993); *In re* Zimmerman, 156 B.R. 192 (Bankr. W.D. Mich. 1993); *see also* Jones v. Arross, 9 F.3d 79 (10th Cir. 1993) (late filed claim in chapter 12 case disallowed, citing *Zimmerman*). And even the courts permitting late-filed claims to be allowed had found that a chapter 13 plan may treat late-filed claims differently than those which were filed on time. *See In re* Hausladen, 146 B.R. 557 (Bankr. D. Minn. 1992). Thus plan provisions separately classifying late claims and providing for little or no dividends to be paid to them should be considered. This issue was largely mooted by the 1994 amendments to the Code, which added 11 U.S.C. § 502(b)(9), specifically providing that late filed claims are, upon objection, to be disallowed. This amendment does create the necessity of objecting to such claims.

246 11 U.S.C. § 502(b)(9). Based upon the wording of this section, an argument can be made that late-filed priority claims are allowed only in chapter 7 cases, because tardy filings are not permitted by the Federal Rules of Bankruptcy Procedure and are authorized only as described in § 726(a) which, under 11 U.S.C. § 103(b), applies only in chapter 7 cases.

247 Fed. R. Bankr. P. 3002(c); *In re* Greenig, 152 F.3d 631 (7th Cir. 1998) (court does not have equitable powers to allow late claim in chapter 12); *In re* Aboody, 223 B.R. 36 (B.A.P. 1st Cir. 1998) (late claim not permissible in chapter 13 even if there was "excusable neglect"); *see also In re* Dennis, 230 B.R. 244 (Bankr. D.N.J. 1999) (creditor whose late claim was disallowed had no standing to object to plan's treatment of part of claim which had been disallowed). If no objection to the claim is filed the claim may well be allowed. By making untimeliness an objection to be raised under § 502(b), Congress may have implicitly provided that if no objection is filed the claim is allowed pursuant to § 502(a). *In re* Jensen, 232 B.R. 118 (Bankr. N.D. Ind. 1999). Thus, if a debtor wants to make sure a claim will be paid and that claim has not been filed by the deadline for claims, the debtor should not object to a late claim, or should file a late claim for the creditor and ask the trustee to cooperate by not objecting to it. *See In re* Miranda, 269 B.R. 737 (Bankr. S.D. Tex. 2001) (if plan provides for payment of all unsecured claims and does not exclude unknown or late-filed claims, late-filed claim to which no objection is made should be paid under plan).

248 *In re* Holm, 931 F.2d 620 (9th Cir. 1991) (creditor's chapter 11 disclosure statement treated as informal claim); *In re* Charter Co., 876 F.2d 861 (11th Cir. 1989) (motion for relief from stay which clearly sets out nature of claim can constitute informal proof of claim); *In re* Haugen Constr. Services, Inc., 876 F.2d 681 (8th Cir. 1989) (creditor's letter to United States trustee explicitly stating nature and amount of claim constitutes amendable informal proof of claim); *In re* Anderson-Walker Indus., Inc., 798 F.2d 1285 (9th Cir. 1986) (informal proof of claim must explicitly state nature and amount of claim and must evidence intent to hold debtor liable); *In re* Sambo's Restaurant's Inc., 754 F.2d 811 (9th Cir. 1985) (requisites of an informal proof of claim); Wilkens v. Simon Bros. Inc., 731 F.2d

---

attachment of writing on which it was based without first granting leave to amend).

242 11 U.S.C. § 502(b) (2). *But see In re* Kielisch, 258 F.3d 315 (4th Cir. 2001) (non-allowability of unmatured interest on non-dischargeable student loan did not mean that post-petition interest on loan was not non-dischargeable).

243 Siegel v. Fed. Home Loan Mortgage Corp., 143 F.3d 525 (9th Cir. 1998); *cf.* County Fuel Co. v. Equitable Bank Corp., 832 F.2d 290 (4th Cir. 1987) (statement in dicta that it is 'doubtful' that a creditor's proof of claim, to which the debtor had not objected, barred the debtor's subsequent suit against the creditor).

244 *In re* Morton, 298 B.R. 301 (B.A.P. 6th Cir. 2003); Hildebrand v. Hays Imports, Inc. (*In re* Johnson), 279 B.R. 218, 224 (Bankr. M.D. Tenn. 2002); *In re* Fryer, 172 B.R. 1020 (Bankr. S.D. Ga. 1994) (TILA objection to creditor's claim was not barred by *res judicata* effect of confirmed plan, as objection did not implicate validity of any plan provision); *see also* Internal Revenue Serv. v. Kolstad (*In re* Kolstad), 928 F.2d 171, 174 (8th Cir. 1991) ("There is no bar date or deadline for filing objections."); *In re* Barton, 249 B.R. 561, 566 (Bankr. E.D. Wash. 2000) ("If Congress had intended objections to claims to be filed prior to Chapter 13 plan confirmation, it would have been a simple matter to write such a deadline into the statute"). *But see In re* Bateman, 331 F.3d 821 (11th Cir. 2003) (although § 502(a) does not provide time limit to file an objection, it must be filed prior to plan confirmation).

245 Fed. R. Bankr. P. 3002(c). Prior to the 1994 amendments to the Code, the rule's dictate that late-filed claims cannot be allowed had been found by some courts to be inconsistent with the Code. *See, e.g., In re* Hausladen, 146 B.R. 557 (Bankr. D. Minn. 1992).

time for filing a claim in a chapter 7, 12, or 13 case are few and they are delimited in the applicable rule.[249] In contrast, the time limits vary on a case-by-case basis in chapter 11 and extensions are available when the failure to act was based on excusable neglect.[250]

An objection to late filed claims is particularly valuable with respect to tax creditors claiming priority in chapter 13, because otherwise those claims must be paid in full.[251] For this reason, and because the IRS sometimes seems to have difficulty responding to bankruptcy filings,[252] much of the litigation on the timeliness of claims involves tax claims in chapter 13.[253] In cases in which a the IRS has attempted to correct its errors by amending a claim it did file on time, courts usually have precluded the IRS from amending the claim for one tax year to include claims for other types of taxes or for the same taxes due in other years.[254]

13.4.3.3 Claims Not Enforceable Against the Debtor

The Code provides that no claim may be allowed to the extent that it is unenforceable against the debtor.[255] This

---

462 (7th Cir. 1984); *see also In re* Unioil, 962 F.2d 988 (10th Cir. 1992) (permitting amendment of claim to state that it was filed by creditor as trustee for another, rather than in his individual capacity, where content of proof of claim was not changed); *In re* Kolstad, 101 B.R. 492 (Bankr. S.D. Tex. 1989) (creditor can amend proof of claim filed by debtor on its behalf even though it did not file a timely proof of claim), *aff'd*, 928 F.2d 171 (5th Cir. 1991). *But see In re* Reliance Equities, 966 F.2d 1338 (10th Cir. 1992) (trustee's awareness that claim existed did not constitute an informal proof of claim that could be amended after bar date for claims); *In re* A.H. Robins Co., 862 F.2d 1092 (4th Cir. 1988) (bare statement of intention to make a claim insufficient as informal proof).

249 Fed. R. Bankr. P. 3002(c), 9006(b)(3); *see In re* Coastal Alaska Lines, 920 F.2d 1428 (9th Cir. 1990) (bankruptcy court had no discretion to enlarge time for filing claim in chapter 7 case; unscheduled creditor with knowledge of the bankruptcy who failed to file timely claim was not entitled to participate in distribution of assets with other timely filed claims); *In re* Shelton, 116 B.R. 453 (Bankr. D. Md. 1990) (trustee's objection to untimely unsecured claim sustained even though no prejudice would result); *see also In re* Gardenhire, 209 F.3d 1145 (9th Cir. 2000) (time period for filing claims did not stop running during time case was erroneously dismissed before case was reinstated); *In re* Johnson, 901 F.2d 513 (6th Cir. 1990) (IRS failed to timely file claim, in case converted to chapter 7, for administrative expenses incurred in superseded chapter 11 case); *In re* Stuart, 31 B.R. 18 (Bankr. D. Conn. 1983) (student loan creditor precluded from amending timely filed claim against wife in joint case to add claim against husband). Significant errors in the notice of the bar date though may provide cause for allowing a late claim. *Compare In re* Herd, 840 F.2d 757 (10th Cir. 1988) (listing of incorrect bar date in chapter 11 case makes notice insufficient); *In re* Johnson, 95 B.R. 197 (Bankr. D. Colo. 1989) (notice sent to "IRS-Ogden, Utah" in chapter 13 case is insufficient and merited allowance of untimely proof of claim) *with In re* Robintech, Inc., 863 F.2d 393 (5th Cir. 1988) (incorrect address on notice does not excuse creditor's late filing absent proof that late receipt caused late filing). Another issue related to timeliness of proofs of claim involves the treatment of creditors who did not receive notice of the bar date. Some courts may allow them additional time to file a proof of claim. *See, e.g., In re* Yoder, 758 F.2d 1114 (6th Cir. 1985). In other cases, debts owed to creditors without timely notice of the bar date may not be discharged. *See In re* Spring Valley Farms, Inc., 863 F.2d 832 (11th Cir. 1989). *See generally* 11 U.S.C. § 523(a)(3); § 14.4.3.3, *infra*. There is, however, a presumption of receipt of any notices mailed by the court.

250 Fed. R. Civ. P. 3003(c)(3), 9006(b)(1). The Supreme Court has defined excusable neglect fairly liberally, to include inadvertence, mistake, or carelessness, in the context of filing a late claim in a chapter 11 case. Pioneer Inv. Services Co. v. Brunswick Associates, 507 U.S. 380, 113 S. Ct. 1489, 123 L. Ed. 2d 74 (1993); *see* Maressa v. A.H. Robins Co., 839 F.2d 220 (4th Cir. 1988); *In re* Int'l Horizons, Inc., 751 F.2d 1213 (11th Cir. 1985); *In re* Pigott, 674 F.2d 1011 (3d Cir. 1982); *see also In re* Pioneer Inv. Services Co., 943 F.2d 673 (6th Cir. 1991) (late claims allowable in chapter 11 based on excusable neglect standard), *aff'd*, 507 U.S. 380 (1993); Chrysler Motors Corp. v.

Schneiderman, 940 F.2d 911 (3d Cir. 1991) (loss of claim filed by regular mail in chapter 11 case does not permit second claim to be filed late based on excusable neglect); *In re* Vertientes Ltd., 845 F.2d 57 (3d Cir. 1988) (listing creditor's claim on schedules in chapter 11 as uncontested does not estop debtor from objecting to late filed proof of claim).

251 *See* § 12.3.5, *supra*.

252 The IRS, like other government units, now has a special extended deadline for filing claims. Under 11 U.S.C. 502(b)(9), claims of government units may be filed until the later of 180 days after the order for relief or the claims bar date provided under Fed. R. Bankr. P. 3002 or 3003.

253 *See In re* Osborne, 76 F.3d 306 (9th Cir. 1996) (IRS claim for payroll taxes disallowed as untimely and could be discharged in chapter 13 case); *In re* Chavis, 47 F.3d 818 (6th Cir. 1995) (untimely proof of [IRS] claim in chapter 13 case disallowed); *In re* Ripley, 926 F.2d 440 (5th Cir. 1991) (objection to late filed claim of IRS denied because taxes were not due pre-petition); *In re* Carr, 134 B.R. 370 (Bankr. D. Neb. 1991) (IRS not permitted to amend claim after confirmation of plan and after court enters order allowing claims); *In re* Garner, 113 B.R. 352 (Bankr. N.D. Ohio 1990) (IRS barred from amending claim thirteen months after confirmation to change claim from unsecured to priority status).

254 United States v. Roberson, 188 B.R. 364 (D. Md. 1995) (IRS precluded from amending existing claim after bar date where supplemental claims involved tax debt for different tax year); *In re* Baker, 129 B.R. 607 (E.D. Mo. 1991) (same); United States v. Owens, 84 B.R. 361 (E.D. Pa. 1988) (IRS cannot amend existing timely filed proof of claim after bar date to include delinquencies for additional tax years); *see also In re* Alliance Operating Corp., 60 F.3d 1174 (5th Cir. 1995) (amendment changing claim from general unsecured claim to priority claim not permitted after deadline for claims had passed); *In re* Taylor, 280 B.R. 711 (Bankr. S.D. Ala. 2001) (creditor could not amend claim long after bar date to change it from unsecured to secured). *But see In re* Tanaka Bros. Farms, Inc., 36 F.3d 996 (10th Cir. 1994) (IRS could amend timely estimated claim to conform to debtor's recently filed tax returns); *In re* Hemingway Transp., Inc., 954 F.2d 1 (1st Cir. 1992); *In re* Unroe, 937 F.2d 346 (7th Cir. 1991) (bankruptcy court has discretion to treat IRS claim for one tax year as notice of intent to collect for a different tax year).

255 11 U.S.C. § 502(b)(1). In determining enforceability, federal common law choice of law rules apply. *See In re* Miller, 292

means that the debtor may assert as objections to a claim any defenses or setoffs the debtor may have with respect to that claim. The objections are then resolved in the bankruptcy forum,[256] which is usually, but not always, the bankruptcy court.[257] If the objections relate to matters such as the extent or validity of a lien, they must be filed by way of complaint.[258] Otherwise, the objection initiates a contested matter.[259] Although a properly filed proof of claim is considered prima facie valid, once some evidence is produced in support of an objection, the burden of proof is on the creditor to substantiate its claim.[260] However, with respect to tax claims, the Supreme Court has held that the burden of proof outside of bankruptcy carries over to bankruptcy proceedings.[261]

In some cases a creditor will file a claim which it knows or should have known is baseless in whole or part. That conduct should be subject to sanctions under Federal Rule of Bankruptcy Procedure 9011,[262] and very likely as an unfair

or deceptive practice as well.[263] Damages and attorney fees should be available under these theories.

The debtor may wish to object to a claim which has been the subject of prior litigation. However, when judgment has been entered by a non-bankruptcy court on a claim, normal rules of *res judicata* and collateral estoppel apply.[264]

In some cases, creditors (and particularly secured creditors) do not file claims to which objections can be filed.[265] In such cases, especially if the debtor seeks a determination of the amount due on the claim, the debtor may file a claim for the amount the debtor believes is due on behalf of the creditor to bring the matter before the court.[266] Under the Rules, this may be done if the creditor does not file a claim on or before the first date set for the meeting of creditors.[267] The court then sends notice of the claim to the creditor, who is given the opportunity to file a substitute claim which would supersede that filed by the debtor. Although superseding claims may not be filed after the bar date, a few courts have allowed creditors to amend the debtor's claim even after the bar date has passed.[268] If such a substitute

B.R. 409 (B.A.P. 9th Cir. 2003) (because choice of law rules dictated following Nevada rather than California law, claim for gambling debt allowed).

256 *See, e.g., In re* Venture Mortgage Fund, Ltd. P'ship, 282 F.3d 185 (2d Cir. 2002) (claims based on usurious loans disallowed); *In re* Guardian Trust Co., 260 B.R. 404 (S.D. Miss. 2000) (neither debtor nor trustee need file administrative request for tax refund or comply with IRS statute of limitations to assert refund claim by way of offset to IRS claim); *In re* Goldberg, 297 B.R. 465 (Bankr. W.D.N.C. 2003) (sustaining objection to student loan claim where school closed one week after debtor enrolled and rejecting argument that debtor had to exhaust administrative remedies); *In re* Dooley, 41 B.R. 31 (Bankr. N.D. Ga. 1984) (successful objection to inadequately documented claim for attorney fees); *In re* Hamby, 19 B.R. 776 (Bankr. N.D. Ala. 1982) (Uniform Commercial Code repossession violations asserted as objections to claim for deficiency).

257 See discussion of discretionary and mandatory withdrawal to district court in § 13.2.5, *supra. See also In re* Ferris, 764 F.2d 1475 (11th Cir. 1985) (debtor's counterclaim raising state consumer law violations is a core proceeding).

258 Fed. R. Bankr. P. 3007.

259 Fed. R. Bankr. P. 9014 governs such proceedings. Because contested matters are governed by Fed. R. Bankr. P. 7041, once an answer to the objection has been filed, there is no right of the objecting party to withdraw the objection without the creditor's consent. *In re* Fairchild, 969 F.2d 866 (10th Cir. 1992). Also, a debtor or trustee should be careful to serve an objection to the claim of the federal government on all parties required to receive service under Bankruptcy Rule 7004, including the attorney general and U.S. attorney, and to comply with Rule 2002(g) requiring service at the address listed in the proof of claim. *See In re* Miller, 16 F.3d 240 (8th Cir. 1994).

260 *In re* Fid. Holding Co., Ltd., 837 F.2d 696 (5th Cir. 1988); *In re* Tesmetges, 87 B.R. 263 (Bankr. S.D.N.Y. 1988); *see also In re* Circle J Dairy, Inc., 112 B.R. 297 (W.D. Ark. 1989) (where claim itself calls into question its amount, it cannot be given prima facie validity); *In re* Koch, 83 B.R. 898 (Bankr. E.D. Pa. 1988) (general standard of proof is a preponderance of the evidence).

261 Raleigh v. Illinois Dep't of Revenue, 530 U.S. 15, 120 S. Ct. 1951, 147 L. Ed. 2d 13 (2000).

262 The rule now covers pleadings filed by unrepresented creditors

and debtors as well as attorneys. A related issue is whether the party listed as creditor or agent for the creditor on the proof of claim has standing to file the claim. One court has held that a servicer of a credit card account is a party in interest that may file a claim and appear on behalf of the creditor. Greer v. O'Dell, 305 F.3d 1297 (11th Cir. 2002); *see also In re* Viencek, 273 B.R. 354 (Bankr. N.D.N.Y. 2002) (mortgage servicing agent has standing to defend against objection to claim).

263 Helpful pleadings on this issue are published in *Suit Against Taxing Agency for Filing Baseless Chapter 13 Proofs of Claim*, National Consumer Law Center, Consumer Law Pleadings, No. 3, § 7.2 (Cumulative CD-Rom and Index Guide). *But see* Holloway v. Household Auto. Fin. Corp., 227 B.R. 501 (N.D. Ill. 1998) (UDAP remedies are preempted by Bankruptcy Code consumer protections). *Holloway* is wrongly decided. *See generally* National Consumer Law Center, Unfair and Deceptive Acts and Practices § 5.1.1.7 (5th ed. 2001 and Supp.).

264 *In re* Baker, 74 F.3d 906 (9th Cir. 1996) (*res judicata* effect of prior final judgment of Tax Court precluded debtor from relitigating tax liability through objection to claim); *In re* Laing, 945 F.2d 354 (10th Cir. 1991) (state court judgment on note must be given preclusive effect upon objections to proof of claim); *see In re* Brady, Tex. Mun. Gas Corp., 936 F.2d 212 (5th Cir. 1991) (state court determination concerning creditor's rights against debtor's successor in interest is entitled to full faith and credit even if erroneous); *cf. In re* Mantz, 343 F.3d 1207 (9th Cir. 2003) (bankruptcy court could consider objection to state tax claim because there had been no final adjudication of tax liability prior to the bankruptcy).

265 It should be noted that no notice to the debtor of filing of a claim is required by the current rules. The only way to be certain as to whether a claim has been filed is to check the bankruptcy court file.

266 11 U.S.C. § 501(c).

267 Fed. R. Bankr. P. 3004. The debtor has until thirty days after the claims bar date to file a proof of claim on behalf of a creditor. *Id.* This time may be extended if the debtor's failure to file timely is based on excusable neglect. Fed. R. Bankr. P. 9006(b); *In re* Davis, 936 F.2d 771 (4th Cir. 1991).

268 Fed. R. Bankr. P. 3004; *In re* Kolstad, 928 F.2d 171 (5th Cir. 1991) (court has discretion to allow IRS to amend debtor's proof

claim is filed, the debtor may then file whatever objections are appropriate. If no superseding claim is filed, the claim filed by the debtor, if allowed by the court, should determine the rights of the parties thereafter.[269] Another approach, which may be preferable if there is a dispute about whether a valid lien exists, is to seek a declaratory judgment that the debtor's proof of claim on behalf of the creditor is valid and binding.[270]

13.4.3.4 Objecting to Overcharges on Mortgage Claims

13.4.3.4.1 Overcharges in general

Because the debtor's main objective in many chapter 13 bankruptcy cases is to cure and reinstate a mortgage, minimizing the cost of reinstatement requires careful review of the creditor's proof of claim to prevent overcharges. Some servicers consistently inflate their claims by miscalculation, misunderstanding the loan contract, or deliberate addition of unauthorized fees. Raising these objections can make an apparently unworkable chapter 13 plan feasible or can provide much more breathing room for a family struggling to afford large plan payments.

When an overcharge appears deliberate, or in situations involving inadvertent overcharges which the servicer fails to correct after due notice, debtor's attorneys should consider seeking unfair trade practice relief (and attorney fees),[271] and in egregious cases, sanctions under Rule 9011. For cases involving interest overcharges, usury claims may also be available.[272] Abusive practices which impact a large group of debtors may be amenable to class action treatment.[273]

Informal discovery on the elements of a creditor's claim can be obtained under the Real Estate Settlement Procedures Act with potential sanctions for failure to provide timely

information. If a borrower sends a "qualified written request" stating the account is in error or a question about the account, a mortgage servicer must within sixty days conduct an investigation if an error is alleged; provide the requested information; make any necessary corrections to the account; and inform the consumer of the actions taken.[274] Once an objection to claim is filed, full discovery under the Federal Rules of Bankruptcy Procedure becomes available.[275]

As the objection would raise issues about the extent of a lien and goes beyond issues of property valuation, it is usually better practice to pursue it as an adversary proceeding.[276]

13.4.3.4.2 Escrow overcharges

One of the most common problems found in reviewing secured claims is abuse in the collection of escrow arrears.[277] Often, this occurs because fees and charges associated with foreclosure are broken out as separate elements of the arrears. At the same time, the servicer has also included those fees and charges in the borrower's escrow account when they were paid out. Based on miscommunication, ignorance, or inattention, these fees can then be double counted in the proof of claim: once as "foreclosure costs" and again as a portion of the amount denominated as "payment arrears."

Similarly, it is fairly common for a servicer to reevaluate each borrower's escrow account on an annual basis. Some servicers take the total escrow arrears, whether or not they have been included in the bankruptcy proof of claim, and include them when they calculate the borrower's new escrow payment going forward. Because those arrears are being paid under the plan, this practice can lead to double or sometimes triple payment (when the escrow arrears are already double counted in the proof of claim).

Proofs of claim should be reviewed for these problems. When the line item for escrow arrears appears to be out of line, (for example, if it is more than the amount of the monthly payment for taxes and insurance multiplied by the

---

of claim after the bar date); *In re* Bishop, 122 B.R. 96 (Bankr. E.D. Mo. 1990) (claim of IRS filed after debtor filed claim for IRS was effective as an amended claim, even though filed after claims bar date).

269 *See also In re* Borne Chem. Co., 691 F.2d 134 (3d Cir. 1982) (court may estimate value of claims in bankruptcy proceeding for purposes of bankruptcy case).

270 *See In re* Kilen, 129 B.R. 538 (Bankr. N.D. Ill. 1991) (debtor can object to the proof of claim it files on behalf of a creditor). If no such action is filed, where the debtor files an unsecured claim on behalf of a creditor which believes it is secured, that creditor may argue later that its lien passed through the case unaffected. In a chapter 13 case, that argument should fail, because the creditor is bound by a chapter 13 plan of which it had notice. *See* § 12.11, *supra*. But the cautious approach is probably to seek a clear determination from the court at the time of the bankruptcy case.

271 *See generally* National Consumer Law Center, Unfair and Deceptive Acts and Practices (5th ed. 2001 and Supp.).

272 National Consumer Law Center, The Cost of Credit: Regulation and Legal Challenges (2d ed. 2000 and Supp.).

273 *See* § 13.7, *infra*.

274 12 U.S.C. § 2605(e)(1)(B)(2); 24 C.F.R. § 3500.21(e)(3); *see* National Consumer Law Center, Repossessions and Foreclosures § 17.2.4.3 (5th ed. 2002 and Supp.). For a sample "qualified written request," see Form 69, Appx. G.8, *infra*.

275 Fed. R. Bankr. P. 7026–7037 as made applicable to contested matters by Fed. R. Bankr. P. 9014.

276 Fed. R. Bankr. P. 7001; *see* § 13.2.4.1, *supra*.

277 Many first mortgage claims include required escrow payments for taxes and insurance. Most lenders also include any other costs charged to the loan in their escrow accounting in order to recover those charges from the borrower. (In some states, consumer escrows associated with mortgage claims are called "impound accounts.") In situations in which modification of mortgage terms is allowed, it may be possible to cancel the escrow account in order to pay the lender only principal and interest. In that event, the debtor would usually have to pay taxes and insurance separately. *See generally* § 11.6.1, *supra*.

number of months the debtor is in arrears), then more information should be requested, by discovery if necessary. At the same time, debtors should be told to be on the alert for unusual changes in their monthly payment amounts.

13.4.3.4.3 Interest overcharges

Several problems related to interest charges can arise as well. A common problem arises when servicers itemize or otherwise include in the proof of claim interest on arrears[278] claims which will accrue post-petition under the plan. In jurisdictions where the trustee automatically calculates and pays that interest, some debtors end up paying double.

In order to prevent this problem, the Code requires that claims for unmatured interest be disallowed.[279] An objection to claim may be necessary. Although many trustees are conscientious about not double paying interest, debtor's counsel cannot rely on the trustee to catch this error.

Another interest charge abuse which has been reported is a secured proof of claim for the entire amount of precomputed interest (for a loan on which the balance is calculated to include precomputed interest for the entire term of the loan under state law). That practice, which includes in the balance interest not yet earned, can undermine plans which propose to modify the secured claim and pay it on an amortization schedule different from that contained in the contract, and it can distort the amount of interest on arrears to which that creditor is entitled.

Even if the credit contract allows precomputed interest, the filing of a claim including such interest should be challenged in bankruptcy as inconsistent with 11 U.S.C. § 1325(a)(5) and § 502(b)(2). At a minimum, the debtor is entitled to have appropriate interest rebates calculated. (In some transactions creditors may argue that these calculations must be made under the very unfair Rule of 78's, but depending upon the contract and state or federal law these arguments can often be defeated, as the Rule of 78's may be abrogated by statute or applicable only in the event of prepayment or other specified event.)[280] If interest on arrears is permitted, the debtor and the trustee will also need to carefully calculate the appropriate interest on arrears payment so that only the arrears generate interest.

13.4.3.4.4 Late charge abuses and other miscrediting of payments

Despite a chapter 13 plan to cure arrears, some creditors continue to treat timely payments received post-petition as if they were late. This occurs based on the industry practice of crediting payments received to the oldest outstanding installment. Although this practice may be appropriate if there is no bankruptcy pending, it is not appropriate in situations where the pre-petition arrears are being paid according to a proof of claim (which may already include late charges for those payments) and the debtor's chapter 13 plan.

Hidden late charges are only one of several pervasive problems with miscrediting payments made to cure a default under a chapter 13 plan.[281] These problems may not be easily detectable without reviewing loan payment records.[282] At a minimum, when a debtor has cured a default, payment records should be reviewed at the close of the case to make sure that they reflect the cure. Debtors should be encouraged to alert attorneys, even after bankruptcy is completed, if they receive communications regarding their mortgage that they do not understand. It is extremely common for illegal charges to be added to a mortgage after a bankruptcy is complete; sometimes they are discovered for the first time only when the debtor receives a pay-off statement. Problems can be remedied as violations of the discharge injunction, violation of the debtor's order of confirmation through contempt proceedings, and as unfair trade practices.[283] Attorney fees should be available in each case.

---

278 This interest is required to be paid based on Rake v. Wade, 508 U.S. 464, 113 S. Ct. 2187, 124 L. Ed. 2d 424 (1993). The requirement of payment of interest on arrears is not applicable to secured claims related to mortgages which were consummated after October 22, 1994 unless the parties' agreement requires that payment. 11 U.S.C. § 1322(e); see § 11.6.2.7.2, *supra*.

279 11 U.S.C. § 502(b)(2).

280 *In re* McMurray, 218 B.R. 867 (Bankr. E.D. Tenn. 1998) (Rule of 78's was only authorized, and was not required, when debtor prepaid loan). See National Consumer Law Center, The Cost of Credit: Regulation and Legal Challenges § 5.6.3 (2d ed. 2000 and Supp.) for a discussion of the Rule and the limited situations in which it continues to be legal.

281 *Debtors Force Mortgage Servicer to Remedy Chapter 13 Violations*, 12 NCLC REPORTS *Bankruptcy and Foreclosures Ed.* 43 (Mar./Apr. 1994).

282 *See In re* Wines, 239 B.R. 703 (Bankr. D.N.J. 1999) (example of case reconciling payments made and proof of claim).

283 See § 12.11, *supra*, and *Suit Against Mortgage Servicer for Disregarding Chapter 13 Plan Payments*, National Consumer Law Center, Consumer Law Pleadings No. 3, § 7.1 (2003 Cumulative CD-Rom and Index Guide) for a helpful sample complaint on this issue. *See also In re* Harris, 297 B.R. 61 (Bankr. N.D. Miss. 2003) (section 105(a) may be used to enforce Bankruptcy Code provisions that prohibit mortgage lender from charging late fees based on delay by trustee in disbursing post-petition mortgage payments); *In re* Turner, 221 B.R. 920 (Bankr. M.D. Fla. 1998) (attorneys fees and costs awarded for contempt based on accounting on secured debt inconsistent with completion of confirmed chapter 11 plan); *In re* McCormack, 203 B.R. 521 (Bankr. D.N.H. 1996) (mortgagee bank held liable for $10,000.00 punitive damages when it did not adjust its computer records to reflect effect of plan confirmation and sent debtor demand letter expressing intent to collect fees that were not due under plan).

13.4.3.4.5 Bankruptcy monitoring fees and other bankruptcy fees

Many mortgage lenders and servicers are now attempting to charge borrowers who file bankruptcy a fee for monitoring the bankruptcy case, even in chapter 7 cases in which the borrower is current on monthly mortgage payments and plans to continue to make monthly payments as they come due. These "monitoring" fees may be $250.00 or more and are automatically assessed to the borrower's account as soon as the bankruptcy is filed. They may include fees for periodic inspections of the property or broker price opinions. Lenders generally assert that these fees are authorized by language in their loan notes that obligates the borrower to pay any costs incurred in defending its security interest.

Other lenders are claiming a right to fees for filing a proof of claim, pursuing motions for relief from stay, objections to confirmation, or for responding to a debtor's objection to claim.[284]

There are several possible bases on which creditors' bankruptcy monitoring fees can be challenged. However, the first problem in some cases is discovering that they exist, because the fees are charged to the debtor's escrow account or to a suspense account, and collected on a going forward basis by adjustment to future payments rather than as elements of a proof of claim. Clients should be alerted to report any correspondence reflecting significant escrow payment changes to determine whether this problem has arisen.

Typically, the contract clause on which the lender relies is a general provision which does not expressly authorize the imposition of "bankruptcy monitoring fees," but which applies more generally to attorney fees and other costs of defending the mortgage in a court action.[285] For example, one large loan servicing company that routinely imposes these fees relies upon the following provision contained in its standard mortgage:

> (9) Litigation. Borrower shall defend this mortgage in any action purporting to affect such property whether or not it affects the lien hereof, or purporting to affect the lien hereof or purporting to affect the rights or powers of Lender, and shall file and prosecute all necessary claims and actions to prevent or recover for any damage to or destruction of such property; and Lender is hereby authorized, without obligation to do so, to prosecute and defend any such action, whether brought by or against Borrower or Lender, or with or without suit, to exercise or enforce any other right, rem-
> edy, or power available or conferred hereunder, whether or not judgment be entered in any action or proceeding; and Lender may appear or intervene in any action or proceeding, and retain counsel therein, and take such action therein, as either may be deemed necessary or advisable, and may settle, compromise or pay the same or any other claims and, in so doing, may expend and advance such sums of money as either may deem necessary. Whether or not Borrower so appears or defends, Borrower on demand shall pay all costs and expenses, including but not limited to reasonable attorney fees of Lender including costs of evidence of title, in any such action or proceeding in which Lender may appear by virtue of being made a party defendant or otherwise, and irrespective of whether the interest of Lender in such property or their respective powers hereunder may be affected by such action, ...

In addition to being an unbargained-for term which is imposed in the boilerplate, this language, upon close reading, does not appear to authorize a bankruptcy monitoring fee. The provision appears to apply only where the borrower or lender defends the mortgage in a case which purports to affect the property, the lien, or the lender's powers or rights, or in actions to enforce the lender's rights, or in actions to recover for damage to or destruction of the property. The borrower's bankruptcy does not affect the property or the lien and is not an action to enforce the lenders' rights.[286]

According to the quoted paragraph, whether or not the borrower defends the action, the borrower is required to pay all of the lender's costs and expenses of any such action *in which the lender appears*, including reasonable attorney fees. Monitoring to determine whether an appearance is necessary does not appear to be covered.

At best, the provision is ambiguous. It is a basic principal of contract law that any ambiguity in a contract is construed against the drafter, in this case the lender.[287] Equally importantly, courts have strictly construed contractual provisions providing for fees and costs.[288]

---

284 *See* § 11.6.2.7.1, *supra*.

285 It is clear that bankruptcy monitoring fees can never be allowed without contractual authorization for charging those fees. *See In re* Hatcher, 208 B.R. 959 (B.A.P. 10th Cir. 1997) (no post-petition attorney fees allowed absent mortgage provision authorizing fees); *In re* LaRoche, 115 B.R. 93 (Bankr. N.D. Ohio 1990).

286 *In re* Thomas, 186 B.R. 470 (Bankr. W.D. Mo. 1995). Even if there is a default, and a case is brought under chapter 13, the bankruptcy arguably does not affect the lender's rights, if the Code protects the lender's claim from being modified under 11 U.S.C. § 1322(b)(2). *In re* Romano, 174 B.R. 342 (Bankr. M.D. Fla. 1994).

287 *In re* Stark, 242 B.R. 866 (Bankr. W.D.N.C. 1999) (bankruptcy monitoring fees disallowed as ambiguous mortgage contract construed against lender).

288 *See, e.g., In re* Sublett 895 F.2d 1381 (11th Cir. 1990); First Brandon Nat'l Bank v. Kerwin-White, 109 B.R. 626 (D. Vt. 1990); *see also In re* Williams, 1998 WL 372656 (Bankr. N.D. Ohio June 10, 1998) (ambiguous contract term inadequate basis to support creditor's request for fees for motion for relief from stay); *In re* Romano, 174 B.R. 342 (Bankr. M.D. Fla. 1994) (interpreting loan note's ambiguous attorney fee provision against the lender/drafter); *cf. In re* Majchrowski, 6 F. Supp. 2d

Of course, the analysis of any particular case will depend on the language of the loan contract at issue. As the language quoted here illustrates, advocates should review the language of the contract closely to determine whether it actually says what the lender claims that it says, and whether it is ambiguous.[289]

If a lender attempts to collect a bankruptcy fee from property of the estate while the automatic stay is in effect by adding the fee to the debtor's account, it has violated Code section 362(a)(3). Section 362(a)(3) prohibits "any act to obtain possession of property of the estate or of property from the estate or to exercise control over property of the estate" while the stay is in effect. In a chapter 13 case, all property the debtor acquires during the entire time the case is pending is property of the estate pursuant to section 1306(a). By seeking payment of this fee directly from the debtor, the lender violates the stay.[290]

In addition, it is an unfair and deceptive practice to state that a fee is authorized by the contract when it is not.[291] It is also unfair and deceptive to impose a fee that is not authorized.[292] Relying on confusing, ambiguous, or mis-

leading contract clauses (which the above-quoted clause certainly is) may also be a unfair or deceptive act or practice (UDAP) violation.[293]

If all the lender is doing is "monitoring" the bankruptcy, that is, receiving court notices, reading them, keeping them, and so forth, then these activities do not constitute the practice of law and should not be compensable as an attorney fee.[294] These routine administrative services are generally not compensable under any reading of typical mortgage provisions.[295]

Several lenders charge a flat rate monitoring fee to all borrowers in bankruptcy. This uniform charge is obviously not based on actual costs or expenses in "monitoring" the borrower's bankruptcy. Instead, it is an attempt to spread costs among all borrowers who file bankruptcy. Contract provisions providing for attorney fees are only enforceable "to the extent that it is shown that the creditor has been damaged by having to pay, or assume the payment of attorney fees or other collection expenses."[296] Similarly, if a lender is charging for other costs based on a contract provision, it should be required to justify the costs and show that they were actually incurred.[297]

In addition to being actually incurred by the lender, the fee must be reasonable and properly documented.[298] If the fee is for services that are unnecessary, then it is not reasonable.[299] In most circumstances it is not necessary for

---

946 (N.D. Ill. 1998) (standard form mortgage provision allows lender to charge a fee for filing proof of claim and is not ambiguous so as to require construction against the drafter).

289 *See In re* Hatala, 295 B.R. 62 (Bankr. D.N.J. 2003) (mortgage provided for fees only in foreclosure and not for fees incurred after foreclosure judgment; fees limited to those permitted by state rules); *In re* Woodham, 174 B.R. 346 (Bankr. M.D. Fla. 1994) (analysis of provision which does not specifically provide for attorneys fees in bankruptcy).

290 *In re* Stark, 242 B.R. 866 (W.D.N.C. 1999) (sanctions imposed for violating stay by attempting to collect inspection and monitoring fees); *In re* Banks, 31 B.R. 173 (Bankr. N.D. Ala. 1982). *But see* Mann v. Chase Manhattan Mortgage Corp., 316 F.3d 1 (1st Cir. 2003) (mortgage company did not violate automatic stay by adding fees to debtor's account if it never attempted to collect those fees from debtor; court glossed over fact that addition of fees increased lien on debtor's property). In order to avoid unknown charges being assessed against a debtor's mortgage account, it may be advisable to file a motion at the end of a chapter 13 case seeking an order that the mortgage default has been cured and the mortgage is current. An example of such a motion can be found in Form 125, Appendix G.11, *infra*. If the debtor does not discover improper charges until after they have been paid, the debtor should still be able to challenge the fees. *See In re* Staggie, 255 B.R. 48 (Bankr. N.D. Idaho 2000) (bankruptcy court has authority under § 506 to review attorney fees of secured creditor even if the collateral has been sold and the fees paid by debtor). In an opinion that was wrongly decided, and may be avoided by counsel through careful drafting of the chapter 13 plan, the Eleventh Circuit rejected a debtor's challenge to a mortgage lender's collection of attorney fees and expenses from mortgage payments made outside the plan because it held that such payments were not property of the estate protected by the automatic stay after confirmation. Telfair v. First Union Mortgage Corp., 216 F.3d 1333 (11th Cir. 2000).

291 *See generally* National Consumer Law Center, Unfair and Deceptive Acts and Practices § 5.2.4.2 (5th ed. 2001 and Supp.).

292 *See generally* National Consumer Law Center, Unfair and Deceptive Acts and Practices § 5.1.1.7 (5th ed. 2001 and Supp.).

293 *See* Michaels v. Amway Corp., 206 Mich. App. 644, 522 N.W.2d 703 (1994).

294 *In re* Thomas, 186 B.R. 470 (Bankr. W.D. Mo. 1995) (lender that filed proof of claim without attorney assistance not entitled to attorney fee); *see* State Unauthorized Practice of Law Comm. v. Paul Mason, 46 F.3d 469 (5th Cir. 1995).

295 *See In re* Thomas, 186 B.R. 470 (W.D. Mo. 1995); *In re* Banks, 31 B.R. 173 (Bankr. N.D. Ala. 1982); *In re* Cipriano, 8 B.R. 697 (Bankr. D.R.I. 1981). *But see In re* Majchrowski, 6 F. Supp. 2d 946 (N.D. Ill. 1998) (standard form mortgage provision allows lender to charge a fee for filing proof of claim and for property inspections associated with foreclosure). The latter court appears to have been hostile to pursuit of these claims in this case as a RICO class action. Incredibly, the court states that the contract authorizes fees even if they are not "reasonable, economical or fair to the borrower."

296 *In re* Banks, 31 B.R. 173, 178 (Bankr. N.D. Ala. 1982) (citing Annotation, 17 A.L.R.2d 288 § 8, at 298 (1951)).

297 *See* Korea First Bank v. Lee, 14 F. Supp. 2d 530 (S.D.N.Y. 1998) (lender can collect no more than it agreed to pay its counsel).

298 *In re* Good, 207 B.R. 686 (Bankr. D. Idaho 1997) (assessing reasonableness of fees charged by mortgage lender); *see In re* Williams, 1998 WL 372656 (Bankr. N.D. Ohio June 10, 1998) (bank failed to meet burden of proving its fees are reasonable, by failing to provide adequate documentation); *cf. In re* Maywood, Inc., 210 B.R. 91 (Bankr. N.D. Tex. 1997) (fees disallowed for lender's bankruptcy monitor in chapter 11 case when the monitor spent the bulk of his time playing games on his laptop computer, reading the newspaper, and practicing his putting). If fees or expenses are to be collected from property of the estate, they should be itemized and requested in an application filed pursuant to Fed. R. Bankr. P. 2016.

299 *See In re* Dalessio, 74 B.R. 721 (B.A.P. 9th Cir. 1987).

the lender to do anything to protect its interest in a bankruptcy case. A lender can adequately monitor a case simply by making sure that it continues to receive payments (which is what the lender does in any event). The Bankruptcy Code and Rules expressly provide for notice if any action is taken which affects its mortgage.[300] A creditor can rely on receiving those notices without any affirmative action to monitor the case.

The fee also may be unreasonable if it exceeds the cost of the services performed.[301] Unreasonable or excessive charges may also violate the requirement of good faith and fair dealing implied in any contractual relationship.[302]

Some state debt collection statutes or regulations apply to creditors as well as debt collectors.[303] (The federal Fair Debt Collection Practices Act applies only to third party collectors.)[304] Most debt collection statutes and regulations prohibit the collection of any amount not authorized by contract or applicable law.[305]

13.4.3.5 Objecting to Claims Filed with Inadequate Documentation

Federal Rule of Bankruptcy Procedure 3001 requires that when a claim is based on a writing, an original or duplicate of the writing must be filed with the proof of claim.[306] Rule 3001(a) states that the proof of claim "shall conform substantially to the appropriate Official Form" and the instructions contained on the claim form (Official Form 10) state that the claimant must attach supporting documents.[307] If the total amount claimed includes interest or other charges, Official Form 10 also requires that the claimant check the appropriate box and attach an itemized statement of all interest or additional charges. An unsubstantiated claim is facially defective and not entitled to the presumption of validity.[308] Without this presumption, a facially defective claim provides evidence to "dispute its own validity" and shall be disallowed upon a general objection unless the creditor introduces evidence that proves the claim.[309]

With the increasing prevalence of debt buyers who buy millions of dollars of consumer credit claims for pennies on the dollar, and who often do not even possess the writings upon which the claims are based, debtors have often successfully objected to proofs of claims that do not comply with the documentation requirements. Rather than attaching cardmember agreements, promissory notes and account statements to proofs of claim, and providing itemized statements of interest and additional charges, debt buyers have been attaching to the claim form a one-page "Accounting Summary" that provides the debtor's name and account number and merely restates the balance owed listed in paragraph 4 on Official Form 10.[310] Proofs of claim are filed in this manner without any actual review of loan documents or account statements. In addition, debt buyers often fail to check the box in paragraph 4 on Official Form 10 that confirms that the total amount claimed includes interest or other charges, even though they are undeniably seeking interest and other charges, and admit this fact by adding language in another section of the claim form: "Claim may include contractual interest and/or late charges." They sometimes also fail to check the most commonly used boxes in paragraph 1 on Official Form 10 for "money loaned," "service performed," or "goods sold," and instead check the "other" box, inserting the description "credit card debt." Some have gone so far as to alter the instructions in paragraph 8 on Official Form 10 under "Supporting Documents" by eliminating the mandatory attachment requirement and adding a self-serving statement that copies of account statements are available upon request.[311]

Courts have found that the purpose of Rule 3001 is subverted by such claims, as the parties charged with policing the claims process are denied necessary information,[312] and that affording *prima facie* validity to such claims can only "lead to abuses of the claim system."[313] Strict compliance with Rule 3001 is necessary to ensure that an appropriate "sifting process" occurs in the evaluation of

---

300 Fed. R. Bankr. P. 3015, 7004, 9014.

301 *See generally* Franks v. Associated Air Ctr. Inc., 663 F.2d 583 (5th Cir. 1982) (gross overcharges violate UDAP); *In re* Staggie, 255 B.R. 48 (Bankr. D. Idaho 2000) (excessive attorney fees sought under § 506(b) disallowed as not reasonable); Russell v. Fid. Consumer Discount Co., 72 B.R. 855 (Bankr. E.D. Pa. 1987) (grossly excessive fee was unconscionable).

302 Burnham v. Mark IV Homes, Inc., 387 Mass. 575, 441 N.E.2d 1027, 1031 (1982); *see* U.C.C. § 1-203.

303 *See* National Consumer Law Center, Fair Debt Collection Ch. 13 (5th ed. 2004).

304 However, the FDCPA does apply if the debt was acquired by the debt collector or mortgage lender (or servicer) at a time when the debt was in default. *See* National Consumer Law Center, Fair Debt Collection (5th ed. 2004).

305 *See, e.g.*, Martinez v. Albuquerque Collection Services, 867 F. Supp. 1495 (D.N.M. 1994) (collection agency violated FDCPA by collecting inflated charges for attorneys fees); West v. Costen, 558 F. Supp. 564 (W.D. Va. 1983) (imposition of service charge on bad check violated FDCPA because no contract or statute permitted charge).

306 Fed. R. Bankr. P. 3001(c). If the writing has been lost or destroyed, a statement describing the loss or destruction must be filed.

307 The instructions state: "You must attach to this proof of claim form copies of documents that show the debtor owes the debt claimed or, if the documents are too lengthy, a summary of those documents. If the documents are not available, you must attach an explanation of why they are not available."

308 *See In re* Consol. Pioneer Mortgage, 178 B.R. 222 (B.A.P. 9th Cir. 1995); *In re* Chain, 255 B.R. 278 (Bankr. D. Conn. 2000); *In re* Lindell Drop Forge Co., 111 B.R. 137 (Bankr. W.D. Mich. 1990).

309 *In re* Circle J Dairy, Inc., 112 B.R. 297, 300 (W.D. Ark 1989).

310 *See In re* Henry, 311 B.R. 813 (Bankr. W.D. Wash. 2004).

311 *See In re* Hughes, 313 B.R. 205 (Bankr. E.D. Mich. 2004).

312 *In re* Trail Ends Lodge, Inc., 51 B.R. 209 (D. Vt. 1985).

313 *In re* Circle J Dairy, Inc., 112 B.R. 297, 301 (W.D. Ark 1989).

claims, otherwise "unmeritorious or excessive claims might dilute the participation of the legitimate claimants."[314] In fact, objections to debt buyers' unsubstantiated claims are often answered with amended claims seeking lower amounts in which questionable fees are removed. In other cases it has been found that the original claims included post-petition interest, were barred by a statute of limitations, or were filed by entities that could not prove they owned the debts.

The debt buyers sometimes contend that credit card issuers and debt buyers do not have to provide documentation if they pursue claims under an "open-account" theory, ignoring the fact that open account claims are typically "founded upon contract" and require proof of the "necessary elements of a contract action."[315] More important, the *theory* upon which a creditor asserts a claim does not determine the need for compliance with Rule 3001's writing and itemization requirements. Rule 3001 does not state that writings must be attached only if the creditor's claim is based on a particular theory, nor does it provide an exception for "open-accounts" or any other theory of liability. Such an exception would of course swallow the rule as just about any claimant could demand presumptive validity of claims filed without documentation simply by stating when challenged that the claim is based on a quasi-contract, *quantum meruit*, or unjust enrichment theory. The plain language of Rule 3001 requires that if the claim is based on a writing, it must be filed with the proof of claim.

And there can be no question that a writing provides the contractual basis for credit card debt.[316] In fact, the typical cardmember agreement is the controlling document that carefully delineates the rights and responsibilities between the card issuer and borrower. It specifies that use of the card is an affirmance of the contract terms contained in the written cardmember agreement (and its periodic amendments). Creditors in most jurisdictions are not permitted to make such an election. An action on an "open-account" may be based on an express or implied contract, but if an enforceable express contract exists between the parties on the relevant subject matter, the creditor cannot recover under an implied contract.[317] Such a ruling is quite appropriate as an implied-in-law contract is a legal fiction that should not be imposed by a court to subvert the express intent of the parties. Moreover, absent the written agreement, credit card lenders have no legal claim to the substantial interest charges, late fees, bad check charges, over-the-limit fees and other costs included in virtually all credit card claims.[318] In addition, pre-judgment interest and costs may not be recovered in many jurisdictions on claims based on *quantum meruit* and implied contract, absent a specific statutory entitlement, because of the unliquidated nature of such claims.[319] Thus, a claim that includes interest filed by a credit card claimant who has disavowed the cardmember agreement is self-contradictory and should be disallowed.

Some debt buyers have also argued that debtors should not be permitted to object to claims when they have listed the amount allegedly owing on their schedules and not noted it as disputed. However, the schedules are not filed for the purposes of claim allowance except in chapter 11 cases.[320] Typically, when debtors complete their schedules they have no way of computing the amounts due under complex credit card contracts and just list the amount stated on a recent statement. However, to avoid such problems if an objection to a claim is anticipated, debtors may wish to mark debts as disputed, or to note that they have no way of verifying the amounts creditors have claimed on monthly statements. In addition, debtors usually have no way of knowing if a claim has been assigned, and often may legitimately object that they have never heard of the debt buyers filing claims in their cases, thus requiring the debt buyers to prove with competent evidence that the claims have in fact been assigned and are owing to them.

13.4.3.6 Reconsideration of Claims

Both Bankruptcy Code § 502(j) and Federal Rule of Bankruptcy Procedure 3008 provide for the reconsideration of previously allowed claims.[321] A motion for reconsideration may be appropriate in a number of circumstances.[322]

---

314 Gardner v. New Jersey, 329 U.S. 565 (1947).

315 Asset Acceptance Corp. v. Proctor, 156 Ohio App. 3d 60, 804 N.E.2d 975 (2004). In addition, the plaintiff must "prove that the contract involves a transaction that usually forms the subject of a book account." *Id.*; *see also* 1 Am. Jur. 2d *Accounts and Accounting* § 8.

316 *See In re* Hughes, 313 B.R. 205 (Bankr. E.D. Mich. 2004); *In re* Henry, 311 B.R. 813 (Bankr. W.D. Wash. 2004).

317 17A Am. Jur. 2d *Contracts* § 13; *e.g.*, Clark-Fitzpatrick v. Long Island, 516 N.E.2d 190 (N.Y. 1987).

318 In *In re Blair*, Civ. No. 02-1140 (Bankr. W.D.N.C. filed Feb. 10, 2004), the court ordered that a credit card issuer may no longer file proofs of claim without itemization. As findings of fact in the Order, claims filed in eighteen separate debtor cases are broken down as between principal and interest and fees. In most all of the claims, interest and fees comprise more than half of the total claim. For example, in Case No. 03-20018, the creditor filed a claim in the amount of $943.58, of which $199.63 is listed as principal and $743.95 is listed as interest and fees. In Case No. 03-100157, a claim of $1011.97 is comprised of $273.33 in principal and $738.64 in interest and fees.

319 22 Am. Jur. 2d *Damages* § 468; *e.g.*, Farmah v. Farmah, 348 N.C. 586, 500 S.E.2d 662 (1998).

320 *See* 11 U.S.C. § 1111(a) (not applicable in other chapters).

321 Pursuant to Rule 2002(g), a motion for reconsideration should ordinarily be served on the claimant at the address listed on the proof of claim. *See In re* Barker, 306 B.R. 339 (Bankr. E.D. Cal. 2004) (notice of reconsideration served on original creditor listed on claim proper because debt buyer assignee failed to update court filing by submitting Rule 3001(e)(1) transfer statement). If the claimant is an insured depository institution, service should also be made by certified mail upon an officer of the institution unless certain requirements have been met. *See* Fed. R. Bankr. P. 7004(h); § 13.3.2.1, *supra*.

322 The debtor may seek reconsideration of a claim even after it has

One situation which arises not infrequently is that of a debtor who cannot maintain the chapter 13 plan payments necessary to keep a motor vehicle. In such a case, the vehicle may be liquidated by the creditor after either a voluntary surrender by the debtor or a repossession. The liquidation results not only in a reduction in the creditor's claim but the creditor becoming unsecured with respect to any deficiency claim. Courts have found such circumstances to be appropriate bases for reconsideration of the creditor's claim to reflect the payment by liquidation and new status as unsecured, often leading to a modification of the chapter 13 plan reducing payments to that creditor.[323]

13.4.4 An Example: Truth in Lending Claims of the Debtor

One common type of claim the debtor might want to bring using these procedures would be an action under the Truth in Lending Act.[324] Such an action could be removed to the bankruptcy court or brought initially in bankruptcy court by a complaint against the creditor, with the cause of action and any proceeds thereof claimed as exempt property (assuming the debtor has exemptions available to cover the amount of property).[325] If the cause of action cannot be claimed as

exempt, it is usually not difficult to persuade a trustee to abandon it, as few trustees are interested in such claims, and that step should be taken.[326]

A number of courts have held that the recovery in such an action must be paid in cash to the debtor/plaintiff and cannot be set off against a debt discharged in the bankruptcy.[327] And when a creditor's claim is fully secured by a non-voidable lien, a successful Truth in Lending claim will at least reduce the amount which must be paid and reward the debtor's counsel with attorney fees.[328] Furthermore, a successful Truth in Lending rescission suit may void the creditor's lien entirely and leave the creditor with an unsecured claim.[329]

---

been paid if sufficient cause exists. *In re* Barker, 306 B.R. 339 (Bankr. E.D. Cal. 2004) (court granted request for reconsideration of claim made by executrix as debtor was in final stages of illness at time claim allowed and paid).

323 *See In re* Zieder, 263 B.R. 114 (Bankr. D. Ariz. 2001); *see also* § 8.7.3 *supra*.

324 15 U.S.C. §§ 1601–1677. *See generally* National Consumer Law Center, Truth in Lending (5th ed. 2003). The trustee in a chapter 13 case could also bring a Truth in Lending action on the debtor's behalf. *In re* Weaver, 632 F.2d 461 (5th Cir. 1980). In cases where the trustee or a debtor-in-possession brings the action, the statute of limitations, if it had not expired as of the filing of the petition, would be extended until two years after the bankruptcy filing. 11 U.S.C. § 108(a); *see* Cunningham v. Healthco, 824 F.2d 1448 (5th Cir. 1987); *see also* Thomas v. GMAC Residential Funding Corp., 309 B.R. 453 (D. Md. 2004) (§ 108(b) extends right of rescission under Truth in Lending Act by sixty days after filing of bankruptcy petition).

325 *See, e.g., In re* Polis, 217 F.3d 899 (7th Cir. 2000) (TILA claim could be valued for exemption purposes based on fair market value, discounted for contingency, on date of bankruptcy petition); Christy v. Heights Fin. Corp., 101 B.R. 542 (C.D. Ill. 1987) (debtor had standing to assert Truth in Lending claim that had been exempted); *In re* Abele, 77 B.R. 460 (E.D. Pa. 1987) (four transactions rescinded under Truth in Lending Act), *aff'd*, 845 F.2d 1009 (3d Cir. 1988); *In re* Ball, 201 B.R. 204 (Bankr. N.D. Ill. 1996) (value of debtor's interest in TILA claim comes into estate, but not enhancement of that value obtained by service as class representative); *In re* Marshall, 121 B.R. 814 (Bankr. C.D. Ill. 1990) (debtor's Truth in Lending claim not compulsory counterclaim which had to be raised prior to confirmation of chapter 13 plan, and in any case failure to assert such a counterclaim would not bar later adversary proceeding against bank as it was exemptible property of the debtor), *aff'd*, 132 B.R. 904 (C.D. Ill. 1991); *In re* Piercy, 18 B.R. 1004 (Bankr.

W.D. Ky. 1982) (Truth in Lending rescission enforced by bankruptcy court); *see also In re* Scrimpsher, 17 B.R. 999 (Bankr. N.D.N.Y. 1982) (debt collection violations raised as counterclaim to dischargeability complaint).

326 *See* Bryson v. Bank of N.Y., 584 F. Supp. 1306 (S.D.N.Y. 1984) (abandonment necessary prior to debtor's Truth in Lending action); Cole v. Pulley, 468 N.E.2d 652 (Mass. App. Ct. 1984) (debtor who filed bankruptcy could not bring actions that were not abandoned by the trustee); *see also* Barletta v. Tedeschi, 121 B.R. 669 (N.D.N.Y. 1990) (closing of case effected abandonment by trustee of debtor's action under Fair Debt Collection Practices Act). For a discussion of abandonment of property by the trustee, see § 11.3.3, *supra*.

327 *See, e.g.*, Griggs v. Provident Consumer Discount Co., 680 F.2d 927 (3d Cir.), *rev'd on other grounds*, 459 U.S. 56 (1982); *In re* Riggs, 623 F.2d 68 (9th Cir. 1980); Newton v. Beneficial Fin. Co., 558 F.2d 731 (5th Cir. 1977) (holding that Truth in Lending damages are meant to penalize the creditor and thus should always be assessed); *In re* Hill, 2 Collier Bankr. Cas. 2d (MB) 84 (M.D. Fla. 1980). *But see* Binick v. Avco Fin. Services of Neb., Inc., 435 F. Supp. 359 (D. Neb. 1977). It should be noted that some of these cases were under the prior Act, which had wording slightly different from the new setoff provision, 11 U.S.C. § 553. Also *In re* Riggs, 623 F.2d 68 (9th Cir. 1980), and other cases cited therein set forth a test of discretion under which a setoff could sometimes be allowed. *See also In re* Johnson, 13 B.R. 185 (Bankr. M.D. Tenn. 1981) (section 553 does not permit setoff against claim abandoned to debtor; section 553 applies only to setoffs against the bankruptcy estate).

328 15 U.S.C. § 1640(a); *see In re* McCausland, 63 B.R. 665 (Bankr. E.D. Pa. 1986).

329 *See* Quenzer v. Advanta Mortgage Corp. USA, 288 B.R. 884 (D. Kan. 2003) (court has discretion to require repayment of principal as condition of voiding lien); *In re* Bell, 309 B.R. 139 (Bankr. E.D. Pa. 2004) (debtor permitted to pay tender obligation, as determined by court after setoff of damages awarded to debtor, over life of chapter 13 plan); *In re* Bilal, 296 B.R. 828 (Bankr. D. Kan. 2003) (debtors effectuated rescission and voiding of mortgage through provisions of confirmed plan); *In re* Williams, 291 B.R. 636 (Bankr. E.D. Pa. 2003) (court treated consumer's tender obligation as unsecured and did not make rescission conditional upon tender but required debtor to classify tender claim separately and pay it in full over life of chapter 13 plan); *In re* Rodrigues, 278 B.R. 683 (Bankr. D.R.I. 2002). *But see* Ray v. Citifinancial Inc., 228 F. Supp. 2d 664 (D. Md. 2002) (bankruptcy court may condition TIL rescission upon tender but also has discretion to reduce or eliminate creditor's lien without requiring tender based on equitable considerations).

Finally, special Truth-in-Lending protections apply to more recent high-rate home-equity loans.[330]

In many cases, however, an action against the creditor for damages may not be possible because of the passage of the one-year statute of limitations applicable to affirmative Truth in Lending actions.[331] And, although the courts of many states have held that Truth in Lending claims may still be asserted defensively in state courts by way of recoupment after the passage of one year, there is a substantial split in authority on that question.[332] Courts in a number of states do not allow a debtor to offset damages arising out of Truth in Lending violations against a creditor's claim for the balance due in a consumer credit transaction.

The availability of objections to claims in bankruptcy court may alleviate this problem in those states that do not allow recoupment.[333] It is clear that recoupment is a matter of procedure, to be determined in the federal courts on the basis of federal law. It is also generally agreed that federal law does permit recoupment,[334] and therefore state decisions barring recoupment should not be applicable in bankruptcy court to objections to claims raising Truth in Lending recoupment. Moreover, under the Truth in Lending Simplification Act, recoupment is specifically permitted unless the applicable procedural law provides otherwise.[335] As the applicable procedural law in bankruptcy court is federal law, there should be little doubt as to the propriety of recoupment to reduce or eliminate creditors' claims. Thus, debtors in states barring recoupment should still be able to make use of that valuable doctrine if they can bring their litigation into the bankruptcy court and their attorneys can collect statutory attorney fees for their efforts.[336] However, the Supreme Court has greatly limited the rights of consumers to invoke the Truth in Lending rescission remedy by way of recoupment after the normal three year period has run.[337]

13.4.5 Habeas Corpus

Another power of the federal courts, which might prove useful on occasion, is the power to issue writs of *habeas corpus*. The Bankruptcy Reform Act of 1978 had expressly granted the power to issue these writs to the bankruptcy courts, but this provision was not retained by the 1984 amendments. Prior to 1978, the Rules of Bankruptcy Procedure had provided that a bankruptcy judge could issue a writ for certain purposes.[338] Thus far a new bankruptcy rule has not been promulgated to fill the statutory gap. In the

---

330 15 U.S.C.§ 1639 (Home Ownership and Equity Protection Act); *see* National Consumer Law Center, Truth in Lending Ch. 9 (5th ed. 2003). If the debtor intends to file an adversary proceeding in a chapter 13 that seeks rescission under TILA, the debtor's schedules and plan should treat the creditor's claim in a manner that is consistent with rescission, and it is advisable that the debtor file the complaint prior to confirmation. *See In re* Mourer, 287 B.R. 889 (Bankr. W.D. Mich. 2003) (denying right to rescind when debtors did not list rescission claim as asset and their confirmed plan treated debt as secured and provided that creditor would retain its lien). An example of a chapter 13 plan providing for TIL rescission can be found in Form 13, Appx. G.3, *infra*.

331 15 U.S.C. § 1640(e). Note, however, that if the limitations period has not expired pre-petition, the period may be tolled or extended by operation of 11 U.S.C. § 108(a). That provision, however, generally only applies when the claim is ultimately brought by the trustee on behalf of the estate. *But see In re* Gaskins, 98 B.R. 328 (Bankr. E.D. Tenn. 1989) (section 108(a) applies to claim brought on behalf of estate by chapter 13 debtor).

332 *Compare* Household Consumer Discount Co. v. Vespaziani, 490 Pa. 209, 415 A.2d 689 (1980) *with* Hewlett v. John Blue Employees Fed. Credit Union, 344 So. 2d 505 (Ala. Civ. App. 1976). Amendments to the law may have undercut some of the cases prohibiting recoupment after the limitations period has run. National Consumer Law Center, Truth in Lending § 7.2.5 (5th ed. 2003).

333 *See, e.g., In re* Jones, 122 B.R. 246 (W.D. Pa. 1990); Werts v. Fed. Nat'l Mortgage Ass'n, 48 B.R. 980 (E.D. Pa. 1985) (filing proof of claim was "action to collect the debt" allowing debtor to file recoupment claim under 15 U.S.C. § 1640(e)); *In re* Hanna, 31 B.R. 424 (Bankr. E.D. Pa. 1983) (debtor allowed to raise Truth in Lending recoupment claim beyond one year statute of limitations because state courts permitted it under doctrine of federal common law); *In re* Galea'i, 31 B.R. 629 (Bankr. D. Haw. 1981); *see also In re* Maxwell, 281 B.R. 101 (Bankr. D. Mass. 2002) (debtor allowed to assert by way of recoupment time-barred claims under the Fair Debt Collection Practices Act against mortgage servicer); *In re* McNinch, 250 B.R. 848 (Bankr. W.D. Pa. 2000) (one-year statute of limitations for Truth In Lending damages claim did not apply to claim asserted by recoupment in response to creditor's proof of claim), *aff'd sub nom.* McNinch v. Harris Trust Sav. Bank, 281 F.3d 222 (3d Cir. 2001); *In re* Remington, 19 B.R. 718 (Bankr. D. Colo.

1982) (debtor allowed to raise claim under Equal Credit Opportunity Act as objection to claim despite fact that two year statute of limitations under that Act had expired); National Consumer Law Center, Truth in Lending § 7.2.5 (5th ed. 2003).

334 Bull v. United States, 295 U.S. 247, 55 S. Ct. 695, 79 L. Ed. 1421 (1937); *In re* Coxson, 43 F.3d 189 (5th Cir. 1995) (applying federal law to permit bankruptcy debtor to assert TILA recoupment against creditor's claim); Pa. R.R. Co. v. Miller, 124 F.2d 160 (5th Cir. 1942).

335 15 U.S.C. § 1640(e).

336 Statutory attorney fees have regularly been awarded after successful recoupment claims. *In re* DiCianno, 58 B.R. 810 (Bankr. E.D. Pa. 1986); United Mission Bank v. Robinson, 7 Kan. App. 2d 120, 638 P.2d 372 (1981); Olinde Hardware & Supply Co. v. London, 387 So. 2d 1246 (La. Ct. App. 1981); Ford v. Defenbaugh, 403 So. 2d 863 (Miss. 1981); Allied Fin. v. Garza, 626 S.W.2d 120 (Tex. App. 1981); National Consumer Law Center, Truth in Lending § 8.9.2.2 (5th ed. 2003).

337 *See* Beach v. Ocwen Fed. Sav. Bank, 523 U.S. 410, 118 S. Ct. 1408, 140 L. Ed 2d 566 (1998) (limiting Truth in Lending right of rescission by recoupment to situations where it is permitted after foreclosure by state law). *But see In re* Fidler, 210 B.R. 411 (Bankr. D. Mass. 1997), *reaffirmed on motion to vacate,* 226 B.R. 734 (Bankr. D. Mass. 1998) (Massachusetts law permitted rescission after three-year period permitted by Truth in Lending Act); *see also* National Consumer Law Center, Truth in Lending § 6.3.3 (5th ed. 2003).

338 Former R. Bankr. P. 913.

absence of a new rule, any writ of *habeas corpus* may have to be issued by the district court.[339]

Such a writ may be issued for a number of purposes. Most important of these is to obtain release of a debtor imprisoned on process in a civil action issued for collection of a debt which is either dischargeable or provided for in the debtor's plan. The most likely cases for use of a writ of *habeas corpus* by consumer clients are those in which a debtor is imprisoned for failure to comply with family support orders issued by a state court. It is an unfortunate fact that, all too often, indigents are jailed for not paying support obligations they are unable to meet.

Often these obligations are owed to a state or local welfare department, which is assigned the right to collect them because the debtor's family has received public assistance. While these obligations may not be discharged in a chapter 7 case,[340] they may be paid through a chapter 13 plan, under the protection of the bankruptcy court.[341]

A less frequent use of the writ of *habeas corpus* is to free those debtors imprisoned through the use of supplementary process and contempt orders which are still available in several states as collection remedies.[342] Similarly, the issue may arise in the context of imprisonment for failure to make payment of court-ordered restitution.[343] Debtors jailed in these proceedings, essentially for not paying their debts, may be able to gain their freedom through the bankruptcy court.[344]

13.5 Abstention

13.5.1 In General

In addition to jurisdiction over a broad array of cases, 28 U.S.C. § 1334 also confers the power to decline to exercise that jurisdiction. The court is allowed to abstain, under 28 U.S.C. § 1334(c), from hearing cases arising under title 11 (the Bankruptcy Code) or arising in or related to cases under title 11, "in the interest of justice, or in the interest of comity with State courts or respect for State law." Moreover, in certain circumstances it is required to abstain upon timely motion of a party.

Rule 5011(b) provides that a request for abstention should be made by motion pursuant to Federal Rule of Bankruptcy Procedure 9014.[345] In core proceedings the bankruptcy court can make a final decision on such a motion. That decision is then appealable to the district court, but no higher unless the appeal challenges a determination that mandatory abstention is not required.[346] In non-core matters, the bankruptcy court can make a recommendation subject to review by the district court pursuant to Federal Rule of Bankruptcy Procedure 9033. No appeal of the district court decision is allowed, unless the decision decides that the mandatory abstention provisions are not applicable.[347]

13.5.2 Mandatory Abstention

As the result of strong pressure from states' rights advocates in the United States Senate, the 1984 bankruptcy amendments introduced another new concept into the bankruptcy jurisdictional scheme—that abstention is mandatory if certain requirements are met.[348] These requirements, set forth in 28 U.S.C. § 1334(c)(2), are:

- A timely motion filed by a party;[349]
- In a proceeding based upon a state law claim or cause of action;

---

339 *See In re* Cornelious, 214 B.R. 588 (Bankr. E.D. Ark. 1997) (bankruptcy court did not have jurisdiction to issue writ of *habeas corpus*). *But see In re* Rainwater, 233 B.R. 126 (Bankr. N.D. Ala. 1999) (writ of *habeas corpus* issued by bankruptcy court), *vacated*, 254 B.R. 273 (N.D. Ala. 2000). In one case the debtor successfully brought an adversary proceeding seeking release from state custody without seeking a writ of *habeas corpus*. The district court affirmed the bankruptcy court's order releasing the debtor. *In re* Hucke, 128 B.R. 675 (D. Or. 1991). Although the court of appeals reversed, Hucke v. Oregon, 992 F.2d 950 (9th Cir. 1993), the reversal was based on grounds other than whether a bankruptcy court could order a debtor's release. Of course, habeas relief may also be available through state court procedures. Marrow v. Williams, 25 Clearinghouse Rev. 717 (Okla. 1991) (*habeas corpus* relief granted to debtor held under state court contempt order requiring payment of divorce debt).

340 11 U.S.C. § 523(a)(5), *as amended by* Pub. L. No. 97-35, § 2335, 95 Stat. 357 (1981). See § 14.4, *infra*, for a further discussion of exceptions to discharge.

341 *See generally* § 12.4, *supra*; Henry J. Sommer & Margaret Doe McGarity, Collier Family Law and the Bankruptcy Code Ch. 8.

342 *See, e.g.*, Juidice v. Vail, 430 U.S. 327, 97 S. Ct. 1211, 51 L. Ed. 2d 376 (1977) (imprisonment on contempt arising out of consumer debt-related proceedings).

343 *See, e.g.*, *In re* Rainwater, 233 B.R. 126 (Bankr. N.D. Ala. 1999). *But see In re* Gruntz, 202 F.3d 1074 (9th Cir. 2000) (*en banc*) (denying release of debtor imprisoned for criminal nonsupport).

344 *But see In re* Bona, 110 B.R. 1012 (Bankr. S.D.N.Y. 1990) (court would not release debtor from prison absent showing that debt on which imprisonment had been obtained was discharge-

able), *aff'd*, 124 B.R. 11 (S.D.N.Y. 1991).

345 Note also that a motion for abstention does not act as a stay of the proceedings in the case, so that if a stay is desired a motion for a stay should be presented to the bankruptcy court pursuant to Fed. R. Bankr. P. 5011(c).

346 28 U.S.C. § 1334(d).

347 28 U.S.C. § 1334(d).

348 *See, e.g.*, Reed v. Miss. Farm Bureau Mut. Ins. Co., 299 B.R. 804 (S.D. Miss. 2003) (remand required when mandatory abstention appropriate); Luevano v. Dow Corning Corp., 183 B.R. 751 (W.D. Tex. 1995) (product liability action against debtor's codefendant was subject to mandatory abstention); Borintex Mfg. Corp. v. Banco Governmental de Fomenta Para Puerto Rico, 102 B.R. 8 (Bankr. D. P.R. 1989) (grounds for mandatory abstention found after action removed from state court).

349 *See In re* AHT Corp., 265 B.R. 379 (Bankr. S.D.N.Y. 2001) (motion filed two-and-a-half months after complaint and only after denial of motion to dismiss was not timely).

- That is a related proceeding and not one arising under title 11 or in a case under title 11;
- Where the claim or cause of action could not have been commenced in a federal court absent section 1334's jurisdiction; and
- An action is commenced and can be timely adjudicated in a state court of appropriate jurisdiction.

The section further provides that it is not intended in any way to limit the applicability of the section 362 automatic stay as it applies to property of the bankruptcy estate. Thus, a decision that mandatory abstention is warranted is not cause for granting relief from the automatic stay.[350]

It is important to note at the outset those proceedings to which mandatory abstention does not apply. Mandatory abstention does not apply to any core proceeding,[351] and is also inapplicable to any proceeding on personal injury tort or wrongful death claims.[352]

Other questions concerning the reach of the mandatory abstention provision do not have clear answers. There is currently no rule to determine when an abstention motion is timely. Until such a rule is promulgated, courts will no doubt use normal standards of reasonableness to decide whether an abstention motion has been filed too late.

Similarly, it may not always be readily apparent when a proceeding is "based upon a state law or cause of action." What happens when a proceeding raises both state and federal claims? Is it bifurcated or is abstention mandatory as to the entire proceeding? Nor is it easy to determine whether a state court proceeding will be "timely adjudicated," either in terms of what would be "timely" or in terms of predicting the timing of state court proceedings. At least one court has held that the party moving for abstention has the burden of proving that the state court action would be timely adjudicated.[353]

Finally, must an action already have been commenced in state court for the section to apply? It has been suggested that this section would permit the district court to conditionally abstain, with the requirement that a state court proceeding be commenced within a short period of time.[354] But courts generally seem to require that the state court action already be commenced for mandatory abstention to be proper.[355]

In any event, the court's decision to abstain under this section is not reviewable by the court of appeals, by appeal or otherwise.[356] This principle probably does not preclude review on the basis that the court did not have jurisdiction in the first instance.[357] By its terms, section 1334(d) does not preclude district court review of a decision to abstain.[358] A decision not to abstain is also not appealable beyond the district court, unless the decision denies a motion for mandatory abstention.

It seems clear that the mandatory abstention provisions were designed primarily to deal with claims of the sort involved in the *Northern Pipeline* case, that is, state law claims of the debtor against non-creditors. These claims arise only occasionally in consumer bankruptcy cases.

13.5.3 Discretionary Abstention

The 1984 amendments preserved the power of the bankruptcy forum to abstain from other proceedings as well. The statute added to the previous language, which allowed abstention "in the interest of justice," language permitting abstention "in the interest of comity with State courts or respect for State law."[359] As these were considerations already taken into account by most courts, it is unclear whether this additional emphasis changed the results in many cases.

The standards to be applied in the use of this discretion are not clear from the statute. The legislative history of the

---

350 *In re* Conejo Enterprises, 96 F.3d 346 (9th Cir. 1996).

351 28 U.S.C. § 1334(c); *In re* S.G. Phillips Constructors, Inc., 45 F.3d 702 (2d Cir. 1995) (mandatory abstention inapplicable with respect to determination of proof of claim filed by creditor); *In re* Ben Cooper, Inc., 924 F.2d 36 (2d Cir. 1991).

352 28 U.S.C. § 157(b)(4).

353 *In re* Burgess, 51 B.R. 300 (Bankr. S.D. Ohio 1985); *see also In re* DeLorean Motor Co., 49 B.R. 900 (Bankr. E.D. Mich. 1985) (thirty to thirty-six months delay in state courts would not permit timely adjudication).

354 *See, e.g.,* Taggart, *The New Bankruptcy Court System*, 30 Prac. Law. 11, 18 (Dec. 1984).

355 *See, e.g., In re* Container Transp., Inc., 86 B.R. 804 (E.D. Pa.

1988); Ram Constr. Co. v. Port Auth. of Allegheny County, 49 B.R. 363 (W.D. Pa. 1985); *In re* Excelite Corp., 49 B.R. 923 (Bankr. N.D. Ga. 1985).

356 28 U.S.C. § 1334(d); *see also In re* Potts, 724 F.2d 47 (6th Cir. 1984). Notwithstanding § 1334(c)(2) a final bankruptcy court order and abstention is reviewable by the district court on appeal pursuant to 28 U.S.C. § 158(a). *See In re* Goerg, 930 F.2d 1563 (11th Cir. 1991) (right of appeal to Article III court of abstention decision under 11 U.S.C. § 305 is constitutionally required). Under the 1994 amendments, 28 U.S.C. § 1334(c) was subdivided into subsections 1334(c) and 1334(d). New § 1334(d) provides that a decision not to abstain under the mandatory abstention provisions on § 1334(c)(2) may be appealed. Legislative drafting errors make it unclear whether discretionary abstention decisions might now be non-appealable.

357 *See* Kennedy, *The Bankruptcy Court Under the New Bankruptcy Law: Its Structure, Jurisdiction, Venue, and Procedure*, 11 St. Mary's L. J. 251, 288–289 (1979); *see also* Pacor, Inc. v. Higgins, 743 F.2d 984 (3d Cir. 1984) (issue of jurisdiction is reviewable even in connection with decision on remand); *In re* Adams Delivery Serv., 24 B.R. 589 (B.A.P. 9th Cir. 1982) (decision to assume jurisdiction of removed proceeding could be reviewed if challenge was aimed at the bankruptcy court's jurisdiction). *But see* Things Remembered v. Petrarca, 516 U.S. 124, 116, S. Ct. 494, 133 L. Ed. 2d 461 (1995) (court of appeals may not review order remanding case based upon defect in procedure or lack of jurisdiction regardless of whether removal was pursuant to 28 U.S.C. § 1452(a) or 28 U.S.C. § 1441(a)).

358 *See* Advisory Committee Note to 1991 Amendment to Fed. R. Bankr. P. 5011.

359 28 U.S.C. § 1334(c)(1).

1978 Act suggested that there may be cases in which it is more appropriate for a state court to hear a particular matter of state law,[360] usually when there is an unsettled question of state law, or a case such as a divorce or child custody matter, which is only tangentially related to the bankruptcy. One possibility in divorce cases is to have the state court decide the marital interests, but to retain jurisdiction over the property for all other purposes.[361]

Courts have also considered whether a duplication of efforts will occur. If certain issues are likely to be litigated in the bankruptcy forum in any case, such as in the allowance of a claim, there is a tendency to retain jurisdiction over those issues for all purposes.[362] This is especially true if the estate cannot be administered without resolution of the dispute[363] or if requiring litigation in courts other than the bankruptcy forum would impose a hardship on the debtor.[364] In some cases, the bankruptcy court may abstain with respect to certain issues, and reserve other issues for its own decision.[365]

Considerations of timing and convenience may also be determinative. If the court feels it is capable of expeditiously resolving a matter, it usually retains the case.[366] Similarly, the court may look to whether it customarily handles the type of question involved, and decline to hear the case if it does not.[367] When issues have been raised after having been fully litigated in a state court action, the court generally defers to the state appeals process, not only to avoid litigation of the same claim, but also as a matter of comity within the federal system.[368] However, when a proceeding concerns property of the estate, over which the district court has exclusive jurisdiction, the bankruptcy forum is normally more appropriate for the litigation of that proceeding.[369]

Obviously, it is important to frame bankruptcy litigation, whether commenced by removal or as an original proceeding, with these considerations in mind. To the extent the case can be framed as one bound up with the bankruptcy's administration and involving matters the bankruptcy forum can expeditiously handle, the chances of staying in the bankruptcy system are improved.

13.6 *In Forma Pauperis* Litigation in Bankruptcy Proceedings

13.6.1 *General Principles*

The possibilities for extensive litigation in connection with bankruptcy cases raise a familiar problem for low-income clients—how to deal with filing fees they cannot afford.[370] Fortunately, under the present fee schedule set by the Administrative Office of the federal courts, there is no filing fee required for adversary complaints filed by debtors.[371] Unfortunately, there are substantial fees or bonds involved for other proceedings, for example, adversary proceedings commenced by non-debtor parties and appeals.[372]

An analysis of the question of *in forma pauperis* filings in bankruptcy court must begin with the fact that, except as provided by statute, a debtor's bankruptcy petition may not be filed without the filing fee. The Supreme Court ruled in *United States v. Kras*,[373] that due process does not require a right to waiver of the basic bankruptcy filing fee for indigents. Congress, when it enacted the Code in 1978, expressly declined to grant such a right statutorily, although it did continue the previous statutory provisions allowing for payment of the fee in installments.[374]

Neither *Kras* nor the Code directly addresses the question of whether either due process or the general federal *in forma pauperis* statute, 28 U.S.C. § 1915, requires fee waivers for indigents in other filings. There are a number of strong arguments why such waivers should be granted, and thus far most courts have been receptive to these arguments.

---

360 H.R. Rep. No. 95-595, at 446 (1977).

361 *See In re* White, 851 F.2d 170 (6th Cir. 1988). *See generally* Henry J. Sommer & Margaret Doe McGarity, Collier Family Law and the Bankruptcy Code Ch. 5.

362 *In re* Lucasa Int'l, Ltd., 6 B.R. 717 (Bankr. S.D.N.Y. 1980); *In re* Bros. Coal Co., 6 B.R. 567 (Bankr. W.D. Va. 1980).

363 *In re* Lucasa Int'l, Ltd., 6 B.R. 717 (Bankr. S.D.N.Y. 1980).

364 *In re* N. Pipeline Constr. Co., 6 B.R. 928 (Bankr. D. Minn. 1980), *rev'd on other grounds*, N. Pipeline Constr. Co. v. Marathon Pipe Line Co., 458 U.S. 50, 102 S. Ct. 2858, 73 L. Ed. 2d 598 (1982).

365 *See, e.g., In re* Al Copeland Enterprises, Inc., 153 F.3d 268 (5th Cir. 1998).

366 *In re* Lucasa Int'l, Ltd., 6 B.R. 717 (Bankr. S.D.N.Y. 1980); *In re* Project Oneco, 3 B.R. 284 (Bankr. D. Colo. 1980).

367 *Compare In re* Cole Associates Inc., 7 B.R. 154 (Bankr. D. Utah 1980) (bankruptcy court routinely hears questions under Uniform Commercial Code) *with* Carver v. Carver, 954 F.2d 1573 (11th Cir. 1992) (state court better able to resolve dispute about debtor's divorce decree obligations).

368 *In re* Moore, 5 B.R. 67 (Bankr. N.D. Tex. 1980); *In re* Tidwell, 4 B.R. 100 (Bankr. N.D. Tex. 1980). See also § 13.2.4.3, *supra*, discussing the Rooker-Feldman doctrine.

369 *In re* S.E. Hornsby & Sons Sand & Gravel Co., 45 B.R. 988 (Bankr. M.D. La. 1985).

---

370 For a more extensive discussion of filing fee waivers in bankruptcy, see Henry J. Sommer, *In Forma Pauperis in Bankruptcy: The Time Has Long Since Come*, 2 Am. Bankr. Inst. L. Rev. 93 (1994).

371 The fee schedule is reproduced in Appendix C, *infra*.

372 However, there is no fee for a child support creditor to file either a motion for relief from the stay or an adversary complaint. *See* Judicial Conference Fee Schedule §§ 6, 21, *reprinted in* Appx. C, *infra*. A child support creditor or a representative of that creditor must file Form B281 in order to qualify for the exemption. A copy of that form may be found in Appendix E, *infra*.

373 409 U.S. 434, 93 S. Ct. 631, 34 L. Ed. 2d 626 (1973).

374 28 U.S.C. § 1930(a). See Chapter 7, *supra*, for a discussion of the procedure for applications to pay filing fees in installments. *But see In re* Reed, 4 B.R. 486 (Bankr. M.D. Tenn. 1980) (filing fees other than initial petition filing fee may not be paid in installments; the debtor did not request waiver of the filing fee in this case, nor was that possibility discussed).

Perhaps the strongest argument arises from the language of the statute itself. While 28 U.S.C. § 1930(a) expressly makes the *in forma pauperis* statute, 28 U.S.C. § 1915, inapplicable to the initial petition filing fees, the sections dealing with other fees contain no such proviso. The logical inference is that Congress intended the distinction and, if this is the case, then even if *Kras* were interpreted to cover all bankruptcy proceedings, Congress could be considered to have granted statutorily what due process did not require.[375] Because the Commission on the Bankruptcy Laws of the United States had recommended the complete overruling of *Kras*,[376] it seems reasonable to assume that Congress moved at least part of the way toward this goal. Congress' loosening of the fee requirements is also reflected in section 727 of the Code, which no longer lists failure to pay the fee as grounds for denial of discharge, and the enactment of 28 U.S.C. § 773(c), which expressly contemplated appeals *in forma pauperis*.[377]

The legislative history also reveals an intention to depart from that portion of the *Kras* holding which was based on statutory interpretation. Besides the denial of discharge previously applicable if fees were not paid, the Supreme Court's decision relied upon the method of financing the bankruptcy courts through the special mechanism of a Referee's Salary and Expense Fund as evidence of Congress' intent to distinguish between bankruptcy courts and other federal courts. The legislative history and the revised statute make clear that this financing method is no longer used, and the bankruptcy fees in general were adjusted "in a manner that treats bankruptcy cases identical with other Federal court cases."[378] Moreover, the House Report on the 1978 Act specifically included, as a subject regarding which procedural rules would have to be drafted, "provisions for in forma pauperis proceedings."[379]

Policy considerations also argue strongly for the allowance of *in forma pauperis* bankruptcy proceedings. One consideration in *Kras* was the fact that the then $50.00 filing fee, which was payable in installments, could supposedly be paid by any debtor and was not onerous. Under the present Code, it may be necessary for an indigent party to become involved in a number of proceedings requiring fees far greater than $50.00, which are probably not payable in installments. Moreover, it makes no sense to require a filing fee for proceedings when the bankruptcy forum has concur-

rent jurisdiction with a state or federal court that would waive the fee. Not only would this policy defeat Congress' purpose of concentrating disputes involving the debtor in the bankruptcy court, but it would also be unfair and irrational.

Finally, the *Kras* holding with respect to due process may be distinguished in many bankruptcy proceedings in which low-income persons are now likely to become involved. At least when the bankruptcy proceeding involves the possible loss of an indigent person's property interest, it can be argued that without a fee waiver that person may be denied property without an opportunity for a hearing. This is unlike the situation in *Kras* where the only thing the debtor could lose was the "privilege" of filing his own bankruptcy petition. It is also a particularly compelling argument when the indigent has been forced into the bankruptcy forum because the court has exclusive jurisdiction over the property involved.[380]

The courts have generally been receptive to *in forma pauperis* proceedings under the Code, adopting some or all of the above arguments. Most reported cases, and several which have not been reported, have accepted the basic principle that bankruptcy proceedings, other than the actual bankruptcy petition, may be instituted *in forma pauperis*.[381] They have also permitted debtors to waive the miscellaneous fees that are now required by the Judicial Conference Fee Schedule upon the initial filing of a case.[382] The costs of

---

375　This inference has been classified under the principle of statutory interpretation known as *expressio unius est exclusio alterius.* Sutherland, Statutory Construction §§ 47.23, 47.24. In the case of a statutory exception, the exception applies only to the section where it appears. *Id.*, at §§ 47.08, 47.11.

376　Comm'n on the Bankr. Laws of the U.S., Commission Report, at 11.

377　28 U.S.C. § 773(c) has since been repealed.

378　124 Cong. Rec. H11,108, (daily ed. Sept. 28, 1978) (remarks of Rep. Edwards); 124 Cong. Rec. S17,425 (daily ed. Oct. 6, 1978) (remarks of Sen. DeConcini).

379　H.R. Rep. No. 95-595, at 307 (1977).

380　Tripati v. United States Bankruptcy Court for the E. District of Texas, 180 B.R. 160 (E.D. Tex. 1995) (constitution requires that an indigent creditor "be afforded an opportunity to be heard before his claims are disposed of"); *see In re* Sarah Allen Home, Inc., 4 B.R. 724 (Bankr. E.D. Pa. 1980) (adopting the due process argument where the bankruptcy court was the only forum available to indigent creditor plaintiffs as well as debtors).

381　*In re* Fitzgerald, 192 B.R. 861 (Bankr. E.D. Va. 1996); *In re* Lindsey, 178 B.R. 895 (Bankr. N.D. Ga. 1995); *In re* Brooks, 175 B.R. 409 (Bankr. S.D. Ala. 1994); *In re* McGinnis, 155 B.R. 294 (Bankr. D.N.H. 1993); *In re* Melendez, 153 B.R. 386 (Bankr. D. Conn. 1993); *In re* Sarah Allen Home, Inc., 4 B.R. 724 (Bankr. E.D. Pa. 1980); *In re* Palestino, 4 B.R. 721 (Bankr. M.D. Fla. 1980); *In re* Weakland, 4 B.R. 114 (Bankr. D. Del. 1980); *see In re* Ravida, 296 B.R. 278 (B.A.P. 1st Cir. 2003) (court had power to waive appeal fees but declined to do so because appeal was frivolous); *In re* Broady, 96 B.R. 221 (Bankr. W.D. Mo. 1988) (frivolous appeal cannot be prosecuted *in forma pauperis*); *In re* Shumate, 91 B.R. 23 (Bankr. W.D. Va. 1988) (although *in forma pauperis* is permissible, debtor living extravagant lifestyle not permitted to appeal *in forma pauperis*); *In re* Moore, 86 B.R. 249 (Bankr. W.D. Okla. 1988) (*in forma pauperis* permitted, but bankruptcy court without authority to order transcription of record *in forma pauperis*); *see also* De-Leon v. Gurda Farms, Inc., 10 B.R. 479 (S.D.N.Y. 1980) (appeal to district court under prior Act allowed without fees pursuant to 28 U.S.C. § 1915(a)).

382　*In re* Stansbury, 226 B.R. 360 (Bankr. E.D. Pa. 1998) (waiving $45.00 in miscellaneous fees due upon filing). The Fee Schedule requires a $39.00 noticing fee in every chapter 7 and chapter 13 case and a $15.00 fee for trustee compensation in every chapter 7 case. Judicial Conference Schedule of Fees §§ 8, 8.1, 8.2,

appeal may also be waived upon a showing of indigence unless the appeal is considered frivolous.[383]

13.6.2 Authority of Bankruptcy Courts to Waive Fees

More recently several cases have concluded that bankruptcy courts are not "courts of the United States" with authority under section 1915(a) to waive fees.[384] Not only is this holding an unduly technical reading of the law, but also it renders the reference to section 1915(a) in section 1930(a) superfluous in violation of normal principles of statutory construction. As several courts disagreeing with these cases have pointed out, it also ignores the fact that bankruptcy courts are units of the district court to which the district court delegates the authority to "enter appropriate orders and judgments."[385] However, even in those jurisdictions with binding authority precluding bankruptcy courts from waiving fees, it may still be possible to direct requests for waivers to the district court (of which the bankruptcy court is a "unit"), which clearly has the necessary authority.[386] Additionally, important due process arguments are still available concerning many fees, particularly for indigent creditors.[387]

13.6.3 Former In Forma Pauperis Pilot Program

The most recent development with respect to the *in forma pauperis* issue was legislation passed in late 1993,[388] creating a pilot program permitting waiver of filing fees in individual chapter 7 cases in six judicial districts[389] and mandating a study of the whole issue of filing fees and *in forma pauperis* bankruptcy filings. The legislation was passed in response to congressional concern about the inequities of prohibiting indigent debtors from obtaining bankruptcy relief even though, in some cases, they may be most in need of it.[390] Several published opinions under the program generally adopted the standards for granting *in forma pauperis* status that are applied in the district court.[391]

Unfortunately, the pilot program expired as of October 1, 1997 and was not renewed. In March, 1998 the Federal Judicial Center issued a favorable report on the program,[392] which showed that it is feasible to provide for *in forma pauperis* filings in bankruptcy court, the only federal court that does not permit them. However, Congress has not yet acted on that report.

---

reprinted in Appx. C, *infra*. A form application for waiver of such fees is found at Form 7, Appendix G.3, *infra*.

383 28 U.S.C. § 1915(a); *see* 28 U.S.C. § 1915(a)(3), (e)(2) (frivolous appeal may not proceed *in forma pauperis*); *see also In re* Perry, 223 B.R. 167 (B.A.P. 8th Cir. 1998) (appeal of dismissal of seventh in a string of chapter 13 cases taken in bad faith and *in forma pauperis* status denied).

384 *In re* Perroton, 958 F.2d 889 (9th Cir. 1992); *In re* Bauckey, 82 B.R. 13 (Bankr. D.N.J. 1988); *see also In re* Jeys, 202 B.R. 153 (B.A.P. 10th Cir. 1996) (bankruptcy appellate panel not a "court of the United States" with power to waive fees under § 1915); *In re* Lamb, 206 B.R. 527 (Bankr. E.D. Mo. 1997) (court does not have necessary authority to appoint counsel for indigent debtor under 28 U.S.C. § 1915(d)); *cf.* O'Connor v. United States Dep't of Energy, 942 F.2d 771 (10th Cir. 1991) (bankruptcy court is "court" with authority to award Equal Access to Justice Act fees).

385 28 U.S.C. § 157(b)(1); *In re* Lassina, 261 B.R. 614 (Bankr. E.D. Pa. 2001); *In re* Lindsey, 178 B.R. 895 (Bankr. N.D. Ga. 1995); *In re* Brooks, 175 B.R. 409 (Bankr. S.D. Ala. 1994); *In re* McGinnis, 155 B.R. 294 (Bankr. D.N.H. 1993); *In re* Melendez, 153 B.R. 386 (Bankr. D. Conn. 1993).

386 *See, e.g., In re* Davis, 899 F.2d 1136 (11th Cir. 1990) (Equal Access to Justice Act fees may be recommended by bankruptcy court for entry of final judgment in district court); *In re* Buck, 157 B.R. 247 (Bankr. W.D. Pa. 1993) (agreeing with *Perroton* but suggesting possibility of seeking relief in district court).

387 *See, e.g., In re* Lassina, 261 B.R. 614 (Bankr. E.D. Pa. 2001); *In re* Sarah Allen Home Inc., 4 B.R. 724 (Bankr. E.D. Pa. 1980).

---

388 Departments of Commerce, Justice and State, The Judiciary, and Related Agencies Appropriations Act, 1994, Pub. L. No. 103-121, § 111(d), 107 Stat. 1153.

389 The pilot districts, which will permit chapter 7 cases to be filed by indigents without any fees during the program, are the Southern District of Illinois, the District of Montana, the Eastern District of New York, the Eastern District of Pennsylvania, the Western District of Tennessee, and the District of Utah. The form to be used in applying for a fee waiver is reproduced in Appendix D, *infra*.

390 For further discussion of the legislation, see Henry J. Sommer, *In Forma Pauperis in Bankruptcy: The Time Has Long Since Come*, 2 Am. Bankr. Inst. L. Rev. 93 (1994).

391 *In re* Stephenson, 205 B.R. 52 (Bankr. E.D. Pa. 1997) (although payment of an attorney fee not an automatic bar to fee waiver, debtor failed to carry burden to establish that she lacks access to sufficient resources to pay the fee); *e.g., In re* Merritt, 186 B.R. 924 (Bankr. S.D. Ill. 1995) (pilot program applied to all fees for chapter 7 debtors, including appeal fees, but debtors not qualified for fee waiver in particular case); *In re* Shannon, 180 B.R. 189 (Bankr. W.D. Tenn. 1995) (debtor who paid $100.00 to attorney not disqualified from receiving fee waiver); *In re* Koren, 176 B.R. 740 (Bankr. E.D. Pa. 1995) (prior payment to attorney not absolute bar to obtaining *in forma pauperis* relief in the pilot program; Fed. R. Bankr. P. 1006(b)(3) is not applicable to pilot program); *In re* Takeshorse, 177 B.R. 99 (Bankr. D. Mont. 1994) (debtor who paid $450.00 attorney fee denied fee waiver); *In re* Clark, 173 B.R. 142 (Bankr. W.D. Tenn. 1994) (debtor carried her burden of proof to establish indigency based on the totality of the circumstances).

392 Wiggins, Implementing and Evaluating the Chapter 7 Filing Fee Waiver Program: Report to the Committee on the Administration of the Bankruptcy System of the Judicial Conference of the United States, Federal Judicial Center (1998).

13.7 Class Actions in Bankruptcy Court

Among the Federal Rules of Civil Procedure incorporated by reference into the Federal Rules of Bankruptcy Procedure is Rule 23, which governs proceedings brought on behalf of or against a class.[393] Thus, there can be little doubt that it is possible and proper to bring class actions in appropriate adversary proceedings.[394] For example, one court has allowed a class dischargeability proceeding on behalf of students who had enrolled in a chapter 11 debtor's fraudulent business schools.[395] Because Federal Rule of Bankruptcy Procedure 9014 permits a court to make the class action rule applicable to contested matters as well, it is even possible that there could be contested matters brought by or against a class.

However, the bankruptcy system is only just beginning to grapple with questions concerning which types of proceedings may properly be heard on a class basis. Perhaps the easiest type of case to allow would be one brought on behalf of a class of debtors, all of whom had filed bankruptcy cases, to enforce some right against another party.[396] Such a case would not involve any particularly difficult questions of jurisdiction because all of the class members would have already submitted to the jurisdiction of the bankruptcy forum. Similarly, it seems appropriate to have a class action or class proof of claim for a determination of common claims arising out of the same transaction or similar transactions.[397] A class proof of claim, however, probably re-

---

393   Fed. R. Bankr. P. 7023. However, Rule 23(f), which permits an interlocutory appeal of class certification by a district court to the court of appeals is not incorporated insofar as it would allow a party to bypass an appeal to a district court or bankruptcy appellate panel. Chrysler Fin. Corp. v. Powe, 312 F.3d 1241 (11th Cir. 2002), *cert. denied*, 538 U.S. 998 (2003).

394   Begley v. Philadelphia Elec. Co., 30 B.R. 469 (E.D. Pa. 1983), *aff'd*, 760 F.2d 46 (3d Cir. 1985); *In re* Fleet, 53 B.R. 833 (Bankr. E.D. Pa. 1985) (class action based on state law could be brought where cause of action was estate property, and debtors' cause of action alleged abuse of bankruptcy system); *see also In re* Salem Mortgage Co., 783 F.2d 626 (6th Cir. 1986) (bankruptcy court has power to enter consent order in consumer class action against debtor mortgage company under the Michigan Consumer Protection Act).

395   *In re* Livaditis, 132 B.R. 897 (Bankr. N.D. Ill. 1991). *But see In re* Hanson, 104 B.R. 261 (Bankr. N.D. Cal. 1989) (class dischargeability proceeding not allowed).

396   Bank United v. Manley, 273 B.R. 229 (N.D. Ala. 2001) (affirming certification of nationwide class of debtors challenging mortgage overcharges); Beck v. Gold Key Lease, Inc., 283 B.R. 163 (Bankr. E.D. Pa. 2002) (finding jurisdiction to certify class limited to district in which discharges issued); *In re* Sims, 278 B.R. 457 (Bankr. E.D. Tenn. 2002) (bankruptcy court has jurisdiction to certify nationwide class of trustees and debtors challenging claims of credit card company that included unmatured interest); *e.g.*, Bessette v. Avco Fin. Services, Inc., 230 F.3d 439 (1st Cir. 2000) (bankruptcy or district court may certify class action seeking enforcement of discharge injunction because statutory injunction under § 524 is uniform in every bankruptcy case); *In re* Tate, 253 B.R. 653 (Bankr. W.D.N.C. 2000) (class action challenging fees improperly included by mortgage company in proofs of claim); *In re* Noletto, 244 B.R. 845 (Bankr. S.D. Ala. 2000) (nationwide class of bankruptcy debtors is permitted); *In re* Coggin, 155 B.R. 934 (Bankr. E.D.N.C. 1993) (class action against creditor seeking to have liens declared void, with enforcement enjoined and damages,

due to noncompliance with state law accounting method); *In re* Watts, 76 B.R. 390 (Bankr. E.D. Pa. 1987) (class action on behalf of bankruptcy debtors challenging discrimination against debtors in mortgage assistance program), *rev'd on other grounds*, 876 F.2d 1090 (3d Cir. 1989); *see also* Malone v. Norwest Fin. Cal., Inc., 245 B.R. 389 (N.D. Cal. 2000) (finding private right of action under § 524 in class action for reaffirmation abuses); Conley v. Sears, Roebuck & Co., 222 B.R. 181 (D. Mass. 1998); *In re* Harris, 280 B.R. 876 (Bankr. S.D. Ala. 2001) (in case challenging attorney fees improperly posted to debtors' mortgage accounts, class certification under Rule 7023(b)(2) was appropriate because most fees had not yet been collected or only partially paid by debtors, and declaratory and injunctive relief removing fees from accounts and providing restitution for those paid was predominant form of relief); *In re* Mosley, 260 B.R. 590 (Bankr. S.D. Ga. 2000) (putative class action challenging $50.00 fee by employer for processing chapter 13 wage order not mooted by refund of $50.00 to chapter 13 trustee). *But see* Dechert v. Cadle Co., 333 F.3d 801 (7th Cir. 2003) (bankruptcy trustee ordinarily not an appropriate class representative); *In re* Singleton, 284 B.R. 322 (D.R.I. 2002) (reversing bankruptcy court ruling that it had jurisdiction to certify nationwide class action); Bessette v. Avco Fin. Services, Inc., 279 B.R. 442 (D.R.I. 2002) (bankruptcy court and district court lack jurisdiction over discharges issued by bankruptcy courts in other districts); *In re* Williams, 244 B.R. 858 (S.D. Ga. 2000) (class action permitted if limited to debtors in judicial district where case filed).

397   *In re* Charter Co., 876 F.2d 861 (11th Cir. 1989) (class proof of claim allowable in bankruptcy); *In re* Am. Reserve Corp., 840 F.2d 487 (7th Cir. 1988); *In re* First Alliance Mortgage Co., 269 B.R. 428 (C.D. Cal. 2001) (class certification granted based on borrowers' class proof of claim for TILA and UDAP claims against debtor-lender); *In re* Birting Fisheries, Inc., 178 B.R. 849 (W.D. Wash. 1995) (class proof of claim permitted for employee wage claims), *aff'd*, 92 F.3d 939 (9th Cir. 1996); *In re* Chateaugay Corp., 104 B.R. 626 (S.D.N.Y. 1989) (class proof of claim permissible for creditors who did not file individual proofs); *In re* Commonpoint Mortgage Co., 283 B.R. 469 (Bankr. W.D. Mich. 2002) (borrowers' class proof of claim certified alleging UDAP and other state law claims against originating lender); *In re* United Companies Fin. Corp., Inc., 276 B.R. 368 (Bankr. D. Del. 2002) (certification of class proof of claim based on debtor's failure to comply with state loan broker law avoids burden of conducting 291 separate claim hearings); *In re* Sheffield, 281 B.R. 24 (Bankr. S.D. Ala. 2000) (certification granted of nationwide class of debtors challenging creditor's failure to adequately disclose attorney fees in proofs of claim, but not on issue of reasonableness of fees); *In re* Retirement Builders, Inc., 96 B.R. 390 (Bankr. S.D. Fla. 1988) (class proof of claim authorized for 2000 claimants in state court class action); *see also In re* Sims, 278 B.R. 457 (Bankr. E.D. Tenn. 2002) (trustee has standing to pursue class objection to claims on behalf of nationwide class of chapter 13 trustees). *But see In re* Standard Metals, 817 F.2d 625 (10th Cir.), *vacated on reh'g and decided on other grounds*, 839 F.2d 1383 (1987);

quires a separate motion to certify the class under the relevant rules, although such a motion may not be necessary if no objection to the claim is filed.[398]

More difficult would be cases in which most class members were not debtors in bankruptcy. For example, if a Truth in Lending class action were brought in connection with a bankruptcy by the debtor who had filed the bankruptcy case, the creditor-defendant might well argue that it would be inappropriate for a bankruptcy court to consider a matter only tangentially related to the bankruptcy case, and that therefore the court has no jurisdiction.[399] The 1984 jurisdictional amendments may lessen this problem as to matters, such as Truth in Lending actions, which could have been brought in federal court regardless of the bankruptcy, but they will probably heighten the concern over state law causes of action brought into the federal system.

Once jurisdiction is established, it seems fairly clear that parties not directly involved in the bankruptcy may become involved in some bankruptcy proceedings.[400] As the Federal Rules of Bankruptcy Procedure contemplate class actions, there is no reason why the same principles would not allow non-debtor class members to be involved in a bankruptcy proceeding. Indeed, the bankruptcy forum may provide a particularly appropriate forum for such actions because of its expertise in commercial and consumer law.

13.8 Involuntary Bankruptcy Cases

Involuntary bankruptcy cases against consumers, in which creditors force the liquidation of debtors' non-exempt assets, were extremely rare under the prior Bankruptcy Act. Although the requirements for commencing an involuntary

bankruptcy have been relaxed somewhat under the Code,[401] such cases continue to be very uncommon.

Creditors are not eager to file involuntary consumer cases for a number of reasons. First, the prerequisites are not easy to meet. A single creditor may file an involuntary case only if the debtor has fewer than twelve unsecured creditors and only if the creditor holds a non-contingent, undisputed, unsecured claim of at least $12,300.00.[402] If the debtor has twelve or more creditors that hold claims which are totally or partially unsecured, three of them, with non-contingent undisputed claims aggregating at least $12,300.00, must join in the petition.[403] The fact that claims subject to bona fide dispute may not be included was made clear by specific language added in the 1984 amendments.[404] Moreover, an involuntary bankruptcy may never be filed against a farmer.[405] It also appears that an involuntary petition cannot be filed against a husband and wife jointly.[406]

Second, creditors are reluctant to force consumers into bankruptcy because of all the advantages (discussed throughout this manual) that consumers can obtain under the Bankruptcy Code. Thus, trying to use bankruptcy to collect

In re Woodmoor Corp., 4 B.R. 186 (Bankr. D. Colo. 1980) (both cases holding that claims must be considered individually).

398 *See* Reid v. White Motor Corp., 886 F.2d 1462 (6th Cir. 1989) (bankruptcy rules permit filing of class proofs of claim, however, claim may be denied for failure to follow procedural requirements of Fed. R. Civ. P. 23 as made applicable by Fed. R. Bankr. P. 7023); *In re* Charter Co., 876 F.2d 861 (11th Cir. 1989) (no motion for class certification is required unless an objection to class proof of claim is filed); *In re* Mortgage & Realty Trust, 125 B.R. 575 (Bankr. C.D. Cal. 1991) (proper in chapter 11 case to wait for deadline for objection to claim to run before filing motion to certify class). Better practice would probably be to file a motion for class certification at or near the time of filing the proof of claim.

399 28 U.S.C. § 1334(b); *see In re* Porter, 295 B.R. 529 (Bankr. E.D. Pa. 2003) (bankruptcy court jurisdiction does not extend over TILA claims of putative class comprised mostly of non-debtors); *In re* Smith, 95 B.R. 286 (Bankr. S.D.N.Y. 1988) (no jurisdiction over individual or class claims arising from IRS tax refund intercept). However it could be argued that the cause of action is property of the estate, and that therefore the court has exclusive jurisdiction over the *debtor's* claim. 28 U.S.C. § 1334(e).

400 *See generally* § 13.4.1.4, *supra*.

401 *See* Donnelly, *The New (Proposed?) Bankruptcy Act: The Development of Its Structural Provisions and Their Impact on the Interests of Consumer Debtors*, 18 Santa Clara L. Rev. 291 (1978).

402 11 U.S.C. § 303(b)(2). This amount is adjusted every three years pursuant to 11 U.S.C. § 104(b). In calculating whether there are more than twelve unsecured creditors for the purpose of determining whether a case may be filed by a single creditor, even relatively small claims must be counted. *See In re* Runyan, 832 F.2d 58 (5th Cir. 1987) (unsecured claim of $600.00 not considered *de minimis*, even assuming *de minimis* claims could be excluded). *Compare In re* Blaine Richards & Co., 10 B.R. 424 (Bankr. E.D.N.Y. 1981) (creditors with small current trade account claims excluded) *with In re* 7H Land & Cattle Co., 6 B.R. 29 (Bankr. D. Nev. 1980) (single creditor must make showing of special circumstances, such as fraud, to be successful petitioner). Creditors also are not permitted to disregard the separate existence of a corporation by asserting that debts of the corporation are debts that can be counted as debts of its principal (absent grounds to pierce the corporate veil). *In re* Sims, 994 F.2d 210 (5th Cir. 1993).

403 11 U.S.C. § 303(b)(1). One court of appeals has held that only some of the petitioning creditors must be fully or partially unsecured. Paradise Hotel Corp. v. Bank of Nova Scotia, 842 F.2d 47 (3d Cir. 1988).

404 11 U.S.C. § 303(b); *see In re* Reid, 773 F.2d 945 (7th Cir. 1985).

405 11 U.S.C. § 303(a). "Farmer" is defined at 11 U.S.C. § 101(20). In determining whether a debtor meets this definition, it has been held that income from the sale of farm machinery to scale back farming was income from a "farming operation," but that land rental income was not. *In re* Armstrong, 812 F.2d 1024 (7th Cir. 1987). It has also been held that an individual retirement account (IRA) distribution was not income from farming despite the fact that IRA contributions came from earlier farm income. *In re* Wagner, 808 F.2d 542 (7th Cir. 1987).

406 *In re* Benny, 842 F.2d 1147 (9th Cir. 1988) (married couple not a "person," only voluntary joint petitions authorized by Code); *In re* Jones, 112 B.R. 770 (Bankr. E.D. Va. 1990); *In re* Calloway, 70 B.R. 175 (Bankr. N.D. Ind. 1986) (joint involuntary petition is improper).

a claim could backfire on the creditor; at best, it only allows the creditor to share the debtor's assets with all other creditors. These assets in many states do not include property that is exempt under the federal bankruptcy exemptions, leaving less for creditors than would be available under state law execution procedures.

Third, bringing an involuntary bankruptcy can be very risky for a petitioning creditor. If the petition is not successful (and the court may dismiss[407] it or abstain[408] from hearing it in some cases), the court is authorized to award to the debtor not only attorney fees and costs, but also compensatory and punitive damages.[409]

In those rare instances in which a consumer is faced with an involuntary bankruptcy petition, the first decision which must be made is whether to contest the case. In some instances, particularly if a creditor has acted without much knowledge of the bankruptcy laws, debtors may be better off going through with the bankruptcy and taking advantage of the numerous protections available to them.[410] In such cases, the debtor would not contest the petition, but might wish to exercise the absolute right to convert the liquidation case to a chapter 13 case.[411]

A debtor who wishes to contest an involuntary petition must file a responsive pleading;[412] otherwise, the petition may be granted by default.[413] It may be possible to raise a number of defenses. If the petition has been filed by only one creditor, the debtor may show that more than twelve creditors holding unsecured claims exist and that therefore one petitioning creditor is not sufficient.[414] Most consumers

have more than twelve creditors, counting utilities, friends, and so forth. However, if the petition is denied on this basis, the court may allow other creditors to intervene to make up the requisite number.[415] When a creditor knows that more than twelve creditors exist, but nonetheless files as a single petitioning creditor, the petition may be dismissed as filed in bad faith.[416] Compensatory and punitive damage claims would then be available against that creditor.[417]

The debtor might also challenge the petition on the grounds that some of the creditors hold contingent claims or claims subject to a bona fide dispute that do not qualify them to file as petitioners.[418] Certain claims, such as unliquidated tort claims and claims against guarantors of notes upon which there has been no default, are pretty clearly disputed, or contingent because they depend upon the occurrence of future events. But claims which are simply unmatured probably are not contingent.[419] In addition, it has been held that if the debtor has a "bona fide" counterclaim or setoff, that claim may serve to extinguish the right of the creditor to join an involuntary petition.[420] Moreover, case law under the

---

407 11 U.S.C. § 707(a).

408 11 U.S.C. § 305(a).

409 11 U.S.C. § 303(i); *see In re* Reid, 854 F.2d 156 (7th Cir. 1988); *see also In re* Am. President Lines, Ltd., 804 F.2d 1307 (D.C. Cir. 1986) (sanctions awarded against creditor for frivolous appeal of dismissal of involuntary bankruptcy).

410 Even if the case is not contested, the debtor may retain its right to challenge the bad faith of the creditors which filed the involuntary petition. *See* Paradise Hotel Corp. v. Bank of Nova Scotia, 842 F.2d 47 (3d Cir. 1988).

411 11 U.S.C. § 706. Section 303 does not provide for involuntary chapter 13 cases, but nothing prevents an involuntary debtor who prefers that chapter from converting. *See also In re* Graham, 21 B.R. 235 (Bankr. N.D. Iowa 1982) (individual debtor could not be involuntarily forced into chapter 11 reorganization). Conversion cures any jurisdictional defects in the original involuntary petition. *In re* Benny, 842 F.2d 1147 (9th Cir. 1988).

412 Fed. R. Bankr. P. 1011(b).

413 *See In re* Nina Merch. Corp., 5 B.R. 743 (Bankr. S.D.N.Y. 1980); *see also In re* Mason, 709 F.2d 1313 (9th Cir. 1983) (defense not raised in answer is waived).

414 This defense must be timely raised by the debtor, because it probably does not go to the jurisdiction of the court. *See In re* Earl's Tire Serv., 6 B.R. 1019 (Bankr. D. Del. 1980). It is also unclear whether every small debt of the debtor must be counted. *See also* King v. Fid. Nat'l Bank of Baton Rouge, 712 F.2d 188 (5th Cir. 1983) (involuntary petition dismissed as to one of two respondent spouses where that spouse not subject to claims of petitioning creditors). *Compare In re* Blaine Richards & Co., 10 B.R. 424 (Bankr. E.D.N.Y. 1981) (creditors with small current

trade account claims excluded) *with In re* 7H Land & Cattle Co., 6 B.R. 29 (Bankr. D. Nev. 1980) (single creditor must make showing of special circumstances, such as fraud, to be successful petitioner).

415 11 U.S.C. § 303(c). Holders of small recurring claims are included in counting the debtor's creditors. *In re* Rassi, 701 F.2d 627 (7th Cir. 1983); *see also In re* Runyan, 832 F.2d 58 (5th Cir. 1987) (even if *de minimis* claims could be excluded, $600.00 and $800.00 claims were not *de minimis*); *In re* Nazarian, 5 B.R. 279 (Bankr. D. Md. 1980); *In re* Kreidler Imp. Corp., 4 B.R. 256 (Bankr. D. Md. 1980); *In re* Trans-High Corp., 3 B.R. 1 (Bankr. S.D.N.Y. 1980).

416 Basin Elec. Power Coop. v. Midwest Processing Co., 769 F.2d 483 (8th Cir. 1985).

417 11 U.S.C. § 303(i).

418 A claim is subject to bona fide dispute if there is an objective basis for either a legal or factual dispute regarding the alleged debt. *In re* Byrd, 357 F.3d 433 (4th Cir. 2004) (debt reduced to judgment may be subject to bona fide dispute if appeal pending or possible on legitimate issue); *In re* BDC 56 Ltd. Liab. Co., 330 F.3d 111 (2d Cir. 2003) (creditor has burden of making prima facie case of no bona fide dispute); *In re* Vortex Finishing Sys., Inc., 262 F.3d 985 (9th Cir. 2001) (bona fide dispute may be legal or factual dispute about whether money is owed), *amended by* 277 F.3d 1057 (9th Cir. 2002); *In re* Rimell, 946 F.2d 1363 (8th Cir. 1991) (debtor has ultimate burden to establish facts demonstrating bona fide dispute and court may conduct some analysis of legal issues to determine whether dispute is bona fide); *In re* Busick, 831 F.2d 745 (7th Cir. 1987); *see also* B.D.W. Associates, Inc. v. Busy Beaver Bldg. Centers Inc., 865 F.2d 65 (3d Cir. 1989); Bartmann v. Maverick Tube Corp., 853 F.2d 1540 (10th Cir. 1988). Note though that if one or more creditors are disqualified, it may be possible for others to join to remedy the deficiency. 11 U.S.C. § 303(c); *see In re* Rimell, 946 F.2d 1363 (8th Cir. 1991).

419 *See In re* All Media Properties, Inc., 5 B.R. 126 (Bankr. S.D. Tex. 1980), *aff'd*, 646 F.2d 193 (5th Cir. 1981).

420 *See In re* BDC 56 Ltd. Liab. Co., 330 F.3d 111 (2d Cir. 2003) (related counterclaims may be considered); *In re* Kreidler Imp. Corp., 4 B.R. 256 (Bankr. D. Md. 1980). *But see In re* Seko Inv., Inc., 156 F.3d 1005 (9th Cir. 1998) (existence of counterclaim

prior Act, holding that a creditor who has received a preference may not join in the petition, probably remains valid under the Code.[421]

The debtor may also contest the basic allegation of the petition, which the creditors have the burden of proving—that the debtor is generally not paying debts as they come due. This is known as the "equity test" of insolvency. Its meaning is not entirely clear, because it is a new concept in American bankruptcy law. It has generally been the rule that even if a debtor is insolvent under a balance sheet test (having liabilities greater than assets) that debtor may still be found to be paying debts as they come due.[422] Moreover, the failure to pay one or only a small percentage of creditors is not considered to be a "general" failure to pay debts as they come due.[423] However, when only a single creditor is not being paid, involuntary bankruptcy has been granted under the following circumstances:

- The creditor is the only creditor of the debtor;
- The creditor is a significant creditor and special circumstances such as fraudulent conduct exist; or
- The debtor admits inability to pay other creditors.[424]

Decisions under the Code have tended to adopt these principles.[425] In determining whether debts are being paid as they come due, the debtor's defenses to the claims can be very important. If the debtor succeeds in such defenses, then the debt has not come due and need not have been paid.[426] Finally, courts have held that making partial payments to all creditors is not paying those debts as they come due[427] although the result might be different if the creditors had agreed to partial payments, because then only those partial payments would be due.

Of course, in defending against an involuntary bankruptcy, the debtor's attorney should aggressively use the weapons the Code provides. By counterclaims, debtors should quickly let petitioning creditors know that they will seek attorney fees and damages under Code section 303(i). Such damages presumably can include compensation for the anxiety and the loss of reputation or credit standing that the debtor will probably suffer as a result of the petition being filed. Discovery should then be available to inquire into issues such as the petitioning creditors' bad faith in filing, and perhaps their assets, which are relevant to awards of punitive damages. And, because involuntary cases against consumers are almost never filed, the court may be sympathetic to a claim for punitive damages when such a drastic remedy is wrongfully invoked. If such damages are sought and awarded in those cases that are filed, involuntary consumer bankruptcies will continue to be rare.

13.9 Dismissal of Bankruptcy Cases

13.9.1 Voluntary Dismissal

Much akin to questions arising regarding debtors who do not wish to be brought into bankruptcy court is the question of when a debtor may extricate himself or herself from a bankruptcy that was voluntarily commenced.

In chapter 13, the answer to this question is simple. Under section 1307(b) of the Code, the debtor may obtain a dismissal upon request in any chapter 13 case that has not been converted from another chapter.[428] Even when creditors oppose dismissal or seek to convert the case, the debtor's election to dismiss must be honored.[429]

does not render claim subject to bona fide dispute when there is no dispute about creditor's claim against debtor).

421 *In re* Kreidler Imp. Corp., 4 B.R. 256 (Bankr. D. Md. 1980).

422 *In re* Cent. Hobron Associates, 41 B.R. 444 (D. Haw. 1984).

423 *In re* Nordbrock, 772 F.2d 397 (8th Cir. 1985); *In re* Dill, 731 F.2d 629 (9th Cir. 1984); *see In re* Concrete Pumping Serv., Inc., 943 F.2d 627 (6th Cir. 1991) (debtor not paying debts as they come due when in default on its only debt; *see also* John Honsberger, *Failure to Pay One's Debts Generally as They Become Due: The Experience of France and Canada*, 54 Am. Bankr. L.J. 153, 156 (1980). *But see In re* Hill, 8 B.R. 779 (Bankr. D. Minn. 1981) (petition granted where three largest creditors not being paid).

424 John Honsberger, *Failure to Pay One's Debts Generally as They Become Due: The Experience of France and Canada*, 54 Am. Bankr. L.J. 153 at 158 (1980).

425 *In re* 7-H Land & Cattle Co., 6 B.R. 29 (Bankr. D. Nev. 1980); *In re* Hill, 5 B.R. 79 (Bankr. D. Minn. 1980); *In re* J. V. Knitting Services, 4 B.R. 597 (Bankr. S.D. Fla. 1980).

426 *In re* All Media Properties, Inc., 5 B.R. 126 (Bankr. S.D. Tex. 1980), *aff'd*, 646 F.2d 193 (5th Cir. 1981); *In re* Kreidler Imp. Corp., 4 B.R. 256 (Bankr. D. Md. 1980).

427 *In re* Duty Free Shops Corp., 6 B.R. 38 (Bankr. S.D. Fla. 1980); *see also In re* Bishop, Baldwin, Rewald, Dillingham & Wong, 779 F.2d 471 (9th Cir. 1986).

428 However, the bankruptcy court may retain jurisdiction to decide adversary proceedings pending at the time of the dismissal. *In re* Pocklington, 21 B.R. 199 (Bankr. S.D. Cal. 1982); *see In re* Nash, 765 F.2d 1410 (9th Cir. 1985); *see also* § 13.2.4.3, *supra*.

429 *In re* Barbieri, 199 F.3d 616 (2d Cir. 1999) (court must dismiss and could not convert case to chapter 7 when debtor had moved to dismiss); *In re* Dulaney, 285 B.R. 10 (D. Colo. 2002); Clearstory & Co. v. Blevins, 225 B.R. 591 (D. Md. 1998); *In re* Eddis, 37 B.R. 217 (E.D. Pa. 1984); *In re* Gillion, 36 B.R. 901 (E.D. Ark. 1984); *In re* Neiman, 257 B.R. 105 (Bankr. S.D. Fla. 2001) (court follows *Barbieri*); *In re* Rebeor, 89 B.R. 314 (Bankr. N.D.N.Y. 1988); *In re* Zarowitz, 36 B.R. 906 (Bankr. S.D.N.Y. 1984); *In re* Benedicktsson, 34 B.R. 349 (Bankr. W.D. Wash. 1983); 8 Collier on Bankruptcy ¶ 1307.03[1] (15th ed. rev.); *see also In re* Cotton, 992 F.2d 311 (11th Cir. 1993) (bankruptcy court could not stay dismissal requested by chapter 12 debtor until after settlement with a major creditor had been confirmed); *In re* Beatty, 162 B.R. 853 (B.A.P. 9th Cir. 1994) (debtor had right to voluntarily dismiss chapter 13 case up until filing, signing, or entry of conversion order). *But see In re* Molitor, 76 F.3d 218 (8th Cir. 1996) (debtor who did not deny filing multiple bankruptcy cases in bad faith could not respond to conversion motion by dismissing chapter 13 case voluntarily).

Chapter 7 cases present a somewhat more complicated picture. The court may dismiss a case only after notice and a hearing,[430] and only for cause.[431] What constitutes cause for dismissal has been a matter of some dispute. A number of courts have held that cause does not exist in cases in which the debtor sought only to refile a petition after paying a favored creditor or to include debts incurred after the first petition was filed.[432] Similarly, debtors who seek to dismiss in order to avoid liquidation of non-exempt property are often unsuccessful.[433] Some courts have required the consent of all creditors for a dismissal to be obtained,[434] although such a blanket rule seems too broad in light of section 707.[435]

Most courts are more liberal, allowing dismissal in any case in which no creditor objects after notice.[436] At least one court has held that cause need not be shown in such cases.[437] These courts have generally conditioned dismissal on payment to the trustee of any expenses incurred,[438] and at least a few have held that the trustee has no standing to object to dismissal if such expenses are paid,[439] though others have held otherwise.[440] As a practical matter there is rarely an objection in no-asset cases.

Another issue which may arise is what happens in a chapter 13 case, which could have been dismissed as of right under section 1307(b), after it is converted to chapter 7. The right to dismiss the case is probably lost upon such a conversion. Thus, before a conversion to chapter 7, it be-

hooves a debtor to consider carefully whether a liquidation bankruptcy is clearly desired. If it is not, or if the debtor is uncertain, it is critical to dismiss the chapter 13 case before an involuntary conversion takes place, so that no dispute about the right to dismiss can arise.[441] The debtor in such a case will then retain the right to file a later chapter 7 case if that is desired, subject to the limitations of 11 U.S.C. § 109(g) if the dismissal follows a request for relief from the automatic stay.[442]

13.9.2 Involuntary Dismissal or Conversion to Chapter 7

13.9.2.1 Typical Causes and Effects of Involuntary Dismissal or Conversion

Involuntary dismissal, in either a chapter 7 or chapter 13 case, may occur for a number of reasons, some of which are listed in sections 707 and 1307(c).[443] Probably the most common causes are failure to pay the filing fees[444] or chapter 13 payments, failure to file appropriate papers, such as the bankruptcy schedules or chapter 13 plan, and failure to appear at a creditors meeting.[445] Often a prelude to such a

---

430 See 11 U.S.C. § 102 for the meaning of "after notice and a hearing."

431 11 U.S.C. § 707(a).

432 *In re* Leach, 130 B.R. 855 (B.A.P. 9th Cir. 1991) (court has discretion to deny motion to dismiss chapter 7 case where debtor intended to refile later when tax liabilities would be dischargeable); *In re* Underwood, 7 B.R. 936 (Bankr. S.D. W. Va. 1980), *aff'd*, 24 B.R. 570 (S.D. W. Va. 1982); *In re* Reynolds, 4 B.R. 703 (Bankr. D. Me. 1980); *In re* Blackman, 3 B.R. 167 (Bankr. S.D. Ohio 1980).

433 *See In re* Maixner, 288 B.R. 815 (B.A.P. 8th Cir. 2003) (desire to save equity to detriment of creditors not cause for dismissal).

434 *In re* Halverson, 6 Bankr. Ct. Dec. (LRP) 241, 1 Collier Bankr. Cas. 2d (MB) 906 (Bankr. W.D. Wis. 1980).

435 *See In re* Simmons, 200 F.3d 738 (11th Cir. 2000) (affirming denial of debtor's motion to dismiss in light of debtor's past abuse of bankruptcy system); *In re* Turpen, 244 B.R. 431 (B.A.P. 8th Cir. 2000) (debtor did not have right to dismiss case in which creditors would be fully paid when creditors objected that debtor might not pay if case dismissed); *In re* Hall, 15 B.R. 913 (B.A.P. 9th Cir. 1981) (affirmative consent of all creditors needed where dismissal prejudiced creditors; notice of dismissal motion should specify "cause" asserted for requesting dismissal).

436 *In re* Gallman, 6 B.R. 1 (Bankr. N.D. Ga. 1980); *In re* Richards, 4 B.R. 85 (Bankr. M.D. Fla. 1980).

437 *In re* Wirick, 3 B.R. 539 (Bankr. E.D. Va. 1980).

438 *In re* Waldman, 5 B.R. 401 (Bankr. S.D.N.Y. 1980).

439 *In re* Wolfe, 12 B.R. 686 (Bankr. S.D. Ohio 1981); *In re* Jackson, 7 B.R. 616 (Bankr. E.D. Tenn. 1980).

440 *See, e.g.,* Penick v. Tice, 732 F.2d 1211 (4th Cir. 1984) (trustee has standing to object on behalf of unsecured creditors).

441 *See In re* Hearn, 18 B.R. 605 (Bankr. D. Neb. 1982) (debtor's motion to dismiss chapter 13 case prevailed over contemporaneously filed and well-founded motion to convert to chapter 7). *But see In re* Graven, 936 F.2d 378 (8th Cir. 1991) (chapter 12 case converted to chapter 7 based on fraudulent concealment of assets despite debtor's prior request to voluntarily dismiss).

442 *See* §§ 3.2.1, 9.7.3.2.1, *supra*.

443 The list of reasons for dismissal is not exclusive. *In re* Gonic Realty Trust, 909 F.2d 624 (1st Cir. 1990) (bankruptcy court not limited to statutorily enumerated grounds for finding "cause" to dismiss or convert chapter 11 case).

444 This suggests one method of obtaining a dismissal in a chapter 7 case in which all of the filing fees have not yet been paid, though a dismissal is not always certain to occur in such cases.

445 The 1986 amendments to the Bankruptcy Code contemplate that the United States trustee will be responsible for prosecuting many motions under § 707 and § 1307(c) including all motions under § 707(a)(3) and § 1307(c)(9) and (10). Although some courts have local rules or procedures providing for "automatic" dismissal if papers are not timely filed, such rules and procedures do not comply with the statute, which requires notice and a hearing before dismissal, or with Fed. R. Bankr. P. 1017(d), which generally requires a contested matter for dismissal of a case. *See In re* Muessel, 292 B.R. 712 (B.A.P. 1st Cir. 2003) (*sua sponte* dismissal case on alternate grounds without notice or a meaningful opportunity for the debtor to be heard on those grounds violated the debtor's fundamental rights to procedural due process and the express requirements of the Bankruptcy Code); *In re* Davis, 275 B.R. 864 (B.A.P. 8th Cir. 2002) (bankruptcy court did not abuse its discretion in dismissing case of incarcerated debtor who made no attempt to make arrangements to conduct creditors meeting by means other than personal appearance); *In re* Dinova, 212 B.R. 437 (B.A.P. 2d Cir. 1997) (case could not be dismissed on *ex parte* order due to debtor's failure to appear at creditors' meeting even though notice of meeting warned that such dismissal would be sought,

dismissal is a court order setting a deadline for the debtor's performance.[446] However, when some reasonable excuse for delay or nonpayment is raised, a motion to dismiss on such grounds is normally denied.[447] When such motions are considered, the debtor's pre-petition conduct is irrelevant.[448] Further, it is clear that such dismissals are discretionary rather than mandatory.[449] The rules require that a debtor be given notice and a hearing prior to a dismissal[450] so that the debtor may argue that there is no basis for dismissal or that the court should exercise its discretion to order some other remedy.[451] Except perhaps in egregious cases of repeated bankruptcies in which the debtor does not follow through, dismissals in such cases usually are without prejudice,[452] subject to the limitations of section 109(g) of the Code.[453] But in a chapter 13 case there is always a possibility that the court might instead convert the case to chapter 7, under section 1307(c), rather than dismiss it.[454]

Dismissal may also occur if the debtor fails to obtain confirmation of a plan, usually when the court has found that the confirmation standards cannot be met.[455] The substantive questions arising in such cases are discussed elsewhere in this manual.[456] Dismissal for this reason generally occurs only when the debtor does not request the opportunity to present an amended plan satisfactory to the court.[457] Absent an amended plan, the debtor is in the same position as if no plan had been filed, a position from which the case cannot proceed, at least under chapter 13.

Occasionally, a creditor in a consumer case will move for dismissal under section 305(a), section 707(a), or 1307(c). The most common ground for such a motion is bad faith, and some courts have ruled that a chapter 13 petition can be dismissed if it was filed in bad faith.[458] Although chapter 7 cases are subject to dismissal in limited circumstances for substantial abuse, only the court or the U.S. trustee can raise that issue.[459] Some creditors seek to circumvent that limitation by moving to have chapter 7 cases dismissed under section 707(a) on the ground that they were filed in bad faith. These motions should be denied as attempts to circumvent the limitation on creditors' motions under section 707(b) which was intended to prevent improper use of claims of abuse by creditors.[460] Additionally, a motion to

---

because notice and hearing not provided as required); *In re* Krueger, 88 B.R. 238 (B.A.P. 9th Cir. 1988) (dismissal of chapter 13 case without notice and hearing violates due process); *In re* Bucurescu, 282 B.R. 124 (S.D.N.Y. 2002) (reversing dismissal based upon the earlier order, without notice and a hearing regarding compliance with order); *In re* Gen. Order Governing Dismissal of Cases, 210 B.R. 941 (Bankr. M.D. Pa. 1997) (statute requires motion by United States trustee for dismissal based upon failure to file required papers).

446 *See* Howard v. Lexington Investments, Inc., 284 F.3d 320 (1st Cir. 2002) (failure to file past due tax returns by deadline set by court); *cf.* Dep't of Treasury v. Galarza Pagan, 279 B.R. 43 (D. P.R. 2002) (refusal to dismiss for failure to file tax returns after confirmation of chapter 13 plans not an abuse of discretion).

447 *See, e.g., In re* Faaland, 37 B.R. 407 (Bankr. D.N.D. 1984). *But see In re* McDonald, 118 F.3d 568 (7th Cir. 1997) (dismissal of case for failure to make first plan payment on time was not abuse of discretion).

448 *In re* Lilley, 91 F.3d 491 (3d Cir. 1996).

449 *In re* Green, 64 B.R. 530 (B.A.P. 9th Cir. 1986); *In re* Smith, 85 B.R. 729 (E.D. Va. 1988).

450 Fed. R. Bankr. P. 1017.

451 *See In re* Wilson, 284 B.R. 109 (B.A.P. 8th Cir. 2002) (abuse of discretion to dismiss for improper venue without notice and opportunity for hearing).

452 11 U.S.C. § 349(a); *cf. In re* Hall, Bayoutree Associates Ltd., 939 F.2d 802 (9th Cir. 1991) (dismissal for improper venue must be without prejudice). Even a dismissal with prejudice does not preclude refiling of a later case when there are changed circumstances. *In re* Smith, 133 B.R. 467 (Bankr. N.D. Ind. 1991). However, it may preclude the discharge of debts that existed at the time of the earlier case. Colonial Auto Ctr. v. Tomlin, 105 F.3d 933 (4th Cir. 1997); *see* 3 Collier on Bankruptcy ¶ 349.02 (15th ed. rev.).

453 *See* §§ 3.2.1, 9.7.3.2.1, *supra.*

454 *See, e.g., In re* Elkin, 5 B.R. 21 (Bankr. S.D. Cal. 1980).

455 *See, e.g., In re* Madden, 1 Collier Bankr. Cas. 2d (MB) 1093 (Bankr. S.D. Ohio 1980); *In re* Fredrickson, 5 B.R. 199 (Bankr. M.D. Fla. 1980); *In re* Cadogan, 4 B.R. 598 (Bankr. W.D. La. 1980). The fact that a debtor's payments are somewhat late and therefore extend beyond the five years prescribed by a plan,

however, is not cause for dismissal. *In re* Black, 78 B.R. 840 (Bankr. S.D. Ohio 1987); § 12.6.5, *supra.*

456 *See* Chapter 12, *supra,* for a discussion of confirmation standards.

457 *In re* Minkes, 237 B.R. 476 (B.A.P. 8th Cir. 1999) (case should not have been dismissed based on original plan being unconfirmable without giving debtor opportunity to argue plan not deficient or propose modified plan).

458 *In re* Alt, 305 F.3d 413 (6th Cir. 2002) (bad faith dismissal of chapter 13 case for knowingly omitting from schedules tax debts that rendered debtor ineligible for relief); *In re* Leavitt, 171 F.3d 1219 (9th Cir. 1999) (bad faith can be cause to dismiss chapter 13 case with prejudice); *In re* Lilley, 91 F.3d 491 (3d Cir. 1996) (lack of good faith can be cause for dismissal of chapter 13 case); *In re* Barrett, 964 F.2d 588 (6th Cir. 1992) (finding that debtor's second chapter 13 filing, when he had insufficient income to support plan, was in bad faith but that third chapter 13 case, after circumstances had changed was not in bad faith); *In re* Love, 957 F.2d 1350 (7th Cir. 1992) (case dismissed where chapter 13 debtor, who had willfully refused to pay pre-petition income taxes as tax protestor, failed to list all of his income and assets and filed case only when IRS began to garnish his wages); *see also In re* Pennino, 299 B.R. 536 (B.A.P. 8th Cir. 2003) (abstention from debtor's sixth bankruptcy case, filed to delay creditor while RICO claims litigated elsewhere, not abuse of discretion); *In re* Cabral, 285 B.R. 563 (B.A.P. 1st Cir. 2002) (bad faith was grounds for reconverting case back to chapter 7). *But see In re* Eastman, 188 B.R. 621 (B.A.P. 9th Cir. 1995) (dismissal under § 305(a) improper unless it benefited debtor as well as creditors).

459 *See* § 13.9.2.2, *infra.*

460 *In re* Padilla, 222 F.3d 1184 (9th Cir. 2000) (bad faith not cause to dismiss chapter 7 case); *In re* Pedigo, 296 B.R. 485 (Bankr. S.D. Ind. 2003) (bad faith not cause for dismissal under § 707(a)); *In re* Bridges, 135 B.R. 36 (Bankr. E.D. Ky. 1991) (denying creditor's motion to dismiss under § 707(a) for "cause" because ability to repay debts is not "cause" for dismissal under that section and creditor was attempting to circumvent prohibition of creditors filing motion to dismiss for

dismiss under either section 707(a) or 1307(c) must be denied for lack of standing if the moving creditor's claim has been or could be disallowed.[461]

13.9.2.2 Dismissal for Substantial Abuse of the Provisions of Chapter 7

Section 707(b) of the Code establishes the "substantial abuse" test. Section 707(b) permits a bankruptcy court to dismiss a chapter 7 case, after notice and a hearing, on its own motion or motion of the United States trustee and not at the request or even the suggestion of any party in interest, if the court finds that granting relief under chapter 7 would be a substantial abuse of its provisions.

Despite the significant theoretical change in philosophy that this section represents, limiting the previously almost absolute right to file a chapter 7 case, its practical effects were meant to be slight, because it was directed at only a tiny percentage of the consumer bankruptcies filed. The purpose of section 707(b) may be ascertained from its lengthy legislative history, which gives important guidance regarding what is and is not intended by the substantial abuse test.

The idea of totally barring a debtor from chapter 7 relief originated in proposals made by the consumer credit industry. These proposals, and the bills that first embodied them,[462] had several key elements. First, dismissal of a bankruptcy petition could be obtained by a creditor filing a motion.[463] Second, dismissal would be ordered in any case in which a consumer could pay a "reasonable portion" of her debts (excluding first mortgage debts), defined as fifty percent of those debts.[464] Third, the determination of this ability to pay would assume a five year repayment period, even if the debts came due in shorter periods.[465] Finally, the

court was to decide these matters based on the debtor's "anticipated future income."[466]

The ultimate legislative product rejected each of these concepts. A case may be dismissed under section 707(b) only by the court acting *sua sponte* after reviewing the petition and schedules, including the schedule of current income and expenditures, or on motion of the United States trustee. The legislative history suggests that this limitation is intended to prevent creditors from using motions to dismiss, or the threat of such motions, to harass or bargain with the debtor,[467] and that if a creditor does request dismissal, the court may not be able to dismiss the case.[468] Although the statute allows the court itself to raise the issue, most courts simply rely on the United States trustee to file motions in cases which might meet the test for substantial abuse.

The final statute also rejected the idea that a chapter 7 case should be dismissed if a debtor could pay only a portion of her debts, or could pay those debts only if they were stretched out over five years. In describing what was meant by the term "substantial abuse" in the Senate version of the bill (which adopted more of the creditor proposals than the final statute), the Senate Report limited the term to those debtors who could meet their debts "without difficulty as they came due."[469] Other portions of the legislative history

---

substantial abuse); *see also In re* Huckfeldt, 39 F.3d 829 (8th Cir. 1994) (court's inquiry under § 707(a) is not into "bad faith" but rather whether cause exists for dismissal); McDow v. Smith, 295 B.R. 69 (E.D. Va. 2003) (ability to pay, by itself, not bad faith warranting dismissal); *In re* Etcheverry, 242 B.R. 503 (D. Colo. 1999) (bad faith not a grounds for dismissal under § 707(a)); *In re* Ryan, 267 B.R. 635 (Bankr. N.D. Iowa 2001) (denying motion to convert case to chapter 11 as attempt to circumvent prohibition of creditor substantial abuse motions); *In re* Khan, 172 B.R. 613 (Bankr. D. Minn. 1994) (question of whether debtor could pay debts was irrelevant to dismissal under § 707(a)). *But see In re* Tamecki, 229 F.3d 205 (3d Cir. 2000) (dismissing chapter 7 case for bad faith on motion of trustee); *In re* Zick, 931 F.2d 1124 (6th Cir. 1991) (creditor's motion to dismiss chapter 7 case for "bad faith" allowed); *see also* § 13.9.2.2, *infra*.

461 *In re* Abijoe Realty Corp., 943 F.2d 121 (1st Cir. 1991).

462 H.R. 4786, 97th Cong. (1981).

463 *Id.* § 3.

464 S. 445, § 203(3), 98th Cong. (1983).

465 *See, e.g.*, S. 2000, § 18(c), 97th Cong. (1982) (setting five-year standard for chapter 13 plans); *Bankruptcy Reform Act of 1978 (future earnings), Hearing Before the Subcomm. on Courts of*

the Senate Comm. on the Judiciary, 97th Cong., pt. 2, at 19 (statement of Robert W. Johnson).

466 H.R. 4786, § 3, 97th Cong. (1981).

467 *See, e.g., Bankruptcy Reform, Hearings Before the Subcomm. on Courts of the Senate Comm. on the Judiciary,* 98th Cong. 280–281 (1983) (statement of Henry J. Sommer).

468 130 Cong. Rec. S7624 (daily ed. June 19, 1984) (remarks of Sen. Metzenbaum); *see In re* Christian, 804 F.2d 46 (3d Cir. 1986) (creditors lack standing to move for dismissal pursuant to § 707(b)); *In re* Natale, 136 B.R. 344 (Bankr. E.D.N.Y. 1992) (creditor had no standing to allege substantial abuse as a grounds for dismissal); *In re* Restea, 76 B.R. 728 (Bankr. D.S.D. 1987) (suggestion of abuse to U.S. trustee nullifies U.S. trustee's subsequent motion); *see also In re* Bridges, 135 B.R. 36 (Bankr. E.D. Ky. 1991) (denying creditor's motion to dismiss under § 707(a) for "cause" because ability to repay debts is not "cause" for dismissal under that section and creditor was attempting to circumvent prohibition of creditors filing motion to dismiss for substantial abuse); *In re* Frisch, 76 B.R. 801 (Bankr. D. Colo. 1987) (creditor may not argue that substantial abuse is "cause" for dismissal under § 707(a); creditor assessed $750.00 legal fees as sanction); *In re* Jones, 60 B.R. 96 (Bankr. W.D. Ky. 1986) (dismissal denied where facts were improperly brought to court's attention by someone acting for a party in interest). *But see In re* Stewart, 215 B.R. 456 (B.A.P. 10th Cir. 1997) (court could hear motion brought by U.S. trustee upon suggestion of creditor), *aff'd*, 175 F.3d 796 (10th Cir. 1999); *In re* Joseph, 208 B.R. 55 (B.A.P. 9th Cir. 1997) (court must hear motion brought by U.S. trustee even though it was based upon referral by panel trustee); *In re* Busbin, 95 B.R. 240 (Bankr. N.D. Ga. 1989) (creditor may bring grounds for motion to dismiss for substantial abuse to the attention of the court).

469 S. Rep. No. 98-65, at 54 (1983).

also show that Congress had no intent to reduce debtors to minimal standards of living to force them to pay their debts.[470]

Finally, Congress rejected the "future income" concept.[471] A court is not to prognosticate about the debtor's prospects for income and expenses over the next five years.[472] It is to look only to the current financial situation of the debtor as reflected in the bankruptcy schedules.

Thus, as it finally emerged from Congress, the substantial abuse test is a narrowly targeted provision. It should affect only a few high income debtors, such as the doctors and professional athletes who so often appeared in creditors' Congressional testimony. Low and even middle income debtors should have little difficulty in arguing that they do not fall within the statute's intended parameters as described above.

However, there still remain substantial questions about how the test should work in practice. For example, if the court raises the issue on its own motion, who will prosecute the court's motion? It is clear that a creditor or trustee may not do so. The statute provides a presumption in favor of granting relief to the debtor, further emphasizing the extraordinary circumstances which must exist before dismissal is appropriate.[473] How will the presumption be overcome? The proceeding is likely to resemble an inquisition, with the court itself questioning the debtor to establish a record.

The 1986 amendments to the Code permit the United States trustee to move for dismissal pursuant to section 707(b). It appears that a U.S. trustee motion would resolve many of the procedural problems which might arise in prosecuting *sua sponte* motions of the court. However, new problems may arise related to creditors' attempts to influence U.S. trustees to bring motions to dismiss.[474] When necessary, debtor's attorneys should consider asking for discovery to investigate creditors' involvement in such motions.

Rule 1017(e) requires that notice of a motion to dismiss on the basis of substantial abuse include all matters to be submitted to or considered by the court at the hearing. Because the Code and the Rules require a hearing prior to dismissal, debtor's counsel has an opportunity to present evidence and arguments which would overcome the court's suspicions related to substantial abuse.[475] A motion under section 707(b) must be made within 60 days following the first date set for the meeting of creditors and cannot be entertained once a discharge is entered.[476] Additionally, failure to properly notice or hold the requisite hearing would certainly be grounds for challenging dismissal pursuant to section 707(b).[477] Although the question is not free from doubt, the legislative history suggests that review in an appeal would be under an error of law, rather than an abuse of discretion standard.[478]

Section 707(b) applies only to debtors whose debts are primarily consumer debts. Thus, for debtors who have incurred most of their debts in business, through investment losses,[479] or through tort liability,[480] the section should not be a problem. A few courts have held that debts secured by real estate are not consumer debts,[481] and in this and other contexts a number of courts have held that tax debts are not

470 See discussion of the chapter 13 ability-to-pay test, § 12.3.3, *supra*.
471 S. Rep. No. 98-65, at 3, 4 (1983); 130 Cong. Rec. H1941 (daily ed. Mar. 26, 1984) (remarks of Rep. Rodino); 130 Cong. Rec. S7624 (daily ed. June 19, 1984) (remarks of Sen. Metzenbaum).
472 *In re* King, 308 B.R. 522 (Bankr. D. Kan. 2004) (court refused to consider potential bonus income).
473 11 U.S.C. § 707(b); *see In re* Pollard, 296 B.R. 531 (Bankr. W.D. Okla. 2003) (presumption requires any doubts to be resolved in favor of debtor).
474 *In re* Restea, 76 B.R. 728 (Bankr. D.S.D. 1987) (suggestion of abuse to U.S. trustee nullifies U.S. trustee's subsequent motion); *see also* § 13.6.3, *supra*. *But see In re* Stewart, 175 F.3d 796 (10th Cir. 1999) (U.S. trustee may make motion after suggestion by creditor); *In re* Kornfield, 164 F.3d 778 (2d Cir. 1999) (creditors and trustees may provide information to U.S. trustee and participate in proceeding once U.S. trustee has made motion); *In re* Clark, 927 F.2d 793 (4th Cir. 1991) (trustee may move to dismiss based on substantial abuse at creditor's suggestion).
475 Fed. R. Bankr. P. 1017(e); *see, e.g., In re* Strong, 84 B.R. 541 (Bankr. N.D. Ind. 1988) (procedure required before *sua sponte* dismissal includes notice to debtor of court's concerns and opportunity for debtor and/or counsel to explain); *In re* Gaukler, 63 B.R. 224 (Bankr. D.N.D. 1986) (court would not impose its own values after proof that debtor's expenses actually included disproportionate religious contributions); *In re* Hamze, 57 B.R. 37 (Bankr. E.D. Mich. 1985) (debtor's disproportionate consumer debt for trip to Lebanon was reasonable in light of explanation that his family's home had been hit by gunshells).
476 Fed. R. Bankr. P. 1017(e); *In re* Cronk, 124 B.R. 759 (Bankr. N.D. Ill. 1990). The United States trustee may, within the sixty-day period, request an extension of the deadline for cause.
477 *See, e.g.,* Cent. Bank of Wooday-Hewitt v. Spark, 61 B.R. 285 (W.D. Tex. 1986).
478 S. Rep. No. 98-65, at 53, 54 (1983). *But see In re* Behlke, 358 F.3d 429 (6th Cir. 2004) (applying abuse of discretion standard).
479 *In re* Stewart, 175 F.3d 796 (10th Cir. 1999) (alimony debts, loan from father-in-law and some student loans used for living expenses were consumer debts); *In re* Booth, 858 F.2d 1051 (5th Cir. 1988) (test for whether a debt is a business obligation is whether debt was incurred with an eye toward profit; court looked to dollar amounts of debts rather than number of creditors to decide if debts primarily consumer debts); *In re* Marshalek, 158 B.R. 704 (Bankr. N.D. Ohio 1993) (debt arising from motor vehicle accident was not consumer debt); *In re* Restea, 76 B.R. 728 (Bankr. D.S.D. 1987) (debts not primarily consumer debts where fifty-three percent of debts were consumer debts); *In re* Bell, 65 B.R. 575 (Bankr. E.D. Mich. 1986) (applying numerical test in comparing amount of consumer debts to amount of business debts); *In re* Campbell, 63 B.R. 702 (Bankr. W.D. Mo. 1986) (principal liability of debtor was business debt); *In re* Almendinger, 56 B.R. 97 (Bankr. N.D. Ohio 1985). *But see In re* Berndt, 127 B.R. 222 (Bankr. D.N.D. 1991) (unsecured credit card debt used to invest in stock market is a consumer debt).
480 *In re* White, 49 B.R. 869 (Bankr. W.D.N.C. 1985).
481 *See, e.g., In re* Restea, 76 B.R. 728 (Bankr. D.S.D. 1987). *But see In re* Kelly, 841 F.2d 908 (9th Cir. 1988).

consumer debts.[482] At least one court has held that this focus on consumer debtors also means that the section should not be applied when the debtor is ineligible for chapter 13, particularly if the debtor also cannot formulate a viable chapter 11 plan.[483]

The cases that have dealt with the substantial abuse test are most notable for their total failure to discuss the legislative history of section 707(b) set forth above, especially the language of the Senate Report.[484] Instead, the courts have focused on high income debtors with extravagant lifestyles, sometimes denying chapter 7 relief even when debtors cannot repay all of their debts.[485]

One early case which did at least approach the drafters' intent was *In re Edwards*,[486] in which the court held that a case should not be dismissed under section 707(b) unless the debtors could afford a three year one-hundred percent chapter 13 plan. The Ninth Circuit Court of Appeals and a number of other courts also seem to have adopted this approach, finding substantial abuse based upon a debtor having income sufficient to fund a one-hundred percent

plan.[487] Other courts have unfortunately developed more expansive definitions of substantial abuse and have dismissed cases even when debtors could pay only some of their debts under a three-year chapter 13 plan.[488] The Sixth Circuit has held that a chapter 7 case may be dismissed for substantial abuse when the debtor could get by and pay one-hundred percent of his debts with "good, old-fashioned belt tightening" and other available state remedies.[489] These

---

482 *E.g., In re* Westberry, 215 F.3d 589 (6th Cir. 2000); *In re* Brashers, 216 B.R. 59 (Bankr. N.D. Okla. 1998). Courts have found that tax debts are not consumer debts for purposes of the codebtor stay. *See* § 9.4.4, *supra*.

483 *In re* Mastroeni, 56 B.R. 456 (Bankr. S.D.N.Y. 1985); *see also In re* Krohn, 886 F.2d 123 (6th Cir. 1989) (the debtor's eligibility for chapter 13 relief is a factor to be considered; however even a debtor ineligible for both chapters 11 and 13 can have chapter 7 case dismissed based on "excesses" and other factors).

484 *But see In re* Attanasio, 218 B.R. 180 (Bankr. N.D. Ala. 1998) (following dictates of legislative history); *In re* Balaja, 190 B.R. 335 (Bankr. N.D. Ill. 1996) (citing legislative history in holding that debtor who has genuine difficulty paying obligations as they come due should be permitted to file chapter 7 case unless debtor deliberately constructed that situation).

485 *See, e.g., In re* Gyurci, 95 B.R. 639 (Bankr. D. Minn. 1989) (debtor had five cars, housekeeper and child in private school); *In re* Kelly, 57 B.R. 536 (Bankr. D. Ariz. 1986) (debtor had annual income from law practice in excess of $60,000.00 so that chapter 13 plan could be funded without undue hardship), *aff'd*, 841 F.2d 908 (9th Cir. 1988); *In re* Kress, 57 B.R. 874 (Bankr. D.N.D. 1985) (debtor had earned income of over $90,000.00); *In re* Grant, 51 B.R. 385 (Bankr. N.D. Ohio 1985) (debtors had income of $40,000.00, expenses for such items as leased Mercedes, $200.00/mo. for telephone, $450.00/mo. for recreation, $500.00/mo. for clothing); *cf. In re* Harris, 279 B.R. 254 (B.A.P. 9th Cir. 2002) (debtors not required to reduce expenses to those allowed by IRS financial collection standards); *In re* Moreland, 284 B.R. 825 (Bankr. W.D. Va. 2002) (debtors' high expenses due to poor choices of occupation and place of residence did not amount to substantial abuse); *In re* Braley, 103 B.R. 758 (Bankr. E.D. Va. 1989) (even the extravagant are entitled to the benefit of chapter 7 relief; Judge Bonney's colorful opinion makes this case a classic), *aff'd*, 110 B.R. 211 (E.D. Va. 1990). *But see In re* Lamanna, 153 F.3d 1 (1st Cir. 1998) (affirming finding of substantial abuse by debtor whose income was about $16,000.00 per year but who had very low expenses because he lived with his parents).

486 50 B.R. 933 (Bankr. S.D.N.Y. 1985).

487 *In re* Kelly, 841 F.2d 908 (9th Cir. 1988); *In re* Harris, 125 B.R. 254 (D.S.D. 1991) (ability to pay one-hundred-fifty percent of debts over three year period warrants dismissal for substantial abuse), *aff'd*, 960 F.2d 74 (8th Cir. 1992); *In re* Piontek, 113 B.R. 17 (Bankr. D. Or. 1990) (chapter 7 debtor's understatement of after tax income and listing of excessive expenses was not bad faith warranting dismissal for substantial abuse; however, case would be dismissed unless converted to chapter 13 because debtors had more than enough income to pay one-hundred percent of debts over three years); *In re* Strange, 85 B.R. 662 (Bankr. S.D. Ga. 1988); *In re* Strong, 84 B.R. 541 (Bankr. N.D. Ind. 1988) (petition dismissed for substantial abuse where nonpetitioning spouse's income would allow one-hundred percent repayment over three years); *In re* Struggs, 71 B.R. 96 (Bankr. E.D. Mich. 1987) (debtor's income sufficient to pay one-hundred percent of debts in as little as nine months); *In re* Day, 77 B.R. 225 (Bankr. D.N.D. 1987) (debtor could pay one-hundred percent debts in two to three years); *see also In re* Walton, 866 F.2d 981 (8th Cir. 1989) (substantial abuse found where debtor's substantial surplus of income over expenses could pay one-hundred percent of debts over *five* years). This latter case appears to stretch the substantial abuse test well beyond its intended bounds, dismissing the petition of a debtor with only a relatively modest income.

488 *E.g., In re* Behlke, 358 F.3d 429 (6th Cir. 2004) (no abuse of discretion to dismiss case of debtor who could pay 14%–23% over three to five years); Fonder v. United States, 974 F.2d 996 (8th Cir. 1992) (finding substantial abuse when debtor could pay at least eighty-nine percent of unsecured debts in three year chapter 13 plan); *In re* Walton, 866 F.2d 981 (8th Cir. 1989) (substantial abuse found where debtor's substantial surplus of income over expenses could pay one-hundred percent of debts over *five* years); *In re* Roth, 108 B.R. 78 (Bankr. W.D. Pa. 1989) (case dismissed where debtors could pay only forty-three percent of unsecured debt in three-year chapter 13 plan).

489 *In re* Krohn, 886 F.2d 123 (6th Cir. 1989) (although income and ability to pay debts alone can justify dismissal, court found additional evidence of bad faith). Given that neither chapter 11 nor chapter 13 relief was available at the time to this debtor in the Sixth Circuit, he would appear to have had no avenue to bankruptcy relief. However the debtor's constitutional claims were denied by the Sixth Circuit. *See also In re* Taylor, 212 F.3d 395 (8th Cir. 2000) (court could consider income from ERISA pension in deciding ability to fund hypothetical chapter 13 plan even though pension was not part of estate); *In re* Koch, 109 F.3d 1285 (6th Cir. 1997) (exempt worker's compensation income could be considered in deciding whether substantial abuse existed); *cf. In re* Mills, 246 B.R. 395 (Bankr. S.D. Cal. 2000) (debtor's voluntary contributions to 401(k) plan should not automatically be considered available to pay creditors and must be examined based on circumstances of case); *In re* Beles, 135 B.R. 286 (Bankr. S.D. Ohio 1991) (interpreting *Krohn* to permit denial of motion to dismiss for substantial abuse where debtors could fund a chapter 13 plan but had struggled to pay debts before bankruptcy and were not in bad faith).

cases have completely lost sight of the congressional intent in enacting the substantial abuse provision. More appropriately, other courts have held that the debtor's ability to fund a chapter 13 plan is not enough by itself to dictate a finding of substantial abuse.[490] Courts have also generally rejected arguments by the United States trustee that debtors should not be supporting stepchildren, elderly relatives, or adult children living in their homes.[491]

Some courts have found substantial abuse in situations in which the debtor was not fully honest in preparing the petition and schedules.[492] A number of these courts have held that a determination of substantial abuse must be based on an examination of the totality of the circumstances.[493] The totality of the circumstances standard, however, has encouraged some judges to make essentially value-based decisions about the purposes of a given debtor's use of credit.[494]

Under a 1998 amendment to section 707(b), enacted in the Religious Liberty and Charitable Donation Protection Act of 1998,[495] one thing the court may not take into consideration is whether a debtor has made or continues to make "charitable contributions"[496] to a "qualified religious or charitable entity or organization."[497] In response to the fears of churches that debtors could be denied bankruptcy relief if they refused to cease tithing or making other contributions, Congress directed the courts to give no weight to such contributions made in the past in deciding section 707(b) motions, or to post-bankruptcy contributions, at least insofar as they "continue." Presumably because of fears that an amendment limited to religious contributions might be found unconstitutional, the new provisions apply to gifts to all charitable organizations qualified for tax deductible contributions under the Internal Revenue Code.[498]

If read too broadly, the substantial abuse test may also be subject to a constitutional challenge. One court has held that the limitation of section 707(b) to consumer debtors would probably violate the Equal Protection Clause unless substantial abuse is interpreted as a codification of the court's general powers to reject bankruptcy filings made in bad faith.[499] The court could see no reason to single out consumer debtors for a future income test, where other debtors were subject only to a bad faith test. Under the bad faith

---

490 *In re* Green, 934 F.2d 568 (4th Cir. 1991) (fact that income exceeds expenses insufficient to establish substantial abuse; court must analyze totality of circumstances); *In re* Harris, 279 B.R. 254 (B.A.P. 9th Cir. 2002) (debtor's ability to pay $4000.00 over thirty-six months, which would pay 3.5% of unsecured claims, did not cause chapter 7 case to be substantial abuse); *In re* Brady, 86 B.R. 616 (W.D. Mo. 1988) (fact that exempt property could fund a one-hundred percent chapter 13 plan not basis for dismissal for substantial abuse); *In re* O'Neill, 301 B.R. 898 (Bankr. D.N.M. 2003) (ability to fund a plan paying 36% to unsecured creditors not grounds for substantial abuse dismissal); *In re* McDonald, 213 B.R. 628 (Bankr. E.D.N.Y. 1997) (no substantial abuse even though debtors' schedules showed $400.00 monthly excess income because many expenses were omitted from schedules and debtors had made great effort to pay debts before filing case); *In re* Adams, 206 B.R. 456, *vacated pursuant to settlement on appeal*, 209 B.R. 874 (Bankr. M.D. Tenn. 1997) (no substantial abuse even though debtors could fund a ninety-two percent plan when debtors had not lived exorbitant lifestyle, were not dishonest, and had tried to make payment plans with creditors); *In re* Fortune, 130 B.R. 525 (Bankr. C.D. Ill. 1991) (ability to pay one-hundred percent of debts in chapter 13 plan, by itself is not substantial abuse); *In re* Keniston, 85 B.R. 202 (Bankr. D.N.H. 1988) (ability to repay debts from future income without more does not constitute substantial abuse); *In re* Deaton, 65 B.R. 663 (Bankr. S.D. Ohio 1986); *see also, e.g., In re* Price, 353 F.3d 1135 (9th Cir. 2004) (finding that debtor has ability to pay debts does not compel dismissal; court has discretion to dismiss); *In re* King, 308 B.R. 522 (Bankr. D. Kan. 2004) (no substantial abuse because $389.00 per month 401(k) contribution for forty-seven-year old debtor and $487.00 per month 401(k) loan repayment found to be reasonable); *In re* Latimer, 82 B.R. 354 (Bankr. E.D. Pa. 1988) (existence of possibly unnecessary expenses such as boarding school for children not sufficient to warrant dismissal for substantial abuse); *In re* Penna, 86 B.R. 171 (Bankr. E.D. Mo. 1988) (no substantial abuse where expenses exceed income, even though some expenses seem unusually high).

491 *See, e.g., In re* King, 308 B.R. 522 (Bankr. D. Kan. 2004) (not unreasonable for debtors to provide $400.00 per month for transportation to twenty-one-year old daughter while away at college); *In re* Marcoux, 301 B.R. 381 (Bankr. D. Conn. 2003) (providing food to stepchildren not an extravagance).

492 *E.g., In re* Kestell, 99 F.3d 146 (4th Cir. 1996) (substantial abuse found because debtor failed to disclose substantial assets and file bankruptcy solely to avoid paying a judgment owed to his former spouse); *In re* Wilson, 125 B.R. 742 (W.D. Mich. 1990) (substantial abuse found where debtor failed to list all her income).

493 *E.g., In re* Green, 934 F.2d 568 (4th Cir. 1991); *In re* Keniston, 85 B.R. 202 (Bankr. D.N.H. 1988); *see In re* Krohn, 886 F.2d 123 (6th Cir. 1989) (appropriate test is totality of circumstances, but ability to repay debts alone can justify finding substantial abuse).

494 *E.g., In re* Krohn, 886 F.2d 123 (6th Cir. 1989) (fact that debtors lived a lifestyle beyond their means is evidence of bad faith).

495 Pub. L. No. 105-183, 112 Stat. 517 (1998).

496 "Charitable contribution" is defined in 11 U.S.C. § 548(d)(3) as a contribution made by a natural person that consists of a financial instrument or cash.

497 "Qualified religious or charitable entity or organization" is defined in 11 U.S.C. § 548(d)(4) as an entity or organization described in section 170(c)(1) or (2) of the Internal Revenue Code.

498 "Qualified religious or charitable entity or organization" is defined in 11 U.S.C. § 548(d)(4) as an entity or organization described in section 170(c)(1) or (2) of the Internal Revenue Code.

499 *In re* Keniston, 85 B.R. 202 (Bankr. D.N.H. 1988). In considering the constitutional question, the court heard arguments by the U.S. attorney and a major creditor group defending the statute and by amicus counsel for the debtor. The decision is thorough and persuasive. *See also In re* Stewart, 215 B.R. 456 (B.A.P. 10th Cir. 1997) (section 707(b) was constitutional as narrowly construed by *Keniston* court), *aff'd*, 175 F.3d 796 (10th Cir. 1999).

interpretation, a consumer debtor's ability to fund a one-hundred percent chapter 13 plan would not by itself be sufficient for dismissal under section 707(b).[500] When there are no factors, other than ability to pay, casting doubt on a debtor's good faith, debtors' attorneys should consider raising equal protection arguments against application of a future income test.

It is safe to say that a dismissal under section 707(b) is without prejudice.[501] If the debtor's circumstances change, she is free to file again at any time.

13.10 Bankruptcy Appeals

13.10.1 Appeals from the Bankruptcy Court

The 1984 amendments to title 28 altered not only the jurisdictional scheme applicable to initial bankruptcy proceedings but also the avenues available for appeals. While these avenues may vary depending upon the judicial district or circuit where a proceeding is litigated, they generally closely resemble the appellate mechanisms which existed prior to 1979.

The usual forum for appeals from decisions of a bankruptcy court is the district court.[502] (While objections to proposed findings of fact and conclusions of law under 28 U.S.C. § 157(c)(1) are also decided by the district court, different rules apply to them.[503]) The provision in the 1978 Act which had allowed a direct appeal to the court of appeals if the parties agreed has been eliminated.[504]

However, the other innovation of the 1978 Act, the bankruptcy appellate panel, has been retained to a limited degree. An appeal that would otherwise go to the district court may be heard by an appellate panel of three bankruptcy judges[505] if all of the following conditions are met:

- The judicial council of the circuit has established a bankruptcy appellate panel;[506]
- The district judges for the district, by majority vote, authorize referral of appeals from that district to the appellate panel;[507] and
- All parties consent.[508]

Most courts have held that decisions of a bankruptcy appellate panel, like decisions of one district judge in a multi-judge district, are not binding on bankruptcy courts in the same circuit.[509]

The Bankruptcy Reform Act of 1994,[510] contained several amendments designed to encourage, but not require the use of bankruptcy appellate panels, referred to in that Act as a judicial circuit's "bankruptcy appellate panel service."[511] Under the amendments, each circuit was required to set up a bankruptcy appellate panel service ("BAPS") unless 1) there were insufficient judicial resources available (for example, not enough bankruptcy judges volunteer or perhaps because of the expense of a BAPS) *or* 2) establishment "would result in undue delay or increased cost to parties" in bankruptcy cases.[512] The legislation resulted in appellate panels being established in about half of the circuits.[513]

As the district judges in a district must still authorize referral of appeals to a BAPS, each district court can veto the use of appellate panels for appeals arising in its district, and some districts have done so. A majority of district judges in a circuit may seek to dissolve a BAPS after at least one year of implementation, or the circuit may reconsider on its own motion after three years. A BAPS judge may not hear an appeal from her own district.[514]

Under current 28 U.S.C. § 158(c), if a bankruptcy appellate panel may hear an appeal, the parties must consent to the panel hearing it. The appellant can elect to go to district court instead. However, this election must be made in a separate written statement filed at the time of filing the appeal.[515] The appellee may elect to go to district court up

---

500 *In re* Keniston, 85 B.R. 202 (Bankr. D.N.H. 1988); *see also* McDow v. Smith, 295 B.R. 69 (E.D. Va. 2003) (ability to pay, by itself, not bad faith warranting dismissal).

501 11 U.S.C. § 349(a).

502 28 U.S.C. § 158(a). The district court may not refer a bankruptcy appeal to a magistrate. Va. Beach Fed. Sav. & Loan Ass'n v. Wood, 901 F.2d 849 (10th Cir. 1990) (magistrates not permitted to enter final decisions in bankruptcy appeals); Minerex Erodel, Inc. v. Sina, Inc., 838 F.2d 781 (5th Cir. 1988); *In re* Elcona Homes Corp., 810 F.2d 136 (7th Cir. 1987). *But see* Hall v. Vance, 887 F.2d 1041 (10th Cir. 1989) (bankruptcy appeal may be referred to magistrate for advisory hearing as long as district court reserves to itself the power to make a final decision).

503 Fed. R. Bankr. P. 9033; *see* § 13.2.5.1, *supra*.

504 *In re* Carter, 759 F.2d 763 (9th Cir. 1985); *In re* Gen. Coffee Corp., 758 F.2d 1406 (11th Cir. 1985); *In re* Exclusive Indus., Inc., 751 F.2d 806 (5th Cir. 1985).

505 A single judge of the appellate panel may not determine the appeal alone. *In re* Caiati, 842 F.2d 1135 (9th Cir. 1988).

506 28 U.S.C. § 158(b)(1). Some but not all circuits have appellate panels. The First Circuit panel hears appeals from all districts in the circuit. The Sixth Circuit appellate panel hears appeals arising only in the Northern and Southern Districts of Ohio. The Eighth Circuit panel hears appeals arising anywhere in the circuit except the districts of North Dakota and South Dakota. The Ninth Circuit panel hears appeals from all districts. The Tenth Circuit's panel hears appeals arising throughout the circuit except for those arising in the District of Colorado.

507 28 U.S.C. § 158(b)(2).

508 28 U.S.C. § 158(b)(1).

509 *In re* Carrozzella & Richardson, 255 B.R. 267 (Bankr. D. Conn. 2000).

510 Pub. L. No. 103-394, 108 Stat. 4106 (1994).

511 28 U.S.C. § 158(b)(1).

512 28 U.S.C. § 158(b)(1).

513 See circuit by circuit discussion above.

514 28 U.S.C. § 158 (b)(5).

515 28 U.S.C. § 158(c)(1)(A); Fed. R. Bankr. P. 8001(e); Official Form 17, Appendix D.5, *infra*. For a sample election form, see

to thirty days after *service* of the notice of appeal.[516] If neither party affirmatively elects to go to district court, the parties are deemed to have consented to a bankruptcy appellate panel hearing the appeal.

An appeal from the bankruptcy court may be taken with respect to any final order. It may also be taken, either to the district court or if appropriate an appellate panel, from an interlocutory order, if leave of the district court or the appellate panel is granted.[517] However, it takes exceptional circumstances to justify an interlocutory appeal,[518] especially given the right to move for withdrawal of a proceeding to the district court prior to the bankruptcy court's decision.[519] It is clear that unlike the district court, the bankruptcy court does not have the power to certify an interlocutory order for immediate appeal.[520] And once an appeal is taken to district court, the district court may not function as a trial level bankruptcy court and presumably may not withdraw the reference.[521]

Thus far, the only court of appeals to rule on the matter has found the bankruptcy appellate panels to be constitutional. Because the decision of the appellate panel is reviewed de novo in any further appeal to the court of appeals, the Ninth Circuit discerned no constitutional infirmity in a panel deciding appeals initially as an adjunct to the court of appeals.[522]

13.10.2 Appeals from the District Court or Appellate Panel

Appeals from the district courts, whether in their trial or appellate capacities and from bankruptcy appellate panels in all matters decided by them, are heard in the courts of appeals.[523] Final decisions, judgments, orders and decrees may be appealed from the district court acting in its appellate capacity or from an appellate panel.[524] It is now clear

---

Form 105, Appx. G.10, *infra. See In re* Ioane, 227 B.R. 181 (B.A.P. 9th Cir. 1998) (statement of election filed after notice of appeal not timely even though notice of appeal was premature and was not deemed filed until date of judgment, which was after statement of election); *In re* Sullivan Jewelry, Inc., 218 B.R. 439 (B.A.P. 8th Cir. 1998) (statement in notice of appeal that appeal was to district court did not satisfy requirement of separate written statement); *In re* County of Orange, 183 B.R. 593 (B.A.P. 9th Cir. 1995); *see also In re* Brown, 273 B.R. 194 (B.A.P. 8th Cir. 2002) (appellate panel did not have jurisdiction over debtor's appeal when creditor had elected to have its closely interwoven appeal from same order heard by district court).

516 28 U.S.C. § 158(c)(1)(B); *see In re* Snell, 237 B.R. 636 (B.A.P. 6th Cir. 1999) (cross-appellants had to file statement with their cross-appeal, so statement filed one day thereafter was not effective, nor was statement in notice of cross-appeal, because it was not a separate statement); *In re* King, 235 B.R. 658 (B.A.P. 10th Cir. 1999) (time runs from date of service of notice of appeal by the court); *In re* Mackey, 232 B.R. 784 (B.A.P. 9th Cir. 1999) (thirty-day period extended by three days under Fed. R. Bankr. P. 9006(e) when notice of appeal served by mail).

517 No certification by the bankruptcy court is required. *In re* Bertoli, 812 F.2d 136 (3d Cir. 1987).

518 *In re* Wood & Locker, Inc., 868 F.2d 139 (5th Cir. 1989); *In re* Nat'l Shoes, 20 B.R. 672 (B.A.P. 1st Cir. 1982); *In re* Hooker Investments, Inc., 122 B.R. 659 (S.D.N.Y. 1991) (interlocutory appeal permitted from order setting bar date for proofs of claim); *see also In re* Chateaugay Corp., 876 F.2d 8 (2d Cir. 1989) (court of appeals has jurisdiction to review a district court decision that a particular order is interlocutory; presumably a reversal would mandate remand to district court for full consideration of the appeal); *In re* Johns-Manville Corp., 42 B.R. 651 (S.D.N.Y. 1984).

519 28 U.S.C. § 157(d).

520 Commerce Bank v. Mountain View Vill., Inc., 5 F.3d 34 (3d Cir. 1993).

521 *In re* Powelson, 878 F.2d 976 (7th Cir. 1989) (writ of mandamus issued directing district court to determine appeal of confirmation order rather than withdraw reference and substitute alternative non-appealable "interim" plan); *see* Dallas v. S.A.G., Inc., 836 F.2d 1307 (11th Cir. 1988) (district court may not open default judgment on appeal when the issue had not been raised

---

before the bankruptcy court); *In re* Davis, 169 B.R. 285 (E.D.N.Y. 1994) (district court deciding appeal could not consider new evidence not presented in bankruptcy court).

522 *In re* Burley, 738 F.2d 981 (9th Cir. 1984); *see also In re* Salter, 279 B.R. 278 (B.A.P. 9th Cir. 2002) (bankruptcy appellate panel was court "established by Act of Congress" and had authority under All Writs Act to issue writ of mandamus). *But see In re* Dartmouth Hous. Nursing Home, Inc., 30 B.R. 56 (B.A.P. 1st Cir. 1983), *aff'd on other grounds*, 726 F.2d 26 (1st Cir. 1984).

523 28 U.S.C. § 158(d). Exceptions are a district court's review of a bankruptcy court order either granting or denying a motion to dismiss or suspend proceedings, 11 U.S.C. § 305(a),(c), and certain decisions to abstain, 28 U.S.C. § 1334(d), or remand, 28 U.S.C. § 1441(e)(5), 1452(b), which may not be reviewed by a court of appeals. *See In re* Axona Int'l Credit & Commerce Ltd., 924 F.2d 31 (2d Cir. 1991).

524 28 U.S.C. § 158(d); *see In re* Kujawa, 323 F.3d 628 (8th Cir. 2003) (bankruptcy appellate panel decision dismissing appeal because order appealed was not a final order was itself a final order that could be appealed); *In re* Johns-Manville Corp., 920 F.2d 121 (2d Cir. 1990) (court of appeals determines first whether bankruptcy court order final and, second, whether district court's disposition rendered matter non-appealable); *In re* Frederick Petroleum Corp., 912 F.2d 850 (6th Cir. 1990) (court of appeals had no jurisdiction unless district court certified that its partial disposition was final under Rule 54(b)). However, in some cases the collateral order doctrine may be invoked to allow appeals of non-final orders. To come within the collateral order doctrine a district court order must conclusively determine a disputed question, resolving an important issue that is completely severed from the merits of the action and effectively unreviewable on appeal from final judgment. *See In re* Looney, 823 F.2d 788 (4th Cir. 1987) (order continuing automatic stay entered without hearing). Several courts of appeal have held that constitutional issues related to the Bankruptcy Code do not present reviewable collateral orders when decided by the district court. *In re* Koerner, 800 F.2d 1358 (5th Cir. 1986); *In re* Moens, 800 F.2d 173 (7th Cir. 1986); *In re* Benny, 791 F.2d 712 (9th Cir. 1986). *But see In re* Parklane/Atlanta Joint Venture, 927 F.2d 532 (11th Cir. 1991) (appeal of interlocutory order withdrawing reference allowed under collateral order doctrine where constitutional issues were asserted as grounds for order).

that district court decisions on appeals of interlocutory bankruptcy orders are also appealable to the court of appeals.[525]

Presumably, the normal federal appellate jurisdictional statutes[526] and rules apply to appeals from the district court when it acts as a trial court or decides cases in which it has received recommended findings from the bankruptcy court.[527] Similarly, the appeals court retains its authority to issue *mandamus* and to exercise its supervisory authority over lower courts in bankruptcy matters originating either in bankruptcy or district court.[528] In at least one case, this supervisory authority was exercised to treat an appeal from

an order found to be interlocutory as a request for a writ of *mandamus* and thereby to hear the appeal on its merits.[529]

13.10.3 What Is a Final Order?

No issue has been more frequently litigated in bankruptcy appeals than the initial jurisdictional issue of whether a final order exists from which an appeal may be taken to the court of appeals, or to a district court or appellate panel without leave of court. There is no statutory provision explaining what is or is not a final order, judgment, or decree, but a wealth of case law does exist. A final order is "one which ends the litigation . . . and leaves nothing for the court to do but execute the judgment."[530]

Generally, the courts of appeal agree that orders granting or denying injunctions, including orders granting or denying relief from the automatic stay, and orders conferring rights in specific property are appealable.[531] Similarly, a district court order reversing a final order of the bankruptcy court is appealable, unless further factual development is necessary.[532] The circuit courts have also considered as final

---

525   28 U.S.C. § 1292(b); Conn. Nat'l Bank v. Germain, 503 U.S. 249, 112 S. Ct. 1146, 117 L. Ed. 2d 391 (1992). However, the district court must clearly indicate its intent to certify the decision for appeal. Askanase v. Livingwell, Inc., 981 F.2d 807 (2d Cir. 1993) (district court's characterization of order as "appealable" without any reference to Fed. R. Civ. P. 54(b) was not sufficient). *But see In re* Watman, 304 B.R. 553 (B.A.P. 1st Cir. 2004) (section 1292(b) does not apply to decisions of a bankruptcy appellate panel reviewing a bankruptcy court decision).

526   28 U.S.C. §§ 1291, 1292.

527   *See* Fed. R. App. P. 6(a); Metro Transp. Co. v. N. Star Reinsurance Co., 912 F.2d 672 (3d Cir. 1990) (where an issue was decided solely by the district court and not as a result of appeal from bankruptcy court, court of appeals would review based on general appellate jurisdictional statutes); *In re* Bishop, Baldwin, Rewald, Dillingham & Wong, 856 F.2d 78 (9th Cir. 1988); *In re* Haw. Corp., 796 F.2d 1139 (9th Cir. 1986); *In re* Manoa Fin. Co., 781 F.2d 1370 (9th Cir. 1986); *In re* Amatex Corp., 755 F.2d 1034 (3d Cir. 1985); *see also In re* Topco, 894 F.2d 727 (5th Cir. 1990) (where district court sits as trial court on bankruptcy matter, thirty-day time limit on appeals governs an appeal to court of appeals, under both 28 U.S.C. § 158(d) and § 1291; Browning v. Navarro, 887 F.2d 553 (5th Cir. 1989) (compliance with time limits in appellate rules required on appeal from interlocutory order of district court sitting as bankruptcy court); *In re* Apex Oil Co., 884 F.2d 343 (8th Cir. 1989) (district court has no jurisdiction over appeal from bankruptcy court order signed by a district judge); *In re* Barrier, 776 F.2d 1298 (5th Cir. 1985) (mandamus jurisdiction); *In re* Orbitec Corp., 520 F.2d 358 (2d Cir. 1975) (party seeking extension of time to file appeal under Fed. R. App. P. 4(a)(5) should file a protective appeal within extension period sought, as neither lower court nor appellate court has power under that rule to permit filing of appeal more than thirty days after original deadline).

528   *See In re* Furlong, 885 F.2d 815 (11th Cir. 1989) (exceptional circumstances justify appeals court in exercising supervisory authority to set aside bankruptcy court judgment where non-participating parties may not have received proper notice); *In re* Powelson, 878 F.2d 976 (7th Cir. 1989) (writ of *mandamus* issued directing district court to determine bankruptcy appeal rather than withdraw reference); *see also In re* Pruitt, 910 F.2d 1160 (3d Cir. 1990) (order withdrawing reference non-appealable, but *mandamus* would issue where district court improperly withdrew reference after bankruptcy court had already dismissed case); *In re* Durability, Inc., 893 F.2d 264 (10th Cir. 1990) (court may retain jurisdiction over appeal of non-final order to allow parties an opportunity to obtain resolution of the remaining issues in bankruptcy court and thus render order final).

529   *In re* Hooker Inv., Inc., 937 F.2d 833 (2d Cir. 1991) (dismissing appeal and denying implied request for *mandamus*).

530   Catlin v. United States, 324 U.S. 229, 65 S. Ct. 631, 89 L. Ed. 911 (1945); *In re* Boca Arena, 184 F.3d 1285 (11th Cir. 1999) (order that does not dispose of all claims of all parties not a final order); *In re* Cont'l Airlines, Inc., 932 F.2d 282 (3d Cir. 1991) (various factors applicable to determination of whether a bankruptcy order is final include impact of issue on assets of bankruptcy estate, whether fact-finding is complete, preclusive effect of decision on merits and judicial economy).

531   *See, e.g.,* FRG, Inc. v. Manley, 919 F.2d 850 (3d Cir. 1990) (order equivalent to denial of motion for relief from stay); *In re* Sonnax Indus., Inc., 907 F.2d 1280 (2d Cir. 1990) (denial of motion for relief from stay); *In re* Apex Oil Co., 884 F.2d 343 (8th Cir. 1989) (denial of motion to lift stay); *In re* W. Electronics, Inc., 852 F.2d 79 (3d Cir. 1988) (denial of motion to lift stay); *In re* La. World Exposition, Inc., 832 F.2d 1391 (5th Cir. 1987) (denial of injunction); Turshen v. Chapman, 823 F.2d 836 (4th Cir. 1987); *In re* Moody, 817 F.2d 365 (5th Cir. 1987) (turnover order); *In re* Sun Valley Foods Co., 801 F.2d 186 (6th Cir. 1986); *In re* Boomgarden, 780 F.2d 657 (7th Cir. 1985); *In re* Kemble, 776 F.2d 802 (9th Cir. 1985); *In re* Feit & Drexler, 760 F.2d 406 (2d Cir. 1985); *In re* Leimer, 724 F.2d 744 (8th Cir. 1984); *In re* Comer, 716 F.2d 168 (3d Cir. 1983); *In re* Maiorino, 691 F.2d 89 (2d Cir. 1982); *see also In re* Fugazy Express, 982 F.2d 769 (2d Cir. 1992) (parties could not agree to act in derogation of the stay and then argue that bankruptcy court order disapproving those actions was a denial of relief from the stay); *In re* Lomas Fin. Corp., 932 F.2d 147 (2d Cir. 1991) (where ambiguity exists on request for injunctive relief, appellate court can direct parties to seek supplemental statement before deciding whether order is final). *But see In re* Henriquez, 261 B.R. 67 (B.A.P. 1st Cir. 2001) (order denying relief from stay not always a final order); *cf. In re* Regency Wood Apartments, Ltd., 686 F.2d 899 (11th Cir. 1982) (district court's reversal of order denying relief from automatic stay not appealable where district court simply directed further proceedings).

532   *In re* Gardner, 810 F.2d 87 (6th Cir. 1987); *In re* Stanton, 766 F.2d 1283 (9th Cir. 1985); *In re* Marin Motor Oil, Inc., 689 F.2d

orders an order to produce allegedly privileged materials,[533] a district court's reversal of an order denying a right to intervene in a proceeding[534] or an order dismissing a dischargeability proceeding,[535] an order confirming a debtor's plan,[536] an order for relief in an involuntary case,[537] an order dismissing an involuntary bankruptcy petition,[538] an order granting priority status,[539] an order avoiding a transfer,[540] an order granting or dismissing a complaint seeking a determination as to ownership of property,[541] an order disallowing an exemption,[542] an order fixing the amount of a creditor's claims,[543] an order granting a default judgment against debtor as a discovery sanction on a complaint to deny discharge,[544] and an order of a district court erroneously concluding that it has no jurisdiction to review a final order of a bankruptcy court.[545] Other orders which have been held final include an order fixing venue for product liability cases,[546] an order confirming a judicial sale of property of the estate,[547] an order regarding obligations upon rejection of a lease,[548] an order holding that a debtor could not designate how payments to the Internal Revenue Service should be credited,[549] an order determining that a lease had not been properly terminated,[550] a decision to abstain from hearing personal injury claims against the debtor,[551] and an order denying a motion to dismiss for bad faith.[552]

There is an apparent split in authority over whether the refusal to confirm a plan, where the case is not dismissed, is appealable.[553] Similar issues would be raised with respect to denial of a motion to modify a plan.[554] An order denying a trustee's motion to convert a case from chapter 13 to chapter 7 has been held non-appealable,[555] as has a district court decision reversing a summary judgment order in favor of a creditor defendant in a preference action,[556] an order denying summary judgment,[557] an order holding a landlord to be adequately protected,[558] orders remanding cases for further consideration, unless the remand is for the bankruptcy court to perform purely ministerial tasks,[559] an order withdrawing

---

445 (3d Cir. 1982); *In re* Cross, 666 F.2d 873 (5th Cir. 1982).

533 *In re* Int'l Horizons, Inc., 689 F.2d 996 (11th Cir. 1982).

534 *In re* Benny, 791 F.2d 712 (9th Cir. 1986); *In re* Marin Motor Oil, Inc., 689 F.2d 445 (3d Cir. 1982).

535 *In re* Dominguez, 51 F.3d 1502 (9th Cir. 1995).

536 *See In re* Maiorino, 691 F.2d 89 (2d Cir. 1982).

537 *In re* McGinnis, 296 F.3d 730 (8th Cir. 2002); *In re* Mason, 709 F.2d 1313 (9th Cir. 1983).

538 *In re* Sweet Transfer & Storage, Inc., 896 F.2d 1189 (9th Cir. 1990).

539 *In re* Olson, 730 F.2d 1109 (8th Cir. 1984); *In re* Saco Local Dev. Corp., 711 F.2d 441 (1st Cir. 1983).

540 *In re* Allen, 816 F.2d 325 (7th Cir. 1987); *In re* Sandy Ridge Oil Co., 807 F.2d 1332 (7th Cir. 1987).

541 Commerce Bank v. Mountain View Vill., Inc., 5 F.3d 34 (3d Cir. 1993) (order determining that rents were not property of the estate); *In re* Ellsworth, 722 F.2d 1448 (9th Cir. 1984); *In re* Bestmann, 720 F.2d 484 (8th Cir. 1983). *But see In re* Morrell, 880 F.2d 855 (5th Cir. 1989) (order determining ownership of property not final when related damage claim remains unresolved).

542 *In re* England, 975 F.2d 1168 (10th Cir. 1992); *In re* Slimick, 928 F.2d 304 (9th Cir. 1990); *In re* Barker, 768 F.2d 191 (7th Cir. 1985); *In re* White, 727 F.2d 884 (9th Cir. 1984); *In re* Woods, 288 B.R. 220 (B.A.P. 8th Cir. 2003). *But see In re* Wisz, 778 F.2d 762 (11th Cir. 1985).

543 *In re* Stoecker, 5 F.3d 1022 (7th Cir. 1993) (order establishing that creditor had secured claim in certain amount); *In re* Moody, 849 F.2d 902 (5th Cir. 1988); *In re* Colley, 814 F.2d 1008 (5th Cir. 1987); *In re* Morse Elec. Co., 805 F.2d 262 (7th Cir. 1986); *see also In re* Unroe, 937 F.2d 346 (7th Cir. 1991) (order denying objection to claim is final even though debtor's contempt proceeding against same creditor remained pending); Walsh Trucking v. Ins. Co. of N. Am., 838 F.2d 698 (3d Cir. 1988) (order expunging creditor's claim is final order).

544 *In re* Golant, 239 F.3d 931 (7th Cir. 2001).

545 *In re* Bestmann, 720 F.2d 484 (8th Cir. 1983).

546 A.H. Robins Co. v. Piccinin, 788 F.2d 994 (4th Cir. 1986).

547 *In re* Met-L-Wood Corp., 861 F.2d 1012 (7th Cir. 1988); *see also In re* Fin. News Network, Inc., 931 F.2d 217 (2d Cir. 1991) (district court's order remanding to bankruptcy court for consideration of competing disqualified bid is not a final order).

548 *In re* Vause, 886 F.2d 794 (6th Cir. 1989) (court may hear appeal by landlord regarding future damages due for rejection of lease even though debtor's pre-petition obligation on lease was not yet fixed); Saravia v. 1736 18th St., N.W. Ltd. P'ship, 844 F.2d 823 (D.C. Cir. 1988) (order relieved debtor of obligation to comply with local housing code).

549 *In re* Technical Knockout Graphics, Inc., 833 F.2d 797 (9th Cir. 1987).

550 *In re* Market Square Inn, Inc., 978 F.2d 116 (3d Cir. 1992).

551 *In re* Pan Am. Corp., 950 F.2d 839 (2d Cir. 1991).

552 Brown v. First Jersey Nat'l Bank, 916 F.2d 120 (3d Cir. 1990). *But see In re* Rega Properties, Ltd., 894 F.2d 1136 (9th Cir. 1990) (order denying motion to dismiss petition as filed in bad faith was not final order). But see also cases cited below finding orders denying motions to dismiss non-appealable.

553 *Compare* Lewis v. Farmers Home Admin., 992 F.2d 767 (8th Cir. 1993) (order denying confirmation of chapter 13 plan and setting forth elements of acceptable plan was not final); *In re* Simons, 908 F.2d 643 (10th Cir. 1990) (denial of confirmation without dismissal of underlying case was not final and appealable); Travelers v. KCC-Leawood Corporate Manor I, 908 F.2d 343 (8th Cir. 1990) (district court order finding that bankruptcy court had implicitly denied confirmation and remanding case to bankruptcy court was not final appealable order); *In re* Maiorino, 691 F.2d 89 (2d Cir. 1982) (refusal to confirm is interlocutory order) *with In re* Foster, 670 F.2d 478 (5th Cir. 1982) (appeal of refusal to confirm plan heard by court of appeals).

554 *See In re* Vincent, 301 B.R. 734 (B.A.P. 8th Cir. 2003) (order denying modification motion not final order).

555 *In re* Kutner, 656 F.2d 1107, 1112 (5th Cir. 1981); *In re* Hayes Bankruptcy, 220 B.R. 57 (N.D. Iowa 1998).

556 *In re* Emerald Oil Co., 694 F.2d 88 (5th Cir. 1982).

557 City of New York v. Exxon Corp., 932 F.2d 1020 (2d Cir. 1991) (order granting partial summary judgment not appealable); *In re* Durability, Inc., 893 F.2d 264 (10th Cir. 1990) (order granting only partial summary judgment); *In re* Smith, 735 F.2d 459 (11th Cir. 1984).

558 *In re* Alchar Hardware, 730 F.2d 1386 (11th Cir. 1984).

559 *In re* St. Charles Preservation Investors, Ltd., 916 F.2d 727 (D.C. Cir. 1990) (order remanding case to bankruptcy court to determine rights and priorities of creditors was not final and appealable); Capital Credit Plan of Tenn., Inc. v. Shaffer, 912 F.2d 749

a case to district court and changing venue,[560] an order refusing to withdraw the reference,[561] an order setting a trial date,[562] an order denying approval of a settlement agreement,[563] an order dismissing one count of a counterclaim,[564] an order denying a motion to dismiss,[565] and an order denying a stay of state court proceedings to a bankruptcy debtor's codefendant.[566] Other orders which have been held non-final include interlocutory sanctions orders,[567] a refusal to permit rejection of a labor contract,[568] an order granting a jury trial in the bankruptcy court,[569] an order denying a jury trial,[570] an order denying motions to compel trustee performance,[571] an order dismissing a claim for punitive damages,[572] an order permitting a prejudgment attachment and the equivalent of a *lis pendens*,[573] an order rejecting an assertion of sovereign immunity,[574] an order granting a stay pending appeal,[575] an order granting an extension of time to file a proof of claim,[576] a discovery order,[577] and an order extending time for filing complaints objecting to chapter 7 discharge.[578]

(4th Cir. 1990) (district court order affirming bankruptcy court order confirming plan and remanding two issues to bankruptcy court for resolution was not final decision); *In re* Bucyrus Grain Co.*, 905 F.2d 1362 (10th Cir. 1990) (district court's reversal of bankruptcy court's grant of relief from stay and remand for determination of amount of creditor's claim required significant further proceedings and was not final); *In re* M.S.V., Inc., 892 F.2d 5 (1st Cir. 1989); *In re* Schneider, 873 F.2d 1155 (8th Cir. 1989) (remand for bankruptcy court to determine proper interest rate not appealable); *In re* Dixie Broad., Inc., 871 F.2d 1023 (11th Cir. 1989) (remand for bankruptcy court to determine whether bankruptcy was brought in bad faith not appealable final order); *In re* Gould & Eberhart Gear Mach. Corp., 852 F.2d 26 (1st Cir. 1988); *In re* Miscott Corp., 848 F.2d 1190 (11th Cir. 1988) (remand for further factual development in regard to award of attorney fees); Bowers v. Conn. Nat'l Bank, 847 F.2d 1019 (2d Cir. 1988); *In re* Briglevich, 847 F.2d 759 (11th Cir. 1988); *In re* Vekco, 792 F.2d 744 (8th Cir. 1986) (but order requiring remand could be final order if only ministerial tasks remain to be performed in the bankruptcy case); *In re* County Mgmt., Inc., 788 F.2d 311 (5th Cir. 1986); *In re* Commercial Contractors, Inc., 771 F.2d 1373 (10th Cir. 1985); *In re* Stanton, 766 F.2d 1283 (9th Cir. 1985); *In re* Fox, 762 F.2d 54 (7th Cir. 1985); *In re* Goldblatt Bros., Inc., 758 F.2d 1248 (7th Cir. 1985); *In re* Riggsby, 745 F.2d 1153 (7th Cir. 1984); *In re* Martinez, 721 F.2d 262 (9th Cir. 1983); *In re* Bassak, 705 F.2d 234 (7th Cir. 1983); *In re* Hansen, 702 F.2d 728 (8th Cir. 1983) (order remanding for de novo trial); *In re* Glover, 697 F.2d 907 (10th Cir. 1983) (order remanding for further consideration of priority issue); *In re* Compton Corp., 889 F.2d 1104 (Temp. Emer. Ct. App. 1989) (order reversing judgment subordinating creditor's claim not final, because bankruptcy court had to determine amount of claim on remand); *see also In re* Harrington, 992 F.2d 3 (1st Cir. 1993) (order remanding case to permit bankruptcy court to docket notice of appeal); *In re* Grey, 902 F.2d 1479 (10th Cir. 1990) (court of appeals had jurisdiction to consider issues raised by debtor even though debtor did not appeal as to those issues until after district court's post-remand order); *In re* Brown, 803 F.2d 120 (3d Cir. 1986) (district court order finding creditor in violation of the automatic stay, but remanding for determination of damages held non-final). *But see In re* Dominguez, 51 F.3d 1502 (9th Cir. 1995) (permitting appeal of order reversing dismissal of a dischargeability proceeding).

560   *In re* Pruitt, 910 F.2d 1160 (3d Cir. 1990) (order withdrawing reference non-appealable, but *mandamus* would issue where district court improperly withdrew reference after bankruptcy court had already dismissed case); *In re* Dalton, 733 F.2d 710 (10th Cir. 1984); *see also In re* U.S. Lines, 216 F.3d 228 (2d Cir. 2000) (determination concerning venue for claims against debtor not final order); *In re* King Mem'l Hosp., 767 F.2d 1508 (11th Cir. 1985) (order withdrawing reference of adversary proceeding). *But see In re* Parklane/Atlanta Joint Venture, 927 F.2d 532 (11th Cir. 1991) (order withdrawing reference in particular case was appealable under collateral order exception to final judgment rule).

561   *In re* The Kissel Co., 105 F.3d 1324 (9th Cir. 1997); Allegheny Int'l v. Allegheny Ludlum Steel Corp., 920 F.2d 1127 (3d Cir. 1990); *In re* Lieb, 915 F.2d 180 (5th Cir. 1990); *In re* Mem'l Estates, 837 F.2d 762 (7th Cir. 1988); *In re* Chateaugay Corp., 826 F.2d 1177 (3d Cir. 1987); *see* § 13.10.2, *supra*.

562   Gold v. Johns-Manville, 723 F.2d 1068 (3d Cir. 1983).

563   *In re* Tidewater Group, Inc., 734 F.2d 794 (11th Cir. 1984).

564   *In re* King City Transit Mix, Inc., 738 F.2d 1065 (9th Cir. 1984); *see also In re* White Beaty View, Inc., 841 F.2d 524 (3d Cir. 1988) (summary judgment against one defendant not a final order where claims against other defendant, counterclaims and crossclaim remain to be decided).

565   *In re* Vlasek, 325 F.3d 955 (7th Cir. 2003); *In re* Allen, 896 F.2d 416 (9th Cir. 1990) (denial of motion to dismiss involuntary case); *In re* Phillips, 844 F.2d 230 (5th Cir. 1988); *In re* Greene County Hosp., 835 F.2d 589 (5th Cir. 1988); *In re* Empresas Noroeste Inc., 806 F.2d 315 (1st Cir. 1986); *In re* Benny, 791 F.2d 712 (9th Cir. 1986); John E. Burns Drilling v. Cent. Bank of Denver, 739 F.2d 1489 (10th Cir. 1984); *see also In re* Bowman, 821 F.2d 245 (5th Cir. 1987) (order reversing dismissal of case); *In re* Andy Frain Services, Inc., 798 F.2d 1113 (7th Cir. 1986) (order refusing to dismiss a chapter 11 case held non-appealable); *In re* 405 N. Bedford Dr. Corp., 778 F.2d 1374 (9th Cir. 1985).

566   Evilsizor v. Eagle-Picher Indus., Inc., 725 F.2d 97 (10th Cir. 1984); Lynch v. Johns-Manville Sales Corp., 701 F.2d 43, 44 (6th Cir. 1983); *see also In re* Hester, 899 F.2d 361 (5th Cir. 1990) (district court order denying stay pending appeal of bankruptcy court order was not final).

567   *In re* Watson, 884 F.2d 879 (5th Cir. 1989) (sanctions order is interlocutory pending final judgment); *In re* Jeanette Corp., 832 F.2d 43 (3d Cir. 1987); *see also In re* Behrens, 900 F.2d 97 (7th Cir. 1990) (order finding violation of discharge injunction not final where bankruptcy court never set amount of damages or fees for which it found creditor liable).

568   *In re* Landmark Hotel & Casino, 872 F.2d 857 (9th Cir. 1989).

569   *In re* Bowers-Siemon Chemicals Co., 123 B.R. 821 (N.D. Ill. 1991).

570   *In re* Popkin & Stern, 105 F.3d 1248 (8th Cir. 1997).

571   Algeran Inc. v. Advance Ross Corp., 759 F.2d 1421 (9th Cir. 1985).

572   *In re* Russell, 957 F.2d 534 (8th Cir. 1992).

573   *In re* Unanue Casal, 998 F.2d 28 (1st Cir. 1993).

574   Pullman Constr. Indus., Inc. v. United States, 23 F.3d 1166 (7th Cir. 1994).

575   *In re* Trans World Airlines, 18 F.3d 208 (3d Cir. 1994).

576   *In re* New Life Health Ctr. Co., 102 F.3d 428 (9th Cir. 1996).

577   *In re* Kujawa, 323 F.3d 628 (8th Cir. 2003).

578   *In re* Aucoin, 35 F.3d 167 (5th Cir. 1994); *In re* Gaines, 932 F.2d 729 (8th Cir. 1991).

13.10.4 Procedure on Appeals

Procedure on appeals from the district court and from the appellate panels is governed by the Federal Rules of Appellate Procedure.[579] For example, an appeal to a court of appeals may be dismissed as to parties who are not named in the notice of appeal.[580] The appellate rules incorporate Federal Rule of Bankruptcy Procedure 8015, however, which applies to motions for rehearing of district court or appellate panel decisions. Such motions must be timely filed pursuant to Federal Rule of Bankruptcy Procedure 9006(a).[581]

The procedure on appeals from the bankruptcy court is governed primarily by the Federal Rules of Bankruptcy Procedure. The statute specifically states that appeals must be taken in the ten-day time period provided by Federal Rule of Bankruptcy Procedure 8002.[582] This ten-day deadline is jurisdictional[583] and cannot be waived, though it may be extended by the bankruptcy court for up to twenty days.[584] If a party files a motion under Federal Rule of Bankruptcy Procedure 9023 or 9024 within ten days after entry of the judgment, the appeal period is ten days from the disposition of that motion.[585] Because the ten-day period includes intervening holidays and weekends, a decision on whether to appeal must be made relatively quickly.[586] A cross-appeal by any other party must be filed within ten days of when a notice of appeal is filed.[587]

Within ten days after filing the notice of appeal, the appellant must file with the clerk of the bankruptcy court, and serve on the appellee, a designation of items to be included in the record on appeal and a statement of issues to be presented.[588] If these materials are not timely filed, the appeal may be dismissed.[589] Within ten days after the appellant's statement is served, the appellee may file and serve a designation of additional items to be included in the record and a counterstatement of issues.[590] The party designating any item to be included in the record must provide the clerk with a copy of that item; otherwise the clerk prepares a copy at that party's expense.[591]

Other Bankruptcy Rules governing appeals[592] pertain to other aspects of the process, including the deadlines for filing briefs, set by Federal Rule of Bankruptcy Procedure 8009(a), and other matters.[593] The deadline for the appel-

---

579 Fed. R. App. P. 6 was amended effective December 1, 1989. The rule as amended controls appeals from final decisions of both district courts and bankruptcy appellate panels. Also amended to encompass bankruptcy appeals were Fed. R. App. P. 1 and 2. A new Form 5 was added for bankruptcy appeals. *See In re* Worcester, 811 F.2d 1224 (9th Cir. 1987).

580 Fed. R. App. P. 3(c); *In re* Unioil, 948 F.2d 678 (10th Cir. 1991); Barnett v. Stern, 909 F.2d 973 (7th Cir. 1990) (failure to name all parties in notice of appeal, even if included in caption, violates Fed. R. App. P. 3(c) and deprives appellate court of jurisdiction over those parties not named).

581 *In re* Eichelberger, 943 F.2d 536 (5th Cir. 1991); *see* Fed. R. App. P. 6(b)(2)(i).

582 28 U.S.C. § 158(c)(2); *see In re* Burns, 322 F.3d 421 (6th Cir. 2003) (failure to file timely notice of appeal of order cannot be remedied by amending notice of appeal of another order); *In re* Arrowhead Estates Dev. Co., 42 F.3d 1306 (9th Cir. 1994) (notice of appeal filed after the bankruptcy court's oral announcement of decision but before its entry is effective).

583 *In re* Mouradnick, 13 F.3d 326 (9th Cir. 1994) (untimely appeal dismissed for lack of jurisdiction); *In re* Souza, 795 F.2d 855 (9th Cir. 1986) (ten day limit to be strictly construed); *In re* Abdallah, 778 F.2d 75 (1st Cir. 1985); *In re* Universal Minerals, 755 F.2d 309 (3d Cir. 1985); *see In re* LBL Sports Ctr., Inc, 684 F.2d 410 (6th Cir. 1982); *In re* Robinson, 640 F.2d 737 (5th Cir. 1981); *In re* Ramsey, 612 F.2d 1220 (9th Cir. 1980). As with non-bankruptcy appeals, the time for appeal begins to run from the date the order is entered on the docket. *See* Reid v. White Motor Corp., 886 F.2d 1462 (6th Cir. 1989) (where order is entered on wrong docket, time for appeal does not begin to run until the mistake is corrected).

584 Fed. R. Bankr. P. 8002(c); *see* Moore v. Hogan, 851 F.2d 1125 (8th Cir. 1988) (request for extension on 21st day after time for appeal had run is untimely); *In re* Bradshaw, 283 B.R. 814 (B.A.P. 1st Cir. 2002) (motion for extension faxed to clerk's office after business hours was untimely); *In re* Betacom of Phoenix, Inc., 250 B.R. 376 (B.A.P. 9th Cir. 2000) (party seeking extension of time need not prove "special circumstances"). However, if the appeal is filed by a prisoner it is deemed filed when it is deposited with prison authorities, addressed to clerk of court with postage paid. *In re* Flanagan, 999 F.2d 753 (3d Cir. 1993).

585 Fed. R. Bankr. P. 8002(b); *In re* Watson, 41 F.3d 493 (9th Cir. 1994). Subsequent motions for reconsideration, though served within ten days of the order denying the initial motion for reconsideration but more than ten days after the original judgment, do not toll the appeal time on the original judgment. *See In re* Columba, 257 B.R. 368 (B.A.P. 1st Cir. 2001).

586 *See* Fed. R. Bankr. P. 9006(a).

587 Fed. R. Bankr. P. 8002(a).

588 Fed. R. Bankr. P. 8006.

589 *In re* CPDC, Inc. 221 F.3d 693 (5th Cir. 2000) (untimely filing of statement of issues and incomplete designation of record did not warrant dismissal of appeal when there was no evidence of prejudice to any party); *In re* M.A. Baheth Constr. Co., 118 F.3d 1082 (5th Cir. 1997); *In re* Bulic, 997 F.2d 299 (7th Cir. 1993) (appeal was properly dismissed when debtors failed to file statement of issues or designation of record within ten days as required by rules and bankruptcy was a bad faith delaying tactic); *In re* Serra Builders, 970 F.2d 1309 (4th Cir. 1992) (appeal could be dismissed when debtor filed designation of the record for appeal fifteen days late); *In re* Fitzsimmons, 920 F.2d 1468 (9th Cir. 1990) (appeal dismissed due to appellant's bad faith conduct in failing to perfect appeal by delaying in designation and preparation of record); *In re* Champion, 895 F.2d 490 (8th Cir. 1990) (it was not abuse of discretion to dismiss appeal where appellant failed to file a designation of items to be included in record and issues to be presented on appeal required by Bankruptcy Rule 8006). *But see In re* SPR Corp., 45 F.3d 70 (4th Cir. 1995) (court should consider issues of bad faith or negligence, explanation for delay, prejudice to other parties, impact of sanction, and other alternative sanctions before dismissing appeal for untimely filing of statement of issues).

590 Fed. R. Bankr. P. 8006.

591 Fed. R. Bankr. P. 8006.

592 Fed. R. Bankr. P. 8001–8019.

593 *In re* Morrissey, 349 F.3d 1187 (9th Cir. 2003) (affirmance due to appellant's egregious violations of rules not an abuse of discretion); Telesphere Communications v. 900 Unlimited, Inc.,

lant's brief is fifteen days after the appeal is docketed in the district court. The appellee's brief, which should also include argument pertinent to any cross-appeal, is due fifteen days after service of the appellant's brief. The appellant may file a reply brief within ten days after the appellee's brief and, if there is a cross appeal, the appellee may file a reply brief with respect to the cross appeal within ten days after the appellant's reply brief is served. However, the language in 28 U.S.C. § 158(c) stating that appeals from bankruptcy courts are to be "taken in the same manner as appeals in civil proceedings generally taken to the courts of appeals from the district courts" could be interpreted otherwise.

Because an appeal does not operate as a stay of the bankruptcy court order that is being appealed, debtor's counsel should carefully consider the need for a motion for a stay at the time of any appeal, especially if there is any potential that the debtor's property may be sold; there is a strong mootness doctrine in bankruptcy appeals.[594] A motion for a stay pending appeal must be presented in the first instance to the trial court.[595]

On most other procedural points, bankruptcy appeals are not significantly different from appeals from any other non-bankruptcy federal order or judgment. The same basic jurisprudential principles apply. For example, new issues generally may not be raised for the first time on appeal from a bankruptcy determination.[596] The appellate court has discretion to take judicial notice of bankruptcy records in the underlying case.[597] Appeals may be dismissed when the party appealing lacks standing to appeal.[598] Claims may be considered abandoned on appeal when they are not briefed.[599]

Under either set of rules, findings of fact by the bankruptcy court are reviewable under a "clearly erroneous" standard.[600] The adoption of this standard, which precludes full review of the case by an Article III court, is a departure from the temporary emergency rule adopted in response to the *Northern Pipeline* case and may give rise to constitutional challenges.

---

177 F.3d 612 (7th Cir. 1999) (no abuse of discretion in dismissal of appeal for failure to file timely brief); Greco v. Stubenberg, 859 F.2d 1401 (9th Cir. 1988) (appeal dismissed for failure to comply with district court deadlines for procuring relevant transcripts); *In re* Tampa Chain Co., 835 F.2d 54 (2d Cir. 1987) (appeal dismissed for failure to file brief for seven months); *In re* Beverly Mfg. Corp., 778 F.2d 666 (11th Cir. 1985) (improper to dismiss for failure to file brief where failure was caused by delay in processing record); *In re* Thompson, 140 B.R. 979 (N.D. Ill. 1992) (appeal dismissed for negligent failure to designate record and issues on appeal), *aff'd*, 4 F.3d 997 (7th Cir. 1993) (table); *see In re* Scheri, 51 F.3d 71 (7th Cir. 1995) (remanding decision to dismiss appeal for failure to file timely brief so district court could explain basis for determination that dismissal was appropriate sanction); *In re* Hill, 775 F.2d 1385 (9th Cir. 1985) (dismissal of appeal for late filing of brief was abuse of discretion absent consideration of lesser sanctions); *In re* Braniff Airways, Inc., 774 F.2d 1303 (5th Cir. 1985) (appeal dismissed where appellant's brief was long overdue); *see also* Nielsen v. Price, 17 F.3d 1276 (10th Cir. 1994) (debtors' duty to designate record and file brief was not stayed by their second bankruptcy filing after the appeal was filed). However, it is important to note that the fifteen-day period for filing a brief after an appeal has been docketed with the district court does not begin to run until the clerk gives notice that the appeal has been docketed. Jewelcor, Inc. v. Asia Commercial Co., 11 F.3d 394 (3d Cir. 1993).

594 *See* 11 U.S.C. § 363(m); *In re* Sullivan Cent. Plaza, I, Ltd., 914 F.2d 731 (5th Cir. 1990) (where creditor was granted relief from stay and foreclosed on property in question, appeal was moot even if no grounds had existed for original relief from stay); *In re* Mann, 907 F.2d 923 (9th Cir. 1990) (debtor's failure to obtain stay of foreclosure sale pending appeal rendered moot appeal of bankruptcy court's ruling on foreclosure action); *In re* Holywell Corp., 901 F.2d 931 (11th Cir. 1990) (where plan was substantially consummated after debtors failed to post appeal bond, appeal of bankruptcy court decision determining amount of creditor's lien was moot); *In re* Crystal Oil Co., 854 F.2d 79 (5th

Cir. 1988) (appeal from confirmation order moot without stay where parties made commitments in reliance on plan); *In re* Onouli-Kona Land Co., 846 F.2d 1170 (9th Cir. 1988); Cent. States, Southeast & Southeast Areas Pension Fund v. Cent. Trans., Inc., 841 F.2d 92 (4th Cir. 1988) (appeal of confirmation order moot because plan was substantially consummated and beyond point of being undone); Miami Ctr. Ltd. P'ship v. Bank of N.Y., 838 F.2d 1547 (11th Cir. 1988) (appeal from confirmation order moot without stay); *In re* Van Ipreen, 819 F.2d 189 (8th Cir. 1987) (sale of collateral rendered appeal moot); *In re* Lashley, 825 F.2d 362 (11th Cir. 1987) (foreclosure sale rendered appeal moot); *In re* Matos, 790 F.2d 864 (11th Cir. 1986). *But see In re* Seidler, 44 F.3d 945 (11th Cir. 1995) (confirmation of chapter 13 plan did not render moot mortgage holder's appeal of order removing mortgage lien from property); *In re* Met-L-Wood Corp., 861 F.2d 1012 (7th Cir. 1988) (fraud is grounds for setting aside judicial sale even though no stay was sought); *In re* Valley Ranches Inc., 823 F.2d 1373 (9th Cir. 1987) (appeal not moot though property had been sold).

595 Fed. R. Bankr. P. 8005; *In re* Ho, 265 B.R. 603 (B.A.P. 9th Cir. 2001).

596 *In re* E.R. Fegert, Inc., 887 F.2d 955 (9th Cir. 1989).

597 *Id.*

598 Holmes v. Silver Wings Aviation, Inc., 881 F.2d 939 (10th Cir. 1989) (debtors may not appeal attorney fee award which will not affect the total amount paid out under their plan).

599 *In re* Brown Family Farms, Inc., 872 F.2d 139 (6th Cir. 1989).

600 Fed. R. Civ. P. 52(a); Fed. R. Bankr. P. 8013; *see, e.g., In re* Branding Iron Motel, Inc., 798 F.2d 396 (10th Cir. 1986); *In re* Pearson Bros. Co., 787 F.2d 1157 (7th Cir. 1986) (discussing the strict standard for reversal of factual determinations of the bankruptcy court embodied by the "clearly erroneous" test); *In re* X-Cel, Inc., 776 F.2d 130 (7th Cir. 1985); *see also In re* Cornelison, 901 F.2d 1073 (11th Cir. 1990) (where confirmation order merely reproduced language of Bankruptcy Code and did not contain findings of fact, remand was required because no findings could be reviewed); *In re* Revco D. S. Inc., 901 F.2d 1359 (6th Cir. 1990) (remand required for factual finding on "good faith" issue).

Chapter 14   The Discharge: Protecting It and Using It

14.1 Introduction

Ultimately, the principal goal of most bankruptcies is the discharge, which frees the debtor from personal liability on almost all debts. It is this clean slate that normally gives debtors the fresh start that bankruptcy is meant to provide. The Bankruptcy Code expanded the protections of the discharge in an effort to help debtors further and to prevent creditors and others from vitiating its benefits.

However, the discharge and its fruits are not quite absolute, nor are they automatic in every bankruptcy case. Under certain limited circumstances the court may deny a discharge, or the discharge may be inapplicable to some debts. Even after it is granted, in rare instances, the discharge may be revoked. Fortunately, many of these occasional pitfalls and roadblocks can be avoided in a well-handled bankruptcy case.

As discussed earlier in this manual,[1] the procedure for obtaining a discharge is normally quite simple. In a chapter 7 case, a discharge order is usually entered a little over sixty days after the first date set for the meeting of creditors, assuming that no objection to discharge has been filed by that time.[2] In a chapter 13 case, the discharge is granted after the debtor completes payments under a confirmed plan or upon the court granting a motion by the debtor for a hardship discharge.[3] In both chapters, the court may choose to hold a discharge hearing, but is not required to do so unless the debtor chooses to reaffirm a debt and the debtor was not represented by an attorney in negotiating the reaffirmation agreement.[4]

This Chapter covers two aspects of the discharge—the difficulties that can arise in obtaining it and the benefits it can provide for consumer clients.

14.2 Objections to Discharge in Chapter 7 Cases

14.2.1 How They Arise

In chapter 7, but not in a chapter 13,[5] a serious obstacle may arise from an objection to the discharge. Such objections, which are quite rare, may be raised in a complaint,[6] filed by the United States trustee, the trustee or a creditor.[7] The complaint must be filed within sixty days of the first date set for the meeting of creditors,[8] unless the court, for cause and based upon a motion filed before that time expires, extends the deadline.[9] Some courts have found that

---

1 *See* § 8.8, *supra*.

2 *See* Fed. R. Bankr. P. 4004(c). Rule 4004(c) also lists several other exceptions to this general rule, such as the filing of a motion under § 707(b) or a request for an extension of time to object to discharge or file such a motion.

3 *See* 11 U.S.C. § 1328.

4 *See* 11 U.S.C. § 524(d).

5 The grounds for denial of discharge listed in section 727 only apply in chapter 7 cases. 11 U.S.C. § 103(b). This may be a good reason to start a case under chapter 13 in some instances, or convert to chapter 13 if problems arise. This is not to say, however, that a chapter 13 discharge could not be opposed on the grounds that the plan had not been completed or that a hardship discharge was not warranted. And, of course, creditors may object earlier to confirmation of the plan. *See* Ch. 12, *supra*.

6 Fed. R. Bankr. P. 7001; *see In re* Markus, 313 F.3d 1146 (9th Cir. 2002) (pro se motion objecting to discharge filed within time limits did not constitute complaint because it did not meet pleading requirements).

7 11 U.S.C. § 727(c)(1). A party whose claim has been disallowed is not a creditor entitled to object to discharge. *In re* Vahlsing, 829 F.2d 565 (5th Cir. 1987); *see also In re* Klinger, 301 B.R. 519 (Bankr. N.D. Ill. 2003) (creditor whose claim had already been found nondischargeable had no standing to seek revocation of discharge). Similarly, one court has held that a party that purchases a claim from a creditor is not itself a creditor entitled to object to discharge. *In re* Beugen, 99 B.R. 961 (B.A.P. 9th Cir. 1989).

8 Fed. R. Bankr. P. 4004(a). These time limits may be waived, however, if the debtor fails to assert untimeliness as a defense. Kontrick v. Ryan, 124 S. Ct. 906, 157 L. Ed. 2d 867 (2004). Also, an amendment filed after the deadline may relate back to the original timely filed complaint in some cases if the amendment is closely connected to the allegations of the original complaint. *In re* Gunn, 111 B.R. 291 (B.A.P. 9th Cir. 1990). At least one appellate court has held that the time limits begin anew if the case is converted from chapter 11 to chapter 7. *In re* Jones, 966 F.2d 169 (5th Cir. 1992). Another has held that expiration of the deadline did not prevent the court from reconsidering its earlier denial of a timely motion for extension of the deadline. Farouki v. Emirates Bank Int'l, Ltd., 14 F.3d 244 (4th Cir. 1994).

9 Fed. R. Bankr. P. 4004 (a), (b). *But see In re* Dominguez, 51 F.3d

the deadline can be subject to extension even if an extension is not sought as required by the rules.[10] In view of the wording of section 727(a) of the Code, it may be possible for the court, *sua sponte*, to deny a discharge, if it knows of facts which would bar the debtor from that relief.[11] However, this almost never happens, because such an active partisanship of the court in a case is out of keeping with its role under the Code as a neutral arbiter of disputes brought before it rather than a participant. While the rules are clear that the objector to a discharge has the burden of proof,[12] how would that burden be carried if the court itself raised the objection?

If a discharge is denied in a chapter 7 case, the effect is quite serious. The debtor loses any non-exempt property to creditors, and creditors that are not paid in full may still pursue the debtor after the bankruptcy for the remaining amounts due. Although property claimed as exempt by the debtor cannot be taken to satisfy these creditors[13] (which might well protect all of the debtor's property), any property acquired after the bankruptcy could be subjected to process.[14]

Some courts have stated that objections to discharge, particularly those involving fraud, must be proved by "clear and convincing" evidence,[15] but those holdings have been called into question by the Supreme Court's decision in *Grogan v. Garner*.[16] At a minimum, the reasons for denying a discharge must be real and substantial and not merely technical and conjectural.[17] And, since *Grogan*, it has been held that the provisions on objections to discharge should be construed liberally in favor of the debtor.[18] Although proof of actual intent to defraud is necessary to prove most objections to discharge, courts have generally held that such proof may be made by circumstantial evidence.[19]

Once an objection to discharge has been filed, it may not be voluntarily dismissed by the objecting party, except after notice to the trustee, United States trustee, and other persons as the court directs, and may be dismissed only on order of the court containing such terms and conditions as the court deems proper.[20] This rule is to ensure that a creditor does not bring an objection to discharge to coerce a settlement with the debtor which only benefits that creditor, and likewise that a debtor, who may lose the discharge of all debts, does not attempt to "buy off" the objecting creditor to preserve that discharge.[21] However, the rule does not absolutely preclude approval of settlements of complaints objecting to discharge, especially if the proceeds of the settlement are paid to the bankruptcy estate.[22]

14.2.2 Grounds for Objecting to Discharge

14.2.2.1 Debtor Is Not an Individual—11 U.S.C. § 727(a)(1)

Of the grounds for denial of discharge that are listed in 11 U.S.C. § 727(a), the first is never applicable in consumer cases. This provision, which prohibits a discharge if the debtor is not an individual, is meant simply to deny a

1502 (9th Cir. 1995) (creditor's memorandum raising issues relating to discharge was sufficient to place chapter 11 debtor on notice of objection, so that later complaint related back to discharge memorandum); 266 B.R. 408 (B.A.P. 8th Cir. 2001) (untimely complaint would be allowed because trustee relied on court order, later set aside, extending time to file discharge objections).

10 *See In re* Moss, 289 F.3d 540 (8th Cir. 2002) (untimely complaint accepted because untimeliness was caused by court's error).

11 11 U.S.C. § 727(c) states that only the trustee or a creditor may object, with the court seemingly limited to acting on request of a party. However, the court may not deny a discharge based on the court's general power under § 105 when the specific grounds listed in § 727 have not been determined. *In re* Yadidi, 274 B.R. 843 (B.A.P. 9th Cir. 2002).

12 Fed. R. Bankr. P. 4005. *But cf. In re* Freedman, 693 F.2d 50 (8th Cir. 1982) (once creditor raises reasonable grounds to support a finding that the debtor committed proscribed acts, debtor has burden of proving that he or she did not do so or did not have requisite intent).

13 11 U.S.C. § 522(c). Of course, the exemptions would not defeat valid non-avoidable liens.

14 That property, though, could conceivably be protected under state exemption laws.

15 *E.g., In re* Mayo, 94 B.R. 315 (Bankr. D. Vt. 1988); *In re* Garcia, 88 B.R. 695 (Bankr. E.D. Pa. 1988). *But see, e.g., In re* Riso, 74 B.R. 750 (Bankr. D.N.H. 1987) (preponderance of the evidence).

16 498 U.S. 279, 111 S. Ct. 654, 112 L. Ed. 2d 755 (1991) (preponderance of the evidence standard applies to exception to dischargeability under 11 U.S.C. § 523(a)). Following *Grogan*, it may still be possible to argue that the clear and convincing standard should apply under section 727, because the consequences of denial of discharge are more severe than those of

making a single debt nondischargeable. *But see In re* Scott, 172 F.3d 959 (7th Cir. 1999) (proof by preponderance of evidence); *In re* Adams, 31 F.3d 389 (6th Cir. 1994) (same); Farouki v. Emirates Bank Int'l, Ltd., 14 F.3d 244 (4th Cir. 1994) (same); *In re* Serafini, 938 F.2d 1156 (10th Cir. 1991) (extending preponderance standard to section 727 based on *Grogan*).

17 *In re* Burgess, 955 F.2d 134 (1st Cir. 1992).

18 Rosen v. Bezner, 996 F.2d 1527 (3d Cir. 1993).

19 *E.g., In re* Chastant, 873 F.2d 89 (5th Cir. 1989); *In re* Sklarin, 69 B.R. 949 (Bankr. S.D. Fla. 1987).

20 Fed. R. Bankr. P. 7041.

21 *See In re* Chalasani, 92 F.3d 1300 (2d Cir. 1996); *In re* Kallstrom, 298 B.R. 753 (B.A.P. 10th Cir. 2003) (affirming refusal to approve settlement in which benefits of settlement went only to objecting creditor); *In re* Traxler, 277 B.R. 699 (Bankr. E.D. Tex. 2002) (refusing to approve settlement that would have made debts to certain creditors non-dischargeable because it produced no benefit to estate or to other general creditors); *In re* Stout, 262 B.R. 862 (Bankr. D. Colo. 2001) (refusing to approve settlement in which debtor paid money to objecting creditor); *see also In re* Diamond, 346 F.3d 224 (1st Cir. 2003) (creditor's threat to seek revocation of debtor's real estate license made during settlement negotiations of § 727 action could be sufficiently coercive as to violate automatic stay).

22 *See In re* Maynard, 269 B.R. 535 (D. Vt. 2001).

discharge to corporations or partnerships.[23] (The prohibition on non-individuals does not apply to the estate of a deceased debtor, which is entitled to the benefits of the debtor's discharge.)[24] The remaining grounds are discussed below in the order in which they appear in the statute.

14.2.2.2 Intentional Concealment, Transfer or Destruction of Property—11 U.S.C. § 727(a)(2)

Probably the most common objection to discharge is that the debtor has intentionally transferred[25] or concealed assets[26] in order to prevent creditors from obtaining access to them in bankruptcy.[27] This blatant type of fraudulent conduct strikes at the very heart of the bankruptcy law, defeating its purpose of distributing non-exempt property to creditors.

Several limitations to this bar to discharge are present both explicitly and implicitly in the statute. First, the debtor must have committed the act with actual intent to hinder, delay, or defraud a creditor or officer of the estate. Thus, the standard for objection is stricter than that contained in many types of fraudulent conveyance provisions under which a constructive intent can be presumed on the basis of the debtor's financial condition. Without this very specific intent, a discharge will not be denied.[28]

Many of the recent cases under this provision have examined the debtor's pre-bankruptcy conversion of non-exempt assets into assets that are exempt in bankruptcy. Several of the decisions turn on whether the exemption planning was done with intent to defraud creditors.[29] Given that the debtor has control over the timing of a voluntary bankruptcy, it would appear to be unfair to require that the debtor maintain non-exempt assets to satisfy creditors' claims in bankruptcy when the debtor could protect those assets under state or federal law by making them exempt before the case is filed.[30] The courts have taken a fairly subjective approach to this issue, depending on the amount of money shielded from creditors, with a good deal of discretion afforded to the trial court.[31]

Exemption planning obviously must be distinguished from the transfer of assets completely out of the debtor's name for little or no consideration, particularly if the debtor has some access to or full use of those assets. The courts have denied a discharge when there has been an obvious dissipation of assets in contemplation of bankruptcy[32] or a suspicious transfer to relatives for little or no consideration.[33] They have even denied a discharge when money

---

23 S. Rep. No. 95-989, at 98 (1978).

24 H.R. Rep. No. 95-595, at 368 (1977); *see* Fed. R. Bankr. P. 1016.

25 "Transfer" is very broadly defined at 11 U.S.C. § 101(54).

26 The "transfer" must be of the debtor's own property. *In re* Thurman, 901 F.2d 839 (10th Cir. 1990).

27 *See, e.g., In re* Adams, 31 F.3d 389 (6th Cir. 1994) (debtors used and made unauthorized post-petition transfers of accounts receivable which were cash collateral); *In re* Perez, 954 F.2d 1026 (5th Cir. 1992) (debtor transferred fifty percent of tax refund attributable to his business to his wife); *In re* Kaiser, 722 F.2d 1574 (2d Cir. 1983).

28 *See, e.g., In re* Dennis, 330 F.3d 696 (5th Cir. 2003) (affirming decision finding that minimal amounts of transfers to minor child showed no intent); *In re* Miller, 39 F.3d 301 (11th Cir. 1994) (motivation for transfer was not fraudulent when debtors were trying to keep business alive and satisfy their largest creditor, who was transferee); Rosen v. Bezner, 996 F.2d 1527 (3d Cir. 1993) (remand for further findings on intent); *In re* Moreno, 892 F.2d 417 (5th Cir. 1990); *In re* Shults, 28 B.R. 395 (B.A.P. 9th Cir. 1983); *In re* Johnson, 80 B.R. 953 (Bankr. D. Minn. 1987) (debtor's intent to prevent creditors from "depriving him of wealth" not fraudulent), *aff'd*, 880 F.2d 78 (8th Cir. 1989); *In re* Dee, 6 B.R. 784 (Bankr. W.D. Pa. 1980) (debtor did not know she was signing a deed when she signed papers at husband's request); *In re* Davis, 3 B.R. 525 (Bankr. D. Md. 1980) (debtor acted solely on advice of counsel); *In re* Viola, 3 B.R. 219 (Bankr. M.D. Fla. 1980) (debtor's purchase of truck in mother's name was result of request by dealership's finance manager); *In re* Vail, 1 B.R. 132 (Bankr. E.D. Pa. 1979) (debtors' transfer of property to children had been planned for fifteen years and was accomplished when debtors were in good financial condition); *see also In re* Swift, 3 F.3d 929 (5th Cir. 1993) (trial court's findings on intent upheld unless clearly

erroneous); McCormick v. Security State Bank, 822 F.2d 806 (8th Cir. 1987) (debtor concealed assets from creditor prior to bankruptcy and purchased a house in name of himself and his wife in clandestine manner).

29 *E.g., In re* Bowyer, 932 F.2d 1100 (5th Cir. 1991) (using savings to pay down mortgage was without requisite intent to defraud creditors); *In re* Johnson, 880 F.2d 78 (8th Cir. 1989) (conversion of property to make use of homestead exemption does not in itself establish fraud absent proof of actual intent to defraud); *In re* Smiley, 864 F.2d 562 (7th Cir. 1989) (conversion of non-exempt assets to exempt assets not in itself fraudulent, absent specific intent to hinder or delay creditors shown by concealment or misrepresentation); Ford v. Poston, 773 F.2d 52 (4th Cir. 1985) (conversion of non-exempt property to exempt property is normally permissible, but a court may find extrinsic elements of fraud); *In re* Carey, 112 B.R. 401 (W.D. Okla. 1989) (debtor's pre-petition conduct in converting, over twenty-one-month period, non-exempt assets into cash which was used to pay mortgage on exempt homestead did not warrant denial of discharge), *aff'd*, 938 F.2d 1073 (10th Cir. 1991); *In re* Crater, 286 B.R. 756 (Bankr. D. Ariz. 2002) (timing of debtors' transfer of property and use of sale proceeds to pay down mortgage did not prove fraudulent intent).

30 For a further discussion of exemption planning see §§ 6.5.2.2 and 10.4.1, *supra*.

31 *See* Frank W. Koger & Sheryl A. Reynolds, *Is Prefiling Engineering Prudent Planning or Section 727 Fraud? (Or, When Does a Pig Become a Hog?)*, 93 Comm. L. J. 465 (1988).

32 *In re* Marcus, 45 B.R. 338 (S.D.N.Y. 1984) (debtor sold property for far less than it was worth); *In re* Kegley, Bankr. L. Rep. (CCH) ¶ 67,397 (Bankr. W.D. Wash. 1980) (debtors used funds for pleasure trip after conferring with attorneys regarding bankruptcy).

33 Cohen v. Bucci, 905 F.2d 1111 (7th Cir. 1990) (denial of discharge where debtor had transferred assets to wife and son); *In re* Chastant, 873 F.2d 89 (5th Cir. 1989) (trust gratuitously created for children suggests fraudulent motive); *In re* Olivier, 819 F.2d 550 (5th Cir. 1987) (debtors concealed beneficial

was "transferred" from a debtor's bank account to the debtor, when it was shown that the transfer was an attempt to avoid attachment of the account and thus hinder creditors.[34] However, if the debtor has recovered substantially all of the property transferred before the bankruptcy is filed and truthfully discloses the transfers, the debtor should not be denied a discharge under this subsection.[35]

Additionally, the challenged action must have taken place within one year prior to the bankruptcy or sometime after the bankruptcy was filed.[36] And it must have involved property that would have been available to creditors. If the debtor had no equity in the property, the bar to discharge is usually not considered applicable.[37] The same result would probably be reached with respect to property that the debtor could claim as exempt.[38]

14.2.2.3 Unjustified Failure to Keep Books or Records As to Finances—11 U.S.C. § 727(a)(3)

The Code provides for denial of discharge if the debtor has "concealed, destroyed, mutilated, falsified, or failed to keep or preserve any recorded information" concerning his or her finances, but only if such act or failure to act was not justified under the circumstances.[39] The exception to the general rule, which excuses the failure to keep records if it was "justified," has prevented the application of this subsection in most consumer cases.

Most consumers, of course, do not keep books and records in the conventional sense. What they have, at most, is a collection of receipts, bills, canceled checks, loan documents, and payment books. Certainly, a consumer debtor who has any of these documents may honestly say that books or records have been kept. And, as this provision is really directed at independent businesses,[40] and perhaps gamblers,[41] even a total lack of records has been excused in the cases of wage-earners and other low-income people.[42] Because this subsection is basically unchanged from the prior Act (except for wording), case law interpreting that Act should still be applicable. As long as the debtor did not have any particular reason to anticipate the need for records

---

interest they retained in home they transferred to parent immediately after automobile accident seven years earlier); Ford v. Poston, 773 F.2d 52 (4th Cir. 1985) (debtor transferred real estate to himself and his wife and extrinsic evidence indicated fraudulent purpose); *see also In re* Aubrey, 111 B.R. 268 (B.A.P. 9th Cir. 1990) (transfer of security interest in assets to third party without credible evidence substantiating debt to third party warranted denial of discharge).

34 *In re* Bernard, 96 F.3d 1279 (9th Cir. 1996) (relying on broad definition of "transfer" to include deposits and withdrawals from bank account).

35 *In re* Adeeb, 787 F.2d 1339 (9th Cir. 1986). *But see In re* Bajgar, 104 F.3d 495 (1st Cir. 1997) (post-petition reconveyance of property back to debtor did not cure pre-petition conveyance found to have been fraudulent); *In re* Davis, 911 F.2d 560 (11th Cir. 1990) (discharge denied where debtor transferred interest in marital home to wife within one year of filing petition even though he retransferred property to himself day before bankruptcy was filed).

36 11 U.S.C. § 727(a)(2)(A); *see In re* Roosevelt, 87 F.3d 311 (9th Cir.), *as amended by* 98 F.3d 1169 (1996) (marital agreement transferring debtor's community property interest was effective upon signing and therefore beyond one year limit). *But see In re* Keeney, 227 F.3d 679 (6th Cir. 2000) (one-year period met by continuing concealment doctrine, because concealment of debtor's secret interest in property continued within year before bankruptcy); *In re* Lawson, 122 F.3d 1237 (9th Cir. 1997) (objection based on deed of trust transferred over one year before petition allowed under continuing concealment doctrine); Rosen v. Bezner, 996 F.2d 1527 (3d Cir. 1993) (continuing concealment could bring transfer that was more than one year prior to petition within scope of section); *In re* Olivier, 819 F.2d 550 (5th Cir. 1987) (same); *In re* Kauffman, 675 F.2d 127 (7th Cir. 1981) (finding continuing concealment of assets more than one year after formal transfer of property where debtor continued to use property as his own).

37 *See, e.g., In re* Harris, 6 B.R. 529 (Bankr. M.D. Tenn. 1980) and cases cited therein.

38 *See, e.g., In re* Lippow, 92 F.2d 619 (7th Cir. 1937) (decided under similar language in prior Act).

---

39 11 U.S.C. § 727(a)(3); *see In re* Cox, 41 F.3d 1294 (9th Cir. 1994) (debtor wife's reliance on husband to keep records was justified under all the circumstances); *see also* Meridian Bank v. Alten, 958 F.2d 1226 (3d Cir. 1992) (debtor has burden of establishing adequate justification).

40 *See, e.g.,* Union Planters Bank v. Connors, 283 F.3d 896 (7th Cir. 2002) (debtors who were sophisticated in business and owned and invested in several enterprises denied discharge for failing to account for large financial transactions); *In re* Juzwiak, 89 F.3d 424 (7th Cir. 1996) (owner of trucking business did not keep records that allowed meaningful reconstruction of debtor's transactions); Meridian Bank v. Alten, 958 F.2d 1226 (3d Cir. 1992) (debtor a sophisticated business person held to a high level of accountability in record keeping; neither small legal practice nor fear of execution by creditors constitutes adequate justification for failure to keep adequate records); *In re* Resnick, 4 B.R. 602 (Bankr. S.D. Fla. 1980) (debtor having no records explaining "loss" of half a million dollars denied discharge).

41 *See In re* Dolin, 799 F.2d 251 (6th Cir. 1986) (debtor's chemical dependency and compulsive gambling did not excuse failure to keep records).

42 *See, e.g., In re* Humphries, 469 F.2d 643 (5th Cir. 1972); Morris Plan Indus. Bank v. Henderson, 131 F.2d 975 (2d Cir. 1942). Certainly, a debtor who customarily and regularly disposes of canceled checks or the like should not be denied a discharge. *In re* Zaidan, 86 B.R. 296 (Bankr. S.D. Fla. 1988); *see also In re* Cox, 41 F.3d 1294 (9th Cir. 1994) (factors to be considered in deciding if failure to keep records is justified by reliance on spouse are debtor's intelligence and education, debtor's experience in business, extent of debtor's involvement in businesses with respect to which debts arose, debtor's reliance on spouse to keep records, including what debtor saw or was told, nature of marital relationship, and any recordkeeping or inquiry duties debtor had under state law).

and there are other ways to ascertain the debtor's financial affairs, this provision should present few problems in consumer cases.

14.2.2.4 Dishonesty in Connection with the Bankruptcy Case—11 U.S.C. § 727(a)(4)

Not surprisingly, debtors who attempt to perpetrate a fraud upon the bankruptcy court are not treated kindly by the Code. Those who make a false oath (commit perjury), present false claims, give or take bribes, or withhold records are denied a discharge.[43] This provision clearly extends to the bankruptcy statements and schedules, which are submitted under oath.

However, like many of the other bars to discharge, the false oath objection is limited by its terms and by case law to the more serious types of cases. The false oath must be in regard to a matter that is material to the proceedings and that could have a real effect on creditors and the estate.[44] The false oath must be intentional; false answers resulting from

carelessness or ignorance do not bar a debtor's discharge.[45] And the false oath must be in connection with the administration of the case itself; fraudulent conduct in connection with a particular debt can be grounds only for an exception to the discharge of that debt.[46]

Finally, a finding that one debtor in a joint case made a false oath does not necessarily bar the other debtor from receiving a discharge.[47] If the joint debtor had no interest in property omitted from the schedules or no knowledge of the facts which were falsely stated, that debtor remains entitled to a discharge.[48]

14.2.2.5 Failure to Explain Loss or Deficiency of Assets—11 U.S.C. § 727(a)(5)

This provision barring discharge is often grouped with the previous two relating to the debtor's honesty with regard to the bankruptcy case. Once a creditor carries its burden of establishing that assets have been lost or dissipated, this section places the burden on the debtor to explain the loss or dissipation.[49] Courts interpreting this section have been

---

43 11 U.S.C. § 727(a)(4); *see, e.g., In re* Keeney, 227 F.3d 679 (6th Cir. 2000) (failure to schedule as asset debtor's secret interest in property purportedly transferred prior to bankruptcy); Farouki v. Emirates Bank Int'l, Ltd., 14 F.3d 244 (4th Cir. 1994) (debtor falsely denied ownership interest in family-owned business); *In re* Calder, 907 F.2d 953 (10th Cir. 1990) (failure to disclose substantial assets in schedules warranted denial of discharge); Williamson v. Fireman's Fund Ins., 828 F.2d 249 (4th Cir. 1987) (false oaths concealed pattern of gratuitous transfers); *In re* Tully, 818 F.2d 106 (1st Cir. 1987) (failing to list assets); *In re* Guadarrama, 284 B.R. 463 (C.D. Cal. 2002) (knowing use of false social security number). The fact that a debtor's bankruptcy discharge may be denied for filing false certifications does not preclude other sanctions that are appropriate, for example, under Fed. R. Bankr. P. 9011, if the debtor files false certifications in an adversary proceeding. *In re* Gioioso, 979 F.2d 956 (3d Cir. 1992).

44 *Compare In re* Beaubouef, 966 F.2d 174 (5th Cir. 1992) (failure to disclose interest in corporation with intent to deceive warranted denial of discharge); Swicegood v. Ginn, 924 F.2d 230 (11th Cir. 1991) (omission from schedules of watch and set of silverware worth $1400.00 was material even though debts to be discharged totaled $861,778.19); *In re* Olson, 916 F.2d 481 (8th Cir. 1990) (debtor's failure to list interest in dinner theater of questionable value and nominally owned by wife was material misrepresentation); *In re* Chalik, 748 F.2d 616 (11th Cir. 1984) (debtor omitted any reference in statement of affairs to 12 corporations with assets of $2.1 million in which he had been involved); *In re* Bell, Jr., 8 B.R. 110 (Bankr. E.D. Va. 1980) (debtor's denial of later-admitted transfer of assets barred discharge) *with In re* Agnew, 818 F.2d 1284 (7th Cir. 1987) (failure to disclose property not subject to claims of creditors did not bar discharge); *In re* Fischer, 4 B.R. 517 (Bankr. S.D. Fla. 1980) (debtor's false statement that he was unemployed would not have affected bankruptcy, so discharge not barred). *But see* Mertz v. Rott, 955 F.2d 596 (8th Cir. 1992) (failure to disclose anticipated estate tax refund, on three separate occasions, justified denial of discharge even though refund was found by lower court to be exempt).

45 *In re* Brown, 108 F.3d 1290 (10th Cir. 1997) (no inference of fraudulent intent when debtor promptly brings mistake to trustee's or court's attention); *In re* Espino, 806 F.2d 1001 (11th Cir. 1986) (failure to list contingent obligation did not bar discharge where no intent to defraud creditors); *see also In re* Varrasso, 37 F.3d 760 (7th Cir. 1994) (circumstantial evidence of intent would rarely be sufficient to grant summary judgment denying discharge); 6 Collier on Bankruptcy ¶ 727.04 (15th ed. rev.); *cf. In re* Sholdra, 249 F.3d 380 (5th Cir. 2001) (doctor who knew he was submitting false information under oath could not blame his attorney's paralegal or his wife who allegedly managed his business); *In re* Bren, 303 B.R. 610 (B.A.P. 8th Cir. 2004) (debtors' signing of oath indicating that one-hundred pages of statements and schedules were true depiction of their complex financial situation when debtors had never read the statements and schedules justified denial of discharge). It may be the debtor's burden to show lack of intent once there is proof of a false oath as to a material fact. *See In re* Tully, 818 F.2d 106 (1st Cir. 1987).

46 *See* § 14.4.3.2, *infra*.

47 *E.g., In re* Montgomery, 86 B.R. 948 (Bankr. N.D. Ind. 1988).

48 *In re* Carp, 340 F.3d 15 (1st Cir. 2003) (wife not automatically an agent of husband or responsible for husband's failure to disclose property; her knowledge and fraudulent intent must be proved).

49 *In re* D'Agnese, 86 F.3d 732 (7th Cir. 1996) (debtor's vague and uncorroborated explanation of what happened to jewelry, crystal and silver worth over $300,000.00 was inadequate); *In re* Hawley, 51 F.3d 246 (11th Cir. 1995) (debtor with no documentation and vague explanations failed to explain satisfactorily loss of $13 million in assets); *In re* Hughes, 873 F.2d 262 (11th Cir. 1989) (case remanded to allow debtor an opportunity to explain loss of assets); *In re* Chalik, 748 F.2d 616 (11th Cir. 1984); *In re* Martin, 698 F.2d 883 (7th Cir. 1983) (although creditor had ultimate burden of proof in proceeding, once evidence of loss or deficiency of assets is presented, debtor has burden of going forward with evidence to explain loss; debtor also could be denied discharge for concealment of such assets where no explanation provided); *In re* Sklarin, 69 B.R. 949

concerned primarily with debtors who previously had large amounts of property or money, a situation which, unfortunately, few consumer clients have ever experienced. In most consumer cases, the obvious use of any diminishing assets was for basic living expenses. Even if this were not the case, this subsection is not intended as a vehicle through which the court may pass judgment on the wisdom of the debtor's expenditures.[50] And the failure of a spouse who took no part in her husband's business to explain a loss of assets will not bar her discharge simply because she filed a joint petition with him.[51]

14.2.2.6 Refusal to Obey Court Orders or to Testify—11 U.S.C. § 727(a)(6)

If the debtor refuses to comply with direct court orders, a discharge may be denied.[52] This unusual situation arises most often when a debtor has been ordered to turn over property which he or she expected to keep in the bankruptcy and that the debtor may no longer even possess. For example, debtors who are poorly advised sometimes spend tax refunds that they receive after filing their cases. When those refunds are not exempt, they constitute property of the estate which the court orders turned over to the trustee. If the debtor is unable to deliver the amount of the refund within a reasonable time, the discharge may be denied. However, not every failure to comply with a court order warrants a denial of discharge.[53]

Debtors who refuse to testify may also be denied a discharge. However, if a debtor properly invokes the privilege against self-incrimination, discharge cannot be denied unless immunity has been offered with respect to the matter concerning which the privilege was invoked.[54] Presumably,

debtors also will not be ordered to answer questions when other privileges are properly invoked.

14.2.2.7 Commission of Prohibited Acts in Connection with Another Bankruptcy Case Concerning an Insider—11 U.S.C. § 727(a)(7)

Debtors who have committed any of the fraudulent acts listed in the previous sections, 11 U.S.C. § 727(a)(2)–(a)(6), within one year before filing their cases, or after filing their cases, are barred from discharge if the act was committed in connection with another case concerning an "insider." The Code defines "insider" to include relatives and partners, as well as partnerships and corporations of which the debtor is a director, officer, or person in control.[55]

Although this section is undoubtedly directed principally at debtors who have been involved in bankrupt corporations and partnerships,[56] it could also be applied to occasional consumer cases. These would most likely involve a husband and wife or other related persons who committed the specified fraudulent acts.[57]

14.2.2.8 Prior Discharge in Chapter 7, Chapter 11, or Their Predecessors—11 U.S.C. § 727(a)(8)

This subsection contains a six-year bar against successive bankruptcy discharges. It is important to note, first of all, that it applies only to prior cases in which a discharge was granted. If a prior bankruptcy case was terminated without a discharge, by a dismissal for example, this objection to discharge may not be raised. (However, in the rare case of dismissal with prejudice, debts listed in the prior case may not be discharged.)[58] Moreover, this section does not bar discharge following prior discharges under chapter 13.[59] And, as with all of the provisions of section 727(a), this section has no applicability in cases in which the debtor

---

(Bankr. S.D. Fla. 1987) (loss of corporate assets which the debtor controlled as alter ego).

50 *In re* Nye, 64 B.R. 759 (Bankr. E.D.N.C. 1986) (requirement of satisfactory explanation required only that debtor explain loss and not that explanation be meritorious). However, the court may require an explanation showing good faith and businesslike conduct. *See* 6 Collier on Bankruptcy ¶ 727.08 (15th ed. rev.); *see also In re* Dolin, 799 F.2d 251 (6th Cir. 1986) (debtor's drug addiction and compulsive gambling were not satisfactory explanations for deficiency of assets).

51 *In re* Suttles, 819 F.2d 764 (7th Cir. 1987); *In re* MacPherson, 101 B.R. 324 (Bankr. M.D. Fla. 1989), *aff'd*, 129 B.R. 259 (M.D. Fla. 1991).

52 11 U.S.C. § 727(a)(6); *e.g.*, *In re* Jones, 966 F.2d 169 (5th Cir. 1992) (debtors disobeyed order of court by assigning interest in insurance proceeds).

53 *In re* Burgess, 955 F.2d 134 (1st Cir. 1992) (failure to file statements and schedules by date set by court did not warrant denial of discharge when there was no evidence of harm to creditors or contumacy).

54 11 U.S.C. § 727(a)(6)(B); *see In re* Martin-Trigona, 732 F.2d 170 (2d Cir. 1984) (use and derivative use immunity are constitutionally coextensive with Fifth Amendment privilege in a bankruptcy hearing; discharge may constitutionally be denied

for failure to testify after grant of immunity); *In re* J.M.V., Inc., 90 B.R. 737 (Bankr. E.D. Pa. 1988) (debtor not required to answer questions from bankruptcy trustee that could form link in chain of evidence to prosecute him; however answers may be compelled if court determines connections between debtor's answers and crimes in question are insufficient to carry burden necessary to sustain privilege).

55 11 U.S.C. § 101(31).

56 *E.g.*, *In re* Watman, 301 F.3d 3 (1st Cir. 2002) (dental practice was "insider" of debtor); *In re* Krehl, 86 F.3d 737 (7th Cir. 1996) (debtor destroyed records of corporation of which he had previously been president).

57 *See, e.g.*, *In re* Mart, 90 B.R. 547 (Bankr. S.D. Fla. 1988).

58 *See* 3 Collier on Bankruptcy ¶ 349.02[2] (15th ed. rev.).

59 See § 14.2.2.9, *infra*, for a discussion of the circumstances in which a chapter 7 discharge is barred following a discharge in chapter 13.

seeks a chapter 13 discharge.[60] Lastly, it should be noted that the six-year period runs from the date the earlier bankruptcy case was commenced, not from the date of the discharge.[61]

14.2.2.9 Prior Discharge Under Chapter 13—11 U.S.C. § 727(a)(9)

The Code also bars a chapter 7 discharge in many cases when a debtor has received a discharge under chapter 13 or its predecessor within the previous six years.[62] Again, this subsection applies only if the earlier case proceeded to a discharge.

A significant exception to this general rule allows a chapter 7 discharge when the previous case completely, or in large part, paid unsecured debts. Thus, if one-hundred percent of the allowed unsecured claims in the previous case were paid, this subsection is not applicable. Similarly, if the actual payments under the previous chapter 13 plan comprised at least seventy percent of the allowed unsecured claims in that case, and the court finds that the plan was proposed by the debtor in good faith and was the debtor's "best effort," a subsequent chapter 7 discharge within six years is not barred. The drafters of the Code anticipated that a debtor could receive this "best effort" determination when the original chapter 13 plan was confirmed.[63]

14.2.2.10 Written Waiver of Discharge—11 U.S.C. § 727(a)(10)

Finally, the court may deny a discharge based upon a court-approved written waiver of discharge executed after the order for relief.[64] Obviously, this section has no applicability to the purported waivers of bankruptcy rights that creditors obtain in granting loans. Given the strict standards set forth for the reaffirmation of even a single debt, discussed later in this chapter, few waivers of discharge are approved.[65]

Probably, the court will approve a waiver of discharge only when it seems likely that no discharge could be granted anyway. Thus, it may be a method of settling a complaint objecting to discharge that would prevent the disclosure of damaging or embarrassing facts about the debtor. Even in such cases, a debtor may be able to obtain a better settlement, excepting only debts to particular creditors from the discharge or compromising the amounts owed in consideration of the settlement.

14.2.2.11 Failure to Pay Filing Fees Is No Longer a Basis for Denial of Discharge

Under the prior Bankruptcy Act, an additional ground for denial of discharge was the failure to pay filing fees. This provision has been eliminated under the Code.

In practical terms, however, the elimination of the provision has resulted in few changes. The original purpose of eliminating this bar to discharge was to allow *in forma pauperis* bankruptcies, in accord with the recommendations of the Bankruptcy Commission.[66] But Congress ultimately decided that the filing fee must be paid.[67] Thus, courts generally dismiss cases in which the filing fee has not been paid, under sections 707(a) or 1307(c) of the Code. In addition, Federal Rule of Bankruptcy Procedure 4004(c)(1)(G) provides that the court is not to grant a discharge until the filing fee has been paid in full.

14.3 Revocation of Discharge

Even more rare than an objection to the debtor's discharge is a complaint seeking revocation of the discharge. Such a complaint must be filed within relatively short time limits and must allege the existence of one of the limited sets of circumstances that allow revocation.

Specifically, the discharge may be revoked only:[68]

---

60 *See* Johnson v. Home State Bank, 501 U.S. 78, 111 S. Ct. 2150, 115 L. Ed. 2d 66 (1991).

61 *See In re* Canganelli, 132 B.R. 369 (Bankr. N.D. Ind. 1991) (where prior case was filed under chapter 13 and converted to chapter 7, original filing date controls). When a case has been converted from another chapter to chapter 7, the relevant date is the date the original bankruptcy petition was filed, not the conversion date. *In re* Burrell, 148 B.R. 820 (Bankr. E.D. Va. 1992).

62 11 U.S.C. § 727(a)(9).

63 124 Cong. Rec. S17,415 (daily ed. Oct. 6, 1978) (remarks of Sen. DeConcini); 8 Collier on Bankruptcy ¶ 1328.06[3] (15th ed. rev.). For this reason, some attorneys include a provision in their form chapter 13 plans that confirmation will constitute a finding that the plan is the debtor's "best effort" within the meaning of section 727(a)(9). For an example of such a provision, see Form 18, Appendix G.3, *supra*.

64 11 U.S.C. § 727(a)(10). In a voluntary case, the order for relief occurs as of the filing of the petition. 11 U.S.C. § 301.

65 *See In re* Martin, 211 B.R. 23 (Bankr. E.D. Ark. 1997) (waiver not approved because debtor did not understand its legal effect).

66 See discussion of *in forma pauperis* bankruptcy proceedings in § 13.6, *supra*.

67 28 U.S.C. § 1930(a).

68 The provisions permitting revocation of a bankruptcy discharge found in the Bankruptcy Code are exclusive and may not be supplemented by other factors which might in other contexts warrant relief from a judgment. *See In re* Zimmerman, 869 F.2d 1126 (8th Cir. 1989); *In re* Rodwell, 280 B.R. 100 (Bankr. D.N.J. 2002) (debtors' failure to respond to trustee's request for information was not within enumerated grounds for revocation of discharge); *see also In re* Markovich, 207 B.R. 909 (B.A.P. 9th Cir. 1997) (debtor not permitted to seek revocation of discharge to convert to chapter 13 after creditor obtained judgment that its debt was nondischargeable); *In re* Wyciskalla, 156 B.R. 579 (Bankr. S.D. Ill. 1993) (debtor had no right to seek revocation of his own discharge because he had reconsidered advisability of his original filing); *In re* Jones, 111 B.R. 674 (Bankr. E.D. Tenn. 1990) (chapter 7 debtor, who had obtained discharge, would not be allowed to convert case to chapter 13 and obtain revocation of chapter 7 discharge). *But see In re*

- If the discharge was obtained through fraud of the debtor, of which the requesting party was unaware until after the discharge;
- If the debtor committed an act described in section 727(d)(2), that is, knowingly and fraudulently failed to report the acquisition of property that would be property of the estate or failed to deliver or surrender such property to the trustee;[69] or
- If the debtor committed an act described in section 727(a)(6), that is, failed to obey an order of the court.[70]

To obtain revocation of a discharge for fraud, it is not sufficient to show that the debtor's fraud rendered a particular debt nondischargeable; the plaintiff must show that the bankruptcy discharge itself would not have been granted but for the fraud.[71] The plaintiff must also allege fraud with particularity, including the time, place and contents of any false representation, as well as its consequences.[72] In addition, the party requesting revocation of discharge must not have learned of the fraud before the discharge was entered.[73] However, courts have also permitted such complaints to be filed if knowledge of the debtor's fraud first came to the plaintiff during the "gap" period before the discharge was granted but after the deadline for objections to discharge.[74]

A complaint raising any of these allegations must be filed within one year of the discharge unless the case is closed after the one year has passed, in which case the second and third grounds set forth above may be raised until the date the case is closed.[75] A closed bankruptcy case must also be reopened for such a complaint to be filed, but the failure of a plaintiff to move to reopen may not be sufficient grounds to defeat the complaint.[76]

Although section 727 does not apply to chapter 13 cases, a creditor or trustee may also move to revoke a chapter 13 discharge within one year of when it was granted if the discharge was obtained by fraud and that fraud was not known by the requesting party until after the discharge was granted.[77] Some courts have also relied on Federal Rule of Bankruptcy Procedure 9024, the equivalent of Federal Rule of Civil Procedure 60, to vacate a discharge when there has been an error in the trustee's handling of the case.[78] It is not clear why, if a trustee has erred to the detriment of a creditor, it would not be more appropriate for the creditor to be compensated by the trustee.

14.4 Exceptions to Discharge

14.4.1 Differences Between Chapter 7 and Chapter 13[79]

Somewhat less serious than an objection to discharge that could prevent a debtor from receiving any discharge at all is

---

Cisneros, 994 F.2d 1462 (9th Cir. 1993) (despite limitations in § 727(d), court could enter order vacating discharge on grounds set forth in Fed. R. Bankr. P. 9024).

69 *E.g., In re* Yonikus, 974 F.2d 901 (7th Cir. 1992) (debtor's failure to report pre-petition personal injury claim warranted revocation of discharge even if it could be claimed as exempt); *see also In re* Putnam, 85 B.R. 881 (Bankr. M.D. Fla. 1988) (refusal to revoke discharge where debtor did not report an asset which he honestly believed had no value to the estate). Where debtors are not clearly put on notice that a turnover of the property is demanded there may not be the knowing and fraudulent intent required by this subsection. *In re* Schwartz, 64 B.R. 285 (Bankr. D.N.H. 1986).

70 11 U.S.C. § 727(d); *see, e.g., In re* Levine, 50 B.R. 587 (Bankr. S.D. Fla. 1985) (debtor failed to obey order to surrender income tax refund check).

71 *In re* Edmonds, 924 F.2d 176 (10th Cir. 1991); *see also In re* Donald, 240 B.R. 141 (B.A.P. 1st Cir. 1999) (less than full disclosure of nature of lawsuit against debtor did not rise to level of fraud).

72 *In re* Edmonds, 924 F.2d 176 (10th Cir. 1991).

73 Mid-Tech Consulting v. Swendra, 938 F.2d 885 (8th Cir. 1991) (creditor knew of omission from schedules before discharge was entered and failed to timely investigate it); *In re* Vereen, 219 B.R. 691 (Bankr. D.S.C. 1997) (complaint dismissed because trustee did not exercise due diligence in investigating possible fraud before discharge); *In re* Kaliana, 202 B.R. 600 (Bankr. N.D. Ill. 1996) (because bank had constructive notice of debtor's hidden bank account, through information in its own files, discharge would not be revoked despite debtor's failure to disclose account).

74 *In re* Emery, 132 F.3d 892 (2d Cir. 1998); *In re* Dietz, 914 F.2d 161 (9th Cir. 1990).

75 11 U.S.C. § 727(e). The one-year period is not tolled by a debtor's fraudulent concealment of assets. *In re* Dolliver, 255 B.R. 251 (Bankr. D. Me. 2000); *In re* Frank, 146 B.R. 851 (Bankr. N.D. Okla. 1992); *see also In re* Bevis, 242 B.R. 805 (Bankr. D.N.H. 1999) (deadline of one year after case closing not extended even if debtor failed to list assets which, therefore, were not administered); *In re* Phillips, 233 B.R. 712 (Bankr. W.D. Tex. 1999) (one-year period not subject to equitable tolling); *In re* Blanchard, 241 B.R. 461 (Bankr. S.D. Cal. 1999) (same).

76 *In re* Leach, 194 B.R. 812 (E.D. Mich. 1996) (reopening necessary, but decision of the bankruptcy court to allow adversary proceeding to go forward deemed tantamount to reopening).

77 11 U.S.C. § 1328(e).

78 *See In re* Midkiff, 342 F.3d 1194 (10th Cir. 2003) (discharge temporarily vacated so trustee could collect debtor's tax refund and distribute it to creditors in accordance with plan); *In re* Cisneros, 994 F.2d 1462 (9th Cir. 1993); *In re* Midkiff, 271 B.R. 383 (B.A.P. 10th Cir. 2002); *In re* Avery, 272 B.R. 718 (Bankr. E.D. Cal. 2002).

79 Note that the exceptions to discharge found in section 523(a) are applicable in chapter 11 cases filed by individuals. 11 U.S.C. § 1141(d)(2). However, none of these exceptions applies when a reorganized corporate debtor receives a chapter 11 discharge. 11 U.S.C. § 1141(d)(1). Because corporations cannot obtain a discharge under chapter 7 because of 11 U.S.C. § 727(a)(1), it is unnecessary to seek to have corporate debts found nondischargeable under that chapter. *See* § 17.5.4.2, *infra*; Garrie v. James L. Gray, Inc., 912 F.2d 808 (5th Cir. 1990) (corporation can only receive a discharge if it reorganizes under chapter 11; 11 U.S.C. § 1141(d)).

the problem of a particular debt that is not covered by the discharge a debtor does receive. When the debtor receives a discharge that is not applicable to all debts, those excepted from discharge can seriously undermine the benefits a bankruptcy would otherwise provide.

One of the important features of chapter 13 is the inapplicability of many of the chapter 7 provisions that exclude certain types of debts from the effect of the discharge. If a debtor earns a chapter 13 discharge by completing a confirmed plan,[80] all debts provided for in the plan are discharged. The only exceptions to that discharge are alimony and support obligations made nondischargeable by 11 U.S.C. § 523(a)(5), debts for educational loans and grants that are nondischargeable under 11 U.S.C. § 523(a)(8), debts for drunk driving debts nondischargeable under 11 U.S.C. § 523(a)(9), certain criminal fines and restitution debts, discussed below,[81] and long-term debts provided for under the section 1322(b)(5) cure provisions, which have a final payment that is due after the last payment of the plan is due.[82] This enhanced discharge for debtors completing a chapter 13 plan is often referred to as the chapter 13 "superdischarge."

However, this discharge cannot be granted unless all claims given priority under 11 U.S.C. § 507, such as alimony, maintenance, or support arrearages and many taxes, are also paid in full, because a plan must normally provide for full payment of such debts.[83] Thus, as a practical matter, priority tax debts too are not dischargeable through a normal chapter 13 discharge.

All of the other debts that are excepted from discharge in a chapter 7 case and are discussed below are included in the normal chapter 13 discharge. This difference, as discussed elsewhere in this manual,[84] can be an important factor in the choice of chapter 13 rather than chapter 7 in some cases, or in a decision to convert from chapter 7 to chapter 13. In view of the inapplicability of most of the exceptions to discharge in chapter 13, courts have ruled that there is no purpose to complaints challenging dischargeability on those inapplicable grounds in chapter 13 cases and have dismissed such complaints.[85] However, some courts have taken the presence of debts that are allegedly nondischargeable under chapter 7 into consideration in ruling upon whether the plan has been filed in good faith.[86]

This difference between chapter 7 and chapter 13 does not exist if the debtor obtains a chapter 13 hardship discharge under section 1328(b). In such cases, the exceptions to discharge are the same as in chapter 7.[87] (The debtor is also excused from the requirement, not present in chapter 7, that all priority debts be paid.)

14.4.2 How Exceptions to Discharge Are Raised

The Bankruptcy Code makes an important distinction between two categories of exceptions to discharge. The first category consists of debts that are excepted from the discharge regardless of whether the issue is raised during the bankruptcy case. The exceptions falling into this category, each of which is discussed below, are those covered by subsections (a)(1), (a)(3), (a)(5), (a)(7), (a)(8), (a)(9), (a)(10), (a)(11), (a)(12), (a)(13), (a)(14), (a)(16), (a)(17) and (a)(18) of section 523. These subsections include exceptions for taxes, debts not listed by the debtor, alimony and support, fines and penalties, student loans, certain debts incurred through drunk driving, debts where a discharge was denied or waived in a prior bankruptcy, debts incurred to pay nondischargeable federal taxes, debts for certain condominium or cooperative assessments, court costs owed by prisoners and certain support debts owed to governmental units. Creditors that hold claims covered by these exceptions are free to assert them against the debtor after the bankruptcy, without the permission of the bankruptcy court.[88]

---

80 *See* Bayshore Nat'l Bank v. Smith, 252 B.R. 107 (E.D. Tex. 2000) (once payments are complete, even if they are completed early, the debtor is entitled to discharge), *aff'd*, 252 F.3d 1357 (5th Cir. 2001) (table); *see also* § 12.3.3.5, *supra* (once payments are complete no party may move to modify plan).

81 *See* § 14.4.3.7, *infra*.

82 11 U.S.C. § 1328(a)(1).

83 11 U.S.C. § 1322(a)(2). However, a priority claim holder may consent to less than full payment, and a priority claim need not be paid if no claim is filed. *See In re* Tomlan, 102 B.R. 790 (E.D. Wash. 1989) (IRS failure to file timely claim deprives it of priority status so that its claim was discharged without full payment under chapter 13 plan), *aff'd*, 907 F.2d 114 (9th Cir. 1990); *In re* Richards, 50 B.R. 339 (E.D. Tenn. 1985); *In re* Riley, 204 B.R. 28 (Bankr. E.D. Ark. 1996) (when debtor's original plan provided for payment of priority tax claim and creditor did not object to modification of plan which omitted payment of tax claim, claim was discharged at conclusion of modified plan); *In re* Goodwin, 58 B.R. 75 (Bankr. D. Me. 1986) (priority tax claim discharged where debtor's plan would have paid claim but timely proof of claim not filed); *see also In re* Hageman, 108 B.R. 1016 (Bankr. N.D. Iowa 1989) (IRS not entitled to be paid post-petition interest on priority claims); *In re* Vlavianos, 71 B.R. 789 (Bankr. W.D. Va. 1986) (court denied IRS motion to amend claim upward at end of case; amounts not in claim were discharged); § 14.4.3.1.2, *infra*.

84 See § 6.3, *supra*, for a discussion of the choice between chapter 7 and chapter 13.

85 *In re* Lewis, 5 B.R. 575 (Bankr. N.D. Ga. 1980); *see also In re* Dole, 7 B.R. 986 (Bankr. D. Idaho 1981) (debt discharged in chapter 13 even after revocation of earlier discharge under Bankruptcy Act). This principle is so clear that an improper dischargeability complaint in chapter 13 might be appropriate grounds for sanctions under 11 U.S.C. § 523(d) or Fed. R. Bankr. P. 9011. Section 523(d) is applicable even to cases to which § 523(a)(2) exceptions to discharge are not.

86 See § 12.3.2, *supra*, for discussion of the "good faith" question.

87 11 U.S.C. § 1328(b). The hardship discharge also does not include long-term debts which were to be cured under the debtor's plan. 11 U.S.C. § 1328(b).

88 However, property claimed as exempt in the bankruptcy may not be reached by such creditors, except those who hold claims

The second category of exceptions consists of debts that are excluded from the discharge only if their nondischargeability is raised and determined during the bankruptcy case. The debts that fall into this category are those specified in subsections (a)(2), (a)(4), (a)(6) and (a)(15) of section 523.[89] These subsections deal with debts incurred by fraud, false pretenses or false financial statements, debts for fraud on the part of fiduciaries, debts for willful and malicious injuries, and debts for certain marital property settlement debts.[90] The rules require that a creditor raise these nondischargeability issues by filing an adversary proceeding.[91]

The deadline for commencing such a proceeding is sixty days after the first date set for the section 341 meeting of creditors.[92] The court gives at least thirty days' notice of this deadline, normally combined with the notice of the meeting of creditors.[93] The deadline may be extended upon motion for cause only if such a motion is filed before the deadline passes.[94] Only a creditor, and not the trustee, is a party in interest entitled to request an extension of the deadline.[95] Such a request must set forth a specific and satisfactory explanation why the creditor is unable to file a timely complaint,[96] and when additional time is granted, it applies only to the creditor who requested it.[97] The court has no discretion to extend the time limit once the deadline has passed.[98] If the creditor does file a dischargeability com-

---

for taxes, alimony, and support, or a student loan or scholarship obtained by fraud. 11 U.S.C. § 522(c).

89 11 U.S.C. § 523(c). This provision contains an exception applicable only to agencies regulating federal depository institutions. A debt under section (a)(2), (a)(4), (a)(6) or (a)(11) may be found nondischargeable outside the normal time limits when owed in some circumstances to a "Federal depository institution regulatory agency" which does not have the ability to "reasonably comply" with the requirement of a timely filed complaint to determine dischargeability. 11 U.S.C. § 523(c)(2). Where there is no ability to "reasonably comply," it is unclear what alternative time limit will apply. *See generally* § 14.4.3.11, *infra.*

90 As the bankruptcy court has exclusive jurisdiction to determine the dischargeability of these debts, a settlement containing a waiver of dischargeability of such debts entered by a non-bankruptcy court is unenforceable. Whitehouse v. La Roche, 277 F.3d 568 (1st. Cir. 2002).

91 Fed. R. Bankr. P. 7001. This means that the adversary rules, Fed. R. Bankr. P. 7001–7087, are applicable. If, for example, the summons and complaint are not served within 120 days as required by Fed. R. Civ. P. 4(j) (made applicable by Fed. R. Bankr. P. 7004(a)) and no good cause is shown the complaint must be dismissed. *In re* Kirkland, 86 F.3d 172 (10th Cir. 1996) (when creditor filed timely dischargeability complaint but failed to make timely service of complaint, complaint was dismissed); *In re* Love, 242 B.R. 169 (E.D. Tenn. 1999); *In re* Heinz, 131 B.R. 38 (Bankr. D. Md. 1991). If the normal requirements for a class action are met, a class action dischargeability complaint may be filed pursuant to Fed. R. Bankr. P. 7023. *See In re* Duck, 122 B.R. 403 (Bankr. N.D. Cal. 1990); § 13.7, *supra.*

92 Fed. R. Bankr. P. 4007(c). In chapter 13 cases in which the debtor seeks a hardship discharge a different deadline is set by the court pursuant to Fed. R. Bankr. P. 4007(d). The deadlines under Rule 4007 are extended, under Bankruptcy Rule 9006(a), to the next workday following a Saturday, Sunday or holiday. *In re* Burns, 102 B.R. 750 (B.A.P. 9th Cir. 1989). The fact that the meeting of creditors is postponed has no effect on the deadline set under Rule 4007(c), which runs from the first date set for the meeting. Some courts had held that this deadline is jurisdictional and could not be waived by a failure to object to an untimely complaint. *In re* Kirsch, 65 B.R. 297 (Bankr. N.D. Ill. 1986). However, the Supreme Court has held that a similar deadline in Rule 4004(a) is not jurisdictional and that the debtor may waive the right to object to an untimely complaint if the debtor fails to assert untimeliness as a defense. Kontrick v. Ryan, 124 S. Ct. 906, 157 L. Ed. 2d 867 (2004). The complaint must be properly filed by the deadline. Mere mailing by the

deadline is not sufficient. *See In re* Strickland, 50 B.R. 16 (Bankr. M.D. Ala. 1985). *But see In re* Coggin, 30 F.3d 1443 (11th Cir. 1994) (disagreeing with cases holding that motion for extension of deadline must be filed and also served by deadline); *In re* Toler, 999 F.2d 140 (6th Cir. 1993) (complaint filed before deadline was timely despite the fact that it was not accompanied by summons as required by local rules). Nor, perhaps, is filing without paying the necessary filing fee sufficient. *See In re* Smolen, 48 B.R. 633 (Bankr. N.D. Ill. 1985). The deadline supplants state statutes of limitations for fraud cases, at least with respect to whether a dischargeability complaint may be brought. *In re* McKendry, 40 F.3d 331 (10th Cir. 1994). This deadline does not apply in some cases in which a federal depository institutions regulatory agency seeks to recover a debt from an "institution-affiliated party" as defined by 11 U.S.C. § 101. 11 U.S.C. § 523(c)(2). *See also In re* Wlaschin, 260 B.R. 306 (Bankr. M.D. Fla. 2000) (deadline extended pursuant to Soldiers' and Sailors' Relief Act).

93 *See* Official Form 9, Appx. D, *infra.*

94 Fed. R. Bankr. P. 4007(c); *In re* Nordin, 299 B.R. 915 (B.A.P. 8th Cir. 2003) (court has no authority to grant motion to extend time if filed after deadline); *see In re* Lewis, 224 B.R. 619 (Bankr. S.D. Ohio 1997) (creditor's claim that more time was needed to pursue settlement negotiations not sufficient cause when debtor's counsel stated no discussion had occurred since meeting of creditors).

95 *In re* Farmer, 786 F.2d 618 (4th Cir. 1986). *But see In re* Brady, 101 F.3d 1165 (6th Cir. 1996) (trustee had standing to seek extension of dischargeability complaint deadline on behalf of creditors).

96 *See In re* Englander, 79 B.R. 897 (B.A.P. 9th Cir. 1988) (complaint which failed to allege specific grounds for nondischargeability permitted when cured by amended complaint after bar date; but plaintiff's attorney sanctioned); *In re* Littell, 58 B.R. 937 (Bankr. S.D. Tex. 1986); *In re* Marino, 195 B.R. 886 (Bankr. N.D. Ill. 1996) (grounds for extension not shown when creditor's attorney had notice of case two months before deadline).

97 *In re* Ichinose, 946 F.2d 1169 (5th Cir. 1991) (order extending time as to one creditor is not implicit extension of deadline as to other creditors). *But see In re* Demos, 57 F.3d 1037 (creditor could rely on extension of deadline granted to trustee when extension order erroneously purported to grant extension for all creditors).

98 *In re* Hill, 811 F.2d 484 (9th Cir. 1987); *In re* Brown, 102 B.R. 187 (B.A.P. 9th Cir. 1989) (court has no discretion to extend the deadline even for extraordinary circumstances such as natural disasters); *In re* Miller, 188 B.R. 1021 (Bankr. S.D. Fla. 1995) (motion filed one day after deadline was not timely even though it was served on debtor on deadline date); *In re* Beam, 73 B.R. 434 (Bankr. S.D. Ohio 1987) (court cannot extend deadline even though an objection was timely, but erroneously, filed in an

plaint, the debtor must respond or a default judgment may be entered, though the court retains its usual discretion to vacate a default judgment on motion.[99]

If a creditor does not file a complaint alleging nondischargeability of its claim before the deadline, or any extension, and the claim is within the categories of exceptions to which the deadline applies under section 523(c), then the claim is permanently discharged. The debtor may then raise the deadline as a complete defense to any later dischargeability action. Even if the creditor did not receive proper notice of the deadline, it is strictly applied by the courts if the creditor had timely notice of the bankruptcy case.[100] The creditor's filing of a motion for relief from the stay or other pleading is not sufficient to put the debtor on notice of issues concerning dischargeability; therefore, the subsequent filing of a dischargeability complaint does not relate back to the date such pleading was filed.[101] Similarly, once the deadline

has run, a creditor may not amend an existing complaint to raise an entirely new ground for nondischargeability.[102] Upon conversion to chapter 7, however, a new period arises for filing complaints.[103]

The rules permit the debtor or any creditor to file a complaint to determine dischargeability of a debt.[104] For the types of discharge exceptions that a creditor need not raise during the bankruptcy case, the debtor may file an adversary proceeding in order to have dischargeability issues settled during the bankruptcy case.[105] The debtor may prefer to resolve dischargeability questions in the bankruptcy court, which is often a more sympathetic forum than the one that might be chosen later by the creditor. (The debtor may also remove a later case brought by the creditor to the bankruptcy forum.)[106] An action may be brought by the debtor seeking a declaratory judgment that a particular debt is dischargeable and an injunction against it being collected. Such a complaint would not be governed by the deadline discussed

---

unrelated case); *see also In re* Kirkland, 86 F.3d 172 (10th Cir. 1996) (when creditor filed timely dischargeability complaint but failed to make timely service of complaint, complaint was dismissed). *But see* Kontrick v. Ryan, 124 S. Ct. 906, 157 L. Ed. 2d 867 (2004) (deadline is not jurisdictional and debtor may waive right to object to untimely complaint by failing to object to Judge's order extending deadline); *In re* Maughan, 340 F.3d 337 (6th Cir. 2003) (wrongly holding that deadline may be equitably tolled based on debtor's behavior); *In re* Albert, 113 B.R. 617 (B.A.P. 9th Cir. 1990) (court may extend deadline pursuant to request made after expiration of original deadline but before expiration of extended deadline.

99 *See In re* Emmerling, 223 B.R. 860 (B.A.P. 2d Cir. 1997); *In re* Lee, 186 B.R. 695 (B.A.P. 9th Cir. 1995).

100 *In re* Williamson, 15 F.3d 1037 (11th Cir. 1994) (creditor did not need to receive specific notice of deadline if it had timely notice of case); *In re* Gordon, 988 F.2d 1000 (9th Cir. 1993) (creditors not entitled to equitable relief from deadline when they had notice fifty-seven days before time period expired); *In re* Green, 876 F.2d 854 (10th Cir. 1989) (actual notice of the bankruptcy filing is sufficient); *In re* Price, 871 F.2d 97 (9th Cir. 1989) (knowledge of the bankruptcy is sufficient); *In re* Alton, 837 F.2d 457 (11th Cir. 1988); Neely v. Marchison, 815 F.2d 345 (5th Cir. 1987); *In re* Bucknum, 105 B.R. 25 (B.A.P. 9th Cir. 1989), *aff'd*, 951 F.2d 204 (9th Cir. 1991); *In re* Ricketts, 80 B.R. 495 (B.A.P. 9th Cir. 1987); *In re* Walker, 103 B.R. 281 (D. Utah 1989). *But see In re* Isaacman, 26 F.3d 629 (6th Cir. 1994) (creditor could file late dischargeability complaint that was within time period stated in erroneous notice from court reasonably relied upon by creditor); *In re* Anwiler, 958 F.2d 925 (9th Cir. 1992) (creditor could file late dischargeability complaint that was within time period stated in erroneous notice from court reasonably relied upon by creditor); *In re* Reichmeier, 130 B.R. 539 (Bankr. W.D. Mo. 1991) (creditor entitled to rely on mistaken notice of deadline, when notice was one day off); *In re* Eliscu, 85 B.R. 480 (Bankr. N.D. Ill. 1988) (creditor with no notice of the case at all not subject to the deadline).

Normally, a certificate of mailing in the bankruptcy court file listing a creditor creates a presumption that the creditor received notice of the case. *In re* Bucknum, 951 F.2d 204 (9th Cir. 1991) (creditors did not overcome presumption merely by stating they did not receive notice).

101 *In re* Goscicki, 207 B.R. 893 (B.A.P. 9th Cir. 1997) (neither adversary cover sheet nor notice to bankruptcy court of poten-

tially nondischargeable claims was substitute for adversary proceeding necessary to challenge dischargeability of debt); *In re* Kennerley, 995 F.2d 145 (9th Cir. 1993) (motion for relief could not be considered equivalent of dischargeability complaint or motion to extend time for filing dischargeability complaint); *In re* McGuirt, 879 F.2d 182 (5th Cir. 1989) (objection to dischargeability does not relate back to date of filing motion for relief); *In re* Harrison, 71 B.R. 457 (Bankr. D. Minn. 1987) (objection to discharge cannot be amended to present grounds for exception to discharge after the deadline has passed); *see In re* Markus, 313 F.3d 1146 (9th Cir. 2002) (pro se motion objecting to discharge filed within time limits did not constitute complaint because it did not meet pleading requirements).

102 *In re* Bercier, 934 F.2d 689 (5th Cir. 1991); *see also In re* Dollar, 257 B.R. 364 (Bankr. S.D. Ga. 2001) (creditor may not amend complaint objecting to discharge to substitute non-dischargeability claim). Also see § 14.4.3.3, *infra*.

103 Fed. R. Bankr. P. 1019(2); *see In re* Marino, 181 F.3d 1142 (9th Cir. 1999) (dismissal of complaint for late filing in chapter 11 did not bar new complaint after case converted to chapter 7); *In re* Goralnick, 81 B.R. 570 (B.A.P. 9th Cir. 1987); Marquette Nat'l Bank v. Richards, 780 F.2d 24 (8th Cir. 1985) (conversion from chapter 11 to chapter 7). But if case is converted from chapter 7 to another chapter and then reconverted to chapter 7, no new time period arises. Fed. R. Bankr. P. 1019(2); *see In re* DiPalma, 94 B.R. 546 (Bankr. N.D. Ill. 1988).

104 Fed. R. Bankr. P. 4007(a). *But see In re* Hamada, 291 F.3d 645 (9th Cir. 2002) (bank that had issued letter of credit as part of collateral for *supersedeas* bond in appeal of judgment for original creditor who had obtained non-dischargeability judgment, and which debtor agreed to indemnify, was not subrogated to rights of original creditor under 11 U.S.C. § 509 because debtor's obligation to bank was purely contractual); *In re* Edmond, 934 F.2d 1304 (4th Cir. 1991) (state consumer protection act gives state's consumer protection agency *parens patriae* standing to bring nondischargeability action on behalf of group of injured consumers).

105 *But cf. In re* Case, 937 F.2d 1014 (5th Cir. 1991) (bankruptcy court may not *sua sponte* address dischargeability of a debt; that is, to declare a debt for attorneys fees in connection with an adversary proceeding nondischargeable).

106 See § 13.4.1, *supra*, for discussion of removing matters within the federal courts' bankruptcy jurisdiction.

above, which is applicable only to those dischargeability complaints that must be filed in the bankruptcy court under section 523(c).[107] The Eleventh Amendment is not a bar to a complaint seeking a determination of dischargeability even if a state agency is named as the defendant.[108]

For some situations in which discharge under the Code is ambiguous, such as certain tax debts to which a time period applies, it is a good idea to clarify with the creditor whether or not it thinks the debt is dischargeable so that problems do not rise after the close of the case. Otherwise the creditor may concede that the debt is dischargeable, but fail to take necessary action to modify its records. An exchange of letters, a stipulation, or a consent order is a useful tool to create a record that will resolve future questions.

Another possibility is to defer the question of dischargeability and to have it resolved later if collection activity is commenced. The discharge can then be interposed as a defense to repayment in the non-bankruptcy forum (or the bankruptcy case can be reopened to address the issue). One advantage of this strategy is that it avoids unnecessary litigation when the creditor is unlikely to commence future collection activities. On the other hand, failure to resolve questions about dischargeability during the bankruptcy creates uncertainty about the scope of the discharge which can seriously undermine the effectiveness of the debtor's fresh start. Once a non-bankruptcy court has ruled on dischargeability the bankruptcy court may not alter that ruling.[109]

14.4.3 Which Debts Are Excepted from Discharge?

14.4.3.1 Taxes—11 U.S.C. § 523(a)(1)

14.4.3.1.1 Taxes that cannot be discharged

Taxes are the debts that are most frequently nondischargeable in bankruptcy cases. However, it is important to realize that not all taxes are nondischargeable.[110] A rather complicated series of cross-references within the Code[111] can be

followed to the conclusion that, basically,[112] only the types of taxes listed below are not discharged in consumer cases:

- Any tax for which a return, if required, was not filed,[113] for which a fraudulent return was filed,[114] or which the debtor attempted to evade;[115]

---

107 Fed. R. Bankr. P. 4007(b) permits such a complaint to be filed at any time.

108 Tennessee Student Assistance Corp. v. Hood, 124 S. Ct. 1905, 158 L. Ed. 2d 764 (2004).

109 *In re* Goetzman, 91 F.3d 1173 (9th Cir. 1996) (Rooker-Feldman doctrine prevents relitigation of questions related to discharge resolved by state court foreclosure judgment against debtors); *see also* § 14.4.4, *infra*.

110 Even if a tax is discharged, liens based on the underlying debt may remain legally enforceable *in rem* claims. *In re* Isom, 901 F.2d 744 (9th Cir. 1990).

111 11 U.S.C. § 523(a)(1) refers to 11 U.S.C. § 507(a)(2) and 507(a)(8), the former of which refers in turn to 11 U.S.C. § 502(f).

112 Not included in the list are some "gap" tax claims arising in involuntary cases, which are provided for in 11 U.S.C. § 502(f). There are special provisions dealing with cases where there has been an offer of compromise (11 U.S.C. § 507(a)(7)(A)(ii)), taxes to be withheld by employers or paid by employers on priority wages (11 U.S.C. § 507(a)(7)(C), (D)), and certain unpaid customs duties (11 U.S.C. § 507(a)(F)). Also not included are sales taxes which are to be collected by some business debtors. *See In re* Shank, 792 F.2d 829 (9th Cir. 1986).

113 A California statute that required debtor to notify state taxing authority that IRS had assessed a deficiency did not require the filing of a new state tax return for purposes of this section. *In re* Jackson, 184 F.3d 1046 (9th Cir. 1999). The substitute return filed by the IRS when a taxpayer is delinquent probably does not constitute a filed return for the purpose of this provision. *In re* Hatton, 220 F.3d 1057 (9th Cir. 2000) (neither substitute return prepared without input from debtor nor installment agreement signed by debtor constituted return); *In re* Bergstrom, 949 F.2d 341 (10th Cir. 1991); *In re* Chapin, 148 B.R. 304 (C.D. Ill. 1992); *In re* Rench, 129 B.R. 649 (Bankr. D. Kan. 1991). Neither does a stipulation settling a disputed case in tax court. *In re* Gushue, 126 B.R. 202 (Bankr. E.D. Pa. 1991). However, if the debtor has signed the substitute return, acknowledging liability, the return is considered to have been filed. *In re* Mathis, 249 B.R. 324 (S.D. Fla. 2000) (forms prepared by IRS with debtor's full cooperation and signed by debtor constituted returns); *In re* Berard, 181 B.R. 653 (Bankr. M.D. Fla. 1995); *In re* Lowrie, 162 B.R. 864 (Bankr. D. Nev. 1994); *In re* Gless, 181 B.R. 414 (Bankr. D. Neb. 1993). Nor should the fact that a substitute return or an assessment has been completed by a taxing authority preclude the honest filing of a return thereafter. *In re* Izzo, 287 B.R. 158 (Bankr. E.D. Mich. 2002); *In re* Woods, 285 B.R. 284 (Bankr. S.D. Ind. 2002). But see cases cited below holding otherwise.

114 *See In re* Dorminy, 301 B.R. 599 (Bankr. M.D. Fla. 2003) (pre-bankruptcy stipulated decision by tax court that debtor liable for fraud penalty did not prevent debtor from litigating fraud issue for purposes of dischargeability).

115 11 U.S.C. § 523(a)(1)(B)(i), (C); Cassidy v. Comm'r, 814 F.2d 477 (7th Cir. 1987). The courts have disagreed on what constitutes "evasion" of taxes. *See In re* Fretz, 244 F.3d 1323 (11th Cir. 2001) (alcoholic doctor who knew he should file returns and had means to pay taxes evaded taxes); *In re* Griffith, 206 F.3d 1389 (11th Cir. 2000) (*en banc*) (exception applies where the debtor engaged in affirmative acts seeking to evade or defeat collection of taxes); *In re* Tudisco, 183 F.3d 133 (2d Cir. 1999) (false affidavit to employer and debtor's knowledge that he had to file returns and pay taxes established *mens rea* required by this exception); *In re* Fegely, 118 F.3d 979 (3d Cir. 1997) (debtor who knew he had duty to file returns, had the wherewithal to pay the taxes due, and intentionally failed to do so had evaded taxes); *In re* Zuhone, 88 F.3d 469 (7th Cir. 1996) (court found long series of complicated transactions designed to evade taxes); *In re* Birkenstock, 87 F.3d 947 (7th Cir. 1996) (debtor husband's actions showed attempts to avoid tax liability, but debtor wife's mere failure to pay back taxes was not evasion); Dalton v. Internal Revenue Serv., 77 F.3d 1297 (10th Cir. 1996)

- Any tax with respect to which a late return was filed within two years before the date of filing of the bankruptcy;[116]
- Taxes on income or gross receipts
  (a) for which a return, if required, was last due within three years of the filing of the bankruptcy,[117] or

(b) assessed within 240 days before filing of the bankruptcy,[118] or
(c) not yet assessed, but assessable after filing of the bankruptcy;[119]

- Property taxes assessed before commencement of the case and last payable without penalty less than one year before filing of the bankruptcy;[120]

(debtor's attempts to conceal assets in order to avoid taxes constituted evasion); *In re* Bruner, 55 F.3d 195 (5th Cir. 1995) (debtors who failed to file returns, failed to pay taxes and attempted to hide income and assets had willfully evaded taxes); *In re* Toti, 24 F.3d 806 (6th Cir. 1994) (debtor has evaded taxes if he voluntarily, consciously and intentionally failed to file returns and pay taxes while living lavish lifestyle; even if evasion was not felonious); *In re* Roper, 294 B.R. 301 (B.A.P. 8th Cir. 2003) (debtor who did not take steps to avoid taxes and who relied on advice of professionals in dealing with IRS did not evade taxes); *In re* Binkley, 242 B.R. 728 (M.D. Fla. 1999) (tax debt discharged for debtor who was not complicit in her husband's fraud); *In re* Brackin, 148 B.R. 953 (Bankr. N.D. Ala. 1992) (evidence did not show that debtor had intentionally claimed non-allowable deductions, but tax on discharge of indebtedness income that debtor never reported was nondischargeable); *In re* Jones, 116 B.R. 810 (Bankr. D. Kan. 1990) (tax debts held nondischargeable when debtor concealed assets); *see also In re* Frosch, 261 B.R. 181 (Bankr. W.D. Pa. 2001) (negligent mistakes on return not evasion); *In re* Howard, 167 B.R. 684 (Bankr. M.D. Fla. 1994) (poor judgment in using funds for purposes other than payment of taxes is not evasion); *In re* Gathwright, 102 B.R. 211 (Bankr. D. Or. 1989) (tax debt found dischargeable where errors were due to sloppiness and lack of understanding of tax code rather than fraud). The decision in Cassidy v. Comm'r was revisited in *In re* Cassidy, 892 F.2d 637 (7th Cir. 1990), where the court held that its earlier dischargeability decision in a tax court appeal was binding on the debtor in a later bankruptcy proceeding.

116 11 U.S.C. § 523(a)(1)(B)(ii); *see In re* Nunez, 232 B.R. 778 (B.A.P. 9th Cir. 1999) (tax forms filed after IRS assessed deficiency qualified as returns when filed in good faith); *In re* Savage, 218 B.R. 126 (B.A.P. 10th Cir. 1998) (amended returns filed after IRS filed substitute returns constituted "returns" for purposes of dischargeability provision); *In re* Ashe, 228 B.R. 457 (C.D. Cal. 1998) (schedule that debtor had provided to IRS, which contained all information necessary to calculate taxes and was signed by debtor constituted "return," even if it was not intended as a return); *In re* Harrison, 226 B.R. 285 (D. Mass. 1997) (late-filed return considered filed on date received by IRS, unlike timely returns which are considered received on date of mailing). *But see In re* Moroney, 352 F.3d 902 (4th Cir. 2003) (income tax forms unjustifiably filed years late, where the IRS has already prepared substitute returns and assessed taxes, do not constitute "returns" for purposes of 11 U.S.C. § 523(a)(1)(B)(i); *In re* Hindenlang, 164 F.3d 1029 (6th Cir. 1999) (tax forms filed after IRS had assessed deficiencies were not "returns" because they were filed too late to have any effect under Internal Revenue Code. Even if a tax is dischargeable as outside this exception, it may nevertheless be nondischargeable as an income tax for which a return is last due within three years of bankruptcy. Etheridge v. Illinois, 127 B.R. 421 (C.D. Ill. 1989). Also, at least some courts have held that the two year period is tolled if the debtor files a bankruptcy case during that period. *E.g., In re* Tibaldo, 187 B.R. 673 (Bankr. C.D. Cal. 1995).

117 This provision was upheld against a constitutional challenge

based on the Equal Protection Clause made by a debtor who had filed his returns late pursuant to a valid extension. *In re* Wood, 866 F.2d 1367 (11th Cir. 1989). The three-year period is tolled during the time that the taxing authority is prevented from collecting taxes by an automatic stay in a prior bankruptcy case. Young v. United States, 535 U.S. 43, 122 S. Ct. 1036, 152 L. Ed. 2d 79 (2002). The three-year period runs from the date an involuntary bankruptcy petition is filed, not date of conversion from chapter 7 to chapter 11. *In re* Rassi, 140 B.R. 490 (Bankr. C.D. Ill. 1992).

118 *See generally In re* Lewis, 199 F.3d 249 (5th Cir. 1999) (state taxes deemed assessed when notice of assessment was given, even though state followed improper procedures); *In re* O'Connell, 246 B.R. 332 (B.A.P. 8th Cir. 2000) (state law definition of assessment was not dispositive of when tax was assessed under § 507(a)(8)(A)); *In re* Hardie, 204 B.R. 944 (S.D. Tex. 1996) (taxes assessed when IRS issued certificate of assessment, not when tax court entered judgment determining deficiency); *In re* King, 122 B.R. 383 (B.A.P. 9th Cir. 1991) (date of assessment depends on specific tax code and practices involved), *aff'd*, 961 F.2d 1423 (9th Cir. 1992); *In re* Hartman, 110 B.R. 951 (D. Kan. 1990) (federal income tax deficiency not assessed immediately upon notice of tax deficiency but only after IRS had taken other steps required by Internal Revenue Code before liability could attach); *In re* Oldfield, 121 B.R. 249 (Bankr. E.D. Ark. 1990) (tax assessed when IRS entered taxes due as determined by tax court on taxpayers' master file and sent notice of deficiency to debtors); *In re* Shotwell, 120 B.R. 163 (Bankr. D. Or. 1990) (tax assessed when summary record signed by assessment officer rather than when returns are filed); *In re* King, 96 B.R. 356 (Bankr. M.D. Fla. 1989). Some courts have held that the time periods are tolled during an earlier bankruptcy case. *In re* Dietz, 116 B.R. 792 (D. Colo. 1990); *In re* Wise, 127 B.R. 20 (Bankr. E.D. Ark. 1991); *In re* Davidson, 120 B.R. 777 (Bankr. D.N.J. 1990). However, the fact that there is now an exception to the automatic stay, 11 U.S.C. § 362(b)(9), which permits assessments during a bankruptcy case may undermine these holdings, at least to the extent they are based on the inability to assess during a bankruptcy case. *Compare* 26 U.S.C. § 6503(b) *with* 11 U.S.C. § 108(b).

119 11 U.S.C. § 523(a)(1)(A), which incorporates 11 U.S.C. § 507(a)(7)(A). *See In re* Aberl, 78 F.3d 241 (6th Cir. 1996) (offer in compromise made prior to assessment does not toll time period for priority status); *In re* King, 961 F.2d 1423 (9th Cir. 1992) (discussing different meaning of "assessment" under California law which, unlike federal law, does not involve creation of a tax lien after notice of deficiency is sent); *In re* Wines, 122 B.R. 804 (Bankr. S.D. Fla. 1991) (although no assessment usually may be made after three years from filing of tax returns, because assessment was prohibited until tax court entered final decision on debtor's petition for redetermination tax was still assessable); *In re* Crist, 85 B.R. 807 (Bankr. N.D. Iowa 1988); *In re* Carter, 74 B.R. 613 (Bankr. E.D. Pa. 1987) (discussion of assessment deadlines).

120 11 U.S.C. § 523(a)(1)(A), which incorporates 11 U.S.C. § 507(a)(7)(B). Some property taxes may acquire lien status.

- Excise taxes[121]
  - (a) On transactions as to which a return was required and last due less than three years before the bankruptcy, or
  - (b) On transactions, as to which no return was required, which occurred less than three years before the bankruptcy;
- Taxes required to be collected or withheld by the debtor, such as employment "trust fund" taxes (income taxes and FICA withholding) or sales taxes.[122]

Any penalties related to the taxes listed above are also nondischargeable, unless the penalty is solely punitive in nature or relates to a transaction that occurred more than three years before the filing of the petition.[123] Erroneous

refunds of nondischargeable taxes are similarly nondischargeable.[124] The treatment of interest is not as clear; but some courts have held that it is dischargeable.[125] However, post-petition interest on nondischargeable tax debts is clearly nondischargeable.[126] And in limited situations, a party who has paid the tax claim of the debtor may become subrogated to the claim and eligible for the same priority and treatment related to dischargeability.[127]

Occasionally, it is not altogether clear whether a particular debt to a governmental entity is a tax subject to these provisions. Courts consider the debt's inherent characteristics, especially whether, or how closely, it is related to a debtor's voluntary use of a service, rather than assessed regardless of the debtor's actions. Thus, when a charge is

---

When they do, they no longer constitute priority debts, nor are they nondischargeable under section 523(a)(1). However, the lien associated with the debt, if unpaid or unavoided, will pass through the bankruptcy unaffected. The penalty necessary to place a tax outside this exception need not be solely a monetary one. *In re* S. Shore Vending, Inc., 25 B.R. 111 (Bankr. D. Mass. 1982) (issuance of a warrant to sell property constitutes a penalty).

121 11 U.S.C. § 523(a)(1)(A), which incorporates 11 U.S.C. § 507(a)(7)(E). A tax may be an excise tax in some circumstances even if it is measured by gross receipts. *In re* Groetken, 843 F.2d 1007 (7th Cir. 1988) (Illinois retailer's occupation tax); *see also In re* Grynberg, 986 F.2d 367 (10th Cir. 1993) (gift taxes were excise taxes); *In re* Suburban Motor Freight, Inc., 998 F.2d 338 (6th Cir. 1993) (unpaid workers compensation premiums, as involuntary exaction applicable to all similarly situated firms, were excise taxes); *In re* C-T of Virginia, 977 F.2d 137 (4th Cir. 1992) (tax imposed upon employer when pension plan assets reverted to employer upon plan's termination was excise tax); New Neighborhoods, Inc. v. W. Va. Workers Compensation Fund, 886 F.2d 714 (4th Cir. 1989) (premiums due the state Workers Compensation Fund are excise taxes under federal law); *In re* Marcucci, 256 B.R. 685 (D.N.J. 2000) (New Jersey vehicle insurance surcharge debt was not an excise tax).

122 11 U.S.C. § 523(a)(1)(A), which incorporates 11 U.S.C. § 507(a)(7)(C). Although such taxes are usually owed by businesses, consumers who have employed others, or who were previously in business may have liabilities for such taxes. *See generally In re* Gust, 197 F.3d 1112 (1st Cir. 1999) (liability imposed on individual based on responsibility to withhold trust fund taxes is a nondischargeable tax). A debtor may request that the bankruptcy court determine whether there is liability for withholding taxes as a "responsible person" with respect to a businesses with which the debtor has been affiliated. Adams v. Coveney, 162 F.3d 23 (1st Cir. 1998) (debtor not liable for corporation's withholding taxes under state law, which was construed to be less strict than federal law); *In re* Macagnone, 253 B.R. 99 (M.D. Fla. 2000); *In re* Newton, 260 B.R. 1 (Bankr. D. Ariz. 2000) (debtor held not liable for responsible person penalty for tax quarter when corporation had insufficient funds to pay taxes); *In re* Schwartz, 192 B.R. 90 (Bankr. D.N.J. 1996) (debtor could initiate proceeding to determine whether he was responsible person even though IRS had not yet claimed that he had such liability).

123 11 U.S.C. § 523(a)(1)(A), which incorporates 11 U.S.C. §§ 507(a)(7)(G), 726(a)(4). Cassidy v. Comm'r, 814 F.2d 477

(7th Cir. 1987). Actually, § 507(a)(7)(G) only applies to income, gross receipts, property, and excise taxes. McKay v. United States, 957 F.2d 689 (9th Cir. 1992) (penalties relating to transactions more than three years old are dischargeable even if underlying taxes are not); Roberts v. United States, 906 F.2d 1440 (10th Cir. 1990) (same); *In re* Burns, 887 F.2d 1541 (11th Cir. 1989) (same); *see In re* Cassidy, 983 F.2d 161 (10th Cir. 1992) (ten percent penalty for premature pension fund withdrawal was non-pecuniary penalty not entitled to priority and not a tax); *In re* Bates, 974 F.2d 1234 (10th Cir. 1992) (punitive tax penalties not entitled to priority); *In re* Hanna, 872 F.2d 829 (8th Cir. 1989) (post-petition penalties are nondischargeable); *In re* Hovan, 172 B.R. 974 (Bankr. W.D. Wash. 1994) (compensatory nature of penalty must be demonstrated by clear statutory language or legislative history), *aff'd*, 96 F.3d 1254 (9th Cir. 1996).

124 Bleak v. United States, 817 F.2d 1368 (9th Cir. 1987); *see also In re* Frontone, 301 B.R. 290 (C.D. Ill. 2003) (erroneous refund claim was nondischargeable to extent it was for taxes that would be nondischargeable, but was otherwise dischargeable). *But see In re* Jackson, 253 B.R. 570 (M.D. Ala. 2000) (erroneous refund was dischargeable because § 507(c) applies only to priority status and not dischargeability).

125 *See In re* Johnson, 146 F.3d 252 (5th Cir. 1998) (debtor liable for post-petition interest on nondischargeable taxes, but not for interest on amounts paid by trustee accruing after such payments had been made); *In re* Hardee, 137 F.3d 337 (5th Cir. 1998) (increase in amount of interest for underpayments arising from tax-motivated transaction was interest and not penalty); *see also In re* Razorback Ready-Mix Concrete Co., 45 B.R. 917 (Bankr. E.D. Ark. 1984). The Seventh Circuit has concluded, however, that pre-petition interest on a nondischargeable tax liability is nondischargeable. *In re* Larson, 862 F.2d 112 (7th Cir. 1988). But interest on dischargeable tax penalties is dischargeable even if the underlying tax debt is not. *In re* Teeslink, 165 B.R. 708 (Bankr. S.D. Ga. 1994). *But see In re* Garcia, 955 F.2d 16 (5th Cir. 1992) (interest on tax debt has same priority as underlying tax debt); *In re* Bates, 974 F.2d 1234 (10th Cir. 1992) (pre-petition interest has same priority as underlying tax debt).

126 *In re* Fullmer, 962 F.2d 1463 (10th Cir. 1992); *In re* Burns, 887 F.2d 1541 (11th Cir. 1989); *In re* Hanna, 872 F.2d 829 (8th Cir. 1989); *In re* Irvin, 129 B.R. 187 (W.D. Mo. 1990) (liability for post-petition interest survives bankruptcy even though pre-petition claim was fully paid by estate); *see also* Bruning v. United States, 376 U.S. 358 (1964).

127 *See In re* Fields, 926 F.2d 501 (5th Cir. 1991); W. Surety Co. v. Waite, 698 F.2d 1177 (11th Cir. 1983); *In re* Allway, 37 B.R. 420 (Bankr. E.D. Pa. 1984) (former spouse).

assessed only when services are used, in proportion to their use, that charge is not a tax.[128] Similarly, if the charge is exacted as punishment for an unlawful act or omission, it is a penalty and not a tax.[129] Nor is the liability under the Internal Revenue Code of a transferee of assets from a taxpayer a tax; it is merely a method of collecting the tax owed by the taxpayer.[130] On the other hand, revenue collected on an *ad valorem* basis from all property holders or for a purpose that confers no particular benefit on the payer would be considered a tax.[131]

In addition, even if a tax is an excise tax, it must be an excise tax "on a transaction" to fall under section 507(a)(7)(E). Thus, an occupation tax is dischargeable despite the fact that it may be an excise tax, because it is not a tax on a transaction.[132]

14.4.3.1.2 Analyzing tax debts to determine dischargeability

In view of the relative intricacy of these provisions, it is always wise to check each particular fact situation against the Code itself. In some cases, when significant amounts of money are involved, it may pay to delay filing until one or more of the time periods listed above has expired. For the purpose of calculating time limits under the various provisions, taxes are found to be payable from the date the relevant tax return is due rather than the date on which quarterly estimated payments are required.[133] It should also

be remembered that, because taxes in many of the categories listed above are priority claims, a chapter 13 plan must normally provide for their full payment.[134]

In analyzing federal income tax debts, it is important to have all the facts, including precise dates, so that the relevant time periods can be calculated accurately. The best way to ensure this is to obtain a transcript from the Internal Revenue Service (IRS). Two types of transcripts are available, an MFTRA-X, which is fairly easily deciphered, and a more detailed MFT-30, which must be decoded. The former, unfortunately, omits information that may be important, such as whether a return listed was a substitute return not filed by the debtor, in which case it does not trigger the time periods triggered by filed returns.

The MFTRA-X can be obtained from the local IRS service center or disclosure office. A letter requesting it should include an IRS form power of attorney signed by the debtor.[135] The debtor can also obtain this transcript in person at the local IRS field office. In an emergency, the IRS will sometimes give some information over the phone and send

128 Bidart Bros. v. California Apple Comm'n, 73 F.3d 925 (9th Cir. 1996) (assessments on apple producers that were kept segregated from general revenues and used for purpose of promoting apple sales were not taxes); *In re* Jenny Lynn Mining Co., 780 F.2d 585 (6th Cir. 1986); *In re* Lorber Indus. of Cal., 675 F.2d 1062 (9th Cir. 1982); *In re* Adams, 40 B.R. 545 (E.D. Pa. 1984); *In re* Mounier, 232 B.R. 186 (Bankr. S.D. Cal. 1998) (ten percent assessment for early withdrawal from retirement plan was not a tax).

129 United States v. Reorganized Fabricators, 518 U.S. 213, 135 L. Ed. 2d. 506, 116 S. Ct. 2106 (1996) (exaction imposed upon employer that fails to correct pension plan deficiency was a penalty, not an excise tax); *In re* Marcucci, 256 B.R. 685 (D.N.J. 2000) (New Jersey vehicle insurance surcharge debt was civil penalty and not an excise tax).

130 *In re* Pert, 201 B.R. 316 (Bankr. M.D. Fla. 1996).

131 *In re* Suburban Motor Freight, Inc., 998 F.2d 338 (6th Cir. 1993) (unpaid workers compensation premiums, as involuntary exaction applicable to all similarly situated firms, were excise taxes); *In re* Dietz, 914 F.2d 161 (9th Cir. 1990) (assessment imposed by Virginia on individuals for operating uninsured vehicle is involuntary pecuniary burden and thus nondischargeable, excise tax; however, a separate service fee was intended to defray administrative costs and was not excluded from discharge); United States v. River Coal Co., 748 F.2d 1103 (6th Cir. 1984); *In re* Lorber Indus. of Cal., 675 F.2d 1062 (9th Cir. 1982).

132 *In re* Templar, 170 B.R. 562 (Bankr. M.D. Pa. 1994). *But see In re* Groetken, 843 F.2d 1007 (7th Cir. 1988) (Illinois retailer's occupation tax was excise tax).

133 *In re* Ripley, 926 F.2d 440 (5th Cir. 1991); *cf.* Moore v. Internal Revenue Serv., 132 B.R. 533 (Bankr. W.D. Pa. 1991) (when

chapter 11 debtor does not elect to divide the taxable year in which the case is filed so that pre-petition taxes are the responsibility of the debtor and not the estate, the entire year's tax obligation is treated as if it arose post-petition).

134 11 U.S.C. § 1322(a)(2); *see* § 12.3.5, *supra*. The holders of such tax claims may agree to different treatment. 11 U.S.C. § 1322(a)(2); *see also In re* Riley, 204 B.R. 28 (Bankr. E.D. Ark. 1996) (tax was provided for in plan when original plan proposed paying priority claim, even though modified plan, not objected to by taxing authority, did not provide for payment). Full payment is not required on a priority claim if it is not filed by the creditor. *See* United States v. Carr, 142 B.R. 351 (D. Neb. 1992) (amended IRS proof of claim not allowed and amounts not included in original claim discharged); *In re* Tomlan, 102 B.R. 790 (E.D. Wash. 1989) (IRS's failure to file timely claim deprives it of priority status so that its claim was discharged without full payment under chapter 13 plan), *aff'd*, 907 F.2d 114 (9th Cir. 1990); *In re* Richards, 50 B.R. 339 (E.D. Tenn. 1985) (IRS claim not allowed and need not be paid where it was not timely filed); *In re* Dixon, 218 B.R. 150 (B.A.P. 10th Cir. 1998) (tax for tax year ending prior to chapter 13 petition was pre-petition claim discharged because no claim filed for such tax, even though return was not yet due when chapter 13 petition was filed); *In re* Rothman, 76 B.R. 38 (Bankr. E.D.N.Y. 1987) (debtor discharged from taxes not included in taxing authorities' claim); *see also* § 14.4.2, *supra*. However, the failure of the government to file a proof of claim in a chapter 7 or chapter 11 case does not affect the dischargeability of a tax debt. *But see In re* Hairopolous, 118 F.3d 1240 (8th Cir. 1997) (unfiled IRS claims not discharged due to lack of notice when only notice of bankruptcy that IRS received before claims bar date was no asset chapter 7 notice sent before conversion to chapter 13); *In re* Grynberg, 986 F.2d 367 (10th Cir. 1993). For this reason, it may be advisable for the debtor to file a claim on behalf of the taxing authority in such cases if assets would be distributed in payment of such claim.

135 The IRS form power of attorney, Form 2848, can be obtained from www.irs.ustreas.gov/forms_pubs/forms.html. In some cases it may be sufficient to supply Form 8821, a tax information authorization, which will not cause all future tax notices to be mailed to the attorney as would a power of attorney.

a transcript more quickly if the debtor's counsel calls the tax practitioner hotline, (866) 860-4259, and immediately sends a power of attorney by facsimile. The MFT-30 takes longer to obtain, usually about two weeks. In complicated cases, a Freedom of Information Act request can be sent to the appropriate IRS disclosure office, requesting the debtor's entire file, including the MFT-30, collection file, notices of deficiency, and records of assessments. However, obtaining these records can take several months.

Once counsel obtains the necessary information, the claim for each tax year must be separately analyzed.[136] First, is there a lien securing the claim? If so, to the extent that the lien is not under-secured and is properly recorded, the tax claim (including interest and penalties) is an allowed secured claim. The lien will probably not be eliminated in chapter 7,[137] even if the tax is dischargeable,[138] although a lien for penalties may be avoidable under section 724(a).[139] In chapter 13, a tax claim is not a priority claim to the extent it is an allowed secured claim. Therefore it is not subject to the requirement of section 1322(a)(2) that it be paid in full. However, if the plan provides for the claim, the taxing authority must receive the present value of its allowed secured claim under section 1325(a)(5)(ii).[140] If the plan does not provide for the secured claim, the taxing authority may seek relief from the automatic stay.[141]

If the debtor filed a tax return, the debt is dischargeable in chapter 7 if all of the following are true:

- The return was filed on time, or the return was filed late, but more than two years before the bankruptcy;
- The tax is not a priority claim (see below); and
- The debtor did not willfully evade taxes.

An unsecured tax claim for which a return has not been filed is never dischargeable in chapter 7, but is dischargeable in chapter 13. Similarly, a tax claim based upon a fraudulently filed return is dischargeable in chapter 13.[142] However, a chapter 13 debtor normally must pay all priority tax claims in full, probably including pre-petition interest but not penalties. Whether the claim is a priority claim depends upon when the debtor's tax return was last due and when the tax was last assessable.

The tax debt is a priority claim if the tax return was last due less than three years before the date of the petition. The due date of the return is normally April 15 (but occasionally the

16th or 17th if the 15th is on a weekend) of the year after the tax year. However, if the debtor obtained an extension, the due date would be the extended deadline. If the debtor was in a prior bankruptcy case during this period, it is normally also extended by the amount of time that case was pending.[143]

A tax debt also is a priority debt if it was assessed within 240 days before the petition, or is assessable after the commencement of the case. Federal income tax is assessed on the date the IRS notifies the taxpayer of a tax claim, or perhaps, on the earlier date that an assessment officer signs a summary record of assessment (Form 23-C).[144] The date of the assessment is normally stated on the IRS transcript and when a return is timely filed it is normally around the time of the return. An assessment may be made within three years[145] of when a return is filed or of the last day the return was due, whichever was later. If an amended tax return is filed, a new 240-day period begins to run for additional taxes assessed. Therefore, if a tax is not otherwise a priority tax, no return or amended return should be filed before the bankruptcy case is filed, because it will trigger a new assessment period. The assessment time period does not begin to run when a substitute return is filed by the IRS.[146] The 240 days is extended by the time during which an offer in compromise made after the assessment[147] is pending plus thirty days.[148] If the debtor was in a prior bankruptcy case during this period, it is normally also extended by the amount of time that case was pending.[149]

Once each year's taxes, interest and penalties are analyzed, they may be categorized as allowed secured claims, unsecured priority claims, claims that are nondischargeable in chapter 7 (which overlap with priority claims), and unsecured claims that are dischargeable in chapter 7. The debtor's counsel can then compute the amounts that would not be discharged in chapter 7 and the amounts that would have to be paid in a chapter 13 case, in order to decide which chapter offers the greater benefit.

---

136 For a more detailed discussion of analyzing tax claims, see M. King, Discharging Taxes in Bankruptcy (1996).

137 See § 10.4.2.6.3, *supra,* for discussion of avoiding tax liens.

138 If the tax is dischargeable, the lien cannot attach to after-acquired property, however. *In re* Dishong, 188 B.R. 51 (Bankr. M.D. Fla. 1995).

139 *See* § 10.4.2.6.8, *supra.*

140 *See* § 11.6.1.3, *supra.*

141 *Id.*

142 *In re* Zieg, 194 B.R. 469 (Bankr. D. Neb. 1996), *aff'd,* 206 B.R. 974 (D. Neb. 1997).

143 Young v. United States, 535 U.S. 43, 122 S. Ct.1036, 152 L. Ed. 2d 79 (2002).

144 Treas. Reg. § 301.6203-1.

145 The period is six years if the return omits over twenty-five percent of reportable gross income.

146 *See* § 14.4.3.1.1, *supra.*

147 United States v. Aberl, 175 B.R. 915 (N.D. Ohio 1994) (language in § 507(a)(8) only extends period for offers in compromise made during the 240-day period), *aff'd,* 78 F.3d 241 (6th Cir. 1996); *In re* Colish, 239 B.R. 670 (Bankr. E.D.N.Y. 1999) (same); *see In re* Romagnolo, 269 B.R. 63 (M.D. Fla. 2001) (discussing length of tolling for defective offer in compromise).

148 11 U.S.C. § 507(a)(8)(A)(ii); *see In re* Klein, 189 B.R. 505 (C.D. Cal. 1995) (letter appealing rejection of offer in compromise was not a new offer in compromise); United States v. Aberl, 175 B.R. 915 (N.D. Ohio 1994) (letter asking reconsideration of offer in compromise that was not form letter prescribed by IRS did not renew offer in compromise), *aff'd,* 78 F.3d 241 (6th Cir. 1996).

149 Young v. United States, 535 U.S. 43, 122 S. Ct. 1036, 152 L. Ed. 2d 79 (2002).

14.4.3.2 Debts Incurred Through False Pretenses, Fraud, or False Financial Statements— 11 U.S.C. § 523(a)(2)

14.4.3.2.1 Overview

While the exception to discharge for taxes is the exception most commonly applicable in consumer cases, the exception dealing with false pretenses, fraud and false financial statements[150] is the one which has given rise to the most litigation. Generally speaking, the Code upholds a creditor's timely-filed complaint seeking a determination that a debt is nondischargeable if the debt is for obtaining money, property, services, or an extension, renewal, or refinancing of credit, by false pretenses, a false representation, fraud, or a false financial statement.[151]

Until recently, litigation concerning this exception had decreased in consumer cases for two reasons. First, debts that are not dischargeable under this subsection in chapter 7 may be discharged in chapter 13. And second, creditors who file nondischargeability complaints based upon this subsection and lose are often required to pay attorney fees to the debtor's counsel, as discussed below.

More recently, however, there has been a surge in claims of fraud by creditors in consumer cases. For the most part, this is due to a concerted effort by the credit card industry to establish that consumers who use a credit card when they do not have a present ability to make substantial payments have committed fraud. The basis for these cases is thus the creditor's claim that a consumer using a credit card makes an implied representation about ability to pay. As will be discussed in more detail below, the vast majority of these cases involve consumers who intend to repay and who believe that they will be able to do so.[152] No misrepresentation is involved. Additionally, because the Supreme Court has made clear that justifiable reliance by the creditor on representations by the debtor is a prerequisite to a claim of fraud,[153] and because there is no such reliance in a credit card transaction, credit card non-dischargeability cases brought on this basis should fail.[154]

14.4.3.2.2 Elements which must be proved by the creditor in cases of alleged false financial statements

14.4.3.2.2.1 Generally

To prevail on a complaint alleging nondischargeability under 11 U.S.C. § 523(a)(2)(B), a creditor must prove that the transaction met every element set out in that subsection.[155] All of the exceptions to discharge are to be construed narrowly.[156] The Supreme Court has held that the creditor has the burden of proof on these issues and that the preponderance of the evidence standard is applicable.[157]

14.4.3.2.2.2 The debtor obtained money, property, services, or an extension, renewal, or refinancing of credit

The first element that the creditor must allege and prove is that the debtor obtained money, property, services, or an extension, renewal, or refinancing of credit through the use of the allegedly false statement. Thus, if the creditor has given up nothing in the transaction, the exception to discharge is not applicable.[158]

The exception applies to the extent that the debt arises from a fraudulent act of the debtor whereby the debtor obtained money or property. Thus, the Supreme Court has held that punitive or multiple damages which arise from

---

150 11 U.S.C. § 523(a)(2).

151 A few courts have held that a creditor may also seek a determination of the amount of liability on the underlying debt in the dischargeability action, or other relief related to collection. *In re Kennedy,* 108 F.3d 1015 (9th Cir. 1997) (bankruptcy court could enter money judgment on disputed state law claim it had found nondischargeable); *In re McLaren,* 3 F.3d 958 (6th Cir. 1993) (creditor could seek determination of amount of liability; debtor who had filed voluntary bankruptcy waived right to jury trial); *Abramowitz v. Palmer,* 999 F.2d 1274 (8th Cir. 1993) (court could impose constructive trust on non-debtor spouse's interest in home in connection with dischargeability case). Note that the standard of proof to establish fraud related to the debt may be "clear and convincing evidence" under state law, while a preponderance standard applies to the issue of nondischargeability. *See* Grogan v. Garner, 498 U.S. 279, 111 S. Ct. 654, 112 L. Ed. 2d 755 (1991).

152 *See* § 14.4.3.2.3.2, *infra.*

153 Field v. Mans, 516 U.S. 59, 116 S. Ct. 437, 133 L. Ed. 2d 351 (1995).

154 *See In re* Alvi, 191 B.R. 724 (Bankr. N.D. Ill. 1996); *In re* Willis, 190 B.R. 866 (Bankr. W.D. Mo.), *aff'd,* 200 B.R. 868 (1996); § 14.4.3.2.3.2, *infra.*

155 *In re* Cohn, 54 F.3d 1108 (3d Cir. 1995); *In re* Kimzey, 761 F.2d 421 (7th Cir. 1985).

156 *See, e.g.,* Kawaauhau v. Geiger, 523 U.S. 57, 118 S. Ct. 974, 140 L. Ed. 2d 90 (1998); Gleason v. Thaw, 236 U.S. 558, 562, 35 S. Ct. 287, 289, 59 L. Ed. 717 (1915) ("exceptions to discharge . . . should be confined to those plainly expressed"); *In re* Ward, 857 F.2d 1082 (6th Cir. 1988); *In re* Black, 787 F.2d 503 (10th Cir. 1986); *In re* Hunter, 780 F.2d 1577 (11th Cir. 1986).

157 Grogan v. Garner, 498 U.S. 279, 111 S. Ct. 654, 112 L. Ed. 2d 755 (1991).

158 *See, e.g., In re* Harlan, 7 B.R. 83 (Bankr. D. Ariz. 1980) (forbearance in suing a co-maker is not property); *In re* Kriger, 2 B.R. 19 (Bankr. D. Or. 1979) (creditor who agreed to stipulate to judgment on alleged debt did not give money or property to debtor simply because judgment was less than that which could have been obtained). *But cf. In re* Van Horne, 823 F.2d 1285 (8th Cir. 1987) (debt nondischargeable when debtor obtained renewal while concealing fact that he intended to divorce creditor's daughter).

such fraud are also nondischargeable.[159] It remains unclear, as it was under the prior Act, whether a transaction is covered by this provision when the money, property, and so forth, is obtained by the debtor for another.[160] It is also unclear to what extent a debtor can be held responsible for actions of a spouse or an agent that were fraudulent.[161]

The most important aspect of this element is its applicability to refinancing transactions, which are very common in the world of consumer credit. By adding the words "extension, renewal, or refinancing of credit, to the extent obtained," Congress intended to include the entire refinanced debt in some, but not all, refinancing transactions. This marked a change in the law that had prevailed in many bankruptcy courts; previously, only the amount of the refinanced loan that was "fresh cash" had been held nondischargeable.

The apparent intent of the provision as now worded is to make the entire refinanced loan nondischargeable, but only in cases when the creditor agreed to refinance because of detrimental reliance on the false financial statement.[162] Thus, despite some unfortunate language in the legislative history[163] which seems at first to indicate that the entire refinanced loan is nondischargeable whenever the original loan was in default at the time of refinancing, there is still room in most cases for the argument that the creditor lost nothing, or even gained something, from refinancing.[164] Using repeated refinancing as a method of business keeps the customer "on the book," over a long period of time, and often results in greater payments of interest, application of the "hidden penalty" in the Rule of 78's,[165] and additional loan servicing charges. Thus, especially in cases in which the refinancing was initially suggested by the creditor,[166] or was required by state law when new funds were advanced,[167] a strong argument may be made that the refinancing itself was not detrimental to the creditor[168] and was not obtained by the consumer as a result of any alleged falsehoods.

A number of courts have adopted these arguments in holding only the "new money" or "fresh cash" nondischargeable.[169] When there has been some payment on a loan that is partially nondischargeable, the payment may, at least in some cases, be apportioned pro-rata by the court between the nondischargeable and dischargeable portions.[170]

The "fresh cash" argument received a substantial boost from the 1984 amendments to the Code. Section 523(a)(2)

---

159   Cohen v. de la Cruz, 523 U.S. 213, 118 S. Ct. 1212, 130 L. Ed. 2d 341 (1998).

160   *See In re* Ashley, 903 F.2d 599 (9th Cir. 1990) (debtor who arranged loan for business in which he had financial interest considered to be recipient of the loan); *In re* Ward, 115 B.R. 532 (W.D. Mich. 1990) (debtor did not obtain benefit where shares of stock received were valueless); *In re* Jacobs, 54 B.R. 791 (Bankr. E.D.N.Y. 1985) (debtor did not share in loan proceeds to his client, so no nondischargeable debt despite fraud); 4 Collier on Bankruptcy ¶ 523.08[1] (15th ed. rev.).

161   *See In re* Bonanzio, 91 F.3d 296 (2d Cir. 1996) (debtor responsible only if debtor knew of fraud, or should have known, and knowingly retained benefit from fraud); *In re* Tsurukawa, 258 B.R. 192 (B.A.P. 9th Cir. 2001) (husband's fraud could not be imputed to spouse unless she knowingly participated in fraud, was a business partner, or stood in agency relationship). *See generally* § 14.4.3.2.3.1, *infra*.

162   *See In re* Campbell, 159 F.3d 963 (6th Cir. 1998) (agreement to forbear from collection was an extension of credit induced by false financial statement); *In re* Siriani, 967 F.2d 302 (9th Cir. 1992) (creditor who renewed bond had to show that it relied to its detriment on false representations by giving up valuable collection remedies).

163   124 Cong. Rec. H11,096 (daily ed. Sept. 28, 1978) (remarks of Rep. Don Edwards), *reprinted in* 1978 U.S.C.C.A.N. 6453. The passage in question states that the entire refinancing is nondischargeable "if the existing loan is in default or the creditor *otherwise* reasonably relies to his detriment" (emphasis added). This implies that if the loan was in default but the creditor did not rely to his detriment as to the refinancing aspect, only the fresh cash would be excepted from discharge. The most sensible reading of the statement in question and the actual language of the statute is that only the new money should be excepted from discharge unless the creditor can prove that it would actually have successfully pursued other remedies to recover more from the debtor, that because of the debtor's falsehoods it gave up on that planned course of action, and that it did not have another opportunity to pursue it later. Otherwise, the creditor could prove no detriment with regard to the refinancing aspect of the new transaction. *In re* Gadberry, 37 B.R. 752 (Bankr. C.D. Ill. 1984); *see also* Zaretsky, *The Fraud Exception to Discharge under the New Bankruptcy Code*, 53 Am. Bankr. L. J. 253, 266, 267 (1979).

164   *But see In re* McFarland, 84 F.3d 943, 947 (7th Cir.) (entire debt nondischargeable based on false financial statement related to refinancing); *In re* Goodrich, 999 F.2d 22 (1st Cir. 1993) (entire amount of loan, not just amount extended after false financial statement, was nondischargeable).

165   *See* Hunt, *The Rule of 78: Hidden Penalty in Consumer Credit Transactions*, 55 B.U. L. Rev. 331 (1975).

166   *See, e.g., In re* Archangeli, 6 B.R. 50 (Bankr. D. Me. 1980) (bank desired consolidation because of its belief that debtor would be better able to make payments to it). *But see In re* McFarland, 84 F.3d 943, 947 (7th Cir. 1996) (entire debt found nondischargeable despite creditor requirement that prior debt be repaid).

167   *In re* Danns, 558 F.2d 114 (2d Cir. 1977). The legislative history assents that § 523(a)(2)(B) codifies *Danns* and states that where state law requires a refinancing, only fresh cash is excepted from discharge, but seems to assume that such requirements only exist when there has been no default. *Id.; see* 124 Cong. Rec. H11,096 (daily ed. Sept. 28, 1978) (remarks of Rep. Dan Edwards). However, such requirements also exist if the loan is in default.

168   *See In re* Gadberry, 37 B.R. 752 (Bankr. C.D. Ill. 1984). *But see In re* Liming, 797 F.2d 895 (10th Cir. 1986) (refinancing does not purge fraud in obtaining original loan).

169   *In re* Greenidge, 75 B.R. 245 (Bankr. M.D. Ga. 1987); *In re* Ojeda, 51 B.R. 91 (Bankr. D.N.M. 1985); *In re* Wright, 52 B.R. 27 (Bankr. W.D. Pa. 1985). *But see In re* McFarland, 84 F.3d 943, 947 (7th Cir. 1996); *In re* Kim, 62 F.3d 1511 (9th Cir. 1995), *aff'g* 163 B.R. 161 (B.A.P. 9th Cir. 1994) (creditor must show only that it had valuable collection remedies that it lost during the loan renewal period).

170   *In re* Hunter, 771 F.2d 1126 (8th Cir. 1985).

was amended by the addition of the words "to the extent obtained" as part of the description of those obligations which are nondischargeable. This seemingly made clear that to the extent that credit had already been obtained previously without fraud or a false financial statement such obligations were not covered by the exception.[171]

A refinancing may also extinguish a basis for nondischargeability arising out of the refinanced transaction. If the refinancing is intended to eliminate the liability on the preexisting note, the debtor may be able to argue that all claims arising from that note are also extinguished.[172] However, the Supreme Court has held that, ordinarily, a settlement of a fraud case that substitutes a new contractual obligation does not eliminate the ability to claim that the underlying debt is non-dischargeable due to fraud.[173] The Court did leave open the possibility that a creditor could be precluded from bringing such a claim if the settlement included a promise that the creditor would not make a claim of non-dischargeability for fraud.[174]

14.4.3.2.2.3 The statement was materially false and in writing

The creditor cannot prevail simply by proving that a debtor's financial statement was false. The financial statement must be in writing.[175] In addition, the financial statement must be *materially* false. Credit card lenders are rarely successful in nondischargeability actions brought under section 523(a)(2)(b) because credit card applications are often taken over the phone and typically contain almost no information about the debtor's financial condition that is relied

upon by the lender in granting credit.[176] Small omissions are usually insufficient to meet this materiality test.[177] Similarly, a false statement that is irrelevant to the decision about whether to grant credit is not material.[178] Thus a debtor contesting this element should be entitled to conduct discovery into the creditor's application evaluation process and credit scoring systems and methods to determine what effect the falsehood actually had.

14.4.3.2.2.4 The statement concerned the financial condition of the debtor or an insider

This requirement is similar to the last. The statement must concern the debtor's financial condition. A recital of false information in a deed or contract is insufficient.[179] A statement having no bearing on the debtor's finances or an insider's[180] finances is not sufficient to bar dischargeability of the debt, no matter how false or distorted.

14.4.3.2.2.5 The creditor reasonably relied upon the false statement

Creditors often cannot meet the test requiring a showing that they reasonably relied on a false financial statement. In reality this test encompasses two elements that the creditor must prove—that the creditor in fact relied on the statement, and that such reliance was reasonable. Whether a creditor reasonably relied on a statement depends on all of the circumstances of the case.[181]

---

171 *But see In re* Gerlach, 897 F.2d 1048 (10th Cir. 1990) (fraud committed to obtain extension of credit made debt nondischargeable to extent court could reasonably estimate amount obtained by the fraud, including old debt extended, renewed or refinanced through fraud).

172 *See In re* Fischer, 116 F.3d 388 (9th Cir. 1997) (agreement that was novation of prior contract eliminated any nondischargeability claims arising out of prior contract); *In re* West, 22 F.3d 775 (7th Cir. 1994) (general release included a release of a nondischargeability claim in bankruptcy, stating, because even if the obligation arising from debtor's embezzlement would have been non-dischargeable due to its fraudulent nature, no allegations of fraud surround the note, and the note substituted a contractual obligation for a tortious one). *But see* United States v. Spicer, 57 F.3d 1152 (D.C. Cir. 1995) (settlement agreement on fraud claim did not extinguish nondischargeability claims grounded in underlying debt).

173 Archer v. Warner, 538 U.S. 314, 123 S. Ct. 1462, 155 L. Ed. 2d 454 (2003); *see also In re* Detrano, 326 F.3d 319 (2d Cir. 2003).

174 Archer v. Warner, 538 U.S. 314, 322, 123 S. Ct. 1468, 155 L. Ed. 2d 463 (2003).

175 *In re* Kaspar, 125 F.3d 1358 (10th Cir. 1997) (credit card application taken over telephone not in writing, even though lender later transferred debtor's answers to a document); Blackwell v. Dabney, 702 F.2d 490 (4th Cir. 1983); *In re* Jackson, 252 B.R. 877 (Bankr. W.D.N.Y. 2000).

176 *In re* Simos, 209 B.R. 193 (Bankr. M.D.N.C. 1997) (claim under section 523(a)(2)(b) denied where lender presented no evidence that application was relied upon). Credit card lenders usually rely upon a credit report in making credit decisions.

177 *Compare In re* Adams, 368 F. Supp. 80 (D.S.D. 1973) (small amounts omitted in proportion to total listed not material) *with In re* Harasymiw, 895 F.2d 1170 (7th Cir. 1990) (failure to disclose $128,000.00 mortgage on property offered as collateral for loan was material); *In re* Barrett, 2 B.R. 296 (Bankr. E.D. Pa. 1980) (omission of $10,000.00 debt changed outcome in formula lender used to determine whether to extend credit).

178 *In re* Furio, 77 F.3d 622 (11th Cir. 1996) (omission of child support obligation from financial statement not materially false when support was taken into account by creditor and decision to grant credit was not affected); *In re* Bogstad, 779 F.2d 370 (7th Cir. 1985) (if lender would have made loan regardless of misrepresentation, then the misrepresentation was not material); *cf. In re* Jordan, 927 F.2d 221 (5th Cir. 1991) (failure to disclose encumbrances on debtor's liquid assets was material omission; bank would never have approved loan if encumbrances had been revealed).

179 *In re* Phillips, 804 F.2d 930 (6th Cir. 1986) (misstatement of acreage in a deed is not a false written statement of debtor's financial condition).

180 "Insider" is defined at 11 U.S.C. § 101(31) and includes relatives of the debtor.

181 *In re* Coston, 987 F.2d 1096 (5th Cir. 1992) (trial court's finding of reasonable reliance based on circumstances would not be overturned unless clearly erroneous).

Thus, when a creditor relies on the consumer's past record of dealing with the creditor or on other information,[182] this standard is not met. If a loan or refinancing is offered and agreed to before the false financial statement is executed, no reliance can be shown.[183] Often, other information possessed by the creditor, such as a credit report, indicates that the financial statement is false, and if the creditor had reason to know that the financial statement was false, it could not have relied upon it.[184] Similarly, if the financial statement was perfunctorily completed for the file and the creditor made no real reference to it in granting credit, no reliance can be shown.[185] This may be the case in some situations in which a lien is taken and the creditor relies on the value of the property subject to the lien rather than on the debtor's ability to make payment.[186]

Even if the creditor shows that it did rely on the statement, that reliance may not have been reasonable. The reasonableness test requires consideration of whether the creditor followed its standard practices in evaluating creditworthiness, whether the creditor followed the standards or customs of the creditor's industry by conducting a commercially reasonable investigation, whether there was a "red flag" that would have alerted a prudent lender to the possibility that the debtor's statement was inaccurate, and whether even minimal investigation would have revealed the debtor's misrepresentations.[187]

If the creditor did not obtain a credit report, or check any information given by the debtor, its reliance may not have met this standard.[188] And if the creditor told the debtor not to worry about listing every single debt owed on the financial statement, it could not have reasonably relied on that statement. Some courts have even held that a creditor may not reasonably rely on a list of debts unless it includes the statement that all debts have been included.[189] In litigating a false financial statement case it is important to obtain discovery with respect to all of the persons involved in the transaction on behalf of the creditor, and what information they did and did not obtain elsewhere. Obviously, if such witnesses are no longer employed by the creditor, it will be difficult for it to prove its case.

14.4.3.2.2.6 The debtor's intent to deceive

Finally, the creditor must prove that the debtor had an actual intent to deceive it through the use of the false financial statement.[190] If the debtor's false disclosure was innocently or negligently made, the debt is dischargeable, although some courts have considered a "reckless indifference" to the truth to be equivalent to intentional falsehood.[191] Thus, debtors who failed to list debts because they

---

182 *In re* Bruce, 214 B.R. 938 (Bankr. E.D.N.Y. 1997) (lender did not rely on loan application omission concerning $400.00 per month obligation as debtors were otherwise qualified for loan based on lender's debt to income ration guideline); *In re* Savich, 82 B.R. 1011 (Bankr. W.D. Mo. 1988) (bank's course of dealing with borrower established that bank ignored the debtor's financial statements which contained misrepresentations); *In re* Lacey, Bankr. L. Rep. (CCH) ¶ 67,715 (Bankr. S.D.N.Y. 1980).

183 *In re* Greene, 65 B.R. 266 (Bankr. M.D. Fla. 1986).

184 *In re* Morris, 223 F.3d 548 (7th Cir. 2000) (when creditor, based on past experience, had doubts about debtor's statements, reliance without further investigation was not reasonable); *In re* Baratta, 272 B.R. 501 (Bankr. M.D. Fla. 2001); *In re* Michael, 265 B.R. 593 (Bankr. W.D. Tenn. 2001) (no reliance when creditor ignored "red flags" based on its knowledge of omissions in financial statement that it helped debtors to prepare and fill out); *In re* Smith, 2 B.R. 276 (Bankr. E.D. Va. 1980); *In re* Schlickman, 6 B.R. 281 (Bankr. D. Mass. 1980); *In re* Lamb, Bankr. L. Rep. (CCH) ¶ 67,202 (Bankr. S.D.N.Y. 1979); *see also In re* Coston, 987 F.2d 1096 (5th Cir. 1992) (creditor's reliance on debtor's statement that retirement account could easily be converted to cash was not reasonable).

185 *In re* Jones, 3 B.R. 410 (Bankr. W.D. Va. 1980).

186 *But see In re* Collins, 946 F.2d 815 (11th Cir. 1991) (it is not unreasonable for creditor to fail to perfect its lien even if the security interest would have fully protected it from injury arising from debtor's false representation).

187 *In re* Cohn, 54 F.3d 1108 (3d Cir. 1995).

188 *In re* Jones, 31 F.3d 659 (8th Cir. 1994) (reliance not reasonable where "red flags" should have alerted creditor to investigate

further); *In re* Kirsh, 973 F.2d 1454 (9th Cir. 1992) (attorney creditor did not show required justifiable reliance in believing debtor's representations regarding liens on property without ordering a title report); *In re* Ward, 857 F.2d 1082 (6th Cir. 1988) (bank did not reasonably rely on misrepresentation in card application where it did not even conduct superficial credit investigation); *In re* Rosel, 63 B.R. 603 (Bankr. W.D. Ky. 1986) (no effort by creditor to check accuracy of information); *In re* Breen, 13 B.R. 965 (Bankr. S.D. Ohio 1981) (creditor did not act reasonably in failing to make credit check). *But see In re* Woolum, 979 F.2d 71 (6th Cir. 1992) (lower court not clearly erroneous in finding that bank could reasonably rely on statements despite the fact that they were incomplete and contained mistakes); *In re* Watson, 958 F.2d 977 (10th Cir. 1992) (reliance without obtaining verification was reasonable where debtor had been introduced to bank by well-respected customer who verbally agreed to guarantee loan); *In re* Jordan, 927 F.2d 221 (5th Cir. 1991) (reasonable reliance found where bank failed to order credit check, because debtor was a well known customer and bank contacted another bank to confirm accuracy of financial statements); *In re* Bonnet, 895 F.2d 1155 (7th Cir. 1989) (even if financial statements should have raised "red flags"; evidence supported conclusion that creditor reasonably relied on false financial statements); *In re* Dallam, 850 F.2d 446 (8th Cir. 1988) (misrepresentation induced action irrespective of reliance); *In re* Phillips, 804 F.2d 930 (6th Cir. 1986) (long term prior relationship may excuse a creditor's failure to check credit information); *In re* Garman, 643 F.2d 1252 (7th Cir. 1980) (creditor reliance reasonable despite absence of further investigation where debtor was a long time customer); *In re* Allen, 65 B.R. 752 (E.D. Va. 1986). The issue of reasonable reliance is reviewed on appeal as a factual finding that is not reversible unless it is clearly erroneous. *In re* Coston, 991 F.2d 257 (5th Cir. 1993) (*en banc*).

189 *See* Dial Fin. v. Duthu, 188 So. 2d 151 (La. Ct. App. 1966).

190 *In re* Martin, 963 F.2d 809 (5th Cir. 1992) (fraud involves moral turpitude or intentional wrong and misrepresentations must be knowingly and fraudulently made).

191 Knoxville Teachers Credit Union v. Parkey, 790 F.2d 490 (6th Cir. 1986) (misrepresentation of liabilities by $4300.00 was

thought a spouse or relative was responsible for paying them have been found to be without intent to deceive.[192] Similarly, debtors who made a good faith effort, but omitted debts such as taxes in answering ambiguous questions, were entitled to discharge of the debts involved.[193] Given good faith, even seriously inaccurate estimates of assets or liabilities do not constitute intentional deception.[194] The debtor may also have simply assumed that the creditor knew of debts from prior statements or other sources. However, it has been held that an intent to deceive can be inferred from the circumstances.[195]

One common defense on the question of intent arises out of the practices of creditors who mislead debtors about the purpose of the financial statement. It is well known, and indeed it was noted in the legislative history of the Code,[196] that some finance companies require a financial statement for future use in bankruptcy proceedings rather than for making the decision to grant credit. These creditors typically provide a form that has very little space for listing debts and they orally advise the debtor not to worry if the list is not complete. Some creditors describe the form as a mere formality or as a list of credit references. Such companies then retain the form for use in a bankruptcy case, in which they challenge the dischargeability of the debt,[197] hoping that the debtor will reaffirm rather than pay an attorney to litigate the matter.

In cases where such conduct can be shown, of course, there is no intent to deceive on the part of the debtor,[198] nor is there reasonable reliance on the part of the creditor. Often, it can be helpful to conduct discovery into the company's practices, and particularly the number of cases in which it has filed complaints seeking to have debts ruled nondischargeable. Finding more than a very few such cases is usually fatal to the creditor's complaint.

14.4.3.2.3 Debts incurred through false pretenses or fraud

14.4.3.2.3.1 Generally

Very similar to cases dealing with false financial statements are complaints challenging dischargeability on the basis of false pretenses, false representations, or actual fraud.[199] These complaints are usually based upon information conveyed by the debtor, orally, in writing, or by conduct, but not in a written financial statement.[200]

A debtor will be denied the discharge of a particular debt under this section if it is shown that the creditor provided money, property, services, or an extension, renewal, or refinancing of credit[201] due to an intentionally and materially false statement by the debtor[202] upon which the creditor justifiably relied.[203] This standard is basically the standard for fraud at common law.[204] However, the fraud must be actual, and not constructive or implied by law.[205]

---

grossly reckless and satisfied the element of intentional deception); Birmingham Trust Nat'l Bank v. Case, 755 F.2d 1474 (11th Cir. 1985); *In re* Martin, 761 F.2d 1163 (6th Cir. 1985) ("grossly reckless disregard" for truth was sufficient to come within exception to discharge); *see also In re* Lansford, 822 F.2d 902 (9th Cir. 1987) (debt nondischargeable as to wife where she signed purchase documents which repeated misrepresentations in husband's financial statement).

192 *In re* Mosley, 4 B.R. 177 (Bankr. S.D. Fla. 1980); *In re* Mausser, 4 B.R. 728 (Bankr. S.D. Fla. 1980).

193 *In re* Miller, 39 F.3d 301 (11th Cir. 1994) (based upon totality of circumstances, bankruptcy court correctly held that there was no intent to deceive when assets were valued on net basis and real estate values were in flux); Gabellini v. Rega, 724 F.2d 579 (7th Cir. 1984) (accounting error not intentional deception); Firstmark Capital Corp. v. Shuback, Bankr. L. Rep. (CCH) ¶ 67,514 (Bankr. W.D. Mo. 1980).

194 *In re* Rosel, 63 B.R. 603 (Bankr. W.D. Ky. 1986).

195 *In re* Young, 995 F.2d 547 (5th Cir. 1993).

196 H.R. Rep. No. 95-595, at 130 (1977).

197 *See, e.g.,* All State Credit Plan, Halihan v. Anderson, 250 So. 2d 806 (La. Ct. App. 1971).

198 *See, e.g., In re* Rosia, 4 B.R. 701 (Bankr. S.D. Fla. 1980) (debtor instructed to state falsely that she owned a home).

199 11 U.S.C. § 523(a)(2)(A).

200 Under the Federal Rules of Civil Procedure, fraud must be pleaded with particularity. A creditor's failure to do so might be grounds to dismiss the complaint. *See In re* Sibley, 71 B.R. 147 (Bankr. D. Mass. 1987) (complaint must appraise debtor of acts that form basis for claim).

201 *See* § 14.4.3.2.2.2, *supra,* for further discussion of whether debtor obtained money, property, services, extension, renewal, or refinancing.

202 The debtor may commit fraud through the agency of another person only if the debtor knew or should have known of the fraud. *See In re* Bonanzio, 91 F.3d 296 (2d Cir. 1996) (debtor responsible only if debtor knew of fraud, or should have known, and knowingly retained benefit from fraud); *In re* Allison, 960 F.2d 481 (5th Cir. 1992) (debt that was nondischargeable with respect to husband held dischargeable with respect to wife who did not participate in transaction); *In re* Walker, 726 F.2d 452 (8th Cir. 1984); *In re* Tsurukawa, 258 B.R. 192 (B.A.P. 9th Cir. 2001) (husband's fraud could not be imputed to spouse unless she knowingly participated in fraud, was a business partner, or stood in agency relationship); *In re* Allen, 65 B.R. 752 (E.D. Va. 1986) (wife who did not sign spouse's false financial statement was not denied discharge of debt). *But see In re* M.M. Winkler & Associates, 239 F.3d 746 (5th Cir. 2001) (fraud imputed to innocent partner even if not carried out in ordinary course of business and innocent partner did not benefit from it); *In re* Ledford, 970 F.2d 1556 (6th Cir. 1992) (fraud of one partner imputed to other general partner where fraud was carried out in ordinary course of partnership's business and other partner profited from fraud); *In re* Luce, 960 F.2d 1277 (5th Cir. 1992) (fraud of one partner committed in ordinary course of partnership's business imputed to other partner).

203 Field v. Mans, 516 U.S. 59, 116 S. Ct. 437, 133 L. Ed. 2d 351 (1995).

204 Field v. Mans, 516 U.S. 59, 116 S. Ct. 437, 133 L. Ed. 2d 351 (1995) (false pretenses, false representation, and actual fraud are common law terms and "they imply elements that the common law has defined them to include.").

205 *See* 124 Cong. Rec. H11,095, H11,096 (daily ed. Sept. 28, 1978); S17,412, S17,413 (daily ed. Oct. 6, 1978) (section 523(a)(2)(A) was intended to codify the holding in Neal v. Clark, 95 U.S. 704, 24 L. Ed. 586 (1877), which interpreted

Thus, debtors who have obtained money in their businesses through deliberate misrepresentations about security interests, or about the use that would be made of the funds, have been denied discharge on those debts.[206] Loans obtained through knowing misrepresentations about other intended activities may also be nondischargeable.[207] In addition, an intentional failure to disclose a material fact may constitute false pretenses. Debtors who fail to disclose significant facts about a transaction, or about unrecorded mortgages on real estate, have been denied discharges of debts incurred in that fashion.[208] However, other courts have held that, absent explicit representations concerning financial condition, there can be no false pretenses or false representations.[209]

Just as with false financial statements, all of the elements of the exception to discharge must be proved in each case. The creditor must prove both intent on the part of the debtor and justifiable reliance on the part of the person who was allegedly deceived.[210] Thus, it is not sufficient to show simply that the debtor wrote a bad check. It must also be shown that the check induced the transfer of money, property, or credit;[211] if it was given in payment of an antecedent debt, no false pretenses exist. Furthermore, the intent requirement is not satisfied unless the debtor knew at the time the check was issued that it would not be honored.[212] In fact,

the Seventh Circuit Court of Appeals has held that a check, by itself, is not even a statement and therefore a bad check cannot be a false statement that gives rise to a nondischargeable claim.[213] In cases in which bad checks are involved, therefore, a creditor must prove some other false pretenses besides the check itself. The fact that a representation or promise later turns out to be one that the debtor does not fulfill is not sufficient to show intent.[214] Otherwise, almost every debt would be nondischargeable under this exception.

The requirement of justifiable reliance, which was enunciated by the Supreme Court in *Field v. Mans*,[215] is slightly different than the test for reasonable reliance used with respect to false financial statements. It judges whether the creditor's reliance on the debtor's false pretenses or false statement was justifiable based upon "the qualities and characteristics of the particular plaintiff, and the circumstances of the particular case."[216] It differs from reasonable reliance, which is an objective standard applicable to all creditors based on community norms.[217]

---

fraud under the Bankruptcy Act to mean actual or positive fraud rather than fraud implied by law).

206 *In re* Miller, 5 B.R. 424 (Bankr. W.D. La. 1980); *In re* Jones, 2 B.R. 46 (Bankr. N.D. Ala. 1979).

207 *In re* Milbank, 1 B.R. 150 (Bankr. S.D.N.Y. 1979) (debtor obtained loan from wife and her father upon representation that he would try to strengthen marriage; loan found nondischargeable upon proof that he was at same time engaged in affair with wife of next door neighbor).

208 *In re* Quintana, 4 B.R. 508 (Bankr. S.D. Fla. 1980); *In re* Flanzbaum, 7 B.R. 826 (Bankr. S.D. Fla. 1980).

209 *In re* Hunter, 780 F.2d 1577 (11th Cir. 1986).

210 *See In re* Slyman, 234 F.3d 1081 (9th Cir. 2000) (home owner's association did not rely on any representation by debtor in providing services which it provided as a matter of course to all home owners); *In re* Rubin, 875 F.2d 755 (9th Cir. 1989) (claimants were entitled to rely on the debtor/real estate agent's misrepresentations based on his position and apparent experience); *In re* Mullet, 817 F.2d 677 (10th Cir. 1987); *In re* Finkel, 21 B.R. 17 (B.A.P. 9th Cir. 1982); *In re* Drake, 5 B.R. 149 (Bankr. D. Idaho 1980) (debtors did not have intent to convert vehicles taken for resale even though they ultimately did not pass on proceeds to the original seller). *But see In re* Allison, 960 F.2d 481 (5th Cir. 1992) (creditor need not prove reasonable reliance under § 523(a)(2) (A)); *In re* Ophaug, 827 F.2d 340 (8th Cir. 1987) (reasonable reliance need not be shown under § 523(a)(2)(A)).

211 *But see In re* Campbell, 159 F.3d 963 (6th Cir. 1998) (agreement to forbear from collection was an extension of credit); Field v. Mans, 157 F.3d 35 (1st Cir. 1998) (fraudulent concealment of sale of property that would have permitted acceleration of mortgage induced non-acceleration which was deemed an extension of credit).

212 *In re* Davis, 246 B.R. 646 (B.A.P. 10th Cir. 2000) (debtor expected to deposit funds in account to pay check), *aff'd in part, vacated in part on other grounds*, 35 Fed. Appx. 826 (10th Cir.

2002); *In re* Burgstaler, 58 B.R.508 (Bankr. D. Minn. 1985) (even if the debtor knew there were insufficient funds to cover the check, no intent may be present if the debtor expected to be able to deposit money in the account before the check was honored); *In re* Denson, 7 B.R. 213 (Bankr. E.D. Va. 1980) (debtor believed he was entitled to draw moneys in excess of the amounts scheduled and did not conceal that excess); *In re* Wise, 6 B.R. 867 (Bankr. M.D. Fla. 1980) (creditor did not reasonably rely on NSF checks (checks returned due to insufficient funds in drawer's account) because debtor had previously submitted such checks, creditor had access to checkbook, creditor made out checks for debtor to sign, and evidence also showed debtor intended to pay); *see also In re* Sibley, 71 B.R. 147 (Bankr. D. Mass. 1987) (allegation that debtor issued check which was dishonored is sufficient to state a claim under § 523(a)(2)(A)).

213 *In re* Scarlata, 979 F.2d 521 (7th Cir. 1992); *see also* Williams v. United States, 458 U.S. 279, 102 S. Ct. 3088, 73 L. Ed. 2d 767 (1982) (issuance of a check is not an implied representation that the payor has sufficient funds in the account to cover the check); *In re* Trevisan, 300 B.R. 708 (Bankr. E.D. Wis. 2003) (check not representation of any kind); *In re* Coatney, 185 B.R. 546 (Bankr. N.D. Ohio 1995).

214 *In re* Ashley, 5 B.R. 262 (Bankr. E.D. Tenn. 1980) (no false representation simply because goods sold proved defective); *In re* Brooks, 4 B.R. 237 (Bankr. S.D. Fla. 1980) (no showing that debtor's implied representation that note would be paid was known to be false at time note was executed); *see also In re* Kroen, 280 B.R. 347 (Bankr. D.N.J. 2002) (alleged promise that debtor would not later seek to discharge debt in bankruptcy was invalid as matter of public policy, so creditor attorney could not have justifiably relied on it).

215 516 U.S. 59, 116 S. Ct. 437, 133 L. Ed. 2d 351 (1995).

216 *Id.*, 516 U.S. at 70, 71; *see In re* Spadoni, 316 F.3d 56 (1st Cir. 2003) (reversing bankruptcy court finding that landlord "should have known" that tenant's promises to pay overdue rent were not reasonable, court of appeals made de novo judgment that reliance was justifiable based on friendship between the parties and other circumstances); Sanford Inst. for Sav. v. Gallo, 156 F.3d 71 (1st Cir. 1998) (due to circumstances of case, creditor justifiably relied on debtor's representations even though it failed to conduct title search which would have revealed fraud).

217 Field v. Mans, 516 U.S. 59, 116 S. Ct. 437, 133 L. Ed. 2d 351 (1995).

14.4.3.2.3.2 Credit cards and other credit use with no intent to pay

The most common allegation of false pretenses is that the debtor obtained money, goods, or services on credit with no intent to pay. As distinguished from debts that the debtor *later* finds himself or herself unable or unwilling to pay, debts incurred through false pretenses were incurred through an intentionally false representation that they would be paid. Because many courts have found that such a representation may be found to have been implied,[218] rather than expressed, it is not surprising that difficult problems of proof can arise as to intent and as to exactly when the debtor decided that the debt would not be paid.

In consumer cases, these issues arise most frequently when credit cards are involved, particularly if there is evidence of an unusual "buying spree" shortly before the bankruptcy. It is not uncommon for creditors to allege that such use of credit constitutes a knowing misrepresentation, upon which they justifiably relied, that the debt could and would be paid.

As the creditor has the burden of proof in such cases, it must produce evidence which proves these allegations. The 1984 and 1994 amendments to the Code made this burden far easier for creditors to meet in certain specified circumstances when a debtor allegedly "loaded up" prior to bankruptcy. In any case in which a debtor incurred consumer debts[219] in excess of $1225.00 to a single creditor for luxury goods or services within sixty days prior to filing a bankruptcy, or cash advances[220] on an open end credit plan[221] of over $1225.00 within sixty days prior to a filing, there is a presumption that the debts were incurred through false pretenses.[222]

"Luxury goods or services" are defined in this subsection as goods and services that are not reasonably acquired for the support or maintenance of the debtor or the debtor's dependents.[223] Therefore, the presumption would not arise if the debtor purchased more than $1225.00 worth of ordinary clothing or a necessary major appliance.[224] Similarly, when a debt is incurred to refinance an earlier debt within sixty days prior to bankruptcy, the presumption does not arise, even if the earlier debt was to purchase luxury goods or services, because those goods and services were not obtained during the sixty-day period.[225] And even when the subsection's standards are met, the presumption is rebuttable. It may be overcome if the debtor can show a sudden change in circumstances after the transaction or that bankruptcy had not been contemplated until after the transaction when the debtor consulted counsel. Indeed, it should be overcome in any case in which the court is convinced that the debtor honestly intended to pay the debt.[226]

The presumption is also not operative unless the creditor files a timely dischargeability complaint. The amendments did not alter Code section 523(c) which, as discussed above,[227] provides that a claim of nondischargeability under section 523(a)(2) is lost if not raised during the bankruptcy case.

---

218 *But see In re* Alvi, 191 B.R. 724 (Bankr. N.D. Ill. 1996) (use of credit card did not involve any representation, either express or implied); *In re* Cox, 182 B.R. 626 (Bankr. D. Mass. 1995) (credit card debt cannot be found nondiscahrgeable based upon implied misrepresentation on intention to pay).

219 "Consumer debt" is defined at 11 U.S.C. § 101(8).

220 *See In re* Manning, 280 B.R. 171 (Bankr. S.D. Ohio 2002) (balance transfer is not a cash advance). Convenience checks are not normally considered cash advances. *See In re* Welch, 208 B.R. 107 (S.D.N.Y. 1997) (cash advance is ATM withdrawal or a check written to cash); *In re* Poor, 219 B.R. 332 (Bankr. D. Me. 1998) (balance transfer was not a "cash advance" under this section); *In re* Cameron, 219 B.R. 531 (Bankr. W.D. Mo. 1998) (same); *In re* Woods, 66 B.R. 984 (Bankr. E.D. Pa. 1986).

221 A single loan from a finance company is not an open-end credit plan. *In re* Hulbert, 150 B.R. 169 (Bankr. S.D. Tex. 1993).

222 11 U.S.C. § 523(a)(2)(C). Pursuant to 11 U.S.C. § 104(b), the dollar amounts in section 523(a)(2)(c) are adjusted every three years. *See generally In re* Koch, 83 B.R. 898 (Bankr. E.D. Pa. 1988).

223 11 U.S.C. § 523(a)(2)(C); *see, e.g., In re* Shaw, 294 B.R. 652 (Bankr. W.D. Pa. 2003) (payments to divorce attorney not for luxury services); *In re* Hall, 228 B.R. 483 (Bankr. M.D. Ga. 1998) (gambling in which debtor engaged, in desperate attempt to pay off casino markers was not in the nature of a "luxury"); *In re* Vernon, 192 B.R. 165 (Bankr. N.D. Ill. 1996) (legal services for divorce proceedings were not luxury services); *In re* Claar, 72 B.R. 319 (Bankr. M.D. Fla. 1987) (lifetime membership to PTL religious theme park); *In re* Herran, 66 B.R. 323 (Bankr. S.D. Fla. 1986) ($1021.00 worth of giftware, cosmetics, fragrances, and clothing); *In re* Hussey, 59 B.R. 573 (Bankr. M.D. Ala. 1986) (three-wheeled vehicle). Cash used to pay other debts is not a luxury good. *In re* Woods, 66 B.R. 984 (Bankr. E.D. Pa. 1986). An unrestricted cash loan is also not covered by this provision, even if it is used to purchase luxury goods. *In re* Neal, 113 B.R. 607 (B.A.P. 9th Cir. 1990).

224 *In re* Larisey, 185 B.R. 877 (Bankr. M.D. Fla. 1995) (air conditioner repair and carpet were not luxury goods or services).

225 *In re* Shurbier, 134 B.R. 922 (Bankr. W.D. Mo. 1991) (loan to repay earlier debt for goods and services did not give rise to presumption); *In re* Smith, 54 B.R. 299 (Bankr. S.D. Iowa 1985).

226 *See In re* Cline, 282 B.R. 493 (Bankr. W.D. Wash. 2002) (because debtor used her account for necessities, and always planned to repay, the presumption of fraud burst and burden of proof reverted to creditor); *In re* Johansen, 160 B.R. 328 (Bankr. W.D. Wis. 1993) (presumption overcome because debtor did not know, when she bought collector edition dolls, that her husband planned to file bankruptcy case and that his attorney would advise joint petition, and debtor had intended to pay for dolls even though she did not have money immediately available); *In re* McDonald, 129 B.R. 279 (Bankr. M.D. Fla. 1991) (presumption overcome by debtor's conduct); *In re* Leaird, 106 B.R. 177 (Bankr. W.D. Wis. 1989) (presumption overcome by proof that debtors made purchases impulsively and did not contemplate bankruptcy until they subsequently became aware of a different debt).

227 *See* § 14.4.2, *supra.*

Obviously, any anticipated problems that might be caused by the presumption may be avoided in most cases by delaying a bankruptcy until after the applicable time period has passed. However, the time period is only relevant to the automatic presumption. Debts incurred prior to that period may still be found nondischargeable for fraud or false pretenses. Eliminating the presumption means simply that the creditor has the burden of going forward, as well as the burden of proof, on all elements of the cause of action in such cases.

To show fraudulent intent, it is not sufficient to prove simply that the debt was incurred and not paid, because that much is true of all dischargeable debts.[228] Usually, absent an admission on the part of the debtor, it is almost impossible to prove the debtor's intent through direct evidence or statements that the debtor has made. These difficulties have led courts to look to circumstantial evidence.

The courts have considered several indicia as strong evidence of fraudulent intent.[229] The first of these is a surge of credit use shortly before the bankruptcy. When a debtor suddenly resigned from her job and left home to travel extensively on credit, without notifying anyone of her whereabouts, it was not hard for the court to infer intent, despite a defense that such activities were the result of mental illness.[230] A debtor who shortly before his bankruptcy charged more than $60,000.00 in luxury items on a trip to France, which was more than his annual income, and who had no assets other than a home that was subject to foreclosure, was found to have had no intent to repay the debt.[231] And a debtor who engaged in an elaborate scheme of "credit card kiting," using one card to make minimum payments on another, was found to have had no intent to repay.[232] Similarly, a debtor who made approximately $1000.00 worth of credit purchases, most of which were gift certificates used not for others but for himself, the court found such behavior more than a little suspicious.[233]

A few courts have gone so far as to say that any substantial use of credit, at least by a sophisticated debtor, at a time when the debtor should have known that he or she would be unable to pay, constitutes false pretenses.[234] But most courts have held that use of the card at a time when the debtor was unable to pay, by itself is not sufficient to show that the debtor lacked intention to repay.[235] The key issue is whether the debtor had a subjective intent, even if unrealistic, to repay. If the debtor intended to repay, the debt should be found dischargeable.[236] One of the primary purposes of credit use is to purchase items the debtor could not otherwise then afford to purchase.[237] Normally, debtors who use credit when they have little income expect their circumstances to improve so they will be able to repay.

A second indication of fraudulent intent is the use of the credit card after it is no longer permitted by the credit contract, either because the credit limit has been exceeded or because the creditor has instructed the debtor to destroy, return, or cease using the card.[238] Some courts have held that such use constitutes intentional false representation to the merchant that the card is being used in compliance with the terms of the contract and is therefore fraudulent by itself.[239] The evidence of fraud has been found stronger for a debtor who ceased to make purchases in excess of $50.00, the amount at which merchants at that time customarily called for credit approval.[240] And, of course, proof that the debtor consulted an attorney or other evidence that bankruptcy was contemplated at the time of the credit use is quite helpful to the creditor's cause.[241]

---

228 *In re* Richards, 196 B.R. 481 (Bankr. E.D. Ark. 1996) (mere draw down of credit limit through cash advances does not prove intention to deceive); *see also In re* Sinclair, 191 B.R. 474 (Bankr. M.D. Fla. 1996) (credit card issuer denied default judgment when sole allegation was that debtor used card eight to nine months before bankruptcy case, with no specific facts indicating fraud); *In re* Roberts, 193 B.R. 828 (Bankr. W.D. Mich. 1996) (default judgment denied when bank offered no evidence of debtor's intent or any other evidence other than charges made).

229 *See generally In re* Dougherty, 84 B.R. 653 (B.A.P. 9th Cir. 1988).

230 *In re* Banasiak, 8 B.R. 171 (Bankr. M.D. Fla. 1981).

231 *In re* Hashemi, 104 F.3d 1122 (9th Cir. 1996).

232 *In re* Eashai, 87 F.3d 1082 (9th Cir. 1996). However, as the concurring opinion points out, the decision does not mean that a debtor commits fraud any time one credit card is used to make a payment on another. Indeed, credit card grantors encourage such "balance transfers."

233 *In re* Ratajczak, 5 B.R. 583 (Bankr. M.D. Fla. 1980).

234 *In re* Kell, 6 B.R. 695 (Bankr. D. Colo. 1980) (debtor obtained new cards after filing chapter 13 case, and after admitting he was "broke," and proceeded to incur new purchases amounting to about $2500.00, paying only about $600.00 of them); *cf. In re* Larson, 136 B.R. 540 (Bankr. D. N.D. 1992) (credit card use even after chapter 11 filing was not fraudulent where debtor did not increase use and continued to make substantial payments on bill and reduced balance).

235 *In re* Sziel, 209 B.R. 712 (Bankr. N.D. Ill. 1997).

236 *In re* Ettell, 188 F.3d 1141 (9th Cir. 1999) (debtor had intent to repay, even if it was objectively unlikely he would be able to do so); *In re* Rembert, 141 F.3d 277 (6th Cir. 1998) (debtor had intent to repay when she took cash advances for gambling); *In re* Anastas, 94 F.3d 1280 (9th Cir. 1996) (nondischargeability determination may not be based solely upon fact that at time debts were incurred debtor was not likely to be able to repay them; additional evidence of fraudulent intent is required).

237 *In re* Hernandez, 208 B.R. 872, 879 (Bankr. W.D. Tex. 1997) (major reason consumers use credit cards is a present lack of ability to repay, and this is also primary reason lenders want consumers to use credit cards).

238 *In re* Brewster, 5 Bankr. Ct. Dec. (LRP) 783 (Bankr. E.D. Va. 1979); *see In re* Dougherty, 84 B.R. 653 (B.A.P. 9th Cir. 1988).

239 *In re* Nolan, 1 B.R. 644 (Bankr. M.D. Fla. 1979); *In re* Cushingberry, 5 Bankr. Ct. Dec. (LRP) 954 (Bankr. E.D. Mich. 1977).

240 *In re* Schartner, 7 B.R. 885 (Bankr. N.D. Ohio 1980). Such evidence, however, is not conclusive. *In re* Dougherty, 84 B.R. 653 (B.A.P. 9th Cir. 1988).

241 *But see In re* Cacho, 137 B.R. 864 (Bankr. N.D. Fla. 1991) (fact

A debtor may raise a number of arguments in defense against such claims. Most courts have held that exceeding the credit limit, without more, is not sufficient to constitute false pretenses.[242] Especially if the creditor has acquiesced in such use of a credit card over a period of months, the creditor should be estopped from later challenging it, or it should be found that the contract was changed by the parties' conduct.[243] Indeed, the Eleventh Circuit Court of Appeals has held that debts incurred through credit card use cannot be excepted from discharge unless the use occurs after an unequivocal revocation of credit card privileges.[244] A debtor's honest belief that she could and would pay, even if that belief is ill-founded, negates any fraudulent intent.[245] An absence of fraudulent intent is also evidenced in many cases by return of the credit cards when that is finally requested.[246]

In addition, a debtor can fairly argue that there was no reliance at the time of the card transaction because the creditor was relying on the express agreement to repay that had occurred when the card was issued, along with its investigation at that time, and because the debtor never communicated with the creditor at the time of the transaction.[247] Justifiable reliance may also be challenged based upon the credit granting investigation and standards used in a particular case. If the creditor knew the debtor had no income at the time the card was granted, or never even asked the debtor's income, a court is unlikely to find justifiable reliance.[248] As with reliance on alleged false financial statements, credit card lenders cannot ignore "red flags" that would cause a prudent lender to question the decision to extend credit.[249] If the debtor immediately begins to use the card primarily for gambling, or to make late payments, and the creditor continues to extend credit, justifiable reliance may be difficult for the creditor to prove.[250] Thus, it is

---

that debtor consulted attorney concerning possible bankruptcy before cash advance was not sufficient to show fraud where debtor made numerous payments of debts after that and did not file until two months later).

242 *In re* Lyon, 8 B.R. 152 (Bankr. D. Me. 1981) (and cases cited therein); *In re* Parker, 1 B.R. 176 (Bankr. E.D. Tenn. 1979).

243 *In re* Lyon, 8 B.R. 152 (Bankr. D. Me. 1981) (and cases cited therein); *see also In re* Chincilla, 202 B.R. 1010 (Bankr. S.D. Fla. 1996) (debtor's exceeding credit limit is not indicia of fraud where lender responded by increasing credit limit with $2000.00 in unsolicited credit).

244 First Nat'l Bank of Mobile v. Roddenberry, 701 F.2d 927 (11th Cir. 1983). This holding may be called into question to some extent by the 1984 addition of section 523(a)(2)(C) to the Code. But those amendments may also be seen as strengthening the argument that defining the extent to which Congress intended pre-bankruptcy credit card usage to be considered fraudulent. *In re* Cox, 182 B.R. 626 (Bankr. D. Mass. 1995).

245 *In re* Lyon, 8 B.R. 152 (Bankr. D. Me. 1981) (and cases cited therein); *In re* Parker, 1 B.R. 176 (Bankr. E.D. Tenn. 1979).

246 *In re* Lyon, 8 B.R. 152 (Bankr. D. Me. 1981) (and cases cited therein); *In re* Parker, 1 B.R. 176 (Bankr. E.D. Tenn. 1979).

247 *In re* Kountry Korner Store, 221 B.R. 265 (Bankr. N.D. Okla. 1998) (creditor which relied only on third party credit reports in granting credit card and had no information about debtor's solvency, budget, work history or assets could not claim justifiable reliance); *In re* Simos, 209 B.R. 188 (Bankr. M.D.N.C. 1997) (creditor who offered no evidence on justifiable reliance could not prevail under § 523(a)(2)); *In re* Christensen, 193 B.R. 863 (N.D. Ill. 1996) (creditor must show more than use of card to show reliance and justifiable nature of reliance; credit card company cannot sit back and doing nothing); *In re* Feld, 203 B.R. 360 (Bankr. E.D. Pa. 1996) (AT & T Universal Card failed to prove justifiable reliance because it sent unsolicited card, took no steps to restrict debtor's use of card, and failed to present evidence on reliance issue); *see also In re* Bird, 224 B.R. 622 (Bankr. S.D. Ohio 1998) (issuance of preapproved loan checks

did not involve justifiable reliance on any representation made by the debtor); *In re* Alvi, 191 B.R. 724 (Bankr. N.D. Ill. 1996) (credit card issuer failed to show actual or justifiable reliance when it passively extended credit on card; it had willingly undergone risk of nonpayment by factoring risk into finance charges); *In re* Willis, 190 B.R. 866 (Bankr. W.D. Mo.) (creditor that failed to offer evidence of justifiable reliance at time of card use did not prove all elements of case; any creditor who knew of debtor's outstanding credit card debt could not have proved justifiable reliance); *In re* Cox, 182 B.R. 626 (Bankr. D. Mass. 1995); *In re* Bui, 188 B.R. 274 (Bankr. N.D. Cal. 1995) (when debt is assigned, creditor must show reasonable reliance at every stage in chain of transactions transferring debtor's account). But see *In re* Mercer, 246 F.3d 391 (5th Cir. 2001) (*en banc*) in which the court held that each use of the card is a new contract and representation of intent to pay and that company could justifiably rely on that representation absent red flags or actual knowledge that it was untrue, essentially reducing dischargeability of credit cards to issue of whether debtor had intent to deceive and whether creditor was aware of red flags, and thus rewarding creditors who do not investigate a debtor's credit and therefore do not discover red flags.

248 *In re* Grause, 245 B.R. 95 (B.A.P. 8th Cir. 2000) (creditor that did nothing more than periodically check FICO credit scores did not justifiably rely when even a cursory look at debtor's situation should have put creditor on notice of her dire straits). But see *In re* Mercer, 246 F.3d 391 (5th Cir. 2001) (*en banc*), (credit card company could justifiably rely on implied representation even though decision to grant credit was based solely on credit reports and not any express representation of debtor).

249 *In re* Akins, 235 B.R. 866 (W.D. Tex. 1999) (debtor obtained approval to use a convenience check up to her full $4000.00 credit limit based on acceptable FICO score even though she had two other credit cards totaling approximately $30,000.00 in debt, or one-hundred-fifty percent of her gross income); *In re* Ellingsworth, 212 B.R. 326 (Bankr. W.D. Mo. 1997) (debtor sent a pre-approved credit card with credit limit of $4000.00 based on FICO score even though she had sixteen other credit cards); *In re* Briese, 196 B.R. 440 (Bankr. W.D. Wis. 1996) (debtors issued a pre-approved credit card with line of $11,500.00, even though bank had conducted a credit check that confirmed debtors' unsecured debt alone exceeded two-thirds of their annual income, a debt-to-income ratio of sixty-six percent).

250 *In re* Reynolds, 221 B.R. 828 (Bankr. N.D. Ala. 1998) (no justifiable reliance when credit card was used almost exclusively for cash advances at local casino over long period); *In re* Stockard, 216 B.R. 237 (Bankr. M.D. Tenn. 1997) (first three payments were at least two weeks late and payments then ceased, but creditor did nothing to limit card use).

important to determine the information that the creditor had when the credit was granted as well as during the time the credit card was used.

There are other factual issues related to credit card dischargeability which can be brought out by thorough discovery.[251] For example, did the creditor have a practice of encouraging consumers with large balances to make additional purchases by increasing their credit limits or by advertising products or services in their billing statements? These practices undermine a creditor's claim that it justifiably relied on the debtor's implied representations about ability to pay, particularly if an increased credit limit is typically granted without a review of the debtor's recent credit record or current income. Similarly, a creditor's practices with respect to accepting minimum payments should be reviewed. If a debtor had the ability to make anticipated minimum payments in the short term, that fact undermines circumstantial evidence which tends to establish that the debtor had no intent to repay.

When cases go to trial, it is important to make a record regarding the debtor's intent at the time of the purchase—usually through the debtor's testimony. For example, if the debtor was unemployed at the time of the purchase, did he or she expect to be reemployed shortly? Was there a reasonable belief that financial difficulties would be temporary? Were the purchases within the debtor's credit limit? Did the debtor have the ability and intent to continue to make the minimum monthly payments despite financial difficulties? Had the debtor had prior financial problems from which he or she recovered that led to a reasonable assumption that these financial difficulties would also be resolved? Had the debtor consulted a bankruptcy attorney before making the purchases? Did the debtor continue to offer partial payments to the creditor which were rejected so that bankruptcy became the only realistic option?

Virtually all debtors have had some financial problems before they file bankruptcy. Most people use credit cards fully expecting that their circumstances will improve so that their debts can be repaid. It is thus inappropriate to use past financial difficulties alone as evidence of fraudulent intent.[252]

14.4.3.2.3.3 Public benefits overpayments

Another type of fraud problem that may arise in the cases of low-income debtors involves past overpayments of social security, unemployment, welfare, or other benefits. In many cases involving such overpayments, the amount that was erroneously paid is deducted from future benefits, often causing considerable hardship.

In determining whether debts for such overpayments should be discharged, the bankruptcy court applies the same standards as in other cases under section 523(a)(2). These standards may be quite different from those applied by the agency that administers the benefits; many such agencies, including the Social Security Administration, may decide to recoup erroneous payments even if the debtor was not at fault or may use a fault standard far less favorable to the debtor than that used in bankruptcy.[253]

Clearly, any overpayment that is the result of an administrative error should be discharged under the bankruptcy standard. No exception to discharge applies solely because the debt is owed to a government agency.[254] Nor would recoupment after bankruptcy be a setoff permitted under 11 U.S.C. § 553, because it would not meet the mutuality requirement, which prohibits a pre-petition debt of the debtor from being setoff against monies that become due to the debtor only after the bankruptcy.[255] Following these principles, and despite the past opposition of the Social Security Administration, courts have consistently held social security overpayments to be dischargeable unless a successful dischargeability challenge is made under 11 U.S.C. § 523.[256] The Social Security Administration's former position that 42 U.S.C. § 407 exempts overpayments from discharge, a position it once memorialized in its claims manual,[257] has been uniformly rejected by the courts.

---

251 See § 14.4.3.2.4, *infra*, and form discovery in Appendix G.11, *infra*. *See generally Litigating the Dischargeability of Credit Card Debts*, 14 NCLC REPORTS *Bankruptcy and Foreclosures* Ed. 10 (Nov./Dec. 1995).

252 *See In re* Mercer, 246 F.3d 391 (5th Cir. 2001) (*en banc*); *In re* Anastas, 94 F.3d 1280 (9th Cir. 1996) (nondischargeability determination may not be based solely upon fact that at time debts were incurred debtor was not likely to be able to repay them; additional evidence of fraudulent intent is required); *In re* Cox, 182 B.R. 626 (Bankr. D. Mass. 1995) (all debtors have history of financial problems which cannot alone establish intent); FCC Bank v. Dobbins, 151 B.R. 509 (W.D. Mo. 1992) (debtor's insolvency at time of credit card use, without more, was not sufficient to render complaint substantially justified).

253 *See In re* Chen, 227 B.R. 614 (D.N.J. 1998) (fraud standard used in state unemployment compensation proceeding was less demanding than that of section 523(a)(2), so finding in such proceeding not entitled to preclusive effect).

254 Some debts owed to government agencies for taxes, or for fines, penalties or forfeitures are nondischargeable under 11 U.S.C. § 523(a)(7). *See* § 14.4.3.1, *supra*; § 14.4.3.7, *infra*.

255 See § 10.4.2.6.7, *supra*, for a discussion of setoffs under section 553. The right to recover money from a state or the federal government based on an improper set-off, however, may be limited based on sovereign immunity. *See* § 13.3.2.2, *supra*. For further discussion of such problems see § 14.5.5.4, *infra*. *See also In re* Soto, 667 F.2d 235 (1st Cir. 1981) (assignment of future wages not a security interest because property acquired post-petition is not subject to pre-petition debts).

256 Rowan v. Morgan, 747 F.2d 1052 (6th Cir. 1984); Lee v. Schweiker, 739 F.2d 870 (3d Cir. 1984); *In re* Neavear, 674 F.2d 1201 (7th Cir. 1982); *see also* McKenney v. City of Cincinnati Retirement Sys., 2 Ohio App. 3d 42, 440 N.E.2d 619 (1981) (obligations to city retirement fund held dischargeable).

257 At one time the Social Security Claims Manual instructed employees to continue recoupment proceedings and to advise claimants and attorneys that "the law requires that future benefits due a person should be withheld to recoup the overpay-

However, debtors who fraudulently obtain benefits by intentionally and falsely representing that they are unemployed will usually be denied a discharge of overpayment if a complaint is filed.[258] Courts are likely to extend this rule to those who do not report new employment, at least if it can be shown that they were aware of their duty to do so, under the theory that such failure constitutes a continuing misrepresentation.[259] Of course, other intentional falsehoods in the application regarding eligibility questions can also lead to an exception of the overpayment from discharge.[260] On the other hand, fraud cannot be assumed simply because a debtor has erroneously received payments while working or because the agency has incorrect information.[261]

14.4.3.2.4 Tactics in cases under 11 U.S.C. § 523(a)(2) and award of attorney fees under 11 U.S.C. § 523(d)

Some creditors file complaints alleging nondischargeability because of a false financial statement, false pretenses, or fraud in hopes that they can obtain a settlement reaffirming all or part of a debt, because some debtors do not defend against such cases. It is important to quickly disabuse a creditor/plaintiff of such notions by making it known that the case will be vigorously defended, quite possibly at the creditor's expense.

The best way to do this is to litigate and negotiate aggressively. It should be remembered that the creditor must plead and prove every element of the case (except when the section 523(a)(2)(C) presumption applies, in which case the creditor has the burden of proof only if the presumption is rebutted.) Further, the rules require fraud to be pleaded with particularity.[262] If these requirements are not met, the debtor may move for dismissal.[263]

The debtor may raise counterclaims as well as defenses in answering the complaint. If the debt itself is not owed because the debtor's rights under consumer credit laws were violated, or for some other reason, dischargeability becomes a moot point.[264] Such challenges to the existence of the debt can also be useful in settling for a lower amount, if that is later desired.

Discovery should be fully pursued. The creditor's practices with respect to obtaining credit reports, credit scoring, filing other dischargeability complaints, and frequently refinancing, encouraging or making a profit from refinancing, may all be relevant. Operations manuals, standardized forms, and other internal documents setting out these practices should be sought if any of them are relevant or could lead to the discovery of relevant information. These inquiries may well serve to put the creditor on the defensive, forcing it to explain why it granted credit in the first place, why it did not obtain a credit report or did not rely on one, why it increased the debtor's credit, why it encourages refinancings and why it challenges dischargeability more than other creditors. The practitioner may also be able to find other consumers who will back up the debtor's assertion as to the creditor's practices in closing loans. Exposure of unethical practices and bad publicity are usually the last things a creditor wants.

In some cases, the creditor may be seeking a determination of nondischargeability for a debt that is not limited to the debt incurred by fraud. Issues concerning refinancings are discussed above.[265] Moreover, if the debt obtained by fraud has been replaced by a newer obligation not obtained through fraud, the newer obligation may well be dischargeable.[266] In other cases, the creditor's asserted liquidated damages can be challenged as unrelated to the alleged fraudulent conduct.[267]

---

ment." POMS § 02215.185. That is no longer current policy.

258 *In re* Kaliff, 2 B.R. 465 (Bankr. D. Ariz. 1979).

259 *Id.*; *In re* Berry, 3 B.R. 430 (Bankr. D. Or. 1980).

260 *In re* Forcier, 7 B.R. 31 (Bankr. D. Ariz. 1980) (student status concealed). Such debts would still be dischargeable in chapter 13. *In re* Jones, 31 B.R. 485 (Bankr. D. Ill. 1983).

261 *Cf. In re* Howell, 4 B.R. 102 (Bankr. M.D. Tenn. 1980) (debt in such circumstances could not automatically be classified separately in chapter 13 plan).

262 Fed. R. Bankr. P. 7009 incorporates Fed. R. Civ. P. 9(b). A motion to dismiss based on failure to plead fraud with particularity may reveal the nature of the circumstantial evidence which the creditor believes supports its claim of intent. Am. Express Travel Related Serv. Co. v. Henein, 257 B.R. 702 (E.D.N.Y. 2001) (affirming dismissal of complaint that did not plead fraud with particularity).

263 *In re* Giuffrida, 302 B.R. 119 (Bankr. E.D.N.Y. 2003) (merely alleging that debtor exceeded credit limit and that debtor's debts exceeded his income when he used credit card did not state a claim under section 523(a)(2)); *In re* Herring, 191 B.R. 317 (Bankr. E.D.N.C. 1995) (credit card issuer's conclusory allegation merely that debtor did not have ability or intention to repay not sufficiently specific because there was no mention of debt-

or's financial condition at relevant times).

264 The bankruptcy court has jurisdiction to determine the validity of the debt as well as its dischargeability. *In re* McLaren, 990 F.2d 850 (6th Cir. 1993); *see In re* Wilder, 178 B.R. 174 (Bankr. E.D. Mo. 1995) (debt that was barred by statute of limitations was not a claim and could not be nondischargeable).

265 *See* § 14.4.3.2.2.2, *supra.*

266 *See In re* West, 22 F.3d 775 (7th Cir. 1995) (when debtor had executed note to employer to repay embezzled funds and employer had agreed not to sue debtor on any obligation other than note, § 523(a)(4) was inapplicable). *But see* Archer v. Warner, 538 U.S. 314, 123 S. Ct. 1462, 155 L. Ed. 2d 454 (2003); United States v. Spicer, 57 F.3d 1152 (D.C. Cir. 1995) (debt that originated through debtor's fraud remained nondischargeable even though there was settlement agreement, regardless of whether agreement included release or waiver of fraud claim).

267 Courts have rejected creditors' attempts to collect attorney fees when they have prevailed in dischargeability cases, even when the underlying contract provides for fees incurred in collection litigation. Collingwood Grain, Inc. v. Coast Trading Co., 744 F.2d 686, 693 (9th Cir. 1984) (fees not awarded when there were no basic contract enforcement issues); *In re* King, 135 B.R. 734 (Bankr. W.D.N.Y. 1992) (Congress did not intend prevailing creditors to collect fees); *In re* LeMaster, 147 B.R. 52 (Bankr. D.

In some cases, it may be appropriate to move for summary judgment. If a creditor has failed to develop through discovery any facts to support its case, given the creditor's burden of proof, the broad allegations of fraud that it may have pleaded in its complaint will be insufficient to prevent summary judgment.[268] Especially if going to trial will involve significant expense, summary judgment may be a good way to cut short the creditor's case.

Finally, the creditor should be reminded of 11 U.S.C. § 523(d) which requires it to pay attorney fees to the debtor if the latter prevails and the creditor's complaint was not "substantially justified."[269] The purpose of this provision is to prevent a creditor from bringing a questionable case to exploit the debtor's need to pay a lawyer to assert a meritorious defense to a dischargeability complaint; thus, whenever a creditor does not have significant evidence to support its claim, the creditor should be obliged to pay the debtor's attorney.[270] Otherwise, the debtor will have lost money even when the case is won.

The "substantially justified" standard was adopted from the Equal Access to Justice Act, 28 U.S.C. § 2412(d). Under that Act courts have held that a losing party must make a strong showing of justification for its claims;[271] there is no requirement that the prevailing party demonstrate the losing party's bad faith.[272] The same is true of 11 U.S.C. § 523(d); Congress clearly rejected creditor proposals to award fees only when bad faith could be demonstrated.[273] It is the creditor's burden to show that fees should not be awarded.[274] Although a creditor may present proof as to "special circumstances" that might warrant a denial of fees, courts have not readily accepted such justifications in light of the purpose of the statute[275]

Indeed, the fact that a creditor failed to diligently investigate the debtor's credit prior to extending credit has been held to be an important factor in deciding that fees should be awarded.[276] One useful tactic, especially if the creditor has sent a letter threatening a dischargeability complaint, is to immediately inform the creditor of the facts supporting the debtor's defense. A better argument can then be made that the creditor's proceeding was not substantially justified in light of the facts available to it either before the case was filed or before significant attorney fees had been incurred. Similarly, a creditor's failure to investigate whether it has a valid nondischargeability claim by attending the section 341 meeting or conducting an examination of the debtor under Bankruptcy Rule 2004 before filing a complaint has often been held sufficient to show that an unsuccessful action was

---

Idaho 1992) (issues were not basic contract enforcement issues, citing Fabian v. W. Bank Farm Credit, 951 F.2d 1149 (9th Cir. 1991)).

268 *In re* Herndon, 193 B.R. 595 (M.D. Fla. 1996) (affidavits submitted by First Card Services in response to summary judgment motion, stating only that debtor did not pay on credit card accounts and restating general allegations of complaint, not sufficient to raise genuine issue of material fact); *see also In re* Sinclair, 191 B.R. 474 (Bankr. M.D. Fla. 1996) (credit card issuer denied default judgment when sole allegation was that debtor used card eight to nine months before bankruptcy case, with no specific facts indicating fraud); *In re* Roberts, 193 B.R. 828 (Bankr. W.D. Mich. 1996) (default judgment denied when bank offered no evidence of debtor's intent or any other evidence other than charges made).

269 *See* Bennett v. Lukens, 131 B.R. 427 (S.D. Ind. 1991) (fees awarded where creditor filed nondischargeability action in state court); *In re* Beam, 73 B.R. 434 (Bankr. S.D. Ohio 1987) (fees awarded where creditor pressed late dischargeability complaint without substantial justification). Previously, fees were recoverable in all cases where they would not be clearly inequitable, a slightly more liberal standard. The fees should be awarded for all hours reasonably expended on the litigation including appellate representation. *In re* Wiencek, 58 B.R. 485 (Bankr. E.D. Va. 1986). *But see In re* Burns, 894 F.2d 361 (10th Cir. 1990) (debtor who successfully defended nondischargeability action not entitled to fees because loan at issue used for investments, was not "consumer debt" within meaning of § 523(d)). *See generally Obtaining Attorneys Fees in Dischargeability Cases,* 15 NCLC REPORTS *Bankruptcy and Foreclosures Ed.* 21 (May/June 1997).

270 Carthage Bank v. Kirkland, 121 B.R. 496 (S.D. Miss. 1990); *In re* Grayson, 199 B.R. 397 (Bankr. W.D. Mo. 1996); *In re* Surbier, 134 B.R. 922 (Bankr. W.D. Mo. 1991).

271 Natural Res. Defense Council v. United States Envtl. Prot. Agency, 703 F.2d 700 (3d Cir. 1983); FCC Bank v. Dobbins, 151 B.R. 509 (W.D. Mo. 1992) (debtor's insolvency at time of

credit card use, without more, was not sufficient to render complaint substantially justified).

272 *See, e.g.,* Fed. Election Comm'n v. Rose, 806 F.2d 1081 (D.C. Cir. 1986); Blitz v. Donovan, 740 F.2d 1241 (D.C. Cir. 1984); *see also In re* Hingson, 954 F.2d 428 (7th Cir. 1992) (traditional equitable principles).

273 *See* H.R. 4786, § 9(b), 97th Cong. (1981), the creditors' proposed bill which would have allowed fees only if bad faith were shown. Cases decided prior to the 1984 amendments also rejected a bad faith requirement. *In re* Carmen, 723 F.2d 16 (6th Cir. 1983); *In re* Majewski, 7 B.R. 904 (Bankr. D. Conn. 1980); *In re* Schlickman, 7 B.R. 139 (Bankr. D. Mass. 1980).

274 *In re* Hunt, 238 F.3d 1098 (9th Cir. 2001) (creditor that presented virtually no evidence that debtor intended to commit fraud failed to meet burden of proof); *In re* McCarthy, 243 B.R. 203 (B.A.P. 1st Cir. 2000).

275 *In re* Stine, 254 B.R. 244 (B.A.P. 9th Cir. 2000) (alleged inaccuracies in schedules which were irrelevant to dischargeability case were not substantial justification, nor were they or the fact that debtor was represented by pro bono counsel special circumstances warranting denial of fees), *aff'd,* 19 Fed. Appx. 626 (9th Cir. 2001); Carthage Bank v. Kirkland, 121 B.R. 496 (S.D. Miss. 1990) (debtor's "hostile and furtive" attitude toward bank did not constitute "special circumstances" warranting denial of attorney fees); *In re* Gross, 149 B.R. 460 (Bankr. E.D. Mich. 1992).

276 *In re* Arroyo, 205 B.R. 984 (Bankr. S.D. Fla. 1997) (where AT & T Universal card gave preapproved and unsolicited card, granted without any evaluation for creditworthiness, no reliance was shown in "six boring hours" of trial; case would have been avoided with minimal investigation by creditor and therefore debtor's counsel awarded $12,200.00 in fees, including $5000.00 fee enhancement); *In re* Leonard, 158 B.R. 839 (Bankr. D. Colo. 1993); *In re* Cordova, 153 B.R. 352 (Bankr. M.D. Fla. 1993).

not substantially justified.[277] However, absent some evidence that suggests a colorable argument for nondischargeability, a creditor does not have an unlimited right to conduct a Rule 2004 examination, which could be used to harass the debtor,[278] especially in view of the right to examine the debtor at the section 341(a) meeting of creditors.

A section 523(d) fee application should be filed within a reasonable time after conclusion of the action.[279] Fees may be awarded even if the debtor failed to specifically request costs and fees in answering the complaint, although careful practice might include the attorney fee claim as a counterclaim to the original action.[280] Section 523(d) has also been construed as authorizing an award of fees for appellate representation.[281]

In addition, attorney fees may be available under other statutory provisions or rules. A frivolous complaint may be grounds for sanctions under Federal Rule of Bankruptcy Procedure 9011, provided the procedures of that rule are followed.[282] And some state statutes provide for consumers to receive fees if they prevail against creditors who have placed attorney fees clauses in their contracts.[283]

The fact that the debtor is represented by a legal services program should not be a factor in a fees determination, because the courts have consistently held such parties to be entitled to statutory attorney fees on the same basis as all others.[284] Nor should the fact that the case was dismissed or dropped by the creditor short of a final judgment after full trial on the merits excuse liability for attorney fees.[285] However, fees awardable against certain governmental units may be limited by the provisions of section 106(a)(3) of the Code.[286]

14.4.3.3 Creditors Not Listed or Scheduled by the Debtor—11 U.S.C. § 523(a)(3)

Debts owed to some creditors that are not listed or scheduled in the bankruptcy case are excepted from the discharge. This exception[287] underscores the importance of filing a complete and accurate list of a client's debts in every case. And at least one court of appeals has held that it applies not only to the schedules themselves, but also to any mailing label matrix required by local rules.[288] Although this exception is expressly applicable only to chapter 7 cases, failure to list a creditor may have similar consequences in a chapter 13 case.[289] Creditors who are never listed and are thus not informed of the bankruptcy need not file a complaint during the bankruptcy case to raise this ground for nondischargeability.

Fortunately, there are a number of exceptions to this exception. The debt is discharged, even though not listed, if the creditor receives actual notice, either from the debtor or from some other source, that the bankruptcy has been filed,[290] and receives that notice in time to file a proof of claim or, if the claim is nondischargeable and a dischargeability complaint is required, in time to file such a com-

277 *In re* Sales, 228 B.R. 748 (B.A.P. 10th Cir. 1999) (credit card issuer which failed to investigate prior to filing complaint and whose only basis for filing complaint was a high balance on account was not substantially justified in filing complaint); *In re* Stahl, 222 B.R. 497 (Bankr. W.D.N.C. 1998) (dischargeability complaint used to coerce settlement found to warrant fees); *In re* Chinchilla, 202 B.R. 1010 (Bankr. S.D. Fla. 1996) (AT & T conducted only minimal and negligent prefiling investigation, using neither the 341 meeting or a Rule 2004 examination); *In re* Grayson, 199 B.R. 397 (Bankr. W.D. Mo. 1996) (AT & T never investigated case by interrogating debtor and never planned to prove its allegations if its complaints were contested and filed solely to extract settlements from debtors; debtors' attorney awarded fees after AT & T voluntarily dismissed its complaint).

278 *In re* Strecker, 251 B.R. 878 (Bankr. D. Colo. 2000).

279 *In re* Wiencek, 58 B.R. 485 (Bankr. E.D. Va. 1986). Fed. R. Civ. P. 54(d), which sets a deadline for fee applications is not incorporated in Fed. R. Bankr. P. 7054.

280 *In re* Bernhardy, 103 B.R. 198 (Bankr. N.D. Ill. 1989).

281 *In re* Wiencek, 58 B.R. 485 (Bankr. E.D. Va. 1986). *But see In re* Vasseli, 5 F.3d 351 (9th Cir. 1993) (section 523(d) does not grant bankruptcy court authority to award fees for appellate representation; however appellate court may award fees under Fed. R. App. P. 38 as sanctions for frivolous appeal).

282 Fed. R. Bankr. P. 9011 was amended in 1997 to conform substantially to Fed. R. Civ. P. 11.

283 *See In re* Baroff, 105 F.3d 439 (9th Cir. 1997) (debtor awarded fees under California statute providing for reciprocal fees); *In re* Mawji, 228 B.R. 321 (Bankr. M.D. Fla. 1999) (fees awarded under Florida law); *see also* § 15.5.3, *infra*.

284 *See, e.g.,* Blum v. Stenson, 465 U.S. 886, 104 S. Ct. 1541, 79 L. Ed. 2d 891 (1984); *In re* Hunt, 238 F.3d 1098 (9th Cir. 2001)

(fact that debtor had pro bono representation did not preclude fees); Rodriguez v. Taylor, 569 F.2d 1231 (3d Cir. 1977); Sellers v. Wollman, 510 F.2d 119 (5th Cir. 1977).

285 *In re* McFadyen, 192 B.R. 328 (Bankr. N.D.N.Y. 1995); *In re* Mull, 122 B.R. 763 (Bankr. W.D. Okla. 1991); *In re* Begley, 12 B.R. 839 (Bankr. D. Conn. 1981).

286 *See* § 13.3.2.2, *supra*.

287 *See* 11 U.S.C. § 523(a)(3).

288 *In re* Adams, 734 F.2d 1094 (5th Cir. 1984). This holding is questionable in general and inapplicable when the debtor provides timely actual notice of the filing to the omitted creditor. *See generally* § 9.5, *supra*.

289 *See* United States Small Bus. Admin. v. Bridges, 894 F.2d 108 (5th Cir. 1990) (failure to schedule debts in chapter 11 case meant they would not be discharged); Reliable Elec. Co. v. Olson Constr. Co., 726 F.2d 620 (10th Cir. 1984) (creditor who had been denied opportunity to comment on chapter 11 plan was not bound by plan); *In re* Pack, 105 B.R. 703 (Bankr. M.D. Fla. 1989) (debt not scheduled in chapter 13 case is not discharged); *see also* Broomall Indus. Inc. v. Data Design Logic Sys., Inc., 786 F.2d 401 (Fed. Cir. 1986) (failure to include potential creditor about which debtor had knowledge precludes discharge of that claim in chapter 11 case).

290 *In re* Barnes, 969 F.2d 526 (7th Cir. 1992) (creditor received actual notice when debtor orally informed him of bankruptcy and debt discharged even though debtor at same time had promised to repay it); Briley v. Hidalgo, 981 F.2d 246 (5th Cir. 1992) (debt to assignee of guarantor was discharged where assignee had actual notice of case).

plaint.[291] Because the deadline for claims is presently ninety days after the first date set for the meeting of creditors (or later), and in many cases there is no deadline under the rules,[292] most creditors can still be notified of the case even if their claims are not discovered until well after the case is filed.[293] Indeed, because under section 726(a)(2)(C) a creditor without notice can receive distributions even if the claim is not filed before the claims bar date, as long as the claim is filed in time to permit payment of the claim, the appropriate deadline for notice when there is a bar date for claims is the last day a claim could be filed in time to receive a distribution.[294] Creditors that claim they were not informed of the time limit for filing a nondischargeability complaint must prove not only that they did not have timely notice, but also that their claims are in fact nondischargeable under one of the listed exceptions.[295] If the debt is nondischargeable under one of those exceptions, section 523(a)(3) permits the creditor without timely notice to bring its dischargeability action at any time.[296]

This exception to the exception applies if the creditor receives actual notice of the case even though the debt is not duly scheduled.[297] However, it is not enough to show that the creditor receives a newspaper that lists bankruptcies, unless perhaps it is also shown that the creditor reads such lists regularly. Sometimes, but not always, notice is imputed if an agent, for example a collection agent or attorney, receives notice.[298] It is safest, therefore, to list the creditor itself in the bankruptcy schedules, though the agent or attorney may also be listed. If a creditor is not scheduled at the outset of a case, the schedules should be amended and the debtor's counsel should be sure to send a copy of the notice of the meeting of creditors to the creditor, by certified mail, to ensure actual notice. If a discharge has already been granted, the debtor may still file an amendment up to the time the case is closed,[299] or even afterward.[300] Even if the schedules are not amended, actual notice sent and received within the time limits should be sufficient under the wording of section 523(a)(3).

If such notice is sent, it is a good idea to provide accurate information about the debtor's address and taxpayer identification number, as well as an account number if possible, to avoid a later dispute about and whether sufficient information was provided for effective notice.

---

291 *See In re* Medaglia, 52 F.3d 451 (2d Cir. 1995) (creditor had timely actual notice of case even though it did not have notice of deadlines); *In re* Dewalt, 961 F.2d 848 (9th Cir. 1992) (notice seven days before deadline was insufficient; notice at least thirty days before deadline required for debt to be discharged); *In re* Sam, 894 F.2d 778 (5th Cir. 1990) (notice eighteen days before deadline for dischargeability complaint was sufficient time); *In re* Compton, 891 F.2d 1180 (5th Cir. 1990) (creditor had actual notice of case in time to file dischargeability complaint); *In re* Green, 876 F.2d 854 (10th Cir. 1989); § 14.4.2, *supra*.

292 Fed. R. Bankr. P. 3002(c).

293 In fact, where a debt does not involve fraud, a creditor may probably be added by amendment even after closing of the case in a no-asset case where no deadline for filing of claims was ever set. *In re* Soult, 894 F.2d 815 (6th Cir. 1990) (debtor entitled to reopen case to add omitted creditor after bar date passed); *In re* Rosinski, 759 F.2d 539 (6th Cir. 1985); *In re* Stark, 717 F.2d 322 (7th Cir. 1983); *In re* Adams, 41 B.R. 933 (D. Me. 1984); *In re* Zablocki, 36 B.R. 779 (Bankr. D. Conn. 1984); *In re* Ratliff, 27 B.R. 465 (Bankr. E.D. Va. 1983); Southwest Fla. Production Credit Ass'n v. Fawl, Bankr. L. Rep. (CCH) ¶ 67,459 (Bankr. S.D. Fla. 1980); *see also In re* Baitcher, 781 F.2d 1529 (11th Cir. 1986) (amendment denied if evidence of debtor's fraud or intentional omission). *But see In re* Laczko, 37 B.R. 676 (B.A.P. 9th Cir. 1984). As discussed later in this section, such an amendment is usually not necessary for the debt to be discharged.

294 *In re* Ricks, 253 B.R. 734 (Bankr. M.D. La. 2000).

295 *In re* Lochrie, 78 B.R. 257 (B.A.P. 9th Cir. 1987); *In re* Anderson, 72 B.R. 783 (Bankr. D. Minn. 1987); *In re* Barrett, 24 B.R. 682 (Bankr. M.D. Tenn. 1982). Although there is a time limit for filing a complaint under section 523(a)(15), it was probably inadvertently omitted from the list in section 523(a)(3). *See In re* Dixon, 280 B.R. 755 (Bankr. M.D. Ga. 2002) (court must follow statute's plain language).

296 *In re* Santiago, 175 B.R. 48 (Bankr. 9th Cir. 1994). The debtor may raise laches as a defense to a § 523 (a)(3) complaint but will have a heavy burden to prove that there has been lack of diligence by the creditor that has prejudiced the debtor. *In re* Beaty, 306 F.3d 914 (9th Cir. 2002); *see also In re* Staffer, 306 F.3d 967 (9th Cir. 2002) (motion to reopen bankruptcy case was not a prerequisite to creditor complaint under § 523(a)(3)).

297 *In re* Presley, 288 B.R. 732 (Bankr. W.D. Va. 2003) (debt discharged, even though improperly scheduled as owed to someone else, because creditor heard about case in time to act). *But see In re* Massa, 187 F.3d 292 (2d Cir. 1999) (when creditor was notified of chapter 13 petition, but never notified that case was converted to chapter 7 or scheduled in time to file a timely dischargeability complaint, creditor had not received adequate notice to protect its rights and could challenge dischargeability for fraud under § 523(a)(3)); *In re* Brown, 267 B.R. 877 (Bankr. W.D. Okla. 2001) (knowledge of debtors' statement that they intended to file a bankruptcy case is not sufficient absent knowledge of actual filing).

298 *See In re* Schicke, 290 B.R. 792 (B.A.P. 10th Cir. 2003) (judgment creditor was properly scheduled in care of attorney who obtained judgment); *In re* Price, 79 B.R. 888 (B.A.P. 9th Cir. 1988), *aff'd*, 871 F.2d 97 (9th Cir. 1989); 4 Collier on Bankruptcy, ¶ 523.09[4][a] (15th ed. rev.); Daniel R. Cowans, Cowans Bankruptcy Law and Practice § 6.35 (6th ed.) (and cases cited therein). *But see* United States Small Bus. Admin. v. Bridges, 894 F.2d 108 (5th Cir. 1990) (knowledge of bankruptcy filing of government agency branch office could not be imputed to separate agency branch office). Notice may not be imputed unless the agent's scope of authority pertains to the collection of the debt involved. Ford Motor Credit Co. v. Weaver, 680 F.2d 451 (6th Cir. 1982). Nor is notice to a creditor's attorney sufficient where there is no indication as to which of the attorney's clients might be the debtor's creditor. Maldonado v. Ramirez, 757 F.2d 48 (3d Cir. 1985).

299 Fed. R. Bankr. P. 1009; *In re* Jones, 22 B.R. 416 (Bankr. M.D. Fla. 1982).

300 Where the deadline for claims has never passed, it may be possible to reopen the case to add creditors. See cases cited above. *See also* 11 U.S.C. § 350. *But see In re* Smith, 21 F.3d 660 (5th Cir. 1994) (debtor could not amend schedules to add creditor four years after petition when claims bar date had passed and creditor had otherwise been prejudiced by delay).

In no-asset cases in which creditors are sent the typical notice that they should not file claims,[301] courts have held that all otherwise dischargeable claims are discharged even if they are not listed in the debtor's schedules.[302] The rationale is that the only notice that the unscheduled creditors holding such claims miss is a notice not to file a proof of claim and a notice of a deadline for dischargeability objections which such creditors do not have. They therefore are not within the terms of section 523(a)(3) and suffer no prejudice from the lack of notice.[303] Many of these courts have held that in such cases there is no need to amend the schedules to add the omitted creditor because the debt is already discharged by operation of law.[304] On the other hand, if a creditor could have filed a valid dischargeability complaint under one of the sections listed in section 523(c), the debt is nondischargeable after the deadline for such complaints passes regardless of whether the schedules are amended.

In other words, under the language of the statute, a creditor in a no asset case is never denied the right to file a timely proof of claim because there is no deadline. Similar logic would suggest that when an otherwise dischargeable debt is not listed in a case involving only partial payments to unsecured creditors, the debt should be nondischargeable only to the extent of that creditor's unpaid pro rata share of the total amount distributed to unsecured creditors, because that is the only harm suffered by the creditor.[305]

If the creditor is duly scheduled, it is irrelevant whether or not it receives notice. The courts have held that minor irregularities, such as misspellings or incorrect amounts listed as due, do not render improper the listing of a particular creditor.[306] Generally, it has been held that if the creditor's identity can be reasonably ascertained, the listing is sufficient.[307] However, listing a creditor's address as that of its attorney, or in care of its attorney, may not be sufficient.[308] Moreover, if the debtor knows that the debt has been assigned, the assignee must be listed as the creditor. And if the debtor lists an incorrect address, the court may inquire whether the debtor exercised reasonable diligence in completing the schedules.[309] If the debtor does not know and cannot, with reasonable diligence, determine[310] a creditor's name or address, the unknown information need not be listed.[311] However, the fact of the debt and whatever information the debtor does know should be listed, along with a statement that the supplied information is the extent of the debtor's knowledge, and perhaps a description of efforts taken to obtain the missing information.[312]

---

301 *See* Official Form 9A, Appx. D, *infra.*

302 *In re* Parker, 313 F.3d 1267 (10th Cir. 2002) (debtor's intent in failing to list claim is irrelevant); *In re* Madaj, 149 F.3d 467 (6th Cir. 1998); Judd v. Wolfe, 78 F.3d 110 (3d Cir. 1996); *In re* Beezley, 994 F.2d 1433 (9th Cir. 1993); *In re* Karras, 165 B.R. 636 (N.D. Ill. 1994) (debt dischargeable in no asset case even if debtor intentionally failed to schedule it); *In re* Anderson, 104 B.R. 427 (Bankr. N.D. Fla. 1989); *In re* Mendiola, 99 B.R. 864 (Bankr. N.D. Ill. 1989); *In re* Smolarick, 56 B.R. 720 (Bankr. W.D. Va. 1986).

303 The same lack of prejudice forms the basis of the argument supporting the reopening of no-asset cases to schedule inadvertently omitted creditors. *See* § 14.4.3.2.3.3, *supra*; *see also In re* Stone, 10 F.3d 285 (5th Cir. 1994) (permitting amendment of claim because no prejudice to creditor who had dischargeable claim in no asset case).

304 *E.g., In re* Parker, 313 F.3d 1267 (10th Cir. 2002) (debtor's intent in failing to list is irrelevant); *In re* Madaj, 149 F.3d 467 (6th Cir. 1998); *In re* Beezley, 994 F.2d 1433 (9th Cir. 1993); *In re* Stecklow, 144 B.R. 314 (Bankr. D. Md. 1992); *In re* Thibodeau, 136 B.R. 7 (Bankr. D. Mass. 1992).

305 *In re* Ladnier, 130 B.R. 335 (Bankr. S.D. Ala. 1991).

306 Kreitlin v. Ferger, 238 U.S. 21, 35 S. Ct. 685, 59 L. Ed. 1184 (1915); 4 Collier on Bankruptcy ¶ 523.09[1], [2] (15th ed. rev.); *see In re* Walker, 125 B.R. 177 (Bankr. E.D. Mich. 1990) (debt properly scheduled when "North Washington St." is listed

rather than "South Washington"). There is no requirement that a corporate creditor be listed at its home office or principal place of business. *In re* Savage, 167 B.R. 22 (Bankr. S.D.N.Y. 1994). However, listing of a totally incorrect address may render a debt not duly scheduled. Ford Motor Credit Co. v. Weaver, 680 F.2d 451 (6th Cir. 1982); *see also In re* Fauchier, 71 B.R. 212 (B.A.P. 9th Cir. 1987).

307 4 Collier on Bankruptcy ¶ 523.09[2] (15th ed. rev.).

308 However, notice to the attorney may be sufficient to constitute actual notice, particularly if there is evidence that the attorney informed his or her client about the bankruptcy. *See In re* Price, 79 B.R. 888 (B.A.P. 9th Cir. 1988), *aff'd*, 871 F.2d 97 (9th Cir. 1989); *see also In re* Land, 215 B.R. 398 (B.A.P. 8th Cir. 1997) (notice to attorney for creditor imputed to creditor because attorney was agent of creditor); *In re* Malandra, 206 B.R. 667 (Bankr. E.D.N.Y. 1997) (notice to creditor counsel who frequently represented clients in bankruptcy was sufficient).

309 *See In re* Faden, 96 F.3d 792 (5th Cir. 1996) (debtor's listing of creditor's parent company's address was more than mere negligence, and debtor intentionally or recklessly failed to provide correct address, so debt not discharged); *In re* Fauchier, 71 B.R. 212 (B.A.P. 9th Cir. 1987) (use of addresses that were two years old). Significantly, the debtors in *Faden* appear to have been sophisticated investors rather than consumer debtors. The same principles should not apply to inadvertent misinformation or negligence. Moreover, the court of appeals in *Faden* did not adequately address why the parent corporation did not pass on the bankruptcy notice to its subsidiary.

310 *See In re* Gelman, 5 B.R. 230 (Bankr. S.D. Fla. 1980).

311 *See* Gen. Collections, Inc. v. Steward, 539 N.E.2d 981 (Ind. Ct. App. 1989) (where creditor dissolved and reformed under new name and at new address without notice to debtor, listing old name and address was sufficient and debt is discharged).

312 The names of creditors may not always be known. The debtor may have engaged in acts with unknown victims. One question which arises in some cases, mostly involving environmental torts or product liability, is whether the debt arises only when injuries manifest themselves. This is important for dischargeability purposes, both so that the injured person knows of his or her claim and so that the debtor knows of the claim in order to give proper notice. The general rule is that injuries become manifest when the claimant discovers the injury and knows or has reason to know the cause. Probably, no claim exists which can be discharged until this occurs. *See In re* Cent. R.R. Co. of N.J., 950 F.2d 887 (3d Cir. 1991); *see also* § 9.4.1, *supra*; § 14.5.1.1, *infra.*

Usually, issues under this exception arise in state courts, which have concurrent jurisdiction to decide them, because the creditor without notice will simply sue to collect its debt. The action may be removed to bankruptcy court, however, once the affirmative defense of the discharge is raised.[313] Even if a default judgment is obtained by the creditor, the debtor should be able to litigate the dischargeability issue in bankruptcy court;[314] if the debtor is correct in asserting that the debt was discharged, the creditor's judgment would be void under 11 U.S.C. § 524(a).

Of course, a claim which is not discharged solely because it was not listed in a chapter 7 case may be included and discharged in a subsequent bankruptcy.[315]

14.4.3.4 Fraud As a Fiduciary, Embezzlement, or Larceny—11 U.S.C. § 523(a)(4)

The fourth exception to discharge involves fraud or defalcation while acting in a fiduciary capacity, or embezzlement or larceny even if not in a fiduciary capacity.[316] The exception based on fraud or defalcation is rarely invoked in cases involving consumers, as few consumers have acted as fiduciaries.[317]

Defalcation has been defined as failure by a trustee to properly account for funds placed in his or her trust.[318] It

seems clear that for this exception to apply the trust relationship involved must be an express or technical trust, and not a constructive trust implied by law in some cases of wrongful conduct.[319] A sales employee who has misappropriated funds is thus not a fiduciary, though a consignee may be one.[320] When a true fiduciary relationship is created by statute, there is little doubt that the section applies.[321]

---

313 See § 13.4.1, *supra*, for a discussion of removal to bankruptcy court.

314 *See In re* McGhan, 288 F.3d 1172 (9th Cir. 2002) (bankruptcy court abused its discretion in refusing to reopen case to decide whether debt was non-dischargeable under § 523(a)(3) and whether discharge injunction was violated; state court's order that debt was not discharged improperly modified bankruptcy court's discharge order).

315 *See In re* Dye, 108 B.R. 135 (Bankr. W.D. Tex. 1989); *see also In re* Samora, 117 B.R. 660 (Bankr. D.N.M. 1990) (debtors may discharge debts scheduled in previous bankruptcy case even though previous case dismissed for failure to obey court order as long as discharge was not waived or denied in previous case).

316 4 Collier on Bankruptcy ¶ 523.10 (15th ed. rev.); *accord, e.g., In re* Kapnison, 65 B.R. 221 (Bankr. D.N.M. 1986).

317 The most common application in consumer cases may be to guardians for elderly persons and executors of estates. *E.g., In re* Messineo, 192 B.R. 597 (Bankr. D.N.H. 1996) (son breached fiduciary duties when, as co-guardian of his elderly mother's estate, he misappropriated her funds and property for his own use).

318 *See, e.g.,* Kwiat v. Doucette, 81 B.R. 184 (D. Mass. 1987); *see also In re* Moreno, 892 F.2d 417 (5th Cir. 1990) (where debtor, while officer of debtor corporation, directed transfer of $200,000.00 to himself and companies in which he owned at least fifty percent interest he acted in fiduciary capacity). Courts have disagreed regarding whether there must be some element of culpability for a defalcation to be nondischargeable or whether all defalcations by fiduciaries are nondischargeable. *Compare In re* Baylis, 313 F.3d 9 (1st Cir. 2002) (defalcation requires some degree of fault, closer to fraud, without necessity of meeting a strict specific intent requirement); *In re* Martin, 161 B.R. 672 (B.A.P. 9th Cir. 1993) (more than negligent defalcation required) *with In re* Uwimana, 274 F.3d 806 (4th Cir. 2001)

(negligence or innocent mistake may be defalcation); *In re* Dauterman, 156 B.R. 976 (Bankr. N.D. Ohio 1993) (defalcation need not be intentional or in bad faith); *In re* Waters, 20 B.R. 277 (Bankr. W.D. Tex. 1982) (intent not an essential element of defalcation, and debt nondischargeable where Texas statute placed upon debtor the responsibility to account for funds).

319 *In re* Banks, 263 F.3d 862 (9th Cir. 2001) (attorney was fiduciary with respect to client trust account); *In re* Garver, 116 F.3d 176 (6th Cir. 1997) (attorney-client relationship without more, such as holding of funds, is not fiduciary relationship); *In re* Gergely, 110 F.3d 1448 (9th Cir. 1997) (fiduciary duties do not arise from doctor-patient relationship); *In re* Cantrell, 88 F.3d 344 (5th Cir. 1996) (exception only applies when there is an express trust and recognizable corpus); *In re* Woldman, 92 F.3d 546 (7th Cir. 1996) (debtor attorney was not fiduciary for attorney who referred personal injury case to him with respect to referring attorney's agreed share of contingent fee; fiduciary obligation must involve substantial inequality in power or knowledge); *In re* Nicholas, 956 F.2d 110 (5th Cir. 1992) (debtor was not a fiduciary under Texas statute that deemed contractor to be "trustee" of funds due to subcontractors absent intent to defraud); *In re* Long, 774 F.2d 875 (8th Cir. 1985); *In re* Teichman, 774 F.2d 1395 (9th Cir. 1985); *In re* Schneider, 99 B.R. 974 (B.A.P. 9th Cir. 1989) (financial advisor who takes control over another's money is a fiduciary pursuant to an express trust); *In re* Schusterman, 108 B.R. 893 (Bankr. D. Conn. 1989) (lottery sales agent had no fiduciary duty under Connecticut law); *In re* Valdes, 98 B.R. 78 (Bankr. M.D. Fla. 1989) (executor in context of a probate proceeding acts as a fiduciary); *In re* Tester, 62 B.R. 486 (Bankr. W.D. Va. 1986) (contract requiring that proceeds of a sale be held "in trust" insufficient to establish fiduciary relationship); *In re* Paley, 8 B.R. 466 (Bankr. E.D.N.Y. 1981) (contract requiring money to be held "in trust" not enough to create fiduciary relationship); *In re* Wise, 6 B.R. 867 (Bankr. M.D. Fla. 1980); *In re* Walker, 7 B.R. 563 (Bankr. M.D. Ga. 1980); *In re* Miles, 5 B.R. 458 (Bankr. E.D. Va. 1980) (contract requiring funds to be held separately not enough to create fiduciary relationship); 4 Collier on Bankruptcy ¶ 523.10[1][c] (15th ed. rev.). *But see In re* Hayes, 183 F.3d 162 (2d Cir. 1999) (attorney-client relationship is fiduciary relationship); *In re* Lewis, 97 F.3d 1182 (9th Cir. 1996) (state law made partners fiduciaries for each other).

320 *In re* Shiller, 21 B.R. 643 (Bankr. D. Idaho 1982) (consignee's debt not dischargeable); 4 Collier on Bankruptcy, ¶ 523.10[1][c] (15th ed. rev.).

321 *In re* McGee, 353 F.3d 537 (7th Cir. 2003) (city ordinance requiring landlord to place tenant's security deposit in segregated account created a fiduciary relationship); *In re* Niles, 106 F.3d 1456 (9th Cir. 1997) (real estate broker who handled client's funds for sales, rentals and loans was a fiduciary); *In re* Short, 818 F.2d 693 (9th Cir. 1987) (debtor who had contractual and statutory duty to pay taxes, maintain books and distribute funds to joint venturers was a fiduciary); *In re* Interstate Agency Inc., 760 F.2d 121 (6th Cir. 1985); *In re* Thomas, 729 F.2d 502 (7th Cir. 1984); *In re* Johnson, 691 F.2d 249 (6th Cir. 1982); Carey Lumber Co. v. Bell, 615 F.2d 370 (5th Cir. 1980); *see*

The terms larceny and embezzlement are also included in this exception in the Code and are applicable to non-fiduciaries as well as fiduciaries. "Larceny" is not necessarily defined in bankruptcy in the same way it is defined in state law.[322] Larceny is defined as a matter of federal common law as taking property from its rightful owner willfully and with fraudulent intent.[323] Embezzlement is the fraudulent appropriation of property belonging to another by a person in lawful possession of that property.[324]

As under 11 U.S.C. § 523(a)(2), it is the creditor's burden to show actual fraudulent intent in order to prove embezzlement.[325] If the debt in question was not actually incurred with such intent, even if it replaced a debt that would have met the tests for fraud, the debt is not excepted from the discharge.[326]

In any case, for this exception to apply, a complaint must be filed during the bankruptcy case within the time limits set by the Bankruptcy Rules.[327] The amount excepted from discharge is equal to the amount misappropriated, rather than any greater amount that may be owed to the creditor.[328]

14.4.3.5 Alimony, Maintenance, or Support Owed to a Spouse, Former Spouse, or Child—11 U.S.C. § 523(a)(5)

14.4.3.5.1 In general

The Code excepts from discharge, both in chapter 7 and chapter 13,[329] alimony, maintenance, or support payments owed to a spouse, former spouse, or child of the debtor[330] in connection with a separation agreement, divorce decree, order of a court of record, administrative determination made by a governmental unit, or property settlement.[331] Interest on such debts is similarly nondischargeable.[332] A 1984 amendment made clear that support order obligations to a child not arising from a marriage, such as those arising in paternity cases, also may not be discharged.[333]

This exception to discharge does not apply to debts for alimony, support or maintenance owed to most other entities, even if they have been assigned by the spouse or child or by operation of law.[334] Thus, debts owed under "palimony" decisions, to persons who were never validly married to the debtor, are not excepted from discharge,[335] nor are debts to putative spouses, for example, spouses in a void

---

Quaif v. Johnson, 4 F.3d 950 (11th Cir. 1993) (insurance agent's statutory duty to segregate insurance premiums made him a fiduciary); *cf. In re* Boyle, 819 F.2d 583 (5th Cir. 1987) (no true trust created by statute); Runnion v. Pedrazzini, 644 F.2d 756 (9th Cir. 1981) (same).

322   *See In re* Lane, 115 B.R. 81 (Bankr. E.D. Va. 1990) (debt arising from conduct which constituted larceny under Virginia law was nevertheless dischargeable); *In re* Goux, 72 B.R. 355 (Bankr. N.D.N.Y. 1987) (debt not due to larceny under Code where debtor obtained possession of funds lawfully, even though debtor had plead guilty to petit larceny); *In re* Storms, 28 B.R. 761 (Bankr. E.D.N.C. 1983).

323   Werner v. Hoffman, 5 F.3d 1170 (8th Cir. 1993) (no larceny found with respect to failure to return creditor's property when debtor's initial possession of property was lawful); *In re* Rose, 934 F.2d 901 (7th Cir. 1991) (debtor took husband's funds from safe deposit box).

324   Werner v. Hoffman, 5 F.3d 1170 (8th Cir. 1993) (no embezzlement found with respect to failure to return creditor's property when debtor did not improperly use creditor's property that was lawfully in debtor's possession); *In re* Conder, 196 B.R. 104 (Bankr. W.D. Wis. 1995) (one cannot embezzle one's own property, so creditor who held only security interest in debtor's property could not claim embezzlement); *In re* Trovato, 145 B.R. 575 (Bankr. N.D. Ill. 1991) (embezzlement shown where debtor saved money for his employer but then deposited funds in his own bank account); *see In re* Belfry, 862 F.2d 661 (8th Cir. 1988) (where creditor had only his own "understanding" that debtor would use funds for certain purpose, embezzlement had not been shown); *see also In re* Wallace, 840 F.2d 762 (10th Cir. 1988) (state court judgment that debtor embezzled funds collaterally estops bankruptcy court from relitigating embezzlement issue).

325   *See, e.g., In re* Weber, 892 F.2d 534 (7th Cir. 1989).

326   *In re* West, 22 F.3d 775 (7th Cir. 1995) (when debtor had executed note to employer to repay embezzled funds and employer had agreed not to sue debtor on any obligation other than note, § 523(a)(4) was inapplicable). *But see* Archer v. Warner, 538 U.S. 314, 123 S. Ct. 1462, 155 L. Ed. 2d 454 (2003).

327   11 U.S.C. § 523(c); Fed. R. Bankr. P. 4007(c); *see* § 14.4.2, *supra*.

328   *In re* Bennett, 989 F.2d 779 (5th Cir. 1993). *But see In re* Bugna,

---

33 F.3d 1054 (9th Cir. 1994) (punitive damages also not discharged).

329   11 U.S.C. §§ 523(a)(5), 1328(a). For a lengthy discussion of this exception, see Henry J. Sommer & Margaret Doe McGarity, Collier Family Law and the Bankruptcy Code, Ch. 6. Because these debts are excepted from discharge in chapter 13, post-petition interest on them is also excepted from discharge, even if the allowed secured claim for the principal is paid in a chapter 13 plan. *In re* Foster, 319 F.3d 495 (9th Cir. 2003); *In re* Crable, 174 B.R. 62 (Bankr. W.D. Ky. 1994).

330   The child need not be a minor and "support" probably includes educational expenses. *See In re* Harrell, 754 F.2d 902 (11th Cir. 1985). However, the child must be a child of the debtor. 253 B.R. 253 (Bankr. W.D. Ark. 2000) (even though state court continued to hold him liable, debtor's debt for support of child determined not to be his by DNA test was not nondischargeable as support for a child of the debtor).

331   A support award entered in a court of record is nondischargeable even if it is not embodied in a divorce decree or marital separation agreement. Shine v. Shine, 802 F.2d 583 (1st Cir. 1986) (suit for separate maintenance).

332   *In re* Foster, 319 F.3d 495 (9th Cir. 2003) (chapter 13 debtor who paid support arrearages in full still owed interest at end of plan).

333   *See In re* Maddigan, 312 F.3d 589 (2d Cir. 2002) (attorney fees awarded to out-of-wedlock mother in custody case were nondischargeable support).

334   *But see In re* Seibert, 914 F.2d 102 (7th Cir. 1990) (debtor father could not discharge court costs of paternity action; expenses of pregnancy and confinement were debts owed to child for support and were also nondischargeable even though payable to person who was neither a spouse or child); *In re* Kemp, 242 B.R. 178 (B.A.P. 8th Cir. 1999) (debt to mother of debtor's child for one half of birth expenses not dischargeable), *aff'd*, 232 F.3d 652 (8th Cir. 2000).

335   *In re* Doyle, 70 B.R. 106 (B.A.P. 9th Cir. 1986).

marriage.[336] Similarly, debts assigned to a former spouse's estate after his or her death are not included in the exception.[337] And in some cases, such as divorce decrees that give the non-debtor spouse a right to pension benefits, courts have ruled that there is no debt to be discharged because the divorce decree granted a vested interest in the pension or other property to that spouse.[338]

14.4.3.5.2 Support debts owed to governmental units

Unfortunately, support rights assigned to public welfare departments in cases in which the debtor's children receive public assistance are included within this exception to discharge.[339] The exception includes both sums owing at the time of the assignment and sums which become due thereafter.[340] All obligations to a spouse, former spouse, or child of the debtor arising out of support orders of any court of record or administrative determinations of a governmental unit are nondischargeable if they have been assigned to a governmental unit.

Moreover, it may be that there need not ever have been an actual assignment of a court order for the debt to be nondischargeable. As part of the 1996 welfare "reform" package, Congress passed several amendments that were apparently intended to overrule prior cases which had required that there be a court order and assignment of the order.[341] First, Congress amended section 523(a)(5) itself, changing the cross-reference to the Social Security Act from section 402(a)(18) to section 408(a)(3). Second, Congress added section 523(a)(18), applicable in chapter 7 cases, which is discussed below.[342] Third, Congress amended section 456(b) of the Social Security Act, which had previously applied only to child support, to provide that a debt owed to a state or municipality that is in the nature of support and that is enforceable under Part IVD of the Social Security Act is not "released" by a discharge in bankruptcy.[343]

Thus, the most a bankruptcy can do with respect to such debts is provide protection during a reasonable payment plan under chapter 13.[344] This protection, however, can be very valuable in areas where overzealous prosecutors and judges harass and even incarcerate those who, because of unemployment or other problems, have allowed their dependents to become public charges.

14.4.3.5.3 Determination of whether debt is in the nature of alimony, maintenance, or support

Most of the disputes under this subsection concern whether the debt is for alimony, maintenance, or support as opposed to being a property settlement debt, which is usually[345] dischargeable.[346] As with any exception to discharge, the burden is on the creditor to establish that the debt is nondischargeable under section 523(a)(5).[347] The legislative history makes clear that this question is to be determined as a matter of federal bankruptcy law, and not state law.[348] The designation of a debt as alimony or property settlement by a state court decree or agreement is not binding in the dischargeability determination; a court can look behind such language to determine the real nature of the debt.[349] However, because state courts have concurrent jurisdiction with respect to dischargeability of such debts, a decision by a state court on a section 523(a)(5) dischargeability issue is probably binding, at least if the issue is actually litigated.[350]

---

336 See *Putative Spousal Support Rights and the Federal Bankruptcy Act*, 25 UCLA L. Rev. 69 (1977); *see also In re Magee*, 111 B.R. 359 (M.D. Fla. 1990).

337 *In re Brunhoff*, 4 B.R. 381 (Bankr. S.D. Fla. 1980); *see also In re Fields*, 23 B.R. 134 (Bankr. D. Colo. 1982) (support arrearage obligation to ex-wife who was also in bankruptcy discharged because the right to collect the arrearage had passed to ex-wife's trustee as part of her estate). However, if an assignment is only for purposes of collection, the exception still applies. *In re Beggin*, 19 B.R. 759 (Bankr. W.D. Wash. 1982), *But see In re Silansky*, 897 F.2d 743 (4th Cir. 1990) (listing divorce judgment for attorney fee as asset in bankruptcy schedules does not constitute an assignment); *In re Combs*, 101 B.R. 609 (B.A.P. 9th Cir. 1989) (where ex-wife died after bankruptcy petition filed, status of debt determined as of petition date).

338 *E.g., In re McCafferty*, 96 F.3d 192 (6th Cir. 1996) (divorce decree dividing pension created separate property interest in pension for non-debtor spouse); *Bush v. Taylor*, 912 F.2d 989 (8th Cir. 1990) (*en banc*); *see also* § 14.4.3.5.3, *infra*.

339 Pub. L. No. 97-35, § 2334, 95 Stat. 863 (1981) (amending 11 U.S.C. § 523(a)(5)(A)).

340 *In re Stovall*, 721 F.2d 1133 (7th Cir. 1983).

341 *See* cases § 14.4.3.17, *infra*.

342 *See* § 14.4.3.17, *infra*.

343 42 U.S.C. § 656(b); *In re Cervantes*, 219 F.3d 955 (9th Cir. 2000) (prejudgment support arrearages non-dischargeable in chapter 13 under 42 U.S.C. § 656(b)).

344 *See* Henry J. Sommer & Margaret Doe McGarity, Collier Family Law and the Bankruptcy Code, Ch. 8. *But see* Caswell v. Lang, 757 F.2d 608 (4th Cir. 1985) (child support arrearages may not be included in chapter 13 plan).

345 Under the 1994 amendments to the Code some property settlement debts are also not dischargeable in chapter 7 cases. 11 U.S.C. § 523(a)(15); *see* § 14.4.3.14, *infra*.

346 In some cases the issue may be whether the support received by a spouse is even a debt of the debtor. *See In re Chandler*, 805 F.2d 555 (5th Cir. 1986) (wife's right to receive portion of ex-husband's military pension was her own property and not his obligation); *see also* § 14.4.3.5.1, *supra*; § 14.4.3.6, *infra*.

347 Tilley v. Jessee, 789 F.2d 1074 (4th Cir. 1986).

348 S. Rep. No. 95-989, at 79 (1978); H.R. Rep. No. 95-595, at 364 (1977).

349 11 U.S.C. § 523(a)(5)(B); Cummings v. Cummings, 244 F.3d 1263 (11th Cir. 2001) (court must look at intent of divorce court in ordering payment labeled as equitable distribution); *In re Goin*, 808 F.2d 1391 (10th Cir. 1987). Therefore, the fact that a party argued in state court that a debt was property settlement for purposes of state law did not estop that party from arguing it was in the nature of support under federal bankruptcy law. *In re Dennis*, 25 F.3d 274 (5th Cir. 1994).

350 *In re Gross*, 722 F.2d 599 (10th Cir. 1983); *In re Peterman*, 5 B.R. 687 (Bankr. E.D. Pa. 1980); *see also In re Comer*, 723 F.2d

The main indicators that courts will look to in determining whether the debt is in the nature of a support payment rather than a property settlement are:

- Whether the payments terminate upon death or remarriage of the spouse receiving them;[351]
- Whether payments are contingent on future earning abilities;
- Whether payments are to be periodic over a long period of time rather than in a lump sum; and
- Whether the payments are designated as being for purposes such as medical care, mortgage, or other needs of the spouse receiving them.

Each of these factors indicates that support, based upon the needs of the obligee spouse, is intended, rather than a property settlement. The existence of those needs at the time of the agreement, by itself, is often sufficient for a finding that an obligation was for the purpose of support.[352] While labels in a divorce decree or settlement are not binding on the court, at least some deference may be given to how the various obligations are labeled in the agreement.[353] Another factor that courts may find relevant is the parties' tax treatment of the payments. A spouse who has taken the benefit of treatment of marital obligations as alimony may be estopped from later contending the obligation was a property settlement.[354] Similarly, an obligee who did not report past payments as alimony income, may be estopped from later claiming the debt is in the nature of alimony.

If the intent of an agreement is to provide support, it is irrelevant whether such support is required under state law.[355] If the court finds, on the other hand, that payments are to compensate for a spouse's property interest, they will be designated as in the nature of a property settlement with dischargeability to be determined under another Code section.[356] Normally, a trial court's findings on such issues will not be disturbed on appeal if the proper legal standards are applied.[357]

Spouses or former spouses often disagree about the nature of a "hold harmless" agreement in which one spouse agrees to pay marital debts and then later claims that they were discharged in a bankruptcy. Whether the responsibility for these debts is more in the nature of a support payment or a property settlement is determined using similar criteria.[358] For these debts to be determined nondischargeable, most courts have held that payment of them must be necessary to support the non-debtor spouse at the time of the agreement

737 (9th Cir. 1984) (*res judicata* also applies as to amount of support found owing by state court). *But see In re* Williams, 3 B.R. 401 (Bankr. N.D. Ga. 1980).

351 *See In re* Morel, 983 F.2d 104 (8th Cir. 1992) (when one portion of award was payable until death or remarriage and other portion was not, the portion not conditioned on the obligee continuing to live as a single person was a dischargeable property settlement).

352 *In re* Werthen, 329 F.3d 269 (1st Cir. 2003) (obligation to pay over percentage of debtor's bonuses, though labeled property settlement, was needed for support of children and payments were to be received roughly until children reached majority); *In re* Benick, 811 F.2d 943 (5th Cir. 1987) (wife needed support); *In re* Yeates, 807 F.2d 874 (10th Cir. 1986) (payments needed to provide basic necessities); *In re* Shaver, 736 F.2d 1314 (9th Cir. 1984) ("property settlement" found in nature of support where wife needed support and divorce decree had no explicit provision for support of wife); *In re* Combs, 101 B.R. 609 (B.A.P. 9th Cir. 1989) (listing eight factors in finding debt for spousal support nondischargeable); *In re* Fox, 6 Bankr. Ct. Dec. (LRP) 709 (Bankr. N.D. Tex. 1980); *see* Henry J. Sommer & Margaret Doe McGarity, Collier Family Law and the Bankruptcy Code, Ch. 6; Schiffer, *The New Bankruptcy Reform Act: Its Implications for Family Law Practitioners*, 19 J. Fam. L. 1, 21 (1980–1981).

353 *See* Tilley v. Jessee, 789 F.2d 1074 (4th Cir. 1986) (settlement agreement structured so as to divide property settlement from alimony given great weight in determining that debt is dischargeable); *In re* Long, 794 F.2d 928 (4th Cir. 1986) (characterization of monetary obligation as alimony in jury award given deference in determining that a debt is nondischargeable); *see also In re* Singer, 787 F.2d 1033 (6th Cir. 1986) (recital in agreement interpreted and given great weight in making determination that an obligation constituted support).

354 Robb v. Fulton, 23 F.3d 895 (4th Cir. 1994); *In re* Davidson, 947 F.2d 1294 (5th Cir. 1991). Such decisions are probably erroneous in looking to this single factor, because the requirements for federal tax deductibility are not exactly the same as the indicia of support under federal bankruptcy law.

355 Richardson v. Edwards, 127 F.3d 97 (D.C. Cir. 1997) (obligation to pay support past children's age of majority in nature of support even though there was no legal duty of support); *In re* Sampson, 997 F.2d 717 (10th Cir. 1993) (listing variety of factors which showed true function and intent of obligation); *In re* Biggs, 907 F.2d 503 (5th Cir. 1990) (debtor's divorce decree obligation to former wife was nondischargeable alimony, even though Texas law did not provide for alimony awards); *In re* Yeates, 807 F.2d 874 (10th Cir. 1986); *In re* Harrell, 754 F.2d 902 (11th Cir. 1985); Boyle v. Donovan, 724 F.2d 681 (8th Cir. 1984).

356 *In re* Ingram, 5 B.R. 232 (Bankr. N.D. Ga. 1980). See § 14.4.3.14, *infra*, for a discussion of nondischargeable property settlements. Alternatively, the debt incurred as a result of a property settlement might be found nondischargeable on some other grounds such as fraud. *See, e.g.,* Edelkind v. Alderman, 106 B.R. 315 (N.D. Ga. 1989) (debtor fraudulently induced his former wife to accept a promissory note and then dishonored the note)*; In re* Brasher, 20 B.R. 408 (Bankr. W.D. Tenn. 1982) (property settlement agreement found fraudulent under 11 U.S.C. § 523(a)(2) where entered into with intent to file bankruptcy after inducing wife to waive alimony).

357 *In re* Brody, 3 F.3d 35 (2d Cir. 1993) (listing factors trial court found showed parties' intent to provide support); *In re* Troup, 730 F.2d 464 (6th Cir. 1984); Boyle v. Donovan, 724 F.2d 681 (8th Cir. 1984); Stout v. Prussel, 691 F.2d 859 (9th Cir. 1982).

358 *See In re* Rice, 94 B.R. 617 (Bankr. W.D. Mo. 1988) (obligation to pay bills and attorney fees and lien on house found to be property settlement where divorce court had separately awarded spousal maintenance); *In re* Campbell, 74 B.R. 805 (Bankr. M.D. Fla. 1987) (property settlement found where debtor's obligations would not terminate on death or remarriage of ex-spouse).

or order.[359] If the debtor spouse has agreed to pay current mortgage, utility, insurance, and tax payments, for example, such payments are normally deemed to be support.[360] This conclusion is bolstered if the non-debtor spouse is unemployed[361] or if the agreement provides for payment through the court, with noncompliance punishable by contempt.[362] Other cases in which courts have found an intent to provide support have involved such debts as payments for life insurance policies that name the debtor's spouse and children as beneficiaries,[363] payments for medical treatment after the divorce,[364] and debts for furniture used by the former spouse and children, when the intent was to relieve the spouse from the burden of paying them, and the spouse waived the right to periodic alimony payments.[365]

The Sixth Circuit Court of Appeals has mandated a several step analysis to determine the dischargeability of a hold harmless obligation under section 523(a)(5).[366] Under this test, the bankruptcy court must look to the intent of the family law court or the intent of the parties themselves as to each loan obligation.[367] If payments were intended as support, the bankruptcy court must then decide whether the payments have the effect of providing support and whether that support is necessary for the daily needs of the spouse and children. If these factors are present, the court must finally decide whether the payments are within the criteria for ability to pay that would normally be applied to support orders. If the amounts are unreasonably excessive, they are dischargeable.

All other circuits to address the issue have rejected the Sixth Circuit approach to the extent that approach looks to current need and the amounts of payments ordered.[368] These courts have generally held that the bankruptcy court should look only to whether the payments due were originally intended to be in the nature of support rather than a property settlement. Once the debt is determined to be one that was originally intended for support, no further inquiry is to be made and the debt must be declared nondischargeable.[369]

On the other hand, if the intent was simply to divide assets and previous liabilities, the debt is not nondischargeable under section 523(a)(5),[370] especially if there is no apparent benefit intended for the other spouse.[371] Such debts may, however, be nondischargeable under section 523(a)(15).[372] If such debts are discharged, any action to collect them is enjoined under section 524 of the Code.[373]

One type of divorce debt that has usually been found to be in the nature of support and thus nondischargeable consists of attorney fees payable by one spouse to the other's attorney, at least when the first spouse has been awarded alimony or support.[374] The attorney fees are sometimes deemed to rise or fall with the determination on the primary debt.[375] Other courts have reasoned that the award of fees is based upon the need of one spouse[376] or the duty of the other to

---

359　*In re* Robinson, 921 F.2d 252 (10th Cir. 1990) (even if non-debtor spouse refinanced a mortgage the debtor agreed to pay, the debtor's obligation would survive and remain nondischargeable); *In re* Warner, 5 B.R. 434 (Bankr. D. Utah 1980); *cf. In re* Edwards, 91 B.R. 95 (Bankr. C.D. Cal. 1988) (state court cannot order debtor to pay spouse's debts discharged in bankruptcy as alimony, support or maintenance).

360　*In re* Gianakas, 917 F.2d 759 (3d Cir. 1990); Sylvester v. Sylvester, 865 F.2d 1164 (10th Cir. 1989); *In re* Tope, 7 B.R. 422 (Bankr. S.D. Ohio 1980); *In re* Henry, 5 B.R. 342 (Bankr. M.D. Fla. 1980). *But see* Richardson v. Edwards, 127 F.3d 97 (D.C. Cir. 1997) (obligation to assume second mortgage not intended as a means of providing support).

361　*In re* Tope, 7 B.R. 422 (Bankr. S.D. Ohio 1980).

362　*In re* Henry, 5 B.R. 342 (Bankr. M.D. Fla. 1980).

363　*In re* Evans, 4 B.R. 232 (Bankr. S.D. Ala. 1980).

364　*In re* Breaux, 8 B.R. 218 (Bankr. W.D. La. 1981).

365　*In re* Coil, 680 F.2d 1170 (7th Cir. 1982); *In re* Sturgell, 7 B.R. 59 (Bankr. S.D. Ohio 1980).

366　*In re* Calhoun, 715 F.2d 1103 (6th Cir. 1983); *see also* Boyle v. Donovan, 724 F.2d 681 (8th Cir. 1984) (court looked to intent of parties, financial situation at time of agreement, and family pattern of life to find obligation in nature of support even where state law did not require support).

367　The Sixth Circuit has since held that in determining the court's intent, once it is shown that there is a direct payment obligation, labeled as maintenance, terminable on death, remarriage or receipt of social security, there is a conclusive presumption that it is intended as support. *In re* Sorah, 163 F.3d 397 (6th Cir. 1998).

368　*E.g.,* Sylvester v. Sylvester, 865 F.2d 1164 (10th Cir. 1989); Forsdick v. Turgeon, 812 F.2d 801 (2d Cir. 1987); Draper v. Draper, 790 F.2d 52 (8th Cir. 1986); *In re* Harrell, 754 F.2d 902 (11th Cir. 1985).

369　*E.g.,* Sylvester v. Sylvester, 865 F.2d 1164 (10th Cir. 1989); Forsdick v. Turgeon, 812 F.2d 801 (2d Cir. 1987); Draper v. Draper, 790 F.2d 52 (8th Cir. 1986); *In re* Harrell, 754 F.2d 902 (11th Cir. 1985).

370　*In re* Williams, 3 B.R. 401 (Bankr. N.D. Ga. 1980) (debtor's car payments and health club membership); *In re* Travis, Bankr. L. Rep. (CCH) ¶ 67,520 (Bankr. W.D. Okla. 1980) (agreement not enforceable by contempt order); *In re* Francisco, 1 B.R. 565 (Bankr. W.D. Va. 1980) (clause about debts distinct from paragraph on support). *But see In re* Kodel, 105 B.R. 729 (Bankr. S.D. Fla. 1989) (debtor's payments to wife from business proceeds found to be support rather than equitable division of business).

371　*In re* Diers, 7 B.R. 18 (Bankr. S.D. Ohio 1980).

372　*See* § 14.4.3.14, *infra*.

373　*In re* Jones, 38 B.R. 690 (N.D. Ohio 1983) (state proceedings to collect on discharged property settlement debt enjoined by bankruptcy court); *In re* Marriage of Williams, 203 Cal. Rptr. 909 (Ct. App. 1984) (attempted setoff of discharged debt).

374　*See* Macy v. Macy, 114 F.3d 1 (1st Cir. 1997); *In re* Catlow, 663 F.2d 960 (9th Cir. 1981). Where the fees are owed by the debtor to an attorney who represented the debtor in seeking an order of child support, the debt is not in the nature of support and is dischargeable. *In re* Rios, 901 F.2d 71 (7th Cir. 1990).

375　*In re* Bell, 5 B.R. 653 (Bankr. W.D. Okla. 1980); Lynn v. Lynn, 91 N.J. 510, 453 A.2d 539 (1982); *see In re* Rice, 94 B.R. 617 (Bankr. W.D. Mo. 1988).

376　*In re* Joseph, 16 F.3d 86 (5th Cir. 1994); *In re* Evans, 2 B.R. 85 (Bankr. W.D. Mo. 1979); *cf. In re* Gibson, 103 B.R. 218 (B.A.P. 9th Cir. 1989) (attorney fee award dischargeable where state court did not appear to have considered need in making it).

support.[377] Generally, pre-Code cases with such holdings[378] are still good law. However, it has also been held that when the fees are payable directly to the attorney they constitute an assigned obligation which is dischargeable.[379] In any case, it appears that the attorney may not be an appropriate party to seek the dischargeability determination.[380]

Courts have also struggled with whether attorney fees incurred in custody proceedings, including fees of attorneys appointed to represent children, are dischargeable. Most courts have found this issue to turn on whether the representation was necessary for the welfare of the child; in such cases the fees have been found nondischargeable.[381] Most of these courts have not addressed, however, the issue of whether the fees are owed to a spouse or child of the debtor, as is also required by section 523(a)(5).[382]

Another frequent situation is that of a divorce decree which has divided the debtor's pension benefits, often through a Qualified Domestic Relations Order. Usually, such pension divisions are deemed to transfer a present interest in the pension benefits to the other spouse, so they do not create a debt that may be later discharged in bankruptcy.[383]

Naturally, bankruptcy debtors and potential debtors, as well as their spouses, will want to keep these principles in mind when negotiating marital settlements. Obtaining a large property settlement in return for reduced alimony may be a short-lived victory if obligations under the former are discharged in bankruptcy soon afterwards. Although some state courts have found discharge of property settlement obligations in bankruptcy to be changed circumstances justifying modification of alimony awards,[384] some of these cases may contravene the Bankruptcy Code's "fresh start" policy.[385]

14.4.3.6 Willful and Malicious Injury—11 U.S.C. § 523(a)(6)

The sixth category of debts excepted from discharge consists of debts for willful and malicious injury by the debtor to another entity or the property of another entity.[386] This exception encompasses a narrow class of tort liabilities, in which the debtor's conduct was both intentional and such that it intended to harm an entity or its property. If the creditor does not have an enforceable claim against the debtor based on the alleged injury, the exception does not apply.[387] In addition, if a contractual obligation has been substituted for the original alleged tort debt, the exception may not apply.[388]

Most of the litigation under this exception has centered on whether specific conduct was willful and malicious. It is

377 *In re* Pelikant, 5 B.R. 404 (Bankr. N.D. Ill. 1980); *In re* Knabe, 8 B.R. 53 (Bankr. S.D. Ind. 1980); *see also In re* Strickland, 90 F.3d 444 (11th Cir. 1996) (attorney fees awarded in post-divorce custody action based on relative need and ability to pay).

378 *See, e.g., In re* Cornish, 529 F.2d 1363 (7th Cir. 1976); *In re* Nunnally, 506 F.2d 1024 (5th Cir. 1975); Damon v. Damon, 283 F.2d 571 (1st Cir. 1960).

379 *In re* Allen, 4 B.R. 617 (Bankr. E.D. Tenn. 1980). *But see In re* Hudson, 107 F.3d 355 (5th Cir. 1997) (fees nondischargeable despite fact that they were awarded directly to attorney); *In re* Spong, 661 F.2d 6 (2d Cir. 1981); *In re* Gwinn, 20 B.R. 233 (B.A.P. 9th Cir. 1982) (fees payable directly to attorney remain nondischargeable); *In re* Knabe, 8 B.R. 53 (Bankr. S.D. Ind. 1980) (holding fees not an assigned debt).

380 *In re* Delillo, 5 B.R. 692 (Bankr. D. Mass. 1980); *In re* Allen, 4 B.R. 617, (Bankr. E.D. Tenn. 1980). *But see In re* Spong, 661 F.2d 6 (2d Cir. 1981); *In re* Gwinn, 20 B.R. 233 (B.A.P. 9th Cir. 1982).

381 *In re* Maddigan, 312 F.3d 589 (2d Cir. 2002) (attorney fees awarded to out-of-wedlock mother in custody case were nondischargeable support); *In re* Chang, 163 F.3d 1138 (9th Cir. 1998) (debts for professional fees in child custody case owed to father and guardian *ad litem* were nondischargeable); Miller v. Gentry, 55 F.3d 1487 (10th Cir. 1995); *In re* Jones, 9 F.3d 878 (10th Cir. 1994) (fees were incurred on behalf of child); *In re* Peters, 964 F.2d 166 (2d Cir. 1992), *aff'g* 133 B.R. 291 (S.D. N.Y. 1991); *cf.* Adams v. Zentz, 963 F.2d 197 (8th Cir. 1992) (case primarily concerned mother's efforts to frustrate father's relationship with child). *But see In re* Lowther, 321 F.3d 946 (10th Cir. 2002) (attorney fee award that would compromise debtor's ability to support children presented unusual circumstances that were an exception to usual dischargeability rule in custody cases).

382 *See generally* Henry J. Sommer & Margaret Doe McGarity, Collier Family Law and the Bankruptcy Code ¶ 6.03[4].

383 *In re* Gendreau, 122 F.3d 815 (9th Cir. 1997); *In re* McCafferty, 96 F.3d 192 (6th Cir. 1996) (divorce decree dividing pension created separate property interest in pension for non-debtor spouse); Bush v. Taylor, 912 F.2d 989 (8th Cir. 1990) (*en banc*);

In re Chandler, 805 F.2d 555 (5th Cir. 1986). *But see In re* Reines, 142 F.3d 970 (7th Cir. 1998) (city pension could not be divided by family court and obligation to pay benefits to former spouse found to be dischargeable).

384 *In re* Myers, 773 P.2d 118 (Wash. Ct. App. 1989); Eckert v. Eckert, 424 N.W.2d 759 (Wis. Ct. App. 1988).

385 Modification issues are discussed in Henry J. Sommer & Margaret Doe McGarity, Collier Family Law and the Bankruptcy Code ¶ 6.10.

386 11 U.S.C. § 523(a)(6). While this exception to discharge is not applicable in chapter 13 cases, the fact that such a debt is not dischargeable in chapter 7 may be found relevant to a determination of whether a chapter 13 plan proposing discharge of such a debt was proposed in good faith. *In re* Lemaire, 898 F.2d 1346 (8th Cir. 1990) (*en banc*); *see* §§ 12.3.2, 12.3.4, *supra*.

387 *In re* Zelis, 66 F.3d 205 (9th Cir. 1995) (creditor that had settled with joint tortfeasor had no claim against debtor and could not have claim held nondischargeable); *In re* Shapiro, 180 B.R. 37 (Bankr. E.D.N.Y. 1995) (creditor whose claim was barred by statute of limitations could not bring dischargeability action); *see also In re* Olson, 262 B.R. 18 (Bankr. D.R.I. 2001) (state victim compensation fund did not have enforceable claim because it had not made payments to victim and could not, in any case, stand in victim's shoes for non-dischargeability action).

388 *But see* Archer v. Warner, 123 S. Ct. 1462, 155 L. Ed. 2d 454 (2003) (creditor not precluded from bringing a non-dischargeability claim by pre-bankruptcy settlement of claim; court left open the possibility of preclusion if settlement includes a promise that creditor will refrain from pursuing non-dischargeability action).

clear, at one end of the spectrum, for example, that assault and battery is willful and malicious.[389] At the other end, negligence, even gross negligence, is not.[390] Thus, few liabilities that arise out of automobile accidents are excepted from discharge under this subsection, regardless of whether the debtor was driving while intoxicated,[391] driving without insurance,[392] or violating various traffic laws.[393] Even a reckless disregard for the safety of others is not sufficient to except the debt from discharge.[394]

The Supreme Court clarified this issue in *Kawaauhau v. Geiger*.[395] The Court held that medical malpractice could not be willful and malicious injury under this section because the word "willful" modified "injury," thus requiring that the actor intended the harmful consequences of the act in question, knowing that they would occur.

Although the case law indicates that a case-by-case analysis must be made to determine whether conduct was willful and malicious, proof of an intentional tort is not enough. The ultimate outcome usually depends on the nature of the act. The intentional setting of a fire is obviously sufficient,[396] but breaches of contractual rights, even if intentional, generally fall short of the standard.[397] Most courts have adopted a definition of willful and malicious injury as one which involves the intentional doing of a wrongful act, which necessarily causes injury, without just cause or excuse.[398]

---

389 *In re* Miera, 926 F.2d 741 (8th Cir. 1991) (debtor judge could not discharge award of compensatory and punitive damages to court reporter for battery consisting of kissing court reporter on mouth without his consent); *In re* Dardar, 620 F.2d 39 (5th Cir. 1980); *see also In re* Braen, 900 F.2d 621 (3d Cir. 1990) (malicious prosecution judgment nondischargeable); *In re* Latch, 820 F.2d 1163 (11th Cir. 1987) (civil theft judgment nondischargeable); *In re* Moberg, 156 B.R. 810 (Bankr. D. Minn. 1993) (sexual assault was willful and malicious); *In re* Gee, 156 B.R. 291 (Bankr. W.D. Wash. 1993) (sexual harassment claim found willful and malicious), *aff'd in part*, 173 B.R. 189 (B.A.P. 9th Cir. 1994).

390 Kawaauhau v. Geiger, 523 U.S. 57, 118 S. Ct. 974, 140 L. Ed. 2d 90 (1998) (doctor's malpractice involving negligent and reckless conduct not covered by § 523(a)(6)); *In re* Kelly, 100 F.3d 110 (9th Cir. 1996), *aff'g* 182 B.R. 255 (B.A.P. 9th Cir. 1995) (showing of legal malpractice is not sufficient to prove willful and malicious conduct); *In re* Delaney, 97 F.3d 800 (5th Cir. 1996) (accidental firing of gun that debtor tapped on car window was not willful and malicious, even though debtor intentionally tapped on window).

391 Cassidy v. Minihan, 794 F.2d 340 (8th Cir. 1986); *In re* Compos, 768 F.2d 1155 (10th Cir. 1985); *In re* Wright, 66 B.R. 403 (Bankr. S.D. Ind. 1986); *In re* Naser, 7 B.R. 116 (Bankr. W.D. Wis. 1980); *In re* Bryson, 3 B.R. 593 (Bankr. N.D. Ill. 1980); *see also In re* Taneff, 190 B.R. 501 (Bankr. W.D.N.Y. 1996) (even high probability of producing harm by selling liquor to intoxicated driver would not be willful and malicious). However, many of these debts are nondischargeable under 11 U.S.C. § 523(a)(9). *See* § 14.4.3.10, *infra*. In other situations where the debtor argues that actions were not willful because of intoxication, there may be issues about whether the debtor was in control of his or her faculties. *See In re* Thirtyacre, 36 F.3d 697 (7th Cir. 1994) (debtor's argument that he was depressed and intoxicated rejected where he had been sober enough to operate car, track and find victim's boyfriend and argue with boyfriend).

392 Pechar v. Moore, 98 B.R. 488 (D. Neb. 1988); *In re* Bex, 143 B.R. 835 (Bankr. E.D. Ky. 1992) (actions of debtors in allowing automobile insurance to lapse did not create willful injury to creditor injured in accident involving debtors' vehicle, because debtors had no intent or knowledge that their son would become involved in accident while they were uninsured).

393 Oregon Ford, Inc. v. Claburn, 89 B.R. 629 (N.D. Ohio 1987) (debtor had driven rented vehicle in excess of lawful speed limit); *In re* Donnelly, 6 B.R. 19 (Bankr. D. Or. 1980).

394 Kawaauhau v. Geiger, 523 U.S. 57, 118 S. Ct. 974, 140 L. Ed. 2d 90 (1998) (doctor's malpractice involving negligent and reckless conduct not covered by § 523(a)(6)); *In re* Quezada, 718 F.2d 121 (5th Cir. 1983); *In re* Warren, 7 B.R. 546 (Bankr. M.D. Ga. 1980); H.R. Rep. No. 95-595, at 363 (1977); S. Rep. No. 95-989, at 77–79 (1978).

395 523 U.S. 57, 118 S. Ct. 974, 140 L. Ed. 2d 90 (1998); *see also In re* Delaney, 97 F.3d 800 (5th Cir. 1996) (accidental firing of gun that debtor tapped on car window was not willful and malicious, even though debtor intentionally tapped on window).

396 *In re* Wuttke, 6 Bankr. Ct. Dec. (LRP) 1304 (Bankr. D.N.J. 1980).

397 *In re* Riso, 978 F.2d 1151 (9th Cir. 1992) (contract giving right of first refusal with respect to sale of property did not give rise to security interest that would constitute property; intentional breach of contract not within exception unless accompanied by willful and malicious tortious conduct); *In re* Mitchell, 227 B.R. 45 (Bankr. S.D.N.Y. 1998) (obligation for past due rent dischargeable; landlord demonstrated only breach of contract); *In re* Brazington, 3 B.R. 309 (Bankr. D. Idaho 1980); *In re* Warren, 7 B.R. 546 (Bankr. M.D. Ga. 1980); *see also In re* Popa, 140 F.3d 317 (1st Cir. 1998) (employer's failure to obtain workers compensation insurance was not willful and malicious injury because there was no intent to injure); *In re* Saylor, 108 F.3d 219 (alleged fraudulent transfer of assets in which creditor did not have a property interest was not willful and malicious injury to property of creditor); *In re* Barriger, 61 B.R. 506 (Bankr. W.D. Tenn. 1986) (allowing insurance to lapse on automobile in which creditor held security interest in violation of the parties' contract not willful or malicious conduct). *But see In re* Bammer, 131 F.3d 788 (9th Cir. 1997) (*en banc*) (debtor caused willful and malicious injury by knowingly participating in scheme to make his mother's assets unavailable to creditors).

398 *E.g., In re* Abbo, 168 F.3d 930 (6th Cir. 1999) (debt for malicious prosecution and abuse of process nondischargeable when debtor had been found to have acted maliciously with intent to injure); *In re* Walker, 48 F.3d 1161 (11th Cir. 1995) (debtor must intend injury or intentionally take action substantially certain to cause injury); *In re* Conte, 33 F.3d 303 (3d Cir. 1994) (debtor must have personally inflicted injury or acted with substantial certainty that injury would result; knowledge that there was a high probability of harm is not sufficient); *In re* Pasek, 983 F.2d 1524 (10th Cir. 1993) (breach of covenant not to compete not willful and malicious because debtor reasonably relied on legal opinion that covenant was not enforceable; statute requires intentional or deliberate injury); *In re* Cecchini, 780 F.2d 1440 (9th Cir. 1986); *see also In re* Karlin, 112 B.R. 319 (B.A.P. 9th Cir. 1990) (inadvertent publication of photographs without subject's permission was excusable under the circumstances and any debt arising from the invasion of privacy was dischargeable); *In re* Strybel, 105 B.R. 22 (B.A.P. 9th Cir.

Under the *Kawaauhau* decision, there are very good arguments that not only must the actions have been very likely to cause injury but that the debtor must also have subjectively known the injury was likely and intended to cause the injury.[399] Because mere reckless disregard as to the truth or falsity of a published statement may support a libel verdict under some circumstances, a court may have to determine whether an obligation based on libel arose from willful or malicious conduct so as to be nondischargeable.[400]

Perhaps the most common attempts to use this exception in consumer cases arise from alleged conversions of a creditor's collateral. It was probably the frequent use of such allegations in cases in which consumers innocently disposed of such property that led to the requirement that the willful and malicious exception be raised during the bankruptcy case if it is to be raised at all.[401]

It is clear, though, that the willful and malicious standard is applicable to conversion cases.[402] Although a technical conversion may occur whenever a debtor disposes of collateral, no matter how small its value, more is required to bring the discharge exception into play.[403] The debt is not excepted from discharge unless the debtor understood that a security interest existed[404] and acted with a specific intent to harm or defraud the creditor.[405] It also is not excepted if the creditor was aware of the debtor's actions and failed to object to them.[406] This is especially true for retailers who know that their credit cards will often be used to purchase gifts and who fail to discourage (and in some cases encourage) that practice.[407] Moreover, if the debt is excepted, it

---

1989) (conduct of psychiatrist in having sexual relations with patient did not give rise to nondischargeable debt); *In re* Meyer, 100 B.R. 301 (D.S.C. 1989) (judgment debt arising from the tort of "criminal conversation" is not dischargeable). An act may be both fraudulent and willful and malicious. *In re* Stokes, 995 F.2d 76 (5th Cir. 1993) (unfair and deceptive practices found willful and malicious).

399 *In re* Moore, 337 F.3d 1125 (10th Cir. 2003) (state court fraud verdict against debtor for misrepresenting insurance coverage was not debt for willful and malicious injury, because debtor did not intend injury to occur); *In re* Su, 290 F.3d 1140 (9th Cir. 2002), *explaining and limiting In re* Jercich, 238 F.3d 1202 (9th Cir. 2001) .

400 *In re* Peck, 295 B.R. 353 (9th Cir. 2003) (false accusation of child molestation was malicious); *In re* Kennedy, 249 F.3d 576 (6th Cir. 2001) (debtors who falsely denied creditor-husband's paternity of child when they had undeniable evidence their claims were untrue committed willful and malicious injury to reputation); Wheeler v. Laudani, 783 F.2d 610 (6th Cir. 1986); *see In re* Yanks, 931 F.2d 42 (11th Cir. 1991) (defamation judgment collaterally estopped debtor in subsequent dischargeability action because malice was actually litigated and determined).

401 11 U.S.C. § 523(c).

402 Printy v. Dean Witter Reynolds, Inc., 110 F.3d 853 (1st Cir. 1997) (debtor who took advantage of broker's computer error to enrich himself at expense of broker committed willful and malicious conversion); Vulcan Coals, Inc. v. Howard, 946 F.2d 1226 (6th Cir. 1991) (allegation of conversion of collateral is sufficient to make out a case under section 523(a)(6)); *In re* Graham, 7 B.R. 5 (Bankr. D. Nev. 1980); *see also In re* Grey, 902 F.2d 1479 (10th Cir. 1990) (debtor's sale of collateral was willful and malicious even though security agreement did not use phrase "after-acquired property"); *In re* Wood, 96 B.R. 993 (B.A.P. 9th Cir. 1988) (debt found nondischargeable where debtor failed to notify spouse of early retirement and converted pension benefits in which she had an interest).

403 Davis v. Aetna Acceptance Co., 293 U.S. 328, 55 S. Ct. 151, 79 L. Ed. 393 (1934); Werner v. Hoffman, 5 F.3d 1170 (8th Cir.

1993) (no willful and malicious injury found with respect to failure to return creditor's property caused by carelessness and poor records); *see* Chrysler Credit Corp. v. Rebhan, 842 F.2d 1257 (11th Cir. 1988) (debtor was actively engaged in management of car dealership which converted proceeds of cars in which the plaintiff had a security interest; implied or constructive malice was found).

404 *In re* Posta, 866 F.2d 364 (10th Cir. 1989) (evidence that debtors were inexperienced in business matters, had never read security agreement and intended to fulfill their loan obligation was sufficient to establish that conversion of collateral was not willful or malicious); *In re* McCune, 85 B.R. 834 (W.D. Mo. 1988) (no willful or malicious conversion where debtor did not understand breach of legal rights which occurred when property was transferred); *In re* Casselli, 4 B.R. 531 (Bankr. C.D. Cal. 1980) (debtor was unaware of security interest when she gave away collateral).

405 *In re* Peklar, 260 F.3d 1035 (9th Cir. 2001) (debtor who removed furniture from property in derogation of landlord's rights did not act willfully and maliciously); *In re* Littleton, 942 F.2d 551 (9th Cir. 1991) (conversion of collateral not willful where debtors were struggling to keep business going and there was no evidence that debtors personally benefited from the sale); *In re* Phillips, 882 F.2d 302 (8th Cir. 1989); *In re* Posta, 866 F.2d 364 (10th Cir. 1989); *In re* Cecchini, 780 F.2d 1440 (9th Cir. 1986) (substituted opinion on denial of rehearing) (debtor acted under mistaken belief in converting checks of another); *In re* Long, 774 F.2d 875 (8th Cir. 1985); St. Paul Fire & Marine Ins. Co. v. Vaughn, 779 F.2d 1003 (4th Cir. 1985); *In re* Logue, 294 B.R. 59 (B.A.P. 8th Cir. 2003) (selling cattle that secured loan was not malicious when proceeds used to feed remaining cattle); *In re* Howard, 6 B.R. 256 (Bankr. M.D. Fla. 1980); *In re* Hawkins, 6 B.R. 97 (Bankr. W.D. Ky. 1980) (debtor sold automobile after it was wrecked and remitted some of proceeds to creditor); *In re* Hodges, 4 B.R. 513 (Bankr. W.D. Va. 1980) (debtor sold equipment to raise money to pay mortgage, not to harm creditor, whom he still intended to pay). *But see In re* Foust, 52 F.3d 766 (8th Cir. 1995) (debt found due to willful and malicious conversion when debtor converted crops securing loans, sold them in distant market, keeping proceeds, and fabricated reports of grain thefts to cover up scheme).

406 *In re* Wolfson, 56 F.3d 52 (11th Cir. 1995) (debtor's belief that creditor acquiesced in his actions, engendered by course of dealing with creditor, was reasonable and supported conclusion that conversion was not willful or malicious).

407 *In re* Goycochea, 192 B.R. 847 (Bankr. D. Md. 1996) (Sears could not claim conversion of collateral when debtor gave goods purchased to others, because Sears had knowledge that goods purchased are often given as gifts and therefore impliedly consented to transfer); *In re* Hodges, 83 B.R. 25 (Bankr. N.D. Cal. 1988) (creditor required to prove that giving away collateral as a gift is an intentional violation of the security agreement).

should be nondischargeable only to the extent of the value of the collateral converted, if that value is less than the debt.[408]

In light of the Supreme Court's decision about punitive damages under section 523(a)(2),[409] there is little doubt that any punitive and multiple damages included in a debt for willful and malicious injury that is not discharged will also be nondischargeable.

Finally, it is clear under the Code that only willful and malicious acts of the debtor, and not those of agents, children, or others, can lead to a finding of nondischargeability.[410] This changes the law from that developed under the prior Bankruptcy Act, which in some cases denied the discharge of debts for willful and malicious acts of partners, children, and others for whom the debtor was legally responsible under state law.[411]

14.4.3.7 Fines and Penalties—11 U.S.C. §§ 523(a)(7), 1328(a)(3)

One of the less frequently applicable exceptions is that for fines and penalties owed to governmental units and for their benefit.[412] To be nondischargeable under this provision the debt must be owed to a governmental unit.[413] By its terms,

this exception is limited to purely punitive, as opposed to compensatory, assessments.[414] However, the Supreme Court in *Kelly v. Robinson*,[415] held that a restitution order in a welfare fraud case constitutes a nondischargeable fine or penalty within the meaning of this section. Similar reasoning has led to some courts holding that a compensatory assessment of costs is nondischargeable.[416] But an examination of the circumstances of other judicial and administrative restitution awards may turn up grounds for distinguishing *Kelly*.[417] The exception may extend to fines

---

408 *In re* Penney, 76 B.R. 160 (Bankr. N.D. Cal. 1987); *see In re* Modicue, 926 F.2d 452 (8th Cir. 1991) (conversion of collateral renders debt nondischargeable to the extent of the value of the collateral at the time of sale); *see also* Epstein, *Collection of U.C.C. Claims in Bankruptcy*, 11 UCC L.J. 295, 303, 304 (1979).

409 Cohen v. De La Cruz, 523 U.S. 213, 118 S. Ct. 1212, 140 L. Ed. 2d 341 (1998).

410 *In re* Maltais, 202 B.R. 807 (Bankr. D. Mass. 1996); *In re* Miller, 196 B.R. 334 (Bankr. E.D. La. 1996) (acts of debtor's minor son in shooting creditor could not be imputed to debtor for purposes of discharge exception); *In re* Albano, 143 B.R. 323 (Bankr. D. Conn. 1992) (restaurant owner's liability to patron injured in altercation with employee found dischargeable). *But see In re* Cecchini, 780 F.2d 1440 (9th Cir. 1986) (partner's acts imputed to debtor).

411 *In re* Eggers, 51 B.R. 452 (Bankr. E.D. Tenn. 1985).

412 11 U.S.C. § 523(a)(7).

413 *In re* Rashid, 210 F.3d 201 (3d Cir. 2000) (federal restitution payable to private victims not within discharge exception); *In re* Towers, 162 F.3d 952 (7th Cir. 1998) (restitution order payable to attorney general for benefit of fraud victims was not for benefit of a governmental unit and therefore was dischargeable, but separate $50,000.00 penalty was nondischargeable); *In re* Pulley, 303 B.R. 81 (D.N.J. 2003) (drunk driving surcharge collected by state for benefit of private creditors was dischargeable); *In re* Wilson, 299 B.R. 380 (Bankr. E.D. Va. 2003) (criminal restitution to pay creditor's damages determined in a civil case was dischargeable); *In re* McNabb, 287 B.R. 820 (Bankr. D. Colo. 2003) (restitution debt owed to private parties not within scope of exception; state could not pass statute to change this result); *In re* Friedman, 253 B.R. 576 (Bankr. S.D. Fla. 2000) (discovery sanction payable to a private party in compensation of pecuniary loss was dischargeable); *In re* Bailey, 202 B.R. 317 (Bankr. D.N.M. 1995) (sanction debt assigned to state university by university officials who debtor

had sued found to be not for benefit of governmental unit, so it was dischargeable); *In re* Strutz, 154 B.R. 508 (Bankr. N.D. Ind. 1993) (attorney fees awarded as sanctions were dischargeable). However, 11 U.S.C. § 523(a)(13), added in 1994, makes all federal criminal restitution orders nondischargeable in chapter 7. *See* § 14.4.3.12, *infra*.

414 *See In re* Hickman, 260 F.3d 400 (5th Cir. 2001) (bail bond forfeiture debt dischargeable); *In re* Collins, 173 F.3d 924 (4th Cir. 1999) (exception covers only fines that are penal in nature; liability of surety on forfeited bail bonds was dischargeable); S. Bend Cmty. School Corp. v. Eggleston, 215 B.R. 1012 (attorney fees and costs awarded in civil case against governmental unit were not within scope of § 523(a)(7)); *In re* Damore, 195 B.R. 40 (Bankr. E.D. Pa. 1996) (liability of debtor on obligation arising from bail bonds posted for other individuals was contractual, not penal). *But see In re* Nam, 273 F.3d 281 (3d Cir. 2001) (bail bond forfeiture judgment against individual who was not a professional bail bondsman was not dischargeable under § 523(a)(7)).

415 479 U.S. 36, 107 S. Ct. 353, 93 L. Ed. 2d 216 (1986); *see also In re* Soderling, 998 F.2d 730 (9th Cir. 1993) (restitution incurred during marriage was a liability of community property under California law); *In re* Warfel, 268 B.R. 205 (B.A.P. 9th Cir. 2001) (criminal restitution, though payable to different governmental unit than the one that imposed it, was nondischargeable).

416 Thompson v. Virginia, 16 F.3d 576 (4th Cir. 1994) (fact that punishment was contingent on costs rendered costs nondischargeable as fines, penalties or forfeitures); *In re* Hollis, 810 F.2d 106 (6th Cir. 1987); Betts v. Att'y Registration & Disciplinary Comm'n, 165 B.R. 870 (N.D. Ill. 1994) (costs imposed for attorney disciplinary proceeding not dischargeable); *In re* Cillo, 165 B.R. 46 (M.D. Fla. 1994) (same); *In re* Garvin, 84 B.R. 824 (Bankr. M.D. Fla. 1988) (cost of prosecution imposed as part of pre-bankruptcy criminal prosecution constitutes a nondischargeable fine). *But see In re* Taggart, 249 F.3d 987 (9th Cir. 2001) (costs, but not monetary sanctions, imposed in attorney disciplinary proceedings were dischargeable).

417 Williams v. Motley, 925 F.2d 741 (4th Cir. 1991) (service fee imposed on uninsured motorists to defray administrative expenses found dischargeable); *In re* Bill, 90 B.R. 651 (Bankr. D.N.J. 1988) (insurance surcharge imposed for traffic violation is a dischargeable debt); *In re* Taite, 76 B.R. 764 (Bankr. C.D. Cal. 1987) (civil restitution order not within scope of § 523(a)(7) but can be within scope of § 523(a)(2)); *In re* Brown, 39 B.R. 820 (Bankr. M.D. Tenn. 1984) (restitution under pretrial diversion program); *In re* Tauscher, 7 B.R. 918 (Bankr. E.D. Wis. 1981) (back pay portion of administrative assessment for violation of Fair Labor Standards Act was dischargeable, but penalty assessment was not); *see also In re* Caggiano, 34 B.R. 449 (Bankr. D. Mass. 1983) (parking fines not dischargeable but surcharge imposed by Registry of Motor Vehicles was dischargeable as a charge to recover pecuniary losses).

imposed by administrative agencies as well as by courts.[418]

In a chapter 13 case, many penalties and fines are dischargeable.[419] In the past, arguments were frequently raised about whether court-imposed payments were debts within the meaning of the Bankruptcy Code. The United States Supreme Court laid most of those arguments to rest by holding that restitution orders imposed as a condition of probation in a criminal proceeding are debts dischargeable in chapter 13.[420] Shortly after it was rendered, this decision was partially overruled by Congress through an amendment creating Code section 1328(a)(3), which makes nondischargeable restitution debts included in a sentence on the debtor's conviction of a crime.[421] Other restitution debts, such as those imposed in pretrial diversion programs, remain dischargeable in chapter 13.

Certain fines, other than federal criminal fines,[422] also remain dischargeable in chapter 13. The 1994 amendments to the Bankruptcy Code made nondischargeable in that chapter fines imposed as part of a sentence upon conviction of a crime.[423] Clearly, civil penalties are not included within this new statutory language. There may also be issues concerning whether parking tickets or traffic tickets remain dischargeable. The answer in a particular case may turn on whether parking or traffic violations are deemed "crimes" under state law. In many states they probably are not, especially if there is state law defining crimes as including only misdemeanors and felonies. There may also be issues regarding whether a "conviction" has occurred in such cases, or whether there has been a "sentence."[424]

In any case, there is no doubt that a debtor may provide for such debts in a chapter 13 plan even if they are nondis-

chargeable. If the debtor does so, the automatic stay should bar collection efforts, such as attempts to revoke the debtor's driver's license or to incarcerate the debtor due to nonpayment. There may be issues regarding whether the debtor can separately classify such debts, similar to issues that now arise with respect to nondischargeable student loans.[425] Also, the debtor may have to file a claim on behalf of the creditor to ensure that the debt is paid.[426]

Not included in either the chapter 7 exception or the chapter 13 exception are two specific kinds of tax penalties. Those penalties relating to a tax which is dischargeable are also dischargeable, as are any tax penalties relating to a transaction or event that occurred more than three years before the filing of the petition.[427] Also not included in either exception are civil awards for multiple and punitive damages.[428] However, such awards may be nondischargeable if the underlying debt is nondischargeable under another provision of section 523(a).[429]

14.4.3.8 Student Loans—11 U.S.C. § 523(a)(8)

14.4.3.8.1 In general

The exception to discharge for student loans resulted from publicity over a supposed flood of bankruptcies in the early 1970s filed by students who were just finishing their education with the purpose of discharging their student loans before they started earning money. The exception has had several different wordings and, as last amended,[430] covers an "educational benefit, overpayment or loan" which is "made, insured or guaranteed by a governmental unit, or made under any program funded in whole or in part by a governmental unit or a nonprofit institution, or for an obli-

---

418 *See In re* Poule, 91 B.R. 83 (B.A.P. 9th Cir. 1988) (civil penalties imposed for debtor's violation of contractor licensing law are nondischargeable fines).

419 Pennsylvania Dep't of Public Welfare v. Davenport, 495 U.S. 552, 110 S. Ct. 2126, 109 L. Ed. 2d 588 (1990); *In re* Young, 10 B.R. 17 (Bankr. S.D. Cal. 1980); *see In re* DeBaecke, 91 B.R. 3 (Bankr. D.N.J. 1988) (insurance surcharges imposed for traffic violations are dischargeable debts in chapter 13 where the offenses occurred pre-petition, even if the surcharges are imposed post-petition); *In re* Colon, 102 B.R. 421 (Bankr. E.D. Pa. 1989) (pre-petition traffic fines are dischargeable in chapter 13; attempts to collect them by post-petition license suspension violate the automatic stay).

420 Pennsylvania Dep't of Public Welfare v. Davenport, 495 U.S. 552, 110 S. Ct. 2126, 109 L. Ed. 2d 588 (1990); *see also* Lugo v. Paulsen, 886 F.2d 602 (3d Cir. 1989) (insurance surcharge levied against individuals convicted of drunk driving is a debt).

421 *See In re* Bova, 326 F.3d 300 (1st Cir. 2003) (fact that injured party sought civil judgment to enforce restitution order did not change fact that debt arose from criminal restitution order and was nondischargeable in chapter 13).

422 *See* 18 U.S.C. § 3613(f).

423 11 U.S.C. § 1328(a)(3). In cases filed prior to the amendments, all fines were dischargeable in chapter 13. *In re* Hardenberg, 42 F.3d 986 (6th Cir. 1994).

424 *See In re* Wilson, 252 B.R. 739 (B.A.P. 8th Cir. 2000) (plea of guilty with deferred sentence of probation was conviction, as determined under federal law).

425 *See* § 12.4.3, *supra*; § 14.4.3.8.5, *infra*; 8 Collier on Bankruptcy ¶ 1322.05[2] (15th ed. rev.).

426 *See* § 8.4.2, *supra*.

427 11 U.S.C. § 523(a)(7)(A), (B); McKay v. United States, 957 F.2d 689 (9th Cir. 1992) (penalties relating to transactions more than three years old are dischargeable even if underlying taxes are not); *In re* Roberts, 906 F.2d 1440 (10th Cir. 1990) (tax penalties dischargeable even if underlying tax liability is nondischargeable, if taxable period was more than three years before bankruptcy filing); *In re* Roberts, 129 B.R. 71 (C.D. Ill. 1991) (debtor need establish grounds for only one of the two exceptions and need not prove both); *In re* Polston, 239 B.R. 277 (Bankr. M.D. Pa. 1999) (penalties were incurred on date tax returns were due but not filed); *see also* § 14.4.3.1.1, *supra*; *cf.* United States v. Amici, 197 B.R. 696 (M.D. Fla. 1996) (penalty for failure to file partnership return did not relate to a tax and therefore was not within the exception to the exception).

428 *In re* Marvin, 139 B.R. 202 (Bankr. E.D. Wis. 1992); *In re* Manley, 135 B.R. 137 (Bankr. W.D. Okla. 1992).

429 Cohen v. De La Cruz, 523 U.S. 213, 118 S. Ct. 1212, 130 L. Ed. 2d 341 (1998).

430 *See* Pub. L. No. 101-647, 104 Stat. 4789 (1990); Pub. L. No. 98-353, 98 Stat. 333 (1984); Pub. L. No. 96-56, 93 Stat. 387 (1979) (amending 11 U.S.C. § 523(a)(8)).

gation to repay funds received as an educational benefit, scholarship or stipend." This language was intended to broaden the scope of the exception to cover most, if not all, student loans made or insured by nonprofit institutions or governmental units,[431] at least when the debtor is the student loan recipient rather than a co-signer.[432] It does not include

debts to educational institutions for tuition, however.[433] Generally, if a student loan debt is nondischargeable, post-petition interest on the debt is also not discharged.[434]

Some courts have held, however, that contractually imposed liquidated damages for nonpayment of student loans are dischargeable, because the penalties are not debts for an "educational loan."[435] And student loan creditors may be denied collection costs and fees as part of their claims where no entitlement exists under relevant regulations or contract provisions.[436]

---

431 The statutory language includes loans from a trust fund administered by a state university. *In re* Shore, 707 F.2d 1337 (11th Cir. 1983). It also includes "scholarships" under the public health service's health professions scholarship program where the student does not fulfill his or her obligation of active duty service. United States Dep't of Health & Human Services v. Smith, 807 F.2d 122 (8th Cir. 1986); *In re* Brown, 59 B.R. 40 (W.D. La. 1986); *see also In re* Murphy, 282 F.3d 868 (5th Cir. 2002) (entire student loan not dischargeable, including portion used for living expenses); *In re* Burks, 244 F.3d 1245 (11th Cir. 2001) (obligation to repay stipend due to failure to complete obligation to teach in "other race" institution after receiving degree was educational loan obligation); T I Fed. Credit Union v. Delbonis, 72 F.3d 921 (1st Cir. 1995) (loan from nonprofit federal credit union nondischargeable; federal credit union was instrumentality of United States); *In re* Merchant, 958 F.2d 738 (6th Cir. 1992) (loan guaranteed by nonprofit institution was nondischargeable); *In re* Bolen, 287 B.R. 127 (D. Vt. 2002) (loan from Law Access program partially funded by non-profit corporation was within scope of section); *In re* Rosen, 179 B.R. 935 (Bankr. D. Or. 1995) (loan made by union training committee was within purview of nondischargeability section); *In re* Hammerstrom, 95 B.R. 160 (Bankr. N.D. Cal. 1989) (student loan made by commercial bank with arrangement that loan was to be purchased by nonprofit guarantee agency is covered by § 523(a)(8)); *In re* Avila, 53 B.R. 933 (Bankr. W.D.N.Y. 1985); *cf. In re* Segal, 57 F.3d 342 (3d Cir. 1995) (when nonprofit hospital paid off debtor's student loan, replacing it with new loans, those new loans were not nondischargeable under this section because they were not made under a "program" of giving educational loans); *In re* Reis, 274 B.R. 46 (Bankr. D. Mass. 2002) (educational loan made by grandparents dischargeable); *In re* Scott, 287 B.R. 470 (Bankr. E.D. Mo. 2002) (loan from for-profit truck driving school was dischargeable); *In re* Jones, 242 B.R. 441 (Bankr. W.D. Tenn. 1999) (debt to for-profit trade school was not within scope of § 523(a)(8)); *In re* Shorts, 209 B.R. 818 (Bankr. D.R.I. 1997) (same); *In re* Simmons, 175 B.R. 624 (Bankr. E.D. Va. 1994) (credit union was not a nonprofit institution and loan was not made pursuant to a program within meaning of § 523(a)(8)); *In re* Sinclair-Ganos, 133 B.R. 382 (Bankr. W.D. Mich. 1991) (credit union not a non-profit institution within meaning of § 523(a)(8)).

432 *See In re* Pryor, 234 B.R. 716 (Bankr. W.D. Tenn. 1999) (exception not applicable to non-student cosigner); *In re* Behr, 80 B.R. 124 (Bankr. N.D. Iowa 1987) (exception not applicable to non-student codebtor); *In re* Meier, 85 B.R. 805 (Bankr. W.D. Wis. 1986) (exception not applicable to accommodation party); *In re* Zobel, 80 B.R. 950 (Bankr. N.D. Iowa 1986) (exception not applicable to co-maker); *In re* Bawden, 55 B.R. 459 (Bankr. M.D. Ala. 1985); *In re* Washington, 41 B.R. 211 (Bankr. E.D. Va. 1984) (exception not applicable to non-student codebtor); *In re* Boylen, 29 B.R. 924 (Bankr. N.D. Ohio 1983); *cf.* H.R. Rep. No. 95-595, at 134 (1977) ("The proponents of an exception to discharge have argued that educational loans are different from most loans, they . . . [rely] for repayment solely on the debtor's future increased income resulting from the education"). *But see In re* Pelkowski, 990 F.2d 737 (3d Cir. 1993) (language of

statute does not limit exception to discharge to exclude parent cosigners); *In re* Varma, 149 B.R. 817 (N.D. Tex. 1992); *In re* Wilcon, 143 B.R. 4 (D. Mass. 1992); *In re* Hammerstrom, 95 B.R. 160 (Bankr. N.D. Cal. 1989) (student loan signed solely by parents nondischargeable); *In re* Taylor, 95 B.R. 550 (Bankr. E.D. Tenn. 1989) (obligation of co-maker spouse who did not receive benefit of loan not dischargeable); *In re* Selmonsky, 93 B.R. 785 (Bankr. N.D. Ga. 1988) (cosigner's obligation on student loan is nondischargeable); *In re* Barth, 86 B.R. 146 (Bankr. W.D. Wis. 1988); *In re* Feenstra, 51 B.R. 107 (Bankr. W.D.N.Y. 1985) (student loan signed solely by parent nondischargeable).

433 *In re* Chambers, 348 F.3d 650 (7th Cir. 2003) (open account for unpaid tuition and fees not a loan); *In re* Mehta, 310 F.3d 308 (3d Cir. 2002); Cazenovia College v. Renshaw 222 F.3d 82 (2d Cir. 2000) (tuition debt not a loan and not part of a program); Manning v. Chambers, 290 B.R. 328 (N.D. Ill. 2003) (applying *Renshaw* and *Mehta*, tuition debt held dischargeable as there was no evidence that parties entered into loan arrangement prior to services being provided); *In re* Nelson, 188 B.R. 32 (D.S.D. 1995) (debt for tuition, room and board to university was not a loan); *In re* Navarro, 284 B.R. 727 (Bankr. C.D. Ca. 2002) (agreement that student would be responsible for tuition and fees was not a promissory note for sum certain and therefore dischargeable); *In re* Johnson, 222 B.R. 783 (Bankr. E.D. Va. 1998) (debt for tuition was not obligation for funds received on a loan and there was no "program" or disbursement of "funds" that would render debt nondischargeable); *In re* Meinhart, 211 B.R. 750 (Bankr. D. Colo. 1997) (debt to school was not an obligation to repay "funds received" as required by statute); *In re* Coole, 202 B.R. 518 (Bankr. D.N.M. 1996) (debt to school for services rendered was not a loan). *But see In re* DePasquale, 225 B.R. 830 (B.A.P. 1st Cir. 1998) (payment agreement for overdue tuition constituted "loan"); *In re* Johnson, 218 B.R. 449 (B.A.P. 8th Cir. 1998) (debtor who signed promissory note to college for unpaid tuition had student loan). *See generally Failure to Pay Tuition Does Not Create Nondischargeable Education Loan*, 17 NCLC REPORTS *Bankruptcy and Foreclosure Ed.* 17 (Mar./Apr. 1999).

434 *In re* Woods, 233 F.3d 324 (5th Cir. 2000); Leeper v. Pennsylvania Higher Educ. Assistance Agency, 49 F.3d 98 (3d Cir. 1995) (post-petition interest not discharged, even after debtor paid pre-petition debt in full through chapter 13 plan); *In re* Pardee, 218 B.R. 916 (B.A.P. 9th Cir. 1998), *aff'd*, 187 F.3d 548 (9th Cir. 1999); *In re* Jordan, 146 B.R. 31 (D. Colo. 1992).

435 *E.g., In re* Lipps, 79 B.R. 67 (Bankr. M.D. Fla. 1987).

436 *In re* McAlpin, 254 B.R. 449 (Bankr. D. Minn. 2000) (collection costs and fees disallowed based on 34 C.F.R. § 674.45(e), when creditor failed to prove they were reasonable and limited to actual or average cost incurred), *rev'd on other grounds*, 263 B.R. 881 (B.A.P. 8th Cir. 2001), *aff'd*, 278 F.3d 866 (8th Cir. 2002).

If a student loan is discharged, the lender should not accept any further payments on the loan, such as payments the lender may receive through a tax intercept program, or even money voluntarily paid by the debtor.[437] Department of Education regulations provide that if a guaranty agency receives any payments on a discharged loan on which the Department of Education previously paid a claim to the agency, the agency must return one-hundred percent of those payments to the sender and notify the borrower that there is no obligation to pay the loan.[438]

14.4.3.8.2 Student loan dischargeability tests

14.4.3.8.2.1 Former seven year test

11 U.S.C. § 523(a)(8) makes student loan debts nondischargeable in bankruptcy cases unless repayment would cause the debtor "undue hardship." This provision is incorporated in chapter 13 by section 1328(a)(2).

Prior to 1998, student loans were dischargeable if they had come due more than seven years prior to the debtor's bankruptcy filing. This exception to the exception was repealed in 1998.[439] *Therefore the seven year provision is applicable only to bankruptcy cases filed before October 7, 1998 and the discussion below applies only to such cases.*

Although student loans usually first become due shortly after graduation,[440] extensions and consolidations can, on occasion, cause confusion as to whether the seven years had passed as of the date of the bankruptcy petition. Generally, the first date that payments became due is the critical point of reference.[441] Later consolidations have been held to start the running of a new seven year period from the date of the first payment on the consolidated loan.[442] On the other hand, a creditor's unilateral changes in the payment schedule,[443] or deferments that are retroactive and not permitted by state regulations,[444] do not change the first payment due date, nor do payment agreements that do not involve cessation of payments.[445] However, courts have suspended the running of the time period when payment has been deferred by re-enrollment after the initial period has begun to run.[446]

There is also some disagreement about whether the seven year period continues to run during a bankruptcy case when collection of the loan may be stayed.[447] Department of Education regulations offer a useful clarification on this issue, providing that the Department will not consider the time a debtor is in bankruptcy to be a suspension of the repayment period if the debtor made payments during the case sufficient to meet the amount owed under the debtor's repayment schedule.[448]

Whether or not there is confusion on the debtor's part about passage of the requisite seven years, it is essential to achieve clarity on this issue with the applicable creditors. In some cases, there will be no dispute because all parties will agree that the loan was dischargeable as it was undeniably more than seven years old. In that event, a stipulation, letter or other confirmation of an agreement is essential because the lending institution, guarantee agency or some other creditor may not keep adequate records reflecting the discharge and therefore seek to collect at some point in the future.[449]

---

437 The protections of the discharge injunction apply. 11 U.S.C. § 524(a)(2); *see* § 14.5, *infra*.

438 34 C.F.R. § 682.402(l).

439 Higher Education Amendments of 1998, Pub. L. No. 105-244, 112 Stat. 1581 (effective October 7, 1998).

440 *See In re* Woodcock, 45 F.3d 363 (10th Cir. 1995) (based upon language of note, debtor's payments first came due nine months after debtor ceased to be matriculated in a program leading to a degree, even though debtor continued to take courses after that).

441 *In re* Scott, 147 F.3d 788 (8th Cir. 1998).

442 Hiatt v. Indiana State Student Assistance Comm'n, 36 F.3d 21 (7th Cir. 1994) (seven years runs from date on which first payment was due on consolidation loan); *In re* McGrath, 143 B.R. 820 (D. Md. 1992), *aff'd*, 8 F.3d 821 (4th Cir. 1993); *In re* Martin, 137 B.R. 770 (Bankr. W.D. Mo. 1992). The argument that the seven year period commences separately for each installment as it becomes due has been uniformly rejected. *See, e.g., In re* Nunn, 788 F.2d 617 (9th Cir. 1986); *see also In re* Mason, 300 B.R. 160 (Bankr. D. Conn. 2003) (consolidation loan obtained by duress held void and unenforceable, permitting debtor to obtain discharge under the former seven-year rule).

443 *In re* Woodcock, 45 F.3d 363 (10th Cir. 1995) (creditor could not unilaterally change the due date of first payment); *In re* Brinzer,

45 B.R. 831 (S.D. W. Va. 1984); *In re* Chisari, 183 B.R. 963 (Bankr. M.D. Fla. 1995) (neither debtor's failure to notify lender of withdrawal from school nor lender's failure to send repayment schedule on time extended due date); *In re* Marlewski, 168 B.R. 378 (Bankr. E.D. Wis. 1994); *In re* Whitehead, 31 B.R. 381 (Bankr. S.D. Ohio 1983); *see In re* Cramley, 21 B.R. 170 (Bankr. E.D. Tenn. 1982) (lender had no right to unilaterally suspend payment period without request of borrower). *But see In re* Woodcock, 144 F.3d 1340 (10th Cir. 1998) (extensions granted at debtor's request stopped running of repayment period, even though debtor was not legally entitled to them).

444 *In re* Manriquez, 207 B.R. 890 (B.A.P. 9th Cir. 1996) (retroactive forbearance agreement signed after seven years had already run did not render loan nondischargeable); *In re* Flynn, 190 B.R. 139 (Bankr. D.N.H. 1995); *In re* Keenam, 53 B.R. 913 (Bankr. D. Conn. 1985).

445 *In re* Salter, 207 B.R. 272 (Bankr. M.D. Fla. 1997) (stipulation changing amount of payments did not constitute a new obligation that would restart the seven-year time period); *In re* Marlewski, 168 B.R. 378 (Bankr. E.D. Wis. 1994).

446 *In re* Kaufman, 9 B.R. 755 (Bankr. E.D. Pa. 1981); *see also In re* Woodcock, 45 F.3d 363 (10th Cir. 1995) (loans became due when debtor ceased to be matriculated due to graduation, even though debtor was part-time student after that, so loans became due nine months after graduation).

447 *In re* Gibson, 184 B.R. 716 (E.D. Va. 1995) (period during which lender was stayed from taking action excluded in computing seven year period), *aff'd*, 86 F.3d 1150 (4th Cir. 1996).

448 34 C.F.R. § 682.402(m)(5).

449 This is especially problematic because Congress has abrogated all statutes of limitations for student loans. *See* National Consumer Law Center, Student Loan Law § 3.2 (2d. ed. 2002 and Supp.).

If there is any dispute about whether the seven years had passed, then a strategic decision must be made about whether to seek a declaratory judgment on dischargeability in the bankruptcy court. The debtor's other potential course of action is to wait and see if the creditor recommences collection efforts following bankruptcy and then raise the discharge defensively in the applicable state or federal forum.[450]

If a bankruptcy court determination is desired, there is no time limit to commence an adversary proceeding to resolve the dischargeability issues. In fact, the applicable rule even speaks of allowing cases to be reopened in order to obtain determinations on issues related to dischargeability.[451]

14.4.3.8.2.2 Undue hardship test

The sole exception to the nondischargeability of student loans is available when excepting the debt from discharge would cause the debtor or the debtor's dependents undue hardship. Courts have long struggled to define the term "undue hardship" found in section 523(a)(8). Although most of the published opinions on the subject agree that "undue" means more than the "garden variety" hardship that arises from the expense of future payments,[452] each judge seems to bring a unique set of values to the process of defining and implementing the applicable standard.

Several circuit courts of appeals have adopted a definition of undue hardship that employs a three-part test.[453] Under this test, undue hardship exists if:

- The debtor cannot maintain, based on current income and expenses, a 'minimal' standard of living for the debtor and the debtor's dependents if forced to repay the loans;

- Additional circumstances exist indicating that this state of affairs is likely to persist for a significant portion of the repayment period of the student loans; and
- The debtor has made good faith efforts to repay the loans.

In general, low-income debtors are most likely to obtain a discharge under this test. Generally speaking, debtors with incomes lower than $25,000.00 (or more for large families)[454] are found to be at a minimal standard of living.[455] They should seek to have the court focus on their income and expenses as the basis for a determination of undue hardship, but debtors need not be at the poverty level to demonstrate undue hardship. Most debtors who have been denied an undue hardship discharge had incomes several times greater than the poverty level.[456] Certainly, any debtor who can demonstrate some personalized misfortune, disability or unique underprivilege should bring that factor to the attention of the court.[457] Similarly, every effort should be

---

450 *See, e.g.,* Indiana Univ. v. Canganelli, 501 N.E.2d 299 (Ill. App. Ct. 1986) (discharge can be raised as a defense to collection of student loans in post-bankruptcy state court proceedings).

451 Fed. R. Bankr. P. 4007(b).

452 *E.g.,* Brunner v. New York State Higher Educ. Services, 831 F.2d 395 (2d Cir. 1987); *In re* Kopf, 245 B.R. 731 (Bankr. D. Me. 2000) (while "garden variety" hardship may not be sufficient, on the other extreme debtors should not be required to prove a "certainty of hopelessness" or "total incapacity").

453 Educ. Credit Mgmt. Corp. v. Polleys, 352 F.3d 1302 (10th Cir. 2004) (test does not require certainty of hopelessness for second prong; good faith prong should not allow imposition of court's values on debtor's life choices); *In re* Cox, 338 F.3d 1238 (11th Cir. 2003); *In re* Pena, 155 F.3d 1108 (9th Cir. 1998); *In re* Faish, 72 F.3d 298 (3d Cir. 1995); *In re* Roberson, 999 F.2d 1132 (7th Cir. 1993); Cheesman v. Tennessee Student Assistance Corp., 25 F.3d 356 (6th Cir. 1994); Brunner v. New York State Higher Educ. Services, 831 F.2d 395 (2d Cir. 1987). Other courts have adopted "totality of the circumstances" test, which does not necessarily conflict with the three-part *Brunner* test but rather expands upon the scope of factors a court may consider. *See* Long v. Educ. Credit Mgmt. Corp., 322 F.3d 549 (8th Cir. 2003); *In re* Kopf, 245 B.R. 731 (Bankr. D. Me. 2000).

454 *E.g., In re* Sweeney, 304 B.R. 360 (Bankr. D. Neb. 2002) (family of six needed $45,000.00 income for minimal standard of living); *see also In re* Cota, 298 B.R. 408 (Bankr. D. Ariz. 2003) (fact that debtor had fathered eleven children was not basis for denying student loan discharge; debtor did not agree to waive his right to procreate when he incurred the student loan obligation); *In re* Mitcham, 293 B.R. 138 (Bankr. N.D. Ohio 2003) (court should not second-guess debtor's decision to take in two grandchildren, or similar decisions such as adoption).

455 *See also In re* Pena, 155 F.3d 1108 (9th Cir. 1998) (discharge granted to childless couple with income of $20,976.00); *In re* Hornsby, 144 F.3d 433 (6th Cir. 1998) (debtors did not need to be at poverty level to show undue hardship); *In re* Cline, 248 B.R. 347 (B.A.P. 8th Cir. 2000) (single woman in good health who earned $25,000.00 and is unlikely to earn more granted discharge); *In re* Nary, 253 B.R. 752 (N.D. Tex. 2000) (income of $48,000.00 for family of five, though 2.2 times poverty standard, would justify discharge based on family expenses if it could not be increased); *In re* Coulson, 253 B.R. 174 (W.D.N.C. 2000) (mother and two children with income of $23,975.00 could not repay loans); *In re* Myers, 280 B.R. 416 (Bankr. S.D. Ohio 2002) (satellite television, related school expenses, and camping expenditures were within minimum standards of living for family with children); *In re* Ivory, 269 B.R. 890 (Bankr. N.D. Ala. 2001) (citing studies showing that income far higher than poverty level is needed for minimal standard of living); *In re* Turretto, 255 B.R. 884 (Bankr. N.D. Cal. 2000) (debtor with one child in her care could not repay loans with income of over $25,000.00); *cf. In re* O'Hearn, 339 F.3d 559 (7th Cir. 2003) (single debtor with no dependents who earned $43,000.00 per year plus benefits, which might increase to $50,000.00, did not meet first prong of *Brunner* test).

456 *E.g., In re* Roberson, 999 F.2d 1132 (7th Cir. 1993) (court found debtor could earn over $30,000.00); *In re* McGinnis, 289 B.R. 257 (Bankr. M.D. Ga. 2003) (debtor need not be at or below poverty level).

457 *See, e.g.,* Educ. Credit Mgmt. Corp. v. Polleys, 352 F.3d 1302 (10th Cir. 2004) (debtor had emotional problems beyond her control); *In re* Cline, 248 B.R. 347 (B.A.P. 8th Cir. 2000) (single woman unable to increase income would need decades to repay $53,000.00 in loans); *In re* Reynolds, 2004 WL 1745835 (D. Minn. Aug. 2, 2004) (upholding discharge of loans owed by law

made to establish lack of job skills, lack of available jobs, disabilities and other factors which make it improbable that a low-income debtor will have better prospects in the future.[458] Debtors who do not demonstrate that they are not likely to earn significantly more in the future are often denied discharge of their loans.[459] The test requiring a good faith effort to pay the loan does not require that repayment actually occurred, although it may require some effort to deal with the loan prior to bankruptcy.[460]

In evaluating student loans that were incurred for vocational school education, two additional considerations related to discharge are appropriate. First, the student's undue hardship argument may be strengthened if the student loan arose from a private vocational school that closed down or defrauded the student. Not only do courts sense the unfairness involved in making a student repay a loan for a valueless education, but also the absence of acquired skills makes it less likely that the debtor will be able to obtain employment that could make possible future loan repayment.[461] In fact, under recent legislation, the debtor may be excused from paying the loan, even without a bankruptcy case or may have a defense to liability on the loan.[462]

Evidence that a student obtained no benefit from their trade school education is relevant to the issue of whether the debtor will be able to pay in the future, because it suggests lack of skills necessary to obtain income for repayment.[463] It is also relevant to the debtor's payment history, because

graduate because of debtor's mental illness even though she possibly could afford to make some payments); *In re* Johnson, 121 B.R. 91 (Bankr. N.D. Okla. 1990) (single mother of two not receiving support); *In re* Reilly, 118 B.R. 38 (Bankr. D. Md. 1990) (debtor was divorced mother of three whose ex-husband was incurably ill and therefore not contributing support); *In re* Zobel, 80 B.R. 950 (Bankr. N.D. Iowa 1986) (unemployed debtors who had made numerous unsuccessful attempts to find work); *In re* Wilcox, 57 B.R. 479 (Bankr. M.D. Ga. 1985) (debtor holding down subsistence job; wife suffering from crippling arthritis and confined to wheelchair); *In re* Dockery, 36 B.R. 41 (Bankr. D. Tenn. 1984) (debtor had suffered severe industrial injuries and several heart attacks); *In re* Diaz, 5 B.R. 253 (Bankr. W.D.N.Y. 1980) (divorced mother of four who had a series of illnesses, heart trouble, and alcoholic problem, need for future surgery, and a husband confined to a mental clinic presented "classic" hardship case); *In re* Bagley, 4 B.R. 248 (Bankr. D. Ariz. 1980) (debtor and husband lived on $560.00 per month earned by him as an Army private and had post-petition debts of over $4000.00 for hospitalization of their baby); *In re* Fonzo, 1 B.R. 722 (Bankr. S.D.N.Y. 1979) (policeman-debtor had expenses exceeding income for himself, wife, and four children). *Compare In re* Gerhardt, 348 F.3d 89 (5th Cir. 2003) (well-educated single musician could obtain additional employment) *with In re* Oyler, 300 B.R. 255 (B.A.P. 6th Cir. 2003) (debtor's choice to work in low-paying field as minister not by itself evidence of bad faith and should not be used against debtor under undue hardship test).

458 *E.g., In re* Price, 25 B.R. 256, 258 (Bankr. W.D. Mo. 1982) (relevant considerations include "whether the education enabled or would enable the debtor to obtain substantially higher income"); *In re* Powelson, 25 B.R. 274 (Bankr. D. Neb. 1982) (vocational degree in hairstyling did not enhance debtor's job skills or employability); *see also In re* Pena, 207 B.R. 919 (B.A.P. 9th Cir. 1997) (debtors did not have to show "exceptional circumstances" to show they were unlikely to improve their financial situation in the future), *aff'd* 155 F.3d 1108 (9th Cir. 1998); *In re* Ordaz, 287 B.R. 912 (Bankr. C.D. Ill. 2002) (consolidation loan that restructured student loan with same lender at end of original ten-year term did not "restart the clock" on a new fifteen-year repayment period for purposes of considering future inability to repay).

459 *E.g., * Goulet v. Educ. Credit Mgmt. Corp., 284 F.3d 773 (7th Cir. 2002) (record devoid of evidence that debtor's problems with alcoholism and a felony conviction prevented debtor from being gainfully employed); *In re* Rifino, 245 F.3d 1083 (9th Cir. 2001) (debtor had Masters degree and was already earning over $27,000.00 with additional increases likely); *In re* Brightful, 267 F.3d 324 (3d Cir. 2001) (debtor who did not introduce evidence showing why she could not use her skills as legal secretary to earn more income denied discharge of loan).

460 *In re* Innes, 284 B.R. 496 (D. Kan. 2002) (failure to make payments does not prevent finding of good faith effort if debtor had no ability to make payments); *In re* Brown, 239 B.R. 204,

209 (S.D. Cal. 1999) (and cases cited therein); *In re* Ivory, 269 B.R. 890 (Bankr. N.D. Ala. 2001) (no bad faith when debtor never had ability to repay loan); *In re* Turretto, 255 B.R. 884 (Bankr. N.D. Cal. 2000); *In re* Coats, 214 B.R. 397 (Bankr. N.D. Okla. 1997); *In re* Hornsby, 201 B.R. 195 (Bankr. W.D. Tenn. 1995), *aff'd* 144 F.3d 433 (6th Cir. 1998); *In re* Maulin, 190 B.R. 153 (Bankr. W.D.N.Y. 1995); *see also In re* Lewis, 276 B.R. 912 (Bankr. C.D. Ill. 2002) (rejecting creditor arguments that only payments made on consolidation loan, and not payments on original loans, could be considered).

461 *See, e.g., In re* Law, 159 B.R. 287 (Bankr. D.S.D. 1993) (repayment of $20,000.00 student loan for two and a half weeks of useless flight training would be undue hardship); *In re* Evans, 131 B.R. 372 (Bankr. S.D. Ohio 1991) (trade school education in word-processing did not put debtor in a position to repay her student loans); *In re* Correll, 105 B.R. 302 (Bankr. W.D. Pa. 1989) (student loan discharged where debtor received no benefit from the education); *In re* Carter, 29 B.R. 228 (Bankr. N.D. Ohio 1983) (loan discharged where debtor did not obtain a marketable skill); *In re* Love, 28 B.R. 475 (Bankr. S.D. Ind. 1983) (college education did not provide marketable skill); *In re* Price, 25 B.R. 256, 258 (Bankr. W.D. Mo. 1982) (relevant considerations include "whether the education enabled or would enable the debtor to obtain substantially higher income"); *In re* Powelson, 25 B.R. 274 (Bankr. D. Neb. 1982) (vocational degree in hairstyling did not enhance debtor's job skills or employability); *In re* Ford, 22 B.R. 442 (Bankr. W.D.N.Y. 1982) (court considered that debtor obtained little benefit from her education); *In re* Littell, 6 B.R. 85 (Bankr. D. Or. 1980) (whether the debtor benefited economically from schooling should be a "substantial factor" in determining whether undue hardship exists).

462 *See* § 14.4.3.8.4, *infra*; National Consumer Law Center, Student Loan Law Chs. 6, 9 (2d ed. 2002 and Supp.). This manual should be consulted for other non-bankruptcy student loan discharges available to debtors in addition to the closed school discharge, such as those based on the debtor's permanent and total disability and a school's false certification of the debtor's eligibility.

463 *E.g., In re* Lewis, 276 B.R. 912 (Bankr. C.D. Ill. 2002) (lack of benefit from uncompleted junior college program considered under second prong of *Brunner* test); *In re* Powelson, 25 B.R. 274 (Bankr. D. Neb. 1982).

the debtor may not have had the ability to make any payments and because a valueless vocational school education is outside the Congressional concern about highly skilled professionals shedding loan obligations prior to a lucrative career.[464]

A further argument related to the dischargeability of trade school loans is that absent discharge, the debtor may be ineligible for future government educational loans.[465] If a discharge is not granted, a low-income student will not be able to go back to school, and will not be able to obtain a decent paying job, making repayment now or in the future an undue hardship.

Sometimes, even in fairly strong hardship cases, student loan creditors offer to take very low payments. While it could be argued that the court should only look to the payments actually due under the terms of the note, such offers of low payments can make it more difficult to assert that the loan, as modified by the creditor, presents a hardship. Perhaps not surprisingly, courts have been attracted to this method of compromising on the outcome of the case, sometimes finding no hardship solely because of the reduced-payments offer. In fact, a few have even devised other solutions short of complete nondischargeability in difficult cases, by reducing the term and/or amount of the loan.[466] The Sixth Circuit Court of Appeals approved a bankruptcy court's order ruling that a debtor's loans were dischargeable, but stayed enforcement of its order for eighteen months to see if the debtor's situation improved.[467] The authority for such actions without the creditor's consent is dubious, because this section of the statute, unlike others, does not use the phrase "to the extent" in describing whether a loan is dischargeable.[468]

In a similar vein, student loan creditors have argued in recent cases that there cannot be undue hardship because the Department of Education's regulations provide for payment relief in the form of Income Contingent Repayment Plans (ICRP).[469] Several courts have found the availability of these repayment plans relevant under the various hardship tests.[470] These courts fail to apply the statute as written, which affords the debtor an opportunity to obtain an absolute discharge, and fail to consider the student loan that the debtor actually has as opposed to some modification of that loan.[471] Most courts have rejected the argument that the availability of an income contingent repayment plan is a defense to student loan dischargeability and have recognized that placing a debtor in a twenty-five-year repayment plan that is not likely to pay off, or sometimes even reduce, the loan does not mitigate the undue hardship the loan would cause.[472] Payments must be made if the debtor's income is even slightly above poverty level, which still does not afford a minimal standard of living.[473] The income contingent repayment plan actually allows the loan balance to go up, with capitalization of some interest and does not prevent the discharge of a remaining balance after twenty-five years from being deemed taxable income to the debtor.[474] If

---

464 *In re* Evans, 131 B.R. 372 (Bankr. S.D. Ohio 1991).

465 *See* National Consumer Law Center, Student Loan Law § 6.1 (2d ed. 2002 and Supp.).

466 *In re* Saxman, 325 F.3d 1168 (9th Cir. 2003) (partial discharge order is permissible); *In re* Hornsby, 144 F.3d 433 (6th Cir. 1998) (partial discharge is permitted under court's equitable powers); *In re* Andresen, 232 B.R. 127 (B.A.P. 8th Cir. 1999) (discharging two of three student loans); *In re* Griffin, 197 B.R. 144 (Bankr. E.D. Okla. 1996) (discharging accrued interest and attorney fees on loans, but not principal); *In re* Hinkle, 200 B.R. 690 (Bankr. W.D. Wash. 1996) (discharging three out of six student loans); *In re* Littell, 6 B.R. 85 (Bankr. D. Or. 1980) (each debtor ordered to pay $10.00 per month for remainder of five year period after initial loan due date); *In re* Hemmen, 7 B.R. 63 (Bankr. N.D. Ala. 1980) (court conditioned discharge of loan on debtor using best efforts to find employment and paying any sums he received in excess of $3,600.00 per year after taxes toward student loan for remainder of five years after loan matured); *see also In re* Cox, 338 F.3d 1238 (11th Cir. 2003) (partial discharge may not be ordered if debtor does not show undue hardship); *In re* Blair, 291 B.R. 514 (B.A.P. 9th Cir. 2003) (partial discharge may not be ordered for debtor who did not satisfy any of the *Brunner* test's three prongs).

467 *In re* Cheesman, 25 F.3d 356 (6th Cir. 1994).

468 Educ. Credit Mgmt. Corp. v. Carter, 279 B.R. 872 (M.D. Ga. 2002); *In re* Pincus, 280 B.R. 303 (Bankr. S.D.N.Y. 2002) (no

language in § 523(a)(8) permits granting of partial discharge); *In re* Skaggs, 196 B.R. 865 (Bankr. W.D. Okla. 1996) (court's authority limited to determination whether entire debt is dischargeable).

469 *See* 20 U.S.C. §§ 1078(m), 1087a; 34 C.F.R. § 685.209(a)(2)(i).

470 *See, e.g., In re* Wallace, 259 B.R. 170 (C.D. Cal. 2000) (remand for further proceedings on impact of ICRP; debtor's lack of diligence in pursing payment plans, even those presented for first time during discharge proceedings, may prove lack of good faith effort to repay the loans); *In re* Standfuss, 245 B.R. 356 (Bankr. E.D. Mo. 2000) ("flexibility" of an ICRP plan considered in determining debtors' ability to repay student loan).

471 *See In re* Kopf, 245 B.R. 731 (Bankr. D. Me. 2000) (no matter how flexible or "humanely executed" such programs may be, they simply are not the equivalent of a discharge).

472 *In re* Ford, 269 B.R. 673 (B.A.P. 8th Cir. 2001); *In re* Adler, 300 B.R. 740 (Bankr. N.D. Cal. 2003) (debtor would face an unaffordable tax liability of $18,000.00 at age seventy-four); *In re* Strand, 298 B.R. 367 (Bankr. D. Minn. 2003) (debtor would be hamstrung into poverty for the rest of his life, precluded from obtaining any credit, and perhaps even from obtaining approval of a rental application, growing hopelessly more insolvent, with no realistic possibility of ever retiring the debt until at the age of seventy-nine, the debt would be forgiven and he would be assessed an enormous income tax liability, probably nondischargeable in bankruptcy); *In re* Cheney, 280 B.R. 648 (N.D. Iowa 2002).

473 *See also In re* Ford, 269 B.R. 673 (B.A.P. 8th Cir. 2001) (availability of ICRP is merely one factor considered in totality of circumstances test and not determinative in case where ICRP would result in sixty-two-year-old woman with arthritic condition carrying large and increasing debt that would not be forgiven until she was eighty-seven years old).

474 *See* 34 C.F.R § 685.209(c)(5); National Consumer Law Center, Student Loan Law § 8.2.2.6 (2d ed. 2002 and Supp.); *see also In re* Durrani, 311 B.R. 496 (Bankr. N.D. Ill. 2004) (unlike discharge in bankruptcy, ICRP discharge may result in substan-

Congress had intended the payment programs to meet all hardship situations, it would have repealed the undue hardship provisions.[475] It has not done so and has, in fact, amended them since those programs were enacted.

14.4.3.8.3 Procedure for dischargeability determination

A proceeding to determine dischargeability of a student loan may be brought at any time.[476] It usually must be commenced by a complaint pursuant to the adversary proceeding rules.[477] A state student loan creditor is not immune from suit under the Eleventh Amendment.[478] The debtor has at least the burden of going forward with proof in such a case, but courts have differed regarding whether the debtor has the ultimate burden of proof, because in other dischargeability proceedings the creditor bears that burden.[479] Alternatively, at least if the student loan creditor does not object, the dischargeability of a student loan may be determined by a provision in the debtor's chapter 13 plan which, if the plan is confirmed and the creditor has been given adequate notice, becomes binding upon the creditor.[480]

Although a debtor has the option of seeking a determination related to dischargeability in a non-bankruptcy forum after the bankruptcy is completed,[481] some state or non-bankruptcy federal courts may be unwilling to make a decision on what they perceive to be a bankruptcy issue

especially if the open question is "undue hardship."[482] If the facts are favorable during the bankruptcy case, the better practice is to seek to have the issue decided in bankruptcy court prior to discharge.[483] If an unfavorable decision is received and circumstances subsequently change for the worse, dischargeability of student loan obligations generally may be relitigated by reopening a prior complaint or bringing a new proceeding even if the debtor's bankruptcy case has been closed.[484]

The Supreme Court has stated that "unless the debtor affirmatively secures a hardship determination, the discharge order will not include a student loan debt."[485] As a practical matter, student loan creditors will continue collection efforts absent such a determination, so it is necessary in any event to obtain a court decision that the loan is dischargeable.

14.4.3.8.4 Raising defenses to student loan debts

If it is not likely that a student loan debt will be found dischargeable (and especially in chapter 13 if payments on the debt are going to be made), the debtor should consider whether there are defenses to the debt, particularly if there was a close relationship between the school and the lender. If possible, the debtor should consider bringing school-related defenses (for example, breach of contract, warranty, fraud or unfair trade practice) to the proof of claim filed by the originating lender or guarantee agency.[486] A decision

---

tial nondischargeable tax liability for debtor because unpaid amount and accrued interest over twenty-five year period treated as income); *In re* Korhonen, 296 B.R. 492 (Bankr. D. Minn. 2003); *In re* Thomsen, 234 B.R. 506 (Bankr. D. Mont. 1999) (debtors will simply replace nondischargeable student loans with another nondischargeable debt in form of income taxes).

475 *See In re* Nanton-Marie, 303 B.R. 228 (Bankr. S.D. Fla. 2003) (nothing in Code requires consideration of ICRP as condition precedent to undue hardship discharge); *In re* Johnson, 299 B.R. 676 (Bankr. M.D. Ga. 2003) (if Congress had intended the question of dischargeability of student loans to be delegated to a non-judicial entity, no matter how fair its formulas and intentions may appear, it could have provided for such); *In re* Alston, 297 B.R. 410 (Bankr. E.D. Pa. 2003) (requiring income contingent repayment agreement as proof of good faith would eviscerate § 523(a)(8)).

476 Fed. R. Bankr. P. 4007(b).

477 Fed. R. Bankr. P. 7001–7087.

478 Tennessee Student Assistance Corp. v. Hood, 124 S. Ct. 1905, 158 L. Ed. 2d 764 (2004); *see* § 13.3.2.2, *supra*.

479 *In re* Fox, 163 B.R. 975 (Bankr. M.D. Pa. 1993) (debtor has burden of going forward but not burden of proof); *In re* Alliger, 78 B.R. (Bankr. E.D. Pa. 1987); *In re* Norman, 25 B.R. 545 (Bankr. S.D. Cal. 1982). *But see* Tennessee Student Assistance Corp. v. Hood, 124 S. Ct. 1905, 158 L. Ed. 2d 764 (2004) (student loans presumptively nondischargeable).

480 *In re* Andersen, 179 F.3d 1253 (10th Cir. 1999). *But see* § 14.4.3.8.5, *infra*.

481 11 U.S.C. § 523(c); Standifer v. Alaska, 3 P.3d 925 (Alaska 2000) (debtor could move to vacate post-bankruptcy default judgment on student loan to obtain determination of undue hardship dischargeability).

482 *See* Massachusetts Higher Educ. Assistance Corp. v. Taylor, 390 Mass. 755, 459 N.E.2d 807 (1984) (implying that if undue hardship claim not raised in bankruptcy court it is waived).

483 Of course, if no decision is obtained in the bankruptcy court for some reason, debtors, in appropriate circumstances, should feel free to raise discharge on the basis of hardship in response to a later collection case. Alternatively, removal of the collection case to the bankruptcy court may be sought. 28 U.S.C. § 1452; Fed. R. Bankr. P. 9027. *See generally* § 13.4.1, *supra*.

484 11 U.S.C. § 350; Fed. R. Bankr. P. 4007(b); *In re* Sobh, 61 B.R. 576 (E.D. Mich. 1986); *see In re* Fisher, 223 B.R. 377 (Bankr. M.D. Fla. 1998) (debtor who had not sought discharge of student loan during bankruptcy could reopen case to seek undue hardship discharge in light of post-bankruptcy accident which reduced her ability to repay). *But see In re* Bugos, 288 B.R. 435 (Bankr. E.D. Va. 2003) (refusing to reopen case to determine undue hardship based on circumstances that arose after bankruptcy petition was filed); *In re* Kapsin, 265 B.R. 778 (Bankr. N.D. Ohio 2001) (refusing to reopen case to consider changed circumstances alleged to cause undue hardship).

485 Tennessee Student Assistance Corp. v. Hood, 124 S. Ct. 1905, 1912, 158 L. Ed. 2d 764 (2004).

486 *See In re* Goldberg, 297 B.R. 465 (Bankr. W.D.N.C. 2003) (debtor who never received check and whose school closed one week after she enrolled received no consideration); 10 NCLC REPORTS *Deceptive Practices and Warranties Ed.* 29 (Sept./ Oct. 1991); National Consumer Law Center, Student Loan Law § 9.5 (2d ed. 2002 and Supp.); *see also* Tipton v. Sec'y of Educ., 768 F. Supp. 540 (S.D. W. Va. 1991); *In re* Mason, 300 B.R. 160 (Bankr. D. Conn. 2003) (consolidation loan obtained by duress held void and unenforceable).

disallowing the claim based on a valid defense is as good or better than a decision that the loan is dischargeable.[487]

14.4.3.8.5 Special issues regarding student loans in chapter 13

In the past, because student loan debts were dischargeable upon completion of a chapter 13 plan, chapter 13 was an attractive option for those who sought to deal with student loan debt burdens. However, changes in the law eliminated many of the advantages of the chapter 13 option. Code section 1328(a)(2) now incorporates section 523(a)(8) by reference so that student loans that would be nondischargeable in chapter 7 are also nondischargeable in chapter 13.

Nevertheless, student loan issues continue to arise in chapter 13 cases that are filed for other reasons. Additionally, in some cases a chapter 13 plan may still provide advantages during the term of the plan, even if the debt is ultimately nondischargeable.

Given that amended section 1328(a) simply incorporates section 523(a)(8), issues of dischargeability of student loans in chapter 13 cases should be treated almost identically to those arising in chapter 7 cases. For example one court addressing dischargeability in chapter 13 determined undue hardship just as if the case had proceeded under chapter 7.[488] The mere fact that the debtor can afford chapter 13 plan payments should not be dispositive of the ability to pay a student loan.[489] In many cases those payments go almost entirely to secured creditors to ensure a debtor continued shelter, transportation to work or other necessities, or are made at great sacrifices that cannot be sustained beyond the plan period.

As in chapter 7, the debtor must affirmatively request a finding of undue hardship for the debt to be found dischargeable during the bankruptcy case. Although a plan provision might provide that confirmation of the plan will constitute a finding that undue hardship exists,[490] such provisions will

probably be disfavored if a party objects.[491] A few courts have even sanctioned counsel for placing such provisions in plans,[492] although such decisions are contrary to both the concept of the chapter 13 plan as a proposal by the debtor which can include any provision not contrary to title 11[493] and the case law which has held that such provisions can be approved and binding.[494] As discussed above, the procedure used in most cases for resolving questions related to dischargeability in bankruptcy is the one set out in Federal Rule of Bankruptcy Procedure 4007 which provides for an adversary proceeding.

As most chapter 13 cases continue for the three to five year length of the plan and because the nondischargeability of student loans can be raised at any time,[495] careful considerations of timing should be brought to bear in order to ensure that the issues are heard when the debtor faces maximum financial pressures. However, some courts may take the position that no determination on dischargeability can be made until the end of the case.[496]

In a few districts, the chapter 13 standing trustee has taken the position that nondischargeable student loan debts must be fully paid in a chapter 13 bankruptcy plan. That position is incorrect. Even if a student loan is not dischargeable, it nevertheless remains an unsecured claim during the bankruptcy case (unless the creditor holds a non-avoided judgment lien), subject to those provisions of the Code applicable to unsecured debts.

For most cases, this means that during the bankruptcy plan, the student loan creditor is entitled to the greater of what it would receive under the best interests of the creditors test[497] or the ability to pay test[498] just like any other unsecured creditor.[499] Certainly, any arguments that a case must

---

487 To the extent the claim is disallowed, the debtor would have a binding judgment that the debt is not owed. Additionally, the creditor would not be entitled to any dividend available from the estate. Finally, attorney fees might be available to counsel to the extent that a determination is based on unfair and deceptive acts or practices or another statute involving fee shifting.

488 *In re* Evans, 131 B.R. 372 (Bankr. S.D. Ohio 1991).

489 *In re* Goranson, 183 B.R. 52 (Bankr. W.D.N.Y. 1995) (income used for plan payments would not be available at end of plan, because major portion of payments was for car payments and other expenses that would continue after the plan).

490 *In re* Andersen, 179 F.3d 1253 (10th Cir. 1999); *see also In re* Pardee, 193 F.3d 1083 (9th Cir. 1999) (creditor bound by confirmed plan provision discharging post-petition interest on student loan). *But see* Banks v. Sallie Mae Servicing Corp., 299 F.3d 296 (4th Cir. 2002) (confirmed plan providing for discharge of post-petition interest violated student loan creditor's due process rights when creditor not served with adversary complaint and summons).

491 *In re* Mammel, 221 B.R. 238 (Bankr. D. Iowa 1998); *In re* Key, 128 B.R. 742 (Bankr. S.D. Ohio 1991).

492 *E.g., In re* Evans, 242 B.R. 407 (Bankr. S.D. Ohio 1999).

493 11 U.S.C. § 1322(b)(10).

494 *See In re* Wright, 279 B.R. 886 (D. Kan. 2002) (sanctions not appropriate unless there was no good faith basis for claim that repayment of student loans would be undue hardship).

495 Fed. R. Bankr. P. 4007(b).

496 *See, e.g., In re* Bender, 368 F.3d 846 (8th Cir. 2004) (student loan discharge determination not ripe for adjudication until conclusion of plan at time of discharge); *In re* Ekenasi, 325 F.3d 541 (4th Cir. 2003) (ordinarily dischargeability proceeding should not be brought until end of chapter 13 case unless there are circumstances under which the *Brunner* factors could be predicted with sufficient certainty earlier in case); *In re* Cleveland, 89 B.R. 69 (B.A.P. 9th Cir. 1988) (decision on dischargeability of HEAL loan cannot be made until close of chapter 13 plan); *In re* Raisor, 180 B.R. 163 (Bankr. E.D. Tex. 1995) (dischargeability based upon undue hardship cannot be determined until end of plan).

497 11 U.S.C. § 1325(a)(4); *see* § 12.3.1, *supra.*

498 11 U.S.C. § 1325(b); *see* § 12.3.3, *supra.*

499 *See In re* Owens, 82 B.R. 960 (Bankr. N.D. Ill. 1988) (potentially nondischargeable HEAL loan may be treated like other unsecured debts during chapter 13); *In re* Gronski, 65 B.R. 932 (Bankr. E.D. Pa. 1986) (same).

be dismissed because the debtor's filing was made in bad faith merely in order to improperly discharge student loans should be put to rest.[500]

Thus, the debtor can propose treatment of a student loan creditor during a bankruptcy plan that is no different than treatment of any other unsecured creditor.[501] The student loan creditor will not be entitled to additional regular payments outside the plan prior to the debtor's discharge.

However, if the student loan is nondischargeable, it is in the debtor's interest to make sure that as much of the loan as possible is paid during the bankruptcy. Frequently this means that the debtor wishes to propose a plan to separately classify the student loan and have it paid at a higher percentage than other unsecured debts.[502] Several judicial decisions have explicitly held that a separate classification in favor of a student loan creditor does not "discriminate unfairly" within the meaning of 11 U.S.C. § 1322(b)(1).[503] At least one court has held that there is a reasonable basis for the separate classification both because the debt is nondischargeable and because absent payment the debtor may be unable to return to school to obtain a degree.[504] And even if separate classification is not permitted, the debtor has the absolute right to provide in the plan for a cure of all defaulted payments and maintenance of current payments under Code section 1322(b)(5) if the loan's last payment is after the plan's last payment.[505]

14.4.3.8.6 Health education assistance loans and other special loan programs

Congress created an additional student loan exception to discharge for certain student loans in the Omnibus Budget Reconciliation Act of 1981. Section 292f(g) of title 42, U.S. Code[506] provides that no bankruptcy discharge may be granted as to a Health Education Assistance Loan (HEAL) within seven years after the date repayment is to begin. During this seven year period no hardship discharge is available for such loans.[507] Even after the seven years, the loan is dischargeable only if the bankruptcy court finds that denial of a discharge would be unconscionable.[508] This nondischargeability provision has been held to apply in chapter 13 as well as in chapter 7.[509] Because the provision contains language making discharge available after seven years based on unconscionability, a discharge should be possible in a chapter 13 case that is filed within seven years of the first repayment due date, if the discharge is not entered until after the seven-year period has expired.[510] Several courts have held that in the context of a chapter 13 plan, the student loan creditor can be treated like other unsecured creditors and that a determination as to discharge can only be made at the conclusion of the plan.[511] Moreover, based on the language of section 523(b), HEAL loans may be dischargeable in a second bankruptcy filing under the more lenient standards of section 523(a) if the prior case resulted in a discharge.[512]

As with section 523(a)(8), the provision making HEAL debts nondischargeable is self-executing. The burden is on the debtor to request and establish grounds for a court to find the loan dischargeable.[513] Courts have held that failure to

---

500 Examples of such cases include: *In re* Stewart, 109 B.R. 998 (D. Kan. 1990); *In re* Makarchuk, 76 B.R. 919 (Bankr. N.D.N.Y. 1987). For other reasons, decisions requiring minimum payments to unsecured creditors beyond those required by the ability to pay or best interest of the creditors tests are obsolete. *See* Education Assistance Corp. v. Zellner, 827 F.2d 1222 (8th Cir. 1987); *In re* Owens, 82 B.R. 960 (Bankr. N.D. Ill. 1998). *See generally* § 12.3, *supra.*

501 Some courts have held, however, that a nondischargeable student loan debt continues to accrue interest during the life of the plan. *See* § 14.4.3.8.1, *supra.*

502 *See generally* § 12.4, *supra.*

503 *In re* Cox, 186 B.R. 744 (Bankr. N.D. Fla. 1995); *In re* Boggan, 125 B.R. 533 (Bankr. N.D. Ill. 1991); *In re* Freshley, 69 B.R. 96 (Bankr. N.D. Ga. 1987). Similarly, separate classification of nondischargeable debts for support arrearages have been allowed. *E.g., In re* Leser, 939 F.2d 669 (8th Cir. 1991); *In re* Storberg, 94 B.R. 144 (Bankr. D. Minn. 1988); *In re* Davidson, 72 B.R. 384 (Bankr. D. Colo. 1987). *But see In re* Groves, 39 F.3d 212 (8th Cir. 1994) (affirming bankruptcy court's refusal to permit separate classification).

504 *In re* Freshley, 69 B.R. 96 (Bankr. N.D. Ga. 1987). See also § 12.4, *supra,* for additional discussion of classification of claims.

505 *In re* Chandler, 210 B.R. 898 (Bankr. D.N.H. 1997); *In re* Sullivan, 195 B.R. 649 (Bankr. W.D. Tex. 1996); *In re* Benner, 156 B.R. 631 (Bankr. D. Minn. 1993). *But see In re* Labib-Kiyarash, 271 B.R. 189 (B.A.P. 9th Cir. 2001) (use of § 1322(b)(5) subject to debtor showing that classification is fair under § 1322(b)(1)); *In re* Thibodeau, 248 B.R. 699 (Bankr. D. Mass. 2000).

506 This section replaces the former applicable provision, 42 U.S.C. § 294f(g).

507 *In re* Hampton, 47 B.R. 47 (Bankr. N.D. Ill. 1985). However, for bankruptcy cases commenced prior to the statute's amendment changing the five-year nondischargeability period to seven years, the five-year period is still applicable. *In re* Barrows, 159 B.R. 86 (Bankr. D.N.H. 1993).

508 42 U.S.C. § 292f(g).

509 *In re* Johnson, 787 F.2d 1179 (7th Cir. 1986).

510 *In re* Nelson, 183 B.R. 972 (Bankr. S.D. Fla. 1995) (also holding that under § 292f(g) the time period was not tolled during forbearance periods). *But see* Ellzey v. United States Dep't of Health & Human Services, 302 B.R. 385 (S.D. Ala. 2003) (time period tolled during prior bankruptcy case).

511 United States v. Lee, 89 B.R. 250 (N.D. Ga. 1987) (debt is conditionally dischargeable during pendency of chapter 13 plan), *aff'd,* 853 F.2d 1547 (11th Cir. 1988); *In re* Cleveland, 89 B.R. 69 (B.A.P. 9th Cir. 1988) (upon completion of chapter 13 plan, issue would be whether non-discharge of loan would be unconscionable); *In re* Battrell, 105 B.R. 65 (Bankr. D. Or. 1989); *In re* Owens, 82 B.R. 960 (Bankr. N.D. Ill. 1988); *see also In re* Gronski, 65 B.R. 932 (Bankr. E.D. Pa. 1986).

512 *In re* Tanski, 195 B.R. 408 (Bankr. E.D. Wis. 1996).

513 United States v. Rushing, 287 B.R. 343 (D.N.J. 2002); United States v. Wood, 925 F.2d 1580 (7th Cir. 1991); *see also* United States v. Erkard, 200 B.R. 152 (N.D. Ohio 1996) (United States,

discharge the loan would be unconscionable if it was "excessive, exorbitant," "lying outside the limits of what is reasonable or acceptable," "shockingly unfair, harsh, or unjust" or "outrageous."[514]

Several other health education programs have similar provisions which make debts arising in those programs nondischargeable.[515] Generally the operation of these provisions is similar to that of the HEAL provisions.

14.4.3.9 Debts Incurred Through Drunk Driving—11 U.S.C. § 523(a)(9)

As a result of increased public concern about the social problem of drunk drivers, the 1984 amendments added an exception to the chapter 7 discharge for debts incurred through drunk driving.[516] A 1990 amendment to the statute made the exception to discharge applicable in chapter 13 cases as well.[517] The same amendment broadened the exception to include unlawful driving while under the influence of a drug or other substance, but also narrowed it to

include only debts for death or personal injury.[518] Thus, debts for property damage are not nondischargeable under section 523(a)(9).[519] The 1990 amendment also removed a former requirement that the debt be evidenced by a judgment to be nondischargeable.

The specific terms of this subsection narrow its scope somewhat. Section 523(a)(9) applies only if the debtor operated a motor vehicle[520] and the operation was unlawful due to intoxication. Courts have disagreed about whether motorboat is a motor vehicle within the meaning of the exception.[521] But it has been held that a snowmobile is a motor vehicle.[522]

At a minimum the language of the subsection also presumably requires that the debtor met the legal standard for intoxication in the jurisdiction where the accident occurred. These standards vary and may not even exist in every jurisdiction. Where they do exist, there may be disputes about how the standard is to be applied, especially if it is not labeled "intoxication."[523] In many cases a judgment or consent decree does not specify whether or not the standard was met, and there is then a question of whether this issue may later be separately litigated to determine dischargeability under this provision.[524] The state courts have concurrent

---

as guarantor of HEAL obligation must be made a party to dischargeability proceeding).

514 United States Dept. of Health and Human Services v. Smitley, 347 F.3d 109 (4th Cir. 2003) (court should determine dischargeability of non-HEAL loans first and then apply HEAL standard to remainder; repayment not unconscionable when debtor could repay in twenty-five-year plan); *In re* Rice, 78 F.3d 1144 (6th Cir. 1996) (nondischarge of HEAL obligation not unconscionable when debtor and his wife had $60,000.00 income and payment would not reduce family's income to anything close to poverty level); Matthews v. Pineo, 19 F.3d 121 (3d Cir. 1994) (nondischarge not unconscionable when debtor chose to move to a small town and earn less than she could elsewhere as physician, rather than fulfill requirement of service in medically underserved area); *In re* Malloy, 155 B.R. 940 (E.D. Va. 1993) (nondischarge not unconscionable in case of debtor who was healthy, college educated and steadily employed); *In re* Nelson, 183 B.R. 972 (Bankr. S.D. Fla. 1995) (nondischarge would be unconscionable based on debtor's psychological and emotional health); Kline v. United States, 155 B.R. 762 (Bankr. W.D. Mo. 1993) (nondischarge would be unconscionable in view of debtor's chronic depression, anxiety and panic disorder); *see also In re* Ascue, 268 B.R. 739 (Bankr. W.D. Va. 2001) (partial discharge, eliminating $300,000.00 in interest on National Health Service Corps loan for debtor whose earnings were limited), *aff'd*, 2002 WL 192561 (W.D. Va. Feb. 7, 2002).

515 *In re* Brown, 79 B.R. 789 (Bankr. N.D. Ill. 1987) (National Health Services Corp. Scholarship Program—42 U.S.C. § 254o(d)); *see also, e.g.,* 37 U.S.C. § 302g(e) (pertaining to refund obligations of military reservist physicians who receive special pay and who terminate their service early). Unlike HEAL loans, these provisions have not been amended to change the five-year absolute bar on discharge to seven years. Provisions relating to such exceptions to discharge are included in Appendix A.2, *infra*.

516 11 U.S.C. § 523(a)(9). This provision has been applied retroactively to judgments entered prior to its effective date. *See In re* Fielder, 799 F.2d 656 (11th Cir. 1986); *see also* Leach v. Reckley, 63 B.R. 724 (S.D. Ind. 1986).

517 11 U.S.C. § 1328(a)(2).

---

518 *See In re* Longhenry, 246 B.R. 234 (Bankr. D. Md. 2000) (loss of consortium is a personal injury). *But see In re* Felski, 277 B.R. 732 (E.D. Mich. 2002) (statutory subrogation claim against uninsured intoxicated motorist arising from injuries in accident would be nondischargeable if accident was caused by intoxicated motorist).

519 *In re* Wiggins, 180 B.R. 676 (M.D. Ala. 1995); *In re* Brisson, 186 B.R. 205 (Bankr. E.D. Va. 1995); *In re* Williams, 175 B.R. 17 (Bankr. M.D. Tenn. 1994).

520 The statute does not cover vicarious liability. *In re* Lewis, 77 B.R. 972 (Bankr. S.D. Fla. 1987) (debt dischargeable where debtor's daughter drove car).

521 *Compare In re* Greenway, 71 F.3d 1177 (5th Cir. 1996) (motorboat is not a motor vehicle) *with* Willison v. Race, 192 B.R. 949 (W.D. Mo. 1996) (motorboat is a motor vehicle within scope of exception).

522 *In re* Dunn, 203 B.R. 414 (E.D. Mich. 1996).

523 *See, e.g.,* Whitson v. Middleton, 898 F.2d 950 (4th Cir. 1990) (evidence as a whole showed intoxication even though no drunk driving charge was made and no breath test administered); *In re* Spencer, 168 B.R. 142 (Bankr. N.D. Tex. 1994) (debt dischargeable where creditor did not show by preponderance of evidence that debtor was intoxicated as defined by Texas law); *In re* Humphrey, 102 B.R. 629 (Bankr. S.D. Ohio 1989) (debtor who had been charged with "driving under the influence" of alcohol found to have been intoxicated based on the evidence as a whole even though state accepted a plea to "reckless operation of a motor vehicle"); *In re* Tuzzolino, 70 B.R. 373 (Bankr. N.D.N.Y. 1987) (various degrees of intoxication are all "legal intoxication" under § 523(a)(9)); *In re* Dougherty, 51 B.R. 987 (Bankr. D. Colo. 1985) (conviction of "driving while ability impaired" came within discharge exception); *see also In re* Barnes, 266 B.R. 397 (B.A.P. 8th Cir. 2001) (discussing admissible evidence of intoxication).

524 *In re* Pahule, 78 B.R. 210 (E.D. Wis. 1987) (bankruptcy court could look to underlying facts of debtor's criminal conviction for driving under influence to find civil judgment within scope

jurisdiction with the bankruptcy forum over any such disputes.

This subsection closes the hole which case law created in the willful and malicious injury exception of section 523(a)(6). It makes clear that drunk driving debts do not fall within the section 523(a)(6) exception, because Congress saw fit to establish a new subsection to deal with them.[525] Thus, if such debts do not fall within the terms of section 523(a)(9), they should be dischargeable. For example, a criminal restitution debt for injuries arising out of judgment based on the debtor operating a vehicle while intoxicated was found nondischargeable under this section.[526] Additionally, one court of appeals has held that an insurance surcharge imposed by a state as a result of a drunk driving conviction is also nondischargeable under section 523(a)(9).[527] However, it is unlikely that the latter decision is still good law after § 523(a)(9) was amended to include only debts for death or personal injury.

14.4.3.10 Debts Which Existed at Time of Denial or Waiver of Discharge in Prior Bankruptcy Cases—11 U.S.C. § 523(a)(10)[528]

11 U.S.C. § 523(a)(10) contains an exception to discharge which is rarely invoked. It is relevant only if the debtor has been denied a discharge in a prior bankruptcy case, which rarely occurs in consumer cases.[529] If the debtor has been denied a discharge, any debt that existed when the prior bankruptcy was filed may not be discharged in a later bankruptcy.

This exception does not apply, however, if discharge was denied in the prior case only because of the six-year bar to consecutive bankruptcies or because of failure to pay filing fees.[530] Nor does it apply when a debt was reaffirmed in a prior bankruptcy case.[531] The sections which concerned these latter two bars to discharge under both the Act and the Code are conspicuously omitted from the list in 11 U.S.C. § 523(a)(10) designating causes for prior denial of discharge which trigger this exception. This exception also does not apply when a previous case was dismissed, with or without prejudice, if a discharge was not waived or denied in that case.[532]

14.4.3.11 Debts Emerging from Responsibilities to Federal Depository Institutions—11 U.S.C. § 523(a)(11) and (12)

The two exceptions to discharge in section 523(a)(11) and (12) are rarely, if ever, applicable in consumer cases. They were added to the Code as part of the Congressional response to the savings and loan crisis in order to help the Federal Deposit Insurance Corporation (FDIC) and other regulators recover assets to pay the cost of the bailout.

Section 523(a)(11) excepts from discharge debts that emerged from fraud or defalcation in a fiduciary capacity[533] related to the debtor's responsibility to a depository institution or credit union when that debt is memorialized in a "final judgment, unreviewable order, consent order, decree or . . . settlement agreement." Section 523(a)(12) excepts debts for malicious or reckless failure to maintain the capital of insured depository institutions, unless such responsibility has been terminated by an act of the applicable regulatory agency.

Section 523(c) was also amended to extend the deadline for regulatory agencies in some cases under sections

---

of § 523(a)(9)), *aff'd*, 849 F.2d 1056 (7th Cir. 1988); *see also In re* Fearn, 295 B.R. 243 (Bankr. S.D. Ohio 2003) (debtor's alleged consumption of alcohol on the same night of a motor vehicle accident does not necessarily mean debt nondischargeable); *In re* Greenwasser, 269 B.R. 918 (Bankr. S.D. Fla. 2001) (denying summary judgment motion based on prior criminal adjudication); *In re* Caffey, 248 B.R. 920 (Bankr. N.D. Ga. 2000) (debt could be found non-dischargeable under this section even if debtor was acquitted in criminal DUI case, because burden of proof was only a preponderance of evidence in bankruptcy proceeding); *In re* Phalen, 145 B.R. 551 (Bankr. N.D. Ohio 1992) (court could find that debtor was driving while under the influence even though debtor plead guilty to a different charge); *In re* Bennett, 80 B.R. 800 (Bankr. E.D. Va. 1988) (debt arising from default judgment entered when debtor was sued for damages resulting from drunk driving is nondischargeable).

525 *See* Cassidy v. Minihan, 794 F.2d 340 (8th Cir. 1986); *In re* Wright, 66 B.R. 403 (Bankr. S.D. Ind. 1986). *But see In re* Adams, 761 F.2d 1422 (9th Cir. 1985).

526 *See In re* Steiger, 159 B.R. 907 (B.A.P. 9th Cir. 1993) (amount of nondischargeable restitution obligation was set in criminal process based on ascertainable damages for vehicular homicide).

527 Lugo v. Paulsen, 886 F.2d 602 (3d Cir. 1989).

528 This section was redesignated 11 U.S.C. § 523(a)(10) (instead of § 523(a)(9)) by the 1986 amendments.

529 See § 14.2, *supra*, for discussion of denial of discharge. This section has also been applied in a case where discharge was

revoked in a prior case. *In re* Klapp, 706 F.2d 998 (9th Cir. 1983).

530 *See* §§ 14.2.2.8, 14.2.2.11, *supra*.

531 *In re* Johnson, 255 B.R. 696 (Bankr. E.D. Mich. 2000) (debt reaffirmed in prior bankruptcy in settlement of dischargeability dispute was not non-dischargeable under § 523(a)(10) unless written waiver of discharge approved by court in prior case provided that debt would be non-dischargeable in future bankruptcy cases); *In re* Lones, 50 B.R. 801 (Bankr. W.D. Ky. 1985).

532 *In re* Samora, 117 B.R. 660 (Bankr. D.N.M. 1990); *see also In re* Logan, 145 B.R. 324 (Bankr. D. Kan. 1992) (order dismissing prior case and denying a discharge for failure to attend creditors' meeting was not a denial of discharge for cause under § 727 that gave rise to an exception to discharge in later case). *But see In re* Smith, 133 B.R. 467 (Bankr. N.D. Ind. 1991) (dismissal with prejudice automatically bars future discharge of debts existing at the time of dismissal based on 11 U.S.C. § 349(a)).

533 Presumably those terms would be defined as they are for cases under 11 U.S.C. § 523(a)(4). *See* § 14.4.3.4, *supra*.

523(a)(2), (4) and (6).[534] The deadline was also purportedly extended for actions to determine nondischargeability under section 523(a)(11), although by its terms that section is not referenced in section 523(c)(1) so it is not clear that a deadline applies.

14.4.3.12 Federal Criminal Restitution—11 U.S.C. § 523(a)(13)

Code section 523(a)(13), enacted as part of a 1994 crime bill, excepts from discharge any order of restitution issued under title 18 of the United States Code, the federal criminal code. As the Supreme Court had already held that criminal restitution generally came within the scope of section 523(a)(7)'s exception for non-compensatory fines, penalties and forfeitures payable to or for the benefit of a governmental unit,[535] this section appears to make only a few additional types of debts nondischargeable. If the federal criminal restitution debt is not payable to or for the benefit of a governmental unit, this section would make it nondischargeable nonetheless. Similarly, if the restitution were found to be compensation for actual pecuniary loss, this section would prevent it from being discharged. However, non-federal criminal restitution debts which do not fall within section 523(a)(7) are not affected by section 523(a)(13).

Section 523(a)(13) is not applicable when the debtor receives a full chapter 13 discharge under Code section 1328(a).[536] But, oddly, the exception to that discharge is in some ways broader than the exceptions to discharge in chapter 7. The chapter 13 exception, in section 1328(a)(3) includes all criminal restitution debts, whether state or federal, imposed in a sentence upon conviction of a crime. However, as discussed elsewhere in this manual,[537] the chapter 13 exception may permit discharge of some restitution debts not dischargeable in chapter 7 if they are not imposed in a sentence upon conviction of a crime.

14.4.3.13 Debts Incurred to Pay Nondischargeable Federal Taxes—11 U.S.C. § 523(a)(14)

At the urging of the credit card industry, Congress enacted section 523(a)(14), which provides that a debt incurred to pay a federal tax that would have been nondischargeable under section 523(a)(1) is nondischargeable to the same extent as the tax debt would have been. Supposedly, this

section was needed to prevent debtors anticipating a bankruptcy from using a credit card to pay nondischargeable taxes and then discharging the credit card debt.

Significantly, the section has no applicability to state or local taxes. It also does not apply in chapter 13, because it was not incorporated in Code section 1328(a).

Although the provision was intended to facilitate the payment of taxes by credit card, it is not limited to credit card payments. Any loan that a lender could show was used to pay taxes probably would be within its scope. However, lenders may not know, in many cases, whether a loan was used to pay taxes unless the loan proceeds check is made out to the tax creditor, for example to pay off a tax lien, or the debtor uses a credit card convenience check made out to the tax creditor.

The new section also creates difficult tracing problems. If taxes are paid by credit card, how are payments on the account after that to be apportioned? In view of the amendment's proponents' arguments that this provision was only to protect against debtors evading the nondischargeability of taxes by borrowing money to pay them, all payments after the credit was incurred to pay taxes should be allocated to the tax charges until those charges are paid. However, creditors undoubtedly will argue for other methods of allocating payments, such as FIFO (first-in, first-out) or prorating them. The issue could become even more confused if the debtor accepted one of the frequent solicitations by credit card companies to pay off the balance on one card using a new card. Of course, in such cases it is unlikely the new card issuer would know that the prior card was used to pay taxes.

Unfortunately, the amendment does little to deter its intended targets, while harming others who are innocent of any intent to manipulate the Code. Debtors who plan their bankruptcy cases and are intent on evading the tax discharge exception can simply obtain cash advances or incur debts to pay other expenses so they can pay their taxes with cash. Alternatively, some may seek to cover their tracks by incurring debt to pay their taxes and then incurring debt from another creditor to pay off the first debt. Because the second lender or credit card issuer will rarely be aware that the debt it paid off was used to pay nondischargeable taxes, the debtor will have achieved the precise result that section 523(a)(14) attempts to prevent. The only debtors likely to be hurt by the nondischargeability provision are those who genuinely want to pay their taxes, incur debts to do so, and later run into financial problems before those debts are paid.

14.4.3.14 Marital Property Settlement Debts That the Debtor Can Afford to Pay—11 U.S.C. § 523(a)(15)

The Bankruptcy Reform Act of 1994 created a new exception to discharge for marital property settlements in

---

534   11 U.S.C. § 523(c)(2). For further discussion of the procedure for determining nondischargeability of various debts, see § 14.4.2, *supra*.

535   *See* § 14.4.3.7, *supra*.

536   Compare 11 U.S.C. § 1328(b) to which § 523(a)(13) is applicable.

537   *See* § 14.4.3.7, *supra*.

limited situations. This exception arose after consistent legislative pressure to make all property settlements non-dischargeable. Various members of Congress had for years introduced bills that would have created that result.

Section 523(a)(15) grew out of a bill which had proposed that property settlement debts "assumed or incurred" be found nondischargeable, if an obligee filed an adversary proceeding under Code section 523(c), unless the court determined that paying the debt would be an undue hardship for the debtor *and* the benefit of the debtor's discharge outweighed the detriment to the obligee.[538] This proposal met opposition on several grounds. First, it was argued that the word "assumed" could be read to mean that when there was a hold harmless agreement the debt to the original creditor (the debt assumed) might be considered nondischargeable, as opposed to the obligation, running to the other party to the marital agreement, to pay that debt.

Second, it was argued that undue hardship was too difficult a test to meet. In the student loan context, some courts have been loathe to find undue hardship in any but the most extreme circumstances.[539] Even a remote chance of income in the future has been found by some courts to prove that repayment would not be an undue hardship. A similar analysis for property settlements could result in a property settlement being nondischargeable and enforceable after bankruptcy, even if that made it impossible for the debtor to provide current support to other dependents.

Third, the proposal would have permitted a vindictive spouse to enforce a property settlement even if did not significantly benefit that spouse, for example, if the obligee spouse had no liability on the assumed debt (perhaps because it had been discharged in bankruptcy).

The provision which was enacted created a more limited exception. The obligee spouse still must file for a determination under section 523(c) during the bankruptcy case in order to have the debt found nondischargeable under the subsection. This fixes a time for the dischargeability determination and prevents the bankruptcy court from becoming a permanent support court constantly assessing the parties' needs. In addition, the word "assumed" was deleted so, as the legislative history also states,[540] the only obligation that is not discharged is that which runs to the spouse, former spouse, or child of the debtor.[541]

Perhaps most importantly, the debt is discharged if the debtor does not have the ability to pay it after providing support for dependents. The language used in the section is identical to that in Code section 1325(b), the ability to pay test in chapter 13.[542] Courts therefore will probably apply similar standards, raising all of the questions that they have dealt with in chapter 13. However, they may also take notice of the circumstances of the obligee spouse, and be more likely to find that the debtor can cut expenses if the obligee spouse has a lower standard of living than the debtor. And courts will take into account the fact that the debtor no longer has to pay other debts which are being discharged in the bankruptcy case.[543] Unlike a determination under section 523(a)(5), which is based upon the parties' finances at the time of the divorce, the court under section 523(a)(15) looks to the current and likely future income and expenses of the debtor,[544] which may involve consideration of the debtor's needs in light of a later marriage or live-in companion.[545] In any event, if the debtor does not have the ability to pay, the analysis is ended and the court never reaches the other prong of the dischargeability test—whether the balance of hardship tips in favor of the debtor.

The second prong provides, because the "and" between the prongs was changed to an "or," that the debt also is discharged if the benefit to the debtor of discharge outweighs the detriment to the non-debtor obligee. This would include situations in which the debt is for an obligation which the non-debtor does not have to pay.[546] The legislative history also mentions that it would include situations in which the non-debtor could easily pay the debt.[547] Finally, some courts have held that the availability of chapter 7 to the obligee may lessen the detriment of discharging the property settlement debt.[548] One tendency emerging in the cases applying this balancing test is the desire of the court to equalize the living standards of the parties, much as a family court would do.[549]

---

538 H.R. 4711, 103d Cong. (1994).

539 *See* § 14.4.3.8, *supra*.

540 H.R. Rep. No. 103-835, at 55 (1994), *reprinted in* 1994 U.S.C.C.A.N. 3340.

541 *In re* Dollaga, 260 B.R. 493 (B.A.P. 9th Cir. 2001) (creditor who was not spouse, former spouse, or child of debtor lacked standing under § 523(a)(15)); *In re* Sanders, 236 B.R. 107 (Bankr. S.D. Ga. 1999) (debt owed to debtor's former divorce attorney not within scope of section); *In re* Finaly, 190 B.R. 312 (Bankr. S.D. Ohio 1995) (creditor that was not spouse, former spouse or child of debtor did not have standing to assert exception).

542 *See* § 12.3.3, *supra*.

543 *In re* Schmitt, 197 B.R. 312 (W.D. Ark. 1996).

544 *In re* Farmer, 250 B.R. 427 (Bankr. M.D. Fla. 2000) (debtor's expenses would soon decline substantially); *In re* Florio, 187 B.R. 654 (Bankr. W.D. Mo. 1995).

545 *In re* Short, 232 F.3d 1018 (9th Cir. 2000) (companion's income may be considered when debtor and companion are financially interdependent or form single economic unit); *In re* Crosswhite, 148 F.3d 879 (7th Cir. 1998); *In re* Adams, 200 B.R. 630 (N.D. Ill. 1996); *In re* Cleveland, 198 B.R. 394 (Bankr. N.D. Ga. 1996).

546 *In re* Craig, 196 B.R. 305 (Bankr. E.D. Va. 1996) (non-debtor spouse had filed chapter 7 case herself).

547 H.R. Rep. No. 103-835, at 54 (1994), *reprinted in* 1994 U.S.C.C.A.N. 3340; *see* Taylor v. Taylor, 199 B.R. 37 (N.D. Ill. 1996) (non-debtor had very high income).

548 *In re* Hill, 184 B.R. 750 (Bankr. N.D. Ill 1995).

549 *E.g., In re* Smither, 194 B.R. 102 (Bankr. W.D. Ky. 1996) (if nondischargeability will cause debtor's living standard to fall materially below non-debtor's, debt will be discharged).

The net result of the subsection should be to prevent the use of bankruptcy simply to evade marital property settlements when the debtor does not have bona fide financial problems. However, it will not prevent the necessity of litigation of yet another issue if the debtor spouse is simply trying to litigate the non-debtor into submission. The fact that the issue must be raised by an adversary proceeding during the bankruptcy also puts a premium on the obligee spouse's attorney being aware of bankruptcy law in this regard.

However, nothing in section 523(a)(15) affects the nondischargeability of debts, whether labeled alimony or property settlement, that in fact are in the nature of alimony, maintenance or support and therefore nondischargeable under section 523(a)(5).[550] An obligee spouse who misses the deadline for a section 523(a)(15) dischargeability complaint is still free to argue, in state court or bankruptcy court, that the debt was nondischargeable because it was in the nature of alimony, maintenance or support.

Also significant is the fact that the exception only applies in chapter 7, 11 and 12 cases and cases of chapter 13 hardship discharges. It was not added to Code section 1328(a), the provision governing chapter 13 discharges after full compliance with a plan. But, non-debtor obligees in chapter 13 are already afforded protections similar to those of section 523(a)(15) through the ability to pay test[551] and the good faith standard[552] applicable to confirmation of a chapter 13 plan.

The new amendment raises several questions of interpretation. First, which party has the burden of proof? Generally, the party asserting an exception to discharge has the burden of proof, and some courts have applied this principle.[553] Most courts, noting the language of the section stating the debt is not dischargeable unless one of the two tests is met, have, as they have with similar language in the student loan exception, put the burden of going forward or the burden of proof on the debtor, at least with respect to proving that one of the two exceptions to the exception are met.[554] Still others have placed the burden of pleading and proving the "affirmative defense" of inability to pay the debt on the debtor

and the burden of proving that the detrimental consequences of the discharge to the creditor outweigh the benefit to the debtor on the creditor.[555]

Courts not wanting to hold the entire debt dischargeable may also seek to achieve compromise results as a few have under the student loan discharge exception.[556] Despite the fact that, unlike many other Bankruptcy Code provisions, section 523(a)(15) does not say that debts are nondischargeable "to the extent that" the debtor can afford to pay them, some courts may try to "split the baby" and discharge part but not all of the debt.[557]

Ordinarily, as in most other dischargeability litigation, no attorney fees are awarded in litigation under section 523(a)(15). However, if a divorce decree provides that fees are to be awarded for enforcement of the decree, a prevailing non-debtor may be awarded fees, at least for litigation of the state law issues of the divorce decree's validity, amount, and enforceability.[558]

14.4.3.15 Debts for Condominium Fees—11 U.S.C. § 523(a)(16)

The Bankruptcy Reform Act of 1994 also enacted a new section 523(a)(16) making nondischargeable condominium and cooperative fees or assessments *if* 1) they become due and payable after the order for relief with respect to the debtor's interest in a dwelling unit with condominium ownership or in a share of a cooperative housing corporation *and* 2) the fees are payable for a "period" during which the debtor physically occupied the dwelling or received rent from a tenant "for such period."

This exception grew out of a split in the case law regarding whether condominium fees were pre-petition debts dischargeable in bankruptcy.[559] The exception does not apply in chapter 13 cases in which the debtor completes a plan, because it was not added to section 1328(a).

There may be disputes under the subsection about what constitutes a period for which fees are nondischargeable. For example, a condominium association with annual or semi-annual fees may argue that the full annual fee is due even if the debtor occupied the property only for a day. However, this argument should fail because the legislative history states the fee is nondischargeable "only to the extent that the fee is payable for time during which the debtor lived in or received rent for the condominium or cooperative unit."[560]

---

550 *See* § 14.4.3.5, *supra.*

551 *See* § 12.3.3, *supra.*

552 11 U.S.C. § 1325(a)(4); *see* § 12.3, *supra.*

553 *E.g., In re* Butler, 186 B.R. 371 (Bankr. D. Vt. 1995).

554 *E.g., In re* Crosswhite, 148 F.3d 879 (7th Cir. 1998) (after non-debtor spouse showed debt was incurred in connection with divorce, debtor had burden of proving inability to pay and detriment to debtor greater than benefit to creditor); *In re* Gamble, 143 F.3d 223 (5th Cir. 1998) (same); *In re* Moeder, 220 B.R. 52 (B.A.P. 8th Cir. 1998) (same); *In re* Jodoin, 209 B.R. 132 (B.A.P. 9th Cir. 1997); *In re* Hill, 184 B.R. 750 (Bankr. N.D. Ill. 1995) (debtor has burden of proof); *In re* Silvers, 187 (Bankr. W.D. Mo. 1995) (debtor has burden of going forward, but not burden of proof); *see* § 14.4.3.8.3, *supra.*

555 *In re* Hesson, 190 B.R. 229 (Bankr. D. Md. 1995).

556 *See* § 14.4.3.8.2.2, *supra.*

557 *In re* Myrvang, 232 1116 (9th Cir. 2000) (court could enter partial discharge and set payment schedule for remainder of debt, but exceeded its equitable powers by providing for large penalty if debtor failed to make payments); *In re* Comisky, 183 B.R. 883 (Bankr. N.D. Cal. 1995).

558 Renfrow v. Draper, 232 F.3d 688 (9th Cir. 2000).

559 *See* § 14.5.1.1, *infra.*

560 H.R. Rep. No. 103-835, at 56 (1994), *reprinted in* 1994

This language in the legislative history should also preclude claims that the debtor "occupied" the premises simply because the debtor's belongings remained there.

The amendment resolves the disputes about whether other condominium or cooperative fees are claims that can be discharged. By specifying that some post-petition fees are claims that cannot be discharged, the new section implicitly undermines decisions holding that such fees were not pre-petition claims.[561] In addition, the legislative history states that, except to the extent made nondischargeable by this section, obligations to pay post-petition fees are dischargeable, and expressly adopts the holding of *In re Rosteck*,[562] which held that because they arose from a pre-petition contract they were pre-petition claims.[563]

Lastly, the amendment contains a savings clause making clear that even if a debt was nondischargeable in a prior bankruptcy case or in a pre-conversion case, it still may be discharged in a later case or converted case filed after the debtor vacated the property, if the conditions of occupancy or rent receipt are no longer present.

14.4.3.16 Costs and Fees in Prisoner Litigation—11 U.S.C. § 523(a)(17)

Yet another exception to the chapter 7 discharge, not applicable in chapter 13, was added by the Prisoner Litigation Reform Act, part of an omnibus budget bill enacted in 1996.[564] Although it is not readily apparent from the wording of the section, the exception is limited to costs and fees that are imposed upon prisoners who seek to file actions *in forma pauperis* in federal courts.

The exception was enacted as part of a larger bill that substantially changed the rights of prisoners to file actions *in forma pauperis* under 28 U.S.C. § 1915. The bill directed federal courts to require any prisoner filing an action to make monthly payments toward fees and costs from the prison account earned by the prisoner. Section 523(a)(17) prohibits prisoners from using chapter 7 to discharge the payments they are ordered to make.

It is this purpose that accounts for the strange wording of section 523(a)(17). The section, prohibits the discharge of "a fee imposed by a court for the filing of a case, motion,

complaint, or appeal or for other costs and expenses assessed with respect to such filings, *regardless of an assertion of poverty by the debtor under section 1915(b) or (f) of title 28, or the debtor's status as a prisoner, as defined in section 1915(h) of title 28."* (emphasis added)

Although, considered out of its legislative context, this section could be read to make nondischargeable all fees, costs or expenses imposed by a court, there is no suggestion in the rest of the legislation or in the conference report that the provision was intended to cover anyone other than prisoners.[565] Indeed, if the intent of Congress was to make nondischargeable all fees, costs, or expenses imposed by courts, there would have been no reason to include the language that is italicized above. Fees, costs, and expenses imposed on prisoners under 28 U.S.C. § 1915 would already have been included along with all other fees, costs, and expenses. As it must be assumed that the italicized language is not mere surplusage, it is clear Congress meant to except from discharge *only* those fees, costs, and expenses that are imposed on a prisoner regardless of an assertion of poverty or the debtor's status as a prisoner.[566]

14.4.3.17 Support Obligations Owed to Governmental Units—11 U.S.C. § 523(a)(18)

Section 523(a)(18), passed as part of the 1996 welfare "reform" legislation,[567] renders nondischargeable a debt owed under state law to a state or municipality that is in the nature of support and enforceable under Part D of Title IV of the Social Security Act.[568] This provision, which is not applicable in chapter 13 cases in which the debtor completes a plan,[569] was apparently part of an attempt to overrule cases which had held that obligation of parents to reimburse states for welfare provided to their dependents were not nondischargeable under section 523(a)(5) if there had never been a court order assigned to the state.[570]

U.S.C.C.A.N. 3340; *see In re* Eno, 269 B.R. 319 (Bankr. M.D. Pa. 2001) (assessment discharged because debtors did not occupy or rent property).

561 *E.g., In re* Rosenfeld, 23 F.3d 833 (4th Cir. 1994).

562 899 F.2d 694 (7th Cir. 1990).

563 *In re* Mattera, 203 B.R. 565 (Bankr. D.N.J. 1997) (chapter 13 discharge eliminated debtor's personal liability for post-petition condominium fees even though she remained owner of condominium after petition). *But see In re* Lozada, 214 B.R. 558 (Bankr. E.D. Va. 1997) (because § 523(a)(16) did not mention post-petition assessments by home owners' associations court was constrained to follow prior Fourth Circuit authority that they were post-petition debts).

564 Pub. L. No. 104-134, 110 Stat. 1321 (1996).

565 *In re* Tepper, 280 B.R. 628 (N.D. Ill. 2002) (citing legislative history); S. Bend Cmty. School Corp. v. Eggleston, 215 B.R. 1012 (N.D. Ind. 1997) (citing legislative history).

566 *In re* Hough, 239 B.R. 412 (B.A.P. 9th Cir. 1999); *In re* Farnsworth, 283 B.R. 503 (Bankr. W.D. Tenn. 2002); *In re* Lopez, 269 B.R. 607 (Bankr. N.D. Tex. 2001); *In re* Tuttle, 224 B.R. 606 (Bankr. W.D. Mich. 1998).

567 Pub. L. No. 104-193, 110 Stat. 2105 (1996).

568 *See also* 42 U.S.C. § 656; *In re* Leibowitz, 218 B.R. 96 (Bankr. C.D. Cal. 1998) (discussion of certain relevant statutory sections in the Social Security Act).

569 11 U.S.C. § 1328(a) was not amended to include this exception among the exceptions to discharge in a case in which the debtor completes a plan. *But see* 42 U.S.C. § 656 (discharge does not "release" debts enforceable under Part IVD, without limitation as to chapter).

570 *E.g., In re* Visness, 57 F.3d 775 (9th Cir. 1995) ; *see In re* Coker, 232 B.R. 182 (C.D. Cal. 1998).

This exception will require careful examination of certain support obligations that may not be otherwise nondischargeable. For the exception to apply, the debt must be in the nature of support and it may be that a reimbursement obligation cannot always be characterized as being in the nature of support. Generally, debts in the nature of support are based on both the needs of the person supported and the ability of the debtor to pay.[571] If the debt is established without taking into consideration ability to pay, it may be considered simply a reimbursement obligation and not a support obligation.

In addition, the debt must be based upon state law and owed to a state or a municipality. If either of these elements is missing, the debt is dischargeable. Finally, the debt must be enforceable under Part D of Title IV of the Social Security Act.[572] Careful scrutiny of those provisions will be necessary to determine if they give enforcement powers with regard to the particular debt involved.

For example, sections of Title IVD speak of the "establishment" of a child support order as distinct from its "enforcement."[573] It may be possible to argue that a child support order is not enforceable unless it was established through a prior order before the bankruptcy petition was filed.[574]

14.4.3.18 Debts Made Nondischargeable by Other Statutes

Congress has passed several other statutory provisions which may make debts nondischargeable in bankruptcy under either chapter 7 or 13. Two statutes making student loan debts nondischargeable in some circumstances outside section 523(a)(8) are discussed above.[575] Similarly, certain obligations arising from retention bonuses or continuation pay paid to military personnel were made nondischargeable when the discharge is entered less than five years from the date the retention or continuation agreement is terminated.[576] To the extent that these provisions contain lan-

guage making them applicable when a discharge is entered within five years, they will not apply in a chapter 13 case which is filed within five years, but where the discharge is not entered until after the five year period has expired.

14.4.3.19 Debts That Were Nondischargeable in a Previous Bankruptcy Case—11 U.S.C. § 523(b)

Section 523(b) provides that certain types of debts that were not discharged in a prior bankruptcy case may be discharged in a later case if they would have been dischargeable under § 523(a) in the later case. The debts enumerated include debts that were previously found nondischargeable under § 523(a)(1), (a)(3), and (a)(8). What these debts have in common (or at least had in common when § 523(b) was enacted)[577] is that they all turn on time periods that may have changed in the later bankruptcy case. For example, § 523(a)(1) looks to whether a return for a prior tax year was filed more than two years before the bankruptcy petition.[578] While that may not have been true in the first case, it may well be true in the later case. Similarly, § 523(a)(3) looks to whether certain debts were scheduled in a case or whether the creditor otherwise had notice in time to participate. If a debt was not dischargeable due to lack of timely scheduling or notice in the first case, it may still be scheduled and therefore be dischargeable in the second case.

However, other debts that were nondischargeable in a prior case cannot be discharged in a later case, except for a case in which a debtor receives a discharge under § 1328(a).[579] In this respect, § 523(b) applies principles of *res judicata*.[580]

Section 523(b) may well allow a debtor with a HEAL loan that was nondischargeable in an earlier case under both

---

571 *See* § 14.4.3.5, *supra*; *see also* Henry J. Sommer & Margaret Doe McGarity, Collier Family Law and the Bankruptcy Code ¶ 6.04.

572 *See In re* Spinks, 233 B.R. 820 (Bankr. S.D. Ill. 1999) (debts under Title IVE for foster care payments are enforceable under Title IVD but creditor failed to establish its debts arose under Title IVE); *In re* Leibowitz, 218 B.R. 96 (Bankr. C.D. Cal. 1998).

573 *E.g.*, 42 U.S.C. §§ 654(4)(B), 659(i).

574 *But see In re* Leibowitz, 217 F.3d 799 (9th Cir. 2000) (obligation to reimburse county for public assistance received by debtor's former spouse and children before entry of support order was non-dischargeable).

575 42 U.S.C. § 292f(g) (Health Education Assistance Loans—HEAL); 42 U.S.C. § 254o(d)(3) (National Health Services Scholarship Program); *see* § 14.4.3.8.6, *supra*; *see also* 42 U.S.C. § 288-5 (incorporating 42 U.S.C. § 254o).

576 37 U.S.C. § 301d(c)(3); *see also* 37 U.S.C. § 302f (obligation of

reserve health specialists who fail to honor agreement to serve in armed forces to refund special bonus pay not dischargeable in bankruptcy with no exceptions); 37 U.S.C. § 317(f)(3) (five year nondischargeable provision related to obligation to refund retention bonuses of military officers who terminate agreement); 37 U.S.C. § 302g(e) (refund obligations of military reservist physicians who receive special pay and who terminate their service early not dischargeable if less than five years after termination); 37 U.S.C. §§ 301e(d)(3), 314(d)(4), 318(h)(3), 319(f)(3), 321(f)(3), 322(f)(4); Pub. L. No. 106-65, § 1705(d)(3), 113 Stat. 512. Such statutes are reprinted in Appendix A.2, *infra*.

577 Prior versions of 11 U.S.C. § 523(a)(8) permitted discharge of student loans if the first payment was due more than five (or later seven) years before the petition.

578 *In re* Cates, 289 B.R. 389 (Bankr. E.D. Ark. 2003).

579 Section 1328(a) discharges all debts provided for by the plan, with certain exceptions. Section 1328(b) discharges all debts provided for in the plan except those provided for under section 1322(b)(5) and those that are non-dischargeable under section 523(a). It does not mention section 523(b).

580 *In re* Paine, 283 B.R. 33 (B.A.P. 9th Cir. 2002).

§ 523(a)(8) and 42 U.S.C. § 292f(g)[581] to seek an undue hardship discharge of that loan under § 523(a)(8) without meeting the stricter requirements for discharge of a HEAL loan. The debtor can argue that the plain language of § 523(b) provides that the loan, which meets the description of that subsection, is dischargeable if the loan is not non-dischargeable under § 523(a)(8) in the second case.[582]

14.4.4 Res Judicata *and Collateral Estoppel in Dischargeability Cases*

One of the more disputed issues in dischargeability litigation has been the extent to which prior state court judgments are binding upon the parties in bankruptcy court through *res judicata* or collateral estoppel. At least some of the questions repeatedly raised in this area have been addressed by the Supreme Court.

In *Brown v. Felsen*,[583] the debtor had entered into a judgment by stipulation in state court, and thereafter filed a bankruptcy case. The creditor then alleged that the debt was incurred through fraud, deceit, and malicious conversion, which would make it nondischargeable. The lower courts, following the rule in the Tenth Circuit, held that the state court stipulation and judgment did not mention fraud and that the bankruptcy court could not go beyond that state court record. Therefore, they held the debt was dischargeable.

The Supreme Court reversed, stating that a creditor should not be required to litigate issues of possible fraud in every state court collection suit just to guard against discharge in a possible later bankruptcy. The Court found that this would frustrate Congressional policy which intended the bankruptcy court to handle dischargeability issues, and held that when the debtor adds the new element of bankruptcy to a dispute the creditor should then have an opportunity to respond by raising dischargeability. Thus, the bankruptcy court was instructed to go outside the state court record to hear evidence on the dischargeability issue.

Brown v. Felsen thereby resolved the question of what to do when a fraud claim had been raised, but not actually litigated or resolved, in prior state litigation. Bankruptcy courts have since had little problem following its holding in that situation.[584]

Slightly different than *Brown* is the case in which the creditor pleaded all of the elements that would give rise to nondischargeability and then obtained a default judgment in state court. Does *res judicata* apply in this situation? The courts have held it does not, based upon *Brown v. Felsen*.[585] *Res judicata* is inapplicable because the dischargeability cause of action is separate and distinct from any state law cause of action.[586] Moreover, Congress intended the dischargeability cause of action to be decided (for certain types of nondischargeability complaints) only in the bankruptcy courts.[587]

The final possibility is the case in which the factual issues necessary to establish a nondischargeable debt were raised, actually litigated and determined in the state court. There the question is whether collateral estoppel, which normally precludes relitigation of factual issues actually litigated and necessarily decided in a prior case, should be applicable to dischargeability cases. In *Brown*, the Supreme Court expressly left this issue open,[588] and lower courts differed on its resolution.

A unanimous Supreme Court answered the question twelve years later, holding that collateral estoppel (also known as issue preclusion) can be applied to permit creditors, who have successfully reduced fraud claims to judgment, to exempt those claims from discharge.[589] Conse-

---

581 *See* § 14.4.3.8.6, *supra.*

582 *See In re* Tanski, 195 B.R. 408 (Bankr. E.D. Wis. 1996).

583 442 U.S. 127, 99 S. Ct. 2205, 60 L. Ed. 2d 767 (1979).

584 *See, e.g., In re* Daley, 776 F.2d 834 (9th Cir. 1985) (a stipulated dismissal of state court fraud claims did not bar dischargeability action); *In re* DiNoto, 46 B.R. 489 (B.A.P. 9th Cir. 1984) (bankruptcy judge free to make own determination as to dischargeability on stipulated judgment debt); *In re* Ashley, 5 B.R. 262 (Bankr. E.D. Tenn. 1980); *In re* Enterkin, Bankr. L. Rep. (CCH) ¶ 67,506 (Bankr. N.D. Ga. 1980); *see also In re* King, 103 F.3d 17 (5th Cir. 1997) (debtor failed to make record establishing that state court judgment in favor of creditor which

failed to award damages on creditor's claim of fraud precluded dischargeability claim based on fraud because there was no evidence that the state court had made findings on the issue of fraud); Greenberg v. Schools, 711 F.2d 152 (11th Cir. 1983) (fact that fraud litigation had been started in state court did not bar dischargeability complaint or extinguish fraud dischargeability claim).

585 *See, e.g., In re* Eskenazi, 6 B.R. 366, 368 (B.A.P. 9th Cir. 1980); *In re* Iannelli, 12 B.R. 561, 563 (Bankr. S.D.N.Y. 1981); Franks v. Thomason, 4 B.R. 814, 821 (Bankr. N.D. Ga. 1980); *In re* McKenna, 4 B.R. 160, 162 (Bankr. N.D. Ill. 1980); *In re* Mallory, 1 B.R. 201 (Bankr. N.D. Ga. 1979); *see also In re* McMillan, 579 F.2d 289 (3d Cir. 1978).

586 *In re* Rahn, 641 F.2d 755 (9th Cir. 1981); *In re* McKenna, 4 B.R. 160 (Bankr. N.D. Ill. 1980); *In re* Richards, 7 B.R. 711 (Bankr. S.D. Fla. 1980); *see also In re* Gibbs, 107 B.R. 492 (Bankr. D.N.J. 1989) (consent judgment entered in district court prior to bankruptcy which included provision that debt would be nondischargeable is not *res judicata*, because district court lacked subject matter jurisdiction over bankruptcy issue before bankruptcy was filed).

587 *In re* Shuler, 722 F.2d 1253 (5th Cir. 1984); Carey Lumber Co. v. Bell, 615 F.2d 370 (5th Cir. 1980); *In re* Houtman, 568 F.2d 651 (9th Cir. 1978); *In re* Eskenazi, 6 B.R. 366 (B.A.P. 9th Cir. 1980).

588 Brown v. Felsen, 442 U.S. 127, 139 n.10, 99 S. Ct. 2205, 60 L. Ed. 2d 767 (1979).

589 Grogan v. Garner, 498 U.S. 279, 111 S. Ct. 654, 112 L. Ed. 2d 755 (1991); *see also In re* Bugna, 33 F.3d 1054 (9th Cir. 1994) (jury verdict finding fraud given collateral estoppel effect in proceeding to establish fraud as a fiduciary under § 523(a)(4); *In re* St. Laurent, 991 F.2d 672 (11th Cir. 1993) (state court fraud judgment given collateral estoppel effect in determining dischargeability under § 523(a)(2)(A)); *In re* Miera, 926 F.2d 741 (8th Cir. 1991) (state court judgment for battery given collateral

quently, collateral estoppel applies when a creditor can produce a record from a non-bankruptcy court proceeding establishing fraud or willful and malicious injury.[590] Similarly, collateral estoppel can apply against a creditor when an issue such as the debtor's malice has been actually litigated and decided in the debtor's favor.[591]

The party seeking collateral estoppel has the burden of making an evidentiary record sufficient to establish that collateral estoppel applies.[592] This would normally require filing the relevant aspects of the non-bankruptcy court record with the bankruptcy court, generally by attaching certified copies to the dischargeability complaint or to a motion for summary judgment. Moreover, for a prior judgment to preclude litigation of dischargeability, all of the elements necessary to the nondischargeability cause of action must have also been necessary to the prior cause of action. If the prior proceeding did not require proof of all of the elements necessary to obtain a judgment that a debt is

nondischargeable, the creditor must prove those elements in the court deciding the dischargeability proceeding.[593]

However, collateral estoppel usually has no applicability if the fraud issue was not actually litigated, that is, if a default judgment was obtained.[594] The effect of a prior

---

estoppel effect to preserve judgment from discharge as a willful and malicious injury); *In re* Braen, 900 F.2d 621 (3d Cir. 1990) (malicious prosecution judgment under New Jersey law given collateral estoppel effect); Cohen v. Bucci, 905 F.2d 1111 (7th Cir. 1990) (prior finding of fraudulent transfer under 11 U.S.C. § 548 precluded debtor from disputing fraudulent intent under § 727(a)(2)(A)). Similarly, collateral estoppel may be applied to findings of fraud contained in a final award entered in an arbitration proceeding. *See In re* O'Neill, 260 B.R. 122 (Bankr. E.D. Tex. 2001).

590 *E.g., In re* Nangle, 274 F.3d 481 (8th Cir. 2001) (prior court orders and jury verdict could only be interpreted as having found debtor's acts to be willful and malicious); *In re* Scarborough, 171 F.3d 638 (8th Cir. 1999) (judgment for malicious prosecution necessarily included finding that debtor acted willfully and maliciously); *In re* McNallen, 62 F.3d 619 (4th Cir. 1995); *In re* Lacy, 947 F.2d 1276 (5th Cir. 1991) (debtor's misrepresentations established in state court proceedings); *In re* Tsamasfyros, 940 F.2d 605 (10th Cir. 1991) (debtor's breach of fiduciary duty established in state court proceeding); *In re* Giangrosso, 145 B.R. 319 (B.A.P. 9th Cir. 1992) (state court judgment given collateral estoppel effect even though jury did not state whether it was based on fraud or conversion, because either theory would render debt nondischargeable); *In re* Smith, 128 B.R. 488 (S.D. Fla. 1991) (consent judgment and state court record used as basis for collateral estoppel).

591 Recoveredge Ltd. P'ship v. Pentecost, 44 F.3d 1284 (5th Cir. 1995) (creditor could not assert under § 523(a)(2) that debtor committed fraud after judgment in earlier action that had been entered on all of creditor's claims except fraud claim); *In re* Menna, 16 F.3d 7 (1st Cir. 1994) (broker could not obtain nondischargeability judgment against debtor after broker had been found liable in action against broker for negligently repeating debtor's fraudulent statements; negligence finding necessarily precluded the broker from arguing it had reasonably relied on debtor's statements); *In re* Picard, 133 B.R. 1 (Bankr. D. Me. 1991) (claim of shooting victim found dischargeable where victim had failed to establish malice in connection with his request for punitive damages in state court).

592 *See In re* Pancake, 106 F.3d 1242 (5th Cir. 1997) (collateral estoppel did not apply because creditor failed to present evidence that the state court held a hearing to determine facts upon entering uncontested judgment).

593 *See In re* Spigel, 260 F.3d 27 (1st Cir. 2001) (state court judgment did not encompass all of the elements required for non-dischargeability); *In re* Harmon, 250 F.3d 1240 (9th Cir. 2001) (state court judgment did not necessarily decide issue of fraud when it could have been entered based on constructive fraud); *In re* Peklar, 260 F.3d 1035 (9th Cir. 2001) (conversion judgment did not establish that debtor who removed furniture from property in derogation of landlord's rights acted willfully and maliciously); *In re* Markowitz, 190 F.3d 455 (6th Cir. 1999) (legal malpractice judgment did not establish willful and malicious injury); *In re* Miller, 156 F.3d 598 (5th Cir. 1998) (state court judgment against debtor did not have collateral estoppel effect in dischargeability action for embezzlement or willful and malicious injury because state cause of action required fewer elements to be proved; conversely, state court verdict for debtor on issue of fiduciary fraud has collateral estoppel effect on dischargeability claim for fraud as a fiduciary, because elements of dischargeability claim were more demanding than state court claim); *In re* Graham, 973 F.2d 1089 (3d Cir. 1992) (tax court consent decree stating that fraud issue was "uncontested" not given collateral estoppel effect when tax court did not make specific fraud finding); *In re* Lewis, 271 B.R. 877 (B.A.P. 10th Cir. 2002) (state disciplinary proceeding against attorney did not establish all of the elements of fraud); Zohlman v. Zoldan, 226 B.R. 767 (S.D.N.Y. 1998) (prior judgment in state court did not preclude debtor from litigating elements of fiduciary defalcation under § 523).

594 *In re* Palmer, 207 F.3d 566 (9th Cir. 2000) (findings in adverse judgment of Tax Court based on facts deemed admitted because debtor did not respond to allegations did not have preclusive effect); *In re* Pancake, 106 F.3d 1242 (5th Cir. 1997) (summary judgment entered after defendant's answer was stricken did not have preclusive effect under Texas law because there was no showing that a hearing to determine facts had been held); *In re* Silva, 190 B.R. 889 (B.A.P. 9th Cir. 1995) (default judgment not given collateral estoppel effect when entered after unopposed summary judgment motion); Stokes v. Vierra, 185 B.R. 341 (N.D. Cal. 1995) (under majority rule of Restatement (Second) of Judgments, §§ 27-29, default judgment does not meet actually litigated test; default judgment for failing to comply with discovery was not actually litigated); *In re* Pelechronis, 186 B.R. 1 (D. Mass. 1995) (default judgment not given collateral estoppel effect if debtor shows good faith excuse for allowing default to occur); Jones v. Ind. Fin. Co., 180 B.R. 531 (S.D. Ind. 1994); *In re* Trevisan, 300 B.R. 708 (Bankr. E.D. Wis. 2003) (small claims court default judgment under bad check statute not entitled to preclusive effect); *In re* Slominski, 229 B.R. 432 (Bankr. D.N.D. 1998) (default judgment finding of conversion, drafted by plaintiff's counsel, not given collateral estoppel effect); *see also In re* Young, 91 F.3d 1367 (10th Cir. 1996) (state court consent decree did not have preclusive effect on dischargeability determination because parties did not express intent that it precluded litigation of issues in bankruptcy case); *In re* Friedman, 200 B.R. 1 (Bankr. D. Mass. 1996) (debtor's plea of guilty to charge of tax evasion not given preclusive effect when debtor maintained he pled guilty to avoid incarceration, but plea could be offered as evidence of evasion); *In re* Prather, 178 B.R. 501 (Bankr. W.D. Wash. 1995) (stipulated fraud judgment not given collateral estoppel effect).

judgment has generally been held to depend on the law of the state in which it was entered.[595] Thus, some courts have given collateral estoppel effect to the facts necessary to a default judgment,[596] or to a judgment entered as a discovery sanction.[597] It is not clear whether stipulated facts can be the basis for collateral estoppel. To the extent such facts are incorporated in a judgment, courts may deem them to be the equivalent of litigated findings of fact. However, a bankruptcy court (or other court deciding issues of dischargeability) is not bound by a stipulation made prior to a bankruptcy case that a debt will not be dischargeable in bankruptcy.[598]

If collateral estoppel does not apply, a creditor must litigate the factual and legal issues in the bankruptcy court.[599] And, all courts agree that collateral estoppel can never bar introduction of evidence when any element of the nondischargeability complaint has not been previously decided.[600]

Whether a creditor can bring a claim based on a whole new cause of action on the same facts supporting a previously litigated dischargeable claim is unclear. That claim is probably barred by *res judicata* when it arises from a common nucleus of operative facts as the actually litigated claims.[601]

A different problem sometimes arises in cases in which the creditor has not yet obtained a judgment on the alleged claim. Obviously, if the claim is not valid in the first place, then the courts need not reach the dischargeability issue. Generally, this means that the court must first decide whether the debt exists,[602] and then determine whether it is dischargeable. While it is clear that bankruptcy courts have jurisdiction to do this, they will occasionally let previously filed proceedings in other courts proceed to their conclusion (at least if they are not removed to bankruptcy court).[603] If the case is tried in the bankruptcy court, then any right to jury trial the debtor has on the issue of liability is preserved and a jury may be demanded in that court.[604]

Finally, *res judicata* principles apply when a court has made a post-petition determination of whether a debt was discharged by a bankruptcy case. Except for debts made

---

595 *In re* Baylis, 217 F.3d 66 (1st Cir. 2000) (state court judgment did not have preclusive effect on issue of bad faith because under Massachusetts law a finding must have been essential to a judgment to have preclusive effect and alternative grounds for judgment not ruled upon in final appellate review were not essential to judgment); *see In re* Sweeney, 276 B.R. 186 (B.A.P. 6th Cir. 2002) (Ohio law permits default judgment to be given collateral estoppel effect only if court knows judgment was based on merits rather than a procedural default). *But see In re* Wald, 208 B.R. 516 (Bankr. N.D. Ala. 1997) (preclusive effect of default judgment should be based on federal collateral estoppel law, not state).

596 *In re* Caton, 157 F.3d 1026 (5th Cir. 1998) (default judgment entered after debtor ceased participating in lawsuit found to have collateral estoppel effect under Illinois law); *In re* Calvert, 105 F.3d 315 (6th Cir. 1997) (default judgment given preclusive effect because it would have had that effect under California law); *In re* Nourbakhsh, 67 F.3d 798 (9th Cir. 1995); *see also In re* Cantrell, 329 F.3d 1119 (9th Cir. 2003) (default judgment does not have collateral estoppel effect under California law if defendant was not personally served and had no knowledge of action; however collateral estoppel may apply if party has actual knowledge that default judgment entered and fails to take action to set it aside); *In re* Garner, 56 F.3d 677 (5th Cir. 1995) (defendant answered complaint but failed to appear for trial); *In re* Bursack, 65 F.3d 51 (6th Cir. 1995) (defendant participated in litigation but did not defend at trial); *In re* Griego, 64 F.3d 580 (10th Cir. 1995) (defendant appeared in litigation but alleged that it was not competently represented); *In re* Thompson, 262 B.R. 407 (B.A.P. 6th Cir. 2001) (magistrate's decision without final judgment not entitled to preclusive effect under Ohio law).

597 *In re* Docteroff, 133 F.3d 210 (3d Cir. 1997) (judgment entered as discovery sanction given collateral estoppel effect); *In re* Ansari, 113 F.3d 17 (4th Cir. 1997) (judgment entered as discovery sanction had collateral estoppel effect under Virginia law); *In re* Gober, 100 F.3d 1195 (5th Cir. 1996) (preclusive effect given to judgment entered as discovery sanction); *In re* Daily, 47 F.3d 365 (9th Cir. 1995); *In re* Bush, 62 F.3d 1319 (11th Cir. 1995).

598 *In re* Huang, 275 F.3d 1173 (9th Cir. 2002) (debtor not precluded from contesting dischargeability proceeding by pre-bankruptcy settlement agreement not to do so). *In re* Cole, 226 B.R. 647 (B.A.P. 9th Cir. 1998). *But see* Saler v. Saler, 217 B.R. 166 (E.D. Pa. 1998) (stipulation in earlier bankruptcy case that debt was not dischargeable given preclusive effect in later bankruptcy case); *In re* Siebert, 302 B.R. 265 (Bankr. N.D. Ohio 2003) (consent judgment in prior bankruptcy case bound debtor in later case).

599 *In re* Raynor, 922 F.2d 1146 (4th Cir. 1991); *In re* Turner, 144 B.R. 47 (Bankr. E.D. Tex. 1992); *In re* Sharp, 119 B.R. 779 (Bankr. D. Idaho 1990); *see also In re* Johns, 158 B.R. 687 (Bankr. N.D. Ohio 1993) (*nolo contendere* plea could not be admitted in support of plaintiff's dischargeability case). *But see* Meyer v. Rigdon, 36 F.3d 1375 (7th Cir. 1994) (different rules apply under § 523(a)(11) because the language of that section makes nondischargeable *any* final judgment arising from debtor's fraud or defalcation while acting as a fiduciary for a financial institution).

600 *See* Massachusetts v. Hale, 618 F.2d 143 (1st Cir. 1980); *In re* Graham, 94 B.R. 386 (Bankr. E.D. Pa. 1987) (questions as to fraud penalty on delinquent taxes not fully litigated, collateral estoppel not applied); *In re* Rambo, 5 Bankr. Ct. Dec. (LRP) 800 (Bankr. M.D. Tenn. 1979).

601 *See In re* Heckert, 272 F.3d 253 (4th Cir. 2001) (creditor could not obtain judgment granting more relief than had already been granted in state court judgment; court could only determine dischargeability of state court judgment). *But see In re* Keller, 106 B.R. 639 (B.A.P. 9th Cir. 1989) (creditor not precluded from arguing that debt was based on willful and malicious conduct where only negligence was pleaded and tried in state court proceeding).

602 Although Grogan v. Garner, 498 U.S. 279, 111 S. Ct. 654, 112 L. Ed. 2d 755 (1991) holds that the preponderance of the evidence standard is applicable to determine nondischargeability in bankruptcy, presumably if a higher evidentiary standard is applicable under state law to establish the debt, for example, a debt for fraud, that higher standard is also applicable to that question if it arises in bankruptcy court.

603 *In re* Harris, 7 B.R. 284 (Bankr. S.D. Fla. 1980).

604 28 U.S.C. § 1411. However, any jury trial may have to be conducted in the district court. *See* § 13.2.7, *supra*.

nondischargeable by sections 523(a)(2), (4), (6), or (15), state courts have concurrent jurisdiction to make dischargeability determinations. Once a state court has found a debt to be dischargeable or nondischargeable, that judgment cannot be challenged in the bankruptcy court.[605] Therefore, if a debtor is concerned that the state court may not fully comprehend the nuances of bankruptcy law, the debtor may wish to remove the proceeding to the bankruptcy court before a judgment is entered.[606]

14.5 The Protections of the Discharge

14.5.1 Effects on Discharged Claims

14.5.1.1 Definition of Claim for Discharge Purposes

With respect to the vast majority of debts discharged in bankruptcy cases, the protections of the discharge can only be described as sweeping. They extend to a wide range of debts—all debts that arose before the order for relief[607] in a chapter 7 case, except those made nondischargeable by a specific provision of title 11 or other federal law.

It is not always clear whether an obligation of a debtor is a pre-petition claim that is discharged. "Debt" is defined as any liability on a claim[608] and "claim" is very broadly defined to include any right to payment or right to an equitable remedy if such remedy gives rise to a right to payment, whether or not such right is reduced to judgment, liquidated, unliquidated, fixed, contingent, matured, unmatured, disputed, undisputed, legal, equitable, secured, or unsecured.[609]

The Supreme Court interpreted these definitions in *Ohio v. Kovacs*,[610] giving them the broad meaning intended by Congress. In *Kovacs*, an injunctive order, which as a practical matter could only be complied with through the pay-

ment of money, was found to be a dischargeable claim.[611] In other cases, however, there may still be disputes as to what constitutes a debt that may be discharged. For example, advances against retirement accounts, often recouped from an employees' wages may be considered to be use of the employee's own money, so that recoupment of wages can continue.[612] In contrast, condominium assessments which arise post-petition have been held to be discharged, because they are contingent, unmatured debts at the time of filing.[613] Courts have differed regarding whether the right to enforce a covenant not to compete is a claim that is dischargeable.[614]

Other disputes arise in numerous contexts in which the debtor's pre-petition conduct has consequences that are undiscovered, or even undiscoverable, until after a petition is filed or a case is closed. Many courts have concluded that such circumstances create cognizable claims in bankruptcy.[615] Whether they are discharged, however, may de-

---

611 *Id.*

612 *See* New York City Employees Retirement Sys. v. Villarie, 648 F.2d 810 (2d Cir. 1981); *In re* Scott, 142 B.R. 126 (Bankr. E.D. Va. 1992) (debtor who borrowed from his pension plan borrowed only from himself and no "debt" existed). These cases should be considered overruled by Johnson v. Home State Bank, 501 U.S. 78, 111 S. Ct. 2150, 115 L. Ed. 2d 66 (1991), because they relied on the principle that the debtor did not have personal liability. *See also In re* B & L Oil Co., 782 F.2d 155 (10th Cir. 1986) (creditor may recoup overpayments made to debtor prior to filing by withholding payment for purchases made from debtor after bankruptcy). *But see In re* Buchferer, 216 B.R. 332 (Bankr. E.D.N.Y. 1997) (pension loan found to be non-recourse secured claim); Soiett v. Veteran's Administration, 92 B.R. 563 (Bankr. D. Me. 1988) (pre-petition advanced sick leave and advanced annual leave gave rise to claims against the debtor which were discharged).

613 *In re* Rosteck, 899 F.2d 694 (7th Cir. 1990); *In re* Elias, 98 B.R. 332 (N.D. Ill. 1989) (debtor entitled to award of attorney fees for enforcing discharge injunction); *In re* Wasp, 137 B.R. 71 (Bankr. M.D. Fla. 1992) (action brought by home owners association to collect fees under pre-petition agreement which had been unmatured at time of bankruptcy filing constituted attempt to collect debt that was discharged); *In re* Turner, 101 B.R. 751 (Bankr. D. Utah 1989). *But see In re* Raymond, 129 B.R. 354 (Bankr. S.D.N.Y. 1991) (post-petition condominium assessments not discharged); *In re* Ryan, 100 B.R. 411 (Bankr. N.D. Ill. 1989) (in order to obtain discharge of condominium assessments debtor must relinquish ownership and possession of unit within reasonable time after filing). Dischargeability of condominium assessments is now specifically governed by 11 U.S.C. § 523(a)(16). *See* § 14.4.3.15, *supra.*

614 *Compare In re* Ward, 194 B.R. 703 (Bankr. D. Mass. 1996) (covenant gives right to dischargeable claim) *with* Kennedy v. Medicap Pharmacies, 267 F.3d 493 (6th Cir. 2001) (covenant not to compete was not a dischargeable claim) *and In re* Hirschorn, 156 B.R. 379 (Bankr. E.D.N.Y. 1993) (covenant is equitable remedy not within the scope of definition of claim).

615 *E.g., In re* Parker, 313 F.3d 1267 (9th Cir. 2002) (legal malpractice claim arose when conduct occurred); Grady v. A.H. Robbins Co., 839 F.2d 198 (4th Cir. 1988) (Dalkon Shield inserted prior to manufacturer's bankruptcy gave rise to a claim subject to the automatic stay, even though no injury was manifested until after the bankruptcy was filed); *see* § 14.4.3.2.4,

---

605 *In re* Swate, 99 F.3d 1282 (5th Cir. 1996) (state court determination that support debt was nondischargeable after debtor's first bankruptcy case given *res judicata* effect in second bankruptcy case); *In re* Whitten, 192 B.R. 10 (Bankr. D. Mass. 1996) (debtor bound by state court determination that condominium fees were not discharged); *see also In re* Goetzman, 91 F.3d 1173 (9th Cir. 1996) (Rooker-Feldman doctrine prevents relitigation of questions related to discharge resolved by state court foreclosure judgment).

606 Removal of cases to bankruptcy court is discussed at § 13.4.1, *supra.*

607 The order for relief occurs upon the filing of a voluntary case. 11 U.S.C. § 301. When a case is converted from chapter 7 to chapter 13 or vice-versa, the conversion constitutes a new order for relief under the new chapter. 11 U.S.C. § 348(b).

608 11 U.S.C. § 101(12).

609 11 U.S.C. § 101(5).

610 469 U.S. 274, 105 S. Ct. 705, 83 L. Ed. 2d 649 (1985).

pend on whether the creditor receives appropriate notice of the bankruptcy.[616]

In chapter 13, the normal discharge covers all "debts," "provided for in the plan," excepting only alimony and support, fines or restitution included in a sentence on the debtor's conviction of a crime, some student loans, some debts connected with intoxicated driving and long-term debts provided for in the plan on which the last payment is due after the last payment under the plan is due.[617] Although it is fairly clear that an unsecured debt is "provided for" even if no payment on that debt is possible in the plan,[618] it is still probably a good idea to include at least a nominal amount for all unsecured creditors in every chapter 13 plan. In chapter 13 too, there may be disputes as to what is a "debt."[619] The Supreme Court has ruled that a restitution order in a criminal case is a "debt,"[620] although Congress thereafter made most restitution debts nondischargeable by enacting section 1328(a)(3).

14.5.1.2 Elimination of Personal Liability and Protections for Property

The discharge operates to eliminate the personal liability of the debtor. It does not eliminate valid liens against the debtor's property that have not been avoided, paid, or modified during the bankruptcy.[621] Thus, a mortgage con-

tinues to be valid after a chapter 7 case, though the creditor can no longer obtain a deficiency judgment against the debtor if the property fails to satisfy the debt. And, if a chapter 13 plan provides for the creditor to retain a lien in order to comply with 11 U.S.C. § 1325(a)(5), that lien remains valid until the allowed claim is paid.

However, as discussed in an earlier chapter,[622] exempt property may not be reached after the case even by most creditors that hold nondischargeable claims. It is protected from any pre-bankruptcy "debt of the debtor," except debts for taxes, alimony and support, and those secured by a lien not voided in the bankruptcy.[623] As "debt" is defined as liability on a claim[624] and "claim against the debtor" includes claims against property of the debtor,[625] it appears that exempt property is also protected against any claim against property of the debtor except those secured by valid liens. In fact, these protections are granted to debtors even in completed cases which do not result in a discharge, because section 522(c) does not make them contingent upon a discharge being granted.

14.5.1.3 Voiding of Judgments

In both chapter 7 and chapter 13 cases, the discharge automatically voids any judgment obtained at any time to the extent such judgment is a determination of the debtor's personal liability on a discharged debt.[626] Thus, even if a creditor proceeded to judgment after the bankruptcy, that judgment would be void *ab initio*.[627] Although this means that the debtor need take no action to protect against such a judgment, the better course would be to seek relief from the judgment as early as possible, perhaps in the bankruptcy court, because even a void judgment may cause various kinds of problems for the debtor until it is stricken. If the

---

supra; see also In re Remington Rand Corp., 836 F.2d 825 (3d Cir. 1988) (creditor may have bankruptcy claim even though no cause of action has accrued on that claim). *But see* Epstein v. Official Comm. of Unsecured Creditors, 58 F.3d 1573 (11th Cir. 1995) (people who might be injured in accidents involving planes manufactured by debtor, but who had no relationship with debtor at time of case, did not hold claims); *In re* Frenville, 744 F.2d 332 (3d Cir. 1984) (absent pre-petition potential for right to payment, no claim exists).

616 *In re* Cent. R.R. Co. of N.J., 950 F.2d 887 (3d Cir. 1991) (claim not manifest until discovered or reasonable person would discover injury); *see* § 14.4.3.3, *supra; see also* City of New York v. N.Y., N.H. & H. R. R. Co., 344 U.S. 293, 73 S. Ct. 299, 97 L. Ed. 333 (1953) (due process requires that creditor be given an opportunity to file a claim prior to discharge).

617 11 U.S.C. § 1328(a). Certain other provisions making government related debts nondischargeable may also be applicable. *See* § 14.4.3.12, *supra.*

618 At least one court of appeals has held that even a plan proposing to pay nothing to unsecured creditors has "provided for" those creditors, because they have notice of the possible discharge of their debts. Lawrence Tractor Co. v. Gregory, 705 F.2d 1118 (9th Cir. 1983). Moreover, the Supreme Court has held that a debt is "provided for" if it is simply referred to or mentioned in a plan. Rake v. Wade, 508 U.S. 464, 473, 113 S. Ct. 2187, 2193, 124 L. Ed. 2d 424, 434, 435 (1993).

619 *See* 11 U.S.C. § 101(12). See discussion above.

620 Pennsylvania Dep't of Public Welfare v. Davenport, 495 U.S. 552, 110 S. Ct. 2126, 109 L. Ed. 2d 588 (1990); *see also In re* Hardenberg, 42 F.3d 986 (6th Cir. 1994) (criminal fines and court costs were debts).

621 Dewsnup v. Timm, 502 U.S. 410, 112 S. Ct. 773, 116 L. Ed. 2d 903 (1992); Chandler Bank of Lyons v. Ray, 804 F.2d 577 (10th

Cir. 1986); Fed. Deposit Ins. Corp. v. Davis, 733 F.2d 1083 (4th Cir. 1983); *see* Johnson v. Home State Bank, 501 U.S. 78, 111 S. Ct. 2150, 115 L. Ed. 2d 66 (1991).

622 *See* § 10.5, *supra.*

623 Also excepted are debts found nondischargeable under § 523(a)(4) and (6) where the liability is to an agency regulating a federal depository institution, 11 U.S.C. § 522(c)(3), and certain educational debts incurred through fraud, 11 U.S.C. § 522(c)(4).

624 11 U.S.C. § 101(12).

625 11 U.S.C. § 102(2).

626 11 U.S.C. § 524(a)(1).

627 *In re* Fernandez-Lopez, 37 B.R. 664 (B.A.P. 9th Cir. 1984) (permitting collateral attack in bankruptcy court on judgment obtained in violation of discharge); L.F. Rothschild & Co. v. Angier, 84 B.R. 274 (D. Mass. 1988); *In re* Dabrowski, 257 B.R. 394 (Bankr. S.D.N.Y 2001) (bankruptcy judge not required to give deference to judgment that was void under § 524(a)(1)); *see In re* Levy, 87 B.R. 107 (Bankr. N.D. Cal. 1988) (state court default judgment on claim that debt was not discharged is void where debt was, in actuality, discharged). *But see* Fed. Deposit Ins. Corp. v. Gulf Life Ins. Co., 737 F.2d 1513 (11th Cir. 1984) (bankruptcy defense rejected where it was pleaded but not proved).

debtor does raise the bankruptcy discharge in the state court and is unsuccessful, it may not be possible to relitigate the issue in the bankruptcy court,[628] so it is usually better to immediately seek enforcement of the discharge in the bankruptcy court, which is more likely to be familiar with the applicable law.

The provision voiding judgments is self-effectuating, and no further action is required by the debtor with respect to judgments already entered.[629] Any diligent record search to check the status of judgments should also turn up the debtor's bankruptcy, which voids all judgments against him or her, at least if all of the proceedings occurred in the same locality. Nonetheless, in some areas it is advisable and customary to notify the court of the discharge or otherwise record its existence where a judgment is recorded.

It is also important to note that the voidness of the judgment extends only to the debtor's personal liability to pay the judgment. To the extent that the judgment acts as a lien on property, that lien is not affected by the bankruptcy unless it is paid or avoided.[630] For this reason, counsel must take advantage of the opportunities in bankruptcy to avoid judgment liens[631] or otherwise to address them as secured claims.[632]

14.5.1.4 The Discharge Injunction

Section 524(a)(2) puts into effect a broad injunction against the commencement or continuation of any action, the employment of process, or any act to collect, recover, or offset any discharged debt as a personal liability of the debtor or from property of the debtor. This section was intended to cover not only legal proceedings, but also any other acts of creditors, such as dunning, harassment, withholding of further credit, threatening or instituting criminal proceedings, and the like, whether directed at the debtor or at anyone else.[633] It has been broadly construed to cover acts

that are related only indirectly to the discharged debt but that could cause harm to the debtor because of the debt's previous existence.[634] Violation of the injunction is contempt, punishable by awards of damages and attorney fees.[635]

---

sum to repay discharged prior loan violates discharge injunction); *In re* Watkins, 240 B.R. 668 (Bankr. E.D.N.Y. 1999) (awarding punitive damages and attorney fees against creditor that conditioned post-discharge loan on debtors agreeing to repay discharged debt); *In re* Mickens, 229 B.R. 114 (Bankr. W.D. Va. 1999) (awarding attorney fees against creditor that facilitated and permitted inclusion of discharged debt in new loan); *In re* Faust, 270 B.R. 310 (Bankr. M.D. Ga. 1998) (referring debtor's account to collection agency was willful violation of discharge injunction); *In re* Lafferty, 229 B.R. 707 (Bankr. N.D. Ohio 1998) (creditor violated discharge injunction by selling discharged accounts receivable without noting debtors' discharges in records sent to purchaser); *In re* Walker, 180 B.R. 834 (Bankr. W.D. La. 1995) (creditor violated injunction by not taking steps to terminate automatic deductions from its employee's wages for debt repayment); *In re* Smurzynski, 72 B.R. 368 (Bankr. N.D. Ill. 1987) (attempt to have debtor sign papers acknowledging total indebtedness in excess of amount received in current transaction); *see also* McGlynn v. Credit Store, 234 B.R. 576 (D.R.I. 1999) (discussing claims against credit card issuers for practice of selling discharged debts to purchasers who would attempt to induce debtors to open new accounts that included discharged debts); Greenwood Trust Co. v. Smith, 212 B.R. 599 (B.A.P. 8th Cir. 1997) (soliciting reaffirmation agreement by direct contact with a represented debtor violates state consumer credit legislation). *But see* Brown v. Pennsylvania State Employees Credit Union, 851 F.2d 81 (3d Cir. 1988) (credit union's letter telling debtor she would be denied future service unless she reaffirmed dischargeable debt does not violate discharge injunction); *In re* Garske, 287 B.R. 537 (B.A.P. 9th Cir. 2002) (telephone calls from secured creditor about whether debtor intended to continue payments in a ride-through jurisdiction did not violate discharge injunction). The debtor in *Brown* might have been more successful in arguing that the credit union was a governmental unit prohibited from discriminating by § 525, an argument she abandoned below. *See In re* Trusko, 212 B.R. 819 (Bankr. D. Md. 1997) (credit union a governmental unit for purposes of a different Code section).

628   *In re* Ferren, 203 F.3d 559 (8th Cir. 2000) (Rooker-Feldman doctrine prohibited bankruptcy court from reviewing state court's determination that creditor had not violated discharge injunction); *cf. In re* Pavelich, 229 B.R. 777 (B.A.P. 9th Cir. 1999) (Rooker-Feldman doctrine did not prevent enforcement of discharge injunction).

629   *See In re* Rourke, 288 B.R. 50 (Bankr. E.D.N.Y. 2003) (because pre-petition judgments were voided by discharge, they could not become liens on property acquired after bankruptcy petition).

630   For a discussion of leases in chapter 13, see § 12.9, *supra.*

631   *See* § 10.4.2.3, *supra.*

632   *See* Ch. 11, *supra.*

633   S. Rep. No. 95-989, at 80 (1978); H.R. Rep. No. 95-595, at 366 (1977); *see In re* Simon, 153 F.3d 991 (9th Cir. 1998) (injunction applied to acts to collect from debtor's non-estate property in a foreign country); *In re* Andrus, 189 B.R. 413 (N.D. Ill. 1995) (creditor found in contempt for erecting signs in his yard intended to pressure debtor into paying discharged debt, notwithstanding creditor's argument that conduct was protected by First Amendment); Van Meter v. Am. State Bank, 89 B.R. 32 (W.D. Ark. 1988) (requiring former debtor to borrow additional

634   *See In re* Warren, 7 B.R. 201 (Bankr. N.D. Ala. 1980) (garnishment proceeding based on discharged debt, where employer had not answered and thus itself became liable for a debt, was enjoined because likely effect of its continuation would be firing of debtor). *But see* Hawxhurst v. Pettibone Corp., 40 F.3d 175 (7th Cir. 1994) (discharge injunction did not prevent creditor from proceeding against debtor's insurers); *In re* Siragusa, 27 F.3d 406 (9th Cir. 1994) (discharge did not prevent state court from modifying alimony order based upon changed circumstances including the discharge of property settlement obligation); *In re* Walker, 927 F.2d 1138 (10th Cir. 1991) (creditor granted relief from discharge injunction to collect debt from state real estate recovery fund; provision allowing recovery fund to suspend debtor's license found unenforceable based on § 525(a)); *In re* Jet Fla. Sys., 883 F.2d 970 (11th Cir. 1989) (creditor granted relief from discharge injunction to obtain judgment in defamation case which would be borne by debtor's insurer and have little or no effect on debtor).

635   *In re* Hardy, 97 F.3d 1384 (11th Cir. 1996) (IRS violation of discharge injunction would be contempt and debtor could seek damages and fees, but damages and fees were limited by

Attempts to collect a discharged debt may also violate other statutes, such as the Fair Debt Collection Practices Act (FDCPA),[636] state debt collection regulations[637] or state tort law.[638]

However, this section does not bar the enforcement of valid security interests against property of the debtor if they have not been paid, modified, or avoided in the bank-

ruptcy.[639] These security interests are limited to property acquired before the bankruptcy regardless of any clause that would otherwise cover after-acquired property.[640] For the same reason, the discharge does not affect other property interests of third parties, such as a portion of the debtor's pension awarded to a former spouse in pre-bankruptcy divorce proceedings.[641] Similarly, many courts have held that the discharge injunction does not bar a suit that is only nominally against the debtor if that suit really seeks to recover from an insurance company, provided no recovery is sought from the debtor.[642]

For debtors with interests in community property, the discharge is even broader; it covers creditors' pre-bankruptcy claims against any after-acquired community property that would have been included in the bankruptcy estate, even if only one spouse has filed a bankruptcy petition.[643]

§ 106(a)); United States v. Kolb, 161 B.R. 30 (N.D. Ill. 1993) (attorney fees awarded against Internal Revenue Service in action to remedy setoff which violated discharge injunction); *In re* Goodfellow, 298 B.R. 358 (Bankr. N.D. Iowa 2003) (letters, telephone calls, and continued reporting of debt to credit reporting agency sanctioned by $5000.00 actual damages and $5000.00 punitive damages); *In re* Harbour Oaks Dev. Corp., 228 B.R. 801 (Bankr. M.D. Fla. 1999) (continuation of foreclosure action in violation of discharge constitutes civil contempt); *In re* Driggers, 204 B.R. 70 (Bankr. N.D. Fla. 1996) (debtors awarded fees and costs after credit card company continued to send bills and dunning letters for discharged debt, plus $500.00 for each future violation); *In re* Thibodaux, 201 B.R. 827 (Bankr. N.D. Ala. 1996) (debtor awarded damages, attorney fees and costs for IRS freezing of post-petition tax refunds to collect discharged taxes); *In re* Lovato, 203 B.R. 747 (Bankr. D. Wyo. 1996) (debtor awarded attorney fees and costs for IRS freezing of post-petition tax refunds to collect discharged taxes); *In re* Kiker, 98 B.R. 103 (Bankr. N.D. Ga. 1988) (IRS' continued efforts to collect discharged tax debt warranted award of attorney fees and costs); *In re* Roush, 88 B.R. 163 (Bankr. S.D. Ohio 1988) (actual damages and attorney fees where creditor did not maintain procedures adequate to prevent collection efforts on discharged debts); Behrens v. Woodhaven Ass'n, 87 B.R. 971 (Bankr. N.D. Ill. 1988) (decision to sue debtors after discharge of pre-petition contract obligation constitutes contempt of court); *In re* Barbour, 77 B.R. 530 (Bankr. E.D.N.C. 1987). See also discussion of contempt sanctions in § 9.6, *supra. But see In re* Grewe, 4 F.3d 299 (4th Cir. 1993) (attorney fees could not be awarded under 26 U.S.C. § 7430(a) in successful action against Internal Revenue Service for violation of discharge injunction because debtors had failed to exhaust administrative remedies).

636   15 U.S.C. §§ 1692e(2)(A)(4), (5), (10), 1692k; *see also* Randolph v. IMBS, Inc., 368 F.3d 726 (7th Cir. 2004) (no irreconcilable conflict exists between FDCPA and Bankruptcy Code, so both statutes can be enforced simultaneously); Molloy v. Primus Auto. Fin. Services, 247 B.R. 804 (C.D. Cal. 2000) (FDCPA claim not preempted by Bankruptcy Code). *See generally* National Consumer Law Center, Fair Debt Collection §§ 5.5.4, 5.5.7, 5.5.8, 5.5.13 (5th ed. 2004).

637   *See also* Sears, Roebuck & Co. v. O'Brien, 178 F.3d 962 (8th Cir. 1999) (Sears violated the Iowa Consumer Credit Code prohibiting creditor contact with a debtor represented by counsel by sending a copy of a letter soliciting a reaffirmation agreement directly to the debtor); Sturm v. Providian Nat. Bank, 242 B.R. 599 (S.D. W. Va. 1999) (creditor violated West Virginia debt collection statute); *In re* Faust, 270 B.R. 310 (Bankr. M.D. Ga. 1998) (creditor violated discharge injunction; debt collector violated FDCPA, but not discharge injunction). *See generally* National Consumer Law Center, Fair Debt Collection § 11.2 (5th ed. 2004).

638   Miele v. Sid Bailey, Inc., 192 B.R. 611 (S.D.N.Y. 1996) (one thousand dollars in damages under FDCPA and $60,000.00 in damages under state tort law awarded against debt collector who repeatedly attempted to collect discharged debt).

639   *See, e.g., In re* Dinatale, 235 B.R. 569 (Bankr. D. Md. 1999) (IRS did not violate discharge injunction by renewing tax lien or contacting debtor about lien, but did violate injunction by attempting to garnish debtor's wages); *In re* Pendlebury, 94 B.R. 120 (Bankr. E.D. Tenn. 1988). However, a court may look behind an action that purports to be one to enforce a security interest to determine whether the true purpose is to collect the debt as a personal liability. Houghton v. Foremost Fin. Services, 724 F.2d 112 (10th Cir. 1983); *In re* Braun, 152 B.R. 466 (N.D. Ohio 1993) (creditor's post-petition suit against debtor violated discharge injunction and attorney held in contempt despite creditor's claim that it sought only damages for post-petition conversion of collateral where suit did not seek to obtain property or its value, but rather sought precise amount previously owed on note); *In re* Evans, 289 B.R. 813 (Bankr. E.D. Va. 2002) (replevin action brought after bank notified that car had been sold to satisfy storage lien and which sought damages and attorney fees was attempt to circumvent discharge injunction); *see also In re* Ramirez, 280 B.R. 252 (C.D. Cal. 2002) (when debtor retained automobile by continuing payments without reaffirmation, creditor did not violate discharge by mailing informational billing statements that were not intended to harass or coerce debtor into making involuntary payments). The mutual setoff of preexisting debts may also still be allowed, because it is considered similar to a security interest under 11 U.S.C. § 553. See § 10.4.2.6.7, *supra*, for a discussion of setoffs. Likewise, true recoupment by an entity that owes money to the debtor is allowed. *See In re* Madigan, 270 B.R. 749 (B.A.P. 9th Cir. 2001) (long-term disability insurer did not have a right to recoupment because discharged overpayment did not arise from same transaction or occurrence as debtor's current claim).

640   11 U.S.C. § 552.

641   Bush v. Taylor, 912 F.2d 989 (8th Cir. 1990) (*en banc*); *In re* Chandler, 805 F.2d 555 (5th Cir. 1986); *In re* Teichman, 774 F.2d 1395 (9th Cir. 1985).

642   *In re* Edgeworth, 993 F.2d 51 (5th Cir. 1993); *In re* Hendrix, 986 F.2d 195 (7th Cir. 1993); Green v. Welsh, 956 F.2d 30 (2d Cir. 1992). *Contra In re* White Motor Credit, 761 F.2d 270 (6th Cir. 1985). But see also cases cited above.

643   11 U.S.C. § 524(c); *In re* Strickland, 153 B.R. 909 (Bankr. D.N.M. 1993) (discharge acted as injunction against any act to collect discharged debt incurred by non-debtor spouse from present or future New Mexico community property, but did not prevent collection from non-debtor spouse's separate property). Generally, section 541(a)(2) provides that community property

The only exceptions to this broad rule are claims excepted from discharge in the debtor spouse's case and claims which would not have been discharged if the non-debtor spouse had filed.[644] Of course, these provisions also mean that all creditors of both spouses should be listed in the schedules to prevent nondischargeability problems under section 523(a)(3), which pertains to unlisted creditors.[645]

Although some courts have held otherwise, the discharge provisions should also give rise to an implied right of action for damages.[646] Unlike claims for contempt, this uniform order need not be enforced by a contempt proceeding in the court that issued it, because debtors are enforcing a statutory right rather than a unique order that requires interpretation by its maker. In addition, there is ample authority to enforce the discharge injunction by requiring disgorgement and other equitable remedies under 11 U.S.C. § 105(a).[647]

14.5.2 Reaffirmation and Security Interests Which Survive Bankruptcy

14.5.2.1 Requirements for Reaffirmation

Some of the most persistent problems under the previous Bankruptcy Act were those arising through the reaffirmation of debts by consumer debtors. By using a variety of coercive levers, such as threats of repossession, collection activities directed at cosigners, and refusal to lend more money without reaffirmation, creditors routinely lured debtors into giving up the protections of their bankruptcy discharges by making new and binding promises to pay debts that had been discharged.[648]

This problem was recognized by both the Bankruptcy Commission, which proposed a total bar against reaffirmation agreements,[649] and Congress.[650] Although the Code does not completely bar reaffirmation agreements, it does restrict them significantly under the theory that reaffirmation is rarely a wise step for the debtor.[651]

Section 524(c) sets forth a number of requirements that must be followed before a reaffirmation is binding.[652] First, there must be an agreement between the debtor and the creditor which is enforceable under applicable non-bankruptcy law. That agreement in most cases is essentially a contract to reaffirm, but the requirements of the Code also apply to other post-petition contracts which effectively constitute a renewed obligation to pay a pre-petition debt.[653] Without an agreement there can be no reaffirmation; in such a case neither the debtor nor the creditor may seek court approval of reaffirmation.[654] The agreement may alter the

---

comes into the bankruptcy estate, even if only one spouse files, if it is under the sole, equal, or joint management and control of the debtor, or to the extent it is liable for a claim against the debtor or both a claim against the debtor and a claim against the debtor's spouse. This means all community property in Arizona, Idaho and New Mexico. *See generally* Henry J. Sommer & Margaret Doe McGarity, Collier Family Law and the Bankruptcy Code, Ch. 4; Pedlar, *Community Property and the Bankruptcy Reform Act of 1978*, 11 St. Mary's L.J. 349 (1979).

644 11 U.S.C. § 524(a)(3), (b). A determination that an objection to the discharge of a non-debtor spouse would have been sustained must be sought by the creditor within the time limits for objecting to the debtor spouse's discharge, unless the non-debtor spouse has previously been denied a discharge within six years. 11 U.S.C. § 524(a)(3), (b); *see In re* Smith, 140 B.R. 904 (Bankr. D.N.M. 1992) (if wrongdoing spouse is in chapter 13 at time of other spouse's chapter 7 case, creditor may only proceed against community property after dismissal of chapter 13 case if it has timely sought a determination of dischargeability as to wrongdoing spouse in innocent spouse's chapter 7 case).

645 *See* § 14.5.5.7, *infra*.

646 *See* § 14.5.5.7, *infra*.

647 *In re* Mickens, 229 B.R. 114 (Bankr. W.D. Va. 1999); *In re* Vazquez, 221 B.R. 222 (Bankr. N.D. Ill. 1998) (actual and punitive damages awarded pursuant to § 105); *see* § 14.5.5.7, *infra. But see* Walls v. Wells Fargo Bank, 276 F.3d 502 (9th Cir. 2002).

648 *See* Butler Consumer Discount Co. v. Cain, 50 B.R. 388 (W.D. Pa. 1985) (new loan after bankruptcy which included prior indebtedness was a reaffirmation); § 14.5.1, *supra*.

649 Comm'n on the Bankr. Laws of the U.S., Commission Report, pt. I at 177, pt. II at 130.

650 H.R. Rep. No. 95-595, at 162–164 (1977).

651 See discussion of advisability of reaffirmation in Chapter 8, *supra*.

652 *See In re* Esposito, 154 B.R. 1011 (Bankr. N.D. Ga. 1993) (creditor violated stay by repossessing property in reliance on reaffirmation agreement negotiated by pro se debtor that was not approved by the court).

653 *In re* Lopez, 345 F.3d 701 (9th Cir. 2002) ("asset retention agreement" which required debtors to pay discharged debt was void reaffirmation); Bennett v. Renwick, 298 F.3d 1059 (9th Cir. 2002) (state court settlement agreement requiring repayment of discharged debt was unenforceable reaffirmation regardless of whether new consideration had been provided); *In re* Getzoff, 180 B.R. 572 (B.A.P. 9th Cir. 1995) (new guaranty of corporate debt by principal who had obtained discharge after prior guaranty was invalid reaffirmation); *In re* Zarro, 268 B.R. 715 (Bankr. S.D.N.Y. 2001) (post-petition settlement agreement that included reaffirmation of debt was unenforceable and judgment based on agreement was void); *In re* Smith, 224 B.R. 388 (Bankr. N.D. Ill. 1998) (addition of discharged debt after discharge to new loan debt constituted invalid reaffirmation); *In re* Artzt, 145 B.R. 866 (Bankr. E.D. Tex. 1992) (absent consideration, note renewing dischargeable debt after bankruptcy filed is an invalid reaffirmation); Schneider v. Curry, 584 So. 2d 86 (Fla. Dist. Ct. App. 1991) (post-petition contract where only consideration is debtor's pre-petition debt found to be invalid reaffirmation). *But see* DuBois v. Ford Motor Credit Co., 276 F.3d 1019 (8th Cir. 2002) (creditor did not violate discharge injunction when debtors voluntarily entered into and paid new car lease that included excess usage charges from previous lease that had been discharged without any coercion by creditor; court did not address question of whether new lease was a void reaffirmation).

654 *In re* Jamo, 283 F.3d 392 (1st Cir. 2002) (creditor cannot be required to agree to reaffirmation on terms to which it does not agree); *In re* Turner, 156 F.3d 713 (7th Cir. 1998) (reaffirmation

terms of the original contract, either in favor of the debtor or the creditor.[655] Only the debtor may actually apply to the court for approval of the reaffirmation, when that is still necessary.[656]

The reaffirmation agreement must be made prior to the discharge. By the terms of 11 U.S.C. § 524(c), a reaffirmation agreement is not enforceable unless entered into before the discharge[657] and unless the court at the discharge hearing, or the attorney who negotiated the agreement for the debtor,[658] has informed the debtor of the right not to enter into the agreement and of the legal effects of the agreement and any default thereunder.[659] Once the discharge has been granted, no reaffirmation is possible,[660] and the discharge may not be revoked to provide for one.[661]

In addition, several other requirements for an enforceable reaffirmation agreement were added by the 1984 and 1994 amendments. The agreement must contain a clear and conspicuous statement advising the debtor that the agreement may be rescinded at any time prior to the discharge or within sixty days after the agreement is filed with the court, whichever is later, by giving notice to the creditor.[662] The agreement must also clearly and conspicuously state that the agreement is not required by bankruptcy law, by any other law or by any other agreement (except for another valid reaffirmation agreement).[663] The agreement must then be filed with the court.[664] And the agreement must not have been rescinded during the time permitted.[665]

---

agreements not valid without creditors' signatures); *In re* Casenove, 306 B.R. 367 (Bankr. M.D. Fla. 2004) (creditor cannot be forced to accept reaffirmation of only portion of secured debt covered by cross-collateralization clause); *In re* Vinson, 5 B.R. 32 (Bankr. N.D. Ga. 1980) (debtor may not unilaterally reaffirm); *In re* Breckenridge, 3 B.R. 141 (Bankr. N.D. Ohio 1980) (there is no agreement to approve if debtors change their minds prior to discharge hearing).

655 *In re* Schott, 282 B.R. 1 (B.A.P. 10th Cir. 2002).

656 *In re* Carlos, 215 B.R. 52 (Bankr. C.D. Cal. 1997); *In re* Newsome, 3 B.R. 626 (Bankr. W.D. Va. 1980); *see also In re* Parker, 193 B.R. 525 (B.A.P. 9th Cir. 1996) (creditor did not have standing to appeal bankruptcy court's disapproval of reaffirmation agreement), *aff'd*, 139 F.3d 668 (9th Cir. 1998).

657 11 U.S.C. § 524(c)(1); *In re* Collins, 243 B.R. 217 (Bankr. D. Conn. 2000) (agreement not made until signed by debtor); *In re* Whitmer, 142 B.R. 811 (Bankr. S.D. Ohio 1992); *In re* Eccleston, 70 B.R. 210 (Bankr. N.D.N.Y. 1986).

658 The 1994 amendments to the Code eliminated the requirement of a discharge hearing in cases where an attorney negotiated a reaffirmation agreement on behalf of the debtor, provided the attorney certifies that the attorney fully advised the debtor of the legal effect and consequences of reaffirmation and of a default under the agreement. 11 U.S.C. § 524(c)(3)(C).

659 11 U.S.C. § 524(c)(5); *In re* Roth, 43 B.R. 484 (N.D. Ill. 1984); *see* Arnhold v. Kyrus, 851 F.2d 738 (4th Cir. 1988) (absence of required admonishments by court invalidates reaffirmation); *In re* Johnson, 148 B.R. 532 (Bankr. N.D. Ill. 1992) (reaffirmation invalid where debtor did not attend discharge hearing and agreement did not advise debtor of rescission rights); *In re* Fisher, 113 B.R. 714 (Bankr. N.D. Okla. 1990) (debtor's failure to attend reaffirmation hearing rendered reaffirmation agreement for debt secured by car unenforceable; therefore, debt was discharged and monies collected by creditor had to be turned over to trustee in subsequent chapter 13 case); *In re* Saeger, 119 B.R. 184 (Bankr. D. Minn. 1990) (reaffirmation agreement not enforceable where no discharge hearing was requested or held); *In re* Churchill, 89 B.R. 878 (Bankr. D. Colo. 1988) (reaffirmation rescindable until after hearing at which court advises debtor of consequences). *But see In re* Sweet, 954 F.2d 610 (10th Cir. 1992) (reaffirmation agreement valid despite debtors' failure to attend reaffirmation hearing where debtors did not claim they did not know about hearing and where hearing occurred more than 60 days after agreement was signed so that debtors no longer had right to rescind agreement and thus hearing could not have affected their obligations); *In re* Richardson, 102 B.R. 254 (Bankr. M.D. Fla. 1989) (although no hearing was held, the debtor is estopped from denying validity of reaffirmation agreement where creditor relied on agreement by not filing timely complaint to determine dischargeability).

660 *In re* Brown, 220 B.R. 101 (Bankr. C.D. Cal. 1998) (debtor's post-bankruptcy agreement to pay creditor in return for forbearance in repossessing necklace was prohibited reaffirmation); *In re* Arnold, 206 B.R. 560 (Bankr. N.D. Ala. 1997) (debtor's post-bankruptcy agreement to pay debt in exchange for promise not to garnish wife's wages was not enforceable even though there was consideration for agreement); *In re* Coots, 4 B.R. 281 (Bankr. S.D. Ohio 1980).

661 *In re* McQuality, 5 B.R. 302 (Bankr. S.D. Ohio 1980). *But see In re* Eccleston, 70 B.R. 210 (Bankr. N.D.N.Y. 1986) (discharge would be vacated only upon showing of explanation for failure to obtain approval of reaffirmation prior to discharge); *In re* Solomon, 15 B.R. 105 (Bankr. E.D. Pa. 1981) (in light of special equities raised, discharge vacated to allow reaffirmation three days after discharge hearing). *See generally* § 14.3, *supra*.

662 11 U.S.C. § 524(c)(2); *see In re* Minor, 115 B.R. 690 (D. Colo. 1990) (when debtor agreed to settle state court action by waiving dischargeability of debt, waiver not a valid reaffirmation where Code's detailed requirements were not met); *In re* Smyth, 277 B.R. 353 (Bankr. N.D. Ohio 2001) (notice of right to rescind inadequate because it did not provide sufficient information on how to rescind); *In re* Roberts, 154 B.R. 967 (Bankr. D. Neb. 1993) (reaffirmation agreement not containing conspicuous language notifying debtors of right to rescind was not valid). *But see In re* Bassett, 285 F.3d 882 (9th Cir. 2002), *cert. denied*, 537 U.S. 1002 (2002). The notice to the debtor of the right to rescind cannot be qualified by language in the agreement which purports to give the creditor the right to keep any payments made pursuant to the agreement before rescission. *In re* Wiley, 224 B.R. 58 (Bankr. N.D. Ill. 1998), *vacated on other grounds*, 237 B.R. 677 (Bankr. N.D. Ill. 1999). A reaffirmation agreement containing such language should be found invalid as not having properly given notice of the right to rescind. Similarly, a reaffirmation agreement on one debt cannot provide that rescission of the agreement rescinds agreements on other debts. *In re* Ireland, 241 B.R. 539 (Bankr. E.D. Mich. 1999).

663 11 U.S.C. § 524(c)(2)(B); *see In re* Noble, 182 B.R. 854 (Bankr. W.D. Wash. 1995) (statement in same type face, size and format as bulk of agreement was not clear and conspicuous).

664 11 U.S.C. § 524(c)(3); *see In re* Davis, 273 B.R. 152 (Bankr. S.D. Ohio 2001) (reopening case for filing of agreement because agreement need not be filed before discharge).

665 11 U.S.C. § 524(c)(4); *see In re* McAuliffe, 180 B.R. 336 (Bankr. D. Me. 1995) (debtor who rescinded reaffirmation entitled to return of all payments to the mortgage company made under the agreement, but had to pay compensation for continued

Finally, in all debt reaffirmations, there are two alternative protective requirements. If an attorney has negotiated the reaffirmation, the agreement filed with the court must be accompanied by the attorney's affidavit that the reaffirmation represents a fully informed and voluntary agreement by the debtor and will not impose an undue hardship on the debtor or the debtor's dependents.[666] The affidavit must also affirm that the attorney advised the debtor of the legal effect and consequences of the agreement and of any default under the agreement.[667]

Because a creditor seeking a reaffirmation is attempting to collect a debt, compliance with state and federal debt collection regulations is also required.[668]

If the agreement was not negotiated by an attorney, the court must approve the agreement as not imposing an undue hardship on the debtor or the debtor's dependents and as being in the debtor's best interests.[669] The only exception to this rule is for reaffirmations of consumer debts secured by real property, to the extent they are secured by that property.[670] It is not clear whether this exception applies in cases in which the agreement is negotiated by an attorney, because the exception appears only in the subsection pertaining to reaffirmations not negotiated by an attorney. The language of section 524(c)(3) suggests that, even if the debt is secured by real property, an attorney for a debtor cannot negotiate a reaffirmation that imposes an undue hardship on the debtor or a dependent of the debtor.

In a number of major cases, courts have found that many creditors had a longstanding practice of obtaining reaffirmation agreements without filing them with the court.[671] This practice rendered the reaffirmations invalid because the agreements fail to meet the requirements of section 524(c)(3).[672] Collection based on such agreements violates the discharge injunction.[673] Other statutory remedies may be available as well.[674]

Class actions against retailers including Sears, May Department Stores, Montgomery Ward and the Federated Department stores have been settled so that money paid on illegal reaffirmation has been repaid to consumers with interest.[675] Some of the settlements also provided for compensatory or punitive damages. For the most part, the settlements were self-executing so that consumers received payments automatically. However, in the case of illegal reaffirmation agreements which are many years old (most of the settlements use 1991 or 1992 as the cut-off date), consumers may need to make affirmative claims as pending cases are resolved. Advocates may wish to let their clients know about the potential for settlement payments, particularly in older cases and whenever there has been an address change which makes it unlikely that the retailer will be able to find clients to mail them their checks.

Abusive reaffirmation procedures remain common. These practices undermine the fresh start and should be resisted whenever possible.[676] Some retailers have responded to court hostility to their overly aggressive reaffirmation tactics, by instead insisting that consumers redeem personal property that is subject to a security interest. As the personal property involved would have little or no value if it were repossessed, the redemption may be an unwise and expen-

---

use of residence during period reaffirmation was in effect); *In re* Davis, 106 B.R. 701 (Bankr. S.D. Ala. 1989) (failure to give creditor notice of intent to rescind reaffirmation agreement within sixty days precluded such rescission). *But see In re* Booth, 242 B.R. 912 (B.A.P. 6th Cir. 2000) (erroneously holding that, although oral rescission normally would be sufficient under section 524(c), agreement valid even though it contained requirement that rescission be in writing).

666 11 U.S.C. § 524(c)(3); *See In re* Adams, 229 B.R. 312 (Bankr. S.D.N.Y. 1999) (unsworn declaration was not a declaration and therefore reaffirmation was void).

667 11 U.S.C. § 524(c)(3).

668 *See* Sears, Roebuck & Co. v. O'Brien, 178 F.3d 962 (8th Cir. 1999); Greenwood Trust Co. v. Smith, 212 B.R. 599 (B.A.P. 8th Cir. 1997) (soliciting reaffirmation agreement by direct contact with a represented debtor violates state debt collection legislation); *see also In re* Machnic, 271 B.R. 789 (Bankr. S.D. W.Va. 2002) (credit card issuer violated state consumer protection law by asking in dischargeability proceeding for costs and attorney fees that were not owed under state law). *See generally* National Consumer Law Center, Fair Debt Collection (5th ed. 2004).

669 11 U.S.C. § 524(c)(6); *see In re* Brown, 95 B.R. 35 (Bankr. E.D. Va. 1989) (approval of reaffirmation agreement denied because creditor had threatened conduct which would violate the Code's antidiscrimination provision). Where the debtor is represented by counsel, the court is less likely to interject itself into these issues. *See In re* Pendlebury, 94 B.R. 120 (Bankr. E.D. Tenn. 1988).

670 It is unclear whether a creditor has a security interest in real property for this purpose if prior liens equal or exceed the value of the property so the creditor is in reality totally under-secured.

671 *See In re* Latanowich, 207 B.R. 326, 336 (Bankr. D. Mass. 1997).

672 *In re* Gardner, 57 B.R. 609 (Bankr. D. Me. 1986) ("An agreement to reaffirm an otherwise dischargeable debt will be binding only if it is made in compliance with section 524(c) and (d)."); *In re* Hovestadt, 193 B.R. 382, 386 (Bankr. D. Mass. 1996); *accord In re* Daily, 47 F.3d 365, 367 (9th Cir. 1995); *In re* Getzoff, 180 B.R. 572, 574, 575 (B.A.P. 9th Cir. 1995); *In re* Bowling, 116 B.R. 659, 664 (Bankr. S.D. Ind. 1990).

673 *In re* Latanowich, 207 B.R. 326, 336 (Bankr. D. Mass. 1997); *In re* Vazquez, 221 B.R. 222 (Bankr. N.D. Ill. 1998) (creditor and attorney for creditor sanctioned for collection actions on debt for which reaffirmation agreement never filed); *In re* Bowling, 116 B.R. 659, 664 (Bankr. S.D. Ind. 1990).

674 *See* § 14.5.1.4, *supra.* Unfair Trade Practice Laws are also implicated. National Consumer Law Center, Unfair and Deceptive Acts and Practices (5th ed. 2001 and Supp.).

675 *See* Mohl, *Sears Admits Missteps in Collecting on Debts*, The Boston Globe, Apr. 10, 1997, at A1. Several cases against major creditors are still pending based on appellate proceedings (in the First, Sixth, Seventh and Ninth Circuits) concerning the availability of a class-wide relief and private remedies under sections 524 and 105. *See* § 14.5.5.7, *infra.*

676 *See generally Abusive Creditor Reaffirmation Practices Require Strong Response*, 15 NCLC REPORTS *Bankruptcy and Foreclosures Ed.* 17 (Mar./Apr. 1997).

sive means for a debtor to retain the property. Creditors that encourage debtors to make this unwise choice now use the redemption process to avoid the procedural requirements and court oversight necessary to obtain a valid reaffirmation.[677] Several courts have asserted authority to review and reject redemption agreements that are unfair to a debtor.[678] Other creditors have attempted to condition reaffirmation of a secured debt on reaffirmation of an unrelated unsecured debt. Such coercive tactics may go beyond the consensual negotiation of a reaffirmation agreement permitted by the automatic stay.[679]

14.5.2.2 The Undue Hardship and Best Interests Tests

Because the tests for approval of reaffirmation of consumer debts not secured by real property were new, the courts had to determine what circumstances are sufficient to satisfy them. To do this evaluation, they looked to a number of factors.

Principally, courts have sought to determine the debtor's reasons for wanting to reaffirm. If the debtor seeks only to satisfy a "moral obligation" or to protect a cosigner, courts have generally found that reaffirmation is not in the debtor's best interests.[680] Reaffirmation agreements in which the only benefit to the debtors is a small amount of new credit have been found to be against the debtors' best interests.[681] Similarly, a reaffirmation coerced under the threat of a

nondischargeability proceeding has been found to be in bad faith.[682] The possibility of undisclosed or unfair pressure from creditors, cosigners, and others has weighed heavily in these cases, and the courts have pointed out that the absence of reaffirmation does not prevent the debtor from voluntarily making whatever payments he or she chooses.[683] It only serves to prevent the debtor from being bound by an agreement to pay should he or she become unable or unwilling to pay.

Cases in which debts are secured by the debtor's property have presented more difficult problems.[684] First, courts have often looked to whether the property was a necessity for the debtor and whether reaffirmation was necessary in order to keep the property.[685] In one case, reaffirmation was allowed on a debt secured by vehicles necessary for the debtor's employment, but denied as to a debt secured by an expensive television.[686] Even with debts secured by necessary property, courts have looked askance at reaffirmation agreements to pay more than the value of the property, absent a showing that some other method, such as redemption, was not possible.[687] Other courts have flatly refused to approve reaffirmations for amounts in excess of the value of the collateral.[688] On occasion, they have also enjoined creditors from attempting to add attorney fees or other fees to the reaffirmed debt.[689] It appears that some agreements have been proposed mainly in cases where the debtor's counsel was lazy, incompetent, or both in not exploring better alternatives for the debtor, and the trend of decisions refusing reaffirmation where such alternatives are available seems clearly correct.

A number of courts have required, by local rule or otherwise, use of a reaffirmation form promulgated by the Administrative Office of United States Courts so that they

---

677 11 U.S.C. § 524(c), (d).

678 Fed. R. Bankr. P. 6008. *In re* White, 231 B.R. 551 (Bankr. D. Vt. 1999) (upholding general order that required filing of redemption agreements); *In re* Lopez, 224 B.R. 439 (Bankr. C.D. Cal. 1998). *But see* Arruda v. Sears, Roebuck & Co., 310 F.3d 13 (1st Cir. 2002) (debtor's post-discharge agreement to pay "value" of collateral in exchange for release of lien, which on its face does not impose personal liability, if not a reaffirmation, at least when debtors agreed to value of property and there was no allegation of harassment or coercion); *In re* Spivey, 265 B.R. 357 (E.D.N.Y. 2001).

679 *But see In re* Jamo, 283 F.3d 392 (1st Cir. 2002) (creditors permitted to refuse reaffirmation not made on their terms, but specific threats in connection with reaffirmation negotiations could be overly coercive), *rev'g* 262 B.R. 159 (B.A.P. 1st Cir. 2001).

680 *In re* Long, 3 B.R. 656 (Bankr. E.D. Va. 1980); *In re* Berkich, 7 B.R. 483 (Bankr. E.D. Pa. 1980); *In re* Avis, 3 B.R. 205 (Bankr. S.D. Ohio 1980); *see also In re* Hirte, 71 B.R. 249 (Bankr. D. Or. 1986) (reaffirmation of unsecured debt which has been discharged to settle nondischargeability claim disapproved where deadline for filing nondischargeability complaint had passed). *But see In re* Kinion, 207 F.3d 751 (5th Cir. 2000) (local rule may not provide that only secured debt can be reaffirmed).

681 *In re* Bain, 223 B.R. 343 (Bankr. N.D. Tex. 1998) (reaffirmation of a $388.00 debt to obtain an additional $12.00 in credit). Some courts have looked to the effective annual percentage rate of the new credit in evaluating the consumer's best interests. *E.g., In re* Bruzzese, 214 B.R. 444 (Bankr. E.D.N.Y. 1997).

682 *In re* Iappini, 192 B.R. 8 (Bankr. D. Mass. 1995) (general statement that Sears' reaffirmation practices are coercive and in bad faith with possibility of sanctions left open in the event of a continuation of those practices).

683 *Id.*; 11 U.S.C. § 524(f); *see also In re* Griffen, 13 B.R. 591 (Bankr. S.D. Ohio 1980) (reaffirmation coerced by threat of illegal post-discharge collection activity). *But see In re* Arnold, 206 B.R. 560 (Bankr. N.D. Ala. 1997) (payments made pursuant to debtor's post-bankruptcy agreement to pay debt in exchange for promise not garnish wife's wages were not voluntary payments).

684 *See also* § 8.8.2, *supra.*

685 *See* §§ 11.5.4, *supra*, and 14.5.3, *infra*, for discussion of whether reaffirmation is necessary in order to retain property when payments are current. *See In re* Ezell, 269 B.R. 768 (Bankr. S.D. Ohio 2001) (refusing approval of reaffirmation of debt secured by vehicle owned by debtor's wife, from whom he was separated).

686 *In re* McGrann, 6 B.R. 612 (Bankr. E.D. Pa. 1980).

687 *In re* Delano, 6 Bankr. Ct. Dec. (LRP) 1280 (Bankr. D. Me. 1980). The court did not mention, although it could have done so, conversion to chapter 13 for payment of the allowed secured claim in installments. *See* Ch. 11, *supra.*

688 *In re* Jenkins, 4 B.R. 651 (Bankr. E.D. Va. 1980).

689 *E.g., In re* Allen, 215 B.R. 503 (Bankr. N.D. Tex 1997).

can be assured of obtaining the information they find necessary to consider a reaffirmation, including copies of the underlying security agreement.[690]

14.5.2.3 Factors to Be Considered by Attorneys Validating Reaffirmation Agreements

Attorneys should be extremely cautious in negotiating and validating reaffirmation agreements under the 1984 and 1994 amendments. There are serious problems of possible malpractice liability if such an agreement later causes harm to the debtor, for example, through the debtor's loss of property if the debtor does not later pay the reaffirmed debt. There is no question that prior to 1979 many debtors entered into ill-advised reaffirmations; the numerous cases in which courts have disapproved reaffirmations since then suggest that attorneys have not always been as wary of reaffirmations as the courts. Although a reaffirmation in which an attorney has filed the requisite declaration no longer requires court approval to be valid, courts nonetheless have the power, under Federal Rule of Bankruptcy Procedure 9011 and section 524(c)(3), to review such declarations and the accompanying reaffirmations.[691]

Thus, it is usually better practice to avoid reaffirmations if at all possible. It is always advisable to verify whether a creditor really has and can document any security interest it claims, as well as the amount due. A detailed letter of inquiry should be sent to any creditor claiming a security interest.[692] Many creditors cannot provide documentation of a security interest and the documentation supplied by others may be insufficient to create a security interest.[693] Although it is not clear that Truth in Lending disclosures are required for reaffirmation agreements by the Truth in Lending Act itself, at least one court has held that they can be required by the court to determine whether reaffirmation is in the debtor's best interest.[694] A form for reaffirmation agreements,

promulgated by the federal Judicial Conference and adopted by local rule in some courts, indicates a similar concern, requiring detailed disclosure of the terms of the reaffirmation.[695] If the court needs such information for reaffirmations that it approves, an attorney deciding whether a reaffirmation is in the debtor's best interest should require no less.

Very often the debtor can obtain the result desired by simply maintaining voluntary payments on a debt without reassuming the legal obligation. For example, a creditor cannot pursue a codebtor if the debtor's payments remain current. And many courts have held that property subject to a security interest may not be repossessed if payments are up to date.[696] If there is any doubt on this issue, a chapter 13 filing should be considered to deal with the secured claim, rather than a reaffirmation.

One way out for an attorney unsure about a possible reaffirmation, perhaps one fervently desired by a client, is to leave the question to the court. If the attorney does not negotiate the reaffirmation agreement, then the procedure for court approval must be followed,[697] relieving the attorney of responsibility for the decision.

14.5.3 Secured Debts Without Reaffirmation

After bankruptcy, for various reasons, secured debts may exist in which neither reaffirmation nor redemption has taken place. This may occur because the debtor does not choose to be personally bound. It may also occur because the creditor refuses to agree to reaffirmation.

In such cases, the question arises whether the creditor may foreclose upon its still-existing lien on a car or a home due to a "bankruptcy clause" which creates an automatic default upon the debtor filing a bankruptcy case even absent a monetary default under the contract. Such contractual default clauses are not favored under the Code,[698] but some creditors have argued that they may still be used to foreclose upon collateral even if there has been no default in payments. Other contractual clauses which generally make impairment of collateral an event of default also should not be enforceable by a secured creditor solely based on the debtor's bankruptcy filing and refusal to reaffirm.[699] Simi-

---

690 *E.g., In re* Brown, 248 B.R. 784 (Bankr. N.D. Ohio 2000). The Administrative Office form is reprinted in Appendix E, *infra.*

691 *See In re* Melendez, 235 B.R. 173 (Bankr. D. Mass. 1999) (attorneys violated their obligations under Rule 9011 by failing to make reasonable inquiry before submitting declarations); *In re* Melendez, 224 B.R. 252 (Bankr. D. Mass. 1998); *In re* Bruzzese, 214 B.R. 444 (Bankr. E.D.N.Y. 1997) (attorney found to have violated Rule 9011 and ethical obligations by signing reaffirmation agreement declaration that was not accurate and did not investigate or explain facts to client); *In re* Izzo, 197 B.R. 11 (Bankr. D.R.I. 1996) (debtor's attorney ordered to show cause why reaffirmation should not be declared void when debtor's expenses exceeded his income even without car payment provided for in agreement).

692 *See* Form 113, Appx. G.11, *infra.*

693 *See, e.g., In re* Immerfall, 216 B.R. 269 (Bankr. D. Minn. 1998) (Sears documents did not create valid security interest); *In re* Carlos, 215 B.R. 52 (Bankr. C.D. Cal. 1997) (documents did not describe collateral with necessary specificity); *see also* § 14.5.3, *infra.*

694 *In re* Kamps, 217 B.R. 836 (Bankr. C.D. Cal. 1998).

695 *See* Appx. E, *infra.*

696 *See* § 11.5.4, *supra;* § 14.5.3, *infra.*

697 11 U.S.C. § 524(c)(6); *see In re* James, 120 B.R. 582 (Bankr. W.D. Okla. 1990) (court would not approve reaffirmation agreement where creditor held unsecured, unliquidated claim; debtor could not bifurcate claim so as to affirm it only to the extent it was secured by debtor's automobile and attorney had not certified, without qualification, that reaffirmation would impose no undue hardship on debtor). *But see In re* Jamo, 283 F.3d 392 (1st Cir. 2002) (absent counsel's approval, a represented debtor cannot reaffirm).

698 *See* 11 U.S.C. §§ 363(l), 365(b)(2), 541(c).

699 *See In re* Parker, 139 F.3d 668 (9th Cir. 1998); *In re* Boodrow,

larly, failure to file the notice of election with respect to retention of secured property, required by 11 U.S.C. § 521(2) does not give a secured creditor the automatic right to repossess collateral.[700]

There are several ways debtors can overcome this potential problem. The best way, usually preferable to reaffirmation, is a redemption agreement that does not provide for reaffirmation. Although it probably cannot be required to do so,[701] a creditor may enter a binding agreement not to foreclose as long as contractual payments are made.[702]

Even when creditors are not willing to enter into such agreements, they will usually take no action against the debtor as long as payments are current. If foreclosure or repossession is attempted, several arguments can be made by the debtor.[703] First, it can be argued that once the debtor's interest in the property had become property of the estate (later to be exempted or abandoned), it was no longer conditioned upon any bankruptcy clause, due to the operation of section 541(c) of the Code which invalidates such clauses as to all property of the estate.[704] Because the debtor is entitled to claim exemptions out of the property of the estate,[705] it follows that the interest claimed as exempt is the estate's interest, freed of the bankruptcy clause. It can also be argued that actions based upon such a clause are unconscionable or not in compliance with the Uniform Commercial Code's requirement of good faith.[706] Some decisions have simply stated, using various reasons, that foreclosure while the debtor is current in payments is not permissible.[707] A final alternative is to file a new chapter 13 case, under which the debtor could retain the property and cure the default.[708] Sometimes the threat of a chapter 13 case or of conversion to that chapter, in which the creditor might be paid less, or more slowly, is enough to persuade a recalcitrant creditor to agree to the debtor's continuing payment without reaffirmation.

If the debtor does fall behind on payments post-petition or post-discharge, the creditor is, of course, entitled to enforce a valid lien. State court defenses may be raised or a new bankruptcy case under chapter 13 may be available as an option. However, the costs of foreclosure, repossession or replevin are pre-petition personal liabilities under the contract and may not be collected from the debtor personally because they have been discharged.[709]

A related problem that has arisen in recent years with increasing frequency concerns the rights of the debtor against credit card issuers asserting a purchase money security interest in goods purchased by credit card. Sears and several other creditors have, at various times, aggressively pursued claimed security interests in the bankruptcy process.[710] The first response to such a claim may be to seek proof of the grounds on which it is asserted. Frequently the creditor has inadequate documentation. Upon obtaining the purported documentation, other questions about the validity of the security interest may also be raised.[711] Finally, in most jurisdictions, a debtor may be advised that there is little risk in ignoring such security interests because the creditor cannot breach the peace to repossess and the debtor may refuse entry to the repossessing agent. Creditors will rarely seek state replevin remedies to obtain an order requiring surrender of the goods, because such procedures are costly in comparison to the value of the used goods. In the rare case in which such an action is undertaken, defenses to repossession may be raised in the replevin action.

A variation of this practice is the attempted use of cross-collateralization (spreader) clauses in contracts such as automobile loan contracts or mortgages which purport to make

---

126 F.3d 43 (2d Cir. 1997); Lowry Fed. Credit Union v. West, 882 F.2d 1543 (10th Cir. 1989).

700 *See In re* Belanger, 962 F.2d 345 (4th Cir. 1992); Lowry Fed. Credit Union v. West, 882 F.2d 1543 (10th Cir. 1989); *see also In re* French, 185 B.R. 910 (Bankr. M.D. Fla. 1995) (debtor who attempted to negotiate reaffirmation agreement but who would not agree to additional attorney fees demanded by creditor had complied with statement of intentions); § 11.4, *supra*. *But see In re* Taylor, 3 F.3d 1512 (11th Cir. 1993).

701 See discussion of redemption in Chapter 11, *supra*.

702 *See In re* Coots, 4 B.R. 281 (Bankr. S.D. Ohio 1980).

703 See also § 11.5.4, *supra*, for discussion of this issue.

704 *In re* Winters, 69 B.R. 145 (Bankr. D. Or. 1986); *In re* Bryant 43 B.R. 189 (Bankr. E.D. Mich. 1984).

705 11 U.S.C. § 522(b).

706 U.C.C. § 1-201(19).

707 Lowry Fed. Credit Union v. West, 882 F.2d 1543 (10th Cir. 1989); Riggs Nat'l Bank v. Perry, 729 F.2d 982 (4th Cir. 1984); *In re* Woodford, 6 Bankr. Ct. Dec. (LRP) 226, 1 Collier Bankr. Cas. 2d (MB) 789 (Bankr. M.D. Fla. 1980); *In re* DeCamp, 4 B.R. 498 (Bankr. M.D. Fla. 1980); *see also In re* Hunter, 121 B.R. 609 (Bankr. N.D. Ala. 1990) (reaffirmation denied where debtor never in default on payments to secured creditor and did not need to reaffirm to retain mobile home subject to security interest); *In re* Carey, 51 B.R. 294 (Bankr. D.D.C. 1985) (repossession enjoined for so long as debtor remained current on her payments). State law anti-forfeiture provisions in statutes or common law may support this argument.

708 11 U.S.C. §§ 1306(b), 1322(b)(3).

709 *In re* McNeil, 128 B.R. 603 (Bankr. E.D. Pa. 1991).

710 These issues have been discussed at length in *Helping Your Client Do The Wash: The Effect in Bankruptcy of PMSI Claims Created By Revolving Credit Accounts*, 12 NCLC REPORTS *Bankruptcy and Foreclosures* Ed. 37 (Jan./Feb. 1994).

711 These may include questions about whether the security interest is valid pursuant to the U.C.C.'s Article 9, whether the contract is an unenforceable adhesion contract, and whether proper accounting practices were used. *See In re* Immerfall, 216 B.R. 269 (Bankr. D. Minn. 1998) (Sears charge slips without underlying credit agreement they purported to incorporate did not prove security interest; description of some items also inadequate); *In re* Carlos, 215 B.R. 52 (Bankr. C.D. Cal. 1997) (property in which Sears alleged security interest was inadequately described in charge slip); § 11.2.2, *supra*. *See generally Helping Your Client Do The Wash: The Effect in Bankruptcy of PMSI Claims Created By Revolving Credit Accounts*, 12 NCLC REPORTS *Bankruptcy and Foreclosures* Ed. 37 (Jan./Feb. 1994). Moreover, no security interest is created if the person signing the charge slip is not the account holder who signed the security agreement.

the property involved security for future advances, such as those on credit cards. There are a variety of arguments against such claims, such as arguments based on whether the debtor knew and intended to create such a security interest, especially when the original contract (which is later assigned) was entered into with a dealer who the debtor would have no reason to believe would make any future advances.[712] A failure to disclose the security interest on the later transaction would probably violate the Truth in Lending Act as well.[713] It may also be that the efforts of the creditor to procure a reaffirmation agreement have violated the automatic stay or other statutes.[714]

14.5.4 Protection Against Discrimination Based on Bankruptcy

In addition to the other protections of the discharge, the Code contains a specific provision barring some types of discrimination based upon a person's bankruptcy or a debt discharged in bankruptcy. Section 525(a) provides that, with a few uncommon exceptions, a governmental unit:[715]

> [M]ay not deny, revoke, suspend, or refuse to renew a license, permit, charter, franchise, or other similar grant to, condition such a grant to, discriminate with respect to such a grant against, deny employment to, terminate the employment

of, or discriminate with respect to employment against, a person that is or has been a debtor under this title or a bankrupt or a debtor under the Bankruptcy Act, or another person with whom such bankrupt or debtor is or has been associated, solely because such bankrupt or debtor is or has been a debtor under this title or a bankrupt or a debtor under the Bankruptcy Act, has been insolvent before the commencement of the case under this title, or during the case but before the debtor is granted or denied a discharge, or has not paid a debt that is dischargeable in the case under this title or that was discharged under the Bankruptcy Act.

It is clear that this provision is directed at governmental units and that it does not cover private entities. But the legislative history also makes clear that the Code is not intended to authorize discrimination by private entities. Rather, Congress thought it best for the courts initially to develop rules with respect to such entities, and gave strong intimations that discrimination not specifically within the terms of section 525 that greatly impeded a debtor's fresh start might be prohibited.[716] To date, case law has been scarce, but the courts have been somewhat receptive to claims of private discrimination.[717] Probably, the strongest cases could be made against quasi-governmental entities such as state bar associations, which are specifically mentioned in the legislative history.[718]

In 1984, another legislative step in this direction was taken with the addition of section 525(b), prohibiting private employers from employment discrimination based on bank-

---

712 *In re* Kim, 256 B.R. 793 (Bankr. S.D. Cal. 2000) (dragnet clause invalid because credit union did not rely on automobile as collateral in providing credit card); *In re* Gibson, 249 B.R. 645 (Bankr. E.D. Pa. 2000) (dragnet clause did not secure unrelated loans); *In re* Wollin, 249 B.R. 555 (Bankr. D. Or. 2000) (dragnet clause invalid because credit card debt not of same class as auto loan); *In re* Fassinger, 246 B.R. 513 (Bankr. W.D. Pa. 2000) (credit union dragnet clause invalid under Pennsylvania "relatedness rule"); *In re* Cushing, 230 B.R. 639 (Bankr. W.D. Pa. 1999) (mortgage note dragnet clause, under which lender argued that credit card debt was secured by mortgage, was invalid); *see also In re* Brooks, 274 B.R. 495 (Bankr. E.D. Tenn. 2002) (credit card debt owed only by wife not secured by mortgage on home owned by both debtors, based on language of mortgage); *In re* Merrill, 258 B.R. 750 (Bankr. W.D. Mo. 2001) (security interest based on future advances not perfected under state law if not noted on certificate of title); National Consumer Law Center, Repossessions and Foreclosures § 3.9 (5th ed. 2002 and Supp.). *But see In re* Conte, 206 F.3d 536 (5th Cir. 2000) (upholding cross-collateral clause).

713 *See* National Consumer Law Center, Truth in Lending §§ 4.6.7.6, 5.5.5.7 (5th ed. 2003).

714 Sears, Roebuck & Co. v. O'Brien, 178 F.3d 962 (8th Cir. 1999) (bankruptcy law does not preempt state consumer credit code provision); *In re* Hurley, 215 B.R. 391 (B.A.P. 8th Cir. 1997) (sending debtors "informational copy" of letter to their attorney seeking reaffirmation violated Iowa Consumer Credit Code prohibition against creditors communicating with represented debtors); *see also* § 9.4.3, *supra*.

715 "Governmental unit" is defined at 11 U.S.C. § 101(27). *See In re* Trusko, 212 B.R. 819 (Bankr. D. Md. 1997) (credit union a governmental unit for purposes of a different Code section).

716 S. Rep. No. 95-989, at 81 (1978); H.R. Rep. No. 95-595, at 367 (1977); *see In re* Macher, 303 B.R. 798 (W.D. Va. 2003) (IRS ordered to consider debtor's offer in compromise under § 105 based on fresh start policy); *In re* Holmes, 298 B.R. 477 (Bankr. M.D. Ga. 2003) (IRS ordered to consider debtor's offer in compromise under § 105 even though not required by § 525); *In re* Golliday, 216 B.R. 407 (Bankr. W.D. Mich. 1998) (although city's termination of debtor's right to sit as rent commissioner found not to violate § 525, it did violate fresh start principles enunciated by Supreme Court and was therefore enjoined).

717 *E.g., In re* Blackwelder Furniture Co., 7 B.R. 328 (Bankr. W.D.N.C. 1980) (preliminary injunction issued requiring private company to continue dealing with corporate debtor according to previous business relationship); *see In re* Bradley, 989 F.2d 802 (5th Cir. 1993) (bankruptcy court must take jurisdiction to determine discrimination claim if there is a potential violation of § 525). *But see* Wilson v. Harris Trust & Sav. Bank, 777 F.2d 1246 (7th Cir. 1985) (section 525 did not apply to private employer prior to 1984 Amendments).

718 *See In re* Oksentowicz, 2004 WL 2110408 (Bankr. E.D. Mich. Sept. 23, 2004) (privately owned apartment complex participating in Section 8 housing program and subject to extensive regulation by the Dep't of Housing and Urban Development was governmental unit); *In re* Marcano, 288 B.R. 324 (Bankr. S.D.N.Y. 2003) (pervasive entwinement of the city in the workings and composition of a nominally private tenant's association justified conclusion that association should be considered an instrumentality of the city and a governmental unit).

ruptcy, insolvency before a bankruptcy, or nonpayment of a debt discharged or dischargeable in a bankruptcy case.[719] This section is most often helpful when employers are unhappy with court orders to deduct chapter 13 payments from a debtor's paycheck and forward them to the chapter 13 trustee. It will also help in those occasional cases in which debtors owe debts to their employers or to persons or institutions closely affiliated with their employers.[720] However, as in any employment discrimination case, there may still be difficult problems of proof as to motivation, particularly when the employer presents alternative reasons for its actions adverse to the debtor. The court may have to evaluate whether the reasons presented are the true motivations for the employer's actions and, if so, whether those reasons are valid.[721]

Yet another step was taken by a 1994 amendment that prohibits discrimination against a debtor seeking a student loan or grant. Section 525(c) prohibits a governmental unit or private entity involved in a student loan program from discriminating based upon a bankruptcy case, insolvency prior to a bankruptcy case, or an unpaid debt that was discharged in a bankruptcy case.

In addition to the question of who may or may not discriminate, there is also a good deal of uncertainty about how broad the scope of section 525(a) really is. What is covered by the phrase "license, permit, charter, franchise, or other similar grant"? Clearly covered are such matters as issuance of drivers' licenses[722] and employment, but what of various public benefits, such as welfare or social security when the agency has been denied recoupment by the discharge.[723] What of utility service provided by public enti-

---

719 *See* Leary v. Warnaco, 251 B.R. 656 (S.D.N.Y. 2000) (provision applied both the current employees and to hiring of new employees). *But see In re* Majewski, 310 F.3d 653 (9th Cir. 2002) (section 525(b) inapplicable when debtor fired before bankruptcy case was filed, even if cause was debtor's intention to file bankruptcy case); Fiorani v. Caci, 192 B.R. 401 (E.D. Va. 1996) (section 525(b) did not extend to hiring); Kepple v. Miller, 257 Ga. App. 784, 572 S.E.2d 687 (2002) (section 525(b) inapplicable to real estate agent who was independent contractor); Pastore v. Medford Sav. Bank, 186 B.R. 553 (D. Mass. 1995) (omission of words "deny employment to" in § 525(b) means that hiring decisions are not covered by that section, because those words do appear in § 525(a)).

720 *See In re* Patterson, 125 B.R. 40 (Bankr. N.D. Ala. 1990) (antidiscrimination provision applied to employer's credit union which denied services to the debtor), *aff'd*, 967 F.2d 505 (11th Cir. 1992); *In re* McNeely, 82 B.R. 628 (Bankr. S.D. Ga. 1987) (antidiscrimination provision applied to entity which refused to do business with independent contractor after claim of that entity's sister corporation was discharged in bankruptcy); *cf.* Mangan v. Cullen, 870 F.2d 1396 (8th Cir. 1989) (district administrator in state court system has qualified official immunity against damage suit for discrimination brought by court reporter who was not given a raise after she discharged state's claim in bankruptcy). *But see* Asquino v. Fed. Deposit Ins. Corp., 196 B.R. 25 (D. Md. 1996) (provision of Federal Deposit Insurance Act precluded review of termination of employment of debtor by F.D.I.C.).

721 *See, e.g.*, Laracuente v. Chase Manhattan Bank, 891 F.2d 17 (1st Cir. 1989) (debtor must show bankruptcy is sole reason for dismissal, bank had valid basis to dismiss bank employee who improperly processed loans for family and friends); Mangan v. Cullen, 870 F.2d 1396 (8th Cir. 1989) (state official had valid nondiscriminatory basis for treating employee differently after she discharged state's claim in bankruptcy); Bell v. Stanford-Corbitt-Bruker, Inc., Bankr. L. Rep. (CCH) ¶ 72,114 (S.D. Ga. 1987) (termination of employment is unlawful if it would not have occurred "but for" the debtor's bankruptcy); *In re* McKibben, 233 B.R. 378 (Bankr. E.D. Tex. 1999) (debtor awarded almost $90,000.00 in lost wages where circumstances belied employer's stated reason for termination); *In re* Sweeney, 113 B.R. 359 (Bankr. N.D. Ohio 1990) (termination from employment, though couched in terms of concern for financial imprudence, was based solely on employee's insolvency and was thus discriminatory); *In re* Vaughter, 109 B.R. 229 (Bankr. W.D. Tex. 1989) (employer's failure to allow bankruptcy debtor to participate in advancement program was discriminatory); *In re* Hop-

kins, 81 B.R. 491 (Bankr. W.D. Ark. 1987) (debtor reinstated with full back pay after she was fired solely for filing bankruptcy); *In re* Hicks, 65 B.R. 980 (Bankr. W.D. Ark. 1986) (bank not permitted to transfer teller due to alleged fear of customer relations problem stemming from teller's bankruptcy when bank had no valid concern about teller's honesty); *In re* Hopkins, 66 B.R. 828 (Bankr. W.D. Ark. 1986) (bank employee could not be terminated on basis of fear of public reaction to employee's bankruptcy where there was no doubt of employee's honesty); *see also* Comeaux v. Brown & Williamson Tobacco Co., 915 F.2d 1264 (9th Cir. 1990) (prospective employer did not discriminate where debtor's bankruptcy status was not sole reason for decision not to hire; employer had told debtor, before learning of chapter 13 filing, that it would not hire him because of credit history); *cf. In re* Arentson, 126 B.R. 236 (Bankr. N.D. Miss. 1991) (bankruptcy court could decide issue of bankruptcy discrimination despite arbitration provision in employment contract).

722 *See In re* Kish, 238 B.R. 271 (Bankr. D.N.J. 1999) (license could not be denied due to nonpayment of discharged insurance "surcharges"); *In re* Brown, 244 B.R. 62 (Bankr. D.N.J. 2000) (denial of driver's license to chapter 13 debtor who was paying dischargeable traffic fines through plan violated § 525); *In re* Colon, 102 B.R. 421 (Bankr. E.D. Pa. 1989) (pre-petition traffic fines are dischargeable in chapter 13; attempts to collect them by post-petition license suspension violate the automatic stay and nondiscrimination provision); *In re* Young, 10 B.R. 17 (Bankr. S.D. Cal. 1980) (state could not deny drivers license due to fine which would be discharged in chapter 13).

723 *See In re* Lech, 80 B.R. 1001 (Bankr. D. Neb. 1987) (government loan agreement with right to extend annually comes within governmental antidiscrimination provision); *In re* Latchaw, 24 B.R. 457 (Bankr. N.D. Ohio 1982) (quasi-governmental transit authority could not take disciplinary action against an employee under policy which prohibited wage garnishment where court ordered employer to pay debtor's wages to chapter 13 trustee); *In re* Rose, 23 B.R. 662 (Bankr. D. Conn. 1982) (home mortgage financing program within scope of § 525); Parker v. Contractors State License Board, 231 Cal. Rptr. 577 (Ct. App. 1986) (contractor's license could not be suspended solely for failure to pay debt to union); *see also In re* Harris, 85 B.R. 858 (Bankr. D. Colo. 1988) (provision of state law which provides that bankruptcy discharge cannot relieve debtor of real estate license suspension violates supremacy clause). *But see* Toth v. Mich. State Hous. Dev. Auth., 136 F.3d 477 (6th Cir. 1998) (§ 525 did

ties? May a deposit be required of debtors who have discharged debts when it is not required of others? Several courts have concluded that in some contexts it is not discriminatory for a governmental entity to deny benefits to a debtor who has discharged a debt, based on the fact that the debtor's need for government assistance is less as a result of the discharge.[724]

The answers to some of these questions can be found in the legislative history,[725] which states that the section is intended to codify the result of *Perez v. Campbell*.[726] In that case, the Supreme Court held that a state could not deny a driver's license due to a debt after that debt had been discharged in bankruptcy, because that denial would impair the debtor's fresh start. Although *Perez* dealt with a driver's license, the "fresh start" principle is equally applicable to virtually any type of public benefit or government action. As discussed below, section 525 has already been broadly interpreted to include the right to live in public housing, and the right to receive a transcript from a university to which a student loan was owed.[727] Denial of various other governmental benefits, services or privileges has also been found discriminatory.[728] It is also clear that the section extends not

just to discrimination based upon the bankruptcy, but also discrimination based upon an unpaid debt that was discharged in bankruptcy.[729] Under section 525, except insofar as creditworthiness is being considered, the debtor should be treated the same as if the discharged debt never existed.[730]

The Supreme Court has interpreted § 525(a) broadly, holding that a court must look behind the alternative alleged motives of a government agency that denies a license.[731] It is not sufficient for the government to say that a license was denied for a "regulatory" purpose if the proximate cause for the denial was the failure to pay a dischargeable debt.[732] The Court made clear that the fact that licenses were also revoked for non-bankruptcy debtors who failed to pay similar debts did not change this fact.[733] The Court specifically rejected the argument, raised by the dissent, that there must be discrimination based upon the debtor's filing bankruptcy, rather than simply non-payment of a dischargeable debt, as contrary to the clear meaning of the statutory language.[734]

One important limitation which should be noted, however, is that the section bars discrimination only when it is solely based upon the bankruptcy or upon nonpayment of a dischargeable debt. Where other factors are involved, unless they can be shown to be pretextual, the debtor will have a difficult case, especially because the legislative history specifically states that factors such as future financial ability may be considered, if applied in a nondiscriminatory fashion.[735] Thus, a financial responsibility law cannot require

---

not extend to denial of credit in state home improvement loan program); Dixon v. United States, 68 F.3d 1253 (10th Cir. 1995) (debtor who did not discharge indemnity obligation to government on VA mortgage could have future eligibility for government guaranteed loans reduced; court held that denial of benefits was not attempt to collect discharged debt and did not discuss § 525(a)); *In re* Watts, 876 F.2d 1090 (3d Cir. 1989) (state mortgage assistance loans not within the scope of § 525); *In re* Goldrich, 771 F.2d 28 (2d Cir. 1985) (student loan not a license, charter or grant within meaning of statute); *In re* Begley, 46 B.R. 707 (E.D. Pa. 1984) (right to have state public utility commission mediate dispute with utility was not license, charter or grant within meaning of section 525), *aff'd*, 760 F.2d 46 (3d Cir. 1985). This holding in *Goodrich* was legislatively overruled by the passage of 11 U.S.C. § 525(c) in 1994.

724 Lee v. Yeutter, 106 B.R. 588 (D. Minn. 1989) (debt restructuring under the Agricultural Credit Act denied), *aff'd*, 917 F.2d 1104 (8th Cir. 1990); *see also In re* Watts, 876 F.2d 1090 (3d Cir. 1989) (state mortgage assistance can be denied on the basis of bankruptcy filing, because the bankruptcy protects the debtor against foreclosure of the mortgage on which assistance is sought).

725 S. Rep. No. 95-989, at 81 (1978); H.R. Rep. No. 95-595, at 366 (1977).

726 402 U.S. 637, 91 S. Ct. 1704, 29 L. Ed. 2d 233 (1971).

727 *See* § 14.5.5, *infra*.

728 *See, e.g., In re* Bradley, 989 F.2d 802 (5th Cir. 1993) (denial of insurance license would be in violation of § 525 if retention of license was conditioned on payment of discharged debt); *In re* Berkelhammer, 279 B.R. 660 (Bankr. S.D.N.Y. 2002) (state could not remove debtor from list of Medicaid-eligible physicians based on non-payment of pre-petition debt); *In re* Jacobs, 149 B.R. 983 (Bankr. N.D. Okla. 1993) (revocation of insurance agent license violated discharge injunction and § 525(a)); *In re* Walker, 927 F.2d 1138 (10th Cir. 1991) (denial of real estate license because of payment by real estate recovery fund to debtor's creditor would violate § 525(a)); *see also* Fed. Communications Comm'n v. NextWave Personal Communications, 537 U.S. 293,

123 S. Ct. 832, 839, 154 L. Ed. 2d 863, 874 (2003); *In re* Exquisito Services, 823 F.2d 151 (5th Cir. 1987) (refusal to renew food service contract violated § 525); *In re* William Tell II, 38 B.R. 327 (N.D. Ill. 1983) (liquor license restored); *In re* Mills, 240 B.R. 689 (Bankr. S.D. W. Va. 1999) (finding that Congress intended broad interpretation to assist debtor's fresh start and holding that IRS refusal to consider offers in compromise from bankruptcy debtors violated § 525); *In re* Coleman Am. Moving Services, 8 B.R. 379 (Bankr. D. Kan. 1980) (Air Force enjoined from discriminating against chapter 11 debtor in contract bidding; term "employment" construed broadly).

729 11 U.S.C. § 525; Henry v. Heyison, 4 B.R. 437 (E.D. Pa. 1980); *In re* Goldrich, 45 B.R. 514 (Bankr. E.D.N.Y. 1984) (barring application of statute denying student loan to any student who had defaulted on previous loan), *rev'd on other grounds*, 771 F.2d 28 (2d Cir. 1985) (scope of section 525 does not include future extensions of credit such as student loans).

730 H.R. Rep. No. 103-835, at 58 (1994), *reprinted in* 1994 U.S.C.C.A.N. 3340.

731 Fed. Communications Comm'n v. NextWave Personal Communications, 537 U.S. 293, 123 S. Ct. 832, 839, 154 L. Ed. 2d 863, 874 (2003).

732 537 U.S. 293, 123 S. Ct. 832, 839, 154 L. Ed. 2d 863, 874, 875 (2003).

733 123 S. Ct. at 841, 842.

734 *Id.*

735 S. Rep. No. 95-989, at 81 (1978); H.R. Rep. No. 95-595, at 367 (1977); *see In re* Smith, 259 B.R. 901 (B.A.P. 2001) (§ 525 not applicable because debtor's public housing lease terminated due to fraud; dictum that there would be no protection under § 525 even if non-payment of rent was only reason); Brookman v. State Bar of Cal., 46 Cal. 3d 1004, 760 P.2d 1023, 251 Cal. Rptr.

only debtors who have filed bankruptcies to obtain insurance. However, if all persons who do not have assets sufficient to pay a judgment are required to obtain insurance, then debtors who filed bankruptcies would not be excepted under section 525(a).[736] And if a debt is not discharged in a bankruptcy, discrimination based upon that debt is not prohibited by this section.[737]

Finally, it should be remembered that in situations when section 525 is not applicable, section 524 may still prevent the challenged action.[738] Whenever it can be shown that the denial or other act directed at a client was intended to coerce payment of the discharged debt, that act is in violation of the injunction in section 524(a) and therefore should be considered a contempt of court.[739]

14.5.5 Particular Problems Relating to Discharge Protections

14.5.5.1 Drivers' Licenses

One of the more common uses of bankruptcy by low-income clients is to prevent the loss of or to regain a driver's licenses that is jeopardized by state financial responsibility laws such as the one dealt with in *Perez v. Campbell*.[740] Typically, such statutes provide that an operator's license, and sometimes vehicle registration, is suspended until a tort judgment arising out of a motor vehicle accident is paid. The Supreme Court held in *Perez* that, if the debt is discharged in bankruptcy, the license can no longer be denied.

Following *Perez*, courts have more recently held that any other discrimination based upon a discharged debt, such as a requirement that special insurance or a bond be purchased before a license can be granted, is also prohibited under the Supremacy Clause because it too would tend to frustrate the Congressional purpose of giving debtors a fresh start.[741]

Similarly, a license cannot be withheld on the basis of nonpayment of traffic tickets which are dischargeable in chapter 13 cases,[742] or of other dischargeable charges arising from driving infractions.[743] In such situations, section 525 has been read to mean that the debtor involved should be treated as if the discharged debt never existed.[744] However, if the license has been suspended or revoked for some reason other than simply the nonpayment of money, such as points assessed after traffic violations, bankruptcy will not resolve that problem.

Thus, for a client who needs a driver's license, but cannot pay a judgment or fines, bankruptcy can be an ideal solution. Especially in areas where use of an automobile is a necessity of life, such a bankruptcy can be a vital service.

14.5.5.2 Student Loans and College Transcripts

One of the persistent problems under the prior Bankruptcy Act concerned college students and graduates who were refused transcripts from educational institutions because of discharged student loans. The case law that had developed under the Act seemed to make a distinction between private institutions and public ones, holding only the latter bound by the Supremacy Clause under *Perez*.[745]

Duffey v. Dollison, 734 F.2d 265 (6th Cir. 1984) (upholding requirement of financial responsibility insurance based upon debt discharged in bankruptcy). The *Duffey* holding is probably no longer good law after the Supreme Court's decision in *NextWave*.

742 Smith v. Pennsylvania Dept. of Transp., 66 B.R. 244 (E.D. Pa. 1986); *In re* Brown, 244 B.R. 62 (Bankr. D.N.J. 2000) (denial of driver's license to chapter 13 debtor who was paying dischargeable traffic fines through plan violated § 525); *In re* Colon, 102 B.R. 421 (Bankr. E.D. Pa. 1989) (attempts to collect pre-petition traffic fines by post-petition license suspension violate the automatic stay and nondiscrimination provision); *In re* Young, 10 B.R. 17 (Bankr. S.D. Cal. 1980). However, not all fines are dischargeable, even in chapter 13. *See* § 14.5.5.5, *infra*. *But see In re* Raphael, 238 B.R. 69 (D.N.J. 1999) (denying injunction against state district court on 11th Amendment grounds and because debts not yet discharged by chapter 13 debtor).

743 *In re* Kish, 238 B.R. 271 (Bankr. D.N.J. 1999) (license could not be denied due to non-payment of discharged insurance "surcharges").

744 Henry v. Heyison, 4 B.R. 437 (E.D. Pa. 1980); *see also In re* Young, 10 B.R. 17 (Bankr. S.D. Cal. 1980) (license could not be denied due to nonpayment of dischargeable fines). *But see* Duffey v. Dollison, 734 F.2d 265 (6th Cir. 1984) (upholding requirement of financial responsibility insurance based upon debt discharged in bankruptcy); *In re* Geiger, 143 B.R. 30 (E.D. Pa. 1992) (restoration of license could be conditioned on payment of $25.00 restoration fee, which was held nondiscriminatory because it was charged whenever a license was restored to a driver), *aff'd*, 993 F.2d 224 (3d Cir. 1993). The *Duffey* holding is probably no longer good law after the Supreme Court's decision in *NextWave*.

745 *Compare* Girardier v. Webster College, 563 F.2d 1267 (8th Cir. 1977) *with* Handsome v. Rutgers Univ., 445 F. Supp. 1362 (D.N.J. 1978).

---

495 (1988) (order that suspended attorney make restitution was not solely because debt was discharged in bankruptcy or because debt not paid; purpose of order was to protect the public from professional misconduct); *In re* Anonymous, 74 N.Y.2d 938, 549 N.E.2d 472 (1989) (denial of application for admission to bar not based solely on applicant's bankruptcy filing).

736 *In re* Norton, 867 F.2d 313 (6th Cir. 1989) (no discrimination found where financial responsibility law is applied equally to every financially irresponsible driver); Henry v. Heyison, 4 B.R. 437 (E.D. Pa. 1980). The *Norton* holding is probably no longer good law after the Supreme Court's decision in *NextWave*.

737 Johnson v. Edinboro State College, 728 F.2d 163 (3d Cir. 1984).

738 *See* § 14.5.1, *supra*.

739 *In re* Olson, 38 B.R. 515 (Bankr. N.D. Iowa 1984) (clinic refusing medical services unless debt "voluntarily" paid after discharge found in contempt); *see* § 14.5.1.4, *supra*.

740 402 U.S. 637, 91 S. Ct. 1704, 29 L. Ed. 2d 233 (1971); *see* Form 86, Appx. G.10, *infra*.

741 Henry v. Heyison, 4 B.R. 437 (E.D. Pa. 1980); *see also In re* Young, 10 B.R. 17 (Bankr. S.D. Cal. 1980) (license could not be denied due to nonpayment of dischargeable fines). *But see*

However, there was considerable scholarly criticism of those cases which denied transcripts as being contrary to the "fresh start" principle of bankruptcy.[746]

Assuming that a transcript can fit within the "license, permit, charter, franchise, or other grant" language, section 525(a) codifies the result of those cases holding a public institution could not deny a transcript.[747]

Similarly, the denial of further student loans by such a public entity based upon the bankruptcy is barred.[748] This principle was clarified and reemphasized by the 1994 enactment of Code section 525(c), which specifically prohibits discrimination with respect to student loans or grants based upon discharge of a prior debt.[749] The Department of Education has also made clear in regulations that students who have discharged prior student loans are eligible for new Pell grants and other non-loan assistance.[750] Following the 1994 amendment to the Code, the Department also clarified that no reaffirmation of a prior debt is required to obtain a new student loan.[751]

And, to the extent that pre-Code cases had held that withholding a transcript was a valid means for a private party to induce payment of a debt,[752] those cases are clearly no longer good law due to the prohibition in section 524 of "any act" to collect a debt after discharge.[753] Indeed, as soon as a bankruptcy case is filed, such acts to collect a debt are prohibited by the automatic stay of section 362.[754]

One additional argument a debtor might face from a private college withholding a transcript is that the school is not trying to coerce payment of the debt, but rather is simply exercising its right to refuse to enter into new transactions, such as providing a transcript, with the debtor. This argument could be attacked directly under *Perez*, as discussed above, by attempting to convince a court to extend the *Perez* doctrine to private entities.[755] It may also be shown to be a pretext to cover up an actual intent to coerce payment. Unlike a creditor who decides not to extend further credit or services, the college puts nothing new at risk in releasing a transcript. The transcript fee is normally paid in advance, and there is no chance whatsoever of creditor harm.[756] Finally, the debtor might argue that the right to a transcript is a property right that is received in conjunction with the degree or with enrollment.[757] If this is the case, and the debtor claims this right as exempt under section 522, then a good argument exists that a creditor may not withhold such property, which is also property of the estate, from the debtor.[758]

Thus, debtors are afforded significant protections with respect to college transcripts under the Code. Since its enactment the courts have largely made this problem a thing of the past.

14.5.5.3 Public and Private Housing

Many of the issues that arise with respect to student loans are also involved in disputes concerning the right to remain in public or private housing after discharge. A strong argument can be made that the right to remain in public housing is in essence a grant of the subsidy which makes possible lower rents. Further, it is well established in case law and HUD regulations that tenants may be evicted from public housing only for valid cause.[759] Thus, it is not surprising that section 525 has been found applicable to bar eviction of

---

746 *See, e.g.*, Comment, *Post Discharge Coercion of Bankrupts by Private Creditors*, 91 Harv. L. Rev. 1336 (1978); Note, *Withholding Transcripts for Non-Payment of Educational Debts: Before and After Bankruptcy*, 15 Willamette L. Rev. 563 (1979).

747 *See In re* Howren, 10 B.R. 303 (Bankr. D. Kan. 1980); *In re* Heath, 3 B.R. 351 (Bankr. N.D. Ill. 1980); Lee v. Board of Higher Ed. in City of New York, 1 B.R. 781 (Bankr. S.D.N.Y. 1979).

748 *But see* Richardson v. Pennsylvania Higher Educ. Assistance Agency, 27 B.R. 560 (E.D. Pa. 1982) (there could be independent reasons for denial of new loans).

749 The legislative history makes clear that this section was meant to clarify what Congress already believed the law to be. H.R. Rep. No. 103-835, at 58 (1994), *reprinted in* 1994 U.S.C.C.A.N. 3340. In addition, there would be no reason for the new section to refer to student loans discharged under the prior Bankruptcy Act, as it does, if the new section were not applicable to bankruptcy cases commenced prior to enactment of the 1994 amendments.

750 58 Fed. Reg. 32,188 (June 8, 1993) (amending 34 C.F.R. 668.7(f)(1)); *see also* 34 C.F.R. § 668.34 (student not considered to be in default if loan was discharged in bankruptcy).

751 *See* 59 Fed. Reg. 61,212 (Nov. 29, 1994) (FFEL loans); 59 Fed. Reg. 61,667 (Dec. 1, 1994) (explaining that reaffirmation no longer required for other loan programs due to change in Bankruptcy Code provisions). A more detailed discussion of these issues is found at National Consumer Law Center, Student Loan Law Ch. 7 (2d ed. 2002 and Supp.).

752 *See* Girardier v. Webster College, 563 F.2d 1267 (8th Cir. 1977).

753 Parraway v. Andrews Univ., 50 B.R. 316 (W.D. Mich. 1984); *see* Op. N.Y. Att'y Gen., *reprinted in* Poverty L. Rep. (CCH) ¶ 31,093 (Jun. 9, 1980). *But cf.* Johnson v. Edinboro State College, 728 F.2d 163 (3d Cir. 1984) (transcript may be denied where student loan debt is *not* discharged).

754 Loyola Univ. v. McClarty, 234 B.R. 386 (E.D. La. 1999); *In re* Parham, 56 B.R. 531 (Bankr. E.D. Pa. 1986); *In re* Howren, 10 B.R. 303 (Bankr. D. Kan. 1980); *In re* Heath, 3 B.R. 351 (Bankr. N.D. Ill. 1980). For discussion of the automatic stay see Chapter 9, *supra*.

755 This argument was urged, with respect to both private and public colleges under the Act, in Girardier v. Webster College, 563 F.2d 1267, 1277 (8th Cir. 1977) (Bright, J. concurring).

756 *See In re* Heath, 3 B.R. 351 (Bankr. N.D. Ill. 1980); Comment, *Postdischarge Coercion of Bankrupts by Private Creditors*, 91 Harv. L. Rev. 1336, 1344 (1979).

757 *See* Handsome v. Rutgers Univ., 445 F. Supp. 1362 (D. N.J. 1978).

758 For a discussion of exemptions see Chapter 10, *supra*.

759 24 C.F.R. § 866.4(l)(1); *see, e.g.*, Tyson v. N.Y. City Hous. Auth., 369 F. Supp. 513 (S.D.N.Y. 1974); *see also In re* Adams, 94 B.R. 838 (Bankr. E.D. Pa. 1989) (household members remaining after lessee vacated public housing unit are entitled to the rights of public housing tenants).

public housing tenants who discharged rent arrearages through bankruptcy.[760] In a case in which continued occupancy is conditioned upon payment of the arrearages, a valid claim may also exist that there are violations of section 524(a).[761]

Like private colleges, private landlords present more difficult problems. In most places, the landlord has no obligation to renew a lease, and the landlord may assert its right to evict the tenant at the end of the lease for any reason, including bankruptcy. The landlord may also argue that the lease was rejected and thus terminated if it was not assumed during the bankruptcy, although this argument should fail.[762] While it is clear that relief from the automatic stay must be obtained to evict during the pendency of the bankruptcy case,[763] after the case the debtor must find some other protection.[764] The same analysis probably applies to private landlords receiving Section 8 subsidies,[765] even though the subsidy could not be terminated by the housing authority directly.

The possible arguments to the contrary are similar to those in the student loan context. The debtor may argue for extension of *Perez* to private entities. If the debtor can show that the landlord has tried to coerce payment of the discharged debt by threatening eviction, protection may also be obtained under section 524(a). In many places the debtor can also assert a right to remain based upon state law. For example in most rent-control jurisdictions and some other jurisdictions the tenant may only be evicted for good cause. It has been held in such areas that when the discharged debt is the only possible basis for the eviction, the eviction must be seen as a means to compel payment and thus enjoined.[766] Similarly, the debtor can argue that the eviction is barred because it is in retaliation for the debtor's exercise of rights granted under the law. At least as long as the debtor posts adequate security for future rent and is otherwise complying with the lease, this argument may well be persuasive. Of course, if a problem with the debtor's landlord is anticipated, the best course of action may be to file a chapter 13 case to take advantage of the additional options under that chapter.[767]

14.5.5.4 Social Security, Welfare, and Other Governmental Benefits

In many instances, debtors have debts to local, state or federal governmental agencies, that arise out of various public benefit programs and that they wish to discharge. These debts may arise out of a general duty to reimburse for such benefits, which exists under some state laws, or out of an overpayment which the debtor is required to repay.

In most cases these debts are clearly dischargeable as, absent certain kinds of fraud, they do not fall within any of the exceptions to discharge.[768] It seems clear that any future denial or recoupment of benefits because of the discharge would fall squarely within the prohibitions of sections 525(a) and/or 524(a).[769]

One situation which may sometimes arise concerns the debtor who has made an agreement to repay interim public assistance benefits received while the debtor is awaiting an award of Supplemental Security Income benefits (SSI). In such cases, federal law provides that the debtor's retroactive benefit check may be sent by the Social Security Adminis-

---

760 *In re* Stolz, 315 F.3d 80 (2d Cir. 2002) (§ 525 trumps any contrary language in § 365); *In re* Curry, 148 B.R. 966 (S.D. Fla. 1992); Gibbs v. Hous. Auth., 76 B.R. 257 (D. Conn. 1983), *aff'g* 9 B.R. 758 (Bankr. D. Conn. 1981); *In re* Pace, 23 Clearinghouse Rev. 1548 (Bankr. W.D. Ky. 1989); *In re* Szymecki, 87 B.R. 14 (Bankr. W.D. Pa. 1988); *In re* Sudler, 71 B.R. 780 (Bankr. E.D. Pa. 1986); *see* Form 84, Appx. G.10, *infra. But see In re* Robinson, 54 F.3d 316 (7th Cir. 1995) (if public housing lease was terminated prior to tenant's bankruptcy, lessor was not required by § 525 to renew lease); *In re* Smith, 259 B.R. 901 (B.A.P. 8th Cir. 2001) (§ 525 not applicable because debtor's public housing lease terminated due to fraud; dictum that there would be no protection under § 525 even if non-payment of rent was only reason); *In re* Valentin, 309 B.R. 715 (Bankr. E.D. Pa. 2004) (§ 525(a) protects only future right to participate in public housing program, not the lease itself); *In re* Lutz, 82 B.R. 699 (Bankr. M.D. Pa. 1988) (landlord who receives subsidy from Dep't of Housing and Urban Development toward debtor's rental is not a public entity subject to the Code's antidiscrimination provision).

761 *See* § 14.5.1, *supra.*

762 See discussion of assumption and rejection of leases in § 12.9, *supra.*

763 For a discussion of the automatic stay see Chapter 9, *supra.*

764 *See* 187 Concourse Associates v. Bunting, 670 N.Y.S.2d 686 (Civ. Ct. 1997) (pre-bankruptcy possessory judgment for apartment not discharged or vacated by bankruptcy).

765 *In re* Lutz, 82 B.R. 699 (Bankr. M.D. Pa. 1988). *But see In re* Oksentowicz, 2004 WL 2110408 (Bankr. E.D. Mich. Sept. 23, 2004) (privately-owned apartment complex participating in Section 8 housing program and subject to extensive regulation by the Dep't of Housing and Urban Development was governmental unit; discrimination found based on owner's refusal to accept debtor's rental application).

766 *In re* Malone, 19 Collier Bankr. Cas. (MB) 163 (Bankr. N.J. 1978); *In re* Smallwood, No. B-78-02468 (Bankr. D.N.J. Oct. 1978), 12 Clearinghouse Rev. 509 (Dec. 1978).

767 For a discussion of leases in chapter 13, see § 12.9, *supra.*

768 *In re* Ramirez, 795 F.2d 1494 (9th Cir. 1986) (debtor had no duty to reimburse state for welfare payments to his former spouse and children where there was no support order or court decree obligating him to provide support); Lee v. Schweiker, 739 F.2d 870 (3d Cir. 1984) (social security overpayment); *In re* Neavear, 674 F.2d 1201 (7th Cir. 1982) (social security overpayments); Baker v. United States, 100 B.R. 80 (M.D. Fla. 1989) (FECA disability benefits); *In re* Olson, 9 B.R. 52 (Bankr. E.D. Wis. 1981) (overpayment of unemployment benefits discharged); *In re* Hudson, 9 B.R. 363 (Bankr. N.D. Ill. 1981) (welfare overpayments allegedly obtained through fraud dischargeable in chapter 13); *see also* § 14.4.3.2.3, *supra.*

769 *In re* Cost, 161 B.R. 856 (Bankr. S.D. Fla. 1993) (attorney fees and costs awarded as sanctions to remedy Social Security Administration's recovery of discharged overpayment through withholding from benefits).

tration to the state welfare department so that the latter may deduct the amount owed under the agreement.[770]

If a bankruptcy is filed by the debtor recipient, the debt to the welfare department should be dischargeable unless the agency successfully argues an exception to discharge.[771] (It should be remembered that certain exceptions, such as fraud and false pretenses may not be raised except in the bankruptcy court and before the deadline set by the rules.)[772] In fact, it is likely that even the contingent liability under the agreement for welfare benefits not yet received can also be discharged, because contingent claims are included in the liabilities covered by the discharge.[773]

Thus, any action taken by the state to collect the debt would be stayed during the bankruptcy case by section 362(a)[774] and afterwards by section 524(a).[775] Moreover, the Social Security Administration could not discriminate against the debtor by sending the retroactive benefit check to the local welfare office, based upon the discharged debt, without violating section 525(a).[776] Finally, to the extent that the transfer has already taken place and was of property acquired within ninety days prior to the case, it would probably constitute a preference avoidable by the debtor or trustee.[777]

14.5.5.5 Criminal Proceedings, Fines, and Incarceration

In some cases, the tricky problem of dealing with criminal or quasi-criminal proceedings during or after bankruptcy may be encountered. During the bankruptcy, such problems may sometimes be dealt with through use of the automatic stay.[778] Both during and after the case, section 525(a) may also be applicable. Assuming that the right to be free from incarceration is a "license,"[779] then the state cannot incarcerate a debtor due to a debt that was discharged.[780] Similarly, driver's license suspensions, based on dischargeable unpaid traffic fines should be found to violate section 525(a).[781] To the extent that it can be shown that a criminal

---

770   42 U.S.C. § 1383(g).

771   *See* § 14.4.3.2.3, *supra*.

772   *See* § 14.4.2, *supra*.

773   Section 727(b) provides for discharge of all "debts" which arose before the bankruptcy. Section 101(12) defines "debt" as "liability on a claim" and section 101(5) defines "claim" to include contingent claims.

774   See discussion of automatic stay under this section in § 9.4, *supra*.

775   *But see In re* Vasquez, 788 F.2d 130 (3d Cir. 1984), *rev'g* 42 B.R. 609 (Bankr. E.D. Pa. 1984). The *Vasquez* decision ignored persuasive arguments that its finding of a common law assignment was contrary to state law. *See also* § 14.5.1, *supra*.

776   *See* § 14.5.3, *supra*. For a discussion of possible limitations on such an action based on sovereign immunity, see § 13.3.2.2, *supra*.

777   11 U.S.C. §§ 522(h), 547. Under section 547(e)(2) and (3), the transfer is made, for purposes of these sections only, when the debtor has acquired rights in the property transferred and the transfer takes effect. However, a debtor seeking to use section 522(h) might have to defend against the argument that the agreement was voluntary. Such an argument would probably be surmounted if the debtor could show that the alternative to signing was starving to death. See § 10.4.2.5, *supra*, for a discussion of these issues. These sections would prove particularly helpful if the welfare department attempted to argue that it had a security interest, a rather doubtful proposition in view of the wording of the regulation and agreements involved. Even if a lien were found to exist, any property acquired after the case was commenced would not be subject to that lien. *See* 11 U.S.C. § 552(a). Some preference actions against state or federal governments may be precluded by sovereign immunity. *See* § 13.3.2.2, *supra*.

778   See § 9.4.6, *supra*, for a discussion of related issues. *See generally In re* Poule, 91 B.R. 83 (B.A.P. 9th Cir. 1988) (comparison of application of automatic stay for restitution with application for fine); *In re* Coulter, 305 B.R. 748 (Bankr. D.S.C. 2003) (although automatic stay did not prohibit state court probation violation hearing, state which had filed a proof of claim for restitution and fees was bound by debtor's confirmed plan providing for their payment).

779   "License" has been defined as the "authority or liberty given to do or forbear any act," the "leave to do a thing which the licensor could prevent," and "permission to do something which without the license would not be allowable." *See* Black's Law Dictionary 1067 (4th ed. rev.).

780   *See generally* Pennsylvania Dep't of Public Welfare v. Davenport, 495 U.S. 552, 110 S. Ct. 2126, 109 L. Ed. 2d 588 (1990). The *Davenport* decision does not fully address whether a judge could have someone imprisoned for the probation violation inherent in not paying a dischargeable restitution order. However, the court's *dicta*, taken together with common sense, strongly suggests that a discharge and/or the automatic stay and/or the confirmed plan must preclude the debtor's incarceration for failure to pay restitution after a chapter 13 case has been filed. In fact, the court specifically found that the exception to the automatic stay for commencement or continuation of criminal proceedings did not encompass the enforcement of obligations arising out of such proceedings. *Id.*, 110 S. Ct. at 2132. In some instances that argument may have to be presented first to the state court sentencing judge. If necessary, emergency *habeas corpus* proceedings could bring the issue before a bankruptcy or other federal judge. *In re* Rainwater, 233 B.R. 126 (Bankr. N.D. Ala. 1999) (writ of *habeas corpus* granted to release debtor from imprisonment for violation of probation by not paying restitution that was provided for in chapter 13 plan), *vacated*, 254 B.R. 273 (N.D. Ala. 2000); *see* § 13.4.5, *supra*. But see Hucke v. Oregon, 992 F.2d 950 (9th Cir. 1993) (revocation of probation after nonpayment of restitution did not violate the automatic stay as attempt to collect debt because state court judge canceled restitution obligation when probation was revoked).

781   *See In re* Colon, 102 B.R. 421 (Bankr. E.D. Pa. 1989) (prepetition traffic fines are dischargeable in chapter 13; attempts to collect them by post-petition license suspension violate the automatic stay); *In re* Young, 10 B.R. 17 (Bankr. S.D. Cal. 1980) (state could not deny drivers license due to fine which would be discharged in chapter 13). Many criminal fines are no longer dischargeable in chapter 13, due to a 1994 amendment to 11 U.S.C. § 1328(a). *See* § 14.4.3.7, *supra*.

or contempt proceeding is for the purpose of collecting a discharged debt,[782] such proceedings are in violation of section 524(a) or (b).[783]

However, as discussed elsewhere in this chapter,[784] the court must first find that the fine or restitution order is a dischargeable debt. The Supreme Court has held that at least some restitution debts are not dischargeable in a chapter 7 case,[785] but such debts may be dischargeable in a chapter 13 case.[786] Similarly, fines are not generally dischargeable in chapter 7, but may be dischargeable in chapter 13.[787]

If those hurdles are overcome, along with such issues as abstention,[788] the bankruptcy forum's authority under 11 U.S.C. § 105, could give debtors significant protections in the many cases in which creditors and local authorities attempt to use criminal or contempt proceedings to coerce payments.[789] However, emotions in such cases may run high, and enforcement of the bankruptcy protections may not always be easy.

14.5.5.6 Tax Consequences of the Discharge

The law is clear that, generally speaking, the discharge of a debt in bankruptcy, unlike most other types of discharge of indebtedness without payment, is excludable from gross income for tax purposes.[790] Nonetheless, some creditors believe that they are required to send a bankruptcy debtor a 1099 Form when a debt is discharged in bankruptcy.[791] Although this problem may eventually disappear as a result

of clarifying tax regulations,[792] and the fact that the current version of Form 1099-C states on its reverse side that "debts canceled in bankruptcy are not includable in your income," it is likely to persist for some time.

These forms cause considerable confusion and harm to debtors. All too often, an unskilled tax preparer will see the 1099 form, assume the debtor had taxable income, and list the amount stated on the form as income on the debtor's tax return. It is also possible, but unlikely, that the Internal Revenue Service will incorrectly seek payment of taxes which are not owed based on a filed 1099.[793] A debtor could thus pay taxes that are not owed, often losing a needed tax refund.

A related problem can occur when a debt was forgiven by the creditor prior to the bankruptcy. The most common example is a deficiency obligation which is forgiven in exchange for a deed in lieu of foreclosure or another type of foreclosure workout. Although the pre-petition forgiveness of debt is technically a taxable event separate from the bankruptcy discharge,[794] it is generally not taxable in the event that the debtor was insolvent.[795] Tax issues can also arise when there is a foreclosure on a mortgage that was obtained after the original purchase of a property; if the mortgage was for more than the original purchase price a capital gain may be created. In most cases, however, the $500,000.00 capital gains exemption for sale of a debtor's principal residence will prevent any tax liability.

In view of the fact that these problems have become more common, attorneys should always advise debtors that the discharge of indebtedness in bankruptcy and most types of forgiveness of debt are not taxable. It is also helpful to recommend that a tax preparer with a question about the law on this issue should be referred to the attorney.

14.5.5.7 Enforcement of the Discharge Protections

In almost every case in which the debtor's discharge rights are being violated, it is wise to take some type of protective action. Even though a judgment obtained on a discharged debt is void,[796] that judgment could also cause illegal but harmful garnishment of the debtor's wages or seizure of the debtor's property. Thus, it is good practice to assert the protections of discharge as early as possible.

---

782 *See In re* Kaping, 13 B.R. 621 (Bankr. D. Or. 1981) (prosecution of criminal nonsupport charge enjoined where principal motivation was to obtain restitution of discharged debts).

783 *See* § 14.5.1, *supra*; *see also In re* Gilliam, 67 B.R. 83 (Bankr. M.D. Tenn. 1986). *But see In re* Daulton, 966 F.2d 1025 (6th Cir. 1992) (where creditors did not seek restitution, their signing of criminal complaint against debtor alleging fraudulent sale of collateral does not violate discharge injunction).

784 *See* § 14.4.3.7, *supra*.

785 Kelly v. Robinson, 479 U.S. 36, 107 S. Ct. 353, 93 L. Ed. 2d 216 (1986).

786 Pennsylvania Dep't of Public Welfare v. Davenport, 495 U.S. 552, 110 S. Ct. 2126, 109 L. Ed. 2d 588 (1990). But see 11 U.S.C. § 1328(a)(3) containing an exception to discharge in chapter 13 applicable to restitution included in a criminal sentence.

787 *See* § 14.4.3.7, *supra*.

788 *See* § 9.4.6, *supra*.

789 *See In re* Lenke, 249 B.R. 1 (Bankr. D. Ariz. 2000) (bankruptcy court had authority to enjoin prosecution if it was disguised effort to collect debt); *In re* Hudson, 9 B.R. 363 (Bankr. N.D. Ill. 1981); Rendleman, *The Bankruptcy Discharge: Toward a Fresher Start*, 58 N.C. L. Rev. 723, 736–741 (1980). *But see* § 9.4.6, *supra*.

790 Internal Revenue Code, 26 U.S.C. § 108(a)(1)(A).

791 Some confusion is possible because there may be tax consequences of pre-petition debt forgiveness, for example, if a deficiency obligation is forgiven in connection with a deed in lieu of foreclosure, as discussed below.

792 26 C.F.R. §§ 1.6050P-0, 1.6050P-1 (indebtedness discharged in bankruptcy required to be reported only if creditor knows that the debt was incurred for business or investment purposes).

793 This would obviously be an IRS error subject to dispute by the debtor.

794 26 U.S.C. § 61(a)(12).

795 26 U.S.C. § 108(a)(1)(B).

796 11 U.S.C. § 524(a)(1); *In re* Cruz, 254 B.R. 801 (Bankr. S.D.N.Y. 2000). *But see* Fed. Deposit Ins. Corp. v. Gulf Life Ins. Co., 737 F.2d 1513 (11th Cir. 1984) (bankruptcy defense rejected where it was pleaded but not proved); § 14.5.1.3, *supra*.

The first decision that arises in such cases is where to enforce the debtor's rights. Although they could be raised in the state forum in which a proceeding is already pending, it is usually preferable to go to the bankruptcy forum, which is likely to be more sympathetic to the debtor's concerns. The bankruptcy court clearly has jurisdiction over any proceeding relating to the debtor's bankruptcy, and in many cases a state court proceeding may be removed to federal district court.[797] If the debtor does litigate the issue in the non-bankruptcy court, there is a risk that any attempt to seek relief from the challenged actions in the bankruptcy court thereafter would be barred.[798]

Several remedies may be possible in the bankruptcy forum (in addition to simply defending a removed action). The federal court may issue a writ of *habeas corpus* to release a debtor incarcerated in state proceedings.[799] An injunction may be issued against private parties or state officials. If the problem is a common one, a class action should be considered, though it might be better to bring an individual case first if the law is unclear.[800] It is probably not necessary to reopen the bankruptcy case to seek remedies for a discharge violation,[801] though that may be the more prudent course. Attorney fees should be available in any action against state or local officials under section 524 or 525.[802] Finally, violators of the section 524(a) injunction can be held in contempt of court.[803] The remedies for civil

contempt can include both damages and attorney fees, even if the contempt is not willful.[804]

The debtor may also assert an implied private right of action under section 524 and seek equitable relief under section 105 of the Bankruptcy Code. Under the principles set forth by the Supreme Court in *Cort v. Ash*,[805] there is every reason to find that Congress intended that such a right of action exist. These issues were well analyzed by the district court in *Malone v. Norwest Financial California, Inc.*,[806] although that decision was later overruled.[807] The *Malone* court held, first, that the enforcement of the bankruptcy discharge is not a matter typically left to state law. Second, the debtors who receive discharge are clearly the specific intended beneficiaries of section 524, not mere incidental beneficiaries. Third, there is evidence of Congressional intent that there be implied remedies: the statute provides for rescission of invalid reaffirmations, for example, and such rescission logically gives rise to actions for enforcing the rescission and restitution. The mere fact that there is an explicit private right of action for violations of section 362, enacted by a later Congress, has no bearing on remedies for violations of section 524, because Congress might have already assumed such a

---

797 28 U.S.C. §§ 1334(b), 1452. See § 13.4.1, *supra*, for a discussion of removal. *See also In re* Myers, 18 B.R. 362 (Bankr. E.D. Va. 1982) (bankruptcy case reopened and creditor fined $10,000.00 for willful violation of discharge injunction).

798 *In re* Ferren, 203 F.3d 559 (8th Cir. 2000) (bankruptcy court lacked jurisdiction over debtor's attack on state court order disbursing foreclosure sale proceeds to judicial lienholders due to Rooker-Feldman doctrine); *cf. In re* Pavelich, 229 B.R. 777 (B.A.P. 9th Cir. 1999) (Rooker-Feldman doctrine did not prevent enforcement of discharge injunction); *In re* Presley, 288 B.R. 732 (Bankr. W.D. Va. 2003) (litigated judgment against debtor was void even though debtor did not raise bankruptcy defense).

799 See § 13.4.5, *supra*, for a discussion of the writ of *habeas corpus* in bankruptcy cases.

800 See § 13.7, *supra*, for a discussion of class actions in bankruptcy.

801 *See In re* Singleton, 269 B.R. 270 (Bankr. D.R.I. 2001), *vacated on other grounds*, 284 B.R. 322 (D.R.I. 2002), and cases cited therein.

802 See discussion of class actions in § 13.7, *supra*, and attorney fees in § 15.5, *infra*.

803 *In re* Hill, 222 B.R. 119 (Bankr. N.D. Ohio 1998) (creditor's calls to debtor after bankruptcy were willful and therefore in contempt of court even though creditor had procedures to prevent violations of discharge, debtor awarded attorney fees); *In re* Tardo, 145 B.R. 862 (E.D. La. 1992) (creditor's attorney found in contempt for seeking to collect attorney fees he would have received under contingent fee agreement with creditor after court rejected his argument that contingent attorney fee was a separate debt which had not been scheduled or discharged); *In re* Esposito, 119 B.R. 305 (Bankr. M.D. Fla. 1990) (unsecured creditor who tricked debtors into payment of dis-

charged debt found in contempt of court and ordered to pay damages and attorney fees); *In re* Barrup, 51 B.R. 318 (Bankr. D. Vt. 1985); *In re* Gallagher, 47 B.R. 92 (Bankr. W.D. Wis. 1985); *see also* § 14.5.1.4, *supra*.

804 *In re* Rosteck, 899 F.2d 694 (7th Cir. 1990) (sanctions imposed against condominium association that had attempted to collect post-petition condominium assessments which were discharged); *In re* Elias, 98 B.R. 332 (N.D. Ill. 1989) (creditor found in contempt even though violation of discharge injunction was not in bad faith, where creditor has knowledge of discharge order); *In re* Atkins, 279 B.R. 639 (Bankr. N.D.N.Y. 2002) ($30,000.00 damages awarded against federal government for attempts to collect discharged loan); *In re* Wasp, 137 B.R. 71 (Bankr. M.D. Fla. 1992) (action brought by home owners association to collect fees under pre-petition agreement which had been unmatured at time of bankruptcy filing constituted contempt); *In re* Burson, 107 B.R. 285 (Bankr. S.D. Cal. 1989) (government violated discharge injunction when it attempted to collect serviceman's repayment obligation; though obligation matured post-petition, government had contingent right to payment at time serviceman filed bankruptcy); *In re* Barrup, 51 B.R. 318 (Bankr. D. Vt. 1985); *In re* Gallagher, 47 B.R. 92 (Bankr. W.D. Wis. 1985); *see* McComb v. Jacksonville Paper Co., 336 U.S. 187, 191 (1949); Borg-Warner Acceptance Corp. v. Hall, 685 F.2d 1306 (11th Cir. 1982); Vuitton et Fils S.A. v. Carousel Handbags, 592 F.2d 126 (2d Cir. 1979); § 9.6, *supra*. Note that a subsequent statutory amendment may have overruled the *Burson* case by making such claims nondischargeable. *See* 37 U.S.C. §§ 301d(c)(3), 317(f)(3); *see also* § 14.5.1.4, *supra*. *But see* 26 U.S.C. § 7433(e), which appears to limit damages for violations of the discharge injunction by the Internal Revenue Service to willful violations.

805 422 U.S. 66, 95 S. Ct. 2080, 45 L. Ed. 2d 26 (1975).

806 245 B.R. 389 (E.D. Cal. 2000); *see also* Molloy v. Primus Auto. Fin. Services, 247 B.R. 804 (C.D. Cal. 2000) (finding private right of action under § 524); Rogers v. Nationscredit Fin. Services, 233 B.R. 98 (N.D. Cal. 1999).

807 Walls v. Wells Fargo Bank, 276 F.3d 502 (9th Cir. 2002).

remedy existed based on the rescission remedies available. Indeed, the Supreme Court has held that the availability of statutory injunctive relief does not limit the corollary equitable powers to order rescission and restitution.[808] And the legislative history shows that Congress intended broad discharge protections for bankruptcy debtors; to restrict those remedies would be inconsistent with that intent. For the same reason, there is no basis for finding that Congress intended to preempt state consumer protection laws or restrict use of other federal consumer protection laws as they apply to bankruptcy debtors.[809]

A number of courts have held that there is no private right of action that allows a class of debtors to pursue relief for violations of the discharge order.[810] Some courts have also held that contempt of the discharge injunction is the only remedy for violations of the discharge and preempts state law remedies.[811] As discussed above, these cases are clearly

wrong given that the discharge injunction is a creation of statute. Unlike other contempt claims, this uniform order need not be enforced solely by an individual contempt proceeding in the court that issued it, because debtors are enforcing a statutory right rather than a unique order that requires interpretation by its maker.[812] Moreover, there is ample authority to enforce the discharge injunction by requiring disgorgement and other equitable remedies under 11 U.S.C. § 105(a).[813]

Reopening of the bankruptcy case may be required to address post-discharge issues, although not all courts require it as a prerequisite to enforcing the discharge. Reopening should be liberally granted where necessary to afford relief for the debtor.[814]

Thus, the bankruptcy forum does not offer assistance to debtors only during their bankruptcy cases. Its expanded reach enables it to provide a full measure of protection as long as it is needed in relation to the bankruptcy and the debts discharged therein. The bankruptcy forum has become one to which consumer debtors can turn to solve many of their problems, applying a law which, unlike most, is designed principally to benefit those unfortunate people who so often find themselves victimized elsewhere.

---

808 *See* California v. Am. Stores, 495 U.S. 271, 110 S. Ct. 1853, 109 L. Ed. 2d 240 (1990) (injunctive relief available under Clayton Act creates power to order other equitable relief including divestiture of acquired assets); Porter v. Warner Holding Co., 328 U.S. 395, 66 S. Ct. 1086, 90 L. Ed. 1332 (1946) (grant of specific equitable powers by statute did not restrict other equitable powers unless statute explicitly so stated).

809 Randolph v. IMBS, Inc., 368 F.3d 726 (7th Cir. 2004) (no irreconcilable conflict exists between Fair Debt Collection Practices Act and Bankruptcy Code, so both statutes can be enforced simultaneously); Sears Roebuck & Co. v. O'Brien, 178 F.3d 962 (8th Cir. 1999) (state debt collection law violated by creditor sending reaffirmation solicitation letter); Molloy v. Primus Auto. Fin. Services, 247 B.R. 804 (C.D. Cal. 2000); *In re* Faust, 270 B.R. 310 (Bankr. M.D. Ga. 1998) (recommending judgment under Fair Debt Collection Practices Act for acts that violated discharge injunction).

810 *E.g., In re* Bassett, 285 F.3d 882 (9th Cir. 2002); Cox v. Zale Del., Inc., 239 F.3d 910 (7th Cir. 2001); Pertuso v. Ford Motor Credit Co., 233 F.3d 417 (6th Cir. 2000); Walls v. Wells Fargo Bank, 255 B.R. 38 (E.D. Cal. 2000); Bessette v. Avco Fin. Services, 230 F.3d 439 (1st Cir. 2000) (the court of appeals found that an action could be brought to remedy discharge violations under 11 U.S.C. § 105).

811 *E.g.,* Cox v. Zale Del., Inc., 239 F.3d 910 (7th Cir. 2001); Pertuso v. Ford Motor Credit Co., 233 F.3d 417 (6th Cir. 2000);

Walls v. Wells Fargo Bank, 255 B.R. 38 (E.D. Cal. 2000); Rogers v. Nationscredit Fin. Services Corp., 233 B.R. 98 (N.D. Cal. 1999), *overruled by* Walls v. Wells Fargo Bank, 276 F.3d 502 (9th Cir. 2002).

812 Bessette v. Avco Fin. Services, Inc., 230 F.3d 439 (1st Cir. 2000) (discharge injunction may be enforced in class action because statutory injunction under § 524 is a uniform order in every bankruptcy case).

813 Bessette v. Avco Fin. Services, Inc., 230 F.3d 439 (1st Cir. 2000) (section 524 may be enforced through section 105); *In re* Mickens, 229 B.R. 114 (Bankr. W.D. Va. 1999); *In re* Vazquez, 221 B.R. 222 (Bankr. N.D. Ill. 1998) (actual and punitive damages awarded pursuant to § 105).

814 *See* Fed. R. Bankr. P. 5010. No filing fee is required to reopen a case if the reopening is for actions related to the debtor's discharge. *See* Judicial Conference Schedule of Fees, reprinted in Appendix C, *infra.*

Chapter 15

Attorney Fees for Debtor's Counsel in Consumer Bankruptcy Cases

15.1 Introduction

A topic of more than passing interest to private attorneys representing consumer debtors is the matter of attorney fees. While the general factors governing decisions concerning what fees to charge and how to collect them can be very similar to those for other types of legal matters, bankruptcy attorney fees are unusual in several ways.

Unlike most clients of private practitioners, bankruptcy clients are always facing serious financial problems. They may have great difficulties in paying even modest fees. These difficulties require counsel to consider alternatives to the typical fee arrangements under which some amount is paid in advance with the remainder billed as services are performed. Such arrangements may be particularly disadvantageous as to unpaid balances owed when the petition is filed; the debt for these pre-bankruptcy services is dischargeable[1] and any attempt to collect the debt would violate the automatic stay imposed by 11 U.S.C. § 362.[2]

Another unusual aspect of bankruptcy attorney fees is the requirement that all such fees be disclosed to the court and approved by the court. While in a typical case this requirement has no impact on the ultimate receipt of fees, special circumstances, as discussed below, can render it important in a particular case.

A third key difference, in chapter 13 cases and in occasional chapter 7 cases involving the liquidation of assets, is the possibility for payment of attorney fees through the court's administration of the bankruptcy. Most typically, this means that fees may be paid as a priority claim through the debtor's chapter 13 plan, an arrangement that provides one solution for the debtor unable to pay all or even part of the fee in advance.

15.2 Initial Fee Arrangements with Clients

15.2.1 The Basic Fee

As in any other matter, it is very important for the attorney and client to discuss and have a clear understanding of fee arrangements as early as possible. Normally, this discussion occurs at the first interview with the debtor. Many attorneys have preprinted retainer agreements or brochures, that they give to clients at this initial consultation, spelling out exactly which services are covered by the attorney's basic fee, and what charges will be made for additional services, should they prove necessary. Naturally, these written materials and all fee arrangements should be consistent with any previous advertisements or representations that the attorney has made.[3]

Many attorneys, as well as some courts in their review of counsel's compensation, begin the process of setting fees by deciding upon a reasonable basic fee for those services necessary in every bankruptcy case.[4] This fee covers the initial consultation and advice to a debtor about alternatives to bankruptcy, consequences of bankruptcy, whether to file, and under what chapter to file. It also encompasses preparation of the initial papers, such as the petition, schedules, statement of affairs and chapter 13 plan, as well as any factual investigation necessary for that task. In addition, the basic fee includes compensation for attendance at the meeting of creditors, chapter 13 confirmation hearing, and discharge hearing (when a discharge hearing is required). Finally, this fee is deemed to encompass ancillary minor and

---

1 *In re* Bethea, 352 F.3d 1125 (7th Cir. 2003) (post-petition collection of pre-petition fees violated automatic stay); *In re* Biggar, 110 F.3d 685 (9th Cir. 1997); *In re* Newkirk, 297 B.R. 457 (Bankr. W.D.N.C. 2002) (obtaining postdated checks for pre-petition fees, to be cashed post-petition, violated automatic stay and created conflict of interest with client; *see also In re* Perez, 177 B.R. 319 (Bankr. D. Neb. 1995) (any reaffirmation of pre-petition debt for attorney fees must comply with all requirements for reaffirmation).

2 See Chapter 9, *supra*, for a general discussion of the automatic stay.

3 *See In re* Stewart, 10 B.R. 472 (Bankr. E.D. Va. 1981) (court reduced fees agreed upon by debtors to level which had been advertised in local publications).

4 *See, e.g., In re* Stewart, 10 B.R. 472 (Bankr. E.D. Va. 1981); *In re* Hill, 5 B.R. 541 (Bankr. C.D. Cal. 1980); *In re* St. Pierre, 4 B.R. 184 (Bankr. D.R.I. 1980); *see also In re* Bancroft, 204 B.R. 548 (Bankr. C.D. Ill. 1997) (attorney who did not personally interview clients or attend meeting of creditors was not providing even minimum level of professional services and was not entitled to attorney fee).

routine tasks and advice to the debtor throughout the course of the case, which are often listed in the applicable local rule.

However, it is clear that the basic fee is not cast in stone and serves more as a guideline for the convenience and efficiency of the court and counsel, permitting prompt approval of fees without a detailed review of the work done. Because fees in bankruptcy cases are to be awarded on the same basis as fees in other cases, counsel is entitled to request more than the court's normal fee, even in a routine case, under the "lodestar method" which provides for compensation at a reasonable hourly rate for time reasonably expended.[5] Nonetheless, counsel seeking to deviate from the basic fee may face a substantial burden in convincing the court that the rates and hours sought are reasonable when other attorneys in the district routinely perform the same services at a lower cost.[6]

15.2.2 Amounts Typically Charged

While there are great variations in the amounts charged to cover these basic services, the range in chapter 7 cases is usually from $500.00 to $1500.00 and many courts set an informal limit between $500.00 and $1000.00.[7] Some at-

torneys and courts consider it appropriate to add a small increment to this fee in joint cases[8] or when other complications make the case more difficult than average to prepare.[9] Similarly, in chapter 13 cases, basic fees generally range from $750.00 to $2000.00,[10] but in complicated cases may be up to $5000.00, or more. Although the presumptive fee maximums set by courts can normally be overcome by additional evidence justifying a higher fee in particular cases, the presumptive fees and procedures for overcoming the presumptions are also subject to judicial review and may be set aside where they are arbitrary or outdated.[11]

For attorneys in doubt regarding what amounts are appropriate in a particular locale, it is usually a good idea to visit the clerk's office and review the fee disclosure statements which have been filed and approved in recent cases. Often, a discussion of the question with a trustee or attorney more experienced in bankruptcy can also prove helpful.

An attorney can usually predict other services that will be necessary, such as motions to avoid liens or the filing of a homestead deed, once the facts of a debtor's case are known. The fees for such services, assuming that they will proceed

---

5 Zolfo, Cooper & Co. v. Sunbeam-Oster Co., 50 F.3d 253 (3d Cir. 1995) (baseline rule for professional fees in bankruptcy cases is for firms to receive their normal rates); *In re* Boddy, 950 F.2d 334 (6th Cir. 1991) (use of $650.00 "normal and customary" fee for bankruptcy case, rather than lodestar method, was abuse of discretion); *In re* Barger, 180 B.R. 326 (Bankr. S.D. Ga. 1995) (lodestar method should be used in chapter 13 case); *see also In re* Zwern, 181 B.R. 80 (Bankr. D. Colo. 1995) (counsel seeking to use lodestar method must submit meaningful time records and task summaries). *But see In re* Eliapo, 298 B.R. 392 (B.A.P. 9th Cir. 2003) (attorney who had opted for standardized "no look" standard fee could not later seek lodestar computation of higher fee for services covered by "no look" fee).

6 *See In re* Peterson, 251 B.R. 359 (B.A.P. 8th Cir. 2000) (reducing hourly rate and number of hours in fee request based on court's perceptions of amounts charged by other local attorneys); *In re* Finlasen, 250 B.R. 446 (Bankr. S.D. Fla. 2000) (reducing fees because time sheets did not indicate date of each entry and there was evidence that they were a form list of time entries); *In re* Thorn, 192 B.R. 52 (Bankr. N.D.N.Y. 1995) (fees reduced to amounts customarily charged when no time records or other evidence introduced to support unusually high fees requested in routine cases).

7 *See In re* Agnew, 144 F.3d 1013 (7th Cir. 1998) (presumptive fee of $575.00 upheld in cases in which attorney offered no evidence that his services were worth more); *In re* Geraci, 138 F.3d 314 (7th Cir. 1998) (presumptive $800.00 fee for no asset chapter 7 case not abuse of discretion); *In re* Sturgeon, 242 B.R. 724 (Bankr. E.D. Okla. 1999) (fee between $500.00 and $750.00 for simple case was presumptively reasonable); *In re* Crivilare, 213 B.R. 721 (Bankr. S.D. Ill. 1997) (presumptively reasonable fee in district for no asset chapter 7 case is $700.00); Geraci v. Hopper, 208 B.R. 907 (Bankr. C.D. Ill. 1997) (attorney required to submit documentation in support of request in excess of presumptively reasonable $800.00 fee for chapter 7

case), *aff'd*, 138 F.3d 314 (7th Cir. 1998); *see also* Jean Braucher, *Lawyers and Consumer Bankruptcy: One Code, Many Cultures*, 67 Am. Bankr. L.J. 501 (1993) (range of fees and median fees charged to chapter 7 clients in four cities studied were: Austin—ranged from $500.00 to $1800.00 with median of $700.00 to $750.00; San Antonio—ranged from $500.00 to $1100.00 with median of $700.00 to $750.00; Cincinnati—ranged from $400.00 to $600.00 with median of $450.00 to $500.00; Dayton—ranged from $250.00 to $600.00 with a median of $300.00 to $350.00).

8 *In re* Stewart, 10 B.R. 472 (Bankr. E.D. Va. 1981) ($85.00 added in joint case).

9 *In re* St. Pierre, 4 B.R. 184 (Bankr. D.R.I. 1981) ($150.00 added for completion of Statement of Affairs for Debtors Engaged in Business).

10 *In re* Migiano, 242 B.R. 759 (Bankr. S.D. Fla. 2000) (chapter 13 fees typically range from $1500.00 to $2500.00); *In re* Howell, 226 B.R. 279 (Bankr. M.D. Fla. 1998) ($1300.00 a reasonable fee for routine chapter 13 case); *In re* Yates, 217 B.R. 296 (Bankr. N.D. Okla. 1998) (detailed fee application and time records required if attorney seeks more than $1300.00 flat fee maximum); *In re* Roffle, 216 B.R. 290 (Bankr. D. Colo. 1998) (presumptive fee for uncomplicated chapter 13 case of $1200.00); *see, e.g., In re* Casull, 139 B.R. 525 (Bankr. D. Colo. 1992) (fee reduced to court's standard fee of $1200.00 because of lack of adequate documentation that higher fee was warranted); *In re* Fricker, 131 B.R. 932 (Bankr. E.D. Pa. 1991) ($1200.00 normal maximum charge for typical chapter 13 case); *see also* Jean Braucher, *Lawyers and Consumer Bankruptcy: One Code, Many Cultures*, 67 Am. Bankr. L.J. 501 (1993) (fees charged to most chapter 13 clients in four cities studied were Austin—$1500.00, San Antonio—$1300.00, Cincinnati—$650.00, Dayton—$650.00).

11 *In re* Kindhart, 160 F.3d 1176 (7th Cir. 1998) (bankruptcy court required to update presumptive fees, which had not been adjusted in ten years); *In re* Ingersoll, 238 B.R. 202 (D. Colo. 1999) (bankruptcy court ordered to change fee procedures which unduly restricted rights to obtain fees above presumptive amounts).

routinely, should also be set in advance. In some cases an agreement for a percentage contingency fee may be appropriate, but no such agreement may override the court's duty to determine whether fees are reasonable. If the agreement produces a fee in excess of the reasonable value of services rendered, the excess portion of the claim may be disallowed.[12]

Lastly, the attorney and client should agree upon an arrangement for fees, usually at an hourly rate prevalent in the community, should complications arise. Such complications might include a motion for relief from the automatic stay, the need to object to a claim, or a dischargeability complaint. In every case the debtor should be advised of all costs likely to be incurred, including the necessary filing fees, as well as possible costs for title searches and appraisals. The attorney must bear in mind, however, that unless withdrawal from the case is permitted the attorney will, in many jurisdictions, be expected to handle all aspects of the case even if the client does not pay these fees.[13]

15.2.3 Method of Payment

In chapter 7 cases, an attorney usually wants to be paid all or most of the fee in advance of the filing. Because the attorney fee is a dischargeable debt and collection efforts are subject to the automatic stay, collection after filing may prove difficult.[14] It does seem clear that payment of the attorney fee prior to filing is not a preference, because the payment is not for an antecedent debt, but rather for work done substantially contemporaneously or to be done in the future.[15]

Although a few courts have held otherwise, fees paid as a pre-petition retainer in advance for post-petition services that the attorney commits to provide also should not be deemed property of the bankruptcy estate.[16] The attorney fee should be deemed earned when the attorney contracts to provide future services in exchange for it.[17] The Supreme Court has generally approved of this method of payment in chapter 7 cases.[18] Alternatively, at a minimum, the fees paid should be deemed subject to a possessory lien that survives the bankruptcy.[19]

A few courts have attempted to draw a distinction between pre-petition and post-petition services. These courts permit an attorney to collect fees after the petition is filed for post-petition services on the theory that the debt for such services is created only when the services are rendered.[20] At least one court has permitted an attorney to take postdated checks from a client for post-petition, but not pre-petition, legal work.[21] Even assuming these courts are correct, most attorneys will not wish to be owed fees after the petition is filed because most of the work in a routine chapter 7 case is done, or should be done, before the petition is filed, and because of the procedural obstacles to withdrawing as counsel once the case is filed if fees are not paid.[22]

Generally, an attorney may not enter into an arrangement with a client to provide only pre-petition services in a

---

12 *In re* Yermakov, 718 F.2d 1465 (9th Cir. 1983).

13 *See, e.g., In re* Egwim, 291 B.R. 559 (Bankr. N.D. Ga. 2003) (attorney expected to represent debtor in all contested matters and adversary proceedings and could not enter into agreement limiting representation to less); *In re* Johnson, 291 B.R. 462 (Bankr. D. Minn. 2003) (attorney could not enter into fee agreement that did not include representation at § 341 meeting).

14 Attorneys in a few jurisdictions have attempted to offer "no money down" chapter 7 cases, arguing that their fees in the bankruptcy cases were not dischargeable and could be collected post-petition. These arguments have generally, and properly, been rejected. *In re* Bethea, 352 F.3d 1125 (7th Cir. 2003) (post-petition collection of pre-petition fees violated automatic stay); *In re* Biggar, 110 F.3d 685 (9th Cir. 1997); *In re* Symes, 174 B.R. 114 (Bankr. D. Ariz. 1994); *see also In re* Newkirk, 297 B.R. 457 (Bankr. W.D.N.C. 2002) (obtaining postdated checks for pre-petition fees, to be cashed post-petition, violated automatic stay and created conflict of interest with client); *In re* Haynes, 216 B.R. 440 (Bankr. D. Colo. 1997) (fee agreement calling for post-petition payments in chapter 7 created conflict of interest and did not reflect fact that most of attorney's work was done pre-petition thereby creating a dischargeable debt); *In re* Martin, 197 B.R. 120 (Bankr. D. Colo. 1996) (fee agreement which permitted the debtor to pay fee through post-petition installments gave rise to conflict of interest and entire fee disallowed).

15 See § 10.4.2.6.4, *supra*, for discussion of avoidable preferences.

16 *In re* Redding, 247 B.R. 474 (B.A.P. 8th Cir. 2000) (fees paid before bankruptcy were from non-estate property absent some other proceeding which rendered funds estate property).

17 *See* Ruan v. Butera, Beausang, Cohen & Brennan, 193 F.3d 210 (3d Cir. 1999) (advance retainer was nonrefundable under state law and became property of attorney when paid); Indian Motorcycle Associates III Ltd. Partnership v. Massachusetts Hous. Fin. Agency, 66 F.3d 1246, 1254, 1255 (1st Cir. 1995); *In re* Jones, 236 B.R. 38 (D. Colo. 1999) (reasonable attorney fees received prior to petition for services to be performed post-petition were not property of the estate).

18 Lamie v. United States Trustee, 124 S. Ct. 1023, 1032 157 L. Ed. 2d 1024, 1036 (2004) ("It appears to be routine for debtors to pay reasonable fees for legal services before filing for bankruptcy to ensure compliance with statutory requirements. See generally Collier Compensation, Employment and Appointment of Trustees and Professionals in Bankruptcy Cases ¶ 3.02[1], p. 3-2 (2002) ("In the majority of cases, the debtor's counsel will accept an individual or a joint consumer chapter 7 case only after being paid a retainer that covers the 'standard fee' and the cost of filing the petition.").").

19 *In re* Century Cleaning Services, 215 B.R. 18 (B.A.P. 9th Cir. 1997), *aff'd on other grounds*, 195 F.3d 1053 (9th Cir. 1999); *In re* Hodes, 289 B.R. 5 (D. Kan. 2003) (debtors' counsel had valid retaining liens against retainers paid pre-petition for post-petition services).

20 *In re* Sanchez, 241 F.3d 1148 (9th Cir. 2001); *In re* Hines, 147 F.3d 1185 (9th Cir. 1998); *In re* McNickle, 274 B.R. 477 (Bankr. S.D. Ohio 2002).

21 *In re* Jastrem, 224 B.R. 125 (Bankr. E.D. Cal. 1998). However, this practice may violate state consumer protection laws.

22 *See In re* Davis, 258 B.R. 510 (Bankr. M.D. Fla. 2001) (denying attorney's motion to withdraw after confirmation even though contract with debtor provided that attorney would represent them only through confirmation).

bankruptcy case.[23] Attempts to have clients reaffirm debts for pre-petition legal work have obvious ethical ramifications, because the attorney's duty to advise the debtor about reaffirmation presents a conflict with her own interest in being paid.[24] Of course, a chapter 7 debtor faced with post-petition litigation in the bankruptcy case may pay legal fees for such litigation from post-petition earnings or other property that is not property of the estate, provided those fees are properly disclosed.[25]

Practically speaking, this means that the debtor also must pay the entire filing fee in advance, because installment filing fee payments are not permitted when the debtor has paid any money or property to an attorney for services in connection with the case.[26] The attorney fee may be paid in ways other than cash from the client. It may be paid by a third party such as a friend or relative. The debtor may also give the attorney a security interest in property or transfer property outright to the attorney. However, the potential for later problems in enforcing the security interest or establishing the fair value of transferred property may make such arrangements inadvisable. They also create the possibility of a conflict of interest between the attorney and the debtor or the estate.[27] When a bankruptcy attorney is a creditor of the estate by virtue of a debt for pre-petition non-bankruptcy-related work, there may be a conflict of interest justifying denial of that attorney's bankruptcy fee.[28]

The remaining method by which an attorney may be compensated is through payment from the debtor's estate. As discussed below,[29] this arrangement is common in chapter 13 cases. It is possible in a chapter 7 case filed by a consumer only if 1) the attorney is specifically appointed by the court to represent the trustee in a particular matter[30] and 2) the debtor has sufficient non-exempt property to pay all priority administrative expenses in full. Because attorneys for chapter 7 debtors rarely are appointed to represent the estate and because debtors, if they receive good advice, normally protect their non-exempt property by converting it to exempt property[31] or by filing a chapter 13 petition,[32] this method of payment in consumer chapter 7 cases is quite rare. Moreover, all attorney fees paid from estate property must be approved in advance.[33]

Attorneys other than the attorney for a debtor in a chapter 7 or chapter 13 case also must be appointed to represent the estate, and this rule can sometimes create pitfalls for unsuspecting non-bankruptcy attorneys, especially attorneys in personal injury cases. When a claim is property of the estate, the estate must file an application to retain counsel to pursue the claim.[34] Often the estate will retain counsel who was handling the case prior to the bankruptcy, especially if that counsel had a fee agreement creating a lien on the proceeds of the claim. But if an attorney pursues a claim belonging to the estate without being appointed to represent the estate, that attorney may be denied all fees in connection with the matter.[35]

---

23 *But see In re* Castorena, 270 B.R. 504 (Bankr. D. Idaho 2001) (permitting fee for work done under agreement to provide pre-petition work only, but reducing fee from $250.00 to $125.00).

24 *In re* Pasco, 220 B.R. 119 (Bankr. D. Colo. 1998) (reaffirmation agreement with attorney did not provide adequate disclosure to client that debt was dischargeable). *But see In re* Nidiver, 217 B.R. 581 (Bankr. D. Neb. 1998) (permitting reaffirmation of attorney fee for pre-petition services due to benefits to debtors of continuing to have counsel represent them; court did not explain why payment for post-petition services would not be sufficient).

25 *See In re* Bressman, 327 F.3d 229 (3d Cir. 2003) (attorneys not required to disgorge fees paid from estate property when they had taken precautions to avoid being paid with estate assets).

26 Fed. R. Bankr. P. 1006(b)(3).

27 *See In re* Martin, 62 B.R. 943 (D. Me. 1986), *aff'd*, 817 F.2d 175 (1st Cir. 1987); *In re* Automend, Inc., 85 B.R. 173 (Bankr. N.D. Ga. 1988).

28 *See In re* Pierce, 809 F.2d 1356 (8th Cir. 1987); *In re* Hargis, 73 B.R. 622 (Bankr. N.D. Tex. 1987).

29 *See* § 15.4, *infra.*

30 Lamie v. United States Trustee, 124 S. Ct. 1023, 1032, 157 L. Ed. 2d 1024, 1036 (2004) (attorney for chapter 7 debtor who has not been appointed to represent estate cannot be paid from estate because amendment to 11 U.S.C. § 330(a) made by the Bank-

ruptcy Reform Act of 1994 deleted reference to "the debtor's attorney" as one of the persons who could be paid professional fees). Fortunately, a new provision, section 330(a)(4)(B), makes clear that the court can award fees to debtors' attorneys in chapters 12 and 13.

31 *See* § 6.5.2.2, *supra,* for a discussion of such exemption planning.

32 *See* § 12.8, *supra,* for a discussion of the debtor's right to retain possession of non-exempt property in a chapter 13 case.

33 11 U.S.C. § 330(a).

34 11 U.S.C. § 327(a); Fed. R. Bankr. P. 2014(a). Special counsel may be appointed to handle a matter on a contingent fee basis. In such cases, the bankruptcy court may not later review the agreed contingent fee to see if it is reasonable, except in cases where it finds that unanticipated developments rendered the original agreement improvident. *In re* Reimers, 972 F.2d 1127 (9th Cir. 1992).

35 *See In re* Anderson, 936 F.2d 199 (5th Cir. 1991) (although attorney may be denied fees for all work done before attorney was appointed, court has discretion to approve employment *nunc pro tunc*); *In re* Alcala, 918 F.2d 99 (9th Cir. 1990); Tanenbaum v. Smith, Friedman & Associates, 289 B.R. 800 (D.N.J. 2002) (bankruptcy court could void settlement of personal injury action that belonged to estate and had not been disclosed; attorney waived retaining lien by surrendering files); *cf. In re* Chaparro Marinez, 293 B.R. 387 (Bankr. N.D. Tex. 2003) (when debtor had successfully exempted personal injury cause of action it ceased to be property of estate and attorney did not have to be appointed by court, or have fees in settlement approved by court).

15.3 Court Supervision of Bankruptcy Attorney Fees

15.3.1 Introduction

One aspect of attorney fees in bankruptcy that is somewhat unusual is the close court supervision of the fees charged. In addition, monitoring and, when appropriate, commenting upon attorney fees applications is one of the primary duties of the United States trustee's office.[36] This supervision of attorney fees in bankruptcy arises mainly from an unfortunate history of abuse and overreaching by the bankruptcy bar.

The purpose of the monitoring is twofold. First, it was designed to prevent bankruptcies in which the debtor has significant assets from becoming boondoggles for the lawyers involved. Scandals in cases where little, if anything, was left for creditors by the time the attorneys finished compensating themselves have left the bankruptcy courts quite sensitive to this problem. Second, the scrutiny of fees paid by the debtor is based upon a recognition that bankruptcy clients are particularly vulnerable to attorney overreaching.[37] Court oversight now prevents much of that overreaching.

15.3.2 Disclosures Required

Hence, both the Code and the Federal Rules of Bankruptcy Procedure have strict requirements for disclosure of all fees. Section 329(a) requires any attorney who represents a debtor in a bankruptcy case, or in connection with a bankruptcy case, to file a statement of all compensation paid or agreed to be paid in connection with services rendered within one year prior to filing, or to be rendered, which are related to the bankruptcy. Such a statement must be filed even if the attorney has charged only for advice or preparation of papers and has not appeared in the bankruptcy case.[38] The same section requires disclosure of the source of all such compensation.[39] It is important to note that the statute requires disclosure of sums already paid as well as money to be paid prospectively. It is improper to list only money which is expected from the estate.

Bankruptcy Rule 2016(b) requires the statement of compensation to be filed within fifteen days after a voluntary petition is filed or at such other time as the court may direct. In addition it must be transmitted to the United States trustee. The failure to file this form may jeopardize an attorney's right to receive any fees at all.[40] The rule also requires a statement regarding whether the attorney has shared or agreed to share such compensation with any other person, and the particulars of any such sharing arrangement, except when the sharing is with another attorney in the same firm.[41] The rules make clear that any sharing in the form of referral or forwarding fees to attorneys who have not performed real service to earn their portion of the fee are not allowed, and can be the basis for the denial of fees for all

---

36 28 U.S.C. § 586(a)(3).

37 *See generally* H.R. Rep. No. 95-595, at 329 (1977); Advisory Committee Note to Fed. R. Bankr. P. 2017.

38 *In re* Zepecki, 277 F.3d 1041 (8th Cir. 2002) (fees for services in connection with pre-petition sale of property were fees for services in contemplation of bankruptcy which had to be disclosed); *In re* Basham, 208 B.R. 926 (B.A.P. 9th Cir. 1997) (attorney who prepared papers for debtors who filed "pro per" but did not file fee disclosure, and who charged excessive fees for services rendered, required to disgorge all fees); *In re* Mayeaux, 269 B.R. 614 (Bankr. E.D. Tex. 2001) (fees paid for assistance in connection with claims of mismanagement and misappropriation were for services in contemplation of bankruptcy and had to be disclosed); *In re* Campbell, 259 B.R. 615 (Bankr. N.D. Ohio 2001) (fees for services in connection with refinancing to complete chapter 13 plan should have been disclosed).

39 This section has been held to also require disclosures by non-attorneys providing services of a legal nature. *In re* Telford, 36 B.R. 92 (B.A.P. 9th Cir. 1984).

40 *In re* Kisseberth, 273 F.3d 714 (6th Cir. 2001) (affirming order requiring disgorgement of fees when disclosure requirements not met); *In re* Downs, 103 F.3d 472 (6th Cir. 1996) (disgorgement of fees is appropriate remedy when fee disclosure requirements not met); *In re* Redding, 263 B.R. 874 (B.A.P. 8th Cir. 2001) (affirming order requiring disgorgement of fees when disclosure requirements not met); *In re* Basham, 208 B.R. 926 (B.A.P. 9th Cir. 1997) (attorney who prepared papers for debtors who filed "pro per" but did not file fee disclosure, and who charged excessive fees for services rendered, required to disgorge all fees); *In re* Bell, 212 B.R. 654 (Bankr. E.D. Cal. 1997) (attorney who failed to file timely fee disclosure, charged excessive fees and failed to disclose potential conflict of interest created by borrowing money on debtors' behalf ordered to disgorge all fees); *In re* Fricker, 131 B.R. 932 (Bankr. E.D. Pa. 1991) (court has discretion to require disgorgement of all fees where disclosure not filed); *see also In re* Park-Helena Corp., 63 F.3d 877 (9th Cir. 1995) (fees denied completely when attorneys failed to disclose source of pre-petition retainer); *In re* Ostas, 158 B.R. 312 (N.D.N.Y. 1993) (attorney ordered to disgorge $1600.00 in fees charged to obtain stay of foreclosure as fees that were not disclosed; fees were "in connection" with bankruptcy case).

41 *See In re* Holmes, 304 B.R. 292 (Bankr. N.D. Miss. 2004) (failing to disclose bonuses paid to non-attorney staff in connection with particular bankruptcy cases violated Rule 2016(b)). Other fee sharing arrangements are generally prohibited under 11 U.S.C. § 504, at least if the compensation is from property of the estate. *See In re* Wright, 290 B.R. 145 (Bankr. C.D. Cal. 2003) (discussing rules for disclosure of payments to "appearance attorney" who attends creditors meeting or hearing); *In re* Greer, 271 B.R. 426 (Bankr. D. Mass. 2002) (it was improper fee-sharing to pay another attorney $50.00 to represent debtors at creditors meeting because merely listing attorney on letterhead and adding attorney to malpractice insurance did not establish "of counsel" relationship); *In re* Palladino, 267 B.R. 825 (Bankr. N.D. Ill. 2001) (disallowing fees sought in fee application for attorneys who were not part of firm hired by debtor and were not hired by debtor).

attorneys involved in the transaction.[42] Similar sorts of fees to non-attorneys are also improper, and must be disclosed to the court, with respect to pre-bankruptcy fees at least, in response to question nine in the Statement of Financial Affairs.[43]

In addition, when compensation is sought from the estate, including payment through the chapter 13 plan, an attorney must provide a detailed statement of the services rendered and expenses incurred[44] to justify the amount requested.[45] Although such a listing is not technically required when the attorney is paid directly by the debtor (except in some jurisdictions by local rule), it is a good idea to furnish a statement of services in such cases as well.[46] Not only does the description of services support the amount of fees requested, it also makes clear to the court what services have not been included, so that there can be no later question regarding whether the attorney fee included particular activities. Indeed, it is usually advisable to include in the statement a specific disclosure of the hourly rate or other arrangements which have been made for such additional services as might become necessary.[47] Finally, Rule 2016(b) requires a supplemental disclosure statement to be filed with the court after any payment or agreement not previously disclosed. The supplemental statement should generally conform to the same standards as the original disclosures.

It is common for local rules (and occasionally local custom) to provide additional specifications for attorney fee disclosures, including special service requirements. Local practice should be reviewed.

15.3.3 Bankruptcy Court Review of Fee Disclosures and Requests

The Bankruptcy Code also follows the approach of the prior rules in requiring the court to review all payments or arrangements between the debtor and her attorney. All fees paid by the debtor that are related to the bankruptcy case are subject to review.[48] Any payments exceeding the reasonable value of services rendered may be ordered returned to either the debtor or the estate, whichever is appropriate.[49] And, of course once the fees are disallowed by the court they cannot be collected directly from the client.[50]

Although the Bankruptcy Rules provide that an order disallowing fees may be made on the court's own motion,[51] it most often occurs after a request by the trustee or the United States trustee. In many districts the court specifically requires the trustee to make a recommendation regarding whether an attorney fee should be approved, and it has been held that reviewing fees is part of the United States trustee's function of supervising the administration of bankruptcy cases.[52] The Executive Office for United States Trustees has announced that it considers the monitoring of debtors' attorneys' fees to be a very important part of the U.S. trustee's job.[53]

One aspect of reviewing fees involves the question of whether the fees charged are reasonable in relation to the services involved. Bankruptcy courts have broad discretion in determining appropriate levels of compensation.[54] As discussed above,[55] most judges have a range of rates that they consider to be fair for the basic services involved in a consumer bankruptcy case. Information as to what this range is should be easy to obtain through a review of fees approved in other cases in the public record of fees on file at the clerk's office.[56] Many judges also have let it be known what they feel is equitable for an uncontested adversary proceeding or other routine tasks.[57] Different courts have a variety of rules regarding such issues as whether fees are

---

42 Advisory Committee Note to Fed. R. Bankr. P. 2016; *see In re* Matis, 73 B.R. 228 (Bankr. N.D.N.Y. 1987).

43 *See* Official Form 7, Appx. D, *infra*.

44 Costs and expenses may be recovered to the extent that they are actual and necessary. *See In re* Nat'l Paragon Corp., 76 B.R. 73 (E.D. Pa. 1987).

45 Fed. R. Bankr. P. 2016(a); *In re* Pinkins, 213 B.R. 818 (Bankr. E.D. Mich. 1997) (fees reduced for failure to submit time records).

46 *See* Form 21, Appx. G.3, *infra*.

47 *Id.*

48 *In re* Walters, 868 F.2d 665 (4th Cir. 1989) (court had power to review fees paid by debtors from exempt property in state court suits against creditor); *In re* Woodward, 229 B.R. 468 (Bankr. N.D. Okla. 1999) (attorney required to disclose fees even if they were passed on to another attorney); *cf. In re* Hargis, 895 F.2d 1025 (5th Cir. 1990) (court had no authority to order disgorgement of fees paid for services not related to bankruptcy case); *In*

re Chaparro Martinez, 293 B.R. 387 (Bankr. N.D. Tex. 2003) (Code provisions regulating attorney fees not applicable to fees relating to debtor's personal injury claim that was not property of debtor's bankruptcy estate).

49 11 U.S.C. § 329(b); *In re* Lee, 884 F.2d 897 (5th Cir. 1989) (court ordered return of fees attorney collected under contingent fee agreement to the extent they exceeded reasonable hourly rate).

50 *See In re* Gantz, 209 B.R. 999 (B.A.P. 10th Cir. 1997) (fees which bankruptcy court denied upon application that they be paid from chapter 13 estate were never due to attorney and could not be collected by attorney directly from client).

51 Fed. R. Bankr. P. 2017(a); *see In re* Busy Beaver Bldg. Centers, Inc., 19 F.3d 833 (3d Cir. 1994) (bankruptcy court has power to review fees *sua sponte* even if neither U.S. trustee nor any other party objects to fees); *In re* Wyslak, 94 B.R. 540 (Bankr. N.D. Ill. 1988).

52 *In re* Pierce, 809 F.2d 1356 (8th Cir. 1987); *In re* Grant, 14 B.R. 567 (Bankr. S.D.N.Y. 1981); *In re* McLeon, 6 B.R. 327 (Bankr. E.D. Va. 1980).

53 Tell, *Chasing the Bankruptcy Bumblers*, Nat. L. J., May 11, 1981, at 1, 26.

54 *See, e.g., In re* Lawler, 807 F.2d 1207 (5th Cir. 1987); *In re* McKeeman, 236 B.R. 667 (B.A.P. 8th Cir. 1999) (reduction in hourly rate to that charged by local attorneys and refusal to grant fees for travel time not an abuse of discretion).

55 *See* § 15.2.2, *supra*.

56 Such a record must be maintained by the class pursuant to Fed. R. Bankr. P. 2013.

57 *See, e.g., In re* Hill, 5 B.R. 541 (Bankr. C.D. Cal. 1980)

allowed for travel time,[58] which costs are compensable, and the rates that will be permitted for costs such as photocopying.

Counsel for debtors should not be afraid, however, to charge more than the basic fee when the work reasonably required in a case warrants a larger fee which the client agrees to pay.[59] The "basic fee" utilized by many courts is only a guideline set for the convenience of the court and counsel. Bankruptcy litigation can be lengthy and complex, and the legislative history of the Code makes clear that Congress intended bankruptcy attorneys to be compensated at the same level as other attorneys in the community handling non-bankruptcy matters of similar difficulty.[60] Previous case law[61] that held that bankruptcy cases were governed by a special "spirit of economy" that dictated lower fees was expressly disapproved.[62] The policy of the Code is to encourage quality representation in bankruptcy by allowing fees which will attract competent practitioners.

Courts also concern themselves with preventing the abuse of the bankruptcy process by attorneys at the expense of debtors or creditors. In pursuit of this goal, bankruptcy judges have remedied conduct that ranges from unfair advertising to incompetence to outright fraud.

For example, the fees of an attorney who had deceptively advertised his fees were limited in all of his cases to the low fees advertised.[63] Other attorneys who failed to attend hearings or cooperate with trustees, misrepresented their fees, and allowed their clients to be seriously prejudiced have been denied all fees and ordered to reimburse their clients for costs incurred.[64] When services rendered have been harmful or worthless to the debtor, all fees have been denied.[65] Similarly, when attorneys have acted unethically in other respects, their requested fees have not been allowed.[66] And when attorneys have failed to accurately disclose the fees charged, those fees have been reduced or denied.[67]

($250.00 a reasonable fee for adversary proceeding to remove judicial liens).

58 *See In re* Braddy, 195 B.R. 365 (Bankr. E.D. Mich. 1996) (attorney permitted full compensation for travel time).

59 *E.g., In re* Shamburger, 189 B.R. 965 (Bankr. N.D. Ala. 1995) (attorney entitled to additional compensation for work performed on novel issues). *See generally In re* Lawler, 807 F.2d 1207 (5th Cir. 1987); *In re* Powerline Oil Co., 71 B.R. 767 (B.A.P. 9th Cir. 1986).

60 *In re* Boddy, 950 F.2d 334 (6th Cir. 1991) (use of $650.00 "normal and customary" fee for bankruptcy case, rather than lodestar method, was abuse of discretion); Grant v. George Schumann Tire & Battery Co., 908 F.2d 874 (11th Cir. 1990) (bankruptcy attorney fees should be calculated by lodestar method and should be no less and no more than fees received for comparable non-bankruptcy work; however, fees should not be awarded on appeal unless the appeal benefited the estate, creditors, or the debtor).

61 *See, e.g., In re* Beverly Crest Convalescent Hosp., Inc., 548 F.2d 817 (9th Cir. 1977); *In re* Paramount Merrick, Inc., 252 F.2d 482, 485 (2d Cir. 1958).

62 124 Cong. Rec. H11,091, H11,092 (daily ed. Sept. 28, 1978) (statement of Rep. Don Edwards); H.R. Rep. No. 95-595, at 329, 330 (1977).

63 *In re* Stewart, 10 B.R. 472 (Bankr. E.D. Va. 1981).

64 *In re* Clark, 223 F.3d 859 (8th Cir. 2000) (attorney who misrepresented that he had done work that was really done by paralegal and collected flat fee designed for work done by attorneys ordered to disgorge fees); *In re* Taylor, 242 B.R. 549

(Bankr. S.D. Ga. 1999) (fee of attorney who failed to attend hearings reduced from $1100.00 to $250.00); *In re* Pinkins, 213 B.R. 818 (Bankr. E.D. Mich. 1997) (fees denied when attorney's legal assistant engaged in unauthorized practice of law, legal assistant signed retention letters and attorney had no contact or direct relationship with clients); *In re* Davila, 210 B.R. 727 (Bankr. S.D. Tex. 1996) (fees ordered disgorged because attorney was not competent, filed inaccurate schedules, failed to disclose fees, inadequately trained and supervised employees and provided little if any accurate legal advice to clients); *In re* Waddell, 21 B.R. 450 (Bankr. N.D. Ga. 1982) (fees limited to $150.00 in chapter 13 cases where attorney abused privilege of filing schedules and statements after petition); *In re* Grant, 14 B.R. 567 (Bankr. S.D.N.Y. 1981); *In re* Wilson, 11 B.R. 986 (Bankr. S.D.N.Y. 1981); *In re* Rivera, 6 B.R. 686 (Bankr. S.D.N.Y. 1980); *see also In re* Pierce, 809 F.2d 1356 (8th Cir. 1987); *In re* Hargis, 73 B.R. 622 (Bankr. N.D. Tex. 1987).

65 *In re* Vargas, 257 B.R. 157 (Bankr. D.N.J. 2001) (debtor's counsel who certified and filed "unwarranted and unsubstantiated" reaffirmation agreements ordered to disgorge fees); *In re* Rutherford, 54 B.R. 784 (Bankr. W.D. Mo. 1985); *In re* Wright, 48 B.R. 172 (Bankr. E.D.N.C. 1985); *In re* Bolton, 43 B.R. 598 (Bankr. E.D.N.Y. 1984) (fees denied for groundless third bankruptcy petition filed one week after second petition dismissed); *In re* Chin, 31 B.R. 314 (Bankr. S.D.N.Y. 1983); *In re* Crestwell, 30 B.R. 619 (Bankr. D.D.C. 1983); *see also In re* Busby, 46 B.R. 15 (Bankr. E.D.N.Y. 1984) (questioning several apparently poor decisions made by attorney who requested $3500.00 fee in chapter 13 case).

66 *In re* Evangeline Ref. Co., 890 F.2d 1312 (5th Cir. 1989) (where facts misrepresented in fee application, all compensation should be denied); *In re* Georgetown of Kettering Ltd., 750 F.2d 536 (6th Cir. 1984) (the application of attorney who represented conflicting interests should have been denied); *In re* Rainwater, 100 B.R. 615 (Bankr. M.D. Ga. 1989) (no compensation for deficient services and attorney sanctioned for filing petition without meeting debtor, reviewing her records, or counseling her about bankruptcy); *In re* Vivado, 94 B.R. 785 (Bankr. D.D.C. 1989) (debtors were not eligible to file case and counsel's action was therefore a sham proceeding); *In re* Costello, 95 B.R. 594 (Bankr. S.D. Ill. 1989) (conflict of interest); *In re* Whitman, 51 B.R. 502 (Bankr. D. Mass. 1985) (fee reduced where law firm overreached by taking a security interest in debtor's major asset); *In re* Smith, 24 B.R. 266 (Bankr. D.D.C. 1982) (failure to explain how the unethical conduct diminished the value of services rendered), *rev'd and remanded in part sub nom. In re* Devers, 33 B.R. 793 (D.D.C. 1983).

67 *In re* Woodward, 229 B.R. 468 (Bankr. N.D. Okla. 1999); *In re* Pair, 77 B.R. 976 (Bankr. N.D. Ga. 1987); *In re* Chambers, 76 B.R. 194 (Bankr. M.D. Fla. 1987); *In re* Whitman, 51 B.R. 502 (Bankr. D. Mass. 1985); *In re* Meyer, 50 B.R. 3 (Bankr. S.D. Fla. 1985); *In re* Weaver, 49 B.R. 190 (Bankr. N.D. Ala. 1985); *see also* Lavender v. Wood Law Firm, 785 F.2d 247 (8th Cir. 1986) (law firm which had not obtained approval for payment of fees in chapter 11 case required to reimburse estate for such fees). *But see In re* Redding, 247 B.R. 474 (B.A.P. 8th Cir. 2000) (reversing disgorgement order based on non-disclosure because

Finally, this supervisory power has been used to police the fees and conduct of non-attorneys who provide debtors with "advice" or "services" in connection with bankruptcy cases, which are then often filed pro se.[68] Either upon motion by the United States trustee, or upon request of disgruntled "clients," section 329 of the Code, combined with remedies available under Code section 110[69] and state unfair trade practice statutes,[70] can be an effective weapon against the unauthorized practice of law and abusive practices of these "clinics," "debt counselors," "typing services" and other operations that prey on the misfortunes of financially troubled debtors.

15.3.4 Making a Record on Fee Issues

Regardless of the way the fee request comes to the court's attention, the matter must be given the same type of careful consideration required by the rules for any other type of proceeding. A final (as opposed to interim) order on fees is a final appealable order.[71] In cases likely to be appealed, all parties must be careful to ensure that there is evidence in the record to support their positions. Although written findings of fact are not necessary in the typical fee request, they are important where a substantial issue is likely to arise. If the bankruptcy court does not make such findings, it should be specifically requested to do so, in order to create an adequate record for appellate review.[72]

When the record evidences the hours reasonably spent and the bankruptcy court gives no specific reason for reducing fees below the amount requested, an appellate court may reverse the reduction of fees as an abuse of discretion.[73]

15.4 Payment of Attorney Fees Through the Chapter 13 Plan

15.4.1 Fees Which Can Be Paid Through a Plan

One important feature of chapter 13 not usually present in consumer chapter 7 cases[74] is the possibility of paying the debtor's attorney from the property of the estate. The opportunity for the debtor to pay all or part of the fee in installments is often the only way a financially strapped client can pay the fee at all. And the fact that the attorney has some assurance, though hardly a complete guarantee, that the fee can be paid in this manner makes him or her more comfortable about taking the client's case without advance payment of all or most of the fee.

Normally the attorney for the debtor classifies her fee among the administrative expenses entitled to priority under 11 U.S.C. § 507(a)(1). Not only does this mean that the fee must be paid in full for the plan to be confirmed under section 1322(a)(2), but it also usually means the fee will be paid before most other creditors receive payment.[75] It also

only issue under § 329 is reasonableness of fees, though court left open possibility of sanctions for rule violation).

68 *In re* Fleet, 95 B.R. 319 (E.D. Pa. 1989); *In re* Webster, 120 B.R. 111 (Bankr. E.D. Wis. 1990) (permanent injunction issued against lay person engaging in unauthorized practice of law and requiring return of monies paid to him by debtor where that person prepared bankruptcy papers, failed to file a statement of compensation, and received fees before the filing fees were paid in full); *In re* Bachman, 113 B.R. 769 (Bankr. S.D. Fla. 1990).

69 This provision contains special requirements for non-attorney bankruptcy petition preparers. *See* § 15.6, *infra.*

70 *In re* Fleet, 95 B.R. 319 (E.D. Pa. 1989); *see also* National Consumer Law Center, Unfair and Deceptive Acts and Practices § 5.1.17.3 (5th ed. 2001 and Supp.).

71 *See In re* Spillane, 884 F.2d 642 (1st Cir. 1989); *cf. In re* Boddy, 950 F.2d 334 (6th Cir. 1991) (interim award became final when it no longer could be modified by the court); *In re* Dahlquist, 751 F.2d 295 (8th Cir. 1985) (interim award became final when bankruptcy case was dismissed).

72 *In re* Botelho, 8 B.R. 305 (B.A.P. 1st Cir. 1981); *see also In re* Clark, 223 F.3d 859 (8th Cir. 2000) (appellant attorney did not provide reviewing court transcript or other record that supported his contentions); *In re* Boddy, 950 F.2d 334 (6th Cir. 1991) (case remanded where court had not discussed how award was calculated under lodestar method); *In re* Pfleghaar, 215 B.R. 394 (B.A.P. 8th Cir. 1997) (attorney entitled to evidentiary hearing before bankruptcy court denied his fee application).

73 *In re* Paster, 119 B.R. 468 (E.D. Pa. 1990) (under "lodestar" method applicable in circuit to bankruptcy fees, where court did not specifically take issue with number of hours reasonably spent and rate was not excessive, reduction of fees was abuse of discretion).

74 A debtor's attorney may not receive compensation from the estate for representing the debtor in a chapter 7 case. Lamie v. United States Trustee, 124 S. Ct. 1023, 1032, 157 L. Ed. 2d 1024, 1036 (2004); *see* § 15.2.3, *supra.* Usually a debtor with non-exempt property should be advised to convert it to exempt property or to file a chapter 13 case. Even if that did not occur, it would normally make more sense to pay the attorney from the non-exempt property prior to the case.

75 11 U.S.C. § 1322(a)(2); *In re* Shorb, 101 B.R. 185 (B.A.P. 9th Cir. 1989) (fees must be paid prior to or concurrently with other claims and cannot be deferred to six months after commencement of payments to unsecured claims); *In re* Parker, 21 B.R. 692 (E.D. Tenn. 1982) (attorney fees may be paid prior to or concurrently with secured and unsecured claims), *aff'g* 15 B.R. 980 (Bankr. E.D. Tenn. 1981); *In re* Harris, 304 B.R. 751 (Bankr. E.D. Mich. 2004) (debtor's plan could provide for payment of priority attorney fees before other creditors; *see also In re* Meadows, 297 B.R. 671 (Bankr. E.D. Mich. 2003) (plan could require trustee to hold $2000.00 in reserve for thirty days after confirmation for payment of anticipated counsel fees). *But see In re* Lasica, 294 B.R. 718 (Bankr. N.D. Ill. 2003) (fees could not be paid through plan if confirmed plan made no provision for paying them). By local rule in some districts, however, attorney fees are customarily paid pro rata with other disbursements to assure the attorney's continued interest in the success of the plan. *See In re* Pedersen, 229 B.R. 445 (Bankr. E.D. Cal. 1999) (local rule required submission of waiver of right to receive fees before creditors if counsel sought to receive

means that, if fees have been approved, they may be paid by the trustee pursuant to section 1326(a)(2) if the case is dismissed before confirmation.[76]

Fees which are not entitled to treatment as administrative expenses must be classified with other unsecured claims. They will be paid less than one hundred cents on the dollar in most plans.

Under Code section 330(a)(4)(B), added by the 1994 amendments, services which are compensable as administrative expenses in a chapter 12 or chapter 13 case include not only services which benefit the bankruptcy estate, but also services necessary for representing the debtor's interests in connection with the bankruptcy case, based on consideration of the benefit and necessity of such services to the debtor. This language would encompass even services outside the bankruptcy court if those services were necessary to successful completion of the case.[77]

It is well established that virtually all of the basic services in a chapter 13 case do benefit the estate, for example, pre-petition advice about bankruptcy, preparation of the initial papers and plan, and attendance at the creditors' meeting and the confirmation hearing. As a practical matter, courts rarely question payment of the entire basic fee as an administrative expense. It also seems quite clear that fees for other activities to preserve the estate or the functioning of the plan, such as objections to claims or modifications of the plan, warrant priority administrative expense treatment.

Because a chapter 13 debtor's attorney is no longer limited to compensation only for services that benefit the estate, as was the case prior to the 1994 amendments, there should be little dispute about the right to compensation for

any work done in legitimate pursuit of the chapter 13 case. When it is necessary to defend against a motion for relief from the automatic stay, the court will normally find that such defense was necessary and for the debtor's benefit. Similarly, defense of a debtor's exemption rights and dischargeability litigation should clearly be compensable under the test laid out in section 330(a)(4)(B).

However, many courts find an abuse of the system when all or almost all of the debtor's plan payments go toward payment of the attorney fee. Such use of chapter 13 as simply a device for collecting fees, with little or no benefit to any creditors, may be looked upon with disfavor as little more than a disguised liquidation and akin to past abuses in which the primary beneficiaries of a bankruptcy plan were the attorneys involved.[78]

15.4.2 Procedure for Obtaining Payment of Fees Through the Plan

The current Bankruptcy Rules provide that an attorney who seeks compensation for services from the estate, that is, through the plan, must file an application for those fees including a detailed statement of services rendered, the time and costs expended,[79] and the amounts requested.[80] The application must also be transmitted to the United States trustee.[81] Some courts require a great deal of specificity in such statements.[82] The same rule requires that this application state all payments made or promised for legal services in connection with the case, the source of such payments made or promised, and whether such payments have been or will be shared with anyone other than an attorney in the applicant's firm.[83] Most courts allow attorney fees for the time spent on the fee application, at least if the time is substantial.[84] Compensation for time spent may be enhanced

---

fees under court's fee guidelines); *In re* Pappas & Rose, Prof'l Corp., 229 B.R. 815 (Bankr. W.D. Okla. 1998) (local rule requiring payment of fees over twenty-four months); *In re* Lanigan, 101 B.R. 530 (Bankr. N.D. Ill. 1986) (bankruptcy court had authority to order payment of fees over life of plan); *see also In re* Townsend, 186 B.R. 248 (Bankr. E.D. Mo. 1994) (payment of fees before mortgage cure was improper if it caused cure to take longer than time permitted by local rule; court did not address question of whether local rule could control substantive issue of length of cure period). Of course, deferring of counsel fees until later in the plan increases the risk that the fees will not be paid in full, and courts that require counsel to defer fees must recognize that it will result in higher fees being charged due to that risk.

76 *In re* Hall, 296 B.R. 707 (Bankr. E.D. Va. 2002) (trustee had obligation to pay allowed fees of debtor's counsel before returning funds to debtor in dismissed case); *In re* Lampman, 276 B.R. 182 (Bankr. W.D. Tex. 2002) (attorney fees may be paid by trustee in dismissed chapter 13 case, but only if fees are allowed by court after debtor and trustee have opportunity to object); *In re* Oliver, 222 B.R. 272 (Bankr. E.D. Va. 1998); *see also In re* Harris, 258 B.R. 8 (Bankr. D. Idaho 2000) (attorney could be paid from funds held by trustee only through request for fees to be allowed as administrative expenses and could not assert charging lien on funds).

77 *See, e.g., In re* Polishuk, 258 B.R. 238 (Bankr. N.D. Okla. 2001) (fees allowed for work in domestic relations court).

78 *In re* San Miguel, 40 B.R. 481 (Bankr. D. Colo. 1984); *see also* Tell, *Chasing the Bankruptcy Bumblers*, Nat. L. J., May 11, 1981, at 1, 26.

79 Costs that are reimbursable may include photocopying, postage, long distance telephone calls, and travel expenses. *In re* Nat'l Paragon Corp., 76 B.R. 73 (E.D. Pa. 1987). A court may not arbitrarily reject certain categories of expenses as non-compensable "overhead" when those expenses are billed to non-bankruptcy clients in the market. *In re* Hillsborough Holdings Corp., 127 F.3d 1398 (11th Cir. 1997).

80 Fed. R. Bankr. P. 2016(a).

81 *Id.*

82 *In re* Beverly Mfg. Corp., 841 F.2d 365 (11th Cir. 1988) (fee application was inadequate because there was no indication of specific nature of each service performed and some entries "lumped" together several different services in one time period); *In re* Newman, 270 B.R. 845 (Bankr. S.D. Ohio 2001) (fees denied for work not documented by contemporaneous time records); *In re* Thacker, 48 B.R. 161 (Bankr. N.D. Ill. 1985); *In re* Horn & Hardart Baking Co., 30 B.R. 938 (Bankr. E.D. Pa. 1983).

83 Fed. R. Bankr. P. 2016(a).

84 *In re* Nucorp Energy, Inc., 764 F.2d 655 (9th Cir. 1985).

for exceptional results, but only if the applicant produces specific evidence showing why such enhancement is necessary to make the award commensurate with non-bankruptcy compensation.[85]

The Code provides that compensation from the estate can be awarded only after notice and hearing.[86] Given the meaning of "notice and a hearing" in the Code,[87] this does not necessarily mean that a hearing must occur. Some type of notice to all parties that fees are sought from the estate is required, giving them an opportunity to request a hearing to raise any questions they might have.[88]

As a practical matter, these provisions mean that the debtor's attorney must apply in some manner for her fees to be approved with notice to all parties interested in the case. In some districts this can be done through a combination of the disclosure statement of fees, if it lists services rendered, and a provision in the plan to be confirmed stating that fees will be paid through the plan. If this method is followed, then notice of the plan should include notice of this plan provision. In other jurisdictions, a separate application must be filed. Normally, the payment of fees through the plan is approved in conjunction with confirmation of the plan.[89]

After confirmation, there are sometimes circumstances which require the debtor's attorney to do other work not originally anticipated. When this occurs, an application for additional fees may be made if the work is compensable from the estate.[90] In many courts, an application and proposed order approving such additional fees can be attached to the pleading filed, especially when it is a fairly simple uncontested matter such as a modification of the plan.[91] However, once the plan has been confirmed, some courts may require a motion to modify the plan if additional attorney fees are requested to be paid through the plan.[92]

15.5 Other Sources of Attorney Fees in Bankruptcy Cases

15.5.1 Overview

An additional source of attorney fees often overlooked by many bankruptcy practitioners is the opposing party.[93] Most practitioners are aware of the Bankruptcy Code provisions that provide for attorney fees to be awarded to prevailing debtors in certain circumstances, such as proceedings to enforce the automatic stay,[94] certain dischargeability complaints,[95] and involuntary bankruptcy petitions.[96] But they are often less knowledgeable about the myriad of other federal and state statutes that provide for attorney fees to prevailing parties. Altogether there are nearly one-hundred such federal statutes, and many more state statutes.[97]

15.5.2 The Civil Rights Attorney's Fees Awards Act of 1976

The most important of these statutes is 42 U.S.C. § 1988, the Civil Rights Attorney's Fees Awards Act of 1976. Despite its title, there are strong arguments that this law applies in every action brought under the Bankruptcy Code against state and local entities or officials.

The Civil Rights Attorney's Fees Awards Act of 1976 prescribes fee awards in every action under 42 U.S.C. § 1983, which in turn is applicable to every denial of federal statutory rights under color of law. The leading case on the subject, *Maine v. Thiboutot*,[98] held that the denial of rights granted by a federal statute, in that instance the Social Security Act, gave rise to a cause of action under section 1983. The Supreme Court held that section 1983 should be interpreted literally: the civil rights statute could be used to enforce any right created by the Constitution or laws of the

---

85 *In re* Manoa Fin. Co., 853 F.2d 687 (9th Cir. 1988).

86 *See also* Fed. R. Bankr. P. 2002(a), requiring twenty-day notice to the debtor, the trustee, and all creditors of an application for compensation or reimbursement of expenses in excess of $1000.00.

87 "After notice and a hearing" is defined at 11 U.S.C. § 102(1).

88 *See* Fed. R. Bankr. P. 2002(a)(7).

89 *See In re* Dewey, 237 B.R. 783 (B.A.P. 10th Cir. 1999) (affirming denial of fees sought by "corrected" application after confirmation because increase in fees sought would have made plan non-confirmable). In some cases, approval of an attorney fee as proper may preclude a later malpractice action by the debtor claiming that the attorney work was inadequate. *See* Grausz v. Englander, 321 F.3d 467 (4th Cir. 2003).

90 *In re* Hanson, 223 B.R. 775 (Bankr. D. Or. 1998) (attorney barred from collecting fees for post-confirmation work if no fee application was filed and approved); *see also In re* Phillips, 219 B.R. 1001 (Bankr. W.D. Tenn. 1998) (attorney could not file post-petition claim for consumer debt under section 1305(a)(2) for post-petition fees).

91 For one form of such an attachment, see Form 22, Appendix G.3, *infra*.

92 *In re* Hallmark, 225 B.R. 192 (Bankr. C.D. Cal. 1998) (modification must be sought where plan provided specific amount for administrative expense attorney fees); *see In re* Black, 116 B.R.

818 (Bankr. W.D. Okla. 1990) (where attorney sought fees six times higher than those provided for in confirmed plan, which would utilize all funds available to unsecured creditors, and no motion to modify plan had been filed, attorney held bound by confirmed plan and application for additional fees denied).

93 A variety of potential opportunities to shift fees are discussed in *Ten Ways to Win Attorneys Fees in Your Bankruptcy Practice (Without Taking A Penny From the Debtor)*, 12 NCLC REPORTS *Bankruptcy and Foreclosures Ed.* 25 (July/Aug. 1993).

94 11 U.S.C. § 362(h); *see* § 9.6, *supra*.

95 11 U.S.C. § 523(d) provides for attorney fees to many debtors who successfully defend against complaints brought under 11 U.S.C. § 523(a)(2). *See* § 14.4.3.2.4, *supra*.

96 11 U.S.C. § 303(i); *see* § 13.8, *supra*.

97 *See generally* Conte & Newberg, Attorney Fee Awards (2d ed.); M. Derfner & A. Wolf, Court Awarded Attorney Fees; E. Larson, Federal Court Awards of Attorney's Fees (1981).

98 448 U.S. 1, 100 S. Ct. 2502, 65 L. Ed. 2d 555 (1980).

United States, regardless of whether the right had a constitutional or civil rights character.[99]

Because the Bankruptcy Code is a federal statute, the *Thiboutot* holding should be applicable. Thus, any denial, under color of law, of rights granted by the Code creates a cause of action under 42 U.S.C. § 1983.[100] If the plaintiff in such a case is successful, attorney fees should be awarded under the Civil Rights Attorneys Fee's Awards Act.[101]

The ramifications of these principles are broad. In every case in which a debtor seeks to enforce bankruptcy rights (arising out of any Code section) against a county-run or municipal utility, or a state or local governmental entity, attorney fees should be available. For example, those claims may rely upon the following provisions:

- Section 525(a), prohibiting discrimination by governmental units against debtors who have filed bankruptcy cases;
- Section 362, providing for the automatic stay;
- Section 366, dealing with utility service; or
- Section 524, dealing with the protections of discharge.

Many of these claims may give rise to fees under Code section 362(h) or contempt theories, so section 1988 will not be necessary.

Damages and fees may also be sought under sections 1983 and 1988 from private parties acting under color of law in concert with government officials.[102] Although debtors' advocates can often receive fee awards under other theories, the possibility of receipt of significant fees under the civil rights acts should not be ignored.[103]

15.5.3 Consumer Protection Statutes

Also common, but all too often neglected, are opportunities in bankruptcy cases to bring actions under various consumer protection statutes providing for attorney fees. A

thorough familiarity with debtors' rights under these statutes can result in substantial, additional fees for bankruptcy attorneys, not to mention important benefits for their clients.

On the federal level, the most important of these statutes is the Truth in Lending Act.[104] Section 130(a) of the Act,[105] which is applicable to every consumer credit transaction, provides for mandatory attorney fees to successful consumer litigants.[106] In view of the fact that the typical consumer debtor has entered into numerous transactions subject to the Act, an attorney handling a substantial number of bankruptcies is quite likely to find many potential Truth in Lending cases in her files.

Other federal consumer protection statutes providing for attorney fees include the Magnuson-Moss Warranty Act,[107] the Fair Debt Collection Practices Act,[108] the Equal Credit Opportunity Act,[109] and the Fair Credit Reporting Act.[110]

Many state laws have similar provisions. These include usury statutes,[111] laws prohibiting unfair and deceptive practices,[112] and laws regulating collection practices or landlord-tenant relationships. A number of states require that if creditors' contracts contain a clause giving them a right to fees if they prevail in litigation with the debtor then that obligation is reciprocal.[113] Bankruptcy practitioners should

---

99 *Id.*, 448 U.S. at 8. *But cf.* Middlesex County Sewerage Auth. v. Nat'l Sea Clammers Ass'n, 453 U.S. 1, 101 S. Ct. 2615, 69 L. Ed. 2d 435 (1981) in which this holding was modified somewhat as to some statutes.

100 Almand v. Benton County, 145 B.R. 608 (W.D. Ark. 1992) (cause of action under § 1983 for violations of automatic stay).

101 *In re* Watts, 93 B.R. 350 (E.D. Pa. 1988), *rev'd on other grounds*, 876 F.2d 1090 (3d Cir. 1989); Higgins v. Philadelphia Gas Works, 54 B.R. 928 (E.D. Pa. 1985); *In re* McKibben, 233 B.R. 378 (Bankr. E.D. Tex. 1999); *In re* Gibbs, 12 B.R. 737 (Bankr. D. Conn. 1981); *In re* Maya, 8 B.R. 202 (Bankr. E. D. Pa. 1981).

102 Almand v. Benton County, 145 B.R. 608 (W.D. Ark. 1992) (cause of action under § 1983 for violations of automatic stay against parties who participated in wrongful execution against debtor's property).

103 However, requests for fees against government entities may now be met with the argument that they must be limited to the rates set forth in 28 U.S.C. § 2412(d)(2)(A) due to the operation of 11 U.S.C. § 106(a)(3). *See* § 15.5.6, *infra.*

104 15 U.S.C. §§ 1601–1677. See § 13.4.4, *supra,* for further discussion of the Truth in Lending Act in bankruptcy cases. See National Consumer Law Center, Truth in Lending (5th ed. 2003) for a detailed explanation of the statute.

105 15 U.S.C. § 1640(a).

106 *See, e.g., In re* Jansen, 47 B.R. 641 (Bankr. D. Ariz. 1985) ($13,104.00 fee for Truth in Lending case).

107 15 U.S.C. §§ 2301–2312. *See generally* National Consumer Law Center, Consumer Warranty Law Ch. 2 (2d ed. 2001 and Supp.).

108 15 U.S.C. §§ 1692–1692o. *See generally* National Consumer Law Center, Fair Debt Collection (5th ed. 2004).

109 15 U.S.C. §§ 1691–1691f. *See generally* National Consumer Law Center, Credit Discrimination (3d ed. 2002 and Supp.).

110 15 U.S.C. §§ 1681–1681t. *See generally* National Consumer Law Center, Fair Credit Reporting (5th ed. 2002 and Supp.).

111 *See generally* National Consumer Law Center, The Cost of Credit: Regulation and Legal Challenges (2d ed. 2000 and Supp.).

112 *See generally* National Consumer Law Center, Unfair and Deceptive Acts and Practices (5th ed. 2001 and Supp.).

113 *See In re* Baroff, 105 F.3d 439 (9th Cir. 1997) (debtor awarded fees under California statute providing for reciprocal fees because nondischargeability proceeding was an action on the contract); *In re* Nealy, 139 B.R. 48 (D.D.C. 1992) (awarding fees incurred in dischargeability proceeding based on contract clause that provided that creditor would pay debtor's fees if debtor prevailed in collection litigation); *In re* Guarnieri, 297 B.R. 365 (Bankr. D. Conn. 2003) (fees awarded for debtors' successful objection to mortgage lender's proof of claim); *In re* Mawji, 228 B.R. 321 (Bankr. M.D. Fla. 1999) (fee granted for successfully defending nondischargeability action based on reciprocity provision in state law); *In re* Pichardo, 186 B.R. 279 (Bankr. M.D. Fla. 1995) (fees awarded to debtor's counsel in student loan dischargeability proceeding under statute providing that, if a contract imposes fees on a debtor who loses in litigation, debtor is entitled to fees from creditor who loses in

become familiar with all such statutes which touch so frequently upon their clients' lives.

In most cases claims under these statutes may be reserved by the debtor as exempt property and then pursued by the debtor in the bankruptcy forum or elsewhere. Even when the debtor cannot exempt such claims, the trustee in a chapter 7 case rarely has either the interest or expertise to pursue them and normally abandons them back to the debtor. In chapter 13 cases, in which the debtor retains control over all property of the estate,[114] there is no reason why such claims may not be immediately pursued if the debtor wishes.

However, counsel representing a chapter 7 debtor with respect to a pre-petition cause of action must pay close attention to the rules regarding representation of the bankruptcy estate. During the bankruptcy case, or at least until the cause of action has been exempted or abandoned and the time for objecting to that treatment has passed, the cause of action belongs to the estate and cannot be pursued without the participation of the trustee and the appointment of debtor's counsel as special counsel for the estate pursuant to Code section 327.[115] In many cases, it may be easier to disclose the cause of action in the schedules and allow the cause of action to remain dormant until the bankruptcy case is over and it is clear that it has been exempted or abandoned, placing it back in the debtor's control.[116]

15.5.4 The Equal Access to Justice Act

In litigation against the federal government, an additional potential source of attorney fees is the Equal Access to Justice Act, 28 U.S.C. § 2412. This Act provides, *inter alia*, for attorney fees when the federal government takes a position, before or during litigation, that is not "substantially justified."[117] The Supreme Court has held that more

than good faith is necessary for the government to meet this test; a position that is "justified in substance or in the main," "having a reasonable basis both in law and in fact," is required.[118] Similar fee provisions apply to litigation with the Internal Revenue Service.[119]

However, the Act provides that fees normally must be awarded at the relatively low rate of $75.00 per hour.[120] This rate may be adjustable, though, at least for inflation.[121] Obviously, despite the lack of prevailing market rates, the possibility of recovering fees in litigation against federal agencies when they are otherwise unavailable can benefit both attorneys and their clients. It has already been utilized in the bankruptcy courts,[122] and in view of the intransigent positions frequently taken by the federal government in bankruptcy cases, it is likely to be applied often.

15.5.5 Other Fee-Shifting Provisions

Fees may be awarded to debtor's counsel when imposed as a sanction against an opposing party or counsel for violation of Federal Rule of Bankruptcy Procedure 9011.[123]

---

litigation). *But see In re* Sheridan, 105 F.3d 1164 (7th Cir. 1997) (chapter 11 debtor could not recover under Florida reciprocal fee statute because dischargeability action was not "action with respect to the contract"); *In re* Johnson, 756 F.2d 738 (9th Cir. 1985) (California statute providing for attorney fees to prevailing party in any action on a contract which contains an attorney fee clause not applicable to motion for relief from automatic stay). The right to fees under such statutes is not preempted by the Bankruptcy Code where the debtor's successful litigation is based on state law claims and defenses. *See In re* Gifford, 256 B.R. 661 (Bankr. D. Conn. 2000) (debtor's claim for attorney fees under state fee-shifting statute not preempted in connection with granting of debtor's objection to mortgage lender's proof of claim based on state law).

114 11 U.S.C. § 1306(b); *see* § 12.8, *supra*.

115 *See* Cuevas-Segarra v. Contreras, 134 F.3d 458 (1st Cir. 1998) (attorneys who settled estate's cause of action without being appointed counsel for estate required to disgorge fees).

116 It is crucial to disclose the cause of action fully, or the debtor may face issues of judicial estoppel. *See* §§ 3.5, 7.3.4.2.2, 10.1.2, *supra*.

117 28 U.S.C. § 2412(d); *see* Dougherty v. Lehman, 711 F.2d 555 (3d Cir. 1983).

118 Pierce v. Underwood, 487 U.S. 552, 108 S. Ct. 2541, 101 L. Ed. 2d 490, 504 (1988).

119 26 U.S.C. § 7430; *see In re* Yochum, 89 F.3d 661 (9th Cir. 1996) (bankruptcy court was "court of the United States" with authority to award fees under 26 U.S.C. § 7430); *In re* Cascade Farms, 34 F.3d 756 (9th Cir. 1994) (district court could order IRS to pay fees to bankruptcy debtor under 26 U.S.C. § 7430); *In re* Germaine, 152 B.R. 619 (B.A.P. 9th Cir. 1993) (bankruptcy court was "court of the United States" for purposes of 26 U.S.C. § 7430); *In re* Chambers, 140 B.R. 233 (N.D. Ill. 1992) (bankruptcy court was "court of the United States" that could award fees under 26 U.S.C. § 7430). *But see In re* Grewe, 4 F.3d 299 (4th Cir. 1993) (fees under 26 U.S.C. § 7430 denied because debtors did not exhaust administrative remedies); *In re* Graham, 981 F.2d 1135 (10th Cir. 1992) (fees could not be awarded under 26 U.S.C. § 7430 if government's position was not substantially unjustified *ab initio*); *In re* Brickell Inv. Corp., 922 F.2d 696 (11th Cir. 1991) (bankruptcy court not a "court of the United States" for purposes of awarding fees under Internal Revenue Code § 7430, 26 U.S.C. § 7430; however, party may seek fees under this section by following procedures for non-core proceedings to obtain judgment of the district court).

120 28 U.S.C. § 2412(d)(1)(C)(2)(A).

121 Natural Res. Defense Council v. United States Envtl. Prot. Agency, 703 F.2d 700 (3d Cir. 1983).

122 O'Connor v. Dep't of Energy, 942 F.2d 771 (10th Cir. 1991) (bankruptcy court had jurisdiction to award fees under Equal Access to Justice Act); *In re* Armstead, 106 B.R. 405 (Bankr. E.D. Pa. 1989); *In re* Hagan, 44 B.R. 59 (Bankr. D.R.I. 1984) (fees awarded against Social Security Administration in case where it pursued its uniformly rejected claim that benefits overpayments are not dischargeable in bankruptcy). *But see In re* Davis, 899 F.2d 1136 (11th Cir. 1990) (bankruptcy court did not have jurisdiction to award fees under Equal Access to Justice Act, and fee award could only be entered by district court upon recommended findings of fact and conclusions of law supplied by bankruptcy court).

123 Fed. R. Bankr. P. 9011 was amended in 1997 to conform substantially to Fed. R. Civ. P. 11. A motion for sanctions may

This principle can provide a basis for attorney fees in a claim objection proceeding, for example, because Rule 9011 imposes an obligation on the claimant to make a reasonable inquiry before filing a proof of claim.[124] Attorneys and unrepresented creditors who submit claims without a proper legal or factual basis are subject to sanctions, which may include an award of attorney fees and expenses to the objecting party.[125] A creditor may be subject to Rule 9011 sanctions without signing a pleading or court document if it has provided false information or failed to correct false information used by its attorney.[126]

Finally, it must be remembered that almost any type of action relating to the debtor's affairs may be brought under the expanded jurisdiction of the bankruptcy forum.[127] It is possible that any one of the wide array of other state and federal fee-shifting statutes could be applicable in a particular case. Even a summary discussion of these statutes is beyond the scope of this manual, and the topic of fee awards has been well-covered elsewhere.[128] Although the courts have differed upon the question of how these fees should be determined, all agree that they must be premised upon fair hourly rates which will serve the statutes' purpose of attracting attorneys to such cases. Suffice it to say that the opportunities for financial rewards in bringing cases of great benefit to consumer clients, even where those clients cannot themselves afford sizeable attorney fees, are enormous.

15.5.6 Limitations on Fee Awards Against Governmental Units

Unfortunately, some limitations were placed on the awarding of attorney fees against at least some governmental units by the Bankruptcy Reform Act of 1994.[129] As part of the price for the abrogation of sovereign immunity, limitations were placed on attorney fees awards. Code section 106(a)(3) states that awards of attorney fees against a governmental unit must be "consistent with the provisions and limitations of" 28 U.S.C. § 2412(d)(2)(A), a subsection of the Equal Access to Justice Act (EAJA).[130]

It is, first of all, unclear whether this provision is simply an exception to the abrogation of sovereign immunity, or whether it goes beyond that. Some governmental units, such as municipalities, never had sovereign immunity and some attorney fees claims (for example, for contempt of court) may be awardable irrespective of sovereign immunity. The structure of the new section 106 suggests that the attorney fee language in section 106(a)(3) is designed to modify and limit the general abrogation language in section 106(a). If that is the case, then the attorney fee limitation should not be applied to situations in which the governmental unit never had sovereign immunity.

In addition, 28 U.S.C. § 2412(d)(2)(A) limits attorney fees against the *federal government* to a rate of $75.00 per hour, which most courts have permitted to be adjusted for inflation since the section's original enactment, so that it is currently significantly higher. This provision should not affect fees awarded against state and local governments. Because 28 U.S.C. § 2412(d) only applies to the federal government, a higher fee award against a state or local government is not inconsistent with that provision.

The amendment can thus be read to make clear that the attorney fee provisions in the Code (for example, § 362(h) and § 523(d)) do not override the Equal Access to Justice Act with respect to rates for fee awards against the federal government in cases where EAJA would otherwise have applied.[131] However, other governmental units may argue that the provision covers all fee awards "against any governmental unit."

15.6 Services Provided by Non-Attorneys

It is not surprising, given the tremendous need for bankruptcy relief among many low-income debtors and the lack of pro bono or affordable bankruptcy attorneys in some areas, that various types of non-attorney operations have sprung up which purport to offer debtors assistance in filing bankruptcy cases. Typically dubbed "typing services," "document preparation services," or "independent paralegals," these entities advertise that they can solve debt problems and prevent evictions and foreclosures without the necessity of an attorney.

not be filed until twenty-one days have passed after it has been served on the respondent, who may withdraw or correct the challenged pleading or paper during that time. *See* Fed. R. Bankr. P. 9011(c)(1)(A).

124 *In re* Dansereau, 274 B.R. 686 (Bankr. W.D. Tex. 2002); *In re* Knox, 237 B.R. 687 (Bankr. N.D. Ill. 1999); *In re* Lenior, 231 B.R. 662 (Bankr. N.D. Ill. 1999).

125 *In re* McAllister, 123 B.R. 393 (Bankr. D. Or. 1991) (Rule 9011 sanctions imposed against state revenue department for filing proof of claim for income taxes not owed); *In re* Hamilton, 104 B.R. 525 (Bankr. M.D. Ga. 1989) (attorney fees awarded to debtor as Rule 9011 sanction against IRS for filing claim for taxes without reasonable inquiry).

126 *In re* Kilgore, 253 B.R. 179 (Bankr. D.S.C. 2000).

127 See Chapter 2, *supra*, for a discussion of bankruptcy court jurisdiction.

128 Conte & Newberg, Attorney Fee Awards (2d ed.); M. Derfner & A. Wolf, Court Awarded Attorney Fees; E. Larson, Federal Court Awards of Attorney's Fee (1981).

129 Pub. L. No. 103-394, 108 Stat. 4106 (1994).

130 *See* Jove Eng'g, Inc. v. Internal Revenue Serv., 92 F.3d 1539 (11th Cir. 1996) (attorney fees could be awarded against I.R.S. for violating automatic stay, but fees had to be consistent with EAJA and 26 U.S.C. § 7430); § 15.5.4, *infra*.

131 The "substantial justification" test which must be met for fees under EAJA is in a separate portion of EAJA that is not referenced in the new § 106(a). Therefore, it is not applicable unless fees are being sought solely under EAJA.

Generally, these non-attorney operations are downright fraudulent, making promises to debtors which they cannot hope to keep and extracting fees which far exceed the value of the work performed. These entities engage in the worst type of consumer fraud, because they are aimed at vulnerable low and moderate income individuals facing financial distress who are desperate for honest help. By promising to stop a foreclosure or eviction, for example, without any real plan for long-term relief, these operators take money which could more appropriately be used to address the consumer's debt problems directly.

The "assistance" provided by even the best non-attorney petition preparer is, in fact, the unauthorized practice of law.[132] It is virtually impossible to properly help someone prepare bankruptcy schedules without giving substantial legal advice. If no legal advice is proffered, then there is little value to the service, schedules are likely to be improperly prepared, and a fee is charged which exceeds the value of inputting information into a computer.

Usually, the advice given is also incorrect or incomplete. Debtors are sent to file bankruptcy petitions with papers that are inadequate or defective, leading to quick dismissals or, at best, a bankruptcy case that does not give the debtor all the relief to which the debtor is entitled. In the worst cases, debtors are not even aware that bankruptcy cases have been filed on their behalf; their signatures are forged by the non-attorney preparer. In some schemes, the only assistance offered by the entity advertising that it can solve debt problems is a referral to a bankruptcy attorney, after the debtor is charged a fee of two hundred dollars or more.[133] And in yet one more variation, an attorney is hired by the non-attorneys with no supervisory responsibilities other than to act as a figurehead and sign papers prepared by the non-attorneys.[134]

The courts have been plagued by the problems caused by these operations for some time. In some areas, such as southern California, they have reached epidemic proportions. They are remedied only when the United States trustee, the court, or consumers take affirmative action to stop them. When challenges are raised, the court can enjoin unlawful practices[135] and require disbursement of funds and damages, either as unlawful fees under the Bankruptcy Code[136] or as damages for unfair and deceptive trade practices.[137] Once such an order is entered, and without being able to engage in unauthorized practice of law or unfair and deceptive practices, few of the non-attorney operations can remain in business without risking contempt sanctions for violation of a court order.[138]

Efforts to regulate the provision of bankruptcy services by non-attorneys received a major boost from enactment of new Code section 110,[139] of the Code, as well as criminal penalties,[140] to deal specifically with the issue of non-attorney petition preparers.

Section 110(a) defines a bankruptcy petition preparer as a person other than an attorney or an employee of an attorney who prepares for compensation a petition or other documents in a bankruptcy case.[141] This definition thus excludes

---

132 Taub v. Weber, 366 F.3d 966 (9th Cir. 2004) (petition preparer's advice regarding the meaning of terms "market value" and "secured claim or exemption" was unauthorized practice of law); *In re* Agyekum, 225 B.R. 695 (B.A.P. 9th Cir. 1998) (preprinted bankruptcy guide and questionnaire used by preparer to assist debtors constituted practice of law); *In re* Doser, 292 B.R. 652 (D. Idaho 2003) (giving debtors an incomplete and inaccurate "bankruptcy overview" prepared by franchisor, "We the People," and telling them that it was reliable was practice of law); *In re* Powell, 266 B.R. 450 (Bankr. N.D. Cal. 2001) (actions in connection with lien avoidance motion were unauthorized practice of law).

133 *See In re* Fleet, 95 B.R. 319 (E.D. Pa. 1989) (finding that such practices were unfair and deceptive).

134 *In re* Hessinger & Associates, 171 B.R. 366 (Bankr. N.D. Cal. 1994), *vacated on other grounds*, 192 B.R. 211 (N.D. Cal. 1996).

135 *In re* Skobinsky, 167 B.R. 45 (E.D. Pa. 1994); *In re* Harris, 152 B.R. 440 (Bankr. W.D. Pa. 1993) ("legal technician" who engaged in unauthorized practice of law enjoined from completing bankruptcy forms for clients); *In re* McCarthy, 149 B.R. 162 (Bankr. S.D. Cal. 1992) (owner of paralegal and typing service enjoined from continuing unauthorized practice of law and from advertising under heading "Legal Clinics" in telephone directory).

136 *In re* Cochran, 164 B.R. 366 (Bankr. M.D. Fla. 1994) (typing service required to disgorge all fees in excess of $50.00 per case, which was deemed to be value of services provided); *In re* Robinson, 162 B.R. 319 (Bankr. D. Kan. 1993) (individuals engaged in unauthorized practice of law required to disgorge all fees received); *In re* Evans, 153 B.R. 960 (Bankr. E.D. Pa. 1993) (legal self-help company required to disgorge all fees in excess of $100.00 value of its services and enjoined from collecting fees of over $100.00 in future; company also ordered to provide all present and future customers with copy of court's opinion); *In re* Harris, 152 B.R. 440 (Bankr. W.D. Pa. 1993) ("legal technician" who engaged in unauthorized practice of law ordered to disgorge all sums received for services); *In re* McCarthy, 149 B.R. 162 (Bankr. S.D. Cal. 1992) (order to remit all fees in case); *In re* Herren, 138 B.R. 989 (Bankr. D. Wyo. 1992) (all fees ordered remitted to debtor); O'Connell v. David, 35 B.R. 141 (Bankr. E.D. Pa. 1983), *modified* 35 B.R. 146 (E.D. Pa. 1983), *aff'd*, 740 F.2d 958 (3d Cir. 1990); *see also In re* Fleet, 95 B.R. 319 (E.D. Pa. 1989) (court has authority to regulate fees paid to non-attorneys in scheme where non-attorneys collected fees for referring debtors to a bankruptcy attorney after numerous deceptive advertisements and statements).

137 *In re* Fleet, 95 B.R. 319 (E.D. Pa. 1989) (triple damages awarded to debtors who had paid money to non-attorneys who deceptively promised to solve debt problems); *In re* Samuels, 176 B.R. 616 (Bankr. M.D. Fla. 1994).

138 *See In re* Guttierez, 248 B.R. 287 (Bankr. W.D. Tex. 2000) (fine for contempt of prior order); *In re* Repp, 218 B.R. 518 (Bankr. D. Ariz. 1998) ($1 million fine for contempt of injunction and failure to pay previous fines).

139 11 U.S.C. § 110.

140 18 U.S.C. § 156.

141 *See In re* Crowe, 243 B.R. 43 (B.A.P. 9th Cir. 2000) (individual who sold self-help book and then prepared bankruptcy petitions for those who had purchased book was preparing petitions for compensation); *In re* Fraga, 210 B.R. 812 (B.A.P. 9th Cir. 1997)

law students and pro bono volunteers who are not compensated.

The new section creates a paper trail to identify and monitor petition preparers. All documents filed must have the preparer's signature, printed name, address and social security number, as well as the social security numbers of all other people who assisted in preparing the document.[142] The Official Bankruptcy Forms have been amended to include a space for this information on each form.[143] In addition, the preparer must, within ten days after the filing of a petition, file a declaration under penalty of perjury of any fees received from or on behalf of the debtor and fees yet to be paid.[144]

The section also contains prohibitions of the most common abuses, including cases in which debtors were not even aware a bankruptcy had been filed on their behalf. The preparer must furnish copies of all documents to the debtor.[145] The preparer may not execute a document on behalf of the debtor.[146] The preparer may not use the word "legal" or similar terms in advertisements.[147] Use of language in an advertisement that implies that legal services will be offered also violates this provision.[148] The court must

disallow and order disgorgement of any fees in excess of the value of services provided.[149] Sometimes, even a small fee is excessive, because petition preparer services, without more, may do the debtor more harm than good. If the services have no value, or a negative value, the entire fee should be disgorged.[150] The preparer may not collect any payment for court fees.[151] Each violation of these provisions, including failure to disgorge excessive fees, is subject to a fine of not more than $500.00.[152]

To encourage enforcement of its provisions, the section creates a cause of action for damages and injunctive relief in addition to the potential fines. The debtor, trustee or a creditor may file a motion for damages, payable to the debtor, if the preparer violates any of the provisions of

---

(corporation that prepared documents for pro se petitions was a petition preparer within definition even though it was owned by an attorney); *In re* Moore, 290 B.R. 287 (Bankr. E.D.N.C. 2003) (franchisor, "We the People," was petition preparer when petition preparer did business under franchisor's name and paid percentage of fees to franchisor); *In re* France, 271 B.R. 748 (Bankr. E.D.N.Y. 2002) (real estate broker who assisted debtor in filing petitions was petition preparer); *see also In re* Desilets, 291 F.3d 925 (6th Cir. 2002) (attorney admitted to federal district court bar could practice in bankruptcy court even if not admitted to state bar for court's jurisdiction so he was not a petition preparer). Related practices that do not involve the provision of bankruptcy services may be subject to state law regulation. *See In re* McNeal, 286 B.R. 910 (Bankr. N.D. Cal. 2002) (treble damages awarded to debtor for foreclosure consultant's violation of state law).

142 11 U.S.C. § 110(b), (c); *see In re* Bohman, 202 B.R. 179 (Bankr. S.D. Fla. 1996) (preparer fined for failing to sign dischargeability complaint prepared for debtor; preparation of complaint held to be unauthorized practice); *In re* Paskel, 201 B.R. 511 (Bankr. E.D. Ark. 1996) (preparer fined $1500.00 for failing to place name and address on three documents); *see also In re* Crawford, 194 F.3d 954 (9th Cir. 1999) (requirement of social security number disclosure not unconstitutional).

143 *See* Official Forms 1, 3, 6, 7, 8, Appx. D, *infra.*

144 11 U.S.C. § 110(h).

145 11 U.S.C. § 110(d).

146 11 U.S.C. § 110(e).

147 11 U.S.C. § 110(f); *In re* Moffett, 263 B.R. 805 (Bankr. W.D. Ky. 2001) (use of "paralegal" in advertisement violated § 110); *In re* Brokenbrough, 197 B.R. 839 (Bankr. S.D. Ohio 1996) (use of word "legal" in telephone listings violated statute); *In re* Burdick, 191 B.R. 529 (Bankr. N.D.N.Y. 1996) (use of word "paralegal" in an advertisement for a petition preparer ruled improper as a similar term to "legal").

148 *In re* Ali, 230 B.R. 477 (Bankr. E.D.N.Y. 1999) (use of term "by law" in flyer describing bankruptcy rights gives debtors the impression that legal services will be offered).

149 11 U.S.C. § 110(h); *In re* Agyekum, 225 B.R. 695 (B.A.P. 9th Cir. 1998) ($173.00 fee excessive, reasonable value of service only $125.00); *In re* Moore, 290 B.R. 287 (Bankr. E.D.N.C. 2003) (fee of $199.00 was excessive and only $80.00 was permitted); *In re* Pavlis, 264 B.R. 57 (Bankr. D.R.I. 2001) (presumed reasonable fee was $30.00 per hour for no more than five hours); *In re* Moffett, 263 B.R. 805 (Bankr. W.D. Ky. 2001) (preparer enjoined from charging more than $20.00 per hour with maximum of $100.00); *In re* Guttierez, 248 B.R. 287 (Bankr. W.D. Tex. 2000) (reasonable fee for typing services was $50.00); *In re* Mullikin, 231 B.R. 750 (Bankr. W.D. Mo. 1999) (reasonable value of petition preparer services found to be $150.00; preparer required to disgorge entire $404.00 fee as sanction); *In re* Ali, 230 B.R. 477 (Bankr. E.D.N.Y. 1999) (reasonable value of preparing skeleton petition without balance of forms necessary to complete case is $25.00); *In re* Burdick, 191 B.R. 529 (Bankr. N.D.N.Y. 1996) (because value of typing a bankruptcy petition is $50.00, fee in excess of that amount ordered returned to debtors); *see also In re* Moore, 232 B.R. 1 (Bankr. D. Me. 1999) (maximum flat fee should be $75.00; paralegal could seek a larger fee if circumstances warrant); *In re* Hartman, 208 B.R. 768 (Bankr. D. Mass. 1997) (fee of $100.00—$20.00 per hour—permissible if schedules competently prepared; incompetence required disgorgement of $625.00 of $675.00 fee).

150 *In re* Pillot, 286 B.R. 157 (Bankr. C.D. Cal. 2002) (value of services which constituted unauthorized practice of law was zero); *In re* Bradshaw, 233 B.R. 315 (Bankr. D.N.J. 1999) (value of defendants' services was "negative" because innocent people relied on defendants' empty promises to their detriment and paid $300.00 for the privilege; entire fee ordered disgorged); *In re* Stacy, 193 B.R. 31 (Bankr. D. Or. 1996) (dismissed petition had no value to debtor).

151 11 U.S.C. § 110(g); *In re* Buck, 290 B.R. 758 (Bankr. C.D. Cal. 2003) (acceptance, for delivery to court, of cashier's check made payable to bankruptcy court violated statute); *In re* McDaniel, 232 B.R. 674 (Bankr. N.D. Tex. 1999); *In re* Green, 197 B.R. 878 (Bankr. D. Ariz. 1996) (preparer fined for delivering money order for filing fee to court); *see also In re* Wallace, 227 B.R. 826 (Bankr. S.D. Ind. 1998) (preparer could neither collect fees nor deliver petition to court because by latter action preparer is controlling the timing of filing because case can not be filed without fees).

152 11 U.S.C. § 110(b)–(h); *see In re* Bradshaw, 233 B.R. 315 (Bankr. D.N.J. 1999) (maximum fine of $500.00 for each document filed without required language); *In re* Cordero, 185 B.R. 882 (Bankr. M.D. Fla. 1995) (fine of $250.00 for each violation of statute).

section 110, or commits any unfair, deceptive or fraudulent act.[153] This permits private parties to bring violations to the attention of the court. In a successful action, the debtor is to be awarded actual damages plus the greater of $2000.00 or twice the amount paid to the petition preparer.[154] A trustee or creditor moving for damages is entitled to an additional $1000.00 in statutory damages.[155]

The "unfair and deceptive" language is from the Federal Trade Commission Act and state unfair and deceptive practices laws, so case law under those statutes should be used in judging preparers' activities.[156] The damage provisions are modeled on the federal Truth in Lending Act damage provisions.[157] As under Truth in Lending, class actions are possible and will be easy to bring for violations giving rise to strict liability, because the proof will consist of the forms filed by the preparer.

The party that brings a successful action is also entitled to attorney fees and costs,[158] which should provide an incentive for attorneys to bring such actions. The court may also enter injunctive relief against specific unfair or deceptive acts by petition preparers.[159] If the court finds that such an injunction would not be sufficient to prevent such conduct, or if the preparer has not paid a fine imposed under section 110, the court may enjoin the person from acting as a petition preparer.[160] Several courts have held that evidence of unauthorized practice of law is sufficient to establish unfair and deceptive conduct in violation of section 110(i) or to justify injunctive relief under section 110(j).[161] A debtor, trustee or creditor may also be awarded attorney fees and costs for successfully seeking injunctive relief.[162]

Fraudulent or misleading advertisements to tenants facing eviction—petition preparers promising that tenants legally can remain in their apartments rent free—have been a recurrent problem in many jurisdictions. Often, the victims of this scam don't know that the bankruptcy only temporarily prevents eviction. In some cases, the tenants are not told that they are filing bankruptcy at all. Recently, a New Jersey court sanctioned and permanently enjoined a ring of petition preparers that repeatedly engaged in these practices from directly or indirectly operating as petition preparers anywhere in the United States.[163]

Finally, to prevent any implication that the new section authorizes non-attorneys to give legal advice or services, section 110(k) states that nothing in the section shall be construed to permit activities otherwise prohibited by law.

Courts and United States trustees have brought numerous actions under these new provisions. In view of the widespread nature of the petition preparer business, new section 110 also offers debtors' attorneys an opportunity to earn attorney fees while at the same time putting an end to unfair and deceptive practices that cause substantial harm to consumer debtors.

---

153 11 U.S.C. § 110(i); *see In re* Doser, 292 B.R. 652 (D. Idaho 2003) (inviting debtors to "chat" with a supervising attorney for "We the People" but not informing them that they cannot rely on that attorney's advice and that attorney does not represent them, was unfair and deceptive); *In re* Moore, 290 B.R. 287 (Bankr. E.D.N.C. 2003) (same); *In re* Landry, 250 B.R. 441 (Bankr. M.D. Fla. 2000) (calling a portion of fee a "membership fee" in a "document preparation club" and failing to disclose that fee was fraudulent and deceptive act).

154 11 U.S.C. § 110(i)(1); *see In re* Gavin, 184 B.R. 670 (E.D. Pa. 1995); *In re* Kangarloo, 250 B.R. 115 (Bankr. C.D. Cal. 2000) (recommending $2050.00 actual damages for cost of proper bankruptcy filing plus $2000.00 statutory damages and plus $1500.00 attorney fees); *In re* Murray, 194 B.R. 651 (Bankr. D. Ariz. 1996) (recommending that debtors be awarded actual damages, statutory damages and attorney fees for unfair and deceptive acts of preparer). The damages must be awarded by the district court, after the bankruptcy court certifies the underlying facts to that court and the moving party then moves for the award in district court. *See* Order Interpreting 11 U.S.C. § 110, 198 B.R. 604 (C.D. Cal. 1996).

155 11 U.S.C. § 110(i)(2); *see In re* Landry, 250 B.R. 441 (Bankr. M.D. Fla. 2000) (awarding $1000.00 minimum damages and attorney fees to trustee).

156 *See generally* National Consumer Law Center, Unfair and Deceptive Acts and Practices (5th ed. 2001 and Supp.).

157 15 U.S.C. § 1640.

158 11 U.S.C. § 110(i)(1)(C).

159 11 U.S.C. § 110(j)(2)(A).

160 11 U.S.C. § 110(j)(2); *see In re* Schweitzer, 196 B.R. 620 (Bankr. M.D. Fla. 1996) (statewide injunction entered precluding preparer from acting as preparer in other bankruptcy cases due to numerous violations); *In re* Gavin, 181 B.R. 814 (Bankr. E.D. Pa. 1995) (injunction against individual acting as a petition preparer in any jurisdiction); *In re* Lyvers, 179 B.R. 837 (Bankr. W.D. Ky. 1995) (injunction against filing any petition or other papers in bankruptcy court for district).

161 *E.g., In re* McDaniel, 232 B.R. 674 (Bankr. N.D. Tex. 1999); *In re* Moore, 232 B.R. 1 (Bankr. D. Me. 1999); *see also In re* Graves, 279 B.R. 266 (B.A.P. 9th Cir. 2002) (court could issue injunction *sua sponte*, but petition preparer must be given notice and opportunity to be heard on issuance of injunction); *In re* Bonarrigo, 282 B.R. 101 (D. Mass. 2002) (violation of previous agreed order delineating what petition preparer could do justified injunction against acting as petition preparers in court's jurisdiction). One court concluded that preparation of a chapter 13 plan by a petition preparer necessarily involves unauthorized practice of law. *In re* Hobbs, 213 B.R. 207 (Bankr. D. Me. 1997).

162 11 U.S.C. § 110(j)(3).

163 *In re* Bradshaw, 233 B.R. 315 (Bankr. D.N.J. 1999).

Chapter 16

Chapter 12 Bankruptcy: Family Farmer Reorganizations

16.1 Introduction

16.1.1 Evolution and Historical Background of Chapter 12

16.1.1.1 Current Status of Chapter 12

Chapter 12 is a blend of consumer and commercial bankruptcy concepts designed to assist family farmers in successful restructuring and reorganization. Chapter 12 became effective on November 26, 1986.[1] Although originally limited to seven years as emergency legislation for family farmers in a time of economic crisis,[2] chapter 12 has been extended several times.[3]

In 1999 Congress extended chapter 12 temporarily, but declined to make it permanent. The extension ran through July 1, 2000.[4] On July 1, 2000, chapter 12 expired. However, on May 11, 2001, Congress passed an eleven-month extension of chapter 12.[5] The eleven months ran retroactively from July 1, 2000 through June 1, 2001. At that point, chapter 12 again expired. Then, on June 26, 2001, Congress passed an additional four-month extension, again running partly retroactively from June 1, 2001, through October 1, 2001.[6] Congress then passed another two extensions: one running from September 30, 2001, through June 1, 2002,

passed on May 7, 2002,[7] and another extension running from May 31, 2002 through January 1, 2003, passed on May 13, 2002.[8] Following those enactments, Congress then passed another two six-month extensions: one extension running from December 31, 2002, through July 1, 2003, and the other running from June 30, 2003, through January 1, 2004.[9] Once again, Congress allowed chapter 12 to expire. Then, on October 25, 2004, Congress passed another extension, again running retroactively, from January 1, 2004 through June 30, 2005.[10] As these laws reenacted chapter 12 retroactively, presumably cases filed in the gap period under other chapters are eligible for conversion.

These temporary extensions of chapter 12 have been designed to create leverage to obtain the votes of members of Congress from farm states for a broader bankruptcy bill that would cover many issues other than chapter 12. It appears likely that chapter 12, now a political football, will eventually be made permanent or will be further extended temporarily in a separate bill.[11]

16.1.1.2 Purpose of Chapter 12

Chapter 12 is not designed to be a panacea to family farmers' economic woes, but is a specific limited remedy which will help some, but not all, farmers. Attorneys utilizing chapter 12 must analyze each farmer's economic situation to determine if a chapter 12 filing is the most appropriate remedy.

Chapter 12's legislative history is instructive in understanding its design, intent and mechanics.[12] Chapter 12

---

1 Section 302, Bankruptcy Judges, United States Trustees, and Family Bankruptcy Act of 1986, Pub. L. No. 99-554, 100 Stat. 3103.

2 Dahlke v. Doering, 94 B.R. 569 (D. Minn. 1989); Travelers Ins. Co. v. Bullington, 89 B.R. 1010 (M.D. Ga. 1988), *aff'd*, 878 F.2d 354 (11th Cir. 1989); *In re* Neff, 89 B.R. 672 (Bankr. S.D. Ohio 1988); *In re* Coffman, 90 B.R. 878 (Bankr. W.D. Tenn. 1988). *See* 132 Cong. Rec. S17,075–S17,093 (daily ed. Oct. 3, 1986); Shapiro, *An Analysis of the Family Farmer Bankruptcy Act of 1986*, 15 Hofstra L. Rev. 353 (Winter 1987).

3 *E.g.*, Pub. L. No. 103-65, 107 Stat. 311 (1993). Pub. L. No. 106-5, 113 Stat. 9 (1999), extended chapter 12 through October 1, 1999.

4 Pub. L. No. 106-70, 113 Stat. 1031 (1999), became effective at the close of the previous extension on October 1, 1999.

5 Pub. L. No. 107-8, 115 Stat. 10 (2001).

6 Pub. L. No. 107-17, 115 Stat. 151 (2001).

7 Pub. L. No. 107-170, 116 Stat. 133 (2002).

8 Pub. L. No. 107-171, 116 Stat. 134 (2002).

9 Pub. L. No. 107-377, 115 Stat. 3115 (2002); Pub. L. No. 108-73, 117 Stat. 891 (2003).

10 Pub. L. No. 108-369, 118 Stat. 1749 (2004).

11 As this is being written, both the House of Representatives and the Senate have separately passed (unenacted) legislation that would make chapter 12 permanent. *See* NCLC REPORTS *Bankruptcy and Foreclosures Ed.* for further updates.

12 *Compare* H.R. 5316 *with* Senate amendments. *See* 132 Cong. Rec. (daily ed. May 6, 1986). What emerged as chapter 12 is different from both proposals in some respects. *See also* H.R. Conf. Rep. No. 99-958 (1986), *reprinted in* 1986 U.S.C.C.A.N. 5247–5252.

arose from Congressional recognition of the imminent crisis in the traditional family farm economy, and the inability of the Bankruptcy Code under existing chapters to furnish most family farmers with substantial assistance in reorganization.

The problems which brought about the need for chapter 12 in substantial measure arose from factors beyond farmers' control. The significant risk involved in farming and natural disasters inherent in crop production make profits and losses highly unpredictable (a problem which makes income and expenditure projections difficult in chapter 12 cases). The decline in prices paid to the farmer for farm products coupled with the rise in farm production costs make farming far less profitable.

Congress has approached the economic problems of farmers from several legislative directions. Chapter 12 is only one approach, and for many farmers merely restructuring under chapter 12 will be an inadequate remedy. Nevertheless, Congress recognized that existing bankruptcy provisions were generally ineffective and unsuitable for farmer reorganization.[13] A bankruptcy chapter exclusively for family farmers has its roots in the Frazier-Lemke Acts which created special bankruptcy provisions for farmers in the 1930s and early 1940s.[14]

16.1.2 Special Bankruptcy Code Protections for Farmers Outside of Chapter 12

In recognition of farmers' special needs and circumstances, Congress built into the 1978 Bankruptcy Reform Act certain protections expressly for farmers.[15] A debtor is a "farmer" under section 101(20) if eighty percent or more of his or her gross income came from a farming operation in the tax year immediately preceding the filing of the debtor's petition.[16] A family farmer is defined generally as someone engaged in farming operations, whose debts do not exceed $1.5 million, at least eighty percent of whose debts arise out of the farming operation (excluding debt on a principal residence), and at least fifty percent of whose gross income comes from farming.[17] An involuntary bankruptcy cannot be initiated against a farmer or family farmer under chapters 7, 11, or 12.[18]

A farmer reorganization case under either chapter 11 or 13 cannot be converted, without the farmer's consent, to a liquidation case under chapter 7.[19] Similarly, absent a finding of fraud,[20] a farmer in chapter 12 cannot be converted to a chapter 7 case.[21] Despite these Code prohibitions on involuntary case commencement or conversion for farmers, some circuits allow the proposal and confirmation of plans which liquidate the debtor under chapter 11 when farmer reorganizations stall. And courts have found that a farmer must make an affirmative assertion of his or her farmer status in response to an involuntary petition or be deemed to have waived that defense.[22]

16.1.3 Farmer Reorganizations Under Chapters Other Than Chapter 12

16.1.3.1 Overview

Before the creation of chapter 12, family farmer reorganizations were limited to chapters 11 and 13 (if the debtor was eligible). These two options are still available to family farmers; family farmers are not compelled to use chapter 12 to reorganize. The option of orderly liquidation and removal

---

13   *See* H.R. Conf. Rep. No. 99-958 (1986), *reprinted in* 1986 U.S.C.C.A.N. 5249–5252.

14   Frazier-Lemke Farm Mortgage Acts Ch. 869, 48 Stat. 1289 (June 28, 1924); Ch. 792, 49 Stat. 942 (Aug. 28, 1935); Ch. 39, ssl, 2, 54 Stat. 40 (Mar. 4, 1940); Norton, *The New Family Farmer Bankruptcy Act*, 3 Prac. Real Estate Lawyer No. 4, 37–44 (July, 1987). The earlier Frazier-Lemke Acts had constitutional problems concerning impairment of property rights under the Fifth Amendment. It has been intimated that the Fifth Amendment problems may also infect chapter 12; *see* United States v. Sec. Indus. Bank, 459 U.S. 70 (1982). However, the cases addressing this issue to date find chapter 12 passes constitutional muster; Albaugh v. Terrell, 93 B.R. 115 (E.D. Mich. 1988); *In re* Kloberdanz, 83 B.R. 767 n.6 (Bankr. D. Colo. 1988); *In re* Bullington, 80 B.R. 590 (Bankr. M.D. Ga. 1987), *aff'd sub nom.* Travelers Ins. Co. v. Bullington, 89 B.R. 1010 (M.D. Ga. 1988), *aff'd*, 878 F.2d 354 (11th Cir. 1989).

15   As early as the Bankruptcy Act of 1898 creditors of a "person engaged chiefly in farming or in tillage of soil" were prevented from forcing that person into an involuntary bankruptcy. Bankruptcy Act of 1898, ch. 541, § 4(b), 30 Stat. 544. This protection against involuntary bankruptcy remains the law today. *See* 11 U.S.C. § 303(a). Protection from involuntary bankruptcy is available to someone defined as a "farmer" under section 101(20) or a "family farmer" as defined under section 101(18).

16   "Farming operation" is defined at 11 U.S.C. § 101(21). *See* 16.2.2.3, *infra*. Section 101(20) has been held not to be jurisdictional for cases in which creditors have sought to put a farmer into an involuntary bankruptcy. *See In re* McCloy, 296 F.3d 370 (5th Cir. 2002) (farmer status must be affirmatively raised as a defense to involuntary bankruptcy, and the status is not jurisdictional); *In re* Frusher, 124 B.R. 331 (D. Kan. 1991) (same).

17   11 U.S.C. § 101(18).

18   11 U.S.C. § 303(a). No involuntary bankruptcy is available for any debtor under chapter 13. *In re* KZK Livestock, Inc., 147 B.R. 452 (Bankr. C.D. Ill. 1992).

19   11 U.S.C. §§ 1112(c), 1307(e).

20   Graven v. Fink, 936 F.2d 378 (8th Cir. 1991).

21   11 U.S.C. § 1208.

22   Potsmeil v. Alexandria Production Credit Ass'n, 42 B.R. 731 (W.D. La. 1984); *In re* Albers, 71 B.R. 39 (Bankr. N.D. Ohio 1987); *In re* Johnson, 4 Collier Bankr. Cas. 2d (MB) 1482 (Bankr. D. Minn. 1981).

of debt is also open to a farmer under chapter 7, and the chapter 7 remedy is an important option for farmers whose reorganization is impossible.

However, chapters 11 and 13 were not originally constructed with the special needs of the farmer debtor in mind and both provide significant barriers to farmer reorganization. A discussion of those problems explains the design of chapter 12 and aids the choice of the best chapter for a farmer needing reorganization.

16.1.3.2 Problems Under Chapter 13 for Farmers

Chapter 13 provides the template for chapter 12; chapter 13's "automatic cram down" feature is its cornerstone.[23] However, chapter 13's ceiling for eligibility of no more than $871,550.00 in liquidated, non-contingent secured debt and no more than $290,525.00 in liquidated, non-contingent unsecured debt[24] makes chapter 13 unavailable for all but the smallest farm operations.[25]

Chapter 13 also requires that the debtor be an "individual with a regular income."[26] This criterion eliminated farms owned by family partnerships and family-owned corporations.

The "regular income" criteria also was interpreted to eliminate farming operations in which the major source of income is crop farming because of the irregularity and infrequence of income. Chapter 13 cases are customarily set up with payments due on a monthly or other relatively frequent basis.[27]

Confirmation of chapter 13 plans also typically do not depend on such reorganizational strategies as sales and recovery of property, long the province and useful tools of chapter 7 trustees and chapter 11 debtors-in-possession.[28] Finally, chapter 13 is not generally well suited to farm cases because chapter 13 plan payments must begin in all cases within thirty days after filing of the plan, unless otherwise ordered by the bankruptcy court.[29]

16.1.3.3 Problems Under Chapter 11 for Farmers

Before enactment of chapter 12, most farmers attempted reorganization under chapter 11. By and large, chapter 11 has proved unsuitable to reorganization of family farms with their peculiar combination of creditors and restructuring needs. Chapter 11 is designed—and typically viewed by a bankruptcy court—as a commercial remedy, and is a costly and cumbersome method for an unsophisticated small business. Chapter 11 reorganizations require relatively complex disclosure statements and plans and several hearings, with the result that much time (both for the attorney and the farmer) and money is spent producing paperwork and making court appearances.[30]

Chapter 11 provides a dual route for confirmation of a reorganization plan, under either section 1129(a) or 1129(b). However, both routes provide obstacles for farmer reorganization. Section 1129(a) provides for creditor approval or rejection by voting on a plan of reorganization. Creditors in classes impaired by the plan in which the creditors will not receive one-hundred percent repayment upon their claims can vote against the plan and thereby block its confirmation. In addition, for section 1129(a) reorganizations most courts require that, upon election by an under-secured creditor, that creditor's indebtedness must be treated and repaid as if *fully* secured.[31] Most farm creditors are under-secured, and repaying these creditors in full, instead of merely the value of their collateral, would make plan feasibility and confirmation virtually impossible.

The second route available for confirmation is the section 1129(b) "cram down." While this route allows for confirmation of plans over creditor objection and for payment of secured creditors at the value of their collateral rather than the face amount of their claims,[32] plan confirmation must follow the "absolute priority" rule. The "absolute priority" rule does not allow owners of property to keep their own-

---

23 11 U.S.C. §§ 1325(a); *see* § 11.6, *supra.*

24 11 U.S.C. § 109(e).

25 The restrictive chapter 13 format has been best utilized by small dairy and livestock operations with a continuous cash flow. *See* Bromley, *The Chapter 12 Family Farm Bankruptcy Law*, 60 Wis. B. Bull. No. 1, 18–20 (Jan. 1987); Comment, *Chapter 13 and the Family Farm*, 3 Bankr. Dev. J. 599 (1986); Matson, *Understanding the New Family Farmer Bankruptcy Act*, 21 U. Rich. L. Rev. 521 (Spring 1987); Shapiro, *An Analysis of the Family Farmer Bankruptcy Act of 1986*, 15 Hofstra L. Rev. 353 (Winter 1987).

26 11 U.S.C. § 109(e).

27 There were instances in which crop farm operation plans were confirmed in chapter 13. *See In re* Fiegi, 61 B.R. 994 (Bankr. D. Or. 1986); *In re* Hines, 7 B.R. 415 (Bankr. D.S.D. 1980).

28 *See* §§ 16.3, 16.4.4.4, *infra*; § 10.4.2, *supra.*

29 11 U.S.C. § 1326(a)(1).

30 For an overview of the problems with farm reorganizations generally under chapter 11, see Frasier, *The New Bankruptcy Code Chapter 12: Friend of the Family Farmer?* 41 Washington State Bar News 29 (Aug. 1987); Matson, *Understanding the New Family Farmer Bankruptcy Act*, 21 U. Rich. L. Rev. 521 (Spring 1987); Norton, *The New Family Farmer Bankruptcy Act*, 3 Prac. Real Estate Lawyer 37 (July, 1987); Shapiro, *An Analysis of the Family Farmer Bankruptcy Act of 1986*, 15 Hofstra L. Rev. 353 (Winter 1987) and the Conference Report (H.R. Conf. Rep. No. 99-958, at 48 (1986)). The filing fee ($230.00, including a $30.00 administrative fee, in chapter 12 versus $830.00 for chapter 11) also makes chapter 11 unattractive for an already cash poor farm operation. 28 U.S.C. § 1930(a); Rowley v. Yarnell, 22 F.3d 190 (8th Cir. 1994); Dahlke v. Doering, 94 B.R. 569 (D. Minn. 1989); *In re* Pianowski, 92 B.R. 225 (Bankr. W.D. Mich. 1988).

31 11 U.S.C. § 1129(a) and 11 U.S.C. § 1111(b)(2). *See, e.g., In re* Baxley, 72 B.R. 195 (Bankr. D.S.C. 1986) (farmer chapter 11); *In re* Hallum, 29 B.R. 343 (Bankr. E.D. Tenn. 1983); *In re* Griffiths, 27 B.R. 873 (Bankr. D. Kan. 1983).

32 11 U.S.C. § 1129(b)(2)(A).

ership interest after confirmation if creditors in all classes ahead of them, for example, secured and general unsecured creditors, receive less than one-hundred percent of their claims.[33] While this rule was once modified in one circuit with regard to farmer debtors in chapter 11, the absolute priority rule still serves as a barrier to chapter 11 reorganization unless sale of the farm is part of the plan.[34]

A final disadvantage of chapter 11 farm reorganization is that some circuits allow proposal and confirmation by creditors of plans which liquidate the farmer in chapter 11 if reorganization efforts stall.[35] In sum, relatively few effective bankruptcy reorganizations, debt restructurings and debt reductions for family farmers have occurred in chapter 11 cases without the cooperation and blessing of a farmer's major creditors.

16.1.4 The Unique Nature of Farm Indebtedness

An attorney who undertakes representation of farmers in financial difficulty should become familiar with the unique structure of the farm economy, its lenders and the non-bankruptcy laws, regulations and policies applicable to farmers. The intricate detail of that structure cannot be adequately covered here, but some comment is appropriate. No analysis of a farmer's situation, financial problems, and potential remedies can be considered complete without surveying the non-bankruptcy options available. Those options include federal options granted by statute, case law, regulations and policies,[36] and may include rights and remedies under state laws.[37] They may also include persuasion and negotiation to arrive at arrangements with creditors not mandated to debtors by right but dictated to both debtor and creditor by good business sense.

Many farmers in financial difficulty will have one or more creditors connected with the federal government or the Farm Credit System: the United States acting through the Farm Service Agency (FSA),[38] or the Small Business Adminis-

tration (SBA); or federal corporations such as Agricultural Credit Banks (ACAs), Federal Land Banks (FLBs)[39] or Production Credit Associations (PCAs). The farmer's attorney should not be dismayed by the presence of government creditors; they receive no deferential treatment in the bankruptcy court except as specific bankruptcy laws may dictate.[40] In fact, it is often easier to deal with the claims of government creditors in the bankruptcy context than outside of it.[41] The anti-discrimination provisions of 11 U.S.C. § 525 also control the conduct of government creditors after the bankruptcy filing.[42]

Each of these creditors—particularly the FSA—has policies, rules and/or regulations governing its operations. In almost all cases in which government creditors are present, the attorney for the farmer can expect that:

- The creditors have relatively detailed financial information about the farmer debtor, primarily generated by close creditor-debtor interaction;
- The creditors have taken or attempted to take security interests that cover most, if not all, of the farmer debtor's assets;
- The debtor and creditor will have had a fairly intimate relationship, and many of their dealings have been oral, for example, permission to sell and use the creditor's collateral; and
- The value of the farmer debtor's assets pledged as security is far below the amount of the creditor's claim. Often it is at the impetus of one of these government-related creditors that a crisis situation has developed prodding the farmer to consider chapter 12.

There are also a number of programs in which the farmer debtor may participate that have an impact upon his or her debt structure; many of these involve government lenders.[43] The farmer's attorney should be aware of these programs, their operation and requirements, their status as actual or

---

33   11 U.S.C. §§ 1129(b)(2)(B)(ii), 1129(b)(2)(C)(ii). *See* 7 Collier on Bankruptcy 1129.03[e] (15th ed. rev.).

34   *In re* Ahlers, 794 F.2d 388 (8th Cir. 1986). The Supreme Court reversed the Eighth Circuit, Norwest Bank v. Ahlers, 485 U.S. 197, 108 S. Ct. 963, 99 L. Ed. 2d 169 (1988), finding in this case that the contribution of labor, experience and expertise could not alter the absolute priority rule.

35   *See* § 16.1.2, *supra.*

36   For example, Farm Service Agency (formerly FmHA) loans are governed by federal administrative debt restructuring provisions. *See* 7 U.S.C. § 2001. Another useful Internet resource is www.flaginc.org.

37   For further information on state mediation remedies, see Bibliography, § 16.9.5, *infra.* Farm attorneys should not forget remedies and requirements that can aid their clients in non-farm federal and state laws, for example, Truth-in-Lending, tort liability, and so forth.

38   Reorganization of the federal government farm agencies has

combined the former Farmers Home Administration (FmHA) and Agricultural Stabilization and Conservation Service (ASCS) into one agency, known as the Farm Service Agency (FSA).

39   Under the Agricultural Credit Act of 1987 at 12 U.S.C. §§ 2011 *et seq.,* the merger of Federal Land Banks produced Farm Credit Banks (FCBs) as successors in interest.

40   The Bankruptcy Code contains a specific partial waiver of sovereign immunity. 11 U.S.C. § 106. *See* 13.3.2.2, *supra.*

41   *See* Ch. 13, *supra. See, e.g.,* Gower v. Farmers Home Admin., 785 F.2d 926 (11th Cir. 1986). For a discussion of these lenders, see Comment, *Chapter 13 and the Family Farm,* 3 Bankr. Dev. J. 599 (1986).

42   *In re* Lech, 80 B.R. 1001 (Bankr. M.D. Tenn. 1988).

43   *See, e.g.,* Note, *Bankruptcy, the U.C.C. and the Farmer: PIK Payments—Heads "General Intangibles," Tails "Proceeds" [In re Schamling, 783 F.2d 680 (7th Cir. 1986)],* 26 Washburn L. J. 178 (1986). An overview of how bankruptcy courts have dealt with certain farm programs under chapters 11 and 12 is at § 16.5.3.7.3, *infra.*

potential property or liabilities of the debtor's estate, their value to the farmer and the estate, *and* how they interact with other lenders and their claims and security interests. The farmer's attorney should also be aware that programs, provisions and protections available for farmers through their lenders may be incorporated into reorganization plans.[44] Should a farmer be forced to choose chapter 7 as a remedy, many of those programs and protections are still available.[45]

Most creditors servicing rural areas, including government creditors, have communications with one another about their common borrowers. It is therefore not surprising that a crisis event precipitated by one creditor, such as acceleration for foreclosure, may become common knowledge in the creditor community long before any public notice occurs. Such knowledge may trigger other crisis events as creditors try to secure repayment before the farmer hits bottom.[46]

16.1.5 Timing a Chapter 12 Filing

The most obvious consideration in making a chapter 12 filing is to forestall a crisis event—for example, foreclosure, repossession—that will destroy the farming operation. Other factors bear on the timing of a chapter 12 bankruptcy—apart from the response to a crisis event—which must factor into the filing decision. For example:

- Eligibility is tied to the gross income in the tax year immediately preceding filing.[47] From this perspective is eligibility a problem that can be eliminated by waiting, or conversely, must filing be accelerated to avoid ineligibility?
- Lien dissolution for crops will be fully effective only if

they have not yet been planted.[48] Should filing be accelerated or forestalled to free crops from unwanted security interests?

- If crops will be harvested pre-confirmation, their harvest value (rather than input value) may have to be accounted for in the liquidation analysis, requiring payments to be significantly higher to unsecured creditors.[49]
- Some property can only be retrieved under 11 U.S.C. §§ 547 and 548, or time limitations expanded under 11 U.S.C. § 108, if the bankruptcy case is properly timed to use the powers of the Code effectively.

16.2 Commencement of a Case

16.2.1 Introduction

Chapter 12 assists *family* farmers to reorganize and rehabilitate. Congress has set out criteria for determining which farmers are eligible to use chapter 12; not every farmer has chapter 12 as an option.

The creation of chapter 12 does not foreclose to eligible farmer debtors the use of any other bankruptcy chapter; chapter 12 is not the exclusive remedy for a farmer who falls within its ambit of eligibility. Indeed, there may be advantages in using chapter 11 instead of chapter 12 for farmer reorganization.[50] Moreover, analysis of the family farmer's overall financial condition and repayment ability may still make chapter 7 liquidation the more desirable—or only—option.

16.2.2 Eligibility for Chapter 12 Relief

16.2.2.1 Definition of "Family Farmer"

Section 109(f) limits the availability of chapter 12 to "family farmers," as defined in sections 101(18) and 101(19). The definition encompasses diverse forms of farm ownership, but excludes large family and investor-owned operations.[51]

Eligibility for chapter 12 relief can be challenged by creditors and/or the chapter 12 trustee by a motion to dismiss or at confirmation by objection. Eligibility is deter-

---

44 Particularly with regard to extensions and moratoria, *see* 132 Cong. Rec. S17,082, S17,083 (Oct. 6, 1986). Additionally, state law should also be consulted, relative to remedies that are available to farmers. For example, before a farm debt may be foreclosed, Iowa law requires mediation. Iowa Code § 654A (1997). *See, e.g., In re* Schaal, 93 B.R. 644 (Bankr. W.D. Ark. 1988) (FmHA Limited Resource Loan); *In re* Kesterson, 94 B.R. 561 (Bankr. W.D. Ark. 1987) (FmHA Limited Resource Loan; but must follow loan limitations and regulations); *In re* Kvamme, 91 B.R. 77 (Bankr. D.N.D. 1988); *In re* Fowler, 83 B.R. 39 (Bankr. D. Mont. 1987); *In re* Big Hook Cattle Co., 77 B.R. 793 (Bankr. D. Mont. 1987); *In re* Alexander, 48 B.R. 110 (Bankr. W.D. Mo. 1985). *See also* § 16.5.7.4, *infra*.

45 *In re* Nelson, 123 B.R. 993 (Bankr. D.S.D. 1991) (a bankruptcy sale of land with FmHA mortgage is the equivalent of foreclosure; debtor is entitled to exercise program rights pre-sale). Some rights, however, do not survive a bankruptcy discharge. *See, e.g.*, Lee v. Yeutter, 917 F.2d 1104 (8th Cir. 1990) (farmer is no longer eligible for FSA administrative debt restructuring after discharge).

46 See discussion at § 16.9.3, *infra*. Pre-petition set-offs are a particular hazard.

47 11 U.S.C. § 101(18)(A).

48 *See* § 16.5.3.2, *infra*.

49 *See, e.g., In re* Musil, 99 B.R. 448 (Bankr. D. Kan. 1988).

50 However, the advent of chapter 12 has diminished the cooperation of creditors and the court in expanding the remedial abilities of chapter 11 for farmers as observed in Norwest v. Ahlers, 794 F.2d 388 (8th Cir. 1986), *rev'd and remanded*, 485 U.S. 197, 108 S. Ct. 963, 99 L. Ed. 2d 169 (1988). *See* § 16.1.3.3, *supra*.

51 *In re* Burke, 81 B.R. 971 (Bankr. S.D. Iowa 1987); *In re* Easton, 79 B.R. 836 (Bankr. N.D. Iowa 1987), *aff'd*, 104 B.R. 111 (N.D. Iowa 1988), *vacated*, 883 F.2d 630 (8th Cir. 1989), *on remand* 118 B.R. 676 (Bankr. N.D. Iowa 1990).

mined as of the filing date of the chapter 12 petition.[52] The burden of proving eligibility rests with the debtor.[53] These eligibility requirements are the subject of inquiry by the chapter 12 trustee at the section 341 meeting of creditors. Some courts have held that these requirements are jurisdictional and subject to strict construction.[54]

The only case to address the issue of whether an estate in probate may be a debtor under chapter 12 has determined that under sections 101(15) and 101(41), it cannot.[55]

16.2.2.2 Income Requirements

16.2.2.2.1 In general

Section 109(f) limits the availability of chapter 12 to a "family farmer with regular annual income," paralleling a chapter 13 requirement of "regular income."[56] "Family farmer with regular annual income" is defined in the Code as a "family farmer whose annual income is sufficiently stable and regular to enable such family farmer to make payments under a plan under chapter 12 of this title," again tracking the chapter 13 definition.[57] There is one significant difference between chapters 12 and 13; the chapter 12 definition refers to regular *annual* income, not merely regular income. This change is designed to embrace clearly crop farmers whose income is erratic during different months of the year. It is likely that, because of the inherent risk in farming, there also will be more elasticity in the concept of stability under chapter 12 than under chapter 13.

The concepts of "regular income" under chapter 13 and "regular annual income" under chapter 12 are closely allied to the feasibility requirements for confirmation in chapters 12 and 13.[58] Existing chapter 13 case law serves as a guide, though not a stricture, to what bankruptcy courts may do under chapter 12.[59]

Income sources have been found relevant only as they affect regularity and stability.[60] Where revenue is from sources outside the debtor's control, such as accounts receivable or promissory notes, regularity and stability do not generally appear.[61] However, several courts have taken into positive account gratuitous payments and income from family members donated to the family farm to shore up its operation, particularly where those non-debtor family members have property at risk in the bankruptcy proceeding.[62]

The regularity of annual income necessary for chapter 12 eligibility can be enhanced by the presence of either off-farm income—provided it does not endanger the income eligibility percentage—or livestock operations which periodically produce relatively predictable income at regular intervals.[63]

16.2.2.2.2 Engaged in a farming operation

A family farmer must be engaged in a "farming operation."[64] "Farming operation" is a term already defined prior to the chapter 12 enactment[65] as *including* "farming, tillage of the soil, dairy farming, ranching, production or raising of crops, poultry, or livestock, and production of poultry or livestock products in an unmanufactured state." The legislative history indicates that this definition is meant to be broad.[66] The Code also states that farming operation "in-

52 *In re* Cross Timbers Ranch, Inc., 151 B.R. 923 (Bankr. W.D. Mo. 1993); *In re* Grey, 145 B.R. 86 (Bankr. D. Kan. 1992) (cannot gain eligibility by filing adversary to capture farm funds to credit for earlier tax years where not otherwise eligible; must be eligible from income data available at filing); *In re* Watford, 92 B.R. 557 (M.D. Ga. 1988), *aff'd in part and vacated in part on other grounds*, 898 F.2d 1525 (11th Cir. 1990); *In re* Williams Land Co.*, 91 B.R. 923 (Bankr. D. Or. 1988).

53 Cottonport Bank v. Dichara, 193 B.R. 798 (W.D. La. 1996); *In re* Voelker, 123 B.R. 749 (Bankr. E.D. Mich. 1990); *In re* Snider, 99 B.R. 374 (Bankr. S.D. Ohio 1989); *In re* Plafcan, 93 B.R. 177 (Bankr. E.D. Ark. 1988).

54 Whaley v. United States, 76 B.R. 95 (N.D. Miss. 1987); *In re* Johnson, 73 B.R. 107 (Bankr. S.D. Ohio 1987); *In re* Stedman, 72 B.R. 49 (Bankr. D.N.D. 1987); *In re* Orr, 71 B.R. 639 (Bankr. E.D.N.C. 1987). The bankruptcy court may also raise the issue of eligibility *sua sponte*. 11 U.S.C. § 105; *In re* Lerch, 85 B.R. 491 (Bankr. N.D. Ill. 1988), *aff'd*, 94 B.R. 998 (N.D. Ill. 1989). *Contra In re* Reak, 92 B.R. 804 (Bankr. E.D. Wis. 1988); *In re* Hettinger, 95 B.R. 110 (Bankr. E.D. Mo. 1989); Anderson & Morris, Chapter 12 Farm Reorganizations (chapter 12 issues must be resolved liberally in favor of debtors). *But see* First Brandon Nat'l Bank v. Kerwin-White, 109 B.R. 626 (D. Vt. 1990) (eligibility is not jurisdictional; it is a defense which is waived if not raised in a timely fashion by a creditor); §§ 16.2.2.3.2, 16.4.7.3.

55 *In re* Estate of Grassman, 91 B.R. 928 (Bankr. D. Or. 1988) (and cases cited therein; although the court takes no position on whether the heirs may file their own partnership case under chapter 12). *See also In re* Erickson, 183 B.R. 189 (Bankr. D. Minn. 1995) (dismissal of case warranted upon debtor's death).

56 *See* 11 U.S.C. § 109(e).

57 *Compare* 11 U.S.C. § 101(19) *with* 11 U.S.C. § 101(30). *See also* § 12.2.2, *supra*; *see* § 16.2.2.1, *supra*.

58 *See* 11 U.S.C. §§ 1225(a)(6), 1325(a)(6).

59 *See, e.g., In re* Hoskins, 74 B.R. 51 (Bankr. C.D. Ill. 1987) (chapter 12); *In re* Campbell, 38 B.R. 193 (Bankr. E.D.N.Y. 1984) (chapter 13); *In re* Tucker, 34 B.R. 257 (Bankr. W.D. Okla. 1983) (chapter 13) (prospective income part of "regularity" determination). See § 12.2.2, *supra*, for a discussion of "regular income" under chapter 13. *See also* § 16.4.1, *infra*.

60 *In re* Mikkelsen Farms, Inc., 74 B.R. 280 (Bankr. D. Or. 1987); *In re* Hoskins, 74 B.R. 51 (Bankr. C.D. Ill. 1987) (chapter 12).

61 *In re* Van Fossen, 82 B.R. 77, (Bankr. W.D. Ark. 1987).

62 *In re* Cheatham, 78 B.R. 104 (Bankr. E.D.N.C. 1987); *In re* Hoskins, 74 B.R. 51 (Bankr. C.D. Ill. 1987); *In re* Campbell, 38 B.R. 193 (Bankr. E.D.N.Y. 1984) (chapter 13); *In re* Cohen, 13 B.R. 350 (Bankr. E.D.N.Y. 1981) (chapter 13) (non-debtor spouse contribution).

63 *In re* Hoskins, 74 B.R. 51 (Bankr. C.D. Ill. 1987).

64 *See* 11 U.S.C. § 101(18)(A), (B).

65 11 U.S.C. § 101(21).

66 *See In re* KZK Livestock, Inc., 147 B.R. 452 (Bankr. C.D. Ill. 1992); *In re* Blanton Smith Corp., 7 B.R. 410 (Bankr. M.D. Tenn. 1980) for a good discussion of this legislative history. *See*

cludes" the above quoted activities, and the Code's rules of construction state that the term "include" is not limiting,[67] so that the operations listed above are exemplary, but not exhaustive.

In assessing whether a debtor has a true farming operation, courts have looked to the actual physical presence and involvement of family members, the ownership of traditional farm assets by the debtor, the permanent cessation of all or part of the farming operation, relationship to actual farm operation or efficiency of an activity, the type of product and its market, and most importantly, if the operation is subject to traditional farm risk.[68] The totality of the circumstances must reflect a farm operation. Cases decided under 11 U.S.C. §§ 101(21) and 303 concerning the definition of "farming operation" are applicable in determining what is a "farming operation" for purposes of chapter 12.[69]

While some non-traditional farms may be within the scope of chapter 12,[70] other non-traditional farming opera-

tions may be barred.[71] Service occupations, where crop growing and other traditional forms of farming are absent or relatively incidental to the business, or where the farm work is primarily performed for other farmers, generally will not be considered "farming operations" with incomes sufficient to qualify for chapter 12 relief.[72]

The question of whether a debtor is "engaged in a farming operation" also arises in the circumstance of farmers who have discontinued or significantly dismantled their own farming operations for the tax year immediately preceding the contemplated chapter 12 filing. Some courts have found that such actions may make the debtor ineligible for chapter 12, regardless of the farmer's history.[73] Others have held that the level of activity of the farmer cannot be dispositive of eligibility, so long as all statutory eligibility requirements are met.[74]

---

also In re Glenn, 181 B.R. 105 (Bankr. E.D. Okla. 1995); *In re* Sugar Pine Ranch, 100 B.R. 28 (Bankr. D. Or. 1989); *In re* Maike, 77 B.R. 832 (Bankr. D. Kan. 1987); *In re* Wolline, 74 B.R. 208 (Bankr. E.D. Wis. 1987).

67 11 U.S.C. § 102(3). What case law which has evolved under chapter 12 also suggests this. *In re* Shepherd, 75 B.R. 501 (Bankr. N.D. Ohio 1987); *In re* Stedman, 72 B.R. 49 (Bankr. D.N.D. 1987). *Compare In re* Wolline, 74 B.R. 208 (Bankr. E.D. Wis. 1987) *with In re* Maike, 77 B.R. 832 (Bankr. D. Kan. 1987).

68 *In re* Howard, 212 B.R. 864 (Bankr. E.D. Tenn. 1997) (non-debtor sons living on farm and owning some part of the farm livestock does not undermine qualification of operation as family farm); *In re* Glenn, 181 B.R. 105 (Bankr. E.D. Okla. 1995); *In re* French, 139 B.R. 476 (Bankr. D.S.D. 1992); *In re* Voelker, 123 B.R. 749 (Bankr. E.D. Mich. 1990) (active involvement in management decisions and shared labor); *In re* Easton, 79 B.R. 836 (Bankr. N.D. Iowa 1987), *aff'd*, 104 B.R. 111 (N.D. Iowa 1988) *vacated*, 883 F.2d 630 (8th Cir. 1989) *on remand* 118 B.R. 676 (Bankr. N.D. Iowa 1990); Fed. Land Bank of Columbia v. McNeal, 77 B.R. 315 (S.D. Ga. 1987), *aff'd*, 848 F.2d 170 (11th Cir. 1988); *In re* Sugar Pine Ranch, 100 B.R. 28 (Bankr. D. Or. 1989); *In re* Maike, 77 B.R. 832 (Bankr. D. Kan. 1987); *In re* Mikkelsen Farms, Inc., 74 B.R. 280 (Bankr. D. Or. 1987); *In re* Tart, 73 B.R. 78 (Bankr. E.D.N.C. 1987); *In re* Rott, 73 B.R. 366 (Bankr. D.N.D. 1987). *See also In re* Garako Farms, Inc., 89 B.R. 506 (Bankr. E.D. Cal. 1988), assessing corporate eligibility, cites additional factors: (1) is the farming operation the principal source of income for the debtor; (2) does the debtor (or corporate officer) live on the property; (3) is the debtor involved in other businesses from which income is received; (4) is the debtor trying to offset income from some other source; (5) is the debtor involved in farming as a tax shelter; (6) does the debtor own or lease the subject property.

69 *In re* Maschhoff, 89 B.R. 768 (Bankr. S.D. Ill. 1988); *In re* McKillips, 72 B.R. 565 (Bankr. N.D. Ill. 1987); *In re* Seabloom, 78 B.R. 543 (Bankr. D. Ill. 1987). One court has even stretched its analysis to embrace cases defining "farmer" under 11 U.S.C. § 522(f)(2) in assessing eligibility. *See In re* Hettinger, 95 B.R. 110 (Bankr. E.D. Mo. 1989).

70 *In re* Watford, 92 B.R. 557 (M.D. Ga. 1988) (catfish farming, by reference to other cases); *In re* Sugar Pine Ranch, 100 B.R. 28 (Bankr. D. Or. 1989) (harvesting of merchantable timber on a

sustained yield basis); *In re* Borg, 88 B.R. 288 (Bankr. D. Mont. 1988) (fox pelting part of farm operation); *In re* SWF, Inc., 83 B.R. 27 (Bankr. S.D. Cal. 1988) (shellfish cultivation operation); *In re* Hill, 83 B.R. 522 (Bankr. E.D. Tenn. 1988) (plant nursery operation); *In re* Wolline, 74 B.R. 208 (Bankr. E.D. Wis. 1987) (riding horse operation which provided financing for traditional farm operation); *In re* Maike, 77 B.R. 832 (Bankr. D. Kan. 1987) (game farm and kennel operation).

71 *In re* Watford, 92 B.R. 557 (M.D. Ga. 1988) (catching and selling stone crabs' claws/development of ponds for recreational use), *aff'd in part and vacated in part*, 898 F.2d 1525 (11th Cir. 1990); Fed. Land Bank of Columbia v. McNeal, 77 B.R. 315 (S.D. Ga. 1987), *aff'd*, 848 F.2d 170 (11th Cir. 1988); *In re* McKillips, 72 B.R. 565 (Bankr. N.D. Ill. 1987).

72 Fed. Land Bank of Columbia v. McNeal, 77 B.R. 315 (S.D. Ga. 1987), *aff'd*, 848 F.2d 170 (11th Cir. 1988); *In re* Cluck, 101 B.R. 691 (Bankr. E.D. Okla. 1989) (horse breeding, training and boarding operation ineligible); *In re* Blackwelder Harvesting Co., 106 B.R. 301 (Bankr. M.D. Fla. 1989) (citrus harvesting services company ineligible); *In re* McKillips, 72 B.R. 565 (Bankr. N.D. Ill. 1987); *In re* Faber, 78 B.R. 934 (Bankr. S.D. Iowa 1987); *In re* Maike, 77 B.R. 832 (Bankr. D. Kan. 1987); *In re* Haschke, 77 B.R. 223 (Bankr. D. Neb. 1987).

73 *In re* Lloyd, 37 F.3d 271 (7th Cir. 1994) (no substantial farming activities); *In re* Lawless, 79 B.R. 850 (W.D. Mo. 1987); *In re* Tart, 73 B.R. 78 (Bankr. E.D.N.C. 1987). The court in *In re* Burke, 81 B.R. 971 (Bankr. S.D. Iowa 1987) opined that the focus of chapter 12 is to continue, not revive farming operations.

74 Cottonport Bank v. Dichara, 193 B.R. 798 (W.D. La. 1996); *In re* Hettinger, 95 B.R. 110 (Bankr. E.D. Mo. 1989); *In re* Fogle, 87 B.R. 493 (Bankr. N.D. Ohio 1988); *In re* Land, 82 B.R. 572 (Bankr. D. Colo. 1988); *In re* Easton, 79 B.R. 836 (Bankr. N.D. Iowa 1987), *aff'd*, 104 B.R. 111 (N.D. Iowa 1988), *vacated*, 883 F.2d 630 (8th Cir. 1989), *on remand,* 118 B.R. 676 (Bankr. N.D. Iowa 1990); *In re* Maike, 77 B.R. 832 (Bankr. D. Kan. 1987); *In re* Indreland, 77 B.R. 268 (Bankr. D. Mont. 1987); *In re* Mikkelsen Farms, Inc., 74 B.R. 280 (Bankr. D. Or. 1987) (leased farm caused by economic conditions can be farming operation). *Cf. In re* Paul, 83 B.R. 709 (Bankr. D.N.D. 1988).

16.2.2.2.3 *Fifty percent of gross income required from the farming operation*

An individual or husband and wife "family farmer" must have received at least fifty percent of his or her gross income (if jointly filed, fifty percent of the gross income of both spouses), in the taxable year immediately preceding the tax year in which the bankruptcy petition is filed from the farming operation.[75] Otherwise, a creditor can move to dismiss the bankruptcy, or persuade the debtor to convert to a different chapter. This fifty percent requirement does not apply to farm partnerships or corporations.

The fifty percent income requirement for family farmers created by the 1986 Amendments compares with an eighty percent income requirement for an individual to qualify as a "farmer" under section 101(20) of the Code.[76] Case law determining whether the eighty percent farm income requirement is met suggests that the percentage requirement may be strictly interpreted for determining eligibility for chapter 12, but may be more flexibly construed in other contexts.[77]

Not all income received by a farmer qualifies as arising from the farming operation. The question of what constitutes income from the "farming operation" has been extensively litigated since the advent of chapter 12. Many courts have accepted the tax characterization of gross income included on a farmer's tax return as dispositive, finding "gross income" to have the same meaning in bankruptcy as in tax laws.[78] Other courts have decided that a straight tax characterization is inappropriate.[79] Some courts have approached it from a middle ground, concluding that the tax approach is acceptable when compatible with chapter 12, but should be abandoned where irreconcilable.[80] All cases find gross farm income is income before deductions for expenses.[81] One court has determined that grain held as inventory, representing potential income, but as yet unliquidated, cannot be counted as income for purposes of eligibility.[82]

Proceeds from the sales of equipment and personal property, if part of the scaling down process, or directly related to the farm operation, are generally considered income from the farm operation.[83]

The courts have been divided on whether rents derived from leases of farm property constitute income from the farming operation for eligibility purposes. The courts have generally found that where the farmer has no involvement with the land rented and where the rent is paid up front and not subject to the regular risks of farming, such rental income is not income from the farm operation.[84] However,

---

75 11 U.S.C. § 101(18). The determination is made from the tax year immediately preceding filing, regardless of whether the current tax year would indicate eligibility or ineligibility. *In re* Nelson, 291 B.R. 861 (Bankr. N.D. Idaho 2003) (debtors who were no longer operating dairy farm at time of confirmation still eligible for chapter 12 relief); *In re* Clark, 288 B.R. 237 (Bankr. D. Kan. 2003) (debtors need only meet income test for taxable year preceding filing and will remain family farmers even if plan is to cease farming operations post-confirmation and enroll in government conservation reserve program); *In re* Fogle, 87 B.R. 493 (Bankr. N.D. Ohio 1988); *In re* Paul, 83 B.R. 709 (Bankr. D.N.D. 1988); *In re* Bergmann, 78 B.R. 911 (Bankr. S.D. Ill. 1987); *In re* Indreland, 77 B.R. 268 (Bankr. D. Mont. 1987). The income must have been actually received, not simply earned, during that tax year examined for eligibility. *In re* Bergmann, 78 B.R. 911 (Bankr. S.D. Ill. 1987).

76 11 U.S.C. § 101(20).

77 *See, e.g.*, Production Credit Ass'n of St. Cloud v. LaFond, 791 F.2d 623 (8th Cir. 1986); Augustine v. United States, 5 Collier Bankr. Cas. 2d (MB) 536 (Bankr. W.D. Pa. 1980), *aff'd*, 675 F.2d 582 (3d Cir. 1982); *In re* Martin, 78 B.R. 593 (Bankr. D. Mont. 1987).

78 *In re* Wagner, 808 F.2d 542 (7th Cir. 1986); *In re* Francks, 1999 WL 565893 (B.A.P. 10th Cir. Aug. 2, 1999); *In re* Lamb, 209 B.R. 759 (Bankr. M.D. Ga. 1997) (partnership income); United States v. Lawless, 79 B.R. 850 (W.D. Mo. 1987); *In re* Gossett, 86 B.R. 941 (Bankr. S.D. Ohio 1988); *In re* Martin, 78 B.R. 593 (Bankr. D. Mont. 1987); *In re* Pratt, 78 B.R. 277 (Bankr. D. Mont. 1987); *In re* Bergmann, 78 B.R. 911 (Bankr. S.D. Ill. 1987); *In re* Shepherd, 75 B.R. 501 (Bankr. N.D. Ohio 1987); *In*

re Nelson, 73 B.R. 363 (Bankr. D. Kan. 1987). *See* analysis in *In re* Brown, 95 B.R. 800 (Bankr. N.D. Okla. 1989) as to applicable tax provisions and nonagricultural businesses. The tax regulations addressed therein indicate that gross farm income does not contemplate reduction for expenses, but that nonagricultural businesses must deduct cost of goods sold from gross sales to reach the gross income figure. 26 U.S.C. § 61(a)(2); Treas. Reg. §§ 1.61-3, 1.61-4.

79 *In re* Barnett, 162 B.R. 535 (Bankr. W.D. Mo. 1993); *In re* Sugar Pine Ranch, 100 B.R. 28 (Bankr. D. Or. 1989); *In re* Burke, 81 B.R. 971 (Bankr. S.D. Iowa 1987); *In re* Wolline, 74 B.R. 208 (Bankr. E.D. Wis. 1987); *In re* Guinnane, 73 B.R. 129 (Bankr. D. Mont. 1987).

80 *In re* Smith, 109 B.R. 241 (Bankr. W.D. Ky. 1989); *In re* Snider, 99 B.R. 374 (Bankr. S.D. Ohio 1989); *In re* Faber, 78 B.R. 934 (Bankr. S.D. Iowa 1987). *In re* Creviston, 157 B.R. 380 (Bankr. S.D. Ohio 1993) uses the following considerations in evaluating whether income is "farm income" for purposes of eligibility: (1) extent to which debtor is involved in operations which produced farm income; (2) historical source of debtor's income; (3) whether challenged income as non-farm is departure from norm (for example, sales, off-farm income to shore up existing operation, and so forth); (4) degree of farming risk; (5) degree to which income producing farm assets are owned by third parties; (6) characterization of challenged income on tax return.

81 Gross income from non-farm business generally means gross profits and not gross receipts. *See In re* Gossett, 86 B.R. 941 (Bankr. S.D. Ohio 1988).

82 *In re* Snider, 99 B.R. 374 (Bankr. S.D. Ohio 1989).

83 *In re* Armstrong, 812 F.2d 1024 (7th Cir. 1987); Cottonport Bank v. Dichara, 193 B.R. 798 (W.D. La. 1996); *In re* Barnett, 162 B.R. 535 (Bankr. W.D. Mo. 1993); *In re* Burke, 81 B.R. 971 (Bankr. S.D. Iowa 1987); *In re* Haschke, 77 B.R. 223 (Bankr. D. Neb. 1987); *In re* Shepherd, 75 B.R. 501 (Bankr. N.D. Ohio 1987); *In re* Welch, 74 B.R. 401 (Bankr. S.D. Ohio 1987).

84 *In re* Armstrong, 812 F.2d 1024 (7th Cir. 1987); *In re* Swanson, 289 B.R. 372 (Bankr. C.D. Ill. 2003); *In re* Krueger, 104 B.R. 223 (Bankr. D. Neb. 1988); *In re* Maschhoff, 89 B.R. 768 (Bankr. S.D. Ill. 1988) (rents from farm houses not considered income from farm operation); *In re* Haschke, 77 B.R. 223 (Bankr. D. Neb. 1987); *In re* Seabloom, 78 B.R. 543 (Bankr.

land rented in the normal course of a farmer's customary on-going operation, where rent payment is subject to traditional farm risks, the lease short-term, rental is to other local family farmers, and the leasing is part of scaling down (not cessation) of the farm, can be considered income from the farming operation for eligibility purposes.[85] Income from rented land where the debtor has played a significant role in or had ownership interest in its crop production generating rent will generally be classified as farm income.[86]

Farmers have traditionally performed some farming-related work for other farmers and family members, referred to as "custom work." The majority of courts have found that payment for this type of work, when a part of the entirety and customary operation of a farmer's operation, to be income from the farming operation.[87] However, marketing and storing, or exclusive provision of trucking or services where not part of the farmer's actual crop production, generally is not.[88] Wages earned by farmers in chapter 12 from corporate family farm operations are farm income for chapter 12 eligibility purposes.[89]

Various other sources of income have been considered by the courts under chapter 12 to determine whether they constitute income from the "farming operation" for eligibility purposes. Reimbursement for preparation of ground, and seed and fertilizer expenses have been found to be farm income, as have crop share income,[90] deficiency payments, and payments from FSA programs.[91] By contrast, loan income, debt forgiveness, business losses, Social Security payments, barter value of goods received from other farms, and IRA withdrawals are not part of farm income.[92] One court has gone so far as to find that both cash rent from farm leasing, although not imbued with traditional farming risk, and hourly wages should still be considered farm income for eligibility purposes based upon the debtor's showing of: (1) active farming history and intent to salvage farm operation for future use; (2) clear and convincing evidence that the renting and liquidation are based on sound business judgment aimed at saving farming business; (3) payment of farm debt with wages.[93]

Unfortunately, the restructuring of some farm operations with heavy income supplementation from non-farm sources prior to the adoption of chapter 12 to insure survival, now will leave some genuine family farmers ineligible for chapter 12. Consequently, farmers may have difficulty meeting the fifty percent requirement where a farm was dormant or rented out during the previous year, or where a failing farm was shored up by off-farm income to a substantial degree. Those farming operations, although active at some time in the past, appear to be eligible for reorganization only under chapter 11 (or in some circumstances chapter 13).

C.D. Ill. 1987); *In re* Tim Wargo & Sons, Inc., 74 B.R. 469 (Bankr. E.D. Ark. 1987), *aff'd*, 869 F.2d 1128 (8th Cir. 1989); *In re Mary Freese Farms, Inc.*, 73 B.R. 508 (Bankr. N.D. Iowa 1987).

85 *In re* Maynard, 295 B.R. 437 (Bankr. S.D.N.Y. 2003); *In re* Howard, 212 B.R. 864 (Bankr. E.D. Tenn. 1997); *In re* Voelker, 123 B.R. 749 (Bankr. E.D. Mich. 1990); *In re* Krueger, 104 B.R. 223 (Bankr. D. Neb. 1988); *In re* Jessen, 82 B.R. 490 (Bankr. S.D. Iowa 1988); *In re* Burke, 81 B.R. 971 (Bankr. S.D. Iowa 1987); *In re* Easton, 79 B.R. 836 (Bankr. N.D. Iowa 1987), *aff'd*, 104 B.R. 111 (N.D. Iowa 1988) *vacated*, 883 F.2d 630 (8th Cir. 1989) *on remand* 118 B.R. 676 (Bankr. N.D. Iowa 1990); *In re* Mikkelsen Farms, Inc., 74 B.R. 280 (Bankr. D. Or. 1987); *In re* Welch, 74 B.R. 401 (Bankr. S.D. Ohio 1987); *In re* Rott, 73 B.R. 366 (Bankr. D.N.D. 1987).

86 *In re* Edwards, 924 F.2d 798 (8th Cir. 1991); *In re* Easton, 118 B.R. 676 (Bankr. N.D. Iowa 1990), *after remand from* 883 F.2d 630 (8th Cir. 1989) (for example, "walked" land during growth, helped to determine how farmed, base also rented, helped to seed, sow and fertilize).

87 *In re* Barnett, 162 B.R. 535 (Bankr. W.D. Mo. 1993); *In re* Maschhoff, 89 B.R. 768 (Bankr. S.D. Ill. 1988) (rents from farm houses not considered income from farm operation); *In re* Welch, 74 B.R. 401 (Bankr. S.D. Ohio 1987); *In re* Guinnane, 73 B.R. 129 (Bankr. D. Mont. 1987); *In re* Martin, 78 B.R. 593 (Bankr. D. Mont. 1987). *Contra In re* Watford, 92 B.R. 557 (M.D. Ga. 1988); *In re* Sugar Pine Ranch, 100 B.R. 28 (Bankr. D. Or. 1989), in *dicta* citing *In re* Hampton, 100 B.R. 535 (Bankr. D. Or. 1987).

88 *In re* Van Air Flying Serv., Inc., 146 B.R. 816 (Bankr. E.D. Ark. 1992); *In re* Watford, 92 B.R. 557 (M.D. Ga. 1988); *In re* Haschke, 77 B.R. 223 (Bankr. D. Neb. 1987).

89 *In re* Lamb, 209 B.R. 759 (Bankr. M.D. Ga. 1997) (partnership income); *In re* Pierce 175 B.R. 153 (Bankr. D. Conn. 1994) (partnership income); *In re* Schaforth, 18 Collier Bankr. Cas. 2d (MB) 149 (Bankr. S.D. Iowa 1987) (Subchapter S corp.); *In re* Schafroth, 81 B.R. 509 (Bankr. S.D. Iowa 1988); *In re* Burke, 81 B.R. 970 (Bankr. S.D. Iowa 1987). *Contra In re* Way, 120 B.R. 81 (Bankr. S.D. Tex. 1990) (director's fees for managing two other farms is not farm income because no risk and farming for others); *In re* Hampton, 100 B.R. 535 (Bankr. D. Or. 1987).

90 *In re* Burke, 81 B.R. 970 (Bankr. S.D. Iowa 1987); *In re* Welch, 74 B.R. 401 (Bankr. S.D. Ohio 1987). *Contra* Tim Wargo & Sons, Inc. v. Equitable Life Assurance Soc'y of the U.S., 74 B.R. 469 (Bankr. E.D. Ark. 1987), *aff'd*, 86 B.R. 150 (E.D. Ark. 1988), *aff'd*, 869 F.2d 1128 (8th Cir. 1989).

91 *In re* Way, 120 B.R. 81 (Bankr. S.D. Tex. 1990); *In re* Fenske, 96 B.R. 244 (Bankr. D.N.D. 1988); *In re* Paul, 83 B.R. 709 (Bankr. D.N.D. 1988); *In re* Jessen, 82 B.R. 490 (Bankr. S.D. Iowa 1988); *In re* Shepherd, 75 B.R. 501 (Bankr. N.D. Ohio 1987); *In re* Welch, 74 B.R. 401 (Bankr. S.D. Ohio 1987).

92 *In re* Wagner, 808 F.2d 542 (7th Cir. 1986); *In re* Francks, 1999 WL 565893 (B.A.P. 10th Cir. Aug. 2, 1999) (loan income); *In re* Koenegstein, 130 B.R. 281 (Bankr. S.D. Ill. 1991); *In re* Smith, 109 B.R. 241 (Bankr. W.D. Ky. 1989) (insurance proceeds/capital gain from destruction of property is not farm income where debtors would not otherwise be eligible for chapter 12); *In re* Dutton, 86 B.R. 651 (Bankr. D. Colo. 1988); *In re* Rott, 73 B.R. 366 (Bankr. D.N.D. 1987).

93 *In re* Hettinger, 95 B.R. 110 (Bankr. E.D. Mo. 1989).

16.2.2.3 Debt Limitations

16.2.2.3.1 In general

A family farmer's aggregate debts cannot exceed $1,500,000.00.[94] The same debt ceiling applies to family farm corporations and partnerships.[95] In a joint case the aggregate debt ceiling applies to both an individual and his or her spouse *together*. Separate petitions cannot be filed by spouses under chapter 12 to escape this debt ceiling limitation, except where liabilities are not joint.[96] Eligibility is generally determined from the debtor's good faith indication of debts in the schedules, not claims filed, although the presumption of the reasonable accuracy of a debtor's schedules is rebuttable.[97]

Unlike chapter 13, the chapter 12 debt limit applies to all debts, including guarantees and contingent debts, and not just non-contingent liquidated debts.[98] Consequently, disputed, contingent and unliquidated indebtedness may either eliminate eligibility or may require, if permitted by the court, swift litigation at a preliminary stage of the bankruptcy proceeding to weed out such claims that may bar eligibility.[99] Courts have intimated that pre-petition com-

promise of debts to achieve chapter 12 eligibility may be acceptable, if done in a legally enforceable and provable manner,[100] but that post-petition compromise[101] or attempt to credit collateral to be surrendered post-petition to achieve eligibility is ineffective.[102]

16.2.2.3.2 Debt arising from the farm operation

Individual or joint family farmers eligible to utilize chapter 12 must have at least eighty percent of their aggregate non-contingent liquidated debt arise from the farming operation owned or operated by the farmer.[103] Mortgage debt, tax indebtedness, and indebtedness arising from the settlement of litigation, where necessary to keep the farm operation, are generally deemed to arise from the farm operation.[104] Indebtedness may be considered as arising from the farming operation under the proper circumstances even if collateralized with non-farm property if: (1) the reason for which the debt was incurred is directly related to the farm operation; and (2) the use of the funds obtained was directly related to the farm operation.[105] Corporate or partnership family farmers must not only meet this requirement, but must also have more than eighty percent of the value of their assets be related to the farming operation.[106] Note that individuals, corporations or partnerships not able to meet these criterion for a "family farmer" may still be able to meet the Code's criteria for a "farmer" which is based solely on whether eighty percent of the debtor's gross

---

94 11 U.S.C. § 101(18)(A).

95 11 U.S.C. § 101(18)(B).

96 If, under state law, liability cannot be apportioned between parties, it cannot be done under chapter 12 as an artifice to meet eligibility requirements. *See, e.g., In re* Walton, 95 B.R. 514 (Bankr. S.D. Ohio 1989); *In re* Marchetto, 24 B.R. 967 (B.A.P. 1st Cir. 1982); *In re* Johnson, 73 B.R. 107 (Bankr. S.D. Ohio 1987); *In re* Welch, 74 B.R. 401 (Bankr. S.D. Ohio 1987); *In re* Anderson, 51 B.R. 532 (Bankr. D.S.D. 1985); *In re* Cronkleton, 18 B.R. 792 (Bankr. S.D. Ohio 1982).

97 *In re* Pearson, 773 F.2d 751 (6th Cir. 1985) (chapter 13); *In re* Williams Land Co., 91 B.R. 923 (Bankr. D. Or. 1988) (under Fed. R. Bankr. P. 3001(f), proofs of claim may also be considered for debt amounts when evaluating eligibility); *In re* Carpenter, 79 B.R. 316 (Bankr. S.D. Ohio 1987); *In re* Labig, 74 B.R. 507 (Bankr. S.D. Ohio 1987) (twenty-seven percent debt understatement excessive).

98 *Compare* 11 U.S.C. § 101(18)(A), (B) *with* 11 U.S.C. §§ 109(e), 303(a). *See In re* Reiners, 846 F.2d 1012 (5th Cir. 1988); *In re* Vaughn, 100 B.R. 423 (Bankr. S.D. Ill. 1989); *In re* Quintana, 107 B.R. 234 (B.A.P. 9th Cir. 1989) (counterclaims cannot be used to reduce indebtedness amount for eligibility purposes). But see the approach taken by the court in *In re* Williams Land Co., 91 B.R. 923 (Bankr. D. Or. 1988), which follows chapter 13 elimination for consideration of disputed, precautionarily scheduled, and intracorporate claims. *In re* Lands, 85 B.R. 83 (Bankr. E.D. Ark. 1988) finds non-recourse loans are not counted for eligibility purposes. *Contra In re* Lindsey, Stephenson & Lindsey, 995 F.2d 626 (5th Cir. 1993) (non-recourse obligation is debt for chapter 12 eligibility determination).

99 *See* § 12.2.2, *supra*; Quintana v. Comm'r of Internal Revenue Serv., 915 F.2d 513 (9th Cir. 1990); *In re* Quintana, 107 B.R. 234 (B.A.P. 9th Cir. 1989) (counterclaims cannot be used to reduce indebtedness amount for eligibility purposes); Whaley v. United States, 76 B.R. 95 (N.D. Miss. 1987); *In re* Cross Timbers Ranch, Inc., 151 B.R. 923 (Bankr. W.D. Mo. 1993); *In re* Vaughn, 100 B.R. 423 (Bankr. S.D. Ill. 1989); *In re* Carpen-

ter, 79 B.R. 316 (Bankr. S.D. Ohio 1987); *In re* Budde, 79 B.R. 35 (Bankr. D. Colo. 1987). At least one chapter 13 case suggests that offsets, counterclaims or disputes are not sufficient to change the character of a debt amount for eligibility purposes. *See In re* Sylvester, 19 B.R. 671 (B.A.P. 9th Cir. 1982).

100 *In re* Budde, 79 B.R. 35 (Bankr. D. Colo. 1987); *In re* Labig, 74 B.R. 507 (Bankr. S.D. Ohio 1987).

101 *In re* Cross Timbers Ranch, Inc., 151 B.R. 923 (Bankr. W.D. Mo. 1993); *In re* Carpenter, 79 B.R. 316 (Bankr. S.D. Ohio 1987); *In re* Labig, 74 B.R. 507 (Bankr. S.D. Ohio 1987).

102 Quintana v. Comm'r of Internal Revenue Serv., 915 F.2d 513 (9th Cir. 1990); *In re* Cross Timbers Ranch, Inc., 151 B.R. 923 (Bankr. W.D. Mo. 1993); *In re* Stedman, 72 B.R. 49 (Bankr. D.N.D. 1987). As one court indicated, the labeling of debt as "disputed" cannot be used to shoehorn a farm operation into eligibility for chapter 12. *In re* Labig, 74 B.R. 507 (Bankr. S.D. Ohio 1987).

103 11 U.S.C. § 101(18)(A).

104 *In re* Marlett, 116 B.R. 703 (Bankr. D. Neb. 1990); *In re* Roberts, 78 B.R. 536 (Bankr. C.D. Ill. 1987); *In re* Rinker, 75 B.R. 65 (Bankr. S.D. Iowa 1987).

105 *In re* Kan Corp., 101 B.R. 726 (Bankr. W.D. Okla. 1988) (whether a debt incurred from a loan "arises out of a farming operation" as required by 11 U.S.C. § 101(18)(B)(ii) is determined by the use made of the loan proceeds, not nature of the collateral or motive of the debtor); *In re* Reak, 92 B.R. 804 (Bankr. E.D. Wis. 1988); *In re* Douglass, 77 B.R. 714 (Bankr. W.D. Mo. 1987).

106 11 U.S.C. § 101(18)(B)(i).

income relates to farming operations.[107] Even if chapter 12 is unavailable, the Code offers such farmers certain special protections.[108] Additionally, if the chapter 12 case was filed in the good faith belief of eligibility, the court may allow conversion to chapter 11.[109]

16.2.2.3.3 Residence exclusion

A family farmer debtor may elect to exclude a debt for his or her principal residence, or that of a member of a family farmer partnership or corporate debtor from the computation of aggregate debt ceiling *unless* the debt arises out of the farming operation.[110] Thus, any indebtedness to a creditor arising solely as a purchase money mortgage on a house and land lot may be excluded. However, as is typically the case, indebtedness on the residence which has been pledged as collateral for credit used for the farming operation must be counted in the aggregate debt computation.

Courts have held the residence exclusion provision applies only to the percentage of indebtedness, and not to exclude the amount of debt to reach the $1,500,000.00 eligibility limit.[111] Chapter 12 does not specify any other form of debt unconnected to the farming operation which can be excluded from the chapter's debt ceiling.

16.2.2.4 Joint Chapter 12 Filings

Joint filings under chapter 12 by both spouses are permitted.[112] A debtor may also file an individual case without including a farmer spouse; or farmer spouses may file individual cases and move for joint administration of the cases, provided each individually meets the eligibility requirements.[113] Most farm loans which are secured by the farmland itself will have both husband and wife as signatories, so that a joint filing is desirable.[114]

Where only one spouse files for chapter 12 relief, the court may assess the income eligibility and apportion income earned based upon state law, or in its absence, upon such basis as is equitable and fair. Where wages or salaries are clearly attributable to one person, for eligibility purposes those wages or salary must be so credited solely to the earning spouse regardless of joint tax filing. However, where both spouses are active family farmers, this may mean a 50-50 split of income earned in the requisite tax year for eligibility purposes.[115]

Joint filings are not permitted for other individuals, although they may be working together in the family farming operation. Unless the operations fall within chapter 12's partnership eligibility criteria, individual chapter 12 cases will be required for each farmer.[116]

16.2.2.5 Additional Eligibility Requirements for Partnerships and Corporate Farmers

Family farm partnerships and corporations are eligible for relief under chapter 12,[117] but these entities must meet several additional eligibility requirements. Partnerships and corporations are eligible to use chapter 12 if the farmer or family conducts the farming operation[118] and more than eighty percent of the value of the assets of the business entity are related to the farming operation. All general partners must give written consent to a chapter 12 filing.[119]

For corporations, chapter 12 eligibility also requires that: (1) more than fifty percent of the corporation's outstanding stock is held by one family and its relatives; and (2) the corporate stock is not publicly traded.[120] The stock in corporate family farmers must be held by natural persons, not other corporate entities.[121]

However, corporations and partnerships need not comply with the fifty percent gross income requirement that applies

---

107 11 U.S.C. § 101(20).

108 *E.g.*, 11 U.S.C. § 303(a), prohibiting involuntary bankruptcies against farmers. *See* § 16.1.2, *supra*.

109 *See* § 16.4.7.3, *infra*. Chapter 12 cases where the debtors are shown to be ineligible are not generally considered void *ab initio*. *In re* Bird, 80 B.R. 861 (Bankr. W.D. Wis. 1987).

110 11 U.S.C. § 101(18)(A), (B).

111 *In re* Reiners, 846 F.2d 1012 (5th Cir. 1988); *In re* Lands, 85 B.R. 83 (Bankr. E.D. Ark. 1988); *In re* Baldwin Farms, 78 B.R. 143 (Bankr. N.D. Ohio 1987); *In re* Henderson Ranches, 75 B.R. 225 (Bankr. D. Idaho 1987).

112 11 U.S.C. § 101(18)(A).

113 *In re* Welch, 74 B.R. 401 (Bankr. S.D. Ohio 1987).

114 Because the codebtor stay applies in chapter 12 only to consumer debts, a creditor may pursue a cosigning spouse who does not participate in a joint filing. However, where the liabilities of the spouses are not joint and where the eligibility ceilings are a problem, separate filings or a single filing may be desirable. *See* §§ 12.2.3.1, 16.2.2.3, *supra*.

115 *In re* Dutton, 86 B.R. 651 (Bankr. D. Colo. 1988).

116 However, separate cases of family members involved in a single farming operation may be consolidated for joint administration by the court. *See In re* Bullington, 80 B.R. 590 (Bankr. M.D. Ga. 1987) (debtors had farmed together as a farm partnership for several years, had commonly owed debts and commonly owned assets, so separately filed cases meshed for coordination of payments), *aff'd sub nom.* Travelers Ins. Co. v. Bullington, 89 B.R. 1010 (M.D. Ga. 1988); *In re* Plafcan, 93 B.R. 177 (Bankr. E.D. Ark. 1988).

117 11 U.S.C. § 101(18)(B). Corporations can be considered farmers under the Code. *Compare In re* Blanton Smith Corp., 7 B.R. 410 (Bankr. M.D. Tenn. 1980) *with In re* Dakota Lay'd Eggs, 57 B.R. 648 (Bankr. D.N.D. 1986).

118 *In re* Tim Wargo & Sons, Inc., 869 F.2d 1128 (8th Cir. 1989) (where debtor is corporate, family member must play active role in farming the land).

119 Fed. R. Bankr. P. 1004(a); *In re* Schaurer Agric. Enterprises, 82 B.R. 911 (Bankr. S.D. Ohio 1988).

120 11 U.S.C. § 101(18)(B).

121 *In re* Tobin Ranch, Inc., 80 B.R. 166 (Bankr. D. Neb. 1987). For an interesting discussion on valuing stock in closely held family farm corporations for liquidation analysis purposes, see *In re* Harper, 157 B.R. 858 (Bankr. E.D. Ark. 1993).

to individual or joint chapter 12 debtors.[122] Partnerships should be cognizable under applicable state law and cannot be formed for the purpose of circumventing the dollar amount requirements for individual chapter 12 eligibility.[123]

Many farming operations have existed as loose or informal joint enterprises, but may not exist as legal partnerships under the relevant law. The clearest indicia of a partnership eligible for chapter 12 relief are written partnership agreements and partnership tax returns.[124] Any partnership seeking chapter 12 relief must clearly distinguish between assets and obligations of the partnership itself and those of the individual partners.[125]

Family farmer partnership and corporations may also have their cases consolidated for joint administration either procedurally or substantively with other chapter 12 debtors. However, all such debtor entities must individually be eligible for relief under chapter 12.[126]

16.2.2.6 Effect of Prior Filings on Eligibility

Where there has been a discharge granted to a debtor in a previous reorganization-type bankruptcy case, there should be no bar to filing a case under chapter 12 save considerations of good faith under section 1225(a)(3). There is no provision in the Bankruptcy Code which contains any specific refiling prohibition in this circumstance.[127] Thus certain cases may warrant a "chapter 19" approach in which a farm homestead debt is restructured after a chapter 7 discharge.

Where a debtor has filed a previous chapter 7 case and received a discharge, then files a chapter 12 case, the bankruptcy court may consider such a refiling evidence of bad faith, although not bad faith per se. The filing of a chapter 7 proceeding prior to a chapter 12 case with the *sole* purpose of reducing indebtedness to the level requisite for chapter 12 eligibility, where the debtor was clearly ineligible before the chapter 7 filing, may result in dismissal by the

court of the subsequent chapter 12 case upon either eligibility or good faith grounds.[128]

Where a debtor has had previous bankruptcy case filings, but none have reached discharge, then the bankruptcy court may consider *sua sponte* or upon motion of the trustee or a party in interest whether such refiling: (1) may be barred by the provisions of section 109(g); or (2) may be an abusive refiling lacking good faith. In the former event, the court may dismiss the improvidently filed chapter 12 case, and the bar to refiling imposed by section 109(g) will be reimposed and will continue to run as if no case had been filed.[129]

In the latter event, the court will consider why previous cases have been aborted, why the debtor failed to comply with statutory requisites, and if there exists any material change in the debtor's circumstances warranting reconsideration of a request for reorganization.[130] In the event a refiling is determined to be abusive, the court will dismiss the case as well as other penalties under appropriate circumstances.[131] It also appears that the fact that a previous case is not closed, although discharge has issued, does not preclude a subsequent repayment/reorganization case filed in good faith.[132]

16.2.3 Initial Schedules, Forms, and Fees

16.2.3.1 Schedules

The schedules for chapter 12 filings must conform to the Official Forms which are reproduced in Appendix D to this manual. Skeletal or abbreviated filings can be used in emergency situations.[133]

Insofar as it is possible and consistent with existing facts, the preparation of the schedules should be done with an eye

---

122 11 U.S.C. § 101(18)(A); *In re* Cross Timbers Ranch, Inc., 151 B.R. 923 (Bankr. W.D. Mo. 1993); *In re* LLL Farms, 111 B.R. 1016 (Bankr. M.D. Ga. 1990).

123 *See* 11 U.S.C. §§ 101(18), 109(f). To be eligible for partnership filing, the farmer should be a cognizable partnership under applicable state law. *In re* Seabloom, 78 B.R. 543 (Bankr. C.D. Ill. 1987). *But see In re* Land, 82 B.R. 572 (Bankr. D. Colo. 1988).

124 *In re* LLL Farms, 111 B.R. 1016 (Bankr. M.D. Ga. 1990) (good discussion of the informal partnership as eligible for chapter 12 relief); *In re* Schauerer Agric. Enterprises, 82 B.R. 911 (Bankr. S.D. Ohio 1988); *In re* Seabloom, 78 B.R. 543 (Bankr. C.D. Ill. 1987).

125 *In re* Eber-Acres Farm, 82 B.R. 889 (Bankr. S.D. Ohio 1987).

126 *In re* Plafcan, 93 B.R. 177 (Bankr. E.D. Ark. 1988); *In re* Williams Land Co., 91 B.R. 923 (Bankr. D. Or. 1988).

127 *In re* Roth, 1994 WL 234532 (Bankr. D.S.D. 1994); *In re* Culbreth, 87 B.R. 225 (Bankr. M.D. Ga. 1988).

128 *In re* Wickliffe, 106 B.R. 470 (Bankr. W.D. Ky. 1989); *In re* Edwards, 87 B.R. 671 (Bankr. W.D. Okla. 1988). These are colloquially referred to as "Chapter 19" filings.

129 *In re* Wilson, 85 B.R. 72 (Bankr. N.D. Ill. 1988) (chapter 13).

130 *In re* Kennedy, 181 B.R. 418 (Bankr. D. Neb. 1995); *In re* Fuhrman, 118 B.R. 72 (Bankr. E.D. Mich. 1990); *In re* Hyman, 82 B.R. 23 (Bankr. D.S.C. 1987).

131 *See* § 16.4.7.2, *infra*.

132 *In re* Saylors, 869 F.2d 1434 (11th Cir. 1989) (chapter 7 to chapter 13); *In re* Schuldies, 122 B.R. 100 (D.S.D. 1990); *In re* Grimes, 117 B.R. 531 (B.A.P. 9th Cir. 1990) (chapter 11 to chapter 12 where chapter 11 was confirmed and debtors discharged, but plan was not substantially consummated); *In re* Miller, 122 B.R. 360 (Bankr. N.D. Iowa 1990); *See* Johnson v. Home State Bank, 501 U.S. 78, 111 S. Ct. 2150, 115 L. Ed. 2d 66 (1991) (chapter 7 followed by chapter 13 case). *Contra In re* Bodine, 113 B.R. 134 (Bankr. W.D.N.Y. 1990); *see in re* Harry and Larry Maronde P'ship, 256 B.R. 913 (Bankr. D. Neb. 2000) (refiling despite another pending case is impermissible if used to circumvent limits on modifying existing confirmed plan);

133 Fed. R. Bankr. P. 1007(c). *See* § 7.2.2, *supra*.

toward their harmony with other documentation produced by the debtor for creditors, for example, financial statements and loan applications.

16.2.3.2 Appointment of Counsel

Because the debtor in chapter 12 operates as a debtor-in-possession and because of the amount of the fees which may be involved, the Code requires the same application process for chapter 12 cases as for chapter 11, with application for appointment of counsel and an order approving the application.[134] Such appointment should be routinely granted unless some conflict of interest or perceived inability competently to represent a debtor due to time constraints or past unacceptable performances is apparent.

Application for appointment as counsel for a family farmer should be done with the initial schedules; otherwise a court may decline compensation for work performed prior to approval of the application or question the ability of counsel to appear on behalf of the debtor.[135] Care should also be taken to obtain court approval for the employment and compensation of all professionals and non-bankruptcy counsel working for debtors.[136]

16.2.3.3 Costs and Attorney Fees

The non-waivable filing fee for a chapter 12 case, whether individual, joint, corporate, or partnership, is two hundred dollars.[137] There is also a $30.00 administrative fee due in every case. Counsel for the chapter 12 debtor should check the local rules and orders of the applicable court for imposition of other charges attendant to a chapter 12 filing. (Fees for the chapter 12 trustee arising from payments under a confirmed chapter 12 plan are discussed at § 16.4.2.2, *infra*.)

Attorney fees for a chapter 12 case are another factor in determining the costs of a filing. Attorney fees arrangements in chapter 12 cases, both as to fees paid pre-petition and post-petition expectations, must be fully and accurately disclosed to the court, as in all other types of bankruptcy cases.[138] These fees are gauged by federal fee standards,[139] and must be consonant with fees charged in the appropriate

legal community and with the number of hours actually expended by the attorney.[140] All fees are subject to review and all post-petition fees are subject to the application process and review by the bankruptcy court.[141] Any fees received post-petition must be reported to the bankruptcy court within fifteen (15) days; however, no fees should be received post-petition without court approval.[142]

16.2.3.4 Other Reports and Documentation

Because bankruptcy schedules and section 341 creditor meetings do not always tell the entire story of a farmer's operations, and currently do not provide enough information for plan projection, other initial documentation will be required from the farmer debtor. The United States trustee or chapter 12 trustee usually requires submission of supplemental information prior to the meeting of creditors.[143] This initial report outlines the history of the farming season, expectations and expenditures, and aids the chapter 12 attorney and farmer, as well as the trustee and creditors, to gauge feasibility at an early stage of the case. If at all possible, the forms should be utilized along with the schedules in the initial analysis of the farming operation *before* a farmer enters chapter 12 and should be filled out at the same time as the initial schedules.

As in chapter 11 cases, the United States trustee or chapter 12 trustee requires monthly or other periodic reports showing income, expenditures, and changes in the farm operation.[144] These reports must be filed in a timely manner within fifteen days after the close of business for a month, must be reflective of *all* transactions of the debtor, and must be drawn from the information in the debtor-in-possession's bank account. Failure to file these reports can result in dismissal of the chapter 12 case.[145] The trustee may also

---

134 *See* 11 U.S.C. §§ 327, 1203. Fed. R. Bankr. P. 2016; *In re* Fulton, 80 B.R. 1009 (Bankr. D. Neb. 1988); *In re* Slack, 73 B.R. 382 (Bankr. W.D. Mo. 1987). Fee disclosure is also required. Fed. R. Bankr. P. 2016(b).

135 *See, e.g., In re* Samford, 102 B.R. 724 (Bankr. E.D. Mo. 1989); *In re* Stacy Farms, 78 B.R. 494 (Bankr. S.D. Ohio 1987); *In re* Willamette Timber Sys., Inc., 54 B.R. 485 (Bankr. D. Or. 1985); *In re* Wolsky, 35 B.R. 481 (Bankr. D.N.D. 1983); *In re* Ladycliff College, 35 B.R. 111 (Bankr. S.D.N.Y. 1983); *In re* Lewis, 30 B.R. 404 (Bankr. E.D. Pa. 1983).

136 11 U.S.C. §§ 327, 328. *In re* Samford, 102 B.R. 724 (Bankr. E.D. Mo. 1989).

137 28 U.S.C. § 1930(a)(5).

138 11 U.S.C. § 329; Fed. R. Bankr. P. 2014, 2016. *See also* Ch. 15, *supra*. However, fees in commercial and quasi-commercial

cases will—and are expected to—run higher than in consumer cases.

139 *See, e.g., In re* Yermakov, 718 F.2d 1465 (9th Cir. 1983); Barber v. Kimbrell's, Inc., 577 F.2d 216 (4th Cir. 1978); Johnson v. Georgia Highway Express, Inc., 488 F.2d 714 (5th Cir. 1974); *In re* Casco Bay Lines, Inc., 25 B.R. 747 (B.A.P. 1st Cir. 1982); *In re* Heller, 105 B.R. 434 (Bankr. N.D. Ill. 1989).

140 *In re* Miller, 288 B.R. 879 (B.A.P. 10th Cir. 2003) (evidence of attorney fee rates in local area supported reduction of attorney's hourly rate).

141 Fed. R. Bankr. P. 2016(a); *In re* Fox, 140 B.R. 761 (Bankr. D.S.D. 1992); *In re* Fulton, 80 B.R. 1009 (Bankr. D. Neb. 1988). *See In re* Combe Farms, Inc., 257 B.R. 48 (Bankr. D. Idaho 2001) (fees reduced because attorney failed to make disclosures required by Rule 2014).

142 Fed. R. Bankr. P. 2016(b); *In re* Brandenburger, 145 B.R. 624 (Bankr. D.S.D. 1992); *In re* Fox, 140 B.R. 761 (Bankr. D.S.D. 1992) (retention of jurisdiction to determine fees after dismissal).

143 U.S. Trustees, Guidelines for Supervision of Chapter 12 cases.

144 *Id.*

145 *In re* Wickersheim, 107 B.R. 177 (Bankr. E.D. Wis. 1989); U.S. Trustees, Guidelines for Supervision of Chapter 12 cases; *In re*

request and require from time to time other reports, documentation, or information from the debtor, including proof of insurance coverage.[146]

16.2.4 Voluntary Conversion from Other Chapters to Chapter 12

This information is important in dealing with the gap periods when chapter 12 is not available, because Congress allowed the chapter to lapse before re-enacting it.

Chapter 7: Section 706(a) provides an absolute right to convert from a chapter 7 bankruptcy to one under chapter 12, provided there has been no previous conversion.

Chapter 11: Section 1112(d), allows conversion from a chapter 11 case to one under chapter 12, with the provision that the court determine that such conversion "is equitable."

Chapter 13: Section 1307(d) allows conversion from chapter 13 to chapter 12 after notice and a hearing.[147] This section does not require that the conversion be "equitable," although that may be an issue if conversion is opposed. Unlike the absolute right to conversion between chapters 7 and 12, the provision for notice and hearing gives creditors and trustees the opportunity to oppose conversion from chapter 13 if the circumstances so warrant.[148]

At minimum, a debtor must be eligible for chapter 12 relief for conversion to be effectuated.[149] If conversion is considered, eligibility will be measured by the tax year immediately preceding the original filing, not the time of conversion.[150]

Reconversion: A farmer debtor who has tried unsuccessfully to reorganize under chapter 11, and converted to chapter 7, may presently believe he or she is eligible for and can reorganize under chapter 12. Reconversion is not an absolute right, but reconversion has been permitted by several courts in their sound discretion after notice and hearing.[151] One court allowed reconversion in a case which originated under chapter 11, converted to chapter 7 and

continued almost two years as a case under chapter 7 before a motion to convert to a case under chapter 12 was made.[152]

Refiling: There is no express prohibition to dismissal and refiling as an alternative to conversion.[153] Several courts have allowed such dismissal to escape the harsh consequences of statutory requirements preventing conversion.[154] However, there are several considerations which may prevent dismissal and refiling from being a viable option for a family farmer debtor who wishes to enjoy the benefits of chapter 12.

First, section 109(g)[155] may prohibit refiling within 180 days of the voluntary dismissal of a pending case if automatic stay litigation has been filed, as it almost always has in chapter 11 farmer cases.[156] Second, if the case to be dismissed is under chapter 7 or 11, dismissal can only be had with court approval after notice and a hearing.[157] Third, a court may not allow dismissal and refiling if the debtor cannot demonstrate a material change in circumstances militating for refiling and good cause for lack of success in the original filing.[158] Finally, one court has declined to allow dismissal of a chapter 11 case where the express purpose of dismissal was chapter 12 refiling. The debtor's chapter 11 case was confirmed and current; the court found that the causes for dismissal found in 11 U.S.C. § 1112(b) do not embrace that circumstance, even when dismissal is sought voluntarily by the debtor.[159]

The bar of section 109(g) or the imminent loss by foreclosure of farmland after the lifting of the automatic stay by the court or by plan provision ("recapture" or "drop dead" provision) in a chapter 11 case pose the problem of whether

---

Goza, 142 B.R. 766 (Bankr. S.D. Miss. 1992) (court can prevent debtor's voluntary dismissal if necessary reports and accounting lacking).

146 U.S. Trustees, Guidelines for Supervision of Chapter 12 cases.

147 *In re* Land, 82 B.R. 572 (Bankr. D. Colo. 1988).

148 *See, e.g., In re* Wulf, 62 B.R. 155 (Bankr. D. Neb. 1986); *In re* Collins, 19 B.R. 209 (Bankr. S.D. Fla. 1982).

149 *In re* Walker, 77 B.R. 803 (Bankr. D. Nev. 1987).

150 11 U.S.C. § 348(a); State Bank of Waubay v. Bisgard, 80 B.R. 491 (D.S.D. 1987); *In re* Cobb, 76 B.R. 557 (Bankr. N.D. Miss. 1987).

151 State Bank of Waubay v. Bisgard, 80 B.R. 491 (D.S.D. 1987) (11 to 7 to 12 reconversion); *In re* Tex. Extrusion Corp., 68 B.R. 712 (N.D. Tex. 1986) (11 to 7 to 11 reconversion); *In re* Walker, 77 B.R. 803 (Bankr. D. Nev. 1987) (11 to 7 to 13 reconversion); *In re* Sensibaugh, 9 B.R. 45 (Bankr. E.D. Va. 1981) (11 to 7 to 13 reconversion). *Contra In re* Richardson, 43 B.R. 636 (Bankr. M.D. Fla. 1984).

152 State Bank of Waubay v. Bisgard, 80 B.R. 491 (D.S.D. 1987); *cf.* Kershaw v. Behm, 81 B.R. 898 (M.D. Tenn. 1988).

153 Travelers Ins. Co. v. Don-Lin Farms, 90 B.R. 48 (W.D.N.Y. 1988) (although ability to refile not addressed); *In re* Reppert, 84 B.R. 37 (Bankr. E.D. Pa. 1988); *In re* Hill, 84 B.R. 623 (Bankr. E.D. Mo. 1988); *In re* Hyman, 82 B.R. 23 (Bankr. D.S.C. 1987); *In re* Mason, 70 B.R. 753 (Bankr. W.D.N.Y. 1987); *In re* McDermott, 77 B.R. 384 (Bankr. N.D.N.Y. 1987) (farmer chapter 11).

154 *See, e.g.,* Travelers Ins. Co. v. Don-Lin Farms, 90 B.R. 48 (W.D.N.Y. 1988) (although ability to refile not addressed); *In re* Reppert, 84 B.R. 37 (Bankr. E.D. Pa 1988); *In re* Gamble, 72 B.R. 75 (Bankr. D. Idaho 1987).

155 *See* § 9.7.3.1.5, *supra.*

156 Many creditors use the strategy of bringing automatic stay litigation at the outset of a case in chapter 11, whether fully warranted or not, to prevent refiling and provide momentum to the case. The court may permit refiling after voluntary dismissal if circumstances so warrant by its powers in 11 U.S.C. § 105. Involuntary dismissal does not prohibit refiling unless expressly with prejudice and mere failure to oppose a motion to dismiss does not equate to a voluntary dismissal. *In re* Glazier, 69 B.R. 666 (Bankr. W.D. Okla. 1987) (in *dicta*); *In re* Ryder, 75 B.R. 890 (Bankr. W.D. La. 1987); *In re* Nelkovski, 46 B.R. 542 (Bankr. N.D. Ill. 1985) (chapter 13). *See* § 3.2.1, *supra*; § 16.4.7, *infra.*

157 11 U.S.C. §§ 707, 1112.

158 *In re* Hyman, 82 B.R. 23 (Bankr. D.S.C. 1987).

159 *In re* Pool, 81 B.R. 20 (Bankr. W.D. Mo. 1987).

a debtor can file an overlapping chapter 12 case before dismissal of the chapter 11. One court has taken such a filing to be a request for conversion;[160] Bankruptcy Rule 1015(a) appears to contemplate the possibility of overlapping petitions.[161] However, where a bar under 109(g) would exist in the event of dismissal and conversion cannot be made, another court has found the overlapping chapter 12 filing to be ineffectual.[162]

16.2.5 What to Expect at the Meeting of Creditors

The meeting of creditors is conducted by the standing chapter 12 trustee or the United States trustee. Depending upon the district, the meeting may be directed by questioning from the trustee, or may be directed by the debtor's attorney.

As eligibility is restricted in chapter 12, a primary focus of the trustee's initial questioning will be the eligibility factors set out in section 101(18). If full disclosure is made in the petition and schedules concerning these eligibility factors, problems from this line of questioning can be kept to a minimum.

As in chapter 11 cases, the debtor will be required to disclose some information concerning the nature of the operation, the reorganizational actions already taken by the debtor, and what may be anticipated in the plan proposal. The trustee and secured creditors should be apprised of the status of secured collateral and insurance thereon. Financing arrangements for the coming year need to be disclosed, either as filed or anticipated to be filed. If sale, return or abandonment of land or equipment is in process or anticipated, that also should be disclosed. The variety and acreage of crops planted should be disclosed, as well as when planting occurred, whether there is a security interest in the crops,[163] and whether the crops are covered by insurance.

As in all other chapters, creditors will be allowed to question the family farmer debtors about their affairs. In most cases, only secured creditors will appear. In preparation of the bankruptcy case itself, and certainly in preparation for the meeting of creditors, the farmer debtor should be able to account for all collateral of secured creditors and the disposition of this collateral.

Creditors may use the meeting of creditors as an opportunity to develop evidence leading to nondischargeability complaints and/or objections to confirmation. If there are significant inconsistencies between previous statements or documents created by the debtor and his or her bankruptcy schedules, this may come out at the meeting. If the debtor has given little thought to the actual mechanics of reorganization or is vague about matters bearing on feasibility, this may also be scrutinized at the meeting.

Time on meeting day should be used as an occasion to confer with and appraise the positions of the creditors and the trustee, ferret out potential problems, to agree to valuations of collateral and/or plan treatment (if possible), and to make creditors and the trustee as comfortable as possible with the debtor's situation and case. All reports and documents should be filed before the meeting, for example, monthly reports due, documents required by the chapter 12 trustee, and any amendments to schedules.

The meeting of creditors can set the tone for the hostility or cooperation of creditors. The more accurate information counsel and debtor can give them, the better creditors may react. If counsel is in a position where it appears information cannot be given without jeopardizing the perceived success of a chapter 12 case and plan, chances increase that the care will be opposed by creditors or the trustee.

16.3 The Family Farmer as Debtor-in-Possession

16.3.1 What Is a Debtor-in-Possession?

The filing of a chapter 12 petition establishes the family farmer debtor as a debtor-in-possession.[164] A debtor-in-possession, often termed a DIP, is a legal fiction created by the Bankruptcy Code, originally under chapter 11.[165] Although it is the individual who operates the farming operation as a DIP, a DIP is a legal entity separate and apart from the actual debtor.

It is the debtor as debtor-in-possession who operates the debtor's business and farming operation. The debtor-in-possession makes the business decisions, applies to the court concerning all operating decisions which require court approval, challenges claims of creditors, controls the property of the estate, and proposes a chapter 12 plan.[166] A DIP has the powers, duties and fiduciary responsibilities of a bankruptcy trustee.[167] Because the DIP is a separate legal entity distinct from the original debtor, the DIP can use all of the avoiding powers bestowed upon a chapter 7 trustee without regard to whether the pre-bankruptcy debtor took any ac-

---

160 *In re* Woloschak, 70 B.R. 498 (Bankr. N.D. Ohio 1987).

161 *See* § 16.2.2.6, *supra*.

162 *In re* Hill, 84 B.R. 623 (Bankr. E.D. Mo. 1988).

163 The lien dissolution provisions of 11 U.S.C. § 552(a) are important here. Creditors should be informed of whether security interests continue in the crops, or if the crops have become clear of lien.

164 11 U.S.C. § 1203.

165 11 U.S.C. §§ 1107, 1108.

166 11 U.S.C. § 1203.

167 *In re* WWG Indus., Inc., 772 F.2d 810 (11th Cir. 1985); Georgia Pacific Corp. v. Sigma Serv. Corp., 712 F.2d 962 (5th Cir. 1983); *In re* Hartman, 102 B.R. 90 (Bankr. N.D. Tex. 1989); *In re* Hollinrake, 93 B.R. 183 (Bankr. S.D. Iowa 1988); *In re* Russell, 60 B.R. 42 (Bankr. W.D. Ark. 1985); *In re* Diamond, 49 B.R. 754 (Bankr. S.D.N.Y. 1985).

tions or made any transfers voluntarily.[168] A DIP has all of a trustee's avoidance powers to recover and recapture property for reorganization.[169]

The DIP also has a trustee's responsibilities in bankruptcy and a fiduciary obligation to creditors to protect and preserve the estate.[170] The DIP must account for all monies and property which are in or come into its possession or control, and must also account for all sums expended by it. The DIP is obligated to make accurate periodic reports to the court and the chapter 12 trustee concerning income, cash flow and expenditures.[171] In addition, a chapter 12 DIP may be required to submit other reports and information to the court, trustee or creditors.[172] All debtors-in-possession are required to open new bank accounts upon filing, and all income and expenditures must be funneled through that account; the account should be labeled so that in addition to the debtor's name, it indicates that the debtor is a chapter 12 debtor-in-possession.[173]

Unlike chapter 11 cases, there is a standing chapter 12 trustee in addition to the DIP who supervises administration and payments under the plan; the trustee must be apprised of all activity in the chapter 12 case, and must be present for some hearings.[174] The chapter 12 trustee's position is akin to that of the chapter 13 trustee.[175]

16.3.2 Tax Years and Tax Duties

Chapter 12 contains a special tax provision which tracks the chapter 11 language[176] creating a new income tax year for a DIP upon filing, and terminating the debtor's old tax year immediately pre-filing. However, this provision applies *only* with regard to state and local taxes and taxing authorities. Congress has not yet amended the Bankruptcy Tax Act to cover chapter 12 debtors and shift tax liability postpetition to the debtor-in-possession.[177]

The Code also provides that the chapter 12 trustee will submit all state and local income tax returns to the appropriate taxing authorities during the pendency of the case.[178] In almost all cases, the chapter 12 trustee will delegate this responsibility back to the actual debtor-in-possession.[179] The periodic report forms which the DIP must file detailing a debtor's financial transactions require disclosure of ongoing tax liability, withholding, and payment. If the farmer debtor has material ongoing tax liability arising because of non-family employees, the court or trustee may require the maintenance of a separate tax and/or payroll account(s) as are militated for chapter 11 debtors-in-possession. Similar to practice under chapter 11, the farmer debtor who proposes a plan under chapter 12 may, upon court authorization, request a determination by the state or local taxing authority of the tax effects of the plan.[180]

If an accountant or other professional is employed by the DIP to do bookkeeping, taxes, or other accounting, application must be made to the bankruptcy court for allowance of employment and payment.[181] The farmer DIP and his or her attorney should also be aware that every plan of reorganization and/or sale has tax consequences for the DIP and/or debtor which should be explored prior to filing and plan formulation and proposal.

16.3.3 Removal of the Farmer As a Debtor-in-Possession

The bankruptcy court, upon request of a party in interest, after notice and a hearing, may remove a family farmer from operating the farm as a debtor-in-possession.[182] Upon the debtor's removal, the standing chapter 12 trustee or an appointee of the United States trustee will operate the farm or recommend that the court dismiss or convert the chapter 12 case as circumstances warrant.[183] The trustee may continue the farm operation with the farmer debtor as an employee, but the trustee is not compelled to do so. The

---

168 *Cf.* 11 U.S.C. § 522(g).

169 8 Collier on Bankruptcy ¶ 1203.02[2] (15th ed. rev.).

170 *In re* Halux, Inc., 665 F.2d 213 (8th Cir. 1981); *In re* J.A.V. Ag., Inc., 154 B.R. 923 (Bankr. W.D. Tex. 1993); *In re* Russell, 60 B.R. 42 (Bankr. W.D. Ark. 1985).

171 *In re* Lawless, 74 B.R. 54 (Bankr. W.D. Mo. 1987), *aff'd*, 79 B.R. 850 (W.D. Mo. 1987); *In re* Paolina, 53 B.R. 399 (Bankr. W.D. Pa. 1985), *aff'd*, 60 B.R. 828 (W.D. Pa. 1986); *In re* Diamond, 49 B.R. 754 (Bankr. S.D.N.Y. 1985).

172 Many trustees require other information to be furnished beyond the schedules so that a clearer picture of the debtor's predicted income and plans can be discerned.

173 This may be good practice. However, the United States Trustee does not have such power to require that the letters "D.I.P." be printed on checks. *E.g.*, *In re* Young, 205 B.R. 894 (Bankr. W.D. Tenn. 1997).

174 11 U.S.C. § 1202(b)(3). *See* § 16.4.2, *infra.*

175 *Cf.* 11 U.S.C. § 1302(b).

176 11 U.S.C. § 1231; *cf.* 11 U.S.C. § 1146.

177 *In re* Powell, 187 B.R. 642, 647 (Bankr. D. Minn. 1995); Bankruptcy Tax Act of 1980, Section 1398 is currently applicable in chapters 11 and 7 only, and then only with regard to

individuals, not corporate or partnership debtors. *See* 26 U.S.C. § 108(d)(8). *In re* Lindsay, 142 B.R. 447 (Bankr. W.D. Okla. 1992). *But see also* special farm provisions at 26 U.S.C. § 108(g).

178 11 U.S.C. § 1231(b).

179 11 U.S.C. § 1231 does not put this obligation on the chapter 12 trustee for corporation or partnership debtors. If § 1203 is read with § 1231, it may always be the duty of DIP to file tax returns.

180 11 U.S.C. § 1231(d). However, this does not include federal taxing authorities. *See* 8 Collier on Bankruptcy ¶ 1146.LH (15th ed. rev.).

181 11 U.S.C. § 327.

182 11 U.S.C. § 1204(a). Compare the conversion provisions of 11 U.S.C. § 1208(d). *See generally* Matson, *Understanding the New Family Farmer Bankruptcy Act*, 21 U. Rich. L. Rev. 521 (Spring 1987).

183 11 U.S.C. § 1204(b)(5). However, the trustee cannot propose a plan under chapter 12; *see also* United States Trustee's Guidelines For Supervision of Chapter 12 Cases.

trustee may hire a farmer/manager if one is needed; to do so the trustee must request permission under section 327 and promptly petition the court for plan modification under section 1229 to reflect the cost and to disclose whether living expenses drawn by the debtor will continue.[184] The court may make the trustee a mere watchdog in more substantive ways than with a DIP in full charge, but without altogether limiting the debtor's decision making.

There is, however, a strong presumption against appointment of a trustee where there is a debtor-in-possession, and appointment of a trustee is regarded as an extraordinary remedy.[185] The reasons for removal of the DIP under chapter 12 track those under chapter 11, although not verbatim.[186] A chapter 12 DIP may be removed for cause, including fraud, dishonesty, incompetence or gross mismanagement, occurring either before or after the commencement of the case.[187] However, unlike chapter 11 cases, a trustee cannot be appointed if the only ground for appointment is the best interests of creditors.[188]

Consequently, most but not all of the case law which has evolved on removal under chapter 11 should be equally applicable to chapter 12 debtors-in-possession.[189] Courts have recognized that every reorganization with a debtor-in-possession suffers from some degree of mismanagement.[190] Nevertheless, in the farm reorganization context many, if not most, bankruptcies are caused by weather-related disasters or matters other than mismanagement. The inability of a debtor to operate a business in its optimal manner due to circumstances beyond the debtor's control or failure of the debtor to pursue all avenues of revenue or recapture of potential property of the estate is generally not such mismanagement.[191] Cause justifying removal includes failure to file appropriate financial information and reports or filing false information,[192] post-petition transfer of assets,[193] commingling of estate and non-estate assets,[194] failure to pay taxes after withholding,[195] cessation of business,[196] or breach of fiduciary duty.[197]

A debtor-in-possession once removed can be restored to DIP status and operation of the farm.[198] This also tracks a similar chapter 11 provision.[199]

16.4 General Principles

16.4.1 Applicability of Chapter 7 and Chapter 13 Concepts to Cases Under Chapter 12

Because the family farmer debtor under chapter 12 is a debtor-in-possession,[200] he or she has all of the powers of a trustee to avoid liens and recover property.[201] Chapters 1, 3 and 5 of the Code also apply to chapter 12 cases unless specifically modified by chapter 12.[202] For example, the following general Code requirements apply to chapter 12:

- The prohibition of involuntary bankruptcies against family farmers;[203]
- Assumption of executory contracts and unexpired leases;[204]
- Expansion of time limits and statutes of limitation;[205]
- Need for approval for sale, use or lease of property including use of cash collateral and new financing;[206]
- Coverage of the automatic stay;[207] and
- Nondischargeability of individual debts.[208]

Any attorney familiar with chapter 13 will recognize the structure of chapter 13 as the template for chapter 12.[209] Except with regard to the disposable income requirement,[210] law developed under chapter 13 is generally controlling in chapter 12 when the statutory language in both chapters is identical.[211] The chapter 12 structure, plan requirements,

184 United States Trustee's Guidelines For Supervision of Chapter 12 Cases.

185 *In re* Jessen, 82 B.R. 490 (Bankr. S.D. Iowa 1988); *In re* H & S Transp. Co., 55 B.R. 786 (Bankr. M.D. Tenn. 1985); *In re* Diamond, 49 B.R. 754 (Bankr. S.D.N.Y. 1985).

186 *Compare* 11 U.S.C. § 1204 *with* 11 U.S.C. § 1104.

187 11 U.S.C. § 1204(a)(2).

188 *Cf.* 11 U.S.C. § 1104(a)(2).

189 *See* § 17.7.4, *infra*.

190 *In re* Jessen, 82 B.R. 490 (Bankr. S.D. Iowa 1988).

191 *Id.*

192 *In re* Lawless, 74 B.R. 54 (Bankr. W.D. Mo. 1987), *aff'd*, 79 B.R. 850 (W.D. Mo. 1987); *In re* Paolina, 53 B.R. 399 (Bankr. W.D. Pa. 1985), *aff'd*, 60 B.R. 828 (W.D. Pa. 1986).

193 *See* Ford v. Postan, 773 F.2d 52 (4th Cir. 1985).

194 *Id.*

195 *In re* St. Louis Globe-Democrat, Inc., 63 B.R. 131 (Bankr. E.D. Mo. 1985).

196 *In re* Russell, 60 B.R. 42 (Bankr. W.D. Ark. 1985).

197 *In re* Diamond, 49 B.R. 754 (Bankr. S.D.N.Y. 1985).

198 11 U.S.C. § 1204(b).

199 11 U.S.C. § 1105.

200 11 U.S.C. § 1203.

201 *See* § 10.4, *supra*.

202 11 U.S.C. § 103(a); *In re* Neff, 89 B.R. 672 (Bankr. S.D. Ohio 1988).

203 11 U.S.C. § 303(a).

204 11 U.S.C. § 365. *See* § 16.4.8, *infra*.

205 11 U.S.C. § 108.

206 11 U.S.C. §§ 363, 364.

207 11 U.S.C. § 362.

208 11 U.S.C. § 523(a).

209 *See In re* Rancho Chamberino, 89 B.R. 597 (W.D. Tex. 1987); *In re* Zurface, 95 B.R. 527 (Bankr. S.D. Ohio 1989); *In re* Anderson, 88 B.R. 877 (Bankr. N.D. Ind. 1988); *In re* Borg, 88 B.R. 288 (Bankr. D. Mont. 1988); *In re* Coffman, 90 B.R. 878 (Bankr. W.D. Tenn. 1988).

210 *See* § 16.5.4.3, *infra*.

211 *In re* White, 25 F.3d 931 (10th Cir. 1994); *In re* Honey, 167 B.R. 540 (W.D. Mo. 1994); *In re* McKinney, 84 B.R. 751 (D. Kan. 1988); *In re* Cook, 148 B.R. 273 (Bankr. W.D. Mich. 1992); *In re* Martin, 130 B.R. 951 (Bankr. N.D. Iowa 1991); *In re* Luchenbill, 112 B.R. 204 (Bankr. E.D. Mich. 1990); *In re*

confirmation standards, property of the estate, and codebtor stay are drawn almost verbatim from chapter 13. Some of the most significant advantages for farmers for chapter 12 over chapter 13 are:

(a) There is a higher debt ceiling for chapter 12 eligibility than under chapter 13;[212]

(b) Indebtedness secured by residential real property and/or the farm homestead can be restructured and the payments thereupon modified and changed from those originally provided by contract;[213]

(c) All secured indebtedness can be—if appropriate— reamortized and repaid over a length of time exceeding the three to five year life of the chapter 12 plan;[214]

(d) Payments can be scheduled to coincide with farm income production periods.

However, certain debts may be dischargeable in chapter 13, but not in chapter 12.[215] Occasionally, this may be a reason to choose chapter 13 over chapter 12.

16.4.2 The Chapter 12 Trustee

16.4.2.1 Role and Standing of the Trustee

The chapter 12 trustee is an administrative officer with duties similar to those of chapter 13 trustees. The chapter 12 trustee may be the United States trustee, a standing chapter 12 trustee appointed by the United States trustee who serves in all chapter 12 cases, or a disinterested person appointed by the United States trustee.[216] Most districts have appointed a special standing chapter 12 trustee for administration of family farmer cases. In other districts with modest chapter 12 activity, the standing chapter 13 trustee also serves as the standing chapter 12 trustee although the administration and distribution of funds are segregated from the chapter 13 operation.

The duties of the chapter 12 trustee closely resemble those of a chapter 13 trustee,[217] but the chapter 12 trustee does not have the duty to investigate the debtor's affairs,[218] unless the court orders the trustee to do so.[219] However, the chapter 12 trustee is empowered to inquire into and examine the affairs of the family farmer debtor to the extent necessary to determine the debtor's eligibility for chapter 12 relief and confirmability of any proposed plan or modified plan.[220] The chapter 12 trustee customarily examines the debtors at the meetings of creditors,[221] and also participates in hearings concerning valuation of property subject to lien, confirmation, plan modification, and sale of property.[222] The trustee may also object to creditors' claims and assist in defining and clarifying issues for the parties and the court.[223]

The chapter 12 trustee, like the chapter 13 trustee, is charged by statute with the duty to monitor plan payments.[224] The failure to make payments under a chapter 12 plan is a default which can result in the trustee's filing of a motion to dismiss.[225] The trustee's duties also include periodic reports to the court and solicitation of reports from the debtor for information which bears on eligibility and the plan's confirmability.[226]

Zurface, 95 B.R. 527 (Bankr. S.D. Ohio 1989); *In re* Mutchler, 95 B.R. 748 (Bankr. D. Mont. 1989); *In re* SWF, Inc., 83 B.R. 27 (Bankr. S.D. Cal. 1988); *In re* Robinson Ranch, Inc., 75 B.R. 606 (Bankr. D. Mont. 1987); *In re* Bigalk, 75 B.R. 561 (Bankr. D. Minn. 1987); *In re* Circle Five, Inc., 75 B.R. 686 (Bankr. D. Idaho 1987).

212 *See* 11 U.S.C. §§ 101(18), 109(f).

213 11 U.S.C. § 1222(b)(2). Harmon v. United States, 101 F.3d 574 (8th Cir. 1996) (lien stripping permitted in chapter 12); *In re* Zabel, 249 B.R. 764 (Bankr. E.D. Wis. 2000). Contrast chapter 13 requirements, Nobelman v. Am. Sav. Bank, 508 U.S. 324, 113 S. Ct. 2106, 124 L. Ed. 2d 228 (1993).

214 11 U.S.C. § 1222(b)(9).

215 The exceptions to discharge contained in 11 U.S.C. § 523(a) are applicable to all discharges under chapter 12, but not to a discharge under § 1328(a). *Compare* 11 U.S.C. § 1228(a) *with* 11 U.S.C. § 1328(a). *See generally* § 14.4.1, *supra*.

216 11 U.S.C. § 1202; Robiner v. Demczyk, 269 B.R. 167 (N.D. Ohio 2001) (U.S. trustee must appoint the chapter 12 trustee, but the chapter 12 trustee may not resign from particular cases without permission from the court; submission of resignation to U.S. trustee is insufficient).

217 *Compare* 11 U.S.C. § 1202 *with* 11 U.S.C. § 1302.

218 *Compare* 11 U.S.C. § 1202(b)(1) *with* 11 U.S.C. § 1302(b)(1).

219 11 U.S.C. § 1202(b)(2). Such examination may be ordered *sua sponte* by the court or upon motion of a creditor. *See, e.g., In re* Graven, 84 B.R. 630 (Bankr. W.D. Mo. 1988).

220 *Compare* 11 U.S.C. § 1202(b) *with* 11 U.S.C. § 704(7); *see also* Executive Office for United States Trustees, Guidelines for Supervision of Chapter 12 Cases, No. 5. *In re* Roesner, 153 B.R. 328 (Bankr. D. Kan. 1993); *In re* Martens, 98 B.R. 530 (Bankr. D. Colo. 1989). But the trustee's power to object may be limited. *See In re* Teigen, 142 B.R. 397 (Bankr. D. Mont. 1992) (trustee cannot object to claims treatment on behalf of creditors which accept plan or fail to object).

221 Executive Office for United States Trustees, Guidelines for Supervision of Chapter 12 Cases, No. 5. 11 U.S.C. § 341 indicates that the United States trustee conducts the meeting, but it is usually his designee, the chapter 12 trustee, who conducts the meeting.

222 *In re* Roesner, 153 B.R. 328 (Bankr. D. Kan. 1993); *In re* Martens, 98 B.R. 530 (Bankr. D. Colo. 1989).

223 11 U.S.C. § 1202(b)(3); *In re* Beard, 45 F.3d 113 (6th Cir. 1995); *In re* Jennings, 190 B.R. 863 (Bankr. W.D. Mo. 1995); *In re* Martens, 98 B.R. 530 (Bankr. D. Colo. 1989).

224 11 U.S.C. §§ 1202(b)(4), 1208 (c)(6).

225 The trustee is a party in interest under 11 U.S.C. § 1208(c), with standing to bring a motion to dismiss. *See, e.g., In re* A-1 Trash Pick-Up, Inc., 802 F.2d 774 (4th Cir. 1986); *In re* Tiana Queen Motel, Inc., 749 F.2d 146 (2d Cir. 1984).

226 11 U.S.C. § 1202(b)(3); Executive Office of United States Trustees, Guidelines for Supervision of Chapter 12 Cases. See discussion of trustee's duties and responsibilities in *In re* Mouser, 99 B.R. 803 (Bankr. S.D. Ohio 1989).

Where a plan so provides, the debtor and affected creditor(s) consent, and the court approves, the chapter 12 trustee may act as a liquidating agent for property of the estate.[227]

The power to pursue avoidance actions appears to remain with the debtor-in-possession, absent removal under 11 U.S.C. § 1204 or by court order under 11 U.S.C. § 1203 limiting the DIP's rights and duties.[228] The role of the trustee post-confirmation may be similarly limited. While the trustee can address fraud under 11 U.S.C. §§ 1202(b)(2), 1228(d), 1230 and 1208(d), any examination must have substantial evidence to generate such a duty after confirmation.[229]

16.4.2.2 Payments Made Through the Chapter 12 Trustee and Trustee Compensation

16.4.2.2.1 General

The compensation of chapter 12 trustees and their offices, like those administering chapter 13 cases, is derived from payments made through the chapter 12 plan.[230] The Code sets out maximum fees to be paid to chapter 12 trustees appointed by the court independent of U.S. trustees: ten percent of the first $450,000.00 and no more than three percent of any additional payments.[231] The trustee can receive fees in a case even if it is not confirmed.[232] Many districts have set the trustee's surcharge at the ten percent maximum.[233] Some districts have adopted split fee schedules, levying a low surcharge on repayment of secured indebtedness under the plan and maximum fees on repayment of unsecured indebtedness.[234]

Consequently, chapter 12 debtors are subject to a much higher surcharge than under chapter 11, where the fees may be less than one percent.[235] A chapter 12 trustee may also be allowed additional administrative fees by the bankruptcy

court.[236] It may be possible to vary the overall percentage due to the chapter 12 trustee for payments under the plan by plan provision or court order, but only if compelling circumstances are demonstrated.[237]

16.4.2.2.2 Challenges to variations in trustee costs paid by different debtors

Since the first chapter 12 plans, debtors have challenged the trustee compensation scheme.[238] These challenges continue to be brought by debtors. For example, raising a direct challenge to the trustee's compensation, the debtors in an Illinois case asked the court to review the reasonableness of the ten percent commission set for their trustee.[239] The debtors argued that the "longstanding policy of the judicial involvement in compensation paid out of a bankruptcy" authorized the court to conduct this review.[240] The debtors further argued that payment of the commission would affect their ability to reorganize and was inconsistent with the legislative intent underlying chapter 12.[241] The court rejected the debtors' request, holding that Congress had vested the executive branch with the authority to set fees and had "eliminated the judiciary's role in overseeing compensation for such trustees."[242] Accordingly the court held that it had "no authority to review the reasonableness" of the fee.[243] The court stated that its decision was in keeping with the majority of courts that have addressed this issue and specifically mentioned three cases.[244] The court cited two cases

---

227 *In re* Lindsay, 142 B.R. 447 (Bankr. W.D. Okla. 1992); *In re* Tyndall, 97 B.R. 266 (Bankr. E.D.N.C. 1989).

228 *In re* Teigen, 123 B.R. 887 (Bankr. D. Mont. 1991).

229 *In re* Gross, 121 B.R. 587 (Bankr. D.S.D. 1990).

230 28 U.S.C. § 586(e). The standing chapter 12 trustee also receives, from the percentage fee, an annual flat compensation not to exceed the annual basic pay for a government employee at GS-16, Step 1. Sections (c) and (d) of 11 U.S.C. § 1202 were repealed upon enactment of § 586(e); § 586(e) has basically the same content but a lower percentage on plan payments over $450,000.00.

231 28 U.S.C. § 586(e)(1)(B)(2).

232 Stahn v. Haeckel, 920 F.2d 555 (8th Cir. 1990).

233 If a district has numerous chapter 12 cases with successful plans filed, it can be anticipated that the percentage there will be lowered.

234 *See, e.g., In re* Caudill, 82 B.R. 969 (Bankr. S.D. Ind. 1988) (one percent on secured, ten percent on unsecured repayment); *In re* Snider Farms, Inc., 83 B.R. 1003 (Bankr. N.D. Ind. 1988) (two percent on secured, ten percent on unsecured repayment).

235 Cost of repayment under chapter 11, in those districts with a United States trustee, are the quarterly charges recently put into

---

place under 28 U.S.C. § 1930(a)(6) keyed to the amount of plan distribution.

236 *See* § 16.2.4, *supra.*

237 *In re* Rott, 73 B.R. 366 (Bankr. D.N.D. 1987); *In re* Meyer, 73 B.R. 457 (Bankr. E.D. Mo. 1987); *In re* Hagensick, 73 B.R. 710 (Bankr. N.D. Iowa 1987); *In re* Tartaglia, 61 B.R. 439 (Bankr. D.R.I. 1986) (and cases cited therein; chapter 13); *In re* Sousa, 46 B.R. 343 (Bankr. D.R.I. 1985) (chapter 13). *Contra In re* Greseth, 78 B.R. 936 (D. Minn. 1987); *In re* Sutton, 91 B.R. 184 (Bankr. M.D. Ga. 1988) (fee set by Attorney General; declines to address whether it can be varied by court); *In re* Citrowske, 72 B.R. 613 (Bankr. D. Minn. 1987). However, several courts have indicated that the ability of the court to vary fees may be only during the phase-in period for the United States Trustee System, and that thereafter only the Attorney General may vary the fees. *See, e.g., In re* Schollett, 980 F.2d 639 (10th Cir. 1992); *In re* Mouser, 99 B.R. 803 (Bankr. S.D. Ohio 1989); *In re* Pianowski, 92 B.R. 225 (Bankr. W.D. Mich. 1988); *In re* Finkbine, 94 B.R. 461 (Bankr. S.D. Ohio 1988); *In re* Erickson P'ship, 77 B.R. 738 (Bankr. D.S.D. 1987).

238 *See, e.g.,* Greseth v. Fed. Land Bank (*In re* Greseth), 78 B.R. 936 (D. Minn. 1987).

239 *In re* Marriott, 156 B.R. 803 (Bankr. S.D. Ill. 1993).

240 *Id.* at 804.

241 *Id.*

242 *Id.* at 805.

243 *Id.*

244 *In re* Schollett, 980 F.2d 639, 645 (10th Cir. 1992); *In re* Savage, 67 B.R. 700, 705, 706 (D.R.I. 1986); *In re* Citrowski, 72 B.R. 613, 615 (Bankr. D. Minn. 1987).

as representing the minority view that authority for judicial review exists.[245]

The fee system has also been challenged as unconstitutional under the uniformity of laws provision of Article I, Section 8, of the United States Constitution.[246] This challenge focused on the practical effect of the statutory maximum, under which some debtors may have to pay a ten percent trustee's fee and others may pay less. The debtors argued that trustee's fees vary between the states, the United States trustee regions and even between different trustees in the same region. Their briefing reported fees of five percent in Nebraska, seven percent in the Northern District of Iowa, and ten percent in the Central District of Illinois. They further alleged that once a standing trustee reaches her statutory maximum compensation, the percentage fee will be reduced, to the advantage of debtors filing subsequently but not debtors who filed previously.

This challenge, however, was also rejected.[247] The court held that the compensation system is "designed to award the trustee reasonable compensation for the services rendered in each case."[248] The court reasoned that historically trustee's fees have always been judged on a reasonableness basis, with no guarantee of uniformity on a debtor-by-debtor basis. The court stated, " [r]easonableness, and not uniformity, is the criterion for expenses of administration."[249] While historically, that has been the approach, the court does not clearly address the "uniformity" requirement in the Constitution. The court also appears to mischaracterize the debtors' argument as demanding uniformity of cost, when in fact, the debtors argued that the present scheme was unconstitutional in that it did not provide a uniform percentage.

16.4.2.2.3 Avoiding the trustee commission for certain payments

Of significant importance to the family farmer is whether all payments are subject to the trustee's percentage commission. Section 586(e)(2) provides that the trustee is to collect her percentage fee from "all payments *received by such individual* [the trustee] *under plans* in the cases under chapter 12 or 13."[250] Some debtors have argued that if they make a payment directly to the creditor, without using the trustee, the trustee's percentage fee should not be assessed. Discussing this issue, the authors of *The Collier Farm Bankruptcy Guide* refer to the "logical inference" that the "trustee may not collect a percentage fee from payments

never received by the trustee but made directly by the debtor." *The Guide* also notes, however, that "[t]his language may have been overlooked by many of the cases."[251] This issue, referred to herein as the direct payment issue, has produced numerous reported decisions, with the result being three lines of cases with conflicting holdings.

One line of cases holds that a debtor is not allowed to make direct payments to impaired creditors, and therefore there is no option of using direct payments to avoid the trustee's fee.[252] However, even under this line of cases, a debtor would be allowed to make direct payments to an unimpaired creditor.[253] One case offered an extension of this approach in holding that a voluntary agreement with a creditor did not constitute an impaired claim for purposes of determining the trustee's fee. The court found that because the agreement was voluntary, and because the claim was not provided for in the plan, the debtor did not need to apply the trustee's percentage fee to payments made to that creditor.[254]

A second line of cases holds that although certain payments to impaired creditors can be made directly by the debtor, the trustee's fee must still be assessed on these payments.[255] A third line finds that direct payments to certain creditors with impaired claims can be made and that the trustees fees do not apply to these direct payments.[256] Providing for direct payments in the plan which may minimize the amount of the surcharge imposition is discussed at § 16.5.6.5, *infra*.

16.4.2.2.4 Does the trustee receive a fee on its fee?

Another trustee compensation issue producing significant litigation and causing a split in authority is whether the chapter 12 trustee should receive her ten percent commission only on payments made by the debtors to their creditors, or whether the ten percent fee also should be computed on the money paid to the trustee herself. It again turns on an interpretation of section 586(e), which provides that the trustee shall collect "such percentage fee from all payments received by such individual under plans in the cases under chapter 12 or 13 of title 11 for which such individual serves as standing trustee."[257]

245 *In re* Melita, 91 B.R. 358, 363 (Bankr. E.D. Pa. 1988); *In re* Sousa, 46 B.R. 343, 346, 347 (Bankr. D.R.I. 1985) ("effectively overruled" by *Savage*).
246 *In re* Westpfahl, 168 B.R. 337 (Bankr. C.D. Ill. 1994).
247 *Westpfahl*, 168 B.R. at 360.
248 *Id.*
249 *Id.*
250 28 U.S.C. § 586(e)(2) (emphasis added).
251 Randy Rogers & Lawrence P. King, The Collier Farm Bankruptcy Guide 4-71 (1994).
252 *See, e.g.,* Fulkrod v. Savage (*In re* Fulkrod), 973 F.2d 801 (9th Cir. 1992); *In re* C.A. Jackson Ranch Co., 181 B.R. 552 (Bankr. E.D. Okla. 1995).
253 *See, e.g., In re* Finkbine, 94 B.R. 461, 464 (Bankr. S.D. Ohio 1988).
254 *In re* Kosmicki, 161 B.R. 828 (Bankr. D. Neb. 1993).
255 *See, e.g., In re* Marriott, 161 B.R. 816 (Bankr. S.D. Ill. 1993).
256 *See, e.g.,* Michel v. Beard (*In re* Beard), 45 F.3d 113 (6th Cir. 1995); Wagner v. Armstrong (*In re* Armstrong), 36 F.3d 723 (8th Cir. 1994); *In re* McCann, 202 B.R. 824 (Bankr. N.D.N.Y. 1996); Westpfahl v. Clark (*In re* Westpfahl), 168 B.R. 337 (Bankr. C.D. Ill. 1994).
257 11 U.S.C. § 586(e).

The Tenth Circuit addressed this issue in *Foulston v. BDT Farms*.[258] The United States trustee's office argued that the standing trustee was to be paid an amount equal to ten percent of all money received by the trustee, that is, ten percent of the amount to be paid to creditors plus ten percent of the trustee's fee itself. This results in a trustee's fee of 11.1111%. The debtors argued that the trustee should receive fees in an amount equal to ten percent of the payments made under the plan to creditors. The Tenth Circuit reversed the lower courts, and gave deference under the *Chevron* standard to the interpretation of the United States trustee's office. The *BDT Farms* decision has received significant criticism and has been specifically rejected in the Eighth Circuit.[259]

16.4.2.3 Role of the Chapter 12 Trustee upon Removal of the Family Farmer As a Debtor-in-Possession

If the bankruptcy court removes the family farmer as the debtor-in-possession,[260] the chapter 12 trustee has all the powers of a chapter 7 trustee or trustee appointed in a chapter 11 case concerning continuation of the business operation.[261] Although in chapter 11 cases the appointment of a trustee usually signals the beginning of the end and eventual liquidation under chapter 11 or conversion to chapter 7, this need not be the case under chapter 12. The chapter 12 trustee can retain the debtor to service the farming operation, even if the debtor no longer makes management decisions. The clear viability of a farm operation is the most compelling argument for the trustee's appointment instead of dismissal.

However, unlike a chapter 11 trustee, a chapter 12 trustee cannot propose a chapter 12 plan.[262] This appears to preclude trustee proposed liquidating plans which have been permitted in some farmer chapter 11 cases.[263]

16.4.3 What Constitutes Property of the Estate

"Property of the estate" in chapter 12 cases is similar to that in chapter 13 cases.[264] In chapter 12, property of the estate subject to administration in the case includes, in addition to all of the debtor's property acquired pre-petition:

- All property which the debtor acquires after the commencement of the case but before the case is closed, dismissed, or converted to a case under chapter 7, whichever happens first;[265] and
- Earnings from services performed by the debtor after the commencement of the case but before the case is closed, dismissed or converted to a case under chapter 7, whichever occurs first.[266]

The debtor remains in possession of all his or her property, except under the following circumstances:

- If the debtor is removed as a debtor-in-possession;
- If a confirmed plan or order confirming a plan otherwise provides;
- If relief from the automatic stay is obtained which may allow removal of property from the debtor by state process; or
- If the debtor affirmatively abandons property pre-confirmation pursuant to section 554.

The property of an active family farmer's estate usually contains types of property with which an attorney who does not work primarily with farmers will be unfamiliar and may overlook. For example, the farmer may:

- Be entitled to payments under government programs;[267]
- Have crop or dairy base, crop allotments, or other price support entitlements which have value, and may be sold or increased;[268]
- Own shares in farmers' cooperatives;
- Participate in conservation, reforestation or loan programs with concomitant obligations for debtor performance;[269]

---

258 21 F.3d 1019 (10th Cir. 1994).

259 Pelofsky v. Wallace, 102 F.3d 350 (8th Cir. 1996). *See also In re* Westpfahl, 168 B.R. 337 (Bankr. C.D. Ill. 1994); *In re* Wallace, 167 B.R. 531 (Bankr. E.D. Mo. 1994); *cf.* Kathleen A. Laughron, *The Standing Chapter 13 Trustee's Percentage Fee: Solving Algebraic Equation*, 24 Creighton L. Rev. 823 (1991).

260 11 U.S.C. § 1204.

261 11 U.S.C. § 1202(b)(5). *See* § 16.3.3, *supra.*

262 *Compare* 11 U.S.C. § 1221 *with* 11 U.S.C. § 1321. Duties of the trustee under 11 U.S.C. § 1204(b)(5), incorporating duties of a debtor-in-possession as in chapter 11, specifically exclude the ability to file a plan as contained in 11 U.S.C. § 1106(a)(5).

263 *See* § 16.1.2, *supra.*

264 *Compare* 11 U.S.C. §§ 541, 1207 *with* 11 U.S.C. § 1306. *See* § 2.6, *supra.*

265 Included are post-petition inheritances and life insurance proceeds. *In re* Hart, 151 B.R. 84 (Bankr. W.D. Tex. 1993); *In re* Cook, 148 B.R. 273 (Bankr. W.D. Mich. 1992) (inheritances and lottery winnings); *In re* Martin, 130 B.R. 951 (Bankr. N.D. Iowa 1991); *In re* Cornell, 95 B.R. 219 (Bankr. W.D. Okla. 1989).

266 11 U.S.C. § 1207(a). *In re* White, 151 B.R. 247 (Bankr. D.N.M. 1993); *In re* Clark, 186 B.R. 249 (Bankr. W.D. Mo. 1995).

267 *E.g., In re* Winterroth, 97 B.R. 454 (Bankr. C.D. Ill. 1988) (PIK certificates). *See* FarmPro Services, Inc. v. Brown, 276 B.R. 620 (D.N.D. 2002) (property of the estate includes crop disaster payments received post-petition by Chapter 12 debtors); *In re* Boyett, 250 B.R. 817 (Bankr. S.D. Ga. 2000) (FSA payments under disaster relief program as property of the estate in chapter 7). *But see In re* Stallings, 290 B.R. 777 (Bankr. D. Idaho 2003) (disaster relief payment received post-petition under program that did not exist until after debtor filed bankruptcy was not property of the estate).

268 *See In re* Kocher, 78 B.R. 844 (Bankr. S.D. Ohio 1987).

269 *See In re* Bremer, 104 B.R. 999 (Bankr. W.D. Mo. 1989) (CRP payments and unharvested crops are property of the estate); *In*

• Be entitled to payments on contracts or rental arrangements due both pre- and post-petition.[270]

All may have value; all are property of the estate which must be accounted for in the debtor's schedules and for plan and confirmation purposes.

Where farmers have established corporate entities which have no independent identity from the individual farmer and where, under state law, the corporate form may be disregarded, the bankruptcy court may also ignore the corporate form and find assets transferred to such a corporation property of an individual debtor's estate.[271]

16.4.4 Exemptions, Lien Avoidance and Recapture Powers

16.4.4.1 Exemptions Available to Family Farmers Under Chapter 12

The exemptions available to individual family farmers under chapter 12 are the same as those available under other bankruptcy chapters.[272] Because most farm indebtedness has been incurred by both farmer and spouse, or has been cosigned by the spouse, many chapter 12 petitions will be joint petitions,[273] permitting the use of two sets of exemptions.[274] Moreover, most courts consider spouses who participate to some degree in the farming operation, either physically or as a record-keeper, a farmer for purposes of exemption.[275]

The fact that a farmer may have other occupations as well as farming does not preclude exemption and lien avoidance of farm implements as tools of trade.[276] In chapter 12, unlike

chapter 7 liquidation, this should not even arise as an issue because of the initial eligibility requirements for chapter 12 relief.

16.4.4.2 Exemptions for "Tools of Trade" and "Livestock"

The federal exemptions and almost all state-formulated exemptions provide protection for "tools of trade."[277] This category is of special interest to farmers, allowing exemption of the tools utilized in the farming operation.[278] In some cases, the exemptions provided by state law for this category of property may be broader and more advantageous than the federal exemption; in states where election between federal and state exemptions is permitted, this should be carefully considered. A minority of courts exempt farm implements as "tools of trade" only if they are smaller, hand-held tools,[279] but the majority view is that farm equipment and implements may be exempted under a functional or "use" test subject to dollar value limitations.[280]

A number of courts have addressed the issue of whether a tools of the trade exemption allows for the exemption of certain types of livestock. The Seventh Circuit did not allow the exemption of a dairy herd as well as a tractor, holding that large capital assets could not be tools of the trade; the exemption was limited to small items, "tools" in the ordinary sense.[281] But the Second Circuit has held that bulls used in a dairy operation fell under the Vermont state "tools

---

re Hunerdosse, 85 B.R. 999 (Bankr. S.D. Iowa 1988); *In re* Claeys, 81 B.R. 985 (Bankr. D.N.D. 1987); *In re* Dunning, 77 B.R. 789 (Bankr. D. Mont. 1987).

270 *In re* Winterroth, 97 B.R. 454 (Bankr. C.D. Ill. 1988).

271 *In re* Nielson, 97 B.R. 269 (Bankr. W.D.N.C. 1989).

272 11 U.S.C. § 522(b). *See* Ch. 10, *supra.* Exemptions are only available to the *individual* family farmer debtor, *not* "family farmers" in partnership or corporate form.

273 As allowed by 11 U.S.C. § 302.

274 11 U.S.C. § 522(b). Except where a state exemption, if chosen or if mandated, allows only one set of exemptions for joint petitioners. *See, e.g.,* Stevens v. Pike County Bank, 829 F.2d 693 (8th Cir. 1987) (Arkansas); *In re* Talmadge, 832 F.2d 1120 (9th Cir. 1987) (California).

275 *See, e.g., In re* Zimmel, 185 B.R. 786 (Bankr. D. Minn. 1995); *In re* Flake, 32 B.R. 360 (Bankr. W.D. Wis. 1983); *In re* Decker, 34 B.R. 640 (Bankr. N.D. Ind. 1983); *In re* Schroeder, 62 B.R. 604 (Bankr. D. Kan. 1986); Middleton v. Farmers State Bank, 45 B.R. 744 (Bankr. D. Minn. 1985); Thorp Credit & Thrift Co. v. Pommerer, 10 B.R. 935 (Bankr. D. Minn. 1981). *See also* Susan A. Schneider, *Who Owns the Family Farm: The Struggle to Determine the Property Rights of Farm Wives,* 14 N. Ill. U. L. Rev. 689 (1994). *Contra In re* Indvik, 118 B.R. 993 (Bankr. N.D. Iowa 1990).

276 *See, e.g., In re* Lampe, 278 B.R. 205 (B.A.P. 10th Cir. 2002); *In*

re Meadows, 75 B.R. 357 (W.D. Va. 1987); *In re* Smith, 78 B.R. 922 (Bankr. S.D. Iowa 1987); *In re* Weinbrenner, 53 B.R. 571 (Bankr. W.D. Wis. 1985); *In re* Rasmussen, 54 B.R. 965 (Bankr. W.D. Mo. 1985). *Contra In re* Samuel, 36 B.R. 312 (Bankr. E.D. Va. 1984). *See generally* §§ 10.2.2.7, 10.4.2.4, *supra,* and § 16.4.4.3, *infra.*

277 *See* § 10.2.2.7, *supra.*

278 Production Credit Ass'n of St. Cloud v. LaFond, 791 F.2d 623 (8th Cir. 1986); Augustine v. United States, 675 F.2d 582 (3d Cir. 1982); *In re* Hrncirik, 138 B.R. 835 (Bankr. N.D. Tex. 1992); *In re* Weinbrenner, 53 B.R. 571 (Bankr. W.D. Wis. 1985) (and cases cited therein); Middleton v. Farmers State Bank, 45 B.R. 744 (Bankr. D. Minn. 1985).

279 *See, e.g., In re* Patterson, 825 F.2d 1140 (7th Cir. 1987) (addressing exemption under federal 11 U.S.C. § 522(d) only); O'Neal v. United States, 20 B.R. 12 (Bankr. E.D. Mo. 1982); Yparrea v. Roswell Production Credit Ass'n, 16 B.R. 33 (Bankr. D.N.M. 1981).

280 Production Credit Ass'n of St. Cloud v. LaFond, 791 F.2d 623 (8th Cir. 1986); Augustine v. United States, 675 F.2d 582 (3d Cir. 1982); *In re* Mutchler, 95 B.R. 748 (Bankr. D. Mont. 1989); *In re* Duss, 79 B.R. 821 (Bankr. W.D. Wis. 1987); *In re* Schyma, 68 B.R. 52 (Bankr. D. Minn. 1985); *In re* Brzezinski, 65 B.R. 336 (Bankr. W.D. Wis. 1985) (farm function); *In re* Thompson, 82 B.R. 985 (Bankr. W.D. Wis. 1988); *In re* Liming, 22 B.R. 740 (Bankr. W.D. Okla. 1982), *rev'd sub nom.* Cent. Nat'l Bank & Trust Co. v. Liming, 797 F.2d 895 (10th Cir. 1986); *In re* Yoder, 32 B.R. 777 (Bankr. W.D. Pa. 1983).

281 *In re* Patterson, 825 F.2d 1140 (7th Cir. 1987).

of the trade" exemption.[282] Similarly, the Tenth Circuit has held that breeding stock could be "tools of the trade."[283]

Another federal and common state exemption of special interest to farmers is for livestock retained by the farmer for personal and family use, for example, consumption or production for the debtor and his or her dependents alone. The emphasis is upon the exclusive family use of the livestock. Livestock which is part of the farming operation in general thus cannot be exempted under this limited provision.[284]

16.4.4.3 Lien Avoidance Under Section 522(f) and the Family Farmer[285]

Section 522(f) lien avoidance provisions for exemptible property and tools of trade impaired by judicial liens and non-possessory, non-purchase money security interests are available for farmers under *all* bankruptcy chapters.[286] In many cases, a farmer will be able to recapture some farm equipment and reduce the amount of repayment to a secured creditor because a blanket non-purchase money interest covers the equipment.[287] Debtors may also be able to avoid liens under these provisions in proceeds after post-petition

sale of equipment.[288] Lien avoidance may also free property for needed sale or trade. Consequently it is important for the farmer's attorney to check security agreements and UCC filings to ascertain whether the security interest is purchase money.[289]

The 1994 amendments at 11 U.S.C. § 522(f)(3) appear to limit lien avoidance related to exempt tools of trade to $5000.00. However, as discussed in an earlier section, the application of this provision is limited by its peculiar wording.[290] A number of courts have held that the $5000.00 limitation does not apply to lien avoidance with respect to exemptions claimed pursuant to state law.[291]

Whenever possible chapter 12 lien avoidance should be undertaken at the outset of the case, because the avoidance of liens can have an effect upon the amount and nature of repayment to creditors and enhance feasibility.[292] However, the Code contains no time limit on such debtor action. In some jurisdictions avoidance of judicial liens may also be accomplished by valuations and provisions in the chapter 12 plan which reduce judgment creditors to unsecured creditors, provided all such creditors have notice of those provisions, an opportunity to object, and the plan is confirmed.[293]

16.4.4.4 Avoidance and Recapture Powers of the Family Farmer Debtor-in-Possession

16.4.4.4.1 In general

A chapter 12 debtor-in-possession has the same powers to avoid liens and recapture property as trustees under chapter 7 and 11 and debtors-in-possession under chapter 11.[294] These avoidance and recapture abilities are analyzed elsewhere in this manual.[295] This subsection concentrates on

---

282　Parrotte v. Sensenich (*In re* Parrotte), 22 F.3d 472 (2d Cir. 1994).

283　*In re* Heape, 886 F.2d 280, 283 (10th Cir. 1989).

284　*In re* Thompson, 750 F.2d 628 (8th Cir. 1984); Patterson v. Abbotsford State Bank, 64 B.R. 120 (W.D. Wis. 1986), *aff'd*, 825 F.2d 1140 (7th Cir. 1987); *In re* Wiford, 105 B.R. 992 (Bankr. N.D. Okla. 1989); *In re* Meadows, 75 B.R. 357 (W.D. Va. 1987); *In re* Simmons, 86 B.R. 160 (Bankr. S.D. Iowa 1988); *In re* Duss, 79 B.R. 821 (Bankr. W.D. Wis. 1987) (hay not household good or tool of trade for exemption purposes); *In re* Eakes, 69 B.R. 497 (Bankr. W.D. Mo. 1987); *In re* Sticha, 60 B.R. 717 (Bankr. D. Minn. 1986); *In re* Newbury, 70 B.R. 1 (Bankr. D. Kan. 1985); *In re* Yoder, 32 B.R. 777 (Bankr. W.D. Pa. 1983). *See In re* Wilson, 738 So. 2d 17 (La. 1999) (answering question certified by the Court of Appeals for the Fifth Circuit, 162 F.3d 378 (1998), the state Supreme Court applied a functional test; animals used for farm work such as a draft horse may be exempt, but animals which produce the product of the farming operation such as dairy cows are not). *Contra In re* Cook, 66 B.R. 3 (Bankr. W.D. Wis. 1985) (cows specialized tools of trade with hay to feed for one year); *In re* Walkington, 42 B.R. 67 (Bankr. W.D. Mich. 1984) (dairy cattle as tools of trade).

285　For a more complete discussion of these lien avoidance provisions, see § 10.4.2, *supra*.

286　Augustine v. United States, 675 F.2d 582 n. 3 (3d Cir. 1982); *In re* Currie, 34 B.R. 745 (D. Kan. 1983); *In re* Simmons, 86 B.R. 160 (Bankr. S.D. Iowa 1988); *In re* Hunerdosse, 85 B.R. 999 (Bankr. S.D. Iowa 1988); *In re* Dykstra, 80 B.R. 128 (Bankr. N.D. Iowa 1987) (chapter 12); *In re* Ptacek, 78 B.R. 986 (Bankr. D.N.D. 1987) (chapter 12). *But see* Farmers State Bank of Oakley v. Schroeder, 62 B.R. 604 (Bankr. D. Kan. 1986).

287　Production Credit Ass'n of St. Cloud v. LaFond, 791 F.2d 623 (8th Cir. 1986) (chapter 7); *In re* Hall, 752 F.2d 582 (11th Cir. 1985) (chapter 13); *In re* Thompson, 750 F.2d 628 (8th Cir. 1984) (chapter 11); *In re* Ptacek, 78 B.R. 986 (Bankr. D.N.D. 1987). *See* § 10.4.2.4, *supra*. However, lien avoidance is tied to exemptibility and only individual family farmers, not corporate or partnership family farmers, can utilize this variety of lien avoidance.

288　*In re* Brzezinski, 65 B.R. 336 (Bankr. W.D. Wis. 1985).

289　The typical security interest taken by Farmers Home Administration is a good example of a blanket security interest which usually is largely non-purchase money, non-possessory. Sovereign immunity does not apply to the federal government for lien avoidance. 11 U.S.C. § 106; Flick v. United States, 47 B.R. 440 (W.D. Pa. 1985).

290　*See* § 10.4.2.4, *supra*; *In re* Zimmel, 185 B.R. 786 (Bankr. D. Minn. 1995).

291　*See, e.g., In re* Ehlen, 202 B.R. 742 (Bankr. W.D. Wis. 1996); *In re* Zimmel, 185 B.R. 786 (Bankr. D. Minn. 1995).

292　One court has allowed the effect of § 522(f) lien avoidance to take place only upon entry of discharge in the chapter 12 case. *In re* Simmons, 86 B.R. 160 (Bankr. S.D. Iowa 1988); *In re* Hunerdosse, 85 B.R. 999 (Bankr. S.D. Iowa 1988). Failure to reserve rights to pursue lien avoidance in negotiated settlements incorporated into chapter 12 plans might result in their loss. *In re* Wickersheim, 107 B.R. 177 (Bankr. E.D. Wis. 1989).

293　*See* § 10.4.2.4, *supra*.

294　11 U.S.C. § 1203; *In re* Teigen, 123 B.R. 887 (Bankr. D. Mont. 1991). *See also* 8 Collier on Bankruptcy ¶ 1203.02[2] (15th ed. rev.). *See generally* Jackson, *Avoiding Powers in Bankruptcy*, 36 Stanford L. Rev. 725 (Feb. 1984).

295　*See* § 10.4.2.6, *supra*.

avoidance and recapture issues of special interest to farmers. It should be remembered that, unlike the situation in consumer bankruptcies, because the family farmer is characterized as a debtor-in-possession, transfers and liens can be avoided for the benefit of the chapter 12 estate without regard to the voluntariness of the transfer or the exemptibility of the property involved.[296]

However, where a debtor has pledged property to enable use of cash collateral during the pendency of chapter 12 case, it may be subsequently impermissible to recapture that property by a form of lien avoidance.[297]

16.4.4.4.2 Recovery of property as a fraudulent transfer[298]

In limited circumstances, farm land which has been lost by forced sale can be recaptured under section 548(a)(2) if its transfer was made for less than reasonably equivalent value; *and*:

- The debtor was insolvent or made insolvent by the transfer;[299] *or*
- The debtor was engaged in business or was about to engage in business or a transaction for which any property remaining with the debtor was an unreasonably small capital;[300] *or*
- The debtor intended to incur debt that would be beyond the debtor's ability to pay.[301]

Section 548(a)(2) embraces pledges for security as well as direct transfers. Transfers can be avoided only if they occurred less than one year pre-petition.[302]

Unfortunately, in *BFP v. Resolution Trust Co.*,[303] the Supreme Court ruled that the price obtained at a "regularly

conducted, non-collusive foreclosure sale is conclusive as to the value of the property." The court concluded that reasonably equivalent value must take into account the circumstances of the transfer, that is, that the property is subject to a forced sale.

In light of *BFP*, section 548 now holds less promise for farmers who have lost property to foreclosure. Attorneys should still evaluate, however, whether a sale was irregular or collusive in some way in order to avoid the application of the court's ruling. Irregularities in the conduct of the sale deprive the foreclosure sale price of its conclusive force under section 548(a)(2)(A) and *BFP*,[304] and may therefore render the transfer avoidable as a fraudulent conveyance "if the price received was not reasonably equivalent to the property's actual value at the time of the sale (which we [the Court] think would be the price that would have been received if the foreclosure sale had proceeded according to law)."[305]

Examples of irregularities in the conduct of the sale include the failure to adequately notice a postponed sale, or to properly advertise the sale, or any other action which discourages competitive bidding at the sale.[306] Collusion may be shown where the lender has an agreement with the purchaser or with potential bidders which is contrary to the interest of the borrower. Under state law, a trustee under a deed of trust, or a mortgagee under a mortgage, has a duty to exercise good faith and diligence in the conducting a foreclosure sale of property.[307] The mortgagee or trustee must remain at arm's length with the buyer,[308] must conduct the sale fairly and limit expenses within reasonable bounds,[309] and must exert reasonable effort to obtain a fair price.[310]

Another open issue is whether the Court's decision in *BFP* applies to forced sales other than foreclosures and to forced transfers which do not involve a sale such as tax sales in many states. The Court's ruling in *BFP* is seemingly inapplicable to this latter type of transfer, because there is no sale by which the "reasonably equivalent value" can be established.[311]

In those limited circumstances where recapture is possible, counsel must weigh the possibility of setting aside the

---

296 *Compare* 11 U.S.C. §§ 522(g), (h).

297 *In re* Gilbert, 147 B.R. 801 (Bankr. W.D. Okla. 1992).

298 *See also* § 10.4.2.6.5, *supra*.

299 11 U.S.C. § 548(a)(2)(B)(i). Insolvency is a modified balance sheet test. *See* 11 U.S.C. § 101(32). In most cases there is no contest concerning the debtor's insolvency; it is readily apparent from the schedules and circumstances. However, where it is not readily apparent, the debtor-in-possession can either demonstrate that the debtor was insolvent at the time of transfer or show such insolvency existed before and after the transfer by retrogression. *See, e.g.,* Kanasky v. Randolph, 27 B.R. 953 (Bankr. D. Conn. 1983). However, it must be remembered that any debt satisfaction by the transfer must be subtracted from the debtor's liabilities for the balance sheet test of insolvency pursuant to 11 U.S.C. § 548(d)(2)(A).

300 11 U.S.C. § 548(a)(2)(B)(ii); *see, e.g.,* Jacobson v. First State Bank of Benson, 48 B.R. 497 (Bankr. D. Minn. 1985).

301 11 U.S.C. § 548(a)(2)(B)(iii).

302 11 U.S.C. § 548(a); unless the state has a similar statute with a longer recapture period which can be utilized by the debtor-in-possession. In the case of a foreclosure where a redemption time is granted by statute, the one year period runs from the time of foreclosure, not the end of redemption. *In re* Hulm, 738 F.2d 323 (8th Cir. 1984).

303 511 U.S. 531, 114 S. Ct. 1757, 128 L. Ed. 2d 556 (1994). *See generally* § 10.4.2.6.5, *supra*.

304 128 L. Ed. 2d at 569.

305 *Id*.

306 *See In re* Bundles, 856 F.2d 815, 824 (7th Cir. 1988).

307 Mills v. Mut. Bldg. & Loan Ass'n, 6 S.E.2d 549 (N.C. 1940).

308 Holman v. Ryon, 56 F.2d 307, 61 App. D.C. 10 (1932) (sale by trustee to his wife at less than adequate price is breach of duty).

309 *See* Am. Jur. 2d *Mortgages* § 758.

310 White v. MacQueen, 360 Ill. 236, 195 N.E. 832 (1935); Harper v. Interstate Brewery Co., 168 Or. 26, 120 P.2d 757 (1942). At least one court has borrowed the U.C.C. standard of commercially reasonable and has applied it to foreclosure sales where the foreclosing lender sought a deficiency judgment, Wansley v. First Nat'l Bank of Vicksburg, 566 So. 2d 1218 (Miss. 1990).

311 *E.g., In re* Grady, 202 B.R. 120 (Bankr. N.D. Iowa 1996) (*BFP* does not apply to forfeiture of real estate installment sales contract); *In re* Butler, 171 B.R. 321 (Bankr. N.D. Ill. 1994). *But see In re* McGrath, 170 B.R. 78 (Bankr. D.N.J. 1994) (applying *BFP* analysis to tax sales).

transfer against the ability of the debtor to make debt service under a chapter 12 plan thereafter.[312]

16.4.4.4.3 Preferential transfers[313]

Several kinds of transfers to farm creditors may be preferential, subject to recapture under section 547(b). Recovery of preferences can provide the farmer with needed working capital, can redistribute the debtor's assets more equitably among creditors, or can go to satisfy secured debts. Payments made to under-secured creditors, where it can be demonstrated that the payments were applied to the unsecured portion of the indebtedness, are recoverable.[314] In addition, the debtor can avoid as preferences extra security added to a loan within ninety days prior to the bankruptcy filing. For example, there may be a preference where a creditor adds as security government benefits due the farmer, but not in existence until the ninety-day preference period.[315] Post-petition transfers may also be recovered by the chapter 12 trustee.[316]

"Insider creditors" are vulnerable for recapture for transfers made for a full year before the bankruptcy filing.[317] For the debtor who chooses to pay relatives who are classified as insiders before his or her regular creditors, the sweep of the insider provision may pose a dilemma of whether the debtor-in-possession should pursue family members for payment, particularly in light of the duty to maximize the estate and treat creditors with an even hand.

The Code lists a number of examples of insider creditors, including persons who have control of the debtor's business.[318] The examples of insider creditors given in the Code are not exclusive,[319] and the Code's legislative history is

helpful: "An insider is one who has a sufficiently close relationship with the debtor that his conduct is made subject to closer scrutiny than those dealing at arms length with the debtor."[320]

Depending on the circumstances, there is an argument that a particular federal agency farm creditor may be characterized as an insider creditor in a farm bankruptcy.[321] Control, for purposes of an insider creditor, means the ability to keep the debtor from acting as well as being able to cause a debtor to act.[322] The close relationship and degree of control exercised by federal agencies with regard to its borrowers can be stunning. Farm Service Agency regulations, for example, set out such control as including: management assistance and supervision of borrowers, direct supervision and continuing analysis of borrower operations in both farm and non-farm activities, supervised bank accounts from which disbursements must be approved and countersigned by FmHA, approval of what creditors to pay from the proceeds of the farm operation, and planning of the current and future operations of borrowers through periodic review, counseling, and preparation of plans and forms.[323]

16.4.4.4.4 Avoidance of improperly perfected security interests

The strong-arm powers of a trustee, applicable to a chapter 12 debtor-in-possession, are discussed elsewhere in this manual.[324] Farmer attorneys are well advised to check a creditor's security interest to determine its bona fide coverage. Security interests which are unperfected prior to filing are avoidable and property can be recovered for use in the estate.[325] As discussed below,[326] creditors may take certain government program benefits as collateral, but the creditor may lose this security to the estate unless the creditor properly characterizes the collateral in the relevant security instruments.[327]

---

312 If the transfer can be avoided, then the underlying note can be deaccelerated for plan treatment. A transfer can be avoided as a whole, although a portion of the property, if appropriate, can be returned to the creditor for debt reduction. However, it is self-defeating to plan to recover the property only to determine that a feasible plan for repayment is not possible.

313 *See generally* § 10.4.2.6.4, *supra.*

314 Small v. Williams, 313 F.2d 29 (4th Cir. 1963); Azar v. Morgan, 301 F.2d 78 (5th Cir. 1962); Mazer v. Aetna Fin. Co., 6 B.R. 449 (Bankr. D.N.M. 1980). Generally, payments are first applied to the unsecured portion of an under-secured debt, but proof of where payments were applied will be necessary where there is cross-collateralization. United States v. Beattie, 31 B.R. 703 (Bankr. W.D.N.C. 1984). However, pre-petition set-offs which have arisen under government liens may not always be regarded as preferential and therefore avoidable. *See, e.g., In re* Stall, 125 B.R. 754 (Bankr. S.D. Ohio 1991); *In re* Remillong, 131 B.R. 727 (Bankr. D. Mont. 1991). *Contra In re* Hankerson, 133 B.R. 711 (Bankr. E.D. Pa. 1991).

315 *In re* Lemley Estate Bus. Trust, 65 B.R. 185 (Bankr. N.D. Tex. 1986).

316 11 U.S.C. § 549. *See In re* Martin, 78 B.R. 599 (Bankr. D. Mont. 1987). *See generally* § 10.4.2.6.6, *supra.*

317 11 U.S.C. § 547(b)(4)(B).

318 11 U.S.C. § 101(31).

319 11 U.S.C. § 102(3); Loftis v. Minar, 4 Collier Bankr. Cas. 2d (MB) 362 (Bankr. D.N.J. 1981).

320 H.R. Rep. No. 95-595, at 25 (1978); S. Rep. No. 95-989, at 312 (1978).

321 Carlson v. Farmers Home Admin., 744 F.2d 621 (8th Cir. 1984) (although FmHA not deemed an insider creditor in that case, it was strictly for lack of factual showing); *see also* United States v. Beattie, 31 B.R. 703 (Bankr. W.D.N.C. 1984) (where the issue was raised but not determined).

322 *In re* Colesville Med. Ctr., Ltd., 6 Collier Bankr. Cas. 2d (MB) 736 (Bankr. D. Md. 1982); Note, *The Term Insider Within § 547(b)(4)(B) of the Bankruptcy Code*, 57 Notre Dame Law. 726 (1982).

323 *See, e.g.,* 7 C.F.R. §§ 1902, 1924.51–1924.60, 1924.74; *see also* Farm and Home Plans and Forms 1962-1.

324 *See generally* §§ 10.4.2.6.2, 10.4.2.6.3, *supra.*

325 11 U.S.C. §§ 544, 545. *See, e.g., In re* Marshall, 239 B.R. 193 (Bankr. S.D. Ill. 1999) (landlord's statutory lien on crops found avoidable); *In re* Hartman, 102 B.R. 90 (Bankr. N.D. Tex. 1989); *In re* Ladd, 106 B.R. 174 (Bankr. C.D. Ill. 1989).

326 *See* § 16.5.3.2, *infra.*

327 For example, some courts have found government program payments under the PIK program to be general intangibles, not

16.4.4.4.5 Redemption and cure

After the commencement of a bankruptcy case, there is a breathing spell when all deadlines are temporarily suspended, and when the debtor-in-possession is given an opportunity to examine the estate, its assets, and any choses in action. Section 108(b) provides that if applicable law, order or agreement fixes the time within which the debtor may file a pleading, demand, notice, proof of claim or loss, cure a default, or perform any similar act, *and* that period has not expired before the filing of the debtor's petition, the debtor-in-possession has sixty additional days from the bankruptcy order for relief to act, unless the time period for acting under other applicable, non-bankruptcy law is longer. If the period under the non-bankruptcy law is longer than sixty days, the debtor-in-possession must act within the time allowed by that law and section 108(b) will not operate to extend the period for performance.

However, if the time for performing the act has expired prior to the filing of the bankruptcy petition, the bankruptcy case will not revive any right forfeited by inaction; section 108(b) will not operate to extend or recreate any right to perform.[328] Consequently, many bankruptcies are short-circuited by the lapse of rights before counsel is consulted and before the petition is filed.

Section 108(b)'s operation is automatic and does not require the debtor-in-possession to take affirmative action to initiate the sixty day period. However, extensions of time for performance beyond the sixty day period are limited.

Chapter 12 allows the debtor to cure defaults through the plan.[329] However, for most courts this curing assumes that the debtor retains both legal title and the equity of redemption, that is, that the debtor-in-possession is still in possession of the property—actually or constructively—and has the right through his or her equity of redemption to cure the default. Once the legal title to the property is surrendered, by foreclosure, repossession or reclamation, a debtor's equity of redemption can cease, and it is replaced by a statutory redemptive right; the existence of a right of redemption is determined by state law.

Many northern farm states have relatively long redemption times (up to a year) for a farmer to redeem his or her farmstead after foreclosure by payment of the foreclosure bid price plus interest. Tax redemption times vary, but may run for several years. Other jurisdictions have severely restricted redemption times or none at all.[330] Federal creditors may not be subject to the extended redemption times of state law.[331]

In this situation, section 108(b) provides additional debtor rights because bankruptcy courts allow debtors to use section 108(b) to redeem collateral, treating this as "curing of default," as allowed by that section.[332] Some courts have taken the view that statutory redemption can be effectuated over the life of a plan and that the debt can be deaccelerated and cured thereunder, leaving only lien rights in the foreclosing creditor or purchaser at foreclosure.[333] Earlier cases also found that section 362(a), rather than 108(b), was applicable and automatically stayed the running of redemptive periods,[334] or that under the proper circumstances a bankruptcy court could use its broad equitable powers under section 105 to extend redemption times.[335] However, the Eighth Circuit has ruled in *Johnson v. First Nat'l Bank of Montevideo*[336] that redemption after foreclosure, as contrasted with deacceleration before foreclosure, requires cure within the compressed time frame of section 108(b).[337]

If redemption is limited to the section 108(b) time frame, performance may be impossible, because refinancing for a chapter 12 debtor of major debt will rarely be forthcoming. Where the redemption can be satisfied by the value of one parcel of land or a portion of land where several parcels have been foreclosed, the bankruptcy court can satisfy the se-

---

proceeds. A financing statement which failed to reserve a security interest in general intangibles, although expressly including proceeds, would be insufficient and the creditor's security interest unperfected. *See* § 16.5.3.2, *infra*; *In re* Ladd, 106 B.R. 174 (Bankr. C.D. Ill. 1989); *In re* Winterroth, 97 B.R. 454 (Bankr. C.D. Ill. 1988); *In re* Kingsley, 73 B.R. 767 (Bankr. D.N.D. 1987); *In re* Bindl, 13 B.R. 148 (Bankr. W.D. Wis. 1982).

328 *See, e.g., In re* Tynan, 773 F.2d 177 (7th Cir. 1985); *In re* Glenn, 760 F.2d 1428 (6th Cir. 1985) (chapter 13); *In re* Heiserman, 78 B.R. 899 (Bankr. C.D. Ill. 1987).

329 11 U.S.C. §§ 1222(b)(2), 1222(b)(3), and (b)(5).

330 Compare the state-mandated redemption times of Minnesota and North Dakota of one year post-foreclosure with the southern statutes in Sun Bank/Suncoast v. Constr. Leasing & Inv. Corp., 20 B.R. 546 (Bankr. M.D. Fla. 1982). Most states also have redemption times which occur after tax lien sales.

331 *See, e.g.,* United States v. Great Plains Gasification Associates, 813 F.2d 193 (8th Cir. 1987); United States v. Elverud, 640 F. Supp. 692 (D.N.D. 1986).

332 *See, e.g.,* Gen. Motors Acceptance Corp. v. English, 20 B.R. 877 (Bankr. E.D. Pa. 1982).

333 Most cases involve personal property. *See* Associates Commercial Corp. v. Attinello, 38 B.R. 609 (Bankr. E.D. Pa. 1984); Robinson v. Ford Motor Corp., 36 B.R. 35 (Bankr. E.D. Ark. 1983); Gen. Motors Acceptance Corp. v. Radden, 35 B.R. 821 (Bankr. E.D. Va. 1983); *In re* Montgomery, 29 B.R. 609 (Bankr. E.D.N.C. 1983). At least one case so far decided under chapter 12 has intimated that redemptive cure might be possible if a plan is proposed and confirmation had before expiration of the redemptive period, proposing restructure under §§ 1222(b)(2), 1222(b)(5) and 1222(b)(9), although it was not possible in that case because of redemptive time expiration. *See In re* Monfortson, 75 B.R. 121 (Bankr. D. Mont. 1987).

334 *See, e.g.,* Moratzka v. Lanesboro State Bank, 8 B.R. 371 (Bankr. D. Minn. 1981).

335 First Nat'l Bank of Montevideo v. Johnson, 19 B.R. 651 (Bankr. D. Minn. 1982).

336 719 F.2d 270 (8th Cir. 1983). *See also In re* Smith, 85 F.3d 1555 (11th Cir. 1996); *In re* Martinson, 731 F.2d 542 (8th Cir. 1984); *In re* Monfortson, 75 B.R. 121 (Bankr. D. Mont. 1987); *In re* Liddell, 75 B.R. 41 (Bankr. D. Mont. 1987). See also cases cited above.

337 More cases and an extended discussion of this issue can be found in National Consumer Law Center, Repossessions and Foreclosures § 20.2 (5th ed. 2002 and Supp.).

cured creditor with return of collateral in such amount as satisfies the creditor's claim.[338]

One interesting prospect is the use of cash collateral for redemption. With approval of the bankruptcy court, if cash collateral is freed early in the bankruptcy, redemption of property necessary for reorganization may be effectuated with a portion of that cash. A replacement lien as contemplated by section 1205(b)(2) can be offered the creditor as adequate protection for use of cash collateral, as the equipment redeemed will be free of lien.

16.4.5 The Automatic Stay and Codebtor Stay in Chapter 12 Cases

16.4.5.1 The Automatic Stay

The automatic stay[339] applies in all respects to chapter 12 cases.[340] Violation of the automatic stay may be addressed by motion under section 362(h) which provides for actual damages, costs and attorney fees as well as punitive damages in appropriate cases or by contempt proceedings and the power of the court under the omnibus provisions of 11 U.S.C. § 105.[341] In recent years, as discussed elsewhere in this manual, questions of sovereign immunity have complicated liability of government creditors for violating the stay. However, for the most part government violations should be subject to the contempt power of the court, with liability for any resultant costs and damages.[342]

The automatic stay is invaluable in stopping foreclosure actions, a primary source of farmer crisis. Because, as a practical matter, the beginning of the foreclosure process alerts other creditors in rural communities to a farmer's problems, who will often immediately move to repossess, attach, levy or set-off, the power of the automatic stay

accompanying chapter 12 filing *before* the eleventh hour can prevent unnecessary—and sometimes irreversible—complications.

16.4.5.2 The Codebtor Stay

The chapter 12 stay for codebtors of family farmers is drawn verbatim from the chapter 13 codebtor stay.[343] The chapter 12 stay is limited to consumer debts not incurred in the ordinary course of a farmer's business, and lasts only so long as the chapter 12 case is active.[344]

Where the stay is lifted to allow pursuit of a codebtor for repayment, the court may subrogate the claim to avoid overpayment and allow the codebtor to stand in the place of the original creditor for payment for the chapter 12 debtor to the extent the debt is paid by the codebtor.[345]

Where motivation for a loan or guarantee/cosigning is for business profit, such as continuation of the family farming operation, and/or the collateral is farm land, that cannot be considered a debt within the protection of the section 1201 codebtor stay.[346] By definition, a family farm corporation cannot incur consumer debt because all debt is of a corporate nature.[347] It may be possible to utilize 11 U.S.C. § 105 to attempt to extend a stay to codebtors where it is essential to the successful reorganization of the debtor, but courts have been reluctant to do so.[348] Absent payment, or a binding provision in a confirmed plan relieving codebtors of liability, valid claims against non-filing codebtors will survive the bankruptcy to the extent that they are not paid.[349]

Upon a creditor's motion to lift the codebtor stay there will be an automatic termination of the codebtor stay without further hearing[350] unless the debtor opposes the motion, in writing within twenty days after the creditor files its motion. Debts with codebtors may be broken out into a separate class or classes for different treatment from general unsecured or secured debts in a chapter 12 plan.[351]

---

338 Chapter 12 specifically contemplates this whole or partial surrender for claim satisfaction. 11 U.S.C. §§ 1222(b)(8) and 1225(a)(5)(C); *In re* B & G Farms, Inc., 82 B.R. 549 (Bankr. D. Mont. 1988); *In re* Indreland, 77 B.R. 268 (Bankr. D. Mont. 1987); *In re* Mikkelsen Farms, Inc., 74 B.R. 280 (Bankr. D. Or. 1987); *In re* O'Farrell, 74 B.R. 421 (Bankr. N.D. Fla. 1987); *In re* Massengill, 73 B.R. 1008 (Bankr. E.D.N.C. 1987); *In re* Lauck, 76 B.R. 717 (Bankr. D. Neb. 1987); *In re* Rott, 73 B.R. 366 (Bankr. D.N.D. 1987).

339 11 U.S.C. § 362(h).

340 11 U.S.C. § 103(a). For a general discussion of the automatic stay, see Chapter 9, *supra*.

341 See § 9.6, *supra*, for discussion of enforcement of the stay and the relationship of section 362(h) to the contempt power.

342 *See* §§ 9.6, 13.3.2.2, *supra*. *In re* Hazelton, 85 B.R. 400 (Bankr. E.D. Mich. 1988), *rev'd*, 96 B.R. 111 (E.D. Mich. 1988); *In re* Ketelsen, 78 B.R. 573 (Bankr. D.S.D. 1987), *aff'd in part and rev'd in part*, 104 B.R. 242 (D.S.D. 1988), *aff'd*, 880 F.2d 990 (9th Cir. 1989); *In re* Woloschak Farms, 74 B.R. 261 (Bankr. N.D. Ohio 1987); *In re* Rinehart, 76 B.R. 746 (Bankr. D.S.D. 1987), *aff'd*, 88 B.R. 1014 (D.S.D. 1988), *aff'd sub nom.* Small Bus. Admin. v. Rinehart, 887 F.2d 165 (8th Cir. 1989) (chapter 11).

343 *Compare* 11 U.S.C. § 1202 *with* 11 U.S.C. § 1301. *See* § 9.4.4, *infra*.

344 11 U.S.C. § 1201(a)(1), (a)(2).

345 *In re* Binstock, 78 B.R. 994 (Bankr. D.N.D. 1987).

346 *In re* Smith, 189 B.R. 11 (Bankr. C.D. Ill. 1995); *In re* SWF, Inc., 83 B.R. 27 (Bankr. S.D. Cal. 1988); *In re* Bigalk, 75 B.R. 561 (Bankr. D. Minn. 1987); *In re* Circle Five, Inc., 75 B.R. 686 (Bankr. D. Idaho 1987).

347 *In re* SWF, Inc., 83 B.R. 27 (Bankr. S.D. Cal. 1988); *In re* Circle Five, Inc., 75 B.R. 686 (Bankr. D. Idaho 1987).

348 *In re* Circle Five, Inc., 75 B.R. 686 (Bankr. D. Idaho 1987); *In re* River Family Farms, Inc., 85 B.R. 816 (Bankr. N.D. Iowa 1987) (discussion of showing necessary for preliminary injunctive relief under § 105).

349 *In re* Lazy D Diamond Ranch, Inc., 4 Fed. Appx. 418 (9th Cir. 2001).

350 11 U.S.C. § 1201(d).

351 11 U.S.C. § 1222(b)(1). *See* 11 U.S.C. § 1322(b)(1); § 12.4.2, *supra*.

16.4.5.3 Grounds for Stay Relief and Adequate Protection[352]

The grounds for stay relief under section 362(d) are applicable to cases under chapter 12:

- Lack of adequate protection or other cause; and
- Lack of equity coupled with a finding that the property at issue is not necessary for effective reorganization and rehabilitation of the debtor.

Lack of adequate protection has been the easiest grounds for a secured creditor to assert to obtain stay relief, or at minimum to obtain payment from debtors pre-confirmation. Two factors in chapter 12 have made this creditor assertion more difficult: (1) the time from filing to plan promulgation and confirmation is short, so that the court is not as concerned with prejudice to the creditor by passage of time; and (2) the concept of adequate protection for creditors has been altered by section 1205.

Adequate protection in section 1205 is tied to the concept of diminution in value of the collateral, rather than complete benefit of that secured creditor's bargain, so that the threshold which the debtor must meet to retain property in the face of an adequate protection argument for stay relief is smaller.

At its outer limit adequate protection requires the fair rental value of the property at issue; however, property which is stable in value may require no further protection.[353] Standing alone and absent true prejudice, failure to make post-petition mortgage payments prior to confirmation will not be sufficient cause for stay relief, given section 1208 and the short time frame for chapter 12 plan promulgation.[354]

However, there are other issues which may be placed under the adequate protection umbrella which can lead to stay relief. Most prominent in farmer cases is the misuse or failure to get permission to use cash collateral.[355] Similarly, conversion of collateral during the pendency of the case is grounds for stay relief.

The other approach of the secured creditor is to show a lack of equity in the collateral, but that showing *must* be coupled with a showing that the property is not necessary for an effective reorganization and rehabilitation of the debtor.[356]

In most family farmer cases, there will be a lack of equity in the property at issue when considered as a whole. However, equity must be evaluated as it applies to an individual creditor by its position as to collateral. For example, a creditor with a first lien of $50,000.00 upon property worth $200,000.00, where there is also a second lien for $170,000.00, may be protected by an equity cushion, although the second lienholder is under-secured.[357] One court has concluded that in no instance can lack of equity for stay relief be demonstrated in a chapter 12 case because of its cramdown provisions.[358]

The demonstration that the property is not necessary for the reorganization of the debtor can subsume the showing that the debtor is not capable of reorganization without liquidation, as well as the lack of need for the property for the farming operation and reorganization.[359]

Whether the property is necessary for the farming operation may depend upon whether the property is an intrinsic part of the farming operation or whether comparable property can be rented or procured for equal or less expenditure.[360] The debtor should attempt to demonstrate both the role of the property in the farming operation and its advantage upon retention. The debtor should also probably address the feasibility of the chapter 12 plan, although on stay motion that showing need not be as extensive as that required for confirmation. To that end, a showing of feasibility with cash flows, projections, and farm history may be required. However, because of the short time frame for confirmation, the consideration of stay relief may be deferred until confirmation.[361]

The final ground for relief from the automatic stay is "cause," a catch-all category for both unsecured and secured creditors showing equitable grounds for relief. Stay relief may be granted after confirmation for plan default affecting secured creditors.[362] Stay relief may be granted an individual creditor for grounds which might also militate for

---

352 *See generally* § 9.7, *supra.*

353 11 U.S.C. § 1205. The concept that an equity cushion can provide adequate protection is applicable to 11 U.S.C. § 361 as well as § 1205. *In re* Novak, 95 B.R. 24 (Bankr. E.D.N.Y. 1989).

354 *In re* Novak, 95 B.R. 24 (Bankr. E.D.N.Y. 1989).

355 *See, e.g., In re* Williams, 61 B.R. 567 (Bankr. N.D. Tex. 1986); *In re* Krisle, 54 B.R. 330 (Bankr. D.S.D. 1985).

356 *In re* Glenn, 181 B.R. 105 (Bankr. E.D. Okla. 1995); *In re* Gore, 113 B.R. 504 (Bankr. E.D. Ark. 1989); *In re* Lewis, 83 B.R. 682 (Bankr. W.D. Mo. 1988). A showing of lack of equity alone is not sufficient. *See, e.g., In re* W.S. Sheppley & Co., 45 B.R. 473 (Bankr. D. Iowa 1984).

357 *In re* Lewis, 83 B.R. 682 (Bankr. W.D. Mo. 1988); *In re* Jug End in the Berkshires, Inc., 46 B.R. 892 (Bankr. D. Mass. 1985).

358 *In re* Lewis, 83 B.R. 682 (Bankr. W.D. Mo. 1988).

359 *In re* Shouse, 95 B.R. 470 (Bankr. W.D. Ky. 1988); *In re* Liona Corp., 68 B.R. 761 (Bankr. E.D. Pa. 1987). *Contra In re* Mellor, 734 F.2d 1396 (9th Cir. 1984); *In re* Hutton 45 B.R. 558 (Bankr. D.N.D. 1984); Trina-Dee, Inc., 26 B.R. 152 (Bankr. E.D. Pa. 1983).

360 The showing is that the property will contribute to the reorganization, but need not be that it is irreplaceable. *In re* Saypol, 31 B.R. 796 (Bankr. S.D.N.Y. 1983). The leasing of a family farm in years previous to the bankruptcy can demonstrate lack of need for reorganization. *In re* Hutton, 45 B.R. 558 (Bankr. D.N.D. 1984).

361 A plan must be proposed within ninety days of filing under chapter 12 (absent extensions); confirmation must be held not less than forty-five days thereafter. However, courts have granted stay relief pre-confirmation for lack of good faith and lack of feasibility. *In re* Ouverson, 79 B.R. 830 (Bankr. N.D. Iowa 1987); *In re* Welsh, 78 B.R. 984 (Bankr. W.D. Mo. 1987).

362 Reinbold v. Dewey County Bank, 942 F.2d 1304 (8th Cir. 1991).

dismissal under section 1208.[363] When stay relief is granted on this or any other grounds, and an appeal is contemplated, a stay pending appeal may be necessary to prevent mootness. If the property at issue is sold pursuant to relief from stay, the appellate court will be usually powerless to reverse the foreclosure.[364]

The automatic stay may also be lifted for cause to allow a creditor to set off an asset or deposit in which it holds an interest against a debtor's pre-petition indebtedness under 11 U.S.C. § 553. For example, courts have allowed payments under certain government conservation programs to be set off against government claims.[365] The stay also may be lifted when contracts or redemptive rights have expired, because the creditor can establish that no interest in the applicable property remains in the debtor's estate.[366]

16.4.6 Nondischargeability and Discharge Bar[367]

The scope of the chapter 12 discharge is similar to that available in chapter 11.[368] Unlike the broader chapter 13 discharge,[369] the confirmation and consummation of a chapter 12 plan will not discharge debts which would be nondischargeable under section 523(a).[370] Unlike the chapter 7 discharge, family farmer corporations and partnerships, as well as individual family farmers, can be granted discharges,[371] and chapter 12 does not include certain bars to a chapter 7 discharge.[372]

Because of the discharge for family farm corporations and partnerships and the cramdown of indebtedness which can be forced upon a creditor, proceedings to determine dischargeability take on a significance in chapter 12 in sharp contrast to their relative uselessness in chapter 11. Chapter 11 has numerous other alternatives for creditors to prevent cramdown; chapter 12 does not apart from objection to confirmation.[373]

Because nondischargeability questions can arise and be litigated in family farmer cases just as in chapters 7 and 11, the family farmer should carefully examine with counsel the farmer's transactions to determine if section 523(a) poses a problem. The presence of a substantial nondischargeable debt may have serious ramifications for the success of the chapter 12 plan. Counsel should review Chapter 14 of this manual, particularly section 14.4, for a further discussion of the types of debt that may be nondischargeable and for the procedures governing determinations of non-dischargeability.

16.4.7 Dismissal and Conversion

16.4.7.1 Voluntary Dismissal

Chapter 12 allows the family farmer debtor, upon his or her own request, to dismiss a chapter 12 proceeding at any time without permission of the court, unless the case is in chapter 12 as a result of a conversion from either chapter 7 or 11.[374] Any waiver of that right of conversion is unenforceable.[375] If the case is a conversion to chapter 12 from either chapter 7 or 11, then court approval upon notice and hearing is required prior to dismissal. The right to refile a chapter 12 after voluntary dismissal is tempered by section 109(g) or any bar expressly provided by bankruptcy court order, discussed earlier in this manual.[376] The failure to oppose a motion to dismiss in a previous case does not equate to a voluntary dismissal for purposes of section 109(g).[377]

Several courts have disregarded the clear language of 11 U.S.C. § 1208(b) allowing dismissal of a chapter 12 case at any time by the debtor. In *In re Tyndall*,[378] the bankruptcy court declined to permit voluntary dismissal under section 1208(b) after plan default without cure where the plan provided for mandatory liquidation of collateral by the

---

363 *See, e.g., In re* Kennedy, 181 B.R. 418 (Bankr. D. Neb. 1995); *In re* Fern Acres, Ltd., 180 B.R. 554 (Bankr. D. Neb. 1995); *In re* Novak, 103 B.R. 403 (Bankr. E.D.N.Y. 1989); *In re* Novak, 95 B.R. 24 (Bankr. E.D.N.Y. 1989); *In re* Ouverson, 79 B.R. 830 (Bankr. N.D. Iowa 1987); *In re* Welsh, 78 B.R. 984 (Bankr. W.D. Mo. 1987); *In re* McMartin Indus., 62 B.R. 718 (Bankr. D. Neb. 1986). *See also In re* Wald, 211 B.R. 359 (Bankr. D.N.D. 1997) (stay relief granted for cause based on chapter 12 debtor's lack of good faith).

364 *See, e.g., In re* Riley, 122 F. Supp. 2d 684 (W.D. Va. 2000) (appeal moot after property sold pursuant to grant of relief from stay and dismissal of chapter 12 case), *aff'd*, 25 Fed. Appx. 149, 2002 WL 15378 (4th Cir. 2002). *See generally* § 13.10.4, *supra*.

365 *In re* Greseth, 78 B.R. 936 (D. Minn. 1987); *In re* Matthieson, 63 B.R. 56 (D. Minn. 1986); *In re* Ratliff, 79 B.R. 930 (Bankr. D. Colo. 1987). See discussion of setoff at § 16.5.3.7.2, *infra*.

366 *In re* Marker Eighty, Inc., 69 B.R. 561 (Bankr. M.D. Fla. 1987); *In re* Beverages Int'l, Ltd., 61 B.R. 966, 971, 972 (Bankr. D. Mass. 1986) (and cases cited therein).

367 *See generally* Ch. 14, *supra*.

368 *Compare* 11 U.S.C. § 727(b) *with* 11 U.S.C. § 1141(d). *See generally* Matson, *Understanding the New Family Farmer Bankruptcy Act*, 21 U. Rich. L. Rev. 521 (Spring 1987).

369 11 U.S.C. § 1328(a).

370 11 U.S.C. § 1228(a).

371 11 U.S.C. § 1228(a), read with 11 U.S.C. §§ 101(18) and 109(f). *Compare* 11 U.S.C. § 727(a)(1).

372 *See* 11 U.S.C. § 727; *cf.* 11 U.S.C. § 1141(d)(3). However, unlike chapter 11, chapter 12 does not usually contemplate that liquidation will take place without conversion.

373 *See, e.g., In re* C & P Gray Farms, 70 B.R. 704 (Bankr. W.D. Mo. 1987) (chapter 11).

374 11 U.S.C. § 1208(b); *In re* Lerch, 85 B.R. 491 (Bankr. N.D. Ill. 1988). *See In re* Davenport, 175 B.R. 355 (Bankr. E.D. Cal. 1994) (section 105 available to sanction debtor rather than prevention of dismissal); *In re* Cotton, 992 F.2d 311 (11th Cir. 1993).

375 11 U.S.C. § 1208(b).

376 *See* Ch. 9, *supra*; *In re* Lerch, 85 B.R. 491 (Bankr. N.D. Ill. 1988).

377 *In re* Gamble, 72 B.R. 75 (Bankr. D. Idaho 1987) (chapter 12).

378 97 B.R. 266 (Bankr. E.D.N.C. 1989).

chapter 12 trustee upon election by the creditor. In spite of the provisions of section 1208(b) making waiver of dismissal unenforceable, that court found the right to dismiss less than absolute when rights gained in reliance upon the bankruptcy are involved.[379] Courts also decline to permit dismissal where the court finds fraud and a motion to convert under 11 U.S.C. § 1208(d) was pending.[380] If the debtor voluntarily dismisses a case with a confirmed chapter 12 plan or the case is dismissed by the court pursuant to section 1208, the question arises whether payments remaining with the trustee or coming to the trustee may be distributed according to the confirmed plan as provided by section 1226(a) or whether they go back to the debtor. In chapter 13 cases, the Ninth Circuit held in *In re Nash*[381] that payments go back to the debtor. The *Nash* case has been distinguished as leading to unfair results in chapter 12 cases where payments are made annually and creditors have been held off through the growing season.[382]

16.4.7.2 Involuntary Dismissal

As in chapters 7, 11 and 13, the failure of the debtor to proceed in the manner mandated by the bankruptcy court, statutes and rules can result in the involuntary dismissal of a chapter 12 case. Any party in interest, including the United States trustee, may move to dismiss a case; the court may also consider dismissal *sua sponte*.[383] Notice and hearing upon such motion is required.[384]

The grounds for dismissal are:

(1) Unreasonable delay or gross mismanagement by the debtor that is prejudicial to creditors;[385]
(2) Nonpayment of filing fees or case charges;
(3) Failure to file timely a plan under chapter 12;[386]
(4) Failure to make timely payments under a confirmed plan;[387]
(5) Denial of plan confirmation and denial of additional time for filing of an additional plan or modification;[388]
(6) Material default in a confirmed plan;
(7) Revocation of confirmation or denial of confirmation of a plan modified after initial conformation;
(8) Termination of a confirmed plan by the plan's terms;
(9) Continuing loss to or diminution of the estate and absence of a reasonable likelihood of rehabilitation;[389]
(10) Commission of fraud by the debtor in connection with the chapter 12 case.[390]

The case can also be dismissed "for cause,"[391] which has been interpreted in other chapters to provide grounds for dismissal in addition to those specifically enumerated in the Code.[392] Such grounds may include lack of good faith,[393] abusive refiling,[394] failure to comply with court orders or

---

379 The court distinguishes the circumstances in *Tyndall* from those in the unreported case *In re Allen*, No. 87-00185-MO8 (Bankr. E.D.N.C. 1988), where the plan provisions apparently provided for possible (but not mandatory) liquidation by the Trustee upon default. *In re Goza*, 142 B.R. 766 (Bankr. S.D. Miss. 1992) (voluntary dismissal not allowed until accounting and reports of income and expense produced for trustee).

380 Fink v. Graven Auction Co. (*In re Estate of Gravan*), 64 F.3d 453 (8th Cir. 1995) *See also In re Molitor*, 76 F.3d 218 (8th Cir. 1996) (chapter 13 debtor not allowed to voluntarily dismiss based on bad faith and pending motion by creditors to convert to chapter 7); Neal v. Western Credit Bank, 181 B.R. 560 (D. Utah 1995); *In re Cotton*, 136 B.R. 888 (M.D. Ga. 1992); *In re Foster*, 121 B.R. 961 (N.D. Tex. 1990), *aff'd*, 945 F.2d 400 (5th Cir. 1991). *But see In re Barbieri*, 182 F.3d 319 (2d Cir. 1999) (right to dismiss is absolute and cannot be overridden even to prevent fraud). *See also* § 13.9.1, *supra*.

381 765 F.2d 1410 (9th Cir. 1985). *See also In re Plata*, 958 F.2d 918 (9th Cir. 1992) (with strong dissent).

382 *In re Samford*, 102 B.R. 724 (Bankr. E.D. Mo. 1989). In one extreme case, the federal government creditor prevailed upon the District Court to issue a pre-judgment attachment upon the funds held by the trustee after dismissal to prevent their return to the debtor. *In re Ethington*, 150 B.R. 48 (Bankr. D. Idaho 1993).

383 *In re Henderson Ranches*, 75 B.R. 225 (Bankr. D. Idaho 1987).

384 11 U.S.C. § 1208(c). *See generally* Matson, *Understanding the New Family Farmer Bankruptcy Act*, 21 U. Rich. L. Rev. 521 (Spring 1987).

385 *See In re Fern Acres, Ltd.*, 180 B.R. 554 (Bankr. D. Neb. 1995); *In re Suthers*, 173 B.R. 570 (W.D. Va. 1994); *In re Hoffman*, 168 B.R. 608 (Bankr. N.D. Ohio 1994); *In re French*, 139 B.R. 476 (Bankr. D.S.D. 1992); *In re Beswick*, 98 B.R. 900 (Bankr. N.D. Ill. 1989), *stay on appeal denied*, 98 B.R. 904 (N.D. Ill. 1989); *In re Rivera Sanchez*, 80 B.R. 6 (Bankr. D. P.R. 1987); *In re Lubbers*, 73 B.R. 440 (Bankr. D. Kan. 1987).

386 *In re Braxton*, 121 B.R. 632 (Bankr. N.D. Fla. 1990); *In re Lawless*, 74 B.R. 54 (Bankr. W.D. Mo. 1987), *aff'd*, 79 B.R. 850 (W.D. Mo. 1987).

387 *In re Gribbins*, 242 B.R. 637 (Bankr. W.D. Ky. 1999).

388 *In re Hoffman*, 168 B.R. 608 (Bankr. N.D. Ohio 1994); *In re Rivera Sanchez*, 80 B.R. 6 (Bankr. D. P.R. 1987).

389 *In re Hoffman*, 168 B.R. 608 (Bankr. N.D. Ohio 1994).

390 11 U.S.C. § 1208(c), (d).

391 11 U.S.C. § 1208(c).

392 *In re Suthers*, 173 B.R. 570 (W.D. Va. 1994) (post-petition debt, sale of collateral, purchase and rental without approval); *In re French*, 139 B.R. 476 (Bankr. D.S.D. 1992); *In re Cardi Ventures, Inc.*, 59 B.R. 18 (Bankr. S.D.N.Y. 1985); *In re Vermont Fiberglass, Inc.*, 38 B.R. 151 (Bankr. D. Vt. 1984); *In re Horizon Hosp., Inc.*, 10 B.R. 672 (Bankr. M.D. Fla. 1981).

393 *In re Burger*, 2000 Bankr. LEXIS 400 (S.D. Ohio 2000) (lack of good faith included effort to misrepresent ownership of property of the estate to obtain the automatic stay, and minimal need for reorganization); *In re Euerle Farms, Inc.*, 861 F.2d 1089 (8th Cir. 1988); *In re Hoffman*, 168 B.R. 608 (Bankr. N.D. Ohio 1994); *In re Fern Acres, Ltd.*, 180 B.R. 554 (Bankr. D. Neb. 1995); *In re Beswick*, 98 B.R. 900 (Bankr. N.D. Ill. 1989), *stay on appeal denied*, 98 B.R. 904 (N.D. Ill. 1989); *In re Hyman*, 82 B.R. 23 (Bankr. D.S.C. 1987); *In re Guglielmo*, 30 B.R. 102 (Bankr. M.D. La. 1983) (chapter 13).

394 *In re Bisso*, 2000 U.S. App. LEXIS 12739 (9th Cir. June 6, 2000) (dismissal based on history of prior filings found within the discretion of the bankruptcy court); Lerch v. Fed. Land Bank of St. Louis, 94 B.R. 998 (N.D. Ill. 1989); *In re Borg*, 105 B.R.

statutory directives,[395] overlapping bankruptcy case filings,[396] failure to make timely filings and performance,[397] and lack of eligibility for chapter 12 relief.[398] The failure of a debtor to pay disposable income under the plan during its life has been used as a foundation for a trustee's motion to dismiss under section 1208(d).[399] Where the time for revocation of confirmation has passed, it may be possible for a trustee alternately to employ section 1208(d).[400]

Dismissals for abusive refiling and/or lack of good faith have been made in some cases with prejudice, either for the period of 180 days specified in section 109(g) or such longer period as the bankruptcy court chooses to impose pursuant to section 105.[401] Abusive refilings have also generated assessment by the bankruptcy court against debtors for costs and expenses of creditors in appropriate circumstances.[402] In assessing multiple filings for abuse, the courts may have sometimes considered cases filed by either or both spouses affecting the same property as intertwined.[403]

All but one of the grounds for dismissal in chapter 12 are drawn from chapter 13,[404] and, in two cases, from chapter 11 (gross mismanagement[405] and continuing loss to the estate and absence of a reasonable likelihood of rehabilitation).[406] The one ground not found in other chapters is involuntary dismissal or conversion because of fraud connected with the chapter 12 case.[407] Additionally, the removal of a debtor-in-possession can provide grounds for dismissal if the trustee cannot practically or economically provide for the management of the farm operation for the benefit of creditors.[408]

16.4.7.3 Voluntary Conversion from Chapter 12 to Other Chapters

Conversion of a case from chapter 12 to another chapter is conditioned upon the premise that the debtor seeking conversion is entitled to be a debtor under the chapter to which conversion is sought.[409] A chapter 12 debtor has an absolute right to convert a pending case to one under chapter 7 for liquidation.[410] Any waiver of that right is unenforceable.[411]

There are no specific provisions allowing the conversion of a chapter 12 case to one under either chapters 11 or 13. Debtors who have filed chapter 12 cases, but find themselves ineligible because of income or debt restrictions, may want to request conversion to chapter 11. Presumably section 1208(e) anticipates the possibility of such conversion, although the absence of specific provision as contained in other sections[412] might be interpreted as precluding or limiting such conversion.[413]

Those courts which have considered this conversion question have not reached a uniform answer. Some have approved the option of conversion from chapter 12 to chapter

56 (Bankr. D. Mont. 1989); *In re* Walton, 95 B.R. 514 (Bankr. S.D. Ohio 1989); *In re* Hyman, 82 B.R. 23 (Bankr. D.S.C. 1987); *In re* McDermott, 77 B.R. 394 (Bankr. N.D.N.Y. 1987) (chapter 11); *In re* Galloway Farms, Inc., 82 B.R. 486 (Bankr. S.D. Iowa 1987); *In re* Ouverson, 79 B.R. 830 (Bankr. N.D. Iowa 1987); *In re* Welsh, 78 B.R. 984 (Bankr. W.D. Mo. 1987); *In re* S Farms One, Inc., 73 B.R. 103 (Bankr. D. Colo. 1987); *In re* Turner, 71 B.R. 120 (Bankr. D. Mont. 1987).

395 *In re* Walton, 95 B.R. 514 (Bankr. S.D. Ohio 1989). *See In re* Gahm, 2000 U.S. App. LEXIS 22736 (6th Cir. Aug. 31, 2000) (failure to comply with terms of order vacating dismissal is grounds for involuntary re-dismissal).

396 *In re* Borg, 105 B.R. 56 (Bankr. D. Mont. 1989). *But see* § 16.2.2.6, *supra.*

397 *In re* Novak, 934 F.2d 401 (2d Cir. 1991); *In re* French, 139 B.R. 476 (Bankr. D.S.D. 1992).

398 *See* § 16.2.2.1, *supra*; *In re* Snider, 99 B.R. 374 (Bankr. S.D. Ohio 1989); *In re* Lawless, 74 B.R. 54 (Bankr. W.D. Mo. 1987), *aff'd*, 79 B.R. 850 (W.D. Mo. 1987).

399 *In re* Kuhlman, 118 B.R. 731 (Bankr. D.S.D. 1990).

400 *In re* Gross, 121 B.R. 587 (Bankr. D.S.D. 1990).

401 *In re* Hildreth, 165 B.R. 429 (Bankr. N.D. Ohio 1994) (failure to provide financial information and to attend confirmation hearing is willfulness under § 109(g)); *In re* Walton, 116 B.R. 536 (Bankr. N.D. Ohio 1990) (dismissal with prejudice for 2 years where abusive refiling, delay of foreclosure, and ineligibility for relief shown on face of schedules); *In re* Walton, 95 B.R. 514 (Bankr. S.D. Ohio 1989); *In re* Lerch, 85 B.R. 491 (Bankr. N.D. Ill. 1988), *aff'd*, 94 B.R. 998 (N.D. Ill. 1989); *In re* Wilson, 85 B.R. 72 (Bankr. N.D. Ill. 1988) (chapter 13); *In re* Hyman, 82 B.R. 23 (Bankr. D.S.C. 1987); *In re* McDermott, 77 B.R. 394 (Bankr. N.D.N.Y. 1987) (chapter 11); *In re* Dyke, 58 B.R. 714 (Bankr. N.D. Ill. 1986) (chapter 13). It is not clear how these cases are reconciled with § 349(a).

402 *In re* Fern Acres, Ltd., 180 B.R. 554 (Bankr. D. Neb. 1995); *In re* McDermott, 77 B.R. 384 (Bankr. N.D.N.Y. 1987); *In re* Hyman, 82 B.R. 23 (Bankr. D.S.C. 1987) (chapter 12); *In re* Kinney, 51 B.R. 840 (Bankr. C.D. Cal. 1985) (chapter 13); *In re* Jones, 41 B.R. 263 (Bankr. C.D. Cal. 1984) (chapter 13).

403 *In re* Ouverson, 79 B.R. 830 (Bankr. N.D. Iowa 1987); *In re* Kinney, 51 B.R. 840 (Bankr. C.D. Cal. 1985) (multiple chapter 11 and 13 filings).

404 11 U.S.C. § 1307.

405 *See* 11 U.S.C. § 1104(a)(1). Gross mismanagement in chapter 11 cases is reason for appointment of a trustee; however, the appointment of a trustee usually signals the beginning of liquidation—a result not possible under chapter 12 with a trustee in control. Gross mismanagement is also a basis for removal of a family farmer as a debtor-in-possession pursuant to 11 U.S.C. § 1204(a); for a discussion of what may constitute gross mismanagement, see § 16.3.3, *supra.*

406 *See* 11 U.S.C. § 1112(b)(1).

407 11 U.S.C. § 1208(d).

408 Executive Office of United States Trustees, Guidelines for Supervision of Chapter 12 Cases.

409 11 U.S.C. § 1208(e).

410 11 U.S.C. § 1208(a).

411 11 U.S.C. § 1208(a).

412 *See* 11 U.S.C. §§ 1112(d), 1307(d), 1307(e), 706(a).

413 *Compare* 11 U.S.C. §§ 1307(d), (e) *with* 11 U.S.C. § 1208. However, equitable considerations such as preservation of avoidance and recapture capacities and lack of prejudice to creditors may persuade courts to allow conversion to other repayment chapters from chapter 12.

11 within the discretion of the bankruptcy judge;[414] others have prohibited such conversion.[415]

If a chapter 12 case is converted to one under chapter 7, then what may be property of the chapter 7 estate comes into question, particularly where assets have been acquired post-petition. The cases to date generally find that determination of property of the estate upon the conversion of a case from chapter 12 where there is no confirmation should be from the date of conversion. This is based upon the rationale that section 1207, with its more specific provisions concerning property of the estate, would control.[416] However, section 348(a) provides that conversion does not affect the date of the order for relief—which triggers section 541(a)—and some cases under chapter 13 provide property of estate as computed from filing, not conversion.[417]

The 1994 Act added 11 U.S.C. § 348(f)(1)(A) concerning property of the estate upon conversion of a case from chapter 13 to chapter 7. The section specifies that the property of the estate in the converted case is the property of the estate as of the date of the original petition which is still in the debtor's control or possession as of the date of conversion.[418] The 1994 Act did not enact a comparable provision for conversions from chapter 12 to chapter 7, and it remains to be seen whether courts analogize this section for application to conversion from chapter 12 or view it as the Congressional intent to exclude chapter 12 from the section.

The authority of the farmer DIP to operate his or her business ends if and when the order of conversion is entered changing the form of bankruptcy to one under chapter 7.[419] Nevertheless, the debtor continues to have the obligation of safeguarding the estate, turning over property, cooperating with the trustee and court, furnishing information, and appearing at examinations and hearings.[420]

16.4.7.4 Involuntary Conversion from Chapter 12 to Chapter 7

Chapter 12 provides that upon the request of a party in interest, after notice and a hearing, a court may convert a chapter 12 case to one under chapter 7 "upon a showing that the debtor has committed fraud in connection with the case."[421] As secured creditors may view this as a weapon to force liquidation, debtors and their counsel should make certain that the debtor's schedules, statements, periodic reports, and other information given to the court and creditors are as accurate as possible. The 1986 Amendments also allow a court to initiate *sua sponte* those actions which parties in interest can request and pursue.[422] This includes conversion of a chapter 12 case to chapter 7.

Involuntary conversion of chapter 12 to 7 might be based upon "fraud in connection with the case." Consequently, debtor's conduct pre-petition should not be grounds for such conversions, particularly because other statutory provisions effectively address alleged pre-petition fraudulent conduct.[423] However, some of the cases to allow such conversion to date found cause for involuntary conversion to chapter 7 from both pre- and post-petition conduct.[424] The standards for conversion for fraud in connection with the case should be similar to the fraud standard used to bar discharge.[425] One court that addressed the burden of proof necessary to persuade a court to convert a case under section 1208(d) has found a clear and convincing showing—not a mere preponderance—was required.[426]

As chapter 12 has aged, a clearer picture of grounds used by some courts to justify conversion under section 1208(d) has emerged. They include willful failure to pay over all disposable income during plan life,[427] and conversion of

---

414 *See, e.g., In re* Lawless, 79 B.R. 850 (W.D. Mo. 1987) (although circumstances in this case persuaded the court to deny permission to convert); *In re* Miller, 177 B.R. 551 (Bankr. N.D. Ohio 1994); *In re* Vaughn, 100 B.R. 423 (Bankr. S.D. Ill. 1989) (over chapter 12 debt limit: allow conversion prejudice to creditors, and otherwise not inequitable); *In re* Bird, 80 B.R. 861 (Bankr. W.D. Mich. 1987); *In re* Baldwin Farms, 78 B.R. 143 (Bankr. N.D. Ohio 1987).

415 *See In re* Roeder Land & Cattle Co., 82 B.R. 536 (Bankr. D. Neb. 1988); *In re* Christy, 80 B.R. 361 (Bankr. E.D. Va. 1987); *In re* Johnson, 73 B.R. 107 (Bankr. S.D. Ohio 1987).

416 *In re* White, 25 F.3d 931 (10th Cir. 1994); *In re* Clark, 186 B.R. 249 (Bankr. W.D. Mo. 1995); *In re* J.A.V. Ag., Inc., 154 B.R. 923 (Bankr. W.D. Tex. 1993); *In re* White, 151 B.R. 247 (Bankr. D.N.M. 1993); *In re* Mutchler, 95 B.R. 748 (Bankr. D. Mont. 1989); Anderson & Morris, Chapter 12 Farm Reorganizations (1987), Conversions & Dismissals, § 3.09.

417 *In re* White, 25 F.3d 931 (10th Cir. 1994). *See* § 8.7.3, *supra.*

418 *See* § 4.7.5, *supra.*

419 *In re* J.A.V. Ag., Inc., 154 B.R. 923 (Bankr. W.D. Tex. 1993); Vregdenhil v. Hoekstra, 773 F.2d 213 (8th Cir. 1985).

420 *In re* J.A.V. Ag., Inc., 154 B.R. 923 (Bankr. W.D. Tex. 1993).

421 11 U.S.C. § 1208(d); Reinbold v. Dewey County Bank, 942 F.2d 1304 (8th Cir. 1991) (constitutionality). *See* § 16.1.2, *supra.*

422 11 U.S.C. § 105.

423 *See, e.g.,* 11 U.S.C. § 523(a)(2) (fraud in creation of indebtedness); 11 U.S.C. § 1225(a)(3) ("good faith" requirement).

424 *In re* Kloubec, 268 B.R. 173 (N.D. Iowa 2001) (fraud found in disclaimer of inheritance, concealment of assets, manipulation of transactions); *In re* Caldwell, 101 B.R. 728 (Bankr. D. Utah 1989); *In re* Graven, 101 B.R. 109 (Bankr. W.D. Mo. 1989), *aff'd sub nom.* Graven v. Fink, 936 F.2d 378 (8th Cir. 1991); *In re* Zurface, 95 B.R. 527 (Bankr. S.D. Ohio 1989). *See also* Fink v. Graven Auction Co. (*In re* Estate of Graven), 64 F.3d 453 (8th Cir. 1995); Graven v. Fink, 196 B.R. 506 (Bankr. W.D. Mo. 1996).

425 *See* 11 U.S.C. § 727(a)(4)(A), (B). Fraud as a measure of conduct runs throughout the Bankruptcy Code. *See, e.g.,* 11 U.S.C. §§ 1144, 1230, 1330 (revocation of confirmation); 11 U.S.C. §§ 1144, 1230(d), 1328(e) (revocation of discharge); 11 U.S.C. § 523(a)(2) (nondischargeability). *In re* Kingsley, 162 B.R. 249 (Bankr. W.D. Mo. 1994).

426 *In re* Caldwell, 101 B.R. 728 (Bankr. D. Utah 1989) (case was converted to chapter 7).

427 *In re* Kuhlman, 118 B.R. 731 (Bankr. D.S.D. 1990).

collateral and fraud in dealing with an individual creditor[428] as well as material misrepresentations.[429]

16.4.8 Executory Contracts and Unexpired Leases[430]

Section 365, where it deals with reorganization and repayment plans, now applies to chapter 12.[431] Executory contracts and unexpired leases should be assumed or rejected by the time of plan proposal, although creditors can force assumption or rejection prior to confirmation.

Rejection of farm equipment leases can be particularly helpful in the chapter 12 paring down process. Most long-term leases are more expensive than either purchasing the equipment outright or leasing services or equipment short-term on an "as needed" basis. This rejection of long term leases should be done at an early stage to avoid unnecessary administrative expenses.[432]

Family farmers should pay particular attention to section 365(d)(4) which requires that leases upon non-residential real property must be assumed within sixty days of the filing of the original petition or that an extension of that period be arranged prior to its expiration.[433] Failure to assume non-residential real property leases within that time means the leases will be deemed rejected and possession must return to the lessor.[434]

Often farmland rented from others and excluding the farmers' residence may be an essential part of the farming operation. Not only is the land available for the farming operation, but it may have allotments or base which increases its value to the farmer above its mere suitability for planting. This important asset to the farm may be lost unless the lease is assumed or assumption at least is initiated and the period for assumption extended. On the other hand, some rented land is merely surplusage to the farm, and the farmer should be encouraged to release that farmland which is a burden to the farming operation or which is not pulling its weight proportionate to its production.

All farm programs in which there is performance remaining (such as some conservation and reforestation programs in which the farmer is a participant through the Farm Service Agency or Commodity Credit Corp.) may also be deemed executory contracts which need to be assumed or rejected under section 365 if they contain mutual obligations.[435]

The contract for deed for purchase by a debtor of farmland also presents a question for treatment as an executory contract or as a security instrument. The nature of the instrument is determined under state law.[436] A majority of jurisdictions have found the contract for deed to be an executory contract, with the concomitant need for treatment under section 365 and plan cure of default under section 365 standards.[437] A minority find that such a contract is a pledge for security rather than an executory contract or that the contract can be modified under a confirmed plan.[438]

16.5 The Chapter 12 Reorganization Process

16.5.1 Introduction

Chapter 13 is the basic template for chapter 12. As a consequence, chapter 13 concepts—for example, feasibility, good faith, devotion of disposable income to repayment of unsecured debt—are often applicable to chapter 12 cases,

428 Reinbold v. Dewey County Bank, 942 F.2d 1304 (8th Cir. 1991).
429 *In re* Kingsley, 162 B.R. 249 (Bankr. W.D. Mo. 1994).
430 *See generally* § 12.9, *supra*.
431 11 U.S.C. § 103(a) as amended by the 1986 Act and Sections 257(j) and (m) of the 1986 Act. 11 U.S.C. § 1222(b)(6); *In re* Rancho Chamberino, 89 B.R. 597 (W.D. Tex. 1987) (cure as in chapter 13; controlled by §§ 1222(b)(6), 365(b) and 365(d)); *In re* Hardie, 100 B.R. 284 (Bankr. E.D.N.C. 1989) (chapter 12 DIP has right to assume or reject executory contracts).
432 11 U.S.C. §§ 503(b)(1)(A), 507(a)(1). *See, e.g.,* Union Leasing Co. v. Peninsula Gunite, Inc., 24 B.R. 593 (B.A.P. 9th Cir. 1982); *In re* Templeton, 154 B.R. 930 (Bankr. W.D. Tex. 1993); *In re* Xonics, Inc., 65 B.R. 69 (Bankr. N.D. Ill. 1986); *see also* 11 U.S.C. § 1222(a)(2).
433 The courts are divided on the timing of § 365(d)(4) and extensions. A minority indicate that the motion for assumption or the motion for extension must be *heard and decided* within sixty days. *E.g., In re* Southwest Aircraft Services, Inc., 53 B.R. 805 (Bankr. C.D. Cal. 1985); *In re* Condo. Admin. Services, Inc., 55 B.R. 792 (Bankr. M.D. Fla. 1985). The majority hold that a motion for extension filed within the sixty-day period, whether resolved or not in that period, is sufficient. *E.g., In re* Am. Health Care Mgmt., 900 F.2d 827 (5th Cir. 1990). *See generally* 3 Collier on Bankruptcy ¶ 365.04[3][c], at 365-35 (15th ed. rev.).
434 11 U.S.C. § 365(d)(4).
435 *See, e.g., In re* Gore, 124 B.R. 75 (Bankr. E.D. Ark. 1990) (program payments are part of executory contract; no entitlement until debtors perform); *In re* Claeys, 81 B.R. 985 (Bankr. D.N.D. 1987); *In re* Ratliff, 79 B.R. 930 (Bankr. D. Colo. 1987); *In re* Carpenter, 79 B.R. 316 (Bankr. S.D. Ohio 1987); *In re* Dunning, 77 B.R. 789 (Bankr. D. Mont. 1987).
436 *In re* Rancho Chamberino, 89 B.R. 597 (W.D. Tex. 1987); *In re* McKinney, 84 B.R. 751 (D. Kan. 1988) (and cases cited therein); *In re* Fitch, 174 B.R. 96 (Bankr. S.D. Ohio 1994).
437 *In re* Rancho Chamberino, 77 B.R. 555 (Bankr. W.D. Tex. 1987), *aff'd,* 89 B.R. 597 (W.D. Tex. 1987) (chapter 12); *In re* Waldron, 65 B.R. 169 (Bankr. N.D. Tex. 1986); *In re* Shaw, 48 B.R. 857 (D.N.M. 1985). *See also In re* Heartline Farms, Inc., 116 B.R. 700 (Bankr. D. Neb. 1990). *But see In re* Hartman, 102 B.R. 90 (Bankr. N.D. Tex. 1989) (title retention contract equals security interest which must be properly perfected).
438 Albaugh v. Terrell, 93 B.R. 115 (E.D. Mich. 1988); *In re* Fitch, 174 B.R. 96 (Bankr. S.D. Ohio 1994); *In re* Reak, 92 B.R. 804 (Bankr. E.D. Wis. 1988); *In re* Flores, 32 B.R. 455 (Bankr. S.D. Tex. 1983) (can use § 1322(b)(10) to modify contract for deed); *In re* Booth, 19 B.R. 53 (Bankr. D. Utah 1982) (lien rather than executory contract).

with adaptation for the unique circumstances of farmers.[439] However, most of the bankruptcy law concerning farmers and reorganization of farming operations has evolved under chapter 11, and much of that case law will be applicable to chapter 12 reorganizations where the issues involved are not related to plan construction and confirmation standards.[440]

16.5.2 Procedure and Timing in Chapter 12 Cases

Only a debtor may propose a plan under a chapter 12.[441] The deadline for a chapter 12 plan proposal is ninety days from the date of the filing of the chapter 12 petition.[442] This is longer than allowed under chapter 13, but considerably shorter than the time provided for debtors in chapter 11.[443] Attorneys must not miss this deadline, unless they first obtain express court approval for the extension of time. Failure to timely file a plan may result in dismissal or conversion.[444] However, chapter 12 has a special provision allowing the ninety-day period to be extended if such extension is "substantially justified."[445] It is thus important to make any request for an extension *before* the ninety-day period has expired.

Extensions of time for chapter 12 plan proposal may not be routinely granted, and most courts will not grant automatic extensions merely upon request.[446] On the other hand, there may be substantial reasons justifying limited extensions, particularly where such extensions may save courts from subsequent inevitable plan modification. Some reasons that can potentially justify limited extension are:

- Potential sale of all or part of the real or personal property of the estate arising close to the time for plan proposal;
- Inability to determine the extent of debtor's participation in government programs which have a material effect on plan payments; and
- Valuation or turnover contests.

The chapter 12 plan may be modified up to the time of confirmation,[447] and even after confirmation, if appropriate.[448] A second plan may be proposed if the first is denied confirmation, with the court's permission.[449] Notice and hearing as appropriate are required for post-confirmation modifications, but only notice is required for pre-confirmation modifications,[450] and then only if a creditor or party in interest is adversely affected.

After the filing of a chapter 12 petition, a meeting of creditors to examine the debtor is scheduled not less than twenty nor more than forty days after the order of relief.[451] Confirmation is the next step, unless intervening motions or applications must be heard.[452] Unlike chapter 11, there are no hearings on disclosure statements, because chapter 12 does not require such statements.

Unlike either chapters 11 or 13, the chapter 12 plan confirmation, after the proposal, is set on an accelerated time frame. A hearing on confirmation must be held within forty-five days of the filing of the chapter 12 plan.[453] The court may extend the time for the confirmation hearing beyond the forty-five-day requirement in the statute if circumstances so require.[454]

---

439 H.R. Rep. No. 99-764, at 48 (1986), *reprinted at* 1986 U.S.C.C.A.N. 5249. *In re* Anderson, 88 B.R. 877 (Bankr. N.D. Ind. 1988); *In re* Borg, 88 B.R. 288 (Bankr. D. Mont. 1988). *See* § 16.4.1, *supra.* However, disposable income is treated very differently under chapter 12, even though the statutory language is identical to chapter 13. *See* 16.5.4.3, *infra.*

440 For example, procurement and approval of financing, leases and their assumption, feasibility factors, use of cash collateral.

441 11 U.S.C. § 1221; *In re* Roesner, 153 B.R. 328 (Bankr. D. Kan. 1993).

442 11 U.S.C. § 1221.

443 *Cf.* 11 U.S.C. § 1121. Although a debtor has an exclusive *right* to file a plan for 120 days under chapter 11, unlike debtors in other chapters he or she is not compelled to do so at risk of dismissal.

444 11 U.S.C. § 1208(c)(3). *In re* Lawless, 79 B.R. 850 (W.D. Mo. 1987); *In re* Offield, 77 B.R. 223 (Bankr. W.D. Mo. 1987); *In re* Lubbers, 73 B.R. 440 (Bankr. D. Kan. 1987); *In re* Rivera Sanchez, 80 B.R. 6 (Bankr. D. P.R. 1987). However, even cases which dismiss for untimely filing find the ninety-day time requirement is not jurisdictional. *See In re* Land, 82 B.R. 572 (Bankr. D. Colo. 1988); *In re* Raylyn Ag, Inc., 72 B.R. 523 (Bankr. S.D. Iowa 1987) (plan filed in 92 days; no dismissal). Conversion can only occur in chapter 12 with debtor consent or under the limited circumstance of fraud under 11 U.S.C. § 1208(d).

445 11 U.S.C. § 1221. Compare 11 U.S.C. § 1121, which merely provides extension "for cause." Yet the time for plan proposal can also be reduced in chapter 11. A plan under chapter 13 must be filed within fifteen days of the filing of the petition unless the court extends that deadline. Fed. R. Bankr. P. 3015.

446 H.R. Rep. No. 99-764, at 50; Frasier, *The New Bankruptcy Code*

Chapter 12: Friend of the Family Farmer? 41 Washington State Bar News 29 (Aug. 1987).

447 11 U.S.C. § 1223. However, modification should be expeditious, not last minute. A plan may be withdrawn and a new one filed if the ninety-day plan promulgation period has not expired. *In re* Ryan, 69 B.R. 599 (Bankr. M.D. Fla. 1987).

448 11 U.S.C. § 1229.

449 11 U.S.C. § 1208(c)(5); *In re* Bentson, 74 B.R. 56 (Bankr. D. Minn. 1987). *See* § 16.6.4, *infra.*

450 11 U.S.C. § 1223(b); 11 U.S.C. § 1229(b)(2). The court can dispense with a hearing under § 1229 if the modification appears to meet confirmation standards and no objection from a party in interest is lodged.

451 Fed. R. Bankr. P. 2003(a).

452 *E.g.,* motion to assume lease(s), application for approval for new financing, application for use of cash collateral, complaint for valuation pursuant to 11 U.S.C. § 506.

453 11 U.S.C. § 1224.

454 *In re* Ivy, 76 B.R. 147 (Bankr. W.D. Mo. 1987); *In re* O'Farrell, 74 B.R. 421 (Bankr. N.D. Fla. 1987). However, the court in *In re* Ryan, 69 B.R. 599 (Bankr. M.D. Fla. 1987) found that a request for extension of the forty-five-day period to "work out problems with creditors" and to file a second amended plan if

To achieve confirmation, valuation issues must be decided at or prior to the time of the confirmation hearing.[455] Although pre-confirmation payments are not usually required, where appropriate, a court can order such payments.[456]

16.5.3 Common Secured Claim Issues in Chapter 12

16.5.3.1 Introduction

Most consumer bankruptcies do not require new financing: the estate is liquidated or regular earnings provide a source of income. By contrast, vital issues in chapter 12 cases for continuation of the family farming operation are financing for the coming year and the use of collateral and proceeds for operating and living expenses.

16.5.3.2 Section 552 Lien Dissolution

Unlike other Code sections,[457] section 552(a) dissolves creditor liens automatically: no act is required to dissolve liens covered by section 552(a) except filing of a bankruptcy petition. Section 552(a) dissolves liens upon property acquired by the debtor's estate or the debtor after the commencement of a case which *but for* the filing of the bankruptcy case would be subject to a valid continuing security interest under an agreement entered into by the debtor pre-petition.[458]

For family farmers, this lien dissolution means that creditors' security interests in the future production of certain types of farm products is automatically eliminated. Most farm creditors who take blanket security interests have liens on future crop production. Although some states' versions of the Uniform Commercial Code require that security interests in crops be renewed each year, most states' versions do not. In these latter states, section 552(a) automatically dissolves security interests in future crops and proceeds therefrom.[459] However, section 552 does not apply to crops which are in the ground at the time the bankruptcy petition is filed,[460] nor does it apply to the proceeds of pre-petition crops, only to crops planted after filing and their proceeds.[461]

Section 552(a) also can dissolve security interests in after-acquired equipment.[462] However, post-petition rents may still be subject to a security interest unless a debtor can show an appropriate equitable basis for their dissolution; if the creditor is over-secured, the court might consider this dissolution proper under section 552(b).[463]

Two decisions in northern states apply section 552(a) lien dissolution to milk and proceeds.[464] However, most courts, relying on the language of section 552(b), hold that section 552(a) does not apply to proceeds, products, offspring, rents or profits of property in which a valid pre-petition security interest attached.[465] Instead, section 552(b) applies, which holds such security interests valid unless the court, based on the equity of the case, orders otherwise.[466]

Another litigated issue is how section 552 applies to farm program payments. This issue was litigated early on with regard to the Payment-in-Kind (PIK) program.[467] Most

---

D.S.D. 1984); *In re* Liebe, 41 B.R. 965 (Bankr. N.D. Iowa 1984) (post-petition PIK payments).

460 *In re* Klaus, 247 B.R. 761 (Bankr. C.D. Ill. 2000); *In re* Vanasdale, 64 B.R. 92 (Bankr. N.D. Ohio 1986); Randall v. Bank of Viola, 58 B.R. 289 (Bankr. C.D. Ill. 1986); *In re* Beck, 61 B.R. 671 (Bankr. D. Neb. 1985).

461 *In re* Smith, 72 B.R. 344 (Bankr. S.D. Ohio 1987); *In re* Wallman, 71 B.R. 125 (Bankr. D.S.D. 1987); *In re* Lorenz, 57 B.R. 734 (Bankr. N.D. Ill. 1986); *In re* Sheehan, 38 B.R. 859 (Bankr. D.S.D. 1984). *But see* Fed. Deposit Ins. Corp. v. Coones, 954 F.2d 596 (10th Cir. 1992) (post-petition crops produced with pre-petition crop funds equal post-petition crops still secured under § 552(b)).

462 *In re* Butler, 97 B.R. 508 (Bankr. E.D. Ark. 1988).

463 11 U.S.C. § 552(b); *In re* Hollinrake, 93 B.R. 183 (Bankr. S.D. Iowa 1988).

464 *In re* Lawrence, 56 B.R. 727 (D. Minn. 1984); *In re* Pigeon, 49 B.R. 657 (Bankr. D.N.D. 1985).

465 Smith v. Dairymen, Inc., 790 F.2d 1107 (4th Cir. 1986); *In re* Neilson, 48 B.R. 273 (D.N.D. 1985); *In re* Rankin, 49 B.R. 565 (Bankr. W.D. Mo. 1985); United States v. Hollie, 42 B.R. 111 (Bankr. M.D. Ga. 1984).

466 Some courts have used the language of § 552(b) which allows the lien dissolution even as to those security interests outlined therein upon "equitable" grounds to dissolve milk assignment liens. *See, e.g., In re* Delbridge, 61 B.R. 484 (Bankr. E.D. Mich. 1986). *See also* United Virginia Bank v. Slab Fork Coastal Co., 784 F.2d 1188 (4th Cir. 1986) (*dicta*). At least two cases have addressed this "equitable" exception and found it to have application where the debtor uses assets which would otherwise be available to unsecured creditors to enhance the value of a secured creditor's collateral. J. Catton Farms, Inc. v. First Nat'l Bank of Chicago, 779 F.2d 1242 (7th Cir. 1985); *In re* Village Properties, Ltd., 723 F.2d 441 (5th Cir. 1984).

467 The PIK program involved giving the farmer certificates for commodities in government storage in exchange for agreeing not to plant their crop. It was a supply reduction program. Some courts treated the payments as though they were proceeds of the nonexistent crop. Therefore, if the crop would have been a pre-petition crop, the proceeds of that crop would be protected under 552(b). Alternatively, the more reasoned analysis found

---

necessary were insufficient cause for extension of the time frame of § 1224. *In re* Braxton, 121 B.R. 632 (Bankr. N.D. Fla. 1990) (debtor's delay in obtaining valuation was not sufficient grounds for extending time for plan proposal).

455 *See* § 16.5.5.2, *infra*.

456 Stahn v. Haeckel, 920 F.2d 555 (8th Cir. 1990).

457 *E.g.*, 11 U.S.C. §§ 545, 547, 548, 554. *See* Fischer v. Pauline Oil & Gas Co., 309 U.S. 294 (1939).

458 *In re* Kucera, 123 B.R. 852 (Bankr. D. Neb. 1990) (§ 552(a) suspends post-petition security interest, but dismissal reinstates it under § 349).

459 *In re* Borg, 88 B.R. 288 (Bankr. D. Mont. 1988); *In re* Hill, 83 B.R. 522 (Bankr. E.D. Tenn. 1988); Randall v. Bank of Viola, 58 B.R. 289 (Bankr. C.D. Ill. 1986); *In re* Lorenz, 57 B.R. 734 (Bankr. N.D. Ill. 1986); *In re* Sheehan, 38 B.R. 859 (Bankr.

courts ruled that PIK payments were not subject to lien dissolution under section 552, whether rights to PIK payments were characterized as proceeds[468] or general intangibles,[469] so long as the creditor had properly perfected its security interest therein.[470]

The courts have been more likely to find interests in other government programs to be subject to section 552(a) lien dissolution, for example, milk diversion program benefits,[471] dairy termination program interests,[472] "sealing" profits,[473] and storage payments.[474] Interests which have been found subject to a continuing lien under section 552(b), in addition to the PIK program, include federal deficiency and disaster payments.[475]

Section 552(a) releases collateral from a security agreement so that:

- The collateral may be repledged to another creditor to secure new financing for the coming crop year;
- The debtor need not get permission to use the proceeds or cash collateral from the sale of the crops;
- The debtor need not provide adequate protection upon the freed crops; and
- The value of crops will not be counted in the calculation of the value of the secured creditor's claim.

16.5.3.3 New Financing and Its Approval

Crop farmers in chapter 12 must give careful thought to obtaining financing for the new crop season. Crop farmers require funding at the beginning of the crop season for seed, fertilizer, pesticides, and some additional funding at harvest before any profit can be realized. For many farmers, diversification into livestock sales provides year-round income sufficient to sustain the operation during periods of crop growth.

Even so, often the family farm operation will need capital from outside sources; counsel should remember there are several new financing sources which may become available to the debtor post-petition. New financing may be obtained by pledging crops freed by section 552(a) lien dissolution. Funding may also be derived from contracts with companies for purchase of the crop at the end of the season; while such contracts fix the price at which the farmer sells the crop (which has disadvantages as well as advantages), the contracts also provide a source of funding for planting and nurture.

However, under section 364 both such financing arrangements must be approved by the bankruptcy court. Court approval is necessary whenever the family farmer desires to incur:

- New secured indebtedness;
- Unsecured indebtedness outside the ordinary course of business; or
- Unsecured indebtedness to which a superpriority would apply.[476]

The debtor should make application as soon as practicable for such approval. The application should recite:

- All terms and conditions of the arrangements sought;
- The fact that similar or better terms and conditions cannot be obtained elsewhere for this farmer debtor;
- The necessity of the arrangement for the continuation of the farming operation;
- Proposed treatment of the creditor providing new financing under the debtor's plan; and
- Whether the arrangement encroaches upon the interests of any other creditors' interests.

In this latter event, court permission and/or creditor permission will be needed to subordinate the original creditor to the new one. Applications for permission to incur secured debt or unsecured debt outside the ordinary course of business must be served upon all creditors and parties in interest at

---

that the payments were general intangibles. Assuming the contract was signed pre-petition, section 552(a) would not apply. It would only cut off an interest in a contract signed post-petition.

468 Wapakoneta Production Credit v. Cupp, 38 B.R. 953 (Bankr. N.D. Ohio 1984); McLemore v. Mid-South Agri-Chemical Corp., 41 B.R. 369 (Bankr. M.D. Tenn. 1984); *In re* Lee, 35 B.R. 663 (Bankr. N.D. Ohio 1983).

469 *In re* Schmaling, 783 F.2d 680 (7th Cir. 1986) (general intangibles); Apple v. Miami Valley Production Credit Ass'n, 804 F.2d 917 (6th Cir. 1986); *In re* Sunberg, 729 F.2d 561 (8th Cir. 1984); *In re* Sumner, 69 B.R. 758 (Bankr. D. Or. 1986).

470 The creditor must have properly perfected its security interest in *that type of collateral* which the court has found the PIK payments to be, or it is subject to avoidance under 11 U.S.C. §§ 544 and 545. *See, e.g., In re* Pressier, 33 B.R. 65 (Bankr. D. Colo. 1983).

471 Tambay Trustee, Inc. v. Agric. Asset Mgmt. Co., 68 B.R. 32 (Bankr. M.D. Fla. 1986). *Contra* United States v. Hollie, 42 B.R. 111 (Bankr. M.D. Ga. 1984).

472 Grunzke v. Sec. State Bank of Wells, 68 B.R. 446 (D. Minn. 1987) (post-petition entry into program).

473 Settles v. United States, 69 B.R. 634 (Bankr. C.D. Ill. 1987).

474 *In re* Sumner, 69 B.R. 758 (Bankr. D. Or. 1986).

475 *In re* Otto Farms, 247 B.R. 757 (Bankr. C.D. Ill. 2000) (loan deficiency payments from the Commodity Credit Corporation); *In re* Norville, 248 B.R. 127 (Bankr. C.D. Ill. 2000) (FSA disaster payments); *In re* Lemos, 243 B.R. 96 (Bankr. D. Idaho 1999) (Crop Loss Disaster Assistance Payments); *In re* Lesmeister, 242 B.R. 920 (Bankr. D.N.D. 1999) (Crop Loss Disaster Assistance Program); *In re* Nivens, 22 B.R. 287 (Bankr. N.D. Tex. 1982).

476 11 U.S.C. §§ 364(b)–(d); *In re* Stacy Farms, 78 B.R. 494 (Bankr. S.D. Ohio 1987). Although § 364 allows the debtor to incur unsecured credit in the ordinary course of business without court approval, every sizable extension of credit to farmers should be submitted to the bankruptcy court for approval.

least fifteen days prior to any hearing thereupon, unless the time is foreshortened by the court.[477]

Certain government deficiency payment programs may require that the debtor receive court permission for treatment of the payments as a superpriority administrative expense for repayment if—and only if—the debtor should fail to comply with the program requisites. This permission requires a section 364 application, notice and order.

16.5.3.4 Use of Cash Collateral

The typical consumer debtor is not concerned with the use of cash collateral except for the consumer's use of checking or savings accounts at creditor institutions.[478] However, the source of a farmer's income for living and operating expenses is often derived directly from sources in which secured creditors have a continuing, post-petition security interest.

Creditors' security interests in crops planted pre-petition survive post-petition, so that a farmer's use of crop proceeds in the normal farm operation must be permitted by the creditor or the court as use of cash collateral.[479] Dairy and livestock operations require continuous capital replenishment for livestock and feed reserves, but the farming operation may be laboring under an assignment of proceeds which hampers the farming operation's cash flow. Nevertheless, the underlying security interest usually makes proceeds of dairy operations and feeder/stockyard operations cash collateral.[480]

Chapter 12 does not change the section 363 requirements for use of cash collateral in which a creditor has a security interest: the debtor must obtain the creditor's permission to use the cash collateral or the court must determine that the debtor is entitled to use the cash collateral in the farming operation subject to the provision of adequate protection for the creditor.[481] However, while chapter 12 does alter the requirements for adequate protection somewhat,[482] standards for determination for what is adequate protection for *cash* collateral remain the same as under 11 U.S.C. § 361(1) and (2).[483] Additionally a confirmed chapter 12 plan, like one under chapter 13, can allow the debtor to use cash collateral subject to the provisions and continued viability of the chapter 12 plan. To do so, unless otherwise agreed by creditors, a plan should make provision for maintenance of a herd or livestock inventory at pre-petition level, with a

value not below the pre-petition amount, and monthly reports and inspection rights to the secured creditor involved.[484]

Debtor's application to use cash collateral must be served upon all creditors and a hearing set thereupon.[485] Because the typical family farmer debtor will need to use cash collateral almost immediately,[486] the application should be filed with the petition or as soon thereafter as practicable. A hearing can be set upon short notice.[487]

What may serve as adequate protection for use of cash collateral (or in the automatic stay context) will differ from case to case, but it should be remembered that adequate protection means prevention of diminution of value of the collateral, not benefit of the bargain. The following is a list of factors contributing to a finding of adequate protection with regard to use of cash collateral:

- Current payments, interest and/or insurance on the collateral;[488]
- Additional security in unencumbered property or second liens;[489]

---

477 *See* Fed. R. Bankr. P. 4001(c).

478 *See* § 11.3.5, *supra*.

479 11 U.S.C. § 363.

480 *See* § 16.5.3.2, *supra*.

481 11 U.S.C. §§ 363(c)(2), 1205; *In re* Stacy Farms, 78 B.R. 494 (Bankr. S.D. Ohio 1987).

482 *See* § 16.5.3.6, *infra*; 11 U.S.C. § 1205.

483 *In re* Stacy Farms, 78 B.R. 494 (Bankr. S.D. Ohio 1987); *In re* Westcamp, 78 B.R. 834 (Bankr. S.D. Ohio 1987).

484 *In re* Watford, 159 B.R. 597 (M.D. Ga. 1993); *In re* Milleson, 83 B.R. 696 (Bankr. D. Neb. 1988); *In re* Underwood, 87 B.R. 594 (Bankr. D. Neb. 1988); *In re* Wobig, 73 B.R. 292 (Bankr. D. Neb. 1987).

485 Fed. R. Bankr. P. 2002(a)(2), 6004(a).

486 The proceeds from cash collateral are the majority of the general operating revenues of a debtor with a dairy or livestock operation and farmers whose crops are not subject to § 552 lien dissolution. A farmer whose loans have been accelerated by the Farmers Home Administration has also had his ability to use proceeds of his farm for living expenses cut off, so that immediate relief is essential.

487 That notice can be as little as 72 hours in emergency situations. *See, e.g., In re* Sheehan, 38 B.R. 859 (Bankr. D.S.D. 1984). Some hearings have been conducted by telephone. *See, e.g., In re* Halls, 79 B.R. 417 (Bankr. S.D. Iowa 1987). Some courts have local rules which provide for emergency hearings concerning cash collateral. Chapter 12 as originally conceived in the Senate had a provision for emergency hearing on cash collateral *ex parte*, but that provision was deleted in conference committee. Under Fed. R. Bankr. P. 4001(b), however, any hearing on the use of cash collateral earlier than fifteen days from service of the motion can only authorize such use as is necessary to avoid irreparable and immediate harm.

488 *In re* Rennich, 70 B.R. 69 (Bankr. D.S.D. 1987).

489 *See In re* TNT Farms, 226 B.R. 436 (Bankr. D. Idaho 1998) (discussion of priority of adequate protection liens issued in connection with cash collateral order). The replacement lien must be comparable to the lien dissipated. For example, bankruptcy courts are split as to whether replacement lien in forthcoming crops (even with crop insurance) is an adequate replacement lien for the use of proceeds from the sale of a previous crop. *See, e.g., In re* Berens, 41 B.R. 524 (Bankr. D. Minn. 1984). *Contra In re* Wiesler, 45 B.R. 871 (D.S.D. 1985) (chapter 11); *In re* Berg, 42 B.R. 335 (D.N.D. 1984) (chapter 11); *In re* Gilbert, 147 B.R. 801 (Bankr. W.D. Okla. 1992); *In re* Stacy Farms, 78 B.R. 494 (Bankr. S.D. Ohio 1987) (chapter 12); *In re* Westcamp, 78 B.R. 834 (Bankr. S.D. Ohio 1987) (chapter 12); *In re* Hoff, 54 B.R. 746 (Bankr. D.N.D. 1985) (chapter 11).

- First distribution under plan of a larger plan payment for cash collateral used;
- Severance of part of property and its conveyance or abandonment to creditor for payment; sale or culling of animals with proceeds to creditor as an immediate payment;
- Additional security interest in property or grain, particularly that upon which the previous lien had dissipated under 11 U.S.C. § 552;
- Continuation of the business itself and livestock maintenance can provide adequate protection, because the collateral may immediately devalue (such as dairy cows) if left unattended and because some collateral will replenish only upon continuation of the farming operation;[490]
- Periodic reports to the individual creditor whose cash collateral is being used;[491]
- Payment of creditor by another party with greater financial stability than the debtor;
- Showing that cash infusion from financing will contribute to a concomitant enhancement in the creditor's interest in secured property;
- Use of the cash collateral to feed and keep live collateral;
- Equity cushion between creditor's interest and value of pledged property;
- Right of inspection to secured creditor to determine levels of security;
- Deposit of cash collateral in interest-bearing account in insured institution.[492]

16.5.3.5 Sale of Property Free and Clear of Liens

One major problem in farm bankruptcies prior to chapter 12 was the inability of farmers to sell a portion of their property free and clear of liens without creditor consent.[493] Such sale can reduce the payments needed for secured debt service and effectuate the paring down process necessary in most farmer reorganizations.

Chapter 12 adds a provision[494] allowing the chapter 12 trustee and the debtor-in-possession[495] to sell farmland or farm equipment free and clear of liens regardless of creditor consent.[496] Any lien affected by the sale attaches to the proceeds.[497] As in all matters under section 363 (sale), the trustee or debtor-in-possession must make application for sale free and clear of liens and notice must be given to all creditors and parties in interest.[498] In practical terms, the sale free and clear can be utilized to:

- Sell unnecessary property;
- Reduce debt service to a secured creditor by applying the proceeds of a sale to the creditor's allowed secured claim;
- Allow sale to friendly entities or relatives of the debtor at a fair value;
- Allow sale to only a portion of farmland rather than an entire parcel.[499]

Debtors may want to sell property free and clear of liens after plan completion but before long-term secured debts are paid and the plan should contemplate and make provision for such sale. Otherwise, if the property is cross-collateralized, sale of a portion of the property free and clear of liens may later be impossible.[500]

16.5.3.6 Adequate Protection in Chapter 12 Cases

Instead of utilizing the adequate protection definition applicable to other bankruptcy chapters,[501] section 1205 creates a special chapter 12 definition of adequate protection for secured creditors.[502] Section 1205 applies to chapter 12

---

490 *In re* Milleson, 83 B.R. 696 (Bankr. D. Neb. 1988); *In re* Underwood, 87 B.R. 594 (Bankr. D. Neb. 1988); *In re* Wobig, 73 B.R. 292 (Bankr. D. Neb. 1987); *In re* Hoff, 54 B.R. 746 (Bankr. D.N.D. 1985) (chapter 11).

491 *In re* Watford, 159 B.R. 597 (M.D. Ga. 1993); *In re* Wobig, 73 B.R. 292 (Bankr. D. Neb. 1987).

492 11 U.S.C. § 1205. *See In re* Gore, 113 B.R. 504 (Bankr. E.D. Ark. 1989); *In re* Westcamp, 78 B.R. 834 (Bankr. S.D. Ohio 1987).

493 11 U.S.C. § 363(f). *See* H.R. Conf. Rep. No. 99-958, at 50 (1986), *reprinted at* 1986 U.S.C.C.A.N. 5251.

494 11 U.S.C. § 1206.

495 Although § 1206 is couched in terms of sale by the trustee, the debtor-in-possession should be able to exercise this same power with court approval by virtue of 11 U.S.C. § 1203 and Congress'

admonition in the legislative history. *See* H.R. Conf. Rep. No. 99-958, at 50 (1986), *reprinted at* 1986 U.S.C.C.A.N. 5251.

496 11 U.S.C. §§ 363(b), (c), 1206. *See also* §§ 16.5.5.3.4, 16.5.5.3.5, *infra*.

497 11 U.S.C. §§ 363(b), (c), 1206. *See also* §§ 16.5.5.3.4, 16.5.5.3.5, *infra*. A creditor is also allowed to bid at any sale, unless forbidden to do so by the court, and if the creditor purchases the property, the successful bid price may be offset against the creditor's claim. *See* H.R. Conf. Rep. No. 99-958, at 50 (1986), *reprinted at* 1986 U.S.C.C.A.N. 5251.

498 Fed. R. Bankr. P. 2002(a)(2) requires twenty-day notice to all creditors, unless the court foreshortens that time.

499 *See* H.R. Conf. Rep. No. 99-959, at 50 (1986), *reprinted at* 1986 U.S.C.C.A.N. 5251: "Most family farmer reorganizations, to be successful, will involve the sale of unnecessary property. This section of the Conference Report allows Chapter 12 debtors to scale down the size of their farming operations by selling unnecessary property." The same goals may also be accomplished in some circumstances by surrender of all or a portion of the property back to the secured creditor. *See also* 16.5.5.3.4, *infra*.

500 *In re* Turner, 84 F.3d 1294 (10th Cir. 1996) (United States is a unitary creditor, and therefore payments due debtors under ASCS program may be off-set against debts owed by the debtor to SBA via an administrative off-set); *In re* Schnakenberg, 195 B.R. 435 (Bankr. D. Neb. 1996).

501 11 U.S.C. § 361.

502 11 U.S.C. § 1205(a); *see also* H.R. Conf. Rep. No. 99-958, at 49, 50 (1986), *reprinted at* 1986 U.S.C.C.A.N. 5251.

cases whenever reference is made to adequate protection under sections 362 (automatic stay and relief therefrom), 363 (sale, use and lease of property and use of cash collateral), and 364 (obtaining credit).

The theme of section 1205 is diminution in value of collateral, not benefit of bargain.[503] As the legislative history expressly indicates, section 1205 does not require the debtor to provide lost opportunity costs.[504]

Adequate protection under chapter 12 can be provided by several methods:

- Cash payments to the extent that the automatic stay or any activity of the debtor results in decrease in the value of property securing a claim or of an entity's ownership interest in property;[505]
- Provision of additional or replacement liens to the extent that the automatic stay or any activity of the debtor results in decrease in the value of property securing a claim or of an entity's ownership interest in property;[506]
- Paying for the use of farmland the reasonable rent customary in the community where the land is located, based upon the rental value, net income and earning capacity of the property;[507]
- Other relief, other than granting of an administrative priority as will adequately protect the value of collateral or property used.[508]

This concept of adequate protection implicitly codifies the concept that an equity cushion alone may serve as adequate

protection for a creditor under proper circumstances.[509] There may be times when no additional adequate protection is required, such as when there is a sufficient equity cushion or when the collateral will not decline in value over time.[510] However, insurance coverage is generally required for adequate protection regardless of value, stability or decline.[511]

Few cases have addressed the concept of fair rental value as adequate protection. One case which has addressed it in some depth is *In re Kocher*.[512] The *Kocher* court found that payment by the debtor of fair rental value constitutes adequate protection per se in a chapter 12 case. It described the following characteristics of fair rental value:

- Section 1205(b)(3) does not require the decline in value anticipated in farmland to be fully offset by rent payments;
- Fair rental value follows the custom in the debtor's farm community; and
- Fair rental value can be periodic, rather than lump sum.[513] For valuation purposes for adequate protection under section 1205, the court may not include the rental from the farm house or expenses attributable thereto since reasonable rental value specifically applies only to use of farmland.[514]

However, the concept of fair rental value applies to pre-confirmation adequate protection. Present value and adequate protection for a secured creditor under a confirmed plan cannot be in the form of rental payments unless the payments are the equivalent of payment for present value of the allowed secured claim.[515]

Some debtors' attorneys have taken a signal from section 1205(b)(3) to attempt to base valuation on rental value of land and a modified income approach to valuation where that approach resulted in a valuation below either a compa-

---

503   *In re* Pretzer, 91 B.R. 428 (Bankr. N.D. Ohio 1988); *In re* Shouse, 95 B.R. 470 (Bankr. W.D. Ky. 1988); *In re* Turner, 82 B.R. 465 (Bankr. W.D. Tenn. 1988); *In re* Westcamp, 78 B.R. 834 (Bankr. S.D. Ohio 1987); *In re* Kocher, 78 B.R. 844 (Bankr. S.D. Ohio 1987); *In re* Mikkelsen Farms, Inc., 74 B.R. 280 (Bankr. D. Or. 1987); *In re* Rennich, 70 B.R. 69 (Bankr. D.S.D. 1987).

504   H.R. Conf. Rep. No. 99-958, at 49 (1986), *reprinted at* 1986 U.S.C.C.A.N. 5250. It expressly eliminated application in chapter 12 of the holdings in *In re* Am. Mariner Indus., Inc., 734 F.2d 426 (9th Cir. 1984) and Grundy Nat'l Bank v. Tandem Mining Corp., 754 F.2d 1436 (4th Cir. 1985). Subsequently in United Sav. Ass'n of Tex. v. Timbers of Inwood Forest Associates, Ltd., 484 U.S. 365, 108 S. Ct. 626, 98 L. Ed. 2d 740 (1988) the Supreme Court overruled *American Mariner* and *Grundy* holding that under-secured creditors are not entitled to lost opportunity costs. *See also In re* Anderson, 88 B.R. 877 (Bankr. N.D. Ind. 1988).

505   11 U.S.C. § 1205(b)(1); *cf.* 11 U.S.C. § 361(1).

506   11 U.S.C. § 1205(b)(2). *See In re* TNT Farms, 226 B.R. 436 (Bankr. D. Idaho 1998) (discussion of priority of adequate protection liens issued in connection with cash collateral order). *Cf.* 11 U.S.C. § 361(2); *In re* Pretzer, 91 B.R. 428 (Bankr. N.D. Ohio 1988).

507   11 U.S.C. § 1205((b)(3). However, rent is not required; the right to rental payment is limited to any demonstrable decrease in value. *In re* Anderson, 88 B.R. 877 (Bankr. N.D. Ind. 1988).

508   11 U.S.C. § 1205(b)(4). *Cf.* 11 U.S.C. § 361(3). *See also* H.R. Conf. Rep. No. 99-958, at 49, 50 (1986), *reprinted at* 1986 U.S.C.C.A.N. 5250, 5251.

509   *See, e.g.,* Walker v. Johnson, 38 B.R. 34 (Bankr. D. Vt. 1983) (and cases cited therein); Aegean Fare, Inc. v. Commonwealth of Massachusetts, Dep't of Revenue, 33 B.R. 745 (Bankr. D. Mass. 1983). *See also In re* Monnier Bros., 755 F.2d 1336 (8th Cir. 1985); *In re* Turner, 82 B.R. 465 (Bankr. W.D. Tenn. 1988); *In re* Mikkelsen Farms, Inc., 74 B.R. 280 (Bankr. D. Or. 1987); *In re* Raylyn Ag, Inc., 72 B.R. 523 (Bankr. S.D. Iowa 1987); *In re* Rennich, 70 B.R. 69 (Bankr. D.S.D. 1987).

510   *In re* Anderson, 137 B.R. 820 (Bankr. D. Colo. 1992); *In re* Anderson, 88 B.R. 877 (Bankr. N.D. Ind. 1988); *In re* Pretzer, 91 B.R. 428 (Bankr. N.D. Ohio 1988); *In re* Shouse, 95 B.R. 470 (Bankr. W.D. Ky. 1988); *In re* Turner, 82 B.R. 465 (Bankr. W.D. Tenn. 1988); *In re* Rennich, 70 B.R. 69 (Bankr. D.S.D. 1987).

511   *In re* Pretzer, 91 B.R. 428 (Bankr. N.D. Ohio 1988).

512   78 B.R. 844 (Bankr. S.D. Ohio 1987).

513   The *Kocher* court observed the rent is "the quintessential measure of the time value of real property" and rent is almost universally paid at intervals. Whether rent can be periodic or should be a lump sum paid up front will be determined on a case by case basis. *Kocher*, 78 B.R. at 851.

514   *In re* Anderson, 88 B.R. 877 (Bankr. N.D. Ind. 1988).

515   *In re* Big Hook Land & Cattle Co., 77 B.R. 793 (Bankr. D. Mont. 1987).

rable sale approach or cost valuation.[516] Some courts have adopted the income approach, but not a straight rental approach, where comparables are few and/or unreliable or the approach appears to result in a truer value. Most courts (and certainly creditors) to date, however, have found themselves more comfortable with fair market value. Even if farmland value is based on a comparable sales approach or cost valuation, there will probably still be a severe cramdown. Courts so far seem reluctant to increase the severity of cramdown by using an evaluation technique which produces a lower secured value.

Adequate protection protects a secured creditor no more than the creditor sought to protect itself pre-bankruptcy.[517] Despite the fact that farm creditors may have a security interest in replenishing collateral,[518] the valuation of the allowed secured claims—both for adequate protection and plan purposes—may take place either at filing[519] or at confirmation.[520] Reevaluation does not continue as replenishing collateral increases or fluctuates.[521]

The legislative history of chapter 12 indicates that the adequate protection concepts applicable to other cases are equally applicable to chapter 12 cases, consistent with the provisions of section 1205.[522] This means that, with the exception of the "indubitable equivalent" standard of 11 U.S.C. § 361(3), the case law which has developed to date in farm bankruptcies under chapter 11 is precedent in chapter 12.

In the typical farm case, cash collateral arises from the products or proceeds of replenishing collateral: milk from dairy cows, pigs from brood sows, and so forth. Because use of the cash collateral to provide feed to the animals in turn replenishes the collateral by more production, the *use* of the cash collateral itself may provide its own adequate protection by maintaining the value of replenishing collateral.[523] Some operating expenses can also be calculated into such use as necessary for the collateral replenishment and maintenance. At least one court has found, however, that adequate protection in the livestock/cash collateral context must include maintenance of an equity cushion equal to that originally bargained for by the creditor.[524]

16.5.3.7 The Relationship of Government Programs and Government Claims

16.5.3.7.1 Overview

In many chapter 12 cases, a major creditor will be the United States government, operating through one or more of its agencies: the Farm Service Agency, and/or the Small Business Administration. At the same time, the debtor may be relying upon government programs for income to support the farming operation and the chapter 12 plan. The nature of the government programs and the ability of the United States as a creditor to control or encroach upon the benefits from those programs has become a significant battleground.

The names of agencies serving as sources of government loans, grants, and other assistance may have changed in recent years, but case law applicable to expired or altered government programs should still be largely relevant. Where case law is dependent on specific regulations rather than broader bankruptcy and other legal principles, careful research requires determination of whether the applicable regulations remain in force.

16.5.3.7.2 Creditors' right to setoff

Under section 553, a creditor may claim or set off against its indebtedness any benefits or property in the creditor's possession or control if; (1) the debt owed to the creditor by the debtor arose before commencement of the bankruptcy case; (2) the claim of the creditor against the debtor also arose before commencement of the bankruptcy case; and (3) the debt and claim are mutual obligations.[525] The provisions of section 553 do not expand the rights of creditors; the

---

516 *See* § 16.5.5.2, *infra.*

517 *In re* Briggs Transp. Co., 780 F.2d 1339 (8th Cir. 1985); *In re* Heatron, Inc., 6 B.R. 493 (Bankr. W.D. Mo. 1980).

518 For example, dairy cows continue to produce milk post-petition, sows continue to produce new litters of pigs post-petition. While the properly perfected lien of a secured creditor may continue in all such post-petition collateral under 11 U.S.C. § 552(b), the amount of the actual allowed secured claim is as it would be on liquidation at filing or the effective date of the plan.

519 *In re* Anderson, 88 B.R. 877 (Bankr. N.D. Ind. 1988) (chapter 12) (measured from time of application for protection except as to cash collateral); *In re* Big Hook Land & Cattle Co., 81 B.R. 1001 (Bankr. D. Mont. 1988); *In re* Pond, 43 B.R. 522 (Bankr. D.N.D. 1984); Aegean Fare, Inc. v. Commonwealth of Massachusetts, Dep't of Revenue, 33 B.R. 745 (Bankr. W.D. Mass. 1983), although for adequate protection purposes evaluation of the extent necessary for a creditor may be measured from the time of application for protection.

520 *See, e.g., In re* Anderson, 88 B.R. 877 (Bankr. N.D. Ind. 1988); *In re* Robinson Ranch, Inc., 75 B.R. 606 (Bankr. D. Mont. 1987); *In re* Mikkelsen Farms, Inc., 74 B.R. 280 (Bankr. D. Or. 1987); *In re* Foster, 79 B.R. 906 (Bankr. D. Mont. 1987); *In re* Cool, 81 B.R. 614 (Bankr. D. Mont. 1987); *In re* Durr, 78 B.R. 221 (Bankr. D.S.D. 1987).

521 *In re* Big Hook Land & Cattle Co., 81 B.R. 1001 (Bankr. D. Mont. 1988); *In re* Wobig, 73 B.R. 292 (Bankr. D. Neb. 1987).

522 1986 U.S.C.C.A.N. 5250.

523 *See, e.g., In re* Vanas, 50 B.R. 988 (Bankr. E.D. Mich. 1985) (and cases cited therein); *In re* Johnson, 47 B.R. 204 (Bankr. W.D. Wis. 1985).

524 *In re* Foertsch, 167 B.R. 555 (Bankr. D.N.D. 1994); *In re* Milleson, 83 B.R. 696 (Bankr. D. Neb. 1988).

525 *In re* Marshall, 240 B.R. 302 (Bankr. S.D. Ill. 1999) (creditor may not set off debt for purchase of goods and services against unearned portion of advance payment for storing grain); *In re* Brooks Farms, 70 B.R. 368 (Bankr. E.D. Wis. 1987); *In re* Hazelton, 85 B.R. 400 (Bankr. E.D. Mich. 1988), *rev'd*, 96 B.R. 111 (E.D. Mich. 1988); *In re* Fred Sanders Co., 33 B.R. 310 (Bankr. E.D. Mich. 1983). *See generally* § 10.4.2.6.7, *supra.*

creditor claiming a right to setoff must be entitled so to do under existing non-bankruptcy law.[526] The ability of a creditor to exercise any right of setoff is tempered by the automatic stay, which prohibits setoff without stay relief or court permission. To attempt setoff without relief or permission subjects a creditor to those penalties available under sections 362(h) and 105.[527]

Moreover, the setoff of mutual debts or claims is not mandatory, and the bankruptcy court can exercise discretion in whether to allow setoff.[528] Some courts hold, particularly where the property is needed for reorganization, that the court may deny a creditor its right of setoff.[529] Other courts rule the opposite.[530]

In many chapter 12 cases, debtors owe government creditors including perhaps the Internal Revenue Service (IRS)), yet they are due benefits from government programs. It is common for government creditors to assert a right of setoff against benefits due a bankruptcy debtor and necessary for the funding of the chapter 12 plan. Bankruptcy courts have taken differing approaches to these issues.

The majority of courts have found that the various agencies of the United States are one entity for setoff purposes and have permitted setoff.[531] Others have found that setoff requested by a government agency is not possible for lack of mutuality, either: (1) because the creditor agency making the claim for setoff is not the same agency providing the benefits;[532] or (2) because the debtor-in-possession (DIP) is not the same entity as the original debtor.[533] No setoff has been allowed where the benefits and debtor's entitlement thereto have arisen wholly post-petition.[534]

Where setoff is allowed, one response is to provide within the plan for repayment of the creditor involved by allowing the setoff automatically from benefits.[535] The plan may also provide for continuing payment of the creditor from setoff by specific grant of that right in post-petition benefits not otherwise subject to setoff. Another response may be to increase the allowed secured claim of the creditor to include the value of the setoff, and request court permission to have present use of the benefits and repayment or reimbursement under the plan pursuant to 11 U.S.C. § 1225(a)(5).[536] How-

---

526 *In re* Hazelton, 85 B.R. 400 (Bankr. E.D. Mich. 1988), *rev'd*, 96 B.R. 111 (E.D. Mich. 1988). *See also In re* Myers, 282 B.R. 478 (B.A.P. 10th Cir. 2002) (federal government denied right of set-off because its claim against debtors had been discharged in prior chapter 7 case).

527 United States v. Ketelsen, 104 B.R. 242 (D.S.D. 1988), *aff'd*, 880 F.2d 990 (9th Cir. 1989); *In re* Britton, 83 B.R. 914 (Bankr. E.D.N.C. 1988); *In re* Hazelton, 85 B.R. 400 (Bankr. E.D. Mich. 1988), *rev'd*, 96 B.R. 111 (E.D. Mich. 1988); *In re* Rinehart, 76 B.R. 746 (Bankr. D.S.D. 1987) (chapter 11), *aff'd*, 88 B.R. 1014 (D.S.D. 1988), *aff'd sub nom.* Small Bus. Admin. v. Rinehart, 887 F.2d 165 (8th Cir. 1989); *In re* Woloschak Farms, 74 B.R. 261 (Bankr. N.D. Ohio 1987). *Cf.* Citizens Bank of Md. v. Strumpf, 116 S. Ct. 286 (1995) (an administrative freeze does not violate the automatic stay).

528 *See* Riggs v. Government Employees Fin. Corp., 623 F.2d 68 (9th Cir. 1980); *In re* Diplomat Electric, Inc., 499 F.2d 342 (5th Cir. 1974); *In re* Julien Co., 116 B.R. 623 (Bankr. W.D. Tenn. 1990); *In re* Nielson, 90 B.R. 172 (Bankr. W.D.N.C. 1988); *In re* Hazelton, 85 B.R. 400 (Bankr. E.D. Mich. 1988) (chapter 12), *rev'd*, 96 B.R. 111 (E.D. Mich. 1988); Artus v. Alaska Dep't of Labor, 16 B.R. 308 (Bankr. D. Alaska 1981).

529 *See In re* Butz, 104 B.R. 128 (Bankr. S.D. Iowa 1989); *In re* Nielson, 90 B.R. 172 (Bankr. W.D.N.C. 1988); *In re* Hazelton, 85 B.R. 400 (Bankr. E.D. Mich. 1988) (chapter 12), *rev'd*, 96 B.R. 111 (E.D. Mich. 1988); *In re* Rinehart, 76 B.R. 746 (Bankr. D.S.D. 1987) (chapter 11), *aff'd*, 88 B.R. 1014 (D.S.D. 1988), *aff'd sub nom.* Small Bus. Admin. v. Rinehart, 887 F.2d 165 (8th Cir. 1989); Allbrand Appliance & Television Co. v. Merdav Trucking Co., 16 B.R. 10 nn.29–31 (Bankr. S.D.N.Y. 1981).

530 *See, e.g.*, N.J. Nat'l Bank v. Gutterman (*In re* Applied Logic Corp.), 576 F.2d 952, 957, 958 (2d Cir. 1978); *In re* Kraus, 261 B.R. 218, 223 (B.A.P. 8th Cir. 2001). Collier on Bankruptcy adheres to this strict interpretation of § 553 rights, stating, "[t]he Bankruptcy Code provides no general equitable mechanism for disallowing rights of setoff that are expressly preserved by section 553." 5 Collier on Bankruptcy ¶ 553.02[3] (15th ed. rev.).

531 United States v. Maxwell, 157 F.3d 1099 (7th Cir. 1998) (federal government a single entity for setoff purposes); *In re* Turner, 84 F.3d 1294 (10th Cir. 1996) (*en banc*); *In re* Greseth 78 B.R. 936 (D. Minn. 1987); *In re* Parrish, 75 B.R. 14 (N.D. Tex 1987); *In re* Matthieson, 63 B.R. 56 (D. Minn. 1986); *In re* Julien Co., 116 B.R. 623 (Bankr. W.D. Tenn. 1990); *In re* Ratliff, 79 B.R. 930 (Bankr. D. Colo. 1987); *In re* Woloschak Farms, 74 B.R. 261 (Bankr. N.D. Ohio 1987).

532 *In re* Hunerdosse, 85 B.R. 999 (Bankr. S.D. Iowa 1988); *In re* Butz, 86 B.R. 595 (Bankr. S.D. Iowa 1988), *rev'd*, No. 88-366-A (S.D. Iowa 1988), *on remand*, 104 B.R. 128 (Bankr. S.D. Iowa 1989) (the court denied the right of setoff to FmHA as inconsistent with the rehabilitative purposes and intent of the Bankruptcy Code and chapter 12 in particular). *In re* Rinehart, 76 B.R. 746 (Bankr. D.S.D. 1987) (chapter 11), *aff'd*, 88 B.R. 1014 (D.S.D. 1988), *aff'd sub nom.* Small Bus. Admin. v. Rinehart, 887 F.2d 165 (8th Cir. 1989); Hill v. FmHA, 19 B.R. 375 (Bankr. N.D. Tex. 1982).

533 *In re* Gore, 124 B.R. 75 (Bankr. E.D. Ark. 1990); *In re* Hill, 19 B.R. 375 (Bankr. N.D Tex. 1982).

534 *In re* Myers, 362 F.3d 667 (10th Cir. 2004) (setoff not allowed because mutual debt between Farm Service Agency and the debtor based on production flexibility contract signed post-petition); *In re* Gerth, 136 B.R. 237 (Bankr. D.N.D. 1990); *In re* Gore, 124 B.R. 75 (Bankr. E.D. Ark. 1990) (program payments are part of executory contract; entitlement accrues only as debtors perform); *In re* Nielson, 90 B.R. 172 (Bankr. W.D.N.C. 1988); *In re* Stephenson, 84 B.R. 74 (Bankr. N.D. Tex. 1988); *In re* Thomas, 84 B.R. 438 (Bankr. N.D. Tex. 1988) (chapter 7); *In re* Lehl, 79 B.R. 880 (Bankr. D. Neb. 1987) (see reference to 7 C.F.R. 770.4(b)(1)–(3) (1987)); *In re* Butz, 86 B.R. 595 (Bankr. S.D. Iowa 1988), *rev'd*, No. 88-366-A (S.D. Iowa 1988), *on remand*, 104 B.R. 128 (Bankr. S.D. Iowa 1989) (court denied the right of setoff to FmHA as inconsistent with the rehabilitative purposes and intent of the Bankruptcy Code and chapter 12 in particular). *Contra In re* Allen, 135 B.R. 856 (Bankr. N.D. Iowa 1992) (allowed setoff of CRP payments against CCC debt).

535 *In re* Greseth, 78 B.R. 936 (D. Minn. 1987).

536 *In re* Thomas, 84 B.R. 438 (Bankr. N.D. Tex. 1988) (chapter 7) (treatment of setoff as secured claim), *aff'd in part, rev'd in part*, 91 B.R. 731 (N.D. Tex. 1988) (appeal did not involve mutuality issue).

ever, where a plan is confirmed providing for treatment of a creditor and that creditor has failed to seek setoff prior to confirmation, or a creditor has failed to assert a right of setoff in its proof of claim, some courts have determined that the creditor has waived any right or claim to setoff.[537]

16.5.3.7.3 Treatment of government programs in the bankruptcy courts

The bankruptcy courts have had to address the operation and ramification of various government farm programs in their relationship to the Bankruptcy Code. The programs are many and varied, and a complete catalogue cannot be made here. The following is a limited enumeration of programs (some of which no longer exist under the given name) that have been described and/or addressed by the bankruptcy courts in various contexts in farm cases.

Specific benefit programs treated in farm bankruptcy cases include:

- Feed Grain Program or Feed Grain and Wheat Program (ASCS/Food Security Act of 1985, 7 U.S.C. §§ 1421, 1444b, 1444e, 1444e-1 and 1461, 7 C.F.R. Parts 713, 770.4(g)); previous Feed Grain, Upland Cotton and Wheat Programs: deficiency payments and conservation programs—
  — description;[538]
  — ability to pledge for past indebtedness;[539]
  — characterization for purposes of determining security interests;[540]
  — setoff.[541]
- Conservation Reserve Program (CRP) (CCC/7 C.F.R. Part 704): contracts—
  — description;[542]
  — characterization for eligibility purposes;[543]
  — characterization for purposes of determining security interests;[544]

- — setoff;[545]
- — value.[546]
- Disaster payments under the Agriculture, Rural Development and Related Agencies Act of 1987 and Farm Disaster Assistance Act of 1987; prior disaster payment acts including 1986 Farm Disaster Program (CCC/7 C.F.R. Parts 713 and 770); generic certificates—
  — description;[547]
  — setoff.[548]
- Price Support and Production Payments (ASCS/CCC); acreage limitation and conservation; deficiency payments—
  — description of "base";[549]
  — executory contracts;[550]
  — setoff.[551]
- 1987 Acreage Reserve Program (ASCS)—
  — setoff.[552]
- Payment in Kind (PIK) Programs: (ASCS/prior to 10/16/86 regulations) (7 U.S.C. §§ 1348, 1444(c), 1445-b-1(e); 16 U.S.C. § 590p, 7 C.F.R. Part 770 (1984))—
  — description;[553]
  — property of the debtor's estate;[554]
  — characterization for purposes of determining security interests;[555]

---

537 *In re* Stephenson, 84 B.R. 74 (Bankr. N.D. Tex. 1988); *In re* Britton, 83 B.R. 914 (Bankr. E.D.N.C. 1988).

538 *In re* Hunerdosse, 85 B.R. 999 (Bankr. S.D. Iowa 1988); *In re* Halls, 79 B.R. 417 (Bankr. S.D. Iowa 1987); *In re* Kruger, 78 B.R. 538 (Bankr. C.D. Ill. 1987); *In re* Hill, 19 B.R. 375 (Bankr. N.D. Tex. 1982).

539 *In re* Halls, 79 B.R. 417 (Bankr. S.D. Iowa 1987).

540 Program deficiency payments not "proceeds": *In re* Hunerdosse, 85 B.R. 999 (Bankr. S.D. Iowa 1988), *aff'd sub nom.* United States v. Hunderdosse, No. 88-364-B (S.D. Iowa Nov. 28, 1988); *In re* Kruger, 78 B.R. 538 (Bankr. C.D. Ill. 1987).

541 No allowance of setoff to FmHA: *In re* Butz, 86 B.R. 595 (Bankr. S.D. Iowa 1988): *In re* Mattice, 81 B.R. 504 (Bankr. S.D. Iowa 1987); *In re* Hill, 19 B.R. 375 (Bankr. N.D. Tex. 1982). *Contra In re* Brooks, 70 B.R. 369 (Bankr. E.D. Wis. 1987).

542 *In re* Arnold, 88 B.R. 917 (Bankr. N.D. Iowa 1988); *In re* Ratliff, 79 B.R. 930 (Bankr. D. Colo. 1987).

543 *In re* Clark, 288 B.R. 237 (Bankr. D. Kan. 2003); *In re* Paul, 83 B.R. 709 (Bankr. D.N.D. 1988).

544 Program payments not "proceeds": *In re* Arnold, 88 B.R. 917 (Bankr. N.D. Iowa 1988); *In re* Ratliff, 79 B.R. 930 (Bankr. D.

Colo. 1987); *In re* Sumner, 69 B.R. 758 (Bankr. D. Or. 1986) (general intangibles, contract rights or accounts). Program payments in the nature of rents and profits: *In re* Arnold, 88 B.R. 917 (Bankr. N.D. Iowa 1988); *In re* Ratliff, 79 B.R. 930 (Bankr. D. Colo. 1987).

545 Setoff allowed to FmHA: *In re* Greseth, 78 B.R. 936 (D. Minn. 1987); *In re* Ratliff, 79 B.R. 930 (Bankr. D. Colo. 1987).

546 *In re* Claeys, 81 B.R. 985 (Bankr. D.N.D. 1987).

547 *In re* Quillen, 97 B.R. 288 (Bankr. W.D. Va. 1989) (chapter 11); *In re* Stephenson, 84 B.R. 74 (Bankr. N.D. Tex. 1988).

548 Setoff allowed to ASCA: *In re* Woloschak Farms, 74 B.R. 261 (Bankr. N.D. Ohio 1987). Setoff denied (post-petition entitlement): *In re* Stephenson, 84 B.R. 74 (Bankr. N.D. Tex. 1988).

549 *In re* Kocher, 78 B.R. 844 (Bankr. S.D. Ohio 1987).

550 *In re* Walat Farms, Inc., 69 B.R. 529 (Bankr. E.D. Mich. 1987).

551 Setoff allowed to FmHA: *In re* Parrish, 75 B.R. 14 (Bankr. N.D. Tex. 1987). *Contra In re* Walat Farms, Inc., 69 B.R. 529 (Bankr. E.D. Mich. 1987).

552 Setoff allowed to ASCS: *In re* Woloschak Farms, 74 B.R. 261 (Bankr. N.D. Ohio 1987); setoff denied to FmHA: *In re* Britton, 83 B.R. 914 (Bankr. E.D.N.C. 1988).

553 *In re* Binning, 45 B.R. 9 (Bankr. S.D. Ohio 1984); *In re* Barton, 37 B.R. 545 (Bankr. E.D. Wash. 1984); *In re* Kruse, 38 B.R. 958 (Bankr. D. Kan. 1983); *In re* Sunberg, 35 B.R. 777 (Bankr. S.D. Iowa 1983), *aff'd*, 729 F.2d 561 (8th Cir. 1984).

554 *In re* Lee, 35 B.R. 663 (Bankr. N.D. Ohio 1983); *In re* Sunberg, 35 B.R. 777 (Bankr. S.D. Iowa 1983), *aff'd*, 729 F.2d 561 (8th Cir. 1984).

555 Program payments in the nature of rents and profits: *In re* Pressier, 33 B.R. 65 (Bankr. D. Colo. 1983). *Contra In re* Liebe, 41 B.R. 965 (Bankr. N.D. Iowa 1983). Program payments in the nature of "proceeds": *In re* J. Catton Farms, Inc., 779 F.2d 1242 (7th Cir. 1985); Osteroos v. Norwest Bank Minot, 604 F. Supp. 848 (D.N.D. 1984); *In re* Judkins, 41 B.R. 369 (Bankr. M.D. Tenn. 1984); *In re* Cupp, 38 B.R. 953 (Bankr. N.D. Ohio 1984); *In re* Kruse, 38 B.R. 958 (Bankr. D. Kan. 1983); *In re*

- Payment in Kind (PIK) Program: (ASCS/ regulations)—
  — characterization for purposes of determining security interests;[556]
  — ability to encumber for pre-existing indebtedness;[557]
- Dairy Termination Program: (CCC/Food Security Act of 1985, 7 U.S.C. § 1446); contracts for slaughter or export—
  — description;[558]
  — property of the debtor's estate;[559]
  — characterization for purposes of determining security interest;[560]
- Milk Diversion Program: (CCC): production reduction—
  — ability to encumber for pre-existing indebtedness;[561]
  — characterization for purposes of determining security interests;[562]
  — setoff.[563]
- "Sealing" grain loan program: (CCC/7 C.F.R. §§ 1421.1 and 1421.2)—

— description;[564]
— characterization for eligibility purposes;[565]
— characterization for purposes of determining security interests;[566]
— setoff.[567]
- Receipt of CCC generic commodity certificates from deficiency program under 7 U.S.C. §§ 1444a and 1445b-4 and 16 U.S.C. § 590h.[568]

Cases have also dealt with some general aspects of farm benefits programs including:

- Farm program benefits generally;[569]
- Deficiency and disaster payments;[570]
- Diversion and abandonment programs;[571]
- Storage programs;[572]
- General anti-discrimination provisions for debtors in or applying for government programs;[573]

Lee, 35 B.R. 663 (Bankr. N.D. Ohio 1983). *Contra In re* Schmaling, 783 F.2d 680 (7th Cir. 1986) (general intangibles or contract rights); *In re* Mattick, 45 B.R. 615 (Bankr. D. Minn. 1985) (general intangibles); *In re* Barton, 37 B.R. 545 (Bankr. E.D. Wash. 1984) (general intangibles); *In re* Lion Farms, Inc., 54 B.R. 241 (Bankr. D. Kan. 1985); *In re* Binning, 45 B.R. 9 (Bankr. S.D. Ohio 1984) (general intangibles); *In re* Schmidt, 38 B.R. 380 (Bankr. D.N.D. 1984) (general intangibles); *In re* Sunberg, 35 B.R. 777 (Bankr. S.D. Iowa 1983), *aff'd*, 729 F.2d 561 (8th Cir. 1984) (general intangibles).

556 Program payments not in the nature of rents and profits: *In re* Butz, 86 B.R. 595 (Bankr. S.D. Iowa 1988), *rev'd*, Civil No. 88-366-A (S.D. Iowa 1988), *on remand*, 104 B.R. 128 (Bankr. S.D. Iowa 1989).

557 Not encumberable: *In re* J. Catton Farms, 779 F.2d 1242 (7th Cir. 1985); *In re* Halls, 79 B.R. 417 (Bankr. S.D. Iowa 1987) (inducement to loan note pledge for pre-existing indebtedness); *In re* Lehl, 79 B.R. 880 (Bankr. D. Neb. 1987).

558 Grunzke v. State Bank of Wells, 68 B.R. 446 (D. Minn. 1987); *In re* Bowling, 64 B.R. 710 (Bankr. W.D. Mo. 1986); *In re* Weyland, 63 B.R. 854 (Bankr. E.D. Wis. 1986).

559 *In re* Bowling, 64 B.R. 710 (Bankr. W.D. Mo. 1986); *In re* Weyland, 63 B.R. 854 (Bankr. E.D. Wis. 1986).

560 Proceeds follows security: *In re* Bowling, 64 B.R. 710 (Bankr. W.D. Mo. 1986) *following In re* Hollie, 42 B.R. 111 (Bankr. M.D. Ga. 1984). *Contra* Grunzke v. State Bank of Wells, 68 B.R. 446 (D. Minn. 1987) (compensation for future income loss); *In re* Weyland, 63 B.R. 854 (Bankr. E.D. Wis. 1986) (general intangibles).

561 No assignment permitted: *In re* Azalea Farms, 68 B.R. 32 (Bankr. M.D. Fla. 1986).

562 Proceeds: *In re* Hollie, 42 B.R. 111 (Bankr. M.D. Ga. 1984). *Contra In re* Azalea Farms, Inc., 68 B.R. 32 (Bankr. M.D. Fla. 1986); *In re* Frasch, 53 B.R. 89 (Bankr. D.S.D. 1985); *In re* Berthold, 54 B.R. 318 (Bankr. D. Minn. 1985) (general intangibles).

563 Setoff permitted to IRS: *In re* Schons, 54 B.R. 665 (Bankr. W.D. Wash. 1985).

564 *In re* Settles, 69 B.R. 634 (Bankr. C.D. Ill. 1987); *In re* George, 62 B.R. 671 (Bankr. C.D. Ill. 1986).

565 Debtor-creditor relationship counts in debt computation: *In re* Stedman, 72 B.R. 49 (Bankr. D.N.D. 1987); counts as farm income: *In re* Jessen, 82 B.R. 490 (Bankr. S.D. Iowa 1988).

566 Proceeds: *In re* George, 62 B.R. 671 (Bankr. C.D. Ill. 1986).

567 No setoff allowed to SBA: *In re* Rinehart, 76 B.R. 746 (Bankr. D.S.D. 1987).

568 *In re* Arnold, 88 B.R. 917 (Bankr. N.D. Iowa 1988) (can be encumbered subject to constraints of 16 U.S.C. §§ 590h(g) as to current crop but not past crop).

569 Characterized as general intangibles: *In re* Hunerdosse, 85 B.R. 999 (Bankr. S.D. Iowa 1988), *aff'd sub nom.* United States v. Hunderdosse, No. 88-364-B (S.D. Iowa Nov. 28, 1988); *In re* Liebe, 41 B.R. 965 (Bankr. N.D. Iowa 1984); *In re* Schmidt, 38 B.R. 380 (Bankr. D.N.D. 1984); *In re* Sunberg, 35 B.R. 777 (Bankr. S.D. Iowa 1983), *aff'd*, 729 F.2d 561 (8th Cir. 1984).

570 As products of crops: *In re* Otto Farms, 247 B.R. 757 (Bankr. C.D. Ill. 2000) (loan deficiency payments from the Commodity Credit Corporation); *In re* Lesmeister, 242 B.R. 920 (Bankr. D.N.D. 1999) (Crop Loss Disaster Assistance Program); *In re* Kingsley, 73 B.R. 767 (Bankr. D. N.D. 1987); proceeds: *In re* Munger, 495 F.2d 511 (9th Cir. 1974); *In re* Kruse, 38 B.R. 958 (Bankr. D. Kan. 1983); Fed. Crop Deficiency Program/setoff allowed: *In re* Matthieson, 63 B.R. 56 (D. Minn. 1986). *Contra In re* Hazelton, 85 B.R. 400 (Bankr. E.D. Mich. 1988), *rev'd*, 96 B.R. 111 (E.D. Mich. 1988).

571 Proceeds: *In re* Munger, 495 F.2d 511 (9th Cir. 1974); *In re* Sumner, 69 B.R. 758 (Bankr. D. Or. 1986); *In re* Nivens, 22 B.R. 287 (Bankr. N.D. Tex. 1982); agreement not to grow/contract right: J. Catton Farms, Inc. v. First Nat'l Bank of Chicago, 779 F.2d 1242 (7th Cir. 1985); diversion agreements and payments/general intangibles: *In re* Kruse, 38 B.R. 958 (Bankr. D. Kan. 1983); setoff not allowed to FmHA: *In re* Hazelton, 85 B.R. 400 (Bankr. E.D. Mich. 1988), *rev'd*, 96 B.R. 111 (E.D. Mich. 1988).

572 *In re* Carpenter, 79 B.R. 316 (Bankr. S.D. Ohio 1987); *In re* Sumner, 69 B.R. 758 (Bankr. D. Or. 1986); *In re* Haffner, 25 B.R. 882 (Bankr. N.D. Ind. 1982).

573 11 U.S.C. § 525; Lee v. Yeutter, 106 B.R. 588 (D. Minn. 1989) (upholding FmHA regulations precluding restructuring after chapter 7 discharge based on questionable finding that discharge eliminated debt obligation), *aff'd*, 917 F.2d 1104 (8th Cir. 1990); *In re* Lech, 80 B.R. 1001 (Bankr. D. Neb. 1987).

Loan and servicing programs which appear in the cases include:

- FmHA Limited Resource Loan Program;[574]
- FmHA 7 U.S.C. § 1981a deferral program;[575]
- Farm Credit Services Land Values Guarantee Program;[576]
- Current Federal Land Bank (FLB) loan programs and borrower classifications;[577] and
- Cotton price support loan program.[578]

While most bankruptcy courts are reluctant to intrude on determinations of qualification for and receipt of benefits,[579] a bankruptcy court may review agency benefit denial and where unfounded, may under appropriate circumstances order payment by turnover of benefits to a debtor.[580]

16.5.4 Treatment of Unsecured Creditors in Chapter 12 Cases

16.5.4.1 Best Interests/Liquidation Analysis

The treatment of unsecured creditors in chapter 12 cases follows the treatment of unsecured creditors in chapter 13. Chapter 12 provisions are drawn verbatim from those in chapter 13, with the result that much law applicable to chapter 13 cases (other than the disposable income test) will be relevant to cases under chapter 12.

Chapter 12 requires that unsecured creditors under a plan receive at least as much or more than they would have received if the debtor had undergone liquidation;[581] this test is discussed elsewhere in this manual.[582] In many farmer bankruptcies, virtually all equity has been pledged to one or more creditors as security; unpledged property is usually exempt. In such cases, unsecured creditors would receive little or nothing upon liquidation.

In some cases, however, debtors have property—particularly real property—which is not part of the exempt farmstead and which has remained unpledged. Although this property may be excluded for purposes of the calculation of eligibility for chapter 12,[583] it cannot be excluded for purposes of the liquidation analysis.

Liquidation analysis is determined "as of the effective date of the plan."[584] Courts have keyed it to the projected effective date of the plan[585] or of the order confirming the plan.[586] The liquidation analysis may embrace post-petition property and program payments.[587] If the court recognized the presence of fraudulent transfers, then it may require the liquidation analysis to include the value of those transfers in its calculation.[588]

Most trustees and courts require the liquidation analysis and percentage for unsecured creditors to be disclosed in the plan;[589] this may be relatively easy to do for dairy and livestock operations, but problematic with crop operations where return is risky and valuation is subject to market factors. If not set forth in the plan, however, the liquidation analysis must be presented in either other documentation or an evidentiary presentation for the court and chapter 12 trustee to determine confirmability.

Some chapter 12 trustees insist on some payment to the unsecured creditors for confirmation. However, the courts that have addressed the issue of zero percent or nominal unsecured distribution plans have clearly indicated that if they truly represent the outcome of the liquidation analysis

---

574 *In re* Schaal, 93 B.R. 644 (Bankr. W.D. Ark. 1988); *In re* Kesterson, 94 B.R. 561 (Bankr. W.D. Ark. 1987); *In re* Doud, 74 B.R. 865 (Bankr. S.D. Iowa 1987).

575 *In re* Kenny, 75 B.R. 515 (Bankr. E.D. Mich. 1987); *In re* Kjeldahl, 52 B.R. 916 (Bankr. D. Minn. 1985); *In re* Beattie, 31 B.R. 703 (Bankr. W.D.N.C. 1984).

576 *In re* Konzak, 78 B.R. 990 (Bankr. D.N.D. 1987).

577 *In re* Neff, 89 B.R. 672 (Bankr. S.D. Ohio 1988).

578 7 U.S.C. § 1444; 7 C.F.R. § 1427 *et seq.*; *In re* Julien Co., 117 B.R. 910 (Bankr. W.D. Tenn. 1990).

579 *See* § 16.4, *supra.*

580 *See, e.g., In re* Quillen, 97 B.R. 288 (Bankr. W.D. Va. 1989) (reversal of denial of ASCS disaster payments in chapter 11 case).

581 11 U.S.C. § 1225(a)(4); *In re* Fortney, 36 F.3d 701 (7th Cir. 1994); *In re* Rott, 94 B.R. 163 (Bankr. D.N.D. 1988); *In re* Nielsen, 86 B.R. 177 (Bankr. E.D. Mo. 1988), *citing* Holytex Carpet Mills v. Tedford, 691 F.2d 392 (8th Cir. 1982).

582 § 12.3.1, *supra. See generally* Matson, *Understanding the New Family Farmer Bankruptcy Act,* 21 U. Rich. L. Rev. 521 (Spring 1987) (example calculation). For an interesting discussion on valuing stock in closely held family farm corporations for liquidation analysis purposes, see *In re* Harper, 156 B.R. 858 (Bankr. E.D. Ark. 1993).

583 *See* § 16.2.2.3.3, *supra.*

584 11 U.S.C. 1225(a)(4).

585 *In re* Hopwood, 124 B.R. 82 (Bankr. E.D. Mo. 1991); *In re* Lupfer Bros., 120 B.R. 1002 (Bankr. W.D. Mo. 1990); *In re* Perdue, 95 B.R. 475 (Bankr. W.D. Ky. 1988); *In re* Musil, 99 B.R. 448 (Bankr. D. Kan. 1988) (debtors cannot redefine effective date; effective date cannot be earlier than the date the first confirmation plan heard). *Contra In re* Nielsen, 86 B.R. 177 (Bankr. E.D. Mo. 1988) (determined from date of petition).

586 Gribbons v. Fed. Land Bank of Louisville, 106 B.R. 113 (W.D. Ky. 1989) (*dicta*); *In re* Foos, 121 B.R. 778 (Bankr. S.D. Ohio 1990); *In re* Bremer, 104 B.R. 999 (Bankr. W.D. Mo. 1989); *In re* Milleson, 83 B.R. 696 (Bankr. D. Neb. 1988).

587 Gribbons v. Fed. Land Bank of Louisville, 106 B.R. 113 (W.D. Ky. 1989) (in *dicta*); *In re* Lupfer Bros., 120 B.R. 1002 (Bankr. W.D. Mo. 1990); *In re* Foos, 121 B.R. 778 (Bankr. S.D. Ohio 1990) (restricted to post-filing but pre-confirmation property; acceptable to exclude growing crops. Exclusion of government payments depends on present entitlement to them); *In re* Bremer, 104 B.R. 999 (Bankr. W.D. Mo. 1989); *In re* Perdue, 95 B.R. 475 (Bankr. W.D. Ky. 1988).

588 *In re* Zurface, 95 B.R. 527 (Bankr. S.D. Ohio 1989). *But see In re* Winterroth, 97 B.R. 454 (Bankr. C.D. Ill. 1988) (absent the pendency of an adversary proceeding to recover a fraudulent conveyance, court cannot rule on its validity or impact).

589 *In re* Snider Farms, Inc., 79 B.R. 801 (Bankr. N.D. Ind. 1987); *In re* Martin, 78 B.R. 598 (Bankr. D. Mont. 1987).

and the disposable income test, such plans may be confirmed.[590] Because of the unique construction of disposable income in chapter 12, however, even if a confirmed plan projects zero percent disposable income, the debtor may be found to have had actual disposable income that must be paid prior to discharge.[591] In the extremely rare instance of the solvent farmer debtor, some courts have indicated that if the liquidation analysis shows assets exceeding the value of one-hundred percent distribution to unsecured creditors, then unsecured creditors must be paid present value on their claims in the same manner as secured creditors.[592]

16.5.4.2 Good Faith Test

Chapter 12 also tracks verbatim the "good faith" test of chapter 13.[593] The good faith test may become the primary tool for creditor opposition to chapter 12 plans, not only by unsecured, but also by secured creditors who may utilize the "good faith" test as a weapon, particularly when a secured creditor is treated unusually.[594] Case law and perspectives developed under chapter 13 regarding "good faith" are relevant to chapter 12 cases.[595]

Despite the fact that the chapter 12 good faith test language is identical to chapter 13, certain unique aspects of chapter 12 should result in courts interpreting the test somewhat differently under chapter 12. For example, chapter 12 allows modification of the rights of holders of farmstead real property interests and the payment of secured creditors over a term exceeding plan life.[596] Courts applying a chapter 12 good faith test may consider the terms and conditions of such modifications and/or repayments in comparison with the other plan aspects, the debtor's financial ability and condition, and market place norms for repayment terms.

Those courts which have addressed good faith in chapter 12 cases have found evidence of lack of good faith where there has been: (1) failure to disclose material assets, transfers and indebtedness;[597] (2) abusive refiling and filing for purposes of delay;[598] (3) transfer of assets to debtor entity pre-petition to avoid foreclosure;[599] (4) failure to file timely schedules and obey court orders[600] (5) filing of a petition without intent or ability to reorganize;[601] and (6) inadequate claim valuation.[602] Abusive refiling with lack of good faith can cause subsequent dismissal *with* prejudice, and in extreme cases potential liability for costs, expenses and attorney fees.[603]

By contrast, courts have not generally determined a lack of good faith from: (1) creating exempt assets from non-exempt assets pre-petition;[604] (2) zero or nominal distribu-

---

590 *See In re* Kjerulf, 82 B.R. 123 (Bankr. D. Or. 1987); *In re* Big Hook Land & Cattle Co., 77 B.R. 793, 795 (Bankr. D. Mont. 1987); *In re* Danelson, 77 B.R. 261 (Bankr. D. Mont. 1987).

591 Rowley v. Yarnall, 22 F.3d 190 (8th Cir. 1994).

592 *In re* Ogle, 261 B.R. 22 (Bankr. D. Idaho 2001) (interest mandated on unsecured claims at federal post-judgment interest rate); *In re* Winter, 151 B.R. 278 (Bankr. W.D. Okla. 1993); *In re* Hansen, 77 B.R. 722 (Bankr. D.N.D. 1987) (chapter 12); *In re* Fursman Ranch, Inc., 38 B.R. 907 (Bankr. W.D. Mo. 1984) (chapter 11 under § 1129(b)(2)(B)); *In re* Christian, 25 B.R. 438 (Bankr. D.N.M. 1982) (chapter 13).

593 11 U.S.C. § 1225(a)(3); *cf.* 11 U.S.C. § 1325(a)(3); *In re* Zurface, 95 B.R. 527 (Bankr. S.D. Ohio 1989). *See also* § 12.3.2, *supra.*

594 *See* §§ 16.5.5.2, 16.5.5.3, *infra,* concerning treatment of secured creditors. Of the factors outlined in *In re* Kitchens, 702 F.2d 885 (11th Cir. 1983), several involve secured creditors, for example, degree of effort, duration of plan (and reamortizations beyond plan life called for by the plan), and circumstances under which debts were contracted and the debtor's dealings with creditors. The "degree of effort" criterion has fallen by the wayside in chapter 13 with the advent of the "disposable income test" in 1984. *See In re* Red, 60 B.R. 113 (Bankr. E.D. Tenn. 1986); 8 Collier on Bankruptcy ¶ 1325.04[1] (15th ed. rev.).

595 *In re* Pearson, 917 F.2d 1215 (9th Cir. 1990); *In re* Carter, 165 B.R. 518 (Bankr. M.D. Fla. 1994); *In re* Luchenbill, 112 B.R. 204 (Bankr. E.D. Mich. 1990) (chapter 12); *In re* Beswick, 98 B.R. 900 (Bankr. N.D. Ill. 1989); *In re* Kloberdanz, 83 B.R. 767 (Bankr. D. Colo. 1988) (adopting the criteria of Flygare v. Boulden, 709 F.2d 1344 (10th Cir. 1983)); *In re* Weldin-Lynn, Inc., 79 B.R. 409 (Bankr. E.D. Ark. 1987). See § 12.3, *supra,* for a discussion of the good faith test in chapter 13.

596 11 U.S.C. §§ 1222(b)(2), (b)(5), (b)(9). *Cf.* 11 U.S.C. § 1322(b)(2).

597 *In re* Luchenbill, 112 B.R. 204 (Bankr. E.D. Mich. 1990); *In re* Welsh, 78 B.R. 984 (Bankr. W.D. Mo. 1987). Not every such failure constitutes bad faith, however: *Contra In re* Nelson, 291 B.R. 861 (Bankr. N.D. Idaho 2003) (debtors' pre-petition sale of cattle without advising secured creditor reflected poor judgment but was not bad faith that would preclude plan confirmation).

598 *In re* Beswick, 98 B.R. 900 (Bankr. N.D. Ill. 1989); *In re* McDermott, 77 B.R. 384 (Bankr. N.D.N.Y. 1987); *In re* Galloway Farms, Inc., 82 B.R. 486 (Bankr. S.D. Iowa 1987).

599 *In re* S Farms One, Inc., 73 B.R. 103 (Bankr. D. Colo. 1987), although filing immediately pre-foreclosure is not in itself bad faith. *See In re* Euerle Farms, Inc., 861 F.2d 1089 (8th Cir. 1988); *In re* Marshall, 108 B.R. 195 (Bankr. C.D. Ill. 1989); *In re* Snider, 99 B.R. 374 (Bankr. S.D. Ohio 1989); *In re* Zurface, 95 B.R. 527 (Bankr. S.D. Ohio 1989); *In re* Land, 82 B.R. 572 (Bankr. D. Colo. 1988); *In re* Weldin-Lynn, Inc., 79 B.R. 409 (Bankr. E.D. Ark. 1987); *In re* Ouverson, 79 B.R. 830 (Bankr. N.D. Iowa 1987) (but can be with other factors); *In re* Route 202 Corp., 37 B.R. 367 (Bankr. E.D. Pa. 1984) (chapter 11).

600 Lerch v. Fed. Land Bank of St. Louis, 94 B.R. 998 (N.D. Ill. 1989); *In re* Turner, 71 B.R. 120 (Bankr. D. Mont. 1987); *In re* S Farms One, Inc., 73 B.R. 103 (Bankr. D. Colo. 1987).

601 *In re* Euerle Farms, Inc., 861 F.2d 1089 (8th Cir. 1988). *See also In re* Wald, 211 B.R. 359 (Bankr. D.N.D. 1997) (lack of good faith found based on prior unsuccessful cases and lack of meaningful change in circumstances).

602 *In re* Euerle Farms, Inc., 861 F.2d 1089 (8th Cir. 1988).

603 *In re* Borg, 105 B.R. 56 (Bankr. D. Mont. 1989); *In re* McDermott, 77 B.R. 384 (Bankr. N.D.N.Y. 1987). Absent court order for cause, however, dismissals are without prejudice except to the extent of limitations in 11 U.S.C. § 109(g). 11 U.S.C. § 349(a). *See* §§ 13.9, 16.4.7.2, *supra.*

604 *In re* McKeag, 77 B.R. 716 (Bankr. D. Neb. 1987) (but the *McKeag* court also found that converting non-exempt assets to exempt assets immediately pre-petition may militate for some plan repayment based upon such converted assets).

tion to unsecured creditors;[605] or surrender of collateral to secured creditors.[606]

Some indicia of good faith in farm cases, as observed in the case of *In re Kloberdanz*,[607] appear to be: (1) a substantially leaner farm operation pared down pre-petition; (2) relatively short payout to principal secured creditors; (3) sharing with secured creditors any upside gain or sales proceeds of farm if sold during plan; (4) demonstrably frugal lifestyle and modest living expenses; (5) substantial work and personal involvement of both debtors in management and day-to-day farm operation.

16.5.4.3 Ability to Pay/Disposable Income Requirement

The chapter 12 disposable income requirement has been lifted verbatim from chapter 13.[608] To obtain confirmation over the objection of the chapter 12 trustee or the holder of an allowed unsecured claim to treatment of the unsecured creditors, a chapter 12 plan must require that the family farmer debtor devote *all* of his or her disposable income for at least three years to repayment under the plan.[609] Absent objection, the disposable income requirement is optional.[610] Failure of a creditor to object upon this basis at confirmation will preclude any subsequent objection upon subsequent modification, unless the debtor proposes a modification prejudicial to the creditor.[611]

There is one very significant difference, however, between how the identical disposable income language has been interpreted in chapter 12 and chapter 13. Considering the identical language in section 1325, courts have held that in the context of a chapter 13 case, projected disposable income is determined as of plan confirmation. The debtor includes reference to disposable income in the proposed plan, and if there is an objection, the debtor is required to "make a best effort" at a three-year projection of disposable income. This "best effort" may become a factor in the good

faith analysis required for confirmation. Under these chapter 13 cases, once the plan has been confirmed, it has a binding effect on the debtor and the creditors. The potential for increases in income beyond that which is projected is handled with a specific provision in the plan addressing this event. The actual amount of projected disposable income cannot be relitigated as a basis for determining dischargeability.

Some courts have not interpreted the disposable income requirement in Chapter 12 this way, however. Without addressing the chapter 13 interpretation, these courts have allowed the issue of disposable income to be raised as an objection to discharge, even when the debtor has met the projections contained in a confirmed plan. A debtor who can be shown to have had *actual* disposable income over the term of the plan that has not been turned over to unsecured creditors can be denied discharge for failing to fulfill the requirements of the plan as required under section 1225.

This interpretation is based on section 1228, the section that sets forth the discharge procedure for chapter 12 bankruptcy. In the typical chapter 12 case, at the end of the chapter 12 plan term, a discharge hearing will be held. If the debtor has completed all of the payments under the terms of the plan, she will request, and will generally receive, an order from the court granting a discharge of debts.

If the court finds that the debtor has not made "all payments under the plan," it can withhold the debtor's discharge pending compliance. The issue that has arisen most frequently as an objection to discharge has been the disposable income requirement under section 1225. In effect, "projected" disposable income has become "actual" disposable income, with the accounting of such income occurring at the end of the plan.[612] One court has provided some helpful discussion for managing this difficult issue during the plan term.[613]

The manner in which the farmer debtor elects to treat secured indebtedness under the plan, (for example, where the debt repayment exceeds plan life), may affect the amount of disposable income available for payment to the unsecured creditors. The farmer debtor may not be able to gauge with clarity the amount available for the unsecured creditors in any one or more years. However, to meet the disposable income requirement on or before objection, a chapter 12 plan should at minimum contain the provision that all of the debtor's disposable income will be devoted to repayment under the plan for at least three years, and provide a rough analysis so that evaluation can be made.[614] The debtor

---

605 *See In re* Kjerulf, 82 B.R. 123 (Bankr. D. Or. 1987); *In re* Big Hook Land & Cattle Co., 77 B.R. 793, 795 (Bankr. D. Mont. 1987); *In re* Citrowske, 72 B.R. 613 (Bankr. D. Minn. 1987).

606 *In re* Kjerulf, 82 B.R. 123 (Bankr. D. Or. 1987); but transfer of collateral back to creditors to help guarantors can be bad faith in corporate context. *In re* Sandy Ridge Dev. Corp., 77 B.R. 69 (Bankr. M.D. La. 1987).

607 83 B.R. 767 (Bankr. D. Colo. 1988).

608 *Compare* 11 U.S.C. § 1225(b)(1) *with* 11 U.S.C. § 1325(b)(1). *See* § 12.3.3, *supra*.

609 11 U.S.C. § 1225(b)(1)(B); *In re* Fortney, 36 F.3d 701 (7th Cir. 1994); *In re* Winterroth, 97 B.R. 454 (Bankr. C.D. Ill. 1988). Spousal income *may* be included in disposable income calculations for feasibility purposes; it is undecided whether it *must* be. *In re* Soper, 152 B.R. 984 (Bankr. D. Kan. 1993).

610 Farm Credit Bank v. Hurd, 108 B.R. 430 (W.D. Tenn. 1989); *In re* Rowley, 143 B.R. 547 (Bankr. D.S.D. 1992), *aff'd*, 22 F.3d 190 (8th Cir. 1994); *In re* Dues, 98 B.R. 434 (Bankr. N.D. Ind. 1989); *In re* Coffman, 90 B.R. 878 (Bankr. W.D. Tenn. 1988).

611 *In re* Coffman, 90 B.R. 878 (Bankr. W.D. Tenn. 1988).

612 *See, e.g.,* Hammrich v. Lovald, 98 F.3d 388 (8th Cir. 1996); Broken Bow Ranch, Inc. v. Farmers Home Admin., 33 F.3d 1005 (8th Cir. 1994); Rowley v. Yarnall, 22 F.3d 190 (8th Cir. 1994); *In re* Coffman, 90 B.R. 878 (Bankr. W.D. Tenn. 1988).

613 *In re* Schmidt, 145 B.R. 983 (Bankr. D.S.D. 1991).

614 A plan with this provision without setting of an amount certain meets confirmation standards. *See, e.g., In re* Coffman, 90 B.R. 878 (Bankr. W.D. Tenn. 1988).

should be able to justify his or her calculation of disposable income on the basis of historical and realistic projected costs.[615]

In chapter 12 cases, as in chapter 13 cases involving a self-employed person or sole proprietorship business, disposable income can be calculated only after deduction from gross income of both reasonable and necessary expenses for the continuation, preservation and operation of the family farm.[616] Such expenses should include taxes, repair costs, equipment upkeep, insurance, replacement livestock where income stream or lien value must be maintained, and reserves for new crop planting and nurture for the coming year.[617]

While chapter 13 case law will be useful on many disposable income questions in chapter 12, some unique aspects of the farmer bankruptcy must be considered. For example, the perspective of bankruptcy courts differ on whether savings can be accumulated under chapter 13 consonant with the disposable income requirement;[618] however, a farmer debtor under chapter 12 who annually plants and harvests crops and who is unable to obtain financing will need to bank part of the proceeds from one year's harvest for planting and expenses in the following year. Also, to account for the increased risk in a farming operation there must be greater elasticity for projected expense calculations, particularly for repair and equipment upkeep, than might be otherwise allowed under chapter 13.[619]

Farmers may have been squeaking by with minimal investment in chemicals, fertilizer, feed, seed and the like, with the result that crop and livestock yields have been substandard and, if so continued, will be inadequate to support a chapter 12 plan. Minimalization of some farm expenses in chapter 12 will result in early plan failure and bad business planning. Budgeting for operating expenses (as contrasted with living expenses) should therefore take into account reasonable—neither optimal nor minimal—expenditures consonant with good farming practices and yields necessary for chapter 12 feasibility. A balance must be struck which economizes expenditure while maximizing return.

16.5.4.4 Treatment of Priority Unsecured Creditors

The Bankruptcy Code at 11 U.S.C. § 507 sets forth several categories of unsecured indebtedness which are accorded priority treatment in both liquidation and reorganization bankruptcies. Priority debts under section 507 are always unsecured. The most common priority debts are recent tax obligations, recent employee wages and benefit plan contributions, and the administrative expenses of a case.

The treatment of priority unsecured indebtedness in chapter 12 is identical to that in chapter 13.[620] Section 1222(a)(2) provides that the plan shall provide for the full payment in deferred cash payments of all priority unsecured indebtedness, unless the holder of the claim agrees to different treatment. The repayment may be over the course of five years, if the plan so provides and is confirmed.[621]

Unlike the provisions of chapter 11,[622] and in contrast to the language used in section 1225(a)(5)(B)(ii) with regard to allowed secured claims, the language of section 1222(a)(2) does not provide for payment at the "present value" of the priority unsecured claim. As a result, interest or discount value need not be added to the repayment of a priority claim.[623] Also in contrast to chapter 11, the payment of

615 *In re* Kloberdanz, 83 B.R. 767 (Bankr. D. Colo. 1988); *In re* Schwarz, 85 B.R. 829 (Bankr. S.D. Iowa 1988). Test is reasonableness: *In re* Coffman, 90 B.R. 878 (Bankr. W.D. Tenn. 1988); *In re* Rott, 94 B.R. 163 (Bankr. D.N.D. 1988).

616 *See* 11 U.S.C. § 1225(b)(2)(A), (B). *In re* Gage, 159 B.R. 272 (Bankr. D.S.D. 1993).

617 *In re* Young, 103 B.R. 1021 (Bankr. S.D. Ind. 1988) ("disposable income" means that part of net operating income *above* what is reasonably necessary to pay the upcoming year's expenses *without* obtaining credit); *In re* Coffman, 90 B.R. 878 (Bankr. W.D. Tenn. 1988). *See In re* Linden, 174 B.R. 769 (C.D. Ill. 1994) (but depreciation is not a proper factor); *In re* Gage, 159 B.R. 272 (Bankr. D.S.D. 1993); *In re* Schmidt, 145 B.R. 983 (Bankr. W.D. Tex. 1993); *In re* Stottlemyer, 146 B.R. 234 (Bankr. W.D. Mo. 1992); *In re* Berger, 61 F.3d 624 (8th Cir. 1995); *In re* Fleshman, 123 B.R. 842 (Bankr. W.D. Mo. 1990). *But see In re* Broken Bow Ranch, Inc., 33 F.3d 1005 (8th Cir. 1994) (court can require debtor to pay more disposable income even if it means borrowing for next crop year); *In re* Bowlby, 113 B.R. 983 (Bankr. S.D. Ill. 1991) (debtors must make showing that they have earnestly explored possibility of producing next year's crop with credit before retention of crop proceeds for next crop year will be allowed).

618 *In re* Red, 60 B.R. 113 (Bankr. E.D. Tenn. 1986) (no savings). *Contra In re* Fries, 68 B.R. 676 (Bankr. E.D. Pa. 1986); *In re* Greer, 60 B.R. 547 (Bankr. C.D. Cal. 1986) (and cases cited therein); 8 Collier on Bankruptcy ¶ 1325.08 (15th ed. rev.).

619 *In re* Coffman, 90 B.R. 878 (Bankr. W.D. Tenn. 1988); *In re* Snider Farms, Inc., 83 B.R. 1003 (Bankr. N.D. Ind. 1988). One court has opined that while there should be a margin for error, it should be built into the projections for expenses rather than as

a separate line item for savings. *In re* Rott, 94 B.R. 163 (Bankr. D.N.D. 1988).

620 11 U.S.C. § 1222(a)(2); 11 U.S.C. § 1322(a)(2). *In re* Krump, 89 B.R. 821 (Bankr. D.S.D. 1988). *See* § 12.3.5, *supra*.

621 11 U.S.C. § 1222(c). One court has allowed a debtor to grant a tax lien on unencumbered property, subject to objection by other creditors, for payment as a secured claim over a longer period while providing for interest. *See In re* C.R. Druse, Sr., Ltd., 82 B.R. 1013 (Bank. D. Neb. 1988); *In re* Palombo, 144 B.R. 516 (Bankr. D. Colo. 1992); *In re* Teigen, 142 B.R. 397 (Bankr. D. Mont. 1992).

622 11 U.S.C. § 1129(a)(9)(B), (C).

623 *In re* Mitchell, 210 B.R. 978 (Bankr. N.D. Tex. 1997) (priority income tax debt); *In re* Bossert, 201 B.R. 553 (Bankr. E.D. Wash. 1996) (same). *See In re* Wakehill Farms, 123 B.R. 774 (Bankr. N.D. Ohio 1990); *In re* Krump, 89 B.R. 821 (Bankr. D.S.D. 1988); *In re* Herr, 80 B.R. 135 (Bankr. S.D. Iowa 1987).

priority administrative expenses is not required immediately upon confirmation or the effective date of the chapter 12 plan.[624]

By definition of the statute, priority debts must be unsecured.[625] If a tax claim qualifies as a secured claim it does not qualify for priority treatment. A tax debt is secured in bankruptcy to the extent a lien securing the debt arises under state or federal law and the lien is unavoidable in bankruptcy.[626] If a tax creditor has a secured claim that is provided for in the plan, it is subject to section 1225(a)(5).

16.5.5 Treatment of Secured Creditors in Chapter 12 Plans

16.5.5.1 Unique Nature of Secured Creditors and Their Security Interests in Farm Cases

The amount which must be paid upon allowed secured claims to insure confirmation in chapter 12 cases is the same as that under chapter 13—one-hundred percent of the present value of their allowed secured claims.[627] Secured creditors in chapter 12 must also retain their lien.[628] In all other aspects, however, chapter 12 allows quite different treatment of secured claims.[629] In particular, the degree of protection provided to creditors in chapter 12 is considerably different and reduced from that accorded secured creditors in other bankruptcy chapters.[630] The material in this subsection must be read together with § 16.5.3, *supra*.

Typically, government and Farm Credit System lenders are the key players in a chapter 12 case. They may be significantly under-secured, so that they are the primary targets of the chapter 12 cramdown. In the typical case, there are also other non-government creditors, for example, local banks or individuals, who may hold security interests in pieces of equipment or vehicles used by the debtor and necessary for the farm operation.

Counsel for the farmer debtor should check the recordation, extent, and accuracy of each and every security interest believed to be involved in a chapter 12 case. Although most secured creditors will comply with all legal requirements to protect their collateral, sometimes a security interest has been improperly formed or remains unrecorded.[631] Inchoate interests are subject to avoidance and will place the farmer debtor in a better posture for reorganization.[632]

624 *In re* Mosbrucker, 227 B.R. 434 (B.A.P. 8th Cir. 1998) (unpaid employee withholding taxes are nondischargeable priority trust fund taxes though labeled penalties by the IRS), *aff'd*, 198 F.3d 250 (8th Cir. 1999). *Cf.* 11 U.S.C. § 1129(a)(9)(A); *see In re* Palombo, 144 B.R. 516 (Bankr. D. Colo. 1992); *In re* Teigen, 142 B.R. 397 (Bankr. D. Mont. 1992); *In re* Citrowske, 72 B.R. 613 (Bankr. D. Minn. 1987). See also discussion of treatment of priority debts at § 16.5.6.3, *infra*.

625 *In re* Stanford, 826 F.2d 353 (5th Cir. 1987); United States v. Neal Pharmacal Co., 789 F.2d 1283 (8th Cir. 1986); *In re* Wrigley, 195 B.R. 914 (Bankr. E.D. Ark. 1996) (county tax liability creates a lien under state law and therefore tax claim is not a priority claim).

626 11 U.S.C. §§ 101(37) and 101(53); *In re* Stanford, 826 F.2d 353 (5th Cir. 1987); *In re* Krump, 89 B.R. 821 (Bankr. D.S.D. 1988).

627 11 U.S.C. § 1225(a)(5); 11 U.S.C. § 1325(a)(5). *In re* Weldin-Lynn, Inc., 79 B.R. 409 (Bankr. E.D. Ark. 1987); *In re* Robinson Ranch, Inc., 75 B.R. 606 (Bankr. D. Mont. 1987); *In re* Edwardson, 74 B.R. 831 (Bankr. D.N.D. 1987); *In re* Hardzog, 74 B.R. 701 (Bankr. W.D. Okla. 1987); *In re* Lenz, 74 B.R. 413 (Bankr. C.D. Ill. 1987); *In re* Janssen Charolais, 73 B.R. 125 (Bankr. D. Mont. 1987); *In re* Hochmuth Farms, Inc., 79 B.R. 266 (Bankr. D. Md. 1987).

628 *See* § 16.6.3.4, *infra*; *In re* Hanna, 915 F.2d 945 (8th Cir. 1990); Albaugh v. Terrell, 93 B.R. 115 (E.D. Mich. 1988); *In re* Batchelor, 97 B.R. 993 (Bankr. E.D. Ark. 1988); *In re* Sealey Bros., 158 B.R. 801 (Bankr. W.D. Mo. 1993) (finds lien partially voided by plan confirmation); *In re* Butler, 97 B.R. 508 (Bankr. E.D. Ark. 1988); *In re* Citrowske, 72 B.R. 613 (Bankr. D. Minn. 1987).

629 *Compare* 11 U.S.C. § 1322(b)(2) *with* 11 U.S.C. §§ 1222(b)(2), (b)(5), (b)(9). *In re* Kline, 94 B.R. 557 (Bankr. N.D. Ind. 1988).

630 *See* § 16.5.3.6, *supra*. The Supreme Court's decision in Dewsnup v. Timm, 502 U.S. 410, 112 S. Ct. 773, 116 L. Ed. 2d 903 (1991), decided under chapter 7, contains some strong language regarding lien splitting and § 506(d); however, § 1225(a)(5) should continue to allow farm reorganizations to utilize cramdown of the claims of under-secured creditors. *See* § 11.7, *supra*. Wade v. Bradford, 39 F.3d 1126 (10th Cir. 1994) (stripdown of residential mortgage permitted in chapter 11); *In re* Broken Bow Ranch, Inc., 33 F.3d 1005 (8th Cir. 1994); *In re* Leverett, 145 B.R. 709 (Bankr. W.D. Okla. 1992); *see also In re* Harmon is 184 B.R. 352 (D.S.D. 1995) (stripdown of liens permitted in chapter 12 under Code section 506), *aff'd*, 101 F.3d 574 (8th Cir. 1996); *In re* Zabel, 249 B.R. 764 (Bankr. E.D. Wis. 2000). Wade v. Bradford, 39 F.3d 1126 (10th Cir. 1994) (stripdown of residential mortgage permitted in chapter 11); *In re* Bowen is 174 B.R. 840 (Bankr. S.D. Ga. 1994). In 1994, Congress addressed this issue by prohibiting stripdown of most residential mortgages in chapter 11, but not in chapter 12. 11 U.S.C. § 1123(b)(5). *Cf.* 11 U.S.C. § 1222(b)(2); Nobelman v. Am. Sav. Bank, 184 U.S. 324, 113 S. Ct. 2106, 124 L. Ed. 2d 228 (1993).

631 The efficacy of creditor perfection is governed by state law in its adaptation of the Uniform Commercial Code and other special laws, such as for registration of liens with state motor vehicle departments. *See* § 16.4.4.4.4, *supra*. See, *e.g., In re* Stout, 284 B.R. 511 (Bankr. D. Kan. 2002) (bank's security agreement did not attach to growing crops planted pre-petition because it failed to provide description of land on which crops were grown; change of law eliminating land description requirement enacted post-petition under Revised Article 9 did not apply); *In re* Buchholz, 224 B.R. 13 (Bankr. D.N.J. 1998) (secured claim disallowed under New Jersey law because it was not properly notarized, claim rendered unsecured). 11 U.S.C. § 502(b)(1) requires that a court disallow a claim to the extent that it is unenforceable against the debtor or property of the debtor. All state law defenses to enforcement, including defenses based on consumer protection laws, thus may be pursued in the objection to claim process.

632 11 U.S.C. § 544. *See* § 10.4.2.6.2, *supra*.

16.5.5.2 The Allowed Secured Claim and Its Valuation

The core of most chapter 12 confirmations and battles with creditors to date, apart from eligibility, has been valuation of the allowed secured claims of the major creditors. Questions of valuation of secured claims are critical because:

- The amount of repayment necessary directly affects feasibility;
- Material provisions of the plan governing the term of repayment and interest hinge on the amount to be repaid;
- Farmers generally are fully enveloped by secured creditors, so that the repayment amount has a bearing both on the disposable income test of section 1225(b) and the liquidation analysis of section 1225(a)(4).

Most farm creditors with extensive security interests have one or more valuations of their security interests. These valuations typically either are done by the person in charge in a creditor's local office or are contracted out to local appraisers.

It is necessary for the debtor's attorney to review the valuation claimed by the secured creditor. The valuation can be obtained either through discovery, informal disclosure, or it may have been previously disclosed to the debtor as part of any proffer of voluntary liquidation or buy out prior to filing. In any event, such valuation is in the creditor's files and should be accessible upon request. If the creditor's valuation appears high, as it probably will, the debtor should have an appraisal done of both real and personal property subject to the security interest prior to filing under chapter 12.

While it may be desirable to come up with a valuation which maximizes the value of the collateral for some purposes such as defense of automatic stay motions, in chapter 12 confirmation, as in chapter 13, the perspective is the reduction of the secured creditor's claim to its optimal low for the one-hundred percent repayment and interest calculation. There may be times, however, when a low valuation should be partially compromised for the sake of expeditious or unopposed confirmation. Section 1225(a)(5)(A) specifically contemplates this course.[633] When valuing security interests, one may need to begin by closely analyzing the loan instruments to determine the scope of the creditor's interest. The loan documents will determine whether the collateral includes, for example, all crops or all livestock or

only a portion. In addition, some security interests will purport to cover real property and/or farm implements.[634]

The valuation of a security interest in chapter 12 under 11 U.S.C. § 506 is at a "going concern" or fair market value, not liquidation value (unless property sale or surrender is proposed), because reorganization and use of the property is contemplated.[635] The point in time at which valuation of the amount of the allowed secured claim—the value of the collateral pledged to the creditor—is determined has been addressed in various ways by the bankruptcy courts. Some freeze the valuation of the allowed secured claim as of the date of the petition's filing;[636] most place valuation as of the effective date of the plan, that is, the date of the confirmation order.[637] Again, the statute specifically states "value, as of the effective date of the plan."[638] Valuation must be based upon actual use, not highest and best use.[639] Possible increase or appreciation in the value of the property over the plan's life is not recoverable as part of a creditor's allowed secured claim.[640]

Valuation of real property may be made by a number of approaches: comparable sales or market value approach,

---

633 *In re* Weldin-Lynn, Inc., 79 B.R. 409 (Bankr. E.D. Ark. 1987); *In re* Durr, 78 B.R. 221 (Bankr. D.S.D. 1987); *In re* Hansen, 77 B.R. 722 (Bankr. D.N.D. 1987).

634 *E.g.*, Mid-Ohio Chem. Co. v. Petry, 140 F. Supp. 2d 828 (S. D. Ohio 2000) (security agreement covered all 1989 crops plus farming equipment).

635 *In re* Felten, 95 B.R. 629 (Bankr. N.D. Iowa 1988) (cannot use valuation formula in Agricultural Credit Act of 1987; *In re* Robinson Ranch, Inc., 75 B.R. 606 (Bankr. D. Mont. 1987) (good discussion of all appraisal methods); *In re* Weldin-Lynn, Inc., 79 B.R. 409 (Bankr. E.D. Ark. 1987); *In re* Citrowske, 72 B.R. 613 (Bankr. D. Minn. 1987); *In re* Foster, 79 B.R. 906 (Bankr. D. Mont. 1987). One court concluded that going concern value for a farm, under the proper circumstances, may be *less* than liquidation value because of use. *In re* Snider Farms, Inc., 79 B.R. 801 (Bankr. N.D. Ind. 1987). *See* Associates Commercial Corp. v. Rash, 117 S. Ct. 1879 (June 16, 1997) (replacement value is appropriate valuation standard for automobile in chapter 13 if debtor intends to use the property). *See generally* § 11.2.2.3, *supra. In re Winthrop Old Farm Nurseries, Inc.*, 50 F.3d 72 (1st Cir. 1995); *In re* McClurkin, 31 F.3d 401 (6th Cir. 1994); *In re* Coker, 973 F.2d 258 (4th Cir. 1992).

636 *In re* Big Hook Land & Cattle Co., 81 B.R. 1001 (Bankr. D. Mont. 1988).

637 *In re* Tunnissen, 216 B.R. 834 (Bankr. D.S.D. 1996); *In re* Rice, 171 B.R. 399 (Bankr. N.D. Ala. 1994); *In re* Braxton, 124 B.R. 870 (Bankr. N.D. Fla. 1991) (value can exclude nursing animals where unmarketable or where they would die absent continuation of the farming operation).

638 11 U.S.C. § 1225(a)(5)(B)(ii).

639 *In re* Caraway, 95 B.R. 466 (Bankr. W.D. Ky. 1988); *In re* Hollinrake, 93 B.R. 183 (Bankr. S.D. Iowa 1988); *In re* Anderson, 88 B.R. 877 (Bankr. W.D. Ind. 1988); legislative history at Sen. Rep. No. 95-989 (1978), *reprinted in* 1978 U.S.C.C.A.N. 5787.

640 *In re* Big Hook Land & Cattle Co., 81 B.R. 1001 (Bankr. D. Mont. 1988); *In re* C.R. Druse, Sr., Ltd., 82 B.R. 1013 (Bankr. D. Neb. 1988); *In re* Wobig, 73 B.R. 292 (Bankr. D. Neb. 1987). This should be remembered when valuing replenishing collateral, for example, livestock and dairy. *In re* Borg, 88 B.R. 288 (Bankr. D. Mont. 1988) (replenishing collateral; no value added for increase in livestock).

cost approach, and/or income approach. Most bankruptcy courts have deemed the comparable sales or market value approach as the most reliable indicia of real property value.[641] However, some courts have found that the lack of recent real property sales in an area and/or the skew attributable to the declining farm economy and increasing foreclosures which affects market value have made the income approach more reliable under the circumstances of a case.[642] Several courts endorse the market value approach, but consider other appraisal approaches to test its efficacy.[643] Although rental may be a component of the basis for the income appraisal approach, courts have indicated that the espousal of a different adequate protection standard in section 1205(b)(3) cannot justify a straight rental value approach to real property valuation.[644]

Appraisals should be sure to contain consideration of *all* items of value. In the case of real property, this must include valuation—or at least consideration—of all base or allotments that run with the land and any contracts which may affect value.[645] Courts may take judicial notice of land values if appropriate documents and publications exist for their geographic areas.[646] In some areas state law may bear on farm land values.[647]

Contested valuation will require expert testimony and may involve documentary evidence and indices involving both the appraisal and typical farm practices and sales. It should also be remembered that the owner of property is competent to testify as to its value.[648] Any previous offers to purchase the property undergoing valuation are also relevant.[649]

Finding reputable and competent farm appraisers for both real and personal property at a cost the debtor can bear may be difficult, particularly where many have been employed on a regular basis by the creditors usually involved in farm bankruptcies.[650] Any critical valuation should be done prepetition, if possible, to allow counsel to evaluate the amount of cramdown possible and to prepare the outline of a plan. Any appraiser and arrangement for compensation made by the debtor post-petition must be approved by the bankruptcy court under 11 U.S.C. § 327.

16.5.5.3 Potential Plan Treatments of Secured Claims

16.5.5.3.1 In general

Secured creditors must be paid one-hundred percent of their allowed secured claims under a chapter 12 plan and be accorded the "present value" of their claim, which means addition of an interest or discount rate over the period for repayment.[651] Nevertheless, treatment of secured indebtedness within a chapter 12 plan can be varied to allow, within recognized commercial and farm lending principles and practices, maximum rescheduling and reamortization to assist the family farmer in reorganization. The debtor is expected to keep collateral adequately insured and to pay required taxes.[652]

The provisions of section 1225(a)(5)(A) allow the debtor and a secured creditor to consent to treatment, regardless of whether such treatment may be authorized under the Code or whether it is similar to pre-petition treatment.[653]

---

641 *In re* Borg, 88 B.R. 288 (Bankr. D. Mont. 1988); *In re* Hollinrake, 93 B.R. 183 (Bankr. S.D. Iowa 1988); *In re* Anderson, 88 B.R. 877 (Bankr. W.D. Ind. 1988) (market value approach should consider adjustments for: (1) any undue "suburbia and urban collar influence;" (2) any excessive disparity between the income approach and the market approach; and (3) any adjustment in location, size/shape, soil/topography, time of sale, and percent of tillable land; (4) downward adjustments for size of parcel; (5) evidence of poor yields based on soil); *In re* Chaney, 87 B.R. 131 (Bankr. D. Mont. 1988); *In re* Snider Farms, Inc., 79 B.R. 801 (Bankr. N.D. Ind. 1987).

642 *In re* Danelson, 77 B.R. 261 (Bankr. D. Mont. 1987); *In re* Cool, 81 B.R. 614 (Bankr. D. Mont. 1987); *In re* McKeag, 77 B.R. 716 (Bankr. D. Neb. 1987).

643 *In re* Borg, 88 B.R. 288 (Bankr. D. Mont. 1988); *In re* Hollinrake, 93 B.R. 183 (Bankr. S.D. Iowa 1988).

644 *In re* Beyer, 72 B.R. 525 (Bankr. D. Colo. 1987); *In re* Snider Farms, Inc., 79 B.R. 801 (Bankr. N.D. Ind. 1987).

645 *See* § 16.4.3, *supra; see also In re* Borg, 88 B.R. 288 (Bankr. D. Mont. 1988) (add value of royalty-producing leases); *In re* Townsend, 90 B.R. 498 (Bankr. M.D. Fla. 1988) (tobacco allotments); *In re* Dunning, 77 B.R. 789 (Bankr. D. Mont. 1987); *In re* Claeys, 81 B.R. 985 (Bankr. D.N.D. 1987); *In re* Ratliff, 79 B.R. 930 (Bankr. D. Colo. 1987).

646 Ahlers v. Norwest Bank of Worthington, 794 F.2d 388 (8th Cir. 1986); *In re* Anderson, 88 B.R. 877 (Bankr. N.D. Ind. 1988); *In re* Snider Farms, Inc., 83 B.R. 977 (Bankr. N.D. Ind. 1988) (judicial notice of land values and interest rates).

647 *In re* Kocher, 78 B.R. 844 (Bankr. S.D. Ohio 1987).

648 *See, e.g.,* Robinson v. Watts Detective Agency, 685 F.2d 729 (1st Cir. 1982); S. Ctr. Livestock Dealer, Inc. v. Securities State Bank of Hedley, 614 F.2d 1056 (5th Cir. 1980).

649 *In re* Weldin-Lynn, Inc., 79 B.R. 409 (Bankr. E.D. Ark. 1987).

650 The Rural Appraisal Manual of the American Society of Farm Managers and Rural Appraisers, Inc. is a good source of information and the Society may be a source of appraisal talent if debtor has difficulty in locating an appraiser.

651 11 U.S.C. § 1225(a)(5). *See In re* Woerner, 214 B.R. 208 (Bankr. D. Neb. 1997) (plan cannot deprive creditor of the value of its lien); *In re* Weldin-Lynn, Inc., 79 B.R. 409 (Bankr. E.D. Ark. 1987) (and cases cited therein); *In re* Claeys, 81 B.R. 985 (Bankr. D.N.D. 1987).

652 *In re* Ames, 973 F.2d 849 (10th Cir. 1992) (plan to pay secured creditor only through results of litigation rejected); *In re* Pretzer, 91 B.R. 428 (Bankr. N.D. Ohio 1988); *In re* Pond, 43 B.R. 522 (Bankr. D.N.D. 1984); *In re* Abbott, 23 B.R. 484 (Bankr. W.D. Okla. 1982). The 1994 amendments added 11 U.S.C. § 362(b)(18), an exception to the automatic stay, which allows for post-petition and *ad valorem* taxes to attach to a debtor's property.

653 *In re* Lyon, 161 B.R. 1013 (Bankr. D. Kan. 1993). *See* § 16.5.5.2, *supra.*

Based upon chapter 12's language and case law in chapters 12 and 13 secured indebtedness which has been accelerated pre-petition can be deaccelerated by the chapter 12 plan.[654] The decisions which have addressed either balloon notes or fully matured notes in the chapter 12 context have found that they may be spread for long-term repayment over a reasonable amortization as if ballooning or maturity had not occurred or would not occur, so long as the creditor retains its lien, in light of section 1222(b)(9).[655]

Chapter 12, however, contains two important departures from chapter 13's treatment of secured creditors:

(1) Chapter 12 allows the repayment of secured creditors, if appropriate, over a period longer than the life of the chapter 12 plan even though the original indebtedness is not so amortized; and

(2) Chapter 12 allows modification of the rights of holders of security interests in *all* real and personal property without regard to its residential nature, so that secured creditors collateralized by the farmstead can be reamortized without the need for cure of default.[656]

The valuation of allowed secured claims proposed by debtor or agreed upon by debtor and creditors must be disclosed in the plan for court evaluation of feasibility and compliance with section 1225(a)(5).[657]

16.5.5.3.2 Amortization and extending plan payments beyond the plan's life

In chapter 12, as in chapter 13, the life of a plan is three to five years. Secured creditors may be paid the value of their allowed secured claim over the life of the plan. As in chapter 13, chapter 12 allows cure of default on all secured indebtedness the term for repayment of which is longer than the plan's life over such longer period as is scheduled for this indebtedness.[658] However, unlike chapter 13, chapter 12 also allows the extension of repayment of secured indebtedness, regardless of original amortization, over a period beyond the life of the chapter 12 plan.[659]

The period of time over which a secured debt can be reamortized or spread must be determined in light of what is commercially reasonable in similar circumstances in the farm economic sector.[660] The following factors are helpful in this determination:

1. *What kind of property collateralizes the original loan?* Repayment on debt collateralized by real property typically can be spread over more lengthy periods, while personal property and livestock repayment is much shorter. If the loan is collateralized by real property, is it farmstead or non-farm residential property?

2. *How long is the useful life (depreciation schedule) of the personal property? How long has the debtor had the property?* The term should be compared with the value of the equipment over time, so that no additional adequate protection for depreciation need be allowed for under the plan.[661]

3. *Is the loan purchase money or non-purchase money?* The more commercially reasonable approach is shorter terms for purchase money than for non-purchase money.

4. *What is the original term on the loan?* How long does the plan propose to extend repayment to the creditor beyond its original bargain? Is the original amortization as good for the debtor as any reamortization would be.

5. *How long can it be anticipated that the debtor will remain farming?* The age of the debtor can be a factor although courts have not found it controlling when approving amortizations which will extend beyond the reasonable life expectancy of the debtor.[662]

6. *How long is the repayment period for loans in the private sector currently being made with the same or similar collateral? How long for government or Farm*

---

654 *In re* Terry, 780 F.2d 894 (11th Cir. 1985) (and cases cited therein); *In re* Taddeo, 685 F.2d 24 (2d Cir. 1982); *In re* Davis, 77 B.R. 312 (Bankr. M.D. Ga. 1987). However, see limitations discussed at § 16.4.4.4.5, *supra.*

655 11 U.S.C. § 1222(b)(2), (b)(5), (b)(9); *In re* Beard, 134 B.R. 239 (Bankr. S.D. Ohio 1991); *In re* Dunning, 77 B.R. 789 (Bankr. D. Mont. 1987); *In re* Martin, 78 B.R. 598 (Bankr. D. Mont. 1987); *In re* Foster, 79 B.R. 906 (Bankr. D. Mont. 1987); *see* § 16.5.5.3.2, *infra.*

656 This is also now a departure from chapter 11 as changed by the 1994 amendments which limits modification of debts secured by residential real property which serves as the debtor's principal residence in much the same manner as chapter 13. *See* 11 U.S.C. § 1123(b)(5); 11 U.S.C. § 1322(b)(2).

657 *In re* Kloberdanz, 83 B.R. 767 (Bankr. D. Colo. 1988); *In re* Rivera Sanchez, 80 B.R. 6 (Bankr. D.R.I. 1987).

658 11 U.S.C. § 1222(b)(5).

659 11 U.S.C. § 1222(b)(9); *In re* Beard, 134 B.R. 239 (Bankr. S.D. Ohio 1991); *In re* Mouser, 99 B.R. 803 (Bankr. S.D. Ohio 1989); *In re* Miller, 98 B.R. 311 (Bankr. N.D. Ohio 1989); *In re* Kline, 94 B.R. 557 (Bankr. N.D. Ind. 1988).

660 *In re* Rose, 135 B.R. 603 (Bankr. N.D. Ind. 1991); *In re* Indreland, 77 B.R. 268 (Bankr. D. Mont. 1987).

661 *In re* Rice, 171 B.R. 399 (Bankr. N.D. Ala. 1994); *In re* Borg, 88 B.R. 288 (Bankr. D. Mont. 1988) (repayment of principal upon collateralized loan must follow depreciation or § 1225(a)(5)(B)(i) lien retention not complied with).

662 *In re* John V. Francks Turkey Co., 1999 Bankr. LEXIS 893 (B.A.P. 10th Cir. Aug. 2, 1999) (twenty-five years allowed although debtor was sixty-two based on commitment of debtor's son to plan); *In re* Howard, 212 B.R. 864 (Bankr. E.D. Tenn. 1997) (twenty-year payment plan too long for debtors who were sixty-two and fifty-seven at time of confirmation). *See, e.g.,* Mulberry Agric. Enterprises, Inc., 113 B.R. 30 (D. Kan. 1990); *In re* Foster, 79 B.R. 906 (Bankr. D. Mont. 1987). *Contra In re* Rose, 135 B.R. 603 (Bankr. N.D. Ind. 1991).

Credit System lenders? What are the maximum and minimum periods typically given?

7. *How long has the repayment period for loans in the private sector historically been for loans with the same or similar collateral? How long for government or Farm Credit System lenders?*

8. *Are the payments under the chapter 12 plan to be made in equal payments, or does the Plan propose a front or end advantage by larger payments? Can a debtor compensate for a longer, less reasonable term by some advantage for the affected creditor?*

9. *What are the policies of the actual lender involved? Does the creditor have the capacity to reamortize, reschedule or defer payments itself? Does it typically restructure loans or have the capacity to do so? What are its typical terms for lending? Is the lender a private individual or an institution?*[663]

10. *How much debt service can the debtor devote to repayment of any individual secured creditors, and all secured creditors, based upon anticipated production, income and expenditures?*

11. *Are balloon notes or notes with disproportionate payments typical for the type of loan being reamortized and rescheduled?* The reamortization can contain a balloon, or can amortize the payments on the loan over a long period of time with a balloon due at a point in time before the end of the scheduled amortization.[664]

12. *Is the creditor willing to agree to a reasonable and feasible amortization period?*

While the following should be viewed only as a rough indicator, generally real estate loans can be amortized over fifteen to twenty years, although under the proper circumstances thirty to forty years may be appropriate.[665] A balloon payment either affecting repayment term and/or both repayment term and amortization (for example, a twenty-year amortization with payoff at ten years) may be proposed if typical and feasible.[666] Reamortization of contracts for deed on real property may demand shorter terms than loans collateralized by real property.[667]

Personal property such as farm equipment may have an outer limit for reamortization of seven years, although circumstances may dictate a shorter or longer period.[668] Livestock may vary with its useful life; dairy cattle, for example, may be as long as seven years, while feeder operations may be less. Continuous replacement and upgrading of a livestock operation may militate for a longer period for repayment.[669]

16.5.5.3.3 Interest rates for secured creditors

Secured creditors in chapter 12 cases are entitled to an interest or discount rate to assure them the present value of their claim when it is paid over time.[670] Different courts had

---

663 *In re* Rose, 135 B.R. 603 (Bankr. N.D. Ind. 1991) (individual lender should be treated differently on amortization than institutional lender); *In re* Koch, 131 B.R. 128 (Bankr. N.D. Iowa 1991).

664 *In re* Smith, 78 B.R. 491 (Bankr. N.D. Tex. 1987) (thirty-year amortization with balloon at twenty years for Federal Land Bank); *In re* Foster, 79 B.R. 906 (Bankr. D. Mont. 1987) (contract for deed maturing post-petition; norm found to be ten to fifteen years or twenty years with balloon at ten years; thirty-year amortization with balloon at fifteen years acceptable). *See, e.g., In re* Nauman, 213 B.R. 355 (B.A.P. 9th Cir. 1997) (evaluation of chapter 12 plan involving negative amortization of secured debt, feasibility is overriding concern).

665 *In re* John V. Francks Turkey Co., 1999 Bankr. LEXIS 893 (B.A.P. 10th Cir. Aug. 2, 1999) (twenty-five years allowed); *In re* Zerr, 167 B.R. 953 (Bankr. D. Kan. 1994) (thirty years allowed); *In re* Miller, 98 B.R. 311 (Bankr. N.D. Ohio 1989); *In re* Hagen, 95 B.R. 708 (Bankr. D.N.D. 1989) (thirty-year amortization in plan as originally confirmed); *In re* Schaal, 93 B.R. 644 (Bankr. W.D. Ark. 1988); *In re* Hart, 90 B.R. 150 (Bankr. E.D.N.C. 1988) (thirty-year amortization under original plan and modification); *In re* Bar L O Farms, West, 87 B.R. 125 (Bankr. D. Idaho 1988) (forty-year amortization); *In re* Chaney,

87 B.R. 131 (Bankr. D. Mont. 1988) (forty-year amortization, *dicta*); *In re* Simmons, 86 B.R. 160 (Bankr. S.D. Iowa 1988) (*dicta*); *In re* Smith, 78 B.R. 491 (Bankr. N.D. Tex. 1987); *In re* Snider Farms, Inc., 79 B.R. 801 and 83 B.R. 1003 (Bankr. N.D. Ind. 1987 and 1988); *In re* Bullington, 80 B.R. 590 (Bankr. M.D. Ga. 1987) (allowed thirty-year amortization on land authorized by § 1225(a)(5)(B) as construed *in pari materia* with § 1222(b)(9)), *aff'd sub nom.* Travelers Ins. Co. v. Bullington, 89 B.R. 1010 (M.D. Ga. 1988), *aff'd* 878 F.2d 354 (11th Cir. 1989); *In re* O'Farrell, 74 B.R. 421 (Bankr. N.D. Fla. 1987); *In re* Lenz, 74 B.R. 413 (Bankr. C.D. Ill. 1987); *In re* Hagensick, 73 B.R. 710 (Bankr. N.D. Iowa 1987); *In re* Janssen Charolais Ranch, Inc., 73 B.R. 125 (Bankr. D. Mont. 1987). *But see In re* Rose, 135 B.R. 603 (Bankr. N.D. Ind. 1991) (thirty-year amortization inappropriate based on age and income); *In re* Lupfer Bros., 120 B.R. 1002 (Bankr. W.D. Mo. 1990) (twenty-five-year amortization too long); *In re* Koch, 131 B.R. 128 (Bankr. N.D. Iowa 1991) (thirty years too long).

666 *See In re* Koch, 131 B.R. 128 (Bankr. N.D. Iowa 1991) (thirty-year amortization with balloon at fifteen years); *In re* LLL Farms, 111 B.R. 1016 (Bankr. M.D. Ga. 1990) (thirty-year amortization with balloon at twenty years).

667 *In re* Foster, 79 B.R. 906 (Bankr. N.D. Mont. 1987); *In re* Martin, 78 B.R. 598 (Bankr. D. Mont. 1987).

668 *In re* Fenske, 96 B.R. 244 (Bankr. D.N.D. 1988) (seven to ten year amortization on equipment (*dicta*)); *In re* Townsend, 90 B.R. 498 (Bankr. M.D. Fla. 1988) (three-year amortization on equipment); *In re* Adam, 92 B.R. 732 (Bankr. E.D. Mich. 1988) (nine-year amortization on equipment where first lien paid off, excellent maintenance record and sufficient budgeting for repair); *In re* Butler, 97 B.R. 508 (Bankr. E.D. Ark. 1988) (twenty years on equipment unacceptable).

669 *In re* Simmons, 86 B.R. 160 (Bankr. S.D. Iowa 1988) (seven to fifteen years on livestock if replaced) (*dicta*); *In re* Foster, 79 B.R. 906 (Bankr. D. Mont. 1987); *In re* Dunning, 77 B.R. 789 (Bankr. D. Mont. 1987).

670 11 U.S.C. § 1225(a)(5)(B)(ii); *In re* Batchelor, 97 B.R. 993 (Bankr. E.D. Ark. 1988); *In re* Weldin-Lynn, Inc., 79 B.R. 409 (Bankr. E.D. Ark. 1987). This is true whether the lien is consensual or by operation of law (and unavoidable). United

taken considerably diverse approaches to the question of what are appropriate interest or discount rates.

Some courts in chapter 12 cases had followed an approach that considered the market rate for the type and quality of loan, not specific to the individual creditor at issue.[671] Other courts preferred to use a "formula" approach that would typically use as a starting point the risk free cost of money, that is, the rate for treasury bills or the prime rate.[672] These courts often added a consideration of a risk factor in addition to market rate, if appropriate to the individual case considering the collateralization and other factors contributing to risk of subsequent default.[673]

The Supreme Court largely resolved this dispute in *Till v. SCS Credit Corp.*[674] The Court held that a formula method is to be used, with the prime rate of interest[675] as the starting point, adjusted by a factor for risk. Although not setting any specific amount for the risk factor, the Court cited cases adding one to three percent to the interest rate, and noted that the rate selected should be "high enough to compensate the creditor for its risk but not so high as to doom the plan."[676] The Court also held that an objecting creditor has the burden of going forward with evidence that the interest rate proposed by the debtor is inadequate.[677]

The pre-confirmation and post-confirmation periods should be distinguished for over-secured farm creditors for interest rates under the rationale in *United States v. Ron Pair Enterprises, Inc.*[678] Over-secured creditors may be entitled to their contract rates during the pre-confirmation period, although not thereafter, as well as reasonable attorney fees under section 506(b).[679]

16.5.5.3.4 Return or surrender of property to secured creditors

One of the most effective tools of reorganization is the paring down of the farm operation by reduction of collateral and its accompanying debt service. One of the primary methods of accomplishing this is return, relinquishment or abandonment to the secured creditor of all or a portion of the creditor's collateral. Such a return or relinquishment operates to reduce the allowed secured claim by the value of the collateral. Chapter 12 permits such relinquishment and credit.[680] How much credit is given to reduce the allowed secured claim of a creditor depends upon the consent of the creditor or the valuation of the collateral by the court.[681] Such return may include surrender of stock or shares owned by the debtor in cooperatives, Federal Land Banks and Production Credit Associations for credit against the secured claim of those creditors; however, generally, surrender to Farm Credit lenders requires their permission under the Agricultural Credit Act of 1987.[682]

---

680 The legislative history clearly contemplates such paring down. *See* 11 U.S.C. § 1225(a)(5)(C); and 11 U.S.C. §§ 1222(b)(7), 1222(b)(8), and 1222(b)(10). *See In re* B & G Farms, Inc., 82 B.R. 549 (Bankr. D. Mont. 1988); *In re* Indreland, 77 B.R. 268 (Bankr. D. Mont. 1987); *In re* Robinson Ranch, Inc., 75 B.R. 606 (Bankr. D. Mont. 1987); *In re* Mikkelsen Farms, Inc., 74 B.R. 280 (Bankr. D. Or. 1987); *In re* O'Farrell, 74 B.R. 421 (Bankr. N.D. Fla. 1987). Rogers & King, Collier Farm Bankruptcy Guide ¶ 4.08[2][d], at 4-114 (1992).

681 *In re* Branch, 127 B.R. 891 (Bankr. N.D. Fla. 1991) (valuation to be made on surrendered property according to disposition and value without remaining property); *In re* Butler, 97 B.R. 508 (Bankr. E.D. Ark. 1988); *In re* Caraway, 95 B.R. 466 (Bankr. W.D. Ky. 1988). *See In re* Grimm, 145 B.R. 994 (Bankr. D.S.D. 1992) (stay relief and disposition of collateral after default does not result of itself in debt satisfaction).

682 *In re* Davenport, 153 B.R. 551 (B.A.P. 9th Cir. 1993); *In re* Carter, 165 B.R. 518 (Bankr. M.D. Fla. 1994) (allows surrender); *In re* Cansler, 99 B.R. 758 (Bankr. W.D. Ky. 1989); *In re* Wright, 103 B.R. 905 (Bankr. M.D. Tenn. 1989); *In re* Neff, 89 B.R. 672 (Bankr. S.D. Ohio 1988) (Agricultural Credit Act of 1987 provisions require cancellation of all but one share of a borrower's statutory stock on a dollar for dollar basis equal to the amount of principal forgiven in any restructuring agreement between the borrower and Federal Land Bank. 12 U.S.C. § 2202(b)); *In re* Greseth, 78 B.R. 936 (D. Minn. 1987); *In re* Arthur, 86 B.R. 98 (Bankr. W.D. Mich. 1988); *In re* Ivy, 86 B.R. 623 (Bankr. W.D. Mo. 1988); *In re* Massengill, 73 B.R. 1008 (Bankr. E.D.N.C. 1987). This has generally not been allowed under chapter 11. *See, e.g., In re* Eisenbarth, 77 B.R. 235 (Bankr. D.N.D. 1987) and *In re* Walker, 48 B.R. 668 (Bankr. D.S.D. 1985). The courts in Ivy and in *In re* Massengill, 73 B.R. 1008 (Bankr. E.D.N.C. 1987) indicated that FLB/PCA stock is to be retired and credited at book value not to exceed par or the face amount pursuant to 12 U.S.C. § 2034(a); *In re* Massengill, which has been cited in most chapter 12 cases allowing stock surrender, has recently been reversed on appeal: Fed. Land Bank of Columbia v. Massengill, 100 B.R. 276 (W.D.N.C. 1989). It holds that surrender of stock in Federal Land Banks and Production Credit Associations for credit upon the secured claim impermissible, refusing to allow bankruptcy law to override

---

States v. Ron Pair Enterprises, Inc., 489 U.S. 235, 109 S. Ct. 1026, 103 L. Ed. 2d 290 (1989).

671 *In re* Fisher, 930 F.2d 1361 (8th Cir. 1991) (finding FmHA entitled to market rate, not lower blended, weighted rate under existing contracts); *In re* Hardzog, 901 F.2d 858 (10th Cir. 1990).

672 *In re* Fowler, 903 F.2d 694 (9th Cir. 1990) (prime rate plus risk factor method approved in chapter 12 case); United States v. Doud, 869 F.2d 1144 (8th Cir. 1989) (chapter 12 case upholding treasury bond plus two percent risk factor as providing a "market rate").

673 United States v. Neal Pharmacal Co., 789 F.2d 1283 (8th Cir. 1986); *In re* Monnier Brothers, 755 F.2d 1336 (8th Cir. 1985); *In re* S. States Motor Homes, 709 F.2d 647 (11th Cir. 1983); *In re* Davenport, 158 B.R. 832 (Bankr. E.D. Cal. 1992) (finds chapter 12 should reduce risk factors).

674 124 S. Ct. 1951, 158 L. Ed. 2d 787 (2004). Although *Till* was a chapter 13 case, the statutory provisions entitling secured creditors to interest are virtually identical in chapters 11, 12, and 13.

675 The prime rate of interest may be found on the Internet at: http://federalreserve.gov/releases/h15/data.htm#top.

676 124 S. Ct. at 1962. *See* § 11.6.1.3.3.5, *supra,* for a discussion of the risk factor.

677 124 S. Ct. at 1961.

678 489 U.S. 235, 109 S. Ct. 1026, 103 L. Ed. 2d 290 (1989).

679 *In re* Foertsch, 167 B.R. 555 (Bankr. D.N.D. 1994).

Valuation of the reduction of the allowed secured claim of the creditor by collateral surrender must be determined by the court or by consent among the parties. That value need not be set by the subsequent sale of the property, although that method can be used. While the value attributed to the property by the creditor itself may help determine value, it will generally not be dispositive and a valuation hearing may be necessary.[683] Offer of return or surrender must be made in good faith.[684]

The farm debtor and attorney must determine at the outset of a chapter 12 case what equipment, property, and even real property is necessary for the farming operation. The choice of what or how much of a creditor's collateral to return or surrender rests in the debtor's discretion.[685] Can equipment be rented or services procured at equivalent prices? Is the farming operation at peak efficiency in relation to its size, or should the operation be pared down to increase its efficiency? Can debt service be reduced to manageable levels by paring down without major sacrifice of production and income?

Chapter 12 apparently also allows debt reduction and satisfaction under a plan by surrender to a secured creditor of property of value which is *not* pledged to the creditor as security.[686] This parallels a debtor's ability to offer a secured creditor a replacement lien on unpledged collateral.[687] In one case, the debtor was allowed to surrender part of the property in full payment of the debt. This is a powerful tool, but one that might not be approved in all situations.[688]

Where tangible property is surrendered to a creditor as payment under a plan, the plan should provide both for the disposition of any surplus after sale by the creditor and for treatment of the creditor's claim in the event of short-fall.[689] However, recent case law indicates that if an under-secured creditor files only a secured claim and fails to amend or seek valuation, then after surrender to the creditor of its collateral there may be no remaining unsecured claim regardless of any deficiency after sale.[690]

16.5.5.3.5 Sale of property free and clear of liens

As discussed in more detail in § 16.5.3.5, *supra*, Chapter 12 has a special provision allowing the sale of collateral in a debtor's estate free and clear of liens regardless of whether the consent of the secured creditor is granted and of whether the sale will bring sufficient funds to satisfy the entirety of the secured creditor's claim.[691] By contrast, sale free and clear of liens can only take place in other bankruptcy chapters under certain more restrictive conditions.[692] Although section 1206 is couched in terms of sale by the trustee, the debtor can sell conditioned upon court permission.[693] Any liens existing on the property before sale will attach to the sale proceeds.[694]

16.5.5.3.6 Replacement liens

Because confirmation of a chapter 12 plan revests property in the debtor, and the secured creditor is bound by the plan after confirmation, under chapter 12 a debtor may be able to propose the substitution of other collateral for existing collateral if that is beneficial for the debtor and non-prejudicial to the creditor.[695] Situations in which replacement liens or substitution of different collateral may be appropriate are:

- Where the debtor needs to sell equipment and replace it with new or better used equipment;
- Where such substitution will allow payment of the allowed secured claim over a period of time longer than consonant with the existing collateral;

---

certain stock ownership requirements of the Farm Credit Act of 1971. *See also In re* Overholt, 125 B.R. 202 (S.D. Ohio 1990); *In re* Shannon, 100 B.R. 913 (S.D. Ohio 1989); *In re* Miller, 106 B.R. 136 (Bankr. N.D. Ohio 1989) (reconsidering and reversing decision at 98 B.R. 311 (1989) which had permitted stock surrender).

683 *In re* Fobian, 951 F.2d 1149 (9th Cir. 1991) (provision for revaluation after confirmation); *In re* Caraway, 95 B.R. 466 (Bankr. W.D. Ky. 1988).

684 *In re* Kerwin, 996 F.2d 552 (2d Cir. 1993) (details considerations re valuation for purposes of surrender and satisfaction); *In re* Braxton, 124 B.R. 870 (Bankr. N.D. Fla. 1991) (scattered, landlocked swamp land parcels proffered for return indicated lack of good faith).

685 *In re* O'Farrell, 74 B.R. 421 (Bankr. N.D. Fla. 1987); *see also In re* Robinson Ranch, 75 B.R. 606 (Bankr. D. Mont. 1987); *In re* Indreland, 77 B.R. 268 (Bankr. D. Mont. 1987).

686 11 U.S.C. § 1222(b)(7); *In re* Kerwin, 996 F.2d 552 (2d Cir. 1993); *In re* Durr, 78 B.R. 221 (Bankr. D.S.D. 1987); *In re* Mikkelsen Farms, Inc. 74 B.R. 280 (Bankr. D. Or. 1987); *In re* Indreland, 77 B.R. 268 (Bankr. D. Mont. 1987).

687 *See* § 16.5.5.3.6, *infra*.

688 *In re* Kerwin, 996 F.2d 552 (2d Cir. 1993).

689 *In re* Kerwin, 996 F.2d 552 (2d Cir. 1993) (surrender may be full debt satisfaction under § 1225(a)(5)(B)(ii)); *In re* Fobian, 951

F.2d 1149 (9th Cir. 1991); *In re* Gore, 113 B.R. 504 (Bankr. E.D. Ark. 1989).

690 *In re* Harrison, 987 F.2d 677 (10th Cir. 1993); *In re* Padget, 119 B.R. 793 (Bankr. D. Colo. 1990) (chapter 13). *Cf. In re* Grimm, 145 B.R. 994 (Bankr. D.S.D. 1992).

691 *See* 11 U.S.C. § 1206; *In re* Brileya, 108 B.R. 444 (Bankr. D. Vt. 1989).

692 *See* 11 U.S.C. § 363(f).

693 *In re* Webb, 932 F.2d 155 (2d Cir. 1991); *In re* Brileya, 108 B.R. 444 (Bankr. D. Vt. 1989).

694 *In re* Brileya, 108 B.R. 444 (Bankr. D. Vt. 1989).

695 11 U.S.C. § 1205(b)(2); 11 U.S.C. § 1222(b)(2). *But see* 11 U.S.C. § 1225(a)(5)(B). *See, e.g., In re* Lairmore, 101 B.R. 681 (Bankr. E.D. Okla. 1988); *In re* Durr, 78 B.R. 221 (Bankr. D.S.D. 1987); *In re* Indreland, 77 B.R. 268 (Bankr. D. Mont. 1987). *But see In re* Stallings, 290 B.R. 777 (Bankr. D. Idaho 2003). The lien retention requirement of section 1225(a)(5)(B)(ii) presents special problems in reorganizing secured debt when the security is livestock that will be sold. This problem is discussed and resolved somewhat in Abbott Bank-Thedford v. Hanna (*In re* Hanna), 912 F.2d 945 (8th Cir. 1990).

- Where the creditor has agreed to replacement; or
- Where additional or replacement collateral will obviate the problem of diminution of collateral value faster than scheduled repayment.[696]

Replacement liens or collateral may be made part of a chapter 12 plan or such replacement may be undertaken prior to plan proposal or confirmation.

16.5.6 Classification of Claims

16.5.6.1 Introduction

The provisions of all bankruptcy chapters in which rehabilitation and reorganization are the goals provide for the division of claims into classifications for administration and repayment.[697] Because the template for chapter 12 is chapter 13, chapter 13 claims classification provides some guide to claims classification in chapter 12.[698] However, because chapter 12 involves commercial as well as consumer debt, claims classification along the more sophisticated lines of chapter 11 may be tolerated if justified under the standards discussed below.[699]

Generally claims of equal rank concerning the same property (whether as collateral or as distribution upon or in lieu of liquidation from general assets) should be included in the same class. Claims of different rank or of the same rank concerning different property should be separately classified. Classification of claims should not be arbitrary, should not do substantial violence to the nature and rights inherent in the claims, and should not uselessly increase the number of classes of creditors.[700]

16.5.6.2 Classification of Codebtor Claims

Chapter 12, like chapter 13, specifically allows the different treatment of unsecured claims on consumer debts with codebtors.[701] Those debts can be placed, for more favorable treatment, in a separate class apart from the general unsecured claims.[702] Debts in such a class are the same debts to which the automatic codebtor stay of section 1201 applies.[703]

Congress did not extend this provision in chapter 12 to encompass business indebtedness. The codebtor classification should not prove very useful in chapter 12 because most consumer debt for farmers is not joint except with a spouse.[704]

16.5.6.3 Classification of the Claims of Unsecured Creditors

Unsecured claims may be classified into different classes for separate treatment in a chapter 12 plan.[705] There is no requirement in the Code that all similar creditors must be grouped into the same class.[706] Another general rule is that unsecured creditors may bear discrimination by classification, but not unfair discrimination.[707]

In addition, section 1222(a)(2) creates at least two classes of unsecured creditors: unsecured creditors entitled to priority treatment under section 507 and other unsecured creditors. Creditors in the priority class of creditors must be paid 100 cents on the dollar on their claims over the life of the plan, unless any creditor consents to different treatment.[708] For most farmer bankruptcies, this class will contain certain tax claims and administrative expenses.[709] Although all priority creditors must receive one-hundred cents on the dollar, it is possible to break out separate classes of priority creditors without impermissible discriminatory treatment. For example, certain administrative expenses may be paid

---

696 The ability to substitute collateral appears to hinge upon: (1) the liquidity of the replacement collateral in comparison to the original collateral; and (2) the risk involved in the replacement collateral in comparison to the original collateral. *See, e.g.*, *In re* Frank, 27 B.R. 748 (Bankr. S.D. Ohio 1983). Concepts which have evolved from evaluating replacement collateral in the adequate protection context are also useful. *See, e.g.*, *In re* O'Connor, 808 F.2d 1393 (10th Cir. 1987); *In re* Schaller, 27 B.R. 959 (W.D. Wis. 1983); *In re* Bear River Orchards, 56 B.R. 976 (Bankr. E.D. Cal. 1986).

697 11 U.S.C. §§ 1122, 1123(a)(1), (a)(4), 1222(a)(3), (b)(1), 1322(a)(3), (b)(1). *See* Fed. R. Bankr. P. 3013.

698 *See* § 12.4, *supra*.

699 Chapter 12 allows classification under the same principles as chapter 11 (11 U.S.C. § 1122) at 11 U.S.C. § 1222(b)(1), but chapter 11 has broader potential for claims classification under the balloting route prescribed by 11 U.S.C. § 1129(a). 11 U.S.C. §§ 1123(a)(1) through (a)(4). The consideration of unfair discrimination comes into play in cramdown. 11 U.S.C. § 1129(b).

700 *See* Anderson, *Classification of Claims and Interests in Reorganization Cases Under the New Bankruptcy Code*, 58 Am. Bankr. L.J. 99 (1984).

701 11 U.S.C. § 1222(b)(1); 11 U.S.C. § 1322(b)(1). *See* § 9.4.4, *supra*, for a discussion of the codebtor stay in chapter 13.

702 *See, e.g.*, Barnes v. Whelan, 689 F.2d 193 (D.C. Cir. 1982); *In re* Dondero, 58 B.R. 847 (Bankr. D. Or. 1986); *In re* Perkins, 55 B.R. 422 (Bankr. N.D. Okla. 1985).

703 For a discussion of the types of debts which may be properly placed in such a codebtor class or must be excluded, see § 16.4.5.2, *supra*.

704 In most cases, this joint debt is farm operation debt which would not be subject to the codebtor stay and which would compel a joint petition under 11 U.S.C. § 302.

705 11 U.S.C. §§ 1222(a)(3), (b)(1).

706 Teamsters Nat'l Freight Indus. Negotiating Committee v. U.S. Truck Co., 800 F.2d 581 (6th Cir. 1986); *In re* Planes, Inc., 48 B.R. 698 (Bankr. N.D. Ga. 1985).

707 *See* § 12.4, *supra*.

708 11 U.S.C. § 1222(a)(2). Unlike cases under chapter 11, administrative expenses need not be paid at confirmation but can be paid over time. *In re* Citrowske, 72 B.R. 613 (Bankr. D. Minn. 1987).

709 11 U.S.C. §§ 507(a)(1), 503547(b).

out of the first distribution under the plan (for example, repayment of crop financing, attorney fees), and other priority claims spread over the plan's life (for example, taxes).

The general unsecured creditors include all remaining creditors in the family farmer's bankruptcy, including the under-secured portion of indebtedness of creditors with collateral.[710] As a general rule, all unsecured claims and the unsecured claims of creditors holding collateral worth less than their indebtedness are placed in one class.[711] However, there may be compelling reasons for breaking some claims into separate classes for different treatment, so long as the plan does not discriminate unfairly among the classes of unsecured creditors.

Unsecured creditors may be divided into separate classes based upon their interplay with the bankruptcy.[712] Chapter 11, with its commercial context and discharge provisions similar to chapter 12, offers a closer analogy than chapter 13 consumer cases. Permitted chapter 11 classes may include trade creditors and creditors upon which the debtor—particularly a rural debtor—must depend for continued credit or services,[713] certain nondischargeable debts,[714] and unsecured portions of the debts of otherwise secured creditors.[715] Yet greater flexibility in claims classification should be available in chapter 12, because there is no voting and thus less incentive for a court to condemn creative classes for supposed gerrymandering.[716]

16.5.6.4 Classification of Secured Creditors

The classification of secured creditors in chapter 12 should follow the same procedure generally used in chapter 11, rather than chapter 13: each secured creditor should be placed in a separate class.[717] This approach is in keeping with the general admonition concerning claims classification that only creditors of equal rank should be placed within the same class. Because there are differences in the collateral or the position of a creditor with regard to its interest in the collateral, each secured creditor's claim will be fundamentally different. Segregation of each secured creditor is advisable because each secured claim will probably differ in its treatment according to:

- Term over which repayment will be effectuated;[718]
- Interest rate;[719]
- Collateralization and lien retention;[720]
- Creditor agreement to a particular treatment;
- Surrender of collateral in whole or part to the creditor.

Because there is no balloting procedure in chapter 12, as there is in chapter 11, this breakout presents no hazard for purposes of balloting or the section 1111(b)(2) election. Remember that creditors that are under-secured have allowed secured claims only to the extent of the value of their collateral.[721] As a result, such creditors must also have a part of their claims classified with the unsecured creditors.[722] A secured creditor with more than one variety of claim, for example, a security interest in farmstead property and a security interest in equipment, may be placed in one class for treatment, or two or more classes based upon different periods for repayment dictated by different collateral.

Although most courts find the anti-discrimination test of 11 U.S.C. § 1222(a)(3), to be generally inapplicable to secured claims,[723] at least one court has determined that it also forbids vastly disproportionate interest and term treatment among secured creditors with similar claims.[724] However, the satisfaction of different secured creditors by partial surrender of collateral with repayment[725] or complete surrender of collateral[726] while other secured creditors are paid

---

710   11 U.S.C. § 506(a). *In re* Hollinrake, 93 B.R. 183 (Bankr. S.D. Iowa 1988).

711   3 Norton Bankr. L. & Prac. § 60.05; *In re* Pine Lake Village, 19 B.R. 819 (Bankr. S.D.N.Y. 1982). *See* First Nat'l Bank v. Allen, 118 F.3d 1289 (8th Cir. 1997) (failure to object to plan which provided for banks' secured claims, but not their unsecured claims constitutes waiver of the unsecured claims).

712   *See* Anderson, *Classification of Claims and Interests in Reorganization Cases Under the New Bankruptcy Code*, 58 Am. Bankr. L.J. 99 (1984); Blair, *Classification of Unsecured Claims in Chapter 11 Reorganizations*, 58 Am. Bankr. L.J. 197 (1984).

713   Brinkley v. Chase Manhattan Mortgage & Realty Trust, 622 F.2d 872 (5th Cir. 1980); *In re* Sutherland, 3 B.R. 420 (Bankr. W.D. Ark. 1980).

714   *In re* Haag, 3 B.R. 649 (Bankr. D. Or. 1980) (child support). *But see In re* May, 1999 Bankr. LEXIS 1750 (Bankr. D. Kan. 1999) (separate classification of debt incurred by fraud was not fair).

715   These may be placed in a different class, but different treatment may be prohibited unless the interests of these creditors are dissimilar to unsecured creditors in general.

716   *Compare In re* Greystone III Joint Venture, 948 F.2d 134 (5th Cir. 1991) *with In re* ZRM-Oklahoma P'ship, 156 B.R. 67 (Bankr. W.D. Okla. 1993).

717   *In re* Robinson Ranch, Inc., 75 B.R. 606 (Bankr. D. Mont. 1987); *In re* Citrowske, 72 B.R. 613 (Bankr. D. Minn. 1987); *In*

re Martin, 66 B.R. 921 (Bankr. D. Mont. 1986) (chapter 11).

718   *See* § 16.5.5.3.2, *supra.*

719   *See* § 16.5.5.3.3, *supra.*

720   *See* §§ 16.5.5.2, 16.5.5.3, *supra.*

721   11 U.S.C. § 506(a); Harmon v. United States, 101 F.3d 574 (8th Cir. 1996) (lien stripping permitted in chapter 12); *In re* Zabel, 249 B.R. 764 (Bankr. E.D. Wis. 2000). *See* § 11.2, *supra.*

722   *See* First Nat'l Bank v. Allen, 118 F.3d 1289 (8th Cir. 1997) (failure to object to plan which provided for banks' secured claims, but not their unsecured claims constitutes waiver of the unsecured claims).

723   *In re* Fortney, 36 F.3d 701 (7th Cir. 1994) (treatment of tax lien can be different from mortgages and on short amortization even if longer treatment would result in increased payments to unsecured creditors); *In re* Harper, 157 B.R. 858 (Bankr. E.D. Ark. 1993); *In re* Bland, 149 B.R. 980 (Bankr. D. Kan. 1992) (cure and restructuring allowed).

724   *In re* Weldin-Lynn, Inc., 79 B.R. 409 (Bankr. E.D. Ark. 1987).

725   *In re* Robinson Ranch, 75 B.R. 606 (Bankr. D. Mont. 1987); *In re* Indreland, 77 B.R. 268 (Bankr. D. Mont. 1987).

726   *In re* B & G Farms, Inc., 82 B.R. 549 (Bankr. D. Mont. 1988).

over time has not been found to be impermissible discrimination among secured creditors.

A statutory lien may be avoidable under 11 U.S.C. §§ 545(3) and 544(a). Hence, like liens avoidable under section 522(f), failure to reduce such a lien to unsecured status can result in more favorable treatment to that creditor where unsecured creditors are not paid in full. This may discriminate unfairly against a class or classes of unsecured creditors in derogation of section 1222(b)(1).[727]

16.5.6.5 Direct Payments Under the Chapter 12 Plan

Payments due under the chapter 12 plan generally must be paid through the office of the chapter 12 trustee for disbursement according to the plan. In the first years under chapter 12 the courts almost uniformly mandated that most payments be funneled through the trustee, because of the start-up costs for new chapter 12 cases and trustees and because of the nature of the chapter 12 plan restructuring of secured and unsecured debt.[728] In those cases, the trustee surcharge in chapter 12 placed a significant burden upon the family farmer debtor because many districts allowed the maximum percentage (ten percent) for trustee's fees.

One approach to reducing this burden is to make some payments due in chapter 12 direct payments without administration by the chapter 12 trustee.[729] Sections 1226(c), 1222(a)(1) and 1225(a)(5)(B)(ii) clearly contemplate this possibility.[730] It should also be remembered that no surcharge will attach to the portion of those secured debts amortized beyond the plan's three to five year life for that period when payment continues after discharge.[731]

It should also be remembered that even the permission to make direct payment may not guarantee reduction of the trustee's surcharge. The court can provide that direct payment be subject to the trustee's surcharge as well,[732] although courts generally do not.[733] Whether the debtor can make the payments directly and whether they are subject to the surcharge has largely been worked out by either controlling district or circuit court precedent.[734]

Some kinds of payments and circumstances lend themselves readily to allowance for direct payment during the life of the plan. For example:

(1) *Attorney Fees*: Arrangements for the payment of attorney fees for work performed after filing *and* duly approved by the bankruptcy court upon application should be paid directly. There is a compelling argument that cost of representation should bear no surcharge for administration.[735]

(2) *Post-petition Debt Repayment*: Where the debtor has received post-petition new financing which will be paid out entirely out of the proceeds of harvest, it makes more sense administratively for the sale proceeds check to be cut to the debtor and creditor, reported to the trustee contemporaneously, but distributed to that creditor directly without trustee administration. The chapter 12 trustee had no real expectation of surcharge from such a post-petition debt at the creation of the chapter 12 case.

(3) *Lump Sum Creditor Payment(s)*: There may be occasions where a creditor or creditors will be paid a large sum upon a claim or claims all at once through a sale free and clear of lien.[736] When this happens, the chapter 12 trustee's

---

727 *In re* Arnold, 88 B.R. 917 (Bankr. N.D. Iowa 1988).

728 *See, e.g., In re* Greseth, 78 B.R. 936 (D. Minn. 1987); *In re* Hildebrandt, 79 B.R. 427 (Bankr. D. Minn. 1987); *In re* Hagensick, 73 B.R. 710 (Bankr. N.D. Iowa 1987) (while some direct payments can be made, they will still be subject to the trustee's surcharge); *In re* Meyer, 73 B.R. 457 (Bankr. E.D. Mo. 1987). Most real property in chapter 12 will be rescheduled and reamortized, so that the direct payment to creditors holding mortgages, deeds to secure debt, or contracts for deed will be different from the original contract; the primary rationale for allowing direct payment to a creditor in chapter 13 was to avoid modification of the rights of such holders. Also, most chapter 12 plans would pay little, if anything, to unsecured creditors so that the percentage payable to compensate the trustee will be minuscule if assessed only upon repayment to unsecured creditors.

729 *See* § 12.4.4, *supra.*

730 *In re* Pianowski, 92 B.R. 225 (Bankr. W.D. Mich. 1988); *In re* Sutton, 91 B.R. 184 (Bankr. M.D. Ga. 1988); *In re* Kline, 94 B.R. 557 (Bankr. N.D. Ind. 1988); *In re* Finkbine, 94 B.R. 461 (Bankr. S.D. Ohio 1988). The Ninth Circuit has held that direct payments may not be made to impaired creditors. *See* Fulkrod v. Barmettler, 126 B.R. 584 (B.A.P. 9th Cir. 1991), *aff'd*, 973 F.2d 801 (9th Cir. 1992).

731 However, chapter 12 plans should make specific provision for this in their treatment of such debts.

732 *See, e.g., In re* BDT Farms, Inc., 21 F.3d 1019 (10th Cir. 1994); *In re* Marriott, 161 B.R. 816 (Bankr. S.D. Ill. 1993); *In re* Oster, 152 B.R. 960 (Bankr. D.N.D. 1993); *In re* Wagner, 159 B.R. 268 (Bankr. D.N.D. 1993), *aff'd*, 36 F.3d 723 (8th Cir. 1994); *In re* Mouser, 99 B.R. 803 (Bankr. S.D. Ohio 1989); *In re* Hagensick, 73 B.R. 710 (Bankr. N.D. Tex. 1987).

733 Haden v. Pelofsky, 212 F.3d 466 (8th Cir. 2000) (no fee due on direct payments); *In re* Wagner, 36 F.3d 723 (8th Cir. 1994); *In re* Schneekloth, 186 B.R. 713 (Bankr. D. Mont. 1995). *See In re* McCann, 202 B.R. 824 (Bankr. N.D.N.Y. 1996) (a direct pay that by-passes trustee fees is permissible "in appropriate cases"); *In re* Cross, 195 B.R. 440 (Bankr. D. Neb. 1996) (Cross II) (plan may provide to pay unsecured creditors directly; 11 U.S.C. § 105 cannot be used to override 11 U.S.C. § 326 and 28 U.S.C. § 586); *In re* Cross, 182 B.R. 42 (Bankr. D. Neb. 1995) (Cross I) (plan may pay secured creditors directly).

734 *See, e.g.,* Wagner v. Armstrong (*In re* Wagner), 36 F.3d 723 (8th Cir. 1994) (direct payments allowed within limits, with no trustee commission thereon); *In re* Fulkrod, 973 F.2d 801 (9th Cir. 1992) (no direct payments allowed). *See* § 16.4.2.2.4, *supra.*

735 *In re* Pianowski, 92 B.R. 225 (Bankr. W.D. Mich. 1988). *But see In re* Beard, 134 B.R. 239 (Bankr. S.D. Ohio 1991) (attorney fees must be paid through plan); *In re* Heller, 105 B.R. 434 (Bankr. N.D. Ill. 1988) (except in rare instances, attorney fees should be paid through trustee because of duty to monitor administrative expenses of estate).

736 11 U.S.C. § 1205; *In re* Schneekloth, 186 B.R. 713 (Bankr. D. Mont. 1995). In fact, this was the rationale in *In re* Sousa, 61

office normally will have had only minimal participation in the sale and the proceeds will be distributed to one or a limited number of creditors holding pre-sale liens. Such a payment is more representative of liquidation than administration, and the chapter 12 trustee has not functioned as a liquidating agent.[737]

(4) *Balloon Payments*: As in cases involving sales free and clear of lien, there may be some creditors who, because of the structure of their indebtedness going into the bankruptcy, or by plan choice, will be paid with a one-time distribution soon after the plan is confirmed. While these will generally be paid out of the debtor's regular operating revenues, the administration required is disproportionate to the trustee's fee.

(5) *Payments on Residential Real Estate Held Apart from the Farmstead*: This has been an area in chapter 13 where many courts have permitted direct payment. In chapter 12, unlike chapter 13, a debtor may modify the terms of notes secured by residential real property, yet most plan treatments of such real estate under chapter 12 will probably leave the terms and conditions of those notes unaltered. As that real estate may be so treated and is apart from the farmstead itself, such indebtedness is more logically treated by direct payment.

(6) *Payments to Lease Creditors Upon Current Obligations*: The trustee may try to require all funds to be paid through his or her office, including lease payments. However, the making of leasehold payments upon current obligations can result in lease default through the administrative delay in the trustee's office which can present problems to the debtor. Because current leasehold obligations (not pre-petition arrearage)[738] are not past indebtedness, there should be no expectation of fee from such future payments.[739]

(7) *Transfers in Kind to Creditors*. Where debt satisfaction is effectuated under the plan by the transfer or surrender either of collateral or unencumbered property other than cash, the lack of trustee involvement should allow direct transfer without attachment of a trustee's fee.[740]

Several courts have determined that secured indebtedness, whether modified by the plan or not, may be paid directly.[741] Other courts have limited direct payments to where the claim is not modified.[742] Some districts have responded to the financial burden created by paying secured indebtedness through the plan by adopting split fee schedules, with a much reduced surcharge on payments to secured creditors.[743]

Some courts have required, when evaluating the allowance of direct payment and claims classification, that direct payments cannot be allowed for some creditors and not others where the claims are substantially similar.[744] Tax and administrative claims, exclusive of fees, should be paid under the plan by the trustee.[745] Generally no direct payments have been permitted to general unsecured creditors.[746] Some courts may restrict cure of defaults and arrearages to payments through the trustee.[747]

Grear, 163 B.R. 524 (Bankr. S.D. Ill. 1994); *In re* Beard, 177 B.R. 74 (S.D. Ohio 1993); *In re* Erickson P'ship, 83 B.R. 725 (D.S.D. 1988); *In re* Cross, 182 B.R. 42 (Bankr. D. Neb. 1995), *aff'd sub nom.* Lydick v. Cross, 197 B.R. 321 (D. Neb. 1996); *In re* Westpfahl, 171 B.R. 330 (Bankr. C.D. Ill. 1994) (application of factors to specific debts); *In re* Westpfahl, 168 B.R. 337 (Bankr. C.D. Ill. 1994) (list of factors for determining when direct payments are permissible in chapter 12); *In re* Wagner, 159 B.R. 288 (Bankr. D.N.D. 1993); *In re* Kosmicki, 161 B.R. 828 (Bankr. D. Neb. 1993); *In re* Teigen, 142 B.R. 397 (Bankr. D. Mont. 1992); *In re* Seamons, 131 B.R. 459 (Bankr. D. Idaho 1991); *In re* Golden, 131 B.R. 201 (Bankr. N.D. Fla. 1991); *In re* Crum, 85 B.R. 878 (Bankr. N.D. Fla. 1988); *In re* Land, 82 B.R. 572 (Bankr. D. Colo. 1988), *aff'd, sub nom.* Bass v. Land, 96 B.R. 311 (D. Colo. 1989); *In re* Lenz, 74 B.R. 413 (Bankr. C.D. Ill. 1987).

742 Direct payments allowed only where secured indebtedness unmodified by the plan: *In re* BDT Farms, Inc., 21 F.3d 1019 (10th Cir. 1994) (allows surrender without surcharge as well); *In re* Foster, 670 F.2d 478 (5th Cir. 1982) (chapter 13); Fulkrod v. Barmettler, 126 B.R. 584 (B.A.P. 9th Cir. 1991), *aff'd* 973 F.2d 801 (9th Cir. 1992); *In re* Marriott, 161 B.R. 816 (Bankr. S.D. Ill. 1993); *In re* Wagner, 159 B.R. 753 (Bankr. D.N.D. 1993); *In re* Oster, 152 B.R. 960 (Bankr. D.N.D. 1993). *In re* Mouser, 99 B.R. 803 (Bankr. S.D. Ohio 1989) (direct payments allowed only to secured creditors where payments are unmodified, no default to cure, and payment extends beyond plan life); *In re* Sutton, 91 B.R. 184 (Bankr. M.D. Ga. 1988); *In re* Kline, 94 B.R. 557 (Bankr. N.D. Ind. 1988); *In re* Hagensick, 73 B.R. 710 (Bankr. N.D. Iowa 1987); *In re* Hildebrandt, 79 B.R. 427 (Bankr. D. Minn. 1987) (direct only where all unmodified secured claims are so paid); *In re* Citrowske, 72 B.R. 613 (Bankr. D. Minn. 1987).

743 *See* § 16.4.2.2, *supra.*

744 *In re* Hildebrandt, 79 B.R. 427 (Bankr. D. Minn. 1987).

745 *In re* Greseth, 78 B.R. 936 (D. Minn. 1987); *In re* Beard, 134 B.R. 239 (Bankr. S.D. Ohio 1991); *In re* Mouser, 99 B.R. 803 (Bankr. S.D. Ohio 1989); *In re* Rott, 94 B.R. 163 (Bankr. D.N.D. 1988); *In re* Kline, 94 B.R. 557 (Bankr. N.D. Ind. 1988).

746 *Compare* § 1225(a)(4) *with* § 1225(a)(5)(B)(ii). *In re* Erickson P'ship, 83 B.R. 725 (D.S.D. 1988); *In re* Cross, 182 B.R. 42 (Bankr. D Neb. 1995) (however, there may be exceptions where unsecured creditors can be paid directly); *In re* Marriott, 161 B.R. 816 (Bankr. S.D. Ill. 1993); *In re* Mouser, 99 B.R. 803 (Bankr. S.D. Ohio 1989); *In re* Kline, 94 B.R. 557 (Bankr. N.D. Ind. 1988).

747 *In re* Kline, 94 B.R. 557 (Bankr. N.D. Ind. 1988).

B.R. 105 (D.R.I. 1986) for a reduced trustee surcharge.

737 However, in some cases the sale will not satisfy all liens or there will be disputes over the claims to the proceeds of sale. In that event, the court should probably order the chapter 12 trustee to become the repository of the disputed funds, so that some administrative tending by the trustee will be necessary. *See, e.g., In re* McClintock, 75 B.R. 612 (Bankr. W.D. Mo. 1987).

738 Any pre-petition arrearage must be cured under the plan pursuant § 1222(b)(3) and (5).

739 *Contra In re* Mouser, 99 B.R. 803 (Bankr. S.D. Ohio 1989).

740 *In re* Mikkelsen Farms, Inc., 74 B.R. 280 (Bankr. D. Or. 1987).

741 Wagner v. Armstrong, 36 F.3d 723 (8th Cir. 1994) (direct payment to impaired secured creditors without trustee surcharge); *In re* Jennings, 190 B.R. 863 (Bankr. W.D. Mo. 1995); *In re* Schneekloth, 186 B.R. 713 (Bankr. D. Mont. 1995); *In re*

The most thorough consideration of direct payments and what policies and factors may be considered in their allowance has come from the bankruptcy court in *In Re Pianowski*.[748] The court detailed a variety of appropriate factors which may justify direct payments. The court in *Pianowski* also required the monitoring of direct payments by inclusion of the following provisions: (a) debtors shall keep accurate records reflecting all direct payments to secured creditors and attorneys, making them available to the trustee and all interested parties during the plan's life; (b) direct payments to creditors must be made by check or other method whereby debtors can conclusively demonstrate timely making; (c) debtors shall file an annual report on a date certain of each year which discloses the amounts, check numbers and dates when direct payments were made, and if a direct payment has not been timely made; (d) in the event debtors fail, neglect or refuse to report, debtors shall be deemed in plan default; upon default, unpaid creditors, trustee or any other interested entity may file appropriate motions.

16.5.7 Feasibility Requirements of Chapter 12 Plans

16.5.7.1 General Observations

Like chapter 13, chapter 12 requires the court to allow confirmation upon a finding that the debtor will be able to make all payments under the plan and comply with all provisions of the plan.[749] Chapter 11 cases also have a similar confirmation requirement,[750] which has been termed the "feasibility" requirement.[751]

In chapter 13, evidence of feasibility may be gleaned from job stability, a realistic budget outlined in the schedules based upon past experience and information, and the full funding of the plan prior to confirmation with payments generally started within thirty days from plan proposal. Chapter 12 does not have the same requirements or indicia of feasibility.[752] The uncertainty of farming and its inherent risks may cloud the feasibility analysis.

It is the debtor's burden to demonstrate feasibility at confirmation,[753] although the debtor is given the benefit of the doubt.[754] The bankruptcy court does not expect feasibility demonstrated to a certainty, but rather that "it appears reasonably probable that the farmer can pay the restructured secured debt, over a reasonable period of time, at a reasonable rate of interest, in light of farm prices and farm programs as of the date of confirmation."[755]

The bankruptcy court is charged with the responsibility to make an informed, independent judgment based upon information and estimates embracing all relevant facts.[756] The court can make substantial inquiry into feasibility even where parties in interest remain silent. In early chapter 12 cases, many courts took the approach of minimizing the feasibility inquiry where creditors have leveled no objections based upon section 1225(a)(6), preferring to allow the debtor to have his or her opportunity at repayment and rehabilitation, and considering shortfall only in the event of default. Yet even these courts expect some debtor showing of evidence concerning plan feasibility.[757]

Bankruptcy courts have recognized that feasibility is more difficult to gauge and projections are more speculative in farm cases because of the high degree of risk and variability of market factors and government subsidy/payment programs.[758] Courts generally only require that projections of both performance and expenditures fall within "reasonable ranges," rather than tight constraints.[759]

---

748 92 B.R. 225 (Bankr. W.D. Mich. 1988).

749 11 U.S.C. § 1225(a)(6).

750 11 U.S.C. § 1129(a)(11).

751 *See* § 12.5, *supra.*

752 Farmer cases to date under chapters 11 and 13 provide guidelines for feasibility consideration. *See* § 16.5.7.2, *infra.*

753 *In re* Ames, 973 F.2d 849 (10th Cir. 1992); *In re* Gough, 190 B.R. 455 (Bankr. M.D. Fla. 1996); *In re* Foertsch, 167 B.R. 555 (Bankr. D.N.D. 1994); *In re* Zurface, 95 B.R. 527 (Bankr. S.D. Ohio 1989); *In re* Adam, 92 B.R. 732 (Bankr. E.D. Mich. 1988); *In re* Crowley, 85 B.R. 76 (Bankr. W.D. Wis. 1988); *In re* Snider Farms, Inc., 83 B.R. 1003 (Bankr. N.D. Ind. 1988); *In re* Eber-Acres Farm, 82 B.R. 889 (Bankr. S.D. Ohio 1987).

754 *In re* Tofsrud, 230 B.R. 862 (Bankr. D.N.D. 1999); *In re* Tate, 217 B.R. 518 (Bankr. E.D. Tex. 1997) (lack of feasibility found even after debtors are given the benefit of the doubt); *In re* Rape, 104 B.R. 741 (W.D.N.C. 1989); *In re* Foertsch, 167 B.R. 555 (Bankr. D.N.D. 1994); *In re* Harper, 157 B.R. 858 (Bankr. E.D. Ark. 1993).

755 *In re* Ames, 973 F.2d 849 (10th Cir. 1992) (plan to pay secured creditor only through results of litigation made plan not feasible); *In re* Ahlers, 794 F.2d 388, 392 (8th Cir. 1986); *In re* Foertsch, 167 B.R. 555 (Bankr. D.N.D. 1994); *In re* Hansen, 77 B.R. 722 (Bankr. D.N.D. 1987).

756 Consolidated Rock Products Co. v. DuBois, 312 U.S. 510 (1941); *In re* Braxton, 124 B.R. 870 (Bankr. N.D. Fla. 1991); *In re* Butler, 97 B.R. 508 (Bankr. E.D. Ark. 1988); *In re* Eber-Acres Farm, 82 B.R. 889 (Bankr. S.D. Ohio 1987); *In re* Weldin-Lynn, Inc., 79 B.R. 409 (Bankr. E.D. Ark. 1987); *In re* Timber Tracts, Inc. 70 B.R. 773 (Bankr. D. Mont. 1987) (chapter 11); *In re* Martin, 66 B.R. 921 (Bankr. D. Mont. 1986) (chapter 11); *In re* Fursman Ranch, 38 B.R. 907 (Bankr. W.D. Mo. 1984).

757 This can be done through the testimony of the debtor at confirmation, through a simple series of questions directed at eligibility, intentions, reorganizational efforts, understanding of the plan, and ability to meet payments. *In re* Braxton, 124 B.R. 870 (Bankr. N.D. Fla. 1991); *In re* Hagen, 95 B.R. 708 (Bankr. D.N.D. 1989).

758 *See, e.g., In re* Fursman Ranch, 38 B.R. 907, 912 (Bankr. W.D. Mo. 1984).

759 *In re* Rape, 104 B.R. 741 (W.D.N.C. 1989); *In re* Dittmer, 82 B.R. 1019 (Bankr. D.N.D. 1988); *In re* Hochmuth Farms, Inc., 79 B.R. 266 (Bankr. D. Md. 1987); *In re* Big Hook Land & Cattle Co., 77 B.R. 793 (Bankr. D. Mont. 1987); *In re* Hansen, 77 B.R. 722 (Bankr. D.N.D. 1987); *In re* Douglass, 77 B.R. 714 (Bankr. W.D. Mo. 1987); *In re* Konzak, 78 B.R. 990 (Bankr. D.N.D. 1987); *In re* Fowler, 83 B.R. 39 (Bankr. D. Mont. 1987); *In re* Reitz, 79 B.R. 934 (Bankr. D. Kan. 1987).

16.5.7.2 Determination of Feasibility

The determination of feasibility for a chapter 12 plan requires an evaluation of the best indicia of plan success—or failure—available to the decision-maker at the time plan confirmation is sought. It is an issue for consideration at confirmation; consideration prior to confirmation would be premature even though a plan's lack of feasibility may be grounds for a chapter 12 case's dismissal.[760]

Confirmation determinations in farm cases under chapters 11 and 13 prior to the advent of chapter 12 provide insight into the courts' analysis of feasibility in farm cases.[761] The following list details factors which have influenced courts concerning feasibility in farm cases. The degree to which inquiry is necessary into these factors is proportionate to the degree of creditor/court interest; certainly not all are anticipated or required to be positive. These factors also provide a good preliminary checklist for inquiry into a debtor's operation pre-petition to determine the likelihood of success in chapter 12.[762]

(1) Debtor's historic cash flow;

(2) Historic and present levels of production and expense;[763]

(3) Earning capacity of the debtor and immediate family;[764]

(4) Inclusion of all expenses in budgeting, including property and other taxes and utilities;[765]

(5) Ability to project realistically, based upon historical performance, crop and/or livestock yields and prices and timetable for realization from sale;[766]

(6) Whether debtor's projections of expenses and income fall within reasonable ranges as gauged by standard studies and measures of same, expert and debtor testimony, and the debtor's and court's experience;[767]

(7) Demonstration of continued sources of economical, financing and feed, seed, custom work (if own equipment is not used), and so forth;[768]

(8) Circumstance(s) which led to previous poor performance or cash flow, and evidence of elimination or mitigation of same;[769]

(9) Maintenance of stability of operation and historic stability record (particularly important in livestock and dairy operations);

(10) Whether debtor's debt and operational burdens have been reduced by sale of property or paring down of farm operation;

(11) Condition of operating equipment and livestock;

(12) Prospects of refinancing all or part of the operation, and/or continued financing for successive years of operation;

(13) Substantial payments made in the past to creditors, particularly secured creditors;[770]

(14) Use of accepted farming methods and characterization of the debtor as a "good" or "poor" manager;[771]

(15) Expectancy and interplay of family donations and donations of money, labor and expertise of money and/or property (seed, feed, livestock, and so forth) during the plan's life;[772]

(16) Labor donation to the farm effort;

(17) Income from outside sources;

---

760 11 U.S.C. § 1208(c)(5). *See, e.g., In re* Woloschak, 70 B.R. 498 (Bankr. N.D. Ohio 1987).

761 *See, e.g., In re* Bartlett, 92 B.R. 142 (E.D.N.C. 1988); *In re* Snider Farms, Inc. 83 B.R. 1003 (Bankr. N.D. Ind. 1988); *In re* Gibson, 61 B.R. 997 (Bankr. D.N.H. 1986); *In re* Cott, 49 B.R. 570 (Bankr. W.D. Mo. 1985); *In re* Hoff, 54 B.R. 746 (Bankr. D.N.D. 1985); *In re* Neff, 60 B.R. 448 (Bankr. N.D. Tex. 1985); *In re* Fursman Ranch, 38 B.R. 907 (Bankr. W.D. Mo. 1984).

762 *See generally* Clarkson v. Cooke Sales & Serv. Co., 767 F.2d 417 (8th Cir. 1985) (chapter 11); *In re* Nauman, 213 B.R. 355 (B.A.P. 9th Cir. 1997) (application of various factors to plan involving negative amortization of secured debt); *In re* Snider Farms, Inc., 83 B.R. 1003 (Bankr. N.D. Ind. 1988).

763 *In re* Rape, 104 B.R. 741 (W.D.N.C. 1989); *In re* Foertsch, 167 B.R. 555 (Bankr. D.N.D. 1994); *In re* Creviston, 157 B.R. 380 (Bankr. S.D. Ohio 1993); *In re* Butler, 101 B.R. 566 (Bankr. E.D. Ark. 1989); *In re* Snider Farms, Inc., 83 B.R. 1003 (Bankr. N.D. Ind. 1988); *In re* Kloberdanz, 83 B.R. 767 (Bankr. D. Colo. 1988); *In re* Crowley, 85 B.R. 76 (Bankr. W.D. Wis. 1988).

764 *In re* Soper, 152 B.R. 984 (Bankr. D. Kan. 1993).

765 *In re* Alvstad, 223 B.R. 733 (Bankr. D.N.D. 1998) (debtor could not establish that cash flow would meet farm expenses together with projected meager living expenses). *See, e.g., In re* Oster, 152 B.R. 960 (Bankr. D.N.D. 1993); *In re* Hagen, 95 B.R. 708 (Bankr. D.N.D. 1989) (modification); *In re* Hochmuth Farms, Inc., 79 B.R. 266 (Bankr. D. Md. 1987); *In re* Big Hook Land & Cattle Co., 77 B.R. 793 (Bankr. D. Mont. 1987); *In re* Hansen, 77 B.R. 722 (Bankr. D.N.D. 1987).

766 *In re* Harper, 157 B.R. 858 (Bankr. E.D. Ark. 1993). *See also In re* Oster, 152 B.R. 960 (Bankr. D.N.D. 1993); *In re* Rott, 94 B.R. 163 (Bankr. D.N.D. 1988); *In re* Douglass, 77 B.R. 714 (Bankr. W.D. Mo. 1987).

767 *See In re* Weber, 297 B.R. 567 (Bankr. N.D. Iowa 2003); *In re* Gough, 190 B.R. 455 (Bankr. M.D. Fla. 1996); *In re* Oster, 152 B.R. 960 (Bankr. D.N.D. 1993); *In re* Townsend, 90 B.R. 498 (Bankr. M.D. Fla. 1988); *In re* Adam, 92 B.R. 732 (Bankr. E.D. Mich. 1988).

768 *In re* Foertsch, 167 B.R. 555 (Bankr. D.N.D. 1994) (written leases versus oral leases as assurance of continuity of operation); *In re* Big Hook Land & Cattle Co., 77 B.R. 793 (Bankr. D. Mont. 1987).

769 *See, e.g., In re* Dittmer, 82 B.R. 1019 (Bankr. D.N.D. 1988).

770 *In re* Gough, 190 B.R. 455 (Bankr. M.D. Fla. 1996); *In re* Fursman Ranch, 38 B.R. 907 (Bankr. W.D. Mo. 1984).

771 *In re* Cluck, 101 B.R. 691 (Bankr. E.D. Okla. 1989).

772 *See, e.g., In re* Cheatham, 78 B.R. 104 (Bankr. E.D.N.C. 1987); *In re* Edwardson, 74 B.R. 831 (Bankr. D.N.D. 1987). *Contra In re* Rott, 94 B.R. 163 (Bankr. D.N.D. 1988).

(18) Income from government payments, contracts and/or subsidies (PIK, ASCS certificates, and so forth);[773]

(19) Presence, maintenance and/or increase of base or allotments to support product prices;

(20) Presence or absence of crop and other insurance, both for income protection and as an item of expense properly projected;[774]

(21) Presence of accounting for next year's crop expenses and reasonable cushion for risk;[775]

(22) Utilization of farm production to minimize family living expenses;[776]

(23) Evidence of maintenance and/or upgrading livestock/dairy herds by introduction or acquisition of new animals;

(24) Monitoring and treatment of operation for peak efficiency, for example, DHIA testing for dairy herds;

(25) Realistic valuation of secured claims and reasonable interest or discount rates for their repayment;[777]

(26) Presence of plan provisions which protect creditors where feasibility is marginal, for example, recapture provisions for return of collateral to a creditor upon plan default;[778]

(27) Resolution or projected resolution of adversary proceedings which have an impact upon plan operation;[779]

(28) Ability to meet lump sum payments or balloon provisions in plan;[780]

(29) Post-petition performance under protection of chapter 12 stay;[781]

(30) Ability to pay post-petition administrative expenses;[782]

(31) Presence or absence of non-dischargeable debts;[783]

(32) Impact of trustee's surcharges.[784]

Some indicia of feasibility are more persuasive than others. For example, crop insurance and outside income provide the kind of stability that minimizes risk. A positive cash flow history and a history of substantial payments to creditors are convincing, but not many farmers have such a recent history. Meaningful reduction of the size of the farming operation, with a concomitant reduction in expenses, is a plus not only for feasibility, but as a demonstration of genuine good faith in attempting reorganization;[785] the operation which has been failing in the past generally needs change above debt reduction to accomplish reorganization and lasting viability.[786] Stricter proof of feasibility may be required where long-term payments are proposed.[787]

To present an effective case on feasibility, the debtor's testimony and available documentary evidence can be proffered. If the plan relies on the efforts of persons other than the debtor, those persons may also be called to testify. Documentary evidence might include appraisals, cash flow statements, and other materials from the farm's records or that of its creditors. Discovery procedures are available under the Rules to enhance access to creditor's records including to obtain familiarity with documents which may be used by creditors to undermine the debtor's case. The court may also take judicial notice of reliable publications which indicate interest rates[788] or land values.[789]

16.5.8 Other Plan Provisions

Section 1222(b)(11) specifically authorizes the inclusion of any appropriate provision in a chapter 12 plan so long as it does not contravene the confirmation standards of sections

---

773 *In re* Kloberdanz, 83 B.R. 767 (Bankr. D. Colo. 1988).

774 *In re* Martin, 66 B.R. 921 (Bankr. D. Mont. 1986) (chapter 11).

775 *In re* Townsend, 90 B.R. 498 (Bankr. M.D. Fla. 1988) (lack of reserves affects feasibility); *In re* Coffman, 90 B.R. 878 (Bankr. W.D. Tenn. 1988); *In re* Snider Farms, Inc., 83 B.R. 1003 (Bankr. N.D. Ind. 1988); *In re* Kocher, 78 B.R. 844 (Bankr. S.D. Ohio 1987); *In re* Hochmuth Farms, Inc., 79 B.R. 266 (Bankr. D. Md. 1987); *In re* Big Hook Land & Cattle Co., 77 B.R. 793 (Bankr. D. Mont. 1987); *In re* Hansen, 77 B.R. 722 (Bankr. D.N.D. 1987); *In re* Douglass, 77 B.R. 714 (Bankr. W.D. Mo. 1987); *In re* Konzak, 78 B.R. 990 (Bankr. D.N.D. 1987); *In re* Fowler, 83 B.R. 39 (Bankr. D. Mont. 1987); *In re* Reitz, 79 B.R. 934 (Bankr. D. Kan. 1987). *Contra In re* Dues, 98 B.R. 434 (Bankr. N.D. Ind. 1989) (failure to build cushion into budget acceptable; an accurate cash flow based on history probably already has some cushion).

776 *In re* Oster, 152 B.R. 960 (Bankr. D.N.D. 1993).

777 *In re* Ames, 973 F.2d 849 (10th Cir. 1992); *In re* Cool, 81 B.R. 614 (Bankr. D. Mont. 1987); *In re* Beyer, 72 B.R. 525 (Bankr. D. Colo. 1987).

778 *In re* Barnett, 162 B.R. 535 (Bankr. W.D. Mo. 1993). *See, e.g.,* *In re* O'Farrell, 74 B.R. 421 (Bankr. N.D. Fla. 1987); however, these can only be suggested in extreme circumstances.

779 *See, e.g., In re* Martin, 78 B.R. 593 (Bankr. D. Mont. 1987); *In re* Edwardson, 74 B.R. 831 (Bankr. D.N.D. 1987); *In re* Bentson, 74 B.R. 56 (Bankr. D. Minn. 1987).

780 *In re* Foertsch, 167 B.R. 555 (Bankr. D.N.D. 1994); *In re* Kuether, 158 B.R. 151 (Bankr. D.N.D. 1993); *In re* Borg, 88 B.R. 288 (Bankr. D. Mont. 1988).

---

781 *In re* Creviston, 157 B.R. 380 (Bankr. S.D. Ohio 1993); *In re* Cluck, 101 B.R. 691 (Bankr. E.D. Okla. 1989).

782 *In re* Winter, 151 B.R. 278 (Bankr. W.D. Okla. 1993).

783 *In re* Oster, 152 B.R. 960 (Bankr. D.N.D. 1993).

784 *Id.*

785 *In re* Kloberdanz, 83 B.R. 767 (Bankr. D. Colo. 1988).

786 Care must be taken to include *all* anticipated and foreseeable expenses. A court cannot confirm a plan with an admitted negative cash flow. *In re* Bartlett, 92 B.R. 142 (E.D.N.C. 1988). *See also In re* Adam, 92 B.R. 732 (Bankr. E.D. Mich. 1988).

787 *In re* Snider Farms, Inc., 83 B.R. 1003 (Bankr. N.D. Ind. 1988).

788 *In re* Crane Automotive, Inc., 88 B.R. 81 (Bankr. W.D. Pa. 1988) (chapter 11 non-farm case; uses Wall Street Journal); *In re* Neff, 89 B.R. 672 (Bankr. S.D. Ohio 1988) (Federal Reserve Bank's Quarterly Survey of Agricultural Credit Conditions at Commercial Banks).

789 *See* § 16.5.5.2, *supra.*

1222 and 1225.[790] This allows for quite a bit of creativity in fashioning a workable chapter 12 plan. Nevertheless, counsel should never let this creativity obscure the primary—and pragmatic—goal of confirmation.

In addition to potential plan treatment of creditors outlined in § 16.5, *supra*, some plan provisions which may or should be included under appropriate circumstances are suggested below.

(1) *Assumption or Rejection of Executory Contracts*: Section 365 provides that, in chapter 12, leases and executory contracts shall be assumed or rejected by the time of confirmation.[791] The plan should specifically reject or assume any leases and executory contracts of the debtors, if they have not already being rejected or assumed by specific action pre-confirmation. If any contracts have been rejected or assumed pre-confirmation, the plan should contain a recitation of that occurrence.

(2) *Provisions for New Financing in Future Plan Years*: The legislative history of chapter 12 specifically contemplates that a plan can anticipate and provide for the incurring of new debt for financing of the farm operation under section 364 and payment of the same under the plan.[792] A plan which provides for yearly distribution, for example, may provide that the financing for each year, as approved by the court, be paid from that distribution as an administrative expense, secured claim, or possibly by direct payment. Similarly, if money is used for capital improvements rather than creditor repayment, a monitoring provision should be included in the plan.[793]

(3) *Provision for Payment of Attorney Fees Through the Plan*: Attorney fees may be treated as an administrative expense under the plan or possibly allowed for direct payment. However, any request for fees to be placed under the plan needs to be accompanied by an application for award of fees and an enumeration of time and work performed to authorize such plan treatment.

(4) *Revesting of Estate Property in Debtor*: Section 1227(b) provides that an order of confirmation will vest property of the estate in the debtor unless the order or plan provides differently. Any distribution or disposition of property which does not vest in the debtor must be enumerated in the plan. The plan may also reiterate the vesting provisions of section 1227(b).

(5) *Payments Through the Trustee and Fees*: Any provisions which seek to have payment to creditors permitted directly rather than through the chapter 12 trustee must be

identified. The plan must specify and explain any request to reduce the chapter 12 trustee's fee in the case, either across the board or concerning selected creditors or transactions.

(6) *Provisions for Use of Cash Collateral During the Life of the Plan*: A plan can provide for the continued use of cash collateral by a debtor during the life of a plan without the continual approval process of section 363, if sale of farm products is in the ordinary course of the debtor's business, for example, dairy, feeder pigs, and so forth. However, the plan should provide for the manner in which the collateral will be sold and the proceeds used, and for the maintenance of pre-confirmation levels of replenishing collateral.[794]

(7) *Disposition of Any Farm Program Attributes or Benefits*: A farmer may be entitled to any number of benefits as a result of federal or other programs. Some of those benefits may be peculiar to the farmer, his or her land, or his or her operation,[795] such as base, allotments, termination program benefits, diversion program benefits, Payment-in-Kind (PIK) program benefits, storage benefits, conservation program contacts, or other kinds of assets. These all have value to the estate and to creditors. If the disposition of those attributes or benefits will be different from complete vesting in the debtor, (for example, allowance of setoff of program benefits for creditor payment during the plan) then the plan should provide for such disposition.[796]

(8) *Recapture or Drop Dead Provisions*: The debtor may include in his or her plan a provision that in the event of plan default, collateral will be relinquished to the secured creditor without further need for action in the federal or state courts. Such a provision was fairly common in chapter 11 cases prior to chapter 12 because many of those cases depended upon the agreement of the secured creditors for confirmation; chapter 12 cases do not so depend. Because of such a provision's drastic—and terminal—effect, such a provision should be agreed to only in exceptional circumstances, only where confirmation cannot be otherwise obtained, and with full knowledge and agreement of the debtor(s).[797] Now that the first wave of defaults and modifications under chapter 12 has begun, the perils of "drop dead" or recapture provisions in confirmed plans have come into sharper focus. Such provisions may be difficult or impossible to modify under section 1229 because they anticipate default.[798] Where a confirmed plan has a recapture provision with mandatory liquidation by the trustee upon

---

790 *In re* Davenport, 153 B.R. 551 (B.A.P. 9th Cir. 1993) (chapter 12 contemplates maximum flexibility in restructuring); *In re* Butler, 97 B.R. 508 (Bankr. E.D. Ark. 1988); *In re* Neff, 89 B.R. 672 (Bankr. S.D. Ohio 1988).

791 11 U.S.C. § 365(d)(2). This section also allows debtors-in-possession those powers by reference to 11 U.S.C. § 1203.

792 H.R. Conf. Rep. No. 99-958, at 48 (1986), *reprinted at* 1986 U.S.C.C.A.N. 5249.

793 *In re* Hansen, 77 B.R. 722 (Bankr. D.N.D. 1987).

794 *See* §§ 16.5.3.4, 16.5.3.6, *supra*.

795 *See* § 16.5.3.2, *supra*.

796 *In re* Greseth, 78 B.R. 936 (D. Minn. 1987).

797 *See, e.g., In re* Gore, 113 B.R. 504 (Bankr. E.D. Ark. 1989) (but such a provision must contain a lifting of the stay); *In re* Hagen, 95 B.R. 708 (Bankr. D.N.D. 1989); *In re* Grogg Farms, Inc., 91 B.R. 482 (Bankr. N.D. Ind. 1988); *In re* Martens, 98 B.R. 530 (Bankr. D. Colo. 1989); *In re* Dittmer, 82 B.R. 1019 (Bankr. D.N.D. 1988); *In re* O'Farrell, 74 B.R. 421 (Bankr. N.D. Fla. 1987); *In re* Erickson P'ship, 77 B.R. 738 (Bankr. D.S.D. 1987).

798 *In re* Grogg Farms, Inc., 91 B.R. 482 (Bankr. N.D. Ind. 1988).

default, one court has not allowed voluntary dismissal under section 1208(b) without curing of the default.[799]

(9) *Moratorium or Deferral*: Existing options for servicing of loans from the federal government may provide for the possibility of a moratorium or deferral of payments, or interest only payments. This moratorium or deferral for repayments during an initial period in a chapter 12 plan, or interest only payments (usually one to three years for servicing on major secured indebtedness), is designed to increase cash flow for building or rebuilding farm operations for later increases in income production, usually in livestock or dairy operations. While not a usual approach to repayment, it appears that in the appropriate case, plans can be confirmed which provide for moratoria or deferral of full repayment, and may be employed for any appropriate creditor, not just those with such loan servicing options in their contracts and policies.[800]

(10) *Reservation of Issues and Alternative Plan Treatment of Creditors*: In some circumstances, confirmation may go forward with some issues unresolved—particularly nondischargeability of individual debts, property surrender or lien avoidance. Because confirmation can set the rights of the debtor and creditors, where issues must survive for resolution after confirmation, the plan should provide for reservation of the issues and alternative treatments of the creditor(s) involved based upon the probable outcomes once the open issues are resolved.[801]

(11) *Prepayment of Indebtedness Without Penalty or Interest*: A few courts have now had some opportunity to assess a variety of innovative provisions proffered by debtors. The bankruptcy courts in Arkansas and Kansas have rejected as unacceptable, provisions which have attempted to: provide for *ex parte* application and granting of moratoria and payment extensions due to unforeseeable circumstances;[802] provide for an "effective date" of the plan significantly different than that provided by statute and case law;[803] include sale provisions for collateral which provide

for consent to sale and partial payment of proceeds;[804] provide for full claim satisfaction (both secured and unsecured) from collateral surrender at any time during the plan's life without a valuation hearing.[805]

(12) *Right of First Refusal Upon Sale*: If property is surrendered by consent of default, the debtor may retain the right to redeem such property by matching the bid accepted by the creditor for sale, if the plan so provides.[806]

(13) *Reservation of Rights to Pursue State Claims*: The plan may minimize the effect of *res judicata* by specifically and expressly preserving claims not intrinsic to the contractual relationship between debtor and a creditor.[807]

16.6 Chapter 12 Plan Confirmation

16.6.1 Overview of the Process

The timetable for confirmation of a chapter 12 plan, after it has been proposed, is shorter than any other chapter—generally no more than forty-five days from proposal.[808] That means that counsel for family farm debtors must expeditiously prepare to address those confirmation issues which can be anticipated as a part of the legitimate inquiry of creditors, the trustee, and the bankruptcy court. As in chapters 11[809] and 13,[810] the Bankruptcy Code provides a statutory checklist for determining confirmability of a plan at sections 1222 and 1225. These sections track the comparable chapter 13 sections, with some exceptions.[811]

The court has an independent duty to review whether the debtor is entitled to confirmation. Without creditor or trustee challenge and strong evidence to the contrary, the bankruptcy court will probably presume good faith and payment of costs and fees under 11 U.S.C. §§ 1225(a)(3) and 1225(a)(2) respectively, but may take evidence regardless of whether an objection is lodged as to the meeting of the best interests, and feasibility tests, particularly where deep com-

---

799 *In re* Tyndall, 97 B.R. 266 (Bankr. E.D.N.C. 1989). *See* § 16.4.7.3, *supra*.

800 *See, e.g., In re* Craven, 97 B.R. 549 (Bankr. W.D. Mo. 1989); *In re* Fowler, 83 B.R. 39 (Bankr. D. Mont. 1987); *In re* Big Hook Land & Cattle Co., 77 B.R. 793 (Bankr. D. Mont. 1987) (plan determined to be not feasible in this decision for other reasons); *In re* Martin, 66 B.R. 921 (Bankr. D. Mont. 1986) (chapter 11). *Contra In re* Cool, 81 B.R. 614 (Bankr. D. Mont. 1987) (no interest deferral). Yet built-in modifications based upon default yet to be experienced which do not provide for notice and hearing to creditors may not be permitted. *In re* Gore, 113 B.R. 504 (Bankr. E.D. Ark. 1989).

801 *See, e.g., In re* Arthur, 86 B.R. 98 (Bankr. W.D. Mich. 1988); *In re* Bentson, 74 B.R. 56 (Bankr. D. Minn. 1987).

802 *In re* Gore, 113 B.R. 504 (Bankr. E.D. Ark. 1989); *In re* Butler, 97 B.R. 508 (Bankr. E.D. Ark. 1988). Yet at least one court has found that a consensual drop-dead provision will not prevent modification under § 1229. *In re* Mader, 108 B.R. 643 (N.D. Ill. 1989).

803 *In re* Musil, 99 B.R. 448 (Bankr. D. Kan. 1988).

804 *In re* Gore, 113 B.R. 504 (Bankr. E.D. Ark. 1989); *In re* Butler, 97 B.R. 508 (Bankr. E.D. Ark. 1988).

805 *In re* Gore, 113 B.R. 504 (Bankr. E.D. Ark. 1989); *In re* Butler, 97 B.R. 508 (Bankr. E.D. Ark. 1988).

806 *In re* Coleman, 125 B.R. 621 (Bankr. D. Mont. 1991).

807 *In re* Mass Farms, Inc., 917 F.2d 1210 (9th Cir. 1990). *Cf. In re* Howe, 913 F.2d 1138 (5th Cir. 1990).

808 11 U.S.C. § 1224. However, the time can be extended beyond the forty-five-day limit for cause. *See* § 16.5.2, *supra*.

809 11 U.S.C. §§ 1123, 1129.

810 11 U.S.C. §§ 1322, 1325.

811 11 U.S.C. § 1222 differs from chapter 13's provision at 11 U.S.C. § 1322 in: when payments must begin under the plan (11 U.S.C. § 1222(b)(1)(B)); allowance of modification of all secured claims (11 U.S.C. § 1222(b)(2)); additional provision for sale of assets as a pivotal part of a confirmed plan (11 U.S.C. § 1222(b)(8)); and allowance of scheduling for repayment of secured debts over a period beyond the life of the plan even if their original terms did not so provide (11 U.S.C. § 1222(b)(9)); *In re* Dues, 98 B.R. 434 (Bankr. N.D. Ind. 1989).

position plans are proposed.[812] The burden of demonstrating confirmability of a chapter 12 plan rests with the debtor.[813] If a creditor files an untimely objection, the court may disregard it absent a showing of excusable neglect on the part of the creditor or fraud on the part of the debtor.[814]

Chapter 13 confirmation hearings tend to be rather cursory, if the plans and pre-confirmation performance on their face indicate confirmability under chapter 13 standards and if there are no objections from parties in interest. Some bankruptcy courts under chapter 12 may also require a minimal demonstration of confirmability if there are no creditor or trustee objections; those districts prefer to deal with debtor inability to reorganize through natural selection and sifting—default and dismissal—rather than front-end sorting. In that event, a simple showing through debtor testimony of the major issues affecting confirmation, discussed below, should suffice. However, many districts show more concern in front-end sorting and so do most creditors. In that event, preparation—particularly pre-petition if possible—is essential to overcome confirmation hurdles.

While the court may permit amendment and modification of the plan upon denial of confirmation, it is not required to give the debtor that opportunity.

Confirmation usually acts as *res judicata* for the debtor and creditors to bar reconsideration of issues addressed by confirmation and the plan, or which should have been considered pre-confirmation.[815] However, confirmation of a plan which provides for payment of a particular unsecured claim is not a basis to allow filing and payment of that claim after the bar date.[816]

16.6.2 Pre-Confirmation Modification

Section 1223 permits modification of the chapter 12 plan at any time before confirmation. The filing of any modification automatically changes the plan without notice, hearing or court approval, and the plan as modified becomes the plan to be considered at confirmation. Any modification must meet the requirements and standards of section 1222 to qualify as a plan modification.

Where the modification is significant or affects the rights of creditors by changing a plan provision upon which creditors would make confirmation decisions, for example, a reduction in the percentage distribution to unsecured creditors, then additional notice is required to all creditors.

While the better practice is to develop the optimum plan from the beginning, organic changes in the debtor's operation, the market, the creditors' agreement or opposition, valuation computations, government programs, or other plan components may make modification—or several modifications—inescapable. It is not unusual, in courts tolerant of such practice, for viable modification to be proffered at confirmation and allowed by later written amendment;[817] however, that availability should not be counted upon.

16.6.3 Major Confirmation Issues in Chapter 12 Cases

16.6.3.1 Eligibility

The design and purpose of chapter 12 put eligibility in sharp focus. The question of eligibility generally will be addressed by a motion to dismiss from the trustee or creditors pre-confirmation, but the fact that no motion is so made never precludes court inquiry *at any time* concerning eligibility. If the court determines at the confirmation hearing that eligibility does not exist, dismissal for lack of jurisdiction rather than denial of confirmation may occur.[818]

---

812 *In re* Eber-Acres Farm, 82 B.R. 889 (Bankr. S.D. Ohio 987). However, a hearing is not mandatory absent timely objection. *In re* Dues, 98 B.R. 434 (Bankr. N.D. Ind. 1989).

813 *In re* Garako Farms, Inc., 98 B.R. 506 (Bankr. E.D. Cal. 1988); *In re* Adam, 92 B.R. 732 (Bankr. E.D. Mich. 1988).

814 *In re* Dues, 98 B.R. 434 (Bankr. N.D. Ind. 1989).

815 11 U.S.C. § 1227(a); First Nat'l Bank v. Allen, 118 F.3d 1289 (8th Cir. 1997) (failure to object to chapter 12 plan which provided for banks' secured claims, but not their unsecured claims constitutes waiver of the unsecured claims); *In re* Harrison, 987 F.2d 677 (10th Cir. 1993); *In re* Webb, 932 F.2d 155 (2d Cir. 1991) (valuation); *In re* Howe, 913 F.2d 1138 (5th Cir. 1990); *In re* Zabel, 249 B.R. 764 (Bankr. E.D. Wis. 2000) (creditor can't challenge plan's treatment of its lien after confirmation; payment made on discharged portion of debt must be returned to the debtor); *In re* Lyon, 161 B.R. 1013 (Bankr. D. Kan. 1993); *In re* Sealey Bros., 158 B.R. 801 (Bankr. W.D. Mo. 1993); *In re* Roesner, 153 B.R. 328 (Bankr. D. Kan. 1993) (trustees fees may be set by confirmation); *In re* Martin, 130 B.R. 951 (Bankr. N.D. Iowa 1991). *But see In re* Holloway, 261 B.R. 490 (M.D. Ala. 2001) (although confirmed plan listed and paid creditor as unsecured, creditor's lien not extinguished by discharge); *In re* Coleman, 104 B.R. 338 (Bankr. D. Mont. 1989) (is *res judicata* as to parties regardless of inconsistent result under other law); *In re* Craven, 97 B.R. 549 (Bankr. W.D. Mo. 1989); *In re* Cooper, 94 B.R. 550 (Bankr. S.D. Ill. 1989) (liquidation analysis); *In re* Grogg Farms, Inc., 91 B.R. 482 (Bankr. N.D. Ind. 1988); *In re* Kesterson, 94 B.R. 561 (Bankr. W.D. Ark. 1987). *See generally* § 12.11, *supra*.

816 *In re* Greenig, 152 F.3d 631 (7th Cir. 1998).

817 However, some courts *require* any modification to be in writing and presented to the court in advance of the confirmation hearing; that is always the best practice. *See, e.g., In re* Hildebrandt, 79 B.R. 427 (Bankr. D. Minn. 1987).

818 *See In re* Glazier, 69 B.R. 666 (Bankr. W.D. Okla. 1987); Mercantile Holdings, Inc. v. Dobkin, 12 B.R. 934 (Bankr. N.D. Ill. 1981). It is possible in some districts for the court to allow conversion from chapter 12 to chapter 11 because of eligibility problems. *See* § 16.4.7.3, *supra*.

16.6.3.2 Feasibility

Section 1225(a)(6) requires that "the debtor will be able to make all payments under the plan and to comply with the plan." Feasibility is the major area where farmer debtors seeking reorganization have encountered close court scrutiny, creditor opposition, and difficulty of proof.

16.6.3.3 Valuation

Central to the computations the court and creditors must make are the valuations assigned (or consented to) for the collateral of secured creditors. It is the rare chapter 12 plan which will (or can) propose repayment at one-hundred cents on the dollar; the typical chapter 12 plan will propose no or *de minimis* distribution to unsecured creditors, so valuation—the amount of allowed secured claims—is critical.

The chapter 12 plan must disclose the valuations of property relied on by the debtor in his or her plan formulation. Those valuations should be taken from appraisals independent of the debtor's own valuation, or valuations reached by agreement with the creditor. Contested valuation can be resolved by adversary proceeding prior to confirmation or at confirmation.[819] Waiting until the confirmation hearing to resolve valuation is risky and problematic, not to mention irksome to most judges; however, sometimes it cannot be helped because of the fast track for chapter 12 confirmation. A discussion of the allowed secured claim and its determination appears at § 16.5.5.2, *supra*. Valuation bears on almost every aspect of plan confirmation and weighs heavily in validating plan treatment of secured creditors and feasibility under section 1225.

Because valuation is pivotal to confirmation and determination of issues under 11 U.S.C. §§ 1225(a)(5) and (a)(6) feasibility, if valuation must be determined by evidentiary hearing rather than consent, confirmation may be deferred until the valuation is determined.[820]

16.6.3.4 Treatment of Secured Creditors

The typical chapter 12 plan will reamortize and reschedule most, if not all, of the family farmer's secured debts; most will be extended beyond the life of the plan as permitted by section 1222(b)(5) and (b)(9). Some creditors will agree to (or simply will not oppose) the treatment proposed. Other secured creditors will contest the terms and/or interest rate proposed by the debtor. The debtor and his or her counsel should be prepared to explain and support the rationale behind the treatment of each secured creditor,[821] and the interplay of the preservation of the creditor's lien.[822]

The plan must delineate the treatment of each secured creditor, amount of allowed secured claim/valuation or secured interest, interest or discount rate to be paid, term of repayment or amortization, and amount to be repaid when plan payments are due. The plan must also provide that secured creditors retain their liens during the life of the plan.[823] However, in most jurisdictions, the plan may provide for the lien to be released when the amount of the allowed secured is fully paid, even if this occurs before the end of the plan term.[824]

16.6.3.5 Liquidation Analysis[825]

The schedules of the family farmer debtor should set out what assets are extant, unencumbered, and non-exempt. However, because the liquidation analysis is a part of the tests for confirmability, some comment and summary information must be provided either as part of the plan, as an attachment to the plan, or as a separate disclosure to the trustee, creditors and the bankruptcy court comparing the chapter 12 plan's treatment of unsecured creditors with their expectations under a hypothetical liquidation of the family farmer debtor.[826]

When unsecured creditors are being paid small percentages of their total claims, the debtor must produce evidence at confirmation that the plan meets the liquidation analysis and best interests test. Where the composition is only moderate, the primary focus shifts from concentration on the liquidation analysis to feasibility.

---

protection for the secured creditor. That showing may include demonstration that the creditor's collateral is replenishing (for example, livestock and offspring), that no or little diminution in value of the collateral will occur over the plan's life, and that the treatment of the debt over time is typical for that kind of debt and collateral. *In re* Adam, 92 B.R. 732 (Bankr. E.D. Mich. 1988); *In re* Milleson, 83 B.R. 696 (Bankr. D. Neb. 1988); *In re* Bartlesmeyer, 78 B.R. 975 (Bankr. W.D. Mo. 1987). *See also In re* Sealey Bros., 158 B.R. 801 (Bankr. W.D. Mo. 1993) (finds lien partially voided by plan confirmation).

823 11 U.S.C. § 1225(a)(5)(B)(i). Albaugh v. Terrell, 93 B.R. 115 (E.D. Mich. 1988); *In re* Batchelor, 97 B.R. 993 (Bankr. E.D. Ark. 1988); *In re* Butler, 97 B.R. 508 (Bankr. E.D. Ark. 1988); *In re* Citrowske, 72 B.R. 613 (Bankr. D. Minn. 1987).

824 *See In re* Lee, 162 B.R. 217 (D. Minn. 1993); *In re* Nicewonger, 192 B.R. 886 (Bankr. N.D. Ohio 1996); *In re* Mandrayar, 174 B.R. 289 (Bankr. S.D. Cal. 1994); *In re* Schultz, 153 B.R. 170 (Bankr. S.D. Miss. 1993). *But see In re* Leverett, 145 B.R. 709 (Bankr. W.D. Okla. 1992). Although these are largely cases under chapter 13, there should be no meaningful distinction under chapter 12. If anything, the case for early voiding of the lien should be better in chapter 12 because there is more authority for modifying the rights of holders of secured claims.

825 For a more detailed discussion of this issue, see § 16.5.4.1, *supra*.

826 *In re* Snider Farms, Inc., 79 B.R. 801 (Bankr. N.D. Ind. 1987); *In re* Martin, 78 B.R. 598 (Bankr. D. Mont. 1987).

---

819 Fed. R. Civ. P. 3012. *In re* Hanna, 915 F.2d 945 (8th Cir. 1990); *In re* Paul, 83 B.R. 709 (Bankr. D.N.D. 1988).

820 *See, e.g., In re* Claeys, 81 B.R. 985 (Bankr. D.N.D. 1987).

821 *See* §§ 16.5.3, 16.5.5, *supra*.

822 The treatment of a secured creditor by a confirmed plan subsumes the provision by the plan of some semblance of adequate

16.6.3.6 Disposable Income Requirement[827]

Most unsecured creditors have little interest in chapter 12 proceedings, reasoning that the typical family farmer is so burdened with secured creditors that there will be no meat left on the bone for them. However, under-secured creditors who are already critically involved with receiving as much as possible on their claims at one-hundred percent will often be quite concerned with the percentage to be paid to the unsecured portion of their claims as will creditors with potentially nondischargeable debts. The disposable income requirement is the flip side to the feasibility question.[828] Assuming feasibility can be readily demonstrated, is the debtor paying as much as he or she can? A creditor cannot force plan extension and devotion of disposable income for more than a three-year period pursuant to section 1222.[829]

The dilemma of feasibility versus the disposable income requirement makes budget and expense projections critical to confirmation. It can be anticipated that family farmer cases will be allowed more expense leeway and savings concomitant with the risk and uncertainty involved in the farm operation. But the disposable income issue is complicated by the courts' interpretation of it as requiring the payment of actual disposable income beyond that projected in the plan.[830]

16.6.3.7 Special Plan Provisions

Any plan provisions which are out of the ordinary or which have a major effect on plan feasibility must bear either scrutiny at confirmation. Such provisions include abandonment or relinquishment of collateral to a secured creditor for debt reduction;[831] sale of property free and clear of lien;[832] plan proposal concerning payments to be made outside the plan or concerning trustee's fees;[833] recapture or "drop dead" provisions which allow a creditor to reclaim property immediately upon default[834] and litigation and its outcome.[835]

16.6.3.8 Reservation of Issues for Determination Post-Confirmation

In some cases, confirmation will be deferred for the outcome of adversary proceedings where their outcome is critical for the analyses which underlie confirmation. Such proceedings may include valuation,[836] technical fraudulent conveyance recovery, and turnover.[837] In other circumstances, confirmation may go forward even with some issues unresolved—particularly nondischargeability under section 523[838] and lien avoidance.[839]

Because confirmation can set the rights of the debtor and creditors,[840] where issues will survive for resolution after confirmation the plan should provide for reservation of the issues and alternative treatments of the creditor(s) involved based upon the probable outcomes of the resolution process. The court should be informed at confirmation of this reservation, not only because it bears on the issue of confirmability but also to insure that no waiver of rights occurs from its status at confirmation.

16.6.4 Denial of Confirmation

In the event confirmation of a chapter 12 plan is denied, the court may dismiss the case under 11 U.S.C. § 1208(c)(5). This is the anticipated route where it appears to the court that no feasible plan can be constructed or where confirmation standards cannot possibly be met given the factual circumstances of a case.

However, the court can allow additional time within which the debtor may propose another plan under chapter 12 or modify the rejected plan to meet confirmation standards and creditor or trustee objection.[841] The court may look to the following factors to determine whether to allow additional time for proposing another plan: (1) when the original plan was filed; (2) how comprehensive and complete the original plan was; (3) reasons for denial of confirmation; (4) likelihood of successful confirmation of new plan and prima facie showing that reorganization is possible; (5) length of time requested to propose another plan;[842] and (6) prior

---

827 For a more detailed discussion of this issue, see § 16.5.4.3, *supra.*

828 *See* § 16.5.7, *supra.*

829 *In re* Grossett, 86 B.R. 941 (Bankr. S.D. Ohio 1988) (chapter 12); *see also In re* Fries, 68 B.R. 676 (Bankr. E.D. Pa. 1986) (chapter 13). *But see In re* Cook, 148 B.R. 273 (Bankr. W.D. Mich. 1992) (where the debtor set no time limitation in original plan for payment to unsecured creditors, the Bankruptcy Court set the plan at 5 years).

830 *See* § 16.5.4.3, *supra.*

831 *See* § 16.5.5.3.4, *supra.*

832 *See* § 16.5.5.3.5, *supra. See, e.g., In re* Schnakenberg, 195 B.R. 435 (Bankr. D. Neb. 1996).

833 *See* § 16.5.6.5, *supra.*

834 *In re* Dittmer, 82 B.R. 1019 (Bankr. D.N.D. 1988); *In re* O'Farrell, 74 B.R. 421 (Bankr. N.D. Fla. 1987); *see also* § 16.5.9.4, *supra.*

835 *See* § 16.4.9, *supra.*

836 *In re* Claeys, 81 B.R. 985 (Bankr. D.N.D. 1987).

837 *In re* Martin, 78 B.R. 593 and 598 (Bankr. D. Mont. 1987).

838 *In re* Bentson, 74 B.R. 56 (Bankr. D. Minn. 1987).

839 *In re* Edwardson, 74 B.R. 831 (Bankr. D.N.D. 1987). *See also In re* Sealey Bros., 158 B.R. 801 (Bankr. W.D. Mo. 1993) (finds line partially voided by plan confirmation). *But see In re* Wickersheim, 107 B.R. 177 (Bankr. E.D. Wis. 1989) (need to reserve right to pursue § 522(f) lien avoidance prior to confirmation).

840 *In re* Lech, 80 B.R. 1001 (Bankr. D. Neb. 1987).

841 11 U.S.C. § 1208(c)(5); *In re* Greseth, 78 B.R. 936 (D. Minn. 1987); *In re* Bentson, 74 B.R. 56 (Bankr. D. Minn. 1987). *But see In re* Weber, 297 B.R. 567 (Bankr. N.D. Iowa 2003) (dismissal appropriate as debtors unable to obtain confirmation after submitting four plans over one-year period).

842 *In re* Bentson, 74 B.R. 56 (Bankr. D. Minn. 1987).

proposal of multiple plans which were not confirmable.[843] A request for additional time may not be routinely granted.

16.7 The Chapter 12 Discharge and Its Operation

16.7.1 Scope of the Chapter 12 Discharge

The chapter 12 discharge is a hybrid of some of the discharge provisions available in other chapters.[844] Like chapters 7 and 11, but unlike chapter 13, the discharge in chapter 12 excepts debts which are nondischargeable pursuant to section 523(a).[845] Like chapter 13, the chapter 12 discharge excepts long-term indebtedness when the maturity date is beyond the life of the chapter 12 plan.[846] The chapter 12 discharge also excepts secured indebtedness upon which repayment exceeds the life of the chapter 12 plan.[847] With these exceptions, the chapter 12 discharge covers all other indebtedness included in the petition and addressed by the plan.[848] Like the chapter 13 discharge,[849] the chapter 12 discharge is granted to the debtor only after completion of the plan provisions and payments.[850] Particular attention must be paid to counseling debtors concerning unpaid non-dischargeable tax debts. Post-petition interest may have continued to accrue thereby creating ongoing risk to an otherwise successfully reorganized farming endeavor.[851]

Federal Rule of Bankruptcy Procedure 3002(c) provides for filing of claims in chapter 12 cases within ninety days of the first date set for the creditors' meeting. To be discharged by a plan, a debt must be provided for by the plan. Creditors may file proofs of claim or a debtor may file for a creditor(s) within the time frame provided by Fed. R. Bankr. P. 3004.[852]

16.7.2 The Hardship Discharge

Like chapter 13,[853] chapter 12 provides for a hardship discharge in the event a debtor cannot reasonably consummate a chapter 12 plan because of circumstances beyond the debtor's control.[854] A debtor seeking a hardship discharge must make affirmative application for it. Notice and a hearing are required for granting of a hardship discharge.[855] The hardship discharge provisions of chapters 12 and 13 are identical, so that case law which has arisen under chapter 13 should be applicable to chapter 12 cases.

At any time after the confirmation of a plan and before the debtor has completed payments under the plan, the court may grant a hardship discharge if the debtor and the aggregate of plan payments already made meet the following three requirements:

1. The debtor has failed to complete plan payments due to circumstances for which the debtor should not be held accountable;
2. The value as of the effective date of the plan of property actually distributed under the plan on account of each allowed unsecured claim is not less than would have been paid under a hypothetical liquidation case; *and*
3. Post-confirmation modification of the plan is not practicable.[856]

The scope of the hardship discharge is the same as the general discharge provided in section 1228(a) and is generally co-extensive with the discharge granted in chapter 7 cases.[857] All unsecured debts are discharged except those: (1) excepted from discharge under section 523(a) as nondischargeable; (2) in which the cure of default or the time for payment of the debt under the plan extends beyond the time of the last payment of the plan as confirmed as provided by section 1222(b)(9); and/or (3) designed to result in the vesting of property in the debtor upon their completion under section 1222(b)(10).[858]

---

843   *In re* Luchenbill, 112 B.R. 204 (Bankr. E.D. Mich. 1990).

844   11 U.S.C. §§ 524, 727(b), 1141(d)(1)(A), 1228(a), 1328(a).

845   11 U.S.C. §§ 727(b), 1141(d)(2). *See In re* Nelson, 255 B.R. 314 (Bankr. D.N.D. 2000) (debt found non-dischargeable under § 523(a)(4) for defalcation in a fiduciary capacity where farmer as trustee farmed and earned profits on trust land without paying rent).

846   11 U.S.C. § 1328(a)(1).

847   11 U.S.C. § 1228(a)(1). The section appears to except debts treated under 11 U.S.C. §§ 1222(b)(5) and (b)(10) from discharge; however, it appears that is a typographical error and the correct citation concerning long-term indebtedness as structured by the plan is 11 U.S.C. § 1222(b)(9). *In re* Eber-Acres Farm, 82 B.R. 889 (Bankr. S.D. Ohio 1987).

848   11 U.S.C. § 1228(a). *But see* § 16.8.2, *infra.*

849   11 U.S.C. § 1328(a).

850   11 U.S.C. § 1228(a). A discharge is to be granted "as soon as practicable after completion by the debtor of all payments under the plan." The payments referred to in § 1228(a) are payments during the plan's life, not long-term secured indebtedness. *In re* Weber, 25 F.3d 413 (7th Cir. 1994); *In re* Gage, 159 B.R. 272 (Bankr. D.S.D. 1993); *In re* Grimm, 145 B.R. 994 (Bankr. D.S.D. 1992); *In re* Butler, 97 B.R. 508 (Bankr. E.D. Ark. 1988).

851   *See generally In re* Cousins, 209 F.3d 38 (1st Cir. 2000) (discussion of non-dischargeable tax debts in chapter 12 context).

---

852   See § 13.4.3, *supra,* for a discussion of time deadlines and late filed claim.

853   11 U.S.C. § 1328(b), (c). *See* § 4.7.2, *supra.*

854   11 U.S.C. § 1228(b), (c). *In re* Roesner, 153 B.R. 328 (Bankr. D. Kan. 1993).

855   11 U.S.C. § 1228(b).

856   *See* 11 U.S.C. § 1229; § 16.8.1, *infra.*

857   11 U.S.C. § 727(b).

858   The literal reading of the 1986 Act excepts from discharge debts under 11 U.S.C. §§ 1222(b)(5) and (b)(10). However, that construction makes no sense and is undoubtedly a typographical error. Commentary, Collier Special Supplement, The Bankruptcy Judges, United States Trustees, and Family Farmer Bankruptcy Act of 1986, p. C-7. The hardship discharge is designed to except long-term secured indebtedness, whether originating

A hardship discharge can be granted prior to the running of the three years of plan life contemplated under chapter 12.[859] Little case law has evolved upon the issue of hardship discharge. However, a hardship discharge is unlikely to be available for a debtor whose conscious choice or decision results in the inability to consummate a chapter 12 plan.[860]

Because farming cases have substantially more risk involved in the production of income that is beyond the debtor's control than in consumer cases, it can be anticipated that hardship discharges will be more common in chapter 12 than in chapter 13. However, there are measures that farmers can take to minimize risk in some circumstances (for example, crop insurance, different farming practices, diversification, and so forth) that courts may consider as positive or negative factors in granting applications for hardship discharges in chapter 12. In sum, the courts look to the effort that the debtor has put forth during the duration of the chapter 12 plan to consider the merit of granting a hardship discharge.

16.7.3 Revocation of Discharge

Revocation of discharge in chapter 12 cases is addressed by 11 U.S.C. § 1228(d). On request of a party in interest and notice and hearing within one year after discharge under this section, the court may revoke such discharge only if such discharge was obtained by the debtor through fraud, and the requesting party did not learn of such fraud until after the discharge was granted. Unlike chapter 11, where the discharge is issued at confirmation, the discharge in a chapter 12 case is issued at the end of the case. Therefore, the knowledge of fraud *must* arise post-discharge and be material to the issuance of the discharge in the case.[861]

16.8 Post-Confirmation Issues

16.8.1 Post-Confirmation Modification of the Chapter 12 Plan

The confirmation of a chapter 12 plan marks the court's approval of the undertaking of reorganization by the family farmer. It is only the beginning. The attorney's responsibility for representation, advice and action does not end at confirmation, but continues throughout the life of the plan.

Section 1229 allows modification of a chapter 12 plan after confirmation, and is patterned after the modification allowed in chapter 13 cases.[862] The debtor is *not* the exclusive party who can offer a post-confirmation modification; section 1229(a) allows the trustee and any holder of an allowed unsecured claim to propose a modification after confirmation.[863] Post-confirmation modification is conditioned upon several requirements:

(1) Any modification of the plan after confirmation must occur before completion of the payments called for under the plan;[864]

(2) The modification can: increase or reduce the amount of payments on claims of a particular class provided for by the plan; extend or reduce the time for payments; or alter the amount of the distribution to a creditor whose claim is provided for by the plan to the extent necessary to take account of any payment of such claim other than under the plan.[865]

(3) Modification must meet the plan confirmation standard of section 1222(a) and 1225(a).[866]

(4) Modification must meet any standards applicable to the modification in section 1222(b).[867]

(5) If the modification does not alter the rights of secured creditors, then a creditor's acceptance or rejection of the original plan is deemed to apply to the modification, unless the secured creditor affirmatively changes its acceptance or rejection upon notification of proposed modification.[868]

---

862 11 U.S.C. § 1329; *In re* Hagen, 95 B.R. 708 (Bankr. D.N.D. 1989). Modification initiated by motion under Bankruptcy Rule 9013, not application. *In re* Hart, 90 B.R. 150 (Bankr. E.D.N.C. 1988). See §§ 4.6, 4.7.3, *supra*.

863 11 U.S.C. § 1229(a). This includes holders of under-secured or partially secured claims. *In re* Cook, 148 B.R. 273 (Bankr. W.D. Mich. 1992). See *In re* Roesner, 153 B.R. 328 (Bankr. D. Kan. 1993); *In re* Koonce, 54 B.R. 643 (Bankr. D.S.C. 1985). However, a modification proposed by any party must meet the same standards for approval of the modification set forth in § 1229.

864 11 U.S.C. § 1229(a); *In re* Cook, 148 B.R. 273 (Bankr. W.D. Mich. 1992); *In re* Moss, 91 B.R. 562 (Bankr. E.D. Cal. 1988) (chapter 13); *In re* Pritchett, 55 B.R. 557 (Bankr. W.D. Va. 1985). This apparently can be beyond the three to five year plan life, if secured debt has been amortized by the plan beyond that time period. See *In re* Schnakenberg, 195 B.R. 435 (Bankr. D. Neb. 1996).

865 11 U.S.C. § 1229(a)(1); *In re* Hart, 90 B.R. 150 (Bankr. E.D.N.C. 1988); *In re* DeMoss, 59 B.R. 90 (Bankr. W.D. La. 1986); *In re* Davis, 34 B.R. 319 (Bankr. E.D. Va. 1983). One court has held that these are the exclusive grounds for modification. Section 1229 cannot be used to make modifications on other bases. *In re* Wruck, 183 B.R. 862 (Bankr. D.N.D. 1995) (cannot change disbursement method by modification).

866 11 U.S.C. § 1229(b)(1). *In re* Roesner, 153 B.R. 328 (Bankr. D. Kan. 1993); *In re* Hagen, 95 B.R. 708 (Bankr. D.N.D. 1989); *In re* Hart, 90 B.R. 150 (Bankr. E.D.N.C. 1988) (feasibility).

867 11 U.S.C. § 1229(b)(1).

868 11 U.S.C. § 1229(b)(1) with reference to 11 U.S.C. § 1223(c). This requirement concerning acceptance and rejection is actu-

---

as such ((b)(5)) or as restructured by the confirmed plan ((b)(9)).

859 *See, e.g., In re* Thornton, 21 B.R. 462 (Bankr. W.D. Va. 1982).

860 *See, e.g., In re* Linden, 174 B.R. 769 (C.D. Ill. 1994) (hardship discharge requires the presence of catastrophic circumstances, more economic hardship causing inability to complete plan is not sufficient); *In re* Fenning, 174 B.R. 475 (Bankr. N.D. Ohio 1994); *In re* Fischer, 23 B.R. 432 (Bankr. W.D. Ky. 1982).

861 *See, e.g., In re* Gross, 121 B.R. 587 (Bankr. D.S.D. 1990). *See generally* § 14.3, *supra*.

(6) The modified plan cannot provide for payments which extend beyond three years from the due date of the first payment under the original plan, although for cause the court can allow extension for up to five years.[869]

Notice and a hearing are required for modification; however, if no objection to modification is lodged, the plan can be implemented as modified as a matter of course without the necessity of formal hearing.[870]

Reasons for modification include illness of the debtor and unforeseen financial difficulties.[871] In the farm context, drought or unexpected damage to crops or livestock outside the control of the debtor may provide justification for modification.[872] The court can, under appropriate circumstances, permit a moratorium on plan payments under such compelling circumstances.[873]

In response to the first chapter 12 filings, the subsequent 1988 drought in much of the country, and the first round of plan defaults, the emerging case law to date concerning post-confirmation modification under section 1229, summarized below, sheds light both upon the acceptance of modification upon default and construction of initial plans under chapter 12.

Most courts have found that no special circumstances are necessary for request of modification; the presence or possibility of default is circumstance enough.[874] For these courts, there is no particular threshold, only a proper showing of changed circumstances.[875]

However, post-confirmation modification is a method of addressing unforeseen difficulties.[876] Circumstances warranting modification must be *unanticipated*.[877] If the debtor proposes modification (in contrast to the trustee or a creditor), the burden of proving that the modification meets confirmation requirements rests with the debtor.[878]

The nature of the circumstances giving rise to the need for modification bears upon the feasibility of any proposed modification.[879] The debtor may have to show that the default was the product of circumstances outside the control of the debtor, not likely to reoccur, and thus likely to be amenable to remedy by modification.[880] Although droughts can recur, they must be viewed as unanticipated and anomalous,[881] justifying modification. Pre-petition defaults cannot be considered upon modification because of the *res judicata* effect of the initial confirmation.[882] A sale or abandonment that could not be consummated under an original plan, where all other plan provisions have been complied with, may be modified.[883]

Post-petition defaults brought about solely by climatic conditions or by failure to consummate a plan provision unrelated to crop or livestock performance (for example, sale of property) must be distinguished from those produced by initial sloppiness (for example failure to do initial valuations correctly, as above) or budget overruns somewhat within the debtor's control. If the post-confirmation default has been occasioned by budget overruns, doubt may be resolved against the debtor.[884] Efforts to satisfy the feasibility requirement on modification must be accompanied by accurate financial data sufficient to overcome the prejudicial effect of preceding year's budget experience.[885]

The nature of bankruptcy proceedings can lead to the inclusion of plan provisions arrived at by consent, which neither the creditor nor debtor could legally insist upon as products of negotiation. Where terms are negotiated, courts may approach modification with caution.[886] A "drop dead"

---

ally a holdover from the balloting procedure and the acceptance and rejection necessary in the confirmation route for chapter 11 plans under 11 U.S.C. § 1129(a). Rejection does not occur in chapters 12 and 13 because of cramdown; however, initial express acceptance by a secured creditor of treatment which does not comport with chapter 12 confirmation standards certainly can occur.

869 11 U.S.C. § 1229(c). *In re* Whitby, 146 B.R. 19 (Bankr. D. Idaho 1992); *In re* Hart, 90 B.R. 150 (Bankr. E.D.N.C. 1988). This does not apply to debts which are reamortized or reamortizable under 11 U.S.C. §§ 1222(b)(5) and (b)(9). The calculation of the time runs from the date the first payment under the original plan was due. *In re* Eves, 67 B.R. 964 (Bankr. N.D. Ohio 1986). The requirement that extension can be had "for cause" to a five-year repayment schedule is taken lightly by some districts, but scrutinized more strictly by others.

870 11 U.S.C. § 102(1); *In re* Eves, 67 B.R. 964 (Bankr. N.D. Ohio. 1986).

871 *See, e.g., In re* DeMoss, 59 B.R. 90 (Bankr. W.D. La. 1986). The change of circumstances need not be egregious, but should be material and substantial. *In re* Pritchett, 55 B.R. 557 (Bankr. W.D. Va. 1985).

872 *In re* Craven, 97 B.R. 549 (Bankr. W.D. Mo. 1989) (drought).

873 *See, e.g.,* Johnson v. Vanguard Holding Co., 708 F.2d 865 (2d Cir. 1983). The availability of moratoria is also a feature of statutes and regulations governing creditor FmHA. *See* 7 U.S.C. § 1981. If caused by drought or disaster, plan modification or cure of plan default can be predicated upon federal payments or insurance payments to be forthcoming as a result of such loss.

874 *In re* Hagen, 95 B.R. 708 (Bankr. D.N.D. 1989).

875 *In re* Grogg Farms, Inc., 91 B.R. 482 (Bankr. N.D. Ind. 1988).

876 *Id.; In re* Hart, 90 B.R. 150 (Bankr. E.D.N.C. 1988).

877 *In re* Cook, 148 B.R. 273 (Bankr. W.D. Mich. 1992) (discussion of modification bases: unforeseeability versus change alone); *In re* Wickersheim, 107 B.R. 177 (Bankr. E.D. Wis. 1989); *In re* Cooper, 94 B.R. 550 (Bankr. S.D. Ill. 1989); *In re* Grogg Farms, Inc., 91 B.R. 482 (Bankr. N.D. Ind. 1988).

878 *In re* Hart, 90 B.R. 150 (Bankr. E.D.N.C. 1988); *In re* Dittmer, 82 B.R. 1019 (Bankr. D.N.D. 1988).

879 *In re* Hagen, 95 B.R. 708 (Bankr. D.N.D. 1989).

880 *Id.*

881 *Id.*

882 *In re* Craven, 97 B.R. 549 (Bankr. W.D. Mo. 1989). Yet that effect might cut both ways: one court has determined that a debtor cannot redo valuations to change the amount due unsecured creditors post-confirmation, based upon failure to do a liquidation analysis properly prior to the confirmation of the initial plan. *In re* Cooper, 94 B.R. 550 (Bankr. S.D. Ill. 1989).

883 *In re* Webb, 932 F.2d 155 (2d Cir. 1991) (modification to allow sale permitted); *In re* Hart, 90 B.R. 150 (Bankr. E.D.N.C. 1988).

884 *In re* Hagen, 95 B.R. 708 (Bankr. D.N.D. 1989).

885 *Id.*

886 *In re* Grogg Farms, Inc., 91 B.R. 482 (Bankr. N.D. Ind. 1988).

or recapture provision may be just such a term.[887] As circumstances warranting modification should be *unanticipated*, if the plan anticipates default, the debtor may not be able to modify the plan to avoid the consequences of that default over the objection of the affected creditor.[888]

One case has determined that because section 1229(b)(1) makes section 1222(b) applicable to modifications, to restrict modification to the three to five year plan life would be contrary to the intent of chapter 12 and would make its provisions significantly inferior to the modification provisions under chapter 11.[889] As a result, the modification in the *Hart* case could extend the life of the plan as modified beyond the original time frame of the plan as initially proposed.

16.8.2 Post-Confirmation Indebtedness

Indebtedness incurred by the debtor after confirmation of a chapter 12 plan must be paid by the debtor separate and apart from the plan and not as a part of the chapter 12 proceeding.[890] Unlike chapter 13, chapter 12 does not have a provision to allow post-petition indebtedness accrued for taxes, approved by the trustee, or incurred upon an emergency basis to be folded back into the plan.[891]

However, due to the special purposes and the rehabilitative nature of chapter 12, it is conceivable that a post-confirmation modification could be proposed under section 1229 which includes post-petition indebtedness so long as undue prejudice did not result to pre-petition creditors.[892] Thus, a debtor may not borrow post-confirmation on a super-priority basis and subordinate the pre-confirmation debt.[893]

If the incurring of post-petition indebtedness can be foreseen prior to confirmation, then it can be placed within the chapter 12 plan itself for original confirmation. For example, if the debtor has been allowed to incur credit pre-confirmation under section 364, to be repaid by the first annual distribution under the plan, the plan can provide that

the debtor can incur similar debt in future years subject to court approval, and if approved, such debt will be treated and repaid in the same manner as the initial post-petition/pre-confirmation debt.[894]

16.8.3 Failure of the Debtor to Comply with Plan Provisions

The failure of the debtor to comply with provisions in a confirmed chapter 12 plan can have the same result under chapter 12 as in chapter 13.[895] The failure to comply with material plan provisions will result in default; material default can result in dismissal of the case by the court pursuant to 11 U.S.C. § 1208(c)(6). The result of dismissal or default can be to place the debtor and creditors back to their pre-confirmation status.[896] Such noncompliance includes not only failure or inability to make plan payments as called for, but also failure to execute other aspects of the plan such as abandonment of property back to a secured creditor, sale of property, and so forth.[897] As detailed in § 8.7.4, *supra*, the debtor's options include plan modification,[898] hardship discharge,[899] conversion to reorganization under chapter 11,[900] conversion to liquidation under chapter 7, and dismissal. However, a court may not be compelled to dismiss simply because a plan is in material default. The causes for dismissal in 11 U.S.C. § 1208(c) require material default caused by the debtor.[901] If default has been caused by factors outside the control of the debtor (drought, catastrophe, and so forth) and in all other aspects the debtor can demonstrate a feasible operation, and a reasonable likelihood of rehabilitation (section 1208(c)(9)), then the chapter 12 plan may be allowed to continue.

---

887 *Id.*

888 *Id.* However, *see In re* Mader, 108 B.R. 643 (N.D. Ill. 1989). Plan had expedited default remedies provision or "drop dead" clause (at option of FLB: conversion, trustee sale or deed delivery). The *Mader* court concluded as a matter of law that its presence in a confirmed plan does not preclude the possibility of modification under § 1229).

889 *In re* Hart, 90 B.R. 150 (Bankr. E.D.N.C. 1988).

890 *See, e.g., In re* Winter, 151 B.R. 278 (Bankr. W.D. Okla. 1993); *In re* Hester, 63 B.R. 607, 609 (Bankr. E.D. Tenn. 1986).

891 *See* 11 U.S.C. § 1305.

892 For example, it might be allowed where the post-petition debt helps bring benefits or revenue back into the estate for payment to pre-petition creditors, or where the post-petition expense itself can be paid from benefits unforeseen at confirmation and arising post-confirmation.

893 *In re* Les Ruggles & Sons, Inc., 222 B.R. 344 (Bankr. D. Neb. 1998).

894 In fact, the legislative history of chapter 12 specifically contemplates that future financing may be anticipated in a chapter 12 plan. *See* H.R. Conf. Rep. 99-958, at 50, 51 (1986), *reprinted at* 1986 U.S.C.C.A.N. 5251, 5252:

   Because Section 1227 is modeled after Section 1327, family farmers may provide in their plans for post-confirmation financing secured by assets that have revested in the debtor. The debtor may also use revested property to the extent it is not encumbered by the plan or order of confirmation to secure post-confirmation credit.

895 *See* 11 U.S.C. §§ 1307 and 1208. However, unlike chapter 13, failure to make payments under the plan or material plan default cannot be cause for involuntary conversion to a chapter 7 case.

896 11 U.S.C. § 349. Farm Credit Bank of Omaha v. Maberry, 1993 WL 93496 (Bankr. D.S.D. 1993).

897 11 U.S.C. § 1208(c)(6).

898 *See* § 16.8.1, *supra*.

899 *See* § 16.7.1, *supra*.

900 *See* § 16.4.7.3, *supra*. The allowance of conversion from chapter 12 to chapter 11 is highly unlikely as an option if the debtor is unable to reorganize under chapter 12 with its more advantageous aspects.

901 11 U.S.C. § 1208(c)(6).

The ability to head off dismissal because of plan default should be relatively easier in chapter 12. The typical chapter 12 plan involving crop and livestock farmers (other than dairy farmers) has plan payments due in relatively long intervals, rather than monthly. By careful placement and spacing of plan payment due dates[902] and monitoring of the farm operation and yield, modification can be proposed within the parameters of confirmation standards *before* non-compliance occurs. Modification after default may not be allowed by some courts.

Good planning on the part of the farmer's attorney can provide alternatives for plan modification in the event of default. Such alternatives may include the surrender of additional real or personal property to decrease the debt load to match the actual production shortfall, the procurement of additional family donations to shore up a plan with a shortfall, additional liquidation of assets to meet plan provisions, or other provisions which lighten the debt burden. A hardship discharge is also possible as a last resort.[903]

16.8.4 Revocation of Confirmation

The confirmation of a chapter 12 plan may be revoked if the order of confirmation was procured by fraud.[904] Revocation must be requested by a party in interest within one hundred eighty days of the entry of the order confirming the plan.[905] Notice and a hearing are required prior to revocation.[906] If confirmation is revoked, then the court will dispose of the chapter 12 case by dismissal, or, if appropriate, by conversion to chapter 7, unless the court allows additional time and the debtor proposes and the court confirms a plan modification.[907]

The provision for confirmation revocation in chapter 12 is drawn verbatim from chapter 13,[908] so that case law developed under chapter 13 should be equally applicable to chapter 12 cases. Chapter 11 also has a provision for revocation of confirmation based upon fraud.[909] As fraud is the sole ground for confirmation revocation in chapter 12 cases, fraud sufficient to warrant revocation should also be sufficient to justify conversion under section 1208(d).[910]

In defining the parameters of fraud which will suffice for confirmation revocation, courts have likened it to fraud sufficient to revoke an individual discharge[911] and fraud under section 523(a)(2).[912] The fraud must be directly connected with procurement of confirmation, as contrasted with other aspects of the case.[913]

The burden upon a party seeking revocation of a confirmation order appears to be to prove that:

- Movant is a party in interest;
- Application to revoke confirmation has been filed within 180 days of entry of the confirmation order;
- There exists fraud in procurement of the plan confirmation, demonstrated by:
  — the debtor made a representation regarding compliance with section 1225 which was materially false;
  — the representation was either known by the debtor to be false, was made without belief in its truth, or was made with reckless disregard for the truth;[914]
  — the representation was made to induce the court to rely upon it;
  — the court did rely upon it; and
  — as a consequence of such reliance, the court entered the confirmation order.[915]

---

902 The payment due dates should mirror the type of operation the family farmer has. For example, dairy operations may make monthly payments to coincide with milk checks. Livestock operations may make quarterly or twice-yearly payments to coincide roughly with sale dates. Crop operations may make yearly payments geared to harvest time. However, in the latter case the payment due date should be sufficiently late to accommodate possible delay in harvest. If the operation is mixed, the plan may provide for several payments at different times during the year to coincide with crop harvesting and livestock sales.

903 11 U.S.C. § 1228(b). *See* 16.7.2, *supra*.

904 11 U.S.C. § 1230(a).

905 11 U.S.C. § 1230(a); Combs v. Combs, 34 B.R. 597 (Bankr. S.D. Ohio 1983). *See* the power of the court to initiate revocation *sua sponte* under the 1986 amendments to 11 U.S.C. § 105. *In re* Davis, 68 B.R. 205 (Bankr. S.D. Ohio 1986). *See also* Chinichian v. Campolongo, 784 F.2d 1440 (9th Cir. 1986) (in a chapter 13 case, partial confirmation could be revoked for bad faith under 11 U.S.C. § 1325); *In re* Gross, 121 B.R. 587 (Bankr. D.S.D. 1990) (strict construction on time period).

906 11 U.S.C. § 1230(a).

907 11 U.S.C. § 1230(b). Conversion would only be appropriate if the debtor requested conversion or if fraud were present; however, the fraud necessary for revocation of confirmation mirrors the fraud sufficient to justify conversion under 11 U.S.C. § 1208(d).

908 *See* 11 U.S.C. § 1330.

909 *See* 11 U.S.C. § 1144. Revocation of confirmation under chapter 11 also revokes discharge.

910 *See, e.g., In re* Krisle, 54 B.R. 330 (Bankr. D.S.C. 1985) (no voluntary dismissal of a chapter 11 case where it found gross misuse of cash collateral); Paccar Financial Corp. v. Pappas, 17 B.R. 662 (Bankr. D. Mass. 1982). Although the *Pappas* court couched its order directing conversion for bad faith, its findings supporting that approach have fraud etched into them.

911 *See* 11 U.S.C. § 1144 and 11 U.S.C. § 727(d)(1).

912 Stamford Mun. Employees Credit Union, Inc. v. Edwards, 67 B.R. 1008 (Bankr. D. Conn. 1986).

913 *In re* Courson, 243 B.R. 288 (Bankr. E.D. Tex. 1999) (failure of creditor to understand plan is insufficient ground for revocation of confirmation). *See generally* for revocation grounds *In re* Moseley, 74 B.R. 791 (Bankr. C.D. Cal. 1987) (and cases surveyed therein); *In re* Scott, 77 B.R. 636 (Bankr. N.D. Ohio 1987); *In re* Hicks, 79 B.R. 45 (Bankr. N.D. Ala. 1987); *In re* Braten Apparel Corp., 21 B.R. 239 (Bankr. S.D.N.Y. 1982), *aff'd*, 742 F.2d 1435 (2d Cir. 1983).

914 Actual, affirmative fraud is required. *In re* Braten Apparel Corp., 21 B.R. 239 (Bankr. S.D.N.Y. 1982), *aff'd*, 742 F.2d 1435 (2d Cir. 1983); Stamford Mun. Employees Credit Union, Inc. v. Edwards, 67 B.R. 1008 (Bankr. D. Conn. 1986).

915 Stamford Mun. Employees Credit Union, Inc. v. Edwards, 67 B.R. 1008 (Bankr. D. Conn. 1986).

The question of whether knowledge of the fraud pre-confirmation and failure to object pre-confirmation upon those grounds will bar later attempts to raise fraud to revoke discharge has been decided both ways under the Bankruptcy Reform Act.[916]

16.9 Bibliography

16.9.1 Introduction

In addition to the articles cited below, also consult the website of the National Center for Agricultural Law, www.nationalaglawcenter.org. Professor Drew Kershen publishes an agriculture law bibliography that is moving to that website.

16.9.2 Chapter 12 Generally

Anderson & Morris, Chapter 12 Farm Reorganizations (1987).

Bauer, *Where You Stand Depends On Where You Sit: A Response to Professor White's Sortie Against Chapter 12*, 13 J. Corp. Law 33 (Fall 1987).

Belcher, *Cramdown under the New Chapter 12 of the Bankruptcy Code: A Boom to the Farmer, a Bust to the Lender?*, 23 Land & Water L. Rev. 227 (1988).

Chatz, Cohen, Feinstein & Morgan, *Farm Bankruptcy and Chapter 12*, 2 Com. L. Bull. 25 (1988).

Dunn, *Bankruptcy Chapter 12: How Many Family Farmers Can It Salvage*, 55 U.M.K.C. L. Rev. 1 (Summer 1987).

Dunn, *Chapter 12 of the United States Bankruptcy Code: Recent Issues and Cases*, 76 Ill. Bar J. 376 (Mar. 1988).

Flaccus & Dixon, *The New Bankruptcy Chapter 12: A Computer Analysis of If and When a Farmer Can Successfully Reorganize*, 41 Ark. L. Rev. 263 (1988).

Horlock, *Chapter 12: Relief for the Family Farmer*, 5 Bankr. Dev. J. 229 (1987).

Hostetler, *Farm Reorganizations under Chapter 12*, 31 Res Gestae 210 (Nov. 1987).

King, *Chapter 12: Adjustment of Debts of a Family Farmer With Regular Income*, 29 S. Tex. L. Rev. 615 (June 1988).

Martin, *Bankruptcy Judges, U.S. Trustee and Family Farmer Bankruptcy Act*, 16 Colo. Law. 221 (Feb. 1987).

Matson, *Understanding the New Family Farmer Bankruptcy Act*, 21 U. Rich. L. Rev. 521 (Spring 1987).

Norton, *The New Family Farmer Bankruptcy Act*, 3 Prac. Real Estate Law. 37 (July 1987).

Rogers & King, Collier Farm Bankruptcy Guide (1992).

Rusch, *Farm Financing Under Revised Article 9*, 73 Am. Bankr. L. J. 211 (Winter 1999).

Sanders, S., *Plan Confirmation under Section 1225 of the Bankruptcy Code Sowing the Seeds of Inconsistency*, 8 Bankr. Dev. J. 291 (1991).

Schneider, *The Family Farmer in Bankruptcy: Recent Developments in Chapter 12*, 3 Drake J. of Agric. L. 161 (Spring 1998).

Schneider, *The Interaction of Agricultural Law and Bankruptcy Law: A Survey of Recent Cases*, 68 N.D. L. Rev. 309 (1992).

Schneider, *Recent Developments in Agricultural Bankruptcy: Judicial Conflict and Legislative Indifference*, 25 U. Memphis L. Rev. 1233 (1995).

Schneider, *Recent Developments in Chapter 12 Bankruptcy*, 24 Ind. L. Rev. 1357 (1991).

Schneider, *Who Owns the Family Farm: The Struggle to Determine the Property Rights of Farm Wives*, 14 N. Ill. U. L. Rev. 689 (1994).

Schneider & Kelley, *Selected Issues of Federal Farm Program Payments in Bankruptcy*, 14 J. Agric. Tax'n & L. 99 (1992).

Shapiro, *An Analysis of the Family Farmer Bankruptcy Act of 1986*, 15 Hofstra L. Rev. 353 (Winter 1987).

Shepard, *Farm Bankruptcy: The New Chapter 12*, 48 Alabama Law. 10 (Jan. 1987).

Tremper, *The Montana Family Farmer Under Chapter 12 Bankruptcy*, 49 Mont. L. Rev. 40 (1988).

Van Patten, *Chapter 12 in Courts*, 38 S.D. L. Rev. 52 (1993).

16.9.3 Creditors' Perspectives of Chapter 12

Armstrong, *The Family Farmer Bankruptcy Act of 1986: An Analysis for Farm Lenders*, 104 Banking L.J. 189 (May/ June 1987).

Dixon & Wegner, *Chapter 11: The Creditor's View of Farm Bankruptcy*, 38 Ala. L. Rev. 509 (Spring 1987).

Eastwood & Ross, *Adequate Protection in Large Farm Bankruptcies*, Norton Annual Survey of Bankruptcy Law 277 (1987).

Hamilton, *Securing Creditor Interests in Federal Farm Program Payments*, 33 S.D. L. Rev. 1 (1988).

Rasor & Wadley, *The Secured Farm Creditor's Interest in Federal Price Supports: Policies and Priorities*, 73 Ky. L.J. 595 (1985).

Rosentrater, *Protecting the Lender's Rights When Farmers File for Bankruptcy*, 29 S.D. L. Rev. 333 (Spring 1984).

---

916 *In re* Braten Apparel Corp., 21 B.R. 239 (Bankr. S.D.N.Y. 1982), *aff'd*, 742 F.2d 1435 (2d Cir. 1983), specifically finds that the language of 11 U.S.C. § 1144 for chapter 11 cases on confirmation revocation eliminates the requirements under the old Bankruptcy Act that knowledge of the grounds for revocation must come to the moving party's knowledge after confirmation. *See also* Official Equity Sec. Holders' Committee v. Wilson Foods Corp., 45 B.R. 776 (Bankr. W.D. Okla. 1985); Stamford Mun. Employees Credit Union, Inc. v. Edwards, 67 B.R. 1008 (Bankr. D. Conn. 1986); *In re* DFD, Inc., 43 B.R. 393 (Bankr. E.D. Pa. 1984)

16.9.4 Farm Bankruptcies in Other Chapters and Prior to Chapter 12

Bland, *Insolvencies in Farming and Agribusiness*, 73 Ky. L.J. 795 (1985).

Flaccus, *A Comparison of Farm Bankruptcies in Chapter 11 and the New Chapter 12*, 11 U. Ark. Little Rock L.J. 49 (1988/89).

Grossman, *Troubled Times for the Farm Debtor Under the Amended Bankruptcy Code*, 38 Okla. L. Rev. 581 (Winter 1985).

Kotis, *Chapter 13 and the Family Farm*, 3 Bankr. Dev. J. 599 (1986).

Kunkel, *Farmers' Relief Under the Bankruptcy Code: Preserving the Farmers' Property*, 29 S.D. L. Rev. 303 (Spring 1984).

Langston, D.R., *A Practical Guide to the Use of Chapter 11 of the Bankruptcy Code in Large Farm and Ranch Reorganization*, 21 Tex. Tech. L. Rev. 2087 (1990).

Note, *The Absolute Priority Rule and the Family Farmer—Setting a Farm Debtor's Priorities Straight: Norwest Bank Worthington v. Ahlers (108 S. Ct. 963)*, 22 Creighton L. Rev. 139 (1988/89).

Scott, *Handling Farm Bankruptcy and Foreclosure—A Debtor's View*, 38 Ala. L. Rev. 701 (Spring 1987).

Waas, *Letting the Lender Have It: Satisfaction of Secured Claims by Abandoning a Portion of the Collateral*, 62 Amer. Bankr. L.J. 97 (Winter 1988).

16.9.5 Farm Law Generally

Bowen, J., *Farm Credit: Is There a Private Right of Action Under the Agricultural Credit Act of 1987?* 43 Okla. L. Rev. 723 (Winter 1990).

Bromley, *The Effect of the Chapter 12 Legislation on Informal Resolution of Farm Debt Problems*, 37 Drake L. Rev. 197 (1987–88).

Evans, J.M., *Agricultural Law: New Directions in Regulation*, 21 Colo. Law 865 (May 1992).

Grossman & Fischer, *The Farm Lease in Bankruptcy: A Comprehensive Analysis*, 59 Notre Dame L. Rev. 598 (1984).

Hambright, *The Agricultural Credit Act of 1987*, 17 Colo. Law. 611 (Apr. 1988).

Hoekstra, B.J., *The Fiduciary Duty Owed by the Farm Credit System Cooperatives to Their Member-Borrowers*, 13 J. Agric. Tax'n & L. 3 (Spring 1991).

Kelley, C.R. & Harbison, J.S., *A Guide to the ASCS Administrative Appeal Process and to the Judicial Review of ASCS Decisions*, 36 S.D. L. Rev. 14 (1991).

Kelley & Hoekstra, *A Guide to Borrower Litigation Against the Farm Credit System and the Rights of Farm Credit System Borrowers*, 66 N.D. L. Rev. 127 (1990).

Kelley & Malasky, *Federal Farm Program Payment-Limitations Law: A Lawyers Guide*, 17 Wm. Mitchell L. Rev. 199 (Winter 1991).

Linden, R.A., *An Overview of the Commodity Credit Corporation and the Procedures and Risks of Litigating Against It*, 11 J. Agric. Tax'n & L. 305 (Winter 1990).

Morse, *Mediation in Debtor-Creditor Relationships*, 20 U. Mich. J.L. Rev. 587 (Winter 1987).

Note, *Avoiding Farm Foreclosure Through Mediation of Agricultural Loan Disputes: An Overview of State and Federal Legislation*, J. Disp. Resol. 355 (1991).

Note, *FmHA Loan Servicing: Alternatives to Foreclosure*, 35 Drake L. Rev. 561 (1985-86).

Pringle, L.N., *The Availability of Small Business Loans for Agricultural and Related Businesses*, 13 J. Agric. Tax'n & L. 134 (Summer 1991).

16.9.6 Security Interests and Financing

Jensen, *Obtaining Operating Capital in a Chapter 12 Farm Reorganization*, 54 Mo. L. Rev. 75 (Winter 1989).

Note, *Bankruptcy, the U.C.C., and the Farmer: PIK Payments—Heads 'General Intangibles', Tails 'Proceeds' [In re Schamling, 783 F.2d 680 (7th Cir. 1986)]*, 26 Washburn L.J. 178 (1986).

Rogers, *The Impairment of Secured Creditors' Rights in Reorganization: A Study of the Relationship Between the Fifth Amendment and the Bankruptcy Clause*, 96 Harv. L. Rev. 973 (1983).

Schneider, *Financing the Agricultural Operation: Recent Developments and Current Trends*, 4 Drake J. of Agric. L. 215 (Spring 1999).

Schneider, *Notes on Agricultural Landlord's Liens Under Revised Article 9 of the Uniform Commercial Code*, 2002 Ark. L. Notes 53.

16.9.7 Tax Consequences

Z.W. Daughtrey, A.W. Varnon, & D.V. Burckel, *Recent Tax Legislation Results in a New Crop of Tax Changes for Farmers*, 12 J. Agric. Tax'n & L. 99 (Summer 1990).

Flaccus, *Taxes, Farmers and Bankruptcy and the 1986 Tax Changes: Much Has Changed, But Much Remains the Same*, 66 Neb. L. Rev. 459 (1987).

Moratzka, *A Farmer's Tax Liability in the Event of Liquidation In or Out of Bankruptcy*, 30 S.D.L. Rev. 198 (Spring 1985).

Nixon, C.J., Richardson, J.W., & Cochran, M.J., *The Impact of Changing Tax Laws on Different-Sized Farming Operations*, 12 J. Agric. Tax'n & L. 268 (Fall 1990).

Chapter 17   Consumers As Creditors in Bankruptcy: Selected Topics

17.1 Introduction

Frequently, consumers have claims against businesses or individuals who file bankruptcy. Sometimes litigation by a consumer or a class of consumers may even motivate a retailer, service provider, finance company, or others to seek shelter in the bankruptcy system. Similarly, tenants may discover that their landlord has filed bankruptcy and services to their building have stopped. And most commonly, a consumer may be a creditor in the bankruptcy of a separated or former spouse.[1]

Several finance company lenders, holding hundreds of thousands of mortgages on the homes of low-income debtors, have recently filed bankruptcy.[2] As many of the affected home owners have claims or defenses to those mortgages, advocates need to understand how bankruptcy can affect these claims and defenses and what tools are available to protect them.[3]

Representing consumers in bankruptcy when they are not debtors involves different perspectives and different legal issues than those that arise when representing consumer debtors. This chapter presents selected topics, which incorporate these perspectives, and discusses some of the issues consumers may face as creditors or parties in interest.

There is voluminous literature on representation of creditors.[4] Most of that literature concerns representation of commercial interests. This chapter focuses primarily on basic concepts and on topics unique to or of special importance to consumers. Where topics overlap those discussed earlier in this manual, there are cross references rather than a repetition of the material.

17.2 Pre-Bankruptcy Strategy

17.2.1 Preparing for the Debtor's Voluntary Bankruptcy

When consumers have claims against persons or entities that are financially shaky, the possibility that the person or entity may file bankruptcy should be considered when pursuing claims and collection of the claims. In many instances, lawyers who have obtained large judgments against an abusive business or landlord find they have merely wasted their time or falsely raised their client's hopes when the judgment debtor files for bankruptcy. The clients become unsecured creditors in a chapter 7 or 11 bankruptcy and the distribution to them is nominal or nonexistent. While there is no way to assure collection in the face of a threatened bankruptcy, there are steps that may help in some cases.

The best approach is to name a defendant in the original suit who is a "deep pocket," someone who is unlikely to go into bankruptcy. In pursuing claims against landlords or other businesses, determine if, in addition to the corporate entity that conducts the business, there is potential liability on the part of individuals involved, parent companies, secured lenders, lawyers, franchisors and others.[5] Also consider what third parties may have obligations to make good on a consumer's claim, such as officer and director liability policy insurers, and state recovery funds[6] for licensed real estate agents or attorneys. A consumer who obtains a judgment should be sure to insist on filing of an appeal bond if the Defendant appeals; the bond surety will then be liable in the event of the defendant's bankruptcy.[7]

Another protective strategy is that when there is potential individual liability (as opposed to corporate liability), pre-bankruptcy litigation should include claims that, if upheld, may be declared nondischargeable if that individual subse-

---

1   While this Chapter will cover some topics relevant to spouses of debtors, a more comprehensive treatment can be found in Henry J. Sommer and Margaret Doe McGarity, Collier Family Law and the Bankruptcy Code.

2   *See* § 17.9, *infra.*

3   *Id.*

4   See texts discussed in § 1.5.3, *supra.* Another text which may be helpful to those new to representation of creditors, although it is oriented to the representation of commercial interests, is Lo-Pucki, Strategies For Creditors in Bankruptcy Proceedings (2d ed. 1991), published by Little Brown and Co.

5   *See* § 17.5.7, *infra*; National Consumer Law Center, Unfair and Deceptive Acts and Practices § 6.1 (5th ed. 2001 and Supp.).

6   *See, e.g.,* Ariz. Rev. Stat. § 32-2186; Cal. Bus. & Prof. Code § 10471 (West) (Chapter 6.5 Real Estate Recovery Program); 63 Pa. Cons. Stat. § 455.801 (Real Estate Licensing Act, Real Estate Recovery Fund).

7   *See, e.g.,* Fed. R. App. P. 8(b).

quently files a bankruptcy case.[8] A finding of nondischargeability will permit the consumer to collect from the debtor's future income and later acquired assets after the debtor's bankruptcy. In consumer cases, nondischargeability claims will generally be based on fraud or false pretenses,[9] on breach of fiduciary duty, embezzlement or larceny,[10] for willful and malicious injury,[11] or injury incurred through drunk driving.[12]

While holdings in other courts will not be binding as *res judicata* to determine dischargeability in bankruptcy court, they may be given effect under the doctrine of collateral estoppel, and in any event, will be persuasive evidence in the bankruptcy court.[13] Care should be taken to have the court make factual findings that could later be used in a bankruptcy proceeding.

Additionally, when settling potentially nondischargeable claims, care should be taken to have the settlement agreement and, if possible, any order entered confirming the settlement recite grounds establishing nondischargeability. For example, in consumer cases involving fraud and other claims, a settlement agreement will be useful in a later nondischargeability case only if the defendant admits liability for fraud. If the plaintiff explicitly releases liability on fraud-based claims in exchange for an admission of liability on other claims that are dischargeable in bankruptcy, that release may undermine the consumer's position if the defendant later files bankruptcy.[14] Similarly, because it is easier to have family support debts found nondischargeable than property settlement obligations,[15] care should be taken in drafting marital separation and divorce agreements. In appropriate cases, these concerns should be addressed aggressively in settlement negotiations.

If a judgment has been obtained or liability admitted, the consumer should collect the debt or at least obtain a lien in the debtor's property to secure the debt as quickly as possible before a possible bankruptcy filing can occur. Speedy collection can be complicated, however, by the trustee's power to avoid as a preference any transfer to creditors (in this case the consumer) ninety days prior to the filing of the bankruptcy if that transfer would put the creditor (in this case the consumer) in a better position than other creditors if the bankruptcy were filed as a chapter 7 and the transfer had not been made.[16]

Thus, if a cash payment is made in full or partial settlement of the debt and the debtor files within ninety days of the payment, the trustee or the debtor in possession may be able to recover the cash from the consumer creditor. Similarly, because of the broad definition of "transfer,"[17] the trustee may be able to void a security interest granted to secure the debt within the ninety days, may recover property levied upon in execution of the judgment, and may recover the proceeds from the sale of the levied goods. As a result, collection efforts may have to tread a fine line between obtaining as much as possible as quickly as possible and not pushing the debtor into bankruptcy.

To avoid the preference problem, explore whether there is any third party who may be required (or willing) to make payment of the debt.[18]

Any settlement for less than the full amount of the debt should include a condition that the reduction in the amount owed only becomes effective at the end of the preference period and that if the payment is recovered as a preference the consumer will be owed the full amount of the debt plus costs and attorney fees.[19]

Similar issues arise when judgment liens are potentially avoidable because they impair a debtor's exemptions.[20] If an individual debtor has more than one attachable parcel of real estate, the lien should be attached to the parcel that would not be eligible for a homestead exemption in a later bankruptcy. The simplest rule of thumb is to make sure that any judgments are in place as a lien on as much property as possible.

17.2.2 Putting the Debtor into Involuntary Bankruptcy

Bankruptcy should also be considered as a potentially favorable collection forum in appropriate circumstances. When consumers as creditors have obtained a large judgment against an abusive business or landlord, and that judgment appears to exceed the judgment debtor's assets, circumstances may lend themselves to filing an involuntary bankruptcy petition against the judgment debtor.[21]

An involuntary petition may be filed under chapter 7 or chapter 11 by three or more creditors with liquidated, non-

---

8 *See* § 17.5.4, *infra.*

9 11 U.S.C. § 532(a)(2); *see* § 14.4.3.2, *supra.*

10 11 U.S.C. § 523(a)(4); *see* § 14.4.3.4, *supra.*

11 11 U.S.C. § 523(a)(6); *see* § 14.4.3.6, *supra.*

12 11 U.S.C. § 523(a)(9); *see* § 14.4.3.9, *supra.*

13 *See* § 14.4.4, *supra.*

14 *See* § 14.4.4, *supra.*

15 *See* §§ 14.4.3.5, 14.4.3.14, *supra.*

16 11 U.S.C. § 547(b); *see* § 10.4.2.6.4, *supra.* For an excellent, more detailed discussion of the implications of § 547(b) for the unsecured creditor prior to bankruptcy upon which the following paragraphs draw heavily, see LoPucki, Strategies For Creditors In Bankruptcy Proceedings, ch. 2 "Representing Unsecured Creditors in the Shadow of Bankruptcy" (2d ed. 1991).

17 "Transfer" is defined in 11 U.S.C. § 101(54). "Transfer" includes granting of security interests and involuntary transfers.

18 *See, e.g., In re* Sun Railings, 5 B.R. 538 (Bankr. S.D. Fla. 1980) (payment was found not be an avoidable preference because the payment was borrowed as an unsecured loan from a third party and paid directly by the third party to the creditor). The limits of this doctrine are discussed in *In re* Neponset River Paper Co., 231 B.R. 829 (B.A.P. 1st Cir. 1999).

19 For an example of such a clause, see LoPucki, Strategies For Creditors In Bankruptcy Proceedings § 2.14.3 (2d Ed. 1991).

20 11 U.S.C. § 522(f); *see* § 10.4.2.3, *supra.*

21 11 U.S.C. § 303. For a more complete discussion of involuntary bankruptcy, see § 13.8, *supra.*

contingent, undisputed,[22] and unsecured claims aggregating at least $12,300.00.[23] If the petition is opposed, the bankruptcy court will hold a hearing, and will enter an order for relief if the debtor is failing to pay its debt(s) as they become due.[24]

An involuntary order for chapter 7 relief can provide many benefits for consumer creditors. It results, among other things, in the appointment of a trustee to take control of the debtor's assets.[25] Creditors can elect a trustee of their own choosing at the meeting of creditors.[26] Forcing an involuntary bankruptcy can trigger useful disclosure requirements as well as other asset discovery procedures.[27] It can also prevent a dishonest debtor from transferring away assets that might have been available to satisfy a judgment and from otherwise mismanaging the business. Similarly, an involuntary case can be used to recover assets that have already been fraudulently transferred.[28] Two other potentially useful powers in an involuntary bankruptcy are the trustee's power to avoid any preferential transfers the debtor has made within the previous ninety days (or within one year to insiders)[29] and the court's power to appoint new management for the debtor.[30]

One example of a case in which consumers as creditors used an involuntary bankruptcy strategy involves a rent-to-own company against whom consumers had obtained a

judgment for usury.[31] Several other unreported cases have involved large mismanaged apartment complexes in which tenants had judgments requiring damage payments and substantial repairs. An involuntary bankruptcy case in the latter situation may force a change of ownership if the debtor has effectively abandoned the building. It may also create opportunities to commence discussions about the future of the building with secured creditors. An involuntary bankruptcy may also be used to bring related parties and their assets before the bankruptcy court when there has been a voluntary bankruptcy by only one of several related parties (partners, spouses, subsidiaries and affiliated corporations, joint owners of real estate, and so forth).

However, advocates should remember that there are substantial risks to an involuntary bankruptcy strategy. The bankruptcy court may require petitioners to post a bond against the debtor's expenses and potential damages to the debtor's business.[32] The penalties for bringing an involuntary bankruptcy that is dismissed include the possibility of compensatory and punitive damages, as well as attorney fees and costs.[33]

17.3 The Automatic Stay

17.3.1 Introduction

In pursuing claims on behalf of consumers, the consumer's attorney must be aware that as soon as an entity has filed a bankruptcy petition, the consumer and the consumer's attorney[34] are subject to the far-reaching impact of the automatic stay.[35] Virtually all legal proceedings against the debtor and other collection efforts must cease until relief is granted by the bankruptcy court. Violators of the stay risk being subject to contempt, actual damages, costs, attorney fees and punitive damages.[36] Moreover, actions taken in violation of the stay are void or at least voidable, even absent notice of the stay.[37] The scope of the stay is discussed in detail in Chapter 9 of this volume.

Formal notice of the filing is *not* required to subject an attorney or creditor to the automatic stay.[38] Once an attorney has received any indication that a bankruptcy has been filed, she should assume the stay is in effect unless the absence of a filing has been verified by inquiry to the bankruptcy court

---

22 On the question of whether the creditor's claims are subject to a bona fide dispute, the bankruptcy court should be willing to give the consumers' earlier judgment effect under the doctrine of collateral estoppel. *In re* DEF Investments, Inc., 186 B.R. 671 (Bankr. D. Minn. 1995).

23 11 U.S.C. § 303(b). The $12,300.00 amount is adjusted periodically for inflation, under 11 U.S.C. § 104. If the debtor has fewer than twelve qualifying creditors, one or more creditors with over $12,300.00 in qualifying claims may file the petition.

24 11 U.S.C. § 303(h)(1). There is a second, alternative basis for entry of an involuntary order for relief that applies in the following, very limited circumstances: when a custodian was appointed for the debtor's assets, or took possession of the debtor's assets, within 120 days before the petition filing, *and* the custodian was *not* a trustee, receiver or agent taking charge of "less than substantially all" of the debtor's assets to enforce a lien. 11 U.S.C. § 303(h)(2). For example, if all of a landlord's buildings were in control of a receiver or liquidator, creditors could seek to preempt the self-help or state law process and obtain the benefits of the bankruptcy law. Appointment of a receiver for only one of a landlord's many buildings, on the other hand, would not meet this criterion.

25 11 U.S.C. § 701.

26 11 U.S.C. § 702.

27 An order for relief in an involuntary case triggers the requirement that schedules and a statement of affairs be filed within fifteen days. Fed. R. Bankr. P. 1007(c). Debtor's examinations are also available under Fed. R. Bankr. P. 2004. An involuntary debtor will not necessarily be cooperative in filing schedules and appearing for questioning, however. *See* § 17.5.8, *infra.*

28 The trustee's powers to avoid transfers are discussed in Chapter 14, *supra.*

29 11 U.S.C. § 547; *see* § 10.4.2.6.4, *supra.*

30 11 U.S.C. § 303(g).

31 *In re* DEF Investments, Inc., 186 B.R. 671 (Bankr. D. Minn. 1995).

32 11 U.S.C. § 303(e).

33 11 U.S.C. § 303(i); *see* § 13.8, *supra.*

34 *See, e.g., In re* Carter, 691 F.2d 390, 391, 392 (8th Cir. 1982) (landlord's attorney in contempt for continuing eviction after receiving notice of the stay).

35 11 U.S.C. § 362; *see* Ch. 9, *supra.*

36 11 U.S.C. § 362(h); *see* § 9.6, *supra.*

37 *See* § 9.6, *supra.*

38 *In re* Carter, 691 F.2d 390 (8th Cir. 1982); Fid. Mortgage Investors v. Camelia Builders, Inc., 550 F.2d 47 (2d Cir. 1976).

or the PACER electronic document system.[39] Upon receipt of notice, the creditor or its attorney is generally obligated to inform any state court in which litigation is pending of the existence of the stay.[40]

17.3.2 Relief from the Stay

In virtually every instance, the bankruptcy court must grant relief from the stay before any litigation or any other action to collect claims from the debtor may be taken. Grounds for relief from stay are discussed in detail elsewhere in this manual.[41] The balance of this section addresses issues that may be specifically applicable to consumers as creditors.

In cases where state or federal (non-bankruptcy) litigation is well advanced, consumers may seek relief from the stay, or abstention, to continue the litigation in the state court for the limited purpose of liquidating the claim.[42] A bankruptcy court may also grant relief from stay to allow a consumer creditor to enforce an order granting injunctive relief in the court that issued it.[43]

Another situation where relief from the stay may be readily granted is where consumers as creditors have a secured claim that is not being adequately protected.[44] Consumers may be secured by judgment liens or, in some cases, by a state law right to set-off mutual claims.

There is an exception to the automatic stay for government agency actions for equitable relief under their police and regulatory powers.[45] For example, public agencies may continue to enforce consumer protection laws,[46] rent regulations,[47] and laws against discrimination.[48] However, public agencies are still stayed from enforcing money judgments, or taking control of the debtor's property through state law liquidation or receivership proceedings.[49]

If the state court litigation is or was commenced by the debtor, (for example, by a bankrupt finance company seeking to foreclose a mortgage, or by a bankrupt landlord seeking to evict a tenant) relief from stay is not necessary to raise defenses in that proceeding, because the action was commenced by the debtor.[50] However, pursuit of counterclaims does require relief from the stay as discussed in more detail in connection with rights of tenants below.[51]

An exception to the automatic stay is also available for collection of alimony, maintenance, or support from property that is not property of the estate.[52] Thus, in a chapter 7 case, post-petition income can be collected by a support creditor, but property of the estate cannot (at least until it has gone out of the estate because it is exempt or abandoned).[53] In a chapter 13 case, because all property acquired by the

---

39 *See, e.g., In re* Carter, 16 B.R. 481 (W.D. Mo. 1981) (where creditor's counsel had doubts about representations of debtor's counsel that filing had been made it was incumbent upon creditor's counsel to verify the filing with the bankruptcy court), *aff'd*, 691 F.2d 390 (8th Cir. 1982).

40 Eskanos & Adler, Prof'l Corp. v. Leetien, 309 F.3d 1210 (9th Cir. 2002) (failure to dismiss or stay pending collection action against debtor was willful violation of stay); *In re* Soares, 107 F.3d 969, 978 (1st Cir. 1997); *In re* Braught, 307 B.R. 399 (Bankr. S.D.N.Y. 2004) (creditor willfully violated stay by failing to take affirmative action to vacate state court judgment entered in violation of stay).

41 *In re* Bison Res., Inc., 230 B.R. 611 (Bankr. N.D. Okla. 1999) (discussing standards applicable to this type of motion). *See* § 9.7, *supra*.

42 *See* §§ 9.7.3.2.1, 13.5, *supra; see also* Davis v. Life Investors Ins. Co., 282 B.R. 186 (S.D. Miss. 2002) (court exercised discretionary abstention because consumer's action against auto dealer and insurance carrier for wrongful denial of credit disability insurance claim was not core proceeding in auto dealer's chapter 11); *In re* Ice Cream Liquidation, Inc., 281 B.R. 154 (Bankr. D. Conn. 2002) (sexual harassment and discrimination claims based on liability of successor corporation were "personal injury tort claims" within meaning of 28 U.S.C. § 157(b) and therefore could not be tried in bankruptcy court; court exercised discretion to lift stay and abstain as to remaining claims); *In re* Pac. Gas & Elec. Co., 279 B.R. 561 (Bankr. N.D. Cal. 2002) (bankruptcy court, not district court, has jurisdiction to decide whether to abstain; abstention and stay relief granted as to 1250 personal injury claims).

43 *E.g., In re* Veit, 227 B.R. 873 (Bankr. S.D. Ind. 1998).

44 *See* § 9.7.3.2.2, *infra*.

45 11 U.S.C. § 362(b)(4).

46 *In re* First Alliance Mortgage Co., 263 B.R. 99 (B.A.P. 9th Cir. 2001) (state may continue to prosecute state court consumer protection action so as to obtain a money judgment for restitution, civil penalties and attorney fees, but enforcement of such judgment would be stayed); *In re* First Alliance Mortgage Co., 264 B.R. 634 (C.D. Cal. 2001) (bankruptcy court order enjoining FTC and state attorneys general from proceeding with consumer protection actions reversed; actions exempt from automatic stay); *In re* Dolen, 265 B.R. 471 (Bankr. M.D. Fla. 2001) (exception to automatic stay under § 362(b)(4) permits FTC to continue prosecution of consumer fraud action against chapter 13 debtor and to enforce preliminary injunction obtained in that action but does not allow use of the injunction to enjoin debtor's use of post-petition earnings); *In re* Nelson, 240 B.R. 802 (Bankr. D. Me. 1999) (state could pursue court action against debtor under consumer protection statutes); *In re* Liss, 59 B.R. 556 (Bankr. N.D. Ill. 1986).

47 *In re* Berry Estates, Inc. 812 F.2d 67 (2d Cir. 1987).

48 Equal Employment Opportunity Comm'n v. Le Bar Bat, Inc., 274 B.R. 66 (S.D.N.Y. 2002) (EEOC enforcement action under Title VII not subject to automatic stay based on § 362(b)(4) to extent that agency acts in the public interest and not simply to benefit individual employees); *In re* Mohawk Greenfield Motel Corp., 239 B.R. 1 (Bankr. D. Mass. 1999).

49 *Compare In re* NextWave Personal Communications, Inc., 244 B.R. 253 (Bankr. S.D.N.Y. 2000) (FCC actions as creditor to collect debt are stayed although FCC has power to take regulatory actions *with In re* Fed. Communications Comm'n, 217 F.3d 125 (2d Cir. 2000) (court of appeals issues mandamus to require bankruptcy court to allow FCC to resell debtor's radio spectrum licenses).

50 *In re* Way, 229 B.R. 11 (B.A.P. 9th Cir. 1998); *see* § 9.4.1, *supra*.

51 *See* § 17.3.4, *infra*. See also sample forms in Appendix G.14, *infra*.

52 11 U.S.C. § 362(b)(2)(B). *See generally* Henry J. Sommer & Margaret Doe McGarity, Collier Family Law and the Bankruptcy Code ¶ 5.03[3]–[6].

53 11 U.S.C. § 522(c)(1) allows exempt property to be pursued for these debts.

debtor is property of the estate, all actions to collect alimony, support or maintenance are usually stayed.[54] Notably, section 362(b)(2)(B) does not permit the commencement or continuation of a proceeding to obtain alimony, maintenance or support, even with respect to property that is not property of the estate. It permits only the collection of payments.

Some judicial proceedings with respect to alimony, maintenance, or support are excepted from the automatic stay under a more narrow provision. Section 362(b)(2)(A) of the Code provides an exception to the stay for the commencement or continuation of proceedings to establish paternity or to establish or modify an order of alimony, maintenance, or support.[55] This exception is carefully worded so that it does not permit proceedings to enforce such orders. However, once a state family court enters an order for current support, the bankruptcy court is likely to permit relief from the stay in most cases in which the debtor does not comply with it.[56]

If actions are inadvertently taken which violate the stay, the court is empowered in limited circumstances to "annul" the stay, which means to grant relief from the stay that applies retroactively.[57] The circumstances in which such relief is granted are generally limited and usually involve duplicitous or bad faith conduct by the debtor, which prejudices the interests of a creditor.[58]

The stay does not bar litigation against co-defendants who are not bankruptcy debtors[59] except certain co-debtors in cases under chapter 12[60] or chapter 13.[61] A consumer plaintiff may wish to add parties, or dismiss the debtor as a party, or both, in order to proceed with otherwise stayed litigation.[62]

17.3.3 Practical Considerations Applicable to Stay Relief Issues

In deciding whether to seek relief from stay, the first question may be whether the consumer as creditor has a legitimate reason to prefer litigating in another forum. Sometimes bankruptcy court may be as good or better for litigation on behalf of creditors as state or federal court.[63] For example, a tenant may prefer to seek restoration of necessary services in a chapter 11 or chapter 13 case in bankruptcy court, where the debtor's obligations to operate property of the estate are implicated and special efforts to accommodate tenants may be made in order to avoid dismissal of the case or appointment of a trustee to manage the property.[64] In general bankruptcy provides a good opportunity to cost-effectively investigate the assets of the debtor and to maximize their use for the benefit of creditors.[65] Moreover, the proof of claim process and other bankruptcy remedies discussed below may make it easier, rather than harder, to find assets of a recalcitrant debtor.

Once a decision is made that relief from stay is the desired remedy, there is a $150.00 filing fee for that motion.[66] No fee is required if the motion is filed by a child support creditor.[67] For the reasons discussed below, the $150.00 fee, when applicable, is waivable upon filing a motion to proceed *in forma pauperis*.[68] The considerations for granting *in forma pauperis* relief are especially valid for low-income creditors because they were dragged involuntarily into the bankruptcy process.[69]

---

54 11 U.S.C. § 1306(a); Carver v. Carver, 954 F.2d 1573 (11th Cir. 1992) (action seeking to collect divorce obligations from chapter 13 debtor's wages violated automatic stay); *In re* Farmer, 150 B.R. 68 (Bankr. N.D. Ala. 1991) (state court order to incarcerate chapter 13 debtor for failing to pay support would violate automatic stay).

55 11 U.S.C. § 362(b)(2)(A).

56 *See generally* Henry J. Sommer & Margaret Doe McGarity, Collier Family Law and the Bankruptcy Code ¶ 5.03[3].

57 11 U.S.C. § 362(d).

58 *See also* Franklin v. Office of Thrift Supervision, 31 F.3d 1020 (10th Cir. 1994) (power to annul stay should rarely be used, probably only in cases of claimants who were honestly ignorant of stay). *See generally In re* Soares, 107 F.3d 969 (1st Cir. 1997) (annulment should not be granted when creditor knew of bankruptcy and failed to inform state court); *In re* Siciliano, 13 F.3d 748 (3d Cir. 1994) (bankruptcy court should not have denied motion for relief from stay applicable retroactively without considering whether grounds for annulment exist); *In re* Albany Partners, Ltd., 749 F.2d 670 (11th Cir. 1984) (lack of good faith on filing may constitute sufficient grounds to annul the stay).

59 *In re* Cont'l Airlines, 203 F.3d 203 (3d Cir. 2000) (bankruptcy court's injunction of shareholders' lawsuits against non-debtor directors and officers found insupportable); Credit Alliance Corp. v. Williams, 851 F.2d 119 (4th Cir. 1988); Fortier v. Dona Anna Plaza Partners, 747 F.2d 1324 (10th Cir. 1984); Austin v. Unarco Indus., Inc., 705 F.2d 1 (1st Cir. 1983); Pitts v. Unarco Indus., Inc., 698 F.2d 313 (7th Cir. 1983); Wedgeworth v. Fibreboard Corp., 706 F.2d 541 (5th Cir. 1983); Williford v. Armstrong World Indus., 715 F.2d 124 (4th Cir. 1983); Rimco Acquisition Co. v. Johnson, 68 F. Supp. 2d 793 (1999) (parent company's bankruptcy does not stay action against wholly owned subsidiary); *see also In re* Am. Hardwoods, Inc., 885

F.2d 621 (9th Cir. 1989) (court lacks power to institute non-automatic stay pursuant to 11 U.S.C. § 105 to protect non-debtor guarantors); *In re* St. Petersburg Hotel Associates, Ltd., 37 B.R. 380 (Bankr. M.D. Fla. 1984) (discussing cases on scope of § 105 to protect non-debtors).

60 11 U.S.C. § 1202; *see* § 16.4.5.2, *supra.*

61 11 U.S.C. § 1301; *see* § 9.4.4, *supra.*

62 *See* § 17.5.7, *infra.*

63 *See* Ch. 13, *supra.*

64 *See* §§ 17.7.4, 17.8.2, *infra.*

65 In addition to the debtor's schedules and other disclosure obligations, § 17.5.8, *infra,* discusses special discovery rights available against a bankruptcy debtor.

66 *See* Judicial Conference Schedule of Fees, Appx. C, *infra,* at ¶ 21. The fee for filing a motion for relief from stay is the same amount as the civil filing fee set by 28 U.S.C. § 1914(a): ($150.00).

67 *See* Judicial Conference Schedule of Fees, Appx. C, *infra,* at ¶ 21. A child support creditor or a representative of that creditor must file Form B281 in order to qualify for the exemption. A copy of the Form may be found in Appendix E, *infra.*

68 *See* § 17.6.2, *infra.* Form pleadings are available in Forms 147 and 148, Appendix G.14, *infra.*

69 *See* § 17.6.2, *infra*; *see also* Tripati v. United States Bankruptcy

17.3.4 *Tenants' Counterclaims Against a Bankrupt Landlord*

One common problem affecting tenants when their landlords file bankruptcy is the need to raise counterclaims to a state court eviction case brought by their landlord. For these purposes it is necessary to distinguish between defenses and counterclaims because a tenant would not be prevented from raising defenses against a landlord's eviction action by the automatic stay.[70] However, relief from the automatic stay is probably required in order to pursue counterclaims that arose pre-petition.[71]

Generally, a two-part process will be necessary to raise counterclaims. First, as eviction cases can proceed quickly, sufficient time must be obtained in the state court process to obtain relief from stay in the bankruptcy court. Usually, this is not a problem because state court judges realize that tenants cannot be expected to fight an eviction without raising their available counterclaims. However, some showing that the counterclaim is not frivolous may be necessary.

Simultaneously, if possible, the tenant should seek relief from stay in the bankruptcy court in order to raise counterclaims.[72] This should be done on an expedited basis, if necessary, to satisfy the state court schedule.

A variety of courts have recognized the need to provide litigants in cases brought by the debtor an opportunity to raise counterclaims to fully defend themselves.[73] Thus relief from stay will usually be granted readily to litigate the debtor's liability on the counterclaims, and allow the counterclaims to be set off against any rent owed by the tenant, but not to enforce any resulting judgment in favor of the tenant against property belonging to the estate.

One further point related to eviction cases brought by bankrupt landlords is that in chapter 7 cases and occasionally in chapter 11, property passes to a trustee.[74] In some cases, the landlord/debtor will nevertheless assert a right to pursue eviction actions against tenants. When that occurs, the debtor is not the real party in interest and cases may be

defended on that basis.[75] The bankruptcy trustee must bring all eviction actions until the property is sold or abandoned.[76]

17.4 Filing a Proof of Claim

17.4.1 *For Individual Consumer Creditors*

Generally speaking, to share in the distribution of the bankruptcy estate, creditors must file a proof of claim. The concept of a "claim" in the Bankruptcy Code is very broad.[77]

As a result, a claim may and should be filed even if the consumer has no judgment against the debtor, has not begun litigation or is not certain of the exact amount of the claim. But even if litigation has begun or a judgment has been obtained outside the bankruptcy proceeding, proof of claim must still be filed in the bankruptcy court.

The claim must be made on Official Form 10[78] or a substantially similar document.[79] The form is relatively simple and self-explanatory. It may be filed by the consumer's attorney[80] and should be filed with the court,[81] not with the trustee unless there is a local rule to the contrary.

In cases under chapter 7, 12, or 13, the proof of claim must be filed within ninety days after the first date set for the meeting of creditors under section 341(a) of the Code.[82] In 1994, Congressional action reinforced the importance of timely filing. Late filed claims are no longer allowable in any jurisdiction.[83]

The first date set for the meeting of creditors, which sets the clock running for the chapter 7, 12 and 13 proof of claim, will be from twenty to sixty days after the filing of the bankruptcy petition.[84] If the debtor listed the consumer as a creditor, the consumer should receive notices of the meeting from the court. Otherwise, the court files must be checked to determine the date.

In a chapter 11 case, the court sets the time for filing of proofs of claim and may extend the time for cause.[85] The

---

Court for E.D. Texas, 180 B.R. 160 (E.D. Tex. 1995) (constitution requires that an indigent creditor "be afforded an opportunity to be heard before his claims are disposed of").

70 *E.g.*, *In re* Way, 229 B.R. 11 (B.A.P. 9th Cir. 1998).

71 *Id.*

72 A form pleading is available in Form 146, Appendix G.14, *infra*. An alternative strategy might be to remove the eviction case to the bankruptcy court and to have it heard in conjunction with proceedings on the tenant's proof of claim for damages. *See* § 13.4.1, *supra*.

73 *E.g.*, *In re* Countryside Manor, Inc., 188 B.R. 489 (Bankr. D. Conn. 1995) (relief from stay granted to allow creditor to file counterclaim in case commenced pre-petition by debtor); *In re* Pro Football Weekly, Inc., 60 B.R. 824 (N.D. Ill. 1986); *see also* Pursifull v. Eakin, 814 F.2d 1501 (10th Cir. 1987) (stay lifted to allow determination in state court of matters related to lease).

74 For a discussion of additional issues facing tenants subject to eviction during their landlord's chapter 11 and chapter 13 cases, see § 17.8.4, *infra*.

75 11 U.S.C. § 363(b), (c); *see* § 2.6, *supra*.

76 11 U.S.C. § 554. For a discussion of abandonment see § 17.8.2, *infra*.

77 11 U.S.C. § 101(5).

78 Reproduced in blank in Appendix D, *infra*.

79 Fed. R. Bankr. P. 3001(a).

80 Fed. R. Bankr. P. 3000(b).

81 Fed. R. Bankr. P. 3002(b), 5005(a).

82 Fed. R. Bankr. P. 3002(c).

83 11 U.S.C. § 502(b)(9). Case law to the contrary has thus been legislatively overruled. *See*, *e.g.*, *In re* Hausladen, 146 B.R. 557 (Bankr. D. Minn. 1992).

84 Fed. R. Bankr. P. 2003(a).

85 Fed. R. Bankr. P. 3003(c)(3). Late filed claims are allowable in chapter 11 cases in the event of "excusable neglect." Fed. R. Bankr. P. 9006(b)(1). The Supreme Court has defined excusable neglect fairly liberally, to include inadvertence, mistake, or carelessness, in the context of filing a late claim in a chapter 11 case. Pioneer Inv. Services Co. v. Brunswick Associates, 507 U.S. 380, 113 S. Ct. 1489, 123 L. Ed. 2d 74 (1993).

time for filing may be set in the chapter 11 plan and will become an order of the court upon confirmation of the plan in place of a separate court order. A creditor whose claim is listed in the schedule of liabilities in a chapter 11 and not listed as disputed, contingent, or unliquidated does not have to file a claim in a chapter 11.[86] Filing a claim is still advisable. In many cases, the debtor will not have valued the claim as high as the creditor would have or given it the priority that the creditor may assert. Further, if the case is converted to a chapter 7, as many chapter 11 cases are, only claims actually filed by the creditor in the chapter 11 are deemed to be filed in the superseding case.[87] At the time of conversion, a new claim date will be set for those who have not previously filed claims.

There are a few exceptions to the timing requirement.[88] The one most likely to be encountered is a "no asset" notice. In a chapter 7 case, if it appears that there will be no assets to be distributed, the notice of the meeting of creditors may indicate that proofs of claim need not be filed, that creditors will be notified if it later appears that there will be assets for distribution, and that notice of a time for filing will then be given.[89]

Certain claims are entitled to priority.[90] They are paid in order of priority set by the Code before payment to general unsecured creditors.[91] In making a proof of claim, take care to claim any available priorities. Priority status is extremely important in a chapter 11 or chapter 13 case. The debtor will not be able to confirm a plan, unless all priority claims are paid in full, immediately in a chapter 11,[92] and over the life of the plan, in chapter 13.[93] Even in a case where the debtor has no assets that are not encumbered by liens, priority unsecured creditors may get paid in full. For example, the

holder of a mortgage on a building may want to sell the building through a chapter 11 plan process, in which case funds must be set aside to pay priority creditors.[94]

Unless there is an objection, a proof of claim is deemed allowed.[95] Therefore, the claim should be for as high an amount and with as high a priority as good faith will permit.

17.4.2 Class Proofs of Claim

When large numbers of consumers are involved, such as in the bankruptcy of a retailer or a large apartment building, or when employees have priority wage claims,[96] the filing of a class proof of claim should be considered.[97] A series of recent cases has now approved class proofs of claim in the Sixth,[98] Seventh,[99] Ninth[100] and Eleventh[101] Circuits, as well as in several district and bankruptcy courts.[102] These cases seem to signal a reversal of an earlier judicial hostility

---

86 Fed. R. Bankr. P. 3003(b)(1); *see In re* FirstPlus Fin., Inc., 248 B.R. 60, 71 (Bankr. N.D. Tex. 2000) (unscheduled creditor must file a claim).

87 Fed. R. Bankr. P. 1019(3). See Advisory Committee Note noting that paragraph three of Fed. R. Bankr. P. 1019 reverses the holding in *In re* Crouthamel Potato Chip Co., 786 F.2d 141 (3d Cir. 1986) which held, under an earlier version of the rule, that all claims scheduled in a chapter 11 were deemed filed in the superseding case.

88 The exceptions are set out in Fed. R. Bankr. P. 3002(c).

89 Fed. R. Bankr. P. 3002(c)(5); *see also In re* Kendavis Holding Co., 249 F.3d 383 (5th Cir. 2001) (employee's claim for pension benefits not discharged even though he had actual knowledge of employer's bankruptcy and did not file claim because employer violated the employee's due process rights by sending letter advising that pension rights would not be affected by the bankruptcy proceeding).

90 11 U.S.C. § 507.

91 The most likely priorities for consumer creditors are administrative expenses for post-petition claims discussed in § 17.5.3, *infra*, the consumer priority discussed in § 17.5.5, *infra*, claims for wages, salaries or commissions, 11 U.S.C. § 507(a)(3), and claims for contributions to employee benefit plans, 11 U.S.C. § 507(a)(4).

92 11 U.S.C. § 1129(a)(9)(B)(ii).

93 11 U.S.C. § 1322(a)(2).

94 On the other hand, if the secured creditor obtains relief from the stay and sells a building under state foreclosure rules, there is no protection for priority claim holders.

95 11 U.S.C. § 502(a); *In re* DeAngelis Tangibles, 238 B.R. 96 (Bankr. M.D. Pa. 1999). For a discussion of objections to proofs of claim, see § 13.4.3, *f*. In some situations, it may be advisable for claimants to seek a withdrawal of the reference so that an objection to the claim may be heard by the district court. *See In re* First Alliance Mortgage Co., 282 B.R. 894 (C.D. Cal. 2001) (permissive withdrawal of reference granted as to 2000 individual borrower claims against debtor-lender because district court had previously withdrawn reference as to government claims). For discussion of withdrawal of reference, see § 13.2.5, *supra*.

96 *In re* Birting Fisheries, Inc., 178 B.R. 849 (W.D. Wash. 1995), *aff'd*, 92 F.3d 939 (9th Cir. 1996) (*per curiam*).

97 *See In re* Longo, 144 B.R. 305 (Bankr. D. Md. 1992) (state education code and regulations give state higher education commission *parens patriae* standing to file proofs of claim against bankrupt vocational school for refunds owed to former students). *See generally* § 13.7, *supra*.

98 Reid v. White Motor Corp., 886 F.2d 1462 (6th Cir. 1989); *see also In re* Commonpoint Mortgage Co., 283 B.R. 469 (Bankr. W.D. Mich. 2002) (borrowers' class proof of claim certified alleging UDAP and other state law claims against originating lender).

99 *In re* Am. Reserve Corp., 840 F.2d 487 (7th Cir. 1988).

100 *In re* Birting Fisheries, Inc., 92 F.3d 939 (9th Cir. 1996); *see also In re* First Alliance Mortgage Co., 269 B.R. 428 (C.D. Cal. 2001) (class certification granted based on borrowers' class proof of claim for TILA and UDAP claims against debtor-lender).

101 *In re* Charter Co., 876 F.2d 866 (11th Cir. 1989).

102 *In re* Chateaugay Corp., 104 B.R. 626 (S.D.N.Y. 1989); *In re* Zenith Laboratories, Inc., 104 B.R. 659 (D.N.J. 1989); *In re* United Companies Fin. Corp., Inc., 276 B.R. 368 (Bankr. D. Del. 2002) (certification of class proof of claim based on debtor's failure to comply with state loan broker law avoids burden of conducting 291 separate claim hearings); *In re* First Interregional Equity Corp., 227 B.R. 358, 366 (Bankr. D.N.J. 1998). *But see In re* United Companies Fin. Corp., Inc., 277 B.R. 596 (Bankr. D. Del. 2002) (class proof of claim based on lender's ECOA violations not certified where individual questions of law and fact predominate).

toward such claims.[103] Courts continue to take a variety of approaches to these cases based on the circumstances.[104] It may be particularly appropriate to allow a class claim or other class treatment in bankruptcy for victims of fraud, when there are insufficient assets to satisfy investors in a Ponzi scheme.[105] Class certification should be available, without a class proof claim, in an adversary proceeding seeking class-wide relief such as imposition of a constructive trust on the debtors' assets.[106]

In preparing a class proof of claim it is prudent to set out factors that fulfill the requirements of Rule 23 of the Federal Rules of Civil Procedure in regard to the prerequisites of a class action. The claim should be filed in the name of a representative or representatives of the class and not in the name of an attorney purporting to represent the class.[107] Authorization of individual class members is not needed.[108] A class proof of claim, however, probably requires a separate motion to certify the class under the relevant rules, although such a motion may not be necessary if no objection to the claim is filed.[109] Some or all of the elements required to certify the class can be established by collateral estoppel if a class has been certified outside the bankruptcy process.[110]

To safeguard the rights of individual claimants in case class certification is denied, all individuals who can easily be identified should be named in their individual and representative capacities. Following up on a class proof of claim may involve additional litigation on behalf of the class. This may include responding to an objection to the claim,[111] possibly proceeding for relief from stay and/or challenging dischargeability[112] as well as any other activities appropriate for bankruptcy creditors as discussed elsewhere in this chapter. To the extent that any litigation on behalf of the class is by adversary proceeding, the formalities of Rule 23 will separately apply.[113] To the extent litigation is commenced by motion, the court has discretion to apply Rule 23.[114]

---

103 *See In re* Standard Metals, 817 F.2d 625 (10th Cir. 1987), *vacated and reversed on other grounds sub nom.* Sheftelman v. Standard Metals Corp., 839 F.2d 1383 (1987); *In re* Charter Co., 876 F.2d 866, 869 n.3 (11th Cir. 1989) (and cases cited therein); *In re* FirstPlus Fin., Inc. 248 B.R. 60 (Bank. N.D. Tex 2000) (class certification denied for consumer claims against finance company, supporting minority view that Rule 3001(b) does not allow class claims); *cf. In re* Edmond, 934 F.2d 1304 (4th Cir. 1991) (state consumer protection act gives state's consumer protection agency *parens patriae* standing to bring nondischargeability action on behalf of group of injured consumers without satisfying requisites of a class action).

104 *See In re* Trebol Motors Distrib. Corp., 211 B.R. 785 (Bankr. D. P.R. 1997) (class proof of claim to enforce pre-petition RICO judgment allowed; appropriate class mirrors that already approved by federal district court in underlying class action), *aff'd*, 220 B.R. 500 (B.A.P. 1st Cir. 1998); *In re* Sacred Heart Hosp. of Norristown, 177 B.R. 16 (Bankr. E.D. Pa. 1995) (court would allow class proof of claim in an appropriate context, but a variety of factors must be considered and allowance should be granted sparingly); *In re* Retirement Builders, Inc., 96 B.R. 390 (Bankr. S.D. Fla. 1988) (important factor is that class certification was previously granted in a non-bankruptcy forum).

105 *See, e.g., In re* First Interregional Equity Corp., 227 B.R. 358 (Bankr. D.N.J. 1998) (investors buying a similar fraudulent investment satisfy commonality prerequisite to class action proceeding).

106 *See In re* Johnson, 80 B.R. 791 (Bankr. E.D. Va.) (class certified and constructive trust imposed), *aff'd*, 960 F.2d 396 (4th Cir. 1992).

107 *See, e.g.,* Reid v. White Motor Corp., 886 F.2d 1462 (6th Cir. 1989) (permitting class proof of claim but denying claim in that case because it was filed by and in name of attorney who was not a representative of the class and who did not file proof that he represented class); *see also In re* First Alliance Mortgage Co., 269 B.R. 428 (C.D. Cal. 2001) (private parties asserting a "representative" claim under California unfair competition law may file class proof of claim on behalf of public, which should be treated same as claim filed by attorney general under *parens patriae* doctrine).

108 *But see In re* FirstPlus Fin., Inc. 248 B.R. 60 (Bank. N.D. Tex 2000) (minority position that Rules 2019 and 3001(b) require authorization).

109 *See* Reid v. White Motor Corp., 886 F.2d 1462 (6th Cir. 1989) (bankruptcy rules permit filing of class proofs of claim, however, claim may be denied for failure to follow procedural requirements of Fed R. Civ. P. 23 as made applicable by Fed. R. Bankr. P. 7023); *In re* Charter Co., 876 F.2d 866 (11th Cir. 1989) (no motion for class certification is required unless an objection to class proof of claim is filed). Better practice would probably be to file a motion for class certification at or near the time of filing the proof of claim.

110 *In re* Lebner, 197 B.R. 180 (Bankr. D. Mass. 1996). Similarly, denial of class status in bankruptcy may be based on denial of certification of the same class in a different court before the debtor filed bankruptcy. *In re* Keck, Mahin & Cate, 253 B.R. 530 (N.D. Ill. 2000).

111 One court has held that absent a class proof of claim, it is inappropriate for individual creditors to respond to objections to their claims by a class response. *In re* Gen. Dev. Corp., 154 B.R. 601 (Bankr. S.D. Fla. 1993).

112 Several courts have allowed class dischargeability proceedings. Anderson v. Cohen, 1995 Bankr. LEXIS 757 (Bankr. E.D. Pa. 1995) (dischargeability determination amounts to declaratory relief, so Rule 23(b)(2) standards apply, rather than Rule 23 (b)(3)); *In re* Iommazzo, 149 B.R. 767 (Bankr. D.N.J. 1993); *In re* Livaditis, 132 B.R. 897 (Bankr. N.D. Ill. 1991); *In re* Duck, 122 B.R. 403 (Bankr. N.D. Cal. 1990); *see also In re* Lebner, 197 B.R. 180 (Bankr. D. Mass. 1996) (class treatment denied only because not all creditors could have brought timely dischargeability proceedings); *In re* Gen. Dev. Corp., 154 B.R. 601 (Bankr. S.D. Fla. 1993) (finding that class treatment is inappropriate in fraud related dischargeability case only because of factual distinctions between each creditor's claims). *But see In re* Hanson, 104 B.R. 261 (Bankr. N.D. Cal. 1989) (class dischargeability proceeding not allowed).

113 Fed. R. Bankr. P. 7023.

114 *See* Fed. R. Bankr. P. 9014 (granting the court discretion to apply various adversary rules to a contested matter); *see also In re* Gen. Dev. Corp., 154 B.R. 601 (Bankr. S.D. Fla. 1993).

17.5 Strategies to Increase the Chance of Recovery

17.5.1 General

Unsecured creditors without priority claims are in the worst position of all creditors in a bankruptcy proceeding. Only in the rarest instance will they receive the full amount of their claim. In most chapter 7 cases, they will receive nothing. Without aggressive advocacy, this may be true even if the consumer creditors were victims of egregious fraud.[115]

Attorneys for consumers whose interests are affected by another party's bankruptcy should seek, wherever possible, to characterize their claims to avoid general unsecured creditor status. Some claims may be secured. Others may be claims to property that is not a part of the bankruptcy estate, such as trust funds. Still other claims may be not be dischargeable against individuals in bankruptcy. Some claims may have priority, such as the consumer priority, or be post-petition claims, which can be claimed as part of the administrative expenses of the bankruptcy estate. Or inequitable conduct by other claimants toward the debtor or the consumer creditors may warrant the subordination of their claims to the consumers' claims.[116] Finally, claims against the entity in bankruptcy may also be pursued against others not in bankruptcy.[117]

17.5.2 Property Which Is Not Part of the Bankruptcy Estate—Trust Funds

17.5.2.1 General

If property held by the entity in bankruptcy is treated as being held in trust for the consumer, it will not be part of the bankruptcy estate, nor will it be subject to the Code's distribution rules. Instead, the consumer can recover the property directly. Trust theories apply not only to property subject to a formal trust agreement, but also in situations where the court may impose a trust, such as where a debtor holds deposits from a consumer or where the debtor has obtained the property by fraud.[118]

"Property of the estate"[119] although broadly defined,[120] does not encompass property held in trust by the debtor for another beneficiary. Subsection 541(d) states that where the debtor holds only legal title and not an equitable interest in property, the equitable interest is not property of the estate. Courts have consistently held under 541(d) that property subject to a trust is excluded from the estate.[121]

If a trust exists, the consumer should be able to have the trust's funds or property[122] separated out of the bankruptcy estate. A court order confirming the existence of a trust and setting it aside for the beneficiary should probably be sought in an adversary proceeding, presumably for a declaratory judgment.[123] As trust property does not belong to the estate,

---

115 *See generally* Vukowich, *Civil Remedies in Bankruptcy for Corporate Fraud*, 6 Am. Bankr. Inst. L.J. 439 (Winter 1998).

116 *See* § 17.5.6, *infra.*

117 These issues are discussed in § 17.5.7, *infra.* No stay would apply automatically to such claims except as to codebtors in chapter 12 and 13. *See* §§ 9.4.4, 16.5.5.1, *supra.* Requests for non-automatic stays as to non-debtor parties in such situations are normally denied. *See* § 9.4.6, *supra.* In some cases an effort must be made to pierce the corporate veil. Such actions can potentially be brought in bankruptcy court. *In re* Haugen Constr. Services, Inc., 104 B.R. 1013, 1019 (D.N.D. 1989); *see In re* Simplified Info. Sys., Inc., 89 B.R. 538, 540 (W.D. Pa. 1988); *see also In re* Lee Way Holding Co., 105 B.R. 404, 412 (Bankr. S.D. Ohio 1989).

118 In Cunningham v. Brown, 265 U.S. 1, 44 S. Ct. 424, 68 L. Ed. 873 (1924), the Supreme Court held that a trust may be imposed in bankruptcy to recover funds belonging to any plaintiff, if those funds are adequately traced to a fraudulent investment scheme. (The case is notable because it emerged out of the original "Ponzi" investment scam.) Despite its age, the case remains good law. *See In re* Johnson, 80 B.R. 791 (Bankr. E.D. Va.) (constructive trust imposed on debtor's assets on behalf of defrauded investors), *aff'd,* 960 F.2d 396 (4th Cir. 1992); *see also* Hoxworth v. Blinder, 74 F.3d 205 (10th Cir. 1996) (constructive trust imposed in favor of a class of investors defrauded by the "penny stock" king of Colorado.) *See generally* Kull, *Restitution in Bankruptcy: Reclamation and Constructive Trust,* 72 Am. Bankr. L.J. 265 (1998); Vukowich, *Consumer and Fraud Victims' Claims in Bankruptcy: Constructive Trusts and the Consumer Priority,* 1988 Ann. Survey of Bankr. Law 129 (Callaghan, 1988) (criticizing use of constructive trusts in bankruptcy).

119 11 U.S.C. § 541.

120 *See* § 2.5, *supra.*

121 *See, e.g., In re* Gen. Coffee Corp., 828 F.2d 699 (11th Cir. 1987) (assets held in constructive trust by debtor for another do not come into bankruptcy estate); Mid-Atlantic Supply v. Three Rivers Aluminum Co., 790 F.2d 1121 (4th Cir. 1986) (property held in trust belongs to beneficiary); *In re* N.S. Garrott & Sons, 772 F.2d 462 (8th Cir. 1985) (estate's interest in property subject to constructive trust); *see also* United States v. Whiting Pools, Inc., 462 U.S. 198, 103 S. Ct. 2309, 2313 n.10, 76 L. Ed. 515 (1983) ("Congress plainly excluded property of others held by the debtor in trust at the time of filing of the petition"); *In re* McCafferty, 96 F.3d 192 (6th Cir. 1996) (divorce decree created an identifiable pre-petition constructive trust in favor of wife on debtor's pension distribution so that the distribution was not part of husband's bankruptcy estate); *In re* Jeter, 73 F.3d 205 (8th Cir. 1996) (general unsecured creditors not entitled to a finding of constructive trust based on a loan transaction when funds lent were not used for their intended purpose); *In re* B.I. Fin. Services Group, Inc., 854 F.2d 351 (9th Cir. 1988); Conn. Gen. Life Ins. v. Universal Ins. Co., 838 F.2d 612 (1st Cir. 1988). *But see In re* Omegas Group, Inc., 16 F.3d 1443 (6th Cir. 1994) (bankruptcy court cannot impose a constructive trust which was not identified pre-petition).

122 However, if the consumer interest is in real estate or other property for which interests must be recorded, the trustee may be able to avoid the trust under § 544. *See* § 10.4.2.6.2, *supra.*

123 Fed. R. Bankr. P. 7001.

relief from stay, for cause, may also be available.[124] Due to the potentially binding impact a confirmed plan, claims that property is held in trust should be raised in chapter 11, 12 or 13 cases before confirmation, including, if necessary, by objecting to the plan.[125] A proof of claim may also be filed reserving all rights to the property and claiming the right to assert alternative remedies as a creditor, if a trust is not ultimately declared.

Low-income consumers have sometimes been victimized when money order sellers have filed bankruptcy after the consumer purchased a money order, but before its intended recipient cashed the money order. Consumer advocates argued aggressively and with some success that money paid for a money order is held in trust for the purpose of paying the intended recipient upon presentation. However, because of the delays in recovering funds based on a trust theory, many consumers experienced hardship when their landlords, mortgage holders or other creditors were not paid.

In 1994 Congress fixed this problem, in part, by excluding from the estate, in most instances, proceeds of sale of a money order sold fourteen days or less before filing bankruptcy.[126] The remedy is only partial because money orders are often purchased long before they are cashed and the purchaser may have no control over how long a money order is held by its recipient. Additionally, in cases involving serious misuse of funds, it is unclear how quickly a remedy can be fashioned to have the money orders paid.

17.5.2.2 Determining the Existence of a Trust

Under section 541, courts look to state law to determine if property is subject to a trust.[127] As one of the standard works on the law of trusts explains:

> Trusts are classified with respect to the manner of their origin. When based upon the expressed intent of the settlor (creator of the trust) they are called express trusts; when they come into existence because of presumed or inferred intent they are given the name of resulting trusts; and when they are created by court action in order to work out justice, without regard to the intent of the parties, they are denominated constructive trusts.[128]

In some cases, the facts may establish an express trust in the consumer's favor. To establish an express trust, the bankruptcy court will look to state law and must find that the consumers as beneficiaries and the debtor as trustee intended to establish an express trust.[129] Intent can be inferred from conduct, although the establishment of a segregated fund is not sufficient alone to prove intent to establish an express trust.[130]

The most useful of the trust classifications for consumer creditors is more likely to be the equitable remedy of constructive trust, which allows courts to impose a trust on property initially held by a debtor or even held by a trustee in bankruptcy. For example, where money or property has been taken from a consumer by fraud, the court may treat the property as being held in trust and not as part of the bankruptcy estate.[131]

As an equitable doctrine, constructive trusts can cover a wide range of situations beyond blatant fraud. "The constructive trust may be defined as a device used by [the courts] to compel one who unfairly holds a property interest to convey that interest to another to whom it justly belongs."[132] Accordingly, a court's willingness to impose a constructive trust is a fact-sensitive process with different fact patterns being stressed as important in different jurisdictions. However, simple failure to repay a debt or misapplication of loaned funds, by itself, is insufficient to create a trust.[133]

A constructive trust may also be imposed on property purchased with funds traced to a defendant's wrongful conduct. This is true even if the wrongfully obtained funds are commingled with legitimate funds to purchase the property.[134] When wrongfully obtained funds, or property bought with such funds, are transferred to a third party, a constructive trust may be imposed unless the third party is a bona

---

124 *In re* Newpower, 233 F.3d 922 (6th Cir. 2000). *See generally* § 17.3, *supra.*

125 *See* Nugent v. Am. Broad. Sys., 1 Fed. Appx. 633 (9th Cir. 2001) (constructive trust claim lost due to confirmation of plan).

126 11 U.S.C. § 541(b)(5); *see In re* Supermarkets of Cheltenham, Inc., 1998 WL 386381 (Bankr. E.D. Pa. July 7, 1998) (turnover ordered of commingled funds paid to money order company by supermarket).

127 *See, e.g., In re* B.I. Fin. Services Group, Inc., 854 F.2d 351 (9th Cir. 1988); *In re* N.S. Garrott & Sons, 772 F.2d 462 (8th Cir. 1985).

128 Bogert, Trusts and Trustees § 1, at 11 (2d ed. 1984).

129 Elliot v. Bumb, 356 F.2d 749 (9th Cir. 1966) (express trust established by agreement); *In re* U.S. Lan Sys. Corp., 235 B.R. 847 (Bankr. E.D. Va. 1999) (wages withheld to pay into 401(k) plan were subject to express statutory trust under ERISA, and when funds were moved to operating account, constructive trust would be imposed).

130 *In re* Tele-Tone Radio Corp., 133 F. Supp. 739 (D.N.J. 1955); Van Denbergh v. Walker, 47 F. Supp. 549 (E.D. Pa. 1942), *aff'd,* 138 F.2d 1023 (3d Cir. 1943); Equitable Life Assurance Soc'y v. Stewart, 12 F. Supp. 186 (W.D.S.C. 1935).

131 *See In re* Johnson, 80 B.R. 791 (Bankr. E.D. Va.) (constructive trust imposed on debtor's assets on behalf of defrauded investors), *aff'd,* 960 F.2d 396 (4th Cir. 1992); *In re* Teltronics Ltd., 649 F.2d 1236 (7th Cir. 1981).

132 Bogert, Trusts and Trustees § 471, at 3 (2d ed. 1982).

133 *In re* Jeter, 73 F.3d 205 (8th Cir. 1996) (general unsecured creditors not entitled to a finding of constructive trust based on a loan transaction when funds lent were not used for their intended purpose).

134 *E.g.,* Church v. Bailey, 90 Cal. App. 2d 501, 203 P.2d 547 (1949).

fide purchaser for value.[135] The source of the funds must, of course, be traced to the wrongdoer.

Potential available underlying causes of action justifying imposition of a constructive trust include statutory claims under RICO,[136] or UDAP,[137] and common law claims for fraud,[138] or conversion.[139] A constructive trust can also be imposed, absent wrongful conduct, simply to prevent unjust enrichment.[140]

By way of illustration of some of the principles discussed here, the plaintiffs in *In re Johnson*,[141] had a class certified and a constructive trust imposed on the defendant's property held by the bankruptcy estate. The debtor, *Johnson*, had sold shares in an industrial wine import venture that did not exist. The scheme ran for six years, through seventeen different limited partnerships and raised about $26 million from more than 400 investors. Proceeds of the scheme, were used, in part, to pay off the early investors.[142]

By the time a bankruptcy case was filed against Johnson, available assets consisted of only approximately 1.6 million dollars. The bankruptcy court certified a class of defrauded investors and imposed a constructive trust on the assets (except for $129,000.00 that could not be traced to the fraudulent scheme). Imposing the trust kept the assets out of the bankruptcy estate. The court found that the plaintiffs were seeking recovery of their own funds, rather than assets belonging to Johnson.

Recently a split of authority has developed about whether constructive trusts (as opposed to express trusts) can be created after a bankruptcy filing. Some courts have concluded that a constructive trust is cognizable only if it is impressed upon assets of the estate, by a court or by operation of statutory law, prior to bankruptcy filing.[143] However, one of the leading courts taking that position has mitigated it somewhat by concluding that relief from the automatic stay may be available to continue a pre-petition action seeking imposition of a constructive trust.[144] Presumably, a constructive trust, if imposed in the non-bankruptcy court could then be recognized by the bankruptcy court.[145] Other courts conclude that the state law of constructive trusts creates the trust from the time of the action giving rise to the trust—so that the trust is in existence before the bankruptcy filing whether it has been judicially identified or not.[146] The latter courts would entertain the possibility of declaring a constructive trust by a determination made after bankruptcy is filed.

This split of authority militates in favor of seeking the imposition of a constructive trust, whenever possible, before a bankruptcy case is filed. In appropriate cases, perhaps even preliminary injunctive relief in the form of a declaration of a trust should be sought in order to prevent a loss to the consumer beneficiary in the event that the wrongdoer files bankruptcy.

If the bankruptcy court is willing to impose a constructive trust post-petition, it will look to state law[147] to find the

---

135 *E.g.*, Church of Jesus Christ of Latter Day Saints v. Jolley, 24 Utah 2d 187 (1970); *see In re* Newpower, 233 F.3d 922 (6th Cir. 2000) (embezzled property belongs to the person(s) from whom it was embezzled; however, if embezzled property is transferred to third parties, constructive trust may be imposed); *see also* Dyll v. Adams, 167 F.3d 945 (5th Cir. 1999) (constructive trust may be imposed on entirely innocent beneficiaries of fraudulent conduct). *See generally* Annotation, *Imposition of Constructive Trust in Property Bought With Stolen or Embezzled Funds*, 38 A.L.R. 3d 1354 (1997). This principle is useful if the transferee files bankruptcy, because the constructive trust keeps the assets out of the estate in that instance. The principle also may be used as an alternative to fraudulent transfer theories when the original constructive trustee files bankruptcy after transferring trust assets for less than their value. One potential advantage may be that recovery of fraudulently transferred assets under the Bankruptcy Code would require sharing those assets with other creditors, while imposition of a constructive trust on behalf of consumers would not. *Cf. In re* Nat'l Liquidators, Inc., 232 B.R. 915 (Bankr. S.D. Ohio 1998) (false profits transferred to early investors in Ponzi scheme recovered as fraudulently transferred and shared among all creditors).

136 County of Cook v. Lynch, 560 F. Supp. 136 (N.D. Ill. 1982).

137 *In re* Teltronics, Ltd., 649 F.2d 1236 (7th Cir. 1981).

138 *In re* Johnson, 80 B.R. 791 (Bankr. E.D. Va.), *aff'd*, 960 F.2d 396 (4th Cir. 1992).

139 Chiu v. Wong, 16 F.3d 306 (8th Cir. 1994).

140 *E.g.*, Clark v. Tibbetts, 167 F.2d 397 (2d Cir. 1948); *In re* Wells, 296 B.R. 728 (Bankr. E.D. Va. 2003) (court invalidated oral purchase agreement but imposed constructive trust in favor of purchaser for payments made towards purchase price).

141 80 B.R. 791 (Bankr. E.D. Va.), *aff'd*, 960 F.2d 396 (4th Cir. 1992).

142 *In re* Johnson, 55 B.R. 800 (Bankr. E.D. Va. 1985).

143 *In re* Union Sec. Mortgage Co., 25 F.3d 338 (6th Cir. 1994); *In re* Omegas Group, Inc., 16 F.3d 1443 (6th Cir. 1994). Alternately, courts have held that the trustee can use the strong-arm powers as a hypothetical bona fide purchaser under 11 U.S.C. § 544 to avoid transfer to a constructive trust, especially if such trust was not created prior to bankruptcy. *See In re* N. Am. Coin & Currency Ltd., 767 F.2d 1573 (9th Cir. 1985); Mullins v. Burtch, 249 B.R. 360 (D. Del. 2000). *But see In re* Morris, 260 F.3d 654 (6th Cir. 2001) (limiting the holding in *Omegas Group, Inc.*).

144 *In re* Newpower, 233 F.3d 922 (6th Cir. 2000).

145 *Id.*; *see also In re* Morris, 260 F.3d 654 (6th Cir. 2001) (explaining *Newpower*).

146 Chiu v. Wong, 16 F.3d 306 (8th Cir. 1994); *In re* Unicom Computer Corp., 13 F.3d 321 (9th Cir. 1994); *see In re* McCafferty, 96 F.3d 192 (6th Cir. 1996) (divorce decree created an identifiable pre-petition constructive trust in favor of wife on debtor's pension distribution so that the distribution was not part of husband's bankruptcy estate); Belisle v. Plunkett, 877 F.2d 512 (7th Cir. 1989) (a constructive trust may survive bankruptcy); *In re* Quality Holstein Leasing, 752 F.2d 1009 (5th Cir. 1985) (same). These cases are supported to some extent by legislative history which refers to at least one instance in which Congress believed that a constructive trust would survive in bankruptcy. H.R. Rep. No. 95-595, at 368 (1977); *see In re* Dameron, 206 B.R. 394 (Bankr. E.D. Va. 1997) (funds received by debtors and placed in accounts pursuant to escrow agreements are not property of the bankruptcy estate), *aff'd*, 155 F.3d 718 (1998).

147 *In re* Longhorn Oil & Gas Co., 64 B.R. 263 (Bankr. S.D. Tex. 1986); Daniel R. Cowans, Cowans Bankruptcy Law and Practice § 9.6, at 73 (1989).

elements necessary.[148] For example, the Supreme Court of Tennessee has declared the constructive trust to be a doctrine of equity under which the courts work out justice in the most efficient manner;[149] and according to recent commentary, a showing of constructive fraud need not be made as a prerequisite for establishing a constructive trust in Tennessee.[150] North Carolina courts are willing to impose constructive trusts when constructive fraud, fiduciary relationships, family relationships or mistake are established.[151] The legislature in South Dakota has codified constructive trusts as an equitable duty to convey property back to an aggrieved party in order to avoid unjust enrichment.[152]

Consumer protection statutes can be used to persuade the court to recognize a constructive trust.[153] Where the debtor has violated such a statute, the consumer could argue that a constructive trust should be imposed to further the legislature's consumer protection policy.[154] For example, some statutes require a merchant to deliver goods or services to prepaid consumers within the time specified by contract or

within thirty days if the merchant's time for performance was unspecified.[155] When a merchant's intervening bankruptcy has halted performance, a constructive trust should be imposed on the funds paid to the merchant by the consumer in order to accomplish the goals of the consumer protection legislation.

Constructive trusts could be imposed where statutes require the merchant debtor to return the consumer's property.[156] For example, a constructive trust could be imposed on consumer payments that must be returned after a consumer's rescission under the federal Truth in Lending Act,[157] state home solicitation sales acts,[158] or state unfair and deceptive practices statutes.[159] Arguments for a constructive trust also apply when tenants retain an interest in security deposits misappropriated by their landlords.[160]

17.5.2.3 Tracing Trust Funds

Consumers attempting to have trusts imposed on funds paid or entrusted are often required to trace the specific funds being claimed.[161] The tracing requirement is considered to be a matter of federal law rather than state law.[162]

The tracing requirement may be a major obstacle to recovering funds when the funds have been commingled and then partially drawn down. Even when those accounts have been replenished with additional deposits, the courts generally apply a "lowest intermediate balance test" which limits any claimant to an amount equal to the lowest balance ever reached in the account after the claimant's funds had been commingled.[163] If the funds have been converted into other

148 *See, e.g., In re* Auto-Train Corp., 53 B.R. 990 (Bankr. D.C. 1985) (breach of fiduciary duty), *aff'd*, 810 F.2d 270 (D.C. Cir. 1987); *In re* Richmond Children's Ctr., Inc., 49 B.R. 262, 267 (S.D.N.Y. 1985) (trust avoids unjust enrichment), *rev'd on other grounds*, 58 B.R. 980 (S.D.N.Y. 1986); *In re* Butts, 46 B.R. 292, 296 (Bankr. N.D. 1985) (confidential relationship breached); *In re* Vt. Real Estate Inv. Trust, 25 B.R. 813, 816 (Bankr. D. Vt. 1982) (honesty and fair dealing standard).

For descriptions of the elements necessary to have the courts impose constructive trusts in various jurisdictions, see Banks, *A Survey of the Constructive Trust in Tennessee*, 12 Mem. St. U. L. Rev. 71 (1981); Comment, *The Status of Implied Trusts in South Dakota*, 8 S.D. L. Rev. 93 (1958); Jennings & Shapiro, *The Minnesota Law of Constructive Trusts & Analogous Equitable Remedies*, 25 Minn. L. Rev. 667 (1941); Lacy, *Constructive Trusts and Equitable Liens in Iowa*, 40 Iowa L. Rev. 107 (1954); Lauerman, *Constructive Trusts and Restitutionary Liens in North Carolina*, 45 N.C. L. Rev. 424 (1966); Note, *Imposition of a Constructive Trust in New England*, 41 B.U. L. Rev. 78 (1961); Notes, *Constructive Trusts in Real Property—Review of Oregon Cases*, 11 Or. L. Rev. 393 (1931); Schuerenberg, *Constructive Trust in Texas*, 21 Baylor L. Rev. 59 (1969); Vanneman, *The Constructive Trust: A Neglected Remedy in Ohio*, 10 U. Cin. L. Rev. 366 (1936).

149 *See* Banks, *A Survey of the Constructive Trust in Tennessee*, 12 Mem. St. U. L. Rev. 71, 79 (1981).

150 *Id.*

151 *See* Lauerman, *Constructive Trusts and Restitutionary Liens in North Carolina*, 45 N.C. L. Rev. 424, 428–439, 444 (1966).

152 *See* Comment, *The Status of Implied Trusts in South Dakota*, 8 S.D. L. Rev. 93 (1958).

153 *See* Schrag & Ratner, *Caveat Emptor—Empty Coffer: The Bankruptcy Law Has Nothing to Offer*, 72 Colum. L. Rev. 1147, 1152 (1972).

154 5 Collier on Bankruptcy ¶ 541.11 (15th ed. rev.); Daniel R. Cowans, Cowans Bankruptcy Law and Practice § 9.6, at 75 (1989); *see, e.g.,* Huffman v. Farros, 275 F.2d 350 (9th Cir. 1960) (constructive trust imposed on license held by trustee in bankruptcy); *In re* D. & B. Elec., Inc., 4 B.R. 263 (Bankr. W.D. Ky. 1980) (state statute creates trust in favor of materialmen); *see also In re* Frosty Morn Meats, 7 B.R. 988 (M.D. Tex. 1980) (federal statute creates express trust for stock breeders).

155 *See, e.g.,* Ala. Code § 8-19-5. For a general discussion of such prohibitions, see National Consumer Law Center, Unfair and Deceptive Acts and Practices § 4.9.2 (5th ed. 2001 and Supp.).

156 5 Collier on Bankruptcy ¶ 541.11 (15th ed. rev.); *see, e.g., In re* Goldberger Inc., 32 F. Supp. 615 (E.D.N.Y. 1940) (sales tax paid to debtor was held by debtor as trustee and therefore did not become property of the estate).

157 15 U.S.C. § 1635; *see* National Consumer Law Center, Truth in Lending Ch. 6 (5th ed. 2003) (rescission rights).

158 *See* National Consumer Law Center, Unfair and Deceptive Acts and Practices § 5.8 (5th ed. 2001 and Supp.).

159 *E.g.,* Ohio Rev. Code Ann § 1345.09 (West). *See generally* National Consumer Law Center, Unfair and Deceptive Acts and Practices § 8.7 (5th ed. 2001 and Supp.).

160 This issue is discussed further below.

161 Cunningham v. Brown, 265 U.S. 1, 44 S. Ct. 424, 68 L. Ed. 873 (1923); Schuyler v. Littlefield, 232 U.S. 707, 34 S. Ct. 466, 58 L. Ed. 806 (1914).

162 Conn. Gen. Life Ins. v. Universal Ins. Co., 838 F.2d 612 (1st Cir. 1988).

163 Schuyler v. Littlefield, 232 U.S. 707, 710, 34 S. Ct. 466, 58 L. Ed. 806 (1914); First Fed. of Mich. v. Barrow, 878 F.2d 912 (6th Cir. 1989); 5 Collier on Bankruptcy ¶ 541.11 (15th ed. rev.); *see In re* Dameron, 206 B.R. 394 (Bankr. E.D. Va. 1997) (funds received by debtors and placed in accounts pursuant to escrow agreements are not property of the bankruptcy estate, despite commingling, to the extent of the lowest intermediate balance in the debtor's account), *aff'd*, 155 F.3d 718 (4th Cir. 1998); *see*

property, the claimant can trace the disbursed funds into the new property.[164]

This requirement for tracing the trust funds and allowing a trust to be imposed on only the lowest balance of funds reached in the trust after a claimant's funds went into the debtor's account, obviously works a hardship on claimants either unable to trace the payments made to a debtor or unfortunate enough to have made their payments prior to a substantial or even total dissipation of funds.[165]

Courts have recognized that in appropriate circumstances, based on the equitable powers under the Code,[166] they can abandon the usual strict tracing requirements of the trust doctrine.[167] Thus, the Seventh Circuit has held that consumers defrauded by a merchant need not trace their funds in the debtor's accounts in order to have the court impose a constructive trust on the funds remaining in the debtor's accounts.[168] Similarly, in those circumstances in which the debtor draws down an account to a balance well below the amount of the claimant's payment to the debtor, but the debtor subsequently replenishes the account from other sources, the bankruptcy court might use its equitable powers to adopt the trust revival doctrine which allows a constructive trust to be imposed on those subsequently deposited funds.[169]

Finally, between competing claimants to the same commingled account, the majority position holds that the most recent contributors to the account have claims superior to the earlier contributors to the account.[170] However, a state law minority position allows distribution among claimants in a commingled account to distribution pro rata regardless of the time of deposit.[171]

17.5.3 Post-Petition Claims As Administrative Expenses

Most consumer claims against businesses in bankruptcy will have arisen before the filing of that bankruptcy petition. But some claims, especially torts which may be of a continuing nature such as debt collection harassment or those involving illegal housing conditions, may continue after the bankruptcy filing or may arise after the filing.[172]

After the filing, not only the property of the debtor, but the proceeds, rents and profits from that property become part of the bankruptcy estate.[173] During the pendency of the bankruptcy case, the business will be operated either by a trustee or more likely by the corporate entity as a "debtor in possession" in a chapter 11[174] or chapter 12[175] or by the individual debtor as a "debtor in possession" in a chapter 12[176] or chapter 13 case.[177] Claims arising after the filing of the petition and prior to confirmation are thus claims against the bankruptcy estate and are considered administrative expenses as a cost or expense of preserving the estate.[178] For example, the post-petition right to return of a security deposit, absent rejection of the lease, has been held to be an administrative expense entitled to priority.[179] Administrative expenses receive the highest priority and are paid before all other unsecured claims.[180]

---

also, e.g., In re Mushroom Transp., 227 B.R. 244, 255 (Bankr. E.D. Pa. 1998) (extended discussion of common law rules applicable to tracing funds).

164 Schuyler v. Littlefield, 232 U.S. 707, 710, 34 S. Ct. 466, 58 L. Ed. 806 (1914); Chiu v. Wong, 16 F.3d 306 (8th Cir. 1994) (constructive trust in property converted from partnership assets traced to homestead); Johnson v. Morris, 175 F.2d 65, 68 (10th Cir. 1949). *See generally* Annotation, *Imposition of Constructive Trust in Property Bought With Stolen or Embezzled Funds*, 38 A.L.R. 3d 1354 (1997).

165 Conn. Gen. Life Ins. v. Universal Ins. Co., 838 F.2d 612 (1st Cir. 1988).

166 11 U.S.C. § 105.

167 *See, e.g., In re* Mahan & Rowsey Inc., 62 B.R. 46, 48 (W.D. Okla. 1985), *aff'd*, 817 F.2d 682 (10th Cir. 1987).

168 *In re* Teltronics Ltd., 649 F.2d 1236 (7th Cir. 1981) Although this case was decided prior to the enactment of the Bankruptcy Code in 1978, none of the changes affected the tracing requirements developed by the courts prior to 1978. Thus, this case and those cited below remain good precedents.

169 *See, e.g., In re* Teltronics Ltd., 649 F.2d 1236 (7th Cir. 1981); *In re* Gottfried Baking Co., 312 F. Supp. 643 (S.D.N.Y. 1970). *But see In re* Dameron, 206 B.R. 394, 403 (Bankr. E.D. Va. 1997) (lowest intermediate balance rule precludes replenishing trust funds with later deposits).

170 *In re* Schmidt, 298 F. 314, 316 (S.D.N.Y. 1923) (Learned Hand, in district court considering a bankruptcy case, holds that most recent depositors withdraw from trust *res* first).

171 People v. Cal. Safe Deposit & Trust Co., 167 P. 388 (Cal. 1917)

(state banking liquidation actions); Gibbs v. Gerberich, 203 N.E.2d 851, 856 (Mass. 1964) (trust case).

172 As to whether a tort claim is pre-petition or post-petition, compare *In re* M. Frenville Co., 744 F.2d 332 (3d Cir. 1984) (where acts occurred pre-petition but cause of action arose post-petition, the claim is post-petition) with *In re* A.H. Robins Co., 63 B.R. 986 (Bankr. E.D. Va. 1986) (contra), *aff'd*, 839 F.2d 198 (4th Cir. 1988). *See also In re* Wheeler, 137 F.3d 299 (5th Cir. 1998) (attorney's malpractice in preparing the bankruptcy petition occurred before the bankruptcy filing so that claim for malpractice claim became property of the estate).

173 11 U.S.C. § 541(b).

174 *See* 11 U.S.C. §§ 1107, 1108 (unless trustee is appointed, debtor has power of trustee including the operation of the debtor's business).

175 11 U.S.C. § 1203 (debtor in possession has functions and duties of trustee including operating the debtor's farm).

176 11 U.S.C. § 1203.

177 11 U.S.C. § 1304 ("Unless the court orders otherwise a [chapter 13] debtor engaged in business may operate the business of the debtor. . . .").

178 11 U.S.C. § 503(b)(1); *In re* Charlesbank Laundry, Inc., 755 F.2d 200 (1st Cir. 1985) (civil fine based on debtor's post-petition conduct granted administrative expense status); *see, e.g., In re* Friendship College Inc., 737 F.2d 430 (4th Cir. 1987) (the term "estate" as used in § 503(b)(1)(B)(i) implies post-petition liabilities); *see also* Reading Co. v. Brown, 391 U.S. 471, 482, 88 S. Ct. 1759, 20 L. Ed. 2d 751 (1968) (post-petition tort claim is administrative expense).

179 *In re* Boston Post Road Ltd. P'ship, 21 F.3d 477 (2d Cir. 1994) (tenants who are owed security deposits have administrative claims which are entitled to priority); *In re* Cantonwood Associates Ltd. P'ship, 138 B.R. 648 (Bankr. D. Mass. 1992) (same).

180 11 U.S.C. § 507(a)(1).

A proof of claim should be filed indicating that the claim arose post-petition, both by setting out the date that the claim accrued and by labeling the claim "administrative" in parentheses. The claim should also indicate that it is a priority claim under section 507(a)(1). A motion or application should then be filed requesting an order designating the claim as an administrative expense under section 503 and ordering payment.

Even administrative expenses, however, are ordinarily paid after secured claims.[181] If, for example, the bankruptcy estate principally consists of an apartment building, and sale of the building does not generate enough funds to pay off the mortgage holders, then neither the administrative expenses nor the unsecured claims will be paid. An exception to this rule exists under section 506(c), which allows certain expenses of preserving and disposing of the secured property to be paid before the secured claim is paid.[182]

Section 506(c) provides that the reasonable and necessary costs of preserving and disposing of property securing an allowed secured claim may be recovered by the trustee, to the extent the expenditure benefits the secured creditor.[183] Claims are made most commonly for continued utility services, other costs of maintaining the business as a going concern, costs of storage of the property and costs of selling the property.[184] Three elements must be shown before an expense qualifies to be paid under section 506(c): 1) the expenditure must be necessary, 2) the amounts expended are reasonable, and 3) the secured creditor benefits from the expenditure.[185]

The usefulness of this provision is limited, however, by the fact that only the trustee may seek to "tax" a secured creditor for expenses of preserving collateral.[186] Earlier cases allowing the party who provided the service or incurred the expense to recover under § 506(c) from the secured creditor are no longer good law.[187] In a case where, for example, tenants have claims for reimbursement of repairs, or utility expenditures, recovery from the secured creditor will require cooperation of the trustee, who might be willing to invoke 506(c) to reimburse the tenants, if doing so will preserve or increase the value of the estate. Still, this provision can be useful to tenants in persuading the trustee

to pay for utilities and essential services to the property out of the secured creditor's funds.

17.5.4 Challenging Dischargeability

17.5.4.1 General

In some circumstances, particular debts may be declared nondischargeable. Such debts remain legally in effect after the bankruptcy and are not subject to the Code's prohibitions on collecting discharged debts.[188] The creditor is free to collect the debt from the future income or later acquired property of the debtor.[189] Whether a particular debt is nondischargeable depends on whether the debtor is an individual or a corporation and the Bankruptcy Code chapter under which the debtor has filed.

17.5.4.2 Individual Debtors in Chapters 7, 11, and 12

17.5.4.2.1 Grounds for a finding of nondischargeability

Where the debtor is an individual who has filed under chapters 7, 11, or 12 or receives a hardship discharge under section 1328(b) of chapter 13,[190] certain categories of debts, set out in section 523(a), are not dischargeable. Generally, those most relevant to cases involving consumers as creditors would be claims based on fraud or false pretenses,[191] fraud as a fiduciary, embezzlement or larceny,[192] alimony, maintenance or support,[193] additional obligations related to dissolution of a marriage under some conditions,[194] willful and malicious injury,[195] or drunk driving.[196] When there has been government enforcement of consumer claims, additional grounds for nondischargeability may apply.[197] And

---

181 *In re* Trim-X, Inc., 695 F.2d 296 (7th Cir. 1982); *In re* Delta Towers, Ltd., 924 F.2d 74 (5th Cir. 1991).

182 *See* 11 U.S.C. § 506(c).

183 *See* 11 U.S.C. § 506(c).

184 *See, e.g., In re* Delta Towers, Ltd., 924 F.2d 74 (5th Cir. 1991) (utility service); *In re* P.C. Ltd., 929 F.2d 203 (5th Cir. 1991) (keeping business going); *In re* McKeesport Steel Castings, Co., 799 F.2d 91 (3d Cir. 1986) (utility service); *In re* Trim-X, Inc., 695 F.2d 296 (7th Cir. 1982) (storage costs).

185 *In re* Delta Towers, Ltd., 924 F.2d 74 (5th Cir. 1991); *In re* Trim-X, Inc., 695 F.2d 296 (7th Cir. 1982).

186 Hartford Underwriters Ins. Co. v. Union Planters Bank, 530 U.S. 1, 120 S. Ct. 1942, 147 L. Ed. 2d 1 (2000).

187 *E.g., In re* Parque Forrestal, Inc., 949 F.2d 504 (1st Cir. 1991).

188 11 U.S.C. § 524; *see* § 14.5, *supra.*

189 Property exempted in the bankruptcy court, however, retains its protection and cannot be seized to satisfy most nondischargeable debts. 11 U.S.C. § 522(c).

190 11 U.S.C. § 1328(b).

191 11 U.S.C. § 532(a)(2); *see* Stokes v. Ferris, 150 B.R. 388 (W.D. Tex. 1992) (state unfair trade practice judgment found to give rise to nondischargeable debt based on fraud, false pretenses and willful and malicious injury), *aff'd*, 995 F.2d 76 (5th Cir. 1993); § 14.4.3.2, *supra.*

192 11 U.S.C. § 523(a)(4); *see In re* Messineo, 192 B.R. 597 (Bankr. D.N.H. 1996) (son breached fiduciary duties when, as co-guardian of his elderly mother's estate, he misappropriated her funds and property for his own use); § 14.4.3.4, *supra.*

193 11 U.S.C. § 523(a)(5); *see* § 14.4.3.5, *supra.*

194 11 U.S.C. § 523(a)(15); *see* § 14.4.3.14, *supra.*

195 11 U.S.C. § 523(a)(6); *see* § 14.4.3.6, *supra.*

196 11 U.S.C. § 523(a)(9); *see* § 14.4.3.9, *supra.*

197 11 U.S.C. § 523(a)(7), (13); *see* §§ 14.4.3.7, 14.4.3.18, *supra.* *See also* United States Dep't of Hous. & Urban Dev. v. Cost Control Mktg. & Sales of Va., 64 F.3d 920 (4th Cir. 1995) (judgment owed to HUD nondischargeable under § 523(a)(7) as

several courts have concluded that dischargeability issues can be raised by a governmental agency on behalf of individual consumers through standing conferred by the *parens patriae* doctrine.[198]

In certain cases more than one ground for nondischargeability will apply.[199] When a consumer has been the victim of an unfair trade practice or outright fraud, nondischargeability claims may be raised under the provision based on fraud,[200] breach of fiduciary duty,[201] willful or malicious

injury[202] or all three. However, the Supreme Court has ruled that only intentional torts can be found nondischargeable for willful and malicious injury.[203] Torts based on reckless or negligent conduct are not within the scope of the exception.[204]

---

long as damages assessed were penal even though damages were measured by consumer's losses and even if some part of judgment would repay consumers for their losses).

198 *In re* Taibbi, 213 B.R. 261 (Bankr. E.D.N.Y. 1997) (county consumer protection agency has *parens patriae* standing to raise dischargeability claims on behalf of consumers); *see also In re* Gorski, 272 B.R. 59 (Bankr. D. Conn. 2002) (state human rights agency having duty to enforce civil rights laws has standing in nondischargeability action involving its award in housing discrimination proceeding even though it is not recipient of award); § 17.4.2, *supra.*

199 *See In re* Stokes, 995 F.2d 76 (5th Cir. 1993) (damages under the Texas consumer protection act found nondischargeable based on both §§ 523(a)(2)(A) and 523(a)(6)).

200 11 U.S.C. § 523(a)(2); *e.g.,* Cohen v. de la Cruz, 523 U.S. 213, 118 S. Ct. 1212, 140 L. Ed. 2d 341 (1998) (actual and punitive damages awarded to tenants based on UDAP for rent overcharges nondischargeable under § 523(a)(2)(A)); *In re* Alport, 144 F.3d 1163 (8th Cir. 1998) (home purchasers claim due to builder's failure to pay subcontractors fell within fraud exception to discharge); Morlang v. Cox, 222 B.R. 83 (W.D. Va. 1998) (debt for money obtained by unlicensed home improvement contractor through misrepresentation that he was authorized to do home improvement work was nondischargeable under 11 U.S.C. § 523(a)(2)); *In re* Fuselier, 211 B.R. 540 (Bankr. W.D. La. 1997) (state fraud and breach of contract damages found nondischargeable under § 523(a)(2)(A) when contractor secured job by falsifying license number and his plan for use of home owners' payments); *In re* Bottone, 209 B.R. 257 (Bankr. D. Mass. 1997) (debtor/home inspector denied summary judgment in nondischargeability case alleging that he knowingly misrepresented condition of home); *In re* George, 205 B.R. 679 (Bankr. D. Conn. 1997) (investment "advisor" who convinced creditors to invest in coins, a condominium and mutual fund could not discharge a state UDAP debt because he had falsely represented his qualifications and objectivity); *In re* Tallant, 207 B.R. 923 (Bankr. E.D. Cal. 1997) (lawyers' misrepresentations in context of attorney/client business transaction found to preclude discharge of debt based on fraud), *aff'd. in part and rev'd. on other grounds*, 218 B.R. 58 (B.A.P. 9th Cir. 1998); *In re* Bebber, 192 B.R. 120 (W.D.N.C. 1995) (false promise that construction project was secured by fraud gave rise to nondischargeable unfair trade practices judgment); *In re* Friedlander, 170 B.R. 472 (Bankr. D. Mass. 1994) (state UDAP damages including multiple (punitive) damages found nondischargeable based on fraud); *In re* Cornner, 191 B.R. 199 (Bankr. N.D. Ala. 1995) (loan broker fraud debt found nondischargeable when deposit was made but no loan was procured); *see also* Keams v. Tempe Technical Inst., 993 F. Supp. 714 (D. Ariz. 1997) (negligent supervision insufficient basis to find debt of trade school's president nondischargeable for fraud).

201 11 U.S.C. § 523(a)(4); *see, e.g., In re* Niles, 106 F.3d 1456 (9th Cir. 1997) (application of § 523(a)(4)); *In re* Storie, 216 B.R. 283, 285 (B.A.P. 10th Cir. 1997) (chapter 7 debtors-general

contractors committed defalcation by negligently failing to pay suppliers with money received from creditors-property owners); *In re* Kohler, 255 B.R. 666 (Bankr. E.D. Pa. 2000) (debt related to abuse of a confidential relationship with an elder found to be a nondischargeable breach of fiduciary duty by collateral estoppel); *In re* Heilman, 241 B.R. 137 (Bankr. D. Md. 1999) (custom home builder was not a fiduciary with respect to home buyer's deposit; opinion includes exhaustive list of cases on whether attorneys, directors, partners, property managers, insurance agents, contractors and homebuilders are "fiduciaries" for purposes of 523(a)(4)); *In re* Young, 208 B.R. 189 (Bankr. S.D. Cal. 1997) (real estate broker had fiduciary duties once funds were entrusted by clients to his care).

202 11 U.S.C. § 523(a)(6); *In re* Nangle, 274 F.3d 481 (8th Cir. 2001) (jury verdict awarding punitive damages under state consumer protection act based on repeated debt collection contacts established that debtor caused willful and malicious injury); *In re* Kennedy, 249 B.R. 576 (6th Cir. 2001) (defamation judgment found nondischargeable on grounds of collateral estoppel); Piccicuto v. Dwyer, 39 F.3d 37 (1st Cir. 1994) (enhanced damages awarded under state unfair trade practice law for willful conduct found nondischargeable on grounds of collateral estoppel under § 523(a)(6)); *In re* Jones, 300 B.R. 133 (B.A.P. 1st Cir. 2003) (state agency damage award against employer based on sexual harassment found nondischargeable on grounds of collateral estoppel under § 523(a)(6)); Zygulski v. Daugherty, 236 B.R. 646 (N.D. Ind. 1999) (husband willfully and maliciously dissipated assets from wife's illegal pyramid scheme, so his debt to victims was found nondischargeable—conversion fulfills the malice requirement); *In re* Guillory, 285 B.R. 307 (Bankr. C.D. Cal. 2002) (debtor's wrongful repossession of truck found to be conversion resulting in willful and malicious injury); *In re* Foushee, 283 B.R. 278 (Bankr. N.D. Iowa 2002) (judgment against debtor-employer for firing employee in violation of whistleblower statute found nondischargeable on grounds of collateral estoppel under § 523(a)(6)); *In re* Paeplow, 217 B.R. 705 (Bankr. D. Vt. 1998) (conversion of security deposit could be willful and malicious injury); *In re* Topakas, 202 B.R. 850 (Bankr. E.D. Pa. 1996) (sexual harassment claim was for willful and malicious injury), *aff'd*, 1997 WL 158197 4107 (E.D. Pa. Mar. 31, 1997). *See generally* Blake, Debts Non-Dischargeable for "Willful and Malicious Injury": Applicability of Bankruptcy Code § 523(a)(6) in a Commercial Setting, 104 Com. L.J. 64 (Spring 1999).

203 Kawaauhau v. Geiger, 523 U.S. 57, 118 S. Ct. 974, 140 L. Ed. 2d 90 (1998); *see In re* Sarbaz, 227 B.R. 298 (B.A.P. 9th Cir. 1998) (*Geiger* standard applies retroactively); *In re* Thomason, 288 B.R. 812 (Bankr. S.D. Ill. 2002) (sexual harassment involving both physical and verbal abuse excepted from discharge); *In re* Mode, 231 B.R. 295 (Bankr. E.D. Ark. 1999) (large judgment against repossessor found to create nondischargeable debt in bankruptcy, when the repossessor had deliberately run over the automobile owner during the repossession attempt).

204 *See In re* Popa, 140 F.3d 317 (1st Cir. 1998) (employer's failure to obtain workers' compensation insurance is not willful because it was not done with the actual intent to cause injury as required by the *Geiger* standard); *In re* Martino, 220 B.R. 129 (Bankr. M.D. Fla. 1998) (employer was not discharged from paying an employee-damages grounded in sexual harassment,

Punitive damages and attorney fees awarded for fraud are nondischargeable, together with actual damages, under 11 U.S.C. § 523(a)(2).[205] The Supreme Court's recent definitive ruling on the punitive damages dischargeability issue arose in the context of a consumer protection claim by tenants against their landlord. The tenants had pled and proved an unfair trade practice claim for illegal rent overcharges, which led to an award of treble damages and attorney fees. The Supreme Court held that § 523(a)(2)(A) "prevents the discharge of all liability arising from fraud and that an award of treble damages therefore falls within the scope of the exception."[206] By this reading, the Court extends protection from discharge not just to multiple and punitive damages, but also to claims for litigation fees and costs and to other foreseeable consequential damages of fraud.[207]

While the *Cohen* ruling will be helpful to creditors with consumer protection claims against an individual that files bankruptcy, it would be incorrect to assume that establishing unfair or deceptive practices under state law will be sufficient to guarantee nondischargeability in bankruptcy, because a bankruptcy debtor may argue that a practice was unfair or deceptive, but not fraudulent.[208] Good practice will continue to require that fraud claims be brought alongside of UDAP claims and proved whenever possible. A non-bankruptcy court resolving UDAP claims should be encouraged to explicitly find fraud when the facts support that outcome. Absent such a finding, there may be a problem trying to use collateral estoppel in a dischargeability case based on the prior judgment.

It is also important to keep in mind that when settling cases with any individual who might later file bankruptcy, language in the settlement agreement absolving them of fraud may preclude a later dischargeability claim. However, the Supreme Court has held that, ordinarily, a settlement of a fraud case that substitutes a new contractual obligation does not eliminate the ability to claim that the underlying debt is nondischargeable due to fraud.[209] At a minimum, the settlement agreement should be neutral on this issue so that it can be litigated, if necessary, in bankruptcy court. If possible, write into the agreement that the settlement is based on fraud, or better yet, that all amounts to be paid are damages for fraud that are not dischargeable in bankruptcy.

Consumer protection claims also give rise to nondischargeability arguments under 11 U.S.C. § 523(a)(4) and (6), provisions which do not require proof of fraud.[210] It is usually prudent to raise these claims together with one based on fraud when litigating the dischargeability of a UDAP claims.

More detail on many issues related to nondischargeability is provided elsewhere in this manual.[211]

17.5.4.2.2 Procedures for obtaining a determination of nondischargeability

The Bankruptcy Code makes an important distinction between two categories of exceptions to discharge. The first category consists of debts that are excepted from the discharge regardless of whether the issue is raised during the bankruptcy case. Debts in this first category include alimony and support, certain debts incurred through drunk driving, and debts where a discharge was denied or waived in a prior bankruptcy. Creditors holding claims covered by these exceptions are free to assert them against the debtor after the bankruptcy, without the permission of the bankruptcy court.

The second category of exceptions consists of debts that are excluded from the discharge only if their nondischargeability is raised and determined during the bankruptcy case. The debts falling into this category are those specified in subsections (a)(2), (a)(4), and (a)(6) of section 523.[212] These subsections deal with debts incurred by false pretenses or false financial statements, claims for breach of fiduciary duty, embezzlement, larceny,[213] and claims for willful and malicious injuries. The Bankruptcy Rules require consumers and other creditors to raise such nondischargeability issues by an adversary proceeding during the bankruptcy case.[214] The deadline for commencing such a proceeding is sixty days after the first date set for the section 341 meeting of creditors.[215] In every case, the court will give at least thirty

---

sex discrimination and defamation because his actions were intended to injure).

205 Cohen v. de la Cruz, 523 U.S. 213, 118 S. Ct. 1212, 140 L. Ed. 2d 341 (1998); *see also In re* Nangle, 274 F.3d 481 (8th Cir. 2001) (state court contempt judgment based on debt collector's failure to comply with prior judgment held nondischargeable under § 523(a)(6)); Scarborough v. Fischer 171 F.3d 638 (8th Cir. 1999) (punitive damages for willful and malicious injury also nondischargeable under § 523(a)(6)).

206 Cohen v. de la Cruz, 523 U.S. 213, 118 S. Ct. 1212, 140 L. Ed. 2d 341 (1998).

207 For example, payments to third parties to correct problems caused by the debtor's fraud may be nondischargeable. *In re* Pleasants, 219 F.3d 372 (4th Cir. 2000) (debtor who misrepresented himself as architect may not discharge consequential damage claims).

208 *See* National Consumer Law Center, Unfair and Deceptive Acts and Practices § 4.2.3 (5th ed. 2001 and Supp.).

209 Archer v. Warner, 538 U.S. 314, 123 S. Ct. 1462, 155 L. Ed. 2d

454 (2003); *see also In re* Detrano, 326 F.3d 319 (2d Cir. 2003).

210 *See* Stokes v. Ferris, 150 B.R. 388 (W.D. Tex. 1992) (state unfair trade practice judgment found to give rise to nondischargeable debt based on willful and malicious injury as well as fraud), *aff'd*, 995 F.2d 76 (5th Cir. 1993).

211 *See* § 14.4, *supra*; *see also* National Consumer Law Center, Unfair and Deceptive Acts and Practices § 6.8 (5th ed. 2001 and Supp.).

212 11 U.S.C. § 523(c).

213 Some consumer scams may come under theft by deception, a form of larceny in many states.

214 Fed. R. Bankr. P. 7001.

215 Fed. R. Bankr. P. 4007(c). The deadline is extended to the next workday following a Saturday, Sunday or holiday. *In re* Burns, 102 B.R. 750 (B.A.P. 9th Cir. 1989). Some courts have held that

days' notice of this deadline, which may be extended upon motion for cause only if such motion is filed before the deadline passes.[216] Normally, this notice is combined with the notice of the meeting of creditors.[217]

If a complaint alleging nondischargeability is not filed before this deadline, or any extension, then the claim is permanently discharged, and the deadline may be raised as a complete defense to any later dischargeability or court action, even if the creditor did not receive proper notice of the deadline.[218] The potentially harsh consequences of the time limit in a consumer case were illustrated in *In re Towers*.[219] The Illinois attorney general failed to raise viable nondischargeability claims based on a state UDAP judgment in a timely way. The court found that nondischargeability arguments under sections (a)(2), (4) and (6) were barred. The court also rejected the state's last ditch attempt to have

the debt found nondischargeable on the alternative basis that a civil restitution order was issued under UDAP which could be found nondischargeable under § 523(a)(7) without a time limit.[220]

State court findings of fact or conclusions of law may provide a basis to collaterally estop the debtor from litigating many of the issues required to establish nondischargeability.[221] If the debt owed to the consumer is unliquidated, the bankruptcy court has jurisdiction not only to find the debt nondischargeable, but also to liquidate the debt and enter judgment.[222]

---

this deadline is jurisdictional and may not be waived by a failure to object to an untimely complaint. *In re Kirsch*, 65 B.R. 297 (Bankr. N.D. Ill. 1986). The complaint must be properly filed by the deadline. Mere mailing by the deadline is not sufficient. *See In re Strickland*, 50 B.R. 16 (Bankr. M.D. Ala. 1985). Nor, perhaps, is filing without paying the necessary filing fee sufficient. *See In re Smolen*, 48 B.R. 633 (Bankr. N.D. Ill. 1985); § 14.4.2, *supra*. When a bankruptcy case is dismissed and reinstated, one court has held that the sixty-day limitation period recommences on the first date, following reinstatement, set for creditors' meeting. *In re Dunlap*, 217 F.3d 311 (5th Cir. 2000).

216 Fed. R. Bankr. P. 4007(c). *In re Taibbi*, 213 B.R. 261 (Bankr. E.D.N.Y. 1997) (county consumer protection agency that levied fine against debtor for deceptive trade practices established cause to extend filing deadline based on need to investigate more than sixty recently filed complaints). Only a creditor, and not the trustee, is a party in interest entitled to request an extension of the deadline. *In re Farmer*, 786 F.2d 618 (4th Cir. 1986). Such a request must set forth a specific and satisfactory explanation why the creditor is unable to file a timely complaint. *In re Englander*, 92 B.R. 425 (B.A.P. 9th Cir. 1988) (complaint which failed to allege specific grounds for nondischargeability permitted when cured by amended complaint after bar date; but plaintiff's attorney sanctioned); *In re Littell*, 58 B.R. 937 (Bankr. S.D. Tex. 1986). The court has no discretion to extend the time limit once the deadline has passed. *In re Hill*, 811 F.2d 484 (9th Cir. 1987); *In re Brown*, 102 B.R. 187 (B.A.P. 9th Cir. 1989) (court has no discretion to extend the deadline even for extraordinary circumstances such as natural disasters); *In re Neese*, 87 B.R. 609 (B.A.P. 9th Cir. 1988); *In re Beam*, 73 B.R. 434 (Bankr. S.D. Ohio 1987) (court cannot extend deadline even though an objection was timely, but erroneously, filed in an unrelated case). *But see In re Kontrick*, 295 F.3d 724 (7th Cir. 2002) (deadline subject to equitable tolling).

217 *See* Official Forms 9A–9I, Appx. D, *infra*.

218 *In re Green*, 876 F.2d 854 (10th Cir. 1989) (actual notice of the bankruptcy filing is sufficient); *In re Price*, 871 F.2d 97 (9th Cir. 1989) (knowledge of the bankruptcy is sufficient); *In re Alton*, 837 F.2d 457 (11th Cir. 1988); *Neeley v. Murchison*, 815 F.2d 345 (5th Cir. 1987); *In re Bucknum*, 105 B.R. 25 (B.A.P. 9th Cir. 1989); *In re Ricketts*, 80 B.R. 495 (B.A.P. 9th Cir. 1987), *aff'd*, 951 F.2d 204 (9th Cir. 1991). *But see In re Eliscu*, 85 B.R. 480 (Bankr. N.D. Ill. 1988) (creditor with no notice of case at all not subject to deadline).

219 162 F.3d 952 (7th Cir. 1998).

220 The court found that the restitution order was not payable for the benefit of a governmental unit, as required under § 523(a)(7). *See also In re Audley*, 268 B.R. 279 (Bankr. D. Kan. 2001) (judgment debt for civil penalties payable to state fund for violations of consumer protection statute nondischargeable under § 523(a)(7)), *aff'd on other grounds*, 275 B.R. 383 (B.A.P. 10th Cir. 2002).

221 *In re Pancake*, 106 F.3d 1242 (5th Cir. 1997) (collateral estoppel not available for Texas default judgment based on breach of fiduciary duty absent evidence of state court hearing at which creditor carried its evidentiary burden); *Piccicuto v. Dwyer*, 39 F.3d 37 (1st Cir. 1994) (unfair trade practice judgment under state law found nondischargeable on grounds of collateral estoppel under § 523(a)(6)); *In re Audley*, 275 B.R. 383 (B.A.P. 10th Cir. 2002) (unfair trade practice judgment based on false representations that goods were made by handicapped workers found nondischargeable on grounds of collateral estoppel under § 523(a)(2)(A)); *In re Markarian*, 228 B.R. 34 (B.A.P. 1st Cir. 1998) (finding of fraud in RICO case could be basis for collateral estoppel in dischargeability proceeding); *In re Krishnamurthy*, 209 B.R. 714, 721, 722 (B.A.P. 9th Cir.) (state court judgment for fraud which included punitive damages collaterally estopped debtors defending nondischargeability claim under § 523(a)(6), because punitive damages could only be awarded in California based on wrongful acts under standard akin to § 523(a)(6)), *aff'd*, 125 F.3d 858 (9th Cir. 1997); *In re Dawson*, 270 B.R. 729 (Bankr. N.D. Iowa 2001) (state court judgment against debtor and her boyfriend contractor based on home improvement fraud given collateral estoppel effect); *In re Busick*, 264 B.R. 518 (Bankr. N.D. Ind. 2001) (state court findings under home improvement fraud statute sufficient to prove nondischargeability for purposes of § 523(a)(2)(A); *In re Mannie*, 258 B.R. 440 (Bankr. N.D. Cal. 2001) (judgment for wrongful employment termination nondischargeable under § 523(a)(6) based on collateral estoppel doctrine; *see* § 14.4.4, *supra*. State agency decisions may also be given collateral estoppel effect. *See In re Jones*, 300 B.R. 133 (B.A.P. 1st Cir. 2003) (discrimination complaint resulting in state agency damage award against employer based on sexual harassment found nondischargeable on grounds of collateral estoppel under § 523(a)(6)).

222 *In re Kennedy*, 108 F.3d 1015 (9th Cir. 1997) (fraud debt owed to consumer creditors by real estate broker properly liquidated and reduced to judgment in the bankruptcy court); *In re McLaren*, 3 F.3d 958 (6th Cir. 1993); *see Cohen v. de la Cruz*, 523 U.S. 213, 118 S. Ct. 1212, 140 L. Ed. 21d 341 (1998) (bankruptcy court found rent overcharge claim of tenants was nondischargeable, and liquidated the claim for treble damages and attorney fees, findings were affirmed by Third Circuit Court of Appeals; the Supreme Court did not review the issue of liquidating the claim amount); *see also In re Santos*, 304 B.R.

523

Sometimes complex procedural issues arise because a debt may be nondischargeable if it is not scheduled by the debtor.[223] This is a limited exception to the discharge that is covered in another section of this manual.[224] Failure to list consumer claims based on fraud or breach of fiduciary duty or failure to notify consumers of a bankruptcy case is a common problem that may impede protecting consumer rights. Nevertheless, if the consumer has actual notice of the bankruptcy, the deadlines for objecting to discharge discussed above will apply and the exception to discharge for unscheduled claims will not.[225]

17.5.4.3 Chapter 13

Unlike chapters 7, 11 and 12, the discharge in a chapter 13 granted by completion of the plan discharges all debts provided for in the plan except:

- Alimony and support obligations made nondischargeable by 11 U.S.C. § 523(a)(5);
- Student loan debts made nondischargeable by section 523(a)(8);
- Drunk driving debts made nondischargable by section 523(a)(9);
- Long-term debts provided for under the section 1322(b)(5) cure provisions on which the initial payment due date occurs after the last payment of the plan is due;[226] and
- Restitution or criminal fines included in a sentence on the debtor's conviction of a crime.

As a result, consumers with claims based on fraud, embezzlement, or willful injury will generally be entitled only to the same distribution as other unsecured creditors.[227]

One possible consumer strategy where someone is using a chapter 13 filing to discharge particularly heinous conduct is to move for dismissal[228] or object to confirmation of the chapter 13 plan on the basis of the absence of good faith.[229] In *In re Smith*,[230] a home repair operator, who had fleeced senior citizens by making unnecessary repairs and had been found liable subsequently for more than $40,000.00, filed under chapter 13. While the judgment debts would not have been dischargeable in a chapter 7 because of the home repair operator's fraudulent conduct, they would have been dischargeable in a chapter 13. The debts from the judgments amounted to about half of his total indebtedness. In the chapter 13 plan, Smith proposed to pay $600.00 over a five-year period toward his total unsecured obligations of about $80,000.00 (including the $40,000.00 owed the consumers he bilked). In reversing confirmation of Smith's chapter 13 plan, the court held that the nature of the debts and the timing of the bankruptcy could be considered in determining the good faith of the filing. The decision recommended that the debts arising from illegal activity be required to have a higher payout.[231]

Any party in interest may object to confirmation of a chapter 13 plan.[232] Creditors will receive at least twenty-five days' notice of the time in which to file objections to the plan.[233] Objections to confirmation must be filed with the court and served on the debtor, the trustee and any other entity designated by the court.[234] Objections are considered contested matters.[235]

17.5.4.4 Corporate or Partnership Debtors

Corporations or partnerships in chapter 7 are not granted a discharge.[236] This exception to discharge is rarely of any value to creditors because a corporation or partnership is unlikely to start up again after going through a chapter 7. However, state law rules concerning successor liability of corporations should be carefully scrutinized. In some cases where corporations are merged or sold in the liquidation process, the successor entity will have some liability on the prior corporation's undischarged obligations.[237]

Corporate or partnership debtors in chapter 12 are treated the same as individual debtors.[238] They are thus subject to

---

639 (Bankr. D.N.J. 2004) (finding district and state courts have greater expertise in evaluating damages in personal injury matters, court declined to liquidate nondischargeable debt).

223 11 U.S.C. § 523(a)(3).

224 *See* § 14.4.3, *supra*.

225 *See id.*

226 11 U.S.C. § 1328(a); *see* § 14.4.1, *supra*. As discussed in that section, as a practical matter priority debts under section 507 must also be paid under the plan.

227 The debtors' plan could theoretically classify nondischargeable unsecured debts separately and pay them more than other unsecured creditors. However, courts have generally disfavored this type of separate classification based on 11 U.S.C. § 1322(b)(1). *See* § 12.4, *supra*.

228 *In re* Mattson, 241 B.R. 629 (Bankr. D. Minn. 1999) (landlord's chapter 13 dismissed for bad faith, in light of pre-petition race discrimination, and fact that bankruptcy was intended primarily to delay payment of nondischargeable judgment in favor of tenants).

229 *See* §§ 12.3.2–12.3.4, *supra*.

230 848 F.2d 813 (7th Cir. 1988); *see also In re* Goddard, 212 B.R. 233 (D.N.J. 1997) (bankruptcy court erred by failing to treat debtor's prefiling misconduct as relevant to a determination of good faith based on the totality of the circumstances).

231 848 F.2d 813 (7th Cir. 1988).

232 11 U.S.C. § 1324.

233 Fed. R. Bankr. P. 2002(b).

234 Fed. R. Bankr. P. 3020(b)(1).

235 Fed. R. Bankr. P. 3020(b)(1), 9014; *see* § 1.4.2, *supra*.

236 11 U.S.C. § 727(a)(1).

237 *See, e.g.*, Lemelle v. Universal Mfg. Corp., 18 F.3d 1268 (5th Cir. 1994) (successor corporation found to have liability under both Alabama and Delaware law); *cf. In re* Nat'l Gypsum Co., 219 F.3d 478 (5th Cir. 2000) (successor corporation not liable).

238 11 U.S.C. § 1228. See § 16.7, *supra*, for a discussion of the chapter 12 discharge.

the exceptions from discharge of section 523. Corporations or partnerships may be granted a discharge in chapter 11 and are not subject to the exceptions of section 523.[239]

An increasingly common issue is whether liability for an undiscovered tort arises pre-petition even if there is no manifestation of injury until after the case is filed or completed. Although there is a split of authority, several courts have held that such liability may not be discharged as a pre-petition claim under the Code's definition of claim, especially where the injured parties could have had no knowledge of their relationship to the debtor while the bankruptcy case was pending.[240]

Related issues arise when a debtor engages in a pattern of conduct that results in separate pre-petition and post-petition claims. One court has held in a case evaluating claims under the Americans with Disabilities Act, that an employer's post-bankruptcy denials of accommodation may be actionable even though the initial denial of accommodation took place prior to bankruptcy and gave rise to a discharged claim.[241]

In the meantime, Congress has ratified the practice of some courts that had confirmed plans transferring liability for undiscovered claims in certain circumstances to trusts for the benefit of potential claimants established under the plan.[242] The circumstances in which such trusts tend to be established are those in which a corporation files bankruptcy knowing of significant potential liabilities, such as asbestos related health claims, before all potential claimants may have manifest symptoms.

17.5.5 The Consumer Priority

Section 507(a)(6) of the Bankruptcy Code provides certain consumers with priority as creditors in bankruptcy proceedings.[243] Consumer creditors are given a sixth priority after claims made by five other categories of preferred creditors.[244] The consumer priority gives individual creditors priority for claims in the amount of $2225.00 for any pre-bankruptcy deposit of money made in connection with the purchase, lease or rental of property or services intended for personal, family or household use, where the goods or services were not delivered or provided.[245] The priority is only available to individuals and is not available for corporations or partnerships.[246] Priority status is especially important in chapter 11, 12 or 13 cases because the plan must pay priority claims in full.[247]

Prior to the adoption of the Code, consumer creditors who could not persuade the bankruptcy court to return deposits paid to bankrupt retailers on some theory such as constructive trust were relegated to unsecured creditor status.[248] The bankruptcies of large retailers such as W.T. Grant, which gave rise to numerous claims by consumers who had given the debtor deposits without being aware that those deposits were not specifically held by the retailer for refund, prompted Congress to act.[249] Commentary by consumer advocates earlier in the decade brought this problem to the attention of the public and Congress.[250] Subsequent commentary explained that a consumer priority was necessary because consumers who did not have the resources to conduct credit checks on retailers before making consumer deposits could not have avoided losses in the bankruptcy of large retailers.[251] Congress met these problems by providing for a consumer priority.[252]

The few reported cases to consider issues pertaining to the consumer priority provisions of the Bankruptcy Code have read section 507(a)(6) broadly.[253] Each member of a house-

---

239 11 U.S.C. § 1141 (d)(1). However, no discharge is granted if the plan amounts to a liquidation, close of business, or if the debtor could have been denied a discharge had the case been filed under chapter 7. 11 U.S.C. § 1141(d)(3). A fuller discussion of chapter 11 procedures together with some potential opportunities to protect the rights of consumer creditors in chapter 11 cases can be found in § 17.7, *infra.*

240 *See, e.g.,* Lemelle v. Universal Mfg. Corp., 18 F.3d 1268 (5th Cir. 1994); *see also In re* Wheeler, 137 F.3d 299 (5th Cir. 1998) (attorney's malpractice in preparing the bankruptcy petition occurred before the bankruptcy filing so that claim for malpractice was property of the estate); *cf.* Jones v. Chemetron Corp., 212 F.3d 199 (3d Cir. 2000); Grady v. A.H. Robins Co., 839 F.2d 198 (4th Cir. 1988) (pre-petition claim arises when the conduct giving rise to the tort occurs even if there is no manifestation pre-petition). *See generally* § 14.5.1, *supra.*

241 O'Loghlin v. County of Orange, 229 F.3d 871 (9th Cir. 2000).

242 11 U.S.C. § 524(g)(1).

243 11 U.S.C. § 507(a)(6).

244 11 U.S.C. § 507(a)(1)–(5).

245 11 U.S.C. § 507(a)(6). The amount of the consumer priority is adjusted for inflation every three years. 11 U.S.C. § 104(b). For cases filed between April 1, 2001 and March 31, 2004, the amount of the priority was $2100.00.

246 Lawyers Edition, Bankruptcy Service § 21.265 at 87 (1981); *In re* Carolina Sales Corp., 43 B.R. 596, 597 (Bankr. E.D.N.C. 1984); *see also In re* Elsinghorst Bros. Co., 180 B.R. 52 (individual members' claims asserted on their behalf by a religious society treated as a priority).

247 11 U.S.C. §§ 1129(a)(9)(B), 1222(a)(2), 1322(a)(2).

248 *Proposed Amendments to the Bankruptcy Act: Hearings on H.R. 31 and 32 Before the Subcomm. on Civil & Constitutional Rights of the House Comm. on the Judiciary,* 94th Cong., Series 27, pt. 3, at 1188 (1976).

249 *Id.;* 4 Collier on Bankruptcy ¶ 507.08[1] (15th ed. rev.); H.R. Rep. No. 95-595, at 188 (1977).

250 *See, e.g.,* Schrag & Ratner, *Caveat Emptor—Empty Coffer: The Bankruptcy Law Has Nothing to Offer,* 72 Colum. L. Rev. 1147 (1972).

251 *See, e.g.,* Carroll, *Priorities & Subordination,* 17 Hous. L. Rev. 223, 235 (1979).

252 4 Collier on Bankruptcy ¶ 507.08[1] (15th ed. rev.); H.R. Rep. No. 95-595, at 188 (1977).

253 *In re* Tart's T.V., Furniture & Appliance Co., 165 B.R. 171 (Bankr. E.D.N.C. 1994) (lump sum payments made for unfulfilled extended warranties give rise to consumer priority claims to the extent of covered repairs as limited by the amount of the available priority); *In re* Terra Distrib. Co., 148 B.R. 598 (Bankr. D. Idaho) (same). *But see In re* Heritage Vill. Church, 137 B.R. 888 (Bankr. D.S.C. 1991) (donator/purchasers of

hold or family has a separate $2225.00 maximum; the family or household is not limited to one priority claim.[254] Courts have interpreted the term "deposit" broadly, to include any payment of money by consumers who had not yet received full performance from the bankrupt seller. This includes situations where the consumer paid in full, rather than in part[255] and cases where the consumer received some of the goods or services.[256] Arguably the priority could also extend to payments by consumers where the merchant attempted delivery of goods or services, but where the consumer has substantial warranty or contract claims such that the merchant's "delivery" could be considered defective or invalid.[257]

Courts have found this priority applicable to a wide variety of transactions, encompassing even transactions that would not ordinarily be considered consumer transactions. The purchase of a yacht for personal use in a lease/purchase transaction has been held to give rise to a consumer priority.[258] Similarly, a transaction in which a wholesale distributor of appliances promoted sales by arranging free trips for participating retailers and allowing individuals to participate in the trips by purchasing tickets, has also been held to fall within section 507(a)(6).[259] In yet another case, in recognizing a consumer priority for deposits given to a residential home builder, the court concluded that Congress did not intend to limit section 507(a)(6) to transactions with retail merchants.[260] And courts have held that the consumer deposit priority applies to security deposits posted by residential tenants.[261] This is likely to be the best potential result if

the deposits have not been segregated and cannot be considered property that is not property of the estate, as discussed above.[262] Finally, students at a vocational school are considered consumers whose contract for lessons is a purchase of services under section 507(a)(6).[263]

A consumer claims a section 507(a)(6) priority at the time the proof of claim is filed.[264] The claim is then deemed allowed unless the debtor in possession, trustee, or a party in interest, such as another creditor, objects to the claim.[265] Upon such objection, after notice and hearing, the court rules on the objection.[266]

17.5.6 Equitable Subordination

Bankruptcy courts possess the power to prevent the consummation of a claimant's fraudulent or otherwise inequitable course of conduct by subordinating that creditor's claims to the claims of other creditors.[267] This principle of equitable subordination is now codified in 11 U.S.C. § 510(c), but it was first developed by the courts.[268] Consumer creditors may be able to use these principles to get their claims paid before the claims of secured or priority creditors in some situations.

Three conditions must be generally be satisfied before equitable subordination of a claim is justified.[269] First, the creditor against whom subordination is sought must have engaged in some sort of inequitable conduct.[270] Transferring

---

time-share at Heritage U.S.A. not entitled to consumer priority status because, having already satisfied their obligation by completing the purchases, their funds were not "deposits" under § 507(a)(6)).

254 *In re* Cont'l Country Club, 64 B.R. 177 (Bankr. M.D. Fla. 1986); *In re* James R. Corbitt Co., 48 B.R. 937 (Bankr. E.D. Va. 1985).

255 *In re* Deangelis Tangibles, Inc. 238 B.R. 96 (M.D. Pa. 1999); *In re* Terra Distrib., Inc. 148 B.R. 598 (Bankr. D. Idaho 1992); *In re* Longo, 144 B.R. 305 (Bankr. D. Md. 1992); *In re* Carolina Sales Corp., 43 B.R. 596 (Bankr. E.D.N.C. 1984).

256 *In re* River Vill. Associates, 161 B.R. 127 (Bankr. E.D. Pa. 1993), *aff'd*, 181 B.R. 795 (E.D. Pa. 1995); *In re* Longo 144 B.R. 305 (Bankr. D. Md. 1992).

257 See *In re* Longo, 144 B.R. 305 (Bankr. D. Md. 1992) (trade school students who did not receive training they paid for).

258 *In re* CSY Yacht Corp., 34 B.R. 215 (Bankr. M.D. Fla. 1983).

259 *In re* Carolina Sales Corp., 43 B.R. 596 (Bankr. E.D.N.C. 1984).

260 *See also In re* Cont'l Country Club, 64 B.R. 177 (Bankr. M.D. Fla. 1986) (down payment on purchase of a mobile home entitled to priority); *In re* James R. Corbitt Co., 48 B.R. 937 (Bankr. E.D. Va. 1985); *cf. In re* Mickelson, 192 B.R. 516 (Bankr. D.N.D. 1996) (purchase of grain drying equipment from seed company is not for personal, family or household use), *aff'd*, 205 B.R. 190 (D.N.D. 1996). *But see In re* Glass, 203 B.R. 61 (Bankr. W.D. Va. 1996) (advance payment on purchase of real property structured by the consumer in the form of a loan to the sellers does not qualify as a deposit).

261 Guarracino v. Hoffman, 246 B.R. 130 (D. Mass. 2000) (security deposit entitled to priority; damages related to mishandling security deposit are not); *In re* River Vill. Associates, 161 B.R.

127 (Bankr. E.D. Pa. 1993), *aff'd on other grounds*, 181 B.R. 795 (E.D. Pa. 1995); *see also In re* Romanus, 1998 Bankr. LEXIS 397 (Bankr. W.D. Pa. 1998) (security deposit and first month rent payment entitled to consumer priority when the debtor/landlord failed to deliver the property in habitable condition). *But see In re* Cimaglia, 50 B.R. 9 (Bankr. S.D. Fla. 1985) (security deposits not within scope of priority for consumer deposits).

262 *See* § 17.5.2, *supra.*

263 *In re* Longo, 144 B.R. 305 (Bankr. D. Md. 1992). For discussion of class proofs of claim in this and other cases, see § 17.4.2, *supra.*

264 11 U.S.C. § 501; Fed. R. Bankr. P. 3001.

265 11 U.S.C. § 502; Fed. R. Bankr. P. 3007.

266 11 U.S.C. § 502(b); *see In re* CSY Yacht Corp., 34 B.R. 215 (Bankr. M.D. Fla. 1983).

267 11 U.S.C. § 510(c); Heiser v. Woodruff, 327 U.S. 726, 66 S. Ct. 853, 90 L. Ed. 970 (1946); Pepper v. Litton, 308 U.S. 295, 60 S. Ct. 238, 84 L. Ed. 281 (1939).

268 4 Collier on Bankruptcy ¶ 510.05 (15th ed. rev.); *see* 11 U.S.C. § 510(c).

269 *See* 4 Collier on Bankruptcy ¶ 510.05 (15th ed. rev.); *In re* Mobile Steel Co., 563 F.2d 692 (5th Cir. 1977).

270 *In re* Mobile Steel Co., 563 F.2d 692 (5th Cir. 1977); *see* United States v. Noland, 517 U.S. 535, 116 S. Ct. 1524, 134 L. Ed. 2d 748 (1996) (courts have no power to reorder priorities set by Congress based on the characteristics of the claim rather than the conduct of the creditor); *see also In re* Rabex of Colo., Inc., 226 B.R. 905 (D. Colo. 1998) (claim based on veil piercing theory against debtor could not be equitably subordinated to claims of other creditors because creditor that pierced corporate veil to obtain claim committed no inequitable conduct).

assets out of the bankrupt corporation without a fair return to the corporation, undercapitalizing the corporation, or insider selling of property to the corporation at inflated prices are all examples of such conduct. Claims of officers, directors, principal shareholders and other fiduciaries, and their immediate families are subject to special scrutiny, because of the potential for abuse of these positions.[271] If an objection to a fiduciary's claim has some substantial factual basis, then the fiduciary has the burden to show the transaction's good faith and its benefit to the corporation.[272] The inequitable conduct need not be related to the claim asserted; rather, any unfair act by the claimant that decreases the other creditors' recovery in the bankruptcy may warrant equitable subordination.[273]

The second condition that must be shown is that the misconduct resulted in injury to the other creditors or conferred an unfair advantage on the claimant.[274] The claim should be subordinated to the extent necessary to offset the harm caused to the debtor and other creditors.[275] But if the amount of the claim exceeds the harm caused, then only part of the claim will be subordinated, as the purpose of equitable subordination is to do justice among the creditors, not to punish the wrongdoer.[276]

Finally, courts have held that equitable subordination of the claim must not be inconsistent with other provisions of the Bankruptcy Code.[277] Two recent Supreme Court cases conclude that courts are not authorized to adjust claims of creditors who have not engaged in inequitable conduct in contravention of the scheme of priorities outlined by Congress.[278] This overrules a line of cases in which IRS penalty claims were subordinated, without fault, to claims of other creditors that had suffered actual losses.[279]

17.5.7 Seeking Defendants Not in Bankruptcy

In addition to pursuing claims against the party in bankruptcy, the consumer's attorney should explore whether there may be other parties not in bankruptcy who can be held liable.[280] Whether the consumer's claims involve torts, contracts or violations of consumer protection statutes, there are a variety of theories for holding the following liable:

- Agents, such as sales personnel and advertising agencies;
- Principals and co-venturers, such as corporations and other business entities;[281]
- Directors, officers, and owners, parent corporations, franchisors;
- Third parties offering the means or assisting in tortious or deceptive schemes;[282]
- Assignees in sales and service transactions and related third-party creditors;
- Secured creditors or investors who financed the venture;[283]
- Bonding companies and other insurers.[284]

Where tenants' claims are concerned, it is possible in some circumstances to hold a non-bankrupt secured creditor responsible for essential services or for injuries due to failure to maintain the property. This should always be possible after foreclosure if the secured creditor has become the owner,[285] but also if the lender has status as mortgagee in possession under state law or if the facts establish that the landlord has control over the property.[286] A related strategy for making a secured creditor responsible for building main-

---

271 Pepper v. Litton, 308 U.S. 295, 60 S. Ct. 238, 84 L. Ed. 281 (1939); *In re* Multipanics, Inc., 622 F.2d 709 (5th Cir. 1980); *In re* Southwest Equip. Rental, Inc., 193 B.R. 276 (E.D. Tenn. 1996) (finding special obligations of insider officers and directors when employees suffer the harm).

272 *In re* Mobile Steel Co., 563 F.2d 692 (5th Cir. 1977).

273 *Id.; In re* Herby's Foods, Inc., 2 F.3d 128 (5th Cir. 1993) (insider creditors' conduct in seeking to buy out undercapitalized company to their own advantage warranted equitable subordination to other unsecured creditor's claims).

274 *In re* Mobile Steel Co., 563 F.2d 692 (5th Cir. 1977); *In re* Westgate-California Corp., 642 F.2d 1174 (9th Cir. 1981).

275 *In re* Mobile Steel Co., 563 F.2d 692 (5th Cir. 1977).

276 *In re* Westgate-California Corp., 642 F.2d 1174 (9th Cir. 1981).

277 *In re* Mobile Steel Co., 563 F.2d 692 (5th Cir. 1977).

278 United States v. Reorganized CF & I Fabricators of Utah, Inc., 518 U.S. 213, 116 S. Ct. 2106, 135 L. Ed. 2d 506 (1996); United States v. Noland, 517 U.S. 535, 116 S. Ct. 1524, 134 L. Ed. 2d 748 (1996).

279 *See* 4 Collier on Bankruptcy ¶ 510.05[2], at 510–15 (15th ed. rev.).

280 No stay would apply automatically to such claims except as to codebtors in chapter 12 and 13. *See* § 9.4.4, 16.5.5.1, *supra*. Requests for non-automatic stays as to non-debtor parties in such situations are normally denied. *See* § 9.4.6, *supra*.

281 In such cases involving corporations it may be necessary to pierce the corporate veil. *See* § 17.5.2.1, *supra*.

282 A civil conspiracy claim may be a useful tool to pursue such third parties. *See* Williams v. Aetna Fin. Co., 83 Ohio St. 3d 464, 700 N.E.3d 859 (1998).

283 *See Case History: Recovering Consumer Deposits From a Bankrupt Furniture Store*, 10 NCLC REPORTS *Bankruptcy and Foreclosures Ed.* 41 (Mar./Apr. 1992).

284 These theories are discussed in National Consumer Law Center, Unfair and Deceptive Acts and Practices Ch. 6 (5th ed. 2001 and Supp.); *see also* Golann, *In Search of Deeper Pockets: Theories of Extended Liability*, 17 Mass. L. Rev. 114 (1986).

285 *See* National Consumer Law Center, Repossessions and Foreclosures § 21.8 (5th ed. 2002 and Supp.).

286 *See, e.g.,* McCorristin v. Salmon Signs, 582 A.2d 1271 (N.J. Super. Ct. App. Div. 1990) (mortgagee in possession steps into shoes of landlord); Thornhill v. Ronnie's I-45 Truck Stop, Inc., 944 S.W.2d 780 (Tex. App. 1997) (secured lender exercising control over property held responsible for injuries due to fire at premises).

tenance in the bankruptcy process is to assert an administrative claim for payment ahead of the secured creditor. This strategy is discussed in § 17.5.3, *supra*.

17.5.8 Rule 2004 Examinations

Section 343 of the Code provides for examination of the debtor at the meeting of creditors. Federal Rule of Bankruptcy Procedure 2004 goes beyond this provision, and allows the examination of *any entity* on motion of any party in interest,[287] as well as the production of documents. Rule 2004 examinations may help consumer creditors discover hidden assets or challenge dischargeability.

The scope of Rule 2004 is the same as section 343: examination must relate to the "acts, conduct or property or to the financial condition of the debtor," to "any matter which may effect the administration of the debtor's estate," or to "the debtor's right to a discharge."[288] Information is subject to discovery if it "fairly tends to establish something which may become important in the administration of the estate."[289] Local practice for requesting a Rule 2004 examination varies. In some courts it is requested *ex parte*, with the party to be examined having a right to quash the subpoena. In other courts, it is requested by a noticed motion.[290]

Depending on the thoroughness of the debtor's schedules and the examination of the debtor at the meeting of creditors, a Rule 2004 deposition may be useful in discovering hidden assets of the debtor. Some consumer creditors, such as tenants, may be aware of assets that the debtor has failed to disclose. Consumers should go over the debtor's schedules carefully and look for assets that might not be accurately reported. A consumer may also use Rule 2004 to see if trust funds have been converted to other property.[291]

An important aspect of Bankruptcy Rule 2004 is its application to "any entity," rather than just the debtor. Thus, in a chapter 11 proceeding, any officer of a debtor corporation is subject to deposition. Another important use is establishing fraudulent conduct necessary to challenge dischargeability. For instance, while the schedules may reveal the debtor's financial condition at the time the petition was filed, Rule 2004 makes it possible to discover the debtor's pre-petition finances. This may enable a consumer to show that the debtor incurred a debt by fraud.[292] Finally, Rule 2004 may be useful in investigating grounds for equitable subordination of claims.[293]

17.6 *In Forma Pauperis*

17.6.1 Need for Consumers As Creditors to Proceed In Forma Pauperis

For low-income persons who have filed bankruptcy, the issue of waiving fees for indigency does not usually arise. 28 U.S.C. § 1930(a) specifically indicates that filing fees may not be waived[294] (although they may be paid in installments[295]). Once a bankruptcy is filed, there is no fee for debtors to file motions or adversary proceedings in bankruptcy court.[296]

For creditors and other parties who are not debtors, however, there are fees—$150.00 to file a complaint, and $150.00 for a motion for relief from the stay.[297] When low-income persons are creditors or are otherwise parties in bankruptcy proceedings, such as when a landlord is in bankruptcy, they may need to proceed *in forma pauperis*.

17.6.2 Seeking In Forma Pauperis Relief

While 28 U.S.C. § 1930(a) is not a model of clarity, most courts have held that its restriction on *in forma pauperis* filings applies only to starting a bankruptcy case, and that the regular federal *in forma pauperis* statute, 28 U.S.C. § 1915, applies to other proceedings.[298]

Nevertheless in many jurisdictions, the clerk's office will be unfamiliar with *in forma pauperis* filings and may not accept them as a matter of course. A sample motion, certification of indigency and order are set out in Appendix G, *infra*.[299] Until local practice is settled, a supporting memorandum should probably be filed whenever a low-income individual seeks *in forma pauperis* relief.

The points to be made in a supporting memorandum are straightforward. 28 U.S.C. § 1915 permits "Any court of the United States" to:

---

287 *See generally In re* Summit Corp., 891 F.2d 1 (1st Cir. 1989) (broad interpretation appropriate in evaluating who can be examined); *In re* M4 Enterprises Inc., 190 B.R. 471 (Bankr. N.D. Ga. 1996) (trustee is party in interest that can be examined).

288 Fed. R. Bankr. P. 2004(b).

289 Ulmer v. United States, 219 F. 641 (6th Cir. 1915). The scope of the permitted examination is very broad. The only restriction is that the examination may not be used to harass the debtor or frivolously waste assets of the estate. *In re* M4 Enterprises Inc., 190 B.R. 471 (Bankr. N.D. Ga. 1996).

290 Note that Rule 2004 is not applicable in the context of an adversary proceeding or contested matter, in which the formal discovery process is available. *See* Fed. R. Bankr. P. 7026, 9014.

291 *See* § 17.5.2.3, *supra*.

292 *See* § 17.5.4, *supra*.

293 *See* § 17.5.6, *supra*.

294 28 U.S.C. § 1930(a) codifies United States v. Kras, 409 U.S. 434, 93 S. Ct. 631, 34 L. Ed. 2d 626 (1973). For a more detailed analysis of *in forma pauperis* in bankruptcy, see § 13.6, *supra*.

295 28 U.S.C. § 1930(a)(6).

296 Judicial Conference Schedule of Fees prescribed pursuant to 28 U.S.C. § 1930(b), reprinted in Appendix C, *infra*.

297 *Id.*

298 *See* § 13.6, *supra*.

299 *See* Forms 81, 82, Appx. G.10, *infra*.

authorize the commencement, prosecution or defense of any suit, action or proceeding, civil or criminal, or appeal therein, without prepayment of fees and costs or security therefor, by a person who makes affidavit that he is unable to pay such costs or give security therefor.

Courts have regularly held that 28 U.S.C. § 1915 applies to fees for proceedings in bankruptcy court other than filing fees. Thus in *In re Shumate*,[300] where a debtor sought leave to appeal a court order *in forma pauperis*, the court held that a bankruptcy court was a "court of the United States" for the purposes of 28 U.S.C. § 1915. The court held further that the limitation of 28 U.S.C. § 1930(a) requiring payment notwithstanding section 1915 applies only, as the statutory language sets out, to "parties commencing a case." The court in *Shumate* followed similar holdings in *In re Moore*,[301] *In re Palestino*,[302] and *In re Sarah Allen Home, Inc.*[303] Other courts have reached the same conclusion.[304]

The legislative intent is clear. While 28 U.S.C. § 1930(a) *expressly* prohibits debtors from proceeding *in forma pauperis* concerning the initial petition filing fees, the bankruptcy sections dealing with other fees contain no such proviso. Thus, 28 U.S.C. § 1930 does not prohibit other bankruptcy proceedings from being *in forma pauperis*.[305]

Unfortunately, the Ninth Circuit and several other courts have concluded that bankruptcy courts are not "courts of the United States" with authority under § 1915(a) to waive fees.[306] Not only are these decisions based on an unduly technical reading of the law, but also they render the reference to § 1915(a) in § 1930(a) superfluous, in violation of normal principles of statutory construction. If bankruptcy courts already are powerless to waive fees, there is no reason to reference section 1915 in section 1930.[307] Further, at least one court has found that bankruptcy courts are "courts of the United States" with power to waive fees.[308] Finally, at least

two bankruptcy courts have concluded that whether or not they are courts of the United States, the District Court is empowered to delegate, pursuant to 28 U.S.C. § 157(b)(1), its own power to waive fees.[309]

Even in those jurisdictions with binding authority precluding bankruptcy courts from waiving fees, it may still be possible to direct requests for waivers to the district court, of which the bankruptcy court is a "unit," and which clearly has the necessary authority. Alternatively, a motion could be directed to the bankruptcy court, with a request that a fee waiver be recommended for final order in the district court.[310]

Additionally, important due process arguments are still available concerning many fees, particularly for indigent creditors.[311] Indigent creditors, such as tenants seeking to preserve a security deposit or other property right, have a due process right to access to court to preserve their property, which is distinguishable from the issues addressed by the Supreme Court in *United States v. Kras*.[312]

Moreover, 28 U.S.C. § 773(c), dealing with appeals from the bankruptcy court, expressly contemplates appeals *in forma pauperis*.[313] The House Report on the Bankruptcy Reform Act of 1978 specifically included, as a subject as to which procedural rules would have to be drafted, "provisions for *in forma pauperis* proceedings."[314]

In jurisdictions where *in forma pauperis* relief is available, applicable procedural requirements must be met. At a minimum, this would include filing an affidavit containing sufficient facts to establish lack of financial resources to pay the filing fee. Such an affidavit might include a household budget. An evidentiary hearing may be available in appro-

---

300 91 B.R. 23 (Bankr. W.D. Va. 1988).

301 86 B.R. 249 (Bankr. W.D. Okla. 1988) (leave to appeal).

302 4 B.R. 721 (Bankr. M.D. Fla. 1980) (leave to initiate adversary proceeding).

303 4 B.R. 724 (Bankr. E.D. Pa. 1980) (leave to initiate adversary proceeding).

304 *See, e.g., In re Jackson*, 86 B.R. 251 (Bankr. N.D. Fla. 1988) (appeal *in forma pauperis* permitted); *In re Weakland*, 4 B.R. 114 (Bankr. D. Del 1980) (fee in adversary proceeding, holding that § 1930(a) limitation on § 1915 applies only to filing fees).

305 *In re Shumate*, 91 B.R. 23 (Bankr. W.D. Va. 1988); *In re Weakland*, 4 B.R. 114 (Bankr. D. Del 1980).

306 *In re Perroton*, 958 F.2d 889 (9th Cir. 1992); *In re Jeys*, 202 B.R. 153 (B.A.P. 9th Cir. 1996); *In re Ennis*, 178 B.R. 192 (Bankr. W.D. Mo. 1995); *In re Bauckey*, 82 B.R. 13 (Bankr. D.N.J. 1988); *see In re Lamb*, 206 B.R. 527 (Bankr. E.D. Mo. 1997) (court does not have necessary authority to appoint counsel for indigent debtor under 28 U.S.C. § 1915(d)).

307 *See In re Moore*, 86 B.R. 249 (Bankr. W.D. Okla. 1988); *In re Palestino*, 4 B.R. 721 (Bankr. M.D. Fla. 1980).

308 *In re Shumate*, 91 B.R. 23 (Bankr. W.D. Va. 1988); *see also O'Connor v. United States Dep't of Energy*, 942 F.2d 771 (10th

Cir. 1991) (bankruptcy court is "court" with authority to award Equal Access to Justice Act fees).

309 *In re Melendez*, 153 B.R. 386 (Bankr. D. Conn. 1993); *In re McGinnis*, 155 B.R. 294 (Bankr. D. N.H. 1993); *see also In re Ushery*, 1999 WL 1579268 (Bankr. D. Del. May 6, 1999).

310 *See, e.g., In re Davis*, 899 F.2d 1136 (11th Cir. 1990) (Equal Access to Justice Act fees may be recommended by bankruptcy court for entry of final judgment in district court). Similar issues arose several years ago concerning the authority of bankruptcy court to make findings of civil contempt. *In re Sequoia Auto Brokers Ltd.*, 827 F.2d 1281 (9th Cir. 1987). Those questions were resolved by granting final authority to district courts on issues of contempt when an objection is raised pursuant to Fed. R. Bankr. R. 9020. *See In re Skinner*, 917 F.2d 444 (10th Cir. 1990); *In re Stephen W. Grosse Prof'l Corp.*, 84 B.R. 377 (Bankr. E.D. Pa. 1988), *aff'd*, 879 F.2d 856 (3d Cir. 1989).

311 *See, e.g., In re Lassina*, 261 B.R. 614 (Bankr. E.D. Pa. 2001) (creditor has right to fee waiver that can be denied for lack of proper evidence of indigency); *In re Sarah Allen Home Inc.*, 4 B.R. 724 (Bankr. E.D. Pa. 1980). *Tripati v. United States Bankruptcy Court for E.D. Texas*, 180 B.R. 160 (E.D. Tex. 1995) (constitution requires that an indigent creditor "be afforded an opportunity to be heard before his claims are disposed of").

312 *See* § 17.5.4.2.1, *supra*.

313 Note, however, that 28 U.S.C. § 773(c) has since been repealed.

314 H.R. Rep. No. 95-595, at 307 (1977).

priate circumstances.[315] An application may be denied if it is not accompanied by an affidavit setting forth the creditor's financial circumstances.[316] Additionally, some courts will examine the merits of the creditor's claim and deny *in forma pauperis* treatment if it concludes that the creditor's position is meritless.[317]

17.7 Chapter 11

17.7.1 Introduction

Consumer attorneys accustomed to using chapters 7 and 13 for their clients may be less familiar with chapter 11, the chapter likely to be utilized by a landlord, retailer or other party against whom consumers have claims. While a chapter 11 case, in theory, is a reorganization,[318] which suggests that at least some of the consumer claims will be paid, in most cases the debtor goes out of business and no payments are made to unsecured creditors.

At the outset of the case, the attorney representing a consumer creditor or group of consumer creditors must assess not only the strength of her clients' claims but also the debtor's financial position and prospects. The initial source of information on the debtor will be the schedules and statement of financial affairs. Other potentially useful sources of information are: (1) the debtor's answers to questions posed at the meeting of creditors[319] and (2) the monthly operating reports which a debtor still operating its business must file with the court.[320] Based on the attorney's assessment of the value of the assets which may be available

to creditors from either liquidation of the debtor or the debtor's potential future operating profits, the attorney will want to set realistic goals for the representation of her consumer creditor clients and plot an appropriate strategy.

The filing of a chapter 11 case presents a number of leverage points for consumer creditors. This section sets out some selected chapter 11 issues of special interest to attorneys representing consumer creditors.[321]

17.7.2 General Role of Creditors and the U.S. Trustee

17.7.2.1 Creditors' Right to Participate in the Case and Vote on the Debtor's Plan

In a chapter 11 case, as in a chapter 13 case, the debtor's fundamental goal is to obtain confirmation of a plan which will favorably adjust the debtor's obligations to pre-bankruptcy creditors. However, there is a fundamental difference between chapter 13 and chapter 11 in the process leading to plan confirmation.

In a chapter 13 case, the debtor is legally entitled to confirmation of the plan if the plan meets certain statutory criteria that are set forth in 11 U.S.C. §§ 1322 and 1325. If these criteria are met, the plan must be confirmed. Ordinarily, creditors do not act collectively in a chapter 13 case. Each creditor individually receives notice and opportunity to be heard concerning the substance of the plan, but can prevent confirmation only by showing that a legal condition under section 1322 or 1325 has not been satisfied.

In a chapter 11 case, the basic principle underlying plan confirmation is not the satisfaction of objective statutory criteria as in chapter 13. Rather, chapter 11 contemplates a process which brings all the affected parties (creditors and the debtor) into a single forum where, subject to certain ground rules set forth in the Code, they are encouraged to determine whether a plan of reorganization satisfying their respective interests can be negotiated. Accordingly, in most cases, plan confirmation is dependent upon the affirmative consent of the creditors. Creditors whose interests are impaired have the opportunity to vote on the proposed chapter 11 plan,[322] to the extent they hold an allowed claim. If a

---

315 *See In re* Lassina, 261 B.R. 614 (Bankr. E.D. Pa. 2001) (creditor's affidavit did not support finding of indigency; *in forma pauperis* request denied for lack of evidence with leave to seek evidentiary hearing).

316 *In re* Fitzgerald, 192 B.R. 861 (Bankr. E.D. Va. 1996) (although creditors may proceed *in forma pauperis* in bankruptcy litigation, application denied for failure to file necessary affidavit); *In re* Barham, 197 B.R. 319 (Bankr. W.D. Mo. 1996). Local Rules may apply. Where there is no local bankruptcy rule, courts may expect that the local district court rules be met.

317 *In re* Merritt, 186 B.R. 924 (Bankr. S.D. Ill. 1995) (appeal cannot be filed *in forma pauperis* if court concludes that appeal has no merit).

318 The Code does, however, provide for "liquidating" chapter 11's in which the debtor sells all or nearly all of its assets. 11 U.S.C. § 1123(b)(4).

319 This opportunity to ask questions of the debtor may be supplemented by a deposition pursuant to Fed. R. Bankr. P. 2004. *See* § 17.5.8, *supra*. The meeting of creditors involves less costs and expense for consumer creditors, but it may not allow for the type of detailed questioning that is available under Rule 2004.

320 The monthly operating report should include a monthly cash flow statement and updated balance sheet. The monthly operating report is required by the U.S. trustee's office in each bankruptcy district pursuant to its powers to "monitor" the administration of bankruptcy cases. For a discussion of the U.S. trustee, see § 17.7.2.2, *infra*.

321 *See also* § 6.3.4, *supra*.

322 *See* 11 U.S.C. §§ 1126, 1129(a)(7)(A), (C). A class of creditors whose interests are not impaired by the plan are deemed to have accepted the plan. 11 U.S.C. § 1126(f). It is not always clear whether a class of creditors is impaired within the meaning of the Code. This issue is usually resolved by an objection to the plan. *See In re* Barakat, 99 F.3d 1520 (9th Cir. 1996) (tenant security deposit claimants not impaired because they would be paid in full); *In re* River Vill. Associates, 181 B.R. 795 (E.D. Pa. 1995) (tenant class not impaired given that one of their choices under the plan is to be repaid the full amount of their security deposits plus interest over a three year period); *cf. In re* Boston Post Road Ltd. P'ship, 21 F.3d 477 (2d Cir. 1994) (tenants who

claim has been objected to, the creditor may request that it be temporarily allowed for purposes of plan voting.[323] If a class of creditors does not vote for the plan, the case may be converted to chapter 7 or dismissed altogether,[324] although there are circumstances under which a plan can be confirmed notwithstanding the vote of a dissenting class.[325]

Because confirmation is ordinarily based on creditor "consent," chapter 11 has enhanced provisions for creditor participation in the case as compared to chapter 13. As under chapter 13, creditors in a chapter 11 case may act individually to protect their interests or otherwise contest the debtor's actions in the chapter 11 case.[326] An individual creditor can receive notice of significant motions or other matters in the chapter 11 case by filing with the court and serving on the debtor's counsel a request for notice pursuant to Federal Rule of Bankruptcy Procedure 2002(i).

In addition, chapter 11 explicitly provides a mechanism for creditors to act collectively through an official creditors' committee.[327] The creditors' committee is empowered to participate in virtually every phase of the chapter 11 case,[328] representing the interests of its constituent class of creditors. The creditors' committee may seek court approval to hire counsel, accountants or other professionals to provide necessary assistance in performing its function.[329] The fees and expenses of committee lawyers and accountants are paid by the debtor as administrative expenses.[330]

17.7.2.2 The United States Trustee

In 1986, after a period of experimentation, Congress established a permanent United States trustee system, covering every state except Alabama and North Carolina.[331] The United States Attorney General appoints United States trustees for twenty-two regions around the country, each region composed of one or more judicial districts.[332] Assistant United States trustees may also be appointed.[333]

The United States trustee is required to "supervise the administration of cases and trustees in cases under chapter 7, 11, or 13."[334] The role of the United States trustee's office is crucial in many chapter 11 cases. It usually monitors the progress of chapter 11 cases to assure that they are properly handled and progress to some conclusion.[335]

The United States trustee convenes and presides at the section 341 meeting of creditors,[336] appoints the creditor committees,[337] may request the appointment of a chapter 11 trustee or examiner, and makes the appointment if one is ordered by the court,[338] and may request the dismissal or conversion of a chapter 11 case.[339] The United States trustee may monitor and comment on plans and disclosure statements in chapter 11.[340] More generally, the United States trustee may raise claims and may appear and be heard in any case or proceeding under chapter 11 (except the United States trustee may not file a chapter 11 plan).[341] The United States trustee will generally require regular cash flow and profit and loss statements from chapter 11 debtors.

With all these powers and the close relationship to the bankruptcy court, the United States trustee can be an important source of information and a critical ally. At the section 341 meeting, the consumer's attorney should be sure to establish contact with the assistant United States trustee assigned to the case, explain the consumer's view, and express an interest, if any, in serving on the creditors' committee, or in forming a separate consumer or tenant committee.[342] Thereafter, contact with the United States Trustee's Office should be maintained and the United States trustee should be provided with copies of information crucial to the consumer's case.

17.7.3 Appointment of a Creditors' Committee

At the meeting of creditors,[343] or perhaps at a separate meeting of creditors holding the largest unsecured claims, the creditors will determine if they wish to form an official creditors' committee. The United States trustee usually

---

are owed security deposits have administrative claims which are entitled to priority and as such are creditors whose claims will be paid in full with no right to vote on the plan).

323   Fed. R. Bankr. P. 3018(a) (final sentence).

324   11 U.S.C. § 1112.

325   *See* 11 U.S.C. § 1129(b).

326   *See* 11 U.S.C. § 1109(b) (any "party in interest" has the right to "appear and be heard on any issue" in a chapter 11 case).

327   *See* § 17.7.3, *infra.*

328   *See* 11 U.S.C. § 1103.

329   *See* 11 U.S.C. § 328(a).

330   11 U.S.C. §§ 330(a), 503(b)(2), 507(a)(1).

331   The Bankruptcy Judges, United States Trustees, and Family Farm Bankruptcy Act of 1986, Pub. L. No. 99-554, 100 Stat. 3088. The provisions concerning the United States Trustee System are codified at 28 U.S.C. §§ 581–589a. See also § 2.7, *supra,* for another discussion of the United States Trustee System.

332   28 U.S.C. § 581.

333   28 U.S.C. § 582.

334   28 U.S.C. § 586a(3). For a complete compilation of the statutory duties of the United States trustee beyond those set out in 28 U.S.C. §§ 581–589a, see 1 Collier on Bankruptcy ¶ 6.22 (15th ed. rev.).

335   *See* 28 U.S.C. § 586a(3)(G) (United States trustee may monitor progress of cases and take appropriate action to prevent undue delay).

336   11 U.S.C. § 341.

337   11 U.S.C. § 1102. See § 17.7.3, *infra,* for a discussion of the appointment of a creditors' committee in chapter 11.

338   11 U.S.C. § 1104. See § 17.7.4, *infra,* for a discussion of the appointment of a trustee or examiner in chapter 11.

339   11 U.S.C. § 1112.

340   28 U.S.C. § 586a(3)(B).

341   11 U.S.C. § 307.

342   *See* § 17.7.3, *infra.*

343   11 U.S.C. § 341; Fed. R. Bankr. P. 2003.

offers membership on the committee to the holders of the largest unsecured claims against the debtor.[344] However, if consumer claims are a significant issue in the case, the U.S. trustee may be willing to appoint a consumer creditor (or her attorney acting as agent) to the committee. As the creditors' committee may seek court approval to hire counsel, accountants, or other professionals to provide necessary assistance to the committee at the estate's expense,[345] there may be some jockeying over who will represent the committee as counsel. If a consumer is appointed to the committee, she may suggest and advocate for a particular attorney to be hired as counsel to the committee.

For consumer creditors and their attorneys, there are both potential advantages and disadvantages to participating in a creditors' committee. A potentially significant, albeit intangible, benefit is the increased status that counsel to the committee has in court proceedings. The position taken on an issue by counsel to the creditors' committee is not simply that of an individual creditor but rather that of the entire class of unsecured creditors and, as such, may be given great weight by the court. Committee members and counsel have access to timely information about the debtor's activities and plan formulation, and a real opportunity to negotiate with the debtor. In addition, counsel to the committee, once approved by the court, may seek compensation for their services from the estate, that is, the debtor, as an administrative expense.[346] Of course, counsel will only be paid if there are assets in the estate, so there is necessarily some risk of non-payment to the attorney.

A drawback of committee status is that the consumer creditor, in her capacity as a committee member, and counsel to the committee undertakes a responsibility to protect the interests of other unsecured creditors. Another drawback is that consumer representatives may be continually outvoted or drowned out by large creditors, typically commercial lenders and bondholders. For these reasons, depending upon the circumstances in the case, a consumer creditor may decide that it is not worthwhile to help form or participate on a committee and that her interest is better served by acting in an individual capacity.

Another alternative, at least where the attorney is representing a substantial number of consumer creditors with similar claims against the debtor, is to request that the court authorize the appointment of a special committee of creditors.[347] This may be appropriate in a case where the consumers have claims that are distinct from those of the other unsecured creditors such as deposit claims with priority status.[348] Although the court may be reluctant to authorize a

special committee when another committee of unsecured creditors has already been appointed due to the added administrative expenses involved, the decision is within the court's discretion.[349] Especially when consumer claims may have a significant impact on the outcome of the case, the court may be willing to appoint a special committee of consumer creditors.

17.7.4 Appointment of a Trustee or an Examiner

17.7.4.1 Introduction

When a chapter 11 case is filed, the debtor ordinarily remains in control of the business as a "debtor in possession."[350] Section 1104(a), however, authorizes the court in some circumstances to appoint a trustee to take over and manage the debtor's affairs.[351] This provision gives consumers powerful leverage against businesses that are mismanaged after filing under chapter 11. For example, tenants may force the appointment of a trustee where a landlord-debtor failed to maintain a building in compliance with state sanitary codes. When a community hospital went into bankruptcy, community groups and others obtained appointment

149 and 150, Appendix G.14, *infra. See generally Case History: Recovering Consumer Deposits From a Bankrupt Furniture Store,* 10 NCLC REPORTS *Bankruptcy and Foreclosures Ed.* 41 (Mar./Apr. 1992).

349 11 U.S.C. § 1102(a)(2). *But see In re* Ctr. Apartments, Ltd., 277 B.R. 747 (Bankr. S.D. Ohio 2001) (court refused to appoint official tenants' committee because named tenants could not establish that they were creditors of debtor-landlord, but encouraged tenants to participate in proceedings as parties in interest pursuant to § 1109(b)).

350 *See* 11 U.S.C. §§ 1101(1) (defining "debtor in possession"), 1107 (giving the debtor in possession most of the powers of a trustee), 1108 (giving a trustee authorization to operate the debtor's business).

351 11 U.S.C. § 1104(a) states:

At any time after the commencement of the case but before confirmation of a plan, on request of a party in interest or the United States trustee, and after notice and a hearing, the court shall order the appointment of a trustee—

(1) for cause, including fraud, dishonesty, incompetence, or gross mismanagement of the affairs of the debtor by current management either before or after the commencement of the case, or similar cause, but not including the number of holders of securities of the debtor or the amount of assets or liabilities of the debtor; or

(2) if such appointment is in the interests of creditors, any equity security holders, and other interests of the estate, without regard to the number of holders of securities of the debtor or the amount of assets or liabilities of the debtor.

344 11 U.S.C. § 1102(b)(1).
345 11 U.S.C. § 328(a).
346 11 U.S.C. § 503(b)(4); *cf. In re* FirstPlus Fin., Inc., 254 B.R. 888 (Bankr. N.D. Tex. 2000) (attorney fees of individual creditors serving on committee are not compensable).
347 11 U.S.C. § 1102(a)(2).
348 11 U.S.C. § 507(a)(6). Form pleadings are available in Forms

of a trustee.[352] Even if unsuccessful, the good faith filing of a motion for a trustee may produce a marked change in the debtor's behavior.

17.7.4.2 General Standards

Section 1104 permits the court on the request of a party in interest or the United States trustee to order the appointment of a trustee "[f]or cause, including fraud, dishonesty, incompetence, or gross mismanagement of the affairs of the debtor by current management either before or after the commencement of the case, or similar cause"; or in the (best) interests of the creditors.[353]

Chapter 11 is designed to allow the debtor-in-possession to retain management and control of the debtor's business operation unless a party in interest can prove that the appointment of a trustee is justified.[354] As the trustee appointment is an extraordinary remedy, a strong presumption exists that the debtor should be permitted to remain in possession absent a showing of need for the appointment of a trustee.[355] But the decision to appoint a trustee under section 1104(a) must be made on a case-by-case basis.[356] Although appointment of a trustee is the exception rather than the rule, the decision to appoint a trustee is within the discretion of the bankruptcy court.[357]

17.7.4.3 Grounds for Appointment of a Trustee Under Section 1104(a)(1)

Section 1104(a)(1) allows appointment of a trustee for "cause," which includes "fraud, dishonesty, incompetence or gross mismanagement," but nothing in the section requires that cause be limited to only those four transgressions. Cases have held that the examples of cause enumerated in section 1104(a)(1) are not exhaustive and the court may thus find that cause exists for a reason not specifically set forth in the statute.[358] Moreover, paragraphs (1) and (2) of subsection (a) can also be applied together in the absence of any enumerated element and the best interest test can be added.[359]

A finding of fraud recognizes the existence of some misrepresentation and requires a breach of the "duty of each to refrain from even attempted deceit of another with whom he deals and the right of the latter to assume he will do so."[360] This cause usually involves a blatant attempt by the debtor to deceive the creditors to the profit of the debtor and the detriment of the creditors. Examples of this type of conduct include where the assets are sold just prior to the filing of the petition with the knowledge that the transfer would be avoided,[361] where assets are siphoned out of the estate by means of a kickback scheme,[362] or where a complete conversion of corporate assets has occurred.[363] Dishonesty appears to be considered by the courts as a lesser form of fraud. Dishonesty may be seen as a certain degree of misrepresentation or breach of fiduciary duty.[364]

Incompetence is related to mismanagement, requiring a showing of a lack of business acumen and ability. However, the mere fact of filing for insolvency under chapter 11 by the debtor, which may be caused by a variety of factors, will not be enough to demonstrate that the debtor is incapable or unsuited to superintend its own reorganization.[365]

Gross mismanagement suggests some extreme ineptitude on the part of management to the detriment of the organization,[366] rising above simple mismanagement to reach the level of cause.[367] Courts generally consider that some mismanagement exists in every insolvency case.[368] While a certain amount of mismanagement of the debtor's affairs prior to the filing date may not be sufficient grounds for an appointment of a trustee and new management will be permitted to identify and correct its mistakes, continuing mismanagement of the affairs of the debtor after the filing date is evidence of the need for an appointment of a trustee.[369] Also, while it is clear that post-petition mismanagement is grounds for appointment of a trustee under this section,[370] conduct before the commencement of the case also can be grounds.[371]

---

352 *In re* St. Mary Hosp., 89 B.R. 503, 504 n.1 (Bankr. E.D. Pa. 1988).

353 11 U.S.C. § 1104(a).

354 *In re* Ionosphere Clubs, Inc., 113 B.R. 164, 167 (Bankr. S.D.N.Y. 1990).

355 *Id.*

356 *In re* Sharon Steel Corp., 871 F.2d 1217, 1226 (3d Cir. 1989).

357 *In re* Sullivan, 108 B.R. 555, 556 (Bankr. E.D. Pa. 1989), *aff'd*, 1992 WL 68613 (E.D. Pa. Mar. 31, 1992).

358 *In re* Cardinal Indus., 109 B.R. 755, 765 (Bankr. S.D. Ohio 1990); *In re* V. Savino Oil & Heating Co., 99 B.R. 518, 525 (Bankr. E.D.N.Y. 1989); *see In re* Ngan Gung Restaurant, Inc., 195 B.R. 593 (S.D.N.Y. 1996) (court has power to appoint a trustee to sanction conduct abusive of the judicial process).

359 7 Collier on Bankruptcy ¶ 1104.02[3][d] (15th ed. rev.).

360 *In re* Garman, 625 F.2d 755 (7th Cir. 1980).

361 *In re* Russell, 60 B.R. 42 (Bankr. W.D. Ark. 1985).

362 *In re* Bibo, 76 F.3d 256 (9th Cir. 1996).

363 *In re* Colby Constr. Inc., 51 B.R. 113, 116 (Bankr. S.D.N.Y. 1985).

364 *See id.*

365 *In re* LaSherene, Inc., 3 B.R. 169, 174–176 (Bankr. N.D. Ga. 1980).

366 *In re* Brown, 31 B.R. 583, 585, 586 (D.D.C. 1983).

367 *In re* Anchorage Boat Sales, Inc., 4 B.R. 635, 645 (Bankr. E.D.N.Y. 1980).

368 *In re* LaSherene, Inc., 3 B.R. 169 (Bankr. N.D. Ga. 1980).

369 *In re* Ionosphere Clubs, Inc., 113 B.R. 164, 168 (Bankr. S.D.N.Y. 1990); *In re* Colby Constr., 51 B.R. 113, 117 (Bankr. S.D.N.Y. 1985).

370 *In re* Stein & Day, Inc., 87 B.R. 290, 294 (Bankr. S.D.N.Y. 1988).

371 *In re* Intercat, Inc., 247 B.R. 911 (Bankr. S.D. Ga. 2000) (evidence of willful infringement of patent rights of another company); *In re* Russell, 60 B.R. 42 (Bankr. W.D. Ark. 1985); *In re* Ford, 36 B.R. 501, 504 (Bankr. W.D. Ky. 1983).

Cause may take a variety of forms. The Tenth Circuit in *In re Oklahoma Refining Co.*,[372] affirmed the bankruptcy court's appointment of a trustee because of the failure to keep adequate records and to file reports, and the existence of a history of transactions with affiliated companies. The Third Circuit found cause under section 1104(a)(1) for appointment of a trustee where there was systematic siphoning of the debtor's assets to other companies under common control on the eve of bankruptcy, and continuing post-petition mismanagement.[373] And a New York bankruptcy court[374] found debtor's pre-petition conduct, post-petition nondisclosures and misrepresentations, and noncompliance with statutory requirements relating to a second corporation which took over the business of the debtor's corporation constituted cause for appointment of a trustee pursuant to section 1104(a)(1). The Fifth Circuit considered whether there are grounds to appoint a trustee when the interests of a electric cooperative's consumer board members (lower utility rates) conflicts with the interests of the cooperative's creditors.[375]

17.7.4.4 Grounds for Appointment of a Trustee Under Section 1104(a)(2)

Even if cause is not established within the meaning of 1104(a)(1), the court may still order the appointment of a trustee pursuant to section 1104(a)(2).[376] Subsection 1104(a)(2) provides a flexible standard for the appointment of a trustee,[377] allowing the court to exercise *equity* powers to appoint a trustee to protect the interests of creditors, equity security holders, and other interests in the debtor's estate.[378] Unlike (a)(1), section (a)(2) may entail the exercise of discretionary powers and equitable considerations; a cost-benefit analysis of the cost of a trustee to the estate compared with the benefits sought to be derived will be a significant aspect of this determination.[379] For example, where the grounds for appointment of a trustee under section 1104(a)(1) were not met, a court has held, in light of the

substantial management fees paid by the debtor corporation to its parent corporation, that the debtor might have claims adverse to the interests of its parent and other related corporation and thus appointed a trustee pursuant to (a)(2).[380]

When proceeding under subsection (a)(2), bankruptcy courts eschew rigid absolutes and look to the practical realities and necessities, considering such factors (in addition to the cost-benefit analysis) as: 1) trustworthiness of the debtor; 2) debtor-in-possession's past and present performance and prospects for the debtor's rehabilitation; 3) debtor's justification for its actions; 4) reliance and harm to other parties; 5) conclusive evidence of detriment to the estate; and 6) business community and creditors' confidence (or lack thereof) in present management.[381] In some cases the court finds the appointment of a trustee was proper under either section 1104(a)(1) or (2).[382]

Another approach to appointing a trustee under (a)(2) is to consider breach of a debtor's fiduciary duty. Several cases have held a breach of fiduciary duty (which is constructive fraud as well) is grounds for a trustee appointment because a debtor-in-possession is a fiduciary for the creditors of the estate and has the same duties as trustees appointed by the court.[383]

17.7.4.5 Appointment of an Examiner

Another mechanism available to creditors under chapter 11 is appointment of an examiner. An examiner has similar investigative powers to a trustee, but does not take over and manage the debtor's affairs.[384] Appointment of an examiner may be particularly useful in cases where there is some evidence of wrongdoing or mismanagement by the debtor but the evidence of fraud or mismanagement is insufficient to convince the court to appoint a trustee.

---

372 838 F.2d 1133 (10th Cir. 1988).

373 *In re* Sharon Steel Corp., 871 F.2d 1217 (3d Cir. 1989).

374 *In re* V. Savino Oil & Heating Co., 99 B.R. 518, 526–528 (Bankr. E.D.N.Y. 1989).

375 *See In re* Cajun Elec. Power Coop., Inc., 69 F.3d 746 (5th Cir. 1995), *modified after reh'g*, 74 F.3d 599 (5th Cir. 1996) (conflict of interest found to go beyond that which is inherent in the structure of rural electrical cooperative).

376 *In re* Cardinal Indus., 109 B.R. 755, 765, 766 (Bankr. S.D. Ohio 1990).

377 *In re* Parker Grande Dev., 64 B.R. 557, 561 (Bankr. S.D. Ind. 1986); *In re* Anchorage Boat Sales, Inc., 4 B.R. 635, 644 (Bankr. E.D.N.Y. 1980).

378 *In re* Nautilus of N.M., Inc., 83 B.R. 784, 789 (Bankr. D.N.M. 1988).

379 *In re* Cardinal Indus., Inc., 109 B.R. 755, 766 (Bankr. S.D. Ohio 1990); *In re* V. Savino Oil & Heating Co., 99 B.R. 518, 525 (Bankr. E.D.N.Y. 1989); *In re* Stein & Day, Inc., 87 B.R. 290, 295 (Bankr. S.D.N.Y. 1988).

380 *In re* L.S. Good & Co., 8 B.R. 312 (Bankr. N.D. W. Va. 1980).

381 *In re* Ionosphere Clubs, Inc., 113 B.R. 164, 168 (Bankr. S.D.N.Y. 1990); *In re* Evans, 48 B.R. 46, 48 (Bankr. W.D. Tex. 1985).

382 *In re* Brown, 31 B.R. 583, 585 (Bankr. D.D.C. 1983).

383 *In re* Nautilus of N.M., Inc., 83 B.R. 784, 789 (Bankr. D.N.M. 1988); *In re* Parker Grande Dev., 64 B.R. 557, 561 (Bankr. S.D. Ind. 1986) (breach of fiduciary duty because debtor-in-possession has such poor skills, ability, training and experience in land management and business acumen, he could not protect and conserve property for the benefit of the creditors); *In re* Russell, 60 B.R. 42, 47 (Bankr. W.D. Ark. 1985); *In re* Ford, 36 B.R. 501, 504 (Bankr. W.D. Ky. 1983) (co-owner president of debtor was incapable of dealing with debtor as fiduciary, and appointed a trustee pursuant to (a)(2)). *Cf. In re* Cardinal Indus., 109 B.R. 755, 766–768 (Bankr. S.D. Ohio 1990) (debtors had not addressed serious deficiencies in recordkeeping processes; evidence established the Unsecured Creditor's Committees' loss of faith in debtors' intentions and abilities to reorganize their affairs; and the cost-benefit analysis was met).

384 *See* 11 U.S.C. § 1106(b).

Section 1104(c) permits the court on request of a party in interest or the United States trustee, to order the appointment of an examiner to investigate "allegations of fraud, dishonesty, incompetence, misconduct, mismanagement, or irregularity in the management of the affairs of the debtor," if the appointment is in the best interests of the creditors or the debtor's fixed unsecured debt exceeds $5,000,000.00.[385] Unsupported allegations of wrongdoing or mismanagement are not generally sufficient to support appointment of an examiner. The courts require that there be a factual basis underlying the need for an independent investigation.[386] However, if the debtor's unsecured debt exceeds $5,000,000.00, the court must appoint an examiner; the court has no discretion.[387] If the debtor's unsecured debt is less than $5,000,000.00, though, appointment is discretionary and the court will weigh the same equitable considerations used to determine whether to appoint a trustee under section 1104(a)(2).[388] Although the standard is the same, the results of the court's cost-benefit analysis under the two provisions may be different, as the costs of employing an examiner are much less than the costs of a trustee, and the nature, extent and duration of the examiner's investigation may be limited by the court.[389]

Examiners are usually appointed to investigate particular subjects or allegations, and to report their findings to the court and the parties in interest.[390] On occasion the courts appoint examiners to perform other tasks, such as to mediate between the debtor and creditors or to prosecute causes of action on the debtor's behalf.[391] The practices and procedure for appointing an examiner are similar to those required for the appointment of a trustee. An examiner's report may provide excellent objective evidence to support subsequent appointment of a trustee, but the Code prohibits appointment of an examiner and a trustee at the same time.[392]

17.7.4.6 Practice and Procedure

An application for appointment of a trustee or an examiner is by motion and may be made by any party in interest or by the United States trustee.[393] Although the motion can be filed at any time, the court may be reluctant to appoint a trustee or an examiner based on pre-petition mismanagement. It may therefore, be preferable to wait for evidence of post-petition misconduct. Once a plan is confirmed, however, the court may lose the power to appoint a trustee, because such an appointment would be inconsistent with the terms of the plan.[394]

Ordinarily, before filing the motion, a record should be built of the debtor's mismanagement. Communications with the debtor or debtor's attorney should be in writing or followed up by confirming letters. Wherever possible, "objective" evidence other than the consumer's experience should be gathered so that the court can be convinced that this is more than a quarrel between the consumer creditor and the debtor. For example, if the debtor is a landlord and the issue is the management of the building, reports should be obtained from state or local housing inspectors documenting the conditions of the building.

The cooperation of the United States trustee can be critical in the success of the motion. Ideally, the United States trustee's office will join in the motion or file a separate supporting motion, but in any event the court is very likely to ask for the opinion of the United States trustee and to give significant weight to that opinion.

As soon as a chapter 11 is filed, the consumer's attorney should make contact with the United States trustee's office, find out which person in the office has been assigned to the case, alert him or her that difficulty is anticipated with the debtor and a motion for appointment of a trustee may be filed. Copies of all correspondence should be sent to the United States trustee's office. Prior to filing the motion, the consumer's attorney should sit down with the United States trustee to present the reasons for filing the motion and request that the United States trustee join in the motion or file a supporting motion.

In considering the motion for appointment of a trustee, the court is not required to conduct a full evidentiary hearing, at least when the record already contains undisputed facts

---

385 11 U.S.C. § 1104(c).

386 *In re* Mechem of Ohio, Inc., 92 B.R. 760 (Bankr. N.D. Ohio 1988); *In re* Gilman Serv., Inc., 46 B.R. 322 (Bankr. D. Mass. 1985); *In re* 1243 20th St., Inc., 6 B.R. 683 (Bankr. D.D.C. 1980); *In re* Leniham, 4 B.R. 209 (Bankr. D.R.I. 1980); *In re* Bel Air Associates Ltd., 4 B.R. 168 (Bankr. W.D. Okla. 1980).

387 *In re* Revco D.S., Inc., 898 F.2d 498 (6th Cir. 1990). *But see In re* Bradlees Stores, 209 B.R. 36 (Bankr. S.D.N.Y. 1997) (failure to request an examiner can be treated as a waiver despite appearance that provision is mandatory).

388 *In re* Gilman Serv., Inc., 46 B.R. 322 (Bankr. D. Mass. 1985); *In re* Leniham, 4 B.R. 209 (Bankr. D.R.I. 1980).

389 *See In re* Mako, Inc., 102 B.R. 809 (Bankr. E.D. Okla. 1988); *In re* Gilman Serv., Inc., 46 B.R. 322 (Bankr. D. Mass. 1985); 7 Collier on Bankruptcy ¶ 1104.03[3] (15th ed. rev.); *see also In re* Revco D.S., Inc., 898 F.2d 498 (6th Cir. 1990) (court has authority to limit scope of examiner's authority).

390 *See, e.g., In re* Carnegie Int'l Corp., 51 B.R. 252 (Bankr. S.D. Ind. 1984) (law professor appointed examiner to investigate debtor causes of action); *In re* 1243 20th St., Inc., 6 B.R. 683 (Bankr. D.D.C. 1980) (examiner appointed to investigate a pre-petition transfer by debtor to a related corporation).

391 *See, e.g., In re* Public Serv. Co. of N.H., 99 B.R. 177 (Bankr. D.N.H. 1989) (examiner appointed to mediate and break deadlock in reorganization plan negotiations).

392 11 U.S.C. § 1104(b); *see also In re* Int'l Distrib. Centers, Inc., 74 B.R. 221 (S.D.N.Y. 1987) (an examiner may not subsequently be made trustee in the same case).

393 11 U.S.C. § 1104(a). A trustee may also be appointed by the court *sua sponte. In re* Bibo, 76 B.R. 256 (9th Cir. 1996).

394 *In re* Am. Preferred Prescription, Inc., 250 B.R. 11 (E.D.N.Y. 2000), *rev'd on other grounds*, 255 F.3d 87 (2d Cir. 2001).

showing that cause exists.[395] The party moving for the appointment has the burden of proof showing "cause" and at least one court has said the evidence supporting the motion must be clear and convincing.[396] Once the court has found that "cause" exists under section 1104, it has no discretion but to appoint a trustee.[397]

Numerous courts have held that appointment of a trustee in a chapter 11 case is an extraordinary remedy.[398] There is generally a bias in favor of allowing the debtor to continue managing the estate, absent a strong showing of fraud, incompetence or mismanagement.[399] Courts often express concern about protecting the interests of creditors by avoiding the administrative costs which appointment a trustee necessarily generates.[400] For these reasons, a request for a trustee will not be appropriate for every case.

The United States trustee's office is required to maintain a panel of persons willing to serve as trustees in chapter 11 cases.[401] Thus, unlike many state court actions for appointment of a receiver where, as a practical matter, the moving party must be prepared to locate a suitable receiver, the aggrieved consumer creditor does not have to recommend a trustee for a chapter 11 bankruptcy. Ordinarily the court will order that the United States trustee appoint a trustee. Ordinarily the trustee will be selected from the United States trustee's panel, but the trustee does not have to be from that panel, and the consumer's attorney may suggest someone else who is suitable.

Finally, although some courts have held an order appointing a trustee in bankruptcy is a procedural order, and thus not a final substantive order that may be reviewed immediately,[402] more recent decisions have held otherwise. In *Committee of Dalkon Shield Claimants v. A.H. Robins Co.*,[403] the Fourth Circuit found an order denying the request for an appointment of a trustee pursuant to section 1104(a) was immediately reviewable as a final decision, even though the order may not have been final in a technical sense. The court also held that as the determination of cause is within the discretion of the fact finder; in the absence of an abuse of discretion, the appellate court will not disturb the lower court's findings.[404]

17.7.5 Objection to Compensation Being Paid to Debtor's Principal

When a business files a chapter 11 bankruptcy, the debtor may continue to pay its employees their salary for the post-petition services rendered. In fact, such employees' right to payment is an administrative expense claim entitled to priority payment.[405] In the case of a small business debtor, there is a potential for the debtor's principal shareholders, partners or proprietors to continue to pay a substantial salary to themselves during post-petition operations, thereby dissipating the remaining assets that would otherwise be available to creditors.

A number of courts have held that the bankruptcy court has the power to determine the propriety of the continued employment of the debtor's principals and to fix the level of their compensation.[406] In some jurisdictions, local rules govern the procedure by which a debtor may obtain authority to continue to pay its principals for post-petition services rendered to the debtor.[407] In evaluating creditor objections to the salaries being paid to officers or principals of the debtor, the general standard employed by the court is the value, in the open market, of the services being provided. This, in turn, requires an evaluation of the salaries paid for equivalent positions in equivalent businesses.[408]

The possibility of a creditor objection to the salary which may be paid to principals of the "opposing party" (the debtor) is an obvious leverage point.[409] Aside from the possibility that the creditor can hit the debtor's principals directly in their "pocketbook," in a hearing on compensation, the court will necessarily consider evidence regarding the debtor's business operations and the principals' responsibilities and conduct. If such evidence puts the debtor in a bad light, it may be useful to present it to the court early in the case as an objection to the principals' compensation, particularly if the evidence may not be sufficient to satisfy the more onerous requirements for the appointment of a trustee.

---

395 *In re* Casco Bay Lines, Inc., 17 B.R. 946, 950 (B.A.P. 1st Cir. 1982).

396 *In re* Ionosphere Clubs, Inc., 113 B.R. 164, 167, 168 (Bankr. S.D.N.Y. 1990).

397 *In re* Okla. Ref. Co., 838 F.2d 1133, 1136 (10th Cir. 1988).

398 *E.g., In re* McCorhill Publ'g, Inc., 73 B.R. 1013 (Bankr. S.D.N.Y. 1987).

399 *E.g., In re* Sharon Steel Corp., 871 F.2d 1217 (3d Cir. 1989).

400 *E.g., In re* McCorhill Publ'g, Inc., 73 B.R. 1013 (Bankr. S.D.N.Y. 1987).

401 28 U.S.C. § 586(a)(1).

402 Albrecht v. Robison, 36 B.R. 913, 915, 916 (D. Utah 1983).

403 828 F.2d 239, 241, 242 (4th Cir. 1987).

404 *Id.; cf. In re* Sharon Steel Corp., 871 F.2d 1217, 1225 (3d Cir. 1989).

405 11 U.S.C. §§ 503(b), 507(a)(1).

406 *E.g., In re* Lynx Transp., Inc., 1999 WL 615366 (Bankr. E.D. Pa. Aug. 11, 1999); *In re* Holly's Inc. 140 B.R. 643, 690, 691 (Bankr. W.D. Mich. 1992); *In re* Zerodec Mega Corp., 39 B.R. 932 (Bankr. E.D. Pa. 1984) (grounding the court's authority in 11 U.S.C. § 327 and § 105).

407 *E.g.,* Local Rule 4002-1 (Bankr. E.D. Pa.) (requiring notice to creditors of the level of compensation to the debtor's principal and providing for a procedure for creditors to object).

408 *E.g., In re* Athos Steel & Aluminum, Inc., 69 B.R. 515 (Bankr. E.D. Pa. 1987).

409 *Cf. In re* Forum Group, Inc., 82 F.3d 159 (7th Cir. 1996) (outgoing directors' golden parachute payments invalidated because outgoing directors recommended new directors so that there was no actual relinquishment of control as required by the golden parachute agreements).

17.7.6 Transfer Avoidance Actions

As a debtor in possession, a chapter 11 debtor has, generally speaking, the same powers as a chapter 7 trustee.[410] These powers include the right to set aside certain pre-petition transfers, including preferences,[411] fraudulent conveyances[412] and transfers avoidable under the "strong-arm" powers.[413]

A creditor actively participating in a chapter 11 case may learn that there are potential transfer avoidance claims that the debtor is not pursuing. This occurs with some regularity because prosecution of the claims would require that the principals or their relatives or other closely connected parties return money or other assets to the debtor for the benefit of all creditors.

For example, a review of the debtor's books and bank records might reveal a pattern of payment by the debtor of the personal expenses (for example, home mortgage) of the principals. Similarly, valuable property may have been transferred for little or no consideration to a family member or to a corporate principal.[414] Such payments and conveyances may be avoidable as fraudulent transfers. Or, in the one year period prior to bankruptcy, the principals may have withdrawn cash from the company in excess of their usual salaries, ostensibly as repayment of "loans" advanced to the debtor. Such transfers may be avoidable as either fraudulent conveyances or preferences. The debtor may have made substantial payments in the one year period prior to bankruptcy to lenders who held claims guaranteed by the debtors' principals. Such payments, too, may be avoidable as preferences.[415]

The investigation and discovery of the existence of these claims, by itself, may lead the chapter 11 debtor to quickly seek a settlement with the active creditor. In the absence of a settlement, if the debtor (as trustee) does not act to recover the transfer, the court can authorize a creditors' committee or individual creditor to prosecute the avoidance action on behalf of the debtor's estate if satisfied that the debtor is not inclined to pursue a potentially meritorious claim.[416] If

successful, the creditor's attorney may seek reasonable counsel fees from the estate.[417] Alternatively, failure to seek recovery of potentially avoidable transfers can be grounds for appointment of an independent trustee.[418] A court-appointed trustee is much more likely than the debtor in possession to investigate and seek relief for abusive transfers of corporate property. If such a trustee has been appointed, information about abusive transfer should be brought to her attention.

17.7.7 Objections to the Debtor's Disclosure Statement

As part of confirmation process the proponent of a chapter 11 plan must file and obtain court approval of a disclosure statement.[419] The disclosure statement is usually filed simultaneously with or shortly after the filing of the plan of reorganization.[420]

The purpose of a disclosure statement is to provide sufficient information to enable creditors to make an informed judgment about the proposed plan.[421] The type of information ordinarily provided in a narrative form in the disclosure statement includes: a brief history of the debtor and its financial operations; a description of the circumstances which resulted in the debtor's financial distress and bankruptcy filing; a summary of the legal and financial events which have occurred since the bankruptcy filing; a chapter 7-type liquidation analysis; a summary of the contents of the plan and the treatment of the different creditor classes; and an explanation of the means by which the debtor expects to carry out the provisions of the plan. As the disclosure statement must be approved by the court upon notice and hearing, the debtor must file a motion seeking court approval and give notice of the motion to all creditors.[422]

A creditor may file objections to the proposed disclosure statement.[423] The disclosure statement hearing is another point in the confirmation process where a creditor may oppose the debtor and, by doing so, gain leverage for more favorable treatment by the debtor. The leverage gained by objection may not be substantial, however, as a debtor may

---

410 11 U.S.C. § 1107(a).

411 11 U.S.C. § 547.

412 11 U.S.C. § 548.

413 11 U.S.C. § 544.

414 *See generally In re* Blatstein, 260 B.R. 698 (E.D. Pa. 2001) (exploring scope of transfers to debtor's wife that may be avoided).

415 Levit v. Ingersoll Rand Fin. Corp., 874 F.2d 1186 (7th Cir. 1989).

416 *In re* The Gibson Group, Inc., 66 F.3d 1436 (6th Cir. 1995) (creditor has standing to bring preference and fraudulent transfer actions after making demand on debtor in possession to bring those actions and having the demand refused); *In re* S.T.N. Enterprises, 779 F.2d 901 (2d Cir. 1985); *In re* Philadelphia Light Supply Co., 39 B.R. 51 (Bankr. E.D. Pa. 1984). Intervention in a pending case which is not being aggressively prosecuted may also be possible. 11 U.S.C. § 1109(b). *See generally*

In re Chalk Line Mfg., 184 B.R. 828 (Bank. N.D. Ala. 1995) (and cases cited therein). *But cf.* Hartford Underwriters Ins. Co. v. Union Planters Bank, 530 U.S. 1, 120 S. Ct. 1942, 147 L. Ed. 2d 1 (2000) (denying a creditor remedy under an analogous Code section; recognizing but not deciding the connection between the issues).

417 11 U.S.C. § 503(b)(3)(B).

418 *See* § 17.7.4, *supra.*

419 11 U.S.C. § 1125(b).

420 Fed. R. Bankr. R. 3016(c).

421 11 U.S.C. § 1125(a).

422 11 U.S.C. § 1125(b); Fed. R. Bankr. P. 3017(a).

423 See Form 152, Appendix G.14, *infra,* for an example of an objection to a disclosure statement.

be perfectly willing to amend the disclosure statement to provide additional information to neutralize creditor objections, at least where the additional information is benign. In some cases, the court might consider objections to the disclosure statement that are based on the alleged legal defects in the substance of the plan itself.[424]

17.7.8 Objections to the Debtor's Plan of Reorganization

After the disclosure statement is approved, the court will issue an order directing the debtor to send out ballots to the creditors for voting on the plan. The court will also schedule a confirmation hearing and set a deadline by which creditors may file objections to the plan. Notice of the confirmation hearing and objection deadline is given to all creditors.[425]

Section 1129(a) of the Code sets out thirteen requirements that must be met for consensual confirmation of a chapter 11 plan. Perhaps the most significant requirement is found in section 1129(a)(8) which provides that every class must either accept the plan or be unimpaired.[426] If this requirement is not met, the plan may not be confirmed under section 1129(a). Thus, the importance of the plan voting is self-evident.

Separate and apart from plan voting, however, any creditor can object to confirmation on any of the other twelve grounds found in section 1129(a), even if the class to which that creditor belongs has voted to accept the plan.[427]

It is beyond the scope of this discussion to discuss comprehensively all of the requirements for confirmation under section 1129(a). However, for a consumer creditor, there are at least two potential objections that may be available. First, if the consumer's claim is a consumer deposit claim entitled to priority under section 507(a)(6) or for certain pre-petition wages or benefits,[428] it must either be: (1) paid in full with interest over the length of the plan even if the consumer's class has accepted a plan containing

less favorable treatment or (2) paid in full on the effective date[429] of the plan if the consumer's class has not accepted the plan.[430] Absent this treatment, the plan is not confirmable. Second, if there is reason to question the debtor's financial ability to make the payments required by the plan, the debtor may assert objections under section 1129(a)(2)[431] and (a)(11).[432] These objections will be heard at the confirmation hearing.

If a plan cannot be confirmed under section 1129(a), a debtor may request confirmation under the chapter 11 "cram down" provision, section 1129(b). To be eligible to request confirmation under section 1129(b), there must be at least one class of creditors that is impaired which has accepted the plan.[433] Then, the plan can be confirmed if it does not discriminate unfairly and is "fair and equitable" as to each class of dissenting creditors.[434] Thus, even if the consumer creditor's class does not accept the plan, the debtor may seek confirmation under section 1129(b).

Section 1129 sets out separate tests for the fair and equitable standard for secured and unsecured creditors. For a plan to be fair and equitable as to secured creditors, the plan must provide for the creditor to retain its lien and receive in deferred cash payments the present value, as of the effective date (that is, confirmation date) of the plan of its allowed secured claim.[435] This is essentially the same requirement as is found under chapter 13.[436]

Usually a consumer creditor will be unsecured. For the plan to be fair and equitable as to a dissenting class of unsecured claims that will not receive a distribution equal to the present value of the allowed unsecured claims, the creditors must receive the same distribution as they would receive in a chapter 7 liquidation and no junior class of creditors or interests can receive any distribution.[437] This

---

424   *In re* Monroe Well Serv., 80 B.R. 324 (Bankr. E.D. Pa. 1987).

425   Fed. R. Bankr. P. 3020(b)(2).

426   Another significant subsection is § 1129(a)(7). Section 1129(a)(7) provides that if a class of claims is impaired, the plan cannot be confirmed unless either every claimant in the class accepts the plan or the distribution to the class under the plan provides the same value that the class would receive in a chapter 7 liquidation. This hypothetical liquidation test, or "best interests of the creditors" test is also found in chapter 13. *See In re* Barakat, 99 F.3d 1520 (9th Cir. 1996) (tenant security deposit claimants were not "impaired" class after debtor assumed leases, because their claims became post-petition priority claims payable in full); 11 U.S.C. § 1325(a)(4).

427   A class of creditors has accepted the plan if creditors holding at least two-thirds in amount and more than one-half in number of the allowed claims of the class have voted to accept the plan. 11 U.S.C. § 1126(c). See Form 153, Appendix G.14, *infra,* for an example of an objection to confirmation of a chapter 11 plan.

428   11 U.S.C. § 507(a)(3).

429   The effective date of the plan is the date that distributions to creditors or other significant actions are scheduled to begin. The term is usually defined in the plan itself, often as shortly after the confirmation order becomes final and unappealable.

430   11 U.S.C. § 1129(a)(9)(B).

431   11 U.S.C. § 1129(a)(2) requires that the plan comply with the applicable provisions of the Code. Section 1123(a)(5) requires that a plan "shall . . . provide adequate means for the plan's implementation."

432   11 U.S.C. § 1129(a)(11) requires that confirmation "is not likely to be followed by the liquidation, or the need for further financial reorganization" unless the plan itself proposes liquidation.

433   *See* 11 U.S.C. § 1129(b)(1).

434   *See* 11 U.S.C. § 1129(b)(1).

435   The amount of the allowed secured claim can be based upon the stripping of an under-secured claim under 11 U.S.C. § 506(a). However, in chapter 11, an under-secured creditor may have the right to elect to be treated as fully secured. *See* 11 U.S.C. § 1111(b). The seminal article on § 1111(b) is Klee, *All You Ever Wanted to Know About Cram Down Under the New Bankruptcy Code,* 53 Am. Bankr. Law J. 133 (1979).

436   *Compare* 11 U.S.C. § 1129(b)(2)(A) *with* 11 U.S.C. § 1325(a)(5)(B).

437   11 U.S.C. § 1129(b)(2)(B).

last requirement, known as the "absolute priority rule," means that the dissenting class of creditors must receive full payment of their allowed claims before the debtor or the owners of the debtor can retain any non-exempt property.[438]

17.7.9 Creditor's Plan of Reorganization

The Bankruptcy Code grants a chapter 11 debtor a time period of 120 days from the entry of the order for relief during which the debtor has the exclusive right to file a plan of reorganization.[439] If the debtor does not file a plan within the 120-day period or if a plan is not confirmed within a 180-day time period following the entry of the order for relief, any party in interest may propose a plan of reorganization.[440] This time limit is intended to give the debtor a reasonable period of time to negotiate a consensual plan with its creditors while at the same time imposing a deadline so that the debtor does not have undue leverage in the negotiations.

It is not uncommon for a debtor to seek an extension of the exclusivity period.[441] Such extensions may be permitted, after notice and hearing "for cause."[442] The debtor seeking an extension must file a motion. Objection to the debtor's motion to extend the exclusivity period can be fertile ground for creditors. The decision by the court on exclusivity is discretionary and often quite fact-specific.[443] The willingness of courts to extend the exclusivity period can vary substantially in different jurisdictions. Active creditor op-

position to the debtor may be grounds for denial of the extension of the exclusivity period, if the objecting creditors can show that further negotiations are unlikely to result in a confirmable consensual plan.[444]

After the exclusivity period has expired, a creditor can propose a plan. This can be a useful strategy where the debtor is no longer operating and the creditors and the debtor cannot agree on the most profitable way of liquidating the debtor's assets. If the debtor is operating, it is difficult to envision how the creditors can practically expect to implement a plan, over the debtor's opposition, that requires some type of future performance by the debtor unless the plan contemplates the replacement of the debtor's management. A creditor proposed plan may then make sense if the creditors prefer that debtor's operations cease and that the assets be liquidated.[445] In at least one instance, a tenant ownership plan was filed and confirmed, with the aid of community development groups experienced in property management and turnarounds of troubled buildings.[446]

A creditor proposed plan must meet all of the same procedural and substantive requirements of a debtor's plan: compliance with the provisions of section 1123(a);[447] approval of a disclosure statement; voting by the creditors; and satisfaction of the confirmation requirements of section 1129.[448] A consumer creditor should give careful thought before undertaking to propose a plan as there can be considerable time and expense involved in shepherding a plan through the confirmation process. At the same time, however, the prospect of a creditor's plan may be extremely helpful in negotiations with the debtor.

17.7.10 Seeking Dismissal or Conversion of a Chapter 11 Case

On request of a party in interest, a chapter 11 case may be dismissed or converted to a case under chapter 7, pursuant to 11 U.S.C. § 1112(b).[449] The standard for either action is "cause," but there are a number of grounds that would constitute such cause set out in the statute. These include "inability to effectuate a plan,"[450] "material default by the debtor with respect to a confirmed plan,"[451] and "unrea-

---

438 Without definitively resolving the issue, the Supreme Court has ruled on whether there is an exception to the absolute priority rule in favor of creditors that contribute "new value" to the reorganizing debtor. Bank of Am. Nat'l Trust & Sav. Ass'n. v. 203 N. LaSalle St. P'ship, 526 U.S. 434, 119 S. Ct. 1411, 143 L. Ed. 2d 607 (1999). The Court concluded that the opportunity to contribute new value (and avoid the effect of the absolute priority rule) cannot be limited exclusively to one group of creditors or equity holders in a reorganizing company. The implication of the opinion is that there is a "new value" exception available once all parties are given a full and fair opportunity to compete to obtain it.

The absolute priority rule was held not to apply to prevent approved rate decreases for member/owners of a rural electric cooperative. *In re* Cajun Elec. Coop., Inc., 185 F.3d 446 (5th Cir. 1999).

439 11 U.S.C. § 1121(b); *see In re* Clamp-All Corp., 233 B.R. 198 (Bankr. D. Mass. 1999) (creditor's claim subordinated as a remedy for violating the exclusivity period by mailing out a proposed alternative plan in the 120-day period).

440 11 U.S.C. § 1121(c)(2), (3).

441 Creditors can also seek to have the exclusivity period shortened. 11 U.S.C. § 1121(d); *see In re* Geriatrics Nursing Home, Inc., 187 B.R. 128 (D.N.J. 1995) (creditor bears heavy burden in seeking premature termination of exclusivity period).

442 11 U.S.C. § 1121(d); *see In re* Express One Int'l, Inc., 194 B.R. 98 (Bankr. E.D. Tex. 1996) (list of factors which courts have identified as relevant to determining whether cause exists).

443 *See, e.g., In re* Express One Int'l, Inc., 194 B.R. 98 (Bankr. E.D. Tex. 1996) (enumerating grounds for extensions).

444 *E.g., In re* Gagel & Gagel, 24 B.R. 674 (Bankr. S.D. Ohio 1982).

445 An alternative way to get to a similar result would be by a motion seeking conversion of the case to chapter 7. 11 U.S.C. § 1112(b).

446 *See Showdown in Minneapolis: How a Member of the Bankruptcy Bar Foiled a Notorious Slumlord*, Consumer Bankr. News (Sept. 3, 1992).

447 11 U.S.C. § 1123(a).

448 11 U.S.C. § 1129.

449 Cases may not be converted to chapter 12 or 13 unless the debtor so requests. 11 U.S.C. § 1112(d).

450 11 U.S.C. § 1112(b)(2); *see, e.g., In re* Koerner, 800 F.2d 1358 (5th Cir. 1986).

451 11 U.S.C. § 1112(b)(8).

sonable delay by the debtor that is prejudicial to creditors"[452] among others. The list in the statute is non-exclusive and the bankruptcy court may also consider other grounds including lack of good faith.[453]

If grounds are shown, the court may either convert or dismiss depending on the best interests of the creditors and the estate. Generally, the choice between conversion or dismissal is considered discretionary, but there are limits on a court's discretion.[454]

Pursuit of a motion to convert or dismiss is a strategic decision that must be made based on the circumstances of the individual case. Such motions should not be undertaken lightly. Most judges are reluctant to convert or dismiss chapter 11 cases early on, absent a showing of extreme misconduct or complete inability to reorganize.[455] When possible, if there are major secured or unsecured creditors whose claims dwarf those of the affected consumers, their position should be solicited in advance of filing a motion. Judges are unlikely to convert or dismiss in the face of opposition to such a motion by the major creditors.

A motion to convert or dismiss is often useful when a case has been pending for a long time without movement toward a confirmable plan. At a minimum, the motion will wake up the debtor and/or the court in order to get the case moving. Alternatively, a motion to dismiss may be a good idea if the creditor can establish inequitable post-petition conduct by the debtor that suggests improper motives in the reorganization process. Often the same conduct that would give rise to a motion to appoint a trustee is also a proper basis for seeking conversion or dismissal under section 1112(b).[456]

Another ground for dismissal of a chapter 11 case is offered by the recent decision of Third Circuit Court of Appeals in *SGL Carbon Corp.*[457] When a solvent company files chapter 11 not to reorganize any debt, but simply to gain a tactical advantage in pending litigation, the bankruptcy may be dismissed on the basis that it was not filed in good faith. The Third Circuit distinguished other chapter 11 cases filed by companies facing mass tort liabilities, on the basis that SGL Carbon Corp. was not facing any prospect of crippling liabilities, or even major disruption to its operations, as a result of the threatened litigation.

17.7.11 Representing Employees and Other Industrial Stakeholders in Chapter 11 Proceedings

17.7.11.1 Introduction

As manufacturing companies face increased pressure to restructure themselves in order to remain competitive (that is, to maximize return on investment), many are turning to chapter 11 as a means of facilitating that restructuring. A chapter 11 filing enables a struggling company to shed less profitable operations and burdensome obligations. This not only affects the company's suppliers, customers, secondary lenders, tort claimants, and so forth, but it can be devastating to the livelihoods of its employees and the economic vitality of its local community. This subsection discusses some of the remedies available to a chapter 11 debtor's employees and community residents, with an emphasis on possible strategies for keeping the debtor's manufacturing facilities operable and for preserving employees' jobs and the local community's economic base.

17.7.11.2 Employee Priority Claims

Section 507(a) provides that certain pre-petition employee wage and benefit claims will be treated with priority. Section 507(a)(3) gives third priority to claims for wages, salaries or commissions earned within ninety days before either the petition filing date or the date of cessation of the debtor's business, whichever occurs first.[458] The maximum amount entitled to priority under this section is $4925.00.[459] This priority extends to vacation, severance and sick leave

---

452 11 U.S.C. § 1112(b)(3).

453 Singer Furniture Acquisition Corp. v. SSMC, Inc., 254 B.R. 46 (M.D. Fla. 2000) (Bilzerian bankruptcy dismissed based on evidence of bad faith including primary motivation of thwarting litigation by secured creditors in another jurisdiction); Quarles v. United States Trustee, 194 B.R. 94 (W.D. Va.), *aff'd*, 86 F.3d 55 (4th Cir. 1996); *In re* Boughton, 243 B.R. 830 (Bankr. M.D. Fla. 1999).

454 *See In re* Superior Siding & Window, Inc., 14 F.3d 240 (4th Cir. 1994) (choice should not be made solely by counting the votes of unsecured creditors).

455 *In re* Macon Prestressed Concrete Co., 61 B.R. 432 (Bankr. M.D. Ga. 1986) (reorganization is the preferred outcome whenever possible). However, when there is evidence that the debtor is using the bankruptcy process for an improper purpose, some courts have found that the case may be dismissed at the outset for lack of good faith. *In re* Albany Partners, Ltd., 749 F.2d 670 (11th Cir. 1984) (lack of good faith on filing is "cause" under § 1112(b)); *cf. In re* Madison Hotel Associates, 749 F.2d 410 (7th Cir. 1984) (good faith prerequisite to plan confirmation is different from good faith requirement on filing).

456 *See* § 17.7.4.3, *supra*.

457 *In re* SGL Carbon Corp., 200 F.3d 154 (3d Cir. 1999); *see also In re* Blumenberg, 263 B.R. 704 (Bankr. E.D. N.Y. 2001) (chapter 11 petition filed with no intention of reorganizing and

for sole purpose of attacking state court judgment was in bad faith and warranted dismissal of converted chapter 7 case); *cf. In re* Muralo Co., 301 B.R. 690 (Bankr. D.N.J. 2003) (refusing to dismiss as bad faith filing, court distinguished *SGL Carbon*).

458 Note that post-petition wages, and so forth, are entitled to administrative priority under 11 U.S.C. § 507(a)(1). *See* § 17.5.3, *supra*.

459 11 U.S.C. § 507(a)(3). The amount of the employee priority is adjusted for inflation every three years. 11 U.S.C. § 104(b). For cases filed between April 1, 2001 and March 31, 2004, the amount of the priority was $4650.00. *See generally In re* Myer, 197 B.R. 875 (Bankr. W.D. Mo. 1996) (priority applies to earned commissions, but not to damages for lost opportunity to

pay.[460] (Pre-petition "trust fund" taxes—that is, employer-withheld income taxes and the employee's share of social security taxes as well as the employer's share—are entitled to eighth priority under section 507(a)(8)).[461]

Some state laws provide for an automatic lien to secure unpaid wages in certain circumstances.[462] Where such a statutory lien has not been avoided under section 545,[463] the claim will be paid before distribution to unsecured priority creditors. Otherwise, any claim for wages earned outside the ninety day time period or in excess of the statutory amount is treated as unsecured, non-priority claim.

Section 507(a)(4) gives a fourth priority to claims for contributions to an employee benefit plan (for example, pension, health, or life insurance plans), arising from services rendered after one hundred and eighty (180) days before either the petition filing date or the date of cessation of the debtor's business, whichever occurs first.[464] The maximum amount allowed for *all claims under each benefit plan* is calculated according to the following formula: (1) multiply the total number of employees covered by the plan by $4925.00, (2) subtract any priority wage claims paid to those employees pursuant to section 507(a)(3), and (3) subtract any other priority benefit claims paid to those employees pursuant to section 507(a)(4).[465] Each claimant is entitled to a pro rata share of the total.

Employer contributions to a trust established for payment of employees' medical benefits are entitled to priority under section 507(a)(4),[466] as are premiums to privately administered employee group insurance plans.[467] There is a split of authority concerning workers' compensation premiums.[468]

An employee asserts priority by filing a proof of claim, and the claim is deemed allowed unless an objection is made and a hearing held.[469] Employees may want to consider filing a class proof of claim,[470] especially for benefit claims under section 507(a)(4).

17.7.11.3 Job Retention Strategies in Chapter 11 Proceedings

17.7.11.3.1 Introduction

When a major employer files for protection under chapter 11, employees and members of the local community will be primarily interested in the prospects for continued operation of the debtor's business. Even employees with wage and benefit claims will usually be more concerned with whether they will have a job to go back to than with whether their pre-petition claims will be fully paid. The job retention strategies available to employees and other interested parties in a chapter 11 proceeding will vary according to the circumstances of each case. A few possibilities will be discussed below.

17.7.11.3.2 Right to intervene

Section 1109(b) states that "[a] party in interest . . . may raise and may appear and may be heard on any issue in a case under this chapter."[471] Creditors, such as employees with wage or benefit claims, are specifically authorized under section 1109 to be heard.[472] A more difficult question is whether non-creditor employees, laid-off employees and representatives of the local community have a sufficient interest to justify intervention.

A party is a "party in interest" if it has a sufficient stake in the outcome of the proceeding to require representation.[473] Where there is a significant economic or similar interest in the outcome of a chapter 11 case, a party who is

earn commissions awarded in court case for breach of employment contract).

460 11 U.S.C. § 507(a)(3); *see In re* Crafts Precision Indus., Inc., 244 B.R. 178 (B.A.P. 1st Cir. 2000) (vacation pay is covered by 507(a)(3), but is not a contribution to an employee benefit plan covered by (a)(4)).

461 11 U.S.C. § 507(a)(8).

462 *See, e.g.,* Cal. Civ. Proc. Code §§ 1204–1208 (West).

463 *See In re* Edgar B, Inc., 200 B.R. 119 (M.D.N.C. 1996) (limit in priority is on the aggregate dollar claim for all employees to the plan; there is no $4000.00 limit for individual employees); *In re* C & S Cartage and Leasing Co., 204 B.R. 565 (Bankr. D. Neb. 1996) (because limit on priority is an aggregate for all employees, individual claim is not barred solely because the individual had already received a priority claim to the extent of $4000.00 for unpaid wages); § 10.4.2.6.3, *supra*.

464 As with wage claims, the entire amount of post-petition benefit claims is entitled to administrative priority under 11 U.S.C. § 507(a)(2). *See* § 17.5.3, *supra*.

465 11 U.S.C. § 507(a)(4).

466 *In re* Structurelite Plastics Corp., 86 B.R. 922 (Bankr. S.D. Ohio 1988).

467 *In re* Saco Local Dev. Corp., 711 F.2d 441 (1st Cir. 1983).

468 *Compare* Employers Ins. of Wausau v. Plaid Pantries, Inc., 10 F.3d 605 (9th Cir. 1993) (workers compensation premium claims entitled to priority) *with In re* Birmingham-Nashville Express, Inc, 224 F.3d 511 (6th Cir. 2000); *In re* HLM Corp., 62 F.3d 224 (8th Cir. 1995) (contra); *In re* S. Star Foods, 144 F.3d 712 (10th Cir. 1998); *In re* Allentown Moving and Storage, 208

B.R. 835 (Bankr. E.D. Pa.), *aff'd*, 214 B.R. 761 (E.D. Pa. 1997). The latter courts have found that these premiums are typically paid to state insurance funds rather than to plans which benefit employees directly so that they are not contributions to an employee benefit plan.

469 *See* § 17.5.5, *supra*.

470 *See* § 17.4.2, *supra*; *see also In re* Birting Fisheries, Inc., 178 B.R. 849 (W.D. Wash. 1995), *aff'd* 92 F.3d 939 (9th Cir. 1996).

471 11 U.S.C. § 1109(b). Note that this section provides the right to be heard in a bankruptcy "case." Whether a party is entitled to intervene in an adversary proceeding is governed by Fed. R. Civ. P. 24, made applicable to bankruptcy proceedings by Fed. R. Bankr. P. 7024. Presumably, the right to be heard pursuant to section 1109(b) is more expansive than the right to intervene under Rule 24.

472 Labor unions and other employee associations also have limited authorization to be heard on the economic soundness of a reorganization plan under Fed. R. Bankr. P. 2018(d).

473 *In re* Kaiser Steel Corp., 998 F.2d 783 (10th Cir. 1993); *In re* Amatex Corp., 755 F.2d 1034 (3d Cir. 1985).

neither a creditor nor a shareholder will be allowed to intervene.[474] The term "party in interest" should be interpreted in light of the legislative history and purposes of the Bankruptcy Code.[475] The legislative history of chapter 11 indicates that Congress sought to encourage greater participation in reorganization cases.[476] Section 1109(b) should be construed liberally so as to effectuate that purpose.[477]

Current and former employees have a clear economic interest in the survival of their employer's business: Their livelihood is at stake. The local community has a similar interest: The local economy suffers through the loss of payroll and a "ripple effect" job loss. As local tax revenues decrease, schools deteriorate, public services are reduced, and residential taxes may increase. Social problems—alcoholism and drug use, divorce, domestic violence, mental health problems—all increase as a result of a large plant shutdown.[478] There is a strong argument that the economic impact of a plant shutdown on the surrounding community creates a sufficient economic interest to allow a representative group of individuals to intervene on behalf of the community at large.

17.7.11.3.3 Opposing a chapter 11 liquidation

Occasionally, the debtor and its major secured creditors will seek court permission to sell assets in order to satisfy secured claims. A sale of all or substantially all of a debtor's assets is known as a liquidating chapter 11. As a business may be worth considerably more as a going concern than in a piecemeal liquidation, holders of junior secured claims, priority claims (such as wages, benefits, and local tax obligations), and unsecured claims may be disadvantaged.[479]

Moreover, the sale of even some of a business' assets may have an adverse effect on the likelihood of a successful reorganization, and therefore threaten the number and quality of jobs that will be retained.

Other than in the ordinary course of business, the chapter 11 debtor in possession may sell property of the estate only after notice and a hearing.[480] If no interested party files a timely objection to a notice of sale, court approval is not required.[481] Such an objection must be filed at least five days prior to any scheduled sale.[482] In ruling on a proposed sale, the court must consider the effect of the property's disposition on future plans of reorganization.[483] Property of the estate should not be sold if it is necessary to an effective reorganization.[484]

The pre-confirmation sale of all or substantially all of a debtor's assets is disfavored. The basic policy behind chapter 11 is that it is generally preferable to allow a business to continue to operate than to liquidate its assets.[485] Only if revival of the business is impossible should liquidation proceed and only then does maximum recovery for creditors become of primary importance.[486] Moreover, such sales potentially circumvent the disclosure and voting requirements that are the very essence of the chapter 11 scheme.[487]

The general rule is that the pre-confirmation sale of all or substantially all of a debtor's assets can take place only when there is a "sound business reason."[488] Implicit in this standard are the following factors: (1) the proportionate value of the asset to the estate as a whole, (2) the amount of time that has elapsed since filing, (3) the likelihood that a plan will be proposed and confirmed in the near future, (4) the effect of the proposed sale on future reorganization, (5) the adequacy of the sale price, (6) whether a sale or lease is proposed, and (7) most importantly, whether the asset is increasing or decreasing in value.[489] Other courts have also required that there be adequate and reasonable notice of the sale and that the sale be conducted in good faith.[490] In no case should a sale be confirmed merely to appease major creditors.[491]

---

474 *In re* Amatex Corp., 755 F.2d 1034 (3d Cir. 1985) (future tort claimants allowed to intervene in order to preserve estate for payment of future claims); *In re* Brown Transp., 118 B.R. 889 (Bankr. N.D. Ga. 1990) (third party allowed to intervene in order to challenge transfer of estate property to competitor); *In re* Hathaway Ranch P'ship, 116 B.R. 208 (Bankr. C.D. Cal. 1990) (debtor's limited partner allowed to intervene); *In re* Wilson, 94 B.R. 886 (Bankr. E.D. Va. 1989) (defendant in civil suit brought by trustee may intervene to challenge abandonment of suit).

475 *In re* Ionosphere Clubs, Inc., 101 B.R. 844 (Bankr. S.D.N.Y. 1989); *see also In re* Ctr. Apartments, Ltd., 277 B.R. 747 (Bankr. S.D. Ohio 2001) (tenants not authorized to serve on creditor's committee nevertheless have right under § 1109(b) to be heard on objection to sale of property and other issues that arise).

476 *In re* Amatex Corp., 755 F.2d 1034 (3d Cir. 1985).

477 *Id.* The right to intervene in a "case" as provided for under § 1109(b) has been construed to include intervention in adversary proceedings. *See In re* Caldor Corp., 303 F.3d 161 (2d Cir. 2002) (section 1109(b) confers on parties in interest an unconditional right to intervene in adversary proceedings).

478 For a modest fee, the Midwest Center for Labor Research (Chicago: (773) 278-5418) can prepare a social costs assessment that will estimate the anticipated monetary cost of a particular plant shutdown on the local community.

479 Anderson & Wright, *Liquidating Plans of Reorganization*, 56 Am. Bankr. L.J. 29 (1982).

480 11 U.S.C. § 363(b).

481 11 U.S.C. § 363(b).

482 Fed. R. Bankr. P. 6004(b).

483 *In re* Lionel Corp., 722 F.2d 1063 (2d Cir. 1983).

484 The standards for relief from automatic stay should be analogous. *See* § 9.7.3.2.3, *supra.*

485 7 Collier on Bankruptcy ¶ 1100.01 (15th ed. rev.).

486 Anderson, Chapter 11 Reorganizations § 1.01, at 1-1, 1-2; Anderson & Wright, *Liquidating Plans of Reorganization*, 56 Am. Bankr. L.J. 29 (1982).

487 *See In re* Braniff Airways, Inc., 700 F.2d 935 (5th Cir. 1985); *In re* Air Beds, Inc., 92 B.R. 419 (B.A.P. 9th Cir. 1988).

488 *In re* Lionel Corp., 722 F.2d 1063 (2d Cir. 1983).

489 *Id.*

490 *In re* Titusville Country Club, 128 B.R. 396 (Bankr. W.D. Pa. 1991).

491 *In re* Lionel Corp., 722 F.2d 1063 (2d Cir. 1983).

17.7.11.3.4 Placing conditions upon approval of a sale of the debtor's business

A court of equity may grant or deny relief upon performance of a condition that will safeguard the public interest.[492] If an interested party files an objection, a sale of the debtor's business requires court approval under section 363(b). This is certainly true of pre-confirmation sales and of auctions held pursuant to a confirmed plan. It is questionable whether a court has discretion to impose conditions upon a sale to a specific purchaser pursuant to a reorganization plan that otherwise meets the requirements for confirmation under section 1129.[493] It could be argued that any such purchaser may only be approved in accordance with public policy considerations under section 1123(a)(7). In any case, whenever a sale of a chapter 11 debtor's business is proposed, interested parties should seek to intervene and ask the court to impose conditions upon that sale in order to safeguard the public interest. One such condition might be a requirement that the property be sold to an entity that intends to keep the business in operation.[494]

In a chapter 11 proceeding, property of the estate need not be sold to the highest bidder.[495] A court may accept a lower bid for a debtor's business, if the higher bidder indicates it would shut the business down. With appropriate proof, the court may consider other issues beyond the money involved.

17.7.11.3.5 Other job retention strategies

In addition to those outlined above, other strategies may be available depending upon the circumstances of a particular case. For instance, if the debtor-in-possession is not operating the business in a sound manner, employees or other interested parties may wish to file a motion to appoint a trustee or examiner.[496] If the debtor has not filed a reorganization plan, it may be possible to file a creditor's plan.[497] Finally, it may be possible for the employees and/or local community to obtain financing to purchase the debtor's business.[498]

17.7.12 Small Business Reorganization Under Chapter 11

In 1994, Congress enacted provisions that are theoretically designed to expedite reorganizations of small businesses. The definition of "small business" precludes use of these provisions by companies primarily engaged in operating real property, or by companies with total non-contingent liquidated debts in excess of two million dollars.[499]

The choice to be treated as a small business must be made by the debtor.[500] There is a sixty-day time frame, that commences upon filing, for making the election.[501] Creditors may argue that small business treatment is improper if the debtor does not meet the Code's definition.[502]

In a chapter 11 case where a debtor elects to be treated as a small business, a party may request that the court order that a creditors' committee not be appointed.[503] This may help the estate save money.

In those cases in which the debtor does elect treatment as a small business, creditors should be aware of more expedited deadlines and procedures. A debtor that elects to be treated as a small business has an exclusivity period of one-hundred days after the order for relief during which only the debtor may file a plan; competing plans must be filed within 160 days.[504] In addition, the court may approve a conditional disclosure statement that can be used to solicit acceptances and rejections, and the court may conduct a combined hearing on the disclosure statement and confirmation of the plan.[505]

17.8 Special Problems of Tenants

17.8.1 General

As the real estate market declines in various parts of the country, owners of private housing[506] occupied by low-income tenants may file bankruptcy. Often, tenants receive no official notice. They may come to their lawyer to complain that the building is no longer receiving services such

---

492 Am. United Mut. Life Ins. Co. v. City of Avon Park, 311 U.S. 138, 61 S. Ct. 157, 85 L. Ed. 91 (1940). Bankruptcy courts are courts of equity, and their proceedings are proceedings in equity. Pepper v. Litton, 308 U.S. 295, 60 S. Ct. 238, 84 L. Ed. 281 (1939).

493 *See* § 17.7.8, *supra.*

494 A creditor whose claim is impaired may also be able to obtain commitments from the debtor in exchange for voting to approve the plan.

495 *In re* Karpe, 84 B.R. 926 (Bankr. M.D. Pa. 1988); *see also* 3 Collier on Bankruptcy ¶ 363.02(1)(g) (15th ed. rev.).

496 *See* § 17.7.4, *supra.*

497 *See* § 17.7.9, *supra.*

498 *See, e.g.,* § 17.8.3, *infra.*

499 11 U.S.C. § 101(51C).

500 11 U.S.C. § 1121(e).

501 Fed. R. Bankr. P. 1020.

502 Cases discussing the chapter 13 debt limits would be relevant. *See* § 12.2.3, *supra.*

503 11 U.S.C. § 1102(a)(3).

504 11 U.S.C. § 1121(e); *see In re* Win Trucking, Inc., 236 B.R. 774 (Bankr. D. Utah 1999) (late filed plan precludes confirmation). *See generally In re* Aspen Limousine Serv., 187 B.R. 989 (Bankr. D. Colo. 1995) (discussion of expediting time periods under small business provisions).

505 11 U.S.C. § 1125(f).

506 Where the building has been constructed with the aid of federal or state programs which earmark some or all units for low or moderate income tenants, tenants may have other rights beyond those discussed in this subsection.

as utilities, trash pick-up and repairs and also to report that no one is collecting the rent. A call to the landlord or the landlord's attorney reveals that the landlord has filed a petition in bankruptcy. This subsection discusses steps to be taken by the tenants' lawyer to protect tenants' rights, with an emphasis on assuring the continuation of needed services.

17.8.2 Maintaining Services When Private Landlords File Chapter 7 Bankruptcy

17.8.2.1 Abandonment by a Chapter 7 Trustee

When the owner believes the building is no longer financially viable, a chapter 7 bankruptcy may be filed.[507] If title to the building is in a corporation or other legal entity which the owner believes insulates him or her from personal liability, the bankruptcy will be in the name of the entity holding title and that entity will the "debtor" in the bankruptcy proceeding. A landlord holding property in her own name may also file under chapter 7, although this will expose all of the landlord's assets to the bankruptcy process and not just the real estate holdings.

Upon the filing of the bankruptcy petition, the property of the debtor, with some inconsequential exceptions, becomes the property of the bankruptcy estate.[508] In theory, the chapter 7 trustee takes over management of the assets of the estate and liquidates them for the benefit of the unsecured creditors.[509] In practice, in a typical apartment building bankruptcy, the only assets of the entity filing bankruptcy will be the building and the land on which it is situated. The real estate will frequently be mortgaged well beyond its value so there is no equity remaining for the unsecured creditors.

Section 554 of the Bankruptcy Code[510] permits the trustee to "abandon" property that is burdensome to the estate or is of inconsequential value and benefit to the estate. Because the building will usually have no equity from which the estate will benefit upon foreclosure and because the rents will be insufficient to meet the mortgage payments and other expenses, the trustee is likely to conclude that the building meets the statutory tests for abandonment.

In theory, abandonment means turning the property back to the debtor.[511] In an apartment building bankruptcy, as a practical matter, abandonment means relieving the trustee of any obligation and clearing the way for the secured lenders to foreclose.

The filing of the chapter 7 bankruptcy is likely to have been an act of desperation on the part of the landlord, brought on by a final realization that the building or buildings are not economically viable, by the threat or actuality of litigation from the tenants, or by all of these factors. As a result, upon filing, the owner may make no arrangement for the continuation of utility or other services or for the management of the building. If the building has low-income tenants, is in bad condition and perhaps is already the subject of dispute between the tenant and the landlord, the trustee's instinct will be to have nothing to do with it.[512] She may immediately file a motion for abandonment and in any event may do nothing about providing services.

Abandonment by the trustee has the potential for leaving the tenants in legal limbo. The foreclosing creditors may do nothing until they have completed state foreclosure proceedings which, depending on state practice, may take from several weeks to several months. The creditors may believe they have no legal right to manage the building prior to the foreclosure, or may wish to avoid responsibility for building maintenance and housing code compliance. The debtor in theory remains responsible until the foreclosure but, by filing bankruptcy, the debtor has renounced any intention of continuing management and will have no interest or incentive to continue. Further, continued involvement by the debtor may be the last thing the tenants want.

17.8.2.2 Legal Theories to Prevent Abandonment

The tenants' attorney has some tools to protect the tenants' interests in this situation. In *Midlantic National Bank v. New Jersey Department of Environmental Protection*,[513] the United States Supreme Court held that a trustee could not abandon property even though it was burdensome to the estate where abandonment would be "in contravention of a state statute or regulation that is reasonably designed to protect the public health or safety from identified haz-

---

507　For a general discussion of chapter 7 bankruptcy see Chapter 3, *supra*.

508　11 U.S.C. § 541.

509　11 U.S.C. § 704.

510　11 U.S.C. § 554.

511　*See, e.g., In re* Franklin Signal Corp., 65 B.R. 268 (D. Minn. 1986) (effect of abandonment is that ownership and control of the asset is reinstated in the debtor with all rights and obligations as before filing a petition in bankruptcy); *In re* Cruseturner, 8 B.R. 581, 591, 592 (Bankr. D. Utah 1981).

512　Among other things, in a deteriorating situation, the trustee may be concerned about personal legal liability as well as the liability of the estate. Although the trustee is generally not personally liable for actions taken in an official capacity, some exposure to liability exists. *See, e.g.,* Yadkin Valley Bank & Trust Co. v. McGee, 819 F.2d 74 (4th Cir. 1987) (trustee may be individually liable for negligence if actions are outside the bounds of the trustee authority and liable within his official capacity when actions are willfully and deliberately in violation of his duties); *In re* Rigden, 795 F.2d 727 (9th Cir. 1986) (trustee liable for negligent violations of duties imposed upon him by law). The expense for short-term liability and other insurance for the building involved may be prohibitive. One possibility is to have the lender cover the building and the trustee under its insurance coverage.

513　474 U.S. 494, 106 S. Ct. 755, 88 L. Ed. 2d 859 (1986).

ards."[514] In a footnote the court added that the violation could not be speculative or indeterminate but must involve "imminent and identifiable harm."[515]

Courts have looked at two factors in evaluating claims under the *Midlantic* doctrine. First, the opposing party must establish that the danger resulting from abandonment is imminent[516] and in violation of law.[517] Second, some courts have stressed there must be resources available to the trustee to alleviate the danger.[518] Where these two factors can be shown, courts will not permit the trustee to abandon the property.[519]

While the *Midlantic* case involved the ownership of a dump containing toxic materials and most of the cases following *Midlantic* have involved some sort of environmental hazard, nothing in the language of the case limits its holding to such hazards. In an unreported West Virginia case,[520] for example, a legal services attorney, arguing on the basis of *Midlantic* and section 959, discussed below, obtained an order requiring the trustee to accept payments from the tenants and Section 8 payments from the public housing authority[521] to restore utility service and to continue to manage the property until such time as the secured party presented an acceptable plan for taking over the management.

Related to the *Midlantic* doctrine are the trustee's obligations under 28 U.S.C. § 959(b):

> [A] trustee, . . . appointed . . . in any court of the United States, . . . shall manage and operate the property in his possession . . . according to the requirements of the valid laws of the State in which such property is situated, in the same manner that the owner or possessor thereof would be bound to do if in possession thereof.

While the Supreme Court in *Midlantic* suggested that section 959(b) might not apply in liquidation, that is, chapter 7 cases, it nevertheless based its decision in part on the policy of section 959(b) that the trustee is bound by local law.[522] In the West Virginia case,[523] the court used section 959(b) as the basis for its authority to order the chapter 7 trustee to manage the building and provide services.

17.8.2.3 Loss of Services Without Abandonment

Where the trustee has not abandoned the property, she may nevertheless not supply needed service. This situation arose in *Saravia v. 1736 18th Street, N.W. Ltd. Partnership*.[524] *Saravia* involved a chapter 11 case in which the debtor in possession,[525] having rejected the tenant leases under section 365(a) of the Bankruptcy Code,[526] attempted to cut off municipal services arguing that because the leases were voided, there was no obligation to provide the services required under the lease. The District of Columbia Circuit flatly rejected the debtor's argument. The court ruled that so long as the District of Columbia, where the housing was located, required the provision of heat and other utility services to tenants under its housing regulations, then, especially in light of the Supreme Court's discussion of section 959(b) in the *Midlantic* case, section 959(b) required the debtor in possession, as trustee, to comply with the District of Columbia housing regulations and provide the required

---

514 *Id.*, 474 U.S. at 507.

515 *Id.*, 474 U.S. at n.9.

516 *In re* Vel Rey Properties, 174 B.R. 859 (Bankr. D.D.C. 1994) (trustee could abandon apartment building because public danger from housing code violations was not imminent); *In re* Smith-Douglass, Inc., 856 F.2d 12 (4th Cir. 1988) (allowing abandonment of fertilizer plant despite presence of environmental violations because the danger was not "imminent"); *In re* Armstrong, 96 B.R. 55 (Bankr. E.D.N.C. 1989) (upon finding of imminent danger, abandonment only permitted conditional upon the debtor setting aside $250,000.00 for the clean up); *In re* Purco, 76 B.R. 523 (Bankr. W.D. Pa. 1987) (court adopts a clear and imminent danger test and finds such danger not present); *In re* Franklin Signal Corp., 65 B.R. 268 (Bankr. D. Minn. 1986) (abandonment of contaminated property permitted because, among other reasons, the danger was not immediate); *In re* Okla. Ref. Co., 63 B.R. 562 (Bankr. W.D. Okla. 1986) (same).

517 *See, e.g., In re* Brio Ref., Inc., 86 B.R. 487 (N.D. Tex. 1988) (upholding abandonment because no known violation of law at the time of abandonment).

518 *See, e.g., In re* Franklin Signal Corp., 65 B.R. 268 (Bankr. D. Minn. 1986) (abandonment of contaminated property permitted because among other reasons trustee had no funds for clean-up); *In re* Okla. Ref. Co., 63 B.R. 562 (Bankr. W.D. Okla. 1986) (abandonment of contaminated property permitted in part because estate had no funds for clean up); *In re* A & T Trailer Park, Inc., 53 B.R. 144 (Bankr. D. Wyo. 1985) (trustee permitted to abandon trailer park not in compliance with environmental laws where estate had no assets to pay for needed expenses); *cf. In re* Smith-Douglass, Inc., 856 F.2d 12 (4th Cir. 1988) (court in dicta disagrees with lower court holding that resources of the estate are irrelevant in determining propriety of abandonment under *Midlantic*).

519 *See, e.g., In re* Stevens, 68 B.R. 774 (D. Me. 1987) (chapter 7 trustee could not abandon drums of contaminated oil, cleanup expenses are priority administrative expenses); *In re* Peerless Plating Co., 70 B.R. 943 (Bankr. W.D. Mich. 1987) (chapter 7 trustee could not abandon metal plating shop over objections of EPA). *But see In re* Vel Rey Properties, 174 B.R. 859 (Bankr. D.D.C. 1994) (trustee not permitted to operate apartment building without compliance with building code in order to maximize return to creditors, but could abandon the property because public danger from the housing code violations was not imminent); *cf. In re* Armstrong, 96 B.R. 55 (Bankr. E.D.N.C. 1989) (debtor in possession in chapter 11 could abandon polluted property only if $250,000.00 set aside for cleanup).

520 Hemetek v. Standish (*In re* Bush), Clearinghouse No. 44,839 (Bankr. S.D. W. Va. 1990).

521 *See* § 17.8.2.4, *infra*.

522 Midlantic Nat'l Bank v. N.J. Dep't of Envtl. Prot., 474 U.S. 494, 505, 106 S. Ct. 755, 761, 762, 88 L. Ed. 2d 859, 868 (1986).

523 *See* Hemetek v. Standish (*In re* Bush), Clearinghouse No. 44,839 (Bankr. S.D. W. Va. 1990).

524 844 F.2d 823 (D.C. Cir. 1988).

525 *See* § 17.7.4.1, *supra*.

526 11 U.S.C. § 365(a).

services. While the trustee in a chapter 7 is unlikely to reject tenant leases,[527] the *Saravia* case is an important precedent illustrating that the principles of *Midlantic* may apply to tenants' rights in housing.[528]

Another useful case in states that allow a debtor to recoup money expended to cure a landlord's default on an obligation to repair and maintain the premises is *In re Flagstaff Realty Trust*.[529] In *Flagstaff*, the Third Circuit concluded that a tenant that had performed pre-petition repairs could recoup any amounts expended from rent even after the debtor filed bankruptcy and rejected the lease. A similar outcome should be possible under 11 U.S.C. § 365(h) for post-petition expenditures for which recoupment is allowed under state law. It may also be possible to work with local government regulatory authorities to enforce building and fire codes. Such enforcement of police and regulatory powers is not stayed by the bankruptcy case.[530]

17.8.2.4 Steps to Take

The clients' immediate concern will be to assure themselves of services to the building. Ordinarily, in a chapter 7 case where the building has been privately developed, there is no reason to oppose foreclosure and sale.[531] The major concern will be to assure that services continue in any interim period and perhaps to assist in the smooth transfer of ownership.

When the tenants' attorney finds that the landlord has filed a chapter 7 bankruptcy petition and services are not being provided, the first thing to do is to call the trustee and discuss the situation.[532] The trustee may well be unaware of what has happened and be willing to cooperate.

The trustee, however, is unlikely to regard the opportunity to manage a building of low-income tenants as a bonanza. The tenants' attorney should stress that the tenants are only asking for assistance in the interim period between the filing and the expected foreclosure on the property and, if it is the case, that they will have no objection to relief from the stay to permit foreclosure.[533]

If the trustee does cooperate, the tenants' attorney may be in the unfamiliar, but nevertheless vital, position of assisting in collecting the rent so that the resources are available to maintain services. The attorney may be able to guide the trustee through the intricacies of Section 8 vouchers and certificates,[534] and LIHEAP[535] payments with which the trustee is unlikely to be familiar. The attorney should also assure her clients and other tenants that it is appropriate to pay their rent to the trustee or the trustee's property manager or designee.

The tenants' attorney should also quickly contact the lender holding the senior security. Like the trustee, the lender's first instincts will not be to join in a quest to provide services to this troubled property. The lender will by now have realized its loan is in trouble and that it is unlikely to recover its money at the foreclosure sale. It will likely consider substantial involvement to be throwing good money after bad and to be exposing itself to needless liability.[536]

---

527 See the discussion of rejection of leases in § 17.8.4, *infra*.

528 *But see In re* Vel Rey Properties, 174 B.R. 859 (Bankr. D.D.C. 1994) (trustee not permitted to operate apartment building without compliance with building code in order to maximize return to creditors, but could abandon the property because public danger from the housing code violations was not imminent).

529 60 F.3d 1031 (3d Cir. 1995).

530 11 U.S.C. § 362(b)(4), (5); *see In re* 1820–1838 Amsterdam Equities, Inc., 191 B.R. 18 (S.D.N.Y. 1996) (bankruptcy court could not interfere with code enforcement by city against debtor's property).

531 If the building has been developed with the aid of federal or state programs which require making some or all units available to low-income tenants, other issues may arise about the status of the subsidy agreements. The tenants may wish to take advantage of the opportunity to gain site control in order to implement a tenant ownership plan, with help from the local community development agency. In such cases, tactics may differ.

532 The trustee in a chapter 7 is more akin to a party in a lawsuit than a court official, so advocates need not be concerned about the propriety of *ex parte* communications.

533 While it will normally be in the tenants' interest to move the foreclosure proceedings along as fast as possible, if there is a possibility that the tenants themselves or a nonprofit community development group might be interested in purchasing the building, tenants may then wish to delay while the feasibility of other ownership is explored.

534 Under Section 8 of the Housing Act of 1937, 42 U.S.C. § 1437f, and the implementing regulations, 24 C.F.R. pt. 800, Section 8 eligible low-income tenants receive rent subsidies. These payments are issued by the local housing authority and paid directly to the landlord so that the landlord receives two checks, one from the tenant and the other from the housing authority. The trustee will have to arrange to be named payee by the housing authority in place of the landlord. For a detailed explanation of the Section 8 program, see National Housing Law Project, HUD Housing Programs: Tenants' Rights (1981 and 1985 Supp.).

535 Under the federal Low Income Home Energy Assistance Program (LIHEAP) agencies administering the program in some states may arrange direct payment of energy assistance benefits to landlords, where heat or electric services are included as part of the rent. *See* 42 U.S.C. § 8624(b)(7). Where landlords are receiving LIHEAP payments directly, the trustee will have to arrange to receive the payments in place of the landlord. For an explanation of the LIHEAP program, see National Consumer Law Center, Access to Utility Service Ch. 7 (2d ed. 2001 and Supp.).

536 As discussed earlier in this Chapter, a secured creditor in some cases may be forced to pay expenses which maintain the value of its security. The trustee might therefore pay for necessary upkeep and force payment of these costs from the secured creditor. *See* § 17.5.3, *supra*. This can provide some leverage to force the secured creditor to participate in reasonably maintaining the property. In addition, state law theories for holding a secured lender responsible may apply. For example, in many states a mortgagee which has constructive possession of a property or which has exercised substantial control over property is potentially liable to tenants. *See, e.g.,* McCorristin v.

Nevertheless, it may be possible to convince the lender that it is in its interest to assist the tenants. If the building is in danger of deterioration because tenants are likely to start moving out, or in danger of vandalism from inadequate security, the value of the building will almost certainly decrease if nothing is done. Keeping the building maintained and fully occupied, the tenants' attorney should argue, will help the lenders as much as the tenants.

If the lender does express some interest, the tenants' attorney should try to get the lender talking to the trustee quickly. Among other things, the lender could arrange for building management, cover the trustee under its liability policy, and post any deposits that might be required to restore utility service or make any needed emergency repairs. Even if no cooperation is anticipated from the lender, it will be helpful at subsequent hearings to know what the lender's approach is going to be.

If the trustee will not cooperate, or has filed and will not withdraw a motion for abandonment, then the tenants must seek relief from the bankruptcy court. While most of the issues could be raised in opposition to a motion for abandonment, the tenants will be in a stronger and clearer position by not only opposing the abandonment, but also asking for affirmative relief in the form of an order enjoining the trustee from failing to provide the needed services. Because the request will be for equitable relief, the tenants must file an adversary proceeding.[537] Where services have already been cut off, tenants may need to ask for a temporary restraining order or for a preliminary injunction.[538]

In preparing for the hearing, it will probably be useful to have the appropriate local health or safety agency inspect the building. That authority should be prepared to testify that no heat or electricity is available and that their absence violates local ordinances or state statutes and poses an imminent threat to health and safety. While most judges would probably be willing to take judicial notice that absence of heat and light is a threat to safety, the inspector's testimony about what building or health codes are being violated will satisfy the *Midlantic* violation of law requirement.

In addition to proving imminent danger, tenants may also have to prove that the resources are available for the trustee to remedy the situation. Tenants should testify about willingness to pay rent. If possible, statements from the local housing authority, the public assistance agency and the local energy assistance agency about the availability of Section 8 payments, public assistance payments and LIHEAP pay-

ments, respectively, should be presented.[539] If the trustee has expressed a reluctance to become involved in the management, it will also be helpful to obtain a statement from a commercial or nonprofit management group expressing a willingness to manage the property and an analysis that the cash flow from the building will be sufficient to provide services and remedy violations.

It is important that the imminent danger part of the tenant's case not prove too much. Testimony that the building is falling down and needs major structural repairs could potentially be harmful because the trustee is then likely to argue that the resources are not available to manage the building.[540]

The judge and the trustee will probably both be wary of any long-term involvement by the trustee. If that is the case, at the hearing the tenants' attorney should stress that the tenants have no objection to the lenders obtaining relief from the stay for the purpose of the foreclosure, and that the tenants are only seeking to assure an orderly transition to new ownership.

Given the relatively informal nature of bankruptcy hearings and the request for equitable relief, the tenants' attorney should be prepared to enter into discussions to fashion some agreement among the tenants, the trustee and the lender.[541] For example, if management of the building is an issue, the tenants might locate a community housing group that would be willing to be hired by the trustee as an interim manager.

If the judge does not grant the relief the tenants seek, the tenants may appeal the decision to the district court or the bankruptcy appellate panel.[542] Before appealing, consider the other alternative of proceeding in state court. For example, if there is a possibility of having a sympathetic state housing court appoint a receiver for the building, that may be better than having the district court judge force an unwilling bankruptcy court judge and trustee to oversee the building. If the decision is to proceed in state court, the tenants should seek an order from the bankruptcy court granting the tenants relief from the automatic stay[543] for that purpose. Even though the building has been abandoned, it is probably still subject to the automatic stay.[544]

Salmon Signs, 582 A.2d 1271 (N.J. Super. Ct. App. Div. 1990) (mortgagee in possession steps into shoes of landlord); Thornhill v. Ronnie's I-45 Truck Stop, Inc., 944 S.W.2d 780 (Tex. App. 1997) (secured lender exercising control over property held responsible for injuries due to fire at premises).

537 For an example, see Hemetek v. Standish (*In re* Bush), Clearinghouse No. 44,839A (Bankr. S.D. W. Va. 1990).

538 *Id.*

539 See discussion above.

540 *See* § 17.8.2.1, *supra.*

541 See, for example, the order in the *Hemetek* case discussed in § 17.8.2.2, *supra,* and *In re* Armstrong, 96 B.R. 55 (Bankr. E.D.N.C. 1989) (abandonment only permitted conditional upon the debtor setting aside $250,000.00 for clean up of hazard).

542 See § 13.10, *supra,* for an explanation of appeals from the bankruptcy court.

543 11 U.S.C. § 362; *see* Ch. 9, § 17.3, *supra.*

544 H.R. Rep. No. 95-595, at 343 (1977), *reprinted in* 1978 U.S.C.C.A.N. 5787, 6299 (property no longer in the estate still subject to the stay if it goes to the debtor); *In re* Cruseturner, 8 B.R. 581 (Bankr. D. Utah 1981) (same).

17.8.2.5 Forcing Abandonment to the Lender

Where there is only one lien holder, another tactic may be to have the court order the property abandoned directly to the lender. Such an order may immediately transfer title to the lender, making the lender responsible for applicable health and safety codes.

Under section 554, the court has authority to order that abandonment be to a party other than the debtor.[545] Tenants could propose abandonment to the lender as an alternative resolution when objecting to the trustee's motion to abandon. Tenants as parties in interest may also bring their own motion for abandonment to the lender.[546] Abandonment to the lender could be proposed as alternative relief to forcing administration of the building by the trustee as discussed in previous subsections. Requesting alternative relief will make it clear to the court that the tenants only interest is assuring that there is a responsible party to manage the building.

The lender may argue that while it may wish to foreclose, it should not be forced to take title to the property. In many cases, the owner will have been in default on the building for many months or even years. Tenants should point out to the court that the lender had ample opportunity to foreclose.

17.8.2.6 Maintaining Services in the Event the Property Has Been Abandoned

Even if the trustee has abandoned the property, there are steps the tenants can take to maintain services. These include forcing the debtor to continue to maintain the property, forming a tenant association to collect voluntary rent and to assume direct responsibility for services, and petitioning to have the property placed under receivership pursuant to state law.

The filing of a bankruptcy petition does not absolve a debtor from the responsibility to maintain rental property on an ongoing basis. The trustee may deem the property abandoned at the end of the case under section 554(c) in which case it reverts to the debtor, unless the court orders otherwise. Once in possession of the abandoned property, the debtor must comply with applicable state laws regarding the use of that property.[547] Even though the debtor may have rejected the lease agreements,[548] if non-bankruptcy requirements for their termination have not been met, a landlord-tenant relationship still exists.[549] The debtor's bankruptcy filing should therefore have no effect on the tenants' ability to use the remedies normally available to them under state law to compel their landlord to maintain services.[550]

If the debtor has rejected the lease agreements, the tenants may also assume management of the rental property themselves, at least until foreclosure. Once the property has been abandoned, there is nothing to prevent the tenants from forming their own association, collecting voluntary rent, and contracting with utility companies for continued services.[551] Many states have laws that prevent utilities from terminating service to rental property without first giving tenants notice and an opportunity to avoid termination by assuming payments.[552]

Finally, the tenants can file a petition in state court to have the rental property placed in receivership. At a minimum, a receiver would collect rent and maintain necessary services to the property. In some states, tenants are given specific statutory authority to petition for receivership.[553] Even in the absence of statutory authority, however, a court in equity can order receivership. For instance, tenants who seek to enjoin their landlord from maintaining rental property in an uninhabitable condition, and who can demonstrate that their landlord is prospectively unable or unwilling to comply with such an injunction, can request that the court appoint a receiver for the property so that compliance is assured. As receivership is an act against the property, rather than the debtor, there is probably no need to seek relief from the automatic stay before pursuing this remedy after the property has been abandoned and is no longer property of the estate.[554]

---

545 11 U.S.C. § 554(c); *see* Dominion Bank of Cumberlands v. Nuckolls, 71 B.R. 593 (W.D. Va. 1987) (after hearing property could be abandoned to creditor); *In re* Maropa Marine Sales Serv. & Storage, Inc., 92 B.R. 547 (Bankr. S.D. Fla. 1988) (property should be abandoned to under-secured creditor, not sold at auction by trustee); *In re* Ware, 59 B.R. 549 (Bankr. N.D. Ohio 1986) (property abandoned to secured creditor); H.R. Rep. No. 95-595, at 377 (1977); Sen. Rep. No. 95-989, at 92 (1978) ("Abandonment may be to any party with a possessory interest in the property abandoned."), *cited with approval in* Ohio v. Kovacs, 469 U.S. 274, 284 n.12, 105 S. Ct. 705, 83 L. Ed. 2d 649, 659 (1985). *But see In re* Manchester Heights Associates, Ltd. P'ship, 165 B.R. 42 (Bankr. W.D. Mo. 1994); *In re* Caron, 50 B.R. 27 (Bankr. N.D. Ga. 1984) ("the procedures of § 554 and Rule 6007 cannot be used to effect turnover, recovery or legal title or possession to any particular creditor").

546 11 U.S.C. § 554(b); Fed. R. Bankr. P. 6007(b).

547 *See* Ohio v. Kovacs, 469 U.S. 274, 105 S. Ct. 705, 83 L. Ed. 2d 649 (1985).

548 *See* § 12.9, *supra*.

549 11 U.S.C. § 365(h)(1)(A)(ii); *see* § 17.8.4, *infra*.

550 *See generally* National Consumer Law Center, Tenants' Rights to Utility Service Ch. 7 (1994).

551 *Id.*; § 6.2, *supra*.

552 *See generally* National Consumer Law Center, Tenants' Rights to Utility Service Ch. 7 (1994); § 17.5.3, *supra*.

553 See, for example, Mass. Gen. Laws ch. 111, § 127(I), which authorizes tenants to petition the courts to enforce the state sanitary code, and specifies various injunctive remedies, including receivership.

554 If the property has not been abandoned, relief from the automatic stay is necessary. *See* 11 U.S.C. § 362(a)(3).

17.8.3 Pursuing Opportunities for Tenant Ownership in a Chapter 7 Bankruptcy

Aside from assuring that services to the rental property are maintained, the tenants may wish to consider what steps they can take to improve their long-term situation. With one absentee landlord in bankruptcy, the tenants may understandably be less than eager to see another absentee landlord buy the property out of foreclosure. If that is the case, tenant ownership strategies should be explored. Chances are, when a residential landlord files for bankruptcy, the rental property has been allowed to deteriorate for some time. Because tenant owners are far more likely to reinvest rent money in the property, tenant ownership may offer the best chance to improve tenants' living conditions.

In some cases, the debtor will not be interested in continued ownership, and the primary mortgage holder will not want to proceed to foreclosure unless it believes there is a potential buyer for the property.[555] Rental property with code violations and organized tenants does not present a very attractive investment opportunity. These circumstances are ripe for tenant ownership. The challenge, of course, is to come up with the financing.

The first step in securing financing for a tenant buyout is to prove that tenants can manage the property at a profit. The best way to do this is to actually manage the property. There are a variety of opportunities for this in a chapter 7 bankruptcy.[556] First, if the trustee has not abandoned the property pursuant to section 554, the tenants can ask the trustee to hire a tenant association to manage it. Alternatively, they could petition the court to abandon the property to such an association.[557] If the property has already been abandoned (and if the leases have been rejected), a tenant association could collect voluntary rent and assume management functions pending foreclosure.[558]

Once the tenants prove they can viably manage the property, the next step is to prepare a business plan and seek financing for a buyout. The primary mortgage holder should be approached. Depending on its chances of finding a commercial buyer for the property, it may be willing to finance a tenant buyout. Local community development corporations (CDCs) should also be approached. CDCs make good partners for exploring financing for low-income

housing development. Finally, it might be possible to find a community development loan fund that exists specifically to finance such ventures.

After financing is secured, there are various ways to go about purchasing the property. The first step should be to contact the debtor and secured creditor(s). If the trustee has not abandoned the property, either of them could propose that the bankruptcy court conduct a sale pursuant to section 363. The secured creditor could also seek relief from the automatic stay in order to pursue foreclosure. The tenants may bid on the property at the foreclosure sale or buy the property from the lender if the lender (as is most often the case) is the high bidder at the foreclosure auction.[559]

17.8.4 Preventing Evictions in Chapter 11 and 13 Proceedings

If the owner believes, however unrealistically, that the property may continue to be economically viable, then the owner may file under chapter 11, or in the case of a small building, under chapter 13.[560] The strategy for tenants may differ when faced with proceedings under chapter 11 or 13.

In a chapter 11 reorganization bankruptcy, the debtor generally continues to operate the business as a "debtor in possession" with the rights and duties of a trustee.[561] A chapter 13 debtor owning a business is similarly treated.[562] In those cases, abandonment is not likely.

In potential "gentrification" situations, landlords in bankruptcy may wish to evict low-income tenants in hopes of replacing them with those of higher income. Tenants whose landlord is in a chapter 11 or 13, or conceivably in a chapter 7, and who are faced with a rejection of the lease under section 365 are given important rights by section 365(h).

If the trustee or debtor in possession rejects the lease, section 365(h) provides that the tenant can retain possession and continue to remain in possession as long as the tenant would have had the right to unilaterally renew the lease under relevant non-bankruptcy law.[563] Section 8 tenants, tenants in rent-controlled housing, or tenants under statutes such as New Jersey's, which requires "cause" for eviction[564] have a right to continued occupancy so long as their rent payments are maintained and other lease provisions not

---

555 A secured lender who assumes any management function (such as collecting rent) or who obtains title to the property through its foreclosure proceeding risks being thrown into a landlord-tenant relationship as a mortgagee in possession. *See, e.g.*, McCorristin v. Salmon Signs, 582 A.2d 1271 (N.J. Super. Ct. App. Div. 1990).

556 In addition to the strategies discussed here, tenants in a chapter 11 case may be able to file a creditors' plan providing for tenant management. *See* § 17.7.9, *supra*.

557 *See* § 17.8.2.5, *supra*.

558 *See* § 17.8.2.6, *supra*.

559 Tenants in a chapter 11 case could also file a creditors' plan providing for tenant ownership. *See* § 17.7.9, *supra*.

560 Chapter 13 is only available to individuals with less than $922,975.00 in secured debt. 11 U.S.C. § 109(e). For cases filed between April 1, 2001 and March 31, 2004, the amount of the secured debt limit was $871,550.00.

561 11 U.S.C. § 1107. *See generally* § 17.7, *supra*.

562 11 U.S.C. § 1304.

563 *See In re* Churchill Properties III, Ltd. P'ship, 197 B.R. 283 (Bankr. N.D. Ill. 1996) (tenant with rejected lease had right to remain in possession even if real property was sold by lessor's trustee).

564 N.J. Stat. Ann. § 2A-18:61.3 (West).

breached. Section 365(h) thus protects tenants from eviction despite a section 365 rejection of their lease. Moreover, if the landlord rejects the lease, section 365(h) provides that the tenant can set off the lease payments up to their full value against the tenant's damages resulting from the rejection.[565]

The 1994 amendments to the Bankruptcy Code, provide new protections for tenants when a debtor rejects a lease. The new provision makes clear that the tenant may not only retain possession, but also that rights appurtenant to that possession are protected.[566] This legislatively overrules cases that had held that possession after lease rejection did not include a variety of ancillary tenant rights under the lease.[567] Finally, the Second Circuit in *In re Berry Estates, Inc.*,[568] has held that filing bankruptcy does not protect a landlord debtor from rent control regulations because the regulations are an exercise of the state police power.

In cases under any chapter, the landlord may be seeking eviction of a tenant/creditor in state court for cause. Where the tenant has counterclaims based, for example, on conditions in the property, relief from stay to raise those claims may be necessary.[569]

A related problem can occur when the trustee or landlord as debtor in possession elects to reject the lease and also sell the rental property under a § 363 asset sale free and clear of the tenants' possessory or other interests in the property.[570] In this situation, § 365(h) should preserve the tenants' benefits under the lease at least for the balance of the lease term, thereby preventing the tenants from being evicted by the new owner and requiring services to be maintained. However, one circuit court of appeals has held that an asset sale under § 363(f) can operate to cut off a tenant's possessory interest notwithstanding the rights provided to tenants under § 365(h).[571] Tenants may seek to avoid the holding in *Qualitech Steel* by arguing that the asset sale has not met all the requirements for approval set out in § 363(f). For example, because a free and clear sale cannot be approved by the bankruptcy court if it would not be permitted under applicable non-bankruptcy law,[572] residential tenants may be able to point to state or federal housing law that prohibits a purchaser from repudiating an existing lease.[573] In addition, the court in *Qualitech Steel* noted that a § 363 asset sale should not be approved if the tenants are not provided with adequate protection of their interests.[574] Unfortunately, this puts the burden on tenants to file an objection to the sale and affirmatively request that their interests be adequately protected.

17.8.5 Security Deposits

In addition to an interest in having services continue despite the initiation of bankruptcy proceedings, the tenants may have an interest in security deposits that the landlord obtained from the tenant at the commencement of the tenancy. As the assets of the estate are stretched to reach the claims of the landlord's creditors, the status of the tenants' security deposits may well become points of contention.

Where tenants have left the building before or during the bankruptcy, the tenants' claim for return of security may be met by countervailing claims that security deposits are property of the debtor's estate. Even when the tenants remain, the trustee may take the position that security deposits commingled with the debtor's funds, or used by the debtor for its own purposes, ceased to be security deposits. In either situation, the tenants risk becoming unsecured creditors for the amount of the security deposit unless the bankruptcy court accepts the tenants' argument that security deposits are entitled to a different status. Tenants may be able to have the deposits treated as not the landlord's property or as property held in trust by the landlord. At the least, they should be able to assert the consumer priority.[575]

---

565 *In re* Milstead, 197 B.R. 33 (Bankr. E.D. Va. 1996) (tenant's claim for relocation damages resulting from debtor's rejection of lease allowed because tenant's duty to mitigate did not require it to remain in possession rather than vacate premises in order to reduce damages).

566 11 U.S.C. § 365(h)(1)(A)(ii); *see In re* Flagstaff Realty Associates, 60 F.3d 1031 (3d Cir. 1995) (debtor retains right of recoupment under lease for improvements made prior to debtor's rejection of lease).

567 *E.g., In re* Carlton Restaurant, Inc., 151 B.R. 353 (Bankr. E.D. Pa. 1993) (preventing a tenant from assigning a lease after lease rejection).

568 812 F.2d 67 (2d Cir. 1987).

569 The process for obtaining that relief is discussed above in § 17.3, *supra*.

570 11 U.S.C. § 363(f); *see* 17.9.3, *infra*.

571 Precision Indus., Inc. v. Qualitech Steel SBQ, Ltd. Liab. Co., 327 F.3d 537 (7th Cir. 2003); *see also In re* Hill, 307 B.R. 821 (Bankr. W.D. Pa. 2004) (following *Qualitech*).

572 11 U.S.C. § 363(f)(1).

573 *E.g., In re* Welker, 163 B.R. 488 (Bankr. N.D. Tex. 1994) (trustee may sell property only after compliance with the Dep't of Housing and Urban Development's statutory and regulatory procedures as § 363(f) does not trump federal housing acts). Because § 363(f) is drafted in the disjunctive, tenants may need to show that each of the five listed statutory conditions has not been satisfied in order to stop a free and clear sale. *See In re* Dundee Equity Corp., 1992 WL 53743 (Bankr. S.D.N.Y. Mar. 6, 1992) (conditions not met because applicable non-bankruptcy law did not permit sale, § 363(f)(1); tenants did not consent to sale, § 363(f)(2); tenants' interest not a lien, § 363(f)(3); trustee did not dispute validity of lease, § 363(f)(4); and no provision of New York law compelled tenants, under circumstances of case, to accept a money satisfaction in lieu of performance, § 363(f)(5)).

574 *See* 11 U.S.C. § 363(e).

575 Guarracino v. Hoffman, 246 B.R. 130 (D. Mass. 2000) (security deposit entitled to priority; damages related to mishandling security deposit are not); *In re* River Vill. Associates, 161 B.R. 127 (Bankr. E.D. Pa. 1993), *aff'd on other grounds*, 181 B.R. 795 (E.D. Pa. 1995); *In re* Wise, 120 B.R. 537 (Bankr. D. Ala. 1990); *see* § 17.5.5, *supra*; *see also In re* Romanus, 1998 Bankr. LEXIS 397 (Bankr. W.D. Pa. 1998) (prepaid security deposit

If the lease is not rejected, the right to the return of a security deposit should be an administrative expense, which is entitled to priority status.[576]

The tenant's best hope for success is to have the bankruptcy court find that the security deposits are not assets of the bankruptcy estate because the deposits were never the landlord's property. A trustee in bankruptcy only succeeds to the debtor's right and title in property.[577] If a claimant challenges the debtor's right to property, the claimant bears the burden of proof on the issue of ownership.[578] The bankruptcy court looks to state law to determine the debtor's right in contested property.[579] Few bankruptcy cases have addressed the issue of whether the security deposits held by a debtor/landlord are assets of the debtor's bankruptcy estate.[580]

State statutory provisions which mandate that landlords maintain security deposits given by residential tenants in escrow accounts specifically established to hold such funds during the term of residential leases offer the best grounds for having security deposits separated from the debtor's property. Some state statutes regulating the collection of deposits from residential tenants explicitly provide that these deposits must be maintained in separate escrow accounts that remain the property of the tenants.[581] A few statutes go further and specifically provide that these escrow deposits remain tenants' property even against claims of a trustee in bankruptcy.[582] A minority of states have taken no legislative action to control the collection of security deposits[583] or have adopted bare-bones statutes which do not specify how the security deposits are to be maintained, but merely mandate that the deposits be returned at the end of the lease term.[584]

The stronger statutes should assure the tenants of recovery. For example, in a New York case in which the lessee was a debtor in bankruptcy and had defaulted under the terms of the lease, the landlord sought to reach the tenant's security deposit ahead of the debtor's general creditors.[585] There the court looked to the state statute that required the maintenance of segregated escrow accounts for tenants' security deposits and found that the deposits remained the tenants' property.[586]

Additional grounds for having the bankruptcy court find that a tenant's security deposit is not an asset of the debtor's estate may be found in particular lease provisions. Many forms of residential leases provide for the payment of security by the tenant at the commencement of the lease, and the establishment of segregated escrow accounts by the landlord to hold those funds. Based on such provisions, tenants can argue that, by contract, the security deposits paid to a landlord pursuant to such lease provisions never become the property of the landlord.

Even in those jurisdictions in which state statutes require that landlords hold security deposits in trust or the lease provides for such accounts, cases are certain to arise where a financially pressed landlord has invaded the trust and dissipated the security deposits. Section 523(a)(4) of the Bankruptcy Code provides that an individual debtor cannot be discharged from a debt arising out of a debtor's embezzlement, larceny, or fraud or defalcation while acting in a fiduciary capacity.[587] This remedy is limited to individual debtors[588] and applies most commonly to a landlord's dissipation of an express trust.[589]

Arguments can be made, based on many states' statutory or common law, that a transfer of property to be held as security creates an express trust within the meaning of section 523(a)(4).[590] The transfer of a security deposit pur-

---

and first month rent payment entitled to consumer priority when the debtor/landlord failed to deliver the property in habitable condition).

576 *In re* Boston Post Road Ltd. P'ship, 21 F.3d 477 (2d Cir. 1994) (tenants who are owed security deposits have administrative claims which are entitled to priority); *In re* Cantonwood Associates Ltd. P'ship, 138 B.R. 648 (Bankr. D. Mass. 1992) (same). See § 12.9, *supra,* for a discussion of assumption or rejection of executory contracts and § 17.5.3, *supra,* for a discussion of post-petition claims as administrative expenses.

577 5 Collier on Bankruptcy ¶ 541.11 (15th ed. rev.); *see* § 17.5.2, *supra.*

578 5 Collier on Bankruptcy ¶ 541.11 (15th ed. rev.).

579 *Id.*; *In re* Contractors Equip. Supply Co., 861 F.2d 241 (9th Cir. 1988) (status of payment of account receivable determined under state law).

580 One adverse case is *In re* Dilberts Leasing & Dev. Corp., 345 F.2d 172 (2d Cir. 1965) (in commercial case where lease did not require segregation of security deposit, tenant held to be general creditor). One helpful case, though decided in another context, held that tenants were not creditors of a debtor-landlord solely based on the latter holding their security deposits because the tenants held title to the deposits under state law. *In re* Ctr. Apartments, Ltd., 277 B.R. 747 (Bankr. S.D. Ohio 2001).

581 *See, e.g.,* Fla. Stat. Ann. § 83.49 (West); Ga. Code Ann. § 44-7-31; Mass. Gen. Laws ch. 186, § 15B(1)(E); N.Y. Gen. Oblig. Law § 7-103 (McKinney).

582 *See, e.g.,* Me. Rev. Stat. Ann. tit. 14, § 6038 (West); Mass. Gen. Laws ch. 186, § 15B(1)(E).

583 Alabama and Mississippi are examples of states not adopting security deposit legislation.

584 *See, e.g.,* Ark. Code Ann. § 18-16-301 (Michie); Ind. Code § 32-7-5-1.

585 *In re* Pal-Playwell Inc., 334 F.2d 389 (2d Cir. 1964).

586 *Id.* at 391.

587 11 U.S.C. § 523(a)(4); *In re* Christian, 172 B.R. 490 (Bankr. D. Mass. 1994); *In re* Wise, 120 B.R. 537 (Bankr. D. Alaska 1990). See § 14.4.3.4, *supra,* for a detailed discussion of dischargeability.

588 An individual debtor may be found responsible in some circumstances for a defalcation by a trust entity or a corporation. *See In re* Lebner, 197 B.R. 180 (Bankr. D. Mass. 1996) (trial necessary to determine if realty trust beneficiary is responsible for actions of trust). *See generally* § 17.5.7, *supra.*

589 *In re* Niles, 106 F.3d 1456 (9th Cir. 1997) (discussing application of § 523(a)(4)); *In re* Angelle, 610 F.2d 1335 (5th Cir. 1980); *In re* Dloogoff, 600 F.2d 166 (8th Cir. 1979); 4 Collier on Bankruptcy ¶ 523.10[1][c] (15th ed. rev.).

590 *In re* McGee, 353 F.3d 537 (7th Cir. 2003) (city ordinance requiring security deposit be held in insured bank account and not commingled with other assets, and providing that funds

suant to a lease agreement creates a trust *res* to be held for the particular purpose of providing security if the tenant violates the lease.[591] Use of those funds for other purposes is then a defalcation within the meaning of the statute.[592] Where such an action is available, it often offers good potential for class certification and class relief.[593] If there is a prior state court judgment establishing a violation of a state law protecting security deposits, that judgment may collaterally estop the debtor on many of the issues required to establish nondischargeability.[594] Tenants may succeed in a nondischargeability action under section 523(a)(4) even if defalcation is not proven when a landlord's misappropriation of the security deposit amounts to embezzlement.[595]

If there is a claim available under a state UDAP statute for misappropriation of security deposits,[596] that claim may create a basis to argue nondischargeability not only under section 523(a)(4), but also under sections 523(a)(2)(A) and 523(a)(6) as well. Section 523(a)(2)(A) covers debts based on fraud or false pretenses and section 523(a)(6) covers willful and malicious injury such as conversion.[597]

Another approach to solving the problem of the depleted trust would be under 28 U.S.C. § 959(b). That statute requires that trustees appointed in federal court comply with state laws affecting any property held by the trustee. In *Saravia v. 1736 18th Street, N.W. Ltd. Partnership*,[598] the D.C. Circuit held a debtor in possession to compliance with local housing regulations based on the obligations imposed on bankruptcy trustees under section 959(b).

No bankruptcy case has yet to hold that either a trustee or debtor in possession must comply with security deposit escrow requirements of state statutes after those escrow funds had been wrongful disbursed. But, based on section 959(b) and *Saravia*, the legal basis for extending the trustees' obligation to a duty to replace dissipated security deposits seems to be within reach and is certainly worth arguing.

In a few jurisdictions, statutes specifically provide that any successors to a landlord that collected security deposits have an obligation to return those deposits to tenants or compensate the tenant with rent credits.[599] Other state statutes impose bonding requirements on landlords that collect statutory established levels of aggregate security deposits.[600] Section 959(b) should require the trustee to return deposits or collect from the bonding company in jurisdictions with this type of legislation. The tenants would also have a claim against the bonding company, which would not be subject to the automatic stay.

Without either a statutory or contractual basis for persuading the bankruptcy court that a tenant's security deposits were not a landlord-debtor's property, an effort may be made to have a constructive trust impressed on the debtor's funds.[601] Landlord-tenant statutes or lease provisions requiring separate accounting for deposits may provide a basis for imposition of a constructive trust even if they fall short of the requirements of an express trust. Even the enactment of a less than adequate state security deposit statute might provide the grounds for a constructive trust. A state statute, for example, might not specify that the security deposits held by the landlord remained the property of the tenant.[602] One could nevertheless argue that a constructive trust ought to be imposed to implement the protection the statute sought to provide. Similarly, a lease provision providing for an escrow or payment of interest on the deposit might supply the basis for arguing that a trust relationship was actually created or implied.

Procedurally, the tenants' attempt to have security deposits excluded from the debtor's estate as property belonging to the tenant, and not property to which the debtor has a right, should be by an adversary proceeding.[603]

---

were to remain property of tenant, created a fiduciary relationship arising from a trust). Courts may refer to a trust imposed pursuant to state common law or statute as a "technical" trust. *E.g., In re* Paeplow, 217 B.R. 705 (Bankr. D. Vt. 1998).

591 *See In re* Christian, 172 B.R. 490 (Bankr. D. Mass. 1994) (security deposit claims and punitive damages award entered against landlord under state law found to be nondischargeable under § 523(a)(4)); *In re* Wise, 120 B.R. 537 (Bankr. D. Alaska 1990); *cf. In re* Lebner, 197 B.R. 180 (Bankr. D. Mass. 1996) (security deposit creates express trust under Massachusetts law, but payment of last month's rent does not).

592 *See In re* McGee, 353 F.3d 537 (7th Cir. 2003) (landlord's unlawful retention of security deposit was defalcation for purposes of § 523(a)(4)); *In re* Bologna, 206 B.R. 628 (D. Mass. 1997) (security deposit law creates fiduciary responsibilities for landlord, but state court judgment which does not address whether landlord was at fault in misappropriating funds cannot collaterally estop landlord on question of whether defalcation occurred); § 14.4.3.4, *supra.*

593 *See* §§ 13.7, 17.4.2, *supra.*

594 *See In re* Christian, 172 B.R. 490 (Bankr. D. Mass. 1994) (collateral estoppel found); *cf. In re* Lebner, 197 B.R. 180 (Bankr. D. Mass. 1996) (discussing limits of collateral estoppel).

595 *In re* Ardolino, 298 B.R. 541 (Bankr. W.D. Pa. 2003) (although no trust established because state law did not require security deposit to be held in escrow account until third year of lease, landlord's misappropriation of funds with fraudulent and deceptive intent was embezzlement for purposes of § 523(a)(4)).

596 See generally National Consumer Law Center, Unfair and Deceptive Acts and Practices § 2.2.6 (5th ed. 2001 and Supp.) for discussion of the application of UDAP laws to residential leases.

597 *See* § 17.5.4, *supra; In re* Cohen, 106 F.3d 52 (3d Cir. 1997) (actual and punitive damages awarded to tenants based on UDAP for rent overcharges nondischargeable under § 523(a)(2)(A)), *aff'd,* 523 U.S. 213 (1998).

---

598 844 F.2d 823 (D.C. Cir. 1988).

599 *E.g.,* Mass. Gen. Laws ch. 186, § 15B(c).

600 Fla. Stat. Ann. § 83.49 (West).

601 *See* § 17.5.2, *supra;* 5 Collier on Bankruptcy ¶ 541.11 (15th ed. rev.). *But see In re* Cimaglia, 50 B.R. 9 (Bankr. S.D. Fla. 1985) (putting security deposits into segregated accounts not sufficient evidence alone to find a trust).

602 *E.g.,* Ind. Code § 32-7-5-1.

603 *See* § 11.3.2, *supra.*

Care should be taken that a proof of claim is also filed. The proof of claim should have a statement reserving all rights to the property and claiming the right to assert alternate remedies. A priority should be asserted under the consumer priority section of the Code[604] when the tenants' proof of claim is filed. This section gives individuals a $2100.00 priority for deposits made in connection with the lease or rental of property.

17.9 Representing Consumers When Lenders File Bankruptcy

17.9.1 Lender Bankruptcies

In recent years, a number of large non-bank lending companies have filed chapter 11 bankruptcy cases,[605] giving rise to numerous new issues in applying bankruptcy law to the anomalous situation where the lender is the debtor, and the borrowers are creditors. Several of these cases involve "subprime" mortgage lenders involved in predatory lending practices, who were defendants in various consumer class actions and government enforcement actions. In at least some cases, the bankruptcy filing appeared to have been filed for the purpose of "laundering" the loans by discharging consumer claims and defenses and selling the loan portfolios or servicing rights to new entities.[606]

Consumer advocates should not be prematurely discouraged when a lender files for bankruptcy. The amounts still payable on all the lender's loans are "assets,"[607] and those funds will come under the supervision of the bankruptcy court and will be distributed according to the rules of the Code. If the lender plans to reorganize, consumer borrowers may have an opportunity to assert claims that must be paid or settled before the reorganization can succeed. A lender bankruptcy may present unexpected opportunities for consumers to receive restitution, or at least some debt reduction relief.

17.9.2 Automatic Stay Issues for Consumer Borrowers

The automatic stay arising when a loan company files a bankruptcy petition affects only legal proceedings against the loan company; it does not stay legal proceedings in which the loan company is plaintiff, such as mortgage foreclosures.[608] The consumer borrower would be stayed from asserting counterclaims, but may assert defenses, including affirmative defenses and recoupment claims up to the amount of the asserted debt.[609] Nothing in section 362 bars a consumer defendant from pursuing discovery, filing motions, and taking any other steps necessary to assert defenses in litigation initiated by a bankrupt lender.

One difficult situation arises in states where non-judicial foreclosure is permitted. A bankrupt lender could send a written notice of sale, and the consumer, who ordinarily would assert defenses by filing an action seeking an injunction of the foreclosure sale, is probably stayed by the lender's bankruptcy. Best practice would be to seek relief from the stay. Such a case would present very strong "cause," under 11 U.S.C. § 362(d)(1), for lifting or modifying the stay, to allow the consumer to assert defenses. The consumer may have to file a motion in the lender's bankruptcy court to modify the stay, which would almost invariably be granted.[610] Such a motion may be filed *in forma pauperis.*[611]

Consumer borrowers with nonpurchase money mortgage loans may have a right to rescind their loans, under the Truth in Lending Act[612] or other consumer protection laws, or on common law grounds such as fraud. The question as to whether sending a written demand to rescind a loan to a bankrupt debtor would violate the section 362(a) presents an interesting issue.

---

604 11 U.S.C. § 507(a)(6); *see* § 17.5.5, *supra.*

605 Bankrupt loan companies have included Conseco Financial, United Companies Lending, Conti Mortgage, First Alliance Mortgage (FAMCO), FirstPlus Financial, and Empire Funding. *See In* re Conseco, Inc., 299 B.R. 875 (N.D. Ill. 2003); *In re* United Co. Fin. Corp., 241 B.R. 521 (Bankr. D. Del. 1999); *In re* Conti Mortgage Co., Bky 00-12184 (Bankr. S.D.N.Y. filed 2000); *In re* First Alliance Mortgage Co., 269 B.R. 428 (C.D. Cal. 2001); *In re* FirstPlus Fin., 248 B.R. 60 (Bankr. N.D. Tex. 2000); *In re* Empire Funding Corp. No. 00-11478 (Bankr. W.D. Tex. filed May 15, 2000); *see also* Cathy Lesser Mansfield, *The Road to Subprime "HEL" Was Paved with Good Congressional Intentions: Usury Deregulation and the Subprime Home Equity Market,* 51 S.C. L. Rev. 473, 530 n.355 (2000); Diane Henriquez, *Troubled Lender Seeks Protection,* New York Times, Mar. 24, 2000, at A-1.

606 Diane Henriquez, Troubled Lender Seeks Protection, New York Times, Mar. 24, 2000, at A-1 (noting that First Alliance Mortgage Co. was solvent, and filed primarily to deal with consumer lawsuits); *cf. In re* SGL Carbon Corp., 200 F.3d 154 (3d Cir. 1999) (chapter 11 dismissed because it was filed by solvent company, solely to gain tactical advantage in antitrust litigation).

607 Some loan companies sell their loans on the secondary market, or securitize them. The bankrupt lender may only retain the right to service the loans or a portion of the excess interest paid by borrowers.

608 Martin-Trigona v. Champion Fed. Sav., 892 F.2d 575, 577 (7th Cir. 1989); *see* § 17.3, *supra.*

609 "There is, in contrast, no policy of preventing persons whom the bankrupt has sued from protecting their legal rights. . . ." *Martin-Trigona,* 892 F.2d at 577.

610 *See In re* Millsap, 141 B.R. 732, 733 (Bankr. D. Idaho 1992) (creditor entitled as a matter of right to stay relief to assert compulsory counterclaim in suit be debtor); *see also* § 17.3, *supra.*

611 *See* § 17.6, *supra.*

612 15 U.S.C. § 1635; *see* National Consumer Law Center, Truth in Lending Ch. 6 (5th ed. 2003).

The better view is that a rescission demand, in itself, does not violate the stay. The transmission of a written rescission notice is necessary to prevent the consumer's rights from expiring,[613] and is equivalent to any party to a contract simply stating the party's belief as to the party's rights under a contract.[614] When the lender disagrees with the borrower, and believes the loan should not be rescinded, the borrower's next step would be to file suit to enforce the rescission. It is that next step, of suing for rescission, which is stayed by the lender's bankruptcy. The statute of limitations to file such a suit for court enforcement of the rescission would be tolled by the bankruptcy.[615] The consumer could follow up the rescission demand with a motion for relief from stay to enforce the rescission, file a proof of claim based on the rescission, and/or assert the rescission as a defense in any foreclosure action.

A bankrupt lender might argue that a rescission demand would amount to an "act to exercise control over property of the estate," that is, the loan, or an "act to collect a claim against the debtor."[616] Terminating a contract with the debtor is in some cases a violation of the stay.[617] A debtor loan company might therefore argue that a rescission notice was equivalent to contract termination, or to an action to set-off mutual debts, stayed by § 362(a)(7). The most cautious approach would therefore be to either file a motion for relief from the stay that includes a rescission demand, or file a proof of claim with the rescission demand. Either action ought to be sufficient to protect the consumer from expiration of the right to rescind.

In some cases the automatic stay will not affect a borrower's efforts to vindicate consumer protection claims, because the debtor loan company does not own the loan outright, but is merely a servicer. This is most common when the consumer's loan has been "securitized," which means that it has been transferred to a trust, along with a large pool of similar loans, and is owned by a trustee on behalf of various investors.[618] The loan company with

whom the consumer is dealing is a servicer, and is paid some portion of the monthly interest as a servicing fee. The servicing loan company may also retain a subordinate interest in a portion of the consumer's loan payments, typically the right to receive excess interest after the trust investors have been paid a guaranteed fixed rate.[619]

The rights of the loan company as servicer, and the trust as owner of the loans, are spelled out in a pooling and servicing agreement (PSA). In many cases, the PSA does not require that the assignment of the consumer loans be perfected (such as by recording a mortgage assignment to the trustee). The originating lender and/or servicer will appear from public records to still be the owner of the loan, and in the case of a mortgage, may foreclose in its own name. Nevertheless, the true owner of the loan is not the servicer, it is the trustee for the investors in the mortgage-backed securities. The servicer's contractual rights do not rise to the level of an ownership interest in the loan.[620]

The consumer borrower is free to take legal action against the trustee as owner of her loan. The automatic stay has no effect on legal action against other parties who are not debtors in bankruptcy.[621] Even if the servicer is bound by the PSA to repurchase a consumer's loan in the event the mortgage is found unenforceable in whole or in part, the loan owner has either a right of contribution against the bankrupt lender, or at best a guarantee. The automatic stay does not ordinarily protect a principal obligor in the guarantor's bankruptcy.[622] If the consumer has initiated legal action against the loan company prior to a bankruptcy, it

---

613 Beach v. Ocwen Fed. Bank, 523 U.S. 410, 118 S. Ct. 1408, 140 L. Ed. 2d 566 (1998).

614 *Cf.* Citizens Bank of Md. v. Strumpf, 516 U.S. 16, 21, 116 S. Ct. 286, 133 L. Ed. 2d 258 (1995) ("temporary refusal to pay [by Bank that held debtor deposits] was neither a taking of possession of respondent's property nor an exercising of control over it, but merely a refusal to perform its promise"); *In re* Smith 737 F.2d 1549 (11th Cir. 1984) (creditor could respond to debtor's rescission demand without violating the stay protecting the consumer debtor).

615 11 U.S.C. § 108(c). However, the borrower should not allow the rescission right to expire. *See In re* Williams, 276 B.R. 394 (Bankr. E.D. Pa. 2002) (lender's bankruptcy does not extend time for borrower to rescind loan under TILA because § 108(c) applies only to filing of action and not exercise of rescission right).

616 11 U.S.C. § 362(a)(3), (6); *see* § 9.4.2, *supra.*

617 *See* § 9.4.2, *supra.*

618 *See* Cathy Lesser Mansfield, *The Road to "HEL" Was Paved with Good Congressional Intentions: Usury Deregulation and*

the Subprime Home Equity Market, 51 S.C. L. Rev. 473, 531, 532 (2000) (growing use of securitization by subprime mortgage lenders in 1990s).

619 *See* Chandler v. Norwest Bank of Minn., 137 F.3d 1053 (8th Cir. 1998) (describes roles of loan originator, loan purchaser, trustee for loan pool, and servicer, noting that the trust itself owns the securitized loans).

620 *In re* Litenda Mortgage Corp., 246 B.R. 185, 193, 194 (Bankr. D.N.J. 1999).

621 *See* §§ 9.4.1, 17.3, *supra.* A primary objective of the parties to the securitization process is that the loans being securitized will not become property of the originating lender's estate if the lender files bankruptcy. To accomplish this, the loans are transferred to a "special purpose entity" (also referred to as a "bankruptcy remote entity") and ultimately held by the trust. The structure of these transactions is carefully designed so that the transfer of assets will be treated as a "true sale" and not reachable by a bankruptcy trustee if the lender files bankruptcy. *See In re* LTV Steel Co., 274 B.R. 278 (Bankr. N.D. Ohio 2001). This supports a consumer borrower's position that the automatic stay issued in the originating lender's bankruptcy should not preclude claims brought against the trustee as owner of the borrower's loan. The bankrupt lender might, however, seek an injunction from the bankruptcy court under 11 U.S.C. § 105. *See* § 9.4.6, *supra.*

622 *See* McCartney v. Integra Nat. Bank N., 106 F.3d 506, 509, 510 (3d Cir. 1997) (noting that in exceptional circumstances bankruptcy court may enjoin action against third party if non-debtor party has no assets, and the action will in effect be against the debtor.); § 17.3.2, *supra.*

may be worthwhile to determine whether a trustee or other assignee should be substituted as the defendant, so that the consumer's litigation can go forward.

In summary, relief from the stay is probably not necessary to:

- Pursue legal action (including counterclaims) against other parties who are not in bankruptcy;
- Assert defenses in litigation brought by the bankrupt lender;
- Notify the lender of the exercise of a valid right to rescind.

Consumer attorneys should also consider the merits of filing a proof of claim, and/or waiting until the consumer's loan is sold by the debtor, as alternatives to immediately seeking relief from the stay. However, when in doubt about the applicability of the stay, the best practice is to move for relief under § 362(d).

17.9.3 Loan Company Sales of Assets Under 11 U.S.C. § 363

In both chapter 7 and chapter 11 cases, but more commonly in the latter, the rights of creditors may be determined not by a liquidation or plan confirmation process, but rather through a sale of some or all of the debtor's assets, free and clear of interests in the property, under 11 U.S.C. § 363(b) and (f).

Although the Bankruptcy Code does not provide for corporate debtors to receive a discharge in chapter 7,[623] and a discharge does not affect the liability of co-defendants,[624] some motions for asset sales under § 363 seek very broad injunctive relief resembling a discharge, and barring creditors from pursuing claims against purchasers and other successors to the debtor. A sale of all or nearly all of the debtor's assets may render the remainder of the bankruptcy proceeding inconsequential. There will be little left to the case apart from distributing the proceeds of the sale (cash or securities in the buyer, typically). More significantly, the purchaser of the assets of a lender may contend that consumers are barred from asserting claims as a result of a § 363 sale.

Successor liability is ordinarily a question of state law.[625] Some bankruptcy courts have entered orders seeking to protect purchasers at § 363 sales from successor liability,[626]

while other courts have questioned the authority under the Bankruptcy Code to do this, especially with regard to claims that were unknown at the time of the bankruptcy, such as product liability claims.[627]

To the extent that a consumer has a claim that arises from the same transaction as the bankruptcy debtor's claim against the consumer, a § 363 sale of assets does not affect the consumer's rights. A consumer borrower's defenses to payment of a delinquent loan owed to a bankrupt loan company should not be affected by a sale of the loan under § 363. The consumer's defenses, so long as they are in the nature of recoupment, define the "property" (the loan) being sold, and are therefore not an "interest" in the property divested by the sale.[628] Thus, a consumer may assert claims defensively, up to the amount of the debt owed by the consumer, against a purchaser of assets, despite a sale "free and clear" under 11 U.S.C. § 363.

17.9.4 Filing a Proof of Claim for a Consumer Borrower

While a consumer's defenses to a loan may be viewed as recoupment defenses, and therefore not a "claim" in the bankruptcy sense, it is still advisable to file a proof of claim in a lender's bankruptcy. The claim, unless objected to, will in some cases allow the consumer to vote on a plan, and/or receive payment from the liquidation or reorganization of the lender. If the lender is not the current holder of the consumer's loan, the consumer can still file any claim arising from the loan origination, for which the lender is individually or jointly liable. However, the consumer should carefully evaluate whether to accept any distribution on the claim if the lender's confirmed chapter 11 plan provides for a release of claims the consumer may have against non-debtor third parties.[629]

A consumer borrower may assert secured status, based on a right of set-off, to the extent the consumer still owes a balance to the lender. If the consumer has affirmative claims against the lender, for example for statutory or punitive damages, state law may allow those claims to be set-off

---

623 11 U.S.C. § 727(a)(1).

624 11 U.S.C. § 524(e).

625 3 Collier on Bankruptcy ¶ 363.02[3], at 363-16 to 363-17 (15th ed. rev.). *See generally* § 17.5.4.4, *supra*.

626 *E.g., In re* Trans World Airlines, Inc., 322 F.3d 283 (3d Cir. 2003) (successor airline not liable for flight attendants' employment discrimination claims that were covered by § 363(f) asset sale order); *In re* All Am. of Ashburn, 56 B.R. 186 (Bankr. N.D. Ga. 1986) (§ 363(f) sale precluded mobile home owners from

bringing product liability claims against purchaser of debtor-manufacturer's assets), *aff'd on other grounds*, 805 F.2d 1515 (11th Cir. 1986).

627 3 Collier on Bankruptcy § 363.02[3], at 363-17 (15th ed. rev.); *see* Nelson v. Tiffany Indus., Inc., 778 F.2d 533 (9th Cir. 1985) (material issues of fact existed, precluding summary judgment, as to whether there was collusive agreement under which successor corporation induced predecessor to file bankruptcy to avoid future tort liability). *See generally In re* Trans World Airlines, Inc., 2001 Bankr. LEXIS 723 (Bankr. D. Del. 2001) (property of airline can be sold free and clear of employment discrimination claims).

628 Folger Adam Sec., Inc. v. DeMatteis/MacGregor, 209 F.3d 252, 260, 261 (3d Cir. 2000).

629 *See* § 17.9.5, *infra*.

against the consumer's loan debt. Set-off rights are protected by § 553 of the Code, and are secured claims under § 506(a).

Under a confirmed chapter 11 plan, the consumer's claim, if allowed, should be paid in full, by immediately reducing the debt owed by the consumer to the lender, by payment of the claim in deferred cash payments, or by having the consumer's claim "attach" to the loan if the loan is sold, that is, allowing the consumer to assert the setoff against the purchaser of the loan.[630] The setoff right should not be adversely affected by a confirmed plan, discharge, or sale of assets.[631]

Some consumer borrowers have priority claims arising from a loan transaction. If the consumer has had payments or loan proceeds set aside in escrow as a deposit for future payments of taxes, insurance, or home repairs, the escrow deposit amounts should come within the consumer deposit priority.[632] Similarly, if part of a loan was applied to a credit insurance premium, the unearned portion of the premium for future months could be regarded as a deposit for which services have not yet been delivered. Arguably, other amounts paid from loan proceeds by the consumer for services that were of no value or were not actually rendered could come within the § 507(a)(6) priority, such as spurious broker or appraisal fees.

17.9.5 Third-Party and Successor Releases and Injunctions

Chapter 11 plans often include provisions in their fine print that attempt to enjoin creditors from pursuing claims against the debtor's potential codefendants in litigation. These third-party release and injunction provisions can leave consumers unable to pursue an otherwise useful strategy, of bypassing the defendant's bankruptcy, by asserting claims against agents, successors, assignees, and other liable third parties. The Bankruptcy Code does not authorize a discharge of a party who is not a debtor,[633] and the courts have generally taken a dim view of chapter 11 plan provisions that appear to result in such a discharge.

For example, in *In re Continental Airlines*, the Third Circuit Court of Appeals refused to enforce a chapter 11 plan provision that would have enjoined a shareholder class action against officers and directors of the bankrupt airline company.[634] The Third Circuit declined to hold that third-party releases are always per se invalid unless consensual, as

other courts have done.[635] Courts that do allow third-party release provisions will consider factors such as whether the third parties have contributed funds to the reorganization, whether the claims are being paid in full or nearly in full, whether the terms of the release have been fully disclosed, and whether the affected creditors have agreed to accept the plan treatment.[636]

The approach adopted by the Seventh Circuit to this "knotty problem" has been to emphasize that non-debtor releases should be "consensual and non-coercive."[637] In approving the release in *In re Specialty Equipment Companies, Inc.*, the Seventh Circuit noted that the debtor's plan permitted each creditor to choose whether to be bound by the release and that only creditors who affirmatively voted to accept the plan would have claims released; a creditor who voted to reject the plan or who abstained from voting could still pursue claims against third-party non-debtors.[638]

As a further limitation on broad releases and injunctions protecting third parties, some courts have held that such orders are permissible only if they are limited to property of the debtor's estate.[639] This should prevent a bankruptcy court from approving an order that releases non-debtor trustee owners of securitized loans from borrower claims. In addition, the bankruptcy court may lack jurisdiction to enjoin an action between non-debtor parties in which one of the parties claims to be protected by a plan release or similar order.[640] In a similar vein, a state court action against a

---

630 *See* 11 U.S.C. § 1129(b)(2)(A). Less favorable treatment is possible only if the class of secured creditors agrees to it, that is, accepts the plan. *See* §§ 1129(a)(8), 1129(b).

631 *See* 3 Collier on Bankruptcy ¶ 363.06[7] (15th ed. rev.).

632 *See* § 17.5.5, *supra*. Also keep in mind the discussion of trust fund theories, § 17.5.2, *supra*.

633 11 U.S.C. § 524(e).

634 *In re* Cont'l Airlines, 203 F.3d 203 (3d Cir. 2000); *see also* § 17.3.2, *supra*.

635 *See, e.g., In re* Lowenschuss, 67 F.3d 1394 (9th Cir. 1995) (chapter 11 plan that released claims against non-debtors could not be confirmed); *In re* Zenith Electronics Corp., 241 B.R. 92 (Bank. D. Del. 1999); *see also* Peter E. Meltzer, Getting out of Jail Free: Can the Bankruptcy Plan Process Be Used to Release Nondebtor Parties?, 71 Am. Bankr. L.J. 1 (1997).

636 *In re* Cont'l Airlines, 203 F.3d at 212, 213.

637 *In re* Specialty Equip. Companies, Inc., 3 F.3d 1043, 1045, 1046 (7th Cir. 1993); *see also In re* Artra Group, Inc., 300 B.R. 699 (Bankr. N.D. Ill. 2003) (court rejected proposed adversary proceeding settlement that included broad injunctive provision seeking to enjoin any entity from pursuing claims in any way related to debtor).

638 *In re* Specialty Equip. Companies, Inc., 3 F.3d 1043, 1045, 1046 (7th Cir. 1993). Although mere acceptance of a plan distribution without an affirmative assent to be bound by a release provision should not cut off further pursuit of claims, a consumer borrower who has filed a proof of claim in a lender's bankruptcy should carefully review any conditions relating to acceptance of a distribution. *See In re* Conseco, Inc., 301 B.R. 525 (Bankr. N.D. Ill. 2003) (court confirmed plan only after third party release was modified to provide that it would bind only those creditors who agreed to be bound, either by voting for the plan or by receiving a distribution under the plan and choosing not to opt out of release); *In re* Arrowmill Dev. Corp., 211 B.R. 497, (Bankr. D.N.J. 1997) (non-debtor must affirmatively assent to release of claim).

639 *E.g.,* Fogel v. Zell, 221 F.3d 955 (7th Cir. 2000); *In re* Artra Group, Inc., 300 B.R. 699 (Bankr. N.D. Ill. 2003).

640 Zerand-Bernal Group, Inc. v. Cox, 23 F.3d 159 (7th Cir. 1994) (bankruptcy court lacked jurisdiction to enjoin product liability suit against purchaser of debtor's assets); *In re* Conseco, Inc.,

non-debtor party that is removed to federal court based on the purported effect of a third-party release should be remanded if the debtor is not a party to the action and if the action will have little or no effect on the debtor's bankruptcy.[641]

In one very limited group of cases, Congress added a special provision to authorize injunctions to protect third parties, including purchasers of the assets of the debtor corporation. This special provision is limited to asbestos claims in chapter 11 cases where a trust has been established to pay off present and future injury claims.[642] The existence of this limited exception suggests that Congress knows how to authorize discharge-like injunctions to protect third parties, and that courts should leave it to Congress to define other circumstances where such discharge provisions might be appropriate.[643]

By way of illustration of some of the principles discussed here, the plaintiff in *Bailey v. Green Tree Servicing Limited Liability Co.*[644] brought an action in state court against the mortgage servicer that had purchased the servicing rights to her mortgage in a § 363(f) asset sale, and against the trustee owner of her securitized mortgage.[645] The servicer and trustee removed the action to federal court and argued in response to a remand motion that the home owner's claims were barred by orders entered in the originating lender's bankruptcy and that the federal court had jurisdiction over the matter as a "core proceeding" based on the originating lender's bankruptcy.[646] The court held that because the alleged servicing misconduct occurred after the § 363(f) sale, the bankruptcy court's sale order could not possibly protect the servicer from claims based on its future, post-acquisition conduct. The court also found that the sale order did not protect the trustee from claims that the loan was unconscionable. Finally, as the plaintiff's state law claims related solely to her mortgage, which was not part of the originating lender's bankruptcy because it had been sold well before the lender filed bankruptcy, the court found that the matter was not a "core proceeding" in the originating lender's bankruptcy and was not within the federal court's jurisdiction, and therefore remanded the case to state court.[647]

---

305 B.R. 281 (Bankr. N.D. Ill. 2004) (court refused to exercise jurisdiction over declaratory judgment action relating to binding affect of release provisions in chapter 11 plan it had confirmed).

641   *See In re* Hotel Mt. Lassen, Inc., 207 B.R. 935 (Bankr. E.D. Cal. 1997) (court held that removed actions are not "related to" debtor's bankruptcy case within meaning of 28 U.S.C. § 1334(b) and must be remanded); *see also* § 13.4.1, *supra*.

642   11 U.S.C. § 524(g).

643   *In re* Lowenschuss, 67 F.3d 1394 (9th Cir. 1995) (amendment adding § 524(g) supports conclusion that § 524(e) does not permit third-party injunctions in non-asbestos cases). See also § 9.4.6, *supra*, regarding limited circumstances when bankruptcy courts may extend automatic stay to non-debtor parties under § 105(a) of the Code.

644   Bailey v. Green Tree Servicing Ltd. Liab. Co., 2004 WL 2347785 (S.D. W. Va. July 23, 2004).

645   The original lender, Conseco Finance, sold the plaintiff's mortgage to a trust, and retained the right to service the loan. Conseco then filed bankruptcy. Conseco sold the servicing rights to Green Tree Servicing in a 363(f) sale, approved by the bankruptcy court.

646   The defendants alleged that the federal court in West Virginia had jurisdiction over the West Virginia state court action, pursuant to 28 U.S.C. § 1334(b) and § 1452, based on the originating lender Conseco's bankruptcy filing in a bankruptcy court in Illinois.

647   Because the court found that it did not have subject matter jurisdiction, it did not reach the plaintiff's argument that the matter should have been remanded on equitable grounds pursuant to 28 U.S.C. § 1452(b).

Bibliography

For a farm bankruptcy bibliography, see § 16.9, supra.

Ackerly, *Tenants by the Entirety Property and the Bankruptcy Reform Act*, 21 Wm. & Mary L. Rev. 701 (1980).

Agin, *Protecting Pension Plans and Individual Retirement Accounts in Bankruptcy*, Boston B.J. 10 (1991).

Ahart, *Enforcing Nondischargeable Money Judgments: The Bankruptcy Courts' Dubious Jurisdiction*, 74 Am. Bankr. L.J. 115 (2000).

Alexander and Slone, *Thinking About the Private Matters in Public Documents: Bankruptcy Privacy in an Electronic Age*, 75 Am. Bankr. L.J. 437 (2001).

Arkinson, *Choosing a Chapter Under the Bankruptcy Code*, 35 Prac. Law. 33 (1989).

Asnes, *Emergency/Expedited Relief Under Section 363 of the Bankruptcy Code: An Overview and Suggested Approach for Improved Resolution of Cash Collateral Disputes*, 1989 Ann. Surv. Bankr. L. 223.

Ayer, *How to Think About Bankruptcy Ethics*, 60 Am. Bankr. L.J. 355 (1986).

Baird & Jackson, *Fraudulent Conveyance Law and Its Proper Domain*, 38 Vand. L. Rev. 829 (1985).

Baird, *Jury Trials After Granfianciera*, 65 Am. Bankr. L.J. 1 (1991).

Baird, *Loss Distribution, Forum Shopping, and Bankruptcy: A Reply to Warren*, 54 U. Chi. L. Rev. 815 (1987).

Ballam, *Kelly v. Robinson, Revisited: Dischargeability of Restitution Obligations in Chapter 13 Bankruptcy Proceedings*, 34 St. Louis U. L.J. 1 (1989).

Bancroft, *Postpetition Interest on Tax Liens in Bankruptcy Proceedings*, 62 Am. Bankr. L.J. 327 (1988).

Barta, *The Impact of Technology on the Bankruptcy Rules*, 70 Am. Bankr. L.J. 287 (1996).

Bermant, Lombard & Wiggins, *A Day in the Life: The Federal Judicial Center's 1988-1989 Bankruptcy Court Time Study*, 65 Am. Bankr. L.J. 491 (1991).

Bhandari & Weiss, *The Increasing Bankruptcy Filing Rate: An Historical Analysis*, 67 Am. Bankr. L.J. 1 (1993).

Bix, *Considering the State Law Consequences of an Allegedly Improper Bankruptcy Filing*, 67 Am. Bankr. L. Rev. 325 (1993).

Black & Herbert, *Bankcard's Revenge: A Critique of the 1984 Consumer Credit Amendments to the Bankruptcy Code*, 19 U. Rich. L. Rev. 845 (1985).

Block-Lieb, *A Comparison of Pro Bono Representation Programs for Consumer Debtors*, 2 Am. Bankr. Inst. L. Rev. 37 (1994).

Bloom, Gorelick & MacKenzie, *Exceptions to Bankruptcy Preferences: Countryman Updated*, 47 Bus. Law. 529 (1992).

Bordewieck, *The Postpetition, Pre-Rejection, Pre-Assumption Status of an Executory Contract*, 59 Am. Bankr. L.J. 197 (1985).

Boren, *An Analysis of Changes in the Use of Chapter 13 Since the Enactment of the Bankruptcy Reform Act of 1978*, 23 Am. Bus. L.J. 451 (1985).

Boshkoff, *As We Forgive Our Debtors in the Classroom*, 65 Ind. L.J. 65 (1989).

Boshkoff, *Bankruptcy-Based Discrimination*, 66 Am. Bankr. L.J. 387 (1992).

Boshkoff, *Limited, Conditional, and Suspended Discharges in Anglo-American Bankruptcy Proceedings*, 131 U. Pa. L. Rev. 69 (1982).

Boshkoff, *Private Parties and Bankruptcy-Based Discrimination*, 62 Ind. L.J. 159 (1986–1987).

Bowles, *Goldilocks, Bankruptcy and Divorce—Are the Adversarial Relationships Too Much, Not Enough or Just Right?*, 21-JUN Am. Bankr. Inst. J. 20 (June 2002).

Bowmar, *Avoidance of Judicial Liens That Impair Exemptions in Bankruptcy: The Workings of 11 U.S.C. § 522 (f)(1)*, 63 Am. Bankr. L.J. 375 (1989).

Brankey & Darr, *Debtor Interests in Pension Plans as Property of the Debtor's Estate*, 28 Am. Bus. L.J. 275 (1990).

Braucher, *An Empirical Study of Debtor Education in Bankruptcy: Impact on Chapter 13 Completion Not Shown*, 9 Am. Bankr. Inst. L. Rev. 557 (2001).

Braucher, *Lawyers and Consumer Bankruptcy: One Code, Many Cultures*, 67 Am. Bankr. L.J. 501 (1993).

Breitowitz, *New Developments in Consumer Bankruptcies: Chapter 7 Dismissal on the Basis of "Substantial Abuse"*, 59 Am. Bankr. L.J. 327 (1985).

Breitowitz, *New Developments in Consumer Bankruptcies: Chapter 7 Dismissal on the Basis of "Substantial Abuse": Second Installment*, 60 Am. Bankr. L.J. 33 (1986).

Broome, *Bankruptcy Appeals: The Wheel is Come Full Circle*, 69 Am. Bankr. L.J. 541 (1995).

Brown, Carpenter & Snow, *Debtors' Counsel Beware: Use of the Doctrine of Judicial Estoppel in Nonbankruptcy Forums*, 75 Am. Bankr. L.J. 197 (2000).

Brunstad, *Appeals of Remand Orders: Limiting Litigation Over Where to Litigate and Some Lessons on Statutory Construction*, 5 J. Bankr. L. & Prac. 323 (1996).

Bucki, *The Automatic Bankruptcy Stay and Real Property Tax Liens*, 66 Am. Bankr. L.J. 233 (1992).

Budnitz, *The Duties Imposed by Bankruptcy Courts Upon Mortgagees at Foreclosure Sales: How to Avoid Avoidance Under Section 548*, 46 Bus. Law. 3 (1991).

Burnett, *Prepetition Waivers of the Automatic Stay: Automatic Enforcement Equals Automatic Trouble*, 5 J. Bankr. L. & Prac. 257 (1996).

Buschman III, *Benefits and Burdens: Post-Petition Performance of Unassumed Executory Contracts*, 5 Bankr. Dev. J. 341 (1988).

Bussel, *Power, Authority, and Precedent in Interpreting the Bankruptcy Code*, 41 UCLA L. Rev. 1063 (1994).

Butler, *A Chapter 13 Trustee Looks at Section 1325(b) of the Bankruptcy Code*, 63 Am. Bankr. L.J. 401 (1989).

Butler, *A Congressman's Reflections on the Drafting of the Bankruptcy Code of 1978*, 21 Wm. & Mary L. Rev. 557 (1980).

Canzoneri, *Residential Mortgages in Declining Markets: The Perils and Potentials of Chapter 13*, 35 Boston B.J. 17 (1991).

Carlson, *Bifurcation of Undersecured Claims in Bankruptcy*, 70 Am. Bankr. L.J. 1 (1996).

Carlson, *Oversecured Creditors Under Bankruptcy Code Section 506(b): The Limits of Postpetition Interest, Attorneys' Fees, and Collection Expenses*, 7 Bankr. Dev. J. 381 (1990).

Carlson, *Undersecured Claims Under Bankruptcy Code Sections 506(a) and 1111(b): Second Looks at Judicial Valuations of Collateral*, 6 Bankr. Dev. J. 253 (1989).

Cataldo, Murphy & Szabo, *Residential Mortgage Bifurcation Under Chapter 13 of the Bankruptcy Code*, 96 Com. L.J. 225 (1991).

Cerne, *Honor Thy Creditors?: The Religious Debtor's Constitutional Conflict with Section 1325(b)*, 98 Com. L.J. 257 (1993).

Chobot, *Anti-Discrimination Under the Bankruptcy Law*, 60 Am. Bankr. L.J. 185 (1986).

Chobot, *Preserving Liens Avoided In Bankruptcy—Limitations And Applications*, 62 Am. Bankr. L.J. 149 (1988).

Coffino, *The Litigious Debtor*, 18 Litig. 41 (Spring 1992).

Cohen, *Chapter 20 Cases: An Appropriate Tool?*, 4 J. Bankr. L. & Prac. 53 (1994).

Cohen & Klee, *Caveat Creditor: The Consumer Debtor Under the Bankruptcy Code*, 58 N.C. L. Rev. 681 (1980).

Coleman, *Individual Consumer "Chapter 20" Cases After Johnson: An Introduction to Nonbusiness Serial Filings Under Chapter 7 and Chapter 13 of the Bankruptcy Code*, 9 Bankr. Dev. J. 357 (1992).

Comment, *Bankruptcy Code Provision Which Limits Dischargeability of Educational Loans Applies to Non-Student Co-Obligor of the Loan*, 23 Seton Hall L. Rev. 1934 (1993).

Comment, *Bankruptcy—Discharge of Debt—Justification of Failure to Maintain Financial Records Rests with the Debtor and Failure to Justify Bars a Debtor's Discharge of Indebtedness Claim*, 22 Seton Hall L. Rev. 1578 (1992).

Comment, *Bankruptcy Estate Planning: Grounds for Denial of Discharge Under Section 727(a)(2)(A)*, 7 Bankr. Dev. J. 199 (1990).

Comment, *Bankruptcy Law—When Creditors Can Force the Sale of a Home Owned by a Debtor and Nondebtor Spouse as Tenants by the Entirety—In re Persky, 893 F.2d 15 (2d Cir. 1989)*, 24 Suffolk U. L. Rev. 790 (1990).

Comment, *Closing the Escape Hatch in the Mandatory Withdrawal Provision of 28 U.S.C. § 157(d)*, 36 UCLA L. Rev. 417 (coauthored by Erich D. Anderson).

Comment, *The Debtor Trap: The Ironies of Section 707(a)*, 7 Bankr. Dev. J. 175 (1990).

Comment, *Equitable Standards of Excusable Neglect: A Critical Analysis of Pioneer Investment Services Co. v. Brunswick Associates Limited Partnership*, 11 Bankr. Dev. J. 181 (1995).

Comment, *"A Fresh Start with Someone Else's Property": Lien Avoidance, the Homestead Exemption and Divorce Property Divisions Under Section 522(f)(1) of the Bankruptcy Code*, 59 Fordham L. Rev. 423 (1990).

Comment, *Johnson v. Home State Bank: Seven Plus Thirteen Can Equal Twenty*, 43 Mercer L. Rev. 1291 (1992).

Comment, *Jury Trials in Bankruptcy: "Give 'Em What They Want,"* 57 Alb. L. Rev. 1157 (1994).

Comment, *Mandatory Abstention Under 28 U.S.C. § 1334(c)(2)*, 4 Bankr. Dev. J. 279 (1987).

Comment, *The Mootness Doctrine in Bankruptcy*, 7 Bankr. Dev. J. 313 (1990).

Comment, *Must Courts Apply Section 109(g)(2) When Debtors Intend No Abuse in an Earlier Dismissal of Their Case?*, 7 Bankr. Dev. J. 103 (1990).

Comment, *In Re Nobelman—A Day Late & A Dollar Unsecured*, 11 Bankr. Dev. J. 127 (1995).

Comment, *Nondischargeability of Educational Debts Under Section 523(A)(8) of the Bankruptcy Code: Equitable Treatment of Cosigners and Guarantors?*, 11 Bankr. Dev. J. 481 (1995).

Comment, *Permissive Withdrawal of Bankruptcy Proceedings Under 28 U.S.C. Section 157(d)*, 11 Bankr. Dev. J. 447 (1995).

Comment, *Postconfirmation Modification of Chapter 13 Plans: A Sheep in Wolf's Clothing*, 9 Bankr. Dev. J. 153 (1992).

Comment, *Property of the Estate After Confirmation of a Chapter 13 Repayment Plan: Balancing Competing Interests*, 65 Wash. L. Rev. 677 (1990).

Comment, *Protecting Non-ERISA Pension Funds From the Reach of Creditors in Bankruptcy*, 11 Bankr. Dev. J. 181 (1995).

Comment, *Providing Adequate Assurance for Utilities Under Section 366*, 9 Bankr. Dev. J. 199 (1992).

Comment, *Recent Decisions, Bankruptcy Law—Creditor Rights to Post-Petition Attorney's Fees Under Section 523(a)(2)—TranSouth Financial Corp. of Florida v. Johnson, 931 F.2d 1505 (11th Cir. 1991)*, 65 Temp. L. Rev. 227 (1992).

Comment, *Sanctions Against the Creditor's Attorney in Non-Reorganization Bankruptcy Proceedings*, 6 Bankr. Dev. J. 481 (1990).

Comment, *Something Every Divorce Attorney Should Know About Bankruptcy Law*, 23 S. Ill. U. L.J. 735 (1999).

Comment, *Toward a Theory of Public Rights: Article III and the Bankruptcy Amendments and Federal Judgeship Act of 1984*, 70 Neb. L. Rev. 555 (1991).

Consumer Bankruptcy: A Roundtable Discussion, 2 Am. Bankr. Inst. L. Rev. 5 (1994).

Cook & Mendales, *The Uniform Fraudulent Transfer Act: An Introductory Critique*, 62 Am. Bankr. L.J. 87 (1988).

Corish & Herbert, *The Debtor's Dilemma: Disposable Income as the Cost of Chapter 13 Discharge in Consumer Bankruptcy*, 47 La. L. Rev. 47 (1986).

Countryman, *Bankruptcy and the Individual Debtor—And a Modest Proposal to Return to the Seventeenth Century*, 32 Cath. U. L. Rev. 809 (1983).

Countryman, *The Bankruptcy Judges: Jurisdiction by Neglect*, 92 Com. L.J. 1 (1987).

Countryman, *Bankruptcy Preferences—Current Law and Proposed Changes*, 11 UCC L.J. 95 (1978).

Countryman, *The Concept of a Voidable Preference in Bankruptcy*, 38 Vand. L. Rev. 713 (1985).

Countryman, *Emergency Rule Compounds Emergency*, 57 Am. Bankr. L.J. 1 (1983).

Countryman, *Is The National Labor Policy Headed For Bankruptcy?*, 1984 Ann. Surv. Bankr. L. 159.

Countryman, *Scrambling to Define Bankruptcy Jurisdiction: the Chief Justice, the Judicial Conference, and the Legislative Process*, 22 Harv. J. on Legis. 1 (1985).

Cristol, Cassidy & Walden, *Exemption Planning: How Far May You Go?*, 48 S.C. L. Rev. 715 (1998).

Cross, *The Application of Section 522(f) of the Bankruptcy Code in Cases Involving Multiple Liens*, 6 Bankr. Dev. J. 309 (1989).

Cross, *Viewing Federal Jurisdiction Through the Looking Glass of Bankruptcy*, 23 Seton Hall L. Rev. 530 (1993).

Cuevas, *Bankruptcy Code Section 544(a) and Constructive Trusts: The Trustee's Strong Arm Powers Should Prevail*, 21 Seton Hall L. Rev. 678 (1991).

Cuevas, *The Consumer Credit Industry, The Consumer Bankruptcy System, Bankruptcy Code Section 707(b) and Justice: A Critical Analysis of the Consumer Bankruptcy System*, 103 Com. L.J. 359 (1998).

Culhane & White, *Debt After Discharge: An Empirical Study of Reaffirmation*, 73 Am. Bankr. L.J. 709 (1999).

Cullen, *Does Anybody Know the Rules in Federal Divorce Court?: A Case for Revision of Bankruptcy Code § 523*, 46 Rutgers L. Rev. 427 (1993).

Cyr, *The Chapter 13 "Good Faith" Tempest: An Analysis and Proposal for Change*, 55 Am. Bankr. L.J. 271 (1981).

DeJarnatt, *In re McCrate: Using Consumer Bankruptcy as a Context for Learning in Advanced Legal Writing*, 50 J. Legal Educ. 50 (2000).

Dickerson, *Bankruptcy Reform: Does the End Justify the Means?*, 75 Am. Bankr. L.J. 243 (2001).

Dickerson, *Family Values and the Bankruptcy Code: A Proposal to Eliminate Bankruptcy Benefits Awarded on the Basis of Marital Status*, 67 Fordham L. Rev. 69 (1998).

Dickerson, *Can Shame, Guilt, or Stigma Be Taught? Why Credit-Focused Debtor Education May Not Work*, 32 Loy. L.A. L. Rev. 945 (1999).

Doherty, *The Interplay Between Bankruptcy and Divorce: Which Former Spouse Deserves the Fresh Start?*, 99 Com. L.J. 192 (1994).

Dole, *Making Due Allowances for Undercollateralized Residential Mortgagees Under Chapter 13 of the Bankruptcy Code*, 1987 Ann. Surv. Bankr. L. 179.

Dole, *Preserving Rights in a Home Through Bankruptcy*, 4 Bankr. Dev. J. 1 (1987).

Domowitz & Sartain, *Incentives and Bankruptcy Chapter Choice: Evidence from the Reform Act*, 28 J. Legal Stud. 461 (1999).

Donald & Latta, *The Dischargeability of Property Settlement and Hold Harmless Agreements in Bankruptcy: An Overview of §523(a)(15)*, 31 Fam. L.Q. 409 (1997).

Drake, *Discharge of Federal Income Taxes in Bankruptcy*, 90 Com. L.J. 466 (1985).

Drake & Morris, *Eligibility for Relief Under Chapter 13*, 57 Am. Bankr. L.J. 195 (1983).

Dreher & Connors, *Fight or Flight: How To Handle a Bankruptcy Stay*, 2 Prac. Litigator 25 (1991).

Duncan, *From Dismemberment to Discharge: The Origins of Modern American Bankruptcy Law*, 100 Com. L.J. 191 (1995).

Dunham, *Pensions and Other Funds in Individual Bankruptcy Cases*, 4 Bankr. Dev. J. 293 (1987).

Dunham & Shimkus, *Tax Claims in Bankruptcy*, 67 Am. Bankr. L.J. 343 (1993).

Effross, *Grammarians At the Gate: The Rehnquist Court's Evolving "Plain Meaning" Approach to Bankruptcy Jurisprudence*, 23 Seton Hall L. Rev. 1636 (1993).

Eisenberg, *Bankruptcy Law in Perspective: A Rejoinder*, 30 UCLA L. Rev. 617 (1983).

Eisenberg, *A Bankruptcy Machine That Would Go of Itself*, 39 Stan. L. Rev. 1519 (1987).

Eisenberg, *Commentary on "On The Nature of Bankruptcy": Bankruptcy and Bargaining*, 75 Va. L. Rev. 205 (1989).

Eisenberg & Gecker, *Due Process and Bankruptcy: A Contradiction in Terms?*, 10 Bankr. Dev. J. 47 (1993–1994).

Elfenbein, *Patterson v. Shumate: Interpretive Error*, 66 Am. Bankr. L.J. 439 (1992).

Ellis, *Protect Your Client's Alimony From Discharge in Bankruptcy*, 36 Prac. Law. 55 (1990).

Epling, *Contractual Cure in Bankruptcy*, 61 Am. Bankr. L.J. 71 (1987).

Epling, *Treatment of Land Sales Contracts Under the New Bankruptcy Code*, 56 Am. Bankr. L.J. 55 (1982).

Epstein, *Chapter 13: Its Operation, Its Statutory Requirements as to Payment to and Classification of Unsecured Claims, and Its Advantages*, 20 Washburn L.J. 1 (1979–1980).

Epstein, *Consequences of Converting a Bankruptcy Case*, 60 Am. Bankr. L.J. 339 (1986).

Epstein & Fuller, *Chapters 11 and 13 of the Bankruptcy Code—Observations on Using Case Authority from One of the Chapters in Proceedings Under the Other*, 38 Vand. L. Rev. 901 (1985).

Fallon, *Of Legislative Courts, Administrative Agencies, and Article III*, 101 Harv. L. Rev. 916 (1988).

Federico, *Dischargeability Proceedings and Default Judgments: Does the Bankruptcy Code Implicitly Repeal the Full Faith and Credit Requirement of 28 U.S.C. § 1738?*, 71 Am. Bankr. L.J. 563 (1997).

Ferguson, *Discourse and Discharge: Linguistic Analysis and Abuse of the "Exemption by Declaration" Process in Bankruptcy*, 70 Am. Bankr. L.J. 55 (1996).

Ferriell, *The Constitutionality of the Bankruptcy Amendments and Federal Judgeship Act of 1984*, 63 Am. Bankr. L.J. 109 (Spring 1989).

Ferriell, *The Preclusive Effect of State Court Decisions in Bankruptcy, First Installment*, 58 Am. Bankr. L.J. 349 (1984).

Ferriell, *The Preclusive Effect of State Court Decisions in Bankruptcy, Second Installment*, 59 Am. Bankr. L.J. 55 (1985).

Filbich & Floyd, *Impact of Bankruptcy on Family Law*, 29 S. Tex. L. Rev. 637 (1988).

Fitzgerald & Arena, *Wrestling With Bankruptcy and Divorce Laws in Property Division and Support Issues*, 6 J. Am. Acad. Matrimonial L. 1 (1990).

Flint, *Bankruptcy Policy: Toward a Moral Justification for Financial Rehabilitation of the Consumer Debtor*, 48 Wash. & Lee L. Rev. 515 (1991).

Fogel, *Executory Contracts and Unexpired Leases in the Bankruptcy Code*, 64 Minn. L. Rev. 341 (1980).

Fortgang & King, *The 1978 Bankruptcy Code: Some Wrong Policy Decisions*, 56 N.Y.U. L. Rev. 1148 (1981).

Fortgang & Mayer, *Valuation in Bankruptcy*, 32 UCLA L. Rev. 1061 (1985).

Fortina & Johnson, *Drafting Settlement Agreements on the Eve of Bankruptcy*, 7 Bankr. Dev. J. 65 (1990).

Franke, *The Code and the Constitution: Fifth Amendment Limits on the Debtor's Discharge in Bankruptcy*, 17 Pepp. L. Rev. 853 (1990).

Frasier, *Caught in a Cycle of Neglect: The Accuracy of Bankruptcy Statistics*, 101 Com. L.J. 307 (1996).

Freeburger & Bowles, *What Divorce Court Giveth, Bankruptcy Court Taketh Away: A Review of the Dischargeability of Marital Support Obligations*, 24 J. Fam. L. 587 (1985–1986).

Frimet, *The Birth of Bankruptcy in the United States*, 96 Com. L.J. 160 (1991).

Garvis & Koger, *If At First You Don't Succeed . . .: An Alternative Remedy After Nordic Village*, 66 Am. Bankr. L.J. 423 (1992).

Gelfand, *How a Community Saved Their Hospitals from Unnecessary Liquidation*, 75 Am. Bankr. L.J. 3 (2001).

Gerson, *A Bankruptcy Exception to Eleventh Amendment Immunity: Limiting the Seminole Tribe Doctrine*, 74 Am. Bankr. L.J. 1 (2000).

Gibson, *Jury Trials and Core Proceedings: The Bankruptcy Judge's Uncertain Authority*, 65 Am. Bankr. L.J. 143 (1991).

Gibson, *Sovereign Immunity in Bankruptcy: The Next Chapter*, 70 Am. Bankr. L.J. 195 (1996).

Giles, *Till Debt Do Us Part: Prebankruptcy Planning*, 14 Fam. Advoc. 22 (1992).

Girth, *The Bankruptcy Reform Process: Maximizing Judicial Control in Wage Earners' Plans*, 11 U. Mich. J.L. Reform 51 (1977).

Girth, *The Role of Empirical Data in Developing Bankruptcy Legislation*, 65 Ind. L.J. 17 (1989).

Gold, *The Dischargeability of Divorce Obligations Under the Bankruptcy Code: Five Faulty Premises in the Application of Section 523(a)(5)*, 39 Case W. Res. L. Rev. 455 (1989).

Goldstein & Lipp, *Practical Tips on Drafting Separation Agreements*, 14 Fam. Advoc. 42 (1992).

Greenfield, *The National Bankruptcy Conference's Position on the Court System Under the Bankruptcy Amendments and Federal Judgeship Act of 1984, and Suggestions for Rules Promulgation*, 23 Harv. J. on Legis. 357 (1986).

Grippando, *Circuit Court Review of Orders on Stays Pending Bankruptcy Appeals to U.S. District Court or Appellate Panels*, 62 Am. Bankr. L.J. 353 (1988).

Gross, *The Debtor as Modern Day Peon: A Problem of Unconstitutional Conditions*, 65 Notre Dame L. Rev. 165 (1990).

Gross, Failure and Forgiveness: Rebalancing the Bankruptcy System (1999).

Gross, *In Forma Pauperis In Bankruptcy: Reflecting On and Beyond United States v. Kras*, 2 Am. Bankr. Inst. L. Rev. 57 (1994).

Gross, *Justice Thurgood Marshall's Bankruptcy Jurisprudence: A Tribute*, 67 Am. Bankr. L.J. 447 (1993).

Gross, *Perceptions and Misperceptions of Reaffirmation Agreements*, 102 Com. L.J. 339 (1997).

Gross, *Preserving a Fresh Start for the Individual Debtor: The Case for Narrow Construction of the Consumer Credit Amendments*, 135 U. Pa. L. Rev. 59 (1988).

Guyerson & Daley, *Propriety of Class Proofs of Claim in Bankruptcy*, 63 Am. Bankr. L.J. 249 (1989).

Haberfelde, *A Reexamination of the Non-Dischargeability of Criminal Restitutive Obligations in Chapter 13 Bankruptcies*, 43 Hastings L.J. 1517 (1992).

Haeussler, *Bankruptcy of the Employer and the Injured Worker*, 1994–95 Ann. Surv. Bankr. L. 241.

Haines, *Getting to Abrogation*, 75 Am. Bankr L.J. 447 (2001).

Hallinan, *The "Fresh Start" Policy in Consumer Bankruptcy: A Historical Inventory and an Interpretive Theory*, 21 U. Rich. L. Rev. 49 (1986).

Harris, *A Reply to Theodore Eisenberg's Bankruptcy Law in Perspective*, 30 UCLA L. Rev. 327 (1982).

Haywood, *The Power of Bankruptcy Courts to Shift Fees under the Equal Access to Justice Act*, 61 U. Chi. L. Rev. 985 (1994).

Henderson, *For Better or for Worse: Liability of Community Property After Bankruptcy*, 29 Idaho L. Rev. 893 (1992–1993).

Hennigan, *Accommodating Regulatory Enforcement and Bankruptcy Protection*, 59 Am. Bankr. L.J. 1 (1985).

Hennigan, *Criminal Restitution and Bankruptcy Law in the Federal System*, 19 Conn. L. Rev. 89 (1986).

Herbert, *Consumer Chapter 11 Proceedings: Abuse or Alternative?*, 91 Com. L.J. 234 (1986).

Herbert, *Once More Unto the Breach, Dear Friends: The 1986 Reforms of the Reformed Bankruptcy Reform Act*, 16 Cap. U. L. Rev. 325 (1987).

Herbert, *The Trustee Versus the Trade Creditor II: The 1984 Amendment to Section 547(c)(2) of the Bankruptcy Code*, 2 Bankr. Dev. J. 201 (1985).

Herbert & Pacitti, *Down and Out in Richmond, Virginia: The Distribution of Assets in Chapter 7 Bankruptcy Proceedings Closed During 1984–1987*, 22 U. Rich. L. Rev. 303 (1988).

Hershner & Boyer, *The Farmer in Distress—Can Bankruptcy Help?*, 1985 Ann. Surv. Bankr. L. 177.

Hertz, *Bankruptcy Code Exemptions: Notes on the Effect of State Law*, 54 Am. Bankr. L.J. 339 (1980).

Heston, *Bankruptcy and Dissolution: Prevention, Action, and Reaction*, 13 Com. Prop. J. 10 (1987).

Howard, *Avoiding Powers and the 1994 Amendments to the Bankruptcy Code*, 69 Am. Bankr. L.J. 259 (1995).

Howard, *Bankruptcy Empiricism: Lighthouse Still No Good*, 17 Bankr. Dev. J. 425 (2001) (book review).

Howard, *A Bankruptcy Primer for the Family Lawyer*, 31 Fam. L.Q. 377 (1997).

Howard, *Multiple Judicial Liens in Bankruptcy: Section 522(f)(1) Simplified*, 67 Am. Bankr. L.J. 151 (1993).

Howard, *Shifting Risk and Fixing Blame, The Vexing Problem of Credit Card Obligations in Bankruptcy*, 75 Am. Bankr. L.J. 63 (2001).

Hughes, *Code Exemptions: Far Reaching Achievement*, 28 DePaul L. Rev. 1025 (1979).

Ishii-Chang, *Litigation and Bankruptcy: The Dilemma of the Codefendant Stay*, 63 Am. Bankr. L.J. 257 (1989).

Jackson, *Avoiding Powers in Bankruptcy*, 36 Stan. L. Rev. 725 (1984).

Jackson, *Bankruptcy, Non-Bankruptcy Entitlements, and the Creditors' Bargain*, 91 Yale L.J. 857 (1982).

Jackson, *The Fresh-Start Policy in Bankruptcy Law*, 98 Harv. L. Rev. 1393 (1985).

Jackson, *Of Liquidation, Continuation, and Delay: An Analysis of Bankruptcy Policy and Nonbankruptcy Rules*, 60 Am. Bankr. L.J. 399 (1986).

Jackson, The Logic and Limits of Bankruptcy Law (1986).

Jackson, *Translating Assets and Liabilities to the Bankruptcy Forum*, 14 J. Legal Stud. 73 (1985).

Jackson & Scott, *On the Nature of Bankruptcy: An Essay on Bankruptcy Sharing and the Creditors' Bargain*, 75 Va. L. Rev. 155 (1989).

Jacoby, *Collecting Debts from the Ill and Injured: The Rhetorical Significance, But Practical Irrelevance, of Culpability and Ability to Pay*, 51 Am. U. L. Rev. 229 (2001).

Jacoby, Sullivan & Warren, *Rethinking the Debates Over Health Care Financing: Evidence from the Bankruptcy Courts*, 76 N.Y.U. L. Rev. 375 (2001).

Jensen-Conklin, *Nondischargeable Debts in Chapter 13: "Fresh Start" or "Haven for Criminals"?*, 7 Bankr. Dev. J. 517 (1990).

Johnson, *Discharging Unscheduled Debts: Creating Equal Justice for Creditors by Restoring Integrity to Section 523(A)(3)*, 10 Bankr. Dev. J. 571 (1994).

Julis, *Classifying Rights and Interests Under the Bankruptcy Code*, 55 Am. Bankr. L.J. 223 (1981).

Kalevitch, *Cheers? The Drunk-Driving Exception to Discharge*, 63 Am. Bankr. L.J. 213 (Spring 1989).

Kalevitch, *Educational Loans in Bankruptcy*, 2 N. Ill. U. L. Rev. 325 (1982).

Kalevitch, *Lien Avoidance on Exemptions: The False Controversy Over Opt-Out*, 44 Okla. L. Rev. 443 (1991).

Kalevitch, *Some Thoughts on Entireties in Bankruptcy*, 60 Am. Bankr. L.J. 141 (1986).

Kauffman & Schupp, *Discharge of Student Loans Under Chapter 13 (Wage Earner Plans) of the Bankruptcy Code*, 93 Com. L.J. 101 (1988).

Kaye, *The Case Against Class Proofs of Claim in Bankruptcy*, 66 N.Y.U. L. Rev. 897 (1991).

Kelch, *An Apology for Plain-Meaning Interpretation of the Bankruptcy Code*, 10 Bankr. Dev. J. 289 (1994).

Kennedy, *Automatic Stay in Bankruptcy*, 11 U. Mich. J.L. Reform 177 (1978).

Kennedy, *Automatic Stays Under the New Bankruptcy Law*, 12 U. Mich. J.L. Reform 1 (1978).

Kennedy, *The Bankruptcy Court Under the New Bankruptcy Law: Its Structure, Jurisdiction, Venue, and Procedure*, 11 St. Mary's L.J. 251 (1979).

Kennedy, *The Commencement of a Case Under the New Bankruptcy Code*, 36 Wash. & Lee L. Rev. 977 (1979).

Kennedy, *Cramdown of the Secured Creditor Under Chapter 13 of the Bankruptcy Code*, 1982 Ann. Surv. Bankr. L. 253.

Kennedy, *Foreword: A Brief History of the Bankruptcy Reform Act*, 58 N.C. L. Rev. 667 (1980).

Kennedy, *Involuntary Fraudulent Transfers*, 9 Cardozo L. Rev. 531 (1987).

Kennedy, *New Bankruptcy Act Impact on Consumer Credit*, 33 Bus. Law. 1059 (1978).

Kennedy, *Secured Creditors Under the Bankruptcy Reform Act*, 15 Ind. L. Rev. 477 (1982).

Kennedy, *Some Comments About the Rules of Bankruptcy Procedure Under the Bankruptcy Reform Act*, 85 Com. L.J. 125 (1980).

Kennedy & Bailey, *Gambling and the Bankruptcy Discharge: An Historical Exegesis and Case Survey*, 11 Bankr. Dev. J. 49 (1995).

Kimmelman, *"Let There Be Light"? The Pitfalls and Possibilities for Utilities Under the Bankruptcy Code*, 57 Am. Bankr. L.J. 155 (1983).

King, *Assuming and Assigning Executory Contracts: A History of Indeterminate "Applicable Law"*, 70 Am. Bankr. L.J. 95 (1996).

King, *The History and Development of the Bankruptcy Rules*, 70 Am. Bankr. L.J. 217 (1996).

King, *Jurisdiction and Procedure Under the Bankruptcy Amendments of 1984*, 38 Vand. L. Rev. 675 (1985).

Klee, *All You Ever Wanted to Know About Cram Down Under the New Bankruptcy Code*, 53 Am. Bankr. L.J. 133 (1979).

Klee, *The Future of the Bankruptcy Rules*, 70 Am. Bankr. L.J. 277 (1996).

Klee, *Legislative History of the New Bankruptcy Code*, 54 Am. Bankr. L.J. 275 (1980).

Klee, *Tithing and Bankruptcy*, 75 Am. Bankr. L. J. 157 (2001).

Klee, Johnson & Wilson, *State Defiance of Bankruptcy Law*, 52 Vand. L. Rev. 1527 (1999).

Klee & Merola, *Ignoring Congressional Intent: Eight Years of Judicial Legislation*, 62 Am. Bankr. L.J. 1 (1988).

Klein, *Bankruptcy Rules Made Easy: A Guide to the Federal Rules of Civil Procedure That Apply in Bankruptcy*, 70 Am. Bankr. L.J. 301 (1996).

Klein, *Bankruptcy Rules Made Easy (2001): A Guide to the Federal Rules of Civil Procedure That Apply in Bankruptcy*, 75 Am. Bankr. L.J. 35 (2001).

Klein, *Consumer Bankruptcy in the Balance: The National Bankruptcy Review Commission's Recommendations Tilt Toward Creditors*, 5 Am. Bankr. Inst. L. Rev. 293 (1997).

Klein, *Means Tested Bankruptcy: What Would it Mean?*, 28 U. Mem. L. Rev. 711 (1998).

Koffler, *The Bankruptcy Clause and Exemption Laws: A Reexamination of the Doctrine of Geographic Uniformity*, 58 N.Y.U. L. Rev. 22 (1983).

Koger & Reynolds, *Is Prefiling Engineering Prudent Planning or Section 727 Fraud? (Or, When Does a Pig Become a Hog?)*, 93 Com. L.J. 465 (1988).

Koger & True, *The Final Word on Excusable Neglect?*, 98 Comm. L.J. 21 (1993).

Korobkin, *"Killing the Husband": Disallowing Contingent Claims for Contribution or Indemnity in Bankruptcy*, 11 Cardozo L. Rev. 737 (1990).

Kosel, *Running the Gauntlet of "Undue Hardship"—The Discharge of Student Loans in Bankruptcy*, 11 Golden Gate U. L. Rev. 457 (1980).

Kovac, *Judgment-Proof Debtors in Bankruptcy*, 65 Am. Bankr. L.J. 675 (1991).

Kratsch & Young, *Criminal Prosecutions and Manipulative Restitution: The Use of State Criminal Courts for Contravention of Debtor Relief*, 1984 Ann. Surv. Bankr. L. 107.

Kripke, *Some Reflections After a Quarter-Century of the Uniform Commercial Code and on the Inception of a New Bankruptcy Code*, 87 Com. L.J. 124 (1982).

Kropp, *The Safety Valve Status of Consumer Bankruptcy Law: The Decline of Unions as a Partial Explanation for the Dramatic Increase in Consumer Bankruptcies*, 7 Va. J. Soc. Pol'y & L. 1 (1999).

Lander, *An Analysis and Comparison of the Nondischargeability Provisions of Chapter 11 and Chapter 13 of the Bankruptcy Code*, 27 St. Louis U. L.J. 639 (1983).

Laurence, *At Home With the Bankruptcy Code: Residential Leases, Installment Real Estate Contracts and Home Mortgages*, 61 Am. Bankr. L.J. 125 (1987).

Lawless & Ferris, *Economics and the Rhetoric of Valuation*, 5 J. Bankr. L. & Prac. 3 (1995).

Lee, *Chapter 13 Nee Chapter XIII*, 53 Am. Bankr. L.J. 303 (1979).

Leonard, *Having Thought About Private Matters: The Federal Courts' Initial Response*, 77 Am. Bankr. L.J. 9 (2003).

Lerch, Gan & Loy, *Should Your Divorce Client File for Bankruptcy?*, 39 [No. 2]Prac. Law. 21 (1993).

Levin, *An Introduction to the Trustee's Avoiding Powers*, 53 Am. Bankr. L.J. 173 (1979).

Litman, *Bankruptcy Status of "ERISA Qualified Pension Plans"—An Epilogue to Patterson v. Shumate*, 9 Am. Bankr. Inst. L. Rev. 637 (2001).

Long, *Religious Exercise as Credit Risk*, 10 Bankr. Dev. J. 119 (1993–1994).

LoPucki, *The Demographics of Bankruptcy Practice*, 63 Am. Bankr. L.J. 289 (1989).

LoPucki, *"Encouraging" Repayment Under Chapter 13 of the Bankruptcy Code*, 18 Harv. J. on Legis. 347 (1981).

Luckett, *Personal Bankruptcies*, 74 Fed. Res. Bull. 591 (Sept. 1988).

Lukey & Morthorst, *Section 109—Who May Be a Debtor*, 1989 Ann. Surv. Bankr. L. 551.

Macey, *Preferences and Fraudulent Transfers Under the Bankruptcy Reform Act of 1978*, 28 Emory L.J. 685 (1979).

Maloy, *Does the New Exception to Discharge in Bankruptcy Give the Marital Creditor a Benefit or a Trompe L'Oeil*, 6 J. Bankr. L. & Prac. 51 (1996).

Maloy, *Should Bankruptcy Be Reserved for People Who Have Money? Or Is the Bankruptcy Court a Court of the United States?*, 7 J. Bankr. L. & Prac. 3 (1997).

Maloy, *Using Bankruptcy Court to Modify Domestic Relations Decrees: Problems Created by § 523(a)(15)*, 31 Fam. L.Q. 433 (1997).

Mann, Republic of Debtors: Bankruptcy in the Age of American Independence (2002).

Matthews, *The Right to Jury Trial in Bankruptcy Courts: Constitutional Implications in the Wake of Granfinanciera, S.A. v. Nordberg*, 65 Am. Bankr. L.J. 43 (1991).

Matthews, *The Scope of Claims Under the Bankruptcy Code*, (Part I), 57 Am. Bankr. L.J. 221 (1982).

Matthews, *The Scope of Claims Under the Bankruptcy Code*, (Part II), 57 Am. Bankr. L.J. 339 (1983).

McCafferty, *The Effect of Bankruptcy on the Debtor's Pending Litigation*, 93 Com. L.J. 214 (1988).

McCoid, *Discharge: The Most Important Development in Bankruptcy History*, 70 Am. Bankr. L.J. 163 (1996).

McCoid, *The Origins of Voluntary Bankruptcy*, 5 Bankr. Dev. J. 361 (1988).

McCoid, *Right to Jury Trial in Bankruptcy: Granfinanciera, S.A. v. Nordberg*, 65 Am. Bankr. L.J. 15 (1991).

McGarity, *Avoidable Transfers Between Spouses and Former Spouses*, 31 Fam. L.Q. 393 (1997).

McGarity, *Who Gets the Retirement Plan?*, 14 Fam. Advoc. 53 (1992).

McIntrye, *A Sociological Perspective on Bankruptcy*, 65 Ind. L.J. 123 (1989–1990).

Merrick, *Chapter 13 of the Bankruptcy Reform Act of 1978*, 56 Denv. L.J. 585 (1979).

Miles, *The Bifurcation of Undersecured Residential Mortgages Under § 1322(b)(2) of the Bankruptcy Code: The Final Resolution*, 67 Am. Bankr. L.J. 207 (1993).

Miles, *A Debtor's Right to Avoid Liens Against Exempt Property Under Section 522 of the Bankruptcy Code: Meaningless or Meaningful?*, 65 Am. Bankr. L.J. 117 (1991).

Morris, *Crime and Discharging Punishment: Criminal Restitution after Davenport*, 2 Faulkner & Gray's Bankr. L. Rev. 50 (Winter 1991).

Morris, *When Are Student Loans Dischargeable?* Faulkner & Gray's Bankr. L. Rev. (Spring 1989).

Morris & Ulrich, *Reaffirmation Under the Consumer Bankruptcy Amendments of 1984: A Loser For All Concerned*, 43 Wash. L. Rev. 111 (1986).

Moss & Gibbs, *The Rise of Consumer Bankruptcy: Evolution, Revolution, or Both*, 73 Am. Bankr. L.J. 311 (1999).

Mueller, *Bankruptcy In Rem Jurisdiction Redefined Within the Constitutional Boundaries Set by Shaffer v. Heitner*, 64 Am. Bankr. L.J. 201 (1990).

Munson, *Discharge of Post-Marital Support Obligations Under the New Bankruptcy Code*, 4 Harv. Women's L.J. 177 (1981).

Murphy, *Can They Do That? The Due Process and Article III Problems of Proposed Findings of Criminal Contempt in Bankruptcy Court*, 78 Minn. L. Rev. 1607 (1994).

Murphy, *The Dischargeability in Bankruptcy of Debts for Alimony and Property Settlements Arising From Divorce*, 14 Pepp. L. Rev. 69 (1986).

Murphy, *Utility Service to Debtors in Bankruptcy*, 16 Cap. U. L. Rev. 507 (1987).

Newborn, *The New Rawlsian Theory of Bankruptcy Ethics*, 16 Cardozo L. Rev. 111 (1994).

Newborn, *Undersecured Creditors in Bankruptcy: Dewsnup, Nobelman, and the Decline of Priority*, 25 Ariz. St. L.J. 547 (1993).

Nichols, *The Poor Need Not Apply: Moralistic Barriers to Bankruptcy's Fresh Start*, 25 Rutgers L.J. 329 (1994).

Nimmer, *Executory Contracts in Bankruptcy: Protecting the Fundamental Terms of the Bargain*, 54 U. Colo. L. Rev. 507 (1983).

Note, *Asset Forfeiture (Modern Anti-Drug Weapon): Is Bankruptcy a "Defense"?*, 25 Tulsa L.J. 617 (1990).

Note, *Class Action—Bankruptcy—Bankruptcy Judge May Exercise Discretion to Allow a Representative to File a Class Proof of Claim in a Bankruptcy Proceeding*, 59 Miss. L.J. 639 (1990).

Note, *Eleventh Amendment Immunity in Bankruptcy: Breaking the Seminole Tribe Barrier*, 75 N.Y.U. L. Rev. 199 (2000).

Note, *Field v. Mans and In re Keim: Excepting Debts from Bankruptcy Discharge and the Difference Between "Experienced Horsemen" and "Reasonable Men,"* 54 Ark. L. Rev. 99 (2001).

Note, *Fifteen Years After Weintraub: Who Controls the Individual's Attorney-Client Privilege in Bankruptcy?*, 80 B.U. L. Rev. 635 (2000).

Note, *"Good Faith" Analysis Under Chapter 13—The Totality of Circumstances Approach: Handeen v. Lemaire*, 23 Creighton L. Rev. 573 (1990).

Note, *Good Faith and Chapter 13 Discharge: How Much Discretion is Too Much?*, 11 Cardozo L. Rev. 657 (1990).

Note, *Jurisprudence and Jurisdiction: Toward a More Flexible Approach to Bankruptcy Interlocutory Appeals*, 67 Fordham L.Rev. 326 (1999).

Note, *The 1984 Bankruptcy Amendments: What Congress Intended by Changing Section 1475 to Section 1412*, 8 Bankr. Dev. J. 553 (1991).

Note, *Property Transfers Under Section 727 of the Bankruptcy Code: Defining the Moment of Transfer*, 72 S. Cal. L. Rev. 1179 (1999).

Note, *Separate Classification of Child Support Arrearages in a Chapter 13 Bankruptcy Plan: In re Leser*, 25 Creighton L. Rev. 977 (1992).

Note, *Separate Classification of Student Loans in Chapter 13*, 73 Wash. U. L.Q. 269 (1995).

Note, *The Supreme Court, Textualism, and the Treatment of Pre-Bankruptcy Code Law*, 79 Geo. L.J. 1831 (1991).

Note, *Suretyship as Adequate Protection in Bankruptcy: The Status of Unsecured Third Party Guaranties Under Section 361 of the Bankruptcy Code*, 12 Cardozo L. Rev. 285 (1990).

Note, *Using Unfiled Dischargeable Tax Liens to Attach to ERISA—Qualified Pension Plan Interests After Patterson v. Shumate*, 14 Bankr. Dev. J. 461 (1998).

Note, *When Creditors Can Force the Sale of a Home Owned by a Debtor and Nondebtor Spouse as Tenants by the Entirety*, 24 Suffolk U. L. Rev. 801 (1990).

Note & Comment, *Confusion Over § 522(d)(11)(D): What Congress Really Meant by Exempting Payments For "Personal Bodily Injury" and Why They Got it Wrong*, 16 Bankr. Dev. J. 503 (2000).

Note & Comment, *The Dischargeability of Student Loans: An Undue Burden?*, 17 Bank. Dev. J. 537 (2001).

Nowka, *Validating a Debtor's Retention of Collateral by Continuing Performance: Removing the Obstructions of 11 U.S.C. § 521(2)(A) and Ipso Facto Clauses*, 6 J. Bankr. L. & Prac. 145 (1997).

Obee & Plouffe, *Privacy in the Federal Bankruptcy Courts*, 14 Notre Dame J.L. Ethics & Pub. Pol'y 1011 (2000).

Ostrow, *Constitutionality of Core Jurisdiction*, 68 Am. Bankr. L.J. 91 (1994).

Parkinson, *The Contempt Power of the Bankruptcy Court Fact or Fiction: The Debate Continues*, 65 Am. Bankr. L.J. 591 (1991).

Parkman, *The Dischargeability of Post-Divorce Financial Obligations Between Spouses: Insights from Bankruptcy in Business Situations*, 31 Fam. L.Q. 493 (1997).

Pedlar, *Community Property and the Bankruptcy Reform Act of 1978*, 11 St. Mary's L.J. 349 (1979).

Petersen, *Prebankruptcy Planning With ERISA—Qualified Pension Plans and Individual Retirement*

Accounts After Patterson v. Shumate, 29 Willamette L. Rev. 893 (1993).

Pitts, *Rights to Future Payment as Property of the Estate Under Section 541 of the Bankruptcy Code*, 64 Am. Bankr. L.J. 61 (1990).

Ponder, *Emerging Marital Property Issues in Bankruptcy Practice*, 13 Com. Prop. J. 32 (1986).

Posner, *The Political Economy of the Bankruptcy Reform Act of 1978*, 96 Mich. L. Rev. 47 (1997).

Price & Rahdert, *Distributing the First Fruits: Statutory and Constitutional Implications of Tithing in Bankruptcy*, 26 U.C. Davis L. Rev. 853 (1993).

Proia, *The Interpretation and Application of Section 707(b) of the Bankruptcy Code*, 93 Com. L.J. 367 (1988).

Rapaport, *Avoiding Judicial Wrath: The Ten Commandments for Bankruptcy Practitioners*, 5 J. Bankr. L. & Prac. 615 (1996).

Rasmussen, *Bankruptcy and the Administrative State*, 42 Hastings L.J. 1567 (1991).

Rasmussen, *A Study of the Costs and Benefits of Textualism: The Supreme Court's Bankruptcy Cases*, 71 Wash. U. L.Q. 535 (1993).

Ravin & Rosen, *The Dischargeability in Bankruptcy of Alimony, Maintenance and Support Obligations*, 60 Am. Bankr. L.J. 1 (1986).

Recent Developments, *Freeze and Recoupment: Methods for Circumventing the Automatic Stay?*, 5 Bankr. Dev. J. 85 (1987).

Recent Developments, *Section 350(b): The Law of Reopening*, 5 Bankr. Dev. J. 63 (1987).

Rendleman, *The Bankruptcy Discharge: Toward a Fresher Start*, 58 N.C. L. Rev. 723 (1980).

Rendleman, *Liquidation Bankruptcy Under the '78 Code*, 21 Wm. & Mary L. Rev. 575 (1980).

Resnick, *The Bankruptcy Rulemaking Process*, 70 Am. Bankr. L.J. 245 (1996).

Resnick, *Prudent Planning or Fraudulent Transfer? The Use of Nonexempt Assets to Purchase or Improve Exempt Property on the Eve of Bankruptcy*, 31 Rutgers L. Rev. 615 (1978).

Resnick & Finkel, *A House May Not Be a Home: Liquidation Under the Bankruptcy Act*, 53 N.Y. St. B.J. 272 (1981).

Resnicoff, *Is It Morally Wrong to Depend on the Honesty of Your Partner or Spouse? Bankruptcy and the Dischargeability of Vicarious Debt*, 42 Case W. Res. L. Rev. 147 (1992).

Rice, *When Bankruptcy Courts Will Enjoin State "Bad Check" Proceedings: The Decline of the Primary Motivation Standard in Favor of the Younger Abstention Doctrine*, 93 Com. L. Rev. 111 (1988).

Ridge & McGlone, *Newly Adopted Uniform Fraudulent Transfer Act*, 99 Dickinson L. Rev. 117 (1994).

Riesenfeld, *Classification of Claims and Interests in Chapter 11 and 13 Cases*, 75 Calif. L. Rev. 1391 (1987).

Rodino & Parker, *The Simplest Solution*, 7 Bankr. Dev. J. 329 (1990).

Roe, *Commentary on "On the Nature of Bankruptcy": Bankruptcy, Priority, and Economics*, 75 Va. L. Rev. 219 (1989).

Rouin, *Abstention Under Section 305: When Is it Appropriate?*, 59 Am. Bankr. L. J. 89 (1985).

Ryman, *Contract Obligation: A Discussion of Morality, Bankruptcy, and Student Debt*, 42 Drake L. Rev. 205 (1993).

Salvin, *Student Loans, Bankruptcy, and the Fresh Start Policy: Must Debtors Be Impoverished to Discharge Educational Loans?*, 71 Tul. L. Rev. 139 (1996).

Scarberry, *Fixtures in Bankruptcy*, 16 Cap. U. L. Rev. 3 (1987).

Scheible, *Bankruptcy and the Modification of Support: Fresh Start, Head Start, or False Start?*, 69 N.C. L. Rev. 577 (1991).

Scheible, *Defining "Support" Under Bankruptcy Law: Revitalization of the "Necessaries" Doctrine*, 41 Vand. L. Rev. 1 (1988).

Schiffer, *The New Bankruptcy Reform Act: Its Implications for Family Law Practitioners*, 19 J. Fam. L. 1 (1980–1981).

Schneyer, *Statutory Liens Under the New Bankruptcy Code—Some Problems Remain*, 55 Am. Bankr. L.J. 1 (1981).

Scholl, *Bankruptcy Court: The Ultimate Consumer Law Forum?*, 44 Bus. Law. 935 (1989).

Schorling & Simons, *Adequate Protection for the Nondebtor Party to Executory Contracts and Unexpired Leases*, 64 Am. Bankr. L.J. 297 (1990).

Schwartzberg, *The Retreat from Pervasive Jurisdiction in Bankruptcy Court*, 7 Bankr. Dev. J. 1 (1990).

Seiden, *Judicial Lien Avoidance and the Homestead Exemption*, 3 J. Bankr. L. & Prac. 320 (1993).

Sepinuck, *Rethinking Unfair Discrimination in Chapter 13*, 74 Am. Bankr. L.J. 341 (2000).

Shanker, *Bankruptcy Asset Theory and Its Application to Executory Contracts*, 1992 Ann. Surv. Bankr. L. 97.

Shanker, *Insuring Payment to Contingent and Unidentified Creditors in Bankruptcy*, 92 Com. L.J. 199 (1992).

Shanker, *A Proposed New Executory Contract Statute*, 1993–1994 Ann. Surv. Bankr. L. 129.

Shanker, *The Treatment of Executory Contracts and Leases in the 1978 Bankruptcy Code*, 25 Prac. Law. 11 (Oct. 1979).

Sheinfeld & Caldwell, *Taxes: An Analysis of the Tax Provisions of the Bankruptcy Code and the Bankruptcy Tax Act of 1980*, 55 Am. Bankr. L.J. 97 (1981).

Shuchman, *The Average Bankrupt: A Description and Analysis of 753 Personal Bankruptcy Filings in Nine States*, 88 Com. L.J. 288 (1983).

Shuchman, *Data on the Durrett Controversy*, 9 Cardozo L. Rev. 605 (1987).

Shuchman, *New Jersey Debtors 1982–1983: An Empirical Study*, 15 Seton Hall L. Rev. 541 (1985).

Shuchman, *Social Science Research on Bankruptcy* (Book Review), 43 Rutgers L. Rev. 185 (1990).

Singer, *Section 523 of the Bankruptcy Code: The Fundamentals of Nondischargeability in Consumer Bankruptcy*, 71 Am. Bankr. L.J. 325 (1997).

D. Skeel, Debt's Dominion: A History of Bankruptcy Law in America (2001).

Skeel, *Vern Countryman and the Path of Progressive (and Populist) Bankruptcy Scholarship*, 113 Harv. L. Rev. 1075 (2000).

Skelton & Harris, *Bankruptcy Jurisdiction and Jury Trials: The Constitutional Nightmare Continues*, 8 Bankr. Dev. J. 469 (1991).

Skoler, *The Elderly and Bankruptcy Relief: Problems Protections and Realities*, 6 Bankr. Dev. J. 121 (1989).

Skoler, *The Status and Protection of Social Security Benefits in Bankruptcy Cases*, 67 Am. Bankr. L.J. 585 (1993).

Slates, *The Unscheduled Creditor in a Chapter 7 No-Asset Case*, 64 Am. Bankr. L.J. 281 (1990).

Smith & Kennedy, *Fraudulent Transfers and Obligations: Issues of Current Interest*, 43 S.C. L. Rev. 709 (1992).

Snow, *Cheers for the Common Law? A Response*, 74 Am. Bankr. L.J. 161 (2000).

Snow, *The Dischargeability of Credit Card Debt: New Developments and the Need for a New Direction*, 72 Am. Bankr. L.J. 63 (1998).

Sommer, *The Automatic Stay Packs a Punch*, 14 Fam. Advoc. 50 (1992).

Sommer, *In Forma Pauperis in Bankruptcy: The Time Has Long Since Come*, 2 Am. Bankr. Inst. L. Rev. 93 (1994).

Sommer, *The New Law of Bankruptcy: A Fresh Start for Legal Services Lawyers*, 13 Clearinghouse Rev. 1 (1979).

Sommer, *The 1984 Changes in Consumer Bankruptcy Law*, 31 Prac. 45 (1985).

H.J. Sommer & M.D. McGarity, Collier Family Law and the Bankruptcy Code (1991).

Sprayregen, *Dischargeability of Personal Income Taxes in Bankruptcy*, 64 Am. Bankr. L.J. 209 (1990).

D. Stanley & M. Girth, Bankruptcy: Problem, Process, Reform (1971).

Stern, *State Exemption Law in Bankruptcy: The Excepted Creditor as a Medium for Appraising Aspects of Bankruptcy Reform*, 33 Rutgers L. Rev. 1 (1980).

Stevenson & Consalus, *Taxing Authorities, Section 506(b) and the "Curious Comma,"* 61 Am. Bankr. L.J. 275 (1987).

Stilson, *The "Overloaded" PMSI in Bankruptcy: A Problem in Search of a Resolution*, 60 Temp. L.Q. 1 (1987).

Stripp, *An Analysis of the Role of the Bankruptcy Judge and the Use of Judicial Time*, 23 Seton Hall L. Rev. 1329 (1993).

Sullivan, *Reply: Limiting Access to Bankruptcy Discharge*, 4 Wis. L. Rev. 1069 (1984).

Sullivan, Warren & Westbrook, As We Forgive Our Debtors: Bankruptcy and Consumer Credit in America (1989).

Sullivan, Warren & Westbrook, *Folklore and Facts: A Preliminary Report from the Consumer Bankruptcy Project*, 60 Am. Bankr. L.J. 293 (1986).

Sullivan, Warren & Westbrook, The Fragile Middle Class: Americans in Debt (2000).

Sullivan, Warren & Westbrook, *From Golden Years to Bankruptcy Years*, Norton Bankr. L. Advisor (July 1998).

Sullivan, Warren & Westbrook, *Laws, Models, and Real People: Choice of Chapter in Personal Bankruptcy*, 13 Law & Soc. Inquiry 661 (1988).

Sullivan, Warren & Westbrook, *Rejoinder: Limiting Access to Bankruptcy Discharge*, 4 Wis. L. Rev. 1087 (1984).

Survey, *The Controversy Surrounding the Jurisdiction of the Bankruptcy Courts*, 5 J. Bankr. L. & Prac. 387 (1996).

Survey, *Has Congress Really Solved the Controversy Surrounding the Jurisdiction of the Bankruptcy Courts?*, 5 J. Bankr. L. & Prac. 481 (1996).

Tabb, *The Bankruptcy Reform Act in the Supreme Court*, 49 U. Pitt. L. Rev. 477 (1988).

Tabb, *The History of the Bankruptcy Laws in the United States*, 3 Am. Bankr. Inst. L. Rev. 5 (1995).

Tabb, *The Scope of the Fresh Start in Bankruptcy: Collateral Conversions and the Dischargeability Debate*, 59 Geo. Wash. L. Rev. (1990).

Tabb & Lawless, *Of Commas, Gerunds, and Conjunctions: The Bankruptcy Jurisprudence of the Rehnquist Court*, 42 Syracuse L. Rev. 823 (1991).

Taggart, *The Bankruptcy Court System*, 59 Am. Bankr. L.J. 231 (1985).

Taggart, *The New Bankruptcy Court System*, 30 Prac. Law. 11 (1984).

Taub, *Section 525—Protection Against Discriminatory Treatment*, 1985 Ann. Surv. Bankr. L. 569.

Towbin, *When Injury Cases Meet Bankruptcy*, 37 Prac. Law. 37 (1991).

Treister, et. al., *The Individual Debtor's Fresh Start under the Bankruptcy Code*, 32 Prac. Law 43 (1986).

Tucker, *The Treatment of Spousal and Support Obligations Under Chapter 13 of the Bankruptcy Reform Act*, 45 Tex. B.J. 1359 (1982).

U.S. General Accounting Office, Greater Oversight and Guidance of Bankruptcy Process Needed (1984).

Vasser, *Bankruptcy Meets Family Law: A Presumptive Approach to Dischargeability of Equitable Distribution Awards*, 5 J. Bankr. L. & Prac. 83 (1995).

Vihon, *Classification of Unsecured Claims: Squaring a Circle?*, 55 Am. Bankr. L.J. 143 (1981).

Vukowich, *Debtor's Exemption Rights Under the Bankruptcy Reform Act*, 58 N.C. L. Rev. 769 (1980).

Vukowich, *Reforming the Bankruptcy Reform Act of 1978: An Alternative Approach*, 71 Geo. L.J. 1129 (1983).

Vukowich, *A Reply to Professor Warren*, 72 Geo. L.J. 1359 (1984).

Ward, *The Supreme Court Diminishes the "Redeeming" Qualities of the Bankruptcy Code in Dewsnup v. Timm*, 1993–1994 Ann. Surv. Bankr. L. 147 (1993).

Warner, *Katchen Up in Bankruptcy: The New Jury Trial Right*, 63 Am. Bankr. L.J. 1 (Winter 1989).

Warren, *Bankrupt Children*, 86 Minn. L. Rev. 1003 (2002).

Warren, *The Bankruptcy Crisis*, 73 Ind. L.J. 1079 (1998).

Warren, *Bankruptcy Policy*, 54 U. Chi. L. Rev. 775 (1987).

Warren, *The Changing Politics of American Bankruptcy Reform*, 37 Osgoode Hall L.J. 189 (1999).

E. Warren & A. Tyagi, The Two Income Trap: Why Middle Class Mothers and Fathers are Going Broke (2003).

Warren, *The Market for Data: The Changing Role of Social Sciences in Shaping the Law*, 2002 Wis. L. Rev. 1 (2002).

Warren, *Reducing Bankruptcy Protection for Consumers: A Response*, 72 Geo. L.J. 1333 (1984).

Warren, *What Is a Women's Issue? Bankruptcy, Commercial law, and Other Gender-Neutral Topics*, 25 Harv. Women's L.J. 19 (2002).

Waxman, *The Bankruptcy Reform Act of 1994*, 11 Bankr. Dev. J. 311 (1994–1995).

Waxman, *Jury Trials After Granfinanciera: Three Proposals for Reform*, 52 Ohio St. L.J. 705 (1991).

Waxman, *Redemption or Reaffirmation: the Debtor's Exclusive Means of Retaining Possession of Collateral in Chapter 7*, 56 U. Pitts. L. Rev. 187 (1994).

Weintraub & Resnick, *Allowance of Claims and Priorities Under the New Bankruptcy Code*, 12 UCC L.J. 291 (1980).

Weintraub & Resnick, *The Bankruptcy Court's Role in Determining Dischargeability of Obligations Owed to a Former Spouse*, 18 UCC L.J. 272 (1986).

Weiss, *Contempt Power of the Bankruptcy Court*, 6 Bankr. Dev. J. 205 (1989).

Weiss, Bhandari & Robins, *An Analysis of State-Wide Variation in Bankruptcy Rates in the United States*, 17 Bankr. Dev. J. 407 (2001).

Welch, *Protect the Rights of the Creditor Spouse*, 14 Fam. Advoc. 36 (1992).

Westbrook, *Empirical Research in Consumer Bankruptcy*, 80 Tex. L. Rev. 2123 (2002).

White, *Calvin and Hobbes in Bankruptcy*, 5 NACTT Q. 18 (1992).

White, *Divorce After the Bankruptcy Reform Act of 1994: Can You Stay Warm After You Split the Blanket*, 29 Creighton L. Rev. 617 (1996).

White, *The Procedural Plight of the Property Settlement Creditor*, 31 Fam. L.Q. 463 (1997).

White, *Spousal and Child Support Payment Provisions in Chapter 13 Plans*, 16 Cap. U. L. Rev. 369 (1987).

White, *Strange Bedfellows: The Uneasy Alliance Between Bankruptcy and Family Law*, 17 N.M. L. Rev. 1 (1987).

Whitford, *Has the Time Come to Repeal Chapter 13?*, 65 Ind. L.J. 85 (1989–1990).

Williams, *Distrust: The Rhetoric and Reality of Means Testing*, 7 Am. Bankr. Inst. L. Rev. 105 (1999).

Williams, *National Bankruptcy Review Commission Tax Recommendations: Individual Debtors, Priorities, and Discharge*, 14 Bankr. Dev. J. 1 (1997).

Williamson & Nixon, *The Malpractice Trap in Divorce Court Liens*, 14 Fam. Advoc. 48 (1992).

Wiseman, *Women in Bankruptcy and Beyond*, 65 Ind. L.J. 107 (1989–1990).

Wolf, *Divorce, Bankruptcy and Metaphysics: Avoidance of Marital Liens Under § 522(f) of the Bankruptcy Code*, 31 Fam. L.Q. 513 (1997).

Wolfe, *Prefiling Engineering and Denial of Discharge: Who Should Slaughter the Hog?*, 96 Com. L.J. 189 (1991).

Wolfson, *Class Actions in Bankruptcy: A Clash of Policies Reconciled*, 5 Bankr. Dev. J. 391 (1988).

Woodward, *Exemptions, Opting Out, and Bankruptcy Reform*, 43 Ohio St. L.J. 335 (1982).

Woodward & Woodward, *Exemptions as an Incentive To Voluntary Bankruptcy: An Empirical Study*, 57 Am. Bankr. L.J. 53 (1983).

Yen, *Bankruptcy and the Low Income Client*, 34 Clearinghouse Rev. 709 (2001).

Zaretsky, *The Fraud Exception to Discharge Under the New Bankruptcy Code*, 53 Am. Bankr. L.J. 253 (1979).

Zeiler, *Section 525(b): Anti-Discrimination Protection for Employees/Debtors in the Private Sector—Is It Illusion or Reality?*, 101 Com. L.J. 152 (1996).

Bankruptcy Statutes

A.1 Selected Provisions of the Bankruptcy Code, 11 U.S.C. §§ 101–1330

Appendix A.1 contains the complete text of chapters 1, 3, and 5, subchapters I and II of chapter 7, subchapters I, II and III of chapter 11, and the complete text of chapters 12 and 13 of title 11 of the United States Code, as amended through July 2004. These statutes may also be found on the CD-Rom accompanying this volume.

CHAPTER 13—ADJUSTMENTS OF DEBTS OF AN INDIVIDUAL WITH REGULAR INCOME

Subchapter I—Officers, Administration, and the Estate

Subchapter II—The Plan

CHAPTER I
GENERAL PROVISIONS

§ 101. Definitions

In this title—

(1) "accountant" means accountant authorized under applicable law to practice public accounting, and includes professional accounting association, corporation, or partnership, if so authorized;

(2) "affiliate" means—

(A) entity that directly or indirectly owns, controls, or holds with power to vote, 20 percent or more of the outstanding voting securities of the debtor, other than an entity that holds such securities—

　(i) in a fiduciary or agency capacity without sole discretionary power to vote such securities; or

　(ii) solely to secure a debt, if such entity has not in fact exercised such power to vote;

(B) corporation 20 percent or more of whose outstanding voting securities are directly or indirectly owned, controlled, or held with power to vote, by the debtor, or by an entity that directly or indirectly owns, controls, or holds with power to vote, 20 percent or more of the outstanding voting securities of the debtor, other than an entity that holds such securities—

　(i) in a fiduciary or agency capacity without sole discretionary power to vote such securities; or

　(ii) solely to secure a debt, if such entity has not in fact exercised such power to vote;

(C) person whose business is operated under a lease or operating agreement by a debtor, or person substantially all of whose property is operated under an operating agreement with the debtor; or

(D) entity that operates the business or substantially all of the property of the debtor under a lease or operating agreement;

[(*3*) (*Redesignated to (21B)*.)]

(4) "attorney" means attorney, professional law association, corporation, or partnership, authorized under applicable law to practice law;

(5) "claim" means—

(A) right to payment, whether or not such right is reduced to judgment, liquidated, unliquidated, fixed, contingent, matured, unmatured, disputed, undisputed, legal, equitable, secured, or unsecured; or

(B) right to an equitable remedy for breach of performance if such breach gives rise to a right to payment, whether or not such right to an equitable remedy is reduced to judgment, fixed, contingent, matured, unmatured, disputed, undisputed, secured, or unsecured;

(6) "commodity broker" means futures commission merchant, foreign futures commission merchant, clearing organization, leverage transaction merchant, or commodity options dealer, as defined in section 761 of this title, with respect to which there is a customer, as defined in section 761 of this title;

(7) "community claim" means claim that arose before the commencement of the case concerning the debtor for which property of the kind specified in section 541(a)(2) of this title is liable, whether or not there is any such property at the time of the commencement of the case;

(8) "consumer debt" means debt incurred by an individual primarily for a personal, family, or household purpose;

(9) "corporation"—

(A) includes—

　(i) association having a power or privilege that a private corporation, but not an individual or a partnership, possesses;

　(ii) partnership association organized under a law that makes only the capital subscribed responsible for the debts of such association;

　(iii) joint-stock company;

　(iv) unincorporated company or association; or

　(v) business trust; but

(B) does not include limited partnership;

(10) "creditor" means—

(A) entity that has a claim against the debtor that arose at the time of or before the order for relief concerning the debtor;

(B) entity that has a claim against the estate of a kind specified in section 348(d), 502(f), 502(g), 502(h) or 502(i) of this title; or

(C) entity that has a community claim;

(11) "custodian" means—

(A) receiver or trustee of any of the property of the debtor, appointed in a case or proceeding not under this title;

(B) assignee under a general assignment for the benefit of the debtor's creditors; or

(C) trustee, receiver, or agent under applicable law, or under a contract, that is appointed or authorized to take charge of property of the debtor for the purpose of enforcing a lien against such property, or for the purpose of general administration of such property for the benefit of the debtor's creditors;

(12) "debt" means liability on a claim;

(12A) "debt for child support" means a debt of a kind specified in section 523(a)(5) of this title for maintenance or support of a child of the debtor;

(13) "debtor" means person or municipality concerning which a case under this title has been commenced;

(14) "disinterested person" means person that—

(A) is not a creditor, an equity security holder, or an insider;

(B) is not and was not an investment banker for any outstanding security of the debtor;

(C) has not been, within three years before the date of the filing of the petition, an investment banker for a security of the debtor, or an attorney for such an investment banker in connection with the offer, sale, or issuance of a security of the debtor;

(D) is not and was not, within two years before the date of the filing of the petition a director, officer or employee of the debtor or of an investment banker specified in subparagraph (B) or (C) of this paragraph; and

(E) does not have an interest materially adverse to the interest of the estate or of any class of creditors or equity security holders, by reason of any direct or indirect relationship to, connection with, or interest in, the debtor or an investment banker specified in subparagraph (B) or (C) of this paragraph, or for any other reason;

(15) "entity" includes person, estate, trust, governmental unit, and United States trustee;

(16) "equity security" means—

(A) share in a corporation, whether or not transferable or denominated "stock," or similar security;

(B) interest of a limited partner in a limited partnership; or

(C) warrant or right, other than a right to convert, to purchase, sell, or subscribe to a share, security, or interest of a kind specified in subparagraph (A) or (B) of this paragraph;

(17) "equity security holder" means holder of an equity security of the debtor;

(18) "family farmer" means—

(A) individual or individual and spouse engaged in a farming operation whose aggregate debts do not exceed $1,500,000 and not less than 80 percent of whose aggregate noncontingent, liquidated debts (excluding a debt for the principal residence of such individual or such individual and spouse unless such debt arises out of a farming operation), on the date the case is filed, arise out of a farming operation owned or operated by such individual or such individual and spouse, and such individual or such individual and spouse receive from such farming operation more than 50 percent of such individual's or such individual and spouse's gross income for the

taxable year preceding the taxable year in which the case concerning such individual or such individual and spouse was filed; or

(B) corporation or partnership in which more than 50 percent of the outstanding stock or equity is held by one family, or by one family and the relatives of the members of such family, and such family or such relatives conduct the farming operation, and

(i) more than 80 percent of the value of its assets consists of assets related to the farming operation;

(ii) its aggregate debts do not exceed $1,500,000 and not less than 80 percent of its aggregate noncontingent, liquidated debts (excluding a debt for one dwelling which is owned by such corporation or partnership and which a shareholder or partner maintains as a principal residence, unless such debt arises out of a farming operation), on the date the case is filed, arise out of the farming operation owned or operated by such corporation or such partnership; and

(iii) if such corporation issues stock, such stock is not publicly traded;

(19) "family farmer with regular annual income" means family farmer whose annual income is sufficiently stable and regular to enable such family farmer to make payments under a plan under chapter 12 of this title;

(20) "farmer" means (except when such term appears in the term "family farmer") person that received more than 80 percent of such person's gross income during the taxable year of such person immediately preceding the taxable year of such person during which the case under this title concerning such person was commenced from a farming operation owned or operated by such person;

(21) "farming operation" includes farming, tillage of the soil, dairy farming, ranching, production or raising of crops, poultry, or livestock, and production of poultry or livestock products in an unmanufactured state;

(21A) "farmout agreement" means a written agreement in which—

(A) the owner of a right to drill, produce, or operate liquid or gaseous hydrocarbons on property agrees or has agreed to transfer or assign all or a part of such right to another entity; and

(B) such other entity (either directly or through its agents or its assigns), as consideration, agrees to perform drilling, reworking, recompleting, testing, or similar or related operations, to develop or produce liquid or gaseous hydrocarbons on the property;

(21B) "Federal depository institutions regulatory agency" means—

(A) with respect to an insured depository institution (as defined in section 3(c)(2) of the Federal Deposit Insurance Act) for which no conservator or receiver has been appointed, the appropriate Federal banking agency (as defined in section 3(q) of such Act);

(B) with respect to an insured credit union (including an insured credit union for which the National Credit Union Administration has been appointed conservator or liquidating agent), the National Credit Union Administration;

(C) with respect to any insured depository institution for which the Resolution Trust Corporation has been appointed conservator or receiver, the Resolution Trust Corporation; and

(D) with respect to any insured depository institution for which the Federal Deposit Insurance Corporation has been appointed conservator or receiver, the Federal Deposit Insurance Corporation;

(22) the term "financial institution"—

(A) means—
  (i) a Federal reserve bank or an entity (domestic or foreign) that is a commercial or savings bank, industrial savings bank, savings and loan association, trust company, or receiver or conservator for such entity and, when any such Federal reserve bank, receiver, conservator, or entity is acting as agent or custodian for a customer in connection with a securities contract, as defined in section 741 of this title, the customer; or
  (ii) in connection with a securities contract, as defined in section 741 of this title, an investment company registered under the Investment Company Act of 1940; and

(B) includes any person described in subparagraph (A) which operates, or operates as, a multilateral clearing organization pursuant to section 409 of the Federal Deposit Insurance Corporation Improvement Act of 1991;

(23) "foreign proceeding" means proceeding, whether judicial or administrative and whether or not under bankruptcy law, in a foreign country in which the debtor's domicile, residence, principal place of business, or principal assets were located at the commencement of such proceeding, for the purpose of liquidating an estate, adjusting debts by composition, extension, or discharge, or effecting a reorganization;

(24) "foreign representative" means duly selected trustee, administrator, or other representative of an estate in a foreign proceeding;

(25) "forward contract" means a contract (other than a commodity contract) for the purchase, sale, or transfer of a commodity, as defined in section 761(8) of this title, or any similar good, article, service, right, or interest which is presently or in the future becomes the subject of dealing in the forward contract trade, or product or byproduct thereof, with a maturity date more than two days after the date the contract is entered into, including, but not limited to, a repurchase transaction, reverse repurchase transaction, consignment, lease, swap, hedge transaction, deposit, loan, option, allocated transaction, unallocated transaction, or any combination thereof or option thereon;

(26) "forward contract merchant" means a person whose business consists in whole or in part of entering into forward contracts as or with merchants in a commodity, as defined in section 761(8) of this title, or any similar good, article, service, right, or interest which is presently or in the future becomes the subject of dealing in the forward contract trade;

(27) "governmental unit" means United States; State; Commonwealth; District; Territory; municipality; foreign state; department,

agency, or instrumentality of the United States (but not a United States trustee while serving as a trustee in a case under this title), a State, a Commonwealth, a District, a Territory, a municipality, or a foreign state; or other foreign or domestic government;

(28) "indenture" means mortgage, deed of trust, or indenture, under which there is outstanding a security, other than a voting-trust certificate, constituting a claim against the debtor, a claim secured by a lien on any of the debtor's property, or an equity security of the debtor;

(29) "indenture trustee" means trustee under an indenture;

(30) "individual with regular income" means individual whose income is sufficiently stable and regular to enable such individual to make payments under a plan under chapter 13 of this title, other than a stockbroker or a commodity broker;

(31) "insider" includes—

(A) if the debtor is an individual—
  (i) relative of the debtor or of a general partner of the debtor;
  (ii) partnership in which the debtor is a general partner;
  (iii) general partner of the debtor; or
  (iv) corporation of which the debtor is a director, officer, or person in control;

(B) if the debtor is a corporation—
  (i) director of the debtor;
  (ii) officer of the debtor;
  (iii) person in control of the debtor;
  (iv) partnership in which the debtor is a general partner;
  (v) general partner of the debtor; or
  (vi) relative of a general partner, director, officer, or person in control of the debtor;

(C) if the debtor is a partnership—
  (i) general partner in the debtor;
  (ii) relative of a general partner in, general partner of, or person in control of the debtor;
  (iii) partnership in which the debtor is a general partner;
  (iv) general partner of the debtor; or
  (v) person in control of the debtor;

(D) if the debtor is a municipality, elected official of the debtor or relative of an elected official of the debtor;

(E) affiliate, or insider of an affiliate as if such affiliate were the debtor; and

(F) managing agent of the debtor;

(32) "insolvent" means—

(A) with reference to an entity other than a partnership and a municipality, financial condition such that the sum of such entity's debts is greater than all of such entity's property, at a fair valuation, exclusive of—
  (i) property transferred, concealed, or removed with intent to hinder, delay, or defraud such entity's creditors; and
  (ii) property that may be exempted from property of the estate under section 522 of this title;

(B) with reference to a partnership, financial condition such that the sum of such partnership's debts is greater than the aggregate of, at a fair valuation—

(i) all of such partnership's property, exclusive of property of the kind specified in subparagraph (A)(i) of this paragraph; and

(ii) the sum of the excess of the value of each general partner's nonpartnership property, exclusive of property of the kind specified in subparagraph (A) of this paragraph, over such partner's nonpartnership debts; and

(C) with reference to a municipality, financial condition such that the municipality is—

(i) generally not paying its debts as they become due unless such debts are the subject of a bona fide dispute; or

(ii) unable to pay its debts as they become due;

(33) "institution-affiliated party"—

(A) with respect to an insured depository institution (as defined in section 3(c)(2) of the Federal Deposit Insurance Act), has the meaning given it in section 3(u) of the Federal Deposit Insurance Act; and

(B) with respect to an insured credit union, has the meaning given it in section 206(r) of the Federal Credit Union Act;

(34) "insured credit union" has the meaning given it in section 101(7) of the Federal Credit Union Act;

(35) "insured depository institution"—

(A) has the meaning given it in section 3(c)(2) of the Federal Deposit Insurance Act; and

(B) includes an insured credit union (except in the case of paragraphs (21B) and (33)(A) of this subsection);

(35A) "intellectual property" means—

(A) trade secret;

(B) invention, process, design, or plant protected under title 35;

(C) patent application;

(D) plant variety;

(E) work of authorship protected under title 17; or

(F) mask work protected under chapter 9 of title 17;

to the extent protected by applicable nonbankruptcy law; and

(36) "judicial lien" means lien obtained by judgment, levy, sequestration, or other legal or equitable process or proceeding;

(37) "lien" means charge against or interest in property to secure payment of a debt or performance of an obligation;

(38) "margin payment" means, for purposes of the forward contract provisions of this title, payment or deposit of cash, a security or other property, that is commonly known in the forward contract trade as original margin, initial margin, maintenance margin, or variation margin, including mark-to-market payments, or variation payments;

(39) "mask work" has the meaning given it in section 901(a)(2) of title 17.

(40) "municipality" means political subdivision or public agency or instrumentality of a State;

(41) "person" includes individual, partnership, and corporation,

but does not include governmental unit, except that a governmental unit that—

(A) acquires an asset from a person—

(i) as a result of the operation of a loan guarantee agreement; or

(ii) as receiver or liquidating agent of a person;

(B) is a guarantor of a pension benefit payable by or on behalf of the debtor or an affiliate of the debtor; or

(C) is the legal or beneficial owner of an asset of—

(i) an employee pension benefit plan that is a governmental plan, as defined in section 414(d) of the Internal Revenue Code of 1986; or

(ii) an eligible deferred compensation plan, as defined in section 457(b) of the Internal Revenue Code of 1986;

shall be considered, for purposes of section 1102 of this title, to be a person with respect to such asset or such benefit;

(42) "petition" means petition filed under section 301, 302, 303, or 304 of this title, as the case may be, commencing a case under this title;

(42A) "production payment" means a term overriding royalty satisfiable in cash or in kind—

(A) contingent on the production of a liquid or gaseous hydrocarbon from particular real property; and

(B) from a specified volume, or a specified value, from the liquid or gaseous hydrocarbon produced from such property, and determined without regard to production costs;

(43) "purchaser" means transferee of a voluntary transfer, and includes immediate or mediate transferee of such a transferee;

(44) "railroad" means common carrier by railroad engaged in the transportation of individuals or property, or owner of trackage facilities leased by such a common carrier;

(45) "relative" means individual related by affinity or consanguinity within the third degree as determined by the common law, or individual in a step or adoptive relationship within such third degree;

(46) "repo participant" means an entity that, on any day during the period beginning 90 days before the date of the filing of the petition, has an outstanding repurchase agreement with the debtor;

(47) "repurchase agreement" (which definition also applies to a reverse repurchase agreement) means an agreement, including related terms, which provides for the transfer of certificates of deposit, eligible bankers' acceptances, or securities that are direct obligations of, or that are fully guaranteed as to principal and interest by, the United States or any agency of the United States against the transfer of funds by the transferee of such certificates of deposit, eligible bankers' acceptances, or securities with a simultaneous agreement by such transferee to transfer to the transferor thereof certificates of deposit, eligible bankers' acceptances, or securities as described above, at a date certain not later than one year after such transfers or on demand, against the transfer of funds;

(48) "securities clearing agency" means person that is registered as a clearing agency under section 17A of the Securities Exchange

Act of 1934, or whose business is confined to the performance of functions of a clearing agency with respect to exempted securities, as defined in section 3(a)(12) of such Act for the purposes of such section 17A;

(49) "security"—

(A) includes—
  (i)   note;
  (ii) stock;
  (iii) treasury stock;
  (iv) bond;
  (v)   debenture;
  (vi) collateral trust certificate;
  (vii) pre-organization certificate or subscription;
  (viii) transferable share;
  (ix) voting-trust certificate;
  (x)   certificate of deposit;
  (xi) certificate of deposit for security;
  (xii) investment contract or certificate of interest or participation in a profit-sharing agreement or in an oil, gas, or mineral royalty or lease, if such contract or interest is required to be the subject of a registration statement filed with the Securities and Exchange Commission under the provisions of the Securities Act of 1933, or is exempt under section 3(b) of such Act from the requirement to file such a statement;
  (xiii) interest of a limited partner in a limited partnership;
  (xiv) other claim or interest commonly known as "security"; and
  (xv) certificate of interest or participation in, temporary or interim certificate for, receipt for, or warrant or right to subscribe to or purchase or sell, a security; but

(B) does not include—
  (i)   currency, check, draft, bill of exchange, or bank letter of credit;
  (ii) leverage transaction, as defined in section 761 of this title;
  (iii) commodity futures contract or forward contract;
  (iv) option, warrant, or right to subscribe to or purchase or sell a commodity futures contract;
  (v)   option to purchase or sell a commodity;
  (vi) contract or certificate of a kind specified in subparagraph A (xii) of this paragraph that is not required to be the subject of a registration statement filed with the Securities and Exchange Commission and is not exempt under section 3(b) of the Securities Act of 1933 from the requirement to file such a statement; or
  (vii) debt or evidence of indebtedness for goods sold and delivered or services rendered;

(50) "security agreement" means agreement that creates or provides for a security interest;

(51) "security interest" means lien created by an agreement;

(51A) "settlement payment" means, for purposes of the forward contract provisions of this title, a preliminary settlement payment, a partial settlement payment, an interim settlement payment, a settlement payment on account, a final settlement payment, a net settlement payment, or any other similar payment commonly used in the forward contract trade;

(51B) "single asset real estate" means real property constituting a single property or project, other than residential real property with fewer than 4 residential units, which generates substantially all of the gross income of a debtor and on which no substantial business is being conducted by a debtor other than the business of operating the real property and activities incidental thereto having aggregate noncontingent, liquidated secured debts in an amount no more than $4,000,000;

(51C) "small business" means a person engaged in commercial or business activities (but does not include a person whose primary activity is the business of owning or operating real property and activities incidental thereto) whose aggregate noncontingent liquidated secured and unsecured debts as of the date of the petition do not exceed $2,000,000;

(52) "State" includes the District of Columbia and Puerto Rico, except for the purpose of defining who may be a debtor under chapter 9 of this title;

(53) "statutory lien" means lien arising solely by force of a statute on specified circumstances or conditions, or lien of distress for rent, whether or not statutory, but does not include security interest or judicial lien, whether or not such interest or lien is provided by or is dependent on a statute and whether or not such interest or lien is made fully effective by statute;

(53A) "stockbroker" means person—

(A) with respect to which there is a customer, as defined in section 741 of this title; and

(B) that is engaged in the business of effecting transactions in securities—
  (i) for the account of others; or
  (ii) with members of the general public, from or for such person's own account;

(53B) "swap agreement" means—

(A) an agreement (including terms and conditions incorporated by reference therein) which is a rate swap agreement, basis swap, forward rate agreement, commodity swap, interest rate option, forward foreign exchange agreement, spot foreign exchange agreement, rate cap agreement, rate floor agreement, rate collar agreement, currency swap agreement, cross-currency rate swap agreement, currency option, any other similar agreement (including any option to enter into any of the foregoing);

(B) any combination of the foregoing; or

(C) a master agreement for any of the foregoing together with all supplements;

(53C) "swap participant" means an entity that, at any time before the filing of the petition, has an outstanding swap agreement with the debtor;

(56A)[1] "term overriding royalty" means an interest in liquid or gaseous hydrocarbons in place or to be produced from particular real property that entitles the owner thereof to a share of production, or the value thereof, for a term limited by time, quantity, or value realized;

---

1 *Editor's Note*: So in original. Paragraph (56A) was inserted between paragraphs (53C) and (53D).

(53D) "timeshare plan" means and shall include that interest purchased in any arrangement, plan, scheme, or similar device, but not including exchange programs, whether by membership, agreement, tenancy in common, sale, lease, deed, rental agreement, license, right to use agreement, or by any other means, whereby a purchaser, in exchange for consideration, receives a right to use accommodations, facilities, or recreational sites, whether improved or unimproved, for a specific period of time less than a full year during any given year, but not necessarily for consecutive years, and which extends for a period of more than three years. A "timeshare interest" is that interest purchased in a timeshare plan which grants the purchaser the right to use and occupy accommodations, facilities, or recreational sites, whether improved or unimproved, pursuant to a timeshare plan;

(54) "transfer" means every mode, direct or indirect, absolute or conditional, voluntary or involuntary, of disposing of or parting with property or with an interest in property, including retention of title as a security interest and foreclosure of the debtor's equity of redemption;

(54A) the term "uninsured State member bank" means a State member bank (as defined in section 3 of the Federal Deposit Insurance Act) the deposits of which are not insured by the Federal Deposit Insurance Corporation; and

(55) "United States," when used in a geographical sense, includes all locations where the judicial jurisdiction of the United States extends, including territories and possessions of the United States;

§ 102. Rules of construction

In this title—

(1) "after notice and a hearing," or a similar phrase—

(A) means after such notice as is appropriate in the particular circumstances, and such opportunity for a hearing as is appropriate in the particular circumstances; but

(B) authorizes an act without an actual hearing if such notice is given properly and if—

(i) such a hearing is not requested timely by a party in interest; or

(ii) there is insufficient time for a hearing to be commenced before such act must be done, and the court authorizes such act;

(2) "claim against the debtor" includes claim against property of the debtor;

(3) "includes" and "including" are not limiting;

(4) "may not" is prohibitive, and not permissive;

(5) "or" is not exclusive;

(6) "order for relief" means entry of an order for relief;

(7) the singular includes the plural;

(8) a definition, contained in a section of this title that refers to another section of this title, does not, for the purpose of such reference, affect the meaning of a term used in such other section; and

(9) "United States trustee" includes a designee of the United States trustee.

§ 103. Applicability of chapters

(a) Except as provided in section 1161 of this title, chapters 1, 3, and 5 of this title apply in a case under chapter 7, 11, 12, or 13 of this title.

(b) Subchapters I and II of chapter 7 of this title apply only in a case under such chapter.

(c) Subchapter III of chapter 7 of this title applies only in a case under such chapter concerning a stockbroker.

(d) Subchapter IV of chapter 7 of this title applies only in a case under such chapter concerning a commodity broker.

(e) Scope of Application.—Subchapter V of chapter 7 of this title shall apply only in a case under such chapter concerning the liquidation of an uninsured State member bank, or a corporation organized under section 25A of the Federal Reserve Act, which operates, or operates as, a multilateral clearing organization pursuant to section 409 of the Federal Deposit Insurance Corporation Improvement Act of 1991.

(f) Except as provided in section 901 of this title, only chapters 1 and 9 of this title apply in a case under such chapter 9.

(g) Except as provided in section 901 of this title, subchapters I, II, and III of chapter 11 of this title apply only in a case under such chapter.

(h) Subchapter IV of chapter 11 of this title applies only in a case under such chapter concerning a railroad.

(i) Chapter 13 of this title applies only in a case under such chapter.

(j) Chapter 12 of this title applies only in a case under such chapter.

§ 104. Adjustment of dollar amounts

(a) The Judicial Conference of the United States shall transmit to the Congress and to the President before May 1, 1985, and before May 1 of every sixth year after May 1, 1985, a recommendation for the uniform percentage adjustment of each dollar amount in this title and in section 1930 of title 28.

(b)(1) On April 1, 1998, and at each 3-year interval ending on April 1 thereafter, each dollar amount in effect under sections 109(e), 303(b), 507(a), 522(d), and 523(a)(2)(C) immediately before such April 1 shall be adjusted—

(A) to reflect the change in the Consumer Price Index for All Urban Consumers, published by the Department of Labor, for the most recent 3-year period ending immediately before January 1 preceding such April 1, and

(B) to round to the nearest $25 the dollar amount that represents such change.

(2) Not later than March 1, 1998, and at each 3-year interval ending on March 1 thereafter, the Judicial Conference of the United States shall publish in the Federal Register the dollar amounts that will become effective on such April 1 under sections 109(e), 303(b), 507(a), 522(d), and 523(a)(2)(C) of this title.

(3) Adjustments made in accordance with paragraph (1) shall not

apply with respect to cases commenced before the date of such adjustments.

§ 105. Power of court

(a) The court may issue any order, process, or judgment that is necessary or appropriate to carry out the provisions of this title. No provision of this title providing for the raising of an issue by a party in interest shall be construed to preclude the court from, sua sponte, taking any action or making any determination necessary or appropriate to enforce or implement court orders or rules, or to prevent an abuse of process.

(b) Notwithstanding subsection (a) of this section, a court may not appoint a receiver in a case under this title.

(c) The ability of any district judge or other officer or employee of a district court to exercise any of the authority or responsibilities conferred upon the court under this title shall be determined by reference to the provisions relating to such judge, officer, or employee set forth in title 28. This subsection shall not be interpreted to exclude bankruptcy judges and other officers or employees appointed pursuant to chapter 6 of title 28 from its operation.

(d) The court, on its own motion or on the request of a party in interest, may—

(1) hold a status conference regarding any case or proceeding under this title after notice to the parties in interest; and

(2) unless inconsistent with another provision of this title or with applicable Federal Rules of Bankruptcy Procedure, issue an order at any such conference prescribing such limitations and conditions as the court deems appropriate to ensure that the case is handled expeditiously and economically, including an order that—
  (A) sets the date by which the trustee must assume or reject an executory contract or unexpired lease; or
  (B) in a case under chapter 11 of this title—
    (i)   sets a date by which the debtor, or trustee if one has been appointed, shall file a disclosure statement and plan;
    (ii) sets a date by which the debtor, or trustee if one has been appointed, shall solicit acceptances of a plan;
    (iii) sets the date by which a party in interest other than a debtor may file a plan;
    (iv) sets a date by which a proponent of a plan, other than the debtor, shall solicit acceptances of such plan;
    (v)   fixes the scope and format of the notice to be provided regarding the hearing on approval of the disclosure statement; or
    (vi) provides that the hearing on approval of the disclosure statement may be combined with the hearing on confirmation of the plan.

§ 106. Waiver of sovereign immunity

(a) Notwithstanding an assertion of sovereign immunity, sovereign immunity is abrogated as to a governmental unit to the extent set forth in this section with respect to the following:

(1) Sections 105, 106, 107, 108, 303, 346, 362, 363, 364, 365, 366, 502, 503, 505, 506, 510, 522, 523, 524, 525, 542, 543, 544, 545, 546, 547, 548, 549, 550, 551, 552, 553, 722, 724, 726, 728, 744, 749, 764, 901, 922, 926, 928, 929, 944, 1107, 1141, 1142, 1143, 1146, 1201, 1203, 1205, 1206, 1227, 1231, 1301, 1303, 1305, and 1327 of this title.

(2) The court may hear and determine any issue arising with respect to the application of such sections to governmental units.

(3) The court may issue against a governmental unit an order, process, or judgment under such sections or the Federal Rules of Bankruptcy Procedure, including an order or judgment awarding a money recovery, but not including an award of punitive damages. Such order or judgment for costs or fees under this title or the Federal Rules of Bankruptcy Procedure against any governmental unit shall be consistent with the provisions and limitations of section 2412(d)(2)(A) of title 28.

(4) The enforcement of any such order, process, or judgment against any governmental unit shall be consistent with appropriate nonbankruptcy law applicable to such governmental unit and, in the case of a money judgment against the United States, shall be paid as if it is a judgment rendered by a district court of the United States.

(5) Nothing in this section shall create any substantive claim for relief or cause of action not otherwise existing under this title, the Federal Rules of Bankruptcy Procedure, or nonbankruptcy law.

(b) A governmental unit that has filed a proof of claim in the case is deemed to have waived sovereign immunity with respect to a claim against such governmental unit that is property of the estate and that arose out of the same transaction or occurrence out of which the claim of such governmental unit arose.

(c) Notwithstanding any assertion of sovereign immunity by a governmental unit, there shall be offset against a claim or interest of a governmental unit any claim against such governmental unit that is property of the estate.

§ 107. Public access to papers

(a) Except as provided in subsection (b) of this section, a paper filed in a case under this title and the dockets of a bankruptcy court are public records and open to examination by an entity at reasonable times without charge.

(b) On request of a party in interest, the bankruptcy court shall, and on the bankruptcy court's own motion, the bankruptcy court may—

(1) protect an entity with respect to a trade secret or confidential research, development, or commercial information; or

(2) protect a person with respect to scandalous or defamatory matter contained in a paper filed in a case under this title.

§ 108. Extension of time

(a) If applicable nonbankruptcy law, an order entered in a nonbankruptcy proceeding, or an agreement fixes a period within which the debtor may commence an action, and such period has not expired before the date of the filing of the petition, the trustee may commence such action only before the later of—

(1) the end of such period, including any suspension of such period occurring on or after the commencement of the case; or

(2) two years after the order for relief.

(b) Except as provided in subsection (a) of this section, if applicable nonbankruptcy law, an order entered in a nonbankruptcy proceeding, or an agreement fixes a period within which the debtor or an individual protected under section 1201 or 1301 of this title may file any pleading, demand, notice, or proof of claim or loss, cure a default, or perform any other similar act, and such period has not expired before the date of the filing of the petition, the trustee may only file, cure, or perform, as the case may be, before the later of—

(1) the end of such period, including any suspension of such period occurring on or after the commencement of the case; or

(2) 60 days after the order for relief.

(c) Except as provided in section 524 of this title, if applicable nonbankruptcy law, an order entered in a nonbankruptcy proceeding, or an agreement fixes a period for commencing or continuing a civil action in a court other than a bankruptcy court on a claim against the debtor, or against an individual with respect to which such individual is protected under section 1201 or 1301 of this title, and such period has not expired before the date of the filing of the petition, then such period does not expire until the later of—

(1) the end of such period, including any suspension of such period occurring on or after the commencement of the case; or

(2) 30 days after notice of the termination or expiration of the stay under section 362, 922, 1201, or 1301 of this title, as the case may be, with respect to such claim.

§ 109. Who may be a debtor

(a) Notwithstanding any other provision of this section, only a person that resides or has a domicile, a place of business, or property in the United States, or a municipality, may be a debtor under this title.

(b) A person may be a debtor under chapter 7 of this title only if such person is not—

(1) a railroad;

(2) a domestic insurance company, bank, savings bank, cooperative bank, savings and loan association, building and loan association, homestead association, a small business investment company licensed by the Small Business Administration under subsection (c) or (d) of section 301 of the Small Business Investment Act of 1958, credit union, or industrial bank or similar institution which is an insured bank as defined in section 3(h) of the Federal Deposit Insurance Act, except that an uninsured State member bank, or a corporation organized under section 25A of the Federal Reserve Act, which operates, or operates as, a multilateral clearing organization pursuant to section 409 of the Federal Deposit Insurance Corporation Improvement Act of 1991 may be a debtor if a petition is filed at the direction of the Board of Governors of the Federal Reserve System; or

(3) a foreign insurance company, bank, savings bank, cooperative bank, savings and loan association, building and loan association, homestead association, or credit union, engaged in such business in the United States.

(c) An entity may be a debtor under chapter 9 of this title if and only if such entity—

(1) is a municipality;

(2) is specifically authorized, in its capacity as a municipality or by name, to be a debtor under such chapter by State law, or by a governmental officer or organization empowered by State law to authorize such entity to be a debtor under such chapter;

(3) is insolvent;

(4) desires to effect a plan to adjust such debts; and

(5)(A) has obtained the agreement of creditors holding at least a majority in amount of the claims of each class that such entity intends to impair under a plan in a case under such chapter;

(B) has negotiated in good faith with creditors and has failed to obtain the agreement of creditors holding at least a majority in amount of the claims of each class that such entity intends to impair under a plan in a case under such chapter;

(C) is unable to negotiate with creditors because such negotiation is impracticable; or

(D) reasonably believes that a creditor may attempt to obtain a transfer that is avoidable under section 547 of this title.

(d) Only a railroad, a person that may be a debtor under chapter 7 of this title (except a stockbroker or a commodity broker), and an uninsured State member bank, or a corporation organized under section 25A of the Federal Reserve Act, which operates, or operates as, a multilateral clearing organization pursuant to section 409 of the Federal Deposit Insurance Corporation Improvement Act of 1991 may be a debtor under chapter 11 of this title.

(e) Only an individual with regular income that owes, on the date of the filing of the petition, noncontingent, liquidated, unsecured debts of less than $307,675[2] and noncontingent, liquidated, secured debts of less than $922,975,[3] or an individual with regular income and such individual's spouse, except a stockbroker or a commodity broker, that owe, on the date of the filing of the petition, noncontingent, liquidated, unsecured debts that aggregate less than $307,675[4] and noncontingent, liquidated, secured debts of less than $922,975[5] may be a debtor under chapter 13 of this title.

(f) Only a family farmer with regular annual income may be a debtor under chapter 12 of this title.

(g) Notwithstanding any other provision of this section, no individual or family farmer may be a debtor under this title who has been a debtor in a case pending under this title at any time in the preceding 180 days if—

---

2 *Editor's Note*: This dollar amount reflects an inflationary adjustment, effective April 1, 2004. For cases commenced before April 1, 2004, the applicable dollar amount is $290,525.

3 *Editor's Note*: This dollar amount reflects an inflationary adjustment, effective April 1, 2004. For cases commenced before April 1, 2004, the applicable dollar amount is $871,550.

4 *Editor's Note*: This dollar amount reflects an inflationary adjustment, effective April 1, 2004. For cases commenced before April 1, 2004, the applicable dollar amount is $290,525.

5 *Editor's Note*: This dollar amount reflects an inflationary adjustment, effective April 1, 2004. For cases commenced before April 1, 2004, the applicable dollar amount is $871,550.

(1) the case was dismissed by the court for willful failure of the debtor to abide by orders of the court, or to appear before the court in proper prosecution of the case; or

(2) the debtor requested and obtained the voluntary dismissal of the case following the filing of a request for relief from the automatic stay provided by section 362 of this title.

§ 110. Penalty for persons who negligently or fraudulently prepare bankruptcy petitions

(a) In this section—

(1) "bankruptcy petition preparer" means a person, other than an attorney or an employee of an attorney, who prepares for compensation a document for filing; and

(2) "document for filing" means a petition or any other document prepared for filing by a debtor in a United States bankruptcy court or a United States district court in connection with a case under this title.

(b)(1) A bankruptcy petition preparer who prepares a document for filing shall sign the document and print on the document the preparer's name and address.

(2) A bankruptcy petition preparer who fails to comply with paragraph (1) may be fined not more than $500 for each such failure unless the failure is due to reasonable cause.

(c)(1) A bankruptcy petition preparer who prepares a document for filing shall place on the document, after the preparer's signature, an identifying number that identifies individuals who prepared the document.

(2) For purposes of this section, the identifying number of a bankruptcy petition preparer shall be the Social Security account number of each individual who prepared the document or assisted in its preparation.

(3) A bankruptcy petition preparer who fails to comply with paragraph (1) may be fined not more than $500 for each such failure unless the failure is due to reasonable cause.

(d)(1) A bankruptcy petition preparer shall, not later than the time at which a document for filing is presented for the debtor's signature, furnish to the debtor a copy of the document.

(2) A bankruptcy petition preparer who fails to comply with paragraph (1) may be fined not more than $500 for each such failure unless the failure is due to reasonable cause.

(e)(1) A bankruptcy petition preparer shall not execute any document on behalf of a debtor.

(2) A bankruptcy petition preparer may be fined not more than $500 for each document executed in violation of paragraph (1).

(f)(1) A bankruptcy petition preparer shall not use the word "legal" or any similar term in any advertisements, or advertise under any category that includes the word "legal" or any similar term.

(2) A bankruptcy petition preparer shall be fined not more than $500 for each violation of paragraph (1).

(g)(1) A bankruptcy petition preparer shall not collect or receive any payment from the debtor or on behalf of the debtor for

the court fees in connection with filing the petition.

(2) A bankruptcy petition preparer shall be fined not more than $500 for each violation of paragraph (1).

(h)(1) Within 10 days after the date of the filing of a petition, a bankruptcy petition preparer shall file a declaration under penalty of perjury disclosing any fee received from or on behalf of the debtor within 12 months immediately prior to the filing of the case, and any unpaid fee charged to the debtor.

(2) The court shall disallow and order the immediate turnover to the bankruptcy trustee of any fee referred to in paragraph (1) found to be in excess of the value of services rendered for the documents prepared. An individual debtor may exempt any funds so recovered under section 522(b).

(3) The debtor, the trustee, a creditor, or the United States trustee may file a motion for an order under paragraph (2).

(4) A bankruptcy petition preparer shall be fined not more than $500 for each failure to comply with a court order to turn over funds within 30 days of service of such order.

(i)(1) If a bankruptcy case or related proceeding is dismissed because of the failure to file bankruptcy papers, including papers specified in section 521(1) of this title, the negligence or intentional disregard of this title or the Federal Rules of Bankruptcy Procedure by a bankruptcy petition preparer, or if a bankruptcy petition preparer violates this section or commits any fraudulent, unfair, or deceptive act, the bankruptcy court shall certify that fact to the district court, and the district court, on motion of the debtor, the trustee, or a creditor and after a hearing, shall order the bankruptcy petition preparer to pay to the debtor—

(A) the debtor's actual damages;

(B) the greater of—

    (i) $2,000; or

    (ii) twice the amount paid by the debtor to the bankruptcy petition preparer for the preparer's services; and

(C) reasonable attorneys' fees and costs in moving for damages under this subsection.

(2) If the trustee or creditor moves for damages on behalf of the debtor under this subsection, the bankruptcy petition preparer shall be ordered to pay the movant the additional amount of $1,000 plus reasonable attorneys' fees and costs incurred.

(j)(1) A debtor for whom a bankruptcy petition preparer has prepared a document for filing, the trustee, a creditor, or the United States trustee in the district in which the bankruptcy petition preparer resides, has conducted business, or the United States trustee in any other district in which the debtor resides may bring a civil action to enjoin a bankruptcy petition preparer from engaging in any conduct in violation of this section or from further acting as a bankruptcy petition preparer.

(2)(A) In an action under paragraph (1), if the court finds that—

    (i) a bankruptcy petition preparer has—

        (I) engaged in conduct in violation of this section or of any provision of this title a violation of which subjects a person to criminal penalty;

    (II) misrepresented the preparer's experience or education as a bankruptcy petition preparer; or

    (III) engaged in any other fraudulent, unfair, or deceptive conduct; and

  (ii) injunctive relief is appropriate to prevent the recurrence of such conduct,

the court may enjoin the bankruptcy petition preparer from engaging in such conduct.

(B) If the court finds that a bankruptcy petition preparer has continually engaged in conduct described in subclause (I), (II), or (III) of clause (i) and that an injunction prohibiting such conduct would not be sufficient to prevent such person's interference with the proper administration of this title, or has not paid a penalty imposed under this section, the court may enjoin the person from acting as a bankruptcy petition preparer.

(3) The court shall award to a debtor, trustee, or creditor that brings a successful action under this subsection reasonable attorney's fees and costs of the action, to be paid by the bankruptcy petition preparer.

(k) Nothing in this section shall be construed to permit activities that are otherwise prohibited by law, including rules and laws that prohibit the unauthorized practice of law.

CHAPTER 3
CASE ADMINISTRATION

Subchapter I—Commencement of a Case

§ 301. Voluntary cases

A voluntary case under a chapter of this title is commenced by the filing with the bankruptcy court of a petition under such chapter by an entity that may be a debtor under such chapter. The commencement of a voluntary case under a chapter of this title constitutes an order for relief under such chapter.

§ 302. Joint cases

(a) A joint case under a chapter of this title is commenced by the filing with the bankruptcy court of a single petition under such chapter by an individual that may be a debtor under such chapter and such individual's spouse. The commencement of a joint case under a chapter of this title constitutes an order for relief under such chapter.

(b) After the commencement of a joint case, the court shall determine the extent, if any, to which the debtors' estates shall be consolidated.

§ 303. Involuntary cases

(a) An involuntary case may be commenced only under chapter 7 or 11 of this title, and only against a person, except a farmer, family farmer, or a corporation that is not a moneyed, business, or commercial corporation, that may be a debtor under the chapter under which such case is commenced.

(b) An involuntary case against a person is commenced by the filing with the bankruptcy court of a petition under chapter 7 or 11 of this title—

(1) by three or more entities, each of which is either a holder of a claim against such person that is not contingent as to liability or the subject of a bona fide dispute, or an indenture trustee representing such a holder, if such claims aggregate at least $12,300[6] more than the value of any lien on property of the debtor securing such claims held by the holders of such claims;

(2) if there are fewer than 12 such holders, excluding any employee or insider of such person and any transferee of a transfer that is voidable under section 544, 545, 547, 548, 549, or 724(a) of this title, by one or more of such holders that hold in the aggregate at least $12,300[7] of such claims;

(3) if such person is a partnership—

  (A) by fewer than all of the general partners in such partnership; or

  (B) if relief has been ordered under this title with respect to all of the general partners in such partnership, by a general partner in such partnership, the trustee of such a general partner, or a holder of a claim against such partnership; or

(4) by a foreign representative of the estate in a foreign proceeding concerning such person.

(c) After the filing of a petition under this section but before the case is dismissed or relief is ordered, a creditor holding an unsecured claim that is not contingent, other than a creditor filing under subsection (b) of this section, may join in the petition with the same effect as if such joining creditor were a petitioning creditor under subsection (b) of this section.

(d) The debtor, or a general partner in a partnership debtor that did not join in the petition, may file an answer to a petition under this section.

(e) After notice and a hearing, and for cause, the court may require the petitioners under this section to file a bond to indemnify the debtor for such amounts as the court may later allow under subsection (i) of this section.

(f) Notwithstanding section 363 of this title, except to the extent that the court orders otherwise, and until an order for relief in the case, any business of the debtor may continue to operate, and the debtor may continue to use, acquire, or dispose of property as if an involuntary case concerning the debtor had not been commenced.

(g) At any time after the commencement of an involuntary case under chapter 7 of this title but before an order for relief in the case, the court, on request of a party in interest, after notice to the debtor and a hearing, and if necessary to preserve the property of the estate or to prevent loss to the estate, may order the United States trustee to appoint an interim trustee under section 701 of this title to take possession of the property of the estate and to operate any business of the debtor. Before an order for relief, the debtor may regain possession of property in the possession of a trustee ordered appointed under this subsection if the debtor files such bond as the court requires, conditioned on the debtor's accounting for and delivering to the trustee, if there is an order for relief in the case,

---

6 *Editor's Note*: This dollar amount reflects an inflationary adjustment, effective April 1, 2004. For cases commenced before April 1, 2004, the applicable dollar amount is $11,625.

7 *Editor's Note*: This dollar amount reflects an inflationary adjustment, effective April 1, 2004. For cases commenced before April 1, 2004, the applicable dollar amount is $11,625.

such property, or the value, as of the date the debtor regains possession, of such property.

(h) If the petition is not timely controverted, the court shall order relief against the debtor in an involuntary case under the chapter under which the petition was filed. Otherwise, after trial, the court shall order relief against the debtor in an involuntary case under the chapter under which the petition was filed, only if—

(1) the debtor is generally not paying such debtor's debts as such debts become due unless such debts are the subject of a bona fide dispute; or

(2) within 120 days before the date of the filing of the petition, a custodian, other than a trustee, receiver, or agent appointed or authorized to take charge of less than substantially all of the property of the debtor for the purpose of enforcing a lien against such property, was appointed or took possession.

(i) If the court dismisses a petition under this section other than on consent of all petitioners and the debtor, and if the debtor does not waive the right to judgment under this subsection, the court may grant judgment—

(1) against the petitioners and in favor of the debtor for—
    (A) costs; or
    (B) a reasonable attorney's fee; or

(2) against any petitioner that filed the petition in bad faith, for—
    (A) any damages proximately caused by such filing; or
    (B) punitive damages.

(j) Only after notice to all creditors and a hearing may the court dismiss a petition filed under this section—

(1) on the motion of a petitioner;

(2) on consent of all petitioners and the debtor; or

(3) for want of prosecution.

(k) Notwithstanding subsection (a) of this section, an involuntary case may be commenced against a foreign bank that is not engaged in such business in the United States only under chapter 7 of this title and only if a foreign proceeding concerning such bank is pending.

§ 304. Cases ancillary to foreign proceedings

(a) A case ancillary to a foreign proceeding is commenced by the filing with the bankruptcy court of a petition under this section by a foreign representative.

(b) Subject to the provisions of subsection (c) of this section, if a party in interest does not timely controvert the petition, or after trial, the court may—

(1) enjoin the commencement or continuation of—
    (A) any action against—
        (i) a debtor with respect to property involved in such foreign proceeding; or
        (ii) such property; or
    (B) the enforcement of any judgment against the debtor with respect to such property, or any act or the commencement or continuation of any judicial proceeding to create or enforce a lien against the property of such estate;

(2) order turnover of the property of such estate, or the proceeds of such property, to such foreign representative; or

(3) order other appropriate relief.

(c) In determining whether to grant relief under subsection (b) of this section, the court shall be guided by what will best assure an economical and expeditious administration of such estate, consistent with—

(1) just treatment of all holders of claims against or interests in such estate;

(2) protection of claim holders in the United States against prejudice and inconvenience in the processing of claims in such foreign proceeding;

(3) prevention of preferential or fraudulent dispositions of property of such estate;

(4) distribution of proceeds of such estate substantially in accordance with the order prescribed by this title;

(5) comity; and

(6) if appropriate, the provision of an opportunity for a fresh start for the individual that such foreign proceeding concerns.

§ 305. Abstention

(a) The court, after notice and a hearing, may dismiss a case under this title, or may suspend all proceedings in a case under this title, at any time if—

(1) the interests of creditors and the debtor would be better served by such dismissal or suspension; or

(2)(A) there is pending a foreign proceeding; and
    (B) the factors specified in section 304(c) of this title warrant such dismissal or suspension.

(b) A foreign representative may seek dismissal or suspension under subsection (a)(2) of this section.

(c) An order under subsection (a) of this section dismissing a case or suspending all proceedings in a case, or a decision not so to dismiss or suspend, is not reviewable by appeal or otherwise by the court of appeals under section 158(d), 1291, or 1292 of title 28 or by the Supreme Court of the United States under section 1254 of title 28.

§ 306. Limited appearance

An appearance in a bankruptcy court by a foreign representative in connection with a petition or request under section 303, 304, or 305 of this title does not submit such foreign representative to the jurisdiction of any court in the United States for any other purpose, but the bankruptcy court may condition any order under section 303, 304, or 305 of this title on compliance by such foreign representative with the orders of such bankruptcy court.

§ 307. United States trustee

The United States trustee may raise and may appear and be heard on any issue in any case or proceeding under this title but may not file a plan pursuant to section 1121(c) of this title.

Subchapter II—Officers

§ 321. Eligibility to serve as trustee

(a) A person may serve as trustee in a case under this title only if such person is—

(1) an individual that is competent to perform the duties of trustee and, in a case under chapter 7, 12, or 13 of this title, resides or has an office in the judicial district within which the case is pending, or in any judicial district adjacent to such district; or

(2) a corporation authorized by such corporation's charter or bylaws to act as trustee, and, in a case under chapter 7, 12, or 13 of this title, having an office in at least one of such districts.

(b) A person that has served as an examiner in the case may not serve as trustee in the case.

(c) The United States trustee for the judicial district in which the case is pending is eligible to serve as trustee in the case if necessary.

§ 322. Qualification of trustee

(a) Except as provided in subsection (b)(1), a person selected under section 701, 702, 703, 1104, 1163, 1202, or 1302 of this title to serve as trustee in a case under this title qualifies if before five days after such selection, and before beginning official duties, such person has filed with the court a bond in favor of the United States conditioned on the faithful performance of such official duties.

(b)(1) The United States trustee qualifies wherever such trustee serves as trustee in a case under this title.

(2) The United States trustee shall determine—
    (A) the amount of a bond required to be filed under subsection (a) of this section; and
    (B) the sufficiency of the surety on such bond.

(c) A trustee is not liable personally or on such trustee's bond in favor of the United States for any penalty or forfeiture incurred by the debtor.

(d) A proceeding on a trustee's bond may not be commenced after two years after the date on which such trustee was discharged.

§ 323. Role and capacity of trustee

(a) The trustee in a case under this title is the representative of the estate.

(b) The trustee in a case under this title has capacity to sue and be sued.

§ 324. Removal of trustee or examiner

(a) The court, after notice and a hearing, may remove a trustee, other than the United States trustee, or an examiner, for cause.

(b) Whenever the court removes a trustee or examiner under subsection (a) in a case under this title, such trustee or examiner shall thereby be removed in all other cases under this title in which such trustee or examiner is then serving unless the court orders otherwise.

§ 325. Effect of vacancy

A vacancy in the office of trustee during a case does not abate any pending action or proceeding, and the successor trustee shall be substituted as a party in such action or proceeding.

§ 326. Limitation on compensation of trustee

(a) In a case under chapter 7 or 11, the court may allow reasonable compensation under section 330 of this title of the trustee for the trustee's services, payable after the trustee renders such services, not to exceed 25 percent on the first $5,000 or less, 10 percent on any amount in excess of $5,000 but not in excess of $50,000, 5 percent on any amount in excess of $50,000 but not in excess of $1,000,000, and reasonable compensation not to exceed 3 percent of such moneys in excess of $1,000,000, upon all moneys disbursed or turned over in the case by the trustee to parties in interest, excluding the debtor, but including holders of secured claims.

(b) In a case under chapter 12 or 13 of this title, the court may not allow compensation for services or reimbursement of expenses of the United States trustee or of a standing trustee appointed under section 586(b) of title 28, but may allow reasonable compensation under section 330 of this title of a trustee appointed under section 1202(a) or 1302(a) of this title for the trustee's services, payable after the trustee renders such services, not to exceed five percent upon all payments under the plan.

(c) If more than one person serves as trustee in the case, the aggregate compensation of such persons for such service may not exceed the maximum compensation prescribed for a single trustee by subsection (a) or (b) of this section, as the case may be.

(d) The court may deny allowance of compensation for services or reimbursement of expenses of the trustee if the trustee failed to make diligent inquiry into facts that would permit denial of allowance under section 328(c) of this title or, with knowledge of such facts, employed a professional person under section 327 of this title.

§ 327. Employment of professional persons

(a) Except as otherwise provided in this section, the trustee, with the court's approval, may employ one or more attorneys, accountants, appraisers, auctioneers, or other professional persons, that do not hold or represent an interest adverse to the estate, and that are disinterested persons, to represent or assist the trustee in carrying out the trustee's duties under this title.

(b) If the trustee is authorized to operate the business of the debtor under section 721, 1202, or 1108 of this title, and if the debtor has regularly employed attorneys, accountants, or other professional persons on salary, the trustee may retain or replace such professional persons if necessary in the operation of such business.

(c) In a case under chapter 7, 12, or 11 of this title, a person is not disqualified for employment under this section solely because of such person's employment by or representation of a creditor, unless there is objection by another creditor or the United States trustee, in which case the court shall disapprove such employment if there is an actual conflict of interest.

(d) The court may authorize the trustee to act as attorney or accountant for the estate if such authorization is in the best interest of the estate.

(e) The trustee, with the court's approval, may employ, for a specified special purpose, other than to represent the trustee in conducting the case, an attorney that has represented the debtor, if in the best interest of the estate, and if such attorney does not represent or hold any interest adverse to the debtor or to the estate with respect to the matter on which such attorney is to be employed.

(f) The trustee may not employ a person that has served as an examiner in the case.

§ 328. Limitation on compensation of professional persons

(a) The trustee, or a committee appointed under section 1102 of this title, with the court's approval, may employ or authorize the employment of a professional person under section 327 or 1103 of this title, as the case may be, on any reasonable terms and conditions of employment, including on a retainer, on an hourly basis, or on a contingent fee basis. Notwithstanding such terms and conditions, the court may allow compensation different from the compensation provided under such terms and conditions after the conclusion of such employment, if such terms and conditions prove to have been improvident in light of developments not capable of being anticipated at the time of the fixing of such terms and conditions.

(b) If the court has authorized a trustee to serve as an attorney or accountant for the estate under section 327(d) of this title, the court may allow compensation for the trustee's services as such attorney or accountant only to the extent that the trustee performed services as attorney or accountant for the estate and not for performance of any of the trustee's duties that are generally performed by a trustee without the assistance of an attorney or accountant for the estate.

(c) Except as provided in section 327(c), 327(e), or 1107(b) of this title, the court may deny allowance of compensation for services and reimbursement of expenses of a professional person employed under section 327 or 1103 of this title if, at any time during such professional person's employment under section 327 or 1103 of this title, such professional person is not a disinterested person, or represents or holds an interest adverse to the interest of the estate with respect to the matter on which such professional person is employed.

§ 329. Debtor's transactions with attorneys

(a) Any attorney representing a debtor in a case under this title, or in connection with such a case, whether or not such attorney applies for compensation under this title, shall file with the court a statement of the compensation paid or agreed to be paid, if such payment or agreement was made after one year before the date of the filing of the petition, for services rendered or to be rendered in contemplation of or in connection with the case by such attorney, and the source of such compensation.

(b) If such compensation exceeds the reasonable value of any such services, the court may cancel any such agreement, or order the return of any such payment, to the extent excessive, to—

(1) the estate, if the property transferred—
    (A) would have been property of the estate; or
    (B) was to be paid by or on behalf of the debtor under a plan under chapter 11, 12, or 13 of this title; or

(2) the entity that made such payment.

§ 330. Compensation of officers

(a)(1) After notice to the parties in interest and the United States trustee and a hearing, and subject to sections 326, 328, and 329, the court may award to a trustee, an examiner, a professional person employed under section 327 or 1103—
    (A) reasonable compensation for actual, necessary services rendered by the trustee, examiner, professional person, or attorney and by any paraprofessional person employed by any such person; and
    (B) reimbursement for actual, necessary expenses.

(2) The court may, on its own motion or on the motion of the United States Trustee, the United States Trustee for the District or Region, the trustee for the estate, or any other party in interest, award compensation that is less than the amount of compensation that is requested.

(3)(A) In determining the amount of reasonable compensation to be awarded, the court shall consider the nature, the extent, and the value of such services, taking into account all relevant factors, including—
    (A) the time spent on such services;
    (B) the rates charged for such services;
    (C) whether the services were necessary to the administration of, or beneficial at the time at which the service was rendered toward the completion of, a case under this title;
    (D) whether the services were performed within a reasonable amount of time commensurate with the complexity, importance, and nature of the problem, issue, or task addressed; and
    (E) whether the compensation is reasonable based on the customary compensation charged by comparably skilled practitioners in cases other than cases under this title.

(4)(A) Except as provided in subparagraph (B), the court shall not allow compensation for—
    (i) unnecessary duplication of services; or
    (ii) services that were not—
        (I) reasonably likely to benefit the debtor's estate; or
        (II) necessary to the administration of the case.

(B) In a chapter 12 or chapter 13 case in which the debtor is an individual, the court may allow reasonable compensation to the debtor's attorney for representing the interests of the debtor in connection with the bankruptcy case based on a consideration of the benefit and necessity of such services to the debtor and the other factors set forth in this section.

(5) The court shall reduce the amount of compensation awarded under this section by the amount of any interim compensation awarded under section 331, and, if the amount of such interim compensation exceeds the amount of compensation awarded under this section, may order the return of the excess to the estate.

(6) Any compensation awarded for the preparation of a fee application shall be based on the level and skill reasonably required to prepare the application.

(b)(1) There shall be paid from the filing fee in a case under chapter 7 of this title $45 to the trustee serving in such case, after such trustee's services are rendered.

(2) The Judicial Conference of the United States—

(A) shall prescribe additional fees of the same kind as prescribed under section 1914(b) of title 28; and

(B) may prescribe notice of appearance fees and fees charged against distributions in cases under this title;

to pay $15 to trustees serving in cases after such trustees' services are rendered. Beginning 1 year after the date of the enactment of the Bankruptcy Reform Act of 1994, such $15 shall be paid in addition to the amount paid under paragraph (1).

(c) Unless the court orders otherwise, in a case under chapter 12 or 13 of this title the compensation paid to the trustee serving in the case shall not be less than $5 per month from any distribution under the plan during the administration of the plan.

(d) In a case in which the United States trustee serves as trustee, the compensation of the trustee under this section shall be paid to the clerk of the bankruptcy court and deposited by the clerk into the United States Trustee System Fund established by section 589a of title 28.

§ 331. Interim compensation

A trustee, an examiner, a debtor's attorney, or any professional person employed under section 327 or 1103 of this title may apply to the court not more than once every 120 days after an order for relief in a case under this title, or more often if the court permits, for such compensation for services rendered before the date of such an application or reimbursement for expenses incurred before such date as is provided under section 330 of this title. After notice and a hearing, the court may allow and disburse to such applicant such compensation or reimbursement.

Subchapter III—Administration

§ 341. Meetings of creditors and equity security holders

(a) Within a reasonable time after the order for relief in a case under this title, the United States trustee shall convene and preside at a meeting of creditors.

(b) The United States trustee may convene a meeting of any equity security holders.

(c) The court may not preside at, and may not attend, any meeting under this section including any final meeting of creditors.

(d) Prior to the conclusion of the meeting of creditors or equity security holders, the trustee shall orally examine the debtor to ensure that the debtor in a case under chapter 7 of this title is aware of—

(1) the potential consequences of seeking a discharge in bankruptcy, including the effects on credit history;

(2) the debtor's ability to file a petition under a different chapter of this title;

(3) the effect of receiving a discharge of debts under this title; and

(4) the effect of reaffirming a debt, including the debtor's knowledge of the provisions of section 524(d) of this title.

§ 342. Notice

(a) There shall be given such notice as is appropriate, including notice to any holder of a community claim, of an order for relief in a case under this title.

(b) Prior to the commencement of a case under this title by an individual whose debts are primarily consumer debts, the clerk shall give written notice to such individual that indicates each chapter of this title under which such individual may proceed.

(c) If notice is required to be given by the debtor to a creditor under this title, any rule, any applicable law, or any order of the court, such notice shall contain the name, address, and taxpayer identification number of the debtor, but the failure of such notice to contain such information shall not invalidate the legal effect of such notice.

§ 343. Examination of the debtor

The debtor shall appear and submit to examination under oath at the meeting of creditors under section 341(a) of this title. Creditors, any indenture trustee, any trustee or examiner in the case, or the United States trustee may examine the debtor. The United States trustee may administer the oath required under this section.

§ 344. Self-incrimination; immunity

Immunity for persons required to submit to examination, to testify, or to provide information in a case under this title may be granted under part V of title 18.

§ 345. Money of estates

(a) A trustee in a case under this title may make such deposit or investment of the money of the estate for which such trustee serves as will yield the maximum reasonable net return on such money, taking into account the safety of such deposit or investment.

(b) Except with respect to a deposit or investment that is insured or guaranteed by the United States or by a department, agency, or instrumentality of the United States or backed by the full faith and credit of the United States, the trustee shall require from an entity with which such money is deposited or invested—

(1) a bond—

(A) in favor of the United States;

(B) secured by the undertaking of a corporate surety approved by the United States trustee for the district in which the case is pending; and

(C) conditioned on—

(i) a proper accounting for all money so deposited or invested and for any return on such money;

(ii) prompt repayment of such money and return; and

(iii) faithful performance of duties as a depository; or

(2) the deposit of securities of the kind specified in section 9303 of title 31;

unless the court for cause orders otherwise.

(c) An entity with which such moneys are deposited or invested is authorized to deposit or invest such moneys as may be required under this section.

§ 346. Special tax provisions

(a) Except to the extent otherwise provided in this section, subsections (b), (c), (d), (e), (g), (h), (i), and (j) of this section apply notwithstanding any State or local law imposing a tax, but subject to the Internal Revenue Code of 1986.

(b)(1) In a case under chapter 7, 12, or 11 of this title concerning an individual, any income of the estate may be taxed under a State or local law imposing a tax on or measured by income only to the estate, and may not be taxed to such individual. Except as provided in section 728 of this title, if such individual is a partner in a partnership, any gain or loss resulting from a distribution of property from such partnership, or any distributive share of income, gain, loss, deduction, or credit of such individual that is distributed, or considered distributed, from such partnership, after the commencement of the case is gain, loss, income, deduction, or credit, as the case may be, of the estate.

(2) Except as otherwise provided in this section and in section 728 of this title, any income of the estate in such a case, and any State or local tax on or measured by such income, shall be computed in the same manner as the income and the tax of an estate.

(3) The estate in such a case shall use the same accounting method as the debtor used immediately before the commencement of the case.

(c)(1) The commencement of a case under this title concerning a corporation or a partnership does not effect a change in the status of such corporation or partnership for the purposes of any State or local law imposing a tax on or measured by income. Except as otherwise provided in this section and in section 728 of this title, any income of the estate in such case may be taxed only as though such case had not been commenced.

(2) In such a case, except as provided in section 728 of this title, the trustee shall make any tax return otherwise required by State or local law to be filed by or on behalf of such corporation or partnership in the same manner and form as such corporation or partnership, as the case may be, is required to make such return.

(d) In a case under chapter 13 of this title, any income of the estate or the debtor may be taxed under a State or local law imposing a tax on or measured by income only to the debtor, and may not be taxed to the estate.

(e) A claim allowed under section 502(f) or 503 of this title, other than a claim for a tax that is not otherwise deductible or a capital expenditure that is not otherwise deductible, is deductible by the entity to which income of the estate is taxed unless such claim was deducted by another entity, and a deduction for such a claim is deemed to be a deduction attributable to a business.

(f) The trustee shall withhold from any payment of claims for wages, salaries, commissions, dividends, interest, or other payments, or collect, any amount required to be withheld or collected under applicable State or local tax law, and shall pay such withheld or collected amount to the appropriate governmental unit at the time and in the manner required by such tax law, and with the same priority as the claim from which such amount was withheld was paid.

(g)(1) Neither gain nor loss shall be recognized on a transfer—
   (A) by operation of law, of property to the estate;
   (B) other than a sale, of property from the estate to the debtor; or
   (C) in a case under chapter 11 or 12 of this title concerning

a corporation, of property from the estate to a corporation that is an affiliate participating in a joint plan with the debtor, or that is a successor to the debtor under the plan, except that gain or loss may be recognized to the same extent that such transfer results in the recognition of gain or loss under section 371 of the Internal Revenue Code of 1986.

(2) The transferee of a transfer of a kind specified in this subsection shall take the property transferred with the same character, and with the transferor's basis, as adjusted under subsection (j)(5) of this section, and holding period.

(h) Notwithstanding sections 728(a) and 1146(a) of this title, for the purpose of determining the number of taxable periods during which the debtor or the estate may use a loss carryover or a loss carryback, the taxable period of the debtor during which the case is commenced is deemed not to have been terminated by such commencement.

(i)(1) In a case under chapter 7, 12, or 11 of this title concerning an individual, the estate shall succeed to the debtor's tax attributes, including—
   (A) any investment credit carryover;
   (B) any recovery exclusion;
   (C) any loss carryover;
   (D) any foreign tax credit carryover;
   (E) any capital loss carryover; and
   (F) any claim of right.

(2) After such a case is closed or dismissed, the debtor shall succeed to any tax attribute to which the estate succeeded under paragraph (1) of this subsection but that was not utilized by the estate. The debtor may utilize such tax attributes as though any applicable time limitations on such utilization by the debtor were suspended during the time during which the case was pending.

(3) In such a case, the estate may carry back any loss of the estate to a taxable period of the debtor that ended before the order for relief under such chapter the same as the debtor could have carried back such loss had the debtor incurred such loss and the case under this title had not been commenced, but the debtor may not carry back any loss of the debtor from a taxable period that ends after such order to any taxable period of the debtor that ended before such order until after the case is closed.

(j)(1) Except as otherwise provided in this subsection, income is not realized by the estate, the debtor, or a successor to the debtor by reason of forgiveness or discharge of indebtedness in a case under this title.

(2) For the purposes of any State or local law imposing a tax on or measured by income, a deduction with respect to a liability may not be allowed for any taxable period during or after which such liability is forgiven or discharged under this title. In this paragraph, "a deduction with respect to a liability" includes a capital loss incurred on the disposition of a capital asset with respect to a liability that was incurred in connection with the acquisition of such asset.

(3) Except as provided in paragraph (4) of this subsection, for the purpose of any State or local law imposing a tax on or measured by income, any net operating loss of an individual or

corporate debtor, including a net operating loss carryover to such debtor, shall be reduced by the amount of indebtedness forgiven or discharged in a case under this title, except to the extent that such forgiveness or discharge resulted in a disallowance under paragraph (2) of this subsection.

(4) A reduction of a net operating loss or a net operating loss carryover under paragraph (3) of this subsection or of basis under paragraph (5) of this subsection is not required to the extent that the indebtedness of an individual or corporate debtor forgiven or discharged—

    (A) consisted of items of a deductible nature that were not deducted by such debtor; or

    (B) resulted in an expired net operating loss carryover or other deduction that—

        (i) did not offset income for any taxable period; and

        (ii) did not contribute to a net operating loss in or a net operating loss carryover to the taxable period during or after which such indebtedness was discharged.

(5) For the purposes of a State or local law imposing a tax on or measured by income, the basis of the debtor's property or of property transferred to an entity required to use the debtor's basis in whole or in part shall be reduced by the lesser of—

    (A)(i) the amount by which the indebtedness of the debtor has been forgiven or discharged in a case under this title; minus

        (ii) the total amount of adjustments made under paragraphs (2) and (3) of this subsection; and

    (B) the amount by which the total basis of the debtor's assets that were property of the estate before such forgiveness or discharge exceeds the debtor's total liabilities that were liabilities both before and after such forgiveness or discharge.

(6) Notwithstanding paragraph (5) of this subsection, basis is not required to be reduced to the extent that the debtor elects to treat as taxable income, of the taxable period in which indebtedness is forgiven or discharged, the amount of indebtedness forgiven or discharged that otherwise would be applied in reduction of basis under paragraph (5) of this subsection.

(7) For the purposes of this subsection, indebtedness with respect to which an equity security, other than an interest of a limited partner in a limited partnership, is issued to the creditor to whom such indebtedness was owed, or that is forgiven as a contribution to capital by an equity security holder other than a limited partner in the debtor, is not forgiven or discharged in a case under this title—

    (A) to any extent that such indebtedness did not consist of items of a deductible nature; or

    (B) if the issuance of such equity security has the same consequences under a law imposing a tax on or measured by income to such creditor as a payment in cash to such creditor in an amount equal to the fair market value of such equity security, then to the lesser of—

        (i) the extent that such issuance has the same such consequences; and

        (ii) the extent of such fair market value.

§ 347. Unclaimed property

(a) Ninety days after the final distribution under section 726, 1226,

or 1326 of this title in a case under chapter 7, 12, or 13 of this title, as the case may be, the trustee shall stop payment on any check remaining unpaid, and any remaining property of the estate shall be paid into the court and disposed of under chapter 129 of title 28.

(b) Any security, money, or other property remaining unclaimed at the expiration of the time allowed in a case under chapter 9, 11, or 12 of this title for the presentation of a security or the performance of any other act as a condition to participation in the distribution under any plan confirmed under section 943(b), 1129, 1173, or 1225 of this title, as the case may be, becomes the property of the debtor or of the entity acquiring the assets of the debtor under the plan, as the case may be.

§ 348. Effect of conversion

(a) Conversion of a case from a case under one chapter of this title to a case under another chapter of this title constitutes an order for relief under the chapter to which the case is converted, but, except as provided in subsections (b) and (c) of this section, does not effect a change in the date of the filing of the petition, the commencement of the case, or the order for relief.

(b) Unless the court for cause orders otherwise, in sections 701(a), 727(a)(10), 727(b), 728(a), 728(b), 1102(a), 1110(a)(1), 1121(b), 1121(c), 1141(d)(4), 1146(a), 1146(b), 1201(a), 1221, 1228(a), 1301(a), and 1305(a) of this title, "the order for relief under this chapter" in a chapter to which a case has been converted under section 706, 1112, 1208, or 1307 of this title means the conversion of such case in such chapter.

(c) Sections 342 and 365(d) of this title apply in a case that has been converted under section 706, 1112, 1208, or 1307 of this title, as if the conversion order were the order for relief.

(d) A claim against the estate or the debtor that arises after the order for relief but before conversion in a case that is converted under section 1112, 1208, or 1307 of this title, other than a claim specified in section 503(b) of this title, shall be treated for all purposes as if such claim had arisen immediately before the date of the filing of the petition.

(e) Conversion of a case under section 706, 1112, 1208, or 1307 of this title terminates the service of any trustee or examiner that is serving in the case before such conversion.

(f)(1) Except as provided in paragraph (2), when a case under chapter 13 of this title is converted to a case under another chapter under this title—

    (A) property of the estate in the converted case shall consist of property of the estate, as of the date of filing of the petition, that remains in the possession of or is under the control of the debtor on the date of conversion; and

    (B) valuations of property and of allowed secured claims in the chapter 13 case shall apply in the converted case, with allowed secured claims reduced to the extent that they have been paid in accordance with the chapter 13 plan.

(2) If the debtor converts a case under chapter 13 of this title to a case under another chapter under this title in bad faith, the property in the converted case shall consist of the property of the estate as of the date of conversion.

§ 349. Effect of dismissal

(a) Unless the court, for cause, orders otherwise, the dismissal of a case under this title does not bar the discharge, in a later case under this title, of debts that were dischargeable in the case dismissed; nor does the dismissal of a case under this title prejudice the debtor with regard to the filing of a subsequent petition under this title, except as provided in section 109(g) of this title.

(b) Unless the court, for cause, orders otherwise, a dismissal of a case other than under section 742 of this title—

(1) reinstates—
   (A) any proceeding or custodianship superseded under section 543 of this title;
   (B) any transfer avoided under section 522, 544, 545, 547, 548, 549, or 724(a) of this title, or preserved under section 510(c)(2), 522(i)(2), or 551 of this title; and
   (C) any lien voided under section 506(d) of this title;

(2) vacates any order, judgment, or transfer ordered, under section 522(i)(1), 542, 550, or 553 of this title; and

(3) revests the property of the estate in the entity in which such property was vested immediately before the commencement of the case under this title.

§ 350. Closing and reopening cases

(a) After an estate is fully administered and the court has discharged the trustee, the court shall close the case.

(b) A case may be reopened in the court in which such case was closed to administer assets, to accord relief to the debtor, or for other cause.

Subchapter IV—Administrative Powers

§ 361. Adequate protection

When adequate protection is required under section 362, 363, or 364 of this title of an interest of an entity in property, such adequate protection may be provided by—

(1) requiring the trustee to make a cash payment or periodic cash payments to such entity, to the extent that the stay under section 362 of this title, use, sale, or lease under section 363 of this title, or any grant of a lien under section 364 of this title results in a decrease in the value of such entity's interest in such property;

(2) providing to such entity an additional or replacement lien to the extent that such stay, use, sale, lease, or grant results in a decrease in the value of such entity's interest in such property; or

(3) granting such other relief, other than entitling such entity to compensation allowable under section 503(b)(1) of this title as an administrative expense, as will result in the realization by such entity of the indubitable equivalent of such entity's interest in such property.

§ 362. Automatic stay

(a) Except as provided in subsection (b) of this section, a petition filed under section 301, 302, or 303 of this title, or an application filed under section 5(a)(3) of the Securities Investor Protection Act of 1970, operates as a stay, applicable to all entities, of—

(1) the commencement or continuation, including the issuance or employment of process, of a judicial, administrative, or other action or proceeding against the debtor that was or could have been commenced before the commencement of the case under this title, or to recover a claim against the debtor that arose before the commencement of the case under this title;

(2) the enforcement, against the debtor or against property of the estate, of a judgment obtained before the commencement of the case under this title;

(3) any act to obtain possession of property of the estate or of property from the estate or to exercise control over property of the estate;

(4) any act to create, perfect, or enforce any lien against property of the estate;

(5) any act to create, perfect, or enforce against property of the debtor any lien to the extent that such lien secures a claim that arose before the commencement of the case under this title;

(6) any act to collect, assess, or recover a claim against the debtor that arose before the commencement of the case under this title;

(7) the setoff of any debt owing to the debtor that arose before the commencement of the case under this title against any claim against the debtor; and

(8) the commencement or continuation of a proceeding before the United States Tax Court concerning the debtor.

(b) The filing of a petition under section 301, 302, or 303 of this title, or of an application under section 5(a)(3) of the Securities Investor Protection Act of 1970, does not operate as a stay—

(1) under subsection (a) of this section, of the commencement or continuation of a criminal action or proceeding against the debtor;

(2) under subsection (a) of this section—
   (A) of the commencement or continuation of an action or proceeding for—
      (i) the establishment of paternity; or
      (ii) the establishment or modification of an order for alimony, maintenance, or support; or
   (B) of the collection of alimony, maintenance, or support from property that is not property of the estate;

(3) under subsection (a) of this section, of any act to perfect, or to maintain or continue the perfection of, an interest in property to the extent that the trustee's rights and powers are subject to such perfection under section 546(b) of this title or to the extent that such act is accomplished within the period provided under section 547(e)(2)(A) of this title;

(4) under paragraph (1), (2), (3), or (6) of subsection (a) of this section, of the commencement or continuation of an action or proceeding by a governmental unit or any organization exercising authority under the Convention on the Prohibition of the Development, Production, Stockpiling and Use of Chemical Weapons and on Their Destruction, opened for signature on January 13, 1993, to enforce such governmental unit's or

organization's police and regulatory power, including the enforcement of a judgment other than a money judgment, obtained in an action or proceeding by the governmental unit to enforce such governmental unit's or organization's police or regulatory power;

(5) [*Abrogated*].

(6) under subsection (a) of this section, of the setoff by a commodity broker, forward contract merchant, stockbroker, financial institutions, or securities clearing agency of any mutual debt and claim under or in connection with commodity contracts, as defined in section 761 of this title, forward contracts, or securities contracts, as defined in section 741 of this title, that constitutes the setoff of a claim against the debtor for a margin payment, as defined in section 101, 741, or 761 of this title, or settlement payment, as defined in section 101 or 741 of this title, arising out of commodity contracts, forward contracts, or securities contracts against cash, securities, or other property held by or due from such commodity broker, forward contract merchant, stockbroker, financial institutions, or securities clearing agency to margin, guarantee, secure, or settle commodity contracts, forward contracts, or securities contracts;

(7) under subsection (a) of this section, of the setoff by a repo participant, of any mutual debt and claim under or in connection with repurchase agreements that constitutes the setoff of a claim against the debtor for a margin payment, as defined in section 741 or 761 of this title, or settlement payment, as defined in section 741 of this title, arising out of repurchase agreements against cash, securities, or other property held by or due from such repo participant to margin, guarantee, secure or settle repurchase agreements;

(8) under subsection (a) of this section, of the commencement of any action by the Secretary of Housing and Urban Development to foreclose a mortgage or deed of trust in any case in which the mortgage or deed of trust held by the Secretary is insured or was formerly insured under the National Housing Act and covers property, or combinations of property, consisting of five or more living units;

(9) under subsection (a), of—

(A) an audit by a governmental unit to determine tax liability;

(B) the issuance to the debtor by a governmental unit of a notice of tax deficiency;

(C) a demand for tax returns; or

(D) the making of an assessment for any tax and issuance of a notice and demand for payment of such an assessment (but any tax lien that would otherwise attach to property of the estate by reason of such an assessment shall not take effect unless such tax is a debt of the debtor that will not be discharged in the case and such property or its proceeds are transferred out of the estate to, or otherwise revested in, the debtor).

(10) under subsection (a) of this section, of any act by a lessor to the debtor under a lease of nonresidential real property that has terminated by the expiration of the stated term of the lease before the commencement of or during a case under this title to obtain possession of such property;

(11) under subsection (a) of this section, of the presentment of a negotiable instrument and the giving of notice of and protesting dishonor of such an instrument;

(12) under subsection (a) of this section, after the date which is 90 days after the filing of such petition, of the commencement or continuation, and conclusion to the entry of final judgment, of an action which involves a debtor subject to reorganization pursuant to chapter 11 of this title and which was brought by the Secretary of Transportation under section 31325 of title 46 (including distribution of any proceeds of sale) to foreclose a preferred ship or fleet mortgage, or a security interest in or relating to a vessel or vessel under construction, held by the Secretary of Transportation under section 207 or title XI of the Merchant Marine Act, 1936, or under applicable State law;

(13) under subsection (a) of this section, after the date which is 90 days after the filing of such petition, of the commencement or continuation, and conclusion to the entry of final judgment, of an action which involves a debtor subject to reorganization pursuant to chapter 11 of this title and which was brought by the Secretary of Commerce under section 31325 of title 46 (including distribution of any proceeds of sale) to foreclose a preferred ship or fleet mortgage in a vessel or a mortgage, deed of trust, or other security interest in a fishing facility held by the Secretary of Commerce under section 207 or title XI of the Merchant Marine Act, 1936;

(14) under subsection (a) of this section, of any action by an accrediting agency regarding the accreditation status of the debtor as an educational institution;

(15) under subsection (a) of this section, of any action by a State licensing body regarding the licensure of the debtor as an educational institution;

(16) under subsection (a) of this section, of any action by a guaranty agency, as defined in section 435(j) of the Higher Education Act of 1965 or the Secretary of Education regarding the eligibility of the debtor to participate in programs authorized under such Act;

(17) under subsection (a) of this section, of the setoff by a swap participant, of any mutual debt and claim under or in connection with any swap agreement that constitutes the setoff of a claim against the debtor for any payment due from the debtor under or in connection with any swap agreement against any payment due to the debtor from the swap participant under or in connection with any swap agreement or against cash, securities, or other property of the debtor held by or due from such swap participant to guarantee, secure or settle any swap agreement; or

(18) under subsection (a) of the creation or perfection of a statutory lien for an ad valorem property tax imposed by the District of Columbia, or a political subdivision of a State, if such tax comes due after the filing of the petition.

(c) Except as provided in subsections (d), (e), and (f) of this section—

(1) the stay of an act against property of the estate under subsection (a) of this section continues until such property is no

longer property of the estate; and

(2) the stay of any other act under subsection (a) of this section continues until the earliest of—

   (A) the time the case is closed;

   (B) the time the case is dismissed; or

   (C) if the case is a case under chapter 7 of this title concerning an individual or a case under chapter 9, 11, 12, or 13 of this title, the time a discharge is granted or denied.

(d) On request of a party in interest and after notice and a hearing, the court shall grant relief from the stay provided under subsection (a) of this section, such as by terminating, annulling, modifying, or conditioning such stay—

(1) for cause, including the lack of adequate protection of an interest in property of such party in interest;

(2) with respect to a stay of an act against property under subsection (a) of this section, if—

   (A) the debtor does not have an equity in such property; and

   (B) such property is not necessary to an effective reorganization; or

(3) with respect to a stay of an act against single asset real estate under subsection (a), by a creditor whose claim is secured by an interest in such real estate, unless, not later than the date that is 90 days after the entry of the order for relief (or such later date as the court may determine for cause by order entered within that 90-day period)—

   (A) the debtor has filed a plan of reorganization that has a reasonable possibility of being confirmed within a reasonable time; or

   (B) the debtor has commenced monthly payments to each creditor whose claim is secured by such real estate (other than a claim secured by a judgment lien or by an unmatured statutory lien), which payments are in an amount equal to interest at a current fair market rate on the value of the creditor's interest in the real estate.

(e) Thirty days after a request under subsection (d) of this section for relief from the stay of any act against property of the estate under subsection (a) of this section, such stay is terminated with respect to the party in interest making such request, unless the court, after notice and a hearing, orders such stay continued in effect pending the conclusion of, or as a result of, a final hearing and determination under subsection (d) of this section. A hearing under this subsection may be a preliminary hearing, or may be consolidated with the final hearing under subsection (d) of this section. The court shall order such stay continued in effect pending the conclusion of the final hearing under subsection (d) of this section if there is a reasonable likelihood that the party opposing relief from such stay will prevail at the conclusion of such final hearing. If the hearing under this subsection is a preliminary hearing, then such final hearing shall be concluded not later than thirty days after the conclusion of such preliminary hearing, unless the 30-day period is extended with the consent of the parties in interest or for a specific time which the court finds is required by compelling circumstances.

(f) Upon request of a party in interest, the court, with or without a hearing, shall grant such relief from the stay provided under subsection (a) of this section as is necessary to prevent irreparable damage to the interest of an entity in property, if such interest will suffer such damage before there is an opportunity for notice and a hearing under subsection (d) or (e) of this section.

(g) In any hearing under subsection (d) or (e) of this section concerning relief from the stay of any act under subsection (a) of this section—

(1) the party requesting such relief has the burden of proof on the issue of the debtor's equity in property; and

(2) the party opposing such relief has the burden of proof on all other issues.

(h) An individual injured by any willful violation of a stay provided by this section shall recover actual damages, including costs and attorneys' fees, and, in appropriate circumstances, may recover punitive damages.

§ 363. Use, sale, or lease of property

(a) In this section, "cash collateral" means cash, negotiable instruments, documents of title, securities, deposit accounts, or other cash equivalents whenever acquired in which the estate and an entity other than the estate have an interest and includes the proceeds, products, offspring, rents, or profits of property and the fees, charges, accounts or other payments for the use or occupancy of rooms and other public facilities in hotels, motels, or other lodging properties subject to a security interest as provided in section 552(b) of this title, whether existing before or after the commencement of a case under this title.

(b)(1) The trustee, after notice and a hearing, may use, sell, or lease, other than in the ordinary course of business, property of the estate.

(2) If notification is required under subsection (a) of section 7A of the Clayton Act in the case of a transaction under this subsection, then—

   (A) notwithstanding subsection (a) of such section, the notification required by such subsection to be given by the debtor shall be given by the trustee; and

   (B) notwithstanding subsection (b) of such section, the required waiting period shall end on the 15th day after the date of the receipt, by the Federal Trade Commission and the Assistant Attorney General in charge of the Antitrust Division of the Department of Justice, of the notification required under such subsection (a), unless such waiting period is extended—

      (i) pursuant to subsection (e)(2) of such section, in the same manner as such subsection (e)(2) applies to a cash tender offer;

      (ii) pursuant to subsection (g)(2) of such section; or

      (iii) by the court after notice and a hearing.

(c)(1) If the business of the debtor is authorized to be operated under section 721, 1108, 1203, 1204, or 1304 of this title and unless the court orders otherwise, the trustee may enter into transactions, including the sale or lease of property of the estate, in the ordinary course of business, without notice or a hearing, and may use property of the estate in the ordinary course of business without notice or a hearing.

(2) The trustee may not use, sell, or lease cash collateral under paragraph (1) of this subsection unless—

(A) each entity that has an interest in such cash collateral consents; or

(B) the court, after notice and a hearing, authorizes such use, sale, or lease in accordance with the provisions of this section.

(3) Any hearing under paragraph (2)(B) of this subsection may be a preliminary hearing or may be consolidated with a hearing under subsection (c) of this section, but shall be scheduled in accordance with the needs of the debtor. If the hearing under paragraph (2)(B) of this subsection is a preliminary hearing, the court may authorize such use, sale, or lease only if there is a reasonable likelihood that the trustee will prevail at the final hearing under subsection (e) of this section. The court shall act promptly on any request for authorization under paragraph (2)(B) of this subsection.

(4) Except as provided in paragraph (2) of this subsection, the trustee shall segregate and account for any cash collateral in the trustee's possession, custody, or control.

(d) The trustee may use, sell, or lease property under subsection (b) or (c) of this section only to the extent not inconsistent with any relief granted under section 362(c), 362(d), 362(e), or 362(f) of this title.

(e) Notwithstanding any other provision of this section, at any time, on request of an entity that has an interest in property used, sold, or leased, or proposed to be used, sold, or leased, by the trustee, the court, with or without a hearing, shall prohibit or condition such use, sale, or lease as is necessary to provide adequate protection of such interest. This subsection also applies to property that is subject to any unexpired lease of personal property (to the exclusion of such property being subject to an order to grant relief from the stay under section 362).

(f) The trustee may sell property under subsection (b) or (c) of this section free and clear of any interest in such property of an entity other than the estate, only if—

(1) applicable nonbankruptcy law permits sale of such property free and clear of such interest;

(2) such entity consents;

(3) such interest is a lien and the price at which such property is to be sold is greater than the aggregate value of all liens on such property;

(4) such interest is in bona fide dispute; or

(5) such entity could be compelled, in a legal or equitable proceeding, to accept a money satisfaction of such interest.

(g) Notwithstanding subsection (f) of this section, the trustee may sell property under subsection (b) or (c) of this section free and clear of any vested or contingent right in the nature of dower or curtesy.

(h) Notwithstanding subsection (f) of this section, the trustee may sell both the estate's interest, under subsection (b) or (c) of this section, and the interest of any co-owner in property in which the debtor had, at the time of the commencement of the case, an undivided interest as a tenant in common, joint tenant, or tenant by the entirety, only if—

(1) partition in kind of such property among the estate and such co-owners is impracticable;

(2) sale of the estate's undivided interest in such property would realize significantly less for the estate than sale of such property free of the interests of such co-owners;

(3) the benefit to the estate of a sale of such property free of the interests of co-owners outweighs the detriment, if any, to such co-owners; and

(4) such property is not used in the production, transmission, or distribution, for sale, of electric energy or of natural or synthetic gas for heat, light, or power.

(i) Before the consummation of a sale of property to which subsection (g) or (h) of this section applies, or of property of the estate that was community property of the debtor and the debtor's spouse immediately before the commencement of the case, the debtor's spouse, or a co-owner of such property, as the case may be, may purchase such property at the price at which such sale is to be consummated.

(j) After a sale of property to which subsection (g) or (h) of this section applies, the trustee shall distribute to the debtor's spouse or the co-owners of such property, as the case may be, and to the estate, the proceeds of such sale, less the costs and expenses, not including any compensation of the trustee, of such sale, according to the interests of such spouse or co-owners, and of the estate.

(k) At a sale under subsection (b) of this section of property that is subject to a lien that secures an allowed claim, unless the court for cause orders otherwise the holder of such claim may bid at such sale, and, if the holder of such claim purchases such property, such holder may offset such claim against the purchase price of such property.

(*l*) Subject to the provisions of section 365, the trustee may use, sell, or lease property under subsection (b) or (c) of this section, or a plan under chapter 11, 12, or 13 of this title may provide for the use, sale, or lease of property, notwithstanding any provision in a contract, a lease, or applicable law that is conditioned on the insolvency or financial condition of the debtor, on the commencement of a case under this title concerning the debtor, or on the appointment of or the taking possession by a trustee in a case under this title or a custodian, and that effects, or gives an option to effect, a forfeiture, modification, or termination of the debtor's interest in such property.

(m) The reversal or modification on appeal of an authorization under subsection (b) or (c) of this section of a sale or lease of property does not affect the validity of a sale or lease under such authorization to an entity that purchased or leased such property in good faith, whether or not such entity knew of the pendency of the appeal, unless such authorization and such sale or lease were stayed pending appeal.

(n) The trustee may avoid a sale under this section if the sale price was controlled by an agreement among potential bidders at such sale, or may recover from a party to such agreement any amount by which the value of the property sold exceeds the price at which such sale was consummated, and may recover any costs, attorneys' fees, or expenses incurred in avoiding such sale or recovering such amount. In addition to any recovery under the preceding sentence, the court may grant judgment for punitive damages in favor of the estate and against any such party that entered into such an agreement in willful disregard of this subsection.

(*o*) In any hearing under this section—

(1) the trustee has the burden of proof on the issue of adequate protection; and

(2) the entity asserting an interest in property has the burden of proof on the issue of the validity, priority, or extent of such interest.

§ 364. Obtaining credit

(a) If the trustee is authorized to operate the business of the debtor under section 721, 1108, 1203, 1204, or 1304 of this title, unless the court orders otherwise, the trustee may obtain unsecured credit and incur unsecured debt in the ordinary course of business allowable under section 503(b)(1) of this title as an administrative expense.

(b) The court, after notice and a hearing, may authorize the trustee to obtain unsecured credit or to incur unsecured debt other than under subsection (a) of this section, allowable under section 503(b)(1) of this title as an administrative expense.

(c) If the trustee is unable to obtain unsecured credit allowable under section 503(b)(1) of this title as an administrative expense, the court, after notice and a hearing, may authorize the obtaining of credit or the incurring of debt—

(1) with priority over any or all administrative expenses of the kind specified in section 503(b) or 507(b) of this title;

(2) secured by a lien on property of the estate that is not otherwise subject to a lien; or

(3) secured by a junior lien on property of the estate that is subject to a lien.

(d)(1) The court, after notice and a hearing, may authorize the obtaining of credit or the incurring of debt secured by a senior or equal lien on property of the estate that is subject to a lien only if—

(A) the trustee is unable to obtain such credit otherwise; and

(B) there is adequate protection of the interest of the holder of the lien on the property of the estate on which such senior or equal lien is proposed to be granted.

(2) In any hearing under this subsection, the trustee has the burden of proof on the issue of adequate protection.

(e) The reversal or modification on appeal of an authorization under this section to obtain credit or incur debt, or of a grant under this section of a priority or a lien, does not affect the validity of any debt so incurred, or any priority or lien so granted, to an entity that extended such credit in good faith, whether or not such entity knew of the pendency of the appeal, unless such authorization and the incurring of such debt, or the granting of such priority or lien, were stayed pending appeal.

(f) Except with respect to an entity that is an underwriter as defined in section 1145(b) of this title, section 5 of the Securities Act of 1933, the Trust Indenture Act of 1939, and any State or local law requiring registration for offer or sale of a security or registration or licensing of an issuer of, underwriter of, or broker or dealer in, a security does not apply to the offer or sale under this section of a security that is not an equity security.

§ 365. Executory contracts and unexpired leases

(a) Except as provided in sections 765 and 766 of this title and in subsections (b), (c), and (d) of this section, the trustee, subject to the court's approval, may assume or reject any executory contract or unexpired lease of the debtor.

(b)(1) If there has been a default in an executory contract or unexpired lease of the debtor, the trustee may not assume such contract or lease unless, at the time of assumption of such contract or lease, the trustee—

(A) cures, or provides adequate assurance that the trustee will promptly cure, such default;

(B) compensates, or provides adequate assurance that the trustee will promptly compensate, a party other than the debtor to such contract or lease, for any actual pecuniary loss to such party resulting from such default; and

(C) provides adequate assurance of future performance under such contract or lease.

(2) Paragraph (1) of this subsection does not apply to a default that is a breach of a provision relating to—

(A) the insolvency or financial condition of the debtor at any time before the closing of the case;

(B) the commencement of a case under this title;

(C) the appointment of or taking possession by a trustee in a case under this title or a custodian before such commencement; or

(D) the satisfaction of any penalty rate or provision relating to a default arising from any failure by the debtor to perform nonmonetary obligations under the executory contract or unexpired lease.

(3) For the purposes of paragraph (1) of this subsection and paragraph (2)(B) of subsection (f), adequate assurance of future performance of a lease of real property in a shopping center includes adequate assurance—

(A) of the source of rent and other consideration due under such lease, and in the case of an assignment, that the financial condition and operating performance of the proposed assignee and its guarantors, if any, shall be similar to the financial condition and operating performance of the debtor and its guarantors, if any, as of the time the debtor became the lessee under the lease;

(B) that any percentage rent due under such lease will not decline substantially;

(C) that assumption or assignment of such lease is subject to all the provisions thereof, including (but not limited to) provisions such as a radius, location, use, or exclusivity provision, and will not breach any such provision contained in any other lease, financing agreement, or master agreement relating to such shopping center; and

(D) that assumption or assignment of such lease will not disrupt any tenant mix or balance in such shopping center.

(4) Notwithstanding any other provision of this section, if there has been a default in an unexpired lease of the debtor, other than a default of a kind specified in paragraph (2) of this subsection, the trustee may not require a lessor to provide

services or supplies incidental to such lease before assumption of such lease unless the lessor is compensated under the terms of such lease for any services and supplies provided under such lease before assumption of such lease.

(c) The trustee may not assume or assign an executory contract or unexpired lease of the debtor, whether or not such contract or lease prohibits or restricts assignment of rights or delegation of duties, if—

(1)(A) applicable law excuses a party, other than the debtor, to such contract or lease from accepting performance from or rendering performance to an entity other than the debtor or the debtor in possession, whether or not such contract or lease prohibits or restricts assignment of rights or delegation of duties; and

  (B) such party does not consent to such assumption or assignment; or

(2) such contract is a contract to make a loan, or extend other debt financing or financial accommodations, to or for the benefit of the debtor, or to issue a security of the debtor;

(3) such lease is of nonresidential real property and has been terminated under applicable nonbankruptcy law prior to the order for relief; or

(4) such lease is of nonresidential real property under which the debtor is lessee of an aircraft terminal or aircraft gate at an airport at which the debtor is the lessee under one or more additional nonresidential leases of an aircraft terminal or aircraft gate and the trustee, in connection with such assumption or assignment, does not assume all such leases or does not assume and assign all of such leases to the same person, except that the trustee may assume or assign less than all of such leases with the airport operator's written consent.

(d)(1) In a case under chapter 7 of this title, if the trustee does not assume or reject an executory contract or unexpired lease of residential real property or of personal property of the debtor within 60 days after the order for relief, or within such additional time as the court, for cause, within such 60-day period, fixes, then such contract or lease is deemed rejected.

(2) In a case under chapter 9, 11, 12, or 13 of this title, the trustee may assume or reject an executory contract or unexpired lease of residential real property or of personal property of the debtor at any time before the confirmation of a plan but the court, on request of any party to such contract or lease, may order the trustee to determine within a specified period of time whether to assume or reject such contract or lease.

(3) The trustee shall timely perform all the obligations of the debtor, except those specified in section 365(b)(2), arising from and after the order for relief under any unexpired lease of nonresidential real property, until such lease is assumed or rejected, notwithstanding section 503(b)(1) of this title. The court may extend, for cause, the time for performance of any such obligation that arises within 60 days after the date of the order for relief, but the time for performance shall not be extended beyond such 60-day period. This subsection shall not be deemed to affect the trustee's obligations under the provisions of subsection (b) or (f) of this section. Acceptance of any

such performance does not constitute waiver or relinquishment of the lessor's rights under such lease or under this title.

(4) Notwithstanding paragraphs (1) and (2), in a case under any chapter of this title, if the trustee does not assume or reject an unexpired lease of nonresidential real property under which the debtor is the lessee within 60 days after the date of the order for relief, or within such additional time as the court, for cause, within such 60-day period, fixes, then such lease is deemed rejected, and the trustee shall immediately surrender such nonresidential real property to the lessor.

(5) Notwithstanding paragraphs (1) and (4) of this subsection, in a case under any chapter of this title, if the trustee does not assume or reject an unexpired lease of nonresidential real property under which the debtor is an affected air carrier that is the lessee of an aircraft terminal or aircraft gate before the occurrence of a termination event, then (unless the court orders the trustee to assume such unexpired leases within 5 days after the termination event), at the option of the airport operator, such lease is deemed rejected 5 days after the occurrence of a termination event and the trustee shall immediately surrender possession of the premises to the airport operator; except that the lease shall not be deemed to be rejected unless the airport operator first waives the right to damages related to the rejection. In the event that the lease is deemed to be rejected under this paragraph, the airport operator shall provide the affected air carrier adequate opportunity after the surrender of the premises to remove the fixtures and equipment installed by the affected air carrier.

(6) For the purposes of paragraph (5) of this subsection and paragraph (f)(1) of this section, the occurrence of a termination event means, with respect to a debtor which is an affected air carrier that is the lessee of an aircraft terminal or aircraft gate—
  (A) the entry under section 301 or 302 of this title of an order for relief under chapter 7 of this title;
  (B) the conversion of a case under any chapter of this title to a case under chapter 7 of this title; or
  (C) the granting of relief from the stay provided under section 362(a) of this title with respect to aircraft, aircraft engines, propellers, appliances, or spare parts, as defined in section 40102(a) of title 49, except for property of the debtor found by the court not to be necessary to an effective reorganization.

(7) Any order entered by the court pursuant to paragraph (4) extending the period within which the trustee of an affected air carrier must assume or reject an unexpired lease of nonresidential real property shall be without prejudice to—
  (A) the right of the trustee to seek further extensions within such additional time period granted by the court pursuant to paragraph (4); and
  (B) the right of any lessor or any other party in interest to request, at any time, a shortening or termination of the period within which the trustee must assume or reject an unexpired lease of nonresidential real property.

(8) The burden of proof for establishing cause for an extension by an affected air carrier under paragraph (4) or the maintenance of a previously granted extension under paragraph (7)(A) and

(B) shall at all times remain with the trustee.

(9) For purposes of determining cause under paragraph (7) with respect to an unexpired lease of nonresidential real property between the debtor that is an affected air carrier and an airport operator under which such debtor is the lessee of an airport terminal or an airport gate, the court shall consider, among other relevant factors, whether substantial harm will result to the airport operator or airline passengers as a result of the extension or the maintenance of a previously granted extension. In making the determination of substantial harm, the court shall consider, among other relevant factors, the level of actual use of the terminals or gates which are the subject of the lease, the public interest in actual use of such terminals or gates, the existence of competing demands for the use of such terminals or gates, the effect of the court's extension or termination of the period of time to assume or reject the lease on such debtor's ability to successfully reorganize under chapter 11 of this title, and whether the trustee of the affected air carrier is capable of continuing to comply with its obligations under section 365(d)(3) of this title.

(10) The trustee shall timely perform all of the obligations of the debtor, except those specified in section 365(b)(2), first arising from or after 60 days after the order for relief in a case under chapter 11 of this title under an unexpired lease of personal property (other than personal property leased to an individual primarily for personal, family, or household purposes), until such lease is assumed or rejected notwithstanding section 503(b)(1) of this title, unless the court, after notice and a hearing and based on the equities of the case, orders otherwise with respect to the obligations or timely performance thereof. This subsection shall not be deemed to affect the trustee's obligations under the provisions of subsection (b) or (f). Acceptance of any such performance does not constitute waiver or relinquishment of the lessor's rights under such lease or under this title.

(e)(1) Notwithstanding a provision in an executory contract or unexpired lease, or in applicable law, an executory contract or unexpired lease of the debtor may not be terminated or modified, and any right or obligation under such contract or lease may not be terminated or modified, at any time after the commencement of the case solely because of a provision in such contract or lease that is conditioned on—

(A) the insolvency or financial condition of the debtor at any time before the closing of the case;

(B) the commencement of a case under this title; or

(C) the appointment of or taking possession by a trustee in a case under this title or a custodian before such commencement.

(2) Paragraph (1) of this subsection does not apply to an executory contract or unexpired lease of the debtor, whether or not such contract or lease prohibits or restricts assignment of rights or delegation of duties, if—

(A)(i) applicable law excuses a party, other than the debtor, to such contract or lease from accepting performance from or rendering performance to the trustee or to an assignee of such contract or lease, whether or not such contract or lease prohibits or restricts assignment of rights or delegation of duties; and

(ii) such party does not consent to such assumption or assignment; or

(B) such contract is a contract to make a loan, or extend other debt financing or financial accommodations, to or for the benefit of the debtor, or to issue a security of the debtor.

(f)(1) Except as provided in subsection (c) of this section, notwithstanding a provision in an executory contract or unexpired lease of the debtor, or in applicable law, that prohibits, restricts, or conditions the assignment of such contract or lease, the trustee may assign such contract or lease under paragraph (2) of this subsection; except that the trustee may not assign an unexpired lease of nonresidential real property under which the debtor is an affected air carrier that is the lessee of an aircraft terminal or aircraft gate if there has occurred a termination event.

(2) The trustee may assign an executory contract or unexpired lease of the debtor only if—

(A) the trustee assumes such contract or lease in accordance with the provisions of this section; and

(B) adequate assurance of future performance by the assignee of such contract or lease is provided, whether or not there has been a default in such contract or lease.

(3) Notwithstanding a provision in an executory contract or unexpired lease of the debtor, or in applicable law that terminates or modifies, or permits a party other than the debtor to terminate or modify, such contract or lease or a right or obligation under such contract or lease on account of an assignment of such contract or lease, such contract, lease, right, or obligation may not be terminated or modified under such provision because of the assumption or assignment of such contract or lease by the trustee.

(g) Except as provided in subsections (h)(2) and (i)(2) of this section, the rejection of an executory contract or unexpired lease of the debtor constitutes a breach of such contract or lease—

(1) if such contract or lease has not been assumed under this section or under a plan confirmed under chapter 9, 11, 12, or 13 of this title, immediately before the date of the filing of the petition; or

(2) if such contract or lease has been assumed under this section or under a plan confirmed under chapter 9, 11, 12, or 13 of this title—

(A) if before such rejection the case has not been converted under section 1112, 1208, or 1307 of this title, at the time of such rejection; or

(B) if before such rejection the case has been converted under section 1112, 1208, or 1307 of this title—

(i) immediately before the date of such conversion, if such contract or lease was assumed before such conversion; or

(ii) at the time of such rejection, if such contract or lease was assumed after such conversion.

(h)(1)(A) If the trustee rejects an unexpired lease of real property under which the debtor is the lessor and—

(i) if the rejection by the trustee amounts to such a breach as would entitle the lessee to treat such lease as terminated by virtue of its terms, applicable nonbankruptcy law, or any agreement made by the lessee, then the lessee under such lease may treat such lease as terminated by the rejection; or

    (ii) if the term of such lease has commenced, the lessee may retain its rights under such lease (including rights such as those relating to the amount and timing of payment of rent and other amounts payable by the lessee and any right of use, possession, quiet enjoyment, subletting, assignment, or hypothecation) that are in or appurtenant to the real property for the balance of the term of such lease and for any renewal or extension of such rights to the extent that such rights are enforceable under applicable nonbankruptcy law.

  (B) If the lessee retains its rights under subparagraph (A)(ii), the lessee may offset against the rent reserved under such lease for the balance of the term after the date of the rejection of such lease and for the term of any renewal or extension of such lease, the value of any damage caused by the nonperformance after the date of such rejection, of any obligation of the debtor under such lease, but the lessee shall not have any other right against the estate or the debtor on account of any damage occurring after such date caused by such nonperformance.

  (C) The rejection of a lease of real property in a shopping center with respect to which the lessee elects to retain its rights under subparagraph (A)(ii) does not affect the enforceability under applicable nonbankruptcy law of any provision in the lease pertaining to radius, location, use, exclusivity, or tenant mix or balance.

  (D) In this paragraph, "lessee" includes any successor, assign, or mortgagee permitted under the terms of such lease.

(2)(A) If the trustee rejects a timeshare interest under a timeshare plan under which the debtor is the timeshare interest seller and—

    (i) if the rejection amounts to such a breach as would entitle the timeshare interest purchaser to treat the timeshare plan as terminated under its terms, applicable nonbankruptcy law, or any agreement made by timeshare interest purchaser, the timeshare interest purchaser under the timeshare plan may treat the timeshare plan as terminated by such rejection; or

    (ii) if the term of such timeshare interest has commenced, then the timeshare interest purchaser may retain its rights in such timeshare interest for the balance of such term and for any term of renewal or extension of such timeshare interest to the extent that such rights are enforceable under applicable nonbankruptcy law.

  (B) If the timeshare interest purchaser retains its rights under subparagraph (A), such timeshare interest purchaser may offset against the moneys due for such timeshare interest for the balance of the term after the date of the rejection of such timeshare interest, and the term of any renewal or extension of such timeshare interest, the value of any damage caused by the nonperformance after the date of such rejection, of any obligation of the debtor under such timeshare plan, but the timeshare interest purchaser shall not have any right against the estate or the debtor on account of any damage

occurring after such date caused by such nonperformance.

(i)(1) If the trustee rejects an executory contract of the debtor for the sale of real property or for the sale of a timeshare interest under a timeshare plan, under which the purchaser is in possession, such purchaser may treat such contract as terminated, or, in the alternative, may remain in possession of such real property or timeshare interest.

(2) If such purchaser remains in possession—

  (A) such purchaser shall continue to make all payments due under such contract, but may, offset against such payments any damages occurring after the date of the rejection of such contract caused by the non-performance of any obligation of the debtor after such date, but such purchaser does not have any rights against the estate on account of any damages arising after such date from such rejection, other than such offset; and

  (B) the trustee shall deliver title to such purchaser in accordance with the provisions of such contract, but is relieved of all other obligations to perform under such contract.

(j) A purchaser that treats an executory contract as terminated under subsection (i) of this section, or a party whose executory contract to purchase real property from the debtor is rejected and under which such party is not in possession, has a lien on the interest of the debtor in such property for the recovery of any portion of the purchase price that such purchaser or party has paid.

(k) Assignment by the trustee to an entity of a contract or lease assumed under this section relieves the trustee and the estate from any liability for any breach of such contract or lease occurring after such assignment.

(*l*) If an unexpired lease under which the debtor is the lessee is assigned pursuant to this section, the lessor of the property may require a deposit or other security for the performance of the debtor's obligations under the lease substantially the same as would have been required by the landlord upon the initial leasing to a similar tenant.

(m) For purposes of this section 365 and sections 541(b)(2) and 362(b)(10), leases of real property shall include any rental agreement to use real property.

(n)(1) If the trustee rejects an executory contract under which the debtor is a licensor of a right to intellectual property, the licensee under such contract may elect—

  (A) to treat such contract as terminated by such rejection if such rejection by the trustee amounts to such a breach as would entitle the licensee to treat such contract as terminated by virtue of its own terms, applicable nonbankruptcy law, or an agreement made by the licensee with another entity; or

  (B) to retain its rights (including a right to enforce any exclusivity provision of such contract, but excluding any other right under applicable nonbankruptcy law to specific performance of such contract) under such contract and under any agreement supplementary to such contract, to such intellectual property (including any embodiment of such intellectual property to the extent protected by applicable nonbankruptcy law), as such rights existed immediately before the case commenced, for—

    (i) the duration of such contract; and

    (ii) any period for which such contract may be extended by the licensee as of right under applicable nonbankruptcy law.

(2) If the licensee elects to retain its rights, as described in paragraph (1)(B) of this subsection, under such contract—

    (A) the trustee shall allow the licensee to exercise such rights;

    (B) the licensee shall make all royalty payments due under such contract for the duration of such contract and for any period described in paragraph (1)(B) of this subsection for which the licensee extends such contract; and

    (C) the licensee shall be deemed to waive—

        (i) any right of setoff it may have with respect to such contract under this title or applicable nonbankruptcy law; and

        (ii) any claim allowable under section 503(b) of this title arising from the performance of such contract.

(3) If the licensee elects to retain its rights, as described in paragraph (1)(B) of this subsection, then on the written request of the licensee the trustee shall—

    (A) to the extent provided in such contract, or any agreement supplementary to such contract, provide to the licensee any intellectual property (including such embodiment) held by the trustee; and

    (B) not interfere with the rights of the licensee as provided in such contract, or any agreement supplementary to such contract, to such intellectual property (including such embodiment) including any right to obtain such intellectual property (or such embodiment) from another entity.

(4) Unless and until the trustee rejects such contract, on the written request of the licensee the trustee shall—

    (A) to the extent provided in such contract or any agreement supplementary to such contract—

        (i) perform such contract; or

        (ii) provide to the licensee such intellectual property (including any embodiment of such intellectual property to the extent protected by applicable nonbankruptcy law) held by the trustee; and

    (B) not interfere with the rights of the licensee as provided in such contract, or any agreement supplementary to such contract, to such intellectual property (including such embodiment), including any right to obtain such intellectual property (or such embodiment) from another entity.

(*o*) In a case under chapter 11 of this title, the trustee shall be deemed to have assumed (consistent with the debtor's other obligations under section 507), and shall immediately cure any deficit under, any commitment by the debtor to a Federal depository institutions regulatory agency (or predecessor to such agency) to maintain the capital of an insured depository institution, and any claim for a subsequent breach of the obligations thereunder shall be entitled to priority under section 507. This subsection shall not extend any commitment that would otherwise be terminated by any act of such an agency.

§ 366. Utility service

(a) Except as provided in subsection (b) of this section, a utility may not alter, refuse, or discontinue service to, or discriminate against, the trustee or the debtor solely on the basis of the commencement of a case under this title or that a debt owed by the debtor to such utility for service rendered before the order for relief was not paid when due.

(b) Such utility may alter, refuse, or discontinue service if neither the trustee nor the debtor, within 20 days after the date of the order for relief, furnishes adequate assurance of payment, in the form of a deposit or other security, for service after such date. On request of a party in interest and after notice and a hearing, the court may order reasonable modification of the amount of the deposit or other security necessary to provide adequate assurance of payment.

CHAPTER 5

CREDITORS, THE DEBTOR, AND THE ESTATE

Subchapter I—Creditors and Claims

§ 501. Filing of proofs of claims or interests

(a) A creditor or an indenture trustee may file a proof of claim. An equity security holder may file a proof of interest.

(b) If a creditor does not timely file a proof of such creditor's claim, an entity that is liable to such creditor with the debtor, or that has secured such creditor, may file a proof of such claim.

(c) If a creditor does not timely file a proof of such creditor's claim, the debtor or the trustee may file a proof of such claim.

(d) A claim of a kind specified in section 502(e)(2), 502(f), 502(g), 502(h) or 502(i) of this title may be filed under subsection (a), (b), or (c) of this section the same as if such claim were a claim against the debtor and had arisen before the date of the filing of the petition.

§ 502. Allowance of claims or interests

(a) A claim or interest, proof of which is filed under section 501 of this title, is deemed allowed, unless a party in interest, including a creditor of a general partner in a partnership that is a debtor in a case under chapter 7 of this title, objects.

(b) Except as provided in subsections (e)(2), (f), (g), (h) and (i) of this section, if such objection to a claim is made, the court, after notice and a hearing, shall determine the amount of such claim in lawful currency of the United States as of the date of the filing of the petition, and shall allow such claim in such amount, except to the extent that—

(1) such claim is unenforceable against the debtor and property of the debtor, under any agreement or applicable law for a reason other than because such claim is contingent or unmatured;

(2) such claim is for unmatured interest;

(3) if such claim is for a tax assessed against property of the estate, such claim exceeds the value of the interest of the estate in such property;

(4) if such claim is for services of an insider or attorney of the debtor, such claim exceeds the reasonable value of such services;

(5) such claim is for a debt that is unmatured on the date of the filing of the petition and that is excepted from discharge under section 523(a)(5) of this title;

(6) if such claim is the claim of a lessor for damages resulting from the termination of a lease of real property, such claim exceeds—

   (A) the rent reserved by such lease, without acceleration, for the greater of one year, or 15 percent, not to exceed three years, of the remaining term of such lease, following the earlier of—

     (i) the date of the filing of the petition; and

     (ii) the date on which such lessor repossessed, or the lessee surrendered, the leased property; plus

   (B) any unpaid rent due under such lease, without acceleration, on the earlier of such dates;

(7) if such claim is the claim of an employee for damages resulting from the termination of an employment contract, such claim exceeds—

   (A) the compensation provided by such contract, without acceleration, for one year following the earlier of—

     (i) the date of the filing of the petition; or

     (ii) the date on which the employer directed the employee to terminate, or such employee terminated, performance under such contract; plus

   (B) any unpaid compensation due under such contract, without acceleration, on the earlier of such dates;

(8) such claim results from a reduction, due to late payment, in the amount of an otherwise applicable credit available to the debtor in connection with an employment tax on wages, salaries, or commissions earned from the debtor; or

(9) proof of such claim is not timely filed, except to the extent tardily filed as permitted under paragraph (1), (2), or (3) of section 726(a) of this title or under the Federal Rules of Bankruptcy Procedure, except that a claim of a governmental unit shall be timely filed if it is filed before 180 days after the date of the order for relief or such later time as the Federal Rules of Bankruptcy Procedure may provide.

(c) There shall be estimated for purpose of allowance under this section—

(1) any contingent or unliquidated claim, the fixing or liquidation of which, as the case may be, would unduly delay the administration of the case; or

(2) any right to payment arising from a right to an equitable remedy for breach of performance.

(d) Notwithstanding subsections (a) and (b) of this section, the court shall disallow any claim of any entity from which property is recoverable under section 542, 543, 550, or 553 of this title or that is a transferee of a transfer avoidable under section 522(f), 522(h), 544, 545, 547, 548, 549, or 724(a) of this title, unless such entity or transferee has paid the amount, or turned over any such property, for which such entity or transferee is liable under section 522(i), 542, 543, 550, or 553 of this title.

(e)(1) Notwithstanding subsections (a), (b), and (c) of this section and paragraph (2) of this subsection, the court shall disallow any claim for reimbursement or contribution of an entity that is liable with the debtor on or has secured the claim of a creditor, to the extent that—

   (A) such creditor's claim against the estate is disallowed;

   (B) such claim for reimbursement or contribution is contingent as of the time of allowance or disallowance of such claim for reimbursement or contribution; or

   (C) such entity asserts a right of subrogation to the rights of such creditor under section 509 of this title.

(2) A claim for reimbursement or contribution of such an entity that becomes fixed after the commencement of the case shall be determined, and shall be allowed under subsection (a), (b), or (c) of this section, or disallowed under subsection (d) of this section, the same as if such claim had become fixed before the date of the filing of the petition.

(f) In an involuntary case, a claim arising in the ordinary course of the debtor's business or financial affairs after the commencement of the case but before the earlier of the appointment of a trustee and the order for relief shall be determined as of the date such claim arises, and shall be allowed under subsection (a), (b), or (c) of this section or disallowed under subsection (d) or (e) of this section, the same as if such claim had arisen before the date of the filing of the petition.

(g) A claim arising from the rejection, under section 365 of this title or under a plan under chapter 9, 11, 12, or 13 of this title, of an executory contract or unexpired lease of the debtor that has not been assumed shall be determined, and shall be allowed under subsection (a), (b), or (c) of this section or disallowed under subsection (d) or (e) of this section, the same as if such claim had arisen before the date of the filing of the petition.

(h) A claim arising from the recovery of property under section 522, 550, or 553 of this title shall be determined, and shall be allowed under subsection (a), (b), or (c) of this section, or disallowed under subsection (d) or (e) of this section, the same as if such claim had arisen before the date of the filing of the petition.

(i) A claim that does not arise until after the commencement of the case for a tax entitled to priority under section 507(a)(8) of this title shall be determined, and shall be allowed under subsection (a), (b), or (c) of this section, or disallowed under subsection (d) or (e) of this section, the same as if such claim had arisen before the date of the filing of the petition.

(j) A claim that has been allowed or disallowed may be reconsidered for cause. A reconsidered claim may be allowed or disallowed according to the equities of the case. Reconsideration of a claim under this subsection does not affect the validity of any payment or transfer from the estate made to a holder of an allowed claim on account of such allowed claim that is not reconsidered, but if a reconsidered claim is allowed and is of the same class as such holder's claim, such holder may not receive any additional payment or transfer from the estate on account of such holder's allowed claim until the holder of such reconsidered and allowed claim receives payment on account of such claim proportionate in value to that already received by such other holder. This subsection does not alter or modify the trustee's right to recover from a creditor any excess payment or transfer made to such creditor.

§ 503. Allowance of administrative expenses

(a) An entity may timely file a request for payment of an administrative expense, or may tardily file such request if permitted by the court for cause.

(b) After notice and a hearing, there shall be allowed administrative expenses, other than claims allowed under section 502(f) of this title, including—

(1)(A) the actual, necessary costs and expenses of preserving the estate, including wages, salaries, or commissions for services rendered after the commencement of the case;

(B) any tax—

(i) incurred by the estate, except a tax of a kind specified in section 507(a)(8) of this title; or

(ii) attributable to an excessive allowance of a tentative carryback adjustment that the estate received, whether the taxable year to which such adjustment relates ended before or after the commencement of the case; and

(C) any fine, penalty, or reduction in credit relating to a tax of a kind specified in subparagraph (B) of this paragraph;

(2) compensation and reimbursement awarded under section 330(a) of this title;

(3) the actual, necessary expenses, other than compensation and reimbursement specified in paragraph (4) of this subsection, incurred by—

(A) a creditor that files a petition under section 303 of this title;

(B) a creditor that recovers, after the court's approval, for the benefit of the estate any property transferred or concealed by the debtor;

(C) a creditor in connection with the prosecution of a criminal offense relating to the case or to the business or property of the debtor;

(D) a creditor, an indenture trustee, an equity security holder, or committee representing creditors or equity security holders other than a committee appointed under section 1102 of this title, in making a substantial contribution in a case under chapter 9 or 11 of this title;

(E) a custodian superseded under section 543 of this title, and compensation for the services of such custodian; or

(F) a member of a committee appointed under section 1102 of this title, if such expenses are incurred in the performance of the duties of such committee;

(4) reasonable compensation for professional services rendered by an attorney or an accountant of an entity whose expense is allowable under paragraph (3) of this subsection, based on the time, the nature, the extent, and the value of such services, and the cost of comparable services other than in a case under this title, and reimbursement for actual, necessary expenses incurred by such attorney or accountant;

(5) reasonable compensation for services rendered by an indenture trustee in making a substantial contribution in a case under chapter 9 or 11 of this title, based on the time, the nature, the extent, and the value of such services, and the cost of comparable services other than in a case under this title; and

(6) the fees and mileage payable under chapter 119 of title 28.

§ 504. Sharing of compensation

(a) Except as provided in subsection (b) of this section, a person receiving compensation or reimbursement under section 503(b)(2) or 503(b)(4) of this title may not share or agree to share—

(1) any such compensation or reimbursement with another person;

or

(2) any compensation or reimbursement received by another person under such sections.

(b)(1) A member, partner, or regular associate in a professional association, corporation, or partnership may share compensation or reimbursement received under section 503(b)(2) or 503(b)(4) of this title with another member, partner, or regular associate in such association, corporation, or partnership, and may share in any compensation or reimbursement received under such sections by another member, partner, or regular associate in such association, corporation, or partnership.

(2) An attorney for a creditor that files a petition under section 303 of this title may share compensation and reimbursement received under section 503(b)(4) of this title with any other attorney contributing to the services rendered or expenses incurred by such creditor's attorney.

§ 505. Determination of tax liability

(a)(1) Except as provided in paragraph (2) of this subsection, the court may determine the amount or legality of any tax, any fine or penalty relating to a tax, or any addition to tax, whether or not previously assessed, whether or not paid, and whether or not contested before and adjudicated by a judicial or administrative tribunal of competent jurisdiction.

(2) The court may not so determine—

(A) the amount or legality of a tax, fine, penalty, or addition to tax if such amount or legality was contested before and adjudicated by a judicial or administrative tribunal of competent jurisdiction before the commencement of the case under this title; or

(B) any right of the estate to a tax refund, before the earlier of—

(i) 120 days after the trustee properly requests such refund from the governmental unit from which such refund is claimed; or

(ii) a determination by such governmental unit of such request.

(b) A trustee may request a determination of any unpaid liability of the estate for any tax incurred during the administration of the case by submitting a tax return for such tax and a request for such a determination to the governmental unit charged with responsibility for collection or determination of such tax. Unless such return is fraudulent, or contains a material misrepresentation, the trustee, the debtor, and any successor to the debtor are discharged from any liability for such tax—

(1) upon payment of the tax shown on such return, if—

(A) such governmental unit does not notify the trustee, within 60 days after such request, that such return has been selected for examination; or

(B) such governmental unit does not complete such an examination and notify the trustee of any tax due, within 180 days after such request or within such additional time as the court, for cause, permits;

(2) upon payment of the tax determined by the court, after notice and a hearing, after completion by such governmental unit of

such examination; or

(3) upon payment of the tax determined by such governmental unit to be due.

(c) Notwithstanding section 362 of this title, after determination by the court of a tax under this section, the governmental unit charged with responsibility for collection of such tax may assess such tax against the estate, the debtor, or a successor to the debtor, as the case may be, subject to any otherwise applicable law.

§ 506. Determination of secured status

(a) An allowed claim of a creditor secured by a lien on property in which the estate has an interest, or that is subject to setoff under section 553 of this title, is a secured claim to the extent of the value of such creditor's interest in the estate's interest in such property, or to the extent of the amount subject to setoff, as the case may be, and is an unsecured claim to the extent that the value of such creditor's interest or the amount so subject to setoff is less than the amount of such allowed claim. Such value shall be determined in light of the purpose of the valuation and of the proposed disposition or use of such property, and in conjunction with any hearing on such disposition or use or on a plan affecting such creditor's interest.

(b) To the extent that an allowed secured claim is secured by property the value of which, after any recovery under subsection (c) of this section, is greater than the amount of such claim, there shall be allowed to the holder of such claim, interest on such claim, and any reasonable fees, costs, or charges provided for under the agreement under which such claim arose.

(c) The trustee may recover from property securing an allowed secured claim the reasonable, necessary costs and expenses of preserving, or disposing of, such property to the extent of any benefit to the holder of such claim.

(d) To the extent that a lien secures a claim against the debtor that is not an allowed secured claim, such lien is void unless—

(1) such claim was disallowed only under section 502(b)(5) or 502(e) of this title; or

(2) such claim is not an allowed secured claim due only to the failure of any entity to file a proof of such claim under section 501 of this title.

§ 507. Priorities

(a) The following expenses and claims have priority in the following order:

(1) First, administrative expenses allowed under section 503(b) of this title, and any fees and charges assessed against the estate under chapter 123 of title 28.

(2) Second, unsecured claims allowed under section 502(f) of this title.

(3) Third, allowed unsecured claims, but only to the extent of $4,925[8] for each individual or corporation, as the case may be, earned within 90 days before the date of the filing of the

petition or the date of the cessation of the debtor's business, whichever occurs first, for—

(A) wages, salaries, or commissions, including vacation, severance, and sick leave pay earned by an individual; or

(B) sales commissions earned by an individual or by a corporation with only 1 employee, acting as an independent contractor in the sale of goods or services for the debtor in the ordinary course of the debtor's business if, and only if, during the 12 months preceding that date, at least 75 percent of the amount that the individual or corporation earned by acting as an independent contractor in the sale of goods or services was earned from the debtor;

(4) Fourth, allowed unsecured claims for contributions to an employee benefit plan—

(A) arising from services rendered within 180 days before the date of the filing of the petition or the date of the cessation of the debtor's business, whichever occurs first; but only

(B) for each such plan, to the extent of—

(i) the number of employees covered by each such plan multiplied by $4,925;[9] less

(ii) the aggregate amount paid to such employees under paragraph (3) of this subsection, plus the aggregate amount paid by the estate on behalf of such employees to any other employee benefit plan.

(5) Fifth, allowed unsecured claims of persons—

(A) engaged in the production or raising of grain, as defined in section 557(b) of this title, against a debtor who owns or operates a grain storage facility, as defined in section 557(b) of this title, for grain or the proceeds of grain, or

(B) engaged as a United States fisherman against a debtor who has acquired fish or fish produce from a fisherman through a sale or conversion, and who is engaged in operating a fish produce storage or processing facility—

but only to the extent of $4,925[10] for each such individual.

(6) Sixth, allowed unsecured claims of individuals, to the extent of $2,225[11] for each such individual, arising from the deposit, before the commencement of the case, of money in connection with the purchase, lease, or rental of property, or the purchase of services, for the personal, family, or household use of such individuals, that were not delivered or provided.

(7) Seventh, allowed claims for debts to a spouse, former spouse, or child of the debtor, for alimony to, maintenance for, or support of such spouse or child, in connection with a separation agreement, divorce decree or other order of a court of record, determination made in accordance with State or territorial law by a governmental unit, or property settlement agreement, but not to the extent that such debt—

---

8 *Editor's Note*: This dollar amount reflects an inflationary adjustment, effective April 1, 2004. For cases commenced before April 1, 2004, the applicable dollar amount is $4,650.

9 *Editor's Note*: This dollar amount reflects an inflationary adjustment, effective April 1, 2004. For cases commenced before April 1, 2004, the applicable dollar amount is $4,650.

10 *Editor's Note*: This dollar amount reflects an inflationary adjustment, effective April 1, 2004. For cases commenced before April 1, 2004, the applicable dollar amount is $4,650.

11 *Editor's Note*: This dollar amount reflects an inflationary adjustment, effective April 1, 2004. For cases commenced before April 1, 2004, the applicable dollar amount is $2,100.

(A) is assigned to another entity, voluntarily, by operation of law, or otherwise; or

(B) includes a liability designated as alimony, maintenance, or support, unless such liability is actually in the nature of alimony, maintenance or support.

(8) Eighth, allowed unsecured claims of governmental units, only to the extent that such claims are for—

(A) a tax on or measured by income or gross receipts—

   (i) for a taxable year ending on or before the date of the filing of the petition for which a return, if required, is last due, including extensions, after three years before the date of the filing of the petition;

   (ii) assessed within 240 days, plus any time plus 30 days during which an offer in compromise with respect to such tax that was made within 240 days after such assessment was pending, before the date of the filing of the petition; or

   (iii) other than a tax of a kind specified in section 523(a)(1)(B) or 523(a)(1)(c) of this title, not assessed before, but assessable, under applicable law or by agreement, after, the commencement of the case;

(B) a property tax assessed before the commencement of the case and last payable without penalty after one year before the date of the filing of the petition;

(C) a tax required to be collected or withheld and for which the debtor is liable in whatever capacity;

(D) an employment tax on a wage, salary, or commission of a kind specified in paragraph (3) of this subsection earned from the debtor before the date of the filing of the petition, whether or not actually paid before such date, for which a return is last due, under applicable law or under any extension, after three years before the date of the filing of the petition;

(E) an excise tax on—

   (i) a transaction occurring before the date of the filing of the petition for which a return, if required, is last due, under applicable law or under any extension, after three years before the date of the filing of the petition; or

   (ii) if a return is not required, a transaction occurring during the three years immediately preceding the date of the filing of the petition;

(F) a customs duty arising out of the importation of merchandise—

   (i) entered for consumption within one year before the date of the filing of the petition;

   (ii) covered by an entry liquidated or reliquidated within one year before the date of the filing of the petition; or

   (iii) entered for consumption within four years before the date of the filing of the petition but unliquidated on such date, if the Secretary of the Treasury certifies that failure to liquidate such entry was due to an investigation pending on such date into assessment of antidumping or countervailing duties or fraud, or if information needed for the proper appraisement or classification of such merchandise was not available to the appropriate customs officer before such date; or

(G) a penalty related to a claim of a kind specified in this paragraph and in compensation for actual pecuniary loss.

(9) Ninth, allowed unsecured claims based upon any commitment by the debtor to a Federal depository institutions regulatory agency (or predecessor to such agency) to maintain the capital of an insured depository institution.

(b) If the trustee, under section 362, 363, or 364 of this title, provides adequate protection of the interest of a holder of a claim secured by a lien on property of the debtor and if, notwithstanding such protection, such creditor has a claim allowable under subsection (a)(1) of this section arising from the stay of action against such property under section 362 of this title, from the use, sale, or lease of such property under section 363 of this title, or from the granting of a lien under section 364(d) of this title, then such creditor's claim under such subsection shall have priority over every other claim under such subsection.

(c) For the purpose of subsection (a) of this section, a claim of a governmental unit arising from an erroneous refund or credit of a tax has the same priority as a claim for the tax to which such refund or credit relates.

(d) An entity that is subrogated to the rights of a holder of a claim of a kind specified in subsection (a)(3), (a)(4), (a)(5), (a)(6), (a)(7), (a)(8), or (a)(9) of this section is not subrogated to the right of the holder of such claim to priority under such subsection.

§ 508. Effect of distribution other than under this title

(a) If a creditor receives, in a foreign proceeding, payment of, or a transfer of property on account of, a claim that is allowed under this title, such creditor may not receive any payment under this title on account of such claim until each of the other holders of claims on account of which such holders are entitled to share equally with such creditor under this title has received payment under this title equal in value to the consideration received by such creditor in such foreign proceeding.

(b) If a creditor of a partnership debtor receives, from a general partner that is not a debtor in a case under chapter 7 of this title, payment of, or a transfer of property on account of, a claim that is allowed under this title and that is not secured by a lien on property of such partner, such creditor may not receive any payment under this title on account of such claim until each of the other holders of claims on account of which such holders are entitled to share equally with such creditor under this title has received payment under this title equal in value to the consideration received by such creditor from such general partner.

§ 509. Claims of codebtors

(a) Except as provided in subsection (b) or (c) of this section, an entity that is liable with the debtor on, or that has secured, a claim of a creditor against the debtor, and that pays such claim, is subrogated to the rights of such creditor to the extent of such payment.

(b) Such entity is not subrogated to the rights of such creditor to the extent that—

(1) a claim of such entity for reimbursement or contribution on account of such payment of such creditor's claim is—

   (A) allowed under section 502 of this title;

   (B) disallowed other than under section 502(e) of this title; or

   (C) subordinated under section 510 of this title; or

(2) as between the debtor and such entity, such entity received the consideration for the claim held by such creditor.

(c) The court shall subordinate to the claim of a creditor and for the benefit of such creditor an allowed claim, by way of subrogation under this section, or for reimbursement or contribution, of an entity that is liable with the debtor on, or that has secured, such creditor's claim, until such creditor's claim is paid in full, either through payments under this title or otherwise.

§ 510. Subordination

(a) A subordination agreement is enforceable in a case under this title to the same extent that such agreement is enforceable under applicable nonbankruptcy law.

(b) For the purpose of distribution under this title, a claim arising from rescission of a purchase or sale of a security of the debtor or of an affiliate of the debtor, for damages arising from the purchase or sale of such a security, or for reimbursement or contribution allowed under section 502 on account of such a claim, shall be subordinated to all claims or interests that are senior to or equal the claim or interest represented by such security, except that if such security is common stock, such claim has the same priority as common stock.

(c) Notwithstanding subsections (a) and (b) of this section, after notice and a hearing, the court may—

(1) under principles of equitable subordination, subordinate for purposes of distribution all or part of an allowed claim to all or part of another allowed claim or all or part of an allowed interest to all or part of another allowed interest; or

(2) order that any lien securing such a subordinated claim be transferred to the estate.

Subchapter II—Debtor's Duties and Benefits

§ 521. Debtor's duties

The debtor shall—

(1) file a list of creditors, and unless the court orders otherwise, a schedule of assets and liabilities, a schedule of current income and current expenditures, and a statement of the debtor's financial affairs;

(2) if an individual debtor's schedule of assets and liabilities includes consumer debts which are secured by property of the estate—

    (A) within thirty days after the date of the filing of a petition under chapter 7 of this title or on or before the date of the meeting of creditors, whichever is earlier, or within such additional time as the court, for cause, within such period fixes, the debtor shall file with the clerk a statement of his intention with respect to the retention or surrender of such property and, if applicable, specifying that such property is claimed as exempt, that the debtor intends to redeem such property, or that the debtor intends to reaffirm debts secured by such property;

    (B) within forty-five days after the filing of a notice of intent under this section, or within such additional time as the court, for cause, within such forty-five day period fixes, the debtor shall perform his intention with respect to such

property, as specified by subparagraph (A) of this paragraph; and

    (C) nothing in subparagraphs (A) and (B) of this paragraph shall alter the debtor's or the trustee's rights with regard to such property under this title;

(3) if a trustee is serving in the case, cooperate with the trustee as necessary to enable the trustee to perform the trustee's duties under this title;

(4) if a trustee is serving in the case, surrender to the trustee all property of the estate and any recorded information, including books, documents, records, and papers, relating to property of the estate, whether or not immunity is granted under section 344 of this title; and

(5) appear at the hearing required under section 524(d) of this title.

§ 522. Exemptions

(a) In this section—

(1) "dependent" includes spouse, whether or not actually dependent; and

(2) "value" means fair market value as of the date of the filing of the petition or, with respect to property that becomes property of the estate after such date, as of the date such property becomes property of the estate.

(b) Notwithstanding section 541 of this title, an individual debtor may exempt from property of the estate the property listed in either paragraph (1) or, in the alternative, paragraph (2) of this subsection. In joint cases filed under section 302 of this title and individual cases filed under section 301 or 303 of this title by or against debtors who are husband and wife, and whose estates are ordered to be jointly administered under Rule 1015(b) of the Federal Rules of Bankruptcy Procedure, one debtor may not elect to exempt property listed in paragraph (1) and the other debtor elect to exempt property listed in paragraph (2) of this subsection. If the parties cannot agree on the alternative to be elected, they shall be deemed to elect paragraph (1), where such election is permitted under the law of the jurisdiction where the case is filed. Such property is—

(1) property that is specified under subsection (d) of this section, unless the State law that is applicable to the debtor under paragraph (2)(A) of this subsection specifically does not so authorize; or, in the alternative,

(2)(A) any property that is exempt under Federal law, other than subsection (d) of this section, or State or local law that is applicable on the date of the filing of the petition at the place in which the debtor's domicile has been located for the 180 days immediately preceding the date of the filing of the petition, or for a longer portion of such 180-day period than in any other place; and

    (B) any interest in property in which the debtor had, immediately before the commencement of the case, an interest as a tenant by the entirety or joint tenant to the extent that such interest as a tenant by the entirety or joint tenant is exempt from process under applicable nonbankruptcy law.

(c) Unless the case is dismissed, property exempted under this section is not liable during or after the case for any debt of the debtor that arose, or that is determined under section 502 of this title as if such debt had arisen, before the commencement of the case, except—

(1) a debt of a kind specified in section 523(a)(1) or 523(a)(5) of this title;

(2) a debt secured by a lien that is—
   (A)(i) not avoided under subsection (f) or (g) of this section or under section 544, 545, 547, 548, 549, or 724(a) of this title; and
   (ii) not void under section 506(d) of this title; or
   (B) a tax lien, notice of which is properly filed;

(3) a debt of a kind specified in section 523(a)(4) or 523(a)(6) of this title owed by an institution-affiliated party of an insured depository institution to a Federal depository institutions regulatory agency acting in its capacity as conservator, receiver, or liquidating agent for such institution; or

(4) a debt in connection with fraud in the obtaining or providing of any scholarship, grant, loan, tuition, discount, award, or other financial assistance for purposes of financing an education at an institution of higher education (as that term is defined in section 101 of the Higher Education Act of 1965 (20 U.S.C. 1001)).

(d) The following property may be exempted under subsection (b)(1) of this section:

(1) The debtor's aggregate interest, not to exceed $18,450[12] in value, in real property or personal property that the debtor or a dependent of the debtor uses as a residence, in a cooperative that owns property that the debtor or a dependent of the debtor uses as a residence, or in a burial plot for the debtor or a dependent of the debtor.

(2) The debtor's interest, not to exceed $2,950[13] in value, in one motor vehicle.

(3) The debtor's interest, not to exceed $475[14] in value in any particular item or $9,850[15] in aggregate value, in household furnishings, household goods, wearing apparel, appliances, books, animals, crops, or musical instruments, that are held primarily for the personal, family, or household use of the debtor or a dependent of the debtor.

(4) The debtor's aggregate interest, not to exceed $1,225[16] in value, in jewelry held primarily for the personal, family, or household use of the debtor or a dependent of the debtor.

(5) The debtor's aggregate interest in any property, not to exceed in value $975[17] plus up to $9,250[18] of any unused amount of the exemption provided under paragraph (1) of this subsection.

(6) The debtor's aggregate interest, not to exceed $1,850[19] in value, in any implements, professional books, or tools, of the trade of the debtor or the trade of a dependent of the debtor.

(7) Any unmatured life insurance contract owned by the debtor, other than a credit life insurance contract.

(8) The debtor's aggregate interest, not to exceed in value $9,850[20] less any amount of property of the estate transferred in the manner specified in section 542(d) of this title, in any accrued dividend or interest under, or loan value of, any unmatured life insurance contract owned by the debtor under which the insured is the debtor or an individual of whom the debtor is a dependent.

(9) Professionally prescribed health aids for the debtor or a dependent of the debtor.

(10) The debtor's right to receive—
   (A) a social security benefit, unemployment compensation, or a local public assistance benefit;
   (B) a veterans' benefit;
   (C) a disability, illness, or unemployment benefit;
   (D) alimony, support, or separate maintenance, to the extent reasonably necessary for the support of the debtor and any dependent of the debtor;
   (E) a payment under a stock bonus, pension, profitsharing, annuity, or similar plan or contract on account of illness, disability, death, age, or length of service, to the extent reasonably necessary for the support of the debtor and any dependent of the debtor, unless—
      (i) such plan or contract was established by or under the auspices of an insider that employed the debtor at the time the debtor's rights under such plan or contract arose;
      (ii) such payment is on account of age or length of service; and
      (iii) such plan or contract does not qualify under section 401(a), 403(a), 403(b), or 408 of the Internal Revenue Code of 1986.

(11) The debtor's right to receive, or property that is traceable to—
   (A) an award under a crime victim's reparation law;
   (B) a payment on account of the wrongful death of an individual of whom the debtor was a dependent, to the extent reasonably necessary for the support of the debtor and any dependent of the debtor;

---

12 *Editor's Note*: This dollar amount reflects an inflationary adjustment, effective April 1, 2004. For cases commenced before April 1, 2004, the applicable dollar amount is $17,425.

13 *Editor's Note*: This dollar amount reflects an inflationary adjustment, effective April 1, 2004. For cases commenced before April 1, 2004, the applicable dollar amount is $2,775.

14 *Editor's Note*: This dollar amount reflects an inflationary adjustment, effective April 1, 2004. For cases commenced before April 1, 2004, the applicable dollar amount is $450.

15 *Editor's Note*: This dollar amount reflects an inflationary adjustment, effective April 1, 2004. For cases commenced before April 1, 2004, the applicable dollar amount is $9,300.

16 *Editor's Note*: This dollar amount reflects an inflationary adjustment, effective April 1, 2004. For cases commenced before April 1, 2004, the applicable dollar amount is $1,150.

17 *Editor's Note*: This dollar amount reflects an inflationary adjustment, effective April 1, 2004. For cases commenced before April 1, 2004, the applicable dollar amount is $925.

18 *Editor's Note*: This dollar amount reflects an inflationary adjustment, effective April 1, 2004. For cases commenced before April 1, 2004, the applicable dollar amount is $8,725.

19 *Editor's Note*: This dollar amount reflects an inflationary adjustment, effective April 1, 2004. For cases commenced before April 1, 2004, the applicable dollar amount is $1,750.

20 *Editor's Note*: This dollar amount reflects an inflationary adjustment, effective April 1, 2004. For cases commenced before April 1, 2004, the applicable dollar amount is $9,300.

(C) a payment under a life insurance contract that insured the life of an individual of whom the debtor was a dependent on the date of such individual's death, to the extent reasonably necessary for the support of the debtor and any dependent of the debtor;

(D) a payment, not to exceed $18,450,[21] on account of personal bodily injury, not including pain and suffering or compensation for actual pecuniary loss, of the debtor or an individual of whom the debtor is a dependent; or

(E) a payment in compensation of loss of future earnings of the debtor or an individual of whom the debtor is or was a dependent, to the extent reasonably necessary for the support of the debtor and any dependent of the debtor.

(e) A waiver of an exemption executed in favor of a creditor that holds an unsecured claim against the debtor is unenforceable in a case under this title with respect to such claim against property that the debtor may exempt under subsection (b) of this section. A waiver by the debtor of a power under subsection (f) or (h) of this section to avoid a transfer, under subsection (g) or (i) of this section to exempt property, or under subsection (i) of this section to recover property or to preserve a transfer, is unenforceable in a case under this title.

(f)(1) Notwithstanding any waiver of exemptions but subject to paragraph (3), the debtor may avoid the fixing of a lien on an interest of the debtor in property to the extent that such lien impairs an exemption to which the debtor would have been entitled under subsection (b) of this section, if such lien is—

(A) a judicial lien, other than a judicial lien that secures a debt—

(i) to a spouse, former spouse, or child of the debtor, for alimony to, maintenance for, or support of such spouse or child, in connection with a separation agreement, divorce decree or other order of a court of record, determination made in accordance with State or territorial law by a governmental unit, or property settlement agreement; and

(ii) to the extent that such debt—

(I) is not assigned to another entity, voluntarily, by operation of law, or otherwise; and

(II) includes a liability designated as alimony, maintenance, or support, unless such liability is actually in the nature of alimony, maintenance or support. or

(B) a nonpossessory, nonpurchase-money security interest in any—

(i) household furnishings, household goods, wearing apparel, appliances, books, animals, crops, musical instruments, or jewelry that are held primarily for the personal, family, or household use of the debtor or a dependent of the debtor;

(ii) implements, professional books, or tools, of the trade of the debtor or the trade of a dependent of the debtor; or

(iii) professionally prescribed health aids for the debtor or a dependent of the debtor.

(2)(A) For the purposes of this subsection, a lien shall be considered to impair an exemption to the extent that the sum of—

(i) the lien,

(ii) all other liens on the property; and

(iii) the amount of the exemption that the debtor could claim if there were no liens on the property;

exceeds the value that the debtor's interest in the property would have in the absence of any liens.

(B) In the case of a property subject to more than 1 lien, a lien that has been avoided shall not be considered in making the calculation under subparagraph (A) with respect to other liens.

(C) This paragraph shall not apply with respect to a judgment arising out of a mortgage foreclosure.

(3) In a case in which State law that is applicable to the debtor—

(A) permits a person to voluntarily waive a right to claim exemptions under subsection (d) or prohibits a debtor from claiming exemptions under subsection (d); and

(B) either permits the debtor to claim exemptions under State law without limitation in amount, except to the extent that the debtor has permitted the fixing of a consensual lien on any property or prohibits avoidance of a consensual lien on property otherwise eligible to be claimed as exempt property;

the debtor may not avoid the fixing of a lien on an interest of the debtor or a dependent of the debtor in property if the lien is a nonpossessory, nonpurchase-money security interest in implements, professional books, or tools of the trade of the debtor or a dependent of the debtor or farm animals or crops of the debtor or a dependent of the debtor to the extent the value of such implements, professional books, tools of the trade, animals, and crops exceeds $5,000.

(g) Notwithstanding sections 550 and 551 of this title, the debtor may exempt under subsection (b) of this section property that the trustee recovers under section 510(c)(2), 542, 543, 550, 551, or 553 of this title, to the extent that the debtor could have exempted such property under subsection (b) of this section if such property had not been transferred, if—

(1)(A) such transfer was not a voluntary transfer of such property by the debtor; and

(B) the debtor did not conceal such property; or

(2) the debtor could have avoided such transfer under subsection (f)(2) of this section.

(h) The debtor may avoid a transfer of property of the debtor or recover a setoff to the extent that the debtor could have exempted such property under subsection (g)(1) of this section if the trustee had avoided such transfer, if—

(1) such transfer is avoidable by the trustee under section 544, 545, 547, 548, 549, or 724(a) of this title or recoverable by the trustee under section 553 of this title; and

(2) the trustee does not attempt to avoid such transfer.

(i)(1) If the debtor avoids a transfer or recovers a setoff under subsection (f) or (h) of this section, the debtor may recover

---

21 *Editor's Note*: This dollar amount reflects an inflationary adjustment, effective April 1, 2004. For cases commenced before April 1, 2004, the applicable dollar amount is $17,425.

in the manner prescribed by, and subject to the limitations of section 550 of this title, the same as if the trustee had avoided such transfer, and may exempt any property so recovered under subsection (b) of this section.

(2) Notwithstanding section 551 of this title, a transfer avoided under section 544, 545, 547, 548, 549, or 724(a) of this title, under subsection (f) or (h) of this section, or property recovered under section 553 of this title, may be preserved for the benefit of the debtor to the extent that the debtor may exempt such property under subsection (g) of this section or paragraph (1) of this subsection.

(j) Notwithstanding subsections (g) and (i) of this section, the debtor may exempt a particular kind of property under subsections (g) and (i) of this section only to the extent that the debtor has exempted less property in value of such kind than that to which the debtor is entitled under subsection (b) of this section.

(k) Property that the debtor exempts under this section is not liable for payment of any administrative expense except—

(1) the aliquot share of the costs and expenses of avoiding a transfer of property that the debtor exempts under subsection (g) of this section, or of recovery of such property, that is attributable to the value of the portion of such property exempted in relation to the value of the property recovered; and

(2) any costs and expenses of avoiding a transfer under subsection (f) or (h) of this section, or of recovery of property under subsection (i)(1) of this section, that the debtor has not paid.

(*l*) The debtor shall file a list of property that the debtor claims as exempt under subsection (b) of this section. If the debtor does not file such a list, a dependent of the debtor may file such a list, or may claim property as exempt from property of the estate on behalf of the debtor. Unless a party in interest objects, the property claimed as exempt on such list is exempt.

(m) Subject to the limitation in subsection (b), this section shall apply separately with respect to each debtor in a joint case.

§ 523. Exceptions to discharge

(a) A discharge under section 727, 1141, 1228(a), 1228(b), or 1328(b) of this title does not discharge an individual debtor from any debt—

(1) for a tax or a customs duty—
  (A) of the kind and for the periods specified in section 507(a)(2) or 507(a)(8) of this title, whether or not a claim for such tax was filed or allowed;
  (B) with respect to which a return, if required—
    (i) was not filed; or
    (ii) was filed after the date on which such return was last due, under applicable law or under any extension, and after two years before the date of the filing of the petition; or
  (C) with respect to which the debtor made a fraudulent return or willfully attempted in any manner to evade or defeat such tax;

(2) for money, property, services, or an extension, renewal, or refinancing of credit, to the extent obtained by—
  (A) false pretenses, a false representation, or actual fraud,

other than a statement respecting the debtor's or an insider's financial condition;
  (B) use of a statement in writing—
    (i) that is materially false;
    (ii) respecting the debtor's or an insider's financial condition;
    (iii) on which the creditor to whom the debtor is liable for such money, property, services, or credit reasonably relied; and
    (iv) that the debtor caused to be made or published with intent to deceive; or
  (C) for purposes of subparagraph (A) of this paragraph, consumer debts owed to a single creditor and aggregating more than $1,225[22] for "luxury goods or services" incurred by an individual debtor on or within 60 days before the order for relief under this title, or cash advances aggregating more than $1,225[23] that are extensions of consumer credit under an open end credit plan obtained by an individual debtor on or within 60 days before the order for relief under this title, are presumed to be nondischargeable; "luxury goods or services" do not include goods or services reasonably acquired for the support or maintenance of the debtor or a dependent of the debtor; an extension of consumer credit under an open end credit plan is to be defined for purposes of this subparagraph as it is defined in the Consumer Credit Protection Act;

(3) neither listed nor scheduled under section 521(1) of this title, with the name, if known to the debtor, of the creditor to whom such debt is owed, in time to permit—
  (A) if such debt is not of a kind specified in paragraph (2), (4), or (6) of this subsection, timely filing of a proof of claim, unless such creditor had notice or actual knowledge of the case in time for such timely filing; or
  (B) if such debt is of a kind specified in paragraph (2), (4), or (6) of this subsection, timely filing of a proof of claim and timely request for a determination of dischargeability of such debt under one of such paragraphs, unless such creditor had notice or actual knowledge of the case in time for such timely filing and request;

(4) for fraud or defalcation while acting in a fiduciary capacity, embezzlement, or larceny;

(5) to a spouse, former spouse, or child of the debtor, for alimony to, maintenance for, or support of such spouse or child, in connection with a separation agreement, divorce decree or other order of a court of record, determination made in accordance with State or territorial law by a governmental unit, or property settlement agreement, but not to the extent that—
  (A) such debt is assigned to another entity, voluntarily, by operation of law, or otherwise (other than debts assigned pursuant to section 408(a)(3) of the Social Security Act, or any such debt which has been assigned to the Federal

---

22 *Editor's Note*: This dollar amount reflects an inflationary adjustment, effective April 1, 2004. For cases commenced before April 1, 2004, the applicable dollar amount is $1,150.

23 *Editor's Note*: This dollar amount reflects an inflationary adjustment, effective April 1, 2004. For cases commenced before April 1, 2004, the applicable dollar amount is $1,150.

Government or to a State or any political subdivision of such State); or

(B) such debt includes a liability designated as alimony, maintenance, or support, unless such liability is actually in the nature of alimony, maintenance, or support;

(6) for willful and malicious injury by the debtor to another entity or to the property of another entity;

(7) to the extent such debt is for a fine, penalty, or forfeiture payable to and for the benefit of a governmental unit, and is not compensation for actual pecuniary loss, other than a tax penalty—

(A) relating to a tax of a kind not specified in paragraph (1) of this subsection; or

(B) imposed with respect to a transaction or event that occurred before three years before the date of the filing of the petition;

(8) for an educational benefit overpayment or loan made, insured or guaranteed by a governmental unit, or made under any program funded in whole or in part by a governmental unit or nonprofit institution, or for an obligation to repay funds received as an educational benefit, scholarship or stipend, unless excepting such debt from discharge under this paragraph will impose an undue hardship on the debtor and the debtor's dependents;

(9) for death or personal injury caused by the debtor's operation of a motor vehicle if such operation was unlawful because the debtor was intoxicated from using alcohol, a drug, or another substance;

(10) that was or could have been listed or scheduled by the debtor in a prior case concerning the debtor under this title or under the Bankruptcy Act in which the debtor waived discharge, or was denied a discharge under section 727(a)(2), (3), (4), (5), (6), or (7) of this title, or under section 14c (1), (2), (3), (4), (6), or (7) of such Act;

(11) provided in any final judgment, unreviewable order, or consent order or decree entered in any court of the United States or of any State, issued by a Federal depository institutions regulatory agency, or contained in any settlement agreement entered into by the debtor, arising from any act of fraud or defalcation while acting in a fiduciary capacity committed with respect to any depository institution or insured credit union;

(12) for malicious or reckless failure to fulfill any commitment by the debtor to a Federal depository institutions regulatory agency to maintain the capital of an insured depository institution, except that this paragraph shall not extend any such commitment which would otherwise be terminated due to any act of such agency; or

(13) for any payment of an order of restitution issued under title 18, United States Code;

(14) incurred to pay a tax to the United States that would be nondischargeable pursuant to paragraph (1);

(15) not of the kind described in paragraph (5) that is incurred by the debtor in the course of a divorce or separation or in connection with a separation agreement, divorce decree or

other order of a court of record, a determination made in accordance with State or territorial law by a governmental unit unless—

(A) the debtor does not have the ability to pay such debt from income or property of the debtor not reasonably necessary to be expended for the maintenance or support of the debtor or a dependent of the debtor and, if the debtor is engaged in a business, for the payment of expenditures necessary for the continuation, preservation, and operation of such business; or

(B) discharging such debt would result in a benefit to the debtor that outweighs the detrimental consequences to a spouse, former spouse, or child of the debtor;

(16) for a fee or assessment that becomes due and payable after the order for relief to a membership association with respect to the debtor's interest in a dwelling unit that has condominium ownership or in a share of a cooperative housing corporation, but only if such fee or assessment is payable for a period during which—

(A) the debtor physically occupied a dwelling unit in the condominium or cooperative project; or

(B) the debtor rented the dwelling unit to a tenant and received payments from the tenant for such period,

but nothing in this paragraph shall except from discharge the debt of a debtor for a membership association fee or assessment for a period arising before entry of the order for relief in a pending or subsequent bankruptcy case;

(17) for a fee imposed by a court for the filing of a case, motion, complaint, or appeal, or for other costs and expenses assessed with respect to such filing, regardless of an assertion of poverty by the debtor under section 1915(b) or (f) of title 28, or the debtor's status as a prisoner, as defined in section 1915(h) of title 28;

(18) owed under State law to a State or municipality that is—

(A) in the nature of support, and

(B) enforceable under part D of title IV of the Social Security Act (42 U.S.C. 601 et seq.); or

(19) that—

(A) is for—

(i) the violation of any of the Federal securities laws (as that term is defined in section 3(a)(47) of the Securities Exchange Act of 1934), any of the State securities laws, or any regulation or order issued under such Federal or State securities laws; or

(ii) common law fraud, deceit, or manipulation in connection with the purchase or sale of any security; and

(B) results from—

(i) any judgment, order, consent order, or decree entered in any Federal or State judicial or administrative proceeding;

(ii) any settlement agreement entered into by the debtor; or

(iii) any court or administrative order for any damages, fine, penalty, citation, restitutionary payment, disgorgement payment, attorney fee, cost, or other payment owed by the debtor.

(b) Notwithstanding subsection (a) of this section, a debt that was excepted from discharge under subsection (a)(1), (a)(3), or (a)(8) of this section, under section 17a(1), 17a(3), or 17a(5) of the Bankruptcy Act, under section 439A of the Higher Education Act of 1965, or under section 733(g) of the Public Health Service Act in a prior case concerning the debtor under this title, or under the Bankruptcy Act, is dischargeable in a case under this title unless, by the terms of subsection (a) of this section, such debt is not dischargeable in the case under this title.

(c)(1) Except as provided in subsection (a)(3)(B) of this section, the debtor shall be discharged from a debt of a kind specified in paragraph (2), (4), (6), or (15) of subsection (a) of this section, unless, on request of the creditor to whom such debt is owed, and after notice and a hearing, the court determines such debt to be excepted from discharge under paragraph (2), (4), (6), or (15) as the case may be, of subsection (a) of this section.

(2) Paragraph (1) shall not apply in the case of a Federal depository institutions regulatory agency seeking, in its capacity as conservator, receiver, or liquidating agent for an insured depository institution, to recover a debt described in subsection (a)(2), (a)(4), (a)(6), or (a)(11) owed to such institution by an institution-affiliated party unless the receiver, conservator, or liquidating agent was appointed in time to reasonably comply, or for a Federal depository institutions regulatory agency acting in its corporate capacity as a successor to such receiver, conservator, or liquidating agent to reasonably comply, with subsection (a)(3)(B) as a creditor of such institution-affiliated party with respect to such debt.

(d) If a creditor requests a determination of dischargeability of a consumer debt under subsection (a)(2) of this section, and such debt is discharged, the court shall grant judgment in favor of the debtor for the costs of, and a reasonable attorney's fee for, the proceeding if the court finds that the position of the creditor was not substantially justified, except that the court shall not award such costs and fees if special circumstances would make the award unjust.

(e) Any institution-affiliated party of a insured depository institution shall be considered to be acting in a fiduciary capacity with respect to the purposes of subsection (a)(4) or (11).

§ 524. Effect of discharge

(a) A discharge in a case under this title—

(1) voids any judgment at any time obtained, to the extent that such judgment is a determination of the personal liability of the debtor with respect to any debt discharged under section 727, 944, 1141, 1228, or 1328 of this title, whether or not discharge of such debt is waived;

(2) operates as an injunction against the commencement or continuation of an action, the employment of process, or an act, to collect, recover or offset any such debt as a personal liability of the debtor, whether or not discharge of such debt is waived; and

(3) operates as an injunction against the commencement or continuation of an action, the employment of process, or an act, to collect or recover from, or offset against, property of the debtor

of the kind specified in section 541(a)(2) of this title that is acquired after the commencement of the case, on account of any allowable community claim, except a community claim that is excepted from discharge under section 523, 1228(a)(1), or 1328(a)(1) of this title, or that would be so excepted, determined in accordance with the provisions of sections 523(c) and 523(d) of this title, in a case concerning the debtor's spouse commenced on the date of the filing of the petition in the case concerning the debtor, whether or not discharge of the debt based on such community claim is waived.

(b) Subsection (a)(3) of this section does not apply if—

(1)(A) the debtor's spouse is a debtor in a case under this title, or a bankrupt or a debtor in a case under the Bankruptcy Act, commenced within six years of the date of the filing of the petition in the case concerning the debtor; and

(B) the court does not grant the debtor's spouse a discharge in such case concerning the debtor's spouse; or

(2)(A) the court would not grant the debtor's spouse a discharge in a case under chapter 7 of this title concerning such spouse commenced on the date of the filing of the petition in the case concerning the debtor; and

(B) a determination that the court would not so grant such discharge is made by the bankruptcy court within the time and in the manner provided for a determination under section 727 of this title of whether a debtor is granted a discharge.

(c) An agreement between a holder of a claim and the debtor, the consideration for which, in whole or in part, is based on a debt that is dischargeable in a case under this title is enforceable only to any extent enforceable under applicable nonbankruptcy law, whether or not discharge of such debt is waived, only if—

(1) such agreement was made before the granting of the discharge under section 727, 1141, 1228, or 1328 of this title;

(2)(A) such agreement contains a clear and conspicuous statement which advises the debtor that the agreement may be rescinded at any time prior to discharge or within sixty days after such agreement is filed with the court, whichever occurs later, by giving notice of rescission to the holder of such claim; and

(B) such agreement contains a clear and conspicuous statement which advises the debtor that such agreement is not required under this title, under nonbankruptcy law, or under any agreement not in accordance with the provisions of this subsection;

(3) such agreement has been filed with the court and, if applicable, accompanied by a declaration or an affidavit of the attorney that represented the debtor during the course of negotiating an agreement under this subsection, which states that—

(A) such agreement represents a fully informed and voluntary agreement by the debtor;

(B) such agreement does not impose an undue hardship on the debtor or a dependent of the debtor; and

(C) the attorney fully advised the debtor of the legal effect and consequences of—

(i) an agreement of the kind specified in this subsection; and

(ii) any default under such an agreement;

(4) the debtor has not rescinded such agreement at any time prior to discharge or within sixty days after such agreement is filed with the court, whichever occurs later, by giving notice of rescission to the holder of such claim;

(5) the provisions of subsection (d) of this section have been complied with; and

(6)(A) in a case concerning an individual who was not represented by an attorney during the course of negotiating an agreement under this subsection, the court approves such agreement as—

    (i) not imposing an undue hardship on the debtor or a dependent of the debtor; and

    (ii) in the best interest of the debtor.

(B) Subparagraph (A) shall not apply to the extent that such debt is a consumer debt secured by real property.

(d) In a case concerning an individual, when the court has determined whether to grant or not to grant a discharge under section 727, 1141, 1228, or 1328 of this title, the court may hold a hearing at which the debtor shall appear in person. At any such hearing, the court shall inform the debtor that a discharge has been granted or the reason why a discharge has not been granted. If a discharge has been granted and if the debtor desires to make an agreement of the kind specified in subsection (c) of this section and was not represented by an attorney during the course of negotiating such agreement, then the court shall hold a hearing at which the debtor shall appear in person and at any such hearing the court shall—

(1) inform the debtor—

    (A) that such an agreement is not required under this title, under nonbankruptcy law, or under any agreement not made in accordance with the provisions of subsection (c) of this section; and

    (B) of the legal effect and consequences of—

        (i) an agreement of the kind specified in subsection (c) of this section; and

        (ii) a default under such an agreement; and

(2) determine whether the agreement that the debtor desires to make complies with the requirements of subsection (c)(6) of this section, if the consideration for such agreement is based in whole or in part on a consumer debt that is not secured by real property of the debtor.

(e) Except as provided in subsection (a)(3) of this section, discharge of a debt of the debtor does not affect the liability of any other entity on, or the property of any other entity for, such debt.

(f) Nothing contained in subsection (c) or (d) of this section prevents a debtor from voluntarily repaying any debt.

(g)(1)(A) After notice and hearing, a court that enters an order confirming a plan of reorganization under chapter 11 may issue, in connection with such order, an injunction in accordance with this subsection to supplement the injunctive effect of a discharge under this section.

    (B) An injunction may be issued under subparagraph (A) to enjoin entities from taking legal action for the purpose of directly or indirectly collecting, recovering, or receiving payment or recovery with respect to any claim or de-mand that, under a plan of reorganization, is to be paid in whole or in part by a trust described in paragraph (2)(B)(i), except such legal actions as are expressly allowed by the injunction, the confirmation order, or the plan of reorganization.

(2)(A) Subject to subsection (h), if the requirements of subparagraph (B) are met at the time an injunction described in paragraph (1) is entered, then after entry of such injunction, any proceeding that involves the validity, application, construction, or modification of such injunction, or of this subsection with respect to such injunction, may be commenced only in the district court in which such injunction was entered, and such court shall have exclusive jurisdiction over any such proceeding without regard to the amount in controversy.

(B) The requirements of this subparagraph are that—

    (i) the injunction is to be implemented in connection with a trust that, pursuant to the plan of reorganization—

        (I) is to assume the liabilities of a debtor which at the time of entry of the order for relief has been named as a defendant in personal injury, wrongful death, or property-damage actions seeking recovery for damages allegedly caused by the presence of, or exposure to, asbestos or asbestos-containing products;

        (II) is to be funded in whole or in part by the securities of 1 or more debtors involved in such plan and by the obligation of such debtor or debtors to make future payments, including dividends;

        (III) is to own, or by the exercise of rights granted under such plan would be entitled to own if specified contingencies occur, a majority of the voting shares of—

            (aa) each such debtor;

            (bb) the parent corporation of each such debtor; or

            (cc) a subsidiary of each such debtor that is also a debtor; and

        (IV) is to use its assets or income to pay claims and demands; and

    (ii) subject to subsection (h), the court determines that—

        (I) the debtor is likely to be subject to substantial future demands for payment arising out of the same or similar conduct or events that gave rise to the claims that are addressed by the injunction;

        (II) the actual amounts, numbers, and timing of such future demands cannot be determined;

        (III) pursuit of such demands outside the procedures prescribed by such plan is likely to threaten the plan's purpose to deal equitably with claims and future demands;

        (IV) as part of the process of seeking confirmation of such plan—

            (aa) the terms of the injunction proposed to be issued under paragraph (1)(A), including any provisions barring actions against third parties pursuant to paragraph (4)(A), are set out in such plan and in any disclosure statement supporting the plan; and

            (bb) a separate class or classes of the claimants

whose claims are to be addressed by a trust described in clause (i) is established and votes, by at least 75 percent of those voting, in favor of the plan; and

    (V) subject to subsection (h), pursuant to court orders or otherwise, the trust will operate through mechanisms such as structured, periodic, or supplemental payments, pro rata distributions, matrices, or periodic review of estimates of the numbers and values of present claims and future demands, or other comparable mechanisms, that provide reasonable assurance that the trust will value, and be in a financial position to pay, present claims and future demands that involve similar claims in substantially the same manner.

(3)(A) If the requirements of paragraph (2)(B) are met and the order confirming the plan of reorganization was issued or affirmed by the district court that has jurisdiction over the reorganization case, then after the time for appeal of the order that issues or affirms the plan—

    (i) the injunction shall be valid and enforceable and may not be revoked or modified by any court except through appeal in accordance with paragraph (6);

    (ii) no entity that pursuant to such plan or thereafter becomes a direct or indirect transferee of, or successor to any assets of, a debtor or trust that is the subject of the injunction shall be liable with respect to any claim or demand made against such entity by reason of its becoming such a transferee or successor; and

    (iii) no entity that pursuant to such plan or thereafter makes a loan to such a debtor or trust or to such a successor or transferee shall, by reason of making the loan, be liable with respect to any claim or demand made against such entity, nor shall any pledge of assets made in connection with such a loan be upset or impaired for that reason;

(B) Subparagraph (A) shall not be construed to—

    (i) imply that an entity described in subparagraph (A) (ii) or (iii) would, if this paragraph were not applicable, necessarily be liable to any entity by reason of any of the acts described in subparagraph (A);

    (ii) relieve any such entity of the duty to comply with, or of liability under, any Federal or State law regarding the making of a fraudulent conveyance in a transaction described in subparagraph (A) (ii) or (iii); or

    (iii) relieve a debtor of the debtor's obligation to comply with the terms of the plan of reorganization, or affect the power of the court to exercise its authority under sections 1141 and 1142 to compel the debtor to do so.

(4)(A)(i) Subject to subparagraph (B), an injunction described in paragraph (1) shall be valid and enforceable against all entities that it addresses.

    (ii) Notwithstanding the provisions of section 524(e), such an injunction may bar any action directed against a third party who is identifiable from the terms of such injunction (by name or as part of an identifiable group) and is alleged to be directly or indirectly liable for the conduct of, claims against, or demands on the debtor to the extent such alleged liability of such third party arises by

reason of—

    (I) the third party's ownership of a financial interest in the debtor, a past or present affiliate of the debtor, or a predecessor in interest of the debtor;

    (II) the third party's involvement in the management of the debtor or a predecessor in interest of the debtor, or service as an officer, director or employee of the debtor or a related party;

    (III) the third party's provision of insurance to the debtor or a related party; or

    (IV) the third party's involvement in a transaction changing the corporate structure, or in a loan or other financial transaction affecting the financial condition, of the debtor or a related party, including but not limited to—

        (aa) involvement in providing financing (debt or equity), or advice to an entity involved in such a transaction; or

        (bb) acquiring or selling a financial interest in an entity as part of such a transaction.

  (iii) As used in this subparagraph, the term "related party" means—

    (I) a past or present affiliate of the debtor;

    (II) a predecessor in interest of the debtor; or

    (III) any entity that owned a financial interest in—

        (aa) the debtor;

        (bb) a past or present affiliate of the debtor; or

        (cc) a predecessor in interest of the debtor.

(B) Subject to subsection (h), if, under a plan of reorganization, a kind of demand described in such plan is to be paid in whole or in part by a trust described in paragraph (2)(B)(i) in connection with which an injunction described in paragraph (1) is to be implemented, then such injunction shall be valid and enforceable with respect to a demand of such kind made, after such plan is confirmed, against the debtor or debtors involved, or against a third party described in subparagraph (A)(ii), if—

    (i) as part of the proceedings leading to issuance of such injunction, the court appoints a legal representative for the purpose of protecting the rights of persons that might subsequently assert demands of such kind, and

    (ii) the court determines, before entering the order confirming such plan, that identifying such debtor or debtors, or such third party (by name or as part of an identifiable group), in such injunction with respect to such demands for purposes of this subparagraph is fair and equitable with respect to the persons that might subsequently assert such demands, in light of the benefits provided, or to be provided, to such trust on behalf of such debtor or debtors or such third party.

(5) In this subsection, the term "demand" means a demand for payment, present or future, that—

(A) was not a claim during the proceedings leading to the confirmation of a plan of reorganization;

(B) arises out of the same or similar conduct or events that gave rise to the claims addressed by the injunction issued under paragraph (1); and

(C) pursuant to the plan, is to be paid by a trust described in paragraph (2)(B)(i).

(6) Paragraph (3)(A)(i) does not bar an action taken by or at the direction of an appellate court on appeal of an injunction issued under paragraph (1) or of the order of confirmation that relates to the injunction.

(7) This subsection does not affect the operation of section 1144 or the power of the district court to refer a proceeding under section 157 of title 28 or any reference of a proceeding made prior to the date of the enactment of this subsection.

(h) Application to existing injunctions. For purposes of subsection (g)—

(1) subject to paragraph (2), if an injunction of the kind described in subsection (g)(1)(B) was issued before the date of the enactment of this Act, as part of a plan of reorganization confirmed by an order entered before such date, then the injunction shall be considered to meet the requirements of subsection (g)(2)(B) for purposes of subsection (g)(2)(A), and to satisfy subsection (g)(4)(A)(ii), if—

  (A) the court determined at the time the plan was confirmed that the plan was fair and equitable in accordance with the requirements of section 1129(b);

  (B) as part of the proceedings leading to issuance of such injunction and confirmation of such plan, the court had appointed a legal representative for the purpose of protecting the rights of persons that might subsequently assert demands described in subsection (g)(4)(B) with respect to such plan; and

  (C) such legal representative did not object to confirmation of such plan or issuance of such injunction; and

(2) for purposes of paragraph (1), if a trust described in subsection (g)(2)(B)(i) is subject to a court order on the date of the enactment of this Act staying such trust from settling or paying further claims—

  (A) the requirements of subsection (g)(2)(B)(ii)(V) shall not apply with respect to such trust until such stay is lifted or dissolved; and

  (B) if such trust meets such requirements on the date such stay is lifted or dissolved, such trust shall be considered to have met such requirements continuously from the date of the enactment of this Act.

§ 525. Protection against discriminatory treatment

(a) Except as provided in the Perishable Agricultural Commodities Act, 1930, the Packers and Stockyards Act, 1921, and section 1 of the Act entitled "An Act making appropriations for the Department of Agriculture for the fiscal year ending June 30, 1944, and for other purposes," approved July 12, 1943, a governmental unit may not deny, revoke, suspend, or refuse to renew a license, permit, charter, franchise, or other similar grant to, condition such a grant to, discriminate with respect to such a grant against, deny employment to, terminate the employment of, or discriminate with respect to employment against, a person that is or has been a debtor under this title or a bankrupt or a debtor under the Bankruptcy Act, or another person with whom such bankrupt or debtor has been associated, solely because such bankrupt or debtor is or has been a debtor under this title or a bankrupt or debtor under the Bankruptcy Act, has been insolvent before the commencement of the case under this title, or during the case but before the debtor is granted or denied a discharge, or has not paid a debt that is dischargeable in the case under this title or that was discharged under the Bankruptcy Act.

(b) No private employer may terminate the employment of, or discriminate with respect to employment against, an individual who is or has been a debtor under this title, a debtor or bankrupt under the Bankruptcy Act, or an individual associated with such debtor or bankrupt, solely because such debtor or bankrupt—

(1) is or has been a debtor under this title or a debtor or bankrupt under the Bankruptcy Act;

(2) has been insolvent before the commencement of a case under this title or during the case but before the grant or denial of a discharge; or

(3) has not paid a debt that is dischargeable in a case under this title or that was discharged under the Bankruptcy Act.

(c)(1) A governmental unit that operates a student grant or loan program and a person engaged in a business that includes the making of loans guaranteed or insured under a student loan program may not deny a grant, loan, loan guarantee, or loan insurance to a person that is or has been a debtor under this title or a bankrupt or debtor under the Bankruptcy Act, or another person with whom the debtor or bankrupt has been associated, because the debtor or bankrupt is or has been a debtor under this title or a bankrupt or debtor under the Bankruptcy Act, has been insolvent before the commencement of a case under this title or during the pendency of the case but before the debtor is granted or denied a discharge, or has not paid a debt that is dischargeable in the case under this title or that was discharged under the Bankruptcy Act.

(2) In this section, "student loan program" means the program operated under part B, D, or E of title IV of the Higher Education Act of 1965 or a similar program operated under State or local law.

Subchapter III—The Estate

§ 541. Property of the estate

(a) The commencement of a case under section 301, 302, or 303 of this title creates an estate. Such estate is comprised of all the following property, wherever located and by whomever held:

(1) Except as provided in subsections (b) and (c)(2) of this section, all legal or equitable interests of the debtor in property as of the commencement of the case.

(2) All interests of the debtor and the debtor's spouse in community property as of the commencement of the case that is—
  (A) under the sole, equal, or joint management and control of the debtor; or
  (B) liable for an allowable claim against the debtor, or for both an allowable claim against the debtor and an allowable claim against the debtor's spouse, to the extent that such interest is so liable.

(3) Any interest in property that the trustee recovers under section 329(b), 363(n), 543, 550, 553, or 723 of this title.

(4) Any interest in property preserved for the benefit of or ordered

transferred to the estate under section 510(c) or 551 of this title.

(5) Any interest in property that would have been property of the estate if such interest had been an interest of the debtor on the date of the filing of the petition, and that the debtor acquires or becomes entitled to acquire within 180 days after such date—

(A) by bequest, devise, or inheritance;

(B) as a result of a property settlement agreement with debtor's spouse, or of an interlocutory or final divorce decree; or

(C) as beneficiary of a life insurance policy or of a death benefit plan.

(6) Proceeds, product, offspring, rents, or profits of or from property of the estate, except such as are earnings from services performed by an individual debtor after the commencement of the case.

(7) Any interest in property that the estate acquires after the commencement of the case.

(b) Property of the estate does not include—

(1) any power that the debtor may exercise solely for the benefit of an entity other than the debtor;

(2) any interest of the debtor as a lessee under a lease of nonresidential real property that has terminated at the expiration of the stated term of such lease before the commencement of the case under this title, and ceases to include any interest of the debtor as a lessee under a lease of nonresidential real property that has terminated at the expiration of the stated term of such lease during the case;

(3) any eligibility of the debtor to participate in programs authorized under the Higher Education Act of 1965 (20 U.S.C. 1001 *et seq.*; 42 U.S.C. 2751 *et seq.*), or any accreditation status or State licensure of the debtor as an educational institution;

(4) any interest of the debtor in liquid or gaseous hydrocarbons to the extent that—

(A)(i) the debtor has transferred or has agreed to transfer such interest pursuant to a farmout agreement or any written agreement directly related to a farmout agreement; and

(ii) but for the operation of this paragraph, the estate could include the interest referred to in clause (i) only by virtue of section 365 or 544(a)(3) of this title; or

(B)(i) the debtor has transferred such interest pursuant to a written conveyance of a production payment to an entity that does not participate in the operation of the property from which such production payment is transferred; and

(ii) but for the operation of this paragraph, the estate could include the interest referred to in clause (i) only by virtue of section 542 of this title; or

(5) any interest in cash or cash equivalents that constitute proceeds of a sale by the debtor of a money order that is made—

(A) on or after the date that is 14 days prior to the date on which the petition is filed; and

(B) under an agreement with a money order issuer that prohibits the commingling of such proceeds with property of the debtor (notwithstanding that, contrary to the agreement, the proceeds may have been commingled with property of the debtor),

unless the money order issuer had not taken action, prior to the filing of the petition, to require compliance with the prohibition.

Paragraph (4) shall not be construed to exclude from the estate any consideration the debtor retains, receives, or is entitled to receive for transferring an interest in liquid or gaseous hydrocarbons pursuant to a farmout agreement.

(c)(1) Except as provided in paragraph (2) of this subsection, an interest of the debtor in property becomes property of the estate under subsection (a)(1), (a)(2), or (a)(5) of this section notwithstanding any provision in an agreement, transfer instrument, or applicable nonbankruptcy law—

(A) that restricts or conditions transfer of such interest by the debtor; or

(B) that is conditioned on the insolvency or financial condition of the debtor, on the commencement of a case under this title, or on the appointment of or taking possession by a trustee in a case under this title or a custodian before such commencement, and that effects or gives an option to effect a forfeiture, modification, or termination of the debtor's interest in property.

(2) A restriction on the transfer of a beneficial interest of the debtor in a trust that is enforceable under applicable nonbankruptcy law is enforceable in a case under this title.

(d) Property in which the debtor holds, as of the commencement of the case, only legal title and not an equitable interest, such as a mortgage secured by real property, or an interest in such a mortgage, sold by the debtor but as to which the debtor retains legal title to service or supervise the servicing of such mortgage or interest, becomes property of the estate under subsection (a)(1) or (2) of this section only to the extent of the debtor's legal title to such property, but not to the extent of any equitable interest in such property that the debtor does not hold.

§ 542. Turnover of property to the estate

(a) Except as provided in subsection (c) or (d) of this section, an entity, other than a custodian, in possession, custody, or control, during the case, of property that the trustee may use, sell, or lease under section 363 of this title, or that the debtor may exempt under section 522 of this title, shall deliver to the trustee, and account for, such property or the value of such property, unless such property is of inconsequential value or benefit to the estate.

(b) Except as provided in subsection (c) or (d) of this section, an entity that owes a debt that is property of the estate and that is matured, payable on demand, or payable on order, shall pay such debt to, or on the order of, the trustee, except to the extent that such debt may be offset under section 553 of this title against a claim against the debtor.

(c) Except as provided in section 362(a)(7) of this title, an entity that has neither actual notice nor actual knowledge of the commencement of the case concerning the debtor may transfer property of the estate, or pay a debt owing to the debtor, in good faith and other than in the manner specified in subsection (d) of this section, to an entity other than the trustee, with the same effect as to the entity making such transfer or payment as if the case under this title concerning the debtor had not been commenced.

(d) A life insurance company may transfer property of the estate or property of the debtor to such company in good faith, with the same effect with respect to such company as if the case under this title concerning the debtor had not been commenced, if such transfer is to pay a premium or to carry out a nonforfeiture insurance option, and is required to be made automatically, under a life insurance contract with such company that was entered into before the date of the filing of the petition and that is property of the estate.

(e) Subject to any applicable privilege, after notice and a hearing, the court may order an attorney, accountant, or other person that holds recorded information, including books, documents, records, and papers, relating to the debtor's property or financial affairs, to turn over or disclose such recorded information to the trustee.

§ 543. Turnover of property by a custodian

(a) A custodian with knowledge of the commencement of a case under this title concerning the debtor may not make any disbursement from, or take any action in the administration of, property of the debtor, proceeds, product, offspring, rents, or profits of such property, or property of the estate, in the possession, custody, or control of such custodian, except such action as is necessary to preserve such property.

(b) A custodian shall—

(1) deliver to the trustee any property of the debtor held by or transferred to such custodian, or proceeds, product, offspring, rents, or profits of such property, that is in such custodian's possession, custody, or control on the date that such custodian acquires knowledge of the commencement of the case; and

(2) file an accounting of any property of the debtor, or proceeds, product, offspring, rents, or profits of such property that, at any time, came into the possession, custody, or control of such custodian.

(c) The court, after notice and a hearing, shall—

(1) protect all entities to which a custodian has become obligated with respect to such property or proceeds, product, offspring, rents, or profits of such property;

(2) provide for the payment of reasonable compensation for services rendered and costs and expenses incurred by such custodian; and

(3) surcharge such custodian, other than an assignee for the benefit of the debtor's creditors that was appointed or took possession more than 120 days before the date of the filing of the petition, for any improper or excessive disbursement, other than a disbursement that has been made in accordance with applicable law or that has been approved, after notice and a hearing, by a court of competent jurisdiction before the commencement of the case under this title.

(d) After notice and hearing, the bankruptcy court—

(1) may excuse compliance with subsection (a), (b), or (c) of this section if the interests of creditors and, if the debtor is not insolvent, of equity security holders would be better served by permitting a custodian to continue in possession, custody, or control of such property, and

(2) shall excuse compliance with subsections (a) and (b)(1) of this section if the custodian is an assignee for the benefit of the debtor's creditors that was appointed or took possession more than 120 days before the date of the filing of the petition, unless compliance with such subsections is necessary to prevent fraud or injustice.

§ 544. Trustee as lien creditor and as successor to certain creditors and purchasers

(a) The trustee shall have, as of the commencement of the case, and without regard to any knowledge of the trustee or of any creditor, the rights and powers of, or may avoid any transfer of property of the debtor or any obligation incurred by the debtor that is voidable by—

(1) a creditor that extends credit to the debtor at the time of the commencement of the case, and that obtains, at such time and with respect to such credit, a judicial lien on all property on which a creditor on a simple contract could have obtained such a judicial lien, whether or not such a creditor exists;

(2) a creditor that extends credit to the debtor at the time of the commencement of the case, and obtains, at such time and with respect to such credit, an execution against the debtor that is returned unsatisfied at such time, whether or not such a creditor exists; or

(3) a bona fide purchaser of real property, other than fixtures, from the debtor, against whom applicable law permits such transfer to be perfected, that obtains the status of a bona fide purchaser and has perfected such transfer at the time of the commencement of the case, whether or not such a purchaser exists.

(b)(1) Except as provided in paragraph (2), the trustee may avoid any transfer of an interest of the debtor in property or any obligation incurred by the debtor that is voidable under applicable law by a creditor holding an unsecured claim that is allowable under section 502 of this title or that is not allowable only under section 502(e) of this title.

(2) Paragraph (1) shall not apply to a transfer of a charitable contribution (as that term is defined in section 548(d)(3)) that is not covered under section 548(a)(1)(B), by reason of section 548(a)(2). Any claim by any person to recover a transferred contribution described in the preceding sentence under Federal or State law in a Federal or State court shall be preempted by the commencement of the case.

§ 545. Statutory liens

The trustee may avoid the fixing of a statutory lien on property of the debtor to the extent that such lien—

(1) first becomes effective against the debtor—
   (A) when a case under this title concerning the debtor is commenced;
   (B) when an insolvency proceeding other than under this title concerning the debtor is commenced;
   (C) when a custodian is appointed or authorized to take possession;
   (D) when the debtor becomes insolvent;
   (E) when the debtor's financial condition fails to meet a specified standard; or

(F) at the time of an execution against property of the debtor levied at the instance of an entity other than the holder of such statutory lien;

(2) is not perfected or enforceable at the time of the commencement of the case against a bona fide purchaser that purchases such property at the time of the commencement of the case, whether or not such a purchaser exists;

(3) is for rent; or

(4) is a lien of distress for rent.

§ 546. Limitations on avoiding powers

(a) An action or proceeding under section 544, 545, 547, 548, or 553 of this title may not be commenced after the earlier of—

(1) the later of—
  (A) 2 years after the entry of the order for relief; or
  (B) 1 year after the appointment or election of the first trustee under section 702, 1104, 1163, 1202, or 1302 of this title if such appointment or such election occurs before the expiration of the period specified in subparagraph (A); or

(2) the time the case is closed or dismissed.

(b)(1) The rights and powers of a trustee under sections 544, 545, and 549 of this title are subject to any generally applicable law that—
  (A) permits perfection of an interest in property to be effective against an entity that acquires rights in such property before the date of perfection; or
  (B) provides for the maintenance or continuation of perfection of an interest in property to be effective against an entity that acquires rights in such property before the date on which action is taken to effect such maintenance or continuation.

(2) If—
  (A) a law described in paragraph (1) requires seizure of such property or commencement of an action to accomplish such perfection, or maintenance or continuation of perfection of an interest in property; and
  (B) such property has not been seized or such an action has not been commenced before the date of the filing of the petition;

such interest in such property shall be perfected, or perfection of such interest shall be maintained or continued, by giving notice within the time fixed by such law for such seizure or such commencement.

(c) Except as provided in subsection (d) of this section, the rights and powers of a trustee under sections 544(a), 545, 547, and 549 of this title are subject to any statutory or common-law right of a seller of goods that has sold goods to the debtor, in the ordinary course of such seller's business, to reclaim such goods if the debtor has received such goods while insolvent, but—

(1) such a seller may not reclaim any such goods unless such seller demands in writing reclamation of such goods—
  (A) before 10 days after receipt of such goods by the debtor; or
  (B) if such 10-day period expires after the commencement of the case, before 20 days after receipt of such goods by the

debtor; and

(2) the court may deny reclamation to a seller with such a right of reclamation that has made such a demand only if the court—
  (A) grants the claim of such a seller priority as a claim of a kind specified in section 503(b) of this title; or
  (B) secures such claim by a lien.

(d) In the case of a seller who is a producer of grain sold to a grain storage facility, owned or operated by the debtor, in the ordinary course of such seller's business (as such terms are defined in section 557 of this title) or in the case of a United States fisherman who has caught fish sold to a fish processing facility owned or operated by the debtor in the ordinary course of such fisherman's business, the rights and powers of the trustee under sections 544(a), 545, 547, and 549 of this title are subject to any statutory or common law right of such producer or fisherman to reclaim such grain or fish if the debtor has received such grain or fish while insolvent, but—

(1) such producer or fisherman may not reclaim any grain or fish unless such producer or fisherman demands, in writing, reclamation of such grain or fish before ten days after receipt thereof by the debtor; and

(2) the court may deny reclamation to such a producer or fisherman with a right of reclamation that has made such a demand only if the court secures such claim by a lien.

(e) Notwithstanding sections 544, 545, 547, 548(a)(1)(B), and 548(b) of this title, the trustee may not avoid a transfer that is a margin payment, as defined in section 101, 741, or 761 of this title, or settlement payment, as defined in section 101 or 741 of this title, made by or to a commodity broker, forward contract merchant, stockbroker, financial institution, or securities clearing agency, that is made before the commencement of the case, except under section 548(a)(1)(A) of this title.

(f) Notwithstanding sections 544, 545, 547, 548(a)(1)(B), and 548(b) of this title, the trustee may not avoid a transfer that is a margin payment, as defined in section 741 or 761 of this title, or settlement payment, as defined in section 741 of this title, made by or to a repo participant, in connection with a repurchase agreement and that is made before the commencement of the case, except under section 548(a)(1)(A) of this title.

(g) Notwithstanding sections 544, 545, 547, 548(a)(1)(B) and 548(b) of this title, the trustee may not avoid a transfer under a swap agreement, made by or to a swap participant, in connection with a swap agreement and that is made before the commencement of the case, except under section 548(a)(1)(A) of this title.

(g)[24] Notwithstanding the rights and powers of a trustee under sections 544(a), 545, 547, 549, and 553, if the court determines on a motion by the trustee made not later than 120 days after the date of the order for relief in a case under chapter 11 of this title and after notice and a hearing, that a return is in the best interests of the estate, the debtor, with the consent of a creditor, may return goods shipped to the debtor by the creditor before the commencement of the case, and the creditor may offset the purchase price of such goods against any claim of the creditor against the debtor that arose

_____

24 *Editor's Note*: So in original. The 1994 Bankruptcy Reform Act added a second § 546(g).

before the commencement of the case.

§ 547. Preferences

(a) In this section—

(1) "inventory" means personal property leased or furnished, held for sale or lease, or to be furnished under a contract for service, raw materials, work in process, or materials used or consumed in a business, including farm products such as crops or live-stock, held for sale or lease;

(2) "new value" means money or money's worth in goods, services, or new credit, or release by a transferee of property previously transferred to such transferee in a transaction that is neither void nor voidable by the debtor or the trustee under any applicable law, including proceeds of such property, but does not include an obligation substituted for an existing obligation;

(3) "receivable" means right to payment, whether or not such right has been earned by performance; and

(4) a debt for a tax is incurred on the day when such tax is last payable without penalty, including any extension.

(b) Except as provided in subsection (c) of this section, the trustee may avoid any transfer of an interest of the debtor in property—

(1) to or for the benefit of a creditor;

(2) for or on account of an antecedent debt owed by the debtor before such transfer was made;

(3) made while the debtor was insolvent;

(4) made—
   (A) on or within 90 days before the date of the filing of the petition; or
   (B) between 90 days and one year before the date of the filing of the petition, if such creditor at the time of such transfer was an insider; and

(5) that enables such creditor to receive more than such creditor would receive if—
   (A) the case were a case under chapter 7 of this title;
   (B) the transfer had not been made; and
   (C) such creditor received payment of such debt to the extent provided by the provisions of this title.

(c) The trustee may not avoid under this section a transfer—

(1) to the extent that such transfer was—
   (A) intended by the debtor and the creditor to or for whose benefit such transfer was made to be a contemporaneous exchange for new value given to the debtor; and
   (B) in fact a substantially contemporaneous exchange;

(2) to the extent that such transfer was—
   (A) in payment of a debt incurred by the debtor in the ordinary course of business or financial affairs of the debtor and the transferee;
   (B) made in the ordinary course of business or financial affairs of the debtor and the transferee; and
   (C) made according to ordinary business terms;

(3) that creates a security interest in property acquired by the debtor—
   (A) to the extent such security interest secures new value that

was—
   (i) given at or after the signing of a security agreement that contains a description of such property as collateral;
   (ii) given by or on behalf of the secured party under such agreement;
   (iii) given to enable the debtor to acquire such property; and
   (iv) in fact used by the debtor to acquire such property; and
   (B) that is perfected on or before 20 days after the debtor receives possession of such property;

(4) to or for the benefit of a creditor, to the extent that, after such transfer, such creditor gave new value to or for the benefit of the debtor—
   (A) not secured by an otherwise unavoidable security interest; and
   (B) on account of which new value the debtor did not make an otherwise unavoidable transfer to or for the benefit of such creditor;

(5) that creates a perfected security interest in inventory or a receivable or the proceeds of either, except to the extent that the aggregate of all such transfers to the transferee caused a reduction, as of the date of the filing of the petition and to the prejudice of other creditors holding unsecured claims, of any amount by which the debt secured by such security interest exceeded the value of all security interests for such debt on the later of—
   (A)(i) with respect to a transfer to which subsection (b)(4)(A) of this section applies, 90 days before the date of the filing of the petition; or
      (ii) with respect to a transfer to which subsection (b)(4)(B) of this section applies, one year before the date of the filing of the petition; or
   (B) the date on which new value was first given under the security agreement creating such security interest;

(6) that is the fixing of a statutory lien that is not avoidable under section 545 of this title;

(7) to the extent such transfer was a bona fide payment of a debt to a spouse, former spouse, or child of the debtor, for alimony to, maintenance for, or support of such spouse or child, in connection with a separation agreement, divorce decree or other order of a court of record, determination made in accordance with State or territorial law by a governmental unit, or property settlement agreement, but not to the extent that such debt—
   (A) is assigned to another entity, voluntarily, by operation of law, or otherwise; or
   (B) includes a liability designated as alimony, maintenance, or support, unless such liability is actually in the nature of alimony, maintenance or support; or

(8) if, in a case filed by an individual debtor whose debts are primarily consumer debts, the aggregate value of all property that constitutes or is affected by such transfer is less than $600.

(d) The trustee may avoid a transfer of an interest in property of the debtor transferred to or for the benefit of a surety to secure reimbursement of such a surety that furnished a bond or other obligation to dissolve a judicial lien that would have been avoidable by the trustee under subsection (b) of this section. The liability of such surety under such bond or obligation shall be discharged to the extent of the value of such property recovered by the trustee or the amount paid to the trustee.

(e)(1) For the purposes of this section—

    (A) a transfer of real property other than fixtures, but including the interest of a seller or purchaser under a contract for the sale of real property, is perfected when a bona fide purchaser of such property from the debtor against whom applicable law permits such transfer to be perfected cannot acquire an interest that is superior to the interest of the transferee; and

    (B) a transfer of a fixture or property other than real property is perfected when a creditor on a simple contract cannot acquire a judicial lien that is superior to the interest of the transferee.

(2) For the purposes of this section, except as provided in paragraph (3) of this subsection, a transfer is made—

    (A) at the time such transfer takes effect between the transferor and the transferee, if such transfer is perfected at, or within 10 days after, such time, except as provided in subsection (c)(3)(B);

    (B) at the time such transfer is perfected, if such transfer is perfected after such 10 days; or

    (C) immediately before the date of the filing of the petition, if such transfer is not perfected at the later of—

        (i) the commencement of the case; or

        (ii) 10 days after such transfer takes effect between the transferor and the transferee.

(3) For the purposes of this section, a transfer is not made until the debtor has acquired rights in the property transferred.

(f) For the purposes of this section, the debtor is presumed to have been insolvent on and during the 90 days immediately preceding the date of the filing of the petition.

(g) For the purposes of this section, the trustee has the burden of proving the avoidability of a transfer under subsection (b) of this section, and the creditor or party in interest against whom recovery or avoidance is sought has the burden of proving the nonavoidability of a transfer under subsection (c) of this section.

§ 548. Fraudulent transfers and obligations

(a)(1) The trustee may avoid any transfer of an interest of the debtor in property, or any obligation incurred by the debtor, that was made or incurred on or within one year before the date of the filing of the petition, if the debtor voluntarily or involuntarily—

    (A) made such transfer or incurred such obligation with actual intent to hinder, delay, or defraud any entity to which the debtor was or became, on or after the date that such transfer was made or such obligation was incurred, indebted; or

    (B)(i) received less than a reasonably equivalent value in exchange for such transfer or obligation; and

        (ii)(I) was insolvent on the date that such transfer was made or such obligation was incurred, or became insolvent as a result of such transfer or obligation;

        (II) was engaged in business or a transaction, or was about to engage in business or a transaction, for which any property remaining with the debtor was an unreasonably small capital; or

        (III) intended to incur, or believed that the debtor would incur, debts that would be beyond the debtor's ability to pay as such debts matured.

(2) A transfer of a charitable contribution to a qualified religious or charitable entity or organization shall not be considered to be a transfer covered under paragraph (1)(B) in any case in which—

    (A) the amount of that contribution does not exceed 15 percent of the gross annual income of the debtor for the year in which the transfer of the contribution is made; or

    (B) the contribution made by a debtor exceeded the percentage amount of gross annual income specified in subparagraph (A), if the transfer was consistent with the practices of the debtor in making charitable contributions.

(b) The trustee of a partnership debtor may avoid any transfer of an interest of the debtor in property, or any obligation incurred by the debtor, that was made or incurred on or within one year before the date of the filing of the petition, to a general partner in the debtor, if the debtor was insolvent on the date such transfer was made or such obligation was incurred, or became insolvent as a result of such transfer or obligation.

(c) Except to the extent that a transfer or obligation voidable under this section is voidable under section 544, 545, or 547 of this title, a transferee or obligee of such a transfer or obligation that takes for value and in good faith has a lien on or may retain any interest transferred or may enforce any obligation incurred, as the case may be, to the extent that such transferee or obligee gave value to the debtor in exchange for such transfer or obligation.

(d)(1) For the purposes of this section, a transfer is made when such transfer is so perfected that a bona fide purchaser from the debtor against whom applicable law permits such transfer to be perfected cannot acquire an interest in the property transferred that is superior to the interest in such property of the transferee, but if such transfer is not so perfected before the commencement of the case, such transfer is made immediately before the date of the filing of the petition.

(2) In this section—

    (A) "value" means property, or satisfaction or securing of a present or antecedent debt of the debtor, but does not include an unperformed promise to furnish support to the debtor or to a relative of the debtor;

    (B) a commodity broker, forward contract merchant, stockbroker, financial institution, or securities clearing agency that receives a margin payment, as defined in section 101, 741 or 761 of this title, or settlement payment, as defined in section 101 or 741 of this title, takes for value to the extent of such payment;

    (C) a repo participant that receives a margin payment, as defined in section 741 or 761 of this title, or settlement payment, as defined in section 741 of this title, in connection with a repurchase agreement, takes for value to the extent of such payment; and

(D) a swap participant that receives a transfer in connection with a swap agreement takes for value to the extent of such transfer.

(3) In this section, the term "charitable contribution" means a charitable contribution, as that term is defined in section 170(c) of the Internal Revenue Code of 1986, if that contribution—

(A) is made by a natural person; and

(B) consists of—

(i) a financial instrument (as that term is defined in section 731(c)(2)(C) of the Internal Revenue Code of 1986); or

(ii) cash.

(4) In this section, the term "qualified religious or charitable entity or organization" means—

(A) an entity described in section 170(c)(1) of the Internal Revenue Code of 1986; or

(B) an entity or organization described in section 170(c)(2) of the Internal Revenue Code of 1986.

§ 549. Postpetition transactions

(a) Except as provided in subsection (b) or (c) of this section, the trustee may avoid a transfer of property of the estate—

(1) that occurs after the commencement of the case; and

(2)(A) that is authorized only under section 303(f) or 542(c) of this title; or

(B) that is not authorized under this title or by the court.

(b) In an involuntary case, the trustee may not avoid under subsection (a) of this section a transfer made after the commencement of such case but before the order for relief to the extent any value, including services, but not including satisfaction or securing of a debt that arose before the commencement of the case, is given after the commencement of the case in exchange for such transfer, notwithstanding any notice or knowledge of the case that the transferee has.

(c) The trustee may not avoid under subsection (a) of this section a transfer of real property to a good faith purchaser without knowledge of the commencement of the case and for present fair equivalent value unless a copy or notice of the petition was filed, where a transfer of such real property may be recorded to perfect such transfer, before such transfer is so perfected that a bona fide purchaser of such property, against whom applicable law permits such transfer to be perfected, could not acquire an interest that is superior to the interest of such good faith purchaser. A good faith purchaser without knowledge of the commencement of the case and for less than present fair equivalent value has a lien on the property transferred to the extent of any present value given, unless a copy or notice of the petition was so filed before such transfer was so perfected.

(d) An action or proceeding under this section may not be commenced after the earlier of—

(1) two years after the date of the transfer sought to be avoided; or

(2) the time the case is closed or dismissed.

§ 550. Liability of transferee of avoided transfer

(a) Except as otherwise provided in this section, to the extent that a transfer is avoided under section 544, 545, 547, 548, 549, 553(b), or 724(a) of this title, the trustee may recover, for the benefit of the estate, the property transferred, or, if the court so orders, the value of such property, from—

(1) the initial transferee of such transfer or the entity for whose benefit such transfer was made; or

(2) any immediate or mediate transferee of such initial transferee.

(b) The trustee may not recover under section (a)(2) of this section from—

(1) a transferee that takes for value, including satisfaction or securing of a present or antecedent debt, in good faith, and without knowledge of the voidability of the transfer avoided; or

(2) any immediate or mediate good faith transferee of such transferee.

(c) If a transfer made between 90 days and one year before the filing of the petition—

(1) is avoided under section 547(b) of this title; and

(2) was made for the benefit of a creditor that at the time of such transfer was an insider;

the trustee may not recover under subsection (a) from a transferee that is not an insider.

(d) The trustee is entitled to only a single satisfaction under subsection (a) of this section.

(e)(1) A good faith transferee from whom the trustee may recover under subsection (a) of this section has a lien on the property recovered to secure the lesser of—

(A) the cost, to such transferee, of any improvement made after the transfer, less the amount of any profit realized by or accruing to such transferee from such property; and

(B) any increase in the value of such property as a result of such improvement, of the property transferred.

(2) In this subsection, "improvement" includes—

(A) physical additions or changes to the property transferred;

(B) repairs to such property;

(C) payment of any tax on such property;

(D) payment of any debt secured by a lien on such property that is superior or equal to the rights of the trustee; and

(E) preservation of such property.

(f) An action or proceeding under this section may not be commenced after the earlier of—

(1) one year after the avoidance of the transfer on account of which recovery under this section is sought; or

(2) the time the case is closed or dismissed.

§ 551. Automatic preservation of avoided transfer

Any transfer avoided under section 522, 544, 545, 547, 548, 549, or 724(a) of this title, or any lien void under section 506(d) of this title, is preserved for the benefit of the estate but only with respect to property of the estate.

§ 552. Postpetition effect of security interest

(a) Except as provided in subsection (b) of this section, property acquired by the estate or by the debtor after the commencement of the case is not subject to any lien resulting from any security agreement entered into by the debtor before the commencement of the case.

(b)(1) Except as provided in sections 363, 506(c), 522, 544, 545, 547, and 548 of this title, if the debtor and an entity entered into a security agreement before the commencement of the case and if the security interest created by such security agreement extends to property of the debtor acquired before the commencement of the case and to proceeds, product, offspring, or profits of such property, then such security interest extends to such proceeds, product, offspring, or profits acquired by the estate after the commencement of the case to the extent provided by such security agreement and by applicable nonbankruptcy law, except to any extent that the court, after notice and a hearing and based on the equities of the case, orders otherwise.

(2) Except as provided in sections 363, 506(c), 522, 544, 545, 547, and 548 of this title, and notwithstanding section 546(b) of this title, if the debtor and an entity entered into a security agreement before the commencement of the case and if the security interest created by such security agreement extends to property of the debtor acquired before the commencement of the case and to amounts paid as rents of such property or the fees, charges, accounts, or other payments for the use or occupancy of rooms and other public facilities in hotels, motels, or other lodging properties, then such security interest extends to such rents and such fees, charges, accounts, or other payments acquired by the estate after the commencement of the case to the extent provided in such security agreement, except to any extent that the court, after notice and a hearing and based on the equities of the case, orders otherwise.

§ 553. Setoff

(a) Except as otherwise provided in this section and in sections 362 and 363 of this title, this title does not affect any right of a creditor to offset a mutual debt owing by such creditor to the debtor that arose before the commencement of the case under this title against a claim of such creditor against the debtor that arose before the commencement of the case, except to the extent that—

(1) the claim of such creditor against the debtor is disallowed;

(2) such claim was transferred, by an entity other than the debtor, to such creditor—

    (A) after the commencement of the case; or

    (B)(i) after 90 days before the date of the filing of the petition; and

      (ii) while the debtor was insolvent; or

(3) the debt owed to the debtor by such creditor was incurred by such creditor—

    (A) after 90 days before the date of the filing of the petition;

    (B) while the debtor was insolvent; and

    (C) for the purpose of obtaining a right of setoff against the debtor.

(b)(1) Except with respect to a setoff of a kind described in sections 362(b)(6), 362(b)(7), 362(b)(14), 365(h), 546(h), or 365(i)(2), of this title, if a creditor offsets a mutual debt owing to the debtor against a claim against the debtor on or within 90 days before the date of the filing of the petition, then the trustee may recover from such creditor the amount so offset to the extent that any insufficiency on the date of such setoff is less than the insufficiency on the later of—

    (A) 90 days before the date of the filing of the petition; and

    (B) the first date during the 90 days immediately preceding the date of the filing of the petition on which there is an insufficiency.

(2) In this subsection, "insufficiency" means amount, if any, by which a claim against the debtor exceeds a mutual debt owing to the debtor by the holder of such claim.

(c) For the purposes of this section, the debtor is presumed to have been insolvent on and during the 90 days immediately preceding the date of the filing of the petition.

§ 554. Abandonment of property of the estate

(a) After notice and a hearing, the trustee may abandon any property of the estate that is burdensome to the estate or that is of inconsequential value and benefit to the estate.

(b) On request of a party in interest and after notice and a hearing, the court may order the trustee to abandon any property of the estate that is burdensome to the estate or that is of inconsequential value and benefit to the estate.

(c) Unless the court orders otherwise, any property scheduled under section 521(1) of this title not otherwise administered at the time of the closing of a case is abandoned to the debtor and administered for purposes of section 350 of this title.

(d) Unless the court orders otherwise, property of the estate that is not abandoned under this section and that is not administered in the case remains property of the estate.

§ 555. Contractual right to liquidate a securities contract

The exercise of a contractual right of a stockbroker, financial institution, or securities clearing agency to cause the liquidation of a securities contract, as defined in section 741 of this title, because of a condition of the kind specified in section 365(e)(1) of this title shall not be stayed, avoided, or otherwise limited by operation of any provision of this title or by order of a court or administrative agency in any proceeding under this title unless such order is authorized under the provisions of the Securities Investor Protection Act of 1970 or any statute administered by the Securities and Exchange Commission. As used in this section, the term "contractual right" includes a right set forth in a rule or bylaw of a national securities exchange, a national securities association, or a securities clearing agency.

§ 556. Contractual right to liquidate a commodities contract or forward contract

The contractual right of a commodity broker or forward contract merchant to cause the liquidation of a commodity contract, as defined in section 761 of this title, or forward contract because of a condition of the kind specified in section 365(e)(1) of this title, and the right to a variation or maintenance margin payment received from a trustee with respect to open commodity contracts or forward contracts, shall not be stayed, avoided, or otherwise limited by operation of any provision of this title or by the order of a court in any proceeding under this title. As used in this section, the term "contractual right" includes a right set forth in a rule or bylaw of a clearing organization or contract market or in a resolution of the governing board thereof and a right, whether or not evidenced in writing, arising under common law, under law merchant or by reason of normal business practice.

§ 557. Expedited determination of interests in, and abandonment or other disposition of grain assets

(a) This section applies only in a case concerning a debtor that owns or operates a grain storage facility and only with respect to grain and the proceeds of grain. This section does not affect the application of any other section of this title to property other than grain and proceeds of grain.

(b) In this section—

(1) "grain" means wheat, corn, flaxseed, grain sorghum, barley, oats, rye, soybeans, other dry edible beans, or rice;

(2) "grain storage facility" means a site or physical structure regularly used to store grain for producers, or to store grain acquired from producers for resale; and

(3) "producer" means an entity which engages in the growing of grain.

(c)(1) Notwithstanding sections 362, 363, 365, and 554 of this title, on the court's own motion the court may, and on the request of the trustee or an entity that claims an interest in grain or the proceeds of grain the court shall, expedite the procedures for the determination of interests in and the disposition of grain and the proceeds of grain, by shortening to the greatest extent feasible such time periods as are otherwise applicable for such procedures and by establishing, by order, a timetable having a duration of not to exceed 120 days for the completion of the applicable procedure specified in subsection (d) of this section. Such time periods and such timetable may be modified by the court, for cause, in accordance with subsection (f) of this section.

(2) The court shall determine the extent to which such time periods shall be shortened, based upon—

(A) any need of an entity claiming an interest in such grain or the proceeds of grain for a prompt determination of such interest;

(B) any need of such entity for a prompt disposition of such grain;

(C) the market for such grain;

(D) the conditions under which such grain is stored;

(E) the costs of continued storage or disposition of such grain;

(F) the orderly administration of the estate;

(G) the appropriate opportunity for an entity to assert an interest in such grain; and

(H) such other considerations as are relevant to the need to expedite such procedures in the case.

(d) The procedures that may be expedited under subsection (c) of this section include—

(1) the filing of and response to—

(A) a claim of ownership;

(B) a proof of claim;

(C) a request for abandonment;

(D) a request for relief from the stay of action against property under section 362(a) of this title;

(E) a request for determination of secured status;

(F) a request for determination of whether such grain or the proceeds of grain—

(i) is property of the estate;

(ii) must be turned over to the estate; or

(iii) may be used, sold, or leased; and

(G) any other request for determination of an interest in such grain or the proceeds of grain;

(2) the disposition of such grain or the proceeds of grain, before or after determination of interests in such grain or the proceeds of grain, by way of—

(A) sale of such grain;

(B) abandonment;

(C) distribution; or

(D) such other method as is equitable in the case;

(3) subject to sections 701, 702, 703, 1104, 1202, and 1302 of this title, the appointment of a trustee or examiner and the retention and compensation of any professional person required to assist with respect to matters relevant to the determination of interests in or disposition of such grain or the proceeds of grain; and

(4) the determination of any dispute concerning a matter specified in paragraph (1), (2), or (3) of this subsection.

(e)(1) Any governmental unit that has regulatory jurisdiction over the operation or liquidation of the debtor or the debtor's business shall be given notice of any request made or order entered under subsection (c) of this section.

(2) Any such governmental unit may raise, and may appear and be heard on, any issue relating to grain or the proceeds of grain in a case in which a request is made, or an order is entered, under subsection (c) of this section.

(3) The trustee shall consult with such governmental unit before taking any action relating to the disposition of grain in the possession, custody, or control of the debtor or the estate.

(f) The court may extend the period for final disposition of grain or the proceeds of grain under this section beyond 120 days if the court finds that—

(1) the interests of justice so require in light of the complexity of the case; and

(2) the interests of those claimants entitled to distribution of grain or the proceeds of grain will not be materially injured by such additional delay.

(g) Unless an order establishing an expedited procedure under subsection (c) of this section, or determining any interest in or approving any disposition of grain or the proceeds of grain, is stayed pending appeal—

(1) the reversal or modification of such order on appeal does not affect the validity of any procedure, determination, or disposition that occurs before such reversal or modification, whether or not any entity knew of the pendency of the appeal; and

(2) neither the court nor the trustee may delay, due to the appeal of such order, any proceeding in the case in which such order is issued.

(h)(1) The trustee may recover from grain and the proceeds of grain the reasonable and necessary costs and expenses allowable under section 503(b) of this title attributable to preserving or disposing of grain or the proceeds of grain, but may not recover from such grain or the proceeds of grain any other costs or expenses.

(2) Notwithstanding section 326(a) of this title, the dollar amounts of money specified in such section include the value, as of the date of disposition, of any grain that the trustee distributes in kind.

(i) In all cases where the quantity of a specific type of grain held by a debtor operating a grain storage facility exceeds ten thousand bushels, such grain shall be sold by the trustee and the assets thereof distributed in accordance with the provisions of this section.

§ 558. Defenses of the estate

The estate shall have the benefit of any defense available to the debtor as against any entity other than the estate, including statutes of limitation, statutes of frauds, usury, and other personal defenses. A waiver of any such defense by the debtor after the commencement of the case does not bind the estate.

§ 559. Contractual right to liquidate a repurchase agreement

The exercise of a contractual right of a repo participant to cause the liquidation of a repurchase agreement because of a condition of the kind specified in section 365(e)(1) of this title shall not be stayed, avoided, or otherwise limited by operation of any provision of this title or by order of a court or administrative agency in any proceeding under this title, unless, where the debtor is a stockbroker or securities clearing agency, such order is authorized under the provisions of the Securities Investor Protection Act of 1970 or any statute administered by the Securities and Exchange Commission. In the event that a repo participant liquidates one or more repurchase agreements with a debtor and under the terms of one or more such agreements has agreed to deliver assets subject to repurchase agreements to the debtor, any excess of the market prices received on liquidation of such assets (or if any such assets are not disposed of on the date of liquidation of such repurchase agreements, at the prices available at the time of liquidation of such repurchase agreements from a generally recognized source or the most recent closing bid quotation from such a source) over the sum of the stated repurchase prices and all expenses in connection with the liquidation of such repurchase agreements shall be deemed property of the estate, subject to the available rights of setoff. As used in this section, the term "contractual right" includes a right set forth in a rule or bylaw, applicable to each party to the repurchase agreement, of a national securities exchange, a national securities association, or a securities clearing agency, and a right, whether or not evidenced in writing, arising under common law, under law merchant or by reason of normal business practice.

§ 560. Contractual right to terminate a swap agreement

The exercise of any contractual right of any swap participant to cause the termination of a swap agreement because of a condition of the kind specified in section 365(e)(1) of this title or to offset or net out any termination values or payment amounts arising under or in connection with any swap agreement shall not be stayed, avoided, or otherwise limited by operation of any provision of this title or by order of a court or administrative agency in any proceeding under this title. As used in this section, the term "contractual right" includes a right, whether or not evidenced in writing, arising under common law, under law merchant, or by reason of normal business practice.

CHAPTER 7
LIQUIDATION

Subchapter I—Officers and Administration

§ 701. Interim trustee

(a)(1) Promptly after the order for relief under this chapter, the United States trustee shall appoint one disinterested person that is a member of the panel of private trustees established under section 586(a)(1) of title 28 or that is serving as trustee in the case immediately before the order for relief under this chapter to serve as interim trustee in the case.

(2) If none of the members of such panel is willing to serve as interim trustee in the case, then the United States trustee may serve as interim trustee in the case.

(b) The service of an interim trustee under this section terminates when a trustee elected or designated under section 702 of this title to serve as trustee in the case qualifies under section 322 of this title.

(c) An interim trustee serving under this section is a trustee in a case under this title.

§ 702. Election of trustee

(a) A creditor may vote for a candidate for trustee only if such creditor—

(1) holds an allowable, undisputed, fixed, liquidated, unsecured claim of a kind entitled to distribution under sections 726(a)(2), 726(a)(3), 726(a)(4), 752(a), 766(h), or 766(i) of this title;

(2) does not have an interest materially adverse, other than an equity interest that is not substantial in relation to such creditor's interest as a creditor, to the interest of creditors entitled to such distribution; and

(3) is not an insider.

(b) At the meeting of creditors held under section 341 of this title, creditors may elect one person to serve as trustee in the case if election of a trustee is requested by creditors that may vote under subsection (a) of this section, and that hold at least 20 percent in amount of the claims specified in subsection (a)(1) of this section that are held by creditors that may vote under subsection (a) of this section.

(c) A candidate for trustee is elected trustee if—

(1) creditors holding at least 20 percent in amount of the claims of a kind specified in subsection (a)(1) of this section that are held by creditors that may vote under subsection (a) of this section vote; and

(2) such candidate receives the votes of creditors holding a majority in amount of claims specified in subsection (a)(1) of this section that are held by creditors that vote for a trustee.

(d) If a trustee is not elected under this section, then the interim trustee shall serve as trustee in the case.

§ 703. Successor trustee

(a) If a trustee dies or resigns during a case, fails to qualify under section 322 of this title, or is removed under section 324 of this title, creditors may elect, in the manner specified in section 702 of this title, a person to fill the vacancy in the office of trustee.

(b) Pending election of a trustee under subsection (a) of this section, if necessary to preserve or prevent loss to the estate, the United States trustee may appoint an interim trustee in the manner specified in section 701(a).

(c) If creditors do not elect a successor trustee under subsection (a) of this section or if a trustee is needed in a case reopened under section 350 of this title, then the United States trustee—

(1) shall appoint one disinterested person that is a member of the panel of private trustees established under section 586(a)(1) of title 28 to serve as trustee in the case; or

(2) may, if none of the disinterested members of such panel is willing to serve as trustee, serve as trustee in the case.

§ 704. Duties of trustee

The trustee shall—

(1) collect and reduce to money the property of the estate for which such trustee serves, and close such estate as expeditiously as is compatible with the best interests of parties in interest;

(2) be accountable for all property received;

(3) ensure that the debtor shall perform his intention as specified in section 521(2)(B) of this title;

(4) investigate the financial affairs of the debtor;

(5) if a purpose would be served, examine proofs of claims and object to the allowance of any claim that is improper;

(6) if advisable, oppose the discharge of the debtor;

(7) unless the court orders otherwise, furnish such information concerning the estate and the estate's administration as is requested by a party in interest;

(8) if the business of the debtor is authorized to be operated, file with the court, with the United States trustee, and with any governmental unit charged with responsibility for collection or determination of any tax arising out of such operation, periodic reports and summaries of the operation of such business, including a statement of receipts and disbursements, and such other information as the United States trustee or the court requires; and

(9) make a final report and file a final account of the administration of the estate with the court and with the United States trustee.

§ 705. Creditors' committee

(a) At the meeting under section 341(a) of this title, creditors that may vote for a trustee under section 702(a) of this title may elect a committee of not fewer than three, and not more than eleven, creditors, each of whom holds an allowable unsecured claim of a kind entitled to distribution under section 726(a)(2) of this title.

(b) A committee elected under subsection (a) of this section may consult with the trustee or the United States trustee in connection with the administration of the estate, make recommendations to the trustee or the United States trustee respecting the performance of the trustee's duties, and submit to the court or the United States trustee any question affecting the administration of the estate.

§ 706. Conversion

(a) The debtor may convert a case under this chapter to a case under chapter 11, 12, or 13 of this title at any time, if the case has not been converted under section 1112, 1208, or 1307 of this title. Any waiver of the right to convert a case under this subsection is unenforceable.

(b) On request of a party in interest and after notice and a hearing, the court may convert a case under this chapter to a case under chapter 11 of this title at any time.

(c) The court may not convert a case under this chapter to a case under chapter 12 or 13 of this title unless the debtor requests such conversion.

(d) Notwithstanding any other provision of this section, a case may not be converted to a case under another chapter of this title unless the debtor may be a debtor under such chapter.

§ 707. Dismissal

(a) The court may dismiss a case under this chapter only after notice and a hearing and only for cause, including—

(1) unreasonable delay by the debtor that is prejudicial to creditors;

(2) nonpayment of any fees or charges required under chapter 123 of title 28; and

(3) failure of the debtor in a voluntary case to file, within fifteen days or such additional time as the court may allow after the filing of the petition commencing such case, the information required by paragraph (1) of section 521, but only on a motion by the United States trustee.

(b) After notice and a hearing, the court, on its own motion or on a motion by the United States trustee, but not at the request or suggestion of any party in interest, may dismiss a case filed by an individual debtor under this chapter whose debts are primarily consumer debts if it finds that the granting of relief would be a substantial abuse of the provisions of this chapter. There shall be a presumption in favor of granting the relief requested by the debtor. In making a determination whether to dismiss a case under this section, the court may not take into consideration whether a debtor has made, or continues to make, charitable contributions (that meet the definition of "charitable contribution" under section 548(d)(3)) to any qualified religious or charitable entity or organization (as that term is defined in section 548(d)(4)).

Subchapter II—Collection, Liquidation, and Distribution of the Estate

§ 721. Authorization to operate business

The court may authorize the trustee to operate the business of the debtor for a limited period, if such operation is in the best interest of the estate and consistent with the orderly liquidation of the estate.

§ 722. Redemption

An individual debtor may, whether or not the debtor has waived the right to redeem under this section, redeem tangible personal property intended primarily for personal, family, or household use, from a lien securing a dischargeable consumer debt, if such property is exempted under section 522 of this title or has been abandoned under section 554 of this title, by paying the holder of such lien the amount of the allowed secured claim of such holder that is secured by such lien.

§ 723. Rights of partnership trustee against general partners

(a) If there is a deficiency of property of the estate to pay in full all claims which are allowed in a case under this chapter concerning a partnership and with respect to which a general partner of the partnership is personally liable, the trustee shall have a claim against such general partner to the extent that under applicable nonbankruptcy law such general partner is personally liable for such deficiency.

(b) To the extent practicable, the trustee shall first seek recovery of such deficiency from any general partner in such partnership that is not a debtor in a case under this title. Pending determination of such deficiency, the court may order any such partner to provide the estate with indemnity for, or assurance of payment of, any deficiency recoverable from such partner, or not to dispose of property.

(c) Notwithstanding section 728(c) of this title, the trustee has a claim against the estate of each general partner in such partnership that is a debtor in a case under this title for the full amount of all claims of creditors allowed in the case concerning such partnership. Notwithstanding section 502 of this title, there shall not be allowed in such partner's case a claim against such partner on which both such partner and such partnership are liable, except to any extent that such claim is secured only by property of such partner and not by property of such partnership. The claim of the trustee under this subsection is entitled to distribution in such partner's case under section 726(a) of this title the same as any other claim of a kind specified in such section.

(d) If the aggregate that the trustee recovers from the estates of general partners under subsection (c) of this section is greater than any deficiency not recovered under subsection (b) of this section, the court, after notice and a hearing, shall determine an equitable distribution of the surplus so recovered, and the trustee shall distribute such surplus to the estates of the general partners in such partnership according to such determination.

§ 724. Treatment of certain liens

(a) The trustee may avoid a lien that secures a claim of a kind specified in section 726(a)(4) of this title.

(b) Property in which the estate has an interest and that is subject to a lien that is not avoidable under this title and that secures an allowed claim for a tax, or proceeds of such property, shall be distributed—

(1) first, to any holder of an allowed claim secured by a lien on such property that is not avoidable under this title and that is senior to such tax lien;

(2) second, to any holder of a claim of a kind specified in sections 507(a)(1), 507(a)(2), 507(a)(3), 507(a)(4), 507(a)(5), or 507(a)(6), or 507(a)(7) of this title, to the extent of the amount of such allowed tax claim that is secured by such tax lien;

(3) third, to the holder of such tax lien, to any extent that such holder's allowed tax claim that is secured by such tax lien exceeds any amount distributed under paragraph (2) of this subsection;

(4) fourth, to any holder of an allowed claim secured by a lien on such property that is not avoidable under this title and that is junior to such tax lien;

(5) fifth, to the holder of such tax lien, to the extent that such holder's allowed claim secured by such tax lien is not paid under paragraph (3) of this subsection; and

(6) sixth, to the estate.

(c) If more than one holder of a claim is entitled to distribution under a particular paragraph of subsection (b) of this section, distribution to such holders under such paragraph shall be in the same order as distribution to such holders would have been other than under this section.

(d) A statutory lien the priority of which is determined in the same manner as the priority of a tax lien under section 6323 of the Internal Revenue Code of 1986 shall be treated under subsection (b) of this section the same as if such lien were a tax lien.

§ 725. Disposition of certain property

After the commencement of a case under this chapter, but before final distribution of property of the estate under section 726 of this title, the trustee, after notice and a hearing, shall dispose of any property in which an entity other than the estate has an interest, such as a lien, and that has not been disposed of under another section of this title.

§ 726. Distribution of property of the estate

(a) Except as provided in section 510 of this title, property of the estate shall be distributed—

(1) first, in payment of claims of the kind specified in, and in the order specified in, section 507 of this title, proof of which is timely filed under section 501 of this title or tardily filed before the date on which the trustee commences distribution under this section;

(2) second, in payment of any allowed unsecured claim, other than a claim of a kind specified in paragraph (1), (3), or (4) of this subsection, proof of which is—
(A) timely filed under section 501(a) of this title;
(B) timely filed under section 501(b) or 501(c) of this title; or
(C) tardily filed under section 501(a) of this title, if—
(i) the creditor that holds such claim did not have notice

or actual knowledge of the case in time for timely filing of a proof of such claim under section 501(a) of this title; and

(ii) proof of such claim is filed in time to permit payment of such claim;

(3) third, in payment of any allowed unsecured claim proof of which is tardily filed under section 501(a) of this title, other than a claim of the kind specified in paragraph (2)(C) of this subsection;

(4) fourth, in payment of any allowed claim, whether secured or unsecured, for any fine, penalty, or forfeiture, or for multiple, exemplary, or punitive damages, arising before the earlier of the order for relief or the appointment of a trustee, to the extent that such fine, penalty, forfeiture, or damages are not compensation for actual pecuniary loss suffered by the holder of such claim;

(5) fifth, in payment of interest at the legal rate from the date of the filing of the petition, on any claim paid under paragraph (1), (2), (3), or (4) of this subsection; and

(6) sixth, to the debtor.

(b) Payment on claims of a kind specified in paragraph (1), (2), (3), (4), (5), (6), (7), or (8) of section 507(a) of this title, or in paragraph (2), (3), (4), or (5) of subsection (a) of this section, shall be made pro rata among claims of the kind specified in each such particular paragraph, except that in a case that has been converted to this chapter under section 1009, 1112, 1208, or 1307 of this title, a claim allowed under section 503(b) of this title incurred under this chapter after such conversion has priority over a claim allowed under section 503(b) of this title incurred under any other chapter of this title or under this chapter before such conversion and over any expenses of a custodian superseded under section 543 of this title.

(c) Notwithstanding subsections (a) and (b) of this section, if there is property of the kind specified in section 541(a)(2) of this title, or proceeds of such property, in the estate, such property or proceeds shall be segregated from other property of the estate, and such property or proceeds and other property of the estate shall be distributed as follows:

(1) Claims allowed under section 503 of this title shall be paid either from property of the kind specified in section 541(a)(2) of this title, or from other property of the estate, as the interest of justice requires.

(2) Allowed claims, other than claims allowed under section 503 of this title, shall be paid in the order specified in subsection (a) of this section, and, with respect to claims of a kind specified in a particular paragraph of section 507(a) of this title or subsection (a) of this section, in the following order and manner:

(A) First, community claims against the debtor or the debtor's spouse shall be paid from property of the kind specified in section 541(a)(2) of this title, except to the extent that such property is solely liable for debts of the debtor.

(B) Second, to the extent that community claims against the debtor are not paid under subparagraph (A) of this paragraph, such community claims shall be paid from property

of the kind specified in section 541 (a)(2) of this title that is solely liable for debts of the debtor.

(C) Third, to the extent that all claims against the debtor including community claims against the debtor are not paid under subparagraph (A) or (B) of this paragraph such claims shall be paid from property of the estate other than property of the kind specified in section 541(a)(2) of this title.

(D) Fourth, to the extent that community claims against the debtor or the debtor's spouse are not paid under subparagraph (A), (B), or (C) of this paragraph, such claims shall be paid from all remaining property of the estate.

§ 727. Discharge

(a) The court shall grant the debtor a discharge, unless—

(1) the debtor is not an individual;

(2) the debtor, with intent to hinder, delay, or defraud a creditor or an officer of the estate charged with custody of property under this title, has transferred, removed, destroyed, mutilated, or concealed, or has permitted to be transferred, removed, destroyed, mutilated, or concealed—

(A) property of the debtor, within one year before the date of the filing of the petition; or

(B) property of the estate, after the date of the filing of the petition;

(3) the debtor has concealed, destroyed, mutilated, falsified, or failed to keep or preserve any recorded information, including books, documents, records, and papers, from which the debtor's financial condition or business transactions might be ascertained, unless such act or failure to act was justified under all of the circumstances of the case;

(4) the debtor knowingly and fraudulently, in or in connection with the case—

(A) made a false oath or account;

(B) presented or used a false claim;

(C) gave, offered, received, or attempted to obtain money, property, or advantage, or a promise of money, property, or advantage, for acting or forbearing to act; or

(D) withheld from an officer of the estate entitled to possession under this title, any recorded information, including books, documents, records, and papers, relating to the debtor's property or financial affairs;

(5) the debtor has failed to explain satisfactorily, before determination of denial of discharge under this paragraph, any loss of assets or deficiency of assets to meet the debtor's liabilities;

(6) the debtor has refused, in the case—

(A) to obey any lawful order of the court, other than an order to respond to a material question or to testify;

(B) on the ground of privilege against self-incrimination, to respond to a material question approved by the court or to testify, after the debtor has been granted immunity with respect to the matter concerning which such privilege was invoked; or

(C) on a ground other than the properly invoked privilege against self-incrimination, to respond to a material question approved by the court or to testify;

(7) the debtor has committed any act specified in paragraph (2), (3), (4), (5), or (6) of this subsection, on or within one year before the date of the filing of the petition, or during the case, in connection with another case, under this title or under the Bankruptcy Act, concerning an insider;

(8) the debtor has been granted a discharge under this section, under section 1141 of this title, or under sections 14, 371, or 476 of the Bankruptcy Act, in a case commenced within six years before the date of the filing of the petition;

(9) the debtor has been granted a discharge under sections 1228 or 1328 of this title, or under sections 660 or 661 of the Bankruptcy Act, in a case commenced within six years before the date of the filing of the petition, unless payments under the plan in such case totaled at least—

(A) 100 percent of the allowed unsecured claims in such case; or

(B)(i) 70 percent of such claims; and

   (ii) the plan was proposed by the debtor in good faith, and was the debtor's best effort; or

(10) the court approves a written waiver of discharge executed by the debtor after the order for relief under this chapter.

(b) Except as provided in section 523 of this title, a discharge under subsection (a) of this section discharges the debtor from all debts that arose before the date of the order for relief under this chapter, and any liability on a claim that is determined under section 502 of this title as if such claim had arisen before the commencement of the case, whether or not a proof of claim based on any such debt or liability is filed under section 501 of this title, and whether or not a claim based on any such debt or liability is allowed under section 502 of this title.

(c)(1) The trustee, a creditor, or the United States trustee may object to the granting of a discharge under subsection (a) of this section.

(2) On request of a party in interest, the court may order the trustee to examine the acts and conduct of the debtor to determine whether a ground exists for denial of discharge.

(d) On request of the trustee, a creditor, or the United States trustee, and after notice and a hearing, the court shall revoke a discharge granted under subsection (a) of this section if—

(1) such discharge was obtained through the fraud of the debtor, and the requesting party did not know of such fraud until after the granting of such discharge;

(2) the debtor acquired property that is property of the estate, or became entitled to acquire property that would be property of the estate, and knowingly and fraudulently failed to report the acquisition of or entitlement to such property, or to deliver or surrender such property to the trustee; or

(3) the debtor committed an act specified in subsection (a)(6) of this section.

(e) The trustee, a creditor, or the United States trustee may request a revocation of a discharge—

(1) under subsection (d)(1) of this section within one year after such discharge is granted; or

(2) under subsection (d)(2) or (d)(3) of this section before the later of—

(A) one year after the granting of such discharge; and

(B) the date the case is closed.

§ 728. Special tax provisions

(a) For the purposes of any State or local law imposing a tax on or measured by income, the taxable period of a debtor that is an individual shall terminate on the date of the order for relief under this chapter, unless the case was converted under section 1112 or 1208 of this title.

(b) Notwithstanding any State or local law imposing a tax on or measured by income, the trustee shall make tax returns of income for the estate of an individual debtor in a case under this chapter or for a debtor that is a corporation in a case under this chapter only if such estate or corporation has net taxable income for the entire period after the order for relief under this chapter during which the case is pending. If such entity has such income, or if the debtor is a partnership, then the trustee shall make and file a return of income for each taxable period during which the case was pending after the order for relief under this chapter.

(c) If there are pending a case under this chapter concerning a partnership and a case under this chapter concerning a partner in such partnership, a governmental unit's claim for any unpaid liability of such partner for a State or local tax on or measured by income, to the extent that such liability arose from the inclusion in such partner's taxable income of earnings of such partnership that were not withdrawn by such partner, is a claim only against such partnership.

(d) Notwithstanding section 541 of this title, if there are pending a case under this chapter concerning a partnership and a case under this chapter concerning a partner in such partnership, then any State or local tax refund or reduction of tax of such partner that would have otherwise been property of the estate of such partner under section 541 of this title—

(1) is property of the estate of such partnership to the extent that such tax refund or reduction of tax is fairly apportionable to losses sustained by such partnership and not reimbursed by such partner; and

(2) is otherwise property of the estate of such partner.

* * *

CHAPTER 11
REORGANIZATION

Subchapter 1—Officers and Administration

§ 1101. Definitions for this chapter

In this chapter—

(1) "dedbtor in possession" means debtor except when a person that has qualified under section 322 of this title is serving as trustee in the case;

(2) "substantial consummation" means—

(A) transfer of all or substantially all of the property proposed by the plan to be transferred;

(B) assumption by the debtor or by the successor to the debtor under the plan of the business or of the management of all or substantially all of the property dealt with by the plan; and

(C) commencement of distribution under the plan.

§ 1102. Creditors' and equity security holders' committees

(a)(1) Except as provided in paragraph (3), as soon as practicable after the order for relief under chapter 11 of this title, the United States trustee shall appoint a committee of creditors holding unsecured claims and may appoint additional committees of creditors or of equity security holders as the United States trustee deems appropriate.

(2) On request of a party in interest, the court may order the appointment of additional committees of creditors or of equity security holders if necessary to assure adequate representation of creditors or of equity security holders. The United States trustee shall appoint any such committee.

(3) On request of a party in interest in a case in which the debtor is a small business and for cause, the court may order that a committee of creditors not be appointed.

(b)(1) A committee of creditors appointed under subsection (a) of this section shall ordinarily consist of the persons, willing to serve, that hold the seven largest claims against the debtor of the kinds represented on such committee, or of the members of a committee organized by creditors before the commencement of the case under this chapter, if such committee was fairly chosen and is representative of the different kinds of claims to be represented.

(2) A committee of equity security holders appointed under subsection (a)(2) of this section shall ordinarily consist of the persons, willing to serve, that hold the seven largest amounts of equity securities of the debtor of the kinds represented on such committee.

§ 1103. Powers and duties of committees

(a) At a scheduled meeting of a committee appointed under section 1102 of this title, at which a majority of the members of such committee are present, and with the court's approval, such committee may select and authorize the employment by such committee of one or more attorneys, accountants, or other agents, to represent or perform services for such committee.

(b) An attorney or accountant employed to represent a committee appointed under section 1102 of this title may not, while employed by such committee, represent any other entity having an adverse interest in connection with the case. Representation of one or more creditors of the same class as represented by the committee shall not per se constitute the representation of an adverse interest.

(c) A committee appointed under section 1102 of this title may—

(1) consult with the trustee or debtor in possession concerning the administration of the case;

(2) investigate the acts, conduct, assets, liabilities, and financial condition of the debtor, the operation of the debtor's business and the desirability of the continuance of such business, and any other matter relevant to the case or to the formulation of a plan;

(3) participate in the formulation of a plan, advise those represented by such committee of such committee's determinations as to any plan formulated, and collect and file with the court

acceptances or rejections of a plan;

(4) request the appointment of a trustee or examiner under section 1104 of this title; and

(5) perform such other services as are in the interest of those represented.

(d) As soon as practicable after the appointment of a committee under section 1102 of this title, the trustee shall meet with such committee to transact such business as may be necessary and proper.

§ 1104. Appointment of trustee or examiner

(a) At any time after the commencement of the case but before confirmation of a plan, on request of a party in interest or the United States trustee, and after notice and a hearing, the court shall order the appointment of a trustee—

(1) for cause, including fraud, dishonesty, incompetence, or gross mismanagement of the affairs of the debtor by current management, either before or after the commencement of the case, or similar cause, but not including the number of holders of securities of the debtor or the amount of assets or liabilities of the debtor; or

(2) if such appointment is in the interest of creditors, any equity security holders, and other interests of the estate, without regard to the number of holders of securities of the debtor or the amount of assets or liabilities of the debtor.

(b) Except as provided in section 1163 of this title, on the request of a party in interest made not later than 30 days after the court orders the appointment of a trustee under subsection (a), the United States trustee shall convene a meeting of creditors for the purpose of electing one disinterested person to serve as trustee in the case. The election of a trustee shall be conducted in the manner provided in subsections (a), (b), and (c) of section 702 of this title.

(c) If the court does not order the appointment of a trustee under this section, then at any time before the confirmation of a plan, on request of a party in interest, or the United States trustee, and after notice and a hearing, the court shall order the appointment of an examiner to conduct such an investigation of the debtor as is appropriate, including an investigation of any allegations of fraud, dishonesty, incompetence, misconduct, mismanagement, or irregularity in the management of the affairs of the debtor of or by current or former management of the debtor, if—

(1) such appointment is in the interests of creditors, any equity security holders, and other interests of the estate; or

(2) the debtor's fixed, liquidated, unsecured debts, other than debts for goods, services, or taxes, or owing to an insider, exceed $5,000,000.

(d) If the court orders the appointment of a trustee or examiner, if a trustee or an examiner dies or resigns during the case or is removed under section 324 of this title, or if a trustee fails to qualify under section 322 of this title, then the United States trustee, after consultation with parties in interest shall appoint, subject to the court's approval, one disinterested person other than the United States trustee to serve as trustee or examiner, as the case may be, in the case.

§ 1105. Termination of trustee's appointment

At any time before confirmation of a plan, on request of a party in interest or the United States trustee, and after notice and a hearing, the court may terminate the trustee's appointment and restore the debtor to possession and management of the property of the estate and of the operation of the debtor's business.

§ 1106. Duties of trustee and examiner

(a) A trustee shall—

(1) perform the duties of a trustee specified in sections 704(2), 704(5), 704(7), 704(8), and 704(9) of this title;

(2) if the debtor has not done so, file the list, schedule, and statement required under section 521(1) of this title;

(3) except to the extent that the court orders otherwise, investigate the acts, conduct, assets, liabilities, and financial condition of the debtor, the operation of the debtor's business and the desirability of the continuance of such business, and any other matter relevant to the case or to the formulation of a plan;

(4) as soon as practicable—

    (A) file a statement of any investigation conducted under paragraph (3) of this subsection, including any fact ascertained pertaining to fraud, dishonesty, incompetence, misconduct, mismanagement, or irregularity in the management of the affairs of the debtor, or to a cause of action available to the estate; and

    (B) transmit a copy or a summary of any such statement to any creditors' committee or equity security holders' committee, to any indenture trustee, and to such other entity as the court designates;

(5) as soon as practicable, file a plan under section 1121 of this title, file a report of why the trustee will not file a plan, or recommend conversion of the case to a case under chapter 7, 12, or 13 of this title or dismissal of the case;

(6) for any year for which the debtor has not filed a tax return required by law, furnish, without personal liability, such information as may be required by the governmental unit with which such tax return was to be filed, in light of the condition of the debtor's books and records and the availability of such information; and

(7) after confirmation of a plan, file such reports as are necessary or as the court orders.

(b) An examiner appointed under section 1104(d) of this title shall perform the duties specified in paragraphs (3) and (4) of subsection (a) of this section, and, except to the extent that the court orders otherwise, any other duties of the trustee that the court orders the debtor in possession not to perform.

§ 1107. Rights, powers, and duties of debtor in possession

(a) Subject to any limitations on a trustee serving in a case under this chapter, and to such limitations or conditions as the court prescribes, a debtor in possession shall have all the rights, other than the right to compensation under section 330 of this title, and powers, and shall perform all the functions and duties, except the duties specified in sections 1106(a)(2), (3), and (4) of this title, of a trustee serving in a case under this chapter.

(b) Notwithstanding section 327(a) of this title, a person is not disqualified for employment under section 327 of this title by a debtor in possession solely because of such person's employment by or representation of the debtor before the commencement of the case.

§ 1108. Authorization to operate business

Unless the court, on request of a party in interest and after notice and a hearing, orders otherwise, the trustee may operate the debtor's business.

§ 1109. Right to be heard

(a) The Securities and Exchange Commission may raise and may appear and be heard on any issue in a case under this chapter, but the Securities and Exchange Commission may not appeal from any judgment, order, or decree entered in the case.

(b) A party in interest, including the debtor, the trustee, a creditors' committee, an equity security holders' committee, a creditor, an equity security holder, or any indenture trustee, may raise and may appear and be heard on any issue in a case under this chapter.

§ 1110. Aircraft equipment and vessels

(a)(1) Except as provided in paragraph (2) and subject to subsection (b), the right of a secured party with a security interest in equipment described in paragraph (3), or of a lessor or conditional vendor of such equipment, to take possession of such equipment in compliance with a security agreement, lease, or conditional sale contract, and to enforce any of its other rights or remedies, under such security agreement, lease, or conditional sale contract, to sell, lease, or otherwise retain or dispose of such equipment, is not limited or otherwise affected by any other provision of this title or by any power of the court.

(2) The right to take possession and to enforce the other rights and remedies described in paragraph (1) shall be subject to section 362 if—

    (A) before the date that is 60 days after the date of the order for relief under this chapter, the trustee, subject to the approval of the court, agrees to perform all obligations of the debtor under such security agreement, lease, or conditional sale contract; and

    (B) any default, other than a default of a kind specified in section 365(b)(2), under such security agreement, lease, or conditional sale contract—

        (i) that occurs before the date of the order is cured before the expiration of such 60-day period;

        (ii) that occurs after the date of the order and before the expiration of such 60-day period is cured before the later of—

            (I) the date that is 30 days after the date of the default; or

            (II) the expiration of such 60-day period; and

        (iii) that occurs on or after the expiration of such 60-day period is cured in compliance with the terms of such security agreement, lease, or conditional sale contract, if a cure is permitted under that agreement, lease, or contract.

(3) The equipment described in this paragraph—

    (A) is—

        (i) an aircraft, aircraft engine, propeller, appliance, or spare part (as defined in section 40102 of title 49) that is subject to a security interest granted by, leased to, or conditionally sold to a debtor that, at the time such transaction is entered into, holds an air carrier operating certificate issued pursuant to chapter 447 of title 49 for aircraft capable of carrying 10 or more individuals or 6,000 pounds or more of cargo; or

        (ii) a documented vessel (as defined in section 30101(1) of title 46) that is subject to a security interest granted by, leased to, or conditionally sold to a debtor that is a water carrier that, at the time such transaction is entered into, holds a certificate of public convenience and necessity or permit issued by the Department of Transportation; and

    (B) includes all records and documents relating to such equipment that are required, under the terms of the security agreement, lease, or conditional sale contract, to be surrendered or returned by the debtor in connection with the surrender or return of such equipment.

(4) Paragraph (1) applies to a secured party, lessor, or conditional vendor acting in its own behalf or acting as trustee or otherwise in behalf of another party.

(b) The trustee and the secured party, lessor, or conditional vendor whose right to take possession is protected under subsection (a) may agree, subject to the approval of the court, to extend the 60-day period specified in subsection (a)(1).

(c)(1) In any case under this chapter, the trustee shall immediately surrender and return to a secured party, lessor, or conditional vendor, described in subsection (a)(1), equipment described in subsection (a)(3), if at any time after the date of the order for relief under this chapter such secured party, lessor, or conditional vendor is entitled pursuant to subsection (a)(1) to take possession of such equipment and makes a written demand for such possession to the trustee.

(2) At such time as the trustee is required under paragraph (1) to surrender and return equipment described in subsection (a)(3), any lease of such equipment, and any security agreement or conditional sale contract relating to such equipment, if such security agreement or conditional sale contract is an executory contract, shall be deemed rejected.

(d) With respect to equipment first placed in service on or before October 22, 1994, for purposes of this section—

(1) the term "lease" includes any written agreement with respect to which the lessor and the debtor, as lessee, have expressed in the agreement or in a substantially contemporaneous writing that the agreement is to be treated as a lease for Federal income tax purposes; and

(2) the term "security interest" means a purchase-money equipment security interest.

§ 1111. Claims and interests

(a) A proof of claim or interest is deemed filed under section 501 of this title for any claim or interest that appears in the schedules filed under section 521(1) or 1106(a)(2) of this title, except a claim or interest that is scheduled as disputed, contingent, or unliquidated.

(b)(1)(A) A claim secured by a lien on property of the estate shall be allowed or disallowed under section 502 of this title the same as if the holder of such claim had recourse against the debtor on account of such claim, whether or not such holder has such recourse, unless—

        (i) the class of which such claim is a part elects, by at least two-thirds in amount and more than half in number of allowed claims of such class, application of paragraph (2) of this subsection; or

        (ii) such holder does not have such recourse and such property is sold under section 363 of this title or is to be sold under the plan.

    (B) A class of claims may not elect application of paragraph (2) of this subsection if—

        (i) the interest on account of such claims in such property is of inconsequential value; or

        (ii) the holder of a claim of such class has recourse against the debtor on account of such claim and such property is sold under section 363 of this title or is to be sold under the plan.

(2) If such an election is made, then notwithstanding section 506(a) of this title, such claim is a secured claim to the extent that such claim is allowed.

§ 1112. Conversion or dismissal

(a) The debtor may convert a case under this chapter to a case under chapter 7 of this title unless—

(1) the debtor is not a debtor in possession;

(2) the case originally was commenced as an involuntary case under this chapter; or

(3) the case was converted to a case under this chapter other than on the debtor's request.

(b) Except as provided in subsection (c) of this section, on request of a party in interest or the United States trustee or bankruptcy administrator, and after notice and a hearing, the court may convert a case under this chapter to a case under chapter 7 of this title or may dismiss a case under this chapter, whichever is in the best interest of creditors and the estate, for cause, including—

(1) continuing loss to or diminution of the estate and absence of a reasonable likelihood of rehabilitation;

(2) inability to effectuate a plan;

(3) unreasonable delay by the debtor that is prejudicial to creditors;

(4) failure to propose a plan under section 1121 of this title within any time fixed by the court;

(5) denial of confirmation of every proposed plan and denial of a request made for additional time for filing another plan or a modification of a plan;

(6) revocation of an order of confirmation under section 1144 of this title, and denial of confirmation of another plan or a modified plan under section 1129 of this title;

(7) inability to effectuate substantial consummation of a confirmed plan;

(8) material default by the debtor with respect to a confirmed plan;

(9) termination of a plan by reason of the occurrence of a condition specified in the plan; or

(10) nonpayment of any fees or charges required under chapter 123 of title 28.

(c) The court may not convert a case under this chapter to a case under chapter 7 of this title if the debtor is a farmer or a corporation that is not a moneyed, business, or commercial corporation, unless the debtor requests such conversion.

(d) The court may convert a case under this chapter to a case under chapter 12 or 13 of this title only if—

(1) the debtor requests such conversion;

(2) the debtor has not been discharged under section 1141(d) of this title; and

(3) if the debtor requests conversion to chapter 12 of this title, such conversion is equitable.

(e) Except as provided in subsections (c) and (f), the court, on request of the United States trustee, may convert a case under this chapter to a case under chapter 7 of this title or may dismiss a case under this chapter, whichever is in the best interest of creditors and the estate if the debtor in a voluntary case fails to file, within fifteen days after the filing of the petition commencing such case or such additional time as the court may allow, the information required by paragraph (1) of section 521, including a list containing the names and addresses of the holders of the twenty largest unsecured claims (or of all unsecured claims if there are fewer than twenty unsecured claims), and the approximate dollar amounts of each of such claims.

(f) Notwithstanding any other provision of this section, a case may not be converted to a case under another chapter of this title unless the debtor may be a debtor under such chapter.

§ 1113. Rejection of collective bargaining agreements

(a) The debtor in possession, or the trustee if one has been appointed under the provisions of this chapter, other than a trustee in a case covered by subchapter IV of this chapter and by title I of the Railway Labor Act, may assume or reject a collective bargaining agreement only in accordance with the provisions of this section.

(b)(1) Subsequent to filing a petition and prior to filing an application seeking rejection of a collective bargaining agreement, the debtor in possession or trustee (hereinafter in this section "trustee" shall include a debtor in possession), shall—

(A) make a proposal to the authorized representative of the employees covered by such agreement, based on the most complete and reliable information available at the time of such proposal, which provides for those necessary modifications in the employees benefits and protections that are necessary to permit the reorganization of the debtor and assures that all creditors, the debtor and all of the affected parties are treated fairly and equitably; and

(B) provide, subject to subsection (d)(3), the representative

of the employees with such relevant information as is necessary to evaluate the proposal.

(2) During the period beginning on the date of the making of a proposal provided for in paragraph (1) and ending on the date of the hearing provided for in subsection (d)(1), the trustee shall meet, at reasonable times, with the authorized representative to confer in good faith in attempting to reach mutually satisfactory modifications of such agreement.

(c) The court shall approve an application for rejection of a collective bargaining agreement only if the court finds that—

(1) the trustee has, prior to the hearing, made a proposal that fulfills the requirements of subsection (b)(1);

(2) the authorized representative of the employees has refused to accept such proposal without good cause; and

(3) the balance of the equities clearly favors rejection of such agreement.

(d)(1) Upon the filing of an application for rejection the court shall schedule a hearing to be held not later than fourteen days after the date of the filing of such application. All interested parties may appear and be heard at such hearing. Adequate notice shall be provided to such parties at least ten days before the date of such hearing. The court may extend the time for the commencement of such hearing for a period not exceeding seven days where the circumstances of the case, and the interests of justice require such extension, or for additional periods of time to which the trustee and representative agree.

(2) The court shall rule on such application for rejection within thirty days after the date of the commencement of the hearing. In the interests of justice, the court may extend such time for ruling for such additional period as the trustee and the employees' representative may agree to. If the court does not rule on such application within thirty days after the date of the commencement of the hearing, or within such additional time as the trustee and the employees' representative may agree to, the trustee may terminate or alter any provisions of the collective bargaining agreement pending the ruling of the court on such application.

(3) The court may enter such protective orders, consistent with the need of the authorized representative of the employee to evaluate the trustee's proposal and the application for rejection, as may be necessary to prevent disclosure of information provided to such representative where such disclosure could compromise the position of the debtor with respect to its competitors in the industry in which it is engaged.

(e) If during a period when the collective bargaining agreement continues in effect, and if essential to the continuation of the debtor's business, or in order to avoid irreparable damage to the estate, the court, after notice and a hearing, may authorize the trustee to implement interim changes in the terms, conditions, wages, benefits, or work rules provided by a collective bargaining agreement. Any hearing under this paragraph shall be scheduled in accordance with the needs of the trustee. The implementation of such interim changes shall not render the application for rejection moot.

(f) No provision of this title shall be construed to permit a trustee to unilaterally terminate or alter any provisions of a collective bargaining agreement prior to compliance with the provisions of this section.

§ 1114. Payment of insurance benefits to retired employees

(a) For purposes of this section, the term "retiree benefits" means payments to any entity or person for the purpose of providing or reimbursing payments for retired employees and their spouses and dependents, for medical, surgical, or hospital care benefits, or benefits in the event of sickness, accident, disability, or death under any plan, fund, or program (through the purchase of insurance or otherwise) maintained or established in whole or in part by the debtor prior to filing a petition commencing a case under this title.

(b)(1) For purposes of this section, the term "authorized representative" means the authorized representative designated pursuant to subsection (c) for persons receiving any retiree benefits covered by a collective bargaining agreement or subsection (d) in the case of persons receiving retiree benefits not covered by such an agreement.

(2) Committees of retired employees appointed by the court pursuant to this section shall have the same rights, powers, and duties as committees appointed under sections 1102 and 1103 of this title for the purpose of carrying out the purposes of sections 1114 and 1129(a)(13) and, as permitted by the court, shall have the power to enforce the rights of persons under this title as they relate to retiree benefits.

(c)(1) A labor organization shall be, for purposes of this section, the authorized representative of those persons receiving any retiree benefits covered by any collective bargaining agreement to which that labor organization is signatory, unless (A) such labor organization elects not to serve as the authorized representative of such persons, or (B) the court, upon a motion by any party in interest, after notice and hearing, determines that different representation of such persons is appropriate.

(2) In cases where the labor organization referred to in paragraph (1) elects not to serve as the authorized representative of those persons receiving any retiree benefits covered by any collective bargaining agreement to which that labor organization is signatory, or in cases where the court, pursuant to paragraph (1) finds different representation of such persons appropriate, the court, upon a motion by any party in interest, and after notice and a hearing, shall appoint a committee of retired employees if the debtor seeks to modify or not pay the retiree benefits or if the court otherwise determines that it is appropriate, from among such persons, to serve as the authorized representative of such persons under this section.

(d) The court, upon a motion by any party in interest, and after notice and a hearing, shall appoint a committee of retired employees if the debtor seeks to modify or not pay the retiree benefits or if the court otherwise determines that it is appropriate, to serve as the authorized representative, under this section, of those persons receiving any retiree benefits not covered by a collective bargaining agreement.

(e)(1) Notwithstanding any other provision of this title, the debtor in possession, or the trustee if one has been appointed under the provisions of this chapter (hereinafter in this section "trustee" shall include a debtor in possession), shall timely pay and shall not modify any retiree benefits, except that—

(A) the court, on motion of the trustee or authorized representative, and after notice and a hearing, may order modification of such payments, pursuant to the provisions of subsections (g) and (h) of this section, or

(B) the trustee and the authorized representative of the recipients of those benefits may agree to modification of such payments,

after which such benefits as modified shall continue to be paid by the trustee.

(2) Any payment for retiree benefits required to be made before a plan confirmed under section 1129 of this title is effective has the status of an allowed administrative expense as provided in section 503 of this title.

(f)(1) Subsequent to filing a petition and prior to filing an application seeking modification of the retiree benefits, the trustee shall—

(A) make a proposal to the authorized representative of the retirees, based on the most complete and reliable information available at the time of such proposal, which provides for those necessary modifications in the retiree benefits that are necessary to permit the reorganization of the debtor and assures that all creditors, the debtor and all of the affected parties are treated fairly and equitably; and

(B) provide, subject to subsection (k)(3), the representative of the retirees with such relevant information as is necessary to evaluate the proposal.

(2) During the period beginning on the date of the making of a proposal provided for in paragraph (1), and ending on the date of the hearing provided for in subsection (k)(1), the trustee shall meet, at reasonable times, with the authorized representative to confer in good faith in attempting to reach mutually satisfactory modifications of such retiree benefits.

(g) The court shall enter an order providing for modification in the payment of retiree benefits if the court finds that—

(1) the trustee has, prior to the hearing, made a proposal that fulfills the requirements of subsection (f);

(2) the authorized representative of the retirees has refused to accept such proposal without good cause; and

(3) such modification is necessary to permit the reorganization of the debtor and assures that all creditors, the debtor, and all of the affected parties are treated fairly and equitably, and is clearly favored by the balance of the equities;

except that in no case shall the court enter an order providing for such modification which provides for a modification to a level lower than that proposed by the trustee in the proposal found by the court to have complied with the requirements of this subsection and subsection (f): *Provided, however,* That at any time after an order is entered providing for modification in the payment of retiree benefits, or at any time after an agreement modifying such benefits is made between the trustee and the authorized representative of the recipients of such benefits, the authorized representative may apply to the court for an order increasing those benefits which order shall be granted if the increase in retiree benefits sought is consistent with the standard set forth in paragraph (3); and: *Provided further,* That neither the trustee nor the authorized representative is precluded from making more than one motion for a modification order governed by this subsection.

(h)(1) Prior to a court issuing a final order under subsection (g) of this section, if essential to the continuation of the debtor's business, or in order to avoid irreparable damage to the estate, the court, after notice and a hearing, may authorize the trustee to implement interim modifications in retiree benefits.

(2) Any hearing under this subsection shall be scheduled in accordance with the needs of the trustee.

(3) The implementation of such interim changes does not render the motion for modification moot.

(i) No retiree benefits paid between the filing of the petition and the time a plan confirmed under section 1129 of this title becomes effective shall be deducted or offset from the amounts allowed as claims for any benefits which remain unpaid, or from the amounts to be paid under the plan with respect to such claims for unpaid benefits, whether such claims for unpaid benefits are based upon or arise from a right to future unpaid benefits or from any benefits not paid as a result of modifications allowed pursuant to this section.

(j) No claim for retiree benefits shall be limited by section 502(b)(7) of this title.

(k)(1) Upon the filing of an application for modifying retiree benefits, the court shall schedule a hearing to be held not later than fourteen days after the date of the filing of such application. All interested parties may appear and be heard at such hearing. Adequate notice shall be provided to such parties at least ten days before the date of such hearing. The court may extend the time for the commencement of such hearing for a period not exceeding seven days where the circumstances of the case, and the interests of justice require such extension, or for additional periods of time to which the trustee and the authorized representative agree.

(2) The court shall rule on such application for modification within 90 days after the date of the commencement of the hearing. In the interests of justice, the court may extend such time for ruling for such additional period as the trustee and the authorized representative may agree to. If the court does not rule on such application within 90 days after the date of the commencement of the hearing, or within such additional time as the trustee and the authorized representative may agree to, the trustee may implement the proposed modifications pending the ruling of the court on such application.

(3) The court may enter such protective orders, consistent with the need of the authorized representative of the retirees to evaluate the trustee's proposal and the application for modification, as may be necessary to prevent disclosure of information provided to such representative where such disclosure could compromise the position of the debtor with respect to its competitors in the industry in which it is engaged.

(*l*) This section shall not apply to any retiree, or the spouse or dependents of such retiree, if such retiree's gross income for the 12 months preceding the filing of the bankruptcy petition equals or exceeds $250,000, unless such retiree can demonstrate to the satisfaction of the court that he is unable to obtain health, medical, life, and disability coverage for himself, his spouse, and his dependents who would otherwise be covered by the employer's insurance plan, comparable to the coverage provided by the employer on the day before the filing of a petition under this title.

Subchapter II—The Plan

§ 1121. Who may file a plan

(a) The debtor may file a plan with a petition commencing a voluntary case, or at any time in a voluntary case or an involuntary case.

(b) Except as otherwise provided in this section, only the debtor may file a plan until after 120 days after the date of the order for relief under this chapter.

(c) Any party in interest, including the debtor, the trustee, a creditors' committee, an equity security holders' committee, a creditor, an equity security holder, or any indenture trustee, may file a plan if and only if—

(1) a trustee has been appointed under this chapter;

(2) the debtor has not filed a plan before 120 days after the date of the order for relief under this chapter; or

(3) the debtor has not filed a plan that has been accepted, before 180 days after the date of the order for relief under this chapter, by each class of claims or interests that is impaired under the plan.

(d) On request of a party in interest made within the respective periods specified in subsections (b) and (c) of this section and after notice and a hearing, the court may for cause reduce or increase the 120-day period or the 180-day period referred to in this section.

(e) In a case in which the debtor is a small business and elects to be considered a small business—

(1) only the debtor may file a plan until after 100 days after the date of the order for relief under this chapter;

(2) all plans shall be filed within 160 days after the date of the order for relief; and

(3) on request of a party in interest made within the respective periods specified in paragraphs (1) and (2) and after notice and a hearing, the court may—
   (A) reduce the 100-day period or the 160-day period specified in paragraph (1) or (2) for cause; and
   (B) increase the 100-day period specified in paragraph (1) if the debtor shows that the need for an increase is caused by circumstances for which the debtor should not be held accountable.

§ 1122. Classification of claims or interests

(a) Except as provided in subsection (b) of this section, a plan may place a claim or an interest in a particular class only if such claim or interest is substantially similar to the other claims or interests of such class.

(b) A plan may designate a separate class of claims consisting only of every unsecured claim that is less than or reduced to an amount that the court approves as reasonable and necessary for administrative convenience.

§ 1123. Contents of plan

(a) Notwithstanding any otherwise applicable nonbankruptcy law, a plan shall—

(1) designate, subject to section 1122 of this title, classes of claims, other than claims of a kind specified in section 507(a)(1), 507(a)(2), or 507(a)(8) of this title, and classes of interests;

(2) specify any class of claims or interests that is not impaired under the plan;

(3) specify the treatment of any class of claims or interests that is impaired under the plan;

(4) provide the same treatment for each claim or interest of a particular class, unless the holder of a particular claim or interest agrees to a less favorable treatment of such particular claim or interest;

(5) provide adequate means for the plan's implementation such as—
  (A) retention by the debtor of all or any part of the property of the estate;
  (B) transfer of all or any part of the property of the estate to one or more entities, whether organized before or after the confirmation of such plan;
  (C) merger or consolidation of the debtor with one or more persons;
  (D) sale of all or any part of the property of the estate, either subject to or free of any lien, or the distribution of all or any part of the property of the estate among those having an interest in such property of the estate;
  (E) satisfaction or modification of any lien;
  (F) cancellation or modification of any indenture or similar instrument;
  (G) curing or waiving of any default;
  (H) extension of a maturity date or a change in an interest rate or other term of outstanding securities;
  (I) amendment of the debtor's charter; or
  (J) issuance of securities of the debtor, or of any entity referred to in subparagraph (B) or (C) of this paragraph, for cash, for property, for existing securities, or in exchange for claims or interests, or for any other appropriate purpose;

(6) provide for the inclusion in the charter of the debtor, if the debtor is a corporation, or of any corporation referred to in paragraph (5)(B) or (5)(C) of this subsection, of a provision prohibiting the issuance of nonvoting equity securities, and providing, as to the several classes of securities possessing voting power, an appropriate distribution of such power among such classes, including, in the case of any class of equity securities having a preference over another class of equity securities with respect to dividends, adequate provisions for the election of directors representing such preferred class in the event of default in the payment of such dividends; and

(7) contain only provisions that are consistent with the interests of creditors and equity security holders and with public policy with respect to the manner of selection of any officer, director, or trustee under the plan and any successor to such officer, director, or trustee.

(b) Subject to subsection (a) of this section, a plan may—

(1) impair or leave unimpaired any class of claims, secured or unsecured, or of interests;

(2) subject to section 365 of this title, provide for the assumption, rejection, or assignment of any executory contract or unexpired lease of the debtor not previously rejected under such section;

(3) provide for—
  (A) the settlement or adjustment of any claim or interest belonging to the debtor or to the estate; or
  (B) the retention and enforcement by the debtor, by the trustee, or by a representative of the estate appointed for such purpose, of any such claim or interest;

(4) provide for the sale of all or substantially all of the property of the estate, and the distribution of the proceeds of such sale among holders of claims or interests;

(5) modify the rights of holders of secured claims, other than a claim secured only by a security interest in real property that is the debtor's principal residence, or of holders of unsecured claims, or leave unaffected the rights of holders of any class of claims; and

(6) include any other appropriate provision not inconsistent with the applicable provisions of this title.

(c) In a case concerning an individual, a plan proposed by an entity other than the debtor may not provide for the use, sale, or lease of property exempted under section 522 of this title, unless the debtor consents to such use, sale, or lease.

(d) Notwithstanding subsection (a) of this section and sections 506(b), 1129(a)(7), and 1129(b) of this title, if it is proposed in a plan to cure a default the amount necessary to cure the default, shall be determined in accordance with the underlying agreement and applicable nonbankruptcy law.

§ 1124. Impairment of claims or interests

Except as provided in section 1123(a)(4) of this title, a class of claims or interests is impaired under a plan unless, with respect to each claim or interest of such class, the plan—

(1) leaves unaltered the legal, equitable, and contractual rights to which such claim or interest entitles the holder of such claim or interest; or

(2) notwithstanding any contractual provision or applicable law that entitles the holder of such claim or interest to demand or receive accelerated payment of such claim or interest after the occurrence of a default—
  (A) cures any such default that occurred before or after the commencement of the case under this title, other than a default of a kind specified in section 365(b)(2) of this title;
  (B) reinstates the maturity of such claim or interest as such maturity existed before such default;
  (C) compensates the holder of such claim or interest for any damages incurred as a result of any reasonable reliance by such holder on such contractual provision or such appli-

cable law; and

(D) does not otherwise alter the legal, equitable, or contractual rights to which such claim or interest entitles the holder of such claim or interest.

§ 1125. Postpetition disclosure and solicitation

(a) In this section—

(1) "adequate information" means information of a kind, and in sufficient detail, as far as is reasonably practicable in light of the nature and history of the debtor and the condition of the debtor's books and records, that would enable a hypothetical reasonable investor typical of holders of claims or interests of the relevant class to make an informed judgment about the plan, but adequate information need not include such information about any other possible or proposed plan; and

(2) "investor typical of holders of claims or interests of the relevant class" means investor having—

(A) a claim or interest of the relevant class;

(B) such a relationship with the debtor as the holders of other claims or interests of such class generally have; and

(C) such ability to obtain such information from sources other than the disclosure required by this section as holders of claims or interests in such class generally have.

(b) An acceptance or rejection of a plan may not be solicited after the commencement of the case under this title from a holder of a claim or interest with respect to such claim or interest unless, at the time of or before such solicitation, there is transmitted to such holder the plan or a summary of the plan, and a written disclosure statement approved, after notice and a hearing, by the court as containing adequate information. The court may approve a disclosure statement without a valuation of the debtor or an appraisal of the debtor's assets.

(c) The same disclosure statement shall be transmitted to each holder of a claim or interest of a particular class, but there may be transmitted different disclosure statements, differing in amount, detail, or kind of information, as between classes.

(d) Whether a disclosure statement required under subsection (b) of this section contains adequate information is not governed by any otherwise applicable non-bankruptcy law, rule, or regulation, but an agency or official whose duty is to administer or enforce such a law, rule, or regulation may be heard on the issue of whether a disclosure statement contains adequate information. Such an agency or official may not appeal from, or otherwise seek review of, an order approving a disclosure statement.

(e) A person that solicits acceptance or rejection of a plan, in good faith and in compliance with the applicable provisions of this title, or that participates, in good faith and in compliance with the applicable provisions of this title, in the offer, issuance, sale, or purchase of a security, offered or sold under the plan, of the debtor, of an affiliate participating in a joint plan with the debtor, or of a newly organized successor to the debtor under the plan, is not liable, on account of such solicitation or participation, for violation of any applicable law, rule, or regulation governing solicitation of acceptance or rejection of a plan or the offer, issuance, sale, or purchase of securities.

(f) Notwithstanding subsection (b), in a case in which the debtor

has elected under section 1121(e) to be considered a small business—

(1) the court may conditionally approve a disclosure statement subject to final approval after notice and a hearing;

(2) acceptances and rejections of a plan may be solicited based on a conditionally approved disclosure statement as long as the debtor provides adequate information to each holder of a claim or interest that is solicited, but a conditionally approved disclosure statement shall be mailed at least 10 days prior to the date of the hearing on confirmation of the plan; and

(3) a hearing on the disclosure statement may be combined with a hearing on confirmation of a plan.

§ 1126. Acceptance of plan

(a) The holder of a claim or interest allowed under section 502 of this title may accept or reject a plan. If the United States is a creditor or equity security holder, the Secretary of the Treasury may accept or reject the plan on behalf of the United States.

(b) For the purposes of subsections (c) and (d) of this section, a holder of a claim or interest that has accepted or rejected the plan before the commencement of the case under this title is deemed to have accepted or rejected such plan, as the case may be, if—

(1) the solicitation of such acceptance or rejection was in compliance with any applicable nonbankruptcy law, rule, or regulation governing the adequacy of disclosure in connection with such solicitation; or

(2) if there is not any such law, rule, or regulation, such acceptance or rejection was solicited after disclosure to such holder of adequate information, as defined in section 1125(a) of this title.

(c) A class of claims has accepted a plan if such plan has been accepted by creditors, other than any entity designated under subsection (e) of this section, that hold at least two-thirds in amount and more than one-half in number of the allowed claims of such class held by creditors, other than any entity designated under subsection (e) of this section, that have accepted or rejected such plan.

(d) A class of interests has accepted a plan if such plan has been accepted by holders of such interests, other than any entity designated under subsection (e) of this section, that hold at least two-thirds in amount of the allowed interests of such class held by holders of such interests, other than any entity designated under subsection (e) of this section, that have accepted or rejected such plan.

(e) On request of a party in interest, and after notice and a hearing, the court may designate any entity whose acceptance or rejection of such plan was not in good faith, or was not solicited or procured in good faith or in accordance with the provisions of this title.

(f) Notwithstanding any other provision of this section, a class that is not impaired under a plan, and each holder of a claim or interest of such class, are conclusively presumed to have accepted the plan, and solicitation of acceptances with respect to such class from the holders of claims or interests of such class is not required.

(g) Notwithstanding any other provision of this section, a class is deemed not to have accepted a plan if such plan provides that the claims or interests of such class do not entitle the holders of such claims or interests to receive or retain any property under the plan on account of such claims or interests.

§ 1127. Modification of plan

(a) The proponent of a plan may modify such plan at any time before confirmation, but may not modify such plan so that such plan as modified fails to meet the requirements of sections 1122 and 1123 of this title. After the proponent of a plan files a modification of such plan with the court, the plan as modified becomes the plan.

(b) The proponent of a plan or the reorganized debtor may modify such plan at any time after confirmation of such plan and before substantial consummation of such plan, but may not modify such plan so that such plan as modified fails to meet the requirements of sections 1122 and 1123 of this title. Such plan as modified under this subsection becomes the plan only if circumstances warrant such modification and the court, after notice and a hearing, confirms such plan as modified, under section 1129 of this title.

(c) The proponent of a modification shall comply with section 1125 of this title with respect to the plan as modified.

(d) Any holder of a claim or interest that has accepted or rejected a plan is deemed to have accepted or rejected, as the case may be, such plan as modified, unless, within the time fixed by the court, such holder changes such holder's previous acceptance or rejection.

§ 1128. Confirmation hearing

(a) After notice, the court shall hold a hearing on confirmation of a plan.

(b) A party in interest may object to confirmation of a plan.

§ 1129. Confirmation of plan

(a) The court shall confirm a plan only if all of the following requirements are met:

(1) The plan complies with the applicable provisions of this title.

(2) The proponent of the plan complies with the applicable provisions of this title.

(3) The plan has been proposed in good faith and not by any means forbidden by law.

(4) Any payment made or to be made by the proponent, by the debtor, or by a person issuing securities or acquiring property under the plan, for services or for costs and expenses in or in connection with the case, or in connection with the plan and incident to the case, has been approved by, or is subject to the approval of, the court as reasonable.

(5)(A)(i) The proponent of the plan has disclosed the identity and affiliations of any individual proposed to serve, after confirmation of the plan, as a director, officer, or voting trustee of the debtor, an affiliate of the debtor participating in a joint plan with the debtor, or a successor to the debtor under the plan; and

(ii) the appointment to, or continuance in, such office of such individual, is consistent with the interests of creditors and equity security holders and with public policy; and

(B) the proponent of the plan has disclosed the identity of any insider that will be employed or retained by the reorganized debtor, and the nature of any compensation for such insider.

(6) Any governmental regulatory commission with jurisdiction, after confirmation of the plan, over the rates of the debtor has approved any rate change provided for in the plan, or such rate change is expressly conditioned on such approval.

(7) With respect to each impaired class of claims or interests—

(A) each holder of a claim or interest of such class—

(i) has accepted the plan; or

(ii) will receive or retain under the plan on account of such claim or interest property of a value, as of the effective date of the plan, that is not less than the amount that such holder would so receive or retain if the debtor were liquidated under chapter 7 of this title on such date; or

(B) if section 1111(b)(2) of this title applies to the claims of such class, each holder of a claim of such class will receive or retain under the plan on account of such claim property of a value, as of the effective date of the plan, that is not less than the value of such holder's interest in the estate's interest in the property that secures such claims.

(8) With respect to each class of claims or interests—

(A) such class has accepted the plan; or

(B) such class is not impaired under the plan.

(9) Except to the extent that the holder of a particular claim has agreed to a different treatment of such claim, the plan provides that—

(A) with respect to a claim of a kind specified in section 507(a)(1) or 507(a)(2) of this title, on the effective date of the plan, the holder of such claim will receive on account of such claim cash equal to the allowed amount of such claim;

(B) with respect to a class of claims of a kind specified in section 507(a)(3), 507(a)(4), 507(a)(5), 507(a)(6), or 507(a)(7) of this title, each holder of a claim of such class will receive—

(i) if such class has accepted the plan, deferred cash payments of a value, as of the effective date of the plan, equal to the allowed amount of such claim; or

(ii) if such class has not accepted the plan, cash on the effective date of the plan equal to the allowed amount of such claim; and

(C) with respect to a claim of a kind specified in section 507(a)(8) of this title, the holder of such claim will receive on account of such claim deferred cash payments, over a period not exceeding six years after the date of assessment of such claim, of a value, as of the effective date of the plan, equal to the allowed amount of such claim.

(10) If a class of claims is impaired under the plan, at least one class of claims that is impaired under the plan has accepted the plan, determined without including any acceptance of the plan by any insider.

(11) Confirmation of the plan is not likely to be followed by the liquidation, or the need for further financial reorganization, of the debtor or any successor to the debtor under the plan, unless such liquidation or reorganization is proposed in the plan.

(12) All fees payable under section 1930 of title 28, as determined by the court at the hearing on confirmation of the plan, have been paid or the plan provides for the payment of all such fees on the effective date of the plan.

(13) The plan provides for the continuation after its effective date of payment of all retiree benefits, as that term is defined in section 1114 of this title, at the level established pursuant to subsection (e)(1)(B) or (g) of section 1114 of this title, at any time prior to confirmation of the plan, for the duration of the period the debtor has obligated itself to provide such benefits.

(b)(1) Notwithstanding section 510(a) of this title, if all of the applicable requirements of subsection (a) of this section other than paragraph (8) are met with respect to a plan, the court, on request of the proponent of the plan, shall confirm the plan notwithstanding the requirements of such paragraph if the plan does not discriminate unfairly, and is fair and equitable, with respect to each class of claims or interests that is impaired under, and has not accepted, the plan.

(2) For the purpose of this subsection, the condition that a plan be fair and equitable with respect to a class includes the following requirements:

(A) With respect to a class of secured claims, the plan provides—

  (i)(I) that the holders of such claims retain the liens securing such claims, whether the property subject to such liens is retained by the debtor or transferred to another entity, to the extent of the allowed amount of such claims; and

    (II) that each holder of a claim of such class receive on account of such claim deferred cash payments totaling at least the allowed amount of such claim, of a value, as of the effective date of the plan, of at least the value of such holder's interest in the estate's interest in such property;

  (ii) for the sale, subject to section 363(k) of this title, of any property that is subject to the liens securing such claims, free and clear of such liens, with such liens to attach to the proceeds of such sale, and the treatment of such liens on proceeds under clause (i) or (iii) of this subparagraph; or

  (iii) for the realization by such holders of the indubitable equivalent of such claims.

(B) With respect to a class of unsecured claims—

  (i) the plan provides that each holder of a claim of such class receive or retain on account of such claim property of a value, as of the effective date of the plan, equal to the allowed amount of such claim; or

  (ii) the holder of any claim or interest that is junior to the claims of such class will not receive or retain under the plan on account of such junior claim or interest any property.

(C) With respect to a class of interests—

  (i) the plan provides that each holder of an interest of such class receive or retain on account of such interest property of a value, as of the effective date of the plan, equal to the greatest of the allowed amount of any fixed liquidation preference to which such holder is entitled, any fixed redemption price to which such holder is entitled, or the value of such interest; or

  (ii) the holder of any interest that is junior to the interests of such class will not receive or retain under the plan on account of such junior interest any property.

(c) Notwithstanding subsections (a) and (b) of this section and except as provided in section 1127(b) of this title, the court may confirm only one plan, unless the order of confirmation in the case has been revoked under section 1144 of this title. If the requirements of subsections (a) and (b) of this section are met with respect to more than one plan, the court shall consider the preferences of creditors and equity security holders in determining which plan to confirm.

(d) Notwithstanding any other provision of this section, on request of a party in interest that is a governmental unit, the court may not confirm a plan if the principal purpose of the plan is the avoidance of taxes or the avoidance of the application of section 5 of the Securities Act of 1933. In any hearing under this subsection, the governmental unit has the burden of proof on the issue of avoidance.

Subchapter III—Postconfirmation Matters

§ 1141. Effect of confirmation

(a) Except as provided in subsections (d)(2) and (d)(3) of this section, the provisions of a confirmed plan bind the debtor, any entity issuing securities under the plan, any entity acquiring property under the plan, and any creditor, equity security holder, or general partner in the debtor, whether or not the claim or interest of such creditor, equity security holder, or general partner is impaired under the plan and whether or not such creditor, equity security holder, or general partner has accepted the plan.

(b) Except as otherwise provided in the plan or the order confirming the plan, the confirmation of a plan vests all of the property of the estate in the debtor.

(c) Except as provided in subsections (d)(2) and (d)(3) of this section and except as otherwise provided in the plan or in the order confirming the plan, after confirmation of a plan, the property dealt with by the plan is free and clear of all claims and interests of creditors, equity security holders, and of general partners in the debtor.

(d)(1) Except as otherwise provided in this subsection, in the plan, or in the order confirming the plan, the confirmation of a plan—

(A) discharges the debtor from any debt that arose before the date of such confirmation, and any debt of a kind specified in section 502(g), 502(h) or 502(i) of this title, whether or not—

  (i) a proof of the claim based on such debt is filed or deemed filed under section 501 of this title;

  (ii) such claim is allowed under section 502 of this title; or

  (iii) the holder of such claim has accepted the plan; and

(B) terminates all rights and interests of equity security holders and general partners provided for by the plan.

(2) The confirmation of a plan does not discharge an individual debtor from any debt excepted from discharge under section 523 of this title.

(3) The confirmation of a plan does not discharge a debtor if-
   (A) the plan provides for the liquidation of all or substantially all of the property of the estate;
   (B) the debtor does not engage in business after consummation of the plan; and
   (C) the debtor would be denied a discharge under section 727(a) of this title if the case were a case under chapter 7 of this title.

(4) The court may approve a written waiver of discharge executed by the debtor after the order for relief under this chapter.

§ 1142. Implementation of plan

(a) Notwithstanding any otherwise applicable nonbankruptcy law, rule, or regulation relating to financial condition, the debtor and any entity organized or to be organized for the purpose of carrying out the plan shall carry out the plan and shall comply with any orders of the court.

(b) The court may direct the debtor and any other necessary party to execute or deliver or to join in the execution or delivery of any instrument required to effect a transfer of property dealt with by a confirmed plan, and to perform any other act, including the satisfaction of any lien, that is necessary for the consummation of the plan.

§ 1143. Distribution

If a plan requires presentment or surrender of a security or the performance of any other act as a condition to participation in distribution under the plan, such action shall be taken not later than five years after the date of the entry of the order of confirmation. Any entity that has not within such time presented or surrendered such entity's security or taken any such other action that the plan requires may not participate in distribution under the plan.

§ 1144. Revocation of an order of confirmation

On request of a party in interest at any time before 180 days after the date of the entry of the order of confirmation, and after notice and a hearing, the court may revoke such order if and only if such order was procured by fraud. An order under this section revoking an order of confirmation shall-

(1) contain such provisions as are necessary to protect any entity acquiring rights in good faith reliance on the order of confirmation; and

(2) revoke the discharge of the debtor.

§ 1145. Exemption from securities laws

(a) Except with respect to an entity that is an underwriter as defined in subsection (b) of this section, section 5 of the Securities Act of 1933 and any State or local law requiring registration for offer or sale of a security or registration or licensing of an issuer of, underwriter of, or broker or dealer in, a security do not apply to-

(1) the offer or sale under a plan of a security of the debtor, of an affiliate participating in a joint plan with the debtor, or of a successor to the debtor under the plan-
   (A) in exchange for a claim against, an interest in, or a claim for an administrative expense in the case concerning, the debtor or such affiliate; or

   (B) principally in such exchange and partly for cash or property;

(2) the offer of a security through any warrant, option, right to subscribe, or conversion privilege that was sold in the manner specified in paragraph (1) of this subsection, or the sale of a security upon the exercise of such a warrant, option, right, or privilege;

(3) the offer or sale, other than under a plan, of a security of an issuer other than the debtor or an affiliate, if—
   (A) such security was owned by the debtor on the date of the filing of the petition;
   (B) the issuer of such security is—
      (i) required to file reports under section 13 or 15(d) of the Securities Exchange Act of 1934; and
      (ii) in compliance with the disclosure and reporting provision of such applicable section; and
   (C) such offer or sale is of securities that do not exceed—
      (i) during the two-year period immediately following the date of the filing of the petition, four percent of the securities of such class outstanding on such date; and
      (ii) during any 180-day period following such two-year period, one percent of the securities outstanding at the beginning of such 180-day period; or

(4) a transaction by a stockbroker in a security that is executed after a transaction of a kind specified in paragraph (1) or (2) of this subsection in such security and before the expiration of 40 days after the first date on which such security was bona fide offered to the public by the issuer or by or through an underwriter, if such stockbroker provides, at the time of or before such transaction by such stockbroker, a disclosure statement approved under section 1125 of this title, and, if the court orders, information supplementing such disclosure statement.

(b)(1) Except as provided in paragraph (2) of this subsection and except with respect to ordinary trading transactions of an entity that is not an issuer, an entity is an underwriter under section 2(11) of the Securities Act of 1933, if such entity—
   (A) purchases a claim against, interest in, or claim for an administrative expense in the case concerning, the debtor, if such purchase is with a view to distribution of any security received or to be received in exchange for such a claim or interest;
   (B) offers to sell securities offered or sold under the plan for the holders of such securities;
   (C) offers to buy securities offered or sold under the plan from the holders of such securities, if such offer to buy is—
      (i) with a view to distribution of such securities; and
      (ii) under an agreement made in connection with the plan, with the consummation of the plan, or with the offer or sale of securities under the plan; or
   (D) is an issuer, as used in such section 2(11), with respect to such securities.

(2) An entity is not an underwriter under section 2(11) of the Securities Act of 1933 or under paragraph (1) of this subsection with respect to an agreement that provides only for—

(A)(i) the matching or combining of fractional interests in securities offered or sold under the plan into whole interests; or

   (ii) the purchase or sale of such fractional interests from or to entities receiving such fractional interests under the plan; or

(B) the purchase or sale for such entities of such fractional or whole interests as are necessary to adjust for any remaining fractional interests after such matching.

(3) An entity other than an entity of the kind specified in paragraph (1) of this subsection is not an underwriter under section 2(11) of the Securities Act of 1933 with respect to any securities offered or sold to such entity in the manner specified in subsection (a)(1) of this section.

(c) An offer or sale of securities of the kind and in the manner specified under subsection (a)(1) of this section is deemed to be a public offering.

(d) The Trust Indenture Act of 1939 does not apply to a note issued under the plan that matures not later than one year after the effective date of the plan.

§ 1146. Special tax provisions

(a) For the purposes of any State or local law imposing a tax on or measured by income, the taxable period of a debtor that is an individual shall terminate on the date of the order for relief under this chapter, unless the case was converted under section 706 of this title.

(b) The trustee shall make a State or local tax return of income for the estate of an individual debtor in a case under this chapter for each taxable period after the order for relief under this chapter during which the case is pending.

(c) The issuance, transfer, or exchange of a security, or the making or delivery of an instrument of transfer under a plan confirmed under section 1129 of this title, may not be taxed under any law imposing a stamp tax or similar tax.

(d) The court may authorize the proponent of a plan to request a determination, limited to questions of law, by a State or local governmental unit charged with responsibility for collection or determination of a tax on or measured by income, of the tax effects, under section 346 of this title and under the law imposing such tax, of the plan. In the event of an actual controversy, the court may declare such effects after the earlier of—

(1) the date on which such governmental unit responds to the request under this subsection; or

(2) 270 days after such request.

***

CHAPTER 12[25]

ADJUSTMENT OF DEBTS OF A FAMILY FARMER WITH REGULAR ANNUAL INCOME

Subchapter I—Officers, Administration, and the Estate

§ 1201. Stay of action against codebtor

(a) Except as provided in subsections (b) and (c) of this section, after the order for relief under this chapter, a creditor may not act, or commence or continue any civil action, to collect all or any part of a consumer debt of the debtor from any individual that is liable on such debt with the debtor, or that secured such debt, unless—

(1) such individual became liable on or secured such debt in the ordinary course of such individual's business; or

(2) the case is closed, dismissed, or converted to a case under chapter 7 of this title.

(b) A creditor may present a negotiable instrument, and may give notice of dishonor of such an instrument.

(c) On request of a party in interest and after notice and a hearing, the court shall grant relief from the stay provided by subsection (a) of this section with respect to a creditor, to the extent that—

(1) as between the debtor and the individual protected under subsection (a) of this section, such individual received the consideration for the claim held by such creditor;

(2) the plan filed by the debtor proposes not to pay such claim; or

(3) such creditor's interest would be irreparably harmed by continuation of such stay.

(d) Twenty days after the filing of a request under subsection (c)(2) of this section for relief from the stay provided by subsection (a) of this section, such stay is terminated with respect to the party in interest making such request, unless the debtor or any individual that is liable on such debt with the debtor files and serves upon such party in interest a written objection to the taking of the proposed action.

§ 1202. Trustee

(a) If the United States trustee has appointed an individual under section 586(b) of title 28 to serve as standing trustee in cases under this chapter and if such individual qualifies as a trustee under section 322 of this title, then such individual shall serve as trustee in any case filed under this chapter. Otherwise, the United States trustee shall appoint one disinterested person to serve as trustee in the case or the United States trustee may serve as trustee in the case if necessary.

---

25 *Editor's Note*: Chapter 12 of the Bankruptcy Code expired on January 1, 2004. However, Pub L. No. 108-369, 118 Stat. 1749 (2004) enacted October 25, 2004, extended chapter 12 through June 30, 2005, with a retroactive effective date of January 1, 2004. Thus newly commenced and pending cases are treated as if chapter 12 had remained in continuous effect. *See* § A.2.10, *infra*.

(b) The trustee shall—

(1) perform the duties specified in sections 704(2), 704(3), 704(5), 704(6), 704(7), and 704(9) of this title;

(2) perform the duties specified in section 1106(a)(3) and 1106(a)(4) of this title if the court, for cause and on request of a party in interest, the trustee, or the United States trustee, so orders;

(3) appear and be heard at any hearing that concerns—
   (A) the value of property subject to a lien;
   (B) confirmation of a plan;
   (C) modification of the plan after confirmation; or
   (D) the sale of property of the estate;

(4) ensure that the debtor commences making timely payments required by a confirmed plan; and

(5) if the debtor ceases to be a debtor in possession, perform the duties specified in sections 704(8), 1106(a)(1), 1106(a)(2), 1106(a)(6), 1106(a)(7), and 1203.

§ 1203. Rights and powers of debtor

Subject to such limitations as the court may prescribe, a debtor in possession shall have all the rights, other than the right to compensation under section 330, and powers, and shall perform all the functions and duties, except the duties specified in paragraphs (3) and (4) of section 1106(a), of a trustee serving in a case under chapter 11, including operating the debtor's farm.

§ 1204. Removal of debtor as debtor in possession

(a) On request of a party in interest, and after notice and a hearing, the court shall order that the debtor shall not be a debtor in possession for cause, including fraud, dishonesty, incompetence, or gross mismanagement of the affairs of the debtor, either before or after the commencement of the case.

(b) On request of a party in interest, and after notice and a hearing, the court may reinstate the debtor in possession.

§ 1205. Adequate protection

(a) Section 361 does not apply in a case under this chapter.

(b) In a case under this chapter, when adequate protection is required under section 362, 363, or 364 of this title of an interest of an entity in property, such adequate protection may be provided by—

(1) requiring the trustee to make a cash payment or periodic cash payments to such entity, to the extent that the stay under section 362 of this title, use, sale, or lease under section 363 of this title, or any grant of a lien under section 364 of this title results in a decrease in the value of property securing a claim or of an entity's ownership interest in property;

(2) providing to such entity an additional or replacement lien to the extent that such stay, use, sale, lease, or grant results in a decrease in the value of property securing a claim or of an entity's ownership interest in property;

(3) paying to such entity for the use of farmland the reasonable rent customary in the community where the property is located, based upon the rental value, net income, and earning capacity of the property; or

(4) granting such other relief, other than entitling such entity to compensation allowable under section 503(b)(1) of this title as an administrative expense, as will adequately protect the value of property securing a claim or of such entity's ownership interest in property.

§ 1206. Sales free of interests

After notice and a hearing, in addition to the authorization contained in section 363(f), the trustee in a case under this chapter may sell property under section 363(b) and (c) free and clear of any interest in such property of an entity other than the estate if the property is farmland or farm equipment, except that the proceeds of such sale shall be subject to such interest.

§ 1207. Property of the estate

(a) Property of the estate includes, in addition to the property specified in section 541 of this title—

(1) all property of the kind specified in such section that the debtor acquires after the commencement of the case but before the case is closed, dismissed, or converted to a case under chapter 7 of this title, whichever occurs first; and

(2) earnings from services performed by the debtor after the commencement of the case but before the case is closed, dismissed, or converted to a case under chapter 7 of this title, whichever occurs first.

(b) Except as provided in section 1204, a confirmed plan, or an order confirming a plan, the debtor shall remain in possession of all property of the estate.

§ 1208. Conversion or dismissal

(a) The debtor may convert a case under this chapter to a case under chapter 7 of this title at any time. Any waiver of the right to convert under this subsection is unenforceable.

(b) On request of the debtor at any time, if the case has not been converted under section 706 or 1112 of this title, the court shall dismiss a case under this chapter. Any waiver of the right to dismiss under this subsection is unenforceable.

(c) On request of a party in interest, and after notice and a hearing, the court may dismiss a case under this chapter for cause, including—

(1) unreasonable delay, or gross mismanagement, by the debtor that is prejudicial to creditors;

(2) nonpayment of any fees and charges required under chapter 123 of title 28;

(3) failure to file a plan timely under section 1221 of this title;

(4) failure to commence making timely payments required by a confirmed plan;

(5) denial of confirmation of a plan under section 1225 of this title and denial of a request made for additional time for filing another plan or a modification of a plan;

(6) material default by the debtor with respect to a term of a confirmed plan;

(7) revocation of the order of confirmation under section 1230 of this title, and denial of confirmation of a modified plan under section 1229 of this title;

(8) termination of a confirmed plan by reason of the occurrence of a condition specified in the plan; or

(9) continuing loss to or diminution of the estate and absence of a reasonable likelihood of rehabilitation.

(d) On request of a party in interest, and after notice and a hearing, the court may dismiss a case under this chapter or convert a case under this chapter to a case under chapter 7 of this title upon a showing that the debtor has committed fraud in connection with the case.

(e) Notwithstanding any other provision of this section, a case may not be converted to a case under another chapter of this title unless the debtor may be a debtor under such chapter.

Subchapter II—The Plan

§ 1221. Filing of plan

The debtor shall file a plan not later than 90 days after the order for relief under this chapter, except that the court may extend such period if the need for an extension is attributable to circumstances for which the debtor should not justly be held accountable.

§ 1222. Contents of plan

(a) The plan shall—

(1) provide for the submission of all or such portion of future earnings or other future income of the debtor to the supervision and control of the trustee as is necessary for the execution of the plan;

(2) provide for the full payment, in deferred cash payments, of all claims entitled to priority under section 507 of this title, unless the holder of a particular claim agrees to a different treatment of such claim; and

(3) if the plan classifies claims and interests, provide the same treatment for each claim or interest within a particular class unless the holder of a particular claim or interest agrees to less favorable treatment.

(b) Subject to subsections (a) and (c) of this section, the plan may—

(1) designate a class or classes of unsecured claims, as provided in section 1122 of this title, but may not discriminate unfairly against any class so designated; however, such plan may treat claims for a consumer debt of the debtor if an individual is liable on such consumer debt with the debtor differently than other unsecured claims;

(2) modify the rights of holders of secured claims, or of holders of unsecured claims, or leave unaffected the rights of holders of any class of claims;

(3) provide for the curing or waiving of any default;

(4) provide for payments on any unsecured claim to be made concurrently with payments on any secured claim or any other unsecured claim;

(5) provide for the curing of any default within a reasonable time and maintenance of payments while the case is pending on any unsecured claim or secured claim on which the last payment is due after the date on which the final payment under the plan is due;

(6) subject to section 365 of this title, provide for the assumption, rejection, or assignment of any executory contract or unexpired lease of the debtor not previously rejected under such section;

(7) provide for the payment of all or part of a claim against the debtor from property of the estate or property of the debtor;

(8) provide for the sale of all or any part of the property of the estate or the distribution of all or any part of the property of the estate among those having an interest in such property;

(9) provide for payment of allowed secured claims consistent with section 1225(a)(5) of this title, over a period exceeding the period permitted under section 1222(c);

(10) provide for the vesting of property of the estate, on confirmation of the plan or at a later time, in the debtor or in any other entity; and

(11) include any other appropriate provision not inconsistent with this title.

(c) Except as provided in subsections (b)(5) and (b)(9), the plan may not provide for payments over a period that is longer than three years unless the court for cause approves a longer period, but the court may not approve a period that is longer than five years.

(d) Notwithstanding subsection (b)(2) of this section and sections 506(b) and 1225(a)(5) of this title, if it is proposed in a plan to cure a default, the amount necessary to cure the default, shall be determined in accordance with the underlying agreement and applicable nonbankruptcy law.

§ 1223. Modification of plan before confirmation

(a) The debtor may modify the plan at any time before confirmation, but may not modify the plan so that the plan as modified fails to meet the requirements of section 1222 of this title.

(b) After the debtor files a modification under this section, the plan as modified becomes the plan.

(c) Any holder of a secured claim that has accepted or rejected the plan is deemed to have accepted or rejected, as the case may be, the plan as modified, unless the modification provides for a change in the rights of such holder from what such rights were under the plan before modification, and such holder changes such holder's previous acceptance or rejection.

§ 1224. Confirmation hearing

After expedited notice, the court shall hold a hearing on confirmation of the plan. A party in interest, the trustee, or the United States trustee may object to the confirmation of the plan. Except for cause, the hearing shall be concluded not later than 45 days after the filing of the plan.

§ 1225. Confirmation of plan

(a) Except as provided in subsection (b), the court shall confirm a plan if—

(1) the plan complies with the provisions of this chapter and with the other applicable provisions of this title;

(2) any fee, charge, or amount required under chapter 123 of title 28, or by the plan, to be paid before confirmation, has been paid;

(3) the plan has been proposed in good faith and not by any means forbidden by law;

(4) the value, as of the effective date of the plan, of property to be distributed under the plan on account of each allowed unsecured claim is not less than the amount that would be paid on such claim if the estate of the debtor were liquidated under chapter 7 of this title on such date;

(5) with respect to each allowed secured claim provided for by the plan—
    (A) the holder of such claim has accepted the plan;
    (B)(i) the plan provides that the holder of such claim retain the lien securing such claim; and
        (ii) the value, as of the effective date of the plan, of property to be distributed by the trustee or the debtor under the plan on account of such claim is not less than the allowed amount of such claim; or
    (C) the debtor surrenders the property securing such claim to such holder; and

(6) the debtor will be able to make all payments under the plan and to comply with the plan.

(b)(1) If the trustee or the holder of an allowed unsecured claim objects to the confirmation of the plan, then the court may not approve the plan unless, as of the effective date of the plan—
    (A) the value of the property to be distributed under the plan on account of such claim is not less than the amount of such claim; or
    (B) the plan provides that all of the debtor's projected disposable income to be received in the three-year period, or such longer period as the court may approve under section 1222(c), beginning on the date that the first payment is due under the plan will be applied to make payments under the plan.

(2) For purposes of this subsection, "disposable income" means income which is received by the debtor and which is not reasonably necessary to be expended—
    (A) for the maintenance or support of the debtor or a dependent of the debtor; or
    (B) for the payment of expenditures necessary for the continuation, preservation, and operation of the debtor's business.

(c) After confirmation of a plan, the court may order any entity from whom the debtor receives income to pay all or any part of such income to the trustee.

§ 1226. Payments

(a) Payments and funds received by the trustee shall be retained by the trustee until confirmation or denial of confirmation of a plan. If a plan is confirmed, the trustee shall distribute any such payment in accordance with the plan. If a plan is not confirmed, the trustee shall return any such payments to the debtor, after deducting—

(1) any unpaid claim allowed under section 503(b) of this title; and

(2) if a standing trustee is serving in the case, the percentage fee fixed for such standing trustee.

(b) Before or at the time of each payment to creditors under the plan, there shall be paid—

(1) any unpaid claim of the kind specified in section 507(a)(1) of this title; and

(2) if a standing trustee appointed under section 1202(c) of this title is serving in the case, the percentage fee fixed for such standing trustee under section 1202(d) of this title.

(c) Except as otherwise provided in the plan or in the order confirming the plan, the trustee shall make payments to creditors under the plan.

§ 1227. Effect of confirmation

(a) Except as provided in section 1228(a) of this title, the provisions of a confirmed plan bind the debtor, each creditor, each equity security holder, and each general partner in the debtor, whether or not the claim of such creditor, such equity security holder, or such general partner in the debtor is provided for by the plan, and whether or not such creditor, such equity security holder, or such general partner in the debtor has objected to, has accepted, or has rejected the plan.

(b) Except as otherwise provided in the plan or the order confirming the plan, the confirmation of a plan vests all of the property of the estate in the debtor.

(c) Except as provided in section 1228(a) of this title and except as otherwise provided in the plan or in the order confirming the plan, the property vesting in the debtor under subsection (b) of this section is free and clear of any claim or interest of any creditor provided for by the plan.

§ 1228. Discharge

(a) As soon as practicable after completion by the debtor of all payments under the plan, other than payments to holders of allowed claims provided for under section 1222(b)(5) or 1222(b)(9) of this title, unless the court approves a written waiver of discharge executed by the debtor after the order for relief under this chapter, the court shall grant the debtor a discharge of all debts provided for by the plan allowed under section 503 of this title or disallowed under section 502 of this title, except any debt—

(1) provided for under section 1222(b)(5) or 1222(b)(9) of this title; or

(2) of the kind specified in section 523(a) of this title.

(b) At any time after the confirmation of the plan and after notice and a hearing, the court may grant a discharge to a debtor that has not completed payments under the plan only if—

(1) the debtor's failure to complete such payments is due to circumstances for which the debtor should not justly be held accountable;

(2) the value, as of the effective date of the plan, of property actually distributed under the plan on account of each allowed unsecured claim is not less than the amount that would have been paid on such claim if the estate of the debtor had been liquidated under chapter 7 of this title on such date; and

(3) modification of the plan under section 1229 of this title is not practicable.

(c) A discharge granted under subsection (b) of this section discharges the debtor from all unsecured debts provided for by the plan or disallowed under section 502 of this title, except any debt—

(1) provided for under section 1222(b)(5) or 1222(b)(9) of this title; or

(2) of a kind specified in section 523(a) of this title.

(d) On request of a party in interest before one year after a discharge under this section is granted, and after notice and a hearing, the court may revoke such discharge only if—

(1) such discharge was obtained by the debtor through fraud; and

(2) the requesting party did not know of such fraud until after such discharge was granted.

(e) After the debtor is granted a discharge, the court shall terminate the services of any trustee serving in the case.

§ 1229. Modification of plan after confirmation

(a) At any time after confirmation of the plan but before the completion of payments under such plan, the plan may be modified, on request of the debtor, the trustee, or the holder of an allowed unsecured claim, to—

(1) increase or reduce the amount of payments on claims of a particular class provided for by the plan;

(2) extend or reduce the time for such payments; or

(3) alter the amount of the distribution to a creditor whose claim is provided for by the plan to the extent necessary to take account of any payment of such claim other than under the plan.

(b)(1) Sections 1222(a), 1222(b), and 1223(c) of this title and the requirements of section 1225(a) of this title apply to any modification under subsection (a) of this section.

(2) The plan as modified becomes the plan unless, after notice and a hearing, such modification is disapproved.

(c) A plan modified under this section may not provide for payments over a period that expires after three years after the time that the first payment under the original confirmed plan was due, unless the court, for cause, approves a longer period, but the court may not approve a period that expires after five years after such time.

§ 1230. Revocation of an order of confirmation

(a) On request of a party in interest at any time within 180 days after the date of the entry of an order of confirmation under section 1225 of this title, and after notice and a hearing, the court may revoke such order if such order was procured by fraud.

(b) If the court revokes an order of confirmation under subsection (a) of this section, the court shall dispose of the case under section 1207 of this title, unless, within the time fixed by the court, the debtor proposes and the court confirms a modification of the plan under section 1229 of this title.

§ 1231. Special tax provisions

(a) For the purpose of any State or local law imposing a tax on or measured by income, the taxable period of a debtor that is an individual shall terminate on the date of the order for relief under this chapter, unless the case was converted under section 706 of this title.

(b) The trustee shall make a State or local tax return of income for the estate of an individual debtor in a case under this chapter for each taxable period after the order for relief under this chapter during which the case is pending.

(c) The issuance, transfer, or exchange of a security, or the making or delivery of an instrument of transfer under a plan confirmed under section 1225 of this title, may not be taxed under any law imposing a stamp tax or similar tax.

(d) The court may authorize the proponent of a plan to request a determination, limited to questions of law, by a State or local governmental unit charged with responsibility for collection or determination of a tax on or measured by income, of the tax effects, under section 346 of this title and under the law imposing such tax, of the plan. In the event of an actual controversy, the court may declare such effects after the earlier of—

(1) the date on which such governmental unit responds to the request under this subsection; or

(2) 270 days after such request.

CHAPTER 13

ADJUSTMENT OF DEBTS OF AN INDIVIDUAL WITH REGULAR INCOME

Subchapter I—Officers, Administration, and the Estate

§ 1301. Stay of action against codebtor

(a) Except as provided in subsections (b) and (c) of this section, after the order for relief under this chapter, a creditor may not act, or commence or continue any civil action, to collect all or any part of a consumer debt of the debtor from any individual that is liable on such debt with the debtor, or that secured such debt, unless—

(1) such individual became liable on or secured such debt in the ordinary course of such individual's business; or

(2) the case is closed, dismissed, or converted to a case under chapter 7 or 11 of this title.

(b) A creditor may present a negotiable instrument, and may give notice of dishonor of such an instrument.

(c) On request of a party in interest and after notice and a hearing, the court shall grant relief from the stay provided by subsection (a) of this section with respect to a creditor, to the extent that—

(1) as between the debtor and the individual protected under subsection (a) of this section, such individual received the consideration for the claim held by such creditor;

(2) the plan filed by the debtor proposes not to pay such claim; or

(3) such creditor's interest would be irreparably harmed by continuation of such stay.

(d) Twenty days after the filing of a request under subsection (c)(2) of this section for relief from the stay provided by subsection (a) of this section, such stay is terminated with respect to the party in interest making such request, unless the debtor or any individual that is liable on such debt with the debtor files and serves upon such party in interest a written objection to the taking of the proposed action.

§ 1302. Trustee

(a) If the United States trustee appoints an individual under section 586(b) of title 28 to serve as standing trustee in cases under this chapter and if such individual qualifies under section 322 of this title, then such individual shall serve as trustee in the case. Otherwise, the United States trustee shall appoint one disinterested person to serve as trustee in the case or the United States trustee may serve as a trustee in the case.

(b) The trustee shall—

(1) perform the duties specified in sections 704(2), 704(3), 704(4), 704(5), 704(6), 704(7) and 704(9) of this title;

(2) appear and be heard at any hearing that concerns—
   (A) the value of property subject to a lien;
   (B) confirmation of a plan; or
   (C) modification of the plan after confirmation;

(3) dispose of, under regulations issued by the Director of the Administrative Office of the United States Courts, moneys received or to be received in a case under chapter XIII of the Bankruptcy Act;

(4) advise, other than on legal matters, and assist the debtor in performance under the plan; and

(5) ensure that the debtor commences making timely payments under section 1326 of this title.

(c) If the debtor is engaged in business, then in addition to the duties specified in subsection (b) of this section, the trustee shall perform the duties specified in sections 1106(a)(3) and 1106(a)(4) of this title.

§ 1303. Rights and powers of debtor

Subject to any limitations on a trustee under this chapter, the debtor shall have, exclusive of the trustee, the rights and powers of a trustee under sections 363(b), 363(d), 363(e), 363(f), and 363(*l*), of this title.

§ 1304. Debtor engaged in business

(a) A debtor that is self-employed and incurs trade credit in the production of income from such employment is engaged in business.

(b) Unless the court orders otherwise, a debtor engaged in business may operate the business of the debtor and, subject to any limitations on a trustee under sections 363(c) and 364 of this title and to such limitations or conditions as the court prescribes, shall have, exclusive of the trustee, the rights and powers of the trustee under such sections.

(c) A debtor engaged in business shall perform the duties of the trustee specified in section 704(8) of this title.

§ 1305. Filing and allowance of postpetition claims

(a) A proof of claim may be filed by any entity that holds a claim against the debtor—

(1) for taxes that become payable to a governmental unit while the case is pending; or

(2) that is a consumer debt, that arises after the date of the order for relief under this chapter, and that is for property or services necessary for the debtor's performance under the plan.

(b) Except as provided in subsection (c) of this section, a claim filed under subsection (a) of this section shall be allowed or disallowed under section 502 of this title, but shall be determined as of the date such claim arises, and shall be allowed under section 502(a), 502(b), or 502(c) of this title, or disallowed under section 502(d) or 502(e) of this title, the same as if such claim had arisen before the date of the filing of the petition.

(c) A claim filed under subsection (a)(2) of this section shall be disallowed if the holder of such claim knew or should have known that prior approval by the trustee of the debtor's incurring the obligation was practicable and was not obtained.

§ 1306. Property of the estate

(a) Property of the estate includes, in addition to the property specified in section 541 of this title—

(1) all property of the kind specified in such section that the debtor acquires after the commencement of the case but before the case is closed, dismissed, or converted to a case under chapter 7, 11, or 12 of this title whichever occurs first; and

(2) earnings from services performed by the debtor after the commencement of the case but before the case is closed, dismissed, or converted to a case under chapter 7, 11, or 12 of this title, whichever occurs first.

(b) Except as provided in a confirmed plan or order confirming a plan, the debtor shall remain in possession of all property of the estate.

§ 1307. Conversion or dismissal

(a) The debtor may convert a case under this chapter to a case under chapter 7 of this title at any time. Any waiver of the right to convert under this subsection is unenforceable.

(b) On request of the debtor at any time, if the case has not been converted under section 706, 1112, or 1208 of this title, the court shall dismiss a case under this chapter. Any waiver of the right to dismiss under this subsection is unenforceable.

(c) Except as provided in subsection (e) of this section, on request of a party in interest or the United States trustee and after notice and a hearing, the court may convert a case under this chapter to a case under chapter 7 of this title, or may dismiss a case under this chapter, whichever is in the best interests of creditors and the estate, for cause, including—

(1) unreasonable delay by the debtor that is prejudicial to creditors;

(2) nonpayment of any fees and charges required under chapter 123 of title 28;

(3) failure to file a plan timely under section 1321 of this title;

(4) failure to commence making timely payments under section 1326 of this title;

(5) denial of confirmation of a plan under section 1325 of this title and denial of a request made for additional time for filing another plan or a modification of a plan;

(6) material default by the debtor with respect to a term of a confirmed plan;

(7) revocation of the order of confirmation under section 1330 of this title, and denial of confirmation of a modified plan under section 1329 of this title;

(8) termination of a confirmed plan by reason of the occurrence of a condition specified in the plan other than completion of payments under the plan;

(9) only on request of the United States trustee, failure of the debtor to file, within fifteen days, or such additional time as the court may allow, after the filing of the petition commencing such case, the information required by paragraph (1) of section 521; or

(10) only on request of the United States trustee, failure to timely file the information required by paragraph (2) of section 521.

(d) Except as provided in subsection (e) of this section, at any time before the confirmation of a plan under section 1325 of this title, on request of a party in interest or the United States trustee and after notice and a hearing, the court may convert a case under this chapter to a case under chapter 11 or 12 of this title.

(e) The court may not convert a case under this chapter to a case under chapter 7, 11, or 12 of this title if the debtor is a farmer, unless the debtor requests such conversion.

(f) Notwithstanding any other provision of this section, a case may not be converted to a case under another chapter of this title unless the debtor may be a debtor under such chapter.

Subchapter II—The Plan

§ 1321. Filing of plan

The debtor shall file a plan.

§ 1322. Contents of plan

(a) The plan shall—

(1) provide for the submission of all or such portion of future earnings or other future income of the debtor to the supervision and control of the trustee as is necessary for the execution of the plan;

(2) provide for the full payment, in deferred cash payments, of all claims entitled to priority under section 507 of this title, unless the holder of a particular claim agrees to a different treatment of such claim; and

(3) if the plan classifies claims, provide the same treatment for each claim within a particular class.

(b) Subject to subsections (a) and (c) of this section, the plan may—

(1) designate a class or classes of unsecured claims, as provided in section 1122 of this title, but may not discriminate unfairly against any class so designated; however, such plan may treat claims for a consumer debt of the debtor if an individual is liable on such consumer debt with the debtor differently than other unsecured claims;

(2) modify the rights of holders of secured claims, other than a claim secured only by a security interest in real property that is the debtor's principal residence, or of holders of unsecured claims, or leave unaffected the rights of holders of any class of claims;

(3) provide for the curing or waiving of any default;

(4) provide for payments on any unsecured claim to be made concurrently with payments on any secured claim or any other unsecured claim;

(5) notwithstanding paragraph (2) of this subsection, provide for the curing of any default within a reasonable time and maintenance of payments while the case is pending on any unsecured claim or secured claim on which the last payment is due after the date on which the final payment under the plan is due;

(6) provide for the payment of all or any part of any claim allowed under section 1305 of this title;

(7) subject to section 365 of this title, provide for the assumption, rejection, or assignment of any executory contract or unexpired lease of the debtor not previously rejected under such section;

(8) provide for the payment of all or part of a claim against the debtor from property of the estate or property of the debtor;

(9) provide for the vesting of property of the estate, on confirmation of the plan or at a later time, in the debtor or in any other entity; and

(10) include any other appropriate provision not inconsistent with this title.

(c) Notwithstanding subsection (b)(2) and applicable nonbankruptcy law—

(1) a default with respect to, or that gave rise to, a lien on the debtor's principal residence may be cured under paragraph (3) or (5) of subsection (b) until such residence is sold at a foreclosure sale that is conducted in accordance with applicable nonbankruptcy law; and

(2) in a case in which the last payment on the original payment schedule for a claim secured only by a security interest in real property that is the debtor's principal residence is due before the date on which the final payment under the plan is due, the plan may provide for the payment of the claim as modified pursuant to section 1325(a)(5) of this title.

(d) The plan may not provide for payments over a period that is longer than three years, unless the court, for cause, approves a longer period, but the court may not approve a period that is longer than five years.

(e) Notwithstanding subsection (b)(2) of this section and sections

506(b) and 1325(a)(5) of this title, if it is proposed in a plan to cure a default, the amount necessary to cure the default, shall be determined in accordance with the underlying agreement and applicable nonbankruptcy law.

§ 1323. Modification of plan before confirmation

(a) The debtor may modify the plan at any time before confirmation, but may not modify the plan so that the plan as modified fails to meet the requirements of section 1322 of this title.

(b) After the debtor files a modification under this section, the plan as modified becomes the plan.

(c) Any holder of a secured claim that has accepted or rejected the plan is deemed to have accepted or rejected, as the case may be, the plan as modified, unless the modification provides for a change in the rights of such holder from what such rights were under the plan before modification, and such holder changes such holder's previous acceptance or rejection.

§ 1324. Confirmation hearing

After notice, the court shall hold a hearing on confirmation of the plan. A party in interest may object to confirmation of the plan.

§ 1325. Confirmation of plan

(a) Except as provided in subsection (b), the court shall confirm a plan if—

(1) the plan complies with the provisions of this chapter and with the other applicable provisions of this title;

(2) any fee, charge, or amount required under chapter 123 of title 28, or by the plan, to be paid before confirmation, has been paid;

(3) the plan has been proposed in good faith and not by any means forbidden by law;

(4) the value, as of the effective date of the plan, of property to be distributed under the plan on account of each allowed unsecured claim is not less than the amount that would be paid on such claim if the estate of the debtor were liquidated under chapter 7 of this title on such date;

(5) with respect to each allowed secured claim provided for by the plan—
  (A) the holder of such claim has accepted the plan;
  (B)(i) the plan provides that the holder of such claim retain the lien securing such claim; and
    (ii) the value, as of the effective date of the plan, of property to be distributed under the plan on account of such claim is not less than the allowed amount of such claim; or
  (C) the debtor surrenders the property securing such claim to such holder; and

(6) the debtor will be able to make all payments under the plan and to comply with the plan.

(b)(1) If the trustee or the holder of an allowed unsecured claim objects to the confirmation of the plan, then the court may not approve the plan unless, as of the effective date of the plan—
  (A) the value of the property to be distributed under the

plan on account of such claim is not less than the amount of such claim; or
  (B) the plan provides that all of the debtor's projected disposable income to be received in the three-year period beginning on the date that the first payment is due under the plan will be applied to make payments under the plan.

(2) For purposes of this subsection, "disposable income" means income which is received by the debtor and which is not reasonably necessary to be expended—
  (A) for the maintenance or support of the debtor or a dependent of the debtor, including charitable contributions (that meet the definition of "charitable contribution" under section 548(d)(3)) to a qualified religious or charitable entity or organization (as that term is defined in section 548(d)(4)) in an amount not to exceed 15 percent of the gross income of the debtor for the year in which the contributions are made; and
  (B) if the debtor is engaged in business, for the payment of expenditures necessary for the continuation, preservation, and operation of such business.

(c) After confirmation of a plan, the court may order any entity from whom the debtor receives income to pay all or any part of such income to the trustee.

§ 1326. Payments

(a)(1) Unless the court orders otherwise, the debtor shall commence making the payments proposed by a plan within 30 days after the plan is filed.

(2) A payment made under this subsection shall be retained by the trustee until confirmation or denial of confirmation of a plan. If a plan is confirmed, the trustee shall distribute any such payment in accordance with the plan as soon as practicable. If a plan is not confirmed, the trustee shall return any such payment to the debtor, after deducting any unpaid claim allowed under section 503(b) of this title.

(b) Before or at the time of each payment to creditors under the plan, there shall be paid—

(1) any unpaid claim of the kind specified in section 507(a)(1) of this title; and

(2) if a standing trustee appointed under section 586(b) of title 28 is serving in the case, the percentage fee fixed for such standing trustee under section 586(e)(1)(B) of title 28.

(c) Except as otherwise provided in the plan or in the order confirming the plan, the trustee shall make payments to creditors under the plan.

§ 1327. Effect of confirmation

(a) The provisions of a confirmed plan bind the debtor and each creditor, whether or not the claim of such creditor is provided for by the plan, and whether or not such creditor has objected to, has accepted, or has rejected the plan.

(b) Except as otherwise provided in the plan or the order confirming the plan, the confirmation of a plan vests all of the property of the estate in the debtor.

(c) Except as otherwise provided in the plan or in the order confirming the plan, the property vesting in the debtor under subsection (b) of this section is free and clear of any claim or interest of any creditor provided for by the plan.

§ 1328. Discharge

(a) As soon as practicable after completion by the debtor of all payments under the plan, unless the court approves a written waiver of discharge executed by the debtor after the order for relief under this chapter, the court shall grant the debtor a discharge of all debts provided for by the plan or disallowed under section 502 of this title, except any debt—

(1) provided for under section 1322(b)(5) of this title;

(2) of the kind specified in paragraph (5), (8) or (9) of section 523(a) or 523(a)(9) of this title; or

(3) for restitution, or a criminal fine, included in a sentence on the debtor's conviction of a crime.

(b) At any time after the confirmation of the plan and after notice and a hearing, the court may grant a discharge to a debtor that has not completed payments under the plan only if—

(1) the debtor's failure to complete such payments is due to circumstances for which the debtor should not justly be held accountable;

(2) the value, as of the effective date of the plan, of property actually distributed under the plan on account of each allowed unsecured claim is not less than the amount that would have been paid on such claim if the estate of the debtor had been liquidated under chapter 7 of this title on such date; and

(3) modification of the plan under section 1329 of this title is not practicable.

(c) A discharge granted under subsection (b) of this section discharges the debtor from all unsecured debts provided for by the plan or disallowed under section 502 of this title, except any debt—

(1) provided for under section 1322(b)(5) of this title; or

(2) of a kind specified in section 523(a) of this title.

(d) Notwithstanding any other provision of this section, a discharge granted under this section does not discharge the debtor from any debt based on an allowed claim filed under section 1305(a)(2) of this title if prior approval by the trustee of the debtor's incurring such debt was practicable and was not obtained.

(e) On request of a party in interest before one year after a discharge under this section is granted, and after notice and a hearing, the court may revoke such discharge only if—

(1) such discharge was obtained by the debtor through fraud; and

(2) the requesting party did not know of such fraud until after such discharge was granted.

§ 1329. Modification of plan after confirmation

(a) At any time after confirmation of the plan but before the completion of payments under such plan, the plan may be modified, upon request of the debtor, the trustee, or the holder of an allowed unsecured claim, to—

(1) increase or reduce the amount of payments on claims of a particular class provided for by the plan;

(2) extend or reduce the time for such payments; or

(3) alter the amount of the distribution to a creditor whose claim is provided for by the plan to the extent necessary to take account of any payment of such claim other than under the plan.

(b)(1) Sections 1322(a), 1322(b), and 1323(c) of this title and the requirements of section 1325(a) of this title apply to any modification under subsection (a) of this section.

(2) The plan as modified becomes the plan unless, after notice and a hearing, such modification is disapproved.

(c) A plan modified under this section may not provide for payments over a period that expires after three years after the time that the first payment under the original confirmed plan was due, unless the court, for cause, approves a longer period, but the court may not approve a period that expires after five years after such time.

§ 1330. Revocation of an order of confirmation

(a) On request of a party in interest at any time within 180 days after the date of the entry of an order of confirmation under section 1325 of this title, and after notice and a hearing, the court may revoke such order if such order was procured by fraud.

(b) If the court revokes an order of confirmation under subsection (a) of this section, the court shall dispose of the case under section 1307 of this title, unless, within the time fixed by the court, the debtor proposes and the court confirms a modification of the plan under section 1329 of this title.

A.2 Other Bankruptcy Statutes

A.2.1 Selected Provisions of Title 28 of the United States Code

TITLE 28—JUDICIARY AND JUDICIAL PROCEDURE

* * *

28 U.S.C. § 151. Designation of bankruptcy courts
28 U.S.C. § 152. Appointment of bankruptcy judges
28 U.S.C. § 153. Salaries; character of service
28 U.S.C. § 154. Division of business; chief judge
28 U.S.C. § 155. Temporary transfer of bankruptcy judges
28 U.S.C. § 156. Staff; expenses
28 U.S.C. § 157. Procedures
28 U.S.C. § 158. Appeals

* * *

28 U.S.C. § 581. United States trustees
28 U.S.C. § 582. Assistant United State trustees
28 U.S.C. § 583. Oath of office

28 U.S.C. § 151. Designation of bankruptcy courts

In each judicial district, the bankruptcy judges in regular active service shall constitute a unit of the district court to be known as the bankruptcy court for that district. Each bankruptcy judge, as a judicial officer of the district court, may exercise the authority conferred under this chapter with respect to any action, suit, or proceeding and may preside alone and hold a regular or special session of the court, except as otherwise provided by law or by rule or order of the district court.

28 U.S.C. § 152. Appointment of bankruptcy judges

(a)(1) The United States court of appeals for the circuit shall appoint bankruptcy judges for the judicial districts established in paragraph (2) in such numbers as are established in such paragraph. Such appointments shall be made after considering the recommendations of the Judicial Conference submitted pursuant to subsection (b). Each bankruptcy judge shall be appointed for a term of fourteen years, subject to the provisions of subsection (e). However, upon the expiration of the term, a bankruptcy judge may, with the approval of the judicial council of the circuit, continue to perform the duties of the office until the earlier of the date which is 180 days after the expiration of the term or the date of the appointment of a successor. Bankruptcy judges shall serve as judicial officers of the United States district court established under Article III of the Constitution.

(2) The bankruptcy judges appointed pursuant to this section shall be appointed for the several judicial districts as follows:

[table omitted]

(3) Whenever a majority of the judges of any court of appeals cannot agree upon the appointment of a bankruptcy judge, the chief judge of such court shall make such appointment.

(4) The judges of the district courts for the territories shall serve as the bankruptcy judges for such courts. The United States court of appeals for the circuit within which such a territorial district court is located may appoint bankruptcy judges under this chapter for such district if authorized to do so by the Congress of the United States under this section.

(b)(1) The Judicial Conference of the United States shall, from time to time, and after considering the recommendations submitted by the Director of the Administrative Office of the United States Courts after such Director has consulted with the judicial council of the circuit involved, determine the official duty stations of bankruptcy judges and places of holding court.

(2) The Judicial Conference shall, from time to time, submit recommendations to the Congress regarding the number of bankruptcy judges needed and the districts in which such judges are needed.

(3) Not later than December 31, 1994, and not later than the end of each 2-year period thereafter, the Judicial Conference of the United States shall conduct a comprehensive review of all judicial districts to assess the continuing need for the bankruptcy judges authorized by this section, and shall report to the Congress its findings and any recommendations for the elimination of any authorized position which can be eliminated when a vacancy exists by reason of resignation, retirement, removal, or death.

(c) Each bankruptcy judge may hold court at such places within the judicial district, in addition to the official duty station of such judge, as the business of the court may require.

(d) With the approval of the Judicial Conference and of each of the judicial councils involved, a bankruptcy judge may be designated to serve in any district adjacent to or near the district for which such bankruptcy judge was appointed.

(e) A bankruptcy judge may be removed during the term for which such bankruptcy judge is appointed, only for incompetence, misconduct, neglect of duty, or physical or mental disability and only by the judicial council of the circuit in which the judge's official duty station is located. Removal may not occur unless a majority of all of the judges of such council concur in the order of removal. Before any order of removal may be entered, a full specification of charges shall be furnished to such bankruptcy judge who shall be accorded an opportunity to be heard on such charges.

28 U.S.C. § 153. Salaries; character of service

(a) Each bankruptcy judge shall serve on a full-time basis and shall receive as full compensation for his services, a salary at an annual rate that is equal to 92 percent of the salary of a judge of the district court of the United States as determined pursuant to section 135, to be paid at such times as the Judicial Conference of the United

States determines.

(b) A bankruptcy judge may not engage in the practice of law and may not engage in any other practice, business, occupation, or employment inconsistent with the expeditious, proper, and impartial performance of such bankruptcy judge's duties as a judicial officer. The Conference may promulgate appropriate rules and regulations to implement this subsection.

(c) Each individual appointed under this chapter shall take the oath or affirmation prescribed by section 453 of this title before performing the duties of the office of bankruptcy judge.

(d) A bankruptcy judge appointed under this chapter shall be exempt from the provisions of subchapter I of chapter 63 of title 5.

28 U.S.C. § 154. Division of businesses; chief judge

(a) Each bankruptcy court for a district having more than one bankruptcy judge shall by majority vote promulgate rules for the division of business among the bankruptcy judges to the extent that the division of business is not otherwise provided for by the rules of the district court.

(b) In each district court having more than one bankruptcy judge the district court shall designate one judge to serve as chief judge of such bankruptcy court. Whenever a majority of the judges of such district court cannot agree upon the designation as chief judge, the chief judge of such district court shall make such designation. The chief judge of the bankruptcy court shall ensure that the rules of the bankruptcy court and of the district court are observed and that the business of the bankruptcy court is handled effectively and expeditiously.

28 U.S.C. § 155. Temporary transfer of bankruptcy judges

(a) A bankruptcy judge may be transferred to serve temporarily as a bankruptcy judge in any judicial district other than the judicial district for which such bankruptcy judge was appointed upon the approval of the judicial council of each of the circuits involved.

(b) A bankruptcy judge who has retired may, upon consent, be recalled to serve as a bankruptcy judge in any judicial district by the judicial council of the circuit within which such district is located. Upon recall, a bankruptcy judge may receive a salary for such service in accordance with regulations promulgated by the Judicial Conference of the United States, subject to the restrictions on the payment of an annuity in section 377 of this title or in subchapter III of chapter 83, and chapter 84, of title 5 which are applicable to such judge.

28 U.S.C. § 156. Staff; expenses

(a) Each bankruptcy judge may appoint a secretary, a law clerk, and such additional assistants as the Director of the Administrative Office of the United States Courts determines to be necessary. A law clerk appointed under this section shall be exempt from the provisions of subchapter I of chapter 63 of title 5, unless specifically included by the appointing judge or by local rule of court.

(b) Upon certification to the judicial council of the circuit involved and to the Director of the Administrative Office of the United States Courts that the number of cases and proceedings pending within the jurisdiction under section 1334 of this title within a judicial district so warrants, the bankruptcy judges for such district may appoint an individual to serve as clerk of such bankruptcy court. The clerk may appoint, with the approval of such bankruptcy judges, and in such number as may be approved by the Director, necessary deputies, and may remove such deputies with the approval of such bankruptcy judges.

(c) Any court may utilize facilities or services, either on or off the court's premises, which pertain to the provision of notices, dockets, calendars, and other administrative information to parties in cases filed under the provisions of title 11, United States Code, where the costs of such facilities or services are paid for out of the assets of the estate and are not charged to the United States. The utilization of such facilities or services shall be subject to such conditions and limitations as the pertinent circuit council may prescribe.

(d) No office of the bankruptcy clerk of court may be consolidated with the district clerk of court office without the prior approval of the Judicial Conference and the Congress.

(e) In a judicial district where a bankruptcy clerk has been appointed pursuant to subsection (b), the bankruptcy clerk shall be the official custodian of the records and dockets of the bankruptcy court.

(f) For purposes of financial accountability in a district where a bankruptcy clerk has been certified, such clerk shall be accountable for and pay into the Treasury all fees, costs, and other monies collected by such clerk except uncollected fees not required by an Act of Congress to be prepaid. Such clerk shall make returns thereof to the Director of the Administrative Office of the United States Courts and the Director of the Executive Office For United States Trustees, under regulations prescribed by such Directors.

28 U.S.C. § 157. Procedures

(a) Each district court may provide that any or all cases under title 11 and any or all proceedings arising under title 11 or arising in or related to a case under title 11 shall be referred to the bankruptcy judges for the district.

(b)(1) Bankruptcy judges may hear and determine all cases under title 11 and all core proceedings arising under title 11 or arising in a case under title 11 referred under subsection (a) of this section, and may enter appropriate orders and judgments, subject to review under section 158 of this title.

(2) Core proceedings include, but are not limited to—
   (A) matters concerning the administration of the estate;
   (B) allowance or disallowance of claims against the estate or exemptions from property of the estate, and estimation of claims or interests for the purposes of confirming a plan under chapter 11, 12, or 13 of title 11 but not the liquidation or estimation of contingent or unliquidated personal injury tort or wrongful death claims against the estate for purposes of distribution in a case under title 11;
   (C) counterclaims by the estate against persons filing claims against the estate;
   (D) orders in respect to obtaining credit;
   (E) orders to turn over property of the estate;
   (F) proceedings to determine, avoid, or recover preferences;
   (G) motions to terminate, annul, or modify the automatic stay;
   (H) proceedings to determine, avoid, or recover fraudulent conveyances;
   (I) determinations as to the dischargeability of particular debts;

(J) objections to discharges;

(K) determinations of the validity, extent, or priority of liens;

(L) confirmations of plans;

(M) orders approving the use or lease of property, including the use of cash collateral;

(N) orders approving the sale of property other than property resulting from claims brought by the estate against persons who have not filed claims against the estate; and

(O) other proceedings affecting the liquidation of the assets of the estate or the adjustment of the debtor-creditor or the equity security holder relationship, except personal injury tort or wrongful death claims.

(3) The bankruptcy judge shall determine, on the judge's own motion or on timely motion of a party, whether a proceeding is a core proceeding under this subsection or is a proceeding that is otherwise related to a case under title 11. A determination that a proceeding is not a core proceeding shall not be made solely on the basis that its resolution may be affected by State law.

(4) Non-core proceedings under section 157(b)(2)(B) of title 28, United States Code, shall not be subject to the mandatory abstention provisions of section 1334(c)(2).

(5) The district court shall order that personal injury tort and wrongful death claims shall be tried in the district court in which the bankruptcy case is pending, or in the district court in the district in which the claim arose, as determined by the district court in which the bankruptcy case is pending.

(c)(1) A bankruptcy judge may hear a proceeding that is not a core proceeding but that is otherwise related to a case under title 11. In such proceeding, the bankruptcy judge shall submit proposed findings of fact and conclusions of law to the district court, and any final order or judgment shall be entered by the district judge after considering the bankruptcy judge's proposed findings and conclusions and after reviewing de novo those matters to which any party has timely and specifically objected.

(2) Notwithstanding the provisions of paragraph (1) of this subsection, the district court, with the consent of all the parties to the proceeding, may refer a proceeding related to a case under title 11 to a bankruptcy judge to hear and determine and to enter appropriate orders and judgments, subject to review under section 158 of this title.

(d) The district court may withdraw, in whole or in part, any case or proceeding referred under this section, on its own motion or on timely motion of any party, for cause shown. The district court shall, on timely motion of a party, so withdraw a proceeding if the court determines that resolution of the proceeding requires consideration of both title 11 and other laws of the United States regulating organizations or activities affecting interstate commerce.

(e) If the right to a jury trial applies in a proceeding that may be heard under this section by a bankruptcy judge, the bankruptcy judge may conduct the jury trial if specially designated to exercise such jurisdiction by the district court and with the express consent of all the parties.

28 U.S.C. § 158. Appeals

(a) The district courts of the United States shall have jurisdiction to hear appeals

(1) from final judgments, orders, and decrees;

(2) from interlocutory orders and decrees issued under section 1121(d) of title 11 increasing or reducing the time periods referred to in section 1121 of such title; and

(3) with leave of the court, from other interlocutory orders and decrees;

of bankruptcy judges entered in cases and proceedings referred to the bankruptcy judges under section 157 of this title. An appeal under this subsection shall be taken only to the district court for the judicial district in which the bankruptcy judge is serving.

(b)(1) The judicial council of a circuit shall establish a bankruptcy appellate panel service composed of bankruptcy judges of the districts in the circuit who are appointed by the judicial council in accordance with paragraph (3), to hear and determine, with the consent of all the parties, appeals under subsection (a) unless the judicial council finds that—

(A) there are insufficient judicial resources available in the circuit; or

(B) establishment of such service would result in undue delay or increased cost to parties in cases under title 11.

Not later than 90 days after making the finding, the judicial council shall submit to the Judicial Conference of the United States a report containing the factual basis of such finding.

(2)(A) a judicial council may reconsider, at any time, the finding described in paragraph (1).

(B) On the request of a majority of the district judges in a circuit for which a bankruptcy appellate panel service is established under paragraph (1), made after the expiration of the 1-year period beginning on the date such service is established, the judicial council of the circuit shall determine whether a circumstance specified in subparagraph (A) or (B) of such paragraph exists.

(C) On its own motion, after the expiration of the 3-year period beginning on the date a bankruptcy appellate panel service is established under paragraph (1), the judicial council of the circuit may determine whether a circumstance specified in subparagraph (A) or (B) of such paragraph exists.

(D) If the judicial council finds that either of such circumstances exists, the judicial council may provide for the completion of the appeals then pending before such service and the orderly termination of such service.

(3) Bankruptcy judges appointed under paragraph (1) shall be appointed and may be reappointed under such paragraph.

(4) If authorized by the Judicial Conference of the United States, the judicial councils of 2 or more circuits may establish a joint bankruptcy appellate panel comprised of bankruptcy judges from the districts within the circuits for which such panel is established, to hear and determine, upon the consent of all the parties, appeals under subsection (a) of this section.

(5) An appeal to be heard under this subsection shall be heard by

a panel of 3 members of the bankruptcy appellate panel service, except that a member of such service may not hear an appeal originating in the district for which such member is appointed or designated under section 152 of this title.

(6) Appeals may not be heard under this subsection by a panel of the bankruptcy appellate panel service unless the district judges for the district in which the appeals occur, by majority vote, have authorized such service to hear and determine appeals originating in such district.

(c)(1) subject to subsection (b), each appeal under subsection (a) shall be heard by a 3-judge panel of the bankruptcy appellate panel service established under subsection (b)(1) unless—

    (A) the appellant elects at the time of filing the appeal; or

    (B) any other party elects, not later than 30 days after service of notice of the appeal;

to have such appeal heard by the district court.

(2) An appeal under subsection (a) and (b) of this section shall be taken in the same manner as appeals in civil proceedings generally are taken to the courts of appeals from the district courts and in the time provided by Rule 8002 of the Bankruptcy Rules.

(d) The courts of appeals shall have jurisdiction of appeals from all final decisions, judgments, orders, and decrees entered under subsections (a) and (b) of this section.

* * *

28 U.S.C. § 581. United States trustees

(a) The Attorney General shall appoint one United States trustee for each of the following regions composed of Federal judicial districts (without regard to section 451):

(1) The judicial districts established for the States of Maine, Massachusetts, New Hampshire, and Rhode Island.

(2) The judicial districts established for the States of Connecticut, New York, and Vermont.

(3) The judicial districts established for the States of Delaware, New Jersey, and Pennsylvania.

(4) The judicial districts established for the States of Maryland, North Carolina, South Carolina, Virginia, and West Virginia and for the District of Columbia.

(5) The judicial districts established for the States of Louisiana and Mississippi.

(6) The Northern District of Texas and the Eastern District of Texas.

(7) The Southern District of Texas and the Western District of Texas.

(8) The judicial districts established for the States of Kentucky and Tennessee.

(9) The judicial districts established for the States of Michigan and Ohio.

(10) The Central District of Illinois and the Southern District of Illinois; and the judicial districts established for the State of Indiana.

(11) The Northern District of Illinois; and the judicial districts established for the State of Wisconsin.

(12) The judicial districts established for the States of Minnesota, Iowa, North Dakota, and South Dakota.

(13) The judicial districts established for the States of Arkansas, Nebraska, and Missouri.

(14) The District of Arizona.

(15) The Southern District of California; and the judicial districts established for the State of Hawaii, and for Guam and the Commonwealth of the Northern Mariana Islands.

(16) The Central District of California.

(17) The Eastern District of California and the Northern District of California; and the judicial district established for the State of Nevada.

(18) The judicial districts established for the States of Alaska, Idaho (exclusive of Yellowstone National Park), Montana (exclusive of Yellowstone National Park), Oregon, and Washington.

(19) The judicial districts established for the States of Colorado, Utah, and Wyoming (including those portions of Yellowstone National Park situated in the States of Montana and Idaho).

(20) The judicial districts established for the States of Kansas, New Mexico, and Oklahoma.

(21) The judicial districts established for the States of Alabama, Florida, and Georgia and for the Commonwealth of Puerto Rico and the Virgin Islands of the United States.

(b) Each United States trustee shall be appointed for a term of five years. On the expiration of his term, a United States trustee shall continue to perform the duties of his office until his successor is appointed and qualifies.

(c) Each United States trustee is subject to removal by the Attorney General.

28 U.S.C. § 582. Assistant United States trustees

(a) The Attorney General may appoint one or more assistant United States trustees in any region when the public interest so requires.

(b) Each assistant United States trustee is subject to removal by the Attorney General.

28 U.S.C. § 583. Oath of Office

Each United States trustee and assistant United States trustee, before taking office, shall take an oath to execute faithfully his duties.

28 U.S.C. § 584. Official stations

The Attorney General may determine the official stations of the United States trustees and assistant United States trustees within the regions for which they were appointed.

28 U.S.C. § 585. Vacancies

(a) The Attorney General may appoint an acting United States trustee for a region in which the office of the United States trustee is vacant. The individual so appointed may serve until the date on which the vacancy is filled by appointment under section 581 of this title or by designation under subsection (b) of this section.

(b) The Attorney General may designate a United States trustee to serve in not more than two regions for such time as the public interest requires.

28 U.S.C. § 586. Duties; supervision by Attorney General

(a) Each United States trustee, within the region for which such United States trustee is appointed, shall—

(1) establish, maintain, and supervise a panel of private trustees that are eligible and available to serve as trustees in cases under chapter 7 of title 11;

(2) serve as and perform the duties of a trustee in a case under title 11 when required under title 11 to serve as trustee in such a case;

(3) supervise the administration of cases and trustees in cases under chapter 7, 11, 12 or 13 of title 11 by, whenever the United States trustee considers it to be appropriate—

  (A)(i) reviewing, in accordance with procedural guidelines adopted by the Executive Office of the United States Trustee (which guidelines shall be applied uniformly by the United States Trustee except when circumstances warrant different treatment), applications filed for compensation and reimbursement under section 330 of title 11; and

    (ii) filing with the court comments with respect to such application and, if the united states trustee considers it to be appropriate, objections to such application.

  (B) monitoring plans and disclosure statements filed in cases under chapter 11 of title 11 and filing with the court, in connection with hearings under sections 1125 and 1128 of such title, comments with respect to such plans and disclosure statements;

  (C) monitoring plans filed under chapters 12 and 13 of title 11 and filing with the court, in connection with hearings under sections 1224, 1229, 1324, and 1329 of such title, comments with respect to such plans;

  (D) taking such action as the United States trustee deems to be appropriate to ensure that all reports, schedules, and fees required to be filed under title 11 and this title by the debtor are properly and timely filed;

  (E) monitoring creditors' committees appointed under title 11;

  (F) notifying the appropriate United States attorney of matters which relate to the occurrence of any action which may constitute a crime under the laws of the United States and, on the request of the United States attorney, assisting the United States attorney in carrying out prosecutions based on such action;

  (G) monitoring the progress of cases under title 11 and taking such actions as the United States trustee deems to be appropriate to prevent undue delay in such progress; and

  (H) monitoring applications filed under section 327 of title 11 and, whenever the United States trustee deems it to be appropriate, filing with the court comments with respect to the approval of such applications;

(4) deposit or invest under section 345 of title 11 money received as trustee in cases under title 11;

(5) perform the duties prescribed for the United States trustee under title 11 and this title, and such duties consistent with title 11 and this title as the Attorney General may prescribe; and

(6) make such reports as the Attorney General directs.

(b) If the number of cases under chapter 12 or 13 of title 11 commenced in a particular region so warrants, the United States trustee for such region may, subject to the approval of the Attorney General, appoint one or more individuals to serve as standing trustee, or designate one or more assistant United States trustees to serve in cases under such chapter. The United States trustee for such region shall supervise any such individual appointed as standing trustee in the performance of the duties of standing trustee.

(c) Each United States trustee shall be under the general supervision of the Attorney General, who shall provide general coordination and assistance to the United States trustees.

(d) The Attorney General shall prescribe by rule qualifications for membership on the panels established by United States trustees under paragraph (a)(1) of this section, and qualifications for appointment under subsection (b) of this section to serve as standing trustee in cases under chapter 12 or 13 of title 11. The Attorney General may not require that an individual be an attorney in order to qualify for appointment under subsection (b) of this section to serve as standing trustee in cases under chapter 12 or 13 of title 11.

(e)(1) The Attorney General, after consultation with a United States trustee that has appointed an individual under subsection (b) of this section to serve as standing trustee in cases under chapter 12 or 13 of title 11, shall fix—

  (A) a maximum annual compensation for such individual consisting of—

    (i) an amount not to exceed the highest annual rate of basic pay in effect for level V of the Executive Schedule; and

    (ii) the cash value of employment benefits comparable to the employment benefits provided by the United States to individuals who are employed by the United States at the same rate of basic pay to perform similar services during the same period of time; and

  (B) a percentage fee not to exceed—

    (i) in the case of a debtor who is not a family farmer, ten percent; or

    (ii) in the case of a debtor who is a family farmer, the sum of—

      (I) not to exceed ten percent of the payments made under the plan of such debtor, with respect to payments in an aggregate amount not to exceed $450,000; and

      (II) three percent of payments made under the plan of such debtor, with respect to payments made after the aggregate amount of payments made under the plan exceeds $450,000;

    based on such maximum annual compensation and the actual, necessary expenses incurred by such individual as standing trustee.

(2) Such individual shall collect such percentage fee from all payments received by such individual under plans in the cases

under chapter 12 or 13 of title 11 for which such individual serves as standing trustee. Such individual shall pay to the United States trustee, and the United States trustee shall deposit in the United States Trustee System Fund—

(A) any amount by which the actual compensation of such individual exceeds 5 per centum upon all payments received under plans in cases under chapter 12 or 13 of title 11 for which such individual serves as standing trustee; and

(B) any amount by which the percentage for all such cases exceeds—

(i) such individual's actual compensation for such cases, as adjusted under subparagraph (A) of paragraph (1); plus

(ii) the actual, necessary expenses incurred by such individual as standing trustee in such cases. Subject to the approval of the Attorney General, any or all of the interest earned from the deposit of payments under plans by such individual may be utilized to pay actual, necessary expenses without regard to the percentage limitation contained in subparagraph (d)(1)(B) of this section.

28 U.S.C. § 587. Salaries

Subject to sections 5315 through 5317 of title 5, the Attorney General shall fix the annual salaries of United States trustees and assistant United States trustees at rates of compensation not in excess of the rate of basic compensation provided for Executive Level IV of the Executive Schedule set forth in section 5315 of title 5, United States Code.

28 U.S.C. § 588. Expenses

Necessary office expenses of the United States trustee shall be allowed when authorized by the Attorney General.

28 U.S.C. § 589. Staff and other employees

The United States trustee may employ staff and other employees on approval of the Attorney General.

28 U.S.C. § 589a. United States Trustee System Fund

(a) There is hereby established in the Treasury of the United States a special fund to be known as the "United States Trustee System Fund" (hereinafter in this section referred to as the "Fund"). Monies in the Fund shall be available to the Attorney General without fiscal year limitation in such amounts as may be specified in appropriations Acts for the following purposes in connection with the operations of United States trustees—

(1) salaries and related employee benefits;

(2) travel and transportation;

(3) rental of space;

(4) communication, utilities, and miscellaneous computer charges;

(5) security investigations and audits;

(6) supplies, books, and other materials for legal research;

(7) furniture and equipment;

(8) miscellaneous services, including those obtained by contract; and

(9) printing.

(b) There shall be deposited in the Fund—

(1) 23.08 per centum of the fees collected under section 1930(a)(1) of this title;

(2) 37.5 per centum of the fees collected under section 1930(a)(3) of this title;

(3) one-half of the fees collected under section 1930(a)(4) of this title;

(4) one-half of the fees collected under section 1930(a)(5);

(5) 60 per centum of the fees collected under section 1930(a)(6) of this title until a reorganization plan is confirmed;

(6) three-fourths of the fees collected under the last sentence of section 1930(a) of this title; and

(7) the compensation of trustees received under section 330(d) of title 11 by the clerks of the bankruptcy courts.

(c) Amounts in the Fund which are not concurrently needed for the purposes specified in subsection (a) shall be kept on deposit or invested in obligations of, or guaranteed by, the United States.

(d) The Attorney General shall transmit to the Congress, not later than 120 days after the end of each fiscal year, a detailed report on the amounts deposited in the Fund and a description of the expenditures made under this section.

(e) There are authorized to be appropriated to the Fund for any fiscal year such sums as may be necessary to supplement amounts deposited under subsection (b) for purposes specified in subsection (a).

* * *

28 U.S.C. § 959. Trustees and receivers suable; management; State laws

(a) Trustees, receivers or managers of any property, including debtors in possession, may be sued, without leave of the court appointing them, with respect to any of their acts or transactions in carrying on business connected with such property. Such actions shall be subject to the general equity power of such court so far as the same may be necessary to the ends of justice, but this shall not deprive a litigant of his right to trial by jury.

(b) Except as provided in section 1166 of title 11, a trustee, receiver or manager appointed in any cause pending in any court of the United States, including a debtor in possession, shall manage and operate the property in his possession as such trustee, receiver or manager according to the requirements of the valid laws of the State in which such property is situated, in the same manner that the owner or possessor thereof would be bound to do if in possession thereof.

28 U.S.C. § 960. Tax liability

Any officers and agents conducting any business under authority of a United States court shall be subject to all Federal, State and local taxes applicable to such business to the same extent as if it were conducted by an individual or corporation.

* * *

28 U.S.C. § 1334. Bankruptcy cases and proceedings

(a) Except as provided in subsection (b) of this section, the district courts shall have original and exclusive jurisdiction of all cases under title 11.

(b) Notwithstanding any Act of Congress that confers exclusive jurisdiction on a court or courts other than the district courts, the district courts shall have original but not exclusive jurisdiction of all civil proceedings arising under title 11, or arising in or related to cases under title 11.

(c)(1) Nothing in this section prevents a district court in the interest of justice, or in the interest of comity with State courts or respect for State law, from abstaining from hearing a particular proceeding arising under title 11 or arising in or related to a case under title 11.

(2) Upon timely motion of a party in a proceeding based upon a State law claim or State law cause of action, related to a case under title 11 but not arising under title 11 or arising in a case under title 11, with respect to which an action could not have been commenced in a court of the United States absent jurisdiction under this section, the district court shall abstain from hearing such proceeding if an action is commenced, and can be timely adjudicated, in a State forum of appropriate jurisdiction.

(d) Any decision to abstain or not abstain made under this subsection (other than a decision not to abstain in a proceeding described in subsection (c)(2)) is not reviewable by appeal or otherwise by the court of appeals under section 158(d), 1291, or 1292 of this title or by the supreme court of the united states under section 1254 of this title. This subsection shall not be construed to limit the applicability of the stay provided for by section 362 of title 11, United States Code, as such section applies to an action affecting the property of the estate in bankruptcy.

(e) The district court in which a case under title 11 is commenced or is pending shall have exclusive jurisdiction of all of the property, wherever located, of the debtor as of the commencement of such case, and of property of the estate.

* * *

28 U.S.C. § 1408. Venue of cases under title 11

Except as provided in section 1410 of this title, a case under title 11 may be commenced in the district court for the district—

(1) in which the domicile, residence, principal place of business in the United States, or principal assets in the United States, of the person or entity that is the subject of such case have been located for the one hundred and eighty days immediately preceding such commencement, or for a longer portion of such one-hundred-and-eighty-day period than the domicile, residence, or principal place of business, in the United States, or principal assets in the United States, of such person were located in any other district; or

(2) in which there is pending a case under title 11 concerning such person's affiliate, general partner, or partnership.

28 U.S.C. § 1409. Venue of proceedings arising under title 11 or arising in or related to cases under title 11

(a) Except as otherwise provided in subsections (b) and (d), a proceeding arising under title 11 or arising in or related to a case under title 11 may be commenced in the district court in which such case is pending.

(b) Except as provided in subsection (d) of this section, a trustee in a case under title 11 may commence a proceeding arising in or related to such case to recover a money judgment of or property worth less than $1,000 or a consumer debt of less than $5,000 only in the district court for the district in which the defendant resides.

(c) Except as provided in subsection (b) of this section, a trustee in a case under title 11 may commence a proceeding arising in or related to such case as statutory successor to the debtor or creditors under section 541 or 544(b) of title 11 in the district court for the district where the State or Federal court sits in which, under applicable nonbankruptcy venue provisions, the debtor or creditors, as the case may be, may have commenced an action on which such proceeding is based if the case under title 11 had not been commenced.

(d) A trustee may commence a proceeding arising under title 11 or arising in or related to a case under title 11 based on a claim arising after the commencement of such case from the operation of the business of the debtor only in the district court for the district where a State or Federal court sits in which, under applicable nonbankruptcy venue provisions, an action on such claim may have been brought.

(e) A proceeding arising under title 11 or arising in or related to a case under title 11, based on a claim arising after the commencement of such case from the operation of the business of the debtor, may be commenced against the representative of the estate in such case in the district court for the district where the State or Federal court sits in which the party commencing such proceeding may, under applicable nonbankruptcy venue provisions, have brought an action on such claim, or in the district court in which such case is pending.

28 U.S.C. § 1410. Venue of cases ancillary to foreign proceedings

(a) A case under section 304 of title 11 to enjoin the commencement or continuation of an action or proceeding in a State or Federal court, or the enforcement of a judgment, may be commenced only in the district court for the district where the State or Federal court sits in which is pending the action or proceeding against which the injunction is sought.

(b) A case under section 304 of title 11 to enjoin the enforcement of a lien against a property, or to require the turnover of property of an estate, may be commenced only in the district court for the district in which such property is found.

(c) A case under section 304 of title 11, other than a case specified in subsection (a) or (b) of this section, may be commenced only in the district court for the district in which is located the principal place of business in the United States, or the principal assets in the United States, of the estate that is the subject of such case.

28 U.S.C. § 1411. Jury trials

(a) Except as provided in subsection (b) of this section, this chapter and title 11 do not affect any right to trial by jury that an individual has under applicable nonbankruptcy law with regard to a personal injury or wrongful death tort claim.

(b) The district court may order the issues arising under section 303 of title 11 to be tried without a jury.

28 U.S.C. § 1412. Change of venue

A district court may transfer a case or proceeding under title 11 to a district court for another district, in the interest of justice or for the convenience of the parties.

* * *

28 U.S.C. § 1452. Removal of claims related to bankruptcy cases

(a) A party may remove any claim or cause of action in a civil action other than a proceeding before the United States Tax Court or a civil action by a governmental unit to enforce such governmental unit's police or regulatory power, to the district court for the district where such civil action is pending, if such district court has jurisdiction of such claim or cause of action under section 1334 of this title.

(b) The court to which such claim or cause of action is removed may remand such claim or cause of action on any equitable ground. An order entered under this subsection remanding a claim or cause of action, or a decision to not remand, is not reviewable by appeal or otherwise by the court of appeals under section 158(d), 1291, or 1292 of this title or by the Supreme Court of the United States under section 1254 of this title.

* * *

28 U.S.C. § 1927. Counsel's liability for excessive costs

Any attorney or other person admitted to conduct cases in any court of the United States or any Territory thereof who so multiplies the proceedings in any case unreasonably and vexatiously may be required by the court to satisfy personally the excess costs, expenses, and attorneys' fees reasonably incurred because of such conduct.

* * *

28 U.S.C. § 1930. Bankruptcy fees

(a) Notwithstanding section 1915 of this title, the parties commencing a case under title 11 shall pay to the clerk of the district court or the clerk of the bankruptcy court, if one has been certified pursuant to section 156(b) of this title, the following filing fees:

(1) For a case commenced under chapter 7 or 13 of title 11, $155.

(2) For a case commenced under chapter 9 of title 11, equal to the fee specified in paragraph (3) for filing a case under chapter 11 of title 11. The amount by which the fee payable under this paragraph exceeds $300 shall be deposited in the fund established under section 1931 of this title.

(3) For a case commenced under chapter 11 of title 11 that does not concern a railroad, as defined in section 101 of title 11, $830.

(4) For a case commenced under chapter 11 of title 11 concerning a railroad, as so defined, $1,000.

(5) For a case commenced under chapter 12 of title 11, $200.

(6) In addition to the filing fee paid to the clerk, a quarterly fee shall be paid to the United States trustee, for deposit in the Treasury, in each case under chapter 11 of title 11 for each quarter (including any fraction thereof) until the case is converted or dismissed, whichever occurs first. The fee shall be $250 for each quarter in which disbursements total less than $15,000; $500 for each quarter in which disbursements total $15,000 or more but less than $75,000; $750 for each quarter in which disbursements total $75,000 or more but less than $150,000; $1,250 for each quarter in which disbursements total $150,000 or more but less than $225,000; $1,500 for each quarter in which disbursements total $225,000 or more but less than $300,000; $3,750 for each quarter in which disbursements total $300,000 or more but less than $1,000,000; $5,000 for each quarter in which disbursements total $1,000,000 or more but less than $2,000,000; $7,500 for each quarter in which disbursements total $2,000,000 or more but less than $3,000,000; $8,000 for each quarter in which disbursements total $3,000,000 or more but less than $5,000,000; $10,000 for each quarter in which disbursements total $5,000,000 or more. The fee shall be payable on the last day of the calendar month following the calendar quarter for which the fee is owed.

(7) In districts that are not part of a United States trustee region as defined in section 581 of this title, the Judicial Conference of the United States may require the debtor in a case under chapter 11 of title 11 to pay fees equal to those imposed by paragraph (6) of this subsection. Such fees shall be deposited as offsetting receipts to the fund established under section 1931 of this title and shall remain available until expended.

An individual commencing a voluntary case or a joint case under title 11 may pay such fee in installments. For converting, on request of the debtor, a case under chapter 7, or 13 of title 11, to a case under chapter 11 of title 11, the debtor shall pay to the clerk of the court a fee of the amount equal to the difference between the fee specified in paragraph (3) and the fee specified in paragraph (1).

(b) The Judicial Conference of the United States may prescribe additional fees in cases under title 11 of the same kind as the Judicial Conference prescribes under section 1914(b) of this title.

(c) Upon the filing of any separate or joint notice of appeal or application for appeal or upon the receipt of any order allowing, or notice of the allowance of, an appeal or a writ of certiorari $5 shall be paid to the clerk of the court, by the appellant or petitioner.

(d) Whenever any case or proceeding is dismissed in any bankruptcy court for want of jurisdiction, such court may order the payment of just costs.

(e) The clerk of the court may collect only the fees prescribed under this section.

* * *

28 U.S.C. § 2075. Bankruptcy rules

The Supreme Court shall have the power to prescribe by general rules, the forms of process, writs, pleadings, and motions, and the practice and procedure in cases under title 11.

Such rules shall not abridge, enlarge, or modify any substantive right.

The Supreme Court shall transmit to Congress not later than May 1 of the year in which a rule prescribed under this section is to become effective a copy of the proposed rule. The rule shall take effect no earlier than december 1 of the year in which it is transmitted to congress unless otherwise provided by law.

* * *

A.2.2 *Selected Provisions of Other Titles of the United States Code*

TITLE 18—CRIMES AND CRIMINAL PROCEDURE

* * *

18 U.S.C. § 151. Definition
18 U.S.C. § 152. Concealment of assets; false oaths and claims; bribery
18 U.S.C. § 153. Embezzlement against estate
18 U.S.C. § 154. Adverse interest and conduct of officers
18 U.S.C. § 155. Fee agreements in cases under title 11 and receiverships
18 U.S.C. § 156. Knowing disregard of bankruptcy law or rule
18 U.S.C. § 157. Bankruptcy fraud

* * *

18 U.S.C. § 1519. Destruction, alteration, or falsification of records in Federal investigations and bankruptcy

* * *

18 U.S.C. § 3057. Bankruptcy investigations

* * *

18 U.S.C. § 3284. Concealment of bankrupt's assets

* * *

18 U.S.C. § 3613. Civil remedies for satisfaction of an unpaid fine

* * *

TITLE 26—INTERNAL REVENUE CODE

* * *

26 U.S.C. § 108. Income from discharge of indebtedness

* * *

26 U.S.C. § 1017. Discharge of indebtedness

* * *

26 U.S.C. § 1398. Rules relating to individuals' title 11 cases
26 U.S.C. § 1399. No separate taxable entities for partnerships, corporations, etc.

* * *

26 U.S.C. § 6321. Lien for taxes
26 U.S.C. § 6322. Period of lien
26 U.S.C. § 6323. Validity and priority against certain persons

* * *

26 U.S.C. § 6658. Coordination with title 11

* * *

26 U.S.C. § 7433(e). Civil damages for certain unauthorized collection actions

* * *

TITLE 37—PAY AND ALLOWANCES OF THE UNIFORMED SERVICES

* * *

37 U.S.C. § 301d(c). Multiyear retention bonus: medical officers of the armed forces
37 U.S.C. § 301e(d). Multiyear retention bonus: dental officers of the armed forces
37 U.S.C. § 302. Special pay: medical officers of the armed forces

* * *

37 U.S.C. § 302g. Special pay: Selected Reserve health care professionals in critically short wartime specialties

* * *

37 U.S.C. § 314(d). Special pay or bonus: qualified enlisted members extending duty at designated locations overseas

* * *

37 U.S.C. § 317(f). Special pay: officers in critical acquisition positions extending period of active duty
37 U.S.C. § 318(h). Special pay: special warfare officers extending period of active duty
37 U.S.C. § 319(f). Special pay: surface warfare officer continuation pay

* * *

37 U.S.C. § 321(f). Special pay: judge advocate continuation pay
37 U.S.C. § 322(f). Special pay: 15-year career status bonus for members entering service on or after August 1, 1986

* * *

TITLE 42—THE PUBLIC HEALTH AND WELFARE

* * *

42 U.S.C. § 254*o*(d), (e). Breach of scholarship contract or loan repayment contract

* * *

42 U.S.C. § 292f(g). Default of borrower

* * *

42 U.S.C. § 297a(c). Loan agreements

* * *

42 U.S.C. § 656(b). Support obligation as obligation to State; amount; discharge in bankruptcy

TITLE 50 APPENDIX—WAR AND NATIONAL DEFENSE

Servicemembers Civil Relief Act

50 U.S.C. app. § 501. Short title
50 U.S.C. app. § 502. Purpose
50 U.S.C. app. § 511. Definitions
50 U.S.C. app. § 512. Jurisdiction and applicability of Act
50 U.S.C. app. § 513. Protection of persons secondarily liable
50 U.S.C. app. § 514. Extension of protections to citizens serving with allied forces
50 U.S.C. app. § 515. Notification of benefits
50 U.S.C. app. § 516. Extension of rights and protections to reserves ordered to report for military service and to persons ordered to report for induction
50 U.S.C. app. § 517. Waiver of rights pursuant to written agreement
50 U.S.C. app. § 518. Exercise of rights under Act not to affect certain future financial transactions

* * *

50 U.S.C. app. § 521. Protection of servicemembers against default judgments
50 U.S.C. app. § 522. Stay of proceedings when servicemember has notice
50 U.S.C. app. § 523. Fines and penalties under contracts

* * *

NATIONAL DEFENSE AUTHORIZATION ACT FOR FISCAL YEAR 2000

Pub. L. No. 106-65, 113 Stat. 512

* * *

Sec. 1705. Stipend and bonus for participants

TITLE 18—CRIMES AND CRIMINAL PROCEDURE

* * *

18 U.S.C. § 151. Definition

As used in this chapter, the term "debtor" means a debtor concerning whom a petition has been filed under Title 11.

18 U.S.C. § 152. Concealment of assets; false oaths and claims; bribery

A person who—

(1) knowingly and fraudulently conceals from a custodian, trustee, marshal, or other officer of the court charged with the control or custody of property, or, in connection with a case under title 11, from creditors or the United States Trustee, any property belonging to the estate of a debtor;

(2) knowingly and fraudulently makes a false oath or account in or in relation to any case under title 11;

(3) knowingly and fraudulently makes a false declaration, certificate, verification, or statement under penalty of perjury as permitted under section 1746 of title 28, in or in relation to any case under title 11;

(4) knowingly and fraudulently presents any false claim for proof against the estate of a debtor, or uses any such claim in any case under title 11, in a personal capacity or as or through an agent, proxy, or attorney;

(5) knowingly and fraudulently receives any material amount of property from a debtor after the filing of a case under title 11, with intent to defeat the provisions of title 11;

(6) knowingly and fraudulently gives, offers, receives, or attempts to obtain any money or property, remuneration, compensation, reward, advantage, or promise thereof for acting or forbearing to act in any case under title 11;

(7) in a personal capacity or as an agent or officer of any person or corporation, in contemplation of a case under title 11 by or against the person or any other person or corporation, or with intent to defeat the provisions of title 11, knowingly and fraudulently transfers or conceals any of his property or the property of such other person or corporation;

(8) after the filing of a case under title 11 or in contemplation thereof, knowingly and fraudulently conceals, destroys, mutilates, falsifies, or makes a false entry in any recorded information (including books, documents, records, and papers) relating to the property or financial affairs of a debtor; or

(9) after the filing of a case under title 11, knowingly and fraudulently withholds from a custodian, trustee, marshal, or other officer of the court or a United States Trustee entitled to its possession, any recorded information (including books, documents, records, and papers) relating to the property or financial affairs of a debtor, shall be fined under this title, imprisoned not more than 5 years, or both.

18 U.S.C. § 153. Embezzlement against estate

(a) Offense.—A person described in subsection (b) who knowingly and fraudulently appropriates to the person's own use, embezzles, spends, or transfers any property or secretes or destroys any document belonging to the estate of a debtor shall be fined under this title, imprisoned not more than 5 years, or both.

(b) Person To Whom Section Applies.—A person described in this subsection is one who has access to property or documents belonging to an estate by virtue of the person's participation in the administration of the estate as a trustee, custodian, marshal, attorney, or other officer of the court or as an agent, employee, or other person engaged by such an officer to perform a service with respect to the estate.

18 U.S.C. § 154. Adverse interest and conduct of officers

A person who, being a custodian, trustee, marshal, or other officer of the court—

(1) knowingly purchases, directly or indirectly, any property of the estate of which the person is such an officer in a case under title 11;

(2) knowingly refuses to permit a reasonable opportunity for the inspection by parties in interest of the documents and accounts relating to the affairs of estates in the person's charge by parties when directed by the court to do so; or

(3) knowingly refuses to permit a reasonable opportunity for the inspection by the United States Trustee of the documents and

accounts relating to the affairs of an estate in the person's charge,

shall be fined under this title and shall forfeit the person's office, which shall thereupon become vacant.

18 U.S.C. § 155. Fee agreements in cases under title 11 and receiverships

Whoever, being a party in interest, whether as a debtor, creditor, receiver, trustee or representative of any of them, or attorney for any such party in interest, in any receivership or case under title 11 in any United States court or under its supervision, knowingly and fraudulently enters into any agreement, express or implied, with another such party in interest or attorney for another such party in interest, for the purpose of fixing the fees or other compensation to be paid to any party in interest or to any attorney for any party in interest for services rendered in connection therewith, from the assets of the estate, shall be fined under this title or imprisoned not more than one year, or both.

18 U.S.C. § 156. Knowing disregard of bankruptcy law or rule

(a) Definitions.—In this section—

"bankruptcy petition preparer" means a person, other than the debtor's attorney or an employee of such an attorney, who prepares for compensation a document for filing.

"document for filing" means a petition or any other document prepared for filing by a debtor in a United States bankruptcy court or a United States district court in connection with a case under this title.

(b) Offense.—If a bankruptcy case or related proceeding is dismissed because of a knowing attempt by a bankruptcy petition preparer in any manner to disregard the requirements of title 11, United States Code, or the Federal Rules of Bankruptcy Procedure, the bankruptcy petition preparer shall be fined under this title, imprisoned not more than 1 year, or both.

18 U.S.C. § 157. Bankruptcy fraud

A person who, having devised or intending to devise a scheme or artifice to defraud and for the purpose of executing or concealing such a scheme or artifice or attempting to do so—

(1) files a petition under title 11;

(2) files a document in a proceeding under title 11; or

(3) makes a false or fraudulent representation, claim, or promise concerning or in relation to a proceeding under title 11, at any time before or after the filing of the petition, or in relation to a proceeding falsely asserted to be pending under such title,

shall be fined under this title, imprisoned not more than 5 years, or both.

* * *

18 U.S.C. § 1519. Destruction, alteration, or falsification of records in Federal investigations and bankruptcy

Whoever knowingly alters, destroys, mutilates, conceals, covers up, falsifies, or makes a false entry in any record, document, or tangible object with the intent to impede, obstruct, or influence the investigation or proper administration of any matter within the jurisdiction of any department or agency of the United States or any case filed under title 11, or in relation to or contemplation of any such matter or case, shall be fined under this title, imprisoned not more than 20 years, or both.

* * *

18 U.S.C. § 3057. Bankruptcy investigations

(a) Any judge, receiver, or trustee having reasonable grounds for believing that any violation under chapter 9 of this title or other laws of the United States relating to insolvent debtors, receiverships or reorganization plans has been committed, or that an investigation should be had in connection therewith, shall report to the appropriate United States attorney all the facts and circumstances of the case, the names of the witnesses and the offense or offenses believed to have been committed. Where one of such officers has made such report, the others need not do so.

(b) The United States attorney thereupon shall inquire into the facts and report thereon to the judge, and if it appears probable that any such offense has been committed, shall without delay, present the matter to the grand jury, unless upon inquiry and examination he decides that the ends of public justice do not require investigation or prosecution, in which case he shall report the facts to the Attorney General for his direction.

* * *

18 U.S.C. § 3284. Concealment of bankrupt's assets

The concealment of assets of a debtor in a case under title 11 shall be deemed to be a continuing offense until the debtor shall have been finally discharged or a discharge denied, and the period of limitations shall not begin to run until such final discharge or denial of discharge.

* * *

18 U.S.C. § 3613. Civil remedies for satisfaction of an unpaid fine

(a) Enforcement.—The United States may enforce a judgment imposing a fine in accordance with the practices and procedures for the enforcement of a civil judgment under Federal law or State law. Notwithstanding any other Federal law (including section 207 of the Social Security Act), a judgment imposing a fine may be enforced against all property or rights to property of the person fined, except that—

(1) property exempt form levy for taxes pursuant to section 6334(a) (1), (2), (3), (4), (5), (6), (7), (8), (10), and (12) of the Internal Revenue Code of 1986 shall be exempt from enforcement of the judgment under Federal law;

(2) section 3014 of chapter 176 of title 28 shall not apply to enforcement under Federal law; and

(3) the provisions of section 303 of the Consumer Credit Protection Act (15 U.S.C. 1673) shall apply to enforcement of the judgment under Federal law or State law.

(b) Termination of Liability.—The liability to pay a fine shall terminate the later of 20 years from the entry of judgment or 20 years after the release from imprisonment of the person fined, or upon the death of the individual fined.

(c) Lien.—A fine imposed pursuant to the provisions of subchapter C of chapter 227 of this title, or an order of restitution made pursuant to sections 2248, 2259, 2264, 2327, 3663, 3663A, or 3664 of this title, is a lien in favor of the United States on all property and rights to property of the person fined as if the liability of the person fined were a liability for a tax assessed under the Internal Revenue Code of 1986. The lien arises on the entry of judgment and continues for 20 years or until the liability is satisfied, remitted, set aside, or is terminated under subsection (b).

(d) Effect of Filing Notice of Lien.—Upon filing of a notice of lien in the manner in which a notice of tax lien would be filed under section 6323(f) (1) and (2) of the Internal Revenue Code of 1986, the lien shall be valid against any purchaser, holder of a security interest, mechanic's lienor or judgment lien creditor, except with respect to properties or transactions specified in subsection (b), (c), or (d) of section 6323 of the Internal Revenue Code of 1986 for which a notice of tax lien properly filed on the same date would not be valid. The notice of lien shall be considered a notice of lien for taxes payable to the United States for the purpose of any State or local law providing for the filing of a notice of a tax lien. A notice of lien that is registered, recorded, docketed, or indexed in accordance with the rules and requirements relating to judgments of the courts of the State where the notice of lien is registered, recorded, docketed, or indexed shall be considered for all purposes as the filing prescribed by this section. The provisions of section 3201(e) of chapter 176 of title 28 shall apply to liens filed as prescribed by this section.

(e) Discharge of Debt Inapplicable.—No discharge of debts in a proceeding pursuant to any chapter of title 11. United States Code, shall discharge liability to pay a fine pursuant to this section, and a lien filed as prescribed by this section shall not be voided in a bankruptcy proceeding.

(f) Applicability to Order of Restitution.—In accordance with section 3664(m)(1)(A) of this title, all provisions of this section are available to the United States for the enforcement of an order or restitution.

TITLE 26—INTERNAL REVENUE CODE

* * *

26 U.S.C. § 108. Income from discharge of indebtedness

(a) Exclusion from gross income.—

(1) In general.—Gross income does not include any amount which (but for this subsection) would be includible in gross income by reason of the discharge (in whole or in part) of indebtedness of the taxpayer if—
  (A) the discharge occurs in a title 11 case,
  (B) the discharge occurs when the taxpayer is insolvent,
  (C) the indebtedness discharged is qualified farm indebtedness, or
  (D) in the case of a taxpayer other than a C corporation, the indebtedness discharged is qualified real property business indebtedness.

(2) Coordination of exclusions.—
  (A) Title 11 exclusion takes precedence.—Subparagraphs (B), (C), and (D) of paragraph (1) shall not apply to a discharge which occurs in a title 11 case.
  (B) Insolvency exclusion takes precedence over qualified farm exclusion and qualified real property business exclu-

sion.—Subparagraphs (C) and (D) of paragraph (1) shall not apply to a discharge to the extent the taxpayer is insolvent.

(3) Insolvency exclusion limited to amount of insolvency.—In the case of a discharge to which paragraph (1)(B) applies, the amount excluded under paragraph (1)(B) shall not exceed the amount by which the taxpayer is insolvent.

(b) Reduction of tax attributes.—

(1) In general.—The amount excluded from gross income under subparagraph (A), (B), or (C) of subsection (a)(1) shall be applied to reduce the tax attributes of the taxpayer as provided in paragraph (2).

(2) Tax attributes affected; order of reduction.—Except as provided in paragraph (5), the reduction referred to in paragraph (1) shall be made in the following tax attributes in the following order:
  (A) NOL.—Any net operating loss for the taxable year of the discharge, and any net operating loss carryover to such taxable year.
  (B) General business credit.—Any carryover to or from the taxable year of a discharge of an amount for purposes for determining the amount allowable as a credit under section 38 (relating to general business credit).
  (C) Minimum tax credit.—The amount of the minimum tax credit available under section 53(b) as of the beginning of the taxable year immediately following the taxable year of the discharge.
  (D) Capital loss carryovers.—Any net capital loss for the taxable year of the discharge, and any capital loss carryover to such taxable year under section 1212.
  (E) Basis reduction.—
    (i) In general.—The basis of the property of the taxpayer.
    (ii) Cross reference.—For provisions for making the reduction described in clause (i), see section 1017.
  (F) Passive activity loss and credit carryovers.—Any passive activity loss or credit carryover of the taxpayer under section 469(b) from the taxable year of the discharge.
  (G) Foreign tax credit carryovers.—Any carryover to or from the taxable year of the discharge for purposes of determining the amount of the credit allowable under section 27.

(3) Amount of reduction.—
  (A) In general.—Except as provided in subparagraph (B), the reductions described in paragraph (2) shall be one dollar for each dollar excluded by subsection (a).
  (B) Credit carryover reduction.—The reductions described in subparagraphs (B), (C), and (G) shall be 33 1/3 cents for each dollar excluded by subsection (a). The reduction described in subparagraph (F) in any passive activity credit carryover shall be 33 1/3 cents for each dollar excluded by subsection (a).

(4) Ordering rules.—
  (A) Reductions made after determination of tax for year.—The reductions described in paragraph (2) shall be made after the determination of the tax imposed by this chapter for the taxable year of the discharge.
  (B) Reductions under subparagraph (A) or (D) of para-

graph (2).—The reductions described in subparagraph (A) or (D) of paragraph (2) (as the case may be) shall be made first in the loss for the taxable year of the discharge and then in the carryovers to such taxable year in the order of the taxable years from which each such carryover arose.

(C) **Reductions under subparagraphs (B) and (G) of paragraph (2).**—The reductions described in subparagraphs (B) and (G) of paragraph (2) shall be made in the order in which carryovers are taken into account under this chapter for the taxable year of the discharge.

(5) **Election to apply reduction first against depreciable property.—**

(A) **In general.**—The taxpayer may elect to apply any portion of the reduction referred to in paragraph (1) to the reduction under section 1017 of the basis of the depreciable property of the taxpayer.

(B) **Limitation.**—The amount to which an election under subparagraph (A) applies shall not exceed the aggregate adjusted bases of the depreciable property held by the taxpayer as of the beginning of the taxable year following the taxable year in which the discharge occurs.

(C) **Other tax attributes not reduced.**—Paragraph (2) shall not apply to any amount to which an election under this paragraph applies.

(c) **Treatment of discharge of qualified real property business indebtedness.—**

(1) **Basis reduction.—**

(A) **In general.**—The amount excluded from gross income under subparagraph (D) of subsection (a)(1) shall be applied to reduce the basis of the depreciable real property of the taxpayer.

(B) **Cross reference.**—For provisions making the reduction described in subparagraph (A), see section 1017.

(2) **Limitations.—**

(A) **Indebtedness in excess of value.**—The amount excluded under subparagraph (D) of subsection (a)(1) with respect to any qualified real property business indebtedness shall not exceed the excess (if any) of—

(i) the outstanding principal amount of such indebtedness (immediately before the discharge), over

(ii) the fair market value of the real property described in paragraph (3)(A) (as of such time), reduced by the outstanding principal amount of any other qualified real property business indebtedness secured by such property (as of such time).

(B) **Overall limitation.**—The amount excluded under subparagraph (D) of subsection (a)(1) shall not exceed the aggregate adjusted bases of depreciable real property (determined after any reductions under subsections (b) and (g)) held by the taxpayer immediately before the discharge (other than depreciable real property acquired in contemplation of such discharge).

(3) **Qualified real property business indebtedness.**—The term "qualified real property business indebtedness" means indebtedness which—

(A) was incurred or assumed by the taxpayer in connection with real property used in a trade or business and is secured by such real property,

(B) was incurred or assumed before January 1, 1993, or if incurred or assumed on or after such date, is qualified acquisition indebtedness, and

(C) with respect to which such taxpayer makes an election to have this paragraph apply.

Such term shall not include qualified farm indebtedness. Indebtedness under subparagraph (B) shall include indebtedness resulting from the refinancing of indebtedness under subparagraph (B) (or this sentence), but only to the extent it does not exceed the amount of the indebtedness being refinanced.

(4) **Qualified acquisition indebtedness.**—For purposes of paragraph (3)(B), the term "qualified acquisition indebtedness" means, with respect to any real property described in paragraph (3)(A), indebtedness incurred or assumed to acquire, construct, reconstruct, or substantially improve such property.

(5) **Regulations.**—The Secretary shall issue such regulations as are necessary to carry out this subsection, including regulations preventing the abuse of this subsection through cross-collateralization or other means.

(d) **Meaning of terms; special rules relating to certain provisions.—**

(1) **Indebtedness of taxpayer.**—For purposes of this section, the term "indebtedness of the taxpayer" means any indebtedness—

(A) for which the taxpayer is liable, or

(B) subject to which the taxpayer holds property.

(2) **Title 11 case.**—For purposes of this section, the term "title 11 case" means a case under title 11 of the United States Code (relating to bankruptcy), but only if the taxpayer is under the jurisdiction of the court in such case and the discharge of indebtedness is granted by the court or is pursuant to a plan approved by the court.

(3) **Insolvent.**—For purposes of this section, the term "insolvent" means the excess of liabilities over the fair market value of assets. With respect to any discharge, whether or not the taxpayer is insolvent, and the amount by which the taxpayer is insolvent, shall be determined on the basis of the taxpayer's assets and liabilities immediately before the discharge.

(4) [*Repealed.*]

(5) **Depreciable property.**—The term "depreciable property" has the same meaning as when used in section 1017.

(6) **Certain provisions to be applied at partner level.**—In the case of a partnership, subsections (a), (b), (c), and (g) shall be applied at the partner level.

(7) **Special rules for S corporation.—**

(A) **Certain provisions to be applied at corporate level.**—In the case of an S corporation, subsections (a), (b), (c), and (g) shall be applied at the corporate level, including by not taking into account under section 1366(a) any amount excluded under subsection (a) of this section.

(B) **Reduction in carryover of disallowed losses and deductions.**—In the case of an S corporation, for purposes of subparagraph (A) of subsection (b)(2), any loss or deduction which is disallowed for the taxable year of the discharge under section 1366(d)(1) shall be treated as a net operating loss for such taxable year. The preceding sentence shall not apply to any discharge to the extent that subsection (a)(1)(D) applies to such discharge.

(C) **Coordination with basis adjustments under section 1367(b)(2).**—For purposes of subsection (e)(6), a shareholder's adjusted basis in indebtedness of an S corporation shall be determined without regard to any adjustments made under section 1367(b)(2).

(8) **Reductions of tax attributes in title 11 cases of individuals to be made by estate.**—In any case under chapter 7 or 11 of title 11 of the United States Code to which section 1398 applies, for purposes of paragraphs (1) and (5) of subsection (b) the estate (and not the individual) shall be treated as the taxpayer. The preceding sentence shall not apply for purposes of applying section 1017 to property transferred by the estate to the individual.

(9) **Time for making election, etc.**—

(A) **Time.**—An election under paragraph (5) of subsection (b) or under paragraph (3)(C) of subsection (c) shall be made on the taxpayer's return for the taxable year in which the discharge occurs or at such other time as may be permitted in regulations prescribed by the Secretary.

(B) **Revocation only with consent.**—An election referred to in subparagraph (A), once made, may be revoked only with the consent of the Secretary.

(C) **Manner.**—An election referred to in subparagraph (A) shall be made in such manner as the Secretary may by regulations prescribe.

(10) **Cross reference.**—For provision that no reduction is to be made in the basis of exempt property of an individual debtor, see section 1017(c)(1).

(e) **General rules for discharge of indebtedness (including discharges not in Title 11 cases or insolvency).**—For purposes of this title—

(1) **No other insolvency exception.**—Except as otherwise provided in this section, there shall be no insolvency exception from the general rule that gross income includes income from the discharge of indebtedness.

(2) **Income not realized to extent of lost deductions.**—No income shall be realized from the discharge of indebtedness to the extent that payment of the liability would have given rise to a deduction.

(3) **Adjustments for unamortized premium and discount.**—The amount taken into account with respect to any discharge shall be properly adjusted for unamortized premium and unamortized discount with respect to the indebtedness discharged.

(4) **Acquisition of indebtedness by person related to debtor.**—

(A) **Treated as acquisition by debtor.**—For purposes of determining income of the debtor from discharge of indebtedness, to the extent provided in regulations prescribed by the Secretary, the acquisition of outstanding indebtedness by a person bearing a relationship to the debtor specified in section 267(b) or 707(b)(1) from a person who does not bear such a relationship to the debtor shall be treated as the acquisition of such indebtedness by the debtor. Such regulations shall provide for such adjustments in the treatment of any subsequent transactions involving the indebtedness as may be appropriate by reason of the application of the preceding sentence.

(B) **Members of family.**—For purposes of this paragraph, sections 267(b) and 707(b)(1) shall be applied as if section 267(c)(4) provided that the family of an individual consists of the individual's spouse, the individual's children, grandchildren, and parents, and any spouse of the individual's children or grandchildren.

(C) **Entities under common control treated as related.**—For purposes of this paragraph, two entities which are treated as a single employer under subsection (b) or (c) of section 414 shall be treated as bearing a relationship to each other which is described in section 267(b).

(5) **Purchase-money debt reduction for solvent debtor treated as price reduction.**—If—

(A) the debt of a purchaser of property to the seller of such property which arose out of the purchase of such property is reduced,

(B) such reduction does not occur—

(i) in a title 11 case, or

(ii) when the purchaser is insolvent, and

(C) but for this paragraph, such reduction would be treated as income to the purchaser from the discharge of indebtedness,

then such reduction shall be treated as a purchase price adjustment.

(6) **Indebtedness contributed to capital.**—Except as provided in regulations, for purposes of determining income of the debtor from discharge of indebtedness, if a debtor corporation acquires its indebtedness from a shareholder as a contribution to capital—

(A) section 118 shall not apply, but

(B) such corporation shall be treated as having satisfied the indebtedness with an amount of money equal to the shareholder's adjusted basis in the indebtedness.

(7) **Recapture of gain on subsequent sale of stock.**—

(A) **In general.**—If a creditor acquires stock of a debtor corporation in satisfaction of such corporation's indebtedness, for purposes of section 1245—

(i) such stock (and any other property the basis of which is determined in whole or in part by reference to the adjusted basis of such stock) shall be treated as section 1245 property,

(ii) the aggregate amount allowed to the creditor—

(I) as deductions under subsection (a) or (b) of section 166 (by reason of the worthlessness or partial worthlessness of the indebtedness), or

(II) as an ordinary loss on the exchange,

shall be treated as an amount allowed as a deduction for depreciation, and

(iii) an exchange of such stock qualifying under section 354(a), 355(a), or 356(a) shall be treated as an exchange to which section 1245(b)(3) applies.

The amount determined under clause (ii) shall be reduced by the amount (if any) included in the creditor's gross income on the exchange.

(B) Special rule for cash basis taxpayers.—In the case of any creditor who computes his taxable income under the cash receipts and disbursements method, proper adjustment shall be made in the amount taken into account under clause (ii) of subparagraph (A) for any amount which was not included in the creditor's gross income but which would have been included in such gross income if such indebtedness had been satisfied in full.

(C) Stock of parent corporation.—For purposes of this paragraph, stock of a corporation in control (within the meaning of section 368(c)) of the debtor corporation shall be treated as stock of the debtor corporation.

(D) Treatment of successor corporation.—For purposes of this paragraph, the term "debtor corporation" includes a successor corporation.

(E) Partnership rule.—Under regulations prescribed by the Secretary, rules similar to the rules of the foregoing subparagraphs of this paragraph shall apply with respect to the indebtedness of a partnership.

(8) Indebtedness satisfied by corporation's stock.—For purposes of determining income of a debtor from discharge of indebtedness, if a debtor corporation transfers stock to a creditor in satisfaction of its indebtedness, such corporation shall be treated as having satisfied the indebtedness with an amount of money equal to the fair market value of the stock.

(9) Discharge of indebtedness income not taken into account in determining whether entity meets REIT qualifications.—Any amount included in gross income by reason of the discharge of indebtedness shall not be taken into account for purposes of paragraphs (2) and (3) of section 856(c).

(10) Indebtedness satisfied by issuance of debt instrument.—
(A) In general.—For purposes of determining income of a debtor from discharge of indebtedness, if a debtor issues a debt instrument in satisfaction of indebtedness, such debtor shall be treated as having satisfied the indebtedness with an amount of money equal to the issue price of such debt instrument.

(B) Issue price.—For purposes of subparagraph (A), the issue price of any debt instrument shall be determined under sections 1273 and 1274. For purposes of the preceding sentence, section 1273(b)(4) shall be applied by reducing the stated redemption price of any instrument by the portion of such stated redemption price which is treated as interest for purposes of this chapter.

(f) Student loans.—

(1) In general.—In the case of an individual, gross income does not include any amount which (but for this subsection) would be includible in gross income by reason of the discharge (in whole or in part) of any student loan if such discharge was pursuant to a provision of such loan under which all or part of the indebtedness of the individual would be discharged if the individual worked for a certain period of time in certain professions for any of a broad class of employers.

(2) Student loan.—For purposes of this subsection, the term "student loan" means any loan to an individual to assist the individual in attending an educational organization described in section 170(b)(1)(A)(ii) made by—

(A) the United States, or an instrumentality or agency thereof,
(B) a State, territory, or possession of the United States, or the District of Columbia, or any political subdivision thereof,
(C) a public benefit corporation—
  (i) which is exempt from taxation under section 501(c)(3),
  (ii) which has assumed control over a State, county, or municipal hospital, and
  (iii) whose employees have been deemed to be public employees under State law, or
(D) any educational organization described in section 170(b)(1)(A)(ii) if such loan is made—
  (i) pursuant to an agreement with any entity described in subparagraph (A), (B), or (C) under which the funds from which the loan was made were provided to such educational organization, or
  (ii) pursuant to a program of such educational organization which is designed to encourage its students to serve in occupations with unmet needs or in areas with unmet needs and under which the services provided by the students (or former students) are for or under the direction of a governmental unit or an organization described in section 501(c)(3) and exempt from tax under section 501(a).

The term "student loan" includes any loan made by an educational organization described in section 170(b)(1)(A)(ii) or by an organization exempt from tax under section 501(a) to refinance a loan to an individual to assist the individual in attending any such educational organization but only if the refinancing loan is pursuant to a program of the refinancing organization which is designed as described in subparagraph (D)(ii).

(3) Exception for discharges on account of services performed for certain lenders.—Paragraph (1) shall not apply to the discharge of a loan made by an organization described in paragraph (2)(D) if the discharge is on account of services performed for either such organization.

(g) Special rules for discharge of qualified farm indebtedness.—

(1) Discharge must be by qualified person.—
(A) In general.—Subparagraph (C) of subsection (a)(1) shall apply only if the discharge is by a qualified person.
(B) Qualified person.—For purposes of subparagraph (A), the term "qualified person" has the meaning given to such term by section 49(a)(1)(D)(iv); except that such term shall include any Federal, State, or local government or agency or instrumentality thereof.

(2) Qualified farm indebtedness.—For purposes of this section, indebtedness of a taxpayer shall be treated as qualified farm indebtedness if—
(A) such indebtedness was incurred directly in connection with the operation by the taxpayer of the trade or business of farming, and
(B) 50 percent or more of the aggregate gross receipts of the taxpayer for the 3 taxable years preceding the taxable year in which the discharge of such indebtedness occurs is attributable to the trade or business of farming.

(3) Amount excluded cannot exceed sum of tax attributes and business and investment assets.—

    (A) In general.—The amount excluded under subparagraph (C) of subsection (a)(1) shall not exceed the sum of—

        (i) the adjusted tax attributes of the taxpayer, and

        (ii) the aggregate adjusted bases of qualified property held by the taxpayer as of the beginning of the taxable year following the taxable year in which the discharge occurs.

    (B) Adjusted tax attributes.—For purposes of subparagraph (A), the term "adjusted tax attributes" means the sum of the tax attributes described in subparagraphs (A), (B), (C), (D), (F), and (G) of subsection (b)(2) determined by taking into account $3 for each $1 of the attributes described in subparagraphs (B), (C), and (G) of subsection (b)(2) and the attribute described in subparagraph (F) of subsection (b)(2) to the extent attributable to any passive activity credit carryover.

    (C) Qualified property.—For purposes of this paragraph, the term "qualified property" means any property which is used or is held for use in a trade or business or for the production of income.

    (D) Coordination with insolvency exclusion.—For purposes of this paragraph, the adjusted basis of any qualified property and the amount of the adjusted tax attributes shall be determined after any reduction under subsection (b) by reason of amounts excluded from gross income under subsection (a)(1)(B).

* * *

26 U.S.C. § 1017. Discharge of indebtedness

(a) General rule.—If—

(1) an amount is excluded from gross income under subsection (a) of section 108 (relating to discharge of indebtedness), and

(2) under subsection (b)(2)(E), (b)(5), or (c)(1) of section 108, any portion of such amount is to be applied to reduce basis,

then such portion shall be applied in reduction of the basis of any property held by the taxpayer at the beginning of the taxable year following the taxable year in which the discharge occurs.

(b) Amount and properties determined under regulations.—

(1) In general.—The amount of reduction to be applied under subsection (a) (not in excess of the portion referred to in subsection (a)), and the particular properties the bases of which are to be reduced, shall be determined under regulations prescribed by the Secretary.

(2) Limitation in Title 11 case or insolvency.—In the case of a discharge to which subparagraph (A) or (B) of section 108(a)(1) applies, the reduction in basis under subsection (a) of this section shall not exceed the excess of—

    (A) the aggregate of the bases of the property held by the taxpayer immediately after the discharge, over

    (B) the aggregate of the liabilities of the taxpayer immediately after the discharge.

The preceding sentence shall not apply to any reduction in basis by reason of an election under section 108(b)(5).

(3) Certain reductions may only be made in the basis of depreciable property.—

    (A) In general.—Any amount which under subsection (b)(5) or (c)(1) of section 108 is to be applied to reduce basis shall be applied only to reduce the basis of depreciable property held by the taxpayer.

    (B) Depreciable property.—For purposes of this section, the term "depreciable property" means any property of a character subject to the allowance for depreciation, but only if a basis reduction under subsection (a) will reduce the amount of depreciation or amortization which otherwise would be allowable for the period immediately following such reduction.

    (C) Special rule for partnership interests.—For purposes of this section, any interest of a partner in a partnership shall be treated as depreciable property to the extent of such partner's proportionate interest in the depreciable property held by such partnership. The preceding sentence shall apply only if there is a corresponding reduction in the partnership's basis in depreciable property with respect to such partner.

    (D) Special rule in case of affiliated group.—For purposes of this section, if—

        (i) a corporation holds stock in another corporation (hereinafter in this subparagraph referred to as the "subsidiary"), and

        (ii) such corporations are members of the same affiliated group which file a consolidated return under section 1501 for the taxable year in which the discharge occurs,

then such stock shall be treated as depreciable property to the extent that such subsidiary consents to a corresponding reduction in the basis of its depreciable property.

    (E) Election to treat certain inventory as depreciable property.—

        (i) In general.—At the election of the taxpayer, for purposes of this section, the term "depreciable property" includes any real property which is described in section 1221(a)(1).

        (ii) Election.—An election under clause (i) shall be made on the taxpayer's return for the taxable year in which the discharge occurs or at such other time as may be permitted in regulations prescribed by the Secretary. Such an election, once made, may be revoked only with the consent of the Secretary.

    (F) Special rules for qualified real property business indebtedness.—In the case of any amount which under section 108(c)(1) is to be applied to reduce basis—

        (i) depreciable property shall only include depreciable real property for purposes of subparagraphs (A) and (C),

        (ii) subparagraph (E) shall not apply, and

        (iii) in the case of property taken into account under section 108(c)(2)(B), the reduction with respect to such property shall be made as of the time immediately before disposition if earlier than the time under subsection (a).

(4) Special rules for qualified farm indebtedness.—

    (A) In general.—Any amount which under subsection

(b)(2)(E) of section 108 is to be applied to reduce basis and which is attributable to an amount excluded under subsection (a)(1)(C) of section 108—

   (i) shall be applied only to reduce the basis of qualified property held by the taxpayer, and

   (ii) shall be applied to reduce the basis of qualified property in the following order:

      (I) First the basis of qualified property which is depreciable property.

      (II) Second the basis of qualified property which is land used or held for use in the trade or business of farming.

      (III) Then the basis of other qualified property.

  (B) Qualified property.—For purposes of this paragraph, the term "qualified property" has the meaning given to such term by section 108(g)(3)(C).

  (C) Certain rules made applicable.—Rules similar to the rules of subparagraphs (C), (D), and (E) of paragraph (3) shall apply for purposes of this paragraph and section 108(g).

(c) Special rules.—

(1) Reduction not to be made in exempt property.—In the case of an amount excluded from gross income under section 108(a)(1)(A), no reduction in basis shall be made under this section in the basis of property which the debtor treats as exempt property under section 522 of title 11 of the United States Code.

(2) Reductions in basis not treated as dispositions.—For purposes of this title, a reduction in basis under this section shall not be treated as a disposition.

(d) Recapture of reductions.—

(1) In general.—For purposes of sections 1245 and 1250—

  (A) any property the basis of which is reduced under this section and which is neither section 1245 property nor section 1250 property shall be treated as section 1245 property, and

  (B) any reduction under this section shall be treated as a deduction allowed for depreciation.

(2) Special rule for section 1250.—For purposes of section 1250(b), the determination of what would have been the depreciation adjustments under the straight line method shall be made as if there had been no reduction under this section.

* * *

26 U.S.C. § 1398. Rules relating to individuals' title 11 cases

(a) Cases to which section applies.—Except as provided in subsection (b), this section shall apply to any case under chapter 7 (relating to liquidations) or chapter 11 (relating to reorganizations) of title 11 of the United States Code in which the debtor is an individual.

(b) Exceptions where case is dismissed, etc.—

(1) Section does not apply where case is dismissed.—This section shall not apply if the case under chapter 7 or 11 of title 11 of the United States Code is dismissed.

(2) Section does not apply at partnership level.—For purposes

of subsection (a), a partnership shall not be treated as an individual, but the interest in a partnership of a debtor who is an individual shall be taken into account under this section in the same manner as any other interest of the debtor.

(c) Computation and payment of tax; basic standard deductions.—

(1) Computation and payment of tax.—Except as otherwise provided in this section, the taxable income of the estate shall be computed in the same manner as for an individual. The tax shall be computed on such taxable income and shall be paid by the trustee.

(2) Tax rates.—The tax on the taxable income of the estate shall be determined under subsection (d) of section 1.

(3) Basic standard deduction.—In the case of an estate which does not itemize deductions, the basic standard deduction for the estate for the taxable year shall be the same as for a married individual filing a separate return for such year.

(d) Taxable year of debtors.—

(1) General rule.—Except as provided in paragraph (2), the taxable year of the debtor shall be determined without regard to the case under title 11 of the United States Code to which this section applies.

(2) Election to terminate debtor's year when case commences.—

  (A) In general.—Notwithstanding section 442, the debtor may (without the approval of the Secretary) elect to treat the debtor's taxable year which includes the commencement date as 2 taxable years—

    (i) the first of which ends on the day before the commencement date, and

    (ii) the second of which begins on the commencement date.

  (B) Spouse may join in election.—In the case of a married individual (within the meaning of section 7703), the spouse may elect to have the debtor's election under subparagraph (A) also apply to the spouse, but only if the debtor and the spouse file a joint return for the taxable year referred to in subparagraph (A)(i).

  (C) No election where debtor has no assets.—No election may be made under subparagraph (A) by a debtor who has no assets other than property which the debtor may treat as exempt property under section 522 of title 11 of the United States Code.

  (D) Time for making election.—An election under subparagraph (A) or (B) may be made only on or before the due date for filing the return for the taxable year referred to in subparagraph (A)(i). Any such election, once made, shall be irrevocable.

  (E) Returns.—A return shall be made for each of the taxable years specified in subparagraph (A).

  (F) Annualization.—For purposes of subsections (b), (c), and (d) of section 443, a return filed for either of the taxable years referred to in subparagraph (A) shall be treated as a return made under paragraph (1) of subsection (a) of section 443.

(3) Commencement date defined.—For purposes of this subsection, the term "commencement date" means the day on which the case under title 11 of the United States Code to which this section applies commences.

(e) Treatment of income, deductions, and credits.—

(1) Estate's share of debtor's income.—The gross income of the estate for each taxable year shall include the gross income of the debtor to which the estate is entitled under title 11 of the United States Code. The preceding sentence shall not apply to any amount received or accrued by the debtor before the commencement date (as defined in subsection (d)(3)).

(2) Debtor's share of debtor's income.—The gross income of the debtor for any taxable year shall not include any item to the extent that such item is included in the gross income of the estate by reason of paragraph (1).

(3) Rule for making determinations with respect to deductions, credits, and employment taxes.—Except as otherwise provided in this section, the determination of whether or not any amount paid or incurred by the estate—
(A) is allowable as a deduction or credit under this chapter, or
(B) is wages for purposes of subtitle C,
shall be made as if the amount were paid or incurred by the debtor and as if the debtor were still engaged in the trades and businesses, and in the activities, the debtor was engaged in before the commencement of the case.

(f) Treatment of transfers between debtor and estate.—

(1) Transfer to estate not treated as disposition.—A transfer (other than by sale or exchange) of an asset from the debtor to the estate shall not be treated as a disposition for purposes of any provision of this title assigning tax consequences to a disposition, and the estate shall be treated as the debtor would be treated with respect to such asset.

(2) Transfer from estate to debtor not treated as disposition.—In the case of a termination of the estate, a transfer (other than by sale or exchange) of an asset from the estate to the debtor shall not be treated as a disposition for purposes of any provision of this title assigning tax consequences to a disposition, and the debtor shall be treated as the estate would be treated with respect to such asset.

(g) Estate succeeds to tax attributes of debtor.—The estate shall succeed to and take into account the following items (determined as of the first day of the debtor's taxable year in which the case commences) of the debtor—

(1) Net operating loss carryovers.—The net operating loss carryovers determined under section 172.

(2) Charitable contributions carryovers.—The carryover of excess charitable contributions determined under section 170(d)(1).

(3) Recovery of tax benefit items.—Any amount to which section 111 (relating to recovery of tax benefit items) applies.

(4) Credit carryovers, etc.—The carryovers of any credit, and all other items which, but for the commencement of the case, would be required to be taken into account by the debtor with respect to any credit.

(5) Capital loss carryovers.—The capital loss carryover determined under section 1212.

(6) Basis, holding period, and character of assets.—In the case of any asset acquired (other than by sale or exchange) by the estate from the debtor, the basis, holding period, and character it had in the hands of the debtor.

(7) Method of accounting.—The method of accounting used by the debtor.

(8) Other attributes.—Other tax attributes of the debtor, to the extent provided in regulations prescribed by the Secretary as necessary or appropriate to carry out the purposes of this section.

(h) Administration, liquidation, and reorganization expenses; carryovers and carrybacks of certain excess expenses.—

(1) Administration, liquidation, and reorganization expenses.—Any administrative expense allowed under section 503 of title 11 of the United States Code, and any fee or charge assessed against the estate under chapter 123 of title 28 of the United States Code, to the extent not disallowed under any other provision of this title, shall be allowed as a deduction.

(2) Carryback and carryover of excess administrative costs, etc., to estate taxable years.—
    (A) Deduction allowed.—There shall be allowed as a deduction for the taxable year an amount equal to the aggregate of (i) the administrative expense carryovers to such year, plus (ii) the administrative expense carrybacks to such year.
    (B) Administrative expense loss, etc.—If a net operating loss would be created or increased for any estate taxable year if section 172(c) were applied without the modification contained in paragraph (4) of section 172(d), then the amount of the net operating loss so created (or the amount of the increase in the net operating loss) shall be an administrative expense loss for such taxable year which shall be an administrative expense carryback to each of the 3 preceding taxable years and an administrative expense carryover to each of the 7 succeeding taxable years.
    (C) Determination of amount carried to each taxable year.—The portion of any administrative expense loss which may be carried to any other taxable year shall be determined under section 172(b)(2), except that for each taxable year the computation under section 172(b)(2) with respect to the net operating loss shall be made before the computation under this paragraph.
    (D) Administrative expense deductions allowed only to estate.—The deductions allowable under this chapter solely by reason of paragraph (1), and the deduction provided by subparagraph (A) of this paragraph, shall be allowable only to the estate.

(i) Debtor succeeds to tax attributes of estate.—In the case of a termination of an estate, the debtor shall succeed to and take into account the items referred to in paragraphs (1), (2), (3), (4), (5), and (6) of subsection (g) in a manner similar to that provided in such paragraphs (but taking into account that the transfer is from the estate to the debtor instead of from the debtor to the estate). In addition, the debtor shall succeed to and take into account the other tax attributes of the estate, to the extent provided in regulations prescribed by the

Secretary as necessary or appropriate to carry out the purposes of this section.

(j) Other special rules.—

(1) Change of accounting period without approval.—Notwithstanding section 442, the estate may change its annual accounting period one time without the approval of the Secretary.

(2) Treatment of certain carrybacks.—

    (A) Carrybacks from estate.—If any carryback year of the estate is a taxable year before the estate's first taxable year, the carryback to such carryback year shall be taken into account for the debtor's taxable year corresponding to the carryback year.

    (B) Carrybacks from debtor's activities.—The debtor may not carry back to a taxable year before the debtor's taxable year in which the case commences any carryback from a taxable year ending after the case commences.

    (C) Carryback and carryback year defined.—For purposes of this paragraph—

        (i) Carryback.—The term "carryback" means a net operating loss carryback under section 172 or a carryback of any credit provided by part IV of subchapter A.

        (ii) Carryback year.—The term "carryback year" means the taxable year to which a carryback is carried.

26 U.S.C. § 1399. No separate taxable entities for partnerships, corporations, etc.

Except in any case to which section 1398 applies, no separate taxable entity shall result from the commencement of a case under title 11 of the United States Code.

* * *

26 U.S.C. § 6321. Lien for taxes

If any person liable to pay any tax neglects or refuses to pay the same after demand, the amount (including any interest, additional amount, addition to tax, or assessable penalty, together with any costs that may accrue in addition thereto) shall be a lien in favor of the United States upon all property and rights to property, whether real or personal, belonging to such person.

26 U.S.C. § 6322. Period of lien

Unless another date is specifically fixed by law, the lien imposed by section 6321 shall arise at the time the assessment is made and shall continue until the liability for the amount so assessed (or a judgment against the taxpayer arising out of such liability) is satisfied or becomes unenforceable by reason of lapse of time.

26 U.S.C. § 6323. Validity and priority against certain persons

(a) Purchasers, holders of security interests, mechanic's lienors, and judgment lien creditors.—The lien imposed by section 6321 shall not be valid as against any purchaser, holder of a security interest, mechanic's lienor, or judgment lien creditor until notice thereof which meets the requirements of subsection (f) has been filed by the Secretary.

(b) Protection for certain interests even though notice filed.— Even though notice of a lien imposed by section 6321 has been filed, such lien shall not be valid—

(1) Securities.—With respect to a security (as defined in subsection (h)(4))—

    (A) as against a purchaser of such security who at the time of purchase did not have actual notice or knowledge of the existence of such lien; and

    (B) as against a holder of a security interest in such security who, at the time such interest came into existence, did not have actual notice or knowledge of the existence of such lien.

(2) Motor vehicles.—With respect to a motor vehicle (as defined in subsection (h)(3)), as against a purchaser of such motor vehicle, if—

    (A) at the time of the purchase such purchaser did not have actual notice or knowledge of the existence of such lien, and

    (B) before the purchaser obtains such notice or knowledge, he has acquired possession of such motor vehicle and has not thereafter relinquished possession of such motor vehicle to the seller or his agent.

(3) Personal property purchased at retail.—With respect to tangible personal property purchased at retail, as against a purchaser in the ordinary course of the seller's trade or business, unless at the time of such purchase such purchaser intends such purchase to (or knows such purchase will) hinder, evade, or defeat the collection of any tax under this title.

(4) Personal property purchased in casual sale.—With respect to household goods, personal effects, or other tangible personal property described in section 6334(a) purchased (not for resale) in a casual sale for less than $1,000, as against the purchaser, but only if such purchaser does not have actual notice or knowledge (A) of the existence of such lien, or (B) that this sale is one of a series of sales.

(5) Personal property subject to possessory lien.—With respect to tangible personal property subject to a lien under local law securing the reasonable price of the repair or improvement of such property, as against a holder of such a lien, if such holder is, and has been, continuously in possession of such property from the time such lien arose.

(6) Real property tax and special assessment liens.—With respect to real property, as against a holder of a lien upon such property, if such lien is entitled under local law to priority over security interests in such property which are prior in time, and such lien secures payment of—

    (A) a tax of general application levied by any taxing authority based upon the value of such property;

    (B) a special assessment imposed directly upon such property by any taxing authority, if such assessment is imposed for the purpose of defraying the cost of any public improvement; or

    (C) charges for utilities or public services furnished to such property by the United States, a State or political subdivision thereof, or an instrumentality of any one or more of the foregoing.

(7) Residential property subject to a mechanic's lien for certain repairs and improvements.—With respect to real property subject to a lien for repair or improvement of a personal residence (containing not more than four dwelling units) occupied by the owner of such residence, as against a mechanic's lienor, but only if the contract price on the contract with the owner is not more than $5,000.

(8) Attorneys' liens.—With respect to a judgment or other amount in settlement of a claim or of a cause of action, as against an attorney who, under local law, holds a lien upon or a contract enforceable against such judgment or amount, to the extent of his reasonable compensation for obtaining such judgment or procuring such settlement, except that this paragraph shall not apply to any judgment or amount in settlement of a claim or of a cause of action against the United States to the extent that the United States offsets such judgment or amount against any liability of the taxpayer to the United States.

(9) Certain insurance contracts.—With respect to a life insurance, endowment, or annuity contract, as against the organization which is the insurer under such contract, at any time—

(A) before such organization had actual notice or knowledge of the existence of such lien;

(B) after such organization had such notice or knowledge, with respect to advances required to be made automatically to maintain such contract in force under an agreement entered into before such organization had such notice or knowledge; or

(C) after satisfaction of a levy pursuant to section 6332(b), unless and until the Secretary delivers to such organization a notice, executed after the date of such satisfaction, of the existence of such lien.

(10) Deposit-secured loans.—With respect to a savings deposit, share, or other account, with an institution described in section 581 or 591, to the extent of any loan made by such institution without actual notice or knowledge of the existence of such lien, as against such institution, if such loan is secured by such account.

(c) Protection for certain commercial transactions financing agreements, etc.—

(1) In general.—To the extent provided in this subsection, even though notice of a lien imposed by section 6321 has been filed, such lien shall not be valid with respect to a security interest which came into existence after tax lien filing but which—

(A) is in qualified property covered by the terms of a written agreement entered into before tax lien filing and constituting—

(i) a commercial transactions financing agreement,

(ii) a real property construction or improvement financing agreement, or

(iii) an obligatory disbursement agreement, and

(B) is protected under local law against a judgment lien arising, as of the time of tax lien filing, out of an unsecured obligation.

(2) Commercial transactions financing agreement.—For purposes of this subsection—

(A) **Definition.**—The term "commercial transactions financing agreement" means an agreement (entered into by a person in the course of his trade or business)—

(i) to make loans to the taxpayer to be secured by commercial financing security acquired by the taxpayer in the ordinary course of his trade or business, or

(ii) to purchase commercial financing security (other than inventory) acquired by the taxpayer in the ordinary course of his trade or business;

but such an agreement shall be treated as coming within the term only to the extent that such loan or purchase is made before the 46th day after the date of tax lien filing or (if earlier) before the lender or purchaser had actual notice or knowledge of such tax lien filing.

(B) **Limitation on qualified property.**—The term "qualified property", when used with respect to a commercial transactions financing agreement, includes only commercial financing security acquired by the taxpayer before the 46th day after the date of tax lien filing.

(C) **Commercial financing security defined.**—The term "commercial financing security" means (i) paper of a kind ordinarily arising in commercial transactions, (ii) accounts receivable, (iii) mortgages on real property, and (iv) inventory.

(D) **Purchaser treated as acquiring security interest.**—A person who satisfies subparagraph (A) by reason of clause (ii) thereof shall be treated as having acquired a security interest in commercial financing security.

(3) Real property construction or improvement financing agreement.—For purposes of this subsection—

(A) **Definition.**—The term "real property construction or improvement financing agreement" means an agreement to make cash disbursements to finance—

(i) the construction or improvement of real property,

(ii) a contract to construct or improve real property, or

(iii) the raising or harvesting of a farm crop or the raising of livestock or other animals.

For purposes of clause (iii), the furnishing of goods and services shall be treated as the disbursement of cash.

(B) **Limitation on qualified property.**—The term "qualified property", when used with respect to a real property construction or improvement financing agreement, includes only—

(i) in the case of subparagraph (A)(i), the real property with respect to which the construction or improvement has been or is to be made,

(ii) in the case of subparagraph (A)(ii), the proceeds of the contract described therein, and

(iii) in the case of subparagraph (A)(iii), property subject to the lien imposed by section 6321 at the time of tax lien filing and the crop or the livestock or other animals referred to in subparagraph (A)(iii).

(4) Obligatory disbursement agreement.—For purposes of this subsection—

(A) **Definition.**—The term "obligatory disbursement agreement" means an agreement (entered into by a person in the course of his trade or business) to make disbursements, but such an agreement shall be treated as coming within the term only to the extent of disbursements which are required to be made by reason of the intervention of the rights of a person other than the taxpayer.

(B) **Limitation on qualified property.**—The term "qualified property", when used with respect to an obligatory disbursement agreement, means property subject to the lien imposed by section 6321 at the time of tax lien filing and (to the extent that the acquisition is directly traceable to the disbursements referred to in subparagraph (A)) property acquired by the taxpayer after tax lien filing.

(C) **Special rules for surety agreements.**—Where the obligatory disbursement agreement is an agreement ensuring the performance of a contract between the taxpayer and another person—

(i) the term "qualified property" shall be treated as also including the proceeds of the contract the performance of which was ensured, and

(ii) if the contract the performance of which was ensured was a contract to construct or improve real property, to produce goods, or to furnish services, the term "qualified property" shall be treated as also including any tangible personal property used by the taxpayer in the performance of such ensured contract.

(d) 45-day period for making disbursements.—Even though notice of a lien imposed by section 6321 has been filed, such lien shall not be valid with respect to a security interest which came into existence after tax lien filing by reason of disbursements made before the 46th day after the date of tax lien filing, or (if earlier) before the person making such disbursements had actual notice or knowledge of tax lien filing, but only if such security interest—

(1) is in property (A) subject, at the time of tax lien filing, to the lien imposed by section 6321, and (B) covered by the terms of a written agreement entered into before tax lien filing, and

(2) is protected under local law against a judgment lien arising, as of the time of tax lien filing, out of an unsecured obligation.

(e) Priority of interest and expenses.—If the lien imposed by section 6321 is not valid as against a lien or security interest, the priority of such lien or security interest shall extend to—

(1) any interest or carrying charges upon the obligation secured,

(2) the reasonable charges and expenses of an indenture trustee or agent holding the security interest for the benefit of the holder of the security interest,

(3) the reasonable expenses, including reasonable compensation for attorneys, actually incurred in collecting or enforcing the obligation secured,

(4) the reasonable costs of insuring, preserving, or repairing the property to which the lien or security interest relates,

(5) the reasonable costs of insuring payment of the obligation secured, and

(6) amounts paid to satisfy any lien on the property to which the lien or security interest relates, but only if the lien so satisfied is entitled to priority over the lien imposed by section 6321,

to the extent that, under local law, any such item has the same priority as the lien or security interest to which it relates.

(f) Place for filing notice; form.—

(1) **Place for filing.**—The notice referred to in subsection (a) shall be filed—

(A) **Under State laws.**—

(i) **Real property.**—In the case of real property, in one office within the State (or the county, or other govern-

mental subdivision), as designated by the laws of such State, in which the property subject to the lien is situated; and

(ii) **Personal property.**—In the case of personal property, whether tangible or intangible, in one office within the State (or the county, or other governmental subdivision), as designated by the laws of such State, in which the property subject to the lien is situated, except that State law merely conforming to or reenacting Federal law establishing a national filing system does not constitute a second office for filing as designated by the laws of such State; or

(B) **With clerk of district court.**—In the office of the clerk of the United States district court for the judicial district in which the property subject to the lien is situated, whenever the State has not by law designated one office which meets the requirements of subparagraph (A); or

(C) **With Recorder of Deeds of the District of Columbia.**—In the office of the Recorder of Deeds of the District of Columbia, if the property subject to the lien is situated in the District of Columbia.

(2) **Situs of property subject to lien.**—For purposes of paragraphs (1) and (4), property shall be deemed to be situated—

(A) **Real property.**—In the case of real property, at its physical location; or

(B) **Personal property.**—In the case of personal property, whether tangible or intangible, at the residence of the taxpayer at the time the notice of lien is filed.

For purposes of paragraph (2)(B), the residence of a corporation or partnership shall be deemed to be the place at which the principal executive office of the business is located, and the residence of a taxpayer whose residence is without the United States shall be deemed to be in the District of Columbia.

(3) **Form.**—The form and content of the notice referred to in subsection (a) shall be prescribed by the Secretary. Such notice shall be valid notwithstanding any other provision of law regarding the form or content of a notice of lien.

(4) **Indexing required with respect to certain real property.**—In the case of real property, if—

(A) under the laws of the State in which the real property is located, a deed is not valid as against a purchaser of the property who (at the time of purchase) does not have actual notice or knowledge of the existence of such deed unless the fact of filing of such deed has been entered and recorded in a public index at the place of filing in such a manner that a reasonable inspection of the index will reveal the existence of the deed, and

(B) there is maintained (at the applicable office under paragraph (1)) an adequate system for the public indexing of Federal tax liens,

then the notice of lien referred to in subsection (a) shall not be treated as meeting the filing requirements under paragraph (1) unless the fact of filing is entered and recorded in the index referred to in subparagraph (B) in such a manner that a reasonable inspection of the index will reveal the existence of the lien.

(5) **National filing systems.**—The filing of a notice of lien shall be governed solely by this title and shall not be subject to any

other Federal law establishing a place or places for the filing of liens or encumbrances under a national filing system.

(g) Refiling of notice.—For purposes of this section—

(1) General rule.—Unless notice of lien is refiled in the manner prescribed in paragraph (2) during the required refiling period, such notice of lien shall be treated as filed on the date on which it is filed (in accordance with subsection (f)) after the expiration of such refiling period.

(2) Place for filing.—A notice of lien refiled during the required refiling period shall be effective only—
(A) if—
(i) such notice of lien is refiled in the office in which the prior notice of lien was filed, and
(ii) in the case of real property, the fact of refiling is entered and recorded in an index to the extent required by subsection (f)(4); and
(B) in any case in which, 90 days or more prior to the date of a refiling of notice of lien under subparagraph (A), the Secretary received written information (in the manner prescribed in regulations issued by the Secretary) concerning a change in the taxpayer's residence, if a notice of such lien is also filed in accordance with subsection (f) in the State in which such residence is located.

(3) Required refiling period.—In the case of any notice of lien, the term "required refiling period" means—
(A) the one-year period ending 30 days after the expiration of 10 years after the date of the assessment of the tax, and
(B) the one-year period ending with the expiration of 10 years after the close of the preceding required refiling period for such notice of lien.

(4) Transitional rule.—Notwithstanding paragraph (3), if the assessment of the tax was made before January 1, 1962, the first required refiling period shall be the calendar year 1967.

(h) Definitions.—For purposes of this section and section 6324—

(1) Security interest.—The term "security interest" means any interest in property acquired by contract for the purpose of securing payment or performance of an obligation or indemnifying against loss or liability. A security interest exists at any time (A) if, at such time, the property is in existence and the interest has become protected under local law against a subsequent judgment lien arising out of an unsecured obligation, and (B) to the extent that, at such time, the holder has parted with money or money's worth.

(2) Mechanic's lienor.—The term "mechanic's lienor" means any person who under local law has a lien on real property (or on the proceeds of a contract relating to real property) for services, labor, or materials furnished in connection with the construction or improvement of such property. For purposes of the preceding sentence, a person has a lien on the earliest date such lien becomes valid under local law against subsequent purchasers without actual notice, but not before he begins to furnish the services, labor, or materials.

(3) Motor vehicle.—The term "motor vehicle" means a self-propelled vehicle which is registered for highway use under the laws of any State or foreign country.

(4) Security.—The term "security" means any bond, debenture, note, or certificate or other evidence of indebtedness, issued by a corporation or a government or political subdivision thereof, with interest coupons or in registered form, share of stock, voting trust certificate, or any certificate of interest or participation in, certificate of deposit or receipt for, temporary or interim certificate for, or warrant or right to subscribe to or purchase, any of the foregoing; negotiable instrument; or money.

(5) Tax lien filing.—The term "tax lien filing" means the filing of notice (referred to in subsection (a)) of the lien imposed by section 6321.

(6) Purchaser.—The term "purchaser" means a person who, for adequate and full consideration in money or money's worth, acquires an interest (other than a lien or security interest) in property which is valid under local law against subsequent purchasers without actual notice. In applying the preceding sentence for purposes of subsection (a) of this section, and for purposes of section 6324—
(A) a lease of property,
(B) a written executory contract to purchase or lease property,
(C) an option to purchase or lease property or any interest therein, or
(D) an option to renew or extend a lease of property,
which is not a lien or security interest shall be treated as an interest in property.

(i) Special rules.—

(1) Actual notice or knowledge.—For purposes of this subchapter, an organization shall be deemed for purposes of a particular transaction to have actual notice or knowledge of any fact from the time such fact is brought to the attention of the individual conducting such transaction, and in any event from the time such fact would have been brought to such individual's attention if the organization had exercised due diligence. An organization exercises due diligence if it maintains reasonable routines for communicating significant information to the person conducting the transaction and there is reasonable compliance with the routine. Due diligence does not require an individual acting for the organization to communicate information unless such communication is part of his regular duties or unless he has reason to know of the transaction and that the transaction would be materially affected by the information.

(2) Subrogation.—Where, under local law, one person is subrogated to the rights of another with respect to a lien or interest, such person shall be subrogated to such rights for purposes of any lien imposed by section 6321 or 6324.

(3) Forfeitures.—For purposes of this subchapter, a forfeiture under local law of property seized by a law enforcement agency of a State, county, or other local governmental subdivision shall relate back to the time of seizure, except that this paragraph shall not apply to the extent that under local law the holder of an intervening claim or interest would have priority over the interest of the State, county, or other local governmental subdivision in the property.

(4) Cost-of-living adjustment.—In the case of notices of liens imposed by section 6321 which are filed in any calendar year after 1998, each of the dollar amounts under paragraph (4) or (7) of subsection (b) shall be increased by an amount equal to.—

(A) such dollar amount, multiplied by

(B) the cost-of-living adjustment determined under section 1(f)(3) for the calendar year, determined by substituting "calendar year 1996" for "calendar year 1992" in subparagraph (B) thereof.

If any amount as adjusted under the preceding sentence is not a multiple of $10, such amount shall be rounded to the nearest multiple of $10.

(j) Withdrawal of notice in certain circumstances.—

(1) In general.—The Secretary may withdraw a notice of a lien filed under this section and this chapter shall be applied as if the withdrawn notice had not been filed, if the Secretary determines that—

(A) the filing of such notice was premature or otherwise not in accordance with administrative procedures of the Secretary,

(B) the taxpayer has entered into an agreement under section 6159 to satisfy the tax liability for which the lien was imposed by means of installment payments, unless such agreement provides otherwise,

(C) the withdrawal of such notice will facilitate the collection of the tax liability, or

(D) with the consent of the taxpayer or the National Taxpayer Advocate, the withdrawal of such notice would be in the best interests of the taxpayer (as determined by the National Taxpayer Advocate) and the United States.

Any such withdrawal shall be made by filing notice at the same office as the withdrawn notice. A copy of such notice of withdrawal shall be provided to the taxpayer.

(2) Notice to credit agencies, etc.—Upon written request by the taxpayer with respect to whom a notice of a lien was withdrawn under paragraph (1), the Secretary shall promptly make reasonable efforts to notify credit reporting agencies, and any financial institution or creditor whose name and address is specified in such request, of the withdrawal of such notice. Any such request shall be in such form as the Secretary may prescribe.

* * *

26 U.S.C. § 6658. Coordination with title 11

(a) Certain failures to pay tax.—No addition to the tax shall be made under section 6651, 6654, or 6655 for failure to make timely payment of tax with respect to a period during which a case is pending under title 11 of the United States Code—

(1) if such tax was incurred by the estate and the failure occurred pursuant to an order of the court finding probable insufficiency of funds of the estate to pay administrative expenses, or

(2) if—

(A) such tax was incurred by the debtor before the earlier of the order for relief or (in the involuntary case) the appointment of a trustee, and

(B)(i) the petition was filed before the due date prescribed by law (including extensions) for filing a return of such tax, or

(ii) the date for making the addition to the tax occurs on or after the day on which the petition was filed.

(b) Exception for collected taxes.—Subsection (a) shall not apply to any liability for an addition to the tax which arises from the failure to pay or deposit a tax withheld or collected from others and required to be paid to the United States.

* * *

26 U.S.C. § 7433. Civil damages for certain unauthorized collection actions

* * *

(e) Actions for violations of certain bankruptcy procedures.—

(1) In general.—If, in connection with any collection of Federal tax with respect to a taxpayer, any officer or employee of the Internal Revenue Service willfully violates any provision of section 362 (relating to automatic stay) or 524 (relating to effect of discharge) of title 11, United States Code (or any successor provision), or any regulation promulgated under such provision, such taxpayer may petition the bankruptcy court to recover damages against the United States.

(2) Remedy to be exclusive.—

(A) **In general.**—Except as provided in subparagraph (B), notwithstanding section 105 of such title 11, such petition shall be the exclusive remedy for recovering damages resulting from such actions.

(B) **Certain other actions permitted.**—Subparagraph (A) shall not apply to an action under section 362(h) of such title 11 for a violation of a stay provided by section 362 of such title; except that—

(i) administrative and litigation costs in connection with such an action may only be awarded under section 7430; and

(ii) administrative costs may be awarded only if incurred on or after the date that the bankruptcy petition is filed.

* * *

TITLE 37—PAY AND ALLOWANCES OF THE UNIFORMED SERVICES

* * *

37 U.S.C. § 301d. Multiyear retention bonus: medical officers of the armed forces

* * *

(c) Refunds.—

(1) Refunds shall be required, on a pro rata basis, of sums paid under this section if the officer who has received the payment fails to complete the total period of active duty specified in the agreement, as conditions and circumstances warrant.

(2) An obligation to reimburse the United States imposed under paragraph (1) is for all purposes a debt owed to the United States.

(3) A discharge in bankruptcy under title 11, United States Code, that is entered less than five years after the termination of an agreement under this section does not discharge the member signing such agreement from a debt arising under such agreement or under paragraph (1). This paragraph applies to any case commenced under title 11 after November 5, 1990.

37 U.S.C. § 301e. Multiyear retention bonus: dental officers of the armed forces

* * *

(d) Refunds.—

(1) Refunds shall be required, on a pro rata basis, of sums paid under this section if the officer who has received the payment fails to complete the total period of active duty specified in the agreement, as conditions and circumstances warrant.

(2) An obligation to reimburse the United States imposed under paragraph (1) is for all purposes a debt owed to the United States.

(3) A discharge in bankruptcy under title 11, United States Code, that is entered less than five years after the termination of an agreement under this section does not discharge the member signing such agreement from a debt arising under such agreement or under paragraph (1). This paragraph applies to any case commenced under title 11 after the date of enactment of the National Defense Authorization Act for Fiscal Year 1998.

37 U.S.C. § 302. Special pay: medical officers of the armed forces

(a) Variable, additional, and board certification special pay.—

(1) An officer who is an officer of the Medical Corps of the Army or the Navy or an officer of the Air Force designated as a medical officer and who is on active duty under a call or order to active duty for a period of not less than one year is entitled to special pay in accordance with this subsection.

(2) An officer described in paragraph (1) who is serving in a pay grade below pay grade O-7 is entitled to variable special pay at the following rates:
  (A) $1,200 per year, if the officer is undergoing medical internship training.
  (B) $5,000 per year, if the officer has less than six years of creditable service and is not undergoing medical internship training.
  (C) $12,000 per year, if the officer has at least six but less than eight years of creditable service.
  (D) $11,500 per year, if the officer has at least eight but less than ten years of creditable service.
  (E) $11,000 per year, if the officer has at least ten but less than twelve years of creditable service.
  (F) $10,000 per year, if the officer has at least twelve but less than fourteen years of creditable service.
  (G) $9,000 per year, if the officer has at least fourteen but less than eighteen years of creditable service.
  (H) $8,000 per year, if the officer has at least eighteen but less than twenty-two years of creditable service.
  (I) $7,000 per year, if the officer has twenty-two or more years of creditable service.

(3) An officer described in paragraph (1) who is serving in a pay grade above pay grade O-6 is entitled to variable special pay at the rate of $7,000 per year.

(4) Subject to subsection (c), an officer entitled to variable special pay under paragraph (2) or (3) is entitled to additional special pay of $15,000 for any twelve-month period during which the officer is not undergoing medical internship or initial residency

training.

(5) An officer who is entitled to variable special pay under paragraph (2) or (3) and who is board certified is entitled to additional special pay at the following rates:
  (A) $2,500 per year, if the officer has less than ten years of creditable service.
  (B) $3,500 per year, if the officer has at least ten but less than twelve years of creditable service.
  (C) $4,000 per year, if the officer has at least twelve but less than fourteen years of creditable service.
  (D) $5,000 per year, if the officer has at least fourteen but less than eighteen years of creditable service.
  (E) $6,000 per year, if the officer has eighteen or more years of creditable service.

(b) Incentive special pay.—

(1) Subject to subsection (c) and paragraph (2) and under regulations prescribed under section 303a(a) of this title, an officer who is entitled to variable special pay under subsection (a)(2) may be paid incentive special pay for any twelve-month period during which the officer is not undergoing medical internship or initial residency training. The amount of incentive special pay paid to an officer under this subsection may not exceed $50,000 for any 12-month period.

(2) An officer is not eligible for incentive special pay under paragraph (1) unless the Secretary concerned has determined that such officer is qualified in the medical profession.

(c) Active-duty agreement.—

(1) An officer may not be paid additional special pay under subsection (a)(4) or incentive special pay under subsection (b) for any twelve-month period unless the officer first executes a written agreement under which the officer agrees to remain on active duty for a period of not less than one year beginning on the date the officer accepts the award of such special pay.

(2) Under regulations prescribed by the Secretary of Defense under section 303a of this title, the Secretary of the military department concerned may terminate at any time an officer's entitlement to the special pay authorized by subsection (a)(4) or (b)(1). If such entitlement is terminated, the officer concerned is entitled to be paid such special pay only for the part of the period of active duty that he served, and he may be required to refund any amount in excess of that entitlement.

(d) Regulations.—Regulations prescribed by the Secretary of Defense under section 303a(a) of this title shall include standards for determining—

(1) whether an officer is undergoing medical internship or initial residency training for purposes of subsections (a)(2)(A), (a)(2)(B), (a)(4), and (b)(1); and

(2) whether an officer is board certified for purposes of subsection (a)(5).

(e) Frequency of payments.—Special pay payable to an officer under paragraphs (2), (3), and (5) of subsection (a) shall be paid monthly. Special pay payable to an officer under subsection (a)(4) or (b)(1) shall be paid annually at the beginning of the twelve-month period for which the officer is entitled to such payment.

(f) Refund for period of unserved obligated service.—An officer who voluntarily terminates service on active duty before the end of the period for which a payment was made to such officer under subsection (a)(4) or (b)(1) shall refund to the United States an amount which bears the same ratio to the amount paid to such officer as the unserved part of such period bears to the total period for which the payment was made.

(g) Determination of creditable service.—For purposes of this section, creditable service of an officer is computed by adding—

(1) all periods which the officer spent in medical internship or residency training during which the officer was not on active duty; and

(2) all periods of active service in the Medical Corps of the Army or Navy, as an officer of the Air Force designated as a medical officer, or as a medical officer of the Public Health Service.

(h) Reserve medical officers special pay.—

(1) A reserve medical officer described in paragraph (2) is entitled to special pay at the rate of $450 a month for each month of active duty, including active duty in the form of annual training, active duty for training, and active duty for special work.

(2) A reserve medical officer referred to in paragraph (1) is a reserve officer who—
 (A) is an officer of the Medical Corps of the Army or the Navy or an officer of the Air Force designated as a medical officer; and
 (B) is on active duty under a call or order to active duty for a period of less than one year.

(i) Effect of discharge in bankruptcy.—A discharge in bankruptcy under title 11 that is entered less than 5 years after the termination of an agreement under this section does not discharge the person signing such agreement from a debt arising under such agreement or under subsection (c)(2) or (f). This paragraph applies to any case commenced under title 11 after September 30, 1985.

* * *

37 U.S.C. § 302g. Special pay: Selected Reserve health care professionals in critically short wartime specialties

(a) Special pay authorized.—An officer of a reserve component of the armed forces described in subsection (b) who executes a written agreement under which the officer agrees to serve in the Selected Reserve of an armed force for a period of not less than one year nor more than three years, beginning on the date the officer accepts the award of special pay under this section, may be paid special pay at an annual rate not to exceed $10,000.

(b) Eligible officers.—An officer referred to in subsection (a) is an officer in a health care profession who is qualified in a specialty designated by regulations as a critically short wartime specialty.

(c) Time for payment.—Special pay under this section shall be paid annually at the beginning of each twelve-month period for which the officer has agreed to serve.

(d) Refund requirement.—An officer who voluntarily terminates service in the Selected Reserve of an armed force before the end of the period for which a payment was made to such officer under this

section shall refund to the United States the full amount of the payment made for the period on which the payment was based.

(e) Inapplicability of discharge in bankruptcy.—A discharge in bankruptcy under title 11 that is entered less than five years after the termination of an agreement under this section does not discharge the person receiving special pay under the agreement from the debt arising under the agreement.

(f) Termination of agreement authority.—No agreement under this section may be entered into after December 31, 2004.

* * *

37 U.S.C. § 314. Special pay or bonus: qualified members extending duty at designated locations overseas

* * *

(d) Repayment of bonus.—

(1) A member who, having entered into a written agreement to extend a tour of duty for a period under subsection (a), receives a bonus payment under subsection (b)(2) for a 12-month period covered by the agreement and ceases during that 12-month period to perform the agreed tour of duty shall refund to the United States the unearned portion of the bonus. The unearned portion of the bonus is the amount by which the amount of the bonus paid to the member exceeds the amount determined by multiplying the amount of the bonus paid by the percent determined by dividing 12 into the number of full months during which the member performed the duty in the 12-month period.

(2) The Secretary concerned may waive the obligation of a member to reimburse the United States under paragraph (1) if the Secretary determines that conditions and circumstances warrant the waiver.

(3) An obligation to repay the United States imposed under paragraph (1) is for all purposes a debt owed to the United States.

(4) A discharge in bankruptcy under title 11 that is entered less than five years after the termination of the agreement does not discharge the member signing the agreement from a debt arising under the agreement or under paragraph (1). This paragraph applies to any case commenced under title 11 or after the date of the enactment of the National Defense Authorization Act for Fiscal Year 1998.[26]

* * *

37 U.S.C. § 317. Special pay: officers in critical acquisition positions extending period of active duty

* * *

(f) Repayment of bonus.—

(1) If an officer who has entered into a written agreement under subsection (a) and who has received all or part of a bonus under this section fails to complete the total period of active duty specified in the agreement, the Secretary concerned may require the officer to repay the United States, on a pro rata basis and to the extent that the Secretary determines conditions and circumstances warrant, all sums paid under this section.

---

26 *Editor's Note*: The date of enactment of the National Defense Authorization Act for Fiscal Year 1998, Pub. L. No. 105-85, 111 Stat. 1629, referred to in § (d)(4), is Nov. 18, 1997.

(2) An obligation to repay the United States imposed under paragraph (1) is for all purposes a debt owed to the United States.

(3) A discharge in bankruptcy under title 11 that is entered less than 5 years after the termination of a written agreement entered into under subsection (a) does not discharge the officer signing the agreement from a debt arising under such agreement or under paragraph (1). This paragraph applies to any case commenced under title 11 after January 1, 1991.

* * *

37 U.S.C. § 318. Special pay: special warfare officers extending period of active duty

* * *

(h) Repayment.—

(1) If an officer who has entered into an agreement under subsection (b) and has received all or part of a retention bonus under this section fails to complete the total period of active duty in special warfare service as specified in the agreement, the Secretary concerned may require the officer to repay the United States, on a pro rata basis and to the extent that the Secretary determines conditions and circumstances warrant, all sums paid the officer under this section.

(2) An obligation to repay the United States imposed under paragraph (1) is for all purposes a debt owed to the United States.

(3) A discharge in bankruptcy under title 11 that is entered less than five years after the termination of an agreement entered into under subsection (b) does not discharge the officer signing the agreement from a debt arising under such agreement or under paragraph (1).

* * *

37 U.S.C. § 319. Special pay: surface warfare officer continuation pay

* * *

(f) Repayment.—

(1) If an officer who has entered into a written agreement under subsection (b) and has received all or part of the amount payable under the agreement fails to complete the total period of active duty as a department head on a surface vessel specified in the agreement, the Secretary of the Navy may require the officer to repay the United States, to the extent that the Secretary of the Navy determines conditions and circumstances warrant, any or all sums paid under this section.

(2) An obligation to repay the United States imposed under paragraph (1) is for all purposes a debt owed to the United States.

(3) A discharge in bankruptcy under title 11 that is entered less than five years after the termination of an agreement entered into under subsection (b) does not discharge the officer signing the agreement from a debt arising under such agreement or under paragraph (1).

* * *

37 U.S.C. § 321. Special pay: judge advocate continuation pay

* * *

(f) Repayment.—

(1) If an officer who has entered into a written agreement under subsection (b) and has received all or part of the amount payable under the agreement fails to complete the total period of active duty specified in the agreement, the Secretary concerned may require the officer to repay the United States, to the extent that the Secretary determines conditions and circumstances warrant, any or all sums paid under this section.

(2) An obligation to repay the United States imposed under paragraph (1) is for all purposes a debt owed to the United States.

(3) A discharge in bankruptcy under title 11 that is entered less than five years after the termination of an agreement entered into under subsection (b) does not discharge the officer signing the agreement from a debt arising under such agreement or under paragraph (1).

* * *

37 U.S.C. § 322. Special pay: 15-year career status bonus for members entering service on or after August 1, 1986

* * *

(f) Repayment of bonus.—

(1) If a person paid a bonus under this section fails to complete a period of active duty beginning on the date on which the election of the person under subsection (a)(1) is received and ending on the date on which the person completes 20 years of active-duty service as described in subsection (a)(2), the person shall refund to the United States the amount that bears the same ratio to the amount of the bonus payment as the uncompleted part of that period of active-duty service bears to the total period of such service.

(2) Subject to paragraph (3), an obligation to reimburse the United States imposed under paragraph (1) is for all purposes a debt owed to the United States.

(3) The Secretary concerned may waive, in whole or in part, a refund required under paragraph (1) if the Secretary concerned determines that recovery would be against equity and good conscience or would be contrary to the best interests of the United States.

(4) A discharge in bankruptcy under title 11 that is entered less than five years after the termination of an agreement under this section does not discharge the member signing such agreement from a debt arising under the agreement or this subsection.

* * *

TITLE 42—THE PUBLIC HEALTH AND WELFARE

42 U.S.C. § 254*o*. Breach of scholarship contract or loan repayment contract

* * *

(d) Cancellation of obligation upon death of individual; waiver or suspension of obligation for impossibility, hardship, or unconscionability; release of debt by discharge in bankruptcy, time limitations—

(1) Any obligation of an individual under the Scholarship Program (or a contract thereunder) or the Loan Repayment Program (or

a contract thereunder) for service or payment of damages shall be canceled upon the death of the individual.

(2) The Secretary shall by regulation provide for the partial or total waiver or suspension of any obligation of service or payment by an individual under the Scholarship Program (or a contract thereunder) or the Loan Repayment Program (or a contract thereunder) whenever compliance by the individual is impossible or would involve extreme hardship to the individual and if enforcement of such obligation with respect to any individual would be unconscionable.

(3)(A) Any obligation of an individual under the Scholarship Program (or a contract thereunder) or the Loan Repayment Program (or a contract thereunder) for payment of damages may be released by a discharge in bankruptcy under title 11 of the United States Code only if such discharge is granted after the expiration of the 7-year period beginning on the first date that payment of such damages is required, and only if the bankruptcy court finds that nondischarge of the obligation would be unconscionable.

(B)(i) Subparagraph (A) shall apply to any financial obligation of an individual under the provision of law specified in clause (ii) to the same extent and in the same manner as such subparagraph applies to any obligation of an individual under the Scholarship or Loan Repayment Program (or contract thereunder) for payment of damages.

(ii) The provision of law referred to in clause (i) is subsection (f) of section 234 of this title, as in effect prior to the repeal of such section by section 408(b)(1) of Public Law 94-484.

(e) Notwithstanding any other provision of Federal or State law, there shall be no limitation on the period within which suit may be filed, a judgment may be enforced, or an action relating to an offset or garnishment, or other action, may be initiated or taken by the Secretary, the Attorney General, or the head of another Federal agency, as the case may be, for the repayment of the amount due from an individual under this section.

* * *

42 U.S.C. § 292f. Default of borrower

* * *

(g) Conditions for discharge of debt in bankruptcy.—Notwithstanding any other provision of Federal or State law, a debt which is a loan insured under the authority of this subpart may be released by a discharge in bankruptcy under any chapter of Title 11, only if such discharge is granted—

(1) after the expiration of the seven-year period beginning on the first date when repayment of such loan is required, exclusive of any period after such date in which the obligation to pay installments on the loan is suspended;

(2) upon a finding by the Bankruptcy Court that the nondischarge of such debt would be unconscionable; and

(3) upon the condition that the Secretary shall not have waived the Secretary's rights to apply subsection (f) of this section to the borrower and the discharged debt.

* * *

42 U.S.C. § 297a. Loan agreements

* * *

(c) Regulatory standards applicable to collection of loans.—

(1) Any standard established by the Secretary by regulation for the collection by schools of nursing of loans made pursuant to loan agreements under this subpart shall provide that the failure of any such school to collect such loans shall be measured in accordance with this subsection. With respect to the student loan fund established pursuant to such agreements, this subsection may not be construed to require such schools to reimburse such loan fund for loans that became uncollectable prior to 1983.

(2) The measurement of a school's failure to collect loans made under this subpart shall be the ratio (stated as a percentage) that the defaulted principal amount outstanding of such school bears to the matured loans of such school.

(3) For purposes of this subsection—

(A) the term "default" means the failure of a borrower of a loan made under this subpart to—

(i) make an installment payment when due; or

(ii) comply with any other term of the promissory note for such loan,

except that a loan made under this subpart shall not be considered to be in default if the loan is discharged in bankruptcy or if the school reasonably concludes from written contacts with the borrower that the borrower intends to repay the loan;

(B) the term "defaulted principal amount outstanding" means the total amount borrowed from the loan fund of a school that has reached the repayment stage (minus any principal amount repaid or cancelled) on loans—

(i) repayable monthly and in default for at least 120 days; and

(ii) repayable less frequently than monthly and in default for at least 180 days;

(C) the term "grace period" means the period of nine months beginning on the date on which the borrower ceases to pursue a full-time or half-time course of study at a school of nursing; and

(D) the term "matured loans" means the total principal amount of all loans made by a school of nursing under this subpart minus the total principal amount of loans made by such school to students who are—

(i) enrolled in a full-time or half-time course of study at such school; or

(ii) in their grace period.

* * *

42 U.S.C. § 656. Support obligation as obligation to State; amount; discharge in bankruptcy

* * *

(b) Nondischargeability—A debt (as defined in section 101 of title 11 of the United States Code) owed under State law to a State (as defined in such section) or municipality (as defined in such section) that is in the nature or support and that is enforceable under this part is not released by a discharge in bankruptcy under title 11 of the United States Code.

TITLE 50 APPENDIX—WAR AND NATIONAL DEFENSE

Servicemembers Civil Relief Act

50 U.S.C. app. § 501. Short title

This Act [sections 501 to 596 of this Appendix] may be cited as the "Servicemembers Civil Relief Act."

50 U.S.C. app. § 502. Purpose

The purposes of this Act are—

(1) to provide for, strengthen, and expedite the national defense through protection extended by this Act to servicemembers of the United States to enable such persons to devote their entire energy to the defense needs of the Nation; and

(2) to provide for the temporary suspension of judicial and administrative proceedings and transactions that may adversely affect the civil rights of servicemembers during their military service.

50 U.S.C. app. § 511. Definitions

For the purposes of this Act:

(1) Servicemember

The term "servicemember" means a member of the uniformed services, as that term is defined in section 101(a)(5) of title 10, United States Code.

(2) Military service

The term "military service" means—

(A) in the case of a servicemember who is a member of the Army, Navy, Air Force, Marine Corps, or Coast Guard—
   (i) active duty, as defined in section 101(d)(1) of title 10, United States Code, and
   (ii) in the case of a member of the National Guard, includes service under a call to active service authorized by the President or the Secretary of Defense for a period of more than 30 consecutive days under section 502(f) of title 32, United States Code, for purposes of responding to a national emergency declared by the President and supported by Federal funds;

(B) in the case of a servicemember who is a commissioned officer of the Public Health Service or the National Oceanic and Atmospheric Administration, active service; and

(C) any period during which a servicemember is absent from duty on account of sickness, wounds, leave, or other lawful cause.

(3) Period of military service

The term "period of military service" means the period beginning on the date on which a servicemember enters military service and ending on the date on which the servicemember is released from military service or dies while in military service.

(4) Dependent

The term "dependent," with respect to a servicemember, means—

(A) the servicemember's spouse;

(B) the servicemember's child (as defined in section 101(4) of title 38, United States Code); or

(C) an individual for whom the servicemember provided more than one-half of the individual's support for 180 days immediately preceding an application for relief under this Act.

(5) Court

The term "court" means a court or an administrative agency of the United States or of any State (including any political subdivision of a State), whether or not a court or administrative agency of record.

(6) State

The term "State" includes—

(A) a commonwealth, territory, or possession of the United States; and

(B) the District of Columbia.

(7) Secretary concerned

The term "Secretary concerned"—

(A) with respect to a member of the armed forces, has the meaning given that term in section 101(a)(9) of title 10, United States Code;

(B) with respect to a commissioned officer of the Public Health Service, means the Secretary of Health and Human Services; and

(C) with respect to a commissioned officer of the National Oceanic and Atmospheric Administration, means the Secretary of Commerce.

(8) Motor vehicle

The term "motor vehicle" has the meaning given that term in section 30102(a)(6) of title 49, United States Code.

50 U.S.C. app. § 512. Jurisdiction and applicability of Act

(a) Jurisdiction

This Act applies to—

(1) the United States;

(2) each of the States, including the political subdivisions thereof; and

(3) all territory subject to the jurisdiction of the United States.

(b) Applicability to proceedings

This Act applies to any judicial or administrative proceeding commenced in any court or agency in any jurisdiction subject to this Act. This Act does not apply to criminal proceedings.

(c) Court in which application may be made

When under this Act any application is required to be made to a court in which no proceeding has already been commenced with respect to the matter, such application may be made to any court which would otherwise have jurisdiction over the matter.

50 U.S.C. app. § 513. Protection of persons secondarily liable

(a) Extension of protection when actions stayed, postponed, or suspended

Whenever pursuant to this Act a court stays, postpones, or suspends (1) the enforcement of an obligation or liability, (2) the prosecution of a suit or proceeding, (3) the entry or enforcement of an order, writ, judgment, or decree, or (4) the performance of any other act, the court may likewise grant such a stay, postponement, or suspension to a surety, guarantor, endorser, accommodation maker, comaker, or other person who is or may be primarily or secondarily subject to the obligation or liability the performance or enforcement of which is stayed, postponed, or suspended.

(b) Vacation or set-aside of judgments

When a judgment or decree is vacated or set aside, in whole or in part, pursuant to this Act, the court may also set aside or vacate, as the case may be, the judgment or decree as to a surety, guarantor, endorser, accommodation maker, comaker, or other person who is or may be primarily or secondarily liable on the contract or liability for the enforcement of the judgment or decree.

(c) Bail bond not to be enforced during period of military service

A court may not enforce a bail bond during the period of military service of the principal on the bond when military service prevents the surety from obtaining the attendance of the principal. The court may discharge the surety and exonerate the bail, in accordance with principles of equity and justice, during or after the period of military service of the principal.

(d) Waiver of rights

(1) Waivers not precluded

This Act does not prevent a waiver in writing by a surety, guarantor, endorser, accommodation maker, comaker, or other person (whether primarily or secondarily liable on an obligation or liability) of the protections provided under subsections (a) and (b). Any such waiver is effective only if it is executed as an instrument separate from the obligation or liability with respect to which it applies.

(2) Waiver invalidated upon entrance to military service

If a waiver under paragraph (1) is executed by an individual who after the execution of the waiver enters military service, or by a dependent of an individual who after the execution of the waiver enters military service, the waiver is not valid after the beginning of the period of such military service unless the waiver was executed by such individual or dependent during the period specified in section 106 [section 516 of this Appendix].

50 U.S.C. app. § 514. Extension of protections to citizens serving with allied forces

A citizen of the United States who is serving with the forces of a nation with which the United States is allied in the prosecution of a war or military action is entitled to the relief and protections provided under this Act if that service with the allied force is similar to military service as defined in this Act. The relief and protections provided to such citizen shall terminate on the date of discharge or release from such service.

50 U.S.C. app. § 515. Notification of benefits

The Secretary concerned shall ensure that notice of the benefits accorded by this Act is provided in writing to persons in military service and to persons entering military service.

50 U.S.C. app. § 516. Extension of rights and protections to reserves ordered to report for military service and to persons ordered to report for induction

(a) Reserves ordered to report for military service

A member of a reserve component who is ordered to report for military service is entitled to the rights and protections of this title and titles II and III [of this Appendix] during the period beginning on the date of the member's receipt of the order and ending on the date on which the member reports for military service (or, if the order is revoked before the member so reports, or the date on which the order is revoked).

(b) Persons ordered to report for induction

A person who has been ordered to report for induction under the Military Selective Service Act (50 U.S.C. App. 451 et seq.) is entitled to the rights and protections provided a servicemember under this title and titles II and III [of this Appendix] during the period beginning on the date of receipt of the order for induction and ending on the date on which the person reports for induction (or, if the order to report for induction is revoked before the date on which the person reports for induction, on the date on which the order is revoked).

50 U.S.C. app. § 517. Waiver of rights pursuant to written agreement

(a) In general

A servicemember may waive any of the rights and protections provided by this Act. In the case of a waiver that permits an action described in subsection (b), the waiver is effective only if made pursuant to a written agreement of the parties that is executed during or after the servicemember's period of military service. The written agreement shall specify the legal instrument to which the waiver applies and, if the servicemember is not a party to that instrument, the servicemember concerned.

(b) Actions requiring waivers in writing

The requirement in subsection (a) for a written waiver applies to the following:

(1) The modification, termination, or cancellation of—
   (A) a contract, lease, or bailment; or
   (B) an obligation secured by a mortgage, trust, deed, lien, or other security in the nature of a mortgage.

(2) The repossession, retention, foreclosure, sale, forfeiture, or taking possession of property that—
   (A) is security for any obligation; or
   (B) was purchased or received under a contract, lease, or bailment.

(c) Coverage of periods after orders received

For the purposes of this section—

(1) a person to whom section 106 [section 516 of this Appendix] applies shall be considered to be a servicemember; and

(2) the period with respect to such a person specified in subsection (a) or (b), as the case may be, of section 106 [section 516 of this Appendix] shall be considered to be a period of military service.

50 U.S.C. app. § 518. Exercise of rights under Act not to affect certain future financial transactions

Application by a servicemember for, or receipt by a servicemember of, a stay, postponement, or suspension pursuant to this Act in the payment of a tax, fine, penalty, insurance premium, or other civil obligation or liability of that servicemember shall not itself (without regard to other considerations) provide the basis for any of the following:

(1) A determination by a lender or other person that the servicemember is unable to pay the civil obligation or liability in accordance with its terms.

(2) With respect to a credit transaction between a creditor and the servicemember—

  (A) a denial or revocation of credit by the creditor;

  (B) a change by the creditor in the terms of an existing credit arrangement; or

  (C) a refusal by the creditor to grant credit to the servicemember in substantially the amount or on substantially the terms requested.

(3) An adverse report relating to the creditworthiness of the servicemember by or to a person engaged in the practice of assembling or evaluating consumer credit information.

(4) A refusal by an insurer to insure the servicemember.

(5) An annotation in a servicemember's record by a creditor or a person engaged in the practice of assembling or evaluating consumer credit information, identifying the servicemember as a member of the National Guard or a reserve component.

(6) A change in the terms offered or conditions required for the issuance of insurance.

* * *

50 U.S.C. app. § 521. Protection of servicemembers against default judgments

(a) Applicability of section

This section applies to any civil action or proceeding in which the defendant does not make an appearance.

(b) Affidavit requirement

(1) Plaintiff to file affidavit

In any action or proceeding covered by this section, the court, before entering judgment for the plaintiff, shall require the plaintiff to file with the court an affidavit—

  (A) stating whether or not the defendant is in military service and showing necessary facts to support the affidavit; or

  (B) if the plaintiff is unable to determine whether or not the defendant is in military service, stating that the plaintiff is unable to determine whether or not the defendant is in military service.

(2) Appointment of attorney to represent defendant in military service

If in an action covered by this section it appears that the defendant is in military service, the court may not enter a judgment until after the court appoints an attorney to represent the defendant. If an attorney appointed under this section to represent a servicemember cannot locate the servicemember, actions by the attorney in the case shall not waive any defense of the servicemember or otherwise bind the servicemember.

(3) Defendant's military status not ascertained by affidavit

If based upon the affidavits filed in such an action, the court is unable to determine whether the defendant is in military service, the court, before entering judgment, may require the plaintiff to file a bond in an amount approved by the court. If the defendant is later found to be in military service, the bond shall be available to indemnify the defendant against any loss or damage the defendant may suffer by reason of any judgment for the plaintiff against the defendant, should the judgment be set aside in whole or in part. The bond shall remain in effect until expiration of the time for appeal and setting aside of a judgment under applicable Federal or State law or regulation or under any applicable ordinance of a political subdivision of a State. The court may issue such orders or enter such judgments as the court determines necessary to protect the rights of the defendant under this Act.

(4) Satisfaction of requirement for affidavit

The requirement for an affidavit under paragraph (1) may be satisfied by a statement, declaration, verification, or certificate, in writing, subscribed and certified or declared to be true under penalty of perjury.

(c) Penalty for making or using false affidavit

A person who makes or uses an affidavit permitted under subsection (b) (or a statement, declaration, verification, or certificate as authorized under subsection (b)(4)) knowing it to be false, shall be fined as provided in title 18, United States Code, or imprisoned for not more than one year, or both.

(d) Stay of proceedings

In an action covered by this section in which the defendant is in military service, the court shall grant a stay of proceedings for a minimum period of 90 days under this subsection upon application of counsel, or on the court's own motion, if the court determines that—

(1) there may be a defense to the action and a defense cannot be presented without the presence of the defendant; or

(2) after due diligence, counsel has been unable to contact the defendant or otherwise determine if a meritorious defense exists.

(e) Inapplicability of section 202 procedures

A stay of proceedings under subsection (d) shall not be controlled by procedures or requirements under section 202 [section 522 of this Appendix].

(f) Section 202 protection

If a servicemember who is a defendant in an action covered by this section receives actual notice of the action, the servicemember may request a stay of proceeding under section 202 [section 522 of this Appendix].

(g) Vacation or setting aside of default judgments

(1) Authority for court to vacate or set aside judgment

If a default judgment is entered in an action covered by this section against a servicemember during the servicemember's period of military service (or within 60 days after termination of or release from such military service), the court entering the judgment shall, upon application by or on behalf of the servicemember, reopen the judgment for the purpose of allowing the servicemember to defend the action if it appears that—

  (A) the servicemember was materially affected by reason of that military service in making a defense to the action; and

(B) the servicemember has a meritorious or legal defense to the action or some part of it.

(2) Time for filing application

An application under this subsection must be filed not later than 90 days after the date of the termination of or release from military service.

(h) Protection of bona fide purchaser

If a court vacates, sets aside, or reverses a default judgment against a servicemember and the vacating, setting aside, or reversing is because of a provision of this Act, that action shall not impair a right or title acquired by a bona fide purchaser for value under the default judgment.

50 U.S.C. app. § 522. Stay of proceedings when servicemember has notice

(a) Applicability of section

This section applies to any civil action or proceeding in which the defendant at the time of filing an application under this section—

(1) is in military service or is within 90 days after termination of or release from military service; and

(2) has received notice of the action or proceeding.

(b) Stay of proceedings

(1) Authority for stay

At any stage before final judgment in a civil action or proceeding in which a servicemember described in subsection (a) is a party, the court may on its own motion and shall, upon application by the servicemember, stay the action for a period of not less than 90 days, if the conditions in paragraph (2) are met.

(2) Conditions for stay

An application for a stay under paragraph (1) shall include the following:

(A) A letter or other communication setting forth facts stating the manner in which current military duty requirements materially affect the servicemember's ability to appear and stating a date when the servicemember will be available to appear.

(B) A letter or other communication from the servicemember's commanding officer stating that the servicemember's current military duty prevents appearance and that military leave is not authorized for the servicemember at the time of the letter.

(c) Application not a waiver of defenses

An application for a stay under this section does not constitute an appearance for jurisdictional purposes and does not constitute a waiver of any substantive or procedural defense (including a defense relating to lack of personal jurisdiction).

(d) Additional stay

(1) Application

A servicemember who is granted a stay of a civil action or proceeding under subsection (b) may apply for an additional stay based on continuing material affect of military duty on the servicemember's ability to appear. Such an application may be made by the servicemember at the time of the initial applica-

tion under subsection (b) or when it appears that the servicemember is unavailable to prosecute or defend the action. The same information required under subsection (b)(2) shall be included in an application under this subsection.

(2) Appointment of counsel when additional stay refused

If the court refuses to grant an additional stay of proceedings under paragraph (1), the court shall appoint counsel to represent the servicemember in the action or proceeding.

(e) Coordination with section 201 [section 521 of this Appendix]

A servicemember who applies for a stay under this section and is unsuccessful may not seek the protections afforded by section 201 [section 521 of this Appendix].

(f) Inapplicability to section 301 [section 531 of this Appendix]

The protections of this section do not apply to section 301 [section 531 of this Appendix].

50 U.S.C. app. § 523. Fines and penalties under contracts

(a) Prohibition of penalties

When an action for compliance with the terms of a contract is stayed pursuant to this Act, a penalty shall not accrue for failure to comply with the terms of the contract during the period of the stay.

(b) Reduction or waiver of fines or penalties

If a servicemember fails to perform an obligation arising under a contract and a penalty is incurred arising from that nonperformance, a court may reduce or waive the fine or penalty if—

(1) the servicemember was in military service at the time the fine or penalty was incurred; and

(2) the ability of the servicemember to perform the obligation was materially affected by such military service.

50 U.S.C. app. § 524. Stay or vacation of execution of judgments, attachments, and garnishments

(a) Court action upon material affect determination

If a servicemember, in the opinion of the court, is materially affected by reason of military service in complying with a court judgment or order, the court may on its own motion and shall on application by the servicemember—

(1) stay the execution of any judgment or order entered against the servicemember; and

(2) vacate or stay an attachment or garnishment of property, money, or debts in the possession of the servicemember or a third party, whether before or after judgment.

(b) Applicability

This section applies to an action or proceeding commenced in a court against a servicemember before or during the period of the servicemember's military service or within 90 days after such service terminates.

50 U.S.C. app. § 525. Duration and term of stays; codefendants not in service

(a) Period of stay

A stay of an action, proceeding, attachment, or execution made pursuant to the provisions of this Act by a court may be ordered for the period of military service and 90 days thereafter, or for any part of that period. The court may set the terms and amounts for such installment payments as is considered reasonable by the court.

(b) Codefendants

If the servicemember is a codefendant with others who are not in military service and who are not entitled to the relief and protections provided under this Act, the plaintiff may proceed against those other defendants with the approval of the court.

(c) Inapplicability of section

This section does not apply to sections 202 and 701 [sections 522 and 591 of this Appendix].

50 U.S.C. app. § 526. Statute of limitations

(a) Tolling of statutes of limitation during military service

The period of a servicemember's military service may not be included in computing any period limited by law, regulation, or order for the bringing of any action or proceeding in a court, or in any board, bureau, commission, department, or other agency of a State (or political subdivision of a State) or the United States by or against the servicemember or the servicemember's heirs, executors, administrators, or assigns.

(b) Redemption of real property

A period of military service may not be included in computing any period provided by law for the redemption of real property sold or forfeited to enforce an obligation, tax, or assessment.

(c) Inapplicability to internal revenue laws

This section does not apply to any period of limitation prescribed by or under the internal revenue laws of the United States.

50 U.S.C. app. § 527. Maximum rate of interest on debts incurred before military service

(a) Interest rate limitation

(1) Limitation to 6 percent

An obligation or liability bearing interest at a rate in excess of 6 percent per year that is incurred by a servicemember, or the servicemember and the servicemember's spouse jointly, before the servicemember enters military service shall not bear interest at a rate in excess of 6 percent per year during the period of military service.

(2) Forgiveness of interest in excess of 6 percent

Interest at a rate in excess of 6 percent per year that would otherwise be incurred but for the prohibition in paragraph (1) is forgiven.

(3) Prevention of acceleration of principal

The amount of any periodic payment due from a servicemember under the terms of the instrument that created an obligation or liability covered by this section shall be reduced by the amount of the interest forgiven under paragraph (2) that is allocable to the period for which such payment is made.

(b) Implementation of limitation

(1) Written notice to creditor

In order for an obligation or liability of a servicemember to be subject to the interest rate limitation in subsection (a), the servicemember shall provide to the creditor written notice and a copy of the military orders calling the servicemember to military service and any orders further extending military service, not later than 180 days after the date of the servicemember's termination or release from military service.

(2) Limitation effective as of date of order to active duty

Upon receipt of written notice and a copy of orders calling a servicemember to military service, the creditor shall treat the debt in accordance with subsection (a), effective as of the date on which the servicemember is called to military service.

(c) Creditor protection

A court may grant a creditor relief from the limitations of this section if, in the opinion of the court, the ability of the servicemember to pay interest upon the obligation or liability at a rate in excess of 6 percent per year is not materially affected by reason of the servicemember's military service.

(d) Interest

As used in this section, the term "interest" includes service charges, renewal charges, fees, or any other charges (except bona fide insurance) with respect to an obligation or liability.

50 U.S.C. app. § 531. Evictions and distress

(a) Court-ordered eviction

(1) In general

Except by court order, a landlord (or another person with paramount title) may not—

(A) evict a servicemember, or the dependents of a servicemember, during a period of military service of the servicemember, from premises—

    (i) that are occupied or intended to be occupied primarily as a residence; and

    (ii) for which the monthly rent does not exceed $2,400, as adjusted under paragraph (2) for years after 2003; or

(B) subject such premises to a distress during the period of military service.

(2) Housing price inflation adjustment

(A) For calendar years beginning with 2004, the amount in effect under paragraph (1)(A)(ii) shall be increased by the housing price inflation adjustment for the calendar year involved.

(B) For purposes of this paragraph—

    (i) The housing price inflation adjustment for any calendar year is the percentage change (if any) by which—

        (I) the CPI housing component for November of the preceding calendar year, exceeds

        (II) the CPI housing component for November of 1984.

    (ii) The term "CPI housing component" means the index published by the Bureau of Labor Statistics of the Department of Labor known as the Consumer Price Index, All Urban Consumers, Rent of Primary Residence, U.S. City Average.

(3) Publication of housing price inflation adjustment

The Secretary of Defense shall cause to be published in the Federal Register each year the amount in effect under paragraph (1)(A)(ii) for that year following the housing price inflation adjustment for that year pursuant to paragraph (2). Such publication shall be made for a year not later than 60 days after such adjustment is made for that year.

(b) Stay of execution

(1) Court authority

Upon an application for eviction or distress with respect to premises covered by this section, the court may on its own motion and shall, if a request is made by or on behalf of a servicemember whose ability to pay the agreed rent is materially affected by military service—

(A) stay the proceedings for a period of 90 days, unless in the opinion of the court, justice and equity require a longer or shorter period of time; or

(B) adjust the obligation under the lease to preserve the interests of all parties.

(2) Relief to landlord

If a stay is granted under paragraph (1), the court may grant to the landlord (or other person with paramount title) such relief as equity may require.

(c) Penalties

(1) Misdemeanor

Except as provided in subsection (a), a person who knowingly takes part in an eviction or distress described in subsection (a), or who knowingly attempts to do so, shall be fined as provided in title 18, United States Code, or imprisoned for not more than one year, or both.

(2) Preservation of other remedies and rights

The remedies and rights provided under this section are in addition to and do not preclude any remedy for wrongful conversion (or wrongful eviction) otherwise available under the law to the person claiming relief under this section, including any award for consequential and punitive damages.

(d) Rent allotment from pay of servicemember

To the extent required by a court order related to property which is the subject of a court action under this section, the Secretary concerned shall make an allotment from the pay of a servicemember to satisfy the terms of such order, except that any such allotment shall be subject to regulations prescribed by the Secretary concerned establishing the maximum amount of pay of servicemembers that may be allotted under this subsection.

(e) Limitation of applicability

Section 202 [section 522 of this Appendix] is not applicable to this section.

50 U.S.C. app. § 532. Protection under installment contracts for purchase or lease

(a) Protection upon breach of contract

(1) Protection after entering military service

After a servicemember enters military service, a contract by the servicemember for—

(A) the purchase of real or personal property (including a motor vehicle); or

(B) the lease or bailment of such property,

may not be rescinded or terminated for a breach of terms of the contract occurring before or during that person's military service, nor may the property be repossessed for such breach without a court order.

(2) Applicability

This section applies only to a contract for which a deposit or installment has been paid by the servicemember before the servicemember enters military service.

(b) Penalties

(1) Misdemeanor

A person who knowingly resumes possession of property in violation of subsection (a), or in violation of section 107 of this Act [section 517 of this Appendix], or who knowingly attempts to do so, shall be fined as provided in title 18, United States Code, or imprisoned for not more than one year, or both.

(2) Preservation of other remedies and rights

The remedies and rights provided under this section are in addition to and do not preclude any remedy for wrongful conversion otherwise available under law to the person claiming relief under this section, including any award for consequential and punitive damages.

(c) Authority of court

In a hearing based on this section, the court—

(1) may order repayment to the servicemember of all or part of the prior installments or deposits as a condition of terminating the contract and resuming possession of the property;

(2) may, on its own motion, and shall on application by a servicemember when the servicemember's ability to comply with the contract is materially affected by military service, stay the proceedings for a period of time as, in the opinion of the court, justice and equity require; or

(3) may make other disposition as is equitable to preserve the interests of all parties.

50 U.S.C. app. § 533. Mortgages and trust deeds

(a) Mortgage as security

This section applies only to an obligation on real or personal property owned by a servicemember that—

(1) originated before the period of the servicemember's military service and for which the servicemember is still obligated; and

(2) is secured by a mortgage, trust deed, or other security in the nature of a mortgage.

(b) Stay of proceedings and adjustment of obligation

In an action filed during, or within 90 days after, a servicemember's period of military service to enforce an obligation described in subsection (a), the court may after a hearing and on its own motion and shall upon application by a servicemember when the servicemember's ability to comply with the obligation is materially affected by military service—

(1) stay the proceedings for a period of time as justice and equity require, or

(2) adjust the obligation to preserve the interests of all parties.

(c) Sale or foreclosure

A sale, foreclosure, or seizure of property for a breach of an obligation described in subsection (a) shall not be valid if made during, or within 90 days after, the period of the servicemember's military service except—

(1) upon a court order granted before such sale, foreclosure, or seizure with a return made and approved by the court; or

(2) if made pursuant to an agreement as provided in section 107 [section 517 of this Appendix].

(d) Penalties

(1) Misdemeanor

A person who knowingly makes or causes to be made a sale, foreclosure, or seizure of property that is prohibited by subsection (c), or who knowingly attempts to do so, shall be fined as provided in title 18, United States Code, or imprisoned for not more than one year, or both.

(2) Preservation of other remedies

The remedies and rights provided under this section are in addition to and do not preclude any remedy for wrongful conversion otherwise available under law to the person claiming relief under this section, including consequential and punitive damages.

50 U.S.C. app. § 534. Settlement of stayed cases relating to personal property

(a) Appraisal of property

When a stay is granted pursuant to this Act in a proceeding to foreclose a mortgage on or to repossess personal property, or to rescind or terminate a contract for the purchase of personal property, the court may appoint three disinterested parties to appraise the property.

(b) Equity payment

Based on the appraisal, and if undue hardship to the servicemember's dependents will not result, the court may order that the amount of the servicemember's equity in the property be paid to the servicemember, or the servicemember's dependents, as a condition of foreclosing the mortgage, repossessing the property, or rescinding or terminating the contract.

50 U.S.C. app. § 535. Termination of residential or motor vehicle leases

(a) Termination by lessee

The lessee on a lease described in subsection (b) may, at the lessee's option, terminate the lease at any time after—

(1) the lessee's entry into military service; or

(2) the date of the lessee's military orders described in paragraph (1)(B) or (2)(B) of subsection (b), as the case may be.

(b) Covered leases

This section applies to the following leases:

(1) Leases of premises

A lease of premises occupied, or intended to be occupied, by a servicemember or a servicemember's dependents for a residential, professional, business, agricultural, or similar purpose if—

(A) the lease is executed by or on behalf of a person who thereafter and during the term of the lease enters military service; or

(B) the servicemember, while in military service, executes the lease and thereafter receives military orders for a permanent change of station or to deploy with a military unit for a period of not less than 90 days.

(2) Leases of motor vehicles

A lease of a motor vehicle used, or intended to be used, by a servicemember or a servicemember's dependents for personal or business transportation if—

(A) the lease is executed by or on behalf of a person who thereafter and during the term of the lease enters military service under a call or order specifying a period of not less than 180 days (or who enters military service under a call or order specifying a period of 180 days or less and who, without a break in service, receives orders extending the period of military service to a period of not less than 180 days); or

(B) the servicemember, while in military service, executes the lease and thereafter receives military orders for a permanent change of station outside of the continental United States or to deploy with a military unit for a period of not less than 180 days.

(c) Manner of termination

(1) In general

Termination of a lease under subsection (a) is made—

(A) by delivery by the lessee of written notice of such termination, and a copy of the servicemember's military orders, to the lessor (or the lessor's grantee), or to the lessor's agent (or the agent's grantee); and

(B) in the case of a lease of a motor vehicle, by return of the motor vehicle by the lessee to the lessor (or the lessor's grantee), or to the lessor's agent (or the agent's grantee), not later than 15 days after the date of the delivery of written notice under subparagraph (A).

(2) Delivery of notice

Delivery of notice under paragraph (1)(A) may be accomplished—

(A) by hand delivery;

(B) by private business carrier; or

(C) by placing the written notice in an envelope with sufficient postage and with return receipt requested, and addressed as designated by the lessor (or the lessor's grantee) or to the lessor's agent (or the agent's grantee), and depositing the written notice in the United States mails.

(d) Effective date of lease termination

(1) Lease of premises

In the case of a lease described in subsection (b)(1) that provides for monthly payment of rent, termination of the lease under subsection (a) is effective 30 days after the first date on which the next rental payment is due and payable after the date on which the notice under subsection (c) is delivered. In the case of any other lease described in subsection (b)(1), termination of the lease under subsection (a) is effective on the last day of the month following the month in which the notice is delivered.

(2) Lease of motor vehicles

In the case of a lease described in subsection (b)(2), termination of the lease under subsection (a) is effective on the day on which the requirements of subsection (c) are met for such termination.

(e) Arrearages and other obligations and liabilities

Rents or lease amounts unpaid for the period preceding the effective date of the lease termination shall be paid on a prorated basis. In the case of the lease of a motor vehicle, the lessor may not impose an early termination charge, but any taxes, summonses, and title and registration fees and any other obligation and liability of the lessee in accordance with the terms of the lease, including reasonable charges to the lessee for excess wear, use and mileage, that are due and unpaid at the time of termination of the lease shall be paid by the lessee.

(f) Rent paid in advance

Rents or lease amounts paid in advance for a period after the effective date of the termination of the lease shall be refunded to the lessee by the lessor (or the lessor's assignee or the assignee's agent) within 30 days of the effective date of the termination of the lease.

(g) Relief to lessor

Upon application by the lessor to a court before the termination date provided in the written notice, relief granted by this section to a servicemember may be modified as justice and equity require.

(h) Penalties

(1) Misdemeanor

Any person who knowingly seizes, holds, or detains the personal effects, security deposit, or other property of a servicemember or a servicemember's dependent who lawfully terminates a lease covered by this section, or who knowingly interferes with the removal of such property from premises covered by such lease, for the purpose of subjecting or attempting to subject any of such property to a claim for rent accruing subsequent to the date of termination of such lease, or attempts to do so, shall be fined as provided in title 18, United States Code, or imprisoned for not more than one year, or both.

(2) Preservation of other remedies

The remedy and rights provided under this section are in addition to and do not preclude any remedy for wrongful conversion otherwise available under law to the person claiming relief under this section, including any award for consequential or punitive damages.

50 U.S.C. app. § 536. Protection of life insurance policy

(a) Assignment of policy protected

If a life insurance policy on the life of a servicemember is assigned before military service to secure the payment of an obligation, the assignee of the policy (except the insurer in connection with a policy loan) may not exercise, during a period of military service of the servicemember or within one year thereafter, any right or option obtained under the assignment without a court order.

(b) Exception

The prohibition in subsection (a) shall not apply—

(1) if the assignee has the written consent of the insured made during the period described in subsection (a);

(2) when the premiums on the policy are due and unpaid; or

(3) upon the death of the insured.

(c) Order refused because of material affect

A court which receives an application for an order required under subsection (a) may refuse to grant such order if the court determines the ability of the servicemember to comply with the terms of the obligation is materially affected by military service.

(d) Treatment of guaranteed premiums

For purposes of this subsection, premiums guaranteed under the provisions of title IV of this Act shall not be considered due and unpaid.

(e) Penalties

(1) Misdemeanor

A person who knowingly takes an action contrary to this section, or attempts to do so, shall be fined as provided in title 18, United States Code, or imprisoned for not more than one year, or both.

(2) Preservation of other remedies

The remedy and rights provided under this section are in addition to and do not preclude any remedy for wrongful conversion otherwise available under law to the person claiming relief under this section, including any consequential or punitive damages.

50 U.S.C. app. § 537. Enforcement of storage liens

(a) Liens

(1) Limitation on foreclosure or enforcement

A person holding a lien on the property or effects of a servicemember may not, during any period of military service of the servicemember and for 90 days thereafter, foreclose or enforce any lien on such property or effects without a court order granted before foreclosure or enforcement.

(2) Lien defined

For the purposes of paragraph (1), the term "lien" includes a lien for storage, repair, or cleaning of the property or effects of a servicemember or a lien on such property or effects for any other reason.

(b) Stay of proceedings

In a proceeding to foreclose or enforce a lien subject to this section, the court may on its own motion, and shall if requested by a servicemember whose ability to comply with the obligation resulting in the proceeding is materially affected by military service—

(1) stay the proceeding for a period of time as justice and equity require; or

(2) adjust the obligation to preserve the interests of all parties.

The provisions of this subsection do not affect the scope of section 303 [section 533 of this Appendix].

(c) Penalties

(1) Misdemeanor

A person who knowingly takes an action contrary to this section, or attempts to do so, shall be fined as provided in title 18, United States Code, or imprisoned for not more than one year, or both.

(2) Preservation of other remedies

The remedy and rights provided under this section are in

addition to and do not preclude any remedy for wrongful conversion otherwise available under law to the person claiming relief under this section, including any consequential or punitive damages.

50 U.S.C. app. § 538. Extension of protections to dependents

Upon application to a court, a dependent of a servicemember is entitled to the protections of this title if the dependent's ability to comply with a lease, contract, bailment, or other obligation is materially affected by reason of the servicemember's military service.

* * *

50 U.S.C. app. § 561. Taxes respecting personal property, money, credits, and real property

(a) Application

This section applies in any case in which a tax or assessment, whether general or special (other than a tax on personal income), falls due and remains unpaid before or during a period of military service with respect to a servicemember's—

(1) personal property (including motor vehicles); or

(2) real property occupied for dwelling, professional, business, or agricultural purposes by a servicemember or the servicemember's dependents or employees—
  (A) before the servicemember's entry into military service; and
  (B) during the time the tax or assessment remains unpaid.

(b) Sale of property

(1) Limitation on sale of property to enforce tax assessment
Property described in subsection (a) may not be sold to enforce the collection of such tax or assessment except by court order and upon the determination by the court that military service does not materially affect the servicemember's ability to pay the unpaid tax or assessment.

(2) Stay of court proceedings
A court may stay a proceeding to enforce the collection of such tax or assessment, or sale of such property, during a period of military service of the servicemember and for a period not more than 180 days after the termination of, or release of the servicemember from, military service.

(c) Redemption

When property described in subsection (a) is sold or forfeited to enforce the collection of a tax or assessment, a servicemember shall have the right to redeem or commence an action to redeem the servicemember's property during the period of military service or within 180 days after termination of or release from military service. This subsection may not be construed to shorten any period provided by the law of a State (including any political subdivision of a State) for redemption.

(d) Interest on tax or assessment

Whenever a servicemember does not pay a tax or assessment on property described in subsection (a) when due, the amount of the tax or assessment due and unpaid shall bear interest until paid at the rate of 6 percent per year. An additional penalty or interest shall not be incurred by reason of nonpayment. A lien for such unpaid tax or assessment may include interest under this subsection.

(e) Joint ownership application

This section applies to all forms of property described in subsection (a) owned individually by a servicemember or jointly by a servicemember and a dependent or dependents.

* * *

50 U.S.C. app. § 581. Inappropriate use of Act

If a court determines, in any proceeding to enforce a civil right, that any interest, property, or contract has been transferred or acquired with the intent to delay the just enforcement of such right by taking advantage of this Act, the court shall enter such judgment or make such order as might lawfully be entered or made concerning such transfer or acquisition.

50 U.S.C. app. § 582. Certificates of service; persons reported missing

(a) Prima facie evidence

In any proceeding under this Act, a certificate signed by the Secretary concerned is prima facie evidence as to any of the following facts stated in the certificate:

(1) That a person named is, is not, has been, or has not been in military service.

(2) The time and the place the person entered military service.

(3) The person's residence at the time the person entered military service.

(4) The rank, branch, and unit of military service of the person upon entry.

(5) The inclusive dates of the person's military service.

(6) The monthly pay received by the person at the date of the certificate's issuance.

(7) The time and place of the person's termination of or release from military service, or the person's death during military service.

(b) Certificates

The Secretary concerned shall furnish a certificate under subsection (a) upon receipt of an application for such a certificate. A certificate appearing to be signed by the Secretary concerned is prima facie evidence of its contents and of the signer's authority to issue it.

(c) Treatment of servicemembers in missing status

A servicemember who has been reported missing is presumed to continue in service until accounted for. A requirement under this Act that begins or ends with the death of a servicemember does not begin or end until the servicemember's death is reported to, or determined by, the Secretary concerned or by a court of competent jurisdiction.

50 U.S.C. app. § 583. Interlocutory orders

An interlocutory order issued by a court under this Act may be revoked, modified, or extended by that court upon its own motion or otherwise, upon notification to affected parties as required by the court.

50 U.S.C. app. § 591. Anticipatory relief

(a) Application for relief

A servicemember may, during military service or within 180

days of termination of or release from military service, apply to a court for relief—

(1) from any obligation or liability incurred by the servicemember before the servicemember's military service; or

(2) from a tax or assessment falling due before or during the servicemember's military service.

(b) Tax liability or assessment

In a case covered by subsection (a), the court may, if the ability of the servicemember to comply with the terms of such obligation or liability or pay such tax or assessment has been materially affected by reason of military service, after appropriate notice and hearing, grant the following relief:

(1) Stay of enforcement of real estate contracts

    (A) In the case of an obligation payable in installments under a contract for the purchase of real estate, or secured by a mortgage or other instrument in the nature of a mortgage upon real estate, the court may grant a stay of the enforcement of the obligation—

        (i) during the servicemember's period of military service; and

        (ii) from the date of termination of or release from military service, or from the date of application if made after termination of or release from military service.

    (B) Any stay under this paragraph shall be—

        (i) for a period equal to the remaining life of the installment contract or other instrument, plus a period of time equal to the period of military service of the servicemember, or any part of such combined period; and

        (ii) subject to payment of the balance of the principal and accumulated interest due and unpaid at the date of termination or release from the applicant's military service or from the date of application in equal installments during the combined period at the rate of interest on the unpaid balance prescribed in the contract or other instrument evidencing the obligation, and subject to other terms as may be equitable.

(2) Stay of enforcement of other contracts

    (A) In the case of any other obligation, liability, tax, or assessment, the court may grant a stay of enforcement—

        (i) during the servicemember's military service; and

        (ii) from the date of termination of or release from military service, or from the date of application if made after termination or release from military service.

    (B) Any stay under this paragraph shall be—

        (i) for a period of time equal to the period of the servicemember's military service or any part of such period; and

        (ii) subject to payment of the balance of principal and accumulated interest due and unpaid at the date of termination or release from military service, or the date of application, in equal periodic installments during this extended period at the rate of interest as may be prescribed for this obligation, liability, tax, or assessment, if paid when due, and subject to other terms as may be equitable.

(c) Affect of stay on fine or penalty

When a court grants a stay under this section, a fine or penalty shall not accrue on the obligation, liability, tax, or assessment for the period of compliance with the terms and conditions of the stay.

* * *

NATIONAL DEFENSE AUTHORIZATION ACT FOR FISCAL YEAR 2000

Pub. L. No. 106-65, 113 Stat. 512

* * *

Sec. 1705. Stipend and bonus for participants.

* * *

(d) Reimbursement under certain circumstances.—

(1) If a participant in the Troops-to-Teachers Program fails to obtain teacher certification or licensure or employment as an elementary or secondary school teacher or vocational or technical teacher as required by the agreement under section 1704(e) or voluntarily leaves, or is terminated for cause, from the employment during the four years of required service in violation of the agreement, the participant shall be required to reimburse the administering Secretary for any stipend paid to the participant under subsection (a) in an amount that bears the same ratio to the amount of the stipend as the unserved portion of required service bears to the four years of required service.

(2) If a participant in the Troops-to-Teachers Program who is paid a bonus under subsection (b) fails to obtain employment for which the bonus was paid as required by the agreement under section 1704(e), or voluntarily leaves or is terminated for cause from the employment during the four years of required service in violation of the agreement, the participant shall be required to reimburse the administering Secretary for any bonus paid to the participant under that subsection in an amount that bears the same ratio to the amount of the bonus as the unserved portion of required service bears to the four years of required service.

(3) The obligation to reimburse the administering Secretary under this subsection is, for all purposes, a debt owing the United States. A discharge in bankruptcy under title 11, United States Code, shall not release a participant from the obligation to reimburse the administering Secretary.

(4) Any amount owed by a participant under this subsection shall bear interest at the rate equal to the highest rate being paid by the United States on the day on which the reimbursement is determined to be due for securities having maturities of ninety days or less and shall accrue from the day on which the participant is first notified of the amount due.

(e) Exceptions to reimbursement requirement.—A participant in the Troops-to-Teachers Program shall be excused from reimbursement under subsection (d) if the participant becomes permanently totally disabled as established by sworn affidavit of a qualified physician. The administering Secretary may also waive reimbursement in cases of extreme hardship to the participant, as determined by the administering Secretary.

* * *

A.2.3 Selected Provisions of Title IV [Transition] of Bankruptcy Act of 1978

(as amended by the Bankruptcy Amendments and Federal Judgeship Act of 1984)

Pub. L. No. 95-598, tit. IV, 92 Stat. 2684 (1978), as amended by Pub. L. No. 98-249, 98 Stat. 116 (1984); Pub. L. No. 98-271, 98 Stat. 163 (1984); Pub. L. No. 98-299, 98 Stat. 214 (1984); Pub. L. No. 98-325, 98 Stat. 268 (1984); Pub. L. No. 98-353, 98 Stat. 343, 345, 364 (1984); Pub. L. No. 98-454, tit. X, 98 Stat. 1745 (1984)

Sec. 401.

(a) The Bankruptcy Act is repealed.

(b) Section 3 of the Act entitled "An Act to amend an Act entitled 'An Act to establish a uniform system of bankruptcy throughout the United States', approved July 1, 1898, and Acts amendatory thereof and supplementary thereto," approved March 3, 1933 (47 Stat. 1482; 11 U.S.C. 101a), is repealed.

(c) Sections 3, 6, and 7 of the Act entitled "An Act to amend an Act entitled 'An Act to establish a uniform system of bankruptcy throughout the United States', approved July 1, 1898, and Acts amendatory thereof and supplementary thereto," approved June 7, 1934 (48 Stat. 923, 924; 11 U.S.C. 76a, 203a, 205a), are repealed.

(d) The sentence beginning "Said section 74" in section 2 of the Act entitled "An Act to amend an Act entitled 'An Act to establish a uniform system of bankruptcy throughout the United States', approved July 1, 1898, and Acts amendatory thereof and supplementary thereto," approved June 7, 1934 (48 Stat. 924; 11 U.S.C. 103a), is repealed.

(e) Subsection (b) of section 4 of the Act entitled "An Act to amend an Act entitled 'An Act to establish a uniform system of bankruptcy throughout the United States', approved July 1, 1898, and Acts amendatory thereof and supplementary thereto," approved June 7, 1934 (48 Stat. 924; 11 U.S.C. 103a), is repealed.

(f) Section 2 of the Act entitled "An Act to amend the Act entitled 'An Act to establish a uniform system of bankruptcy throughout the United States', approved July 1, 1898, as amended and supplemented," approved June 5, 1936 (49 Stat. 1476; 11 U.S.C. 93a), is repealed.

(g) Section 3 of the Act entitled "An Act to amend the Interstate Commerce Act, as amended, and for other purposes," approved April 9, 1948 (62 Stat. 167; 11 U.S.C. 208), is repealed.

Sec. 402.

(a) Except as otherwise provided in this title, this Act shall take effect on October 1, 1979.

(b) Except as provided in subsections (c) and (d) of this section, the amendments made by title II of this Act shall not be effective.

(c) The amendments made by sections 210, 214, 219, 220, 222, 224, 225, 228, 229, 235, 244, 245, 246, 249, and 251 of this Act shall take effect on October 1, 1979.

(d) The amendments made by sections 217, 218, 230, 247, 302, 314(j), 317, 327, 328, 338, and 411 of this Act shall take effect on the date of enactment of this Act.

(e) [*Repealed. Pub. L. No. 98-454, tit. X, § 1001, 98 Stat. 1745 (1984).*]

Sec. 403.

(a) A case commenced under the Bankruptcy Act, and all matters and proceedings in or relating to any such case, shall be conducted and determined under such Act as if this Act had not been enacted, and the substantive rights of parties in connection with any such bankruptcy case, matter, or proceeding shall continue to be governed by the law applicable to such case, matter, or proceeding as if the Act had not been enacted.

(b) Notwithstanding subsection (a) of this section, sections 1165, 1167, 1168, 1169, and 1171 of title 11 of the United States Code, as enacted by section 101 of this Act, apply to cases pending under section 77 of the Bankruptcy Act (11 U.S.C. 205) on the date of enactment of this Act in which the trustee has not filed a plan of reorganization.

(c) The repeal made by section 401(a) of this Act does not affect any right of a referee in bankruptcy, United States bankruptcy judge, or survivor of a referee in bankruptcy or United States bankruptcy judge to receive any annuity or other payment under the civil service retirement laws.

(d) The amendments made by section 314 of this Act do not affect the application of chapter 9, chapter 96, section 2516, section 3057, or section 3284 of title 18 of the United States Code to any act of any person—

(1) committed before October 1, 1979; or

(2) committed after October 1, 1979, in connection with a case commenced before such date.

(e) Notwithstanding subsection (a) of this section—

(1) a fee may not be charged under section 40c(2)(a) of the Bankruptcy Act in a case pending under such Act after September 30, 1979, to the extent that such fee exceeds $200,000;

(2) a fee may not be charged under section 40c(2)(b) of the Bankruptcy Act in a case in which the plan is confirmed after September 30, 1978, or in which the final determination as to the amount of such fee is made after September 30, 1979, notwithstanding an earlier confirmation date, to the extent that such fee exceeds $100,000;

(3) after September 30, 1979, all moneys collected for payment into the referees' salary and expense fund in cases filed under the Bankruptcy Act shall be collected and paid into the general fund of the Treasury; and

(4) any balance in the referees' salary and expense fund in the Treasury on October 1, 1979, shall be transferred to the general fund of the Treasury and the referees' salary and expense fund account shall be closed.

A.2.4 Selected Provisions of the Bankruptcy Amendments and Federal Judgeship Act of 1984

Pub. L. No. 98-353, 98 Stat. 343 (1984)

Sec. 106.

(a) Notwithstanding section 152 of title 28, United States Code, as added by this Act, the term of office of a bankruptcy judge who is serving on the date of enactment of this Act is extended to and expires four years after the date such bankruptcy judge was last appointed to such office or on October 1, 1986, whichever is later.

(b)(1) Notwithstanding section 153(a) of title 28, United States Code, as added by this Act, and notwithstanding subsection (a) of this section, a bankruptcy judge serving on a part-time basis on the date of enactment of this Act may continue to serve on such basis for a period not to exceed two years from the date of enactment of this Act.

(2) Notwithstanding the provisions of section 153(b) of title 28, United States Code, a bankruptcy judge serving on a part-time basis may engage in the practice of law but may not engage in any other practice, business, occupation, or employment inconsistent with the expeditious, proper, and impartial performance of such bankruptcy judge's duties as a judicial officer. The Judicial Conference of the United States may promulgate appropriate rules and regulations to implement this paragraph.

Sec. 113.

Section 402(b) of the Act of November 6, 1978 (Public Law 95-598; 92 Stat. 2682), is amended by striking out "shall take effect on June 28, 1984" and inserting in lieu thereof "shall not be effective."

Sec. 115.

(a) On the date of the enactment of this Act the appropriate district court of the United States shall have jurisdiction of—

(1) cases, and matters and proceedings in cases, under the Bankruptcy Act that are pending immediately before such date in the bankruptcy courts continued by section 404(a) of the Act of November 6, 1978 (Public Law 95-598; 92 Stat. 2687), and

(2) cases under title 11 of the United States Code, and proceedings arising under title 11 of the United States Code or arising in or related to cases under title 11 of the United States Code, that are pending immediately before such date in the bankruptcy courts continued by section 404(a) of the Act of November 6, 1978 (Public Law 95-598; 92 Stat. 2687).

(b) On the date of the enactment of this Act, there shall be transferred to the appropriate district court of the United States appeals from final judgments, orders, and decrees of the bankruptcy courts pending immediately before such date in the bankruptcy appellate panels appointed under section 405(c) of the Act of November 6, 1978 (Public Law 95-598; 92 Stat. 2685 [sic]).

Sec. 121.[27]

(a) Section 402 of the Act entitled "An Act to establish a uniform Law on the Subject of Bankruptcies" (Public Law 95-598) is amended in subsections (b) and (e) by striking out "June 28, 1984" each place it appears and inserting in lieu thereof "the date of enactment of the Bankruptcy Amendments and Federal Judgeship Act of 1984."

(b) Section 404 of such Act is amended in subsections (a) and (b) by striking out "June 27, 1984" each place it appears and inserting in lieu thereof "the day before the date of enactment of the Bankruptcy Amendments and Federal Judgeship Act of 1984."

(c) Section 406 of such Act is amended by striking out "June 27, 1984" each place it appears and inserting in lieu thereof "the day before the date of enactment of the Bankruptcy Amendments and Federal Judgeship Act of 1984."

(d) Section 409 of such Act is amended by—

(1) striking out "June 28, 1984" each place it appears and inserting in lieu thereof "the day before the date of enactment of the Bankruptcy Amendments and Federal Judgeship Act of 1984"; and

(2) striking out "June 27, 1984" each place it appears and inserting in lieu thereof "the day before the date of enactment of the Bankruptcy Amendments and Federal Judgeship Act of 1984."

(e) The term of office of any bankruptcy judge who was serving on June 27, 1984, is extended to and shall expire at the end of the day of enactment of this Act.

(f) Section 8339(n) of title 5, United States Code, is amended by striking out "June 28, 1984" and inserting in lieu thereof "the date of enactment of the Bankruptcy Amendments and Federal Judgeship Act of 1984."

(g) Section 8331(22) of title 5, United States Code, is amended by striking out "June 27, 1984" and inserting in lieu thereof "the day before the date of enactment of the Bankruptcy Amendments and Federal Judgeship Act of 1984."

Sec. 122.

(a) Except as otherwise provided in this section, this title and the amendments made by this title shall take effect on the date of the enactment of this Act.

(b) Section 1334(c)(2) of title 28, United States Code, and section 1411(a) of title 28, United States Code, as added by this Act, shall not apply with respect to cases under title 11 of the United States Code that are pending on the date of enactment of this Act, or to proceedings arising in or related to such cases.

(c) Sections 108(b), 113, and 121(e) shall take effect on June 27, 1984.

---

27 Subsections (a) through (d) of section 121, Pub. L. No. 98-353, 98 Stat. 343 (1984) were not executed, as a reflection of the probable intent of Congress. Other sections of the same act (Pub. L. No. 98-353, §§ 113, 114, 98 Stat. 343 (1984)), which were executed, also amended section 402(b), and repealed sections 404, 406, and 409, of Pub. L. No. 95-598, 92 Stat. 2684 (1978).

A.2.5 Selected Provisions of Title III [Transition and Administrative Provisions] of Bankruptcy Judges, United States Trustees, and Family Farmer Bankruptcy Act of 1986 (as amended by the Judicial Improvements Act of 1990)

Pub. L. No. 99-554, 100 Stat. 3088 (1986), as amended by Pub. L. No. 101-650, 104 Stat. 5089 (1990).

Sec. 301. Incumbent United States Trustees.

(a) Area for Which Appointed—Notwithstanding any paragraph of section 581(a) of title 28, United States Code, as in effect before the effective date of this Act, a United States trustee serving in such office on the effective date of this Act shall serve the remaining term of such office as United States trustee for the region specified in a paragraph of such section, as amended by this Act, that includes the site at which the primary official station of the United States trustee is located immediately before the effective date of this Act.

(b) Term of Office—Notwithstanding section 581(b) of title 28, United States Code, as in effect before the effective date of this Act, the term of office of any United States trustee serving in such office on the date of the enactment of this Act shall expire—

(1) 2 years after the expiration date of such term of office under such section, as so in effect, or

(2) 4 years after the date of the enactment of this Act, whichever occurs first.

Sec. 302. Effective Dates; Application of Amendments.

(a) General Effective Date—Except as provided in subsections (b), (c), (d), (e), and (f), this Act and the amendments made by this Act shall take effect 30 days after the date of the enactment of this Act.

(b) Amendments Relating to Bankruptcy Judges and Incumbent United States Trustees—Subtitle A of title I, and sections 301 and 307(a), shall take effect on the date of the enactment of this Act.

(c) Amendments Relating to Family Farmers—

(1) The amendments made by subtitle B of title II shall not apply with respect to cases commenced under title 11 of the United States Code before the effective date of this Act.

(2) Section 1202 of title 11 of the United States Code (as added by the amendment made by section 255 of this Act) shall take effect on the effective date of this Act and before the amendment made by section 227 of this Act.

(3) Until the amendments made by subtitle A of title II of this Act become effective in a district and apply to a case, for purposes of such case—

    (A)(i)   any reference in section 326(b) of title 11 of the United States Code to chapter 13 of title 11 of the United States Code shall be deemed to be a reference to chapter 12 or chapter 13 of title 11 of the United States Code,

        (ii)   any reference in such section 326(b) to section 1302(d) of title 11 of the United States Code shall be deemed to be a reference to section 1302(d) of title 11 of the United States Code or section 586(b) of title 28 of the United States Code, and

       (iii)   any reference in such section 326(b) to section 1302(a) of title 11 of the United States Code shall be deemed to be a reference to section 1202(a) or section 1302(a) of title 11 of the United States Code, and

    (B)(i)   the first two references in section 1202(a) of title 11 of the United States Code (as added by the amendment made by section 255 of this Act) to the United States trustee shall be deemed to be a reference to the court, and

        (ii)   any reference in such section 1202(a) to section 586(b) of title 28 of the United States Code shall be deemed to be a reference to section 1202(c) of title 11 of the United States Code (as so added).

(d) Application of Amendments to Judicial Districts—

(1) Certain Regions not Currently Served by United States Trustees—

(A) The amendments made by subtitle A of title II of this Act, and section 1930(a)(6) of title 28 of the United States Code (as added by section 117(4) of this Act), shall not—

    (i)   become effective in or with respect to a judicial district specified in subparagraph (B) until, or

    (ii)   apply to cases while pending in such district before, the expiration of the 270-day period beginning on the effective date of this Act or of the 30-day period beginning on the date the Attorney General certifies under section 303 of this Act the region specified in a paragraph of section 581(a) of title 28, United States Code, as amended by section 111(a) of this Act, that includes such district, whichever occurs first.

(B) Subparagraph (A) applies to the following:

    (i)   The judicial district established for the Commonwealth of Puerto Rico.

    (ii)   The District of Connecticut.

    (iii)   The judicial districts established for the State of New York (other than the Southern District of New York).

    (iv)   The District of Vermont.

    (v)   The judicial districts established for the State of Pennsylvania.

    (vi)   The judicial district established for the Virgin Islands of the United States.

    (vii)   The District of Maryland.

    (viii)   The judicial districts established for the State of North Carolina.

    (ix)   The District of South Carolina.

    (x)   The judicial districts established for the State of West Virginia.

    (xi)   The Western District of Virginia.

    (xii)   The Eastern District of Texas.

    (xiii)   The judicial districts established for the State of Wisconsin.

    (xiv)   The judicial districts established for the State of Iowa.

(xv)   The judicial districts established for the State of New Mexico.

(xvi)   The judicial districts established for the State of Oklahoma.

(xvii) The District of Utah.

(xviii) The District of Wyoming (including those portions of Yellowstone National Park situated in the States of Montana and Idaho).

(xix)   The judicial districts established for the State of Alabama.

(xx)   The judicial districts established for the State of Florida.

(xxi)   The judicial districts established for the State of Georgia.

(2) Certain Remaining Judicial Districts not Currently Served by United States Trustees—

(A) The amendments made by subtitle A of title II of this Act, and section 1930(a)(6) of title 28 of the United States Code (as added by section 117(4) of this Act), shall not—

(i)   become effective in or with respect to a judicial district specified in subparagraph (B) until, or

(ii) apply to cases while pending in such district before, the expiration of the 2-year period beginning on the effective date of this Act or of the 30-day period beginning on the date the Attorney General certifies under section 303 of this Act the region specified in a paragraph of section 581(a) of title 28, United States Code, as amended by section 111(a) of this Act, that includes such district, whichever occurs first.

(B) Subparagraph (A) applies to the following:

(i)   The judicial districts established for the State of Louisiana.

(ii)   The judicial districts established for the State of Mississippi.

(iii) The Southern District of Texas and the Western District of Texas.

(iv)   The judicial districts established for the State of Kentucky.

(v)   The judicial districts established for the State of Tennessee.

(vi)   The judicial districts established for the State of Michigan.

(vii) The judicial districts established for the State of Ohio.

(viii) The judicial districts established for the State of Illinois (other than the Northern District of Illinois).

(ix)   The judicial districts established for the State of Indiana.

(x)   The judicial districts established for the State of Arkansas.

(xi)   The judicial districts established for the State of Nebraska.

(xii) The judicial districts established for the State of Missouri.

(xiii) The District of Arizona.

(xiv) The District of Hawaii.

(xv)   The judicial district established for Guam.

(xvi) The judicial district established for the Commonwealth of the Northern Mariana Islands.

(xvii) The judicial districts established for the State of California (other than the Central District of California).

(xviii) The District of Nevada.

(xix)   The District of Alaska.

(xx)   The District of Idaho.

(xxi)   The District of Montana.

(xxii) The District of Oregon.

(xxiii) The judicial districts established for the State of Washington.

(3) Judicial Districts for the States of Alabama and North Carolina—

(A) Notwithstanding paragraphs (1) and (2), and any other provision of law, the amendments made by subtitle A of title II of this Act, and section 1930(a)(6) of title 28 of the United States Code (as added by section 117(4) of this Act), shall not—

(i)   become effective in or with respect to a judicial district specified in subparagraph (E) until, or

(ii) apply to cases while pending in such district before, such district elects to be included in a bankruptcy region established in section 581(a) of title 28, United States Code, as amended by section 111(a) of this Act, or October 1, 2002, whichever occurs first, except that the amendment to Section 105(a) of title 11, United States Code, shall become effective as of the date of the enactment of the Federal Courts Study Committee Implementation Act of 1990.

(B) Any election under subparagraph (A) shall be made upon a majority vote of the chief judge of such district and each bankruptcy judge in such judicial district in favor of such election.

(C) Notice that an election has been made under subparagraph (A) shall be given, not later than 10 days after such election, to the Attorney General and the appropriate Federal Circuit Court of Appeals for such district.

(D) Any election made under subparagraph (A) shall become effective on the date the amendments made by subtitle A of title II of this Act become effective in the region that includes such district or 30 days after the Attorney General receives the notice required under subparagraph (C), whichever occurs later.

(E) Subparagraph (A) applies to the following:

(i)   The judicial districts established for the State of Alabama.

(ii) The judicial districts established for the State of North Carolina.

(F)(i) Subject to clause (ii), with respect to cases under chapters 7, 11, 12, and 13 of title 11, United States Code—

(I)   commenced before the effective date of this Act, and

(II) pending in a judicial district in the State of Alabama or the State of North Carolina before any election made under subparagraph (A) by such district becomes effective or October 1, 2002, whichever occurs first, the amendments made by section 113 and subtitle A of title II of this Act, and section 1930(a)(6) of title 28 of the United States Code (as added by section 117(4) of this Act), shall not apply until October 1, 2003, or the expiration of the 1-year period beginning on the date such election becomes effective, whichever occurs first.

(ii) For purposes of clause (i), the amendments made by section 113 and subtitle A of title II of this Act, and section 1930(a)(6) of title 28 of the United States Code (as added by section 117(4) of this Act), shall not apply with respect to a case under chapter 7, 11, 12, or 13 of title 11, United States Code, if—

    (I) the trustee in the case files the final report and account of administration of the estate, required under section 704 of such title, or

    (II) a plan is confirmed under section 1129, 1225, or 1325 of such title, before October 1, 2003, or the expiration of the 1-year period beginning on the date such election becomes effective, whichever occurs first.

(G) Notwithstanding section 589a of title 28, United States Code, as added by section 115 of this Act, funds collected as a result of the amendments made by section 117 of this Act in a judicial district in the State of Alabama or the State of North Carolina under section 1930(a) of title 28, United States Code, before the date the amendments made by subtitle A of title II of this Act take effect in such district shall be deposited in the general receipts of the Treasury.

(H) The repeal made by section 231 of this Act shall not apply in or with respect to the Northern District of Alabama until March 1, 1987, or the effective date of any election made under subparagraph (A) by such district, whichever occurs first.

(I) In any judicial district in the State of Alabama or the State of North Carolina that has not made the election described in subparagraph (A), any person who is appointed under regulations issued by the Judicial Conference of the United States to administer estates in cases under title 11 of the United States Code may—

    (i) establish, maintain, and supervise a panel of private trustees that are eligible and available to serve as trustees in cases under title 11, United States Code, and

    (ii) supervise the administration of cases and trustees in cases under chapters 7, 11, 12, and 13 of title 11, United States Code, until the amendments made by subtitle A of title II take effect in such district.

(e) Application of United States Trustee System and Quarterly Fees to Certain Cases—

(1) In General—Subject to paragraph (2), with respect to cases under chapters 7, 11, 12, and 13 of title 11, United States Code—

(A) commenced before the effective date of this Act, and

(B) pending in a judicial district referred to in section 581(a) of title 28, United States Code, as amended by section 111(a) of this Act, for which a United States trustee is not authorized before the effective date of this Act to be appointed, the amendments made by section 113 and subtitle A of title II of this Act, and section 1930(a)(6) of title 28 of the United States Code (as added by section 117(4) of this Act), shall not apply until the expiration of the 3-year period beginning on the effective date of this Act, or of the 1-year

period beginning on the date the Attorney General certifies under section 303 of this Act the region specified in a paragraph of such section 581(a), as so amended, that includes such district, whichever occurs first.

(2) Amendments Inapplicable—For purposes of paragraph (1), the amendments made by section 113 and subtitle A of title II of this Act, and section 1930(a)(6) of title 28 of the United States Code (as added by section 117(4) of this Act), shall not apply with respect to a case under chapter 7, 11, 12, or 13 of title 11, United States Code, if—

(A) the trustee in the case files the final report and account of administration of the estate, required under section 704 of such title, or

(B) a plan is confirmed under section 1129, 1225, or 1325 of such title, before the expiration of the 3-year period, or the expiration of the 1-year period, specified in paragraph (1), whichever occurs first.

(3) Rule of Construction Regarding Fees for Cases—This Act and the amendments made by section 117(4) of this Act shall not be construed to require the payment of a fee under paragraph (6) of section 1930(a) of title 28, United States Code, in a case under title 11 of the United States Code for any conduct or period occurring before such paragraph becomes effective in the district in which such case is pending.

(f) Repeal of Chapter 12 of Title 11—Chapter 12 of title 11 of the United States Code is repealed on October 1, 1998.[28] All cases commenced or pending under chapter 12 of title 11, United States Code, and all matters and proceedings in or relating to such cases; shall be conducted and determined under such chapter as if such chapter had not been repealed. The substantive rights of parties in connection with such cases, matters, and proceedings shall continue to be governed under the laws applicable to such cases, matters, and proceedings as if such chapter had not been repealed.

Sec. 303. Certification of Judicial Districts; Notice and Publication of Certification.

(a) Certification by Attorney General—The Attorney General may certify in writing a region specified in a paragraph of section 581(a) of title 28, United States Code (other than paragraph (16)), as amended by section 111(a) of this Act, to the appropriate court of appeals of the United States, for the purpose of informing such court that certain amendments made by this Act will become effective in accordance with section 302 of this Act.

(b) Notice and Publication of Certification—Whenever the Attorney General transmits a certification under subsection (a), the Attorney General shall simultaneously—

(1) transmit a copy of such certification to the Speaker of the House of Representatives and to the President pro tempore of the Senate, and

(2) publish such certification in the Federal Register.

---

28 Family Farm Bankruptcies, Extension, Pub. L. No. 103-65, § 1, 107 Stat. 311 (1993), extended the period during which chapter 12 of title 11 of the United States Code remains in effect. The original repeal date was October 1, 1993. For information on the current status of chapter 12, see Appx. A.2.10, *infra.*

Sec. 305. Application of Certain Bankruptcy Rules.

(a) Rules Relating to the United States Trustee System—If a United States trustee is not authorized, before the effective date of this Act, to be appointed for a judicial district referred to in section 581(a) of title 28, United States Code, as amended by section 111(a) of this Act, then part X of the Bankruptcy Rules shall not apply to cases in such district until the amendments made by subtitle A of title II of this Act become effective under section 302 of this Act in such district.

(b) Rules Relating to Chapter 12 of Title 11—The rules prescribed under section 2075 of title 28, United States Code, and in effect on the date of the enactment of this Act shall apply to cases filed under chapter 12 of title 11, United States Code, to the extent practicable and not inconsistent with the amendments made by title II of this Act.

A.2.6 Provisions Related to Effective Date of 1990 and 1991 Student Loan Dischargeability Issues

Student Loan Default Prevention Initiative Act of 1990, Pub. L. No. 101-508, tit. III, § 3007, 104 Stat. 1388

Sec. 3007. Amendments to Bankruptcy Laws.

(a) Automatic Stay and Property of the Estate—

(1) Section 362(b) of title 11, United States Code, is amended—
    (A) in paragraph (12), by striking "or" at the end thereof;
    (B) in paragraph (13), by striking the period at the end thereof and inserting a semicolon; and
    (C) by inserting immediately following paragraph (13) the following new paragraphs:
        "(14) under subsection (a) of this section, of any action by an accrediting agency regarding the accreditation status of the debtor as an educational institution;
        "(15) under subsection (a) of this section, of any action by a State licensing body regarding the licensure of the debtor as an educational institution; or
        "(16) under subsection (a) of this section, of any action by a guaranty agency, as defined in section 435(j) of the Higher Education Act of 1965 (20 U.S.C. 1001 *et seq.*) or the Secretary of Education regarding the eligibility of the debtor to participate in programs authorized under such Act.".

(2) Section 541(b) of title 11, United States Code, is amended—
    (A) in paragraph (1), by striking "or" at the end thereof;
    (B) in paragraph (2), by striking the period at the end thereof and inserting a semicolon and "or"; and
    (C) by adding at the end thereof the following new paragraph:
        "(3) any eligibility of the debtor to participate in programs authorized under the Higher Education Act of 1965 (20 U.S.C. 1001 *et seq.*; 42 U.S.C. 2751 *et seq.*), or any accreditation status or State licensure of the debtor as an educational institution."

(3) The amendments made by this subsection shall be effective upon date of enactment of this Act.

(b) Treatment of Certain Education Loans in Bankruptcy Proceedings—

(1) Section 1328(a)(2) of title 11, United States Code, is amended by striking "section 523(a)(5)" and inserting "paragraph (5) or (8) of section 523(a)."

(2) The amendment made by paragraph (1) shall not apply to any case under the provisions of title 11, United States Code, commenced before the date of the enactment of this Act.

Federal Debt Collection Procedures Act of 1990, Pub. L. No. 101-647, tit. XXXVI, 104 Stat. 4964

Sec. 3621.

Section 523(a)(8) of title 11, United States Code, is amended—

(1) by striking "for an educational" and all that follows through "unless," and inserting the following: "for an educational benefit overpayment or loan made, insured or guaranteed by a governmental unit, or made under any program funded in whole or in part by a governmental unit or nonprofit institution, or for an obligation to repay funds received as an educational benefit, scholarship or stipend, unless"; and

(2) by amending subparagraph (A) to read as follows:
    "(A) such loan, benefit, scholarship, or stipend overpayment first became due more than 7 years (exclusive of any applicable suspension of the repayment period) before the date of the filing of the petition; or."

A.2.7 Selected Provisions of the Judicial Improvements Act of 1990

Pub. L. No. 101-650, 104 Stat. 5089

Sec. 317. Bankruptcy Administrator Program.

(a) Extension.—Section 302(d)(3) of the Bankruptcy Judges, United States Trustees, and Family Farmer Bankruptcy Act of 1986 (Public Law 99-554; 28 U.S.C. 581 note) is amended—

(1) in subparagraph (A)(ii), by striking out "October 1, 1992" and inserting in lieu thereof "October 1, 2002";

(2) in subparagraph (F)(i)(II), by striking out "October 1, 1992" and inserting in lieu thereof "October 1, 2002";

(3) in subparagraph (F)(i), by striking out "October 1, 1993" and inserting in lieu thereof "October 1, 2003"; and

(4) in subparagraph (F)(ii), by striking out "October 1, 1993" and inserting in lieu thereof "October 1, 2003".

(b) Standing.—A bankruptcy administrator may raise and may appear and be heard on any issue in any case under title 11, United States Code, but may not file a plan pursuant to section 1121(c) of such title.

(c) Power of the Court.—Section 302(d)(3)(A)(ii) of the Bankruptcy Judges, United States Trustees, and Family Farmer Bankruptcy Act of 1986, as amended by subsection (a), is further amended by inserting before the period at the end thereof the following: ", except that the amendment to section 105(a) of title 11, United States Code, shall become effective as of the date of the enactment of the Federal Courts Study Committee Implementation Act of 1990".

A.2.8 Selected Provisions of the Bankruptcy Reform Act of 1994

Pub. L. No. 103-394, 108 Stat. 4106

Sec. 105. Participation by Bankruptcy Administrator at Meetings of Creditors and Equity Security Holders.

(a) Presiding Officer.—A bankruptcy administrator appointed under section 302(d)(3)(I) of the Bankruptcy Judges, United States Trustees, and Family Farmer Bankruptcy Act of 1986 (28 U.S.C. 581 note; Public Law 99-554; 100 Stat. 3123), as amended by section 317(a) of the Federal Courts Study Committee Implementation Act of 1990 (Public Law 101-650; 104 Stat. 5115), or the bankruptcy administrator's designee may preside at the meeting of creditors convened under section 341(a) of title 11, United States Code. The bankruptcy administrator or the bankruptcy administrator's designee may preside at any meeting of equity security holders convened under section 341(b) of title 11, United States Code.

(b) Examination of the Debtor.—The bankruptcy administrator or the bankruptcy administrator's designee may examine the debtor at the meeting of creditors and may administer the oath required under section 343 of title 11, United States Code.

Sec. 304. Protection of Child Support and Alimony.

* * *

(g) Appearance Before Court.—Child support creditors or their representatives shall be permitted to appear and intervene without charge, and without meeting any special local court rule requirement for attorney appearances, in any bankruptcy case or proceeding in any bankruptcy court or district court of the United States if such creditors or representatives file a form in such court that contains information detailing the child support debt, its status, and other characteristics.

Sec. 702. Effective Date; Application of Amendments.

(a) Effective Date.—Except as provided in subsection (b), this Act shall take effect on the date of the enactment of this Act.

(b) Application of Amendments.—

(1) Except as provided in paragraph (2), the amendments made by this Act shall not apply with respect to cases commenced under title 11 of the United States Code before the date of the enactment of this Act.

(2)(A) Paragraph (1) shall not apply with respect to the amendment made by section 111.

(B) The amendments made by sections 113 and 117 shall apply with respect to cases commenced under title 11 of the United States Code before, on, and after the date of the enactment of this Act.

(C) Section 1110 of title 11, United States Code, as amended by section 201 of this Act, shall apply with respect to any lease, as defined in such section 1110(c) as so amended, entered into in connection with a settlement of any proceeding in any case pending under title 11 of the United States Code on the date of the enactment of this Act.

(D) The amendments made by section 305 shall apply only to agreements entered into after the date of enactment of this Act.

A.2.9 Selected Provision of the Federal Courts Improvements Act of 2000

Pub. L. No. 106-518, 114 Stat. 2410

Sec. 501. Extensions Relating to Bankruptcy Administrator program.

Section 302(d)(3) of the Bankruptcy Judges, United States Trustees, and Family Farmer Bankruptcy Act of 1986 (28 U.S.C. 581 note) is amended—

(1) in subparagraph (A), in the matter following clause (ii), by striking "or October 1, 2002, whichever occurs first,"; and

(2) in subparagraph (F)—
    (A) in clause (i)—
        (i) in subclause (II), by striking "or October 1, 2002, whichever occurs first"; and
        (ii) in the matter following subclause (II)—
            (I) by striking "October 1, 2003, or"; and
            (II) by striking ", whichever occurs first"; and
    (B) in clause (ii), in the matter following subclause (II)—
        (i) by striking "October 1, 2003, or"; and
        (ii) by striking ", whichever occurs first".

A.2.10 Reenactment of Bankruptcy Code Chapter 12

Reenactment from October 1, 1999 to July 1, 2000

Pub. L. 105-277, div. C, tit. I, § 149, 112 Stat. 2681 (1998), as amended by Pub. L. No. 106-5, 113 Stat. 9 (1999) and by Pub. L. No. 106-70, 113 Stat. 1031 (1999)]

Sec. 149.

(a) Chapter 12 of title 11 of the United States Code, as in effect on September 30, 1999, is hereby reenacted for the period beginning on October 1, 1999, and ending on July 1, 2000.

(b) All cases commenced or pending under chapter 12 of title 11, United States Code, as reenacted under subsection (a), and all matters and proceedings in or relating to such cases, shall be conducted and determined under such chapter as if such chapter were continued in effect after July 1, 2000. The substantive rights of parties in connection with such cases, matters, and proceedings shall continue to be governed under the law applicable to such cases, matters, and proceedings as if such chapter were continued in effect after July 1, 2000.

The amendments made by section 1 [Pub. L. No. 106-70, § 1, 113 Stat. 1031] shall take effect on October 1, 1999.

Reenactment from July 1, 2000 to June 1, 2001

Pub. L. No. 107-8, 115 Stat. 10 (2001)

Sec. 1. Amendments.

Section 149 of title I of division C of Public Law 105-277, as amended by Public Law 106-5 and Public Law 106-70, is amended—

(1) by striking "July 1, 2000" each place it appears and inserting "June 1, 2001"; and

(2) in subsection (a)—
   (A) by striking "September 30, 1999" and inserting "June 30, 2000"; and
   (B) by striking "October 1, 1999" and inserting "July 1, 2000".

Sec. 2. Effective Date.

The amendments made by section 1 shall take effect on July 1, 2000.

Reenactment from June 1, 2001 to October 1, 2001

Pub. L. No. 107-17, 115 Stat. 151 (2001)

Sec. 1. Amendments.

Section 149 of title I of division C of Public Law 105-277, as amended by Public Law 106-5, Public Law 106-70, and Public Law 107-8, is amended—

(1) by striking "June 1, 2001" each place it appears and inserting "October 1, 2001", and

(2) in subsection (a)—
   (A) by striking "June 30, 2000" and inserting "May 31, 2001", and
   (B) by striking "July 1, 2000" and inserting "June 1, 2001".

Sec. 2. Effective Date.

The amendments made by section 1 shall take effect on June 1, 2001.

Reenactment from September 30, 2001 to June 1, 2002

Pub. L. No. 107-170, 116 Stat. 133 (2002)

Sec. 1. Amendments.

Section 149 of title I of division C of Public Law 105-277, as amended by Public Laws 106-5, 106-70, 107-8, and 107-17, is amended—

(1) by striking "October 1, 2001" each place it appears and inserting "June 1, 2002"; and

(2) in subsection (a)—
   (A) by striking "May 31, 2001" and inserting "September 30, 2001"; and
   (B) by striking "June 1, 2001" and inserting "October 1, 2001".

Sec. 2. Effective Date.

The amendments made by section 1 shall take effect on October 1, 2001.

Reenactment from May 31, 2002 to January 1, 2003

Pub. L. No. 107-171, § 10814, 116 Stat. 134 (2002)

Sec. 10814. 7-Month Extension of Chapter 12 of Title 11 of the United States Code.

(a) Amendments.—Section 149 of title I of division C of Public Law 105-277 is amended—

(1) by striking "June 1, 2002" each place it appears and inserting "January 1, 2003"; and

(2) in subsection (a)—
   (A) by striking "September 30, 2001" and inserting "May 31, 2002"; and
   (B) by striking "October 1, 2001" and inserting "June 1, 2002".

(b) Effective Date.—The amendments made by subsection (a) shall take effect on June 1, 2002.

Reenactment from December 31, 2002 to July 1, 2003

Pub. L. No. 107-377, 115 Stat. 3115 (2002)

Sec. 1. Short Title.

This Act may be cited as the "Protection of Family Farmers Act of 2002".

Sec. 2. Six-Month Extension of Period for Which Chapter 12 of Title 11 of the United States Code Is Reenacted.

(a) Amendments.—Section 149 of title I of division C of Public Law 105-277 is amended—

(1) by striking "January 1, 2003" each place it appears and inserting "July 1, 2003"; and

(2) in subsection (a)—
   (A) by striking "May 31, 2002" and inserting "December 31, 2002"; and
   (B) by striking "June 1, 2002" and inserting "January 1, 2003".

(b) Effective Date.—The amendments made by subsection (a) shall take effect on January 1, 2003.

Reenactment from June 30, 2003 to January 1, 2004

Pub. L. No. 108-73, § 2(a), 117 Stat. 891 (2003)

Sec. 1. Short Title.

This Act may be cited as the "Family Farmer Bankruptcy Relief Act of 2003."

Sec. 2. Six-Month Extension of Period for Which Chapter 12 of Title 11, United States Code, Is Reenacted.

(a) Amendments—Section 149 of title I of division C of Public Law 105-277 (11 U.S.C. 1201 note) is amended—

(1) by striking "July 1, 2003" each place it appears and inserting "January 1, 2004"; and

(2) in subsection (a)—
   (A) by striking "December 31, 2002" and inserting "June 30, 2003"; and
   (B) by striking "January 1, 2003" and inserting "July 1, 2003."

(b) Effective Date—The amendments made by subsection (a) take effect on July 1, 2003.

Reenactment from January 1, 2004 to June 30, 2005

Pub. L. No. 108-369, 118 Stat. 1749 (2004)

Sec. 1. Short Title.

This Act may be cited as the "Family Farmer Bankruptcy Relief Act of 2004."

Sec. 2. Eighteen-Month Extension of Period for Which Chapter 12 of Title 11, United States Code, Is Reenacted.

(a) Amendments—Section 149 of title I of division C of Public Law 105-277 (11 U.S.C. 1201 note) is amended—

(1) by striking "January 1, 2004" each place it appears and inserting "July 1, 2005"; and

(2) in subsection (a)—
   (A) by striking "June 30, 2003" and inserting "December 31, 2003"; and
   (B) by striking "July 1, 2003." and inserting "January 1, 2004."

(b) Effective Date—The amendments made by subsection (a) take effect on January 1, 2004.

Appendix B   Federal Rules of Bankruptcy Procedure

This appendix reprints a complete, integrated set of the Rules of Practice and Procedure in Bankruptcy, current through the 2004 amendments that became effective December 1, 2004. These rules may also be found on the CD-Rom accompanying this volume.

Based on amendments to the Federal Rules of Civil Procedure which became effective on December 1, 2000, all of the federal discovery rules, including the disclosure requirements contained in Federal Rule of Civil Procedure 26, are applicable in every district and bankruptcy court. Bankruptcy courts are no longer authorized to alter or opt out of these requirements by local rule. However, see Federal Rule of Bankruptcy Procedure 9014(c), as amended in 2004, for an exception to the applicability of parts of Federal Rule of Civil Procedure 26.

TABLE OF CONTENTS

RULES OF PRACTICE AND PROCEDURE IN BANKRUPTCY

PART X (ABROGATED)

RULES OF PRACTICE AND PROCEDURE IN BANKRUPTCY

Rule 1001. Scope of Rules and Forms; Short Title

The Bankruptcy Rules and Forms govern procedure in cases under title 11 of the United States Code. The rules shall be cited as the Federal Rules of Bankruptcy Procedure and the forms as the Official Bankruptcy Forms. These rules shall be construed to secure the just, speedy, and inexpensive determination of every case and proceeding.

PART I

COMMENCEMENT OF CASE; PROCEEDINGS RELATING TO PETITION AND ORDER FOR RELIEF

Rule 1002. Commencement of Case

(a) PETITION. A petition commencing a case under the Code shall be filed with the clerk.

(b) TRANSMISSION TO UNITED STATES TRUSTEE. The clerk shall forthwith transmit to the United States trustee a copy of the petition filed pursuant to subdivision (a) of this rule.

Rule 1003. Involuntary Petition

(a) TRANSFEROR OR TRANSFEREE OF CLAIM. A transferor or transferee of a claim shall annex to the original and each copy of the petition a copy of all documents evidencing the transfer, whether transferred unconditionally, for security, or otherwise, and a signed statement that the claim was not transferred for the purpose of commencing the case and setting forth the consideration for and terms of the transfer. An entity that has transferred or acquired a claim for the purpose of commencing a case for liquidation under chapter 7 or for reorganization under chapter 11 shall not be a qualified petitioner.

(b) JOINDER OF PETITIONERS AFTER FILING. If the answer to an involuntary petition filed by fewer than three creditors avers the existence of 12 or more creditors, the debtor shall file with the answer a list of all creditors with their addresses, a brief statement of the nature of their claims, and the amounts thereof. If it appears that there are 12 or more creditors as provided in § 303(b) of the Code, the court shall afford a reasonable opportunity for other creditors to join in the petition before a hearing is held thereon.

Rule 1004. Involuntary Petition Against a Partnership

After filing of an involuntary petition under § 303(b)(3) of the Code, (1) the petitioning partners or other petitioners shall promptly send to or serve on each general partner who is not a petitioner a copy of the petition; and (2) the clerk shall promptly issue a summons for service on each general partner who is not a petitioner. Rule 1010 applies to the form and service of the summons.

Rule 1004.1. Petition for an Infant or Incompetent Person

If an infant or incompetent person has a representative, including a general guardian, committee, conservator, or similar fiduciary, the representative may file a voluntary petition on behalf of the infant or incompetent person. An infant or incompetent person who does not have a duly appointed representative may file a voluntary petition by next friend or guardian ad litem. The court shall appoint a guardian ad litem for an infant or incompetent person who is a debtor and is not otherwise represented or shall make any other order to protect the infant or incompetent debtor.

Rule 1005. Caption of Petition

The caption of a petition commencing a case under the Code shall contain the name of the court, the title of the case, and the docket number. The title of the case shall include the following information about the debtor: name, employer identification number, last four digits of the social security number, any other federal tax idenfitication number, and all other names used within six years before filing the petition. If the petition is not filed by the debtor, it shall include all names used by the debtor which are known to petitioners.

Rule 1006. Filing Fee

(a) GENERAL REQUIREMENT. Every petition shall be accompanied by the prescribed filing fee except as provided in subdivision (b) of this rule. For the purpose of this rule, "filing fee" means the filing fee prescribed by 28 U.S.C. § 1930(a)(1)-(a)(5) and any other fee prescribed by the Judicial Conference of the United States under 28 U.S.C. § 1930(b) that is payable to the clerk upon the commencement of a case under the Code.

(b) PAYMENT OF FILING FEE IN INSTALLMENTS.

(1) *Application for Permission to Pay Filing Fee in Installments.* A voluntary petition by an individual shall be accepted for filing if accompanied by the debtor's signed application stating that the debtor is unable to pay the filing fee except in installments. The application shall state the proposed terms of the installment payments and that the applicant has neither paid any money nor transferred any property to an attorney for services in connection with the case.

(2) *Action on Application.* Prior to the meeting of creditors, the court may order the filing fee paid to the clerk or grant leave to pay in installments and fix the number, amount and dates of payment. The number of installments shall not exceed four, and the final installment shall be payable not later than 120 days after filing the petition. For cause shown, the court may extend the time of any installment, provided the last installment is paid not later than 180 days after filing the petition.

(3) *Postponement of Attorney's Fees.* The filing fee must be paid in full before the debtor or chapter 13 trustee may pay an attorney or any other person who renders services to the debtor in connection with the case.

Rule 1007. Lists, Schedules, and Statements; Time Limits

(a) LIST OF CREDITORS AND EQUITY SECURITY HOLDERS, AND CORPORATE OWNERSHIP STATEMENT.

(1) *Voluntary Case.* In a voluntary case, the debtor shall file with the petition a list containing the name and address of each creditor unless the petition is accompanied by a schedule of liabilities. If the debtor is a corporation, other than a governmental unit, the debtor shall file with the petition a corporate ownership statement containing the information described in Rule 7007.1. The debtor shall file a supplemental statement promptly upon any change in circumstances that renders the corporate ownership statement inaccurate.

(2) *Involuntary Case.* In an involuntary case, the debtor shall file within 15 days after entry of the order for relief, a list containing the name and address of each creditor unless a schedule of liabilities has been filed.

(3) *Equity Security Holders.* In a chapter 11 reorganization case, unless the court orders otherwise, the debtor shall file within 15 days after entry of the order for relief a list of the debtor's equity security holders of each class showing the number and kind of interests registered in the name of each holder, and the last known address or place of business of each holder.

(4) *Extension of Time*. Any extension of time for the filing of the lists required by this subdivision may be granted only on motion for cause shown and on notice to the United States trustee and to any trustee, committee elected pursuant to § 705 or appointed pursuant to § 1102 of the Code, or other party as the court may direct.

(b) SCHEDULES AND STATEMENTS REQUIRED.

(1) Except in a chapter 9 municipality case, the debtor, unless the court orders otherwise, shall file schedules of assets and liabilities, a schedule of current income and expenditures, a schedule of executory contracts and unexpired leases, and a statement of financial affairs, prepared as prescribed by the appropriate Official Forms.

(2) An individual debtor in a chapter 7 case shall file a statement of intention as required by § 521(2) of the Code, prepared as prescribed by the appropriate Official Form. A copy of the statement of intention shall be served on the trustee and the creditors named in the statement on or before the filing of the statement.

(c) TIME LIMITS. The schedules and statements, other than the statement of intention, shall be filed with the petition in a voluntary case, or if the petition is accompanied by a list of all the debtor's creditors and their addresses, within 15 days thereafter, except as otherwise provided in subdivisions (d), (e), (f), and (h) of this rule. In an involuntary case the schedules and statements, other than the statement of intention, shall be filed by the debtor within 15 days after entry of the order for relief. Schedules and statements filed prior to the conversion of a case to another chapter shall be deemed filed in the converted case unless the court directs otherwise. Any extension of time for the filing of the schedules and statements may be granted only on motion for cause shown and on notice to the United States trustee and to any committee elected under § 705 or appointed under § 1102 of the Code, trustee, examiner, or other party as the court may direct. Notice of an extension shall be given to the United States trustee and to any committee, trustee, or other party as the court may direct.

(d) LIST OF 20 LARGEST CREDITORS IN CHAPTER 9 MUNICIPALITY CASE OR CHAPTER 11 REORGANIZATION CASE. In addition to the list required by subdivision (a) of this rule, a debtor in a chapter 9 municipality case or a debtor in a voluntary chapter 11 reorganization case shall file with the petition a list containing the name, address and claim of the creditors that hold the 20 largest unsecured claims, excluding insiders, as prescribed by the appropriate Official Form. In an involuntary chapter 11 reorganization case, such list shall be filed by the debtor within 2 days after entry of the order for relief under § 303(h) of the Code.

(e) LIST IN CHAPTER 9 MUNICIPALITY CASES. The list required by subdivision (a) of this rule shall be filed by the debtor in a chapter 9 municipality case within such time as the court shall fix. If a proposed plan requires a revision of assessments so that the proportion of special assessments or special taxes to be assessed against some real property will be different from the proportion in effect at the date the petition is filed, the debtor shall also file a list showing the name and address of each known holder of title, legal or equitable, to real property adversely affected. On motion for cause shown, the court may modify the requirements of this subdivision and subdivision (a) of this rule.

(f) STATEMENT OF SOCIAL SECURITY NUMBER. An individual debtor shall submit a verified statement that sets out the debtor's social security number, or states that the debtor does not have a social security number. In a voluntary case, the debtor shall submit the statement with the petition. In an involuntary case, the debtor shall submit the statement within 15 days after the entry of the order for relief.

(g) PARTNERSHIP AND PARTNERS. The general partners of a debtor partnership shall prepare and file the schedules of the assets and liabilities, schedule of current income and expenditures, schedule of executory contracts and unexpired leases, and statement of financial affairs of the partnership. The court may order any general partner to file a statement of personal assets and liabilities within such time as the court may fix.

(h) INTERESTS ACQUIRED OR ARISING AFTER PETITION. If, as provided by § 541(a)(5) of the Code, the debtor acquires or becomes entitled to acquire any interest in property, the debtor shall within 10 days after the information comes to the debtor's knowledge or within such further time the court may allow, file a supplemental schedule in the chapter 7 liquidation case, chapter 11 reorganization case, chapter 12 family farmer's debt adjustment case, or chapter 13 individual debt adjustment case. If any of the property required to be reported under this subdivision is claimed by the debtor as exempt, the debtor shall claim the exemptions in the supplemental schedule. The duty to file a supplemental schedule in accordance with this subdivision continues notwithstanding the closing of the case, except that the schedule need not be filed in a chapter 11, chapter 12, or chapter 13 case with respect to property acquired after entry of the order confirming a chapter 11 plan or discharging the debtor in a chapter 12 or chapter 13 case.

(i) DISCLOSURE OF LIST OF SECURITY HOLDERS. After notice and hearing and for cause shown, the court may direct an entity other than the debtor or trustee to disclose any list of security holders of the debtor in its possession or under its control, indicating the name, address and security held by any of them. The entity possessing this list may be required either to produce the list or a true copy thereof, or permit inspection or copying, or otherwise disclose the information contained on the list.

(j) IMPOUNDING OF LISTS. On motion of a party in interest and for cause shown the court may direct the impounding of the lists filed under this rule, and may refuse to permit inspection by any entity. The court may permit inspection or use of the lists, however, by any party in interest on terms prescribed by the court.

(k) PREPARATION OF LIST, SCHEDULES, OR STATEMENTS ON DEFAULT OF DEBTOR. If a list, schedule, or statement, other than a statement of intention, is not prepared and filed as required by this rule, the court may order the trustee, a petitioning creditor, committee, or other party to prepare and file any of these papers within a time fixed by the court. The court may approve reimbursement of the cost incurred in complying with such an order as an administrative expense.

(*l*) TRANSMISSION TO UNITED STATES TRUSTEE. The clerk shall forthwith transmit to the United States trustee a copy of every list, schedule, and statement filed pursuant to subdivision (a)(1), (a)(2), (b), (d), or (h) of this rule.

(m) INFANTS AND INCOMPETENT PERSONS. If the debtor knows that a person on the list of creditors or schedules is an infant or incompetent person, the debtor also shall include the name, address, and legal relationship of any person upon whom process would be served in an adversary proceeding against the infant or incompetent person in accordance with Rule 7004(b)(2).

Rule 1008. Verification of Petitions and Accompanying Papers

All petitions, lists, schedules, statements and amendments thereto shall be verified or contain an unsworn declaration as provided in 28 U.S.C. § 1746.

Rule 1009. Amendments of Voluntary Petitions, Lists, Schedules and Statements

(a) GENERAL RIGHT TO AMEND. A voluntary petition, list, schedule, or statement may be amended by the debtor as a matter of course at any time before the case is closed. The debtor shall give notice of the amendment to the trustee and to any entity affected thereby. On motion of a party in interest, after notice and a hearing, the court may order any voluntary petition, list, schedule, or statement to be amended and the clerk shall give notice of the amendment to entities designated by the court.

(b) STATEMENT OF INTENTION. The statement of intention may be amended by the debtor at any time before the expiration of the period provided in § 521(2)(B) of the Code. The debtor shall give notice of the amendment to the trustee and to any entity affected thereby.

(c) TRANSMISSION TO UNITED STATES TRUSTEE. The clerk shall forthwith transmit to the United States trustee a copy of every amendment filed pursuant to subdivision (a) or (b) of this rule.

Rule 1010. Service of Involuntary Petition and Summons; Petition Commencing Ancillary Case

On the filing of an involuntary petition or a petition commencing a case ancillary to a foreign proceeding the clerk shall forthwith issue a summons for service. When an involuntary petition is filed, service shall be made on the debtor. When a petition commencing an ancillary case is filed, service shall be made on the parties against whom relief is sought pursuant to § 304(b) of the Code and on any other parties as the court may direct. The summons shall be served with a copy of the petition in the manner provided for service of a summons and complaint by Rule 7004(a) or (b). If service cannot be so made, the court may order that the summons and petition be served by mailing copies to the party's last known address, and by at least one publication in a manner and form directed by the court. The summons and petition may be served on the party anywhere. Rule 7004(e) and Rule 4(*l*) F.R. Civ. P. apply when service is made or attempted under this rule.

Rule 1011. Responsive Pleading or Motion in Involuntary and Ancillary Cases

(a) WHO MAY CONTEST PETITION. The debtor named in an involuntary petition or a party in interest to a petition commencing a case ancillary to a foreign proceeding may contest the petition. In the case of a petition against a partnership under Rule 1004, a nonpetitioning general partner, or a person who is alleged to be a general partner but denies the allegation, may contest the petition.

(b) DEFENSES AND OBJECTIONS; WHEN PRESENTED. Defenses and objections to the petition shall be presented in the manner prescribed by Rule 12 F.R. Civ. P. and shall be filed and served within 20 days after service of the summons, except that if service is made by publication on a party or partner not residing or found within the state in which the court sits, the court shall prescribe the time for filing and serving the response.

(c) EFFECT OF MOTION. Service of a motion under Rule 12(b) F.R. Civ. P. shall extend the time for filing and serving a responsive pleading as permitted by Rule 12(a) F.R. Civ. P.

(d) CLAIMS AGAINST PETITIONERS. A claim against a petitioning creditor may not be asserted in the answer except for the purpose of defeating the petition.

(e) OTHER PLEADINGS. No other pleadings shall be permitted, except that the court may order a reply to an answer and prescribe the time for filing and service.

Rule 1012. (Abrogated)

Rule 1013. Hearing and Disposition of Petition in Involuntary Cases

(a) CONTESTED PETITION. The court shall determine the issues of a contested petition at the earliest practicable time and forthwith enter an order for relief, dismiss the petition, or enter any other appropriate order.

(b) DEFAULT. If no pleading or other defense to a petition is filed within the time provided by Rule 1011, the court, on the next day, or as soon thereafter as practicable, shall enter an order for the relief requested in the petition.

(c) [Abrogated]

Rule 1014. Dismissal and Change of Venue

(a) DISMISSAL AND TRANSFER OF CASES.

(1) *Cases Filed in Proper District.* If a petition is filed in a proper district, on timely motion of a party in interest, and after hearing on notice to the petitioners, the United States trustee, and other entities as directed by the court, the case may be transferred to any other district if the court determines that the transfer is in the interest of justice or for the convenience of the parties.

(2) *Cases Filed in Improper District.* If a petition is filed in an improper district, on timely motion of a party in interest and after hearing on notice to the petitioners, the United States trustee, and other entities as directed by the court, the case may be dismissed or transferred to any other district if the court determines that transfer is in the interest of justice or for the convenience of the parties.

(b) PROCEDURE WHEN PETITIONS INVOLVING THE SAME DEBTOR OR RELATED DEBTORS ARE FILED IN DIFFERENT COURTS. If petitions commencing cases under the Code are filed in different districts by or against (1) the same debtor, or (2) a partnership and one or more of its general partners, or (3) two or more general partners, or (4) a debtor and an affiliate, on motion filed in the district in which the petition filed first is pending and after hearing on notice to the petitioners, the United States trustee, and other entities as directed by the court, the court may determine, in the interest of justice or for the convenience of the parties, the district or districts in which the case or cases should proceed. Except as otherwise ordered by the court in the district in which the petition filed first is pending, the proceedings on the other petitions shall be stayed by the courts in which they have been filed until the determination is made.

Rule 1015. Consolidation or Joint Administration of Cases Pending in Same Court

(a) CASES INVOLVING SAME DEBTOR. If two or more petitions are pending in the same court by or against the same debtor, the court may order consolidation of the cases.

(b) CASES INVOLVING TWO OR MORE RELATED DEBT-ORS. If a joint petition or two or more petitions are pending in the same court by or against (1) a husband and wife, or (2) a partnership and one or more of its general partners, or (3) two or more general partners, or (4) a debtor and an affiliate, the court may order a joint administration of the estates. Prior to entering an order the court shall give consideration to protecting creditors of different estates against potential conflicts of interest. An order directing joint administration of individual cases of a husband and wife shall, if one spouse has elected the exemptions under § 522(b)(1) of the Code and the other has elected the exemptions under § 522(b)(2), fix a reasonable time within which either may amend the election so that both shall have elected the same exemptions. The order shall notify the debtors that unless they elect the same exemptions within the time fixed by the court, they will be deemed to have elected the exemptions provided by § 522(b)(1).

(c) EXPEDITING AND PROTECTIVE ORDERS. When an order for consolidation or joint administration of a joint case or two or more cases is entered pursuant to this rule, while protecting the rights of the parties under the Code, the court may enter orders as may tend to avoid unnecessary costs and delay.

Rule 1016. Death or Incompetency of Debtor

Death or incompetency of the debtor shall not abate a liquidation case under chapter 7 of the Code. In such event the estate shall be administered and the case concluded in the same manner, so far as possible, as though the death or incompetency had not occurred. If a reorganization, family farmer's debt adjustment, or individual's debt adjustment case is pending under chapter 11, chapter 12, or chapter 13, the case may be dismissed; or if further administration is possible and in the best interest of the parties, the case may proceed and be concluded in the same manner, so far as possible, as though the death or incompetency had not occurred.

Rule 1017. Dismissal or Conversion of Case; Suspension

(a) VOLUNTARY DISMISSAL; DISMISSAL FOR WANT OF PROSECUTION OR OTHER CAUSE. Except as provided in §§ 707(a)(3), 707(b), 1208(b), and 1307(b) of the Code, and in Rule 1017(b), (c), and (e), a case shall not be dismissed on motion of the petitioner, for want of prosecution or other cause, or by consent of the parties, before a hearing on notice as provided in Rule 2002. For the purpose of the notice, the debtor shall file a list of creditors with their addresses within the time fixed by the court unless the list was previously filed. If the debtor fails to file the list, the court may order the debtor or another party to prepare and file it.

(b) DISMISSAL FOR FAILURE TO PAY FILING FEE.

(1) If any installment of the filing fee has not been paid, the court may, after a hearing on notice to the debtor and the trustee, dismiss the case.

(2) If the case is dismissed or closed without full payment of the filing fee, the installments collected shall be distributed in the same manner and proportions as if the filing fee had been paid in full.

(c) DISMISSAL OF VOLUNTARY CHAPTER 7 OR CHAPTER 13 CASE FOR FAILURE TO TIMELY FILE LIST OF CREDITORS, SCHEDULES, AND STATEMENT OF FINANCIAL AFFAIRS. The court may dismiss a voluntary chapter 7 or chapter 13 case under § 707(a)(3) or § 1307(c)(9) after a hearing on notice served by the United States trustee on the debtor, the trustee, and any other entities as the court directs.

(d) SUSPENSION. The court shall not dismiss a case or suspend proceedings under § 305 before a hearing on notice as provided in Rule 2002(a).

(e) DISMISSAL OF AN INDIVIDUAL DEBTOR'S CHAPTER 7 CASE FOR SUBSTANTIAL ABUSE. The court may dismiss an individual debtor's case for substantial abuse under § 707(b) only on motion by the United States trustee or on the court's own motion and after a hearing on notice to the debtor, the trustee, the United States trustee, and any other entities as the court directs.

(1) A motion to dismiss a case for substantial abuse may be filed by the United States trustee only within 60 days after the first date set for the meeting of the creditors under § 341(a), unless on request filed by the United States trustee before the time expired, the court for cause extends the time for filing the motion to dismiss. The United States trustee shall set forth in the motion all matters to be submitted to the court for its consideration at the hearing.

(2) If the hearing is set on the court's own motion, notice of the hearing shall be served on the debtor no later than 60 days after the first date set for the meeting of creditors under § 341(a). The notice shall set forth all matters to be considered by the court at the hearing.

(f) PROCEDURE FOR DISMISSAL, CONVERSION, OR SUSPENSION.

(1) Rule 9014 governs a proceeding to dismiss or suspend a case, or to convert a case to another chapter, except under §§ 706(a), 1112(a), 1208(a) or (b), or 1307(a) or (b).

(2) Conversion or dismissal under §§ 706(a), 1112(a), 1208(b), or 1307(b) shall be on motion filed and served as required by Rule 9013.

(3) A chapter 12 or chapter 13 case shall be converted without court order when the debtor files a notice of conversion under §§ 1208(a) or 1307(a). The filing date of the notice becomes the date of the conversion order for the purposes of applying § 348(c) and Rule 1019. The clerk shall promptly transmit a copy of the notice to the United States trustee.

Rule 1018. Contested Involuntary Petitions; Contested Petitions Commencing Ancillary Cases; Proceedings to Vacate Order for Relief; Applicability of Rules in Part VII Governing Adversary Proceedings

The following rules in Part VII apply to all proceedings relating to a contested involuntary petition, to proceedings relating to a contested petition commencing a case ancillary to a foreign proceeding, and to all proceedings to vacate an order for relief: Rules 7005, 7008-7010, 7015, 7016, 7024-7026, 7028-7037, 7052, 7054, 7056, and 7062, except as otherwise provided in Part I of these rules and unless the court otherwise directs. The court may direct that other rules in Part VII shall also apply. For the purposes of this rule a reference in the Part VII rules to adversary proceedings shall be read as a reference to proceedings relating to a contested involuntary petition, or contested ancillary petition, or proceedings to vacate an order for relief. Reference in the Federal Rules of Civil Procedure to the complaint shall be read as a reference to the petition.

Rule 1019. Conversion of Chapter 11 Reorganization Case, Chapter 12 Family Farmer's Debt Adjustment Case, or Chapter 13 Individual's Debt Adjustment Case to Chapter 7 Liquidation Case

When a chapter 11, chapter 12, or chapter 13 case has been converted or reconverted to a chapter 7 case:

(1) *Filing of Lists, Inventories, Schedules, Statements.*

    (A) Lists, inventories, schedules, and statements of financial affairs theretofore filed shall be deemed to be filed in the chapter 7 case, unless the court directs otherwise. If they have not been previously filed, the debtor shall comply with Rule 1007 as if an order for relief had been entered on an involuntary petition on the date of the entry of the order directing that the case continue under chapter 7.

    (B) If a statement of intention is required, it shall be filed within 30 days after entry of the order of conversion or before the first date set for the meeting of creditors, whichever is earlier. The court may grant an extension of time for cause only on the written motion filed, or oral request made during a hearing, before the time has expired. Notice of an extension shall be given to the United States trustee and to any committee, trustee, or other party as the court may direct.

(2) *New Filing Periods.* A new time period for filing claims, a complaint objecting to discharge, or a complaint to obtain a determination of dischargeability of any debt shall commence pursuant to Rules 3002, 4004, or 4007, provided that a new time period shall not commence if a chapter 7 case had been converted to a chapter 11, 12, or 13 case and thereafter reconverted to a chapter 7 case and the time for filing claims, a complaint objecting to discharge, or a complaint to obtain a determination of the dischargeability of any debt, or any extension thereof, expired in the original chapter 7 case.

(3) *Claims Filed before Conversion.* All claims actually filed by a creditor before conversion of the case are deemed filed in the chapter 7 case.

(4) *Turnover of Records and Property.* After qualification of, or assumption of duties by the chapter 7 trustee, any debtor in possession or trustee previously acting in the chapter 11, 12, or 13 case shall, forthwith, unless otherwise ordered, turn over to the chapter 7 trustee all records and property of the estate in the possession or control of the debtor in possession or trustee.

(5) *Filing Final Report and Schedule of Postpetition Debts.*

    (A) *Conversion of Chapter 11 or Chapter 12 Case.* Unless the court directs otherwise, if a chapter 11 or chapter 12 case is converted to chapter 7, the debtor in possession or, if the debtor is not a debtor in possession, the trustee serving at the time of conversion, shall:

        (i) not later than 15 days after conversion of the case, file a schedule of unpaid debts incurred after the filing of the petition and before the conversion of the case, including the name and address of each holder of a claim; and

        (ii) not later than 30 days after conversion of the case, file and transmit to the United States trustee a final report and account;

    (B) *Conversion of Chapter 13 Case.* Unless the court directs otherwise, if a chapter 13 case is converted to chapter 7,

        (i) the debtor, not later than 15 days after the conversion of the case, shall file a schedule of unpaid debts incurred

after the filing of the petition and before conversion of the case, including the name and address of each older of a claim; and

        (ii) the trustee, not later than 30 days after conversion of the case, shall file and transmit to the United States trustee a final report and account;

    (C) *Conversion After Confirmation of A Plan.* Unless the court orders otherwise, if a chapter 11, chapter 12, or chapter 13 case is converted to chapter 7 after confirmation of a plan, the debtor shall file:

        (i) a schedule of property not listed in the final report and account acquired after the filing of the petition but before conversion, except if the case is converted from chapter 13 to chapter 7 and § 348(f)(2) does not apply;

        (ii) a schedule of unpaid debts not listed in the final report and account incurred after confirmation but before the conversion; and

        (iii) a schedule of executory contracts and unexpired leases entered into or assumed after the filing of the petition but before conversion.

    (D) *Transmission to United States Trustee.* The clerk shall forthwith transmit to the United States trustee a copy of every schedule filed pursuant to Rule 1019(5).

(6) *Postpetition Claims; Preconversion Administrative Expenses; Notice.* A request for payment of an administrative expense incurred before conversion of the case is timely filed under § 503(a) of the Code if it is filed before conversion or a time fixed by the court. If the request is filed by a governmental unit, it is timely if it is filed before conversion or within the later of a time fixed by the court or 180 days after the date of conversion. A claim of a kind specified in § 348(d) may be filed in accordance with Rules 3001(a)–(d) and 3002. Upon the filing of the schedule of unpaid debts incurred after the commencement of the case and before conversion, the clerk, or some other person as the court may direct, shall give notice to those entities listed on the schedule of the time for filing a request for payment of an administrative expense and, unless a notice of insufficient assets to pay a dividend is mailed in accordance with Rule 2002(e), the time for filing a claim of a kind specified in § 348(d).

(7) [Abrogated]

Rule 1020. Election to be Considered a Small Business in a Chapter 11 Reorganization Case

In a chapter 11 reorganization case, a debtor that is a small business may elect to be considered a small business by filing a written statement of election not later than 60 days after the date of the order for relief.

PART II

OFFICERS AND ADMINISTRATION; NOTICES; MEETINGS; EXAMINATIONS; ELECTIONS; ATTORNEYS AND ACCOUNTANTS

Rule 2001. Appointment of Interim Trustee Before Order for Relief in a Chapter 7 Liquidation Case

(a) APPOINTMENT. At any time following the commencement of an involuntary liquidation case and before an order for relief, the court on written motion of a party in interest may order the appointment of an interim trustee under § 303(g) of the Code. The motion shall set forth the necessity for the appointment and may be granted only after hearing on notice to the debtor, the petitioning creditors, the United States trustee, and other parties in interest as the court may designate.

(b) BOND OF MOVANT. An interim trustee may not be appointed under this rule unless the movant furnishes a bond in an amount approved by the court, conditioned to indemnify the debtor for costs, attorney's fee, expenses, and damages allowable under § 303(i) of the Code.

(c) ORDER OF APPOINTMENT. The order directing the appointment of an interim trustee shall state the reason the appointment is necessary and shall specify the trustee's duties.

(d) TURNOVER AND REPORT. Following qualification of the trustee selected under § 702 of the Code, the interim trustee, unless otherwise ordered, shall (1) forthwith deliver to the trustee all the records and property of the estate in possession or subject to control of the interim trustee and, (2) within 30 days thereafter file a final report and account.

Rule 2002. Notices to Creditors, Equity Security Holders, United States, and United States Trustee

(a) TWENTY-DAY NOTICES TO PARTIES IN INTEREST. Except as provided in subdivisions (h), (i), and (*l*) of this rule, the clerk or some other person as the court may direct, shall give the debtor, the trustee, all creditors and indenture trustees at least 20 days' notice by mail of:

(1) the meeting of creditors under § 341 or § 1104(b) of the Code, which notice, unless the court orders otherwise, shall include the debtor's employer identification number, social security number, and any other federal taxpayer identification number;

(2) a proposed use, sale, or lease of property of the estate other than in the ordinary course of business, unless the court for cause shown shortens the time or directs another method of giving notice;

(3) the hearing on approval of a compromise or settlement of a controversy other than approval of an agreement pursuant to Rule 4001(d), unless the court for cause shown directs that notice not be sent;

(4) in a chapter 7 liquidation, a chapter 11 reorganization case, or a chapter 12 family farmer debt adjustment case, the hearing on the dismissal of the case or the conversion of the case to another chapter, unless the hearing is under § 707(a)(3) or § 707(b) or is on dismissal of the case for failure to pay the filing fee;

(5) the time fixed to accept or reject a proposed modification of a plan;

(6) a hearing on any entity's request for compensation or reimbursement of expenses if fee request exceeds $1000;

(7) the time fixed for filing proofs of claims pursuant to Rule 3003(c); and

(8) the time fixed for filing objections and the hearing to consider confirmation of a chapter 12 plan.

(b) TWENTY-FIVE-DAY NOTICES TO PARTIES IN INTEREST. Except as provided in subdivision (l) of this rule, the clerk, or some other person as the court may direct, shall give the debtor, the trustee, all creditors and indenture trustees not less than 25 days notice by mail of (1) the time fixed for filing objections and the hearing to consider approval of a disclosure statement; and (2) the

time fixed for filing objections and the hearing to consider confirmation of a chapter 9, chapter 11, or chapter 13 plan.

(c) CONTENT OF NOTICE.

(1) *Proposed Use, Sale, or Lease of Property.* Subject to Rule 6004 the notice of a proposed use, sale, or lease of property required by subdivision (a)(2) of this rule shall include the time and place of any public sale, the terms and conditions of any private sale and the time fixed for filing objections. The notice of a proposed use, sale, or lease of property, including real estate, is sufficient if it generally describes the property.

(2) *Notice of Hearing on Compensation.* The notice of a hearing on an application for compensation or reimbursement of expenses required by subdivision (a)(6) of this rule shall identify the applicant and the amounts requested.

(3) *Notice of Hearing on Confirmation When Plan Provides for an Injunction.* If a plan provides for an injunction against conduct not otherwise enjoined under the Code, the notice required under Rule 2002(b)(2) shall:

(A) include in conspicuous language (bold, italic, or underlined text) a statement that the plan proposes an injunction;

(B) describe briefly the nature of the injunction; and

(C) identify the entities that would be subject to the injunction.

(d) NOTICE TO EQUITY SECURITY HOLDERS. In a chapter 11 reorganization case, unless otherwise ordered by the court, the clerk, or some other person as the court may direct, shall in the manner and form directed by the court give notice to all equity security holders of (1) the order for relief; (2) any meeting of equity security holders held pursuant to § 341 of the Code; (3) the hearing on the proposed sale of all or substantially all of the debtor's assets; (4) the hearing on the dismissal or conversion of a case to another chapter; (5) the time fixed for filing objections to and the hearing to consider approval of a disclosure statement; (6) the time fixed for filing objections to and the hearing to consider confirmation of a plan; and (7) the time fixed to accept or reject a proposed modification of a plan.

(e) NOTICE OF NO DIVIDEND. In a chapter 7 liquidation case, if it appears from the schedules that there are no assets from which a dividend can be paid, the notice of the meeting of creditors may include a statement to that effect; that it is unnecessary to file claims; and that if sufficient assets become available for the payment of a dividend, further notice will be given for the filing of claims.

(f) OTHER NOTICES. Except as provided in subdivision (1) of this rule, the clerk, or some other person as the court may direct, shall give the debtor, all creditors, and indenture trustees notice by mail of: (1) the order for relief; (2) the dismissal or the conversion of the case to another chapter, or the suspension of proceedings under § 305; (3) the time allowed for filing claims pursuant to Rule 3002; (4) the time fixed for filing a complaint objecting to the debtor's discharge pursuant to § 727 of the Code as provided in Rule 4004; (5) the time fixed for filing a complaint to determine the dischargeability of a debt pursuant to § 523 of the Code as provided in Rule 4007; (6) the waiver, denial, or revocation of a discharge as provided in Rule 4006; (7) entry of an order confirming a chapter 9, 11, or 12 plan; and (8) a summary of the trustee's final report in a chapter 7 case if the net proceeds realized exceed $1,500. Notice of the time fixed for accepting or rejecting a plan pursuant to Rule 3017(c) shall be given in accordance with Rule 3017(d).

(g) ADDRESSING NOTICES.

(1) Notices required to be mailed under Rule 2002 to a creditor, indenture trustee, or equity security holder shall be addressed as such entity or an authorized agent has directed in its last request filed in the particular case. For purposes of this subdivision—

(A) a proof of claim filed by a creditor or indenture trustee that designates a mailing address constitutes a filed request to mail notices to that address, unless a notice of no dividend has been given under Rule 2002(e) and a later notice of possible dividend under Rule 3002(c)(5) has not been given; and

(B) a proof of interest filed by an equity security holder that designates a mailing address constitutes a filed request to mail notices to that address.

(2) If a creditor or indenture trustee has not filed a request designating a mailing address under Rule 2002(g)(1), the notices shall be mailed to the address shown on the list of creditors or schedule of liabilities, whichever is filed later. If an equity security holder has not filed a request designating a mailing address under Rule 2002(g)(1), the notices shall be mailed to the address shown on the list of equity security holders.

(3) If a list or schedule filed under Rule 1007 includes the name and address of a legal representative of an infant or incompetent person, and a person other than that representative files a request or proof of claim designating a name and mailing address that differs from the name and address of the representative included in the list or schedule, unless the court orders otherwise, notices under Rule 2002 shall be mailed to the representative included in the list or schedules and to the name and address designated in the request or proof of claim.

(h) NOTICES TO CREDITORS WHOSE CLAIMS ARE FILED. In a chapter 7 case, after 90 days following the first date set for the meeting of creditors under § 341 of the Code, the court may direct that all notices required by subdivision (a) of this rule be mailed only to the debtor, the trustee, all indenture trustees, creditors that hold claims for which proofs of claim have been filed, and creditors, if any, that are still permitted to file claims by reason of an extension granted pursuant to Rule 3002(c)(1) or (c)(2). In a case where notice of insufficient assets to pay a dividend has been given to creditors pursuant to subdivision (e) of this rule, after 90 days following the mailing of a notice of the time for filing claims pursuant to Rule 3002(c)(5), the court may direct that notices be mailed only to the entities specified in the preceding sentence.

(i) NOTICES TO COMMITTEES. Copies of all notices required to be mailed pursuant to this rule shall be mailed to the committees elected under § 705 or appointed under § 1102 of the Code or to their authorized agents. Notwithstanding the foregoing subdivisions, the court may order that notices required by subdivision (a)(2), (3) and (6) of this rule be transmitted to the United States trustee and be mailed only to the committees elected under § 705 or appointed under § 1102 of the Code or to their authorized agents and to the creditors and equity security holders who serve on the trustee or debtor in possession and file a request that all notices be mailed to them. A committee appointed under § 1114 shall receive copies of all notices required by subdivisions (a)(1), (a)(5), (b), (f)(2), and (f)(7), and such other notices as the court may direct.

(j) NOTICES TO THE UNITED STATES. Copies of notices required to be mailed to all creditors under this rule shall be mailed (1) in a chapter 11 reorganization case, to the Securities and Exchange Commission at any place the Commission designates, if the Commission has filed either a notice of appearance in the case or a written request to receive notices; (2) in a commodity broker case, to the Commodity Futures Trading Commission at Washington, D.C.; (3) in a chapter 11 case to the Internal Revenue Service at its address set out in the register maintained under Rule 5003(e) for the district in which the case is pending; (4) if the papers in the case disclose a debt to the United States other than for taxes, to the United States attorney for the district in which the case is pending and to the department, agency, or instrumentality of the United States through which the debtor became indebted; or (5) if the filed papers disclose a stock interest of the United States, to the Secretary of the Treasury at Washington, D.C.

(k) NOTICES TO UNITED STATES TRUSTEE. Unless the case is a chapter 9 municipality case or unless the United States trustee requests otherwise, the clerk, or some other person as the court may direct, shall transmit to the United States trustee notice of the matters described in subdivisions (a)(2), (a)(3), (a)(4), (a)(8), (b), (f)(1), (f)(2), (f)(4), (f)(6), (f)(7), and (f)(8) of this rule and notice of hearings on all applications for compensation or reimbursement of expenses. Notices to the United States trustee shall be transmitted within the time prescribed in subdivision (a) or (b) of this rule. The United States trustee shall also receive notice of any other matter if such notice is requested by the United States trustee or ordered by the court. Nothing in these rules requires the clerk or any other person to transmit to the United States trustee any notice, schedule, report, application or other document in a case under the Securities Investor Protection Act, 15 U.S.C. § 78aaa *et seq.*

(*l*) NOTICE BY PUBLICATION. The court may order notice by publication if it finds that notice by mail is impracticable or that it is desirable to supplement the notice.

(m) ORDERS DESIGNATING MATTER OF NOTICES. The court may from time to time enter orders designating the matters in respect to which, the entity to whom, and the form and manner in which notices shall be sent except as otherwise provided by these rules.

(n) CAPTION. The caption of every notice given under this rule shall comply with Rule 1005. The caption of every notice required to be given by the debtor to a creditor shall include the information require to be in the notice by § 342(c) of the Code.

(o) NOTICE OF ORDER FOR RELIEF IN CONSUMER CASE. In a voluntary case commenced by an individual debtor whose debts are primarily consumer debts, the clerk or some other person as the court may direct shall give the trustee and all creditors notice by mail of the order for relief within 20 days from the date thereof.

Rule 2003. Meeting of Creditors or Equity Security Holders

(a) DATE AND PLACE. In a chapter 7 liquidation or a chapter 11 reorganization case, the United States trustee shall call a meeting of creditors to be held no fewer than 20 and no more than 40 days after the order for relief. In a chapter 12 family farmer debt adjustment case, the United States trustee shall call a meeting of creditors to be held no fewer than 20 and no more than 35 days after the order for relief. In a chapter 13 individual's debt adjustment case, the United States trustee shall call a meeting of creditors to be held no fewer than 20 and no more than 50 days after the order for relief. If there is an appeal from or a motion to vacate the order for relief, or if there is a motion to dismiss the case, the United States trustee may set a later date for the meeting. The meeting may be held at a regular place for holding court or at any other place designated by the United States trustee within the district convenient for the parties in interest. If the United States trustee designates a place for the meeting which is not regularly staffed by the United States trustee or an assistant who may preside at the meeting, the meeting may be held not more than 60 days after the order for relief.

(b) ORDER OF MEETING.

(1) *Meeting of Creditors.* The United States trustee shall preside at the meeting of creditors. The business of the meeting shall include the examination of the debtor under oath and, in a chapter 7 liquidation case, may include the election of a creditors' committee and, if the case is not under subchapter V of chapter 7, the election of a trustee. The presiding officer shall have the authority to administer oaths.

(2) *Meeting of Equity Security Holders.* If the United States trustee convenes a meeting of equity security holders pursuant to § 341(b) of the Code, the United States trustee shall fix a date for the meeting and shall preside.

(3) *Right To Vote.* In a chapter 7 liquidation case, a creditor is entitled to vote at a meeting if, at or before the meeting, the creditor has filed a proof of claim or a writing setting forth facts evidencing a right to vote pursuant to § 702(a) of the Code unless objection is made to the claim or the proof of claim is insufficient on its face. A creditor of a partnership may file a proof of claim or writing evidencing a right to vote for the trustee for the estate of a general partner notwithstanding that a trustee for the estate of the partnership has previously qualified. In the event of an objection to the amount or allowability of a claim for the purpose of voting, unless the court orders otherwise, the United States trustee shall tabulate the votes for each alternative presented by the dispute and, if resolution of such dispute is necessary to determine the result of the election, the tabulations for each alternative shall be reported to the court.

(c) RECORD OF MEETING. Any examination under oath at the meeting of creditors held pursuant to § 341(a) of the Code shall be recorded verbatim by the United States trustee using electronic sound recording equipment or other means of recording, and such record shall be preserved by the United States trustee and available for public access until two years after the conclusion of the meeting of creditors. Upon request of any entity, the United States trustee shall certify and provide a copy or transcript of such recording at the entity's expense.

(d) REPORT OF ELECTION AND RESOLUTION OF DISPUTES IN A CHAPTER 7 CASE.

(1) *Report of Undisputed Election.* In a chapter 7 case, if the election of a trustee or a member of a creditor's committee is not disputed, the United States trustee shall promptly file a report of the election, including the name and address of the person or entity elected and a statement that the election is undisputed.

(2) *Disputed Election.* If the election is disputed, the United States trustee shall promptly file a report stating that the election is disputed, informing the court of the nature of the dispute, and listing the name and address of the candidate elected under any alternative presented by the dispute. No later than the date on which the report is filed, the United States trustee shall mail a copy of the report to any party in interest that has made a request to receive a copy of the report. Pending disposition by the court of a disputed election for trustee, the interim trustee shall continue in office. Unless a motion for the resolution of the dispute is filed no later than 10 days after the United States trustee files a report of a disputed election for trustee, the interim trustee shall serve as trustee in the case.

(e) ADJOURNMENT. The meeting may be adjourned from time to time by announcement at the meeting of the adjourned date and time without further written notice.

(f) SPECIAL MEETINGS. The United States trustee may call a special meeting of creditors on request of a party in interest or on the United States trustee's own initiative.

(g) FINAL MEETING. If the United States trustee calls a final meeting of creditors in a case in which the net proceeds realized exceed $1,500, the clerk shall mail a summary of the trustee's final account to the creditors with a notice of the meeting, together with a statement of the amount of the claims allowed. The trustee shall attend the final meeting and shall, if requested, report on the administration of the estate.

Rule 2004. Examination

(a) EXAMINATION ON MOTION. On motion of any party in interest, the court may order the examination of any entity.

(b) SCOPE OF EXAMINATION. The examination of an entity under this rule or of the debtor under § 343 of the Code may relate only to the acts, conduct, or property or to the liabilities and financial condition of the debtor, or to any matter which may affect the administration of the debtor's estate, or to the debtor's right to a discharge. In a family farmer's debt adjustment case under chapter 12, an individual's debt adjustment case under chapter 13, or a reorganization case under chapter 11 of the Code, other than for the reorganization of a railroad, the examination may also relate to the operation of any business and the desirability of its continuance, the source of any money or property acquired or to be acquired by the debtor for purposes of consummating a plan and the consideration given or offered therefor, and any other matter relevant to the case or to the formulation of a plan.

(c) COMPELLING ATTENDANCE AND PRODUCTION OF DOCUMENTS. The attendance of an entity for examination and for the production of documents, whether the examination is to be conducted within or without the district in which the case is pending, may be compelled as provided in Rule 9016 for the attendance of a witness at a hearing or trial. As an officer of the court, an attorney may issue and sign a subpoena on behalf of the court for the district in which the examination is to be held if the attorney is admitted to practice in that court or in the court in which the case is pending.

(d) TIME AND PLACE OF EXAMINATION OF DEBTOR. The court may for cause shown and on terms as it may impose order the debtor to be examined under this rule at any time or place it designates, whether within or without the district wherein the case is pending.

(e) MILEAGE. An entity other than a debtor shall not be required to attend as a witness unless lawful mileage and witness fee for one day's attendance shall be first tendered. If the debtor resides more than 100 miles from the place of examination when required to appear for an examination under this rule, the mileage allowed by law to a witness shall be tendered for any distance more than 100 miles from the debtor's residence at the date of the filing of the first petition commencing a case under the Code or the residence at the time the debtor is required to appear for the examination, whichever is the lesser.

Rule 2005. Apprehension and Removal of Debtor to Compel Attendance for Examination

(a) ORDER TO COMPEL ATTENDANCE FOR EXAMINA-TION. On motion of any party in interest supported by an affidavit alleging (1) that the examination of the debtor is necessary for the proper administration of the estate and that there is reasonable cause to believe that the debtor is about to leave or has left the debtor's residence or principal place of business to avoid exami-nation, or (2) that the debtor has evaded service of a subpoena or of an order to attend for examination, or (3) that the debtor has willfully disobeyed a subpoena or order to attend for examination, duly served, the court may issue to the marshal, or some other officer authorized by law, an order directing the officer to bring the debtor before the court without unnecessary delay. If, after hearing, the court finds the allegations to be true, the court shall thereupon cause the debtor to be examined forthwith. If necessary, the court shall fix conditions for further examination and for the debtor's obedience to all orders made in reference thereto.

(b) REMOVAL. Whenever any order to bring the debtor before the court is issued under this rule and the debtor is found in a district other than that of the court issuing the order, the debtor may be taken into custody under the order and removed in accordance with the following rules:

(1) If the debtor is taken into custody under the order at a place less than 100 miles from the place of issue of the order, the debtor shall be brought forthwith before the court that issued the order.

(2) If the debtor is taken into custody under the order at a place 100 miles or more from the place of issue of the order, the debtor shall be brought without unnecessary delay before the nearest available United States magistrate judge, bankruptcy judge, or district judge. If, after hearing, the magistrate judge, bankruptcy judge, or district judge finds that an order has issued under this rule and that the person in custody is the debtor, or if the person in custody waives a hearing, the magistrate judge, bankruptcy judge, or district judge shall order removal, and the person in custody shall be released on conditions ensuring prompt appearance before the court that issued the order to compel the attendance.

(c) CONDITIONS OF RELEASE. In determining what condi-tions will reasonably assure attendance or obedience under subdi-vision (a) of this rule or appearance under subdivision (b) of this rule, the court shall be governed by the provisions and policies of title 18, U.S.C., § 3146(a) and (b).

Rule 2006. Solicitation and Voting of Proxies in Chapter 7 Liquidation Cases

(a) APPLICABILITY. This rule applies only in a liquidation case pending under chapter 7 of the Code.

(b) DEFINITIONS.

(1) *Proxy*. A proxy is a written power of attorney authorizing any entity to vote the claim or otherwise act as the owner's attorney in fact in connection with the administration of the estate.

(2) *Solicitation of Proxy*. The solicitation of a proxy is any com-munication, other than one from an attorney to a regular client who owns a claim or from an attorney to the owner of a claim who has requested the attorney to represent the owner, by which a creditor is asked, directly or indirectly, to give a proxy after or in contemplation of the filing of a petition by or against the debtor.

(c) AUTHORIZED SOLICITATION.

(1) A proxy may be solicited only by (A) a creditor owning an allowable unsecured claim against the State on the date of the filing of the petition; (B) a committee elected pursuant to § 705 of the Code; (C) a committee of creditors selected by a majority in number and amount of claims of creditors (i) whose claims are not contingent or unliquidated; (ii) who are not disqualified from voting under § 702(a) of the Code; and (iii) who were present or represented at a meeting of which all creditors having claims of over $500 or the 100 creditors having the largest claims had at least five days notice in writing and of which meeting written minutes were kept and are available reporting the names of the creditors present or rep-resented and voting and the amounts of their claims; or (D) a bona fide trade or credit association, but such association may solicit only creditors who were its members or subscribers in good standing and had allowable unsecured claims on the date of the filing of the petition.

(2) A proxy may be solicited only in writing.

(d) SOLICITATION NOT AUTHORIZED. This rule does not permit solicitation (1) in any interest other than that of general creditors; (2) by or on behalf of any custodian; (3) by the interim trustee or by or on behalf of any entity not qualified to vote under § 702(a) of the Code; (4) by or on behalf of an attorney at law; or (5) by or on behalf of a transferee of a claim for collection only.

(e) DATA REQUIRED FROM HOLDERS OF MULTIPLE PROXIES. At any time before the voting commences at any meeting of creditors pursuant to § 341(a) of the Code, or at any other time as the court may direct, a holder of two or more proxies shall file and transmit to the United States trustee a verified list of the proxies to be voted and a verified statement of the pertinent facts and circumstances in connection with the execution and delivery of each proxy, including:

(1) a copy of the solicitation;

(2) identification of the solicitor, the forwarder, if the forwarder is neither the solicitor nor the owner of the claim, and the proxyholder, including their connections with the debtor and with each other. If the solicitor, forwarder, or proxyholder is an association, there shall also be included a statement that the creditors whose claims have been solicited and the creditors whose claims are to be voted were members or subscribers in good standing and had allowable unsecured claims on the date of the filing of the petition. If the solicitor, forwarder, or proxyholder is a committee of creditors, the statement shall also set forth the date and place the committee was organized, that the committee was organized in accordance with clause (B) or (C) of paragraph (c)(1) of this rule, the members of the committee, the amounts of their claims, when the claims were acquired, the amounts paid therefor, and the extent to which the claims of the committee members are secured or entitled to priority;

(3) a statement that no consideration has been paid or promised by the proxyholder for the proxy;

(4) a statement as to whether there is any agreement and, if so, the particulars thereof, between the proxyholder and any other entity for the payment of any consideration in connection with voting the proxy, or for the sharing of compensation with any entity, other than a member or regular associate of the proxyholder's law firm, which may be allowed the trustee or any entity for services rendered in the case, or for the employment of any person as attorney, accountant, appraiser, auctioneer, or other employee for the estate;

(5) if the proxy was solicited by an entity other than the proxyholder, or forwarded to the holder by an entity who is neither a solicitor of the proxy nor the owner of the claim, a statement signed and verified by the solicitor or forwarder that no consideration has been paid or promised for the proxy, and whether there is any agreement, and, if so, the particulars thereof, between the solicitor or forwarder and any other entity for the payment of any consideration in connection with voting the proxy, or for sharing compensation with any entity, other than a member or regular associate of the solicitor's or forwarder's law firm which may be allowed the trustee or any entity for services rendered in the case, or for the employment of any person as attorney, accountant, appraiser, auctioneer, or other employee for the estate;

(6) if the solicitor, forwarder, or proxyholder is a committee, a statement signed and verified by each member as to the amount and source of any consideration paid or to be paid to such member in connection with the case other than by way of dividend on the member's claim.

(f) ENFORCEMENT OF RESTRICTIONS ON SOLICITATION. On motion of any party in interest or on its own initiative, the court may determine whether there has been a failure to comply with the provisions of this rule or any other impropriety in connection with the solicitation or voting of a proxy. After notice and a hearing the court may reject any proxy for cause, vacate any order entered in consequence of the voting of any proxy which should have been rejected, or take any other appropriate action.

Rule 2007. Review of Appointment of Creditors' Committee Organized Before Commencement of the Case

(a) MOTION TO REVIEW APPOINTMENT. If a committee appointed by the United States trustee pursuant to § 1102(a) of the Code consists of the members of a committee organized by creditors before the commencement of a chapter 9 or chapter 11 case, on motion of a party in interest and after a hearing on notice to the United States trustee and other entities as the court may direct, the court may determine whether the appointment of the committee satisfies the requirements of § 1102(b)(1) of the Code.

(b) SELECTION OF MEMBERS OF COMMITTEE. The court may find that a committee organized by unsecured creditors before the commencement of a chapter 9 or chapter 11 case was fairly chosen if:

(1) it was selected by a majority in number and amount of claims of unsecured creditors who may vote under § 702(a) of the Code and were present in person or represented at a meeting of which all creditors having unsecured claims of over $1,000 or the 100 unsecured creditors having the largest claims had at least five days notice in writing, and of which meeting written

minutes reporting the names of the creditors present or represented and voting and the amounts of their claims were kept and are available for inspection;

(2) all proxies voted at the meeting for the elected committee were solicited pursuant to Rule 2006 and the lists and statements required by subdivision (e) thereof have been transmitted to the United States trustee; and

(3) the organization of the committee was in all other respects fair and proper.

(c) FAILURE TO COMPLY WITH REQUIREMENTS FOR APPOINTMENT. After a hearing on notice pursuant to subdivision (a) of this rule, the court shall direct the United States trustee to vacate the appointment of the committee and may order other appropriate action if the court finds that such appointment failed to satisfy the requirements of § 1102(b)(1) of the Code.

Rule 2007.1. Appointment of Trustee or Examiner in a Chapter 11 Reorganization Case

(a) ORDER TO APPOINT TRUSTEE OR EXAMINER. In a chapter 11 reorganization case, a motion for an order to appoint a trustee or an examiner under § 1104(a) or § 1104(c) of the Code shall be made in accordance with Rule 9014.

(b) ELECTION OF TRUSTEE.

(1) *Request for an Election.* A request to convene a meeting of creditors for the purpose of electing a trustee in a chapter 11 reorganization case shall be filed and transmitted to the United States trustee in accordance with Rule 5005 within the time prescribed by § 1104(b) of the Code. Pending court approval of the person elected, any person appointed by the United States trustee under § 1104(d) and approved in accordance with subdivision (c) of this rule shall serve as trustee.

(2) *Manner of Election and Notice.* An election of a trustee under § 1104(b) of the Code shall be conducted in the manner provided in Rules 2003(b)(3) and 2006. Notice of the meeting of creditors convened under § 1104(b) shall be given as provided in Rule 2002. The United States trustee shall preside at the meeting. A proxy for the purpose of voting in the election may be solicited only by a committee of creditors appointed under § 1102 of the Code or by any other party entitled to solicit a proxy pursuant to Rule 2006.

(3) *Report of Election and Resolution of Disputes.*

(A) Report of Undisputed Election. If the election is not disputed, the United States trustee shall promptly file a report of the election, including the name and address of the person elected and a statement that the election is undisputed. The United States trustee shall file with the report an application for approval of the appointment in accordance with subdivision (c) of this rule. The report constitutes appointment of the elected person to serve as trustee, subject to court approval, as of the date of entry of the order approving the appointment.

(B) Disputed Election. If the election is disputed, the United States trustee shall promptly file a report stating that the election is disputed, informing the court of the nature of the dispute, and listing the names and address of any candidate elected under any alternative presented by the dispute. The report shall be accompanied by a verified statement by each candidate elected under each alternative presented by the dispute, setting forth the person's connections with the debtor, creditors, and other party in interest, their respective attorneys and accountants, the United Stats trustee, and any person employed in the office of the United States trustee. Not later than the date on which the report of the disputed election is filed, the United States trustee shall mail a copy of the report and each verified statement to any party in interest that has made a request to convene a meeting under § 1104(b) or to receive a copy of the report, and to any committee appointed under § 1102 of the Code. Unless a motion for the resolution of the dispute is filed not later than 10 days after the United States trustee files the report, any person appointed by the United States trustee under § 1104(d) and approved in accordance with subdivision (c) of this rule shall serve as trustee. If a motion for the resolution of the dispute is timely filed, and the court determines the result of the election and approves the person elected, the report will constitute appointment of the elected person as of the date of entry of the order approving the appointment.

(c) APPROVAL OF APPOINTMENT. An order approving the appointment of a trustee elected under § 1104(b) or appointed under § 1104(d), or the appointment of an examiner under § 1104(d) of the Code, shall be made on application of the United States trustee. The application shall state the name of the person appointed and, to the best of the applicant's knowledge, all the person's connections with the debtor, creditors, any other parties in interest, their respective attorneys and accountants, the United States trustee, and persons employed in the office of the United States trustee. Unless the person has been elected under § 1104(b), the application shall state the names of the parties in interest with whom the United States trustee consulted regarding the appointment. The application shall be accompanied by a verified statement of the person appointed setting forth the person's connections with the debtor, creditors, any other party in interest, their respective attorneys and accountants, the United States trustee, and any person employed in the office of the United States trustee.

Rule 2008. Notice to Trustee of Selection

The United States trustee shall immediately notify the person selected as trustee how to qualify and, if applicable, the amount of the trustee's bond. A trustee that has filed a blanket bond pursuant to Rule 2010 and has been selected as trustee in a chapter 7, chapter 12, or chapter 13 case that does not notify the court and the United States trustee in writing of rejection of the office within five days after receipt of notice of selection shall be deemed to have accepted the office. Any other person selected as trustee shall notify the court and the United States trustee in writing of acceptance of the office within five days after receipt of notice of selection or shall be deemed to have rejected the office.

Rule 2009. Trustees for Estates When Joint Administration Ordered

(a) ELECTION OF SINGLE TRUSTEE FOR ESTATES BEING JOINTLY ADMINISTERED. If the court orders a joint administration of two or more estates under Rule 1015(b), creditors may elect a single trustee for the estates being jointly administered, unless the case is under subchapter V of chapter 7 of the Code.

(b) RIGHT OF CREDITORS TO ELECT SEPARATE TRUSTEE. Notwithstanding entry of an order for joint administration under Rule 1015(b) the creditors of any debtor may elect a separate trustee for the estate of the debtor as provided in § 702 of the Code, unless the case is under subchapter V of chapter 7.

(c) APPOINTMENT OF TRUSTEES FOR ESTATES BEING JOINTLY ADMINISTERED.

(1) *Chapter 7 Liquidation Cases.* Except in a case governed by subchapter V of chapter 7, the United States trustee may appoint one or more interim trustees for estates being jointly administered in chapter 7 cases.

(2) *Chapter 11 Reorganization Cases.* If the appointment of a trustee is ordered, the United States trustee may appoint one or more trustees for estates being jointly administered in chapter 11 cases.

(3) *Chapter 12 Family Farmer's Debt Adjustment Cases.* The United States trustee may appoint one or more trustees for estates being jointly administered in chapter 12 cases.

(4) *Chapter 13 Individual's Debt Adjustment Cases.* The United States trustee may appoint one or more trustees for estates being jointly administered in chapter 13 cases.

(d) POTENTIAL CONFLICTS OF INTEREST. On a showing that creditors or equity security holders of the different estates will be prejudiced by conflicts of interest of a common trustee who has been elected or appointed, the court shall order the selection of separate trustees for estates being jointly administered.

(e) SEPARATE ACCOUNTS. The trustee or trustees of estates being jointly administered shall keep separate accounts of the property and distribution of each estate.

Rule 2010. Qualification by Trustee; Proceeding on Bond

(a) BLANKET BOND. The United States trustee may authorize a blanket bond in favor of the United States conditioned on the faithful performance of official duties by the trustee or trustees to cover (1) a person who qualifies as trustee in a number of cases, and (2) a number of trustees each of whom qualifies in a different case.

(b) PROCEEDING ON BOND. A proceeding on the trustee's bond may be brought by any party in interest in the name of the United States for the use of the entity injured by the breach of the condition.

Rule 2011. Evidence of Debtor in Possession or Qualification of Trustee

(a) Whenever evidence is required that a debtor is a debtor in possession or that a trustee has qualified, the clerk may so certify and the certificate shall constitute conclusive evidence of that fact.

(b) If a person elected or appointed as trustee does not qualify within the time prescribed by § 322(a) of the Code, the clerk shall so notify the court and the United States trustee.

Rule 2012. Substitution of Trustee or Successor Trustee; Accounting

(a) TRUSTEE. If a trustee is appointed in a chapter 11 case or the debtor is removed as debtor in possession in a chapter 12 case, the trustee is substituted automatically for the debtor in possession as a party in any pending action, proceeding, or matter.

(b) SUCCESSOR TRUSTEE. When a trustee dies, resigns, is removed, or otherwise ceases to hold office during the pendency of a case under the Code (1) the successor is automatically substituted as a party in any pending action, proceeding, or matter; and (2) the successor trustee shall prepare, file, and transmit to the United States trustee an accounting of the prior administration of the estate.

Rule 2013. Public Record of Compensation Awarded to Trustees, Examiners, and Professionals

(a) RECORD TO BE KEPT. The clerk shall maintain a public record listing fees awarded by the court (1) to trustees and attorneys, accountants, appraisers, auctioneers and other professionals employed by trustees, and (2) to examiners. The record shall include the name and docket number of the case, the name of the individual or firm receiving the fee and the amount of the fee awarded. The record shall be maintained chronologically and shall be kept current and open to examination by the public without charge. "Trustees," as used in this rule, does not include debtors in possession.

(b) SUMMARY OF RECORD. At the close of each annual period, the clerk shall prepare a summary of the public record by individual or firm name, to reflect total fees awarded during the preceding year. The summary shall be open to examination by the public without charge. The clerk shall transmit a copy of the summary to the United States trustee.

Rule 2014. Employment of Professional Persons

(a) APPLICATION FOR AN ORDER OF EMPLOYMENT. An order approving the employment of attorneys, accountants, appraisers, auctioneers, agents, or other professionals pursuant to § 327, § 1103, or § 1114 of the Code shall be made only on application of the trustee or committee. The application shall be filed and, unless the case is a chapter 9 municipality case, a copy of the application shall be transmitted by the applicant to the United States trustee. The application shall state the specific facts showing the necessity for the employment, the name of the person to be employed, the reasons for the selection, the professional services to be rendered, any proposed arrangement for compensation, and, to the best of the applicant's knowledge, all of the person's connections with the debtor, creditors, any other party in interest, their respective attorneys and accountants, the United States trustee, or any person employed in the office of the United States trustee. The application shall be accompanied by a verified statement of the person to be employed setting forth the person's connections with the debtor, creditors, any other party in interest, their respective attorneys and accountants, the United States trustee, or any person employed in the office of the United States trustee.

(b) SERVICES RENDERED BY MEMBER OR ASSOCIATE OF FIRM OF ATTORNEYS OR ACCOUNTANTS. If, under the Code and this rule, a law partnership or corporation is employed as an attorney, or an accounting partnership or corporation is employed as an accountant, or if a named attorney or accountant is employed, any partner, member, or regular associate of the partnership, corporation or individual may act as attorney or accountant so employed, without further order of the court.

Rule 2015. Duty to Keep Records, Make Reports, and Give Notice of Case

(a) TRUSTEE OR DEBTOR IN POSSESSION. A trustee or debtor in possession shall

(1) in a chapter 7 liquidation case and, if the court directs, in a chapter 11 reorganization case file and transmit to the United States trustee a complete inventory of the property of the debtor within 30 days after qualifying as a trustee or debtor in possession, unless such an inventory has already been filed;

(2) keep a record of receipts and the disposition of money and property received;

(3) file the reports and summaries required by § 704(8) of the Code which shall include a statement, if payments are made to employees, of the amounts of deductions for all taxes required to be withheld or paid for and in behalf of employees and the place where these amounts are deposited;

(4) as soon as possible after the commencement of the case, give notice of the case to every entity known to be holding money or property subject to withdrawal or order of the debtor, including every bank, savings or building and loan association, public utility company, and landlord with whom the debtor has a deposit, and to every insurance company which has issued a policy having a cash surrender value payable to the debtor, except that notice need not be given to any entity who has knowledge or has previously been notified of the case;

(5) in a chapter 11 reorganization case, on or before the last day of the month after each calendar quarter during which there is a duty to pay fees under 28 U.S.C. § 1930(a)(6), file and transmit to the United States trustee a statement of any disbursements made during that quarter and of any fees payable under 28 U.S.C. § 1930(a)(6) for that quarter.

(b) CHAPTER 12 TRUSTEE AND DEBTOR IN POSSESSION. In a chapter 12 family farmer's debt adjustment case, the debtor in possession shall perform the duties prescribed in clauses (2)-(4) of subdivision (a) of this rule and, if the court directs, shall file and transmit to the United States trustee a complete inventory of the property of the debtor within the time fixed by the court. If the debtor is removed as debtor in possession, the trustee shall perform the duties of the debtor in possession prescribed in this paragraph.

(c) CHAPTER 13 TRUSTEE AND DEBTOR.

(1) *Business Cases.* In a chapter 13 individual's debt adjustment case, when the debtor is engaged in business, the debtor shall perform the duties prescribed by clauses (2)-(4) of subdivision (a) of this rule and, if the court directs, shall file and transmit to the United States trustee a complete inventory of the property of the debtor within the time fixed by the court.

(2) *Nonbusiness Cases.* In a chapter 13 individual's debt adjustment case, when the debtor is not engaged in business, the trustee shall perform the duties prescribed by clause (2) of subdivision (a) of this rule.

(d) TRANSMISSION OF REPORTS. In a chapter 11 case the court may direct that copies or summaries of annual reports and copies or summaries of other reports shall be mailed to the creditors, equity security holders, and indenture trustees. The court may also direct the publication of summaries of any such reports. A copy of every report or summary mailed or published pursuant to this subdivision shall be transmitted to the United States trustee.

Rule 2016. Compensation for Services Rendered and Reimbursement of Expenses

(a) APPLICATION FOR COMPENSATION OR REIM-BURSEMENT. An entity seeking interim or final compensation for services, or reimbursement of necessary expenses, from the estate shall file an application setting forth a detailed statement of (1) the services rendered, time expended and expenses incurred, and (2) the amounts requested. An application for compensation shall include a statement as to what payments have theretofore been made or promised to the applicant for services rendered or to be rendered in any capacity whatsoever in connection with the case, the source of the compensation so paid or promised, whether any compensation previously received has been shared and whether an agreement or understanding exists between the applicant and any other entity for the sharing of compensation received or to be received for services rendered in or in connection with the case, and the particulars of any sharing of compensation or agreement or understanding therefor, except that details of any agreement by the applicant for the sharing of compensation as a member or regular associate of a firm of lawyers or accountants shall not be required. The requirements of this subdivision shall apply to an application for compensation for services rendered by an attorney or accountant even though the application is filed by a creditor or other entity. Unless the case is a chapter 9 municipality case, the applicant shall transmit to the United States trustee a copy of the application.

(b) DISCLOSURE OF COMPENSATION PAID OR PROM-ISED TO ATTORNEY FOR DEBTOR. Every attorney for a debtor, whether or not the attorney applies for compensation, shall file and transmit to the United States trustee within 15 days after the order for relief, or at another time as the court may direct, the statement required by § 329 of the Code including whether the attorney has shared or agreed to share the compensation with any other entity. The statement shall include the particulars of any such sharing or agreement to share by the attorney, but the details of any agreement for the sharing of the compensation with a member or regular associate of the attorney's law firm shall not be required. A supplemental statement shall be filed and transmitted to the United States trustee within 15 days after any payment or agreement not previously disclosed.

(c) DISCLOSURE OF COMPENSATION PAID OR PROM-ISED TO BANKRUPTCY PETITION PREPARER. Every bankruptcy petition preparer for a debtor shall file a declaration under penalty of perjury and transmit the declaration to the United States trustee within 10 days after the date of the filing of the petition, or at another time as the court may direct, as required by § 110(h)(1). The declaration must disclose any fee, and the source of any fee, received from or on behalf of the debtor within 12 months of the filing of the case and all unpaid fees charged to the debtor. The declaration must describe the services performed and documents prepared or caused to be prepared by the bankruptcy petition preparer. A supplemental statement shall be filed within 10 days after any payment or agreement not previously disclosed.

Rule 2017. Examination of Debtor's Transactions with Debtor's Attorney

(a) PAYMENT OR TRANSFER TO ATTORNEY BEFORE ORDER FOR RELIEF. On motion by any party in interest or on the court's own initiative, the court after notice and a hearing may determine whether any payment of money or any transfer of property by the debtor, made directly or indirectly and in contemplation of the filing of a petition under the Code by or against the debtor or before entry of the order for relief in an involuntary case, to an attorney for services rendered or to be rendered is excessive.

(b) PAYMENT OR TRANSFER TO ATTORNEY AFTER ORDER FOR RELIEF. On motion by the debtor, the United States trustee, or on the court's own initiative, the court after notice and a hearing may determine whether any payment of money or any transfer of property, or any agreement therefor, by the debtor to an attorney after entry of an order for relief in a case under the Code is excessive, whether the payment or transfer is made or is to be made directly, or indirectly, if the payment, transfer, or agreement therefor is for services in any way related to the case.

Rule 2018. Intervention; Right to Be Heard

(a) PERMISSIVE INTERVENTION. In a case under the Code, after hearing on such notice as the court directs and for cause shown, the court may permit any interested entity to intervene generally or with respect to any specified matter.

(b) INTERVENTION BY ATTORNEY GENERAL OF A STATE. In a chapter 7, 11, 12, or 13 case, the Attorney General of a State may appear and be heard on behalf of consumer creditors if the court determines the appearance is in the public interest, but the Attorney General may not appeal from any judgment, order, or decree in the case.

(c) CHAPTER 9 MUNICIPALITY CASE. The Secretary of the Treasury of the United States may, or if requested by the court shall, intervene in a chapter 9 case. Representatives of the state in which the debtor is located may intervene in a chapter 9 case with respect to matters specified by the court.

(d) LABOR UNIONS. In a chapter 9, 11, or 12 case, a labor union or employees' association, representative of employees of the debtor, shall have the right to be heard on the economic soundness of a plan affecting the interests of the employees. A labor union or employees' association which exercises its right to be heard under this subdivision shall not be entitled to appeal any judgment, order, or decree relating to the plan, unless otherwise permitted by law.

(e) SERVICE ON ENTITIES COVERED BY THIS RULE. The court may enter orders governing the service of notice and papers on entities permitted to intervene or be heard pursuant to this rule.

Rule 2019. Representation of Creditors and Equity Security Holders in Chapter 9 Municipality and Chapter 11 Reorganization Cases

(a) DATA REQUIRED. In a chapter 9 municipality or chapter 11 reorganization case, except with respect to a committee appointed pursuant to § 1102 or 1114 of the Code, every entity or committee representing more than one creditor or equity security holder and, unless otherwise directed by the court, every indenture trustee, shall file a verified statement setting forth

(1) the name and address of the creditor or equity security holder;

(2) the nature and amount of the claim or interest and the time of acquisition thereof unless it is alleged to have been acquired more than one year prior to the filing of the petition;

(3) a recital of the pertinent facts and circumstances in connection with the employment of the entity or indenture trustee, and, in

the case of a committee, the name or names of the entity or entities at whose instance, directly or indirectly, the employment was arranged or the committee was organized or agreed to act; and

(4) with reference to the time of the employment of the entity, the organization or formation of the committee, or the appearance in the case of any indenture trustee, the amounts of claims or interests owned by the entity, the members of the committee or the indenture trustee, the times when acquired, the amounts paid therefor, and any sales or other disposition thereof.

The statement shall include a copy of the instrument, if any, whereby the entity, committee, or indenture trustee is empowered to act on behalf of creditors or equity security holders. A supplemental statement shall be filed promptly, setting forth any material changes in the facts contained in the statement filed pursuant to this subdivision.

(b) FAILURE TO COMPLY; EFFECT. On motion of any party in interest or on its own initiative, the court may

(1) determine whether there has been a failure to comply with the provisions of subdivision (a) of this rule or with any other applicable law regulating the activities and personnel of any entity, committee, or indenture trustee or any other impropriety in connection with any solicitation and, if it so determines, the court may refuse to permit that entity, committee, or indenture trustee or any other impropriety in connection with any solicitation and, if it so determines, the court may refuse to permit that entity, committee, or indenture trustee to be heard further or to intervene in the case;

(2) examine any representation provision of a deposit agreement, proxy, trust mortgage, trust indenture, or deed of trust, or committee or other authorization, and any claim or interest acquired by any entity or committee in contemplation or in the course of a case under the Code and grant appropriate relief; and

(3) hold invalid any authority, acceptance, rejection, or objection given, procured, or received by an entity or committee who has not complied with this rule or with § 1125(b) of the Code.

Rule 2020. Review of Acts by United States Trustee

A proceeding to contest any act or failure to act by the United States trustee is governed by Rule 9014.

PART III

CLAIMS AND DISTRIBUTION TO CREDITORS AND EQUITY INTEREST HOLDERS; PLANS

Rule 3001. Proof of Claim

(a) FORM AND CONTENT. A proof of claim is a written statement setting forth a creditor's claim. A proof of claim shall conform substantially to the appropriate Official Form.

(b) WHO MAY EXECUTE. A proof of claim shall be executed by the creditor or the creditor's authorized agent except as provided in Rules 3004 and 3005.

(c) CLAIM BASED ON A WRITING. When a claim, or an interest in property of the debtor securing the claim, is based on a writing, the original or a duplicate shall be filed with the proof of claim. If the writing has been lost or destroyed, a statement of the circumstances of the loss or destruction shall be filed with the claim.

(d) EVIDENCE OF PERFECTION OF SECURITY INTEREST. If a security interest in property of the debtor is claimed, the proof of claim shall be accompanied by evidence that the security interest has been perfected.

(e) TRANSFERRED CLAIM.

(1) *Transfer of Claim Other Than for Security Before Proof Filed.* If a claim has been transferred other than for security before proof of the claim has been filed, the proof of claim may be filed only by the transferee or an indenture trustee.

(2) *Transfer of Claim Other Than for Security After Proof Filed.* If a claim other than one based on a publicly traded note, bond, or debenture has been transferred other than for security after the proof of claim has been filed, evidence of the transfer shall be filed by the transferee. The clerk shall immediately notify the alleged transferor by mail of the filing of the evidence of transfer and that objection thereto, if any, must be filed within 20 days of the mailing of the notice or within any additional time allowed by the court. If the alleged transferor files a timely objection and the court finds, after notice and a hearing, that the claim has been transferred other than for security, it shall enter an order substituting the transferee for the transferor. If a timely objection is not filed by the alleged transferor, the transferee shall be substituted for the transferor.

(3) *Transfer of Claim for Security Before Proof Filed.* If a claim other than one based on a publicly traded note, bond, or debenture has been transferred for security before proof of the claim has been filed, the transferor or transferee or both may file a proof of claim for the full amount. The proof shall be supported by a statement setting forth the terms of the transfer. If either the transferor or the transferee files a proof of claim, the clerk shall immediately notify the other by mail of the right to join in the filed claim. If both transferor and transferee file proofs of the same claim, the proofs shall be consolidated. If the transferor or transferee does not file an agreement regarding its relative rights respecting voting of the claim, payment of dividends thereon, or participation in the administration of the estate, on motion by a party in interest and after notice and a hearing, the court shall enter such orders respecting these matters as may be appropriate.

(4) *Transfer of Claim for Security After Proof Filed.* If a claim other than one based on a publicly traded note, bond, or debenture has been transferred for security after the proof of claim has been filed, evidence of the terms of the transfer shall be filed by the transferee. The clerk shall immediately notify the alleged transferor by mail of the filing of the evidence of transfer and that objection thereto, if any, must be filed within 20 days of the mailing of the notice or within any additional time allowed by the court. If a timely objection is filed by the alleged transferor, the court, after notice and a hearing, shall determine whether the claim has been transferred for security. If the transferor or transferee does not file an agreement regarding its relative rights respecting voting of the claim, payment of dividends thereon, or participation in the administration of the estate, on motion by a party in interest and after notice and a hearing, the court shall enter such orders respecting these matters as may be appropriate.

(5) *Service of Objection or Motion; Notice of Hearing.* A copy of an objection filed pursuant to paragraph (2) or (4) or a motion filed pursuant to paragraph (3) or (4) of this subdivision together with a notice of a hearing shall be mailed or otherwise

delivered to the transferor or transferee, whichever is appropriate, at least 30 days prior to the hearing.

(f) EVIDENTIARY EFFECT. A proof of claim executed and filed in accordance with these rules shall constitute prima facie evidence of the validity and amount of the claim.

(g) To the extent not inconsistent with the United States Warehouse Act or applicable State law, a warehouse receipt, scale ticket, or similar document of the type routinely issued as evidence of title by a grain storage facility, as defined in section 557 of title 11, shall constitute prima facie evidence of the validity and amount of a claim of ownership of a quantity of grain.

Rule 3002. Filing Proof of Claim or Interest

(a) NECESSITY FOR FILING. An unsecured creditor or an equity security holder must file a proof of claim or interest in accordance with this rule for the claim or interest to be allowed, except as provided in Rules 1019(3), 3003, 3004 and 3005.

(b) PLACE OF FILING. A proof of claim or interest shall be filed in accordance with Rule 5005.

(c) TIME FOR FILING. In a chapter 7 liquidation, chapter 12 family farmer's debt adjustment, or chapter 13 individual's debt adjustment case, a proof of claim is timely filed if it is filed not later than 90 days after the first date set for the meeting of creditors called under § 341(a) of the Code, except as follows:

(1) A proof of claim filed by a governmental unit is timely filed if it is filed not later than 180 days after the date of the order for relief. On motion of a governmental unit before the expiration of such period and for cause shown, the court may extend the time for filing of a claim by the governmental unit.

(2) In the interest of justice and if it will not unduly delay the administration of the case, the court may extend the time for filing a proof of claim by an infant or incompetent person or the representative of either.

(3) An unsecured claim which arises in favor of an entity or becomes allowable as a result of a judgment may be filed within 30 days after the judgment becomes final if the judgment is for the recovery of money or property from that entity or denies or avoids the entity's interest in property. If the judgment imposes a liability which is not satisfied, or a duty which is not performed within such period or such further time as the court may permit, the claim shall not be allowed.

(4) A claim arising from the rejection of an executory contract or unexpired lease of the debtor may be filed within such time as the court may direct.

(5) If notice of insufficient assets to pay a dividend was given to creditors pursuant to Rule 2002(e), and subsequently the trustee notifies the court that payment of a dividend appears possible, the clerk shall notify the creditors of that fact and that they may file proofs of claim within 90 days after the mailing of the notice.

Rule 3003. Filing Proof of Claim or Equity Security Interest in Chapter 9 Municipality or Chapter 11 Reorganization Cases

(a) APPLICABILITY OF RULE. This rule applies in chapter 9 and 11 cases.

(b) SCHEDULE OF LIABILITIES AND LIST OF EQUITY SECURITY HOLDERS.

(1) *Schedule of Liabilities.* The schedule of liabilities filed pursuant to § 521(1) of the Code shall constitute prima facie evidence of the validity and amount of the claims of creditors, unless they are scheduled as disputed, contingent, or unliquidated. It shall not be necessary for a creditor or equity security holder to file a proof of claim or interest except as provided in subdivision (c)(2) of this rule.

(2) *List of Equity Security Holders.* The list of equity security holders filed pursuant to Rule 1007(a)(3) shall constitute prima facie evidence of the validity and amount of the equity security interests and it shall not be necessary for the holders of such interests to file a proof of interest.

(c) FILING PROOF OF CLAIM.

(1) *Who May File.* Any creditor or indenture trustee may file a proof of claim within the time prescribed by subdivision (c)(3) of this rule.

(2) *Who Must File.* Any creditor or equity security holder whose claim or interest is not scheduled or scheduled as disputed, contingent, or unliquidated shall file a proof of claim or interest within the time prescribed by subdivision (c)(3) of this rule; any creditor who fails to do so shall not be treated as a creditor with respect to such claim for the purposes of voting and distribution.

(3) *Time for Filing.* The court shall fix and for cause shown may extend the time within which proofs of claim or interest may be filed. Notwithstanding the expiration of such time, a proof of claim may be filed to the extent and under the conditions stated in Rule 3002(c)(2), (c)(3), and (c)(4).

(4) *Effect of Filing Claim or Interest.* A proof of claim or interest executed and filed in accordance with this subdivision shall supersede any scheduling of that claim or interest pursuant to § 521(1) of the Code.

(5) *Filing by Indenture Trustee.* An indenture trustee may file a claim on behalf of all known or unknown holders of securities issued pursuant to the trust instrument under which it is trustee.

(d) PROOF OF RIGHT TO RECORD STATUS. For the purposes of Rules 3017, 3018 and 3021 and for receiving notices, an entity who is not the record holder of a security may file a statement setting forth facts which entitle that entity to be treated as the record holder. An objection to the statement may be filed by any party in interest.

Rule 3004. Filing of Claims by Debtor or Trustee

If a creditor fails to file a proof of claim on or before the first date set for the meeting of creditors called pursuant to § 341(a) of the Code, the debtor or trustee may do so in the name of the creditor, within 30 days after expiration of the time for filing claims prescribed by Rule 3002(c) or 3003(c), whichever is applicable. The clerk shall forthwith mail notice of the filing to the creditor, the debtor and the trustee. A proof of claim filed by a creditor pursuant to Rule 3002 or Rule 3003(c), shall supersede the proof filed by the debtor or trustee.

Rule 3005. Filing of Claim, Acceptance, or Rejection by Guarantor, Surety, Indorser, or Other Codebtor

(a) FILING OF CLAIM. If a creditor has not filed a proof of claim pursuant to Rule 3002 or 3003(c), an entity that is or may be liable with the debtor to that creditor, or who has secured that creditor, may, within 30 days after the expiration of the time for filing claims prescribed by Rule 3002(c) or 3003(c) whichever is applicable, execute and file a proof of claim in the name of the creditor, if known, or if unknown, in the entity's own name. No distribution shall be made on the claim except on satisfactory proof that the original debt will be diminished by the amount of distribution. A proof of claim filed by a creditor pursuant to Rule 3002 or 3003(c) shall supersede the proof of claim filed pursuant to the first sentence of this subdivision.

(b) FILING OF ACCEPTANCE OR REJECTION; SUBSTITUTION OF CREDITOR. An entity which has filed a claim pursuant to the first sentence of subdivision (a) of this rule may file an acceptance or rejection of a plan in the name of the creditor, if known, or if unknown, in the entity's own name but if the creditor files a proof of claim within the time permitted by Rule 3003(c) or files a notice prior to confirmation of a plan of the creditor's intention to act in the creditor's own behalf, the creditor shall be substituted for the obligor with respect to that claim.

Rule 3006. Withdrawal of Claim; Effect on Acceptance or Rejection of Plan

A creditor may withdraw a claim as of right by filing a notice of withdrawal, except as provided in this rule. If after a creditor has filed a proof of claim an objection is filed thereto or a complaint is filed against that creditor in an adversary proceeding, or the creditor has accepted or rejected the plan or otherwise has participated significantly in the case, the creditor may not withdraw the claim except on order of the court after a hearing on notice to the trustee or debtor in possession, and any creditors' committee elected pursuant to § 705(a) or appointed pursuant to § 1102 of the Code. The order of the court shall contain such terms and conditions as the court deems proper. Unless the court orders otherwise, an authorized withdrawal of a claim shall constitute withdrawal of any related acceptance or rejection of a plan.

Rule 3007. Objections to Claims

An objection to the allowance of a claim shall be in writing and filed. A copy of the objection with notice of the hearing thereon shall be mailed or otherwise delivered to the claimant, the debtor or debtor in possession and the trustee at least 30 days prior to the hearing. If an objection to a claim is joined with a demand for relief of the kind specified in Rule 7001, it becomes an adversary proceeding.

Rule 3008. Reconsideration of Claims

A party in interest may move for reconsideration of an order allowing or disallowing a claim against the estate. The court after a hearing on notice shall enter an appropriate order.

Rule 3009. Declaration and Payment of Dividends in a Chapter 7 Liquidation Case

In a chapter 7 case, dividends to creditors shall be paid as promptly as practicable. Dividend checks shall be made payable to and mailed to each creditor whose claim has been allowed, unless a power of attorney authorizing another entity to receive dividends has been executed and filed in accordance with Rule 9010. In that event, dividend checks shall be made payable to the creditor and to

the other entity and shall be mailed to the other entity.

Rule 3010. Small Dividends and Payments in Chapter 7 Liquidation, Chapter 12 Family Farmer's Debt Adjustment, and Chapter 13 Individual's Debt Adjustment Cases

(a) CHAPTER 7 CASES. In a chapter 7 case no dividend in an amount less than $5 shall be distributed by the trustee to any creditor unless authorized by local rule or order of the court. Any dividend not distributed to a creditor shall be treated in the same manner as unclaimed funds as provided in § 347 of the Code.

(b) CHAPTER 12 AND CHAPTER 13 CASES. In a chapter 12 or chapter 13 case no payment in an amount less than $15 shall be distributed by the trustee to any creditor unless authorized by local rule or order of the court. Funds not distributed because of this subdivision shall accumulate and shall be paid whenever the accumulation aggregates $15. Any funds remaining shall be distributed with the final payment.

Rule 3011. Unclaimed Funds in Chapter 7 Liquidation, Chapter 12 Family Farmer's Debt Adjustment, and Chapter 13 Individual's Debt Adjustment Cases

The trustee shall file a list of all known names and addresses of the entities and the amounts which they are entitled to be paid from remaining property of the estate that is paid into court pursuant to § 347(a) of the Code.

Rule 3012. Valuation of Security

The court may determine the value of a claim secured by a lien on property in which the estate has an interest on motion of any party in interest and after a hearing on notice to the holder of the secured claim and any other entity as the court may direct.

Rule 3013. Classification of Claims and Interests

For the purposes of the plan and its acceptance, the court may, on motion after hearing on notice as the court may direct, determine classes of creditors and equity security holders pursuant to §§ 1122, 1222(b)(1), and 1322(b)(1) of the Code.

Rule 3014. Election Under § 1111(b)(2) By Secured Creditor in Chapter 9 Municipality or Chapter 11 Reorganization Case

An election of application of § 1111(b)(2) of the Code by a class of secured creditors in a chapter 9 or 11 case may be made at any time prior to the conclusion of the hearing on the disclosure statement or within such later time as the court may fix. If the disclosure statement is conditionally approved pursuant to Rule 3017.1, and a final hearing on the disclosure statement is not held, the election of application of § 1111(b)(2) may be made not later than the date fixed pursuant to Rule 3017.1(a)(2) or another date the court may fix. The election shall be in writing and signed unless made at the hearing on the disclosure statement. The election, if made by the majorities required by § 1111(b)(1)(A)(i), shall be binding on all members of the class with respect to the plan.

Rule 3015. Filing, Objection to Confirmation, and Modification of a Plan in a Chapter 12 Family Farmer's Debt Adjustment or a Chapter 13 Individual's Debt Adjustment Case

(a) CHAPTER 12 PLAN. The debtor may file a chapter 12 plan with the petition. If a plan is not filed with the petition, it shall be filed within the time prescribed by § 1221 of the Code.

(b) CHAPTER 13 PLAN. The debtor may file a chapter 13 plan with the petition. If a plan is not filed with the petition, it shall be filed within 15 days thereafter, and such time may not be further extended except for cause shown and on notice as the court may direct. If a case is converted to chapter 13, a plan shall be filed within 15 days thereafter, and such time may not be further extended except for cause shown and on notice as the court may direct.

(c) DATING. Every proposed plan and any modification thereof shall be dated.

(d) NOTICE AND COPIES. The plan or a summary of the plan shall be included with each notice of the hearing on confirmation mailed pursuant to Rule 2002. If required by the court, the debtor shall furnish a sufficient number of copies to enable the clerk to include a copy of the plan with the notice of the hearing.

(e) TRANSMISSION TO UNITED STATES TRUSTEE. The clerk shall forthwith transmit to the United States trustee a copy of the plan and any modification thereof filed pursuant to subdivision (a) or (b) of this rule.

(f) OBJECTION TO CONFIRMATION; DETERMINATION OF GOOD FAITH IN THE ABSENCE OF AN OBJECTION. An objection to confirmation of a plan shall be filed and served on the debtor, the trustee, and any other entity designated by the court, and shall be transmitted to the United States trustee, before confirmation of the plan. An objection to confirmation is governed by Rule 9014. If no objection is timely filed, the court may determine that the plan has been proposed in good faith and not by any means forbidden by law without receiving evidence on such issues.

(g) MODIFICATION OF PLAN AFTER CONFIRMATION. A request to modify a plan pursuant to § 1229 or § 1329 of the Code shall identify the proponent and shall be filed together with the proposed modification. The clerk, or some other person as the court may direct, shall give the debtor, the trustee, and all creditors not less than 20 days notice by mail of the time fixed for filing objections and, if an objection is filed, the hearing to consider the proposed modification, unless the court orders otherwise with respect to creditors who are not affected by the proposed modification. A copy of the notice shall be transmitted to the United States trustee. A copy of the proposed modification, or a summary thereof, shall be included with the notice. If required by the court, the proponent shall furnish a sufficient number of copies of the proposed modification, or a summary thereof, to enable the clerk to include a copy with each notice. Any objection to the proposed modification shall be filed and served on the debtor, the trustee, and any other entity designated by the court, and shall be transmitted to the United States trustee. An objection to a proposed modification is governed by Rule 9014.

Rule 3016. Filing of Plan and Disclosure Statement in a Chapter 9 Municipality or Chapter 11 Reorganization Case

(a) IDENTIFICATION OF PLAN. Every proposed plan and any modification thereof shall be dated and, in a chapter 11 case, identified with the name of the entity or entities submitting or filing it.

(b) DISCLOSURE STATEMENT. In a chapter 9 or 11 case, a disclosure statement pursuant to § 1125 or evidence showing compliance with § 1126(b) of the Code shall be filed with the plan or within a time fixed by the court.

(c) INJUNCTION UNDER A PLAN. If a plan provides for an injunction against conduct not otherwise enjoined under the Code, the plan and disclosure statement shall describe in specific and conspicuous language (bold, italic, or underlined text) all acts to be enjoined and identify the entities that would be subject to the injunction.

Rule 3017. Court Consideration of Disclosure Statement in a Chapter 9 Municipality or Chapter 11 Reorganization Case

(a) HEARING ON DISCLOSURE STATEMENT AND OBJECTIONS. Except as provided in Rule 3017.1, after a disclosure statement is filed in accordance with Rule 3016(b), the court shall hold a hearing on at least 25 days' notice to the debtor, creditors, equity security holders and other parties in interest as provided in Rule 2002 to consider the disclosure statement and any objections or modifications thereto. The plan and the disclosure statement shall be mailed with the notice of the hearing only to the debtor, any trustee or committee appointed under the Code, the Securities and Exchange Commission, and any party in interest who requests in writing a copy of the statement or plan. Objections to the disclosure statement shall be filed and served on the debtor, the trustee, any committee appointed under the Code and any other entity designated by the court, at any time before the disclosure statement is approved or by an earlier date as the court may fix. In a chapter 11 reorganization case, every notice, plan, disclosure statement, and objection required to be served or mailed pursuant to this subdivision shall be transmitted to the United States trustee within the time provided in this subdivision.

(b) DETERMINATION ON DISCLOSURE STATEMENT. Following the hearing the court shall determine whether the disclosure statement should be approved.

(c) DATES FIXED FOR VOTING ON PLAN AND CONFIRMATION. On or before approval of the disclosure statement, the court shall fix a time within which the holders of claims and interests may accept or reject the plan and may fix a date for the hearing on confirmation.

(d) TRANSMISSION AND NOTICE TO UNITED STATES TRUSTEE, CREDITORS, AND EQUITY SECURITY HOLDERS. Upon approval of a disclosure statement,—except to the extent that the court orders otherwise with respect to one or more unimpaired classes of creditors or equity security holders—the debtor in possession, trustee, proponent of the plan, or clerk as the court orders shall mail to all creditors and equity security holders, and in a chapter 11 reorganization case shall transmit to the United States trustee,

(1) the plan or a court-approved summary of the plan;

(2) the disclosure statement approved by the court;

(3) notice of the time within which acceptances and rejections of the plan may be filed; and

(4) any other information as the court may direct, including any court opinion approving the disclosure statement or a court-approved summary of the opinion.

In addition, notice of the time fixed for filing objections and the hearing on confirmation shall be mailed to all creditors and equity security holders in accordance with Rule 2002(b), and a form of ballot conforming to the appropriate Official Form shall be mailed to creditors and equity security holders entitled to vote on the plan. If the court opinion is not transmitted or only a summary of the plan is transmitted, the court opinion or the plan shall be provided on request of a party in interest at the plan proponent's expense. If the court orders that the disclosure statement and the plan or a summary of the plan shall not be mailed to any unimpaired class, notice that the class is designated in the plan as unimpaired and notice of the name and address of the person from whom the plan or summary of the plan and disclosure statement may be obtained upon request and at the plan proponent's expense, shall be mailed to members of the unimpaired class together with the notice of the time fixed for filing objections to and the hearing on confirmation. For the purposes of this subdivision, creditors and equity security holders shall include holders of stock, bonds, debentures, notes, and other securities of record on the date the order approving the disclosure statement is entered or another date fixed by the court, for cause, after notice and a hearing.

(e) TRANSMISSION TO BENEFICIAL HOLDERS OF SECURITIES. At the hearing held pursuant to subdivision (a) of this rule, the court shall consider the procedures for transmitting the documents and information required by subdivision (d) of this rule to beneficial holders of stock, bonds, debentures, notes, and other securities, determine the adequacy of the procedures, and enter any orders the court deems appropriate.

(f) NOTICE AND TRANSMISSION OF DOCUMENTS TO ENTITIES SUBJECT TO AN INJUNCTION UNDER A PLAN. If a plan provides for an injunction against conduct not otherwise enjoined under the Code and an entity that would be subject to the injunction is not a creditor or equity security holder, at the hearing held under Rule 3017(a), the court shall consider procedures for providing the entity with:

(1) at least 25 days' notice of the time fixed for filing objections and the hearing on confirmation of the plan containing the information described in Rule 2002(c)(3); and

(2) to the extent feasible, a copy of the plan and disclosure statement.

Rule 3017.1. Court Consideration of Disclosure Statement in a Small Business Case

(a) CONDITIONAL APPROVAL OF DISCLOSURE STATEMENT. If the debtor is a small business and has made a timely election to be considered a small business in a chapter 11 case, the court may, on application of the plan proponent, conditionally approve a disclosure statement filed in accordance with Rule 3016(b). On or before conditional approval of the disclosure statement, the court shall:

(1) fix a time within which the holders of claims and interests may accept or reject the plan;

(2) fix a time for filing objections to the disclosure statement;

(3) fix a date for the hearing on final approval of the disclosure statement to be held if a timely objection is filed; and

(4) fix a date for the hearing on confirmation.

(b) APPLICATION OF RULE 3017. Rule 3017(a), (b), (c), and (e) do not apply to a conditionally approved disclosure statement. Rule 3017(d) applies to a conditionally approved disclosure statement, except that conditional approval is considered approval of the disclosure statement for the purpose of applying Rule 3017(d).

(c) FINAL APPROVAL.

(1) *Notice.* Notice of the time fixed for filing objections and the hearing to consider final approval of the disclosure statement shall be given in accordance with Rule 2002 and may be combined with notice of the hearing on confirmation of the plan.

(2) *Objections.* Objections to the disclosure statement shall be filed, transmitted to the United States trustee, and served on the debtor, the trustee, any committee appointed under the Code and any other entity designated by the court at any time before final approval of the disclosure statement or by an earlier date as the court may fix.

(3) *Hearing.* If a timely objection to the disclosure statement is filed, the court shall hold a hearing to consider final approval before or combined with the hearing on confirmation of the plan.

Rule 3018. Acceptance or Rejection of Plan in a Chapter 9 Municipality or a Chapter 11 Reorganization Case

(a) ENTITIES ENTITLED TO ACCEPT OR REJECT PLAN; TIME FOR ACCEPTANCE OR REJECTION. A plan may be accepted or rejected in accordance with § 1126 of the Code within the time fixed by the court pursuant to Rule 3017. Subject to subdivision (b) of this rule, an equity security holder or creditor whose claim is based on a security of record shall not be entitled to accept or reject a plan unless the equity security holder or creditor is the holder of record of the security on the date the order approving the disclosure statement is entered or on another date fixed by the court, for cause, after notice and a hearing. For cause shown, the court after notice and hearing may permit a creditor or equity security holder to change or withdraw an acceptance or rejection. Notwithstanding objection to a claim or interest, the court after notice and hearing may temporarily allow the claim or interest in an amount which the court deems proper for the purpose of accepting or rejecting a plan.

(b) ACCEPTANCES OR REJECTIONS OBTAINED BEFORE PETITION. An equity security holder or creditor whose claim is based on a security of record who accepted or rejected the plan before the commencement of the case shall not be deemed to have accepted or rejected the plan pursuant to § 1126(b) of the Code unless the equity security holder or creditor was the holder of record of the security on the date specified in the solicitation of such acceptance or rejection for the purposes of such solicitation. A holder of a claim or interest who has accepted or rejected a plan before the commencement of the case under the Code shall not be deemed to have accepted or rejected the plan if the court finds after notice and hearing that the plan was not transmitted to substantially all creditors and equity security holders of the same class, that an unreasonably short time was prescribed for such creditors and equity security holders to accept or reject the plan, or that the solicitation was not in compliance with § 1126(b) of the Code.

(c) FORM OF ACCEPTANCE OR REJECTION. An acceptance or rejection shall be in writing, identify the plan or plans accepted or rejected, be signed by the creditor or equity security holder or an authorized agent, and conform to the appropriate Official Form. If more than one plan is transmitted pursuant to Rule 3017, an acceptance or rejection may be filed by each creditor or equity security holder for any number of plans transmitted and if acceptances are filed for more than one plan, the creditor or equity security holder may indicate a preference or preferences among the plans so accepted.

(d) ACCEPTANCE OR REJECTION BY PARTIALLY SE-CURED CREDITOR. A creditor whose claim has been allowed in part as a secured claim and in part as an unsecured claim shall be entitled to accept or reject a plan in both capacities.

Rule 3019. Modification of Accepted Plan Before Confirmation in a Chapter 9 Municipality or Chapter 11 Reorganization Case

In a chapter 9 or chapter 11 case, after a plan has been accepted and before its confirmation, the proponent may file a modification of the plan. If the court finds after hearing on notice to the trustee, any committee appointed under the Code, and any other entity designated by the court that the proposed modification does not adversely change the treatment of the claim of any creditor or the interest of any equity security holder who has not accepted in writing the modification, it shall be deemed accepted by all creditors and equity security holders who have previously accepted the plan.

Rule 3020. Deposit; Confirmation of Plan in a Chapter 9 Municipality or a Chapter 11 Reorganization Case

(a) DEPOSIT. In a chapter 11 case, prior to entry of the order confirming the plan, the court may order the deposit with the trustee or debtor in possession of the consideration required by the plan to be distributed on confirmation. Any money deposited shall be kept in a special account established for the exclusive purpose of making the distribution.

(b) OBJECTION TO AND HEARING ON CONFIRMATION IN A CHAPTER 9 OR CHAPTER 11 CASE.

(1) *Objection.* An objection to confirmation of the plan shall be filed and served on the debtor, the trustee, the proponent of the plan, any committee appointed under the Code, and any other entity designated by the court, within a time fixed by the court. Unless the case is a chapter 9 municipality case, a copy of every objection to confirmation shall be transmitted by the objecting party to the United States trustee within the time fixed for filing objections. An objection to confirmation is governed by Rule 9014.

(2) *Hearing.* The court shall rule on confirmation of the plan after notice and hearing as provided in Rule 2002. If no objection is timely filed, the court may determine that the plan has been proposed in good faith and not by any means forbidden by law without receiving evidence on such issues.

(c) ORDER OF CONFIRMATION.

(1) The order of confirmation shall conform to the appropriate Official Form. If the plan provides for an injunction against conduct not otherwise enjoined under the Code, the order of confirmation shall (1) describe in reasonable detail all acts enjoined; (2) be specific in its terms regarding the injunction; and (3) identify the entities subject to the injunction.

(2) Notice of entry of the order of confirmation shall be mailed promptly to the debtor, the trustee, creditors, equity security

holders, other parties in interest, and, if known, to any identified entity subject to an injunction provided for in the plan against conduct not otherwise enjoined under the Code.

(3) Except in a chapter 9 municipality case, notice of entry of the order of confirmation shall be transmitted to the United States trustee as provided in Rule 2002(k).

(d) RETAINED POWER. Notwithstanding the entry of the order of confirmation, the court may issue any other order necessary to administer the estate.

(e) STAY OF CONFIRMATION ORDER. An order confirming a plan is stayed until the expiration of 10 days after the entry of the order, unless the court orders otherwise.

Rule 3021. Distribution Under Plan

Except as provided in Rule 3020(e), after a plan is confirmed, distribution shall be made to creditors whose claims have been allowed, to interest holders whose interests have not been disallowed, and to indenture trustees who have filed claims under Rule 3003(c)(5) that have been allowed. For purposes of this rule, creditors include holders of bonds, debentures, notes, and other debt securities, and interest holders include the holders of stock and other equity securities, of record at the time of commencement of distribution, unless a different time is fixed by the plan or the order confirming the plan.

Rule 3022. Final Decree in Chapter 11 Reorganization Case

After an estate is fully administered in a chapter 11 reorganization case, the court, on its own motion or on motion of a party in interest, shall enter a final decree closing the case.

PART IV

THE DEBTOR; DUTIES AND BENEFITS

Rule 4001. Relief from Automatic Stay; Prohibiting or Conditioning the Use, Sale, or Lease of Property; Use of Cash Collateral; Obtaining Credit; Agreements

(a) RELIEF FROM STAY; PROHIBITING OR CONDITIONING THE USE, SALE, OR LEASE OF PROPERTY.

(1) *Motion.* A motion for relief from an automatic stay provided by the Code or a motion to prohibit or condition the use, sale, or lease of property pursuant to § 363(e) shall be made in accordance with Rule 9014 and shall be served on any committee elected pursuant to § 705 or appointed pursuant to § 1102 of the Code or its authorized agent, or, if the case is a chapter 9 municipality case or a chapter 11 reorganization case and no committee of unsecured creditors has been appointed pursuant to § 1102, on the creditors included on the list filed pursuant to Rule 1007(d), and on such other entities as the court may direct.

(2) *Ex Parte Relief.* Relief from a stay under § 362(a) or a request to prohibit or condition the use, sale, or lease of property pursuant to § 363(e) may be granted without prior notice only if (A) it clearly appears from specific facts shown by affidavit or by a verified motion that immediate and irreparable injury, loss, or damage will result to the movant before the adverse party or the attorney for the adverse party can be heard in opposition, and (B) the movant's attorney certifies to the court in writing the efforts, if any, which have been made to give notice and the reasons why notice should not be required. The

party obtaining relief under this subdivision and § 362(f) or § 363(e) shall immediately give oral notice thereof to the trustee or debtor in possession and to the debtor and forthwith mail or otherwise transmit to such adverse party or parties a copy of the order granting relief. On two days notice to the party who obtained relief from the stay without notice or on shorter notice to that party as the court may prescribe, the adverse party may appear and move reinstatement of the stay or reconsideration of the order prohibiting or conditioning the use, sale, or lease of property. In that event, the court shall proceed expeditiously to hear and determine the motion.

(3) *Stay of Order*. An order granting a motion for relief from an automatic stay made in accordance with Rule 4001(a)(1) is stayed until the expiration of 10 days after the entry of the order, unless the court orders otherwise.

(b) USE OF CASH COLLATERAL.

(1) *Motion; Service*. A motion for authorization to use cash collateral shall be made in accordance with Rule 9014 and shall be served on any entity which has an interest in the cash collateral, on any committee elected pursuant to § 705 or appointed pursuant to § 1102 of the Code or its authorized agent, or, if the case is a chapter 9 municipality case or a chapter 11 reorganization case and no committee of unsecured creditors has been appointed pursuant to § 1102, on the creditors included on the list filed pursuant to Rule 1007(d), and on such other entities as the court may direct.

(2) *Hearing*. The court may commence a final hearing on a motion for authorization to use cash collateral no earlier than 15 days after service of the motion. If the motion so requests, the court may conduct a preliminary hearing before such 15 day period expires, but the court may authorize the use of only that amount of cash collateral as is necessary to avoid immediate and irreparable harm to the estate pending a final hearing.

(3) *Notice*. Notice of hearing pursuant to this subdivision shall be given to the parties on whom service of the motion is required by paragraph (1) of this subdivision and to such other entities as the court may direct.

(c) OBTAINING CREDIT.

(1) *Motion; Service*. A motion for authority to obtain credit shall be made in accordance with Rule 9014 and shall be served on any committee elected pursuant to § 705 or appointed pursuant to § 1102 of the Code or its authorized agent, or, if the case is a chapter 9 municipality case or a chapter 11 reorganization case and no committee of unsecured creditors has been appointed pursuant to § 1102, on the creditors included on the list filed pursuant to Rule 1007(d), and on such other entities as the court may direct. The motion shall be accompanied by a copy of the agreement.

(2) *Hearing*. The court may commence a final hearing on a motion for authority to obtain credit no earlier than 15 days after service of the motion. If the motion so requests, the court may conduct a hearing before such 15 day period expires, but the court may authorize the obtaining of credit only to the extent necessary to avoid immediate and irreparable harm to the estate pending a final hearing.

(3) *Notice*. Notice of hearing pursuant to this subdivision shall be given to the parties on whom service of the motion is required by paragraph (1) of this subdivision and to such other entities as the court may direct.

(d) AGREEMENT RELATING TO RELIEF FROM THE AUTOMATIC STAY, PROHIBITING OR CONDITIONING THE USE, SALE, OR LEASE OF PROPERTY, PROVIDING ADEQUATE PROTECTION, USE OF CASH COLLATERAL, AND OBTAINING CREDIT.

(1) *Motion; Service*. A motion for approval of an agreement (A) to provide adequate protection, (B) to prohibit or condition the use, sale, or lease of property, (C) to modify or terminate the stay provided for in § 362, (D) to use cash collateral, or (E) between the debtor and an entity that has a lien or interest in property of the estate pursuant to which the entity consents to the creation of a lien senior or equal to the entity's lien or interest in such property shall be served on any committee elected pursuant to § 705 or appointed pursuant to § 1102 of the Code or its authorized agent, or, if the case is a chapter 9 municipality case or a chapter 11 reorganization case and no committee of unsecured creditors has been appointed pursuant to § 1102, on the creditors included on the list filed pursuant to Rule 1007(d), and on such other entities as the court may direct. The motion shall be accompanied by a copy of the agreement.

(2) *Objection*. Notice of the motion and the time within which objections may be filed and served on the debtor in possession or trustee shall be mailed to the parties on whom service is required by paragraph (1) of this subdivision and to such other entities as the court may direct. Unless the court fixes a different time, objections may be filed within 15 days of the mailing of notice.

(3) *Disposition; Hearing*. If no objection is filed, the court may enter an order approving or disapproving the agreement without conducting a hearing. If an objection is filed or if the court determines a hearing is appropriate, the court shall hold a hearing on no less than five days' notice to the objector, the movant, the parties on whom service is required by paragraph (1) of this subdivision and such other entities as the court may direct.

(4) *Agreement in Settlement of Motion*. The court may direct that the procedures prescribed in paragraphs (1), (2), and (3) of this subdivision shall not apply and the agreement may be approved without further notice if the court determines that a motion made pursuant to subdivisions (a), (b), or (c) of this rule was sufficient to afford reasonable notice of the material provisions of the agreement and opportunity for a hearing.

Rule 4002. Duties of Debtor

In addition to performing other duties prescribed by the Code and rules, the debtor shall:

(1) attend and submit to an examination at the times ordered by the court;

(2) attend the hearing on a complaint objecting to discharge and testify, if called as a witness;

(3) inform the trustee immediately in writing as to the location of real property in which the debtor has an interest and the name and address of every person holding money or property subject to the debtor's withdrawal or order if a schedule of property has not yet been filed pursuant to Rule 1007;

(4) cooperate with the trustee in the preparation of an inventory, the examination of proofs of claim, and the administration of the estate; and

(5) file a statement of any change of the debtor's address.

Rule 4003. Exemptions

(a) CLAIM OF EXEMPTIONS. A debtor shall list the property claimed as exempt under § 522 of the Code on the schedule of assets required to be filed by Rule 1007. If the debtor fails to claim exemptions or file the schedule within the time specified in Rule 1007, a dependent of the debtor may file the list within 30 days thereafter.

(b) OBJECTING TO A CLAIM OF EXEMPTIONS. A party in interest may file an objection to the list of property claimed as exempt only within 30 days after the meeting of creditors held under § 341(a) is concluded or within 30 days after any amendment to the list or supplemental schedules is filed, whichever is later. The court may, for cause, extend the time for filing objections if, before the time to object expires, a party in interest files a request for an extension. Copies of the objections shall be delivered or mailed to the trustee, the person filing the list, and the attorney for that person.

(c) BURDEN OF PROOF. In any hearing under this rule, the objecting party has the burden of proving that the exemptions are not properly claimed. After hearing on notice, the court shall determine the issues presented by the objections.

(d) AVOIDANCE BY DEBTOR OF TRANSFERS OF EXEMPT PROPERTY. A proceeding by the debtor to avoid a lien or other transfer of property exempt under § 522(f) of the Code shall be by motion in accordance with Rule 9014.

Rule 4004. Grant or Denial of Discharge

(a) TIME FOR FILING COMPLAINT OBJECTING TO DISCHARGE; NOTICE OF TIME FIXED. In a chapter 7 liquidation case a complaint objecting to the debtor's discharge under § 727(a) of the Code shall be filed no later than 60 days after the first date set for the meeting of creditors under § 341(a). In a chapter 11 reorganization case, the complaint shall be filed no later than the first date set for the hearing on confirmation. At least 25 days' notice of the time so fixed shall be given to the United States trustee and all creditors as provided in Rule 2002(f) and (k), and to the trustee and the trustee's attorney.

(b) EXTENSION OF TIME. On motion of any party in interest, after hearing on the notice, the court may for cause extend the time to file a complaint objecting to discharge. The motion shall be filed before the time is expired.

(c) GRANT OF DISCHARGE.

(1) In a chapter 7 case, on expiration of the time fixed for filing a complaint objecting to discharge and the time fixed for filing a motion to dismiss the case pursuant to Rule 1017(e), the court shall forthwith grant the discharge unless:

(A) the debtor is not an individual,

(B) a complaint objecting to the discharge has been filed,

(C) the debtor has filed a waiver under § 727(a)(10),

(D) a motion to dismiss the case pursuant to § 707 is pending,

(E) a motion to extend the time for filing a complaint objecting to discharge is pending,

(F) a motion to extend the time for filing a motion to dismiss the case under Rule 1017(e)(1) is pending, or

(G) the debtor has not paid in full the filing fee prescribed by 28 U.S.C. § 1930(a) and any other fee prescribed by the

Judicial Conference of the United States under 28 U.S.C. § 1930(b) that is payable to the clerk upon the commencement of a case under the Code.

(2) Notwithstanding Rule 4004(c)(1), on motion of the debtor, the court may defer the entry of an order granting a discharge for 30 days and, on motion within that period, the court may defer entry of the order to a date certain.

(d) APPLICABILITY OF RULES IN PART VII. A proceeding commenced by a complaint objecting to discharge is governed by Part VII of these rules.

(e) ORDER OF DISCHARGE. An order of discharge shall conform to the appropriate Official Form.

(f) REGISTRATION IN OTHER DISTRICTS. An order of discharge that has become final may be registered in any other district by filing a certified copy of the order in the office of the clerk of that district. When so registered the order of discharge shall have the same effect as an order of the court of the district where registered.

(g) NOTICE OF DISCHARGE. The clerk shall promptly mail a copy of the final order of discharge to those specified in subdivision (a) of this rule.

Rule 4005. Burden of Proof in Objecting to Discharge

At the trial on a complaint objecting to a discharge, the plaintiff has the burden of proving the objection.

Rule 4006. Notice of No Discharge

If an order is entered denying or revoking a discharge or if a waiver of discharge is filed, the clerk, after the order becomes final or the waiver is filed shall promptly give notice thereof to all creditors in the manner provided in Rule 2002.

Rule 4007. Determination of Dischargeability of a Debt

(a) PERSONS ENTITLED TO FILE COMPLAINT. A debtor or any creditor may file a complaint to obtain a determination of the dischargeability of any debt.

(b) TIME FOR COMMENCING PROCEEDING OTHER THAN UNDER § 523(c) OF THE CODE. A complaint other than under § 523(c) may be filed at any time. A case may be reopened without payment of an additional filing fee for the purpose of filing a complaint to obtain a determination under this rule.

(c) TIME FOR FILING COMPLAINT UNDER § 523(C) IN A CHAPTER 7 LIQUIDATION, CHAPTER 11 REORGANIZATION, OR A CHAPTER 12 FAMILY FARMER'S DEBT ADJUSTMENT CASE; NOTICE OF THE TIME FIXED. A complaint to determine the dischargeability of a debt under § 523(c) shall be filed no later than 60 days after the first date set for the meeting of the creditors under § 341(a). The court shall give all creditors no less than 30 days' notice of the time so fixed in the manner provided in Rule 2002. On motion of a party in interest, after hearing on notice, the court may for cause extend the time fixed under this subdivision. The motion shall be filed before the time has expired.

(d) TIME FOR FILING COMPLAINT UNDER § 523(C) IN CHAPTER 13 INDIVIDUAL'S DEBT ADJUSTMENT CASE; NOTICE OF TIME FIXED. On motion by a debtor for a discharge under § 1328(b), the court shall enter an order fixing the time to file a complaint to determine the dischargeability of any debt under

§ 523(c) and shall give no less than 30 days' notice of the time fixed to all creditors in the manner provided in Rule 2002. On motion of any party in interest, after hearing on notice, the court may for cause extend the time fixed under this subdivision. The motion shall be filed before the time has expired.

(e) APPLICABILITY OF RULES IN PART VII. A proceeding commenced by a complaint filed under this rule is governed by Part VII of these rules.

Rule 4008. Discharge and Reaffirmation Hearing

Not more than 30 days following the entry of an order granting or denying a discharge, or confirming a plan in a chapter 11 reorganization case concerning an individual debtor and on not less than 10 days notice to the debtor and the trustee, the court may hold a hearing as provided in § 524(d) of the Code. A motion by the debtor for approval of a reaffirmation agreement shall be filed before or at the hearing.

PART V

COURTS AND CLERKS

Rule 5001. Courts and Clerks' Offices

(a) COURTS ALWAYS OPEN. The courts shall be deemed always open for the purpose of filing any pleading or other proper paper, issuing and returning process, and filing, making, or entering motions, orders and rules.

(b) TRIALS AND HEARINGS; ORDERS IN CHAMBERS. All trials and hearings shall be conducted in open court and so far as convenient in a regular court room. All other acts or proceedings may be done or conducted by a judge in chambers and at any place either within or without the district; but no hearing, other than one ex parte, shall be conducted outside the district without the consent of all parties affected thereby.

(c) CLERK'S OFFICE. The clerk's office with the clerk or a deputy in attendance shall be open during business hours on all days except Saturdays, Sundays and the legal holidays listed in Rule 9006(a).

Rule 5002. Restrictions on Approval of Appointments

(a) APPROVAL OF APPOINTMENT OF RELATIVES PROHIBITED. The appointment of an individual as a trustee or examiner pursuant to § 1104 of the Code shall not be approved by the court if the individual is a relative of the bankruptcy judge approving the appointment or the United States trustee in the region in which the case is pending. The employment of an individual as an attorney, accountant, appraiser, auctioneer, or other professional person pursuant to §§ 327, 1103, or 1114 shall not be approved by the court if the individual is a relative of the bankruptcy judge approving the employment. The employment of an individual as attorney, accountant, appraiser, auctioneer, or other professional person pursuant to §§ 327, 1103, or 1114 may be approved by the court if the individual is a relative of the United States trustee in the region in which the case is pending, unless the court finds that the relationship with the United States trustee renders the employment improper under the circumstances of the case. Whenever under this subdivision an individual may not be approved for appointment or employment, the individual's firm, partnership, corporation, or any other form of business association or relationship, and all members, associates and professional employees thereof also may not be approved for appointment or employment.

(b) JUDICIAL DETERMINATION THAT APPROVAL OF APPOINTMENT OR EMPLOYMENT IS IMPROPER. A bankruptcy judge may not approve the appointment of a person as a trustee or examiner pursuant to § 1104 of the Code or approve the employment of a person as an attorney, accountant, appraiser, auctioneer, or other professional person pursuant to §§ 327, 1103, or 1114 of the Code if that person is or has been so connected with such judge or the United States trustee as to render the appointment or employment improper.

Rule 5003. Records Kept By the Clerk

(a) BANKRUPTCY DOCKETS. The clerk shall keep a docket in each case under the Code and shall enter thereon each judgment, order, and activity in that case as prescribed by the Director of the Administrative Office of the United States Courts. The entry of a judgment or order in a docket shall show the date the entry is made.

(b) CLAIMS REGISTER. The clerk shall keep in a claims register a list of claims filed in a case when it appears that there will be a distribution to unsecured creditors.

(c) JUDGMENTS AND ORDERS. The clerk shall keep, in the form and manner as the Director of the Administrative Office of the United States Courts may prescribe, a correct copy of every final judgment or order affecting title to or lien on real property or for the recovery of money or property, and any other order which the court may direct to be kept. On request of the prevailing party, a correct copy of every judgment or order affecting title to or lien upon real or personal property or for the recovery of money or property shall be kept and indexed with the civil judgments of the district court.

(d) INDEX OF CASES; CERTIFICATE OF SEARCH. The clerk shall keep indices of all cases and adversary proceedings as prescribed by the Director of the Administrative Office of the United States Courts. On request, the clerk shall make a search of any index and papers in the clerk's custody and certify whether a case or proceeding has been filed in or transferred to the court or if a discharge has been entered in its records.

(e) REGISTER OF MAILING ADDRESSES OF FEDERAL AND STATE GOVERNMENTAL UNITS. The United States or the state or territory in which the court is located may file a statement designating its mailing address. The clerk shall keep, in the form and manner as the Director of the Administrative Office of the United States Courts may prescribe, a register that includes these mailing addresses, but the clerk is not required to include in the register more than one mailing address for each department, agency, or instrumentality of the United States or the state or territory. If more than one address for a department, agency, or instrumentality is included in the register, the clerk shall also include information that would enable a user of the register to determine the circumstances when each address is applicable, and mailing notice to only one applicable address is sufficient to provide effective notice. The clerk shall update the register annually, effective January 2 of each year. The mailing address in the register is conclusively presumed to be a proper address for the governmental unit, but the failure to use that mailing address does not invalidate any notice that is otherwise effective under applicable law.

(f) OTHER BOOKS AND RECORDS OF THE CLERK. The clerk shall also keep such other books and records as may be required by the Director of the Administrative Office of the United States Courts.

Rule 5004. Disqualification

(a) DISQUALIFICATION OF JUDGE. A bankruptcy judge shall be governed by 28 U.S.C. § 455, and disqualified from presiding over the proceeding or contested matter in which the disqualifying circumstance arises or, if appropriate, shall be disqualified from presiding over the case.

(b) DISQUALIFICATION OF JUDGE FROM ALLOWING COMPENSATION. A bankruptcy judge shall be disqualified from allowing compensation to a person who is a relative of the bankruptcy judge or with whom the judge is so connected as to render it improper for the judge to authorize such compensation.

Rule 5005. Filing and Transmittal of Papers

(a) FILING.

(1) *Place of Filing.* The lists, schedules, statements, proofs of claim or interest, complaints, motions, applications, objections and other papers required to be filed by these rules, except as provided in 28 U.S.C. § 1409, shall be filed with the clerk in the district where the case under the Code is pending. The judge of that court may permit the papers to be filed with the judge, in which event the filing date shall be noted thereon, and they shall be forthwith transmitted to the clerk. The clerk shall not refuse to accept for filing any petition or other paper presented for the purpose of filing solely because it is not presented in proper form as required by these rules or any local rules or practices.

(2) *Filing by Electronic Means.* A court may by local rule permit documents to be filed, signed, or verified by electronic means that are consistent with technical standards, if any, that the Judicial Conference of the United States establishes. A document filed by electronic means in compliance with a local rule constitutes a written paper for the purpose of applying these rules, the Federal Rules of Civil Procedure made applicable by these rules, and § 107 of the Code.

(b) TRANSMITTAL TO THE UNITED STATES TRUSTEE.

(1) The complaints, motions, applications, objections and other papers required to be transmitted to the United States trustee by these rules shall be mailed or delivered to an office of the United States trustee, or to another place designated by the United States trustee, in the district where the case under the Code is pending.

(2) The entity, other than the clerk, transmitting a paper to the United States trustee shall promptly file as proof of such transmittal a verified statement identifying the paper and stating the date on which it was transmitted to the United States trustee.

(3) Nothing in these rules shall require the clerk to transmit any paper to the United States trustee if the United States trustee requests in writing that the paper not be transmitted.

(c) ERROR IN FILING OR TRANSMITTAL. A paper intended to be filed with the clerk but erroneously delivered to the United States trustee, the trustee, the attorney for the trustee, a bankruptcy judge, a district judge, or the clerk of the district court shall, after the date of its receipt has been noted thereon, be transmitted forthwith to the clerk of the bankruptcy court. A paper intended to be transmitted to the United States trustee but erroneously delivered to the clerk, the trustee, the attorney for the trustee, a bankruptcy judge, or the clerk of the district court shall, after the date of its receipt has been noted thereon, be transmitted forthwith to the United States trustee. In the interest of justice, the court may order that a paper erroneously delivered shall be deemed filed with the clerk or transmitted to the United States trustee as of the date of its original delivery.

Rule 5006. Certification of Copies of Papers

The clerk shall issue a certified copy of the record of any proceeding in a case under the Code or of any paper filed with the clerk on payment of any prescribed fee.

Rule 5007. Record of Proceedings and Transcripts

(a) FILING OF RECORD OR TRANSCRIPT. The reporter or operator of a recording device shall certify the original notes of testimony, tape recording, or other original record of the proceeding and promptly file them with the clerk. The person preparing any transcript shall promptly file a certified copy.

(b) TRANSCRIPT FEES. The fees for copies of transcripts shall be charged at rates prescribed by the Judicial Conference of the United States. No fee may be charged for the certified copy filed with the clerk.

(c) ADMISSIBILITY OF RECORD IN EVIDENCE. A certified sound recording or a transcript of a proceeding shall be admissible as prima facie evidence to establish the record.

Rule 5008. (Abrogated)

Rule 5009. Closing Chapter 7 Liquidation, Chapter 12 Family Farmer's Debt Adjustment, and Chapter 13 Individual's Debt Adjustment Cases

If in a chapter 7, chapter 12, or chapter 13 case the trustee has filed a final report and final account and has certified that the estate has been fully administered, and if within 30 days no objection has been filed by the United States trustee or a party in interest, there shall be a presumption that the estate has been fully administered.

Rule 5010. Reopening Cases

A case may be reopened on motion of the debtor or other party in interest pursuant to § 350(b) of the Code. In a chapter 7, 12, or 13 case a trustee shall not be appointed by the United States trustee unless the court determines that a trustee is necessary to protect the interests of creditors and the debtor or to insure efficient administration of the case.

Rule 5011. Withdrawal and Abstention from Hearing a Proceeding

(a) WITHDRAWAL. A motion for withdrawal of a case or proceeding shall be heard by a district judge.

(b) ABSTENTION FROM HEARING A PROCEEDING. A motion for abstention pursuant to 28 U.S.C. § 1334(c) shall be governed by Rule 9014 and shall be served on the parties to the proceeding.

(c) EFFECT OF FILING OF MOTION FOR WITHDRAWAL OR ABSTENTION. The filing of a motion for withdrawal of a case or proceeding or for abstention pursuant to 28 U.S.C. § 1334(c) shall not stay the administration of the case or any proceeding therein before the bankruptcy judge except that the bankruptcy judge may stay, on such terms and conditions as are proper, proceedings pending disposition of the motion. A motion for a stay ordinarily shall be presented first to the bankruptcy judge. A motion for a stay or relief from a stay filed in the district court shall state why it has not been presented to or obtained from the bankruptcy judge. Relief granted by the district judge shall be on such terms and conditions as the judge deems proper.

PART VI

COLLECTION AND LIQUIDATION OF THE ESTATE

Rule 6001. Burden of Proof as to Validity of Postpetition Transfer

Any entity asserting the validity of a transfer under § 549 of the Code shall have the burden of proof.

Rule 6002. Accounting by Prior Custodian of Property of the Estate

(a) ACCOUNTING REQUIRED. Any custodian required by the Code to deliver property in the custodian's possession or control to the trustee shall promptly file and transmit to the United States trustee a report and account with respect to the property of the estate and the administration thereof.

(b) EXAMINATION OF ADMINISTRATION. On the filing and transmittal of the report and account required by subdivision (a) of this rule and after an examination has been made into the superseded administration, after notice and a hearing, the court shall determine the propriety of the administration, including the reasonableness of all disbursements.

Rule 6003. (Abrogated)

Rule 6004. Use, Sale, or Lease of Property

(a) NOTICE OF PROPOSED USE, SALE, OR LEASE OF PROPERTY. Notice of a proposed use, sale, or lease of property, other than cash collateral, not in the ordinary course of business shall be given pursuant to Rule 2002(a)(2), (c)(1), (i), and (k) and, if applicable, in accordance with § 363(b)(2) of the Code.

(b) OBJECTION TO PROPOSAL. Except as provided in subdivisions (c) and (d) of this rule, an objection to a proposed use, sale, or lease of property shall be filed and served not less than five days before the date set for the proposed action or within the time fixed by the court. An objection to the proposed use, sale, or lease of property is governed by Rule 9014.

(c) SALE FREE AND CLEAR OF LIENS AND OTHER INTERESTS. A motion for authority to sell property free and clear of liens or other interests shall be made in accordance with Rule 9014 and shall be served on the parties who have liens or other interests in the property to be sold. The notice required by subdivision (a) of this rule shall include the date of the hearing on the motion and the time within which objections may be filed and served on the debtor in possession or trustee.

(d) SALE OF PROPERTY UNDER $2,500. Notwithstanding subdivision (a) of this rule, when all of the nonexempt property of the estate has an aggregate gross value less than $2,500, it shall be sufficient to give a general notice of intent to sell such property

other than in the ordinary course of business to all creditors, indenture trustees, committees appointed or elected pursuant to the Code, the United States trustee and other persons as the court may direct. An objection to any such sale may be filed and served by a party in interest within 15 days of the mailing of the notice, or within the time fixed by the court. An objection is governed by Rule 9014.

(e) HEARING. If a timely objection is made pursuant to subdivision (b) or (d) of this rule, the date of the hearing thereon may be set in the notice given pursuant to subdivision (a) of this rule.

(f) CONDUCT OF SALE NOT IN THE ORDINARY COURSE OF BUSINESS.

(1) *Public or Private Sale.* All sales not in the ordinary course of business may be by private sale or by public auction. Unless it is impracticable, an itemized statement of the property sold, the name of each purchaser, and the price received for each item or lot or for the property as a whole if sold in bulk shall be filed on completion of a sale. If the property is sold by an auctioneer, the auctioneer shall file the statement, transmit a copy thereof to the United States trustee, and furnish a copy to the trustee, debtor in possession, or chapter 13 debtor. If the property is not sold by an auctioneer, the trustee, debtor in possession, or chapter 13 debtor shall file the statement and transmit a copy thereof to the United States trustee.

(2) *Execution of Instruments.* After a sale in accordance with this rule the debtor, the trustee, or debtor in possession, as the case may be, shall execute any instrument necessary or ordered by the court to effectuate the transfer to the purchaser.

(g) STAY OF ORDER AUTHORIZING USE, SALE, OR LEASE OF PROPERTY. An order authorizing the use, sale, or lease of property other than cash collateral is stayed until the expiration of 10 days after entry of the order, unless the court orders otherwise.

Rule 6005. Appraisers and Auctioneers

The order of the court approving the employment of an appraiser or auctioneer shall fix the amount or rate of compensation. No officer or employee of the Judicial Branch of the United States or the United States Department of Justice shall be eligible to act as appraiser or auctioneer. No residence or licensing requirement shall disqualify an appraiser or auctioneer from employment.

Rule 6006. Assumption, Rejection or Assignment of an Executory Contract to Unexpired Leases

(a) PROCEEDING TO ASSUME, REJECT, OR ASSIGN. A proceeding to assume, reject, or assign an executory contract or unexpired lease, other than as part of a plan, is governed by Rule 9014.

(b) PROCEEDING TO REQUIRE TRUSTEE TO ACT. A proceeding by a party to an executory contract or unexpired lease in a chapter 9 municipality case, chapter 11 reorganization case, chapter 12 family farmer's debt adjustment case, or chapter 13 individual's debt adjustment case, to require the trustee, debtor in possession, or debtor to determine whether to assume or reject the contract or lease is governed by Rule 9014.

(c) NOTICE. Notice of a motion made pursuant to subdivision (a) or (b) of this rule shall be given to the other party to the contract or lease, to other parties in interest as the court may direct, and, except in a chapter 9 municipality case, to the United States trustee.

(d) STAY OF ORDER AUTHORIZING ASSIGNMENT. An order authorizing the trustee to assign an executory contract or unexpired lease under § 365(f) is stayed until the expiration of 10 days after the entry of the order, unless the court orders otherwise.

Rule 6007. Abandonment or Disposition of Property

(a) NOTICE OF PROPOSED ABANDONMENT OR DISPOSITION; OBJECTIONS; HEARING. Unless otherwise directed by the court, the trustee or debtor in possession shall give notice of a proposed abandonment or disposition of property to the United States trustee, all creditors, indenture trustees and committees elected pursuant to § 705 or appointed pursuant to § 1102 of the Code. A party in interest may file and serve an objection within 15 days of the mailing of the notice, or within the time fixed by the court. If a timely objection is made, the court shall set a hearing on notice to the United States trustee and to other entities as the court may direct.

(b) MOTION BY PARTY IN INTEREST. A party in interest may file and serve a motion requiring the trustee or debtor in possession to abandon property of the estate.

(c) [Abrogated]

Rule 6008. Redemption of Property from Lien or Sale

On motion by the debtor, trustee, or debtor in possession and after hearing on notice as the court may direct, the court may authorize the redemption of property from a lien or from a sale to enforce a lien in accordance with applicable law.

Rule 6009. Prosecution and Defense of Proceedings by Trustee or Debtor in Possession

With or without court approval, the trustee or debtor in possession may prosecute or may enter an appearance and defend any pending action or proceeding by or against the debtor, or commence and prosecute any action or proceeding in behalf of the estate before any tribunal.

Rule 6010. Proceeding to Avoid Indemnifying Lien or Transfer to Surety

If a lien voidable under § 547 of the Code has been dissolved by the furnishing of a bond or other obligation and the surety thereon has been indemnified by the transfer of, or the creation of a lien upon, nonexempt property of the debtor, the surety shall be joined as a defendant in any proceeding to avoid the indemnifying transfer or lien. Such proceeding is governed by the rules in Part VII.

PART VII

ADVERSARY PROCEEDINGS

Rule 7001. Scope of the Rules of Part VII

An adversary proceeding is governed by the rules of this Part VII. The following are adversary proceedings:

(1) a proceeding to recover money or property, other than a proceeding to compel a debtor to deliver property to the trustee, or a proceeding under § 554(b) or § 725 of the Code, Rule 2017, or Rule 6002;

(2) a proceeding to determine the validity, priority, or extent of a lien or other interest in property, other than a proceeding under Rule 4003(d);

(3) a proceeding to obtain approval under § 363(h) for the sale of both the interest of the estate and of a co-owner in property;

(4) a proceeding to object to or revoke a discharge;

(5) a proceeding to revoke an order of confirmation of a chapter 11, chapter 12, or chapter 13 plan;

(6) a proceeding to determine the dischargeability of a debt;

(7) a proceeding to obtain an injunction or other equitable relief, except when a chapter 9, chapter 11, chapter 12, or chapter 13 plan provides for the relief;

(8) a proceeding to subordinate any allowed claim or interest, except when a chapter 9, chapter 11, chapter 12, or chapter 13 plan provides for subordination;

(9) a proceeding to obtain a declaratory judgment relating to any of the foregoing; or

(10) a proceeding to determine a claim or cause of action removed under 28 U.S.C. § 1452.

Rule 7002. References to Federal Rules of Civil Procedure

Whenever a Federal Rule of Civil Procedure applicable to adversary proceedings makes reference to another Federal Rule of Civil Procedure, the reference shall be read as a reference to the Federal Rule of Civil Procedure as modified in this Part VII.

Rule 7003. Commencement of Adversary Proceeding

Rule 3 F.R. Civ. P. applies in adversary proceedings.

Rule 7004. Process; Service of Summons, Complaint

(a) SUMMONS; SERVICE; PROOF OF SERVICE. Rule 4(a), (b), (c)(1), (d)(1), (e)-(j), (*l*), and (m) F.R. Civ. P. applies in adversary proceedings. Personal service pursuant to Rule 4(e)-(j) F.R. Civ. P. may be made by any person at least 18 years of age who is not a party, and the summons may be delivered by the clerk to any such person.

(b) SERVICE BY FIRST CLASS MAIL. Except as provided in subdivision (h), in addition to the methods of service authorized by Rule 4(e)-(j) F.R. Civ. P., service may be made within the United States by first class mail postage prepaid as follows:

(1) Upon an individual other than an infant or incompetent, by mailing a copy of the summons and complaint to the individual's dwelling house or usual place of abode or to the place where the individual regularly conducts a business or profession.

(2) Upon an infant or an incompetent person, by mailing a copy of the summons and complaint to the person upon whom process is prescribed to be served by the law of the state in which service is made when an action is brought against such a defendant in the courts of general jurisdiction of that state. The summons and complaint in that case shall be addressed to the person required to be served at that person's dwelling house or usual place of abode or at the place where the person regularly conducts a business or profession.

(3) Upon a domestic or foreign corporation or upon a partnership or other unincorporated association, by mailing a copy of the summons and complaint to the attention of an officer, a managing or general agent, or to any other agent authorized by appointment or by law to receive service of process and, if the

agent is one authorized by statute to receive service and the statute so requires, by also mailing a copy to the defendant.

(4) Upon the United States, by mailing a copy of the summons and complaint addressed to the civil process clerk at the office of the United States attorney for the district in which the action is brought and by mailing a copy of the summons and complaint to the Attorney General of the United States at Washington, District of Columbia, and in any action attacking the validity of an order of an officer or an agency of the United States not made a party, by also mailing a copy of the summons and complaint to that officer or agency. The court shall allow a reasonable time for service pursuant to this subdivision for the purpose of curing the failure to mail a copy of the summons and complaint to multiple officers, agencies, or corporations of the United States if the plaintiff has mailed a copy of the summons and complaint either to the civil process clerk at the office of the United States attorney or to the Attorney General of the United States.

(5) Upon any officer or agency of the United States, by mailing a copy of the summons and complaint to the United States as prescribed in paragraph (4) of this subdivision and also to the officer or agency. If the agency is a corporation, the mailing shall be as prescribed in paragraph (3) of this subdivision of this rule. The court shall allow a reasonable time for service pursuant to this subdivision for the purpose of curing the failure to mail a copy of the summons and complaint to multiple officers, agencies, or corporations of the United States if the plaintiff has mailed a copy of the summons and complaint either to the civil process clerk at the office of the United States attorney or to the Attorney General of the United States. If the United States trustee is the trustee in the case and service is made upon the United States trustee solely as trustee, service may be made as prescribed in paragraph (10) of this subdivision of this rule.

(6) Upon a state or municipal corporation or other governmental organization thereof subject to suit, by mailing a copy of the summons and complaint to the person or office upon whom process is prescribed to be served by the law of the state in which service is made when an action is brought against such a defendant in the courts of general jurisdiction of that state, or in the absence of the designation of any such person or office by state law, then to the chief executive officer thereof.

(7) Upon a defendant of any class referred to in paragraph (1) or (3) of this subdivision of this rule, it is also sufficient if a copy of the summons and complaint is mailed to the entity upon whom service is prescribed to be served by any statute of the United States or by the law of the state in which service is made when an action is brought against such a defendant in the court of general jurisdiction of that state.

(8) Upon any defendant, it is also sufficient if a copy of the summons and complaint is mailed to an agent of such defendant authorized by appointment or by law to receive service of process, at the agent's dwelling house or usual place of abode or at the place where the agent regularly carries on a business or profession and, if the authorization so requires, by mailing also a copy of the summons and complaint to the defendant as provided in this subdivision.

(9) Upon the debtor, after a petition has been filed by or served upon the debtor and until the case is dismissed or closed, by mailing a copy of the summons and complaint to the debtor at the address shown in the petition or statement of affairs or to such other address as the debtor may designate in a filed writing and, if the debtor is represented by an attorney, to the attorney at the attorney's post-office address.

(10) Upon the United States trustee, when the United States trustee is the trustee in the case and service is made upon the United States trustee solely as trustee, by mailing a copy of the summons and complaint to an office of the United States trustee or another place designated by the United States trustee in the district where the case under the Code is pending.

(c) SERVICE BY PUBLICATION. If a party to an adversary proceeding to determine or protect rights in property in the custody of the court cannot be served as provided in Rule 4(e)-(j) F.R. Civ. P. or subdivision (b) of this rule, the court may order the summons and complaint to be served by mailing copies thereof by first class mail postage prepaid, to the party's last known address and by at least one publication in such manner and form as the court may direct.

(d) NATIONWIDE SERVICE OF PROCESS. The summons and complaint and all other process except a subpoena may be served anywhere in the United States.

(e) SUMMONS: TIME LIMIT FOR SERVICE WITHIN THE UNITED STATES. Service made under rule 4(e), (g), (h)(1), (i), or (j)(2) F.R. Civ. P. shall be by delivery of the summons and complaint within 10 days after the summons is issued. If service is by any authorized form of mail, the summons and complaint shall be deposited in the mail within 10 days after the summons is issued. If a summons is not timely delivered or mailed, another summons shall be issued and served. This subdivision does not apply to service in a foreign country.

(f) PERSONAL JURISDICTION. If the exercise of jurisdiction is consistent with the Constitution and laws of the United States, serving a summons or filing a waiver of service in accordance with this rule or the subdivisions of Rule 4 F.R. Civ. P. made applicable by these rules is effective to establish personal jurisdiction over the person of any defendant with respect to a case under the Code or a civil proceeding arising under the Code, or arising in or related to a case under the Code.

(g) [Abrogated]

(h) SERVICE OF PROCESS ON AN INSURED DEPOSITORY INSTITUTION.—Service on an insured depository institution (as defined in section 3 of the Federal Deposit Insurance Act) in a contested matter or adversary proceeding shall be made by certified mail addressed to an officer of the institution unless—

(1) the institution has appeared by its attorney, in which case the attorney shall be served by first class mail;

(2) the court orders otherwise after service upon the institution by certified mail of notice of an application to permit service on the institution by first class mail sent to an officer of the institution designated by the institution; or

(3) the institution has waived in writing its entitlement to service by certified mail by designating an officer to receive service.

Rule 7005. Service and Filing of Pleadings and Other Papers

Rule 5 F.R. Civ. P. applies in adversary proceedings.

Rule 7007. Pleadings Allowed

Rule 7 F.R. Civ. P. applies in adversary proceedings.

Rule 7007.1. Corporate Ownership Statement

(a) REQUIRED DISCLOSURE. Any corporation that is a party to an adversary proceeding, other than the debtor or a governmental unit, shall file two copies of a statement that identifies any corporation, other than a governmental unit, that directly or indirectly owns 10% or more of any class of the corporation's equity interests, or states that there are no entities to report under this subdivision.

(b) TIME FOR FILING. A party shall file the statement required under Rule 7007.1(a) with its first pleading in an adversary proceeding. A party shall file a supplemental statement promptly upon any change in circumstances that this rule requires the party to identify or disclose.

Rule 7008. General Rules of Pleading

(a) APPLICABILITY OF RULE 8 F.R. CIV. P. Rule 8 F.R. Civ. P. applies in adversary proceedings. The allegation of jurisdiction required by Rule 8(a) shall also contain a reference to the name, number, and chapter of the case under the Code to which the adversary proceeding relates and to the district and division where the case under the Code is pending. In an adversary proceeding before a bankruptcy judge, the complaint, counterclaim, cross-claim, or third-party complaint shall contain a statement that the proceeding is core or non-core and, if non-core, that the pleader does or does not consent to entry of final orders or judgment by the bankruptcy judge.

(b) ATTORNEY'S FEES. A request for an award of attorney's fees shall be pleaded as a claim in a complaint, cross-claim, third-party complaint, answer, or reply as may be appropriate.

Rule 7009. Pleading Special Matters

Rule 9 F.R. Civ. P. applies in adversary proceedings.

Rule 7010. Form of Pleadings.

Rule 10 F.R. Civ. P. applies in adversary proceedings, except that the caption of each pleading in such a proceeding shall conform substantially to the appropriate Official Form.

Rule 7012. Defenses and Objections—When and How Presented—By Pleading or Motion—Motion for Judgment on the Pleadings

(a) WHEN PRESENTED. If a complaint is duly served, the defendant shall serve an answer within 30 days after the issuance of the summons, except when a different time is prescribed by the court. The court shall prescribe the time for service of the answer when service of a complaint is made by publication or upon a party in a foreign country. A party served with a pleading stating a cross-claim shall serve an answer thereto within 20 days after service. The plaintiff shall serve a reply to a counterclaim in the answer within 20 days after service of the answer or, if a reply is ordered by the court, within 20 days after service of the order, unless the order otherwise directs. The United States or an officer or agency thereof shall serve an answer to a complaint within 35 days after the issuance of the summons, and shall serve an answer to a cross-claim, or a reply to a counterclaim, within 35 days after service upon the United States attorney of the pleading in which the claim is asserted. The service of a motion permitted under this rule alters these periods of time as follows, unless a different time is fixed by order of the court: (1) if the court denies the motion or postpones its disposition until the trial on the merits, the responsive pleading shall be served within 10 days after notice of the court's action; (2) if the court grants a motion for a more definite statement, the responsive pleading shall be served within 10 days after the service of a more definite statement.

(b) APPLICABILITY OF RULE 12(b)–(h) F.R. Civ. P. Rule 12(b)–(h) F.R. Civ. P. applies in adversary proceedings. A responsive pleading shall admit or deny an allegation that the proceeding is core or non-core. If the response is that the proceeding is non-core, it shall include a statement that the party does or does not consent to entry of final orders or judgment by the bankruptcy judge. In non-core proceedings final orders and judgments shall not be entered on the bankruptcy judge's order except with the express consent of the parties.

Rule 7013. Counterclaim and Cross-Claim

Rule 13 F.R. Civ. P. applies in adversary proceedings, except that a party sued by a trustee or debtor in possession need not state as a counterclaim any claim that the party has against the debtor, the debtor's property, or the estate, unless the claim arose after the entry of an order for relief. A trustee or debtor in possession who fails to plead a counterclaim through oversight, inadvertence, or excusable neglect, or when justice so requires, may by leave of court amend the pleading, or commence a new adversary proceeding or separate action.

Rule 7014. Third-Party Practice

Rule 14 F.R. Civ. P. applies in adversary proceedings.

Rule 7015. Amended and Supplemental Pleadings

Rule 15 F.R. Civ. P. applies in adversary proceedings.

Rule 7016. Pre-Trial Procedure; Formulating Issues

Rule 16 F.R. Civ. P. applies in adversary proceedings.

Rule 7017. Parties Plaintiff and Defendant; Capacity

Rule 17 F.R. Civ. P. applies in adversary proceedings, except as provided in Rule 2010(b).

Rule 7018. Joinder of Claims and Remedies

Rule 18 F.R. Civ. P. applies in adversary proceedings.

Rule 7019. Joinder of Persons Needed for Just Determination

Rule 19 F.R. Civ. P. applies in adversary proceedings, except that (1) if an entity joined as a party raises the defense that the court lacks jurisdiction over the subject matter and the defense is sustained, the court shall dismiss such entity from the adversary proceedings and (2) if an entity joined as a party properly and timely raises the defense of improper venue, the court shall determine, as provided in 28 U.S.C. § 1412, whether that part of the proceeding involving the joined party shall be transferred to another district, or whether the entire adversary proceeding shall be transferred to another district.

Rule 7020. Permissive Joinder of Parties

Rule 20 F.R. Civ. P. applies in adversary proceedings.

Rule 7021. Misjoinder and Non-Joinder of Parties

Rule 21 F.R. Civ. P. applies in adversary proceedings.

Rule 7022. Interpleader

Rule 22(1) F.R. Civ. P. applies in adversary proceedings.

Rule 7023. Class Proceedings

Rule 23 F.R. Civ. P. applies in adversary proceedings.

Rule 7023.1. Derivative Proceedings by Shareholders

Rule 23.1 F.R. Civ. P. applies in adversary proceedings.

Rule 7023.2. Adversary Proceedings Relating to Unincorporated Associations

Rule 23.2 F.R. Civ. P. applies in adversary proceedings.

Rule 7024. Intervention

Rule 24 F.R. Civ. P. applies in adversary proceedings.

Rule 7025. Substitution of Parties

Subject to the provisions of Rule 2012, Rule 25 F.R. Civ. P. applies in adversary proceedings.

Rule 7026. General Provisions Governing Discovery

Rule 26 F.R. Civ. P. applies in adversary proceedings.

Rule 7027. Depositions Before Adversary Proceedings or Pending Appeal

Rule 27 F.R. Civ. P. applies in adversary proceedings.

Rule 7028. Persons Before Whom Depositions May Be Taken

Rule 28 F.R. Civ. P. applies in adversary proceedings.

Rule 7029. Stipulations Regarding Discovery Procedure

Rule 29 F.R. Civ. P. applies in adversary proceedings.

Rule 7030. Depositions Upon Oral Examination

Rule 30 F.R. Civ. P. applies in adversary proceedings.

Rule 7031. Deposition Upon Written Questions

Rule 31 F.R. Civ. P. applies in adversary proceedings.

Rule 7032. Use of Depositions in Adversary Proceedings

Rule 32 F.R. Civ. P. applies in adversary proceedings.

Rule 7033. Interrogatories to Parties

Rule 33 F.R. Civ. P. applies in adversary proceedings.

Rule 7034. Production of Documents and Things and Entry Upon Land for Inspection and Other Purposes

Rule 34 F.R. Civ. P. applies in adversary proceedings.

Rule 7035. Physical and Mental Examination of Persons

Rule 35 F.R. Civ. P. applies in adversary proceedings.

Rule 7036. Requests for Admission

Rule 36 F.R. Civ. P. applies in adversary proceedings.

Rule 7037. Failure to Make Discovery: Sanctions

Rule 37 F.R. Civ. P. applies in adversary proceedings.

Rule 7040. Assignment of Cases for Trial

Rule 40 F.R. Civ. P. applies in adversary proceedings.

Rule 7041. Dismissal of Adversary Proceedings

Rule 41 F.R. Civ. P. applies in adversary proceedings, except that a complaint objecting to the debtor's discharge shall not be dismissed at the plaintiff's instance without notice to the trustee, the United States trustee, and such other persons as the court may direct, and only on order of the court containing terms and conditions which the court deems proper.

Rule 7042. Consolidation of Adversary Proceedings; Separate Trials

Rule 42 F.R. Civ. P. applies in adversary proceedings.

Rule 7052. Findings by the Court

Rule 52 F.R. Civ. P. applies in adversary proceedings.

Rule 7054. Judgments; Costs

(a) JUDGMENTS. Rule 54(a)-(c) F.R. Civ. P. applies in adversary proceedings.

(b) COSTS. The court may allow costs to the prevailing party except when a statute of the United States or these rules otherwise provides. Costs against the United States, its officers and agencies shall be imposed only to the extent permitted by law. Costs may be taxed by the clerk on one day's notice; on motion served within five days thereafter, the action of the clerk may be reviewed by the court.

Rule 7055. Default

Rule 55 F.R. Civ. P. applies in adversary proceedings.

Rule 7056. Summary Judgment

Rule 56 F.R. Civ. P. applies in adversary proceedings.

Rule 7062. Stay of Proceedings to Enforce a Judgment

Rule 62 F.R.Civ.P. applies in adversary proceedings.

Rule 7064. Seizure of Person or Property

Rule 64 F.R. Civ. P. applies in adversary proceedings.

Rule 7065. Injunctions

Rule 65 F.R. Civ. P. applies in adversary proceedings, except that a temporary restraining order or preliminary injunction may be issued on application of a debtor, trustee, or debtor in possession without compliance with Rule 65(c).

Rule 7067. Deposit in Court

Rule 67 F.R. Civ. P. applies in adversary proceedings.

Rule 7068. Offer of Judgment

Rule 68 F.R. Civ. P. applies in adversary proceedings.

Rule 7069. Execution

Rule 69 F.R. Civ. P. applies in adversary proceedings.

Rule 7070. Judgment for Specific Acts; Vesting Title

Rule 70 F.R. Civ. P. applies in adversary proceedings and the court may enter a judgment divesting the title of any party and vesting title in others whenever the real or personal property involved is within the jurisdiction of the court.

Rule 7071. Process in Behalf of and Against Persons Not Parties

Rule 71 F.R. Civ. P. applies in adversary proceedings.

Rule 7087. Transfer of Adversary Proceeding

On motion and after a hearing, the court may transfer an adversary proceeding or any part thereof to another district pursuant to 28 U.S.C. § 1412, except as provided in Rule 7019(2).

PART VIII

APPEALS TO DISTRICT COURT OR BANKRUPTCY APPELLATE PANEL

Rule 8001. Manner of Taking Appeal; Voluntary Dismissal

(a) APPEAL AS OF RIGHT; HOW TAKEN. An appeal from a final judgment, order, or decree of a bankruptcy judge to a district court or bankruptcy appellate panel as permitted by 28 U.S.C. § 158(a)(1) or (a)(2) shall be taken by filing a notice of appeal with the clerk within the time allowed by Rule 8002. An appellant's failure to take any step other than timely filing a notice of appeal does not affect the validity of the appeal, but is ground only for such action as the district court or bankruptcy appellate panel deems appropriate, which may include dismissal of the appeal. The notice of appeal shall (1) conform substantially to the appropriate Official Form, (2) contain the names of all parties to the judgment, order, or decree appealed from and the names, addresses, and telephone numbers of their respective attorneys, and (3) be accompanied by the prescribed fee. Each appellant shall file a sufficient number of copies of the notice of appeal to enable the clerk to comply promptly with Rule 8004.

(b) APPEAL BY LEAVE; HOW TAKEN. An appeal from an interlocutory judgment, order, or decree of a bankruptcy judge as permitted by 28 U.S.C. § 158(a)(3) shall be taken by filing a notice of appeal, as prescribed in subdivision (a) of this rule, accompanied by a motion for leave to appeal prepared in accordance with Rule 8003 and with proof of service in accordance with Rule 8008.

(c) VOLUNTARY DISMISSAL.

(1) *Before Docketing*. In an appeal has not been docketed, the appeal may be dismissed by the bankruptcy judge on the filing of a stipulation for dismissal signed by all the parties, or on motion and notice by the appellant.

(2) *After Docketing*. If an appeal has been docketed and the parties to the appeal sign and file with the clerk of the district court or the clerk of the bankruptcy appellate panel an agreement that the appeal be dismissed and pay any court costs or fees that may be due, the clerk of the district court or the clerk of the bankruptcy appellate panel shall enter an order dismissing the appeal. An appeal may also be dismissed on motion of the appellant on terms and conditions fixed by the district court or bankruptcy appellate panel.

(d) [Abrogated]

(e) ELECTION TO HAVE APPEAL HEARD BY DISTRICT COURT INSTEAD OF BANKRUPTCY APPELLATE PANEL. An election to have an appeal heard by the district court under 28 U.S.C. § 158(c)(1) may be made only by a statement of election contained in a separate writing filed within the time prescribed by 28 U.S.C. § 158(c)(1).

Rule 8002. Time for Filing Notice of Appeal

(a) TEN-DAY PERIOD. The notice of appeal shall be filed with the clerk within 10 days of the date of the entry of the judgment, order, or decree appealed from. If a timely notice of appeal is filed by a party, any other party may file a notice of appeal within 10 days of the date on which the first notice of appeal was filed, or within the time otherwise prescribed by this rule, whichever period last expires. A notice of appeal filed after the announcement of a decision or order but before entry of the judgment, order, or decree shall be treated as filed after such entry and on the day thereof. If a notice of appeal is mistakenly filed with the district court or the bankruptcy appellate panel, the clerk of the district court or the clerk of the bankruptcy appellate panel shall note thereon the date on which it was received and transmit it to the clerk and it shall be deemed filed with the clerk on the date so noted.

(b) EFFECT OF MOTION ON TIME FOR APPEAL. If any party makes a timely motion of a type specified immediately below, the time for appeal for all parties runs from the entry of the order disposing of the last such motion outstanding. This provision applies to a timely motion:

(1) to amend or make additional findings of fact under Rule 7052, whether or not granting the motion would alter the judgment;

(2) to alter or amend the judgment under Rule 9023; or

(3) for a new trial under Rule 9023,

(4) for relief under Rule 9024 if the motion is filed no later than 10 days after the entry of judgment. A notice of appeal filed after announcement or entry of judgment, order, or decree but before disposition of any of the above motions is ineffective to appeal from the judgment, order, or decree, or part thereof, specified in the notice of appeal, until the entry of the order disposing of the last such motion outstanding. Appellate review of an order disposing of any of the above motions requires the party, in compliance with Rule 8001, to amend a previously filed notice of appeal. A party intending to challenge an alteration or amendment of the judgment, order, or decree shall file a notice, or an amended notice, of appeal within the time prescribed by this Rule 8002 measured from

the entry of the order disposing of the last such motion outstanding. No additional fees will be required for filing an amended notice.

(c) EXTENSION OF TIME FOR APPEAL.

(1) The bankruptcy judge may extend the time for filing the notice of appeal by any party, unless the judgment, order, or decree appealed from:

(A) grants relief from an automatic stay under § 362, § 922, § 1201, or § 1301;

(B) authorizes the sale or lease of property or the use of cash collateral under § 363;

(C) authorizes the obtaining of credit under § 364;

(D) authorizes the assumption or assignment of an executory contract or unexpired lease under § 365;

(E) approves a disclosure statement under § 1125; or

(F) confirms a plan under § 943, § 1129, § 1225, or § 1325 of the Code.

(2) A request to extend the time for filing a notice of appeal must be made by written motion filed before the time for filing a notice of appeal has expired, except that such a motion filed not later than 20 days after the expiration of the time for filing a notice of appeal may be granted upon a showing of excusable neglect. An extension of time for filing a notice of appeal may not exceed 20 days from the expiration of the time for filing a notice of appeal otherwise prescribed by this rule or 10 days from the date of entry of the order granting the motion, whichever is later.

Rule 8003. Leave to Appeal

(a) CONTENT OF MOTION; ANSWER. A motion for leave to appeal under 28 U.S.C. § 158(a) shall contain: (1) a statement of the facts necessary to an understanding of the questions to be presented by the appeal; (2) a statement of those questions and of the relief sought; (3) a statement of the reasons why an appeal should be granted; and (4) a copy of the judgment, order, or decree complained of and of any opinion or memorandum relating thereto. Within 10 days after service of the motion, an adverse party may file with the clerk an answer in opposition.

(b) TRANSMITTAL; DETERMINATION OF MOTION. The clerk shall transmit the notice of appeal, the motion for leave to appeal and any answer thereto to the clerk of the district court or the clerk of the bankruptcy appellate panel as soon as all parties have filed answers or the time for filing an answer has expired. The motion and answer shall be submitted without oral argument unless otherwise ordered.

(c) APPEAL IMPROPERLY TAKEN REGARDED AS A MOTION FOR LEAVE TO APPEAL. If a required motion for leave to appeal is not filed, but a notice of appeal is timely filed, the district court or bankruptcy appellate panel may grant leave to appeal or direct that a motion for leave to appeal be filed. The district court or the bankruptcy appellate panel may also deny leave to appeal but in so doing shall consider the notice of appeal as a motion for leave to appeal. Unless an order directing that a motion for leave to appeal be filed provides otherwise, the motion shall be filed within 10 days of entry of the order.

Rule 8004. Service of the Notice of Appeal

The clerk shall serve notice of the filing of a notice of appeal by mailing a copy thereof to counsel of record of each party other than the appellant or, if a party is not represented by counsel, to the party's last known address. Failure to serve notice shall not affect the validity of the appeal. The clerk shall note on each copy served the date of the filing of the notice of appeal and shall note in the docket the names of the parties to whom copies are mailed and the date of the mailing. The clerk shall forthwith transmit to the United States trustee a copy of the notice of appeal, but failure to transmit such notice shall not affect the validity of the appeal.

Rule 8005. Stay Pending Appeal

A motion for a stay of the judgment, order, or decree of a bankruptcy judge, for approval of a supersedeas bond, or for other relief pending appeal must ordinarily be presented to the bankruptcy judge in the first instance. Notwithstanding Rule 7062 but subject to the power of the district court and the bankruptcy appellate panel reserved hereinafter, the bankruptcy judge may suspend or order the continuation of other proceedings in the case under the Code or make any other appropriate order during the pendency of an appeal on such terms as will protect the rights of all parties in interest. A motion for such relief, or for modification or termination of relief granted by a bankruptcy judge, may be made to the district court or the bankruptcy appellate panel, but the motion shall show why the relief, modification, or termination was not obtained from the bankruptcy judge. The district court or the bankruptcy appellate panel may condition the relief it grants under this rule on the filing of a bond or other appropriate security with the bankruptcy court. When an appeal is taken by a trustee, a bond or other appropriate security may be required, but when an appeal is taken by the United States or an officer or agency thereof or by direction of any department of the Government of the United States a bond or other security shall not be required.

Rule 8006. Record and Issues on Appeal

Within 10 days after filing the notice of appeal as provided by Rule 8001(a), entry of an order granting leave to appeal, or entry of an order disposing of the last timely motion outstanding of a type specified in Rule 8002(b), whichever is later, the appellant shall file with the clerk and serve on the appellee a designation of the items to be included in the record on appeal and a statement of the issues to be presented. Within 10 days after the service of the appellant's statement, the appellee may file and serve on the appellant a designation of additional items to be included in the record on appeal and, if the appellee has filed a cross appeal, the appellee as cross appellant shall file and serve a statement of the issues to be presented on the cross appeal and a designation of additional items to be included in the record. A cross appellee may, within 10 days of service of the cross appellant's statement, file and serve on the cross appellant a designation of additional items to be included in the record. The record on appeal shall include the items so designated by the parties, the notice of appeal, the judgment, order, or decree appealed from, and any opinion, findings of fact, and conclusions of law of the court. Any party filing a designation of the items to be included in the record shall provide to the clerk a copy of the items designated or, if the party fails to provide the copy, the clerk shall prepare the copy at the party's expense. If the record designated by any party includes a transcript of any proceeding or a part thereof, the party shall immediately after filing the designation deliver to the reporter and file with the clerk a written request for the transcript and make satisfactory arrangements for payment of its cost. All parties shall take any other action necessary to enable the clerk to assemble and transmit the record.

Rule 8007. Completion and Transmission of the Record; Docketing of the Appeal

(a) DUTY OF REPORTER TO PREPARE AND FILE TRANSCRIPT. On receipt of a request for a transcript, the reporter shall acknowledge on the request the date it was received and the date on which the reporter expects to have the transcript completed and shall transmit the request, so endorsed, to the clerk or the clerk of the bankruptcy appellate panel. On completion of the transcript the reporter shall file it with the clerk and, if appropriate, notify the clerk of the bankruptcy appellate panel. If the transcript cannot be completed within 30 days of receipt of the request the reporter shall seek an extension of time from the clerk or the clerk of the bankruptcy appellate panel and the action of the clerk shall be entered in the docket and the parties notified. If the reporter does not file the transcript within the time allowed, the clerk or the clerk of the bankruptcy appellate panel shall notify the bankruptcy judge.

(b) DUTY OF CLERK TO TRANSMIT COPY OF RECORD; DOCKETING OF APPEAL. When the record is complete for purposes of appeal, the clerk shall transmit a copy thereof forthwith to the clerk of the district court or the clerk of the bankruptcy appellate panel. On receipt of the transmission the clerk of the district court or the clerk of the bankruptcy appellate panel shall enter the appeal in the docket and give notice promptly to all parties to the judgment, order, or decree appealed from of the date on which the appeal was docketed. If the bankruptcy appellate panel directs that additional copies of the record be furnished, the clerk of the bankruptcy appellate panel shall notify the appellant and, if the appellant fails to provide the copies, the clerk shall prepare the copies at the expense of the appellant.

(c) RECORD FOR PRELIMINARY HEARING. If prior to the time the record is transmitted a party moves in the district court or before the bankruptcy appellate panel for dismissal, for a stay pending appeal, for additional security on the bond on appeal or on a supersedeas bond, or for any intermediate order, the clerk at the request of any party to the appeal shall transmit to the clerk of the district court or the clerk of the bankruptcy appellate panel a copy of the parts of the record as any party to the appeal shall designate.

Rule 8008. Filing and Service

(a) FILING. Papers required or permitted to be filed with the clerk of the district court or the clerk of the bankruptcy appellate panel may be filed by mail addressed to the clerk, but filing is not timely unless the papers are received by the clerk within the time fixed for filing, except that briefs are deemed filed on the day of mailing. An original and one copy of all papers shall be filed when an appeal is to the district court; an original and three copies shall be filed when an appeal is to a bankruptcy appellate panel. The district court or bankruptcy appellate panel may require that additional copies be furnished. Rule 5005(a)(2) applies to papers filed with the clerk of the district court or the clerk of the bankruptcy appellate panel if filing by electronic means is authorized by local

rule promulgated pursuant to Rule 8018.

(b) SERVICE OF ALL PAPERS REQUIRED. Copies of all papers filed by any party and not required by these rules to be served by the clerk of the district court or the clerk of the bankruptcy appellate panel shall, at or before the time of filing, be served by the party or a person acting for the party on all other parties to the appeal. Service on a party represented by counsel shall be made on counsel.

(c) MANNER OF SERVICE. Service may be personal or by mail. Personal service includes delivery of the copy to a clerk or other responsible person at the office of counsel. Service by mail is complete on mailing.

(d) PROOF OF SERVICE. Papers presented for filing shall contain an acknowledgment of service by the person served or proof of service in the form of a statement of the date and manner of service and of the names of the persons served, certified by the person who made service. The clerk of the district court or the clerk of the bankruptcy appellate panel may permit papers to be filed without acknowledgment or proof of service but shall require the acknowledgment or proof of service to be filed promptly thereafter.

Rule 8009. Briefs and Appendix; Filing and Service

(a) BRIEFS. Unless the district court or the bankruptcy appellate panel by local rule or by order excuses the filing of briefs or specifies different time limits:

(1) The appellant shall serve and file a brief within 15 days after entry of the appeal on the docket pursuant to Rule 8007.

(2) The appellee shall serve and file a brief within 15 days after service of the brief of appellant. If the appellee has filed a cross appeal, the brief of the appellee shall contain the issues and argument pertinent to the cross appeal, denominated as such, and the response to the brief of the appellant.

(3) The appellant may serve and file a reply brief within 10 days after service of the brief of the appellee, and if the appellee has cross-appealed, the appellee may file and serve a reply brief to the response of the appellant to the issues presented in the cross appeal within 10 days after service of the reply brief of the appellant. No further briefs may be filed except with leave of the district court or the bankruptcy appellate panel.

(b) APPENDIX TO BRIEF. If the appeal is to a bankruptcy appellate panel, the appellant shall serve and file with the appellant's brief excerpts of the record as an appendix, which shall include the following:

(1) The complaint and answer or other equivalent pleadings;

(2) Any pretrial order;

(3) The judgment, order, or decree from which the appeal is taken;

(4) Any other orders relevant to the appeal;

(5) The opinion, findings of fact, or conclusions of law filed or delivered orally by the court and citations of the opinion if published;

(6) Any motion and response on which the court rendered decision;

(7) The notice of appeal;

(8) The relevant entries in the bankruptcy docket; and

(9) The transcript or portion thereof, if so required by a rule of the bankruptcy appellate panel.

An appellee may also serve and file an appendix which contains material required to be included by the appellant but omitted by appellant.

Rule 8010. Form of Briefs; Length

(a) FORM OF BRIEFS. Unless the district court or the bankruptcy appellate panel by local rule otherwise provides, the form of brief shall be as follows:

(1) *Brief of the Appellant*. The brief of the appellant shall contain under appropriate headings and in the order here indicated:

  (A) A table of contents, with page references, and a table of cases alphabetically arranged, statutes and other authorities cited, with references to the pages of the brief where they are cited.

  (B) A statement of the basis of appellate jurisdiction.

  (C) A statement of the issues presented and the application standard of appellate review.

  (D) A statement of the case. The statement shall first indicate briefly the nature of the case, the course of the proceedings, and the disposition in the court below. There shall follow a statement of the facts relevant to the issues presented for review, with appropriate references to the record.

  (E) An argument. The argument may be preceded by a summary. The argument shall contain the contentions of the appellant with respect to the issues presented, and the reasons therefor, with citations to the authorities, statutes and parts of the record relied on.

  (F) A short conclusion stating the precise relief sought.

(2) *Brief of the Appellee*. The brief of the appellee shall conform to the requirements of paragraph (1)(A)–(E) of this subdivision, except that a statement of the basis of appellate jurisdiction, of the issues, or of the case need not be made unless the appellee is dissatisfied with the statement of the appellant.

(b) REPRODUCTION OF STATUTES, RULES, REGULATIONS, OR SIMILAR MATERIAL. If determination of the issues presented requires reference to the Code or other statutes, rules, regulations, or similar material, relevant parts thereof shall be reproduced in the brief or in an addendum or they may be supplied to the court in pamphlet form.

(c) LENGTH OF BRIEFS. Unless the district court or the bankruptcy appellate panel by local rule or order otherwise provides, principal briefs shall not exceed 50 pages, and reply briefs shall not exceed 25 pages, exclusive of pages containing the table of contents, tables of citations and any addendum containing statutes, rules, regulations, or similar material.

Rule 8011. Motions

(a) CONTENT OF MOTIONS; RESPONSE; REPLY. A request for an order or other relief shall be made by filing with the clerk of the district court or the clerk of the bankruptcy appellate panel a motion for such order or relief with proof of service on all other parties to the appeal. The motion shall contain or be accompanied by any matter required by a specific provision of these rules governing such a motion, shall state with particularity the grounds on which it is based, and shall set forth the order or relief sought. If a motion is supported by briefs, affidavits or other papers, they shall be served and filed with the motion. Any party may file a response in opposition to a motion other than one for a procedural order within seven days after service of the motion, but the district

court or the bankruptcy appellate panel may shorten or extend the time for responding to any motion.

(b) DETERMINATION OF MOTIONS FOR PROCEDURAL ORDERS. Notwithstanding subdivision (a) of this rule, motions for procedural orders, including any motion under Rule 9006, may be acted on at any time, without awaiting a response thereto and without hearing. Any party adversely affected by such action may move for reconsideration, vacation, or modification of the action.

(c) DETERMINATION OF ALL MOTIONS. All motions will be decided without oral argument unless the court orders otherwise. A motion for a stay, or for other emergency relief may be denied if not presented promptly.

(d) EMERGENCY MOTIONS. Whenever a movant requests expedited action on a motion on the ground that, to avoid irreparable harm, relief is needed in less time than would normally be required for the district court or bankruptcy appellate panel to receive and consider a response, the word "Emergency" shall precede the title of the motion. The motion shall be accompanied by an affidavit setting forth the nature of the emergency. The motion shall state whether all grounds advanced in support thereof were submitted to the bankruptcy judge and, if any grounds relied on were not submitted, why the motion should not be remanded to the bankruptcy judge for reconsideration. The motion shall include the office addresses and telephone numbers of moving and opposing counsel and shall be served pursuant to Rule 8008. Prior to filing the motion, the movant shall make every practicable effort to notify opposing counsel in time for counsel to respond to the motion. The affidavit accompanying the motion shall also state when and how opposing counsel was notified or if opposing counsel was not notified why it was not practicable to do so.

(e) POWER OF A SINGLE JUDGE TO ENTERTAIN MOTIONS. A single judge of a bankruptcy appellate panel may grant or deny any request for relief which under these rules may properly be sought by motion, except that a single judge may not dismiss or otherwise decide an appeal or a motion for leave to appeal. The action of a single judge may be reviewed by the panel.

Rule 8012. Oral Argument

Oral argument shall be allowed in all cases unless the district judge or the judges of the bankruptcy appellate panel unanimously determine after examination of the briefs and record, or appendix to the brief, that oral argument is not needed. Any party shall have an opportunity to file a statement setting forth the reason why oral argument should be allowed.

Oral argument will not be allowed if: (1) the appeal is frivolous; (2) the dispositive issue or set of issues has been recently authoritatively decided; or (3) the facts and legal arguments are adequately presented in the briefs and record and the decisional process would not be significantly aided by oral argument.

Rule 8013. Disposition of Appeal; Weight Accorded Bankruptcy Judge's Findings of Fact

On an appeal the district court or bankruptcy appellate panel may affirm, modify, or reverse a bankruptcy judge's judgment, order, or decree or remand with instructions for further proceedings. Findings of fact, whether based on oral or documentary evidence, shall not be set aside unless clearly erroneous, and due regard shall be given to the opportunity of the bankruptcy court to judge the credibility of the witnesses.

Rule 8014. Costs

Except as otherwise provided by law, agreed to by the parties, or ordered by the district court or the bankruptcy appellate panel, costs shall be taxed against the losing party on an appeal. If a judgment is affirmed or reversed in part, or is vacated, costs shall be allowed only as ordered by the court. Costs incurred in the production of copies of briefs, the appendices, and the record and in the preparation and transmission of the record, the cost of the reporter's transcript, if necessary for the determination of the appeal, the premiums paid for cost of supersedeas bonds or other bonds to preserve rights pending appeal and the fee for filing the notice of appeal shall be taxed by the clerk as costs of the appeal in favor of the party entitled to costs under this rule.

Rule 8015. Motion for Rehearing

Unless the district court or the bankruptcy appellate panel by local rule or by court order otherwise provides, a motion for rehearing may be filed within 10 days after entry of the judgment of the district court or the bankruptcy appellate panel. If a timely motion for rehearing is filed, the time for appeal to the court of appeals for all parties shall run from the entry of the order denying rehearing or the entry of a subsequent judgment.

Rule 8016. Duties of Clerk of District Court and Bankruptcy Appellate Panel

(a) ENTRY OF JUDGMENT. The clerk of the district court or the clerk of the bankruptcy appellate panel shall prepare, sign and enter the judgment following receipt of the opinion of the court or the appellate panel or, if there is no opinion, following the instruction of the court or the appellate panel. The notation of a judgment in the docket constitutes entry of judgment.

(b) NOTICE OF ORDERS OR JUDGMENTS; RETURN OF RECORD. Immediately on the entry of a judgment or order the clerk of the district court or the clerk of the bankruptcy appellate panel shall transmit a notice of the entry to each party to the appeal, to the United States trustee, and to the clerk, together with a copy of any opinion respecting the judgment or order, and shall make a note of the transmission in the docket. Original papers transmitted as the record on appeal shall be returned to the clerk on disposition of the appeal.

Rule 8017. Stay of Judgment of District Court or Bankruptcy Appellate Panel

(a) AUTOMATIC STAY OF JUDGMENT ON APPEAL. Judgments of the district court or the bankruptcy appellate panel are stayed until the expiration of 10 days after entry, unless otherwise ordered by the district court or the bankruptcy appellate panel.

(b) STAY PENDING APPEAL TO THE COURT OF APPEALS. On motion and notice to the parties to the appeal, the district court or the bankruptcy appellate panel may stay its judgment pending an appeal to the court of appeals. The stay shall not extend beyond 30 days after the entry of the judgment of the district court or the bankruptcy appellate panel unless the period is extended for cause shown. If before the expiration of a stay entered pursuant to this subdivision there is an appeal to the court of appeals by the party who obtained the stay, the stay shall continue until final disposition by the court of appeals. A bond or other security may be required as a condition to the grant or continuation of a stay of the judgment. A bond or other security may be required if a trustee obtains a stay but a bond or security shall not be required if a stay is obtained by the United States or an officer or agency thereof or at the direction of any department of the Government of the United States.

(c) POWER OF COURT OF APPEALS NOT LIMITED. This rule does not limit the power of a court of appeals or any judge thereof to stay proceedings during the pendency of an appeal or to suspend, modify, restore, or grant an injunction during the pendency of an appeal or to make any order appropriate to preserve the status quo or the effectiveness of the judgment subsequently to be entered.

Rule 8018. Rules by Circuit Councils and District Courts; Procedure Where There Is No Controlling Law

(a) LOCAL RULES BY CIRCUIT COUNCILS AND DISTRICT COURTS.

(1) Circuit councils which have authorized bankruptcy appellate panels pursuant to 28 U.S.C. § 158(b) and the district courts may, acting by a majority of the judges of the council or district court, make and amend rules governing practice and procedure for appeals from orders or judgments of bankruptcy judges to the respective bankruptcy appellate panel or district court consistent with—but not duplicative of—Acts of Congress and the rules of this Part VIII. Local rules shall confirm to any uniform numbering system prescribed by the Judicial Conference of the United States. Rule 83 F.R. Civ. P. governs the procedure for making and amending rules to govern appeals.

(2) A local rule imposing a requirement of form shall not be enforced in a manner that causes a party to lose rights because of a negligent failure to comply with the requirement.

(b) PROCEDURE WHEN THERE IS NO CONTROLLING LAW. A bankruptcy appellate panel or district judge may regulate practice in any manner consistent with federal law, these rules, Official Forms, and local rules of the circuit council or district court. No sanction or other disadvantage may be imposed for noncompliance with any requirement not in federal law, federal rules, Official Forms, or the local rules of the circuit council or district court unless the alleged violator has been furnished in the particular case with actual notice of the requirement.

Rule 8019. Suspension of Rules in Part VIII

In the interest of expediting decision or for other cause, the district court or the bankruptcy appellate panel may suspend the requirements or provisions of the rules in Part VIII, except Rules 8001, 8002, and 8013, and may order proceedings in accordance with the direction.

Rule 8020. Damages and Costs for Frivolous Appeal

If a district court or bankruptcy appellate panel determines that an appeal from an order, judgment, or decree of a bankruptcy judge is frivolous, it may, after a separately filed motion or notice from the district court or bankruptcy appellate panel and reasonable opportunity to respond, award just damages and single or double costs to the appellee.

PART IX

GENERAL PROVISIONS

Rule 9001. General Definitions

The definitions of words and phrases in § 101, § 902 and § 1101 and the rules of construction in § 102 of the Code govern their use in these rules. In addition, the following words and phrases used in these rules have the meanings indicated:

(1) "Bankruptcy clerk" means a clerk appointed pursuant to 28 U.S.C. § 156(b).

(2) "Bankruptcy Code" or "Code" means title 11 of the United States Code.

(3) "Clerk" means bankruptcy clerk, if one has been appointed, otherwise clerk of the district court.

(4) "Court" or "judge" means the judicial officer before whom a case or proceeding is pending.

(5) "Debtor." When any act is required by these rules to be performed by a debtor or when it is necessary to compel attendance of a debtor for examination and the debtor is not a natural person: (A) if the debtor is a corporation, "debtor" includes, if designated by the court, any or all of its officers, members of its board of directors or trustees or of a similar controlling body, a controlling stockholder or member, or any other person in control; (B) if the debtor is a partnership, "debtor" includes any or all of its general partners or, if designated by the court, any other person in control.

(6) "Firm" includes a partnership or professional corporation of attorneys or accountants.

(7) "Judgment" means any appealable order.

(8) "Mail" means first class, postage prepaid.

(9) "Regular associate" means any attorney regularly employed by, associated with, or counsel to an individual or firm.

(10) "Trustee" includes a debtor in possession in a chapter 11 case.

(11) "United States trustee" includes an assistant United States trustee and any designee of the United States trustee.

Rule 9002. Meanings of Words in the Federal Rules of Civil Procedure When Applicable to Cases Under the Code

The following words and phrases used in the Federal Rules of Civil Procedure made applicable to cases under the Code by these rules have the meanings indicated unless they are inconsistent with the context:

(1) "Action" or "civil action" means an adversary proceeding or, when appropriate, a contested petition, or proceedings to vacate an order for relief or to determine any other contested matter.

(2) "Appeal" means an appeal as provided by 28 U.S.C. § 158.

(3) "Clerk" or "clerk of the district court" means the court officer responsible for the bankruptcy records in the district.

(4) "District court," "trial court," "court," "district judge," or "judge" means bankruptcy judge if the case or proceeding is pending before a bankruptcy judge.

(5) "Judgment" includes any order appealable to an appellate court.

Rule 9003. Prohibition of Ex Parte Contacts

(a) GENERAL PROHIBITION. Except as otherwise permitted by applicable law, any examiner, any party in interest, and any attorney, accountant, or employee of a party in interest shall refrain from ex parte meetings and communications with the court concerning matters affecting a particular case or proceeding.

(b) UNITED STATES TRUSTEE. Except as otherwise permitted by applicable law, the United States trustee and assistants to and employees or agents of the United States trustee shall refrain from ex parte meetings and communications with the court concerning matters affecting a particular case or proceeding. This rule does not preclude communications with the court to discuss general problems of administration and improvement of bankruptcy administration, including the operation of the United States trustee system.

Rule 9004. General Requirements of Form

(a) LEGIBILITY; ABBREVIATIONS. All petitions, pleadings, schedules and other papers shall be clearly legible. Abbreviations in common use in the English language may be used.

(b) CAPTION. Each paper filed shall contain a caption setting forth the name of the court, the title of the case, the bankruptcy docket number, and a brief designation of the character of the paper.

Rule 9005. Harmless Error

Rule 61 F.R. Civ. P. applies in cases under the Code. When appropriate, the court may order the correction of any error or defect or the cure of any omission which does not affect substantial rights.

Rule 9006. Time

(a) COMPUTATION. In computing any period of time prescribed or allowed by these rules or by the Federal Rules of Civil Procedure made applicable by these rules, by the local rules, by order of court, or by any applicable statute, the day of the act, event, or default from which the designated period of time begins to run shall not be included. The last day of the period so computed shall be included, unless it is a Saturday, a Sunday, or a legal holiday, or, when the act to be done is the filing of a paper in court, a day on which weather or other conditions have made the clerk's office inaccessible, in which event the period runs until the end of the next day which is not one of the aforementioned days. When the period of time prescribed or allowed is less than 8 days, intermediate Saturdays, Sundays, and legal holidays shall be excluded in the computation. As used in this rule and in Rule 5001(c), "legal holiday" includes New Year's Day, Birthday of Martin Luther King, Jr., Washington's Birthday, Memorial Day, Independence Day, Labor Day, Columbus Day, Veterans Day, Thanksgiving Day, Christmas Day, and any other day appointed as a holiday by the President or the Congress of the United States, or by the state in which the court is held.

(b) ENLARGEMENT.

(1) *In General.* Except as provided in paragraphs (2) and (3) of this subdivision, when an act is required or allowed to be done at or within a specified period by these rules or by a notice given thereunder or by order of court, the court for cause shown may at any time in its discretion (1) with or without motion or notice order the period enlarged if the request therefor is made before the expiration of the period originally prescribed or as extended by a previous order or (2) on motion made after the expiration of the specified period permit the act

to be done where the failure to act was the result of excusable neglect.

(2) *Enlargement Not Permitted.* The court may not enlarge the time for taking action under Rules 1007(d), 2003(a) and (d), 7052, 9023, and 9024.

(3) *Enlargement Limited.* The court may enlarge the time for taking action under Rules 1006(b)(2), 1017(e), 3002(c), 4003(b), 4004(a), 4007(c), 8002, and 9033, only to the extent and under the conditions stated in those rules.

(c) REDUCTION.

(1) *In General.* Except as provided in paragraph (2) of this subdivision, when an act is required or allowed to be done at or within a specified time by these rules or by a notice given thereunder or by order of court, the court for cause shown may in its discretion with or without motion or notice order the period reduced.

(2) *Reduction Not Permitted.* The court may not reduce the time for taking action pursuant to Rules 2002(a)(7), 2003(a), 3002(c), 3014, 3015, 4001(b)(2), (c)(2), 4003(a), 4004(a), 4007(c), 8002, and 9033(b).

(d) FOR MOTIONS—AFFIDAVITS. A written motion, other than one which may be heard ex parte, and notice of any hearing shall be served not later than five days before the time specified for such hearing, unless a different period is fixed by these rules or by order of the court. Such an order may for cause shown be made on ex parte application. When a motion is supported by affidavit, the affidavit shall be served with the motion; and, except as otherwise provided in Rule 9023, opposing affidavits may be served not later than one day before the hearing, unless the court permits them to be served at some other time.

(e) TIME OF SERVICE. Service of process and service of any paper other than process or of notice by mail is complete on mailing.

(f) ADDITIONAL TIME AFTER SERVICE BY MAIL OR UNDER RULE 5(b)(2)(C) OR (D) F. R. CIV. P. When there is a right or requirement to do some act or undertake some proceedings within a prescribed period after service of a notice or other paper and the notice or paper other than process is served by mail or under Rule 5(b)(2)(C) or (D) F. R. Civ. P., three days shall be added to the prescribed period.

(g) GRAIN STORAGE FACILITY CASES. This rule shall not limit the court's authority under § 557 of the Code to enter orders governing procedures in cases in which the debtor is an owner or operator of a grain storage facility.

Rule 9007. General Authority to Regulate Notices

When notice is to be given under these rules, the court shall designate, if not otherwise specified herein, the time within which, the entities to whom, and the form and manner in which the notice shall be given. When feasible, the court may order any notices under these rules to be combined.

Rule 9008. Service or Notice By Publication

Whenever these rules require or authorize service or notice by publication, the court shall, to the extent not otherwise specified in these rules, determine the form and manner thereof, including the newspaper or other medium to be used and the number of publications.

Rule 9009. Forms

The Official Forms prescribed by the Judicial Conference of the United States shall be observed and used with alterations as may be appropriate. Forms may be combined and their contents rearranged to permit economies in their use. The Director of the Administrative Office of the United States Courts may issue additional forms for use under the Code. The forms shall be construed to be consistent with these rules and the Code.

Rule 9010. Representation and Appearances; Powers of Attorney

(a) AUTHORITY TO ACT PERSONALLY OR BY ATTORNEY. A debtor, creditor, equity security holder, indenture trustee, committee or other party may (1) appear in a case under the Code and act either in the entity's own behalf or by an attorney authorized to practice in the court, and (2) perform any act not constituting the practice of law, by an authorized agent, attorney in fact, or proxy.

(b) NOTICE OF APPEARANCE. An attorney appearing for a party in a case under the Code shall file a notice of appearance with the attorney's name, office address and telephone number, unless the attorney's appearance is otherwise noted in the record.

(c) POWER OF ATTORNEY. The authority of any agent, attorney in fact, or proxy to represent a creditor for any purpose other than the execution and filing of a proof of claim or the acceptance or rejection of a plan shall be evidenced by a power of attorney conforming substantially to the appropriate Official Form. The execution of any such power of attorney shall be acknowledged before one of the officers enumerated in 28 U.S.C. § 459, § 953, Rule 9012, or a person authorized to administer oaths under the laws of the state where the oath is administered.

Rule 9011. Signing of Papers; Representations to the Court; Sanctions; Verification and Copies of Papers

(a) SIGNATURE. Every petition, pleading, written motion, and other paper, except a list, schedule, or statement, or amendments thereto, shall be signed by at least one attorney of record in the attorney's individual name. A party who is not represented by an attorney shall sign all papers. Each paper shall state the signer's address and telephone number, if any. An unsigned paper shall be stricken unless omission of the signature is corrected promptly after being called to the attention of the attorney or party.

(b) REPRESENTATIONS TO THE COURT. By presenting to the court (whether by signing, filing, submitting, or later advocating) a petition, pleading, written motion, or other paper, an attorney or unrepresented party is certifying that to the best of the person's knowledge, information, and belief, formed after an inquiry reasonable under the circumstances,—

(1) it is not being presented for any improper purpose, such as to harass or to cause unnecessary delay or needless increase in the cost of litigation;

(2) the claims, defenses, and other legal contentions therein are warranted by existing law or by a nonfrivolous argument for the extension, modification, or reversal of existing law or the establishment of new law;

(3) the allegations and other factual contentions have evidentiary support or, if specifically so identified, are likely to have evidentiary support after a reasonable opportunity for further

investigation or discovery; and

(4) the denials of factual contentions are warranted on the evidence or, if specifically so identified, are reasonably based on a lack of information or belief.

(c) SANCTIONS. If, after notice and a reasonable opportunity to respond, the court determines that subdivision (b) has been violated, the court may, subject to the conditions stated below, impose an appropriate sanction upon the attorneys, law firms, or parties that have violated subdivision (b) or are responsible for the violation.

(1) *How Initiated.*

   (A) By Motion. A motion for sanctions under this rule shall be made separately from other motions or requests and shall describe the specific conduct alleged to violate subdivision (b). It shall be served as provided in Rule 7004. The motion for sanctions may not be filed with or presented to the court unless, within 21 days after service of the motion (or such other period as the court may prescribe), the challenged paper, claim, defense, contention, allegation, or denial is not withdrawn or appropriately corrected, except that this limitation shall not apply if the conduct alleged is the filing of a petition in violation of subdivision (b). If warranted, the court may award to the party prevailing on the motion the reasonable expenses and attorney's fees incurred in presenting or opposing the motion. Absent exceptional circumstances, a law firm shall be held jointly responsible for violations committed by its partners, associates, and employees.

   (B) On Court's Initiative. On its own initiative, the court may enter an order describing the specific conduct that appears to violate subdivision (b) and directing an attorney, law firm, or party to show cause why it has not violated subdivision (b) with respect thereto.

(2) *Nature of Sanction: Limitations.* A sanction imposed for violation of this rule shall be limited to what is sufficient to deter repetition of such conduct or comparable conduct by others similarly situated. Subject to the limitations in subparagraphs (A) and (B), the sanction may consist of, or include, directives of a nonmonetary nature, an order to pay a penalty into court, or, if imposed on motion and warranted for effective deterrence, an order directing payment to the movant of some or all of the reasonable attorneys' fees and other expenses incurred as a direct result of the violation.

   (A) Monetary sanctions may not be awarded against a represented party for a violation of subdivision (b)(2).

   (B) Monetary sanctions may not be awarded on the court's initiative unless the court issues its order to show cause before a voluntary dismissal or settlement of the claims made by or against the party which is, or whose attorneys are, to be sanctioned.

(3) *Order.* When imposing sanctions, the court shall describe the conduct determined to constitute a violation of this rule and explain the basis for the sanction imposed.

(d) INAPPLICABILITY TO DISCOVERY. Subdivisions (a) through (c) of this rule do not apply to disclosures and discovery requests, responses, objections, and motions that are subject to the provisions of Rules 7026 through 7037.

(e) VERIFICATION. Except as otherwise specifically provided by these rules, papers filed in a case under the Code need not be verified. Whenever verification is required by these rules, an unsworn declaration as provided in 28 U.S.C. § 1746 satisfies the requirement of verification.

(f) COPIES OF SIGNED OR VERIFIED PAPERS. When these rules require copies of a signed or verified paper, it shall suffice if the original is signed or verified and the copies are conformed to the original.

Rule 9012. Oaths and Affirmations

(a) PERSONS AUTHORIZED TO ADMINISTER OATHS. The following persons may administer oaths and affirmations and take acknowledgments: a bankruptcy judge, clerk, deputy clerk, United States trustee, officer authorized to administer oaths in proceedings before the courts of the United States or under the laws of the state where the oath is to be taken, or a diplomatic or consular officer of the United States in any foreign country.

(b) AFFIRMATION IN LIEU OF OATH. When in a case under the Code an oath is required to be taken, a solemn affirmation may be accepted in lieu thereof.

Rule 9013. Motions: Form and Service

A request for an order, except when an application is authorized by these rules, shall be by written motion, unless made during a hearing. The motion shall state with particularity the grounds therefor, and shall set forth the relief or order sought. Every written motion other than one which may be considered ex parte shall be served by the moving party on the trustee or debtor in possession and on those entities specified by these rules or, if service is not required or the entities to be served are not specified by these rules, the moving party shall serve the entities the court directs.

Rule 9014. Contested Matters

(a) MOTION. In a contested matter not otherwise governed by these rules, relief shall be requested by motion, and reasonable notice and opportunity for hearing shall be afforded the party against whom relief is sought. No response is required under this rule unless the court directs otherwise.

(b) SERVICE. The motion shall be served in the manner provided for service of a summons and complaint by Rule 7004. Any paper served after the motion shall be served in the manner provided by Rule 5(b) F.R. Civ. P.

(c) APPLICATION OF PART VII RULES. Except as otherwise provided in this rule, and unless the court directs otherwise, the following rules shall apply: 7009, 7017, 7021, 7025, 7026, 7028-7037, 7041, 7042, 7052, 7054-7056, 7064, 7069, and 7071. The following subdivisions of Fed. R. Civ. P. 26, as incorporated by Rule 7026, shall not apply in a contested matter unless the court directs otherwise: 26(a)(1) (mandatory disclosure), 26(a)(2) (disclosures regarding expert testimony) and 26(a)(3) (additional pretrial disclosure), and 26(f) (mandatory meeting before scheduling conference/discovery plan). An entity that desires to perpetuate testimony may proceed in the same manner as provided in Rule 7027 for the taking of a deposition before an adversary proceeding. The court may at any stage in a particular matter direct that one or more of the other rules in Part VII shall apply. The court shall give the parties notice of any order issued under this paragraph to afford them a reasonable opportunity to comply with the procedures prescribed by the order.

(d) TESTIMONY OF WITNESSES. Testimony of witnesses with respect to disputed material factual issues shall be taken in the same manner as testimony in an adversary proceeding.

(e) ATTENDANCE OF WITNESSES. The court shall provide procedures that enable parties to ascertain at a reasonable time before any scheduled hearing whether the hearing will be an evidentiary hearing at which witnesses may testify.

Rule 9015. Jury Trials

(a) APPLICABILITY OF CERTAIN FEDERAL RULES OF CIVIL PROCEDURE. Rules 38, 39, and 47–51 F.R. Civ. P., and Rule 81 (c) F.R. Civ. P. insofar as it applies to jury trials, apply in cases and proceedings, except that a demand made pursuant to Rule 38(b) F.R. Civ. P. shall be filed in accordance with Rule 5005.

(b) CONSENT TO HAVE TRIAL CONDUCTED BY BANK-RUPTCY JUDGE. If the right to a jury trial applies, a timely demand has been file pursuant to Rule 38(b) F.R. Civ. P., and the bankruptcy judge has been specially designated to conduct the jury trial, the parties may consent to have a jury trial conducted by a bankruptcy judge under 28 U.S.C. § 157(e) by jointly or separately filing a statement of consent within any applicable time limits specified by local rule.

Rule 9016. Subpoena

Rule 45 F.R. Civ. P. applies in cases under the Code.

Rule 9017. Evidence

The Federal Rules of Evidence and Rules 43, 44 and 44.1 F.R. Civ. P. apply in cases under the Code.

Rule 9018. Secret, Confidential, Scandalous, or Defamatory Matter

On motion or on its own initiative, with or without notice, the court may make any order which justice requires (1) to protect the estate or any entity in respect of a trade secret or other confidential research, development, or commercial information, (2) to protect any entity against scandalous or defamatory matter contained in any paper filed in a case under the Code, or (3) to protect governmental matters that are made confidential by statute or regulation. If an order is entered under this rule without notice, any entity affected thereby may move to vacate or modify the order, and after a hearing on notice the court shall determine the motion.

Rule 9019. Compromise and Arbitration

(a) COMPROMISE. On motion by the trustee and after notice and a hearing, the court may approve a compromise or settlement. Notice shall be given to creditors, the United States trustee, the debtor, and indenture trustees as provided in Rule 2002 and to any other entity as the court may direct.

(b) AUTHORITY TO COMPROMISE OR SETTLE CON-TROVERSIES WITHIN CLASSES. After a hearing on such notice as the court may direct, the court may fix a class or classes of controversies and authorize the trustee to compromise or settle controversies within such class or classes without further hearing or notice.

(c) ARBITRATION. On stipulation of the parties to any controversy affecting the estate the court may authorize the matter to be submitted to final and binding arbitration.

Rule 9020. Contempt Proceedings

Rule 9014 governs a motion for an order of contempt made by the United States trustee or a party in interest.

Rule 9021. Entry of Judgment

Except as otherwise provided herein, Rule 58 F.R. Civ. P. applies in cases under the Code. Every judgment entered in an adversary proceeding or contested matter shall be set forth on a separate document. A judgment is effective when entered as provided in Rule 5003. The reference in Rule 58 F.R. Civ. P. to Rule 79(a) F.R. Civ. P. shall be read as a reference to Rule 5003 of these rules.

Rule 9022. Notice of Judgment or Order

(a) JUDGMENT OR ORDER OF BANKRUPTCY JUDGE. Immediately on the entry of a judgment or order the clerk shall serve a notice of the entry in the manner provided in Rule 5(b) F.R. Civ. P. on the contesting parties and on other entities as the court directs. Unless the case is a chapter 9 municipality case, the clerk shall forthwith transmit to the United States trustee a copy of the judgment or order. Service of the notice shall be noted in the docket. Lack of notice of the entry does not affect the time to appeal or relieve or authorize the court to relieve a party for failure to appeal within the time allowed, except as permitted in Rule 8002.

(b) JUDGMENT OR ORDER OF DISTRICT JUDGE. Notice of a judgment or order entered by a district judge is governed by Rule 77(d) F.R. Civ. P. Unless the case is a chapter 9 municipality case, the clerk shall forthwith transmit to the United States trustee a copy of the judgment or order entered by a district judge.

Rule 9023. New Trials; Amendment of Judgments

Rule 59 F.R. Civ. P. applies in cases under the Code, except as provided in Rule 3008.

Rule 9024. Relief From Judgment or Order

Rule 60 F.R. Civ. P. applies in cases under the Code except that (1) a motion to reopen a case under the Code or for the reconsideration of an order allowing or disallowing a claim against the estate entered without a contest is not subject to the one year limitation prescribed in Rule 60(b), (2) a complaint to revoke a discharge in a chapter 7 liquidation case may be filed only within the time allowed by § 727(e) of the Code, and (3) a complaint to revoke an order confirming a plan may be filed only within the time allowed by § 1144, § 1230, or § 1330.

Rule 9025. Security: Proceedings Against Sureties

Whenever the Code or these rules require or permit the giving of security by a party, and security is given in the form of a bond or stipulation or other undertaking with one or more sureties, each surety submits to the jurisdiction of the court, and liability may be determined in an adversary proceeding governed by the rules in Part VII.

Rule 9026. Exceptions Unnecessary

Rule 46 F.R. Civ. P. applies in cases under the Code.

Rule 9027. Removal

(a) NOTICE OF REMOVAL.

(1) WHERE FILED; FORM AND CONTENT. A notice of removal shall be filed with the clerk for the district and division within which is located the state or federal court where the civil action is pending. The notice shall be signed pursuant to Rule 9011 and contain a short and plain statement of the facts which entitle the party filing the notice to remove, contain a statement that upon removal of the claim or cause of action the proceeding is core or non-core and, if non-core, that the party filing the notice does or does not consent to entry of final orders or judgment by the bankruptcy judge, and be accompanied by a copy of all process and pleadings.

(2) TIME FOR FILING; CIVIL ACTION INITIATED AFTER COMMENCEMENT OF THE CASE UNDER THE CODE. If the claim or cause of action in a civil action is pending when a case under the Code is commenced, a notice of removal may be filed only within the longest of (A) 90 days after the order for relief in the case under the Code, (B) 30 days after entry of an order terminating a stay, if the claim or cause of action in a civil action has been stayed under § 362 of the Code, or (C) 30 days after a trustee qualifies in a chapter 11 reorganization case but no later than 180 days after the order for relief.

(3) TIME FOR FILING; CIVIL ACTION INITIATED AFTER COMMENCEMENT OF THE CASE UNDER THE CODE. If a claim or cause of action is asserted in another court after the commencement of a case under the Code, a notice of removal may be filed with the clerk only within the shorter of (A) 30 days after receipt, through service or otherwise, of a copy of the initial pleading setting forth the claim or cause of action sought to be removed, or (B) 30 days after receipt of the summons if the initial pleading has been filed with the court but not served with the summons.

(b) NOTICE. Promptly after filing the notice of removal, the party filing the notice shall serve a copy of it on all parties to the removed claim or cause of action.

(c) FILING IN NON-BANKRUPTCY COURT. Promptly after filing the notice of removal, the party filing the notice shall file a copy of it with the clerk of the court from which the claim or cause of action is removed. Removal of the claim or cause of action is effected on such filing of a copy of the notice of removal. The parties shall proceed no further in that court unless and until the claim or cause of action is remanded.

(d) REMAND. A motion for remand of the removed claim or cause of action shall be governed by Rule 9014 and served on the parties to the removed claim or cause of action.

(e) PROCEDURE AFTER REMOVAL.

(1) After removal of a claim or cause of action to a district court the district court or, if the case under the Code has been referred to a bankruptcy judge of the district, the bankruptcy judge, may issue all necessary orders and process to bring before it all proper parties whether served by process issued by the court from which the claim or cause of action was removed or otherwise.

(2) The district court or, if the case under the Code has been referred to a bankruptcy judge of the district, the bankruptcy judge, may require the party filing the notice of removal to file with the clerk copies of all records and proceedings relating to the claim or cause of action in the court from which the claim or cause of action was removed.

(3) Any party who has filed a pleading in connection with the removed claim or cause of action, other than the party filing the notice of removal, shall file a statement admitting or denying any allegation in the notice of removal that upon removal of the claim or cause of action the proceeding is core or non-core. If the statement alleges that the proceeding is non-core, it shall state that the party does or does not consent to entry of final orders or judgment by the bankruptcy judge. A statement required by this paragraph shall be signed pursuant to Rule 9011 and shall be filed not later than 10 days after the filing of the notice of removal. Any party who files a statement pursuant to this paragraph shall mail a copy to every other party to the removed claim or cause of action.

(f) PROCESS AFTER REMOVAL. If one or more of the defendants has not been served with process, the service has not been perfected prior to removal, or the process served proves to be defective, such process or service may be completed or new process issued pursuant to Part VII of these rules. This subdivision shall not deprive any defendant on whom process is served after removal of the defendant's right to move to remand the case.

(g) APPLICABILITY OF PART VII. The rules of Part VII apply to a claim or cause of action removed to a district court from a federal or state court and govern procedure after removal. Repleading is not necessary unless the court so orders. In a removed action in which the defendant has not answered, the defendant shall answer or present the other defenses or objections available under the rules of Part VII within 20 days following the receipt through service or otherwise of a copy of the initial pleading setting forth the claim for relief on which the action or proceeding is based, or within 20 days following the service of summons on such initial pleading, or within five days following the filing of the notice of removal, whichever period is longest.

(h) RECORD SUPPLIED. When a party is entitled to copies of the records and proceedings in any civil action or proceeding in a federal or a state court, to be used in the removed civil action or proceeding, and the clerk of the federal or state court, on demand accompanied by payment or tender of the lawful fees, fails to deliver certified copies, the court may, on affidavit reciting the facts, direct such record to be supplied by affidavit or otherwise. Thereupon the proceedings, trial and judgment may be had in the court, and all process awarded, as if certified copies has been filed.

(i) ATTACHMENT OR SEQUESTRATION; SECURITIES. When a claim or cause of action is removed to a district court, any attachment or sequestration of property in the court from which the claim or cause of action was removed shall hold the property to answer the final judgment or decree in the same manner as the property would have been held to answer final judgment or decree had it been rendered by the court from which the claim or cause of action was removed. All bonds, undertakings, or security given by either party to the claim or cause of action prior to its removal shall remain valid and effectual notwithstanding such removal. All injunctions issued, orders entered and other proceedings had prior to removal shall remain in full force and effect until dissolved or modified by the court.

Rule 9028. Disability of a Judge

Rule 63 F.R. Civ. P. applies in cases under the Code.

Rule 9029. Local Bankruptcy Rules Procedure When There is No Controlling Law

(a) LOCAL BANKRUPTCY RULES.

(1) Each district court acting by a majority of its district judges may make and amend rules governing practice and procedure in all cases and proceedings within the district court's bankruptcy jurisdiction which are consistent with—but not duplicative of—Acts of Congress and these rules and which do not prohibit or limit the use of the Official Forms. Rule 83 F.R. Civ. P. governs the procedure for making local rules. A district court may authorize the bankruptcy judges of the district, subject to any limitation or condition it may prescribe and the requirements of 83 F.R. Civ. P., to make and amend rules of practice and procedure which are consistent with—but not duplicative of—Acts of Congress and with these rules and which do not prohibit or limit the use of the Official Forms. Local rules shall conform to any uniform numbering system prescribed by the Judicial Conference of the United States.

(2) A local rule imposing a requirement of form shall not be enforced in a manner that causes a party to lose rights because of a negligent failure to comply with the requirement.

(b) PROCEDURE WHEN THERE IS NO CONTROLLING LAW. A judge may regulate practice in any manner consistent with federal law, these rules, Official Forms, and local rules of the district. No sanction or other disadvantage may be imposed for noncompliance with any requirement not in federal law, federal rules, Official Forms, or the local rules of the district unless the alleged violator has been furnished in the particular case with actual notice of the requirement.

Rule 9030. Jurisdiction and Venue Unaffected

These rules shall not be construed to extend or limit the jurisdiction of the courts or the venue of any matters therein.

Rule 9031. Masters Not Authorized

Rule 53 F.R. Civ. P. does not apply in cases under the Code.

Rule 9032. Effect of Amendment of Federal Rules of Civil Procedure

The Federal Rules of Civil Procedure which are incorporated by reference and made applicable by these rules shall be the Federal Rules of Civil Procedure in effect on the effective date of these rules and as thereafter amended, unless otherwise provided by such amendment or by these rules.

Rule 9033. Review of Proposed Findings of Fact and Conclusions of Law in Non-Core Proceedings

(a) SERVICE. In non-core proceedings heard pursuant to 28 U.S.C. § 157(c)(1), the bankruptcy judge shall file proposed findings of fact and conclusions of law. The clerk shall serve forthwith copies on all parties by mail and note the date of mailing on the docket.

(b) OBJECTIONS: TIME FOR FILING. Within 10 days after being served with a copy of the proposed findings of fact and conclusions of law a party may serve and file with the clerk written objections which identify the specific proposed findings or conclusions objected to and state the grounds for such objection. A party may respond to another party's objections within 10 days after being served with a copy thereof. A party objecting to the bankruptcy judge's proposed findings or conclusions shall arrange promptly for the transcription of the record, or such portions of it as all parties may agree upon or the bankruptcy judge deems sufficient, unless the district judge otherwise directs.

(c) EXTENSION OF TIME. The bankruptcy judge may for cause extend the time for filing objections by any party for a period not to exceed 20 days from the expiration of the time otherwise prescribed by this rule. A request to extend the time for filing objections must be made before the time for filing objections has expired, except that a request made no more than 20 days after the expiration of the time for filing objections may be granted upon a showing of excusable neglect.

(d) STANDARD OF REVIEW. The district judge shall make a de novo review upon the record or, after additional evidence, of any portion of the bankruptcy judge's findings of fact or conclusions of law to which specific written objection has been made in accordance with this rule. The district judge may accept, reject, or modify the proposed findings of fact or conclusions of law, receive further evidence, or recommit the matter to the bankruptcy judge with instructions.

Rule 9034. Transmittal of Pleadings, Motion Papers, Objections, and Other Papers to the United States Trustee

Unless the United States trustee requests otherwise or the case is a chapter 9 municipality case, any entity that files a pleading, motion, objection, or similar paper relating to any of the following matters shall transmit a copy thereof to the United States trustee within the time required by these rules for service of the paper:

(a) a proposed use, sale, or lease of property of the estate other than in the ordinary course of business;

(b) the approval of a compromise or settlement of a controversy;

(c) the dismissal or conversion of a case to another chapter;

(d) the employment of professional persons;

(e) an application for compensation or reimbursement of expenses;

(f) a motion for, or approval of an agreement relating to, the use of cash collateral or authority to obtain credit;

(g) the appointment of a trustee or examiner in a chapter 11 reorganization case;

(h) the approval of a disclosure statement;

(i) the confirmation of a plan;

(j) an objection to, or waiver or revocation of, the debtor's discharge;

(k) any other matter in which the United States trustee requests copies of filed papers or the court orders copies transmitted to the United States trustee.

Rule 9035. Applicability of Rules in Judicial Districts in Alabama and North Carolina

In any case under the Code that is filed in or transferred to a district in the State of Alabama or the State of North Carolina and in which a United States trustee is not authorized to act, these rules apply to the extent that they are not inconsistent with any federal statute effective in the case.

Rule 9036. Notice by Electronic Transmission

Whenever the clerk or some other person as directed by the court is required to send notice by mail and the entity entitled to receive the notice requests in writing that, instead of notice by mail, all or part of the information required to be contained in the notice be sent by a specified type of electronic transmission, the court may direct the clerk or other person to send the information by such electronic transmission. Notice by electronic transmission is complete, and the sender shall have fully complied with the requirement to send notice, when the sender obtains electronic confirmation that the transmission has been received.

Appendix C Bankruptcy Court Miscellaneous Fee Schedule

The fee schedule is issued by the Judicial Conference of the United States in accordance with 28 U.S.C. § 1930(b). It became effective November 1, 2003. This schedule may also be found on the CD-Rom accompanying this volume.

Following are fees to be charged for services to be performed by clerks of the bankruptcy courts. No fees are to be charged for services rendered on behalf of the United States, with the exception of those specifically prescribed in items 1, 3, and 5, or to bankruptcy administrators appointed under Public Law No. 99-554, § 302(d)(3)(I). No fees under this schedule shall be charged to federal agencies or programs which are funded from judiciary appropriations, including, but not limited to, agencies, organizations, and individuals providing services authorized by the Criminal Justice Act, 18 U.S.C. § 3006A.

(1) For reproducing any record or paper, $.50 per page. This fee shall apply to paper copies made from either: (1) original documents; or (2) microfiche or microfilm reproductions of the original records. This fee shall apply to services rendered on behalf of the United States if the record or paper requested is available through electronic access.

(2) For certification of any document or paper, whether the certification is made directly on the document or by separate instrument, $9. For exemplification of any document or paper, twice the amount of the charge for certification.

(3) For reproduction of recordings of proceedings, regardless of the medium, $26, including the cost of materials. This fee shall apply to services rendered on behalf of the United States, if the reproduction of the recording is available electronically.

(4) For amendments to a debtor's schedules of creditors, lists of creditors, matrix, or mailing lists, $26 for each amendment, provided the bankruptcy judge may, for good cause, waive the charge in any case.

(5) For every search of the records of the bankruptcy court conducted by the clerk of the bankruptcy court or a deputy clerk, $26 per name or item searched. This fee shall apply to services rendered on behalf of the United States if the information requested is available through electronic access.

(6) For filing a complaint, a fee shall be collected in the same amount as the filing fee prescribed in 28 U.S.C. § 1914(a) for instituting any civil action other than a writ of habeas corpus. If the United States, other than a United States trustee acting as a trustee in a case under title 11, or a debtor is the plaintiff, no fee is required. If a trustee or debtor in possession is the plaintiff, the fee should be payable only from the estate and to the extent there is any estate realized. If a child support creditor or its representative is the plaintiff, and if such plaintiff files the form required by § 304(g) of the Bankruptcy Reform Act of 1994, no fee is required.

(7) For filing or indexing any document not in a case or proceeding for which a filing fee has been paid, $39.

(8) In all cases filed under title 11, the clerk shall collect from the debtor or the petitioner a miscellaneous administrative fee of $39. This fee may be paid in installments in the same manner that the filing fee may be paid in installments, consistent with the procedure set forth in Federal Rule of Bankruptcy Procedure 1006.

(9) Upon the filing of a petition under chapter 7 of the Bankruptcy Code, the petitioner shall pay $15 to the clerk of the court for payment to trustees serving in cases as provided in 11 U.S.C. § 330(b)(2). An application to pay the fee in installments may be filed in the manner set forth in Federal Rule of Bankruptcy Procedure 1006(b).

(10) Upon the filing of a motion to convert a case to chapter 7 of the Bankruptcy Code, the movant shall pay $15 to the clerk of court for payment to trustees serving in cases as provided in 11 U.S.C. § 330(b)(2). Upon the filing of a notice of conversion pursuant to section 1208(a) or section 1307(a) of the Code, $15 shall be paid to the clerk of the court for payment to trustees serving in cases as provided in 11 U.S.C. § 330(b)(2). If the trustee serving in the case before the conversion is the movant, the fee shall be payable only from the estate that exists prior to conversion.

(11) For filing a motion to reopen a Bankruptcy Code case, a fee shall be collected in the same amount as the filing fee prescribed by 28 U.S.C. § 1930(a) for commencing a new case on the date of reopening, unless the reopening is to correct an administrative error or for actions related to the debtor's discharge. The court may waive this fee under appropriate circumstances or may defer payment of the fee from trustees pending discovery of additional assets.

(12) For each microfiche sheet of film or microfilm jacket copy of any court record, where available, $5.

(13) For retrieval of a record from a Federal Records Center, National Archives, or other storage location removed from the place of business of the court, $45.

(14) For a check paid into the court which is returned for lack of funds, $45.

(15) For docketing a proceeding on appeal or review from a final judgment of a bankruptcy judge pursuant to 28 U.S.C. § 158(a) and (b), the fee shall be the same amount as the fee for docketing a case on appeal or review to the appellate court as required by Item 1 of the Courts of Appeals Miscellaneous Fee Schedule. A separate fee shall be paid by each party filing a notice of appeal in the bankruptcy court, but parties filing a joint notice of appeal in the bankruptcy court are required to pay only one fee. If a trustee or debtor in possession is the appellant, the fee should be payable only from the estate and to the extent there is any estate realized.

(16) For filing a petition ancillary to a foreign proceeding under 11 U.S.C. § 304, the fee shall be the same amount as the fee for a case commenced under chapter 11 of title 11 as required by 28 U.S.C. § 1930(a)(3).

(17) The court may charge and collect fees commensurate with the cost of providing copies of the local rules of court. The court may also distribute copies of the local rules without charge.

(18) The clerk shall assess a charge for the handling of registry funds deposited with the court, to be assessed from interest earnings and in accordance with the detailed fee schedule issued by the Director of the Administrative Office of the United States Courts.

(19) When a joint case filed under § 302 of title 11 is divided into two separate cases at the request of the debtor(s), a fee shall be charged equal to the current filing fee for the chapter under which the joint case was commenced.

(20) For filing a motion to terminate, annul, modify, or condition the automatic stay provided under § 362(a) of title 11, a motion to compel abandonment of property of the estate pursuant to Rule 6007(b) of the Federal Rules of Bankruptcy Procedure, or a motion to withdraw the reference of a case or proceeding under 28 U.S.C. § 157(d), a fee shall be collected in the amount of the filing fee prescribed in 28 U.S.C. § 1914(a) for instituting any civil action other than a writ of habeas corpus. If a child support creditor or its representative is the movant, and if such movant files the form required by § 304(g) of the Bankruptcy Reform Act of 1994, no fee is required.

(21) For docketing a cross appeal from a bankruptcy court determination, the fee shall be the same amount as the fee for docketing a case on appeal or review to the appellate court as required by Item 1 of the Courts of Appeals Miscellaneous Fee Schedule. If a trustee or debtor in possession is the appellant, the fee should be payable only from the estate and to the extent there is any estate realized.

Appendix D   Official Bankruptcy Forms

Blank Official Forms Contained in This Appendix

D.1 Introduction

Appendix D reprints selected Official Bankruptcy Forms in blank, preceded by explanatory comments. These blank forms are available as Acrobat (PDF) files on the CD-Rom accompanying this volume. Of more significance, the CD-Rom also includes *Bankruptcy Forms* software, by Law Disks, that allows practitioners to complete many of the Official Forms on their computer in Microsoft Word or in WordPerfect. This software is explained in more detail in Appendix D.4, *infra.*

Appendix F contains completed Official Forms for a sample bankruptcy case, with annotations explaining why the forms were completed in this fashion. These completed forms can also be found in PDF format on the CD-Rom accompanying this volume.

In addition to the Official Forms, the Administrative Office of the United States Courts has issued a number of other forms for use in bankruptcy cases. Several of these forms are reprinted in blank in Appendix E, *infra,* and are also found in PDF format on the CD-Rom accompanying this volume. Over one-hundred other bankruptcy pleadings developed by the authors of this volume are found in Appendix G, *infra,* and on the CD-Rom accompanying this volume, in both PDF and Microsoft Word format, allowing them to be copied and pasted into a word-processing program.

D.2 Permitted Alterations to the Official Forms

Federal Rule of Bankruptcy Procedure 9009 provides that the Official Forms "shall be observed and used," but permits "alteration as may be appropriate." *See* H.R. Doc. No. 102-80, at 525 (1991). The use of the Official Forms has been held to be subject to a "rule of substantial compliance." *Id.* If a document uses a different format, but contains all of the information required by the Official Form, that document will generally meet the standard of substantial compliance. Reprinted below is the Official Forms Introduction and General Instructions, as promulgated by the Judicial Conference in 1991. Only reprinted is that portion of the Introduction still found on the Judicial Conference of the United States' website, www.uscourts.gov:

> Bankruptcy Rule 9009 of the Federal Rules of Bankruptcy Procedure states that the Official Forms prescribed by the Judicial Conference of the United States "shall be observed and used." The Official Forms, accordingly, are obligatory in character.
>
> Rule 9009 expressly permits the user of the Official Forms to make such "alterations as may be appropriate," and the use of the Official Forms has been held to be subject to a "rule of substantial compliance." Some rules, for example, Fed. R. Bankr. P. 3001(a), specifically state that the filed document need only "conform substantially" to the Official Form. A document for which an Official Form is prescribed generally will meet the standard of substantial compliance if the document contains the complete substance, that is, all of the information required by the Official Form.
>
> Rule 9009 also expressly permits the contents of Official Forms to be rearranged, and the format of the Official Forms traditionally has been quite flexible. The forms of the voluntary petition, the

schedules, and the statement of financial affairs are printed and sold by private publishers. Design features such as type face, type size, layout, and side and top margins were not prescribed by the Judicial Conference, but rather left to the professional judgment of each publisher.

> A great deal of variation, accordingly, has developed. Some publishers also add forms that are not official but which have been drafted by the publisher. A form for a chapter 13 plan, for example, frequently is included with commercially printed packages of forms for filing cases under chapter 13, although there is no Official Form for this purpose. The variety of formats has accelerated since the introduction of computer software for generating the petitions, schedules, and statements of affairs. It is the policy of the Judicial Conference that such diversity is desirable and should be encouraged.
>
> The sheer volume of bankruptcy cases, however, has compelled the Judicial Conference, for the first time, to prescribe the format of certain Official Forms. In particular, the format of Form 1, the Voluntary Petition, now is prescribed. This format is designed to assist the clerk of the bankruptcy court to enter the case in the court's computer database and ensures that all required information is available to both the clerk and the United States trustee at the inception of the case. The rule of substantial compliance continues to apply, however. Accordingly, publishers may vary the size and style of the type and may alter the size and shape of the boxes on the form, within the bounds of that rule.
>
> The Official Forms of the petitions, schedules, and statement of financial affairs (Forms 1, 5, 6, and 7), are to be printed on one side of the paper only. Each page is to be pre-punched with two holes at the top, and sufficient top margin allowed so that neither caption nor text is destroyed or obscured. Compliance with these standards will facilitate both the securing of the papers in the case file and review of the file by the public.
>
> Although Rule 9009 permits alteration, for most of the Official Forms, alteration will be appropriate only in rare circumstances. The special forms for chapter 11 cases, on the other hand, seldom will be used without alterations. Forms 12 through 15, while legally sufficient in any chapter 11 case, are intended by the Judicial Conference, and most often will be used, as a framework for drafting a document specially tailored to the particular case. These alterations generally will take the form of additions to the prescribed elements.
>
> Rule 9009 provides for a balance of prescribed substance, to which full adherence is expected in all but the most unusual cases, and flexible formatting, under which requirements are kept to the minimum necessary for proper operation of the courts and the bankruptcy system. While Rule

9009 recognizes the overall need for flexibility, Rule 9029 makes it clear that the Official Forms must be accepted in every bankruptcy court.

* * *

D.3 Annotations to Official Bankruptcy Forms

Official Bankruptcy Form 1—Voluntary Petition

Official Form 1 is the petition used to commence a voluntary case under chapter 7, 11, 12, or 13 of the Bankruptcy Code. Exhibit C concerning whether the debtor owns property that poses a threat of immediate harm to the public health or safety is also reprinted.

The petition should include other names used by the debtor(s), such as trade names, business names, married names, and maiden names, to help creditors identify the debtor when they receive notices of the bankruptcy filing. The form now requires the reporting of only the last four digits of the debtor's social security number or other taxpayer identification number. The form requires both a street address and any separate mailing address, as well as any separate addresses used by a joint debtor.

The petition must be accompanied by filing fees totaling $209 for chapter 7 cases and $194 for chapter 13 cases, unless an application and order to pay the fee in installments (Official Form 3) is filed. Certain portions of these fees may be waivable by the courts for indigent debtors, because they are imposed under 28 U.S.C. § 1930(b). *See* § 13.6, *supra.* Husband and wife need pay only a single filing fee if they file jointly. The petition, whether filed under chapter 7 or chapter 13, must be accompanied by the schedules and statement of affairs (Official Forms 6 and 7). If filed under chapter 13, a plan will also be required.

Alternatively, the debtor at this stage can file the petition with only a List of Creditors. Consult local rules for other possible requirements or variations. A more detailed discussion of the debtor's petition, together with additional filing requirements, is contained in § 7.3, *supra.*

Official Bankruptcy Form 3—Application and Order to Pay Filing Fees in Installments

Official Form 3 is an application and order to pay filing fees in installments, and may be filed pursuant to 28 U.S.C. § 1930(a) and Federal Rule of Bankruptcy Procedure 1006(b). Local rules may require that this application be filed in duplicate. No filing fee need be paid at the time the petition is filed if the petition is accompanied by this form. No more than four installments may be proposed, to be paid over no more than 120 days after the petition is filed. However this time, upon debtor's application, may be ex-

tended for cause to 180 days. The proposed terms of payment should normally specify the dates payments will be due, for example:

$59.00 on February 1, 2005
$50.00 on March 1, 2005
$50.00 on April 1, 2005
$50.00 on May 1, 2005

Local practice should be checked. Paying filing fees in installments is discussed further in § 7.3.8, *supra.*

The Order provided in Official Form 3 should accompany the application to pay filing fees in installments. This Application and Order may be used only if no money or property has been paid to the debtor's attorney or any other person for services in connection with the bankruptcy or any other pending bankruptcy case, and no such payments may be made until the filing fee has been paid in full. *See* Fed. R. Bankr. P. 1006(b)(3). The dates of the proposed payments are to be inserted in the application and are then incorporated by reference in the Order.

Official Bankruptcy Form 6—Schedules

These schedules are used to comply with section 521(1) of the Bankruptcy Code and Fedederal Rule of Bankruptcy Procedure 1007(b). Official Form 6 must be filed by all debtors without regard to the chapter under which they have filed.

Schedules A, B, D, E and F constitute the schedules of assets and liabilities. Schedule G addresses executory contracts and unexpired leases. Schedule H addresses codebtors. Schedules I and J constitute the schedules of current income and current expenditures for individual and joint debtors.

Following the summary sheet, the schedules of assets appear first, followed by the schedules of liabilities. This order corresponds to the usual pattern by which trustees and creditors review these documents.

Instructions to Schedules D, E, and F now inform the debtor that the debtor's account number with a listed creditor should be provided whenever practicable, but it is not required that the number be provided. Certain dollar amounts in Schedule E have been adjusted for inflation, effective April 1, 2004, and will again be adjusted effective April 1, 2007.

Leasehold interests in both real and personal property should be reported in Schedule G. This information should not be repeated in the schedules of assets. But note that even though interests in executory contracts and leases are not listed in Schedules A or B, they still can be exempt property for purposes of Schedule C (for example, Illinois law specifically includes leasehold interests in the homestead exemption). See generally the discussion of executory contracts and leases in § 12.9, *supra.*

Official Bankruptcy Form 6—Declaration

Debtors are required to attest to the accuracy of all schedules submitted to the court. All non-attorney bankruptcy petition preparers are required to identify themselves.

Official Bankruptcy Form 7—Statement of Financial Affairs

This form should be completed by all debtors. Questions should be answered by either furnishing information or checking the box labeled "None." Official Form 7 now requires the debtor to disclose only the last four digits of the debtor's social security or other taxpayer identification number. In addition, those items that require the listing of any account number now require disclosure only of the last four digits. Questions 16 through 21 should be answered only by consumer debtors who are or have been in business. Bankruptcy petition preparers must disclose the information requested.

Official Bankruptcy Form 8—Chapter 7 Individual Debtor's Statement of Intention

Federal Rule of Bankruptcy Procedure 1007(b)(2) requires the debtor to serve a copy of this statement on the trustee and all creditors named in the statement. The Advisory Committee note accompanying the 1997 changes to this form states that "the form is not intended to take a position regarding whether the options stated on the form are the only choices available to the debtor. Compare *Lowry Federal Credit Union v. West*, 882 F.2d 1543 (10th Cir. 1989), with *In re Taylor*, 3 F.3d 1512 (11th Cir. 1993)."

Official Bankruptcy Form 9—Notice of Bankruptcy Case, Meeting of Creditors, and Deadlines

This form will generally be prepared by the clerk of the bankruptcy court. It facilitates the process of notifying creditors of the filing of the petition, the meeting of creditors, and certain deadlines in the case. This form also provides notice of the claims filing period provided to "a governmental unit." This appendix only reprints the versions of Form 9 applicable to most consumer cases. The CD-Rom accompanying this volume reprints all of the versions of Form 9:

- 9A—Chapter 7 Individual or Joint Debtor No Asset Case
- 9B—Chapter 7 Corporation or Partnership No Asset Case
- 9C—Chapter 7 Individual or Joint Debtor Asset Case
- 9D—Chapter 7 Corporation or Partnership Asset Case
- 9E—Chapter 11 Individual or Joint Debtor Case

- 9E (Alternate)—Chapter 11 Individual or Joint Debtor Case
- 9F—Chapter 11 Corporation or Partnership Case
- 9F (Alternate)—Chapter 11 Corporation or Partnership Case
- 9G—Chapter 12 Individual or Joint Debtor Family Farmer Case
- 9H—Chapter 12 Corporation or Partnership Family Farmer Case
- 9I—Chapter 13 Case

Forms 9E (Alternate) and 9F (Alternate) are for use in districts that set a deadline for filing a claim in a chapter 11 case. Official Forms 9A–9I provide for disclosure of all names used by the debtor during the prior six years. The forms request the debtor's full employer identification number, if any, as well as the last four digits of the debtor's social security number. The case file only shows the last four digits of the social security number, while copies going to the trustees and creditors show the complete number.

Official Bankruptcy Form 10—Proof of Claim

A proof of claim is used to file a claim on behalf of a creditor. See § 17.4, *supra*, for a general discussion of proofs of claim. This form allows for future additions to section 507(a) of the Bankruptcy Code. It also clarifies that the amount of the claim should include only pre-petition arrearages and charges. Official Form 10 requires a wage, salary, or other compensation creditor to disclose only the last four digits of the creditor's social security number. Certain dollar amounts were adjusted for inflation, effective April 1, 2004. These same amounts will again be adjusted effective April 1, 2007.

Official Bankruptcy Form 16A—Caption (Full)

This form sets out the caption for the case. Pursuant to Federal Rules of Bankruptcy Procedure 9004(b) and 1005, Official Form 16A includes the title of the case, the debtor's name, all names the debtor used within six years prior to the commencement of the case, and the last four digits of the debtor's social security and tax identification numbers. The full caption form also notes the chapter of the Bankruptcy Code under which the case is filed. This form of caption is prescribed for use on the petition, the notice of the meeting of creditors, the order of discharge, and the documents relating to a chapter 11 plan (Official Forms 1, 9, 12, 13, 14, 15, and 18). *See* Fed. R. Bankr. P. 2002(m).

Official Bankruptcy Form 16B—Caption (Short Title)

The short title form of caption is prescribed for general use in filing papers in bankruptcy cases. It should not be used on the petition, the notice of the meeting of creditors, the order of discharge, and the documents relating to a chapter 11 plan (Official Forms 1, 9, 12, 13, 14, 15, and 18), which require the full caption set out in Official Form 16A. *See* Fed. R. Bankr. P. 2002(m). The title specifies that this form can be used when section 342(c) of the Bankruptcy Code is not applicable.

Official Bankruptcy Form 16C—Caption of Complaint in Adversary Proceeding Filed by a Debtor

This form is now abrogated. Instead, debtors use Official Form 16D.

Official Bankruptcy Form 16D—Caption for Use in Adversary Proceeding

This form should be used by debtors in adversary proceedings, as Official Form 16C is now abrogated. When used in this manner, Official Form 16D should be altered to include the debtor's address and last four digits of the debtor's social security number. The debtor's complete social security number should be included on copies furnished to creditors when section 342(c) of the Bankruptcy Code is applicable.

Official Bankruptcy Form 17—Notice of Appeal

This form, used for appeals under 28 U.S.C. § 158(a) or (b) from a judgment, order, or decree of a bankruptcy judge, indicates that a final order may be entered in cases other than adversary proceedings. A party who wishes to appeal to the district court rather than to a bankruptcy appellate panel must make that election on a separate statement of election at the time of filing the appeal. The form also provides flexibility to permit certain immediate appeals. The form now provides notice that no filing fee is required if a child support creditor or its representative is the appellant and files a form.

Official Bankruptcy Form 18—Discharge of Debtor in a Chapter 7 Case

This form provides for cases commenced by voluntary or involuntary petitions.

Official Bankruptcy Form 19—Certification and Signature of Non-Attorney Bankruptcy Petition Preparer (See 11 U.S.C. § 110)

This form requires a non-attorney bankruptcy petition preparer to sign all "documents for filing" that the preparer prepares for compensation. The preparer must also disclose certain required information and provide the debtor with a copy of the document. This form should be used in connection with any document that the preparer prepares for filing by a debtor.

Official Bankruptcy Form 20A—Notice of Motion or Objection

Official Bankruptcy Form 20B—Notice of Objection to Claim

The following Advisory Committee note accompanying the 1997 adoption of these forms states: "These notices will be sent by the movant unless local rules provide for some other entity to give notice. . . . [T]he signature line will be adapted to identify the actual sender of the notice in each circumstance. All adaptations of the form should carry out the intent to give notice of applicable procedures in easily understood language."

Official Bankruptcy Form 21—Statement of Social Security Number

Because other forms now just indicate the last four digits of the social security number, this new form provides the debtor's full social security number. The statement is submitted by the debtor with the petition and schedules but is not made a part of the official court file. Therefore, the debtor's full social security number is not available to the general public or over the Internet. The debtor's full social security number provided on this Statement is included in the notice of the section 341(a) meeting mailed to creditors.

D.4 *Bankruptcy Forms* Software on the Companion CD-Rom

D.4.1 General

The CD-Rom accompanying this volume contains simple software which will allow you to create bankruptcy petitions and schedules as Microsoft Word or WordPerfect files. The philosophy of these *Bankruptcy Forms*, from Law Disks[1] software, is that every law firm and legal aid office should have the ability to file a computerized bankruptcy petition.[2] These forms are intentionally simple, as NCLC cannot provide technical support, and such support should not be necessary with these forms.[3]

---

1 Law Disks, www.lawdisks.com, is an independent software publisher which assists NCLC by organizing NCLC's Acrobat (PDF) materials on CD-Rom, and by providing the *Bankruptcy Forms* software.
2 *Bankruptcy Forms* are for use only by attorneys: the forms do not contain all the required disclosures for non-attorney petition preparers.
3 For technical support, please send e-mail to support@lawdisks.com.

When you insert the CD-Rom into your CD-Rom drive, a pop-up menu appears. Click on the START button, then click on the button for "Bankruptcy Forms Software." The software provides users with a choice of either filling in the forms using Microsoft Word or WordPerfect, depending upon which word processor the user owns. The standard Microsoft Word option is compatible with Word 97, 2000, 2002 (XP), and 2003. The standard WordPerfect option is compatible with WordPerfect 8, 9, 10, or 11. *Bankruptcy Forms* also offers options for older versions of Word (such as versions 2, 6, 7, or 95) or WordPerfect (such as versions 6 or 7 for Windows, or 5.1 for DOS).[4]

D.4.2 Microsoft Word 97, 2000, 2002 (XP), and 2003

If you click on the button for the Microsoft Word version of "Petition/Schedules," then you will be asked if you wish to open Microsoft Word (yes), and then asked if you wish to enable macros (yes).[5] You may need to click on a blinking Microsoft Word icon at the bottom of the screen.

A copy of the bankruptcy petition, schedules, and social security form will then open in Microsoft Word. You can save this blank document to your Word templates folder[6] or, if so desired, you can just save it as a Word document, repeating the process for each new case you file. You fill in this document using the normal Word editing tools, and then save it with a different name, such as Petition_Garcia.doc, to a folder such as "\My Documents\."

You can delete unneeded pages (such as the Application to Pay Filing Fee in Installments) by selecting (highlighting) the text, then clicking on the Delete key. You can separate the social security numbers page by selecting the text, then clicking on Edit, and then on Cut. Then open a new blank document, click on Edit, and then on Paste.

Most of the schedules use the Table function to create the rows and columns. To add an extra horizontal row for an additional creditor, place the cursor in the next to last row (*not* the Total row), then click on Table, then on Insert, and then on Rows Above.

To make a mailing list, sometimes known as the matrix, in Microsoft Word, select each left column in schedules D, E, and F as needed, then click on Edit and then on Copy. Move the cursor to the end of the schedules, then click the [CTRL] and [ENTER] keys together to create a new page. Then click on Edit and then on Paste Cells. Now select the pasted cells, click on Table, then on Convert, then on Table to Text. This procedure eliminates the cell lines.

To save the mailing list as an ASCII text file (.txt) for submission on diskette or for use in electronic filing (ECF), you simply select the mailing list matrix, click on Edit and then on Copy. Then click on File, then on New, then on New Blank Document. When the blank document appears, click on Edit and then on Paste. Now you have just the mailing list in its own file. Click on File and then on Save As. *Important*: in the list "Save as Type," you must change the type to "Text only .txt," which is one of the choices in the drop down list. Give the document a unique name, then click on the Save button, and now you have an ASCII text file of the mailing list.

In the Microsoft Word version of the forms, the first two pages are "protected," meaning that you must type answers within the gray form fields. You can type outside those fields by clicking on the "UnprotectBcy" menu. If you do this, be careful not to delete any of the gray form fields. Click on "ProtectBcy" when done. While the Word document is protected, you can click on the menu item "UpdateBcy" to insert the names of the debtors, attorney and Court throughout the schedules.

D.4.3 WordPerfect 8, 9, 10, and 11

If you click on the button for the WordPerfect version of "Petition/Schedules," you will be asked if you wish to open WordPerfect (yes). A copy of the bankruptcy petition, schedules, and social security form will then open in WordPerfect. You can use this "Instant Copy" feature to:

- get a copy of any of the forms from the CD-Rom at anytime;
- customize the blank form and copy to your hard drive; or
- open the CD-Rom file: \LawDisks\Blank_Bcy_Petition.wpd, then customize it for your firm and court, and then save it as a model blank form in your document folder.

Editing is done by normal WordPerfect editing tools. The methods for adding extra rows and making the mailing list matrix are similar to those described for the Microsoft Word version, above.[7]

---

4 *Bankruptcy Forms* is not compatible with Microsoft Works.

5 To ensure that Microsoft Word macros (useful programs) work, in Word click on Tools, then on Macro, then on Security, and then set the Security Level to "Medium." On the "Trusted Sources" tab check the yes box, to trust installed templates and add-ins, which will allow them to function.

6 Click on File, then on Save As, but then choose the file type "Word Template." This ought to save a copy to Word's Templates folder. You can check the location of the Templates folder by clicking on Tools, then on Options, then on File Locations, then on User Templates, and then on Modify. Do not modify the location, just write it down for reference. To use a template, click on File, then on New, then on (General Templates), and then click on "Bankrupt.dot" to bring up a blank copy of the template on the screen.

7 The WordPerfect version of *Bankruptcy Forms* however does not have macros, nor form fields, nor the "UpdateBcy" macro due to technical problems relating to different WordPerfect

D.4.4 WordPerfect 5.1 for DOS, WordPerfect 6 and 7 for Windows, Microsoft Word 2, 6, 7, and 95

The CD-Rom contains instructions specifying which files to use if you have an older version of WordPerfect or Microsoft Word. These instructions can be found by clicking on bookmarks on the left side of the "Instant Copy" page (from START, click on "Bankruptcy Forms Software").

D.4.5 Chapter 13 Plan; Local Forms

The Administrative Office of the United States Courts does not have an official form for a chapter 13 plan. Several examples of attorney-drafted chapter 13 plans are included in Appendix G, *infra*. Practitioners should check their bankruptcy court's local rules to see if a specific form of chapter 13 plan is required in that jurisdiction. Most bankruptcy courts have websites, which can be found at www.uscourts.gov/links.html.

Always check a court's website for local forms, as some courts have added local requirements in chapter 7 cases as well. Typically, local forms will be in Acrobat (PDF) format on the local bankruptcy court's website. The *Bankruptcy Forms* on the CD-Rom accompanying this volume are copies of the official bankruptcy forms of the Administrative Office of the United States Courts, but do not contain local variations.

D.4.6 Other Forms Included in Bankruptcy Forms

The "Business Questions" button will retrieve the business questions from the Statement of Financial Affairs, as well as Exhibit A (concerning business ownership, stock). The "Captions" button produces a caption which can be used for an adversary proceeding, or a motion, with some editing. The Proof of Claim form is for a creditor to file in a chapter 13 or an asset case.

D.5 Electronic Case Filing (ECF)

D.5.1 Overview

At present two-thirds of the bankruptcy courts are requiring, or at least allowing, the filing of bankruptcy forms electronically, and that number is growing rapidly. The trend has been that after Electronic Case Filing (ECF) has been in use for a year or two in a court its use in that court becomes

mandatory. ECF saves bankruptcy attorneys time and postage. ECF is particularly useful for emergency petitions, especially for attorneys who reside at a distance from the courthouse.

The forms produced by the *Bankruptcy Forms* software may be used with electronic filing, as can forms generated in any other manner. Whatever format in which the documents were created, they must be converted to Adobe Acrobat (PDF) format before filing. This format is similar to an electronic photograph of the original document. An exception to the PDF requirement is that generally the creditor mailing list must be in ASCII text (.txt) format.

Some bankruptcy courts require attorneys to participate in training about how to use ECF or give attorneys practice petitions to file before an attorney is certified to file using ECF. Once an attorney is using ECF, then all pleadings, such as adversary complaints, motions, and so forth, must be filed exclusively in Acrobat PDF format via the ECF system.

Once the forms have been converted to PDF format, log onto the bankruptcy court's ECF website, fill in basic data about the debtor, and locate/attach the PDF petition/schedules file and the mailing list text (.txt) file. Click on the final button, and the files are sent over the Internet to the bankruptcy court's website. The court gives the petitioner an instant case number as proof of filing, and future communication from the court arrives via e-mail, so one receives instant notice of events in the case.

D.5.2 Converting Documents to PDF Format

The principal method of creating PDF files is to use the "full" Adobe Acrobat program (which retails for about $250 and is different than the free Acrobat Reader program widely available on the Internet.) When the full version of Adobe Acrobat is installed on a computer, any file can be duplicated as an Acrobat file by clicking on File and then on Print, and choosing Acrobat PDF or Acrobat Distiller as the "printer driver." Acrobat does not print out a paper copy of the file, rather it takes the original file and makes an Acrobat file, which will have the same file name but include the extension ".pdf." The original file is not changed. Now you have both the original file and a PDF copy.

There are ways of avoiding the $250 cost for the full Acrobat program. WordPerfect versions 9, 10, and 11 have an internal PDF generator that comes free with the word processor (click on File and then on Publish to PDF). Some of the specialized bankruptcy programs also include a PDF converter to create a PDF copy of the petition for you. However, such users will likely find that they still need to buy the full version of Adobe Acrobat in order to create the pleadings not covered by the software, such as custom motions, complaints, and adversary proceedings.

---

macro versions, and the difficulty of recompiling WordPerfect macros when files on CD-Rom must necessarily be read-only.

Free or low-cost PDF converters offered by third party (non-Adobe) software vendors are available on the Internet. For example, see www.primopdf.com for a free PDF print driver which makes PDF files. For best quality on the screen, however, the full Adobe Acrobat program is better than the free converters.

Scanning is another way to make a PDF file. A scanner is hardware which copies pieces of paper into electronic files, including PDF format. In general, the bankruptcy courts discourage submission of scanned documents in ECF because the resulting files are much larger than the ones created by converting a word-processed document into a PDF file, and thus take up excessive space on the court's computer system.

Consequently, the best practice is not to scan in the forms themselves. Instead, scan into PDF only exhibits such as mortgages or contracts which only exist as images on paper, and not as word-processing files.

One exception to this rule is that some courts want the page with the debtor's signature to be scanned into PDF. In other bankruptcy courts, nothing on a petition needs to be scanned, and the court accepts signatures in the format of "S/Attorney Signature" and "S/Debtor Signature."[8] Check the bankruptcy court's local rules. See www.uscourts.gov/links.html for weblinks to the individual bankruptcy courts.

---

8 Using the free *Bankruptcy Forms* software available on the CD-Rom accompanying this volume, this task can be performed easily in the WordPerfect version. In the Microsoft Word version, you must click on "UnProtectBcy" to add the S/ signatures. More automated software is available for purchase from Law Disks, at www.lawdisks.com.

D.6 Blank Official Bankruptcy Forms

(Official Form 1) (12/03)

FORM B1	United States Bankruptcy Court _____District of_____	Voluntary Petition

Name of Debtor (if individual, enter Last, First, Middle):	Name of Joint Debtor (Spouse) (Last, First, Middle):
All Other Names used by the Debtor in the last 6 years (include married, maiden, and trade names):	All Other Names used by the Joint Debtor in the last 6 years (include married, maiden, and trade names):
Last four digits of Soc. Sec. No./Complete EIN or other Tax I.D. No. (if more than one, state all):	Last four digits of Soc. Sec.No./Complete EIN or other Tax I.D. No. (if more than one, state all):
Street Address of Debtor (No. & Street, City, State & Zip Code):	Street Address of Joint Debtor (No. & Street, City, State & Zip Code):
County of Residence or of the Principal Place of Business:	County of Residence or of the Principal Place of Business:
Mailing Address of Debtor (if different from street address):	Mailing Address of Joint Debtor (if different from street address):

Location of Principal Assets of Business Debtor (if different from street address above):

Information Regarding the Debtor (Check the Applicable Boxes)

Venue (Check any applicable box)

☐ Debtor has been domiciled or has had a residence, principal place of business, or principal assets in this District for 180 days immediately preceding the date of this petition or for a longer part of such 180 days than in any other District.

☐ There is a bankruptcy case concerning debtor's affiliate, general partner, or partnership pending in this District.

Type of Debtor (Check all boxes that apply)	**Chapter or Section of Bankruptcy Code Under Which the Petition is Filed** (Check one box)
☐ Individual(s) ☐ Railroad ☐ Corporation ☐ Stockbroker ☐ Partnership ☐ Commodity Broker ☐ Other_____ ☐ Clearing Bank	☐ Chapter 7 ☐ Chapter 11 ☐ Chapter 13 ☐ Chapter 9 ☐ Chapter 12 ☐ Sec. 304 - Case ancillary to foreign proceeding
Nature of Debts (Check one box) ☐ Consumer/Non-Business ☐ Business	**Filing Fee** (Check one box) ☐ Full Filing Fee attached ☐ Filing Fee to be paid in installments (Applicable to individuals only)
Chapter 11 Small Business (Check all boxes that apply) ☐ Debtor is a small business as defined in 11 U.S.C. § 101 ☐ Debtor is and elects to be considered a small business under 11 U.S.C. § 1121(e) (Optional)	Must attach signed application for the court's consideration certifying that the debtor is unable to pay fee except in installments. Rule 1006(b). See Official Form No. 3.

Statistical/Administrative Information (Estimates only)   THIS SPACE IS FOR COURT USE ONLY

☐ Debtor estimates that funds will be available for distribution to unsecured creditors.

☐ Debtor estimates that, after any exempt property is excluded and administrative expenses paid, there will be no funds available for distribution to unsecured creditors.

Estimated Number of Creditors	1-15	16-49	50-99	100-199	200-999	1000-over
	☐	☐	☐	☐	☐	☐

Estimated Assets								
$0 to $50,000	$50,001 to $100,000	$100,001 to $500,000	$500,001 to $1 million	$1,000,001 to $10 million	$10,000,001 to $50 million	$50,000,001 to $100 million	More than $100 million	
☐	☐	☐	☐	☐	☐	☐	☐	

Estimated Debts								
$0 to $50,000	$50,001 to $100,000	$100,001 to $500,000	$500,001 to $1 million	$1,000,001 to $10 million	$10,000,001 to $50 million	$50,000,001 to $100 million	More than $100 million	
☐	☐	☐	☐	☐	☐	☐	☐	

Voluntary Petition (This page must be completed and filed in every case)	Name of Debtor(s):

Prior Bankruptcy Case Filed Within Last 6 Years (If more than one, attach additional sheet)

Location Where Filed:	Case Number:	Date Filed:

Pending Bankruptcy Case Filed by any Spouse, Partner or Affiliate of this Debtor (If more than one, attach additional sheet)

Name of Debtor:	Case Number:	Date Filed:
District:	Relationship:	Judge:

Signatures

Signature(s) of Debtor(s) (Individual/Joint)

I declare under penalty of perjury that the information provided in this petition is true and correct.
[If petitioner is an individual whose debts are primarily consumer debts and has chosen to file under chapter 7] I am aware that I may proceed under chapter 7, 11, 12 or 13 of title 11, United States Code, understand the relief available under each such chapter, and choose to proceed under chapter 7.
I request relief in accordance with the chapter of title 11, United States Code, specified in this petition.

X _____
Signature of Debtor

X _____
Signature of Joint Debtor

_____
Telephone Number (If not represented by attorney)

_____
Date

Signature of Attorney

X _____
Signature of Attorney for Debtor(s)

_____
Printed Name of Attorney for Debtor(s)

_____
Firm Name

_____
Address

_____
Telephone Number

_____
Date

Signature of Debtor (Corporation/Partnership)

I declare under penalty of perjury that the information provided in this petition is true and correct, and that I have been authorized to file this petition on behalf of the debtor.

The debtor requests relief in accordance with the chapter of title 11, United States Code, specified in this petition.

X _____
Signature of Authorized Individual

_____
Printed Name of Authorized Individual

_____
Title of Authorized Individual

_____
Date

Exhibit A

(To be completed if debtor is required to file periodic reports (e.g., forms 10K and 10Q) with the Securities and Exchange Commission pursuant to Section 13 or 15(d) of the Securities Exchange Act of 1934 and is requesting relief under chapter 11)

☐   Exhibit A is attached and made a part of this petition.

Exhibit B

(To be completed if debtor is an individual whose debts are primarily consumer debts)

I, the attorney for the petitioner named in the foregoing petition, declare that I have informed the petitioner that [he or she] may proceed under chapter 7, 11, 12, or 13 of title 11, United States Code, and have explained the relief available under each such chapter.

X _____
Signature of Attorney for Debtor(s)   Date

Exhibit C

Does the debtor own or have possession of any property that poses or is alleged to pose a threat of imminent and identifiable harm to public health or safety?

☐   Yes, and Exhibit C is attached and made a part of this petition.
☐   No

Signature of Non-Attorney Petition Preparer

I certify that I am a bankruptcy petition preparer as defined in 11 U.S.C. § 110, that I prepared this document for compensation, and that I have provided the debtor with a copy of this document.

_____
Printed Name of Bankruptcy Petition Preparer

_____
Social Security Number (Required by 11 U.S.C.§ 110(c).)

_____
Address

Names and Social Security numbers of all other individuals who prepared or assisted in preparing this document:

If more than one person prepared this document, attach additional sheets conforming to the appropriate official form for each person.

X _____
Signature of Bankruptcy Petition Preparer

_____
Date

A bankruptcy petition preparer's failure to comply with the provisions of title 11 and the Federal Rules of Bankruptcy Procedure may result in fines or imprisonment or both 11 U.S.C. §110; 18 U.S.C. §156.

Form B1, Exhibit C (9/01)

United States Bankruptcy Court
District of

In re _____

    Debtor(s)

                          Case No: _____
                          Chapter: _____

Exhibit C to Voluntary Petition

1. Identify and briefly describe all real and personal property owned by or in possession of the debtor that, to the best of the debtor's knowledge, poses or is alleged to pose a threat of imminent and identifiable harm to the public health or safety (attach additional sheets if necessary).

2. With respect to each parcel of real property or item of personal property identified in question 1, describe the nature and location of the dangerous condition, whether environmental or otherwise, that poses or is alleged to pose a threat of imminent and identifiable harm to public health or safety (attach additional sheets if necessary).

Official Form 3
(12/03)

United States Bankruptcy Court

_____ District Of _____

In re _____,   Case No. _____
                            Debtor

Chapter _____

APPLICATION TO PAY FILING FEE IN INSTALLMENTS

1.   In accordance with Fed. R. Bankr. P. 1006, I apply for permission to pay the Filing Fee amounting to $_____ in installments.

2.   I certify that I am unable to pay the Filing Fee except in installments.

3.   I further certify that I have not paid any money or transferred any property to an attorney for services in connection with this case and that I will neither make any payment nor transfer any property for services in connection with this case until the filing fee is paid in full.

4.   I propose the following terms for the payment of the Filing Fee.*

$ _____   Check one ☐   With the filing of the petition, or
                                  ☐   On or before _____

$ _____   on or before _____

$ _____   on or before _____

$ _____   on or before _____

*   The number of installments proposed shall not exceed four (4), and the final installment shall be payable not later than 120 days after filing the petition. For cause shown, the court may extend the time of any installment, provided the last installment is paid not later than 180 days after filing the petition. Fed. R. Bankr. P. 1006(b)(2).

5.   I understand that if I fail to pay any installment when due my bankruptcy case may be dismissed and I may not receive a discharge of my debts.

_____   _____
Signature of Attorney   Date   Signature of Debtor   Date
                                             (In a joint case, both spouses must sign.)

_____   _____
Name of Attorney   Signature of Joint Debtor (if any)   Date

CERTIFICATION AND SIGNATURE OF NON-ATTORNEY BANKRUPTCY PETITION PREPARER (See 11 U.S.C. § 110)

   I certify that I am a bankruptcy petition preparer as defined in 11 U.S.C. § 110, that I prepared this document for compensation, and that I have provided the debtor with a copy of this document. I also certify that I will not accept money or any other property from the debtor before the filing fee is paid in full.

_____   _____
Printed or Typed Name of Bankruptcy Petition Preparer   Social Security No.
                                                            (Required by 11 U.S.C. § 110(c).)

_____

_____
Address

Names and Social Security numbers of all other individuals who prepared or assisted in preparing this document:

If more than one person prepared this document, attach additional signed sheets conforming to the appropriate Official Form for each person.

x_____   _____
Signature of Bankruptcy Petition Preparer   Date

A bankruptcy petition preparer's failure to comply with the provisions of title 11 and the Federal Rules of Bankruptcy Procedure may result in fines or imprisonment or both. 11 U.S.C. § 110; 18 U.S.C. § 156.

Official Form 3 continued
(9/97)

United States Bankruptcy Court
_____ District Of _____

In re _____,
              Debtor

Case No. _____

Chapter _____

ORDER APPROVING PAYMENT OF FILING FEE IN INSTALLMENTS

IT IS ORDERED that the debtor(s) may pay the filing fee in installments on the terms proposed in the foregoing application.

IT IS FURTHER ORDERED that until the filing fee is paid in full the debtor shall not pay any money for services in connection with this case, and the debtor shall not relinquish any property as payment for services in connection with this case.

BY THE COURT

Date: _____

_____
United States Bankruptcy Judge

UNITED STATES BANKRUPTCY COURT

_____ District of _____

In re _____,   Case No. _____

         Debtor   (If known)

SUMMARY OF SCHEDULES

Indicate as to each schedule whether that schedule is attached and state the number of pages in each. Report the totals from Schedules A, B, D, E, F, I, and J in the boxes provided. Add the amounts from Schedules A and B to determine the total amount of the debtor's assets. Add the amounts from Schedules D, E, and F to determine the total amount of the debtor's liabilities.

NAME OF SCHEDULE	ATTACHED (YES/NO)	NO. OF SHEETS	AMOUNTS SCHEDULED		
			ASSETS	LIABILITIES	OTHER
A - Real Property			$		
B - Personal Property			$		
C - Property Claimed as Exempt					
D - Creditors Holding Secured Claims				$	
E - Creditors Holding Unsecured Priority Claims				$	
F - Creditors Holding Unsecured Nonpriority Claims				$	
G - Executory Contracts and Unexpired Leases					
H - Codebtors					
I - Current Income of Individual Debtor(s)					$
J - Current Expenditures of Individual Debtor(s)					$
Total Number of Sheets of ALL Schedules					
Total Assets			$		
Total Liabilities				$	

In re _____ ,   Case No. _____
                    Debtor   (If known)

SCHEDULE A -- REAL PROPERTY

Except as directed below, list all real property in which the debtor has any legal, equitable, or future interest, including all property owned as a co-tenant, community property, or in which the debtor has a life estate. Include any property in which the debtor holds rights and powers exercisable for the debtor's own benefit. If the debtor is married, state whether husband, wife, or both own the property by placing an "H," "W," "J," or "C" in the column labeled "Husband, Wife, Joint, or Community." If the debtor holds no interest in real property, write "None" under "Description and Location of Property."
    Do not include interests in executory contracts and unexpired leases on this schedule. List them in Schedule G -- Executory Contracts and Unexpired Leases.
    If an entity claims to have a lien or hold a secured interest in any property, state the amount of the secured claim. See Schedule D. If no entity claims to hold a secured interest in the property, write "None" in the column labeled "Amount of Secured Claim."
    If the debtor is an individual or if a joint petition if filed, state the amount of any exemption claimed in the property only in Schedule C -- Property Claimed as Exempt.

DESCRIPTION AND LOCATION OF PROPERTY	NATURE OF DEBTOR'S INTEREST IN PROPERTY	H, W, J, or C	CURRENT MARKET VALUE OF DEBTOR'S INTEREST IN PROPERTY, WITHOUT DEDUCTING ANY SECURED CLAIM OR EXEMPTION	AMOUNT OF SECURED CLAIM
		Total	$	

(Report also on Summary of Schedules.)

SCHEDULE B -- PERSONAL PROPERTY

Except as directed below, list all personal property of the debtor of whatever kind. If the debtor has no property in one or more of the categories, place an "x" in the appropriate position in the column labeled "None." If additional space is needed in any category, attach a separate sheet properly identified with the case name, case number, and the number of the category. If the debtor is married, state whether husband, wife, or both own the property by placing an "H," "W," "J," or "C" in the column labeled "Husband, Wife, Joint, or Community." If the debtor is an individual or a joint petition is filed, state the amount of any exemptions claimed only in Schedule C -- Property Claimed as Exempt.
    Do not list interests in executory contracts and unexpired leases on this schedule. List them in Schedule G -- Executory Contracts and Unexpired Leases.
    If the property is being held for the debtor by someone else, state that person's name and address under "Description and Location of Property."

TYPE OF PROPERTY	N O N E	DESCRIPTION AND LOCATION OF PROPERTY	H, W, J, or C	CURRENT MARKET VALUE OF DEBTOR'S INTEREST IN PROPERTY, WITHOUT DEDUCTING ANY SECURED CLAIM OR EXEMPTION
1. Cash on hand.				
2. Checking, savings or other financial accounts, certificates of deposit, or shares in banks, savings and loan, thrift, building and loan, and homestead associations, or credit unions, brokerage houses, or cooperatives.				
3. Security deposits with public utilities, telephone companies, landlords, and others.				

In re _____,   Case No. _____
                  Debtor   (If known)

SCHEDULE B -- PERSONAL PROPERTY
(Continuation Sheet)

TYPE OF PROPERTY	N O N E	DESCRIPTION AND LOCATION OF PROPERTY	H, W, J, or C	CURRENT MARKET VALUE OF DEBTOR'S INTEREST IN PROPERTY, WITHOUT DEDUCTING ANY SECURED CLAIM OR EXEMPTION
4. Household goods and furnishings, including audio, video, and computer equipment.				
5. Books; pictures and other art objects; antiques; stamp, coin, record, tape, compact disc, and other collections or collectibles.				
6. Wearing apparel.				
7. Furs and jewelry.				
8. Firearms and sports, photographic, and other hobby equipment.				
9. Interests in insurance policies. Name insurance company of each policy and itemize surrender or refund value of each.				
10. Annuities. Itemize and name each issuer.				
11. Interests in IRA, ERISA, Keogh, or other pension or profit sharing plans. Itemize.				
12. Stock and interests in incorporated and unincorporated businesses. Itemize.				
13. Interests in partnerships or joint ventures. Itemize.				
14. Government and corporate bonds and other negotiable and non-negotiable instruments.				
15. Accounts receivable.				
16. Alimony, maintenance, support, and property settlements to which the debtor is or may be entitled. Give particulars.				
17. Other liquidated debts owing debtor including tax refunds. Give particulars.				
18. Equitable or future interests, life estates, and rights or powers exercisable for the benefit of the debtor other than those listed in Schedule of Real Property.				
19. Contingent and noncontingent interests in estate of a decedent, death benefit plan, life insurance policy, or trust.				
20. Other contingent and unliquidated claims of every nature, including tax refunds, counterclaims of the debtor, and rights to setoff claims. Give estimated value of each.				
21. Patents, copyrights, and other intellectual property. Give particulars.				
22. Licenses, franchises, and other general intangibles. Give particulars.				
23. Automobiles, trucks, trailers, and other vehicles and accessories.				
24. Boats, motors, and accessories.				
25. Aircraft and accessories.				

In re _____,   Case No. _____
                    Debtor   (If known)

SCHEDULE B -- PERSONAL PROPERTY
(Continuation Sheet)

TYPE OF PROPERTY	N O N E	DESCRIPTION AND LOCATION OF PROPERTY	H, W, J, or C	CURRENT MARKET VALUE OF DEBTOR'S INTEREST IN PROPERTY, WITHOUT DEDUCTING ANY SECURED CLAIM OR EXEMPTION
26. Office equipment, furnishings, and supplies.				
27. Machinery, fixtures, equipment, and supplies used in business.				
28. Inventory.				
29. Animals.				
30. Crops -- growing or harvested. Give particulars.				
31. Farming equipment and implements.				
32. Farm supplies, chemicals, and feed.				
33. Other personal property of any kind not already listed. Itemize.				

_____ Continuation sheets attached   TOTAL $ _____

(Include amounts from any continuation sheets attached. Report total also on Summary of Schedules.)

SCHEDULE C -- PROPERTY CLAIMED AS EXEMPT

Debtor elects the exemption to which debtor is entitled under:
(Check one)

_____ 11 U.S.C. § 522(b)(1):   Exemptions provided in 11 U.S.C. § 522(d). **Note: These exemptions are available only in certain states.**

_____ 11 U.S.C. § 522(b)(2):   Exemptions available under applicable nonbankruptcy federal laws, state or local law where the debtor's domicile has been located for the 180 days immediately preceding the filing of the petition, or for a longer portion of the 180-day period than in any other place, and the debtor's interest as a tenant by the entirety or joint tenant to the extent the interest is exempt from process under applicable nonbankruptcy law.

DESCRIPTION OF PROPERTY	SPECIFY LAW PROVIDING EACH EXEMPTION	VALUE OF CLAIMED EXEMPTION	CURRENT MARKET VALUE OF PROPERTY WITHOUT DEDUCTING EXEMPTION
	Total	$	

In re _____,   Case No. _____
                  Debtor   (If known)

SCHEDULE D -- CREDITORS HOLDING SECURED CLAIMS

State the name, mailing address, including zip code, and last four digits of any account number, if any, of all entities holding claims secured by property of the debtor as of the date of filing of the petition. The complete account number of any account the debtor has with the creditor is useful to the trustee and the creditor and may be provided if the debtor chooses to do so. List creditors holding all types of secured interests such as judgment liens, garnishments, statutory liens, mortgages, deeds of trust, and other security interests. List creditors in alphabetical order to the extent practicable. If all secured creditors will not fit on this page, use the continuation sheet provided.

If any entity other than a spouse in a joint case may be jointly liable on a claim, place an "X" in the column labeled "Codebtor," include the entity on the appropriate schedule of creditors, and complete Schedule H -- Codebtors. If a joint petition if filed, state whether husband, wife, both of them, or the marital community may be liable on each claim by placing an "H," "W," "J," or "C" in the column labeled "Husband, Wife, Joint, or Community."

If the claim is contingent, place an "X" in the column labeled "Contingent." If the claim is unliquidated, place an "X" in the column labeled "Unliquidated." If the claim is disputed, place an "X" in the column labeled "Disputed." (You may need to place an "X" in more than one of these three columns.)

Report the total of all claims listed on this schedule in the box labeled "Total" on the last sheet of the completed schedule. Report this total also on the Summary of Schedules.

___ Check here if debtor has no creditors holding secured claims to report on this Schedule D.

CREDITOR'S NAME, MAILING ADDRESS INCLUDING ZIP CODE, AND ACCOUNT NUMBER (See instructions above.)	C O D E B T O R	H, W, J, or C	DATE CLAIM WAS INCURRED, NATURE OF LIEN, AND DESCRIPTION AND MARKET VALUE OF PROPERTY SUBJECT TO LIEN	C O N T I N G E N T	U N L I Q.	D I S P U T E D	AMOUNT OF CLAIM WITHOUT DEDUCTING VALUE OF COLLATERAL	UNSECURED PORTION, IF ANY
ACCOUNT NO.								
			VALUE $					
ACCOUNT NO.								
			VALUE $					
ACCOUNT NO.								
			VALUE $					

____ continuation sheets attached

	Subtotal (Total of this page)	$
	Total (Use only on last page)	$

(Report total also on Summary of Schedules)

Form B6E
(04/04)

In re _____,   Case No._____
                          Debtor   (if known)

SCHEDULE E - CREDITORS HOLDING UNSECURED PRIORITY CLAIMS

A complete list of claims entitled to priority, listed separately by type of priority, is to be set forth on the sheets provided. Only holders of unsecured claims entitled to priority should be listed in this schedule. In the boxes provided on the attached sheets, state the name, mailing address, including zip code, and last four digits of the account number, if any, of all entities holding priority claims against the debtor or the property of the debtor, as of the date of the filing of the petition. The complete account number of any account the debtor has with the creditor is useful to the trustee and the creditor and may be provided if the debtor chooses to do so.

If any entity other than a spouse in a joint case may be jointly liable on a claim, place an "X" in the column labeled "Codebtor," include the entity on the appropriate schedule of creditors, and complete Schedule H-Codebtors. If a joint petition is filed, state whether husband, wife, both of them or the marital community may be liable on each claim by placing an "H,""W,""J," or "C" in the column labeled "Husband, Wife, Joint, or Community."

If the claim is contingent, place an "X" in the column labeled "Contingent." If the claim is unliquidated, place an "X" in the column labeled "Unliquidated." If the claim is disputed, place an "X" in the column labeled "Disputed." (You may need to place an "X" in more than one of these three columns.)

Report the total of claims listed on each sheet in the box labeled "Subtotal" on each sheet. Report the total of all claims listed on this Schedule E in the box labeled "Total" on the last sheet of the completed schedule. Repeat this total also on the Summary of Schedules.

☐ Check this box if debtor has no creditors holding unsecured priority claims to report on this Schedule E.

TYPES OF PRIORITY CLAIMS (Check the appropriate box(es) below if claims in that category are listed on the attached sheets)

☐ **Extensions of credit in an involuntary case**

Claims arising in the ordinary course of the debtor's business or financial affairs after the commencement of the case but before the earlier of the appointment of a trustee or the order for relief. 11 U.S.C. § 507(a)(2).

☐ **Wages, salaries, and commissions**

Wages, salaries, and commissions, including vacation, severance, and sick leave pay owing to employees and commissions owing to qualifying independent sales representatives up to $4,925* per person earned within 90 days immediately preceding the filing of the original petition, or the cessation of business, whichever occurred first, to the extent provided in 11 U.S.C. § 507(a)(3).

☐ **Contributions to employee benefit plans**

Money owed to employee benefit plans for services rendered within 180 days immediately preceding the filing of the original petition, or the cessation of business, whichever occurred first, to the extent provided in 11 U.S.C. § 507(a)(4).

☐ **Certain farmers and fishermen**

Claims of certain farmers and fishermen, up to $4,925* per farmer or fisherman, against the debtor, as provided in 11 U.S.C. § 507(a)(5).

☐ **Deposits by individuals**

Claims of individuals up to $2,225* for deposits for the purchase, lease, or rental of property or services for personal, family, or household use, that were not delivered or provided. 11 U.S.C. § 507(a)(6).

Form B6E
(04/04)

In re _____ ,   Case No._____
                Debtor   (if known)

☐ **Alimony, Maintenance, or Support**

   Claims of a spouse, former spouse, or child of the debtor for alimony, maintenance, or support, to the extent provided in 11 U.S.C. § 507(a)(7).

☐ **Taxes and Certain Other Debts Owed to Governmental Units**

   Taxes, customs duties, and penalties owing to federal, state, and local governmental units as set forth in 11 U.S.C. § 507(a)(8).

☐ **Commitments to Maintain the Capital of an Insured Depository Institution**

   Claims based on commitments to the FDIC, RTC, Director of the Office of Thrift Supervision, Comptroller of the Currency, or Board of Governors of the Federal Reserve System, or their predecessors or successors, to maintain the capital of an insured depository institution. 11 U.S.C. § 507 (a)(9).

* Amounts are subject to adjustment on April 1, 2007, and every three years thereafter with respect to cases commenced on or after the date of adjustment.

_____ continuation sheets attached

Form B6E - Cont.
(04/04)

In re _____,   Case No. _____
          Debtor   **(If known)**

SCHEDULE E - CREDITORS HOLDING UNSECURED PRIORITY CLAIMS
(Continuation Sheet)

TYPE OF PRIORITY _____

CREDITOR'S NAME, MAILING ADDRESS INCLUDING ZIP CODE, AND ACCOUNT NUMBER (See instructions.)	CODEBTOR	HUSBAND, WIFE, JOINT, OR COMMUNITY	DATE CLAIM WAS INCURRED AND CONSIDERATION FOR CLAIM	CONTINGENT	UNLIQUIDATED	DISPUTED	AMOUNT OF CLAIM	AMOUNT ENTITLED TO PRIORITY
ACCOUNT NO.								
ACCOUNT NO.								
ACCOUNT NO.								
ACCOUNT NO.								
ACCOUNT NO.								

Sheet no. ___ of ___ sheets attached to Schedule of Creditors
Holding Priority Claims

Subtotal ➤ $ _____
(Total of this page)
Total ➤ $ _____
(Use only on last page of the completed Schedule E.)
(Report total also on Summary of Schedules)

757

Form B6F (12/03)

In re _____, **Case No.** _____

                         Debtor   **(If known)**

SCHEDULE F- CREDITORS HOLDING UNSECURED NONPRIORITY CLAIMS

State the name, mailing address, including zip code, and last four digits of any account number, of all entities holding unsecured claims without priority against the debtor or the property of the debtor, as of the date of filing of the petition. The complete account number of any account the debtor has with the creditor is useful to the trustee and the creditor and may be provided if the debtor chooses to do so. Do not include claims listed in Schedules D and E. If all creditors will not fit on this page, use the continuation sheet provided.

If any entity other than a spouse in a joint case may be jointly liable on a claim, place an "X" in the column labeled "Codebtor," include the entity on the appropriate schedule of creditors, and complete Schedule H - Codebtors. If a joint petition is filed, state whether husband, wife, both of them, or the marital community maybe liable on each claim by placing an "H," "W," "J," or "C" in the column labeled "Husband, Wife, Joint, or Community."

If the claim is contingent, place an "X" in the column labeled "Contingent." If the claim is unliquidated, place an "X" in the column labeled "Unliquidated." If the claim is disputed, place an "X" in the column labeled "Disputed." (You may need to place an "X" in more than one of these three columns.)

Report total of all claims listed on this schedule in the box labeled "Total" on the last sheet of the completed schedule. Report this total also on the Summary of Schedules.

☐ Check this box if debtor has no creditors holding unsecured claims to report on this Schedule F.

CREDITOR'S NAME, MAILING ADDRESS INCLUDING ZIP CODE, AND ACCOUNT NUMBER (See instructions, above.)	CODEBTOR	HUSBAND, WIFE, JOINT, OR COMMUNITY	DATE CLAIM WAS INCURRED AND CONSIDERATION FOR CLAIM. IF CLAIM IS SUBJECT TO SETOFF, SO STATE.	CONTINGENT	UNLIQUIDATED	DISPUTED	AMOUNT OF CLAIM
ACCOUNT NO.							
ACCOUNT NO.							
ACCOUNT NO.							
ACCOUNT NO.							

_____continuation sheets attached

                                              Subtotal ➤ $_____

                                                 Total ➤ $_____

(Report also on Summary of Schedules)

Form B6F - Cont.
(12/03)

In re _____,   **Case No.** _____

            Debtor   **(If known)**

SCHEDULE F - CREDITORS HOLDING UNSECURED NONPRIORITY CLAIMS
(Continuation Sheet)

CREDITOR'S NAME, MAILING ADDRESS INCLUDING ZIP CODE, AND ACCOUNT NUMBER	CODEBTOR	HUSBAND, WIFE, JOINT, OR COMMUNITY	DATE CLAIM WAS INCURRED AND CONSIDERATION FOR CLAIM. IF CLAIM IS SUBJECT TO SETOFF, SO STATE.	CONTINGENT	UNLIQUIDATED	DISPUTED	AMOUNT OF CLAIM
ACCOUNT NO.							
ACCOUNT NO.							
ACCOUNT NO.							
ACCOUNT NO							
ACCOUNT NO.							

Sheet no. ___ of ___ sheets attached to Schedule of   Subtotal ➤ $
Creditors Holding Unsecured Nonpriority Claims   (Total of this page)
                                                              Total ➤ $
(Use only on last page of the completed Schedule F.)
(Report total also on Summary of Schedules)

759

In re _____,   Case No. _____
                          Debtor   (If known)

SCHEDULE G -- EXECUTORY CONTRACTS AND UNEXPIRED LEASES

Describe all executory contracts of any nature and all unexpired leases of real or personal property. Include any timeshare interests.
State nature of debtor's interest in contract, i.e., "Purchaser," Agent," etc. State whether debtor is the lessor or lessee of a lease.
Provide the names and complete mailing addresses of all other parties to each lease or contract described.
NOTE: A party listed on this schedule will not receive notice of the filing of this case unless the party is also scheduled in the appropriate schedule of creditors.

___ Check here if debtor has no executory contracts or unexpired leases.

NAME AND MAILING ADDRESS, INCLUDING ZIP CODE, OF OTHER PARTIES TO LEASE OR CONTRACT.	DESCRIPTION OF CONTRACT OR LEASE AND NATURE OF DEBTOR'S INTEREST. STATE WHETHER LEASE IS FOR NONRESIDENTIAL REAL PROPERTY. STATE CONTRACT NUMBER OF ANY GOVERNMENT CONTRACT.

SCHEDULE H -- CODEBTORS

Provide the information requested concerning any person or entity, other than a spouse in a joint case, that is also liable on any debts listed by debtor in the schedules of creditors. Include all guarantors and co-signers. In community property states, a married debtor not filing a joint case should report the name and address of the nondebtor spouse on this schedule. Include all names used by the nondebtor spouse during the six years immediately preceding the commencement of this case.

___ Check here if debtor has no codebtors.

NAME AND ADDRESS OF CODEBTOR	NAME AND ADDRESS OF CREDITOR

In re _____ ,　　　Case No. _____
　　　　　　　　　　Debtor　　　　　　　　　　　　　　　　　　　　　　　(If known)

SCHEDULE I -- CURRENT INCOME OF INDIVIDUAL DEBTOR(S)

The column labeled "Spouse" must be completed in all cases filed by joint debtors and by a married debtor in a chapter 12 or 13 case whether or not a joint petition is filed, unless the spouses are separated and a joint petition is not filed.

Debtor's Marital Status:	DEPENDENTS OF DEBTOR AND SPOUSE	
	RELATIONSHIP	AGE

Employment:	DEBTOR	SPOUSE
Occupation:		
Name of Employer:		
How long employed:		
Address of Employer:		

Income: (Estimate of average monthly income)	DEBTOR	SPOUSE
Current monthly gross wages, salary, and commissions (pro rate if not paid monthly.)	$_____	$_____
Estimated monthly overtime	$_____	$_____
SUBTOTAL	$_____	$_____
LESS PAYROLL DEDUCTIONS		
a. Payroll taxes and social security	$_____	$_____
b. Insurance	$_____	$_____
c. Union dues	$_____	$_____
d. Other (Specify: _____)	$_____	$_____
SUBTOTAL OF PAYROLL DEDUCTIONS	$_____	$_____
TOTAL NET MONTHLY TAKE HOME PAY	$_____	$_____
Regular income from operation of business or profession or farm (attach detailed statement)	$_____	$_____
Income from real property	$_____	$_____
Interest and dividends	$_____	$_____
Alimony, maintenance or support payments payable to the debtor for the debtor's use or that of dependents listed above.	$_____	$_____
Social security or other government assistance (Specify) _____	$_____	$_____
Pension or retirement income	$_____	$_____
Other monthly income (Specify) _____	$_____	$_____
_____	$_____	$_____
TOTAL MONTHLY INCOME	$_____	$_____

TOTAL COMBINED MONTHLY INCOME　$_____　(Report also on Summary of Schedules)

Describe any increase or decrease of more than 10% in any of the above categories anticipated to occur within the year following the filing of this document:

In re _____,   Case No. _____

Debtor   (If known)

SCHEDULE J -- CURRENT EXPENDITURES OF INDIVIDUAL DEBTOR(S)

Complete this schedule by estimating the average monthly expenses of the debtor and the debtor's family. Pro rate any payments made bi-weekly, quarterly, semi-annually, or annually to show monthly rate.

___ Check here if a joint petition is filed and debtor's spouse maintains a separate household. Complete a separate schedule of expenditures labeled "Spouse."

Rent or home mortgage payment (include lot rented for mobile home)		$ _____
Are real estate taxes included?	Yes _____ No _____	
Is property insurance included?	Yes _____ No _____	
Utilities Electricity and heating fuel		$ _____
Water and sewer		$ _____
Telephone		$ _____
Other _____		$ _____
Home maintenance (repairs and upkeep)		$ _____
Food		$ _____
Clothing		$ _____
Laundry and dry cleaning		$ _____
Medical and dental expenses		$ _____
Transportation (not including car payments)		$ _____
Recreation, clubs and entertainment, newspapers, magazines, etc.		$ _____
Charitable contributions		$ _____
Insurance (not deducted from wages or included in home mortgage payments)		
Homeowner's or renter's		$ _____
Life		$ _____
Health		$ _____
Auto		$ _____
Other _____		$ _____
Taxes (not deducted from wages or included in home mortgage payments)		
(Specify) _____		$ _____
Installment payments: (In chapter 12 and 13 cases, do not list payments to be included in the plan)		
Auto		$ _____
Other _____		$ _____
Other _____		$ _____
Alimony, maintenance, and support paid to others		$ _____
Payments for support of additional dependents not living at your home		$ _____
Regular expenses from operation of business, profession, or farm (attach detailed statement)		$ _____
Other _____		$ _____

TOTAL MONTHLY EXPENSES (Report also on Summary of Schedules) $ _____

(FOR CHAPTER 12 AND 13 DEBTORS ONLY)

Provide the information requested below, including whether plan payments are to be made bi-weekly, monthly, annually, or at some other regular interval.

A. Total projected monthly income	$ _____
B. Total projected monthly expenses	$ _____
C. Excess income (A minus B)	$ _____
D. Total amount to be paid into plan each _____	$ _____
(interval)	

In re _____,   Case No. _____

               Debtor   (If known)

DECLARATION CONCERNING DEBTOR'S SCHEDULES

DECLARATION UNDER PENALTY OF PERJURY BY INDIVIDUAL DEBTOR

      I declare under penalty of perjury that I have read the foregoing summary and schedules, consisting of _____ sheets, (total shown on summary page plus 1), and that they are true and correct to the best of my knowledge, information, and belief.

Date _____   Signature: _____

                                                      Debtor

Date _____   Signature: _____

                                                 (Joint Debtor, if any)

                      [If joint case, both spouses must sign]

CERTIFICATION AND SIGNATURE OF NON-ATTORNEY BANKRUPTCY PETITION PREPARER
(See 11 U.S.C. § 110)

      I certify that I am a bankruptcy petition preparer as defined in 11 U.S.C. § 110, that I prepared this document for compensation, and that I have provided the debtor with a copy of this document.

_____   _____

Printed or Typed Name of Bankruptcy Petition Preparer   Social Security No.
                                                             (Required by 11 U.S.C. § 110(c).)

_____

_____

Address

Names and Social Security numbers of all other invididuals who prepared or assisted in preparing this document:

If more than one person prepared this document, attach additional sheets conforming to the appropriate Official Form for each person.

X_____   _____

  Signature of Bankruptcy Petition Preparer   Date

A bankruptcy petition preparer's failure to comply with the provisions of title 11 and the Federal Rules of Bankruptcy Procedure may result in fines or imprisonment or both. 11 U.S.C. § 110; 18 U.S.C. § 156.

Form 7
(12/03)

FORM 7. STATEMENT OF FINANCIAL AFFAIRS

UNITED STATES BANKRUPTCY COURT

_____ DISTRICT OF _____

In re: _____,   Case No. _____
                    (Name)   (if known)
                              Debtor

STATEMENT OF FINANCIAL AFFAIRS

This statement is to be completed by every debtor. Spouses filing a joint petition may file a single statement on which the information for both spouses is combined. If the case is filed under chapter 12 or chapter 13, a married debtor must furnish information for both spouses whether or not a joint petition is filed, unless the spouses are separated and a joint petition is not filed. An individual debtor engaged in business as a sole proprietor, partner, family farmer, or self-employed professional, should provide the information requested on this statement concerning all such activities as well as the individual's personal affairs.

Questions 1 - 18 are to be completed by all debtors. Debtors that are or have been in business, as defined below, also must complete Questions 19 - 25. **If the answer to an applicable question is "None," mark the box labeled "None."** If additional space is needed for the answer to any question, use and attach a separate sheet properly identified with the case name, case number (if known), and the number of the question.

DEFINITIONS

"In business." A debtor is "in business" for the purpose of this form if the debtor is a corporation or partnership. An individual debtor is "in business" for the purpose of this form if the debtor is or has been, within the six years immediately preceding the filing of this bankruptcy case, any of the following: an officer, director, managing executive, or owner of 5 percent or more of the voting or equity securities of a corporation; a partner, other than a limited partner, of a partnership; a sole proprietor or self-employed.

"Insider." The term "insider" includes but is not limited to: relatives of the debtor; general partners of the debtor and their relatives; corporations of which the debtor is an officer, director, or person in control; officers, directors, and any owner of 5 percent or more of the voting or equity securities of a corporate debtor and their relatives; affiliates of the debtor and insiders of such affiliates; any managing agent of the debtor. 11 U.S.C. § 101.

_____

1.   Income from employment or operation of business

None
☐

State the gross amount of income the debtor has received from employment, trade, or profession, or from operation of the debtor's business from the beginning of this calendar year to the date this case was commenced. State also the gross amounts received during the **two years** immediately preceding this calendar year. (A debtor that maintains, or has maintained, financial records on the basis of a fiscal rather than a calendar year may report fiscal year income. Identify the beginning and ending dates of the debtor's fiscal year.) If a joint petition is filed, state income for each spouse separately. (Married debtors filing under chapter 12 or chapter 13 must state income of both spouses whether or not a joint petition is filed, unless the spouses are separated and a joint petition is not filed.)

AMOUNT   SOURCE (if more than one)

2. Income other than from employment or operation of business

None

☐

State the amount of income received by the debtor other than from employment, trade, profession, or operation of the debtor's business during the **two years** immediately preceding the commencement of this case. Give particulars. If a joint petition is filed, state income for each spouse separately. (Married debtors filing under chapter 12 or chapter 13 must state income for each spouse whether or not a joint petition is filed, unless the spouses are separated and a joint petition is not filed.)

AMOUNT   SOURCE

---

3. Payments to creditors

None

☐

a. List all payments on loans, installment purchases of goods or services, and other debts, aggregating more than $600 to any creditor, made within **90 days** immediately preceding the commencement of this case. (Married debtors filing under chapter 12 or chapter 13 must include payments by either or both spouses whether or not a joint petition is filed, unless the spouses are separated and a joint petition is not filed.)

NAME AND ADDRESS OF CREDITOR	DATES OF PAYMENTS	AMOUNT PAID	AMOUNT STILL OWING

None

☐

b. List all payments made within **one year** immediately preceding the commencement of this case to or for the benefit of creditors who are or were insiders. (Married debtors filing under chapter 12 or chapter 13 must include payments by either or both spouses whether or not a joint petition is filed, unless the spouses are separated and a joint petition is not filed.)

NAME AND ADDRESS OF CREDITOR AND RELATIONSHIP TO DEBTOR	DATE OF PAYMENT	AMOUNT PAID	AMOUNT STILL OWING

---

4. Suits and administrative proceedings, executions, garnishments and attachments

None

☐

a. List all suits and administrative proceedings to which the debtor is or was a party within **one year** immediately preceding the filing of this bankruptcy case. (Married debtors filing under chapter 12 or chapter 13 must include information concerning either or both spouses whether or not a joint petition is filed, unless the spouses are separated and a joint petition is not filed.)

CAPTION OF SUIT AND CASE NUMBER	NATURE OF PROCEEDING	COURT OR AGENCY AND LOCATION	STATUS OR DISPOSITION

None
☐

b. Describe all property that has been attached, garnished or seized under any legal or equitable process within **one year** immediately preceding the commencement of this case. (Married debtors filing under chapter 12 or chapter 13 must include information concerning property of either or both spouses whether or not a joint petition is filed, unless the spouses are separated and a joint petition is not filed.)

NAME AND ADDRESS OF PERSON FOR WHOSE BENEFIT PROPERTY WAS SEIZED	DATE OF SEIZURE	DESCRIPTION AND VALUE OF PROPERTY

---

5. Repossessions, foreclosures and returns

None
☐

List all property that has been repossessed by a creditor, sold at a foreclosure sale, transferred through a deed in lieu of foreclosure or returned to the seller, within **one year** immediately preceding the commencement of this case. (Married debtors filing under chapter 12 or chapter 13 must include information concerning property of either or both spouses whether or not a joint petition is filed, unless the spouses are separated and a joint petition is not filed.)

NAME AND ADDRESS OF CREDITOR OR SELLER	DATE OF REPOSSESSION, FORECLOSURE SALE, TRANSFER OR RETURN	DESCRIPTION AND VALUE OF PROPERTY

---

6. Assignments and receiverships

None
☐

a. Describe any assignment of property for the benefit of creditors made within **120 days** immediately preceding the commencement of this case. (Married debtors filing under chapter 12 or chapter 13 must include any assignment by either or both spouses whether or not a joint petition is filed, unless the spouses are separated and a joint petition is not filed.)

NAME AND ADDRESS OF ASSIGNEE	DATE OF ASSIGNMENT	TERMS OF ASSIGNMENT OR SETTLEMENT

None
☐

b. List all property which has been in the hands of a custodian, receiver, or court-appointed official within **one year** immediately preceding the commencement of this case. (Married debtors filing under chapter 12 or chapter 13 must include information concerning property of either or both spouses whether or not a joint petition is filed, unless the spouses are separated and a joint petition is not filed.)

NAME AND ADDRESS OF CUSTODIAN	NAME AND LOCATION OF COURT CASE TITLE & NUMBER	DATE OF ORDER	DESCRIPTION AND VALUE OF PROPERTY

7. Gifts

None ☐

List all gifts or charitable contributions made within **one year** immediately preceding the commencement of this case except ordinary and usual gifts to family members aggregating less than $200 in value per individual family member and charitable contributions aggregating less than $100 per recipient. (Married debtors filing under chapter 12 or chapter 13 must include gifts or contributions by either or both spouses whether or not a joint petition is filed, unless the spouses are separated and a joint petition is not filed.)

NAME AND ADDRESS OF PERSON OR ORGANIZATION	RELATIONSHIP TO DEBTOR, IF ANY	DATE OF GIFT	DESCRIPTION AND VALUE OF GIFT

8. Losses

None ☐

List all losses from fire, theft, other casualty or gambling within **one year** immediately preceding the commencement of this case **or since the commencement of this case**. (Married debtors filing under chapter 12 or chapter 13 must include losses by either or both spouses whether or not a joint petition is filed, unless the spouses are separated and a joint petition is not filed.)

DESCRIPTION AND VALUE OF PROPERTY	DESCRIPTION OF CIRCUMSTANCES AND, IF LOSS WAS COVERED IN WHOLE OR IN PART BY INSURANCE, GIVE PARTICULARS	DATE OF LOSS

9. Payments related to debt counseling or bankruptcy

None ☐

List all payments made or property transferred by or on behalf of the debtor to any persons, including attorneys, for consultation concerning debt consolidation, relief under the bankruptcy law or preparation of a petition in bankruptcy within **one year** immediately preceding the commencement of this case.

NAME AND ADDRESS OF PAYEE	DATE OF PAYMENT, NAME OF PAYOR IF OTHER THAN DEBTOR	AMOUNT OF MONEY OR DESCRIPTION AND VALUE OF PROPERTY

10. Other transfers

None ☐

List all other property, other than property transferred in the ordinary course of the business or financial affairs of the debtor, transferred either absolutely or as security within **one year** immediately preceding the commencement of this case. (Married debtors filing under chapter 12 or chapter 13 must include transfers by either or both spouses whether or not a joint petition is filed, unless the spouses are separated and a joint petition is not filed.)

NAME AND ADDRESS OF TRANSFEREE, RELATIONSHIP TO DEBTOR	DATE	DESCRIBE PROPERTY TRANSFERRED AND VALUE RECEIVED

11. Closed financial accounts

None ☐   List all financial accounts and instruments held in the name of the debtor or for the benefit of the debtor which were closed, sold, or otherwise transferred within **one year** immediately preceding the commencement of this case. Include checking, savings, or other financial accounts, certificates of deposit, or other instruments; shares and share accounts held in banks, credit unions, pension funds, cooperatives, associations, brokerage houses and other financial institutions. (Married debtors filing under chapter 12 or chapter 13 must include information concerning accounts or instruments held by or for either or both spouses whether or not a joint petition is filed, unless the spouses are separated and a joint petition is not filed.)

NAME AND ADDRESS OF INSTITUTION	TYPE OF ACCOUNT, LAST FOUR DIGITS OF ACCOUNT NUMBER, AND AMOUNT OF FINAL BALANCE	AMOUNT AND DATE OF SALE OR CLOSING

12. Safe deposit boxes

None ☐   List each safe deposit or other box or depository in which the debtor has or had securities, cash, or other valuables within **one year** immediately preceding the commencement of this case. (Married debtors filing under chapter 12 or chapter 13 must include boxes or depositories of either or both spouses whether or not a joint petition is filed, unless the spouses are separated and a joint petition is not filed.)

NAME AND ADDRESS OF BANK OR OTHER DEPOSITORY	NAMES AND ADDRESSES OF THOSE WITH ACCESS TO BOX OR DEPOSITORY	DESCRIPTION OF CONTENTS	DATE OF TRANSFER OR SURRENDER, IF ANY

13. Setoffs

None ☐   List all setoffs made by any creditor, including a bank, against a debt or deposit of the debtor within **90 days** preceding the commencement of this case. (Married debtors filing under chapter 12 or chapter 13 must include information concerning either or both spouses whether or not a joint petition is filed, unless the spouses are separated and a joint petition is not filed.)

NAME AND ADDRESS OF CREDITOR	DATE OF SETOFF	AMOUNT OF SETOFF

14. Property held for another person

None ☐   List all property owned by another person that the debtor holds or controls.

NAME AND ADDRESS OF OWNER	DESCRIPTION AND VALUE OF PROPERTY	LOCATION OF PROPERTY

15. Prior address of debtor

None ☐ If the debtor has moved within the **two years** immediately preceding the commencement of this case, list all premises which the debtor occupied during that period and vacated prior to the commencement of this case. If a joint petition is filed, report also any separate address of either spouse.

ADDRESS	NAME USED	DATES OF OCCUPANCY

---

16. Spouses and Former Spouses

None ☐ If the debtor resides or resided in a community property state, commonwealth, or territory (including Alaska, Arizona, California, Idaho, Louisiana, Nevada, New Mexico, Puerto Rico, Texas, Washington, or Wisconsin) within the **six-year period** immediately preceding the commencement of the case, identify the name of the debtor's spouse and of any former spouse who resides or resided with the debtor in the community property state.

NAME

---

17. Environmental Information.

For the purpose of this question, the following definitions apply:

"Environmental Law" means any federal, state, or local statute or regulation regulating pollution, contamination, releases of hazardous or toxic substances, wastes or material into the air, land, soil, surface water, groundwater, or other medium, including, but not limited to, statutes or regulations regulating the cleanup of these substances, wastes, or material.

"Site" means any location, facility, or property as defined under any Environmental Law, whether or not presently or formerly owned or operated by the debtor, including, but not limited to, disposal sites.

"Hazardous Material" means anything defined as a hazardous waste, hazardous substance, toxic substance, hazardous material, pollutant, or contaminant or similar term under an Environmental Law

---

None ☐ a. List the name and address of every site for which the debtor has received notice in writing by a governmental unit that it may be liable or potentially liable under or in violation of an Environmental Law. Indicate the governmental unit, the date of the notice, and, if known, the Environmental Law:

SITE NAME AND ADDRESS	NAME AND ADDRESS OF GOVERNMENTAL UNIT	DATE OF NOTICE	ENVIRONMENTAL LAW

None ☐ b. List the name and address of every site for which the debtor provided notice to a governmental unit of a release of Hazardous Material. Indicate the governmental unit to which the notice was sent and the date of the notice.

SITE NAME AND ADDRESS	NAME AND ADDRESS OF GOVERNMENTAL UNIT	DATE OF NOTICE	ENVIRONMENTAL LAW

None □ c. List all judicial or administrative proceedings, including settlements or orders, under any Environmental Law with respect to which the debtor is or was a party. Indicate the name and address of the governmental unit that is or was a party to the proceeding, and the docket number.

NAME AND ADDRESS OF GOVERNMENTAL UNIT	DOCKET NUMBER	STATUS OR DISPOSITION

18 . Nature, location and name of business

None □ a. If the debtor is an individual, list the names, addresses, taxpayer identification numbers, nature of the businesses, and beginning and ending dates of all businesses in which the debtor was an officer, director, partner, or managing executive of a corporation, partnership, sole proprietorship, or was a self-employed professional within the **six years** immediately preceding the commencement of this case, or in which the debtor owned 5 percent or more of the voting or equity securities within the **six years** immediately preceding the commencement of this case.

If the debtor is a partnership, list the names, addresses, taxpayer identification numbers, nature of the businesses, and beginning and ending dates of all businesses in which the debtor was a partner or owned 5 percent or more of the voting or equity securities, within the **six years** immediately preceding the commencement of this case.

If the debtor is a corporation, list the names, addresses, taxpayer identification numbers, nature of the businesses, and beginning and ending dates of all businesses in which the debtor was a partner or owned 5 percent or more of the voting or equity securities within the **six years** immediately preceding the commencement of this case.

NAME	TAXPAYER I.D. NO. (EIN)	ADDRESS	NATURE OF BUSINESS	BEGINNING AND ENDING DATES

None □ b. Identify any business listed in response to subdivision a., above, that is "single asset real estate" as defined in 11 U.S.C. § 101.

NAME	ADDRESS

The following questions are to be completed by every debtor that is a corporation or partnership and by any individual debtor who is or has been, within the **six years** immediately preceding the commencement of this case, any of the following: an officer, director, managing executive, or owner of more than 5 percent of the voting or equity securities of a corporation; a partner, other than a limited partner, of a partnership; a sole proprietor or otherwise self-employed.

*(An individual or joint debtor should complete this portion of the statement **only** if the debtor is or has been in business, as defined above, within the six years immediately preceding the commencement of this case. A debtor who has not been in business within those six years should go directly to the signature page.)*

19. Books, records and financial statements

None ☐   a.   List all bookkeepers and accountants who within the **two years** immediately preceding the filing of this bankruptcy case kept or supervised the keeping of books of account and records of the debtor.

NAME AND ADDRESS   DATES SERVICES RENDERED

None ☐   b.   List all firms or individuals who within the **two years** immediately preceding the filing of this bankruptcy case have audited the books of account and records, or prepared a financial statement of the debtor.

NAME   ADDRESS   DATES SERVICES RENDERED

None ☐   c.   List all firms or individuals who at the time of the commencement of this case were in possession of the books of account and records of the debtor. If any of the books of account and records are not available, explain.

NAME   ADDRESS

None ☐   d.   List all financial institutions, creditors and other parties, including mercantile and trade agencies, to whom a financial statement was issued within the **two years** immediately preceding the commencement of this case by the debtor.

NAME AND ADDRESS   DATE ISSUED

20. Inventories

None ☐   a.   List the dates of the last two inventories taken of your property, the name of the person who supervised the taking of each inventory, and the dollar amount and basis of each inventory.

                                           DOLLAR AMOUNT OF INVENTORY
DATE OF INVENTORY   INVENTORY SUPERVISOR   (Specify cost, market or other basis)

None ☐   b.   List the name and address of the person having possession of the records of each of the two inventories reported in a., above.

                                      NAME AND ADDRESSES OF CUSTODIAN
DATE OF INVENTORY   OF INVENTORY RECORDS

21 . Current Partners, Officers, Directors and Shareholders

None
☐

a. If the debtor is a partnership, list the nature and percentage of partnership interest of each member of the partnership.

NAME AND ADDRESS   NATURE OF INTEREST   PERCENTAGE OF INTEREST

None
☐

b. If the debtor is a corporation, list all officers and directors of the corporation, and each stockholder who directly or indirectly owns, controls, or holds 5 percent or more of the voting or equity securities of the corporation.

                                                          NATURE AND PERCENTAGE
NAME AND ADDRESS   TITLE   OF STOCK OWNERSHIP

22 . Former partners, officers, directors and shareholders

None
☐

a. If the debtor is a partnership, list each member who withdrew from the partnership within **one year** immediately preceding the commencement of this case.

NAME   ADDRESS   DATE OF WITHDRAWAL

None
☐

b. If the debtor is a corporation, list all officers, or directors whose relationship with the corporation terminated within **one year** immediately preceding the commencement of this case.

NAME AND ADDRESS   TITLE   DATE OF TERMINATION

23 . Withdrawals from a partnership or distributions by a corporation

None
☐

If the debtor is a partnership or corporation, list all withdrawals or distributions credited or given to an insider, including compensation in any form, bonuses, loans, stock redemptions, options exercised and any other perquisite during **one year** immediately preceding the commencement of this case.

NAME & ADDRESS   AMOUNT OF MONEY
OF RECIPIENT,   DATE AND PURPOSE   OR DESCRIPTION
RELATIONSHIP TO DEBTOR   OF WITHDRAWAL   AND VALUE OF PROPERTY

24. Tax Consolidation Group.

None
☐

If the debtor is a corporation, list the name and federal taxpayer identification number of the parent corporation of any consolidated group for tax purposes of which the debtor has been a member at any time within the **six-year period** immediately preceding the commencement of the case.

NAME OF PARENT CORPORATION   TAXPAYER IDENTIFICATION NUMBER (EIN)

---

25. Pension Funds.

None
☐

If the debtor is not an individual, list the name and federal taxpayer identification number of any pension fund to which the debtor, as an employer, has been responsible for contributing at any time within the **six-year period** immediately preceding the commencement of the case.

NAME OF PENSION FUND   TAXPAYER IDENTIFICATION NUMBER (EIN)

---

* * * * * *

[If completed by an individual or individual and spouse]

I declare under penalty of perjury that I have read the answers contained in the foregoing statement of financial affairs and any attachments thereto and that they are true and correct.

Date _____   Signature _____
                                      of Debtor

Date _____   Signature_____
                                      of Joint Debtor
                                      (if any)

_____

[If completed on behalf of a partnership or corporation]

I, declare under penalty of perjury that I have read the answers contained in the foregoing statement of financial affairs and any attachments thereto and that they are true and correct to the best of my knowledge, information and belief.

Date _____   Signature _____

                                      _____
                                      Print Name and Title

[An individual signing on behalf of a partnership or corporation must indicate position or relationship to debtor.]

_____ continuation sheets attached

Penalty for making a false statement: Fine of up to $500,000 or imprisonment for up to 5 years, or both. 18 U.S.C. § 152 and 3571

CERTIFICATION AND SIGNATURE OF NON-ATTORNEY BANKRUPTCY PETITION PREPARER (See 11 U.S.C. § 110)

I certify that I am a bankruptcy petition preparer as defined in 11 U.S.C. § 110, that I prepared this document for compensation, and that I have provided the debtor with a copy of this document.

_____
Printed or Typed Name of Bankruptcy Petition Preparer

Social Security No.
(Required by 11 U.S.C. § 110(c).)

_____

_____
Address

Names and Social Security numbers of all other individuals who prepared or assisted in preparing this document:

If more than one person prepared this document, attach additional signed sheets conforming to the appropriate Official Form for each person.

X _____   _____
Signature of Bankruptcy Petition Preparer   Date

A bankruptcy petition preparer's failure to comply with the provisions of title 11 and the Federal Rules of Bankruptcy Procedure may result in fines or imprisonment or both. 18 U.S.C. § 156.

Official Form 8
(12/03)

United States Bankruptcy Court
_____ District Of _____

In re _____,
       Debtor

Case No. _____

Chapter 7

CHAPTER 7 INDIVIDUAL DEBTOR'S STATEMENT OF INTENTION

1. I have filed a schedule of assets and liabilities which includes consumer debts secured by property of the estate.

2. I intend to do the following with respect to the property of the estate which secures those consumer debts:

   a. *Property to Be Surrendered.*

Description of Property   **Creditor's name**

   b. *Property to Be Retained*   *[Check any applicable statement.]*

Description of Property	Creditor's Name	Property is claimed as exempt	Property will be redeemed pursuant to 11 U.S.C. § 722	Debt will be reaffirmed pursuant to 11 U.S.C. § 524(c)

Date: _____

_____
Signature of Debtor

CERTIFICATION OF NON-ATTORNEY BANKRUPTCY PETITION PREPARER (See 11 U.S.C. § 110)

I certify that I am a bankruptcy petition preparer as defined in 11 U.S.C. § 110, that I prepared this document for compensation, and that I have provided the debtor with a copy of this document.

_____   _____
Printed or Typed Name of Bankruptcy Petition Preparer   Social Security No.
(Required by 11 U.S.C. § 110(c).)

_____

_____
Address

Names and Social Security Numbers of all other individuals who prepared or assisted in preparing this document.

If more than one person prepared this document, attach additional signed sheets conforming to the appropriate Official Form for each person.

X_____   _____
Signature of Bankruptcy Petition Preparer   Date

A bankruptcy petition preparer's failure to comply with the provisions of title 11 and the Federal Rules of Bankruptcy Procedure may result in fine or imprisonment or both. 11 U.S.C. § 110; 18 U.S.C. § 156.

FORM B9A (Chapter 7 Individual or Joint Debtor No Asset Case (12/03)

UNITED STATES BANKRUPTCY COURT	_____ **District of** _____

Notice of
Chapter 7 Bankruptcy Case, Meeting of Creditors, & Deadlines

[A chapter 7 bankruptcy case concerning the debtor(s) listed below was filed on _____ (date).]

or [A bankruptcy case concerning the debtor(s) listed below was originally filed under chapter _____ on _____ (date) and was converted to a case under chapter 7 on_____.]

You may be a creditor of the debtor. **This notice lists important deadlines.** You may want to consult an attorney to protect your rights. All documents filed in the case may be inspected at the bankruptcy clerk's office at the address listed below. NOTE: The staff of the bankruptcy clerk's office cannot give legal advice.

See Reverse Side For Important Explanations.

Debtor(s) (name(s) and address):	Case Number:
	Last four digits of Soc. Sec. No./Complete EIN or other Taxpayer I.D.No.:
All Other Names used by the Debtor(s) in the last 6 years (include married, maiden, and trade names):	Bankruptcy Trustee (name and address):
Attorney for Debtor(s) (name and address): Telephone number:	Telephone number:

Meeting of Creditors:

Date: /   /   Time: (   ) A.M.   Location: _____
                                   (   ) P.M.

Deadlines: Papers must be *received* by the bankruptcy clerk's office by the following deadlines:

Deadline to File a Complaint Objecting to Discharge of the Debtor *or* to Determine Dischargeability of Certain Debts:

Deadline to Object to Exemptions: Thirty (30) days after the *conclusion* of the meeting of creditors.

Creditors May Not Take Certain Actions

The filing of the bankruptcy case automatically stays certain collection and other actions against the debtor and the debtor's property. If you attempt to collect a debt or take other action in violation of the Bankruptcy Code, you may be penalized.

Please Do Not File A Proof of Claim Unless You Receive a Notice To Do So.

Address of the Bankruptcy Clerk's Office:	For the Court:
	Clerk of the Bankruptcy Court:
Telephone number:	
Hours Open:	Date:

EXPLANATIONS

Filing of Chapter 7 Bankruptcy Case	A bankruptcy case under chapter 7 of the Bankruptcy Code (title 11, United States Code) has been filed in this court by or against the debtor(s) listed on the front side, and an order for relief has been entered.
Creditors May Not Take Certain Actions	Prohibited collection actions are listed in Bankruptcy Code § 362. Common examples of prohibited actions include contacting the debtor by telephone, mail or otherwise to demand repayment; taking actions to collect money or obtain property from the debtor; repossessing the debtor's property; starting or continuing lawsuits or foreclosures; and garnishing or deducting from the debtor's wages.
Meeting of Creditors	A meeting of creditors is scheduled for the date, time and location listed on the front side. *The debtor (both spouses in a joint case) must be present at the meeting to be questioned under oath by the trustee and by creditors.* Creditors are welcome to attend, but are not required to do so. The meeting may be continued and concluded at a later date without further notice.
Do Not File a Proof of Claim at This Time	There does not appear to be any property available to the trustee to pay creditors. *You therefore should not file a proof of claim at this time.* If it later appears that assets are available to pay creditors, you will be sent another notice telling you that you may file a proof of claim, and telling you the deadline for filing your proof of claim.
Discharge of Debts	The debtor is seeking a discharge of most debts, which may include your debt. A discharge means that you may never try to collect the debt from the debtor. If you believe that the debtor is not entitled to receive a discharge under Bankruptcy Code § 727(a) *or* that a debt owed to you is not dischargeable under Bankruptcy Code § 523(a)(2), (4), (6), or (15), you must start a lawsuit by filing a complaint in the bankruptcy clerk's office by the "Deadline to File a Complaint Objecting to Discharge of the Debtor or to Determine Dischargeability of Certain Debts" listed on the front side. The bankruptcy clerk's office must receive the complaint and the required filing fee by that Deadline.
Exempt Property	The debtor is permitted by law to keep certain property as exempt. Exempt property will not be sold and distributed to creditors. The debtor must file a list of all property claimed as exempt. You may inspect that list at the bankruptcy clerk's office. If you believe that an exemption claimed by the debtor is not authorized by law, you may file an objection to that exemption. The bankruptcy clerk's office must receive the objection by the "Deadline to Object to Exemptions" listed on the front side.
Bankruptcy Clerk's Office	Any paper that you file in this bankruptcy case should be filed at the bankruptcy clerk's office at the address listed on the front side. You may inspect all papers filed, including the list of the debtor's property and debts and the list of the property claimed as exempt, at the bankruptcy clerk's office.
Legal Advice	The staff of the bankruptcy clerk's office cannot give legal advice. You may want to consult an attorney to protect your rights.

—Refer To Other Side For Important Deadlines and Notices—

FORM B9C (Chapter 7 Individual or Joint Debtor Asset Case) (12/03)

UNITED STATES BANKRUPTCY COURT	_____ District of _____

Notice of
Chapter 7 Bankruptcy Case, Meeting of Creditors, & Deadlines

[A chapter 7 bankruptcy case concerning the debtor(s) listed below was filed on _____ (date).]

or [A bankruptcy case concerning the debtor(s) listed below was originally filed under chapter _____ on _____ (date) and was converted to a case under chapter 7 on_____.]

You may be a creditor of the debtor. **This notice lists important deadlines.** You may want to consult an attorney to protect your rights. All documents filed in the case may be inspected at the bankruptcy clerk's office at the address listed below. NOTE: The staff of the bankruptcy clerk's office cannot give legal advice.

See Reverse Side For Important Explanations.

Debtor(s) (name(s) and address):	Case Number:
	Last four digits of Soc. Sec. No./Complete EIN or other Taxpayer I.D. No.:
All Other Names used by the Debtor(s) in the last 6 years (include married, maiden, and trade names):	Bankruptcy Trustee (name and address):
Attorney for Debtor(s) (name and address):

Telephone number: | Telephone number: |

Meeting of Creditors:

Date: /   /   Time: (   ) A.M.   Location:
                                          (   ) P.M.

Deadlines: Papers must be *received* by the bankruptcy clerk's office by the following deadlines:

Deadline to File a Proof of Claim:

For all creditors (except a governmental unit):   For a governmental unit:

Deadline to File a Complaint Objecting to Discharge of the Debtor or to Determine Dischargeability of Certain Debts:

Deadline to Object to Exemptions: Thirty (30) days after the *conclusion* of the meeting of creditors.

Creditors May Not Take Certain Actions:

The filing of the bankruptcy case automatically stays certain collection and other actions against the debtor and the debtor's property. If you attempt to collect a debt or take other action in violation of the Bankruptcy Code, you may be penalized.

Address of the Bankruptcy Clerk's Office:	**For the Court:**
	Clerk of the Bankruptcy Court:
Telephone number:	
Hours Open:	Date:

EXPLANATIONS

Filing of Chapter 7 Bankruptcy Case	A bankruptcy case under chapter 7 of the Bankruptcy Code (title 11, United States Code) has been filed in this court by or against the debtor(s) listed on the front side, and an order for relief has been entered.
Creditors May Not Take Certain Actions	Prohibited collection actions are listed in Bankruptcy Code § 362. Common examples of prohibited actions include contacting the debtor by telephone, mail or otherwise to demand repayment; taking actions to collect money or obtain property from the debtor; repossessing the debtor's property; starting or continuing lawsuits or foreclosures; and garnishing or deducting from the debtor's wages.
Meeting of Creditors	A meeting of creditors is scheduled for the date, time and location listed on the front side. *The debtor (both spouses in a joint case) must be present at the meeting to be questioned under oath by the trustee and by creditors.* Creditors are welcome to attend, but are not required to do so. The meeting may be continued and concluded at a later date without further notice.
Claims	A Proof of Claim is a signed statement describing a creditor's claim. If a Proof of Claim form is not included with this notice, you can obtain one at any bankruptcy clerk's office. If you do not file a Proof of Claim by the "Deadline to File a Proof of Claim" listed on the front side, you might not be paid any money on your claim against the debtor in the bankruptcy case. To be paid you must file a Proof of Claim even if your claim is listed in the schedules filed by the debtor.
Discharge of Debts	The debtor is seeking a discharge of most debts, which may include your debt. A discharge means that you may never try to collect the debt from the debtor. If you believe that the debtor is not entitled to receive a discharge under Bankruptcy Code § 727(a) *or* that a debt owed to you is not dischargeable under Bankruptcy Code § 523(a)(2), (4), (6), or (15), you must start a lawsuit by filing a complaint in the bankruptcy clerk's office by the "Deadline to File a Complaint Objecting to Discharge of the Debtor or to Determine Dischargeability of Certain Debts" listed on the front side. The bankruptcy clerk's office must receive the complaint and the required filing fee by that Deadline.
Exempt Property	The debtor is permitted by law to keep certain property as exempt. Exempt property will not be sold and distributed to creditors. The debtor must file a list of all property claimed as exempt. You may inspect that list at the bankruptcy clerk's office. If you believe that an exemption claimed by the debtor is not authorized by law, you may file an objection to that exemption. The bankruptcy clerk's office must receive the objection by the "Deadline to Object to Exemptions" listed on the front side.
Liquidation of the Debtor's Property and Payment of Creditors' Claims	The bankruptcy trustee listed on the front of this notice will collect and sell the debtor's property that is not exempt. If the trustee can collect enough money, creditors may be paid some or all of the debts owed to them, in the order specified by the Bankruptcy Code. To make sure you receive any share of that money, you must file a Proof of Claim, as described above.
Bankruptcy Clerk's Office	Any paper that you file in this bankruptcy case should be filed at the bankruptcy clerk's office at the address listed on the front side. You may inspect all papers filed, including the list of the debtor's property and debts and the list of the property claimed as exempt, at the bankruptcy clerk's office.
Legal Advice	The staff of the bankruptcy clerk's office cannot give legal advice. You may want to consult an attorney to protect your rights.

—Refer To Other Side For Important Deadlines and Notices—

FORM B9I (Chapter 13 Case) (12/03)

UNITED STATES BANKRUPTCY COURT   _____ District of _____

Notice of
Chapter 13 Bankruptcy Case, Meeting of Creditors, & Deadlines

[The debtor(s) listed below filed a chapter 13 bankruptcy case on _____ (date).]

or [A bankruptcy case concerning the debtor(s) listed below was originally filed under chapter _____ on _____ (date) and was converted to a case under chapter 13 on_____.]

You may be a creditor of the debtor. **This notice lists important deadlines.** You may want to consult an attorney to protect your rights. All documents filed in the case may be inspected at the bankruptcy clerk's office at the address listed below. NOTE: The staff of the bankruptcy clerk's office cannot give legal advice.

See Reverse Side For Important Explanations.

Debtor(s) (name(s) and address):	Case Number:
	Last four digits of Soc. Sec. No./Complete EIN or other Taxpayer I.D. No.:
All Other Names used by the Debtor(s) in the last 6 years (include married, maiden, and trade names):	Bankruptcy Trustee (name and address):
Attorney for Debtor(s) (name and address): Telephone number:	Telephone number:

Meeting of Creditors:

Date: /   /   Time: (   ) A.M.   Location:
                                          (   ) P.M.

Deadlines: Papers must be *received* by the bankruptcy clerk's office by the following deadlines:

Deadline to File a Proof of Claim:

For all creditors (except a governmental unit):   For a governmental unit:

Deadline to Object to Exemptions:
Thirty (30) days after the *conclusion* of the meeting of creditors.

Filing of Plan, Hearing on Confirmation of Plan

[The debtor has filed a plan. The plan or a summary of the plan is enclosed. The hearing on confirmation will be held:
Date: _____ Time: _____ Location: _____]

or [The debtor has filed a plan. The plan or a summary of the plan and notice of confirmation hearing will be sent separately.]

or [The debtor has not filed a plan as of this date. You will be sent separate notice of the hearing on confirmation of the plan.]

Creditors May Not Take Certain Actions:

The filing of the bankruptcy case automatically stays certain collection and other actions against the debtor, debtor's property, and certain codebtors. If you attempt to collect a debt or take other action in violation of the Bankruptcy Code, you may be penalized.

Address of the Bankruptcy Clerk's Office: Telephone number:	**For the Court:** Clerk of the Bankruptcy Court:
Hours Open:	Date:

EXPLANATIONS

Filing of Chapter 13 Bankruptcy Case	A bankruptcy case under chapter 13 of the Bankruptcy Code (title 11, United States Code) has been filed in this court by the debtor(s) listed on the front side, and an order for relief has been entered. Chapter 13 allows an individual with regular income and debts below a specified amount to adjust debts pursuant to a plan. A plan is not effective unless confirmed by the bankruptcy court. You may object to confirmation of the plan and appear at the confirmation hearing. A copy or summary of the plan [is included with this notice] *or* [will be sent to you later], and [the confirmation hearing will be held on the date indicated on the front of this notice] *or* [you will be sent notice of the confirmation hearing]. The debtor will remain in possession of the debtor's property and may continue to operate the debtor's business, if any, unless the court orders otherwise.
Creditors May Not Take Certain Actions	Prohibited collection actions against the debtor and certain codebtors are listed in Bankruptcy Code § 362 and § 1301. Common examples of prohibited actions include contacting the debtor by telephone, mail or otherwise to demand repayment; taking actions to collect money or obtain property from the debtor; repossessing the debtor's property; starting or continuing lawsuits or foreclosures; and garnishing or deducting from the debtor's wages.
Meeting of Creditors	A meeting of creditors is scheduled for the date, time and location listed on the front side. *The debtor (both spouses in a joint case) must be present at the meeting to be questioned under oath by the trustee and by creditors.* Creditors are welcome to attend, but are not required to do so. The meeting may be continued and concluded at a later date without further notice.
Claims	A Proof of Claim is a signed statement describing a creditor's claim. If a Proof of Claim form is not included with this notice, you can obtain one at any bankruptcy clerk's office. If you do not file a Proof of Claim by the "Deadline to File a Proof of Claim" listed on the front side, you might not be paid any money on your claim against the debtor in the bankruptcy case. To be paid you must file a Proof of Claim even if your claim is listed in the schedules filed by the debtor.
Discharge of Debts	The debtor is seeking a discharge of most debts, which may include your debt. A discharge means that you may never try to collect the debt from the debtor.
Exempt Property	The debtor is permitted by law to keep certain property as exempt. Exempt property will not be sold and distributed to creditors, even if the debtor's case is converted to chapter 7. The debtor must file a list of all property claimed as exempt. You may inspect that list at the bankruptcy clerk's office. If you believe that an exemption claimed by the debtor is not authorized by law, you may file an objection to that exemption. The bankruptcy clerk's office must receive the objection by the "Deadline to Object to Exemptions" listed on the front side.
Bankruptcy Clerk's Office	Any paper that you file in this bankruptcy case should be filed at the bankruptcy clerk's office at the address listed on the front side. You may inspect all papers filed, including the list of the debtor's property and debts and the list of property claimed as exempt, at the bankruptcy clerk's office.
Legal Advice	The staff of the bankruptcy clerk's office cannot give legal advice. You may want to consult an attorney to protect your rights.

—Refer To Other Side For Important Deadlines and Notices—

FORM B10 (Official Form 10) (04/04)

UNITED STATES BANKRUPTCY COURT _____ DISTRICT OF _____		PROOF OF CLAIM
Name of Debtor	Case Number	

NOTE: This form should not be used to make a claim for an administrative expense arising after the commencement of the case. A "request" for payment of an administrative expense may be filed pursuant to 11 U.S.C. § 503.

Name of Creditor (The person or other entity to whom the debtor owes money or property): Name and address where notices should be sent: Telephone number:	☐ Check box if you are aware that anyone else has filed a proof of claim relating to your claim. Attach copy of statement giving particulars. ☐ Check box if you have never received any notices from the bankruptcy court in this case. ☐ Check box if the address differs from the address on the envelope sent to you by the court.	THIS SPACE IS FOR COURT USE ONLY
Account or other number by which creditor identifies debtor:	Check here ☐ replaces if this claim a previously filed claim, dated:_____ ☐ amends	

1. Basis for Claim

☐ Goods sold
☐ Services performed
☐ Money loaned
☐ Personal injury/wrongful death
☐ Taxes
☐ Other _____

☐ Retiree benefits as defined in 11 U.S.C. § 1114(a)
☐ Wages, salaries, and compensation (fill out below)
Last four digits of SS #: _____
Unpaid compensation for services performed

from _____ to _____
(date)   (date)

2. Date debt was incurred:	**3. If court judgment, date obtained:**

4. Total Amount of Claim at Time Case Filed: $ _____ _____ _____ _____
(unsecured)   (secured)   (priority)   (Total)

    If all or part of your claim is secured or entitled to priority, also complete Item 5 or 7 below.

☐ Check this box if claim includes interest or other charges in addition to the principal amount of the claim. Attach itemized statement of all interest or additional charges.

5. Secured Claim.

☐ Check this box if your claim is secured by collateral (including a right of setoff).

Brief Description of Collateral:

☐ Real Estate   ☐ Motor Vehicle
☐ Other_____

Value of Collateral: $_____

Amount of arrearage and other charges at time case filed included in secured claim, if any: $_____

6. Unsecured Nonpriority Claim $_____

☐ Check this box if: a) there is no collateral or lien securing your claim, or b) your claim exceeds the value of the property securing it, or if c) none or only part of your claim is entitled to priority.

7. Unsecured Priority Claim.

☐ Check this box if you have an unsecured priority claim

Amount entitled to priority $_____
Specify the priority of the claim:

☐ Wages, salaries, or commissions (up to $4,925),* earned within 90 days before filing of the bankruptcy petition or cessation of the debtor's business, whichever is earlier - 11 U.S.C. § 507(a)(3).
☐ Contributions to an employee benefit plan - 11 U.S.C. § 507(a)(4).
☐ Up to $2,225* of deposits toward purchase, lease, or rental of property or services for personal, family, or household use - 11 U.S.C. § 507(a)(6).
☐ Alimony, maintenance, or support owed to a spouse, former spouse, or child - 11 U.S.C. § 507(a)(7).
☐ Taxes or penalties owed to governmental units-11 U.S.C. § 507(a)(8).
☐ Other - Specify applicable paragraph of 11 U.S.C. § 507(a)(___).
Amounts are subject to adjustment on 4/1/07 and every 3 years thereafter with respect to cases commenced on or after the date of adjustment.

8. Credits: The amount of all payments on this claim has been credited and deducted for the purpose of making this proof of claim.

9. Supporting Documents: *Attach copies of supporting documents,* such as promissory notes, purchase orders, invoices, itemized statements of running accounts, contracts, court judgments, mortgages, security agreements, and evidence of perfection of lien. DO NOT SEND ORIGINAL DOCUMENTS. If the documents are not available, explain. If the documents are voluminous, attach a summary.

10. Date-Stamped Copy: To receive an acknowledgment of the filing of your claim, enclose a stamped, self-addressed envelope and copy of this proof of claim

THIS SPACE IS FOR COURT USE ONLY

Date	Sign and print the name and title, if any, of the creditor or other person authorized to file this claim (attach copy of power of attorney, if any):

Penalty for presenting fraudulent claim: Fine of up to $500,000 or imprisonment for up to 5 years, or both. 18 U.S.C. §§ 152 and 3571.

FORM B10 (Official Form 10) (04/04)

INSTRUCTIONS FOR PROOF OF CLAIM FORM

The instructions and definitions below are general explanations of the law. In particular types of cases or circumstances, such as bankruptcy cases that are not filed voluntarily by a debtor, there may be exceptions to these general rules.

—— DEFINITIONS ——

Debtor

The person, corporation, or other entity that has filed a bankruptcy case is called the debtor.

Creditor

A creditor is any person, corporation, or other entity to whom the debtor owed a debt on the date that the bankruptcy case was filed.

Proof of Claim

A form telling the bankruptcy court how much the debtor owed a creditor at the time the bankruptcy case was filed (the amount of the creditor's claim). This form must be filed with the clerk of the bankruptcy court where the bankruptcy case was filed.

Secured Claim

A claim is a secured claim to the extent that the creditor has a lien on property of the debtor (collateral) that gives the creditor the right to be paid from that property before creditors who do not have liens on the property.

Examples of liens are a mortgage on real estate and a security interest in a car, truck, boat, television set, or other item of property. A lien may have been obtained through a court proceeding before the bankruptcy case began; in some states a court judgment is a lien. In addition, to the extent a creditor also owes money to the debtor (has a right of setoff), the creditor's claim may be a secured claim. (See also *Unsecured Claim*.)

Unsecured Claim

If a claim is not a secured claim it is an unsecured claim. A claim may be partly secured and partly unsecured if the property on which a creditor has a lien is not worth enough to pay the creditor in full.

Unsecured Priority Claim

Certain types of unsecured claims are given priority, so they are to be paid in bankruptcy cases before most other unsecured claims (if there is sufficient money or property available to pay these claims). The most common types of priority claims are listed on the proof of claim form. Unsecured claims that are not specifically given priority status by the bankruptcy laws are classified as *Unsecured Nonpriority Claims.*

Items to be completed in Proof of Claim form (if not already filled in)

Court, Name of Debtor, and Case Number:

Fill in the name of the federal judicial district where the bankruptcy case was filed (for example, Central District of California), the name of the debtor in the bankruptcy case, and the bankruptcy case number. If you received a notice of the case from the court, all of this information is near the top of the notice.

Information about Creditor:

Complete the section giving the name, address, and telephone number of the creditor to whom the debtor owes money or property, and the debtor's account number, if any. If anyone else has already filed a proof of claim relating to this debt, if you never received notices from the bankruptcy court about this case, if your address differs from that to which the court sent notice, or if this proof of claim replaces or changes a proof of claim that was already filed, check the appropriate box on the form.

1. Basis for Claim:

Check the type of debt for which the proof of claim is being filed. If the type of debt is not listed, check "Other" and briefly describe the type of debt. If you were an employee of the debtor, fill in the last four digits of your social security number and the dates of work for which you were not paid.

2. Date Debt Incurred:

Fill in the date when the debt first was owed by the debtor.

3. Court Judgments:

If you have a court judgment for this debt, state the date the court entered the judgment.

4. Total Amount of Claim at Time Case Filed:

Fill in the applicable amounts, including the total amount of the entire claim. If interest or other charges in addition to the principal amount of the claim are included, check the appropriate place on the form and attach an itemization of the interest and charges.

5. Secured Claim:

Check the appropriate place if the claim is a secured claim. You must state the type and value of property that is collateral for the claim, attach copies of the documentation of your lien, and state the amount past due on the claim as of the date the bankruptcy case was filed. A claim may be partly secured and partly unsecured. (See DEFINITIONS, above).

6. Unsecured Nonpriority Claim:

Check the appropriate place if you have an unsecured nonpriority claim, sometimes referred to as a "general unsecured claim". (See DEFINITIONS, above.) If your claim is partly secured and partly unsecured, state here the amount that is unsecured. If part of your claim is entitled to priority, state here the amount **not** entitled to priority.

7. Unsecured Priority Claim:

Check the appropriate place if you have an unsecured priority claim, and state the amount entitled to priority. (See DEFINITIONS, above). A claim may be partly priority and partly nonpriority if, for example, the claim is for more than the amount given priority by the law. Check the appropriate place to specify the type of priority claim.

8. Credits:

By signing this proof of claim, you are stating under oath that in calculating the amount of your claim you have given the debtor credit for all payments received from the debtor.

9. Supporting Documents:

You must attach to this proof of claim form copies of documents that show the debtor owes the debt claimed or, if the documents are too lengthy, a summary of those documents. If documents are not available, you must attach an explanation of why they are not available.

Official Form 16A
(12/03)

Form 16A. CAPTION (FULL)

United States Bankruptcy Court

_____ District Of _____

In re _____,   )
       Set forth here all names including married,   )
       maiden, and trade names used by debtor within   )
       last 6 years.]   )
                              Debtor   )   Case No. _____
)

Address _____   )
)
       _____   )   Chapter _____

Employer's Tax Identification (EIN) No(s). [if any]:_____   )
_____   )
Last four digits of Social Security No(s).:_____   )

[Designation of Character of Paper]

Official Form 16B
12/94

FORM 16B. CAPTION (SHORT TITLE)

(May be used if 11 U.S.C. § 342(c) is not applicable)

United States Bankruptcy Court

_____ District Of _____

In re _____,
      Debtor

                         Case No. _____

                         Chapter _____

[Designation of Character of Paper]

Official Form 16D
12/04

Form 16D. CAPTION FOR USE IN ADVERSARY PROCEEDING

United States Bankruptcy Court
_____ District Of _____

In re   _____,   )
                        Debtor   )   Case No. _____
)
        _____,   )   Chapter _____
                        Plaintiff   )
)
        v.   )
)
        _____,   )   Adv. Proc. No. _____
                        Defendant   )

COMPLAINT [*or* other Designation]

[If used in a Notice of Appeal (see Form 17) or other notice filed and served by a debtor, this caption must be altered to include the debtor's address and Employer's Tax Identification Number(s) or last four digits of Social Social Security Number(s) as in Form 16A.]

Official Form 17
(12/04)

United States Bankruptcy Court

_____ District Of _____

In re _____,
            Debtor

Case No. _____

Chapter _____

[Caption as in Form 16A, 16B, or 16D, as appropriate]

NOTICE OF APPEAL

_____, the plaintiff [*or* defendant *or* other party] appeals under 28 U.S.C. § 158(a) or (b) from the judgment, order, or decree of the bankruptcy judge (describe) entered in this adversary proceeding [*or other proceeding, describe type*] on the _____ day of _____,_____.
                                                                                        (month)   (year)
         The names of all parties to the judgment, order, or decree appealed from and the names, addresses, and telephone numbers of their respective attorneys are as follows:

Dated: _____

Signed: _____
             Attorney for Appellant (or Appellant, if not represented by
             an Attorney)

Attorney Name: _____

Address: _____

_____

Telephone No: _____

         If a Bankruptcy Appellate Panel Service is authorized to hear this appeal, each party has a right to have the appeal heard by the district court. The appellant may exercise this right only by filing a separate statement of election at the time of the filing of this notice of appeal. Any other party may elect, within the time provided in 28 U.S.C. § 158(c), to have the appeal heard by the district court.

         If a child support creditor or its representative is the appellant, and if the child support creditor or its representative files the form specified in § 304(g) of the Bankruptcy Reform Act of 1994, no fee is required.

Form B18 (Official Form 18)
(9/97)

Form 18.   DISCHARGE OF DEBTOR
IN A CHAPTER 7 CASE

[Caption as in Form 16A]

DISCHARGE OF DEBTOR

It appearing that the debtor is entitled to a discharge, **IT IS ORDERED:** The debtor is granted a discharge

under section 727 of title 11, United States Code, (the Bankruptcy Code).

Dated: _____

BY THE COURT

_____

United States Bankruptcy Judge.

SEE THE BACK SIDE OF THIS ORDER FOR IMPORTANT INFORMATION

Form 18 continued
(9/97)

EXPLANATION OF A BANKRUPTCY DISCHARGE
IN A CHAPTER 7 CASE

This court order grants a discharge to the person named as the debtor. It is not a dismissal of the case and it does not determine how much money, if any, the trustee will pay to creditors.

Collection of Discharged Debts Prohibited

The discharge prohibits any attempt to collect from the debtor a debt which has been discharged. For example, a creditor is not permitted to contact the debtor by mail, phone or otherwise, to file or to continue a lawsuit, to attach wages or other property, or to take any other action to collect a discharged debt from the debtor. *[In a case involving community property:]* [There are also special rules that protect certain community property owned by the debtor's spouse, even if that spouse did not file a bankruptcy case.] A creditor who violates this order can be required to pay damages and attorneys fees to the debtor.

However, a creditor may have the right to enforce a valid lien, such as a mortgage or security interest, against the debtor's property after the bankruptcy, if that lien was not avoided or eliminated in the bankruptcy case. Also, a debtor may voluntarily pay any debt which has been discharged.

Debts That are Discharged

The chapter 7 discharge order eliminates a debtor's legal obligation to pay a debt that is discharged. Most, but not all, types of debts are discharged if the debt existed on the date the bankruptcy case was filed. (If this case was begun under a different chapter of the Bankruptcy Code and converted to chapter 7, the discharge applies to debts owed when the bankruptcy case was converted.)

Debts that are Not Discharged

Some of the common types of debts which are <u>not</u> discharged in a chapter 7 bankruptcy case are:

a. Debts for most taxes;

b. Debts in the nature of alimony, maintenance, or support;

c. Debts for most student loans;

d. Debts for most fines, penalties, forfeitures, or criminal restitution obligations;

e. Debts for personal injuries or death caused by the debtor's operation of a motor vehicle while intoxicated;

f. Some debts which are not properly listed by the debtor;

g. Debts that the bankruptcy court specifically has decided or will decide in this bankruptcy case are not discharged;

h. Debts for which the debtor has given up the discharge protections by signing a reaffirmation agreement in compliance with the Bankruptcy Code requirements for reaffirmation of debts.

This information is only a general summary of the bankruptcy discharge. There are exceptions to these general rules. Because the law is complicated, you may want to consult an attorney to determine the exact effect of the discharge in this case.

FORM 19.   CERTIFICATION AND SIGNATURE OF NON-ATTORNEY BANKRUPTCY PETITION PREPARER (See 11 U.S.C. § 110)

[CAPTION AS IN FORM 16B.]

CERTIFICATION AND SIGNATURE OF NON-ATTORNEY BANKRUPTCY PETITION PREPARER (See 11 U.S.C. § 110)

I certify that I am a bankruptcy petition preparer as defined in 11 U.S.C. § 110, that I prepared this document for compensation, and that I have provided the debtor with a copy of this document.

_____

Printed or Typed Name of Bankruptcy Petition Preparer

_____

Social Security No.
(Required by 11 U.S.C. § 110(c).)

_____

_____

Address

Names and Social Security numbers of all other individuals who prepared or assisted in preparing this document:

If more than one person prepared this document, attach additional signed sheets conforming to the appropriate Official Form for each person.

X _____   _____
Signature of Bankruptcy Petition Preparer   Date

A bankruptcy petition preparer's failure to comply with the provisions of title 11 and the Federal Rules of Bankruptcy Procedure may result in fines or imprisonment or both. 11 U.S.C. § 110; 18 U.S.C. § 156.

Form B20A (Official Form 20A)
(9/97)

Form 20A. Notice of Motion or Objection

[Caption as in Form 16A]

NOTICE OF [MOTION TO   ] [OBJECTION TO   ]

_____ has filed papers with the court to [relief sought in the motion or objection].

Your rights may be affected. **You should read these papers carefully and discuss them with your attorney, if you have one in this bankruptcy case. (If you do not have an attorney, you may wish to consult one.)**

If you do not want the court to [relief sought in the motion or objection], or if you want the court to consider your views on the [motion] [objection] then on or before _____(date), you or your attorney must:

[File with the court a written request for a hearing {*or, if the court requires a written response, an answer, explaining your position*} at:

{address of the bankruptcy clerk's office}

If you mail your {request} {response} to the court for filing, you must mail it early enough so the court will **receive** it on or before the date stated above.

You must also mail a copy to:

{movant's attorney's name and address}

{names and addresses of others to be served}]

[Attend the hearing scheduled to be held on _____(date), _____(year) at _____a.m./p.m. in Courtroom _____, United States Bankruptcy Court, {address}].

[Other steps required to oppose a motion or objection under local rule or court order.]

If you or your attorney do not take these steps, the court may decide that you do not oppose the relief sought in the motion or objection and may enter an order granting that relief.

Date: _____   Signature: _____
                               Name:
                               Address:

Form B20B (Official Form 20B)
(9/97)

FORM 20B. Notice of Objection to Claim

[Caption as in Form 16A]

NOTICE OF OBJECTION TO CLAIM

_____ has filed an objection to your claim in this bankruptcy case.

<u>Your claim may be reduced, modified or eliminated.</u> You should read these papers carefully and discuss them with your attorney, if you have one.

If you do not want the court to eliminate or change your claim, then on or before _____(date), you or your lawyer must:

{If required by local rule or court order.}

[File with the court a written response to the objection, explaining your position, at:

{address of the bankruptcy clerk's office}

If you mail your response to the court for filing, you must mail it early enough so that the court will **receive** it on or before the date stated above.

You must also mail a copy to:

{objector's attorney's name and address}

{names and addresses of others to be served}].

Attend the hearing on the objection, scheduled to be held on _____(date), ____(year), at _____ a.m./p.m. in Courtroom _____, United States Bankruptcy Court, {address}.

If you or your attorney do not take these steps, the court may decide that you do not oppose the objection to your claim.

Date: _____   Signature: _____
                              Name:
                              Address:

Form B 21 Official Form 21
(12/03)

FORM 21. STATEMENT OF SOCIAL SECURITY NUMBER

[*Caption as in Form 16A.*]

STATEMENT OF SOCIAL SECURITY NUMBER(S)

1.Name of Debtor (enter Last, First, Middle):_____
(Check the appropriate box and, if applicable, provide the required information.)

       / /Debtor has a Social Security Number and it is: _ _ _-_ _-_ _ _ _
                             (If more than one, state all.)
       / /Debtor does not have a Social Security Number.

2.Name of Joint Debtor (enter Last, First, Middle):_____
(Check the appropriate box and, if applicable, provide the required information.)

       / /Joint Debtor has a Social Security Number and it is: _ _ _-_ _-_ _ _ _
                             (If more than one, state all.)
       / /Joint Debtor does not have a Social Security Number.

I declare under penalty of perjury that the foregoing is true and correct.

            X _____
                       Signature of Debtor   Date

            X _____
                       Signature of Joint Debtor   Date

Joint debtors must provide information for both spouses.
Penalty for making a false statement: Fine of up to $250,000 or up to 5 years imprisonment or both. 18 U.S.C. §§ 152 and 3571.

Selected Forms Promulgated by the Administrative Office of the U.S. Courts

Reproducible Forms Contained in This Appendix

This appendix contains selected forms promulgated by the Administrative Office of the United States Courts that are relevant to consumer bankruptcies. These forms are:

E.1 Introduction

This appendix contains reproducible forms for use in bankruptcy cases, when no Official Form has been prescribed. The Judicial Conference of the United States has approved and encourages the use of privately published forms when no Official Form is required. *See* H.R. Doc. No. 102-80, at 525 (1991). Practitioners should check local rules for further guidance.

Extraneous headings, numbers, and notes have been eliminated from these forms, and instructions and explanatory comments follow this introduction. Please note that some of the forms consist of several pages. These blank forms are available as Acrobat (PDF) files on the CD-Rom accompanying this volume. For reproducible Official Bank-

ruptcy Forms, see Appendix D, *supra*.

Notice to Individual Consumer Debtor

11 U.S.C. § 342(b) requires the clerk of the bankruptcy court to give each consumer debtor a notice indicating each chapter under which such individual may proceed, prior to the filing of the petition. The acknowledgment of notice from the clerk regarding types of relief available, which had been required in most jurisdictions to satisfy section 342(b), is no longer in use, except possibly in a few locations where required as a matter of local practice. It is a good idea to check with the local clerk's office.

Apparently, it is contemplated that the requirements of section 342(b) are now met by that portion of Official Form 1 in which a chapter 7 debtor certifies awareness of the various chapters under which she may proceed, and a represented debtor's attorney certifies that she explained the relief available under each chapter. In any event, it is extremely doubtful that failure to file or receive the acknowledgment of notice, even in those places where it is still required, would invalidate a bankruptcy petition. *See* § 7.3.3, *supra*.

Statement of Attorney Compensation Under Bankruptcy Rule 2016(b), and Disclosure of Compensation of Attorney for Debtor

Pursuant to Fed. R. Bankr. P. 2016(b) and section 329 of the Code, a debtor's attorney must file, within fifteen days after the order for relief or as the court directs, a statement disclosing compensation paid or promised, including a description of any fee-sharing agreements. Within fifteen days of any additional payment or agreement a supplement to the statement must be filed. The first of the two forms reprinted here is provided for use in cases in which the lawyer has agreed to provide legal services without charge. The second form is for use when the attorney has accepted, or has made an agreement to accept, compensation.

Adversary Proceeding Cover Sheet

The bankruptcy Adversary Proceeding Cover Sheet, promulgated by the Administrative Office of the U.S. Courts, is required to initiate every adversary proceeding, primarily for statistical purposes. It is quite unlikely that anything stated in the form will have any effect on the proceedings, except the designation of the bankruptcy case to which the matter is related. Normally, in most courts, the adversary proceeding will then be referred to the bankruptcy judge handling the bankruptcy case. Generally, the form should be completed in the same manner as the comparable form used in U.S. district court. Some courts allow submission of a photocopy of this form, but other courts may require that the original form, obtainable from the clerk of the bankruptcy court, be filed.

Summons and Notice of Trial in an Adversary Proceeding, Summons in an Adversary Proceeding

A copy of the summons, once completed with the caption, dates, and so forth, must be served upon the defendant(s) within ten days of its issuance. A copy of the complaint must be served with the summons. Fed. R. Bankr. P. 7004, which incorporates portions of Fed. R. Civ. P. 4, sets out detailed rules for the issuance and service of the summons. Service is normally permitted by first-class mail, in the manner and to the parties prescribed by Fed. R. Bankr. P. 7004, except for certain depository institutions which are served by certified mail pursuant to Fed. R. Bankr. P. 7004(h). If ten days pass before service, the summons may have to be reissued. The court may dismiss the action if the summons and complaint are not served within 120 days of the filing of the complaint. Some bankruptcy courts require a completed summons form, with only the case number and dates left blank, to be filed along with the complaint. Blank copies

may be obtained from the clerk of the bankruptcy court, and some jurisdictions allow a photocopy of the form to be used. The caption should list the name of the bankruptcy case, as well as the parties to the adversary proceeding, the bankruptcy number, and the adversary proceeding number. After service is completed, the certificate of service on the reverse side of the summons should be filled out and filed with the court. Some courts may have local rules of practice with respect to these matters.

Third-Party Summons

See the annotations to the Summons and Notice of Trial in an Adversary Proceeding, above. Additionally, Fed. R. Bankr. P. 7014, which incorporates by reference Fed. R. Civ. P. 14, provides that if the third-party complaint is served more than ten days after the defendant serves an answer to the primary complaint, the defendant must obtain court approval prior to service. A motion on notice to all of the parties of the original adversary proceeding should be used to obtain court approval.

Subpoena for Rule 2004 Examination, Subpoena in an Adversary Proceeding, Subpoena in a Case Under the Bankruptcy Code

The three subpoena forms are reprinted here. These subpoenas will be issued by attorneys as "officers of the court," rather than by the clerk of the court.

Order Discharging Debtor After Completion of Chapter 13 Plan

Upon confirming the debtor's chapter 13 plan, the court may use this form to discharge all debts provided for by the plan or disallowed under 11 U.S.C. § 502. This form also provides that certain debts are non-dischargeable.

Order Discharging Debtor Before Completion of Chapter 13 Plan

This form is used to discharge unsecured debts when a debtor has not completed all payments necessary under the plan. The court may use this form to discharge all debts provided for by the plan or disallowed under 11 U.S.C. § 502. This form also provides that certain debts are non-dischargeable.

Order Discharging Debtor After Completion of Chapter 12 Case

Upon confirming the debtor's chapter 12 plan, the court may use this form to discharge all debts provided for by the plan or disallowed under 11 U.S.C. § 502. This form also provides that certain debts are non-dischargeable.

Order Discharging Debtor Before Completion of Chapter 12 Plan

This form is used to discharge unsecured debts when a debtor has not completed all payments necessary under the plan. The court may use this form to discharge all debts provided for by the plan or disallowed under 11 U.S.C. § 502. This form also provides that certain debts are nondischargeable.

Disclosure of Compensation of Bankruptcy Petition Preparer

This form requires the non-attorney bankruptcy petition preparer to disclose fully the amount and source of compensation for services, as well as providing an itemization of documents prepared and the services rendered.

Reaffirmation Agreement

This form may be used when a debtor has agreed to reaffirm a debt under section 524(c). As this form contains detailed information about the terms of the reaffirmation, it will help to ensure that the reaffirmation represents a fully informed agreement by the debtor and will assist the bankruptcy court in determining whether reaffirmation is in the debtor's best interest.

In a memorandum to bankruptcy judges and clerks announcing the new form, dated June 17, 1999, the Administrative Office stated that use of the form is "strongly recommended." Some courts have adopted local rules requiring its use. The Administrative Office also indicated in the memorandum that the new form incorporates certain requirements imposed by the Bankruptcy Reform Act of 1994 and also adopts many suggestions included in the National Bankruptcy Review Commission's final report issued on October 20, 1997.

Appearance of Child Support Creditor or Representative

This form may be used by a child support creditor or the authorized representative of a child support creditor to file an appearance in a bankruptcy case. The filing of such appearance will enable the child support creditor or representative to be added to the list of creditors that the court will use for the mailing of notices, even when such creditor was not listed in the schedules filed by the debtor. It should also ensure that such creditor will continue to receive the notices to creditors required by Fed. R. Bankr. P. 2002, even when such creditor has not filed a proof of claim. By filing this form, such creditor will not be charged a fee for filing certain motions. *See* Appx. C, *supra* (Judicial Conference Schedule of Fees). The information relating to the child support obligation may be of interest to the court or the trustee in determining the feasibility of a chapter 13 plan.

United States Bankruptcy Court

_____ District of _____

NOTICE TO INDIVIDUAL CONSUMER DEBTOR

The purpose of this notice is to acquaint you with the four chapters of the federal Bankruptcy Code under which you may file a bankruptcy petition. The bankruptcy law is complicated and not easily described. Therefore, you should seek the advice of an attorney to learn of your rights and responsibilities under the law should you decide to file a petition with the court. Neither the judge nor the court's employees may provide you with legal advice.

Chapter 7: Liquidation ($155 filing fee plus $30 administrative fee plus $15 trustee surcharge)

1. Chapter 7 is designed for debtors in financial difficulty who do not have the ability to pay their existing debts.

2. Under chapter 7 a trustee takes possession of all your property. You may claim certain of your property as exempt under governing law. The trustee then liquidates the property and uses the proceeds to pay your creditors according to priorities of the Bankruptcy Code.

3. The purpose of filing a chapter 7 case is to obtain a discharge of your existing debts. If, however, you are found to have committed certain kinds of improper conduct described in the Bankruptcy Code, your discharge may be denied by the court, and the purpose for which you filed the bankruptcy petition will be defeated.

4. Even if you receive a discharge, there are some debts that are not discharged under the law. Therefore, you may still be responsible for such debts as certain taxes and student loans, alimony and support payments, criminal restitution, and debts for death or personal injury caused by driving while intoxicated from alcohol or drugs.

5. Under certain circumstances you may keep property that you have purchased subject to a valid security interest. Your attorney can explain the options that are available to you.

Chapter 13: Repayment of All or Part of the Debts of an Individual with Regular Income ($155 filing fee plus $30 administrative fee)

1. Chapter 13 is designed for individuals with regular income who are temporarily unable to pay their debts but would like to pay them in installments over a period of time. You are only eligible for chapter 13 if your debts do not exceed certain dollar amounts set forth in the Bankruptcy Code.

2. Under chapter 13 you must file a plan with the court to repay your creditors all or part of the money that you owe them, using your future earnings. Usually, the period allowed by the court to repay your debts is three years, but not more than five years. Your plan must be approved by the court before it can take effect.

3. Under chapter 13, unlike chapter 7, you may keep all your property, both exempt and non-exempt, as long as you continue to make payments under the plan.

4. After completion of payments under your plan, your debts are discharged except alimony and support payments, student loans, certain other debts including criminal restitution and debts for death or personal injury caused by driving while intoxicated from alcohol or drugs, and long term secured obligations.

Chapter 11: Reorganization ($800 filing fee plus $30 administrative fee)

Chapter 11 is designed primarily for the reorganization of a business but is also available to consumer debtors. Its provisions are quite complicated, and any decision by an individual to file a chapter 11 petition should be reviewed with an attorney.

Chapter 12: Family Farmer ($200 filing fee plus $30 administrative fee)

Chapter 12 is designed to permit family farmers to repay their debts over a period of time from future earnings and is in many ways similar to a chapter 13. The eligibility requirements are restrictive, limiting its use to those whose income arises primarily from a family-owned farm.

I, the debtor, affirm that I have read this notice.

_____   _____   _____
Date   Signature of Debtor   Case Number

United States Bankruptcy Court

_____ **District of** _____

In re _____

                                                    Bankruptcy Case No. _____

Debtor _____

STATEMENT OF ATTORNEY COMPENSATION
UNDER BANKRUPTCY RULE 2016(b)

Pursuant to Bankruptcy Rule 2016(b), the undersigned, attorney for the debtor(s) herein, states that s/he has received no compensation for services rendered or to be rendered. The debtor(s) is/are being provided legal services at no charge, and it has been agreed that there will be no compensation for services rendered paid to the undersigned or any other party.

_____   _____
            Date   *Attorney for Debtor(s)*

United States Bankruptcy Court

_____ **District of** _____

In re _____

                                   Bankruptcy Case No. _____

Debtor _____

DISCLOSURE OF COMPENSATION OF ATTORNEY FOR DEBTOR

1. Pursuant to 11 U.S.C. § 329(a) and Bankruptcy Rule 2016(b), I certify that I am the attorney for the above-named debtor(s) and that compensation paid to me within one year before the filing of the petition in bankruptcy, or agreed to be paid to me, for services rendered or to be rendered on behalf of the debtor(s) in contemplation of or in connection with the bankruptcy case is as follows:

    For legal services, I have agreed to accept . . . . $ _____

    Prior to the filing of this statement I have received . . . . $ _____

    Balance Due . . . . $ _____

2. The source of the compensation paid to me was:

        ☐ Debtor   ☐ Other (specify)

3. The source of compensation to be paid to me is:

        ☐ Debtor   ☐ Other (specify)

4. ☐ I have not agreed to share the above-disclosed compensation with any other person unless they are members and associates of my law firm.

    ☐ I have agreed to share the above-disclosed compensation with a person or persons who are not members or associates of my law firm. A copy of the agreement, together with a list of the names of the people sharing in the compensation, is attached.

5. In return for the above-disclosed fee, I have agreed to render legal service for all aspects of the bankruptcy case, including:

    a. Analysis of the debtor's financial situation, and rendering advice to the debtor in determining whether to file a petition in bankruptcy;

    b. Preparation and filing of any petition, schedules, statement of affairs and plan which may be required;

    c. Representation of the debtor at the meeting of creditors and confirmation hearing, and any adjourned hearings thereof;

DISCLOSURE OF COMPENSATION OF ATTORNEY FOR DEBTOR (Continued)

   d. Representation of the debtor in adversary proceedings and other contested bankruptcy matters;

   e. [Other provisions as needed]

6. By agreement with the debtor(s), the above-disclosed fee does not include the following services:

CERTIFICATION

   I certify that the foregoing is a complete statement of any agreement or arrangement for payment to me for representation of the debtor(s) in this bankruptcy proceeding.

_____   _____
                    Date   *Signature of Attorney*

                                                                _____
                                                                              Name of law firm

---

B 104 (Rev. 2/92)	**ADVERSARY PROCEEDING COVER SHEET** (Instructions on Reverse)	ADVERSARY PROCEEDING NUMBER (Court Use Only)

PLAINTIFFS	**DEFENDANTS**
ATTORNEYS (Firm Name, Address, and Telephone No.)	ATTORNEYS (If Known)

PARTY (check one box only)　☐ 1 U.S. PLAINTIFF　☐ 2 U.S. DEFENDANT　☐ 3 U.S. NOT A PARTY

CAUSE OF ACTION (WRITE A BRIEF STATEMENT OF CAUSE OF ACTION, INCLUDING ALL U.S. STATUTES INVOLVED)

NATURE OF SUIT
(Check the one most appropriate box only)

☐ 454　To Recover Money or Property
☐ 435　To Determine Validity, Priority, or Extent of a Lien or Other Interest in Property
☐ 458　To obtain approval for the sale of both the interest of the estate and of a co-owner in property
☐ 424　To object or to revoke a discharge 11 U.S.C. § 727

☐ 455　To revoke an order of confirmation of a Ch. 11, Ch. 12 or Ch. 13 Plan
☐ 426　To determine the dischargeability of a debt 11 U.S.C. § 523　　459
☐ 434　To obtain an injunction or other equitable relief
☐ 457　To subordinate any allowed claim or interest except where such subordination is provided in a plan

☐ 456　To obtain a declaratory judgment relating to any of foregoing causes of action
　　To determine a claim or cause of
☐ 　　action removed to a bankruptcy court
☐ 　　498 Other (specify)
☐ 　　499 Hardship Discharge (student loan)

ORIGIN OF PROCEEDINGS (Check one box only.)	☐1 Original Proceeding	☐2 Removed Proceeding	☐4 Reinstated or Reopened	☐5 Transferred from Another Bankruptcy Court	☐ CHECK IF THIS IS A CLASS ACTION UNDER F.R.C.P. 23

DEMAND	NEAREST THOUSAND $	OTHER RELIEF SOUGHT	☐ JURY DEMAND

BANKRUPTCY CASE IN WHICH THIS ADVERSARY PROCEEDING ARISES

NAME OF DEBTOR	BANKRUPTCY CASE NO.
DISTRICT IN WHICH CASE IS PENDING	DIVISIONAL OFFICE	NAME OF JUDGE

RELATED ADVERSARY PROCEEDING (IF ANY)

PLAINTIFF	DEFENDANT	ADVERSARY PROCEEDING NO.
DISTRICT	DIVISIONAL OFFICE	NAME OF JUDGE

FILING FEE　(Check one box only.)	☐ FEE ATTACHED	☐ FEE NOT REQUIRED	☐ FEE IS DEFERRED

DATE	PRINT NAME	SIGNATURE OF ATTORNEY (OR PLAINTIFF)

ADVERSARY PROCEEDING COVER SHEET (Reverse Side)

This cover sheet must be completed by the plaintiff's attorney (or by the plaintiff if the plaintiff is not represented by an attorney) and submitted to the Clerk of the court upon the filing of a complaint initiating an adversary proceeding.

The cover sheet and the information contained on it *do not* replace or supplement the filing and service of pleadings or other papers as required by law, the Bankruptcy Rules, or the local rules of court. This form is required for the use of the clerk of the court to initiate the docket sheet and to prepare necessary indices and statistical records. A separate cover sheet must be submitted to the clerk of the court for each complaint filed. The form is largely self explanatory.

Parties. The names of the parties to the adversary proceeding *exactly* as they appear on the complaint. Give the names and addresses of the attorneys if known. Following the heading "Party," check the appropriate box indicating whether the United States is a party named in the complaint.

Cause of Action. Give a brief description of the cause of action including all federal statutes involved. For example, "Complaint seeking damages for failure to disclose information, Consumer Credit Protection Act, 15 U.S.C. § 1601 et seq.," or "Complaint by trustee to avoid a transfer of property by the debtor, 11 U.S.C. § 544."

Nature of Suit. Place an "X" in the appropriate box. Only one box should be checked. If the cause fits more than one category of suit, select the most definitive.

Origin of Proceedings. Check the appropriate box to indicate the origin of the case:

> 1. Original Proceeding.
> 2. Removed from a State or District Court.
> 4. Reinstated or Reopened.
> 5. Transferred from Another Bankruptcy Court.

Demand. On the next line, state the dollar amount demanded in the complaint in thousands of dollars. For $1,000 enter "1," for $10,000 enter "10," for $100,000 enter "100," if $1,000,000, enter "1000." If $10,000,000 or more, enter "9999." If the amount is less than $1,000, enter "0001." If no monetary demand is made, enter "XXXX." If the plaintiff is seeking non-monetary relief, state the relief sought, such as injunction or foreclosure of a mortgage.

Bankruptcy Case In Which This Adversary Proceeding Arises. Enter the name of the debtor and the docket number of the bankruptcy case from which the proceeding now being filed arose. Beneath, enter the district and divisional office where the case was filed, and the name of the presiding judge.

Related Adversary Proceedings. State the names of the parties and the six digit adversary proceeding number from any adversary proceeding concerning the same two parties or the same property currently pending in any bankruptcy court. On the next line, enter the district where the related case is pending, and the name of the presiding judge.

Filing Fee. Check one box. The fee must be paid upon filing unless the plaintiff meets one of the following exceptions. The fee is not required if the plaintiff is the United States government or the debtor. If the plaintiff is the trustee or a debtor in possession, and there are no liquid funds in the estate, the filing fee may be deferred until there are funds in the estate. (In the event no funds are ever recovered for the estate, there will be no fee.) There is no fee for adding a party after the adversary proceeding has been commenced.

Signature. This cover sheet must be signed by the attorney of record in the box on the right of the last line of the form. If the plaintiff is represented by a law firm, a member of the firm must sign. If the plaintiff is *pro se*, that is, not represented by an attorney, the plaintiff must sign.

The name of the signatory must be printed in the box to the left of the signature. The date of the signing must be indicated in the box on the far left of the last line.

United States Bankruptcy Court

_____ **District of** _____

In re _____

           Debtor

           Bankruptcy Case No. _____

           Plaintiff

           Adversary Proceeding No. _____

           Defendant

SUMMONS AND NOTICE OF TRIAL IN AN ADVERSARY PROCEEDING

YOU ARE SUMMONED and required to submit a motion or answer to the complaint which is attached to this summons to the clerk of the bankruptcy court within 30 days after the date of issuance of this summons, except that the United States and its offices and agencies shall submit a motion or answer to the complaint within 35 days.

Address of Clerk

At the same time, you must also serve a copy of the motion or answer upon the plaintiff's attorney.

Name and Address of Plaintiff's Attorney

If you make a motion, your time to answer is governed by Bankruptcy Rule 7012.

YOU ARE NOTIFIED that a trial of the proceeding commenced by the filing of the complaint will be held at the following time and place.

Address	Room
	Date and Time

IF YOU FAIL TO RESPOND TO THIS SUMMONS, YOUR FAILURE WILL BE DEEMED TO BE YOUR CONSENT TO ENTRY OF A JUDGMENT BY THE BANKRUPTCY COURT AND JUDGMENT BY DEFAULT MAY BE TAKEN AGAINST YOU FOR THE RELIEF DEMANDED IN THE COMPLAINT.

_____
Clerk of the Bankruptcy Court

_____   By: _____

      Date   *Deputy Clerk*

I, _____ , certify that I am, and at all times during the service of process

(name)

was, not less than 18 years of age and not a party to the matter concerning which service of process was made.
I further certify that the service of this summons and a copy of the complaint was made _____
by:

(date)

☐ Mail service: Regular, first class United States mail, postage fully pre-paid, addressed to:

☐ Personal Service: By leaving the process with defendant or with an officer or agent of defendant at:

☐ Residence Service: By leaving the process with the following adult at:

☐ Publication: The defendant was served as follows: [Describe briefly]

☐ State Law: The defendant was served pursuant to the laws of the State of _____ ,
as follows: [Describe briefly]

(name of state)

Under penalty of perjury, I declare that the foregoing is true and correct.

_____   _____
Date   *Signature*

Print Name		
Business Address		
City	State	Zip

United States Bankruptcy Court

_____ **District of** _____

In re _____

                Debtor

                Plaintiff

                Defendant

Bankruptcy Case No. _____

Adversary Proceeding No. _____

SUMMONS IN AN ADVERSARY PROCEEDING

YOU ARE SUMMONED and required to submit a motion or answer to the complaint which is attached to this summons to the clerk of the bankruptcy court within 30 days after the date of issuance of this summons, except that the United States and its offices and agencies shall submit a motion or answer to the complaint within 35 days.

> Address of Clerk

At the same time, you must also serve a copy of the motion or answer upon the plaintiff's attorney.

> Name and Address of Plaintiff's Attorney

If you make a motion, your time to answer is governed by Bankruptcy Rule 7012.

IF YOU FAIL TO RESPOND TO THIS SUMMONS, YOUR FAILURE WILL BE DEEMED TO BE YOUR CONSENT TO ENTRY OF A JUDGMENT BY THE BANKRUPTCY COURT AND JUDGMENT BY DEFAULT MAY BE TAKEN AGAINST YOU FOR THE RELIEF DEMANDED IN THE COMPLAINT.

_____
Clerk of the Bankruptcy Court

_____
Date

By: _____
Deputy Clerk

CERTIFICATE OF SERVICE

I, _____ , certify that I am, and at all times during the service of process
(name)
was, not less than 18 years of age and not a party to the matter concerning which service of process was made.
I further certify that the service of this summons and a copy of the complaint was made _____
by: (date)

☐ Mail service: Regular, first class United States mail, postage fully pre-paid, addressed to:

☐ Personal Service: By leaving the process with defendant or with an officer or agent of defendant at:

☐ Residence Service: By leaving the process with the following adult at:

☐ Publication: The defendant was served as follows: [Describe briefly]

☐ State Law: The defendant was served pursuant to the laws of the State of _____ ,
as follows: [Describe briefly]   (name of state)

Under penalty of perjury, I declare that the foregoing is true and correct.

_____   _____
Date   *Signature*

Print Name		
Business Address		
City	State	Zip

United States Bankruptcy Court

_____ **District of** _____

In re _____

                    Debtor

                    Bankruptcy Case No. _____

                    Plaintiff

                    Defendant and Third-Party Plaintiff

                    Adversary Proceeding No. _____

                    Third-Party Defendant

THIRD-PARTY SUMMONS

YOU ARE SUMMONED and required to submit a motion or answer to the third-party complaint which is attached to this summons to the clerk of the bankruptcy court within 30 days after the date of issuance of this summons, except that the United States and its offices and agencies shall submit a motion or answer to the third-party complaint within 35 days.

Address of Clerk

At the same time, you must also serve a copy of the motion or answer upon Plaintiff's attorney.

Name and Address of Plaintiff's Attorney

At the same time, you must also serve a copy of the motion or answer upon Defendant and Third-Party Plaintiff's Attorney.

Name and Address of Attorney

If you make a motion, your time to answer is governed by Bankruptcy Rule 7012. If you are also being served with a copy of the complaint of the plaintiff you have the option of not answering the plaintiff's complaint **unless** this is an admiralty or maritime case subject to the provisions of Federal Rules of Civil Procedure 9(h) and 14(c), in which case you are required to submit a motion or an answer to both the plaintiff's complaint and the third-party complaint, and to serve a copy of your motion or answer upon the appropriate parties.

IF YOU FAIL TO RESPOND TO THIS SUMMONS, YOUR FAILURE WILL BE DEEMED TO BE YOUR CONSENT TO ENTRY OF A JUDGMENT BY THE BANKRUPTCY COURT AND JUDGMENT BY DEFAULT MAY BE TAKEN AGAINST YOU FOR THE RELIEF DEMANDED IN THE THIRD-PARTY COMPLAINT.

                    _____

                    Clerk of the Bankruptcy Court

_____   By: _____

      Date   *Deputy Clerk*

CERTIFICATE OF SERVICE

I, _____ , certify that I am, and at all times during the service of process
    (name)
was, not less than 18 years of age and not a party to the matter concerning which service of process was made.
I further certify that the service of this summons and a copy of the complaint was made _____
by: (date)

☐ Mail service: Regular, first class United States mail, postage fully pre-paid, addressed to:

☐ Personal Service: By leaving the process with defendant or with an officer or agent of defendant at:

☐ Residence Service: By leaving the process with the following adult at:

☐ Publication: The defendant was served as follows: [Describe briefly]

☐ State Law: The defendant was served pursuant to the laws of the State of _____ ,
    as follows: [Describe briefly]   (name of state)

Under penalty of perjury, I declare that the foregoing is true and correct.

_____   _____
            Date   *Signature*

Print Name		
Business Address		
City	State	Zip

United States Bankruptcy Court

_____ District of _____

In re _____ ,

                 Debtor

To:

SUBPOENA FOR RULE 2004 EXAMINATION

Case No. _____

Chapter _____

☐ YOU ARE COMMANDED to appear pursuant to a court order issued under Rule 2004, Fed.R.Bankr.P., at the place, date, and time specified below to testify at the taking of a deposition in the above case.

PLACE	DATE AND TIME

☐ YOU ARE COMMANDED to produce and permit inspection and copying of the following documents or objects at the place, date, and time specified below (list documents or objects):

PLACE	DATE AND TIME

ISSUING OFFICER SIGNATURE AND TITLE	DATE

ISSUING OFFICER'S NAME, ADDRESS AND PHONE NUMBER

PROOF OF SERVICE

	DATE	PLACE
SERVED		

SERVED ON (PRINT NAME)	MANNER OF SERVICE

SERVED BY (PRINT NAME)	TITLE

DECLARATION OF SERVER

I declare under penalty of perjury under the laws of the United States of America that the foregoing information contained in the Proof of Service is true and correct.

Executed on _____

_____   _____
DATE   SIGNATURE OF SERVER

_____
ADDRESS OF SERVER

_____

Rule 45, Fed.R.Civ.P., Parts (c) & (d) made applicable in cases under the Bankruptcy Code by Rule 9016, Fed.R.Bankr.P.

(c) PROTECTION OF PERSONS SUBJECT TO SUBPOENAS.

(1) A party or an attorney responsible for the issuance and service of a subpoena shall take reasonable steps to avoid imposing undue burden or expense on a person subject to that subpoena. The court on behalf of which the subpoena was issued shall enforce this duty and impose upon the party or attorney in breach of this duty an appropriate sanction, which may include, but is not limited to, lost earnings and a reasonable attorney's fee.

(2)(A) A person commanded to produce and permit inspection and copying of designated books, papers, documents or tangible things, or inspection of premises need not appear in person at the place of production or inspection unless commanded to appear for deposition, hearing or trial.

(B) Subject to paragraph (d)(2) of this rule, a person commanded to produce and permit inspection and copying may, within 14 days after service of the subpoena or before the time specified for compliance if such time is less than 14 days after service, serve upon the party or attorney designated in the subpoena written objection to inspection or copying of any or all of the designated materials or of the premises. If objection is made, the party serving the subpoena shall not be entitled to inspect and copy the materials or inspect the premises except pursuant to an order of the court by which the subpoena was issued. If objection has been made, the party serving the subpoena may, upon notice to the person commanded to produce, move at any time for an order to compel the production. Such an order to compel production shall protect any person who is not a party or an officer of a party from significant expense resulting from the inspection and copying commanded.

(3)(A) On timely motion, the court by which a subpoena was issued shall quash or modify the subpoena if it

(i) fails to allow reasonable time for compliance;
(ii) requires a person who is not a party or an officer of a party to travel to a place more than 100 miles from the place where that person resides, is employed or regularly transacts business in person, except that, subject to the provisions of clause (c)(3)(B)(iii) of this rule, such a person may in order to attend trial be commanded to travel from any such place within the state in which the trial is held, or

(iii) requires disclosure of privileged or other protected matter and no exception or waiver applies, or
(iv) subjects a person to undue burden.

(B) If a subpoena

(i) requires disclosure of a trade secret or other confidential research, development, or commercial information, or
(ii) requires disclosure of an unretained expert's opinion or information not describing specific events or occurrences in dispute and resulting from the expert's study made not at the request of any party, or
(iii) requires a person who is not a party or an officer of a party to incur substantial expense to travel more than 100 miles to attend trial, the court may, to protect a person subject to or affected by the subpoena, quash or modify the subpoena or, if the party in whose behalf the subpoena is issued shows a substantial need for the testimony or material that cannot be otherwise met without undue hardship and assures that the person to whom the subpoena is addressed will be reasonably compensated, the court may order appearance or production only upon specified conditions.

(d) DUTIES IN RESPONDING TO SUBPOENA.

(1) A person responding to a subpoena to produce documents shall produce them as they are kept in the usual course of business or shall organize and label them to correspond with the categories in the demand.

(2) When information subject to a subpoena is withheld on a claim that it is privileged or subject to protection as trial preparation materials, the claim shall be made expressly and shall be supported by a description of the nature of the documents, communications, or things not produced that is sufficient to enable the demanding party to contest the claim.

United States Bankruptcy Court

_____ DISTRICT OF_____

In re _____ ,
　　　　　　Debtor

　　　　　　Plaintiff,

　　　　　　V.

　　　　　　Defendant,

To:

**SUBPOENA IN
AN ADVERSARY PROCEEDING**

Case No. _____

Chapter _____

Adv. Proc. No. _____

☐ YOU ARE COMMANDED to appear in the United States Bankruptcy Court at the place, date, and time specified below to testify in the above adversary proceeding.

PLACE	COURTROOM
	DATE AND TIME

☐ YOU ARE COMMANDED to appear at the place, date, and time specified below to testify at the taking of a deposition in the above adversary proceeding.

PLACE	DATE AND TIME

☐ YOU ARE COMMANDED to produce and permit inspection and copying of the following documents or objects at the place, date, and time specified below (list documents or objects):

PLACE	DATE AND TIME

☐ YOU ARE COMMANDED to permit inspection of the following premises at the date and time specified below.

PREMISES	DATE AND TIME

　　Any subpoenaed organization not a party to this adversary proceeding shall designate one or more officers, directors, or managing agents, or other persons who consent to testify on its behalf, and may set forth, for each person designated, the matters on which the person will testify, Fed.R.Civ.P. 30(b)(6) made applicable in adversary proceedings by Rule 7030, Fed.R.Bankr.P.

ISSUING OFFICER SIGNATURE AND TITLE	DATE

ISSUING OFFICER'S NAME, ADDRESS AND PHONE NUMBER

PROOF OF SERVICE

SERVED	DATE	PLACE

SERVED ON (PRINT NAME)	MANNER OF SERVICE

SERVED BY (PRINT NAME)	TITLE

DECLARATION OF SERVER

I declare under penalty of perjury under the laws of the United States of America that the foregoing information contained in the Proof of Service is true and correct.

Executed on

_____   _____
                    DATE   SIGNATURE OF SERVER

                                          _____
                                          ADDRESS OF SERVER

                                          _____

Rule 45, Fed.R.Civ.P., Parts (c) & (d) made applicable in cases under the Bankruptcy Code by Rule 9016, Fed.R.Bankr.P.

(c) PROTECTION OF PERSONS SUBJECT TO SUBPOENAS.

(1) A party or an attorney responsible for the issuance and service of a subpoena shall take reasonable steps to avoid imposing undue burden or expense on a person subject to that subpoena. The court on behalf of which the subpoena was issued shall enforce this duty and impose upon the party or attorney in breach of this duty an appropriate sanction, which may include, but is not limited to, lost earnings and a reasonable attorney's fee.

(2)(A) A person commanded to produce and permit inspection and copying of designated books, papers, documents or tangible things, or inspection of premises need not appear in person at the place of production or inspection unless commanded to appear for deposition, hearing or trial.

(B) Subject to paragraph (d)(2) of this rule, a person commanded to produce and permit inspection and copying may, within 14 days after service of the subpoena or before the time specified for compliance if such time is less than 14 days after service, serve upon the party or attorney designated in the subpoena written objection to inspection or copying of any or all of the designated materials or of the premises. If objection is made, the party serving the subpoena shall not be entitled to inspect and copy the materials or inspect the premises except pursuant to an order of the court by which the subpoena was issued. If objection has been made, the party serving the subpoena may, upon notice to the person commanded to produce, move at any time for an order to compel the production. Such an order to compel production shall protect any person who is not a party or an officer of a party from significant expense resulting from the inspection and copying commanded.

(3)(A) On timely motion, the court by which a subpoena was issued shall quash or modify the subpoena if it

(i) fails to allow reasonable time for compliance;
(ii) requires a person who is not a party or an officer of a party to travel to a place more than 100 miles from the place where that person resides, is employed or regularly transacts business in person, except that, subject to the provisions of clause (c)(3)(B)(iii) of this rule, such a person may in order to attend trial be commanded to travel from any such place within the state in which the trial is held, or
(iii) requires disclosure of privileged or other protected matter and no exception or waiver applies, or
(iv) subjects a person to undue burden.

(B) If a subpoena

(i) requires disclosure of a trade secret or other confidential research, development, or commercial information, or
(ii) requires disclosure of an unretained expert's opinion or information not describing specific events or occurrences in dispute and resulting from the expert's study made not at the request of any party, or
(iii) requires a person who is not a party or an officer of a party to incur substantial expense to travel more than 100 miles to attend trial, the court may, to protect a person subject to or affected by the subpoena, quash or modify the subpoena or, if the party in whose behalf the subpoena is issued shows a substantial need for the testimony or material that cannot be otherwise met without undue hardship and assures that the person to whom the subpoena is addressed will be reasonably compensated, the court may order appearance or production only upon specified conditions.

(d) DUTIES IN RESPONDING TO SUBPOENA.

(1) A person responding to a subpoena to produce documents shall produce them as they are kept in the usual course of business or shall organize and label them to correspond with the categories in the demand.

(2) When information subject to a subpoena is withheld on a claim that it is privileged or subject to protection as trial preparation materials, the claim shall be made expressly and shall be supported by a description of the nature of the documents, communications, or things not produced that is sufficient to enable the demanding party to contest the claim.

United States Bankruptcy Court

_____ DISTRICT OF_____

In re _____ ,

           Debtor

**SUBPOENA IN A CASE UNDER
THE BANKRUPTCY CODE**

Case No. _____

To:

Chapter _____

☐ YOU ARE COMMANDED to appear in the United States Bankruptcy Court at the place, date, and time specified below to testify in the above case.

PLACE	COURTROOM
	DATE AND TIME

☐ YOU ARE COMMANDED to appear at the place, date, and time specified below to testify at the taking of a deposition in the above case.

PLACE	DATE AND TIME

☐ YOU ARE COMMANDED to produce and permit inspection and copying of the following documents or objects at the place, date, and time specified below (list documents or objects):

PLACE	DATE AND TIME

☐ YOU ARE COMMANDED to permit inspection of the following premises at the date and time specified below.

PREMISES	DATE AND TIME

    Any subpoenaed organization not a party to this proceeding shall designate one or more officers, directors, or managing agents, or other persons who consent to testify on its behalf, and may set forth, for each person designated, the matters on which the person will testify, Fed.R.Civ.P. 30(b)(6) made applicable to this proceeding by Rule 7030, Fed.R.Bankr.P. See Rules 1018 and 9014, Fed.R.Bankr.P.

ISSUING OFFICER SIGNATURE AND TITLE	DATE

ISSUING OFFICER'S NAME, ADDRESS AND PHONE NUMBER

PROOF OF SERVICE

	DATE	PLACE
SERVED		

SERVED ON (PRINT NAME)	MANNER OF SERVICE

SERVED BY (PRINT NAME)	TITLE

DECLARATION OF SERVER

I declare under penalty of perjury under the laws of the United States of America that the foregoing information contained in the Proof of Service is true and correct.

Executed on

_____

DATE

_____

SIGNATURE OF SERVER

_____

ADDRESS OF SERVER

Rule 45, Fed.R.Civ.P., Parts (c) & (d) made applicable in cases under the Bankruptcy Code by Rule 9016, Fed.R.Bankr.P.

(c) PROTECTION OF PERSONS SUBJECT TO SUBPOENAS.

(1) A party or an attorney responsible for the issuance and service of a subpoena shall take reasonable steps to avoid imposing undue burden or expense on a person subject to that subpoena. The court on behalf of which the subpoena was issued shall enforce this duty and impose upon the party or attorney in breach of this duty an appropriate sanction, which may include, but is not limited to, lost earnings and a reasonable attorney's fee.

(2)(A) A person commanded to produce and permit inspection and copying of designated books, papers, documents or tangible things, or inspection of premises need not appear in person at the place of production or inspection unless commanded to appear for deposition, hearing or trial.

(B) Subject to paragraph (d)(2) of this rule, a person commanded to produce and permit inspection and copying may, within 14 days after service of the subpoena or before the time specified for compliance if such time is less than 14 days after service, serve upon the party or attorney designated in the subpoena written objection to inspection or copying of any or all of the designated materials or of the premises. If objection is made, the party serving the subpoena shall not be entitled to inspect and copy the materials or inspect the premises except pursuant to an order of the court by which the subpoena was issued. If objection has been made, the party serving the subpoena may, upon notice to the person commanded to produce, move at any time for an order to compel the production. Such an order to compel production shall protect any person who is not a party or an officer of a party from significant expense resulting from the inspection and copying commanded.

(3)(A) On timely motion, the court by which a subpoena was issued shall quash or modify the subpoena if it

(i) fails to allow reasonable time for compliance;

(ii) requires a person who is not a party or an officer of a party to travel to a place more than 100 miles from the place where that person resides, is employed or regularly transacts business in person, except that, subject to the provisions of clause (c)(3)(B)(iii) of this rule, such a person may in order to attend trial be commanded to travel from any such place within the state in which the trial is held, or

(iii) requires disclosure of privileged or other protected matter and no exception or waiver applies, or

(iv) subjects a person to undue burden.

(B) If a subpoena

(i) requires disclosure of a trade secret or other confidential research, development, or commercial information, or

(ii) requires disclosure of an unretained expert's opinion or information not describing specific events or occurrences in dispute and resulting from the expert's study made not at the request of any party, or

(iii) requires a person who is not a party or an officer of a party to incur substantial expense to travel more than 100 miles to attend trial, the court may, to protect a person subject to or affected by the subpoena, quash or modify the subpoena or, if the party in whose behalf the subpoena is issued shows a substantial need for the testimony or material that cannot be otherwise met without undue hardship and assures that the person to whom the subpoena is addressed will be reasonably compensated, the court may order appearance or production only upon specified conditions.

(d) DUTIES IN RESPONDING TO SUBPOENA.

(1) A person responding to a subpoena to produce documents shall produce them as they are kept in the usual course of business or shall organize and label them to correspond with the categories in the demand.

(2) When information subject to a subpoena is withheld on a claim that it is privileged or subject to protection as trial preparation materials, the claim shall be made expressly and shall be supported by a description of the nature of the documents, communications, or things not produced that is sufficient to enable the demanding party to contest the claim.

(7/99)

United States Bankruptcy Court

_____ District Of _____

In re

Case No. _____

Debtor*

Address: Chapter 13

Social Security No(s).:
Employer's Tax I.D. No(s). [if any]:

DISCHARGE OF DEBTOR AFTER COMPLETION
OF CHAPTER 13 PLAN

It appearing that the debtor is entitled to a discharge,

IT IS ORDERED:

The debtor is granted a discharge under section 1328(a) of title 11, United States Code, (the Bankruptcy Code).

BY THE COURT

Dated: _____   _____
                                                      United States Bankruptcy Judge

SEE THE BACK OF THIS ORDER FOR IMPORTANT INFORMATION.

Set forth all names, including trade names, used by the debtor within the last 6 years. (Federal Rule of Bankruptcy Procedure 1005).

Form B 18W continued
7/99

EXPLANATION OF BANKRUPTCY DISCHARGE
IN A CHAPTER 13 CASE

This court order grants a discharge to the person named as the debtor after the debtor has completed all payments under the chapter 13 plan. It is not a dismissal of the case.

Collection of Discharged Debts Prohibited

The discharge prohibits any attempt to collect from the debtor a debt that has been discharged. For example, a creditor is not permitted to contact a debtor by mail, phone, or otherwise, to file or continue a lawsuit, to attach wages or other property, or to take any other action to collect a discharged debt from the debtor. *[In a case involving community property:]* [There are also special rules that protect certain community property owned by the debtor's spouse, even if that spouse did not file a bankruptcy case.] A creditor who violates this order can be required to pay damages and attorney's fees to the debtor.

However, a creditor may have the right to enforce a valid lien, such as a mortgage or security interest, against the debtor's property after the bankruptcy, if that lien was not avoided or eliminated in the bankruptcy case. Also, a debtor may voluntarily pay any debt that has been discharged.

Debts That are Discharged

The chapter 13 discharge order eliminates a debtor's legal obligation to pay a debt that is discharged. Most, but not all, types of debts are discharged if the debt is provided for by the chapter 13 plan or is disallowed by the court pursuant to section 502 of the Bankruptcy Code.

Debts that are Not Discharged

Some of the common types of debts which are not discharged in a chapter 13 bankruptcy case are:

a. Debts that are in the nature of alimony, maintenance, or support;

b. Debts for most student loans;

c. Debts for most fines, penalties, forfeitures, or criminal restitution obligations;

d. Debts for personal injuries or death caused by the debtor's operation of a motor vehicle while intoxicated;

e. Debts provided for under section 1322(b)(5) of the Bankruptcy Code and on which the last payment is due after the date on which the final payment under the plan was due; and

f. Debts for certain consumer purchases made after the bankruptcy case was filed if prior approval by the trustee of the debtor's incurring the debt was practicable but was not obtained.

This information is only a general summary of the bankruptcy discharge. There are exceptions to these general rules. Because the law is complicated, you may want to consult an attorney to determine the exact effect of the discharge in this case.

B 18WH
(7/99)

United States Bankruptcy Court

_____ District Of _____

In re

Case No. _____

Debtor*

Address: Chapter 13

Social Security No(s).:
Employer's Tax I.D. No(s). [if any]:

DISCHARGE OF DEBTOR BEFORE COMPLETION
OF CHAPTER 13 PLAN

It appearing that the debtor is entitled to a discharge,

IT IS ORDERED:

The debtor is granted a discharge under section 1328(b) of title 11, United States Code, (the Bankruptcy Code).

BY THE COURT

Dated: _____   _____
                                    United States Bankruptcy Judge

SEE THE BACK OF THIS ORDER FOR IMPORTANT INFORMATION.

EXPLANATION OF BANKRUPTCY DISCHARGE
IN A CHAPTER 13 CASE BEFORE COMPLETION OF PLAN PAYMENTS

This court order grants a discharge to the person named as the debtor. After notice and a hearing, the court has determined that the debtor is entitled to a discharge pursuant to section 1328(b) of the Bankruptcy Code without completing all of the payments under the chapter 13 plan. Because this discharge is granted pursuant to the hardship provisions of section 1328(b), it is referred to as a chapter 13 "hardship discharge." This order is not the dismissal of the case.

Collection of Discharged Debts Prohibited

The discharge prohibits any attempt to collect from the debtor a debt that has been discharged. For example, a creditor is not permitted to contact a debtor by mail, phone, or otherwise, to file or continue a lawsuit, to attach wages or other property, or to take any other action to collect a discharged debt from the debtor. *[In a case involving community property:]* [There are also special rules that protect certain community property owned by the debtor's spouse, even if that spouse did not file a bankruptcy case.] A creditor who violates this order can be required to pay damages and attorney's fees to the debtor.

However, a creditor may have the right to enforce a valid lien, such as a mortgage or security interest, against the debtor's property after the bankruptcy, if that lien was not avoided or eliminated in the bankruptcy case. Also, a debtor may voluntarily pay any debt that has been discharged.

Debts That Are Discharged

The chapter 13 "hardship discharge" order eliminates a debtor's legal obligation to pay a debt that is discharged. Most, but not all, types of debts are discharged if the debt is provided for by the chapter 13 plan or is disallowed by the court pursuant to section 502 of the Bankruptcy Code.

Debts that are Not Discharged

Some of the common types of debts which are not eliminated by chapter 13 "hardship discharge" are:

a. Debts for most taxes;

b. Debts that are in the nature of alimony, maintenance, or support;

c. Debts for most student loans;

e. Debts provided for under section 1322(b)(5) of the Bankruptcy Code and on which the last payment is due after the date on which the final payment under the plan was due;

e. Debts for certain consumer purchases made after the bankruptcy case was filed if prior approval by the trustee of the debtor's incurring the debt was practicable but was not obtained;

f. Debts for most fines, penalties, forfeitures, or criminal restitution obligations;

g. Debts for personal injuries or death caused by the debtor's operation of a motor vehicle while intoxicated;

h. Some debts which were not properly listed by the debtor;

i. Debts that the bankruptcy court specifically has decided or will decide in this bankruptcy case are not discharged; and

j. Debts for which the debtor has given up the discharge protections by signing a reaffirmation agreement in compliance with the Bankruptcy Code requirements for reaffirmation of debts.

This information is only a general summary of the bankruptcy discharge. There are exceptions to these general rules. Because the law is complicated, you may want to consult an attorney to determine the exact effect of the discharge in this case.

Form B 18F
7/99

United States Bankruptcy Court

_____ District Of _____

In Re   Case No. _____

Debtor*

Address: Chapter 12

Social Security No(s).:
Employers's Tax I.D. No(s). [if any]:

DISCHARGE OF DEBTOR AFTER COMPLETION
OF CHAPTER 12 CASE

It appearing that the debtor is entitled to a discharge,

IT IS ORDERED:

The debtor is granted a discharge under section 1228(a) of title 11, United States Code, (the Bankruptcy Code).

BY THE COURT

Dated: _____   _____
                                          United States Bankruptcy Judge

SEE THE BACK OF THIS ORDER FOR IMPORTANT INFORMATION.

Set forth all names, including trade names, used by the debtor within the last 6 years. (Federal Rule of Bankruptcy Procedure 1005).

EXPLANATION OF BANKRUPTCY DISCHARGE
IN A CHAPTER 12 CASE

This court order grants a discharge to the person named as the debtor after the debtor has fulfilled all requirements under the chapter 12 plan. It is not a dismissal of the case.

Collection of Discharged Debts Prohibited

The discharge prohibits any attempt to collect from the debtor a debt that has been discharged. For example, a creditor is not permitted to contact a debtor by mail, phone, or otherwise, to file or continue a lawsuit, to attach wages or other property, or to take any other action to collect a discharged debt from the debtor. *[In a case involving community property:]* [There are also special rules that protect certain community property owned by the debtor's spouse, even if that spouse did not file a bankruptcy case.] A creditor who violates this order can be required to pay damages and attorney's fees to the debtor.

However, a creditor may have the right to enforce a valid lien, such as a mortgage or security interest, against the debtor's property after the bankruptcy, if that lien was not avoided or eliminated in the bankruptcy case. Also, a debtor may voluntarily pay any debt that has been discharged.

Debts That are Discharged

The chapter 12 discharge order eliminates a debtor's legal obligation to pay a debt that is discharged. Most, but not all, types of debts are discharged if the debt is provided for by the chapter 12 plan or is disallowed by the court pursuant to section 502 of the Bankruptcy Code.

Debts that are Not Discharged

Some of the common types of debts which are not discharged in a chapter 12 bankruptcy case are:

a. Debts for most taxes;

b. Debts that are in the nature of alimony, maintenance, or support;

c. Debts for most student loans;

d. Debts provided for under sections 1222(b)(5), (b)(9), or (b)(10) of the Bankruptcy Code and on which the last payment or other transfer is due after the date on which the final payment under the plan was due;

e. Debts for most fines, penalties, forfeitures, or criminal restitution obligations;

f. Debts for personal injuries or death caused by the debtor's operation of a motor vehicle while intoxicated;

g. Some debts which were not properly listed by the debtor; and

h. Debts that the bankruptcy court specifically has decided or will decide in this bankruptcy case are not discharged.

This information is only a general summary of the bankruptcy discharge. There are exceptions to these general rules. Because the law is complicated, you may want to consult an attorney to determine the exact effect of the discharge in this case.

Form B 18FH
7/99

United States Bankruptcy Court

_____ District Of _____

In Re

Case No. _____

Debtor*

Address:

Chapter 12

Social Security No(s).:
Employers's Tax I.D. Nos. [if any]:

DISCHARGE OF DEBTOR BEFORE COMPLETION
OF CHAPTER 12 PLAN

It appearing that the debtor is entitled to a discharge,

IT IS ORDERED:

The debtor is granted a discharge under section 1228(b) of title 11, United States Code, (the Bankruptcy Code).

BY THE COURT

Dated: _____

_____
United States Bankruptcy Judge

SEE THE BACK OF THIS ORDER FOR IMPORTANT INFORMATION.

Set forth all names, including trade names, used by the debtor within the last 6 years. (Federal Rule of Bankruptcy Procedure 1005).

Form B 18FH continued
7/99

EXPLANATION OF BANKRUPTCY DISCHARGE BEFORE COMPLETION
OF PLAN PAYMENTS IN A CHAPTER 12 CASE

This court order grants a discharge to the person named as the debtor. After notice and a hearing, the court has determined that the debtor is entitled to a discharge pursuant to section 1228(b) of the Bankruptcy Code without completing all of the requirements under the chapter 12 plan. Because this discharge is granted pursuant to the hardship provisions of section 1228(b), it is referred to as a chapter 12 "hardship discharge." This order is not the dismissal of the case.

Collection of Discharged Debts Prohibited

The discharge prohibits any attempt to collect from the debtor a debt that has been discharged. For example, a creditor is not permitted to contact a debtor by mail, phone, or otherwise, to file or continue a lawsuit, to attach wages or other property, or to take any other action to collect a discharged debt from the debtor. *[In a case involving community property:]* [There are also special rules that protect certain community property owned by the debtor's spouse, even if that spouse did not file a bankruptcy case.] A creditor who violates this order can be required to pay damages and attorney's fees to the debtor.

However, a creditor may have the right to enforce a valid lien, such as a mortgage or security interest, against the debtor's property after the bankruptcy, if that lien was not avoided or eliminated in the bankruptcy case. Also, a debtor may voluntarily pay any debt that has been discharged.

Debts That are Discharged

The chapter 12 "hardship discharge" eliminates a debtor's legal obligation to pay a debt that is discharged. Most, but not all, types of debts are discharged if the debt is provided for by the chapter 12 plan or is disallowed by the court payment to section 502 of the Bankruptcy Code.

Debts that are Not Discharged

Some of the common types of debts which a<u>re </u>not eliminated by in a chapter 12 "hardship discharge" are:

a. Debts for most taxes;

b. Debts that are in the nature of alimony, maintenance, or support;

c. Debts for most student loans;

d. Debts provided for under sections 1222(b)(5), (b)(9), or (b)(10) of the Bankruptcy Code and on which the last payment or other transfer is due after the date on which the final payment under the plan was due;

e. Debts for most fines, penalties, forfeitures, or criminal restitution obligations;

f. Debts for personal injuries or death caused by the debtor's operation of a motor vehicle while intoxicated;

g. Some debts which were not properly listed by the debtor;

h. Debts that the bankruptcy court specifically has decided or will decide in this bankruptcy case are not discharged; and

i. Debts for which the debtor has given up the discharge protections by signing a reaffirmation agreement in compliance with the Bankruptcy Code requirements for reaffirmation of debts.

This information is only a general summary of the bankruptcy discharge. There are exceptions to these general rules. Because the law is complicated, you may want to consult an attorney to determine the exact effect of the discharge in this case.

B 18W

UNITED STATES BANKRUPTCY COURT
_____DISTRICT OF_____

In re   Bankruptcy Case No.

Debtor   Chapter _____
Address:
Social Security No(s):
Employer's Tax Identification No(s). [if any]:

DISCLOSURE OF COMPENSATION OF BANKRUPTCY
PETITION PREPARER

1.   Under 11 U.S.C. § 110(h), I declare under penalty of perjury that I am not an attorney or employee of an attorney, that I prepared or caused to be prepared one or more documents for filing by the above-named debtor(s) in connection with this bankruptcy case, and that compensation paid to me within one year before the filing of the bankruptcy petition, or agreed to be paid to me, for services rendered on behalf of the debtor(s) in contemplation of or in connection with the bankruptcy case is as follows:

For document preparation services, I have agreed to accept . . . . $_____
Prior to the filing of this statement I have received . . . . $_____
Balance Due . . . . $_____

2.   I have prepared or caused to be prepared the following documents (itemized):

and provided the following services (itemize):

3.   The source of the compensation paid to me was:
           ☐ Debtor   ☐ Other (specify)

4.   The source of compensation to be paid to me is:
           ☐ Debtor   ☐ Other (specify)

5.   The foregoing is a complete statement of any agreement or arrangement for payment to me for preparation of the petition filed by the debtor(s) in this bankruptcy case.

6.   To my knowledge no other person has prepared for compensation a document for filing in connection with this bankruptcy case except as listed below:
           NAME   SOCIAL SECURITY NUMBER

DECLARATION OF BANKRUPTCY PETITION PREPARER

I declare under penalty of perjury that the foregoing is true and correct to the best of my knowledge, information, and belief.

X_____   _____   _____
          Signature   Social Security Number   Date
Name (Print):
Address:

Form B240
3/99

REAFFIRMATION AGREEMENT

UNITED STATES BANKRUPTCY COURT
_____ DISTRICT OF _____

Debtor's Name	Bankruptcy Case No.
	Chapter
Creditor's Name and Address	

<u>Instructions:</u>   1) Attach a copy of all court judgments, security agreements, and evidence of their perfection.
          2) File all the documents by mailing them or delivering them to the Clerk of the Bankruptcy Court.

NOTICE TO DEBTOR:

This agreement <u>gives up the protection of your bankruptcy discharge</u> for this debt.

<u>As a result of this agreement, the creditor may be able to take your property or wages</u> if you do not pay the agreed amounts. The creditor may also act to collect the debt in other ways.

<u>You may rescind (cancel) this agreement at any time before the bankruptcy court enters a discharge order or within 60 days after this agreement is filed with the court, whichever is later,</u> by notifying the creditor that the agreement is canceled.

<u>You are not required to enter into this agreement by any law.</u> It is not required by the Bankruptcy Code, by any other law, or by any contract (except another reaffirmation agreement made in accordance with Bankruptcy Code § 524(c)).

<u>You are allowed to pay this debt without signing this agreement.</u> However, if you do not sign this agreement and are later unwilling or unable to pay the full amount, the creditor will not be able to collect it from you. The creditor also will not be allowed to take your property to pay the debt unless the creditor has a lien on that property.

If the creditor has a lien on your personal property, you may have a right to <u>redeem</u> the property and eliminate the lien by making a single payment to the creditor equal to the current value of the property, as agreed by the parties or determined by the court.

This agreement is not valid or binding unless it is filed with the clerk of the bankruptcy court. If you were not represented by an attorney during the negotiation of this reaffirmation agreement, the agreement cannot be enforced by the creditor unless 1) you have attended a reaffirmation hearing in the bankruptcy court, and 2) the agreement has been approved by the bankruptcy court. (Court approval is not required if this is a consumer debt secured by a mortgage or other lien on your real estate.)

REAFFIRMATION AGREEMENT

The debtor and creditor named above agree to reaffirm the debt described in this agreement as follows.

THE DEBT

Total Amount of Debt When Case was Filed $_____

Total Amount of Debt Reaffirmed $_____

  Above total includes the following:

   Interest Accrued to Date of Agreement $_____
   Attorneys Fees $_____
   Late Fees $_____
   Other Expenses or Costs Relating to the
   Collection of this Debt (Describe) $_____

Annual Percentage Rate (APR)   _____%

Amount of Monthly Payment $_____

Date Payments Start   _____

Total Number of Payments to be made   _____

Total of Payments if paid according to schedule   _____

Date Any Lien Is to Be Released if paid   _____
according to schedule

The debtor agrees that any and all remedies available to the creditor under the security agreement remain available.

All additional Terms Agreed to by the Parties (if any):

_____

Payments on this debt [were][were not] in default on the date on which this bankruptcy case was filed.

This agreement differs from the original agreement with the creditor as follows:

_____

_____

CREDITOR'S STATEMENT CONCERNING AGREEMENT AND SECURITY/COLLATERAL (IF ANY)

Description of collateral. <u>If applicable, list manufacturer, year and model.</u> _____

_____

Value $ _____

Basis or Source for Valuation   _____

Current Location and Use of Collateral   _____

Expected Future Use of Collateral   _____

Check Applicable Boxes:

[]   Any lien described herein is valid and perfected.

[]   This agreement is part of a settlement of a dispute regarding the dischargeability of this debt under section 523 of the Bankruptcy Code (11 U.S.C. § 523) or any other dispute. The nature of the dispute is _____.

DEBTOR'S STATEMENT OF EFFECT OF AGREEMENT ON DEBTOR'S FINANCES

My Monthly Income (take home pay plus any other income received) is $ _____.

My current monthly expenses total $ _____, not including any payment due under this agreement or any debt to be discharged in this bankruptcy case.

I believe this agreement [will][will not] impose a hardship on me or my dependents.

DEBTOR'S STATEMENT CONCERNING DECISION TO REAFFIRM

I agreed to reaffirm this debt because _____

_____

I believe this agreement is in my best interest because _____

_____

I [considered][did not consider] redeeming the collateral under section 722 of the Bankruptcy Code (11 U.S.C. § 722). I choose not to redeem because _____

_____

CERTIFICATION OF ATTACHMENTS

Any documents which created and perfected the security interest or lien [are][are not] attached. [*If documents are not attached:* The documents which created and perfected the security interest or lien are not attached because

_____

_____.]

SIGNATURES

_____   _____
(Signature of Debtor)   (Name of Creditor)

Date _____   _____
                                                          (Signature of Creditor Representative)

                                                          Date _____

_____
(Signature of Joint Debtor)

Date _____

CERTIFICATION BY DEBTOR'S ATTORNEY (IF ANY)

I hereby certify that 1) this agreement represents a fully informed and voluntary agreement by the debtor(s); 2) this agreement does not impose a hardship on the debtor or any dependent of the debtor; and 3) I have fully advised the debtor of the legal effect and consequences of this agreement and any default under this agreement.

_____   _____
(Signature of Debtor's Attorney, if any)   Date

Form B 281. Appearance of Child Support Creditor or Representative

B 281
(12/94)

UNITED STATES BANKRUPTCY COURT
_____ DISTRICT OF _____

In re_____   Bankruptcy Case No. _____
      Debtor   Chapter _____
Address:
Social Security No(s).:
Employer's Tax Identification No(s). [if any]:

APPEARANCE OF CHILD SUPPORT CREDITOR*
OR REPRESENTATIVE

I certify under penalty of perjury that I am a child support creditor* of the above-named debtor, or the authorized representative of such child support creditor, with respect to the child support obligation which is set out below.

      Name:
      Organization:
      Address:

      Telephone Number:

_____   X _____
Date   Child Support Creditor* or Authorized Representative

Summary of Child Support Obligation

Amount in arrears: If Child Support has been assigned:

$ _____   Amount of Support which is owed under assignments:

Amount currently due per week or per month: $ _____
on a continuing basis:

                                        Amount owed primary child support creditor
$ _____   (balance not assigned):
 (per week) (per month)

                                        $ _____

Attach an itemized statement of account

---

* Child support creditor includes both creditor to whom the debtor has a primary obligation to pay child support as well as any entity to whom such support has been assigned, if pursuant to Section 402(a)(26) of the Social Security Act or if such debt has been assigned to the Federal Government or to any State or political subdivision of a State.

Sample Completed Bankruptcy Schedules to Institute Case

Sample Completed Official Forms with Annotations Contained in This Appendix

Appendix F contains completed Official Forms for a sample bankruptcy case, with annotations explaining why the forms were completed in this fashion. These completed forms can also be found in Adobe Acrobat (PDF) format on the CD-Rom accompanying this volume. Of more significance, the CD-Rom also includes *Bankruptcy Forms* software, by Law Disks, that allows practitioners to complete many of the Official Forms on their computer in Microsoft Word or in WordPerfect. This software is explained in more detail in Appendix D.4, *supra.*

FORM B1 (12/03)	UNITED STATES BANKRUPTCY COURT DISTRICT OF MASSACHUSETTS	Voluntary Petition

Name of debtor (if individual, enter Last, First, Middle): **Debtor, Joseph A.**	Name of Joint Debtor (Spouse)(Last, First, Middle) **Debtor, Josephine S.**
All Other Names used by the Debtor in the last 6 years (include married, maiden, and trade names): **Joe Debtor**[1]	All Other Names used by the Joint Debtor in the last 6 years (include married, maiden, and trade names): **Josephine Debtor**
Last four digits of Soc. Sec./Complete EIN or other Tax ID No. (if more than one, state all): **1234**	Last four digits of Soc. Sec./Complete EIN or other Tax ID No.. (if more than one, state all): **4321**
Street Address of Debtor (No. & Street, City, State, & Zip Code) **100 Main Street** **Warren, Massachusetts 02345**	Street Address of Joint Debtor (No. & St., City, State & Zip Code) **100 Main Street** **Warren, Massachusetts 02345**
County of Residence or of the Principal Place of Business: **Nassau**	County of Residence or of the Principal Place of Business: **Nassau**
Mailing Address of Debtor (if different from street address):	Mailing Address of Joint Debtor (if different from street address):
Location of Principal Assets of Business Debtor (if different from street address above):	

Information Regarding the Debtor (Check the Applicable Boxes)

Venue: (Check any applicable box)
☒   Debtor has been domiciled or has had a residence, principal place of business, or principal assets in this District for 180 days immediately preceding the date of this petition or for a longer part of such 180 days than in any other District.
☐   There is a bankruptcy case concerning debtor's affiliate, general partner, or partnership pending in this District.

Type of Debtor (Check all boxes that apply)	**Chapter or Section of Bankruptcy Code Under Which the Petition is filed** (Check one box)
☒ Individual(s) ☐ Railroad	☐ Chapter 7 ☐ Chapter 11 ☒ Chapter 13
☐ Corporation ☐ Stockbroker	☐ Chapter 9 ☐ Chapter 12
☐ Partnership ☐ Commodity Broker	☐ Sec. 304- Case ancillary to foreign proceeding
☐ Other _____ ☐ Clearing Bank	

Nature of Debts (Check one box) ☒ Consumer/Non-Business ☐ Business	**Filing Fee** (Check one box)
Chapter 11 Small Business (Check all boxes that apply) ☐ Debtor is a small business as defined in 11 U.S.C. § 101 ☐ Debtor is and elects to be considered a small business under 11 U.S.C. § 1121(e)(Optional)	☐ Full Filing Fee attached ☒ Filing Fee to be paid in installments (Applicable to individuals only) Must attach signed application for the court's consideration certifying that the debtor is unable to pay fee except in installments. Rule 1006(e). See Official Form No. 3.[2]

Statistical/Administrative Information (estimates only)[3]
☒   Debtor estimates that funds will be available for distribution to unsecured creditors.
☐   Debtor estimates that, after any exempt property is excluded and administrative expenses paid, there will be no funds available for distribution to unsecured creditors.

THIS SPACE IS FOR COURT USE ONLY

Estimated Number of Creditors

1-15	16-49	50-99	100-199	200-999	1000-over
☒	☐	☐	☐	☐	☐

Estimated Assets

$0 to $50,000	$50,001 to $100,000	$100,001 to $500,000	$500,001 to $1 million	$1,000,001 to $10 million	$10,000,001 to $50 million	$50,000,001 to $100 million	More than $100 million
☐	☐	☒	☐	☐	☐	☐	☐

Estimated Debts

$0 to $50,000	$50,001 to $100,000	$100,001 to $500,000	$500,001 to $1 million	$1,000,001 to $10 million	$10,000,001 to $50 million	$50,000,001 to $100 million	More than $100 million
☐	☐	☒	☐	☐	☐	☐	☐

Form Published by: Law Disks, 734 Franklin Avenue, Garden City, NY 11530   www.lawdisks.com

Voluntary Petition (This page must be completed and filed in every case.)	Name of Debtor(s): Joseph A. Debtor, Josephine S. Debtor	**FORM B1**, Page 2

Prior Bankruptcy Case Filed Within the last 6 Years (if more than one, attach additional sheet.)		
Location Where filed: **Massachusetts**	Case Number: **95-34567**	Date Filed: **September 10, 2000**[4]

Pending Bankruptcy Case Filed by any Spouse, Partner, or Affiliate of this Debtor (If more than one, attach additional sheet)		
Name of Debtor: n/a	Case Number:	Date Filed:
District:	Relationship:	Judge:

Signatures

Signature(s) of Debtor(s) (Individual/Joint)

I declare under penalty of perjury that the information provided in this petition is true and correct. [If the petitioner is an individual whose debts are primarily consumer debts and has chosen to file under chapter 7] I am aware that I may proceed under chapter 7, 11, 12, or 13 of title 11, United States Code, understand the relief available under each such chapter, and choose to proceed under chapter 7 .

I request relief in accordance with the chapter of title 11, United States Code, specified in this petition.

X_____
Joseph A. Debtor, Debtor

X_____
Josephine S. Debtor, Joint Debtor

_____
Telephone Number (If not represented by attorney)

December 1, 2004_____
Date

Signature of Attorney[5]

X_____
Signature of Attorney for Debtor(s)
Print below: Attorney Name, Code, Firm, Address, Telephone No:
Linda Lawyer Bar Number/Code: **67890**
250 First Street
Warren, Massachusetts 02345
(617) 525-1000

December 1, 2004_____
Date

Signature of Debtor (Corporation/Partnership)

I declare under penalty of perjury that the information provided in this petition is true and correct, and that I have been authorized to file this petition on behalf of the debtor.

The debtor requests relief in accordance with the chapter of title 11, United States Code, specified in this petition.

X_____
Signature of Authorized Individual

_____
Printed Name of Authorized Individual

_____
Title of Authorized Individual

_____
Date

Exhibit A

(To be completed if the Debtor is required to file periodic reports (e.g., forms 10K and 10Q with the Securities and Exchange Commission pursuant to Section 13 or 15(d) of the Securities Exchange Act of 1934 and is requesting relief under chapter 11)

☐ Exhibit A is attached and made a part of this petition.

Exhibit B

(To be completed if Debtor is an individual whose debts are primarily consumer debts.)

I, the attorney for the petitioner named in the foregoing petition, declare that I have informed the petitioner that [he or she] may proceed under chapter 7, 11, 12, or 13 of title 11, United States Code, and have explained the relief available under each chapter.

X_____   December 1, 2004_____
Linda Lawyer, Attorney for Debtor(s)   Date

Exhibit C

Does the debtor own or have possession of any property that poses or is alleged to pose a threat of imminent and identifiable harm to public health or safety?

☐ Yes, and Exhibit C is attached and made part of this petition.
☒ No

Signature of Non-Attorney Petition Preparer

I certify that I am a bankruptcy petition preparer as defined in 11 U.S.C. § 110, that I prepared this document for compensation, and that I have provided the debtor with a copy of this document.

_____
Printed Name of Bankruptcy Petition Preparer

_____
Social Security Number (required by 11 U.S.C. § 110(c))

_____
Address

Name and Social Security Numbers of all other individuals who prepared or assisted in preparing this document:

If more than one person prepared this document, attach additional sheets conforming to the appropriate official form for each person.

X_____
Signature of Bankruptcy Petition Preparer   Date

A bankruptcy petition preparer's failure to comply with the provisions of title 11 and the Federal Rules of Bankruptcy Procedure may result in fines or imprisonment or both 11 U.S.C. §110; 18 U.S.C. §156.

[Publisher's Note: This form is NOT intended to be used by nonattorney bankruptcy-petition preparers: Schedules do not contain all disclosures required for use by nonattorney bankruptcy-petition preparers.]

Form B1, Exhibit C (9/01)

United States Bankruptcy Court
District of Massachusetts

In re Joseph A. Debtor, Josephine S. Debtor
      Debtor(s)

                                Case No: 04-55780
                                Chapter: 13

Exhibit C to Voluntary Petition[6]

1. Identify and briefly describe all real and personal property owned by or in possession of the debtor that, to the best of the debtor's knowledge, poses or is alleged to pose a threat of imminent and identifiable harm to the public health or safety (attach additional sheets if necessary).

    N/A

2. With respect to each parcel of real property or item of personal property identified in question 1, describe the nature and location of the dangerous condition, whether environmental or otherwise, that poses or is alleged to pose a threat of imminent and identifiable harm to public health or safety (attach additional sheets if necessary).

    N/A

Form B 21 Official Form 21
(12/03)

FORM 21. STATEMENT OF SOCIAL SECURITY NUMBER[7]

UNITED STATES BANKRUPTCY COURT
DISTRICT OF MASSACHUSETTS

In re: Joseph A. Debtor, Josephine S. Debtor   Case No:
              Debtors

STATEMENT OF SOCIAL SECURITY NUMBER(S)

1. Name of Debtor.(enter Last, First, Middle):   Joseph A. Debtor
(Check the appropriate box and, if applicable, provide the required information.)

       [X] Debtor has a Social Security Number and it is: 000-00-1234
           (If more than one, state all.)
       [ ] Debtor does not have a Social Security Number.

2. Name of Joint debtor (enter Last, First, Middle):   Josephine S. Debtor
(Check the appropriate box and: if applicable, provide the required information)

       [X] Joint Debtor has a Social Security Number and it is: 000-00-4321
           (If more than one, state all.)
       [ ] Joint debtor does not have a Social Security Number

I declare under penalty of perjury that the foregoing is true and correct.

x _____
Signature of Debtor Joseph A. Debtor   Date

x _____
Signature of Joint Debtor Josephine S. Debtor   Date

_____

* *Joint debtors must provide information for both spouses.*
Penalty for making a false statement: Fine of up to $250,000 or up to 5 years imprisonment or both.
18 U.S.C. §§ 152 and 3571.

Chevrolet Finance Co.
248 Springfield Co. Park
Springfield, MA 02134

Debt Collectors, Inc.
19 Dunning Drive
Buffalo, NY 14203

David & Deborah Debtor
114 Main Street
Warren, MA 02345

Easy Credit Co.
165 Main Street
Warren, MA 02345

Fast Finance Co.
1234 Main Street
Warren, MA 02345

First Express Card
P.O. Box 39670
Phoenix, AZ 85067

Halliday Health Spa
1576 Main Street
Warren, MA 02345

Internal Revenue Service
432 Columbia Street
Boston, MA 02105

Mass. National Bank VISA
234 Main Street
Warren, MA 02345

Massachusetts Electric Co.
Electric Co. Park
Warren, MA 02345

Steven A. Debtor
234 City Street
Boston, MA 02109

Warren Bank Mortgage Co.
656 Bank Street Park
Springfield, MA 02333

Warren Hospital
958 Main Street
Warren, MA 02345

Warren Water Co.
523 Main Street
Warren, MA 02345

Annotations to Completed Official Form 1, Voluntary Petition

The petition is the document which commences the case. See § 7.3.2, *supra*, for a general discussion about filling out the petition. See also the Judicial Conference Introduction and Instructions in Appendix D (preceding the Official Forms), *supra*, which provides general instructions for filling out and reproducing the forms.

Note that there is no longer any distinction between the basic chapter 7 and chapter 13 forms. The sample completed forms reproduced here are the initial forms for a chapter 13 filing.

1 Particular attention should be paid to listing all names under which the debtor has incurred the debts which are listed in the petition.

2 *See* § 7.3.2, *supra*; Official Form 3, Appx. D, *supra*. This option cannot be used if the debtor has paid any money to an attorney or any other person in connection with the case.

3 Although the best available estimates should be used, it is clear that there are no penalties for inaccurate estimates.

4 In limited situations, a prior bankruptcy may preclude filing a new case. 11 U.S.C. § 109(g); *see* §§ 3.2.1, 9.7.3.1.5, *supra*.

5 Note that if the debtor is an individual with primarily consumer debts, the debtor's attorney will have to execute the petition in two places, here and also on Exhibit B.

6 This form Exhibit C does not need to be filed if the debtors answer "no" to the question on the petition about possessing hazardous property.

7 This Statement of Social Security Number is submitted by the debtor with the petition and schedules but is not made a part of the official court file. Therefore, the debtor's full social security number is not available to the general public or over the Internet.

UNITED STATES BANKRUPTCY COURT
DISTRICT OF MASSACHUSETTS

In re: Joseph A. Debtor, Josephine S. Debtor   Case No:
          Debtors

APPLICATION TO PAY FILING FEE IN INSTALLMENTS

1.   In accordance with Fed. R. Bankr. P. 1006, I apply for permission to pay the Filing Fee, amounting to $ 194 in installments.

2.   I certify that I am unable to pay the filing fee except in installments.

3.   I further certify that I have not paid any money or transferred any property to an attorney for services in connection with this case and that I will neither make any payment nor transfer any property for services in connection with the case until the filing fee is paid in full.

4.   I propose the following terms for the payment of the Filing Fee.*
      $ 59.00   Check One   [X]   With the filing of the petition, or
                                          [ ]   On or before:
      $ 45.00   on or before: 30 days after the filing of the petition
      $ 45.00   on or before: 60 days after the filing of the petition
      $ 45.00   on or before: 90 days after the filing of the petition
      * The number of installments proposed shall not exceed four (4), and the final installment shall be payable not later than 120 days after filing the petition. For cause shown, the court may extend the time of any installment, provided the last installment is paid not later than 180 days after filing the petition. Fed. R. Bankr. P. 1006(b)(2).

5.   I understand that if I fail to pay any installment when due my bankruptcy case may be dismissed and I may not receive a discharge of my debts.

_____   _____
Joseph A. Debtor, Debtor   Date:

(In a joint case, both spouses must sign)

_____   _____
Josephine S. Debtor, Joint Debtor   Date:

_____   _____
Linda Lawyer, Attorney   Date:
- -
ORDER APPROVING PAYMENT OF FILING FEE IN INSTALLMENTS

IT IS ORDERED that the debtor(s) may pay the filing fee in installments on the terms proposed in the foregoing application.

IT IS FURTHER ORDERED that until the filing fee is paid in full the debtor shall not pay any money for services in connection with this case, and the debtor shall not relinquish any property as payment for services in connection with this case.

BY THE COURT

Date: _____   _____
                                        United States Bankruptcy Judge

Annotations to Completed Official Form 3, Application and Order to Pay Filing Fee in Installments

The installment filing fee process is available to those who cannot afford to pay the full fee at the outset of the case. It is only available if the debtors have not transferred money or property to an attorney or any other person in connection with the case.

Although it is common to pay the first installment at the time of filing, nothing in the Code or Rules requires any payment when the petition is filed. It is perfectly appropriate to propose that the whole fee be paid in installments due after the case has been commenced. The only limits in the rule are that the number of installments may not exceed four and the final installment must be paid within 120 days after filing the petition. The court, for cause, can extend the period to 180 days. Fed. R. Bankr. P. 1006(b).

UNITED STATES BANKRUPTCY COURT
DISTRICT OF MASSACHUSETTS

In re: Joseph A. Debtor, Josephine S. Debtor[8]
          Debtor(s)   Case No:

SUMMARY OF SCHEDULES

Indicate as to each schedule whether that schedule is attached and state the number of pages in each. Report the totals from schedules A, B, C, D, E, F, G, H, I and J in the boxes provided. Add the amounts from Schedules A and B to determine the total amount of the debtor's assets. Add the amounts from Schedules D, E, and F to determine the total amount of the debtor's liabilities.

NAME OF SCHEDULE	ATTACHED	NO. SHEETS	ASSETS	LIABILITIES	OTHER
A — Real Property	Yes	1	$125,000		
B — Personal Property	Yes	2	$8,860		
C — Property Claimed as Exempt	Yes	1			
D — Creditors Holding Secured Claims	Yes	1		$155,148	
E — Creditors Holding Unsecured Priority Claims	Yes	2		$715	
F — Creditors Holding Unsecured Nonpriority Claims	Yes	2		$7,859	
G — Executory Contracts and Unexpired Leases	Yes	1			
H — Codebtors	Yes	1			
I — Current Income of Individual Debtor(s)	Yes	1			$1,801
J — Current Expenditures of Individual Debtor(s)	Yes	2			$1,553
Total number of sheets in all Schedules ➤		14			
Total Assets ➤			$133,360		
Total Liabilities ➤				$163,722	

SCHEDULE A- REAL PROPERTY

Except as directed below, list all real property in which the debtor has any legal, equitable, or future interest, including all property owned as a co-tenant, community property, or in which the debtor has a life estate. Include any property in which the debtor holds rights and powers excercisable for the debtor's own benefit. If the debtor is married, state whether husband, wife, or both own the property by placing an "H","W","J", or "C" in the third column labeled "Husband, Wife, Joint or Community." if the debtor holds no interest in real property, write "None" under "Description and Location of Property."

Do not include interests in executory contracts and unexpired leases on this schedule. List them in Schedule G-Executory Contracts and Unexpired Leases.

If an entity claims to have a lien or hold a security interest in any property, state the amount of the secured claim. See Schedule D. If no entity claims to hold a secured interest in the property, write "None" in the column labeled "Amount of Secured Claim."

If the debtor is an individual or if a joint petition is filed, state the amount of any exemption claimed in the property only in Schedule C— Property Claimed as Exempt.

DESCRIPTION AND LOCATION OF PROPERTY	NATURE OF DEBTOR'S INTEREST IN PROPERTY	HUSB WIFE JOINT COM.	CURRENT MARKET VALUE OF DEBTOR'S INTEREST IN PROPERTY WITHOUT DEDUCTING ANY SECURED CLAIM OR EXEMPTION	AMOUNT OF SECURED CLAIM
Debtors' Residence 100 Main Street, Warren, MA Single family frame ranch-style home.[9]	Owners evidenced by deed recorded at Nassau County Deed Book, No. 23152, p. 635 dated 4/1/90, held by the debtors as tenants by the entireties.[10]	J	$125,000*[11]	$150,000[12]
			$125,000	TOTAL

* The total market value of this entireties property is given. The interest of each debtor, which cannot be sold or assigned without the other's consent, is worth considerably less than one-half this amount.[13]

SCHEDULE B— PERSONAL PROPERTY

Except as directed below, list all personal property of the debtor of whatever kind. If the debtor has no property in one or more of the categories, place an "X" in the appropriate position in the column labeled "None." If additional space is needed in any category, attach a separate sheet properly identified with the case name, case number, and the number of the category. If the debtor is married, state whether husband, wife, or both own the property by placing an "H," "W," "J," or "C" in the column labeled "Husband, Wife, Joint, or Community." If the debtor is an individual or a joint petition is filed, state the amount of any exemptions claimed only in Schedule C— Property Claimed as Exempt.

Do not list interests in executory contracts and unexpired leases on this schedule. List them in Schedule G— Executory Contracts and Unexpired Leases.

If the property is being held for the debtor by someone else, state that person's name and address under "Description and Location of Property."

TYPE OF PROPERTY	NONE	DESCRIPTION AND LOCATION OF PROPERTY	HUSB. WIFE JOINT COMM.	CURRENT MARKET VALUE OF DEBTOR'S INTEREST IN PROPERTY, WITHOUT DEDUCTION OF ANY SECURED CLAIM OR EXEMPTION	
1. Cash on hand.	1b.	1c. Cash held by debtors	1d. J	1e.	$70
2. Checking, savings or other financial accounts, certificates of deposit, or shares in banks, savings and loan, thrift, building and loan, and homestead associations, or credit unions, brokerage houses, or cooperatives.	2b.	2c. Massachusetts National Bank 234 Main Street Warren, MA 02345 Account #23422-2242[14]	2d. J	2e.	$230
3. Security deposits with public utilities, telephone companies, landlords, and others.	3b. X	3c.	3d.	3e.	
4. Household goods and furnishings, including audio, video, and computer equipment.[15]	4b.	4c. a. 32" Color T.V. (5 yrs. old)[16] b. Home computer (3 yrs. old) c. Refrigerator d. Stove e. Pool table and equipment f. Living room set g. 2 Bedroom sets h. Miscellaneous household items (none worth more than $450)[18]	4d. J J J J H J J J	4e.	$100[17] $250 $100 $100 $150 $150 $200 $1,200
5. Books; pictures and other art objects; antiques; stamp, coin, record, tape, compact disc, and other collections or collectibles.	5b. X	5c.	5d.	5e.	
6. Wearing apparel.	6b.	6c. a. misc. used clothing b. misc. used clothing	6d. W H	6e.	$200 $200
7. Furs and jewelry.	7b.	7c. a. wedding ring and misc. costume jewelry b. two watches c. wedding ring	7d. W J H	7e.	$300 $125 $200
8. Firearms and sports, photographic, and other hobby equipment.	8b. X	8c.	8d.	8e.	

9. Interests in insurance policies. Name insurance company of each policy and itemize surrender or refund value of each.	9b. X	9c.	9d.	9e.
10. Annuities. Itemize and name each issuer.	10b. X	10c.	10d.	10e.
11. Interests in IRA, ERISA, Keogh, or other pension or profit sharing plans. Itemize.	11b.	11c. ERISA QUALIFIED PENSION PLAN (held by Joseph Debtor's employer, not part of bankruptcy estate)[19]	11d. H	11e. $2,800
12. Stock and interests in incorporated and unincorporated businesses. Itemize.	12b. X	12c.	12d.	12e.
13. Interests in partnerships or joint ventures. Itemize.	13b. X	13c.	13d.	13e.
14. Government and corporate bonds and other negotiable and non-negotiable instruments.	14b. X	14c.	14d.	14e.
15. Accounts receivable.	15b. X	15c.	15d.	15e.
16. Alimony, maintenance, support, and property settlements to which the debtor is or may be entitled. Give particulars.	16b. X	16c.	16d.	16e.
17. Other liquidated debts owing debtor including tax refunds. Give particulars.	17b.	17c. Anticipated 2004 Income Tax Refund[20]	17d.	17e. $500
18. Equitable or future interests, life estates, and rights or powers exercisable for the benefit of the debtor other than those listed in Schedule of Real Property.	18b. X	18c.	18d.	18e.
19. Contingent and noncontingent interests in estate of a decedent, death benefit plan, life insurance policy, or trust.	19b. X	19c.	19d.	19e.
20. Other contingent and unliquidated claims of every nature, including tax refunds, counterclaims of the debtor, and rights to setoff claims. Give estimated value of each.	20b.	20c. a. unliquidated truth-in-lending claim against East Credit Co.[21] b. unliquidated unfair trade practice claim against Fast Finance Co.[23]	20d. J J	20e. unknown[22] unknown
21. Patents, copyrights, and other intellectual property. Give particulars.	21b. X	21c.	21d.	21e.
22. Licenses, franchises, and other general intangibles. Give particulars.	22b. X	22c.	22d.	22e.
23. Automobiles, trucks, trailers, and other vehicles and accessories.	23b.	23c. 1995 Chevy Caprice (held by Chevrolet Finance Co. at We Get 'em Repo Co., 501 Main Street, Warren, MA.)[24]	23d. J	23e. $1,350
24. Boats, motors, and accessories.	24b. X	24c.	24d.	24e.
25. Aircraft and accessories.	25b. X	25c.	25d.	25e.
26. Office equipment, furnishings, and supplies.	26b. X	26c.	26d.	26e.

27. Machinery, fixtures, equipment, and supplies used in business.	27b. X	27c.		27d.	27e.
28. Inventory.	28b. X	28c.		28d.	28e.
29. Animals.	29b. X	29c.		29d.	29e.
30. Crops— growing or harvested. give particulars.	30b. X	30c.		30d.	30e.
31. Farming equipment and implements.	31b. X	31c.		31d.	31e.
32. Farm supplies, chemicals, and feed.	32b. X	32c.		32d.	32e.
33. Other personal property of any kind not already listed. Itemize.	33b.	33c. Wages held by debtor's employer, Allied Factories, pursuant to wage garnishment[25]		33d. H	33e. $635
		2 continuation sheets attached	Total	$	8,860

Include amounts from any continuation sheets attached.
Report also on Summary of Schedules.

* All property at debtor's residence unless otherwise noted.

SCHEDULE C— PROPERTY CLAIMED AS EXEMPT[26]

Debtor(s) elect(s) the exemption to which the debtor(s) is entitled under:

[X] 11 U.S.C. §522(b)(1)[27] Federal exemptions provided in 11 U.S.C. §522(d). Note: these exemptions are available *only in certain states.*
[ ] 11 U.S.C. §522(b)(2) Exemptions available under applicable nonbankruptcy federal laws, state or local laws where the debtor's domicile has been located for the 180 days immediately preceding the filing of the petition, or for a longer portion of the 180 day period than in any other place, and the debtor's interest as a tenant by the entirety or joint tenant to the extent the interest is exempt from process under applicable nonbankruptcy law. Specifically, debtor selects the exemptions of the state of: _____

Description of Property	Specify Law Providing Each Exemption	Value of Claimed Exemption	Current Market Value of Property Without Deducting Exemptions
Debtor's Home (Although this property is fully encumbered by security interests, the debtors claim the value of their possessory interest in the property as exempt.)[28]	§ 522 (d) (1)	$10,000[29]	$125,000
1995 Chevy Caprice (fully encumbered)[30]	§ 522 (d) (2)	$1,350	$1,350
Misc. Used Clothing (H)[31]	§ 522 (d) (3)	$200	$200
Misc. Used Clothing (W)	§ 522 (d) (3)	$200	$200
Misc. Household goods listed in Schedule B[32]	§ 522 (d) (3)	$2,250	$2,250
Jewelry listed in Schedule B	§ 522 (d) (4)	$625	$625
Cash held by debtors	§ 522 (d) (5)[33]	$70	$70
Anticipated 2004 Tax Refund	§ 522 (d) (5)	$500	$500
MA National Bank Account	§ 522 (d) (5)	$230	$230
Unliquidated unfair trade practice claim against Fast Finance Co.[34]	§ 522 (d) (5) § 522 (d) (11)[35]	$5,000	unknown
Unliquidated truth-in-lending claim against Easy Credit Co.	§ 522 (d) (5) § 522 (d) (11)[36]	$5,000	unknown
ERISA Qualified Pension Plan (The pension does not come into the estate by virtue of 11 U.S.C. Sec. 541(c) (2). The exemption is claimed in the alternative.)[37]	§ 522 (d) (10)	$2,800	$2,800
Wages held by employer	§ 522 (d) (5)	$635	$635
		Total: $28,860	

*Unless specifically stated otherwise, the debtors claim 100% of their interest in each item listed in this Schedule as exempt.

SCHEDULE D— CREDITORS HOLDING SECURED CLAIMS

State the name, mailing address, including zip code, and the last four digits of any account number of all entities holding claims secured by property of the debtor as of the date of filing of the petition. The complete account number of any account the debtor has with the creditor is useful to the trustee and the creditor and may be provided if the debtor chooses to do so. List creditors holding all types of secured interests such as judgment liens, garnishments, statutory liens, mortgages, deeds of trust, and other security interests. List creditors in alphabetical order to the extent practicable. If all secured creditors will not fit on this page, use the continuation sheet provided.

If any entity other than a spouse in a joint case may be jointly liable on a claim, place an "X" in the column labeled "Codebtor," include the entity on the appropriate schedule of creditors, and complete Schedule H— Codebtors. If a joint petition is filed, state whether husband, wife, both of them or the marital community may be liable on each claim by placing an "H," "W," "J," or "C," in the column labeled "Husband, Wife, Joint or Community" (Abbreviated: H,W,J,C).

If the claim is contingent, place an "X" in the column labeled "Contingent." If the claim is unliquidated, place an "X" in the column labeled "Unliquidated." If the claim is Disputed, place an "X" in the column labeled Disputed. You may need to place an X in more than one of these three columns.

Report the total of all claims listed on this Schedule D in the box labeled "Total" on the last sheet of the completed Schedule. Report this total also on the Summary of Schedules.

Creditor's Name and Mailing Address Including Zip Code[38]	CODEBTOR	HWJC	Date Claim Was Incurred, Nature of Lien, and Description and Market Value of Property Subject to Lien	CONTINGENT	UNLIQUIDATED	DISPUTED	Amount of Claim Without Deducting Value of Collateral	Unsecured Portion If Any
Acct No: 222-332-33 Warren Bank Mortgage Co. 656 Bank Co. Park Springfield, MA 02333		J	April 1, 1996; mortgage on debtor's residence; VALUE $125,000[39]				$95,500 ($2,912 arrears to be paid in plan)[40]	$0
Acct No: 98434 Fast Finance Co. 1234 Main Street Warren, MA 02345	X[41]	J	May 3, 2002; debt consolidation loan; mortgage on debtor's residence; VALUE $125,000			X[42]	$55,000[43]	$25,500[44]
Acct No: 34343 Chevrolet Finance Co.[45] 248 Finance Co. Park Springfield, MA 02134		J	September 14, 2001; auto loan; 1995 Chevy Caprice; VALUE $1,350			X	$2,300	$950
Acct No: 4324-23-54355 Mass. National Bank VISA 234 Main Street Warren, MA 02345		J	May 2001; judgment lien on debtor's wages; VALUE $635			X	$2,348	$1,713
							Subtotal: $155,148	
							$155,148	TOTAL

(Report total also on Summary of Schedules)

SCHEDULE E— CREDITORS HOLDING UNSECURED PRIORITY CLAIMS

A complete list of claims entitled to priority, listed separately by type of priority, is to be set forth on the sheets provided. Only holders of unsecured claims entitled to priority should be listed in this schedule. In the boxes provided on the attached sheets, state the name and mailing address, including zip code, and the last four digits of the account number, if any, of all entities holding priority claims against the debtor or property of the debtor, as of the date of the filing of the petition. The complete account number of any account the debtor has with the creditor is useful to the trustee and the creditor and may be provided if the debtor chooses to do so.

If any entity other than a spouse in a joint case may be jointly liable on a claim, place an "X" in the column labeled "Codebtor," include the entity in the appropriate schedule of creditors, and complete Schedule HC Codebtors. If a joint petition is filed, state whether husband, wife, both of them, or the marital community may be liable on each claim by placing an "H", "W", "J", or "C" in the column labeled "Husband, Wife, Joint, or Community."

If the claim is contingent, place an "X" in the column labeled "Contingent." If the claim is unliquidated, place an "X" in the column labeled "Unliquidated." If the claim is disputed, place an "X" in the column labeled "Disputed." (You may need to place an X in more than one of these three columns.)

Report the total of claims listed on each sheet in the box labeled "Subtotal" on each sheet. Report the total of all claims listed on this Schedule E in the box labeled "Total" on the last sheet of the completed schedule. Repeat this total also on the Summary of Schedules.

☐   Check this box if debtor has no creditors holding unsecured claims to report on this Schedule E.

TYPES OF PRIORITY CLAIMS (Check the appropriate box(es) below if claims in that category are listed on the attached sheets)

☐   **Extensions of credit in an involuntary case**.

Claims arising in the ordinary course of the debtor's business or financial affairs after the commencement of the case but before the earlier of the appointment of a trustee or the order for relief. 11 U.S.C. § 507(a)(2).

☐   **Wages, salaries, and commissions**

Wages, salaries and commissions, including vacation, severance, and sick leave pay owing to employees and commissions owing to qualifying independent sales representatives up to $4,925* per person earned within 90 days immediately preceding the filing of the original petition, or the cessation of business, whichever occurred first, to the extent provided in 11 U.S.C. § 507(a)(3).

☐   **Contributions to employee benefit plans**

Money owed to employee benefit plans for services rendered within 180 days immediately preceding the filing of the original petition, or the cessation of business, whichever occurred first, to the extent provided in 11 U.S.C. § 507(a)(4).

☐   **Certain farmers and fishermen**

Claims of certain farmers and fishermen, up to a maximum of $4,925* per farmer or fisherman, against the debtor, as provided in 11 U.S.C. § 507(a)(5).

☐   **Deposits by individuals**

Claims of individuals up to a maximum of $2,225* for deposits for the purchase, lease, or rental of property or services for personal, family or household use, that were not delivered or provided. 11 U.S.C. § 507(a)(6).

☐   **Alimony, Maintenance or Support**

Claims of a spouse, former spouse, or child of the debtor for alimony, maintenance or support, to the extent provided in 11 U.S.C. § 507(a)(7).

☑   **Taxes and Certain Other Debts Owed to Governmental Units**

Taxes, custom duties, and penalties owing to federal, state, and local governmental units as set forth in 11 U.S.C. § 507(a)(8).

☐   **Commitments to Maintain the Capital of an Insured Depository Institution**

Claims based on commitments to the FDIC, RTC, Director of the Office of Thrift Supervision, Comptroller of the Currency, or Board of Governors of the Federal Reserve System, or their predecessors or successors, to maintain the capital of an insured depository institution. 11 U.S.C. § 507(a)(9).

* Amounts are subject to adjustment on April 1, 2004, and every three years thereafter with respect to cases commenced after the date of adjustment.

Creditor's Name and Mailing Address Including Zip Code	C O D E B T O R	H W J C	Date Claim Was Incurred, and Consideration for Claim	C O N T I N G E N T	U N L I Q U I D A T E D	D I S P U T E D	Total Amount of Claim	Amount Entitled to Priority
Acct No: Internal Revenue Service 432 Columbia Ave. Boston, MA 02105		J	April, 2003; 2002 taxes[46] April, 1999; 1998 taxes				$715	$348[47]
Acct No:								
Acct No:								
Acct No:								
Acct No:								
Acct No:								

$715 TOTAL

(Report total also on Summary of Schedules)

SCHEDULE F— CREDITORS HOLDING UNSECURED NONPRIORITY CLAIMS

State the name, mailing address,, including zip code, and the last four digits of any account number of all entities holding unsecured claims without priority against the debtor or property of the debtor, as of the date of the filing of the petition. The complete account number of any account the debtor has with the creditor is useful to the trustee and the creditor and may be provided if the debtor chooses to do so. Do not include claims listed in Schedules D and E. If all creditors will not fit on this page, use continuation sheets.

If any entity other than a spouse in a joint case may be jointly liable on a claim, place an "X" in the column labeled "Codebtor," include the entity in the appropriate schedule of creditors, and complete Schedule H— Codebtors. If a joint petition is filed, state whether husband, wife, both of them, or the marital community may be liable on each claim by placing an "H," "W," "J," or "C" in the column labeled "HWJC" for "Husband, Wife, Joint, or Community."

If the claim is contingent, place an "X" in the column labeled "CONTINGENT." If the claim is unliquidated, place an "X" in the column labeled "UNLIQUIDATED." If the claim is disputed, place an "X" in the column labeled "DISPUTED." You may need to place an X in more than one of these three columns. Report the total of all claims listed on this Schedule E in the box labeled "Total" on the last sheet of the completed schedule. Report this total also in the Summary of Schedules.

Creditor's Name and Mailing Address Including Zip Code	CODEBTOR	HWJC	Date Claim Was Incurred And Consideration for Claim If Claim is Subject to Setoff, so State	CONTINGENT	UNLIQUIDATED	DISPUTED	Amount of Claim
Acct No: Warren Hospital 958 Main Street Warren, MA 02345		J	April 27, 2003; medical services[48]				$2,789
Acct No: 4324-23-54355 First Express Card P.O. Box 39670 Phoenix, AZ 85067		J	Various dates, credit card purchases			X[49]	$2,250 approx.[50]
Acct No: Debt Collectors, Inc.[51] 19 Dunning Dr. Buffalo, NY 14203		J	Same as above (collection agent for First Express Card)			X	same as above
Acct No: 3455555-55567776 Massachusetts Electric Co.[52] Electric Co. Park Warren, MA 02345		J	April, 1996; utility service				$790
Acct No:[53] Easy Credit Co. 165 Main Street Warren, MA 02345		J	May 27, 2003; personal loan. This claim is subject to setoff.[54]			X	$789

Acct No: Steven A. Debtor[55] 234 City Street Boston, MA 02109		J	June 27, 2004; personal loan.				$500
Acct No: Warren Water Co. 523 Main Street Warren, MA 02345		J	April, 1996; utility service			X	$341
Acct No: David & Deborah Debtor[56] 114 Main Street Warren, MA 02345		J	Same as debt listed in Schedule D to Fast Finance Co.; contingent liability to codebtors on that claim.	X		X	
Acct No: Halliday Health Spa[57] 1576 Main Street Warren, MA 02345		J	April 30, 2003; executory contract for health spa				$400
							$7,859 TOTAL

(Report total also on Summary of Schedules)

SCHEDULE G— EXECUTORY CONTRACTS AND UNEXPIRED LEASES

Describe all executory contracts of any nature and all unexpired leases of real or personal property. Include any timeshare interests.

State nature of debtor's interest in contract, i.e, "Purchaser," "Agent" etc. State whether the debtor is lessor or lessee of a lease.

Provide the name and complete mailing address of all other parties to each lease or contract described.

NOTE: a party listed on this schedule will not receive notice of the filing of this case unless the party is also scheduled in the appropriate schedule of creditors.

Name and Mailing Address, including Zip Code, of Other Parties to Lease or Contract	Description of Contract or Lease and Nature of Debtor's Interest. State Whether Lease is for Nonresidential real property. State Contract Number of any Government Contract
Halliday Health Spa 576 Main Street Warren, MA 02345	36 month contract to use weight room and pool at health spa; monthly payments of $56 terminated 3/04.[58]

SCHEDULE H— CODEBTORS

Provide the information requested concerning any person or entity, other than a spouse in a joint case, that is also liable on any debts listed by debtor in the schedules of creditors. Include all guarantors and co-signors. In community property states, a married debtor not filing a joint case should report the name and address of the nondebtor spouse in this schedule. Include all names used by the nondebtor spouse during the six years immediately preceding the commencement of the case.

Name and Address of Codebtor	Name and Address of Creditor
David & Deborah Debtor[59] 114 Main Street Warren, MA 02345	Fast Finance Co. 234 Main Street Warren, MA 02345

SCHEDULE I— CURRENT INCOME OF INDIVIDUAL DEBTORS

The column labeled "spouse" must be completed in all cases filed by joint debtors and by a married debtor in a Chapter 12 or 13 case whether or not a joint petition is filed, unless the spouses are separated and a joint petition is not filed.

Debtor's Marital Status:	Dependents of Debtor and Spouse	
	RELATIONSHIP daughter son	AGE 3 1

EMPLOYMENT:	Debtor	Spouse
Occupation, Name of Employer:	maintenance worker, Allied Factories	cashier (part-time), Big Box Stores
How long employed:	2 years	6 mos.
Address of employer:	777 Main Street Warren, MA 02345	35 Mall Ln. Warren, MA 02345

Income: (Estimate of average monthly income) Current monthly gross wages, salary, and commissions (Pro rate if not paid monthly)	DEBTOR	SPOUSE
	$1,205	$516
Estimated monthly overtime	$150	$0
SUBTOTAL	$1,355	$516
LESS PAYROLL DEDUCTIONS a. Payroll taxes and Social Security	$140	$50
b. Insurance	$35	$0
c. Union dues	$22	$0
d. Other (Specify)	$0	$0
SUBTOTAL OF PAYROLL DEDUCTIONS	$197	$50
TOTAL NET MONTHLY TAKE HOME PAY	$1,158	$466
Regular income from operation of business/profession/farm (attach statement)	$0	$0
Income from real property	$0	$0
Interest and dividends	$0	$0
Alimony, maintenance, or support payments payable to the debtor for the debtor's use or that of the dependents listed above	$0	$0
Social security or other governmental assistance Specify: Food Stamps	$0	$57[60]
Pension or retirement income	$0	$0
Other monthly income (Specify): Debtor: Odd jobs	$120[61]	$0
TOTAL MONTHLY INCOME	$1,278	$523
TOTAL COMBINED MONTHLY INCOME	$ 1,801	(Report also on Summary of Schedules)

Describe any increase or decrease of more than 10% in any of the above categories anticipated to occur within the year following the filing of this document. None[62]

SCHEDULE J— CURRENT EXPENDITURES OF INDIVIDUAL DEBTORS
Complete this schedule by estimating the average monthly expenses of the debtor and the debtor's family.
Prorate any payments made bi-weekly, quarterly, semi-annually or annually to show monthly rate.

Rent, home mortgage, or mobile-home lot rent Are real estate taxes included? Yes __X__ No _____	$728.00[63]
Is property insurance included? Yes __X__ No _____	
Utilities Electricity and heating fuel	$61.00[64]
Water and sewer	$32.00
Telephone	$28.00
Other utilities: Cable T.V.	$20.00
Home Maintenance, repairs, upkeep	$25.00
Food	$375.00[65]
Clothing	$40.00
Laundry, dry cleaning	$20.00
Medical and dental expenses (Employer-paid health insurance)[66]	$15.00
Transportation (not including car payments)	$50.00
Recreation, clubs, entertainment, newspapers, magazines	$30.00
Charitable contributions	$25.00
Insurance (not deducted from wages or inc. in mortgage pmt) Homeowner's or renter's	$0.00
Life	$0.00
Health	$0.00
Auto	$54.00[67]
Other insurance:	$0.00
Taxes (not deducted from wages or included in home mortgage) Specify:	$0.00
Installment payments (in Chapters 12 and 13, do not list payments to be included in the plan)	$0.00
Auto payment:	$0.00
Other payment:	$0.00
Alimony, maintenance, and support paid to others	$0.00
Payments for support of additional dependents not living at the debtor's home	$0.00
Regular expenses from operation of business, profession, or farm (attach detailed statement)	$0.00
Other expenses: Baby Formula and Diapers, Cigarettes	$50.00[68]
TOTAL MONTHLY EXPENSES (report also on Summary of Schedules)	$1,553.00[69]

DECLARATION CONCERNING DEBTOR'S SCHEDULES

DECLARATION UNDER PENALTY OF PERJURY BY INDIVIDUAL DEBTOR

I declare under penalty of perjury that I have read the foregoing summary and schedules, consisting of __16__ sheets (Total shown on summary page plus 1) and that they are true and correct to the best of my knowledge, information and belief.

Date __October 27, 2004__   Signature   _____

Joseph A. Debtor

Date __October 27, 2004__   Signature   _____

Josephine S. Debtor

(In joint case, both debtors must sign)

- -

DECLARATION UNDER PENALTY ON BEHALF OF A CORPORATION

I, the _____ (the president or other officer or an authorized agent of the corporation or a member or an authorized agent of the partnership) of the _____ (corporation or partnership) named as debtor in this case, declare under penalty of perjury that I have read the foregoing summary and schedules, consisting of ____ sheets (Total shown on summary page plus 1), and that I declare that they are true and correct to the best of my knowledge, information and belief.

Date _____

Signature

(Print or type the name of individual signing for debtor)

(An individual signing on behalf of a partnership or corporation must indicate position or relationship to debtor.)

- -

Penalty for making a false statement or concealing property: Fine of up to $500,000 or imprisonment for up to 5 years or both. 18 U.S.C. §§ 152 and 3571.

Annotations to Completed Official Form 6, Schedules

Official Form 6 contains the debtor's bankruptcy schedules. It must be filed in all cases. For a general discussion of Official Form 6, see § 7.3.4, *supra*.

Summary of Schedules

The Summary of Schedules is fairly straightforward. It merely reports totals from Schedules A through J. In some jurisdictions, local rules or practice may require that this form follow Schedules A through J in the packet for filing.

    8 Each schedule requires the debtor's name and case number. The case number will not be available if the schedules are filed at the same time as the petition and can be left blank.

Schedule A

Schedule A is a list of the debtor's real property. For a general discussion of Schedule A, see § 7.3.4.2, *supra*.

    9 A basic description, including the street address for the property, is usually sufficient. In some districts, local practice will require the full legal description.

  10 The debtor should describe the interest, such as "owner," "holder of life estate," or "holder of equitable interest under land contract." The exact book and page number of the deed may not be necessary.

  11 The value of the property can be the debtor's best estimate. Often the valuation is selected from a range of good faith choices in a manner consistent with the debtor's best interests and the overall goals of the case. For a further discussion of valuation, see §§ 9.7.3.3, 11.2.2, *supra*.

  12 This is the total amount of secured claims against the property consistent with Schedule D, *infra*. When the amount of the secured claims exceeds the value of the property in chapter 13, a debtor may seek to avoid the liens to the extent they exceed the value of the collateral. *See* §§ 11.2, 11.7, *supra*.

  13 It is sometimes difficult to value an undivided interest which cannot be alienated by one debtor. For example, does one of the two tenants by the entirety in a $10,000.00 property have an interest worth $5000.00 if that interest could not be sold by that tenant? Generally, it is best to list one-half of the value of such a property, with a note explaining that the interest could not be sold by the debtor for that much, because the trustee may partition under 11 U.S.C. § 363(h). For property that the debtor owns with other individuals, the debtor should list a value that represents the debtor's proportional interest and provide an explanation of that interest.

Schedule B

Schedule B is the statement of the debtor's personal property. For a general discussion of Schedule B, see § 7.3.4.2, *supra*.

  14 If the debtor has funds in a bank account, credit union, brokerage house, pension, or other savings instruments when the bankruptcy is filed, then they must be listed as assets in item 2. If they cannot be exempted, then the debtor should consider converting them to exempt property, if possible, prior to the bankruptcy. On occasion, a trustee will request records of bank accounts to see if there has been a rapid, unexplained dissipation of assets. If the bank has a right of set-off and might "freeze" the account upon filing, funds should be withdrawn prior to the case if possible.

  15 Courts vary widely in the specificity they require here. In general, a debtor should list separately each major appliance and anything of exceptional value. Some courts will allow all items of small value in a room to be called a "set." Obviously, there is some limit when it comes to listing each utensil. If there is a very long list of household goods, it may be typed separately, included as an appendix to the Schedules, and incorporated here by reference.

  16 A note such as this one which explains a low valuation is often useful.

  17 Generally, the values for used furniture and similar household items can be quite low. Clients should be asked for "garage sale" value.

  18 There is usually no need to list every last plate, cup, and saucer. Some sort of catch-all for miscellaneous items is usually a good idea. A catch-all may be important if there is a later loss covered by insurance. *See* Payne v. Wood, 775 F.2d 202 (7th Cir. 1985).

  19 Although ERISA-qualified pension plans are not property of the estate under 11 U.S.C. § 541(c)(2), they are nevertheless personal property of the debtor which must be listed. *See* § 2.5.2, *supra*.

  20 Even overpayments of wage withholding which are still in the hands of the employer should probably be listed here and exempted if possible. Local practice should be checked. In many places only anticipated refunds for prior tax years need be listed. *See* § 2.5.3, *supra*.

  21 If the debtor intends to claim any cause of action as exempt, it is very important to list it both in Schedule B and in Schedule C. If a claim is exempted, once the time for objecting to exemptions has run, the debtor may pursue the claim. *See* § 10.3, *supra*. The debtor's failure to list causes of action or claims may preclude the debtor from pursuing them after bankruptcy under the doctrine of judicial estoppel. *See* § 7.3.4.2.1, *supra*. Occasionally, a future interest in public benefits may be specifically exempted to pursue a particular litigation strategy. In such cases, the right to receive the public benefits should be listed as an asset. Technically, it is usually property of the estate, but as it has no value to the trustee, it is not ordinarily listed.

  22 If the value of property is truly unknown, it is often best to simply state the value as "unknown," leaving it to the trustee and creditors to assess the value on their own. *See* § 7.3.4.2.2, *supra*.

  23 Even if the debtor expects only to use a claim defensively (for example, as a defense to a mortgage company's secured proof of claim), it is a good idea to list the claim.

  24 The debtor retains an interest in repossessed property which should be listed, particularly if the debtor intends to seek its return. Property which has been repossessed or seized is property of the estate to the extent of the debtor's interest in it. If the debtor has an interest then it should be turned over under 11 U.S.C. § 542, and the debtor has a right to possession under 11 U.S.C. § 1306. *See* §§ 9.9, 12.8, *supra*. In addition, many transfers of property which may be claimed as exempt may be nullified by the debtor or the trustee. *See* § 10.4, *supra*.

  25 Wages garnished pre-petition should be listed in Schedule B and exempted on Schedule C if an exemption is available. Wages in excess of $600.00 that were garnished during the ninety-day period before the bankruptcy filing may be recovered as a preference pursuant to section 547. If the debtor retains a property interest in the wages under state law and can claim them as exempt, the debtor may be able to recover wages less than $600.00 or garnished more than ninety days pre-petition by using the lien avoidance provisions under section 522(f). *See* § 10.4.2.6.4, *supra*.

Schedule C

Schedule C is a list of the debtor's exemptions. All possible good faith exemptions should be listed, because if no party in interest files a timely objection, the exemptions will be allowed as listed. *See* § 10.3, *supra*. The goal, if possible, is to list all of the debtor's property as exempt. For this reason it is a good idea to compare carefully Schedules B and C to ascertain that nothing in Schedule B is inadvertently left off Schedule C. However, if mistakes are made, it is possible to amend easily. Fed. R. Bankr. P. 1009. For a general discussion of Schedule C, see § 7.3.4.2, *supra*.

26 It is important to check the total, as well as individual items on Schedule C, against the other schedules to be sure that as much property as possible has been claimed as exempt. Usually this total will be all property. The totals may differ, as here, due to deduction for undisputed security interests.

It also may be important to specify that the debtor is exempting the debtor's entire interest in the property listed. *See, e.g., In re Hyman*, 967 F.2d 1316 (9th Cir. 1992). While in most cases a fair reading of the other schedules listing the amount of the exemption as the total value of the debtor's interest in the property should make clear that the debtor indeed did intend to claim as exempt that total value of her interest, it may be safest to specify this fact on Schedule C itself.

It is recommended that a note be added at the bottom of Schedule C stating: "Unless specifically stated otherwise, the debtors claim 100% of their interest in each item listed in this Schedule as exempt." *See* § 7.3.4.2, *supra*.

27 *See* § 10.2.1, *supra*. If a husband and wife file jointly, both spouses must take the same set of exemptions in a state which has not foreclosed use of the federal exemptions.

28 The right to live in the property has value and should be exempted even when the debtors have no equity in the property. It is also advisable to assert an available exemption in the event that liens on the property are avoided during the bankruptcy.

29 The value listed in this schedule should be the debtor's equity in the property, not its full value (here, because the debtors have no equity, the estimated value of their possessory interest is listed). If there is a dispute with respect to the secured creditor's claim, it is best to claim the highest possible equity within the allowed exemptions, so that there is no chance of some equity not being claimed as exempt if the debtor successfully disputes the claim. Although Fed. R. Bankr. P. 1009 provides that the schedules may be amended at any time, some courts have limited amendments to exemption claims. *See* § 10.3, *supra*. The value should generally be the same as that listed in Schedules A and B, except for deduction of undisputed security interests. In close cases in which insufficient exemptions are available, slightly less than the full equity might be claimed, because a trustee is unlikely to sell a property to realize an amount so small it will cover only the costs of the sale. However, check local trustee practices.

It may also be a good idea to state here that the debtors are claiming the full value of their interest in the property as exempt.

30 Although the automobile is fully encumbered and has been repossessed, the debtors' retained interest has value which should be exempted. Because the debtors have no equity, the value of their interest can be listed as nominal. An alternative approach would be to assign a value to the interest of the debtors for use of the recovered property, or to assert the highest possible equity within the allowed exemption if it will not be used for any other property. See note concerning claimed value of debtor's house, above.

31 Each debtor is entitled to a separate set of exemptions in a joint case, though both spouses must choose the same exemption scheme. In some instances involving solely-owned property, the debtor claiming the exemption should be identified.

32 Most courts will allow this type of incorporation by reference.

33 The wild-card exemption is $925.00 plus one-half the unused homestead for each debtor pursuant to 11 U.S.C. § 522(d)(5). As the debtors here have each used only $5000.00 of their homestead, they retain a substantial additional wild-card exemption.

34 By exempting this property, the debtor will have full rights to litigate the cause of action if no objections are raised. *See* § 10.3, *supra*.

35 Although it may be a stretch, there is probably a good faith argument that some unfair and deceptive acts and practices (UDAP) damages may be exempted as compensation for personal bodily injury or for loss of future income under 11 U.S.C. § 522(d)(11)(D) or (E). There is no reason not to list that exemption in the alternative.

36 This section is an alternative basis for the exemption, as explained above.

37 When there are two theories which prevent creditors from reaching an item of property, they may be listed in the alternative.

Schedule D

Schedule D is a list of the debtor's secured debts. For a general discussion of Schedule D, see § 7.3.4.3, *supra*.

38 Some courts require that creditors be numbered and/or alphabetized on the schedules. In addition, most courts require the debtor to submit along with the petition a list or matrix of all creditors in the case, which is used to prepare mailing labels for notices to creditors. The names and addresses are typically listed in a column and there may be specific requirements as to the type size and font that may be used. Check local practice.

39 This amount is the full fair market value of the property. It should correspond to Schedules A and B.

40 Some courts require a separate listing of the arrears when the plan proposes to cure arrears. Check local practice.

41 The existence of codebtors should be indicated here with their names and addresses listed in Schedule H.

42 If there is any doubt, list the claim as disputed to preserve the debtors' right to raise issues about the validity of the claim later.

43 This amount is the full amount of the claim even though it exceeds the value of the collateral.

44 This amount is the amount by which this creditor's claim exceeds the value of the collateral. In chapter 13, it may be possible to avoid the lien to the extent that it exceeds the value of the collateral or otherwise to limit the claim to the value of the collateral, though this is more difficult with loans secured by the debtors' principal residence. *See* §§ 11.2, 11.7, *supra*.

45 Chevrolet Finance Co. is a secured creditor and must be listed as such even though the collateral has been repossessed.

Schedule E

This is a list of the debtor's unsecured priority creditors. For a general discussion of Schedule E, see § 7.3.4.3, *supra*. For a discussion of priority debts in chapter 13 cases, see § 12.3.5, *supra*.

46 Not all tax debts are priority debts. Check 11 U.S.C. § 507(a)(7) in each instance. Remember also that if a tax creditor holds a lien for the debt, the tax debt is not a priority claim because it is not unsecured as required by section 507(a)(7). Different debts to the Internal Revenue Service may be listed on different schedules.

47 The total tax debt may include amounts which are no longer subject to priority. The amount entitled to priority should be listed in this column.

Schedule F

This is a list of the debtor's general unsecured creditors. The rule of thumb is "when in doubt, list it." Failure to list a claim may prevent discharge. *See* § 14.4.3.3, *supra*. For a general discussion of Schedule F, see § 7.3.4.3, *supra*.

48 The exact date the claim was incurred should be listed if that information is available. Otherwise, listing the month and year, or simply the year, should suffice.

49 It is less critical to list disputes in this schedule, because normally all unsecured debts are discharged, except those listed in 11 U.S.C. § 523(a). *See* Ch. 14, *supra*. However, the debtor may have an interest in objecting to unsecured claims in a chapter 13 case, as the amount of the claim will affect the percentage distribution to unsecured creditors and may reduce the amount needed to be paid by the debtor under certain types of plans. If there is any doubt about the debtors' liability or the amount of the claim, list the claim as disputed to preserve the debtors' right to assert an objection to the claim later.

50 The debtor should attempt to list the amount of the debt as precisely as possible, though the listed amount need not be exact. If the only figure the debtor has is an approximation, this may be noted on the schedules by adding "approx." after the amount.

51 For an obligation that is owed to two separate creditors, it is a good idea to include both creditors in the schedule. The debtor may enter the creditors' names separately in two boxes with a notation that it is the same debt so that it does not affect the total. This approach is also useful with respect to an obligation assigned to another entity or to a collection agency for purposes of collection. Including both the original creditor and the collection agency or assignee in both the schedule and the mailing matrix ensures that both get notice of the bankruptcy and that any claim of either of them is discharged.

52 Utility debts are often omitted by accident, particularly if the accounts are more or less current. Technically, there is almost always some debt owed, and unless a current bill has just been paid, it should be listed.

53 When there is no account number or it is unknown, the debt should be listed anyway, with the account number left blank. There is no requirement that the account number be listed in order to have the debt discharged.

54 The debtor has a potential truth-in-lending set-off, which is listed in Schedule B as property and exempted in Schedule C. The debt is also listed as disputed based on the truth-in-lending claim.

55 All debts must be listed, even debts to relatives. The debtor, of course, may still pay back such debts later if she chooses to do so.

56 It is good practice to include the contingent liability to cosigners as a debt to avoid any claim that the codebtors did not receive notice of the case and that the debt was not discharged. The debt should be listed only once to avoid a distortion caused by double-counting. When mortgages are guaranteed by the Veterans Administration, Federal Housing Administration, or private mortgage insurance, those agencies are considered sureties and should be listed.

57 The amounts due on an executory contract should be listed as an unsecured debt.

Schedule G

Schedule G is the debtor's statement of executory contracts and unexpired leases. For a general discussion of this form, see § 7.3.4.4, *supra*. For a general discussion of unexpired leases and executory contracts, see § 12.9, *supra*.

58 Even though the debtor may consider an executory contract terminated when she stops using benefits under the contract, if the term of the contract is not completed then it should be listed here. An unsecured claim should also be listed in Schedule F. *See* § 12.9, *supra*.

Schedule H

Schedule H is a list of codebtors, other than a spouse in a joint case, who are obligated on any of the debtor's debts. For a general discussion of this form, see § 7.3.4.5, *supra*.

59 Although there may be resistance to listing family members, there is no ground for not doing so. Some debtors may take comfort in chapter 13 cases in the availability of a limited codebtor stay. 11 U.S.C. § 1301; *see* § 9.4.4, *supra*.

Schedule I

Schedule I is the debtor's current income statement. For a general discussion of Schedule I, see § 7.3.4.6, *supra*.

60 Non-cash income such as food stamps or a utility allowance should be listed as income and offset by a relevant expense in the same amount in the appropriate category in Schedule J.

61 All of the debtor's outside sources of income should be listed. In chapter 13, absent enumeration of outside sources of income, it may appear that the debtor is unable to support plan payments.

62 If a change is listed, such as, for example, commencement of unemployment income, it may be necessary to account for the anticipated change in the chapter 13 plan. Alternatively, the debtor may file a modified plan when the income change occurs. *See* § 8.7.3, *supra*.

Schedule J

Schedule J is the debtor's statement of expenses. For a general discussion of Schedule J, see § 7.3.4.6, *supra*.

63 Any amount which the debtor will pay on mortgages direct to the mortgage-holders should be listed here. Amounts to be paid under the plan should not be listed.

64 The estimates here are future *average* monthly expenses and not necessarily what the debtor is accustomed to paying. Often the debtor has paid more than her average monthly charge in the past, due to an old default. Similarly, if reasonable conservation measures can be taken, the debtor may be able to lower future payments and thereby free up money for a chapter 13 plan.

65 The food expense is often difficult for the debtor to estimate. It should include all food costs including, for example, the cost of eating lunches out.

66 A note is sometimes necessary to explain why a debtor has few medical or other expenses. The amount listed represents co-payments for office visits and medications.

67 If the debtor owns a car, the absence of auto insurance costs may give rise to a creditor allegation that a car loan claim is not "adequately protected." The debtor should be advised of that risk in such a situation and should consider buying insurance if possible.

68 These are examples of frequently omitted expenses. In general, the debtors should be carefully questioned about forgotten expenses because such expenses can make a plan unworkable or can reduce the amount necessary to meet the ability to pay test. *See* § 12.3.3, *supra*.

69 This amount must be worked out upon formulating the debtors' chapter 13 plan. *See* § 7.3.7, *supra*. The excess of income over expenses should, if at all possible, be slightly higher than the payments, so the plan is capable of meeting the feasibility standard under 11 U.S.C. § 1325(a)(6). However, if the excess is substantially greater than payments, the plan may not meet the "ability to pay" test of 11 U.S.C. § 1325(b). *See generally* § 12.3.3, *supra*.

UNITED STATES BANKRUPTCY COURT
DISTRICT OF MASSACHUSETTS

In re: Joseph A. Debtor, Josephine S. Debtor   Debtor(s)   Case No.

STATEMENT OF FINANCIAL AFFAIRS

This statement is to be completed by every debtor. Spouses filing a joint petition may file a single statement on which the information for both spouses is combined. If the case is filed under Chapter 12 or Chapter 13, a married debtor must furnish information for both spouses whether or not a joint petition is filed, unless the spouses are separated and a joint petition is not filed. An individual debtor engaged in business as a sole proprietor, partner, family farmer, or self-employed professional should provide the information requested on this statement concerning all such activities as well as the individual's personal affairs.

Questions 1-18 are to be completed by all debtors. Debtors that are or have been in business, as defined below, must also complete Questions 19-25. Each question must be answered. If the answer to any question is "None," or the question is not applicable, mark the box labeled "None." If additional space is needed for the answer to any question, use and attach a separate sheet properly identified with the case name, case number (if known), and the number of the question.

Definitions

"In business." A debtor is "in business" for the purpose of this form if the debtor is a corporation or partnership. An individual debtor is "in business" for the purpose of this form if the debtor is or has been within the six years immediately preceding the filing of this bankruptcy case, any of the following: an officer, director, managing executive, or owner of 5 percent or more of the voting or equity securities of a corporation; a partner, other than a limited partner, of a partnership; a sole proprietor or self employed.

"Insider." The term "insider" includes but is not limited to: relatives of the debtor, general partners of the debtor and their relatives; corporations of which the debtor is an officer, director or person in control; officers, directors, and owner of 5 percent or more of the voting or equity securities of a corporate debtor and their relatives; affiliates of the debtor and insiders of such affiliates; any managing agent of the debtor. 11 U.S.C. § 101.

1. Income from employment or operation of business

State the gross amount of income the debtor has received from employment, trade or profession, or from operation of the debtor's business from the beginning of this calendar year to the date this case was commenced. State also the gross amounts received during the two years immediately preceding this calendar year. (A debtor that maintains, or has maintained, financial records on the basis of a fiscal rather than a calendar year may report fiscal year income. Identify the beginning and ending dates of the debtor's fiscal year. If a joint petition is filed, state income for each spouse separately. (Married debtors filing under chapter 12 or chapter 13 must state income of both spouses whether or not a joint petition is filed, unless the spouses are separated, and a joint petition is not filed.)

AMOUNT[70]   SOURCE (if more than one)

Joseph Debtor:
$13,500.00   2004 YTD wages from Allied Factories
$15,500.00   2003 wages from Allied Factories
$15,100.00   2002 wages from Allied Factories
$1,440.00   2004 odd jobs for corner grocer

Josephine Debtor:
$5,100.00   2004 YTD wages from Big Box Stores
$2,700.00   2003 telephone polling

2. Income other than from employment or operation of business

State the amount of income received by the debtor other than from employment trade or profession, or operation of the debtor's business during the two years immediately preceding the commencement of the case. Give particulars. If a joint petition is filed, state income for each spouse separately. (Married debtors filing under chapter 12 or chapter 13 must state income of both spouses whether or not a joint petition is filed, unless the spouses are separated, and a joint petition is not filed.)

AMOUNT   SOURCE

$312[71]   Josephine Debtor 2003 Food Stamps

3. Payments to creditors[72]

　　　　a. List all payments on loans, installment purchases of goods or services, and other debts, aggregating more than $600 to any creditor, made within 90 days immediately preceding the commencement of this case. (Married debtors filing under chapter 12 or chapter 13 must state payments by either or both spouses whether or not a joint petition is filed, unless the spouses are separated, and a joint petition is not filed.)

NAME AND ADDRESS OF CREDITOR	DATES OF PAYMENTS	AMOUNT PAID	AMOUNT STILL OWING
Massachusetts National Bank VISA	8/15/04	$145	
234 Main Street	9/10/04	$200	
Warren, MA 02345	9/15/04	$145	
	10/15/04	$145	
	TOTAL:	$635	$1713

　　　　b. List all payments made within one year immediately preceding the commencement of this case to or for the benefit of creditors who were insiders. (Married debtors filing under chapter 12 or chapter 13 must include payments of either or both spouses whether or not a joint petition is filed, unless the spouses are separated, and a joint petition is not filed.)

NAME AND ADDRESS OF CREDITOR RELATIONSHIP TO DEBTOR	DATES OF PAYMENTS	AMOUNT PAID	AMOUNT STILL OWING

[X] NONE

4. Suits and administrative proceedings, executions, garnishments and attachments[73]

　　　　a. List all suits and administrative proceedings to which the debtor is or was a party within one year immediately preceding the filing of this case. (Married debtors filing under chapter 12 or chapter 13 must include information concerning either or both spouses whether or not a joint petition is filed, unless the spouses are separated, and a joint petition is not filed.)

CAPTION OF SUIT AND CASE NUMBER	NATURE OF PROCEEDING	COURT/AGENCY AND LOCATION	STATUS OR DISPOSITION
Massachusetts National Bank VISA v. Debtor, 99-0333	Debt Collection	Massachusetts Superior Court	Judgment for Plaintiff: $2,348.39

　　　　b. Describe all property that has been attached, garnished, or seized under any legal or equitable process within one year immediately preceding the commencement of this case. (Married debtors filing under chapter 12 or chapter 13 must include information concerning property of either or both spouses whether or not a joint petition is filed, unless the spouses are separated, and a joint petition is not filed.)

NAME AND ADDRESS OF PERSON FOR WHOSE BENEFIT PROPERTY WAS SEIZED	DATE OF SEIZURE	DESCRIPTION AND VALUE OF PROPERTY
Massachusetts National Bank VISA[74] 234 Main Street Warren, MA 02345	2004	Wages, $635.00

5. Repossessions, foreclosures and returns[75]

　　　　List all property that has been repossessed by a creditor, sold at foreclosure sale, transferred through a deed in lieu of foreclosure or returned to a seller within one year immediately preceding the commencement of this case. (Married debtors filing under chapter 12 or chapter 13 must include information concerning either or both spouses whether or not a joint petition is filed, unless the spouses are separated, and a joint petition is not filed.)

NAME AND ADDRESS OF CREDITOR OR SELLER	DATE OF REPOSSESSION, FORECLOSURE, SALE TRANSFER OR RETURN	DESCRIPTION AND VALUE OF PROPERTY
Chevrolet Finance Co. 248 Finance Co. Park Springfield, MA 02134	September 22, 2004	1989 Chevy Caprice $1,350.00

6. Assignments and receiverships[76]

      a. Describe any assignment of property for the benefit of creditors made within 120 days immediately preceding the commencement of this case. (Married debtors filing under chapter 12 or chapter 13 must include any assignments by either or both spouses whether or not a joint petition is filed, unless the spouses are separated, and a joint petition is not filed.)

NAME AND ADDRESS OF ASSIGNEE	DATE OF ASSIGNMENT	TERMS OF ASSIGNMENT OR SETTLEMENT

[X] NONE

      b. List all property which has been in the hands of a custodian, receiver, or court-appointed official within one year immediately preceding the commencement of this case. (Married debtors filing under chapter 12 or chapter 13 must include information concerning property of either or both spouses whether or not a joint petition is filed, unless the spouses are separated, and a joint petition is not filed.)

NAME AND ADDRESS OF CUSTODIAN	NAME, LOCATION OF COURT, CASE TITLE AND NUMBER	DATE OF ORDER	DESCRIPTION, VALUE OF PROPERTY

[X] NONE

7. Gifts[77]

      List all gifts or charitable contributions made within one year immediately preceding the commencement of this case except ordinary and usual gifts to family members aggregating less than $200 in value per individual family member and charitable contributions aggregating less than $100 per recipient. (Married debtors filing under chapter 12 or chapter 13 must include gifts or contributions by either or both spouses whether or not a joint petition is filed, unless the spouses are separated and a joint petition is not filed.)

NAME AND ADDRESS OF PERSON OR ORGANIZATION	RELATIONSHIP TO DEBTOR, IF ANY	DATE OF GIFT	DESCRIPTION AND VALUE OF GIFT

[X] NONE

8. Losses[78]

      List all losses from fire, theft, other casualty or gambling within one year immediately preceding the commencement of this case or since the commencement of this case. (Married debtors filing under chapter 12 or chapter 13 must include losses by either or both spouses whether or not a joint petition is filed, unless the spouses are separated and a joint petition is not filed.)

DESCRIPTION AND VALUE OF PROPERTY	DESCRIPTION OF CIRCUMSTANCES, AND IF LOSS WAS COVERED IN WHOLE OR IN PART BY INSURANCE, GIVE PARTICULARS	DATE OF LOSS

[X] NONE

9. Payments related to debt counseling or bankruptcy[79]

      List all payments made or property transferred by or on behalf of the debtor to any persons, including attorneys, for consultation concerning debt consolidation, relief under the bankruptcy law or preparation of a petition in bankruptcy within one year immediately preceding the commencement of this case.

NAME AND ADDRESS OF PAYEE	DATE OF PAYMENT, NAME OF PAYOR, IF OTHER THAN DEBTOR	AMOUNT OF MONEY, OR DESCRIPTION AND VALUE OF PROPERTY
Easy Pay Debt Counseling Service 848 Main Street Warren, MA 02345	August 21, 2004	$350.00

10. Other transfers[80]

List all other property, other than property transferred in the ordinary course of the business or financial affairs of the debtor, transferred either absolutely or as security within one year immediately preceding the commencement of this case. (Married debtors filing under chapter 12 or chapter 13 must include transfers by either or both spouses whether or not a joint petition is filed, unless the spouses are separated and a joint petition is not filed.)

NAME AND RELATIONSHIP OF
TRANSFEREE; RELATIONSHIP TO DEBTOR   DATE

DESCRIBE PROPERTY TRANSFERRED
AND VALUE RECEIVED

[X] NONE

11. Closed financial accounts[81]

List all financial accounts and instruments held in the name of the debtor or for the benefit of the debtor which were closed, sold or otherwise transferred within one year immediately preceding the commencement of this case. Include checking, saving, or other financial accounts, certificates of deposit, or other instruments; shares and share accounts held in banks, credit unions, pension funds, cooperatives, associations and brokerage houses and other financial institutions. (Married debtors filing under chapter 12 or chapter 13 must include information concerning accounts or instruments held by either or both spouses whether or not a joint petition is filed, unless the spouses are separated and a joint petition is not filed.)

NAME AND ADDRESS OF INSTITUTION

TYPE OF ACCOUNT; LAST FOUR
DIGITS OF ACCOUNT NUMBER, AND
AMOUNT OF FINAL BALANCE

AMOUNT AND DATE OF
SALE OR CLOSING

[X] NONE

12. Safe deposit boxes[82]

List each safe deposit or other box or depository in which the debtor has or had securities, cash or other valuables within one year immediately preceding the commencement of this case. (Married debtors filing under chapter 12 or chapter 13 must include boxes or depositories of either or both spouses whether or not a joint petition is filed, unless the spouses are separated and a joint petition is not filed.)

NAME AND ADDRESS OF BANK OR
OTHER INSTITUTION

NAMES AND ADDRESSES OF
THOSE WITH ACCESS TO
BOX OR DEPOSITORY

DESCRIPTION OF
CONTENTS

DATE OF TRANSFER
OR SURRENDER, IF
ANY

[X] NONE

13. Setoffs[83]

List all setoffs made by any creditor, including a bank, against a debt or deposit of the debtor within 90 days preceding the commencement of this case. (Married debtors filing under chapter 12 or chapter 13 must include information concerning either or both spouses whether or not a joint petition is filed, unless the spouses are separated and a joint petition is not filed.)

NAME AND ADDRESS OF CREDITOR   DATE OF SETOFF   AMOUNT OF SETOFF

[X] NONE

14. Property held for another person[84]

List all property owned by another person that the debtor holds or controls.

LOCATION OF
PROPERTY

NAME AND ADDRESS OF OWNER   DESCRIPTION AND VALUE OF PROPERTY   PROPERTY

NAME AND ADDRESS OF OWNER	DESCRIPTION AND VALUE OF PROPERTY	LOCATION OF PROPERTY
John D. Debtor[85] 100 Main Street Warren, MA 02345	$392.00 Bank Account (Trust Account for Minor Child)	First National Bank of MA

15. Prior address of debtor[86]

If the debtor has moved within two years immediately preceding the commencement of this case, list all premises which the debtor occupied during that period and vacated prior to the commencement of this case. If a joint petition is filed, report also any separate address of either spouse.

ADDRESS   NAME USED   DATES OF OCCUPANCY

[X] NONE

16. Spouses and Former Spouses

If the debtor resided in a community property state, commonwealth, or territory (including Alaska, Arizona, California, Idaho, Louisiana, Nevada, New Mexico, Puerto Rico, Texas, Washington, or Wisconsin) within the six-year period immediately preceding the commencement of the case, identify the name of the debtor's spouse and of any former spouse who resides or resided with the debtor in the community property state.

NAME

[X] NONE

17. Environmental Information

For the purposes of this question, the following definitions apply:

An "Environmental Law" means any federal, state or local statute or regulation regulating pollution, contamination, releases of hazardous or toxic substances, wastes or materials into the air, land, soil, surface water, groundwater, or other medium, including but not limited to, statutes or regulations regulating the cleanup of these substances, wastes, or material.

A "Site" means any location, facility, or property as defined by any Environmental Law, whether or not presently or formerly owned or operated by the debtor, including but not limited to, disposal sites.

A "Hazardous Material" means anything defined as a hazardous waste, hazardous substance, toxic substance, hazardous material, pollutant, or contaminant or similar term under an Environmental Law.

a. List the name and address of every site for which the debtor has received notice in writing by a governmental unit that it may be liable or potentially liable under or in violation of an Environmental Law. Indicate the governmental unit, the date of the notice, and , if known, the Environmental Law.

SITE NAME AND ADDRESS	NAME AND ADDRESS OF GOVERNMENTAL UNIT	DATE OF NOTICE	ENVIRONMENTAL LAW

[X] NONE

b. List the name and address of every site for which the debtor has received notice in writing by a governmental unit that it may be liable or potentially liable under or in violation of an Environmental Law. Indicate the governmental unit, the date of the notice, and, if known, the Environmental Law.

SITE NAME AND ADDRESS	NAME AND ADDRESS OF GOVERNMENTAL UNIT	DATE OF NOTICE	ENVIRONMENTAL LAW

[X] NONE

c. List all judicial or administrative proceedings, including settlements or orders, under any Environmental Law with respect to which the debtor is or was a party. Indicate the name and address of the governmental unit that is or was a party to the proceeding, and the docket number.

NAME AND ADDRESS OF GOVERNMENTAL UNIT	DOCKET NUMBER	STATUS OR DISPOSITION

[X] NONE

18. Nature, location and name of business

       a. If the debtor is an individual, list the names, addresses, taxpayer identification numbers, nature of the business, and beginning and ending dates of all businesses in which the debtor was an officer, director, partner, or managing executive of a corporation, partnership, sole proprietorship or was a self-employed professional within the six years immediately preceding the commencement of this case, or in which the debtor owned 5 percent or more of the voting or equity securities within the six years immediately preceding the commencement of this case.

       If the debtor is a partnership, list the names, addresses, taxpayer identification numbers, nature of the business, and beginning and ending dates of all businesses in which the debtor was a partner or owned 5 percent or more of the voting or equity securities, within the six years immediately preceding the commencement of this case.

       If the debtor is a corporation, list the names, addresses, taxpayer identification numbers, nature of the businesses, and beginning and ending dates of all businesses in which the debtor was a partner or owned 5 percent or more of the voting or equity securities, within the six years immediately preceding the commencement of this case.

NAME	TAXPAYER I.D. NUMBER	ADDRESS	NATURE OF BUSINESS	BEGINNING AND ENDING DATES
[X] NONE				

       b. Identify any business listed in response to subdivision a., above, that is "single asset real estate" as defined in 11 U.S.C. § 101.

NAME   ADDRESS

       The following questions [numbers 19 - 25] are to be completed by every debtor that is a corporation or partnership and by any individual debtor who is or has been, within six years immediately preceding the commencement of this case, any of the following: an officer, director, managing executive, or owner of more than 5 percent of the voting securities of a corporation, a partner, other than a limited partner, of a partnership; a sole proprietor, or otherwise self-employed.

       (An individual or joint debtor should complete this portion of the statement only if the debtor is or has been in business, as defined above, within six years immediately preceding the commencement of this case. A debtor who has not been in business within those six years should go directly to the signature page.)

Questions 19 to 25 Not applicable/Omitted.

* * * * * *

[To be completed by individual or individual and spouse]

I declare under penalty of perjury that I have read the answers contained in the foregoing statement of financial affairs and any attachments thereto and that they are true and correct.

Date: October 27, 2004   _____
                                   Joseph A. Debtor

Date: October 27, 2004   _____
                                   Josephine S. Debtor

Penalty for making a false statement: Fine of up to $500,000 or imprisonment for up to 5 years, or both. 18 U.S.C. §152 and 3571.

****

[To be completed on behalf of a partnership or corporation]

I declare under penalty of perjury that I have read the answers contained in the foregoing statement of financial affairs and any attachments thereto, and that they are true to the best of my knowledge, information, and belief.

Date: _____   _____
                     Signature

                     _____
                     Print Name and Title
[An individual signing on behalf of a partnership or corporation must indicate position or relationship to debtor.]

_____ Continuation sheets attached
Penalty for making a false statement: Fine of up to $500,000 or imprisonment for up to 5 years, or both. 18 U.S.C. §§ 152 and 3571.

Publisher's Note:

The "Certification and Signature of Non-attorney Bankruptcy Petition Preparer" (see 11 U.S.C. § 110)
which is required to be signed by a non-attorney bankruptcy petition preparer here,
has been OMITTED because this product is not knowingly sold to non-attorney bankruptcy petition preparers.
Bankruptcy Forms should NOT be used by non-attorney petition preparers.

* * * * * *

Annotations to Completed Official Form 7, Statement of Financial Affairs

Official Form 7 contains the debtor's statement of financial affairs. It must be filed in all cases. Items 1–18 must be completed by all debtors. Items 19–25 are to be completed by debtors that are or have been in business. For a general discussion of Official Form 7, see § 7.3.5, *supra*. If the answer to any question is "None," the box marked "None" must be checked.

70 This question should be answered with the debtor's gross, not net, income. However, a note of explanation may be warranted if large expenses offset much of the gross income.

71 This category can include income from a variety of sources, such as Social Security benefits, public assistance payments, income tax refunds, alimony and child support, and interest, dividends, pensions, and rents.

72 See discussion accompanying § 7.3.5, *supra*.

73 See discussion accompanying § 7.3.5, *supra*. Remember that a judgment may result in a lien on property which would make that creditor secured. If such a judgment lien impairs exempt property, it may be avoidable pursuant to 11 U.S.C. § 522(f)(1). *See* § 10.4.2.3, *supra*. If taken within the ninety days prior to the bankruptcy, it may constitute an avoidable preference. *See* § 10.4.2.6.4, *supra*.

74 The seizure of wages may constitute an avoidable preference. *See* § 10.4.2.6.4, *supra*.

75 Property repossessed may still be property of the estate if the debtor retains some interest, such as equity or a right of redemption. In such cases, it should be turned over under 11 U.S.C. § 542. *See* § 9.9, *supra*. Note that this question only pertains to repossessions and returns to sellers and secured parties. It includes voluntary returns as well as involuntary repossessions.

76 Property in the hands of a custodian may be recovered in certain circumstances. *See* 11 U.S.C. § 543.

77 See discussion accompanying § 7.3.5, *supra*.

78 See discussion of question 8 in § 7.3.5, *supra*. Any pending insurance claims based on a loss listed here should also be included on Schedule B.

79 See discussion accompanying § 7.3.5, *supra*.

80 See discussion accompanying § 7.3.5, *supra*. The granting of a security interest is a transfer which should be listed here if not listed elsewhere in the statement of financial affairs.

81 See discussion of question 11 in § 7.3.5, *supra*.

82 See discussion of question 12 in § 7.3.5, *supra*.

83 See discussion of question 13 in § 7.3.5, *supra*.

84 See discussion of question 14 in § 7.3.5, *supra*.

85 Trust interests should be listed here if someone other than the debtor is the sole beneficiary of the trust. It may also be a good idea to list the debtor's legal interest as trustee as personal property in Schedule B.

86 See discussion of question 15 in § 7.3.5, *supra*.

UNITED STATES BANKRUPTCY COURT
DISTRICT OF MASSACHUSETTS

In re: Joseph A. Debtor, Josephine S. Debtor
           Debtor(s)   Case No:

CHAPTER 7 INDIVIDUAL DEBTOR'S STATEMENT OF INTENTION

1.   I have filed a schedule of assets and liabilities which includes consumer debts secured by property of the estate.

2.   I intend to do the following with respect to the property of the estate which secures those consumer debts:

       a. Property to be Surrendered.

           Description of Property   Creditor's name

       b. Property to Be Retained.   [Check any applicable statement]

Description of Property	Creditor's Name	Property is claimed as exempt	Property will be redeemed pursuant to 11 U.S.C. § 722[87]	Debt will be reaffirmed pursuant to 11 U.S.C. § 524(c)[88]
Household good, books, pictures, and clothing	Friendly Finance	X (Lien to be avoided pursuant to § 522 (f))[89]		
Refrigerator	Bill's Appliance Store		X	
Automobile	Chrysler Finance Co.	X (Retain with continuing payments)[90]		

Date: October 27, 2004

                                    _____
                                    Joseph A. Debtor, Debtor
                                    100 Main Street
                                    Warren, MA 02345

Date: October 27, 2004

                                    _____
                                    Josephine S. Debtor, Debtor
                                    100 Main Street
                                    Warren, MA 02345

Annotations to Completed Official Form 8, Debtor's Statement of Intention

This form is required by 11 U.S.C. § 521(2)(A), and must be filed within thirty days after the petition is filed, or on or before the date of the meeting of creditors, whichever is earlier. The court, for cause and within that time period, may extend the deadline. The form's purpose is to advise secured creditors of certain intentions of the debtor in regard to property securing consumer debts. The form is probably required only in chapter 7 cases. See § 7.3.6, *supra*, for a general discussion of this form and its effects.

The Official Form requires that property securing all consumer debts be listed, along with the creditors' names. The debtor's intention is also to be noted by checking the appropriate places where applicable. In many cases the debtor may not wish to check any of the choices given, if none of them reflects the debtor's intent. For example, the debtor may wish to claim her interest in the property as exempt and simply let the lien ride through the bankruptcy unaffected, if it cannot be avoided and the debtor cannot redeem pursuant to section 722. The Official Form was revised in 1997 to make clear that the form is not intended to take a position on whether the options listed are exclusive. *See* § 7.3.6, *supra*. The statement must be served on the trustee and each creditor holding security for a consumer debt. Fed. R. Bankr. P. 1007(b)(3). The statement of intention is not binding and may be amended as a matter of course at any time before the deadline for performance of the intention set forth in 11 U.S.C. § 521(2)(B), which is forty-five days after the statement of intention, unless it is extended by the court. *See* § 7.3.6, *supra*. The Official Form is for an individual debtor and should be modified for a joint filing.

Note that because the preceding forms are for a hypothetical chapter 13 case, no Statement of Intention is required. Therefore the answers given here do not correspond with the information provided in completed Official Forms 1, 3, 6, and 7, *supra*.

87 See § 11.5, *supra*, for a discussion of redemption.

88 Reaffirmation is almost always inadvisable. *See* § 14.5.2.3, *supra*.

89 See § 10.4.2, *supra*, for a discussion of lien avoidance. Checking the box "property is claimed as exempt" is sufficient, though the debtor may include a more specific statement that the lien is to be avoided.

90 The three options given in Official Form 8 are not the only choices available to retain property. For example, many courts have held that as long as payments are maintained on a secured loan, there is no need to reaffirm and the creditor would not be permitted to repossess. In circuits where this option is available, the debtor may simply leave all of the boxes blank on the basis that there is no applicable statement or may include a statement such as "retain with continuing payments." *See* §§ 11.5.4, 14.5.3, *supra*. Alternatively, if the trustee abandons the property, it could be redeemed even if it is not exempt. Usually property which is fully encumbered or nearly so will be abandoned. *See* § 11.5, *supra*.

Sample Bankruptcy Pleadings and Other Forms

G.1 Introduction

This Appendix contains over one-hundred consumer bankruptcy pleadings and other forms. All captions have been deleted in favor of references to Official Forms 16A, 16B, and 16D, which are contained in Appendix D, *supra*. These pleadings are also found in both Adobe Acrobat (PDF) format and Microsoft Word format on the CD-Rom accompanying this volume. These pleadings should be edited using your word-processing program in order to fit the particulars of an actual case.

IMPORTANT NOTE CONCERNING CAPTIONS OF PLEADINGS AND OTHER NOTICES TO CREDITORS:

11 U.S.C. § 342(c) requires that all notices required to be given by the debtor to a creditor under the Code, a rule, an applicable law, or an order of court contain the debtor's name, address and taxpayer identification number (usually a social security number). Official Form 16A reflects this requirement, but has been amended to require disclosure of only the last four digits of the debtor's social security number. A debtor can fulfill the section 342(c) requirement by including the debtor's complete social security number on only the creditor's copy of any notice or summons the debtor may serve on the creditor. Official Form 16B is available for captions of pleadings which do not fall within the 11 U.S.C. § 342(c) requirement. Official Form 16D is designated for complaints filed by persons other than the debtor, though it should be used by debtors in adversary proceedings as Official Form 16C is now abrogated. When used in this manner, Official Form 16D should be altered to include the debtor's address and last four digits of the debtor's social security number (and the debtor's complete social security number on the creditor's copy). Please see Appendix D, *supra*, to review the Official Form captions. For forms in this Appendix containing captions, please use the necessary revised caption.

When section 342(c) applies to a notice sent by letter, the required information should be included in the letter. Many of the notices contained in this Appendix are not required by law so 11 U.S.C. § 342(c) does not apply. However, some lawyers, in an excess of caution, may wish to include the debtor's address and social security number in all notices to be certain of compliance.

Although a good faith effort to comply with the Code is required, note that section 342(c) states that failure to include the required information "shall not invalidate the legal effect of such notice."

IMPORTANT NOTE CONCERNING SERVICE OF PROCESS ON INSURED DEPOSITORY INSTITUTIONS

By amendment to Federal Rule of Bankruptcy Procedure 7004, contested matters and adversary proceeding which must be served on insured depository institutions must be served by certified mail. *See* Fed. R. Bankr. P. 7004(h). The rule contains exceptions which apply in certain limited situations. *See generally* § 13.3.2.1, *supra*. Note that Federal Rule of Bankruptcy Procedure 9014 makes this service rule applicable to service of contested matters (that is, motions not otherwise governed by the Rules).

Pleadings and Other Forms Contained in This Appendix

G.12 Conversion, Dismissal and Modification of Plan After Confirmation

G.13 Farm Reorganization

G.14 Consumers As Creditors

G.2 Pre-Filing Forms

Form 1 Pre-Filing Notification to Creditors of Representation[1]

Re: [*debtor(s)*]

Dear Sir/Madam:

Please be advised that this office represents the above-captioned individual(s) with respect to [*his, her, their*] alleged debt to [*creditor*]. We are presently preparing a bankruptcy petition which will shortly be filed.

We are requesting that all further communications concerning this matter be directed to us. If you have any questions concerning the above, please feel free to call me. Thank you for your cooperation in this matter.

Very truly yours,

Form 2 Notification to Creditor Seeking Information As to Account[2]

Re: [*debtor(s)*]

Dear Sir/Madam:

Please be advised that this office represents the above-captioned individual(s) with respect to [*his, her, their*] alleged debt to [*creditor*]. We are presently preparing a bankruptcy petition which will shortly be filed.

Enclosed please find an Information Release Authorization for the above-captioned individual(s). As we are interested in having the most current and accurate information possible, please forward the information listed in the authorization as soon as possible. It is especially important that we know if there is any security or judgment for the debt owed to you, so that we may know which debts will have to be paid after bankruptcy. If we do not hear from you, we may have to assume there was no security for this debt.

We are requesting that all further communications concerning this matter be directed to us. If you have any questions concerning the above, please feel free to call me. Thank you for your cooperation in this matter.

Very truly yours,

Information Release Authorization

To: [*creditor—bank*]

This will authorize you to deliver to _____ a full statement with respect to the following facts concerning:

[*debtor*]
[*address*]
Account No. [*number*]

who is a debtor/depositor of yours.

Depositor:
    Total amount of deposit and accrued interest.

Debtor:
1. Total amount borrowed;
2. Installment amount;
3. Reason owed;
4. Security interest (if recorded state where and when);
5. Amounts and number of installments in arrears;
6. Present balance;
7. Interest or other costs;
8. Any assignment of debt and to whom;
9. Legal action pending and attorney involved;
10. Photostatic copies of all papers relevant to the transaction or transactions;
11. Date debt incurred; and
12. Codebtors or cosigners.

Thank you for your cooperation in this request.

[*signature*]
Debtor

---

1 This letter should be sent to any creditors who have been bothering the client, if not to all creditors. It should succeed in ending creditor contacts with the client. If a creditor communicates with the debtor after receipt of this letter, an unfair trade practice claim may arise (which could be claimed as exempt if it arises before the petition is filed). If a collection agency is involved, the communication may give rise to damages under the Fair Debt Collection Practices Act, 15 U.S.C. §§ 1692–1692*o.*

2 This letter requests information for cases in which the schedules or statement cannot be completed because the debtor's records are incomplete. An information release authorization, signed by the debtor, may not be necessary, depending on local practices. However, to save the necessity of another letter, it should be included if there is some doubt as to whether the creditor or bank will release information without it. If it is not included, the information requested should be specified in the letter itself. Creditors, of course, do not always cooperate in furnishing information. Additionally some care should be taken because certain creditors, when they know bankruptcy is imminent, will hasten actions (often creating preferences, see § 10.4.2.6.4, *supra*), which would violate the automatic stay after the filing.

G.3 Initial Forms

The Official Forms necessary to commence a case are contained in Appendix D, *supra*. Those forms are reproducible and may be copied, filled out, and submitted to the bankruptcy court. Sample completed Official Forms are contained in Appendix F, *supra*.

Certain other non-official forms may also be necessary to commence a case, pursuant to the Federal Rules of Bankruptcy Procedure and the Bankruptcy Code. These include a list of creditors, required by Federal Rule of Bankruptcy Procedure 1007(a) (if the debtor does not file a schedule of liabilities at the outset of a case); a disclosure of compensation, required by Federal Rule of Bankruptcy Procedure 2016(b); and a notice to consumer debtors, required by 11 U.S.C. § 342(b). These non-official forms are contained in a reproducible format in Appendix E, *supra*.

In addition, check your local rules and local practice to determine if there are other forms necessary to file at the outset of a case in your jurisdiction.

Form 3 Motion and Order for Extension of Time to File Schedules and Statement of Affairs[3]

[Caption: Official Form 16A][4]

Motion for Extension of Time to File Schedules and Statement of Affairs

The Debtor moves this Court as follows:

1. On April 6, 2000, the Debtor filed a voluntary petition in bankruptcy which halted an execution sale of his real property.

2. The schedules and statement of affairs are due on April 21, 2000.

3. The Debtor will need an additional twenty (20) days to prepare the schedules and statement of affairs, because of the need to gather all the necessary information from creditors.

WHEREFORE, the Debtor requests that this Court grant an extension of twenty (20) days, until May 11, 2000, to prepare and file his schedules and statement of affairs pursuant to Rule 1007(c) of the Federal Rules of Bankruptcy Procedure.

Date: *[signature]*
                                Attorney for Debtor

---

3 This form may be used if the debtor cannot file schedules and a statement of affairs within fifteen days of the petition as required. The application is governed by Fed. R. Bankr. P. 1007(c) and 3015. Any extension of time under those rules may be granted only on motion for cause shown, and on notice to the trustee. Use of this form should be adapted to reflect any cause for delay in the particular case involved.

4 Official Form 16A is contained in Appendix D, *supra*. While this motion and several other pleadings in this Appendix may not be required to be served by the debtor on creditors pursuant to explicit provisions of the Code or Bankruptcy Rules, local rules may so require. Thus, in order to comply with 11 U.S.C. § 342(c), it is advisable to use Official Form 16A, which includes the debtor's address and the last four digits of the debtor's social security number. The legislative history of the amendment notes, however, that bankruptcy courts may waive the requirement in compelling circumstances such as the need of a domestic violence victim to conceal her residence for safety reasons. *See* 140 Cong. Rec. H10,764 (daily ed. Oct. 4, 1994) (remarks of Rep. Brooks).

[Caption: Official Form 16A]

Order Granting Additional Time to File Schedules and Statement of Affairs[5]

It is ORDERED that the Debtor herein shall have until May 11, 2000, to file schedules and a statement of affairs.

Date: *[signature]*
                      United States Bankruptcy Judge

Form 4 Motion and Order for Extension of Time to File Chapter 13 Schedules, Statement of Affairs, and Chapter 13 Plan[6]

[Caption: Official Form 16A]

Motion for Extension of Time to File Chapter 13 Schedules, Statement of Affairs, and Chapter 13 Plan

The Debtor moves the Court as follows:

1. On April 6, 2000, the Debtor filed a voluntary petition in bankruptcy which halted the execution sale of his real property.

2. The chapter 13 schedules, statement of affairs and chapter 13 plan are due on April 21, 2000.

3. The Debtor will need an additional twenty (20) days to prepare the statement and plan, because of the need to gather all the necessary information from creditors.

4. The Debtor requests that this Court grant an extension of twenty (20) days, until May 11, 2000, to prepare and file his chapter 13 schedules, statement of affairs and chapter 13 plan, pursuant to Rule 3015 of the Federal Rules of Bankruptcy Procedure.

Date: *[signature]*
                        Attorney for Debtor

[Caption: Official Form 16A]

Order Granting Additional Time to File Chapter 13 Schedules, Statement of Affairs and Chapter 13 Plan

It is ORDERED that the Debtor herein shall have until May 11, 2000, to file his chapter 13 schedules, statement of affairs and chapter 13 plan.

Date: *[signature]*
                      United States Bankruptcy Judge

---

5 Most courts require a proposed order, such as this form, to accompany the Motion for Extension of Time to File Schedules and Statement of Affairs. In the many jurisdictions where the debtor does not serve copies of court orders, Official Form 16B may be acceptable as a caption.

6 This form may be used if the debtor cannot file a chapter 13 statement and chapter 13 plan within fifteen days of the petition as required. This application is governed by Fed. R. Bankr. P. 1007(c) and 3015. Any extension of time under these rules may be granted only on motion for cause shown, and on notice to the trustee. Use of this form should be adapted to reflect the cause of delay in the particular case involved.

Form 5　Application and Order for Additional Extension of Time to File Chapter 13 Schedules, Statement of Affairs, and Chapter 13 Plan[7]

[*Caption: Official Form 16A*]

Application for Additional Extension of Time to File Chapter 13 Schedules, Statement of Affairs, and Chapter 13 Plan

Debtor, [*debtor*], by his attorney, respectfully represents:

1. Debtor filed a voluntary petition under chapter 13 of the Bankruptcy Code on April 6, 2000.

2. Debtor's petition was prepared and filed quickly in order to stay the execution of a judgment against Debtor's residential real estate scheduled for April 6, 2000. Therefore, Debtor was unable to gather all the necessary documents for completing the chapter 13 schedules, statement of affairs and plan when the petition was filed. Debtor filed an Application for Extension of Time to File Chapter 13 Schedules, Statement of Affairs and Chapter 13 Plan and an extension of time was granted until May 11, 2000.

3. On April 23, 2000, Debtor's wife went into labor and was hospitalized for the birth of a child.

4. During the next few days, Debtor will have little opportunity to take the steps necessary to complete the chapter 13 statement and plan on time.

5. It is requested that the Court grant the Debtor an additional extension of time so that counsel can complete the necessary forms.

6. This application is not made for the purposes of delay and no creditor will suffer any prejudice if Debtor is granted an additional extension of time.

WHEREFORE, Debtor requests that this Court grant him an extension of time until May 31, 2000, in which to file his chapter 13 schedules, statement of affairs and chapter 13 plan.

Date:　　　　　　　　　　　　　　　　　　　[*signature*]
　　　　　　　　　　　　　　　　　　　　　Attorney for Debtor

[*Caption: Official Form 16A*]

Order

AND NOW, this [*date*] day of [*month*], 2000, upon consideration of Debtor's Application for an Additional Extension of Time to File Chapter 13 Schedules, Statement of Affairs and Chapter 13 Plan, it is hereby ORDERED and DECREED that said Application is GRANTED. Debtor shall have until May 31, 2000 to file his chapter 13 schedules, statement of affairs and chapter 13 plan.

Date:　　　　　　　　　　　　　　　　　　　[*signature*]
　　　　　　　　　　　　　　　United States Bankruptcy Judge

Form 6　Motion to Keep Prior Name Confidential[8]

[*Caption: Official Form 16A*]

Debtor, by her counsel, hereby moves that she be excused from disclosing on her bankruptcy petition a former name used within

the past six years. In support of her motion she avers:

1. Debtor's former husband, with whom she lived in a different state, was extremely abusive toward her.

2. The abuse included [for example, a gun to her head and threatening to kill her, and resulted in back injuries, lacerations and bruises.]

3. The debtor obtained court orders for protection from abuse, but the abuse nonetheless continued.

4. Eventually, the debtor obtained, in [*date*] a court order changing her name to [*current name*] and she moved to her current address.

5. None of the debtor's debts were incurred using her former name.

6. Debtor's former husband builds computers and is a computer hacker, and debtor is afraid that if her former name appears in any computer database, her life and the life of her child will be in danger.

7. No entity will be prejudiced by the failure of the debtor to disclose her former name.

WHEREFORE, the debtor prays that she be permitted to file this case without disclosing her former name.

Date:　　　　　　　　　　　　　　　　　　　[*signature*]
　　　　　　　　　　　　　　　　　　　　　Attorney for Debtor

Form 7　Application and Order for Waiver of Miscellaneous Fees

[*Caption: Official Form 16A*]

Application for Waiver of Miscellaneous Administrative Fee[9]

1. The debtors filed a voluntary chapter _____ bankruptcy petition contemporaneously with this application.

2. The debtors believe they are entitled to relief under chapter _____ .

3. The debtors are indigent and are unable to pay the miscellaneous administrative fee or give security therefor.

4. The debtors' income consists of $[*amount*] in benefits.

5. The debtors have [*number*] children dependent upon them for support.

6. The debtors' basic monthly expenses exceed their income.

7. The debtors' income is below the national poverty level as established by the Office of Management and Budget.

8. The debtors do not have any stocks, bonds, bank accounts, or

---

7　This form may be used to obtain additional extensions of time for cause shown. The application is governed by Fed. R. Bankr. P. 1007(c) and 3015. Any extension of time under those rules

may be granted only on motion for cause shown, and on notice to the trustee. This form may be adapted for chapter 7 cases as well.

8　Official Form 1, Voluntary Petition, requires the debtor to list all names used by the debtor in the six years prior to filing. This form may be used when the debtor has a substantial need to keep these names confidential, such as for safety reasons relating to domestic violence.

9　This form may be used to obtain a waiver of the $39.00 miscellaneous administrative fee normally payable upon the filing of a chapter 7 or chapter 13 case. The form can be modified to also seek waiver of the $15.00 trustee surcharge applicable in chapter 7 cases. These fee waivers should be available pursuant to 28 U.S.C. § 1915, although some courts have held that a bankruptcy court does not have the power to waive such a fee. See § 13.6, *supra*. Different courts may also have varying requirements regarding the specificity of the statement of the debtor's financial situation.

other liquid assets from which they can pay the miscellaneous administrative fee.

9. The debtors own no real estate other than their residence, in which they have no equity and which is subject to foreclosure.

10. The debtors do not own an automobile or any item of household furnishings worth more than $200.00.

11. There are no family or friends who could provide funds to the debtors for payment of the miscellaneous administrative fee.

12. The debtors' rights under Title 11 will be prejudiced if the debtors' petition and schedules are not accepted for filing or if their bankruptcy is dismissed for failure to pay the miscellaneous administrative fee.

WHEREFORE, the debtors request that this Court waive payment of the miscellaneous administrative fee and permit them to proceed with their bankruptcy without payment of the fee or security therefor.

[*signature*]
Attorney for Debtors

VERIFICATION

I, [*debtor*], verify under penalty of perjury that the foregoing is true and correct.

[*signature*]
Debtor

Executed on: [*date*]

[*Caption: Official Form 16B*]

Order to Waive Miscellaneous Administrative Fee

AND NOW, this [*date*] day of [*month*], [*year*], upon consideration of the debtors' application to waive the miscellaneous administrative fee for the filing of their bankruptcy petition, it is hereby ordered that the fee is waived and the debtors are permitted to proceed with their bankruptcy without payment of the miscellaneous administrative fee.

Date:

[*signature*]
United States Bankruptcy Judge

Form 8 Debtors' Chapter 13 Plan[10]

[*Caption: Official Form 16A*]

Debtors' Chapter 13 Plan

---

10 This chapter 13 plan is a far cry from the simplicity of former Official Form 13-6, devised for use under the old Chapter XIII. Some of the provisions of this plan are controversial and may not be accepted by all courts. See generally Chapter 12, *supra*, for a discussion of issues arising in chapter 13 cases.

Many districts now require a form plan by local rule or administrative order. When that is the case, provisions from this plan can be incorporated into the required form or a supplemental document containing provisions from this plan may be attached. Advocates should not allow their clients' substantive rights to be limited by a restrictive required format.

This plan is written so that most of its provisions can be used without change in most chapter 13 cases. Cases which are out of the ordinary may require a radically different approach. For example, a plan may be largely funded out of the sale of specified property of the debtor by the trustee or debtor, as provided in the plan. 11 U.S.C. § 1322(b)(8); *see* Form 12,

1. If the instant estate were liquidated under chapter 7 of the Bankruptcy Code, the allowed unsecured claimants would be paid $0.00.[11]

2. Under this plan the allowed unsecured claimants will receive not less than that amount.

3. The Debtors[12] shall submit to the supervision and control of the trustee the following sums:[13]

a. During the first year of the plan:[14] $120.00 monthly;

b. During the second, third, fourth and fifth years of the plan: $190.00 monthly.[15]

4. The various claims of the Debtors' creditors shall be classified as follows:[16]

a. Class one: Claims filed and allowed which are entitled to priority under 11 U.S.C. § 507.[17] The administrative expenses are the only priority claims contemplated by this plan. Any creditor entitled to priority under section 507 of the Bankruptcy Code contrary to the provisions of this plan shall be deemed to have agreed to waive any such priority, unless

---

Appx. G.3, *infra*. It may also provide for an order that the debtor's employer submit a portion of the debtor's wages to the court. Some courts may require that such an order be part of the plan in most cases.

In some districts the debtor is required to furnish a copy of the plan to be mailed to each creditor. Bankruptcy courts in some districts also require a form summarizing the plan provisions to be filed with every case. Counsel should check local rules and practice regarding whether such a form is required. The chapter 13 plan must be filed with the petition or within fifteen days thereafter, unless the time is extended for cause shown. *See* Forms 4, 5, Appx. G.3, *supra*.

11 These paragraphs, while probably not absolutely necessary, give the court the basic information necessary to decide whether the "best interests of creditors" test is met. *See* § 12.3.1, *supra*.

12 The plan may provide for the debtor's employer, or some other entity, to submit payments instead of the debtor.

13 The plan must provide for the submission to the trustee of such portion of the debtor's income as is necessary for the execution of the plan. Probably, this means that at least some part of the debtor's income must be submitted. *See In re* Terry, 630 F.2d 634 (8th Cir. 1980).

14 There is no requirement that the same amount be submitted throughout the plan. The plan may anticipate increased income (if it does not happen, the plan can always be modified). However, the good faith or feasibility of a plan providing for a large balloon payment at the end may well be questioned unless there is a basis for expecting such a payment is likely to be fulfilled.

15 Payments may be made at such intervals as the debtor chooses. Payments must begin, however, within thirty days after the plan is filed, unless the court orders otherwise. 11 U.S.C. § 1326(a); *see* § 8.3.9, *supra*. Creditors, however, will be paid by the trustee according to the trustee's own schedule. Many trustees make distributions only two or three times a year.

16 See § 12.4, *supra*, for discussion of permissible classifications in a chapter 13 plan.

17 All priority claims must be paid in full under the plan. 11 U.S.C. § 1322(a)(2). However, no interest need be provided unless necessary under the standards of 11 U.S.C. § 1325(a)(4) or § 1325(a)(5). This class will normally include the trustee's fees and expenses of nine to ten percent of the amounts paid through the trustee, as well as the fee of the debtor's attorney, if that fee is to be paid through the plan. Local practice may require the amount of this fee to be specified in the plan.

such entity objects to the plan.[18]

b. Class two: All allowed secured claims secured by a lien which is not avoidable by the Debtors under 11 U.S.C. § 522, except for the first mortgage held by [*creditor*] and any allowed secured claim of the City of _____ .[19] These creditors will retain their liens until their allowed secured claims are paid in full, and shall be deemed to have accepted this plan unless they object to the plan.[20]

c. Class three: The allowed secured claim held by Mortgage Co., which shall be cured pursuant to paragraph 6 below.

d. Class four: All other claims against the debtors that are timely filed [except for the first mortgage held by [*creditor*] and any allowed secured claim of the City of _____ .[21]

e. Class five: The allowed secured claims of the City of _____ .[22]

5. The payments received by the trustee from the Debtors pursuant to this plan shall be distributed as follows:[23]

a. Class one claims: The amount paid by the Debtors to the trustee shall be distributed first to the class one administrative claims, pro rata, until they are paid in full. Any other priority claimants shall be paid only after the class two and class four claims are paid in full.

b. Class two and class three claims: After the application of the appropriate amount each month to the class one administrative claims, the entire amount of the monthly payment remaining in the hands of the trustee shall be distributed, pro rata, to the holders of the class two claims until each such claimant shall have received 100% of the amount allowed on each claim and to the payment of arrears on the class three claim until such arrears are paid in full.[24]

c. Class four claims: After the application of the appropriate amount each month to the class one, class two and class three claims, the entire amount of the monthly payment remaining in the hands of the trustee shall be distributed, pro rata, to the holders of the class four claims.[25]

d. Class five claims: The class five claims are not being paid under this plan, and there shall be no distribution to the holders of such claims.[26]

6. The current payments on the first mortgage on the Debtors' home, held by [*creditor*], will be paid by the Debtors directly to that creditor and will not be paid under the plan.[27] The Debtors will cure the default on that mortgage within a reasonable period of time by making payments on the arrears through the trustee.[28] Upon completion of the payment of the arrears, the debtors will be reinstated on the original payment schedule for the mortgage as if no default had ever occurred, except for the amount of any default in current payments to be made after commencement of this case which has not been cured by that date. The term "arrears," for all purposes under this plan, shall mean the amount of arrears stated in the aforesaid mortgage holder's proof of claim, unless the debtors at any time dispute that amount, in which case arrears will mean the amount ultimately decided by the Court or agreed to by the parties.[29]

---

18 It is not totally clear that this sentence is permissible. A priority creditor must be paid in full unless it agrees to different treatment. *See* § 12.3.5, *supra*. Silence may or may not constitute such an agreement, even with this provision in the plan.

19 This class is basically that of creditors whose claims remain secured despite the debtor's avoiding powers. Normally the debtor will want to pay these debts, because the liens thereon will otherwise remain after the bankruptcy. However, a chapter 13 plan need not provide for every secured claim.

20 There is substantial case law that a creditor who does not object to the plan has accepted the plan. *See* § 11.6.1.2.1. Language putting a creditor on notice of this fact would bolster the argument that this is correct.

21 This class consists of general unsecured claims, which need be paid only in an amount not less than the amount of the debtor's nonexempt property, an amount which may be minimal. However, some courts have held minimal payment plans not to be in good faith. *See* § 12.3, *supra*. This class may be further subdivided into small and large claims if the debtor decides to do so in order to quickly pay off small claims first.

22 This paragraph creates a separate class for a secured claim which is provided for by the plan.

23 This distribution scheme pays priority claims first, allowed secured claims second, and any remaining amounts to unsecured claims. Specific amounts are usually impossible to designate because of disputes with respect to the amounts of some claims and the uncertainty about which unsecured claims are to be filed. The general language in this paragraph may be used without change in every plan similar in design to this one.

24 This paragraph specifies that the arrearages on the mortgage shall be paid pro rata with the allowed secured claims being paid under the plan.

25 It is a good idea to have at least some payment to unsecured creditors, because unless a creditor has a right to receive something under the plan, it may argue that it has not been "provided for" under the plan and that its claims therefore are not discharged pursuant to 11 U.S.C. § 1328(a). These issues can be avoided altogether by proposing even minimal payments. *See* § 12.3, *supra*.

26 This paragraph specifies that certain secured claims are not being provided for in the plan. The debtor is not required to provide for all secured claims in the plan. *See* § 11.6.1.3.3.3, *supra*.

27 Payments "outside the plan" are those made directly to the creditors rather than through the trustee. They are especially advantageous to the debtor with respect to large debts such as mortgages because they save the trustee's commission. For the same reason, they are sometimes opposed by trustees. *See* § 12.4.4, *supra*.

28 The cure of a mortgage default within a reasonable period of time is permitted by 11 U.S.C. § 1322(b)(5). This paragraph may be objected to by creditors as it does not specify the amount of time for a cure. It is generally advantageous for the debtor not to bind himself or herself to a specific payment schedule if that can be avoided. Often, however, such a schedule is negotiated to forestall or settle litigation seeking relief from the automatic stay.

29 This paragraph fleshes out what it means to cure a mortgage default. It is intended to help prevent problems arising after completion of a chapter 13 plan in which a creditor alleges that the amount paid through the plan did not cure the default. *See* § 11.6.2.8, *supra*. Creditors are likely to seek interest on arrears following Rake v. Wade, 508 U.S. 464, 113 S. Ct. 2187, 124 L. Ed. 2d 228 (1993). The holding in the *Rake* case will not apply to mortgages made after October 22, 1994 so that no interest on arrears on those mortgages will be required unless it is authorized by the mortgage and state law. *See* § 11.6.2.7, *supra*. Some courts may require that such interest be included as an element of the debtor's plan. This provision makes clear that the debtor may in most cases object to the creditor's calculation of its arrearage. An objection is necessary in most cases as often the creditor's calculation is inconsistent with the amount provided for that creditor under the plan. *See* § 13.4.3, *supra*.

7. To the extent that any claim is fully or partially unsecured pursuant to 11 U.S.C. § 506(a), that portion of the claim which is unsecured shall be provided for as a class four (unsecured) claim under this plan. Creditors holding such claims shall retain their liens only to the extent of their allowed secured claims. To the extent that the allowed secured claim is paid during this case or thereafter, such creditors' liens shall be reduced. Once the allowed secured claim has been paid in full, either during or after the pendency of this case, the creditor holding such claim shall promptly mark any lien securing such claim as satisfied in the appropriate public records.[30]

8. By failing to object to this plan, or any modification thereof, all creditors holding claims agree not to make any effort to collect their claims from any cosigners that may exist, so long as this case remains pending.[31]

9. Confirmation of this plan shall constitute a finding that the plan constitutes the Debtors' best effort under all the circumstances to pay their creditors, within the meaning of 11 U.S.C. § 727(a)(9).[32]

10. Confirmation of this plan shall constitute a finding in accordance with 11 U.S.C. § 1322 that there is cause for extending the plan beyond three years. Confirmation shall also constitute approval of such extension. Such extension is essential to the success of the plan. Without it the plan would fail and no claims would be paid in full.[33]

11. The current defaults by the Debtors on the class two and class three claims are waived and the defaults on the class two claims shall be cured by payments to this plan.[34]

12. The title to the property of the estate shall revest in the Debtors upon termination of this plan, and the Debtors shall have sole right to use and possession thereof during the pendency of this case,[35] including the right to use, sell or lease such property in the ordinary course of the Debtors' affairs.

13. Confirmation of this plan shall constitute a finding and order that due to the Debtors' low income, the trustee's fee should not exceed 10% of each monthly payment, even if that amount is less than $5.00 per month.[36]

14. Upon confirmation of this plan, no creditor may assess the debtor or the debtor's estate for attorney fees and/or collection costs arising during the plan, except as authorized by contract and upon approval of the Court after notice to the Debtor. Unless approved by the Court for payment under this paragraph, the Debtor shall have no liability for any such fees and costs arising during the plan, and there shall be no *in rem* liability of property at any time held by the debtor's estate. Any application for approval of fees or costs under this paragraph shall meet the requirements of Fed. R. Bankr. P. 2016(a).[37]

15. Any money or property acquired by either the trustee or the Debtors or refunded from the trustee's percentage fees,[38] while this case is pending shall be deemed exempt property of the debtors if exemptible, and shall be forthwith delivered to the Debtors.[39]

16. If the Debtors default after filing of the petition, on any payment to a utility entitled to adequate assurance under 11 U.S.C. § 366, then that debt shall, upon application of said utility, become a class one claim under this plan. This priority shall be deemed adequate assurance of the utility's future payments.[40]

17. The following executory contracts are rejected,[41] with the

---

30 This provision is designed to protect the debtor's right to bifurcate claims under 11 U.S.C. § 506(a) and to treat separately the allowed secured claim and allowed unsecured claim. It is drafted to avoid resort to 11 U.S.C. § 506(d) and the issues created by *Dewsnup v. Timm*, 502 U.S. 410, 112 S. Ct. 773, 116 L. Ed. 2d 903 (1992). *See* §§ 11.2, 11.7, *supra*. In those jurisdictions which have expressly held that § 506(d) may be employed to reduce or eliminate liens in chapter 13 despite *Dewsnup*, this plan language may be less important. Creditors may object if this provision is read to apply to mortgages protected by 11 U.S.C. § 1322(b)(2). *See* Nobelman v. Am. Sav. Bank, 508 U.S. 324, 113 S. Ct. 2106, 124 L. Ed. 2d 228 (1993).

31 This provision, extending the codebtor stay to situations in which it would not otherwise exist, was held permissible and valid as against creditors who had not objected to it in *In re Weaver*, 8 B.R. 803 (Bankr. S.D. Ohio 1981). *See also In re Bonanno*, 78 B.R. 52 (Bankr. E.D. Pa. 1987). *But see In re Britts*, 18 B.R. 203 (Bankr. N.D. Ohio 1982) (creditor not bound by such a clause unless he specifically adopts plan after notice of clause); *In re* Rolland, 20 B.R. 931 (Bankr. W.D.N.Y. 1982) (clause is inconsistent with provisions of chapter 13).

32 A chapter 7 case may be filed within six years of a chapter 13 case only if the chapter 13 plan paid 100% of the allowed unsecured claims or if it paid 70% of the allowed unsecured claims and was the debtor's best effort. 11 U.S.C. § 727(a)(9). The legislative history contemplates that the debtor may seek a finding that the plan was a "best effort" at the time of the original chapter 13 case. 124 Cong. Rec. H11,098 (daily ed. Sept. 28, 1978) (remarks of Rep. Edwards).

33 The court must specifically find cause for and approve any plan over three years in length. 11 U.S.C. § 1322(c). The rules are unclear as to whether the plan may provide for confirmation being deemed such a finding as provided in this clause. Some courts require a separate application for such an extended plan to be filed.

34 This provision is based upon 11 U.S.C. § 1322(b)(3). It is not

totally clear whether any type of default, including a non-economic default, may be waived under that subsection, although that appears to be its meaning. Nor is it certain that a plan can cure a default merely by stating, as here, that completion of the plan shall be a cure.

35 This paragraph is based upon 11 U.S.C. § 1327(c), which states that except as otherwise provided in the plan, property of the estate revests in the debtor as of confirmation. In some cases it may be preferable to defer the revesting of certain property until the end of the plan. *See* § 9.4.2, *supra*. This paragraph also specifically deals with the issue of the right to use property of the estate, giving sole right to such use to the debtor. See generally discussion of use of property in § 12.8, *supra*.

36 Unless the court orders otherwise, the trustee is entitled to a minimum fee of $5.00 per month. 11 U.S.C. § 330(c). This paragraph will probably suffice as the court-ordered exception to the rule.

37 This language is intended to avoid the holding in Telfair v. First Union Mortgage Corp., 216 F.3d 1333 (11th Cir. 2000).

38 In some districts, when trustees find they have collected an amount greater than that necessary to meet their compensation and expenses, they refund those excess fees to the debtor. This paragraph makes clear that such refunds should be paid to the debtor rather than to creditors.

39 This provision covers the problem of new property coming into the estate under 11 U.S.C. § 1306(a). It also deals with the question of how property turned over to the trustee under 11 U.S.C. § 542 can be obtained by the debtor. *See* § 9.9, *supra*.

40 This paragraph, at least in a well-funded plan, may be deemed to provide adequate assurance to a utility under 11 U.S.C. § 366 without the payment of any security deposit. *See* § 9.8, *supra*.

41 The plan may assume or reject executory contracts. 11 U.S.C. § 1322(b)(7).

refunds of prepaid charges claimed as exempt property:

  a. All credit life, disability, and property insurance contracts to which the Debtors is/are part(y)(ies).[42]

  b. Membership in [*name*] Health Spa.

18. The following liens are avoided pursuant to section 522(f):[43]

  a. Judicial lien arising out of judgment in favor of [*name*] Finance Company, at [*name*] Court, No. [*number*].

  b. Non-possessory, non-purchase money security interest in Debtors' household goods held by [*name*] Finance Company.

19. Upon completion of this plan, all debts listed in the Debtors' schedules or provided for by this plan, except those excepted by 11 U.S.C. § 1328(a) shall be discharged.[44]

20. If prior to the expiration of the period set forth in paragraph 3 of this plan all filed claims entitled to payment under this plan are paid in full, this plan shall terminate on that date.[45]

Date: [*signature(s)*]
                                      Debtors

Acceptances may be sent to:[46]

Form 9 Order Confirming Chapter 13 Plan[47]

[*Caption: Official Form 16A*]

Order Confirming Chapter 13 Plan

The Debtor's plan having been filed on [*date*], and the plan having been available to creditors [*or: transmitted to creditors*], the Court after hearing on notice has determined that:

1. The plan complies with the provisions of chapter 13 and all other applicable provisions of title 11 of the United States Code;

2. The filing fee and all other amounts required to be paid to date have been paid;

3. The plan has been proposed in good faith and not by any means forbidden by law;

4. The value as of the effective date of the plan, of property to be distributed under the plan on account of each allowed unsecured claim is not less than the amount that would be paid on such claims if the estate of the Debtor were liquidated under chapter 7 of the Bankruptcy Code on such date;

5. The Debtor will be able to make all payments under the plan and to comply with the plan.

It is ORDERED that:

1. The Debtor's chapter 13 plan is confirmed.

2. The Debtor shall pay to the trustee on the first day of [*month*], 2000, and the first day of each month thereafter for [*number*] months, the amounts specified in the Debtor's plan.

3. The trustee shall make payments in accordance with the Debtor's plan.

Date: [*signature*]
                  United States Bankruptcy Judge

Form 10 Motion for Payover Order in Chapter 13[48]

[*Caption: Official Form 16A*]

Motion for Payover Order

The above-named Debtor respectfully represents that:

1. Debtor has filed a petition under chapter 13 of title 11 U.S.C. and proposes to pay debts out of future earnings or wages.

2. Debtor has claimed certain exemptions but has also submitted such portion of his future earnings or other future income to the control of the trustee as is necessary for the execution of the plan.

3. Debtor has proposed a plan under which a portion of his future earnings or wages is to be paid to the trustee for the benefit of creditors, in the amount of $[*amount*] per [*time period*].

---

42 It is not totally clear that such contracts are executory. *See* § 12.9, *supra*.

43 Many courts allow avoidance of liens under section 522(f) in the chapter 13 plan. Most require that the individual liens be specified, as here. A few may allow a simple statement that "all liens avoidable under 11 U.S.C. § 522(f) are avoided." Under the Federal Rules of Bankruptcy Procedure, however, a separate motion may be necessary to avoid a lien. *See* Fed. R. Bankr. P. 4003(d); *In re* McKay, 732 F.2d 44 (3d Cir. 1984).

44 This paragraph is probably unnecessary unless the plan has a possibility of no payments to unsecured creditors. In such cases, it may provide protection against later arguments that unsecured creditors were not discharged under 11 U.S.C. § 1328(a) because they were not "provided for" in the plan.

45 In some cases only a few creditors file claims and the payments originally contemplated exceed those necessary to pay all claims in full. This provision obviates the necessity of filing a motion to modify the plan by shortening the period of payments, in that it shortens the plan automatically.

46 Acceptances are no longer a significant part of the chapter 13 process, because creditors have no right to vote on the plan. Many debtor's attorneys do not even bother to solicit acceptances in most cases. However, a plan's acceptance by a priority or secured creditor may still be critical under 11 U.S.C. § 1322(a)(2) or § 1325(a)(5). This plan does not contain a specific provision dealing with post-petition debts. If the debtor anticipates such debts being paid by the plan such a provision may be included initially, stating generally that they will be paid, with amounts submitted to the trustee increased accordingly. In many cases, it is easier to amend the plan if and when the debtor decides to pay specific post-petition debts through the plan.

47 This is one example of an order confirming a chapter 13 plan. Some courts may require a form of order confirming the plan to be submitted at the confirmation hearing. Local rules or practice should be checked.

48 Pursuant to 11 U.S.C. § 1325(c) the court may, after confirmation, order any entity from whom the debtor receives income to pay all or part of such income to the trustee. Such an order can be directed against a governmental unit (except the Social Security Administration), but most typically will be directed to the debtor's employer.

Although section 1325(c) speaks only of orders after confirmation, the statute now requires payments to the trustee to begin before confirmation, and many courts will grant a payover order prior to confirmation. In some places, if payments are to start only after confirmation, a plan provision providing for a payover order and a confirmation order including a payover order may be allowed in lieu of a separate motion such as this one. These forms are adapted from those provided by Mitchell W. Miller, Esq., Philadelphia, PA.

Payover orders are discussed generally in § 12.6.1, *supra*. They are advisable primarily for debtors who feel they do not have the discipline to maintain payments on their own, or when a creditor objects on the basis of feasibility because the debtor has failed to make payments in prior bankruptcies. They also may be sought by the trustee if the debtor is not keeping up with payments as scheduled.

4. The principal source of money for the payment of said claims, demands and debts will be a portion of the future earnings or wages of Debtor, payable by [*employer*], his employer.

5. Debtor's employer should be ordered to deduct from Debtor's future earnings or wages the periodic amount proposed by the plan filed herein, and to pay said amount forthwith to the standing chapter 13 trustee appointed by your Honorable Court and continue such periodic deductions and payments until such time as the plan submitted by Debtor is consummated, or until further order of the Court.

WHEREFORE, Debtor prays that your Honorable Court enter the Order attached hereto directing Debtor's employer to make payments as outlined therein.

[*signature*]   [*signature*]
Debtor   Attorney for Debtor

APPROVED:

[*signature*]
United States Bankruptcy Judge

Form 11 Order to Pay Wages to the Trustee in Chapter 13[49]

[*Caption: Official Form 16A*]

Order to Pay Wages to the Trustee

Upon representation of the trustee, or other interested party, the Courts finds:

The above-named Debtor has pending in this Court a case under chapter 13 of the title 11 U.S.C. and, pursuant to the provisions of said statute and of the Debtor's plan, the Debtor has submitted such portion of his future earnings or income to the control of the trustee as is necessary for the execution of the plan; and

Under the provisions of 11 U.S.C. § 1325(c) an entity may be required, upon Order of this Court, to pay over such portion of the wages, earnings or income of the Debtor as may be needed to effectuate said plan, and that such an Order is necessary and proper, now therefore,

IT IS ORDERED, that, for a period of [*number*] months, or until further Order of this Court, [*debtor's employer*] deduct from the earnings or income of said Debtor the sum of $[*amount*] each [*time period*] pay period beginning on the next pay day following the receipt of this Order and deduct a similar amount for each pay period thereafter, including any period for which the Debtor receives periodic or lump sum payment for or on account of vacation, termination or other benefits arising out of present or past employment of the Debtor, and forthwith remit the sums so deducted to:

[*trustee*]

IT IS FURTHER ORDERED that all earnings, wages and income of the Debtor, except the amounts required to be withheld by the provisions of any laws of the United States, the laws of any state or political subdivision, or by any insurance, pension or union dues agreement between said entity and the Debtor, or by Order of this Court, be paid to the aforesaid Debtor in accordance with the entity's usual payroll procedure.

IT IS FURTHER ORDERED that no deductions for or on account of any garnishment, wage assignment, credit union or other purpose not specifically authorized by this Court be made from the earnings of said Debtor.

IT IS FURTHER ORDERED that this Order supersedes previous orders, if any, made to the subject entity in this or any previous case.

Date: [*signature*]
United States Bankruptcy Judge

Form 12 Chapter 13 Plan Providing for Liquidation of Debtor's Interest in Residence[50]

[*Caption: Official Form 16A*]

Chapter 13 Plan of Debtor

1. If the instant estate were liquidated under chapter 7 of the Bankruptcy Code, the allowed unsecured claimants would be paid $0.00.

2. Under this plan the allowed unsecured claimants will receive not less than that amount.

3. The Debtor shall submit to the supervision and control of the trustee, the following sum: $10.00 per month for eighteen months.

4. The various claims of the Debtor's creditors shall be classified as follows:

a. Class one: Claims filed and allowed which are entitled to priority under 11 U.S.C. § 507. The administrative costs are the only priority claims contemplated by this plan. Any creditor entitled to priority under section 507 of the Bankruptcy Code contrary to the provisions of this plan shall be deemed to have waived any such priority, unless such entity objects to the plan.

b. Class two: Claims filed and allowed which are secured by a lien which is not avoidable by the Debtor under 11 U.S.C. § 522. Class two creditors will retain their liens until their allowed secured claims are paid in full, and shall be deemed to have accepted this plan unless they object to the plan.

---

49 See notes to Form 10, Appendix G.3, *supra*.

50 See notes to Form 8, Appendix G.3, *supra*, for general discussion of chapter 13 plans. In some cases the debtor may be unable to afford to remain in his or her home. One option for such a debtor is to sell the home to realize accumulated equity. While this can often be done without a bankruptcy, it is sometimes necessary to file a case in order to avoid a foreclosure sale at which the house would be sold for much less than its true value. Bankruptcy may also allow the avoidance of liens under section 522 or the trustee's avoiding powers, which would increase the debtor's equity and/or allow for payments to unsecured creditors. Finally, it may be necessary to use the trustee's partition powers under 11 U.S.C. § 363(h) to sell the home when a co-tenant refuses to agree to the sale.

Chapter 13 specifically provides that a plan may liquidate property of the debtor. 11 U.S.C. § 1322(b)(8). This plan is one example of how to do this. In order to obtain a specific order that will allow the sale to go through it may also be necessary to file a Complaint to Sell Property Free and Clear of Liens. *See* Form 56, Appx. G.8, *infra*. This plan, for less than thirty-six months, may be subject to a successful objection if all unsecured claims are not paid in full under the ability-to-pay test of 11 U.S.C. § 1325(b). *See* § 12.6.3, *supra*.

c. Class three: All other claims against the debtor that are timely filed.

5. The payments received by the trustee from the Debtor pursuant to this plan shall be distributed as follows:

   a. Class one claims: The amount paid by the Debtor to the trustee shall be distributed first to the class one claims, pro rata, until they are paid in full.

   b. Class two claims: After the application of the appropriate amount each month to the class one claims, the entire amount of the payments remaining in the hands of the trustee shall be distributed in monthly installments, pro rata, to the holders of the class two claims until each such claimant shall receive 100% of the amount allowed on each such claim.

   c. Class three claims: After the application of the appropriate amount each month to the class one and class two claims, the entire amount of the monthly payment remaining in the hands of the trustee shall be distributed in monthly installments, pro rata, to the holders of the class three claims.

6. As part of this plan, and subject to court approval of the sale,[51] the Debtor and her husband shall also liquidate the Debtor's interest in her home at [*address*] paying creditors secured by that property in full.

7. The nonexempt value of the residence shall be paid to the trustee and applied to the claims of the class three creditors, after payment of the trustee's fees.

8. By failing to object to this plan, or any modification thereof, all creditors holding claims agree not to make any effort to collect their claims from any co-signers that may exist, so long as this case remains pending.

9. Confirmation of this plan shall constitute a finding that the plan constitutes the Debtor's best effort under all the circumstances to pay the creditors, within the meaning of 11 U.S.C. § 727(a)(9).

10. The current defaults by the Debtor on the class two claims are waived and shall be cured by the completion of this plan.

11. The title to the property of the estate shall revest in the Debtor upon the confirmation of this plan, and the Debtor shall have sole right to use and possession thereof.

12. Upon *ex parte* application, for good cause shown, the Debtor may alter the amount or timing of payments under this plan. Such modifications shall be permitted if they are reasonable and if they do not decrease the total amount of money that will be paid out under the plan.

13. Any other money or property acquired by either the trustee or the Debtor while this case is pending shall be deemed exempt property of the Debtor, if exemptible, and will be forthwith delivered to the Debtor.

14. If the Debtor defaults, after filing of this petition, on any payment to a utility entitled to adequate assurance under 11 U.S.C. § 366, then the debt shall, upon application of said utility, become a class one claim under this plan. This priority shall be deemed adequate assurance of the utility's right to future payments.

15. Upon completion of this plan, all debts listed in the Debtor's schedules or provided for by this plan, except those excepted by 11 U.S.C. § 1328(a) shall be discharged.

Date: [*signature*]
                                                    Debtor

---

51 11 U.S.C. §§ 363(b), 1303.

Form 13 Chapter 13 Plan Providing for Filing of Adversary Proceeding Involving Predatory Mortgage Lending Claims[52]

[*Caption: Official Form 16A*]

Chapter 13 Plan of Debtors

1. If the instant estate were liquidated under Chapter 7 of the Bankruptcy Code, the allowed unsecured claimants would be paid $0.00. Under this Plan, the allowed unsecured claimants will receive not less than that amount.

2. The Debtors shall submit to the supervision and control of the trustee $150.00 per month for the thirty-six (36) months of the Plan. The total sum to be submitted is $5400.00.

3. The various claims of the Debtors' creditors shall be classified as follows:

   a. *CLASS 1*—Claims filed and allowed which are entitled to priority under 11 U.S.C. § 507. The administrative costs of the trustee are the only priority claims contemplated by this plan. Any creditor entitled to priority under § 507 of the Bankruptcy Code contrary to the provisions of this plan shall be deemed to have waived any such priority, unless such entity objects to the plan before confirmation.

   b. *CLASS 2*—The allowed secured claim of [*name of mortgage holder*], as the holder of the mortgage on Debtors' home, [*address*], dated [*date*].

   c. *CLASS 3*—All other allowed secured claims against the Debtors other than the Class 2 claim that are timely filed, including any secured claims filed by the [*name of local municipality*] for property taxes and/or water-sewer service.

   d. *CLASS 4*—All unsecured claims against the Debtors that are timely filed.

   e. *CLASS 5*—All other claims against the Debtors that are not timely filed.

4. The payments received by the trustee from the Debtors pursuant to this plan shall be distributed as follows:

   a. *CLASS 1 CLAIMS*: The amount paid by the Debtors to the trustee shall be distributed first to the Class 1 claims, pro rata, until they are paid in full.

   b. *CLASS 2 CLAIMS:* After application of the appropriate amount each month to the Class 1 claims, the amount of the monthly payment remaining in the hands of the trustee shall be distributed to the holder of the Class 2 claim until 100% of its allowed secured claim is paid. The consumer loan transaction upon which this claim is based was a predatory mortgage loan that the Debtors are contesting in an adversary proceeding filed in this bankruptcy, which shall be adjudicated by this Court.[53] Debtors have rescinded the mortgage

---

52 This Chapter 13 plan may be used if the debtor intends to file an adversary proceeding against a mortgage holder seeking enforcement of the debtor's rescission rights under the Truth in Lending Act. *See* § 13.4.4, *supra*.

53 This language can be helpful in defeating a mortgage holder's attempt to seek referral of the adversary proceeding to arbitration if an arbitration clause was included in the mortgage loan documents. *See* Ernst & Young, L.L.P. v. Baker O'Neal Holdings, Inc., 304 F.3d 753 (7th Cir. 2002) (creditor's right to enforce arbitration agreement superseded by terms of confirmed plan, which provided that court retained jurisdiction to "adju-

pursuant to the Truth in Lending Act and anticipate that the Class 2 claimant shall have only an allowed unsecured claim or a greatly reduced secured claim. The funds paid to the Trustee are designed to provide additional adequate protection to the Class 2 claimant until the validity and extent of the mortgage lien is determined by the Court. In the event this bankruptcy case is dismissed prior to the resolution of the adversary action, the net amount of the adequate protection funds in the hands of the trustee shall be paid to the Class 2 creditor. The Class 2 creditor shall be deemed to have accepted this Plan unless it objects to the Plan.

c. *CLASS 3 CLAIMS:* The Class 3 claims are provided for as follows: No payments shall be made by the trustee to the holders of Class 3 claims. Any lien held by a Class 3 creditor, including the [*name of local municipality*], shall be retained by the creditor and such lien shall pass through this bankruptcy intact. The Debtors shall make arrangements to pay Class 3 claims outside this plan.

d. *CLASS 4 CLAIMS:* After application of the appropriate amount to the holders of Class 1 and 2 claims, the trustee shall distribute all other amounts, pro rata, to the holders of the allowed Class 4 claims.

e. *CLASS 5 CLAIMS:* The Class 5 claims are provided for as follows: There shall be no distribution to the holders of Class 5 claims.

5. The Debtors will be responsible for securing and maintaining homeowner's insurance and for the payment of real estate taxes as of the date of confirmation. These payments are not to be paid by any creditor of Debtors.

6. To the extent that any claim is fully or partially unsecured pursuant to 11 U.S.C. § 506(a), that portion of the claim which is unsecured shall be provided for as a Class 3 (unsecured) claim under this Plan. Creditors holding such claims shall retain their liens only to the extent of their allowed secured claims.

7. To the extent that any allowed secured claim is paid during this case or thereafter, such creditors' liens shall be extinguished. Once the allowed secured claim has been paid in full, either during or after the pendency of this case, the claim shall be entirely extinguished and the creditor holding such claim shall promptly mark any lien securing such claims as satisfied in the appropriate public records. The term "allowed secured claim," for all purposes under this Plan, shall mean the amount of the total due stated in the proof of claim unless the Debtors at any time disputes that amount, in which case the allowed secured claim will mean the amount ultimately decided by the Court or agreed to by the parties.

8. By failing to object to this Plan, or any modification or amendment thereof, all creditors holding claims agree not to make any effort to collect their claims from any co-debtors that may exist, so long as this case remains pending.

9. Confirmation of this plan shall constitute a finding that the plan constitutes the Debtors best effort under all the circumstances to pay creditors, within the meaning of 11 U.S.C. § 727(a)(9).

10. The title to the property of the estate shall remain with the trustee and shall not revest in the Debtors until the termination of this plan. The Debtors shall have sole right to use and possession

thereof during the pendency of this case, including the right to use, sell, or lease such property in the ordinary course of the Debtors' affairs.

11. Confirmation of this plan shall constitute a finding and order that, due to the Debtors low income, the trustee's fee should not exceed 10 percent of each monthly payment to the trustee, even if that amount is less than $5.00 per month.

12. Any money or property acquired by either the trustee or the Debtors or refunded from the trustee's percentage fees, while this case is pending, shall be deemed exempt property of the Debtors, if exemptible, and shall be forthwith delivered to the Debtors.

13. Upon completion of this plan, all debts listed in the Debtors' Schedules or provided for by this plan, except those excepted by 11 U.S.C. § 1328(a), shall be discharged.

14. If, prior to the expiration of the period set forth in Paragraph 2 of this plan, all filed claims entitled to payment under this plan are paid in full, this plan shall terminate on that date.

Date: [*signature(s)*]
Debtors

Form 14 Chapter 13 Plan Assuming Residential Lease[54]

[*Caption: Official Form 16A*]

Chapter 13 Plan of Debtor

1. If the instant estate were liquidated under chapter 7 of the Bankruptcy Code, the allowed unsecured claimants would be paid $0.00.

2. Under this plan the allowed unsecured claimants will receive not less than that amount.

3. The Debtor shall submit to the supervision and control of the trustee, in the form of a certified check or money order, the following assets of the estate:

a. All money received by the Debtor in satisfaction of the Debtor's contingent and unliquidated claim against the owner of the [*name*] Apartments relating to the rental of Apartment [*number*], and the condition of that apartment.[55] It is anticipated that the amount, without deduction for setoffs, should be at least $600.00.

b. During the first eight months of the plan: twenty dollars ($20.00) per month.[56]

c. During the ninth through the thirty-sixth month of the plan: forty dollars ($40.00) per month.

4. The various claims of the Debtor's creditors shall be classified as follows:

a. Class one: Claims filed and allowed which are entitled to priority under 11 U.S.C. § 507. The administrative costs and

---

dicate" adversary proceeding). For a discussion of the bankruptcy court's discretion to deny referral to arbitration in core proceedings, see National Consumer Law Center, *Consumer Arbitration Agreements* § 5.2.3 (3d ed. 2003).

54 A chapter 13 plan may sometimes be necessary to protect a debtor's rights under a lease, allowing the debtor to cure a default and assume the lease. *See* § 12.9.2, *supra*. This plan is an example of such a plan.

55 A plan may provide for property, tangible or intangible, to be used to satisfy debts.

56 A plan may provide for graduated payments, as long as they are feasible. Often it is necessary to have low payments in the first few months so the debtor can pay utility and other deposits, as well as to make other budgetary adjustments.

payments pursuant to paragraph 8, *infra*, are the only priority claims contemplated by this plan. Any creditor entitled to priority under section 507 of the Bankruptcy Code contrary to the provisions of this plan shall be deemed to have waived any such priority, unless such entity objects to the plan.

   b. Class two: Claims filed and allowed in favor of the owner of the [*name*] Apartments, [*address*], for money owed as the result of the Debtor's default in her obligation to pay rent pursuant to the lease of the residential premises located at Apartment [*number*], [*address*].[57] These creditors shall be deemed to have accepted this plan unless they object to the plan.

   c. Class three: All other claims against the debtor that are timely filed.

5. The payments received by the trustee from the Debtor pursuant to this plan shall be distributed as follows:

   a. Class two claims: The entire amount of the payments in the hands of the trustee shall be distributed in monthly installments, to the [*name*] Apartments, the holder of the class two claim until such claimant shall receive 100% of the amount allowed on its claim.

   b. Class one claims: After the application of the appropriate amount to the holder of the class two claim, the entire amount of the payments remaining in the hands of the trustee shall be paid in monthly installments, pro rata, to the holders of class one claims until they are paid in full.

   c. Class three claims: After the application of the appropriate amount each month to the class one claims, the entire amount of the monthly payment remaining in the hands of the trustee shall be distributed in monthly installments, pro rata, to the holders of the class three claims until each such claimant shall have received 100% of the amount allowed or until the money in the hands of the trustee is exhausted, whichever first occurs.

6. The Debtor shall assume the Debtor's lease for the use as a residence of the residential premises located at [*address*]. Confirmation of this plan shall constitute a judicial finding that said lease is assumable by the Debtor and shall constitute judicial approval of the assumption of the lease by the Debtor.

7. Pursuant to 11 U.S.C. § 1322(b)(3) the past defaults of the Debtor under her lease with the [*name*] Apartments are waived. Such defaults as may exist shall be cured by the payments under this plan.

8. The Debtor's right to possession of said residential premises shall vest in the Debtor upon judicial confirmation of this plan, and shall continue until termination of this plan.

9. By failing to object to this plan, or any modification thereof, all creditors holding claims agree not to make any effort to collect their claims from any co-signers that may exist, so long as this case remains pending.

10. Confirmation of this plan shall constitute a finding that the plan constitutes the Debtor's best effort under all the circumstances to pay the creditors, within the meaning of 11 U.S.C. § 727(a)(9), and a finding that the plan is proposed in good faith.

11. Upon notice and hearing for good cause shown, the Debtor may alter the amount or timing of the payments under this plan. Such modifications shall be permitted if they are reasonable and if they do not decrease the total amount of money that will be paid out under the plan, the total amount that will be paid out to the class one claimants or the total amount that will be paid out to the class two claimants.

12. Any money or property acquired by either the trustee or the Debtor while this case is pending shall be deemed exempt property of the Debtor, if exemptible, and will be forthwith delivered to the Debtor.

13. If the Debtor defaults, after filing of her petition, on any payment to a utility entitled to adequate assurance under 11 U.S.C. § 366(b), then the debt shall, upon application of said utility, become a class one claim under this plan. This priority, upon judicial confirmation, shall be deemed adequate assurance of the utility's right to future payments.

14. Confirmation of this plan shall constitute a judicial finding that the [*name*] Apartments has not suffered any actual pecuniary loss from the Debtor's default under the lease other than the default itself which is being cured under this plan.

15. Confirmation of this plan shall not deprive the Debtor of her remedies under state law for the breach by the owners of the [*name*] Apartments of their duties under state law.

16. Upon completion of this plan, all debts listed in the Debtor's schedules or provided for by this plan, except those excepted by 11 U.S.C. § 1328(a), shall be discharged.

17. Upon completion of this plan, all sums remaining in the hands of the trustee shall be returned to the Debtor.

18. This plan shall be deemed completed when all filed and allowed claims are paid in full or upon completion of the payments listed above, whichever first occurs.

19. Confirmation of this plan shall constitute an order binding every creditor of the Debtor and enjoining each such creditor from taking any action inconsistent with this plan and from proceeding with any claim against the Debtor in any forum other than the Bankruptcy Court.

20. Confirmation of this plan shall constitute a finding that the Debtor's continued possession of Apartment [*number*], [*address*], is essential for the success of the plan and that without it the plan would fail and no claim would be paid in full.

21. Upon confirmation of this plan, as assurance of the payment of future rents which are determined to be legitimately owing to [*name*] Apartments, Debtor shall give to [*name*] Apartments a security deposit of one month's rent, to be returned at the termination of this plan.[58] Confirmation of this plan shall constitute a determination that such security deposit constitutes adequate assurance of future payments for all purposes.

Date: [*signature*]
                                         Attorney for Debtor

---

57 A plan assuming a lease must provide for a prompt cure of the arrearages. 11 U.S.C. § 365(D)(1)(A). The debtor may contest the amount of the arrearages, however, if there are defenses to the lessor's claim.

58 To assume a lease a debtor must provide adequate assurance of future performance. 11 U.S.C. § 365(b)(1)(C).

Form 15 Chapter 13 Debtor's Motion to Assume Lease[59]

[*Caption: Official Form 16A*]

Debtor's Motion to Assume Lease

The Debtor, by her counsel, hereby moves to assume the lease for the rental premises at [*address*]. In support of this motion she avers:

1. The Debtor is a tenant in the premises at [*address*]. A copy of the Debtor's lease is attached hereto as Exhibit A [*omitted*].

2. As a chapter 13 debtor, she is entitled to assume the lease pursuant to 11 U.S.C. §§ 365, 1322(b)(7).[60]

3. Her chapter 13 plan provides for assumption of the lease and cure of any delinquent rent pursuant to the lease.

WHEREFORE, Debtor prays that her Motion to Assume the Lease be granted.

Date: [*signature*]
                              Attorney for Debtor

Form 16 Chapter 13 Bankruptcy Checklist from Debtor's Attorney to Debtor[61]

Re: Bankruptcy No. [*number*]

Dear [*name*]:

On [*date*] our office filed a chapter 13 bankruptcy petition on your behalf. The court number of your bankruptcy case is [*number*]; please make a careful note of it and include it on all payments made to the bankruptcy trustee and the clerk of the bankruptcy court.

As we have explained to you, the filing of this bankruptcy places an automatic stay upon the attempts of your creditors to collect debts owed by you. In order that you get the maximum benefit from

your bankruptcy, I am writing to make sure you understand exactly what is required by you during the months ahead.

Mortgage Payments

According to your chapter 13 plan, you must pay your current monthly mortgage payments directly to your mortgage company as they become due each month. Payments to your mortgage company should begin in [*month*]. If your current mortgage payment does not include an escrow for taxes and insurance, you must continue to keep your home insured and pay any tax bills that come due.

Do *not* pay any past due amounts as that delinquency is being cured by your payments to the bankruptcy trustee.

Payments to the Chapter 13 Trustee

You must also make monthly payments to the bankruptcy trustee of:

$[*amount*]/month from [*date*] to [*date*]
$[*amount*]/month from [*date*] to [*date*]

These payments must be in the form of a money order made payable to:

[*trustee*]
[*address*]

Always place your name, address and bankruptcy number on each payment and keep a *receipt* for every payment you make in case any disputes arise.

Court Costs

The cost of filing a bankruptcy petition is $194.00. This fee cannot be waived. However, you have been allowed to pay this cost in four installments. These installments are due as follows:

$50.00 is due on [*date*];
$50.00 is due on [*date*];
$47.00 is due on [*date*];
$47.00 is due on [*date*].

Make all payments for court costs in the form of a money order made payable to "Clerk, U.S. Bankruptcy Court," and mail them to:

Clerk, U.S. Bankruptcy Court
U.S. Courthouse, Room [*number*]
[*address*]

Always place your name, address and bankruptcy number on each money order and remember to keep a receipt of each payment in a safe place in case any disputes arise.

If you do not make all of the payments described above, your bankruptcy case may be dismissed or your mortgage company may be allowed to foreclose on its mortgage. Therefore, if you are unable to keep up with payments you should call me so I can advise you on whether there are any ways to deal with your problem.

---

59 When a chapter 13 debtor intends to cure a default under a lease, some courts may require a motion even though 11 U.S.C. § 1322(b)(7) and Fed. R. Bankr. P. 6006 appear to allow assumption of an executory contract to occur by plan provision. When a motion is desired or required, a motion in the form here should suffice. Generally, the motion will have to be made in conjunction with a plan to make the payments necessary to cure the defaults under the lease to be assumed. However, occasionally the debtor may be current on the lease or may have funds which do not belong to the estate which can be used to cure the default. In that event, the motion should so state. *See* § 12.9, *supra.*

60 *See* § 12.9, *supra.* In a chapter 13 case, the debtor may generally assume a lease at any time up to plan confirmation. 11 U.S.C. § 365(d)(2).

61 This letter serves to confirm and clarify for the debtor in a chapter 13 case the various payments that must be made. It can be adapted as circumstances of different cases require. Debtors are understandably confused by all of the payments they must make to different places. Payments in the wrong form or to the wrong party are not uncommon. A letter such as this one, to which the debtor can always refer, eliminates most problems. A similar, but much shorter letter can also be sent in chapter 7 cases. *See* Form 17, Appx. G.3, *infra.* This form is adapted from one created by Eric Frank, Esq., Philadelphia, PA.

Utility Service

Your gas, electric, phone or water company may request a security deposit for service after the bankruptcy if you listed a debt to them in your bankruptcy papers. While your bankruptcy will wipe out any bills you owed them up until the date you filed, the utilities are entitled to a deposit for continued service. If you receive a request for a deposit and feel it is too high, or if you will have difficulty paying it on time, please call our office right away.

Other Things You Should Know

The next thing to happen in your case will probably be a hearing called the meeting of creditors. You will soon receive a notice from the court of the date and time of that hearing. Please call me when you receive that notice or any other legal papers.

In the meantime, remember not to make payments to any other creditors for debts which arose prior to your bankruptcy unless instructed to do so by our office. Also, do not enter into any new credit transaction without first checking with me.

We understand that bankruptcy can be confusing. Therefore, if you have any questions at all or if you do not understand exactly what you must do, please call our office at [*number*]. We will be happy to answer all of your questions.

> [*signature*]
> Attorney

Form 17 Chapter 7 Information Sheet from Attorney to Debtor[62]

> Re: Bankruptcy No. [*number*]

Dear [*name*]:

On [*date*] our office filed a chapter 7 bankruptcy petition on your behalf. The court number of your bankruptcy case is [*number*]; please make a careful note of it and include it on all payments made to the clerk of the bankruptcy court.

As I have explained to you, the filing of this bankruptcy places an automatic stay upon the attempts of your creditors to collect debts owed by you. In order that you get the maximum benefit from your bankruptcy, I am writing to make sure you understand exactly what is required by you during the months ahead.

Filing Fees

The bankruptcy court has approved our request to have you pay the mandatory $209.00 bankruptcy filing fee in installments. Your payments are due as follows:

> $59.00 is due on or before [*date*]
> $50.00 is due on or before [*date*]
> $50.00 is due on or before [*date*]
> $50.00 is due on or before [*date*]

All payments must be made by money order and they should be made payable to "Clerk, U.S. District Court." On your money order, make sure to write (1) your name and address and (2) your bankruptcy number. *Please* keep a copy of the money order by retaining the carbon copy or by photocopying the money order. Sometimes the clerk does lose money orders, and your copy or carbon of your money order will be some proof that you in fact paid the court. Remember, if you miss a payment, the bankruptcy court may dismiss your case. If you send a self-addressed stamped envelope the clerk will send you a receipt which will be absolute proof of your payment.

The money order can be handed in personally or it can be mailed to:

> Clerk, U.S. Bankruptcy Court
> U.S. Courthouse, Room [*number*]
> [*address*]

Utility Service

Your gas, electric, phone or water company may request a security deposit for service after the bankruptcy if you listed a debt to them in your bankruptcy papers. While your bankruptcy will wipe out any bills you owed them up until the date you filed, the utilities are entitled to a deposit for continued service. If you receive a request for a deposit and feel it is too high, or if you will have difficulty paying it on time, please call our office right away.

Mortgage and Auto Payments

If you have a mortgage and/or auto loan and you want to keep your home and/or auto, try to continue to make payments to your mortgage company and/or auto lender. Remember, chapter 7 bankruptcy does not wipe out your mortgage or auto loan. Also, if your mortgage payment does not include an escrow for taxes and insurance, you should continue to keep your home insured and pay any tax bills that come due. If you are unable to keep up with these payments, or if your mortgage company or auto lender will not accept your payments, please call our office right away.

Other Things You Should Know

The next thing to happen in your case will probably be a hearing called the meeting of creditors. You will soon receive a notice from the court of the date and time of that hearing. Please call me when you receive that notice or any other legal papers.

In the meantime, remember not to make payments to any other creditors unless instructed to do so by our office.

Bankruptcy can be confusing. Therefore, if you have any questions at all or if you do not understand exactly what you must do, please call our office at [*number*]. We will be happy to answer all of your questions.

> [*signature*]
> Attorney

---

62 This letter serves to confirm and clarify information given to the debtor in a chapter 7 case. It can be adapted as circumstances require. Such a letter usually eliminates confusion about the various payments debtors must make and what will occur next. A similar letter can be sent in chapter 13 cases. *See* Form 16, Appx. G.3, *supra*.

Form 18 Debtor's First Amended Chapter 13 Plan[63]

[*Caption: Official Form 16A*]

First Amended Chapter 13 Plan of the Debtor

1. If the instant estate were liquidated under chapter 7 of the Bankruptcy Code, the allowed unsecured claimants would be paid $0.00.

2. Under this plan the allowed unsecured claimants will receive not less than that amount.

3. The Debtor shall submit to the supervision and control of the trustee the following sums:

a. During the first year of the plan: $115.00 monthly;

b. During the second, third, fourth and fifth year of the plan: $135.00 monthly.

4. The various claims of the Debtor's creditors shall be classified as follows:

a. Class one: Claims filed and allowed which are entitled to priority under 11 U.S.C. § 507. The administrative expenses are the only priority claims contemplated by this plan. Any creditor entitled to priority under section 507 of the Bankruptcy Code contrary to the provisions of this plan shall be deemed to have agreed to waive any such priority, unless such entity objects to the plan before the first meeting of creditors.

b. Class two: Claims filed and allowed which are secured by a lien which is not avoidable by the debtor under 11 U.S.C. § 522, except for the first mortgage held by [*name*] Mortgage Company. These creditors will retain their liens until allowed secured claims are paid in full and shall be deemed to have accepted this plan unless they object to the plan.

c. Class three: All other claims against the debtor that are timely filed.

d. Class four: All other claims against the debtor that are not timely filed.

5. The payments received by the trustee from the Debtor pursuant to this plan shall be distributed as follows:

a. Class one claims: The amount paid by the Debtor to the trustee shall be distributed first to the class one claims, pro rata, until they are paid in full.

b. Class two claims: After the application of the appropriate amount each month to the class one claims, the entire amount of the monthly payment remaining in the hands of the trustee shall be distributed, pro rata, to the holders of the class two claims until each such claimant shall have received 100% of the arrears allowed on each such claim, as necessary to cure any existing default.

c. Class three claims: After the application of the appropriate amount each month to the class one and class two claims, the entire amount of the monthly payment remaining in the hands of the trustee shall be distributed, pro rata, to the holders of the class three claims.

d. Class four claims: The class four claims are provided for by this plan as follows: There shall be no distribution to the holders of class four claims.[64]

6. The first mortgage on the Debtor's home, held by [*name*] Mortgage Company, will be paid by the Debtor directly to that creditor and will not be paid under the plan. The Debtor will cure the default on that mortgage within a reasonable period of time.

7. To the extent that any claim is fully or partially unsecured pursuant to 11 U.S.C. § 506(a), that portion of the claim which is unsecured shall be provided for as a class three (unsecured) claim under this plan. Creditors holding such claims shall retain their liens only to the extent of their allowed secured claim. To the extent that the allowed secured claim is paid during this case or thereafter, such creditors' liens shall be reduced. Once the allowed secured claim has been paid in full, either during or after the pendency of this case, the creditor holding such claim shall promptly mark any lien securing such claim as satisfied in the appropriate public records.[65]

8. By failing to object to this plan, or any modification thereof, all creditors holding claims agree not to make any effort to collect their claims from any cosigners that may exist, so long as this case remains pending.

9. Confirmation of this plan shall constitute a finding that the plan constitutes the Debtor's best effort under all the circumstances to pay creditors, within the meaning of 11 U.S.C. § 727(a)(9).

10. Confirmation of this plan shall constitute a finding in accordance with 11 U.S.C. § 1322 that there is cause for extending the plan beyond three years. Confirmation shall also constitute approval of such extension. Such extension is essential to the success of the plan. Without it the plan would fail and no claims would be paid in full.

11. The current defaults by the Debtor on the class two and the Debtor's first mortgage claims are waived and shall be cured by the completion of this plan.

12. The title to the property of the estate shall revest in the Debtor upon confirmation of this plan, and the Debtor shall have sole right to use and possession thereof.

13. Upon *ex parte* application, for good cause shown, the Debtor may alter the amount of timing of the payments under this plan.

---

63 The debtor may file one or more amended plans as of course prior to confirmation. Such plans should be designated as the first amended plan, second amended plan, and so forth. After confirmation, modification may be subject to notice and hearing requirements under 11 U.S.C. § 1329(b)(2). This would seem to require an application by the debtor. *See* Form 128, Appx. G.12, *infra.*

64 This paragraph specifically provides for late filed claims, giving them no distribution. Without such a paragraph, there might be an argument that a late filed claim is entitled to receive funds under section 1325(a)(4) or 1325(b). Inclusion of this paragraph should prevent a late filing claimant from raising such arguments because the plan would be binding on that claimant. *See* § 13.4.3, *supra.*

65 This provision is designed to protect the debtor's right to bifurcate claims under 11 U.S.C. § 506(a) and to treat separately the allowed secured claim and allowed unsecured claim. It is drafted to avoid resort to 11 U.S.C. § 506(d) and the issues created by Dewsnup v. Timm, 502 U.S. 410, 112 S. Ct. 773, 116 L. Ed. 2d 903 (1992). *See* §§ 11.2, 11.7, *supra.* In those jurisdictions which have expressly held that section 506(d) may be employed to reduce or eliminate liens in chapter 13 despite *Dewsnup*, this plan language may be less important.

Such modifications shall be permitted if they are reasonable and if they do not decrease the total amount of money that will be paid out under the plan.

14. Confirmation of the plan shall constitute a finding and order that due to the Debtor's low income, the trustee's fee should not exceed 0% of each monthly payment, even if that amount is less than $5.00 per month.

15. Any money or property acquired by either the trustee or the Debtor, or refunded from the trustee's percentage fees, while this case is pending shall be deemed exempt property of the Debtor, if exemptible, and shall be forthwith delivered to the Debtor.

16. If the Debtor defaults, after filing of his petition, on any payment to a utility entitled to adequate assurance under 11 U.S.C. § 366, then that debt shall, upon application of said utility, become a class one claim under this plan. This priority shall be deemed adequate assurance of the utility's future payments.

17. The following executory contracts are rejected, with the refunds of prepaid charges claimed as exempt property:

    a. All credit life, disability and property insurance contracts to which the Debtor is a party.

    b. Membership in [*name*] Health Spa.

18. The following liens are avoided pursuant to section 522(f):

    a. Judicial lien arising out of judgment in favor of [*name*] Finance Company, at [*name*] Court, No. [*number*].

    b. Non-possessory, non-purchase money security interest in Debtor's household goods held by [*name*] Finance Company.

19. Upon completion of this plan, all debts listed in the Debtor's schedules or provided for by this plan, except those excepted by 11 U.S.C. § 1328(a) shall be discharged.

20. If, prior to the expiration of the period set forth in paragraph 3 of this plan all filed claims provided for in this plan are paid in full, this plan shall terminate on that date.

Date: [*signature*]
                                        Debtor

Form 19 Debtor's Amendment of Schedules[66]

[Caption: Official Form 16A]

Debtor's Amendment of Schedules

The Debtor in the above-captioned case hereby amends schedules D and E by substituting the attached amended schedules for those originally filed, pursuant to Fed. R. Bankr. P. 1009.

Date: [*signature*]
                              Attorney for Debtors

Certificate of Service

I, [*name*], attorney for the Debtor, hereby certify that a copy of the foregoing amendment to the schedules or statement of the Debtor has this day been served upon the trustee in this case and the following affected creditors, [*names*], by first-class mail.

Date: [*signature*]
                              Attorney for Debtors

Debtor's Verification

I declare under penalty of perjury that I have read the attached amendments and that they are true and correct to the best of my knowledge, information or belief.

Date: [*signature*]
                                    Debtor

Form 20 Application and Order for Waiver of Filing Fee to Amend Debtor's Schedule of Creditors[67]

[Caption: Official Form 16A]

Application for Waiver of Fee to Amend Debtor's Schedules

1. Applicant filed a voluntary chapter 7 petition bankruptcy on [*date*].

2. Applicant has discovered additional creditors she wishes to list on her schedules.

3. The Applicant's rights under title 11 will be prejudiced if the Debtor's Schedules are not amended.

4. The Applicant is indigent and unable to pay the filing fee for the amendment of her schedules.[68]

WHEREFORE, Applicant prays that this Court waive payment of the fee as permitted by the Judicial Conference Schedule of Fees under 28 U.S.C. § 1930(b).

Date: [*signature*]
                                    Debtor

[Caption: Official Form 16A]

Order to Waive Filing Fees for the Amendment of Debtor's Schedules

The Debtor having applied for waiver of filing fees for the amendment of her schedules:

It is ORDERED that the Debtor be permitted to file an amendment to her schedules without payment of the filing fee.

Date: [*signature*]
                          United States Bankruptcy Judge

---

66 Federal Rule of Bankruptcy Procedure 1009 allows amendment as a matter of course by filing the amendment (with the same number of copies as the original) and giving notice to the trustee and any entity affected thereby. A certificate of service listing parties in interest who are served is useful as record evidence of compliance with the rule. Any amendment to the schedules or statements must be verified by the debtor, Fed. R. Bankr. P. 1008, and filed in the same number of copies as required for the original, Fed. R. Bankr. P. 1009.

67 The schedule of filing fees adopted by the Administrative Office of United States Courts requires a fee of $26.00 for an amendment to the schedule of creditors. *See* Appx. C, *supra*. The Administrative Office's fee schedule specifically provides that this fee may be waived by the court for good cause. *See* § 13.6, *supra*.

68 Some courts may require the debtor to attach a more specific affidavit setting forth information about financial circumstances supporting the application.

Form 21 Statement by Debtor's Attorney of Fees Charged[69]

[Caption: Official Form 16A]

Statement Under Bankruptcy Rule 2016(b)

The attorney for the Debtor in this case hereby states that the following arrangements have been made with the Debtor for payment of counsel fees:[70]

1. The total fee to be paid by the Debtor will be $900.00.

2. The source of the fee is:

a. Social Security benefits of Debtor, $800.00;

b. Gift from Debtor's mother, $100.00.

3. This fee covers the following bankruptcy services:

a. Interview and investigation of facts;

b. Counseling on alternative remedies available and consequences of bankruptcy;

c. Preparation and filing of statements, schedules, chapter 13 plan, and other initial papers;

d. Representation at section 341(a) meeting;

e. Representation at confirmation hearing;

f. Representation at discharge hearing;

g. Counseling and advice during and after the case;

h. Letters and telephone calls regarding the case;

i. Two motions to avoid liens under section 522(f).

4. The Debtor has also agreed that if any other services should become necessary, and the Debtor chooses to employ the same counsel, those services will be rendered at a rate of $125.00 per hour.

5. There has been no agreement to share the fees in this case with any other entity, and no fees have been or will be shared with any other entity.

Date: *[signature]*
                                          Attorney for Debtor

Form 22 Application for Counsel Fees[71]

[Caption: Official Form 16A]

Application For Counsel Fees

[Name], Esquire, counsel for the Debtors herein, hereby applies for the approval of attorney fees with the unpaid balance to be paid through the Debtors' chapter 13 plan.

1. The following services have been performed for the Debtors, or will be performed at the appropriate time:

a. Interview and investigation of facts;

b. Counseling on alternative remedies available and consequences of bankruptcy;

c. Preparation and filing of chapter 13 statement; chapter 13 plan, and other initial papers;

d. Representation at section 341(a) meeting;

e. Representation at confirmation hearing;

f. Representation at discharge hearing;

g. Counseling and advice during and after the case;

h. Letters and telephone calls regarding the case;

i. Two motions to avoid liens under section 522(f);

2. The Debtors have agreed to pay a total of $1000.00 for these services, which is a fair and reasonable fee.

3. The Debtors have thus far paid a $200.00 retainer to their attorney, and have agreed that the remainder of their attorney fees may be paid through their chapter 13 plan as an administrative expense.

WHEREFORE, the Court is respectfully requested to enter an Order directing the payment of $800.00 to the undersigned counsel for the Debtors as an administrative expense in the Debtors' chapter 13 plan.

Date: *[signature]*
                                          Attorney for Debtors

G.4 Automatic Stay

Form 23 Letter to Creditors Giving Notice of Stay[72]

[creditor][73]
[address]

                                          Re:*[debtor]*
                                 Bankr. No.*[number]*
                              District of *[name]*
                                 [debtor address]
                          [social security number]

---

which means that one way or another all parties must be notified of the request and given an opportunity to object. *See generally* Ch. 15, *supra*.

72 This letter should be sent to any creditor who may take action against the debtor, shortly after the bankruptcy is filed and before the court's notice of filing and date of the first meeting is sent. It should prevent repossessions, court actions, harassing collection activity, and so forth. The letter may be adapted for specific circumstances as needed. It should be sent by certified mail so there is evidence that the creditor has received notice of the stay for any later enforcement proceeding. Though not required by 11 U.S.C. § 342(c), the debtor's address and social security number should be included so as to avoid any claim of confusion by creditor in the event enforcement proceedings are initiated. *See* § 9.5, *supra*.

In some localities a letter or other notice of this nature is filed in courts where actions concerning the debtor are pending. Technically, no such notice should be required to effectuate the stay, which is automatic under federal law. However, in some cases, it may be wiser to follow local practice than to challenge it.

73 For purposes of proof, it may be advantageous to send this type of letter by certified mail.

---

69 This statement is required in every bankruptcy case so the court can exercise its duty to oversee counsel fees. It is normally filed along with the schedules or chapter 13 statement, although the applicable rules allow filing within fifteen days of the filing of the order for relief (the date of filing in a voluntary bankruptcy case). Fed. R. Bankr. P. 2016(b). A supplemental statement must be filed within fifteen days after any new payment or agreement not previously disclosed. *Id. See generally* Ch. 15, *supra*.

70 If no fees are being charged, use the form contained in Appendix E, *supra*.

71 In some districts it is necessary to file a separate application for approval of compensation for the debtors' attorney through the chapter 13 plan. Sometimes such an application, if required, can be combined with the disclosure of fees under Fed. R. Bankr. P. 2016(a). In any case, whether fees are sought through a plan provision or a separate application, fees can be paid from the estate (that is, through the plan) only after notice and a hearing,

Dear Sir/Madam:

Please be advised that I represent [*debtor*].

On [*date*], a voluntary petition pursuant to chapter _____ of the Bankruptcy Code was filed on [*debtor*]'s behalf at the court and number indicated above.

Pursuant to 11 U.S.C. § 362(a) you are automatically stayed by the filing of this petition from taking any action to collect any debt from my client or from enforcing any lien against [*debtor*]. A violation of the stay may be actionable pursuant to 362(h) or as contempt of court and punished accordingly.

[*signature*]
Attorney for Debtor

Form 24 Complaint Seeking Damages for Violation of Automatic Stay and Unfair Trade Practices[74]

[*Caption: Official Form 16D*][75]

Complaint

1. On August 21, 2004, the Plaintiff/Debtor commenced a voluntary case under chapter 7 of the Bankruptcy Code, by filing a petition which has been assigned No. [*number*] in this Court.

2. This Court has jurisdiction to hear this matter under 28 U.S.C. § 1334, because it arises in that case and is related to it. This proceeding is a core proceeding.

3. The Defendant was named in Schedule A-3 of the petition as a creditor without security or priority. The Defendant is a creditor of the Debtor by virtue of [*describe debt*].

4. The Defendant is also a creditor of the Debtor within the meaning of [*cite provision(s) of state debt collection or unfair trade practices law*].

5. Within several days of May 28, 2004, the undersigned counsel for the Debtor telephoned the Defendant and informed its agent and employee, Ms. [*name*], that the Debtor was represented by counsel, that counsel was attempting to assist the Debtor in making satisfactory arrangements with creditors, and that the Defendant was not to have any further contact with the Debtor directly.

6. On or about July 15, 2004, an agent or employee of the Defendant, whose name sounded to the Debtor like "Ms. [*name*]" telephoned the Debtor personally, attempting to collect her debt to the Defendant.[76]

7. An order for relief was entered in this case on August 21, 2004, pursuant to 11 U.S.C. § 301, thus triggering an automatic stay, pursuant to 11 U.S.C. § 362(a), of all debt collection against the Debtor.

8. On August 25, 2004, the undersigned counsel for the Debtor sent a first class letter to the Defendant, informing it of the filing of the petition and describing the provisions of section 362(a). A copy of that letter is attached hereto as Exhibit A [*omitted*], along with a return receipt showing receipt by Defendant.[77]

9. On September 10, 2004, the Defendant by its agent and employee, Ms. [*name*], sent a letter to the Debtor at her home address, a copy of which is attached as Exhibit B [*omitted*], attempting to collect the debt owing from the Debtor to the Defendant.

10. On September 12, 2004, at 3:00 P.M., Ms. [*name*] endeavored to collect the debt by telephoning the Debtor directly at her place of employment. Failing to reach her, she left the message: "Personal. Please call."

11. At no time did any agent or employee of the Defendant communicate or attempt to communicate with the Debtor's undersigned counsel, although the Defendant knew or had reason to know that the Debtor was represented by him as an attorney with respect to her debt, and the Defendant knew or could readily ascertain the address of the attorney.

WHEREFORE, the Plaintiff/Debtor prays that this Court will enter an Order:

a. Declaring the Defendant guilty of civil contempt by violating the automatic stay granted herein on August 21, 2004, for its actions on September 10 and 12, 2004;[78]

b. Declaring that the Defendant violated the rights of the Debtor as secured by [*cite provision(s) of state law*] by its actions on or about July 15, 2004, and September 10 and 12, 2004;[79]

c. Awarding the Plaintiff/Debtor damages in the amount of $100.00 for each violation, as provided in [*cite provision(s) of state law*]; and

d. Awarding the Plaintiff compensatory and punitive damages, plus attorney fees and costs pursuant to 11 U.S.C. § 362(h) and for contempt of Court; and

e. Granting such additional relief as it deems necessary or proper.

Date:

[*signature*]
Attorney for Plaintiff/Debtor

---

74 Although contempt might be sought by an application, it probably can also be sought by complaint, especially when other relief sought on the same facts requires an adversary proceeding. Fed. R. Bankr. P. 7001 requires an adversary proceeding to seek all types of relief under non-bankruptcy law. For a general discussion of adversary proceeding complaints, see notes to Form 83, Appendix G.10, *infra*. For a general discussion of the automatic stay and remedies for violations, see Chapter 9, *supra*.

75 Official Form 16D is the caption for adversary proceedings. It can be found in Appendix D, *supra*.

76 Note that the creditor's pre-petition action in violation of the state unfair trade practices or debt collection laws gives rise to a cause of action which is property of the debtor's bankruptcy estate. For the debtor to act on it, it must be either exempted or abandoned. *See* Chs. 3, 11, *supra*.

77 *See* Form 23, Appx. G.4, *supra*.

78 Violation of the automatic stay by a party with actual notice constitutes contempt of court. Specific remedies including punitive damages are also provided by 11 U.S.C. § 362(h) for willful violations.

79 Unlawful collection actions may be found to be unfair trade practices, under state unfair trade practice statutes and regulations, giving rise to a damage claim. In this case, contacting the debtor both after notice of representation by counsel and also after notice of the stay could be considered unfair practices.

Form 25 Motion Seeking Relief for Violations of the Automatic Stay by Governmental Agency[80]

[*Caption: Official Form 16A*]

Motion for Contempt for Violations of the Automatic Stay

Debtor, [*debtor*], by his counsel, hereby requests that this Court hold Respondents [*first respondent*], [*second respondent*], [*third respondent*], and the Veterans Administration in contempt of Court, assigning the following reasons therefore:

I.

1. Debtor [*name*] is an individual residing at [*address*].

2. Respondent [*first respondent*], is Chief of the Finance Division of the Veterans Administration's Regional Office located at [*address*]. As such, he is responsible for administering the payment of claims for veterans' pension benefits in the Philadelphia area.

3. Respondent [*second respondent*] is the Director of the Veterans Administration's Regional Office located at [*address*]. As such, he is the head regional officer responsible for administering the payment of veterans' pension benefits in the Philadelphia area.

4. Respondent [*third respondent*] is the Administrator of Veterans' Affairs, the chief administrative officer of the Veterans Administration. Her office is located in Washington, D.C.

5. Respondent Veterans Administration (hereinafter referred to as "VA") is an agency of the United States whose principal office is in Washington, D.C. and which has the responsibility of administering veterans' pension benefits.

II.

6. Prior to March 2004, Debtor was receiving monthly veterans' disability pension benefits in the amount of five hundred sixteen dollars ($516.00).

7. On February 9, 2004, the VA Center in Philadelphia sent him a notice that the recent adjustment in his benefits resulted in an overpayment of one thousand three hundred fifty-six dollars and thirty-seven cents ($1356.37).

8. On July 7, 2004, Respondent [*first respondent*] sent Debtor a letter advising him that his overpayment totaled two thousand nine hundred fifty-eight dollars and eighty-seven cents ($2958.87) without any explanation of the basis for the new figure.

9. From April 2004 until the present, Respondents have completely withheld payment of Debtor's veterans' disability pension benefits in an effort to collect from Debtor the alleged overpayment.

10. Because the VA ceased sending the Debtor his benefit checks, the Debtor was forced to obtain welfare benefits of only two hundred sixty-two dollars ($262.00) per month and was unable to meet his expenses and his bills.

11. On September 23, 2004, Debtor filed a voluntary petition in bankruptcy under chapter 7 in this Court.

12. In Schedule A-3 accompanying the petition, Debtor listed an unsecured debt to the VA in the amount of two thousand nine hundred fifty-eight dollars and eighty-seven cents ($2958.87).

13. By certified letter on September 25, 2004, Debtor's counsel informed Respondents of the filing of the bankruptcy petition and Respondents' obligation to cease all efforts to recover the alleged overpayment. (A copy of this letter is attached hereto as "Exhibit A.")

14. Despite the filing of the bankruptcy petition and the notice thereof given to Respondents, Respondents nevertheless withheld Debtor's veterans' disability benefits in October, 2004.

15. By certified letter on October 26, 2004, Debtor's counsel advised respondents that the withholding of Debtor's checks was unlawful and informed Respondents that unless the monthly benefits were restored by November 1, 2004, Debtor would seek a remedy in this Court. (A copy of this letter is attached hereto as "Exhibit B" [*omitted*].)

16. To date, Respondents have neither responded to the above letters nor resumed payment of Debtor's monthly benefits.

17. Due to the interruption of his benefits, Debtor has been unable to meet his expenses for his basic life necessities such as food, shelter and utilities.

III.

18. By continuing to withhold payment of Debtor's veterans' disability pension checks in order to collect the alleged overpayment from Debtor, Respondents have violated the automatic stay provisions of the Bankruptcy Code, including but not limited to:

a. 11 U.S.C. § 362(a)(1); and

b. 11 U.S.C. § 362(a)(6).

IV.

19. Debtor requests that this Court:

a. Hold Respondents in contempt of court for violating 11 U.S.C. § 362;

b. Order Respondents to restore Debtor's October and November, 2004 benefits within ten (10) days;

c. Fine Respondents if benefits have not been restored within ten (10) days in an amount necessary to compensate for damages to the Debtor;

---

80 A motion such as this one may be used to enforce the automatic stay in cases in which, after a petition has been filed, a government agency refuses to cease recouping benefits on account of a pre-bankruptcy overpayment. The debtor may also wish to request relief under 11 U.S.C. § 362(h). A complaint is not normally necessary, because the injunction of the automatic stay is already in effect and no further injunction need be sought. The motion procedure has been held to meet the requirements of due process. *See, e.g., In re* Zumbrun, 88 B.R. 250 (B.A.P. 9th Cir. 1988). However, it may be advantageous in some cases to seek injunctive or declaratory relief and use the slightly greater formality of an adversary proceeding. Many courts will also desire proposed orders to be presented with all motions. Local practice should be checked.

See general discussion of the automatic stay in Chapter 9, *supra*, and of public benefit overpayment dischargeability in § 14.5.5.4, *supra*. See also Form 79, Appendix G.9, *infra*, seeking to recover funds withheld through pre-bankruptcy recoupments.

A further issue in cases involving government defendants is sovereign immunity. These issues are discussed in §§ 9.6 and 13.3.2.2, *supra*.

d. Award compensatory and punitive damages, sanctions and attorney fees for contempt of court and pursuant to 11 U.S.C. § 362(h) to the Debtor;[81] and

e. Order all other relief as is just and proper.

Date: [*signature*]
                                              Attorney for Debtor

"Exhibit A"

Veterans Administration
[*address*]
Attn: [*first respondent*], Chief, Finance Division
                                          Re: [*debtor*]
                                          [*address*]
                                          [*social security no.*]

Dear Mr. [*name*]:

Please be advised that I represent the above-captioned individual who has filed a voluntary petition in bankruptcy in the [*district name*] District of [*state*]. The petition, Bankruptcy No. [*number*], was filed on September 23, 2004 and a copy is enclosed.

The Veterans Administration (VA), which has claimed that it overpaid [*debtor*], is listed as a creditor in this Petition. Pursuant to the automatic stay provisions of the Bankruptcy Code, 11 U.S.C. § 362, the filing of a Petition operates as a stay of any action to collect or recover a claim against [*debtor*] that arose before the filing of the Petition. Accordingly, the VA is obligated to cease all efforts to recover the overpayment and may not reduce [*debtor*]'s monthly benefit check to recoup the overpayment.

This means that the VA must reinstate his monthly benefit check immediately.

If you have any questions concerning your legal obligations set forth above, please contact me.

                                             [*signature*]
                                          Attorney for Debtor

Form 26 Motion for Expedited Hearing on Contempt Motion[82]

[*Caption: Official Form 16A*]

Motion for Expedited Hearing

Debtor, [*name*], by his counsel, hereby requests that the Bankruptcy Court hold an expedited hearing upon his Motion to hold the Veterans Administration (VA) and various VA officials in contempt for violating the automatic stay provisions of 11 U.S.C. § 362(a) and assigns the following reasons for this request:

1. Debtor has filed a Motion for Contempt with the Court directed against the VA and various VA officials;

2. The VA claims to have overpaid the Debtor and is therefore a creditor of the Debtor;

3. Prior to the overpayment claim, the Debtor had been receiving disability benefits from the VA;

4. The VA has been and continues to withhold the Debtor's entire monthly benefit check in order to recover on its overpayment claim even after receiving notification of the Debtor's filing of a bankruptcy petition;

5. The complete cessation of disability benefits by the VA contravenes the automatic stay provisions of 11 U.S.C. § 362(a);

6. The actions of the VA have forced the Debtor, his wife and her daughter to go on welfare which only provides them with two hundred sixty-two dollars ($262.00) per month;

7. These welfare benefits are insufficient for the needs of the Debtor and his family;

8. The Debtor needs a prompt hearing on his Motion for Contempt so that, if the motion is granted, he can resume receiving his proper monthly benefits.

WHEREFORE, Debtor requests that he be granted an expedited hearing on his Motion for Contempt.

Date: [*signature*]
                                              Attorney for Debtor

---

81 Given that section 106(a)(3) prohibits an award of punitive damages, relief in this case might be limited to compensatory damages. However, because the exclusion for "punitive damages" found in this section should be given its normal meaning and not be read to prohibit all monetary sanctions that are not compensatory in nature, the debtor should still seek an award of "sanctions" for contempt. Also, if section 106(a)(3) is construed simply as an exception to the abrogation of sovereign immunity, an award of punitive damages may still be appropriate against some governmental units, such as municipalities, which never had immunity, or in actions for contempt, in which sovereign immunity is generally not implicated.

Section 106(a)(3) also limits awards of attorney fees and costs to those available under 28 U.S.C. § 2412(d)(2)(A) (Equal Access to Justice Act). Once again, it can be argued that this provision is simply an exception to the abrogation of sovereign immunity and therefore not applicable to entities which would not ordinarily have immunity or in situations such as contempt of court. Moreover, as 28 U.S.C. § 2412(d)(2)(A) applies only to claims against the federal government, section 106(a)(3) would seem not to apply to fees awarded against state and local governments. See discussion of sovereign immunity in §§ 9.6, 13.3.2.2, *supra*.

---

82 When cases involve funds used by the debtor for the basic expenses of daily life, expedited relief may be necessary, depending upon the timetable of a particular court for hearing motions. The motion for expedited relief presented here can be used in these circumstances, or in any situation in which it is important that a motion be heard quickly. The debtor should also give the other parties prompt notice of such a motion. In an adversary proceeding it would be necessary to seek a temporary restraining order or a preliminary injunction.

Form 27 Complaint Seeking Contempt Remedies and Recovery of Property from IRS[83]

[*Caption: Official Form 16D*]

Complaint

1. This Complaint seeks to remedy a violation of the automatic stay due to the seizure of the Debtors' income tax refund by Defendant to collect on a pre-petition debt.

2. This Court has jurisdiction over this matter pursuant to 28 U.S.C. § 1334. This matter is a core proceeding.

3. The Debtors filed a petition under chapter 7 on March 10, 2004.

4. On May 28, 2004 the Debtors were sent a notice by defendant Internal Revenue Service (IRS) informing them that an income tax refund of $625.00 due to them had been seized by the IRS to partially satisfy a pre-petition debt to the Department of Education.[84] A copy of that notice is attached hereto as Exhibit A [*omitted*].

5. On June 15, 2004 the Debtors' counsel sent a letter to Defendant Internal Revenue Service advising it of the bankruptcy, demanding return of the funds that had been seized and that there be no further seizures. A copy of that letter is attached as Exhibit B [*omitted*].

6. Despite that letter, Defendants have failed to return the money which was seized from the Debtor.

7. Once Defendant IRS was notified of the bankruptcy, its failure to rectify its violation of the stay was a willful violation of the stay.

8. The monies seized were property of the Debtors' estate, claimed as exempt, and the transfer is avoidable under 11 U.S.C. §§ 522(h) and 549. The transfer is also avoidable as a remedy for the defendant's contempt.

WHEREFORE, the Debtors pray that the Court order that:

1. Defendant IRS return to the Debtors all of the monies seized by them;

2. Defendant IRS be held in contempt of Court;

3. Defendant IRS pay damages and attorney fees to the Debtors; and

4. Such other relief as is just and proper.

Date: [*signature*]

                             Attorney for Debtors/Plaintiffs

Form 28 Answer to Motion for Relief from Automatic Stay[85]

[*Caption: Official Form 16A*]

Answer to Motion of [*name*] Finance Company For Relief from Automatic Stay[86]

The Debtors in this matter, by counsel, answer the Motion for Relief from Stay of [*name*] Finance Company as follows:

First Defense[87]

Paragraphs 1 and 2 are admitted. It is also admitted that the liens averred are presently recorded. All of the remaining factual allegations are denied.

Second Defense

By way of recoupment the Debtors have the following claim under the Truth in Lending Act, 15 U.S.C. §§ 1601–1666j ("Act"). This claim, when offset against Movant's claim reduces the amount owing to Movant to zero:[88]

1. Movant [*name*] Finance Company, in the ordinary course of its business, regularly extends consumer credit to its customers.

2. On or about November 9, 1998, the Debtors entered into a consumer credit transaction with [*name*] Finance Company, the terms of which are embodied in the Note, Security Agreement and Disclosure Statement attached hereto as Exhibit A [*omitted*].

---

83 A complaint for contempt may be pursued in a case against a government entity when there are still concerns, even after the 1994 amendments to section 106(a), that a sovereign immunity defense might limit the statutory remedies under 11 U.S.C. § 362(h). Under section 106(a), sovereign immunity is expressly abrogated with respect to a broad range of statutory provisions, including virtually all of the provisions which normally give rise to claims against the government in bankruptcy. Both federal sovereign immunity and state Eleventh Amendment immunity were abrogated by the amendments, thus overruling *Hoffman v. Connecticut Department of Income Maintenance* and *United States v. Nordic Village Inc.* Because of the potential limitations on punitive damages and attorney fees when sovereign immunity is implicated, as discussed in the notes to Form 25, Appendix G.4, *supra*, it is advisable to include a contempt claim when appropriate. *See also* § 13.3.2.2, *supra*. The ability of Congress to abrogate the states' Eleventh Amendment immunity was severely limited by the Supreme Court's decision in Seminole Tribe of Florida v. Florida, 517 U.S. 44, 116 S. Ct. 1114, 134 L. Ed. 2d 252 (1996) so it is questionable whether the provisions of section 106 abrogating states' immunity from suit are valid.

There is another alternative for avoiding federal sovereign immunity under the "Tucker" Act and the "Little Tucker" Act, 28 U.S.C. §§ 1491, 1346(a)(2). *See* § 13.3.2.2, *supra*.

84 The debtor may seek to recover that amount as an unauthorized post-petition transfer. *See* § 10.4.2.6.6, *supra*. It is now clear that such a claim for recovery of property using the trustee's avoiding powers would not be barred by a sovereign immunity defense under section 106(a) of the Code. The sovereign immunity issues need to be reviewed carefully in each instance because they may, in part, preclude the debtor's claim to recover property using the trustee's avoiding powers. *See* § 13.3.2.2, *supra*.

85 For a general discussion of tactics in responding to a motion seeking relief from the automatic stay, see § 9.7.3, *supra*. If an answer is filed, the following considerations are pertinent.

86 The title of the pleading should specify the particular motion to which it responds.

87 No answer to the motion for relief from the automatic stay is required unless the Court orders otherwise. Fed. R. Bankr. P. 9014. Sometimes it is still advisable to file one, even when not required, to define the issues as the debtor wishes. Factual allegations may be denied as a first defense. Federal practice requires only a general denial with respect to facts which are not admitted.

88 A defense or counterclaim to the creditor's claim should be at least considered, if not actually decided, in the stay litigation, because it is necessary to determine what interest the creditor has before it can be decided whether there is adequate protection or cause for relief from the stay. See discussion of defenses and counterclaims in § 9.7.3.1.3, *supra*.

3. In the course of this transaction, Movant violated the Act and Regulation Z, 12 C.F.R. § 226, by failing to clearly and conspicuously make numerous required disclosures, including but not limited to:

    a. The correct finance charge;

    b. The correct annual percentage rate;

    c. The correct amount financed;

    d. The security interests taken.

4. By reason of these violations, Movant is indebted to Debtors in the amount of $2000.00, under 15 U.S.C. § 1640.

Third Defense

This Court may not hear this matter in that the motion was not properly served upon Debtors as required by the Federal Rules of Bankruptcy Procedure.[89]

Fourth Defense

The mortgage held by Movant is invalid in that it should have been terminated upon the Debtors' rescission of the transaction pursuant to the Truth in Lending Act, 15 U.S.C. § 1635.[90]

Fifth Defense

The Debtors have substantial equity in their property and Movant has been afforded adequate protection of its interest.[91]

Sixth Defense

Even if Movant is entitled to relief from the stay, the stay should not be terminated. The Court should grant less drastic relief by conditioning or modifying the stay.[92]

Seventh Defense

Movant has not shown the irreparable harm necessary to justify lifting the stay with respect to its foreclosure.[93]

Eighth Defense

Movant's motion is barred by laches.[94]

Ninth Defense

Movant is not entitled to the relief it seeks because its lien is subject to avoidance under 11 U.S.C. § 506 [*or other applicable code provision*].[95]

---

89 See Fed. R. Bankr. P. 8011, 9013 and local rules related to service of motions. Defenses based on jurisdiction may be raised in the answer to the motion. The defense of jurisdiction over the person or improper service is probably waived if not raised.

90 If the party seeking relief from the stay has no interest deserving of protection, then relief should not be granted.

91 For discussion of adequate protection see § 9.7.3.2.2, *supra*.

92 The court does not have to terminate the stay if the prerequisites of 11 U.S.C. § 362(d) are met. It may maintain the stay and simply modify or condition it.

93 Irreparable harm is a general concept applicable to injunction proceedings including, presumably, those concerning the automatic stay.

94 While laches is probably not a strong defense in most cases, pointing out the movant's delay may vitiate the court's concern as to the urgency of the matter.

95 *See* § 10.4.2, *supra*. Although counterclaims may not be asserted in response to a motion, it is often advisable to file a

WHEREFORE, Debtors pray that the motion be dismissed.

Date: [*signature*]
                                    Attorney for Debtors

Form 29 Motion for Sanctions Pursuant to Rule 9011 for Baseless Motion for Relief from Automatic Stay[96]

[Caption: Official Form 16A]

Motion for Sanctions Against [*name*] Mortgage Company For Filing Baseless Motion for Relief[97]

Debtor, [*debtor*], hereby moves this Court for an order imposing sanctions on [*name*] Mortgage Company and its attorneys pursuant to Fed. R. Bankr. P. 9011. In support of this motion, Debtor states the following:

1. The Debtor filed the instant voluntary petition under chapter 13 of the Bankruptcy Code on [*date*].

2. [*name*] Mortgage Company is the current holder [*or servicer*] of the mortgage on the debtor's home.

3. The Debtor has made all payments required under her chapter 13 Plan, which was confirmed on [*date*].

4. [*name*] Mortgage Company filed a motion for relief from the automatic stay on or about [*date*], alleging that the Debtor has failed to make her ongoing post-petition mortgage payments. Specifically, [*name*] Mortgage Company alleged that the debtor failed to make the monthly payments due for [*months*].

5. As will be proven by the Debtor at the hearing on the motion for relief, the allegations contained in [*name*] Mortgage Company's motion were made without evidentiary support and without conducting an inquiry reasonable under the circumstances.

6. As a result of [*name*] Mortgage Company's baseless motion, the Debtor has had to incur costs and attorney fees, and has had to take time from work to meet with her attorney, in order to respond

---

    complaint raising the debtor's claims and seek its consolidation with the stay litigation. Special care on these issues is required because of the time constraints placed upon the court by 11 U.S.C. § 362(e). It may be critical to raise and/or prove that the lien could be avoided in response to the creditor's motion for relief. *See In re* Munoz, 83 B.R. 334 (Bankr. E.D. Pa. 1988); Form 31, Appx. G.4, *infra*.

96 Attorneys and unrepresented creditors who file motions for relief without a proper legal or factual basis may be subject to sanctions under Fed. R. Bankr. P. 9011. A creditor may be subject to Rule 9011 sanctions without signing a pleading or court document if it has provided false information or failed to correct false information used by its attorney. *See In re* Kilgore, 253 B.R. 179 (Bankr. D.S.C. 2000).

97 This motion may be served along with an answer to the motion for relief (Form 28, Appx. G.4, *supra*), but may not be filed earlier than twenty-one days before it has been served on the respondent, who may withdraw or correct the motion for relief during that time. *See* Fed. R. Bankr. P. 9011(c)(1)(A). It may be advisable for the debtor to seek a continuance of any hearing on the motion for relief scheduled during the twenty-one-day period to allow time for the safe-harbor period to pass. The creditor's failure to provide discovery or responses to a "qualified written request" under RESPA (see Form 69, Appx. G.8, *infra*) may provide the grounds for requesting an extension.

to the motion and prepare for the upcoming hearing on stay relief. The Debtor has also suffered emotional distress based on the threatened loss of her home.

WHEREFORE, based on this Court's authority under Fed. R. Bankr. P. 9011, section 105 of the Bankruptcy Code, and 28 U.S.C. § 1927, the Debtor requests this Court impose sanctions against [*name*] Mortgage Company and its attorneys and award Debtor damages, costs, attorney fees, and such other relief as is just and proper.

Date: [*signature*]
                                         Attorney for Debtors

Form 30 Answer to Motion of Landlord for Relief from Automatic Stay[98]

[*Caption: Official Form 16A*]

Answer to Motion of Landlord for Relief from Automatic Stay

1. Admitted.
2. Admitted.
3. Admitted.
4. Admitted.
5. Admitted.
6. Admitted.
7. Denied insofar as the averment states the conclusion of law that the Debtor has "failed" to pay rent. Admitted insofar as it is alleged that the Debtor has not paid the monthly rental of $100.00 since August, 2003, up to and including the present time.[99]
8. Denied insofar as it is alleged that "on or about December 16, 2003 . . ." the Movant filed a claim. Movant filed his claim in municipal court on December 3, 2003. Denied insofar as it is averred that "He [movant] obtained a judgment for rent then due and possession requiring the tenant to vacate within five (5) days." Debtor alleges that the judgment, if any, was void on its face. Debtor is without knowledge or information sufficient to form a response to the allegation that the alleged judgment required "the tenant to vacate within five (5) days."
9. Admitted.
10. Admitted.

---

98 A request for relief from the automatic stay is made by motion, Fed. R. Bankr. P. 4001, 9014, and no answer is required unless the court orders otherwise. In many jurisdictions, however, the court issues an order requiring an answer and indicates that relief will otherwise be ordered by default. Other jurisdictions require an answer by local rule. For these reasons an answer to a motion for relief is generally advisable. A counterclaim is not permissible, but a companion adversary proceeding may be advisable. See § 9.7.3, *supra*, for discussion of defending against motions for relief from the automatic stay and the possible defenses in landlord-tenant cases. This answer shows how appropriate landlord-tenant claims may be raised in this context for resolution by the bankruptcy court. Obviously, other claims and defenses may be applicable to particular cases. This form is adapted from pleadings in *In re* Lewis, 15 B.R. 643 (Bankr. E.D. Pa. 1981).

99 Paragraph 7 contains very specific denials of facts alleged. Such specific denials are not required under federal pleading rules but may be made if counsel wishes to emphasize assertions contrary to those in the motion.

Affirmative Defenses

First Affirmative Defense: Movant's Interest in the Property Is Adequately Protected and Movant Has No Cause for Relief from the Stay

11. The Movant filed a Certificate of Registration with the [*city*] Department of Licenses And Inspections on December 2, 2003, pursuant to [*city*] Housing Code [*cite provision of local housing code*].
12. The Movant filed a Landlord and Tenant Complaint in Municipal Court, Claim No. [*number*], on December 3, 2003, referring in his Complaint to the December 2, 2003 registration date. A copy of the Landlord and Tenant Complaint is attached hereto as "Exhibit A" [*omitted*]. The complaint sets forth, *inter alia*, a claim for rent from August, 2003 to December, 2003 totalling $500.00.
13. On December 8, 2003 Inspector [*name*] of the City of [*city*] Department of Licenses And Inspections visited [*address of property*] and conducted an inspection of the building for housing code violations.
14. On December 12, 2003 Inspector [*name*] issued a Violation Notice to Movant, which listed thirteen (13) violations of the [*city*] Code of General Ordinances. A copy of the Violation Notice is attached hereto as "Exhibit B" [*omitted*].
15. Subsequently a hearing was held in the municipal court. Both the Movant herein and [*debtor*] appeared.
16. The Debtor alleges that at said hearing she explained to the judge the nature of the housing code violations, to which explanation the Movant offered no defenses. Debtor was instructed by the judge that no rent was due unless the housing code violations were removed.
17. On December 18, 2003, a hearing was conducted in the said Municipal Court case. The Debtor received no notice of the hearing. Judgment by default was entered in favor of the Movant.
18. On March 24, 2004, the Debtor filed a petition in bankruptcy under chapter 7.
19. On April 8, 2004, Inspector [*name*] of the City Of [*city*] Department of Licenses And Inspections conducted a re-inspection of the premises at [*address of property*].
20. Inspector [*name*] has reported that none of the thirteen violations had been removed as of April 8, 2004.
21. The Debtor has established a rent escrow account, in favor of Plaintiff, in the amount of $200.00.
22. In light of said violations of the [*city*] Housing Code the fair market value rent for [*address of property*] is forty dollars ($40.00) per month for the period in question.
23. Movant's interest in the leasehold premises is adequately protected because:
   a. The Debtor has placed $200.00 in a rent escrow account in favor of the Movant, and, if rent is due to the Movant for the time from August, 2003 to the present, that amount does not exceed $320.00.
   b. The Debtor is ready and able to deposit into the Court on a monthly basis the fair market value of the leasehold premises for the duration of the stay. Such monthly deposits should be substantially less than $100.00 each month and possibly a nominal amount. Such payments are within the Debtor's means.
   c. Because the property cannot be re-rented in case the Debtor is evicted, the Movant has no expectation of future rental

income flowing from the property until the housing code violations are removed [*cite local code provision*].

d. The Debtor's chapter 13 plan will assume the lease and promptly cure and default.[100]

24. Movant has no cause for relief from the stay because:

a. Movant's judgment for rent and possession was entered by mistake of the municipal court.

b. Movant's money judgment is void on the face of the municipal court record because the Movant has not registered for the period from August, 2003 to December 2, 2004. See "Exhibit A" [*omitted*]. Accordingly, the Municipal Court has no jurisdiction to enter a judgment for past due rent [*cite local code provision*].

c. Movant's judgment or possession is void because at the time of the alleged termination of the lease there were outstanding violations of the housing code [*cite local code provision*].

d. Movant's judgment is void in that it was entered into without giving the Debtor notice or an opportunity to defend.

Second Affirmative Defense: The Leasehold Is Necessary to an Effective Reorganization

25. Paragraphs 1 through 24 are incorporated herein by reference.

26. On August 19, 2003 the Debtor converted her chapter 7 petition in bankruptcy to a chapter 13 petition. The Debtor did so pursuant to 11 U.S.C. § 706(a).

27. The Debtor's leasehold interest in the premises and possession thereof is necessary to an effective reorganization, because the Debtor has not been able to find in the current housing market another leasehold that both fits within her limited budget and is also large enough for her family of seven. Further, if the Debtor is forced to move, then she will be forced to pay substantially more to house her family and herself. She will therefore not have the necessary resources to complete her chapter 13 plan successfully nor pay her moving expenses.

Third Affirmative Defense: Implied Warranty of Habitability

28. Paragraphs 1 through 24 are incorporated herein by reference.

29. The subject premises contain material violations of the Movant's implied warranty of habitability. Said violations, listed in "Exhibit B" attached hereto [*omitted*], render the premises uninhabitable and, accordingly, the amount of rent due should be reduced.

30. Said violations cause the liability of the Debtor for rent to be governed by the fair market value of the percentage of her leasehold interest that can be used, which is approximately forty percent (40%) of the original contract price.

31. Debtor has the right under [*cite local code provision*] law to withhold all rent and retain possession of the leasehold premises until the material breaches of the implied warranty of habitability are corrected.

Fourth Affirmative Defense: Conditioning of the Stay

32. Paragraphs 1 through 24 are incorporated herein by reference.

33. If this Honorable Court finds that relief from the stay is in order, then it is proper for this Court to order relief insofar as conditioning of the stay to continue upon the Debtor's providing adequate protection to the interest of the Movant.

34. The measure of the adequate protection should be the fair market value of the premises paid on a monthly basis pending disposition of the Debtor's petition in bankruptcy.

WHEREFORE, the Debtor prays that this Court:

1. Deny the motion for relief from the automatic stay;

2. Declare the fair rental value of the premises to be forty dollars per month;

3. Order Movant to correct all housing code violations at the premises forthwith;

4. Order any other relief that the Court deems just and proper.

Date: [*signature*]
                                          Attorney for Debtor

Form 31 Answer to Motion for Relief from Automatic Stay Raising Avoidability of Transfer to Plaintiff[101]

[Caption: Official Form 16A]

Answer to Motion of [*name*] Mortgage Company for Relief from Automatic Stay

1–4. Admitted.

5–9. It is admitted that Movant filed a complaint in mortgage foreclosure, obtained a "snap" default judgment, and that a sheriff sale was held as indicated. It is also admitted that the property was sold to the Movant. The remaining factual allegations are denied.

10–13. Admitted, except that Movant's response to the petition to open was filed on or about January 25, 2004.

14. Denied. Debtor's equity in the property is about $4000.00. Debtor's debt to Movant is less than $5000.00, and the liens set

---

100 *See* Form 14, Appx. G.3, *supra.*

---

101 A request for relief from the automatic stay is made by motion, Fed. R. Bankr. P. 4001, 9014, and no answer is required unless the Court orders otherwise. In many jurisdictions, however, the court issues an order requiring an answer and indicates that relief will otherwise be ordered by default. Other jurisdictions require an answer by local rule. For these reasons an answer to a motion for relief is generally advisable. A counterclaim is not permissible but a companion offensive adversary proceeding by the debtor may be advisable. See § 9.7.3, *supra*, for general discussion of defending against motions for relief from the automatic stay.

The debtor's defense to a motion for relief from the stay sometimes depends upon the outcome of other issues that must be litigated in the bankruptcy court, such as the avoidance of a transfer or defenses to a creditor's claim. *See generally In re* Munoz, 83 B.R. 334 (Bankr. E.D. Pa. 1988). A useful strategy is to try to consolidate all of these issues, raising the debtor's claims and defenses in the stay litigation and seeking consolidation with other cases that the debtor may have filed with the bankruptcy court.

This answer, for example, is adapted from the pleadings in *In re* Jones, 20 B.R. 988 (Bankr. E.D. Pa. 1982), a case in which the debtor avoided an earlier transfer of title to a creditor that had foreclosed on a mortgage. The avoidance of the transfer was raised by a complaint (see Form 80, Appx. G.9, *infra*). The debtor was able to successfully place before the court and litigate the complaint by consolidating that action with the stay litigation.

forth by Movant are either incorrect or subject to avoidance.

15. Denied. No transfer of Debtor's interest in the property took place as a result of the sheriff sale because the terms of the sale were not complied with prior to the order for relief in the instant bankruptcy and because the passage of title was stayed. Any transfer of Debtor's interest that might have taken place is subject to avoidance by Debtor pursuant to 11 U.S.C. §§ 522(h) and 544(a)(3) or 11 U.S.C. § 548. Debtor's equity in the property is between $3000.00 and $5000.00.[102]

16. Denied. Movant's secured claim is less than $5000.00.

17. Admitted.

18. Denied.

19. Denied. Debtor has submitted a plan and an amended plan both of which comport with the requirements of 11 U.S.C. §§ 1322 and 1325.

20. Denied. To date Movant has paid not less than $1567.65 to the standing trustee under the terms of his plans.

21. Admitted that Movant sent the letters which it attached as an exhibit to its pleading. Denied that either Debtor or his attorney have not been cooperative.

22. Denied. Debtor has submitted a plan and an amended plan in accordance with the provisions of chapter 13 of the Bankruptcy Code. Debtor has done nothing to intentionally delay the confirmation of that plan.

23. Denied. Debtor has not acted in bad faith and has caused Movant no loss, injury or damage. Movant's interest in [*address of property*] is adequately protected by both a large equity cushion in the property and by the provisions of Debtor's chapter 13 plan.

Affirmative Defenses

24. [*Address of property*] (hereinafter "the property") is [*debtor*]'s residence and has been since 1973.

25. [*Debtor*]'s interest in the property is exempt pursuant to 11 U.S.C. § 522(d)(1) and (d)(5) to the extent that the value of that interest does not exceed $15,800.00.

26. On or about September 10, 2002, the fair market value of the property was not less than $15,000.00.

27. At the September 10, 2002, sheriff's sale, [*debtor*]'s home was "sold" to Movant's attorney on the writ for a "bid" of $5800.00, plus settlement costs.

28. Any transfer of the Debtor's interest in the property was stayed by an order signed by the Honorable [*judge*] on October 5, 2002.

29. Notice of Debtor's bankruptcy petition was given Movant by letter to its attorney dated January 29, 2003.

30. As of the date of the bankruptcy, [*debtor*] held at least record legal title to the property with a right to possession subject to the mortgage and judgment of Movant and to the contingent equitable interest of Movant as the prevailing execution bidder.

31. As of the date of the filing the terms of the sheriff's sale had not been complied with, as part of the sheriff's fees remained unpaid.

32. On January 24, 2003, pursuant to 11 U.S.C. § 541(a)(1) and (a)(7), Debtor's interest in the property became a part of his estate in bankruptcy.

33. On March 6, 2003, the Honorable [*judge*], Judge of the [*name*] Court issued an order authorizing a deed transferring title to the Debtor's home to Movant's assignee.

34. Said order, to the extent it authorized a transfer of Debtor's interest in the property, was violative of 11 U.S.C. § 362(a)(1), (a)(2) and (a)(3).

35. On or about March 25, 2003, Movant, by its attorney, in violation of 11 U.S.C. § 362(a)(1), (a)(2) and (a)(3), completed the terms of the sheriff's sale, and had the sheriff issue a deed purporting to transfer title to the property to the Veterans Administration ("V.A.").

36. A deed purporting to transfer title to the property to the V.A. was recorded May 22, 2003.

37. By letter to Movant, the V.A. refused to accept the deed to the property.

38. The purported transfer of title to the property to the V.A. is void or avoidable for each of the following reasons:

a. The transfer was refused by the V.A.;

b. The purported transfer was accomplished at Movant's insistence in violation of the injunction found in 11 U.S.C. § 362(a)(1), (2), (3), (4), (5) and (6); and

c. The transfer was accomplished after the commencement of the bankruptcy but was not authorized under the Bankruptcy Code or by order of the Bankruptcy Court, 11 U.S.C. § 549(a).

39. Pursuant to 11 U.S.C. §§ 522(h) and 544(a)(3), any transfer of Debtor's interest in the property that may have occurred by virtue of said sheriff's sale may be avoided by Debtor.

40. Any transfer of Debtor's interest in the property which may have occurred by virtue of the sheriff's sale may also be avoided by Debtor pursuant to 11 U.S.C. §§ 522(h) and 548(a)(2)(A) and (B)(i) as a fraudulent conveyance.[103]

41. Debtor's continued use and occupancy of the property is necessary for Debtor's completion of his chapter 13 plan.

42. Movant's interest in the property is adequately protected in that Movant has the first lien on the property and the fair market value of the property is at least $6000.00 more than Movant's lien.

43. Movant's request for relief from the automatic stay is barred by laches in that it waited almost eighteen months before requesting relief.

44. Movant has not shown the irreparable harm necessary to justify lifting the stay.

45. Even if Movant is entitled to relief from the stay the stay should not be terminated; the stay may be modified or conditioned to insure Movant any protection which it may lack.

WHEREFORE, Debtor prays that the motion be denied.

Date: [*signature*]
                                          Attorney for Debtor

---

102 The use of section 548(a) to avoid sheriffs' or foreclosure sales for less than reasonably equivalent value was drastically curtailed by the Supreme Court in *BFP v. Resolution Trust Co.* For further discussion of this issue, see § 10.4.2.6.5, *supra*.

103 The use of section 548(a) to avoid sheriffs' or foreclosure sales for less than reasonably equivalent value was drastically curtailed by the Supreme Court in *BFP v. Resolution Trust Co.* For further discussion of this issue, see § 10.4.2.6.5, *supra*.

Form 32 Debtor's Answer to Motion for Relief from Codebtor Stay[104]

[Caption: Official Form 16A]

Debtor's Answer to [*name*] Credit Company's Motion for Relief from the Codebtor Stay

The Debtor, by her counsel, hereby answers [*name*] Credit Company's Motion for Relief from the Codebtor Stay as follows:

1. Admitted that the Debtor's plan provides for total payments of $1500.00 to [*name*] Credit Company.

2. Denied that [*name*] Credit Company's claim is $2500.00. The claim is only $1500.00 because it must be reduced by the Debtor's Truth in Lending Act recoupment claim of $1000.00.[105] An objection to [*name*] Credit Company's claim has already been filed with this Court.[106]

3. Denied that amount will not pay the claim of [*name*] Credit Company in full. On the contrary, [*name*] Credit Company's claim is only $1500.00 for the reasons set forth above.

WHEREFORE, the Debtor prays that the Motion for Relief from the Codebtor Stay be denied.

Date: *[signature]*
                                             Attorney for Debtor

Form 33 Debtor's Objection to Relief from the Co-debtor Stay[107]

[Caption: Official Form 16A]

Debtor's Objection to Relief From the Co-debtor Stay

[*Debtor*], Debtor in the above-captioned case, hereby objects to the action proposed in [*name*] Credit Company's Motion for Relief from the Co-debtor Stay.

Date: *[signature]*
                                             Attorney for Debtor

Form 34 Answer to Application for Abandonment of Real Estate[108]

[Caption: Official Form 16A]

Debtor's Answer to Application for Abandonment of Real Estate Pursuant to Section 554 of the Bankruptcy Code

1. Admitted.
2. Admitted.
3. Admitted.
4. Admitted.
5. Admitted.
6. a. Admitted.
   b. Admitted.
   c. Admitted.
   d. Admitted.
   e. Admitted.
   f. Denied.
7. Denied.
8. Denied.
9. Denied.
10. Denied.

First Defense

11. The encumbrances which have priority over the mortgage of [*creditor*] (hereinafter "Creditor") secure debts in excess of the fair market value of Debtor's real estate.

12. Accordingly, Creditor's lien is void pursuant to 11 U.S.C. § 506(d) and its claim is a general unsecured claim.

13. On January 6, 2004, Debtor filed a complaint in this Court seeking relief under 11 U.S.C. § 506. [*debtor*] v. [*creditor*], Bankruptcy No. [*number*], Adversary No. [*number*].

14. Creditor is not a party in interest under 11 U.S.C. § 554 and has no standing to seek an order of abandonment.[109]

---

104 The most common ground for creditors seeking relief from the codebtor stay is that the plan does not propose to pay their claims in full. 11 U.S.C. § 1301(c)(2). On this ground only, if the debtor does not file and serve a "written objection" to the creditor's motion within twenty days after it is filed, relief from the co-debtor stay is automatic, without the necessity of the creditor taking a default. 11 U.S.C. § 1301(d). Although a formal answer may not be necessary, it is often a good idea to set forth the debtor's case. *But see* Form 33, Appx. G.4, *infra.*

105 The most likely cause of a dispute over whether a claim will be paid in full is a dispute over the amount of the claim. Debtors' defenses, such as recoupment under the Truth in Lending Act, will not be readily recognized by creditors.

106 It is usually good strategy to take the offensive against a creditor that has filed or is likely to file for relief from the stay, by filing a proceeding against the creditor, which can usually then be consolidated with the stay proceeding.

107 If no formal answer to a motion for relief from the co-debtor stay is ordered by the court or desired by debtor's counsel, an objection such as this one, filed and served on the creditor requesting relief within twenty days, will prevent the automatic relief from the stay otherwise provided by 11 U.S.C. § 1301(d).

108 As discussed in Chapters 9 and 11, *supra*, creditors sometimes try to avoid the requirements of 11 U.S.C. § 362 by seeking the abandonment of property in which they claim an interest. An answer to such an application or motion may not always be required under Fed. R. Bankr. P. 9014. Under Fed. R. Bankr. P. 6007, when abandonment is sought by a creditor, a hearing is not required if it is not requested or if an answer or objection is not filed. Thus, if the debtor wishes to raise specific defenses, it is often a good idea to file an answer in any case.

Besides the general argument that abandonment cannot be a substitute for the lifting of the stay (the debtor is usually still protected after abandonment by 11 U.S.C. § 362(a)(5)) this pleading illustrates other defenses which may be raised. This form is adapted from litigation documents provided by Eric L. Frank, Esq., Philadelphia, PA.

109 This defense is based upon the voidness of a lien under 11 U.S.C. § 506(d). An unsecured creditor has no interest in seeking abandonment of property unless, perhaps, the property is burdensome to the estate so as to reduce that creditor's potential dividend. Only a "party in interest" may seek abandonment under 11 U.S.C. § 554(b). Counsel should note that this defense may no longer be available to the debtor in a chapter 7 case in light of the Supreme Court's decision in *Dewsnup v. Timm. See* § 11.2, *supra.*

Second Defense

15. Debtor resides at [*address*] with her five dependent children.

16. This property has been claimed as exempt property pursuant to 11 U.S.C. § 522(d)(1).

17. It would be inappropriate to abandon said property during the pendency of this case because the property is necessary to the rehabilitation of the Debtor.[110]

Third Defense

18. The trustee is a necessary party to an application for abandonment pursuant to 11 U.S.C. § 554.

19. The trustee has not been joined in nor notified of this proceeding.[111]

WHEREFORE, Debtor requests that this Court deny the application for abandonment.

Date: [*signature*]
                           Attorney for Debtor

Form 35 Motion to Reimpose Stay After Relief from Stay Has Been Granted[112]

[Caption: Official Form 16A]

Debtor's Motion for Reimposition of Stay as to Property of the Estate

Debtor hereby moves for reimposition of a stay with respect to her residential property at [*address*] which is property of the estate, and in support thereof avers as follows:

1. On August 21, 2003, this court entered an Order terminating the automatic stay with respect to the Debtor's residence in favor of [*name*] Mortgage Company ("Mortgage Company").

2. The Debtor's residence is and at all times relevant to this case has been an asset included in the Debtor's bankruptcy estate.

3. The Order granting relief from the stay was based solely on evidence that the Debtor did not have property insurance covering

the interest of Mortgage Company in the property. The Court found that the interest of Mortgage Company was not adequately protected.

4. As set forth in the accompanying affidavit of the Debtor, as of the date of this motion the debtor has obtained insurance covering Mortgage Company's interest in the Debtor's residence. A copy of the insurance policy is attached to this motion as Exhibit A [*omitted*].

5. To the extent that Mortgage Company has an interest in the debtor's estate, such interest is adequately protected pursuant to the Bankruptcy Code.

WHEREFORE, the Debtor requests that this Court reimpose a stay applicable to [*name*] Mortgage Company protecting the Debtor's residence.

Date: [*signature*]
                           Attorney for Debtor

G.5 Turnover of Property

Form 36 Letter Demanding Turnover of Property[113]

[*creditor*] Motors[114]
[*address*]

                         Re: [*debtor*]
              Bankruptcy No. [*number*]
                    [*address*]
           [*social security number*]

Dear Sir/Madam:

Please be advised that I represent [*debtor*], who has filed a chapter 13 bankruptcy petition with the United States Bankruptcy Court. [*Debtor*] informs me that you are presently holding property of hers, namely a 1998 Volkswagen. Pursuant to section 542 of the Bankruptcy Code, you are obligated to turn that property over immediately to either the chapter 13 trustee or [*debtor*], as that property has been claimed as exempt.

Please call me if you wish to discuss this, or arrange for the transfer of the property.

                        [*signature*]
                          Attorney for Debtor

---

110 Property may be abandoned if it is burdensome to the estate or of inconsequential value to the estate. Because exempt property is property of the estate under the Bankruptcy Code (see Ch. 10, *supra*), a broad reading of value to estate should include value, as exempt property, to the debtor's rehabilitation, particularly in a chapter 13 case.

111 If a necessary party is not joined to an adversary proceeding, the action may be dismissed. Fed. R. Bankr. P. 7019. Similar considerations can be applied here, because the trustee must ultimately be the party subject to the court's order to abandon under 11 U.S.C. § 554(b).

112 In some cases after stay relief has been granted, the debtor may have grounds to have the stay reimposed. Usually this means that the debtor will have remedied whatever problem served as grounds for relief from the stay in the first instance. In some jurisdictions, courts will enter an order vacating the order granting relief from stay; others will simply enter an order reimposing the "automatic stay," and finally some courts will enter a new "non-automatic" stay applicable to the creditor pursuant to 11 U.S.C. § 105. These last courts recognize that the reimposed stay is not automatic and they generally look to general equitable standards for granting a stay. *See* § 9.4.6, *supra*.

113 This letter may be used in situations such as when property has been repossessed or is being held pursuant to a possessory lien. It may lead to the possessor requesting adequate protection of its interest in the property. See generally the discussion of turnover requirements in § 9.9, *supra*. Often the creditor will agree to return the property to the debtor rather than go through the trustee. It is clear in chapter 13 cases that the debtor has the right to possess the property while the case is pending. 11 U.S.C. § 1306(b).

114 For purposes of proof, it may be advantageous to send this type of letter by certified mail.

Form 37 Complaint Seeking Turnover of Property[115]

[Caption: Official Form 16D][116]

Complaint Seeking Turnover of Property Pursuant to 11 U.S.C. § 542

1. Plaintiff is the Debtor in the above-captioned chapter 13 case. This Court thus has jurisdiction over this proceeding, which arises in a case under the Bankruptcy Code and concerns property of the Debtor, pursuant to 28 U.S.C. § 1334. This proceeding is a core proceeding.

2. Certain of Plaintiff's exempt property, which is property of the estate as defined by 11 U.S.C. § 541, to wit, an automobile in which she has an interest, is in the possession of Defendant.

3. At the time her petition was filed, Debtor gave notice of the filing to Defendant, a copy of which is attached hereto as Exhibit A [*omitted*].[117]

4. Upon receipt of this notice, Defendant was required pursuant to 11 U.S.C. § 542, to turn over this exempt property to the trustee in this case.

5. The trustee has not acted to recover this exempt property of the Debtor.

6. Under 11 U.S.C. § 1306, the Debtor is entitled to possession of all property of the estate.[118]

7. Plaintiff has offered to provide adequate protection for the interest of Defendant through the purchase of collision insurance, providing a replacement lien on the property, and cash payments in excess of any depreciation.[119]

8. Nonetheless, Defendant has refused to turn over the property as required by 11 U.S.C. § 542.

WHEREFORE, Plaintiff prays that this Court:

a. Order Defendant forthwith to turn over Debtor's automobile to the trustee or the Debtor;

b. Find that Defendant is in contempt of Court for violating 11 U.S.C. §§ 362 and 542;[120]

c. Award Plaintiff, pursuant to 11 U.S.C. §§ 105(a) and 362(h) damages, reasonable attorney fees, costs, and punitive damages for this complaint;[121] and

d. Order such other relief as is just and proper.

Date: *[signature]*
Attorney for Debtor

Form 38 Motion for Enforcement of Turnover Order and to Hold Defendant in Contempt of Court[122]

[Caption: Official Form 16D][123]

Motion for Enforcement of Turnover Order and to Hold Defendant in Contempt of Court

The Plaintiffs, [*debtors*], Debtors in the above-captioned bankruptcy case, hereby move for an Order that the United States Marshal enforce the earlier Order of this Court and that Defendant [*name*] Storage Company be held in contempt of Court. In support of this motion they aver:

1. This adversary proceeding was originally brought due to the failure of Defendant [*name*] to fulfill its obligations to turn over the Plaintiffs' household goods and clothing under 11 U.S.C. § 542.

2. After proper service, on September 21, 2003, this Court entered a default judgment in the matter, due to Defendant's failure to file a response to the Complaint, and ordered Defendant to turn over the Debtors' possessions. A copy of that Order is attached hereto as Exhibit A [*omitted*].

3. Since that time, the Plaintiffs/Debtors have attempted to have Defendant comply with the Order, with no success.

4. The Order was served on Defendant first by regular mail on September 29, 2003, and then by certified mail, mailed by the Debtors, which was signed for and received on October 16, 2003.

5. Defendant has continued to refuse to comply with the Order of this Court since that time.

6. As a result, Plaintiffs have had to live for over two months without virtually all of their furniture and clothing, which Defendant is holding.

WHEREFORE, Plaintiffs pray that this Court order:

1. That Defendant [*name*] Storage Company be held in contempt of Court;[124]

---

115 A proceeding to recover property must be brought as an adversary proceeding. Fed. R. Bankr. P. 7001. For general discussion of complaints in adversary proceedings, see notes to Form 83, Appendix G.10, *infra*. Under 11 U.S.C. §§ 542 and 543, entities in possession of property that the debtor may exempt, or the trustee may use, sell, or lease, must turn over such property. *See generally* § 9.9, *supra*.

116 In some jurisdictions courts require that the trustee be joined as a party defendant whenever the debtor seeks to make use of the trustee's avoiding powers. The trustee may have some interest in the property if it is ultimately concluded that it is not fully exempt.

117 *See* Form 36, Appx. G.5, *supra*.

118 See discussions of possession of exempt property and property of the estate in Chapters 10 and 12, *supra*. As discussed there, the debtor has a somewhat clearer right to immediate possession in chapter 13.

119 This paragraph anticipates a request for adequate protection which the holder is often entitled to make under 11 U.S.C. § 363(e).

120 It is not totally clear that a failure to follow the turnover provisions is contempt. However, there is a good argument that such actions are essentially the same as violations of the automatic stay because both provisions are meant to be self-effectuating. Exer-

cising control over property of the estate is a violation of the automatic stay, 11 U.S.C. § 362(a)(3). *See* § 9.9.2, *supra*.

121 Attorney fees may be awarded if it can be shown that defendant acted in bad faith or possibly if it acted in willful disregard of its obligations.

122 When a complaint seeking turnover of property (Form 37, Appx. G.5, *supra*) is filed and an order for turnover is entered, the defendant usually complies with the order; occasionally, however, further enforcement proceedings are necessary. A motion to have the defendant held in contempt, such as this one, is appropriate. A motion for contempt is governed by Fed. R. Bankr. P. 9020. For discussion of turnover requirements see § 9.9, *supra*. For discussion of contempt, see § 13.2.8, *supra*.

123 The motion should contain the caption of the adversary proceeding giving rise to the order of which the debtor is seeking enforcement.

124 A separate notice procedure may be a prerequisite to a finding of contempt under Fed. R. Bankr. P. 9020(b).

2. That the United States Marshal be directed to secure entry to the premises where Plaintiffs' belongings are stored, by force if necessary, so that Plaintiffs may recover possession of those items at a time to be arranged between Plaintiffs and the United States Marshal Service, with the Marshal's costs to be borne by Plaintiffs;[125]

3. That any claim of [*defendant*] be deemed satisfied as a sanction for its contempt and the costs which Plaintiffs have incurred; and that Plaintiffs be awarded compensatory and punitive damages;[126]

4. That [*defendant*] be ordered to pay $2500.00 attorney fees for the costs of this proceeding; and

5. Such other relief as is just and proper.

Date: [*signature*]
                               Attorney for Plaintiffs

G.6 Utilities

Form 39 Letter to Utility Company Giving Notice of Stay and Requirements of 11 U.S.C. § 366[127]

[*creditor—utility*]
[*address*]

                   RE: [*debtor*]
           Account No. [*number*]
       Bankruptcy No. [*number*]
                  [*address*]
       [*social security number*]

Dear Sir/Madam:

Please be advised that I represent [*debtor*].

On [*date*], the above-named individual filed a voluntary petition under chapter _____ of the Bankruptcy Code in the Bankruptcy Court for the [*district name*] District of [*state*], at Bankruptcy No. [*number*].

Pursuant to the automatic stay provision of the Bankruptcy Code, 11 U.S.C. § 362, the filing of a petition operates as a stay of any action to collect or recover a claim against [*debtor*] that arose before the filing of the petition. Accordingly, you are obliged to cease all collection efforts with respect to the account. In addition, pursuant to 11 U.S.C. § 366, you may not alter, refuse, or discon-

tinue service, or discriminate against my client(s) with respect to service on the basis that any debt owed for service prior to the date of the bankruptcy was not paid when due, or on the basis of the bankruptcy.

I believe that the existing security deposit you are holding on my client's account should provide [*utility*] with adequate assurance under 11 U.S.C. § 366(b). If I fail to hear from you by [*date*], I will assume that you are not seeking any additional adequate assurance of payment.

If you have any questions concerning your legal obligations set forth above, please contact me.

Thank you for your attention to the foregoing.

Date: [*signature*]
                             Attorney for Debtor

Form 40 Letter to Utility Company Giving Notice of Conversion from Chapter 13 to Chapter 7[128]

[*creditor—utility*]
[*address*]

                   Re: [*debtor*]
           Account No. [*number*]
       Bankruptcy No. [*number*]
                  [*address*]
       [*social security number*]

Dear Sir/Madam:

As you know, on [*date*] the above-named individual filed a voluntary petition in bankruptcy under chapter 13 in the United States Bankruptcy Court for the [*district name*] District of [*state*] at Bankruptcy No. [*number*].

I am writing to advise you that on [*date*] the debtor exercised his right to convert his case to a chapter 7 bankruptcy. Enclosed is a copy of the notice of conversion filed with the court [*omitted*].

Under the Bankruptcy Code, any claim against the debtor that arose between the initial filing of the bankruptcy on [*filing date*] and the conversion of the case on [*date*] must now be treated as if the claim arose immediately before [*filing date*], pursuant to 11 U.S.C. § 348(d). This means that the conversion of the bankruptcy case operates as a stay of any action to recover a claim against the debtor that arose after the initial filing of the chapter 13 petition, but before the conversion to chapter 7. Accordingly, you are obliged to cease all collection efforts with respect to the current obligation on the debtor's account and may not terminate service due to that obligation.

---

125 Because the bankruptcy court is a federal court, its orders are enforced by the United States Marshal Service. The Marshal charges fees which, ultimately, should be recoverable from the defendant. However, to expedite matters the plaintiff may have to pay them initially as other court costs are paid.

126 Damages and attorney fees may be awarded in contempt proceedings. *See* § 9.6, *supra*.

127 This letter should be sent immediately after filing if a utility shutoff is imminent, or has already occurred. It should prevent any shutoff, at least for twenty days, after which, in some cases, the utility may demand a deposit. Because some courts have held that the burden is on the debtor to obtain an agreement from the utility on adequate assurance, or seek court intervention, within the twenty-day period to avoid termination of service, it is advisable for counsel to raise the issue in this letter. See discussion of 11 U.S.C. §§ 362 and 366 in Chapter 9, *supra*.

128 If a debtor who converts from chapter 13 to chapter 7 has utility arrearages which have accrued since the filing of the chapter 13 petition, it is important to notify the utility of the conversion, because those arrearages are dischargeable in the converted case. 11 U.S.C. § 348(d). Presumably, the utility may again require adequate assurance under 11 U.S.C. § 366(b). See discussion of conversion with respect to utilities at § 9.8, *supra*.

A converting debtor who is not in arrears may not wish to send a letter such as this one because it may trigger a demand for a deposit that she should not have to pay. See discussion at § 9.8, *supra*. However, the utility should be notified of the conversion by the court, in any case, under 11 U.S.C. § 348(c).

If you have any questions concerning your legal obligations set forth above, please contact me.

Thank you for your attention to the foregoing.

[*signature*]
Attorney for Debtor

Form 41 Complaint to Enjoin Termination of Utility Service for Nonpayment of Deposit by Debtor Current on Her Utility Payments[129]

[*Caption: Official Form 16D*]

Complaint to Enjoin Termination of Utility Service for Nonpayment of Deposit by Debtor Current on Her Utility Payments

1. This action is brought by Plaintiff, [*debtor*], Debtor in the above-captioned bankruptcy case, to enforce her rights to continued electric service under the Bankruptcy Code and state law.

2. This Court has jurisdiction of this case under 28 U.S.C. § 1334. This proceeding is a core proceeding.

3. On April 1, 2004, Plaintiff filed a voluntary petition in this Court seeking relief under chapter 7 of the Bankruptcy Code.

4. At the time she filed her petition, Plaintiff was completely current in her payments for electric utility service from Defendant, as she has always been in the past, and therefore did not list a debt to Defendant in her schedules.

5. Nonetheless, shortly after she filed her petition, Plaintiff received from Defendant a demand for a security deposit of fifty dollars, an amount which was many times greater than the eight to ten dollar cost of her average monthly usage. A copy of this demand is attached hereto as Exhibit A [*omitted*].

6. Plaintiff's counsel then spoke with Defendant's counsel to determine whether there was any mistake in sending such a demand to a customer who has always been current in her bill and owed no overdue debt to Defendant at the time of the petition.

7. Defendant's counsel stated that there had been no mistake and that it was Defendant's policy to demand such a deposit from every bankruptcy debtor regardless of whether any overdue bill was owing.

8. Defendant's demand of a deposit from Plaintiff is not authorized by 11 U.S.C. § 366 because 11 U.S.C. § 366(a) prohibits discrimination based solely upon a bankruptcy.

9. Defendant's demand constitutes a form of discrimination against the Debtor solely on account of her bankruptcy, which impairs the "fresh start" Congress intended her to have.[130]

10. Defendant's demand of a deposit from a ratepayer current in her bills is contrary to state public utility regulations at [*cite to state regulatory provision*].[131]

11. Defendant's demand of a deposit, which would have to be paid from the Plaintiff's savings, is an action to obtain possession of property of the estate in violation of 11 U.S.C. § 362(a)(3).

12. Defendant's demand for a deposit bears no rational relationship to Plaintiff's average monthly bill.[132]

Prayer for Relief

WHEREFORE, Plaintiff prays that this Court enter a judgment:

1. Declaring that the Defendant's demand of a security deposit from Plaintiff is not permitted by 11 U.S.C. § 366;

2. Enjoining Defendant from terminating Plaintiff's electric service for failure to pay the security deposit; and

3. Ordering such other relief as is just and proper.

Date: [*signature*]
Attorney for Debtor

Form 42 Complaint Seeking Reconnection of Utility Service and Damages[133]

[*Caption: Official Form 16D*]

Complaint Seeking Reconnection of Utility Service and Damages

1. This action is brought by the Debtor/Plaintiff seeking reconnection of her utility service by the Defendant together with damages for the period of time since the bankruptcy filing during which the Debtor and her family have been without heat.

2. This Court has jurisdiction over this matter pursuant to 28 U.S.C. § 1334. This matter is a core proceeding.

3. The Debtors filed a petition under chapter 7 on March 10, 2004.

4. On the date of filing, the Debtor was without gas service, because Defendant utility had terminated the service based on an unpaid bill.

5. The Debtor listed the debt to Defendant, in the amount of $232.86, in her bankruptcy schedules as a general unsecured obligation.

---

129 Some utility companies have adopted a practice of demanding adequate assurance by way of a deposit from every bankruptcy debtor, regardless of whether that debtor had any unpaid bill at the time of filing. There are a number of reasons why this should be considered improper and enjoined. See discussion in § 9.8, *supra*.

The debtor's counsel should seek assurance from the utility that service will not be terminated while an action such as this one is pending. If such assurance cannot be obtained, a motion for a temporary restraining order may be necessary. The debtor could also pay the deposit under protest and litigate the matter of whether it should be refunded because the utility was not entitled to it.

A proceeding for injunctive relief must be brought as an adversary proceeding. Fed. R. Bankr. P. 7001. For a general discussion of complaints in adversary proceedings, see notes to Form 83, Appendix G.10, *infra*. This form is adapted from pleadings in *In re* Demp, 22 B.R. 331 (Bankr. E.D. Pa. 1981).

130 This claim is based upon the general "fresh start" theory of 11 U.S.C. § 525, as well as the anti-discrimination thrust of 11 U.S.C. § 366(a) and (b). In the case of a governmental utility, a debtor may rely directly upon 11 U.S.C. § 525.

131 State public utility regulations often govern deposits outside of bankruptcy. If 11 U.S.C. § 366(b) is inapplicable, then such regulations would continue to be the relevant law.

132 As an alternative claim, the amount of the deposit may be challenged. *See* Form 43, Appx. G.6, *infra*.

133 In some cases, the utility may have terminated service to the debtor pre-petition. In that event the debtor should be able to have the service restored immediately on filing bankruptcy. *See* § 9.8.1, *supra*. If, after a reasonable request, the utility refuses to reconnect the debtor, an adversary proceeding like the one here may be appropriate. Counsel will almost always want to request injunctive relief with the complaint.

6. On March 10, 2004, after filing the petition, the Debtor called the Defendant, notified it of the bankruptcy and requested reconnection. She was informed that she could not be reconnected unless she paid or made an agreement to pay the back bill.

7. On March 11, 2004, the Debtor, by counsel, informed the Defendant of the bankruptcy in writing and requested that the Debtor's service be reconnected immediately. A copy of that letter is attached hereto as Exhibit A [*omitted*].

8. As of the date of this Complaint, neither the Debtor nor her attorney had received any response to that letter.

9. As a matter of policy, the Defendant does not charge new customers a security deposit prior to initiating service. A copy of the relevant portions of the Defendant's tariff and customer service regulations is attached hereto as Exhibit B [*omitted*].[134]

10. The Debtor and her family have been without heat for the eight days since her bankruptcy petition was filed causing great hardship and danger to the family's health. The only source of heat for the family has been one five-year-old kerosene stove.

11. The Defendant's conduct violates its obligations under 11 U.S.C. § 366(a) because it is refusing service to the Debtor solely on the basis that a debt owed by the Debtor before the Order for Relief was not paid when due.

WHEREFORE, the Debtor requests that this Court:

a. Immediately enter injunctive relief requiring that the Defendant restore gas service to the Debtor[135];

b. Enter an award of damages, costs and attorney fees pursuant to 11 U.S.C. §§ 366, 362(h);[136] and

c. Order such other relief as the Court deems just in the circumstances of this case.

Date: [*signature*]
                                                                       Attorney for Debtor/Plaintiff

Form 43 Motion for Modification of Security Deposit for Utility Service[137]

[*Caption: Official Form 16A*]

Motion for Modification of Security Deposit for Utility Service

Pursuant to 11 U.S.C. § 366, the Debtors, by their counsel, hereby seek a determination as to what security will provide

[*creditor—utility*] with adequate assurance of future payment. In support of this application, they allege that:

1. Debtors filed a voluntary chapter 7 petition in this court on [*date*].

2. [*Creditor—utility*] has demanded a security deposit of $200.00 to continue gas heating service.

3. The amount demanded is excessive in that it is almost three times the Debtors' average monthly bill of $70.00.

4. The equivalent of one average monthly bill, i.e. $70.00, will provide adequate assurance of future payment, because in the event of non-payment, the Defendant is authorized by law to shut off service after following procedures which, diligently pursued, require about one month to exhaust.

WHEREFORE, the Debtors pray this Court to enter an Order declaring that payment of a security deposit by the Debtors in the amount of $70.00, payable in two equal monthly installments, shall be adequate assurance of future payment under 11 U.S.C. § 366.

Date: [*signature*]
                                                                       Attorney for Debtors

G.7 Steps After Filing

Form 44 Letter Advising Belatedly-Added Creditor of Meeting of Creditors[138]

[*creditor*]
[*address*]

                                                                       Re: [*debtor*]
                                                        Bankruptcy No. [*number*]
                                                                       [*address*]
                                                        [*social security number*]

Dear [*name*]:

Please be advised that this office represents the above-named individual who is indebted to you in the amount of $[*amount*].

On April 1, 2000, [*debtor*] filed a petition in bankruptcy in the United States Bankruptcy Court for the [*district name*] District of [*state*]. A copy of the Notice of First Meeting of Creditors is enclosed, as is a copy of the amended schedule on which your claim is listed.

If you have any questions about this matter you should contact the bankruptcy court or your own attorney, immediately.

Date: [*signature*]
                                                                       Attorney for Debtor

---

134 In some cases, the utility's tariff may actually authorize the taking of deposits from new customers but as a matter of practice, the utility does not make such demands. In this case, counsel may attempt to obtain an affidavit from a consumer complaint representative of the local public utilities commission describing the utility's practice.

135 When appropriate a motion for a temporary restraining order or a preliminary injunction and a request for expedited consideration should be filed with the complaint.

136 If the utility is run by a government entity, claims under 42 U.S.C. § 1983 may be added.

137 The rights of utilities to security deposits under 11 U.S.C. § 366 are discussed in Chapter 9, *supra*. This motion, requesting a court determination prior to the expiration of the twenty-day period, is one approach to disputes regarding the amount necessary to provide "adequate assurance" under that section. It is unlikely that the utility will terminate service while such an action is pending, even after the twenty-day period. Another,

more conservative approach would be to pay the amount demanded by the utility and then seek to have the deposit lowered by the court.

138 This letter may be used when the schedules are amended to add a creditor after the notice of the section 341 meeting has been mailed by the clerk. It provides, to the extent time permits, actual notice to a creditor not originally listed in order to preclude a later claim that the debt was not discharged under 11 U.S.C. § 523(a)(3). See discussion of this exception to discharge in § 14.4.3.3, *supra*. In order to have proof that the creditor received actual notice, the letter should be sent by certified mail, return receipt requested.

Form 45 Chapter 7 Section 341(a) Meeting Questions[139]

- Are there any creditors or parties in interest here today?
- Debtor, I have handed you a debtor's oath form and now asked you to verify your signature on that form. Is that your signature?
- In signing the form you are indicating that the statements you are about to give will be true and correct under penalty of perjury. Do you understand that?
- I note for the record that the attorney representing the debtor in this proceeding is [*name*].
- I asked previously are there any creditors of the debtor or other parties in interest in the courtroom today for this case and I hear no response.
- Please state your full name and current address.
- Do you rent or own your home?
- What is your spouse's name?
- When were you married?
- What was her (your) maiden name?
- Did you ever have another name?
- Have you filed a petition seeking relief under the Bankruptcy Code?
- I show you your petition and ask if that is your petition.
- Did your spouse file a joint petition with you?
- [*If no joint petition was filed*] Does your spouse have notice of these proceedings?
- Is your spouse present today?
- Is he or she responsible for any of the debts listed?
- I have handed you a copy of your petition and ask whether you recognize this as the petition you executed and filed with this court.
- Is that your signature at the bottom?
- When signing this petition, did you review its contents and assure that all the information contained in the petition was true and correct?
- Have you ever filed a bankruptcy proceeding before?
- If you did, did you receive a discharge? If so, when?
- Have you made any voluntary or involuntary transfers of real or personal property within the last year?
- Are any of these credit card claims?
- Have you returned the credit cards or destroyed them?
- Do you understand the potential consequences of seeking a discharge in bankruptcy and its possible effects on your credit rating?[140]

- Are you aware that you may be able to file under a different chapter of the bankruptcy code?
- Do you understand the effect of receiving a discharge?
- Do you understand what it means to reaffirm a debt and that you are under no obligation to reaffirm any debts?
- Does schedule E contain a complete list of all your creditors having priority? If none, state none.
- Does schedule D contain a complete list of all your creditors having security? If none, state none.
- Does schedule F contain a complete list of all your unsecured creditors? If none, state none.
- Does schedule A contain a complete list of all your real property? If none, state none.
- Does schedule B contain a complete list of your personal property? If none, state none.
- Have you voluntarily or involuntarily transferred any real estate or personal property within twelve months before you filed your petition?
- Does schedule C contain a list of all property claimed as exempt and indicate the statutory provisions providing for those exemptions?
- Does the summary of schedules contain a complete and accurate total of your property and debts?
- Are you currently employed and, if so, by whom?
- Has your attorney filed a disclosure of fees?
- Is that the correct amount that you will pay your attorney for representing you in this matter?
- What caused your financial difficulties?
- Are those difficulties continuing or have they ended?
- Have you paid filing fees and costs?
- Are there any creditors or other parties in interest who wish to ask any questions?
- Thank you.

Form 46 Section 341(a) Questions from United States Trustee Chapter 7 Handbook[141]

Required Statements/Questions

1. State your name and current address for the record.

2. Have you read the Bankruptcy Information Sheet provided by the United States Trustee?

3. Did you sign the petition, schedules, statements, and related documents you filed with the court? Did you read the petition, schedules, statements, and related documents before you signed them and is the signature your own?

4. Please provide your picture ID and social security number card for review.

a. If the documents are in agreement with the petition, a suggested statement for the record is:

---

139 These questions are typical of those asked by the presiding officer, usually the trustee, at the 11 U.S.C. § 341(a) meeting of creditors in a chapter 7 case. However, practice varies widely in different districts and even within districts. As anyone may attend such a meeting, advocates are advised to watch several meetings in their district to be able to prepare clients for the questions likely to be asked. For a general discussion of the section 341(a) meeting, see Chapter 8, *supra*.

140 This question and the next three questions are intended to comply with the requirements placed upon the trustee by the amendments to 11 U.S.C. § 341(d). *See* § 3.4, *supra*. In most courts, this information in given to the debtor in writing and the requirement is satisfied by the trustee simply asking at the meeting if the debtor has read and understood the statement. *See* Form 47, Appx. G.7, *infra*. Counsel should ensure that the debtor has read the statement in advance of the meeting.

---

141 These questions were prepared by the United States Trustees office to be used by private trustees in conducting § 341(a) meetings. *See* Executive Office of the U.S. Trustees, United States Dep't of Justice, Handbook for Chapter 7 Trustees (July 1, 2002). The handbook notes that the first ten statements and questions are required. Trustees are instructed to ensure that the debtor answers the substance of each of the ten questions on the record. The trustee may exercise discretion and judgment in varying the wording of the statements and questions if the substance of the questions is covered.

"I have viewed the original drivers license (or other type of original photo ID) and original social security card (or other original document used for proof) and they match the name and social security number on the petition."

b. If the documents are not in agreement with the petition, a suggested statement for the record is:

"I have viewed the original social security card (or other original document used for proof) and the number is 000-00-000. It does not match the number on the petition. I have instructed the debtor (or debtor's counsel) to file an amended petition by [date], serve all creditors and the trustee, and send a 'Notice of Correction of Social Security Number in Bankruptcy Filing' and a copy of the amended petition to the three major credit reporting agencies, and to the United States Trustee."

c. When the documents do not match the petition, the trustee shall attempt to ascertain why. The trustee also shall ask if the debtor has ever obtained credit or benefits, such as Medicaid or employment, using this social security number or any other social security number.

d. If the debtor did not bring proof of identity and social security number, the trustee needs to determine why.

5. Are you personally familiar with the information contained in the petition, schedules, statements and related documents?

6. To the best of your knowledge, is the information contained in the petition, schedules, statements, and related documents true and correct?

7. Are there any errors or omissions to bring to my, or the court's, attention at this time?

8. Are all of your assets identified on the schedules?

9. Have you listed all of your creditors on the schedules?

10. Have you previously filed bankruptcy? (If so, the trustee must obtain the case number and the discharge information to determine the debtor(s) discharge eligibility.)

Sample General Questions
(to be asked when deemed appropriate)

1. Do you own or have any interest whatsoever in any real estate?

If owned: When did you purchase the property? How much did the property cost? What are the mortgages encumbering it? What do you estimate the present value of the property to be? Is that the whole value or your share? How did you arrive at that value?

If renting: Have you ever owned the property in which you live and/or is its owner in any way related to you?

2. Have you made any transfers of any property or given any property away within the last one year period (or such longer period as applicable under state law)?

If yes: What did you transfer? To whom was it transferred? What did you receive in exchange? What did you do with the funds?

3. Does anyone hold property belonging to you?

If yes: Who holds the property and what is it? What is its value?

4. Do you have a claim against anyone or any business? If there are large medical debts, are the medical bills from injury? Are you the plaintiff in any lawsuit? What is the status of each case and who is representing you?

5. Are you entitled to life insurance proceeds or an inheritance as a result of someone's death?

If yes: Please explain the details. If you become a beneficiary of anyone's estate within six months of the date your bankruptcy petition was filed, the trustee must be advised within ten days through your counsel of the nature and extent of the property you will receive. Fed. R. Bankr. P. 1007(h).

6. Does anyone owe you money?

If yes: Is the money collectible? Why haven't you collected it? Who owes the money and where are they?

7. Have you made any large payments, over $600.00, to anyone in the past year?

8. Were federal income tax returns filed on a timely basis? When was the last return filed? Do you have copies of the federal income tax returns? At the time of the filing of your petition, were you entitled to a tax refund from the federal or state government ?

If yes: Inquire as to amounts.

9. Do you have a bank account, either checking or savings?

If yes: In what banks and what were the balances as of the date you filed your petition?

10. When you filed your petition, did you have:

a. any cash on hand?

b. any U.S. Savings Bonds?

c. any other stocks or bonds?

d. any Certificates of Deposit?

e. a safe deposit box in your name or in anyone else's name?

11. Do you own an automobile?

If yes: What is the year, make, and value? Do you owe any money on it? Is it insured?

12. Are you the owner of any cash value life insurance policies?

If yes: State the name of the company, face amount of the policy, cash surrender value, if any, and the beneficiaries.

13. Do you have any winning lottery tickets?

14. Do you anticipate that you might realize any property, cash or otherwise, as a result of a divorce or separation proceeding?

15. Regarding any consumer debts secured by your property, have you filed the required Statement of Intention with respect to the exemption, retention, or surrender of that secured property? Please provide a copy of the statement to the trustee. Have you performed that intention?

16. Have you been engaged in any business during the last six years?

If yes: Where and when? What happened to the assets of the business?

In cases in which debtors are engaged in business, the following questions should be considered:

1. Who was responsible for maintaining financial records?

2. Which of the following records were maintained?

    a. Cash receipts journal

    b. Cash disbursements journal

    c. General journal

    d. Accounts receivable ledger

    e. Accounts payable ledger

    f. Payroll ledger

    g. Fixed asset ledger

    h. Inventory ledger

    i. General ledger

    j. Balance sheet, income statement, and cash flow statements

3. Where are each of the foregoing records now located?

4. Who was responsible for preparing financial statements?

5. How often were financial statements prepared?

6. For what periods are financial statements available?
7. Where are such financial statements now located?
8. Was the business on a calendar year or a fiscal year?
9. Were federal income tax returns filed on a timely basis? When was the last return filed?
10. Do you have copies of the federal income tax returns? Who does have the copies?
11. What outside accountants were employed within the last three years?
12. Do you have copies of the reports of such accountants? Who does have copies?
13. What bank accounts were maintained within the last three years?
14. Where are the bank statements and cancelled checks now located?
15. What insurance policies were in effect within the last year? What kind, and why?
16. From whom can copies of such insurance policies be obtained?
17. If the business is incorporated, where are the corporate minutes?
18. Is the debtor owed any outstanding accounts receivable? From whom? Are they collectible?
19. Is there any inventory, property, or equipment remaining?

Form 47 Statement of Information Required by 11 U.S.C. § 341[142]

STATEMENT OF INFORMATION REQUIRED BY 11 U.S.C. § 341

INTRODUCTION

Pursuant to the Bankruptcy Reform Act of 1994, the Office of the United States Trustee, United States Department of Justice, has prepared this information sheet to help you understand some of the possible consequences of filing a bankruptcy petition under chapter 7 of the Bankruptcy Code. This information is intended to make you aware of—

(1) the potential consequences of seeking a discharge in bankruptcy, including the effects on credit history;
(2) the effect of receiving a discharge of debts;
(3) the effect of reaffirming a debt; and
(4) your ability to file a petition under a different chapter of the Bankruptcy Code.

There are many other provisions of the Bankruptcy Code that may affect your situation. This information sheet contains only general principles of law and is not a substitute for legal advice. If you have questions or need further information as to how the bankruptcy laws apply to your specific case, you should consult with your lawyer.

---

142 This form was prepared by the United States Trustee's office to comply with the informational requirements of 11 U.S.C. § 341(d). It may be used by many trustees as a supplement to information provided orally. Other trustees may use it without an attempt to make an oral presentation on the issues. Because the information provided is limited, debtor's counsel may want to supplement the information or respond to client's questions either before or after the meeting of creditors.

WHAT IS A DISCHARGE?

The filing of a chapter 7 petition is designed to result in a discharge of most of the debts you listed on your bankruptcy schedules. A discharge is a court order that says you do not have to repay your debts, but there are a number of exceptions. Debts which may not be discharged in your chapter 7 case include, for example, most taxes, child support, alimony, and student loans; court-ordered fines and restitution; debts obtained through fraud or deception; and personal injury debts caused by driving while intoxicated or taking drugs. Your discharge may be denied entirely if you, for example, destroy or conceal property; destroy, conceal or falsify records; or make a false oath. Creditors cannot ask you to pay any debts which have been discharged. You can only receive a chapter 7 discharge once every six (6) years.

WHAT ARE THE POTENTIAL EFFECTS OF A DISCHARGE?

The fact that you filed bankruptcy can appear on your credit report for as long as 10 years. Thus, filing a bankruptcy petition may affect your ability to obtain credit in the future. Also, you may not be excused from repaying any debts that were not listed on your bankruptcy schedules or that you incurred after you filed bankruptcy.

WHAT ARE THE EFFECT OF REAFFIRMING A DEBT?

After you file your petition, a creditor may ask you to reaffirm a certain debt or you may seek to do so on your own. Reaffirming a debt means that you sign and file with the court a legally enforceable document, which states that you promise to repay all or a portion of the debt that may otherwise have been discharged in your bankruptcy case. Reaffirmation agreements must generally be filed with the court within 60 days after the first meeting of creditors.

Reaffirmation agreements are strictly voluntary—they are not required by the Bankruptcy Code or other state or federal law. You can voluntarily repay any debt instead of signing a reaffirmation agreement, but there may be valid reasons for wanting to reaffirm a particular debt.

Reaffirmation agreements must not impose an undue burden on you or your dependents and must be in your best interest. If you decide to sign a reaffirmation agreement, you may cancel it at any time before the court issues your discharge order *or* within sixty (60) days after the reaffirmation agreement was filed with the court, whichever is later. If you reaffirm a debt and fail to make the payments required in the reaffirmation agreement, the creditor can take action against you to recover any property that was given as security for the loan and you may remain personally liable for any remaining debt.

OTHER BANKRUPTCY OPTIONS

You have a choice in deciding what chapter of the Bankruptcy Code will best suit your needs. Even if you have already filed for relief under chapter 7, you may be eligible to convert your case to a different chapter.

Chapter 7 is the liquidation chapter of the Bankruptcy Code. Under chapter 7, a trustee is appointed to collect and sell, if economically feasible, all property you own that is not exempt from these actions.

Chapter 11 is the reorganization chapter most commonly used by businesses, but it is also available to individuals. Creditors vote on whether to accept or reject a plan, which also must be approved by the court. While the debtor normally remains in control of the assets, the court can order the appointment of a trustee to take possession and control of the business.

Chapter 12 offers bankruptcy relief to those who qualify as family farmers. Family farmers must propose a plan to repay their creditors over a three-to-five year period and it must be approved by the court. Plan payments are made through a chapter 12 trustee, who also monitors the debtors' farming operations during the pendency of the plan.

Finally, chapter 13 generally permits individuals to keep their property by repaying creditors out of their future income. Each chapter 13 debtor writes a plan which must be approved by the bankruptcy court. The debtor must pay the chapter 13 trustee the amounts set forth in their plan. Debtors receive a discharge after they complete their chapter 13 repayment plan. Chapter 13 is only available to individuals with regular income whose debts do not exceed $1,000,000.00 ($250,000.00 in unsecured debts and $750,000.00 in secured debts).

AGAIN, PLEASE SPEAK TO YOUR LAWYER IF YOU NEED FURTHER INFORMATION OR EXPLANATION, INCLUDING HOW THE BANKRUPTCY LAWS RELATE TO YOUR SPECIFIC CASE.

Form 48 Chapter 13 Section 341(a) Meeting Questions[143]

- Are there any creditors or parties in interest here today?
- Debtor, I have handed you a debtor's oath form and ask you to verify your signature on that form. Is that your signature?
- In signing the form you are indicating that the statements you are about to give will be true and correct under penalty of perjury. Do you understand that?
- I note for the record that the attorney representing the debtor in this proceeding is [*name*].
- I asked previously are there any creditors of the debtor or other parties in interest in the courtroom today for this case and I hear no response.
- Please state your full name and current address.
- Do you rent or own your home?
- Are you married?
- What is your spouse's name?
- When were you married?
- What was her (your) maiden name?
- Did you ever have another name?
- Have you filed a petition seeking relief under the Bankruptcy Code?
- I show you your petition and ask if that's your petition?
- Did your spouse file a joint petition with you?
- Is your spouse present today?
- I have handed you a copy of your petition and ask whether you recognize this as the petition you executed and filed with this court?
- Is that your signature at the bottom?

- When signing this petition did you review its contents and assure that all the information contained in the petition was true and correct?
- Have you ever filed a bankruptcy proceeding before?
- If so, under what chapter and what was the result?
- Counsel, do you have any changes in this petition or plan?
- Were you employed on the date you filed your petition?
- Are you still employed at the same job or profession?
- Has your income situation from that employment changed since you filed the petition?
- Do your chapter 13 schedules provide an explanation of your current income before and after deductions?
- Do your chapter 13 schedules provide an explanation of your current monthly budget?
- I ask you if there are any changes in that?
- Do your chapter 13 schedules contain a list of the following:
  a. All your real property? If none, state none.
  b. Is this a list of all of your personal property?
  c. Is it a complete list?
  d. Does this statement show all of your bank accounts and safe deposit boxes?
  e. All your automobiles or automotive vehicles?
- Do your schedules show the relevant subsections of section 522 under which your property is claimed as exempt?
- Have you made any voluntary or involuntary transfers of real or personal property within the last year?
- Has your counsel filed a disclosure of fee statement?
- Is that the amount you have agreed to pay your attorney in connection with the case?
- Do your schedules contain all of your creditors having priority?
- Are there any creditors holding security?
- Do they show all of your unsecured claims?
- Are any of these credit card claims?
- Have you returned the credit cards?
- Specifically how does this plan propose to pay your creditors?
- Have you paid filing fees and costs?
- Are there any creditors or other parties in interest who wish to ask any questions?
- Thank you.

Form 49 Section 341(a) Questions from United States Trustee Chapter 13 Handbook[144]

Section 341(A) Meeting Of Creditors (Individual Debtors)

Required Statements/Questions

1. State your name and current address for the record.

2. Have you read the Bankruptcy Information Sheet provided by the United States Trustee?

---

143 These questions are typical of those asked by the presiding officer, usually the trustee, at the 11 U.S.C. § 341(a) meeting of creditors in a chapter 13 case. However, practice varies widely in different districts and even within districts. As anyone may attend such a meeting, advocates are advised to watch several meetings in their district to be able to prepare clients for the questions likely to be asked. For a general discussion of the section 341(a) meeting, see Chapter 8, *supra*.

144 These questions were prepared by the United States Trustees office to be used by private trustees in conducting § 341(a) meetings. *See* Executive Office of the U.S. Trustees, United States Dep't of Justice, Handbook for Chapter 13 Trustees (July 1, 2002). The handbook notes that the first ten statements and questions are required. Trustees are instructed to ensure that the debtor answers the substance of each of the ten questions on the record. The trustee may exercise discretion and judgment in varying the wording of the statements and questions if the substance of the questions is covered.

3. Did you sign the petition, schedules, statements, and related documents you filed with the court? Did you read the petition, schedules, statements, and related documents before you signed them and is the signature your own?

4. Please provide your picture ID and social security number card for review.

    a. If the documents are in agreement with the petition, a suggested statement for the record is:

      "I have viewed the original drivers license (or other type of original photo ID) and original social security card (or other original document used for proof) and they match the name and social security number on the petition."

    b. If the documents are not in agreement with the petition, a suggested statement for the record is:

      "I have viewed the original social security card (or other original document used for proof) and the number is 000-00-000. It does not match the number on the petition. I have instructed the debtor (or debtor's counsel) to file an amended petition by [date], serve all creditors and the standing trustee, and send a 'Notice of Correction of Social Security Number in Bankruptcy Filing' and a copy of the amended petition to the three major credit reporting agencies, and to the United States Trustee."

    c. When the documents do not match the petition, the standing trustee shall attempt to ascertain why. The standing trustee also shall ask if the debtor has ever obtained credit or benefits, such as Medicaid or employment, using this social security number or any other social security number.

    d. If the debtor did not bring proof of identity and social security number, the standing trustee needs to determine why.

5. Are you personally familiar with the information contained in the petition, schedules, statements and related documents?

6. To the best of your knowledge, is the information contained in the petition, schedules, statements, and related documents true and correct?

7. Are there any errors or omissions to bring to my, or the court's, attention at this time?

8. Are all of your assets identified on the schedules?

9. Have you listed all of your creditors on the schedules?

10. Have you filed bankruptcy before using the social security number you presented today, the social security number on the petition or any other social security number not issued by the Social Security Administration? (If so, the standing trustee must obtain the case number and the discharge information to determine the debtor(s) discharge eligibility.)

Sample General Questions
(to be asked when deemed appropriate)

1. Do you own or have any interest whatsoever in any real estate?

If owned: When did you purchase the property? How much did the property cost? What are the mortgages encumbering it? What do you estimate the present value of the property to be? Is that the whole value or your share? How did you arrive at that value?

If renting: Have you ever owned the property in which you live and/or is its owner in any way related to you?

2. Have you made any transfers of any property or given any property away within the last one year period (or such longer period as applicable under state law)?

If yes: What did you transfer? To whom was it transferred? What did you receive in exchange? What did you do with the funds?

3. Does anyone hold property belonging to you?

If yes: Who holds the property and what is it? What is its value?

4. Do you have a claim against anyone or any business? If there are large medical debts, are the medical bills from injury? Are you the plaintiff in any lawsuit? What is the status of each case and who is representing you?

5. Are you entitled to life insurance proceeds or an inheritance as a result of someone's death?

If yes: Please explain the details. If you become a beneficiary of anyone's estate within six months of the date your bankruptcy petition was filed, the trustee must be advised within ten days through your counsel of the nature and extent of the property you will receive.

6. Does anyone owe you money?

If yes: Is the money collectible? Why haven't you collected it? Who owes the money and where are they?

7. Have you made any large payments, over $600.00, to anyone in the past year?

8. Were federal income tax returns filed on a timely basis? When was the last return filed? Do you have copies of the federal income tax returns? At the time of the filing of your petition, were you entitled to a tax refund from the federal or state government?

If yes: Inquire as to amounts.

9. Do you have a bank account, either checking or savings?

If yes: In what banks and what were the balances as of the date you filed your petition?

10. When you filed your petition, did you have:

    a. any cash on hand?

    b. any U.S. savings bonds?

    c. any other stocks or bonds?

    d. any certificates of deposit?

    e. a safe deposit box in your name or in anyone else's name?

11. Do you own an automobile?

If yes: What is the year, make, and value? Do you owe any money on it? Is it insured?

12. Are you the owner of any cash value life insurance policies?

If yes: State the name of the company, face amount of the policy, cash surrender value, if any, and the beneficiaries.

13. Do you have any winning lottery tickets?

14. Do you anticipate that you might realize any property, cash or otherwise, as a result of a divorce or separation proceeding?

15. Have you been engaged in any business during the last six years?

If yes: Where and when? What happened to the assets of the business?

16. Have you seen a credit counselor within the last year?

Form 50 Debtor's Motion to Excuse Appearance and to Conduct Meeting of Creditors by Interrogatories[145]

[Caption: Official Form 16B]

Debtor's Motion to Excuse Appearance and to Conduct Meeting of Creditors by Interrogatories

Debtor, by her attorney, hereby requests this Court to excuse her appearance at a meeting of creditors in this case and to permit the meeting of creditors to be conducted by interrogatories and in support thereof avers as follows:

1. The Debtor is a 73-year-old disabled individual who filed bankruptcy pursuant to chapter 13 of the Bankruptcy Code on March 5, 2004.

2. Due to a stroke suffered by the Debtor after filing bankruptcy, the Debtor is hospitalized and unable to travel.

3. The Debtor's physical problems prevent her from attending a section 341 meeting of creditors.

4. The meeting of creditors in this bankruptcy case was originally scheduled for July 2, 2004, at which time counsel for the Debtor informed the trustee that the Debtor could not appear because of her physical problems.

5. No creditors appeared on July 2, 2004, at the scheduled meeting of creditors.

6. Written interrogatories are attached and labeled Exhibit B *[omitted]* regarding the Debtor's bankruptcy schedules and financial affairs.

7. The trustee has been contacted concerning this motion and she has stated that she has no objection.[146]

WHEREFORE, the Debtor requests that this motion be approved, that the requirement of an appearance at a meeting of creditors be waived and that in lieu thereof the Debtor be permitted to submit answers to the interrogatories in the form attached to this motion.

Date: *[signature]*
                                          Attorney for Debtor

Form 51 Interrogatories to Debtor in Lieu of Attendance at Meeting of Creditors[147]

[Caption: Official Form 16B]

Interrogatories to Debtor in Lieu of Attendance at Meeting of Creditors Under § 341(a) of the Bankruptcy Code

1. Please state your full name and current address.

2. Do you rent or own your home?

3. Have you filed a petition seeking relief under the Bankruptcy Code?

4. When signing the petition, did you review its contents and assure that all the information contained in the petition was true and correct?

5. Does your signature appear at the bottom of the petition?

6. Have you ever filed a bankruptcy proceeding before?

7. Has your income situation changed since you filed the petition?

8. Does your chapter 13 statement correctly list the following:
   a. All your real property?
   b. All your personal property?

9. Does your chapter 13 statement show the relevant subsections of section 522 under which your property is claimed as exempt?

10. Have you made any voluntary or involuntary transfers of real or personal property within the last year?

11. Does your schedule of debts contain a complete list of all your creditors having priority?

12. Does your schedule of debts contain a complete list of all your creditors having security?

13. Does your schedule of debts contain a complete list of all your unsecured creditors?

14. Are any of your debts credit card claims?

15. Have you returned the credit cards or destroyed them?

16. Has your attorney filed a disclosure of fees?

17. Have you paid filing fees and costs?

18. Are you current in your payments to the chapter 13 standing trustee?

I declare under penalty of perjury that the foregoing answers are true and correct to the best of my knowledge, belief and understanding.

Date: *[signature]*
                                          Debtor

Form 52 Report of Trustee[148]

[Caption: Official Form 16B]

Report of Trustee and Order Approving Trustee's Report Setting Aside Certain Property to the Debtor, Discharging Trustee and Closing Case

AND NOW, this *[date]* day of *[month]*, *[year]*, the following Report is made:

1. The below-named person was duly appointed to serve as the interim trustee pursuant to section 701 of title 11, United States Code.

---

145 When debtors are physically unable to attend a meeting of creditors, courts will generally approve a meeting process by written interrogatories. *See* § 8.4.3, *supra*.

146 The trustee's consent is not required but is helpful when it can be obtained.

147 This form should be adapted to local practice and to questions appropriate to the chapter under which the debtor is proceeding. It may be a good idea to allow the trustee to review it in advance and to add or delete questions as appropriate.

148 This form is former Official Form 33. The report of the trustee is generally the method by which the court is informed that the trustee does not object to the claim of exemptions. See discussion in § 10.3, *supra*. As the Federal Rules of Bankruptcy Procedure no longer require a report of the trustees, there is no longer an official form for the report and in many districts none is filed. Similarly there is no longer a rule requiring a debtor to answer any report filed. Issues formerly raised in trustee's reports are now litigated as objections to exemptions. *See* Fed. R. Bankr. P. 4003(b), (c). Probably, if a trustee's report is filed and it disagrees with the debtor's exemption claim, it will be heard by the court as an objection to the debtor's exemptions.

2. A meeting of creditors has been held in the above matter pursuant to section 341 of title 11, United States Code, and the meeting was concluded.

3. At the meeting of creditors a trustee was not elected pursuant to section 702 of title 11, United States Code.

4. The Debtor was examined by the clerk, United States Bankruptcy Court, and/or the trustee. The Debtor was available for examination by any creditor, indenture trustee, or any other party in interest.

5. The trustee has neither received nor paid any money on account of the estate in this matter.

6. The trustee has made a diligent inquiry into the whereabouts of property belonging to the estate in this matter.

7. The clerk, United States Bankruptcy Court, and/or the trustee examined the Debtor as to the property listed in the schedules attached to the petition and exemptions claimed by the Debtor pursuant to section 522 of title 11 of the United States Code.

8. The trustee is of the conclusion that the exemptions claimed are authorized by and do not exceed the provisions of section 522.

9. The trustee is of the conclusion that there are no assets in the estate over and above the exemptions claimed by the Debtor and recommends that the exemptions be allowed as claimed and that the respective property be set aside to the Debtor.

10. The trustee has no information or other basis on which to make recommendation that a discharge of the Debtor not be granted.

11. The disclosure statement filed by Debtor's counsel indicates a total fee of $[*amount*].

In my opinion, the fee is reasonable.   [ ]

In my opinion, the fee should be reviewed. [ ]

12. The trustee requests that this report be approved as a final report and account and that the trustee be discharged from office.

Date: [*signature*]
                                                              Trustee

Order

AND NOW, this [*date*] day of [*month*], [*year*], it appearing that the trustee in the above-entitled matter has filed a report of no assets and that the interim trustee has performed all other duties required in the administration of the Debtor's estate; it is OR-DERED that the report be and is hereby approved; that the trustee be discharged and relieved of any trust; and this case be, and the same hereby is, closed.

Date: [*signature*]
                                        United States Bankruptcy Judge

G.8 Claims

Form 53 Priority Proof of Claim by Debtor[149]

[Caption: Official Form 16A]

Priority Proof of Claim by Debtor

1. The undersigned, who is filing this proof of claim, is the Debtor in this case.

---

149 This form is a proof of claim for a debt entitled to priority, such as taxes. *See* Official Form 11, Appx. D, *supra*. It should be filed

2. This claim is filed in the name of [*creditor*], of [*address*], who asserts a claim against the Debtor in the sum of $[*amount*].

3. The consideration for this debt or the ground for this liability is as follows: [*describe consideration*].

4. This claim consists of $[*amount—principal*] in principal amount and $[*amount—additional charges*] in additional charges.

5. No judgment has been rendered on this claim.

6. The amount of all payments on this claim has been credited and deducted for the purpose of making this proof of claim.

7. This claim is not subject to any setoff or counterclaim.

8. No security interest is held for this claim.

9. This claim is a priority claim for the full amount as a tax claim within the terms of 11 U.S.C. § 507(a)(7).

Date: [*signature*]
                                               Attorney for Debtor

[Attach: Certificate of Service on creditor]

Form 54 Proof of Secured Claim by Debtor[150]

[Caption: Official Form 16A]

Proof of Secured Claim by Debtor

1. The undersigned, who is filing this proof of claim on behalf of the holder of claims against Debtor, is the Debtor in this case.

2. This claim is filed in the name of [*creditor*], of [*address*], who asserts a secured claim against the Debtor in the amount of $[*amount*].

3. The consideration for this debt or the basis of Debtor's liability is as follows: [*describe consideration*].

4. This claim consists of $[*amount—principal*] in principal amount and $[*amount—additional charges*] in additional charges.

5. The writing upon which this claim is founded is attached hereto [*omitted*].

6. No judgment has been rendered on this claim.

7. The amount of all payments on this claim has been credited and deducted for the purpose of making this proof of claim.

8. This claim is not subject to any setoff or counterclaim.

9. No security interest is held for this claim except that the holder of the claim holds a lien on the following property of debtor: [*list property*].

---

in a chapter 7 case when assets are to be distributed, for priority claimants holding claims which are otherwise non-discharge-able. This is true of most tax claims. *See* § 14.4.3.1, *supra*. It generally should not be filed in chapter 13 cases in which most priority claims, including tax claims, are dischargeable. *See* § 14.4.1, *supra*. When a creditor does not file a proof of claim before the first date set for the meeting of creditors, the debtor may file a claim on that creditor's behalf until thirty days after the creditors' bar date for claims. Fed. R. Bankr. P. 3004.

150 This form is for a secured claim, which the debtor will usually want paid prior to unsecured claims in a chapter 13 case. Secured claims (and all other claims) must be filed by ninety days after the first date set for the section 341(a) meeting of the creditors. Fed. R. Bankr. P. 3002(c); *see also* Official Form 11, Appx. D, *supra*. When a creditor does not file a proof of claim before the first date set for the meeting of creditors, the debtor may file a claim on that creditor's behalf until thirty days after the bar date for claims. Fed. R. Bankr. P. 3004.

10. Claimant asserts the security interest under the writing referred to in paragraph 5 hereof.

11. This claim is a general unsecured claim, except to the extent that the security interest described in paragraph 9 hereof is sufficient to satisfy the claim.

Date:　　　　　　　　　　　　　　　　　　　*[signature]*
　　　　　　　　　　　　　　　　　　　Attorney for Debtor

[Attach: Certificate of Service on creditor]

Form 55　Proof of Unsecured Claim by Debtor[151]

[Caption: Official Form 16A]

Proof of Claim by Debtor

1. *[Debtor]*, who is filing this proof of claim through her attorney, is the Debtor in this case and resides at *[address]*.

2. The claim is filed in the name of *[creditor]*, of *[address]*, which asserts a claim against the Debtor in the amount of $5491.20.

3. The ground for this alleged liability is as follows: a personal loan advanced to the Debtor and her husband, on or about June 24, 2002.

4. A copy of the writing on which this claim is founded is attached hereto *[omitted]*.

5. No judgment has been rendered on this claim except: a default judgment entered against Debtor's husband only, at *[name]* Court, Number *[number]*.

6. The amount of all payments on this claim has been credited and deducted for the purpose of making this proof of claim.

7. This claim is not subject to any setoff or counterclaim.

8. No security interest is held for this claim except: two (2) mortgages against *[address of property]*, recorded in the Department of Records, *[address]* at *[number]* on October 17, 1994 and *[number]* on June 27, 2002.

9. The fair market value of the Debtor's residence is $65,000.00.

10. The Debtor's residence is also subject to a first mortgage and a second mortgage which have priority over *[creditors]*'s mortgage. The first and second mortgages exceed the fair market value of the Debtor's residence.

11. This claim is a general unsecured claim because the security interest described in Paragraph 8 above is not sufficient to satisfy the claim.

Date:　　　　　　　　　　　　　　　　　　　*[signature]*
　　　　　　　　　　　　　　　　　　　Attorney for Debtor

[Attach: Certificate of Service on creditor]

151　This can also be used in cases of undersecured claims, when the debtor seeks to have all or part of the lien declared void under 11 U.S.C. § 506(d). However, if the creditor's mortgage claim is partially secured solely by the debtor's principal residence, an attempt to bifurcate the claim will fail under the *Nobelman* decision. See discussion in § 11.7, *supra*, and Form 68, Appendix G.8, *infra. See also* Official Form 11, Appx. D, *supra*.

Form 56　Motion to Sell Property Free and Clear of Liens[152]

[Caption: Official Form 16D]

Motion to Sell Property Free and Clear of Liens

1. This action is brought by Plaintiff *[debtor]*, Debtor in the above-captioned proceeding, to obtain this Court's permission for the sale of her home free and clear of liens.

2. This Court has exclusive jurisdiction over the property in question under 28 U.S.C. § 1334. This is a core matter.

3. The residence of the Debtor at *[address]*, is presently worth approximately $75,000.00 and is owned jointly with her husband.

4. Said real estate is encumbered by a first mortgage held by Defendant *[name]* Savings and Loan in the amount of approximately $60,000.00, and a second mortgage held by Defendant *[name]* Finance Company in the amount of approximately $10,000.00.

5. The Debtor has claimed her interest in the property, worth approximately $5000.00, as fully exempt in her bankruptcy.

6. The Debtor is unable to maintain current payments on the mortgages and wishes to sell her home, with the proceeds to be applied first to payment of the mortgage balances and then, from the Debtor's share, as follows: $500.00, if such amount remains, to the trustee to fund her chapter 13 plan, and the remaining amount, up to the maximum allowable exemption of $18,450.00, to the Debtor.

7. Such a sale, which would realize the full value of the home, would not prejudice the rights of any party, and would allow those lienholders with liens not avoidable to realize their security.

152　In some cases a debtor may wish to sell, often through a liquidation provision of a chapter 13 plan, a property on which mortgage payments are no longer affordable, to prevent the loss of equity and other ramifications of a foreclosure sale.

　　For several reasons a motion such as this one may be necessary to sell property of the debtor. First, the order obtained makes clear that the property is sold free of the bankruptcy with the bankruptcy court's approval. Many title insurance companies insist on such clarification.

　　The motion would also be necessary if there were a possibility that liens on the property would exceed its value. Only by getting a court order that a buyer would take free of all liens could a sale be effectuated in such circumstances, because few buyers would be interested in taking property encumbered by liens. Such a motion could also include counts avoiding certain liens, including judicial liens under 11 U.S.C. § 522(f). See § 10.4, *supra*, for a discussion of the debtor's avoiding powers.

　　The prayer for relief and proposed order in a motion of this nature should be as specific as possible as to the distribution of the process of the sale, in order to avoid later questions at settlement. A form such as this one may be used in conjunction with a chapter 13 plan with a provision for sale of the debtor's property, such as Form 10, Appendix G.3, *supra*.

　　Bankruptcy Rule 6004(c), added by the 1987 amendments, requires proceedings seeking to sell property free and clear of liens and other interests to be brought as motions pursuant to Rule 9014. The motion must be served on all parties who have liens or other interests in the property to be sold. Fed. R. Bankr. P. 6004(c). Notice of the motion must include the date of the hearing and the time by which objections may be filed and served. *Id.*

WHEREFORE, the Debtor prays that this Court enter an Order permitting the sale of the Debtor's home free and clear of liens, the proceeds being applied first to payment of outstanding mortgages, with the first $500.00 of the Debtor's share of the proceeds, if any, paid to the trustee, and the remaining portion of that share, if any, paid to the Debtor.

Date: [*signature*]
                                            Attorney for Plaintiff

Form 57 Debtor's Motion to Redeem Property Pursuant to 11 U.S.C. § 722[153]

[*Caption: Official Form 16A*]

Debtor's Motion to Redeem Property Pursuant to 11 U.S.C. § 722

1. Movant is one of the Debtors in the above-captioned chapter 7 case. This matter is a core matter.

2. Among the dischargeable consumer debts listed in the petition filed herein was a loan from [*creditor*] secured by an automobile owned by Movant.

3. The automobile, a 1995 Chevrolet Chevette, has been claimed as exempt by Movant under 11 U.S.C. § 522(d)(2), and is used by her for personal and family purposes.

4. The present value of the automobile is fifteen hundred dollars ($1500.00).

5. Movant wishes to redeem the vehicle pursuant to 11 U.S.C. § 722 by paying to the creditor the value of the property, but the creditor has not agreed to her request that this be done.

6. No assets of the estate will be used by the Debtor in redeeming this property.

WHEREFORE, Movant prays this Court to order [*creditor*] to remove and mark satisfied any encumbrance or security interest in Movant's vehicle upon payment to [*creditor*] of fifteen hundred dollars ($1500.00).

Date: [*signature*]
                                             Attorney for Debtor

Form 58 Agreement for Redemption of Property[154]

[*Caption: Official Form 16A*]

Agreement for Redemption of Property

It is hereby agreed, by and between the Debtor in this bankruptcy case and [*creditor*], holder of a purchase money security interest in the Debtor's automobile, that:

1. The value of the said automobile is $1000.00.

2. The security interest of [*creditor*] is valid and enforceable despite the Debtor's bankruptcy case.

3. For so long as the Debtor continues to make payments of $75.00 per month on the said obligation, [*creditor*] will, in consideration for such payments, take no action to repossess or foreclose its security.

4. Such payments will continue until the amount of $1000.00, plus interest computed at the same annual percentage rate as in the original contract between the parties, is paid.

5. At such time, [*creditor*] will take all steps necessary to terminate its security interest in the automobile.

Date: [*signature*]
                                             Attorney for Debtor

Date: [*signature*]
                                            Attorney for Creditor

Form 59 Objection to Proof of Claim[155]

[*Caption: Official Form 16A*]

Objection to Proof of Claim

Debtor, by counsel, objects to Proof of Claim Number Three, filed by [*creditor*] in the amount of $2,139.37 and assigns the following reasons for same:

1. The proof of claim does not comply with Federal Rule of Bankruptcy Procedure 3001(c) because although the claim is alleged to be founded upon an instrument in writing, the instrument itself is not attached to the proof of claim nor is a copy of the instrument attached to the proof of claim.

2. Debtor scheduled the claim of [*creditor*] in the amount of $800.00 and admits owing that amount but does not admit owing the amount filed by Creditor nor does Debtor, in fact, owe anything in excess of the amount scheduled.

3. The proof of claim should be expunged to the extent that it is attempting to obtain post-petition interest in violation of section 502(b)(2) of the Bankruptcy Code.

4. The claim of [*creditor*] is subject to recoupment in the amount of $2000.00 due to the Claimant's violations of the Truth in Lending Act, 15 U.S.C. §§ 1601–1666j, in failing to clearly or accurately disclose the amount financed in this transaction.

---

153 This form may be used to effectuate the debtor's right to redeem under 11 U.S.C. § 722. Fed. R. Bankr. P. 6008 provides that authorization for redemption is obtained by motion. If an order is submitted it should include a directive that the creditor release all security interests. Creditors may argue that valuation standards in the redemption context must be at replacement value based on Associates Commercial Corp. v. Rash, 520 U.S. 953, 117 S. Ct. 1879, 138 L. Ed. 2d 148 (1997). This argument should fail because, upon redemption, the creditor will be paid in a lump sum and so will not experience any risk associated

with the debtor's continuing use of the property. For a general discussion of redemption, see § 11.5, *supra*.

154 This agreement will, if the creditor is willing, allow redemption in installments without reaffirmation of the debt. It protects against repossession so long as payments are kept current. There is some doubt whether a creditor may be forced to take installment payments, but often creditors will agree to do so, for example, as part of a general compromise settlement on issues of value. See discussion of redemption in § 11.5, *supra*.

155 For various reasons, debtors may wish to object to unsecured claims in some chapter 13 cases, especially if such claims are priority claims or if the creditor will cause problems by filing a motion under the ability to pay test. See § 12.3.3, *supra*. The objection may raise any defense the debtor has (11 U.S.C. § 506(b)(1)) or may raise noncompliance with the Code or the Federal Rules of Bankruptcy Procedure. See general discussion of objections to claims in § 13.4.3, *supra*.

WHEREFORE, Debtor respectfully requests that your Honorable Court disallow the proof of claim filed by [*creditor*], and order such other and further relief as is just and proper.

Date: [*signature*]
                                Attorney for Debtor

Form 60 Objection to Undocumented Credit Card Claim[156]

[*Caption: Official Form 16A*]

Objection to Proof of Claim

Debtors, by counsel, object to Proof of Claim Number Four, filed by [*claimant*] in the amount of $3408.59 and assigns the following reasons for same:

1. The proof of claim does not comply with Federal Rule of Bankruptcy Procedure 3001(c) because the claim is based on written credit card agreement, but neither an original nor copy of the credit card agreement or any other supporting documents are attached to the proof of claim.

2. An itemization of interest and other charges is not attached to the proof of claim as required by the instructions to Official Form 10 even though the claim amount of $3408.59 is alleged to include interest and other charges. The claimant also failed to check the appropriate box on the claim form indicating that the claim includes such charges.

3. Attached to the claim form is a one-page "Accounting Summary" that merely restates the balance owed listed in paragraph 4 on Official Form 10 and purports to include billing statement information for the month preceding the filing of the claim. This "Accounting Summary" fails provide an account transaction summary or other information that would show how the total amount claimed has been calculated.

4. Debtors scheduled the claim of [*claimant*] in the amount of $3000.00 and listed the debt as disputed.[157]

5. As a result of [*claimant's*] failure to comply with Federal Rule of Bankruptcy Procedure 3001(c), its proof of claim is not entitled to *prima facie* validity.

6. [*Claimant*] is a buyer of bankruptcy debt that has repeatedly filed, through its attorneys, undocumented and unsubstantiated proofs of claim in this Court and in bankruptcy courts nationwide. Debtors' counsel has previously advised [*claimant*] that attorney fees would be sought if such claims continued to be filed in violation of Federal Rule of Bankruptcy Procedure 3001(c).

WHEREFORE, Debtors respectfully request that this Court disallow the proof of claim filed by [*claimant*], award attorney fees

pursuant to 28 U.S.C. § 1927 and 11 U.S.C. § 105 for the prosecution of this objection, and order such other and further relief as is just and proper.

Date: [*signature*]
                               Attorney for Debtors

Form 61 Order Disallowing Undocumented Claim

[*Caption: Official Form 16D*]

Order

AND NOW, this [*date*] day of [*month*], [*year*], upon consideration of the Debtors' objection and the proceedings thereon it is hereby ORDERED, ADJUDGED AND DECREED:

1. The claim filed by [*claimant*] is disallowed.

2. [*Claimant*] and its attorney shall pay to the Debtor's attorney the sum of $1000.

3. [*Claimant*] and its attorney shall be subject to sanctions and further attorneys fees for the filing in this case or any other case before this Court a proof of claim that does not comply with Federal Rule of Bankruptcy Procedure 3001(c) and which fails to include:

a) supporting documentation such as the credit card agreement and any other agreement authorizing the charges and fees included in the claim;

b) an itemization of the total amount claimed separately listing principal, interest, late fees, over-limit charges, bad check fees, and other charges;

c) a sufficient number of monthly account statements to show how the total amount claimed has been calculated.

Date: [*signature*]
                          United States Bankruptcy Judge

Form 62 Objection to Frivolous Priority Claim and Request for Sanctions[158]

[*Caption: Official Form 16A*]

Debtor's Objection to the Claim of the Traffic Court and Request for Sanctions

The Debtors, [*debtors*], by their counsel, hereby object to the claim filed by the [*city*] Traffic Court in the above-captioned case. The grounds for their objection are as follows:

1. The claim was filed as a priority claim.

2. There is no basis for the traffic court to claim that it has priority status in this bankruptcy.

3. The Claimant has repeatedly filed frivolous priority proofs of claim in this Court and Debtors' counsel has previously advised Claimant that attorney fees would be sought if such claims continued to be filed.[159]

---

156 A proof of claim based on a writing that is not supported by attached documentation or otherwise fails to comply with Fed. R. Bankr. P. 3001 is facially defective and not entitled to a presumption of validity. *See* § 13.4.3.4, *supra*.

157 The failure to list a debt as disputed on the bankruptcy schedules should not bar a debtor from later filing a claim objection because the schedules are not filed for the purposes of claim allowance, except in chapter 11 cases. However, to avoid a dispute on this issue, debtors may wish to mark debts as disputed, or to note that they have no way of verifying the amounts creditors have claimed on monthly statements.

---

158 A form such as this one may be used when an obviously frivolous claim is filed.

159 If a party persists in filing frivolous pleadings, a record should be made of efforts to remedy the problem before seeking sanctions.

WHEREFORE, the Debtors pray that the claim be disallowed as a priority claim and allowed only as a general unsecured claim, and that they be awarded attorney fees of $500.00 pursuant to 28 U.S.C. § 1927 for the prosecution of this objection.[160]

Date: [*signature*]
                                                Attorney for Plaintiff

Form 63 Complaint Objecting to Secured Claims for Failure to Comply with Truth in Lending Act and HUD Mortgage Servicing Requirements[161]

[*Caption: Official Form 16D*]

Complaint

1. This adversary proceeding is brought by the Debtor pursuant to 11 U.S.C. § 502, to object to the allowed secured claim of Defendant [*creditor*] on the basis that a portion of its claim is unenforceable against the Debtor under applicable law, and to assert counterclaims against Defendant.

2. This Court has jurisdiction in that this matter is a core proceeding, under 11 U.S.C. § 1334 and 28 U.S.C. § 157(b)(2)(B) and (C).[162]

3. On October 15, 2004, the Plaintiff/Debtor filed a chapter 13 case in this Court.

4. On November 18, 2004, Defendant filed a secured claim in the amount of $3744.00 which stated that this amount was the amount owed on the mortgage by the Debtor.

5. The amount claimed is excessive and should be disallowed to the extent that it is subject to the defenses and counterclaims set forth below.

I. Truth in Lending Act

6. The transaction upon which this claim is based was a consumer credit transaction subject to the federal Truth in Lending Act, 15 U.S.C. §§ 1601–1666j ("Act"), and Regulation Z thereunder, 12 C.F.R. § 226.

7. In the course of the transaction, Defendant failed to properly make all of the disclosures required by the Act and Regulation Z.[163]

8. As a result of this failure, Defendant is liable to Plaintiff in the amount of $2000.00 plus attorney fees and costs, which must be deducted from its claim by way of recoupment.

II. Failure to Comply with HUD Regulations

9. The mortgage on which this action was brought is a mortgage insured by the Federal Housing Administration.

10. Due to that fact, Defendant was bound to comply with rules and regulations of the Department of Housing and Urban Development.

11. The applicable regulations required Defendant to service this mortgage, and to offer and accept reasonable forbearance arrangements to avoid foreclosure when Plaintiff became delinquent in her payments.

12. Defendant failed to comply with these obligations; it not only did not offer forbearance to Plaintiff, but also refused reasonable repayment proposals made by her.

13. As a result, the commencement of a foreclosure action by Defendant was improper, and all attorney fees and costs incurred in connection with the foreclosure cannot be charged to Plaintiff. Therefore, the claim should be further disallowed, to the extent of these fees and costs of $1525.00.

III. Unfair Trade Practices

14. The allegations of paragraphs 9 through 13 above are incorporated herein by reference.

15. The failure to reasonably forbear from foreclosure, as required by HUD regulations, constituted an unfair trade practice in violation of the Unfair Trade Practices Law, [*cite provision(s) of state law*] for which [*creditor*] is liable for triple the damages incurred by Plaintiff, that is, the attorney fees and costs for which she has been held liable.[164]

IV. Excessive Attorney Fees

16. The Defendant's claim requests attorney fees and costs of $1525.00 These attorney fees and costs are unreasonably high, and exceed the amount due under the mortgage and note which place a five percent (5%) limit on attorney fees.

---

160 A separate motion for sanctions under Rule 9011 may also be served on the claimant and filed with the court together with this Objection no sooner than twenty-one days after service, provided that the claimant has not withdrawn the claim during the twenty-one-day period. *See* Fed. R. Bankr. P. 9011(c)(1)(A).

161 This complaint illustrates a more abbreviated form with which to raise Truth in Lending violations than Form 65, Appendix G.8, *infra*. See generally notes to Form 65, Appendix G.8, *infra*, for discussion of the principles involved in such complaints. The complaint also raises a defense to costs and fees incurred in a foreclosure pursued in a manner prohibited by regulations governing the servicing of Federal Housing Administration (FHA) mortgages. Similar claims can be raised in regard to Veterans Administration mortgages. Numerous courts have held that equitable relief can be granted from such foreclosures. *See*, *e.g.*, Bankers Life Co. v. Denton, 120 Ill. App. 576, 458 N.E.2d 203 (1983); Associated E. Mortgage Co. v. Young, 163 N.J. Super. 315 (Super. Ct. Ch. Div. 1978); Fed. Nat'l Mortgage Ass'n v. Ricks, 372 N.Y.S.2d 485 (Sup. Ct. 1975); *see also* Brown v. Lynn, 380 F. Supp. 986, 990 (N.D. Ill. 1974). Finally, the complaint challenges attorney fees sought in excess of the amount permitted by 11 U.S.C. § 506(b), which allows only those provided for in the parties' agreement, to the extent they are reasonable. *See* § 11.6.2, *supra*.

162 A proceeding to allow or disallow a claim or raise counterclaims to a claim is a core proceeding. 28 U.S.C. § 157(b)(2)(B), (C).

---

163 In some cases a debtor may have no recollection of receiving any Truth in Lending disclosures. In such cases, it is appropriate to allege that proper disclosures were not made. If a creditor then provides a copy of disclosures that appear to have been provided the debtor, this allegation can be dropped. This allegation would also encompass a claim that the disclosures were deficient.

164 The failure to follow applicable law or to disclose material facts about customers' rights can be an unfair or deceptive practice. *See generally* National Consumer Law Center, Unfair and Deceptive Acts and Practices § 4.2.14 (5th ed. 2001 and Supp.).

V. Prayer for Relief

WHEREFORE, Plaintiff prays that:

1. The claim of [*creditor*] be disallowed as currently filed;

2. The allowed secured claim be determined to be $219.00;

3. She be awarded her attorney fees and costs herein;

4. She be awarded triple damages in the amount of $4575.00 under the Unfair Trade Practices Law, [*cite provision(s) of state law*]; and

5. The Court order such other relief as is just and proper.

Date: [*signature*]
Attorney for Debtor

Form 64 Complaint Objecting to Secured Claim and Seeking to Enforce Truth in Lending Rescission[165]

[*Caption: Official Form16D*]

Complaint to Determine Validity and/or Extent of Secured Claim

Preliminary Statement

1. This is a complaint challenging the validity and/or extent of the Defendant's proof of claim on the basis of the Truth in Lending Act, 15 U.S.C. §§ 1601–1666j, and alternatively on the ground that it is excessive and without foundation. Debtor/Plaintiff seeks a determination that she has properly rescinded any security interest held on her property by Defendant and that Defendant has no valid secured or unsecured claim. In addition, Debtor/Plaintiff seeks damages for Defendant's failure to rescind under the Truth in Lending Act.

Jurisdiction

2. Jurisdiction of the Bankruptcy Court in this matter is provided by 28 U.S.C. §§ 1334 and 157, as amended, and the Order of Reference made by the district court for this district dated July 25, 1984.

3. This is a core proceeding.

Parties

4. Debtor/plaintiff, [*debtor*], is an adult individual residing at [*address*]. [*Debtor*] is a debtor in this Court, having filed a petition pursuant to chapter 13 of the Bankruptcy Code on March 20, 2004.

5. Plaintiff, [*trustee*], is the Chapter 13 Standing Trustee for this case. [*Trustee*], as trustee, is listed as a nominal plaintiff at his request.

6. Defendant, [*name*], is a corporation whose principal place of business is at [*address*].

---

165 This complaint form may be used to seek enforcement of Truth in Lending rescission claims. In some jurisdictions more specificity about the claimed violations may be necessary. Other consumer defenses to the mortgage or bankruptcy lien avoidance theories may also be joined to this complaint. It may make sense to mix and match appropriate theories from this and the other objections to claims in this appendix. Note also that whenever the defendant is an insured depository institution, special service requirements apply. Fed. R. Bankr. P. 7004(h).

Factual Allegations

7. The Debtor/Plaintiff entered into a loan transaction with the Defendant on or about October 6, 2002 ("the transaction").

8. A true and correct copy of the Truth in Lending disclosures given by Defendant to the Debtor/Plaintiff in the transaction is attached hereto and marked Exhibit A [*omitted*].

9. Defendant obtained a mortgage on Debtor/Plaintiff's home in connection with the transaction.

10. On or about January 11, 2004, the Debtor/Plaintiff, through her attorney, notified Defendant that she was exercising her right to rescind the transaction pursuant to the Truth in Lending Act. A true and correct copy of the letter by which Debtor/Plaintiff exercised her rescission rights is attached hereto and marked Exhibit B [*omitted*].

11. The Defendant failed to implement the Debtor/Plaintiff's rescission of the transaction within twenty days as required by the Truth in Lending Act.

12. On or about May 16, 2004 the Defendant filed a secured proof of claim in this bankruptcy case in the total amount of $14,353.74.

13. The proof of claim filed by Defendant includes interest, insurance, appraisal and attorney fee charges which are not authorized by contract or applicable law.

Claims

I. "TILA"

14. At all times relevant hereto Defendant was a creditor within the meaning of the Truth in Lending Act ("TILA"), 15 U.S.C. §§ 1601–1666j.

15. The Debtor/Plaintiff's transactions with Defendant were consumer credit transactions within the meaning of TILA.

16. In connection with the transaction, Defendant failed to provide the Debtor/Plaintiff with a disclosure statement in conformity with TILA.

17. The disclosure statement provided by Defendant to Debtor/Plaintiff fails to set forth accurately the finance charge, amount financed and annual percentage rate in the transaction.

18. The disclosure statement provided by Defendant to Debtor/Plaintiff fails to set forth properly the payment schedule for the transaction.

19. By reason of Defendant's failure to provide a proper disclosure statement, Debtor/Plaintiff retained a right to rescind the transaction for three years from the date of the transaction.

20. Debtor/Plaintiff properly exercised her right to rescind the transaction in a timely fashion.

21. The Debtor/Plaintiff is entitled to a determination that any security interest held by Defendant in her residence is void.

22. The Debtor/Plaintiff is entitled to a determination that Defendant holds no valid secured or unsecured claim.

23. The Debtor/Plaintiff is entitled to an award of $2000.00 affirmative damages together with costs and attorney fees for Defendant's failure to rescind the transaction in conformity with TILA.

24. The Debtor/Plaintiff is entitled to recoup $2000.00 from Defendant's proof of claim, if any, for Defendant's violations of the Truth in Lending Act.

II. The Claim is Excessive and Must Be Disallowed in Part

25. To the extent that Defendant's claim is excessive or unsupported by contract or applicable law, it must be disallowed.

Request for Relief

The Debtor/Plaintiff requests that this Court:

a. Assume jurisdiction of this proceeding;

b. Declare that the Debtor/Plaintiff validly rescinded the transaction;

c. Declare that any mortgages held by Defendant on the Debtor/Plaintiff's property are void and unenforceable;

d. Determine that Defendant has no allowed secured claim and no allowed unsecured claim in this bankruptcy case;

e. Award Debtor/Plaintiff $2000.00 in statutory damages for Defendant's failure to rescind and recoupment of $2000.00 for Defendant's disclosure violations pursuant to TILA, 15 U.S.C. § 1640;

f. Order that Defendant return all money paid to it in connection with the transaction;

g. Award Debtor's counsel reasonable attorney fees and costs pursuant to the TILA, 15 U.S.C. § 1640;

h. Award such other relief as the Court deems appropriate and just.

Date: [*signature*]
                                      Attorney for Debtor/Plaintiff

Form 65 Alternative Complaint Objecting to Secured Claim on the Basis of Truth in Lending Rescission[166]

[*Caption: Official Form 16D*]

Complaint Objecting to Secured Claim

1. On December 26, 2003, Debtor herein filed a voluntary petition under chapter 13 of the Bankruptcy Code. Therefore, this Court has jurisdiction over this proceeding pursuant to 28 U.S.C. § 1334. This proceeding is a core proceeding.

---

166 An objection to a claim challenging the extent or validity of a lien must be filed as an adversary proceeding. Fed. R. Bankr. P. 3007. For a general discussion of complaints in adversary proceedings, see notes to Form 83, Appendix G.10, *infra*. Such an objection may raise the validity of a lien under 11 U.S.C. § 506(d), when the creditor is undersecured, subject to the limitations imposed by the *Dewsnup* and *Nobelman* decisions, or when there are other reasons why the lien is invalid, such as a rescission under the Truth in Lending Act. *See* Form 64, Appx. G.8, *supra*; Form 68, Appx. G.8, *infra*. For a discussion of section 506, see Chapter 11, *supra*. For a discussion of litigating other claims, see Chapter 13, *supra*.

   This complaint raises violations of the Truth in Lending requirements applicable after October 1, 1982, under the Truth in Lending Simplification and Reform Act. Title VI of Pub. L. No. 96-221, 94 Stat. 132 (1980). Prior to October 1, 1982, creditors were subject to different disclosure requirements. *See* National Consumer Law Center, Truth in Lending (5th ed. 2003). This form is adapted from pleadings by Irwin Trauss, Esq., Philadelphia, PA.

2. Debtor's first modified plan provides for payment of 100% of the Debtor's allowed secured and priority claims and for payment of 74% of the Debtor's unsecured claims if sufficient funds are left over after payment of the secured and priority claims.

3. On or about August 4, 2002, the Debtor entered into a consumer loan transaction with [*creditor*], (hereinafter "Defendant").

4. Defendant is a creditor within the meaning of the Truth in Lending Act and Regulation Z, 12 C.F.R. § 226.2(17).

5. In connection with the transaction Defendant took a security interest in Debtor's home at [*address*].

6. In violation of 12 C.F.R. § 226.23(b) Defendant did not, at the consummation of the loan transaction, give the Debtor two copies of a notice of her right to rescind the transaction.

7. In violation of 12 C.F.R. § 226.23(c) Defendant did not delay the distribution of the proceeds of the loan until after the rescission period that had elapsed, but immediately distributed the proceeds of the loan.

8. In connection with the consumer loan transaction Defendant gave to Plaintiff two copies of the disclosure statement, a copy of which is attached hereto as Exhibit A [*omitted*].

9. Said disclosure statement does not contain all of the material disclosures required by the federal Truth in Lending Act and by Regulation Z, and is missing, *inter alia*, the following material disclosures:

a. The disclosure statement fails to include the cost of credit life and disability insurance in the finance charge even though:

   i. Such insurance was required by Plaintiff as a condition of the loan; and even though:

   ii. The Debtor did not give a separately signed indication of her desire for *each* insurance. 12 C.F.R. § 226.4(d)(1)(iii).

b. The notice fails to disclose the service charge as a prepaid finance charge as required by 12 C.F.R. § 226.18(c).

c. The notice fails to itemize the components of the amount financed as required by 12 C.F.R. § 226.18(c).

d. As a result of the failure to properly disclose the above-mentioned items as finance charges the notice misstates the amount financed, the finance charge and the APR.

e. In violation of 12 C.F.R. § 226.17(a) the notice misleadingly states that credit insurance was not required by the lender when in fact it was a specific precondition of the loan, and Defendant would not extend credit if credit insurance was not purchased.

10. On or about October 28, 2003, Debtor, pursuant to 12 C.F.R. § 226.23(a), rescinded the entire consumer loan transaction by sending to Defendant a Notice of Rescission, a copy of which is attached hereto as Exhibit B.

11. On or about April 23, 2004, Defendant filed a proof of claim in the amount of $947.30.

12. In its proof Defendant claimed to be secured for the entire amount of its claim by an interest in [*address of debtor's home*].

13. Defendant's claim against the Debtor is not secured as the Debtor's exercise of her right of rescission rendered any security interest Defendant might have had in [*address of debtor's home*] void.

14. Defendant's claim is excessive and cannot be allowed for more than $14.28 for the following reasons:

a. After rescission, the Debtor is liable at most for the principal amount of the rescinded loan exclusive of finance charges, insurance charges and all other charges, 12 C.F.R. § 226.23, 11 U.S.C. § 502(b)(1), in this case not more than $675.62;

b. Of this amount, $675.62, Debtor has already paid not less than $270.34, 11 U.S.C. § 502(b)(1);

c. Against the $405.28 remaining, Debtor has a recoupment in the amount of $391.00, or twice the finance charge, under section 130 of the Truth in Lending Act, 15 U.S.C. § 1640, leaving a balance of not more than $14.28 owing to Defendant.

WHEREFORE, Debtor prays that Defendant's security interest in [*address of debtor's home*] be declared void, that the claim of Defendant be classified as wholly unsecured, that the claim be allowed for not more than $14.28, that attorney fees and costs be awarded pursuant to 15 U.S.C. § 1640 and that the Court order such additional relief as is necessary in the interest of justice.

Date: [*signature*]
               Attorney for Debtor/Plaintiff

Exhibit B

October 28, 2003

[*creditor*]
[*address*]   RE: [*debtor*]
                     [*creditor*]
           Date of Loan: 8/4/02
          Total of payments: $912.00
       Loan secured by mortgage on:
       [*address of debtor's home*]

Notice of Rescission

Dear Sir or Madam:

Please be advised that I represent [*debtor*]. On or about August 4, 2002, [*debtor*] entered into the above-referenced consumer loan transaction with [*creditor*]. A security interest in [*debtor*]'s home at the captioned address was taken as security for this loan. At the time the loan transaction was consummated the proceeds of the loan were immediately distributed. In violation of 12 C.F.R. § 226.23(c) the proceeds were not withheld in order to enable [*debtor*] to exercise her right of rescission. When the transaction was consummated [*debtor*] was not given two copies of her notice of her right to rescission. The disclosure form that was given to [*debtor*], in an attempt to comply with 12 C.F.R. § 226.18, omitted several material disclosures required by the federal Truth in Lending Act. Some of the omissions are enumerated in the list attached to this letter.

Please be advised that pursuant to section 125 of the federal Truth in Lending Act, 15 U.S.C. § 1635, and pursuant to section 226.23(a) of Regulation Z, 12 C.F.R. § 226.23, [*debtor*] is rescinding the above-referenced consumer loan transaction. This letter constitutes NOTICE OF RESCISSION.

Please return to [*debtor*] all of the money which has been paid to [*creditor*] in connection with the above-referenced consumer loan transaction. This includes all payments of interest, all payments of principal, all discount charges, all service charges, and all charges for insurance taken out in connection with the loan. Under section 226.23(d) of Regulation Z, 12 C.F.R. § 226.23(d), you have twenty days from the receipt of this notice in which to return this money to [*debtor*] and to take all action necessary to terminate the

security interests which were created by the transaction. This includes, but is not limited to, the mortgage taken in [*debtor*]'s residence at [*address*].

Please send the appropriate amount of money as well as confirmation of the termination of all security interests to this office no later than November 7, 2003.

I look forward to your prompt reply.

                   [*signature*]
                 Attorney for Debtor

Certified mail # [*number*]

Copy also sent to addressee by first class mail.

Following is a partial list of the material disclosures which were not made to [*debtor*] in connection with the transaction described in the foregoing letter:

a. The disclosure statement fails to include the cost of credit life and disability insurance in the finance charge even though:

     i. Such insurance was required by Plaintiff as a condition of the loan; and even though

     ii. [*Debtor*] did not give a separately signed indication of her desire for such insurance. 12 C.F.R. § 226.4(d)(1)(iii).

b. As a result of the failure to properly disclose the above-mentioned items as finance charges the notice misstates the amount financed, the finance charge and the APR.

c. In violation of 12 C.F.R. § 226.6 the notice misleadingly states that credit insurance was not required by the lender when in fact it was a specific precondition of the loan, and Plaintiff would not extend credit if credit insurance was not purchased.

Form 66   Judgment Order Disallowing Secured Claim

[Caption: Official Form 16D]

Order

AND NOW, this [*date*] day of [*month*], [*year*], upon consideration of the Debtor's complaint and the proceedings thereon it is hereby ORDERED, ADJUDGED AND DECREED:

1. That the security interest claimed by [*creditor*] in [*address of debtor's home*], dated August 4, 2002 and recorded in the Department of Records of [*county*] in Mortgage Book No. [*number*], page [*number*], is void, and

2. That the claim of [*creditor*] be classified as an unsecured claim and allowed in the amount of $14.28.

3. [*Creditor*] is directed to take all actions necessary to have the security interest released and removed from the mortgage book of [*county*].

Date: [*signature*]
             United States Bankruptcy Judge

Form 67 Complaint Objecting to Secured Claim on the Basis of Usury and Warranty Defenses[167]

[Caption: Official Form 16D]

Complaint I. Preliminary Statement

1. This is an action by a consumer debtor against a finance company asserting usury claims under the state Unfair Trade Practices and Consumer Protection Act, *[citation]*, and for breach of warranty.

II. Jurisdiction

2. Jurisdiction is provided by 28 U.S.C. § 1334.

3. This proceeding is a core matter.

III. Parties

4. Plaintiff is the Debtor in the above-captioned bankruptcy case. He resides at *[address]*.

5. Defendant *[name]* Mortgage Company ("Mortgage Co.") is a mortgage company organized and existing under the laws of *[state]* and, at all relevant times hereto, was doing business at *[address]*.

6. Defendant *[name]* Bank ("Bank") is a national bank organized under the laws of the United States doing business at *[address]*, and is either the successor in interest to Mortgage Co. or the assignee of Mortgage Co.'s rights and obligations in the consumer credit transaction which is the subject of this proceeding.

IV. Factual Allegations

7. Mortgage Co. is the entity to which the debt arising from the consumer credit transaction is initially payable on the face of the evidence of indebtedness.

8. Bank is the current holder of the mortgage and/or other security interests taken in the subject transaction.

9. At all relevant times hereto, Mortgage Co. and a home improvement contractor believed to be trading as *[name]* Builders were engaged in a business relationship in connection with the financing of home improvements.

10. Pursuant to said business relationship, the contractor

a. had knowledge of Mortgage Co.'s credit terms and business practices;

b. supplied Mortgage Co. with loan customers;

c. supplied Mortgage Co. with loan information and otherwise participated in the preparation of loan documents; and

d. received a fee, commission or other consideration from Mortgage Co.

11. On or about April 9, 2000, Debtor entered into a home improvement installment sales contract with the contractor for the installation, *inter alia*, of storm doors and windows on their house.

---

167 This complaint raises state law usury and warranty claims against a mortgage holder in bankruptcy court. These issues may be raised in a complaint challenging a proof of claim or affirmatively to determine claims affecting the validity and extent of the mortgage. Consumer defenses may vary widely from state to state and therefore this complaint must be adapted to fit applicable law.

That contract was assigned to Mortgage Co. A copy of the contract is attached hereto as Exhibit "A" *[omitted]*.

12. After the completion of the work on the outside of their home, the contractor representative showed Debtor and his wife some new carpeting for the inside of their home and they agreed to purchase the carpeting.

13. In the course of his sales presentation, the contractor's representative represented and guaranteed that the carpet would never stain, would remain thick and plush and would never wear down.

14. Debtor and his wife then agreed to purchase the carpet.

15. In return for a referral fee, the contractor then contacted Mortgage Co. and made arrangements for Mortgage Co. to provide the financing in the transaction.

16. Subsequently, on May 20, 2000, a representative of Mortgage Co. came to Debtor's home to have Debtor and his wife sign the necessary papers for the purchase of the carpet on credit.

17. As a result of the visit from the Mortgage Co. representative, Debtor and his wife entered into a consumer credit transaction with Mortgage Co. to finance the purchase of the carpeting from their home. The Debtor also agreed to refinance their prior loan from Mortgage Co. The new transaction was at an interest rate substantially higher than the original loan from Mortgage Co.

18. In the transaction, Mortgage Co. acquired a security interest in *[address]*, real property owned by Debtor and used as his principal residence.

19. The representations made by the contractor regarding the quality of the carpet were not true. In fact, the carpet was of inferior quality, retained stains and wore down substantially within a few months.

V. Statement of Claims

First Claim—State Deceptive Practices Statute

20. The transaction described above constituted a home improvement sales finance transaction within the meaning of *[cite provision of state law]*.

21. By writing the transaction as a personal loan under the *[state]* Consumer Discount Company Act, *[citation]*, a statute containing a substantially higher interest rate, Mortgage Co. committed an unfair and deceptive act within the meaning of UDAP.

WHEREFORE, Debtor requests damages in an amount equal to three times the additional interest charged in the transaction and a reasonable attorney fee.

Second Claim—Breach of Express Warranty

22. The contractor breached his express warranty to Debtor.

23. Under the terms of Debtor's contract with Defendants, they are subject to all claims and defenses which Debtor could assert against the contractor.

24. As a proximate result of the breach of express warranty, Debtor has suffered actual damages.

WHEREFORE, Debtor requests that the Court award him damages in an amount equal to the difference between the value of the carpet as warranted and the value as delivered, plus incidental and consequential damages.

Third Claim—Breach of Implied Warranty of Merchantability

25. The contractor, as a merchant dealing in carpeting, warranted as a matter of law that the carpet was merchantable as fit for ordinary purposes and could pass in the trade without objection.

26. The carpet was not merchantable at the time of delivery, could not pass in the trade without objection and was not fit for ordinary purposes.

27. As a proximate result of the breach of the implied warranty of merchantability, Debtor has suffered actual damages.

WHEREFORE, Debtor requests that the Court award him damages in an amount equal to the difference between the value of the carpet as warranted and the value as delivered, plus incidental and consequential damages.

Fourth Claim—Breach of Implied Warranty of Fitness for Particular Purpose

28. The contractor impliedly warranted that the carpet was fit for use in a property in which a family with small children reside.

29. The carpet was not fit for that particular purpose.

30. As a result of the breach of the implied warranty of fitness for particular purpose, Debtor has suffered actual damages.

WHEREFORE, Debtor requests that the Court award him damages in an amount equal to the difference between the value of the carpet as warranted and the value as delivered, plus incidental and consequential damages.

Date: [*signature*]
                             Attorney for Debtor/Plaintiff

Form 68   Complaint or Motion to Determine Value of Security and Creditor's Allowed Secured Claim[168]

[*Caption: Official Form 16D*]

Debtor's Complaint Pursuant to 11 U.S.C. § 506(a) and Bankruptcy Rule 3012 to Determine the Value of Security and Creditor's Allowed Secured Claim

The Debtor, by her attorney, requests that this Court, pursuant to 11 U.S.C. § 506(a) and Bankruptcy Rule 3012 determine the value of the interest of the [*name*] Mortgage Company in the Debtor's real estate and determine the amount of [*name*] Mortgage Company allowed secured claim. In support of this complaint the Debtor states as follows:

1. The Debtor filed the instant voluntary petition under chapter 13 of the Bankruptcy Code on June 3, 2004.

2. The Court has jurisdiction over this proceeding pursuant to 28 U.S.C. §§ 1334 and 157(b)(2)(K). This is a core proceeding.

3. At the time the Debtor filed the instant bankruptcy petition and at the present time the value of the Debtor's interest in the real estate was and is approximately $55,000.00.

4. The Debtor's interest in the real estate is subject to a lien arising out of a mortgage dated January 31, 1996 in favor of [*name*] Bank in the amount of $48,000.00.

5. The Debtor's interest in the real estate is further encumbered by a municipal lien in favor of the City of [*city*] for real estate taxes in the amount of $3500.00. The lien of the City of [*city*] is a statutory lien with first priority, regardless of the date of its recording.

6. [*Name*] Mortgage Company filed a secured proof of claim in the instant case on or about November 25, 2004, in the amount of $25,000.00 based on a mortgage dated January 10, 2000.

7. The lien securing the claim of [*name*] Mortgage Company is junior to the liens listed above, which liens total in excess of $51,500.00.

8. The value of the interest of [*name*] Mortgage Company in the estate's interest in the real estate is no more than $3500.00.

9. Pursuant to 11 U.S.C. § 506(a), the allowable secured claim of [*name*] Mortgage Company is no more than $3500.00.

10. The balance of any claim of [*name*] Mortgage Company is an allowable only as unsecured claim.

11. In addition to a security interest in the debtor's residence [*name*] Mortgage Co. has a security interest in personal property belonging to the debtor [*and/or*] in rents payable to the debtor as owner of the property. [*Name*] Mortgage Co. is not entitled to the protections of 11 U.S.C. § 1322(b)(2).[169]

WHEREFORE the Debtor prays this Court to:

a. Value the interest of the [*name*] Mortgage Company in the real estate at $3500.00.

b. Determine the allowed secured claim of [*name*] Mortgage Company to be $3500.00 pursuant to 11 U.S.C. § 506(a) with the balance allowed as an unsecured claim only.

c. Grant such other relief as may be necessary and proper under the law.

Date: [*signature*]
                             Attorney for Debtor

---

168 This is a complaint form to determine a creditor's allowed secured claim under 11 U.S.C. § 506(a) in light of the Supreme Court's decision in Dewsnup v. Timm, 502 U.S. 410, 112 S. Ct. 77, 116 L. Ed. 2d 903 (1992). *See* § 11.2, *supra*. Whether this issue needs to be brought as a motion pursuant to Fed. R. Bankr. P. 3012 or as an adversary proceeding will probably vary from jurisdiction to jurisdiction. Best practice, when any doubt exists, will be to file this action as an adversary proceeding subject to the adversary rules. Fed. R. Bankr. P. 7001–7087. This form is easily adaptable to either practice. The standard for valuation will be affected by the Supreme Court's decision in Associates Commercial Corp. v. Rash, 520 U.S. 953, 117 S. Ct. 1879, 138 L. Ed. 2d 148 (1997). *See* § 11.2.2.3.2, *supra*; *Resolving Valuation Issues After Rash*, 16 NCLC REPORTS *Bankruptcy and Foreclosures Ed.* 1 (July/Aug. 1997).

169 This additional paragraph may now be necessary in some jurisdictions when seeking bifurcation of a residential mortgage because of the Supreme Court's decision in Nobelman v. Am. Sav. Bank, 508 U.S. 324, 113 S. Ct. 2106, 124 L. Ed. 2d 228 (1993). It also may be possible to argue that the protections of 11 U.S.C. § 1322 (b)(2) are an affirmative defense which must raised by the creditor. *See generally* §§ 11.2.1, 11.7, *supra*.

Form 69 Qualified Written Request Under RESPA to Obtain Mortgage Loan Information[170]

[*date*]

[*mortgage company or servicer*]

RE: [*debtor*]
    [*debtor's address*]
    [*social security number*]
    [*bankruptcy number:*]
    [*file date:*]
    [*account number*]

To Whom It May Concern:

Please treat this letter as a **"qualified written request"** under the Real Estate Settlement Procedures Act, 12 U.S.C. section 2605(e). I am making this request on behalf of my client, [*client*], based on her dispute of the amount alleged to be due and owing contained in the [*mortgage company's*] notice of default and/or proof of claim filed in [*client's*] chapter 13 bankruptcy. Specifically, I am requesting a breakdown of the following pre-bankruptcy and post-bankruptcy information:

1. The monthly principal and interest payment, and monthly escrow payment prior to [*date of bankruptcy filing*].

2. The monthly principal and interest payment, and monthly escrow payment subsequent to [*date of bankruptcy filing*].

3. The total unpaid principal, interest and escrow balances due and owing as of [*date of bankruptcy filing*].

4. For all payments received during the twelve (12) months prior to [*date of bankruptcy filing*], indicate the amount of the payment, the date received, the date posted to the account, how the payment was applied or credited (indicating the portion, if any, applied or credited to principal, interest, escrow or suspense), and the month to which the payment was applied. If interest is calculated using a daily accrual accounting method, indicate for each payment the number of days that elapsed from the prior payment application date.

5. The amount, payment date, purpose, and recipient of all foreclosure expenses, late charges, NSF check charges, appraisal fees, property inspection/preservation fees, legal fees, recoverable corporate advances, and other expenses or costs that have been charged and/or assessed to [*client's*] mortgage account in the eighteen (18) months prior to [*date of bankruptcy filing*],

6. The amount, payment date, purpose, and recipient of all foreclosure expenses, late charges, NSF check charges, appraisal fees, property inspection/preservation fees, force placed insurance charges, legal fees, bankruptcy/proof of claim fees, recoverable corporate advances, and other expenses or costs that have been charged and/or assessed to [*client's*] mortgage account subsequent to [*date of bankruptcy filing*].

7. The amount, payment date, purpose, and recipient of all escrow account items, including but not limited to taxes, water and sewer charges, and forced placed or other insurance premiums, charged and/or assessed to [*client's*] mortgage account in the eighteen (18) months prior to [*date of bankruptcy filing*].

8. A breakdown of the current escrow payment showing how it was calculated and the reasons for any increase or decrease in the eighteen (18) months prior to [*date of bankruptcy filing*].

9. The balance in the escrow account as of [*date of bankruptcy filing*].

10. The balance in any suspense account as of [*date of bankruptcy filing*] and the reason why such funds were deposited in said account.

11. The current interest rate on [*client's*] mortgage account.

Finally, if you are not the current holder of the note and mortgage relating to [*client's*] mortgage account, please provide the name and address of said holder and indicate your relationship to this entity.

Thank you for taking the time to acknowledge and answer this request as required by the Real Estate Settlement Procedures Act (section 2605(e)).

Very truly yours,

[*Attorney*]

Form 70 Motion for Order Directing Claimant to Appear for Rule 2004 Examination[171]

[*Caption: Official Form 16A*]

Motion for Order Directing [*name*] Mortgage Company to Appear for Examination and Produce Documents

The Debtor hereby requests, pursuant to Federal Rule of Bankruptcy Procedure 2004, that [*name*] Mortgage Company be directed to designate an officer, agent, or other person to appear for examination with respect to the proof of claim it has filed in this matter, and to produce the documents requested on Exhibit A attached hereto In support of this motion, Debtor states as follows:

1. The Debtor filed the instant voluntary petition under chapter 13 of the Bankruptcy Code on [*date*].

2. [*Name*] Mortgage Company is the current holder [*or servicer*] of the mortgage on the debtor's home.

3. [*Name*] Mortgage Company filed a secured proof of claim in the instant case on or about [*date*] in the amount of $105,037.85, claiming an arrearage owed of $26,315.11. The proof of claim does not include an itemization of the various charges comprising the arrearage amount, though it contains a notation that the amount includes "corporate advances" in excess of $8000.00.

4. The Debtor disputes the amount claimed as an arrearage on the mortgage account and believes that the amount includes charges that are not authorized by the mortgage contract or are otherwise unlawful. The Debtor also believes that the claim may

---

170 This form letter may be used to conduct informal discovery on the elements of a creditor's claim based on the Real Estate Settlement Procedures Act (RESPA), 12 U.S.C. § 2605. It can be helpful in uncovering hidden overcharges on mortgage claims. *See* § 13.4.3.4, *supra*. For a detailed discussion of the RESPA servicing requirements, see Chapter 19 of NCLC's Repossessions and Foreclosures (5th ed. 2002 and Supp.).

171 If the debtor disputes a mortgage arrearage or other creditor claim, and is unable to obtain necessary information or a response to a qualified written request (see Form 69, Appx. G.8, *supra*) prior to confirmation, this form may be used to seek an order to conduct an examination of a creditor representative under Fed. R. Bankr. P. 2004. If granted, the debtor should also have a subpoena issued and served in accordance with Fed. R. Bankr. P. 9016.

include post-petition attorney fees that have not been properly disclosed or approved by this Court.

5. The Debtor has attempted to obtain information necessary to evaluate the claim by serving upon [*name*] Mortgage Company a **"qualified written request"** under the Real Estate Settlement Procedures Act, 12 U.S.C. section 2605(e), but [*name*] Mortgage Company has not responded.

6. It is necessary for the Debtor to examine a representative of [*name*] Mortgage Company to obtain an explanation of and documents related to the arrearage claim amount so as to determine whether sufficient grounds exist to object to the claim prior to the confirmation hearing presently scheduled for [*date*].

WHEREFORE, the Debtor requests that this motion be granted.

Date: [*signature*]
                                        Attorney for Debtor

Exhibit A

Debtor's Request for Production of Documents Directed to [*name*] Mortgage Company

The Debtor, [*name*], by her counsel, and pursuant to Fed. R. Bankr. P. 2004, makes this request for production of documents directed to [*name*] Mortgage Company. Defendant is requested to produce the documents described below at the Rule 2004 examination to be held as ordered by the Bankruptcy Court.

DEFINITIONS

1. The term "person(s)" means all entities, and, without limiting the generality of the foregoing, includes natural persons, joint owners, associations, companies, partnerships, joint ventures, corporations, trusts and estates.

2. The term "document(s)" means all written, printed, recorded or graphic matter, photographic matter or sound reproductions, video tapes and/or films, however produced or reproduced, pertaining in any manner to the subject matter indicated, including computer tapes, discs, or other electronically stored data.

3. The terms "you" and "your" refer to [*name*] Mortgage Company and all agents, employees, officers, and other representatives acting on its behalf.

4. The term "Debtor" refers to [*name*].

5. The term "[*name*] law firm" refers to "[*name*], LLC" and all agents, employees, officers and other representatives acting on its behalf.

6. The terms "mortgage" and "mortgages" refer to residential mortgages owned or serviced by [*name*] Mortgage Company.

7. The term "bankruptcy related fees" refers to any fees or other charges billed, assessed or charged to mortgagors and/or their mortgage accounts in connection with or as a result of the bankruptcy filing of the mortgagor.

8. The terms "and" and "or" shall be interpreted conjunctively and disjunctively, to give the interrogatories the broadest interpretation.

9. The singular shall include the plural, and the plural shall include the singular.

Document Requests

1. All documents that relate to your purchase or acquisition of the Debtor's mortgage.

2. All documents that you received or sent relating to the Debtor and/or her mortgage account.

3. All documents, by type, that you sent or received on a regular periodic basis (weekly, monthly, annually, and so forth) relating to the Debtor's mortgage.

4. All documents, including servicing guidelines, handbooks or other manuals, which evidence how you protected your security interest as a mortgagee in regard to the Debtor's mortgage.

5. All documents that relate to or constitute a file maintained by you with respect to the mortgage and/or note signed by the Debtor, including, but not limited to, any account statements, correspondence, and other information with respect to the Debtor's mortgage and/or loan.

6. Documents evidencing the application of each payment the Debtor made on her mortgage and/or loan.

7. Documents evidencing each assessment of interest, fees and/or other charges on the Debtor's mortgage account.

8. Documents identifying all formulas and/or calculations used to determine the amount of any fees and/or other charges assessed, imposed or charged to the Debtor mortgage account to protect your security interest as a mortgagee.

9. Documents identifying all formulas and/or calculations used to determine the amount of any bankruptcy related fees charged to the Debtor.

10. All documents that refer to, reflect, or concern each assessment or addition of any bankruptcy related fees to the Debtor's mortgage account.

11. All documents that refer to, reflect, or concern communications between you and the [*name*] law firm in regard to the Debtor and/or the Debtor's mortgage.

12. All documents that refer to, reflect, or concern communications between the [*name*] law firm and the Debtor.

13. All documents that constitute, refer to, or concern any agreement or other understanding between you and the [*name*] law firm concerning work performed or to be performed by the [*name*] law firm for you or on your behalf.

14. All documents that refer to, reflect, or concern the work performed by the [*name*] law firm concerning the Debtor and/or Debtor's mortgage.

15. All documents that refer to, reflect, or concern any pleading, proof of claim, or other document filed by the [*name*] law firm in the Debtor's bankruptcy cases.

16. All documents that refer to, reflect, or concern the payment of any fees to the [*name*] law firm concerning the Debtor and/or Debtor's mortgage.

17. All documents related to and leading up to your decision to assess bankruptcy related fees on the Debtor's mortgage without seeking bankruptcy court approval including, *inter alia*, all reports, studies, memoranda, organizational minutes, files and notes discussing this issue.

18. All documents related to your determination that it was not required to seek bankruptcy court approval before assessing bankruptcy related fees on the Debtor's mortgage including, *inter alia*, all reports, studies, memoranda, organizational minutes, files and notes discussing this issue.

19. All documents related to your implementation of policies concerning the assessment or collection of bankruptcy related fees including, *inter alia*, all reports, studies, memoranda, organizational minutes, files and notes discussing this issue.

20. A sample of all form notices, statements or other documents that are or have been used to notify mortgagors that they are or have been assessed bankruptcy related fees.

21. A sample of all form notices, statements or other documents that are or have been sent to mortgagors in an attempt to collect bankruptcy related fees.

22. All documents identifying past and present policies and procedures related to the assessment or collection of bankruptcy related fees.

23. All documents, including reports, studies, memoranda, organizational minutes, files and notes addressing the assessment or collection of bankruptcy related fees.

24. Documents identifying all system(s) that you use or have used, at any time from January 1, 1990 to the present, to file documents you receive and/or send relating to each of the mortgages you own or service.

Form 71 Order Directing Claimant to Appear for Rule 2004 Examination

[Caption: Official Form 16A]

Order Directing [*name*] Mortgage Company to Appear for Examination and Produce Documents

AND NOW, this [*date*] day of [*month*], [*year*], upon the Debtor's motion to conduct an examination of [*name*] Mortgage Company,

It is hereby ORDERED and DECREED that [*name*] Mortgage Company is directed to appear, by and through an officer, agent or other person it shall designate, at [*address*] on [*date*] at [*time*], for examination pursuant to Bankruptcy Rule 2004(a) with respect to the debtor's mortgage account and the proof of claim filed by [*name*] Mortgage Company in this matter, or as to any matter which may affect the confirmation of the Debtor's chapter 13 plan or administration of this case. The [*name*] Mortgage Company is also directed to produce at the time and location of the examination the documents requested on Exhibit A attached to the Debtor's motion.

Date: *[signature]*
                        United States Bankruptcy Judge

Form 72 Complaint Objecting to Mortgage Servicer's Claim Based on RESPA and FDCPA Violations

[Caption: Official Form 16D]

Complaint

Preliminary Statement

1. This action is brought by the Debtor, [*name*], against the mortgage company that holds and services a mortgage on her home, the [*name*] Federal Bank.

2. Defendant [*name*] Federal Bank has refused to honor a Modification Agreement entered into between the parties and as a result has overcharged the Debtor and failed to properly credit payments on her mortgage account. In addition to its breach of contract, Defendant has engaged in abusive, deceptive and unfair debt collection practices in violation of the Fair Debt Collection Practices Act (FDCPA), 15 U.S.C. §§ 1692–1692*o*.

3. Defendant [*name*] Federal Bank has also failed to make appropriate corrections to the mortgage account despite Debtor's dispute of the overcharges and misapplication of payments, in violation of the mortgage servicer provisions of the Real Estate Settlement Procedures Act (RESPA), 12 U.S.C. § 2605.

Jurisdiction

4. This court has jurisdiction over this matter pursuant to 28 U.S.C. §§ 1334 and 157. This action is a core proceeding.

Parties

5. Debtor [*name*] is an individual who resides at [*address*] in Laguna Vista, California.

6. Defendant [*name*] Federal Bank (hereinafter "Defendant [*name*]") is a corporation with its principal place of business in Irving, Texas. At all times material to this action, Defendant [*name*] regularly transacted business in the State of California.

7. Defendant [*name*] is a "debt collector" of the Debtor's "debt" as those terms are defined in the FDCPA, 15 U.S.C. § 1692a.

8. Defendant [*name*] is a loan "servicer" of the Debtor's "federally related mortgage loan" as those terms are defined in the RESPA, 12 U.S.C. § 2602(1) and 12 U.S.C. § 2605(i)(2).

Factual Allegations

9. On [*date*], the Debtor borrowed $50,000.00 for the purchase of her home from the Merchants Bank. The Note signed by the Debtor was secured by a mortgage on her home.

10. Defendant [*name*] subsequently became the owner of the subject Note and Mortgage (hereinafter referred to as the "original Loan"). At the time Defendant [*name*] obtained an interest in the Debtor's original Loan, Defendant [*name*] deemed the mortgage account to be in default and serviced the account as a debt in default.

11. In March, 2000, Defendant [*name*] initiated foreclosure proceedings against the Debtor claiming that she was in default on the original Loan.

12. Prior to this time, the Debtor had attempted to resolve a long-standing dispute with Defendant [*name*] over whether payments she had made had been properly credited to her account.

13. Unable to resolve this dispute, the Debtor filed a chapter 13 bankruptcy in the United States Bankruptcy Court on April 15, 2000. In the chapter 13 proceeding, the Debtor sought to obtain a determination of the proper balance owed on her account and to cure any default found to exist with payments through her chapter 13 plan.

14. On August 21, 2001, the Debtor and Defendant [*name*] entered into a consent order in the bankruptcy court resolving the Debtor's objection to Defendant [*name*]'s proof of claim. This consent order provided that parties would enter into agreement modifying the Debtor's original Loan.

15. This agreement also provided that the parties would have a period of thirty (30) days before entering into the modification agreement in order to resolve any disputes concerning the outstanding balance owed under the original Loan.

16. The Debtor and Defendant [*name*] subsequently entered into a Modification Agreement, effective November 1, 2001. A copy of the Modification Agreement is attached as Exhibit A.

17. In the "Recital" section of the Modification Agreement, the parties acknowledged that the Debtor was in default on the original Loan and that Defendant [*name*] was "entitled to demand" payment of a principal balance on the original Loan of over $85,000.00, plus "interest, and all other charges."

18. The parties further acknowledged that despite the default and based on the Debtor's request to modify the original Loan, the Defendant [*name*] agreed to adjust the terms of the original Loan, including "total amount due."

19. In accordance with these acknowledgments, the parties specifically agreed in Paragraph 3(d) of the Modification Agreement that the "New Principal Balance" that the Debtor would "now owe" on her loan was $85,000.00.

20. The intention of the parties as evidenced by the terms of the Modification Agreement was that the Debtor's loan was reinstated as current and that the total outstanding balance, including all accrued interest, charges and fees owing on the loan as of the effective date, was stipulated to be $85,000.00.

21. Although the Debtor believed that she owed less than $85,000.00, she agreed to this amount and signed the Modification Agreement in order to achieve a final resolution of her dispute with Defendant [*name*] over the amount owed on her mortgage account.

22. In Paragraph 12 of the Modification Agreement, the parties additionally agreed that the loan modification was a "Final Agreement" and that it "constitutes the entire agreement between you and [*name*], supercedes all previous negotiations and discussions. . . ."

23. After the Modification Agreement became effective on November 1, 2001, the Debtor began making her new monthly payments of $671.73 as provided for under the Modification Agreement.

24. Despite the Debtor's timely payments each month and her full compliance with the terms of the Modification Agreement, Defendant [*name*], through its attorneys, sent the Debtor a foreclosure notice on June 15, 2002 and on July 10, 2002. Copies of these Notices are attached as Exhibits B and C respectively.

25. In response, the Debtor, through her attorney, sent Defendant [*name*] a letter dated August 15, 2002, seeking information about the Debtor's mortgage account and disputing that her account was in default.

26. On January 25, 2003, Defendant [*name*] sent the Debtor a response stating that sometime "after the Modification Agreement was completed," Defendant [*name*] had received invoices from its attorneys for fees in the amount of $6701.92 relating to the Debtor's earlier bankruptcy case.

27. The response further stated that upon receiving the invoices, Defendant [*name*] assessed the legal fees to the Debtor's loan balance and then applied the Debtor's payments made on the Modification Agreement to cover these pre-modification fees.

28. A history of the Debtor's account provided with the response suggests that Defendant [*name*] paid some or all of the invoices and assessed the attorney fee charges to the Debtor's account on November 11, 2001.

29. At no time prior to the execution of the Modification Agreement by the Debtor on October 14, 2001, or its effective date on November 1, 2001, did Defendant [*name*] advise the Debtor that, contrary to the plain terms of the Modification Agreement, it

believed that the Debtor would be responsible for paying outstanding legal fees separate from her obligations under the Modification Agreement, or that Defendant [*name*] had not waived any claim for outstanding legal fees by signing the Modification Agreement.

30. At no time during the Debtor's first chapter 13 bankruptcy, or at any time thereafter, did Defendant [*name*] or its attorneys seek or obtain bankruptcy court approval of an award of attorney fees against the Debtor.

31. Defendant [*name*]'s refusal to honor the terms of the Modification Agreement by charging and collecting extraneous fees not agreed to by the parties, and its actions in improperly declaring defaults and pursing a wrongful foreclosure of the Debtor's home, have caused the Debtor to suffer severe emotional distress and mental anguish. Defendant [*name*]'s actions have also damaged the Debtor's credit rating and caused her to incur expenses in seeking redress against Defendant's wrongful acts.

32. Unable to resolve her dispute with Defendant [*name*], the Debtor was forced to file this second chapter 13 bankruptcy to stop the foreclosure of her home.

Count I—Breach of Contract

33. The allegations of paragraphs 1–32 above are realleged and incorporated herein by reference.

34. Defendant [*name*] breached its contractual obligations to the Debtor in at least the following ways:

a. By failing to apply all payments received from the Debtor after November 1, 2001 to the principal and interest accrued after that date on the Debtor's mortgage account according to the terms of the original Loan and Modification Agreement;

b. By assessing to the Debtor's mortgage account charges and fees not agreed to between the parties;

c. By improperly allocating payments received from the Debtor after November 1, 2001 to fees and charges not agreed to between the parties;

d. By assessing late payment charges to the Debtor's mortgage account after November 1, 2001 contrary to the terms of the original Loan and Modification Agreement;

e. By declaring the Debtor to be in default of the original Loan and Modification Agreement when no such default exists;

f. By initiating foreclosure proceedings contrary to the terms of the original Loan and Modification Agreement.

Count II—Violation of Real Estate Settlement Procedures Act

35. The allegations of paragraphs 1–32 above are realleged and incorporated herein by reference.

36. On August 15, 2002, the Debtor, though her attorney, sent Defendant [*name*] a "qualified written request" as that term is defined under RESPA, 12 U.S.C. § 2605(e)(1)(B), regarding the crediting of payments on her mortgage account. In the qualified written request, the Debtor specified her reasons for belief that the account was not in default and requested that Defendant [*name*] correct the error. The Debtor also requested that Defendant [*name*] provide her with information and documentation supporting its claim that the Debtor's account was in default.

37. Defendant [*name*] violated RESPA, 12 U.S.C. § 2605(e)(1)(A), by failing to provide a written response acknowledging receipt of the Debtor's qualified written request no later than 20 days after receipt of the request.

38. Defendant [*name*] violated RESPA, 12 U.S.C. § 2605(e)(2)(A), by failing to make appropriate corrections to the Debtor's account in response to the qualified written request, including the crediting of any late charges or penalties, and failing to transmit written notice of such corrections to the Debtor no later than sixty (60) days after receipt of the Debtor's qualified written request.

39. Defendant [*name*] violated RESPA, 12 U.S.C. § 2605(e)(2)(C), by failing to provide the Debtor with the information and documentation requested, or an explanation why the information sought was unavailable, no later than sixty (60) days after receipt of the Debtor's qualified written request.

40. Defendant [*name*] violated RESPA, 12 U.S.C. § 2605(e)(2), by refusing to cease its collection efforts and foreclosure proceedings after receiving the Debtor's qualified written request.

41. Upon information and belief, Defendant [*name*] violated RESPA, 12 U.S.C. 2605(e)(3), by providing information to consumer reporting agencies regarding overdue payments allegedly owed by the Debtor that were related to her qualified written request.

42. Defendant [*name*] has engaged in a pattern or practice of non-compliance with the requirements of the mortgage servicer provisions of RESPA as set forth in 12 U.S.C. § 2605.

Count III—Violation of the Fair Debt Collection Practices Act

43. The allegations of paragraphs 1–32 above are realleged and incorporated herein by reference.

44. Defendant [*name*] violated the FDCPA, 15 U.S.C. § 1692f, by using unfair and unconscionable means to collect the debt owed by the Debtor, including the collecting and attempting to collect of interest and other charges, fees and expenses not authorized by the original Loan and Modification Agreement, or otherwise legally chargeable to the Debtor, as more fully set forth above.

45. Defendant [*name*] violated the FDCPA, 15 U.S.C. § 1692e(2), by misrepresenting the character, amount and legal status of the Debtor's debt.

46. Defendant [*name*] violated the FDCPA, 15 U.S.C. §§ 1692e(5)and 1692f(6), by threatening to foreclose on the Debtor's home even though Defendant [*name*] has no present right to possession of the property under its security agreement, and by threatening to take other action prohibited by law.

47. Defendant [*name*] violated the FDCPA, 15 U.S.C. § 1692g(a)(1), by failing to accurately and fully state in communications to the Debtor "the amount of the debt."

Prayer for Relief

WHEREFORE, the Debtor respectfully requests that this Court:

A. Assume jurisdiction over this action;

B. Declare that the Defendant [*name*] is in breach of the original Loan and Modification Agreement and that Debtor is current and not in default on the terms of the original Loan and Modification Agreement;

C. Enjoin the Defendant [*name*] from collecting or attempting to collect any attorney fees or other charges incurred prior to the effective date of the Modification Agreement that were not included the "New Principal Balance" specified in the Modification Agreement;

D. Disallow the Proof of Claim filed by Defendant [*name*] to the extent it seeks payment of any pre-petition arrearage;

E. Award actual and compensatory damages, including those for mental anguish, in an amount to be determined at trial;

F. Award punitive or exemplary damages in an amount to be determined at trial;

G. Declare that Defendant [*name*] violated RESPA, enjoin Defendant from committing any future violations of the Act, and award the Debtor actual damages and $1000.00 in statutory damages pursuant to 12 U.S.C. § 2605(f);

H. Declare that Defendant [*name*] violated the FDCPA, enjoin Defendant from committing any future violations of the Act, and award the Debtor actual damages and $1000.00 in statutory damages pursuant to 15 U.S.C. § 1692k;

I. Award Debtor reasonable attorney fees and litigation expenses, plus costs of suit, pursuant to 12 U.S.C. § 2605(f) and 15 U.S.C. § 1692k(3);

J. Grant such other or further relief as is appropriate.

Date: [*signature*]
                                    Attorney for Debtor

Form 73 Request for Approval of Post-Petition Consumer Debt[172]

[Caption: Official Form 16A]

Request for Approval of Post-petition Consumer Debt

The Debtor hereby requests that the trustee approve a post-petition consumer debt on the following grounds:

1. The Debtor's automobile, a 1993 Ford Escort, was recently totally destroyed in an accident.

2. Without this automobile Debtor [*debtor*] has no way to travel to his job, and has missed several days of work, using up his vacation time.

3. The Debtor has negotiated a loan from the First National Bank in the amount of $1200.00, to purchase a used automobile from his neighbors.

4. The proposed loan has payments of $50.00 per month over thirty-six months, which Debtor can afford to pay without modifying his plan.

5. The proposed post-petition consumer debt is necessary for the Debtor's continued performance under his plan.

WHEREFORE, the Debtor requests that the trustee approve the proposed post-petition debt as described above.

Date: [*signature*]
                                    Attorney for Debtor

Approved:
[*signature*]
Chapter 13 Trustee

---

172 Normally the chapter 13 debtor should obtain the trustee's approval before entering into a post-petition credit obligation. Such a claim may then or later be provided for in the plan. 11 U.S.C. §§ 1305, 1328(d); *see* § 8.7.2, *supra*. If the case is converted to a chapter 7 case, such a post-petition claim may be treated as if it arose before the case and may be discharged. 11 U.S.C. § 348(d). This form has a space for the trustee to indicate approval of the debt. The trustee may request a self-addressed stamped envelope for return of the form.

G.9 Exemptions and Lien Avoidance

Form 74 Motion to Avoid Judicial Lien on Residential Real Estate[173]

[Caption: Official Form 16A]

Motion to Avoid Lien

1. Debtors, [*debtor—husband*], and [*debtor—wife*], his wife, commenced this case on [*date*], by filing the above-numbered voluntary petition for relief under chapter 7 of title 11, United States Code.

2. This motion is filed pursuant to 11 U.S.C. § 522(f) to avoid and cancel a judicial lien held by the [*creditor*] on real property used as the Debtors' residence.

3. In January, 1995, Plaintiff/Debtors received a loan of $7216.00 from [*creditor*]. On or about May 30, 2003, [*creditor*] obtained a judicial lien in and on the real property used as Debtors' residence at [*address*]. The said judicial lien is entered of record as follows:

June Term, 2003, No. 851: $7216.00.

4. The Debtors' interest in the property referred to in the preceding paragraph and encumbered by the lien does not exceed $15,000.00 in value and has been claimed as fully exempt in their bankruptcy case.[174]

5. The existence of [*creditor*]'s lien on Debtors' real property impairs exemptions to which the Debtors would be entitled under 11 U.S.C. § 522(b).

WHEREFORE, Debtors pray for an Order against [*creditor*] for the cancellation and avoidance of the judicial liens on their residential real estate, and for such additional or alternative relief as may be just and proper.

---

173 Fed. R. Bankr. P. 4003(d) provides that debtors proceeding under 11 U.S.C. § 522(f) to avoid judicial liens or household goods security interests shall proceed by motion rather than complaint. Fed. R. Bankr. P. 9013 requires service of a motion by the moving party on the trustee and on others as the court may direct. Normally, the creditor holding the lien would be the only other party served. If the creditor holding the lien is an insured depository institution, service generally will not be effective unless an officer of the institution is served by certified mail. *See* Fed. R. Bankr. P. 7004(h); *In re* Hamlett, 322 F.3d 342 (4th Cir. 2003). Many courts have local rules as to service, the amount of time for filing a response (if one is necessary), and certifications of service. Many courts will not schedule a hearing on the matter unless it is contested by the creditor, but will instead simply grant the relief requested. For a discussion of judicial lien avoidance, see § 10.4.2.3, *supra*.

174 This motion contemplates a case in which the property subject to the lien is fully exemptible. If the lien covers property which cannot be exempted as well, the motion should specify what property, or portion of the property should be relieved of the lien. Responding to several cases which had misconstrued the lien avoidance provisions, Congress amended section 522(f) in 1994 to specifically set forth an arithmetic formula for determining whether a lien can be avoided. The amendment overrules cases which had limited the availability of lien avoidance in certain situations. *See* § 10.4.2.3, *supra*.

Date: *[signature]*
Attorney for Debtors

Form 75 Order Avoiding Lien on Residential Real Estate

[Caption: Official Form 16A]

Order Avoiding Lien

AND NOW, this [*date*] day of [*month*], [*year*], upon the Debtors' motion to avoid and cancel a judicial lien which impairs an exemption of the Debtors,

It is hereby ORDERED AND DECREED that the judicial lien held by [*creditor*], in and on Debtors' residential real estate at [*address*], entered of record at June Term, 2003, No. [*number*] be and hereby is canceled.

It is further ORDERED that [*creditor*] is directed forthwith to take all steps necessary and appropriate to release the said judicial lien and remove it from the local judgment index.[175]

Date: *[signature]*
United States Bankruptcy Judge

Form 76 Motion to Avoid Non-Possessory, Non-Purchase Money Security Interest[176]

[Caption: Official Form 16A]

Motion to Avoid Non-Possessory Non-Purchase Money Security Interest

1. Debtors, [*debtors*], commenced this case on [*date*] by filing a voluntary petition for relief under chapter 7 of Title 11 of the United States Code.

2. On or about April 29, 2002, Debtors borrowed two thousand six hundred sixty-four dollars ($2664.00) from [*creditor*]. As security for the loan [*creditor*] insisted upon, and Debtors executed, a note and security agreement granting to [*creditor*] a security interest in and on the Debtors' personal property, which consisted of household furnishings, appliances, books, and musical instruments which are held primarily for the family and household use of the Debtors and their dependents.

3. All such possessions of Debtors have been claimed as fully exempt in their bankruptcy case.

4. The money borrowed from [*creditor*] does not represent any part of the purchase money of any of the articles covered in the security agreement executed by the Debtors, and all of the articles so covered remain in the possession of Debtors.

---

175 The order here puts the burden on the creditor to correct public records to reflect termination of the lien. However, it is often simpler for the debtor's attorney to simply file the lien avoidance order in the records where the lien exists, and this order is suitable for filing in local records offices.

The order also contemplates a case when the property is fully exemptible. If only some of the property is exemptible, the order must be modified to specify what portion of the lien is avoided.

176 See notes to Form 74, Appendix G.9, *supra*. See also § 10.4.2.4, *supra*.

5. The existence of [*creditor*]'s lien on Debtors' household and personal goods impairs exemptions to which the Debtors would be entitled under 11 U.S.C. § 522(b).

WHEREFORE, Debtors pray for an Order avoiding the security interest on their personal and household goods, and for such additional or alternative relief as may be just and proper.

Date: [*signature*]
                                              Attorney for Debtors

Form 77 Order Avoiding Non-Possessory, Non-Purchase Money Security Interest

[Caption: Official Form 16A]

Order Avoiding Non-Possessory, Non-Purchase Money Security Interest

AND NOW, this [*date*] day of [*month*], [*year*], upon the motion to avoid and cancel a security interest which impaired an exemption of the Debtors,

It is hereby ORDERED and DECREED that the non-possessory, non-purchase money security of [*creditor*] in Debtors' household and personal goods be, and hereby is, declared null and void.

Date: [*signature*]
                                    United States Bankruptcy Judge

Form 78 Complaint to Set Aside Preference[177]

[Caption: Official Form 16D]

Complaint to Set Aside Preference

1. This case was commenced by Debtor/Plaintiff, [*debtor*], by filing a voluntary petition under chapter 7 of the Bankruptcy Code on [*date*].

2. This complaint is filed, pursuant to 11 U.S.C. § 522(h), to set aside a transfer of the Debtor's exempt property to Defendant, [*creditor*]. This Court has jurisdiction under 28 U.S.C. § 1334. This proceeding is a core proceeding.

3. On [*date*], a date less than ninety days prior to the commencement of this case, Defendant [*creditor*] caused to be issued an attachment of the debtor's wages from Debtor's employer, [*name and address of debtor's employer*].

4. Pursuant to this garnishment, for payment of an antecedent debt to Defendant, Defendant collected $750.00.

5. The Debtor could have exempted those funds in this case had they been recovered by the trustee as a preference under 11 U.S.C. § 547.

6. The trustee has not attempted to avoid this transfer.

---

177 This complaint, or one which is similar, may be used by the debtor under 11 U.S.C. § 522(h) to set aside preferential transfers if the property may be claimed as exempt. See discussion in § 10.4, *supra*. It pleads the elements of a preference under 11 U.S.C. § 547. For a general discussion of complaints in adversary proceedings, see notes to Form 83, Appendix G.10, *infra*.

   Similar complaints may be used by the debtor to utilize other trustee avoiding powers through 11 U.S.C. § 522(h). However, a preference of less than $600.00 may not be recovered in a case filed by an individual debtor.

7. The aforesaid transfer to Defendant was not voluntary nor did the Debtor conceal any of the property involved.

8. The transfer to Defendant on account of the antecedent debt to it, while the Debtor was insolvent, enabled Defendant to receive more than it would have received if the transfer had not been made, because the Defendant would have received no dividend in the Debtor's bankruptcy case.

WHEREFORE, the Plaintiffs pray for judgment against the Defendant ordering it to return the $750.00 obtained by it as described above and ordering such other and further relief as is just and proper.

Date: [*signature*]
                                              Attorney for Debtors

Form 79 Complaint to Set Aside Preference and/or Setoff by Governmental Agency Recouping Overpayments of Benefits[178]

[Caption: Official Form 16D]

Complaint to Set Aside Preference and/or Setoff

I. Preliminary Statement

1. This is an action under the Bankruptcy Code, 11 U.S.C. §§ 101–1330, to set aside a preference and/or setoff which occurred when Defendants withheld veterans' pension benefits from the Debtor within ninety (90) days of his filing a voluntary petition in bankruptcy.

II. Jurisdiction

2. This Court has jurisdiction pursuant to 28 U.S.C. § 1334. This proceeding is a core proceeding.

III. Parties

3. Plaintiff, [*debtor*], is an individual who resides at [*address*]. He is the Debtor in this bankruptcy case.

---

178 A proceeding by the debtor to set aside a preference or recover a setoff of otherwise exemptible property must be brought as an adversary proceeding. Fed. R. Bankr. P. 7001. For a general discussion of complaints in adversary proceedings, see notes to Form 83, Appendix G.10, *infra*.

   This complaint or one which is similar may be used to recover benefits withheld by an agency within the three months prior to bankruptcy when benefits have been withheld to recoup an alleged overpayment. It may be adapted for cases involving social security, welfare, unemployment or other benefits, if those benefits could have been exempted. See discussion of the debtor's avoiding powers in § 10.4, *supra*, and the discussion of cases holding such overpayments ordinarily to be dischargeable debts in Chapter 14, *supra*. However, one court of appeals has held that a pre-bankruptcy recovery of an overpayment by the Social Security Administration may not be reversed. *See* Lee v. Schweiker, 739 F.2d 870 (3d Cir. 1984). See also Forms 24 and 25, Appendix G.4, *supra*, which may be utilized to prevent recoupment after the petition is filed.

   An additional issue which may arise is the extent of a governmental defendant's sovereign immunity, but an action to recover a setoff under section 522 such as in this case is now clearly allowed under section 106(a), subject to the limitations discussed in § 13.3.2.2, *supra*.

4. Defendant Veterans Administration is an agency of the United States whose principal offices are in Washington, DC, and which has the responsibility for administering veterans' pension benefits.

5. Defendant [*defendant—administrator*] is the current Administrator of Veterans Affairs, the chief administrative officer of the Veterans Administration. His office is located in Washington, DC.

6. Defendant [*defendant—director*] is the Director of the Veterans Administration Regional Office and Insurance Center in Philadelphia, PA. As such, he is responsible for administering claims for veterans' pension benefits in the Philadelphia area.

7. Defendant [*defendant—chief*] is Chief of the Finance Division of the Veterans Administration Regional Office in Philadelphia. As such he is responsible for administering the payment of claims for veterans' pension benefits in the Philadelphia area.

IV. Factual Allegations

8. Prior to May, 2004, Plaintiff [*debtor*] was receiving a monthly veterans' disability pension.

9. The Veterans Administration subsequently determined that Plaintiff had been overpaid two thousand nine hundred fifty-eight dollars and eighty-seven cents ($2958.87).

10. Beginning in May, 2004, Defendants withheld Plaintiff's entire monthly pension and intended to continue withholding the pension benefits each month until the overpayment had been recouped.

11. Plaintiff received no pension benefits in July, August, September, 2004. Had he received benefits in those months, he would have received two hundred thirty-eight dollars and twenty-five cents ($238.25) in July, two hundred thirty-eight dollars and twenty-five cents ($238.25) in August, and two hundred forty-four dollars and ninety-one cents ($244.91) in September, totaling seven hundred twenty-one dollars and forty-one cents ($721.41).

12. On September 23, 2004, Plaintiff filed a voluntary petition in bankruptcy under chapter 7 in this Court.

13. In Schedule F, accompanying his bankruptcy petition, Plaintiff listed the Veterans Administration as an unsecured creditor and listed the unsecured debt owed to the Veterans Administration in the amount of two thousand nine hundred fifty-eight dollars and eighty-seven cents ($2958.87), the amount Plaintiff allegedly has been overpaid.

14. In Schedule B Plaintiff listed the amount of benefits which Defendants withheld in July, August, and September, 2004, as a preference which was property of his estate.[179]

15. In Schedule C, Plaintiff listed as exempt, *inter alia*, the funds which the Defendants withheld for the months of July, August, and September, 2004.

16. The Veterans Administration has not objected to Plaintiff's exemption claim nor has it challenged the dischargeability[180] of its unsecured debt.

17. This bankruptcy is a no-asset case. None of the unsecured creditors received any distribution from the property of the Debtor's estate.

V. Claims

First Claim

18. The actions of Defendants in withholding benefits in July, August, and September, 2004, to which Plaintiff was entitled, in order to recover a prior overpayment made to Plaintiff has enabled Defendants to obtain a preference[181] under 11 U.S.C. § 547 in that:
   a. The transfer of Plaintiff's property was for the benefit of his creditor, the Veterans Administration;
   b. The transfer was made on account of a debt owed by Plaintiff to the Veterans Administration which arose prior to transfer of his property and prior to the filing of his bankruptcy petition;
   c. The transfer was made while the Debtor was insolvent;
   d. The transfer was made within ninety (90) days of the filing of Plaintiff's petition in bankruptcy; and
   e. The transfer enabled the Veterans Administration to receive more than it would have received in a chapter 7 proceeding if the transfer had not been made and this creditor had received payments on its claim to the extent provided by the Code.

19. Pursuant to 11 U.S.C. § 522(h), Plaintiff may avoid this transfer to the Veterans Administration because it involves property which will be exempt if the transfer is avoided, the trustee has not avoided this transfer, and the transfer was not a voluntary transfer by the Debtor.

Second Claim

20. The actions of Defendants in withholding benefits in July, August, and September, 2004, represent a setoff under 11 U.S.C. § 553 which occurred within ninety (90) days of the filing of Plaintiff's bankruptcy petition, while the Debtor was insolvent, and which lessened the insufficiency between Defendants' claim and the Plaintiff's claim. In the alternative, the Defendants acted for the purpose of obtaining a right to setoff against Plaintiff.

21. Pursuant to 11 U.S.C. § 522(h) Plaintiff may recover this setoff because the trustee has not done so, the property would be exempt, and the transfer was not a voluntary transfer by the Debtor.

WHEREFORE, Plaintiff requests that this Court:
1. Take jurisdiction of this matter;
2. Avoid the transfer as a preference or allow the Debtor to recover the setoff pursuant to 11 U.S.C. § 522(h);
3. Order the Defendant to return seven hundred twenty-one dollars and forty-one cents ($721.41) to Plaintiff; and
4. Grant such other relief as this Court deems just and proper.

Date: [*signature*]
                         Attorney for Debtor/Plaintiff

---

179 It is probably not necessary to list the benefits to be recovered as property in the schedules or to claim them as exempt therein, because the statute allows avoidance when the benefits "could have" been exempted but for the transfer. 11 U.S.C. § 522(h). However, there is no harm in listing them or amending schedules to list them and claiming them as exempt, in order to be safe.

180 The dischargeability of the debt would not provide a defense to this complaint, but the fact that no objection on those lines was raised furthers the debtor's arguments that this debt is an ordinary unsecured claim.

181 The recoupment of benefits is more likely to be held a setoff than a preference, but a cautious approach would require pleading both theories in the alternative. A setoff recovery is not governed by the $600.00 minimum set by 11 U.S.C. § 547(a)(7).

Form 80 Complaint to Set Aside Foreclosure Sale for Less Than Reasonably Equivalent Value and to Remedy Mortgagee's Contempt[182]

[Caption: Official Form 16D]

Complaint to Avoid Transfer of Real Property for Contempt and for Relief from Defendants' Contempt

1. [*Debtor*], Plaintiff and Debtor, filed a petition under chapter 13 of the Bankruptcy Code on January 24, 2004. He resides at [*address*] and has resided there continuously since January 1983.

2. This Court therefore has jurisdiction over this matter pursuant to 28 U.S.C. § 1334. This proceeding is a core proceeding.

3. [*Creditor*], a Defendant herein, is servicing agent for the mortgage on Debtor's residence at [*address*].

4. Veterans Administration (hereinafter "VA"), a Defendant herein, is the guarantor of the mortgage on the Debtor's residence.

5. [*Defendant—sheriff*], Sheriff (hereinafter "Sheriff"), a Defendant herein, is the Sheriff of [*name*] County.

6. Some time in 2000, due to various financial and family problems, Debtor was unable to meet his mortgage payments and [*creditor*] commenced an action in mortgage foreclosure in the Common Pleas Court of [*name*] County.

7. [*Creditor*] obtained a default judgment against Debtor and a writ of execution was obtained on July 5, 2002.

---

182 A proceeding to recover property must be brought as an adversary proceeding. Fed. R. Bankr. P. 7001. For a general discussion of complaints in adversary proceedings, see notes to Form 83, Appendix G.10, *infra*.

This complaint addresses two aspects of a foreclosure sale situation. The debtor seeks to utilize the trustee's avoiding powers under 11 U.S.C. § 548 to set aside a foreclosure sale for less than reasonably equivalent value. See § 10.4.2.6.5, *supra*, for discussion of use of this power in foreclosure sale situations. It also asserts that the debtor's residual interest of legal title prior to the final completion of the sale was protected by the automatic stay, and that therefore a transfer of that interest violated the automatic stay and was avoidable under 11 U.S.C. § 549.

The use of section 548(a)(2) to avoid foreclosure sales for less than reasonably equivalent value was drastically curtailed by the Supreme Court in BFP v. Resolution Trust Co., 511 U.S. 531, 114 S. Ct. 1757, 128 L. Ed. 566 (1994). That case held that a regularly conducted non-collusive foreclosure sale may not be avoided under section 548. Thus, the cause of action based on section 548(a)(2) in this form requires proof that the sale was collusive or not regularly conducted. For further discussion of these issues, see § 10.4.2.6.5 *supra*.

This form was adapted from the pleadings in *In re* Jones, 20 B.R. 988 (Bankr. E.D. Pa. 1982). See also Form 31, Appendix G.5, *supra*, which is a form for an Answer to Mortgagee's Complaint for Relief from the Automatic Stay in such a situation.

It is also possible to argue that a sale need not be set aside under section 548 when it does not meet state law requirements, but rather that it is simply void under state law. *See, e.g., In re* Edry, 201 B.R. 604 (Bankr. D. Mass. 1996). When that argument is available a complaint seeking a declaratory judgment that the property involved is the property of the estate and seeking turnover, if necessary, is likely to be the appropriate procedure.

---

8. Pursuant to the writ of execution, a sheriff's sale of Debtor's residence was scheduled on September 10, 2002.

9. The sale was held on a day during which a hurricane had closed all travel routes to the place of sale. No bidders other than the attorney on the writ of execution appeared.

10. The highest bidder at the sale was [*creditor*]'s attorney, the attorney on the writ of execution.

11. The price bid by [*creditor*] to obtain Debtor's residence was fifteen thousand, eight hundred dollars ($15,800.00), even though Debtor's residence had a market value of thirty-five thousand dollars ($35,000.00).

12. Shortly after the sale, near the end of September, 1989, Debtor contacted counsel for advice and representation.

13. On or about October 13, 2002, Debtor's counsel filed a Petition to Open Default Judgment and Set Aside Sheriff's Sale in the foreclosure action.

14. As a result of the aforementioned petition, an Order was issued staying any action (specifically, the passing of the deed) by the Sheriff with respect to the September 10th sale. A copy of the Order was served on the Sheriff.

15. Debtor's chapter 13 petition was filed with this Court on January 24, 2004. As of that date, the terms of sale had not been complied with and Debtor had both record legal title and a possessory interest in his residence. The Debtor's interest in his residence became part of his estate pursuant to 11 U.S.C. § 541(a)(1).

16. Debtor's counsel notified [*creditor*]'s counsel of the chapter 13 petition by telephone and by letter.

17. On or about March 6, 2004, forty days after the filing of the chapter 13 petition, an Order was issued by Judge [*name*] of the Common Pleas Court, who was unaware of the proceedings in this Court, denying the Debtor's Petition to Open Judgment, and affirming the sheriff sale and allowing a deed to transfer title of Debtor's residence to the administrator of Veterans' Affairs.

18. Shortly after receipt of Judge [*name*]'s Order, Debtor's counsel filed a Motion to Vacate the Order.

19. In violation of the automatic stay provisions, [*creditor*]'s attorney, acting as execution purchaser, paid all remaining sheriff costs and fees and obtained a sheriff's deed purporting to transfer all of Debtor's interest in the property to the VA.

20. On or about March 31, 2004, in violation of the automatic stay provisions of the Bankruptcy Code, the Sheriff issued a deed purporting to transfer the property to the VA.

21. On or about April 23, 2004, the VA refused to accept the transfer of the property, thus rendering the transfer void under state law.

22. [*Creditor*]'s present counsel has indicated that the sheriff's deed is presently within his possession.

Claims

First Claim: Violation of Section 548 of Bankruptcy Code as Fraudulent Conveyance

23. At the sheriff's sale, [*creditor*] and VA paid $15,800.00 for Debtor's residence, which was less than a reasonably equivalent value for Debtor's interest in his residence, which interest was valued at $15,000.00. Based on the weather conditions, the sale was not regularly conducted within the meaning of the law. The Debtor was insolvent at the time of the transfer. This transaction is voidable pursuant to 11 U.S.C. §§ 522(h) and 548(a)(2).

*Second Claim: Purported Transfer Is Void as Matter
of State Law*

24. Any transfer of Debtor's interest in his residence is void as a matter of state law as the VA, the purported transferee, refused to accept the transfer.

*Third Claim: Violation of Section 549 of Bankruptcy Code,
Post-petition Transaction*

25. Any transfer of Debtor's interest in his residence which was property of his chapter 13 estate that occurred after the filing of his chapter 13 petition and was not authorized by this Court is subject to avoidance by Debtor pursuant to 11 U.S.C. §§ 522(h) and 549(a).

*Fourth Claim: Violation of Section 362 of Bankruptcy Code,
Automatic Stay*

26. Any attempted transfer by a creditor of Debtor's interest in his residence, which was property of his chapter 13 estate, that occurred after the filing of his chapter 13 petition was in violation of the automatic stay provisions of the Bankruptcy Code, 11 U.S.C. § 362(a).

Prayer for Relief

WHEREFORE, Plaintiff/Debtor requests that this Honorable Court:
1. Assume jurisdiction of this case.
2. Order that:
   a. The sheriff's sale of Debtor's residence be avoided pursuant to 11 U.S.C. §§ 522(h) and 549(a), or 11 U.S.C. § 548(a)(2);
   b. Defendants take all necessary steps to reflect the avoidance of the sale within thirty days to restore legal title to Debtor;
   c. The transfer be preserved for the benefit of the Debtor; and
   d. The Debtor's interest in the property is property of his estate that is exempt property pursuant to 11 U.S.C. § 522(d)(1) and (5).
3. Declare that [*creditor*] has violated and is in contempt of the automatic stay under 11 U.S.C. § 362, and order it to pay damages resulting from its contempt together with attorney fees and punitive damages pursuant to 11 U.S.C. § 362(h); and
4. Grant any other relief which this Court deems necessary and proper.

Date: [*signature*]
                                                   Attorney for Debtor

G.10 Litigation

Form 81 Motion for Leave to Proceed *In Forma Pauperis*[183]

[*Caption: Official Form 16D*]

Motion for Leave to Proceed *In Forma Pauperis*

Plaintiff moves this Court, by his attorney, for an Order permitting him to file this action *in forma pauperis* without the prepay-

---

183 The filing of adversary proceedings *in forma pauperis* is dis-

ment of fees and costs or security therefor, pursuant to 28 U.S.C. § 1915, because he is unable to pay such fees and costs or give security therefor, as is shown by the attached certification.

Date: [*signature*]
                                                   Attorney for Debtor

[*Caption: Official Form 16D*]

**Certification in Support of Motion to Proceed
*In Forma Pauperis***

Plaintiff [*name*] hereby certifies that:
1. He is the Plaintiff in the above-titled action.
2. He believes he is entitled to bring, and intends to bring this action in the United States Bankruptcy Court for the [*district name*] District of [*state*] against the above-named Defendant.
3. He has been informed by his attorney and believes that he is entitled to the relief sought in this action.
4. He has read and knows the contents of the complaint and believes them to be true.
5. He has no substantial assets which could be liquidated to pay the filing fee herein.
6. His sole income consists of $318.00 per month from the Department of Public Assistance for himself and his one child.
7. Because of his poverty, he is unable to pay the costs of this action or to give security therefor.

WHEREFORE, Plaintiff prays that he may have leave to proceed in this action without being required to prepay costs or fees or give security therefor.

I hereby certify that the foregoing is true and correct under penalty of perjury.

Date: [*signature*]
                                                             Plaintiff

Form 82 *In Forma Pauperis* Order

[*Caption: Official Form 16D*]

Order

This matter, having come before the undersigned Judge on the motion of the Plaintiff for leave to proceed with this action *in forma pauperis*, and it appearing to the Court that Plaintiff is entitled to the relief she seeks through this motion, it is hereby

ORDERED, that Plaintiff is authorized to proceed with this action *in forma pauperis*, without being required to pay any fees or costs or to give security therefor.

Date: [*signature*]
                                          United States Bankruptcy Judge

---

cussed in § 13.6, *supra.* Fortunately, no filing fee is required of debtors filing such proceedings, so these forms are now necessary only for non-debtor plaintiffs (except in rare cases in which defendants might have costs) and in cases in which debtors must file appeals. This form, or any similar forms used in the district court for obtaining *in forma pauperis* status under 28 U.S.C. § 1915, should accomplish that result in bankruptcy courts as well. Local practice may vary to some extent as to the specificity required with respect to the plaintiff's financial situation.

Form 83 Complaint: Class Action Adversary Proceeding Raising Claims Under Stay, Discharge, and Exemption Provisions As Well As 42 U.S.C. § 1983[184]

[*Caption: Official Form 16D*]

Complaint[185]

I. Preliminary Statement[186]

1. This is a class action brought under the Bankruptcy Code, 11 U.S.C. §§ 101–1330 (hereinafter "the Code"), and the emergency energy assistance provisions of the Economic Opportunity Act of 1964, as amended, 42 U.S.C. § 2809(a)(5),[187] seeking declaratory and injunctive relief for the individual Plaintiffs and the Class they represent. Plaintiffs also raise their claims under 42 U.S.C. § 1983.

II. Jurisdiction[188]

2. Jurisdiction is conferred on this Court by 28 U.S.C. § 1334 in that this proceeding arises under title 11 of the United States Code, arises in and is related to the above-captioned chapter 7 case under title 11, and concerns property of the Debtors in that case. This proceeding is a core proceeding.

3. Plaintiffs' action for declaratory relief is authorized by 28 U.S.C. §§ 2201 and 2202.[189]

III. Parties[190]

4. Plaintiffs [*first debtor*] and [*second debtor*], husband and wife, are individuals who reside at [*address*], and are the Debtors in this bankruptcy case.

5. Defendant [*name*] Gas Works (hereinafter "GW") is the "brand name" for real and personal property owned by the City of [*city*] which is used to furnish gas service to customers. GW is managed by Defendant [*name*] Facilities Management Company (hereinafter "FMC").

6. Defendant FMC is a nonprofit corporation organized by the City of [*city*] for the purpose of operating GW for the sole and exclusive benefit of the City.

7. Defendant [*name*] Gas Commission (hereinafter "GC") is an agency of the City[191] of [*city*] charged with the duty of overseeing and regulating the general operations of GW by FMC including but not limited to determination of rates for gas and the establishment of standards for customer service. GC is the repository of all power not specifically granted to FMC.

8. [*Defendant—assistant vice president*] is the Assistant Vice President for Customer Activities of FMC and GW and is directly responsible, *inter alia*, for the operation of the Collection and Meter Reading Department of GW and FMC, including all collection activity carried out, the crediting of customer payments, and termination of service.[192]

---

184 This form is adapted from the complaint filed in *In re* Maya, 8 B.R. 202 (Bankr. E.D. Pa. 1981). This note and the following notes to this form provide information that apply to practice in adversary proceedings generally, and should be consulted when reference is made to any of the adversary proceeding forms which follow this one. However, as should be clear from the differences in those forms, there is no single correct way to draft a pleading.

As discussed in Chapter 13, *supra*, most significant bankruptcy litigation is conducted in the form of adversary proceedings. See Fed. R. Bankr. P. 7001 for the types of actions which must be commenced as adversary proceedings. These proceedings are governed by Fed. R. Bankr. P. 7001–7087, which, with a few exceptions, are identical to the Federal Rules of Civil Procedure.

As the adversary rules are so similar to the civil procedure rules, authorities discussing the civil procedure rules are generally excellent sources of information that may be cited as persuasive on the interpretation of the adversary rules.

185 Fed. R. Bankr. P. 7008 incorporates Fed. R. Civ. P. 8, providing that all adversary proceedings originally filed in bankruptcy court be commenced by a complaint.

186 In actions in which the issues are somewhat complex or the complaint is lengthy, a preliminary statement is useful to give the reader of the complaint an overview of the action. It is not required, however, by the rules. If included, it may state generally the actions challenged, the statutes relied upon, and the relief sought.

187 Note that the benefit program which this complaint addresses no longer exists.

188 Fed. R. Bankr. P. 7008 provides that the complaint shall contain a short and plain statement of the grounds on which the court's jurisdiction depends as well as a reference to the name, number and chapter of the case under the Bankruptcy Code to which the adversary proceeding relates and the district and division where the case is pending. It may be necessary in some courts to state all of this information more specifically in this paragraph rather than simply referring to the caption as is done here. However, other than the substantive merits of the jurisdictional claims, courts rarely pay much attention to this paragraph. It also may not be necessary to spell out, as is done here, why the various jurisdictional provisions apply. A statement of the applicable statutory provisions will normally suffice.

Fed. R. Bankr. P. 7008 requires every complaint, counterclaim, or third-party complaint to contain a statement that the proceeding is either core or non-core. If the proceeding is alleged to be non-core, the pleading must also state whether the party filing it consents to the entry of a final order or judgment in the matter by the bankruptcy judge. See § 13.2.4, *supra*, for discussion of these jurisdictional issues.

189 This statement with respect to declaratory relief is not specifically required because 28 U.S.C. §§ 2201, 2202 are not jurisdictional provisions.

190 The complaint should contain a set of paragraphs identifying each of the parties. These paragraphs may, as here, briefly describe the parties' relation to the lawsuit. If the addresses of parties are not stated in the caption, they should normally be stated in these paragraphs.

191 In an action under 42 U.S.C. § 1983, it is important to indicate that the entities sued are involved in state action through their relation to state or local governmental units.

192 Defendants generally should include all entities whose presence in the case might be necessary to obtain the relief sought. For example, some courts require that the trustee be designated as a defendant whenever the debtor seeks to exercise the trustee's avoiding powers. In addition, when designating defendants, plaintiffs should give consideration to problems which might be posed by sovereign immunity and/or the Eleventh Amendment in the case of state officials (see § 13.3.2.2, *supra*), what parties may be necessary to facilitate discovery, and the requirements of 42 U.S.C. § 1983 if that section is pleaded.

To deal with Eleventh Amendment and/or sovereign immunity problems, it is usually desirable to sue named individual

9. [*Defendant—manager*] is the Manager of the Collection and Meter Reading Department of FMC and GW and is directly responsible for the operation of the department, including but not limited to all collection activity carried out by FMC and GW, the crediting of customer payments, and terminations of service.

IV. Class Action Allegations[193]

10. This action is brought as a class action pursuant to Federal Rule of Bankruptcy Procedure 7023 and Federal Rule of Civil Procedure 23(b)(2) because Defendants have acted on grounds generally applicable to the Class, thereby making appropriate declaratory and injunctive relief for the Class as a whole.

11. The Plaintiff Class consists of all individuals who (1) are or in the future will be customers receiving gas service from Defendants or any of them; (2) have filed or in the future will file a petition for relief under the Code listing Defendants or any of them

---

officials. If such officials have acted illegally, they are deemed to be stripped of their official character, because they are not authorized to so act. *Ex Parte* Young, 209 U.S. 123, 28 S. Ct. 441, 52 L. Ed. 714 (1908). 42 U.S.C. § 1983, when applicable, authorizes relief against "persons" which clearly includes individual officials. In cases in which specific policies are challenged, "persons" can also include municipalities. Monell v. Dep't of Social Services, 436 U.S. 658, 98 S. Ct. 2018, 56 L. Ed. 2d 611 (1978). By suing public officers in their official capacities as well, plaintiffs may insure that the action will continue if the original official sued is replaced by another. Fed. R. Civ. P. 25(d)(1) is incorporated in Fed. R. Bankr. P. 7025, providing a very convenient mechanism for substitution of parties.

In many cases it may be useful to designate organizational or agency defendants, as well as subordinate officials for discovery and enforcement purposes. If a corporation, partnership, association, or agency is a defendant, Fed. R. Civ. P. 30(b)(6) provides a mechanism for the opposing party to force that entity to locate a deponent best able to provide information on matters designated in a notice of deposition. In addition, parties generally do not have to be served with subpoenas or witness fees in order to secure their attendance at depositions. As statements of parties, their depositions may more easily be introduced into evidence. Finally, subordinate officials or entities may be more likely to obey a court order which is specifically directed to them. If they do not, they can more easily be held in contempt than if the order is directed only at their superiors.

193 Fed. R. Bankr. P. 7023 incorporates Fed. R. Civ. P. 23. In a class action it is generally advisable to identify the class specifically and to allege compliance with the class action rules. The local rules of many courts require such allegations, sometimes in greater detail than they are made here.

A class action has a number of advantages in some cases. It can serve the goal of efficiency by solving the problems of numerous clients in a single case. It also prevents the defendants from granting relief simply to the plaintiff in an individual action in order to moot his or her case while continuing the challenged practice with respect to others. *See* Deposit Guar. Nat'l Bank v. Roper, 445 U.S. 326, 100 S. Ct. 1166, 63 L. Ed. 2d 427 (1980). If relief is ordered on a class-wide basis, then a violation of the order with respect to any class member can be challenged as contempt of court.

See generally the discussion of class actions in § 13.7, *supra*. See also Newberg on Class Actions (3d ed.) for exhaustive treatment of virtually all class action issues, as well as National Consumer Law Center, Consumer Class Actions: A Practical Litigation Guide (5th ed. 2002 and Supp.).

---

as an unsecured creditor; and (3) subsequent to the filing of the bankruptcy petition received or will receive governmental benefits under the Emergency Crisis Assistance Program (hereinafter "ECAP") or similar government benefit programs which pay the benefits directly or indirectly to Defendants or any of them on behalf of the individual Class member.

12. The Class is so numerous that joinder of all members is impracticable.

13. The claims of the named Plaintiffs are typical of those of the Class.

14. The following questions of law and fact are common to all members of the Plaintiff Class: whether Defendants, by applying vendor payments from ECAP or other government benefit programs, made on behalf of a bankruptcy debtor and received by Defendants after the filing of the bankruptcy petition, to satisfy a debt incurred before the filing of the petition violate:

    a. section 362 of the Code, 11 U.S.C. § 362;

    b. section 525 of the Code, 11 U.S.C. § 525;

    c. section 524 of the Code, 11 U.S.C. § 524;

    d. section 522 of the Code, 11 U.S.C. § 522(c), when the benefits are claimed as exempt property; and

    e. the Economic Opportunity Act, as amended, 42 U.S.C. § 2809(a)(5) and the ECAP regulations promulgated thereunder.

15. Plaintiffs' attorneys have the experience necessary to competently protect and vigorously represent all members of this Class and Plaintiffs will adequately represent the interests of the Class and have no conflict of interest with other Class members.

V. Factual Allegations[194]

16. In approximately February 1991, Defendants began supplying gas service to Plaintiffs at their residence. The gas service has been supplied since that date without interruption.

17. On or about December 21, 2002, Plaintiffs applied for benefits under ECAP and were found eligible for benefits.

18. ECAP is a federal assistance program funded under section 222(a)(5) of the Economic Opportunity Act, as amended, 42 U.S.C. § 2809(a)(5). The purpose of the program is to make funds available to poor and low-income households suffering energy-related crises caused by the high cost of energy. ECAP provides grants to eligible persons under which payments are made directly or indirectly to vendors and suppliers of energy-related fuel, goods and services on behalf of the eligible persons. Payments under the program are not conditioned upon the existence of a debt owed to

---

194 Factual allegations are to be made in accordance with Fed. R. Bankr. P. 7008, which generally incorporates Fed. R. Civ. P. 8. All that is required is a "short and plain statement of the claim." Each averment is to be simple, concise, and direct. Facts and legal theories may be alleged in the alternative even if they are inconsistent. Thus the facts need not be extensive, though care should be taken to assure that all of the elements of the cause of action are averred. Such averments are to be in numbered paragraphs, the content of each limited as far as practicable to a statement of a single set of circumstances.

One useful way to clearly present a case with more than one legal theory is to allege the facts first, following them with a separate claim for each theory, as is done in this complaint. Documents may be appended to the complaint as exhibits and, under Fed. R. Bankr. P. 7010, incorporating Fed. R. of Civ. P. 10, are considered a part of the complaint for all purposes.

the vendor and supplier. Payments may be made to establish a line of credit for the eligible persons. *See* 45 C.F.R. § 1601.70-3(a); 45 C.F.R. § 1601.70-8.[195]

19. On January 3, 2004, Plaintiffs filed a petition for relief under the Code.

20. In the bankruptcy proceeding, Plaintiffs listed an obligation to Defendants for gas service provided prior to the filing of the bankruptcy petition.

21. On January 3, 2004, the date Plaintiffs filed their bankruptcy petition, their debt to Defendants was approximately $162.48.

22. On March 3, 2004, Defendants received a payment of $300.00 which constituted Plaintiffs' ECAP emergency energy assistance grant.

23. In their schedules, as amended, Plaintiffs claimed this payment and their entitlement to it as exempt property under 11 U.S.C. § 522.

24. Defendants applied the payment to satisfy the debt Plaintiffs incurred before the filing of their bankruptcy petition.

VI. Statement of Claim[196]

First Claim

25. By applying the vendor payment made by ECAP on Plaintiffs' behalf to satisfy the debt Plaintiffs had incurred before the filing of the bankruptcy petition, Defendants violated the automatic stay provision of the Code, 11 U.S.C. § 362.[197]

Second Claim

26. By applying the vendor payment made by ECAP on Plaintiffs' behalf to satisfy the debt Plaintiffs had incurred before the filing of the bankruptcy petition, Defendants violated the anti-discrimination provision of the Code, 11 U.S.C. § 525.[198]

Third Claim

27. By applying the vendor payment made by ECAP on Plaintiffs' behalf to satisfy the debt Plaintiffs had incurred before the filing of the bankruptcy petition, Defendants violated the discharge provision of the Code, 11 U.S.C. § 524.[199]

Fourth Claim

28. By applying the vendor payment made by ECAP on Plaintiffs' behalf and claimed as exempt by them, to satisfy the debt incurred by Plaintiffs before the filing of their bankruptcy petition, Defendants violated the exemption provision of the Code, 11 U.S.C. § 522(c).[200]

Fifth Claim

29. By applying the vendor payment made by ECAP on Plaintiffs' behalf to satisfy a debt which was dischargeable by their bankruptcy and thus not payable by them as part of their energy costs, Defendants misappropriated that payment in violation of the ECAP regulations, 45 C.F.R. § 1601.70, which provide for payments only to respond to energy needs of poor households.[201]

Sixth Claim

30. By depriving Plaintiffs of their rights guaranteed to them by federal law as set forth above, Defendants, acting under color of law, have violated 42 U.S.C. § 1983 and are subject to relief appropriate to remedy that violation.[202]

VII. Relief[203]

WHEREFORE, Plaintiffs request that this Court:

1. Take jurisdiction of this case;

2. Certify that plaintiff class as set forth in paragraphs 10 through 15 above;[204]

3. Enter judgment and grant relief declaring[205] that Defendants' practice of applying payments under ECAP or other government benefit programs on behalf of a debtor who has filed a bankruptcy petition that are received by Defendants after the filing of the debtor's bankruptcy petition to satisfy a debt incurred before the filing of the petition violates:

   a. 11 U.S.C. § 362;
   b. 11 U.S.C. § 525;
   c. 11 U.S.C. § 524;
   d. 11 U.S.C. § 522(c);
   e. 45 C.F.R. §§ 1601.70-1 *et seq.*; and
   f. 42 U.S.C. § 1983.

---

195 This kind of explanation of the law is sometimes helpful in explaining the case through the complaint but is not necessary.

196 Fed. R. Civ. P. 10(b), incorporated in Fed. R. Bankr. P. 7010, requires each claim founded upon a separate transaction or occurrence to be stated in a separate count "whenever a separation facilitates the clear presentation of the matters set forth." One way of doing this is by making each claim after the factual allegations, as in this example.

197 The automatic stay prohibits any act to collect a debt against the debtors, or to obtain possession of property of the estate. 11 U.S.C. § 362(a); *see* Ch. 9, *supra.*

198 Municipal utilities are governmental units as defined in 11 U.S.C. § 101(27), and are thus prohibited from discriminating against the debtor based upon a debt discharged in bankruptcy. 11 U.S.C. § 525(a). In this case, by applying the vendor payment to the pre-bankruptcy debt, rather than giving the credit which would have been due if that debt had not been considered, defendants have discriminated. *See* Chs. 9, 14, *supra.*

199 Once the debtor's debt is discharged, 11 U.S.C. § 524(b) provides an injunction against any act to collect, recover, or offset the debt as a personal liability of the debtor.

---

200 Exempt property may not be pursued to collect any pre-petition debt after bankruptcy unless that debt falls within the exceptions made by 11 U.S.C. § 522(c).

201 Claims other than Bankruptcy Code claims may be raised in bankruptcy court, either by themselves or in conjunction with claims under the Code, so long as they arise in a bankruptcy case or are related to such a case, or to the property of the debtor as of the commencement of the case. 28 U.S.C. § 1334. But see § 13.2, *supra*, for limitations on bankruptcy court jurisdiction.

202 The availability of 42 U.S.C. § 1983 to remedy state actions in violation of rights guaranteed by the Bankruptcy Code is discussed in § 15.5.2, *supra.*

203 Normally, a complaint will end with a prayer for relief stating what action the court is requested to take. *See* Fed. R. Civ. P. 8(a) (incorporated in Fed. R. Bankr. P. 7008). This is often colloquially known as the "Wherefore Clause."

204 Often a separate motion is required by local rule or practice specifically requesting class certification.

205 This is one form of request for declaratory relief.

4. Enjoin Defendants, their successors in office, agents, employees, and all other persons in active concert and participation with them[206] from continuing their practice of crediting payments under ECAP or other government benefit programs to satisfy debts incurred prior to the filing of a debtor's bankruptcy petition.

5. Order Defendants, their successors in office, agents, employees, and all other persons in active concert and participation with them to credit payments received under ECAP or other government benefit programs made on behalf of Plaintiffs and all Class members solely to debts incurred subsequent to the filing of the Class member's bankruptcy petition.

6. Award Plaintiffs their attorney fees herein;[207] and

7. Grant such other relief as shall be just and proper.[208]

Date:
[*signature*]
Attorney for Plaintiffs[209]

Form 84 Complaint to Prohibit Eviction from Public Housing Based upon Dischargeable Debt for Rent[210]

[*Caption: Official Form 16D*]

Complaint

1. This is an action brought under section 525(a) of the Bankruptcy Code (11 U.S.C. § 525(a)), seeking a declaration that the

termination of the Plaintiff's tenancy by the Defendants is null and void, and an order directing the Defendants to continue to lease to Plaintiff and to enjoin the Defendants from discriminating against Plaintiff based upon any debt that is dischargeable or discharged under the Bankruptcy Code or attempting to evict Plaintiff on the basis of such a debt.

2. Jurisdiction is conferred on this Court by 28 U.S.C. § 1471 in that this proceeding arises in and is related to the above-captioned chapter 7 case under title 11 and concerns the rights of the debtor in that case. This proceeding is a core proceeding.

3. Plaintiff's action for declaratory relief is authorized by 28 U.S.C. §§ 2201 and 2202.

4. Plaintiff [*debtor*] resides at [*address*] and is the debtor in this bankruptcy case.

5. The [*name*] Housing Authority (hereinafter "HA") is a public body, corporate and politic, with offices at [*address*]. It exercises the public powers of the Commonwealth as an agency and has the statutory right to sue and be sued.

6. [*Defendant—general manager*] is the General Manager of HA and is responsible for the management, direction, and administration of the affairs of HA and the acts of its agents and employees while acting within the scope of their employment.

7. [*Defendant—site manager*] is Manager of scattered sites of HA and is responsible for the direction and administration of the site in which the Plaintiff resides.

8. Plaintiff is and has been, prior to the filing of her bankruptcy petition, a resident of subsidized housing, a form of government grant.

9. On March 20, 2004, the Plaintiff filed a voluntary petition for relief under the Bankruptcy Code.

10. In the bankruptcy case, Plaintiff listed as an unsecured debt an obligation to Defendant HA for rent owed prior to the filing of the bankruptcy petition.

11. On March 20, 2004, the date of the Plaintiff's petition, her debt to HA was $484.00.

12. The Defendants, by letter of February 29, 2004 from [*defendant—site manager*], notified the Plaintiff that her right to live in subsidized housing would be terminated effective April 2, 2004, and allowed her thirty days to vacate the premises.

13. The stated reason for the termination and eviction was nonpayment of the rent debt which is dischargeable in the bankruptcy case.

Claim

14. Under 11 U.S.C. § 525(a) the Defendants may not refuse to lease to Plaintiff because she is or has been a debtor under the Bankruptcy Code.

15. Defendants are further prohibited by 11 U.S.C. § 525(a) from refusing to lease to Plaintiff because she has not paid a debt that is dischargeable or discharged under the Bankruptcy Code.

16. By depriving the Plaintiff of her rights guaranteed to her by federal law as set forth above, Defendants, acting under color of law, would violate 42 U.S.C. § 1983 and would be subject to relief appropriate to that violation.

WHEREFORE, Plaintiff requests that this Court:

1. Take jurisdiction of this case;

---

206 If an order specifying these persons is obtained, enforcement by contempt may be somewhat easier. However, normally enforcement proceedings will be brought against the officials named in the complaint or their successors. Agents of the defendants are generally bound by an injunction in any case under Fed. R. Civ. P. 65(d), incorporated in Fed. R. Bankr. P. 7065, provided they receive actual notice of the order.

207 Under the "American Rule," attorney fees are not normally awarded to prevailing parties, except in special circumstances. Here, fees are sought under 42 U.S.C. § 1988. Certain provisions of the Bankruptcy Code also authorize the awarding of fees. *See* Ch. 15, *supra.*

208 This type of catch-all prayer is usually included in case other types of relief are later found appropriate. Case law on the subject generally permits the court to go beyond the prayer for relief even if this request is not included.

209 Fed. R. Bankr. P. 9011 provides that every pleading filed by a party represented by an attorney shall be signed by at least one attorney of record in his or her individual name, whose address shall be stated. The signature of an attorney to any pleading, motion, or application constitutes a certification that he or she has read the paper, that to the best of his or her knowledge, information and belief, there is good ground to support it, and that it is not interposed for delay or other improper purpose. The complaint need not be verified by the plaintiff or any other person.

210 A complaint such as this one may be used to seek declaratory and injunctive relief against a public housing lessor's attempts to evict the debtor. The complaint seeks relief under 11 U.S.C. § 525(a) which prohibits discrimination against bankruptcy debtors. *See* § 14.5.5.3, *supra.* The complaint also seeks relief under 42 U.S.C. § 1983. *See* § 15.5.2, *supra.* An alternative method of proceeding would be to assume the public housing lease in a chapter 13 case. However, the debtor would have to promptly cure a rent default if the lease is assumed. *See* § 12.9.2, *supra.* For a general discussion of complaints in adversary proceedings, see notes to Form 83, Appendix G.10, *supra.*

2. Enter judgment and grant relief declaring that Defendants' termination of the Plaintiff's right to live in subsidized housing for reason of an unpaid debt dischargeable under the Bankruptcy Act is a violation of 11 U.S.C. § 525(a);

3. Order Defendants, their successors in office, agents, employees, and all other persons in active concert and participation with them to continue the Plaintiff's lease;

4. Enjoin Defendants, their successors in office, agents, employees, and all other persons in active concert and participation with them from pursuing their claim against the Plaintiff outside the bankruptcy process or seeking to evict the Plaintiff based upon that claim;

5. Award Plaintiff her attorney fees herein;[211]

6. Grant such other relief as shall be proper and just.

Date: [*signature*]

                           Attorney for Plaintiff

Form 85 Complaint Seeking Review of Administrative Action[212]

[Caption: Official Form 16D]

Complaint

1. This action is filed by Plaintiff, Debtor in the above-captioned chapter 13 case, to seek this Court's review of the decision of Defendants to deny relief under the HUD assignment program. This Court has jurisdiction under 28 U.S.C. § 1334 and this matter is a core proceeding.[213]

2. Defendants are the United States Department of Housing and Urban Development ("HUD") and [*defendant—secretary*], the Secretary of Housing and Urban Development, who has responsibility for the operation and policies of HUD. He is sued in his individual and official capacities.

3. Plaintiff first applied to HUD for assignment relief with respect to her problems on an FHA-insured mortgage in June, 1991, through her lender, who believed she met the requirements for assignment relief.

4. In July, 2004, Plaintiff received a letter preliminarily denying relief, and requesting further information, which is attached hereto as Exhibit A [*omitted*].

5. Plaintiff provided the requested information to the best of her ability, giving ample evidence that she met the regulatory requirements for assignment relief.

6. Nonetheless, in August, 2004, Plaintiff was denied assignment relief, essentially because Plaintiff did not submit certain documents, by a letter attached as Exhibit B [*omitted*].

7. The denial of assignment relief was erroneous as a matter of law, arbitrary and capricious, an abuse of discretion, and not supported by substantial evidence, and should be reversed by this Court.[214]

WHEREFORE, Plaintiff prays that:

1. Defendants be ordered to accept Plaintiff's request for an assignment.

2. Plaintiff be awarded attorney fees under 28 U.S.C. § 2412.[215]

3. This Court order such other relief as is just and proper.

Date: [*signature*]

                           Attorney for Plaintiff

Form 86 Complaint Seeking Restoration of Driver's License[216]

[Caption: Official Form 16D]

Complaint

1. Debtor brings this action to enjoin Defendant [*state*] Department of Transportation and Defendant: [*defendant—secretary*] from suspending Debtor's driver's license because of his nonpayment of pre-petition debts, and to obtain sanctions for contempt.

2. This Court has jurisdiction of this case proceeding under 28 U.S.C. §§ 1331 and 157(b)(2). This proceeding is a core proceeding.

3. Plaintiff is an individual residing in [*city*].

4. Defendant [*state*] Department of Transportation is a state government agency.[217] [*Defendant—secretary*] is the Secretary of Transportation, and has the duty of directing the issuance of driver's licenses in [*state*].

5. In early 2004, Defendants suspended Plaintiff's drivers license solely because he had not paid a motor vehicle judgment in favor of [*judgment-holder*], entered in [*city*] Municipal Court, [*number*].

6. On September 11, 2004, Defendants issued a second license suspension notice to Plaintiff this time because of failure to pay a Connecticut traffic ticket, incurred April 15, 2004.

---

211 Attorney fees are available on the claim under 42 U.S.C. § 1983. *See* § 15.5.2, *supra*.

212 In 1996, Congress curtailed the HUD assignment program. A complaint such as this one can be still be used as a model for actions seeking administrative review of state or federal agency action. For a general discussion of complaints in adversary proceedings, see notes to Form 83, Appendix G.10, *supra*.

213 Normally, administrative review of HUD assignment denials would be had in district court. However, it is clear that the broad jurisdiction of the bankruptcy court would include such matters. *See* § 13.4.2, *supra*. This type of proceeding probably is a core proceeding to the adjustment of the debtor-creditor relationship, because HUD is a contingent creditor as guarantor of the insured mortgage. 28 U.S.C. § 157(b)(2)(O). However, a court might find it to be a non-core proceeding.

214 Review of administrative actions, when applicable, is governed by the Administrative Procedures Act.

215 If the plaintiff prevails in an action against the federal government and the government's position was not substantially justified, attorney fees may be awarded under the Equal Access to Justice Act. *See* § 15.5.4, *supra*.

216 This complaint may be used by chapter 13 debtors to seek restoration of driver's licenses revoked solely due to failure to pay traffic tickets, which are dischargeable debts in chapter 13. The complaint seeks relief under 11 U.S.C. § 362(a) because the continued suspension is an effort to coerce payment of the debts, and 11 U.S.C. § 525(a) because the defendants are discriminating against the debtor based solely upon the nonpayment of dischargeable debts. *See* § 14.5.5.1, *supra*. The complaint also seeks relief under 42 U.S.C. § 1983 because of the state action involved. *See* § 15.5.2, *supra*. For a general discussion of complaints in adversary proceedings, see notes to Form 83, Appendix G.10, *supra*. This form is adopted from pleadings in Smith v. Pa. Dep't of Transp., 66 B.R. 244 (E.D. Pa. 1986).

217 *See* § 13.3.2.2, *supra*, for a discussion of applicable sovereign immunity issues.

7. On June 11, 2004, the Plaintiff filed this bankruptcy petition under chapter 13. The Debtor's statement lists both debts which are the basis for the license suspensions.

8. On June 26, 2004, and again on October 7, 2004, Debtor's counsel wrote to Defendant requesting reinstatement of the Debtor's driver's license (letters attached as Exhibits A and B).

9. Defendant [*state*] Department of Transportation has taken no action to restore Plaintiff's driver's license.

10. Plaintiff needs his license to obtain employment, and has suffered loss of wages because of Defendant's wrongful refusal to reinstate his license.

11. Defendant is violating the automatic stay, 11 U.S.C. § 362, by conditioning restoration of Plaintiff's license on his payment of pre-petition debts.

12. Defendant is violating 11 U.S.C. § 525(a) and 42 U.S.C. § 1983 by denying Plaintiff his license solely because of his failure to pay debts which are dischargeable in this chapter 13 bankruptcy.

WHEREFORE, Plaintiff [*debtor*] requests that this Court:

1. Assume jurisdiction of the case;

2. Order Defendants to restore Plaintiff's driver's license immediately;

3. Hold Defendants in contempt of the automatic stay;

4. Award Plaintiff damages[218] and attorney fees;[219] and

5. Grant such other relief as is just and proper.

Date: [*signature*]
                    Attorney for Plaintiff

Exhibit A

[*attorney*]
Legal Department
[*state*] Department of Transportation
[*address*]   October 7, 2004
                 RE: [*debtor*]
                  [*address*]
      Operator's License [*number*]

Dear [*attorney*]:

I represent [*debtor*], who filed a chapter 13 bankruptcy petition on June 11, 2004, in the [*district name*] of [*state*], Docket No. [*number*]. [*Debtor*]'s license is currently under suspension because of his failure to pay a traffic citation from Connecticut. There is another suspension because of failure to pay a motor vehicle judgment held by [*judgment-holder*]. Both of these debts have been listed in [*debtor*]'s chapter 13 statement.

Please take all necessary action to cancel these suspensions and clear [*debtor*]'s record. As you know, the Bankruptcy Code, 11 U.S.C. §§ 362 and 525, prohibits the Department of Transportation from taking any action, including license suspension, to collect a debt. This includes action related to debts [*debtor*] owes to other parties as well as to the Department of Transportation. Section 525 also prohibits any government entity from denying a license to a bankruptcy debtor because of his failure to pay a pre-petition debt.

If I do not receive confirmation from you that the suspensions

have been canceled within fifteen (15) days, I intend to seek relief from the bankruptcy court, including sanctions for contempt. Time is of the essence, because [*debtor*] needs his license to obtain employment.

                    [*signature*]
                    Attorney

Exhibit B

[*name—administrator*]
[*state*]
Financial Responsibility Division
[*address*]   [*date*]
                 Re: [*debtor*]
                  [*address*]
      Operator's License [*number*]

Dear [*name*]:

I represent the above individual whose license was suspended due to an unpaid motor vehicle judgment. [*Debtor*] has filed a chapter 13 bankruptcy petition. Under his chapter 13 plan, this creditor in the motor vehicle case will receive payments in accordance with the requirements of the Bankruptcy Code. Therefore, [*debtor*] seeks reinstatement of his operator's privileges.

In support of this application, I enclose:

1. a copy of [*debtor*]'s bankruptcy petition;

2. a copy of the bankruptcy statements confirming that the motor vehicle judgment was duly listed as an unsecured debt in the bankruptcy case;

3. [*debtor*]'s sworn declaration that he does not operate his car, because his insurance was canceled when his license was canceled; and

4. a money order payable to your office in the amount of $25.00.

[*Debtor*] is a truck driver by trade. In order to complete his chapter 13 plan, he needs to obtain his license within the next two (2) months. Please take immediate action to issue him a license. If I can be of any assistance, please do not hesitate to call. Thank you.

                    [*signature*]
                    Attorney

Form 87 Complaint Seeking Damages in Non-Core Adversary Proceeding Against a Non-Creditor for Unfair Debt Collection Practices[220]

[Caption: Official Form 16D]

Complaint

I. Introduction

1. This is an action for actual and statutory damages brought by an individual consumer for Defendant's violation of the Fair Debt Collection Practices Act, 15 U.S.C. §§ 1692–1692*o* (hereinafter referred to as "FDCPA") and the [*state*] Deceptive Practices Law,

---

218 Damages are available under 42 U.S.C. § 1983, as well as for violations of the automatic stay, under 11 U.S.C. § 362(b), and as a remedy for contempt. *See* § 9.6, *supra*.

219 Award of attorney fees is mandatory when the plaintiff prevails on a claim under 42 U.S.C. § 1983. *See* § 15.5.2, *supra*.

220 As a proceeding to recover money an action against a party who is not a creditor asserting claims under state and federal non-bankruptcy law should be brought as an adversary proceeding. For a general discussion of complaints in adversary proceedings, see notes to Form 83, Appendix G.10, *supra*. See generally Chapter 13, *supra* for discussion of litigation consumer claims of the debtor in bankruptcy court.

[*state*] General Laws [*cite provision*] (hereinafter referred to as "state act"), which prohibit debt collectors from engaging in abusive, deceptive and unfair practices.[221]

II. Jurisdiction[222]

2. Jurisdiction is conferred on this court by 28 U.S.C. § 1334 in that this proceeding arises in and is related to the above-captioned chapter 13 case under title 11, and concerns property of the debtor in that case. This matter is a non-core proceeding; the Plaintiff consents to the entry of final order in this proceeding by the Bankruptcy Judge.[223]

III. Parties

3. Plaintiff is a debtor under title 11 in the above-captioned case.

4. Defendant is a natural person engaged in the business of collecting debts in this state with his principal place of business in Pennsylvania.

5. Defendant, using the mails, regularly attempts to collect debts alleged to be due another.

IV. Factual Allegations

6. On June 19, 1998, Plaintiff entered into a consumer loan transaction with [*name*] Consumer Discount Company (hereinafter referred to as "Company").

7. Pursuant to this transaction, the Plaintiff gave Company a security interest in her residential real property at [*address*].

8. On or about September 17, 2003, Defendant mailed to the Plaintiff a collection letter which is attached hereto as Plaintiff's "Exhibit A" [*omitted*] and incorporated herein.

9. The above-mentioned letter threatened suit within one week of the date of the letter unless Plaintiff made payment in full of $207.50.

10. Plaintiff was unable to make payment of the full amount of $207.50 within one week of the date of the letter and therefore made no payment.

11. No legal action was taken by Defendant within one week of the date of the Defendant's letter.

---

221 In addition to the federal Fair Debt Collection Practices Act, all states have unfair and deceptive practices statutes which limit debt collection practices. Damages may normally be sought under both state and federal law. *See generally* National Consumer Law Center, Fair Debt Collection (5th ed. 2004).

222 The debtor may pursue this action if it is exempt or abandoned by the trustee. If abandoned it would presumably have to be brought other than in bankruptcy court because it would not be related to the bankruptcy case. *See* Barletta v. Tedeschi, 121 B.R. 669 (N.D.N.Y. 1990).

223 Every pleading must allege whether the proceeding is a core or non-core proceeding. Fed. R. Bankr. P. 7008(a). In a non-core proceeding, every pleading must state whether the pleader consents to entry of final orders by the bankruptcy judge. *Id.* A proceeding seeking damages for emotional distress due to unfair collection practices is not a personal injury or wrongful death claim which must be tried in district court under 28 U.S.C. § 157(b)(5). Littles v. Lieberman, 75 B.R. 240 (Bankr. E.D. Pa. 1987). This form is adapted from pleadings drafted by Margaret E. Taylor, Esq. and Mary Jeffery, Esq., Philadelphia, PA.

12. As a result of the Defendant's act, Plaintiff suffered extreme fright, became severely agitated, lost sleep, experienced episodes of crying, suffered an aggravation of pre-existing physical infirmity, and incurred medical expenses.

V. First Claim for Relief

13. Plaintiff realleges and incorporates by reference paragraphs 1 through 12 above as if fully set out herein.

14. Defendant violated the FDCPA. Defendant's violations include but are not limited to:

a. representation or implication that nonpayment of the debt would result in the imminent sale of property when such action would not have been lawful and the debt collector did not intend to take such action, 15 U.S.C. § 1692e(4);

b. threat to take legal action that could not have been legally taken and that was not intended to be taken, 15 U.S.C. § 1692e(5); and

c. failure to provide Plaintiff within five days of the Defendant's initial communication a validation notice as required by 15 U.S.C. § 1692g.

15. As a result of the above violations of the FDCPA, the Defendant is liable to the Plaintiff in the sum of Plaintiff's actual damages, statutory damages of $1000.00 and attorney fees.

VI. Second Claim for Relief

16. Plaintiff realleges and incorporates by reference paragraphs 1 through 15 above as if fully set out herein.

17. Defendant violated the state act. Defendant's violations of the state act include, but are not limited to the following:

a. representation or implication that nonpayment of the debt would result in the imminent sale of property when such action would not have been lawful and the debt collector did not intend to take such action; and

b. threat to take legal action that could not have been legally taken and that was not intended to be taken.

18. Defendant's act, as described above, was done intentionally with the purpose of coercing Plaintiff to pay the alleged debt.

19. As a result of the above violations of the state act, the Defendant is liable to the Plaintiff for triple the Plaintiff's actual damages.

WHEREFORE, Plaintiff respectfully prays that judgment be entered against the Defendant in the amount of:

a. triple her actual damages pursuant to [*state*] General Laws [*provision*];

b. $1000.00 statutory damages pursuant to 15 U.S.C. § 1692k;

c. costs and reasonable attorney fees pursuant to 15 U.S.C. § 1692k; and

d. for such other and further relief as may be just and proper.

Date: [*signature*]

Attorney for Debtor/Plaintiff

Form 88 Motion for Abandonment of Property by Trustee[224]

[Caption: Official Form 16A]

Motion for Abandonment of Property by Trustee

1. Debtor, [*name*], commenced this case on [*date*] by filing a voluntary petition for relief under chapter 7 of the Bankruptcy Code.

2. Listed on Schedule B of the debtor's bankruptcy schedules is a claim against [*creditor/collector*] for violations of the Fair Debt Collection Practices Act, 15 U.S.C. §§ 1692–1692*o* and the [*state*] Deceptive Practices Law, [*cite provision*].

3. The debtor has listed this property as a contingent, unliquidated claim having a value of $1500.00. The debtor has also claimed this property as fully exempt in her bankruptcy schedules.

4. The Trustee has not objected to the debtor's claim of exemption in this property.

5. The property so listed is burdensome to the estate and/or is of inconsequential value and benefit to the estate.

WHEREFORE, the Debtor requests, pursuant to § 554(b) of the Bankruptcy Code, that this Court enter an Order providing that the Trustee shall abandon said property.

Date: [*signature*]
                                 Attorney for Debtor

Form 89 Debtor's Motion for Expedited Discovery[225]

[Caption: Official Form 16D]

Debtors' Motion for Expedited Discovery

Debtors hereby move that discovery in this contested matter be expedited. As grounds for this motion, Debtors aver:

1. This action was commenced by filing of a motion on February 1, 2004.

2. An evidentiary hearing on the matter is scheduled for February 27, 2004.

3. It is not possible for discovery to be conducted before the trial date if normal time limits are allowed.

4. Discovery by Debtors will substantially aid in preparation of their case and also shorten the time required for trial of the case, perhaps even eliminating the necessity of a trial.

WHEREFORE, Debtors pray that full responses to their discovery requests (Request for Production of Documents and Request for Admissions) be delivered to the office of their counsel no later than 5:00 P.M., February 22, 2004.

Date: [*signature*]
                                 Attorney for Debtors

Form 90 Plaintiff's Request for Documents[226]

[Caption: Official Form 16D]

Plaintiffs' Request for Documents

Plaintiffs request, pursuant to Rule 7034 of the Federal Rules of Bankruptcy Procedure, that Defendant produce a copy of each of the following documents to be sent to the office of Plaintiffs' attorney within thirty (30) days of this request.

"Document" means and includes any printed, typewritten or handwritten matter of whatever character including specifically, but not exclusively and without limiting the generality of the foregoing, letters, desk or other calendars, memoranda, telegrams, cables, reports, charts, business records, personal records, accountants' statements, bank statements, handwritten notes, minutes of meetings, notes of meetings or conversations, catalogs, written agreements, checks, receipts, invoices, bills, and any carbon or other copies of such materials.

1. All contracts between Plaintiffs and Defendant including notes, judgment notes, security agreements, mortgages, and insurance agreements.[227]

2. All credit applications or credit reports pertaining to Plaintiffs' account.[228]

---

224 Under § 554(c), property that is scheduled under § 512(1) and not otherwise administered by the trustee is abandoned to the debtor upon the closing of the bankruptcy case. In the case of property consisting of legal claims, the debtor may wish to initiate a lawsuit or continue with pending litigation before the bankruptcy case is closed. A motion under § 554(b) can be filed requesting that the trustee abandon the property. Counsel should ensure that proper notice is provided and that other procedural requirements in Fed. Bankr. P. 6007 are satisfied.

225 The time limits for stay litigation in 11 U.S.C. § 362(e) make discovery under the normal time limits impossible. A motion, such as this one, is permitted under Fed. R. Bankr. P. 7034 and 7035, which incorporate Fed. R. Civ. P. 34 and 35, and permit the court to allow a shorter time for answering discovery. It serves to put a good deal of pressure on the plaintiff in stay litigation to settle or agree to postponement of the hearing.

   Practitioners should note the changes to discovery practice imposed by amended Federal Rules of Civil Procedure 26–37 which are applicable in some jurisdictions. In particular, note the new prerequisites to traditional formal discovery contained in amended Rule 26, including the duty of voluntary or automatic disclosure in Rule 26(a). These form discovery requests may need to be adjusted to reflect these new rules and/or the results of automatic disclosures made pursuant to the rules when the amended discovery rules are applicable.

226 This request for documents form may be used in most consumer litigation both in and out of bankruptcy court. It seeks all of the documents typically involved in a consumer credit transaction, including those which may lead to further discovery or claims of the debtor against the creditor.

   Practitioners should note the changes to discovery practice imposed by amended Federal Rules of Civil Procedure 26–37 which are applicable in some jurisdictions. In particular, note the new prerequisites to traditional formal discovery contained in amended Rule 26, including the duty of voluntary or automatic disclosure in Rule 26(a). These form discovery requests may need to be adjusted to reflect these new rules and/or the results of automatic disclosures made pursuant to the rules.

227 Security agreements may sometimes be helpful in showing security other than a mortgage for purposes of 11 U.S.C. § 1322(b)(2) so that a secured creditor's rights may be modified. Insurance agreements may give rise to various claims by the debtor with respect to unfair practices in selling credit insurance.

228 Credit applications may show violations of the Equal Credit Opportunity Act, 15 U.S.C. §§ 1691–1691f. Obtaining credit reports for improper purposes violates the Fair Credit Reporting Act, 15 U.S.C. §§ 1681–1681t.

3. All disclosure statements given to Plaintiffs or other notices of their rights.[229]

4. All ledger cards or ledger sheets or other documents reflecting payments, charges, and costs incurred on Plaintiffs' account as well as any document related to any settlement with the Plaintiffs in any transaction.[230]

5. All correspondence concerning Plaintiffs' account.[231]

6. All telephone log sheets or other internal memoranda or notes concerning Plaintiffs' account.

7. All fee agreements between Defendant and its attorneys or other documents relating to such fees.[232]

8. All operating manuals, memoranda, or other documents concerning internal procedures of Defendant.[233]

9. All agreements, correspondence, or other documents concerning credit life, accident or property insurance on the Plaintiffs' account including any master or overall contracts, agreements, or other documents relating to the overall cost, commission on, or other details of any group insurance policy applicable to Plaintiffs.[234]

10. All records of attorney fees actually incurred or paid with respect of Plaintiffs' account.

11. All documents reflecting the identity or value of any security or collateral which you claim in connection with Plaintiffs' account.

12. All other documents pertaining to Plaintiffs' account.

13. All of the above-enumerated documents with respect to any previous transactions between Plaintiffs and Defendant.[235]

Date: [*signature*]
Attorney for Plaintiffs

Form 91 Defendant's Request for Admissions[236]

[*Caption: Official Form 16D*]

Defendants' Request for Admissions

Defendants request Plaintiff to admit, pursuant to Federal Rule of Bankruptcy Procedure 7036, for the purpose of this action only,

the truth of the following statements of fact or of application of law to fact:

1. The fair market value of Defendants' home, without any deduction for any mortgages or liens thereon, is in excess of thirty-five thousand dollars ($35,000.00) and less than forty thousand dollars ($40,000.00).

2. With the exception of the Plaintiff's lien, the validity of which is in dispute, all of the other liens on Defendants' home are voidable under 11 U.S.C. § 522(f)(2).

Date: [*signature*]
Attorney for Defendants

Form 92 Petition for Writ of *Habeas Corpus*[237]

[*Caption: Official Form 16D*]

Petition for Writ of *Habeas Corpus*

1. Petitioner is the debtor in this chapter 13 bankruptcy case. The Court has jurisdiction over this matter under 28 U.S.C. § 1334. This is a core proceeding.

2. Respondent is the superintendent of the [*name*] County Jail.

3. Petitioner has been detained at that jail and is in Respondent's custody on process in the civil action[238] brought by the [*name*] County Department of Public Welfare to collect spousal support payments which were assigned to the Department.

4. All of the said spousal support payments are listed in the chapter 13 schedules and are provided for[239] in Petitioner's chapter 13 plan.

---

229 Disclosure statements may contain violations of the Truth in Lending Act, 15 U.S.C. §§ 1601–1666j, or state statutes.

230 These materials may reveal improper charges or the failure to credit payments made.

231 These documents typically contain evidence of contacts with the debtor, some of which may constitute unfair collection practices.

232 These documents may be used to challenge claims for attorney fees as unreasonable or unfair.

233 If operating manuals or other internal documents are obtained, they will often suggest other avenues to explore with respect to the procedures followed by the creditor with respect to the debtor's case.

234 Insurance agreements may give rise to various claims by the debtor with respect to unfair practices in selling credit insurance.

235 Many consumer transactions are preceded by a series of earlier transactions between the parties, and may be refinancings of such transactions. The documents in the earlier transactions may show other violations of the debtor's rights, or render disclosures made in the current transaction inaccurate, for example, when a security interest was taken in an earlier transaction as to

all future transactions, but was not disclosed in the later transaction.

236 A request for admissions with respect to the valuation of property can be a useful tool in a variety of proceedings, including stay litigation, redemption proceedings, and proceedings concerning exemptions. If an opposing party fails to admit the truth of a matter requested and the party requesting the admission thereafter proves the truth of that matter, the court is required to award the requesting party expenses, including attorney fees, unless certain exceptions stated in Fed. R. Civ. P. 37(c), incorporated in Fed. R. Bankr. P. 7037, apply. Thus, in many cases it may be possible to recover the costs of an appraisal or other proof of value which would otherwise be paid by the debtor. Not only facts but also statements of application of law to fact may be included in a request for admissions.

Practitioners should note the changes to discovery practice imposed by amended Federal Rules of Civil Procedure 26–37 which are applicable in some jurisdictions. In particular, note the new prerequisites to traditional formal discovery contained in amended Rule 26, including the duty of voluntary or automatic disclosure in Rule 26(a). These form discovery requests may need to be adjusted to reflect these new rules and/or the results of automatic disclosures made pursuant to the rules.

237 This is one form of a petition for a writ of *habeas corpus*. For a discussion of the bankruptcy court's *habeas corpus* powers, see § 13.4.5, *supra*. Because those powers are unclear at present, it may be advisable to file initially in the district court. The clerk of either court may be consulted if necessary.

238 The court may order release of a debtor imprisoned in a civil action.

239 The debtor may have been imprisoned for the collection of a debt that is dischargeable or provided for in a plan under the Bankruptcy Code.

5. No other application for this writ has heretofore been made to any other court or judge.

WHEREFORE, Petitioner prays, pursuant to 28 U.S.C. § 2255 that:

1. This Court give notice to Respondent that this petition has been filed and that any answer to it showing cause why Petitioner should not be released must be filed within three (3) days.

2. This Court order the Respondent to release Petitioner forthwith pending the final determination of this petition.

3. In the event no answer is filed, this Court enter a final order that Respondent release Petitioner from his custody.

4. In the event an answer is filed a hearing be held within three (3) days thereafter and that after that hearing this Court enter a final order that Respondent release Petitioner from his custody.

Date: [*signature*]
                                   Attorney for Debtor

Form 93 Application for Default Judgment[240]

[Caption: Official Form 16D]

Application for Default Judgment

Plaintiffs hereby apply to this Court to enter default judgment in favor of Plaintiffs and against the Defendant granting all relief requested in Plaintiff's complaint on the ground that, without excuse, Defendant has failed to answer or otherwise defend as to the complaint of the Plaintiffs,[241] a copy of which is attached hereto as Exhibit A[242] [*omitted*]. The Defendant is not in the military service of the United States, as more particularly shown by the certification of [*attorney*], Esquire, attached hereto as Exhibit B[243] [*omitted*].

Date: [*signature*]
                                Attorney for Plaintiffs

Form 94 Order for Default Judgment

[Caption: Official Form 16D]

Order

AND NOW, this [*date*] day of [*month*], [*year*], upon finding that Defendant has failed to answer or otherwise defend as to the complaint of the Plaintiffs, and upon this Court's finding that the allegations of the complaint are sufficient to state a good claim for relief, it is hereby ORDERED, ADJUDGED and DECREED that:

The mortgage lien, held by Defendant [*creditor*] on Plaintiffs' residence be, and hereby is, declared void.

It is further ORDERED that Defendant shall take all steps necessary to reflect the effect of this Order in the public records where said lien is recorded.

Date: [*signature*]
                        United States Bankruptcy Judge

Form 95 Request for Default Judgment by Clerk[244]

[Caption: Official Form 16D]

Request for Default Judgment by Clerk

To the Clerk of the United States
Bankruptcy Court:

Upon the affidavit attached hereto kindly enter judgment by default against [*creditor*], Defendant in the above-captioned action, for $1000.00 together with interest and costs of suit.

Date: [*signature*]
                                Attorney for Debtor

Declaration

[*Attorney for plaintiff/debtor*] being duly sworn, deposes and says that she is attorney for the Plaintiff, and as such, is authorized to make this declaration on behalf of the Plaintiff; that she has read the Complaint filed in this action and knows the contents thereof and that the same is true of her own knowledge; that the amount due Plaintiff from Defendant as set forth in the complaint, less any payments on account received, is $1000.00; that the Defendant is not an infant or incompetent person; that the Defendant is not in the military services of the United States; and that the disbursements sought to be taxed have been made in this action or will necessarily be made or incurred therein.

I declare under penalty of perjury that the foregoing is true and correct.[245]

Date: [*signature*]
                                Attorney for Plaintiff

---

240   Fed. R. Bankr. P. 7055 incorporates Fed. R. Civ. P. 55, requiring a request to the court for entry of a default judgment in many adversary proceedings. If an answer has been required to a motion filed under Fed. R. Bankr. P. 9014, then Fed. R. Bankr. P. 7055 would permit a default judgment in that type of proceeding as well. A default judgment may not be entered against the United States or an officer or agency thereof unless the claimant establishes her claim or right to relief by evidence satisfactory to the court.

241   Failure, without excuse, to respond to a complaint is grounds for a default judgment under Fed. R. Bankr. P. 7055.

242   Attaching the complaint makes it easier for the court to ascertain readily that the order sought is warranted.

243   This certification is required by the Servicemembers Civil Relief Act, 50 U.S.C. app. §§ 501–596.

244   Fed. R. Bankr. P. 7055, applicable in both adversary proceedings and contested matters (see Fed. R. Bankr. P. 9014), fully incorporates Fed. R. Civ. P. 55. Under that rule a default judgment may be entered by the clerk if the claim is for a sum certain or a sum which can by computation be made certain and if the defendant is not an infant or incompetent person. In all other cases, application must be made to the court for a default judgment. *See* Forms 91, 92, Appx. G.10, *supra*. No default judgment may be entered against the United States unless the claim is established by evidence satisfactory to the court. Fed. R. Civ. P. 55(e).

245   This statement is necessary under federal law to constitute an affidavit. 28 U.S.C. § 1746. No additional verification or notarization is required.

Form 96 Default Judgment by Clerk

[Caption: Official Form 16D]

Default Judgment

The Defendant [*creditor*] having failed to plead or otherwise defend in this action and its default having been entered,

NOW, upon application of the Plaintiff and upon declaration that Defendant is indebted to Plaintiff in the sum of $1000.00, that Defendant has been defaulted for failure to appear and that Defendant is not an infant or incompetent person, and is not in the military service of the United States, it is hereby

ORDERED, ADJUDGED AND DECREED that Plaintiff recover of Defendant the sum of $1000.00 together with interest and costs of suit.

Date: *[signature]*
                                                        Clerk

Form 97 Notice of Removal[246]

[Caption: Official Form 16D]

Notice of Removal

The Debtor [*debtor*], by counsel, hereby gives notice of removal on the following grounds:

1. On July 15, 2004, an action was filed against the Debtor in the [*name*] Court of [*state*]. This action, now pending at docket number [*number*], is entitled [*caption*].

2. In the above-referenced action the Plaintiff is seeking foreclosure of its mortgage on the Debtor's home, possession of the premises, and attorney fees.

3. The Debtor has answered the complaint raising several defenses.

4. On September 1, 2004, the Debtor filed a petition for relief in this Court under chapter 13 of the Bankruptcy Code.

5. The Debtor has a right to remove the above-described state court action because it is a civil action over which this Court has jurisdiction and which is removable under 28 U.S.C. § 1409. The removed action would be a core proceeding in the Bankruptcy Court.[247]

6. A copy of all process and pleadings in the state court action is attached hereto.

WHEREFORE, the Debtor prays that the case of [*caption*] be removed to this Court.

Date: *[signature]*
                                          Attorney for Debtor

[Attach certificate of service on opposing party and trustee][248]

Form 98 Plaintiff's Motion for Withdrawal of Proceeding to the District Court[249]

[Caption: Official Form 16D]

Plaintiff's Motion for Withdrawal of Proceeding to the District Court

Plaintiff [*debtor*] hereby moves, pursuant to 28 U.S.C. § 157(d), for the withdrawal of this adversary proceeding from the Bankruptcy Court to the District Court. As grounds for this motion he avers:

1. This adversary proceeding is an objection to a secured claim raising questions under the federal Truth in Lending Act, 15 U.S.C. §§ 1601–1666j.

2. As such, it requires consideration of both title 11 and other laws of the United States regulating activities affecting interstate commerce.[250]

3. There is also a proceeding already pending in this Court seeking rescission of the same credit transaction as that involved in this proceeding, and raising some of the same issues, at No. [*number*].[251]

WHEREFORE, Plaintiff prays that this proceeding be withdrawn from the Bankruptcy Court to this Court.

Date: *[signature]*
                                        Attorney for Plaintiff

---

246 A party may remove to the district court any pending action over which that court has jurisdiction, 28 U.S.C. § 1452, provided a notice of removal is filed within the time limits set by Fed. R. Bankr. P. 9027. The 1984 bankruptcy amendments, in accordance with the jurisdictional scheme making the bankruptcy court a part of the district court, provide that removal is to the district court, which would normally then refer the matter to the bankruptcy court. Initially, then, the notice of removal is probably addressed to the district court. However, when a bankruptcy clerk has been appointed, filing with the bankruptcy court as a unit of the district court is contemplated. *See In re* Hendersonville Homes, 84 B.R. 510 (M.D. Tenn. 1988).

   The notice of removal should contain a short and plain statement of the facts that entitle the filing party to removal, together with a copy of all the pleadings. Filing of a notice of removal initiates an adversary proceeding. Fed. R. Bankr. P. 9027(g). The notice must be served on all parties to the removed claim pursuant to Fed. R. Bankr. P. 9027(b) and must be filed in the court from which removal is sought pursuant to Rule 9027(c). If a motion for remand is filed, it is heard initially by the bankruptcy judge, unless the district court orders otherwise. The bankruptcy judge makes a report and recommendation to the district court, to which the parties are entitled to object in the manner provided in Fed. R. Bankr. P. 9033(b). *See* Fed. R. Bankr. P. 9027(e). *See generally* § 13.4.1, *supra*.

247 Fed. R. Bankr. P. 9027(a)(1) requires a statement of whether the removed action is a core or non-core proceeding. If a non-core proceeding, the party seeking removal must state whether it would consent to a final order or judgment being entered by the bankruptcy judge.

248 This certificate should also properly certify compliance with Fed. R. Bankr. P. 9027(c), which requires filing in the non-bankruptcy court from which the action is removed.

249 Under 28 U.S.C. § 157(d) the district court may withdraw all or part of a case or proceeding from the bankruptcy court, on its own motion or on motion of a party. Withdrawal on timely motion is mandatory when resolution of a proceeding requires consideration of both title 11 and other federal laws regulating organizations or activities affecting interstate commerce. 28 U.S.C. § 157(d); *see* § 13.2.5, *supra*.

250 This paragraph sets forth grounds for mandatory withdrawal. As discussed in the text, it is unclear how much consideration of a federal statute other than the Bankruptcy Code is sufficient grounds for withdrawal. *See* § 13.2.5.2, *supra*. Counsel's position on this question may depend on which forum is preferable for a given case.

251 This paragraph sets forth grounds which might justify discretionary withdrawal to conserve judicial resources.

Form 99 Motion for Determination That Proceeding Is a Core Proceeding[252]

[*Caption: Official Form 16D*]

Motion for Determination That Proceeding Is a Core Proceeding

[*Debtor*], Plaintiff herein, moves this Court, pursuant to 28 U.S.C. § 157(b)(3), to determine that this matter is a core proceeding. In support of this motion he avers:

1. This adversary proceeding seeks to enjoin [*creditor*] from repossessing Debtor's automobile, pursuant to the bankruptcy clause in its contract, after this case is concluded and the automatic stay is no longer in effect.

2. As such, it is a proceeding affecting the adjustment of the debtor-creditor relationship and a core proceeding pursuant to 28 U.S.C. § 157(b)(2)(O).

WHEREFORE, Plaintiff prays that this Court determine that this proceeding is a core proceeding.

Date: [*signature*]
          Attorney for Plaintiff

Form 100 Stipulation That Matter May Be Determined by Bankruptcy Court[253]

[*Caption: Official Form 16D*]

Stipulation That Matter May Be Determined by Bankruptcy Court

It is hereby stipulated, by and between the parties and pursuant to 28 U.S.C. § 157(c)(2), that the Bankruptcy Court may hear this adversary proceeding and enter a final judgment in this matter notwithstanding the fact that it may be a non-core proceeding.

Date: [*signature*]
          Attorney for Plaintiff

Date: [*signature*]
          Attorney for Defendant

Form 101 Plaintiff's Objections to Findings of Fact and Conclusions of Law[254]

[*Caption: Official Form 16D*]

Plaintiff's Objections to Findings of Fact and Conclusions of Law

Plaintiff [*debtor*] hereby objects to the proposed findings of fact and conclusions of law submitted by the Bankruptcy Court in this proceeding.

The Plaintiff's specific objections are as follows:

1. The conclusion of law that the Defendant did not violate the Fair Debt Collection Practices Act by sending the notice marked as Exhibit P-1 is contrary to law.

2. The finding of fact that Plaintiff suffered no damages in this case is contrary to the evidence presented at trial.

Date: [*signature*]
          Attorney for Debtor

Form 102 Motion for Leave to Appeal Interlocutory Order[255]

[*Caption: Official Form 16A or 16D*][256]

Motion for Leave to Appeal Interlocutory Order to District Court (or Bankruptcy Appellate Panel)

---

252 The bankruptcy court must determine, on its own motion or timely motion of a party, whether a proceeding is a core proceeding. 28 U.S.C. § 157(b)(3). However, it is not clear that this decision must be a formal determination of record and frequently, in practice, it is not. In order to resolve doubts, such as whether objections or an appeal will be necessary to bring the matter before the district court, it may be advisable to file a motion for a formal determination. As there are no rules setting guidelines as to timeliness, such a motion should be filed as early in the proceeding as possible. The specific decision on whether the matter is a core proceeding might then also be subject to appeal or objections to the district court, and there would be no question that the issue was not waived. (As a jurisdictional matter, it might not be possible to waive the right to a district court trial; however, failure to raise the issue could be deemed an implied consent to bankruptcy court jurisdiction.) See § 13.2.4, *supra*, for further discussion of jurisdiction.

253 Despite the fact that a proceeding is not a core proceeding, the parties may submit to bankruptcy court jurisdiction by express consent. 28 U.S.C. § 157(c)(2). Such a stipulation, which allows the bankruptcy court to enter a final judgment on order, may be advisable to resolve doubts as to the nature of the proceeding or to limit the expenditures of resources that would be necessary in a de novo consideration by the district court. All parties must join in the stipulation. *See generally* § 13.2.4, *supra*. The same effect will be achieved if all parties consent to a final judgment or order by the bankruptcy court in their pleadings pursuant to Fed. R. Bankr. P. 7008(a) and 7012(b).

254 In a non-core proceeding the bankruptcy court must submit proposed findings of fact and conclusions of law to the district court. 28 U.S.C. § 157(c)(1). A party may obtain de novo review only if timely and specific objections are filed. Objections must be filed within ten days after the proposed findings and conclusions are served upon a party by the clerk of the bankruptcy court, identifying the specific findings or conclusions objected to and stating the grounds for the objection. The objections are filed with the clerk of the bankruptcy court if one exists. Any other party then has ten days from the service of the objections to respond to them. Fed. R. Bankr. P. 9033(b). The time for filing objections may be extended for cause, pursuant to Fed. R. Bankr. P. 9033(c). See generally §§ 13.2.4, 13.10, *supra*, for further discussion.

255 Use Official Form 18 in Appendix D, *supra*, to appeal final orders. Unlike final orders, interlocutory orders may only be appealed with leave of the appellate court. 28 U.S.C. § 158(a). This form may be used to obtain permission to appeal. It should be filed with the clerk of the court to which applicant wishes to appeal and must be filed within ten days of the order of the bankruptcy court accompanied by a notice of appeal. Fed. R. Bankr. P. 8003. Procedure thereafter is governed by Fed. R. Bankr. P. 8003.

Under Fed. R. Bankr. P. 8003, the motion must contain a statement of the facts necessary to an understanding of the questions involved, a statement of the questions presented and the relief sought, a statement with respect to why leave to appeal should be granted, and a copy of the order appealed from along with any opinion or memorandum related to it.

256 The applicable caption is that of the order appealed from.

Defendant, [*debtor*], hereby applies for leave to appeal an interlocutory order of the Bankruptcy Court. In support of this application he avers:

1. This case was commenced as a voluntary case under chapter 13 of the Bankruptcy Code.

2. Shortly after the case was commenced, [*creditor*] filed a motion to lift the automatic stay under 11 U.S.C. § 362.

3. In response to the motion, [*debtor*] promptly moved for an order which would permit expedited discovery before the scheduled trial date.

4. The Bankruptcy Court denied the Debtor's motion, in effect denying any discovery, except by depositions, which the Debtor cannot afford to pay for. A copy of this order is attached hereto as Exhibit A [*omitted*].

5. The question presented by this appeal is whether a debtor may be denied all discovery prior to the hearing on a motion for relief from the automatic stay.

6. The Debtor seeks an order reversing the denial of this motion and ordering expedited discovery.

7. Without such discovery, the Debtor will be seriously harmed in that he will be unable to adequately prepare or present his case as to why he and his family should not be evicted from their home.

WHEREFORE, Defendant Debtor prays that he be granted leave to appeal from the interlocutory order of the Bankruptcy Court, so that order may be reviewed prior to completion of litigation of the motion for relief from the automatic stay.

Date: [*signature*]
                              Attorney for Debtor

Form 103 Motion for Stay of Order Pending Appeal[257]

[*Caption: Official Form 16A or 16D*][258]

Motion for Stay Pending Appeal of Order Granting Relief from Automatic Stay[259]

The Debtor, [*debtor*], hereby moves this Court, pursuant to Fed. R. Bankr. P. 8005, for a stay of an order of the Bankruptcy Court. In support of this motion, Debtor states:

1. This case was commenced as a voluntary case under chapter 13 of the Bankruptcy Code.

2. Shortly after the case was commenced, [*creditor*] filed a motion to lift the automatic stay under 11 U.S.C. § 362.

3. In response to the motion, Debtor filed an objection to the motion and a separate adversary complaint alleging that the mortgage held by [*creditor*] is invalid in that it should have been

terminated upon the Debtor's rescission of the mortgage transaction pursuant to the Truth in Lending Act, 15 U.S.C. § 1635. A copy of this Objection and Adversary Complaint are attached hereto as Exhibit A and Exhibit B respectively [*omitted*].

4. On [*date*], the Bankruptcy Court entered an Order overruling the Debtor's objection and terminating the automatic stay with respect to the Debtor's residence in favor of [*creditor*]. A copy of this Order is attached hereto as Exhibit C [*omitted*].

5. On [date], the Debtor timely filed a notice of appeal from the Order granting relief from stay.

6. The Debtor's residence is and at all times necessary to this case and to the successful reorganization of the Debtor, and has been an asset included in the Debtor's bankruptcy estate.

7. The Debtor has substantial equity in her residence and [*creditor*] has been afforded adequate protection of its interest.

8. If the Order permitting [*creditor*] to foreclose on the property is not stayed pending appeal, the Debtor will be left without a remedy as her appeal will become moot, and she will suffer irreparable harm.

WHEREFORE, Debtor respectfully requests that the Order entered on [*date*] be stayed pending appeal and that such other appropriate relief be ordered during the pendency of the appeal on such terms that will protect the Debtor's rights and interest in the property.

Date: [*signature*]
                              Attorney for Debtor

Form 104 Stipulation for Appeal to Bankruptcy Appellate Panel[260]

[*Caption: Official Form 16B or 16D*][261]

Stipulation for Appeal to Bankruptcy Appellate Panel

The parties to this proceeding, by their counsel, hereby stipulate and agree that any appeal from the Final Order of [*date*] may be taken to the Bankruptcy Appellate Panel for the [*number*] Circuit, pursuant to 28 U.S.C. § 158(b).

Date: [*signature*]
                              Attorney for Plaintiff

Date: [*signature*]
                              Attorney for Defendant

---

257 Under Fed. R. Bankr. P. 8005, this motion should ordinarily be filed in the first instance with the bankruptcy court. If denied by the bankruptcy court, this same motion may then be filed with the district court or the bankruptcy appellate panel, and should indicate why the relief was not obtained from the bankruptcy court.

258 The applicable caption is that of the order appealed from.

259 Fed. R. Bankr. P. 4001(a)(3) provides that an order granting relief from the automatic stay is stayed for ten days after entry unless the court orders otherwise. If an appeal is contemplated, the debtor should object to any language in the court's order shortening the normal ten-day period and ensure that this motion for stay is filed before the order becomes effective.

260 Consent to have an appeal heard by an appellate panel may be given in a stipulation such as this one or in separate statements by each party. The consent may also be contained in a notice of appeal or cross-appeal. In any case all necessary consents must be filed before transmittal of the record or within thirty days of filing of the appeal, whichever is later. Fed. R. Bankr. P. 8001(e). Local rules pertaining to appellate panels may alter or add to these requirements. Fed. R. Bankr. P. 8001(e), 8018.

261 The applicable caption is that of the order appealed from.

Form 105 Appellant's Election Form[262]

[*Caption: Official Form 16B or 16D*]

Appellant's Election Form

In accordance with this appeal of the Order or Judgment of the United States Bankruptcy Court, District of _____ dated _____, Doc. No. _____ , the Appellant, [*name*], hereby elects to have this appeal heard by the Bankruptcy Appellate Panel for the_____ Circuit.

[*alternate election*]

In accordance with this appeal of the Order or Judgment of the United States Bankruptcy Court, District of _____ dated _____ , Doc. No. _____, the Appellant, [*name*], hereby elects to opt out of the Bankruptcy Appellate Panel for the _____ Circuit and requests that this appeal be heard by the United States District Court for the District of _____ .

Date: [*signature*]
                                           Attorney for Appellant

G.11 Discharge and Reaffirmation

Form 106 Complaint to Determine Dischargeability of Student Loan[263]

[*Caption: Official Form 16D*]

Complaint to Determine Dischargeability of Student Loan

1. The Debtor filed this case under chapter 7 of the Bankruptcy Code on September 1, 2004. This Court thus has jurisdiction over this action under 28 U.S.C. § 1334. This proceeding is a core proceeding.

2. One of the unsecured debts owing by the Debtor and listed in Schedule F is a student loan owing to Defendant [*creditor*].

3. The Defendant [*director*] is the executive director of the [*creditor*] and is responsible for the overall operation of the guaranteed student loan program.[264]

4. This loan was incurred to pay expenses at [*school*].

5. Subsequent to beginning coursework at that school, the Debtor learned that the school had lost its accreditation and that none of its recent graduates had obtained the employment for which they were trained due to that loss.

6. The Debtor was unable to transfer to any other educational program, and was also refused any refund of the tuition paid by the student loan.

7. Since that time, the Debtor has been unemployed, and the sole source of income for herself and her two children has been public assistance in the amount of $[*amount*], which barely suffices for the necessities of life.

8. The Debtor has no current or anticipated available income or resources with which to pay the aforementioned loan and any payments on that loan could be made only at great hardship to the Debtor and her children.

WHEREFORE, the Debtor prays that this Court enter an Order declaring the student loan debt of the Debtor to be dischargeable in this bankruptcy case.

Date: [*signature*]
                                            Attorney for Debtor

Form 107 Debtor's Answer to Complaint Seeking Determination of Nondischargeability[265]

[*Caption: Official Form 16D*]

Debtor's Answer to Complaint Seeking Determination of Nondischargeability[266]

First Defense

The Debtor admits the allegations of paragraphs 1 and 2. The Debtor admits that this proceeding is a core proceeding. The remaining allegations of the complaint are denied.[267]

---

262 In districts that have a Bankruptcy Appellate Panel (BAP), all appeals are determined by the BAP unless the appellant files with the notice of appeal a separate written statement indicating an election to have the appeal determined by the district court. *See* 11 U.S.C. § 158(c)(1); Fed. R. Bankr. P. 8001(e). The appellee or any other party may file a similar written statement within thirty days of service of the notice of appeal.

263 Both debtors and creditors may seek determinations with respect to the dischargeability of debts, either during or after the bankruptcy (however, there are deadlines for certain creditor complaints; see Fed. R. Bankr. P. 4007(c); 11 U.S.C. § 523(c)). Such determinations must be sought by way of adversary proceedings. Fed. R. Bankr. P. 7001. For a discussion of complaints in adversary proceedings see notes to Form 83, Appendix G.10, *supra*.

   Debtors may want such determinations to settle an issue likely to be disputed later, or to obtain an explicit court order enjoining a creditor with whom difficulties are anticipated. For a discussion of dischargeability in general as well as the law relating to student loans, see Chapter 14, *supra*.

264 If the student loan creditor is a governmental entity that may claim Eleventh Amendment immunity, it had previously been desirable to sue named individual officials rather than the entity itself. *See Ex Parte* Young, 209 U.S. 123, 28 S. Ct. 441, 52 L. Ed. 714 (1908). This procedure is no longer necessary as the Supreme Court's decision in Tennessee Student Assistance Corp. v. Hood, 124 S. Ct. 1905, 158 L. Ed. 2d 764 (2004) now clearly establishes that the debtor may sue the state directly when seeking a dischargeability determination. *See* § 13.3.2.2, *supra*. However, naming the head of the relevant agency may still be useful for other purposes.

265 An answer must normally be filed within thirty days of the issuance of the summons. Fed. R. Bankr. P. 7012. For a general discussion of dischargeability questions and false financial statement issues, see Chapter 14, *supra*.

266 The pleading may also be designated simply as "Answer."

267 Factual allegations may be denied as a first defense. Fed. R. Civ. P. 8, incorporated in Fed. R. Bankr. P. 7008, permits general denials.

Second Defense

This complaint was not filed within the deadline set by the Federal Rules of Bankruptcy Procedure for dischargeability complaints and therefore must be dismissed.[268]

Third Defense

The Debtor asserts that even if the Court finds that this refinancing transaction involved a false financial statement, the Plaintiff encouraged the refinancing and did not give up any remedies it would otherwise have utilized had there been no refinancing. Therefore, only the amount of the loan which exceeded the amount refinanced would be nondischargeable.[269]

Counterclaim[270]

1. The position of the Creditor in this matter is not substantially justified.

2. In refinancing the loan, the Creditor violated state deceptive practices law section [*cite provision of state law*] and the Truth in Lending Act, 15 U.S.C. §§ 1601–1666j.

WHEREFORE, the Debtor prays that this Court enter an Order:

1. Dismissing the complaint of Plaintiff [*creditor*], and declaring the debt in question dischargeable.

2. Awarding the Debtor attorney fees and costs, pursuant to 11 U.S.C. § 523(d).[271]

3. Awarding the Debtor compensatory and punitive damages on her counterclaim.

Date:

[*signature*]
Attorney for Debtor

Form 108 Interrogatories Directed to Lender Regarding Debtor's Alleged False Financial Statement(s)[272]

[*Caption: Official Form 16D*]

Interrogatories Directed to Plaintiff Lender Regarding the Defendant Debtor's Alleged False Financial Statement(s)[273]

Definitions[274]

As used herein the following terms shall have the following meaning:

"Document" means and includes any printed, typewritten or handwritten matter of whatever character including specifically, but not exclusively and without limiting the generality of the foregoing, letters, desk or other calendars, memoranda, telegrams, cables, reports, charts, business records, personal records, accountants' statements, bank statements, handwritten notes, minutes of meetings, notes of meetings or conversations, catalogs, written agreements, checks, receipts, invoices, bills, and any carbon or other copies of such materials.

"Person" means and includes natural persons, public and private corporations, associations and any other type of entity, and the agents, employees, officers, deputies and representatives thereof.

"Identify" when used in reference to a contract, instrument, or other document means to:

a. State the type of document, for example, installment contract, credit application, recourse agreement, letter, memorandum, or notes;

b. State the date of document;

c. State the name of the originator thereof;

d. State the name of each signatory thereto;

e. State the name and address of its present custodian;

f. State the reason, in detail, for preparing the document or writing;

g. State the subject or subjects covered by the document or writing; and

h. State the name(s), business address(es), and title(s) of the person or persons to whom the document or writing was directed.

Interrogatories

1. State the gross amount of the loan to Defendants including interest and other charges.

2. State the net amount of the loan, less interest and any other charges.

3. State the amount of cash paid to Defendants.

4. State the amount paid to others, and identify each such entity.

5. State the amount paid on any other account with Plaintiff.

6. State the number of prior loans and other transactions with Defendant with details of all of them.[275]

---

268 The deadlines for the filing of dischargeability complaints under 11 U.S.C. § 523(c) are set pursuant to Fed. R. Bankr. P. 4007(c) and stated in the notice of the meeting of creditors. A creditor may seek an extension of time beyond such deadlines only for cause.

269 For a discussion of this and other defenses in refinancing cases, see § 14.4.3.2, *supra*.

270 A counterclaim may be pleaded under Fed. R. Bankr. P. 7013 and may be strategically important in settlement or litigation of the matter. Compulsory counterclaims are barred from later litigation if not raised here. Fed. R. Bankr. P. 7013.

271 In a creditor's complaint under 11 U.S.C. § 523(a)(2), the debtor is entitled to attorney fees if the court finds that the creditor's position was not substantially justified, unless special circumstances would make such an award unjust. 11 U.S.C. § 523(d).

272 Interrogatories such as these seek much of the information which may be helpful in defending a false financial statement

case. Others may, of course, be added. *See* Ch. 14, *supra*.

Practitioners should note the changes to discovery practice imposed by amended Federal Rules of Civil Procedure 26–37 which are applicable in some jurisdictions. In particular, note the new prerequisites to traditional formal discovery contained in amended Rule 26, including the duty of voluntary or automatic disclosure in Rule 26(a). These form discovery requests may need to be adjusted to reflect these new rules and/or the results of automatic disclosures made pursuant to the rules. This form is adapted from interrogatories drafted by Professor Philip Shuchman, Rutgers Law School.

273 This document may be entitled simply Defendant's Interrogatories to Plaintiff if there are only two parties to the proceeding.

274 These definitions may be used generally in interrogatories or adapted as necessary.

275 If the loan is a refinancing, the plaintiff may have relied on past dealings or information rather than the alleged false statement. Also, there are some arguments that only the new money is non-dischargeable (hence questions 3–5).

7. State the frequency with which Plaintiff obtains credit reports.[276]

8. State whether the Plaintiff obtained credit reports on Defendants, and if so, when, from whom, and with regard to which transactions.

9. State the details of such credit reports.

10. State the number of Plaintiff's borrowers who filed petitions in bankruptcy during this year and the preceding year.

11. State the number of section 523(a)(2) actions which were threatened and how many were actually brought by Plaintiff in that period.

12. State the names and addresses of the borrowers and docket numbers of both the preceding categories.[277]

13. Identify all other documents related to any loan from Plaintiff to Defendants.

14. Identify all persons present when the loan was consummated, giving name, position, and present address.[278]

Date: [*signature*]
                                Attorney for Debtor

Form 109 Defendant's Requests for Production of Documents in Dischargeability Case Based on Credit Card Fraud[279]

[*Caption: Official Form 16D*]

Defendant's First Requests for Production of Documents

Defendant requests, pursuant to Bankruptcy Rule 7034 and Fed. R. Civ. P. 34, that plaintiff produce each of the following documents to be delivered to the office of defendant's attorney for

---

276 A creditor who has obtained a credit report may have relied upon that rather than the alleged false statement. It may also have had information that should have put the creditor on notice that there were discrepancies between the two documents warranting further investigation or precluding reliance on the statement. Alternatively, if the creditor did not obtain a report, it may be found to have engaged in imprudent business practices which would have made any reliance unreasonable.

277 These questions go to the issue of whether the creditor makes a practice of deliberately obtaining false financial statements in order to later bring dischargeability complaints.

278 This question is to determine what witnesses, if any, the creditor may produce to testify to the creditor's version of the transaction. It may turn out that the creditor no longer employs the people who completed the transaction on its behalf.

279 These requests for production of documents are designed for a case in which a credit card lender has alleged that the debtor has committed fraud in the use of a credit card under 11 U.S.C. § 523(a)(2). *See generally Litigating the Dischargeability of Credit Card Debts,* 14 NCLC REPORTS *Bankruptcy and Foreclosures Ed.* 10 (Nov./Dec. 1995).

Practitioners should note the changes to discovery practice imposed by amended Federal Rules of Civil Procedure 26–37 which are applicable in some jurisdictions. In particular, note the new prerequisites to traditional formal discovery contained in amended Rule 26, including the duty of voluntary or automatic disclosure in Rule 26(a). These form discovery requests may need to be adjusted to reflect these new rules and/or the results of automatic disclosures made pursuant to the rules.

inspection and copying within the time limits set forth in the aforementioned rules.

Definitions and Instructions

A. "Documents" means all writings of any kind, including the originals and all non-identical copies, whether different from the originals by reason of any notation made on such copies or otherwise, including but not limited to correspondence, memoranda, notes, diaries, desk or other calendars, statistics, charts, summaries, pamphlets, books, interoffice and intraoffice communications, notations of any sort of conversations, written agreements, bulletins, printed matter, computer printouts, teletypes, telefax, invoices, worksheets, all drafts, alterations, modifications, changes and amendments of any of the foregoing, graphic or oral records or representations of any kind (including, without limitation, tapes, cassettes, discs, recordings and computer memories).

B. The word "person(s)" means all entities and, without limiting the generality of the foregoing, includes natural persons, joint owners, associations, companies, partnerships, joint ventures, corporations, trusts and estates.

C. If your response to any request herein is that the documents are not in your possession or custody, describe in detail the unsuccessful efforts you made to locate the records.

D. If your response to any request herein is that the documents are not in your control, identify who has control and location of the records.

E. If a request herein for production seeks a specific document or an itemized category which is not in your possession, control or custody, provide any documents you have that contain all or part of the information contained in the requested document or category.

F. All requests shall be deemed to include any documents made by, held by or maintained in the files of any predecessor, successor, employee, agent or assignee of either defendant.

G. The term "the transaction(s)" or the account(s) when used without qualification herein means the transactions and accounts between or among plaintiff and the defendant and all related activities.

H. Identify the source of each of the documents you produce.

I. Each of the following Requests is intended to be continuing and Defendant hereby demand that, in the event at any later date you obtain any additional documents responsive to these requests that they be supplied in a timely manner.

Requests for Production

1. For any information provided in your answers to interrogatories,[280] all documents, diagrams, photographs, drawings, calculations or other demonstrative documents which are identified therein or which form the basis for your responses.

2. All documents maintained by plaintiff related to the accounts relevant to this action including but not limited to credit applications, contracts, charge slips, transaction records, payment records, account ledgers, calculations of interest due, correspondence, notices, internal memoranda, and records of telephone contacts.

3. All documents maintained by plaintiff concerning the defendant or transactions between the plaintiff and the defendant.

---

280 *See* Form 110, Appx. G.11, *infra.*

4. All documents maintained by plaintiff concerning its decision to grant credit to the defendant and the basis on which that decision was made.

5. All documents maintained by plaintiff related to its evaluation of the defendant's credit-worthiness at any time.

6. All documents maintained by plaintiff concerning collection activity related to the defendant's accounts.

7. All documents maintained by plaintiff concerning the amount of the monthly minimum payment due on the defendant's accounts at any time.

8. All documents maintained by plaintiff concerning decisions made by plaintiff to accept or reject charges on the defendant's accounts.

9. All documents maintained by plaintiff concerning decisions about the credit limits provided to the defendant.

10. All documents maintained by plaintiff concerning any attempts it made to revoke defendant's permission to use his credit accounts.

11. All documents mailed to the defendant by the plaintiff at any time, including but not limited to, bills, account statements, promotional material, advertisements, and offers of additional credit.

12. All documents concerning plaintiff's policies related to granting credit to consumers.

13. All documents concerning plaintiff's policies related to determining credit-worthiness of potential consumer borrowers.

14. All documents concerning plaintiff's policies related to accepting or rejecting charges on consumer's credit accounts.

15. All documents concerning plaintiff's policies related to accepting or rejecting cash advances on consumer's credit accounts.

16. All documents concerning plaintiff's policies related to setting the minimum payment due on a consumer credit account.

17. All documents reflecting plaintiff's policies related to making decisions about filing complaints to determine dischargeability in bankruptcy cases.

18. All documents reflecting plaintiff's policies related to revoking or terminating consumer credit accounts.

19. All documents reflecting plaintiff's policies related to setting credit limits for consumer credit accounts.

20. All documents which were reviewed by plaintiff in making its decision concerning whether to file this adversary proceeding.

21. All documents which you intend to use or introduce in the trial of this proceeding.

Date: [*signature*]
                                   Attorney for Debtor(s)

Form 110 Defendant's Interrogatories in Dischargeability Case Based on Credit Card Fraud[281]

[*Caption: Official Form 16D*]

Defendant's First Set of Interrogatories

Defendant requests that the plaintiff answer under oath, in accordance with Fed. R. Bankr. P. 7033 and Fed. R. Civ. P. 33, the

following interrogatories within the time set forth in the foregoing rules.

Definitions and Instructions

As used herein the following terms shall have the following meaning:

A. "Document" means all writings of any kind, including the originals and all non-identical copies, whether different from the originals by reason of any notation made on such copies or otherwise, including but not limited to correspondence, memoranda, notes, diaries, desk or other calendars, statistics, letters, telegrams, minutes, business records, personal records, accountants' statements, bank statements, contracts, reports, studies, checks, statements, receipts, invoices, bills, return charts, summaries, pamphlets, books, interoffice and intra-office communications, notations of any sort of conversations or meetings, telephone call meetings or other communications, written agreements, bulletins, printed matter, computer printouts, teletypes, telefax, invoices, worksheets, all drafts, alterations, modifications, changes and amendments of any of the foregoing, graphic or oral records or representations of any kind (including, without limitation, tapes, cassettes, discs, recordings, and computer memories).

B. "Act" as used herein includes acts of every kind and description.

C. "Identify" or "describe" when used in reference to a contract, instrument, record or other document means to state:

a. The type of document (for example, installment, letter, memorandum, notes, and so forth);

b. The date of the document;

c. The name of each signatory thereto;

d. The name and address of its present custodian;

e. The reason, in detail, for preparing the document;

f. The subject or subjects covered by the document;

g. The name(s), business address(es), and title(s), of the person(s) to whom the document writing was directed; and

h. The name(s), business address(es), and title(s), of the person(s) who originated the document.

D. "Identify" as used herein in connection with a "person" or "persons" means to state the names, titles, the present employers of such "person" or "persons," the relationship of such person to Defendant, and such person's current business address and business telephone number.

E. The term "identify" as used herein in connection with an "act" means:

a. Furnish the date and place of the act;

---

281 These interrogatories are designed for a case in which a credit card lender has alleged that the debtor has committed fraud in

the use of a credit card under 11 U.S.C. § 523(a)(2). *See generally Litigating the Dischargeability of Credit Card Debts,* 14 NCLC REPORTS *Bankruptcy and Foreclosures Ed.* 10 (Nov./Dec. 1995).

Practitioners should note the changes to discovery practice imposed by amended Federal Rules of Civil Procedure 26–37 which are applicable in some jurisdictions. In particular, note the new prerequisites to traditional formal discovery contained in amended Rule 26, including the duty of voluntary or automatic disclosure in Rule 26(a). These form discovery requests may need to be adjusted to reflect these new rules and/or the results of automatic disclosures made pursuant to the rules.

b. Identify the person acting, the person for whom the act was performed, and the person against whom the act was directed; and

c. Describe, in detail, the act.

F. The terms "describe" or "state" as used herein means:

a. Describe or state fully by reference to underlying facts rather than by ultimate facts or conclusions of fact of law;

b. Particularize as to:

1. Time;
2. Place; and
3. Manner.

G. The term "oral communication" means and includes any face-to-face conversation, meeting, conference, telephone conversation or telephone conference.

H. "Person" or "persons" means and includes all natural persons, public and private corporations, association and any other type of entity and the agents, employees, officers, deputies and representatives thereof.

I. The term "you" or "your" shall refer to plaintiff.

J. All requests shall be deemed to include any documents made by, held by or maintained in the files of any predecessor, successor, employee, agent or assignee of either defendant.

K. The term "the transaction(s)" or the account(s) when used without qualification herein means the transactions and accounts between or among plaintiff and the defendant and all related activities.

L. If the space provided at each Interrogatory for your answer is not sufficient, use additional sheets, numbered consecutively after each such Interrogatory, and inserted in proper order in all copies filed and served. For example, in the case of Interrogatory No. 1, any additional sheet(s) for your answers should be numbered 1-A, 1-B, 1-C, and so forth.

M. Each of the following Interrogatories is intended to be a continuing Interrogatory, and Debtors hereby demand that, in the event at any later date you obtain any additional facts, or forms any conclusions, opinions or contentions different from those set forth in the answers to these Interrogatories, you shall amend your answers to such Interrogatories promptly and sufficiently in advance of any trial, to fully set forth such differences.

Interrogatories

1. Identify each person participating in the preparation of the answers to these interrogatories by stating the complete name, position or title, business and residential address of each person or persons and indicate the subject matter with respect to which he or she provided answers.

2. You have made the allegation that the debtor obtained funds from you by false pretenses. Please state with particularity the nature of the false pretenses alleged including but not limited to any information provided to you which you allege was inaccurate in whole or in part and the basis on which you have formed the belief that such information was inaccurate.

3. You have made the allegation that the debtor obtained funds from you by false representations. Please state with particularity the exact representations of which you complain stating with particularity to whom the representations were made, the date of the representation, and how you claim to have been deceived.

4. You have made the allegation that the debtor obtained funds from you by actual fraud. Please state with particularity the nature of the actual fraud.

5. (a) For what purpose do you claim that the debtor borrowed money from you? (b) Identify any and all documents (including receipts, invoices and canceled checks) which evidence the use of loan proceeds.

6. State with particularity all steps taken by you to determine the credit-worthiness of the defendant. Identify any persons who participated in determining that the defendant was credit-worthy.

7. Identify all representations made by defendant to the plaintiff including date and time of representation, manner in which the representation was transmitted to you, substance of representation, and identify person to whom made by name, address, job title, and telephone number.

8. Identify every document containing any relevant facts to the complaint in this adversary proceeding and state with particularity what particular relevant facts each such document contains.

9. You have made the allegation that at the time the Defendant obtained credit he did not intend to repay it. State with particularity any facts in you possession that would support the allegation.

10. Identify any credit policies you maintain which were violated by the defendant in connection with use of his accounts. State how such policies were communicated to the defendant and identify any documents by which such policies were communicated.

11. Identify the means you used to verify the defendant's income, expenses, assets, or liabilities at any time, including but not limited to the nature, dates, extent, persons involved, and analysis of that verification. Identify any documents obtained in the verification process.

12. Identify your policies concerning decisions about the credit-worthiness of account holders and state with particularity how they were applied to the defendant and his accounts.

13. Identify your policies concerning revocation of charge privileges and state with particularity how they were applied to the defendant and his accounts.

14. Identify the date on which you believe the following events occurred and state with particularity any charges on the accounts you allege were made after those dates:

a. the defendant consulted a bankruptcy attorney;
b. the defendant had a reduction in income;
c. the defendant formulated his purported intent not to repay;
d. the defendant violated the terms of his credit agreement.

15. To the extent you are alleging that the defendant's misconduct giving rise to your claim of non-dischargeability is based on conduct other than a specific misrepresentation or is based on a representation implied by defendant's course of actions, identify:

a. the nature of the conduct or course of actions;
b. the nature of any such implied representations;
c. the person or person(s) to whom each implied representation was made or who drew a conclusion therefrom;
d. the date on which such implications or conclusions were made;
e. the basis for any conclusion drawn from such representations; and
f. the manner in which such conclusions were recorded or memorialized.

16. Identify all of your employees who you claim had personal contact with the defendant at any time in connection with his accounts.

17. Identify all persons who you claim have knowledge of the facts alleged in your complaint stating their name, address, telephone number, occupation, title, and a brief statement of the information that you claim that they have.

18. State the number of your borrowers who filed bankruptcy this year and in each of the previous two calendar years.

19. State the number of actions you brought under 11 U.S.C. § 523(a)(2) this year and in each of the previous two calendar years.

20. Is it plaintiff's position that every use of plaintiff's credit card by a borrower who does not later repay the debt is a fraudulent representation upon which plaintiff justifiably relies?

21. If your answer to interrogatory 21 is no, state each fact which distinguishes defendant's use of your credit card.

22. What percentage of plaintiff's credit card accounts were charged off, in whole or in part, in each of the last two years?

23. How much were plaintiff's net profits from its credit card operations in each of the last two years?

24. How many unsolicited credit card offers did plaintiff mail in each of the last two years?

25. State the name and address of each witness you intend to call at trial of this matter and describe the substance of their testimony.

Date: [*signature*]
                          Attorney for Debtor

Form 111 Defendant's Requests for Admissions in Dischargeability Case Based on Credit Card Fraud[282]

[*Caption: Official Form 16D*]

Defendant's First Set of Requests for Admissions

Defendant requests plaintiff to admit, pursuant to Fed. R. Bankr. P. 7036 and Fed. R. Civ. P. 36, for the purposes of this action only, the truth of the following statements of fact or application of law to fact:

1. Plaintiff solicited the defendant to enter into credit contracts.

2. Plaintiff sent a credit application to the defendant in connection with each account.

3. Defendant returned credit applications to the plaintiff after which credit was approved.

4. Plaintiff has no specific basis on which to claim that any information contained in any credit application by the defendant was inaccurate.

5. Plaintiff did not independently verify any of the information contained in defendants' credit application.

---

282 These requests for admissions are designed for a case in which a credit card lender has alleged that the debtor has committed fraud in the use of a credit card under 11 U.S.C. § 523(a)(2). *See generally Litigating the Dischargeability of Credit Card Debts*, 14 NCLC REPORTS *Bankruptcy and Foreclosures Ed.* 10 (Nov./Dec. 1995).

Practitioners should note the changes to discovery practice imposed by amended Federal Rules of Civil Procedure 26–37 which are applicable in some jurisdictions. In particular, note the new prerequisites to traditional formal discovery contained in amended Rule 26, including the duty of voluntary or automatic disclosure in Rule 26(a). These form discovery requests may need to be adjusted to reflect these new rules and/or the results of automatic disclosures made pursuant to the rules.

6. No employee or agent of the plaintiff had personal contact with the defendant by telephone or any other means of oral communication at any time with respect to the accounts.

7. The defendant's right to use his accounts was not revoked before he filed bankruptcy.

8. Plaintiff did not reject any charges or cash advances made by the defendant on his accounts.

9. Plaintiff does not individually review each use of an account by a customer, but rather routinely allows use until such time as that customer exceeds the applicable credit limit or until the account is revoked.

10. Plaintiff did not seek a credit report concerning the defendant at any time after the accounts were opened.

11. Plaintiff did not seek verification of income or employment concerning the defendant at any time after the accounts were opened.

12. Plaintiff did not attend the meeting of creditors in the defendant's bankruptcy case and did not conduct a deposition of the defendant at any time prior to filing this adversary proceeding.[283]

13. One common use of credit is to obtain goods and services for which the borrower does not have the immediate ability to pay.

Date: [*signature*]
                       Attorney for Debtor(s)

Form 112 Debtor's Application for a Hardship Discharge[284]

[*Caption: Official Form 16A*]

Debtor's Motion for a Hardship Discharge

The Debtor, by his counsel, hereby moves for the entry of a hardship discharge pursuant to 11 U.S.C. § 1328(b). In support of this motion he avers that:

1. This chapter 13 plan was filed on January 15, 1997.

2. The Debtor's chapter 13 plan was confirmed on May 1, 1999.

3. Since that date the Debtor has made regular monthly payments to the trustee in the full amounts provided for by the plan.

4. The value, as of the effective date of the plan, of the amounts distributed to the unsecured creditors under the plan has not been less than the amounts which those creditors would have been paid on their claims had the estate of the Debtor been liquidated under chapter 7 on that date.

5. On July 7, 2003, the Debtor, through no fault of his own, was laid off along with ten other people at his place of employment.

6. No modification of the plan is practicable because the Debtor's present income is barely sufficient to pay daily living expenses and is not sufficient to pay even the creditors entitled to priority who must be paid under the plan.

---

283 This addresses the plaintiff's good faith basis for its claims and the right to attorney fees under 11 U.S.C. § 523(d).

284 11 U.S.C. § 1328(b) provides that the debtor may obtain a hardship discharge if the debtor cannot complete the plan due to circumstances beyond her control, if modification is impracticable, and if the "best interests of creditors test" has been met, that is, if unsecured creditors have received the equivalent of what they would have gotten in a chapter 7 liquidation. For a discussion of the hardship discharge and other alternatives for the debtor who cannot complete the plan, see § 8.7.4, *supra*.

WHEREFORE, the Debtor prays that this Court grant him a discharge pursuant to 11 U.S.C. § 1328(b).

Date: [*signature*]
Attorney for Debtor

Form 113 Letter to Creditor Concerning Proposed Reaffirmation Agreement[285]

[*creditor*]

Re: [*debtor*]

[*bankruptcy number*]
[*account number*]
[*social security number*]

Dear [*creditor*]:

Please be advised that I represent the above debtor. I am writing in response to your letter dated January 5, 1998, in which you have requested that my client enter into a reaffirmation agreement. In order to fully advise my client about the legal effect and consequences of a reaffirmation agreement, [and to satisfy Local Rule _____ of the United States Bankruptcy Court for District of _____],[286] I will need additional information.

My client's account was listed as a general unsecured claim on her bankruptcy schedules because she did not have documentation showing that you properly acquired or have retained a purchase money security interest (PMSI) in the goods purchased on the account in accordance with [*state*] law. As your proposed reaffirmation agreement requests that I represent to the Court that you retain a PMSI, please provide the following information:[287]

1) All documents signed by my client at the time the account was established in which my client agreed to create a PMSI as defined by [*U.C.C. 9-107 or other state law*]. Please also include a copy of the credit account agreement or any other documents which indicate the method of allocation of payments made on the account;

2) All documents signed by my client at the time of purchase which granted to you a PMSI in the items purchased, and with regard to prior purchases, establishes my client's intention to continue any PMSI in goods financed by an earlier transaction;

3) All documents showing the dates and amounts of all charges (including interest and late fees) and payments made on my client's account for the two year period preceding the filing of my client's bankruptcy petition. In the event that you are still claiming a PMSI in any items purchased more than two years before the bankruptcy filing, kindly provide all such documentation from the time the items were purchased. This documentation should reflect the actual allocation of payments made on the account in reference to the specific items purchased.

Please provide the following additional information so that I may fully advise my client with respect to your reaffirmation request.

1) A description of all collateral, including the manufacturer, year, model and any other pertinent identifying information;

2) The original purchase price of the collateral (excluding sales tax, service contracts and extended warranties);

3) The balance currently owed on the account;

4) The present market value of the collateral, and a description of the method used to determine this value;

5) If interest is to be charged in connection with the reaffirmation agreement and/or additional charge privileges are to be extended, a statement setting forth the annual percentage rate, any annual or other fees imposed for the availability of the account, any minimum finance charges or transaction charges, any minimum payments, any applicable grace period, the balance-computation method, the due date for payments, and any late payment or over-the-limit charges;

6) If the reaffirmed amount is to be paid over a fixed term under the reaffirmation agreement, a statement setting forth the schedule of payments, including the number of payments, the amount of each payment, and the timing of payments scheduled to complete payment under the proposed agreement.

Upon receipt of the above-requested information, I will consult with my client about her options. If you fail to respond to this letter, I shall assume that you have accepted my client's classification of your claim as unsecured. If you have any questions concerning the above, please give me a call.

Sincerely,

[*signature*]
Attorney for Debtor(s)

Form 114 Reaffirmation Agreement[288]

[*Caption: Official Form 16A*]

Reaffirmation Agreement

[*Debtor*], the Debtor in the above-captioned bankruptcy case, and [*creditor*] hereby agree that:

---

285 It is not uncommon for creditors to press for reaffirmation based on the threat of repossession of personal property. This letter is useful to resist unnecessary reaffirmations. The creditor may not have a valid security interest. By asking for proof of the facts necessary to support a proposed reaffirmation, an advocate may learn that there is no credible threat of repossession. In some cases the creditor will not respond and will stop pressing for reaffirmation.

286 Some jurisdictions have local rules setting requirements for attorneys that sign the attorney affidavit pursuant to 11 U.S.C. § 524(c)(3). This may be another justification for requesting information as a prerequisite to recommending reaffirmation.

287 These requests seek to obtain information necessary to establishing that the creditor is asserting a valid secured claim.

288 Although it should be avoided whenever possible, through the use of voluntary repayments or agreements to redeem (such as Form 58, Appx. G.8, *supra*), it is sometimes necessary for a debtor to reaffirm a debt. For example, a debtor may be in default on an automobile loan under which the creditor has the power to repossess after the bankruptcy if no agreement is reached. Reaffirmation may be necessary to induce the creditor to waive the default and modify the payment terms.

As an alternative to this form, advocates may wish to use the form Reaffirmation Agreement promulgated by the Administrative Office of the United States Courts, which is reproduced in Appendix E, *supra*. Use of the Administrative Office form may be required in some districts by local rule.

1. [*Debtor*], subject to the approval of the Bankruptcy Court and his statutory right to rescind, hereby reaffirms his debt of $2140.00 to [*creditor*], secured by a 1998 Ford currently valued at $3000.00.[289]

2. This debt will be paid in installments of eighty dollars ($80.00) per month, at twelve percent (12%) simple interest, until it has been paid in full.[290]

3. [*Creditor*] agrees to waive all previous and current defaults on this debt.[291]

4. [*Creditor*] further agrees that it will not act to repossess the vehicle securing this debt unless the Debtor is more than thirty days in default under this agreement.[292]

5. [*Creditor*] further agrees that, in the event of any deficiency judgment arising out of this transaction, it will not execute against the Debtor's wages.

THIS AGREEMENT MAY BE CANCELED BY THE DEBTOR AT ANY TIME BEFORE [*date sixty days after filing with court*] OR THE DATE OF THE BANKRUPTCY DISCHARGE IF THAT DATE IS AFTER [*date*][293] BY GIVING NOTICE TO [*creditor*].

THIS AGREEMENT IS NOT REQUIRED UNDER THE BANKRUPTCY CODE, UNDER NON-BANKRUPTCY LAW, OR UNDER ANY AGREEMENT NOT IN ACCORDANCE WITH THE PROVISIONS OF 11 U.S.C. § 524.[294]

Date: [*signature*]
                                                            [*debtor*]

                                                         [*signature*]
                                        Attorney for Debtor

                                                         [*signature*]
                        Attorney [*or Agent*] for [*creditor*]

Form 115 Declaration in Support of Reaffirmation Agreement[295]

[*Caption: Official Form 16A*]

Declaration in Support of Reaffirmation Agreement

[*Attorney for debtor*], attorney for the Debtor in the above-captioned case, hereby declares that:

1. I have represented [*debtor*] in this bankruptcy case and in negotiating the foregoing reaffirmation agreement.

2. I have fully explained the agreement to the Debtor and he understands it fully, as well as the following possible adverse consequences:[296]

a. He must pay a debt that he is not legally obligated to pay;

b. If he defaults, his automobile may be repossessed and he may be subject to a deficiency judgment;

c. If he defaults his wages may be garnished;

d. If he defaults his home may be sold at an execution sale;

e. If he defaults his credit may be further impaired;

f. If he defaults he may be subject to collection activity on the debt.

3. The Debtor has voluntarily entered into the agreement without pressure or coercion from any source.

4. I have fully examined the current financial circumstances of the Debtor and all dependents of the Debtor and the agreement does not impose an undue hardship on the Debtor or any of his dependents.[297]

I declare under penalty of perjury that the facts stated herein are true and correct.

Date: [*signature*]
                                        Attorney for Debtor

---

289 It should almost never be necessary to reaffirm a debt for more than the value of the collateral and some bankruptcy courts would not approve such a reaffirmation, because the debt could be reduced by a redemption, chapter 13 cramdown, or use of 11 U.S.C. § 506. See § 14.5.2, *supra*, for discussion of requirements for reaffirmation and Chapter 11, *supra*, for discussion of ways to reduce the debt in such circumstances.

290 It may be possible to negotiate better terms as part of the reaffirmation agreement. In any case, debtor's counsel should carefully negotiate the rate of interest.

291 A waiver of default is the consideration often sought by the debtor, and should be specifically provided for in the agreement.

292 Other moderating provisions such as a payment grace period and limitations on deficiency judgments should also be included if possible. Some states prohibit deficiency judgments. In those states, reaffirmation may have little effect unless the creditor is unwilling or unable to foreclose upon the collateral to collect the debt.

293 Insert date at least sixty days after date agreement will be filed. 11 U.S.C. § 524(c)(4). Although a statement that "the agreement may be canceled within sixty days after filing with the court" is probably sufficient to meet the sixty-day portion of the clause, giving a specific date is much more meaningful to the debtor, who may not know the date of filing. If the date of filing is not known when the agreement is signed, the latest possible date should be used to assure that no fewer than sixty days are afforded.

294 These clauses, in a clear and conspicuous form, are required by 11 U.S.C. § 524(c)(2). Without them the reaffirmation agreement is not valid.

295 Under the 1984 Amendments to the Bankruptcy Code, a reaffirmation of a consumer debt need not be approved by the court if an attorney represents the debtor in negotiating the agreement and the attorney files an affidavit stating that the agreement is a fully informed and voluntary agreement by the debtor and does not impose an undue hardship on the debtor or the debtor's dependents.

Attorneys should be wary of signing such affidavits, because the potential for liability, if the agreement does prove to pose a hardship, is not insignificant. It is perfectly appropriate to leave the matter to the court, which would still have to approve reaffirmations of debts not secured by real property if the debtor wants to reaffirm and the affidavit is not filed. See Form 116, Appx. G.11, *infra*.

Whether or not an affidavit is signed, it is also important to make sure that the creditor follows through and meets the requirements for an enforceable reaffirmation agreement—including filing the agreement with the court. If the creditor does not meet those requirements, the reaffirmation agreement is void. Collection on void reaffirmation agreements violates the discharge injunction. See § 14.5.2.1, *supra*.

296 It is a good idea to spell out the possible adverse consequences that have been explained to the debtor in order to show that there is a fully informed agreement. The 1994 amendments to 11 U.S.C. § 524(c)(3)(C) require that the declaration state that the attorney fully advised the debtor of the legal effect and consequences of the reaffirmation and any possible default.

297 The only way to honestly state that the agreement does not pose an undue hardship to the debtor or any dependents is to fully examine their circumstances.

Form 116 Application for Approval of Reaffirmation Agreement[298]

[*Caption: Official Form 16A*]

Application for Approval of Reaffirmation Agreement Pursuant to 11 U.S.C. § 524(c)

The Debtors in this case hereby apply for approval of their reaffirmation agreement with [*creditor*]. In support of this application they aver that:

1. They wish to reaffirm their debt with [*creditor*] to the extent it is secured by their automobile, a 1995 Chevrolet, to redeem that property under 11 U.S.C. § 722.

2. The automobile is presently worth $600.00.

3. The reaffirmation agreement, signed by the parties and providing for the payment of $600.00 plus twelve percent (12%) interest in twenty-four (24) monthly installments, is attached hereto [*omitted*].

4. The agreement is in the best interests of the Debtors, who need the automobile to commute to work.

5. The agreement does not impose a hardship on the Debtors or their dependents in that the Debtors' current monthly income is $500.00 per month and their expenses are $400.00 per month.

WHEREFORE, the Debtors pray that the reaffirmation of the aforesaid debt be approved.

Date: [*signature*]
                                                        Attorney for Debtor

Form 117 Order Approving Reaffirmation Agreement[299]

[*Caption: Official Form 16A*]

Order

AND NOW, this [*date*] day of [*month*], [*year*], the Court having found that the reaffirmation agreement proposed by the Debtors is in the best interests of the Debtor and does not pose a hardship on the Debtor or the Debtor's dependents, it is hereby ordered that the reaffirmation agreement with [*creditor*] is approved.

Date: [*signature*]
                                       United States Bankruptcy Judge

Form 118 Letter to Client After Discharge[300]

Dear [*client*]:

You should have received by now, as we did, a copy of your discharge in bankruptcy. This document certifies that you have been discharged from liability for payment of any and all debts which are made dischargeable by the Bankruptcy Code.

This does not mean that you can ignore any creditor's attempt to collect these debts. If any of your creditors try to collect a debt which you listed on your bankruptcy petition, you should contact us or another attorney so that you may assert your rights under the Bankruptcy Code and receive the full protection of your discharge.

The discharge also protects you from many types of discrimination based in your bankruptcy or the debts you eliminated in the bankruptcy. Generally, no government agency or employer can treat you differently than other people just because you filed a bankruptcy case or because of the debts you did not pay before the bankruptcy.

It is also important for you to be aware of your rights when applying for credit in the future. There are laws which protect your rights. If any of these laws are violated, you may be entitled to sue the creditor for damages, as well as make him pay your attorney fees.

The Equal Credit Opportunity Act forbids the discrimination of granting credit, when such discrimination is based on race, color, religion, national origin, sex, marital status, age, or the fact that any of your income derives from a public assistance program such as welfare, social security or unemployment compensation.

The Equal Credit Opportunity Act states that a creditor may not, either orally or in writing, discourage a person from making or pursuing an application for credit on any of the forbidden grounds. Generally, a creditor may not ask information about a spouse or request the signature of your spouse or a cosigner except in limited circumstances. Please call me if you need further details about a request for a cosigner.

Once you apply for credit, whether orally or in writing, the creditor must give you a written notice within thirty (30) days stating specific reasons why credit is being denied, and setting forth your rights under the Equal Credit Opportunity Act. Do not allow yourself to be discouraged from submitting an application; insist on a written statement of reasons for denial.

If a creditor does a credit check on you, it must disclose whether a denial of credit is based on information from a credit reporting agency, together with the name and address of that agency. The credit reporting agency must then disclose to you the nature and substance of all information in its files. If bankruptcy has been filed, the credit agency may keep that record for ten (10) years; as to other debts, the record may be kept for seven (7) years, except that any debts which have been discharged in bankruptcy should no longer be reported as having a balance owed and instead should be reported with a zero balance.

If you dispute the accuracy of any information which the credit reporting agency has in its file, you can ask the credit agency to reinvestigate. This request should be made in writing using the

---

298 In order to reaffirm a consumer debt not secured by real property, the debtor must obtain the court's approval at the discharge hearing unless an affidavit similar to Form 115, Appendix G.11, *supra*, is filed by the debtor's attorney. Most courts require a written application to be filed prior to that hearing, so local practice should be checked. The agreement may only be approved if it is in the best interests of the debtor and does not impose an undue hardship on the debtor or a dependent of the debtor. 11 U.S.C. § 524(c)(6)(A). See discussion of reaffirmation in § 14.5.2, *supra*.

299 This form of order may be used with an application for approval of reaffirmation.

300 This letter, or something like it, should be sent to clients after the discharge is granted to close a case. It explains the necessity for invoking the protections of the discharge, and outlines some of the client's rights in applying for future credit. It may have to be modified to provide for unusual circumstances in some cases.

agency's dispute form or your own simple letter. You should keep a copy of whatever you send. The agency must reinvestigate by at least asking the source of the information to respond to your dispute. If the source cannot or does not verify the disputed information, it should be removed from your credit report. If the reinvestigation does not resolve the dispute, you should contact our office. You may also submit a short statement in writing telling your side of the story. In all future reports, the credit agency must note your dispute. The credit agency will send out a corrected record to anyone who inquired about your credit within six (6) months before the correction.

If you think you are going to have problems in applying for credit, you should take a witness with you to make sure that your rights, as outlined above, are being observed. The creditor has no right to insist that your witness cosign for you, and you should be sure that this does not happen.

The discharge in bankruptcy completes the matter which we were handling for you. Unless we hear that you have some other legal problem, your case will be closed. I hope your bankruptcy succeeds in providing you with a new start and that you will be able to avoid future financial difficulties.

Date:

[*signature*]
Attorney

Form 119 Complaint to Recover SSI Benefits Collected by State As Reimbursement for Pre-Bankruptcy Welfare Debt[301]

[*Caption: Official Form 16D*]

Complaint

1. Plaintiff [*debtor*] was a Debtor in the above-captioned voluntary petition under chapter 7 of title 11, United States Code. This

Court therefore has jurisdiction under 28 U.S.C. § 1334. This proceeding is a core proceeding.

2. This Complaint is filed by Plaintiff under 11 U.S.C. § 524 to remedy violations of that section by the Defendant State of [*state*] Department of Public Welfare, and [*defendant—administrator*], individually and in his official capacity as Secretary of that department.

3. Among the debts discharged by Order of October 9, 2004 in Plaintiff's bankruptcy case was a debt to Defendant State of [*state*] Department of Public Welfare for public assistance received while he awaited a determination by the Social Security Administration as to his eligibility for Social Security and Supplemental Security Income benefits.

4. This debt was never reaffirmed under the provisions of 11 U.S.C. § 524(c).

5. At the time of the commencement of the case, Plaintiff had not yet been approved for SSI benefits.

6. Plaintiff was found eligible for SSI benefits on March 27, 2002.

7. Despite the discharge, when Plaintiff was found eligible for Supplemental Security Income benefits he was notified that his retroactive benefits check was being sent by the Social Security Administration to Defendants to repay the debt for public assistance which had been discharged. A copy of this notice is attached hereto as Exhibit A [*omitted*].

8. On information and belief, Defendants have since acted to collect the discharged debt from Plaintiff's retroactive SSI benefits.

9. Such action to collect a discharged debt violated the injunction of 11 U.S.C. § 524(a) and Defendants are now wrongfully holding Plaintiff's property.

10. Such action by Defendants also constituted a denial of Plaintiff's federal statutory rights under color of law, and therefore violated 42 U.S.C. § 1983.[302]

Prayer for Relief

WHEREFORE, Plaintiff prays that this Court enter an Order:

a. Declaring that Defendants have violated the injunction provisions of 11 U.S.C. § 524(a);

b. Requiring that Defendants forthwith deliver to Plaintiff the full amount forwarded to it by the Social Security Administration;[303]

---

301 A proceeding to recover property must be brought as an adversary proceeding. Fed. R. Bankr. P. 7001. For a general discussion of complaints in adversary proceedings see notes to Form 83, Appendix G.10, *supra*.

   A complaint such as this one may be necessary for a debtor who files a bankruptcy case during the pendency of an application for Supplemental Security Income benefits (SSI). The SSI statute authorizes a state to obtain from the applicant a reimbursement authorization which permits the Social Security Administration to forward the initial SSI check, including retroactive benefits, directly to the state, which then deducts its reimbursement and remits the balance to the recipient. 42 U.S.C. § 1382(g)(I). Because the debt to the welfare department is dischargeable, such action to collect it by the state after a bankruptcy would violate 11 U.S.C. § 362 if taken during the case, and 11 U.S.C. § 524 if taken after the discharge. Technically, in each instance it is contempt of court.

   Because there is a preexisting court order staying collection action, there should not be any difficulty with state claims based on sovereign immunity or the Eleventh Amendment. *See generally* § 13.3.2.2, *supra*. Nor should the fact that the SSI statute provides states with a method of collection make their debts any less dischargeable. There is no conflict between that statute and the Bankruptcy Code, because the SSI statute states only that Social Security *may* honor the reimbursement authorization. See discussion in Chapter 14, *supra*.

   An additional claim that could be made in a case with these facts would be one under 11 U.S.C. § 525 against the Social Security Administration for discrimination based upon a discharged debt. See § 14.5.5.4, *supra*, for a discussion of prohibited discrimination. In this case, the Social Security Administration would not have sent the check to the state welfare department if the recipient had not owed any money to the welfare department. By sending it to someone other than the recipient, Social Security has treated the debtor with a discharged debt differently solely because he once owed money to the state. This complaint is adapted from papers in *In re Coughlin*, 48 B.R. 191 (Bankr. E.D. Pa. 1985).

302 Violations of the Bankruptcy Code by state and local officials should be encompassed within 42 U.S.C. § 1983. *See* § 15.5.2, *supra*.

303 This particular complaint is pleaded cautiously, seeking only a return of the funds taken and no additional sanctions for contempt. Once debtors' rights in this area become more well-established, such sanctions would be more appropriate.

c. Awarding Plaintiff attorney fees and costs herein;[304] and

d. Granting such other relief as is just and equitable.

Date: *[signature]*
                           Attorney for Plaintiff

Form 120 Complaint Seeking Contempt Remedies for Violation of the Automatic Stay and Discharge Injunction[305]

[Caption: Official Form 16D]

Complaint

1. This complaint is filed by the Debtor in the above-captioned chapter 7 case. This Court thus has jurisdiction over this proceeding, which arises in a case under the Bankruptcy Code and concerns property of the Debtor, pursuant to 28 U.S.C. § 1334. This proceeding is a core proceeding.

2. The Defendant received notice of Plaintiff's bankruptcy petition, a copy of which is attached and labeled as Exhibit A *[omitted]*.

3. After this case was filed, Plaintiff requested his diploma and asked why he had not received it. Defendant indicated that plaintiff would be sent the diploma only if he paid a pre-petition tuition debt.

4. Defendant's failure to provide the diploma and its demand that the balance of the debt be paid in order to obtain the diploma constituted unlawful collection actions in willful violation of the automatic stay of 11 U.S.C. § 362(a).

5. Plaintiff's debts were discharged in case number *[number]*, by the Order of this Court on May 28, 2003, pursuant to 11 U.S.C. § 524. Defendant's claims fall within the scope of that discharge.

6. Defendant's continued attempts to collect the debt, through its refusal to release the diploma, constitute willful violations of the discharge injunction of 11 U.S.C. § 524.

WHEREFORE, Plaintiff prays that this Court:

a. Order Defendant forthwith to deliver Plaintiff's diploma to him;

b. Find that Defendant is in contempt of Court for violating 11 U.S.C. §§ 362 and 524;

c. Award Plaintiff damages, costs and attorney fees pursuant to 11 U.S.C. § 362(h) and 11 U.S.C. § 105(a); and

d. Order such other relief as is just and proper.

Date: *[signature]*
                          Attorney for Debtor/Plaintiff

Form 121 Complaint to Enjoin Discriminatory Denial of Guaranteed Student Loan[306]

[Caption: Official Form 16D]

Complaint

I. Preliminary Statement

1. This is an action brought by Plaintiff *[debtor]*, a bankruptcy debtor who has received his discharge, seeking declaratory and injunctive relief to invalidate certain policies of and regulations promulgated by the Higher Education Assistance Agency ("HEAA") as violative of federal bankruptcy law, 11 U.S.C. § 525(c), 42 U.S.C. § 1983, and the Supremacy Clause of the United States Constitution.

II. Jurisdiction

2. Jurisdiction for this action is conferred by 28 U.S.C. § 1334. This proceeding is a core proceeding.

III. Parties

3. *[Debtor]* is an individual residing at *[address]*.

4. Defendant HEAA is a public corporation and government instrumentality of the Commonwealth of *[state]* whose corporate purpose is to improve the higher education opportunities of *[state]* residents by granting scholarships and guaranteeing loans to such persons to assist them in meeting their expenses of higher education. *[Cite provision(s) of state law]*.

5. Defendant *[defendant—director]* is the Executive Director of HEAA and is responsible for the overall operations of HEAA, including the enforcement of HEAA regulations codified at *[cite provision(s) of state law]*.[307]

6. Defendant *[defendant—deputy director]* is the Deputy Director of HEAA and is responsible for the operation of HEAA's guaranteed student loan program, including the enforcement of HEAA regulations codified at *[cite provision(s) of state law]*.

IV. Facts

7. Plaintiff attended undergraduate school at the University of *[name]* from the fall term of 1988 to the spring term of 1990.

8. During this period, Plaintiff received student loans guaranteed by HEAA in the total amount of approximately $5874.00.

9. After leaving school, Plaintiff was financially unable to repay his student loans.

10. On March 12, 1996, Plaintiff filed a voluntary petition in bankruptcy under chapter 13 of the Bankruptcy Code, Bkr. No. *[number]*.

11. By Order dated June 29, 2003, the Bankruptcy Court ordered Plaintiff released from all his dischargeable debts, including his obligation to HEAA.[308]

---

304 Attorney fees are sought pursuant to 42 U.S.C. § 1988. *See* Ch. 15, *supra*. They may also be available in some circumstances under the Equal Access to Justice Act. *See* § 15.5.4, *supra*.

305 This complaint seeks remedies for the defendant's violations of the discharge injunction. 11 U.S.C. § 524(a); *see* § 14.5, *supra*. In many cases a complaint of this type will require a separate motion to reopen the bankruptcy case. *See* Form 133, Appx. G.12, *infra*.

306 The 1994 amendments to section 525 clarify that requiring reaffirmation of discharged student loans as a condition for the eligibility for new student loans or grants violates the anti-discrimination provisions of the Code. *See* § 14.5.5.2, *supra*. A proceeding to obtain an injunction must be brought as an adversary proceeding. Fed. R. Bankr. P. 7001. For a general discussion of complaints in adversary proceedings, see notes to Form 83, Appendix G.10, *supra*.

307 In order to avoid any claims of sovereign immunity, it may be advisable to sue only the executive director or other officer and seek prospective injunctive relief. *See Ex parte Young*, 209 U.S. 123, 28 S. Ct. 441, 52 L. Ed. 714 (1908); § 13.3.2.2, *supra*.

308 Although a bankruptcy court clearly has jurisdiction over a

12. During the spring term of 2003 Plaintiff returned to the University of [*name*] to complete the twelve credits he needed for his undergraduate degree.

13. To finance his education, Plaintiff applied for an HEAA higher education grant.

14. HEAA denied Plaintiff's grant application based upon section [*number*] of its regulations, [*cite provision of state law*].

15. In 2003, Plaintiff also applied for an HEAA guaranteed student loan.

16. Plaintiff graduated from the University of [*name*] in May 2004, with a B.A. in political science and philosophy.

17. When this action was filed, Plaintiff had been accepted for admission into several law schools commencing the fall term of 2004.

18. On or about June 21, 2004, Plaintiff filed an application through [*name*] Bank, [*address*], for an HEAA guaranteed student loan to assist the financing of his law school education at University of [*name*] Law School. The application has been approved by [*name*] Bank and is pending before HEAA.

19. On August 11, 2004, Plaintiff was accepted for admission into the University of [*name*] Law School.

20. Plaintiff has applied for financial aid from the University of [*name*] Law School.

21. The University of [*name*] Law School will provide $4000.00 assistance in loans and grants and requires that Plaintiff obtain a guaranteed student loan of at least $4,700.00.

22. Plaintiff is in the process of applying for an HEAA student loan for the University of [*name*] Law School and expects that the application will be received by HEAA by August 31, 2004.

23. Pursuant to [*cite provision(s) of state law*], Plaintiff is ineligible for an HEAA guaranteed student loan due to his debt on the prior loans, even though his obligation has been discharged in bankruptcy.

24. Unless Plaintiff obtains a guaranteed student loan he will be unable to attend law school and he will suffer irreparable harm.

V. Statement of Claims

A. First Claim

25. Defendants' policy of denying guaranteed student loans to individuals who have discharged in bankruptcy prior student loans which were in default constitutes discrimination against Plaintiff because he was a debtor under the Bankruptcy Code or because Plaintiff has not paid a debt that was discharged under the Bankruptcy Code, in violation of 11 U.S.C. § 525(c).

B. Second Claim

26. Defendants' policy of denying guaranteed student loans to individuals who have discharged in bankruptcy prior student loans which were in default violates 11 U.S.C. § 524 in that it fails to give Plaintiff a "fresh start" and it fails to treat Plaintiff as if he had never had a liability arising from that debt. Therefore, the policy violates the Supremacy Clause of the United States Constitution, Article VI, Clause 2.

27. By denying Plaintiff his rights guaranteed by federal law, that is, the Bankruptcy Code and the United States Constitution,

Defendants acting under color of law have violated 42 U.S.C. § 1983.

VI. Prayer for Relief

WHEREFORE, Plaintiff requests that this Court:

a. Take jurisdiction of this case;

b. Enter judgment and grant relief declaring that [*cite provision(s) of state law*] and Defendants' practice of denying guaranteed student loans to individuals who have discharged prior student loans in bankruptcy violates:

i. 11 U.S.C. § 525(c);

ii. 42 U.S.C. § 1983;

iii. 11 U.S.C. § 524; and

iv. The Supremacy Clause of the United States Constitution.

c. Enjoin Defendants from continuing the practice of denying Plaintiff guaranteed student loans, pursuant to [*cite provision(s) of state laws*], due to his prior loans which have been discharged in bankruptcy;

d. Order Defendants to process Plaintiff's application for a guaranteed student loan without consideration of or discrimination based upon Plaintiff's prior loans which have been discharged in bankruptcy;

e. Award Plaintiff's counsel a reasonable attorney fee; and

f. Grant Plaintiff all such other relief as shall be just and proper.

Date: [*signature*]

Attorney for Plaintiff

Declaration[309]

I, [*debtor*], the Plaintiff in the above-captioned action, certify under penalty of perjury that the foregoing is true and correct to the best of my knowledge, information and belief.

Date: [*signature*]

Debtor

Form 122 Motion for Preliminary Relief in Complaint to Enjoin Discriminatory Denial of Guaranteed Student Loan[310]

[Caption: Official Form 16D]

Plaintiff's Motion For Temporary Restraining Order and/or Preliminary Injunction

Plaintiff [*debtor*], by his attorney, hereby moves this Court, pursuant to Federal Rule of Bankruptcy Procedure 7065 and Federal Rule of Civil Procedure 65 for a Temporary Restraining Order and/or Preliminary Injunction against Defendants Higher Education Assistance Agency, [*defendant—director*], and [*defen-*

---

dispute such as this one, some bankruptcy judges require a complaint to be accompanied by a motion to reopen a bankruptcy case which has been concluded. 11 U.S.C. § 350.

309 A verified complaint or affidavit is required as a prerequisite to a temporary restraining order. Fed. R. Civ. P. 65(b). In this case, a trial was held prior to the time when the need for preliminary relief arose, but that is not often true. Often, the court will schedule a special hearing to adduce the necessary facts if time permits.

310 This request for preliminary injunctive relief may be filed with a complaint such as the one provided here in Form 121, Appx. G.11, *supra*.

dant—deputy director] on the basis of:

1. Plaintiff's verified Complaint.

2. Plaintiff's verified Motion for a Temporary Restraining Order and/or Preliminary Injunction against Defendant Higher Education Assistance Agency.

3. The evidentiary hearing held on August 20, 2004.

Without immediate relief from this Court, Plaintiff will suffer irreparable harm.

WHEREFORE, Plaintiff requests that this Court grant Plaintiff's Motion for Temporary Restraining Order and/or Preliminary Injunction.

Date: [signature]
           Attorney for Plaintiff

[Attach: Certificate of Service][311]

Form 123 Proposed Order for Preliminary Relief in Complaint to Enjoin Discriminatory Denial of Guaranteed Student Loan

[Caption: Official Form 16D]

Order[312]

AND NOW, this [date] day of [month], [year], upon consideration of Plaintiff's verified Motion for Temporary Restraining Order and/or Preliminary Injunction, verified Amended Complaint, and the evidentiary hearing held on August 20, 2004, it is hereby ORDERED and DECREED that the Motion is GRANTED.

Defendants HEAA, [defendant—director] and [defendant—deputy director] are enjoined from enforcing Higher Education Assistance Agency's policy of denying Plaintiff guaranteed student loans, pursuant to [cite provision(s) of state law], due to Plaintiff's prior loans discharged in bankruptcy. Defendants HEAA, [defen-

---

311 A certificate of service or of efforts to notify opponents, or of why notice should not be required, is required prior to issuance of a temporary restraining order. Fed. R. Civ. P. 65(b).

312 A proposed order should normally be presented to the court. Some courts prefer findings of fact necessary for issuance of an order to be included (for example, that without the order specific types of irreparable harm will occur). This complaint and the accompanying papers are appropriate for use when a government agency refuses to process a guaranteed student loan because a previous student loan has been discharged. Similar complaints, modified where appropriate, could be used to remedy other types of governmental discrimination.

 Many such cases, involving benefits or employment, may pose a pressing need for relief. The Federal Rules of Bankruptcy Procedure generally parallel the Federal Rules of Civil Procedure in this respect. Therefore, treatises and form books on federal practice may be consulted for further discussion of practice in seeking temporary restraining orders and preliminary injunctions.

 This complaint raises claims under both 11 U.S.C. § 525 and the general doctrine of Perez v. Campbell, 402 U.S. 637, 91 S. Ct. 1704, 29 L. Ed. 2d 233 (1971). See generally § 14.5, supra. The complaint seeks attorney fees under 42 U.S.C. § 1988. See discussion of attorney fees in § 15.5.2, supra. This complaint and the accompanying forms are adapted from those used in In re Richardson, 15 B.R. 925 (Bankr. E.D. Pa. 1981), rev'd in part, 27 B.R. 560 (E.D. Pa. 1982).

---

dant—director] and [defendant—deputy director] are ordered to process Plaintiff's application for a guaranteed student loan in the ordinary course of business without consideration of or discrimination based upon Plaintiff's prior loans which have been discharged in bankruptcy.

This Order shall continue in effect pending final determination of this action by the Court.

Date: [signature]
       United States Bankruptcy Judge

Form 124 Class Action Complaint Seeking Remedies for Coercive Collection Practices Involving Discharged Debt

[Caption: Official Form 16D]

Class Action Complaint

Introduction

1. This action seeks redress for the unlawful and deceptive practices committed by the Bankruptcy Collection Network and its attorney, in connection with their efforts to collect debts discharged by debtors in bankruptcy. Defendants' conduct involves falsely threatening debtors with a wide array of legal actions which it has no intention of taking, ostensibly under the guise of enforcement of security interests, the sole purpose of which is to coerce the payment of discharged debts. Plaintiffs seek monetary, declaratory and injunctive relief for themselves and the class they represent based on Defendants' violations of 11 U.S.C. § 362(h) and § 524, and the Fair Debt Collection Practices Act, 15 U.S.C. § 1692–1692o.

Jurisdiction

2. This court has jurisdiction over this matter pursuant to 28 U.S.C. § 1334. This action is a core proceeding.

Parties

3. Plaintiff A.J.A. is an individual who resides at [address].

4. Plaintiff S.R.S. is an individual who resides at [address].

5. Plaintiff E.T.E. is an individual who resides at [address].

6. Defendant Bankruptcy Collection Network ("BCN") is a Delaware corporation with its principal place of business located at [address]. BCN purchases from retailers of consumer goods and services the retail installment contracts and revolving charge accounts of consumers who have filed bankruptcy. The accounts purchased by BCN are in default at the time of purchase. The principal purpose of BCN is the collection through the use of the mails and telephones of these delinquent accounts it has purchased from creditors to which the debts were originally owed. BCN also regularly collects or attempts to collect debts which are owed or due another, or alleged to be owed or due another. BCN is accordingly a "debt collector" as defined by 15 U.S.C. § 1692a(6).

7. Defendant [firm name], is a California professional corporation with its principal place of business located at [address]. The principal purpose of Defendant attorneys is the collection through the use of the mails and telephones of debts which are owed or due another, or alleged to be owed or due another, by debtors in bankruptcy, and as such it is a "debt collector" as defined by 15 U.S.C. § 1692a(6).

Class Action Allegations

8. Plaintiffs bring this action on behalf of themselves and all others similarly situated pursuant to Fed. R. Civ. P. 23(a), 23(b)(1), (b)(2) and (b)(3) because Defendants, in regularly acting pursuant to the actions challenged herein, have acted on grounds generally applicable to the class, thereby making appropriate relief for the class as a whole. Further, prosecution of this case by individual class members could create the risk of inconsistent adjudications which could establish incompatible standards of conduct for defendants or impede the ability of other class members to protect their interests. Finally, there are questions of law and fact which predominate over those pertaining to individual class members only.

9. The Plaintiff class consists of all individuals:

a. who filed a petition for relief under the Bankruptcy Code;

b. who listed as a debt a credit account which was subsequently assigned by the creditor to Defendant BCN, and;

c. who, subsequent to the filing of the bankruptcy petition, were subjected to Defendants' collection practices and were sent letters similar to those sent to Plaintiffs herein.

10. The class is so numerous, numbering at least in the thousands, that joinder of all class members is impracticable. A class action is the only feasible method of adjudicating the rights of the affected debtors, and absent allowance of a certification of a class action a failure of justice will result.

11. The claims of the named Plaintiffs are typical of those of the class. They are bankruptcy debtors whose entitlement to the benefits of a bankruptcy discharge have been or are being threatened by the actions of the Defendants.

12. The questions of law and fact common to all class members, which predominate over those pertaining to individual class members, are limited to (a) whether Defendants engage in the acts and practices complained of, (b) whether Defendants are in contempt of bankruptcy court automatic stay and discharge injunction orders, and (c) whether Defendants' acts and omissions in attempting to collect discharged debts and other charges which are not due are in violation of the Fair Debt Collection Practices Act.

13. Plaintiffs will fairly and adequately represent the interests of the class and have no conflicts of interest with other class members. Plaintiffs' attorney has the experience necessary to competently and vigorously represent all members of the class.

14. A class action is superior to other available methods for the fair and efficient adjudication of this controversy in that (a) the class necessarily consists of persons in unfavorable economic circumstances who are not able to pay to maintain individual actions against Defendants, (b) many class members lack the sophistication to recognize that Defendants' practices are unlawful and to retain counsel, (c) many class members will accede to Defendants' unlawful collection demands and attempt to pay Defendants for fear of losing consumer goods based on Defendants' false threats that it will repossess or take other action against the alleged secured property, and (d) there is no reason that the courts should be burdened with multiple lawsuits challenging Defendants' practices.

Facts

Facts Relating to A.J.A.

15. On September 14, 1995, Plaintiff A.J.A. sought protection from his creditors by filing a Chapter 7 bankruptcy in the [*court*].

16. As part of the schedules filed with his bankruptcy petition, A.J.A. listed an account due XXX Jewelers.

17. On or about October 31, 1995, XXX Jewelers assigned A.J.A.'s account to Defendant BCN.

18. On December 21, 1995, A.J.A. was granted a discharge of all dischargeable debts pursuant to 11 U.S.C. § 524, including his obligation to XXX Jewelers and its assignee, Defendant BCN.

19. On April 22, 1996, Defendant attorneys sent A.J.A. a letter indicating that BCN's collection file on him had been transferred to the attorneys law firm. A copy of the letter is attached hereto and incorporated herein as Exhibit A [*omitted*].

20. The letter also informed A.J.A. that a "motion/complaint" had been prepared and that it would be filed against him within "four (4) days" if he did not contact BCN.

21. Included with the letter as attachments were two documents having the appearance of legal pleadings. The first document, with a caption listing BCN as the plaintiff and A.J.A. as the defendant, was entitled "NOTICE OF INTENTION TO FILE SUIT AND OF INCREASED COSTS AND ATTORNEY FEES." A copy of the Notice is attached hereto and incorporated herein as Exhibit B [*omitted*].

22. This Notice signed by Defendant Attorney attorneys advised A.J.A. that his client BCN intended to file suit and that A.J.A. "may become liable for actual costs and attorney fees."

23. The second document included with the letter had the appearance of a court complaint and was entitled "COMPLAINT ON SECURITY AGREEMENT (PURCHASE MONEY) FOR POSSESSION OF SECURITY AFTER DISCHARGE IN BANKRUPTCY C.C.SECTION 3379 AND 3380; C.C.P. SECTION 667; 11 U.S.C. SECTION 362(C)." The caption listed on the Complaint represented that it would be filed in the Municipal Court for the State of California. A copy of the Complaint is attached hereto and incorporated herein as Exhibit C [*omitted*].

24. At all times relevant to this matter A.J.A. has not resided in California and the XXX Jewelers contract was not signed in California.

25. In the Complaint, Defendants allege that a written agreement which more fully describes and identifies the security for the XXX Jewelers credit account is attached as an exhibit but no such agreement was included in the documents sent to A.J.A.

26. In the prayer for relief, the Complaint seeks a return of the alleged secured property or alternatively a money judgment against A.J.A. in the amount of $400.00 based on the claimed value of the security, as well as a judgment for damages for "detention of the security," interest and costs of suit.

27. Although A.J.A. did not contact Defendant attorneys or BCN upon receipt of the correspondence, the draft Complaint was not filed within the four-day period as threatened and, upon information and belief, was not filed in the California municipal court or any other court.

28. None of the correspondence received by A.J.A. from Defendants stated that it was being sent by a debt collector or contained a notice of the right to obtain validation of the debt.

Facts Relating to S.R.S.

29. On February 16, 1996, Plaintiff S.R.S. sought protection from his creditors by filing a Chapter 7 bankruptcy in the [*court*].

30. As part of the schedules filed with his bankruptcy petition, S.R.S. listed an account due Circus City.

31. On June 16, 1996, S.R.S. was granted a discharge of all dischargeable debts pursuant to 11 U.S.C. § 524, including his obligation to Circus City.

32. On or about March 10, 1997, approximately nine months after S.R.S. received his discharge, his account with Circus City was assigned to Defendant BCN.

33. On April 8, 1997, Defendant attorneys sent S.R.S. a letter indicating that BCN had retained the attorneys law firm for representation in "its post-bankruptcy repossession actions." A copy of the letter is attached hereto and incorporated herein as Exhibit D [*omitted*].

34. The letter also informed S.R.S. that if he did not contact BCN immediately, Defendant attorneys would seek repossession of the collateral or a judgment for its value and damages for "your wrongful retention of the collateral."

35. On April 24, 1997, S.R.S. was sent a second letter by Defendant attorneys stating that the law firm had prepared a "motion/complaint" which would be filed within seven days by "local counsel" if he did not contact BCN.

36. Included with the letter as an attachment was a document having the appearance of a court complaint and was entitled "COMPLAINT ON SECURITY AGREEMENT (PURCHASE MONEY) FOR POSSESSION OF SECURITY AFTER DISCHARGE IN BANKRUPTCY; 11 U.S.C. SECTION 362(C)." The caption listed on the Complaint stated that it was intended to be filed in a Municipal Court and left blank the state of filing creating the impression that the complaint may be filed in a state other than the state where plaintiff resides. A copy of the Complaint is attached hereto and incorporated herein as Exhibit E [*omitted*].

37. In the Complaint, Defendants allege that a written agreement which more fully describes and identifies the security for the Circus City credit account is attached as an exhibit but no such agreement was included in the documents sent to S.R.S.

38. In the prayer for relief, the Complaint seeks a return of the alleged secured property or alternatively a money judgment against S.R.S. in the amount of $2505.00 based on the claimed value of the security, as well as a judgment for damages for "detention of the security," interest, and costs of suit.

39. Although S.R.S. did not contact Defendant attorneys or BCN upon receipt of the correspondence, the draft Complaint was not filed within the seven-day period as threatened and, upon information and belief, was not filed in the courts of the state where plaintiff resides or any other court.

40. On May 6, 1997, Defendant attorneys sent S.R.S. a letter with attachments identical in form and substance to Exhibits A–C sent to Plaintiff A.J.A. The legal action threatened in that letter was also not taken against S.R.S.

41. None of the correspondence received by A.J.A. from Defendants stated that it was being sent by a debt collector or contained a notice of the right to obtain validation of the debt.

Facts Relating to E.T.E.

42. On June 19, 1996, Plaintiff E.T.E. sought protection from her creditors by filing a Chapter 7 bankruptcy in the [*court*].

43. As part of the schedules filed with her bankruptcy petition, E.T.E. listed an account due XXX Jewelers.

44. Sometime following E.T.E.'s bankruptcy filing, her account with XXX Jewelers was assigned to Defendant BCN.

45. On August 13, 1996, Defendant attorneys sent E.T.E.'s counsel a letter indicating that the attorneys firm had been retained by BCN. The letter demanded that debtor's counsel amend E.T.E.'s schedules to list the claim of XXX Jewelers as a secured claim. Defendant attorneys also stated that a motion to "force surrender of the property" would be filed within seven days if debtor's counsel did not contact BCN. Finally, the letter also threatened that Bankruptcy Rule 11 sanctions would be sought if debtor's counsel did not comply. A copy of the letter is attached hereto and incorporated herein as Exhibit F [*omitted*].

46. On November 24, 1996, E.T.E. was granted a discharge of all dischargeable debts pursuant to 11 U.S.C. § 524, including her obligation to XXX Jewelers and its assignee, Defendant BCN.

47. On October 25, 1996, E.T.E. was sent a letter from Defendant BCN stating that if she intended to retain the property, she would either need to make a lump-sum cash payment for its fair market value, or enter into an agreement for monthly payments on the "remaining amount owed." A copy of the letter is attached hereto and incorporated herein as Exhibit G [*omitted*].

48. Included with the letter as an attachment was a document entitled "POST DISCHARGE PROPERTY RETENTION AGREEMENT." Under the proposed agreement, E.T.E. would be required to pay the sum of $1613.86, the claimed value of the collateral, together with interest at 18%, by making payments of $65.00 per month until paid in full. The agreement required that E.T.E. acknowledge that the agreement was not to be considered a reaffirmation agreement. A copy of the Agreement is attached hereto and incorporated herein as Exhibit H [*omitted*].

49. On September 12, 1996, E.T.E.'s counsel was sent a second letter from Defendant attorneys stating that because E.T.E.'s bankruptcy schedules had not been amended and as she failed to comply with 11 U.S.C. § 521 (2)(A) and (B), Defendant attorneys would file a complaint seeking a revocation of E.T.E.'s discharge and sanctions if she did not contact BCN within ten days. A copy of the letter is attached hereto and incorporated herein as Exhibit I [*omitted*].

50. Included with the letter as an attachment was a document having the appearance of a court complaint and was entitled "COMPLAINT FOR: 1. DECLARATORY RELIEF; 2. TO REVOKE DEBTOR'S DISCHARGE (11 U.S.C. 727(d); AND REQUEST FOR SANCTIONS AGAINST DEBTOR." The caption listed on the Complaint represented that it would be filed in this court. A copy of the Complaint is attached hereto and incorporated herein as Exhibit J [*omitted*].

51. Although neither E.T.E. or her counsel contacted Defendant attorneys or BCN upon receipt of the correspondence, the draft Complaint was not filed after the ten-day period expired as threatened or at any subsequent time.

52. None of the correspondence received by E.T.E. or her counsel from Defendants stated that it was being sent by a debt collector or contained a notice of the right to obtain validation of the debt.

First Claim—Willful Violation of the Automatic Stay

53. The allegations of paragraphs 1–52 above are realleged and incorporated herein by reference.

54. The actions of Defendants in this case, in seeking and collecting payments from Plaintiffs and class members to satisfy debts incurred before the filing of their bankruptcy cases and by falsely and deceptively threatening various forms of legal action, are in violation of the automatic stay entered in Plaintiffs' and class members' bankruptcy cases, entitle Plaintiffs and class members to the relief afforded under 11 U.S.C. § 362(h), and additionally constitute contempt of bankruptcy court orders.

WHEREFORE, Plaintiffs respectfully request that this Court enter judgment in favor of Plaintiffs and the class and against the Defendants as follows:

(1) Declaring that Defendants' policies and practices are unlawful and in willful violation of 11 U.S.C. § 362, and in contempt of court;

(2) Enjoining Defendants from continuing its policies and practices;

(3) Ordering Defendants to refund all monies collected pursuant to its policies and practices with interest thereon at the lawful rate;

(4) Awarding exemplary or punitive damages against Defendants in an amount sufficient to deter further unlawful conduct;

(5) Awarding Plaintiffs reasonable attorney fees and litigation expenses, plus costs of suit;

(6) Granting such other or further relief as is appropriate.

Second Claim—Willful Violation of Discharge Injunction

55. The allegations of paragraphs 1–52 above are realleged and incorporated herein by reference.

56. The actions of Defendants in this case, in seeking and collecting payments on discharged debts by falsely and deceptively threatening various forms of legal actions, are in violation of the discharge injunction orders entered in Plaintiffs' and class members' bankruptcy cases pursuant to 11 U.S.C. § 524, and constitute contempt of bankruptcy court orders.

WHEREFORE, Plaintiffs respectfully request that this Court enter judgment in favor of Plaintiffs and the class and against the Defendants as follows:

(1) Declaring that Defendants' policies and practices are unlawful and in willful violation of 11 U.S.C. § 524, and in contempt of court;

(2) Enjoining Defendants from continuing its policies and practices;

(3) Ordering Defendants to refund all monies collected pursuant to its policies and practices with interest thereon at the lawful rate;

(4) Awarding exemplary or punitive damages against Defendants in an amount sufficient to deter further unlawful conduct;

(5) Awarding Plaintiffs reasonable attorney fees and litigation expenses, plus costs of suit;

(6) Granting such other or further relief as is appropriate.

Third Claim—Violation of the FDCPA

57. The allegations of paragraphs 1–52 above are realleged and incorporated herein by reference.

58. The foregoing acts and omissions by Defendants constitute violations of the FDCPA, which include, but are not limited to, the following:

(a) The Defendants violated 15 U.S.C. §§ 1692e(2)(A), (4), (5), (9), (10), (13) and 1692f(6) by misrepresenting the imminence of legal action and making other false and misleading representations;

(b) The Defendants violated 15 U.S.C. §§ 1692e(11) and 1692g by failing to provide the required notices in communications with the Plaintiffs;

(c) The Defendants violated 15 U.S.C. § 1692f(1) by collecting or attempting to collect amounts not permitted by law and by otherwise using unfair and unconscionable methods.

WHEREFORE, Plaintiffs respectfully request that this Court enter judgment in favor of Plaintiffs and the class and against the Defendants as follows:

(1) Declaring that Defendants' policies and practices are unlawful;

(2) Enjoining Defendants from continuing its policies and practices;

(3) Ordering Defendants to refund all monies collected pursuant to its policies and practices with interest thereon at the lawful rate;

(4) Awarding actual and statutory damages against Defendants pursuant to 11 U.S.C. § 1692k;

(5) Awarding Plaintiffs reasonable attorney fees and litigation expenses, plus costs of suit;

(6) Granting such other or further relief as is appropriate.

Date: *[signature]*
                                   Attorney for Plaintiff

Form 125 Motion for Order Declaring Mortgage Loan Current[313]

[Caption: Official Form 16A]

Motion for Order Declaring Mortgage Default Has Been Cured and That Loan Is Current

The debtors move the Court pursuant to Sections 1322, 1327, and 1328 of the Bankruptcy Code, for the entry of an order in this case to declare the mortgage loan currently serviced by [*name of mortgage holder or servicer*] to have been cured by the completion of the debtors' chapter 13 plan and to be current as of the date of

---

313 The chapter 13 plan, under section 1327, is binding on all creditors so that, if a debtor completes a plan providing for the cure of a mortgage default, that default must be deemed cured. Nonetheless, some mortgage holders routinely assess charges to debtors' accounts immediately after completion of a chapter 13 case in connection with alleged defaults that occurred before or during the chapter 13 case, charges that have not been approved by the Court and of which debtors were never previously notified. It is often helpful to file a motion like this one shortly before the case is closed to obtain an order that such charges are not permitted.

entry of the Discharge Order in this case. In support of their motion the debtors aver:

1. This case was commenced by the filing of a petition with the Clerk of this court on [*date of petition*].

2. The debtors' chapter 13 plan provided for a cure of the debtor's mortgage delinquency and the maintenance of current mortgage payments during the plan pursuant to 11 U.S.C. § 1322(b)(5).

3. The debtors' mortgage delinquency was determined by the allowance of mortgagee's proof of claim in the amount of [*amount of delinquency as set forth in proof of claim or determined by court*].

4. The debtors' chapter 13 plan providing for payment of that amount and maintenance of current payments by the debtor was confirmed by order of this Court and is binding on [*name of mortgage holder or servicer*] under 11 U.S.C. § 1327.

5. After the debtors completed their plan payments, the trustee filed a Final Report in this case on [*date*].

6. The amount established as the arrearage to be cured by the debtors on their mortgage has been paid, according to the Final Report of the trustee.

7. The debtors have made all of their post-petition mortgage payments to [*name of mortgage holder or servicer*] up to and including the date of the filing of this motion.

8. The court has not, since confirmation of the plan, approved any further expenses, fees, or charges in connection with the claim of [*name of mortgage holder or servicer*].

WHEREFORE, the debtors request this Court to declare:

1. That the debtors' mortgage loan has been cured so that it is current as of the effective date of the debtors' discharge and the debtors' remaining balance due is the amount that would have existed if their default had never occurred.

2. That any amounts for charges, fees, or expenses that [*name of mortgage holder or servicer*] may allege the debtors to owe as of the date of the discharge in connection with any default on their mortgage or otherwise, that have not been approved by this Court through the allowance of the claim of [*name of mortgage holder or servicer*] or otherwise, be deemed cured by completion of the plan and therefore canceled and discharged by the discharge order.

3. That any attempt to collect any of these discharged charges, fees, or expenses be deemed to be a willful violation of the discharge injunction and contempt of the orders of this Court.

4. That the debtors be afforded such other and further relief as is just and proper.

Date: [*signature*]
                 Attorney for Debtors

Form 126 Order Declaring Mortgage Loan Current[314]

[*Caption: Official Form 16A*]

Order Declaring Mortgage Default Has Been Cured and That Loan Is Current

AND NOW, this [*date*] day of [*month*], [*year*], upon the motion of debtors and after notice and an opportunity for a hearing, it is

hereby ordered and declared that:

1. The debtors' mortgage loan has been cured by completion of their chapter 13 plan so that it is current as of the effective date of the debtors' discharge, and the debtors' remaining balance due is the amount that would have existed if their default had never occurred;

2. Any amounts for charges, fees, or expenses that [*name of mortgage holder or servicer*] may allege the debtors to owe as of the date of the discharge in connection with any default on their mortgage or otherwise, that have not been approved by this Court through the allowance of the claim of [*name of mortgage holder or servicer*] or otherwise, be deemed cured by completion of the plan and therefore canceled and discharged by the discharge order.

3. Any attempt to collect any of these discharged charges, fees or expenses shall be deemed to be a willful violation of the discharge injunction and contempt of the orders of this Court.

Date: [*signature*]
             United States Bankruptcy Judge

Form 127 Complaint Challenging Misapplication of Mortgage Payments in Chapter 13 Case[315]

[*Caption: Official Form C*]

Complaint

Introduction

1. This action is filed by the Plaintiff to remedy Defendant [*creditor's*] disregard for the provisions of the debtor's confirmed chapter 13 bankruptcy plan, resulting in overcharges being assessed and collected on the debtor's mortgage account. This action seeks a declaration that the Defendant's claim has been paid in full, a turnover of funds overpaid to the Defendant, and damages as sanctions for contempt of this Court's orders, for unfair trade practices and contract violations under state law.

Jurisdiction

2. This Court has jurisdiction over this matter pursuant to 28 U.S.C. § 1334. This action is a core proceeding.

Parties

3. Plaintiff/debtor [*name*] is an individual who resides at [*address*].

4. Defendant [*creditor*] is a corporation doing business at [*address*].

---

314   After this order has been entered, practitioners may wish to send the mortgage holder or servicer a request for a pay-off statement or a qualified written request under the Real Estate Settlement

Procedures Act, 12 U.S.C. § 2605, to determine whether any improper charges have been assessed to the mortgage account. See Form 69, Appendix G.8, *supra*, for a sample qualified written request.

315   This complaint challenges the pervasive practice by mortgage lenders and servicers of miscrediting payments made to cure a default under a chapter 13 plan. *See* § 13.4.3.4, *supra*. Although this complaint was prepared for filing in an individual action, it could be redrafted to include class certification allegations where appropriate.

Facts

5. Plaintiff is a debtor in this chapter 13 case, which was filed on October 17, 2000.

6. On December 11, 2000, the Defendant's predecessor in interest, [*assignor*], prepared a proof of claim for filing in this matter. As an itemization of the claim, an "Amended Attachment" form was filed with the proof of claim, a copy of which is incorporated herein and attached hereto as Exhibit A [*omitted*].

7. Pursuant to this proof of claim and attachment, the Defendant sought payment of a claim for a pre-petition mortgage arrearage in the total amount of $14,511.60. In addition to the thirteen mortgage payments claimed to be in arrears, this amount included pre-petition legal fees and expenses, late fees and a pre-computed interest amount based on the total arrearage calculated to be repaid over a period of sixty months.

8. As a separate itemization on the claim form, the Defendant also listed a figure representing the total payoff on the mortgage account in the amount of $114,715.54.

9. On December 15, 2000, this Court entered an Order confirming Plaintiff's chapter 13 plan, which provided for a cure of the default by payment of the arrears through the chapter 13 trustee and maintenance of current payments on the mortgage by the debtor during the pendency of the plan. Accordingly, the Defendant was required to use an accounting procedure in which all post-petition mortgage payments made to the Defendant should have been applied to current payments due and owing and all payments made by the trustee should have been applied separately to the arrearage amount.

10. Although the Plaintiff initially fell behind on her post-petition mortgage payments to Defendant, these payments were brought fully up to date prior to the confirmation hearing.

11. The Plaintiff has remained current with her payments to the trustee since they first came due in November, 1997. From the monies paid to the trustee, disbursements in the amount of $6134.66 had been made by the trustee on the Defendant's claim as of January, 2003.

12. In February, 2003, Plaintiff notified the Defendant that she intended to sell her home and a mortgage pay-off statement was requested. At that time, the Plaintiff was current on her post-petition mortgage and trustee payments.

13. On February 20, 2003, the Defendant prepared a pay-off statement seeking payment of $134,212.47 on the Plaintiff's mortgage account. Despite the substantial payments made to the Defendant under the Plaintiff's chapter 13 plan, the amount claimed to be owed by the Defendant had actually increased by approximately $20,000.00 since the initial filing of this case. A copy of the pay-off statement is attached hereto as Exhibit B [*omitted*] and incorporated herein by reference.

14. On March 12, 2003, a closing on the sale of the Plaintiff's home was conducted. As part of the sale proceeds, the sum of $135,112.35 was paid to the Defendant on the subject mortgage account.

15. In connection with the payoff of the Plaintiff's mortgage account, the Defendant demanded and Plaintiff was required to pay an amount far in excess of that which should have been charged had her payments during this chapter 13 case been properly applied.

16. Defendant's actions occurred as a result of its regular policies and practices of failing to properly adjust its accounting procedures and records to take into account the provisions of chapter 13 plans and any stipulations or court decisions concerning its claims that take place during bankruptcy cases.

17. The result of these actions and policies and practices is that Defendant:

(a) Coerced the payment of money from the Plaintiff in violation of the terms of the Plaintiff's chapter 13 plan and the order confirming the plan.

(b) Violated 11 U.S.C. § 1327, under which the plan is binding on all creditors.

(c) Coerced the payment of money that was not owed.

(d) Deprived the Plaintiff of the benefits and protections of the Bankruptcy Code.

18. The Plaintiff has been damaged in that she has had to pay amounts to Defendant that she did not owe.

19. Defendant's actions and its policies and practices are deceptive, insofar as they involve the intentional concealment of the fact that Defendant did not properly account for the Plaintiff's bankruptcy plan and payments and involve deceptive demands by Defendant or payment of amounts that were not owed.

First Claim

20. The allegations of paragraphs 1–19 above are realleged and incorporated herein by reference.

21. The actions of Defendant in this case were in willful violation of the confirmation order of this Court, the Plaintiff's chapter 13 plan, and 11 U.S.C. § 1327, and therefore Defendant is in contempt of this Court's orders.

WHEREFORE, Plaintiff prays that this Court enter a Judgment in her favor and against the Defendant as follows:

(a) Declaring that Defendant's actions are unlawful, and in contempt of court;

(b) Ordering Defendant to refund to the Plaintiff all monies unlawfully collected pursuant to its actions;

(c) Awarding reasonable attorney fees and litigation expenses, costs of suit, and punitive damages pursuant to 11 U.S.C. § 105(a);

(d) Granting such other or further relief as is appropriate.

Second Claim

22. The allegations of paragraphs 1–19 above are realleged and incorporated herein by reference.

23. To the extent Defendant sought to enforce its mortgage and recover pre-petition amounts that were not included in its allowed secured claim, it demanded and collected pre-petition debts in willful violation of the automatic stay, 11 U.S.C. § 362.

WHEREFORE, Plaintiff prays that this Court enter a Judgment in her favor and against the Defendant as follows:

(a) Declaring that Defendant's actions are unlawful, and in contempt of court;

(b) Ordering Defendant to refund to the Plaintiff all monies unlawfully collected pursuant to its actions;

(c) Awarding reasonable attorney fees and litigation expenses, costs of suit, and punitive damages pursuant to 11 U.S.C. §§ 105(a) and 362(h);

(d) Granting such other or further relief as is appropriate.

Third Claim

24. The allegations of paragraphs 1–19 above are realleged and incorporated herein by reference.

25. Defendant's actions and its policies and practices set forth herein violate the [*state*] Consumer Protection Act, [*cite provision*], in that they, *inter alia*:

(a) Deceptively claim that money is due which is not in fact owed;

(b) Deceptively conceal that payments made by the Plaintiff were not being properly applied and accounted for pursuant to the Plaintiff's plan and confirmation order.

WHEREFORE, Plaintiff prays that this Court enter a Judgment in her favor and against the Defendant as follows:

(a) Declaring that Defendant's actions and its policies and practices are unlawful, and in contempt of court;

(b) Ordering Defendant to refund to the Plaintiff all monies collected pursuant to its actions and policies and practices;

(c) Awarding actual and treble damages pursuant to [*state statute*];

(d) Awarding reasonable attorney fees and litigation expenses, plus costs of suit, pursuant to [*state statute*];

(e) Granting such other or further relief as is appropriate.

Fourth Claim

26. The allegations of paragraphs 1–48 above are realleged and incorporated herein by reference.

27. Defendant obtained money from the Plaintiff in a manner contrary to equity and good conscience and under circumstances constituting unjust enrichment.

28. Defendant obtained money from the Plaintiff in a manner contrary to and in breach of the Note and Mortgage entered into between the parties.

WHEREFORE, Plaintiff prays that this Court enter a Judgment in her favor and against the Defendant as follows:

(a) Ordering Defendant to refund to the Plaintiff all monies unlawfully collected pursuant to its actions;

(b) Awarding actual damages for Defendant's breach of contract;

(c) Granting such other or further relief as is appropriate.

Date: [*signature*]

Attorney for Plaintiff

G.12 Conversion, Dismissal and Modification of Plan After Confirmation

Form 128 Motion to Modify Plan After Confirmation[316]

[*Caption: Official Form 16A*]

Motion to Modify Plan After Confirmation

The Debtors, by their attorney, hereby move to modify their chapter 13 plan. In support of this motion they aver:

1. Their chapter 13 plan presently calls for them to pay $400.00 per month to the trustee.

2. Because of unanticipated financial problems, including loss of income and the necessity of installing a new roof on their home, the Debtors have fallen behind on their payments and feel it would be difficult to catch up and maintain payments over the next year at the level originally called for by the plan.

3. The Debtors anticipate that Ms. Debtor will soon be employed, adding to the income of the family.

4. A proposed modified plan is attached hereto and labeled Exhibit A [*omitted*].

5. Under the modified plan the Debtors would reduce their payments to $150.00 monthly for the next year and then resume payments of $400.00 monthly in the final year of the plan. The plan as modified meets the requirements of the Bankruptcy Code.

WHEREFORE, the Debtors pray that they be permitted to amend their plan to conform to the attached amended plan pursuant to 11 U.S.C. § 1329, reducing their payments by $150.00 for the next year and increasing their payments in the final year of the plan.

Date: [*signature*]

Attorney for Debtor

Form 129 Motion to Modify Plan to Terminate Plan

[*Caption: Official Form 16A*]

Motion to Modify Plan

The Debtors hereby apply to modify their chapter 13 plan on the following grounds:

1. The Debtors' chapter 13 plan was confirmed by this Court on April 5, 2002, providing for sixty monthly payments of one hundred dollars ($100.00).

2. On September 13, 2004, a fire occurred in the Debtors' home destroying much of their property.

3. The Debtors did not have insurance which would compensate for the loss of that property, and have had to expend considerable sums to replace it.

4. Because of these increased expenses the Debtors have no disposable income available for payments to the trustee under their plan.

5. The payments already made under the Debtors' plan meet all the mandatory requirements of chapter 13.

WHEREFORE, the Debtors pray that the Court allow them to modify their chapter 13 plan so that it terminates as of the last payment which was made.

Date: [*signature*]

Attorney for Debtors

---

316 This form and the following Form 129, Appendix G.12, *infra*, are motions to modify the debtor's proposed chapter 13 plan pursuant to 11 U.S.C. § 1329. *See* § 8.7.3, *supra*. Bankruptcy Rule 3015(g) requires the filing of a motion, along with the proposed modification or summary thereof. At least twenty days notice shall then be provided by the clerk, or sometimes by the moving party if local rules so require, to the trustee, the United States Trustee, and the creditors, of the time for filing objections and of a hearing to consider any objections.

Form 130 Motion to Modify Plan to Surrender Vehicle[317]

[*Caption: Official Form 16A*]

Motion to Modify Plan to Provide for Surrender of Vehicle and Reclassification of Secured Creditor's Claim

The Debtor, [*name*], hereby moves to modify her Chapter 13 plan on the following grounds:

1. The Debtor's Chapter 13 plan was confirmed by this Court on April 5, 2002, providing for monthly payments of five-hundred dollars ($500.00).

2. One of the secured claims provided for under the debtor's confirmed plan is the claim held by [*creditor*], which is secured by a 1998 Dodge Caravan. Approximately three-hundred dollars ($300.00) of her monthly plan payment is currently devoted to paying this secured claim.

3. On September 12, 2003, one of the debtor's employers informed her that her work hours would be reduced, resulting in a reduction of her work hours from 65 hours to 45 hours per week, also resulting in a drop of two-hundred dollars ($200.00) per week in the Debtor's income.

4. The Debtor has also been notified by her primary employer that her contribution for health insurance coverage would increase by fifty dollars ($50.00) per month beginning January 1, 2004.

5. Because of her decreased income and additional expenses, the Debtor can no longer afford to pay five-hundred dollars ($500.00) per month under the plan to the trustee.

6. The Debtor is able to pay two-hundred dollars ($200.00) per month under her plan to the trustee.

7. The debtor's father is purchasing a new vehicle and is prepared to give his current vehicle to the debtor without charge.

8. The debtor has at all times properly maintained the Dodge Caravan and it is currently in good working order. The debtor's usage of the Dodge Caravan has been under normal conditions and it currently has less than 20,000 miles.

WHEREFORE, the Debtor requests that this Court allow her to modify her chapter 13 plan by:

   a. surrendering the Dodge Caravan to [*creditor*] in full satisfaction of its secured claim;

   b. providing for payment to [*creditor*] of any deficiency resulting from the sale of the collateral as an unsecured claim;

   c. reducing the monthly payments under the plan from $500.00 to $200.00 for the remainder of the plan's duration.

Date: [*signature*]
                   Attorney for Debtor

Date: [*signature*]
                           Debtor

---

317 Courts are divided on whether this type of modification is permissible. *See* § 8.7.3, *supra*. The more reasoned approach is to consider modifications as proposed in this motion on a case-by-case basis rather than adopting a general rule that such modifications are never permitted. *See In re* Jock, 95 B.R. 75 (Bankr. M.D. Tenn. 1989). It is therefore important that the modification be proposed in good faith.

Form 131 Motion to Modify Plan to Permit Mortgage Refinancing to Pay Off Plan

[*Caption: Official Form 16A*]

Motion to Modify Plan to Permit Mortgage Refinancing to Pay Off Plan

The Debtor, [*name*], hereby moves to modify her chapter 13 plan on the following grounds:

1. The Debtor's chapter 13 plan was confirmed by this Court on [*date*], providing for sixty monthly payments of varying amounts.

2. The Debtor has made the payments to the trustee under her plan for over thirty-six months.

3. The Debtor's home is in need of unexpected major repairs, including a new boiler for heating, for which she will have great difficulty paying while maintaining her plan obligations.

4. The Debtor believes that, due to the increased equity in her home, she can obtain a refinancing of her mortgage that will be sufficient to pay for these repairs and also fund the remaining payments under her plan, while at the same time lowering her mortgage interest rate and substantially lowering her current monthly payment obligations under the plan.

5. The Debtor seeks to modify her plan, as provided in paragraph 4 of the Amended Chapter 13 Plan attached hereto, to provide her an option to refinance her mortgage and use the proceeds to make her remaining plan payments.

6. If the Debtor completes her payments by refinancing, all of the mandatory requirements of chapter 13 would still be satisfied.

WHEREFORE, the Debtor requests that this Court enter an Order approving the modification and approving the debtor's Amended Chapter 13 Plan.

Date: [*signature*]
                   Attorney for Debtor

Form 132 Debtor's Amended Plan Permitting Mortgage Refinancing to Pay Off Plan

[*Caption: Official Form 16A*]

Amended Chapter 13 Plan Permitting Mortgage Refinancing to Pay Off Plan

1. If the instant estate were liquidated under chapter 7 of the Bankruptcy Code, the allowed unsecured claimants would be paid $0.00.

2. Under this plan the allowed unsecured claimants will receive not less than that amount.

3. The Debtor shall submit to the supervision and control of the trustee the following sums:

   a. During the first year of the plan: $500.00 monthly;

   b. During the 13th through 15th months of the plan: $600.00 monthly;

   c. During the 16th through 24th months of the plan: $700.00 monthly;

   d. During the third year of the plan: $840.00 monthly;

   e. During the fourth year of the plan: $1255.00 monthly;

   f. During the fifth year of the plan: $1505.00 monthly.

4. After the thirty-sixth month of this plan, the Debtor shall have the option of refinancing her mortgage and using funds obtained

through such refinancing to make the payments set forth above that have not yet been made, as well as any post-petition arrears on the mortgage. The remaining payments due from the trustee at the time of any such refinancing on the allowed secured claim of [*mortgage company*] may be paid directly to [*mortgage company*] at the closing on the refinancing loan, and the amount due to be paid by the Debtor under the plan shall be reduced by that amount plus the trustee's anticipated commission on that amount. If there is any dispute regarding the amount necessary to complete the plan and pay off the mortgage, the Debtor may pay the amount demanded by the mortgage holder and thereafter seek in the bankruptcy court a refund of any overpayment and a determination of whether the mortgage holder has complied with the plan's terms and the terms of the earlier stipulation settling the adversary proceeding between the Debtor and the mortgage company. [*Mortgage company*]'s failure to comply with the binding terms of the plan and stipulation shall be deemed contempt of court.

5. The various claims of the Debtor's creditors shall be classified as follows:

    a. Class one: Claims filed and allowed which are entitled to priority under 11 U.S.C. § 507(a)(1).

    b. Class two: The pre-petition arrearages on the allowed secured claim held by [*mortgage company*].

    c. Class three: All other priority claims.

    d. Class four: All other claims against the debtors that are timely filed except for the first mortgage held by [*mortgage company*], priority claims, and any allowed secured claim of the City of Philadelphia.

    e. Class five: The allowed secured claims of the City of Philadelphia.

    f. Class six: All other claims against the debtor that are not timely filed.

6. The payments received by the trustee from the Debtor pursuant to this plan shall be distributed as follows:

    a. Class one claims: The amount paid by the Debtor to the trustee shall be distributed first to the class one administrative claims, pro rata, until they are paid in full. Any other priority claimants shall be paid only after the class two claims are paid in full.

    b. Class two claims: After the application of the appropriate amount each month to the class one administrative claims, the entire amount of the monthly payment remaining in the hands of the trustee shall be distributed, pro rata, to the holders of the class two claims until each such claimant shall have received 100% of the amount allowed on each claim for arrears.

    c. Class three claims: After the application of the appropriate amount each month to the class one and class two claims, the entire amount of the monthly payment remaining in the hands of the trustee shall be distributed, pro rata, to the holders of the class three claims.

    d. Class four claims: After the application of the appropriate amount each month to the class one, class two, and class three claims, the entire amount of the monthly payment remaining in the hands of the trustee shall be distributed, pro rata, to the holders of the class four claims.

    e. The Class five claims are not provided for by this plan, and there shall be no distribution to the holders of such claims.

    f. Class six claims: The class six claims are provided for by this plan as follows: There shall be no distribution to the holders of class six claims.

7. The current payments on the first mortgage on the Debtor's home, held by [*mortgage company*], will be paid by the Debtor directly to that creditor and will not be paid under the plan, except as provided above for post-petition arrears. The Debtor will cure the pre-petition defaults on that mortgage within a reasonable period of time by making payments on the arrears through the trustee. Upon completion of the payment of the arrears, the Debtor will be reinstated on the original payment schedule for the mortgage as if no default had ever occurred, except for the amount of any default in current payments to be made after commencement of this case which has not been cured by that date. The term "arrears," for all purposes under this plan, shall mean the amount of arrears stated in the aforesaid mortgage holder's amended proof of claim.

8. To the extent that any claim is fully or partially unsecured pursuant to 11 U.S.C. § 506(a), that portion of the claim which is unsecured shall be provided for as a class four (unsecured) claim under this plan. Creditors holding such claims shall retain their liens only to the extent of their allowed secured claims. To the extent that the allowed secured claim is paid during this case or thereafter, such creditors' liens shall be reduced. Once the allowed secured claim has been paid in full, either during or after the pendency of this case, the creditor holding such claim shall promptly mark any lien securing such claim as satisfied in the appropriate public records.

9. By failing to object to this plan, or any modification thereof, all creditors holding claims agree not to make any effort to collect their claims from any cosigners that may exist, so long as this case remains pending.

10. Confirmation of this plan shall constitute a finding that the plan constitutes the Debtor's best effort under all the circumstances to pay their creditors, within the meaning of 11 U.S.C. § 727(a)(9).

11. Confirmation of this plan shall constitute a finding in accordance with 11 U.S.C. § 1322 that there is cause for extending the plan beyond three years. The Debtor shall have until sixty months from the date of confirmation to complete payments under this plan. Confirmation shall also constitute approval of such extension. Such extension is essential to the success of the plan. Without it the plan would fail and no claims would be paid in full.

12. The current defaults by the Debtor on the class two claims shall be cured by payments under this plan.

13. The title to the property of the estate shall revest in the Debtors upon termination of this plan, and the Debtor shall have sole right to use and possession thereof during the pendency of this case, including the right to use, sell, or lease such property in the ordinary course of the Debtor's affairs.

14. Any money or property acquired by either the trustee or the Debtor or refunded from the trustee's percentage fees, while this case is pending shall be deemed exempt property of the Debtor if exemptible, and shall be forthwith delivered to the Debtor.

15. Upon completion of this plan, all debts listed in the Debtor's schedules or provided for by this plan, except those excepted by 11 U.S.C. § 1328(a), shall be discharged.

16. If prior to the expiration of the period set forth in paragraph 3 of this plan all filed claims entitled to payment under this plan are paid in full, this plan shall terminate on that date.

Date: [*signature*]
                                      Debtor

Form 133 Debtor's Notice to Convert Case From Chapter 13 to Chapter 7[318]

[Caption: Official Form 16A]

Debtor's Notice to Convert Case from Chapter 13 to Chapter 7

The Debtors, pursuant to 11 U.S.C. § 1307(a), hereby elect to convert the above-captioned chapter 13 case to a case under chapter 7 of the Bankruptcy Code. The Debtors are entitled to convert their case because:

1. This case, filed on *[filing date]*, is a case under chapter 13 of the Bankruptcy Code.

2. The Debtors are eligible to be debtors under chapter 7 of the Bankruptcy Code.

WHEREFORE, the Debtors pray for relief under chapter 7 of the Bankruptcy Code.

Date: *[signature]*
                                    Attorney for Debtors

Form 134 Supplemental Schedule of Debts Arising After Filing of the Petition, But Prior to Conversion to Chapter 7[319]

[Caption: Official Form 16A]

Supplemental Schedule of Debts Arising After Filing of the Petition, But Prior to Conversion to Chapter 7

Pursuant to Fed. R. Bankr. P. 1019(5), the following debts arose subsequent to the filing date of the petition in this matter, and prior to the date on which this case was converted to a case under chapter 7:

Creditor	Basis of Debt	Amount	
United Gas Works	Gas service to Debtor's residence	$1062.58	*[date incurred]*
City of Hope	Water service to Debtor's residence	$668.81	*[date incurred]*
Allied Collection	Consumer purchase	$294.89	*[date incurred]*
	TOTAL	$2026.28	

Date: *[signature]*
                                    Attorney for Debtor

Form 135 Debtor's Motion to Convert Chapter 7 Case to Chapter 13[320]

[Caption: Official Form 16A]

Debtor's Motion to Convert Case to Chapter 13

The Debtors, pursuant to 11 U.S.C. § 706(a), hereby elect to convert the above-captioned chapter 7 case to a case under chapter 13 of the Bankruptcy Code. The Debtors are entitled to convert their case because:

1. This case, filed on *[filing date]*, has not been previously converted under sections 1112 or 1307 of the Bankruptcy Code.

2. The Debtors are eligible to be debtors under chapter 13 of the Bankruptcy Code.

WHEREFORE, the Debtors pray for relief under chapter 13 of the Bankruptcy Code.

Date: *[signature]*
                                    Attorney for Debtors

Form 136 Debtor's Motion to Dismiss Chapter 13 Case[321]

[Caption: Official Form 16A]

Debtor's Motion to Dismiss Chapter 13 Case

The Debtors, pursuant to 11 U.S.C. § 1307(b), hereby elect to dismiss the above-captioned chapter case. The Debtors are entitled to dismiss their case because:

---

318   The debtor has an absolute one-time right to convert a case filed under chapter 7 to a chapter 13 case and may always convert from chapter 13 to chapter 7. 11 U.S.C. §§ 706(a), 1307(a). The filing of this form effectuates conversion of the case without a court order. Fed. R. Bankr. P. 1017(d). However, some courts may require an application procedure or some other formalities such as submission of a proposed order.

   If a case is converted to chapter 13, Fed. R. Bankr. P. 3015(b) requires that the debtor file a plan fifteen days after conversion, which deadline may only be extended upon motion for cause shown. Amendments to Fed. R. Bankr. P. 1017(d) also clarify that the date of the filing of a notice of conversion from chapter 13 to chapter 7 is treated as the date of the conversion order. Supplemental schedules should always be filed in any case in which new debts have arisen since the chapter 13 petition, which would be dischargeable in the chapter 7 case. 11 U.S.C. § 348(d); *see* Form 134, Appx. G.12, *infra.*

   As a conversion terminates the trustee's duties in the case, 11 U.S.C. § 348(e), a copy of the form filed should be mailed to the trustee. After a debtor has converted from chapter 13 to chapter 7, court permission is required for further conversion.

319   This schedule is required when a debtor converts a case from chapter 11, 12, or 13 to chapter 7. Fed. R. Bankr. P. 1019(5). It is useful to the debtor to file this schedule particularly when it will include debts which will be dischargeable under 11 U.S.C. § 348(d). Often forgotten are new utility arrearages arising post-petition. *See also* Form 40, Appx. G.5, *supra.*

320   See notes to Form 133, Appendix G.12, *supra.* Although a motion is required to convert pursuant to 11 U.S.C. § 706(a), the proceeding is not considered a contested matter pursuant to Fed. R. Bankr. P. 9014. *See* Fed. R. Bankr. P. 1017(d). A simple form of order should probably be submitted as well.

321   Although the debtor has the absolute right to dismiss a chapter 13 case which has not been converted, a motion to the court is required, presumably so the court can verify that indeed the debtor has not previously converted the case. Fed. R. Bankr. P. 1017(d). However, the dismissal is not considered a contested matter. *Id.* Nonetheless, some courts may require an application procedure and/or submission of a proposed order. Such a dismissal would be without prejudice, except as provided in 11 U.S.C. § 109(g), and the parties are basically returned to the positions they held prior to the case. 11 U.S.C. § 349(b); *see* § 4.7.5, *supra.*

1. This case, filed on [*filing date*], is a case under chapter 13 of the Bankruptcy Code.

2. This case has not been previously converted under section 706 or 1112 of the Bankruptcy Code.

Date: [*signature*]
Attorney for Debtors

Form 137 Debtor's Motion to Dismiss Chapter 7 Case[322]

[*Caption: Official Form 16A*]

Debtor's Motion to Dismiss Chapter 7 Case

The Debtors in the above-mentioned case, by their attorney, pursuant to 11 U.S.C. § 707, hereby move to dismiss their bankruptcy case for the following reasons:

1. A voluntary petition under chapter 7 of the Bankruptcy Code was filed by the Debtors on [*filing date*].

2. No complaints objecting to discharge or to determine the dischargeability of any debt have been filed in the case.

3. The Debtors have realized that filing a chapter 7 case was a mistake, made because they were unaware of the value of certain family heirlooms which they had inherited prior to the case, and which are sufficiently valuable so that they may not be claimed as exempt.

4. No creditor has filed a claim in this case.

5. The Debtors are willing to compensate the trustee for any expenses incurred herein.

WHEREFORE, the Debtors pray that this bankruptcy case be dismissed without prejudice.

Date: [*signature*]
Attorney for Debtors

Form 138 Debtor's Motion to Reopen Case[323]

[*Caption: Official Form 16A*]

Debtor's Motion to Reopen Case

The Debtor, by counsel, requests that the above-captioned case be reopened pursuant to 11 U.S.C. § 350(b) in order to accord relief

to the Debtor and in support thereof avers as follows:

1. The Debtor filed bankruptcy pursuant to chapter 7 of the Bankruptcy Code on May 1, 2002, and received a discharge pursuant to 11 U.S.C. § 727 on September 10, 2002.

2. Among the debts listed in the Debtor's petition and discharged in this bankruptcy case was a debt in the amount of $550.00 to [*hospital*].

3. [*Hospital*] received notice of the discharge on or about September 10, 2002.

4. In January, 2003, the Debtor began receiving calls from [*collection agency*] which represented that it was collecting the [*hospital*] debt.

5. The Debtor informed [*collection agency*] of the discharge by telephone and by letter, but nevertheless continued to receive collection calls and letters.

6. The Debtor has prepared an action against [*hospital*] and [*collection agency*] for contempt for violation of the discharge injunction applicable to this case by virtue of 11 U.S.C. § 524(a). A copy of that action is attached hereto and labeled Exhibit A [*omitted*].

WHEREFORE, the Debtor requests that this case be reopened to allow the Debtor to file and prosecute an action against [*hospital*] and [*collection agency*] for violation of the discharge injunction.

Date: [*signature*]
Attorney for Debtor

G.13 Farm Reorganization[324]

Form 139 Debtor's Motion for Permission to Apply for ASCS Programs[325]

[*Caption: Official Form 16A*]

Motion for Order Approving Debtor's Application to Participate in ASCS Programs and Request for Expedited Hearing

COMES NOW [*family farmer/debtor*] and moves the Court to enter the Order approving Debtor's application to participate in ASCS Programs, in support of which, the Debtor shows that the Agricultural Stabilization Conservation Service requires the entry of such Order as a prerequisite for participation in ASCS Programs,

---

322 The debtor does not have the absolute right to dismiss a chapter 7 case and must obtain court permission for such a dismissal. See discussion of dismissals in § 13.9, *supra*. The case may be dismissed only for cause and after notice and hearing. 11 U.S.C. § 707. Notice will normally be given to the trustee and all creditors, either by the debtor or the court. Local practice should be checked. A dismissal generally places all parties in the positions they were in prior to the bankruptcy, 11 U.S.C. § 349, and is without prejudice, except as provided in 11 U.S.C. § 109(g).

323 11 U.S.C. § 350 provides that a case may be reopened, *inter alia*, to "accord relief to the debtor." In many cases the debtor will seek relief after the case is closed related to the scope or the enforcement of the discharge. *See* §§ 14.4.3.3, 14.5, *supra*. As the discharge can also be raised defensively in non-bankruptcy forums, the debtor will have to choose in those cases between requesting reopening or proceeding armed with the discharge outside the bankruptcy case. Other problems may also sometimes require that a case be reopened, including, for example,

questions about the scope or effect of an order of the bankruptcy court, questions about newly discovered pre-bankruptcy transfers which the debtor may seek to avoid, and even occasionally disputes about the scope of exempt property.

324 These farm reorganization forms are adapted from a form book funded by the Nebraska Legal Aid Society through a grant from the Public Welfare Foundation. They were drafted by Legal Aid Society staff members Annette Higby, John Thomas, and Jan Stansberry. The form book, which includes more forms than are reprinted here, is available from the Nebraska Legal Aid Society.

325 This form is a motion for an order permitting an application to the Agricultural Stabilization Conservation Service. Most farmers will either want to continue to participate in ASCS programs or sign up to participate after the bankruptcy filing. The ASCS requires the bankruptcy court order as a prerequisite for participation.

and that the Debtor's participation in the ASCS programs is in the best interests of the creditors and of the estate.

An expedited hearing is warranted because [*family farmer/debtor*]'s participation in these programs is essential to [*his, her, their*] operation. A copy of this Motion and Request for Expedited Hearing has been sent to all interested parties.

Date:　　　　　　　　　　　　　　　[*signature*]
　　　　　　　　　　　　　　　　　　　　　Debtor

Date:　　　　　　　　　　　　　　　[*signature*]
　　　　　　　　　　　　　　　　　Attorney for Debtor

Form 140　Order Authorizing Debtor-in-Possession to Apply for ASCS Programs[326]

[*Caption: Official Form 16A*]

Order Authorizing Debtor-in-Possession to Apply for ASCS Programs

[*Family farmer/debtor*], as debtor-in-possession, has filed an application with the Court for authorization to participate in programs administered by the Agricultural Stabilization Conservation Service (ASCS), United States Department of Agriculture.

As a prerequisite for participation, the Agricultural Stabilization Conservation Service requires that if the conditions for compliance with its programs are not met, then all sums which become due from Debtor to ASCS as a result shall be treated as a loan with priority under 11 U.S.C. §§ 364(c) and 507(b). ASCS further requires that it be granted a first lien interest in any collateral pledged pursuant to its programs under 11 U.S.C. § 364(c)(2).

All the conditions and requirements mentioned in this order shall be required for the duration of any contracts made with ASCS.

In the case of some programs such as the Conservation Reserve Program and the Agricultural Conservation Program, these requirements and obligations, along with penalties, must be given priority for a ten (10) year period.

It appears to the Court that participation in ASCS programs is in the best interest of the estate and the creditors. Notice has been properly given to all creditors, and no objections being filed, participation by the Debtor-in-Possession is hereby authorized, provided the Debtor-in-Possession qualifies for such programs under the usual terms and conditions thereof, and Debtor-in-Possession is authorized to grant to ASCS a security interest under 11 U.S.C. § 364(c)(2) in collateral required by ASCS. This authorization recognizes and provides that in the event the conditions for compliance with the respective programs are not met by the Debtor-in-Possession, all payments or advances, together with liquidated damages and interest, will be repaid as required by the Agricultural Stabilization Conservation Service on a priority basis in accordance with 11 U.S.C. §§ 364(c) and 507(b).

Date:　　　　　　　　　　　　　　　[*signature*]
　　　　　　　　　　　　United States Bankruptcy Judge

Form 141　Motion for Authority to Obtain Secured Credit[327]

[*Caption: Official Form 16A*]

Motion for Authority to Obtain Secured Credit and Request for Expedited Hearing

1. [*Family farmer/debtors*] filed a petition under chapter 12 of Title 11, United States Code on [*filing date*], and are currently Debtors-in-Possession.

2. The Debtors-in-Possession conduct a farming operation at [*address*].

3. The Debtors-in-Possession obtained pre-petition from the [*creditor*] an operating advance of $[*amount—advance*] on a $[*amount—note*] master note for the [*year*] production season. Such advances are fully secured by property of the estate; a second mortgage in the Debtors' interest in the [*describe property*] in [*county*], [*state*], and a properly perfected lien on the Debtors' equipment and crops in inventory.

4. The [*family farmer/debtors*] propose that all post-petition advances made by the [*creditor*] under the above-described master note together with interest at [*interest rate*]% per annum be secured by a first and priority lien on the [*year*] crop to the extent of advances made.

5. The Debtors propose that the [*creditor*] be granted a first lien on the [*year*] crop pursuant to 11 U.S.C. § 364(c)(2) and a priority lien pursuant to section 364(d)(1) ahead of any claims arising from a mortgage, rents and profits clause, or right to a receivership but for the filing of the chapter 12 petition.

6. An expedited hearing is warranted to insure that advances necessary to put in the [*year*] crop are adequately protected and timely.

WHEREFORE, the Debtors move this honorable Court for an Order authorizing the Debtors to obtain secured credit as described in this motion.

Date:　　　　　　　　　　　　　　　[*signature*]
　　　　　　　　　　　　　　　　　Attorney for Debtors

Form 142　Cash Collateral Stipulation[328]

[*Caption: Official Form 16A*]

Cash Collateral Stipulation

[*Family farmer/debtors*], the Family Farmer/Debtors, and [*lender 1*], a secured creditor, and [*lender 2*], a secured creditor, stipulate:

1. [*Lender 1*] has a blanket lien on all machinery, livestock and crops of the [*family farmer/debtors*].

326　This form of order should be submitted with the Motion for Permission to Apply for ASCS Programs, Form 139, Appendix G.13, *supra*.

327　Operating lenders will be more likely to continue lending to a chapter 12 debtor if their post-petition advances are secured. The following motion and order provide for a first priority crop lien to the extent of the advances made.

328　A farmer's use of cash collateral must be approved by the creditor or the court. The following is a stipulation between the chapter 12 debtor and the creditor, approving the use of cash collateral and the granting of a replacement lien. *See* § 16.5.3.4, *supra*.

2. [*Lender 2*] has a second lien on all machinery, livestock and crops of the [*family farmer/debtors*].

3. The [*family farmer/debtors*] have an ongoing livestock feeding operation requiring periodic and timely sales of livestock. There is a need to purchase feed, as well as provide utilities, veterinary care, and generally continue to meet the needs of the livestock operation over the course of the next several months.

4. The [*family farmer/debtors*] must presently meet the expense of putting in the [*year*] crop including the purchase of seed, fertilizer and fuel.

5. The [*family farmer/debtors*] must rely on cash collateral to meet the expenses associated with caring for their livestock and putting in their crop.

6. The [*family farmer/debtors*] shall account in writing to the chapter 12 trustee for all such expenditures and receipts and provide a copy of such accounting to the [*lender 1*] and the [*lender 2*].

7. It is in the best interests of the chapter 12 estate and the secured creditors that this operation be kept in good condition, that the crop be put in, and that the sales of livestock are made in a timely fashion.

It is therefore STIPULATED: that the [*family farmer/debtors*] may utilize proceeds from the sale of livestock, including two checks dated [*date*], made to the order of [*family farmer/debtors*], the [*lender 1*] and the [*lender 2*] in the amounts of $[*amount*] and $[*amount*]; that the [*family farmer/debtors*] may utilize proceeds from the sale of [*number*] bushels of [*crop*]; and any cash proceeds received under the government's [*year*] and [*year*] price support and production adjustment programs. The Debtors may use such proceeds to meet the normal and customary operating expenses associated with putting in a crop and caring for the livestock.

It is further STIPULATED: that the [*lender 1*] shall be given a replacement lien in the form of a first lien on the [*year*] crop to the extent of cash collateral used; that the [*lender 1*] shall retain its lien on the Debtor's livestock; and the [*family farmer/debtors*] shall insure the [*year*] crop.

It is further STIPULATED: that the [*family farmer/debtors*] will incur no major expense without the prior written consent of [*lender 1*].

Date: [*signature*]
                              Attorney for Debtors

Date: [*signature*]
                                         [*lender 1*]

Date: [*signature*]
                                         [*lender 2*]

Form 143 Chapter 12 Plan[329]

[*Caption: Official Form 16A*]

Chapter 12 Plan

Table of Contents

1. Good Faith
2. History of Operation
3. Assets and Liabilities
4. Valuation of Property
5. Liquidation Analysis
6. Four Year Income and Expense Trend Sheet
7. Secured Creditors
8. Exemptions
9. Operation and Post-petition Financing
10. Payments Through the Plan
11. Schedule of Payments
12. Probable Tax Consequences
13. Disposable Income
14. Executory Contracts
15. Miscellaneous Provisions
16. Discharge

[*Debtor 1*] and [*debtor 2*], Family Farmer/Debtor(s), propose the following chapter 12 plan under 11 U.S.C. §§ 1221 and 1222.

1. *Good Faith*

The Family Farmer/Debtor(s), represent that it is within their ability to carry out this plan and that it is submitted in good faith.

2. *History of Operation*

The Family Farmer/Debtor(s) are ages [*age 1*] and [*age 2*], and were married on [*date*]. They have [*number*] children: [*list names and ages of children*].

The Family Farmer/Debtor(s) commenced their farming operation in [*location and type of operation*]. The Family Farmer/Debtor(s) currently operate [*location and type of operation*]. [*as appropriate*:]

The Family Farmer/Debtor(s) expanded their operation [*describe each expansion*].

The Family Farmer/Debtor(s) modified their operation [*describe each modification*].

The Family Farmer/Debtor(s) have identified the problem areas in their operation as [*describe problem*] and have taken the following steps to correct these problems:
[*state correction and success*].

The Family Farmer/Debtor(s) sought off-farm employment in [*year*].

3. *Assets and Liabilities*

The Family Farmer/Debtor(s) have filed schedules of all assets and liabilities and said schedules are incorporated herein by reference thereto.

4. *Valuation of Property*

The basis of valuation of property is as follows:
The real estate was appraised by [*appraiser*], a licensed real estate appraiser, on [*date*]. The equipment, livestock, and farm products were appraised by [*appraiser*], an auctioneer, on [*date*]. The Family Farmer/Debtor(s) are unaware if their valuation is different from the valuation of any creditor's proof of claim at this time.

5. *Liquidation Analysis*

The Family Farmer/Debtor(s) believe the following is an accurate liquidation analysis assuming immediate voluntary sale by the chapter 7 trustee paying the standard costs of liquidation.

---

329 A chapter 12 plan is required in every case. 11 U.S.C. § 1221. The requirements of the plan are set out in 11 U.S.C. § 1222. *See* § 16.5, *supra.*

Liquidation Analysis

Real Property

Farm   *No. of Acres to be Sold*   *$ per Acre*   *Total*

1.

2.

Non-Farm   *Value*

1.

2.

Liquidation Costs   *Amount*

Publication Costs

Auctioneer Fees

Closing Costs (abstracting, and so forth)

Trustee's Fees, Trustee's Atty's Fees

Other

Total: $[amount]

Net Value $[amount]

Less taxes: $[amount]

Less claim of [creditor]: $[amount]

Balance available to unsecured creditors: $[amount]

Equipment

[list farm equipment]

Liquidation Costs   *Amount*

Publication Costs

Auctioneer and Clerks' Fees

Trustee's Fees, Trustee's Atty's Fees

Other

Total: $[amount]

Net Value $[amount]

Less claimed exemption of [exemption]: $[amount]

Less claim of [creditor]: $[amount]

Balance available to unsecured creditors: $[amount]

Livestock

A. Feeder

Number	*Weight*	*Value*
[no.]pigs	[no.] at [lbs.] cwt.	
[no.]pigs	[no.] at [lbs.] cwt.	
[no.]pigs	[no.] at [lbs.] cwt.	
[no.]steers	[no.] at [lbs.] cwt.	
[no.]heifers	[no.] at [lbs.] cwt.	
[no.]calves	[no.] at [lbs.] cwt.	

Total:

B. Breeding

Number	*Weight*	*Value*
[no.]Sows	[no.] at [lbs.] cwt.	
[no.]Gilts	[no.] at [lbs.] cwt.	
[no.]Boars	[no.] at [lbs.] cwt.	
[no.]Cows	[no.] at [lbs.] cwt.	
[no.]Bulls	[no.] at [lbs.] cwt.	
[no.]Heifers	[no.] at [lbs.] cwt.	
[no.]Calves	[no.] at [lbs.] cwt.	

Total:

Liquidation Costs   *Amount*

Trucking Costs

Commission Fees

Trustee's Fees, Trustee's Atty's Fees

Other

Total: $[amount]

Net Value   Total: $[amount]

Less claim of [creditor]: $[amount]

Balance available to unsecured creditors: $[amount]

Crops

Type/Bu.	*Stored Crops*	*Price/Bu.*	*Value*
1.			
2.			
3.			
4.			

Liquidation Costs   *Amount*

Trucking Costs

Storage Charges

Penalties, Interest Due

Trustee's Fees, Trustee's Atty's Fees

Other

Total: $[amount]

Net Value $[amount]

Less claim of [creditor]: $[amount]

Balance available to unsecured creditors: $[amount]

Sealed Crops

Type/Bu.	*Year of Production*	*Price/Bu.*	*Value*
1.			
2.			
3.			

Total: $[amount]

Less Claim of [creditor]: $[amount]

Balance available to unsecured creditors: $[amount]

Vehicles

Type/Model	Year	$ on Sale
1.		
2.		

Total: $[*amount*]

Less claim of [*creditor*]: $[*amount*]

Less claimed exemption of [*exemption*]: $[*amount*]

Balance available to unsecured creditors: $[*amount*]

Miscellaneous Assets	**Amount**
Cash	
Stock	
Contract Rights	
Credit Payments	
Commodity Certificates	
Other	

Total: $[*amount*]

Liquidation Costs	Amount
Brokerage Fees	
Trustee's Fees, Trustee's Atty's Fees	
Other	

Total: $[*amount*]

Net Value	$[*amount*]

Less claimed exemption of [*exemption*]: $[*amount*]

Less claim of [*creditor*]: $[*amount*]

Balance available to unsecured creditors: $[*amount*]

Liquidation Analysis Summary

	Amount
Real Property, Balance available	
Equipment, Balance available	
Livestock, Balance available	
Crop, Balance available	
Miscellaneous Assets, Balance available	

Total: $[*amount*]

6. *Four Year Income and Expense Trend Sheet*

The Family Farmer/Debtors' farm income and expense trend sheets for the previous four years are attached hereto. The Family Farmer/Debtors' Schedule F forms for the previous four years are attached hereto.

The Family Farmer/Debtors' non-farm income for the tax year preceding the filing of this petition was $[*amount*].

7. *Secured Creditors*

A. The Family Farmer/Debtor(s) shall retain the [*number of acres*] acre parcel of farmland legally described as [*legal description*], and shall pay to the [*first lien holder*] outside the plan the total sum of $[*allowed claim*] together with interest at [*percentage interest rate*]% per annum from the

date of confirmation in equally amortized payments over a [*number of years*] year period of $[*annual payment*] commencing on the first year anniversary of confirmation. The [*first lien holder*] shall retain its lien on the above-described real estate until all such payments are made, whereupon the Family Farmer/Debtor(s) shall own the real estate free and clear of any interest of the [*first lien holder*]. The Family Farmer/Debtor(s) may prepay at anytime and in any amount without penalty.

The Family Farmer/Debtor(s) shall pay to the [*second lien holder*] outside the plan, the total sum of $[*allowed claim*], being the appraised value of the real estate less taxes owing against it and less the claim of [*first lien holder*], together with interest rate at [*percentage interest rate*]% per annum from the date of confirmation in equally amortized payments over a [*number of years*] period of $[*annual payment*], commencing on [*date of payment*].

The [*second lien holder*] shall retain its lien on the above-described property until all such payments are made, whereupon, the Family Farmer/Debtor(s) shall own the real estate free and clear of any interest of the [*second lien holder*]. The Family Farmer/Debtor(s) may prepay at any time and in any amount without penalty.

B. Joint Debtors/Co-signatures

The Family Farmer/Debtor(s) will retain the real estate legally described as [*legal description*]. The Family Farmer/Debtor(s) shall surrender [*assets*], having a value of $[*amount*], which shall be applied to their principal. Family Farmer/Debtor(s) will pay the [*creditor*] the total sum of $[*amount*], being its remaining debt and the value of its secured claim, with interest at the contract rate and shall not allow such payments to become in default. As long as such payments are made, [*creditor*] shall not act or commence any civil action to collect all or any part of this debt from [*co-signers*].

C. The Family Farmer/Debtor(s) shall retain their line of farm equipment, livestock and crops in inventory. The first $[*amount of exemption*] in value of the equipment is claimed as exempt. The Family Farmer/Debtor(s) shall pay to the [*creditor*] outside the plan the total sum of $[*amount allowed secured claim*] together with interest at [*percentage interest rate*]% per annum in equally amortized payments of $[*annual payment*] over a [*number of years*] year period commencing on [*date*] and ending [*date*]. The creditor shall retain its lien upon the above-described property until all such payments are made, whereupon, the Family Farmer/Debtor(s) shall own the real estate free and clear of any interest of the [*creditor*]. The Family Farmer/Debtor(s) may prepay at any time and in any amount without penalty.

Upon confirmation the [*creditor*] shall file amended financing statements terminating any interest in after-acquired property acquired by the debtor post petition and consequently cut off by the operation of 11 U.S.C. § 552(a).

D. The Family Farmer/Debtor(s) shall relinquish [*security property*] to the [*creditor*] which may, following confirmation, repossess the property at its own convenience.

8. *Exemptions*

The Family Farmer/Debtor(s) select the property described in their Schedule B-4 as exempt pursuant to the laws of the State of [*state*].

Upon confirmation of the plan, the Family/Farmer Debtor(s)' exemptions shall be deemed allowed and they shall own their exempt property free and clear of the claims of creditors, including the chapter 12 trustee.

Should the claimed exemptions be disallowed, the Family Farmer/Debtor(s) will pay the value thereof to the trustee, if the property is otherwise free from liens, and retain the property. If the claimed exemption is disallowed and the property is subject to a perfected lien, the Family Farmer/Debtor(s) will either surrender such property to the secured creditor, or pay the value thereof to such creditor outside the plan as otherwise provided herein and the payments to the trustee will be reduced pro rata.

9. *Operation and Post-petition Financing*

　A. The Family Farmer/Debtor(s)' cash flow projection for the year beginning [*date*], and ending [*date*], is as follows:

Amount

1. Beginning Cash Balance

Operating Sales

Amount

2. Crops

3. Livestock & Livestock Products

4. Other (Custom Work, Govt. Pmts. and so forth)

5. Breeding Livestock

6. Machinery & Equipment

7. Other

8. Non-farm Income

9. **Total Cash Available** (Add lines 1–8)

Operating Expense

Amount

10. Labor Hired

11. Repairs & Maintenance

12. Rents & Leases

13. Feed Purchased

14. Seeds and Plants

15. Fertilizer, Lime & Chemicals

16. Machine Hire

17. Supplies

18. Livestock Expense (Breeding, Vet, and so forth)

19. Gas, Fuel, Oil

20. Storage, Warehousing

21. Taxes (Real Estate & Pers. Property)

22. Insurance (Property, Liability, Hail)

23. Utilities (Electricity, Telephone)

24. Freight & Trucking

25. Auto (if not included in other items)

26. Feeder Livestock (purchased for resale)

27. Miscellaneous

Capital Expense

Amount

28. Breeding Livestock

29. Machinery repair

30. Building repair

31. Other

32. Family Living Expense

33. Income Tax & Social Security

34. Plan—Secured and Priority Payments; Principal and Interest

35. Fees and Administration

36. Trustee Fees

37. **Total Cash Required** (Add lines 10–36)

　B. The assumptions, upon which the cash-flow projection is based, are as follows:

Crop Income:

Crop	*Farm*	*Acre/Yield*	*Total*	*Price*	*Income*

[*complete as appropriate*]

Crop Expenses:

Seed	*Acres*	*$ per Acre*	*Total Cost*

[*complete as appropriate*]

Fertilizer

Crop	*Acres*	*$ per Acre*	*Total Cost*

[*complete as appropriate*]

Chemicals

Crop	*Acres*	*$ per Acre*	*Total Cost*

[*complete as appropriate*]

Livestock Income:

Livestock or Poul-try (List by Kind)	*No. of Head to be Sold*	*Estimated Total Income*

[*complete as appropriate*]

Livestock Kind/No.	*Period on Feed*	*Feed Cost per Animal*	*Total Cost*

[*complete as appropriate*]

Custom Feeding:

Kind	*No. of Head*	*Cents per Day*	*Estimated Income*

[*completed as appropriate*]

Dairy Income:

Average No. Cows	Average Production per Cow	$ per cwt.	Estimated Income

[*complete as appropriate*]

C. The Family Farmer/Debtors' credit needs for the duration of the plan shall be met by purchasing goods on open account. In addition, the Family Farmer/Debtor(s) shall utilize cash collateral from the sale of [*security property*]. The debtor(s) shall maintain a minimum value in remaining collateral of 110% of the remaining balance due on the [*creditor*]'s allowed secured claim. The Debtor(s) shall file monthly reports of inventory and values and shall permit inspection by the secured creditor or the Trustee at any time upon reasonable notice. So long as the Family Farmer/Debtor(s) maintain a value of 110% of the creditor's balance due, the creditor shall release its security interest in cash collateral to be used under this plan, by endorsing checks made jointly to debtor and creditor. *See In re* Wobig, 73 B.R. 292 (Bankr. D. Neb. 1987).

Alternative Paragraph:

The Family Farmer/Debtor(s) intend to meet their credit needs for the [*year*] crop season by borrowing operations funds from the [*creditor*]. Upon notice, hearing and authorization by the Court, [*creditor*] shall be granted a lien on the [*year*] crop to the extent of advances made post petition, pursuant to 11 U.S.C. Sections 364(c)(2) and 364(d)(10).

10. *Payments Through the Plan*

The Family Farmer/Debtor(s) will pay to the chapter 12 trustee the total sum of $[*amount*] from which the trustee will

a. Chapter 12 trustee fees and commissions, not to exceed $[*amount*], in each year of the three-year plan, in equal installments of $[*installment amount*] commencing on [*date*] and ending on [*date*].

b. Priority claims, as follows: [*list priority claims*].

11. *Schedule of Payments*

Unless the Court orders otherwise, the Family Farmer/Debtor(s) propose to make the following payments to creditors and to the trustee:

Name of Creditor	Amount of Payment	Dates of Payment	Under the Plan (Yes/No)
1.			
2.			
3.			
4.			

The Debtor(s) expect to incur $[*amount*] per year in expenses for attorney, accounting, and tax services rendered. The accounting, tax service, financial counseling service, attorney fees, and income tax and social security taxes will be paid as operating expenses outside the plan. The Family Farmer/Debtor(s) will also incur income, social security and real estate taxes after filing their petition herein which will be paid as operating expenses outside the plan.

12. *Probable Tax Consequences*

The probable tax consequences from the sale of [*assets*] as provided in this plan are: [*describe*]. Any income tax consequences arising from the discharge of indebtedness income will occur, if at all, in [*year*], upon the discharge of unsecured debt. There will be no tax consequences during the period of the plan.

13. *Disposable Income*

All of the Family Farmer/Debtors' projected disposable income to be received in the three-year period beginning on [*date*] will be applied to make payments under the plan; specifically, the Family Farmer/Debtor(s) will pay to the trustee the total sum of $[*amount*], payable as follows: [*describe*].

14. *Executory Contracts*

The Family Farmer/Debtor(s) shall [*assume/reject/assign*] the [*executory contract/unexpired lease*] as follows: [*describe*].

15. *Miscellaneous Provisions*

A. The trustee from time to time, during the period of the plan, may increase or reduce the amount of installments or may extend or shorten the time of such installments, when the circumstances of the Debtors so warrant or require, provided that any moratorium on payments or reduction in the amount, in excess of a period of 90 days, must be with Court approval.

B. Secured creditors shall retain their respective liens until all payments are made to them or until the collateral is sold as provided in this plan and the proceeds are paid to the creditor as provided in this plan.

C. If there is a dispute as to the value or interest rate of any secured claim, then the Family Farmer/Debtor(s) will pay the value of that secured claim, together with interest as finally determined by the Court. To the extent the payments to the secured creditor increase, the payments to the trustee should decrease.

D. The Family Farmer/Debtor(s) submit all or such portion of their future income to the supervision and control of the trustee as is necessary for the execution of the plan.

E. The Family Farmer/Debtor(s) shall make full payment, through the plan, in deferred cash payments, of all claims entitled to priority under section 507.

16. *Discharge*

Upon completion by the Family Farmer/Debtor(s) of all payments under the plan, other than payments to secured creditors, the Court shall grant the Family Farmer/Debtor(s) a discharge of all unsecured debts. Upon completion by the Family Farmer/Debtor(s) of all payments to each respective secured creditor, the Family Farmer/Debtor(s) shall be discharged of that creditor's debt.

Date: [*signature*]
                                                  Debtor(s)

Date: [*signature*]
                                      Attorney for Debtor(s)

Form 144 Order Confirming Chapter 12 Plan[330]

[*Caption: Official Form 16A*]

Order Confirming Plan

On [*date*], this matter came on for confirmation hearing. [*Attorney for debtor*] appeared on behalf of the debtor. [*Trustee*] appeared as trustee. The Court finds:

1. No objections have been filed against the plan [or: *All objections to confirmation of the plan have been resolved*].

2. The plan as amended complies with the applicable provision of chapter 12 and the Bankruptcy Code.

3. The plan has been proposed in good faith and not by any means forbidden by law.

4. The value, as of the effective date of the plan, of property to be distributed by the trustee or the Debtors under the plan on account of each allowed unsecured claim is not less than the amount that would be paid on such claim if the estate of the Debtors were liquidated under chapter 7 of this title on such date.

5. With respect to each allowed secured claim provided for by the plan:

    a. The holder of such claim has accepted the plan; or

    b. (1) The plan provides that the holder of such claim retain the lien securing such claim; and

        (2) the value as of the effective date of the plan, of property to be distributed by the trustee or the Debtor under the plan on account of such claim is not less than the allowed amount of such claim; or

    c. The Debtor surrenders the property securing such claim to such holder; and

6. The Debtor will be able to make all payments under the plan as amended and to comply with the plan as amended.

7. The value of the real estate to be retained by the Debtor is as follows:

    a. [*legal description*]

    b. [*legal description*]

8. The Debtor shall retain livestock and equipment valued at $[*amount*].

THEREFORE, it is so ORDERED that the Chapter 12 Plan, as amended, is confirmed.

Date: [*signature*]

            United States Bankruptcy Judge

Form 145 Disposable Income Affidavit for Chapter 12 Cases[331]

[*Caption: Official Form 16A*]

Disposable Income Affidavit for Period
[*beginning date*] to [*ending date*]

1. Cash Balance, ending _____ $_____

2. Loan funds injected into farming operation $_____

---

3. OPERATING INCOME: $_____

4. Crop: Cotton $_____

5. Crop: Oats $_____

6. Crop: Peanuts $_____

7. Crop: Watermelon $_____

8. Crop: Wheat $_____

9. Crop: Soybean $_____

9A. Crop: Squash $_____

9B. Crop: Hay $_____

10. Livestock: Swine sales $_____

11. Custom work $_____

12. Non-farm income (including Social Security and Medicare)
    $_____

13. Family donations $_____

14. Crop/property insurance receipts $_____

15. Commodity Credit Corp. receipts $_____

16. ASCS receipts $_____

17. Other receipts due to crop failure or damage
    $_____

18. Receipts for losses of livestock $_____

18A. Receipts from Coop memberships $_____

19. TOTAL RECEIPTS FROM OPERATIONS:
    $_____

20. CAPITAL INCOME: $_____

21. OPERATING EXPENSES:

22. Labor-Hired $_____

23. Machine hire $_____

24. Fertilizer/chemicals $_____

25. Seed and plants $_____

26. Feed and feed supplements $_____

27. Livestock for resale $_____

28. Gasoline, fuel and oil (farm) $_____

29. Repairs, parts & maintenance $_____

30. Utilities and telephone
(home and farm: excludes home gas) $_____

31. Insurance $_____

32. Taxes $_____

32A. Recording fees $_____

33. Rent and leases $_____

34. Interest $_____

---

330 This is a form of order which may be submitted at the time of confirmation if required.

331 This form may be required by the United States Trustee or the chapter 12 trustee to establish disposable income from a farm operation. *See* § 16.2.3.4, *supra*.

35. Storage and warehousing $_____

36. Freight and truck $_____

37. Farm spraying $_____

38. Supplies/hardware/building $_____

39. Livestock breeding fees $_____

40. Veterinary fees & medicine $_____

41. Other livestock fees (pig purchase) $_____

42. Miscellaneous membership fees, ASCS charges, bank charges $_____

43. TOTAL OPERATING EXPENSES: $_____

44. HOUSEHOLD OPERATING EXPENSES:

45. Rent $_____

46. Utilities $_____

47. Food, clothing, laundry & cleaning newspapers & periodicals $_____

48. Medical and drug expenses $_____

49. Insurance $_____

50. Transportation $_____

51. Recreation $_____

52. Church tithes, social and professional dues, union dues $_____

53. Income taxes $_____

54. Alimony, maintenance and support payments $_____

55. Other payments for support of dependents $_____

56. Child care $_____

57. Other $_____

58. TOTAL HOUSEHOLD OPERATING EXPENSES $_____

59. CAPITAL EXPENSES/PURCHASES $_____

60. Livestock $_____

61. Principal and interest payment loans (including Chapter 12 Trustee payments) $_____

62. Machinery and equipment $_____

63. Land clearing, ditching, fencing, building, and so forth $_____

64. TOTAL CAPITAL EXPENSES: $_____

65. TOTAL EXPENDITURES: $_____

66. CASH BALANCE AT END OF REPORTING PERIOD: Needed for family living expenses $_____

67. DISPOSABLE INCOME: $_____

Affidavit

State of [*state*]
County of [*county*]

Before me, the undersigned Notary Public in and for the County of [*county*], State of [*state*], personally appeared [*debtor*], Debtor, and upon oath duly sworn says that the information contained in the above affidavit is true and correct to the best of his knowledge, information and belief.

This [*date*] day of [*month*], [*year*].

[*signature*]
Debtor

[*signature*]
Notary Public
My commission expires:

[*signature*]
Unofficial Witness

Certification

I hereby certify that I have reviewed the above disposable income statement to be filed with the United States Bankruptcy Court and the same is true and correct to the best of my knowledge, information and belief.

[*signature*]
Debtor's Attorney

G.14 Consumers As Creditors

Form 146 Motion for Relief from Stay by Tenant to Raise Counterclaims to Eviction[332]

[*Caption: Official Form 16A*]

Motion for Relief from Stay

Movant by her counsel, requests that this Court modify the stay pursuant to 11 U.S.C. § 362(d)(1) to permit her to pursue claims in a state court action against the Debtors. In support of her motion she states:

1. The Debtors filed bankruptcy under chapter 11 in this case. An order for relief was entered and proceedings against the Debtors and their estate were stayed as provided in 11 U.S.C. § 362(a) as of [*date*].

2. Movant is the Defendant/Tenant in [*caption*], Housing Court No. [*number*], the state court case in which the Debtors seek to evict her from her apartment.

3. Movant has meritorious counterclaims necessary to her defense and other meritorious counterclaims in the state court case including:

a. breach of warranty;

b. negligent failure to maintain the premises;

---

332 When a bankrupt landlord seeks to evict a tenant outside the bankruptcy process, the tenant's counterclaims may be stayed. *See* Ch. 9, *supra*. This motion seeks relief from the stay in order to raise counterclaims which would constitute defenses to eviction, but not to enforce a money judgment against the debtor. Enforcement of the judgment would have to be done in the bankruptcy process.

c. retaliation;

d. violation of state law by failing to provide hot water, and by the accumulation of unmade repairs, including infestation of roaches;

e. violation of state law related to unfair trade practices;

f. intentional infliction of emotional distress;

g. failure to put the security deposit in a bank account secured from attachment and liability by the Debtors' creditors.

4. Movant's ability to defend her eviction depends in part on her right to raise counterclaims because under state law success on any of her counterclaims will provide a defense to her eviction in the state court case.

5. The issues in the state court case consist entirely of state landlord-tenant law and state consumer protection issues.

6. The state court case has been set for trial May 30, 1995.

7. Pursuit of Movant's defenses and counterclaims in the state court case will not hinder, burden, delay or be inconsistent with this case.

WHEREFORE, Movant requests that the stay pursuant to 11 U.S.C. § 362 be modified to permit her:

a. to defend in the state court case;

b. to pursue her counterclaims in that case to judgment; and,

c. to pursue any appeal therefrom; but,

d. not to enforce any judgments so obtained.

Date: [*signature*]
                                  Attorney for Petitioner

Form 147 *In Forma Pauperis* Petition and Memorandum of Law in Support[333]

[*Caption: Official Form 16A or 16D*][334]

Motion for Leave to Proceed *In Forma Pauperis*

Petitioner moves this Court, by her attorney, for an Order permitting her to file this Motion for Relief from Automatic Stay *in forma pauperis* without the prepayment of fees and costs or security therefor, pursuant to 28 U.S.C. § 1915, because she is unable to pay such fees and costs or give security therefor, as is shown by the attached certification.

Date: [*signature*]
                                  Attorney for Petitioner

[*Caption: Official Form 16A*]

Certification in Support of Motion to Proceed *In Forma Pauperis*

Movant hereby certifies that:

1. She is a tenant of the Debtor. She has raised substantial and meritorious counterclaims in an eviction action brought against her by the Debtor and she believes she is entitled to the relief sought.

2. She is the moving party in this Motion for Relief from Automatic Stay in which she is seeking permission to litigate her claims in the state court eviction action.

3. She has no substantial assets which could be liquidated to pay the filing fee herein.

4. Her sole income consists of Aid to Families with Dependent Children ("AFDC") benefits.

5. Because of her poverty, she is unable to pay the costs of this action or to give security therefor.

WHEREFORE, Petitioner prays that she may have leave to proceed with this Motion without being required to prepay costs or fees or give security therefor.

I hereby certify that the foregoing is true and correct under penalty of perjury.

Date: [*signature*]
                                           Petitioner

[*Caption: Official Form 16A or 16D*][335]

Memorandum in Support of Motion of Movant for Leave to Proceed *In Forma Pauperis*[336]

I. Indigents May Proceed in Bankruptcy Court *In Forma Pauperis* Under 28 U.S.C. § 1915

A. 28 U.S.C. § 1915 applies to proceedings in Bankruptcy Court.

28 U.S.C. § 1915 permits "Any court of the United States" to:

> authorize the commencement, prosecution or defense of any suit, action or proceeding, civil or criminal or appeal therein, without prepayment of fees and costs or security therefor, by a person who makes affidavit that he is unable to pay such costs or give security therefor.

Courts have regularly held that 28 U.S.C. § 1915 applies to fees for proceedings in bankruptcy court other than filing fees for the bankruptcy petition itself. Thus in *In re* Shumate, 91 B.R. 23 (Bankr. W.D. Va. 1988), in which a debtor sought leave to appeal a court order *in forma pauperis*, the court held that a bankruptcy court was a "court of the United States" for the purposes of 28 U.S.C. § 1915. The court held further that the limitation of 28 U.S.C. § 1930(a), requiring payment notwithstanding, section 1915, applies only, as the statutory language sets out, to "parties commencing a case."

The court in *Shumate* followed similar holdings in *In re* Moore, 86 B.R. 249 (W.D. Okla. 1988) (leave to appeal); *In re* Palestino, 4 B.R. 721 (Bankr. M.D. Fla. 1980) (leave to initiate adversary proceeding); *In re* Sarah Allen Home, Inc., 4 B.R. 724 (Bankr. E.D. Pa. 1980) (same). Other courts have reached the same conclusion. *See, e.g., In re* Melendez, 153 B.R. 386 (Bankr. D. Conn. 1993) (court has power to waive fees); *In re* McGinnis, 155 B.R. 294 (Bankr. D. N.H. 1993)(same); *In re* Jackson, 86 B.R. 251 (Bankr. N.D. Fla. 1988) (appeal *in forma pauperis* permitted); *In re*

---

333 There is normally a charge for a motion for relief from stay or to file an adversary proceeding. See Judicial Conference Schedule of Fees, found in Appendix C, *supra*. This is an application to waive those fees on behalf of an indigent creditor.

334 This form may be used in connection with a motion for relief from stay or an adversary proceeding. It should be captioned accordingly (that is, Official Form 16D should be used for adversary proceedings).

335 This form may be used in connection with a motion for relief from stay or an adversary proceeding. It should be captioned accordingly (that is, Official Form 16D should be used for adversary proceedings).

336 Obviously, this memorandum should be updated with current law as well as with cases from the relevant jurisdiction.

Weakland, 4 B.R. 115 (Bankr. D. Del. 1980) (fee in adversary proceeding, holding that section 1930(a) limitation on section 1915 applies only to filing fees).

Most of the few cases denying a right to proceed *in forma pauperis* have been cases on which clear independent grounds for denial existed. For example, in *In re* Broady, 96 B.R. 221 (Bankr. W.D. Mo. 1988) the court found the appellant was not indigent and that her appeal was "plainly frivolous." *Cf. In re* Odessa Mfg. Corp.*, 97 B.R. 1000 (Bankr. W.D. Mo. 1989) (no showing of indigency of appellant); *In re* Ghermann, 105 B.R. 712 (Bankr. S.D. Fla. 1989) (fees requested to be waived not subject to section 1915). *But see In re* Perroton, 958 F.2d 889 (9th Cir. 1992) (bankruptcy court lacks power to grant *in forma pauperis* motion).

B. The limitations of 28 U.S.C. § 1930(a) apply only to fees for commencing a case.

While 28 U.S.C. § 1930(a) expressly makes the *in forma pauperis* statute, 28 U.S.C. § 1915, inapplicable to the initial petition filing fees, the sections dealing with other fees contain no such proviso. Thus, 28 U.S.C. § 1930 does not prohibit other bankruptcy proceedings to be *in forma pauperis*. *In re* Shumate, 91 B.R. 23 (Bankr. W.D. Va. 1988); *In re* Weakland, 4 B.R. 115 (Bankr. D. Del. 1980).

Other parts of the Bankruptcy Reform Act of 1978 which enacted 28 U.S.C. section 1930 and the legislative history of the Act show that the section 1930(a) limitation on *in forma pauperis* actions is not intended to go beyond the fee for commencing a case. 28 U.S.C. § 773(c) dealing with appeals from the bankruptcy court expressly contemplates appeals *in forma pauperis*. The House Report on the 1978 Act specifically included, as a subject as to which procedural rules would have to be drafted, "provisions for in forma pauperis proceedings." H.R. Rep. No. 95-595, at 307 (1977).

II. Movant is Unable to Afford the Fee But Must Have the Right to Raise Counterclaims to Defend Her Eviction

Movant's affidavit demonstrates her indigency in that her sole income consist of AFDC benefits. She seeks only the right to proceed in a court proceeding not initiated by her and in which she has meritorious defenses and counterclaims.

Success on any of her counterclaims will provide a defense to her eviction in state court. State law provides that:

> There shall be no recovery of possession under this chapter if the amount found by the court to be due the landlord equals or is less than the amount found to be due the tenant or occupant by reason of any counterclaim or defense under this section. If the amount found to be due the landlord exceeds the amount to be due the tenant or occupant, there shall be no recovery of possession if the tenant or occupant, within one week after having received written notice from the court of the balance due, pays the clerk the balance due the landlord, together with interest and costs of suit.

Thus Movant's ability to defend her claim to her tenancy depends on the granting of her motion for leave to proceed *in forma pauperis*.

Date: _____ [*signature*]
Attorney for Petitioner

Form 148 Complaint to Determine Dischargeability of Tenant's Claims Against Landlord[337]

[Caption: Official Form 16D]

Complaint

1. This is an action for an accounting of security deposit funds paid to the Debtor pre-petition and to determine the dischargeability of certain debts pursuant to 11 U.S.C. § 523(a)(4),(6).

2. This Court has jurisdiction over this matter by virtue of 28 U.S.C. § 1334 and 28 U.S.C. § 157. This is a core proceeding pursuant to 28 U.S.C. § 157(b)(2).

3. The Plaintiffs are tenants who reside in a building which is owned and maintained by the Debtor.

4. As a condition of their tenancy, each Plaintiff paid a security deposit to the Debtor in the amount of $500.00. The Plaintiffs' receipts for said funds are attached and marked Exhibit A [*omitted*]. Said deposits were to be held by the Debtor to protect the Debtor from noncompliance with lease terms.

5. State law and the terms of the lease contract require that the landlord maintain said security deposits in a segregated account for the benefit of the Plaintiffs.

6. The security deposits were given to the landlord to be held in trust pending their disposition pursuant to state law.

7. The security deposits constitute escrows within the meaning of state law.

8. The Debtor had and continues to have a fiduciary responsibility with respect to the security deposits under state law.

9. The Debtor failed to properly maintain said security deposits in a separate account as required by law, has commingled said funds with other property and has otherwise failed to maintain the funds as required by law.

Claims

10. To the extent, if any, that security deposit payments can be traced, said funds are not included in the estate and must be held aside for the exclusive claims of the Plaintiffs in this action.[338]

11. To the extent that said funds have been commingled or used for other than their intended purposes, the Debtor has committed fraud or defalcation in a fiduciary capacity such that Plaintiffs' claims against the Debtor for the return of said funds are nondischargeable pursuant to 11 U.S.C. § 523(a)(4).

12. To the extent that said funds have been commingled or used for other than their intended purpose, the Debtor has done willful and malicious injury to property of the Plaintiffs such that Plaintiffs' claims against the Debtor for the return of said funds are non-dischargeable pursuant to 11 U.S.C. § 523(a)(6).

WHEREFORE, the Plaintiffs request that this Court assume jurisdiction of this case and order that:

---

337 This complaint seeks an accounting of a tenant's security deposit payments, or in the alternative that claims arising from failure to return the security deposits are non-dischargeable. These non-dischargeability issues under § 523 are applicable only to individual debtors. *See generally* § 17.8.5, *supra*.

338 This allegation may depend on state statutory law, the terms of the lease, or the common law related to escrow in the applicable jurisdiction.

a. The Debtor account for all security deposits paid by the Plaintiffs;

b. Funds which can be traced to security deposits paid by the Plaintiffs are outside the Debtor's bankruptcy estate and are subject to the exclusive claims of the Plaintiffs in this case;

c. Any claims which the Plaintiffs have for return of their security deposit are nondischargeable under 11 U.S.C. § 523(a)(4) or (6); and

d. Plaintiffs are entitled to such other relief as this Court deems necessary in the interest of justice.

Date: [*signature*]
                                              Attorney for Plaintiffs

Form 149 Motion for Appointment of Committee of Tenants[339]

[*Caption: Official Form 16A*]

Motion for Appointment of a Committee of Tenants

The Motion of [*tenant*] of [*building*] at [*address*], and other tenants of [*building*], whose names and addresses appear on Exhibit "A" hereto [*omitted*], respectfully represents:

1. The Debtor is a corporation which owns [*building*].

2. Movant, and the other persons whose names appear on Exhibit "A" hereto [*omitted*], are tenants and creditors of the Debtor. They seek to have their rights to safe, sanitary and habitable living conditions adequately represented.

3. The Debtor filed a voluntary petition under chapter 11 of the Bankruptcy Code on May 19, 1998.

4. Prior to the bankruptcy the Movants had informally organized to address issues related to inadequate maintenance of the building.

5. By appointing a committee of tenants in this proceeding, there will be an official spokesperson for the interests of the tenants. This will be of material assistance to this Court, the Debtor and the trustee. It will also be helpful in investigating the conduct of the Debtor in managing and operating the building.

6. The interests of the tenants are not being adequately represented in this proceeding. These interests must be protected to assure the safety and well-being of the tenants. The tenants have several claims against the Debtor which are stayed pursuant to 11 U.S.C. § 362(a). The conditions at the building have been in substantial violation of the state Sanitary Code, and in breach of the warranty of habitability at least since September, 2003, due to conscious neglect by the Debtor. The tenants have sought injunctive relief and compensatory and consequential damages in a state court proceeding. On May 27, 2004, the state court allowed the tenants' motion for provisional certification of class and for pre-

liminary injunctive relief. The court has ordered the Debtor to perform numerous repairs at the building.

7. The tenants' interests differ substantially from those of other creditors in this proceeding. In addition to a financial interest in the estate of the Debtor, the tenants' interests are related to their basic need for safe, sanitary, and decent housing at the building.

8. A committee of tenants is needed also to aid in the formulation of a plan, to protect their interests as creditors of the Debtor, and to assure that the Debtor's residential property is operated in accord with applicable state law. Without a plan to adequately address the egregious conditions at the building, the tenants will continue to be subject to unsanitary, unsafe, and life threatening conditions.

WHEREFORE, the moving parties herein pray that this Court order the appointment of a Committee of Tenants in this case, and for such other relief as is just.

Date: [*signature*]
                                              Attorney for Movants

Form 150 Expedited Motion for Appointment of Committee of Consumer Creditors[340]

[*Caption: Official Form 16A*]

Expedited Motion for Appointment of Committee of Consumer Creditors

Movant, by her attorneys, hereby requests that the Court order the appointment of a committee of consumer creditors on the following grounds:

1. Movant is a creditor of the Debtor.

2. Movant's claim arises from her pre-petition payment of $1150.00 to the Debtor for home furniture which was never delivered.

3. Movant's claim is entitled to priority, at least in part, pursuant to 11 U.S.C. § 507(a)(6).

4. There are a minimum of 150 to 200 other consumers who made pre-petition deposit payments to the Debtor for furniture or other goods for personal, family or household use that was not delivered (hereinafter "consumer creditors").

5. Approximately seventy (70) consumer creditors have already filed priority claims in this Bankruptcy Court.

6. The precise number of consumer creditors is unknown because the Debtor failed to identify any such creditors on its schedules and statement of affairs.

7. At the meeting of creditors held on February 5, 2004, the Debtor's attorney stated that the names and addresses of all the consumer claimants were not identified because the Debtor's records have been seized by law enforcement authorities.

8. According to the schedules filed by the Debtor, there are no assets in the bankruptcy estate available for distribution to unsecured creditors.

---

339 This form is a motion for appointment of a committee of tenants in a chapter 11 case. *See* 11 U.S.C. § 1102(a)(2). Two important elements of such a motion are pleading the reasons why other committees cannot adequately represent the interests of tenants and the reasons why tenants have an interest in the estate. Most often the relevant predicate for the first point will be that tenants have an interest in the maintenance of their building which is separate from the interest of other creditors. On the second point, the tenants most often will be interested in the estate based on liquidated or unliquidated pre-petition claims related to security deposits or poor conditions at the property.

---

340 This form is a motion to appoint a committee of consumer creditors in a case involving a large number of deposits by consumers to a furniture store prior to the store's bankruptcy. *See* 11 U.S.C. § 1102(a)(2). Again, as with Form 149, Appendix G.14, *supra*, it is important to differentiate the consumers' interests from those of other unsecured creditors.

9. The U.S. Trustee has not appointed a committee of general unsecured creditors or a committee of consumer creditors.

10. Presently, the interests of the consumer creditors are not represented in this case.

11. In the apparent absence of any unencumbered assets in this bankruptcy estate and the absence of any creditors' committee, a committee of consumer creditors is necessary to protect the interests of consumer creditors. Many consumer creditors paid their deposits as many as six months before the Debtor ceased operating its business, thus raising serious questions about propriety of the conduct of the Debtor and its principals. A committee of consumer creditors will be of material assistance in conducting an investigation into the affairs of the Debtor and in pursuing any appropriate legal actions to recover funds which may have been wrongfully diverted from the estate or which may otherwise be subject to recovery by the estate.

12. The consumer creditors require their own committee as their claims are entitled to priority, at least in part, and their interests are diverse from those of the general unsecured creditors.

13. The appointment of a committee of consumer creditors will not drain the estate of assets which would otherwise be available for distribution to creditors as it appears no such assets presently exist. In essence, there will be no estate unless the Court appoints the committee and the committee can create an estate.

14. Due to the possible misconduct on the part of the Debtor and/or its principals or others, the public interest and the integrity of the bankruptcy process requires that there be a meaningful inquiry into the facts of this case. Such inquiry may not take place unless this Court appoints a committee of consumer creditors.

WHEREFORE, Movant requests that the Court order the appointment of a committee of consumer creditors in this case.

Reasons for Expedited Treatment of This Motion

15. Movant, by her counsel, learned on Wednesday, February 13, 2004, at 4:45 p.m. that the U.S. Trustee would not be appointing a creditors' committee of any kind.

16. A hearing on a Motion for Relief from Stay Filed which has been filed by a secured creditor is presently scheduled for February 27, 2004.

17. From the information presently available, it appears that the secured creditor's motion seeks relief to proceed against the principal assets of the Debtor. The outcome of the February 27, 2004, hearing may substantially affect the ability of the consumer creditors to recover the furniture which, pursuant to the Uniform Commercial Code, they purchased and which they own free and clear of any interest of the secured creditor or the Debtor.

18. It is critical to the interests of the consumer creditors that they be represented at the February 27, 2004, hearing. Therefore, expedited treatment of this motion is needed.

19. Due to the hearing scheduled for February 27, 2004, Movant requests that a hearing be scheduled by the Court no later than Wednesday, February 20, 2004.

WHEREFORE, Movant requests that the Court order the appointment of a committee of consumer creditors and that her motion be considered on an expedited basis.

Date: [*signature*]
                                                Attorney for Movant

Form 151 Statement of Attorney Pursuant to Rule 2019[341]

[*Caption: Official Form 16A*]

Statement of Attorney for Tenants Pursuant to Rule 2019

[*Attorney for tenants*], as attorney for tenants of the above-named Debtors, makes the following statement pursuant to Rule 2019 of the Federal Rules of Bankruptcy Procedure:

1. I am the attorney for the tenants whose names, addresses, the nature of claim, amount of claim and time of acquisition are as follows: [*omitted*].[342]

2. I have been retained by the above-named persons to provide legal representation for matters arising from their tenancies at a building which is property of the estate. My employment was arranged [*omitted*].[343]

3. I am empowered under the terms of a written retainer to represent the above-named Plaintiffs (see attached) [*retainer omitted*].

4. My sole involvement in this case is my representation of the tenants. I do not own, nor have I ever owned, any claim whatever against the Debtor in this case.

Date: [*signature*]
                                                Attorney for Tenants

Form 152 Objection to Chapter 11 Disclosure Statement[344]

[*Caption: Official Form 16A*]

Objections of the Official Committee of Consumer Creditors to Debtor's Disclosure Statement

The Official Committee of Consumer Creditors, by its attorneys, hereby objects to the disclosure statement filed by the Debtor in this case on the following grounds:

1. The Debtor failed to give parties in interest twenty-five days' notice of the time for filing objections to the disclosure statement, as required by Rule 2002(b) of the Federal Rules of Bankruptcy Procedure.

2. The disclosure statement is not in plain English understandable by large numbers of consumer creditors to whom it is directed,

---

341 When a committee is not appointed pursuant to 11 U.S.C. § 1102 or § 1114, an attorney representing a number of tenants or other consumer creditors acting as a group is probably required to file a statement pursuant to Fed. R. Bankr. P. 2019. Failure to comply may invalidate actions taken on behalf of the group.

342 *See* Fed. R. Bankr. P. 2019(a)(1), (2), (4).

343 *See* Fed. R. Bankr. P. 2019(a)(3).

344 A chapter 11 debtor is required to file a disclosure statement prior to soliciting acceptances of a plan. 11 U.S.C. § 1125; Fed. R. Bankr. P. 3016. The disclosure statement must contain adequate information about the debtor and the plan within the meaning of section 1125(a). This form objects to a disclosure statement on behalf of a committee of consumer creditors. *See* 11 U.S.C. § 1125(b); Fed. R. Bankr. P. 3017. An objection may also be filed on behalf of an individual creditor.

who are not knowledgeable in commercial transactions or bankruptcy law. The disclosure statement seems to be designed to obfuscate rather than disclose.

3. The disclosure statement does not tell consumer creditors or other creditors anything about the likelihood of their receiving distributions as priority creditors under the plan, much less that there is little likelihood of any distributions to general unsecured creditors.

4. The disclosure statement does not inform its readers that the Debtor has not found any appropriate party to serve as a disbursing agent and that without such a disbursing agent the plan is not feasible.

5. The disclosure statement does not inform creditors that the plan cannot be confirmed if it is rejected by any consumer creditor.

6. The disclosure statement does not inform creditors that without the acceptance of creditors holding allowed secured claims the plan cannot be confirmed, and that such creditors have not to date accepted the plan.

7. The disclosure statement inaccurately states that a priority consumer creditor may be denied the right to vote on the plan based simply on the unfounded assertion that such creditor is not impaired because the Debtor "will attempt to complete the furniture orders."

8. The disclosure statement fails to inform creditors that an official committee has been appointed to represent consumer creditors and that consumer creditors may address questions about the plan to that committee.

9. The disclosure statement fails to inform creditors that information about the Debtor is unavailable due to the fact that the Debtor's principal has refused to answer any questions by invoking the Fifth Amendment.

10. The disclosure statement inaccurately states that the Debtor will receive a discharge, when such discharge is unavailable in a liquidating plan.

11. The disclosure statement refers to a cash fund to be created by a secured creditor, without giving any information about the size of such fund or whether the creditor has agreed to create such a fund.

12. The disclosure statement fails to disclose that the Debtor's plan would eliminate consumer creditors' claims against the secured creditor.

13. The disclosure statement fails to disclose the likely results of a liquidation.

14. The disclosure statement states that the plan provides for assumption of consumer creditors' contracts, when in fact the plan proposes altering those contracts by requiring consumers to pay the remainder of the purchase price on their furniture prior to delivery and by providing delivery that is so untimely that it would be considered an independent breach of the contract, and not a prompt cure as required by the Bankruptcy Code.

15. The disclosure statement should be disapproved because the Debtor's plan is not confirmable.

WHEREFORE, the Official Committee of Consumer Creditors prays that the Debtor's disclosure statement be disapproved.

Date:　　　　　　　　　　　　　　　　　　　*[signature]*
　　　　　　　　　　　　　　　　　　　Attorney for Creditors

Form 153　Objection to Confirmation of Chapter 11 Plan[345]

[Caption: Official Form 16A]

The Official Committee of Consumer Creditors' Objections to Confirmation of the Debtor's Proposed Chapter 11 Plan

The Official Committee of Consumer Creditors, by its attorney, hereby objects to the chapter 11 plan proposed by the Debtor. The bases for the objections are as follows:

1. The plan does not propose to pay priority claims in full if they do not consent to other treatment, as required by 11 U.S.C. § 1129(a)(9). As many holders of priority claims will not consent to such treatment, this defect alone bars confirmation.

2. The plan is not feasible in that no appropriate person has agreed to act as a disbursing agent for the Debtor. In fact, the committee does not believe that the Debtor has approached any governmental agency about acting as disbursing agent or that any such agency would perform the role envisioned by the Debtor.

3. The plan is not feasible in that the Debtor does not have the means to complete furniture orders as proposed, as the remaining balances on most of the orders would not be sufficient to pay the Debtor's cost of obtaining the furniture.

4. The plan unlawfully attempts to release the claims of consumer creditors against a third-party secured creditor of the Debtor.

5. The plan does not pay claims with priority under 11 U.S.C. § 507(a)(6) in full before paying claims with lower priority, and improperly places all priority claims in the same class.

6. The plan is not filed in good faith and is filed solely for purposes of delay.

WHEREFORE, the committee prays that confirmation of the plan be denied.

Date:　　　　　　　　　　　　　　　　　　　*[signature]*
　　　　　　　　　　　　　　　　　　　Attorney for Creditors

Form 154　Complaint Seeking Subordination of Secured Creditor's Claims[346]

[Caption: Official Form 16D]

Complaint

1. This adversary proceeding is brought by Plaintiffs, consumer creditors of the Debtor, to establish the priority of their rights against the Debtor's property over the rights of the creditor, which claims to have first lien priority with respect to the Debtor's property ("the secured creditor"). Plaintiffs assert that, because the secured creditor knew or should have known of the past history of questionable business practices on the part of the Debtor and/or its principals, and under principles of the Uniform Commercial Code, Plaintiffs' rights in the property of the Debtor should be found to have priority over those of the secured creditor.

345　This form objects to a chapter 11 plan on the grounds that it is not in compliance with 11 U.S.C. §§ 1123, 1129. It is filed pursuant to Fed. R. Bankr. P. 3020(b).

346　This complaint raises several theories for subordinating the claims of a secured creditor in property of the debtor to those of unsecured consumers. *See* § 17.5.6, *supra.*

2. This Court has jurisdiction over this proceeding under 28 U.S.C. § 1334. This proceeding is a core proceeding.

3. Plaintiffs are individuals who made pre-petition deposit payments to the Debtor for furniture or other household goods which the Debtor never delivered.

4. Subsequent to their dealings with the Debtor, in trying to obtain delivery of the furniture they had ordered, Plaintiffs learned that the Debtor had engaged in a variety of unfair and deceptive practices in the course of its business before closing down its operation.

5. Among other practices, the Debtor had taken deposits from numerous consumers without the ability or intent to deliver the merchandise ordered by those consumers. In the course of so doing, the Debtor made numerous false statements to Plaintiffs and others about their furniture orders.

6. Plaintiffs have learned that the Debtor never even ordered the furniture for which some consumers paid deposits amounting to thousands of dollars.

7. Plaintiffs have also learned that the principals of the Debtor operated a very similar business several years earlier, which similarly took deposits from numerous consumers for merchandise and then abruptly closed down and filed a bankruptcy case without ever delivering that merchandise.

8. The secured creditor knew or should have known of the Debtor's prior business practices when it extended credit to the Debtor.

9. The secured creditor knew or should have known of the Debtor's practices in operating because it extended credit and was in a position to police the Debtor's behavior.

First Claim

10. Some of the furniture specifically ordered by Plaintiffs may be presently stored in a warehouse containing some of the Debtor's property, which is under the control of the secured creditor.

11. As to all such furniture, Plaintiffs have rights superior to those of the secured creditor under section 9-307 of the Uniform Commercial Code, as buyers in the ordinary course of business of identified goods.

Second Claim

12. The rights of the secured creditor in the Debtor's property should be subordinated to those of Plaintiffs in this bankruptcy case, pursuant to 11 U.S.C. § 510.

Third Claim

13. The furniture held by the Debtor is held in constructive trust for Plaintiffs, and their rights in the property pursuant to that trust are superior to those of the secured creditor.

Fourth Claim

14. The secured creditor's actions in lending to the Debtor and permitting it to carry out its scheme caused damages to Plaintiffs in the amount of their lost deposits.

15. The secured creditor's actions in failing to take steps to prevent the Debtor from defrauding consumers breached the standard of care owed to customers of a borrower, resulting in damages to Plaintiffs.

16. The secured creditor is therefore liable to Plaintiffs for the damages they suffered due to the Debtor's conduct and therefore should not have priority over them with respect to the Debtor's property.

Prayer for Relief

WHEREFORE, Plaintiffs pray that this Court enter an Order:

1. Declaring that Plaintiffs have rights superior to those of Defendant secured creditor in the Debtor's property;

2. Ordering such other relief as is just and proper.

Date: [*signature*]
                                                          Attorney for Plaintiffs

Appendix H Bankruptcy Questionnaire[1]

Bankruptcy is a right provided by law to people who are deeply in debt and in need of a fresh start. Bankruptcy will discharge many of your debts and you will not have to pay them, except, in some cases, secured debts for the purchase of particular merchandise or debts on which you gave a mortgage or put up other property as collateral.

The law allows you to keep some money and most types of necessary property in bankruptcy. To receive this protection, it is necessary that you list all items asked for in the following questions: if you do not list an item, that item will not be protected in bankruptcy. You must also list *everyone* to whom you owe money. If you leave out one of your creditors, you may have to pay the money to that creditor or you may lose your right to bankruptcy. It may also be considered a crime if you intentionally give false information or leave out information. If you have any questions about whether you can keep certain property or whether you should list a debt, write that question down and remember to ask the lawyer. We know this questionnaire is long. Preparing your bankruptcy papers properly takes a lot of time and a lot of information. If we work together on this, we can protect your family from great hardship and give you the new start the law intends you to have.

There is a filing fee of $209.00 which must be paid to the court ($194.00 if your case is filed under chapter 13). If you do not have the money at the time you file, the court may allow you up to four months to pay the fee in installments. You must attend two hearings and pay the filing fee to get a discharge.

(1) Fill out *every* question on all pages. Wherever you are given a choice of YES or NO on these forms, check either YES or NO, whichever is correct. Please fill out these pages as well as you can. We will help with any questions you don't understand.

(2) Write clearly or typewrite your answers. We *must* be able to read them.

(3) Wherever the name of a person or firm is asked for, give the *full address. Make the address accurate.* Your discharge from each debt depends upon your giving a complete and correct address.

(4) If you do not know the exact amount you owe, fill in a *HIGH* estimate. Do *not* leave the amount blank and do not say "don't know."

(5) Wherever you need more room, turn the page over and put the information on the back together with the number of the question.

(6) List *every creditor and everybody* that has had anything to do with your debts, including cosigners. Please include accurate account numbers. If a bill you owe has been sent to a collection agency or any attorney, list *both* the person you originally owed *and* the collection agency or any attorney, giving the *full* address of each. If the collection agency has an attorney, list the person you originally owed, the collection agency, and the attorney, giving the full address of each.

(7) Whenever a question asks you to be prepared to give details, gather all papers concerning the matter, including bills and collection letters, and bring them with you when you return this form. In any event, be sure to bring with you the following items (unless they don't apply to you):

(a) Picture identification card and Social Security card or other document containing your social security number;

(b) Deeds and mortgages on your house or other real estate;

(c) Any insurance policies;

(d) Any papers relating to past bankruptcies and Wage Earner Plans (Chapter 13);

(e) Copies of tax returns for past two years, and copies of your last several pay check stubs;

(f) Copies of your last several bank statements and copies of statements from any other deposit accounts, such as a credit union or brokerage account, including IRAs, 401(k)s, and other pension accounts;

(g) Legal papers, lawsuits, divorce papers, separation agreements, alimony orders, and child support orders;

(h) Any appraisals or tax assessment papers;

(i) Any other papers you have concerning any of your debts; and

(j) Any lease or installment sale ("lease purchase" or "rent-to-own") agreements for housing (apartment, house, mobile home) or other property (cars, televisions, etc.) that you have signed and that are still in effect or not fully paid.

---

[1] This questionnaire is based in part on a form developed by New Haven Legal Assistance. This questionnaire is also available in Microsoft Word and Adobe Acrobat (PDF) format on the CD-Rom accompanying this volume. Use the PDF format if you wish to reprint the questionnaire, and the Word format if you want to edit the document using your word-processing program.

Complete All Questions. If you and your spouse are not living together, and there is no possibility that your spouse will file bankruptcy along with you, you don't have to answer the questions about your spouse.

1. **Name and Residence Information:**
A. Your full name: _____
    Your spouse's full name: _____
B. Your Social Security Number: _____
    Your spouse's Social Security Number: _____
C. Your date of birth and age: _____
    Your spouse's date of birth and age: _____
D. List any other names used by you or your spouse (including maiden name), or other ways you have signed your names to papers and checks during the last six years:
    _____
    _____
    _____
    _____
E. Current Address: _____
                                        (Street)

    _____   _____   _____
        (City)   (County)   (Zip Code)
F. Telephone Number: _____
G. List all addresses you have had in the last two years, the dates when you lived there, and the name you used while living there. If husband and wife are filing bankruptcy together, list addresses for each for the last two years (include street, town, and zip code).
    Addresses   *Dates*   *Name Used*
    _____
    _____
    _____
    _____
    _____

2. **Prior Bankruptcy:** Have you ever been involved before in a bankruptcy (chapter 7 or chapter 13 wage earner plan)? Yes___ No___. If yes, bring *all* papers from the case to our office.

3. **Occupation and Income:**
A. Usual type of work: _____
B. Name and address of current employer: _____
    _____
C. Spouse's usual type of work: _____
D. Name and address of spouse's current employer: _____
E. How long have you been at your current job?: _____ Your spouse? _____
F. List all income received so far this year and in the last two years by you or your spouse:
    Income Received   *Source* (Names and addresses of   *By Whom*
    (Give gross income as   employers or specify social security,   (Self or
    reported on tax returns)   welfare, unemployment, investments, etc.) spouse)
    So far this year: _____

    Last year: _____

    Year before last: _____

G. Have you or your spouse been in business by yourself or with others during the last six years?
    YES _____ NO _____. If yes, give the dates, name of the business, its address, and the names of others in business with you or your spouse. _____
    _____
    _____

H.   Are there any debts from your former business?
     YES ___ NO ___. If YES, list them in questions 32 and 33 and give details here:
     _____
     _____

I.   (1) If you employed anyone (such as regular employees, cleaning people, gardeners, babysitters), do you still
          owe them wages? YES ___ NO ___. If YES, give name and address of employee, dates worked, amount
          owed, and work done. _____
          _____
          _____

     (2) Has anyone given you money to purchase property or services that you were unable to provide?
          YES ___ NO ___. If YES, give details: _____
          _____
          _____

J.   Have you ever been on welfare within the past two years? YES ___ NO ___. Has anyone in your immediate
     family? YES ___ NO ___. If YES to either question, specify the persons, dates, amounts received, and places
     (if state welfare, name the state, if local welfare, name the city or county).
     _____
     _____
     _____

K.   Have you ever received or been told you have received more money from the government than you were
     supposed to (such as social security, welfare, unemployment compensation, food stamps, etc.)?
     YES _____ NO _____. If YES, give details: _____
     _____
     _____

L.   Do you have any vacation time that is due you from your employer? YES _____ NO _____.
     If YES, how much is due? _____
M.   Do you have an IRA or any other pension plan? YES ____ NO _____. If YES, give details: _____
     _____
     _____

N.   Are you the beneficiary of a trust or future interest? YES _____ NO _____. If YES, give details: _____
     _____
     _____

O.   Do you expect to receive more than a small amount of money or property at any time in the near future by way
     of gift or life insurance proceeds? YES _____ NO _____. If YES, give details: _____
     _____
     _____

P.   (1) Do you expect to inherit any money or property in the near future? YES ___ NO ___.
          If YES, give details: _____
          _____

     (2) Has anyone died and left you anything (including insurance benefits)? YES __ NO ___.
          If YES, give details: _____
          _____

4.   **Taxes:** (***Bring a copy of your income tax forms with you to our office.***)
A.   Have you received any tax refunds this year? YES ___ NO ___.   State $ _____ Federal $ _____
B.   What income tax refunds do you expect to receive this year?   State $ _____ Federal $ _____
C.   Does this amount include an Earned Income Credit? YES _____ NO _____.
D.   Have you already filed for the refund? YES _____ NO _____.
E.   When do you expect to receive the tax refund? _____
F.   Do you know if anyone intends to take or intercept your tax refund? YES __ NO __. If yes, give details.
     _____

G.   Did you sign an agreement or refund anticipation loan with a tax preparer to get your refund early?
     YES _____ NO _____.
H.   (1) Is any other person (such as your spouse) entitled to part of your refund? YES ___ NO ___.
     (2) Have you filed income tax returns every year for the last seven years? YES ___ NO ___.

(3) Do you owe any taxes to the United States? YES ___ NO ___. If YES, give the name and address of the department or agency to which the tax is owing, the kind of tax that is owing, and the years for which the tax is owing: _____
_____
_____

(4) Do you owe any taxes to any states? YES _____ NO _____. If YES, give the name of the state and the department or agency therein, the address of the department or agency, the kind of tax that is owing, and the years for which the tax is owing: _____
_____

(5) Do you owe any taxes to a county, district, or city? YES _____ NO _____. If YES, give the name of the county, district, or city, the kind of tax that is owing, and the years for which the tax is owing:
_____
_____

(6) Besides taxes, do you owe any other money to any branch of the United States Government (e.g., FHA, VA, repossessions or loans, withholding taxes [if you were in business], or money owed Small Business Administration)? YES _____ NO _____. If YES, give the name of the branch, its address, the amount owing, and why it is owed: _____
_____
_____

5. Debts Repaid:

A. If you have made any payments totaling more than $600 to a creditor within the last ninety days, give the name of the creditor and the dates and amount of the payments:

Creditor's Name & Address	Is the Creditor a Relative?	Payment Dates	Amount of Payment

Please make sure to bring any payment books you have with you.

B. Have you made any payments within the last year to creditors who are or were insiders (relatives or business partners)? YES _____ NO _____. If YES, give details:
_____
_____

C. (1) Have you ever had a student loan or cosigned for someone else's student loan? YES ___ NO ___.
      If YES to either question, please state:
   (2) Who lent you the money? _____
   (3) What school was the loan for? _____
   (4) Did the student finish the course of study at the school? YES _____ NO _____. If NO, why not?
      _____
   (6) Who is trying to collect the debt? _____
   (7) How much have you paid on the debt (include any tax refund intercepts)? _____
   (8) Has anyone else made payments on the debt? YES ___ NO _____. How much? $_____

6. Suits: (Bring in all papers relating to any suits or criminal cases.)

A. Have you ever been sued by any person, company, or organization? YES ___ NO _____. If YES, state:

Case Name	Case No.	Name and Address of Court	Type of Case	Result of Case

B. Have any court suits resulted in a lien being placed on your property? YES _____ NO _____.
C. Have you ever sued any person, company, or organization? YES ___ NO _____. If yes, state:

Case Name	Case No.	Name and Address of Court	Type of Case	Result of Case

D. Do you have any criminal charges or convictions? YES _____ NO _____. If yes, state:

Case No.   *Name of Court*   *Charges*   *Result of Case*   *Do You Owe Fines or Restitution?*

_____

_____

_____

E. Have you been involved in any administrative agency cases (unemployment compensation, worker's compensation, etc.) in the past 12 months? YES _____ NO _____. If yes, state:

Case Name   *Case No.*   *Agency's Name and Address*   *Type of Case*   *Result of Case*

_____

_____

_____

F. Do you have any possible reason for suing someone for damage to your property or for injuries to yourself or other members of your family? YES _____ NO _____. If YES, who could you sue, how much money is involved, and why could you sue? _____

_____

_____

7. Garnishment, Attachment, and Sheriff's Sale

A. Have you ever had any property listed for or sold at a foreclosure, tax sale, or sheriff's sale, or levied upon? YES _____ NO _____. If YES, bring any papers concerning those actions to the office and state:

What Property Was Sold   *Value of*   *Date*   *Name and Address of Creditor*
or Listed for Sale   *Property*

_____

_____

_____

B. Has money from your pay check or bank account been garnished, or taken or frozen by a creditor, including your bank or credit union, because of a debt? YES _____ NO _____. If YES, give the following:

Name and Address of Creditor   *Amount Taken*   *Dates*
Who Received the Money

_____

_____

_____

8. Repossessions and Returns

A. Have you had any property or merchandise repossessed during the last year? YES _____ NO _____.
If YES, bring all papers including all letters telling you of the repossession or sale.

Description of   *Month & Year*   *Who Repossessed Item*   *Value of Property*
Property   *of Repossession*   *(Name, Address)*   *When Repossessed*

_____

_____

B. Have you voluntarily returned any property or merchandise to the seller in the past year?
YES _____ NO _____. If YES, state:

Description of   *Month & Year*   *Seller's Name and*   *Value of Property*
Property   *of Return to Seller*   *Address*   *at Time of Return*

_____

_____

9. Property of Yours Held by Someone Else:

A. Does any other person have any of your property? (This includes any check you may have given to a payday lender or check cashing service.) YES _____ NO _____. If YES, list the following:

Type of   *Value*   *Being Held By*   *Why Is This Person*
Property   *(Name and Address)*   *Holding the Property?*

_____

_____

B.   Have you given or made an assignment of any of your property for the benefit of your creditors or any settlements with your creditors within the past two years? YES _____ NO _____. If YES, give the name and address of the creditor and the terms and conditions under which you gave the property to the creditor or made an agreement with the creditor: _____

_____

C.   Is any of your property in the hands of a court-appointed person (a receiver), or in the hands of a person who is holding it for your benefit and use (a trustee)? If YES, give details: _____

_____

_____

D.   Is any of your property in the possession of a pawnbroker, storage company or repairman?

YES_____ NO _____. If YES, describe and give its value: _____

_____

_____

_____

10.   **Gifts and Transfers:**

Have you made sales of property, mortgages, gifts, or transfers of any substantial property or cash within the last four years? YES_____ NO _____. If YES, give the following:

Name of Person Who Received Property	*Description of Property*	*Month and Year of Gift or Sale*	*Was Sale or Gift to a Relative?*

11.   **Losses:**

A.   Did you lose any substantial amount of money as a result of fire, theft, or gambling during the last year?

YES _____ NO _____. If YES, state the following:

What Caused the Loss?	*Value of the Money or Property That Was Lost*	*Date of the Loss*

B.   Did insurance pay for any part of the loss? YES__ NO__. If YES, what was date of payment? _____
How much was paid? $ _____

12.   **Payments or Transfers to Attorney or Debt Consultants:**

A.   Give the date, name, and address of any attorney or bankruptcy consultant (petition preparer, typing service, document preparation service, independent paralegal) you have consulted during the past year:

_____

B.   Give the reason for which you consulted the attorney or bankruptcy consultant: _____

_____

C.   How much have you paid the attorney or bankruptcy consultant? $ _____

D.   Did you promise to pay money to the attorney or bankruptcy consultant? YES _____ NO _____. If YES, give the amount and terms of the agreement: _____

_____

E.   Have you consulted anyone else about your debts in the past year? YES _____ NO _____. If YES, give name, address, and amount(s) paid for the service: _____

_____

F.   Did any of your debts result from a refinancing or a consolidation loan? YES ___ NO ___. If YES, which ones?

_____

Please be sure to bring all papers for these loans with you.

13. Closed Bank Accounts:
Have you or your spouse had your name on any bank account (such as savings, checking, certificates of deposit) during the past 12 months that is now closed? YES __ NO __. If YES, state:

Bank's Name and Address	Acct. No.	Type of Account (Savings/Checking)	Names of Others on Account	Date Closed	Final Balance

14. Safe Deposit Boxes:
Have you or your spouse had a safe deposit box during the last year? YES _____ NO _____.
If YES, list the name and address of the bank, the name and address of everyone who had access to the box, the contents of the box and, if you no longer have the box, the date it was closed:

_____

_____

_____

15. Property Held for Another Person: Do you have any money, property, furniture, etc. that belongs to another person or that you are holding for the benefit of someone else (in trust)? YES ____ NO____. If YES, what is the property, who owns it, and what is it worth? Include name and address of the owners:

Type of Property	Value	Owned By	Address	Relative? (Yes or No)

At what address are you keeping this property? _____

16. Leases: Have you had an auto lease, rent-to-own, or rental-purchase transaction in the past four years?
YES _____ NO _____. If YES, give details: _____

_____

_____

_____

17. Cooperatives: Are you a member of any type of cooperative (housing, food, agricultural, etc.)? If YES, give details:

_____

_____

_____

18. Alimony, Child Support, and Property Settlements:

A. Have you had any previous marriages? YES __ NO __. If YES, what is the name of your former spouse?

_____

Please be sure that any debts from prior marriages which were never paid are listed with your other debts.

B. Does anybody owe you any money or child support? YES _____ NO _____.
Who? _____ How much? $_____

C. Have you ever been ordered to pay child support? YES ____ NO ____.
Alimony? YES ____ NO ____.
Property Settlement? YES ____ NO ____.
If yes to any question, state:
(1) To whom do you make the payments? _____
(2) Are you behind in your payments? _____
(3) Are the persons you are required to support this way on welfare? _____
(4) Do you have any family court hearings coming up? If yes, explain and give dates:

_____

_____

D. Do you expect to be involved in a property settlement with your spouse in the near future?
YES _____ NO _____.

19. **Accidents and Driver's License:**
A.   Have you been involved in a vehicle accident in the last four years? YES ____ NO ____.
B.   Has your vehicle been involved in an accident in the last four years? YES ____ NO ____.
C.   Have your children ever injured anyone else or their property? YES ____ NO ____.
D.   Have you ever lost your driver's license? YES ____ NO ____. If YES, give details:
_____
_____
_____

20. **Cosigners and Debts Incurred for Other People:**
A.   Were there any cosigners for you on any of the debts you have listed in these forms?
YES _____ NO _____. If YES, give the cosigner's name and address, and which debts were cosigned:
_____

B.   Have you ever been the cosigner on someone else's loan or debt which hasn't been paid off?
YES __ NO __. If yes, list the following for each debt:

Creditor's Name and Address	*Date of Debt*	*Amount Owing*	*Name and Address of Person You Cosigned For*

C.   Have you borrowed any money for someone else's benefit? YES _____ NO _____. If YES, list the following
unless you are sure that loan or debt has been paid:

Creditor's Name and Address	*Collection Agent or Attorneys*	*Date of Debt and Which Spouse Owes*	*For What*	*Current Amount of Claim*

D.   If you put up any of your property as collateral on a debt you cosigned, list the following:

Creditor	*Type of Property*	*How Much the Property Is Worth Now*

21. **Credit Card and Finance Company Debts**
A.   Have you obtained cash advances of more than $1000 or used any credit card to purchase more than $1000 worth
of goods or services in the last sixty days? YES _____ NO _____. If YES, give details: _____
_____

B.   Have you ever gone over your credit limit on any credit cards? YES ___ NO ___. If YES, give details:
_____

C.   If any of your debts listed on this form are owed to finance companies, did you sign an agreement that listed
some of your property (such as a second television or VCR) and stated that the property would be security or
collateral for the loan? YES _____ NO _____. If YES, which ones?
_____

D.   Do you owe money on a payday loan or for a check cashing service? YES ___ NO ___. If YES give details:
_____
_____

22. Secured Debts (Answer Every Question). Do you owe any money for any property or goods which can be repossessed or foreclosed if you fail to make payments? YES _____ NO _____. Have you agreed with any creditor that it can take any of your possessions from you, such as your car or your furniture, if you don't keep up with your payments? YES _____ NO _____. Do you have any mortgages or liens on your property? YES _____ NO _____. For all these debts, give the following information, including the full name and address of the creditor AND the attorney or collection agency.

Names and Addresses of Creditor, Collection Agency, & Attorney	Acct. No.	Date & Purpose of Debt	What Property Is Collateral or Subject to Lien?	Current Value of Property	Original Amount Owed	Current Balance	Monthly Payment & No. of Payments Behind	Who Owes? (Which Spouse? Co-signers?)

If the collateral is a home or a car, do you have insurance on the property? YES _____ NO _____.

Is any of the collateral located somewhere other than your home? YES _____ NO _____. If YES, describe: _____

Do you dispute any of these debts? YES _____ NO _____. If yes, which ones? _____

Do you have an FHA, FmHA or VA Mortgage? _____

23. **Unsecured Debts:** List all creditors, including creditors who have judgments or whose claims you dispute. Anyone who you think may have a claim against you must be listed even if the claim is old. **For each debt, please give all information requested. If a collection agency or an attorney is involved, list it and the person or company you originally owed.**

Creditor's Name and Address	Name and Address of Collection Agency and Attorney, If Any	Account No.	Date of Debt	What Is Debt For?	Current Amount of Claim	Which Spouse Owes?	Any Co-signers?

Do you dispute any of these debts? YES _____ NO _____. If YES, which ones? _____

Now review all the debts you have listed on this page and the last. Have you forgotten any:

medical bills?
credit card bills?
store charges?
cable T.V. bills?
payday loans?

mail order bills?
judgments?
loan companies?
debts you cosigned?
provided to your dependents?

schools?
student loans?
welfare debts?
back rent?

condominium assessments?
traffic tickets or parking tickets?
criminal restitution debts?
bills for goods or services?
bills owed to old landlords?

utility or telephone bills?
loans from relatives?
money owed to creditors who repossessed your property?

24. **Asset Listing:**

(If you are married and living with your spouse, designate any items listed below that are not jointly owned.)

A.   REAL PROPERTY:

(1)   Do you own real estate? YES _____ NO _____. Describe and give the location of all real property (lot, house, condominium, cooperative, land, burial plot, etc.) in which you hold an interest:

_____

_____

_____

(2)   Co-owners: _____

(3)   Outstanding mortgage balance: _____

(4)   Name of mortgage company: _____

(5)   Purchase price: _____ Year purchased: _____

(6)   Present value of your house: _____

(7)   Are there any other mortgages? YES __ NO __. If YES, give the name and address of each company:

_____

_____

(8)   Is any mortgage insured by the FHA, VA, or a private mortgage insurance company?

YES _____ NO _____. If YES, give details: _____

B.   PERSONAL PROPERTY:

(1)   Cash on hand: $_____

(2)   Do you have any deposits of money in banks, savings and loan associations, or credit unions? If YES, list the name and address of the bank, savings and loan association, or credit union, and the amount:

_____

_____

(3)   Have you given a security deposit to any landlord, utility, or anyone else? YES _____ NO _____. If YES, list the name and address of the person or company and the amount:

_____

_____

(4)   List your major property items such as stove, refrigerator, TV, sewing machine, furniture, guns, etc., giving approximate age and value (what you could get for it if you sold it). (These goods usually can be protected, but you must list them to protect them.)

Item	*Approximate Age*	*Value (What You Could Get for It If You Sold It)*

If any of the above items are being financed through a company, list the item and the name and address of the company below: _____

_____

_____

(5)   Give an estimate of the value (what you could get for it if you sold it) of the following:

All your furniture not already listed: $_____ All your clothing: $_____ All minor appliances not already listed: $_____ All your household goods not already listed (dishes, utensils, food, etc.): $_____

(6)   List each item of jewelry that you own, and an estimate of its value (what you could get for it if you sold it):

_____

C.   CARS, MOBILE HOMES, TRAILERS AND BOATS:

Do you have any cars, trucks, mobile homes, boats, trailers, or motorcycles? YES _____ NO _____. If YES, give the year, make, model, value, who is financing it, and amount owed:

_____

_____

_____

D.   OTHER PROPERTY:

Do you own any life insurance policies? YES _____ NO _____.

If YES, list insurance company's name and address: _____

_____

How long have you had each policy? _____

Cash surrender value: _____

Do you have any other insurance, including credit insurance? YES _____ NO _____. If YES, describe:

_____

Do you expect to receive any money from any insurance in the near future? YES _____ NO _____. If YES, give details: _____

_____

Do you own any stocks? YES _____ NO _____. Value: $_____

Do you own any bonds (including U.S. Savings Bonds)? YES ____ NO ____. Value: $_____

Do you own any machinery, tools, or fixtures used in your business or work? YES ____ NO ____. If YES, list and state what you could sell it for: _____

_____

Do you have any animals or pets? YES _____ NO _____. If YES, describe and give value (what you could sell them for): _____

_____

_____

Do you have any right to receive commissions or other payments from any previous job you have held? YES _____ NO _____. Does anyone owe you any money? YES _____ NO _____. If YES to either, state names, addresses and amounts owed: _____

_____

Do you have any books, prints or pictures, stamps or coins, or sports equipment of substantial value? YES _____ NO _____. If YES, describe and estimate their value: _____

_____

_____

Do you have any stock in trade (inventory)? YES ____ NO ____. If YES, describe and estimate the value:

_____

Do you own anything else not mentioned above? YES _____ NO _____. If YES, describe and state its value (what you could sell it for): _____

_____

_____

Does any of the property that you own or possess pose a threat of harm to public health or safety? YES _____ NO _____.

Is the threat imminent? YES _____ NO _____.

Has anyone ever alleged that any of the property that you own or possess poses a threat of imminent harm to public health or safety? YES _____ NO _____.

Was the threat alleged to be imminent? YES _____ NO _____.

Give details regarding any threat or alleged threat to public health or safety, including identification of property and nature of potential harm or alleged harm. _____

_____

_____

_____

25. Budget Information

A. Do you currently receive your pay or other income (check one)

	YOU	YOUR SPOUSE
WEEKLY	_____	_____
EVERY 2 WEEKS	_____	_____
MONTHLY	_____	_____
OTHER	_____	_____

B. What is the gross amount received in wages or other income (before taxes or other deductions)?

	YOU	YOUR SPOUSE
	_____	_____

C. What deductions, if any, are taken out?

	YOU	YOUR SPOUSE
Taxes	_____	_____
Insurance	_____	_____
Union dues	_____	_____
Other (identify: _____)	_____	_____

D. What is the usual amount of your check (take-home pay)?

	YOU	YOUR SPOUSE
	_____	_____

E. Is your job subject to seasonal or other changes?

YOU	YES _____	NO _____
YOUR SPOUSE	YES _____	NO _____

F. What was your gross income (reported on W-2 form and tax return) for last year?

	YOU	YOUR SPOUSE
	_____	_____

G. List all dependents of either spouse.

	NAME	AGE	RELATIONSHIP
YOU	_____	_____	_____
	_____	_____	_____
YOUR SPOUSE	_____	_____	_____
	_____	_____	_____

H. Do you expect your income to increase or decrease more than 10% in the next year? YES ____ NO _____.

J. Do you expect to have any major expenses (like medical bills) in the near future? YES____ NO_____.
    If YES, describe: _____
    _____

K. Does either spouse or do your children receive income from any source other than jobs, alimony, maintenance, or support listed above (such as public assistance, unemployment compensation, social security, SSI, pension, etc.)? YES _____ NO _____. If YES, list:

Source of Income	*To Whom Payable*	*Amount per Month*
_____	_____	_____
_____	_____	_____
_____	_____	_____

L. Is your family eligible for food stamps? YES _____ NO _____.
    If YES, how much in food stamps do you receive per month? $_____.

M.   Monthly Expenses. (Give <u>realistic</u> estimates. If your expenses add up to more than the income you have listed, or less than your income, be prepared to explain why.)

What are your average monthly expenses for:

Rent or mortgage   _____
     Are real estate taxes included? ___
     Is property tax included? ___
Electricity   _____
Heat   _____
Water   _____
Telephone   _____
Other utilities   _____
Home maintenance (repairs and upkeep)   _____
Food (cash you spend on food)   _____
Amount of food stamps you spend   _____
Clothing   _____
Laundry and cleaning   _____
Medications   _____
Other medical and dental expenses   _____
Public transportation   _____
Automobile upkeep   _____
Gasoline and oil   _____
Newspapers, magazines, school books   _____
Recreation   _____
Charitable contributions   _____
Club and union dues (not deducted from wages)   _____
Insurance (not deducted from wages)
     Homeowner's or renter's   _____
     Life   _____
     Health   _____
     Auto   _____
     Other _____   _____
Taxes (not deducted from wages
     or included in mortgage payment)   _____
Installment payments
     Vehicle   _____
     Other _____   _____
     Other _____   _____
Alimony, maintenance or support payments   _____
Other payments for support of dependents   _____
Expenses for operating your business   _____
Other expenses (list types of expenses) (e.g.,
     home maintenance, cable T.V., school)
     Identify: _____   _____
     _____   _____
     _____   _____

Appendix I	# Bankruptcy Client Handouts

I.1 Introduction

This appendix contains four client handouts. The National Consumer Law Center provides copyright permission for individuals and organizations to copy or adapt these handouts for distribution without charge to consumers. No permission is granted to include these materials in other publications for sale.

To facilitate adaption of these materials, they are also found in both Microsoft Word and Adobe Acrobat (PDF) format on the CD-Rom accompanying this volume. Copy them into a word-processing program and edit them to meet individual needs.

I.2 Answers to Common Bankruptcy Questions
I.3 Your Legal Rights During and After Bankruptcy: Making the Most of Your Bankruptcy Discharge
I.4 Using Credit Wisely After Bankruptcy
I.5 Advice on Filing a Chapter 7 Bankruptcy

Additional Client Resources

NCLC Guide to Surviving Debt is NCLC's most popular book, with a new edition due out in early 2005. *NCLC Guide to Surviving Debt* provides precise, practical advice on how to deal with an overwhelming debt load, including such topics as:

- Bankruptcy rights;
- Dealing with debt collectors;
- What consumers need to know about their credit rating;
- Which debts to pay first;
- Refinancing do's and don'ts;
- Saving a home from foreclosure;
- Automobile repossessions;
- Evictions and utility shutoffs;
- Credit card debt;
- Student loans.

A number of bankuptcy practitioners and credit counselors purchase bulk-discounted quantities of this book to distribute to clients, by calling (617) 542-9595. Consumers can also purchase individual copies by calling the same telephone number or by ordering securely on-line at www.consumerlaw.org.

The second and third handouts, Appendices I.3 and I.4, *infra*, are available in bulk in color, nicely designed, printed, and folded. While supplies last, there will be a modest charge for such bulk orders. Contact NCLC Publications at (617) 542-9595.

A large number of additional consumer education brochures are found on the CD-Rom accompanying this volume, and are also available free of charge at www.consumerlaw.org.

Credits

The first handout, Appendix I.2, *infra*, is adapted from a pamphlet prepared by Legal Services, Inc., under a grant from the Pennsylvania Law Coordination Center, and from National Consumer Law Center, *NCLC Guide to Surviving Debt*.

The fourth handout, Appendix I.5, *infra*, is adapted from a form developed by John T. Orcutt, Esq., in Raleigh, North Carolina. Other client forms, checklists and practice documents prepared by Mr. Orcutt are available on his firm's website, www.johnorcutt.com/hdfiles.htm.

I.2 Answers to Common Bankruptcy Questions

A decision to file for bankruptcy should be made only after determining that bankruptcy is the best way to deal with your financial problems. This brochure cannot explain every aspect of the bankruptcy process. If you still have questions after reading it, you should speak with an attorney familiar with bankruptcy or a paralegal working for an attorney.

What Is Bankruptcy?

Bankruptcy is a legal proceeding in which a person who cannot pay his or her bills can get a fresh financial start. The right to file for bankruptcy is provided by federal law, and all bankruptcy cases are handled in federal court. Filing bankruptcy immediately stops all of your creditors from seeking to collect debts from you, at least until your debts are sorted out according to the law.

What Can Bankruptcy Do for Me?

Bankruptcy may make it possible for you to:

- Eliminate the legal obligation to pay most or all of your debts. This is called a "discharge" of debts. It is designed to give you a fresh financial start.
- Stop foreclosure on your house or mobile home and allow you an opportunity to catch up on missed payments. (Bankruptcy does not, however, automatically eliminate mortgages and other liens on your property without payment.)
- Prevent repossession of a car or other property, or force the creditor to return property even after it has been repossessed.
- Stop wage garnishment, debt collection harassment, and similar creditor actions to collect a debt.
- Restore or prevent termination of utility service.
- Allow you to challenge the claims of creditors who have committed fraud or who are otherwise trying to collect more than you really owe.

What Bankruptcy Cannot Do

Bankruptcy cannot, however, cure every financial problem. Nor is it the right step for every individual. In bankruptcy, it is usually *not* possible to:

- Eliminate certain rights of "secured" creditors. A "secured" creditor has taken a mortgage or other lien on property as collateral for the loan. Common examples are car loans and home mortgages. You *can* force

secured creditors to take payments over time in the bankruptcy process and bankruptcy *can* eliminate your obligation to pay any additional money if your property is taken. Nevertheless, you generally cannot keep the collateral unless you continue to pay the debt.
- Discharge types of debts singled out by the bankruptcy law for special treatment, such as child support, alimony, certain other debts related to divorce, most student loans, court restitution orders, criminal fines, and some taxes.
- Protect cosigners on your debts. When a relative or friend has co-signed a loan, and the consumer discharges the loan in bankruptcy, the cosigner may still have to repay all or part of the loan.
- Discharge debts that arise after bankruptcy has been filed.

What Different Types of Bankruptcy Cases Should I Consider?

There are four types of bankruptcy cases provided under the law:

- *Chapter 7* is known as "straight" bankruptcy or "liquidation." It requires a debtor to give up property which exceeds certain limits called "exemptions," so the property can be sold to pay creditors.
- *Chapter 11*, known as "reorganization," is used by businesses and a few individual debtors whose debts are very large.
- *Chapter 12* is reserved for family farmers.
- *Chapter 13* is called "debt adjustment." It requires a debtor to file a plan to pay debts (or parts of debts) from current income.

Most people filing bankruptcy will want to file under either chapter 7 or chapter 13. Either type of case may be filed individually or by a married couple filing jointly.

Chapter 7 (Straight Bankruptcy)

In a bankruptcy case under chapter 7, you file a petition asking the court to discharge your debts. The basic idea in a chapter 7 bankruptcy is to wipe out (discharge) your debts in exchange for your giving up property, except for "exempt" property which the law allows you to keep. In most cases, all of your property will be exempt. But property which is not exempt is sold, with the money distributed to creditors.

If you want to keep property like a home or a car and are behind on the payments on a mortgage or car loan, a chapter 7 case probably will not be the right choice for you. That is because chapter 7 bankruptcy does not eliminate the right of mortgage holders or car loan creditors to take your property to cover your debt.

Chapter 13 (Reorganization)

In a chapter 13 case you file a "plan" showing how you will pay off some of your past-due and current debts over three to five years. The most important thing about a chapter 13 case is that it will allow you to keep valuable property—especially your home and car—which might otherwise be lost, if you can make the payments which the bankruptcy law requires to be made to your creditors. In most cases, these payments will be at least as much as your regular monthly payments on your mortgage or car loan, with some extra payment to get caught up on the amount you have fallen behind.

You should consider filing a chapter 13 plan if you

(1) own your home and are in danger of losing it because of money problems;

(2) are behind on debt payments, but can catch up if given some time;

(3) have valuable property which is not exempt, but you can afford to pay creditors from your income over time.

You will need to have enough income in chapter 13 to pay for your necessities and to keep up with the required payments as they come due.

What Does It Cost to File for Bankruptcy?

It now costs $209 to file for bankruptcy under chapter 7 and $194 to file for bankruptcy under chapter 13, whether for one person or a married couple. The court may allow you to pay this filing fee in installments if you cannot pay all at once. If you hire an attorney you will also have to pay the attorney's fees you agree to.

What Property Can I Keep?

[*Note to the Attorney: This answer is accurate for states that permit the federal exemptions. For states which have opted out of federal exemptions, the answer must be adapted to indicate that the debtor's exemptions are those specified by state law.*]

In a chapter 7 case, you can keep all property which the law says is "exempt" from the claims of creditors. You can choose between your exemptions under your state law or under federal law. In many cases, the federal exemptions are better.

Federal exemptions include:

- $18,450 in equity in your home;
- $2950 in equity in your car;
- $475 per item in any household goods up to a total of $9850;
- $1850 in things you need for your job (tools, books, etc.);

- $975 in any property, plus part of the unused exemption in your home, up to $9250;
- Your right to receive certain benefits such as social security, unemployment compensation, veteran's benefits, public assistance, and pensions—regardless of the amount.

The amounts of the exemptions are doubled when a married couple files together.

In determining whether property is exempt, you must keep a few things in mind. The value of property is not the amount you paid for it, but what it is worth now. Especially for furniture and cars, this may be a lot less than what you paid or what it would cost to buy a replacement.

You also only need to look at your equity in property. This means that you count your exemptions against the full value minus any money that you owe on mortgages or liens. For example, if you own a $50,000 house with a $40,000 mortgage, you count your exemptions against the $10,000 which is your equity if you sell it.

While your exemptions allow you to keep property even in a chapter 7 case, your exemptions do not make any difference to the right of a mortgage holder or car loan creditor to take the property to cover the debt if you are behind. In a chapter 13 case, you can keep all of your property if your plan meets the requirements of the bankruptcy law. In most cases you will have to pay the mortgages or liens as you would if you didn't file bankruptcy.

What Will Happen to My Home and Car If I File Bankruptcy?

In most cases you will not lose your home or car during your bankruptcy case as long as your equity in the property is fully exempt. Even if your property is not fully exempt, you will be able to keep it, if you pay its non-exempt value to creditors in chapter 13.

However, some of your creditors may have a "security interest" in your home, automobile or other personal property. This means that you gave that creditor a mortgage on the home or put your other property up as collateral for the debt. Bankruptcy does not make these security interests go away. If you don't make your payments on that debt, the creditor may be able to take and sell the home or the property, during or after the bankruptcy case.

There are several ways that you can keep collateral or mortgaged property after you file bankruptcy. You can agree to keep making your payments on the debt until it is paid in full. Or you can pay the creditor the amount that the property you want to keep is worth. In some cases involving fraud or other improper conduct by the creditor, you may be able to challenge the debt. If you put up your household goods as collateral for a loan (other than a loan to purchase the goods), you can usually keep your property without making any more payments on that debt.

Can I Own Anything After Bankruptcy?

Yes! Many people believe they cannot own anything for a period of time after filing for bankruptcy. This is not true. You can keep your exempt property and anything you obtain after the bankruptcy is filed. However, if you receive an inheritance, a property settlement, or life insurance benefits within 180 days after filing for bankruptcy, that money or property may have to be paid to your creditors if the property or money is not exempt.

Will Bankruptcy Wipe Out All My Debts?

Yes, with some exceptions. Bankruptcy will not normally wipe out:

(1) money owed for child support or alimony, fines, and some taxes;

(2) debts not listed on your bankruptcy petition;

(3) loans you got by knowingly giving false information to a creditor, who reasonably relied on it in making you the loan;

(4) debts resulting from "willful and malicious" harm;

(5) student loans owed to a school or government body, except if the court decides that payment would be an undue hardship;

(6) mortgages and other liens which are not paid in the bankruptcy case (but bankruptcy will wipe out your obligation to pay any additional money if the property is sold by the creditor).

Will I Have to Go to Court?

In most bankruptcy cases, you only have to go to a proceeding called the "meeting of creditors" to meet with the bankruptcy trustee and any creditor who chooses to come. Most of the time, this meeting will be a short and simple procedure where you are asked a few questions about your bankruptcy forms and your financial situation.

Occasionally, if complications arise, or if you choose to dispute a debt, you may have to appear before a judge at a hearing. If you need to go to court, you will receive notice of the court date and time from the court and/or from your attorney.

Will Bankruptcy Affect My Credit?

There is no clear answer to this question. Unfortunately, if you are behind on your bills, your credit may already be bad. Bankruptcy will probably not make things any worse.

The fact that you've filed a bankruptcy can appear on your credit record for ten years. But since bankruptcy wipes out your old debts, you are likely to be in a better position to pay your current bills, and you may be able to get new credit.

What Else Should I Know?

Utility services—Public utilities, such as the electric company, cannot refuse or cut off service because you have filed for bankruptcy. However, the utility can require a deposit for future service and you do have to pay bills which arise after bankruptcy is filed.

Discrimination—An employer or government agency cannot discriminate against you because you have filed for bankruptcy.

Driver's license—If you lost your license solely because you couldn't pay court-ordered damages caused in an accident, bankruptcy will allow you to get your license back.

Co-signers—If someone has co-signed a loan with you and you file for bankruptcy, the co-signer may have to pay your debt. If you file a chapter 13, you may be able to protect co-signers, depending upon the terms of your chapter 13 plan.

How Do I Find a Bankruptcy Attorney?

As with any area of the law, it is important to carefully select an attorney who will respond to your personal situation. The attorney should not be too busy to meet you individually and to answer questions as necessary.

The best way to find a trustworthy bankruptcy attorney is to seek recommendations from family, friends or other members of the community, especially any attorney you know and respect. You should carefully read retainers and other documents the attorney asks you to sign. You should not hire an attorney unless he or she agrees to represent you throughout the case.

In bankruptcy, as in all areas of life, remember that the person advertising the cheapest rate is not necessarily the best. Many of the best bankruptcy lawyers do not advertise at all.

Paying for debt counseling is almost never a good idea. There is almost nothing that a paid debt counselor can offer other than a recommendation about whether bankruptcy is appropriate and a list of highly priced debt consolidation lenders. There is no good reason to pay someone for this service. A reputable attorney will generally provide counseling on whether bankruptcy is the best option. This avoids the double charge of having to pay a counselor and then an attorney. If bankruptcy is not the right answer for you, a good attorney will offer a range of other suggestions.

Document preparation services also known as "typing services" or "paralegal services" involve non-lawyers who offer to prepare bankruptcy forms for a fee. Problems with these services often arise because non-lawyers cannot offer advice on difficult bankruptcy cases and they offer no services once a bankruptcy case has begun. There are also many shady operators in this field, who give bad advice and defraud consumers.

When first meeting a bankruptcy attorney, you should be prepared to answer the following questions:

- What types of debt are causing you the most trouble?
- What are your significant assets?
- How did your debts arise and are they secured?
- Is any action about to occur to foreclose or repossess property or to shut off utility service?
- What are your goals in filing the case?

Can I File Bankruptcy Without an Attorney?

Although it may be possible for some people to file a bankruptcy case without an attorney, it is not a step to be taken lightly. The process is difficult and you may lose property or other rights if you do not know the law. It takes patience and careful preparation. Chapter 7 (straight bankruptcy) cases are easier. Very few people have been able to successfully file chapter 13 (debt adjustment) cases on their own.

Remember: The law often changes. Each case is different. This pamphlet is meant to give you general information and not to give you specific legal advice.

I.3 Your Legal Rights During and After Bankruptcy: Making the Most of Your Bankruptcy Discharge

About Bankruptcy

Bankruptcy is a choice that may help if you are facing serious financial problems. You may be able to cancel your debts, stop collection calls, and get a fresh financial start. Although bankruptcy can help with some financial problems, its effects are not permanent. If you choose bankruptcy, you should take advantage of the fresh start it offers and then make careful decisions about future borrowing and credit, so you won't ever need to file bankruptcy again!

How Long Will Bankruptcy Stay on My Credit Report?

The results of your bankruptcy case will be part of your credit record for *ten (10) years*. The ten years are counted from the date you filed your bankruptcy.

This does not mean you can't get a house, a car, a loan, or a credit card for ten years. In fact, you can probably get credit even before your bankruptcy is over! The question is, how much interest and fees will you have to pay? And, can you afford your monthly payments, so you don't begin a new cycle of painful financial problems.

Which Debts Do I Still Owe After Bankruptcy?

When your bankruptcy is completed, many of your debts are "discharged." This means they are canceled and you are no longer legally obligated to pay them.

However, certain types of debts are NOT discharged in bankruptcy. The following debts are among the debts that generally may not be canceled by bankruptcy:

- *Alimony, maintenance or support for a spouse or children.*
- *Student loans.* Almost no student loans are canceled by bankruptcy. But you can ask the court to discharge the loans if you can prove that paying them is an "undue hardship." Occasionally, student loans can be canceled for reasons not related to your bankruptcy when, for example, the school closed before you completed the program or if you have become disabled. There are also many options for reducing your monthly payments on student loans, even if you can't discharge them. For more information, look at *NCLC Guide to Surviving Debt.*

- *Money borrowed by fraud or false pretenses.* A creditor may try to prove in court during your bankruptcy case that you lied or defrauded them, so that your debt cannot be discharged. A few creditors (mainly credit card companies) accuse debtors of fraud even when they have done nothing wrong. Their goal is to scare honest families so that they agree to reaffirm the debt. You should never agree to reaffirm a debt if you have done nothing wrong. If the company files a fraud case and you win, the court may order the company to pay your lawyer's fees
- *Most taxes.* The vast majority of tax debts cannot be discharged. However, this can be a complicated issue. If you have tax debts you will need to discuss these issues with your lawyer.
- *Most criminal fines, penalties and restitution orders.* This exception includes even minor fines, including traffic tickets.
- *Drunk driving injury claims.*

If you have debts that may not be discharged, you should discuss with your lawyer whether filing or converting to a chapter 13 may help.

Do I Still Owe Secured Debts (Mortgages, Car Loans) After Bankruptcy?

Yes and No. The term "secured debt" applies when you give the lender a mortgage, deed of trust or lien on property as collateral for a loan. The most common types of secured debts are home mortgages and car loans. The treatment of secured debts after bankruptcy can be confusing.

Bankruptcy cancels your personal legal obligation to pay a debt, even a secured debt. This means the secured creditor can't sue you after a bankruptcy to collect the money you owe.

But, and this is a big "but," the creditor can still take back their collateral if you don't pay the debt. For example, if you are behind on a car loan or home mortgage, the creditor can ask the bankruptcy court for permission to repossess your car or foreclose on the home. Or the creditor can just wait until your bankruptcy is over and then do so. Although a secured creditor can't sue you if you don't pay, that creditor can usually take back the collateral.

For this reason, if you want to keep property that is collateral for a secured debt, you will need to catch up on the payments and continue to make them during and after bankruptcy, keep any required insurance, and you may have to reaffirm the loan.

What Is Reaffirmation?

Although you filed bankruptcy to cancel your debts, you have the option to sign a written agreement to "reaffirm" a debt. If you choose to reaffirm, you agree to be *legally obligated* to pay the debt despite bankruptcy. If you reaffirm, the debt is not canceled by bankruptcy. If you fall behind on a reaffirmed debt, you can get collection calls, be sued, and possibly have your pay attached or other property taken.

Reaffirming a debt is a serious matter. You should never agree to a reaffirmation without a very good reason.

Do I Have to Reaffirm Any Debts?

No. Reaffirmation is always optional. It is not required by bankruptcy law or any other law. If a creditor tries to pressure you to reaffirm, remember you can always say no.

Can I Change My Mind After I Reaffirm a Debt?

Yes. You can cancel any reaffirmation agreement for *sixty (60) days* after it is filed with the court. You can also cancel at any time before your discharge order. To cancel a reaffirmation agreement, you must notify the creditor in writing. You do not have to give a reason. Once you have canceled, the creditor must return any payments you made on the agreement.

Also, remember that a reaffirmation agreement has to be in writing, has to be signed by your lawyer or approved by the judge, and has to be made before your bankruptcy is over. Any other reaffirmation agreement is not valid.

Do I Have to Reaffirm on the Same Terms?

No. A reaffirmation is a new contract between you and the lender. You should try to get the creditor to agree to better terms such as a lower balance or interest rate. You can also try to negotiate a reduction in the amount you owe. The lender may refuse but it is always worth a try.

Should I Reaffirm?

If you are thinking about reaffirming, *the first question should always be whether you can afford the monthly payments.* Reaffirming any debt means that you are agreeing to make the payments every month, and to face the consequences if you don't.

If you have any doubts whether you can afford the payments, do not reaffirm. Caution is always a good idea when you are giving up your right to have a debt canceled.

Before reaffirming, *always consider your other options.* For example, instead of reaffirming a car loan you can't afford, can you get by with a less costly used car for a while?

Some offers to reaffirm may seem attractive at first. Let's say a department store lets you keep your credit card if you reaffirm $1000 out of the $2000 you owed before bankruptcy. They say it will cost you only $25 per month and they will also give you a $500 line of credit for new purchases. What they might not tell you is that they will give you a new credit card in a few months even if you do not reaffirm. More importantly, though, you should understand that you are agreeing to repay $1000 plus interest that the law says you can have legally canceled. This is a big price to pay for $500 in new credit.

Do I Have Other Options for Secured Debts?

You may be able to keep the collateral on a secured debt by paying the creditor in a lump sum the amount the item is worth rather than what you owe on the loan. This is your right under the bankruptcy law to "redeem" the collateral.

Redeeming collateral can save you hundreds of dollars. Since furniture, appliances and other household goods go down in value quickly once they are used, you may redeem them for a lot less than their original cost or what you owe on the account.

You may have another option if the creditor did not loan you the money to buy the collateral, like when a creditor takes a lien on household goods you already have. You may be able to ask the court to "avoid" this kind of lien. This will make the debt unsecured.

Do I Have to Reaffirm Car Loans, Home Mortgages?

If you are behind on a car loan or a home mortgage and you can afford to catch up, you can reaffirm and possibly keep your car or home. If the lender agrees to give you the time you need to get caught up on a default, this may be a good reason to reaffirm. But if you were having trouble staying current with your payments before bankruptcy and your situation has not improved, reaffirmation may be a mistake. The collateral is likely to be repossessed or foreclosed anyway after bankruptcy, because your obligation to make payments continues. If you have reaffirmed, you could then be required to pay the difference between what the collateral is sold for and what you owe.

If you are up to date on your loan, you may not need to reaffirm to keep your car or home. Some lenders will let you keep your property without signing a reaffirmation as long as you continue to make your payments. In some parts of the country, you have this as a legal right. Check with your lawyer.

And What About Credit Cards and Department Store Cards?

It is almost never a good idea to reaffirm a credit card. Reaffirming means you will pay bills that your bankruptcy would normally wipe out. That can be a very high price to pay for the convenience of a credit card. Try paying cash for a while. Then in a few years, you can probably get a new credit card, that won't come with *a large unpaid balance*!

If you do reaffirm, try to get something in return, like a lower balance, no interest on the balance, or a reasonable interest rate on any new credit. Don't be stuck paying 18-21 percent or higher!

Some department store credit cards may be secured. The things you buy with the credit card may be collateral. The store might tell you that they will repossess what you bought, such as a TV, VCR, or sofa, if you do not reaffirm the debt. Most of the time, stores will not repossess used merchandise. So, after a bankruptcy, it is much less likely that a department store would repossess "collateral" than a car lender.

However, repossession is possible. You have to decide how important the item is to you or your family. If you can replace it cheaply or live without it, then you should not reaffirm. You can still shop at the store by paying cash, and the store may offer you a new credit card even if you don't reaffirm. (Just make sure that your old balance is not added into the new account.)

For Example

Some offers to reaffirm may seem attractive at first. Let's say a department store lets you keep your credit card if you reaffirm $1000 out of the $2000 you owed before bankruptcy. They say it will cost you only $25 per month and they will also give you a $500 line of credit for new purchases. What they might not tell you is that they will give you a new credit card in a few months even if you do not reaffirm. More importantly, though, you should understand that you are agreeing to repay $1000 plus interest that the law says you can have legally canceled. This is a big price to pay for $500 in new credit.

I.4 Using Credit Wisely After Bankruptcy

Beware of Credit Offers Aimed at Recent Bankruptcy Filers

"Disguised" Reaffirmation Agreement

Carefully read any credit card or other credit offer from a company that claims to represent a lender you listed in your bankruptcy or own a debt you discharged. This may be from a debt collection company that is trying to trick you into reaffirming a debt. The fine print of the credit offer or agreement will likely say that you will get new credit, but only if some or all of the balance from the discharged debt is added to the new account.

"Secured" Credit Card

Another type of credit marketed to recent bankruptcy filers as a good way to reestablish credit involves "secured" credit cards. These are cards where the balances are secured by a bank deposit. The card allows you a credit limit up to the amount you have on deposit in a particular bank account. If you can't make the payments, you lose the money in the account. They may be useful to establish that you can make regular monthly payments on a credit card after you have had trouble in the past. But since almost everyone now gets unsecured credit card offers even after previous financial problems, there is less reason to consider allowing a creditor to use your bank deposits as collateral. It is preferable not to tie up your bank account.

Credit Repair Companies

Beware of companies that claim: "We can erase bad credit." These companies rarely offer valuable services for what they charge, and are often an outright scam. The truth is that no one can erase bad credit information from your report if it is accurate. And if there is old or inaccurate information on your credit report, you can correct it yourself for free.

Avoid High Cost Predatory Lenders

Don't assume that because you filed bankruptcy you will have to get credit on the worst terms. If you can't get credit on decent terms right after bankruptcy, it may be better to wait. Most lenders will not hold the bankruptcy against you if after a few years you can show that you have avoided problems and can manage your debts.

Be wary of auto dealers, mortgage brokers and lenders who advertise: "Bankruptcy? Bad Credit? No Credit? No Problem!" They may give you a loan after bankruptcy, but at a very high cost. The extra costs and fees on these loans can make it impossible for you to keep up the loan payments. Getting this kind of loan can ruin your chances to rebuild your credit.

Mortgage Loans

If you own your home, some home improvement contractors, loan brokers and mortgage lenders may offer to give you a home equity loan despite your credit history. These loans can be very costly and can lead to serious financial problems and even the loss of your home. Avoid mortgage lenders that:

- Charge excessive interest rates, "points," brokers' fees and other closing costs;
- Require that you refinance your current lower interest mortgage or pay off other debts;
- Add on unnecessary and costly products, like credit insurance;
- Make false claims of low monthly payments based on a "teaser" variable interest rate;
- Include a "balloon" payment term that requires you to pay all or most of the loan amount in a lump sum as the last payment;
- Charge a prepayment penalty if you pay off the loan early;
- Change the terms at closing;
- Make false promises that the rate will be reduced later if you make timely payments;
- Pressure you to keep refinancing the loan for no good reason once you get it.

Small Loans

It is always best to save some money to cover unexpected expenses so you can avoid borrowing. But if you are in need of a small loan, avoid the following high cost loans:

Payday loans

Some "check cashers" and finance companies offer to take a personal check from you and hold it without cashing it for one or two weeks. In return, they will give you an amount of cash that is less than the amount of your check. The difference between the amount of your check and the cash you get back in return is interest that the lender is charging you. These payday loans are very costly. For example, if you write a $256 check and the lender gives you $200 back as a loan for two weeks, the $56 you pay equals a 728-percent interest rate! And if you don't have the money to cover the check, the lender will either sue you or try to get you to write another check in a larger amount. If you choose to write another check, the lender gets more money from you and you get further into debt.

Auto title loans

For many years, pawn shops have made small high-interest loans in exchange for property. A new type of "pawn" is being made by title lenders who will give you a small loan at very high-interest rates (from 200 percent to 800 percent) if you let them hold your car title as collateral for the loan. If you fall behind on the payments, the lender can repossess your car and sell it.

Rent-to-own

By renting a TV, furniture or appliance from a rent-to-own company, you will often pay three or four times more than what it would cost to buy. The company may make even more profit on you because the item you are buying may be previously used and returned. And if you miss a payment, the company may repossess the item leaving with you no credit for the payments you made.

Tax refund anticipation loans

Some tax return preparers offer to provide an "instant" tax refund by arranging for loans based on the expected refund. The loan is for a very short period of time between when the return is filed and when you would expect to get your refund. Like other short-term loans, the fees may seem small but amount to an annual interest rate of 200 percent or more. It is best to patient and wait for the refund.

What You Can Do to Avoid Problems

- *If you don't want it, don't get it.* If you have doubts about whether you really need the loan or service, or whether you can afford it, don't let yourself get talked into it by a salesperson using high-pressure tactics. You can always walk away from a bad deal, even at the last minute.
- *Shop around.* You may qualify for a loan with normal rates from a reputable bank or credit union. Don't forget that high-cost lenders are counting on your belief that you cannot get credit on better terms elsewhere. Do not let feelings of embarrassment about your past problems stop you from shopping around for the best credit terms.
- *Compare credit terms.* Do not consider just the monthly payment. Compare the interest rate by looking at the

"annual percentage rate," as this takes into account other fees and finance charges added on the loan. Make sure you know exactly what fees are being charged for credit and why.

- *Read before you sign.* If you have questions, get help from a qualified professional to review the paperwork. A lender that will not let you get outside help should not be trusted.
- *If you give a lender a mortgage in a refinancing deal, remember your cancellation rights.* In home mortgage refinancings, federal law gives you a right to cancel for three days after you sign the papers. Exercise these rights if you feel you signed loan papers and got a bad deal. Don't let the lender talk you out of cancelling.
- *Get help early.* If you begin to have financial problems, or you are thinking of consolidating unmanageable debts, get help first from a local non-profit housing or debt counseling agency.

Ten Things to Think About Before Getting a New Credit Card

1. Don't apply for a credit card until you are ready.

Unfortunately, bankruptcy may not have permanently resolved all of your financial problems. It is a bad idea to apply for new credit before you can afford it.

2. Avoid accepting too many offers.

There is rarely a good reason to have more than one or two credit cards. Having too much credit can lead to bad decisions and unmanageable debts, and it will lower your credit rating. This can make it harder for you to get other lower interest rate loans. Avoid accepting a credit card just to get a discount at a store or a "free" gift.

3. Remember that lenders are looking for people who run up big balances, because those consumers pay the most interest.

You may find that credit card companies are pursuing you aggressively by mail and phone even though you filed bankruptcy. Do not view this as a sign that you can afford more credit. The lender may have a marketing profile telling them you are someone who is likely to carry a big credit card balance and pay a good deal of interest. Or they may see you as a good credit risk because you cannot file a Chapter 7 bankruptcy again for quite a few years.

4. Interest rate is important in choosing a card but not the only consideration.

You should always try to get a card with an interest rate as low as possible. But it is rarely a good idea to take a new card just because of a low rate. The rate only matters if you carry a balance from month to month. Also, the rate can easily change, with or without a reason. Remember that even the best credit cards are expensive unless you pay your balance in full every month. And other credit terms can add to your cost, like annual fees, late charges, over-the-limit fees, account set-up fees, cash advance fees, and the method of calculating balances. Sometimes a credit card that appears cheaper is actually more expensive.

5. Beware of temporary "teaser" rates. A teaser rate is an artificially low initial rate that applies only for a limited time.

Most teaser rates are good only for six months or less. After that, the rate automatically goes up. Remember that, if you build up a balance under the teaser rate, the much higher permanent rate will apply when you repay the bill. This means that the permanent long-term rate on the card is much more important than the temporary rate.

6. If your rate is variable, understand how it may change.

Variable interest rates can be very confusing. Some variable rate terms can make your rate go up steeply over time. Read the credit contract to understand how and when your rate may change. And don't be misled by advertisements that claim "fixed rate," as this may mean the rate is fixed only until the lender decides to change it again.

7. Check terms related to late payment charges and penalty rates of interest.

Most credit card contracts have terms in the small print for late charges or penalty interest rates that increase if you make even a single late payment. Try to avoid cards with late fees as high as $25–$35 or penalty interest rates of 21–24 percent or higher. Even if you are not having financial problems, these terms may become important, because they apply equally to accidental late payments.

8. Get a card with a grace period and learn the billing method.

It is important to understand how you will be billed. Look for a card with a grace period that lets you pay off the balance each month without interest. If the card does not have a grace period and interest will apply from the date of your purchase, a low interest rate may actually be higher than it looks. The terms of the grace period are also important, as it may not apply to balance transfers and cash advances. And look out for different interest rates that may apply depending upon the type of charge: these usually include a higher rate for cash advances.

9. Don't accept a card just because you qualify for a high credit limit.

It is easy to assume that because a card offer includes a high credit limit, this means the lender thinks you can afford more credit. In fact, the opposite may be true. Lenders often give high credit limits to consumers hoping that they think will carry a bigger balance and pay more interest. You must evaluate whether you can afford more credit based on your individual circumstances.

10. Always read both the disclosures and the credit contract.

You will find disclosures about the terms of a credit card offer, usually in small print on the reverse or at the bottom of the offer. Review these carefully. However, the law does not require that all relevant information be disclosed. For this reason, you must also read your credit contract, which comes with the card. This will include terms such as late payment fees, default rates of interest, and a description of the billing method. Since these terms are not easy to understand, you may want to call the lender for an explanation. Or better yet, refuse credit with too many complex provisions, because those terms are likely to work to your disadvantage.

Ten Things to Think About Before Using Your Credit Card

1. Establish a realistic budget.

Before using a credit card after bankruptcy, try paying cash for a while. This will help you learn how much money you need each month to pay the basic necessities. Don't forget to budget for the payments on any debts you reaffirmed in your bankruptcy.

2. It is important not to use credit cards to make up for a budget shortfall.

Credit card debt is expensive. Sometimes credit cards are so easy to use that people forget they are loans. Be sure to charge only things you really need and plan to pay the balance off in full each month. If you find you are constantly using your card without being able to pay the bill in full each month, you need to consider that you are using cards to finance an unaffordable lifestyle.

3. If you get into financial trouble, do not make it worse by using credit cards to make ends meet.

If you find that you are using credit cards to get through a period of financial difficulty, it is likely that additional credit will only make things worse. For example, if you use cash advances on your credit card to pay bills, the interest due will only add to your debt burden sooner rather than later.

4. Don't get hooked on minimum payments.

Credit card lenders usually offer an optional "minimum payment" in their monthly billing. These are usually set very low (usually 2 percent of the balance), barely covering the monthly interest charge. If you pay only the minimum, chances are that you will be paying your debt very slowly or not at all, and you may think you are managing the debt when you are really getting in over your head. For example, if you make only the monthly minimum payments to pay off a $1000 balance at a 17 percent interest rate, it will take over 7 years to pay your debt! If you are also making new purchases every month while making minimum payments, your debt will grow and take even longer to pay off. This means that your monthly interest obligations will increase and you will have less money in the monthly budget for necessities.

5. Don't run up the balance based on a temporary "teaser" interest rate.

Money borrowed during a temporary rate period of 6 percent is likely to be paid back at a much higher permanent rate of 15 percent or more. Also be careful about juggling cards to take advantage of teaser rates and balance transfer options. It takes a great deal of time and effort to take advantage of terms designed to be temporary. Remember that all teaser rate offers are designed to get you locked into the higher rate for the long term, because that is how the lender makes the most money.

6. Avoid the special services and programs credit card lenders offer to bill to your card.

You are likely to get many mail offers and telemarketer calls from your credit card lender about special services such as credit card fraud protection plans, credit report

protection, travel clubs, life and unemployment insurance, and other similar offers. These products are generally overpriced. It is best to throw out and refuse these offers, or at a minimum, treat them with a high degree of caution. And avoid "free trial" offers as you will be billed automatically if you forget to cancel the service.

7. If you can afford to do so, always make your credit card payments on time.

Be careful to avoid late payment charges and penalty rates if you can do so while still paying higher priority debts. Bad problems get worse fast when you have a new higher interest rate and late charge to pay during a time of financial difficulty. Most lenders will waive a late charge or default interest rate one time only. It is worth calling to ask for a waiver if you make a late payment accidentally or with a good excuse.

8. Know exactly when the grace period ends.

The grace period usually ends on the payment "due date," which may change every month. Many lenders do not mail bills until late in the grace period, so your payment may be due quite soon after you receive the bill. This also means that the grace period may be less than a full month, usually about 20-25 days. Some lenders are slow in posting payments or have strange rules about deadlines (like payments received after 10:00 a.m. on the due date are considered late). Try to mail your payment well before the due date so there will be no question it gets there on time. Paying credit cards on time not only saves you interest and late fees but is a good way to improve your credit rating after bankruptcy.

9. Beware of unsolicited increases by a credit card lender to your credit card limit.

Some lenders increase your credit limit even when you have not asked for more credit. Avoid using the full credit line as your debt can easily spiral out of control. And going over the credit limit even by a few dollars can be very costly as you will likely be charged an over-the-limit fee and a higher penalty interest rate.

10. If you do take a credit card and discover terms you do not like: Cancel!

You can always cancel any credit card at any time. Although you will be responsible for any balance due at the time of cancellation, you should not keep using a card after you discover that its terms are unfavorable.

I.5 Advice on Filing a Chapter 7 Bankruptcy

Your Next Appointment with us:

_____ at _____

Total Fee Due *Before Filing* in Chapter 7:

_____

CHAPTER 7—THINGS TO DO BEFORE WE FILE YOUR CASE

(1) Payments You Need to Bring Into Our Office to Get Your Case Filed:

$ _____

Total Fee must be paid *in full* to our office before your case can be filed with the Court.

(2) Paperwork and Money: Complete the "BANK-RUPTCY QUESTIONNAIRE" form and bring in your payments as scheduled. This way we can get your case filed as quickly as possible. Filing will stop the harassment and help protect you from losing property you want to keep.

(3) Don't Listen to Your Creditors: Creditors may tell you horror stories about bankruptcy, but all they are trying to do is to keep you from filing so that they won't take a loss. Don't listen to them. If you have questions about bankruptcy, call and ask us.

(4) Don't Get Advice from Your Friends or Even Your Family About Bankruptcy. Friends and family always mean well, but they don't have the training or experience to tell you how bankruptcy really works or to answer your questions about bankruptcy. Think about it. We're the experts and you are hiring us to work for you. So make us work. Call us with all your questions and concerns, and keep calling until we have answered all your questions and concerns. Every question you have is important. Every concern you have is important. Remember: We handle bankruptcy cases all the time. Use us to get your answers.

(5) Don't Pay on Debts, Except the Ones We Tell You to Pay: Many clients leave our office and pay on debts that don't need to be paid. This is a waste of money that could be better used to take care of you and your family. Make sure you read and follow the instructions in the next two paragraphs. Call us with any questions.

(6) Debts to Pay: Of the debts we talked about (other than your normal monthly expenses for food, gas for the car, insurance, etc.) keep paying *only* on the following debts.

If you are behind on these debts and the creditor has a lien on your property, you must get these debts up-to-date before we file your case if you want to be guaranteed the right to keep your collateral:

_____

_____

_____

(7) Debts Not to Pay and What to Say: Stop paying the rest of the debts we talked about and if they call you, tell them: "I cannot pay." Tell them: "Do whatever you need to do." Then hang up the phone. *DO NOT LET ANY CREDITOR INTO YOUR HOME.* If something bad happens, or if you receive any legal papers or other papers you do not understand, call us for help.

(8) Your Present Bank/Credit Union: If you owe money to a bank or credit union: (1) Stop putting money into your checking and savings accounts with that institution, and (2) immediately get all monies out of those accounts. After you file bankruptcy, the bank or credit union may try to grab any money left on account, applying it to pay any debt you owe. Besides, after you file bankruptcy, if you owe the bank or credit union money, they may want to get rid of you as a customer. Therefore, if you want to make sure you have a checking account for the future, open up a new checking account in a different bank or credit union before we file your bankruptcy case. However, make sure you pick an institution where you do *not* owe any money.

(9) Stop Making Payments on Your Credit Counseling Program. Once you make the decision to file bankruptcy, it makes no sense to continue making payments on this type of program. Stop making payments immediately. That money can be better used to take care of your family or to get the money in to us so that we can finish your bankruptcy filing. Dealing with automatic withdrawals: If your credit counseling program is taking money out of your bank account or directly out of your paycheck, immediately take whatever steps are necessary to stop the withdrawals. If you have any questions, call us.

(10) Stop Using Your Credit Cards. If you continue to use any of your credit cards after you come to see us, you could be accused of fraud and, in the extreme, it could also negatively affect your right to get a bankruptcy discharge. So, stop using the credit cards *right now*. Don't think the creditors are going to miss anything. The creditors are very good at picking up on debts incurred just before bankruptcy. Lastly, please keep this in mind: The goal is to get you out of debt, not deeper in debt, AND we are here to help. Call us before you do something you might regret.

(11) Credit Report: In most cases, much like a car dealership, we will pull your credit report. We use this to: (1) Help get complete information about your debts, (2) to make sure we don't miss something important, and (3) to find out how good or bad it reads, so that we can better advise you. You will need to fill out and sign a "CREDIT REPORT AUTHORIZATION" form. The cost is $ _____ per credit report.

(12) Military Allotments: Immediately stop the allotment for each of the following creditors:

_____

_____

_____

(13) Possibly Dischargeable Taxes: Also, bring in your tax returns *and* all letters, tax liens, notices of levy or garnishment, or other documents you can find concerning the taxes you owe for the following years. We need this information to determine whether or not you can get rid of these taxes by filing bankruptcy:

_____, _____,

_____, _____,

_____, _____.

(14) _____ **Record Search**: Please be advised that, although we are performing a judgment search with _____ , our office will not be searching individual County or DMV records to find out what judgment, tax, or other liens may be on file against you or your property. For purposes of filing this case, we will depend solely on the information provided by _____ and what you provide us. If you own any real property *or* owe a lot of taxes, it may be advisable for you to search, or hire someone to search, all lien records with DMV or in Counties in which you live, have lived, or own property. Undisclosed liens against your property have not been taken into account in advising you concerning your decision to file bankruptcy. Furthermore, some liens against your property will survive your bankruptcy discharge and may later interfere with your ability to dispose of such property.

(15) Extremely Important—Papers We Need to See: When you bring back in your paperwork, also bring in *all letters*, *documents*, *court papers* and *bills* you have received from the creditors, the collection agencies and attorneys. Also bring in any papers from when you bought your home or obtained a mortgage or other loan. *Bring in everything*. We will go through it.

(16) Information About Your Income: Bring in your (1) tax returns for the last two years *and* (2) pay stubs for at least the last month for each and every job you have.

(17) Agreements with Creditors: Bring in all the agreements you have signed with the following creditors. The attorney needs to review these documents:

_____

_____

_____

(18) Giving Up Your Home? If, as part of your case, you own (which means the title is in your name) and have decided to give up your home (in bankruptcy, we call it "surrender") to either (1) get out from under mortgage payments that are too high or (2) get rid of a home for which the mortgage payoffs exceed the value of the home, *please remember this*: The home is yours to live in until [*Note to Attorney: insert time when debtor could be evicted from property after foreclosure*]. Therefore, if you need a place to live, just stay in your home until the end of the inevitable foreclosure. Just because you have decided to give up the home does NOT mean you have to move out immediately. If the intent is to give up the home, you can stop making mortgage payments and continue to live in the home, because you cannot be evicted until [*Note to Attorney: insert time when debtor could be evicted from property after foreclosure*]. In most cases, this is a number of months. By living in your home for this time period, hopefully you can save up money to make an easier transition to another residence. To figure out when you need to move out of your home, keep track of the foreclosure paperwork served on you. [*Note to Attorney: describe steps in foreclosure process*].

(19) Unless We Give You the O.K.:

Don't Give Away Any Money/Don't Pay Any Friends or Relatives/Don't Give Away, Sell, Transfer, or Trade in Any Vehicles, Equipment, Accounts, Land, Houses, or Other Property. If you want to get rid of some money or property, first check with us. That's why we're here. Maybe what you want to do is perfectly O.K., but why take a chance? Call us before you do it. Otherwise, you might be doing something that is totally unnecessary or, worse, you might be doing something illegal or which could cause big problems in your bankruptcy case.

Don't Let Your Family or Anyone Else Pay Off Any of Your Bills or Put Any Property in Your Name. Again, what you or your family are thinking of doing may be perfectly O.K., but maybe NOT. It could be the worst possible thing to do. Don't take a chance. You don't have to be the expert. You have us. Call us first, before, not after, you or your family do something you might regret.

Don't Buy Any Vehicles or Other Large Items of Personal Property: Such purchases could cause problems in your case. Be on the safe side. Check with us first.

Don't Take Any More Loans Against Your 401-K Retirement Plan. This money is protected. As a general rule, you want to leave it alone. Check with us first.

(20) Other: _____

I HAVE READ, UNDERSTAND, AND HAVE RE-CEIVED A COPY OF THIS NOTICE.

_____

Client Signature

_____

Client Signature

WE ARE HERE TO HELP. CALL US IF YOU HAVE ANY PROBLEMS.

WHAT HAPPENS AFTER YOUR CHAPTER 7 CASE IS FILED?

HOW CREDITORS ARE NOTIFIED

After you sign your final papers, your case will be sent to the Bankruptcy Court for filing. After the Court receives it, the Court will prepare and mail you a notice which confirms the filing and schedules the meeting of creditors in your case. At the same time, the Court will send this notice to each of your creditors. This usually takes between ten days and three weeks. Once the creditor receives the notice, the creditor is supposed to stop sending bills, stop calling, and stop trying to collect money.

Creditor Calls: After your case is filed, to make sure the creditor has notice of the bankruptcy, you should tell each creditor who calls me that you have filed bankruptcy and the bankruptcy case number (located on the Court notice, or available from your attorney). Once you tell a creditor these things, it is unlawful for the creditor to call. Giving notice to the creditor over the telephone is just as binding under the law as the written notice sent by the Court. If you continue to receive calls from a creditor, you should then bring the matter to the attention of your attorney.

Creditor Bills: If you receive more than one bill from a creditor after you file, you should mark on the second bill "I have filed bankruptcy" and "It is unlawful for you to continue billing me." You should then mail the bill back to the creditor at the same address listed on the bill and, if you have already received the Court notice, include with the bill a *copy* of the Court notice (which tells the creditor the case number and where the case is filed). If you continue to receive bills from a creditor, unless it is a creditor you are

supposed to keep paying (see following sections of this notice), you should send the bill to your attorney, with a note asking the attorney to take whatever steps are necessary to get the creditor to stop the unlawful conduct.

REQUIRED MONTHLY PAYMENTS

Although some of your debts will be discharged as a result of filing a Chapter 7 bankruptcy, there are certain debts which you must continue to pay so that you have the right to keep the collateral which secures those debts. You must make regular payments on the following debts, each and every month, *as the payments become due,* and send these payments directly to the creditor. The creditor might not send you a bill or book but, if you do not keep the payments up-to-date, the creditor can take steps to take your property away.

Creditor	*Creditor*	*Creditor*
_____	_____	_____
_____	_____	_____
_____	_____	_____
_____	_____	_____

Important: If you ever lose collateral to one of these creditors due to non-payment or otherwise, you are still protected by the bankruptcy. Unless you signed a Reaffirmation Agreement during the bankruptcy, the only thing the creditor gets is the money it receives from selling the collateral and nothing more.

INSURANCE

If you are keeping a home, mobile home, or car, on which you still owe money, you must keep the property properly insured. You must also keep the creditor to whom you owe such money informed and up-to-date regarding insurance coverage. If you do not keep such property insured, the creditor can take steps to take the property.

PAYROLL DEDUCTION

If you are paying any loans by payroll deduction or automatic deductions from a bank account, you need to read this information carefully. Usually, this only applies to credit union loans, but it can apply to other types of loans as well.

After you file bankruptcy, any lender collecting payments by using a payroll deduction is supposed to stop taking money out of your paycheck. Sometimes, however, they forget to stop the deduction. Even when they do remember, it usually takes about a month for them to get the deduction stopped. You must keep an eye on your paycheck stub. If any money is taken out of my paycheck after the case is filed, you should immediately contact the lender to make sure they have taken steps to stop the deduction. In addition, the lender must refund any money it has collected since the date the case was filed with the Bankruptcy Court. In the meantime, if you have informed your attorney of the automatic deduction, as soon as your attorney receives proof from the Bankruptcy Court that the case has been filed, the attorney's office will send out a letter telling the lender that you have filed and reminding them of their duty to stop all payroll deductions.

If you want to continue making payments by payroll deduction on one or more of the secured loans that you intend to keep up-to-date—for instance, on a house or car loan—you will need to start up a new payroll deduction with the lender.

If you are making payments by automatic deductions from your bank account, you must notify the bank in writing to stop those payments, unless you want the payments to continue because the debt is one which you must continue to pay.

DEBTS NOT ELIMINATED BY BANKRUPTCY

Certain debts are not eliminated by bankruptcy. There are too many types of such debts to list them all here. Some of the most common include:

Student Loans. Student loans are usually not dischargeable in bankruptcy, except in cases of undue hardship. If you have a student loan, be sure to discuss with your attorney whether there is any chance you can eliminate it in the bankruptcy. If you cannot, you will continue to owe money on that loan.

Most Taxes. Most taxes will not be discharged (eliminated) by a chapter 7 bankruptcy case. You should discuss with your attorney what taxes you will still owe after bankruptcy. The bankruptcy will however stop collection upon these taxes until you receive a bankruptcy discharge. Even so, interest and penalties on non-dischargeable taxes will continue to accrue. Filing bankruptcy also will not get rid of any new taxes which become due after you file bankruptcy.

Alimony and/or Child Support. Debts in the nature of alimony or child support are not dischargeable in bankruptcy; therefore, you will continue to owe all such debts.

Other Divorce-Related Debts. Many times, Separation Agreements or Court Orders will obligate a former spouse to pay and remain responsible for the payment of certain other debts (such as credit card debts) which, if you don't pay, will fall back on an ex-spouse for payment. These debts may be dischargeable in bankruptcy, but your ex-spouse may have the right to ask the Bankruptcy Court to make a determination that one or more these debts are not dischargeable, or he or she may take the position in a family court proceeding after your bankruptcy case that the debts were not discharged.

PROPERTY ACQUIRED BY INHERITANCE, DIVORCE DECREE, OR MARITAL SEPARATION AGREEMENT

The advisability of filing a Chapter 7 bankruptcy is based on the amount of property you own at the time of filing. If, on or before the expiration of the first six (6) months after your case is filed, you obtain or become "entitled" to additional property or even a greater interest in a piece of property by reason of inheritance, divorce decree, equitable distribution order, or a marital separation agreement, you may stand to lose some of the property so acquired. *If you acquire or become entitled to any property from an inheritance, life insurance proceeds, or a marital property settlement in the six months after filing, you should immediately notify your attorney.*

There may be nothing you can do to keep from inheriting property, but you should not voluntarily enter into any marital separation agreement or proceed with the finalization of any divorce or equitable distribution proceedings during this period of time without first checking with your bankruptcy attorney regarding how it will affect your case.

CREDIT REPORTS

Your Credit Report: After you file a bankruptcy case, the credit bureaus will report that you have filed "bankruptcy." Your attorney does not control how or when this information shows up on the credit report. Sometimes the information does not get reported in an accurate manner, in which case you have a right to require the credit bureaus to correct all errors brought to their attention. However, you do not have the right to change information that is accurate but negative. At the same time, you do have the right to place on your credit report a hundred-word explanation of your circumstances. It is advisable to obtain a copy of your credit report directly from the credit bureau about six months after the bankruptcy case gets filed to examine it for errors. All debts that have been discharged should show a zero balance and have a notation that they were discharged. If there are errors on the credit report, you need to write each credit bureau and request corrections. You can also request corrections over the Internet. For this purpose, the following is the information necessary to contact the three major credit bureaus:

[Attorney: Insert credit bureau contact information]

Your Co-Signer's Credit Report: If a debt is discharged, a cosigner who has not filed bankruptcy will continue to owe it. There may be a notation placed on the credit report of anyone who has co-signed or guaranteed a debt for you that you have filed bankruptcy. Usually, this takes the form of words to the effect that a debt "was included in the bankruptcy of another." Sometimes the information is written in a manner that gives the inaccurate impression that the co-signer has also filed for bankruptcy. In such event, if the co-signer has not filed bankruptcy, the co-signer has the right to require the credit bureau to correct the error. Lastly, although in some circumstances it may be illegal for a creditor to try to collect from your co-signer—for instance, during a Chapter 13 case with respect to co-signed "consumer" debts—the bankruptcy law does not prohibit the reporting of accurate but negative information on the co-signer's credit report stating that the debt is or has become delinquent.

LEASES

If you are leasing a motor vehicle, business equipment, apartment, commercial building, or household goods, and want to keep the items, you need to keep the lease payments up-to-date. (However, if you have a "rent-to-own" contract this may not be true. Consult your attorney about your rights.) In most, situations, the lessor just wants the payments and not the property so, if you keep the lease payments up-to-date, the lessor will not try to take back the leased property. However, there is no guarantee in this regard, and there is a risk that you will lose the property if you do not come to an agreement with the lessor.

PROPERTY BEING SURRENDERED

When you "surrender" property back to a creditor in a bankruptcy case, this simply means that you don't have to pay that creditor any more money. It does not mean that the property is automatically taken out of your name. In many situations, when you "surrender" property in a bankruptcy case, the creditor will promptly foreclose or repossess the property. However, there is no guarantee that the creditor will do so. Until something happens to get the property out of your name, you will still owe any debts—such as real or personal property taxes that come due with respect to the property—because the property is still in your name. Therefore, if the creditor does not quickly foreclose or repossess upon the property that you surrender, you may want to contact the creditor to find out why. Of course if a creditor never takes action to assert its rights, you may continue to use the property.

TAX REFUNDS

Any tax refunds you are entitled to as of the date the bankruptcy case is filed are considered "property of the estate." If the refund has not been claimed as exempt in your case (ask your attorney if you are not sure), the trustee assigned to the case has the right to demand that the tax refunds be paid over to him or her for distribution to creditors. *If you are required to pay over your tax refund and you do not do so, you could be denied the benefits of your bankruptcy case.*

CLAIMS OR LAWSUITS YOU HAVE AGAINST OTHER PEOPLE

It is your responsibility to notify your attorney if, at any time during the case, you realize you have a claim or lawsuit against any other person or company (1) which was not listed in your schedules and (2) the basis for which arose before the filing of the bankruptcy case. The failure to notify your attorney could result in that claim being lost and the lawsuit arising from the claim, if any, being dismissed. However, without further written agreement, notifying your attorney does not mean that your attorney will represent you regarding any such claim or lawsuit.

REMEMBER: Bankruptcy laws are complicated and this summary cannot explain every possible detail of bankruptcy. If you have questions, please consult your attorney.

I HAVE READ, UNDERSTAND, AND HAVE RECEIVED A COPY OF THIS NOTICE.

Dated:

_____

Name of Client

_____

Name of Second Client

Index

References are to sections

MEETING OF CREDITORS (SECTION 341(a))
adjournments, 10.3.4
advice to clients, 8.2, 8.4.1
attendance, 8.4.2
chapter 7 bankruptcies
  after meeting, 3.5, 8.5
  notice, 3.3
  oral examination of debtor by trustee, 1.1.2.4, 3.4, 8.4.2
  procedures, 3.4
chapter 12 bankruptcies
  generally, 16.2.5
  time, 16.5.2
chapter 13 bankruptcies
  notice, 4.3
  procedures, 4.4
events prior to, 8.3
notice, Official Form 9, Appx. D.6
preparation for, 8.4.1
procedure at, 8.4.2
sample pleadings and forms, Appx. G.7

MILITARY RETENTION BONUSES
dischargeability, 14.4.3.18

MINORS
bankruptcy filing
  chapter 7, 3.2.1.1
  chapter 13, 4.2.1

MODIFICATION
chapter 12 plans, *see* CHAPTER 12 PLANS (FAMILY FARMERS)
chapter 13 plans, *see* CHAPTER 13 PLANS
cure, status as, 11.6.1.2.3
secured claims, *see* CRAMDOWN

MONEY ORDER COMPANIES
bankruptcy, effect on consumers, 17.5.2.1

MONITORING FEES
challenging, 13.4.3.4.5

MORTGAGES
see also LIENS; SECURITY INTERESTS
bankrupt lenders, 17.9
chapter 13 right to cure, 11.6.2
modification, 11.6.1.2
objecting to overcharges, 13.4.3.4
refinancing during chapter 13, 12.6.6
spreader clauses, 14.5.3

MOTOR VEHICLES
federal exemption, 10.2.2.1, 10.2.2.3
impaired driving debts, 14.4.3.9
motorboats, status, 14.4.3.9
right of redemption, use, 11.5.5
snowmobiles, status, 14.4.3.9
title pawn transactions, 11.9
valuation, 5.3.4, 11.2.2.3.2

MUTUAL DEBTS
setoffs, 10.4.2.6.7

NATIONAL BANKRUPTCY REVIEW COMMISSION
establishment, 1.1.2.4

NATIONAL CONSUMER LAW CENTER (NCLC)
bankruptcy manual, *see* CONSUMER BANKRUPTCY LAW AND PRACTICE (NCLC MANUAL)

consulting service, 1.3.3.2
Guide to Surviving Debt, 6.1.2

NON-ATTORNEYS
see also BANKRUPTCY PETITION PREPARERS
fees to, disclosure, 15.3.2, 15.3.3, 15.6
role in bankruptcy case, 5.1.2, 15.6
unauthorized practice of law, 15.6

NON-CORE PROCEEDINGS
see also PROCEEDINGS IN BANKRUPTCY
core proceedings, distinction, 13.2.4.2, 13.2.4.3
procedures, 13.2.4.4

NON-PURCHASE MONEY SECURITY INTERESTS
see also SECURITY INTERESTS
avoidance, 10.4.2.4, 10.4.2.10

NOTICE
clerk of bankruptcy court, available relief, 7.3.3
creditors, to, 13.3.2.1, 14.4.3.3
  mailing label matrix, *see* MATRIX (MAILING LABELS)
individual consumer debtor, form, Appx. E
Official Form 9, Appx. D.6
pre-filing forms, Appx. G.2
removal to bankruptcy court, 13.4.1.2

OBJECTIONS
chapter 7 discharge, 14.2
chapter 13 plans, 4.4, 8.6, 11.6.1.3.3.6, 12.3.3.2
claims by creditors, 3.5.3, 4.4, 8.3.6, 13.3.2.4, 13.4.3
exemptions claimed, 8.5, 10.3.3, 10.3.4
failure to raise, effect, 13.4.3.1
mortgage overcharges, 13.4.3.4
recoupment claims, raising as, 13.3.2.4
sample pleadings, Appx. G.8
secured claims, 11.2.2.1, 11.6.1.3.3.4

OFFICIAL BANKRUPTCY FORMS
see also BANKRUPTCY FORMS
amendments to, 1.4.3
annotations, Appx. D.3
bankruptcy petition preparers, information on, 15.6
chapter 13 plans, Appx. 4.5
family farmer reorganizations, application, 16.2.3.1
general principles, 7.1.1
initial forms
  amendments to, 8.3.2
  chapter 7, 3.2.2
  chapter 13, 4.2.2, Appx. 4.5
  preparing, 7.3
obtaining, 7.1.2
reproducible forms, reprinted, Appx. D.6
revised, 7.1.2
sample completed forms, Appx. F
substantial compliance, 1.4.3, 7.3.1
  computer programs, 7.1.3
  permitted alterations, Appx. D.2
  precise compliance not necessary, 7.1.2, 7.3.1
voluntary petition, *see* PETITIONS IN BANKRUPTCY

PACER SYSTEM
bankruptcy court dockets, access, 2.4.1, 5.3.4

PAPERS
see BANKRUPTCY FORMS

PRACTICE TIPS (*cont.*)
attorney fees, *see* ATTORNEY FEES AND COSTS
bankruptcy court advantages, 13.3
chapter 12 plans
   direct payments, 16.5.6.5
   feasibility, 16.5.7.2
   provisions, 16.5.8
chapter 13 plans
   successive filings, 12.10
   unexpired leases or executory contracts, 12.9.4
client handout, common questions, Appx. I
computerization, 7.1.3, Appx. D.4
counseling the debtor, 6
   advantages and disadvantages of bankruptcy, 6.2
   choosing type of bankruptcy, 6.3
   exemption planning, 6.5.2.2
   explaining bankruptcy, 6.1.2
   explaining options 6.1.1
   pre-bankruptcy transfers, 6.5.2.1, 6.5.3.2
   spousal filing, 6.4
   timing, 6.5
declaration concerning schedules, 7.3.4.7
delay of petition as tactic, 6.5.3.3
discharge orders, retention, 8.8.1
dischargeability complaints, 14.4.3.2.4
electronic case filing, Appx. D.5
exemption planning, 6.5.2.2, 10.4.1
facts and information, 5
   frequently missed info, 5.3.3
   full and accurate, need for, 5.4
   importance of getting, 5.2
   methods of gathering, 5.3
   other sources, 5.3.4
   questionnaire, 5.3.2
   web resources, 5.3.4
involuntary bankruptcies, generally, 13.8
landlord bankruptcy
   maintaining services, 17.8.2
   preventing abandonment, 17.8.2.2
   tenant ownership, 17.8.3
litigation advantages of bankruptcy, 6.2.1.6
meeting of creditors, 8.4.1
multiple cases, 7.2.3
NCLC consulting service, 1.3.3.2
NCLC Guide to Surviving Debt, 6.1.2
NCLC manual
   see also CONSUMER BANKRUPTCY LAW AND PRACTICE
      (NCLC MANUAL)
   using, 5.1.1
non-attorneys, role, 5.1.2
preparing and filing papers, 7
   forms, 7.2.1, 7.3
   generally, 7.1
   signing and verification, 7.4
   time considerations, 7.2
reaffirmation agreements, 14.5.2.2
sample pleadings and forms, Appx. G
stay litigation
   other tactics, 9.7.3.3.2
   stays pending appeal, 9.7.3.3.3
   valuation problems, 9.7.3.3.1
subsequent to filing, 8
   administration of chapter 13 plans, 8.7
   advice to clients, 8.2
   after discharge, 8.9
   after meeting of creditors, 8.5, 8.6
   confirmation hearings, 8.6
   discharge and discharge hearing, 8.8
   events prior to meeting of creditors, 8.3
   generally, 8.1
   meeting of creditors, 8.4

PRE-BANKRUPTCY TRANSFERS
avoidance by debtor
   consumer as creditor, chapter 11, 17.7.6
   exempt property, principles, 10.4.2.1
   farmers, 16.4.4.4
   judicial liens, 10.4.2.3
   non-purchase money security interests, 10.4.2.4
   pre-Code liens, 10.4.2.10
   procedures, 8.3.3, 10.4.2.2
   property recovered by trustee, 10.4.2.5
   sample pleadings, Appx. G.9
   trustee's powers, use, 10.4.2.6, 10.4.2.7
avoidance by trustee
   fraudulent transfers, 10.4.2.6.5
   liens securing penalties, 10.4.2.6.8
   preferences, 10.4.2.6.4.1, 10.4.2.6.4.2, 16.4.4.4.3
   setoffs, 10.4.2.6.7
   statutory liens, 10.4.2.6.3
   strong-arm clause, 10.4.2.6.2
   voluntary transfers, 10.4.2.6.1
avoided transfers, preservation, 10.4.2.9
cash advances, 6.5.2.1
charitable donations, 1.1.2.5, 10.4.2.6.2, 10.4.2.6.5, 13.9.2.2
check, by, date of transfer, 10.4.2.6.6
definition of transfer, 10.4.2.1
discharge, denial, 14.2.2.2
exempt property, avoidance, 8.3.3, Appx. G.9
exemption planning, 6.5.2.2
fraudulent conveyances, 6.5.2.1
luxury goods or services, 6.5.2.1
preferences, 6.5.2.1, 6.5.3.2

PREFERENCES
attorney fees paid in advance, status, 15.2.3
avoidance
   chapter 11, 17.7.6
   chapter 12, 16.4.4.4.3
   exceptions, 10.4.2.6.4.2
   generally, 10.4.2.6.4.1
   pre-bankruptcy, 6.5.2.1, 6.5.3.2
   sample pleadings, Appx. G.9
consumers as creditors, 17.2.1
exceptions, 10.4.2.6.4.2
pre-bankruptcy, avoidance, 6.5.2.1, 6.5.3.2
security interests, status, 10.4.2.6.4.2, 10.4.2.6.4.3

PRINCIPAL RESIDENCE
see also HOMESTEADS; MORTGAGES
capital gains exemption, 11.3.4
chapter 12, exclusion from debt ceiling, 16.2.2.3.3
chapter 13 cramdown, exemption, 11.6.1.2
right to cure default, 11.6.1.2.3, 11.6.2

PRIOR BANKRUPTCIES
automatic stay, effect, 9.7.3.1.5
chapter 7, 3.2.1.2, 6.2.2.8.2, 14.2.2.8, 14.2.2.9
chapter 12, 16.2.2.6

SETOFFS
see also COUNTERCLAIMS
allowed secured claims, 11.2.1
automatic stay, effect, 9.4.3
avoidance, 10.4.2.6.7
bank account freezes, 11.3.5
family farmer reorganizations, government creditors, 16.5.3.7.2
governmental units, 13.3.2.2
lender bankruptcies, 17.9.4
mutual debts, 10.4.2.6.7
post discharge, 10.5
recoupment claims, 10.4.2.6.7, 13.3.2.4
right to, 10.4.2.6.7

SMALL BUSINESSES
chapter 11 reorganizations, 17.7.12

SOCIAL SECURITY BENEFITS
see also PUBLIC BENEFITS
discharge protections, 14.5.5.4
federal exemption, 10.2.2.11
overpayments, dischargeability, 14.4.3.2.3.3
wage orders, attachment, 12.6.1

SOCIAL SECURITY NUMBERS
see STATEMENT OF SOCIAL SECURITY NUMBER

SOVEREIGN IMMUNITY
attorney fee awards, relationship, 15.5.6
Bankruptcy Code, abrogation, 1.1.2.4, 9.6, 13.3.2.2
stripdown not violation of, 11.2.1.1
Tucker Act application, 13.3.2.2

SPENDTHRIFT TRUSTS
bankruptcy estate, exclusion, 2.5.2

SPOUSES
see also CODEBTORS; JOINT BANKRUPTCIES; JOINT
    PROPERTY
chapter 13 eligibility, 4.2.1, 6.3.2, 12.2.2
considerations favoring chapter 7, 6.3.2
fraudulent actions, liability of debtor, 14.4.3.2.2.2
joint filings, considerations, 6.4
listing in schedule, 7.3.4.5
marital property settlements, *see* MARITAL PROPERTY
    SETTLEMENTS
statement of financial affairs, 7.3.5
support obligations, *see* SUPPORT OBLIGATIONS

SPREADER CLAUSES
validity, 14.5.3

STATEMENT OF FINANCIAL AFFAIRS
see also BANKRUPTCY FORMS
generally, 7.3.5
Official Form 7, Appx. D.6
sample completed form, Appx. F

STATEMENT OF INTENTION
see also BANKRUPTCY FORMS
conversion from chapter 13, 4.7.4
generally, 11.4
Official Form 8, Appx. D.6
  annotations, Appx. D.3
performance, 3.5, 4.7.4, 11.4
preparing and filing, 7.3.6
sample completed form, Appx. F

STATEMENT OF SOCIAL SECURITY NUMBER
see also BANKRUPTCY FORMS
chapter 7, 3.4, 7.2.1
chapter 13, 4.4, 7.2.1
emergency bankruptcies, 7.2.2
Official Form 21, Appx. D.6
  annotations, Appx. D.3
privacy issues, 7.3.2

STATUTE OF LIMITATIONS
see also TIME LIMITS
avoidance actions, 10.4.2.2, 10.4.2.7
fraudulent conveyances, 10.4.2.6.5
recovery actions, 10.4.2.2, 10.4.2.8
student loans, 14.4.3.8.2
tax reach backs, 6.5.3.4
TIL claims, 13.4.4
tolling, 10.4.2.7

STATUTORY LIENS
see also LIENS
avoidance, 10.4.2.6.3
chapter 13 cramdown, application, 11.6.1.2.4
preferences, exception, 10.4.2.6.4.2
valuation of property, 11.2.2.3.4

STAY OF PROCEEDINGS
see AUTOMATIC STAY

STRAIGHT BANKRUPTCY
see CHAPTER 7 LIQUIDATIONS

STRIPDOWN
see also CRAMDOWN
chapter 13 plans, 11.2.1.3, 11.2.2
government claims, 11.2.1.1
limitations on, 11.6.1.2
non-recourse loans, 11.2.1.2

STUDENT LOANS
chapter 13 classification, 12.4.3
chapter 13 issues, 14.4.3.8.5
defenses, raising, 14.4.3.8.4
discharge issues
  discharge protections, 14.5.5.2
  dischargeability, 14.4.1, 14.4.3.8
  hardship discharge, 14.4.3.8.3
  related provisions, Appx. A.2.6
  sample pleadings, Appx. G.11
HEAL debts, 14.4.3.8.6
reaffirmation agreements, 14.5.5.2
related provisions, Appx. A.2.2, Appx. A.2.6

SUBPOENAS
forms, Appx. E

SUBSTANTIAL ABUSE
dismissal, 13.9.2.2

SUBSTANTIVE CONSOLIDATION
joint bankruptcy, differences, 6.4

SUPPORT OBLIGATIONS
see also DIVORCE; MARITAL PROPERTY SETTLEMENTS
automatic stay, application, 9.4.5, 17.3.2
avoidance, 10.4.2.3.1, 10.4.2.3.2, 10.4.2.6.4.2
chapter 13 classification, 12.4.3
dischargeability, 14.4.1, 14.4.3.5, 14.4.3.17
federal exemption, 10.2.2.11

Quick Reference to the Consumer Credit and Sales Legal Practice Series

References are to sections in *all* manuals in NCLC's Consumer Credit and Sales Legal Practice Series. References followed by "S" appear only in a supplement.

Readers should also consider another search option available at *www.consumerlaw.org/keyword*. There, users can search all sixteen NCLC manuals for a case name, party name, statutory or regulatory citation, or *any* other word, phrase, or combination of terms. The search engine provides the title and page number of every occurrence of that word or phrase within each of the NCLC manuals. Further search instructions and tips are provided on the web site.

The Quick Reference to the Consumer Credit and Sales Legal Practice Series pinpoints where to find specific topics analyzed in the NCLC manuals. References are to individual manual or supplement sections. For more information on these volumes, see *What Your Library Should Contain* at the beginning of this volume, or go to www.consumerlaw.org.

This Quick Reference is a speedy means to locate key terms in the appropriate NCLC manual. More detailed indexes are found at the end of the individual NCLC volumes. Both the detailed contents pages and the detailed indexes for each manual are also available at NCLC's web site, www.consumerlaw.org.

NCLC *strongly recommends*, when searching for PLEADINGS on a particular subject, that users refer to the *Index Guide* accompanying *Consumer Law Pleadings on CD-Rom*, and <u>not</u> to this *Quick Reference*. Another option is to search for pleadings directly on the *Consumer Law Pleadings* CD-Rom or on the *Consumer Law in a Box* CD-Rom, using the finding tools that are provided on the CD-Roms themselves.

The finding tools found on *Consumer Law in a Box* are also an effective means to find statutes, regulations, agency interpretations, legislative history, and other primary source material found on NCLC's CD-Roms. Other search options are detailed at page vii, *supra*.

Abbreviations

AUS	=	Access to Utility Service (3d ed. 2004)
Auto	=	Automobile Fraud (2d ed. 2003 and 2004 Supp.)
Arbit	=	Consumer Arbitration Agreements (4th ed. 2004)
CBPL	=	Consumer Banking and Payments Law (2d ed. 2002 and 2004 Supp.)
Bankr	=	Consumer Bankruptcy Law and Practice (7th ed. 2004)
CCA	=	Consumer Class Actions: A Practical Litigation Guide (5th ed. 2002 and 2004 Supp.)
CLP	=	Consumer Law Pleadings, Numbers One Through Ten (2004)
COC	=	The Cost of Credit (2d ed. 2000 and 2004 Supp.)
CD	=	Credit Discrimination (3d ed. 2002 and 2004 Supp.)
FCR	=	Fair Credit Reporting (5th ed. 2002 and 2004 Supp.)
FDC	=	Fair Debt Collection (5th ed. 2004)
Repo	=	Repossessions and Foreclosures (5th ed. 2002 and 2004 Supp.)
Stud	=	Student Loan Law (2d ed. 2002 and 2004 Supp.)
TIL	=	Truth in Lending (5th ed. 2003 and 2004 Supp.)
UDAP	=	Unfair and Deceptive Acts and Practices (6th ed. 2004)
Warr	=	Consumer Warranty Law (2d ed. 2001 and 2004 Supp.)

References are to sections in *all* manuals in NCLC's Consumer Credit and Sales Legal Practice Series

Finance Companies—COC Ch 2; UDAP §§ 2.2.1, 5.1.5

Flipping—COC § 6.1; UDAP § 5.1.5

Flood Damage to Vehicle—Auto § 2.1.3

Food Advertising—UDAP § 5.11.2

Food Stamps, Electronic Payment—CBPL Ch 6

Forbearance of Student Loans—Stud § 2.3

Force-Placed Auto Insurance—UDAP § 5.3.11; COC § 8.3.5.4.2; TIL § 3.9.4.4.2

Foreclosure—Repo

Foreclosure, False Threat—Repo Ch 6

Foreclosure, Government-Held Mortgages—Repo Ch 18

Foreclosure, Preventing Through Bankruptcy—Bankr Ch 9, §§ 10.4.2.6.4, 11.5, 11.6; Repo Ch 20

Foreclosure, Preventing Through Refinancing—COC § 6.5; Repo § 17.9.2

Foreclosure, Preventing Through Rescission—TIL Ch 6; Repo § 16.7.3.1

Foreclosure, Preventing Through Workouts—Repo Ch 17

Foreclosure, Setting Aside—Repo § 21.1

Foreclosure, Special Problems for Elderly—Repo § 16.10

Foreclosure, Summary of State Laws—Repo App I

Foreclosures and UDAP—UDAP § 5.1.1.5; Repo § 16.7.1.1

Forged Signatures, Indorsements—CBPL § 1.2

Franchises—UDAP §§ 2.2.9.2, 5.13.1

Fraud—UDAP; Warr § 11.4

Fraud and Arbitration—Arbit Ch 4

FRB Official Staff Commentary on Reg. B—CD App C

FRB Official Staff Commentary on Reg. M—TIL App I.3

FRB Official Staff Commentary on Reg. Z—TIL App C

Free Offers—UDAP § 4.6.4

Freezer Meats—UDAP § 5.7.2

FTC (Federal Trade Commission)—UDAP

FTC Act, No Private Action Under—UDAP § 9.1

FTC Cooling Off Period Rule—UDAP § 5.8.2, App B.3

FTC Credit Practices Rule—Repo § 3.4.2; UDAP § 5.1.1.2, App B.1; FDC § 8.4.2

FTC Debt Collection Law—FDC Ch 8

FTC FCR Enforcement Actions—FCR App H

FTC FCR Official Staff Commentary—FCR App C

FTC FDCPA Official Staff Commentary—FDC § 3.2.6, App C

FTC Funeral Rule—UDAP § 5.11.5, App B.5

FTC Holder Rule—UDAP § 6.6, App B.2

FTC Mail or Telephone Order Merchandise Rule—UDAP § 5.8.1.1, App B.4

FTC Staff Letters on FCR—FCR App D

FTC Staff Letters on FDCPA—FDC § 3.2.5, App B

FTC Telemarketing Sales Rule—UDAP App D.2.1

FTC Telephone and Dispute Resolution Rule—UDAP App D.2.2

FTC Used Car Rule—UDAP § 5.4.3.2, App B.6; Warr § 14.7, App D

Funds Availability—CBPL § 1.8

Funerals—UDAP § 5.11.5

Furniture Sales—UDAP § 5.7.3

Future Advance Clauses—Repo § 3.9

Future Service Contracts—UDAP § 5.10

GAP Insurance—TIL §§ 3.7.10, 3.9.4.7

Garnishment—FDC § 5.5.7, Ch 12, App D

Garnishment of Bank Account—CBPL § 1.10

Garnishment to Repay Student Loans—Stud § 5.3, App B.1.2A

Gas Service—AUS § 1.2.1; UDAP § 5.6.9

Gasoline, Price Gouging—UDAP § 5.6.8.5

Government Benefits—FCR §§ 2.3.6.8, 5.2.7

Government Checks—CBPL § 1.1.8.4, Ch 5

Government Collection Practices—FDC Ch 13; Stud Ch 4

Gramm-Leach-Bliley Act—COC §§ 3.10S, 8.4.1.5.2; FCR § 1.5.3

Gray Market Sales—Auto § 1.4.11; Warr § 13.7

Guaranteed Student Loans—Stud

Guarantees—UDAP § 5.2.7.3

Guarantors—*See* Cosigners

Handguns—UDAP § 5.7.9

Handicapped, Discrimination Against—CD § 3.5.2

Handouts for Client—*See* Client Handouts

Health Care Bills—FDC Ch 14; Bankr § 6.2.2.4.1

Health Care Plans, Misrepresentations—UDAP § 5.11.6

Health Care Treatment, Discrimination In—CD § 2.2.2.6

Health Cures, Misrepresentations—UDAP § 5.11

Health Spas—UDAP § 5.10.3

Hearing Aids—UDAP § 5.11.1

Heating Fuel—AUS §§ 1.2, 1.6; UDAP § 5.6.8

HELC—TIL § 5.11

Hidden Interest—COC Ch 7; TIL § 3.10

High Pressure Sales—UDAP § 4.8

Hill-Burton Act Compliance—UDAP § 5.11.5

Holder in Due Course—UDAP § 6.6; COC §§ 10.6.1, 10.7.2.3

Home Builders—UDAP § 5.5.5.2

Home Equity Lines of Credit—TIL § 5.11

Home Equity Loans—TIL Ch 9

Home Foreclosure—*See* Foreclosure

Home Heating Fuel—AUS §§ 1.2, 1.6; UDAP § 5.6.8

Home Improvement Practices—TIL § 6.5.3; UDAP § 5.6.1; Warr § 17.7, Apps I.3, K.4

Home Mortgage Disclosure Act—CD § 4.4.5

Home Mortgage, Rescission of—TIL Ch 6, App E.3

Home Owners' Loan Act—COC § 3.5S

Home Owners Warranty Program—UDAP § 5.5.5.2

Home Ownership & Equity Protection Act—TIL Ch 9, App E.4; COC § 11.3.2; Repo §§ 16.7.3.5, 14.11.3.2

Homes and UDAP—UDAP §§ 2.2.5, 5.5.5

Homes, Warranties—Warr § 1.4.3

Homestead Exemptions, Bankruptcy—Bankr § 10.2.2.2

Horizontal Privity—Warr § 6.3

Hospital Bills—FDC Ch 14

House Warranties—Warr Ch 16

Household Goods, Bankruptcy Exemption—Bankr §§ 10.2.2.4, 10.4.2.4

Household Goods Security Interest—Repo § 3.4; UDAP §§ 5.1.1.2; 5.1.1.5; TIL § 4.6.7

Household Goods Security Interest, Credit Property Insurance on—COC § 8.5.4.4

Houses and UDAP—UDAP §§ 2.2.5, 5.5

HOW Program—UDAP § 5.5.5.5.2

HUD—*See* Department of Housing and Urban Development

Identity Theft—FCR § 13.5.5

Illegal Conduct—UDAP §§ 4.3.9, 9.5.8

Illegality as Contract Defense—UDAP § 9.5.8

Immigrant Consultants, Deceptive Practices—UDAP § 5.12.2

Immigrant Status, Discrimination Based On—CD § 3.3.3.3

Implied Warranties—Warr Ch 4

Improvident Extension of Credit—UDAP § 5.1.4

Incomplete Information in Consumer Reports—FCR Ch 7

Inconvenient Venue—*See* Venue

Indian Tribal Law, Bankruptcy Exemptions—Bankr § 10.2.3.1

Industrial Loan Laws—COC Ch 2

Infancy—*See* Minority

Infliction of Emotional Distress—FDC § 10.2

In Forma Pauperis Bankruptcy Pilot Program—Bankr § 13.6.2

In Forma Pauperis Filings in Bankruptcy—Bankr §§ 13.6, 17.6

Informal Dispute Resolution—Warr § 2.8

Injunctions—UDAP § 8.6; FDC §§ 6.12, 12.6.2, 13.3

References are to sections in *all* manuals in NCLC's Consumer Credit and Sales Legal Practice Series

References are to sections in *all* manuals in NCLC's Consumer Credit and Sales Legal Practice Series

NOTES

NOTES

NOTES

About the Companion CD-Rom

CD-Rom Supersedes All Prior CD-Roms

This CD-Rom supersedes all CD-Roms and disks accompanying *Consumer Bankruptcy Law and Practice* (6th ed. 2000) and its supplements. Discard all prior CDs and disks, including *Bankruptcy Forms Disk*. This 2004 CD-Rom contains everything found on the earlier CDs and disks and contains much additional and updated material.

What Is on the CD-Rom

For a detailed listing of the CD's contents, see the CD-Rom Contents section on page xxxv of this book. Highlights and new additions include:

- Law Disks' *Bankruptcy Forms* that allows completion of the petition, schedules, and certain other forms on a word processor:[1]
  - The Petition, as amended effective December 1, 2004;
  - Application and Order to Pay Filing Fee in Installments;
  - The Official Form 6 Schedules, as amended;
  - The Official Form 7 Statement of Financial Affairs;
  - The Individual Debtor's Statement of Intention;
  - The Proof of Claim Form, with current amendments; and
  - Captions;
- 150 other bankruptcy pleadings;
- A number of other blank official forms and forms promulgated by the Administrative Office of the U.S. Courts, all up-to-date;
- The Bankruptcy Code and other bankruptcy statutes;
- The Rules of Bankruptcy Procedure and Fee Schedule;
- A bankruptcy questionnaire to facilitate debtor representation; and
- Client handouts answering common bankruptcy questions and numerous other consumer education brochures.

How to Use the CD-Rom

The CD's pop-up menu quickly allows you to use the CD—just place the CD into its drive and click on the "Start NCLC CD" button that will pop up in the middle of the screen. You can also access the CD by clicking on a desktop icon that you can create using the pop-up menu.[2] For detailed installation instructions, see *One-Time Installation* below.

All the CD-Rom's information is available in PDF (Acrobat) format, making the information:

- Highly readable (identical to the printed pages in the book);
- Easily navigated (with bookmarks, "buttons," and Internet-style forward and backward searches);
- Easy to locate with keyword searches and other quick-search techniques across the whole CD-Rom; and
- Easy to paste into a word processor.

While much of the material is also found on the CD-Rom in word processing format, we strongly recommend you use the material in PDF format—not only because it is easiest to use, contains the most features, and includes more material, but also because you can easily switch back to a word processing format when you prefer.

Acrobat Reader 5 and 6.0.1 come free of charge with the CD-Rom. **We strongly recommend that new Acrobat users read the Acrobat tutorial on the Home Page. It takes two minutes and will really pay off.**

How to Find Documents in Word Processing Format

Most pleadings and other practice aids are also available in Microsoft Word format to make them more easily adaptable for individual use. (Current versions of WordPerfect are able to convert the Word documents upon opening them.) The CD-Rom offers several ways to find those word processing documents. One option is simply to browse to the folder on the CD-Rom containing all the word processing

---

1 *Bankruptcy Forms* is for attorneys only, and does NOT include required statements for non-attorney "bankruptcy petition preparers."

2 Alternatively, click on the D:\Start.pdf file on "My Computer" or open that file in Acrobat—always assuming "D:" is the CD-Rom drive on your computer.

files and open the desired document from your standard word processing program, such as Word or WordPerfect. All word processing documents are in the D:\WP_Files folder, if "D:" is the CD-Rom drive,[3] and are further organized by book title. Documents that appear in the book are named after the corresponding appendix; other documents have descriptive file names.

Another option is to navigate the CD in PDF format, and, when a particular document is on the screen, click on the corresponding bookmark for the "Word version of . . ." This will automatically run Word, WordPerfect for Windows, or *any other word processor* that is associated with the ".DOC" extension, and then open the word processing file that corresponds to the Acrobat document.[4]

How to Use Law Disks' *Bankruptcy Forms*

This CD makes it easier than ever before to use Law Disks' *Bankruptcy Forms*. Just click on the Bankruptcy Forms Software button, and then click on the button for the form you wish to fill out, either in Word or Corel Wordperfect. Save the resulting file under a new name and print it out. There is no need to install the software to your hard drive.

Links are provided for information about specific local bankruptcy rules available on the Internet. In addition, a button provides information on electronic filing of bankruptcy forms.

Restricted Technical Support for Law Disks' *Bankruptcy Forms*

Bankruptcy Forms *is provided as a public service and as a bonus, so that law offices can file the basic bankruptcy forms using their word processors. This version of* Bankruptcy Forms *is unsupported software, which means: you may use the program, for your own use, without paying any additional charge. However, because you have received a working* Bankruptcy Forms *program at nominal cost, **there is no technical support provided**.*

This software allows insertion on most word processors of required information directly into the forms. Technical support should not be necessary. Please do not call NCLC with technical questions. If you feel you need technical support, you can purchase it from Law Disks, 734 Franklin Ave., Garden City, NY 11530, Tel. and FAX (516) 741-5740, support@lawdisks.com. For more information, visit Law

Disks' web site at www.lawdisks.com or open the file "LawDisks" in the LAWDISKS subdirectory of this CD-Rom.

Important Information Before Opening the CD-Rom Package

Before opening the CD-Rom package, please read this information. Opening the package constitutes acceptance of the following described terms. In addition, the *book* is not returnable once the seal to the *CD-Rom* has been broken.

The CD-Rom is copyrighted and all rights are reserved by the National Consumer Law Center, Inc. No copyright is claimed to the text of statutes, regulations, excerpts from court opinions, or any part of an original work prepared by a United States Government employee. *Bankruptcy Forms* is copyrighted 1991–2004 by Law Disks, all rights reserved. *Bankruptcy Forms* is the property of Law Disks.

You may not commercially distribute the CD-Rom or otherwise reproduce, publish, distribute or use the disk in any manner that may infringe on any copyright or other proprietary right of the National Consumer Law Center or Law Disks. Nor may you otherwise transfer the disk or this agreement to any other party unless that party agrees to accept the terms and conditions of this agreement. You may use the disk on only one computer and by one user at a time.

The CD-Rom is warranted to be free of defects in materials and faulty workmanship under normal use for a period of ninety days after purchase. If a defect is discovered in the disk during this warranty period, a replacement disk can be obtained at no charge by sending the defective disk, postage prepaid, with information identifying the purchaser, to National Consumer Law Center, Publications Department, 77 Summer Street, 10th Floor, Boston, MA 02110. After the ninety-day period, a replacement will be available on the same terms, but will also require a $20 prepayment.

The National Consumer Law Center makes no other warranty or representation, either express or implied, with respect to this disk, its quality, performance, merchantability, or fitness for a particular purpose. In no event will the National Consumer Law Center be liable for direct, indirect, special, incidental, or consequential damages arising out of the use or inability to use the disk. The exclusion of implied warranties is not effective in some states, and thus this exclusion may not apply to you.

Except as stated above, *Bankruptcy Forms* is sold AS IS, THERE ARE NO WARRANTIES, THERE IS NO WARRANTY OF MERCHANTABILITY, NOR ANY WARRANTY OF FITNESS FOR ANY PARTICULAR PURPOSE. ALL LIABILITY RESULTING FROM HOW THE USER FILLS IN THE FORM IS DISCLAIMED. Some states do not allow the disclaimer of implied warranties, so this disclaimer may not apply to you. *Bankruptcy Forms* is

---

3 The CD-Rom drive could be any letter following "D:" depending on your computer's configuration.

4 For instructions on how to associate WordPerfect to the ".DOC" extension, go to the CD-Rom's home page and click on "How to Use/Help," then "Word Files."

an electronic form. Law Disks and NCLC have no control over how you fill in the form, and have no attorney-client relationship with you or with your clients. Using *Bankruptcy Forms* will be considered acceptance of the conditions above.

System Requirements

Use of this CD-Rom requires a Windows-based PC with a CD-Rom drive. (Macintosh users report success using NCLC CDs, but the CD has been tested only on Windows-based PCs.) The CD-Rom's features are optimized with Acrobat Reader 5 or later. Acrobat Reader versions 5 and 6.0.1 are included free on this CD-Rom, and either will work with this CD-Rom as long as it is compatible with your version of Windows. Acrobat Reader 5 is compatible with Windows 95/98/Me/NT/2000/XP, while Acrobat Reader 6.0.1 is compatible with Windows 98SE/Me/NT/2000/XP. If you already have Acrobat Reader 6.0, we *highly* recommend you install version 6.0.1 from this CD because a bug

in version 6.0 interferes with optimum use of this CD-Rom. The Microsoft Word versions of pleadings and practice aids can be used with any reasonably current word processor (1995 or later).

One-Time Installation

When the CD-Rom is inserted in its drive, a menu will pop up automatically. (Please be patient if you have a slow CD-Rom drive; this will only take a few moments.) If you do not already have Acrobat Reader 5 or 6.0.1, first click the "Install Acrobat Reader" button. Do not reboot, but then click on the "Make Shortcut Icon" button. (You need not make another shortcut icon if you already have done so for another NCLC CD.) Then reboot and follow the *How to Use the CD-Rom* instructions above.

[*Note*: If the pop-up menu fails to appear, go to "My Computer," right-click "D:" if that is the CD-Rom drive, and select "Open." Then double-click on "Read_Me.txt" for alternate installation and use instructions.]